Peterson's Graduate Programs in the Physical Sciences, Mathematics, Agricultural Sciences, the Environment & Natural Resources

2012

PETERSON'S
Publishing

About Peterson's Publishing

To succeed on your lifelong educational journey, you will need accurate, dependable, and practical tools and resources. That is why Peterson's is everywhere education happens. Because whenever and however you need education content delivered, you can rely on Peterson's to provide the information, know-how, and guidance to help you reach your goals. Tools to match the right students with the right school. It's here. Personalized resources and expert guidance. It's here. Comprehensive and dependable education content—delivered whenever and however you need it. It's all here.

For more information, contact Peterson's, 2000 Lenox Drive, Lawrenceville, NJ 08648; 800-338-3282 Ext. 54229; or find us online at www.petersonspublishing.com.

Facebook® and Facebook logos are registered trademarks of Facebook, Inc., which was not involved in the production of this book and makes no endorsement of this product.

Bernadette Webster, Director of Publishing; Jill C. Schwartz, Editor; Ken Britschge, Research Project Manager; Nicole Gallo, Amy L. Weber, Research Associates; Phyllis Johnson, Software Engineer; Ray Golaszewski, Publishing Operations Manager; Linda M. Williams, Composition Manager; Karen Mount, Fulfillment Coordinator; Danielle Vreeland, Shannon White, Client Relations Representatives

Peterson's Publishing makes every reasonable effort to obtain accurate, complete, and timely data from reliable sources. Nevertheless, Peterson's and the third-party data suppliers make no representation or warranty, either expressed or implied, as to the accuracy, timeliness, or completeness of the data or the results to be obtained from using the data, including, but not limited to, its quality, performance, merchantability, or fitness for a particular purpose, non-infringement or otherwise.

Neither Peterson's Publishing nor the third-party data suppliers warrant, guarantee, or make any representations that the results from using the data will be successful or will satisfy users' requirements. The entire risk to the results and performance is assumed by the user.

ISSN 1093-8443
ISBN-13: 978-0-7689-3283-6
ISBN-10: 0-7689-3283-1

Printed in the United States of America

10 9 8 7 6 5 4 3 2 1   14 13 12

Forty-sixth Edition

By producing this book on recycled paper (40% post-consumer waste) 42 trees were saved.

Sustainability—Its Importance to Peterson's Publishing

What does sustainability mean to Peterson's Publishing? As a leading publisher, we are aware that our business has a direct impact on vital resources—most especially the trees that are used to make our books. Peterson's Publishing is proud that its products are certified by the Sustainable Forestry Initiative (SFI) and that all of its books are printed on paper that is 40 percent post-consumer waste using vegetable-based ink.

Being a part of the Sustainable Forestry Initiative (SFI) means that all of our vendors—from paper suppliers to printers—have undergone rigorous audits to demonstrate that they are maintaining a sustainable environment.

Peterson's Publishing continuously strives to find new ways to incorporate sustainability throughout all aspects of its business.

CONTENTS

SPECIAL ADVERTISING SECTION

Thomas Jefferson University School of Population Health

University of Medicine and Dentistry of New Jersey

Saint Louis University

St. Mary's University

The Winston Preparatory Schools

vi   www.facebook.com/petersonspublishing

Peterson's Graduate Programs in the Physical Sciences, Mathematics, Agricultural Sciences, the Environment & Natural Resources 2012

A Note from the Peterson's Editors

The six volumes of Peterson's *Graduate and Professional Programs*, the only annually updated reference work of its kind, provide wide-ranging information on the graduate and professional programs offered by accredited colleges and universities in the United States, U.S. territories, and Canada and by those institutions outside the United States that are accredited by U.S. accrediting bodies. More than 44,000 individual academic and professional programs at more than 2,200 institutions are listed. Peterson's *Graduate and Professional Programs* have been used for more than forty years by prospective graduate and professional students, placement counselors, faculty advisers, and all others interested in postbaccalaureate education.

Graduate & Professional Programs: An Overview contains information on institutions as a whole, while the other books in the series are devoted to specific academic and professional fields:

Graduate Programs in the Humanities, Arts & Social Sciences
Graduate Programs in the Biological Sciences
Graduate Programs in the Physical Sciences, Mathematics, Agricultural Sciences, the Environment & Natural Resources
Graduate Programs in Engineering & Applied Sciences
Graduate Programs in Business, Education, Health, Information Studies, Law & Social Work

The books may be used individually or as a set. For example, if you have chosen a field of study but do not know what institution you want to attend or if you have a college or university in mind but have not chosen an academic field of study, it is best to begin with the Overview guide.

Graduate & Professional Programs: An Overview presents several directories to help you identify programs of study that might interest you; you can then research those programs further in the other books in the series by using the Directory of Graduate and Professional Programs by Field, which lists 500 fields and gives the names of those institutions that offer graduate degree programs in each.

For geographical or financial reasons, you may be interested in attending a particular institution and will want to know what it has to offer. You should turn to the Directory of Institutions and Their Offerings, which lists the degree programs available at each institution. As in the Directory of Graduate and Professional Programs by Field, the level of degrees offered is also indicated.

All books in the series include advice on graduate education, including topics such as admissions tests, financial aid, and accreditation. **The Graduate Adviser** includes two essays and information about accreditation. The first essay, "The Admissions Process," discusses general admission requirements, admission tests, factors to consider when selecting a graduate school or program, when and how to apply,

and how admission decisions are made. Special information for international students and tips for minority students are also included. The second essay, "Financial Support," is an overview of the broad range of support available at the graduate level. Fellowships, scholarships, and grants; assistantships and internships; federal and private loan programs, as well as Federal Work-Study; and the GI bill are detailed. This essay concludes with advice on applying for need-based financial aid. "Accreditation and Accrediting Agencies" gives information on accreditation and its purpose and lists institutional accrediting agencies first and then specialized accrediting agencies relevant to each volume's specific fields of study.

With information on more than 44,000 graduate programs in 500 disciplines, Peterson's *Graduate and Professional Programs* give you all the information you need about the programs that are of interest to you in three formats: **Profiles** (capsule summaries of basic information), **Displays** (information that an institution or program wants to emphasize), and **Close-Ups** (written by administrators, with more expansive information than the **Profiles**, emphasizing different aspects of the programs). By using these various formats of program information, coupled with **Appendixes** and **Indexes** covering directories and subject areas for all six books, you will find that these guides provide the most comprehensive, accurate, and up-to-date graduate study information available.

At the end of the book, you'll find a special section of ads placed by Peterson's preferred clients. Their financial support makes it possible for Peterson's Publishing to continue to provide you with the highest-quality educational exploration, test-prep, financial aid, and career-preparation resources you need to succeed on your educational journey.

Find Us on Facebook®

Join the grad school conversation on Facebook® at www.facebook.com/petersonspublishing. Peterson's expert resources are available to help you as you search for the right graduate program for you.

Peterson's publishes a full line of resources with information you need to guide you through the graduate admissions process. Peterson's publications can be found at college libraries and career centers and your local bookstore or library—or visit us on the Web at www.petersonspublishing.com. Peterson's books are now also available as eBooks.

Colleges and universities will be pleased to know that Peterson's helped you in your selection. Admissions staff members are more than happy to answer questions, address specific problems, and help in any way they can. The editors at Peterson's wish you great success in your graduate program search!

THE GRADUATE ADVISER

The Admissions Process

Generalizations about graduate admissions practices are not always helpful because each institution has its own set of guidelines and procedures. Nevertheless, some broad statements can be made about the admissions process that may help you plan your strategy.

Factors Involved in Selecting a Graduate School or Program

Selecting a graduate school and a specific program of study is a complex matter. Quality of the faculty; program and course offerings; the nature, size, and location of the institution; admission requirements; cost; and the availability of financial assistance are among the many factors that affect one's choice of institution. Other considerations are job placement and achievements of the program's graduates and the institution's resources, such as libraries, laboratories, and computer facilities. If you are to make the best possible choice, you need to learn as much as you can about the schools and programs you are considering before you apply.

The following steps may help you narrow your choices.

- Talk to alumni of the programs or institutions you are considering to get their impressions of how well they were prepared for work in their fields of study.
- Remember that graduate school requirements change, so be sure to get the most up-to-date information possible.
- Talk to department faculty members and the graduate adviser at your undergraduate institution. They often have information about programs of study at other institutions.
- Visit the Web sites of the graduate schools in which you are interested to request a graduate catalog. Contact the department chair in your chosen field of study for additional information about the department and the field.
- Visit as many campuses as possible. Call ahead for an appointment with the graduate adviser in your field of interest and be sure to check out the facilities and talk to students.

General Requirements

Graduate schools and departments have requirements that applicants for admission must meet. Typically, these requirements include undergraduate transcripts (which provide information about undergraduate grade point average and course work applied toward a major), admission test scores, and letters of recommendation. Most graduate programs also ask for an essay or personal statement that describes your personal reasons for seeking graduate study. In some fields, such as art and music, portfolios or auditions may be required in addition to other evidence of talent. Some institutions require that the applicant have an undergraduate degree in the same subject as the intended graduate major.

Most institutions evaluate each applicant on the basis of the applicant's total record, and the weight accorded any given factor varies widely from institution to institution and from program to program.

The Application Process

You should begin the application process at least one year before you expect to begin your graduate study. Find out the application deadline for each institution (many are provided in the **Profile** section of this guide). Go to the institution's Web site and find out if you can apply online. If not, request a paper application form. Fill out this form thoroughly and neatly. Assume that the school needs all the information it is requesting and that the admissions officer will be sensitive to the neatness and overall quality of what you submit. Do not supply more information than the school requires.

The institution may ask at least one question that will require a three- or four-paragraph answer. Compose your response on the assumption that the admissions officer is interested in both what you think and how you express yourself. Keep your statement brief and to the point, but, at the same time, include all pertinent information about your past experiences and your educational goals. Individual statements vary greatly in style and content, which helps admissions officers differentiate among applicants. Many graduate departments give considerable weight to the statement in making their admissions decisions, so be sure to take the time to prepare a thoughtful and concise statement.

If recommendations are a part of the admissions requirements, carefully choose the individuals you ask to write them. It is generally best to ask current or former professors to write the recommendations, provided they are able to attest to your intellectual ability and motivation for doing the work required of a graduate student. It is advisable to provide stamped, preaddressed envelopes to people being asked to submit recommendations on your behalf.

Completed applications, including references, transcripts, and admission test scores, should be received at the institution by the specified date.

Be advised that institutions do not usually make admissions decisions until all materials have been received. Enclose a self-addressed postcard with your application, requesting confirmation of receipt. Allow at least ten days for the return of the postcard before making further inquiries.

If you plan to apply for financial support, it is imperative that you file your application early.

ADMISSION TESTS

The major testing program used in graduate admissions is the Graduate Record Examinations (GRE) testing program, sponsored by the GRE Board and administered by Educational Testing Service, Princeton, New Jersey.

The Graduate Record Examinations testing program consists of a General Test and eight Subject Tests. The General Test measures critical thinking, verbal reasoning, quantitative reasoning, and analytical writing skills. It is offered as an Internet-based test (iBT) in the United States, Canada, and many other countries.

The typical computer-based General Test consists of one 30-minute verbal reasoning section, one 45-minute quantitative reasoning sections, one 45-minute issue analysis (writing) section, and one 30-minute argument analysis (writing) section. In addition, an unidentified verbal or quantitative section that doesn't count toward a score may be included and an identified research section that is not scored may also be included.

The Subject Tests measure achievement and assume undergraduate majors or extensive background in the following eight disciplines:

- Biochemistry, Cell and Molecular Biology
- Biology
- Chemistry
- Computer Science
- Literature in English
- Mathematics
- Physics
- Psychology

The Subject Tests are available three times per year as paper-based administrations around the world. Testing time is approximately 2 hours and 50 minutes. You can obtain more information about the GRE by visiting the ETS Web site at www.ets.org or consulting the *GRE Information and Registration Bulletin*. The *Bulletin* can be obtained at many undergraduate colleges. You can also download it from the ETS Web site or obtain it by contacting Graduate Record Examinations, Educational Testing Service, P.O. Box 6000, Princeton, NJ 08541-6000; phone: 609-771-7670.

If you expect to apply for admission to a program that requires any of the GRE tests, you should select a test date well in advance of the

application deadline. Scores on the computer-based General Test are reported within ten to fifteen days; scores on the paper-based Subject Tests are reported within six weeks.

Another testing program, the Miller Analogies Test (MAT), is administered at more than 500 Controlled Testing Centers, licensed by Harcourt Assessment, Inc., in the United States, Canada, and other countries. The MAT computer-based test is now available. Testing time is 60 minutes. The test consists of 120 partial analogies. You can obtain the *Candidate Information Booklet,* which contains a list of test centers and instructions for taking the test, from http://www.milleranalogies.com or by calling 800-622-3231 (toll-free).

Check the specific requirements of the programs to which you are applying.

How Admission Decisions Are Made

The program you apply to is directly involved in the admissions process. Although the final decision is usually made by the graduate dean (or an associate) or the faculty admissions committee, recommendations from faculty members in your intended field are important. At some institutions, an interview is incorporated into the decision process.

A Special Note for International Students

In addition to the steps already described, there are some special considerations for international students who intend to apply for graduate study in the United States. All graduate schools require an indication of competence in English. The purpose of the Test of English as a Foreign Language (TOEFL) is to evaluate the English proficiency of people who are nonnative speakers of English and want to study at colleges and universities where English is the language of instruction. The TOEFL is administered by Educational Testing Service (ETS) under the general direction of a policy board established by the College Board and the Graduate Record Examinations Board.

The TOEFL iBT assesses the four basic language skills: listening, reading, writing, and speaking. It was administered for the first time in September 2005, and ETS continues to introduce the TOEFL iBT in selected cities. The Internet-based test is administered at secure, official test centers. The testing time is approximately 4 hours. Because the TOEFL iBT includes a speaking section, the Test of Spoken English (TSE) is no longer needed.

The TOEFL is also offered in the paper-based format in areas of the world where Internet-based testing is not available. The paper-based TOEFL consists of three sections—listening comprehension, structure and written expression, and reading comprehension. The testing time is approximately 3 hours. The Test of Written English (TWE) is also given. The TWE is a 30-minute essay that measures the examinee's ability to compose in English. Examinees receive a TWE score separate from their TOEFL score. The *Information Bulletin* contains information on local fees and registration procedures.

Additional information and registration materials are available from TOEFL Services, Educational Testing Service, P.O. Box 6151, Princeton, New Jersey 08541-6151. Phone: 609-771-7100. Web site: www.toefl.org.

International students should apply especially early because of the number of steps required to complete the admissions process. Furthermore, many United States graduate schools have a limited number of spaces for international students, and many more students apply than the schools can accommodate.

International students may find financial assistance from institutions very limited. The U.S. government requires international applicants to submit a certification of support, which is a statement attesting to the applicant's financial resources. In addition, international students *must* have health insurance coverage.

Tips for Minority Students

Indicators of a university's values in terms of diversity are found both in its recruitment programs and its resources directed to student success. Important questions: Does the institution vigorously recruit minorities for its graduate programs? Is there funding available to help with the costs associated with visiting the school? Are minorities represented in the institution's brochures or Web site or on their faculty rolls? What campus-based resources or services (including assistance in locating housing or career counseling and placement) are available? Is funding available to members of underrepresented groups?

At the program level, it is particularly important for minority students to investigate the "climate" of a program under consideration. How many minority students are enrolled and how many have graduated? What opportunities are there to work with diverse faculty and mentors whose research interests match yours? How are conflicts resolved or concerns addressed? How interested are faculty in building strong and supportive relations with students? "Climate" concerns should be addressed by posing questions to various individuals, including faculty members, current students, and alumni.

Information is also available through various organizations, such as the Hispanic Association of Colleges & Universities (HACU), and publications such as *Diverse Issues in Higher Education* and *Hispanic Outlook* magazine. There are also books devoted to this topic, such as *The Multicultural Student's Guide to Colleges* by Robert Mitchell.

4   www.facebook.com/petersonspublishing

Peterson's Graduate Programs in the Physical Sciences, Mathematics, Agricultural Sciences, the Environment & Natural Resources 2012

Financial Support

The range of financial support at the graduate level is very broad. The following descriptions will give you a general idea of what you might expect and what will be expected of you as a financial support recipient.

Fellowships, Scholarships, and Grants

These are usually outright awards of a few hundred to many thousands of dollars with no service to the institution required in return. Fellowships and scholarships are usually awarded on the basis of merit and are highly competitive. Grants are made on the basis of financial need or special talent in a field of study. Many fellowships, scholarships, and grants not only cover tuition, fees, and supplies but also include stipends for living expenses with allowances for dependents. However, the terms of each should be examined because some do not permit recipients to supplement their income with outside work. Fellowships, scholarships, and grants may vary in the number of years for which they are awarded.

In addition to the availability of these funds at the university or program level, many excellent fellowship programs are available at the national level and may be applied for before and during enrollment in a graduate program. A listing of many of these programs can be found at the Council of Graduate Schools' Web site: http://www.cgsnet.org. There is a wealth of information in the "Programs" and "Awards" sections.

Assistantships and Internships

Many graduate students receive financial support through assistantships, particularly involving teaching or research duties. It is important to recognize that such appointments should not be viewed simply as employment relationships but rather should constitute an integral and important part of a student's graduate education. As such, the appointments should be accompanied by strong faculty mentoring and increasingly responsible apprenticeship experiences. The specific nature of these appointments in a given program should be considered in selecting that graduate program.

TEACHING ASSISTANTSHIPS

These usually provide a salary and full or partial tuition remission and may also provide health benefits. Unlike fellowships, scholarships, and grants, which require no service to the institution, teaching assistantships require recipients to provide the institution with a specific amount of undergraduate teaching, ideally related to the student's field of study. Some teaching assistants are limited to grading papers, compiling bibliographies, taking notes, or monitoring laboratories. At some graduate schools, teaching assistants must carry lighter course loads than regular full-time students.

RESEARCH ASSISTANTSHIPS

These are very similar to teaching assistantships in the manner in which financial assistance is provided. The difference is that recipients are given basic research assignments in their disciplines rather than teaching responsibilities. The work required is normally related to the student's field of study; in most instances, the assistantship supports the student's thesis or dissertation research.

ADMINISTRATIVE INTERNSHIPS

These are similar to assistantships in application of financial assistance funds, but the student is given an assignment on a part-time basis, usually as a special assistant with one of the university's administrative offices. The assignment may not necessarily be directly related to the recipient's discipline.

RESIDENCE HALL AND COUNSELING ASSISTANTSHIPS

These assistantships are frequently assigned to graduate students in psychology, counseling, and social work, but they may be offered to students in other disciplines, especially if the student has worked in this capacity during his or her undergraduate years. Duties can vary from being available in a dean's office for a specific number of hours for consultation with undergraduates to living in campus residences and being responsible for both counseling and administrative tasks or advising student activity groups. Residence hall assistantships often include a room and board allowance and, in some cases, tuition assistance and stipends. Contact the Housing and Student Life Office for more information.

Health Insurance

The availability and affordability of health insurance is an important issue and one that should be considered in an applicant's choice of institution and program. While often included with assistantships and fellowships, this is not always the case and, even if provided, the benefits may be limited. It is important to note that the U.S. government requires international students to have health insurance.

The GI Bill

This provides financial assistance for students who are veterans of the United States armed forces. If you are a veteran, contact your local Veterans Administration office to determine your eligibility and to get full details about benefits. There are a number of programs that offer educational benefits to current military enlistees. Some states have tuition assistance programs for members of the National Guard. Contact the VA office at the college for more information.

Federal Work-Study Program (FWS)

Employment is another way some students finance their graduate studies. The federally funded Federal Work-Study Program provides eligible students with employment opportunities, usually in public and private nonprofit organizations. Federal funds pay up to 75 percent of the wages, with the remainder paid by the employing agency. FWS is available to graduate students who demonstrate financial need. Not all schools have these funds, and some only award them to undergraduates. Each school sets its application deadline and work-study earnings limits. Wages vary and are related to the type of work done. You must file the Free Application for Federal Student Aid (FAFSA) to be eligible for this program.

Loans

Many graduate students borrow to finance their graduate programs when other sources of assistance (which do not have to be repaid) prove insufficient. You should always read and understand the terms of any loan program before submitting your application.

FEDERAL DIRECT LOANS

Federal Direct Stafford Loans. The Federal Direct Stafford Loan Program offers low-interest loans to students with the Department of Education acting as the lender.

There are two components of the Federal Stafford Loan program. Under the *subsidized* component of the program, the federal government pays the interest on the loan while you are enrolled in graduate school on at least a half-time basis, during the six-month grace period after you drop below half-time enrollment, as well as during any period of deferment. Under the *unsubsidized* component of the program, you pay the interest on the loan from the day proceeds are issued. Eligibility for the federal subsidy is based on demonstrated financial need as determined by the financial aid office from the information you provide on the FAFSA. A cosigner is not required, since the loan is not based on creditworthiness.

Although *unsubsidized* Federal Direct Stafford Loans may not be as desirable as *subsidized* Federal Direct Stafford Loans from the student's perspective, they are a useful source of support for those who may not qualify for the subsidized loans or who need additional financial assistance.

Graduate students may borrow up to $20,500 per year through the Direct Stafford Loan Program, up to a cumulative maximum of $138,500, including undergraduate borrowing. This may include up to $8,500 in *subsidized* Direct Stafford Loans annually, depending on eligibility, up to a cumulative maximum of $65,500, including undergraduate borrowing. The amount of the loan borrowed through the *unsubsidized* Direct Stafford Loan Program equals the total amount of the loan (as much as $20,500) minus your eligibility for a *subsidized* Direct Loan (as much as $8,500). You may borrow up to the cost of attendance at the school in which you are enrolled or will attend, minus estimated financial assistance from other federal, state, and private sources, up to a maximum of $20,500.

Direct Stafford Loans made on or after July 1, 2006, carry a fixed interest rate of 6.8% both for in-school and in-repayment borrowers.

A fee is deducted from the loan proceeds upon disbursement. Loans with a first disbursement on or after July 1, 2010, have a borrower origination fee of 1 percent. The Department of Education offers a 0.5 percent origination fee rebate incentive. Borrowers must make their first twelve payments on time in order to retain the rebate.

Under the *subsidized* Federal Direct Stafford Loan Program, repayment begins six months after your last date of enrollment on at least a half-time basis. Under the *unsubsidized* program, repayment of interest begins within thirty days from disbursement of the loan proceeds, and repayment of the principal begins six months after your last enrollment on at least a half-time basis. Some borrowers may choose to defer interest payments while they are in school. The accrued interest is added to the loan balance when the borrower begins repayment. There are several repayment options.

Federal Perkins Loans. The Federal Perkins Loan is available to students demonstrating financial need and is administered directly by the school. Not all schools have these funds, and some may award them to undergraduates only. Eligibility is determined from the information you provide on the FAFSA. The school will notify you of your eligibility.

Eligible graduate students may borrow up to $6,000 per year, up to a maximum of $40,000, including undergraduate borrowing (even if your previous Perkins Loans have been repaid). The interest rate for Federal Perkins Loans is 5 percent, and no interest accrues while you remain in school at least half-time. There are no guarantee, loan, or disbursement fees. Repayment begins nine months after your last date of enrollment on at least a half-time basis and may extend over a maximum of ten years with no prepayment penalty.

Federal Direct Graduate PLUS Loans. Effective July 1, 2006, graduate and professional students are eligible for Graduate PLUS loans. This program allows students to borrow up to the cost of attendance, less any other aid received. These loans have a fixed interest rate of 7.9 percent, and interest begins to accrue at the time of disbursement. The PLUS loans do involve a credit check; a PLUS borrower may obtain a loan with a cosigner if his or her credit is not good enough. Grad PLUS loans may be deferred while a student in school and for the six months following a drop below half-time enrollment. For more information, contact your college financial aid office.

Deferring Your Federal Loan Repayments. If you borrowed under the Federal Direct Stafford Loan Program, Federal Direct PLUS Loan Program, or the Federal Perkins Loan Program for previous undergraduate or graduate study, your payments may be deferred when you return to graduate school, depending on when you borrowed and under which program.

There are other deferment options available if you are temporarily unable to repay your loan. Information about these deferments is provided at your entrance and exit interviews. If you believe you are eligible for a deferment of your loan payments, you must contact your lender or loan servicer to request a deferment. The deferment must be filed prior to the time your payment is due, and it must be refiled when it expires if you remain eligible for deferment at that time.

SUPPLEMENTAL (PRIVATE) LOANS

Many lending institutions offer supplemental loan programs and other financing plans, such as the ones described here, to students seeking additional assistance in meeting their education expenses. Some loan programs target all types of graduate students; others are designed specifically for business, law, or medical students. In addition, you can use private loans not specifically designed for education to help finance your graduate degree.

If you are considering borrowing through a supplemental or private loan program, you should carefully consider the terms and be sure to "read the fine print." Check with the program sponsor for the most current terms that will be applicable to the amounts you intend to borrow for graduate study. Most supplemental loan programs for graduate study offer unsubsidized, credit-based loans. In general, a credit-ready borrower is one who has a satisfactory credit history or no credit history at all. A creditworthy borrower generally must pass a credit test to be eligible to borrow or act as a cosigner for the loan funds.

Many supplemental loan programs have minimum and maximum annual loan limits. Some offer amounts equal to the cost of attendance minus any other aid you will receive for graduate study. If you are planning to borrow for several years of graduate study, consider whether there is a cumulative or aggregate limit on the amount you may borrow. Often this cumulative or aggregate limit will include any amounts you borrowed and have not repaid for undergraduate or previous graduate study.

The combination of the annual interest rate, loan fees, and the repayment terms you choose will determine how much you will repay over time. Compare these features in combination before you decide which loan program to use. Some loans offer interest rates that are adjusted monthly, some quarterly, some annually. Some offer interest rates that are lower during the in-school, grace, and deferment periods and then increase when you begin repayment. Some programs include a loan "origination" fee, which is usually deducted from the principal amount you receive when the loan is disbursed and must be repaid along with the interest and other principal when you graduate, withdraw from school, or drop below half-time study. Sometimes the loan fees are reduced if you borrow with a qualified cosigner. Some programs allow you to defer interest and/or principal payments while you are enrolled in graduate school. Many programs allow you to capitalize your interest payments; the interest due on your loan is added to the outstanding balance of your loan, so you don't have to repay immediately, but this increases the amount you owe. Other programs allow you to pay the interest as you go, which reduces the amount you later have to repay. The private loan market is very competitive, and your financial aid office can help you evaluate these programs.

Applying for Need-Based Financial Aid

Schools that award federal and institutional financial assistance based on need will require you to complete the FAFSA and, in some cases, an institutional financial aid application.

If you are applying for federal student assistance, you **must** complete the FAFSA. A service of the U.S. Department of Education,

6   www.facebook.com/petersonspublishing

Peterson's Graduate Programs in the Physical Sciences, Mathematics, Agricultural Sciences, the Environment & Natural Resources 2012

the FAFSA is free to all applicants. Most applicants apply online at www.fafsa.ed.gov. Paper applications are available at the financial aid office of your local college.

After your FAFSA information has been processed, you will receive a Student Aid Report (SAR). If you provided an e-mail address on the FAFSA, this will be sent to you electronically; otherwise, it will be mailed to your home address.

Follow the instructions on the SAR if you need to correct information reported on your original application. If your situation changes after you file your FAFSA, contact your financial aid officer to discuss amending your information. You can also appeal your financial aid award if you have extenuating circumstances.

If you would like more information on federal student financial aid, visit the FAFSA Web site or download the most recent version of *Funding Education Beyond High School: The Guide to Federal Student Aid* at http://studentaid.ed.gov/students/publications/student_guide/index.html. This guide is also available in Spanish.

The U.S. Department of Education also has a toll-free number for questions concerning federal student aid programs. The number is 1-800-4-FED AID (1-800-433-3243). If you are hearing impaired, call toll-free, 1-800-730-8913.

Summary

Remember that these are generalized statements about financial assistance at the graduate level. Because each institution allots its aid differently, you should communicate directly with the school and the specific department of interest to you. It is not unusual, for example, to find that an endowment vested within a specific department supports one or more fellowships. You may fit its requirements and specifications precisely.

Peterson's Graduate Programs in the Physical Sciences, Mathematics, Agricultural Sciences, the Environment & Natural Resources 2012

www.facebook.com/petersonspublishing   **7**

Accreditation and Accrediting Agencies

Colleges and universities in the United States, and their individual academic and professional programs, are accredited by nongovernmental agencies concerned with monitoring the quality of education in this country. Agencies with both regional and national jurisdictions grant accreditation to institutions as a whole, while specialized bodies acting on a nationwide basis—often national professional associations—grant accreditation to departments and programs in specific fields.

Institutional and specialized accrediting agencies share the same basic concerns: the purpose an academic unit—whether university or program—has set for itself and how well it fulfills that purpose, the adequacy of its financial and other resources, the quality of its academic offerings, and the level of services it provides. Agencies that grant institutional accreditation take a broader view, of course, and examine university-wide or college-wide services with which a specialized agency may not concern itself.

Both types of agencies follow the same general procedures when considering an application for accreditation. The academic unit prepares a self-evaluation, focusing on the concerns mentioned above and usually including an assessment of both its strengths and weaknesses; a team of representatives of the accrediting body reviews this evaluation, visits the campus, and makes its own report; and finally, the accrediting body makes a decision on the application. Often, even when accreditation is granted, the agency makes a recommendation regarding how the institution or program can improve. All institutions and programs are also reviewed every few years to determine whether they continue to meet established standards; if they do not, they may lose their accreditation.

Accrediting agencies themselves are reviewed and evaluated periodically by the U.S. Department of Education and the Council for Higher Education Accreditation (CHEA). Recognized agencies adhere to certain standards and practices, and their authority in matters of accreditation is widely accepted in the educational community.

This does not mean, however, that accreditation is a simple matter, either for schools wishing to become accredited or for students deciding where to apply. Indeed, in certain fields the very meaning and methods of accreditation are the subject of a good deal of debate. For their part, those applying to graduate school should be aware of the safeguards provided by regional accreditation, especially in terms of degree acceptance and institutional longevity. Beyond this, applicants should understand the role that specialized accreditation plays in their field, as this varies considerably from one discipline to another. In certain professional fields, it is necessary to have graduated from a program that is accredited in order to be eligible for a license to practice, and in some fields the federal government also makes this a hiring requirement. In other disciplines, however, accreditation is not as essential, and there can be excellent programs that are not accredited. In fact, some programs choose not to seek accreditation, although most do.

Institutions and programs that present themselves for accreditation are sometimes granted the status of candidate for accreditation, or what is known as "preaccreditation." This may happen, for example, when an academic unit is too new to have met all the requirements for accreditation. Such status signifies initial recognition and indicates that the school or program in question is working to fulfill all requirements; it does not, however, guarantee that accreditation will be granted.

Institutional Accrediting Agencies—Regional

MIDDLE STATES ASSOCIATION OF COLLEGES AND SCHOOLS
Accredits institutions in Delaware, District of Columbia, Maryland, New Jersey, New York, Pennsylvania, Puerto Rico, and the Virgin Islands.
Dr. Elizabeth Sibolski, President
Middle States Commission on Higher Education
3624 Market Street, Second Floor West
Philadelphia, Pennsylvania 19104
Phone: 267-284-5000
Fax: 215-662-5501
E-mail: info@msche.org
Web: www.msche.org

NEW ENGLAND ASSOCIATION OF SCHOOLS AND COLLEGES
Accredits institutions in Connecticut, Maine, Massachusetts, New Hampshire, Rhode Island, and Vermont.
Barbara E. Brittingham, Director
Commission on Institutions of Higher Education
209 Burlington Road, Suite 201
Bedford, Massachusetts 01730-1433
Phone: 781-271-0022
Fax: 781-271-0950
E-mail: kwillis@neasc.org
Web: www.neasc.org

NORTH CENTRAL ASSOCIATION OF COLLEGES AND SCHOOLS
Accredits institutions in Arizona, Arkansas, Colorado, Illinois, Indiana, Iowa, Kansas, Michigan, Minnesota, Missouri, Nebraska, New Mexico, North Dakota, Ohio, Oklahoma, South Dakota, West Virginia, Wisconsin, and Wyoming.
Dr. Sylvia Manning, President
The Higher Learning Commission
230 South LaSalle Street, Suite 7-500
Chicago, Illinois 60604-1413
Phone: 312-263-0456
Fax: 312-263-7462
E-mail: smanning@hlcommission.org
Web: www.ncahlc.org

NORTHWEST COMMISSION ON COLLEGES AND UNIVERSITIES
Accredits institutions in Alaska, Idaho, Montana, Nevada, Oregon, Utah, and Washington.
Dr. Sandra E. Elman, President
8060 165th Avenue, NE, Suite 100
Redmond, Washington 98052
Phone: 425-558-4224
Fax: 425-376-0596
E-mail: selman@nwccu.org
Web: www.nwccu.org

SOUTHERN ASSOCIATION OF COLLEGES AND SCHOOLS
Accredits institutions in Alabama, Florida, Georgia, Kentucky, Louisiana, Mississippi, North Carolina, South Carolina, Tennessee, Texas, and Virginia.
Belle S. Wheelan, President
Commission on Colleges
1866 Southern Lane
Decatur, Georgia 30033-4097
Phone: 404-679-4500
Fax: 404-679-4558
E-mail: questions@sacscoc.org
Web: www.sacscoc.org

WESTERN ASSOCIATION OF SCHOOLS AND COLLEGES
Accredits institutions in California, Guam, and Hawaii.
Ralph A. Wolff, President and Executive Director
Accrediting Commission for Senior Colleges and Universities
985 Atlantic Avenue, Suite 100
Alameda, California 94501
Phone: 510-748-9001
Fax: 510-748-9797
E-mail: www.wascsenior.org/contact
Web: www.wascweb.org/contact

Institutional Accrediting Agencies—Other

ACCREDITING COUNCIL FOR INDEPENDENT COLLEGES AND SCHOOLS
Albert C. Gray, Ph.D., Executive Director and CEO
750 First Street, NE, Suite 980
Washington, DC 20002-4241
Phone: 202-336-6780
Fax: 202-842-2593
E-mail: info@acics.org
Web: www.acics.org

DISTANCE EDUCATION AND TRAINING COUNCIL (DETC)
Accrediting Commission
Michael P. Lambert, Executive Director
1601 18th Street, NW, Suite 2
Washington, DC 20009
Phone: 202-234-5100
Fax: 202-332-1386
E-mail: Brianna@detc.org
Web: www.detc.org

Specialized Accrediting Agencies

[Only *Graduate & Professional Programs: An Overview* of *Peterson's Graduate and Professional Programs* Series includes the complete list of specialized accrediting groups recognized by the U.S. Department of Education and the Council on Higher Education Accreditation (CHEA). The list in this book is abridged.]

DIETETICS
Ulric K. Chung, Ph.D., Executive Director
American Dietetic Association
Commission on Accreditation for Dietetics Education (CADE-ADA)
120 South Riverside Plaza, Suite 2000
Chicago, Illinois 60606-6995
Phone: 800-877-1600
Fax: 312-899-4817
E-mail: cade@eatright.org
Web: www.eatright.org/cade

FORESTRY
Michael T. Goergen, Jr.
Executive Vice-President and CEO
Society of American Foresters (SAF)
5400 Grosvenor Lane
Bethesda, Maryland 20814-2198
Phone: 301-897-8720 Ext. 123
Fax: 301-897-3690
E-mail: goergenm@safnet.org
Web: www.safnet.org

10   www.facebook.com/petersonspublishing

Peterson's Graduate Programs in the Physical Sciences, Mathematics, Agricultural Sciences, the Environment & Natural Resources 2012

How to Use These Guides

As you identify the particular programs and institutions that interest you, you can use both the *Graduate & Professional Programs: An Overview* volume and the specialized volumes in the series to obtain detailed information.

- *Graduate Programs in the Physical Sciences, Mathematics, Agricultural Sciences, the Environment & Natural Resources*
- *Graduate Programs in Engineering & Applied Sciences*
- *Graduate Programs the Humanities, Arts & Social Sciences*
- *Graduate Programs in the Biological Sciences*
- *Graduate Programs in Business, Education, Health, Information Studies, Law & Social Work*

Each of the specialized volumes in the series is divided into sections that contain one or more directories devoted to programs in a particular field. If you do not find a directory devoted to your field of interest in a specific volume, consult "Directories and Subject Areas" (located at the end of each volume). After you have identified the correct volume, consult the "Directories and Subject Areas in This Book" index, which shows (as does the more general directory) what directories cover subjects not specifically named in a directory or section title.

Each of the specialized volumes in the series has a number of general directories. These directories have entries for the largest unit at an institution granting graduate degrees in that field. For example, the general Engineering and Applied Sciences directory in the *Graduate Programs in Engineering & Applied Sciences* volume consists of Profiles for colleges, schools, and departments of engineering and applied sciences.

General directories are followed by other directories, or sections, that give more detailed information about programs in particular areas of the general field that has been covered. The general Engineering and Applied Sciences directory, in the previous example, is followed by nineteen sections with directories in specific areas of engineering, such as Chemical Engineering, Industrial/Management Engineering, and Mechanical Engineering.

Because of the broad nature of many fields, any system of organization is bound to involve a certain amount of overlap. Environmental studies, for example, is a field whose various aspects are studied in several types of departments and schools. Readers interested in such studies will find information on relevant programs in the *Graduate Programs in the Biological Sciences* volume under Ecology and Environmental Biology; in the *Graduate Programs in the Physical Sciences, Mathematics, Agricultural Sciences, the Environment & Natural Resources* volume under Environmental Management and Policy and Natural Resources; in the *Graduate Programs in Engineering & Applied Sciences* volume under Energy Management and Policy and Environmental Engineering; and in the *Graduate Programs in Business, Education, Health, Information Studies, Law & Social Work* volume under Environmental and Occupational Health. To help you find all of the programs of interest to you, the introduction to each section within the specialized volumes includes, if applicable, a paragraph suggesting other sections and directories with information on related areas of study.

Directory of Institutions with Programs in the Physical Sciences, Mathematics, Agricultural Sciences, the Environment & Natural Resources

This directory lists institutions in alphabetical order and includes beneath each name the academic fields in which each institution offers graduate programs. The degree level in each field is also indicated, provided that the institution has supplied that information in response to Peterson's Annual Survey of Graduate and Professional Institutions.

An M indicates that a master's degree program is offered; a D indicates that a doctoral degree program is offered; a P indicates that the first professional degree is offered; an O signifies that other advanced degrees (e.g., certificates or specialist degrees) are offered; and an * (asterisk) indicates that a **Close-Up** and/or **Display** is located in this volume. See the index, "Close-Ups and Displays," for the specific page number.

Profiles of Academic and Professional Programs in the Specialized Volumes

Each section of **Profiles** has a table of contents that lists the Program Directories, **Displays**, and **Close-Ups**. Program Directories consist of the **Profiles** of programs in the relevant fields, with **Displays** following if programs have chosen to include them. **Close-Ups,** which are more individualized statements, again if programs have chosen to submit them, are also listed.

The **Profiles** found in the 500 directories in the specialized volumes provide basic data about the graduate units in capsule form for quick reference. To make these directories as useful as possible, **Profiles** are generally listed for an institution's smallest academic unit within a subject area. In other words, if an institution has a College of Liberal Arts that administers many related programs, the **Profile** for the individual program (e.g., Program in History), not the entire College, appears in the directory.

There are some programs that do not fit into any current directory and are not given individual **Profiles**. The directory structure is reviewed annually in order to keep this number to a minimum and to accommodate major trends in graduate education.

The following outline describes the **Profile** information found in the guides and explains how best to use that information. Any item that does not apply to or was not provided by a graduate unit is omitted from its listing. The format of the **Profiles** is constant, making it easy to compare one institution with another and one program with another.

Identifying Information. The institution's name, in boldface type, is followed by a complete listing of the administrative structure for that field of study. (For example, University of Akron, Buchtel College of Arts and Sciences, Department of Theoretical and Applied Mathematics, Program in Mathematics.) The last unit listed is the one to which all information in the **Profile** pertains. The institution's city, state, and zip code follow.

Offerings. Each field of study offered by the unit is listed with all postbaccalaureate degrees awarded. Degrees that are not preceded by a specific concentration are awarded in the general field listed in the unit name. Frequently, fields of study are broken down into subspecializations, and those appear following the degrees awarded; for example, "Offerings in secondary education (M.Ed.), including English education, mathematics education, science education." Students enrolled in the M.Ed. program would be able to specialize in any of the three fields mentioned.

Professional Accreditation. Some **Profiles** indicate whether a program is professionally accredited. Because it is possible for a program to receive or lose professional accreditation at any time, students entering fields in which accreditation is important to a career should verify the status of programs by contacting either the chairperson or the appropriate accrediting association.

Jointly Offered Degrees. Explanatory statements concerning programs that are offered in cooperation with other institutions are included in the list of degrees offered. This occurs most commonly on a regional basis (for example, two state universities offering a cooperative Ph.D. in special education) or where the specialized nature of the institutions encourages joint efforts (a J.D./M.B.A. offered by a law school at an institution with no formal business programs and an institution with a business school but lacking a law school). Only

programs that are truly cooperative are listed; those involving only limited course work at another institution are not. Interested students should contact the heads of such units for further information.

Part-Time and Evening/Weekend Programs. When information regarding the availability of part-time or evening/weekend study appears in the **Profile**, it means that students are able to earn a degree exclusively through such study.

Postbaccalaureate Distance Learning Degrees. A postbaccalaureate distance learning degree program signifies that course requirements can be fulfilled with minimal or no on-campus study.

Faculty. Figures on the number of faculty members actively involved with graduate students through teaching or research are separated into full-and part-time as well as men and women whenever the information has been supplied.

Students. Figures for the number of students enrolled in graduate and professional programs pertain to the semester of highest enrollment from the 2010–11 academic year. These figures are broken down into full-and part-time and men and women whenever the data have been supplied. Information on the number of matriculated students enrolled in the unit who are members of a minority group or are international students appears here. The average age of the matriculated students is followed by the number of applicants, the percentage accepted, and the number enrolled for fall 2010.

Degrees Awarded. The number of degrees awarded in the calendar year is listed. Many doctoral programs offer a terminal master's degree if students leave the program after completing only part of the requirements for a doctoral degree; that is indicated here. All degrees are classified into one of four types: master's, doctoral, first professional, and other advanced degrees. A unit may award one or several degrees at a given level; however, the data are only collected by type and may therefore represent several different degree programs.

Degree Requirements. The information in this section is also broken down by type of degree, and all information for a degree level pertains to all degrees of that type unless otherwise specified. Degree requirements are collected in a simplified form to provide some very basic information on the nature of the program and on foreign language, thesis or dissertation, comprehensive exam, and registration requirements. Many units also provide a short list of additional requirements, such as fieldwork or an internship. For complete information on graduation requirements, contact the graduate school or program directly.

Entrance Requirements. Entrance requirements are broken down into the four degree levels of master's, doctoral, first professional, and other advanced degrees. Within each level, information may be provided in two basic categories: entrance exams and other requirements. The entrance exams are identified by the standard acronyms used by the testing agencies, unless they are not well known. Other entrance requirements are quite varied, but they often contain an undergraduate or graduate grade point average (GPA). Unless otherwise stated, the GPA is calculated on a 4.0 scale and is listed as a minimum required for admission. Additional exam requirements/recommendations for international students may be listed here. Application deadlines for domestic and international students, the application fee, and whether electronic applications are accepted may be listed here. Note that the deadline should be used for reference only; these dates are subject to change, and students interested in applying should always contact the graduate unit directly about application procedures and deadlines.

Expenses. The typical cost of study for the 2010–11 academic year is given in two basic categories: tuition and fees. Cost of study may be quite complex at a graduate institution. There are often sliding scales for part-time study, a different cost for first-year students, and other variables that make it impossible to completely cover the cost of study for each graduate program. To provide the most usable information, figures are given for full-time study for a full year where available and for part-time study in terms of a per-unit rate (per credit, per semester hour, etc.). Occasionally, variances may be noted in tuition and fees for reasons such as the type of program, whether courses are taken during the day or evening, whether courses are at the master's or doctoral level, or other institution-specific reasons. Expenses are usually subject to change; for exact costs at any given time, contact your chosen schools and programs directly. Keep in mind that the tuition of Canadian institutions is usually given in Canadian dollars.

Financial Support. This section contains data on the number of awards administered by the institution and given to graduate students during the 2010–11 academic year. The first figure given represents the total number of students receiving financial support enrolled in that unit. If the unit has provided information on graduate appointments, these are broken down into three major categories: fellowships give money to graduate students to cover the cost of study and living expenses and are not based on a work obligation or research commitment, research assistantships provide stipends to graduate students for assistance in a formal research project with a faculty member, and teaching assistantships provide stipends to graduate students for teaching or for assisting faculty members in teaching undergraduate classes. Within each category, figures are given for the total number of awards, the average yearly amount per award, and whether full or partial tuition reimbursements are awarded. In addition to graduate appointments, the availability of several other financial aid sources is covered in this section. Tuition waivers are routinely part of a graduate appointment, but units sometimes waive part or all of a student's tuition even if a graduate appointment is not available. Federal Work-Study is made available to students who demonstrate need and meet the federal guidelines; this form of aid normally includes 10 or more hours of work per week in an office of the institution. Institutionally sponsored loans are low-interest loans available to graduate students to cover both educational and living expenses. Career-related internships or fieldwork offer money to students who are participating in a formal off-campus research project or practicum. Grants, scholarships, traineeships, unspecified assistantships, and other awards may also be noted. The availability of financial support to part-time students is also indicated here.

Some programs list the financial aid application deadline and the forms that need to be completed for students to be eligible for financial awards. There are two forms: FAFSA, the Free Application for Federal Student Aid, which is required for federal aid, and the CSS PROFILE®.

Faculty Research. Each unit has the opportunity to list several keyword phrases describing the current research involving faculty members and graduate students. Space limitations prevent the unit from listing complete information on all research programs. The total expenditure for funded research from the previous academic year may also be included.

Unit Head and Application Contact. The head of the graduate program for each unit is listed with academic title and telephone and fax numbers and e-mail address if available. In addition to the unit head, many graduate programs list a separate contact for application and admission information, which follows the listing for the unit head. If no unit head or application contact is given, you should contact the overall institution for information on graduate admissions.

Displays and Close-Ups

The **Displays** and **Close-Ups** are supplementary insertions submitted by deans, chairs, and other administrators who wish to offer an additional, more individualized statement to readers. A number of graduate school and program administrators have attached a **Display** ad near the **Profile** listing. Here you will find information that an institution or program wants to emphasize. The **Close-Ups** are by their very nature more expansive and flexible than the **Profiles**, and the administrators who have written them may emphasize different aspects of their programs. All of the **Close-Ups** are organized in the same way (with the exception of a few that describe research and training opportunities instead of degree programs), and in each one you will find information on the same basic topics, such as programs of study, research facilities, tuition and fees, financial aid, and application procedures. If an institution or program has submitted a **Close-Up**, a boldface cross-reference appears below its **Profile**. As with the **Displays**, all of the **Close-Ups** in the guides have been submitted by choice; the absence of a **Display** or **Close-Up** does not reflect any type of editorial judgment on the part of Peterson's, and their presence in the guides should not be taken as an indication of status, quality, or approval. Statements regarding a university's objectives and accomplishments are a reflection of its own beliefs and are not the opinions of the Peterson's editors.

12 www.facebook.com/petersonspublishing

Peterson's Graduate Programs in the Physical Sciences, Mathematics, Agricultural Sciences, the Environment & Natural Resources 2012

Appendixes

This section contains two appendixes. The first, "Institutional Changes Since the 2011 Edition," lists institutions that have closed, merged, or changed their name or status since the last edition of the guides. The second, "Abbreviations Used in the Guides," gives abbreviations of degree names, along with what those abbreviations stand for. These appendixes are identical in all six volumes of *Peterson's Graduate and Professional Programs*.

Indexes

There are three indexes presented here. The first index, "Close-Ups and Displays," gives page references for all programs that have chosen to place **Close-Ups** and **Displays** in this volume. It is arranged alphabetically by institution; within institutions, the arrangement is alphabetical by subject area. It is not an index to all programs in the book's directories of **Profiles**; readers must refer to the directories themselves for **Profile** information on programs that have not submitted the additional, more individualized statements. The second index, "Directories and Subject Areas in Other Books in This Series", gives book references for the directories in the specialized volumes and also includes cross-references for subject area names not used in the directory structure, for example, "Computing Technology (see Computer Science)." The third index, "Directories and Subject Areas in This Book," gives page references for the directories in this volume and cross-references for subject area names not used in this volume's directory structure.

Data Collection Procedures

The information published in the directories and **Profiles** of all the books is collected through Peterson's Annual Survey of Graduate and Professional Institutions. The survey is sent each spring to nearly 2,400 institutions offering postbaccalaureate degree programs, including accredited institutions in the United States, U.S. territories, and Canada and those institutions outside the United States that are accredited by U.S. accrediting bodies. Deans and other administrators complete these surveys, providing information on programs in the 500 academic and professional fields covered in the guides as well as overall institutional information. While every effort has been made to ensure the accuracy and completeness of the data, information is sometimes unavailable or changes occur after publication deadlines. All usable information received in time for publication has been included. The omission of any particular item from a directory or **Profile** signifies either that the item is not applicable to the institution or program or that information was not available. **Profiles** of programs scheduled to begin during the 2011–12 academic year cannot, obviously, include statistics on enrollment or, in many cases, the number of faculty members. If no usable data were submitted by an institution, its name, address, and program name appear in order to indicate the availability of graduate work.

Criteria for Inclusion in This Guide

To be included in this guide, an institution must have full accreditation or be a candidate for accreditation (preaccreditation) status by an institutional or specialized accrediting body recognized by the U.S. Department of Education or the Council for Higher Education Accreditation (CHEA). Institutional accrediting bodies, which review each institution as a whole, include the six regional associations of schools and colleges (Middle States, New England, North Central, Northwest, Southern, and Western), each of which is responsible for a specified portion of the United States and its territories. Other institutional accrediting bodies are national in scope and accredit specific kinds of institutions (e.g., Bible colleges, independent colleges, and rabbinical and Talmudic schools). Program registration by the New York State Board of Regents is considered to be the equivalent of institutional accreditation, since the board requires that all programs offered by an institution meet its standards before recognition is granted. A Canadian institution must be chartered and authorized to grant degrees by the provincial government, affiliated with a chartered institution, or accredited by a recognized U.S. accrediting body. This guide also includes institutions outside the United States that are accredited by these U.S. accrediting bodies. There are recognized specialized or professional accrediting bodies in more than fifty different fields, each of which is authorized to accredit institutions or specific programs in its particular field. For specialized institutions that offer programs in one field only, we designate this to be the equivalent of institutional accreditation. A full explanation of the accrediting process and complete information on recognized institutional (regional and national) and specialized accrediting bodies can be found online at www.chea.org or at www.ed.gov/admins/finaid/accred/index.html.

NOTICE: Certain portions of or information contained in this book have been submitted and paid for by the educational institution identified, and such institutions take full responsibility for the accuracy, timeliness, completeness and functionality of such contents. Such portions or information include (i) each display ad that comprises a half page of information covering a single educational institution or program and (ii) each two-page description or Close-Up of a graduate school or program that appear in the different sections of this guide. The "Close-Ups and Displays" are listed in various sections throughout the book.

DIRECTORY OF INSTITUTIONS WITH PROGRAMS IN THE PHYSICAL SCIENCES, MATHEMATICS, AGRICULTURAL SCIENCES, THE ENVIRONMENT & NATURAL RESOURCES

ACADIA UNIVERSITY

Applied Mathematics	M
Chemistry	M
Geology	M
Statistics	M

ADELPHI UNIVERSITY

Environmental Management and Policy	M*

AIR FORCE INSTITUTE OF TECHNOLOGY

Applied Mathematics	M,D
Applied Physics	M,D
Astrophysics	M,D
Environmental Management and Policy	M
Optical Sciences	M,D
Planetary and Space Sciences	M,D

ALABAMA AGRICULTURAL AND MECHANICAL UNIVERSITY

Agricultural Sciences— General	M,D
Agronomy and Soil Sciences	M,D
Animal Sciences	M,D
Applied Physics	M,D
Environmental Sciences	M,D
Food Science and Technology	M,D
Optical Sciences	M,D
Physics	M,D
Plant Sciences	M,D

ALABAMA STATE UNIVERSITY

Environmental Sciences	M,D
Geology	M,D
Geosciences	M,D
Mathematics	M,O

ALASKA PACIFIC UNIVERSITY

Environmental Sciences	M

ALBANY STATE UNIVERSITY

Water Resources	M

ALCORN STATE UNIVERSITY

Agricultural Sciences— General	M
Agronomy and Soil Sciences	M
Animal Sciences	M

AMERICAN PUBLIC UNIVERSITY SYSTEM

Environmental Management and Policy	M

AMERICAN UNIVERSITY

Applied Statistics	M,O
Chemistry	M,O
Environmental Management and Policy	M,D,O
Environmental Sciences	M,O
Marine Sciences	M
Mathematics	M,O
Natural Resources	M,D,O
Statistics	M,O

THE AMERICAN UNIVERSITY IN CAIRO

Chemistry	M

AMERICAN UNIVERSITY OF BEIRUT

Agronomy and Soil Sciences	M
Animal Sciences	M
Aquaculture	M
Biostatistics	M
Chemistry	M
Computational Sciences	M

Environmental Management and Policy	M
Environmental Sciences	M,D
Food Science and Technology	M
Geology	M
Mathematics	M
Physics	M
Plant Sciences	M
Statistics	M

ANDREWS UNIVERSITY

Mathematics	M

ANGELO STATE UNIVERSITY

Agricultural Sciences— General	M
Animal Sciences	M

ANTIOCH UNIVERSITY NEW ENGLAND

Environmental Management and Policy	M,D
Environmental Sciences	M,D

ANTIOCH UNIVERSITY SEATTLE

Environmental Management and Policy	M

APPALACHIAN STATE UNIVERSITY

Environmental Management and Policy	M
Mathematics	M

ARIZONA STATE UNIVERSITY

Applied Mathematics	M,D,O
Astrophysics	M,D
Atmospheric Sciences	M,D,O
Chemistry	M,D
Environmental Management and Policy	M
Environmental Sciences	M,D,O
Geology	M,D
Geosciences	M,D
Mathematics	M,D
Physics	M,D
Planetary and Space Sciences	M,D
Statistics	M,D,O

ARKANSAS STATE UNIVERSITY

Agricultural Sciences— General	M,O
Chemistry	M,O
Environmental Sciences	M,D
Mathematics	M

ARKANSAS TECH UNIVERSITY

Fish, Game, and Wildlife Management	M

AUBURN UNIVERSITY

Agricultural Sciences— General	M,D
Agronomy and Soil Sciences	M,D
Analytical Chemistry	M,D
Animal Sciences	M,D
Applied Mathematics	M,D
Aquaculture	M,D
Chemistry	M,D
Fish, Game, and Wildlife Management	M,D
Food Science and Technology	M,D
Forestry	M,D
Geology	M
Horticulture	M,D
Hydrology	M,D
Inorganic Chemistry	M,D
Mathematics	M,D
Natural Resources	M,D
Organic Chemistry	M,D
Physical Chemistry	M,D
Physics	M,D
Statistics	M,D

AURORA UNIVERSITY

Mathematics	M

BALL STATE UNIVERSITY

Chemistry	M
Geology	M
Mathematics	M
Natural Resources	M
Physics	M
Statistics	M

BARD COLLEGE

Atmospheric Sciences	M,O
Environmental Management and Policy	M,O

BAYLOR UNIVERSITY

Chemistry	M,D
Environmental Management and Policy	M
Environmental Sciences	D
Geology	M,D
Geosciences	M,D
Limnology	M,D
Mathematics	M,D
Physics	M,D
Statistics	M,D

BEMIDJI STATE UNIVERSITY

Environmental Management and Policy	M
Mathematics	M

BERNARD M. BARUCH COLLEGE OF THE CITY UNIVERSITY OF NEW YORK

Mathematical and Computational Finance	M
Statistics	M

BOISE STATE UNIVERSITY

Animal Sciences	M
Environmental Management and Policy	M
Geology	M,D
Geophysics	M,D
Geosciences	M

BOSTON COLLEGE

Chemistry	M,D
Geology	M
Geophysics	M
Inorganic Chemistry	M,D
Mathematics	D
Organic Chemistry	M,D
Physical Chemistry	M,D
Physics	M,D

BOSTON UNIVERSITY

Astronomy	M,D
Biostatistics	M,D
Chemistry	M,D,O
Environmental Management and Policy	M,D,O
Food Science and Technology	M
Geosciences	M,D,O
Mathematical and Computational Finance	M,D
Mathematics	M,D
Photonics	M,D
Physics	M,D,O*

BOWIE STATE UNIVERSITY

Applied Mathematics	M

BOWLING GREEN STATE UNIVERSITY

Applied Statistics	M,D
Chemistry	M,D
Geology	M
Geophysics	M
Mathematics	M,D
Physics	M
Statistics	M,D

BRADLEY UNIVERSITY

Chemistry	M

BRANDEIS UNIVERSITY

Chemistry	M,D
Inorganic Chemistry	M,D
Mathematics	M,D,O
Organic Chemistry	M,D
Physical Chemistry	M,D
Physics	M,D

BRIGHAM YOUNG UNIVERSITY

Agricultural Sciences— General	M,D
Analytical Chemistry	M,D
Animal Sciences	M,D
Applied Statistics	M
Astronomy	M,D
Chemistry	M,D
Environmental Sciences	M,D
Fish, Game, and Wildlife Management	M,D
Food Science and Technology	M
Geology	M
Mathematics	M,D
Physics	M,D
Plant Sciences	M,D
Statistics	M

BROCK UNIVERSITY

Chemistry	M,D
Geosciences	M
Mathematics	M
Physics	M
Statistics	M

BROOKLYN COLLEGE OF THE CITY UNIVERSITY OF NEW YORK

Chemistry	M,D
Geology	M,D
Geosciences	M,O
Mathematics	M,D
Physics	M,D

BROWN UNIVERSITY

Applied Mathematics	M,D
Biostatistics	M,D
Chemistry	M,D
Environmental Management and Policy	M
Geosciences	M,D
Mathematics	M,D
Physics	M,D

BRYN MAWR COLLEGE

Chemistry	M,D*
Mathematics	M,D*
Physics	M,D*

BUCKNELL UNIVERSITY

Chemistry	M
Mathematics	M

BUFFALO STATE COLLEGE, STATE UNIVERSITY OF NEW YORK

Chemistry	M

CALIFORNIA INSTITUTE OF TECHNOLOGY

Applied Mathematics	M,D
Applied Physics	M,D
Astronomy	D
Chemistry	M,D
Computational Sciences	M,D
Geochemistry	M,D
Geology	M,D
Geophysics	M,D
Mathematics	D
Physics	D
Planetary and Space Sciences	M,D

CALIFORNIA POLYTECHNIC STATE UNIVERSITY, SAN LUIS OBISPO

Agricultural Sciences—General	M
Chemistry	M
Forestry	M
Mathematics	M
Natural Resources	M

CALIFORNIA STATE POLYTECHNIC UNIVERSITY, POMONA

Agricultural Sciences—General	M
Applied Mathematics	M
Chemistry	M
Environmental Sciences	M
Mathematics	M

CALIFORNIA STATE UNIVERSITY, BAKERSFIELD

Geology	M
Hydrology	M

CALIFORNIA STATE UNIVERSITY CHANNEL ISLANDS

Mathematics	M

CALIFORNIA STATE UNIVERSITY, CHICO

Environmental Sciences	M
Geology	M
Geosciences	M
Hydrogeology	M
Hydrology	M

CALIFORNIA STATE UNIVERSITY, DOMINGUEZ HILLS

Environmental Sciences	M

CALIFORNIA STATE UNIVERSITY, EAST BAY

Applied Mathematics	M
Biostatistics	M
Chemistry	M
Environmental Sciences	M
Geology	M
Marine Sciences	M
Mathematics	M
Statistics	M

CALIFORNIA STATE UNIVERSITY, FRESNO

Animal Sciences	M
Chemistry	M
Food Science and Technology	M
Geology	M
Marine Sciences	M
Mathematics	M
Physics	M
Plant Sciences	M
Viticulture and Enology	M

CALIFORNIA STATE UNIVERSITY, FULLERTON

Applied Mathematics	M
Chemistry	M
Environmental Management and Policy	M
Environmental Sciences	M
Geochemistry	M
Geology	M
Mathematics	M
Physics	M

CALIFORNIA STATE UNIVERSITY, LONG BEACH

Applied Mathematics	M,D
Applied Statistics	M
Chemistry	M

Food Science and Technology	M
Geology	M
Geophysics	M
Mathematics	M
Physics	M

CALIFORNIA STATE UNIVERSITY, LOS ANGELES

Analytical Chemistry	M
Applied Mathematics	M
Chemistry	M
Geology	M
Inorganic Chemistry	M
Mathematics	M
Organic Chemistry	M
Physical Chemistry	M
Physics	M

CALIFORNIA STATE UNIVERSITY, MONTEREY BAY

Marine Sciences	M
Water Resources	M

CALIFORNIA STATE UNIVERSITY, NORTHRIDGE

Applied Mathematics	M
Chemistry	M
Environmental Sciences	M
Geology	M
Mathematics	M
Physics	M

CALIFORNIA STATE UNIVERSITY, SACRAMENTO

Chemistry	M
Marine Sciences	M
Mathematics	M
Statistics	M

CALIFORNIA STATE UNIVERSITY, SAN BERNARDINO

Chemistry	M
Environmental Sciences	M
Mathematics	M

CALIFORNIA STATE UNIVERSITY, SAN MARCOS

Mathematics	M

CARLETON UNIVERSITY

Chemistry	M,D
Geosciences	M,D
Mathematics	M,D
Physics	M,D

CARNEGIE MELLON UNIVERSITY

Applied Mathematics	M,D
Applied Physics	M,D
Chemistry	M,D
Computational Sciences	M,D
Inorganic Chemistry	M,D
Mathematical and Computational Finance	M,D
Mathematics	M,D
Organic Chemistry	M,D
Physics	M,D
Statistics	M,D
Theoretical Chemistry	M,D

CASE WESTERN RESERVE UNIVERSITY

Applied Mathematics	M,D
Astronomy	M,D
Biostatistics	M,D
Chemistry	M,D
Geology	M,D
Geosciences	M,D
Mathematics	M,D
Physics	M,D
Statistics	M,D

THE CATHOLIC UNIVERSITY OF AMERICA

Physics	M,D

CENTRAL CONNECTICUT STATE UNIVERSITY

Chemistry	M,O
Geosciences	M,O
Mathematics	M,O
Physics	M,O
Statistics	M,O

CENTRAL EUROPEAN UNIVERSITY

Applied Mathematics	M,D
Environmental Management and Policy	M,D

CENTRAL MICHIGAN UNIVERSITY

Chemistry	M
Mathematics	M,D
Physics	M,D

CENTRAL WASHINGTON UNIVERSITY

Chemistry	M
Geology	M
Mathematics	M
Natural Resources	M

CHAPMAN UNIVERSITY

Food Science and Technology	M

CHICAGO STATE UNIVERSITY

Mathematics	M

CHRISTOPHER NEWPORT UNIVERSITY

Applied Physics	M
Chemistry	M
Environmental Sciences	M
Physics	M

CITY COLLEGE OF THE CITY UNIVERSITY OF NEW YORK

Atmospheric Sciences	M,D
Chemistry	M,D
Environmental Sciences	M,D
Geosciences	M,D
Mathematics	M
Physics	M,D

CLAREMONT GRADUATE UNIVERSITY

Applied Mathematics	M,D
Computational Sciences	M,D
Mathematics	M,D
Statistics	M,D

CLARK ATLANTA UNIVERSITY

Chemistry	M,D
Mathematics	M
Physics	M

CLARKSON UNIVERSITY

Chemistry	M,D
Environmental Sciences	M,D
Mathematics	M,D
Physics	M,D

CLARK UNIVERSITY

Chemistry	M,D
Environmental Management and Policy	M
Physics	M,D

CLEMSON UNIVERSITY

Agricultural Sciences—General	M,D
Animal Sciences	M,D
Applied Mathematics	M,D
Aquaculture	M,D

Astronomy	M,D
Astrophysics	M,D
Atmospheric Sciences	M,D
Chemistry	M,D
Computational Sciences	M,D
Environmental Management and Policy	M,D
Environmental Sciences	M,D
Fish, Game, and Wildlife Management	M,D
Food Science and Technology	M,D
Forestry	M,D
Hydrogeology	M
Mathematics	M,D
Physics	M,D
Plant Sciences	M,D
Statistics	M,D

CLEVELAND STATE UNIVERSITY

Analytical Chemistry	M,D
Chemistry	M,D
Condensed Matter Physics	M
Environmental Management and Policy	M,O
Environmental Sciences	M,D
Inorganic Chemistry	M,D
Mathematics	M
Optical Sciences	M
Organic Chemistry	M,D
Physical Chemistry	M,D
Physics	M

COASTAL CAROLINA UNIVERSITY

Marine Sciences	M

THE COLLEGE AT BROCKPORT, STATE UNIVERSITY OF NEW YORK

Computational Sciences	M
Environmental Sciences	M
Mathematics	M

COLLEGE OF CHARLESTON

Environmental Sciences	M
Marine Sciences	M
Mathematics	M,O

COLLEGE OF STATEN ISLAND OF THE CITY UNIVERSITY OF NEW YORK

Environmental Sciences	M

COLLEGE OF THE ATLANTIC

Environmental Management and Policy	M

THE COLLEGE OF WILLIAM AND MARY

Chemistry	M
Computational Sciences	M
Marine Sciences	M,D
Physics	M,D

COLORADO SCHOOL OF MINES

Applied Physics	M,D
Chemistry	M,D
Environmental Sciences	M,D
Geochemistry	M,D
Geology	M,D
Geophysics	M,D
Mathematics	M,D
Physics	M,D

COLORADO STATE UNIVERSITY

Agricultural Sciences—General	M,D
Agronomy and Soil Sciences	M,D
Animal Sciences	M,D
Atmospheric Sciences	M,D
Chemistry	M,D
Fish, Game, and Wildlife Management	M,D

*M—master's degree; P—first professional degree; D—doctorate; O—other advanced degree; *—Close-Up and / or Display*

Peterson's Graduate Programs in the Physical Sciences, Mathematics, Agricultural Sciences, the Environment & Natural Resources 2012

www.facebook.com/petersonspublishing   **17**

Food Science and Technology	M,D
Forestry	M,D
Geosciences	M,D
Horticulture	M,D
Hydrology	M,D
Mathematics	M,D
Natural Resources	M,D
Physics	M,D
Plant Sciences	M,D
Range Science	M,D
Statistics	M,D
Water Resources	M,D

COLORADO STATE UNIVERSITY–PUEBLO

Chemistry	M

COLUMBIA UNIVERSITY

Applied Mathematics	M,D,O
Applied Physics	M,D,O*
Astronomy	M,D
Atmospheric Sciences	M,D
Biostatistics	M,D
Chemical Physics	M,D
Chemistry	M,D
Environmental Management and Policy	M
Environmental Sciences	M*
Geochemistry	M,D
Geodetic Sciences	M,D
Geophysics	M,D
Geosciences	M,D
Inorganic Chemistry	M,D
Mathematics	M,D
Meteorology	M
Oceanography	M,D
Organic Chemistry	M,D
Physics	M,D
Planetary and Space Sciences	M,D
Statistics	M,D

COLUMBUS STATE UNIVERSITY

Environmental Sciences	M

CONCORDIA UNIVERSITY (CANADA)

Chemistry	M,D
Environmental Management and Policy	M,O
Mathematics	M,D
Physics	M,D

CORNELL UNIVERSITY

Agronomy and Soil Sciences	M,D
Analytical Chemistry	D
Animal Sciences	M,D
Applied Mathematics	M,D
Applied Physics	M,D
Applied Statistics	M,D
Astronomy	D
Astrophysics	D
Atmospheric Sciences	M,D
Biometry	M,D
Chemical Physics	D
Chemistry	D
Computational Sciences	M,D
Environmental Management and Policy	M,D
Environmental Sciences	M,D
Fish, Game, and Wildlife Management	M,D
Food Science and Technology	M,D
Forestry	M,D
Geochemistry	M,D
Geology	M,D
Geophysics	M,D
Geosciences	M,D
Horticulture	M,D
Hydrology	M,D
Inorganic Chemistry	D
Limnology	D
Marine Geology	M,D
Marine Sciences	M,D

Mathematics	D
Mineralogy	M,D
Natural Resources	M,D
Oceanography	D
Organic Chemistry	D
Paleontology	M,D
Physical Chemistry	D
Physics	M,D
Planetary and Space Sciences	D
Plant Sciences	M,D
Statistics	M,D
Theoretical Chemistry	D
Theoretical Physics	M,D

CREIGHTON UNIVERSITY

Atmospheric Sciences	M
Physics	M

DALHOUSIE UNIVERSITY

Agricultural Sciences—General	M
Applied Mathematics	M,D
Chemistry	M,D
Environmental Management and Policy	M
Food Science and Technology	M,D
Geosciences	M,D
Marine Affairs	M
Mathematics	M,D
Natural Resources	M
Oceanography	M,D
Physics	M,D
Statistics	M,D

DARTMOUTH COLLEGE

Astronomy	M,D
Chemistry	D
Geosciences	M,D
Mathematics	D
Physics	M,D

DELAWARE STATE UNIVERSITY

Applied Mathematics	M,D
Chemistry	M
Mathematics	M
Natural Resources	M
Optical Sciences	M,D
Physics	M,D
Plant Sciences	M
Theoretical Physics	D

DEPAUL UNIVERSITY

Applied Mathematics	M,O
Applied Physics	M
Applied Statistics	M,O
Chemistry	M
Mathematical and Computational Finance	M,D
Mathematics	M,O
Physics	M

DOWLING COLLEGE

Mathematics	M

DREW UNIVERSITY

Chemistry	M
Physics	M

DREXEL UNIVERSITY

Biostatistics	M,D,O
Chemistry	M,D
Environmental Management and Policy	M
Environmental Sciences	M,D
Food Science and Technology	M
Hydrology	M,D
Mathematics	M,D
Physics	M,D

DUKE UNIVERSITY

Biostatistics	M
Chemistry	D

Environmental Management and Policy	M,D
Environmental Sciences	M,D
Forestry	M
Geology	M,D
Marine Affairs	M
Marine Sciences	M
Mathematics	D
Natural Resources	M,D
Optical Sciences	M
Paleontology	D
Photonics	M
Physics	M,D
Statistics	D
Water Resources	M

DUQUESNE UNIVERSITY

Chemistry	M,D
Environmental Management and Policy	M,O
Environmental Sciences	M,O
Mathematics	M

EAST CAROLINA UNIVERSITY

Applied Mathematics	M
Chemistry	M
Geology	M
Marine Affairs	D
Mathematics	M
Natural Resources	D
Physics	M,D

EASTERN ILLINOIS UNIVERSITY

Chemistry	M
Mathematics	M

EASTERN KENTUCKY UNIVERSITY

Chemistry	M
Geology	M,D
Mathematics	M

EASTERN MICHIGAN UNIVERSITY

Applied Statistics	M
Chemistry	M
Geosciences	M
Mathematics	M
Physics	M
Water Resources	M,O

EASTERN NEW MEXICO UNIVERSITY

Analytical Chemistry	M
Chemistry	M
Inorganic Chemistry	M
Mathematics	M
Organic Chemistry	M
Physical Chemistry	M

EASTERN WASHINGTON UNIVERSITY

Mathematics	M

EAST TENNESSEE STATE UNIVERSITY

Biostatistics	M,D,O
Chemistry	M
Mathematics	M
Paleontology	M

ÉCOLE POLYTECHNIQUE DE MONTRÉAL

Applied Mathematics	M,D,O
Optical Sciences	M,D,O

ELIZABETH CITY STATE UNIVERSITY

Mathematics	M

EMORY UNIVERSITY

Biostatistics	M,D
Chemistry	D
Condensed Matter Physics	D
Mathematics	M,D
Physics	D

EMPORIA STATE UNIVERSITY

Geosciences	M,O
Mathematics	M

THE EVERGREEN STATE COLLEGE

Environmental Management and Policy	M

FAIRFIELD UNIVERSITY

Mathematics	M

FAIRLEIGH DICKINSON UNIVERSITY, COLLEGE AT FLORHAM

Chemistry	M

FAIRLEIGH DICKINSON UNIVERSITY, METROPOLITAN CAMPUS

Chemistry	M
Mathematics	M

FAYETTEVILLE STATE UNIVERSITY

Mathematics	M

FISK UNIVERSITY

Chemistry	M
Physics	M

FLORIDA AGRICULTURAL AND MECHANICAL UNIVERSITY

Agricultural Sciences—General	M
Animal Sciences	M
Chemistry	M
Environmental Sciences	M,D
Food Science and Technology	M
Physics	M,D
Plant Sciences	M

FLORIDA ATLANTIC UNIVERSITY

Applied Mathematics	M,D
Chemistry	M,D
Environmental Management and Policy	M,O
Environmental Sciences	M
Geology	M,D
Geosciences	M,D
Mathematics	M,D
Physics	M,D
Statistics	M,D

FLORIDA GULF COAST UNIVERSITY

Environmental Management and Policy	M
Environmental Sciences	M

FLORIDA INSTITUTE OF TECHNOLOGY

Applied Mathematics	M,D
Chemistry	M,D
Environmental Management and Policy	M,D
Environmental Sciences	M,D
Meteorology	M,D
Oceanography	M,D
Physics	M,D
Planetary and Space Sciences	M,D

FLORIDA INTERNATIONAL UNIVERSITY

Biostatistics	M,D
Chemistry	M,D
Environmental Management and Policy	M
Environmental Sciences	M
Geosciences	M,D
Mathematics	M
Physics	M,D
Statistics	M

Peterson's Graduate Programs in the Physical Sciences, Mathematics, Agricultural Sciences, the Environment & Natural Resources 2012

FLORIDA STATE UNIVERSITY

Analytical Chemistry	M,D
Applied Mathematics	M,D
Applied Statistics	M,D
Biostatistics	M,D
Chemistry	M,D
Computational Sciences	M,D
Environmental Sciences	M,D
Food Science and Technology	M,D
Geology	M,D
Geophysics	D
Inorganic Chemistry	M,D
Marine Sciences	M,D
Mathematical and Computational Finance	M,D
Mathematics	M,D
Meteorology	M,D
Oceanography	M,D
Organic Chemistry	M,D
Physical Chemistry	M,D
Physics	M,D*
Statistics	M,D,O

FORT HAYS STATE UNIVERSITY

Geology	M
Geosciences	M

FORT VALLEY STATE UNIVERSITY

Animal Sciences	M

FRAMINGHAM STATE UNIVERSITY

Food Science and Technology	M

FROSTBURG STATE UNIVERSITY

Fish, Game, and Wildlife Management	M

FURMAN UNIVERSITY

Chemistry	M

GANNON UNIVERSITY

Environmental Sciences	M,O

GEORGE MASON UNIVERSITY

Applied Physics	M,D
Atmospheric Sciences	D
Biostatistics	M,D,O
Chemistry	M,D
Computational Sciences	M,D,O
Environmental Management and Policy	M,D,O
Environmental Sciences	M,D,O
Geosciences	M,D,O
Mathematics	M,D,O
Physics	M,D
Statistics	M,D,O

GEORGETOWN UNIVERSITY

Analytical Chemistry	D
Biostatistics	M
Chemistry	D
Inorganic Chemistry	D
Mathematics	M
Organic Chemistry	D
Physical Chemistry	D
Statistics	M
Theoretical Chemistry	D

THE GEORGE WASHINGTON UNIVERSITY

Analytical Chemistry	M,D
Applied Mathematics	M,D
Biostatistics	M,D
Chemistry	M,D
Environmental Management and Policy	M
Inorganic Chemistry	M,D
Mathematics	M,D
Organic Chemistry	M,D
Physical Chemistry	M,D

Physics	M,D
Statistics	M,D,O

GEORGIA HEALTH SCIENCES UNIVERSITY

Biostatistics	M,D

GEORGIA INSTITUTE OF TECHNOLOGY

Applied Mathematics	M,D
Atmospheric Sciences	M,D
Chemistry	M,D
Environmental Management and Policy	M,D
Environmental Sciences	M,D
Geochemistry	M,D
Geophysics	M,D
Geosciences	M,D
Marine Sciences	M,D
Mathematical and Computational Finance	M,D
Mathematics	M,D
Meteorology	M,D
Natural Resources	M,D
Oceanography	M,D
Physics	M,D
Planetary and Space Sciences	M,D
Statistics	M,D

GEORGIAN COURT UNIVERSITY

Mathematics	M,O

GEORGIA SOUTHERN UNIVERSITY

Biostatistics	M,D
Mathematics	M

GEORGIA STATE UNIVERSITY

Astronomy	D
Chemistry	M,D
Geology	M
Geosciences	M,O
Hydrogeology	M,O
Mathematics	M,D
Physics	M,D
Statistics	M,D

GODDARD COLLEGE

Environmental Management and Policy	M

GOVERNORS STATE UNIVERSITY

Analytical Chemistry	M

GRADUATE SCHOOL AND UNIVERSITY CENTER OF THE CITY UNIVERSITY OF NEW YORK

Chemistry	D
Environmental Sciences	D
Geosciences	D
Mathematics	D
Physics	D

GRAND VALLEY STATE UNIVERSITY

Biostatistics	M

GREEN MOUNTAIN COLLEGE

Environmental Management and Policy	M

HAMPTON UNIVERSITY

Applied Mathematics	M
Atmospheric Sciences	M,D
Chemistry	M
Computational Sciences	M
Physics	M,D
Planetary and Space Sciences	M,D
Statistics	M

HARDIN-SIMMONS UNIVERSITY

Environmental Management and Policy	M
Mathematics	M,D

HARVARD UNIVERSITY

Applied Mathematics	M,D
Applied Physics	M,D
Astronomy	D
Astrophysics	D
Biostatistics	M,D
Chemical Physics	D
Chemistry	D*
Environmental Management and Policy	M,O
Environmental Sciences	M
Forestry	M
Geosciences	M,D
Inorganic Chemistry	D
Mathematics	D
Organic Chemistry	D
Physical Chemistry	D
Physics	D
Planetary and Space Sciences	M,D
Statistics	M,D
Theoretical Physics	D

HAWAI'I PACIFIC UNIVERSITY

Marine Sciences	M*

HOFSTRA UNIVERSITY

Chemistry	M,O
Geology	M,O
Geosciences	M,O
Physics	M,O

HOWARD UNIVERSITY

Analytical Chemistry	M,D
Applied Mathematics	M,D
Atmospheric Sciences	M,D
Chemistry	M,D
Environmental Sciences	M,D
Inorganic Chemistry	M,D
Mathematics	M,D
Organic Chemistry	M,D
Physical Chemistry	M,D
Physics	M,D

HUMBOLDT STATE UNIVERSITY

Environmental Management and Policy	M
Environmental Sciences	M
Fish, Game, and Wildlife Management	M
Forestry	M
Geology	M
Natural Resources	M
Water Resources	M

HUNTER COLLEGE OF THE CITY UNIVERSITY OF NEW YORK

Applied Mathematics	M
Biostatistics	M
Chemistry	M,D
Environmental Sciences	M,O
Geosciences	M,O
Mathematics	M
Physics	M,D

ICR GRADUATE SCHOOL

Astrophysics	M
Geology	M
Geophysics	M

IDAHO STATE UNIVERSITY

Applied Physics	M,D
Chemistry	M
Environmental Management and Policy	M
Environmental Sciences	M,O
Geology	M,O
Geophysics	M,O

Geosciences	M,O
Hydrology	M,O
Mathematics	M,D
Physics	M,D

ILLINOIS INSTITUTE OF TECHNOLOGY

Analytical Chemistry	M,D
Applied Mathematics	M,D
Chemistry	M,D
Environmental Management and Policy	M
Food Science and Technology	M
Mathematical and Computational Finance	M
Physics	M,D

ILLINOIS STATE UNIVERSITY

Agricultural Sciences—General	M
Chemistry	M
Hydrogeology	M
Hydrology	M
Mathematics	M
Plant Sciences	M,D

INDIANA STATE UNIVERSITY

Mathematics	M

INDIANA UNIVERSITY BLOOMINGTON

Analytical Chemistry	M,D
Applied Mathematics	M,D
Astronomy	M,D
Astrophysics	M,D
Chemistry	M,D
Environmental Management and Policy	M,D,O
Environmental Sciences	M,D*
Geochemistry	M,D
Geology	M,D
Geophysics	M,D
Geosciences	M,D
Hydrogeology	M,D
Inorganic Chemistry	M,D
Mathematics	M,D
Mineralogy	M,D
Organic Chemistry	M,D
Physical Chemistry	M,D
Physics	M,D
Statistics	M,D

INDIANA UNIVERSITY NORTHWEST

Environmental Sciences	M,O

INDIANA UNIVERSITY OF PENNSYLVANIA

Applied Mathematics	M
Chemistry	M
Mathematics	M
Physics	M

INDIANA UNIVERSITY–PURDUE UNIVERSITY FORT WAYNE

Applied Mathematics	M,O
Applied Statistics	M,O
Mathematics	M,O

INDIANA UNIVERSITY–PURDUE UNIVERSITY INDIANAPOLIS

Applied Mathematics	M,D
Applied Statistics	M
Chemistry	M,D
Geology	M,D
Geosciences	M,D
Mathematics	M,D
Physics	M,D

INDIANA UNIVERSITY SOUTH BEND

Applied Mathematics	M

*M—master's degree; P—first professional degree; D—doctorate; O—other advanced degree; *—Close-Up and/or Display*

Peterson's Graduate Programs in the Physical Sciences, Mathematics, Agricultural Sciences, the Environment & Natural Resources 2012

www.facebook.com/petersonspublishing   **19**

INSTITUTO TECNOLOGICO DE SANTO DOMINGO

Environmental Management and Policy	M,D,O
Environmental Sciences	M,D,O
Marine Sciences	M,D,O
Mathematics	M,D,O
Natural Resources	M,D,O

INSTITUTO TECNOLÓGICO Y DE ESTUDIOS SUPERIORES DE MONTERREY, CAMPUS CIUDAD DE MÉXICO

Environmental Sciences	M,D

INSTITUTO TECNOLÓGICO Y DE ESTUDIOS SUPERIORES DE MONTERREY, CAMPUS ESTADO DE MÉXICO

Environmental Management and Policy	M,D

INSTITUTO TECNOLÓGICO Y DE ESTUDIOS SUPERIORES DE MONTERREY, CAMPUS IRAPUATO

Environmental Management and Policy	M,D

INSTITUTO TECNOLÓGICO Y DE ESTUDIOS SUPERIORES DE MONTERREY, CAMPUS MONTERREY

Agricultural Sciences—General	M,D
Applied Statistics	M,D
Chemistry	M,D
Organic Chemistry	M,D

INTER AMERICAN UNIVERSITY OF PUERTO RICO, METROPOLITAN CAMPUS

Environmental Management and Policy	M

INTER AMERICAN UNIVERSITY OF PUERTO RICO, SAN GERMÁN CAMPUS

Applied Mathematics	M
Environmental Sciences	M
Water Resources	M

IOWA STATE UNIVERSITY OF SCIENCE AND TECHNOLOGY

Agricultural Sciences—General	M,D
Agronomy and Soil Sciences	M,D
Animal Sciences	M,D
Applied Mathematics	M,D
Applied Physics	M,D
Astronomy	M,D
Astrophysics	M,D
Biostatistics	M,D
Chemistry	M,D
Condensed Matter Physics	M,D
Environmental Sciences	M,D
Fish, Game, and Wildlife Management	M,D
Food Science and Technology	M,D
Forestry	M,D
Geology	M,D
Geosciences	M,D
Horticulture	M,D
Mathematics	M,D
Meteorology	M,D
Natural Resources	M,D
Physics	M,D
Statistics	M,D

JACKSON STATE UNIVERSITY

Chemistry	M,D
Environmental Sciences	M,D
Mathematics	M

JACKSONVILLE STATE UNIVERSITY

Mathematics	M

JAMES MADISON UNIVERSITY

Mathematics	M
Statistics	M

JOHN CARROLL UNIVERSITY

Mathematics	M

THE JOHNS HOPKINS UNIVERSITY

Applied Mathematics	M,D,O
Applied Physics	M,O
Astronomy	D
Biostatistics	M,D
Chemistry	D
Environmental Management and Policy	M,O
Environmental Sciences	M
Geosciences	M,D
Mathematical and Computational Finance	M,D
Mathematics	D
Physics	D
Statistics	M,D

KANSAS STATE UNIVERSITY

Agricultural Sciences—General	M,D
Agronomy and Soil Sciences	M,D
Analytical Chemistry	M,D
Animal Sciences	M,D
Chemistry	M,D
Food Science and Technology	M,D
Geology	M
Horticulture	M,D
Inorganic Chemistry	M,D
Mathematics	M,D
Organic Chemistry	M,D
Physical Chemistry	M,D
Range Science	M,D
Statistics	M,D

KEAN UNIVERSITY

Environmental Management and Policy	M

KENNESAW STATE UNIVERSITY

Applied Statistics	M

KENT STATE UNIVERSITY

Analytical Chemistry	M,D
Applied Mathematics	M,D
Chemical Physics	M,D
Chemistry	M,D*
Geology	M,D
Inorganic Chemistry	M,D
Mathematics	M,D
Organic Chemistry	M,D
Physical Chemistry	M,D
Physics	M,D

KENTUCKY STATE UNIVERSITY

Aquaculture	M
Environmental Sciences	M

LAKEHEAD UNIVERSITY

Chemistry	M
Forestry	M,D
Geology	M
Mathematics	M
Physics	M

LAMAR UNIVERSITY

Chemistry	M
Environmental Management and Policy	M,D
Mathematics	M

LAURENTIAN UNIVERSITY

Analytical Chemistry	M
Applied Physics	M

Chemistry	M
Environmental Sciences	M
Geology	M,D
Natural Resources	M,D
Organic Chemistry	M
Physical Chemistry	M
Theoretical Chemistry	M

LEHIGH UNIVERSITY

Applied Mathematics	M,D
Chemistry	M,D
Computational Sciences	M,D
Environmental Management and Policy	M,O
Environmental Sciences	M,D
Geology	M,D
Geosciences	M,D
Mathematics	M,D
Photonics	M,D
Physics	M,D
Statistics	M,D

LEHMAN COLLEGE OF THE CITY UNIVERSITY OF NEW YORK

Mathematics	M
Plant Sciences	D

LOMA LINDA UNIVERSITY

Biostatistics	M,D,O
Geosciences	M,D

LONG ISLAND UNIVERSITY, BROOKLYN CAMPUS

Chemistry	M

LONG ISLAND UNIVERSITY, C.W. POST CAMPUS

Applied Mathematics	M
Environmental Management and Policy	M
Geosciences	M
Mathematics	M

LOUISIANA STATE UNIVERSITY AND AGRICULTURAL AND MECHANICAL COLLEGE

Agricultural Sciences—General	M,D
Agronomy and Soil Sciences	M,D
Animal Sciences	M,D
Applied Statistics	M
Astronomy	M,D
Astrophysics	M,D
Chemistry	M,D
Environmental Management and Policy	M
Environmental Sciences	M,D
Fish, Game, and Wildlife Management	M,D
Food Science and Technology	M,D
Forestry	M,D
Geology	M,D
Geophysics	M,D
Horticulture	M,D
Marine Affairs	M,D
Mathematics	M,D
Natural Resources	M,D
Oceanography	M,D
Physics	M,D
Statistics	M

LOUISIANA STATE UNIVERSITY HEALTH SCIENCES CENTER

Biostatistics	M,D

LOUISIANA TECH UNIVERSITY

Chemistry	M
Mathematics	M
Physics	M,D
Statistics	M

LOYOLA MARYMOUNT UNIVERSITY

Environmental Sciences	M

LOYOLA UNIVERSITY CHICAGO

Applied Statistics	M
Chemistry	M,D
Mathematics	M
Statistics	M

MARQUETTE UNIVERSITY

Analytical Chemistry	M,D
Chemical Physics	M,D
Chemistry	M,D
Computational Sciences	M,D
Inorganic Chemistry	M,D
Mathematics	M,D
Organic Chemistry	M,D
Physical Chemistry	M,D
Water Resources	M,D,O

MARSHALL UNIVERSITY

Chemistry	M
Environmental Sciences	M
Mathematics	M
Physics	M

MARYLHURST UNIVERSITY

Environmental Management and Policy	M
Natural Resources	M

MASSACHUSETTS COLLEGE OF PHARMACY AND HEALTH SCIENCES

Chemistry	M,D
Organic Chemistry	M

MASSACHUSETTS INSTITUTE OF TECHNOLOGY

Atmospheric Sciences	M,D
Chemistry	D
Computational Sciences	M
Environmental Sciences	M,D,O
Geochemistry	M,D
Geology	M,D
Geophysics	M,D
Geosciences	M,D
Hydrology	M,D,O
Inorganic Chemistry	D
Marine Geology	M,D
Mathematics	D
Oceanography	M,D,O
Organic Chemistry	M,D,O
Physical Chemistry	D
Physics	M,D
Planetary and Space Sciences	M,D

MCGILL UNIVERSITY

Agricultural Sciences—General	M,D,O
Agronomy and Soil Sciences	M,D
Animal Sciences	M,D
Applied Mathematics	M,D
Atmospheric Sciences	M,D
Biostatistics	M,D,O
Chemistry	M,D
Computational Sciences	M,D
Environmental Management and Policy	M,D
Fish, Game, and Wildlife Management	M,D
Food Science and Technology	M,D
Forestry	M,D
Geosciences	M,D
Mathematics	M,D
Meteorology	M,D
Natural Resources	M,D
Oceanography	M,D
Physics	M,D
Planetary and Space Sciences	M,D
Plant Sciences	M,D,O
Statistics	M,D,O

20   www.facebook.com/petersonspublishing

Peterson's Graduate Programs in the Physical Sciences, Mathematics, Agricultural Sciences, the Environment & Natural Resources 2012

MCMASTER UNIVERSITY

Analytical Chemistry	M,D
Applied Statistics	M
Astrophysics	D
Chemical Physics	M,D
Chemistry	M,D
Geochemistry	M,D
Geology	M,D
Geosciences	M,D
Inorganic Chemistry	M,D
Mathematics	M,D
Organic Chemistry	M,D
Physical Chemistry	M,D
Physics	D
Statistics	M

MCNEESE STATE UNIVERSITY

Agricultural Sciences—	
General	M
Chemistry	M
Environmental Sciences	M
Mathematics	M
Statistics	M

MEDICAL COLLEGE OF WISCONSIN

Biostatistics	D*

MEDICAL UNIVERSITY OF SOUTH CAROLINA

Biostatistics	M,D
Marine Sciences	D

MEMORIAL UNIVERSITY OF NEWFOUNDLAND

Aquaculture	M
Chemistry	M,D
Computational Sciences	M
Condensed Matter Physics	M,D
Environmental Sciences	M
Fish, Game, and Wildlife	
Management	M,O
Food Science and	
Technology	M,D
Geology	M,D
Geophysics	M,D
Geosciences	M,D
Marine Affairs	M,D,O
Marine Sciences	M,O
Mathematics	M,D
Oceanography	M,D
Physics	M,D
Statistics	M,D

MERCER UNIVERSITY

Environmental Sciences	M

MIAMI UNIVERSITY

Chemistry	M,D
Computational Sciences	M
Environmental Sciences	M
Geology	M,D
Mathematics	M
Physics	M
Plant Sciences	M,D
Statistics	M

MICHIGAN STATE UNIVERSITY

Agricultural Sciences—	
General	M,D
Agronomy and Soil	
Sciences	M,D
Animal Sciences	M,D
Applied Mathematics	M,D
Applied Statistics	M,D
Astronomy	M,D
Astrophysics	M,D
Chemical Physics	M,D
Chemistry	M,D
Environmental Sciences	M,D
Fish, Game, and Wildlife	
Management	M,D
Food Science and	
Technology	M,D

Forestry	M,D
Geosciences	M,D
Horticulture	M,D
Mathematics	M,D
Natural Resources	M,D
Physics	M,D
Plant Sciences	M,D
Statistics	M,D

MICHIGAN TECHNOLOGICAL UNIVERSITY

Atmospheric Sciences	D
Chemistry	M,D
Computational Sciences	D
Environmental Management	
and Policy	M,D
Forestry	M,D
Geology	M,D
Geophysics	M
Mathematics	M,D
Physics	M,D

MIDDLE TENNESSEE STATE UNIVERSITY

Biostatistics	M
Chemistry	M,D
Food Science and	
Technology	M
Geosciences	O
Mathematics	M,D

MINNESOTA STATE UNIVERSITY MANKATO

Astronomy	M
Environmental Sciences	M
Mathematics	M
Physics	M
Statistics	M

MISSISSIPPI COLLEGE

Chemistry	M
Mathematics	M

MISSISSIPPI STATE UNIVERSITY

Agricultural Sciences—	
General	M,D
Agronomy and Soil	
Sciences	M,D
Animal Sciences	M,D
Applied Physics	M,D
Atmospheric Sciences	M,D
Chemistry	M,D
Fish, Game, and Wildlife	
Management	M,D
Food Science and	
Technology	M,D
Forestry	M,D
Geosciences	M,D
Horticulture	M,D
Mathematics	M,D
Physics	M,D
Plant Sciences	M,D
Statistics	M,D

MISSOURI STATE UNIVERSITY

Agricultural Sciences—	
General	M
Chemistry	M
Environmental Management	
and Policy	M
Geology	M
Geosciences	M
Mathematics	M
Natural Resources	M
Plant Sciences	M

MISSOURI UNIVERSITY OF SCIENCE AND TECHNOLOGY

Applied Mathematics	M,D
Chemistry	M,D
Geochemistry	M,D
Geology	M,D
Geophysics	M,D
Hydrology	M,D

Mathematics	M,D
Physics	M,D
Statistics	M,D
Water Resources	M,D

MISSOURI WESTERN STATE UNIVERSITY

Chemistry	M

MONMOUTH UNIVERSITY

Mathematical and	
Computational Finance	M

MONTANA STATE UNIVERSITY

Agricultural Sciences—	
General	M,D
Animal Sciences	M,D
Chemistry	M,D
Environmental Sciences	M,D
Fish, Game, and Wildlife	
Management	M,D
Geosciences	M,D
Mathematics	M,D
Natural Resources	M
Physics	M,D
Plant Sciences	M,D
Range Science	M,D
Statistics	M,D

MONTANA TECH OF THE UNIVERSITY OF MONTANA

Geochemistry	M
Geology	M
Geosciences	M
Hydrogeology	M

MONTCLAIR STATE UNIVERSITY

Applied Mathematics	M,D,O
Chemistry	M,O
Environmental Management	
and Policy	M,D
Environmental Sciences	M,D,O
Food Science and	
Technology	M,O
Geosciences	M,D,O
Statistics	M,D,O

MONTEREY INSTITUTE OF INTERNATIONAL STUDIES

Environmental Management	
and Policy	M

MOREHEAD STATE UNIVERSITY

Agricultural Sciences—	
General	M
Environmental Management	
and Policy	M

MORGAN STATE UNIVERSITY

Chemistry	M
Mathematics	M

MOUNT ALLISON UNIVERSITY

Chemistry	M

MURRAY STATE UNIVERSITY

Agricultural Sciences—	
General	M
Chemistry	M
Environmental Sciences	M
Geosciences	M
Hydrology	M
Mathematics	M
Statistics	M

NAROPA UNIVERSITY

Environmental Management	
and Policy	M

NAVAL POSTGRADUATE SCHOOL

Applied Mathematics	M,D
Applied Physics	M,D

Mathematics	M,D
Meteorology	M,D
Oceanography	M,D
Physics	M,D

NEW JERSEY INSTITUTE OF TECHNOLOGY

Applied Mathematics	M
Applied Physics	M,D
Applied Statistics	M
Biostatistics	M
Chemistry	M,D
Environmental Management	
and Policy	M
Environmental Sciences	M,D
Mathematics	D

NEW MEXICO HIGHLANDS UNIVERSITY

Chemistry	M
Fish, Game, and Wildlife	
Management	M

NEW MEXICO INSTITUTE OF MINING AND TECHNOLOGY

Applied Mathematics	M,D
Astrophysics	M,D
Atmospheric Sciences	M,D
Chemistry	M,D
Environmental Sciences	M,D
Geochemistry	M,D
Geology	M,D
Geophysics	M,D
Geosciences	M,D
Hydrology	M,D
Mathematical Physics	M,D
Mathematics	M,D
Physics	M,D

NEW MEXICO STATE UNIVERSITY

Agricultural Sciences—	
General	M
Animal Sciences	M,D
Applied Statistics	M,D
Astronomy	M,D
Chemistry	M,D
Environmental Sciences	M,D
Fish, Game, and Wildlife	
Management	M
Geology	M
Horticulture	M,D
Mathematics	M,D
Physics	M,D
Plant Sciences	M,D
Range Science	M,D

THE NEW SCHOOL: A UNIVERSITY

Environmental Management	
and Policy	M

NEW YORK INSTITUTE OF TECHNOLOGY

Environmental Management	
and Policy	M,O

NEW YORK UNIVERSITY

Chemistry	M,D
Environmental Management	
and Policy	M
Food Science and	
Technology	M,D
Mathematical and	
Computational Finance	M,D
Mathematics	M,D
Physics	M,D
Statistics	M,D

NICHOLLS STATE UNIVERSITY

Mathematics	M

NORFOLK STATE UNIVERSITY

Optical Sciences	M

---

*M—master's degree; P—first professional degree; D—doctorate; O—other advanced degree; *—Close-Up and / or Display*

*Peterson's Graduate Programs in the Physical Sciences, Mathematics,
Agricultural Sciences, the Environment & Natural Resources 2012*

www.facebook.com/petersonspublishing **21**

NORTH CAROLINA AGRICULTURAL AND TECHNICAL STATE UNIVERSITY

Agricultural Sciences—General	M
Agronomy and Soil Sciences	M
Animal Sciences	M
Chemistry	M
Environmental Sciences	M
Optical Sciences	M,D
Plant Sciences	M

NORTH CAROLINA CENTRAL UNIVERSITY

Applied Mathematics	M
Chemistry	M
Geosciences	M
Mathematics	M
Physics	M

NORTH CAROLINA STATE UNIVERSITY

Agricultural Sciences—General	M,D,O
Agronomy and Soil Sciences	M,D
Animal Sciences	M,D
Applied Mathematics	M,D
Atmospheric Sciences	M,D
Biomathematics	M,D
Chemistry	M,D
Fish, Game, and Wildlife Management	M,D
Food Science and Technology	M,D
Forestry	M,D
Geosciences	M,D
Horticulture	M,D,O
Marine Sciences	M,D
Mathematical and Computational Finance	M
Mathematics	M,D
Meteorology	M,D
Natural Resources	M,D
Oceanography	M,D
Physics	M,D
Statistics	M,D

NORTH DAKOTA STATE UNIVERSITY

Agricultural Sciences—General	M,D
Agronomy and Soil Sciences	M,D
Animal Sciences	M,D
Applied Mathematics	M,D
Applied Statistics	M,D,O
Chemistry	M,D
Environmental Sciences	M,D
Food Science and Technology	M,D
Mathematics	M,D
Natural Resources	M,D
Physics	M,D
Plant Sciences	M,D
Range Science	M,D
Statistics	M,D,O

NORTHEASTERN ILLINOIS UNIVERSITY

Chemistry	M
Environmental Management and Policy	M
Mathematics	M

NORTHEASTERN UNIVERSITY

Analytical Chemistry	M,D
Applied Mathematics	M,D
Chemistry	M,D
Inorganic Chemistry	M,D
Mathematics	M,D
Organic Chemistry	M,D
Physical Chemistry	M,D
Physics	M,D

NORTHERN ARIZONA UNIVERSITY

Applied Physics	M
Applied Statistics	M,O
Atmospheric Sciences	M
Chemistry	M
Environmental Management and Policy	M
Environmental Sciences	M
Forestry	M,D
Geology	M
Mathematics	M,O
Meteorology	M
Physics	M
Statistics	M,O

NORTHERN ILLINOIS UNIVERSITY

Chemistry	M,D
Geology	M,D
Mathematics	M,D
Physics	M,D
Statistics	M

NORTHWESTERN UNIVERSITY

Applied Mathematics	M,D
Astronomy	M,D
Astrophysics	M,D
Chemistry	D
Geology	M,D
Geosciences	M,D
Mathematics	D
Physics	M,D
Statistics	M,D

NORTHWEST MISSOURI STATE UNIVERSITY

Agricultural Sciences—General	M

NOVA SCOTIA AGRICULTURAL COLLEGE

Agricultural Sciences—General	M
Agronomy and Soil Sciences	M
Animal Sciences	M
Aquaculture	M
Environmental Management and Policy	M
Environmental Sciences	M
Food Science and Technology	M
Horticulture	M
Water Resources	M

NOVA SOUTHEASTERN UNIVERSITY

Environmental Sciences	M
Marine Affairs	M
Marine Sciences	M
Oceanography	M,D

OAKLAND UNIVERSITY

Applied Mathematics	M,D
Applied Statistics	M
Chemistry	M,D
Environmental Sciences	M,D
Mathematics	M
Physics	M,D
Statistics	O

OGI SCHOOL OF SCIENCE & ENGINEERING AT OREGON HEALTH & SCIENCE UNIVERSITY

Environmental Sciences	M,D

THE OHIO STATE UNIVERSITY

Agricultural Sciences—General	M,D
Agronomy and Soil Sciences	M,D
Animal Sciences	M,D
Astronomy	M,D
Atmospheric Sciences	M,D
Biostatistics	M,D
Chemical Physics	M,D
Chemistry	M,D
Environmental Sciences	M,D
Food Science and Technology	M,D
Geodetic Sciences	M,D
Geology	M,D
Horticulture	M,D
Mathematics	M,D
Natural Resources	M,D
Optical Sciences	P,M,D
Physics	M,D
Statistics	M,D

OHIO UNIVERSITY

Astronomy	M,D
Environmental Management and Policy	M
Geochemistry	M
Geology	M
Geophysics	M
Hydrogeology	M
Mathematics	M,D
Physics	M,D*

OKLAHOMA STATE UNIVERSITY

Agricultural Sciences—General	M,D
Agronomy and Soil Sciences	M,D
Animal Sciences	M,D
Applied Mathematics	M,D
Chemistry	M,D
Environmental Sciences	M,D,O
Food Science and Technology	M,D
Forestry	M,D
Geology	M,D
Horticulture	M,D
Mathematics	M,D
Natural Resources	M,D
Photonics	M,D,O
Physics	M,D
Plant Sciences	M,D,O
Statistics	M,D

OLD DOMINION UNIVERSITY

Analytical Chemistry	M,D
Chemistry	M,D
Marine Affairs	M
Mathematics	M,D
Oceanography	M,D
Organic Chemistry	M,D
Physical Chemistry	M,D
Physics	M,D

OREGON HEALTH & SCIENCE UNIVERSITY

Biostatistics	M
Environmental Sciences	M,D

OREGON STATE UNIVERSITY

Agricultural Sciences—General	M,D
Agronomy and Soil Sciences	M,D
Analytical Chemistry	M,D
Animal Sciences	M,D
Applied Physics	M,D
Atmospheric Sciences	M,D
Chemistry	M,D
Environmental Sciences	M,D
Fish, Game, and Wildlife Management	M,D
Food Science and Technology	M,D
Forestry	M,D
Geology	M,D
Geophysics	M,D
Geosciences	M,D
Horticulture	M,D
Inorganic Chemistry	M,D
Marine Affairs	M
Marine Sciences	M
Mathematics	M,D

Oceanography	M,D
Organic Chemistry	M,D
Physical Chemistry	M,D
Physics	M,D
Range Science	M,D
Statistics	M,D

PACE UNIVERSITY

Environmental Management and Policy	M
Environmental Sciences	M

PENN STATE HARRISBURG

Environmental Sciences	M

PENN STATE UNIVERSITY PARK

Acoustics	M,D
Agricultural Sciences—General	M,D
Agronomy and Soil Sciences	M,D
Animal Sciences	M,D
Applied Mathematics	M,D
Astronomy	M,D
Astrophysics	M,D
Chemistry	M,D
Environmental Management and Policy	M
Environmental Sciences	M
Food Science and Technology	M,D
Forestry	M,D
Geosciences	M,D
Horticulture	M,D
Mathematics	M,D
Meteorology	M,D
Physics	M,D
Statistics	M,D

PITTSBURG STATE UNIVERSITY

Applied Physics	M
Chemistry	M
Mathematics	M
Physics	M

PLYMOUTH STATE UNIVERSITY

Environmental Management and Policy	M
Meteorology	M

POINT PARK UNIVERSITY

Environmental Management and Policy	M

POLYTECHNIC INSTITUTE OF NYU

Applied Physics	M,D
Chemistry	M,D
Environmental Sciences	M
Mathematical and Computational Finance	M,O
Mathematics	M,D

POLYTECHNIC INSTITUTE OF NYU, LONG ISLAND GRADUATE CENTER

Chemistry	M

POLYTECHNIC INSTITUTE OF NYU, WESTCHESTER GRADUATE CENTER

Chemistry	M
Mathematical and Computational Finance	M,O

POLYTECHNIC UNIVERSITY OF PUERTO RICO

Environmental Management and Policy	M

POLYTECHNIC UNIVERSITY OF PUERTO RICO, MIAMI CAMPUS

Environmental Management and Policy	M

POLYTECHNIC UNIVERSITY OF PUERTO RICO, ORLANDO CAMPUS

Environmental Management and Policy	M

PONTIFICAL CATHOLIC UNIVERSITY OF PUERTO RICO

Chemistry	M
Environmental Sciences	M

PORTLAND STATE UNIVERSITY

Chemistry	M,D
Environmental Management and Policy	M,D
Environmental Sciences	M,D
Geology	M,D
Mathematics	M,D,O
Physics	M,D
Statistics	M,D

PRAIRIE VIEW A&M UNIVERSITY

Agricultural Sciences— General	M
Agronomy and Soil Sciences	M
Animal Sciences	M
Chemistry	M
Mathematics	M

PRESCOTT COLLEGE

Environmental Management and Policy	M

PRINCETON UNIVERSITY

Applied Mathematics	D
Astronomy	D
Astrophysics	D
Atmospheric Sciences	D
Chemistry	M,D*
Computational Sciences	D
Geosciences	D
Mathematics	D
Oceanography	D
Photonics	D
Physics	D
Plasma Physics	D

PURDUE UNIVERSITY

Agricultural Sciences— General	M,D
Agronomy and Soil Sciences	M,D
Analytical Chemistry	M,D
Animal Sciences	M,D
Aquaculture	M,D
Atmospheric Sciences	M,D
Chemistry	M,D
Environmental Management and Policy	M,D
Fish, Game, and Wildlife Management	M,D
Food Science and Technology	M,D
Forestry	M,D
Geosciences	M,D
Horticulture	M,D
Inorganic Chemistry	M,D
Mathematics	M,D
Natural Resources	M,D
Organic Chemistry	M,D
Physical Chemistry	M,D
Physics	M,D
Statistics	M,D,O

PURDUE UNIVERSITY CALUMET

Mathematics	M

QUEENS COLLEGE OF THE CITY UNIVERSITY OF NEW YORK

Chemistry	M
Environmental Sciences	M
Geology	M
Mathematics	M
Physics	M,D

QUEEN'S UNIVERSITY AT KINGSTON

Chemistry	M,D
Geology	M,D
Mathematics	M,D
Physics	M,D
Statistics	M,D

RENSSELAER POLYTECHNIC INSTITUTE

Acoustics	M,D
Analytical Chemistry	M,D
Applied Mathematics	M
Chemistry	M,D
Environmental Management and Policy	D
Geology	M,D
Inorganic Chemistry	M,D
Mathematics	M,D
Organic Chemistry	M,D
Physical Chemistry	M,D
Physics	M,D

RHODE ISLAND COLLEGE

Mathematics	M,O

RICE UNIVERSITY

Applied Mathematics	M,D
Applied Physics	M,D
Astronomy	M,D
Biostatistics	M,D
Chemistry	M,D
Computational Sciences	M,D
Environmental Management and Policy	M
Environmental Sciences	M,D
Geophysics	M
Geosciences	M,D
Inorganic Chemistry	M,D
Mathematical and Computational Finance	M,D
Mathematics	D
Organic Chemistry	M,D
Physical Chemistry	M,D
Physics	M,D
Statistics	M,D

THE RICHARD STOCKTON COLLEGE OF NEW JERSEY

Computational Sciences	M
Environmental Sciences	M

RIVIER COLLEGE

Mathematics	M

ROCHESTER INSTITUTE OF TECHNOLOGY

Applied Mathematics	M
Applied Statistics	M,O
Astrophysics	M,D
Chemistry	M
Environmental Management and Policy	M
Environmental Sciences	M
Optical Sciences	M,D
Statistics	M,O

ROOSEVELT UNIVERSITY

Chemistry	M
Mathematics	M

ROSE-HULMAN INSTITUTE OF TECHNOLOGY

Optical Sciences	M

ROWAN UNIVERSITY

Mathematics	M

ROYAL MILITARY COLLEGE OF CANADA

Chemistry	M,D
Environmental Sciences	M,D
Mathematics	M
Physics	M

ROYAL ROADS UNIVERSITY

Environmental Management and Policy	M,O

RUTGERS, THE STATE UNIVERSITY OF NEW JERSEY, CAMDEN

Chemistry	M
Mathematics	M

RUTGERS, THE STATE UNIVERSITY OF NEW JERSEY, NEWARK

Analytical Chemistry	M,D
Applied Physics	M,D
Chemistry	M,D
Environmental Sciences	M,D
Geology	M
Inorganic Chemistry	M,D
Mathematics	D
Organic Chemistry	M,D
Physical Chemistry	M,D

RUTGERS, THE STATE UNIVERSITY OF NEW JERSEY, NEW BRUNSWICK

Animal Sciences	M,D
Applied Mathematics	M,D
Applied Statistics	M,D
Astronomy	M,D
Atmospheric Sciences	M,D
Biostatistics	M,D
Chemistry	M,D
Condensed Matter Physics	M,D
Environmental Sciences	M,D
Food Science and Technology	M,D
Geology	M,D
Horticulture	M,D
Inorganic Chemistry	M,D
Mathematics	M,D
Oceanography	M,D
Organic Chemistry	M,D
Physical Chemistry	M,D
Physics	M,D
Statistics	M,D
Theoretical Physics	M,D
Water Resources	M,D

SACRED HEART UNIVERSITY

Chemistry	M

ST. CLOUD STATE UNIVERSITY

Applied Statistics	M
Environmental Management and Policy	M
Mathematics	M

ST. FRANCIS XAVIER UNIVERSITY

Chemistry	M
Geology	M
Geosciences	M
Physics	M

ST. JOHN'S UNIVERSITY (NY)

Applied Mathematics	M
Chemistry	M
Mathematics	M
Statistics	M

SAINT JOSEPH COLLEGE

Chemistry	M

SAINT JOSEPH'S UNIVERSITY

Mathematics	M,O

SAINT LOUIS UNIVERSITY

Chemistry	M,D
Geophysics	M,D
Geosciences	M,D
Mathematics	M,D
Meteorology	M,D

SAINT MARY-OF-THE-WOODS COLLEGE

Environmental Management and Policy	M

SAINT MARY'S UNIVERSITY (CANADA)

Astronomy	M,D

ST. THOMAS UNIVERSITY

Geosciences	M,D,O
Planetary and Space Sciences	M,D,O

SAINT XAVIER UNIVERSITY

Mathematics	M

SALEM STATE UNIVERSITY

Mathematics	M

SAMFORD UNIVERSITY

Environmental Management and Policy	M

SAM HOUSTON STATE UNIVERSITY

Agricultural Sciences— General	M
Chemistry	M
Computational Sciences	M
Mathematics	M
Statistics	M

SAN DIEGO STATE UNIVERSITY

Applied Mathematics	M
Astronomy	M
Biometry	M
Biostatistics	M,D
Chemistry	M,D
Computational Sciences	M,D
Geology	M
Mathematics	M,D
Physics	M
Statistics	M

SAN FRANCISCO STATE UNIVERSITY

Chemistry	M
Environmental Management and Policy	M
Geosciences	M
Marine Sciences	M
Mathematics	M
Natural Resources	M
Physics	M

SAN JOSE STATE UNIVERSITY

Applied Mathematics	M
Chemistry	M
Environmental Management and Policy	M
Geology	M
Marine Sciences	M
Mathematics	M
Meteorology	M
Physics	M
Statistics	M

SANTA CLARA UNIVERSITY

Applied Mathematics	M
Mathematical and Computational Finance	M

---

*M—master's degree; P—first professional degree; D—doctorate; O—other advanced degree; *—Close-Up and / or Display*

Peterson's Graduate Programs in the Physical Sciences, Mathematics, Agricultural Sciences, the Environment & Natural Resources 2012

www.facebook.com/petersonspublishing   **23**

SAVANNAH STATE UNIVERSITY

Marine Sciences — M

THE SCRIPPS RESEARCH INSTITUTE

Chemistry — D

SETON HALL UNIVERSITY

Analytical Chemistry — M,D
Chemistry — M,D
Inorganic Chemistry — M,D
Organic Chemistry — M,D
Physical Chemistry — M,D

SHIPPENSBURG UNIVERSITY OF PENNSYLVANIA

Environmental Management and Policy — M

SIMON FRASER UNIVERSITY

Applied Mathematics — M,D
Chemical Physics — M,D
Chemistry — M,D
Computational Sciences — M,D
Environmental Management and Policy — M,D
Geosciences — M,D
Mathematics — M,D
Physics — M,D
Statistics — M,D

SLIPPERY ROCK UNIVERSITY OF PENNSYLVANIA

Environmental Management and Policy — M

SMITH COLLEGE

Chemistry — M
Mathematics — O

SOUTH DAKOTA SCHOOL OF MINES AND TECHNOLOGY

Atmospheric Sciences — M,D
Environmental Sciences — D
Geology — M,D
Paleontology — M,D
Physics — M,D

SOUTH DAKOTA STATE UNIVERSITY

Agricultural Sciences—
General — M,D
Agronomy and Soil Sciences — M,D
Animal Sciences — M,D
Chemistry — M,D
Computational Sciences — M,D
Fish, Game, and Wildlife Management — M,D
Food Science and Technology — M,D
Geosciences — D
Mathematics — M,D
Physics — M
Plant Sciences — M,D
Statistics — M,D

SOUTHEASTERN LOUISIANA UNIVERSITY

Chemistry — M
Mathematics — M
Physics — M

SOUTHEAST MISSOURI STATE UNIVERSITY

Chemistry — M
Environmental Management and Policy — M
Environmental Sciences — M
Mathematics — M

SOUTHERN ARKANSAS UNIVERSITY–MAGNOLIA

Agricultural Sciences—
General — M

SOUTHERN CONNECTICUT STATE UNIVERSITY

Chemistry — M
Mathematics — M

SOUTHERN ILLINOIS UNIVERSITY CARBONDALE

Agricultural Sciences—
General — M
Agronomy and Soil Sciences — M
Animal Sciences — M
Applied Physics — M,D
Chemistry — M,D
Environmental Sciences — D
Forestry — M
Geology — M,D
Horticulture — M
Mathematics — M,D
Physics — M,D
Plant Sciences — M
Statistics — M,D

SOUTHERN ILLINOIS UNIVERSITY EDWARDSVILLE

Chemistry — M
Environmental Management and Policy — M
Environmental Sciences — M
Mathematics — M

SOUTHERN METHODIST UNIVERSITY

Applied Mathematics — M,D
Chemistry — M,D
Computational Sciences — M,D
Environmental Sciences — M,D
Geology — M,D
Geophysics — M,D
Mathematics — M,D
Physics — M,D
Statistics — M,D

SOUTHERN UNIVERSITY AND AGRICULTURAL AND MECHANICAL COLLEGE

Agricultural Sciences—
General — M
Analytical Chemistry — M
Chemistry — M
Environmental Sciences — M
Forestry — M
Inorganic Chemistry — M
Mathematics — M
Organic Chemistry — M
Physical Chemistry — M
Physics — M

STANFORD UNIVERSITY

Applied Physics — M,D
Chemistry — D
Computational Sciences — M,D
Environmental Management and Policy — M
Environmental Sciences — M,D,O
Geophysics — M,D
Geosciences — M,D,O
Mathematical and Computational Finance — M,D
Mathematics — M,D
Physics — D
Statistics — M,D

STATE UNIVERSITY OF NEW YORK AT BINGHAMTON

Analytical Chemistry — M,D
Applied Physics — M,D

Chemistry — M,D
Geology — M,D
Inorganic Chemistry — M,D
Mathematics — M,D
Organic Chemistry — M,D
Physical Chemistry — M,D
Physics — M,D
Statistics — M,D

STATE UNIVERSITY OF NEW YORK AT FREDONIA

Chemistry — M
Mathematics — M

STATE UNIVERSITY OF NEW YORK AT NEW PALTZ

Chemistry — M
Geosciences — M

STATE UNIVERSITY OF NEW YORK AT OSWEGO

Chemistry — M

STATE UNIVERSITY OF NEW YORK COLLEGE AT CORTLAND

Mathematics — M

STATE UNIVERSITY OF NEW YORK COLLEGE AT ONEONTA

Geosciences — M

STATE UNIVERSITY OF NEW YORK COLLEGE AT POTSDAM

Mathematics — M

STATE UNIVERSITY OF NEW YORK COLLEGE OF ENVIRONMENTAL SCIENCE AND FORESTRY

Chemistry — M,D
Environmental Management and Policy — M,D
Environmental Sciences — M,D
Fish, Game, and Wildlife Management — M,D
Forestry — M,D
Geodetic Sciences — M,D
Natural Resources — M,D
Organic Chemistry — M,D
Plant Sciences — M,D
Water Resources — M,D

STEPHEN F. AUSTIN STATE UNIVERSITY

Chemistry — M
Environmental Sciences — M
Forestry — M,D
Geology — M
Mathematics — M
Physics — M
Statistics — M

STEVENS INSTITUTE OF TECHNOLOGY

Analytical Chemistry — M,D,O
Applied Mathematics — M
Applied Statistics — O
Chemistry — M,D,O
Hydrology — M,D,O
Marine Affairs — M
Mathematics — M,D
Organic Chemistry — M,D,O
Photonics — M,D,O
Physical Chemistry — M,D,O
Physics — M,D,O
Statistics — M,O

STONY BROOK UNIVERSITY, STATE UNIVERSITY OF NEW YORK

Applied Mathematics — M,D
Astronomy — D
Atmospheric Sciences — M,D

Chemistry — M,D
Environmental Management and Policy — M,O
Geosciences — M,D
Marine Affairs — M
Marine Sciences — M,D
Mathematics — M,D
Physics — M,D
Statistics — M,D

SUL ROSS STATE UNIVERSITY

Animal Sciences — M
Fish, Game, and Wildlife Management — M
Geology — M
Range Science — M

SYRACUSE UNIVERSITY

Applied Statistics — M
Chemistry — M,D
Geology — M,D
Mathematics — M,D
Physics — M,D

TARLETON STATE UNIVERSITY

Agricultural Sciences—
General — M
Environmental Sciences — M
Mathematics — M

TAYLOR UNIVERSITY

Environmental Sciences — M

TEMPLE UNIVERSITY

Applied Mathematics — M,D
Chemistry — M,D
Computational Sciences — M,D
Geology — M
Mathematics — M,D
Physics — M,D*
Statistics — M,D

TENNESSEE STATE UNIVERSITY

Agricultural Sciences—
General — M
Chemistry — M
Mathematics — M

TENNESSEE TECHNOLOGICAL UNIVERSITY

Chemistry — M,D
Environmental Sciences — D
Fish, Game, and Wildlife Management — M
Mathematics — M

TEXAS A&M INTERNATIONAL UNIVERSITY

Mathematics — M
Physics — M

TEXAS A&M UNIVERSITY

Agricultural Sciences—
General — M,D
Agronomy and Soil Sciences — M,D
Animal Sciences — M,D
Applied Physics — M,D
Chemistry — M,D
Fish, Game, and Wildlife Management — M,D
Food Science and Technology — M,D
Forestry — M,D
Geology — M,D
Geophysics — M,D
Horticulture — M,D
Mathematics — M,D
Meteorology — M,D
Natural Resources — M,D
Oceanography — M,D
Physics — M,D
Plant Sciences — M,D
Range Science — M,D
Statistics — M,D

24 www.facebook.com/petersonspublishing

Peterson's Graduate Programs in the Physical Sciences, Mathematics, Agricultural Sciences, the Environment & Natural Resources 2012

TEXAS A&M UNIVERSITY AT GALVESTON

Marine Sciences	M

TEXAS A&M UNIVERSITY–COMMERCE

Agricultural Sciences— General	M
Chemistry	M
Geosciences	M
Mathematics	M
Physics	M

TEXAS A&M UNIVERSITY–CORPUS CHRISTI

Applied Mathematics	M
Aquaculture	M
Environmental Sciences	M
Marine Sciences	D
Mathematics	M

TEXAS A&M UNIVERSITY–KINGSVILLE

Agricultural Sciences— General	M,D
Agronomy and Soil Sciences	M,D
Animal Sciences	M
Chemistry	M
Fish, Game, and Wildlife Management	M,D
Geology	M
Mathematics	M
Plant Sciences	M,D
Range Science	M

TEXAS CHRISTIAN UNIVERSITY

Astrophysics	M,D
Chemistry	M,D
Environmental Sciences	M
Geology	M
Inorganic Chemistry	M,D
Mathematics	M,D
Organic Chemistry	M,D
Physical Chemistry	M,D
Physics	M,D

TEXAS SOUTHERN UNIVERSITY

Chemistry	M
Environmental Management and Policy	M,D
Mathematics	M

TEXAS STATE UNIVERSITY–SAN MARCOS

Applied Mathematics	M
Chemistry	M
Environmental Management and Policy	M
Fish, Game, and Wildlife Management	M
Mathematics	M,D
Physics	M

TEXAS TECH UNIVERSITY

Agricultural Sciences— General	M,D
Agronomy and Soil Sciences	M,D
Animal Sciences	M,D
Applied Physics	M,D
Atmospheric Sciences	M,D
Chemistry	M,D
Environmental Management and Policy	D
Environmental Sciences	M,D
Fish, Game, and Wildlife Management	M,D
Food Science and Technology	M,D
Geosciences	M,D
Horticulture	M,D
Mathematics	M,D

Natural Resources	M,D
Physics	M,D
Plant Sciences	M,D
Range Science	M,D
Statistics	M,D

TEXAS WOMAN'S UNIVERSITY

Chemistry	M
Food Science and Technology	M,D
Mathematics	M

THOMPSON RIVERS UNIVERSITY

Environmental Sciences	M

TOWSON UNIVERSITY

Applied Mathematics	M
Applied Physics	M
Environmental Management and Policy	M
Environmental Sciences	M,O

TRENT UNIVERSITY

Chemistry	M
Environmental Management and Policy	M,D
Physics	M

TROPICAL AGRICULTURE RESEARCH AND HIGHER EDUCATION CENTER

Agricultural Sciences— General	M,D
Environmental Management and Policy	M,D
Forestry	M,D
Water Resources	M,D

TROY UNIVERSITY

Environmental Management and Policy	M

TUFTS UNIVERSITY

Analytical Chemistry	M,D
Animal Sciences	M
Biostatistics	M,D
Chemistry	M,D
Environmental Management and Policy	M,D,O
Environmental Sciences	M,D
Inorganic Chemistry	M,D
Mathematics	M,D
Organic Chemistry	M,D
Physical Chemistry	M,D
Physics	M,D

TULANE UNIVERSITY

Applied Mathematics	M,D
Biostatistics	M,D
Chemistry	M,D
Mathematics	M,D
Physics	D
Statistics	M,D

TUSKEGEE UNIVERSITY

Agronomy and Soil Sciences	M
Animal Sciences	M
Chemistry	M
Environmental Sciences	M
Food Science and Technology	M
Plant Sciences	M

UNIVERSIDAD AUTONOMA DE GUADALAJARA

Environmental Management and Policy	M,D

UNIVERSIDAD DE LAS AMÉRICAS–PUEBLA

Food Science and Technology	M

UNIVERSIDAD DEL TURABO

Chemistry	M,D
Environmental Management and Policy	M,D
Environmental Sciences	M,D

UNIVERSIDAD METROPOLITANA

Environmental Management and Policy	M
Natural Resources	M

UNIVERSIDAD NACIONAL PEDRO HENRIQUEZ URENA

Agricultural Sciences— General	M
Animal Sciences	M
Environmental Sciences	M
Horticulture	M
Natural Resources	M

UNIVERSITÉ DE MONCTON

Astronomy	M
Chemistry	M
Food Science and Technology	M
Mathematics	M
Physics	M

UNIVERSITÉ DE MONTRÉAL

Chemistry	M,D
Environmental Management and Policy	O
Mathematical and Computational Finance	M,D,O
Mathematics	M,D,O
Physics	M,D
Statistics	M,D,O

UNIVERSITÉ DE SHERBROOKE

Chemistry	M,D,O
Environmental Sciences	M,O
Mathematics	M,D
Physics	M,D

UNIVERSITÉ DU QUÉBEC À CHICOUTIMI

Environmental Management and Policy	M
Geosciences	M
Mineralogy	D

UNIVERSITÉ DU QUÉBEC À MONTRÉAL

Atmospheric Sciences	M,D,O
Chemistry	M,D
Environmental Sciences	M,D,O
Geology	M,D,O
Geosciences	M,D,O
Mathematics	M,D
Meteorology	M,D,O
Mineralogy	M,D,O
Natural Resources	M,D,O

UNIVERSITÉ DU QUÉBEC À RIMOUSKI

Fish, Game, and Wildlife Management	M,D,O
Marine Affairs	M,O
Oceanography	M,D

UNIVERSITÉ DU QUÉBEC À TROIS-RIVIÈRES

Chemistry	M
Environmental Sciences	M,D
Mathematics	M
Physics	M,D

UNIVERSITÉ DU QUÉBEC EN ABITIBI-TÉMISCAMINGUE

Environmental Sciences	M,D
Forestry	M,D
Natural Resources	M,D

UNIVERSITÉ DU QUÉBEC, INSTITUT NATIONAL DE LA RECHERCHE SCIENTIFIQUE

Environmental Management and Policy	M,D
Geosciences	M,D
Hydrology	M,D

UNIVERSITÉ LAVAL

Agricultural Sciences— General	M,D,O
Agronomy and Soil Sciences	M,D
Animal Sciences	M,D
Chemistry	M,D
Environmental Management and Policy	M,D,O
Environmental Sciences	M,D
Food Science and Technology	M,D
Forestry	M,D
Geodetic Sciences	M,D
Geology	M,D
Geosciences	M,D
Mathematics	M,D
Oceanography	D
Physics	M,D
Statistics	M

UNIVERSITY AT ALBANY, STATE UNIVERSITY OF NEW YORK

Atmospheric Sciences	M,D
Biostatistics	M,D
Chemistry	M,D
Environmental Management and Policy	M
Environmental Sciences	M
Geology	M,D
Geosciences	M,D
Mathematics	M,D
Physics	M,D
Statistics	M,D,O

UNIVERSITY AT BUFFALO, THE STATE UNIVERSITY OF NEW YORK

Biostatistics	M,D
Chemistry	M,D
Environmental Sciences	M,D,O
Geology	M,D
Geosciences	M,D,O
Mathematics	M,D
Physics	M,D

THE UNIVERSITY OF AKRON

Applied Mathematics	M,D
Chemistry	M,D
Geology	M
Geophysics	M
Geosciences	M
Mathematics	M
Physics	M
Statistics	M

THE UNIVERSITY OF ALABAMA

Applied Mathematics	M,D
Applied Statistics	M,D
Geology	M,D
Mathematics	M,D
Physics	M,D

THE UNIVERSITY OF ALABAMA AT BIRMINGHAM

Applied Mathematics	D
Biostatistics	M,D
Chemistry	M,D
Mathematics	M
Physics	M,D

---

*M—master's degree; P—first professional degree; D—doctorate; O—other advanced degree; *—Close-Up and/or Display*

Peterson's Graduate Programs in the Physical Sciences, Mathematics, Agricultural Sciences, the Environment & Natural Resources 2012

www.facebook.com/petersonspublishing

25

THE UNIVERSITY OF ALABAMA IN HUNTSVILLE

Applied Mathematics	M,D
Atmospheric Sciences	M,D
Chemistry	M
Environmental Sciences	M,D
Mathematics	M,D
Optical Sciences	M,D
Photonics	M,D
Physics	M,D

UNIVERSITY OF ALASKA ANCHORAGE

Environmental Sciences	M

UNIVERSITY OF ALASKA FAIRBANKS

Astrophysics	M,D
Atmospheric Sciences	M,D
Chemistry	M,D
Computational Sciences	M,D
Environmental Management and Policy	M,D
Environmental Sciences	M,D
Fish, Game, and Wildlife Management	M,D
Geology	M,D
Geophysics	M,D
Limnology	M,D
Marine Sciences	M,D
Mathematics	M,D
Natural Resources	M,D
Oceanography	M,D
Physics	M,D
Statistics	M,D
Water Resources	M,D

UNIVERSITY OF ALBERTA

Agricultural Sciences— General	M,D
Agronomy and Soil Sciences	M,D
Applied Mathematics	M,D,O
Astrophysics	M,D
Biostatistics	M,D,O
Chemistry	M,D
Condensed Matter Physics	M,D
Environmental Management and Policy	M,D
Environmental Sciences	M,D
Forestry	M,D
Geophysics	M,D
Geosciences	M,D
Mathematical and Computational Finance	M,D,O
Mathematical Physics	M,D,O
Mathematics	M,D,O
Natural Resources	M,D
Physics	M,D
Statistics	M,D,O

THE UNIVERSITY OF ARIZONA

Agricultural Sciences— General	M,D
Agronomy and Soil Sciences	M,D
Animal Sciences	M,D
Applied Mathematics	M,D
Applied Physics	M
Astronomy	M,D
Atmospheric Sciences	M,D
Biostatistics	D
Chemistry	D
Environmental Sciences	M,D
Fish, Game, and Wildlife Management	M,D
Forestry	M,D
Geosciences	M,D
Hydrology	M,D
Mathematics	M,D
Optical Sciences	M,D
Physics	M,D
Planetary and Space Sciences	M,D
Plant Sciences	M,D
Range Science	M,D

Statistics	M,D
Water Resources	M,D

UNIVERSITY OF ARKANSAS

Agricultural Sciences— General	M,D
Agronomy and Soil Sciences	M,D
Animal Sciences	M,D
Applied Physics	M,D
Chemistry	M,D
Food Science and Technology	M,D
Geology	M
Horticulture	M
Mathematics	M,D
Photonics	M,D
Physics	M,D
Planetary and Space Sciences	M,D
Plant Sciences	D
Statistics	M

UNIVERSITY OF ARKANSAS AT LITTLE ROCK

Applied Mathematics	M,O
Applied Statistics	M,O
Chemistry	M
Geosciences	O
Mathematics	M,O

UNIVERSITY OF ARKANSAS AT MONTICELLO

Forestry	M
Natural Resources	M

UNIVERSITY OF ARKANSAS AT PINE BLUFF

Aquaculture	M
Fish, Game, and Wildlife Management	M

THE UNIVERSITY OF BRITISH COLUMBIA

Agricultural Sciences— General	M,D
Agronomy and Soil Sciences	M,D
Animal Sciences	M,D
Applied Mathematics	M,D
Astronomy	M,D
Atmospheric Sciences	M,D
Chemistry	M,D
Food Science and Technology	M,D
Forestry	M,D
Geology	M,D
Geophysics	M,D
Marine Sciences	M,D
Mathematics	M,D
Natural Resources	M,D
Oceanography	M,D
Physics	M,D
Plant Sciences	M,D
Statistics	M,D

UNIVERSITY OF CALGARY

Analytical Chemistry	M,D
Astronomy	M,D
Chemistry	M,D
Environmental Management and Policy	M,D,O
Geology	M,D
Geophysics	M,D
Inorganic Chemistry	M,D
Mathematics	M,D
Organic Chemistry	M,D
Physical Chemistry	M,D
Physics	M,D
Statistics	M,D
Theoretical Chemistry	M,D

UNIVERSITY OF CALIFORNIA, BERKELEY

Applied Mathematics	D
Astrophysics	D

Biostatistics	M,D
Chemistry	D
Environmental Management and Policy	M,D,O
Environmental Sciences	M,D
Forestry	M,D
Geology	M,D
Geophysics	M,D
Mathematics	M,D
Natural Resources	M,D
Physics	D
Range Science	M
Statistics	M,D

UNIVERSITY OF CALIFORNIA, DAVIS

Agricultural Sciences— General	M
Agronomy and Soil Sciences	M,D
Animal Sciences	M,D
Applied Mathematics	M,D
Atmospheric Sciences	M,D
Biostatistics	M,D
Chemistry	M,D
Environmental Sciences	M,D
Food Science and Technology	M,D
Geology	M,D
Horticulture	M
Hydrology	M,D
Mathematics	M,D
Physics	M,D
Statistics	M,D
Viticulture and Enology	M,D

UNIVERSITY OF CALIFORNIA, IRVINE

Chemistry	M,D
Geosciences	M,D
Mathematics	M,D
Physics	M,D
Statistics	M,D

UNIVERSITY OF CALIFORNIA, LOS ANGELES

Astronomy	M,D
Astrophysics	M,D
Atmospheric Sciences	M,D
Biomathematics	M,D
Biometry	M,D*
Biostatistics	M,D
Chemistry	M,D
Environmental Sciences	M,D
Geochemistry	M,D
Geology	M,D
Geophysics	M,D
Geosciences	M,D
Mathematics	M,D
Physics	M,D
Planetary and Space Sciences	M,D
Statistics	M,D

UNIVERSITY OF CALIFORNIA, MERCED

Applied Mathematics	M,D
Chemistry	M,D
Environmental Sciences	M,D
Physics	M,D

UNIVERSITY OF CALIFORNIA, RIVERSIDE

Agronomy and Soil Sciences	M,D
Applied Statistics	M,D
Chemistry	M,D
Environmental Sciences	M,D
Geology	M,D
Mathematics	M,D
Physics	M,D
Plant Sciences	M,D
Statistics	M,D
Water Resources	M,D

UNIVERSITY OF CALIFORNIA, SAN DIEGO

Applied Mathematics	M,D
Applied Physics	M,D
Chemistry	M,D
Geosciences	D
Marine Sciences	M
Mathematics	M,D
Oceanography	D
Photonics	M,D
Physics	M,D
Statistics	M,D

UNIVERSITY OF CALIFORNIA, SAN FRANCISCO

Chemistry	D

UNIVERSITY OF CALIFORNIA, SANTA BARBARA

Applied Mathematics	M,D
Applied Statistics	M,D
Chemistry	M,D
Computational Sciences	M,D
Environmental Management and Policy	M,D
Environmental Sciences	M,D
Geology	M,D
Geophysics	M,D
Geosciences	M,D
Marine Sciences	M,D
Mathematical and Computational Finance	M,D
Mathematics	M,D
Photonics	M,D
Physics	D
Statistics	M,D

UNIVERSITY OF CALIFORNIA, SANTA CRUZ

Applied Mathematics	M,D
Astronomy	D
Astrophysics	D
Chemistry	M,D
Environmental Management and Policy	D
Geosciences	M,D
Marine Sciences	M,D
Mathematics	M,D
Physics	M,D
Planetary and Space Sciences	M,D
Statistics	M,D

UNIVERSITY OF CENTRAL ARKANSAS

Applied Mathematics	M
Mathematics	M

UNIVERSITY OF CENTRAL FLORIDA

Applied Mathematics	M,D,O
Chemistry	M,D,O
Mathematics	M,D,O
Optical Sciences	M,D
Photonics	M,D
Physics	M,D
Statistics	M,O

UNIVERSITY OF CENTRAL MISSOURI

Applied Mathematics	M,D
Environmental Management and Policy	M,D
Mathematics	M,D

UNIVERSITY OF CENTRAL OKLAHOMA

Applied Mathematics	M
Chemistry	M
Mathematics	M
Physics	M
Statistics	M

UNIVERSITY OF CHICAGO

Applied Mathematics	M,D

26   www.facebook.com/petersonspublishing

Peterson's Graduate Programs in the Physical Sciences, Mathematics, Agricultural Sciences, the Environment & Natural Resources 2012

Astronomy	M,D
Astrophysics	M,D
Atmospheric Sciences	M,D
Chemistry	D
Environmental Management and Policy	M,D
Environmental Sciences	M,D
Geophysics	M,D
Geosciences	M,D
Mathematical and Computational Finance	M
Mathematics	M,D
Paleontology	M,D
Physics	M,D
Planetary and Space Sciences	M,D
Statistics	M,D

UNIVERSITY OF CINCINNATI

Analytical Chemistry	M,D
Applied Mathematics	M,D
Biostatistics	M,D
Chemistry	M,D
Environmental Sciences	M,D
Geology	M,D
Inorganic Chemistry	M,D
Mathematics	M,D
Organic Chemistry	M,D
Physical Chemistry	M,D
Physics	M,D
Statistics	M,D

UNIVERSITY OF COLORADO AT COLORADO SPRINGS

Applied Mathematics	M,D
Chemistry	M
Environmental Sciences	M
Mathematics	M,D
Physics	M

UNIVERSITY OF COLORADO BOULDER

Applied Mathematics	M,D
Astrophysics	M,D
Atmospheric Sciences	M,D
Chemical Physics	M,D
Chemistry	M,D
Environmental Management and Policy	M,D
Geology	M,D
Geophysics	M,D
Hydrology	M,D
Mathematical Physics	M,D
Mathematics	M,D
Oceanography	M,D
Optical Sciences	M,D
Physics	M,D
Plasma Physics	M,D

UNIVERSITY OF COLORADO DENVER

Applied Mathematics	M,D
Biostatistics	M,D
Chemistry	M
Environmental Management and Policy	M,D
Environmental Sciences	M
Hydrology	M,D
Mathematics	M
Water Resources	M

UNIVERSITY OF CONNECTICUT

Agricultural Sciences— General	M,D
Agronomy and Soil Sciences	M,D
Animal Sciences	M,D
Applied Mathematics	M
Chemistry	M,D
Geology	M,D
Marine Sciences	M,D
Mathematical and Computational Finance	M
Mathematics	M,D
Natural Resources	M,D
Oceanography	M,D

Physics	M,D
Plant Sciences	M,D
Statistics	M,D

UNIVERSITY OF DAYTON

Applied Mathematics	M
Chemistry	M
Environmental Management and Policy	M,D
Mathematical and Computational Finance	M
Optical Sciences	M,D

UNIVERSITY OF DELAWARE

Agricultural Sciences— General	M,D
Agronomy and Soil Sciences	M,D
Animal Sciences	M,D
Applied Mathematics	M,D
Astronomy	M,D
Chemistry	M,D
Environmental Management and Policy	M,D
Fish, Game, and Wildlife Management	M,D
Food Science and Technology	M,D
Geology	M,D
Horticulture	M
Marine Affairs	M,D
Marine Geology	M,D
Marine Sciences	M,D
Mathematics	M,D
Natural Resources	M
Oceanography	M,D
Physics	M,D
Plant Sciences	M,D
Statistics	M

UNIVERSITY OF DENVER

Applied Physics	M,D
Astronomy	M,D
Chemistry	M,D
Environmental Management and Policy	M,O
Mathematics	M,D
Natural Resources	M,O
Physics	M,D
Statistics	M

UNIVERSITY OF DETROIT MERCY

Chemistry	M

THE UNIVERSITY OF FINDLAY

Environmental Management and Policy	M

UNIVERSITY OF FLORIDA

Agricultural Sciences— General	M,D
Agronomy and Soil Sciences	M,D
Animal Sciences	M,D
Aquaculture	M,D
Astronomy	M,D
Biostatistics	M
Chemistry	M,D
Fish, Game, and Wildlife Management	M,D
Food Science and Technology	M,D
Forestry	M,D
Geology	M,D
Geosciences	M,D
Horticulture	M,D
Limnology	M,D
Marine Sciences	M,D
Mathematics	M,D
Natural Resources	M,D
Physics	M,D
Plant Sciences	D
Statistics	M,D
Water Resources	M,D

UNIVERSITY OF GEORGIA

Agricultural Sciences— General	M,D
Agronomy and Soil Sciences	M,D
Analytical Chemistry	M,D
Animal Sciences	M,D
Applied Mathematics	M,D
Biostatistics	M
Chemistry	M,D
Food Science and Technology	M,D
Forestry	M,D
Geology	M,D
Horticulture	M,D
Inorganic Chemistry	M,D
Marine Sciences	M,D
Mathematics	M,D
Natural Resources	M,D
Organic Chemistry	M,D
Physical Chemistry	M,D
Physics	M,D
Plant Sciences	M,D
Statistics	M,D

UNIVERSITY OF GUAM

Environmental Sciences	M

UNIVERSITY OF GUELPH

Agricultural Sciences— General	M,D,O
Agronomy and Soil Sciences	M,D
Animal Sciences	M,D
Applied Mathematics	M,D
Applied Statistics	M,D
Aquaculture	M
Atmospheric Sciences	M,D
Chemistry	M,D
Environmental Management and Policy	M,D
Environmental Sciences	M,D
Food Science and Technology	M,D
Horticulture	M,D
Mathematics	M,D
Natural Resources	M,D
Physics	M,D
Statistics	M,D

UNIVERSITY OF HAWAII AT HILO

Environmental Sciences	M

UNIVERSITY OF HAWAII AT MANOA

Agricultural Sciences— General	M,D
Animal Sciences	M
Astronomy	M,D
Chemistry	M,D
Environmental Management and Policy	M,D,O
Food Science and Technology	M
Geochemistry	M,D
Geology	M,D
Geophysics	M,D
Horticulture	M,D
Hydrogeology	M,D
Marine Geology	M,D
Marine Sciences	O
Mathematics	M,D
Meteorology	M,D
Natural Resources	M,D
Oceanography	M,D
Physics	M,D
Planetary and Space Sciences	M,D
Plant Sciences	M,D

UNIVERSITY OF HOUSTON

Applied Mathematics	M,D
Atmospheric Sciences	M,D
Chemistry	M,D
Geology	M,D

Geophysics	M,D
Mathematics	M,D
Physics	M,D
Planetary and Space Sciences	M,D

UNIVERSITY OF HOUSTON–CLEAR LAKE

Chemistry	M
Environmental Management and Policy	M
Environmental Sciences	M
Mathematics	M
Physics	M
Statistics	M

UNIVERSITY OF IDAHO

Agronomy and Soil Sciences	M,D
Animal Sciences	M,D
Chemistry	M,D
Environmental Sciences	M,D
Fish, Game, and Wildlife Management	M,D
Food Science and Technology	M,D
Geology	M,D
Hydrology	M
Mathematics	M,D
Natural Resources	M,D
Physics	M,D
Plant Sciences	M,D
Statistics	M
Water Resources	M,D

UNIVERSITY OF ILLINOIS AT CHICAGO

Applied Mathematics	M,D
Biostatistics	M,D
Chemistry	M,D
Geology	M,D
Geosciences	M,D
Mathematical and Computational Finance	M,D
Mathematics	M,D
Physics	M,D
Statistics	M,D

UNIVERSITY OF ILLINOIS AT SPRINGFIELD

Environmental Management and Policy	M
Environmental Sciences	M

UNIVERSITY OF ILLINOIS AT URBANA–CHAMPAIGN

Agricultural Sciences— General	M
Agronomy and Soil Sciences	M,D
Animal Sciences	M,D
Applied Mathematics	M,D
Applied Statistics	M,D
Astronomy	M,D
Atmospheric Sciences	M,D
Chemical Physics	M,D
Chemistry	M,D
Environmental Sciences	M,D
Food Science and Technology	M,D
Geology	M,D
Geosciences	M,D
Mathematics	M,D
Natural Resources	M,D
Physics	M,D
Statistics	M,D

THE UNIVERSITY OF IOWA

Applied Mathematics	D
Astronomy	M
Biostatistics	M,D
Chemistry	M,D
Computational Sciences	D
Geosciences	M,D
Mathematics	M,D

*M—master's degree; P—first professional degree; D—doctorate; O—other advanced degree; *—Close-Up and / or Display*

Peterson's Graduate Programs in the Physical Sciences, Mathematics, Agricultural Sciences, the Environment & Natural Resources 2012

www.facebook.com/petersonspublishing

27

Physics	M,D
Statistics	M,D,O

THE UNIVERSITY OF KANSAS

Astronomy	M,D
Atmospheric Sciences	M,D
Biostatistics	M,D
Chemistry	M,D
Computational Sciences	M,D
Environmental Sciences	M,D
Geology	M,D
Mathematics	M,D
Physics	M,D

UNIVERSITY OF KENTUCKY

Agricultural Sciences—General	M,D
Agronomy and Soil Sciences	M,D
Animal Sciences	M,D
Applied Mathematics	M,D
Astronomy	M,D
Chemistry	M,D
Forestry	M
Geology	M,D
Mathematics	M,D
Physics	M,D
Plant Sciences	M
Statistics	M,D

UNIVERSITY OF LETHBRIDGE

Agricultural Sciences—General	M,D
Chemistry	M,D
Computational Sciences	M,D
Environmental Sciences	M,D
Mathematics	M,D
Physics	M,D

UNIVERSITY OF LOUISIANA AT LAFAYETTE

Geology	M
Mathematics	M,D
Physics	M

UNIVERSITY OF LOUISVILLE

Analytical Chemistry	M,D
Applied Mathematics	M,D
Biostatistics	M,D
Chemical Physics	M,D
Chemistry	M,D
Inorganic Chemistry	M,D
Mathematics	M,D
Organic Chemistry	M,D
Physical Chemistry	M,D
Physics	M,D

UNIVERSITY OF MAINE

Agricultural Sciences—General	M,D,O
Agronomy and Soil Sciences	M,D
Animal Sciences	M
Astronomy	M
Chemistry	M,D
Environmental Management and Policy	M,D
Environmental Sciences	M,D
Fish, Game, and Wildlife Management	M,D
Food Science and Technology	M,D
Forestry	M,D
Geology	M,D
Geosciences	M,D
Horticulture	M
Marine Affairs	M
Marine Sciences	M,D
Mathematics	M
Natural Resources	M,D
Oceanography	M,D
Physics	M,D
Plant Sciences	M,D
Water Resources	M,D

THE UNIVERSITY OF MANCHESTER

Analytical Chemistry	M,D
Applied Mathematics	M,D
Astronomy	M,D
Astrophysics	M,D
Atmospheric Sciences	M,D
Chemistry	M,D
Condensed Matter Physics	M,D
Environmental Management and Policy	M,D
Environmental Sciences	M,D
Geochemistry	M,D
Geosciences	M,D
Inorganic Chemistry	M,D
Mathematical and Computational Finance	M,D
Mathematics	M,D
Natural Resources	M,D
Organic Chemistry	M,D
Paleontology	M,D
Physical Chemistry	M,D
Physics	M,D
Plant Sciences	M,D
Statistics	M,D
Theoretical Chemistry	M,D
Theoretical Physics	M,D

UNIVERSITY OF MANITOBA

Agricultural Sciences—General	M,D
Agronomy and Soil Sciences	M,D
Animal Sciences	M,D
Chemistry	M,D
Computational Sciences	M
Environmental Sciences	M,D
Food Science and Technology	M,D
Geology	M,D
Geophysics	M,D
Horticulture	M,D
Mathematics	M,D
Natural Resources	M,D
Physics	M,D
Plant Sciences	M,D
Statistics	M,D

UNIVERSITY OF MARYLAND, BALTIMORE

Biostatistics	M,D
Environmental Sciences	M,D
Marine Sciences	M,D

UNIVERSITY OF MARYLAND, BALTIMORE COUNTY

Applied Mathematics	M,D
Applied Physics	M,D
Astrophysics	M,D
Atmospheric Sciences	M,D
Biostatistics	M,D
Chemistry	M,D
Environmental Management and Policy	M,D
Environmental Sciences	M,D
Marine Sciences	M,D
Optical Sciences	M,D
Physics	M,D
Planetary and Space Sciences	M
Statistics	M,D

UNIVERSITY OF MARYLAND, COLLEGE PARK

Agricultural Sciences—General	P,M,D
Analytical Chemistry	M,D
Animal Sciences	M,D
Applied Mathematics	M,D
Astronomy	M,D
Biostatistics	M,D
Chemical Physics	M,D
Chemistry	M,D
Environmental Sciences	M,D
Food Science and Technology	M,D
Geology	M,D
Horticulture	M,D
Inorganic Chemistry	M,D

Marine Sciences	M,D
Mathematics	M,D
Meteorology	M,D
Natural Resources	M,D
Oceanography	M,D
Organic Chemistry	M,D
Physical Chemistry	M,D
Physics	M,D
Statistics	M,D

UNIVERSITY OF MARYLAND EASTERN SHORE

Agricultural Sciences—General	M,D
Environmental Sciences	M,D
Food Science and Technology	M,D
Marine Sciences	M,D

UNIVERSITY OF MARYLAND UNIVERSITY COLLEGE

Environmental Management and Policy	M,O

UNIVERSITY OF MASSACHUSETTS AMHERST

Agronomy and Soil Sciences	M,D
Animal Sciences	M,D
Applied Mathematics	M
Astronomy	M,D
Biostatistics	M,D
Chemistry	M,D
Environmental Management and Policy	M,D
Fish, Game, and Wildlife Management	M,D
Food Science and Technology	M,D
Forestry	M,D
Geosciences	M,D
Marine Sciences	M,D
Mathematics	M,D
Physics	M,D
Plant Sciences	M,D
Statistics	M,D
Water Resources	M,D

UNIVERSITY OF MASSACHUSETTS BOSTON

Applied Physics	M
Chemistry	M
Environmental Sciences	D
Marine Sciences	D

UNIVERSITY OF MASSACHUSETTS DARTMOUTH

Acoustics	M,D,O
Chemistry	M,D
Environmental Management and Policy	M,O
Marine Sciences	M,D
Physics	M

UNIVERSITY OF MASSACHUSETTS LOWELL

Analytical Chemistry	M,D
Applied Mathematics	M,D
Applied Physics	M,D
Atmospheric Sciences	M,D
Chemistry	M,D
Computational Sciences	M,D
Environmental Management and Policy	M,D,O
Environmental Sciences	M,D,O
Inorganic Chemistry	M,D
Mathematics	M,D
Optical Sciences	M,D
Organic Chemistry	M,D
Physics	M,D

UNIVERSITY OF MEDICINE AND DENTISTRY OF NEW JERSEY

Biostatistics	M,D,O
Environmental Sciences	D

UNIVERSITY OF MEMPHIS

Analytical Chemistry	M,D
Applied Mathematics	M,D
Applied Statistics	M,D
Biostatistics	M
Chemistry	M,D
Geology	M,D,O
Geophysics	M,D,O
Inorganic Chemistry	M,D
Mathematics	M,D
Organic Chemistry	M,D
Physical Chemistry	M,D
Physics	M
Statistics	M,D

UNIVERSITY OF MIAMI

Chemistry	M,D
Environmental Management and Policy	M,D
Fish, Game, and Wildlife Management	M,D
Geophysics	M,D
Inorganic Chemistry	M,D
Marine Affairs	M
Marine Geology	M,D
Marine Sciences	M,D
Mathematics	M,D
Meteorology	M,D
Oceanography	M,D
Organic Chemistry	M,D
Physical Chemistry	M,D
Physics	M,D

UNIVERSITY OF MICHIGAN

Analytical Chemistry	D
Applied Physics	D
Applied Statistics	M,D
Astronomy	D
Astrophysics	D
Atmospheric Sciences	M,D
Biostatistics	M,D
Chemistry	D
Environmental Management and Policy	M,D
Environmental Sciences	M,D
Geology	M,D
Inorganic Chemistry	D
Marine Sciences	M,D
Mathematics	M,D
Natural Resources	M,D
Organic Chemistry	D
Physical Chemistry	D
Physics	M,D
Planetary and Space Sciences	M,D
Statistics	M,D

UNIVERSITY OF MICHIGAN–DEARBORN

Applied Mathematics	M
Computational Sciences	M
Environmental Sciences	M

UNIVERSITY OF MINNESOTA, DULUTH

Applied Mathematics	M
Chemistry	M
Computational Sciences	M
Geology	M,D
Physics	M

UNIVERSITY OF MINNESOTA, TWIN CITIES CAMPUS

Agricultural Sciences—General	M,D
Agronomy and Soil Sciences	M,D
Animal Sciences	M,D
Astronomy	M,D
Astrophysics	M,D
Biostatistics	M,D
Chemistry	M,D
Computational Sciences	M,D
Environmental Management and Policy	M

Peterson's Graduate Programs in the Physical Sciences, Mathematics,
Agricultural Sciences, the Environment & Natural Resources 2012

Food Science and	
Technology	M,D
Geology	M,D
Geophysics	M,D
Mathematics	M,D
Natural Resources	M,D
Physics	M,D
Plant Sciences	M,D
Statistics	M,D
Water Resources	M,D

UNIVERSITY OF MISSISSIPPI

Chemistry	M,D
Mathematics	M,D
Physics	M,D

UNIVERSITY OF MISSOURI

Agricultural Sciences—	
General	M,D,O
Agronomy and Soil	
Sciences	M,D
Analytical Chemistry	M,D
Animal Sciences	M,D
Applied Mathematics	M
Astronomy	M,D
Atmospheric Sciences	M,D
Chemistry	M,D
Fish, Game, and Wildlife	
Management	M,D
Food Science and	
Technology	M,D
Forestry	M,D
Geology	M,D
Horticulture	M,D
Inorganic Chemistry	M,D
Mathematics	M,D
Natural Resources	M
Organic Chemistry	M,D
Physical Chemistry	M,D
Physics	M,D
Plant Sciences	M,D
Statistics	M,D

UNIVERSITY OF MISSOURI–KANSAS CITY

Analytical Chemistry	M,D
Chemistry	M,D
Geology	M,D
Geosciences	M,D
Inorganic Chemistry	M,D
Mathematics	M,D
Organic Chemistry	M,D
Physical Chemistry	M,D
Physics	M,D
Statistics	M,D

UNIVERSITY OF MISSOURI–ST. LOUIS

Applied Mathematics	M,D
Applied Physics	M,D
Astrophysics	M,D
Chemistry	M,D
Inorganic Chemistry	M,D
Mathematics	M,D
Organic Chemistry	M,D
Physical Chemistry	M,D
Physics	M,D

THE UNIVERSITY OF MONTANA

Analytical Chemistry	M,D
Chemistry	M,D
Environmental Management	
and Policy	M
Environmental Sciences	M
Fish, Game, and Wildlife	
Management	M,D
Forestry	M,D
Geology	M,D
Geosciences	M,D
Inorganic Chemistry	M,D
Mathematics	M,D
Natural Resources	M,D
Organic Chemistry	M,D
Physical Chemistry	M,D

UNIVERSITY OF NEBRASKA AT OMAHA

Mathematics	M

UNIVERSITY OF NEBRASKA–LINCOLN

Agricultural Sciences—	
General	M,D
Agronomy and Soil	
Sciences	M,D
Analytical Chemistry	M,D
Animal Sciences	M,D
Astronomy	M,D
Chemistry	M,D
Food Science and	
Technology	M,D
Geosciences	M,D
Horticulture	M,D
Inorganic Chemistry	M,D
Mathematics	M,D
Natural Resources	M,D
Organic Chemistry	M,D
Physical Chemistry	M,D
Physics	M,D
Statistics	M,D

UNIVERSITY OF NEVADA, LAS VEGAS

Astronomy	M,D
Chemistry	M,D
Environmental Sciences	M,D,O
Geosciences	M,D
Mathematics	M,D
Physics	M,D
Water Resources	M

UNIVERSITY OF NEVADA, RENO

Agricultural Sciences—	
General	M,D
Animal Sciences	M
Atmospheric Sciences	M,D
Chemical Physics	D
Chemistry	M,D
Environmental Management	
and Policy	M
Environmental Sciences	M,D
Geochemistry	M,D
Geology	M,D
Geophysics	M,D
Hydrogeology	M,D
Hydrology	M,D
Mathematics	M
Physics	M,D

UNIVERSITY OF NEW BRUNSWICK FREDERICTON

Chemistry	M,D
Environmental Management	
and Policy	M,D
Forestry	M,D
Geodetic Sciences	M,D,O
Geology	M,D
Hydrology	M,D
Mathematics	M,D
Physics	M,D
Statistics	M,D
Water Resources	M,D

UNIVERSITY OF NEW BRUNSWICK SAINT JOHN

Natural Resources	M

UNIVERSITY OF NEW ENGLAND

Marine Sciences	M

UNIVERSITY OF NEW HAMPSHIRE

Animal Sciences	M,D
Applied Mathematics	M,D,O
Chemistry	M,D
Environmental Management	
and Policy	M
Fish, Game, and Wildlife	
Management	M
Forestry	M

Geochemistry	M
Geology	M
Geosciences	M
Hydrology	M
Marine Sciences	M
Mathematics	M,D,O
Natural Resources	M,D
Oceanography	M,D,O
Physics	M,D
Statistics	M,D,O
Water Resources	M

UNIVERSITY OF NEW HAVEN

Computational Sciences	M,O
Environmental Management	
and Policy	M,O
Environmental Sciences	M,O
Geosciences	M,O

UNIVERSITY OF NEW MEXICO

Chemistry	M,D
Computational Sciences	O
Environmental Management	
and Policy	M
Geosciences	M,D
Mathematics	M,D
Natural Resources	M,D
Optical Sciences	M,D
Physics	M,D
Planetary and Space	
Sciences	M,D
Statistics	M,D
Water Resources	M

UNIVERSITY OF NEW ORLEANS

Chemistry	M,D
Environmental Sciences	M
Geosciences	M
Mathematics	M
Physics	M,D

THE UNIVERSITY OF NORTH CAROLINA AT CHAPEL HILL

Astronomy	M,D
Astrophysics	M,D
Atmospheric Sciences	M,D
Biostatistics	M,D
Chemistry	M,D
Environmental Management	
and Policy	M,D
Environmental Sciences	M,D
Geology	M,D
Marine Sciences	M,D
Mathematics	M,D
Physics	M,D
Statistics	M,D

THE UNIVERSITY OF NORTH CAROLINA AT CHARLOTTE

Applied Mathematics	M,D
Applied Physics	M,D
Chemistry	M,D
Geosciences	M,D
Mathematical and	
Computational Finance	M
Mathematics	M,D
Optical Sciences	M,D

THE UNIVERSITY OF NORTH CAROLINA AT GREENSBORO

Chemistry	M
Mathematics	M,D

THE UNIVERSITY OF NORTH CAROLINA WILMINGTON

Chemistry	M
Environmental Management	
and Policy	M
Geology	M
Geosciences	M
Marine Sciences	M,D
Mathematics	M

UNIVERSITY OF NORTH DAKOTA

Atmospheric Sciences	M,D
Chemistry	M,D
Fish, Game, and Wildlife	
Management	M,D
Geology	M,D
Geosciences	M,D
Mathematics	M
Physics	M,D
Planetary and Space	
Sciences	M

UNIVERSITY OF NORTHERN BRITISH COLUMBIA

Environmental Management	
and Policy	M,D,O
Mathematics	M,D,O
Natural Resources	M,D,O

UNIVERSITY OF NORTHERN COLORADO

Applied Statistics	M,D
Chemistry	M,D
Geosciences	M
Mathematics	M,D

UNIVERSITY OF NORTHERN IOWA

Applied Mathematics	M
Applied Physics	M
Chemistry	M
Environmental Sciences	M
Geosciences	M
Mathematics	M
Natural Resources	M
Physics	M

UNIVERSITY OF NORTH FLORIDA

Mathematics	M
Statistics	M

UNIVERSITY OF NORTH TEXAS

Chemistry	M,D
Environmental Sciences	M,D
Mathematics	M,D
Physics	M,D

UNIVERSITY OF NORTH TEXAS HEALTH SCIENCE CENTER AT FORT WORTH

Biostatistics	M,D

UNIVERSITY OF NOTRE DAME

Applied Mathematics	M,D
Chemistry	M,D
Geosciences	M,D
Inorganic Chemistry	M,D
Mathematics	M,D
Organic Chemistry	M,D
Physical Chemistry	M,D
Physics	M,D

UNIVERSITY OF OKLAHOMA

Chemistry	M,D
Environmental Sciences	M,D
Geology	M,D
Geophysics	M,D
Mathematics	M,D*
Meteorology	M,D
Natural Resources	M,D
Physics	M,D

UNIVERSITY OF OKLAHOMA HEALTH SCIENCES CENTER

Biostatistics	M,D

UNIVERSITY OF OREGON

Chemistry	M,D
Environmental Management	
and Policy	M,D
Geology	M,D
Mathematics	M,D
Physics	M,D

*M—master's degree; P—first professional degree; D—doctorate; O—other advanced degree; *—Close-Up and / or Display*

Peterson's Graduate Programs in the Physical Sciences, Mathematics, Agricultural Sciences, the Environment & Natural Resources 2012

www.facebook.com/petersonspublishing   29

UNIVERSITY OF OTTAWA

Chemistry	M,D
Geosciences	M,D
Mathematics	M,D
Physics	M,D
Statistics	M,D

UNIVERSITY OF PENNSYLVANIA

Applied Mathematics	D
Astrophysics	M,D
Biostatistics	M,D
Chemistry	M,D
Computational Sciences	D
Environmental Management and Policy	M
Environmental Sciences	M,D
Geosciences	M,D
Mathematics	M,D
Physics	M,D
Statistics	M,D

UNIVERSITY OF PITTSBURGH

Applied Mathematics	M,D
Applied Statistics	M,D
Biostatistics	M,D
Chemistry	M,D*
Environmental Management and Policy	M,O
Geology	M,D
Mathematics	M,D
Physics	M,D
Planetary and Space Sciences	M,D
Statistics	M,D

UNIVERSITY OF PRINCE EDWARD ISLAND

Chemistry	M

UNIVERSITY OF PUERTO RICO, MAYAGÜEZ CAMPUS

Agricultural Sciences—General	M
Agronomy and Soil Sciences	M
Animal Sciences	M
Applied Mathematics	M
Chemistry	M,D
Computational Sciences	M
Food Science and Technology	M
Geology	M
Horticulture	M
Marine Sciences	M,D
Mathematics	M
Physics	M
Statistics	M

UNIVERSITY OF PUERTO RICO, MEDICAL SCIENCES CAMPUS

Biostatistics	M

UNIVERSITY OF PUERTO RICO, RÍO PIEDRAS

Chemistry	M,D
Environmental Management and Policy	M
Environmental Sciences	M,D
Mathematics	M,D
Physics	M,D

UNIVERSITY OF REGINA

Analytical Chemistry	M,D
Chemistry	M,D
Geology	M,D
Inorganic Chemistry	M,D
Mathematics	M,D
Organic Chemistry	M,D
Physics	M,D
Statistics	M,D
Theoretical Chemistry	M,D

UNIVERSITY OF RHODE ISLAND

Animal Sciences	M,D
Applied Mathematics	M,D,O
Aquaculture	M,D
Chemistry	M,D
Environmental Management and Policy	M,D
Environmental Sciences	M,D
Fish, Game, and Wildlife Management	M,D
Food Science and Technology	M,D
Geosciences	M,D
Marine Affairs	M,D
Marine Sciences	M,D
Mathematics	M,D
Natural Resources	M,D
Oceanography	M,D,O
Physics	M,D
Plant Sciences	M,D
Statistics	M,D,O

UNIVERSITY OF ROCHESTER

Applied Mathematics	
Astronomy	
Biostatistics	M,D
Chemistry	M,D
Geology	M,D
Geosciences	M,D
Mathematics	
Optical Sciences	M,D,O
Physics	
Statistics	M,D

UNIVERSITY OF SAN DIEGO

Marine Affairs	M
Marine Sciences	M

UNIVERSITY OF SAN FRANCISCO

Chemistry	M
Natural Resources	M

UNIVERSITY OF SASKATCHEWAN

Agricultural Sciences—General	M,D,O
Agronomy and Soil Sciences	M,D,O
Animal Sciences	M,D
Chemistry	M,D
Environmental Sciences	M
Food Science and Technology	
Geology	M,D,O
Mathematics	M,D
Physics	M,D
Plant Sciences	M,D
Statistics	M,D

THE UNIVERSITY OF SCRANTON

Chemistry	M

UNIVERSITY OF SOUTH AFRICA

Agricultural Sciences—General	M,D
Environmental Management and Policy	M,D
Environmental Sciences	M,D
Horticulture	M,D
Natural Resources	M,D
Statistics	M,D

UNIVERSITY OF SOUTH ALABAMA

Marine Sciences	M,D
Mathematics	M

UNIVERSITY OF SOUTH CAROLINA

Applied Statistics	M,D,O
Astronomy	M,D
Biostatistics	M,D
Chemistry	M,D
Environmental Management and Policy	M
Geology	M,D
Geosciences	M,D
Marine Sciences	M,D
Mathematics	M,D
Physics	M,D
Statistics	M,D,O

THE UNIVERSITY OF SOUTH DAKOTA

Chemistry	M,D
Computational Sciences	M,D
Mathematics	M
Physics	M,D
Statistics	M,D

UNIVERSITY OF SOUTHERN CALIFORNIA

Applied Mathematics	M,D
Biostatistics	M,D
Chemistry	D
Food Science and Technology	M,D,O
Geosciences	M,D
Marine Sciences	M,D
Mathematical and Computational Finance	M,D
Mathematics	M,D
Oceanography	M,D
Physical Chemistry	D
Physics	M,D
Statistics	M,D
Water Resources	M,D,O

UNIVERSITY OF SOUTHERN MAINE

Statistics	M

UNIVERSITY OF SOUTHERN MISSISSIPPI

Analytical Chemistry	M,D
Biostatistics	M
Chemistry	M,D
Computational Sciences	M,D
Geology	M,D
Hydrology	M,D
Inorganic Chemistry	M,D
Marine Sciences	M,D
Mathematics	M,D
Organic Chemistry	M,D
Physical Chemistry	M,D
Physics	M,D

UNIVERSITY OF SOUTH FLORIDA

Analytical Chemistry	M,D
Applied Physics	M,D
Biostatistics	M,D
Chemistry	M,D
Environmental Management and Policy	M
Environmental Sciences	M,D
Geology	M,D
Inorganic Chemistry	M,D
Marine Sciences	M,D
Mathematics	M,D
Oceanography	M,D
Organic Chemistry	M,D
Physical Chemistry	M,D
Physics	M,D
Statistics	M,D

THE UNIVERSITY OF TENNESSEE

Agricultural Sciences—General	M,D
Analytical Chemistry	M,D
Animal Sciences	M,D
Applied Mathematics	M,D
Chemical Physics	M,D
Chemistry	M,D
Environmental Management and Policy	M,D
Fish, Game, and Wildlife Management	M
Food Science and Technology	M,D
Forestry	M
Geology	M,D
Inorganic Chemistry	M,D
Mathematics	M,D
Organic Chemistry	M,D
Physical Chemistry	M,D
Physics	M,D
Plant Sciences	M
Statistics	M,D
Theoretical Chemistry	M,D

THE UNIVERSITY OF TENNESSEE AT CHATTANOOGA

Computational Sciences	M,D
Environmental Sciences	M

THE UNIVERSITY OF TENNESSEE AT MARTIN

Agricultural Sciences—General	M
Food Science and Technology	M

THE UNIVERSITY OF TENNESSEE SPACE INSTITUTE

Applied Mathematics	M
Physics	M,D

THE UNIVERSITY OF TEXAS AT ARLINGTON

Applied Mathematics	M,D
Chemistry	M,D
Environmental Sciences	M,D
Geology	M,D
Mathematics	M,D
Physics	M,D

THE UNIVERSITY OF TEXAS AT AUSTIN

Analytical Chemistry	M,D
Applied Mathematics	M,D
Applied Physics	M,D
Astronomy	M,D
Chemistry	M,D
Computational Sciences	M,D
Geology	M,D
Geosciences	M,D
Inorganic Chemistry	M,D
Marine Sciences	M,D
Mathematics	M,D
Natural Resources	M
Organic Chemistry	M,D
Physical Chemistry	M,D
Physics	M,D
Statistics	M

THE UNIVERSITY OF TEXAS AT BROWNSVILLE

Mathematics	M
Physics	M

THE UNIVERSITY OF TEXAS AT DALLAS

Applied Mathematics	M,D
Chemistry	M,D
Geochemistry	M,D
Geophysics	M,D
Geosciences	M,D
Hydrogeology	M,D
Mathematics	M,D
Paleontology	M,D
Physics	M,D
Statistics	M,D

THE UNIVERSITY OF TEXAS AT EL PASO

Chemistry	M,D
Computational Sciences	M,D
Environmental Sciences	M,D
Geology	M,D
Geophysics	M
Mathematics	M
Physics	M
Statistics	M

THE UNIVERSITY OF TEXAS AT SAN ANTONIO

Applied Mathematics	M
Applied Statistics	M,D
Chemistry	M,D*
Environmental Sciences	M,D*
Geology	M
Mathematics	M
Physics	M,D
Statistics	M,D

30   www.facebook.com/petersonspublishing

Peterson's Graduate Programs in the Physical Sciences, Mathematics,
Agricultural Sciences, the Environment & Natural Resources 2012

THE UNIVERSITY OF TEXAS AT TYLER

Mathematics	M

THE UNIVERSITY OF TEXAS HEALTH SCIENCE CENTER AT HOUSTON

Biomathematics	M,D
Biostatistics	M,D

THE UNIVERSITY OF TEXAS OF THE PERMIAN BASIN

Geology	M

THE UNIVERSITY OF TEXAS–PAN AMERICAN

Chemistry	M
Mathematics	M

UNIVERSITY OF THE DISTRICT OF COLUMBIA

Applied Statistics	M

UNIVERSITY OF THE INCARNATE WORD

Mathematics	M
Statistics	M

UNIVERSITY OF THE PACIFIC

Water Resources	P,M,D

UNIVERSITY OF THE SCIENCES IN PHILADELPHIA

Chemistry	M,D

UNIVERSITY OF THE VIRGIN ISLANDS

Environmental Sciences	M
Marine Sciences	M

THE UNIVERSITY OF TOLEDO

Analytical Chemistry	M,D
Applied Mathematics	M,D
Biostatistics	M,O
Chemistry	M,D
Environmental Sciences	M
Geology	M
Geosciences	M
Inorganic Chemistry	M,D
Mathematics	M,D
Organic Chemistry	M,D
Physical Chemistry	M,D
Physics	M,D
Statistics	M,D

UNIVERSITY OF TORONTO

Astronomy	M,D
Astrophysics	M,D
Chemistry	M,D
Environmental Sciences	M,D
Forestry	M,D
Geology	M,D
Mathematical and Computational Finance	M
Mathematics	M,D
Physics	M,D
Statistics	M,D

UNIVERSITY OF TULSA

Applied Mathematics	
Chemistry	M,D
Geosciences	M,D
Mathematics	M
Physics	M

UNIVERSITY OF UTAH

Atmospheric Sciences	M,D
Biostatistics	M,D
Chemical Physics	M,D
Chemistry	M,D
Computational Sciences	M
Environmental Sciences	M
Geology	M,D
Geophysics	M,D
Mathematics	M,D
Physics	M,D
Statistics	M,D

UNIVERSITY OF VERMONT

Agricultural Sciences—General	M,D
Agronomy and Soil Sciences	M,D
Animal Sciences	M,D
Biostatistics	M
Chemistry	M,D
Food Science and Technology	D
Forestry	M,D
Geology	M
Horticulture	M,D
Mathematics	M,D
Natural Resources	M,D
Physics	M
Plant Sciences	M,D
Statistics	M

UNIVERSITY OF VICTORIA

Astronomy	M,D
Astrophysics	M,D
Chemistry	M,D
Condensed Matter Physics	M,D
Geophysics	M,D
Geosciences	M,D
Mathematics	M,D
Oceanography	M,D
Physics	M,D
Statistics	M,D
Theoretical Physics	M,D

UNIVERSITY OF VIRGINIA

Astronomy	M,D
Chemistry	M,D
Environmental Sciences	M,D
Mathematics	M,D
Physics	M,D
Statistics	M,D

UNIVERSITY OF WASHINGTON

Applied Mathematics	M,D
Applied Physics	M,D
Astronomy	M,D
Atmospheric Sciences	M,D
Biostatistics	M,D
Chemistry	M,D
Computational Sciences	M,D
Environmental Management and Policy	M,D
Fish, Game, and Wildlife Management	M,D
Forestry	M,D
Geology	M,D
Geophysics	M,D
Horticulture	M,D
Hydrology	M,D
Marine Affairs	M,O
Marine Geology	M,D
Mathematics	M,D
Natural Resources	M,D
Oceanography	M,D
Physics	M,D
Statistics	M,D

UNIVERSITY OF WATERLOO

Applied Mathematics	M,D
Biostatistics	M,D
Chemistry	M,D
Environmental Management and Policy	M
Geosciences	M,D
Mathematics	M,D
Physics	M,D
Statistics	M,D

THE UNIVERSITY OF WESTERN ONTARIO

Applied Mathematics	M,D
Astronomy	M,D
Biostatistics	M,D
Chemistry	M,D
Environmental Sciences	M,D
Geology	M,D
Geophysics	M,D
Geosciences	M,D
Mathematics	M,D
Physics	M,D
Plant Sciences	M,D
Statistics	M,D

UNIVERSITY OF WEST FLORIDA

Applied Statistics	M
Environmental Sciences	M
Marine Affairs	M
Mathematics	M

UNIVERSITY OF WEST GEORGIA

Applied Mathematics	M
Mathematics	M

UNIVERSITY OF WINDSOR

Chemistry	M,D
Environmental Sciences	M,D
Geosciences	M,D
Mathematics	M,D
Physics	M,D
Statistics	M,D

UNIVERSITY OF WISCONSIN–GREEN BAY

Environmental Management and Policy	M
Environmental Sciences	M

UNIVERSITY OF WISCONSIN–LA CROSSE

Marine Sciences	M

UNIVERSITY OF WISCONSIN–MADISON

Agricultural Sciences—General	M,D
Agronomy and Soil Sciences	M,D
Animal Sciences	M,D
Astronomy	D
Atmospheric Sciences	M,D
Biometry	M
Chemistry	M,D
Environmental Sciences	M,D
Fish, Game, and Wildlife Management	M,D
Food Science and Technology	M,D
Forestry	M,D
Geology	M,D
Geophysics	M,D
Horticulture	M,D
Limnology	M,D
Marine Sciences	M,D
Mathematics	D
Natural Resources	M,D
Oceanography	M,D
Physics	M,D
Plant Sciences	M,D
Statistics	M,D
Water Resources	M

UNIVERSITY OF WISCONSIN–MILWAUKEE

Chemistry	M,D
Geochemistry	M,D
Geology	M,D
Mathematics	M,D
Physics	M,D
Water Resources	M,D

UNIVERSITY OF WISCONSIN–RIVER FALLS

Agricultural Sciences—General	M

UNIVERSITY OF WISCONSIN–STEVENS POINT

Natural Resources	M

UNIVERSITY OF WISCONSIN–STOUT

Food Science and Technology	M

UNIVERSITY OF WYOMING

Agricultural Sciences—General	M,D
Agronomy and Soil Sciences	M,D
Animal Sciences	M,D
Atmospheric Sciences	M,D
Chemistry	M,D
Food Science and Technology	M
Geology	M,D
Geophysics	M,D
Mathematics	M,D
Natural Resources	M,D
Range Science	M,D
Statistics	M,D
Water Resources	M,D

UTAH STATE UNIVERSITY

Agricultural Sciences—General	M,D
Agronomy and Soil Sciences	M,D
Animal Sciences	M,D
Applied Mathematics	M,D
Chemistry	M,D
Environmental Management and Policy	M,D
Fish, Game, and Wildlife Management	M,D
Food Science and Technology	M,D
Forestry	M,D
Geology	M
Mathematics	M,D
Meteorology	M,D
Natural Resources	M
Physics	M,D
Plant Sciences	M,D
Range Science	M,D
Statistics	M,D
Water Resources	M,D

VANDERBILT UNIVERSITY

Analytical Chemistry	M,D
Astronomy	M,D
Chemistry	M,D
Environmental Management and Policy	M,D
Environmental Sciences	M
Inorganic Chemistry	M,D
Mathematics	M,D
Organic Chemistry	M,D
Physical Chemistry	M,D
Physics	M,D
Theoretical Chemistry	M,D

VERMONT LAW SCHOOL

Environmental Management and Policy	M,O

VILLANOVA UNIVERSITY

Applied Statistics	M
Chemistry	M
Mathematics	M

VIRGINIA COMMONWEALTH UNIVERSITY

Analytical Chemistry	M,D
Applied Mathematics	M
Applied Physics	M
Biostatistics	M,D
Chemical Physics	M,D
Chemistry	M,D
Environmental Management and Policy	M

*M—master's degree; P—first professional degree; D—doctorate; O—other advanced degree; *—Close-Up and/or Display*

Inorganic Chemistry — M,D
Mathematics — M
Organic Chemistry — M,D
Physical Chemistry — M,D
Physics — M
Statistics — M

VIRGINIA POLYTECHNIC INSTITUTE AND STATE UNIVERSITY

Agricultural Sciences—
  General — M
Agronomy and Soil
  Sciences — M,D
Animal Sciences — M,D
Chemistry — M,D
Environmental Management
  and Policy — M,D,O
Environmental Sciences — M,D,O
Fish, Game, and Wildlife
  Management — M,D
Food Science and
  Technology — M,D,O
Forestry — M,D,O
Geosciences — M,D
Horticulture — M,D
Hydrology — M,D,O
Mathematics — M,D
Natural Resources — M,O
Physics — M,D
Statistics — M,D
Water Resources — M,D,O

VIRGINIA STATE UNIVERSITY

Agricultural Sciences—
  General — M
Mathematics — M
Physics — M
Plant Sciences — M

WAKE FOREST UNIVERSITY

Analytical Chemistry — M,D
Chemistry — M,D
Inorganic Chemistry — M,D
Mathematics — M
Organic Chemistry — M,D
Physical Chemistry — M,D
Physics — M,D

WASHINGTON STATE UNIVERSITY

Agricultural Sciences—
  General — M
Agronomy and Soil
  Sciences — M,D
Animal Sciences — M,D
Applied Mathematics — M,D
Applied Statistics — M
Chemistry — M,D
Environmental Sciences — M,D
Food Science and
  Technology — M,D
Geology — M,D
Geosciences — M,D
Horticulture — M,D
Mathematics — M,D
Natural Resources — M,D
Physics — M,D
Statistics — M

WASHINGTON STATE UNIVERSITY TRI-CITIES

Chemistry — M,D
Environmental Sciences — M,D

WASHINGTON STATE UNIVERSITY VANCOUVER

Environmental Sciences — M

WASHINGTON UNIVERSITY IN ST. LOUIS

Chemistry — D

Geosciences — M,D
Mathematics — M,D
Physics — D
Planetary and Space
  Sciences — M,D
Statistics — M,D

WAYNE STATE UNIVERSITY

Applied Mathematics — M,D
Chemistry — M,D
Food Science and
  Technology — M,D
Geology — M
Mathematics — M,D
Physics — M,D
Statistics — M,D

WEBSTER UNIVERSITY

Environmental Management
  and Policy — M,D,O

WESLEYAN UNIVERSITY

Astronomy — M
Chemical Physics — M,D
Chemistry — M,D
Environmental Sciences — M
Geosciences — M
Inorganic Chemistry — M,D
Mathematics — M,D*
Organic Chemistry — M,D
Physics — M,D
Theoretical Chemistry — M,D

WESLEY COLLEGE

Environmental Management
  and Policy — M

WEST CHESTER UNIVERSITY OF PENNSYLVANIA

Applied Statistics — M,O
Astronomy — M,O
Chemistry — O
Geology — M,O
Geosciences — M,O
Mathematics — M,O
Planetary and Space
  Sciences — M,O

WESTERN CAROLINA UNIVERSITY

Chemistry — M
Mathematics — M

WESTERN CONNECTICUT STATE UNIVERSITY

Environmental Sciences — M
Geosciences — M
Mathematics — M
Planetary and Space
  Sciences — M

WESTERN ILLINOIS UNIVERSITY

Applied Mathematics — M,O
Chemistry — M
Mathematics — M,O
Physics — M

WESTERN KENTUCKY UNIVERSITY

Agricultural Sciences—
  General — M
Chemistry — M
Computational Sciences — M
Geology — M
Geosciences — M
Mathematics — M
Physics — M

WESTERN MICHIGAN UNIVERSITY

Applied Mathematics — M
Chemistry — M,D

Computational Sciences — M
Geosciences — M,D
Mathematics — M,D
Physics — M,D
Statistics — M,D

WESTERN WASHINGTON UNIVERSITY

Chemistry — M
Environmental Sciences — M
Geology — M
Marine Sciences — M
Mathematics — M

WEST TEXAS A&M UNIVERSITY

Agricultural Sciences—
  General — M,D
Animal Sciences — M
Chemistry — M
Environmental Sciences — M
Mathematics — M
Plant Sciences — M

WEST VIRGINIA UNIVERSITY

Agricultural Sciences—
  General — M,D
Agronomy and Soil
  Sciences — D
Analytical Chemistry — M,D
Animal Sciences — M,D
Applied Mathematics — M,D
Applied Physics — M,D
Chemical Physics — M,D
Chemistry — M,D
Condensed Matter Physics — M,D
Environmental Management
  and Policy — M,D
Fish, Game, and Wildlife
  Management — M
Food Science and
  Technology — M,D
Forestry — M,D
Geology — M,D
Geophysics — M,D
Horticulture — M,D
Hydrogeology — M,D
Inorganic Chemistry — M,D
Mathematics — M,D
Natural Resources — M,D
Organic Chemistry — M,D
Paleontology — M,D
Physical Chemistry — M,D
Physics — M,D
Plant Sciences — D
Plasma Physics — M,D
Statistics — M,D
Theoretical Chemistry — M,D
Theoretical Physics — M,D

WICHITA STATE UNIVERSITY

Applied Mathematics — M,D
Chemistry — M,D
Environmental Sciences — M
Geology — M
Mathematics — M,D

WILFRID LAURIER UNIVERSITY

Chemistry — M
Environmental Management
  and Policy — M,D
Environmental Sciences — M,D
Mathematics — M

WILKES UNIVERSITY

Mathematics — M

WILLAMETTE UNIVERSITY

Environmental Management
  and Policy — M

WOODS HOLE OCEANOGRAPHIC INSTITUTION

Geochemistry — M,D,O
Geophysics — M,D,O
Marine Geology — M,D,O
Oceanography — M,D,O

WORCESTER POLYTECHNIC INSTITUTE

Applied Mathematics — M,D,O
Applied Statistics — M,D,O
Chemistry — M,D
Mathematics — M,D,O
Physics — M,D

WRIGHT STATE UNIVERSITY

Applied Mathematics — M
Applied Statistics — M
Chemistry — M
Environmental Sciences — M,D
Geology — M
Geophysics — M
Mathematics — M
Physics — M

YALE UNIVERSITY

Applied Mathematics — M,D
Applied Physics — M,D
Astronomy — M,D
Astrophysics — M,D
Atmospheric Sciences — D
Biostatistics — M,D,O
Chemistry — D
Environmental Management
  and Policy — M,D
Environmental Sciences — M,D
Forestry — M,D
Geochemistry — D
Geology — D
Geophysics — D
Geosciences — D
Inorganic Chemistry — D
Mathematics — M,D
Meteorology — D
Oceanography — D
Organic Chemistry — D
Paleontology — D
Physical Chemistry — D
Physics — D
Planetary and Space
  Sciences — M,D
Statistics — M,D
Theoretical Chemistry — D

YORK UNIVERSITY

Applied Mathematics — M,D
Astronomy — M,D
Chemistry — M,D
Environmental Management
  and Policy — M,D
Geosciences — M,D
Mathematics — M,D
Physics — M,D
Planetary and Space
  Sciences — M,D
Statistics — M,D

YOUNGSTOWN STATE UNIVERSITY

Analytical Chemistry — M
Applied Mathematics — M
Chemistry — M
Environmental Management
  and Policy — M,O
Inorganic Chemistry — M
Mathematics — M
Organic Chemistry — M
Physical Chemistry — M
Statistics — M

32   www.facebook.com/petersonspublishing

*Peterson's Graduate Programs in the Physical Sciences, Mathematics,
Agricultural Sciences, the Environment & Natural Resources 2012*

ACADEMIC AND PROFESSIONAL PROGRAMS IN THE PHYSICAL SCIENCES

Section 1
Astronomy and Astrophysics

This section contains a directory of institutions offering graduate work in astronomy and astrophysics. Additional information about programs listed in the directory but not augmented by an in-depth entry may be obtained by writing directly to the dean of a graduate school or chair of a department at the address given in the directory.

For programs offering related work, see also in this book *Geosciences, Meteorology and Atmospheric Sciences,* and *Physics.* In the other guides in this series:

Graduate Programs in the Biological Sciences
See *Biological and Biomedical Sciences and Biophysics*
Graduate Programs in Engineering & Applied Sciences
See *Aerospace/Aeronautical Engineering, Energy and Power Engineering (Nuclear Engineering), Engineering and Applied Sciences,* and *Mechanical Engineering and Mechanics*

CONTENTS

Program Directories

Close-Up and Display

Astronomy

Boston University, Graduate School of Arts and Sciences, Department of Astronomy, Boston, MA 02215. Offers MA, PhD. *Students:* 45 full-time (23 women); includes 8 minority (1 American Indian or Alaska Native, non-Hispanic/Latino; 2 Asian, non-Hispanic/Latino; 3 Hispanic/Latino; 2 Two or more races, non-Hispanic/Latino), 7 international. Average age 28. 64 applicants, 30% accepted, 6 enrolled. In 2010, 8 master's awarded. Terminal master's awarded for partial completion of doctoral program. *Degree requirements:* For master's, one foreign language, comprehensive exam, thesis or alternative; for doctorate, one foreign language, comprehensive exam, thesis/dissertation. *Entrance requirements:* For master's and doctorate, GRE General Test, GRE Subject Test (physics), 3 letters of recommendation. Additional exam requirements/recommendations for international students: Required—TOEFL (minimum score 550 paper-based; 213 computer-based). *Application deadline:* For fall admission, 1/15 for domestic and international students. Application fee: $70. *Expenses:* Tuition: Full-time $39,314; part-time $1228 per credit. Required fees: $40 per semester. *Financial support:* In 2010–11, 1 fellowship with full tuition reimbursement (averaging $19,300 per year), 30 research assistantships with full tuition reimbursements (averaging $18,800 per year), 9 teaching assistantships with full tuition reimbursements (averaging $18,800 per year) were awarded; Federal Work-Study and unspecified assistantships also available. Support available to part-time students. Financial award application deadline: 1/15; financial award applicants required to submit FAFSA. *Unit head:* James Jackson, Chairman, 617-353-6499, Fax: 617-353-6463, E-mail: jackson@bu.edu. *Application contact:* Laura Wipf, Department Administrator, 617-363-2625, Fax: 617-353-5704, E-mail: lwipf@bu.edu.

Brigham Young University, Graduate Studies, College of Physical and Mathematical Sciences, Department of Physics and Astronomy, Provo, UT 84602-1001. Offers physics (MS, PhD); physics and astronomy (PhD). Part-time programs available. *Faculty:* 29 full-time (2 women). *Students:* 34 full-time (4 women); includes 2 Asian, non-Hispanic/Latino; 1 Hispanic/Latino. Average age 29. 20 applicants, 50% accepted, 9 enrolled. In 2010, 8 master's, 4 doctorates awarded. Terminal master's awarded for partial completion of doctoral program. *Degree requirements:* For master's, thesis; for doctorate, thesis/dissertation, qualifying exam. *Entrance requirements:* For master's and doctorate, GRE Subject Test (physics) General GRE Required, minimum GPA of 3.0 in last 60 hours, ecclesiastical endorsement. Additional exam requirements/recommendations for international students: Required—TOEFL (minimum score 580 paper-based; 85 iBT), IELTS (minimum score 7). *Application deadline:* For fall admission, 1/15 priority date for domestic and international students. Application fee: $50. Electronic applications accepted. *Expenses:* Tuition: Full-time $5580; part-time $310 per credit hour. Tuition and fees vary according to program and student's religious affiliation. *Financial support:* In 2010–11, 37 students received support, including 27 research assistantships with full tuition reimbursements available (averaging $19,730 per year), 15 teaching assistantships with full tuition reimbursements available (averaging $18,780 per year); fellowships with full tuition reimbursements available, institutionally sponsored loans and tuition waivers (full) also available. Support available to part-time students. Financial award application deadline: 1/15. *Faculty research:* Acoustics; atomic, molecular, and optical physics; theoretical and mathematical physics; condensed matter; astrophysics and plasma. Total annual research expenditures: $2 million. *Unit head:* Dr. Ross L. Spencer, Chair, 801-422-2341, Fax: 801-422-0553, E-mail: ross_spencer@byu.edu. *Application contact:* Dr. J. Ward Moody, Graduate Coordinator, 801-422-4347, Fax: 801-422-0553, E-mail: jmoody@byu.edu.

California Institute of Technology, Division of Physics, Mathematics and Astronomy, Department of Astronomy, Pasadena, CA 91125-0001. Offers PhD. *Degree requirements:* For doctorate, one foreign language, thesis/dissertation, candidacy and final exams. *Entrance requirements:* For doctorate, GRE General Test, GRE Subject Test. Additional exam requirements/recommendations for international students: Required—TOEFL. *Faculty research:* Observational and theoretical astrophysics, cosmology, radio astronomy, solar physics.

Case Western Reserve University, School of Graduate Studies, Department of Astronomy, Cleveland, OH 44106. Offers MS, PhD. Part-time programs available. *Faculty:* 4 full-time (2 women), 4 part-time/adjunct (1 woman). *Students:* 1 full-time (0 women), all international. Average age 25. 11 applicants, 9% accepted, 0 enrolled. *Degree requirements:* For doctorate, comprehensive exam, thesis/dissertation. *Entrance requirements:* For doctorate, GRE General Test, GRE Subject Test (physics). Additional exam requirements/recommendations for international students: Required—TOEFL (minimum score 550 paper-based; 213 computer-based; 79 iBT). *Application deadline:* For fall admission, 1/15 for domestic students. Applications are processed on a rolling basis. Application fee: $50. Electronic applications accepted. *Financial support:* Fellowships, research assistantships available. Financial award application deadline: 2/15; financial award applicants required to submit FAFSA. *Faculty research:* Ground-based optical astronomy, high- and low-dispersion spectroscopy, theoretical astrophysics, galactic structure. *Unit head:* Prof. James Christopher Mihos, Chair, 216-368-3729, Fax: 216-368-5406, E-mail: mihos@case.edu. *Application contact:* Agnes Torontalli, Department Assistant, 216-368-3728, Fax: 216-368-5406, E-mail: agnes@case.edu.

Clemson University, Graduate School, College of Engineering and Science, Department of Physics and Astronomy, Clemson, SC 29634. Offers physics (MS, PhD), including astronomy and astrophysics, atmospheric physics, biophysics. Part-time programs available. *Faculty:* 25 full-time (4 women), 2 part-time/adjunct (0 women). *Students:* 63 full-time (19 women); includes 3 Black or African American, non-Hispanic/Latino, 26 international. Average age 27. 66 applicants, 92% accepted, 21 enrolled. In 2010, 2 master's, 6 doctorates awarded. Terminal master's awarded for partial completion of doctoral program. *Degree requirements:* For master's, thesis or alternative; for doctorate, thesis/dissertation. *Entrance requirements:* For master's and doctorate, GRE General Test. Additional exam requirements/recommendations for international students: Required—TOEFL. *Application deadline:* For fall admission, 1/15 priority date for domestic students; for spring admission, 9/15 priority date for domestic students. Applications are processed on a rolling basis. Application fee: $70 ($80 for international students). Electronic applications accepted. *Expenses:* Tuition, state resident: full-time $6492; part-time $400 per credit hour. Tuition, nonresident: full-time $13,634; part-time $800 per credit hour. Required fees: $262 per semester. Part-time tuition and fees vary according to course load and program. *Financial support:* In 2010–11, 58 students received support, including 1 fellowship with full and partial tuition reimbursement available (averaging $16,000 per year), 26 research assistantships with partial tuition reimbursements available (averaging $13,559 per year), 43 teaching assistantships with partial tuition reimbursements available (averaging $14,097 per year); career-related internships or fieldwork, institutionally sponsored loans, scholarships/grants, health care benefits, and unspecified assistantships also available. Support available to part-time students. Financial award application deadline: 6/1; financial award applicants required to submit FAFSA. *Faculty research:* Radiation physics, solid-state physics, nuclear physics, radar and lidar studies of atmosphere. Total annual research expenditures: $2.4 million. *Unit head:* Dr. Peter Barnes, Chair, 864-656-3419, Fax: 864-656-0805, E-mail: peterb@clemson.edu. *Application contact:* Dr. Murray Daw, Graduate Coordinator, 864-656-6702, Fax: 864-656-0805, E-mail: physgradinfo-l@clemson.edu.

Columbia University, Graduate School of Arts and Sciences, Division of Natural Sciences, Department of Astronomy, New York, NY 10027. Offers M Phil, MA, PhD. Part-time programs available. *Degree requirements:* For doctorate, thesis/dissertation. *Entrance requirements:* For master's and doctorate, GRE General Test, major in astronomy or physics. Additional exam requirements/recommendations for international students: Required—TOEFL. *Faculty research:* Theoretical astrophysics, x-ray astronomy, radio astronomy.

Cornell University, Graduate School, Graduate Fields of Arts and Sciences, Field of Astronomy and Space Sciences, Ithaca, NY 14853-0001. Offers astronomy (PhD); astrophysics (PhD);

general space sciences (PhD); infrared astronomy (PhD); planetary studies (PhD); radio astronomy (PhD); radiophysics (PhD); theoretical astrophysics (PhD). *Faculty:* 25 full-time (2 women). *Students:* 28 full-time (11 women); includes 3 Asian, non-Hispanic/Latino; 1 Hispanic/Latino, 7 international. Average age 26. 88 applicants, 24% accepted, 2 enrolled. In 2010, 3 doctorates awarded. *Degree requirements:* For doctorate, comprehensive exam, thesis/dissertation. *Entrance requirements:* For doctorate, GRE General Test, GRE Subject Test (physics), 3 letters of recommendation. Additional exam requirements/recommendations for international students: Required—TOEFL (minimum score 600 paper-based; 250 computer-based; 77 iBT). *Application deadline:* For fall admission, 1/15 for domestic students. Application fee: $80. Electronic applications accepted. *Expenses:* Tuition: Full-time $29,500. Required fees: $76. Tuition and fees vary according to degree level and program. *Financial support:* In 2010–11, 2 fellowships with full tuition reimbursements, 17 research assistantships with full tuition reimbursements, 9 teaching assistantships with full tuition reimbursements were awarded; institutionally sponsored loans, scholarships/grants, health care benefits, tuition waivers (full and partial), and unspecified assistantships also available. Financial award applicants required to submit FAFSA. *Faculty research:* Observational astrophysics, planetary sciences, cosmology, instrumentation, gravitational astrophysics. *Unit head:* Director of Graduate Studies, 607-255-4341. *Application contact:* Graduate Field Assistant, 607-255-4341, E-mail: oconnor@astro.cornell.edu.

Dartmouth College, Arts and Sciences Graduate Programs, Department of Physics and Astronomy, Hanover, NH 03755. Offers MS, PhD. Terminal master's awarded for partial completion of doctoral program. *Degree requirements:* For master's, thesis; for doctorate, thesis/dissertation. *Entrance requirements:* For master's and doctorate, GRE General Test, GRE Subject Test. Additional exam requirements/recommendations for international students: Required—TOEFL. *Faculty research:* Matter physics, plasma and beam physics, space physics, astronomy, cosmology.

Georgia State University, College of Arts and Sciences, Department of Physics and Astronomy, Program in Astronomy, Atlanta, GA 30302-3083. Offers PhD. *Degree requirements:* For doctorate, 2 foreign languages, thesis/dissertation, exam. *Entrance requirements:* For doctorate, GRE General Test, GRE Subject Test. Additional exam requirements/recommendations for international students: Required—TOEFL. Electronic applications accepted. *Faculty research:* Extragalactic photometry, theoretical astrophysics, young stellar objects.

Harvard University, Graduate School of Arts and Sciences, Department of Astronomy, Cambridge, MA 02138. Offers astronomy (PhD); astrophysics (PhD). *Degree requirements:* For doctorate, thesis/dissertation, paper, research project, 2 semesters of teaching. *Entrance requirements:* For doctorate, GRE General Test, GRE Subject Test (physics). Additional exam requirements/recommendations for international students: Required—TOEFL. Electronic applications accepted. *Expenses:* Tuition: Full-time $34,976. Required fees: $1166. Full-time tuition and fees vary according to program. *Faculty research:* Atomic and molecular physics, electromagnetism, solar physics, nuclear physics, fluid dynamics.

Indiana University Bloomington, University Graduate School, College of Arts and Sciences, Department of Astronomy, Bloomington, IN 47405-7000. Offers astronomy (MA, PhD); astrophysics (PhD). *Faculty:* 9 full-time (5 women), 1 part-time/adjunct (0 women). *Students:* 21 full-time (7 women); includes 2 minority (1 American Indian or Alaska Native, non-Hispanic/Latino; 1 Two or more races, non-Hispanic/Latino), 1 international. Average age 29. 40 applicants, 5% accepted, 2 enrolled. In 2010, 4 master's, 3 doctorates awarded. Terminal master's awarded for partial completion of doctoral program. *Degree requirements:* For master's, thesis or alternative, oral exam; for doctorate, comprehensive exam, thesis/dissertation, oral defense. *Entrance requirements:* For master's and doctorate, GRE General Test, GRE Subject Test (physics), BA or BS in science. Additional exam requirements/recommendations for international students: Required—TOEFL. *Application deadline:* For fall admission, 1/15 for domestic students, 12/1 for international students; for spring admission, 9/1 for domestic students. Application fee: $55 ($65 for international students). Electronic applications accepted. *Financial support:* In 2010–11, 6 students received support, including 3 fellowships with full tuition reimbursements available (averaging $15,000 per year), 8 research assistantships with full tuition reimbursements available (averaging $16,547 per year), 9 teaching assistantships with full tuition reimbursements available (averaging $14,008 per year); Federal Work-Study and tuition waivers (full and partial) also available. Support available to part-time students. Financial award application deadline: 1/15. *Faculty research:* Stellar and galaxy dynamics, stellar chemical abundancies, galaxy evolution, observational cosmology, astrophsical disk. *Unit head:* Dr. Catherine Pilachowski, Chair, 812-855-6913, Fax: 812-855-8725, E-mail: catyp@astro.indiana.edu. *Application contact:* Christina Lirot, Department Manager, 812-855-6912, Fax: 812-855-8725, E-mail: clirot@indiana.edu.

Iowa State University of Science and Technology, Graduate College, College of Liberal Arts and Sciences, Department of Physics and Astronomy, Ames, IA 50011. Offers applied physics (MS, PhD); astrophysics (MS, PhD); condensed matter physics (MS, PhD); high energy physics (MS, PhD); nuclear physics (MS, PhD); physics (MS, PhD). Part-time programs available. *Faculty:* 48 full-time (4 women), 4 part-time/adjunct (0 women). *Students:* 97 full-time (19 women), 6 part-time (0 women); includes 3 Asian, non-Hispanic/Latino, 53 international. 179 applicants, 32% accepted, 18 enrolled. In 2010, 4 master's, 11 doctorates awarded. Terminal master's awarded for partial completion of doctoral program. *Degree requirements:* For master's, thesis (for some programs); for doctorate, thesis/dissertation. *Entrance requirements:* For master's and doctorate, GRE General Test, GRE Subject Test (physics). Additional exam requirements/recommendations for international students: Required—TOEFL (minimum score 550 paper-based; 79 iBT), IELTS (minimum score 6.5). *Application deadline:* For fall admission, 2/15 priority date for domestic and international students; for spring admission, 10/15 for domestic and international students. Applications are processed on a rolling basis. Application fee: $40 ($90 for international students). Electronic applications accepted. *Financial support:* In 2010–11, 54 research assistantships with full and partial tuition reimbursements (averaging $12,890 per year), 34 teaching assistantships with full and partial tuition reimbursements (averaging $13,928 per year) were awarded; fellowships, Federal Work-Study, institutionally sponsored loans, scholarships/grants, health care benefits, and unspecified assistantships also available. Support available to part-time students. Financial award application deadline: 2/15. *Faculty research:* Condensed-matter physics, including superconductivity and new materials; high-energy and nuclear physics; astronomy and astrophysics; atmospheric and environmental physics. Total annual research expenditures: $8.8 million. *Unit head:* Dr. Joseph Shinar, Chair, 515-294-3455, Fax: 515-294-6027, E-mail: phys_astro@iastate.edu. *Application contact:* Dr. Steven Kawaler, Director of Graduate Education, 515-294-9728, E-mail: phys_astro@iastate.edu.

The Johns Hopkins University, Zanvyl Krieger School of Arts and Sciences, Henry A. Rowland Department of Physics and Astronomy, Baltimore, MD 21218-2699. Offers astronomy (PhD); physics (PhD). *Faculty:* 30 full-time (2 women), 14 part-time/adjunct (3 women). *Students:* 105 full-time (18 women); includes 6 minority (3 Asian, non-Hispanic/Latino; 1 Hispanic/Latino; 2 Two or more races, non-Hispanic/Latino), 48 international. Average age 26. 258 applicants, 19% accepted, 49 enrolled. In 2010, 8 doctorates awarded. *Degree requirements:* For doctorate, comprehensive exam, thesis/dissertation, minimum B- average on required coursework. *Entrance requirements:* For doctorate, GRE General Test, GRE Subject Test. Additional exam requirements/recommendations for international students: Required—TOEFL (minimum score 600 paper-based; 250 computer-based; 100 iBT), IELTS. *Application deadline:* For fall admission, 1/15 for domestic and international students. Application fee: $75. Electronic applications accepted. *Financial support:* In 2010–11, 107 students received support, including 4 fellow-

ships with full tuition reimbursements available (averaging $26,000 per year), 55 research assistantships with full tuition reimbursements available (averaging $26,000 per year), 48 teaching assistantships with full tuition reimbursements available (averaging $19,500 per year); career-related internships or fieldwork, Federal Work-Study, institutionally sponsored loans, tuition waivers (partial), and unspecified assistantships also available. Financial award application deadline: 4/15; financial award applicants required to submit FAFSA. *Faculty research:* High-energy physics, condensed-matter, astrophysics, particle and experimental physics, plasma physics. Total annual research expenditures: $24.9 million. *Unit head:* Dr. Daniel H. Reich, Chair, 410-516-7346, Fax: 410-516-7239, E-mail: dhr@pha.jhu.edu. *Application contact:* Carmelita D. King, Academic Affairs Administrator, 410-516-7344, Fax: 410-516-7239, E-mail: jazzy@pha.jhu.edu.

Louisiana State University and Agricultural and Mechanical College, Graduate School, College of Basic Sciences, Department of Physics and Astronomy, Baton Rouge, LA 70803. Offers astronomy (PhD); astrophysics (PhD); medical physics (MS); physics (MS, PhD). *Faculty:* 47 full-time (5 women), 1 part-time/adjunct (0 women). *Students:* 99 full-time (24 women), 4 part-time (0 women); includes 1 Black or African American, non-Hispanic/Latino; 1 Asian, non-Hispanic/Latino; 3 Hispanic/Latino, 43 international. Average age 27. 103 applicants, 17% accepted, 14 enrolled. In 2010, 9 master's, 12 doctorates awarded. Terminal master's awarded for partial completion of doctoral program. *Degree requirements:* For master's, thesis or alternative; for doctorate, thesis/dissertation. *Entrance requirements:* For master's and doctorate, GRE General Test, minimum GPA of 3.0. Additional exam requirements/recommendations for international students: Required—TOEFL (minimum score 550 paper-based; 213 computer-based; 79 iBT) or IELTS (minimum score 6.5). *Application deadline:* For fall admission, 1/25 priority date for domestic students, 5/15 for international students; for spring admission, 10/15 for international students. Applications are processed on a rolling basis. Application fee: $50 ($70 for international students). Electronic applications accepted. *Financial support:* In 2010–11, 103 students received support, including 15 fellowships with full tuition reimbursements available (averaging $16,537 per year), 48 research assistantships with full and partial tuition reimbursements available (averaging $20,677 per year), 40 teaching assistantships with full and partial tuition reimbursements available (averaging $18,525 per year); Federal Work-Study, institutionally sponsored loans, health care benefits, tuition waivers (full and partial), and unspecified assistantships also available. Financial award application deadline: 3/15; financial award applicants required to submit FAFSA. *Faculty research:* Experimentation and numerical relativity, condensed matter astrophysics, quantum computing, medical physics. Total annual research expenditures: $8.8 million. *Unit head:* Dr. Michael Cherry, Chair, 225-578-2261, Fax: 225-578-5855, E-mail: cherry@phys.lsu.edu. *Application contact:* Arnell Dangerfield, Administrative Coordinator, 225-578-1193, Fax: 225-578-5855, E-mail: adanger@lsu.edu.

Michigan State University, The Graduate School, College of Natural Science, Department of Physics and Astronomy, East Lansing, MI 48824. Offers astrophysics and astronomy (MS, PhD); physics (MS, PhD). *Entrance requirements:* Additional exam requirements/recommendations for international students: Required—TOEFL (minimum score 550 paper-based; 213 computer-based), Michigan State University ELT (minimum score 85), Michigan English Language Assessment Battery (minimum score 83). Electronic applications accepted. *Faculty research:* Nuclear and accelerator physics, high energy physics, condensed matter physics, biophysics, astrophysics and astronomy.

Minnesota State University Mankato, College of Graduate Studies, College of Science, Engineering and Technology, Department of Physics and Astronomy, Mankato, MN 56001. Offers MS. *Students:* 2 full-time (0 women), 4 part-time (1 woman). *Degree requirements:* For master's, one foreign language, comprehensive exam, thesis or alternative. *Entrance requirements:* For master's, minimum GPA of 3.0 during previous 2 years, recommendation letters. Additional exam requirements/recommendations for international students: Required—TOEFL. *Application deadline:* For fall admission, 7/1 priority date for domestic students; for spring admission, 11/1 for domestic students. Applications are processed on a rolling basis. Application fee: $40. Electronic applications accepted. *Financial support:* Research assistantships, teaching assistantships with full tuition reimbursements, Federal Work-Study and unspecified assistantships available. Support available to part-time students. Financial award application deadline: 3/15; financial award applicants required to submit FAFSA. *Unit head:* Dr. Youwen Xu, Chairperson, 507-389-5742. *Application contact:* 507-389-2321, E-mail: grad@mnsu.edu.

New Mexico State University, Graduate School, College of Arts and Sciences, Department of Astronomy, Las Cruces, NM 88003-8001. Offers MS, PhD. Part-time programs available. *Faculty:* 9 full-time (2 women). *Students:* 33 full-time (13 women), 3 part-time (2 women); includes 1 minority (Asian, non-Hispanic/Latino), 1 international. Average age 28. 54 applicants, 94% accepted, 7 enrolled. In 2010, 6 master's, 2 doctorates awarded. Terminal master's awarded for partial completion of doctoral program. *Degree requirements:* For master's, thesis (for some programs); for doctorate, thesis/dissertation. *Entrance requirements:* For master's and doctorate, GRE General Test, GRE Subject Test (advanced physics). Additional exam requirements/recommendations for international students: Required—TOEFL. *Application deadline:* For fall admission, 2/15 priority date for domestic and international students. Applications are processed on a rolling basis. Application fee: $30 ($50 for international students). Electronic applications accepted. *Expenses:* Tuition, state resident: full-time $4536; part-time $242 per credit. Tuition, nonresident: full-time $15,816; part-time $712 per credit. Required fees: $636 per term. *Financial support:* In 2010–11, 16 research assistantships with tuition reimbursements (averaging $13,781 per year), 11 teaching assistantships with partial tuition reimbursements (averaging $14,650 per year) were awarded; scholarships/grants, health care benefits, and unspecified assistantships also available. Financial award application deadline: 3/1. *Faculty research:* Planetary systems, accreting binary stars, stellar populations, galaxies, interstellar medium. *Unit head:* Dr. James Murphy, Head, 575-646-5333, Fax: 575-646-1602, E-mail: murphy@nmsu.edu. *Application contact:* Dr. James Murphy, Head, 575-646-5333, Fax: 575-646-1602, E-mail: murphy@nmsu.edu.

Northwestern University, The Graduate School, Judd A. and Marjorie Weinberg College of Arts and Sciences, Department of Physics and Astronomy, Evanston, IL 60208. Offers astrophysics (PhD); physics (MS, PhD). Admissions and degrees offered through The Graduate School. *Degree requirements:* For doctorate, thesis/dissertation, qualifying exam. *Entrance requirements:* For doctorate, GRE General Test, GRE Subject Test. Additional exam requirements/recommendations for international students: Required—TOEFL. *Faculty research:* Nuclear and particle physics, condensed-matter physics, nonlinear physics, astrophysics.

The Ohio State University, Graduate School, College of Arts and Sciences, Division of Natural and Mathematical Sciences, Department of Astronomy, Columbus, OH 43210. Offers MS, PhD. *Faculty:* 20. *Students:* 11 full-time (5 women), 13 part-time (4 women); includes 1 Two or more races, non-Hispanic/Latino, 7 international. Average age 25. In 2010, 2 master's, 5 doctorates awarded. *Degree requirements:* For master's, comprehensive exam, thesis; for doctorate, comprehensive exam, thesis/dissertation. *Entrance requirements:* For master's and doctorate, GRE General Test, GRE Subject Test (physics). Additional exam requirements/recommendations for international students: Required—TOEFL (minimum score 600 paper-based; 250 computer-based). *Application deadline:* For fall admission, 8/15 priority date for domestic students, 7/1 priority date for international students; for winter admission, 12/1 priority date for domestic students, 11/1 priority date for international students; for spring admission, 3/1 priority date for domestic students, 2/1 priority date for international students. Applications are processed on a rolling basis. Application fee: $40 ($50 for international students). Electronic applications accepted. *Expenses:* Tuition, state resident: full-time $10,605. Tuition, nonresident: full-time $26,535. Tuition and fees vary according to course load and program. *Financial support:* Fellowships, research assistantships, teaching assistantships, Federal Work-Study and institutionally sponsored loans available. Support available to part-time students. *Unit head:* Bradley M. Peterson, Chair, 614-292-1773, E-mail: peterson@astronomy.ohio-state.edu. *Application contact:* 614-292-9444, Fax: 614-292-3895, E-mail: domestic.grad@osu.edu.

Ohio University, Graduate College, College of Arts and Sciences, Department of Physics and Astronomy, Athens, OH 45701. Offers astronomy (MS, PhD); physics (MS, PhD). Part-time programs available. *Faculty:* 27 full-time (3 women), 5 part-time/adjunct (1 woman). *Students:* 85 full-time (29 women); includes 1 Hispanic/Latino, 66 international. Average age 27. 125 applicants, 38% accepted, 21 enrolled. In 2010, 7 master's, 9 doctorates awarded. Terminal master's awarded for partial completion of doctoral program. *Degree requirements:* For master's, thesis or alternative; for doctorate, comprehensive exam, thesis/dissertation. *Entrance requirements:* For master's and doctorate, minimum GPA of 3.0. Additional exam requirements/recommendations for international students: Required—TOEFL (minimum score 600 paper-based; 250 computer-based; 100 iBT), IELTS (minimum score 7), TWE (minimum score 4). *Application deadline:* For fall admission, 2/1 priority date for domestic and international students. Applications are processed on a rolling basis. Application fee: $0. Electronic applications accepted. *Financial support:* In 2010–11, 1 fellowship with tuition reimbursement (averaging $22,205 per year), 42 research assistantships with full tuition reimbursements (averaging $23,908 per year), 31 teaching assistantships with full tuition reimbursements (averaging $21,726 per year) were awarded; scholarships/grants and unspecified assistantships also available. Financial award application deadline: 4/1. *Faculty research:* Nuclear physics, condensed-matter physics, nonlinear systems, astrophysics, biophysics. Total annual research expenditures: $4.3 million. *Unit head:* Dr. Joseph Shields, Chair, 740-593-0336, Fax: 740-593-0433, E-mail: shields@helios.phy.ohiou.edu. *Application contact:* Dr. Marcus Boettcher, Graduate Admissions Chair, 740-593-1714, Fax: 740-593-0433, E-mail: gradapp@phy.ohiou.edu.

See display on page 193 and Close-Up on page 217.

Penn State University Park, Graduate School, Eberly College of Science, Department of Astronomy and Astrophysics, State College, University Park, PA 16802-1503. Offers MS, PhD. *Unit head:* Dr. Eric D. Feigelson, Assistant Department Head, 814-865-0162, Fax: 814-863-3399. *Application contact:* Cynthia E. Nicosia, Director, Graduate Enrollment Services, 814-865-1795, Fax: 814-865-4627, E-mail: cey1@psu.edu.

Princeton University, Graduate School, Department of Astrophysical Sciences, Princeton, NJ 08544-1019. Offers astronomy (PhD); plasma physics (PhD). *Degree requirements:* For doctorate, thesis/dissertation. *Entrance requirements:* For doctorate, GRE General Test, GRE Subject Test (physics). Additional exam requirements/recommendations for international students: Required—TOEFL (minimum score 600 paper-based; 250 computer-based). Electronic applications accepted. *Faculty research:* Theoretical astrophysics, cosmology, galaxy formation, galactic dynamics, interstellar and intergalactic matter.

Rice University, Graduate Programs, Wiess School of Natural Sciences, Department of Physics and Astronomy, Houston, TX 77251-1892. Offers nanoscale physics (MS); physics and astronomy (PhD); science teaching (MST). Part-time programs available. *Degree requirements:* For master's, thesis (for some programs); for doctorate, thesis/dissertation, minimum B average. *Entrance requirements:* For master's, GRE General Test; for doctorate, GRE General Test, GRE Subject Test. Additional exam requirements/recommendations for international students: Required—TOEFL (minimum score 600 paper-based; 250 computer-based; 90 iBT). Electronic applications accepted. *Faculty research:* Optical physics; ultra cold atoms; membrane electr-statics, peptides, proteins and lipids; solar astrophysics; stellar activity; magnetic fields; young stars.

Rutgers, The State University of New Jersey, New Brunswick, Graduate School-New Brunswick, Department of Physics and Astronomy, Piscataway, NJ 08854-8097. Offers astronomy (MS, PhD); biophysics (PhD); condensed matter physics (MS, PhD); elementary particle physics (MS, PhD); intermediate energy nuclear physics (MS); nuclear physics (MS, PhD); physics (MST); surface science (PhD); theoretical physics (MS, PhD). Part-time programs available. Terminal master's awarded for partial completion of doctoral program. *Degree requirements:* For master's, comprehensive exam, thesis or alternative; for doctorate, comprehensive exam, thesis/dissertation. *Entrance requirements:* For master's and doctorate, GRE General Test, GRE Subject Test. Additional exam requirements/recommendations for international students: Required—TOEFL (minimum score 560 paper-based). Electronic applications accepted. *Expenses:* Tuition, state resident: full-time $7200; part-time $600 per credit. Tuition, nonresident: full-time $11,124; part-time $927 per credit. *Faculty research:* Astronomy, high energy, condensed matter, surface, nuclear physics.

Saint Mary's University, Faculty of Science, Department of Astronomy and Physics, Halifax, NS B3H 3C3, Canada. Offers astronomy (M Sc, PhD). Part-time programs available. *Degree requirements:* For master's, thesis optional; for doctorate, comprehensive exam, thesis/dissertation. *Entrance requirements:* For master's, honors degree with minimum GPA of 3.0. Additional exam requirements/recommendations for international students: Required—TOEFL. *Faculty research:* Young stellar objects, interstellar medium, star clusters, galactic structure, early-type galaxies.

San Diego State University, Graduate and Research Affairs, College of Sciences, Department of Astronomy, San Diego, CA 92182. Offers MS. *Degree requirements:* For master's, thesis. *Entrance requirements:* For master's, GRE General Test, letters of reference. Additional exam requirements/recommendations for international students: Required—TOEFL. Electronic applications accepted. *Faculty research:* CCD, classical and dwarf novae, photometry, interactive binaries.

Stony Brook University, State University of New York, Graduate School, College of Arts and Sciences, Department of Physics and Astronomy, Program in Astronomy, Stony Brook, NY 11794. Offers PhD. *Degree requirements:* For doctorate, thesis/dissertation. *Entrance requirements:* For doctorate, GRE General Test, minimum GPA of 3.0. Additional exam requirements/recommendations for international students: Required—TOEFL. *Application deadline:* For fall admission, 1/15 for domestic students. Application fee: $100. *Expenses:* Tuition, state resident: full-time $8370; part-time $349 per credit. Tuition, nonresident: full-time $13,780; part-time $574 per credit. Required fees: $994. *Financial support:* Fellowships, research assistantships, teaching assistantships available. Financial award application deadline: 2/1. *Unit head:* Dr. Laszlo Mihaly, Chair, 631-632-8100, Fax: 631-632-8176, E-mail: laszlo.mihaly@stonybrook.edu. *Application contact:* Dr. Jacobus Verbaarschot, Director, 631-403-0754, Fax: 631-632-8176, E-mail: jacobus.verbaarschot@stonybrook.edu.

Université de Moncton, Faculty of Science, Department of Physics and Astronomy, Moncton, NB E1A 3E9, Canada. Offers M Sc. Part-time programs available. *Degree requirements:* For master's, thesis. *Entrance requirements:* For master's, proficiency in French. Electronic applications accepted. *Faculty research:* Thin films, optical properties, solar selective surfaces, microgravity and photonic materials.

The University of Arizona, College of Science, Department of Astronomy, Tucson, AZ 85721. Offers MS, PhD. *Faculty:* 24 full-time (4 women), 3 part-time/adjunct (0 women). *Students:* 36 full-time (14 women), 7 part-time (1 woman); includes 1 Hispanic/Latino; 1 Two or more races, non-Hispanic/Latino, 7 international. Average age 27. 116 applicants, 12% accepted, 4 enrolled. In 2010, 1 master's, 4 doctorates awarded. *Degree requirements:* For doctorate, thesis/dissertation. *Entrance requirements:* For doctorate, GRE General Test, GRE Subject Test (physics), minimum GPA of 3.5, 3 letters of recommendation. Additional exam requirements/recommendations for international students: Required—TOEFL (minimum score 550 paper-

Astronomy

The University of Arizona (continued)

based; 213 computer-based; 79 iBT). *Application deadline:* For fall admission, 1/15 for domestic students, 12/1 for international students. Applications are processed on a rolling basis. Application fee: $75. Electronic applications accepted. *Expenses:* Tuition, state resident: full-time $7692. *Financial support:* In 2010–11, 37 research assistantships with full tuition reimbursements (averaging $22,481 per year), 9 teaching assistantships with full tuition reimbursements (averaging $17,203 per year) were awarded; scholarships/grants, health care benefits, and unspecified assistantships also available. *Faculty research:* Astrophysics, submillimeter astronomy, infrared astronomy, NICMOS, SIRTF. Total annual research expenditures: $79.3 million. *Unit head:* Dr. Peter A. Strittmatter, Head, 520-621-6524, Fax: 520-621-1532, E-mail: pstrittm@as.arizona.edu. *Application contact:* Erin L. Carlson, Administrative Associate, 520-621-6538, Fax: 520-621-1532, E-mail: ecarlson@as.arizona.edu.

The University of British Columbia, Faculty of Science, Program in Astronomy, Vancouver, BC V6T 1Z1, Canada. Offers M Sc, PhD. Tuition charges are reported in Canadian dollars. *Expenses:* Tuition, area resident: Full-time $4179 Canadian dollars. International tuition: $7344 Canadian dollars full-time.

University of Calgary, Faculty of Graduate Studies, Faculty of Science, Department of Physics and Astronomy, Calgary, AB T2N 1N4, Canada. Offers M Sc, PhD. Part-time programs available. *Degree requirements:* For master's, thesis; for doctorate, thesis/dissertation, oral candidacy exam, written qualifying exam. *Entrance requirements:* For master's and doctorate, GRE General Test, GRE Subject Test. Additional exam requirements/recommendations for international students: Required—TOEFL (minimum score 550 paper-based; 213 computer-based). Electronic applications accepted. *Faculty research:* Astronomy and astrophysics, mass spectrometry, atmospheric physics, space physics, medical physics.

University of California, Los Angeles, Graduate Division, College of Letters and Science, Department of Physics and Astronomy, Program in Astronomy, Los Angeles, CA 90095. Offers MAT, MS, PhD. *Students:* 18 full-time (8 women); includes 2 minority (1 Asian, non-Hispanic/Latino; 1 Hispanic/Latino), 1 international. Average age 25. 69 applicants, 22% accepted, 3 enrolled. In 2010, 3 master's, 5 doctorates awarded. Terminal master's awarded for partial completion of doctoral program. *Degree requirements:* For master's, comprehensive exam; for doctorate, thesis/dissertation, oral and written qualifying exams. *Entrance requirements:* For master's, GRE General Test, GRE Subject Test (physics), minimum GPA of 3.0, statement of purpose, BS in related field; for doctorate, GRE General Test, GRE Subject Test (physics), BS in related field, minimum undergraduate GPA of 3.0. *Application deadline:* For fall admission, 12/15 for domestic and international students. Application fee: $70 ($90 for international students). Electronic applications accepted. *Financial support:* In 2010–11, 13 fellowships with full and partial tuition reimbursements, 20 research assistantships with full and partial tuition reimbursements, 10 teaching assistantships with full and partial tuition reimbursements were awarded; Federal Work-Study, institutionally sponsored loans, scholarships/grants, health care benefits, tuition waivers (full and partial), and unspecified assistantships also available. Financial award application deadline: 3/1; financial award applicants required to submit FAFSA. *Unit head:* Dr. James Rosenzweig, Chair, 310-206-4541, E-mail: rosenzweig@physics.ucla.edu. *Application contact:* Carol Finn, Graduate Counselor, 310-825-2307, E-mail: apply@physics.ucla.edu.

University of California, Santa Cruz, Division of Graduate Studies, Division of Physical and Biological Sciences, Department of Astronomy and Astrophysics, Santa Cruz, CA 95064. Offers PhD. *Students:* 37 full-time (18 women), 1 (woman) part-time; includes 8 minority (4 Asian, non-Hispanic/Latino; 4 Hispanic/Latino), 7 international. Average age 26. 131 applicants, 19% accepted, 8 enrolled. In 2010, 3 doctorates awarded. *Degree requirements:* For doctorate, one foreign language, thesis/dissertation, qualifying exam. *Entrance requirements:* For doctorate, GRE General Test, GRE Subject Test. Additional exam requirements/recommendations for international students: Required—TOEFL (minimum score 550 paper-based; 220 computer-based; 83 iBT); Recommended—IELTS (minimum score 8). *Application deadline:* For fall admission, 1/5 for domestic and international students. Application fee: $70 ($90 for international students). Electronic applications accepted. *Financial support:* Fellowships, research assistantships, teaching assistantships, institutionally sponsored loans and tuition waivers available. Financial award applicants required to submit FAFSA. *Faculty research:* Solar system and the Milky Way to the most distant galaxies in the Universe, fundamental questions of cosmology. *Unit head:* Maria Sliwinski, Graduate Program Coordinator, 831-459-2844, Fax: 831-459-5265, E-mail: sliwinsk@ucsc.edu. *Application contact:* Maria Sliwinski, Graduate Program Coordinator, 831-459-2844, Fax: 831-459-5265, E-mail: sliwinsk@ucsc.edu.

University of Chicago, Division of the Physical Sciences, Department of Astronomy and Astrophysics, Chicago, IL 60637-1513. Offers MS, PhD. Terminal master's awarded for partial completion of doctoral program. *Degree requirements:* For master's, comprehensive exam, thesis optional, candidacy exam; for doctorate, comprehensive exam, thesis/dissertation, dissertation for publication. *Entrance requirements:* For master's, department candidacy examination, minimum GPA of 3.0; for doctorate, GRE General Test, GRE Subject Test, minimum GPA of 3.0. Additional exam requirements/recommendations for international students: Required—TOEFL (minimum score 600 paper-based; 250 computer-based); Recommended—IELTS. Electronic applications accepted. *Faculty research:* Quasi-stellar object absorption lines, fluid dynamics, interstellar matter, particle physics, cosmology.

University of Delaware, College of Arts and Sciences, Department of Physics and Astronomy, Newark, DE 19716. Offers MS, PhD. Part-time programs available. Terminal master's awarded for partial completion of doctoral program. *Degree requirements:* For master's, thesis; for doctorate, thesis/dissertation. *Entrance requirements:* For master's and doctorate, GRE General Test, GRE Subject Test. Additional exam requirements/recommendations for international students: Required—TOEFL (minimum score 600 paper-based; 250 computer-based). Electronic applications accepted. *Faculty research:* Magnetoresistance and magnetic materials, ultrafast optical phenomena, superfluidity, elementary particle physics, stellar atmospheres and interiors.

University of Denver, Faculty of Natural Sciences and Mathematics, Department of Physics and Astronomy, Denver, CO 80208. Offers MS, PhD. Part-time programs available. *Faculty:* 10 full-time (2 women), 1 part-time/adjunct (0 women). *Students:* 7 full-time (2 women), 10 part-time (3 women); includes 2 minority (1 Asian, non-Hispanic/Latino; 1 Hispanic/Latino), 2 international. Average age 28. 28 applicants, 36% accepted, 5 enrolled. In 2010, 1 doctorate awarded. Terminal master's awarded for partial completion of doctoral program. *Degree requirements:* For master's, thesis optional; for doctorate, thesis/dissertation. *Entrance requirements:* For master's and doctorate, GRE General Test; GRE Subject Test in physics (strongly preferred). Additional exam requirements/recommendations for international students: Required—TOEFL (minimum score 550 paper-based; 80 iBT). *Application deadline:* For fall admission, 3/1 priority date for domestic students. Applications are processed on a rolling basis. Application fee: $60. Electronic applications accepted. *Expenses:* Tuition: Full-time $35,604; part-time $29,670 per year. Required fees: $687 per year. Tuition and fees vary according to program. *Financial support:* In 2010–11, 11 research assistantships with full and partial tuition reimbursements (averaging $19,299 per year), 7 teaching assistantships with full and partial tuition reimbursements (averaging $19,299 per year) were awarded; career-related internships or fieldwork, Federal Work-Study, institutionally sponsored loans, scholarships/grants, and unspecified assistantships also available. Support available to part-time students. Financial award application deadline: 3/1; financial award applicants required to submit FAFSA. *Faculty research:* Atomic and molecular beams and collisions, infrared astronomy, acoustic emission from stressed solids, nano materials. *Unit head:* Dr. Davor Balzar, Chair, 303-871-2238, E-mail: davor.balzar@du.edu. *Application contact:* Barbara Stephen, Assistant to the Chair, 303-871-2238, E-mail: barbara.stephen@du.edu.

University of Florida, Graduate School, College of Liberal Arts and Sciences, Department of Astronomy, Gainesville, FL 32611. Offers MS, PhD. *Faculty:* 21 full-time (3 women). *Students:* 34 full-time (9 women), 2 part-time (1 woman); includes 1 Asian, non-Hispanic/Latino; 3 Hispanic/Latino, 13 international. Average age 28. 58 applicants, 9% accepted, 5 enrolled. In 2010, 3 master's, 3 doctorates awarded. Terminal master's awarded for partial completion of doctoral program. *Degree requirements:* For master's, thesis (terminal MS); for doctorate, one foreign language, comprehensive exam, thesis/dissertation. *Entrance requirements:* For master's and doctorate, GRE General Test, GRE Physics Subject Test, minimum GPA of 3.0. Additional exam requirements/recommendations for international students: Required—TOEFL (minimum score 550 paper-based; 213 computer-based; 80 iBT), IELTS (minimum score 6). *Application deadline:* For fall admission, 1/20 for domestic and international students. Applications are processed on a rolling basis. Application fee: $30. Electronic applications accepted. *Expenses:* Tuition, state resident: full-time $10,915.92. Tuition, nonresident: full-time $28,309. *Financial support:* In 2010–11, 41 students received support, including 17 fellowships, 10 research assistantships (averaging $20,507 per year), 14 teaching assistantships (averaging $22,577 per year); tuition waivers (full) and unspecified assistantships also available. Financial award application deadline: 1/31; financial award applicants required to submit FAFSA. *Faculty research:* Solar systems, stars and stellar populations, star formation and interstellar medium, structure and evolution of galaxies, extragalactic astronomy and cosmology, extrasolar planets and instrumentation. *Unit head:* Rafael Guzman, PhD, Chair, 352-392-2052 Ext. 212, Fax: 352-392-5089, E-mail: guzman@astro.ufl.edu. *Application contact:* Anthony H. Gonzalez, PhD, Graduate Coordinator, 352-392-2052 Ext. 233, Fax: 352-392-5089, E-mail: anthony@astro.ufl.edu.

University of Hawaii at Manoa, Graduate Division, College of Natural Sciences, Department of Physics and Astronomy, Program in Astronomy, Honolulu, HI 96822. Offers MS, PhD. Part-time programs available. *Faculty:* 53 full-time (8 women). *Students:* 38 full-time (12 women); includes 8 minority (1 American Indian or Alaska Native, non-Hispanic/Latino; 4 Asian, non-Hispanic/Latino; 1 Native Hawaiian or other Pacific Islander, non-Hispanic/Latino; 2 Two or more races, non-Hispanic/Latino), 10 international. Average age 28. 98 applicants, 17% accepted, 5 enrolled. In 2010, 3 master's, 9 doctorates awarded. *Degree requirements:* For master's, thesis optional; for doctorate, comprehensive exam, thesis/dissertation. *Entrance requirements:* For master's and doctorate, GRE General Test. Additional exam requirements/recommendations for international students: Required—TOEFL (minimum score 560 paper-based; 220 computer-based; 83 iBT), IELTS (minimum score 5). *Application deadline:* For fall admission, 12/31 for domestic and international students. Application fee: $60. *Financial support:* In 2010–11, 38 students received support, including 1 fellowship (averaging $1,100 per year), 33 research assistantships (averaging $24,981 per year), 4 teaching assistantships (averaging $22,140 per year). Total annual research expenditures: $29.3 million. *Application contact:* David Sanders, Graduate Chair, 808-956-8101, Fax: 808-956-4532, E-mail: sandersd@hawaii.edu.

University of Illinois at Urbana–Champaign, Graduate College, College of Liberal Arts and Sciences, Department of Astronomy, Champaign, IL 61820. Offers astronomy (PhD). *Faculty:* 11 full-time (1 woman). *Students:* 20 full-time (7 women), 12 part-time (5 women); includes 3 Asian, non-Hispanic/Latino, 14 international. 43 applicants, 9% accepted, 4 enrolled. In 2010, 3 master's, 4 doctorates awarded. *Entrance requirements:* For master's and doctorate, GRE General Test, minimum GPA of 3.0. Additional exam requirements/recommendations for international students: Required—TOEFL (minimum score 550 paper-based; 213 computer-based). *Application deadline:* Applications are processed on a rolling basis. Application fee: $75 ($90 for international students). Electronic applications accepted. *Financial support:* In 2010–11, 2 fellowships, 18 research assistantships, 12 teaching assistantships were awarded; tuition waivers (full and partial) also available. *Unit head:* You-Hua Chu, Chair, 217-333-5535, Fax: 217-244-7638, E-mail: yhchu@illinois.edu. *Application contact:* Jeri Cochran, Administrative Assistant, 217-333-9784, Fax: 217-244-7638, E-mail: jcochran@illinois.edu.

The University of Iowa, Graduate College, College of Liberal Arts and Sciences, Department of Physics and Astronomy, Program in Astronomy, Iowa City, IA 52242-1316. Offers MS. *Degree requirements:* For master's, thesis optional, exam. *Entrance requirements:* For master's, GRE General Test, minimum GPA of 3.0. Additional exam requirements/recommendations for international students: Required—TOEFL (minimum score 550 paper-based; 213 computer-based; 81 iBT). Electronic applications accepted.

The University of Kansas, Graduate Studies, College of Liberal Arts and Sciences, Department of Physics and Astronomy, Lawrence, KS 66045. Offers computational physics and astronomy (MS); physics (MS, PhD). *Students:* 39 full-time (9 women), 4 part-time (1 woman); includes 2 minority (1 Black or African American, non-Hispanic/Latino; 1 Hispanic/Latino), 13 international. Average age 28. 41 applicants, 29% accepted, 5 enrolled. In 2010, 2 master's, 2 doctorates awarded. Terminal master's awarded for partial completion of doctoral program. *Degree requirements:* For master's, thesis (for some programs); for doctorate, comprehensive exam, thesis/dissertation, computer skills, communication skills. *Entrance requirements:* For master's and doctorate, GRE Subject Test (physics), undergraduate degree. Additional exam requirements/recommendations for international students: Required—TOEFL. *Application deadline:* For fall admission, 5/1 priority date for domestic and international students; for spring admission, 11/15 for domestic and international students. Applications are processed on a rolling basis. Application fee: $55 ($65 for international students). Electronic applications accepted. *Expenses:* Tuition, state resident: full-time $7092; part-time $295.50 per credit hour. Tuition, nonresident: full-time $16,590; part-time $691.25 per credit hour. Required fees: $858; $71.49 per credit hour. Tuition and fees vary according to course load, campus/location and program. *Financial support:* Fellowships with full and partial tuition reimbursements, research assistantships with full and partial tuition reimbursements, teaching assistantships with full and partial tuition reimbursements, health care benefits and unspecified assistantships available. Financial award application deadline: 5/1. *Faculty research:* Condensed-matter, cosmology, elementary particles, nuclear physics, space physics, astrophysics, astrobiology, biophysics, high energy. *Unit head:* Dr. Stephen J. Sanders, Chair, 785-864-4626, Fax: 785-864-5262. *Application contact:* Tess Gratton, Graduate Admission Specialist, 785-864-4626, Fax: 785-864-5262, E-mail: physics@ku.edu.

University of Kentucky, Graduate School, College of Arts and Sciences, Program in Physics and Astronomy, Lexington, KY 40506-0032. Offers physics (MS, PhD). *Degree requirements:* For master's, comprehensive exam, thesis optional; for doctorate, comprehensive exam, thesis/dissertation. *Entrance requirements:* For master's, GRE General Test, minimum undergraduate GPA of 2.75; for doctorate, GRE General Test, minimum graduate GPA of 3.0. Additional exam requirements/recommendations for international students: Required—TOEFL (minimum score 550 paper-based; 213 computer-based). Electronic applications accepted. *Faculty research:* Astrophysics, active galactic nuclei, and radio astronomy; Rydbert atoms, and electron scattering; TOF spectroscopy, hyperon interactions and muons; particle theory, lattice gauge theory, quark, and skyrmion models.

University of Maine, Graduate School, College of Education and Human Development, Interdisciplinary Program in Teaching, Orono, ME 04469. Offers earth sciences (MST); generalist (MST); mathematics (MST); physics and astronomy (MST). *Students:* 10 full-time (7 women), 20 part-time (17 women); includes 1 minority (Black or African American, non-Hispanic/Latino). Average age 40. 13 applicants, 46% accepted, 6 enrolled. In 2010, 17 master's awarded. *Entrance requirements:* For master's, GRE General Test, MAT. Application fee: $65. *Expenses:* Tuition, state resident: full-time $400. Tuition, nonresident: full-time $1050. *Unit head:* Dr. Susan McKay, Director, 207-581-1016. *Application contact:* Scott G. Delcourt, Associate Dean of the Graduate School, 207-581-3219, Fax: 207-581-3232, E-mail: graduate@maine.edu.

38 www.facebook.com/petersonspublishing

Peterson's Graduate Programs in the Physical Sciences, Mathematics, Agricultural Sciences, the Environment & Natural Resources 2012

The University of Manchester, School of Physics and Astronomy, Manchester, United Kingdom. Offers astronomy and astrophysics (M Sc, PhD); biological physics (M Sc, PhD); condensed matter physics (M Sc, PhD); nonlinear and liquid crystals physics (M Sc, PhD); nuclear physics (M Sc, PhD); particle physics (M Sc, PhD); photon physics (M Sc, PhD); physics (M Sc, PhD); theoretical physics (M Sc, PhD).

University of Maryland, College Park, Academic Affairs, College of Computer, Mathematical and Natural Sciences, Department of Astronomy, College Park, MD 20742. Offers MS, PhD. Part-time and evening/weekend programs available. *Faculty:* 85 full-time (19 women), 10 part-time/adjunct (2 women). *Students:* 39 full-time (14 women); includes 4 minority (all Asian, non-Hispanic/Latino), 12 international. 116 applicants, 22% accepted, 7 enrolled. In 2010, 2 master's, 4 doctorates awarded. Terminal master's awarded for partial completion of doctoral program. *Degree requirements:* For master's, thesis or alternative, written exam; for doctorate, thesis/dissertation, research project. *Entrance requirements:* For master's, GRE General Test, GRE Subject Test (physics), minimum GPA of 3.0, 3 letters of recommendation; for doctorate, GRE General Test, GRE Subject Test (physics), 3 letters of recommendation. *Application deadline:* For fall admission, 1/15 for domestic and international students. Applications are processed on a rolling basis. Application fee: $75. Electronic applications accepted. *Expenses:* Tuition, area resident: Part-time $471 per credit hour. Tuition, state resident: part-time $471 per credit hour. Tuition, nonresident: part-time $1016 per credit hour. Required fees: $337 per term. *Financial support:* In 2010–11, 3 fellowships with full tuition reimbursements (averaging $14,933 per year), 23 research assistantships with tuition reimbursements (averaging $21,264 per year), 13 teaching assistantships with tuition reimbursements (averaging $19,082 per year) were awarded; career-related internships or fieldwork, Federal Work-Study, and scholarships/grants also available. Support available to part-time students. Financial award applicants required to submit FAFSA. *Faculty research:* Solar radio astronomy, plasma and high-energy astrophysics, galactic and extragalactic astronomy. Total annual research expenditures: $24.3 million. *Unit head:* Stuart N. Vogel, Chair, 301-405-1508, Fax: 301-314-9067, E-mail: svogel@umd.edu. *Application contact:* Dr. Charles A. Caramello, Dean of Graduate School, 301-405-0358, Fax: 301-314-9305, E-mail: ccaramel@umd.edu.

University of Massachusetts Amherst, Graduate School, College of Natural Sciences, Department of Astronomy, Amherst, MA 01003. Offers MS, PhD. Part-time programs available. *Faculty:* 16 full-time (3 women). *Students:* 21 full-time (6 women), 5 part-time (1 woman); includes 4 minority (1 American Indian or Alaska Native, non-Hispanic/Latino; 2 Hispanic/Latino; 1 Two or more races, non-Hispanic/Latino), 14 international. Average age 28. 48 applicants, 23% accepted, 5 enrolled. In 2010, 6 master's, 3 doctorates awarded. Terminal master's awarded for partial completion of doctoral program. *Degree requirements:* For master's, thesis or alternative; for doctorate, comprehensive exam, thesis/dissertation. *Entrance requirements:* For master's and doctorate, GRE General Test, GRE Subject Test (physics). Additional exam requirements/recommendations for international students: Required—TOEFL (minimum score 550 paper-based; 213 computer-based; 80 iBT), IELTS (minimum score 6.5). *Application deadline:* For fall admission, 2/1 for domestic and international students; for spring admission, 10/1 for domestic and international students. Applications are processed on a rolling basis. Application fee: $50 ($65 for international students). Electronic applications accepted. *Expenses:* Tuition, state resident: full-time $2640. Required fees: $8282. One-time fee: $357 full-time. *Financial support:* In 2010–11, 1 fellowship with full tuition reimbursement (averaging $14,469 per year), 22 research assistantships with full tuition reimbursements (averaging $13,951 per year), 11 teaching assistantships with full tuition reimbursements (averaging $8,558 per year) were awarded; career-related internships or fieldwork, Federal Work-Study, scholarships/grants, traineeships, health care benefits, tuition waivers (full), and unspecified assistantships also available. Support available to part-time students. Financial award application deadline: 2/1; financial award applicants required to submit FAFSA. *Unit head:* Dr. William M. Irvine, Graduate Program Director, 413-545-2194, Fax: 413-545-4223. *Application contact:* Jean M. Ames, Supervisor of Admissions, 413-545-0722, Fax: 413-577-0010, E-mail: gradadm@grad.umass.edu.

University of Michigan, Horace H. Rackham School of Graduate Studies, College of Literature, Science, and the Arts, Department of Astronomy, Ann Arbor, MI 48109-1042. Offers astronomy and astrophysics (PhD). *Faculty:* 20 full-time (5 women). *Students:* 29 full-time (12 women); includes 1 Black or African American, non-Hispanic/Latino; 4 Asian, non-Hispanic/Latino. 122 applicants, 9% accepted, 3 enrolled. In 2010, 3 doctorates awarded. Terminal master's awarded for partial completion of doctoral program. *Degree requirements:* For doctorate, thesis/dissertation, oral defense of dissertation, preliminary exam. *Entrance requirements:* For doctorate, GRE General Test, GRE Subject Test (physics). Additional exam requirements/recommendations for international students: Required—TOEFL. *Application deadline:* For fall admission, 1/5 for domestic and international students. Application fee: $65 ($75 for international students). Electronic applications accepted. *Expenses:* Tuition, state resident: full-time $17,784; part-time $1116 per credit hour. Tuition, nonresident: full-time $35,944; part-time $2125 per credit hour. International tuition: $35,994 full-time. Required fees: $95 per semester. Tuition and fees vary according to course load, degree level and program. *Financial support:* In 2010–11, 5 fellowships with full tuition reimbursements (averaging $22,800 per year), 23 research assistantships with full tuition reimbursements (averaging $22,800 per year), 13 teaching assistantships with full tuition reimbursements (averaging $22,800 per year) were awarded; institutionally sponsored loans, scholarships/grants, health care benefits, and unspecified assistantships also available. Financial award applicants required to submit FAFSA. *Faculty research:* Extragalactic and galactic astronomy, cosmology, star and planet formation, high energy astrophysics. Total annual research expenditures: $2.1 million. *Unit head:* Dr. Joel Bregman, Chair and Professor, 734-764-3440, Fax: 734-763-6317, E-mail: jbregman@umich.edu. *Application contact:* Brian M. Cox, Administrative Assistant, 734-764-3440, Fax: 734-763-6317, E-mail: bmcox@umich.edu.

University of Minnesota, Twin Cities Campus, Institute of Technology, School of Physics and Astronomy, Department of Astronomy, Minneapolis, MN 55455-0213. Offers astrophysics (MS, PhD). Terminal master's awarded for partial completion of doctoral program. *Degree requirements:* For master's, thesis optional; for doctorate, thesis/dissertation. *Entrance requirements:* For master's and doctorate, GRE General Test, GRE Subject Test. *Faculty research:* Evolution of stars and galaxies; the interstellar medium; cosmology; observational, optical, infrared, and radio astronomy; computational astrophysics.

University of Missouri, Graduate School, College of Arts and Sciences, Department of Physics and Astronomy, Columbia, MO 65211. Offers MS, PhD. *Faculty:* 34 full-time (9 women), 1 (woman) part-time/adjunct. *Students:* 31 full-time (7 women), 17 part-time (3 women); includes 2 minority (1 Asian, non-Hispanic/Latino; 1 Two or more races, non-Hispanic/Latino), 27 international. Average age 29. 66 applicants, 17% accepted, 11 enrolled. In 2010, 5 master's, 5 doctorates awarded. Terminal master's awarded for partial completion of doctoral program. *Degree requirements:* For doctorate, one foreign language, comprehensive exam, thesis/dissertation. *Entrance requirements:* For master's and doctorate, GRE General Test, minimum GPA of 3.0. Additional exam requirements/recommendations for international students: Required—TOEFL (minimum score 550 paper-based; 213 computer-based; 80 iBT). *Application deadline:* For fall admission, 3/15 priority date for domestic students. Applications are processed on a rolling basis. Application fee: $45 ($60 for international students). Electronic applications accepted. *Financial support:* In 2010–11, 35 research assistantships with full tuition reimbursements, 10 teaching assistantships with full tuition reimbursements were awarded; institutionally sponsored loans, health care benefits, and unspecified assistantships also available. *Faculty research:* Experimental and theoretical condensed-matter physics, biological physics, astronomy/astrophysics. *Unit head:* Dr. Peter Pfeifer, Department Chair, 573-882-2335, E-mail: pfeiferp@missouri.edu. *Application contact:* Dr. Carsten Ullrich, Director of Graduate Studies, 573-882-3335, E-mail: ullrichc@missouri.edu.

University of Nebraska–Lincoln, Graduate College, College of Arts and Sciences, Department of Physics and Astronomy, Lincoln, NE 68588. Offers astronomy (MS, PhD); physics (MS, PhD). *Degree requirements:* For master's, thesis optional; for doctorate, comprehensive exam, thesis/dissertation. *Entrance requirements:* For master's and doctorate, GRE General Test. Additional exam requirements/recommendations for international students: Required—TOEFL (minimum score 550 paper-based; 213 computer-based). Electronic applications accepted. *Faculty research:* Electromagnetics of solids and thin films, photoionization, ion collisions with atoms, molecules and surfaces, nanostructures.

University of Nevada, Las Vegas, Graduate College, College of Science, Department of Physics, Las Vegas, NV 89154-4002. Offers astronomy (MS, PhD); physics (MS, PhD). Part-time programs available. *Faculty:* 16 full-time (0 women), 6 part-time/adjunct (2 women). *Students:* 22 full-time (3 women), 1 part-time (0 women); includes 11 minority (1 Hispanic/Latino; 10 Two or more races, non-Hispanic/Latino), 9 international. Average age 29. 12 applicants, 42% accepted, 5 enrolled. In 2010, 7 master's, 2 doctorates awarded. *Degree requirements:* For master's, thesis, oral exam; for doctorate, comprehensive exam, thesis/dissertation. *Entrance requirements:* For master's and doctorate, GRE General Test. Additional exam requirements/recommendations for international students: Required—TOEFL (minimum score 550 paper-based; 213 computer-based; 80 iBT), IELTS (minimum score 7). *Application deadline:* For fall admission, 8/1 priority date for domestic and international students; for spring admission, 10/1 priority date for domestic and international students. Applications are processed on a rolling basis. Application fee: $60 ($95 for international students). Electronic applications accepted. *Expenses:* Tuition, area resident: Part-time $239.50 per credit. Tuition, state resident: part-time $239.50 per credit. Tuition, nonresident: part-time $503 per credit. Required fees: $108 per semester. Tuition and fees vary according to course load, program and reciprocity agreements. *Financial support:* In 2010–11, 13 research assistantships with partial tuition reimbursements (averaging $16,395 per year), 15 teaching assistantships with partial tuition reimbursements (averaging $12,856 per year) were awarded; institutionally sponsored loans, scholarships/grants, health care benefits, and unspecified assistantships also available. Financial award application deadline: 3/1. *Faculty research:* Gamma-ray bursters astrophysics, cosmology and dark matter astrophysics, experimental high pressure physics, theoretical condensed matter physics, laser-plasma atomic physics. Total annual research expenditures: $5 million. *Unit head:* Dr. Tao Pang, Chair/Professor, 702-895-4454, Fax: 702-895-0804, E-mail: pang@physics.unlv.edu. *Application contact:* Graduate College Admissions Evaluator, 702-895-3320, Fax: 702-895-4180, E-mail: gradcollege@unlv.edu.

The University of North Carolina at Chapel Hill, Graduate School, College of Arts and Sciences, Department of Physics and Astronomy, Chapel Hill, NC 27599. Offers physics (MS, PhD). Terminal master's awarded for partial completion of doctoral program. *Degree requirements:* For master's, comprehensive exam; for doctorate, comprehensive exam, thesis/dissertation. *Entrance requirements:* For master's and doctorate, GRE General Test, minimum GPA of 3.0. Electronic applications accepted. *Faculty research:* Observational astronomy, fullerenes, polarized beams, nanotubes, nucleosynthesis in stars and supernovae, superstring theory, ballistic transport in semiconductors, gravitation.

University of Rochester, School of Arts and Sciences, Department of Physics and Astronomy, Program in Physics and Astronomy, Rochester, NY 14627.

University of South Carolina, The Graduate School, College of Arts and Sciences, Department of Physics and Astronomy, Columbia, SC 29208. Offers IMA, MAT, MS, PSM, PhD. IMA and MAT offered in cooperation with the College of Education. Part-time programs available. Terminal master's awarded for partial completion of doctoral program. *Degree requirements:* For master's, comprehensive exam, thesis; for doctorate, one foreign language, comprehensive exam, thesis/dissertation. *Entrance requirements:* For master's and doctorate, GRE General Test, GRE Subject Test. Additional exam requirements/recommendations for international students: Required—TOEFL (minimum score 570 paper-based; 230 computer-based; 75 iBT). Electronic applications accepted. *Faculty research:* Condensed matter, intermediate-energy nuclear physics, foundations of quantum mechanics, astronomy/astrophysics.

The University of Texas at Austin, Graduate School, College of Natural Sciences, Department of Astronomy, Austin, TX 78712-1111. Offers MA, PhD. *Entrance requirements:* For master's and doctorate, GRE General Test, GRE Subject Test (physics). Additional exam requirements/recommendations for international students: Required—TOEFL. Electronic applications accepted. *Faculty research:* Stars, interstellar medium, galaxies, planetary astronomy, cosmology.

University of Toronto, School of Graduate Studies, Physical Sciences Division, Department of Astronomy and Astrophysics, Toronto, ON M5S 1A1, Canada. Offers M Sc, PhD. Part-time programs available. *Degree requirements:* For doctorate, thesis/dissertation, qualifying exam, thesis defense. *Entrance requirements:* For master's, minimum B average, bachelor's degree in astronomy or equivalent, 3 letters of reference; for doctorate, GRE General Test, minimum B+ average, master's degree in astronomy or equivalent, demonstrated research competence, 3 letters of reference.

University of Victoria, Faculty of Graduate Studies, Faculty of Science, Department of Physics and Astronomy, Victoria, BC V8W 2Y2, Canada. Offers astronomy and astrophysics (M Sc, PhD); condensed matter physics (M Sc, PhD); experimental particle physics (M Sc, PhD); medical physics (M Sc, PhD); ocean physics (M Sc, PhD); theoretical physics (M Sc, PhD). *Degree requirements:* For master's, thesis; for doctorate, comprehensive exam, thesis/dissertation, candidacy exam. *Entrance requirements:* For master's and doctorate, GRE. Additional exam requirements/recommendations for international students: Required—TOEFL (minimum score 575 paper-based; 233 computer-based), IELTS (minimum score 7). Electronic applications accepted. *Faculty research:* Old stellar populations; observational cosmology and large scale structure; cp violation; atlas.

University of Virginia, College and Graduate School of Arts and Sciences, Department of Astronomy, Charlottesville, VA 22903. Offers MS, PhD. *Faculty:* 15 full-time (2 women). *Students:* 34 full-time (13 women), 1 (woman) part-time, 11 international. Average age 26. 70 applicants, 26% accepted, 8 enrolled. In 2010, 3 master's, 5 doctorates awarded. *Degree requirements:* For master's, comprehensive exam, thesis or alternative; for doctorate, comprehensive exam, thesis/dissertation. *Entrance requirements:* For master's and doctorate, GRE General Test, GRE Subject Test. Additional exam requirements/recommendations for international students: Required—TOEFL (minimum score 650 paper-based; 250 computer-based; 90 iBT), IELTS (minimum score 7). *Application deadline:* For fall admission, 12/31 for domestic and international students. Applications are processed on a rolling basis. Application fee: $60. Electronic applications accepted. *Financial support:* Fellowships, research assistantships, teaching assistantships available. Financial award application deadline: 12/3; financial award applicants required to submit FAFSA. *Unit head:* John Hawley, Chair, 434-924-7494, Fax: 434-924-3104, E-mail: jh8h@virginia.edu. *Application contact:* Craig Sarazin, Chair, Graduate Admissions, 434-924-7494, Fax: 434-924-3104, E-mail: gradadm@mail.astro.virginia.edu.

University of Washington, Graduate School, College of Arts and Sciences, Department of Astronomy, Seattle, WA 98195. Offers MS, PhD. Terminal master's awarded for partial completion of doctoral program. *Degree requirements:* For doctorate, thesis/dissertation. *Entrance requirements:* For master's and doctorate, GRE General Test, GRE Subject Test, minimum GPA of 3.0. Additional exam requirements/recommendations for international students: Required—TOEFL. *Faculty research:* Solar system dust, space astronomy, high-energy astrophysics, galactic and extragalactic astronomy, stellar astrophysics.

The University of Western Ontario, Faculty of Graduate Studies, Physical Sciences Division, Department of Physics and Astronomy, Program in Astronomy, London, ON N6A 5B8, Canada.

Astronomy

The University of Western Ontario (continued)
Offers M Sc, PhD. Terminal master's awarded for partial completion of doctoral program. *Degree requirements:* For master's, thesis optional; for doctorate, comprehensive exam, thesis/dissertation. *Entrance requirements:* For master's, GRE Subject Test (physics), honors B Sc degree, minimum B average (Canadian), A—(international); for doctorate, M Sc degree, minimum B average (Canadian), A—(international). Additional exam requirements/recommendations for international students: Required—TOEFL (minimum score 580 paper-based; 237 computer-based). *Faculty research:* Observational and theoretical astrophysics spectroscopy, photometry, spectro-polarimetry, variable stars, cosmology.

University of Wisconsin–Madison, Graduate School, College of Letters and Science, Department of Astronomy, Madison, WI 53706-1380. Offers PhD. *Degree requirements:* For doctorate, comprehensive exam, thesis/dissertation. *Entrance requirements:* For doctorate, GRE General Test, GRE Subject Test (physics), bachelor's degree in related field. Additional exam requirements/recommendations for international students: Required—TOEFL. Electronic applications accepted. *Expenses:* Tuition, state resident: full-time $9887.36; part-time $617.96 per credit. Tuition, nonresident: full-time $24,054; part-time $1503.40 per credit. Required fees: $67.63 per credit. Tuition and fees vary according to reciprocity agreements. *Faculty research:* Kinematics, evolution of galaxies, cosmic distance, scale and large-scale structures, interstellar intergalactic medium, star formation and evolution, solar system chemistry and dynamics.

Vanderbilt University, Graduate School, Department of Physics and Astronomy, Nashville, TN 37240-1001. Offers astronomy (MS); physics (MA, MAT, MS, PhD). *Faculty:* 33 full-time (3 women). *Students:* 71 full-time (19 women), 1 part-time (0 women); includes 6 Black or African American, non-Hispanic/Latino; 2 Asian, non-Hispanic/Latino; 4 Hispanic/Latino. Average age 28. 179 applicants, 18% accepted, 15 enrolled. In 2010, 6 master's, 9 doctorates awarded. *Degree requirements:* For master's, thesis; for doctorate, comprehensive exam, thesis/dissertation, final and qualifying exams. *Entrance requirements:* For master's, GRE General Test; for doctorate, GRE General Test, GRE Subject Test. Additional exam requirements/recommendations for international students: Required—TOEFL (minimum score 570 paper-based; 230 computer-based; 88 iBT). *Application deadline:* For fall admission, 1/15 for domestic and international students. Application fee: $0. Electronic applications accepted. *Financial support:* Fellowships with full and partial tuition reimbursements, research assistantships with full tuition reimbursements, teaching assistantships with full tuition reimbursements, career-related internships or fieldwork, Federal Work-Study, and institutionally sponsored loans available. Financial award application deadline: 1/15; financial award applicants required to submit CSS PROFILE or FAFSA. *Faculty research:* Experimental and theoretical physics, free electron laser, living-state physics, heavy-ion physics, nuclear structure. *Unit head:* Robert J. Scherrer, PhD, Chair, 615-322-2828, Fax: 615-343-7263, E-mail: robert.scherrer@vanderbilt.edu. *Application contact:* Julia Velkovska, PhD, Director of Graduate Studies, 615-322-0656, Fax: 615-343-7263, E-mail: julia.velkovska@vanderbilt.edu.

Wesleyan University, Graduate Programs, Department of Astronomy, Middletown, CT 06459. Offers MA. *Faculty:* 3 full-time (0 women). *Students:* 4 full-time (2 women). Average age 24. 20 applicants, 10% accepted, 2 enrolled. In 2010, 2 master's awarded. *Degree requirements:* For master's, thesis. *Entrance requirements:* For master's, GRE General Test, GRE Subject Test. Additional exam requirements/recommendations for international students: Required—TOEFL. *Application deadline:* For fall admission, 3/1 for domestic and international students. Application fee: $0. Electronic applications accepted. *Expenses:* Tuition: Full-time $43,404. Required fees: $830. *Financial support:* In 2010–11, 4 teaching assistantships with full tuition reimbursements were awarded. Financial award application deadline: 4/15; financial award applicants required to submit FAFSA. *Faculty research:* Observational-theoretical astronomy and astrophysics. *Unit head:* Dr. Edward Moran, Chairman, 860-685-3739, E-mail: emoran@wesleyan.edu. *Application contact:* Linda Shettleworth, Information Contact, 860-685-2130, E-mail: shettleworth@wesleyan.edu.

West Chester University of Pennsylvania, Office of Graduate Studies, College of Arts and Sciences, Department of Geology and Astronomy, West Chester, PA 19383. Offers earth-space science (Teaching Certificate); general science (Teaching Certificate); geoscience (MA). Part-time and evening/weekend programs available. *Students:* 7 full-time (2 women), 20 part-time (11 women); includes 1 minority (Black or African American, non-Hispanic/Latino). Average age 33. 14 applicants, 86% accepted, 6 enrolled. In 2010, 7 master's awarded. *Degree requirements:* For master's, comprehensive exam (for some programs), thesis optional. *Entrance requirements:* For master's, minimum GPA of 2.5. Additional exam requirements/recommendations for international students: Required—TOEFL (minimum score 550 paper-based; 213 computer-based; 80 iBT). *Application deadline:* For fall admission, 4/15 priority date for domestic students, 3/15 for international students; for spring admission, 10/15 for domestic students, 9/1 for international students. Applications are processed on a rolling basis. Application fee: $35. Electronic applications accepted. *Expenses:* Tuition, state resident: full-time $6966; part-time $387 per credit. Tuition, nonresident: full-time $11,146; part-time $619 per credit. Required fees: $1614.40; $133.24 per credit. Part-time tuition and fees vary according to campus/location. *Financial support:* Unspecified assistantships available. Support available to part-time students. Financial award application deadline: 2/15; financial award applicants required to submit FAFSA. *Faculty research:* Developing and using a meteorological data station. *Unit head:* Dr. Marc Gagne, Chair, 610-436-2727, E-mail: mgagne@wcupa.edu. *Application contact:* Dr. Steven Good, Graduate Coordinator, 610-436-2203, E-mail: sgood@wcupa.edu.

Yale University, Graduate School of Arts and Sciences, Department of Astronomy, New Haven, CT 06520. Offers astronomy (PhD); solar and terrestrial physics (PhD). *Degree requirements:* For doctorate, thesis/dissertation. *Entrance requirements:* For doctorate, GRE General Test, GRE Subject Test (physics).

York University, Faculty of Graduate Studies, Faculty of Science and Engineering, Program in Physics and Astronomy, Toronto, ON M3J 1P3, Canada. Offers M Sc, PhD. Part-time and evening/weekend programs available. *Degree requirements:* For master's, thesis or alternative; for doctorate, comprehensive exam, thesis/dissertation. Electronic applications accepted.

Astrophysics

Air Force Institute of Technology, Graduate School of Engineering and Management, Department of Engineering Physics, Dayton, OH 45433-7765. Offers applied physics (MS, PhD); electro-optics (MS, PhD); materials science (PhD); nuclear engineering (MS, PhD); space physics (MS). Part-time programs available. *Degree requirements:* For master's, thesis; for doctorate, thesis/dissertation. *Entrance requirements:* For master's and doctorate, GRE General Test, minimum GPA of 3.0, U.S. citizenship. *Faculty research:* High-energy lasers, space physics, nuclear weapon effects, semiconductor physics.

Arizona State University, College of Liberal Arts and Sciences, School of Earth and Space Exploration, Tempe, AZ 85287-1404. Offers astrophysics (MS, PhD); exploration systems design (PhD); geological sciences (MS, PhD). PhD in exploration systems design is offered in collaboration with the Fulton Schools of Engineering. *Faculty:* 43 full-time (4 women), 2 part-time/adjunct (1 woman). *Students:* 89 full-time (32 women), 16 part-time (8 women); includes 12 minority (2 American Indian or Alaska Native, non-Hispanic/Latino; 4 Asian, non-Hispanic/Latino; 6 Hispanic/Latino), 18 international. Average age 30. 181 applicants, 28% accepted, 28 enrolled. In 2010, 6 master's, 7 doctorates awarded. Terminal master's awarded for partial completion of doctoral program. *Degree requirements:* For master's, thesis, interactive Program of Study (iPOS) submitted before completing 50 percent of required credit hours; for doctorate, thesis/dissertation, interactive Program of Study (iPOS) submitted before completing 50 percent of required credit hours. *Entrance requirements:* For master's and doctorate, GRE, minimum GPA of 3.0 or equivalent in last 2 years of work leading to bachelor's degree. Additional exam requirements/recommendations for international students: Required—TOEFL, IELTS, or Pearson Test of English. *Application deadline:* For fall admission, 1/15 for domestic and international students; for spring admission, 10/1 for domestic and international students. Applications are processed on a rolling basis. Application fee: $70 ($90 for international students). Electronic applications accepted. *Expenses:* Tuition, state resident: full-time $8510; part-time $608 per credit. Tuition, nonresident: full-time $16,542; part-time $919 per credit. Required fees: $339; $110 per credit. Part-time tuition and fees vary according to course load. *Financial support:* In 2010–11, 52 research assistantships with full and partial tuition reimbursements (averaging $15,804 per year), 42 teaching assistantships with full and partial tuition reimbursements (averaging $15,169 per year) were awarded; fellowships with full tuition reimbursements, career-related internships or fieldwork, Federal Work-Study, institutionally sponsored loans, scholarships/grants, and tuition waivers (full and partial) also available. Financial award application deadline: 3/1; financial award applicants required to submit FAFSA. Total annual research expenditures: $18.8 million. *Unit head:* Dr. Kip Hodges, Director, 480-965-5331, Fax: 480-965-8102, E-mail: kvhodges@asu.edu. *Application contact:* Graduate Admissions, 480-965-6113.

Clemson University, Graduate School, College of Engineering and Science, Department of Physics and Astronomy, Clemson, SC 29634. Offers physics (MS, PhD), including astronomy and astrophysics, atmospheric physics, biophysics. Part-time programs available. *Faculty:* 25 full-time (4 women), 2 part-time/adjunct (0 women). *Students:* 63 full-time (19 women); includes 3 Black or African American, non-Hispanic/Latino, 26 international. Average age 27. 66 applicants, 92% accepted, 21 enrolled. In 2010, 2 master's, 6 doctorates awarded. Terminal master's awarded for partial completion of doctoral program. *Degree requirements:* For master's, thesis or alternative; for doctorate, thesis/dissertation. *Entrance requirements:* For master's and doctorate, GRE General Test. Additional exam requirements/recommendations for international students: Required—TOEFL. *Application deadline:* For fall admission, 1/15 priority date for domestic students; for spring admission, 9/15 priority date for domestic students. Applications are processed on a rolling basis. Application fee: $70 ($80 for international students). Electronic applications accepted. *Expenses:* Tuition, state resident: full-time $6492; part-time $400 per credit hour. Tuition, nonresident: full-time $13,634; part-time $800 per credit hour. Required fees: $262 per semester. Part-time tuition and fees vary according to course load and program. *Financial support:* In 2010–11, 58 students received support, including 1 fellowship with full and partial tuition reimbursement available (averaging $16,000 per year), 26 research assistantships with partial tuition reimbursements available (averaging $13,559 per year), 43 teaching assistantships with partial tuition reimbursements available (averaging $14,097 per year); career-related internships or fieldwork, institutionally sponsored loans, scholarships/grants, health care benefits, and unspecified assistantships also available. Support available to part-time students. Financial award application deadline: 6/1; financial award applicants required to submit FAFSA. *Faculty research:* Radiation physics, solid-state physics, nuclear physics, radar and lidar studies of atmosphere. Total annual research expenditures: $2.4 million. *Unit head:* Dr. Peter Barnes, Chair, 864-656-3419, Fax: 864-656-0805, E-mail: peterb@clemson.edu. *Application contact:* Dr. Murray Daw, Graduate Coordinator, 864-656-6702, Fax: 864-656-0805, E-mail: physgradinfo-l@clemson.edu.

Cornell University, Graduate School, Graduate Fields of Arts and Sciences, Field of Astronomy and Space Sciences, Ithaca, NY 14853-0001. Offers astronomy (PhD); astrophysics (PhD); general space sciences (PhD); infrared astronomy (PhD); planetary studies (PhD); radio astronomy (PhD); radiophysics (PhD); theoretical astrophysics (PhD). *Faculty:* 25 full-time (2 women). *Students:* 28 full-time (11 women); includes 3 Asian, non-Hispanic/Latino; 1 Hispanic/Latino, 7 international. Average age 26. 88 applicants, 24% accepted, 2 enrolled. In 2010, 3 doctorates awarded. *Degree requirements:* For doctorate, comprehensive exam, thesis/dissertation. *Entrance requirements:* For doctorate, GRE General Test, GRE Subject Test (physics), 3 letters of recommendation. Additional exam requirements/recommendations for international students: Required—TOEFL (minimum score 600 paper-based; 250 computer-based; 77 iBT). *Application deadline:* For fall admission, 1/15 for domestic students. Application fee: $80. Electronic applications accepted. *Expenses:* Tuition: Full-time $29,500. Required fees: $76. Tuition and fees vary according to degree level and program. *Financial support:* In 2010–11, 2 fellowships with full tuition reimbursements, 17 research assistantships with full tuition reimbursements, 9 teaching assistantships with full tuition reimbursements were awarded; institutionally sponsored loans, scholarships/grants, health care benefits, tuition waivers (full and partial), and unspecified assistantships also available. Financial award applicants required to submit FAFSA. *Faculty research:* Observational astrophysics, planetary sciences, cosmology, instrumentation, gravitational astrophysics. *Unit head:* Director of Graduate Studies, 607-255-4341. *Application contact:* Graduate Field Assistant, 607-255-4341, E-mail: oconnor@astro.cornell.edu.

Harvard University, Graduate School of Arts and Sciences, Department of Astronomy, Cambridge, MA 02138. Offers astronomy (PhD); astrophysics (PhD). *Degree requirements:* For doctorate, thesis/dissertation, paper, research project, 2 semesters of teaching. *Entrance requirements:* For doctorate, GRE General Test, GRE Subject Test (physics). Additional exam requirements/recommendations for international students: Required—TOEFL. Electronic applications accepted. *Expenses:* Tuition: Full-time $34,976. Required fees: $1166. Full-time tuition and fees vary according to program. *Faculty research:* Atomic and molecular physics, electromagnetism, solar physics, nuclear physics, fluid dynamics.

ICR Graduate School, Graduate Programs, Santee, CA 92071. Offers astro/geophysics (MS); biology (MS); geology (MS); science education (MS). Part-time programs available. *Degree requirements:* For master's, comprehensive exam (for some programs), thesis (for some programs). *Entrance requirements:* For master's, minimum undergraduate GPA of 3.0, bachelor's degree in science or science education. *Faculty research:* Age of the earth, limits of variation, catastrophe, optimum methods for teaching.

Indiana University Bloomington, University Graduate School, College of Arts and Sciences, Department of Astronomy, Bloomington, IN 47405-7000. Offers astronomy (MA, PhD); astrophysics (PhD). *Faculty:* 9 full-time (5 women), 1 part-time/adjunct (0 women). *Students:* 21 full-time (7 women); includes 2 minority (1 American Indian or Alaska Native, non-Hispanic/Latino; 1 Two or more races, non-Hispanic/Latino), 1 international. Average age 29. 40

40 www.facebook.com/petersonspublishing

Peterson's Graduate Programs in the Physical Sciences, Mathematics, Agricultural Sciences, the Environment & Natural Resources 2012

applicants, 5% accepted, 2 enrolled. In 2010, 4 master's, 3 doctorates awarded. Terminal master's awarded for partial completion of doctoral program. *Degree requirements:* For master's, thesis or alternative, oral exam; for doctorate, comprehensive exam, thesis/dissertation, oral defense. *Entrance requirements:* For master's and doctorate, GRE General Test, GRE Subject Test (physics), BA or BS in science. Additional exam requirements/recommendations for international students: Required—TOEFL. *Application deadline:* For fall admission, 1/15 for domestic students, 12/1 for international students; for spring admission, 9/1 for domestic students. Application fee: $55 ($65 for international students). Electronic applications accepted. *Financial support:* In 2010–11, 6 students received support, including 3 fellowships with full tuition reimbursements available (averaging $15,000 per year), 8 research assistantships with full tuition reimbursements available (averaging $16,547 per year), 9 teaching assistantships with full tuition reimbursements available (averaging $14,008 per year); Federal Work-Study and tuition waivers (full and partial) also available. Support available to part-time students. Financial award application deadline: 1/15. *Faculty research:* Stellar and galaxy dynamics, stellar chemical abundancies, galaxy evolution, observational cosmology, astrophsical disk. *Unit head:* Dr. Catherine Pilachowski, Chair, 812-855-6913, Fax: 812-855-8725, E-mail: catyp@astro.indiana.edu. *Application contact:* Christina Lirot, Department Manager, 812-855-6912, Fax: 812-855-8725, E-mail: clirot@indiana.edu.

Iowa State University of Science and Technology, Graduate College, College of Liberal Arts and Sciences, Department of Physics and Astronomy, Ames, IA 50011. Offers applied physics (MS, PhD); astrophysics (MS, PhD); condensed matter physics (MS, PhD); high energy physics (MS, PhD); nuclear physics (MS, PhD); physics (MS, PhD). Part-time programs available. *Faculty:* 48 full-time (4 women), 4 part-time/adjunct (0 women). *Students:* 97 full-time (19 women), 6 part-time (0 women); includes 3 Asian, non-Hispanic/Latino, 53 international. 179 applicants, 32% accepted, 18 enrolled. In 2010, 4 master's, 11 doctorates awarded. Terminal master's awarded for partial completion of doctoral program. *Degree requirements:* For master's, thesis (for some programs); for doctorate, thesis/dissertation. *Entrance requirements:* For master's and doctorate, GRE General Test, GRE Subject Test (physics). Additional exam requirements/recommendations for international students: Required—TOEFL (minimum score 550 paper-based; 79 iBT), IELTS (minimum score 6.5). *Application deadline:* For fall admission, 2/15 priority date for domestic and international students; for spring admission, 10/15 for domestic and international students. Applications are processed on a rolling basis. Application fee: $40 ($90 for international students). Electronic applications accepted. *Financial support:* In 2010–11, 54 research assistantships with full and partial tuition reimbursements (averaging $12,890 per year), 34 teaching assistantships with full and partial tuition reimbursements (averaging $13,928 per year) were awarded; fellowships, Federal Work-Study, institutionally sponsored loans, scholarships/grants, health care benefits, and unspecified assistantships also available. Support available to part-time students. Financial award application deadline: 2/15. *Faculty research:* Condensed-matter physics, including superconductivity and new materials; high-energy and nuclear physics; astronomy and astrophysics; atmospheric and environmental physics. Total annual research expenditures: $8.8 million. *Unit head:* Dr. Joseph Shinar, Chair, 515-294-3455, Fax: 515-294-6027, E-mail: phys_astro@iastate.edu. *Application contact:* Dr. Steven Kawaler, Director of Graduate Education, 515-294-9728, E-mail: phys_astro@iastate.edu.

Louisiana State University and Agricultural and Mechanical College, Graduate School, College of Basic Sciences, Department of Physics and Astronomy, Baton Rouge, LA 70803. Offers astronomy (PhD); astrophysics (PhD); medical physics (MS); physics (MS, PhD). *Faculty:* 47 full-time (5 women), 1 part-time/adjunct (0 women). *Students:* 99 full-time (24 women), 4 part-time (0 women); includes 1 Black or African American, non-Hispanic/Latino; 1 Asian, non-Hispanic/Latino; 3 Hispanic/Latino, 43 international. Average age 27. 103 applicants, 17% accepted, 14 enrolled. In 2010, 9 master's, 12 doctorates awarded. Terminal master's awarded for partial completion of doctoral program. *Degree requirements:* For master's, thesis or alternative; for doctorate, thesis/dissertation. *Entrance requirements:* For master's and doctorate, GRE General Test, minimum GPA of 3.0. Additional exam requirements/recommendations for international students: Required—TOEFL (minimum score 550 paper-based; 213 computer-based; 79 iBT) or IELTS (minimum score 6.5). *Application deadline:* For fall admission, 1/25 priority date for domestic students, 5/15 for international students; for spring admission, 10/15 for international students. Applications are processed on a rolling basis. Application fee: $50 ($70 for international students). Electronic applications accepted. *Financial support:* In 2010–11, 103 students received support, including 15 fellowships with full tuition reimbursements available (averaging $16,537 per year), 48 research assistantships with full and partial tuition reimbursements available (averaging $20,677 per year), 40 teaching assistantships with full and partial tuition reimbursements available (averaging $18,525 per year); Federal Work-Study, institutionally sponsored loans, health care benefits, tuition waivers (full and partial), and unspecified assistantships also available. Financial award application deadline: 3/15; financial award applicants required to submit FAFSA. *Faculty research:* Experimentation and numerical relativity, condensed matter astrophysics, quantum computing, medical physics. Total annual research expenditures: $8.8 million. *Unit head:* Dr. Michael Cherry, Chair, 225-578-2261, Fax: 225-578-5855, E-mail: cherry@phys.lsu.edu. *Application contact:* Arnell Dangerfield, Administrative Coordinator, 225-578-1193, Fax: 225-578-5855, E-mail: adanger@lsu.edu.

McMaster University, School of Graduate Studies, Faculty of Science, Department of Physics and Astronomy, Hamilton, ON L8S 4M2, Canada. Offers astrophysics (PhD); physics (PhD). Part-time programs available. *Degree requirements:* For doctorate, comprehensive exam, thesis/dissertation. *Entrance requirements:* For doctorate, minimum B+ average. Additional exam requirements/recommendations for international students: Required—TOEFL (minimum score 550 paper-based; 213 computer-based). *Faculty research:* Condensed matter, astrophysics, nuclear, medical, nonlinear dynamics.

Michigan State University, The Graduate School, College of Natural Science, Department of Physics and Astronomy, East Lansing, MI 48824. Offers astrophysics and astronomy (MS, PhD); physics (MS, PhD). *Entrance requirements:* Additional exam requirements/recommendations for international students: Required—TOEFL (minimum score 550 paper-based; 213 computer-based), Michigan State University ELT (minimum score 85), Michigan English Language Assessment Battery (minimum score 83). Electronic applications accepted. *Faculty research:* Nuclear and accelerator physics, high energy physics, condensed matter physics, biophysics, astrophysics and astronomy.

New Mexico Institute of Mining and Technology, Graduate Studies, Department of Physics, Socorro, NM 87801. Offers astrophysics (MS, PhD); atmospheric physics (MS, PhD); instrumentation (MS); mathematical physics (PhD). *Degree requirements:* For master's, thesis optional; for doctorate, thesis/dissertation. *Entrance requirements:* For master's, GRE General Test; for doctorate, GRE General Test, GRE Subject Test. Additional exam requirements/recommendations for international students: Required—TOEFL (minimum score 540 paper-based; 207 computer-based). *Faculty research:* Cloud physics, stellar and extragalactic processes.

Northwestern University, The Graduate School, Judd A. and Marjorie Weinberg College of Arts and Sciences, Department of Physics and Astronomy, Evanston, IL 60208. Offers astrophysics (PhD); physics (MS, PhD). Admissions and degrees offered through The Graduate School. *Degree requirements:* For doctorate, thesis/dissertation, qualifying exam. *Entrance requirements:* For doctorate, GRE General Test, GRE Subject Test. Additional exam requirements/recommendations for international students: Required—TOEFL. *Faculty research:* Nuclear and particle physics, condensed-matter physics, nonlinear physics, astrophysics.

Penn State University Park, Graduate School, Eberly College of Science, Department of Astronomy and Astrophysics, State College, University Park, PA 16802-1503. Offers MS, PhD. *Unit head:* Dr. Eric D. Feigelson, Assistant Department Head, 814-865-0162, Fax: 814-863-3399. *Application contact:* Cynthia E. Nicosia, Director, Graduate Enrollment Services, 814-865-1795, Fax: 814-865-4627, E-mail: cey1@psu.edu.

Princeton University, Graduate School, Department of Astrophysical Sciences, Princeton, NJ 08544-1019. Offers astronomy (PhD); plasma physics (PhD). *Degree requirements:* For doctorate, thesis/dissertation. *Entrance requirements:* For doctorate, GRE General Test, GRE Subject Test (physics). Additional exam requirements/recommendations for international students: Required—TOEFL (minimum score 600 paper-based; 250 computer-based). Electronic applications accepted. *Faculty research:* Theoretical astrophysics, cosmology, galaxy formation, galactic dynamics, interstellar and intergalactic matter.

Rochester Institute of Technology, Graduate Enrollment Services, College of Science, Health Sciences and Sustainability, Department of Astrophysical Sciences and Technology, Rochester, NY 14623-5603. Offers MS, PhD. *Students:* 11 full-time (3 women), 3 part-time (0 women); includes 1 Black or African American, non-Hispanic/Latino; 2 Hispanic/Latino, 4 international. Average age 31. 24 applicants, 29% accepted, 5 enrolled. In 2010, 1 doctorate awarded. Terminal master's awarded for partial completion of doctoral program. *Degree requirements:* For master's, comprehensive exam, thesis. *Entrance requirements:* For master's, GRE. Additional exam requirements/recommendations for international students: Required—TOEFL (minimum score 550 paper-based; 213 computer-based; 79 iBT) or IELTS (minimum score 6.5). *Application deadline:* For fall admission, 1/15 priority date for domestic and international students. Application fee: $50. *Expenses:* Tuition: Full-time $33,234; part-time $924 per credit hour. Required fees: $219. *Financial support:* In 2010–11, 8 students received support; fellowships with full and partial tuition reimbursements available, research assistantships with full and partial tuition reimbursements available, teaching assistantships with full and partial tuition reimbursements available, Federal Work-Study, scholarships/grants, health care benefits, and unspecified assistantships available. *Faculty research:* Supermassive black holes, dark energy, gravitational waves, supernovae, massive stars, the galactic center, star formation, clusters of galaxies, active galactic nuclei, astro-informatics, computational astrophysics, instrument and detector development. *Unit head:* Dr. Andrew Robinson, Graduate Program Director, 585-475-2726, E-mail: axrsps@rit.edu. *Application contact:* Diane Ellison, Assistant Vice President, Graduate Enrollment Services, 585-475-2229, Fax: 585-475-7164, E-mail: gradinfo@rit.edu.

Texas Christian University, College of Science and Engineering, Department of Physics and Astronomy, Fort Worth, TX 76129-0002. Offers physics (MA, MS, PhD), including astrophysics (PhD), business (PhD), physics (PhD); PhD/MBA. Terminal master's awarded for partial completion of doctoral program. *Degree requirements:* For master's, comprehensive exam, thesis; for doctorate, comprehensive exam, thesis/dissertation, paper submitted to scientific journal. *Entrance requirements:* For master's and doctorate, GRE General Test, minimum GPA of 3.0. Additional exam requirements/recommendations for international students: Required—TOEFL (minimum score 600 paper-based). *Application deadline:* For fall admission, 2/1 for domestic and international students; for spring admission, 10/1 for domestic and international students. Applications are processed on a rolling basis. Application fee: $50. Electronic applications accepted. *Expenses:* Tuition: Full-time $18,720; part-time $1040 per credit hour. Tuition and fees vary according to course load and program. *Financial support:* In 2010–11, 11 teaching assistantships (averaging $18,000 per year) were awarded; tuition waivers also available. Financial award application deadline: 2/1. *Unit head:* Dr. T. W. Zerda, Chairperson, 817-257-7375 Ext. 7124, Fax: 817-257-7742, E-mail: t.zerda@tcu.edu. *Application contact:* Dr. Yuri Strzhemechny, Assistant Professor, 817-257-7375 Ext. 5793, Fax: 817-257-7742, E-mail: y.strzhemechny@tcu.edu.

University of Alaska Fairbanks, College of Natural Sciences and Mathematics, Department of Physics, Fairbanks, AK 99775-5920. Offers computational physics (MS); physics (MAT, MS, PhD); space physics (MS, PhD). Part-time programs available. *Faculty:* 5 full-time (1 woman). *Students:* 28 full-time (6 women); includes 2 minority (1 Black or African American, non-Hispanic/Latino; 1 American Indian or Alaska Native, non-Hispanic/Latino), 8 international. Average age 29. 28 applicants, 36% accepted, 10 enrolled. In 2010, 1 master's, 2 doctorates awarded. Terminal master's awarded for partial completion of doctoral program. *Degree requirements:* For master's, comprehensive exam, thesis or alternative; for doctorate, comprehensive exam, thesis/dissertation, oral defense. *Entrance requirements:* Additional exam requirements/recommendations for international students: Required—TOEFL (minimum score 550 paper-based; 213 computer-based; 80 iBT). *Application deadline:* For fall admission, 6/1 for domestic students, 3/1 for international students; for spring admission, 10/15 for domestic students, 9/1 for international students. Applications are processed on a rolling basis. Application fee: $60. Electronic applications accepted. *Expenses:* Tuition, state resident: full-time $5688; part-time $316 per credit. Tuition, nonresident: full-time $11,628; part-time $646 per credit. Required fees: $289 per semester. Tuition and fees vary according to course load and reciprocity agreements. *Financial support:* In 2010–11, 18 research assistantships with tuition reimbursements (averaging $12,399 per year), 9 teaching assistantships with tuition reimbursements (averaging $18,259 per year) were awarded; fellowships with tuition reimbursements, Federal Work-Study, scholarships/grants, health care benefits, and unspecified assistantships also available. Support available to part-time students. Financial award application deadline: 2/15; financial award applicants required to submit FAFSA. *Faculty research:* Atmospheric and ionospheric radar studies, space plasma theory, magnetospheric dynamics, space weather and auroral studies, turbulence and complex systems. *Unit head:* Ataur Chowdhury, Chair, 907-474-7339, Fax: 907-474-6130, E-mail: physics@uaf.edu. *Application contact:* Ataur Chowdhury, Chair, 907-474-7339, Fax: 907-474-6130, E-mail: physics@uaf.edu.

University of Alberta, Faculty of Graduate Studies and Research, Department of Physics, Edmonton, AB T6G 2E1, Canada. Offers astrophysics (M Sc, PhD); condensed matter (M Sc, PhD); geophysics (M Sc, PhD); medical physics (M Sc, PhD); subatomic physics (M Sc, PhD). *Degree requirements:* For master's, thesis; for doctorate, thesis/dissertation. *Entrance requirements:* For master's and doctorate, minimum GPA of 7.0 on a 9.0 scale. Additional exam requirements/recommendations for international students: Required—TOEFL. *Faculty research:* Cosmology, astroparticle physics, high-intermediate energy, magnetism, superconductivity.

University of California, Berkeley, Graduate Division, College of Letters and Science, Department of Astrophysics, Berkeley, CA 94720-1500. Offers PhD. *Degree requirements:* For doctorate, thesis/dissertation, qualifying exam. *Entrance requirements:* For doctorate, GRE General Test, GRE Subject Test, minimum GPA of 3.0, 3 letters of recommendation. *Faculty research:* Theory, cosmology, radio astronomy, extra solar planets, infrared instrumentation.

University of California, Los Angeles, Graduate Division, College of Letters and Science, Department of Earth and Space Sciences, Program in Geophysics and Space Physics, Los Angeles, CA 90095. Offers MS, PhD. *Students:* 30 full-time (17 women); includes 2 minority (both Asian, non-Hispanic/Latino), 14 international. Average age 26. 51 applicants, 24% accepted, 4 enrolled. In 2010, 4 master's, 6 doctorates awarded. Terminal master's awarded for partial completion of doctoral program. *Degree requirements:* For master's, comprehensive exams or thesis; for doctorate, thesis/dissertation, oral and written qualifying exams. *Entrance requirements:* For master's, GRE General Test, minimum GPA of 3.0, bachelor's degree in related field; for doctorate, GRE General Test, minimum undergraduate GPA of 3.0, bachelor's degree in related field. *Application deadline:* For fall admission, 1/15 for domestic and international students. Application fee: $70 ($90 for international students). Electronic applications accepted. *Financial support:* In 2010–11, 31 fellowships with full and partial tuition reimbursements, 29 research assistantships with full and partial tuition reimbursements, 7 teaching assistantships with full and partial tuition reimbursements were awarded; Federal Work-Study, institutionally sponsored loans, scholarships/grants, health care benefits, tuition waivers (full and partial), and unspecified assistantships also available. Financial award application deadline:

Astrophysics

University of California, Los Angeles (continued)

3/1; financial award applicants required to submit FAFSA. *Unit head:* Dr. Craig E. Manning, Chair, 310-206-3290, E-mail: manning@ess.ucla.edu. *Application contact:* Departmental Office, 310-825-3917, E-mail: holbrook@ess.ucla.edu.

University of California, Santa Cruz, Division of Graduate Studies, Division of Physical and Biological Sciences, Department of Astronomy and Astrophysics, Santa Cruz, CA 95064. Offers PhD. *Students:* 37 full-time (18 women), 1 (woman) part-time; includes 8 minority (4 Asian, non-Hispanic/Latino; 4 Hispanic/Latino), 7 international. Average age 26. 131 applicants, 19% accepted, 8 enrolled. In 2010, 3 doctorates awarded. *Degree requirements:* For doctorate, one foreign language, thesis/dissertation, qualifying exam. *Entrance requirements:* For doctorate, GRE General Test, GRE Subject Test. Additional exam requirements/recommendations for international students: Required—TOEFL (minimum score 550 paper-based; 220 computer-based; 83 iBT); Recommended—IELTS (minimum score 8). *Application deadline:* For fall admission, 1/5 for domestic and international students. Application fee: $70 ($90 for international students). Electronic applications accepted. *Financial support:* Fellowships, research assistantships, teaching assistantships, institutionally sponsored loans and tuition waivers available. Financial award applicants required to submit FAFSA. *Faculty research:* Solar system and the Milky Way to the most distant galaxies in the Universe, fundamental questions of cosmology. *Unit head:* Maria Sliwinski, Graduate Program Coordinator, 831-459-2844, Fax: 831-459-5265, E-mail: sliwinsk@ucsc.edu. *Application contact:* Maria Sliwinski, Graduate Program Coordinator, 831-459-2844, Fax: 831-459-5265, E-mail: sliwinsk@ucsc.edu.

University of Chicago, Division of the Physical Sciences, Department of Astronomy and Astrophysics, Chicago, IL 60637-1513. Offers MS, PhD. Terminal master's awarded for partial completion of doctoral program. *Degree requirements:* For master's, comprehensive exam, thesis optional, candidacy exam; for doctorate, comprehensive exam, thesis/dissertation, dissertation for publication. *Entrance requirements:* For master's, department candidacy examination, minimum GPA of 3.0; for doctorate, GRE General Test, GRE Subject Test, minimum GPA of 3.0. Additional exam requirements/recommendations for international students: Required—TOEFL (minimum score 600 paper-based; 250 computer-based); Recommended—IELTS. Electronic applications accepted. *Faculty research:* Quasi-stellar object absorption lines, fluid dynamics, interstellar matter, particle physics, cosmology.

University of Colorado Boulder, Graduate School, College of Arts and Sciences, Department of Astrophysical and Planetary Sciences, Boulder, CO 80309. Offers astrophysics (MS, PhD); planetary science (MS, PhD). *Faculty:* 20 full-time (3 women). *Students:* 48 full-time (14 women); includes 3 minority (1 American Indian or Alaska Native, non-Hispanic/Latino; 2 Asian, non-Hispanic/Latino), 4 international. Average age 26. 140 applicants, 9 enrolled. In 2010, 10 master's, 7 doctorates awarded. Terminal master's awarded for partial completion of doctoral program. *Degree requirements:* For master's, comprehensive exam, thesis or alternative; for doctorate, one foreign language, thesis/dissertation. *Entrance requirements:* For master's, GRE General Test, GRE Subject Test, minimum undergraduate GPA of 3.0; for doctorate, GRE General Test, GRE Subject Test. *Application deadline:* For fall admission, 1/15 priority date for domestic students, 12/1 for international students. Applications are processed on a rolling basis. Application fee: $50 ($60 for international students). *Financial support:* In 2010–11, 13 fellowships (averaging $22,199 per year), 33 research assistantships (averaging $17,541 per year) were awarded; tuition waivers (full) also available. Support available to part-time students. Financial award application deadline: 1/15. *Faculty research:* Stellar and extragalactic astrophysics cosmology, space astronomy, planetary science. Total annual research expenditures: $31.2 million.

The University of Manchester, School of Physics and Astronomy, Manchester, United Kingdom. Offers astronomy and astrophysics (M Sc, PhD); biological physics (M Sc, PhD); condensed matter physics (M Sc, PhD); nonlinear and liquid crystals physics (M Sc, PhD); nuclear physics (M Sc, PhD); particle physics (M Sc, PhD); photon physics (M Sc, PhD); physics (M Sc, PhD); theoretical physics (M Sc, PhD).

University of Maryland, Baltimore County, Graduate School, College of Natural and Mathematical Sciences, Department of Physics, Program in Applied Physics, Baltimore, MD 21250. Offers astrophysics (PhD); optics (MS, PhD); quantum optics (PhD); solid state physics (MS, PhD). Part-time programs available. *Faculty:* 24 full-time (3 women), 18 part-time/adjunct (2 women). *Students:* 31 full-time (10 women), 3 part-time (0 women); includes 3 Black or African American, non-Hispanic/Latino, 15 international. Average age 24. 28 applicants, 43% accepted, 7 enrolled. In 2010, 4 master's, 4 doctorates awarded. Terminal master's awarded for partial completion of doctoral program. *Degree requirements:* For master's, thesis optional; for doctorate, comprehensive exam, thesis/dissertation. *Entrance requirements:* For master's, GRE General Test, minimum GPA of 3.0; for doctorate, GRE General Test, GRE Subject Test, minimum GPA of 3.0. Additional exam requirements/recommendations for international students: Required—TOEFL. *Application deadline:* For fall admission, 5/31 for domestic and international students; for spring admission, 11/30 for domestic students. Applications are processed on a rolling basis. Application fee: $50. Electronic applications accepted. *Financial support:* In 2010–11, 30 students received support, including 4 fellowships with full tuition reimbursements available (averaging $27,000 per year), 14 research assistantships with full tuition reimbursements available (averaging $24,000 per year), 12 teaching assistantships with full tuition reimbursements available (averaging $22,000 per year); career-related internships or fieldwork, scholarships/grants, health care benefits, and unspecified assistantships also available. Support available to part-time students. Financial award application deadline: 5/31. *Faculty research:* Astrophysics, atmospheric physics, nanophysics, optics, quantum optics and quantum information. Total annual research expenditures: $4.8 million. *Unit head:* Dr. Todd Pittman, EdD, Graduate Program Director, 410-455-2513, Fax: 410-455-1072, E-mail: todd.pittman@umbc.edu. *Application contact:* Dr. Lazlo L. Takacs, Director, 410-455-2524, Fax: 410-455-1072, E-mail: takacs@umbc.edu.

University of Michigan, Horace H. Rackham School of Graduate Studies, College of Literature, Science, and the Arts, Department of Astronomy, Ann Arbor, MI 48109-1042. Offers astronomy and astrophysics (PhD). *Faculty:* 20 full-time (5 women). *Students:* 29 full-time (12 women); includes 1 Black or African American, non-Hispanic/Latino; 4 Asian, non-Hispanic/Latino. 122 applicants, 9% accepted, 3 enrolled. In 2010, 3 doctorates awarded. Terminal master's awarded for partial completion of doctoral program. *Degree requirements:* For doctorate, thesis/dissertation, oral defense of dissertation, preliminary exam. *Entrance requirements:* For doctorate, GRE General Test, GRE Subject Test (physics). Additional exam requirements/recommendations for international students: Required—TOEFL. *Application deadline:* For fall admission, 1/5 for domestic and international students. Application fee: $65 ($75 for international students). Electronic applications accepted. *Expenses:* Tuition, state resident: full-time $17,784; part-time $1116 per credit hour. Tuition, nonresident: full-time $35,944; part-time $2125 per credit hour. International tuition: $35,994 full-time. Required fees: $95 per semester. Tuition and fees vary according to course load, degree level and program. *Financial support:* In 2010–11, 5 fellowships with full tuition reimbursements (averaging $22,800 per year), 23 research assistantships with full tuition reimbursements (averaging $22,800 per year), 13 teaching assistantships with full tuition reimbursements (averaging $22,800 per year) were awarded; institutionally sponsored loans, scholarships/grants, health care benefits, and unspecified assistantships also available. Financial award applicants required to submit FAFSA. *Faculty research:* Extragalactic and galactic astronomy, cosmology, star and planet formation, high energy astrophysics. Total annual research expenditures: $2.1 million. *Unit head:* Dr. Joel Bregman, Chair and Professor, 734-764-3440, Fax: 734-763-6317, E-mail: jbregman@umich.edu. *Application contact:* Brian M. Cox, Administrative Assistant, 734-764-3440, Fax: 734-763-6317, E-mail: bmcox@umich.edu.

University of Minnesota, Twin Cities Campus, Institute of Technology, School of Physics and Astronomy, Department of Astronomy, Minneapolis, MN 55455-0213. Offers astrophysics (MS, PhD). Terminal master's awarded for partial completion of doctoral program. *Degree requirements:* For master's, thesis optional; for doctorate, thesis/dissertation. *Entrance requirements:* For master's and doctorate, GRE General Test, GRE Subject Test. *Faculty research:* Evolution of stars and galaxies; the interstellar medium; cosmology; observational, optical, infrared, and radio astronomy; computational astrophysics.

University of Missouri–St. Louis, College of Arts and Sciences, Department of Physics and Astronomy, St. Louis, MO 63121. Offers physics (MS, PhD), including applied physics (MS), astrophysics (MS). Part-time and evening/weekend programs available. *Faculty:* 12 full-time (2 women), 4 part-time/adjunct (1 woman). *Students:* 10 full-time (2 women), 13 part-time (4 women), 2 international. Average age 34. 17 applicants, 29% accepted, 4 enrolled. In 2010, 3 master's, 3 doctorates awarded. Terminal master's awarded for partial completion of doctoral program. *Degree requirements:* For master's, thesis optional; for doctorate, thesis/dissertation. *Entrance requirements:* For master's, GRE General Test; for doctorate, GRE General Test, 2 letters of recommendation. Additional exam requirements/recommendations for international students: Required—TOEFL (minimum score 550 paper-based; 213 computer-based). *Application deadline:* For fall admission, 7/1 for domestic and international students; for spring admission, 12/1 for domestic students, 11/1 for international students. Application fee: $35 ($40 for international students). Electronic applications accepted. *Expenses:* Tuition, state resident: full-time $5522; part-time $306.80 per credit hour. Tuition, nonresident: full-time $14,253; part-time $792.10 per credit hour. Required fees: $658; $49 per credit hour. One-time fee: $12. Tuition and fees vary according to program. *Financial support:* In 2010–11, 4 research assistantships with full and partial tuition reimbursements (averaging $16,125 per year), 10 teaching assistantships with full and partial tuition reimbursements (averaging $14,815 per year) were awarded; fellowships with full tuition reimbursements, career-related internships or fieldwork also available. Financial award applicants required to submit FAFSA. *Faculty research:* Biophysics, atomic physics, nonlinear dynamics, materials science. *Unit head:* Dr. Phil Fraundorf, Director of Graduate Studies, 314-516-5931, Fax: 314-516-6152, E-mail: fraundorfp@msx.umsl.edu. *Application contact:* 314-516-5458, Fax: 314-516-6996, E-mail: gradadm@umsl.edu.

The University of North Carolina at Chapel Hill, Graduate School, College of Arts and Sciences, Department of Physics and Astronomy, Chapel Hill, NC 27599. Offers physics (MS, PhD). Terminal master's awarded for partial completion of doctoral program. *Degree requirements:* For master's, comprehensive exam; for doctorate, comprehensive exam, thesis/dissertation. *Entrance requirements:* For master's and doctorate, GRE General Test, minimum GPA of 3.0. Electronic applications accepted. *Faculty research:* Observational astronomy, fullerenes, polarized beams, nanotubes, nucleosynthesis in stars and supernovae, superstring theory, ballistic transport in semiconductors, gravitation.

University of Pennsylvania, School of Arts and Sciences, Graduate Group in Physics and Astronomy, Philadelphia, PA 19104. Offers medical physics (MS); physics (PhD). Part-time programs available. *Faculty:* 44 full-time (5 women), 17 part-time/adjunct (1 woman). *Students:* 109 full-time (27 women), 1 part-time (0 women); includes 10 Asian, non-Hispanic/Latino; 2 Hispanic/Latino, 22 international. 373 applicants, 13% accepted, 20 enrolled. In 2010, 22 master's, 14 doctorates awarded. *Degree requirements:* For doctorate, thesis/dissertation, oral, preliminary, and final exams. *Entrance requirements:* For doctorate, GRE General Test, GRE Subject Test (recommended). Additional exam requirements/recommendations for international students: Required—TOEFL. *Application deadline:* For fall admission, 12/1 priority date for domestic students. Application fee: $70. Electronic applications accepted. *Expenses:* Tuition: Full-time $25,660; part-time $4758 per course. Required fees: $2152; $270 per course. Tuition and fees vary according to course load, degree level and program. *Financial support:* Fellowships, research assistantships, teaching assistantships, institutionally sponsored loans, scholarships/grants, traineeships, health care benefits, and unspecified assistantships available. Financial award application deadline: 12/15. *Faculty research:* Astrophysics, condensed matter experiment, condensed matter theory, particle experiment, particle theory. Total annual research expenditures: $7.3 million. *Unit head:* Larry Gladney, Department Chair, Physics and Astronomy, 215-898-8152, E-mail: gladney@sas.upenn.edu. *Application contact:* Millicent Minnick, Academic Coordinator, 215-898-3125, E-mail: admiss@physics.upenn.edu.

University of Toronto, School of Graduate Studies, Physical Sciences Division, Department of Astronomy and Astrophysics, Toronto, ON M5S 1A1, Canada. Offers M Sc, PhD. Part-time programs available. *Degree requirements:* For doctorate, thesis/dissertation, qualifying exam, thesis defense. *Entrance requirements:* For master's, minimum B average, bachelor's degree in astronomy or equivalent, 3 letters of reference; for doctorate, GRE General Test, minimum B+ average, master's degree in astronomy or equivalent, demonstrated research competence, 3 letters of reference.

University of Victoria, Faculty of Graduate Studies, Faculty of Science, Department of Physics and Astronomy, Victoria, BC V8W 2Y2, Canada. Offers astronomy and astrophysics (M Sc, PhD); condensed matter physics (M Sc, PhD); experimental particle physics (M Sc, PhD); medical physics (M Sc, PhD); ocean physics (M Sc, PhD); theoretical physics (M Sc, PhD). *Degree requirements:* For master's, thesis; for doctorate, comprehensive exam, thesis/dissertation, candidacy exam. *Entrance requirements:* For master's and doctorate, GRE. Additional exam requirements/recommendations for international students: Required—TOEFL (minimum score 575 paper-based; 233 computer-based), IELTS (minimum score 7). Electronic applications accepted. *Faculty research:* Old stellar populations; observational cosmology and large scale structure; cp violation; atlas.

Yale University, Graduate School of Arts and Sciences, Department of Astronomy, New Haven, CT 06520. Offers astronomy (PhD); solar and terrestrial physics (PhD). *Degree requirements:* For doctorate, thesis/dissertation. *Entrance requirements:* For doctorate, GRE General Test, GRE Subject Test (physics).

Section 2
Chemistry

This section contains a directory of institutions offering graduate work in chemistry, followed by in-depth entries submitted by institutions that chose to prepare detailed program descriptions. Additional information about programs listed in the directory but not augmented by an in-depth entry may be obtained by writing directly to the dean of a graduate school or chair of a department at the address given in the directory.

For programs offering related work, see also in this book *Geosciences* and *Physics.* In the other guides in this series:

Graduate Programs in the Biological Sciences

See *Biological and Biomedical Sciences, Biochemistry, Biophysics, Nutrition,* and *Pharmacology and Toxicology*

Graduate Programs in Engineering & Applied Sciences

See *Engineering and Applied Sciences; Agricultural Engineering; Chemical Engineering; Geological, Mineral/Mining, and Petroleum Engineering; Materials Sciences and Engineering;* and *Pharmaceutical Engineering*

Graduate Programs in Business, Education, Health, Information Studies, Law & Social Work

See *Pharmacy and Pharmaceutical Sciences*

CONTENTS

Program Directories

Close-Ups and Displays

Analytical Chemistry

Auburn University, Graduate School, College of Sciences and Mathematics, Department of Chemistry and Biochemistry, Auburn University, AL 36849. Offers analytical chemistry (MS, PhD); biochemistry (MS, PhD); inorganic chemistry (MS, PhD); organic chemistry (MS, PhD); physical chemistry (MS, PhD). Part-time programs available. *Faculty:* 27 full-time (6 women). *Students:* 39 full-time (20 women), 21 part-time (8 women); includes 4 Black or African American, non-Hispanic/Latino; 1 Asian, non-Hispanic/Latino; 1 Hispanic/Latino, 41 international. Average age 28. 54 applicants, 11% accepted, 3 enrolled. In 2010, 1 master's, 13 doctorates awarded. *Degree requirements:* For master's, thesis (for some programs); for doctorate, thesis/dissertation, oral and written exams. *Entrance requirements:* For master's and doctorate, GRE General Test. *Application deadline:* For fall admission, 7/7 for domestic students; for spring admission, 11/24 for domestic students. Applications are processed on a rolling basis. Application fee: $50 ($60 for international students). Electronic applications accepted. *Expenses:* Tuition, state resident: full-time $7002. Tuition, nonresident: full-time $21,898. International tuition: $22,116 full-time. Required fees: $892. Tuition and fees vary according to course load and program. *Financial support:* Fellowships, research assistantships, teaching assistantships available. Financial award application deadline: 3/15; financial award applicants required to submit FAFSA. *Unit head:* Dr. J. V. Ortiz, Chair, 334-844-4043, Fax: 334-844-4043. *Application contact:* Dr. George Flowers, Dean of the Graduate School, 334-844-2125.

Brigham Young University, Graduate Studies, College of Physical and Mathematical Sciences, Department of Chemistry and Biochemistry, Provo, UT 84602. Offers biochemistry (MS, PhD); chemistry (MS, PhD). *Faculty:* 33 full-time (2 women). *Students:* 105 full-time (44 women); includes 1 Asian, non-Hispanic/Latino; 1 Hispanic/Latino; 2 Native Hawaiian or other Pacific Islander, non-Hispanic/Latino, 44 international. Average age 28. 72 applicants, 58% accepted, 23 enrolled. In 2010, 5 master's, 11 doctorates awarded. *Degree requirements:* For master's, thesis; for doctorate, thesis/dissertation, qualifying exam. *Entrance requirements:* For master's and doctorate, GRE General Test, minimum GPA of 3.0 in last 60 hours. Additional exam requirements/recommendations for international students: Required—TOEFL (minimum score 580 paper-based; 237 computer-based; 85 iBT); Recommended—TWE. *Application deadline:* For fall admission, 2/1 priority date for domestic and international students. Applications are processed on a rolling basis. Application fee: $50. Electronic applications accepted. *Expenses:* Tuition: Full-time $5580; part-time $310 per credit hour. Tuition and fees vary according to program and student's religious affiliation. *Financial support:* In 2010–11, 105 students received support, including 10 fellowships with full tuition reimbursements available (averaging $21,250 per year), 56 research assistantships with full tuition reimbursements available (averaging $21,250 per year), 29 teaching assistantships with full tuition reimbursements available (averaging $21,250 per year); institutionally sponsored loans, scholarships/grants, health care benefits, tuition waivers (full), and unspecified assistantships also available. Financial award application deadline: 2/1. *Faculty research:* Separation science, molecular recognition, organic synthesis and biomedical application, biochemistry and molecular biology, molecular spectroscopy. Total annual research expenditures: $5.6 million. *Unit head:* Dr. Gregory F. Burton, Chair, 801-422-4917, Fax: 801-422-0153, E-mail: gburton@byu.edu. *Application contact:* Dr. Matthew R. Linford, Graduate Coordinator, 801-422-1699, Fax: 801-422-0153, E-mail: mrlinford@byu.edu.

California State University, Los Angeles, Graduate Studies, College of Natural and Social Sciences, Department of Chemistry and Biochemistry, Los Angeles, CA 90032-8530. Offers analytical chemistry (MS); biochemistry (MS); chemistry (MS); inorganic chemistry (MS); organic chemistry (MS); physical chemistry (MS). Part-time and evening/weekend programs available. *Faculty:* 5 part-time/adjunct (1 woman). *Students:* 19 full-time (15 women), 24 part-time (12 women); includes 21 minority (3 Black or African American, non-Hispanic/Latino; 8 Asian, non-Hispanic/Latino; 10 Hispanic/Latino), 9 international. Average age 30. 22 applicants, 100% accepted, 10 enrolled. In 2010, 7 master's awarded. *Degree requirements:* For master's, one foreign language, comprehensive exam or thesis. *Entrance requirements:* Additional exam requirements/recommendations for international students: Required—TOEFL. *Application deadline:* For fall admission, 5/1 for domestic and international students. Applications are processed on a rolling basis. Application fee: $55. *Financial support:* Federal Work-Study available. Support available to part-time students. Financial award application deadline: 3/1. *Faculty research:* Intercalation of heavy metal, carborane chemistry, conductive polymers and fabrics, titanium reagents, computer modeling and synthesis. *Unit head:* Dr. Robert L. Vellanoweth, Chair, 323-343-2300, Fax: 323-343-6490, E-mail: rvellan@calstatela.edu. *Application contact:* Dr. Allan Muchlinski, Dean of Graduate Studies, 323-343-3820 Ext. 3827, Fax: 323-343-5653, E-mail: amuchli@exchange.calstatela.edu.

Cleveland State University, College of Graduate Studies, College of Sciences and Health Professions, Department of Chemistry, Cleveland, OH 44115. Offers analytical chemistry (MS); clinical chemistry (MS); clinical/bioanalytical chemistry (PhD), including cellular and molecular medicine, clinical chemistry, clinical/bioanalytical chemistry; environmental chemistry (MS); inorganic chemistry (MS); pharmaceutical/organic chemistry (MS); physical chemistry (MS). Part-time and evening/weekend programs available. *Faculty:* 13 full-time (0 women), 1 (woman) part-time/adjunct. *Students:* 58 full-time (29 women), 42 part-time (17 women); includes 4 Black or African American, non-Hispanic/Latino; 3 Asian, non-Hispanic/Latino; 1 Hispanic/Latino, 70 international. Average age 28. 76 applicants, 74% accepted, 16 enrolled. In 2010, 4 master's, 15 doctorates awarded. *Degree requirements:* For master's, thesis optional; for doctorate, comprehensive exam, thesis/dissertation. *Entrance requirements:* For master's and doctorate, GRE General Test. Additional exam requirements/recommendations for international students: Required—TOEFL (minimum score 525 paper-based; 197 computer-based; 65 iBT). *Application deadline:* For fall admission, 1/15 priority date for domestic and international students. Applications are processed on a rolling basis. Application fee: $30. Electronic applications accepted. *Expenses:* Tuition, state resident: full-time $8447; part-time $469 per credit hour. Tuition, nonresident: full-time $16,020; part-time $890 per credit hour. Required fees: $50. *Financial support:* In 2010–11, 44 students received support, including 5 fellowships with full tuition reimbursements available (averaging $30,000 per year), 13 research assistantships with full tuition reimbursements available (averaging $20,000 per year), 24 teaching assistantships with full tuition reimbursements available (averaging $18,500 per year); scholarships/grants and unspecified assistantships also available. Financial award application deadline: 1/15. *Faculty research:* Bioanalytical techniques and molecular diagnostics, glycoproteomics and antithrombotic agents, drug discovery and innovation, analytical pharmacology, inflammatory disease research. Total annual research expenditures: $3 million. *Unit head:* Dr. David J. Anderson, Interim Chair, 216-687-2467, Fax: 216-687-9298, E-mail: d.anderson@csuohio.edu. *Application contact:* Richelle P. Emery, Administrative Coordinator, 216-687-2457, Fax: 216-687-9298, E-mail: r.emery@csuohio.edu.

Cornell University, Graduate School, Graduate Fields of Arts and Sciences, Field of Chemistry and Chemical Biology, Ithaca, NY 14853-0001. Offers analytical chemistry (PhD); bio-organic chemistry (PhD); biophysical chemistry (PhD); chemical biology (PhD); chemical physics (PhD); inorganic chemistry (PhD); materials chemistry (PhD); organic chemistry (PhD); organometallic chemistry (PhD); physical chemistry (PhD); polymer chemistry (PhD); theoretical chemistry (PhD). *Faculty:* 46 full-time (3 women). *Students:* 163 full-time (63 women); includes 10 Asian, non-Hispanic/Latino; 3 Hispanic/Latino, 49 international. Average age 24. 340 applicants, 36% accepted, 48 enrolled. In 2010, 31 doctorates awarded. *Degree requirements:* For doctorate, comprehensive exam, thesis/dissertation. *Entrance requirements:* For doctorate, GRE General Test, GRE Subject Test (chemistry), 3 letters of recommendation. Additional exam requirements/recommendations for international students: Required—TOEFL (minimum score 600 paper-based; 250 computer-based; 77 iBT). *Application deadline:* For fall admission, 1/10 for domestic students. Application fee: $80. Electronic applications accepted. *Expenses:* Tuition: Full-time $29,500. Required fees: $76. Tuition and fees vary according to degree level and program. *Financial support:* In 2010–11, 19 fellowships with full tuition reimbursements, 69 research assistantships with full tuition reimbursements, 68 teaching assistantships with full tuition reimbursements were awarded; institutionally sponsored loans, scholarships/grants, health care benefits, tuition waivers (full and partial), and unspecified assistantships also available. Financial award applicants required to submit FAFSA. *Faculty research:* Analytical, organic, inorganic, physical, materials, chemical biology. *Unit head:* Director of Graduate Studies, 607-255-4139, Fax: 607-255-4137. *Application contact:* Graduate Field Assistant, 607-255-4139, Fax: 607-255-4137, E-mail: chemgrad@cornell.edu.

Eastern New Mexico University, Graduate School, College of Liberal Arts and Sciences, Department of Physical Sciences, Portales, NM 88130. Offers chemistry (MS), including analytical, biochemistry, inorganic, organic, physical. Part-time programs available. *Faculty:* 3 full-time (0 women). *Students:* 7 full-time (2 women), 2 part-time (1 woman), 6 international. Average age 32. 10 applicants, 40% accepted, 4 enrolled. In 2010, 3 master's awarded. *Degree requirements:* For master's, thesis optional, seminar, oral and written comprehensive exams. *Entrance requirements:* For master's, ACS placement examination, minimum GPA of 3.0; 2 letters of recommendation; personal statement of career goals; bachelor's degree with one year minimum each of general, organic, and analytical chemistry. Additional exam requirements/recommendations for international students: Required—TOEFL (minimum score 550 paper-based; 213 computer-based; 79 iBT), IELTS (minimum score 6). *Application deadline:* For fall admission, 7/20 priority date for domestic students, 6/20 priority date for international students; for spring admission, 12/15 priority date for domestic students, 11/15 priority date for international students. Applications are processed on a rolling basis. Application fee: $10. Electronic applications accepted. *Expenses:* Tuition, state resident: full-time $3210; part-time $130 per credit hour. Tuition, nonresident: full-time $8652; part-time $360.50 per credit hour. Required fees: $1212; $50.50 per credit hour. Tuition and fees vary according to course load. *Financial support:* In 2010–11, 1 research assistantship with partial tuition reimbursement (averaging $8,500 per year), 9 teaching assistantships with partial tuition reimbursements (averaging $8,500 per year) were awarded; career-related internships or fieldwork and unspecified assistantships also available. Support available to part-time students. Financial award application deadline: 3/1; financial award applicants required to submit FAFSA. *Faculty research:* Synfuel, electrochemistry, protein chemistry. *Unit head:* Dr. Juacho Yan, Graduate Coordinator, 575-562-2174, Fax: 575-562-2192, E-mail: juacho.yan@enmu.edu. *Application contact:* Sharon Potter, Department Secretary, Chemistry/Physical Sciences, 575-562-2174, Fax: 575-562-2192, E-mail: sharon.potter@enmu.edu.

Florida State University, The Graduate School, College of Arts and Sciences, Department of Chemistry and Biochemistry, Tallahassee, FL 32306-4390. Offers analytical chemistry (MS, PhD); biochemistry (MS, PhD); inorganic chemistry (MS, PhD); materials chemistry (PhD); organic chemistry (MS, PhD); physical chemistry (MS, PhD). *Faculty:* 38 full-time (5 women), 3 part-time/adjunct (0 women). *Students:* 142 full-time (46 women), 8 part-time (4 women); includes 12 minority (6 Black or African American, non-Hispanic/Latino; 3 Asian, non-Hispanic/Latino; 3 Hispanic/Latino), 68 international. Average age 25. 299 applicants, 17% accepted, 19 enrolled. In 2010, 10 master's, 20 doctorates awarded. Terminal master's awarded for partial completion of doctoral program. *Degree requirements:* For master's, comprehensive exam (for some programs), thesis (for some programs), cumulative exams; for doctorate, comprehensive exam (for some programs), thesis/dissertation, cumulative exams. *Entrance requirements:* For master's and doctorate, GRE General Test, minimum B average in undergraduate course work. Additional exam requirements/recommendations for international students: Required—TOEFL (minimum score 550 paper-based; 213 computer-based; 80 iBT). *Application deadline:* For fall admission, 12/15 priority date for domestic and international students; for spring admission, 9/15 for domestic and international students. Applications are processed on a rolling basis. Application fee: $30. Electronic applications accepted. *Expenses:* Tuition, state resident: full-time $8238.24. *Financial support:* In 2010–11, 150 students received support, including fellowships with full tuition reimbursements available (averaging $20,000 per year), 50 research assistantships with full tuition reimbursements available (averaging $20,000 per year), 100 teaching assistantships with full tuition reimbursements available (averaging $20,000 per year). Financial award application deadline: 12/15; financial award applicants required to submit FAFSA. *Faculty research:* Materials synthesis including polymers, natural products; catalysis, NMR; mass spectrometry; optical spectroscopy, scattering techniques, computational chemistry, separation technology; nanostructured materials including metallic, semiconducting and magnetic nanocrystals; nanoscience interfaced with biology; supramolecular materials for solar energy conversion. Total annual research expenditures: $5.6 million. *Unit head:* Dr. Timothy Logan, Chairman, 850-644-1244, Fax: 850-644-8281, E-mail: gradinfo@chem.fsu.edu. *Application contact:* Dr. Tyler McQuade, Chair, Graduate Admissions Committee, 888-525-9286, Fax: 850-644-0465, E-mail: gradinfo@chem.fsu.edu.

Georgetown University, Graduate School of Arts and Sciences, Department of Chemistry, Washington, DC 20057. Offers analytical chemistry (PhD); biochemistry (PhD); computational chemistry (PhD); inorganic chemistry (PhD); materials chemistry (PhD); organic chemistry (PhD); physical chemistry (PhD); theoretical chemistry (PhD). Terminal master's awarded for partial completion of doctoral program. *Degree requirements:* For doctorate, comprehensive exam, thesis/dissertation. *Entrance requirements:* For doctorate, GRE General Test. Additional exam requirements/recommendations for international students: Required—TOEFL.

The George Washington University, Columbian College of Arts and Sciences, Department of Chemistry, Washington, DC 20052. Offers analytical chemistry (MS, PhD); inorganic chemistry (MS, PhD); materials science (MS, PhD); organic chemistry (MS, PhD); physical chemistry (MS, PhD). Part-time and evening/weekend programs available. *Faculty:* 15 full-time (4 women), 5 part-time/adjunct (2 women). *Students:* 21 full-time (10 women), 10 part-time (5 women); includes 3 Asian, non-Hispanic/Latino; 1 Hispanic/Latino, 9 international. Average age 28. 33 applicants, 45% accepted, 7 enrolled. In 2010, 4 master's, 2 doctorates awarded. Terminal master's awarded for partial completion of doctoral program. *Degree requirements:* For master's, comprehensive exam, thesis or alternative; for doctorate, thesis/dissertation, general exam. *Entrance requirements:* For master's and doctorate, GRE General Test, interview, minimum GPA of 3.0. Additional exam requirements/recommendations for international students: Required—TOEFL (minimum score 550 paper-based; 213 computer-based; 80 iBT). *Application deadline:* For fall admission, 1/15 priority date for domestic and international students; for spring admission, 9/1 priority date for domestic and international students. Applications are processed on a rolling basis. Application fee: $75. Electronic applications accepted. *Financial support:* In 2010–11, 27 students received support; fellowships with tuition reimbursements available, research assistantships, teaching assistantships with tuition reimbursements available, Federal Work-Study and tuition waivers available. Financial award application deadline: 1/15. *Unit head:* Dr. Michael King, Chair, 202-994-6488. *Application contact:* Information Contact, 202-994-6121, E-mail: gwchem@gwu.edu.

Governors State University, College of Arts and Sciences, Program in Analytical Chemistry, University Park, IL 60466-0975. Offers MS. Part-time and evening/weekend programs available. *Degree requirements:* For master's, thesis or alternative. *Expenses:* Tuition, state resident: full-time $5400; part-time $225 per credit hour. Tuition, nonresident: full-time $16,200; part-time $675 per credit hour. Required fees: $1358; $46 per credit hour. $126 per term. Tuition and fees vary according to degree level and program. *Faculty research:* Electrochemistry, photochemistry, spectrochemistry, biochemistry.

Howard University, Graduate School, Department of Chemistry, Washington, DC 20059-0002. Offers analytical chemistry (MS, PhD); atmospheric (MS, PhD); biochemistry (MS, PhD);

environmental (MS, PhD); inorganic chemistry (MS, PhD); organic chemistry (MS, PhD); physical chemistry (MS, PhD). Terminal master's awarded for partial completion of doctoral program. *Degree requirements:* For master's, comprehensive exam, thesis, teaching experience; for doctorate, comprehensive exam, thesis/dissertation, teaching experience. *Entrance requirements:* For master's, GRE General Test, minimum GPA of 2.7; for doctorate, GRE General Test, minimum GPA of 3.0. Additional exam requirements/recommendations for international students: Required—TOEFL. Electronic applications accepted. *Faculty research:* Synthetic organics, materials, natural products, mass spectrometry.

Illinois Institute of Technology, Graduate College, College of Science and Letters, Department of Biological, Chemical and Physical Sciences, Chemistry Division, Chicago, IL 60616. Offers analytical chemistry (M Ch); chemistry (M Chem, MS, PhD); materials and chemical synthesis (M Ch). Part-time and evening/weekend programs available. Postbaccalaureate distance learning degree programs offered (no on-campus study). *Faculty:* 13 full-time (5 women), 2 part-time/adjunct (0 women). *Students:* 29 full-time (11 women), 46 part-time (20 women); includes 26 minority (1 Black or African American, non-Hispanic/Latino; 2 Asian, non-Hispanic/Latino; 23 Hispanic/Latino), 23 international. Average age 30. 157 applicants, 46% accepted, 18 enrolled. In 2010, 11 master's, 3 doctorates awarded. Terminal master's awarded for partial completion of doctoral program. *Degree requirements:* For master's, comprehensive exam, thesis (for some programs); for doctorate, comprehensive exam, thesis/dissertation. *Entrance requirements:* For master's, GRE General Test (minimum score 1000 Quantitative and Verbal, 2.5 Analytical Writing), minimum undergraduate GPA of 3.0; for doctorate, GRE General Test (minimum score 1100 Quantitative and Verbal, 3.0 Analytical Writing), GRE Subject Test, minimum undergraduate GPA of 3.0. Additional exam requirements/recommendations for international students: Required—TOEFL (minimum score 523 paper-based; 213 computer-based; 70 iBT); Recommended—IELTS. *Application deadline:* For fall admission, 5/1 for domestic and international students; for spring admission, 10/15 for domestic and international students. Applications are processed on a rolling basis. Application fee: $40. Electronic applications accepted. *Expenses:* Tuition: Full-time $18,576; part-time $1032 per credit hour. Required fees: $583 per semester. One-time fee: $150. Tuition and fees vary according to program and student level. *Financial support:* In 2010–11, 2 fellowships with full and partial tuition reimbursements (averaging $7,750 per year), 3 research assistantships with full and partial tuition reimbursements (averaging $5,950 per year), 13 teaching assistantships with full and partial tuition reimbursements (averaging $7,173 per year) were awarded; Federal Work-Study, institutionally sponsored loans, scholarships/grants, health care benefits, tuition waivers (partial), and unspecified assistantships also available. Support available to part-time students. Financial award applicants required to submit FAFSA. *Faculty research:* Synthesis and analysis of inorganic nanoparticles; synthetic and mechanistic organic chemistry; synthesis of penicillin-related compounds; design, synthesis and property studies of nanomaterials for applications in chemical sensing, energy storage and biomedical usage; scanning probe microscopy. Total annual research expenditures: $356,146. *Unit head:* Dr. Rong Wang, Associate Chair, 312-567-3121, Fax: 312-567-3494, E-mail: wangr@iit.edu. *Application contact:* Deborah Gibson, Director, Graduate Admission, 866-472-3448, Fax: 312-567-3138, E-mail: inquiry.grad@iit.edu.

Indiana University Bloomington, University Graduate School, College of Arts and Sciences, Department of Chemistry, Bloomington, IN 47405. Offers analytical chemistry (PhD); chemical biology chemistry (PhD); chemistry (MAT); inorganic chemistry (PhD); materials chemistry (PhD); organic chemistry (PhD); physical chemistry (PhD). *Faculty:* 42 full-time (4 women). *Students:* 224 full-time (77 women); includes 19 minority (7 Black or African American, non-Hispanic/Latino; 1 American Indian or Alaska Native, non-Hispanic/Latino; 8 Asian, non-Hispanic/Latino; 3 Hispanic/Latino), 68 international. Average age 27. 270 applicants, 39% accepted, 31 enrolled. In 2010, 1 master's, 20 doctorates awarded. Terminal master's awarded for partial completion of doctoral program. *Degree requirements:* For master's, thesis; for doctorate, thesis/dissertation. *Entrance requirements:* For master's and doctorate, GRE General Test, GRE Subject Test. Additional exam requirements/recommendations for international students: Required—TOEFL. *Application deadline:* For fall admission, 1/15 priority date for domestic students, 12/15 for international students. Applications are processed on a rolling basis. Application fee: $55 ($65 for international students). *Financial support:* In 2010–11, 200 students received support, including 10 fellowships with full tuition reimbursements available, 76 research assistantships with full tuition reimbursements available, 111 teaching assistantships with full tuition reimbursements available; Federal Work-Study and institutionally sponsored loans also available. *Faculty research:* Synthesis of complex natural products, organic reaction mechanisms, organic electrochemistry, transitive-metal chemistry, solid-state and surface chemistry. Total annual research expenditures: $7.7 million. *Unit head:* David Giedroc, Chairperson, 812-855-6239, E-mail: chemchair@indiana.edu. *Application contact:* Daneil Mindiola, Director of Graduate Admissions, 812-855-2069, Fax: 812-855-8385, E-mail: mindiola@indiana.edu.

Kansas State University, Graduate School, College of Arts and Sciences, Department of Chemistry, Manhattan, KS 66506. Offers analytical chemistry (MS); biological chemistry (MS); chemistry (PhD); inorganic chemistry (MS); materials chemistry (MS); organic chemistry (MS); physical chemistry (MS). Terminal master's awarded for partial completion of doctoral program. *Degree requirements:* For master's, thesis; for doctorate, thesis/dissertation. *Entrance requirements:* For master's and doctorate, GRE, minimum GPA of 3.0. Additional exam requirements/recommendations for international students: Required—TOEFL (minimum score 550 paper-based; 213 computer-based). Electronic applications accepted. *Faculty research:* Inorganic chemistry, organic and biological chemistry, analytical chemistry, physical chemistry, materials chemistry and nanotechnology.

Kent State University, College of Arts and Sciences, Department of Chemistry and Biochemistry, Kent, OH 44242-0001. Offers analytical chemistry (MS, PhD); biochemistry (MS, PhD); chemistry (MA); inorganic chemistry (MS, PhD); organic chemistry (MS, PhD); physical chemistry (MS, PhD). Terminal master's awarded for partial completion of doctoral program. *Degree requirements:* For master's, comprehensive exam, thesis; for doctorate, comprehensive exam, thesis/dissertation. *Entrance requirements:* For master's and doctorate, placement exam, GRE General Test, GRE Subject Test (recommended), minimum GPA of 2.75. Additional exam requirements/recommendations for international students: Required—TOEFL (minimum score 525 paper-based; 71 iBT). Electronic applications accepted. *Expenses:* Tuition, state resident: full-time $7866; part-time $437 per credit hour. Tuition, nonresident: full-time $14,022; part-time $779 per credit hour. *Faculty research:* Biological chemistry, materials chemistry, molecular spectroscopy.

See Display on page 57 and Close-Up on page 101.

Laurentian University, School of Graduate Studies and Research, Programme in Chemistry and Biochemistry, Sudbury, ON P3E 2C6, Canada. Offers analytical chemistry (M Sc); biochemistry (M Sc); environmental chemistry (M Sc); organic chemistry (M Sc); physical/theoretical chemistry (M Sc). Part-time programs available. *Degree requirements:* For master's, thesis or alternative. *Entrance requirements:* For master's, honors degree with minimum second class. *Faculty research:* Cell cycle checkpoints, kinetic modeling, toxicology to metal stress, quantum chemistry, biogeochemistry metal speciation.

Marquette University, Graduate School, College of Arts and Sciences, Department of Chemistry, Milwaukee, WI 53201-1881. Offers analytical chemistry (MS, PhD); bioanalytical chemistry (MS, PhD); biophysical chemistry (MS, PhD); chemical physics (MS, PhD); inorganic chemistry (MS, PhD); organic chemistry (MS, PhD); physical chemistry (MS, PhD). Part-time programs available. *Faculty:* 27 full-time (3 women), 1 part-time/adjunct (0 women). *Students:* 33 full-time (12 women), 16 part-time (3 women); includes 4 minority (2 Black or African American, non-Hispanic/Latino; 2 Asian, non-Hispanic/Latino), 37 international. Average age 29. 25 applicants, 92% accepted, 10 enrolled. In 2010, 2 master's, 1 doctorate awarded. Terminal master's awarded for partial completion of doctoral program. *Degree requirements:* For master's, comprehensive exam; for doctorate, thesis/dissertation, cumulative exams. *Entrance requirements:* For master's and doctorate, GRE Subject Test (optional), official transcripts from all current and previous colleges/universities except Marquette, three letters of recommendation from individuals familiar with the applicant's academic work. Additional exam requirements/recommendations for international students: Required—TOEFL (minimum score 530 paper-based; 78 computer-based). *Application deadline:* Applications are processed on a rolling basis. Application fee: $50. Electronic applications accepted. *Expenses:* Tuition: Full-time $16,290; part-time $905 per credit hour. Tuition and fees vary according to program. *Financial support:* In 2010–11, 2 fellowships, 4 research assistantships, 27 teaching assistantships were awarded; Federal Work-Study, institutionally sponsored loans, scholarships/grants, and tuition waivers (full and partial) also available. Support available to part-time students. Financial award application deadline: 2/15. *Faculty research:* Inorganic complexes, laser Raman spectroscopy, organic synthesis, synthetic bioinorganic chemistry, electro-active organic molecules. Total annual research expenditures: $1.2 million. *Unit head:* Dr. Michael Ryan, Chair, 414-288-3537, Fax: 414-288-7066. *Application contact:* Dr. Mark Steinmetz, Director of Graduate Studies, 414-288-7374, Fax: 414-288-7066.

McMaster University, School of Graduate Studies, Faculty of Science, Department of Chemistry, Hamilton, ON L8S 4M2, Canada. Offers analytical chemistry (M Sc, PhD); chemical physics (M Sc, PhD); chemistry (M Sc, PhD); inorganic chemistry (M Sc, PhD); organic chemistry (M Sc, PhD); physical chemistry (M Sc, PhD); polymer chemistry (M Sc, PhD). Part-time programs available. Terminal master's awarded for partial completion of doctoral program. *Degree requirements:* For master's, thesis; for doctorate, comprehensive exam, thesis/dissertation. *Entrance requirements:* For master's, minimum B+ average. Additional exam requirements/recommendations for international students: Required—TOEFL (minimum score 550 paper-based; 213 computer-based).

Northeastern University, College of Science, Department of Chemistry and Chemical Biology, Boston, MA 02115-5096. Offers analytical chemistry (PhD); chemistry (MS, PhD); inorganic chemistry (PhD); organic chemistry (PhD); physical chemistry (PhD). Part-time and evening/weekend programs available. *Faculty:* 24 full-time (5 women), 7 part-time/adjunct (0 women). *Students:* 98 full-time (58 women), 31 part-time (15 women). 190 applicants, 32% accepted, 34 enrolled. In 2010, 16 master's, 6 doctorates awarded. Terminal master's awarded for partial completion of doctoral program. *Degree requirements:* For master's, thesis (for some programs); for doctorate, thesis/dissertation, qualifying exam in specialty area. *Entrance requirements:* Additional exam requirements/recommendations for international students: Required—TOEFL. *Application deadline:* For fall admission, 2/1 priority date for domestic and international students. Applications are processed on a rolling basis. Application fee: $50. Electronic applications accepted. *Financial support:* In 2010–11, 41 research assistantships with tuition reimbursements (averaging $18,285 per year), 38 teaching assistantships with tuition reimbursements (averaging $18,285 per year) were awarded; fellowships with tuition reimbursements, career-related internships or fieldwork, Federal Work-Study, scholarships/grants, tuition waivers (partial), and unspecified assistantships also available. Financial award application deadline: 3/1; financial award applicants required to submit FAFSA. *Faculty research:* Bioanalysis, biorganic and medicinal chemistry, biophysical chemistry, nanomaterials, proteonics. *Unit head:* Dr. Robert Hanson, Graduate Coordinator, 617-373-3313, Fax: 617-373-8795, E-mail: chemistry-grad-info@neu.edu. *Application contact:* Jo-Anne Dickinson, Admissions Contact, 617-373-5990, Fax: 617-373-7281, E-mail: gsas@neu.edu.

Old Dominion University, College of Sciences, Program in Chemistry, Norfolk, VA 23529. Offers analytical chemistry (MS); biochemistry (MS); chemistry (PhD); environmental chemistry (MS); organic chemistry (MS); physical chemistry (MS). Part-time and evening/weekend programs available. *Faculty:* 14 full-time (5 women), 2 part-time/adjunct (0 women). *Students:* 36 full-time (22 women), 1 part-time (0 women); includes 3 minority (1 Black or African American, non-Hispanic/Latino; 1 Asian, non-Hispanic/Latino; 1 Hispanic/Latino), 16 international. Average age 29. 35 applicants, 60% accepted, 8 enrolled. In 2010, 6 master's, 2 doctorates awarded. *Degree requirements:* For master's, comprehensive exam, thesis. *Entrance requirements:* For master's, GRE General Test, minimum GPA of 3.0 in major, 2.5 overall; for doctorate, GRE General Test. Additional exam requirements/recommendations for international students: Required—TOEFL. *Application deadline:* For fall admission, 7/1 for domestic students, 1/15 for international students; for spring admission, 11/1 for domestic students, 8/15 for international students. Applications are processed on a rolling basis. Application fee: $30. Electronic applications accepted. *Expenses:* Tuition, state resident: full-time $8592; part-time $358 per credit. Tuition, nonresident: full-time $21,672; part-time $903 per credit. Required fees: $119 per semester. One-time fee: $50. *Financial support:* In 2010–11, 6 students received support, including fellowships (averaging $18,000 per year), research assistantships with tuition reimbursements available (averaging $21,000 per year), teaching assistantships with tuition reimbursements available (averaging $18,000 per year); career-related internships or fieldwork, scholarships/grants, and unspecified assistantships also available. Financial award application deadline: 2/15; financial award applicants required to submit FAFSA. *Faculty research:* Biogeochemistry, materials chemistry, bioanalytical chemistry, computational chemistry, organic chemistry. Total annual research expenditures: $2.6 million. *Unit head:* Dr. Craig A. Bayse, Graduate Program Director, 757-683-4097, Fax: 757-683-4628, E-mail: chemgpd@odu.edu. *Application contact:* Valerie DeCosta, Grants and Graduate Program Assistant, 757-683-6979, Fax: 757-683-4628, E-mail: chemgpd@odu.edu.

Oregon State University, Graduate School, College of Science, Department of Chemistry, Corvallis, OR 97331. Offers analytical chemistry (MS, PhD); chemistry (MA, MAIS); inorganic chemistry (MS, PhD); nuclear and radiation chemistry (MS, PhD); organic chemistry (MS, PhD); physical chemistry (MS, PhD). Part-time programs available. Terminal master's awarded for partial completion of doctoral program. *Degree requirements:* For master's, one foreign language, thesis; for doctorate, one foreign language, thesis/dissertation. *Entrance requirements:* For master's and doctorate, minimum GPA of 3.0 in last 90 hours of course work. Additional exam requirements/recommendations for international students: Required—TOEFL. *Faculty research:* Solid state chemistry, enzyme reaction mechanisms, structure and dynamics of gas molecules, chemiluminescence, nonlinear optical spectroscopy.

Purdue University, Graduate School, College of Science, Department of Chemistry, West Lafayette, IN 47907. Offers analytical chemistry (MS, PhD); biochemistry (MS, PhD); chemical education (MS, PhD); inorganic chemistry (MS, PhD); organic chemistry (MS, PhD); physical chemistry (MS, PhD). Terminal master's awarded for partial completion of doctoral program. *Degree requirements:* For master's, thesis; for doctorate, thesis/dissertation. *Entrance requirements:* Additional exam requirements/recommendations for international students: Required—TOEFL. Electronic applications accepted.

Rensselaer Polytechnic Institute, Graduate School, School of Science, Program in Chemistry, Troy, NY 12180-3590. Offers analytical chemistry (MS, PhD); biochemistry (MS, PhD); inorganic chemistry (MS, PhD); organic chemistry (MS, PhD); physical chemistry (MS, PhD); polymer chemistry (MS, PhD). Part-time and evening/weekend programs available. *Faculty:* 16 full-time (2 women). *Students:* 42 full-time (18 women), 3 part-time (1 woman); includes 1 Black or African American, non-Hispanic/Latino; 4 Asian, non-Hispanic/Latino, 16 international. Average age 24. 139 applicants, 16% accepted, 6 enrolled. In 2010, 5 master's, 8 doctorates awarded. Terminal master's awarded for partial completion of doctoral program. *Degree requirements:* For master's, thesis (for some programs); for doctorate, comprehensive exam, thesis/dissertation. *Entrance requirements:* For master's, GRE General Test, GRE Subject Test (strongly recommended); for doctorate, GRE General Test, GRE Subject Test (chemistry or biochemistry strongly recommended). Additional exam requirements/recommendations for

Peterson's Graduate Programs in the Physical Sciences, Mathematics, Agricultural Sciences, the Environment & Natural Resources 2012

www.facebook.com/petersonspublishing 45

Analytical Chemistry

Rensselaer Polytechnic Institute (continued)
international students: Required—TOEFL (minimum score 570 paper-based; 230 computer-based; 88 iBT). *Application deadline:* For fall admission, 2/1 priority date for domestic students; for spring admission, 11/15 for domestic students. Applications are processed on a rolling basis. Application fee: $75. Electronic applications accepted. *Expenses:* Tuition: Full-time $39,600; part-time $1650 per credit. Required fees: $1896. *Financial support:* In 2010–11, 1 fellowship with full tuition reimbursement (averaging $23,000 per year), 12 research assistantships with full tuition reimbursements (averaging $23,000 per year), 23 teaching assistantships with full tuition reimbursements (averaging $23,000 per year) were awarded; institutionally sponsored loans and tuition waivers (full and partial) also available. Financial award application deadline: 2/1. *Faculty research:* Synthetic polymer and biopolymer chemistry, physical chemistry of polymeric systems, bioanalytical chemistry, synthetic and computational drug design, protein folding and protein design. Total annual research expenditures: $1.1 million. *Unit head:* Dr. Curtis M. Breneman, Chair, 518-276-3264, Fax: 518-276-4887, E-mail: brenec@rpi.edu. *Application contact:* Sharon E. Gardner, Graduate Program Administrator, 518-276-2140, Fax: 518-276-4887, E-mail: derris@rpi.edu.

Rutgers, The State University of New Jersey, Newark, Graduate School, Program in Chemistry, Newark, NJ 07102. Offers analytical chemistry (MS, PhD); biochemistry (MS, PhD); inorganic chemistry (MS, PhD); organic chemistry (MS, PhD); physical chemistry (MS, PhD). Part-time and evening/weekend programs available. *Faculty:* 13 full-time (3 women). *Students:* 29 full-time (14 women), 32 part-time (19 women); includes 2 Black or African American, non-Hispanic/Latino; 30 Asian, non-Hispanic/Latino; 3 Hispanic/Latino. 153 applicants, 45% accepted, 17 enrolled. In 2010, 4 master's, 9 doctorates awarded. Terminal master's awarded for partial completion of doctoral program. *Degree requirements:* For master's, thesis optional, cumulative exams; for doctorate, thesis/dissertation, exams, research proposal. *Entrance requirements:* For master's and doctorate, GRE General Test, minimum undergraduate B average. Additional exam requirements/recommendations for international students: Required—TOEFL. *Application deadline:* For fall admission, 7/1 priority date for domestic students; for spring admission, 12/1 for domestic students. Applications are processed on a rolling basis. Application fee: $60. Electronic applications accepted. *Expenses:* Tuition, state resident: part-time $600 per credit. Tuition, nonresident: full-time $10,694. *Financial support:* In 2010–11, 35 students received support, including 5 fellowships (averaging $18,000 per year), 6 research assistantships with full and partial tuition reimbursements available (averaging $23,112 per year), 20 teaching assistantships with full and partial tuition reimbursements available (averaging $23,112 per year); Federal Work-Study and institutionally sponsored loans also available. Financial award application deadline: 3/1. *Faculty research:* Medicinal chemistry, natural products, isotope effects, biophysics and biorganic approaches to enzyme mechanisms, organic and organometallic synthesis. *Unit head:* Prof. Frank Jordan, Chairman and Program Director, 973-353-5741, Fax: 973-353-1264, E-mail: frjordan@andromeda.rutgers.edu. *Application contact:* Jason Hand, Director of Admissions, 973-353-5205, Fax: 973-353-1440.

Seton Hall University, College of Arts and Sciences, Department of Chemistry and Biochemistry, South Orange, NJ 07079-2697. Offers analytical chemistry (MS, PhD); biochemistry (MS, PhD); chemistry (MS); inorganic chemistry (MS, PhD); organic chemistry (MS, PhD); physical chemistry (MS, PhD). Part-time and evening/weekend programs available. Terminal master's awarded for partial completion of doctoral program. *Degree requirements:* For master's, thesis optional; for doctorate, comprehensive exam, thesis/dissertation. *Entrance requirements:* Additional exam requirements/recommendations for international students: Required—TOEFL. Electronic applications accepted. *Faculty research:* DNA metal reactions; chromatography; bioinorganic, biophysical, organometallic, polymer chemistry; heterogeneous catalyst; synthetic organic and carbohydrate chemistry.

Southern University and Agricultural and Mechanical College, Graduate School, College of Sciences, Department of Chemistry, Baton Rouge, LA 70813. Offers analytical chemistry (MS); biochemistry (MS); environmental sciences (MS); inorganic chemistry (MS); organic chemistry (MS); physical chemistry (MS). *Degree requirements:* For master's, thesis. *Entrance requirements:* For master's, GMAT or GRE General Test. Additional exam requirements/recommendations for international students: Required—TOEFL (minimum score 525 paper-based; 193 computer-based). *Faculty research:* Synthesis of macrocyclic ligands, latex accelerators, anticancer drugs, biosensors, absorption isotheums, isolation of specific enzymes from plants.

State University of New York at Binghamton, Graduate School, School of Arts and Sciences, Department of Chemistry, Binghamton, NY 13902-6000. Offers analytical chemistry (PhD); chemistry (MA, MS); inorganic chemistry (PhD); organic chemistry (PhD); physical chemistry (PhD). Part-time programs available. *Faculty:* 15 full-time (4 women), 3 part-time/adjunct (2 women). *Students:* 28 full-time (8 women), 29 part-time (17 women); includes 2 Black or African American, non-Hispanic/Latino; 4 Asian, non-Hispanic/Latino; 2 Hispanic/Latino, 34 international. Average age 29. 35 applicants, 40% accepted, 9 enrolled. In 2010, 5 master's, 8 doctorates awarded. Terminal master's awarded for partial completion of doctoral program. *Degree requirements:* For master's, thesis or alternative, oral exam, seminar presentation; for doctorate, thesis/dissertation, cumulative exams. *Entrance requirements:* For master's and doctorate, GRE General Test, GRE Subject Test. Additional exam requirements/recommendations for international students: Required—TOEFL (minimum score 550 paper-based; 213 computer-based; 80 iBT). *Application deadline:* For fall admission, 1/15 priority date for domestic and international students; for spring admission, 10/15 priority date for domestic and international students. Applications are processed on a rolling basis. Application fee: $60. Electronic applications accepted. *Financial support:* In 2010–11, 51 students received support, including 5 fellowships with full tuition reimbursements available (averaging $18,000 per year), 9 research assistantships with full tuition reimbursements available (averaging $18,000 per year), 35 teaching assistantships with full tuition reimbursements available (averaging $18,000 per year); career-related internships or fieldwork, Federal Work-Study, institutionally sponsored loans, scholarships/grants, health care benefits, tuition waivers (full), and unspecified assistantships also available. Financial award application deadline: 2/15; financial award applicants required to submit FAFSA. *Unit head:* Dr. Wayne E. Jones, Chairperson, 607-777-2421, E-mail: wjones@binghamton.edu. *Application contact:* Catherin Smith, Recruiting and Admissions Coordinator, 607-777-2151, Fax: 607-777-2501, E-mail: cmsmith@binghamton.edu.

Stevens Institute of Technology, Graduate School, Charles V. Schaefer Jr. School of Engineering, Department of Chemistry, Chemical Biology and Biomedical Engineering, Hoboken, NJ 07030. Offers analytical chemistry (PhD, Certificate); bioinformatics (PhD, Certificate); biomedical chemistry (Certificate); biomedical engineering (M Eng, Certificate); chemical biology (MS, PhD, Certificate); chemical physiology (Certificate); chemistry (MS, PhD); organic chemistry (PhD); physical chemistry (PhD); polymer chemistry (PhD, Certificate). Part-time and evening/weekend programs available. Postbaccalaureate distance learning degree programs offered (no on-campus study). *Students:* 66 full-time (35 women), 25 part-time (7 women); includes 2 Black or African American, non-Hispanic/Latino; 14 Asian, non-Hispanic/Latino; 8 Hispanic/Latino, 31 international. Average age 26. 109 applicants, 68% accepted.Terminal master's awarded for partial completion of doctoral program. *Degree requirements:* For master's, thesis or alternative; for doctorate, one foreign language, thesis/dissertation; for Certificate, project or thesis. *Entrance requirements:* Additional exam requirements/recommendations for international students: Required—TOEFL. *Application deadline:* Applications are processed on a rolling basis. Application fee: $50. Electronic applications accepted. *Financial support:* Fellowships, research assistantships, teaching assistantships available. Financial award application deadline: 4/1. *Faculty research:* Biochemical reaction engineering, polymerization engineering, reactor design, biochemical process control and synthesis. *Unit head:* Philip Leopold, Director, 201-216-8957, Fax: 201-216-8196, E-mail: pleopold@stevens.edu. *Application contact:* Graduate Admissions, 800-496-4935, Fax: 201-216-8044, E-mail: gradadmissions@stevens.edu.

Tufts University, Graduate School of Arts and Sciences, Department of Chemistry, Medford, MA 02155. Offers analytical chemistry (MS, PhD); bioorganic chemistry (MS, PhD); environmental chemistry (MS, PhD); inorganic chemistry (MS, PhD); organic chemistry (MS, PhD); physical chemistry (MS, PhD). Terminal master's awarded for partial completion of doctoral program. *Degree requirements:* For master's, thesis optional; for doctorate, thesis/dissertation. *Entrance requirements:* For master's and doctorate, GRE General Test, GRE Subject Test. Additional exam requirements/recommendations for international students: Required—TOEFL (minimum score 600 paper-based; 250 computer-based; 80 iBT). Electronic applications accepted. *Expenses:* Tuition: Full-time $39,624; part-time $3962 per course. Required fees: $40 per year. Full-time tuition and fees vary according to degree level, program and student level. Part-time tuition and fees vary according to course load.

University of Calgary, Faculty of Graduate Studies, Faculty of Science, Department of Chemistry, Calgary, AB T2N 1N4, Canada. Offers analytical chemistry (M Sc, PhD); applied chemistry (M Sc, PhD); inorganic chemistry (M Sc, PhD); organic chemistry (M Sc, PhD); physical chemistry (M Sc, PhD); polymer chemistry (M Sc, PhD); theoretical chemistry (M Sc, PhD). *Degree requirements:* For master's, thesis; for doctorate, thesis/dissertation, candidacy exam. *Entrance requirements:* For master's, minimum GPA of 3.0; for doctorate, honors B Sc degree with minimum GPA of 3.7 or M Sc with minimum GPA of 3.3. Additional exam requirements/recommendations for international students: Required—TOEFL (minimum score 580 paper-based; 237 computer-based). Electronic applications accepted. *Faculty research:* Chemical analysis, chemical dynamics, synthesis theory.

University of Cincinnati, Graduate School, McMicken College of Arts and Sciences, Department of Chemistry, Cincinnati, OH 45221. Offers analytical chemistry (MS, PhD); biochemistry (MS, PhD); inorganic chemistry (MS, PhD); organic chemistry (MS, PhD); physical chemistry (MS, PhD); polymer chemistry (MS, PhD); sensors (PhD). Part-time and evening/weekend programs available. Terminal master's awarded for partial completion of doctoral program. *Degree requirements:* For master's, thesis optional; for doctorate, comprehensive exam, thesis/dissertation. *Entrance requirements:* For master's and doctorate, GRE General Test. Additional exam requirements/recommendations for international students: Required—TOEFL (minimum score 580 paper-based; 237 computer-based). Electronic applications accepted. *Faculty research:* Biomedical chemistry, laser chemistry, surface science, chemical sensors, synthesis.

University of Georgia, College of Arts and Sciences, Department of Chemistry, Athens, GA 30602. Offers analytical chemistry (MS, PhD); inorganic chemistry (MS, PhD); organic chemistry (MS, PhD); physical chemistry (MS, PhD). *Faculty:* 27 full-time (3 women). *Students:* 149 full-time (46 women), 3 part-time (1 woman); includes 5 Black or African American, non-Hispanic/Latino; 8 Asian, non-Hispanic/Latino; 1 Hispanic/Latino; 1 Two or more races, non-Hispanic/Latino, 58 international. 176 applicants, 38% accepted, 27 enrolled. In 2010, 6 master's, 20 doctorates awarded. Terminal master's awarded for partial completion of doctoral program. *Degree requirements:* For master's, thesis; for doctorate, one foreign language, thesis/dissertation. *Entrance requirements:* For master's and doctorate, GRE General Test. Additional exam requirements/recommendations for international students: Required—TOEFL (minimum score 213 computer-based). *Application deadline:* For fall admission, 7/1 priority date for domestic students; for spring admission, 11/15 for domestic students. Application fee: $50. Electronic applications accepted. *Expenses:* Tuition, state resident: full-time $7200; part-time $344 per credit hour. Tuition, nonresident: full-time $21,900; part-time $944 per credit hour. Tuition and fees vary according to course load and program. *Financial support:* Fellowships, research assistantships, teaching assistantships, unspecified assistantships available. *Unit head:* Dr. Jon Amster, Head, 706-542-2726, E-mail: jamster@uga.edu. *Application contact:* Dr. George F. Majetich, Graduate Coordinator, 706-542-1966, Fax: 706-542-9454, E-mail: majetich@chem.uga.edu.

University of Louisville, Graduate School, College of Arts and Sciences, Department of Chemistry, Louisville, KY 40292-0001. Offers analytical chemistry (MS, PhD); biochemistry (MS, PhD); chemical physics (PhD); inorganic chemistry (MS, PhD); organic chemistry (MS, PhD); physical chemistry (MS, PhD). *Faculty:* 21 full-time (4 women). *Students:* 55 full-time (24 women), 4 part-time (0 women); includes 1 Black or African American, non-Hispanic/Latino; 1 Asian, non-Hispanic/Latino, 42 international. Average age 29. 79 applicants, 27% accepted, 7 enrolled. In 2010, 7 master's, 5 doctorates awarded. Terminal master's awarded for partial completion of doctoral program. *Degree requirements:* For master's, variable foreign language requirement, comprehensive exam, thesis optional; for doctorate, variable foreign language requirement, comprehensive exam, thesis/dissertation. *Entrance requirements:* For master's, BA or BS courseowork; for doctorate, none, BA or BS coursework. Additional exam requirements/recommendations for international students: Required—TOEFL. *Application deadline:* For fall admission, 3/15 for domestic and international students; for winter admission, 9/15 for domestic and international students. Applications are processed on a rolling basis. Application fee: $50. Electronic applications accepted. *Expenses:* Tuition, state resident: full-time $9144; part-time $508 per credit hour. Tuition, nonresident: full-time $19,026; part-time $1057 per credit hour. Tuition and fees vary according to program and reciprocity agreements. *Financial support:* In 2010–11, 33 teaching assistantships with full tuition reimbursements (averaging $22,000 per year) were awarded; fellowships with full tuition reimbursements, research assistantships with full tuition reimbursements, career-related internships or fieldwork, scholarships/grants, traineeships, health care benefits, and unspecified assistantships also available. Support available to part-time students. Financial award application deadline: 3/15. *Faculty research:* Computational chemistry, biophysics nuclear magnetic resonance, synthetic organic chemistry, synthetic inorganic chemistry, medicinal chemistry, protein chemistry, enzymology, nanochemistry, electrochemistry, analytical chemistry, synthetic biology, bioinformatics. Total annual research expenditures: $2.5 million. *Unit head:* Dr. Richard J. Wittebort, Professor and Chair. *Application contact:* Sherry Nalley, Administrator, 502-852-6798.

The University of Manchester, School of Chemical Engineering and Analytical Science, Manchester, United Kingdom. Offers biocatalysis (M Phil, PhD); chemical engineering (M Phil, PhD); chemical engineering and analytical science (M Phil, D Eng, PhD); colloids, crystals, interfaces and materials (M Phil, PhD); environment and sustainable technology (M Phil, PhD); instrumentation (M Phil, PhD); multi-scale modeling (M Phil, PhD); process integration (M Phil, PhD); systems biology (M Phil, PhD).

University of Maryland, College Park, Academic Affairs, College of Computer, Mathematical and Natural Sciences, Department of Chemistry and Biochemistry, Chemistry Program, College Park, MD 20742. Offers analytical chemistry (MS, PhD); inorganic chemistry (MS, PhD); organic chemistry (MS, PhD); physical chemistry (MS, PhD). Part-time and evening/weekend programs available. *Students:* 128 full-time (65 women), 5 part-time (1 woman); includes 14 Black or African American, non-Hispanic/Latino; 3 Asian, non-Hispanic/Latino; 3 Hispanic/Latino; 2 Two or more races, non-Hispanic/Latino, 62 international. 398 applicants, 16% accepted, 22 enrolled. In 2010, 3 master's, 16 doctorates awarded. Terminal master's awarded for partial completion of doctoral program. *Degree requirements:* For master's, thesis optional; for doctorate, thesis/dissertation, 2 seminar presentations, oral exam. *Entrance requirements:* For master's and doctorate, GRE General Test, GRE Subject Test (recommended), minimum GPA of 3.0, 3 letters of recommendation. Additional exam requirements/recommendations for international students: Required—TOEFL. *Application deadline:* For fall admission, 2/1 for domestic and international students. Applications are processed on a rolling basis. Application fee: $75. Electronic applications accepted. *Expenses:* Tuition, area resident: Part-time $471 per credit hour. Tuition, state resident: part-time $471 per credit hour. Tuition, nonresident: part-time $1016 per credit hour. Required fees: $337 per term. *Financial support:* In 2010–11, 9 fellowships with full tuition reimbursements (averaging $24,410 per year), 48 research

assistantships (averaging $19,514 per year), 64 teaching assistantships (averaging $19,155 per year) were awarded. Financial award applicants required to submit FAFSA. *Faculty research:* Environmental chemistry, nuclear chemistry, lunar and environmental analysis, x-ray crystallography. *Unit head:* Dr. Michael Doyle, Chairperson, 301-405-1795, Fax: 301-314-2779, E-mail: mdoyle3@umd.edu. *Application contact:* Dean of Graduate School, 301-405-0358, Fax: 301-314-9305.

University of Massachusetts Lowell, College of Arts and Sciences, Department of Chemistry, Lowell, MA 01854-2881. Offers analytical chemistry (PhD); biochemistry (PhD); chemistry (MS, PhD); environmental studies (PhD); green chemistry (PhD); inorganic chemistry (PhD); organic chemistry (PhD); polymer science (MS). Terminal master's awarded for partial completion of doctoral program. *Degree requirements:* For master's, thesis; for doctorate, 2 foreign languages, thesis/dissertation. *Entrance requirements:* For master's and doctorate, GRE General Test. Electronic applications accepted.

University of Memphis, Graduate School, College of Arts and Sciences, Department of Chemistry, Memphis, TN 38152. Offers analytical chemistry (MS, PhD); computational chemistry (MS, PhD); inorganic chemistry (MS, PhD); organic chemistry (MS, PhD); physical chemistry (MS, PhD). Part-time programs available. *Faculty:* 6 full-time (1 woman). *Students:* 39 full-time (16 women), 5 part-time (3 women); includes 8 minority (6 Black or African American, non-Hispanic/Latino; 2 Asian, non-Hispanic/Latino), 6 international. Average age 28. 37 applicants, 30% accepted, 8 enrolled. In 2010, 3 master's, 5 doctorates awarded. Terminal master's awarded for partial completion of doctoral program. *Degree requirements:* For master's, comprehensive exam, thesis or alternative; for doctorate, comprehensive exam, thesis/dissertation. *Entrance requirements:* For master's and doctorate, GRE General Test, admission to Graduate School plus 32 undergraduate hours in chemistry. Additional exam requirements/recommendations for international students: Required—TOEFL. *Application deadline:* For fall admission, 7/1 for domestic students, 5/1 for international students; for winter admission, 9/15 for international students; for spring admission, 12/1 for domestic students. Applications are processed on a rolling basis. Application fee: $35 ($60 for international students). Electronic applications accepted. *Financial support:* In 2010–11, 12 students received support; research assistantships with full tuition reimbursements available, teaching assistantships with full tuition reimbursements available, Federal Work-Study, scholarships/grants, and unspecified assistantships available. Financial award application deadline: 2/15; financial award applicants required to submit FAFSA. *Faculty research:* Computational chemistry, materials chemistry, organic/polymer synthesis, drug design/delivery, water chemistry. *Unit head:* Dr. Abby L. Parrill, Professor and Chair, 901-678-2638, Fax: 901-678-3447, E-mail: aparrill@memphis.edu. *Application contact:* Dr. Gary Emmert, Associate Professor and Graduate Coordinator, 901-678-2636, Fax: 901-678-3447, E-mail: gemmert@memphis.edu.

University of Michigan, Horace H. Rackham School of Graduate Studies, College of Literature, Science, and the Arts, Department of Chemistry, Ann Arbor, MI 48109-1055. Offers analytical chemistry (PhD); chemical biology (PhD); inorganic chemistry (PhD); material chemistry (PhD); organic chemistry (PhD); physical chemistry (PhD). *Faculty:* 39 full-time (8 women). *Students:* 201 full-time (106 women); includes 19 minority (1 Black or African American, non-Hispanic/Latino; 12 Asian, non-Hispanic/Latino; 4 Hispanic/Latino; 2 Two or more races, non-Hispanic/Latino), 60 international. Average age 26. 565 applicants, 38% accepted, 39 enrolled. In 2010, 58 doctorates awarded. *Degree requirements:* For doctorate, thesis/dissertation, oral defense of dissertation, organic cumulative proficiency exams. *Entrance requirements:* For doctorate, GRE General Test, GRE Subject Test (recommended), 3 letters of recommendation. Additional exam requirements/recommendations for international students: Required—TOEFL (minimum score 560 paper-based; 220 computer-based; 84 iBT). *Application deadline:* For fall admission, 1/15 for domestic students, 12/15 for international students. Applications are processed on a rolling basis. Application fee: $0 ($75 for international students). Electronic applications accepted. *Expenses:* Tuition, state resident: full-time $17,784; part-time $1116 per credit hour. Tuition, nonresident: full-time $35,944; part-time $2125 per credit hour. International tuition: $35,994 full-time. Required fees: $95 per semester. Tuition and fees vary according to course load, degree level and program. *Financial support:* In 2010–11, 201 students received support, including 23 fellowships with full tuition reimbursements available (averaging $25,905 per year), 54 research assistantships with full tuition reimbursements available (averaging $25,905 per year), 118 teaching assistantships with full tuition reimbursements available (averaging $25,905 per year); career-related internships or fieldwork, scholarships/grants, traineeships, health care benefits, and unspecified assistantships also available. *Faculty research:* Biological catalysis, protein engineering, chemical sensors, de novo metalloprotein design, supra-molecular architecture. *Unit head:* Dr. Carol A. Fierke, Chair, 734-763-9681, Fax: 734-647-4847. *Application contact:* Margarita Bekiares, Graduate Program Coordinator, 734-764-7278, Fax: 734-647-4865, E-mail: chemadmissions@umich.edu.

University of Missouri, Graduate School, College of Arts and Sciences, Department of Chemistry, Columbia, MO 65211. Offers analytical chemistry (MS, PhD); inorganic chemistry (MS, PhD); organic chemistry (MS, PhD); physical chemistry (MS, PhD). *Faculty:* 30 full-time (6 women), 2 part-time/adjunct (0 women). *Students:* 92 full-time (35 women), 5 part-time (1 woman); includes 5 minority (2 Black or African American, non-Hispanic/Latino; 2 Asian, non-Hispanic/Latino; 1 Hispanic/Latino), 46 international. Average age 27. 99 applicants, 21% accepted, 19 enrolled. In 2010, 3 master's, 16 doctorates awarded. *Degree requirements:* For master's, thesis; for doctorate, one foreign language, comprehensive exam, thesis/dissertation. *Entrance requirements:* For master's, GRE General Test, minimum GPA of 3.0; for doctorate, GRE General Test (minimum score: Verbal 450, Quantitative 600, Analytical 3), minimum GPA of 3.0. Additional exam requirements/recommendations for international students: Required—TOEFL (minimum score 600 paper-based; 250 computer-based; 100 iBT). *Application deadline:* For fall admission, 4/1 priority date for domestic students; for winter admission, 10/15 for domestic students. Applications are processed on a rolling basis. Application fee: $45 ($60 for international students). Electronic applications accepted. *Financial support:* In 2010–11, 9 fellowships with full tuition reimbursements, 15 research assistantships with full tuition reimbursements, 78 teaching assistantships with full tuition reimbursements were awarded; institutionally sponsored loans, traineeships, health care benefits, and unspecified assistantships also available. *Faculty research:* Analytical, organic, biological, physical, inorganic and radiochemistry. *Unit head:* Dr. Jerry Atwood, Department Chair, 573-882-8374, E-mail: atwoodj@missouri.edu. *Application contact:* Jerry Brightwell, Administrative Assistant, 573-884-6832, E-mail: brightwellj@missouri.edu.

University of Missouri–Kansas City, College of Arts and Sciences, Department of Chemistry, Kansas City, MO 64110-2499. Offers analytical chemistry (MS, PhD); inorganic chemistry (MS, PhD); organic chemistry (MS, PhD); physical chemistry (MS, PhD); polymer chemistry (MS, PhD). PhD (interdisciplinary) offered through the School of Graduate Studies. Part-time and evening/weekend programs available. *Faculty:* 17 full-time (3 women). *Students:* 5 part-time (2 women); includes 1 minority (Black or African American, non-Hispanic/Latino). Average age 37. 19 applicants, 37% accepted, 1 enrolled. In 2010, 4 master's awarded. *Degree requirements:* For master's, thesis (for some programs); for doctorate, thesis/dissertation. *Entrance requirements:* For master's, equivalent of American Chemical Society approved bachelor's degree in chemistry; for doctorate, GRE General Test, equivalent of American Chemical Society approved bachelor's degree in chemistry. Additional exam requirements/recommendations for international students: Required—TOEFL (minimum score 550 paper-based; 213 computer-based; 80 iBT), TWE. *Application deadline:* For fall admission, 4/15 for domestic and international students; for spring admission, 10/15 for domestic and international students. Applications are processed on a rolling basis. Application fee: $45 ($50 for international students). Electronic applications accepted. *Expenses:* Tuition, state resident: full-time $5522.40; part-time $306.80 per credit hour. Tuition, nonresident: full-time $7128; part-time $792 per credit hour. Required fees: $261.15 per term. *Financial support:* In 2010–11, 7

research assistantships with partial tuition reimbursements (averaging $18,311 per year), 16 teaching assistantships with partial tuition reimbursements (averaging $16,906 per year) were awarded; Federal Work-Study, institutionally sponsored loans, and scholarships/grants also available. Support available to part-time students. Financial award application deadline: 3/1; financial award applicants required to submit FAFSA. *Faculty research:* Molecular spectroscopy, characterization and synthesis of materials and compounds, computational chemistry, natural products, drug delivery systems and anti-tumor agents. Total annual research expenditures: $729,815. *Unit head:* Dr. Kathleen V. Kilway, Chair, 816-235-2289, Fax: 816-235-5502. *Application contact:* Graduate Recruiting Committee, 816-235-2272, Fax: 816-235-5502, E-mail: umkc-chemdept@umkc.edu.

The University of Montana, Graduate School, College of Arts and Sciences, Department of Chemistry, Missoula, MT 59812-0002. Offers chemistry (MS, PhD), including environmental/analytical chemistry, inorganic chemistry, organic chemistry, physical chemistry. Terminal master's awarded for partial completion of doctoral program. *Degree requirements:* For master's, thesis (for some programs); for doctorate, thesis/dissertation. *Entrance requirements:* For master's and doctorate, GRE General Test. Additional exam requirements/recommendations for international students: Required—TOEFL (minimum score 575 paper-based; 230 computer-based). *Faculty research:* Reaction mechanisms and kinetics, inorganic and organic synthesis, analytical chemistry, natural products.

University of Nebraska–Lincoln, Graduate College, College of Arts and Sciences, Department of Chemistry, Lincoln, NE 68588. Offers analytical chemistry (PhD); biochemistry (PhD); chemistry (MS); inorganic chemistry (PhD); materials chemistry (PhD); organic chemistry (PhD); physical chemistry (PhD). *Degree requirements:* For master's, one foreign language, thesis optional, departmental qualifying exam; for doctorate, one foreign language, comprehensive exam, thesis/dissertation, departmental qualifying exams. *Entrance requirements:* For master's and doctorate, GRE. Additional exam requirements/recommendations for international students: Required—TOEFL (minimum score 550 paper-based; 213 computer-based). Electronic applications accepted. *Faculty research:* Bioorganic and bioinorganic chemistry, biophysical and bioanalytical chemistry, structure-function of DNA and proteins, organometallics, mass spectrometry.

University of Regina, Faculty of Graduate Studies and Research, Faculty of Science, Department of Chemistry and Biochemistry, Regina, SK S4S 0A2, Canada. Offers analytical/environmental chemistry (M Sc, PhD); biophysics of biological interfaces (M Sc, PhD); enzymology/chemical biology (M Sc, PhD); inorganic/organometallic chemistry (M Sc, PhD); signal transduction and mechanisms of cancer cell regulation (M Sc, PhD); supramolecular organic photochemistry and photophysics (M Sc, PhD); synthetic organic chemistry (M Sc, PhD); theoretical/computational chemistry (M Sc, PhD). *Faculty:* 10 full-time (2 women). *Students:* 19 full-time (9 women), 2 part-time (1 woman). 20 applicants, 40% accepted. In 2010, 2 master's, 1 doctorate awarded. *Degree requirements:* For master's, thesis; for doctorate, thesis/dissertation. *Entrance requirements:* Additional exam requirements/recommendations for international students: Required—TOEFL (minimum score 580 paper-based; 80 iBT). *Application deadline:* Applications are processed on a rolling basis. Application fee: $100. Electronic applications accepted. Tuition and fees charges are reported in Canadian dollars. *Expenses:* Tuition, area resident: Full-time $3244.50 Canadian dollars; part-time $180.25 Canadian dollars per credit hour. International tuition: $4744.50 Canadian dollars full-time. Required fees: $494 Canadian dollars; $115.25 Canadian dollars per credit hour. $115.25 Canadian dollars per semester. Tuition and fees vary according to program. *Financial support:* In 2010–11, 3 fellowships (averaging $20,000 per year), 2 research assistantships (averaging $17,250 per year), 8 teaching assistantships (averaging $6,965 per year) were awarded; scholarships/grants also available. Financial award application deadline: 6/15. *Faculty research:* Asymmetric synthesis and methodology, theoretical and computational chemistry, biophysical biochemistry, analytical and environmental chemistry, chemical biology. *Unit head:* Dr. Lynn Mihichuk, Head, 306-585-4793, Fax: 306-337-2409, E-mail: lynn.mihichuk@uregina.ca. *Application contact:* Dr. Tanya Dahms, Graduate Program Coordinator, 306-585-4246, Fax: 306-337-2409, E-mail: tanya.dahms@uregina.ca.

University of Southern Mississippi, Graduate School, College of Science and Technology, Department of Chemistry and Biochemistry, Hattiesburg, MS 39406-0001. Offers analytical chemistry (MS, PhD); biochemistry (MS, PhD); inorganic chemistry (MS, PhD); organic chemistry (MS, PhD); physical chemistry (MS, PhD). *Faculty:* 16 full-time (4 women). *Students:* 23 full-time (11 women), 1 part-time (0 women); includes 1 Black or African American, non-Hispanic/Latino, 11 international. Average age 29. 35 applicants, 20% accepted, 5 enrolled. In 2010, 3 master's, 8 doctorates awarded. *Degree requirements:* For master's, comprehensive exam, thesis; for doctorate, comprehensive exam, thesis/dissertation. *Entrance requirements:* For master's, GRE General Test, minimum GPA of 2.75 in last 60 hours; for doctorate, GRE General Test, minimum GPA of 3.5. Additional exam requirements/recommendations for international students: Required—TOEFL, IELTS. *Application deadline:* For fall admission, 3/1 priority date for domestic students, 3/1 for international students. Applications are processed on a rolling basis. Application fee: $50. *Financial support:* In 2010–11, 3 research assistantships with full tuition reimbursements (averaging $17,000 per year), 19 teaching assistantships with full tuition reimbursements (averaging $20,700 per year) were awarded; fellowships, Federal Work-Study, institutionally sponsored loans, scholarships/grants, health care benefits, and unspecified assistantships also available. Support available to part-time students. Financial award application deadline: 3/15; financial award applicants required to submit FAFSA. *Faculty research:* Plant biochemistry, photo chemistry, polymer chemistry, x-ray analysis, enzyme chemistry. *Unit head:* Dr. Sabine Heinhorst, Chair, 601-266-4701, Fax: 601-266-6075. *Application contact:* Dr. Sabine Heinhorst, Graduate Coordinator, 601-266-4702, Fax: 601-266-6075.

University of South Florida, Graduate School, College of Arts and Sciences, Department of Chemistry, Tampa, FL 33620-9951. Offers analytical chemistry (MS, PhD); biochemistry (MS, PhD); computational chemistry (MS, PhD); environmental chemistry (MS, PhD); inorganic chemistry (MS, PhD); organic chemistry (MS); physical chemistry (MS, PhD); polymer chemistry (PhD). Part-time programs available. *Faculty:* 15 full-time (1 woman). *Students:* 120 full-time (42 women), 9 part-time (2 women); includes 7 Black or African American, non-Hispanic/Latino; 8 Asian, non-Hispanic/Latino; 8 Hispanic/Latino, 62 international. Average age 29. 1,118 applicants, 4% accepted, 20 enrolled. In 2010, 4 master's, 14 doctorates awarded. Terminal master's awarded for partial completion of doctoral program. *Degree requirements:* For master's, comprehensive exam, thesis (for some programs); for doctorate, 2 foreign languages, comprehensive exam, thesis/dissertation. *Entrance requirements:* For master's, GRE General Test or GMAT, minimum GPA of 3.0. Additional exam requirements/recommendations for international students: Required—TOEFL (minimum score 550 paper-based; 213 computer-based). *Application deadline:* For fall admission, 2/15 priority date for domestic students, 1/2 priority date for international students; for spring admission, 10/1 priority date for domestic students, 6/1 priority date for international students. Applications are processed on a rolling basis. Application fee: $30. Electronic applications accepted. *Financial support:* In 2010–11, 39 research assistantships (averaging $14,359 per year), 99 teaching assistantships with tuition reimbursements (averaging $15,094 per year) were awarded; unspecified assistantships also available. Financial award application deadline: 6/30. *Faculty research:* Synthesis, bio-organic chemistry, bioinorganic chemistry, environmental chemistry, NMR. Total annual research expenditures: $3.9 million. *Unit head:* Dr. Randy Larsen, Chairperson, 813-974-4129, Fax: 813-974-3203, E-mail: rlarsen@cas.usf.edu. *Application contact:* Patricia Muisener, Director, 813-974-1730, Fax: 813-974-3203, E-mail: muisener@cas.usf.edu.

The University of Tennessee, Graduate School, College of Arts and Sciences, Department of Chemistry, Knoxville, TN 37996. Offers analytical chemistry (MS, PhD); chemical physics

Peterson's Graduate Programs in the Physical Sciences, Mathematics, Agricultural Sciences, the Environment & Natural Resources 2012

www.facebook.com/petersonspublishing   **47**

Analytical Chemistry

The University of Tennessee (continued)
(PhD); environmental chemistry (MS, PhD); inorganic chemistry (MS, PhD); organic chemistry (MS, PhD); physical chemistry (MS, PhD); polymer chemistry (MS, PhD); theoretical chemistry (PhD). Part-time programs available. Terminal master's awarded for partial completion of doctoral program. *Degree requirements:* For master's, thesis; for doctorate, thesis/dissertation. *Entrance requirements:* For master's and doctorate, GRE General Test, minimum GPA of 2.7. Additional exam requirements/recommendations for international students: Required—TOEFL. Electronic applications accepted. *Expenses:* Tuition, state resident: full-time $7440; part-time $414 per credit hour. Tuition, nonresident: full-time $22,478; part-time $1250 per credit hour. Required fees: $922; $43 per credit hour. Tuition and fees vary according to program.

The University of Texas at Austin, Graduate School, College of Natural Sciences, Department of Chemistry and Biochemistry, Austin, TX 78712-1111. Offers analytical chemistry (MA, PhD); biochemistry (MA, PhD); inorganic chemistry (MA, PhD); organic chemistry (MA, PhD); physical chemistry (MA, PhD). *Entrance requirements:* For master's and doctorate, GRE General Test.

The University of Toledo, College of Graduate Studies, College of Natural Sciences and Mathematics, Department of Chemistry, Toledo, OH 43606-3390. Offers analytical chemistry (MS, PhD); biological chemistry (MS, PhD); inorganic chemistry (MS, PhD); organic chemistry (MS, PhD); physical chemistry (MS, PhD). Part-time programs available. *Faculty:* 24. *Students:* 63 full-time (22 women), 4 part-time (2 women); includes 2 minority (1 Asian, non-Hispanic/Latino; 1 Hispanic/Latino), 45 international. Average age 27. 111 applicants, 17% accepted, 16 enrolled. In 2010, 4 master's, 6 doctorates awarded. *Degree requirements:* For master's, thesis; for doctorate, thesis/dissertation. *Entrance requirements:* For master's and doctorate, GRE General Test, GRE Subject Test, A minimum 2.7 cumulative point-hour ratio (on a 4.0 scale) for all previous academic work. Three letters of recommendation, a statement of purpose, and transcripts from all prior institutions attended. Additional exam requirements/recommendations for international students: Required—TOEFL (minimum score 550 paper-based; 213 computer-based; 80 iBT), IELTS (minimum score 6.5). *Application deadline:* For fall admission, 1/15 priority date for domestic and international students. Applications are processed on a rolling basis. Application fee: $45 ($75 for international students). Electronic applications accepted. *Expenses:* Tuition, state resident: full-time $11,426; part-time $476 per credit hour. Tuition, nonresident: full-time $21,660; part-time $903 per credit hour. One-time fee: $62. *Financial support:* Fellowships with tuition reimbursements, research assistantships with full tuition reimbursements, teaching assistantships with full tuition reimbursements, Federal Work-Study, institutionally sponsored loans, scholarships/grants, tuition waivers (full), and unspecified assistantships available. Support available to part-time students. *Faculty research:* Enzymology, materials chemistry, crystallography, theoretical chemistry. *Unit head:* Dr. Alan Pinkerton, Chair, 419-530-7902, Fax: 419-530-4033, E-mail: alan.pinkerton@utoledo.edu. *Application contact:* Graduate School Office, 419-530-4723, Fax: 419-530-4724, E-mail: grdsch@utnet.utoledo.edu.

Vanderbilt University, Graduate School, Department of Chemistry, Nashville, TN 37240-1001. Offers analytical chemistry (MAT, MS, PhD); inorganic chemistry (MAT, MS, PhD); organic chemistry (MAT, MS, PhD); physical chemistry (MAT, MS, PhD); theoretical chemistry (MAT, MS, PhD). *Faculty:* 21 full-time (3 women). *Students:* 121 full-time (43 women); includes 18 minority (8 Black or African American, non-Hispanic/Latino; 1 American Indian or Alaska Native, non-Hispanic/Latino; 3 Asian, non-Hispanic/Latino; 1 Hispanic/Latino; 5 Two or more races, non-Hispanic/Latino). Average age 26. 373 applicants, 23% accepted, 39 enrolled. In 2010, 4 master's, 17 doctorates awarded. Terminal master's awarded for partial completion of doctoral program. *Degree requirements:* For master's, thesis; for doctorate, thesis/dissertation, area, qualifying, and final exams. *Entrance requirements:* For master's and doctorate, GRE General Test, GRE Subject Test (recommended). Additional exam requirements/recommendations for international students: Required—TOEFL (minimum score 570 paper-based; 230 computer-based; 88 iBT). *Application deadline:* For fall admission, 1/15 for domestic and international students. Application fee: $0. Electronic applications accepted. *Financial support:* Fellowships with full and partial tuition reimbursements, research assistantships with full tuition reimbursements, teaching assistantships with full tuition reimbursements, Federal Work-Study, institutionally sponsored loans, scholarships/grants, traineeships, and health care benefits available. Financial award application deadline: 1/15; financial award applicants required to submit CSS PROFILE or FAFSA. *Faculty research:* Chemical synthesis; mechanistic, theoretical, bioorganic, analytical, and spectroscopic chemistry. *Unit head:* Mike P. Stone, PhD, Chair, 615-322-2589, Fax: 615-343-1234, E-mail: michael.p.stone@vanderbilt.edu. *Application contact:* Charles M. Lukehart, PhD, Director of Graduate Studies, 615-322-2861, Fax: 615-343-1234, E-mail: charles.m.lukehart@vanderbilt.edu.

Virginia Commonwealth University, Graduate School, College of Humanities and Sciences, Department of Chemistry, Richmond, VA 23284-9005. Offers analytical chemistry (MS, PhD); chemical physics (PhD); inorganic chemistry (MS, PhD); organic chemistry (MS, PhD); physical chemistry (MS, PhD). Part-time programs available. *Students:* 51 full-time (23 women), 14 part-time (6 women); includes 7 minority (3 Black or African American, non-Hispanic/Latino; 2 Asian, non-Hispanic/Latino; 1 Hispanic/Latino; 1 Two or more races, non-Hispanic/Latino), 26 international. 76 applicants, 33% accepted, 10 enrolled. In 2010, 6 master's, 5 doctorates awarded. Terminal master's awarded for partial completion of doctoral program. *Degree requirements:* For master's, thesis; for doctorate, thesis/dissertation, comprehensive cumulative exams, research proposal. *Entrance requirements:* For master's, GRE General Test, 30 undergraduate credits in chemistry; for doctorate, GRE General Test. Additional exam requirements/recommendations for international students: Required—Either TOEFL (minimum score: paper-based 600, computer-based 250) or IELTS (6.5). *Application deadline:* For fall admission, 3/15 for domestic students; for spring admission, 11/15 for domestic students. Applications are processed on a rolling basis. Application fee: $50. Electronic applications accepted. *Expenses:* Tuition, state resident: full-time $4308; part-time $479 per credit hour. Tuition, nonresident: full-time $8942; part-time $994 per credit hour. Required fees: $2000; $85 per credit hour. Tuition and fees vary according to course level, course load, degree level, campus/location and program. *Financial support:* Fellowships, research assistantships, teaching assistantships, career-related internships or fieldwork and institutionally sponsored loans available. Support available to part-time students. Financial award application deadline: 7/1; financial award applicants required to submit FAFSA. *Faculty research:* Physical, organic, inorganic, analytical, and polymer chemistry; chemical physics. *Unit head:* Dr. Scott Gronert, Chair, 804-828-1298, Fax: 804-828-8599, E-mail: sgronert@vcu.edu. *Application contact:* Dr. Maryanne M. Collinson, Chair, Graduate Recruiting and Admissions Committee, 804-828-7509, E-mail: mselshal@vcu.edu.

Wake Forest University, Graduate School of Arts and Sciences, Department of Chemistry, Winston-Salem, NC 27109. Offers analytical chemistry (MS, PhD); inorganic chemistry (MS, PhD); organic chemistry (MS, PhD); physical chemistry (MS, PhD). Part-time programs available. *Degree requirements:* For master's, one foreign language, comprehensive exam, thesis; for doctorate, 2 foreign languages, comprehensive exam, thesis/dissertation. *Entrance requirements:* For master's and doctorate, GRE General Test. Additional exam requirements/recommendations for international students: Required—TOEFL (minimum score 213 computer-based). Electronic applications accepted.

West Virginia University, Eberly College of Arts and Sciences, Department of Chemistry, Morgantown, WV 26506. Offers analytical chemistry (MS, PhD); inorganic chemistry (MS, PhD); organic chemistry (MS, PhD); physical chemistry (MS, PhD); theoretical chemistry (MS, PhD). Part-time programs available. Postbaccalaureate distance learning degree programs offered (no on-campus study). Terminal master's awarded for partial completion of doctoral program. *Degree requirements:* For master's, thesis; for doctorate, thesis/dissertation. *Entrance requirements:* For master's, GRE General Test, GRE Subject Test (recommended), minimum GPA of 2.5; for doctorate, GRE General Test, GRE Subject Test (recommended), minimum GPA of 2.75. Additional exam requirements/recommendations for international students: Required—TOEFL. Electronic applications accepted. *Faculty research:* Analysis of proteins, drug interactions, solids and effluents by advanced separation methods; new synthetic strategies for complex organic molecules; synthesis and structural characterization of metal complexes for polymerization catalysis, nonlinear science, spectroscopy.

Youngstown State University, Graduate School, College of Science, Technology, Engineering and Mathematics, Department of Chemistry, Youngstown, OH 44555-0001. Offers analytical chemistry (MS); biochemistry (MS); chemistry education (MS); inorganic chemistry (MS); organic chemistry (MS); physical chemistry (MS). Part-time programs available. *Degree requirements:* For master's, thesis. *Entrance requirements:* For master's, bachelor's degree in chemistry, minimum GPA of 2.7. Additional exam requirements/recommendations for international students: Required—TOEFL. *Faculty research:* Analysis of antioxidants, chromatography, defects and disorder in crystalline oxides, hydrogen bonding, novel organic and organometallic materials.

Chemistry

Acadia University, Faculty of Pure and Applied Science, Department of Chemistry, Wolfville, NS B4P 2R6, Canada. Offers M Sc. *Faculty:* 2 full-time (0 women). *Students:* 2 full-time (0 women), 5 part-time (3 women). Average age 26. 8 applicants, 13% accepted, 1 enrolled. *Degree requirements:* For master's, thesis. *Entrance requirements:* Additional exam requirements/recommendations for international students: Required—TOEFL (minimum score 580 paper-based; 237 computer-based; 93 iBT), IELTS (minimum score 6.5). *Application deadline:* For fall admission, 2/1 for domestic and international students. Applications are processed on a rolling basis. Application fee: $50. *Financial support:* Research assistantships, teaching assistantships, scholarships/grants and unspecified assistantships available. Financial award application deadline: 2/1. *Faculty research:* Atmospheric chemistry, chemical kinetics, bioelectrochemistry of proteins, self-assembling monolayers. *Unit head:* Dr. Jeffrey Banks, Head, 902-585-1242, Fax: 902-585-1114, E-mail: jeffrey.banks@acadiau.ca. *Application contact:* Avril Bird, Secretary, 902-585-1242, Fax: 902-585-1114, E-mail: avril.bird@acadiau.ca.

American University, College of Arts and Sciences, Department of Chemistry, Washington, DC 20016-8014. Offers chemistry (MS); pre-medical (Certificate); toxicology (MS, Certificate). Part-time and evening/weekend programs available. *Faculty:* 8 full-time (3 women), 2 part-time/adjunct (1 woman). *Students:* 7 full-time (3 women), 36 part-time (25 women); includes 4 minority (3 Black or African American, non-Hispanic/Latino; 1 Asian, non-Hispanic/Latino). Average age 25. 6 applicants, 67% accepted, 2 enrolled. In 2010, 2 master's awarded. *Degree requirements:* For master's, comprehensive exam, thesis, tool of research in foreign language or statistics. *Entrance requirements:* For master's, GRE. Additional exam requirements/recommendations for international students: Required—TOEFL. *Application deadline:* For fall admission, 2/1 priority date for domestic students; for spring admission, 10/1 priority date for domestic students. Applications are processed on a rolling basis. Application fee: $80. *Financial support:* In 2010–11, 33 students received support; fellowships, research assistantships with full and partial tuition reimbursements available, teaching assistantships with full and partial tuition reimbursements available, career-related internships or fieldwork, Federal Work-Study, institutionally sponsored loans, scholarships/grants, traineeships, tuition waivers (full and partial), unspecified assistantships, and service awards available. Financial award application deadline: 2/1. *Faculty research:* AIDS, chemical damage to DNA, organic reaction mechanisms, chromatography in environmental samples. *Unit head:* Dr. James E. Girard, Chair, 202-885-1791, E-mail: jgirard@american.edu. *Application contact:* Kathleen Clowery, Director, Graduate Admissions, 202-885-3621, Fax: 202-885-1505.

The American University in Cairo, School of Sciences and Engineering, Department of Chemistry, Cairo, Egypt. Offers food chemistry (M Chem). *Degree requirements:* For master's, thesis. *Entrance requirements:* For master's, bachelor[0092]s degree in chemistry or related discipline with minimum GPA of 3.0.

American University of Beirut, Graduate Programs, Faculty of Arts and Sciences, Beirut, Lebanon. Offers anthropology (MA); Arabic language and literature (MA); archaeology (MA); biology (MS); chemistry (MS); computational science (MS); computer science (MS); economics (MA); education (MA); English language (MA); English literature (MA); environmental policy planning (MSES); financial economics (MAFE); geology (MS); history (MA); mathematics (MA, MS); Middle Eastern studies (MA); philosophy (MA); physics (MS); political studies (MA); psychology (MA); public administration (MA); sociology (MA); statistics (MA, MS). Part-time programs available. *Faculty:* 229 full-time (98 women), 136 part-time/adjunct (79 women). *Students:* 158 full-time (104 women), 263 part-time (171 women). Average age 25. 356 applicants, 59% accepted, 127 enrolled. In 2010, 57 master's awarded. *Degree requirements:* For master's, one foreign language, comprehensive exam, thesis (for some programs). *Entrance requirements:* For master's, GRE, letter of recommendation. Additional exam requirements/recommendations for international students: Required—TOEFL (minimum score 600 paper-based; 250 computer-based; 97 iBT), IELTS (minimum score 7). *Application deadline:* For fall admission, 4/30 for domestic and international students; for spring admission, 11/1 for domestic and international students. Application fee: $50. *Expenses:* Tuition: Full-time $12,294; part-time $683 per credit. Required fees: $499; $499 per credit. Tuition and fees vary according to course load and program. *Financial support:* In 2010–11, 33 students received support. Career-related internships or fieldwork, institutionally sponsored loans, scholarships/grants, health care benefits, and unspecified assistantships available. Financial award application deadline: 2/4; financial award applicants required to submit FAFSA. *Faculty research:* Modern and contemporary world theatre; mineralogy, petrology, and geochemistry; cell differentiation and transformation; combinatorial technologies; philosophy of action; continental philosophy; Phoenician epigraphy; nascent complex societies and urbanism; the economies of the Arab world; environmental economics; tectonophysics; host-parasite interactions; innate immunity; insect-plant interactions; history of the Ottoman archives; decentralization; transparency and corruption. Total annual research expenditures: $622,243. *Unit head:* Dr. Patrick McGreevy, Dean, 961-137-4374 Ext. 3800, Fax: 961-174-4461, E-mail: pm07@aub.edu.lb. *Application contact:* Dr. Salim Kanaan, Director, Admissions Office, 961-135-0000 Ext. 2594, Fax: 961-175-0775, E-mail: sk00@aub.edu.lb.

Arizona State University, College of Liberal Arts and Sciences, Department of Chemistry and Biochemistry, Tempe, AZ 85287-1604. Offers biochemistry (MS, PhD); chemistry (MS, PhD);

nanoscience (PSM). *Faculty:* 68 full-time (16 women), 10 part-time/adjunct (6 women). *Students:* 180 full-time (59 women), 9 part-time (4 women); includes 13 minority (1 Black or African American, non-Hispanic/Latino; 10 Asian, non-Hispanic/Latino; 1 Hispanic/Latino; 1 Two or more races, non-Hispanic/Latino), 96 international. Average age 26. 505 applicants, 19% accepted, 45 enrolled. In 2010, 9 master's, 22 doctorates awarded. Terminal master's awarded for partial completion of doctoral program. *Degree requirements:* For master's, thesis, interactive Program of Study (iPOS) submitted before completing 50 percent of required credit hours; for doctorate, comprehensive exam, thesis/dissertation, interactive Program of Study (iPOS) submitted before completing 50 percent of required credit hours. *Entrance requirements:* For master's and doctorate, GRE, minimum GPA of 3.0 or equivalent in last 2 years of work leading to bachelor's degree. Additional exam requirements/recommendations for international students: Required—TOEFL, IELTS, or Pearson Test of English. *Application deadline:* For fall admission, 1/15 priority date for domestic and international students. Applications are processed on a rolling basis. Application fee: $70 ($90 for international students). Electronic applications accepted. *Expenses:* Tuition, state resident: full-time $8510; part-time $608 per credit. Tuition, nonresident: full-time $16,542; part-time $919 per credit. Required fees: $339; $110 per credit. Part-time tuition and fees vary according to course load. *Financial support:* In 2010–11, 77 research assistantships with full and partial tuition reimbursements (averaging $17,448 per year), 97 teaching assistantships with full and partial tuition reimbursements (averaging $17,637 per year) were awarded; fellowships with full tuition reimbursements, career-related internships or fieldwork, Federal Work-Study, institutionally sponsored loans, scholarships/grants, health care benefits, and tuition waivers (full and partial) also available. Financial award application deadline: 3/1. Total annual research expenditures: $18.2 million. *Unit head:* Dr. William Petuskey, Chair, 480-965-4430, Fax: 480-965-8607, E-mail: wpetuskey@asu.edu. *Application contact:* Graduate Admissions, 480-965-6113.

Arkansas State University, Graduate School, College of Sciences and Mathematics, Department of Chemistry and Physics, Jonesboro, State University, AR 72467. Offers chemistry (MS); chemistry education (MSE, SCCT). Part-time programs available. *Faculty:* 8 full-time (3 women), 2 part-time/adjunct (1 woman). *Students:* 6 full-time (3 women), 13 part-time (6 women); includes 2 minority (both Black or African American, non-Hispanic/Latino), 11 international. Average age 26. 15 applicants, 80% accepted, 8 enrolled. In 2010, 4 master's awarded. *Degree requirements:* For master's, comprehensive exam, thesis or alternative; for SCCT, comprehensive exam. *Entrance requirements:* For master's, GRE General Test or MAT, appropriate bachelor's degree, official transcript, immunization records, valid teaching certificate (MSE); for SCCT, GRE General Test or MAT, interview, master's degree, official transcript, immunization records. Additional exam requirements/recommendations for international students: Required—TOEFL (minimum score 550 paper-based; 213 computer-based; 79 iBT), IELTS (minimum score 6), PTE: Pearson Test of English Academic (56). *Application deadline:* For fall admission, 7/1 for domestic and international students; for spring admission, 11/15 for domestic students, 11/14 for international students. Applications are processed on a rolling basis. Application fee: $30 ($40 for international students). Electronic applications accepted. *Expenses:* Tuition, state resident: full-time $3888; part-time $216 per credit hour. Tuition, nonresident: full-time $9918; part-time $551 per credit hour. International tuition: $8376 full-time. Required fees: $932; $49 per credit hour. $25 per term. One-time fee: $30. Tuition and fees vary according to course load and program. *Financial support:* In 2010–11, 5 students received support; teaching assistantships, career-related internships or fieldwork, scholarships/grants, and unspecified assistantships available. Financial award application deadline: 7/1; financial award applicants required to submit FAFSA. *Unit head:* Dr. William Burns, Interim Chair, 870-972-3086, Fax: 870-972-3089, E-mail: wburns@astate.edu. *Application contact:* Dr. Andrew Sustich, Dean of the Graduate School, 870-972-3029, Fax: 870-972-3857, E-mail: sustich@astate.edu.

Auburn University, Graduate School, College of Sciences and Mathematics, Department of Chemistry and Biochemistry, Auburn University, AL 36849. Offers analytical chemistry (MS, PhD); biochemistry (MS, PhD); inorganic chemistry (MS, PhD); organic chemistry (MS, PhD); physical chemistry (MS, PhD). Part-time programs available. *Faculty:* 27 full-time (6 women). *Students:* 39 full-time (20 women), 21 part-time (8 women); includes 4 Black or African American, non-Hispanic/Latino; 1 Asian, non-Hispanic/Latino; 1 Hispanic/Latino), 41 international. Average age 28. 54 applicants, 11% accepted, 3 enrolled. In 2010, 1 master's, 13 doctorates awarded. *Degree requirements:* For master's, thesis (for some programs); for doctorate, thesis/dissertation, oral and written exams. *Entrance requirements:* For master's and doctorate, GRE General Test. *Application deadline:* For fall admission, 7/7 for domestic students; for spring admission, 11/24 for domestic students. Applications are processed on a rolling basis. Application fee: $50 ($60 for international students). Electronic applications accepted. *Expenses:* Tuition, state resident: full-time $7002. Tuition, nonresident: full-time $21,898. International tuition: $22,116 full-time. Required fees: $892. Tuition and fees vary according to course load and program. *Financial support:* Fellowships, research assistantships, teaching assistantships available. Financial award application deadline: 3/15; financial award applicants required to submit FAFSA. *Unit head:* Dr. J. V. Ortiz, Chair, 334-844-4043, Fax: 334-844-4043. *Application contact:* Dr. George Flowers, Dean of the Graduate School, 334-844-2125.

Ball State University, Graduate School, College of Sciences and Humanities, Department of Chemistry, Muncie, IN 47306-1099. Offers MA, MS. *Faculty:* 10. *Students:* 4 full-time (2 women), 17 part-time (9 women); includes 1 Black or African American, non-Hispanic/Latino; 1 American Indian or Alaska Native, non-Hispanic/Latino; 1 Asian, non-Hispanic/Latino; 1 Two or more races, non-Hispanic/Latino), 6 international. Average age 22. 19 applicants, 37% accepted, 5 enrolled. In 2010, 6 master's awarded. *Entrance requirements:* For master's, GRE General Test. Application fee: $50. *Expenses:* Tuition, state resident: full-time $6160; part-time $299 per credit hour. Tuition, nonresident: full-time $16,020; part-time $783 per credit hour. Required fees: $2278; $95 per credit hour. *Financial support:* In 2010–11, 1 research assistantship with full tuition reimbursement (averaging $11,200 per year), 12 teaching assistantships with full tuition reimbursements (averaging $10,533 per year) were awarded. Financial award application deadline: 3/1. *Faculty research:* Synthetic and analytical chemistry, biochemistry, theoretical chemistry. *Unit head:* Dr. Patti Lang, Interim Chair, 765-285-8060, Fax: 765-285-2351, E-mail: plang@bsu.edu. *Application contact:* Dr. James Poole, Associate Provost for Research and Dean of the Graduate School, 765-285-8071, E-mail: jpoole@bsu.edu.

Baylor University, Graduate School, College of Arts and Sciences, Department of Chemistry and Biochemistry, Waco, TX 76798. Offers chemistry (MS, PhD). Part-time programs available. *Faculty:* 14 full-time (2 women). *Students:* 48 full-time (23 women), 2 part-time (1 woman); includes 6 minority (2 Asian, non-Hispanic/Latino; 2 Hispanic/Latino; 2 Two or more races, non-Hispanic/Latino), 17 international. In 2010, 3 master's, 11 doctorates awarded. Terminal master's awarded for partial completion of doctoral program. *Degree requirements:* For master's, thesis; for doctorate, comprehensive exam, thesis/dissertation. *Entrance requirements:* For master's and doctorate, GRE General Test, GRE Subject Test. Additional exam requirements/recommendations for international students: Required—TOEFL. *Application deadline:* For fall admission, 8/1 for domestic students. Applications are processed on a rolling basis. Application fee: $25. *Financial support:* In 2010–11, 20 students received support; fellowships, research assistantships, teaching assistantships, Federal Work-Study, institutionally sponsored loans, and tuition waivers (full) available. Support available to part-time students. *Unit head:* Dr. Charles Garner, Graduate Program Director, 254-710-6862, Fax: 254-710-2403, E-mail: charles_garner@baylor.edu. *Application contact:* Nancy Kallas, Admin Asst., 254-710-6844, Fax: 254-710-2403, E-mail: nancy_kallas@baylor.edu.

Boston College, Graduate School of Arts and Sciences, Department of Chemistry, Chestnut Hill, MA 02467-3800. Offers biochemistry (PhD); inorganic chemistry (PhD); organic chemistry (PhD); physical chemistry (PhD); science education (MST). Part-time programs available. *Degree requirements:* For doctorate, thesis/dissertation, qualifying exam. *Entrance requirements:* For doctorate, GRE General Test, GRE Subject Test. Additional exam requirements/recommendations for international students: Required—TOEFL (minimum score 600 paper-based; 250 computer-based; 100 iBT). Electronic applications accepted.

Boston University, Graduate School of Arts and Sciences, Department of Chemistry, Boston, MA 02215. Offers MA, PhD. *Students:* 112 full-time (50 women), 1 (woman) part-time; includes 11 minority (2 American Indian or Alaska Native, non-Hispanic/Latino; 4 Asian, non-Hispanic/Latino; 5 Hispanic/Latino), 40 international. Average age 26. 193 applicants, 18% accepted, 14 enrolled. In 2010, 23 master's, 11 doctorates awarded. Terminal master's awarded for partial completion of doctoral program. *Degree requirements:* For master's, one foreign language; for doctorate, one foreign language, comprehensive exam, thesis/dissertation. *Entrance requirements:* For master's and doctorate, GRE General Test, GRE Subject Test (recommended), 3 letters of recommendation. Additional exam requirements/recommendations for international students: Required—TOEFL (minimum score 550 paper-based; 213 computer-based). *Application deadline:* For fall admission, 1/1 for domestic and international students; for spring admission, 10/15 for domestic and international students. Application fee: $70. Electronic applications accepted. *Expenses:* Tuition: Full-time $39,314; part-time $1228 per credit. Required fees: $40 per semester. *Financial support:* In 2010–11, 4 fellowships with full tuition reimbursements (averaging $19,300 per year), 48 research assistantships with full tuition reimbursements (averaging $18,800 per year), 61 teaching assistantships with full tuition reimbursements (averaging $18,800 per year) were awarded; Federal Work-Study, scholarships/grants, and tuition waivers (full) also available. Support available to part-time students. Financial award application deadline: 1/1; financial award applicants required to submit FAFSA. *Unit head:* John Straub, Chairman, 617-353-2498, Fax: 617-353-6466, E-mail: straub@bu.edu. *Application contact:* Sarah Coenen, Academic Administrator, 617-353-2503, Fax: 617-353-6466, E-mail: scoenen@bu.edu.

Boston University, School of Education, Boston, MA 02215. Offers counseling (Ed M, CAGS), including community, school, sport psychology; counseling psychology (Ed D); curriculum and teaching (Ed M, Ed D, CAGS), including early childhood (Ed D), educational media and technology (Ed D), English and language arts (Ed D), mathematics (Ed D), physical education and coaching (Ed D), science (Ed D), social studies education (Ed D), special education (Ed D); developmental studies (Ed D), including literacy and language, reading education; developmental studies in literacy and language education (Ed M, CAGS); early childhood education (Ed M, CAGS); education of the deaf (Ed M, CAGS); educational leadership and development (Ed D), including educational administration (Ed M, Ed D, CAGS), higher education administration (Ed M, Ed D, CAGS); educational media and technology (Ed M, CAGS); elementary education (Ed M); English and language arts (Ed M, CAGS); English education (MAT); health education (Ed M, CAGS); Latin and classical studies (MAT); mathematics education (Ed M, MAT, CAGS); mathematics for teaching (MMT); modern foreign language education (MAT), including French, Spanish; physical education and coaching (Ed M, CAGS); policy, planning, and administration (Ed M, CAGS), including community education leadership, educational administration (Ed M, Ed D, CAGS), higher education administration (Ed M, Ed D, CAGS); reading education (Ed M, CAGS); science education (Ed M, MAT, CAGS), including biology (MAT), chemistry (MAT), earth science (MAT), general science (MAT), physics (MAT); social studies education (Ed M, MAT, CAGS), including history (MAT), political science (MAT); special education (Ed M, Ed D, CAGS), including disability studies (Ed M), moderate disabilities (Ed M), severe disabilities (Ed M), special education administration (Ed M); teaching English as a second language (Ed M, CAGS). Part-time programs available. *Faculty:* 57 full-time, 39 part-time/adjunct. *Students:* 245 full-time (191 women), 376 part-time (274 women); includes 83 minority (14 Black or African American, non-Hispanic/Latino; 2 American Indian or Alaska Native, non-Hispanic/Latino; 28 Asian, non-Hispanic/Latino; 31 Hispanic/Latino; 2 Native Hawaiian or other Pacific Islander, non-Hispanic/Latino; 6 Two or more races, non-Hispanic/Latino), 79 international. Average age 30. 1,270 applicants, 66% accepted, 292 enrolled. In 2010, 273 master's, 15 doctorates, 7 other advanced degrees awarded. Terminal master's awarded for partial completion of doctoral program. *Degree requirements:* For master's, thesis (for some programs); for doctorate, comprehensive exam, thesis/dissertation; for CAGS, comprehensive exam. *Entrance requirements:* For master's and CAGS, GRE General Test or Miller Analogies Test (MAT); for doctorate, GRE General Test. Additional exam requirements/recommendations for international students: Required—TOEFL, IELTS. *Application deadline:* For fall admission, 1/15 priority date for domestic and international students; for spring admission, 9/15 priority date for domestic and international students. Applications are processed on a rolling basis. Application fee: $70. Electronic applications accepted. *Expenses:* Tuition: Full-time $39,314; part-time $1228 per credit. Required fees: $40 per semester. *Financial support:* In 2010–11, 276 students received support, including 31 fellowships with full tuition reimbursements available, 16 research assistantships, 26 teaching assistantships with partial tuition reimbursements available; career-related internships or fieldwork, Federal Work-Study, and scholarships/grants also available. Support available to part-time students. Financial award applicants required to submit FAFSA. *Faculty research:* Deaf studies, social emotional learning, civic engagement and education, STEM education, pre-college educational pipelines. Total annual research expenditures: $2.6 million. *Unit head:* Dr. Hardin Coleman, Dean, 617-353-3213. *Application contact:* Dana Fernandez, Director of Enrollment, 617-353-4237, Fax: 617-353-8937, E-mail: sedgrad@bu.edu.

Bowling Green State University, Graduate College, College of Arts and Sciences, Center for Photochemical Sciences, Bowling Green, OH 43403. Offers PhD. *Degree requirements:* For doctorate, comprehensive exam, thesis/dissertation. *Entrance requirements:* For doctorate, GRE General Test. Additional exam requirements/recommendations for international students: Required—TOEFL. Electronic applications accepted. *Faculty research:* Laser-initiated photopolymerization, spectroscopic and kinetic studies, optoelectronics of semiconductor multiple quantum wells, electron transfer processes, carotenoid pigments.

Bowling Green State University, Graduate College, College of Arts and Sciences, Department of Chemistry, Bowling Green, OH 43403. Offers MAT, MS. Part-time programs available. *Degree requirements:* For master's, thesis or alternative. *Entrance requirements:* For master's, GRE General Test. Additional exam requirements/recommendations for international students: Required—TOEFL. Electronic applications accepted. *Faculty research:* Organic, inorganic, physical, and analytical chemistry; biochemistry; surface science.

Bradley University, Graduate School, College of Liberal Arts and Sciences, Department of Chemistry and Biochemistry, Peoria, IL 61625-0002. Offers chemistry (MS). Part-time and evening/weekend programs available. *Degree requirements:* For master's, comprehensive exam, thesis. *Entrance requirements:* For master's, 2 letters of recommendation. Additional exam requirements/recommendations for international students: Required—TOEFL (minimum score 550 paper-based; 213 computer-based; 79 iBT).

Brandeis University, Graduate School of Arts and Sciences, Department of Chemistry, Waltham, MA 02454. Offers inorganic chemistry (MS, PhD); organic chemistry (MS, PhD); physical chemistry (MS, PhD). *Faculty:* 26 full-time (14 women). *Students:* 43 full-time (14 women); includes 1 Black or African American, non-Hispanic/Latino, 27 international. 115 applicants, 25% accepted, 14 enrolled. In 2010, 9 master's, 8 doctorates awarded. Terminal master's awarded for partial completion of doctoral program. *Degree requirements:* For master's, thesis, 1 year of residency; for doctorate, one foreign language, thesis/dissertation, 3 years of residency, 2 seminars, qualifying exams. *Entrance requirements:* For master's and doctorate, GRE General Test, resume, letters of recommendation. Additional exam requirements/recommendations for international students: Required—TOEFL (minimum score 600 paper-based; 250 computer-based; 100 iBT); Recommended—IELTS (minimum score 7). *Application deadline:* For fall admission, 1/15 priority date for domestic students. Applications are processed on a rolling basis. Application fee: $75. Electronic applications accepted. *Financial support:* In

Peterson's Graduate Programs in the Physical Sciences, Mathematics, Agricultural Sciences, the Environment & Natural Resources 2012

www.facebook.com/petersonspublishing   **49**

Chemistry

Brandeis University (continued)
2010–11, 23 fellowships with full tuition reimbursements (averaging $24,500 per year), 14 research assistantships with full tuition reimbursements (averaging $24,500 per year), teaching assistantships with partial tuition reimbursements (averaging $3,200 per year) were awarded; scholarships/grants and health care benefits also available. Financial award application deadline: 4/15; financial award applicants required to submit FAFSA. *Faculty research:* Oscillating chemical reactions, molecular recognition systems, protein crystallography, synthesis of natural product spectroscopy and magnetic resonance. *Unit head:* Dr. Judith Herzfeld, Chair, Graduate Program in Chemistry, 781-736-2540, Fax: 781-736-2516, E-mail: herzfeld@brandeis.edu. *Application contact:* Charlotte Haygazian, Graduate Department Coordinator, 781-736-2500, Fax: 781-736-2516, E-mail: chemadm@brandeis.edu.

Brigham Young University, Graduate Studies, College of Physical and Mathematical Sciences, Department of Chemistry and Biochemistry, Provo, UT 84602. Offers biochemistry (MS, PhD); chemistry (MS, PhD). *Faculty:* 33 full-time (2 women). *Students:* 105 full-time (44 women); includes 1 Asian, non-Hispanic/Latino; 1 Hispanic/Latino; 2 Native Hawaiian or other Pacific Islander, non-Hispanic/Latino, 44 international. Average age 28. 72 applicants, 58% accepted, 23 enrolled. In 2010, 5 master's, 11 doctorates awarded. *Degree requirements:* For master's, thesis; for doctorate, thesis/dissertation, qualifying exam. *Entrance requirements:* For master's and doctorate, GRE General Test, minimum GPA of 3.0 in last 60 hours. Additional exam requirements/recommendations for international students: Required—TOEFL (minimum score 580 paper-based; 237 computer-based; 85 iBT); Recommended—TWE. *Application deadline:* For fall admission, 2/1 priority date for domestic and international students. Applications are processed on a rolling basis. Application fee: $50. Electronic applications accepted. *Expenses:* Tuition: Full-time $5580; part-time $310 per credit hour. Tuition and fees vary according to program and student's religious affiliation. *Financial support:* In 2010–11, 105 students received support, including 10 fellowships with full tuition reimbursements available (averaging $21,250 per year), 56 research assistantships with full tuition reimbursements available (averaging $21,250 per year), 29 teaching assistantships with full tuition reimbursements available (averaging $21,250 per year); institutionally sponsored loans, scholarships/grants, health care benefits, tuition waivers (full), and unspecified assistantships also available. Financial award application deadline: 2/1. *Faculty research:* Separation science, molecular recognition, organic synthesis and biomedical application, biochemistry and molecular biology, molecular spectroscopy. Total annual research expenditures: $5.6 million. *Unit head:* Dr. Gregory F. Burton, Chair, 801-422-4917, Fax: 801-422-0153, E-mail: gburton@byu.edu. *Application contact:* Dr. Matthew R. Linford, Graduate Coordinator, 801-422-1699, Fax: 801-422-0153, E-mail: mrlinford@byu.edu.

Brock University, Faculty of Graduate Studies, Faculty of Mathematics and Science, Program in Chemistry, St. Catharines, ON L2S 3A1, Canada. Offers M Sc, PhD. Part-time programs available. *Degree requirements:* For master's, thesis; for doctorate, thesis/dissertation. *Entrance requirements:* For master's, honors B Sc in chemistry; for doctorate, M Sc. Additional exam requirements/recommendations for international students: Required—TOEFL (minimum score 550 paper-based; 213 computer-based; 80 iBT), IELTS (minimum score 6.5), TWE (minimum score 4). Electronic applications accepted. *Faculty research:* Bioorganic chemistry, trace element analysis, organic synthesis, electrochemistry, structural inorganic chemistry.

Brooklyn College of the City University of New York, Division of Graduate Studies, Department of Chemistry, Brooklyn, NY 11210-2889. Offers MA, PhD. Part-time programs available. *Students:* 3 full-time (1 woman), 18 part-time (7 women); includes 11 minority (4 Black or African American, non-Hispanic/Latino; 6 Asian, non-Hispanic/Latino; 1 Hispanic/Latino), 2 international. Average age 30. 11 applicants, 82% accepted, 6 enrolled. In 2010, 1 master's awarded. *Degree requirements:* For master's, one foreign language, thesis or alternative, 30 credits. *Entrance requirements:* For master's, 2 letters of recommendation. Additional exam requirements/recommendations for international students: Required—TOEFL (minimum score 500 paper-based; 173 computer-based; 61 iBT). *Application deadline:* For fall admission, 3/1 priority date for domestic students, 2/1 priority date for international students; for spring admission, 11/1 priority date for domestic students, 10/1 priority date for international students. Applications are processed on a rolling basis. Application fee: $125. Electronic applications accepted. *Expenses:* Tuition, state resident: full-time $7360; part-time $310 per credit hour. Tuition, nonresident: full-time $13,800; part-time $575 per credit hour. Required fees: $190 per semester. *Financial support:* Teaching assistantships, Federal Work-Study, institutionally sponsored loans, and scholarships/grants available. Support available to part-time students. Financial award application deadline: 5/1; financial award applicants required to submit FAFSA. Total annual research expenditures: $25,000. *Unit head:* Dr. Malgorzata Ciszkowska, Chairperson, 718-951-5458, E-mail: malgcisz@brooklyn.cuny.edu. *Application contact:* Hernan Sierra, Graduate Admissions Coordinator, 718-951-4536, Fax: 718-951-4506, E-mail: grads@brooklyn.cuny.edu.

Brooklyn College of the City University of New York, Division of Graduate Studies, School of Education, Program in Middle Childhood Education (Science), Brooklyn, NY 11210-2889. Offers biology (MA); chemistry (MA); earth science (MA); general science (MA); physics (MA). Part-time and evening/weekend programs available. *Students:* 3 full-time (1 woman), 74 part-time (46 women); includes 29 minority (12 Black or African American, non-Hispanic/Latino; 8 Asian, non-Hispanic/Latino; 9 Hispanic/Latino), 4 international. Average age 32. 29 applicants, 97% accepted, 21 enrolled. In 2010, 24 master's awarded. *Entrance requirements:* For master's, LAST, interview, previous course work in education and mathematics, resume, 2 letters of recommendation, essay. Additional exam requirements/recommendations for international students: Required—TOEFL (minimum score 500 paper-based; 173 computer-based; 61 iBT). *Application deadline:* For fall admission, 7/15 priority date for domestic students, 6/1 priority date for international students; for spring admission, 11/15 priority date for domestic students, 10/1 priority date for international students. Applications are processed on a rolling basis. Application fee: $125. Electronic applications accepted. *Expenses:* Tuition, state resident: full-time $7360; part-time $310 per credit hour. Tuition, nonresident: full-time $13,800; part-time $575 per credit hour. Required fees: $190 per semester. *Financial support:* Federal Work-Study, institutionally sponsored loans, and scholarships/grants available. Support available to part-time students. Financial award application deadline: 5/1; financial award applicants required to submit FAFSA. *Faculty research:* Geometric thinking, mastery of basic facts, problem-solving strategies, history of mathematics. *Unit head:* Dr. Jennifer Adams, Program Head, 718-951-5214, E-mail: jadams@brooklyn.cuny.edu. *Application contact:* Hernan Sierra, Graduate Admissions Coordinator, 718-951-4536, Fax: 718-951-4506, E-mail: grads@brooklyn.cuny.edu.

Brown University, Graduate School, Department of Chemistry, Providence, RI 02912. Offers biochemistry (PhD); chemistry (AM, Sc M, PhD). *Degree requirements:* For master's, thesis; for doctorate, one foreign language, thesis/dissertation, cumulative exam.

Bryn Mawr College, Graduate School of Arts and Sciences, Department of Chemistry, Bryn Mawr, PA 19010-2899. Offers MA, PhD. *Faculty:* 6. *Students:* 2 full-time (1 woman), 6 part-time (2 women). Average age 28. 12 applicants, 42% accepted, 2 enrolled. *Degree requirements:* For master's, one foreign language, thesis; for doctorate, 2 foreign languages, comprehensive exam, thesis/dissertation. *Entrance requirements:* For master's and doctorate, GRE General Test, GRE Subject Test. Additional exam requirements/recommendations for international students: Required—TOEFL (minimum score 600 paper-based; 250 computer-based). *Application deadline:* For fall admission, 1/3 for domestic and international students. Application fee: $50. *Financial support:* In 2010–11, 1 research assistantship with full tuition reimbursement (averaging $15,000 per year), 4 teaching assistantships with partial tuition reimbursements (averaging $14,000 per year) were awarded; Federal Work-Study, scholarships/grants, and tuition waivers (partial) also available. Support available to part-time students. Financial award application deadline: 1/3. *Unit head:* Dr. William Malachowski, Chair, 610-526-5104. *Application contact:* Lea R. Miller, Secretary, 610-526-5072, Fax: 610-526-5076, E-mail: lrmiller@brynmawr.edu.

See Display on next page and Close-Up on page 97.

Bucknell University, Graduate Studies, College of Arts and Sciences, Department of Chemistry, Lewisburg, PA 17837. Offers MA, MS. Part-time programs available. *Degree requirements:* For master's, thesis. *Entrance requirements:* For master's, GRE General Test, GRE Subject Test, minimum GPA of 2.8. Additional exam requirements/recommendations for international students: Required—TOEFL. *Expenses:* Tuition: Full-time $36,992; part-time $4624 per course.

Buffalo State College, State University of New York, The Graduate School, Faculty of Natural and Social Sciences, Department of Chemistry, Buffalo, NY 14222-1095. Offers chemistry (MA); secondary education (MS Ed), including chemistry. Part-time and evening/weekend programs available. *Degree requirements:* For master's, thesis (for some programs), project. *Entrance requirements:* For master's, minimum GPA of 2.6, New York teaching certificate (MS Ed). Additional exam requirements/recommendations for international students: Required—TOEFL (minimum score 550 paper-based; 213 computer-based).

California Institute of Technology, Division of Chemistry and Chemical Engineering, Program in Chemistry, Pasadena, CA 91125-0001. Offers MS, PhD. Part-time and evening/weekend programs available. Postbaccalaureate distance learning degree programs offered (minimal on-campus study). *Faculty:* 30 full-time (5 women). *Students:* 211 full-time (80 women). Average age 26. 367 applicants, 25% accepted, 27 enrolled. In 2010, 4 master's, 32 doctorates awarded. Terminal master's awarded for partial completion of doctoral program. *Degree requirements:* For master's, thesis; for doctorate, thesis/dissertation. *Entrance requirements:* Additional exam requirements/recommendations for international students: Required—TOEFL; Recommended—IELTS, TWE. *Application deadline:* For fall admission, 1/1 for domestic and international students. Application fee: $80. Electronic applications accepted. *Financial support:* Fellowships, research assistantships, teaching assistantships, Federal Work-Study, institutionally sponsored loans, scholarships/grants, traineeships, health care benefits, and unspecified assistantships available. Financial award application deadline: 1/1. *Unit head:* Prof. Jacqueline K. Barton, Chair, Chemistry and Chemical Engineering, 626-395-3646, Fax: 626-568-8824, E-mail: jkbarton@caltech.edu. *Application contact:* Agnes Tong, Option Secretary, 626-395-6111, E-mail: agnest@caltech.edu.

California Polytechnic State University, San Luis Obispo, College of Science and Mathematics, Department of Chemistry and Biochemistry, San Luis Obispo, CA 93407. Offers polymers and coating science (MS). Part-time programs available. *Students:* 3 full-time (0 women), 7 part-time (3 women); includes 2 minority (1 Black or African American, non-Hispanic/Latino; 1 Asian, non-Hispanic/Latino). Average age 24. 5 applicants, 80% accepted, 1 enrolled. *Degree requirements:* For master's, comprehensive oral exam. *Entrance requirements:* For master's, minimum GPA of 2.5 in last 90 quarter units of course work. Additional exam requirements/recommendations for international students: Required—TOEFL (minimum score 550 paper-based; 213 computer-based) or IELTS (minimum score 6). *Application deadline:* For fall admission, 7/1 for domestic students, 11/30 for international students; for winter admission, 11/1 for domestic students, 6/30 for international students; for spring admission, 2/1 for domestic students. Applications are processed on a rolling basis. Application fee: $55. Electronic applications accepted. *Expenses:* Tuition, state resident: full-time $5386; part-time $3124 per year. Tuition, nonresident: full-time $11,160; part-time $248 per unit. Required fees: $2250; $614 per term. One-time fee: $2250 full-time; $1842 part-time. *Financial support:* Career-related internships or fieldwork, Federal Work-Study, and scholarships/grants available. Support available to part-time students. Financial award application deadline: 3/2; financial award applicants required to submit FAFSA. *Faculty research:* Polymer physical chemistry and analysis, polymer synthesis, coatings formulation. *Unit head:* Dr. Ray Fernando, Graduate Coordinator, 805-756-2395, Fax: 805-756-5500, E-mail: rhfernan@calpoly.edu. *Application contact:* Dr. James Maraviglia, Assistant Vice President for Admissions, Recruitment and Financial Aid, 805-756-2311, Fax: 805-756-5400, E-mail: admissions@calpoly.edu.

California State Polytechnic University, Pomona, Academic Affairs, College of Science, Program in Chemistry, Pomona, CA 91768-2557. Offers MS. Part-time programs available. *Students:* 4 full-time (3 women), 13 part-time (8 women); includes 6 minority (2 Asian, non-Hispanic/Latino; 2 Hispanic/Latino; 2 Two or more races, non-Hispanic/Latino), 3 international. Average age 27. 30 applicants, 50% accepted, 6 enrolled. *Degree requirements:* For master's, thesis. *Entrance requirements:* For master's, GRE General Test. *Application deadline:* For fall admission, 5/1 priority date for domestic students; for winter admission, 10/15 priority date for domestic students; for spring admission, 1/20 priority date for domestic students. Applications are processed on a rolling basis. Application fee: $55. Electronic applications accepted. *Expenses:* Tuition, state resident: full-time $5386; part-time $2850 per year. Tuition, nonresident: full-time $12,082; part-time $248 per credit. Required fees: $577; $248 per credit. $577 per year. Tuition and fees vary according to course load and program. *Financial support:* In 2010–11, 2 students received support. Career-related internships or fieldwork, Federal Work-Study, and institutionally sponsored loans available. Support available to part-time students. Financial award application deadline: 3/2; financial award applicants required to submit FAFSA. *Unit head:* Dr. Tim C. Corcoran, Assistant Professor, 909-869-3660, Fax: 909-869-4344, E-mail: tccorcoran@csupomona.edu. *Application contact:* Scott J. Duncan, Director, Admissions, 909-869-3258, Fax: 909-869-4529, E-mail: sjduncan@csupomona.edu.

California State University, East Bay, Office of Academic Programs and Graduate Studies, College of Science, Department of Chemistry, Hayward, CA 94542-3000. Offers biochemistry (MS); chemistry (MS). *Faculty:* 5 full-time (3 women). *Students:* 18 full-time (10 women), 26 part-time (8 women); includes 2 Black or African American, non-Hispanic/Latino; 16 Asian, non-Hispanic/Latino; 2 Hispanic/Latino, 10 international. Average age 29. 44 applicants, 70% accepted, 18 enrolled. In 2010, 15 master's awarded. *Degree requirements:* For master's, comprehensive exam or thesis. *Entrance requirements:* For master's, minimum GPA of 2.5 in field during previous 2 years of course work. Additional exam requirements/recommendations for international students: Required—TOEFL (minimum score 550 paper-based; 213 computer-based). *Application deadline:* For fall admission, 6/30 for domestic and international students. Application fee: $55. Electronic applications accepted. *Financial support:* Fellowships, career-related internships or fieldwork, Federal Work-Study, institutionally sponsored loans, and scholarships/grants available. Support available to part-time students. Financial award application deadline: 3/2; financial award applicants required to submit FAFSA. *Unit head:* Dr. Ann McPartland, Chair, 510-885-3452, Fax: 510-885-4675, E-mail: ann.mcpartland@csueastbay.edu. *Application contact:* Dr. Donna Wiley, Interim Associate Director, 510-885-2928, Fax: 510-885-4777, E-mail: donna.wiley@csueastbay.edu.

California State University, Fresno, Division of Graduate Studies, College of Science and Mathematics, Department of Chemistry, Fresno, CA 93740-8027. Offers MS. Part-time programs available. *Degree requirements:* For master's, thesis or alternative. *Entrance requirements:* For master's, GRE General Test, minimum GPA of 2.5. Additional exam requirements/recommendations for international students: Required—TOEFL. Electronic applications accepted. *Faculty research:* Genetics, viticulture, DNA, soils, molecular modeling, analysis of quinone.

California State University, Fullerton, Graduate Studies, College of Natural Science and Mathematics, Department of Chemistry and Biochemistry, Fullerton, CA 92834-9480. Offers chemistry (MS); geochemistry (MS). Part-time programs available. *Students:* 7 full-time (3 women), 21 part-time (13 women); includes 8 Asian, non-Hispanic/Latino; 3 Hispanic/Latino, 5 international. Average age 27. 52 applicants, 44% accepted, 8 enrolled. In 2010, 10 master's awarded. *Degree requirements:* For master's, thesis, departmental qualifying exam. *Entrance requirements:* For master's, minimum GPA of 2.5 in last 60 units of course work, major in chemistry or related field. Application fee: $55. *Financial support:* Research assistantships,

50 www.facebook.com/petersonspublishing

Peterson's Graduate Programs in the Physical Sciences, Mathematics, Agricultural Sciences, the Environment & Natural Resources 2012

Chemistry

BRYN MAWR
COLLEGE

Graduate Program in Chemistry

Why Bryn Mawr Chemistry?

Small, supportive atmosphere

Committed to building teaching skills

Excellent facilities

Cutting-edge research

Great location

Discover for yourself what Bryn Mawr has to offer!

plan your visit at:

www.brynmawr.edu/chemistry/graduate

teaching assistantships, career-related internships or fieldwork, Federal Work-Study, institutionally sponsored loans, and scholarships/grants available. Support available to part-time students. Financial award application deadline: 3/1; financial award applicants required to submit FAFSA. *Unit head:* Dr. Christopher Meyer, Chair, 657-278-3621. *Application contact:* Admissions/Applications, 657-278-2371.

California State University, Long Beach, Graduate Studies, College of Natural Sciences and Mathematics, Department of Chemistry and Biochemistry, Long Beach, CA 90840. Offers biochemistry (MS); chemistry (MS). Part-time programs available. *Faculty:* 14 full-time (2 women). *Students:* 17 full-time (9 women), 23 part-time (9 women); includes 1 Black or African American, non-Hispanic/Latino; 8 Asian, non-Hispanic/Latino; 4 Hispanic/Latino, 13 international. Average age 26. 74 applicants, 62% accepted, 21 enrolled. In 2010, 9 master's awarded. *Degree requirements:* For master's, thesis, departmental qualifying exam. *Application deadline:* For fall admission, 6/1 for domestic students. Applications are processed on a rolling basis. Application fee: $55. Electronic applications accepted. *Financial support:* Research assistantships, teaching assistantships, Federal Work-Study, institutionally sponsored loans, scholarships/grants, and unspecified assistantships available. Financial award application deadline: 3/2. *Faculty research:* Enzymology, organic synthesis, molecular modeling, environmental chemistry, reaction kinetics. *Unit head:* Dr. Jeffrey Cohlberg, Chair, 562-985-4944, Fax: 562-985-8557, E-mail: cohlberg@csulb.edu. *Application contact:* Dr. Lijuan Li, Graduate Advisor, 562-985-5068, Fax: 562-985-8557, E-mail: lli@csulb.edu.

California State University, Los Angeles, Graduate Studies, College of Natural and Social Sciences, Department of Chemistry and Biochemistry, Los Angeles, CA 90032-8530. Offers analytical chemistry (MS); biochemistry (MS); chemistry (MS); inorganic chemistry (MS); organic chemistry (MS); physical chemistry (MS). Part-time and evening/weekend programs available. *Faculty:* 5 part-time/adjunct (1 woman). *Students:* 19 full-time (15 women), 24 part-time (12 women); includes 21 minority (3 Black or African American, non-Hispanic/Latino; 8 Asian, non-Hispanic/Latino; 10 Hispanic/Latino), 9 international. Average age 30. 22 applicants, 100% accepted, 10 enrolled. In 2010, 7 master's awarded. *Degree requirements:* For master's, one foreign language, comprehensive exam or thesis. *Entrance requirements:* Additional exam requirements/recommendations for international students: Required—TOEFL. *Application deadline:* For fall admission, 5/1 for domestic and international students. Applications are processed on a rolling basis. Application fee: $55. *Financial support:* Federal Work-Study available. Support available to part-time students. Financial award application deadline: 3/1. *Faculty research:* Intercalation of heavy metal, carborane chemistry, conductive polymers and fabrics, titanium reagents, computer modeling and synthesis. *Unit head:* Dr. Robert L. Vellanoweth, Chair, 323-343-2300, Fax: 323-343-6490, E-mail: rvellan@calstatela.edu. *Application contact:* Dr. Allan Muchlinski, Dean of Graduate Studies, 323-343-3820 Ext. 3827, Fax: 323-343-5653, E-mail: amuchli@exchange.calstatela.edu.

California State University, Northridge, Graduate Studies, College of Science and Mathematics, Department of Chemistry and Biochemistry, Northridge, CA 91330. Offers biochemistry (MS); chemistry (MS), including chemistry, environmental chemistry. *Degree requirements:* For master's, thesis. *Entrance requirements:* For master's, GRE General Test or minimum GPA of 3.0. Additional exam requirements/recommendations for international students: Required—TOEFL. Electronic applications accepted.

California State University, Sacramento, Graduate Studies, College of Natural Sciences and Mathematics, Department of Chemistry, Sacramento, CA 95819. Offers MS. Part-time programs available. *Degree requirements:* For master's, thesis or alternative, departmental qualifying exam, writing proficiency exam. *Entrance requirements:* For master's, minimum GPA of 2.5 during previous 2 years of course work, BA in chemistry or equivalent. Additional exam requirements/recommendations for international students: Required—TOEFL. Electronic applications accepted.

California State University, San Bernardino, Graduate Studies, College of Social and Behavioral Sciences, Program in Environmental Sciences, San Bernardino, CA 92407-2397. Offers MS.

Carleton University, Faculty of Graduate Studies, Faculty of Science, Department of Chemistry, Ottawa, ON K1S 5B6, Canada. Offers M Sc, PhD. Programs offered jointly with University of Ottawa. *Degree requirements:* For master's, thesis; for doctorate, comprehensive exam, thesis/dissertation. *Entrance requirements:* For master's, honors degree; for doctorate, M Sc. Additional exam requirements/recommendations for international students: Required—TOEFL. *Faculty research:* Bioorganic chemistry, analytical toxicology, theoretical and physical chemistry, inorganic chemistry.

Carnegie Mellon University, Mellon College of Science, Department of Chemistry, Pittsburgh, PA 15213-3891. Offers biotechnology and management (MS); chemistry (PhD), including bioinorganic, bioorganic, organic and materials, biophysics and spectroscopy, computational and theoretical, polymer; colloids, polymers and surfaces (MS). Part-time programs available. Terminal master's awarded for partial completion of doctoral program. *Degree requirements:* For doctorate, thesis/dissertation, departmental qualifying and oral exams, teaching experience. *Entrance requirements:* For master's, GRE General Test; for doctorate, GRE General Test, GRE Subject Test. Additional exam requirements/recommendations for international students: Required—TOEFL. Electronic applications accepted. *Faculty research:* Physical and theoretical chemistry, chemical synthesis, biophysical/bioinorganic chemistry.

Case Western Reserve University, School of Graduate Studies, Department of Chemistry, Cleveland, OH 44106. Offers MS, PhD. Part-time programs available. *Faculty:* 21 full-time (5 women). *Students:* 86 full-time (36 women), 6 part-time (4 women); includes 1 Black or African American, non-Hispanic/Latino; 4 Asian, non-Hispanic/Latino, 61 international. Average age 27. 304 applicants, 7% accepted, 20 enrolled. In 2010, 3 master's, 14 doctorates awarded. Terminal master's awarded for partial completion of doctoral program. *Degree requirements:* For master's, thesis optional; for doctorate, thesis/dissertation. *Entrance requirements:* For master's and doctorate, GRE General Test, GRE Subject Test. Additional exam requirements/recommendations for international students: Required—TOEFL (minimum score 550 paper-based; 213 computer-based; 79 iBT). *Application deadline:* Applications are processed on a rolling basis. Application fee: $8. Electronic applications accepted. *Financial support:* Fellowships, research assistantships, teaching assistantships, unspecified assistantships available. Financial award application deadline: 2/15. *Faculty research:* Electrochemistry, synthetic chemistry, chemistry of life process, spectroscopy, kinetics. *Unit head:* Mary Barkley, Chair, 216-368-3622, Fax: 216-368-3006, E-mail: mary.barkley@case.edu. *Application contact:* Julie Ilhan, Graduate Affairs Coordinator, 216-368-5030, Fax: 216-368-3006, E-mail: julie.ilhan@case.edu.

Central Connecticut State University, School of Graduate Studies, School of Arts and Sciences, Department of Chemistry and Biochemistry, New Britain, CT 06050-4010. Offers natural sciences (MS). Part-time and evening/weekend programs available. *Students:* 1 applicant, 100% accepted, 0 enrolled. In 2010, 1 other advanced degree awarded. *Degree requirements:* For Certificate, qualifying exam. *Entrance requirements:* Additional exam requirements/recommendations for international students: Required—TOEFL. *Application deadline:* For fall admission, 7/1 for domestic students; for spring admission, 12/1 for domestic students. Applications are processed on a rolling basis. Application fee: $50. Electronic applications accepted. *Expenses:* Tuition, area resident: Full-time $5012; part-time $470 per credit. Tuition, state resident: full-time $7518; part-time $482 per credit. Tuition, nonresident: full-time $13,962; part-time $482 per credit. Required fees: $3772. One-time fee: $62 part-time. *Unit head:* Dr. Thomas Burkholder, Chair, 860-832-2675. *Application contact:* Dr. Thomas Burkholder, Chair, 860-832-2675.

Chemistry

Central Michigan University, College of Graduate Studies, College of Science and Technology, Department of Chemistry, Mount Pleasant, MI 48859. Offers chemistry (MS); teaching chemistry (MA), including teaching college chemistry, teaching high school chemistry. Part-time programs available. *Faculty:* 9 full-time (3 women), 2 part-time/adjunct (1 woman). *Students:* 6 full-time (2 women), 15 part-time (3 women); includes 1 Black or African American, non-Hispanic/Latino, 9 international. Average age 28. *Degree requirements:* For master's, comprehensive exam, thesis or alternative. *Entrance requirements:* For master's, GRE. *Application deadline:* For fall admission, 6/1 for international students; for spring admission, 10/1 for international students. Applications are processed on a rolling basis. Application fee: $35 ($45 for international students). Electronic applications accepted. *Expenses:* Tuition, state resident: full-time $8208; part-time $456 per credit hour. Tuition, nonresident: full-time $13,788; part-time $766 per credit hour. One-time fee: $25. *Financial support:* Fellowships with tuition reimbursements, research assistantships with tuition reimbursements, teaching assistantships with tuition reimbursements, career-related internships or fieldwork, Federal Work-Study, unspecified assistantships, and out-of-state merit awards, non-resident graduate awards available. Financial award application deadline: 2/1. *Faculty research:* Analytical and organic-inorganic chemistry, biochemistry, catalysis, dendrimer and polymer studies, nanotechnology. *Unit head:* Dr. David Ash, Chairperson, 989-774-3981, Fax: 989-774-3883, E-mail: ash1de@cmich.edu. *Application contact:* Dr. Dillip Mohanty, Graduate Program Coordinator, 989-774-6445, Fax: 989-774-3883, E-mail: mohan1dk@cmich.edu.

Central Washington University, Graduate Studies and Research, College of the Sciences, Department of Chemistry, Ellensburg, WA 98926. Offers MS. Part-time programs available. *Degree requirements:* For master's, thesis. *Entrance requirements:* For master's, GRE General Test, minimum GPA of 3.0. Additional exam requirements/recommendations for international students: Required—TOEFL (minimum score 550 paper-based; 213 computer-based; 79 iBT).

Christopher Newport University, Graduate Studies, Department of Teacher Preparation, Newport News, VA 23606-2998. Offers art (PK-12) (MAT); biology (6-12) (MAT); chemistry (6-12) (MAT); computer science (6-12) (MAT); elementary (PK-6) (MAT); English (6-12) (MAT); English as second language (PK-12) (MAT); French (PK-12) (MAT); history and social science (6-12) (MAT); mathematics (6-12) (MAT); music (PK-12) (MAT), including choral, instrumental; physics (6-12) (MAT); Spanish (PK-12) (MAT). Part-time and evening/weekend programs available. *Faculty:* 22 full-time (15 women), 10 part-time/adjunct (8 women). *Students:* 69 full-time (60 women), 10 part-time (6 women); includes 5 minority (1 Black or African American, non-Hispanic/Latino; 2 Hispanic/Latino; 2 Two or more races, non-Hispanic/Latino). Average age 24. 4 applicants, 100% accepted, 3 enrolled. In 2010, 86 master's awarded. *Degree requirements:* For master's, comprehensive exam, thesis or alternative. *Entrance requirements:* For master's, PRAXIS I, minimum GPA of 3.0. Additional exam requirements/recommendations for international students: Required—TOEFL (minimum score 580 paper-based; 237 computer-based; 92 iBT). *Application deadline:* For fall admission, 4/1 for international students; for spring admission, 10/15 for domestic students, 10/1 for international students. Applications are processed on a rolling basis. Application fee: $50. Electronic applications accepted. *Expenses:* Tuition, state resident: part-time $418 per credit hour. Tuition, nonresident: part-time $769 per credit hour. *Financial support:* In 2010–11, 3 research assistantships with full and partial tuition reimbursements (averaging $2,000 per year) were awarded; career-related internships or fieldwork, Federal Work-Study, and unspecified assistantships also available. Support available to part-time students. Financial award application deadline: 3/1; financial award applicants required to submit FAFSA. *Faculty research:* Early literacy development, instructional innovations, professional teaching standards, multicultural issues, aesthetic education. *Unit head:* Dr. Marsha Sprague, Director, 757-594-7388, Fax: 757-594-7803, E-mail: msprague@cnu.edu. *Application contact:* Lyn Sawyer, Associate Director, Graduate Admissions, 757-594-7544, Fax: 757-594-7649, E-mail: gradstdy@cnu.edu.

City College of the City University of New York, Graduate School, College of Liberal Arts and Science, Division of Science, Department of Chemistry, Program in Chemistry, New York, NY 10031-9198. Offers MA, PhD. PhD program offered jointly with Graduate School and University Center of the City University of New York. Terminal master's awarded for partial completion of doctoral program. *Degree requirements:* For doctorate, one foreign language, thesis/dissertation. *Entrance requirements:* For master's and doctorate, GRE. Additional exam requirements/recommendations for international students: Required—TOEFL (minimum score 500 paper-based; 173 computer-based). *Faculty research:* Laser spectroscopy, bioorganic chemistry, polymer chemistry and crystallography, electroanalytical chemistry, ESR of metal clusters.

Clark Atlanta University, School of Arts and Sciences, Department of Chemistry, Atlanta, GA 30314. Offers MS, PhD. Part-time programs available. *Faculty:* 7 full-time (0 women). *Students:* 17 full-time (11 women), 18 part-time (9 women); includes 24 Black or African American, non-Hispanic/Latino; 1 American Indian or Alaska Native, non-Hispanic/Latino, 5 international. Average age 30. 13 applicants, 92% accepted, 11 enrolled. In 2010, 2 master's, 2 doctorates awarded. *Degree requirements:* For master's, one foreign language, thesis; for doctorate, 2 foreign languages, thesis/dissertation. *Entrance requirements:* For master's, GRE General Test, minimum GPA of 2.5; for doctorate, GRE General Test, GRE Subject Test, minimum graduate GPA of 3.0. Additional exam requirements/recommendations for international students: Required—TOEFL (minimum score 500 paper-based; 173 computer-based; 61 iBT). *Application deadline:* For fall admission, 4/1 for domestic and international students; for spring admission, 11/1 for domestic and international students. Applications are processed on a rolling basis. Application fee: $40 ($55 for international students). *Expenses:* Tuition: Full-time $12,942; part-time $719 per credit hour. Required fees: $710; $355 per semester. *Financial support:* In 2010–11, 6 teaching assistantships were awarded; fellowships, research assistantships, career-related internships or fieldwork, Federal Work-Study, scholarships/grants, traineeships, and unspecified assistantships also available. Support available to part-time students. Financial award application deadline: 4/30; financial award applicants required to submit FAFSA. *Unit head:* Dr. Cass Parker, Chairperson, 404-880-6858, E-mail: cparker@cau.edu. *Application contact:* Michelle Clark-Davis, Graduate Program Admissions, 404-880-6605, E-mail: cauadmissions@cau.edu.

Clarkson University, Graduate School, School of Arts and Sciences, Department of Chemistry and Biomolecular Science, Potsdam, NY 13699. Offers chemistry (MS, PhD). Part-time programs available. *Faculty:* 24 full-time (6 women), 2 part-time/adjunct (both women). *Students:* 39 full-time (13 women), 27 international. Average age 27. 77 applicants, 31% accepted, 9 enrolled. In 2010, 1 master's, 5 doctorates awarded. *Degree requirements:* For doctorate, comprehensive exam, thesis/dissertation, departmental qualifying exam. *Entrance requirements:* For master's and doctorate, GRE, transcripts of all college coursework, three letters of recommendation; resume and personal statement (recommended). Additional exam requirements/recommendations for international students: Required—TOEFL, TSE recommended. *Application deadline:* For fall admission, 1/30 priority date for domestic and international students; for spring admission, 9/1 priority date for domestic and international students. Applications are processed on a rolling basis. Application fee: $25 ($35 for international students). Electronic applications accepted. *Expenses:* Tuition: Part-time $1136 per credit hour. *Financial support:* In 2010–11, 36 students received support, including 4 fellowships with full tuition reimbursements available (averaging $21,580 per year), 17 research assistantships with full tuition reimbursements available (averaging $21,580 per year), 15 teaching assistantships with full tuition reimbursements available (averaging $21,580 per year); scholarships/grants, tuition waivers (partial), and unspecified assistantships also available. *Faculty research:* Biomagnetic glasses, dispersed particles, enzyme logic systems, ionic toothbrush, magnetic nanofibers, polysilicon laminates. Total annual research expenditures: $2 million. *Unit head:* Dr. Phillip Christiansen, Chair, 315-268-2389, Fax: 315-268-6610, E-mail: pac@clarkson.edu. *Application contact:* Jennifer Reed, Graduate School Coordinator, School of Arts and Sciences, 315-268-3802, Fax: 315-268-3989, E-mail: sciencegrad@clarkson.edu.

Clark University, Graduate School, Department of Chemistry, Worcester, MA 01610-1477. Offers MA, PhD. *Faculty:* 8 full-time (1 woman). *Students:* 20 full-time (9 women), 1 part-time (0 women); includes 1 minority (Asian, non-Hispanic/Latino), 12 international. Average age 25. 46 applicants, 28% accepted, 8 enrolled. In 2010, 1 master's, 3 doctorates awarded. Terminal master's awarded for partial completion of doctoral program. *Degree requirements:* For master's, thesis or alternative; for doctorate, one foreign language, thesis/dissertation. *Entrance requirements:* For master's and doctorate, GRE General Test. Additional exam requirements/recommendations for international students: Required—TOEFL. *Application deadline:* For fall admission, 2/15 priority date for domestic students. Applications are processed on a rolling basis. Application fee: $50. *Expenses:* Tuition: Full-time $37,000; part-time $1156 per credit hour. Required fees: $30; $1156 per credit hour. *Financial support:* In 2010–11, fellowships with tuition reimbursements (averaging $19,825 per year), 6 research assistantships with full tuition reimbursements (averaging $19,825 per year), 13 teaching assistantships with full tuition reimbursements (averaging $19,825 per year) were awarded; tuition waivers (full) also available. *Faculty research:* Nuclear chemistry, molecular biology simulation, NMR studies, anthrax edema, biochemistry. Total annual research expenditures: $500,000. *Unit head:* Dr. Frederick Greenaway, Chair, 508-793-7116. *Application contact:* Rene Baril, Department Secretary, 528-793-7173, Fax: 528-793-8861, E-mail: chemistry@clarku.edu.

Clemson University, Graduate School, College of Engineering and Science, Department of Chemistry, Clemson, SC 29634. Offers MS, PhD. *Faculty:* 27 full-time (4 women), 5 part-time/adjunct (0 women). *Students:* 92 full-time (36 women), 4 part-time (1 woman); includes 6 Black or African American, non-Hispanic/Latino; 3 Asian, non-Hispanic/Latino; 1 Hispanic/Latino; 1 Two or more races, non-Hispanic/Latino, 39 international. Average age 30. 118 applicants, 32% accepted, 17 enrolled. In 2010, 1 master's, 10 doctorates awarded. *Degree requirements:* For master's, one foreign language, thesis; for doctorate, one foreign language, thesis/dissertation. *Entrance requirements:* For master's and doctorate, GRE General Test. Additional exam requirements/recommendations for international students: Required—TOEFL. *Application deadline:* For fall admission, 3/1 for domestic students, 4/15 for international students; for spring admission, 9/15 for international students. Applications are processed on a rolling basis. Application fee: $70 ($80 for international students). Electronic applications accepted. *Expenses:* Tuition, state resident: full-time $6492; part-time $400 per credit hour. Tuition, nonresident: full-time $13,634; part-time $800 per credit hour. Required fees: $262 per semester. Part-time tuition and fees vary according to course load and program. *Financial support:* In 2010–11, 91 students received support, including 4 fellowships with full and partial tuition reimbursements available (averaging $6,771 per year), 20 research assistantships with partial tuition reimbursements available (averaging $20,297 per year), 85 teaching assistantships with partial tuition reimbursements available (averaging $17,342 per year); career-related internships or fieldwork, institutionally sponsored loans, scholarships/grants, health care benefits, and unspecified assistantships also available. Support available to part-time students. Financial award applicants required to submit FAFSA. *Faculty research:* Fluorine chemistry, organic synthetic methods and natural products, metal and non-metal clusters, analytical spectroscopies, polymers. Total annual research expenditures: $3.6 million. *Unit head:* Dr. Stephen E. Creager, Chair, 864-656-3065, Fax: 864-656-6613, E-mail: screage@clemson.edu. *Application contact:* Dr. Steve Stuart, Coordinator, 864-656-5013, Fax: 864-656-6613, E-mail: ss@clemson.edu.

Cleveland State University, College of Graduate Studies, College of Sciences and Health Professions, Department of Chemistry, Cleveland, OH 44115. Offers analytical chemistry (MS); clinical chemistry (MS); clinical/bioanalytical chemistry (PhD), including cellular and molecular medicine, clinical chemistry, clinical/bioanalytical chemistry; environmental chemistry (MS); inorganic chemistry (MS); pharmaceutical/organic chemistry (MS); physical chemistry (MS). Part-time and evening/weekend programs available. *Faculty:* 13 full-time (0 women), 1 (woman) part-time/adjunct. *Students:* 58 full-time (29 women), 42 part-time (17 women); includes 4 Black or African American, non-Hispanic/Latino; 3 Asian, non-Hispanic/Latino; 1 Hispanic/Latino, 70 international. Average age 28. 76 applicants, 74% accepted, 16 enrolled. In 2010, 4 master's, 15 doctorates awarded. *Degree requirements:* For master's, thesis optional; for doctorate, comprehensive exam, thesis/dissertation. *Entrance requirements:* For master's and doctorate, GRE General Test. Additional exam requirements/recommendations for international students: Required—TOEFL (minimum score 525 paper-based; 197 computer-based; 65 iBT). *Application deadline:* For fall admission, 1/15 priority date for domestic and international students. Applications are processed on a rolling basis. Application fee: $30. Electronic applications accepted. *Expenses:* Tuition, state resident: full-time $8447; part-time $469 per credit hour. Tuition, nonresident: full-time $16,020; part-time $890 per credit hour. Required fees: $50. *Financial support:* In 2010–11, 44 students received support, including 5 fellowships with full tuition reimbursements available (averaging $30,000 per year), 13 research assistantships with full tuition reimbursements available (averaging $20,000 per year), 24 teaching assistantships with full tuition reimbursements available (averaging $18,500 per year); scholarships/grants and unspecified assistantships also available. Financial award application deadline: 1/15. *Faculty research:* Bioanalytical techniques and molecular diagnostics, glycoproteomics and antithrombotic agents, drug discovery and innovation, analytical pharmacology, inflammatory disease research. Total annual research expenditures: $3 million. *Unit head:* Dr. David J. Anderson, Interim Chair, 216-687-2467, Fax: 216-687-9298, E-mail: d.anderson@csuohio.edu. *Application contact:* Richelle P. Emery, Administrative Coordinator, 216-687-2457, Fax: 216-687-9298, E-mail: r.emery@csuohio.edu.

The College of William and Mary, Faculty of Arts and Sciences, Department of Chemistry, Williamsburg, VA 23187-8795. Offers MA, MS. *Faculty:* 15 full-time (4 women), 3 part-time/adjunct (0 women). *Students:* 10 full-time (6 women); includes 1 minority (Black or African American, non-Hispanic/Latino). Average age 25. 15 applicants, 53% accepted, 7 enrolled. In 2010, 4 master's awarded. *Degree requirements:* For master's, comprehensive exam, thesis (for some programs). *Entrance requirements:* For master's, GRE, minimum GPA of 2.5. Additional exam requirements/recommendations for international students: Required—TOEFL. *Application deadline:* For fall admission, 3/1 priority date for domestic and international students. Applications are processed on a rolling basis. Application fee: $45. Electronic applications accepted. *Expenses:* Tuition, state resident: full-time $6400; part-time $345 per credit hour. Tuition, nonresident: full-time $19,720; part-time $920 per credit hour. Required fees: $4368. *Financial support:* In 2010–11, 10 students received support, including 6 research assistantships with full tuition reimbursements available, 4 teaching assistantships with full tuition reimbursements available (averaging $15,400 per year); health care benefits and unspecified assistantships also available. Financial award application deadline: 5/1; financial award applicants required to submit FAFSA. *Faculty research:* Organic, physical, polymer and analytic chemistry; biochemistry. Total annual research expenditures: $827,892. *Unit head:* Dr. Chris Abelt, Chair, 757-221-2540, Fax: 757-221-2715, E-mail: cjabel@wm.edu. *Application contact:* Dr. Deborah C. Bebout, Graduate Director, 757-221-2558, Fax: 757-221-2715, E-mail: dcbebo@wm.edu.

Colorado School of Mines, Graduate School, Department of Chemistry and Geochemistry, Program in Chemistry, Golden, CO 80401. Offers applied chemistry (PhD); chemistry (MS). Part-time programs available. *Students:* 44 full-time (20 women), 3 part-time (1 woman); includes 4 Asian, non-Hispanic/Latino; 2 Hispanic/Latino, 12 international. Average age 28. 51 applicants, 55% accepted, 18 enrolled. In 2010, 5 master's, 1 doctorate awarded. *Degree requirements:* For master's, thesis (for some programs); for doctorate, comprehensive exam, thesis/dissertation. *Entrance requirements:* For master's and doctorate, GRE General Test. Additional exam requirements/recommendations for international students: Required—TOEFL (minimum score 550 paper-based; 213 computer-based; 80 iBT). *Application deadline:* For fall admission, 1/15 priority date for domestic and international students; for spring admission, 10/15 priority date for domestic and international students. Application fee: $50 ($70 for

international students). Electronic applications accepted. *Expenses:* Tuition, state resident: full-time $11,550; part-time $641 per credit. Tuition, nonresident: full-time $25,980; part-time $1444 per credit. Required fees: $1874; $937 per semester. *Financial support:* In 2010–11, fellowships with full tuition reimbursements (averaging $20,000 per year), research assistantships with full tuition reimbursements (averaging $20,000 per year), teaching assistantships with full tuition reimbursements (averaging $20,000 per year) were awarded; scholarships/grants, health care benefits, and unspecified assistantships also available. Financial award application deadline: 1/15; financial award applicants required to submit FAFSA. *Unit head:* Dr. Dan Knauss, Department Head, 303-273-3625 Ext. 303, Fax: 303-273-3629. *Application contact:* Prof. Tina Voelker, Associate Professor, 303-273-3152, Fax: 303-273-3629, E-mail: tvoelker@mines.edu.

Colorado State University, Graduate School, College of Natural Sciences, Department of Chemistry, Fort Collins, CO 80523-1872. Offers MS, PhD. Postbaccalaureate distance learning degree programs offered (no on-campus study). *Faculty:* 28 full-time (8 women), 2 part-time/adjunct (0 women). *Students:* 53 full-time (22 women), 96 part-time (34 women); includes 20 minority (1 Black or African American, non-Hispanic/Latino; 6 Asian, non-Hispanic/Latino; 8 Hispanic/Latino; 5 Two or more races, non-Hispanic/Latino), 13 international. Average age 27. 55 applicants, 55% accepted, 29 enrolled. In 2010, 6 master's, 12 doctorates awarded. Terminal master's awarded for partial completion of doctoral program. *Degree requirements:* For master's, comprehensive exam (for some programs), thesis (for some programs); for doctorate, thesis/dissertation, oral comprehensive exam. *Entrance requirements:* For master's, GRE General Test, minimum GPA of 3.0; 3 letters of recommendation; for doctorate, GRE General Test, minimum GPA of 3.0; 2 transcripts; 3 letters of recommendation; statement of purpose. Additional exam requirements/recommendations for international students: Required—TOEFL (minimum score 550 paper-based; 213 computer-based; 80 iBT). *Application deadline:* For fall admission, 2/1 priority date for domestic and international students; for spring admission, 9/15 priority date for domestic and international students. Applications are processed on a rolling basis. Application fee: $50. Electronic applications accepted. *Expenses:* Tuition, state resident: full-time $7434; part-time $413 per credit. Tuition, nonresident: full-time $19,022; part-time $1057 per credit. Required fees: $1729; $88 per credit. *Financial support:* In 2010–11, 37 fellowships (averaging $23,186 per year), 84 research assistantships with full tuition reimbursements (averaging $15,272 per year), 69 teaching assistantships with full tuition reimbursements (averaging $14,287 per year) were awarded; health care benefits also available. Financial award application deadline: 1/15; financial award applicants required to submit FAFSA. *Faculty research:* Analytical chemistry, inorganic chemistry, organic chemistry, physical chemistry, materials and biological chemistry. Total annual research expenditures: $6.4 million. *Unit head:* Dr. Ellen R. Fisher, Department Head, 970-491-6292, Fax: 970-491-1801, E-mail: ellen.fisher@colostate.edu. *Application contact:* Kathy Gibson, Graduate Contact, 970-491-0502, Fax: 970-491-1801, E-mail: kathy.gibson@colostate.edu.

Colorado State University–Pueblo, College of Science and Mathematics, Pueblo, CO 81001-4901. Offers applied natural science (MS), including biochemistry, biology, chemistry. Part-time and evening/weekend programs available. *Degree requirements:* For master's, comprehensive exam (for some programs), thesis (for some programs), internship report (if non-thesis). *Entrance requirements:* For master's, GRE General Test (minimum score 1000), 2 letters of reference, minimum GPA of 3.0. Additional exam requirements/recommendations for international students: Required—TOEFL (minimum score 500 paper-based; 173 computer-based), IELTS (minimum score 5). *Faculty research:* Fungal cell walls, molecular biology, bioactive materials synthesis, atomic force microscopy-surface chemistry, nanoscience.

Columbia University, Graduate School of Arts and Sciences, Division of Natural Sciences, Department of Chemistry, New York, NY 10027. Offers chemical physics (M Phil, PhD); inorganic chemistry (M Phil, MA, PhD); organic chemistry (M Phil, MA, PhD); MD/PhD. *Degree requirements:* For master's, one foreign language, teaching experience, oral/written exams (M Phil); for doctorate, one foreign language, thesis/dissertation. *Entrance requirements:* For master's and doctorate, GRE General Test, GRE Subject Test. Additional exam requirements/recommendations for international students: Required—TOEFL. *Faculty research:* Biophysics.

Concordia University, School of Graduate Studies, Faculty of Arts and Science, Department of Chemistry and Biochemistry, Montréal, QC H3G 1M8, Canada. Offers chemistry (M Sc, PhD). *Degree requirements:* For master's, thesis; for doctorate, thesis/dissertation. *Entrance requirements:* For master's, honors degree in chemistry; for doctorate, M Sc in biochemistry, biology, or chemistry. *Faculty research:* Bioanalytical, bio-organic, and inorganic chemistry; materials and solid-state chemistry.

Cornell University, Graduate School, Graduate Fields of Arts and Sciences, Field of Chemistry and Chemical Biology, Ithaca, NY 14853-0001. Offers analytical chemistry (PhD); bio-organic chemistry (PhD); biophysical chemistry (PhD); chemical biology (PhD); chemical physics (PhD); inorganic chemistry (PhD); materials chemistry (PhD); organic chemistry (PhD); organometallic chemistry (PhD); physical chemistry (PhD); polymer chemistry (PhD); theoretical chemistry (PhD). *Faculty:* 46 full-time (3 women). *Students:* 163 full-time (63 women); includes 10 Asian, non-Hispanic/Latino; 3 Hispanic/Latino, 49 international. Average age 24. 340 applicants, 36% accepted, 48 enrolled. In 2010, 31 doctorates awarded. *Degree requirements:* For doctorate, comprehensive exam, thesis/dissertation. *Entrance requirements:* For doctorate, GRE General Test, GRE Subject Test (chemistry), 3 letters of recommendation. Additional exam requirements/recommendations for international students: Required—TOEFL (minimum score 600 paper-based; 250 computer-based; 77 iBT). *Application deadline:* For fall admission, 1/10 for domestic students. Application fee: $80. Electronic applications accepted. *Expenses:* Tuition: Full-time $29,500. Required fees: $76. Tuition and fees vary according to degree level and program. *Financial support:* In 2010–11, 19 fellowships with full tuition reimbursements, 69 research assistantships with full tuition reimbursements, 68 teaching assistantships with full tuition reimbursements were awarded; institutionally sponsored loans, scholarships/grants, health care benefits, tuition waivers (full and partial), and unspecified assistantships also available. Financial award applicants required to submit FAFSA. *Faculty research:* Analytical, organic, inorganic, physical, materials, chemical biology. *Unit head:* Director of Graduate Studies, 607-255-4139, Fax: 607-255-4137. *Application contact:* Graduate Field Assistant, 607-255-4139, Fax: 607-255-4137, E-mail: chemgrad@cornell.edu.

Dalhousie University, Faculty of Science, Department of Chemistry, Halifax, NS B3H 4R2, Canada. Offers M Sc, PhD. Part-time programs available. Terminal master's awarded for partial completion of doctoral program. *Degree requirements:* For master's, thesis; for doctorate, thesis/dissertation. *Entrance requirements:* Additional exam requirements/recommendations for international students: Required—TOEFL (minimum score 600 paper-based; 237 computer-based; 92 iBT), IELTS (minimum score 7). Electronic applications accepted. *Faculty research:* Analytical, inorganic, organic, physical, and theoretical chemistry.

Dartmouth College, Arts and Sciences Graduate Programs, Department of Chemistry, Hanover, NH 03755. Offers PhD. *Degree requirements:* For doctorate, thesis/dissertation, departmental qualifying exams. *Entrance requirements:* For doctorate, GRE General Test, GRE Subject Test. Additional exam requirements/recommendations for international students: Required—TOEFL. Electronic applications accepted. *Faculty research:* Organic and polymer synthesis, bioinorganic chemistry, magnetic resonance parameters.

Delaware State University, Graduate Programs, Department of Chemistry, Program in Chemistry, Dover, DE 19901-2277. Offers MS. *Entrance requirements:* For master's, GRE. Additional exam requirements/recommendations for international students: Required—TOEFL (minimum score 550 paper-based). Electronic applications accepted.

DePaul University, College of Liberal Arts and Sciences, Department of Chemistry, Chicago, IL 60614. Offers biochemistry (MS); chemistry (MS); polymer chemistry and coatings technology (MS). Part-time and evening/weekend programs available. *Degree requirements:* For master's, thesis (for some programs), oral exam (for select programs). *Entrance requirements:* For master's, GRE Subject Test (chemistry), GRE General Test, BS in chemistry or equivalent. Additional exam requirements/recommendations for international students: Required—TOEFL (minimum score 590 paper-based; 243 computer-based). Electronic applications accepted. *Faculty research:* Computational chemistry, organic synthesis, inorganic synthesis, polymer synthesis, biochemistry.

Drew University, Caspersen School of Graduate Studies, Program in Education, Madison, NJ 07940-1493. Offers biology (MAT); chemistry (MAT); English (MAT); French (MAT); Italian (MAT); math (MAT); physics (MAT); social studies (MAT); Spanish (MAT); theatre arts (MAT). Part-time programs available. *Entrance requirements:* For master's, transcripts, personal statement, recommendations. Additional exam requirements/recommendations for international students: Required—TOEFL, TWE. *Expenses:* Contact institution.

Drexel University, College of Arts and Sciences, Department of Chemistry, Philadelphia, PA 19104-2875. Offers MS, PhD. Part-time programs available. Terminal master's awarded for partial completion of doctoral program. *Degree requirements:* For master's, thesis optional; for doctorate, one foreign language, thesis/dissertation. *Entrance requirements:* For master's and doctorate, GRE. Additional exam requirements/recommendations for international students: Required—TOEFL. Electronic applications accepted. *Faculty research:* Inorganic, analytical, organic, physical, and atmospheric polymer chemistry.

Duke University, Graduate School, Department of Chemistry, Durham, NC 27708. Offers PhD. *Faculty:* 23 full-time. *Students:* 93 full-time (46 women); includes 3 Black or African American, non-Hispanic/Latino, 34 international. 218 applicants, 28% accepted, 19 enrolled. In 2010, 14 doctorates awarded. *Degree requirements:* For doctorate, one foreign language, thesis/dissertation. *Entrance requirements:* For doctorate, GRE General Test, GRE Subject Test (recommended). Additional exam requirements/recommendations for international students: Required—TOEFL (minimum score 550 paper-based; 213 computer-based; 83 iBT), IELTS (minimum score 7). *Application deadline:* For fall admission, 12/8 priority date for domestic and international students. Application fee: $75. Electronic applications accepted. *Financial support:* Fellowships, research assistantships, teaching assistantships available. Financial award application deadline: 12/8. *Unit head:* Baldwin Steve, Director of Graduate Studies, 919-660-1503, Fax: 919-660-1605, E-mail: caroline.morris@duke.edu. *Application contact:* Elizabeth Hutton, Director of Admissions, 919-684-3913, Fax: 919-684-2277, E-mail: grad-admissions@duke.edu.

Duquesne University, Bayer School of Natural and Environmental Sciences, Department of Chemistry and Biochemistry, Pittsburgh, PA 15282-0001. Offers chemistry (MS, PhD). Part-time programs available. *Faculty:* 15 full-time (4 women). *Students:* 51 full-time (22 women), 2 part-time (0 women); includes 4 minority (3 Black or African American, non-Hispanic/Latino; 1 Hispanic/Latino), 14 international. Average age 30. 53 applicants, 42% accepted, 13 enrolled. In 2010, 1 master's, 5 doctorates awarded. Terminal master's awarded for partial completion of doctoral program. *Degree requirements:* For master's, thesis (for some programs); for doctorate, thesis/dissertation. *Entrance requirements:* For master's, GRE General Test, BS in chemistry or related field, 3 letters of recommendation; for doctorate, GRE General Test, BS in chemistry or related field, statement of purpose, official transcripts, 3 letters of recommendation with recommendation forms. Additional exam requirements/recommendations for international students: Required—TOEFL (minimum score 100 iBT). *Application deadline:* For fall admission, 2/15 priority date for domestic students, 2/15 for international students; for spring admission, 10/1 priority date for domestic students, 10/1 for international students. Applications are processed on a rolling basis. Application fee: $0 ($40 for international students). Electronic applications accepted. *Expenses:* Contact institution. *Financial support:* In 2010–11, 48 students received support, including 1 fellowship with tuition reimbursement available (averaging $21,900 per year), 17 research assistantships with full tuition reimbursements available (averaging $21,400 per year), 30 teaching assistantships with full tuition reimbursements available (averaging $21,400 per year); scholarships/grants and unspecified assistantships also available. Financial award application deadline: 5/31. *Faculty research:* Computational physical chemistry, bioinorganic chemistry, analytical chemistry, biophysics, synthetic organic chemistry. *Unit head:* Dr. Ralph Wheeler, Chair, 412-396-6341, Fax: 412-396-5683, E-mail: Wheeler7@duq.edu. *Application contact:* Heather Costello, Graduate Academic Advisor, 412-396-6339, Fax: 412-396-4881, E-mail: costelloh@duq.edu.

East Carolina University, Graduate School, Thomas Harriot College of Arts and Sciences, Department of Chemistry, Greenville, NC 27858-4353. Offers MS. Part-time programs available. *Degree requirements:* For master's, one foreign language, comprehensive exam, thesis. *Entrance requirements:* For master's, GRE General Test. Additional exam requirements/recommendations for international students: Required—TOEFL. *Expenses:* Tuition, state resident: full-time $3130; part-time $391.25 per credit hour. Tuition, nonresident: full-time $13,817; part-time $1727.13 per credit hour. Required fees: $1916; $239.50 per credit hour. Tuition and fees vary according to campus/location and program. *Faculty research:* Organometallic, natural-product syntheses; chemometrics; electroanalytical method development; microcomputer adaptations for handicapped students.

Eastern Illinois University, Graduate School, College of Sciences, Department of Chemistry, Charleston, IL 61920-3099. Offers MS. *Degree requirements:* For master's, thesis. *Entrance requirements:* For master's, GRE General Test.

Eastern Kentucky University, The Graduate School, College of Arts and Sciences, Department of Chemistry, Richmond, KY 40475-3102. Offers MS. Part-time and evening/weekend programs available. *Entrance requirements:* For master's, GRE General Test, minimum GPA of 2.5. *Faculty research:* Organic synthesis, surface chemistry, inorganic chemistry, analytical chemistry.

Eastern Michigan University, Graduate School, College of Arts and Sciences, Department of Chemistry, Ypsilanti, MI 48197. Offers MS. Part-time and evening/weekend programs available. *Faculty:* 22 full-time (9 women). *Students:* 4 full-time (2 women), 27 part-time (14 women); includes 3 minority (1 Black or African American, non-Hispanic/Latino; 1 American Indian or Alaska Native, non-Hispanic/Latino; 1 Asian, non-Hispanic/Latino), 19 international. Average age 28. 53 applicants, 43% accepted, 9 enrolled. In 2010, 11 master's awarded. *Degree requirements:* For master's, thesis. *Entrance requirements:* For master's, GRE General Test. Additional exam requirements/recommendations for international students: Required—TOEFL. *Application deadline:* For fall admission, 8/1 for domestic students, 5/1 for international students; for winter admission, 12/1 for domestic students, 8/1 for international students; for spring admission, 4/1 for domestic students, 3/1 for international students. Applications are processed on a rolling basis. Application fee: $35. *Financial support:* Fellowships, research assistantships with full tuition reimbursements, teaching assistantships with full tuition reimbursements, career-related internships or fieldwork, Federal Work-Study, institutionally sponsored loans, scholarships/grants, tuition waivers (partial), and unspecified assistantships available. Support available to part-time students. Financial award applicants required to submit FAFSA. *Unit head:* Dr. Ross Nord, Department Head, 734-487-0106, Fax: 734-487-1496, E-mail: ross.nord@emich.edu. *Application contact:* Dr. Timothy Brewer, Graduate Coordinator, 734-487-9613, Fax: 734-487-1496, E-mail: tbrewer@emich.edu.

Eastern New Mexico University, Graduate School, College of Liberal Arts and Sciences, Department of Physical Sciences, Portales, NM 88130. Offers chemistry (MS), including analytical, biochemistry, inorganic, organic, physical. Part-time programs available. *Faculty:* 3 full-time (0 women). *Students:* 7 full-time (2 women), 2 part-time (1 woman), 6 international.

Chemistry

Eastern New Mexico University (continued)
Average age 32. 10 applicants, 40% accepted, 4 enrolled. In 2010, 3 master's awarded. *Degree requirements:* For master's, thesis optional, seminar, oral and written comprehensive exams. *Entrance requirements:* For master's, ACS placement examination, minimum GPA of 3.0; 2 letters of recommendation; personal statement of career goals; bachelor's degree with one year minimum each of general, organic, and analytical chemistry. Additional exam requirements/recommendations for international students: Required—TOEFL (minimum score 550 paper-based; 213 computer-based; 79 iBT), IELTS (minimum score 6). *Application deadline:* For fall admission, 7/20 priority date for domestic students, 6/20 priority date for international students; for spring admission, 12/15 priority date for domestic students, 11/15 priority date for international students. Applications are processed on a rolling basis. Application fee: $10. Electronic applications accepted. *Expenses:* Tuition, state resident: full-time $3210; part-time $130 per credit hour. Tuition, nonresident: full-time $8652; part-time $360.50 per credit hour. Required fees: $1212; $50.50 per credit hour. Tuition and fees vary according to course load. *Financial support:* In 2010–11, 1 research assistantship with partial tuition reimbursement (averaging $8,500 per year), 9 teaching assistantships with partial tuition reimbursements (averaging $8,500 per year) were awarded; career-related internships or fieldwork and unspecified assistantships also available. Support available to part-time students. Financial award application deadline: 3/1; financial award applicants required to submit FAFSA. *Faculty research:* Synfuel, electrochemistry, protein chemistry. *Unit head:* Dr. Juacho Yan, Graduate Coordinator, 575-562-2174, Fax: 575-562-2192, E-mail: juacho.yan@enmu.edu. *Application contact:* Sharon Potter, Department Secretary, Chemistry/Physical Sciences, 575-562-2174, Fax: 575-562-2192, E-mail: sharon.potter@enmu.edu.

East Tennessee State University, School of Graduate Studies, College of Arts and Sciences, Department of Chemistry, Johnson City, TN 37614. Offers MS. Part-time and evening/weekend programs available. *Faculty:* 7 full-time (1 woman). *Students:* 24 full-time (8 women), 8 part-time (4 women); includes 4 minority (2 Black or African American, non-Hispanic/Latino; 1 Asian, non-Hispanic/Latino; 1 Two or more races, non-Hispanic/Latino), 18 international. Average age 29. 37 applicants, 57% accepted, 9 enrolled. In 2010, 6 master's awarded. *Degree requirements:* For master's, comprehensive exam, thesis. *Entrance requirements:* Additional exam requirements/recommendations for international students: Required—TOEFL (minimum score 550 paper-based; 213 computer-based; 79 iBT). *Application deadline:* For fall admission, 6/1 priority date for domestic students, 4/30 for international students; for spring admission, 11/1 for domestic students, 9/30 for international students. Application fee: $25 ($35 for international students). Electronic applications accepted. *Financial support:* In 2010–11, 9 teaching assistantships with full tuition reimbursements (averaging $8,000 per year) were awarded; research assistantships with full tuition reimbursements, career-related internships or fieldwork, institutionally sponsored loans, scholarships/grants, and unspecified assistantships also available. Financial award application deadline: 7/1; financial award applicants required to submit FAFSA. *Faculty research:* Development of luminescence techniques for chemical analysis, new functional materials and biosensor technology, synthesis of theoretically significant organic molecules and synthetic metals, synthesis and study of phosphatase enzyme models. Total annual research expenditures: $12,500. *Unit head:* Dr. Jeffrey G. Wardeska, Interim Chair, 423-439-4367, Fax: 423-439-5835, E-mail: rd1jeff@etsu.edu. *Application contact:* Admissions and Records Clerk, 423-439-4221, Fax: 423-439-5624, E-mail: gradsch@etsu.edu.

Emory University, Laney Graduate School, Department of Chemistry, Atlanta, GA 30322-1100. Offers PhD. *Degree requirements:* For doctorate, comprehensive exam, thesis/dissertation. *Entrance requirements:* For doctorate, GRE General Test, 3 letters of recommendation, curriculum vitae. Additional exam requirements/recommendations for international students: Required—TOEFL. Electronic applications accepted. *Expenses:* Tuition: Full-time $33,800. Required fees: $1300. *Faculty research:* Organometallic synthesis and catalysis, synthesis of natural products, x-ray crystallography, mass spectrometry, analytical neurochemistry.

Fairleigh Dickinson University, College at Florham, Maxwell Becton College of Arts and Sciences, Department of Chemistry and Geological Sciences, Program in Chemistry, Madison, NJ 07940-1099. Offers MS. *Students:* 61 full-time (26 women), 20 part-time (9 women), 74 international. Average age 24. 122 applicants, 80% accepted, 27 enrolled. In 2010, 49 master's awarded. *Application deadline:* Applications are processed on a rolling basis. Application fee: $40. *Application contact:* Susan Brooman, University Director, Graduate Admissions, 973-443-8905, Fax: 973-443-8088, E-mail: grad@fdu.edu.

Fairleigh Dickinson University, Metropolitan Campus, University College: Arts, Sciences, and Professional Studies, School of Natural Sciences, Program in Chemistry, Teaneck, NJ 07666-1914. Offers MS. *Students:* 27 full-time (15 women), 26 international. Average age 23. 105 applicants, 34% accepted, 10 enrolled. In 2010, 37 master's awarded. *Application deadline:* Applications are processed on a rolling basis. Application fee: $40. *Application contact:* Susan Brooman, University Director of Graduate Admissions, 201-692-2554, Fax: 201-692-2560, E-mail: globaleducation@fdu.edu.

Fairleigh Dickinson University, Metropolitan Campus, University College: Arts, Sciences, and Professional Studies, School of Natural Sciences, Program in Cosmetic Science, Teaneck, NJ 07666-1914. Offers MS. *Students:* 3 applicants, 0% accepted, 0 enrolled. *Application contact:* Susan Brooman, University Director of Graduate Admissions, 201-692-2554, Fax: 201-692-2560, E-mail: globaleducation@fdu.edu.

Fisk University, Division of Graduate Studies, Department of Chemistry, Nashville, TN 37208-3051. Offers MA. Part-time programs available. *Degree requirements:* For master's, comprehensive exam, thesis. *Entrance requirements:* For master's, GRE General Test, minimum GPA of 3.0. Electronic applications accepted. *Faculty research:* Environmental studies, lithium compound synthesis, HIU compound synthesis.

Florida Agricultural and Mechanical University, Division of Graduate Studies, Research, and Continuing Education, College of Arts and Sciences, Department of Chemistry, Tallahassee, FL 32307-3200. Offers MS. *Degree requirements:* For master's, comprehensive exam, thesis optional. *Entrance requirements:* For master's, GRE General Test, minimum GPA of 3.0.

Florida Atlantic University, Charles E. Schmidt College of Science, Department of Chemistry and Biochemistry, Boca Raton, FL 33431-0991. Offers chemistry (MS, MST, PhD). Part-time programs available. *Faculty:* 18 full-time (4 women). *Students:* 28 full-time (14 women), 4 part-time (1 woman); includes 4 minority (1 Black or African American, non-Hispanic/Latino; 3 Hispanic/Latino), 14 international. Average age 29. 30 applicants, 20% accepted, 5 enrolled. In 2010, 3 master's, 2 doctorates awarded. Terminal master's awarded for partial completion of doctoral program. *Degree requirements:* For master's, thesis; for doctorate, comprehensive exam, thesis/dissertation. *Entrance requirements:* For master's, GRE General Test, minimum GPA of 3.0; for doctorate, GRE, minimum GPA of 3.0. Additional exam requirements/recommendations for international students: Required—TOEFL. *Application deadline:* For fall admission, 7/1 priority date for domestic students, 2/15 priority date for international students; for spring admission, 11/1 priority date for domestic students, 7/15 priority date for international students. Applications are processed on a rolling basis. Application fee: $30. *Expenses:* Tuition, area resident: Part-time $319.96 per credit. Tuition, state resident: part-time $319.96 per credit. Tuition, nonresident: part-time $926.42 per credit. *Financial support:* Fellowships, research assistantships with full tuition reimbursements, teaching assistantships with full tuition reimbursements, Federal Work-Study available. *Faculty research:* Polymer synthesis and characterization, spectroscopy, geochemistry, environmental chemistry, biomedical chemistry. *Unit head:* Dr. Ramaswamy Narayanan, Chair, 561-297-2093, Fax: 561-297-2759, E-mail: rnarayan@fau.edu. *Application contact:* Dr. Salvatore D. Lepore, Professor, 561-297-0330, Fax: 561-297-2759, E-mail: slepore@fau.edu.

Florida Institute of Technology, Graduate Programs, College of Science, Department of Chemistry, Melbourne, FL 32901-6975. Offers biochemistry (MS); chemistry (MS, PhD). Part-time programs available. *Faculty:* 6 full-time (0 women). *Students:* 33 full-time (13 women), 2 part-time (1 woman); includes 1 minority (Black or African American, non-Hispanic/Latino), 23 international. Average age 28. 59 applicants, 59% accepted, 14 enrolled. In 2010, 4 master's, 1 doctorate awarded. Terminal master's awarded for partial completion of doctoral program. *Degree requirements:* For master's, comprehensive exam, thesis, research proposal, thesis and oral examination in defense of the thesis, Proficiency Examination; for doctorate, comprehensive exam, thesis/dissertation, oral defense of dissertation, dissertation research publishable to standards, complete original research study. *Entrance requirements:* For master's, proficiency exams, minimum GPA of 3.0; for doctorate, minimum GPA of 3.3, resume, 3 letters of recommendation, statement of objectives. Additional exam requirements/recommendations for international students: Required—TOEFL (minimum score 550 paper-based; 213 computer-based; 79 iBT). *Application deadline:* For fall admission, 4/1 for international students; for spring admission, 9/30 for international students. Applications are processed on a rolling basis. Application fee: $50. Electronic applications accepted. *Expenses:* Tuition: Part-time $1040 per credit hour. Tuition and fees vary according to campus/location. *Financial support:* In 2010–11, 5 research assistantships with full and partial tuition reimbursements (averaging $13,581 per year), 15 teaching assistantships with full and partial tuition reimbursements (averaging $10,973 per year) were awarded; career-related internships or fieldwork, institutionally sponsored loans, tuition waivers (partial), unspecified assistantships, and tuition remissions also available. Support available to part-time students. Financial award application deadline: 3/1; financial award applicants required to submit FAFSA. *Faculty research:* Energy storage applications, marine and organic chemistry, stereochemistry, medicinal chemistry, environmental chemistry. Total annual research expenditures: $718,486. *Unit head:* Dr. Michael W. Babich, Department Head, 321-674-8046, Fax: 321-674-8951, E-mail: babich@fit.edu. *Application contact:* Cheryl A. Brown, Associate Director of Graduate Admissions, 321-674-7581, Fax: 321-723-9468, E-mail: cbrown@fit.edu.

Florida International University, College of Arts and Sciences, Department of Chemistry, Chemistry Program, Miami, FL 33199. Offers MS, PhD. *Students:* Average age 26. In 2010, 4 master's, 3 doctorates awarded. *Degree requirements:* For master's, thesis; for doctorate, comprehensive exam, thesis/dissertation. *Entrance requirements:* For master's and doctorate, GRE, minimum GPA of 3.0, 3 letters of recommendation. Additional exam requirements/recommendations for international students: Required—TOEFL (minimum score 550 paper-based; 213 computer-based). *Application deadline:* For fall admission, 6/1 for domestic students, 4/1 for international students; for spring admission, 10/1 for domestic students, 9/1 for international students. Applications are processed on a rolling basis. Application fee: $30. Electronic applications accepted. *Financial support:* Fellowships, research assistantships, teaching assistantships, Federal Work-Study, institutionally sponsored loans, and scholarships/grants available. Financial award application deadline: 3/1; financial award applicants required to submit FAFSA. *Unit head:* Dr. Kenneth Furton, Dean, 305-348-2864, Fax: 305-348-4172, E-mail: furtonk@fiu.edu. *Application contact:* Nanett Rojas, Coordinator of Graduate Admissions, 305-348-7442, Fax: 305-348-7441, E-mail: gradadm@fiu.edu.

Florida State University, The Graduate School, College of Arts and Sciences, Department of Chemistry and Biochemistry, Tallahassee, FL 32306-4390. Offers analytical chemistry (MS, PhD); biochemistry (MS, PhD); inorganic chemistry (MS, PhD); materials chemistry (PhD); organic chemistry (MS, PhD); physical chemistry (MS, PhD). *Faculty:* 38 full-time (5 women), 3 part-time/adjunct (0 women). *Students:* 142 full-time (46 women), 8 part-time (4 women); includes 12 minority (6 Black or African American, non-Hispanic/Latino; 3 Asian, non-Hispanic/Latino; 3 Hispanic/Latino), 68 international. Average age 25. 299 applicants, 17% accepted, 19 enrolled. In 2010, 10 master's, 20 doctorates awarded. Terminal master's awarded for partial completion of doctoral program. *Degree requirements:* For master's, comprehensive exam (for some programs), thesis (for some programs), cumulative exams; for doctorate, comprehensive exam (for some programs), thesis/dissertation, cumulative exams. *Entrance requirements:* For master's and doctorate, GRE General Test, minimum B average in undergraduate course work. Additional exam requirements/recommendations for international students: Required—TOEFL (minimum score 550 paper-based; 213 computer-based; 80 iBT). *Application deadline:* For fall admission, 12/15 priority date for domestic and international students; for spring admission, 9/15 for domestic and international students. Applications are processed on a rolling basis. Application fee: $30. Electronic applications accepted. *Expenses:* Tuition, state resident: full-time $8238.24. *Financial support:* In 2010–11, 150 students received support, including fellowships with full tuition reimbursements available (averaging $20,000 per year), 50 research assistantships with full tuition reimbursements available (averaging $20,000 per year), 100 teaching assistantships with full tuition reimbursements available (averaging $20,000 per year). Financial award application deadline: 12/15; financial award applicants required to submit FAFSA. *Faculty research:* Materials synthesis including polymers, natural products; catalysis, NMR; mass spectrometry; optical spectroscopy, scattering techniques, computational chemistry, separation technology; nanostructured materials including metallic, semiconducting and magnetic nanocrystals; nanoscience interfaced with biology; supramolecular materials for solar energy conversion. Total annual research expenditures: $5.6 million. *Unit head:* Dr. Timothy Logan, Chairman, 850-644-1244, Fax: 850-644-8281, E-mail: gradinfo@chem.fsu.edu. *Application contact:* Dr. Tyler McQuade, Chair, Graduate Admissions Committee, 888-525-9286, Fax: 850-644-0465, E-mail: gradinfo@chem.fsu.edu.

Furman University, Graduate Division, Department of Chemistry, Greenville, SC 29613. Offers MS. *Faculty:* 9 full-time (3 women). *Students:* 2 full-time (0 women). Average age 23. In 2010, 6 master's awarded. *Degree requirements:* For master's, comprehensive exam, thesis. *Entrance requirements:* For master's, GRE General Test, GRE Subject Test. *Application deadline:* For fall admission, 8/1 for domestic and international students; for spring admission, 12/10 for domestic and international students. Applications are processed on a rolling basis. Application fee: $50. *Financial support:* In 2010–11, 2 fellowships (averaging $4,350 per year) were awarded; research assistantships, scholarships/grants and unspecified assistantships also available. Financial award application deadline: 7/1; financial award applicants required to submit FAFSA. *Faculty research:* Computer-assisted chemical analysis, DNA-metal interactions, laser-initiated reactions, nucleic acid chemistry and biochemistry. *Unit head:* Dr. Lon B. Knight, Professor, 864-294-3372, Fax: 864-294-3559, E-mail: lon.knight@furman.edu. *Application contact:* Myra Crumley, Information Contact, 864-294-2056, Fax: 864-294-3559, E-mail: myra.crumley@furman.edu.

George Mason University, College of Science, Department of Chemistry and Biochemistry, Fairfax, VA 22030. Offers chemistry (MS); chemistry and biochemistry (PhD). *Faculty:* 18 full-time (3 women), 6 part-time/adjunct (4 women). *Students:* 15 full-time (7 women), 36 part-time (15 women); includes 16 minority (1 Black or African American, non-Hispanic/Latino; 11 Asian, non-Hispanic/Latino; 4 Hispanic/Latino), 4 international. Average age 28. 49 applicants, 51% accepted, 16 enrolled. In 2010, 15 master's awarded. *Degree requirements:* For master's, thesis or alternative. *Entrance requirements:* For master's, GRE General Test, minimum GPA of 3.0 in last 60 hours of course work. Additional exam requirements/recommendations for international students: Required—TOEFL (minimum score 570 paper-based; 230 computer-based; 88 iBT). *Application deadline:* For fall admission, 5/1 for domestic students; for spring admission, 11/1 for domestic students. Application fee: $100. Electronic applications accepted. *Expenses:* Tuition, state resident: full-time $8192; part-time $440 per credit hour. Tuition, nonresident: full-time $22,952; part-time $1055 per credit hour. Required fees: $2364; $99 per credit hour. *Financial support:* In 2010–11, 13 students received support, including 2 fellowships (averaging $18,000 per year), 11 teaching assistantships (averaging $11,804 per year);

career-related internships or fieldwork, Federal Work-Study, scholarships/grants, unspecified assistantships, and health care benefits (full-time research or teaching assistantship recipients) also available. Financial award application deadline: 3/1; financial award applicants required to submit FAFSA. Total annual research expenditures: $84,592. *Unit head:* Gregory Foster, Chairperson, 703-993-1070, Fax: 703-993-1055, E-mail: gfoster@gmu.edu. *Application contact:* Dr. Tim Born, Associate Dean for Graduate Programs, 703-993-4171, Fax: 703-993-9034, E-mail: tborn@gmu.edu.

Georgetown University, Graduate School of Arts and Sciences, Department of Chemistry, Washington, DC 20057. Offers analytical chemistry (PhD); biochemistry (PhD); computational chemistry (PhD); inorganic chemistry (PhD); materials chemistry (PhD); organic chemistry (PhD); physical chemistry (PhD); theoretical chemistry (PhD). Terminal master's awarded for partial completion of doctoral program. *Degree requirements:* For doctorate, comprehensive exam, thesis/dissertation. *Entrance requirements:* For doctorate, GRE General Test. Additional exam requirements/recommendations for international students: Required—TOEFL.

The George Washington University, Columbian College of Arts and Sciences, Department of Chemistry, Washington, DC 20052. Offers analytical chemistry (MS, PhD); inorganic chemistry (MS, PhD); materials science (MS, PhD); organic chemistry (MS, PhD); physical chemistry (MS, PhD). Part-time and evening/weekend programs available. *Faculty:* 15 full-time (4 women), 5 part-time/adjunct (2 women). *Students:* 21 full-time (10 women), 10 part-time (5 women); includes 3 Asian, non-Hispanic/Latino; 1 Hispanic/Latino, 9 international. Average age 28. 33 applicants, 45% accepted, 7 enrolled. In 2010, 4 master's, 2 doctorates awarded. Terminal master's awarded for partial completion of doctoral program. *Degree requirements:* For master's, comprehensive exam, thesis or alternative; for doctorate, thesis/dissertation, general exam. *Entrance requirements:* For master's and doctorate, GRE General Test, interview, minimum GPA of 3.0. Additional exam requirements/recommendations for international students: Required—TOEFL (minimum score 550 paper-based; 213 computer-based; 80 iBT). *Application deadline:* For fall admission, 1/15 priority date for domestic and international students; for spring admission, 9/1 priority date for domestic and international students. Applications are processed on a rolling basis. Application fee: $75. Electronic applications accepted. *Financial support:* In 2010–11, 27 students received support; fellowships with tuition reimbursements available, research assistantships, teaching assistantships with tuition reimbursements available, Federal Work-Study and tuition waivers available. Financial award application deadline: 1/15. *Unit head:* Dr. Michael King, Chair, 202-994-6488. *Application contact:* Information Contact, 202-994-6121, E-mail: gwchem@gwu.edu.

Georgia Institute of Technology, Graduate Studies and Research, College of Sciences, School of Chemistry and Biochemistry, Atlanta, GA 30332-0001. Offers MS, MS Chem, PhD. Terminal master's awarded for partial completion of doctoral program. *Degree requirements:* For master's, thesis (for some programs); for doctorate, thesis/dissertation. *Entrance requirements:* For master's and doctorate, GRE General Test, GRE Subject Test, minimum GPA of 2.7. Additional exam requirements/recommendations for international students: Required—TOEFL. Electronic applications accepted. *Faculty research:* Inorganic, organic, physical, and analytical chemistry.

Georgia State University, College of Arts and Sciences, Department of Chemistry, Atlanta, GA 30302-3083. Offers MS, PhD. Part-time programs available. Terminal master's awarded for partial completion of doctoral program. *Degree requirements:* For master's, one foreign language, comprehensive exam, thesis or alternative, oral defense or approved non-thesis paper; for doctorate, one foreign language, comprehensive exam, thesis/dissertation, oral defense. *Entrance requirements:* For master's, GRE General Test; for doctorate, GRE General Test, 3 letters of recommendation, departmental supplemental form. Additional exam requirements/recommendations for international students: Required—TOEFL (minimum score 550 paper-based; 213 computer-based; 90 iBT). Electronic applications accepted. *Faculty research:* RNA/DNA, enzymology, drug design/discovery, biochemical-biophysical studies.

Graduate School and University Center of the City University of New York, Graduate Studies, Program in Chemistry, New York, NY 10016-4039. Offers PhD. *Degree requirements:* For doctorate, one foreign language, thesis/dissertation. *Entrance requirements:* For doctorate, GRE General Test. Additional exam requirements/recommendations for international students: Required—TOEFL. Electronic applications accepted.

Hampton University, Graduate College, Department of Chemistry, Hampton, VA 23668. Offers MS. Part-time and evening/weekend programs available. *Degree requirements:* For master's, thesis. *Entrance requirements:* For master's, GRE General Test.

Harvard University, Graduate School of Arts and Sciences, Department of Chemistry and Chemical Biology, Cambridge, MA 02138. Offers biochemical chemistry (PhD); inorganic chemistry (PhD); organic chemistry (PhD); physical chemistry (PhD). *Degree requirements:* For doctorate, thesis/dissertation, cumulative exams. *Entrance requirements:* For doctorate, GRE General Test, GRE Subject Test. Additional exam requirements/recommendations for international students: Required—TOEFL. *Expenses:* Tuition: Full-time $34,976. Required fees: $1166. Full-time tuition and fees vary according to program.

See Close-Up on page 99.

Hofstra University, School of Education, Health, and Human Services, Programs in Teaching—Secondary Education, Hempstead, NY 11549. Offers business education (MS Ed); English education (MA, MS Ed); foreign language and TESOL (MS Ed); foreign language education (MA, MS Ed), including French, German, Russian, Spanish; mathematics education (MA, MS Ed); science education (MA, MS Ed), including biology, chemistry, earth science, geology, physics; secondary education (Advanced Certificate); social studies education (MA, MS Ed). Part-time and evening/weekend programs available. Postbaccalaureate distance learning degree programs offered (minimal on-campus study). *Students:* 114 full-time (74 women), 61 part-time (36 women); includes 7 Black or African American, non-Hispanic/Latino; 1 American Indian or Alaska Native, non-Hispanic/Latino; 8 Asian, non-Hispanic/Latino; 10 Hispanic/Latino; 1 Native Hawaiian or other Pacific Islander, non-Hispanic/Latino. Average age 27. 153 applicants, 90% accepted, 59 enrolled. In 2010, 102 master's, 11 other advanced degrees awarded. *Degree requirements:* For master's, one foreign language, comprehensive exam (for some programs), thesis (for some programs), exit project, electronic portfolio, student teaching, fieldwork, curriculum project; for Advanced Certificate, 3 foreign languages, comprehensive exam (for some programs), thesis project. *Entrance requirements:* For master's, 2 letters of recommendation, teacher certification (MA), essay; for Advanced Certificate, 2 letters of recommendation, essay, interview and/or portfolio. Additional exam requirements/recommendations for international students: Required—TOEFL (minimum score 550 paper-based; 213 computer-based; 80 iBT). *Application deadline:* Applications are processed on a rolling basis. Application fee: $70 ($75 for international students). Electronic applications accepted. *Expenses:* Tuition: Full-time $18,000; part-time $1000 per credit hour. Required fees: $970; $145 per term. Tuition and fees vary according to program. *Financial support:* In 2010–11, 108 students received support, including 14 fellowships with full and partial tuition reimbursements available (averaging $3,943 per year), 1 research assistantship with full and partial tuition reimbursement available (averaging $6,574 per year); career-related internships or fieldwork, Federal Work-Study, institutionally sponsored loans, scholarships/grants, tuition waivers (full and partial), unspecified assistantships, and scholarships also available. Support available to part-time students. Financial award applicants required to submit FAFSA. *Faculty research:* Appropriate content and pedagogy in secondary school disciplines, adolescent development, secondary school organization, alternative secondary school programs. *Unit head:* Dr. Esther Fusco, Chairperson, 516-463-7704, Fax: 516-463-6196, E-mail: catezf@hofstra.edu. *Application contact:* Carol Drummer, Dean of Graduate Admissions, 516-463-4876, Fax: 516-463-4664, E-mail: gradstudent@hofstra.edu.

Howard University, Graduate School, Department of Chemistry, Washington, DC 20059-0002. Offers analytical chemistry (MS, PhD); atmospheric (MS, PhD); biochemistry (MS, PhD); environmental (MS, PhD); inorganic chemistry (MS, PhD); organic chemistry (MS, PhD); physical chemistry (MS, PhD). Terminal master's awarded for partial completion of doctoral program. *Degree requirements:* For master's, comprehensive exam, thesis, teaching experience; for doctorate, comprehensive exam, thesis/dissertation, teaching experience. *Entrance requirements:* For master's, GRE General Test, minimum GPA of 2.7; for doctorate, GRE General Test, minimum GPA of 3.0. Additional exam requirements/recommendations for international students: Required—TOEFL. Electronic applications accepted. *Faculty research:* Synthetic organics, materials, natural products, mass spectrometry.

Hunter College of the City University of New York, Graduate School, School of Arts and Sciences, Department of Chemistry, New York, NY 10021-5085. Offers biochemistry (MA, PhD); chemistry (PhD). Part-time programs available. *Faculty:* 4 full-time (3 women). *Students:* 1 full-time (0 women), 13 part-time (7 women); includes 1 Black or African American, non-Hispanic/Latino; 5 Asian, non-Hispanic/Latino, 1 international. Average age 25. 5 applicants, 80% accepted, 3 enrolled. *Degree requirements:* For master's, comprehensive exam or thesis. *Entrance requirements:* For master's, GRE General Test, 1 year of course work in chemistry, quantitative analysis, organic chemistry, physical chemistry, biology, biochemistry lecture and laboratory. Additional exam requirements/recommendations for international students: Required—TOEFL. *Application deadline:* For fall admission, 4/1 for domestic students; for spring admission, 11/1 for domestic students. Application fee: $125. *Financial support:* Teaching assistantships, tuition waivers (partial) available. Support available to part-time students. *Faculty research:* Theoretical chemistry, vibrational optical activity, Raman spectroscopy. *Unit head:* Dr. Gary J. Quigley, Chairperson, 212-772-5330, E-mail: gary.quilgley@hunter.cuny.edu. *Application contact:* William Zlata, Director for Graduate Admissions, 212-772-4482, Fax: 212-650-3336, E-mail: admissions@hunter.cuny.edu.

Idaho State University, Office of Graduate Studies, College of Arts and Sciences, Department of Chemistry, Pocatello, ID 83209-8023. Offers MNS, MS. MS students must enter as undergraduates. Part-time programs available. *Degree requirements:* For master's, comprehensive exam, thesis (for some programs). *Entrance requirements:* For master's, GRE General Test, minimum GPA of 3.0 in all upper-division classes; 1 semester of calculus, inorganic chemistry, and analytical chemistry; 1 year of physics, organic chemistry and physical chemistry. Additional exam requirements/recommendations for international students: Required—TOEFL (minimum score 550 paper-based; 213 computer-based; 80 iBT). Electronic applications accepted. *Faculty research:* Low temperature plasma, organic chemistry, physical chemistry, inorganic chemistry, analytical chemistry.

Illinois Institute of Technology, Graduate College, College of Science and Letters, Department of Biological, Chemical and Physical Sciences, Chemistry Division, Chicago, IL 60616. Offers analytical chemistry (M Ch); chemistry (M Chem, MS, PhD); materials and chemical synthesis (M Ch). Part-time and evening/weekend programs available. Postbaccalaureate distance learning degree programs offered (no on-campus study). *Faculty:* 13 full-time (5 women), 2 part-time/adjunct (0 women). *Students:* 29 full-time (11 women), 46 part-time (20 women); includes 26 minority (1 Black or African American, non-Hispanic/Latino; 2 Asian, non-Hispanic/Latino; 23 Hispanic/Latino), 23 international. Average age 30. 157 applicants, 46% accepted, 18 enrolled. In 2010, 11 master's, 3 doctorates awarded. Terminal master's awarded for partial completion of doctoral program. *Degree requirements:* For master's, comprehensive exam, thesis (for some programs); for doctorate, comprehensive exam, thesis/dissertation. *Entrance requirements:* For master's, GRE General Test (minimum score 1000 Quantitative and Verbal, 2.5 Analytical Writing), minimum undergraduate GPA of 3.0; for doctorate, GRE General Test (minimum score 1100 Quantitative and Verbal, 3.0 Analytical Writing), GRE Subject Test, minimum undergraduate GPA of 3.0. Additional exam requirements/recommendations for international students: Required—TOEFL (minimum score 523 paper-based; 213 computer-based; 70 iBT); Recommended—IELTS. *Application deadline:* For fall admission, 5/1 for domestic and international students; for spring admission, 10/15 for domestic and international students. Applications are processed on a rolling basis. Application fee: $40. Electronic applications accepted. *Expenses:* Tuition: Full-time $18,576; part-time $1032 per credit hour. Required fees: $583 per semester. One-time fee: $150. Tuition and fees vary according to program and student level. *Financial support:* In 2010–11, 2 fellowships with full and partial tuition reimbursements (averaging $7,750 per year), 3 research assistantships with full and partial tuition reimbursements (averaging $5,950 per year), 13 teaching assistantships with full and partial tuition reimbursements (averaging $7,173 per year) were awarded; Federal Work-Study, institutionally sponsored loans, scholarships/grants, health care benefits, tuition waivers (partial), and unspecified assistantships also available. Support available to part-time students. Financial award applicants required to submit FAFSA. *Faculty research:* Synthesis and analysis of inorganic nanoparticles; synthetic and mechanistic organic chemistry; synthesis of penicillin-related compounds; design, synthesis and property studies of nanomaterials for applications in chemical sensing, energy storage and biomedical usage; scanning probe microscopy. Total annual research expenditures: $356,146. *Unit head:* Dr. Rong Wang, Associate Chair, 312-567-3121, Fax: 312-567-3494, E-mail: wangr@iit.edu. *Application contact:* Deborah Gibson, Director, Graduate Admission, 866-472-3448, Fax: 312-567-3138, E-mail: inquiry.grad@iit.edu.

Illinois State University, Graduate School, College of Arts and Sciences, Department of Chemistry, Normal, IL 61790-2200. Offers MS. *Degree requirements:* For master's, thesis. *Entrance requirements:* For master's, GRE General Test, minimum GPA of 2.6 in last 60 hours of course work. *Faculty research:* Solid-state and solution behavior of lanthanide scorpionates and porphyrinoids; CAREER: Versatile Vanadium: biology, materials science and education through its diverse coordinator carbaporphyrins and other highly modified porphyrinoid systems; oxadiazines: structurally novel templates for catalytic asymmetric synthesis.

Indiana University Bloomington, University Graduate School, College of Arts and Sciences, Department of Chemistry, Bloomington, IN 47405. Offers analytical chemistry (PhD); chemical biology chemistry (PhD); chemistry (MAT); inorganic chemistry (PhD); materials chemistry (PhD); organic chemistry (PhD); physical chemistry (PhD). *Faculty:* 42 full-time (4 women). *Students:* 224 full-time (77 women); includes 19 minority (7 Black or African American, non-Hispanic/Latino; 1 American Indian or Alaska Native, non-Hispanic/Latino; 8 Asian, non-Hispanic/Latino; 3 Hispanic/Latino), 68 international. Average age 27. 270 applicants, 39% accepted, 31 enrolled. In 2010, 1 master's, 20 doctorates awarded. Terminal master's awarded for partial completion of doctoral program. *Degree requirements:* For master's, thesis; for doctorate, thesis/dissertation. *Entrance requirements:* For master's and doctorate, GRE General Test, GRE Subject Test. Additional exam requirements/recommendations for international students: Required—TOEFL. *Application deadline:* For fall admission, 1/15 priority date for domestic students, 12/15 for international students. Applications are processed on a rolling basis. Application fee: $55 ($65 for international students). *Financial support:* In 2010–11, 200 students received support, including 10 fellowships with full tuition reimbursements available, 76 research assistantships with full tuition reimbursements available, 111 teaching assistantships with full tuition reimbursements available; Federal Work-Study and institutionally sponsored loans also available. *Faculty research:* Synthesis of complex natural products, organic reaction mechanisms, organic electrochemistry, transitive-metal chemistry, solid-state and surface chemistry. Total annual research expenditures: $7.7 million. *Unit head:* David Giedroc, Chairperson, 812-855-6239, E-mail: chemchair@indiana.edu. *Application contact:* Daneil Mindiola, Director of Graduate Admissions, 812-855-2069, Fax: 812-855-8385, E-mail: mindiola@indiana.edu.

Indiana University of Pennsylvania, School of Graduate Studies and Research, College of Natural Sciences and Mathematics, Department of Chemistry, Program in Chemistry, Indiana,

Chemistry

Indiana University of Pennsylvania (continued)
PA 15705-1087. Offers MA, MS. Part-time programs available. *Faculty:* 8 full-time (2 women). *Students:* 10 full-time (4 women), 1 part-time (0 women). Average age 30. 18 applicants, 28% accepted, 2 enrolled. In 2010, 3 master's awarded. *Degree requirements:* For master's, thesis optional. *Entrance requirements:* For master's, 2 letters of recommendation. Additional exam requirements/recommendations for international students: Required—TOEFL. *Application deadline:* For fall admission, 7/1 priority date for domestic students; for spring admission, 11/1 for domestic students. Applications are processed on a rolling basis. Application fee: $40. *Financial support:* In 2010–11, 5 research assistantships with full and partial tuition reimbursements (averaging $5,718 per year) were awarded. Financial award application deadline: 3/15; financial award applicants required to submit FAFSA. *Unit head:* Dr. Keith Kyler, Graduate Coordinator, 724-357-5702, E-mail: keith.kyler@iup.edu. *Application contact:* Dr. Lawrence Kupchella, Graduate Coordinator, 724-357-5702, E-mail: lkup@iup.edu.

Indiana University–Purdue University Indianapolis, School of Science, Department of Chemistry and Chemical Biology, Indianapolis, IN 46202-2896. Offers MS, PhD, MD/PhD. MD/PhD offered jointly with Indiana University School of Medicine and Purdue University. Part-time and evening/weekend programs available. *Faculty:* 10 full-time (2 women). *Students:* 19 full-time (7 women), 20 part-time (7 women); includes 5 minority (2 Asian, non-Hispanic/Latino; 1 Hispanic/Latino; 2 Two or more races, non-Hispanic/Latino), 8 international. Average age 31. 14 applicants, 79% accepted, 11 enrolled. In 2010, 7 master's awarded. Terminal master's awarded for partial completion of doctoral program. *Degree requirements:* For master's, thesis (for some programs); for doctorate, thesis/dissertation. *Entrance requirements:* For master's and doctorate, minimum GPA of 3.0. Additional exam requirements/recommendations for international students: Required—TOEFL. *Application deadline:* Applications are processed on a rolling basis. Application fee: $55 ($65 for international students). *Financial support:* In 2010–11, 3 fellowships with partial tuition reimbursements (averaging $13,500 per year), 13 teaching assistantships with partial tuition reimbursements (averaging $17,440 per year) were awarded; research assistantships with partial tuition reimbursements, career-related internships or fieldwork, institutionally sponsored loans, tuition waivers (partial), and cooperative positions also available. Financial award application deadline: 3/1. *Faculty research:* Analytical, biological, inorganic, organic, and physical chemistry. Total annual research expenditures: $1.6 million. *Unit head:* Jay A. Siegel, Chair, 317-274-6872. *Application contact:* Eric Long, Associate Chair, 317-274-6888, Fax: 317-274-4701, E-mail: long@chem.iupui.edu.

Instituto Tecnológico y de Estudios Superiores de Monterrey, Campus Monterrey, Graduate and Research Division, Program in Natural and Social Sciences, Monterrey, Mexico. Offers biotechnology (MS); chemistry (MS, PhD); communications (MS); education (MA). Part-time programs available. *Degree requirements:* For master's, one foreign language, thesis; for doctorate, one foreign language, thesis/dissertation. *Entrance requirements:* For master's, EXADEP; for doctorate, EXADEP, master's degree in related field. Additional exam requirements/recommendations for international students: Required—TOEFL. *Faculty research:* Cultural industries, mineral substances, bioremediation, food processing, CQ in industrial chemical processing.

Iowa State University of Science and Technology, Graduate College, College of Liberal Arts and Sciences, Department of Chemistry, Ames, IA 50011. Offers MS, PhD. *Faculty:* 32 full-time (6 women), 4 part-time/adjunct (1 woman). *Students:* 176 full-time (64 women), 8 part-time (2 women); includes 2 Black or African American, non-Hispanic/Latino; 4 Asian, non-Hispanic/Latino; 2 Hispanic/Latino, 89 international. 69 applicants, 64% accepted, 33 enrolled. In 2010, 6 master's, 26 doctorates awarded. *Degree requirements:* For master's, thesis; for doctorate, thesis/dissertation. *Entrance requirements:* Additional exam requirements/recommendations for international students: Required—TOEFL (minimum score 550 paper-based; 89 iBT), IELTS (minimum score 6.5). *Application deadline:* For fall admission, 2/1 priority date for domestic and international students. Application fee: $40 ($90 for international students). Electronic applications accepted. *Financial support:* In 2010–11, 88 research assistantships with full and partial tuition reimbursements (averaging $9,296 per year), 74 teaching assistantships with full and partial tuition reimbursements (averaging $11,502 per year) were awarded; fellowships, scholarships/grants, health care benefits, and unspecified assistantships also available. *Unit head:* Dr. Jacob Petrich, Chair, 515-294-7812, Fax: 515-294-0105, E-mail: chemgrad@iastate.edu. *Application contact:* Dr. Theresa Windus, Director of Graduate Education, 800-521-6134, E-mail: chemgrad@iastate.edu.

Jackson State University, Graduate School, College of Science, Engineering and Technology, Department of Chemistry and Biochemistry, Jackson, MS 39217. Offers MS, PhD. Part-time and evening/weekend programs available. *Faculty:* 14 full-time (4 women). *Students:* 21 full-time (12 women), 22 part-time (13 women); includes 25 Black or African American, non-Hispanic/Latino; 1 Asian, non-Hispanic/Latino; 1 Hispanic/Latino; 1 Two or more races, non-Hispanic/Latino, 13 international. Average age 30. In 2010, 11 master's, 7 doctorates awarded. *Degree requirements:* For master's, comprehensive exam, thesis; for doctorate, comprehensive exam, thesis/dissertation. *Entrance requirements:* For master's, GRE General Test; for doctorate, MAT. Additional exam requirements/recommendations for international students: Required—TOEFL (minimum score 520 paper-based; 195 computer-based; 67 iBT). *Application deadline:* For fall admission, 3/1 priority date for domestic students, 3/1 for international students; for spring admission, 10/1 for domestic and international students. Applications are processed on a rolling basis. Application fee: $25. *Expenses:* Tuition, state resident: full-time $5050; part-time $281 per credit hour. Tuition, nonresident: full-time $12,380; part-time $689 per credit hour. *Financial support:* Career-related internships or fieldwork, Federal Work-Study, scholarships/grants, and unspecified assistantships available. Support available to part-time students. Financial award application deadline: 3/1; financial award applicants required to submit FAFSA. *Faculty research:* Electrochemical and spectroscopic studies on charge transfer and energy transfer processes, spectroscopy of trapped molecular ions, respirable mine dust. *Unit head:* Dr. Hangtao Yu, Chair, 601-968-2171, Fax: 601-973-3730, E-mail: yu@jsums.edu. *Application contact:* Sharlene Wilson, Director of Graduate Admissions, 601-979-2455, Fax: 601-979-4325, E-mail: sharlene.f.wilson@jsums.edu.

The Johns Hopkins University, Zanvyl Krieger School of Arts and Sciences, Chemistry-Biology Interface Program, Baltimore, MD 21218-2699. Offers PhD. *Faculty:* 32 full-time (6 women). *Students:* 16 full-time (10 women); includes 5 minority (1 Black or African American, non-Hispanic/Latino; 1 American Indian or Alaska Native, non-Hispanic/Latino; 2 Asian, non-Hispanic/Latino; 1 Hispanic/Latino), 1 international. Average age 25. 77 applicants, 23% accepted, 3 enrolled.Terminal master's awarded for partial completion of doctoral program. *Degree requirements:* For doctorate, comprehensive exam, thesis/dissertation, 8 one-semester courses, literature seminar, research proposal. *Entrance requirements:* For doctorate, GRE General Test, GRE Subject Test in biochemistry, cell and molecular biology, biology or chemistry (strongly recommended), 3 letters of recommendation, interview. *Application deadline:* For fall admission, 1/15 for domestic and international students. Applications are processed on a rolling basis. Application fee: $75. Electronic applications accepted. *Financial support:* Fellowships, teaching assistantships, Federal Work-Study, scholarships/grants, health care benefits, and unspecified assistantships available. Financial award application deadline: 4/15; financial award applicants required to submit FAFSA. *Faculty research:* Enzyme mechanisms, inhibitors, and metabolic pathways; DNA replication, damaged, and repair; using small molecules to probe signal transduction, gene regulation, angiogenesis, and other biological processes; synthetic methods and medicinal chemistry; synthetic modeling of metalloenzymes. *Unit head:* Dr. Marc Greenberg, Director, 410-516-8095, Fax: 410-516-7044, E-mail: mgreenberg@jhu.edu. *Application contact:* Lauren Riker, Academic Coordinator, 410-516-7427, Fax: 410-516-8420, E-mail: lriker@jhu.edu.

The Johns Hopkins University, Zanvyl Krieger School of Arts and Sciences, Department of Chemistry, Baltimore, MD 21218-2699. Offers PhD. *Faculty:* 24 full-time (4 women), 1 part-time/adjunct (0 women). *Students:* 105 full-time (35 women); includes 10 minority (3 Black or African American, non-Hispanic/Latino; 1 American Indian or Alaska Native, non-Hispanic/Latino; 4 Asian, non-Hispanic/Latino; 1 Hispanic/Latino; 1 Two or more races, non-Hispanic/Latino), 33 international. Average age 23. 158 applicants, 14% accepted, 22 enrolled. In 2010, 17 doctorates awarded. Terminal master's awarded for partial completion of doctoral program. *Degree requirements:* For doctorate, comprehensive exam, thesis/dissertation, 8 one-semester courses, literature seminar. *Entrance requirements:* For doctorate, GRE General Test, GRE Subject Test. Additional exam requirements/recommendations for international students: Required—TOEFL (minimum score 600 paper-based; 250 computer-based), IELTS. *Application deadline:* For fall admission, 1/2 for domestic and international students. Applications are processed on a rolling basis. Application fee: $60. Electronic applications accepted. *Financial support:* Fellowships, teaching assistantships, Federal Work-Study, scholarships/grants, health care benefits, and unspecified assistantships available. Financial award application deadline: 4/15; financial award applicants required to submit FAFSA. *Faculty research:* Experimental physical, biophysical, inorganic/materials, organic/bioorganic theoretical. Total annual research expenditures: $6.6 million. *Unit head:* Dr. John Toscano, Chair, 410-516-6534, E-mail: jtoscano@jhu.edu. *Application contact:* Jean Goodwin, Academic Program Coordinator, 410-516-7791, Fax: 410-516-8420, E-mail: jeang@jhu.edu.

Kansas State University, Graduate School, College of Arts and Sciences, Department of Chemistry, Manhattan, KS 66506. Offers analytical chemistry (MS); biological chemistry (MS); chemistry (PhD); inorganic chemistry (MS); materials chemistry (MS); organic chemistry (MS); physical chemistry (MS). Terminal master's awarded for partial completion of doctoral program. *Degree requirements:* For master's, thesis; for doctorate, thesis/dissertation. *Entrance requirements:* For master's and doctorate, GRE, minimum GPA of 3.0. Additional exam requirements/recommendations for international students: Required—TOEFL (minimum score 550 paper-based; 213 computer-based). Electronic applications accepted. *Faculty research:* Inorganic chemistry, organic and biological chemistry, analytical chemistry, physical chemistry, materials chemistry and nanotechnology.

Kent State University, College of Arts and Sciences, Department of Chemistry and Biochemistry, Kent, OH 44242-0001. Offers analytical chemistry (MS, PhD); biochemistry (MS, PhD); chemistry (MA); inorganic chemistry (MS, PhD); organic chemistry (MS, PhD); physical chemistry (MS, PhD). Terminal master's awarded for partial completion of doctoral program. *Degree requirements:* For master's, comprehensive exam, thesis; for doctorate, comprehensive exam, thesis/dissertation. *Entrance requirements:* For master's and doctorate, placement exam, GRE General Test, GRE Subject Test (recommended), minimum GPA of 2.75. Additional exam requirements/recommendations for international students: Required—TOEFL (minimum score 525 paper-based; 71 iBT). Electronic applications accepted. *Expenses:* Tuition, state resident: full-time $7866; part-time $437 per credit hour. Tuition, nonresident: full-time $14,022; part-time $779 per credit hour. *Faculty research:* Biological chemistry, materials chemistry, molecular spectroscopy.

See Display on next page and Close-Up on page 101.

Lakehead University, Graduate Studies, Faculty of Social Sciences and Humanities, Department of Chemistry, Thunder Bay, ON P7B 5E1, Canada. Offers M Sc. Part-time and evening/weekend programs available. *Degree requirements:* For master's, thesis, oral examination. *Entrance requirements:* For master's, minimum B+ average. Additional exam requirements/recommendations for international students: Required—TOEFL. *Faculty research:* Physical inorganic chemistry, photochemistry, physical chemistry.

Lamar University, College of Graduate Studies, College of Arts and Sciences, Department of Chemistry and Physics, Beaumont, TX 77710. Offers chemistry (MS). Part-time programs available. *Faculty:* 11 full-time (3 women). *Students:* 20 full-time (13 women), 14 part-time (6 women); includes 1 Hispanic/Latino, 27 international. Average age 25. 46 applicants, 72% accepted, 3 enrolled. In 2010, 14 master's awarded. *Degree requirements:* For master's, thesis, practicum. *Entrance requirements:* For master's, GRE General Test, minimum GPA of 2.5 in last 60 hours of course work. Additional exam requirements/recommendations for international students: Required—TOEFL, TWE. *Application deadline:* For fall admission, 8/1 for domestic students, 7/1 for international students; for spring admission, 12/1 for domestic students, 11/1 for international students. Applications are processed on a rolling basis. Application fee: $25 ($50 for international students). *Expenses:* Tuition, state resident: full-time $4160; part-time $208 per credit hour. Tuition, nonresident: full-time $10,360; part-time $518 per credit hour. *Financial support:* In 2010–11, 6 students received support, including 5 teaching assistantships with partial tuition reimbursements available (averaging $9,000 per year); tuition waivers (partial) and unspecified assistantships also available. Financial award application deadline: 4/1. *Faculty research:* Environmental chemistry, surface chemistry, polymer chemistry, organic synthesis, computational chemistry. *Unit head:* Dr. Richard S. Lumpkin, Chair, 409-880-8267, Fax: 409-880-8270, E-mail: lumpkines@hal.lamar.edu. *Application contact:* Dr. Paul Bernazzani, Graduate Advisor, 409-880-8272, Fax: 409-880-8270, E-mail: bernazzapx@hal.lamar.edu.

Laurentian University, School of Graduate Studies and Research, Programme in Chemistry and Biochemistry, Sudbury, ON P3E 2C6, Canada. Offers analytical chemistry (M Sc); biochemistry (M Sc); environmental chemistry (M Sc); organic chemistry (M Sc); physical/theoretical chemistry (M Sc). Part-time programs available. *Degree requirements:* For master's, thesis or alternative. *Entrance requirements:* For master's, honors degree with minimum second class. *Faculty research:* Cell cycle checkpoints, kinetic modeling, toxicology to metal stress, quantum chemistry, biogeochemistry metal speciation.

Lehigh University, College of Arts and Sciences, Department of Chemistry, Bethlehem, PA 18015. Offers MS, PhD. Part-time programs available. Postbaccalaureate distance learning degree programs offered (no on-campus study). *Faculty:* 15 full-time (2 women), 1 part-time/adjunct (0 women). *Students:* 39 full-time (20 women), 92 part-time (43 women); includes 12 minority (4 Black or African American, non-Hispanic/Latino; 1 American Indian or Alaska Native, non-Hispanic/Latino; 3 Asian, non-Hispanic/Latino; 4 Hispanic/Latino), 12 international. Average age 30. 64 applicants, 47% accepted, 23 enrolled. In 2010, 31 master's, 1 doctorate awarded. Terminal master's awarded for partial completion of doctoral program. *Degree requirements:* For master's, comprehensive exam, thesis; for doctorate, comprehensive exam, thesis/dissertation. *Entrance requirements:* Additional exam requirements/recommendations for international students: Required—TOEFL (minimum score 230 computer-based; 85 iBT). *Application deadline:* For fall admission, 1/15 priority date for domestic and international students. Applications are processed on a rolling basis. Application fee: $75. Electronic applications accepted. *Financial support:* In 2010–11, 3 fellowships with full tuition reimbursements (averaging $25,000 per year), 8 research assistantships with full tuition reimbursements (averaging $25,000 per year), 19 teaching assistantships with full tuition reimbursements (averaging $25,000 per year) were awarded; career-related internships or fieldwork, Federal Work-Study, institutionally sponsored loans, scholarships/grants, tuition waivers (full and partial), and unspecified assistantships also available. Support available to part-time students. Financial award application deadline: 1/15. *Faculty research:* Materials chemistry, biological chemistry, surface chemistry, nano science. Total annual research expenditures: $3.5 million. *Unit head:* Prof. Robert A. Flowers, Professor & Danser Distinguished Chair of Chemistry, 610-758-3470, Fax: 610-758-6536, E-mail: rof2@lehigh.edu. *Application contact:* Dr. Rebecca Miller, Graduate Coordinator, 610-758-3471, Fax: 610-758-6536, E-mail: inluchem@lehigh.edu.

Long Island University, Brooklyn Campus, Richard L. Conolly College of Liberal Arts and Sciences, Department of Chemistry, Brooklyn, NY 11201-8423. Offers MS. Part-time and evening/weekend programs available. *Degree requirements:* For master's, thesis or alternative. *Entrance requirements:* For master's, 2 letters of recommendation. Additional exam requirements/recommendations for international students: Required—TOEFL (minimum score 500 paper-

56 www.facebook.com/petersonspublishing

Peterson's Graduate Programs in the Physical Sciences, Mathematics, Agricultural Sciences, the Environment & Natural Resources 2012

Chemistry

based; 173 computer-based). Electronic applications accepted. *Faculty research:* Clinical chemistry, free radicals, heats of hydrogenation.

Louisiana State University and Agricultural and Mechanical College, Graduate School, College of Basic Sciences, Department of Chemistry, Baton Rouge, LA 70803. Offers MS, PhD. Part-time programs available. *Faculty:* 28 full-time (6 women). *Students:* 153 full-time (64 women), 2 part-time (0 women); includes 32 Black or African American, non-Hispanic/Latino; 5 Asian, non-Hispanic/Latino; 1 Hispanic/Latino; 1 Two or more races, non-Hispanic/Latino, 68 international. Average age 29. 163 applicants, 31% accepted, 21 enrolled. In 2010, 2 master's, 20 doctorates awarded. Terminal master's awarded for partial completion of doctoral program. *Degree requirements:* For master's, thesis (for some programs); for doctorate, thesis/dissertation, general exam. *Entrance requirements:* For master's and doctorate, GRE General Test, minimum GPA of 3.0. Additional exam requirements/recommendations for international students: Required—TOEFL (minimum score 550 paper-based; 213 computer-based; 79 iBT) or IELTS (minimum score 6.5). *Application deadline:* For fall admission, 3/1 priority date for domestic students, 5/15 for international students; for spring admission, 8/1 for domestic students, 10/15 for international students. Applications are processed on a rolling basis. Application fee: $25. Electronic applications accepted. *Financial support:* In 2010–11, 152 students received support, including 19 fellowships with full tuition reimbursements available (averaging $19,531 per year), 59 research assistantships with full and partial tuition reimbursements available (averaging $21,789 per year), 75 teaching assistantships with full and partial tuition reimbursements available (averaging $22,353 per year); career-related internships or fieldwork, Federal Work-Study, scholarships/grants, traineeships, and unspecified assistantships also available. Support available to part-time students. Financial award application deadline: 7/1; financial award applicants required to submit FAFSA. *Faculty research:* Materials, biological, environmental. Total annual research expenditures: $7.2 million. *Unit head:* Dr. Andrew Maverick, Chair, 225-578-3462, Fax: 225-578-3458, E-mail: maverick@lsu.edu. *Application contact:* Dr. John Pojman, Director of Graduate Studies, 225-578-7202, Fax: 225-578-3458, E-mail: japojman@lsu.edu.

Louisiana Tech University, Graduate School, College of Engineering and Science, Department of Chemistry, Ruston, LA 71272. Offers MS. Part-time programs available. *Degree requirements:* For master's, thesis. *Entrance requirements:* For master's, GRE General Test, minimum GPA of 3.0 in last 60 hours. Additional exam requirements/recommendations for international students: Required—TOEFL. *Faculty research:* Vibrational spectroscopy, quantum studies of chemical reactions, enzyme kinetics, synthesis of transition metal compounds, NMR spectrometry.

Loyola University Chicago, Graduate School, Department of Chemistry, Chicago, IL 60660. Offers MS, PhD. Part-time and evening/weekend programs available. *Faculty:* 14 full-time (2 women). *Students:* 29 full-time (15 women), 10 part-time (5 women); includes 8 minority (4 Black or African American, non-Hispanic/Latino; 2 Asian, non-Hispanic/Latino; 1 Hispanic/Latino; 1 Native Hawaiian or other Pacific Islander, non-Hispanic/Latino), 6 international. Average age 30. 52 applicants, 31% accepted, 7 enrolled. In 2010, 2 master's, 3 doctorates awarded. Terminal master's awarded for partial completion of doctoral program. *Degree requirements:* For master's, thesis (for some programs); for doctorate, comprehensive exam, thesis/dissertation. *Entrance requirements:* For master's and doctorate, GRE General Test, GRE Subject Test. Additional exam requirements/recommendations for international students: Required—TOEFL (minimum score 550 paper-based; 213 computer-based). *Application deadline:* For fall admission, 8/1 priority date for domestic students; for spring admission, 12/1 for domestic students. Applications are processed on a rolling basis. Application fee: $50. Electronic applications accepted. *Expenses:* Tuition: Full-time $14,940; part-time $830 per credit hour. Required fees: $87 per semester. Part-time tuition and fees vary according to course load and program. *Financial support:* In 2010–11, 19 students received support, including 3 fellowships with full tuition reimbursements available (averaging $16,000 per year), 16 teaching assistantships with full tuition reimbursements available (averaging $18,000 per year); research assistantships with full and partial tuition reimbursements available, Federal Work-Study, scholarships/grants, traineeships, and unspecified assistantships also available. Financial award application deadline: 2/1; financial award applicants required to submit FAFSA. *Faculty research:* Magnetic resonance of membrane/protein systems, organometallic catalysis, novel synthesis of natural products. Total annual research expenditures: $682,510. *Unit head:* Dr. Richard Holz, Chair, 773-508-7045, Fax: 773-508-3086, E-mail: rholz1@luc.edu. *Application contact:* Stacey N. Lind, Graduate Program Coordinator, 773-508-3104, Fax: 773-508-3086, E-mail: slind@luc.edu.

Marquette University, Graduate School, College of Arts and Sciences, Department of Chemistry, Milwaukee, WI 53201-1881. Offers analytical chemistry (MS, PhD); bioanalytical chemistry (MS, PhD); biophysical chemistry (MS, PhD); chemical physics (MS, PhD); inorganic chemistry (MS, PhD); organic chemistry (MS, PhD); physical chemistry (MS, PhD). Part-time programs available. *Faculty:* 27 full-time (3 women), 1 part-time/adjunct (0 women). *Students:* 33 full-time (12 women), 16 part-time (3 women); includes 4 minority (2 Black or African American, non-Hispanic/Latino; 2 Asian, non-Hispanic/Latino), 37 international. Average age 29. 25 applicants, 92% accepted, 10 enrolled. In 2010, 2 master's, 1 doctorate awarded. Terminal master's awarded for partial completion of doctoral program. *Degree requirements:* For master's, comprehensive exam; for doctorate, thesis/dissertation, cumulative exams. *Entrance requirements:* For master's and doctorate, GRE Subject Test (optional), official transcripts from all current and previous colleges/universities except Marquette, three letters of recommendation from individuals familiar with the applicant's academic work. Additional exam requirements/recommendations for international students: Required—TOEFL (minimum score 530 paper-based; 78 computer-based). *Application deadline:* Applications are processed on a rolling basis. Application fee: $50. Electronic applications accepted. *Expenses:* Tuition: Full-time $16,290; part-time $905 per credit hour. Tuition and fees vary according to program. *Financial support:* In 2010–11, 2 fellowships, 4 research assistantships, 27 teaching assistantships were awarded; Federal Work-Study, institutionally sponsored loans, scholarships/grants, and tuition waivers (full and partial) also available. Support available to part-time students. Financial award application deadline: 2/15. *Faculty research:* Inorganic complexes, laser Raman spectroscopy, organic synthesis, synthetic bioinorganic chemistry, electro-active organic molecules. Total annual research expenditures: $1.2 million. *Unit head:* Dr. Michael Ryan, Chair, 414-288-3537, Fax: 414-288-7066. *Application contact:* Dr. Mark Steinmetz, Director of Graduate Studies, 414-288-7374, Fax: 414-288-7066.

Marshall University, Academic Affairs Division, College of Science, Department of Chemistry, Huntington, WV 25755. Offers MS. *Faculty:* 9 full-time (3 women). *Students:* 4 full-time (1 woman), 1 (woman) part-time, 1 international. Average age 24. In 2010, 5 master's awarded. *Degree requirements:* For master's, thesis. Application fee: $40. *Financial support:* Career-related internships or fieldwork available. *Unit head:* Dr. Michael Casteliani, Chairperson, 304-696-6486, E-mail: castella@marshall.edu. *Application contact:* Dr. John Hubbard, Information Contact, 304-696-2430, Fax: 304-746-1902, E-mail: hubbard@marshall.edu.

Massachusetts College of Pharmacy and Health Sciences, Graduate Studies, Program in Medicinal Chemistry, Boston, MA 02115-5896. Offers MS, PhD. *Students:* 5 full-time (2 women), 1 part-time (0 women); includes 1 minority (Asian, non-Hispanic/Latino), 5 international. Average age 29. 14 applicants, 57% accepted, 1 enrolled. In 2010, 1 doctorate awarded. Terminal master's awarded for partial completion of doctoral program. *Degree requirements:* For master's, thesis, oral defense of thesis; for doctorate, one foreign language, comprehensive exam, thesis/dissertation, oral defense of dissertation, qualifying exam. *Entrance requirements:* For master's and doctorate, GRE General Test, minimum GPA of 3.0. Additional exam requirements/recommendations for international students: Required—TOEFL (minimum score 550 paper-based; 213 computer-based; 79 iBT). *Application deadline:* For fall admission, 2/1 priority date

Peterson's Graduate Programs in the Physical Sciences, Mathematics, Agricultural Sciences, the Environment & Natural Resources 2012

www.facebook.com/petersonspublishing   **57**

Chemistry

Massachusetts College of Pharmacy and Health Sciences *(continued)*
for domestic and international students. Application fee: $70. Electronic applications accepted. *Financial support:* Fellowships with partial tuition reimbursements, research assistantships with partial tuition reimbursements, teaching assistantships with full tuition reimbursements, tuition waivers (partial) and unspecified assistantships available. Financial award application deadline: 3/15. *Faculty research:* Analytical chemistry, medicinal chemistry, organic chemistry, neurochemistry. *Unit head:* Dr. Ahmed Mehanna, Professor, Medicinal Chemistry, 617-732-2955, E-mail: ahmed.mehanna@mcphs.edu. *Application contact:* Brian Barilone, Coordinator of Graduate Admission, 617-879-5032, E-mail: admissions@mcphs.edu.

Massachusetts Institute of Technology, School of Science, Department of Chemistry, Cambridge, MA 02139. Offers biological chemistry (PhD, Sc D); inorganic chemistry (PhD, Sc D); organic chemistry (PhD, Sc D); physical chemistry (PhD, Sc D). *Faculty:* 29 full-time (7 women). *Students:* 227 full-time (78 women); includes 44 minority (5 Black or African American, non-Hispanic/Latino; 1 American Indian or Alaska Native, non-Hispanic/Latino; 27 Asian, non-Hispanic/Latino; 9 Hispanic/Latino; 2 Two or more races, non-Hispanic/Latino), 65 international. Average age 25. 516 applicants, 25% accepted, 55 enrolled. In 2010, 34 doctorates awarded. *Degree requirements:* For doctorate, comprehensive exam, thesis/dissertation, 2 terms as a teaching assistant. *Entrance requirements:* For doctorate, GRE General Test. Additional exam requirements/recommendations for international students: Required—IELTS (minimum score 7); Recommended—TOEFL (minimum score 600 paper-based; 250 computer-based). *Application deadline:* For fall admission, 12/15 for domestic and international students. Application fee: $75. Electronic applications accepted. *Expenses:* Tuition: Full-time $38,940; part-time $605 per unit. Required fees: $272. *Financial support:* In 2010–11, 213 students received support, including 66 fellowships with tuition reimbursements available (averaging $33,072 per year), 123 research assistantships with tuition reimbursements available (averaging $29,440 per year), 38 teaching assistantships with tuition reimbursements available (averaging $31,275 per year); Federal Work-Study, institutionally sponsored loans, scholarships/grants, health care benefits, and unspecified assistantships also available. *Faculty research:* Synthetic organic and inorganic chemistry; biomolecular reactions and structure; multidimensional spectroscopy and chemical dynamics; inorganic, organometallic, and organic chemical catalysis; materials chemistry including surface science, nanoscience and polymers. Total annual research expenditures: $32.1 million. *Unit head:* Prof. Sylvia T. Ceyer, Department Head, 617-253-1803, Fax: 617-258-7500. *Application contact:* Graduate Administrator, 617-253-1845, Fax: 617-258-0241, E-mail: chemgradeducation@mit.edu.

McGill University, Faculty of Graduate and Postdoctoral Studies, Faculty of Science, Department of Chemistry, Montréal, QC H3A 2T5, Canada. Offers chemical biology (M Sc, PhD); chemistry (M Sc, PhD).

McMaster University, School of Graduate Studies, Faculty of Science, Department of Chemistry, Hamilton, ON L8S 4M2, Canada. Offers analytical chemistry (M Sc, PhD); chemical physics (M Sc, PhD); chemistry (M Sc, PhD); inorganic chemistry (M Sc, PhD); organic chemistry (M Sc, PhD); physical chemistry (M Sc, PhD); polymer chemistry (M Sc, PhD). Part-time programs available. Terminal master's awarded for partial completion of doctoral program. *Degree requirements:* For master's, thesis; for doctorate, comprehensive exam, thesis/dissertation. *Entrance requirements:* For master's, minimum B+ average. Additional exam requirements/recommendations for international students: Required—TOEFL (minimum score 550 paper-based; 213 computer-based).

McNeese State University, Doré School of Graduate Studies, College of Science, Department of Chemistry, Program in Environmental and Chemical Sciences, Lake Charles, LA 70609. Offers chemistry (MS); chemistry/environmental science education (MS). Evening/weekend programs available. *Faculty:* 6 full-time (1 woman). *Students:* 12 full-time (6 women), 2 part-time (both women); includes 3 minority (all Black or African American, non-Hispanic/Latino), 8 international. In 2010, 6 master's awarded. *Degree requirements:* For master's, comprehensive exam, thesis or alternative. *Entrance requirements:* For master's, GRE. *Application deadline:* For fall admission, 5/15 priority date for domestic and international students; for spring admission, 10/15 priority date for domestic and international students. Applications are processed on a rolling basis. Application fee: $20 ($30 for international students). Tuition and fees vary according to course load. *Financial support:* Application deadline: 5/1. *Unit head:* Dr. Bruce C. Wyman, Coordinator, 337-475-5669, Fax: 337-475-5677, E-mail: wyman@mcneese.edu. *Application contact:* Dr. Bruce C. Wyman, Coordinator, 337-475-5669, Fax: 337-475-5677, E-mail: wyman@mcneese.edu.

Memorial University of Newfoundland, School of Graduate Studies, Department of Chemistry, St. John's, NL A1C 5S7, Canada. Offers chemistry (M Sc, PhD); instrumental analysis (M Sc). Part-time programs available. *Degree requirements:* For master's, thesis, research seminar, American Chemical Society Exam; for doctorate, comprehensive exam, thesis/dissertation, seminars, oral thesis defense, American Chemical Society Exam. *Entrance requirements:* For master's, B Sc or honors degree in chemistry (preferred); for doctorate, master's degree in chemistry or honors bachelor's degree. Electronic applications accepted. *Faculty research:* Analytical/environmental chemistry; medicinal electrochemistry; inorganic, marine, organic, physical, and theoretical/computational chemistry, environmental science and instrumental analysis.

Miami University, Graduate School, College of Arts and Science, Department of Chemistry and Biochemistry, Oxford, OH 45056. Offers MS, PhD. *Students:* 68 full-time (30 women), 1 part-time (0 women); includes 4 minority (2 Black or African American, non-Hispanic/Latino; 1 Asian, non-Hispanic/Latino; 1 Hispanic/Latino), 35 international. Average age 26. In 2010, 4 master's, 7 doctorates awarded. *Entrance requirements:* For master's, minimum undergraduate GPA of 3.0 during previous 2 years or 2.75 overall; for doctorate, minimum undergraduate GPA of 2.75, 3.0 graduate. Additional exam requirements/recommendations for international students: Required—TOEFL. *Application deadline:* Applications are processed on a rolling basis. Application fee: $50. Electronic applications accepted. *Expenses:* Tuition, state resident: full-time $11,616; part-time $484 per credit hour. Tuition, nonresident: full-time $25,656; part-time $1069 per credit hour. Required fees: $528. *Financial support:* Fellowships with full tuition reimbursements, research assistantships with full tuition reimbursements, teaching assistantships with full tuition reimbursements, Federal Work-Study, institutionally sponsored loans, tuition waivers (full), and unspecified assistantships available. Financial award application deadline: 3/1; financial award applicants required to submit FAFSA. *Unit head:* Dr. Chris Makaroff, Chair, 513-529-1659, E-mail: makaroca@muohio.edu. *Application contact:* Dr. Michael Crowder, Professor, 513-529-7274, E-mail: crowdermw@muohio.edu.

Michigan State University, The Graduate School, College of Natural Science, Department of Chemistry, East Lansing, MI 48824. Offers chemical physics (PhD); chemistry (MS, PhD); chemistry-environmental toxicology (PhD); computational chemistry (MS). *Entrance requirements:* Additional exam requirements/recommendations for international students: Required—TOEFL. Electronic applications accepted. *Faculty research:* Analytical chemistry, inorganic and organic chemistry, nuclear chemistry, physical chemistry, theoretical and computational chemistry.

Michigan State University, National Superconducting Cyclotron Laboratory, East Lansing, MI 48824. Offers chemistry (PhD); physics (PhD).

Michigan Technological University, Graduate School, College of Sciences and Arts, Department of Chemistry, Houghton, MI 49931. Offers MS, PhD. Part-time programs available. Terminal master's awarded for partial completion of doctoral program. *Degree requirements:* For master's, thesis; for doctorate, comprehensive exam, thesis/dissertation. *Entrance requirements:* Additional exam requirements/recommendations for international students: Required—TOEFL (minimum score 550 paper-based; 213 computer-based). Electronic applica-

tions accepted. *Faculty research:* Inorganic chemistry, physical/theoretical chemistry, bio/organic chemistry, polymer/materials chemistry, analytical/environmental chemistry.

Middle Tennessee State University, College of Graduate Studies, College of Basic and Applied Sciences, Department of Chemistry, Murfreesboro, TN 37132. Offers MS, DA. Part-time and evening/weekend programs available. Postbaccalaureate distance learning degree programs offered. *Faculty:* 21 full-time (8 women). *Students:* 29 part-time (13 women); includes 4 Black or African American, non-Hispanic/Latino; 8 Asian, non-Hispanic/Latino. Average age 28. 26 applicants, 42% accepted, 11 enrolled. In 2010, 3 master's, 1 doctorate awarded. *Degree requirements:* For master's, one foreign language, comprehensive exam, thesis. *Entrance requirements:* For master's and doctorate, GRE General Test. Additional exam requirements/recommendations for international students: Required—TOEFL (minimum score 525 paper-based; 195 computer-based; 71 iBT) or IELTS (minimum score 6). *Application deadline:* For fall admission, 6/1 for domestic and international students. Applications are processed on a rolling basis. Application fee: $25 ($30 for international students). Electronic applications accepted. *Expenses:* Tuition, state resident: full-time $4632. Tuition, nonresident: full-time $11,520. *Financial support:* In 2010–11, 25 students received support. Institutionally sponsored loans available. Support available to part-time students. Financial award application deadline: 5/1; financial award applicants required to submit FAFSA. *Faculty research:* Chemical education; computational chemistry and visualization; materials science and surface modifications; biochemistry, antibiotics and leukemia; environmental chemistry and toxicology. *Unit head:* Dr. Preston J. MacDougall, Interim Chair, 615-898-2956, Fax: 615-898-5182, E-mail: pmacdoug@mtsu.edu. *Application contact:* Dr. Michael Allen, Dean and Vice Provost for Research, 615-898-2840, Fax: 615-904-8020, E-mail: mallen@mtsu.edu.

Mississippi College, Graduate School, College of Arts and Sciences, School of Science and Mathematics, Department of Chemistry and Biochemistry, Clinton, MS 39058. Offers MCS, MS. Part-time programs available. *Degree requirements:* For master's, comprehensive exam, thesis (for some programs). *Entrance requirements:* For master's, GRE. Additional exam requirements/recommendations for international students: Recommended—IELTS. Electronic applications accepted.

Mississippi State University, College of Arts and Sciences, Department of Chemistry, Mississippi State, MS 39762. Offers chemistry (MS, PhD); interdisciplinary sciences (MA), including chemistry. MA program is only available online. *Faculty:* 12 full-time (0 women), 1 part-time adjunct (0 women). *Students:* 50 full-time (16 women), 7 part-time (1 woman); includes 2 minority (1 Black or African American, non-Hispanic/Latino; 1 Asian, non-Hispanic/Latino), 41 international. Average age 30. 116 applicants, 10% accepted, 10 enrolled. In 2010, 3 doctorates awarded. Terminal master's awarded for partial completion of doctoral program. *Degree requirements:* For master's, thesis, comprehensive oral or written exam; for doctorate, thesis/dissertation, comprehensive oral or written exam. *Entrance requirements:* For master's, minimum GPA of 2.75 on last two years of undergraduate courses; for doctorate, minimum GPA of 2.75. Additional exam requirements/recommendations for international students: Required—TOEFL (minimum score 475 paper-based; 153 computer-based). *Application deadline:* For fall admission, 7/1 for domestic students, 5/1 for international students; for spring admission, 11/1 for domestic students, 9/1 for international students. Applications are processed on a rolling basis. Application fee: $40. Electronic applications accepted. *Expenses:* Tuition, state resident: full-time $2730.50; part-time $304 per credit hour. Tuition, nonresident: full-time $6901; part-time $767 per credit hour. *Financial support:* In 2010–11, 9 research assistantships with full tuition reimbursements (averaging $16,835 per year), 41 teaching assistantships with full tuition reimbursements (averaging $17,092 per year) were awarded; Federal Work-Study, institutionally sponsored loans, scholarships/grants, and unspecified assistantships also available. Financial award application deadline: 4/1; financial award applicants required to submit FAFSA. *Faculty research:* Spectroscopy, fluorometry, organic and inorganic synthesis, electrochemistry. Total annual research expenditures: $4.8 million. *Unit head:* Dr. Edwin A. Lewis, Department Head, 662-325-3584, Fax: 662-325-1618, E-mail: elewis@chemistry.msstate.edu. *Application contact:* Dr. Stephen Foster, Graduate Coordinator, 662-325-8854, E-mail: grad@chemistry.msstate.edu.

Missouri State University, Graduate College, College of Natural and Applied Sciences, Department of Chemistry, Springfield, MO 65897. Offers chemistry (MS); natural and applied science (MNAS), including chemistry (MNAS, MS Ed); secondary education (MS Ed), including chemistry (MNAS, MS Ed). Part-time programs available. *Degree requirements:* For master's, comprehensive exam, thesis. *Entrance requirements:* For master's, GRE General Test (MS, MNAS), minimum undergraduate GPA of 3.0 (MS and MNAS), 9-12 teacher certification (MS Ed). Additional exam requirements/recommendations for international students: Required—TOEFL (minimum score 550 paper-based; 213 computer-based; 79 iBT). Electronic applications accepted. *Expenses:* Tuition, state resident: full-time $3348; part-time $186 per credit hour. Tuition, nonresident: full-time $6696; part-time $372 per credit hour. Required fees: $238 per semester. Tuition and fees vary according to course level, course load and program. *Faculty research:* Polyethylene glycol derivatives, electrochemiluminescence of environmental systems, enzymology, environmental organic pollutants, DNA repair via NMR.

Missouri University of Science and Technology, Graduate School, Department of Chemistry, Rolla, MO 65409. Offers MS, MST, PhD. Terminal master's awarded for partial completion of doctoral program. *Degree requirements:* For doctorate, one foreign language, thesis/dissertation. *Entrance requirements:* For master's, GRE (minimum score 600 quantitative, 3 writing), minimum GPA of 3.0; for doctorate, GRE (minimum score: quantitative 600, writing 3.5), minimum GPA of 3.0. Additional exam requirements/recommendations for international students: Required—TOEFL (minimum score 550 paper-based; 213 computer-based). Electronic applications accepted. *Faculty research:* Structure and properties of materials; bioanalytical, environmental, and polymer chemistry.

Missouri Western State University, Program in Applied Science, St. Joseph, MO 64507-2294. Offers chemistry (MAS); engineering technology management (MAS); human factors and usability testing (MAS); information technology management (MAS). *Expenses:* Tuition, state resident: full-time $5544; part-time $308 per credit hour. Tuition, nonresident: full-time $10,206; part-time $567 per credit hour. Required fees: $30 per semester. One-time fee: $45 full-time.

Montana State University, College of Graduate Studies, College of Letters and Science, Department of Chemistry and Biochemistry, Bozeman, MT 59717. Offers biochemistry (MS, PhD); chemistry (MS, PhD). Part-time programs available. *Faculty:* 16 full-time (3 women), 14 part-time/adjunct (7 women). *Students:* 2 full-time (0 women), 71 part-time (25 women); includes 6 minority (1 Black or African American, non-Hispanic/Latino; 3 Asian, non-Hispanic/Latino; 2 Two or more races, non-Hispanic/Latino), 9 international. Average age 27. 42 applicants, 74% accepted, 17 enrolled. In 2010, 3 master's, 8 doctorates awarded. *Degree requirements:* For master's, comprehensive exam, thesis (for some programs); for doctorate, comprehensive exam, thesis/dissertation. *Entrance requirements:* For master's and doctorate, GRE General Test, transcripts, letter of recommendation. Additional exam requirements/recommendations for international students: Required—TOEFL (minimum score 550 paper-based; 213 computer-based), GRE Subject Test. *Application deadline:* For fall admission, 7/15 priority date for domestic students, 5/15 priority date for international students; for spring admission, 12/1 priority date for domestic students, 10/1 priority date for international students. Applications are processed on a rolling basis. Application fee: $30. Electronic applications accepted. *Expenses:* Tuition, state resident: full-time $5553.90. Tuition, nonresident: full-time $14,646. Required fees: $1233. *Financial support:* In 2010–11, 70 students received support, including 4 fellowships with tuition reimbursements available (averaging $22,000 per year), 31 research assistantships with tuition reimbursements available (averaging $22,000 per year), 35 teaching assistantships with tuition reimbursements available (averaging $22,000 per year); tuition waivers (full) and federal loans also available. Financial award application deadline:

3/1; financial award applicants required to submit FAFSA. *Faculty research:* Proteomics, nano-materials chemistry, computational chemistry, optical spectroscopy, photochemistry. Total annual research expenditures: $12.3 million. *Unit head:* Dr. David Singel, Interim Department Head, 406-994-3960, Fax: 406-994-5407, E-mail: rchds@montana.edu. *Application contact:* Dr. Carl A. Fox, Vice Provost for Graduate Education, 406-994-4145, Fax: 406-994-7433, E-mail: gradstudy@montana.edu.

Montclair State University, The Graduate School, College of Science and Mathematics, Department of Chemistry and Biochemistry, Montclair, NJ 07043-1624. Offers chemistry (MS, Certificate), including biochemistry (MS), chemical business (MS), chemistry (MS); pharmaceutical biochemistry (MS); MS/MBA. Part-time and evening/weekend programs available. *Faculty:* 14 full-time (2 women), 4 part-time/adjunct (3 women). *Students:* 16 full-time (9 women), 27 part-time (14 women); includes 3 Black or African American, non-Hispanic/Latino; 4 Asian, non-Hispanic/Latino; 4 Hispanic/Latino, 5 international. Average age 28. 23 applicants, 65% accepted, 12 enrolled. In 2010, 6 master's awarded. *Degree requirements:* For master's, comprehensive exam. *Entrance requirements:* For master's, GRE General Test, 24 credits of course work in undergraduate chemistry, 2 letters of recommendation. Additional exam requirements/recommendations for international students: Required—TOEFL (minimum score 83 iBT) or IELTS. *Application deadline:* For fall admission, 6/1 for international students; for spring admission, 10/1 for international students. Applications are processed on a rolling basis. Application fee: $60. Electronic applications accepted. *Expenses:* Tuition, state resident: part-time $501.34 per credit. Tuition, nonresident: part-time $773.88 per credit. Required fees: $71.15 per credit. *Financial support:* In 2010–11, 8 research assistantships with full tuition reimbursements (averaging $7,000 per year) were awarded; Federal Work-Study, scholarships/grants, and unspecified assistantships also available. Support available to part-time students. Financial award application deadline: 3/1; financial award applicants required to submit FAFSA. *Faculty research:* Antimicrobial compounds, marine bacteria. *Unit head:* Dr. Marc Kasner, Chair, 973-655-6864. *Application contact:* Amy Aiello, Director of Graduate Admissions and Operations, 973-655-5147, E-mail: graduate.school@montclair.edu.

Morgan State University, School of Graduate Studies, School of Computer, Mathematical, and Natural Sciences, Department of Chemistry, Baltimore, MD 21251. Offers MS. *Degree requirements:* For master's, comprehensive exam, thesis, oral defense of thesis. *Entrance requirements:* For master's, GRE General Test, minimum GPA of 2.5.

Mount Allison University, Department of Chemistry, Sackville, NB E4L 1E4, Canada. Offers M Sc. *Degree requirements:* For master's, thesis. *Entrance requirements:* For master's, honors degree in chemistry. *Faculty research:* Biophysical chemistry of model biomembranes, organic synthesis, fast-reaction kinetics, physical chemistry of micelles.

Murray State University, College of Science, Engineering and Technology, Program in Chemistry, Murray, KY 42071. Offers MS. Part-time programs available. *Degree requirements:* For master's, comprehensive exam (for some programs), thesis (for some programs). *Entrance requirements:* For master's, GRE General Test. Additional exam requirements/recommendations for international students: Required—TOEFL. *Faculty research:* Environmental, organic, biochemistry, analytical.

New Jersey Institute of Technology, Office of Graduate Studies, College of Science and Liberal Arts, Department of Chemistry and Environmental Science, Program in Chemistry, Newark, NJ 07102. Offers MS, PhD. Part-time and evening/weekend programs available. *Students:* 39 full-time (24 women), 9 part-time (5 women); includes 1 Black or African American, non-Hispanic/Latino; 4 Asian, non-Hispanic/Latino; 2 Hispanic/Latino, 33 international. Average age 27. 84 applicants, 25% accepted, 13 enrolled. In 2010, 7 master's, 1 doctorate awarded. Terminal master's awarded for partial completion of doctoral program. *Degree requirements:* For master's, thesis optional; for doctorate, thesis/dissertation. *Entrance requirements:* For master's, GRE General Test; for doctorate, GRE General Test, minimum graduate GPA of 3.5. Additional exam requirements/recommendations for international students: Required—TOEFL (minimum score 550 paper-based; 213 computer-based; 79 iBT). *Application deadline:* For fall admission, 6/5 priority date for domestic students, 4/1 for international students; for spring admission, 11/15 for domestic and international students. Applications are processed on a rolling basis. Application fee: $65. Electronic applications accepted. *Expenses:* Tuition, state resident: full-time $14,724; part-time $818 per credit. Tuition, nonresident: full-time $20,304; part-time $1128 per credit. Required fees: $2272; $209 per credit. $103 per semester. One-time fee: $312 full-time; $212 part-time. *Financial support:* Fellowships with full and partial tuition reimbursements, research assistantships with full and partial tuition reimbursements, teaching assistantships with full and partial tuition reimbursements, career-related internships or fieldwork, Federal Work-Study, institutionally sponsored loans, and unspecified assistantships available. Financial award application deadline: 3/15. *Faculty research:* Medical instrumentation, prosthesis design, biodegradation of hazardous waste, orthopedic biomechanics, image processing. *Unit head:* Dr. Somenath Mitra, Chair, 973-596-5611, E-mail: somenath.mitra@njit.edu. *Application contact:* Kathryn Kelly, Director of Admissions, 973-596-3300, Fax: 973-596-3461, E-mail: admissions@njit.edu.

New Mexico Highlands University, Graduate Studies, College of Arts and Sciences, Department of Natural Sciences, Las Vegas, NM 87701. Offers chemistry (MS); life science (MS). Part-time programs available. *Faculty:* 21 full-time (10 women). *Students:* 23 full-time (8 women), 11 part-time (6 women); includes 1 American Indian or Alaska Native, non-Hispanic/Latino; 20 Hispanic/Latino, 11 international. Average age 28. 14 applicants, 93% accepted, 7 enrolled. In 2010, 4 master's awarded. *Degree requirements:* For master's, comprehensive exam, thesis. *Entrance requirements:* For master's, minimum undergraduate GPA of 3.0. Additional exam requirements/recommendations for international students: Required—TOEFL (minimum score 540 paper-based; 207 computer-based). *Application deadline:* For fall admission, 8/1 priority date for domestic students. Applications are processed on a rolling basis. Application fee: $15. *Expenses:* Tuition, state resident: full-time $2544. Required fees: $624; $132 per credit hour. *Financial support:* In 2010–11, 17 students received support. Career-related internships or fieldwork, Federal Work-Study, institutionally sponsored loans, scholarships/grants, tuition waivers (full and partial), and unspecified assistantships available. Support available to part-time students. Financial award application deadline: 3/1. *Faculty research:* Invasive organisms in managed and wildland ecosystems, juniper and pinyon ecology and management, vegetation and community structure, big game management, quantitative forestry. *Unit head:* Dr. Mary Shaw, Department Head, 505-454-3407, E-mail: shaw_mary@nmhu.edu. *Application contact:* Diane Trujillo, Administrative Assistant, Graduate Studies, 505-454-3266, Fax: 505-426-2117, E-mail: dtrujillo@nmhu.edu.

New Mexico Institute of Mining and Technology, Graduate Studies, Department of Chemistry, Socorro, NM 87801. Offers biochemistry (MS); chemistry (MS); environmental chemistry (PhD); explosives technology and atmospheric chemistry (PhD). Part-time programs available. *Degree requirements:* For master's, thesis; for doctorate, thesis/dissertation. *Entrance requirements:* For master's, GRE General Test; for doctorate, GRE General Test, GRE Subject Test. Additional exam requirements/recommendations for international students: Required—TOEFL (minimum score 540 paper-based; 207 computer-based). Electronic applications accepted. *Faculty research:* Organic, analytical, environmental, and explosives chemistry.

New Mexico State University, Graduate School, College of Arts and Sciences, Department of Chemistry and Biochemistry, Las Cruces, NM 88003-8001. Offers chemistry (MS, PhD). Part-time programs available. *Faculty:* 14 full-time (3 women), 1 (woman) part-time/adjunct. *Students:* 48 full-time (11 women), 3 part-time (0 women); includes 8 minority (1 Black or African American, non-Hispanic/Latino; 1 American Indian or Alaska Native, non-Hispanic/Latino; 1 Asian, non-Hispanic/Latino; 5 Hispanic/Latino), 36 international. Average age 29. 61 applicants, 97% accepted, 17 enrolled. In 2010, 8 master's, 4 doctorates awarded. *Degree requirements:* For master's, comprehensive exam, thesis; for doctorate, comprehensive exam, thesis/dissertation. *Entrance requirements:* For master's and doctorate, GRE, BS in chemistry or biochemistry, minimum GPA of 3.0. Additional exam requirements/recommendations for international students: Required—TOEFL (minimum score 600 paper-based; 250 computer-based). *Application deadline:* For fall admission, 7/1 priority date for domestic students, 3/1 priority date for international students; for spring admission, 11/1 for domestic students. Applications are processed on a rolling basis. Application fee: $30 ($50 for international students). Electronic applications accepted. *Expenses:* Tuition, state resident: full-time $4536; part-time $242 per credit. Tuition, nonresident: full-time $15,816; part-time $712 per credit. Required fees: $636 per term. *Financial support:* In 2010–11, 17 research assistantships with tuition reimbursements (averaging $13,247 per year), 29 teaching assistantships with tuition reimbursements (averaging $16,454 per year) were awarded; fellowships with tuition reimbursements, career-related internships or fieldwork, Federal Work-Study, and health care benefits also available. Support available to part-time students. Financial award application deadline: 4/1. *Faculty research:* Clays, surfaces, and water structure; electroanalytical and environmental chemistry; organometallic synthesis and organobiomimetics; molecular genetics, DNA recombination mechanisms, and NMR spectroscopy of protein interactions; spectroscopy and reaction kinetics. *Unit head:* Dr. Glenn D. Kuehn, Head, 575-646-5877, Fax: 575-646-2649, E-mail: gkuehn@nmsu.edu. *Application contact:* Dr. Cynthia Zoski, Associate Professor, Chemistry, 575-646-5292, Fax: 575-646-2649, E-mail: czoski@nmsu.edu.

New York University, Graduate School of Arts and Science, Department of Chemistry, New York, NY 10012-1019. Offers MS, PhD. *Faculty:* 23 full-time (1 woman). *Students:* 95 full-time (38 women), 6 part-time (4 women); includes 1 Black or African American, non-Hispanic/Latino; 3 Asian, non-Hispanic/Latino; 5 Hispanic/Latino, 70 international. Average age 28. 156 applicants, 35% accepted, 16 enrolled. In 2010, 14 master's, 15 doctorates awarded. *Degree requirements:* For master's, thesis or alternative; for doctorate, one foreign language, thesis/dissertation. *Entrance requirements:* For master's and doctorate, GRE General Test, GRE Subject Test. Additional exam requirements/recommendations for international students: Required—TOEFL. *Application deadline:* For fall admission, 12/15 for domestic students. Application fee: $90. *Financial support:* Fellowships with tuition reimbursements, research assistantships with tuition reimbursements, teaching assistantships with tuition reimbursements, career-related internships or fieldwork, Federal Work-Study, institutionally sponsored loans, scholarships/grants, health care benefits, and unspecified assistantships available. Financial award application deadline: 12/15; financial award applicants required to submit FAFSA. *Faculty research:* Biomolecular chemistry, theoretical and computational chemistry, physical chemistry, nanotechnology, bio-organic chemistry. *Unit head:* Michael Ward, Chair, 212-998-8400, Fax: 212-260-7905, E-mail: grad.chem@nyu.edu. *Application contact:* Marcus Weck, Director of Graduate Studies, 212-998-8400, Fax: 212-260-7905, E-mail: grad.chem@nyu.edu.

North Carolina Agricultural and Technical State University, Graduate School, College of Arts and Sciences, Department of Chemistry, Greensboro, NC 27411. Offers MS. Part-time and evening/weekend programs available. *Degree requirements:* For master's, comprehensive exam, thesis or alternative, qualifying exam. *Entrance requirements:* For master's, GRE General Test, minimum GPA of 3.0. *Faculty research:* Tobacco pesticides.

North Carolina Central University, Division of Academic Affairs, College of Science and Technology, Department of Chemistry, Durham, NC 27707-3129. Offers MS. *Degree requirements:* For master's, one foreign language, comprehensive exam, thesis. *Entrance requirements:* For master's, GRE, minimum GPA of 3.0 in major, 2.5 overall. Additional exam requirements/recommendations for international students: Required—TOEFL.

North Carolina State University, Graduate School, College of Physical and Mathematical Sciences, Department of Chemistry, Raleigh, NC 27695. Offers MS, PhD. Part-time programs available. Terminal master's awarded for partial completion of doctoral program. *Degree requirements:* For master's, thesis (for some programs); for doctorate, thesis/dissertation. *Entrance requirements:* For master's and doctorate, GRE General Test (recommended). Electronic applications accepted. *Faculty research:* Biological chemistry, electrochemistry, organic/inorganic materials, natural products, organometallics.

North Dakota State University, College of Graduate and Interdisciplinary Studies, College of Science and Mathematics, Department of Biochemistry and Molecular Biology, Program in Chemistry, Fargo, ND 58108. Offers MS, PhD. *Students:* 32 full-time (11 women), 2 part-time (1 woman); includes 2 Asian, non-Hispanic/Latino; 1 Two or more races, non-Hispanic/Latino, 16 international. 38 applicants, 45% accepted, 12 enrolled. In 2010, 1 master's, 5 doctorates awarded. *Unit head:* Dr. John Hershberger, Chair, 701-231-7678, Fax: 701-231-8831, E-mail: john.hershberger@ndsu.edu. *Application contact:* Dr. Seth Rasmussen, Chair, Graduate Admissions, 701-231-8747, Fax: 701-231-8831, E-mail: seth.rasmussen@ndsu.edu.

Northeastern Illinois University, Graduate College, College of Arts and Sciences, Department of Chemistry, Program in Chemistry, Chicago, IL 60625-4699. Offers MS. Part-time and evening/weekend programs available. *Faculty:* 7 full-time (2 women), 4 part-time/adjunct (0 women). *Students:* 9 full-time (1 woman), 3 part-time (0 women); includes 5 minority (3 Black or African American, non-Hispanic/Latino; 2 Asian, non-Hispanic/Latino), 2 international. Average age 35. 11 applicants, 100% accepted. In 2010, 6 master's awarded. *Degree requirements:* For master's, comprehensive exam, final exam or thesis. *Entrance requirements:* For master's, 2 semesters of chemistry, calculus, organic chemistry, physical chemistry, and physics; 1 semester analytic chemistry; minimum GPA of 2.75. Additional exam requirements/recommendations for international students: Required—TOEFL (minimum score 550 paper-based; 213 computer-based; 79 iBT). *Application deadline:* For fall admission, 4/1 priority date for domestic students; for spring admission, 8/15 for domestic students. Applications are processed on a rolling basis. Application fee: $25. Electronic applications accepted. *Financial support:* In 2010–11, 9 students received support, including 2 research assistantships with full tuition reimbursements available (averaging $6,600 per year); career-related internships or fieldwork, Federal Work-Study, institutionally sponsored loans, and tuition waivers (full and partial) also available. Support available to part-time students. Financial award applicants required to submit FAFSA. *Faculty research:* Liquid chromatographic separation of pharmaceuticals, Diels-Alder reaction products, organogermanium chemistry, mass spectroscopy.

Northeastern University, College of Science, Department of Chemistry and Chemical Biology, Boston, MA 02115-5096. Offers analytical chemistry (PhD); chemistry (MS, PhD); inorganic chemistry (PhD); organic chemistry (PhD); physical chemistry (PhD). Part-time and evening/weekend programs available. *Faculty:* 24 full-time (5 women), 7 part-time/adjunct (0 women). *Students:* 98 full-time (58 women), 31 part-time (15 women). 190 applicants, 32% accepted, 34 enrolled. In 2010, 16 master's, 6 doctorates awarded. Terminal master's awarded for partial completion of doctoral program. *Degree requirements:* For master's, thesis (for some programs); for doctorate, thesis/dissertation, qualifying exam in specialty area. *Entrance requirements:* Additional exam requirements/recommendations for international students: Required—TOEFL. *Application deadline:* For fall admission, 2/1 priority date for domestic and international students. Applications are processed on a rolling basis. Application fee: $50. Electronic applications accepted. *Financial support:* In 2010–11, 41 research assistantships with tuition reimbursements (averaging $18,285 per year), 38 teaching assistantships with tuition reimbursements (averaging $18,285 per year) were awarded; fellowships with tuition reimbursements, career-related internships or fieldwork, Federal Work-Study, scholarships/grants, tuition waivers (partial), and unspecified assistantships also available. Financial award application deadline: 3/1; financial award applicants required to submit FAFSA. *Faculty research:* Bioanalysis, biorganic and medicinal chemistry, biophysical chemistry, nanomaterials, proteomics. *Unit head:* Dr. Robert Hanson, Graduate Coordinator, 617-373-3313, Fax: 617-373-8795, E-mail: chemistry-grad-

Chemistry

Northeastern University (continued)

info@neu.edu. *Application contact:* Jo-Anne Dickinson, Admissions Contact, 617-373-5990, Fax: 617-373-7281, E-mail: gsas@neu.edu.

Northern Arizona University, Graduate College, College of Engineering, Forestry and Natural Sciences, Department of Chemistry and Biochemistry, Flagstaff, AZ 86011. Offers chemistry (MS). Part-time programs available. *Faculty:* 15 full-time (8 women). *Students:* 14 full-time (8 women), 2 part-time (1 woman); includes 5 minority (3 American Indian or Alaska Native, non-Hispanic/Latino; 2 Hispanic/Latino), 2 international. Average age 27. 10 applicants, 60% accepted, 5 enrolled. In 2010, 3 master's awarded. *Degree requirements:* For master's, thesis. *Entrance requirements:* For master's, minimum GPA of 3.0. Additional exam requirements/recommendations for international students: Required—TOEFL (minimum score 550 paper-based; 213 computer-based; 80 iBT), IELTS (minimum score 7). *Application deadline:* For fall admission, 3/1 priority date for domestic and international students; for spring admission, 10/1 priority date for domestic and international students. Applications are processed on a rolling basis. Application fee: $65. Electronic applications accepted. *Financial support:* In 2010–11, 6 research assistantships with partial tuition reimbursements (averaging $9,874 per year), 12 teaching assistantships with partial tuition reimbursements (averaging $12,390 per year) were awarded; Federal Work-Study, scholarships/grants, health care benefits, tuition waivers (full and partial), and unspecified assistantships also available. Financial award applicants required to submit FAFSA. *Faculty research:* Biochemistry of exercise, organic and inorganic mechanism studies, inhibition of ice mutation, polymer separation. Total annual research expenditures: $261,191. *Unit head:* Dr. Cindy Browder, Chair, 928-523-9062, E-mail: cindy.browder@nau.edu. *Application contact:* Julie Gillette, Administrative Associate, 928-523-7079, Fax: 928-523-8111, E-mail: chemistry@nau.edu.

Northern Illinois University, Graduate School, College of Liberal Arts and Sciences, Department of Chemistry and Biochemistry, De Kalb, IL 60115-2854. Offers chemistry (MS, PhD). *Faculty:* 16 full-time (1 woman), 3 part-time/adjunct (1 woman). *Students:* 40 full-time (20 women), 3 part-time (0 women); includes 1 Black or African American, non-Hispanic/Latino; 2 Asian, non-Hispanic/Latino; 1 Hispanic/Latino, 14 international. Average age 27. 59 applicants, 39% accepted, 5 enrolled. In 2010, 10 master's, 12 doctorates awarded. Terminal master's awarded for partial completion of doctoral program. *Degree requirements:* For master's, comprehensive exam, thesis optional, research seminar; for doctorate, one foreign language, thesis/dissertation, candidacy exam, dissertation defense, research seminar. *Entrance requirements:* For master's, GRE General Test, bachelor's degree in mathematics or science, minimum GPA of 2.75; for doctorate, GRE General Test, bachelor's degree in mathematics or science; minimum undergraduate GPA of 2.75, 3.2 graduate. Additional exam requirements/recommendations for international students: Required—TOEFL (minimum score 550 paper-based; 213 computer-based). *Application deadline:* For fall admission, 6/1 for domestic students, 5/1 for international students; for spring admission, 11/1 for domestic students, 10/1 for international students. Applications are processed on a rolling basis. Application fee: $30. Electronic applications accepted. *Expenses:* Tuition, state resident: full-time $7200; part-time $300 per credit hour. Tuition, nonresident: full-time $14,400; part-time $600 per credit hour. Required fees: $79 per credit hour. *Financial support:* In 2010–11, 8 research assistantships with full tuition reimbursements, 31 teaching assistantships with full tuition reimbursements were awarded; fellowships with full tuition reimbursements, career-related internships or fieldwork, Federal Work-Study, scholarships/grants, tuition waivers (full), and unspecified assistantships also available. Support available to part-time students. Financial award applicants required to submit FAFSA. *Faculty research:* Viscoelastic properties of polymers, lig and buding tocytochrome coxidases, computational inorganic chemistry, chemistry of organosilanes. *Unit head:* Dr. Jon Carnahan, Chair, 815-753-1181, Fax: 815-753-4802, E-mail: carnahan@niu.edu. *Application contact:* Dr. Jon Carnahan, Chair, 815-753-1181, Fax: 815-753-4802, E-mail: carnahan@niu.edu.

Northwestern University, The Graduate School, Judd A. and Marjorie Weinberg College of Arts and Sciences, Department of Chemistry, Evanston, IL 60208. Offers PhD. Admissions and degrees offered through The Graduate School. *Degree requirements:* For doctorate, thesis/dissertation. *Entrance requirements:* For doctorate, GRE General Test, GRE Subject Test (chemistry). Additional exam requirements/recommendations for international students: Required—TOEFL. Electronic applications accepted. *Faculty research:* Inorganic, organic, physical, environmental, materials, and chemistry of life processes.

Oakland University, Graduate Study and Lifelong Learning, College of Arts and Sciences, Department of Chemistry, Rochester, MI 48309-4401. Offers biological sciences: health and environmental chemistry (PhD); chemistry (MS). *Degree requirements:* For master's, thesis; for doctorate, thesis/dissertation. *Entrance requirements:* For master's, minimum GPA of 3.0 for unconditional admission; for doctorate, GRE Subject Test, minimum GPA of 3.0 for unconditional admission. Additional exam requirements/recommendations for international students: Required—TOEFL (minimum score 550 paper-based; 213 computer-based). Electronic applications accepted. *Faculty research:* Chemistry of free radical species generated from biological intermediates; fate of toxic organic compounds in the environment; electroanalytical and surface chemistry at solid/liquid interface; computational modeling of intermolecular interactions and surface phenomena; metabolism and biological activity of modified fatty acids and xenobiotic carboxylic acids; physiologic and pathologic mechanisms that modulate immune responses.

The Ohio State University, Graduate School, College of Arts and Sciences, Division of Natural and Mathematical Sciences, Department of Chemistry, Columbus, OH 43210. Offers MS, PhD. *Faculty:* 39. *Students:* 63 full-time (23 women), 143 part-time (55 women); includes 6 Black or African American, non-Hispanic/Latino; 1 American Indian or Alaska Native, non-Hispanic/Latino; 7 Asian, non-Hispanic/Latino; 2 Hispanic/Latino; 2 Two or more races, non-Hispanic/Latino, 92 international. Average age 26. In 2010, 18 master's, 37 doctorates awarded. *Degree requirements:* For master's, thesis optional; for doctorate, thesis/dissertation. *Entrance requirements:* For master's and doctorate, GRE General Test, GRE Subject Test (chemistry). Additional exam requirements/recommendations for international students: Required—TOEFL (minimum score 600 paper-based; 250 computer-based). *Application deadline:* For fall admission, 8/15 priority date for domestic students, 7/1 priority date for international students; for winter admission, 12/1 priority date for domestic students, 11/1 priority date for international students; for spring admission, 3/1 priority date for domestic students, 2/1 priority date for international students. Applications are processed on a rolling basis. Application fee: $40 ($50 for international students). Electronic applications accepted. *Expenses:* Tuition, state resident: full-time $10,605. Tuition, nonresident: full-time $26,535. Tuition and fees vary according to course load and program. *Financial support:* Fellowships, research assistantships, teaching assistantships, Federal Work-Study and institutionally sponsored loans available. Support available to part-time students. *Unit head:* Malcolm Chisholm, Chair, 614-292-3979, E-mail: chair@chemistry.ohio-state.edu. *Application contact:* 614-292-9444, Fax: 614-292-3895, E-mail: domestic.grad@osu.edu.

Oklahoma State University, College of Arts and Sciences, Department of Chemistry, Stillwater, OK 74078. Offers MS, PhD. *Faculty:* 21 full-time (1 woman), 1 (woman) part-time/adjunct. *Students:* 7 full-time (2 women), 47 part-time (20 women); includes 2 Black or African American, non-Hispanic/Latino; 1 Hispanic/Latino, 33 international. Average age 29. 98 applicants, 18% accepted, 7 enrolled. In 2010, 1 master's, 6 doctorates awarded. *Degree requirements:* For master's, thesis; for doctorate, comprehensive exam, thesis/dissertation. *Entrance requirements:* For master's and doctorate, GRE or GMAT. Additional exam requirements/recommendations for international students: Required—TOEFL (minimum score 550 paper-based; 79 iBT). *Application deadline:* For fall admission, 3/1 priority date for international students; for spring admission, 8/1 priority date for international students. Applications are processed on a rolling basis. Application fee: $40 ($75 for international students). Electronic applications accepted. *Expenses:* Tuition, state resident: full-time $3716; part-time $154.85 per credit hour. Tuition, nonresident: full-time $14,892; part-time $621 per credit hour. Required fees: $2044; $85.20 per credit hour. One-time fee: $50. Tuition and fees vary according to course load and campus/location. *Financial support:* In 2010–11, 21 research assistantships (averaging $18,254 per year), 33 teaching assistantships (averaging $18,826 per year) were awarded; career-related internships or fieldwork, Federal Work-Study, scholarships/grants, health care benefits, tuition waivers (partial), and unspecified assistantships also available. Support available to part-time students. Financial award application deadline: 3/1; financial award applicants required to submit FAFSA. *Faculty research:* Materials science, surface chemistry, and nanoparticles; theoretical physical chemistry; synthetic and medicinal chemistry; bioanalytical chemistry; electromagnetic (UV, VIS, IR, Raman), mass, and x-ray spectroscopes. *Unit head:* Dr. Jeffery L. White, Interim Head, 405-744-5920, Fax: 405-744-6007. *Application contact:* Dr. Gordon Emslie, Dean, 405-744-6368, Fax: 405-744-0355, E-mail: grad-i@okstate.edu.

Old Dominion University, College of Sciences, Program in Chemistry, Norfolk, VA 23529. Offers analytical chemistry (MS); biochemistry (MS); chemistry (PhD); environmental chemistry (MS); organic chemistry (MS); physical chemistry (MS). Part-time and evening/weekend programs available. *Faculty:* 14 full-time (5 women), 2 part-time/adjunct (0 women). *Students:* 36 full-time (22 women), 1 part-time (0 women); includes 3 minority (1 Black or African American, non-Hispanic/Latino; 1 Asian, non-Hispanic/Latino; 1 Hispanic/Latino), 16 international. Average age 29. 35 applicants, 60% accepted, 8 enrolled. In 2010, 6 master's, 2 doctorates awarded. *Degree requirements:* For master's, comprehensive exam, thesis. *Entrance requirements:* For master's, GRE General Test, minimum GPA of 3.0 in major, 2.5 overall; for doctorate, GRE General Test. Additional exam requirements/recommendations for international students: Required—TOEFL. *Application deadline:* For fall admission, 7/1 for domestic students, 1/15 for international students; for spring admission, 11/1 for domestic students, 8/15 for international students. Applications are processed on a rolling basis. Application fee: $30. Electronic applications accepted. *Expenses:* Tuition, state resident: full-time $8592; part-time $358 per credit. Tuition, nonresident: full-time $21,672; part-time $903 per credit. Required fees: $119 per semester. One-time fee: $50. *Financial support:* In 2010–11, 6 students received support, including fellowships (averaging $18,000 per year), research assistantships with tuition reimbursements available (averaging $21,000 per year), teaching assistantships with tuition reimbursements available (averaging $18,000 per year); career-related internships or fieldwork, scholarships/grants, and unspecified assistantships also available. Financial award application deadline: 2/15; financial award applicants required to submit FAFSA. *Faculty research:* Biogeochemistry, materials chemistry, bioanalytical chemistry, computational chemistry, organic chemistry. Total annual research expenditures: $2.6 million. *Unit head:* Dr. Craig A. Bayse, Graduate Program Director, 757-683-4097, Fax: 757-683-4628, E-mail: chemgpd@odu.edu. *Application contact:* Valerie DeCosta, Grants and Graduate Program Assistant, 757-683-6979, Fax: 757-683-4628, E-mail: chemgpd@odu.edu.

Old Dominion University, Darden College of Education, Programs in Secondary Education, Norfolk, VA 23529. Offers biology (MS Ed); chemistry (MS Ed); English (MS Ed); instructional technology (MS Ed); library science (MS Ed); secondary education (MS Ed). *Accreditation:* NCATE. Part-time and evening/weekend programs available. Postbaccalaureate distance learning degree programs offered (minimal on-campus study). *Faculty:* 20 full-time (16 women). *Students:* 80 full-time (46 women), 101 part-time (61 women); includes 37 minority (22 Black or African American, non-Hispanic/Latino; 2 Asian, non-Hispanic/Latino; 6 Hispanic/Latino; 1 Native Hawaiian or other Pacific Islander, non-Hispanic/Latino; 6 Two or more races, non-Hispanic/Latino). Average age 32. 67 applicants, 79% accepted, 53 enrolled. In 2010, 105 master's awarded. *Degree requirements:* For master's, comprehensive exam, thesis. *Entrance requirements:* For master's, GRE General Test or MAT, PRAXIS I (for licensure), minimum GPA of 2.8, teaching certificate. Additional exam requirements/recommendations for international students: Required—TOEFL. *Application deadline:* For fall admission, 6/1 for domestic and international students; for winter admission, 11/1 for domestic and international students; for spring admission, 3/1 for domestic and international students. Applications are processed on a rolling basis. Application fee: $50. Electronic applications accepted. *Expenses:* Tuition, state resident: full-time $8592; part-time $358 per credit. Tuition, nonresident: full-time $21,672; part-time $903 per credit. Required fees: $119 per semester. One-time fee: $50. *Financial support:* In 2010–11, 56 students received support, including fellowships (averaging $15,000 per year), 2 research assistantships with tuition reimbursements available (averaging $9,000 per year), 3 teaching assistantships with tuition reimbursements available (averaging $12,500 per year); career-related internships or fieldwork, Federal Work-Study, institutionally sponsored loans, scholarships/grants, and tuition waivers (partial) also available. Support available to part-time students. Financial award application deadline: 2/15; financial award applicants required to submit FAFSA. *Faculty research:* Use of technology, writing project for teachers, geography teaching, reading. *Unit head:* Dr. Robert Lucking, Graduate Program Director, 757-683-5545, Fax: 757-683-5862, E-mail: rlucking@odu.edu. *Application contact:* Dr. Robert Lucking, Graduate Program Director, 757-683-5545, Fax: 757-683-5862, E-mail: rlucking@odu.edu.

Oregon State University, Graduate School, College of Science, Department of Chemistry, Corvallis, OR 97331. Offers analytical chemistry (MS, PhD); chemistry (MA, MAIS); inorganic chemistry (MS, PhD); nuclear and radiation chemistry (MS, PhD); organic chemistry (MS, PhD); physical chemistry (MS, PhD). Part-time programs available. Terminal master's awarded for partial completion of doctoral program. *Degree requirements:* For master's, one foreign language, thesis; for doctorate, one foreign language, thesis/dissertation. *Entrance requirements:* For master's and doctorate, minimum GPA of 3.0 in last 90 hours of course work. Additional exam requirements/recommendations for international students: Required—TOEFL. *Faculty research:* Solid state chemistry, enzyme reaction mechanisms, structure and dynamics of gas molecules, chemiluminescence, nonlinear optical spectroscopy.

Penn State University Park, Graduate School, Eberly College of Science, Department of Chemistry, State College, University Park, PA 16802-1503. Offers MS, PhD. *Unit head:* Dr. Ayusman Sen, Head, 814-865-1383, Fax: 814-863-8403, E-mail: axs20@psu.edu. *Application contact:* Dana Coval-Dinant, Graduate Student Recruiting Manager, 814-865-1383, Fax: 814-865-3228, E-mail: dmc6@psu.edu.

Pittsburg State University, Graduate School, College of Arts and Sciences, Department of Chemistry, Pittsburg, KS 66762. Offers MS. *Degree requirements:* For master's, thesis or alternative.

Polytechnic Institute of NYU, Department of Chemical and Biological Sciences, Major in Chemistry, Brooklyn, NY 11201-2990. Offers MS. Part-time and evening/weekend programs available. *Students:* 15 full-time (6 women), 19 part-time (12 women); includes 1 Black or African American, non-Hispanic/Latino; 2 Asian, non-Hispanic/Latino; 1 Hispanic/Latino, 17 international. Average age 29. 39 applicants, 56% accepted, 10 enrolled. In 2010, 12 master's awarded. *Degree requirements:* For master's, comprehensive exam (for some programs), thesis (for some programs). *Entrance requirements:* For master's, GRE General Test, GRE Subject Test. Additional exam requirements/recommendations for international students: Required—TOEFL (minimum score 550 paper-based; 213 computer-based; 80 iBT); Recommended—IELTS (minimum score 6.5). *Application deadline:* For fall admission, 7/31 priority date for domestic students, 4/30 priority date for international students; for spring admission, 12/31 priority date for domestic students, 10/30 priority date for international students. Applications are processed on a rolling basis. Application fee: $75. Electronic applications accepted. *Expenses:* Tuition: Full-time $21,492; part-time $1194 per credit. Required fees: $385 per semester. Tuition and fees vary according to course load. *Financial support:* Fellowships, research assistantships, teaching assistantships, institutionally sponsored loans,

scholarships/grants, and unspecified assistantships available. Support available to part-time students. Financial award applicants required to submit FAFSA. *Faculty research:* Optical rotation of light by plastic films, supramolecular chemistry, unusual stereochemical opportunities, polyaniline copolymers. *Unit head:* Dr. Bruce Garetz, Department Head, 718-260-3287, E-mail: bgaretz@poly.edu. *Application contact:* JeanCarlo Bonilla, Dir. Graduate Enrollment Management, 718-260-3182, Fax: 718-260-3624, E-mail: gradinfo@poly.edu.

Polytechnic Institute of NYU, Department of Chemical and Biological Sciences, Major in Materials Chemistry, Brooklyn, NY 11201-2990. Offers PhD. Part-time and evening/weekend programs available. *Students:* 7 full-time (3 women), 11 part-time (3 women), 16 international. 30 applicants, 40% accepted, 1 enrolled. *Degree requirements:* For doctorate, comprehensive exam, thesis/dissertation. *Entrance requirements:* Additional exam requirements/recommendations for international students: Required—TOEFL (minimum score 550 paper-based; 213 computer-based; 80 iBT); Recommended—IELTS (minimum score 6.5). *Application deadline:* For fall admission, 7/31 priority date for domestic students, 4/30 priority date for international students; for spring admission, 12/31 priority date for domestic students, 10/30 priority date for international students. Applications are processed on a rolling basis. Application fee: $75. Electronic applications accepted. *Expenses:* Tuition: Full-time $21,492; part-time $1194 per credit. Required fees: $385 per semester. Tuition and fees vary according to course load. *Financial support:* Fellowships, research assistantships, teaching assistantships, institutionally sponsored loans, scholarships/grants, and unspecified assistantships available. Support available to part-time students. Financial award applicants required to submit FAFSA. *Unit head:* Dr. Bruce Garetz, Department Head, 718-260-3287, E-mail: bgaretz@poly.edu. *Application contact:* JeanCarlo Bonilla, Director, Graduate Enrollment Management, 718-260-3182, Fax: 718-260-3624, E-mail: gradinfo@poly.edu.

Polytechnic Institute of NYU, Long Island Graduate Center, Graduate Programs, Department of Chemical and Biological Sciences, Major in Chemistry, Melville, NY 11747. Offers MS. *Students:* 17 applicants, 82% accepted, 13 enrolled. *Degree requirements:* For master's, comprehensive exam (for some programs), thesis (for some programs). *Entrance requirements:* Additional exam requirements/recommendations for international students: Required—TOEFL (minimum score 550 paper-based; 213 computer-based; 80 iBT); Recommended—IELTS (minimum score 6.5). *Application deadline:* For fall admission, 7/31 priority date for domestic students, 4/30 priority date for international students; for spring admission, 12/31 priority date for domestic students, 11/30 priority date for international students. Applications are processed on a rolling basis. Application fee: $75. Electronic applications accepted. *Expenses:* Tuition: Full-time $21,492; part-time $1194 per credit. Required fees: $385 per semester. Tuition and fees vary according to course load. *Financial support:* Institutionally sponsored loans, scholarships/grants, and unspecified assistantships available. Support available to part-time students. *Unit head:* Prof. Bruce A. Garetz, Department Head, 718-260-3287, E-mail: bgaretz@poly.edu. *Application contact:* JeanCarlo Bonilla, Director of Graduate Enrollment Management, 718-260-3182, Fax: 718-260-3624, E-mail: gradinfo@poly.edu.

Polytechnic Institute of NYU, Westchester Graduate Center, Graduate Programs, Department of Chemical and Biological Sciences, Major in Chemistry, Hawthorne, NY 10532-1507. Offers MS. *Students:* 1 part-time (0 women). Average age 36. In 2010, 2 master's awarded. *Degree requirements:* For master's, comprehensive exam (for some programs), thesis (for some programs). *Entrance requirements:* Additional exam requirements/recommendations for international students: Required—TOEFL (minimum score 550 paper-based; 213 computer-based; 80 iBT); Recommended—IELTS (minimum score 6.5). *Application deadline:* For fall admission, 7/31 priority date for domestic students, 4/30 priority date for international students; for spring admission, 12/31 priority date for domestic students, 11/30 priority date for international students. Applications are processed on a rolling basis. Application fee: $75. Electronic applications accepted. *Expenses:* Tuition: Full-time $21,492; part-time $1194 per credit. Required fees: $385 per semester. Tuition and fees vary according to course load. *Financial support:* Institutionally sponsored loans, scholarships/grants, and unspecified assistantships available. Support available to part-time students. *Unit head:* Dr. Bruce A. Garetz, Department Head, 718-260-3287, E-mail: bgaretz@poly.edu. *Application contact:* JeanCarlo Bonilla, Director of Graduate Enrollment Management, 718-260-3182, Fax: 718-260-3624, E-mail: gradinfo@poly.edu.

Pontifical Catholic University of Puerto Rico, College of Sciences, Department of Chemistry, Ponce, PR 00717-0777. Offers MS. Part-time and evening/weekend programs available. *Degree requirements:* For master's, thesis. *Entrance requirements:* For master's, GRE General Test, 2 letters of recommendation, minimum GPA of 3.0, minimum 37 credits in chemistry. Electronic applications accepted.

Portland State University, Graduate Studies, College of Liberal Arts and Sciences, Department of Chemistry, Portland, OR 97207-0751. Offers MA, MS, PhD. Part-time programs available. *Faculty:* 17 full-time (4 women), 4 part-time/adjunct (all women). *Students:* 48 full-time (22 women), 8 part-time (4 women); includes 2 Asian, non-Hispanic/Latino; 1 Two or more races, non-Hispanic/Latino, 30 international. Average age 29. 48 applicants, 54% accepted, 16 enrolled. In 2010, 2 master's, 1 doctorate awarded. *Degree requirements:* For master's, one foreign language, thesis; for doctorate, one foreign language, thesis/dissertation, cumulative exams, seminar presentations. *Entrance requirements:* For master's, GRE General Test, GRE Subject Test, minimum GPA of 3.0 in upper-division course work or 2.75 overall, 2 letters of recommendation. Additional exam requirements/recommendations for international students: Required—TOEFL (minimum score 550 paper-based; 213 computer-based). *Application deadline:* For fall admission, 2/1 priority date for domestic and international students; for winter admission, 9/1 priority date for domestic and international students; for spring admission, 11/1 priority date for domestic and international students. Applications are processed on a rolling basis. Application fee: $50. *Expenses:* Tuition, state resident: full-time $8505; part-time $315 per credit. Tuition, nonresident: full-time $13,284; part-time $492 per credit. Required fees: $1482; $21 per credit. $99 per term. One-time fee: $120. Part-time tuition and fees vary according to course load and program. *Financial support:* Research assistantships with full tuition reimbursements, teaching assistantships with full tuition reimbursements, career-related internships or fieldwork, Federal Work-Study, scholarships/grants, tuition waivers (partial), and unspecified assistantships available. Support available to part-time students. Financial award application deadline: 3/1; financial award applicants required to submit FAFSA. *Faculty research:* Synthetic inorganic chemistry, atmospheric chemistry, organic photochemistry, enzymology, analytical chemistry. Total annual research expenditures: $4.5 million. *Unit head:* Kevin A. Reynolds, Chair, 503-725-8757, Fax: 503-725-3888, E-mail: reynoldsk@pdx.edu. *Application contact:* Abbey Lawrence, Department Secretary, 503-725-8756, Fax: 503-725-3888, E-mail: aslawren@pdx.edu.

Prairie View A&M University, College of Arts and Sciences, Department of Chemistry, Prairie View, TX 77446-0519. Offers MS. Part-time and evening/weekend programs available. *Faculty:* 3 full-time (1 woman). *Students:* 2 full-time (1 woman), 7 part-time (6 women); includes 7 Black or African American, non-Hispanic/Latino, 2 international. Average age 32. In 2010, 1 master's awarded. *Degree requirements:* For master's, thesis. *Entrance requirements:* For master's, GRE General Test. *Application deadline:* For fall admission, 4/1 for domestic students; for spring admission, 10/1 for domestic students. Applications are processed on a rolling basis. Application fee: $50. Electronic applications accepted. *Expenses:* Tuition, state resident: full-time $3586.14; part-time $119.06 per credit hour. Tuition, nonresident: part-time $511.23 per credit hour. *Financial support:* In 2010–11, 5 students received support, including 1 fellowship (averaging $12,000 per year), 2 research assistantships (averaging $12,000 per year), 2 teaching assistantships (averaging $12,000 per year); career-related internships or fieldwork, Federal Work-Study, institutionally sponsored loans, and tuition waivers (full and partial) also available. Support available to part-time students. Financial award application deadline: 4/1; financial award applicants required to submit FAFSA. *Faculty research:* Material science, environmental characterization (surface phenomena), activation of plasminogens, polymer modifications, organic synthesis. Total annual research expenditures: $114,895. *Unit head:* Dr. Remi R. Oki, Head, 936-261-2616, Fax: 936-261-3105, E-mail: aroki@pvamu.edu. *Application contact:* Dr. Remi R. Oki, Head, 936-261-2616, Fax: 936-261-3105, E-mail: aroki@pvamu.edu.

Princeton University, Graduate School, Department of Chemistry, Princeton, NJ 08544-1019. Offers chemistry (PhD); industrial chemistry (MS). *Degree requirements:* For doctorate, thesis/dissertation, general exams. *Entrance requirements:* For master's, GRE General Test; for doctorate, GRE General Test, GRE Subject Test (recommended). Additional exam requirements/recommendations for international students: Required—TOEFL (minimum score 250 computer-based). Electronic applications accepted. *Faculty research:* Chemistry of interfaces, organic synthesis, organometallic chemistry, inorganic reactions, biostructural chemistry.

See Display on next page and Close-Up on page 105.

Purdue University, Graduate School, College of Science, Department of Chemistry, West Lafayette, IN 47907. Offers analytical chemistry (MS, PhD); biochemistry (MS, PhD); chemical education (MS, PhD); inorganic chemistry (MS, PhD); organic chemistry (MS, PhD); physical chemistry (MS, PhD). Terminal master's awarded for partial completion of doctoral program. *Degree requirements:* For master's, thesis; for doctorate, thesis/dissertation. *Entrance requirements:* Additional exam requirements/recommendations for international students: Required—TOEFL. Electronic applications accepted.

Queens College of the City University of New York, Division of Graduate Studies, Mathematics and Natural Sciences Division, Department of Chemistry and Biochemistry, Flushing, NY 11367-1597. Offers biochemistry (MA); chemistry (MA). Part-time and evening/weekend programs available. *Faculty:* 14 full-time (4 women). *Students:* 2 full-time (0 women), 8 part-time (4 women); includes 1 Black or African American, non-Hispanic/Latino; 5 Asian, non-Hispanic/Latino, 2 international. 13 applicants, 38% accepted, 2 enrolled. In 2010, 6 master's awarded. *Degree requirements:* For master's, comprehensive exam. *Entrance requirements:* For master's, GRE, previous course work in calculus and physics, minimum GPA of 3.0. Additional exam requirements/recommendations for international students: Required—TOEFL. *Application deadline:* For fall admission, 4/1 for domestic students; for spring admission, 11/1 for domestic students. Applications are processed on a rolling basis. Application fee: $125. *Financial support:* Career-related internships or fieldwork, Federal Work-Study, institutionally sponsored loans, and tuition waivers (partial) available. Support available to part-time students. Financial award application deadline: 4/1; financial award applicants required to submit FAFSA. *Unit head:* Dr. William Hersh, Chairperson, 718-997-4144. *Application contact:* Graduate Adviser, 718-997-4100.

Queen's University at Kingston, School of Graduate Studies and Research, Faculty of Arts and Sciences, Department of Chemistry, Kingston, ON K7L 3N6, Canada. Offers M Sc, PhD. Part-time programs available. *Degree requirements:* For master's, thesis (for some programs); for doctorate, comprehensive exam, thesis/dissertation. *Entrance requirements:* Additional exam requirements/recommendations for international students: Required—TOEFL (minimum score 580 paper-based). *Faculty research:* Medicinal/biological chemistry, materials chemistry, environmental/analytical chemistry, theoretical/computational chemistry.

Rensselaer Polytechnic Institute, Graduate School, School of Science, Program in Chemistry, Troy, NY 12180-3590. Offers analytical chemistry (MS, PhD); biochemistry (MS, PhD); inorganic chemistry (MS, PhD); organic chemistry (MS, PhD); physical chemistry (MS, PhD); polymer chemistry (MS, PhD). Part-time and evening/weekend programs available. *Faculty:* 16 full-time (2 women). *Students:* 42 full-time (18 women), 3 part-time (1 woman); includes 1 Black or African American, non-Hispanic/Latino; 4 Asian, non-Hispanic/Latino, 16 international. Average age 24. 139 applicants, 16% accepted, 6 enrolled. In 2010, 5 master's, 8 doctorates awarded. Terminal master's awarded for partial completion of doctoral program. *Degree requirements:* For master's, thesis (for some programs); for doctorate, comprehensive exam, thesis/dissertation. *Entrance requirements:* For master's, GRE General Test, GRE Subject Test (strongly recommended); for doctorate, GRE General Test, GRE Subject Test (chemistry or biochemistry strongly recommended). Additional exam requirements/recommendations for international students: Required—TOEFL (minimum score 570 paper-based; 230 computer-based; 88 iBT). *Application deadline:* For fall admission, 2/1 priority date for domestic students; for spring admission, 11/15 for domestic students. Applications are processed on a rolling basis. Application fee: $75. Electronic applications accepted. *Expenses:* Tuition: Full-time $39,600; part-time $1650 per credit. Required fees: $1896. *Financial support:* In 2010–11, 1 fellowship with full tuition reimbursement (averaging $23,000 per year), 12 research assistantships with full tuition reimbursements (averaging $23,000 per year), 23 teaching assistantships with full tuition reimbursements (averaging $23,000 per year) were awarded; institutionally sponsored loans and tuition waivers (full and partial) also available. Financial award application deadline: 2/1. *Faculty research:* Synthetic polymer and biopolymer chemistry, physical chemistry of polymeric systems, bioanalytical chemistry, synthetic and computational drug design, protein folding and protein design. Total annual research expenditures: $1.1 million. *Unit head:* Dr. Curtis M. Breneman, Chair, 518-276-3264, Fax: 518-276-4887, E-mail: brenec@rpi.edu. *Application contact:* Sharon E. Gardner, Graduate Program Administrator, 518-276-2140, Fax: 518-276-4887, E-mail: derris@rpi.edu.

Rice University, Graduate Programs, Wiess School of Natural Sciences, Department of Chemistry, Houston, TX 77251-1892. Offers chemistry (MA); inorganic chemistry (PhD); organic chemistry (PhD); physical chemistry (PhD). Terminal master's awarded for partial completion of doctoral program. *Degree requirements:* For master's, thesis; for doctorate, thesis/dissertation. *Entrance requirements:* For master's and doctorate, GRE General Test, minimum GPA of 3.0. Additional exam requirements/recommendations for international students: Required—TOEFL (minimum score 600 paper-based; 250 computer-based; 90 iBT). Electronic applications accepted. *Faculty research:* Nanoscience, biomaterials, nanobioinformatics, fullerene pharmaceuticals.

Rochester Institute of Technology, Graduate Enrollment Services, College of Science, Health Sciences and Sustainability, Department of Chemistry, Rochester, NY 14623-5603. Offers MS. Part-time and evening/weekend programs available. Postbaccalaureate distance learning degree programs offered (minimal on-campus study). *Students:* 7 full-time (4 women), 8 part-time (4 women); includes 1 Asian, non-Hispanic/Latino, 3 international. Average age 30. 37 applicants, 22% accepted, 5 enrolled. In 2010, 6 master's awarded. *Degree requirements:* For master's, thesis. *Entrance requirements:* For master's, GRE, minimum GPA of 3.0. Additional exam requirements/recommendations for international students: Required—TOEFL (minimum score 550 paper-based; 213 computer-based; 79 iBT) or IELTS (minimum score 6.5). *Application deadline:* For fall admission, 2/15 priority date for domestic and international students; for winter admission, 11/1 for domestic students; for spring admission, 2/1 for domestic students. Applications are processed on a rolling basis. Application fee: $50. Electronic applications accepted. *Expenses:* Tuition: Full-time $33,234; part-time $924 per credit hour. Required fees: $219. *Financial support:* In 2010–11, 13 students received support; fellowships with full and partial tuition reimbursements available, research assistantships with full and partial tuition reimbursements available, teaching assistantships with full and partial tuition reimbursements available, career-related internships or fieldwork, scholarships/grants, and unspecified assistantships available. Support available to part-time students. Financial award applicants required to submit FAFSA. *Faculty research:* Organic polymer chemistry, magnetic resonance and imaging, inorganic coordination polymers, biophysical chemistry, physical polymer chemistry. *Unit head:* Dr. Paul Rosenberg, Department Head, 585-475-2497, Fax: 585-475-7800, E-mail: lprsch@

Chemistry

Princeton University

Department of Chemistry

Frick Chemistry Laboratory

Princeton, NJ 08544

Taking Chemistry Into the Future

www.princeton.edu/chemistry

Rochester Institute of Technology (continued)
rit.edu. *Application contact:* Diane Ellison, Assistant Vice President, Graduate Enrollment Services, 585-475-2229, Fax: 585-475-7164, E-mail: gradinfo@rit.edu.

Rochester Institute of Technology, Graduate Enrollment Services, College of Science, Health Sciences and Sustainability, Department of Medical Sciences, Rochester, NY 14623-5603. Offers clinical chemistry (MS). Part-time programs available. *Students:* 4 full-time (1 woman), 9 part-time (1 woman), 10 international. Average age 30. 17 applicants, 47% accepted, 4 enrolled. In 2010, 3 master's awarded. *Degree requirements:* For master's, thesis. *Entrance requirements:* For master's, minimum GPA of 3.0. Additional exam requirements/recommendations for international students: Required—TOEFL (minimum score 575 paper-based; 233 computer-based; 90 iBT) or IELTS (minimum score 6.5). *Application deadline:* For fall admission, 2/15 priority date for domestic and international students. Applications are processed on a rolling basis. Application fee: $50. *Expenses:* Tuition: Full-time $33,234; part-time $924 per credit hour. Required fees: $219. *Financial support:* In 2010–11, 4 students received support; research assistantships with partial tuition reimbursements available, teaching assistantships with partial tuition reimbursements available, career-related internships or fieldwork, institutionally sponsored loans, scholarships/grants, and unspecified assistantships available. Support available to part-time students. Financial award applicants required to submit FAFSA. *Faculty research:* Pathology, forensic science, clinical chemistry. *Unit head:* James Aumer, Professor and Director of Clinical Chemistry, 585-475-2526, E-mail: jcascl@rit.edu. *Application contact:* Diane Ellison, Assistant Vice President, Graduate Enrollment Services, 585-475-2229, Fax: 585-475-7164, E-mail: gradinfo@rit.edu.

Roosevelt University, Graduate Division, College of Arts and Sciences, Department of Biological, Chemical, and Physical Sciences, Chicago, IL 60605. Offers biotechnology and chemical science (MS). Part-time and evening/weekend programs available. *Degree requirements:* For master's, thesis optional. *Entrance requirements:* For master's, minimum GPA of 2.7, undergraduate course work in science and mathematics. *Faculty research:* Phase-transfer catalysts, bioinorganic chemistry, long chain dicarboxylic acids, organosilicon compounds, spectroscopic studies.

Royal Military College of Canada, Division of Graduate Studies and Research, Science Division, Department of Chemistry and Chemical and Materials Engineering, Kingston, ON K7K 7B4, Canada. Offers chemical engineering (M Eng, MA Sc, PhD); chemistry (M Sc, PhD). *Degree requirements:* For master's, for doctorate, comprehensive exam, thesis/dissertation. *Entrance requirements:* For master's, honour's degree with second-class standing; for doctorate, master's degree. Electronic applications accepted.

Rutgers, The State University of New Jersey, Camden, Graduate School of Arts and Sciences, Program in Chemistry, Camden, NJ 08102. Offers MS. Part-time and evening/weekend programs available. *Faculty:* 5 full-time (1 woman), 1 part-time/adjunct (0 women). *Students:* 3 full-time (1 woman), 11 part-time (7 women); includes 3 Asian, non-Hispanic/Latino, 1 international. Average age 31. 17 applicants, 59% accepted, 7 enrolled. In 2010, 4 master's awarded. *Degree requirements:* For master's, comprehensive exam, thesis (for some programs), 30 credits. *Entrance requirements:* For master's, GRE (for assistantships), 3 letters of recommendation; statement of personal, professional and academic goals; chemistry or related undergraduate degree (preferred). Additional exam requirements/recommendations for international students: Required—TOEFL, IELTS; Recommended—TWE. *Application deadline:* For fall admission, 3/1 priority date for domestic students; for spring admission, 12/1 priority date for domestic students. Applications are processed on a rolling basis. Application fee: $65. Electronic applications accepted. *Expenses:* Tuition, state resident: full-time $4963; part-time $319 per credit. Tuition, nonresident: full-time $10,493; part-time $680 per credit. *Financial support:* In 2010–11, 6 students received support, including 3 fellowships with partial tuition reimbursements available (averaging $1,400 per year), 2 teaching assistantships with full tuition reimbursements available (averaging $26,000 per year); research assistantships, Federal Work-Study, scholarships/grants, tuition waivers (partial), and unspecified assistantships also available. Financial award application deadline: 3/15; financial award applicants required to

submit FAFSA. *Faculty research:* Organic and inorganic synthesis, enzyme biochemistry, trace metal analysis, theoretical and molecular modeling. Total annual research expenditures: $201,339. *Unit head:* Dr. Georgia A. Arbuckle-Keil, Director, 856-225-6142, Fax: 856-225-6506, E-mail: arbuckle@camden.rutgers.edu. *Application contact:* Dr. Georgia A. Arbuckle-Keil, Director, 856-225-6142, Fax: 856-225-6506, E-mail: arbuckle@camden.rutgers.edu.

Rutgers, The State University of New Jersey, Newark, Graduate School, Program in Chemistry, Newark, NJ 07102. Offers analytical chemistry (MS, PhD); biochemistry (MS, PhD); inorganic chemistry (MS, PhD); organic chemistry (MS, PhD); physical chemistry (MS, PhD). Part-time and evening/weekend programs available. *Faculty:* 13 full-time (3 women). *Students:* 29 full-time (14 women), 32 part-time (19 women); includes 2 Black or African American, non-Hispanic/Latino; 30 Asian, non-Hispanic/Latino; 3 Hispanic/Latino. 153 applicants, 45% accepted, 17 enrolled. In 2010, 4 master's, 9 doctorates awarded. Terminal master's awarded for partial completion of doctoral program. *Degree requirements:* For master's, thesis optional, cumulative exams; for doctorate, thesis/dissertation, exams, research proposal. *Entrance requirements:* For master's and doctorate, GRE General Test, minimum undergraduate B average. Additional exam requirements/recommendations for international students: Required—TOEFL. *Application deadline:* For fall admission, 7/1 priority date for domestic students; for spring admission, 12/1 for domestic students. Applications are processed on a rolling basis. Application fee: $60. Electronic applications accepted. *Expenses:* Tuition, state resident: part-time $600 per credit. Tuition, nonresident: full-time $10,694. *Financial support:* In 2010–11, 35 students received support, including 5 fellowships (averaging $18,000 per year), 6 research assistantships with full and partial tuition reimbursements available (averaging $23,112 per year), 20 teaching assistantships with full and partial tuition reimbursements available (averaging $23,112 per year); Federal Work-Study and institutionally sponsored loans also available. Financial award application deadline: 3/1. *Faculty research:* Medicinal chemistry, natural products, isotope effects, biophysics and bioorganic approaches to enzyme mechanisms, organic and organometallic synthesis. *Unit head:* Prof. Frank Jordan, Chairman and Program Director, 973-353-5741, Fax: 973-353-1264, E-mail: frjordan@andromeda.rutgers.edu. *Application contact:* Jason Hand, Director of Admissions, 973-353-5205, Fax: 973-353-1440.

Rutgers, The State University of New Jersey, New Brunswick, Graduate School-New Brunswick, Department of Chemistry and Chemical Biology, Piscataway, NJ 08854-8097. Offers biological chemistry (MS, PhD); inorganic chemistry (MS, PhD); organic chemistry (MS, PhD); physical chemistry (MS, PhD). Part-time and evening/weekend programs available. Terminal master's awarded for partial completion of doctoral program. *Degree requirements:* For master's, thesis or alternative, exam; for doctorate, thesis/dissertation, 1 year residency. *Entrance requirements:* For master's and doctorate, GRE General Test, GRE Subject Test. Additional exam requirements/recommendations for international students: Required—TOEFL. Electronic applications accepted. *Expenses:* Tuition, state resident: full-time $7200; part-time $600 per credit. Tuition, nonresident: full-time $11,124; part-time $927 per credit. *Faculty research:* Biophysical organic/bioorganic, inorganic/bioinorganic, theoretical, and solid-state/surface chemistry.

Rutgers, The State University of New Jersey, New Brunswick, Graduate School-New Brunswick, Department of Environmental Sciences, Piscataway, NJ 08854-8097. Offers air pollution and resources (MS, PhD); aquatic biology (MS, PhD); aquatic chemistry (MS, PhD); atmospheric science (MS, PhD); chemistry and physics of aerosol and hydrosol systems (MS, PhD); environmental chemistry (MS, PhD); environmental microbiology (MS, PhD); environmental toxicology (PhD); exposure assessment (PhD); fate and effects of pollutants (MS, PhD); pollution prevention and control (MS, PhD); water and wastewater treatment (MS, PhD); water resources (MS, PhD). Terminal master's awarded for partial completion of doctoral program. *Degree requirements:* For master's, comprehensive exam, thesis or alternative, oral final exam; for doctorate, comprehensive exam, thesis/dissertation, thesis defense, qualifying exam. *Entrance requirements:* For master's and doctorate, GRE General Test. Additional exam requirements/recommendations for international students: Required—TOEFL. Electronic applications accepted. *Expenses:* Tuition, state resident: full-time $7200; part-time $600 per credit. Tuition, nonresident: full-time $11,124; part-time $927 per credit. *Faculty research:* Biological waste treatment; contaminant fate and transport; air, soil and water quality.

62   www.facebook.com/petersonspublishing

Peterson's Graduate Programs in the Physical Sciences, Mathematics, Agricultural Sciences, the Environment & Natural Resources 2012

Sacred Heart University, Graduate Programs, College of Arts and Sciences, Department of Chemistry, Fairfield, CT 06825-1000. Offers MS. Part-time and evening/weekend programs available. *Degree requirements:* For master's, thesis optional. *Entrance requirements:* For master's, bachelor's degree in related area, minimum GPA of 2.75. Additional exam requirements/recommendations for international students: Required—TOEFL (minimum score 550 paper-based; 213 computer-based; 75 iBT). Electronic applications accepted.

St. Francis Xavier University, Graduate Studies, Department of Chemistry, Antigonish, NS B2G 2W5, Canada. Offers M Sc. *Degree requirements:* For master's, thesis. *Entrance requirements:* Additional exam requirements/recommendations for international students: Required—TOEFL (minimum score 580 paper-based; 236 computer-based). *Faculty research:* Photoelectron spectroscopy, synthesis and properties of surfactants, nucleic acid synthesis, transition metal chemistry, colloids.

St. John's University, St. John's College of Liberal Arts and Sciences, Department of Chemistry, Queens, NY 11439. Offers MS. Part-time and evening/weekend programs available. *Students:* 18 full-time (12 women), 10 part-time (7 women); includes 16 minority (3 Black or African American, non-Hispanic/Latino; 7 Asian, non-Hispanic/Latino; 3 Hispanic/Latino; 3 Two or more races, non-Hispanic/Latino), 9 international. Average age 28. 22 applicants, 41% accepted, 7 enrolled. In 2010, 4 master's awarded. *Degree requirements:* For master's, comprehensive exam, thesis optional. *Entrance requirements:* For master's, minimum GPA of 3.0. Additional exam requirements/recommendations for international students: Required—TOEFL (minimum score 600 paper-based; 250 computer-based; 100 iBT), IELTS (minimum score 5.5). *Application deadline:* For fall admission, 5/1 priority date for domestic and international students; for spring admission, 11/1 priority date for domestic and international students. Applications are processed on a rolling basis. Application fee: $70. Electronic applications accepted. *Expenses:* Tuition: Full-time $17,100; part-time $950 per credit. Required fees: $340; $170 per semester. Tuition and fees vary according to program. *Financial support:* Research assistantships, teaching assistantships, scholarships/grants available. Support available to part-time students. Financial award application deadline: 3/1; financial award applicants required to submit FAFSA. *Faculty research:* Synthesis and reactions of a-lactams, NMR spectroscopy or nucleosides, analytical chemistry, environment chemistry and photochemistry of transition metal complexes. *Unit head:* Dr. Richard Rosso, Chair, 718-990-5216, E-mail: rossor@stjohns.edu. *Application contact:* Kathleen Davis, Director of Graduate Admission, 718-990-1601, Fax: 718-990-5686, E-mail: gradhelp@stjohns.edu.

Saint Joseph College, Department of Chemistry, West Hartford, CT 06117-2700. Offers biochemistry (MS); chemistry (MS). Part-time and evening/weekend programs available. Post-baccalaureate distance learning degree programs offered. *Students:* 2 full-time (1 woman), 30 part-time (18 women); includes 3 Black or African American, non-Hispanic/Latino; 2 Asian, non-Hispanic/Latino; 2 Hispanic/Latino. *Degree requirements:* For master's, comprehensive exam, thesis optional. *Entrance requirements:* For master's, 2 letters of recommendation. *Application deadline:* Applications are processed on a rolling basis. Application fee: $50. Electronic applications accepted. *Expenses:* Tuition: Full-time $11,340; part-time $630 per credit. Required fees: $540; $30 per credit. Tuition and fees vary according to course load, campus/location and program. *Financial support:* Career-related internships or fieldwork and unspecified assistantships available. Support available to part-time students. Financial award applicants required to submit FAFSA. *Application contact:* Graduate Admissions Office, 860-231-5261, E-mail: graduate@sjc.edu.

Saint Louis University, Graduate Education, College of Arts and Sciences and Graduate Education, Department of Chemistry, St. Louis, MO 63103-2097. Offers MS, MS-R, PhD. Part-time and evening/weekend programs available. *Degree requirements:* For master's, thesis; for doctorate, comprehensive exam, thesis/dissertation. *Entrance requirements:* For master's, letters of recommendation, resume, interview; for doctorate, letters of recommendation, resumé, interview, transcripts, goal statement. Additional exam requirements/recommendations for international students: Required—TOEFL (minimum score 550 paper-based; 213 computer-based; 80 iBT). Electronic applications accepted. *Faculty research:* Photochemistry, energy, materials, biomaterials, nanomaterials.

Sam Houston State University, College of Arts and Sciences, Department of Chemistry, Huntsville, TX 77341. Offers MS. Part-time programs available. *Faculty:* 1 (woman) part-time/adjunct. *Students:* 9 full-time (6 women); includes 1 Asian, non-Hispanic/Latino; 1 Hispanic/Latino, 4 international. Average age 25. 3 applicants, 33% accepted, 0 enrolled. In 2010, 6 master's awarded. *Degree requirements:* For master's, thesis (for some programs). *Entrance requirements:* For master's, GRE General Test. Additional exam requirements/recommendations for international students: Required—TOEFL (minimum score 550 paper-based; 213 computer-based; 79 iBT). *Application deadline:* For fall admission, 8/1 for domestic and international students; for spring admission, 12/1 for domestic and international students. Applications are processed on a rolling basis. Application fee: $20. *Expenses:* Tuition, state resident: full-time $1363; part-time $163 per credit hour. Tuition, nonresident: full-time $3856; part-time $473 per credit hour. *Financial support:* Research assistantships, teaching assistantships, Federal Work-Study, institutionally sponsored loans, and tuition waivers (partial) available. Support available to part-time students. Financial award application deadline: 5/31; financial award applicants required to submit FAFSA. *Unit head:* Dr. Rick Norman, Chair, 936-294-1527, Fax: 936-294-4996, E-mail: chm_ren@shsu.edu. *Application contact:* Dr. Thomas Chasteen, Advisor, 936-294-1971, E-mail: chm_tgc@shsu.edu.

San Diego State University, Graduate and Research Affairs, College of Sciences, Department of Chemistry, San Diego, CA 92182. Offers MA, MS, PhD. PhD offered jointly with University of California, San Diego. Terminal master's awarded for partial completion of doctoral program. *Degree requirements:* For doctorate, thesis/dissertation. *Entrance requirements:* For master's, GRE General Test, bachelor's degree in related field, 3 letters of reference; for doctorate, GRE General Test, GRE Subject Test. Additional exam requirements/recommendations for international students: Required—TOEFL. Electronic applications accepted. *Faculty research:* Nonlinear, laser, and electrochemistry; surface reaction dynamics; catalysis, synthesis, and organometallics; proteins, enzymology, and gene expression regulation.

San Francisco State University, Division of Graduate Studies, College of Science and Engineering, Department of Chemistry and Biochemistry, San Francisco, CA 94132-1722. Offers chemistry (MS), including biochemistry. Part-time programs available. *Application deadline:* Applications are processed on a rolling basis. Electronic applications accepted. *Unit head:* Dr. Jane DeWitt, Chair, 415-338-1288, Fax: 415-338-2384, E-mail: gradchem@sfsu.edu. *Application contact:* Dr. Bruce Manning, Graduate Coordinator, 415-338-1288, Fax: 415-338-2384, E-mail: gradchem@sfsu.edu.

San Jose State University, Graduate Studies and Research, College of Science, Department of Chemistry, San Jose, CA 95192-0001. Offers MA, MS. Part-time and evening/weekend programs available. *Degree requirements:* For master's, thesis or alternative. *Entrance requirements:* For master's, GRE. Electronic applications accepted. *Faculty research:* Intercalated compounds, organic/biochemical reaction mechanisms, complexing agents in biochemistry, DNA repair, metabolic inhibitors.

The Scripps Research Institute, Kellogg School of Science and Technology, La Jolla, CA 92037. Offers chemical and biological sciences (PhD). *Faculty:* 163 full-time (35 women). *Students:* 222 full-time (78 women). 494 applicants, 20% accepted, 32 enrolled. *Degree requirements:* For doctorate, thesis/dissertation. *Entrance requirements:* For doctorate, GRE General Test, GRE Subject Test, 3 letters of recommendation. Additional exam requirements/recommendations for international students: Required—TOEFL. *Application deadline:* For fall admission, 12/1 for domestic and international students. Application fee: $0. Electronic applications accepted. *Expenses:* Tuition: Full-time $5000. *Financial support:* Fellowships, institutionally sponsored loans, tuition waivers (full), and annual stipends available. *Faculty research:* Molecular structure and function, plant biology, immunology, bioorganic chemistry and molecular design, synthetic organic chemistry and natural product synthesis. *Unit head:* Dr. James R. Williamson, Dean of Graduate and Postdoctoral Studies, 858-784-8469, Fax: 858-784-2802, E-mail: gradprgm@scripps.edu. *Application contact:* Marylyn Rinaldi, Administrative Director, 858-784-8469, Fax: 858-784-2802, E-mail: mrinaldi@scripps.edu.

Seton Hall University, College of Arts and Sciences, Department of Chemistry and Biochemistry, South Orange, NJ 07079-2697. Offers analytical chemistry (MS, PhD); biochemistry (MS, PhD); chemistry (MS); inorganic chemistry (MS, PhD); organic chemistry (MS, PhD); physical chemistry (MS, PhD). Part-time and evening/weekend programs available. Terminal master's awarded for partial completion of doctoral program. *Degree requirements:* For master's, thesis optional; for doctorate, comprehensive exam, thesis/dissertation. *Entrance requirements:* Additional exam requirements/recommendations for international students: Required—TOEFL. Electronic applications accepted. *Faculty research:* DNA metal reactions; chromatography; bioinorganic, biophysical, organometallic, polymer chemistry; heterogeneous catalyst; synthetic organic and carbohydrate chemistry.

Simon Fraser University, Graduate Studies, Faculty of Science, Department of Chemistry, Burnaby, BC V5A 1S6, Canada. Offers chemical physics (PhD); chemistry (PhD). *Degree requirements:* For master's, thesis; for doctorate, thesis/dissertation. *Entrance requirements:* For master's, minimum GPA of 3.0. Additional exam requirements/recommendations for international students: Required—TOEFL (minimum score 600 paper-based; 250 computer-based; 100 iBT). Electronic applications accepted. *Faculty research:* Organic chemistry, nuclear chemistry, physical chemistry, inorganic chemistry, theoretical chemistry.

Smith College, Graduate and Special Programs, Department of Chemistry, Northampton, MA 01063. Offers MAT. Part-time programs available. *Faculty:* 9 full-time (6 women). *Entrance requirements:* For master's, GRE General Test, GRE Subject Test. Additional exam requirements/recommendations for international students: Required—TOEFL (minimum score 590 paper-based; 243 computer-based; 97 iBT). *Application deadline:* For fall admission, 4/1 for domestic students, 1/15 for international students; for spring admission, 12/1 for domestic students. Application fee: $60. *Expenses:* Tuition: Full-time $14,520; part-time $1210 per credit. *Financial support:* Career-related internships or fieldwork and institutionally sponsored loans available. Support available to part-time students. Financial award application deadline: 1/15; financial award applicants required to submit CSS PROFILE or FAFSA. *Unit head:* Kate Queeney, Chair, 413-585-3835, E-mail: kqueeney@smith.edu. *Application contact:* Ruth Morgan, Administrative Assistant, 413-585-3050, Fax: 413-585-3054, E-mail: gradstdy@smith.edu.

South Dakota State University, Graduate School, College of Arts and Science, Department of Chemistry, Brookings, SD 57007. Offers MS, PhD. *Degree requirements:* For master's, thesis, oral exam; for doctorate, thesis/dissertation, preliminary oral and written exams, research tool. *Entrance requirements:* For master's, bachelor's degree in chemistry or closely related discipline; for doctorate, bachelor's degree in chemistry or closely related discipline. Additional exam requirements/recommendations for international students: Required—TOEFL (minimum score 580 paper-based; 237 computer-based; 92 iBT). *Faculty research:* Environmental chemistry, computational chemistry, organic synthesis and photochemistry, novel material development and characterization.

Southeastern Louisiana University, College of Science and Technology, Program in Integrated Science and Technology, Hammond, LA 70402. Offers chemistry (MS); computer science (MS); information technology (MS); mathematics (MS); physics (MS). Part-time and evening/weekend programs available. *Faculty:* 11 full-time (3 women). *Students:* 13 full-time (5 women), 11 part-time (2 women); includes 1 minority (Asian, non-Hispanic/Latino), 8 international. Average age 32. 13 applicants, 46% accepted, 4 enrolled. In 2010, 5 master's awarded. *Degree requirements:* For master's, thesis (for some programs), 33-36 hours. *Entrance requirements:* For master's, GRE (minimum combined score 850), 2 letters of reference; minimum GPA of 2.75; 30 hours of course work including chemistry, physics, industrial technology, or mathematics. Additional exam requirements/recommendations for international students: Required—TOEFL (minimum score 500 paper-based; 173 computer-based; 61 iBT). *Application deadline:* For fall admission, 7/15 priority date for domestic students, 6/1 priority date for international students; for spring admission, 12/1 priority date for domestic students, 10/1 priority date for international students. Applications are processed on a rolling basis. Application fee: $20 ($30 for international students). Electronic applications accepted. *Expenses:* Tuition, state resident: full-time $3533. Tuition, nonresident: full-time $12,002. Required fees: $907. Tuition and fees vary according to degree level. *Financial support:* In 2010–11, 7 students received support, including 7 research assistantships (averaging $10,100 per year); career-related internships or fieldwork, Federal Work-Study, institutionally sponsored loans, and unspecified assistantships also available. Support available to part-time students. Financial award application deadline: 5/1; financial award applicants required to submit FAFSA. *Faculty research:* Computational statistics, medicinal chemistry, machine learning, optical interferometry,strength of materials and structure. *Unit head:* Dr. Ken Li, Coordinator, 985-549-3822, Fax: 985-549-2099, E-mail: kli@selu.edu. *Application contact:* Sandra Meyers, Graduate Admissions Analyst, 985-549-5620, Fax: 985-549-5632, E-mail: admissions@selu.edu.

Southeast Missouri State University, School of Graduate Studies, Department of Chemistry, Cape Girardeau, MO 63701-4799. Offers applied chemistry (MNS). Part-time programs available. *Faculty:* 8 full-time (1 woman). *Students:* 20 full-time (11 women), 7 part-time (2 women); includes 3 minority (2 Black or African American, non-Hispanic/Latino; 1 Asian, non-Hispanic/Latino), 19 international. Average age 25. 21 applicants, 57% accepted, 10 enrolled. In 2010, 4 master's awarded. *Degree requirements:* For master's, comprehensive exam (for some programs), thesis (for some programs), scholarly paper; 6 hours research/internship. *Entrance requirements:* For master's, GRE General Test, minimum GPA of 2.75 for last 30 semester hours of undergraduate science or math courses; 2 letters of recommendation; minimum C grade in selected chemistry courses. Additional exam requirements/recommendations for international students: Required—TOEFL (minimum score 550 paper-based; 213 computer-based; 79 iBT); Recommended—IELTS (minimum score 6). *Application deadline:* For fall admission, 8/1 for domestic students, 6/1 for international students; for spring admission, 11/21 for domestic students, 10/1 for international students. Applications are processed on a rolling basis. Application fee: $25 ($35 for international students). Electronic applications accepted. *Expenses:* Tuition, state resident: full-time $4698; part-time $261 per credit hour. Tuition, nonresident: full-time $8379; part-time $465.50 per credit hour. *Financial support:* In 2010–11, 21 students received support, including 11 teaching assistantships with full tuition reimbursements available (averaging $7,600 per year); career-related internships or fieldwork, Federal Work-Study, institutionally sponsored loans, scholarships/grants, tuition waivers (full), and unspecified assistantships also available. Financial award application deadline: 6/30; financial award applicants required to submit FAFSA. *Faculty research:* Crystallography, trace metal detection, electrochemistry of metalloporphyrins, organic reactions with supported reagents, synthesis of molecules of biological interest. *Unit head:* Dr. Philip W. Crawford, Chairperson and Professor, 573-651-2166, Fax: 573-986-6433, E-mail: pcrawford@semo.edu. *Application contact:* Gail Amick, Administrative Secretary, 573-651-2049, Fax: 573-651-2001, E-mail: gamick@semo.edu.

Southern Connecticut State University, School of Graduate Studies, School of Arts and Sciences, Department of Chemistry, New Haven, CT 06515-1355. Offers MS. Part-time and evening/weekend programs available. *Faculty:* 6 full-time (1 woman). *Students:* 11 part-time (5 women); includes 2 Asian, non-Hispanic/Latino; 1 Hispanic/Latino, 1 international. 16 applicants, 25% accepted, 3 enrolled. In 2010, 1 master's awarded. *Degree requirements:* For master's, thesis or alternative. *Entrance requirements:* For master's, interview, undergraduate work in

Chemistry

Southern Connecticut State University (continued)
chemistry. *Application deadline:* Applications are processed on a rolling basis. Application fee: $50. Electronic applications accepted. *Expenses:* Tuition, state resident: full-time $5137; part-time $518 per credit. Tuition, nonresident: part-time $542 per credit. Required fees: $4008; $55 per semester. Tuition and fees vary according to program. *Financial support:* Teaching assistantships available. Financial award application deadline: 4/15; financial award applicants required to submit FAFSA. *Unit head:* Dr. Gregory Kowalczyk, Chairperson, 203-392-6268, Fax: 203-392-6396, E-mail: kowalczykg1@southernct.edu. *Application contact:* Dr. Robert Snyder, Graduate Coordinator, 203-392-6263, E-mail: snyderr1@southernct.edu.

Southern Illinois University Carbondale, Graduate School, College of Science, Department of Chemistry and Biochemistry, Carbondale, IL 62901-4701. Offers MS, PhD. Part-time programs available. Terminal master's awarded for partial completion of doctoral program. *Degree requirements:* For master's, one foreign language, thesis; for doctorate, variable foreign language requirement, thesis/dissertation. *Entrance requirements:* For master's, minimum GPA of 2.7; for doctorate, GRE General Test, minimum GPA of 3.25. Additional exam requirements/recommendations for international students: Required—TOEFL. *Faculty research:* Materials, separations, computational chemistry, synthetics.

Southern Illinois University Edwardsville, Graduate School, College of Arts and Sciences, Department of Chemistry, Edwardsville, IL 62026-0001. Offers MS. Part-time and evening/weekend programs available. *Faculty:* 18 full-time (3 women). *Students:* 13 full-time (2 women), 22 part-time (7 women); includes 2 minority (1 Black or African American, non-Hispanic/Latino; 1 Hispanic/Latino), 11 international. Average age 26. 47 applicants, 49% accepted. In 2010, 15 master's awarded. *Degree requirements:* For master's, thesis (for some programs), research paper. *Entrance requirements:* Additional exam requirements/recommendations for international students: Required—TOEFL (minimum score 550 paper-based; 213 computer-based; 79 iBT), IELTS (minimum score 6.5). *Application deadline:* For fall admission, 7/22 for domestic students, 6/1 for international students; for spring admission, 12/9 for domestic students, 10/1 for international students. Applications are processed on a rolling basis. Application fee: $30. Electronic applications accepted. *Expenses:* Tuition, state resident: full-time $6012; part-time $1503 per semester. Tuition, nonresident: full-time $15,030; part-time $3758 per semester. Required fees: $1711; $675 per semester. *Financial support:* In 2010–11, 8 research assistantships with full tuition reimbursements (averaging $8,064 per year), 29 teaching assistantships with full tuition reimbursements (averaging $8,064 per year) were awarded; fellowships with full tuition reimbursements, career-related internships or fieldwork, Federal Work-Study, institutionally sponsored loans, scholarships/grants, and unspecified assistantships also available. Support available to part-time students. Financial award application deadline: 3/1; financial award applicants required to submit FAFSA. *Unit head:* Dr. Sadegh Khazaeli, Program Director, 618-650-2042, E-mail: skhazae@siue.edu. *Application contact:* Dr. Sadegh Khazaeli, Program Director, 618-650-2042, E-mail: skhazae@siue.edu.

Southern Methodist University, Dedman College, Department of Chemistry, Dallas, TX 75275-0314. Offers MS, PhD. *Faculty:* 12 full-time (2 women). *Students:* 20 full-time (10 women); includes 9 Asian, non-Hispanic/Latino; 1 Hispanic/Latino, 10 international. Average age 26. 20 applicants, 60% accepted, 10 enrolled. In 2010, 2 doctorates awarded. Terminal master's awarded for partial completion of doctoral program. *Degree requirements:* For master's, thesis; for doctorate, comprehensive exam, thesis/dissertation. *Entrance requirements:* For master's, GRE General Test, bachelor's degree in chemistry, minimum GPA of 3.0; for doctorate, GRE General Test, bachelor's degree in chemistry or closely related field, minimum GPA of 3.0. Additional exam requirements/recommendations for international students: Required—TOEFL (minimum score 550 paper-based; 213 computer-based; 80 iBT). *Application deadline:* For fall admission, 2/28 priority date for domestic and international students. Applications are processed on a rolling basis. Application fee: $75. Electronic applications accepted. *Financial support:* In 2010–11, 20 students received support, including 4 research assistantships with full tuition reimbursements available (averaging $22,000 per year), 16 teaching assistantships with full tuition reimbursements available (averaging $22,000 per year); fellowships, scholarships/grants, health care benefits, and unspecified assistantships also available. Financial award application deadline: 2/28. *Faculty research:* Materials/polymer, medicinal/bioorganic, theoretical and computational, organic/inorganic/organometallic synthesis, inorganic polymer chemistry. Total annual research expenditures: $1 million. *Unit head:* Dr. Elfi Kraka, Chair, 214-768-2480, Fax: 214-768-4089, E-mail: ekraka@smu.edu. *Application contact:* Dr. Michael Lattman, Graduate Adviser, 214-768-2467, Fax: 214-768-4089, E-mail: mlattman@smu.edu.

Southern University and Agricultural and Mechanical College, Graduate School, College of Sciences, Department of Chemistry, Baton Rouge, LA 70813. Offers analytical chemistry (MS); biochemistry (MS); environmental sciences (MS); inorganic chemistry (MS); organic chemistry (MS); physical chemistry (MS). *Degree requirements:* For master's, thesis. *Entrance requirements:* For master's, GMAT or GRE General Test. Additional exam requirements/recommendations for international students: Required—TOEFL (minimum score 525 paper-based; 193 computer-based). *Faculty research:* Synthesis of macrocyclic ligands, latex accelerators, anticancer drugs, biosensors, absorption isotheums, isolation of specific enzymes from plants.

Stanford University, School of Humanities and Sciences, Department of Chemistry, Stanford, CA 94305-5080. Offers PhD. *Degree requirements:* For doctorate, thesis/dissertation. *Entrance requirements:* For doctorate, GRE General Test, GRE Subject Test. Additional exam requirements/recommendations for international students: Required—TOEFL. Electronic applications accepted. *Expenses:* Tuition: Full-time $38,700; part-time $860 per unit. One-time fee: $200 full-time.

State University of New York at Binghamton, Graduate School, School of Arts and Sciences, Department of Chemistry, Binghamton, NY 13902-6000. Offers analytical chemistry (PhD); chemistry (MA, MS); inorganic chemistry (PhD); organic chemistry (PhD); physical chemistry (PhD). Part-time programs available. *Faculty:* 15 full-time (4 women), 3 part-time/adjunct (2 women). *Students:* 28 full-time (8 women), 29 part-time (17 women); includes 2 Black or African American, non-Hispanic/Latino; 4 Asian, non-Hispanic/Latino; 2 Hispanic/Latino, 34 international. Average age 29. 35 applicants, 40% accepted, 9 enrolled. In 2010, 5 master's, 8 doctorates awarded. Terminal master's awarded for partial completion of doctoral program. *Degree requirements:* For master's, thesis or alternative, oral exam, seminar presentation; for doctorate, thesis/dissertation, cumulative exams. *Entrance requirements:* For master's and doctorate, GRE General Test, GRE Subject Test. Additional exam requirements/recommendations for international students: Required—TOEFL (minimum score 550 paper-based; 213 computer-based; 80 iBT). *Application deadline:* For fall admission, 1/15 priority date for domestic and international students; for spring admission, 10/15 priority date for domestic and international students. Applications are processed on a rolling basis. Application fee: $60. Electronic applications accepted. *Financial support:* In 2010–11, 51 students received support, including 5 fellowships with full tuition reimbursements available (averaging $18,000 per year), 9 research assistantships with full tuition reimbursements available (averaging $18,000 per year), 35 teaching assistantships with full tuition reimbursements available (averaging $18,000 per year); career-related internships or fieldwork, Federal Work-Study, institutionally sponsored loans, scholarships/grants, health care benefits, tuition waivers (full), and unspecified assistantships also available. Financial award application deadline: 2/15; financial award applicants required to submit FAFSA. *Unit head:* Dr. Wayne E. Jones, Chairperson, 607-777-2421, E-mail: wjones@binghamton.edu. *Application contact:* Catherin Smith, Recruiting and Admissions Coordinator, 607-777-2151, Fax: 607-777-2501, E-mail: cmsmith@binghamton.edu.

State University of New York at Fredonia, Graduate Studies, Department of Chemistry and Biochemistry, Fredonia, NY 14063-1136. Offers chemistry (MS); curriculum and instruction science education (MS Ed). Part-time and evening/weekend programs available. *Degree requirements:* For master's, thesis optional. *Expenses:* Tuition, state resident: full-time $8370; part-time $349 per credit hour. Tuition, nonresident: full-time $13,250; part-time $552 per credit hour. Required fees: $1328; $55.15 per credit hour.

State University of New York at New Paltz, Graduate School, School of Education, Department of Secondary Education, New Paltz, NY 12561. Offers adolescence education: biology (MAT, MS Ed); adolescence education: chemistry (MAT, MS Ed); adolescence education: earth science (MAT, MS Ed); adolescence education: English (MAT, MS Ed); adolescence education: French (MAT, MS Ed); adolescence education: social studies (MAT, MS Ed); adolescence education: Spanish (MAT, MS Ed); second language education (MS Ed). *Accreditation:* NCATE. Part-time and evening/weekend programs available. *Faculty:* 7 full-time (5 women), 7 part-time/adjunct (5 women). *Students:* 84 full-time (49 women), 78 part-time (52 women); includes 1 Black or African American, non-Hispanic/Latino; 4 Asian, non-Hispanic/Latino; 20 Hispanic/Latino; 2 Two or more races, non-Hispanic/Latino, 1 international. Average age 30. 122 applicants, 75% accepted, 68 enrolled. In 2010, 88 master's awarded. *Degree requirements:* For master's, comprehensive exam (for some programs), portfolio. *Entrance requirements:* For master's, minimum GPA of 3.0, New York state teaching certificate (MS Ed). Additional exam requirements/recommendations for international students: Required—TOEFL (minimum score 550 paper-based; 213 computer-based; 80 iBT), IELTS (minimum score 6.5). *Application deadline:* For fall admission, 3/1 priority date for domestic students, 3/1 for international students; for spring admission, 10/1 priority date for domestic students, 10/1 for international students. Application fee: $50. Electronic applications accepted. *Expenses:* Tuition, state resident: full-time $8370; part-time $349 per credit hour. Tuition, nonresident: full-time $13,780; part-time $574 per credit hour. Required fees: $1165; $33.80 per credit hour. $175 per term. Tuition and fees vary according to program. *Financial support:* In 2010–11, 13 students received support, including 5 fellowships (averaging $5,000 per year), 3 research assistantships with partial tuition reimbursements available (averaging $5,000 per year); Federal Work-Study, institutionally sponsored loans, and tuition waivers (full) also available. Financial award application deadline: 8/1; financial award applicants required to submit FAFSA. *Unit head:* Dr. Devon Duhaney, Chair, 845-257-2850, E-mail: duhaneyd@newpaltz.edu. *Application contact:* Caroline Murphy, Graduate Admissions Advisor, 845-257-3285, Fax: 845-257-3284, E-mail: gradschool@newpaltz.edu.

State University of New York at Oswego, Graduate Studies, College of Liberal Arts and Sciences, Department of Chemistry, Oswego, NY 13126. Offers MS. Part-time programs available. *Faculty:* 7 full-time (2 women). *Students:* 7 full-time (4 women), 1 (woman) part-time; includes 1 Hispanic/Latino, 1 international. Average age 25. 6 applicants, 83% accepted. In 2010, 5 master's awarded. *Degree requirements:* For master's, comprehensive exam, thesis. *Entrance requirements:* For master's, GRE General Test, GRE Subject Test, BA or BS in chemistry. Additional exam requirements/recommendations for international students: Required—TOEFL (minimum score 560 paper-based; 220 computer-based). *Application deadline:* For fall admission, 4/1 for domestic and international students; for spring admission, 10/1 for domestic and international students. Applications are processed on a rolling basis. Application fee: $50. *Expenses:* Tuition, state resident: full-time $8370; part-time $349 per credit hour. Tuition, nonresident: full-time $13,780; part-time $574 per credit hour. Required fees: $853; $22.59 per credit hour. *Financial support:* In 2010–11, 7 students received support, including 7 teaching assistantships with full tuition reimbursements available (averaging $11,000 per year); research assistantships with full tuition reimbursements available, career-related internships or fieldwork, Federal Work-Study, institutionally sponsored loans, scholarships/grants, health care benefits, and unspecified assistantships also available. Support available to part-time students. Financial award application deadline: 4/1; financial award applicants required to submit FAFSA. *Unit head:* Dr. Lawrence Fuller, Chair, 315-312-3048. *Application contact:* Dr. Fehmi Damkaci, Graduate Coordinator, 315-312-2698, E-mail: fehmi.damkaci@oswego.edu.

State University of New York College of Environmental Science and Forestry, Department of Chemistry, Syracuse, NY 13210-2779. Offers biochemistry (MPS, MS, PhD); environmental and forest chemistry (MPS, MS, PhD); organic chemistry (MPS); organic chemistry of natural products (MS, PhD); polymer chemistry (MPS, MS, PhD). *Degree requirements:* For master's, thesis; for doctorate, comprehensive exam, thesis/dissertation. *Entrance requirements:* For master's and doctorate, GRE General Test, GRE Subject Test, minimum GPA of 3.0. Additional exam requirements/recommendations for international students: Required—TOEFL (minimum score 550 paper-based; 213 computer-based; 80 iBT), IELTS (minimum score 6). Electronic applications accepted. *Expenses:* Tuition, state resident: full-time $8370; part-time $349 per credit hour. Tuition, nonresident: full-time $13,780. Required fees: $30.30 per credit hour. $20 per year. *Faculty research:* Polymer chemistry, biochemistry.

Stephen F. Austin State University, Graduate School, College of Sciences and Mathematics, Department of Chemistry, Nacogdoches, TX 75962. Offers MS. Part-time programs available. *Degree requirements:* For master's, comprehensive exam. *Entrance requirements:* For master's, GRE General Test, minimum GPA of 2.8 in last 60 hours, 2.5 overall. Additional exam requirements/recommendations for international students: Required—TOEFL. *Faculty research:* Synthesis and chemistry of ferrate ion, properties of fluoroberyllates, polymer chemistry.

Stevens Institute of Technology, Graduate School, Charles V. Schaefer Jr. School of Engineering, Department of Chemistry, Chemical Biology and Biomedical Engineering, Hoboken, NJ 07030. Offers analytical chemistry (PhD, Certificate); bioinformatics (PhD, Certificate); biomedical chemistry (Certificate); biomedical engineering (M Eng, Certificate); chemical biology (MS, PhD, Certificate); chemical physiology (Certificate); chemistry (MS, PhD); organic chemistry (PhD); physical chemistry (PhD); polymer chemistry (PhD, Certificate). Part-time and evening/weekend programs available. Postbaccalaureate distance learning degree programs offered (no on-campus study). *Students:* 66 full-time (35 women), 25 part-time (7 women); includes 2 Black or African American, non-Hispanic/Latino; 14 Asian, non-Hispanic/Latino; 8 Hispanic/Latino, 31 international. Average age 26. 109 applicants, 68% accepted.Terminal master's awarded for partial completion of doctoral program. *Degree requirements:* For master's, thesis or alternative; for doctorate, one foreign language, thesis/dissertation; for Certificate, project or thesis. *Entrance requirements:* Additional exam requirements/recommendations for international students: Required—TOEFL. *Application deadline:* Applications are processed on a rolling basis. Application fee: $50. Electronic applications accepted. *Financial support:* Fellowships, research assistantships, teaching assistantships available. Financial award application deadline: 4/1. *Faculty research:* Biochemical reaction engineering, polymerization engineering, reactor design, biochemical process control and synthesis. *Unit head:* Philip Leopold, Director, 201-216-8957, Fax: 201-216-8196, E-mail: pleopold@stevens.edu. *Application contact:* Graduate Admissions, 800-496-4935, Fax: 201-216-8044, E-mail: gradadmissions@stevens.edu.

Stony Brook University, State University of New York, Graduate School, College of Arts and Sciences, Department of Chemistry, Stony Brook, NY 11794. Offers MS, PhD. *Faculty:* 35 full-time (7 women), 4 part-time/adjunct (2 women). *Students:* 187 full-time (76 women), 6 part-time (3 women); includes 4 Black or African American, non-Hispanic/Latino; 16 Asian, non-Hispanic/Latino; 7 Hispanic/Latino, 110 international. Average age 28. 398 applicants, 35% accepted, 52 enrolled. In 2010, 13 master's, 14 doctorates awarded. Terminal master's awarded for partial completion of doctoral program. *Degree requirements:* For master's, thesis; for doctorate, one foreign language, thesis/dissertation. *Entrance requirements:* For master's and doctorate, GRE General Test. Additional exam requirements/recommendations for international students: Required—TOEFL. *Application deadline:* For fall admission, 1/15 for domestic students. Application fee: $100. *Expenses:* Tuition, state resident: full-time $8370; part-time $349 per credit. Tuition, nonresident: full-time $13,780; part-time $574 per credit. Required fees: $994. *Financial support:* In 2010–11, 116 research assistantships, 66 teaching assistantships were awarded; fellowships also available. Total annual research expenditures:

$10 million. *Unit head:* Prof. Ben Hsiao, Chairman, 631-632-7880, Fax: 631-632-7960. *Application contact:* Prof. Ben Hsiao, Chairman, 631-632-7880, Fax: 631-632-7960.

Syracuse University, College of Arts and Sciences, Program in Chemistry, Syracuse, NY 13244. Offers MS, PhD. *Students:* 67 full-time (32 women), 4 part-time (0 women); includes 6 minority (4 Asian, non-Hispanic/Latino; 2 Hispanic/Latino), 23 international. Average age 26. 98 applicants, 41% accepted, 14 enrolled. In 2010, 8 master's, 14 doctorates awarded. *Degree requirements:* For master's, one foreign language, comprehensive exam, thesis (for some programs); for doctorate, one foreign language, comprehensive exam, thesis/dissertation. *Entrance requirements:* For master's and doctorate, GRE General Test. Additional exam requirements/recommendations for international students: Required—TOEFL (minimum score 100 iBT). *Application deadline:* For fall admission, 3/15 priority date for domestic and international students. Application fee: $75. Electronic applications accepted. *Expenses:* Tuition: Part-time $1162 per credit. *Financial support:* Fellowships with full tuition reimbursements, research assistantships with full and partial tuition reimbursements, teaching assistantships with full tuition reimbursements available. Financial award application deadline: 1/1; financial award applicants required to submit FAFSA. *Faculty research:* Synthetic organic chemistry, biophysical spectroscopy, solid state in organic chemistry, biochemistry, organometallic chemistry. *Unit head:* Dr. Karin Ruhlandt, Chair, 315-443-4109, Fax: 315-443-4070. *Application contact:* Joyce Lagoe, Information Contact, 315-443-4109, E-mail: jalagoe@syr.edu.

Temple University, College of Science and Technology, Department of Chemistry, Philadelphia, PA 19122-6096. Offers MA, PhD. Evening/weekend programs available. *Faculty:* 22 full-time (3 women). *Students:* 71 full-time (22 women), 37 part-time (12 women); includes 3 Black or African American, non-Hispanic/Latino; 5 Asian, non-Hispanic/Latino, 65 international. 94 applicants, 37% accepted, 15 enrolled. In 2010, 9 master's, 4 doctorates awarded. Terminal master's awarded for partial completion of doctoral program. *Degree requirements:* For master's, thesis (for some programs); for doctorate, thesis/dissertation, teaching experience. *Entrance requirements:* For master's and doctorate, GRE General Test, minimum GPA of 3.0. Additional exam requirements/recommendations for international students: Required—TOEFL (minimum score 550 paper-based; 213 computer-based; 79 iBT). *Application deadline:* For fall admission, 2/15 for domestic students, 12/15 for international students; for spring admission, 9/15 for domestic students, 8/1 for international students. Applications are processed on a rolling basis. Application fee: $50. Electronic applications accepted. *Financial support:* Fellowships, research assistantships, teaching assistantships available. Financial award application deadline: 1/15; financial award applicants required to submit FAFSA. *Faculty research:* Polymers, nonlinear optics, natural products, materials science, enantioselective synthesis. Total annual research expenditures: $691,921. *Unit head:* Dr. Robert Levis, Chair, 215-204-5241, Fax: 215-204-1532, E-mail: rjlevis@temple.edu. *Application contact:* Dr. Robert Levis, Chair, 215-204-5241, Fax: 215-204-1532, E-mail: rjlevis@temple.edu.

Tennessee State University, The School of Graduate Studies and Research, College of Arts and Sciences, Department of Chemistry, Nashville, TN 37209-1561. Offers MS. Part-time programs available. *Degree requirements:* For master's, thesis optional. *Entrance requirements:* For master's, GRE General Test. Electronic applications accepted.

Tennessee Technological University, Graduate School, College of Arts and Sciences, Department of Chemistry, Cookeville, TN 38505. Offers MS. Part-time programs available. *Faculty:* 16 full-time (1 woman). *Students:* 8 full-time (3 women), 6 part-time (1 woman); includes 1 Black or African American, non-Hispanic/Latino; 6 Asian, non-Hispanic/Latino; 1 Hispanic/Latino. Average age 28. 14 applicants, 43% accepted, 1 enrolled. In 2010, 5 master's awarded. *Degree requirements:* For master's, thesis. *Entrance requirements:* For master's, GRE. Additional exam requirements/recommendations for international students: Required—TOEFL (minimum score 550 paper-based; 79 iBT), IELTS (minimum score 5.5). *Application deadline:* For fall admission, 8/1 for domestic students, 5/1 for international students; for spring admission, 2/1 for domestic students, 10/1 for international students. Application fee: $25 ($30 for international students). *Expenses:* Tuition, state resident: full-time $7934; part-time $388 per credit hour. Tuition, nonresident: full-time $19,758; part-time $962 per credit hour. *Financial support:* In 2010–11, 1 research assistantship (averaging $10,000 per year), 6 teaching assistantships (averaging $7,500 per year) were awarded; career-related internships or fieldwork also available. Financial award application deadline: 4/1. *Unit head:* Dr. Jeffrey Boles, Interim Chairperson, 931-372-3421, Fax: 931-372-3434, E-mail: jboles@tntech.edu. *Application contact:* Shelia K. Kendrick, Coordinator of Graduate Admissions, 931-372-3808, Fax: 931-372-3497, E-mail: skendrick@tntech.edu.

Tennessee Technological University, Graduate School, College of Arts and Sciences, Department of Environmental Sciences, Cookeville, TN 38505. Offers biology (PhD); chemistry (PhD). *Students:* 9 full-time (4 women), 6 part-time (2 women); includes 3 Black or African American, non-Hispanic/Latino; 2 Asian, non-Hispanic/Latino; 2 Hispanic/Latino. 14 applicants, 21% accepted, 1 enrolled. In 2010, 4 doctorates awarded. *Degree requirements:* For doctorate, comprehensive exam, thesis/dissertation. *Entrance requirements:* For doctorate, GRE. Additional exam requirements/recommendations for international students: Required—TOEFL (minimum score 550 paper-based; 79 iBT), IELTS (minimum score 5.5). *Application deadline:* For fall admission, 8/1 for domestic students, 5/1 for international students; for spring admission, 12/1 for domestic students, 10/2 for international students. Application fee: $25 ($30 for international students). Electronic applications accepted. *Expenses:* Tuition, state resident: full-time $7934; part-time $388 per credit hour. Tuition, nonresident: full-time $19,758; part-time $962 per credit hour. *Financial support:* In 2010–11, 5 research assistantships (averaging $10,000 per year), 3 teaching assistantships (averaging $10,000 per year) were awarded; fellowships also available. Financial award application deadline: 4/1. *Unit head:* Dr. Dal Ensor, Director. *Application contact:* Shelia K. Kendrick, Coordinator of Graduate Admissions, 931-372-3808, Fax: 931-372-3497, E-mail: skendrick@tntech.edu.

Texas A&M University, College of Science, Department of Chemistry, College Station, TX 77843. Offers MS, PhD. *Faculty:* 44. *Students:* 282 full-time (102 women), 7 part-time (4 women); includes 8 Black or African American, non-Hispanic/Latino; 1 American Indian or Alaska Native, non-Hispanic/Latino; 10 Asian, non-Hispanic/Latino; 16 Hispanic/Latino, 139 international. Average age 24. In 2010, 7 master's, 40 doctorates awarded. Terminal master's awarded for partial completion of doctoral program. *Degree requirements:* For master's, thesis; for doctorate, thesis/dissertation. *Entrance requirements:* For master's and doctorate, GRE General Test. Additional exam requirements/recommendations for international students: Required—TOEFL. *Application deadline:* For fall admission, 3/1 priority date for domestic students. Applications are processed on a rolling basis. Electronic applications accepted. *Financial support:* In 2010–11, fellowships with full tuition reimbursements (averaging $21,600 per year), research assistantships with full tuition reimbursements (averaging $18,600 per year), teaching assistantships with full tuition reimbursements (averaging $18,600 per year) were awarded. Financial award application deadline: 3/1; financial award applicants required to submit FAFSA. *Faculty research:* Biological chemistry, spectroscopy, structure and bonding, reactions and mechanisms, theoretical chemistry. *Unit head:* Dr. David Russell, Head, 979-845-3345, E-mail: russell@chem.tamu.edu. *Application contact:* Dr. Michael P. Rosynek, Graduate Advisor, 979-845-2233, Fax: 979-845-4719, E-mail: rosynek@chem.tamu.edu.

Texas A&M University–Commerce, Graduate School, College of Arts and Sciences, Department of Chemistry, Commerce, TX 75429-3011. Offers M Ed, MS. Part-time programs available. *Degree requirements:* For master's, comprehensive exam, thesis (for some programs). *Entrance requirements:* For master's, GRE General Test. Electronic applications accepted. *Faculty research:* Analytical organic.

Texas A&M University–Kingsville, College of Graduate Studies, College of Arts and Sciences, Department of Chemistry, Kingsville, TX 78363. Offers MS. Part-time programs available. *Degree requirements:* For master's, comprehensive exam, thesis or alternative. *Entrance requirements:* For master's, GRE General Test, minimum GPA of 3.0. Additional exam requirements/recommendations for international students: Required—TOEFL. *Faculty research:* Organic heterocycles, amino alcohol complexes, rare earth arsine complexes.

Texas Christian University, College of Science and Engineering, Department of Chemistry, Fort Worth, TX 76129-0002. Offers biochemistry (MS, PhD); chemistry (MA); inorganic (MS, PhD); organic (MS, PhD); physical (MS, PhD). Part-time and evening/weekend programs available. *Faculty:* 11 full-time (2 women), 1 (woman) part-time/adjunct. *Students:* 19 full-time (9 women), 2 part-time (both women); includes 1 American Indian or Alaska Native, non-Hispanic/Latino; 3 Asian, non-Hispanic/Latino; 4 Hispanic/Latino, 9 international. Average age 24. 23 applicants, 26% accepted, 5 enrolled. In 2010, 3 doctorates awarded. *Degree requirements:* For master's, thesis; for doctorate, thesis/dissertation, literature seminar, cumulative exams, research progress report, original proposal. *Entrance requirements:* For master's and doctorate, GRE General Test. Additional exam requirements/recommendations for international students: Required—TOEFL. *Application deadline:* For fall admission, 3/1 priority date for domestic and international students; for spring admission, 9/1 priority date for domestic and international students. Applications are processed on a rolling basis. Application fee: $50. Electronic applications accepted. *Expenses:* Tuition: Full-time $18,720; part-time $1040 per credit hour. Tuition and fees vary according to course load and program. *Financial support:* Fellowships, teaching assistantships, unspecified assistantships available. Financial award application deadline: 3/1. *Faculty research:* Phase transitions and transport properties of bio/macromolecular solutions, nanoscale biomaterials, electronic structure theory, synthetic methodology and total synthesis of natural products, chemistry and biology of (bio)polymers. *Unit head:* Dr. Robert Neilson, Chairperson; Professor, 817-257-7345, Fax: 817-257-5851, E-mail: r.neilson@tcu.edu. *Application contact:* Dr. Sergei V. Rzyuba, Director of Graduate Studies; Assistant Professor, 817-257-6218, Fax: 817-257-5851, E-mail: s.dzyuba@tcu.edu.

Texas Southern University, School of Science and Technology, Department of Chemistry, Houston, TX 77004-4584. Offers MS. *Faculty:* 4 full-time (1 woman), 1 part-time/adjunct (0 women). *Students:* 6 full-time (5 women), 4 part-time (3 women); includes 6 Black or African American, non-Hispanic/Latino; 3 Asian, non-Hispanic/Latino, 1 international. Average age 29. 7 applicants, 100% accepted, 5 enrolled. *Degree requirements:* For master's, one foreign language, comprehensive exam, thesis. *Entrance requirements:* For master's, GRE General Test, minimum GPA of 2.5. Additional exam requirements/recommendations for international students: Required—TOEFL. *Application deadline:* For fall admission, 7/1 for domestic and international students; for spring admission, 11/1 for domestic and international students. Applications are processed on a rolling basis. Application fee: $50 ($75 for international students). Electronic applications accepted. *Expenses:* Tuition, state resident: full-time $1875; part-time $100 per credit hour. Tuition, nonresident: full-time $6641; part-time $343 per credit hour. Tuition and fees vary according to course level, course load and degree level. *Financial support:* In 2010–11, 1 research assistantship (averaging $2,250 per year), 4 teaching assistantships (averaging $3,488 per year) were awarded; fellowships, scholarships/grants and unspecified assistantships also available. Financial award application deadline: 5/1. *Faculty research:* Analytical and physical chemistry, geochemistry, inorganic chemistry, biochemistry, organic chemistry. *Unit head:* Dr. John Sapp, Chair, 713-313-7831, E-mail: sapp_jb@tsu.edu. *Application contact:* Delois Smith-Johnson, Administrative Secretary, 713-313-7831, E-mail: johnson_ds@tsu.edu.

Texas State University–San Marcos, Graduate School, College of Science, Department of Chemistry and Biochemistry, Program in Chemistry, San Marcos, TX 78666. Offers MA, MS. *Faculty:* 10 full-time (2 women). *Students:* 6 full-time (1 woman), 3 part-time (1 woman); includes 2 minority (1 Black or African American, non-Hispanic/Latino; 1 Hispanic/Latino), 1 international. Average age 30. 12 applicants, 67% accepted, 2 enrolled. In 2010, 4 master's awarded. *Degree requirements:* For master's, comprehensive exam, thesis (for some programs). *Entrance requirements:* For master's, minimum GPA of 2.75 in last 60 hours of course work. Additional exam requirements/recommendations for international students: Required—TOEFL (minimum score 550 paper-based; 213 computer-based; 78 iBT). *Application deadline:* For fall admission, 6/15 for domestic students, 6/1 for international students; for spring admission, 10/15 for domestic students, 10/1 for international students. Applications are processed on a rolling basis. Application fee: $40 ($90 for international students). *Expenses:* Tuition, state resident: full-time $6024; part-time $251 per credit hour. Tuition, nonresident: full-time $13,536; part-time $564 per credit hour. Required fees: $1776; $50 per credit hour. $306 per semester. *Financial support:* In 2010–11, 4 students received support, including 7 teaching assistantships (averaging $4,844 per year); research assistantships, career-related internships or fieldwork, Federal Work-Study, institutionally sponsored loans, scholarships/grants, health care benefits, and unspecified assistantships also available. Support available to part-time students. Financial award application deadline: 4/1; financial award applicants required to submit FAFSA. *Faculty research:* Metal ions in biological systems, cancer chemotherapy, absorption of pesticides on solid surfaces, polymer chemistry, biochemistry of nucleic acids. *Unit head:* Dr. Chad Booth, Graduate Advisor, 512-245-2156, Fax: 512-245-2374, E-mail: chadbooth@txstate.edu. *Application contact:* Dr. J. Michael Willoughby, Dean of Graduate School, 512-245-2581, Fax: 512-245-8365, E-mail: gradcollege@txstate.edu.

Texas Tech University, Graduate School, College of Arts and Sciences, Department of Chemistry and Biochemistry, Lubbock, TX 79409. Offers chemistry (MS, PhD). Part-time programs available. *Faculty:* 21 full-time (2 women), 1 (woman) part-time/adjunct. *Students:* 96 full-time (40 women), 4 part-time (0 women); includes 2 Black or African American, non-Hispanic/Latino; 2 Asian, non-Hispanic/Latino; 4 Hispanic/Latino, 70 international. Average age 26. 176 applicants, 28% accepted, 22 enrolled. In 2010, 5 master's, 22 doctorates awarded. *Degree requirements:* For master's, thesis; for doctorate, thesis/dissertation. *Entrance requirements:* For master's and doctorate, GRE General Test, diagnostic examination in area of specialization. Additional exam requirements/recommendations for international students: Required—TOEFL (minimum score 550 paper-based; 213 computer-based; 79 iBT). *Application deadline:* For fall admission, 6/1 priority date for domestic students, 1/15 priority date for international students; for spring admission, 9/1 priority date for domestic students, 6/15 priority date for international students. Applications are processed on a rolling basis. Application fee: $50 ($75 for international students). Electronic applications accepted. *Expenses:* Tuition, state resident: full-time $5495.76; part-time $228.99 per credit hour. Tuition, nonresident: full-time $12,936; part-time $538.99 per credit hour. Required fees: $2674; $36 per credit hour. $905 per semester. *Financial support:* In 2010–11, 98 students received support, including 26 research assistantships with partial tuition reimbursements available (averaging $5,852 per year), 29 teaching assistantships with partial tuition reimbursements available (averaging $7,542 per year). Financial award application deadline: 4/15; financial award applicants required to submit FAFSA. *Faculty research:* Theoretical and computational chemistry, plant biochemistry and chemical biology, materials and supramolecular chemistry, nanotechnology, spectroscopic analysis. Total annual research expenditures: $4.4 million. *Unit head:* Dr. Carol Korzeniewski, Chair, 806-742-3067, Fax: 806-742-1289, E-mail: carol.korzeniewski@ttu.edu. *Application contact:* Carly Jenkins, Senior Business Assistant, 806-742-3057, Fax: 806-742-4890, E-mail: carly.jenkins@ttu.edu.

Texas Woman's University, Graduate School, College of Arts and Sciences, Department of Chemistry and Physics, Denton, TX 76201. Offers chemistry (MS). Part-time programs available. *Faculty:* 10 full-time (4 women), 1 part-time/adjunct (0 women). *Students:* 4 full-time (3 women), 4 part-time (all women); includes 1 Hispanic/Latino, 2 international. Average age 28. 3 applicants, 33% accepted, 0 enrolled. In 2010, 2 master's awarded. *Degree requirements:* For master's, comprehensive exam, thesis. *Entrance requirements:* For master's, GRE General Test (preferred minimum score 400 verbal, 550 quantitative), bachelor's degree in chemistry or equivalent, 2 reference contacts. Additional exam requirements/recommendations for inter-

Peterson's Graduate Programs in the Physical Sciences, Mathematics, Agricultural Sciences, the Environment & Natural Resources 2012

www.facebook.com/petersonspublishing 65

Texas Woman's University (continued)
national students: Required—TOEFL (minimum score 550 paper-based; 213 computer-based; 79 iBT). *Application deadline:* For fall admission, 7/1 priority date for domestic students, 3/1 for international students; for spring admission, 12/1 priority date for domestic students, 7/1 for international students. Applications are processed on a rolling basis. Application fee: $50 ($75 for international students). Electronic applications accepted. *Expenses:* Tuition, state resident: full-time $3834; part-time $213 per credit hour. Tuition, nonresident: full-time $9468; part-time $526 per credit hour. Required fees: $1247; $220 per credit hour. *Financial support:* In 2010–11, 6 students received support, including 6 research assistantships (averaging $13,248 per year), 2 teaching assistantships (averaging $13,248 per year); career-related internships or fieldwork, Federal Work-Study, institutionally sponsored loans, scholarships/grants, traineeships, health care benefits, and unspecified assistantships also available. Support available to part-time students. Financial award application deadline: 3/1; financial award applicants required to submit FAFSA. *Faculty research:* Glutathione synthetase, conformational properties of DNA quadruplexes, constriction and analysis of aqueous enzyme phase diagrams, development of metallopolymers, basic chemical research. Total annual research expenditures: $102,821. *Unit head:* Dr. Richard Sheardy, Chair, 940-898-2550, Fax: 940-898-2548, E-mail: rsheardy@mail.twu.edu. *Application contact:* Dr. Samuel Wheeler, Assistant Director of Admissions, 940-898-3188, Fax: 940-898-3081, E-mail: wheelersr@twu.edu.

Trent University, Graduate Studies, Program in Applications of Modeling in the Natural and Social Sciences, Department of Chemistry, Peterborough, ON K9J 7B8, Canada. Offers M Sc. Part-time programs available. *Degree requirements:* For master's, thesis. *Entrance requirements:* For master's, honours degree. *Faculty research:* Synthetic-organic chemistry, mass spectrometry and ion storage.

Tufts University, Graduate School of Arts and Sciences, Department of Chemistry, Medford, MA 02155. Offers analytical chemistry (MS, PhD); bioorganic chemistry (MS, PhD); environmental chemistry (MS, PhD); inorganic chemistry (MS, PhD); organic chemistry (MS, PhD); physical chemistry (MS, PhD). Terminal master's awarded for partial completion of doctoral program. *Degree requirements:* For master's, thesis optional; for doctorate, thesis/dissertation. *Entrance requirements:* For master's and doctorate, GRE General Test, GRE Subject Test. Additional exam requirements/recommendations for international students: Required—TOEFL (minimum score 600 paper-based; 250 computer-based; 80 iBT). Electronic applications accepted. *Expenses:* Tuition: Full-time $39,624; part-time $3962 per course. Required fees: $40 per year. Full-time tuition and fees vary according to degree level, program and student level. Part-time tuition and fees vary according to course load.

Tulane University, School of Science and Engineering, Department of Chemistry, New Orleans, LA 70118-5669. Offers MS, PhD. Terminal master's awarded for partial completion of doctoral program. *Degree requirements:* For master's, thesis; for doctorate, thesis/dissertation. *Entrance requirements:* For master's, GRE General Test, minimum B average in undergraduate course work; for doctorate, GRE General Test. Additional exam requirements/recommendations for international students: Required—TOEFL. Electronic applications accepted. *Faculty research:* Enzyme mechanisms, organic synthesis, photochemistry, theory of polymer dynamics.

Tuskegee University, Graduate Programs, College of Agricultural, Environmental and Natural Sciences, Department of Chemistry, Tuskegee, AL 36088. Offers MS. *Faculty:* 6 full-time (1 woman). *Students:* 12 full-time (9 women); includes 6 Black or African American, non-Hispanic/Latino, 4 international. Average age 31. In 2010, 4 master's awarded. *Degree requirements:* For master's, thesis. *Entrance requirements:* For master's, GRE General Test. Additional exam requirements/recommendations for international students: Required—TOEFL (minimum score 500 paper-based; 69 computer-based). *Application deadline:* For fall admission, 7/15 for domestic students. Applications are processed on a rolling basis. Application fee: $25 ($35 for international students). *Expenses:* Tuition: Full-time $16,100; part-time $665 per credit hour. Required fees: $650. *Financial support:* Fellowships, teaching assistantships, Federal Work-Study and institutionally sponsored loans available. Support available to part-time students. Financial award application deadline: 4/15. *Unit head:* Dr. Gregory Pritchett, Head, 334-727-8836. *Application contact:* Dr. Robert L. Laney, Vice President/Director Admissions and Enrollment Management, 334-727-8580, Fax: 334-727-5750, E-mail: planey@tuskegee.edu.

Universidad del Turabo, Graduate Programs, Programs in Science and Technology, Gurabo, PR 00778-3030. Offers environmental analysis (MSE), including environmental chemistry; environmental management (MSE), including pollution management; environmental science (D Sc), including environmental biology. *Entrance requirements:* For master's, GRE, EXADEP, interview.

Université de Moncton, Faculty of Science, Department of Chemistry and Biochemistry, Moncton, NB E1A 3E9, Canada. Offers biochemistry (M Sc); chemistry (M Sc). Part-time programs available. *Degree requirements:* For master's, one foreign language, thesis. *Entrance requirements:* For master's, minimum GPA of 3.0. Electronic applications accepted. *Faculty research:* Environmental contaminants, natural products synthesis, nutraceutical, organic catalysis, molecular biology of cancer.

Université de Montréal, Faculty of Arts and Sciences, Department of Chemistry, Montréal, QC H3C 3J7, Canada. Offers M Sc, PhD. *Degree requirements:* For master's, thesis; for doctorate, thesis/dissertation, general exam. *Entrance requirements:* For master's, B Sc in chemistry or the equivalent; for doctorate, M Sc in chemistry or equivalent. Electronic applications accepted. *Faculty research:* Analytical, inorganic, physical, and organic chemistry.

Université de Sherbrooke, Faculty of Sciences, Department of Chemistry, Sherbrooke, QC J1K 2R1, Canada. Offers M Sc, PhD, Diploma. *Degree requirements:* For master's, thesis; for doctorate, thesis/dissertation. *Entrance requirements:* For doctorate, master's degree. Electronic applications accepted. *Faculty research:* Organic, electro-, theoretical, and physical chemistry.

Université du Québec à Montréal, Graduate Programs, Program in Chemistry, Montréal, QC H3C 3P8, Canada. Offers M Sc, PhD. M Sc offered jointly with Université du Québec à Trois-Rivières. Part-time programs available. *Degree requirements:* For master's, thesis. *Entrance requirements:* For master's, appropriate bachelor's degree or equivalent and proficiency in French.

Université du Québec à Trois-Rivières, Graduate Programs, Program in Chemistry, Trois-Rivières, QC G9A 5H7, Canada. Offers M Sc. Part-time programs available. *Degree requirements:* For master's, thesis. *Entrance requirements:* For master's, appropriate bachelor's degree, proficiency in French.

Université Laval, Faculty of Sciences and Engineering, Department of Chemistry, Programs in Chemistry, Québec, QC G1K 7P4, Canada. Offers M Sc, PhD. Part-time programs available. Terminal master's awarded for partial completion of doctoral program. *Degree requirements:* For master's, thesis; for doctorate, comprehensive exam, thesis/dissertation. *Entrance requirements:* For master's and doctorate, knowledge of French, comprehension of written English. Electronic applications accepted.

University at Albany, State University of New York, College of Arts and Sciences, Department of Chemistry, Albany, NY 12222-0001. Offers MS, PhD. *Degree requirements:* For master's, one foreign language, thesis, major field exam; for doctorate, 2 foreign languages, thesis/dissertation, cumulative exams, oral proposition. *Entrance requirements:* For doctorate, GRE. Additional exam requirements/recommendations for international students: Required—TOEFL (minimum score 550 paper-based; 213 computer-based). Electronic applications accepted. *Faculty research:* Synthetic, organic, and inorganic chemistry; polymer chemistry; ESR and NMR spectroscopy; theoretical chemistry; physical biochemistry.

University at Albany, State University of New York, School of Public Health, Department of Environmental Health Sciences, Albany, NY 12222-0001. Offers environmental and analytical chemistry (MS, PhD); environmental and occupational health (MS, PhD); toxicology (MS, PhD). *Degree requirements:* For master's, thesis; for doctorate, comprehensive exam, thesis/dissertation. *Entrance requirements:* For master's and doctorate, GRE General Test, GRE Subject Test, 3 letters of reference. Additional exam requirements/recommendations for international students: Required—TOEFL (minimum score 600 paper-based; 213 computer-based). Electronic applications accepted. *Faculty research:* Xenobiotic metabolism, neurotoxicity of halogenated hydrocarbons, pharmac/toxicogenomics, environmental analytical chemistry.

University at Buffalo, the State University of New York, Graduate School, College of Arts and Sciences, Department of Chemistry, Buffalo, NY 14260. Offers chemistry (MA, PhD); medicinal chemistry (MS, PhD). Part-time programs available. *Faculty:* 30 full-time (4 women), 2 part-time/adjunct (both women). *Students:* 136 full-time (51 women), 3 part-time (2 women); includes 8 Black or African American, non-Hispanic/Latino; 2 Asian, non-Hispanic/Latino; 5 Hispanic/Latino, 39 international. Average age 26. 235 applicants, 25% accepted, 24 enrolled. In 2010, 9 master's, 13 doctorates awarded. Terminal master's awarded for partial completion of doctoral program. *Degree requirements:* For master's, thesis or alternative, project; for doctorate, thesis/dissertation, synopsis proposal. *Entrance requirements:* For master's and doctorate, GRE General Test. Additional exam requirements/recommendations for international students: Required—TOEFL (minimum score 550 paper-based; 213 computer-based; 79 iBT). *Application deadline:* For fall admission, 3/1 priority date for domestic students, 3/1 for international students; for spring admission, 11/1 priority date for domestic students. Applications are processed on a rolling basis. Application fee: $75. Electronic applications accepted. *Financial support:* In 2010–11, 6 students received support, including 6 fellowships with full tuition reimbursements available (averaging $22,080 per year), 40 research assistantships with full tuition reimbursements available (averaging $22,080 per year), 78 teaching assistantships with full tuition reimbursements available (averaging $22,080 per year); Federal Work-Study, institutionally sponsored loans, and unspecified assistantships also available. Financial award application deadline: 6/15; financial award applicants required to submit FAFSA. *Faculty research:* Synthesis, measurements, structure theory, translation. Total annual research expenditures: $9.5 million. *Unit head:* Dr. Luis A. Colon, Chairman, 716-645-6824, Fax: 716-645-6963, E-mail: chechair@buffalo.edu. *Application contact:* Dr. Steven T. Diver, Director of Graduate Studies, 716-645-4208, Fax: 716-645-6963, E-mail: diver@buffalo.edu.

The University of Akron, Graduate School, Buchtel College of Arts and Sciences, Department of Chemistry, Akron, OH 44325. Offers MS, PhD. Part-time and evening/weekend programs available. *Faculty:* 20 full-time (2 women), 2 part-time/adjunct (1 woman). *Students:* 60 full-time (30 women), 1 (woman) part-time; includes 4 minority (2 Black or African American, non-Hispanic/Latino; 2 Hispanic/Latino), 31 international. Average age 28. 75 applicants, 27% accepted, 7 enrolled. In 2010, 2 master's, 7 doctorates awarded. Terminal master's awarded for partial completion of doctoral program. *Degree requirements:* For master's, thesis, seminar presentation; for doctorate, comprehensive exam, thesis/dissertation, cumulative exams, oral exam, defense of dissertation. *Entrance requirements:* For master's, baccalaureate degree in chemistry, biochemistry, or a related field, minimum GPA of 2.75, 3 letters of recommendation, statement of purpose; for doctorate, baccalaureate degree in chemistry, biochemistry, or a related field, minimum GPA of 2.75, three letters of recommendation, statement of purpose. Additional exam requirements/recommendations for international students: Required—TOEFL (minimum score 550 paper-based; 213 computer-based; 79 iBT). *Application deadline:* For fall admission, 6/1 for domestic and international students; for spring admission, 11/15 for domestic and international students. Application fee: $30 ($40 for international students). *Expenses:* Tuition, state resident: full-time $6800; part-time $378 per credit hour. Tuition, nonresident: full-time $11,644; part-time $647 per credit hour. Required fees: $1265. One-time fee: $30 full-time. *Financial support:* In 2010–11, 18 research assistantships with full tuition reimbursements, 41 teaching assistantships with full tuition reimbursements were awarded; tuition waivers (partial) also available. *Faculty research:* NMR and mass spectrometric characterization of biological and synthetic polymers, synthesis and characterization of new organic and inorganic material, metals in medicine, enzymalogy of gene regulation, high-resolution spectroscopy and ultrafast characterization of organic materials. Total annual research expenditures: $1.5 million. *Unit head:* Dr. Kim Calvo, Chair, 330-972-6135, E-mail: kcalvo@uakron.edu. *Application contact:* Dr. Kim Calvo, Chair, 330-972-6135, E-mail: kcalvo@uakron.edu.

The University of Alabama at Birmingham, College of Arts and Sciences, Program in Chemistry, Birmingham, AL 35294. Offers MS, PhD. *Students:* 38 full-time (18 women), 1 (woman) part-time; includes 6 minority (3 Black or African American, non-Hispanic/Latino; 3 Asian, non-Hispanic/Latino), 16 international. Average age 28. 33 applicants, 27% accepted, 8 enrolled. In 2010, 8 master's, 1 doctorate awarded. *Degree requirements:* For master's, thesis (for some programs); for doctorate, thesis/dissertation. *Entrance requirements:* For master's and doctorate, GRE General Test. Additional exam requirements/recommendations for international students: Required—TOEFL. *Application deadline:* Applications are processed on a rolling basis. *Expenses:* Tuition, state resident: full-time $5482. Tuition, nonresident: full-time $12,430. Tuition and fees vary according to program. *Financial support:* In 2010–11, 10 fellowships with full tuition reimbursements (averaging $18,700 per year), 4 research assistantships with full tuition reimbursements (averaging $18,700 per year), 11 teaching assistantships with full tuition reimbursements (averaging $18,700 per year) were awarded; career-related internships or fieldwork, Federal Work-Study, institutionally sponsored loans, health care benefits, and unspecified assistantships also available. Support available to part-time students. Financial award application deadline: 5/1; financial award applicants required to submit FAFSA. *Faculty research:* Drug discovery and synthesis, structural biochemistry and physical biochemistry, synthesis and characterization of advanced materials and polymers. Total annual research expenditures: $707,000. *Unit head:* Dr. David E. Graves, Chair, 205-975-5381, Fax: 205-934-2543, E-mail: dgraves@uab.edu. *Application contact:* Julie Bryant, Director of Graduate Admissions, 205-934-8227, Fax: 205-934-8413, E-mail: jbryant@uab.edu.

The University of Alabama in Huntsville, School of Graduate Studies, College of Science, Department of Chemistry, Huntsville, AL 35899. Offers MS. Part-time and evening/weekend programs available. *Faculty:* 12 full-time (1 woman), 1 (woman) part-time/adjunct. *Students:* 8 full-time (5 women), 6 part-time (2 women); includes 2 minority (1 Black or African American, non-Hispanic/Latino; 1 American Indian or Alaska Native, non-Hispanic/Latino), 3 international. Average age 29. 19 applicants, 79% accepted, 11 enrolled. In 2010, 2 master's awarded. *Degree requirements:* For master's, comprehensive exam, thesis or alternative, oral and written exams. *Entrance requirements:* For master's, GRE General Test, minimum GPA of 3.0. Additional exam requirements/recommendations for international students: Required—TOEFL (minimum score 550 paper-based; 213 computer-based; 62 iBT). *Application deadline:* For fall admission, 7/15 for domestic students, 4/1 for international students; for spring admission, 11/30 for domestic students, 9/1 for international students. Applications are processed on a rolling basis. Application fee: $40 ($50 for international students). Electronic applications accepted. *Expenses:* Tuition, state resident: full-time $7250; part-time $407.75 per credit hour. Tuition, nonresident: full-time $17,358; part-time $970.05 per credit hour. Required fees: $246.80 per semester. Tuition and fees vary according to course load and program. *Financial support:* In 2010–11, 9 students received support, including 8 teaching assistantships with full tuition reimbursements available (averaging $10,783 per year); career-related internships or fieldwork, Federal Work-Study, institutionally sponsored loans, scholarships/grants, health care benefits, tuition waivers, and unspecified assistantships also available. Support available to part-time students. Financial award application deadline: 4/1; financial award applicants required to submit FAFSA. *Faculty research:* Kinetics and bonding, organic nonlinear optical materials, x-ray crystallography, crystal growth in space, polymers, Raman spectroscopy. Total annual research expenditures: $2 million. *Unit head:* Dr. William Setzer, Chair, 256-824-6153,

Fax: 256-824-6349, E-mail: setzerw@uah.edu. *Application contact:* Kathy Biggs, Graduate Studies Admissions Manager, 256-824-6199, Fax: 256-824-6405, E-mail: deangrad@uah.edu.

University of Alaska Fairbanks, College of Natural Sciences and Mathematics, Department of Chemistry and Biochemistry, Fairbanks, AK 99775-6160. Offers biochemistry and molecular biology (MS, PhD); chemistry (MA, MS); environmental chemistry (MS, PhD). Part-time programs available. *Faculty:* 9 full-time (1 woman). *Students:* 33 full-time (17 women), 4 part-time (2 women); includes 8 minority (1 Black or African American, non-Hispanic/Latino; 2 American Indian or Alaska Native, non-Hispanic/Latino; 2 Asian, non-Hispanic/Latino; 3 Two or more races, non-Hispanic/Latino), 6 international. Average age 31. 38 applicants, 34% accepted, 10 enrolled. In 2010, 3 master's, 4 doctorates awarded. *Degree requirements:* For master's, comprehensive exam, thesis or alternative; for doctorate, comprehensive exam, thesis/dissertation, oral defense. *Entrance requirements:* Additional exam requirements/recommendations for international students: Required—TOEFL (minimum score 550 paper-based; 213 computer-based). *Application deadline:* For fall admission, 6/1 for domestic students, 3/1 for international students; for spring admission, 10/15 for domestic students, 9/1 for international students. Applications are processed on a rolling basis. Application fee: $60. Electronic applications accepted. *Expenses:* Tuition, state resident: full-time $5688; part-time $316 per credit. Tuition, nonresident: full-time $11,628; part-time $646 per credit. Required fees: $289 per semester. Tuition and fees vary according to course load and reciprocity agreements. *Financial support:* In 2010–11, 15 research assistantships with tuition reimbursements (averaging $12,459 per year), 16 teaching assistantships with tuition reimbursements (averaging $14,968 per year) were awarded; fellowships with tuition reimbursements, Federal Work-Study, scholarships/grants, health care benefits, and unspecified assistantships also available. Support available to part-time students. Financial award application deadline: 7/1; financial award applicants required to submit FAFSA. *Faculty research:* Atmospheric aerosols, cold adaptation, hibernation and neuroprotection, liganogated ion channels, arctic contaminants. *Unit head:* Bill Simpson, Department Chair, 907-474-5510, Fax: 907-474-5640, E-mail: fychem@uaf.edu. *Application contact:* Bill Simpson, Department Chair, 907-474-5510, Fax: 907-474-5640, E-mail: fychem@uaf.edu.

University of Alberta, Faculty of Graduate Studies and Research, Department of Chemistry, Edmonton, AB T6G 2E1, Canada. Offers M Sc, PhD. Part-time programs available. Terminal master's awarded for partial completion of doctoral program. *Degree requirements:* For master's, thesis; for doctorate, thesis/dissertation. *Entrance requirements:* For master's and doctorate, minimum GPA of 6.5 on 9.0 scale. *Expenses:* Contact institution. *Faculty research:* Synthetic inorganic and organic chemistry, chemical biology and biochemical analysis, materials and surface chemistry, spectroscopy and instrumentation, computational chemistry.

The University of Arizona, College of Science, Department of Chemistry and Biochemistry, Tucson, AZ 85721. Offers biochemistry (PhD); chemistry (PhD). Part-time programs available. *Faculty:* 33 full-time (6 women), 4 part-time/adjunct (1 woman). *Students:* 201 full-time (85 women), 14 part-time (8 women); includes 25 minority (2 Black or African American, non-Hispanic/Latino; 1 American Indian or Alaska Native, non-Hispanic/Latino; 2 Asian, non-Hispanic/Latino; 9 Hispanic/Latino; 1 Native Hawaiian or other Pacific Islander, non-Hispanic/Latino; 10 Two or more races, non-Hispanic/Latino), 85 international. Average age 30. 124 applicants, 31% accepted, 34 enrolled. In 2010, 21 doctorates awarded. *Degree requirements:* For doctorate, comprehensive exam, thesis/dissertation. *Entrance requirements:* For doctorate, GRE General Test, 3 letters of recommendation, statement of purpose. Additional exam requirements/recommendations for international students: Required—TOEFL (minimum score 550 paper-based; 213 computer-based; 79 iBT). *Application deadline:* For fall admission, 2/1 for domestic students, 1/1 for international students; for spring admission, 10/15 for domestic and international students. Applications are processed on a rolling basis. Application fee: $75. Electronic applications accepted. *Expenses:* Tuition, state resident: full-time $7692. *Financial support:* In 2010–11, 66 research assistantships with full tuition reimbursements (averaging $24,083 per year), 112 teaching assistantships with full tuition reimbursements (averaging $23,402 per year) were awarded; institutionally sponsored loans, scholarships/grants, health care benefits, tuition waivers (partial), and unspecified assistantships also available. Financial award applicants required to submit FAFSA. *Faculty research:* Analytical, inorganic, organic, physical chemistry, biological chemistry. Total annual research expenditures: $11.6 million. *Unit head:* Mark A. Smith, Head, 520-621-2115, Fax: 520-621-8407, E-mail: msmith@u.arizona.edu. *Application contact:* Lori Boyd, 800-545-5814, Fax: 520-621-8407, E-mail: chemistry@arizona.edu.

University of Arkansas, Graduate School, J. William Fulbright College of Arts and Sciences, Department of Chemistry and Biochemistry, Fayetteville, AR 72701-1201. Offers chemistry (MS, PhD). *Students:* 23 full-time (10 women), 38 part-time (14 women), 24 international. 39 applicants, 49% accepted. In 2010, 3 master's, 6 doctorates awarded. *Degree requirements:* For master's, one foreign language, thesis; for doctorate, one foreign language, thesis/dissertation. *Application deadline:* For fall admission, 4/1 for international students; for spring admission, 10/1 for international students. Applications are processed on a rolling basis. Application fee: $40 ($50 for international students). Electronic applications accepted. *Financial support:* In 2010–11, 9 fellowships with tuition reimbursements, 24 research assistantships, 34 teaching assistantships were awarded; career-related internships or fieldwork and Federal Work-Study also available. Support available to part-time students. Financial award application deadline: 4/1; financial award applicants required to submit FAFSA. *Unit head:* Dr. Bill Durham, Departmental Chairperson, 479-575-4601, Fax: 479-575-4049, E-mail: cehminfo@uark.edu. *Application contact:* Graduate Admissions, 479-575-6246, Fax: 479-575-5908, E-mail: gradinfo@uark.edu.

University of Arkansas at Little Rock, Graduate School, College of Science and Mathematics, Department of Chemistry, Little Rock, AR 72204-1099. Offers MA, MS. Part-time and evening/weekend programs available. *Degree requirements:* For master's, thesis (MS). *Entrance requirements:* For master's, minimum GPA of 2.7.

The University of British Columbia, Faculty of Science, Program in Chemistry, Vancouver, BC V6T 1Z1, Canada. Offers M Sc, PhD. Terminal master's awarded for partial completion of doctoral program. *Degree requirements:* For master's, thesis; for doctorate, comprehensive exam, thesis/dissertation. *Entrance requirements:* For master's and doctorate, GRE General Test, GRE Subject Test. Additional exam requirements/recommendations for international students: Required—TOEFL (minimum score 580 paper-based; 237 computer-based). Electronic applications accepted. Tuition charges are reported in Canadian dollars. *Expenses:* Tuition, area resident: Full-time $4179 Canadian dollars. International tuition: $7344 Canadian dollars full-time. *Faculty research:* Organic, physical, analytical, inorganic, and bio-chemical projects.

University of Calgary, Faculty of Graduate Studies, Faculty of Science, Department of Chemistry, Calgary, AB T2N 1N4, Canada. Offers analytical chemistry (M Sc, PhD); applied chemistry (M Sc, PhD); inorganic chemistry (M Sc, PhD); organic chemistry (M Sc, PhD); physical chemistry (M Sc, PhD); polymer chemistry (M Sc, PhD); theoretical chemistry (M Sc, PhD). *Degree requirements:* For master's, thesis; for doctorate, thesis/dissertation, candidacy exam. *Entrance requirements:* For master's, minimum GPA of 3.0; for doctorate, honors B Sc degree with minimum GPA of 3.7 or M Sc with minimum GPA of 3.3. Additional exam requirements/recommendations for international students: Required—TOEFL (minimum score 580 paper-based; 237 computer-based). Electronic applications accepted. *Faculty research:* Chemical analysis, chemical dynamics, synthesis theory.

University of California, Berkeley, Graduate Division, College of Chemistry, Department of Chemistry, Berkeley, CA 94720-1500. Offers PhD. *Degree requirements:* For doctorate, thesis/dissertation, qualifying exam. *Entrance requirements:* For doctorate, GRE General Test, GRE Subject Test, minimum GPA of 3.0, 3 letters of recommendation. Additional exam requirements/recommendations for international students: Required—TOEFL. Electronic applications accepted. *Faculty research:* Analytical bioinorganic, bio-organic, biophysical environmental, inorganic and organometallic.

University of California, Davis, Graduate Studies, Graduate Group in Agricultural and Environmental Chemistry, Davis, CA 95616. Offers MS, PhD. *Degree requirements:* For master's, thesis; for doctorate, thesis/dissertation. *Entrance requirements:* For master's and doctorate, GRE General Test, minimum GPA of 3.0. Additional exam requirements/recommendations for international students: Required—TOEFL (minimum score 550 paper-based; 213 computer-based). Electronic applications accepted.

University of California, Davis, Graduate Studies, Program in Chemistry, Davis, CA 95616. Offers MS, PhD. Terminal master's awarded for partial completion of doctoral program. *Degree requirements:* For master's, thesis; for doctorate, thesis/dissertation. *Entrance requirements:* For master's, minimum GPA of 3.0; for doctorate, GRE, minimum GPA of 3.0. Additional exam requirements/recommendations for international students: Required—TOEFL (minimum score 550 paper-based; 213 computer-based). Electronic applications accepted. *Faculty research:* Analytical, biological, organic, inorganic, and theoretical chemistry.

University of California, Irvine, School of Physical Sciences, Department of Chemistry, Irvine, CA 92697. Offers chemical and material physics (PhD); chemical and materials physics (MS); chemistry (MS, PhD). *Students:* 197 full-time (78 women), 1 part-time (0 women); includes 36 minority (2 Black or African American, non-Hispanic/Latino; 24 Asian, non-Hispanic/Latino; 7 Hispanic/Latino; 3 Two or more races, non-Hispanic/Latino), 32 international. Average age 27. 298 applicants, 48% accepted, 44 enrolled. In 2010, 14 master's, 26 doctorates awarded. *Degree requirements:* For doctorate, thesis/dissertation. *Entrance requirements:* For master's and doctorate, GRE General Test, GRE Subject Test, minimum GPA of 3.0. Additional exam requirements/recommendations for international students: Required—TOEFL (minimum score 550 paper-based; 213 computer-based). *Application deadline:* For fall admission, 1/15 priority date for domestic students, 1/15 for international students. Applications are processed on a rolling basis. Application fee: $80 ($100 for international students). Electronic applications accepted. *Financial support:* Fellowships, research assistantships with full tuition reimbursements, teaching assistantships, institutionally sponsored loans, traineeships, health care benefits, and unspecified assistantships available. Financial award application deadline: 3/1; financial award applicants required to submit FAFSA. *Faculty research:* Analytical, organic, inorganic, physical, and atmospheric chemistry; biogeochemistry and climate; synthetic chemistry. *Unit head:* Dr. Scott Rychnovsky, Chair, 949-824-8292, Fax: 949-824-6379, E-mail: srychnov@uci.edu. *Application contact:* Jaime M. Albano, Graduate Affairs Officer, 949-824-4261, Fax: 949-824-8571, E-mail: jmalbano@uci.edu.

University of California, Los Angeles, Graduate Division, College of Letters and Science, Department of Chemistry and Biochemistry, Program in Chemistry, Los Angeles, CA 90095. Offers MS, PhD. *Students:* 212 full-time (81 women); includes 65 minority (3 Black or African American, non-Hispanic/Latino; 39 Asian, non-Hispanic/Latino; 21 Hispanic/Latino; 2 Two or more races, non-Hispanic/Latino), 39 international. Average age 26. 313 applicants, 41% accepted, 41 enrolled. In 2010, 26 master's, 28 doctorates awarded. Terminal master's awarded for partial completion of doctoral program. *Degree requirements:* For master's, comprehensive exam or thesis; for doctorate, thesis/dissertation, oral and written exams, 1 year teaching experience. *Entrance requirements:* For master's, GRE General Test, GRE Subject Test, minimum GPA of 3.0; for doctorate, GRE General Test, GRE Subject Test, minimum undergraduate GPA of 3.0. *Application deadline:* For fall admission, 1/15 for domestic and international students. Application fee: $70 ($90 for international students). Electronic applications accepted. *Financial support:* In 2010–11, 215 fellowships with full and partial tuition reimbursements, 134 research assistantships with full and partial tuition reimbursements, 155 teaching assistantships with full and partial tuition reimbursements were awarded; Federal Work-Study, scholarships/grants, health care benefits, tuition waivers (full and partial), and unspecified assistantships also available. Financial award applicants required to submit FAFSA. *Unit head:* Dr. Albert Courey, 310-825-2530, E-mail: courey@chem.ucla.edu. *Application contact:* Departmental Office, 310-825-1490, E-mail: chemgrad@chem.ucla.edu.

University of California, Merced, Division of Graduate Studies, School of Natural Sciences, Merced, CA 95343. Offers applied mathematics (MS, PhD); biological engineering and small-scale technologies (MS, PhD); environmental systems (MS, PhD); mechanical engineering and applied mechanics (MS, PhD); physics and chemistry (PhD); quantitative and systems biology (MS, PhD).

University of California, Riverside, Graduate Division, Department of Chemistry, Riverside, CA 92521-0403. Offers MS, PhD. *Faculty:* 27 full-time (5 women). *Students:* 132 full-time (49 women); includes 21 minority (3 Black or African American, non-Hispanic/Latino; 6 Asian, non-Hispanic/Latino; 11 Hispanic/Latino; 1 Native Hawaiian or other Pacific Islander, non-Hispanic/Latino), 48 international. Average age 27. 277 applicants, 28% accepted, 35 enrolled. In 2010, 17 master's, 13 doctorates awarded. Terminal master's awarded for partial completion of doctoral program. *Degree requirements:* For master's, qualifying exams or thesis; for doctorate, thesis/dissertation, qualifying exams, 3 quarters of teaching experience, research proposition. *Entrance requirements:* For master's and doctorate, GRE General Test, minimum GPA of 3.0. Additional exam requirements/recommendations for international students: Required—TOEFL (minimum score 550 paper-based; 213 computer-based; 80 iBT). *Application deadline:* For fall admission, 1/5 for domestic and international students; for winter admission, 12/1 for domestic students, 4/1 for international students; for spring admission, 3/1 for domestic students, 10/1 for international students. Applications are processed on a rolling basis. Application fee: $80 ($100 for international students). Electronic applications accepted. *Financial support:* In 2010–11, 132 students received support, including 13 fellowships with full tuition reimbursements available (averaging $17,838 per year), 33 research assistantships with full tuition reimbursements available (averaging $23,352 per year), 86 teaching assistantships with full tuition reimbursements available (averaging $22,803 per year); career-related internships or fieldwork, Federal Work-Study, institutionally sponsored loans, and tuition waivers (full and partial) also available. Financial award application deadline: 2/1; financial award applicants required to submit FAFSA. *Faculty research:* Analytical, inorganic, organic, and physical chemistry; chemical physics. Total annual research expenditures: $4 million. *Unit head:* Prof. Eric L. Chronister, Chair, 951-827-3288, Fax: 951-827-4713, E-mail: eric.chronister@ucr.edu. *Application contact:* Prof. Christopher J. Bardeen, Graduate Advisor, 951-827-2723, Fax: 951-827-4713, E-mail: christopher.bardeen@ucr.edu.

University of California, San Diego, Office of Graduate Studies, Department of Chemistry and Biochemistry, La Jolla, CA 92093. Offers chemistry (MS, PhD). *Degree requirements:* For doctorate, thesis/dissertation. *Entrance requirements:* For doctorate, GRE General Test, GRE Subject Test. Electronic applications accepted.

University of California, San Francisco, School of Pharmacy and Graduate Division, Chemistry and Chemical Biology Graduate Program, San Francisco, CA 94143. Offers PhD. *Faculty:* 45 full-time (9 women). *Students:* 42 full-time (20 women); includes 3 Black or African American, non-Hispanic/Latino; 8 Asian, non-Hispanic/Latino; 6 Hispanic/Latino, 4 international. Average age 27. 111 applicants, 19% accepted, 9 enrolled. In 2010, 8 doctorates awarded. *Degree requirements:* For doctorate, thesis/dissertation. *Entrance requirements:* For doctorate, GRE General Test, GRE Subject Test, minimum GPA of 3.0. Additional exam requirements/recommendations for international students: Required—TOEFL (minimum score 550 paper-based; 213 computer-based; 80 iBT). *Application deadline:* For fall admission, 12/1 for domestic and international students. Applications are processed on a rolling basis. Application fee: $70 ($90 for international students). Electronic applications accepted. *Financial support:* In 2010–11, 48 students received support, including 41 fellowships with partial tuition reimbursements

Chemistry

University of California, San Francisco *(continued)*
available (averaging $19,365 per year), 16 research assistantships with full tuition reimbursements available (averaging $27,000 per year), 2 teaching assistantships with partial tuition reimbursements available (averaging $16,000 per year); institutionally sponsored loans, scholarships/grants, traineeships, and tuition waivers (full) also available. Financial award application deadline: 5/15. *Faculty research:* Biochemistry, macromolecular structure, cellular and molecular pharmacology, physical chemistry and computational biology, synthetic chemistry. *Unit head:* Dr. Charles S. Craik, Director, 415-476-8146, E-mail: craik@cgl.ucsf.edu. *Application contact:* Christine Olson, Senior Administrative Analyst, 415-476-1914, Fax: 415-514-1546, E-mail: olson@cmp.ucsf.edu.

University of California, Santa Barbara, Graduate Division, College of Letters and Sciences, Division of Mathematics, Life, and Physical Sciences, Department of Chemistry and Biochemistry, Santa Barbara, CA 93106-9510. Offers chemistry (MA, MS, PhD). *Faculty:* 19 full-time (3 women), 13 part-time/adjunct (2 women). *Students:* 152 full-time (50 women); includes 3 Black or African American, non-Hispanic/Latino; 1 American Indian or Alaska Native, non-Hispanic/Latino; 28 Asian, non-Hispanic/Latino; 7 Hispanic/Latino; 1 Native Hawaiian or other Pacific Islander, non-Hispanic/Latino. Average age 27. 276 applicants, 32% accepted, 21 enrolled. In 2010, 5 master's, 22 doctorates awarded. Terminal master's awarded for partial completion of doctoral program. *Degree requirements:* For master's, comprehensive exam (for some programs), thesis (for some programs); for doctorate, comprehensive exam, thesis/dissertation. *Entrance requirements:* For master's and doctorate, GRE, 3 letters of recommendation, statement of purpose, resume/curriculum vitae, transcripts. Additional exam requirements/recommendations for international students: Required—TOEFL (minimum score 550 paper-based; 80 iBT), IELTS. *Application deadline:* For fall admission, 12/15 priority date for domestic and international students. Application fee: $70 ($90 for international students). *Financial support:* In 2010–11, 152 students received support, including 81 fellowships with full and partial tuition reimbursements available (averaging $7,897 per year), 101 research assistantships with full and partial tuition reimbursements available (averaging $13,449 per year), 85 teaching assistantships with full and partial tuition reimbursements available (averaging $11,956 per year); career-related internships or fieldwork, Federal Work-Study, institutionally sponsored loans, scholarships/grants, traineeships, health care benefits, tuition waivers (full and partial), and unspecified assistantships also available. Support available to part-time students. Financial award application deadline: 12/15; financial award applicants required to submit FAFSA. *Faculty research:* Organic, inorganic, physical, and materials chemistry, biochemistry. *Unit head:* Dr. Fredrick W. Dahlquist, Department Chair, 805-893-5326, Fax: 805-893-4120, E-mail: dahlquist@chem.ucsb.edu. *Application contact:* Mallarie A. Stevens, Graduate Program Advisor, 805-893-5675, Fax: 805-893-4120, E-mail: gradprog@chem.ucsb.edu.

University of California, Santa Cruz, Division of Graduate Studies, Division of Physical and Biological Sciences, Department of Chemistry and Biochemistry, Santa Cruz, CA 95064. Offers MS, PhD. *Students:* 87 full-time (31 women), 3 part-time (1 woman); includes 20 minority (5 Asian, non-Hispanic/Latino; 12 Hispanic/Latino; 3 Two or more races, non-Hispanic/Latino), 10 international. Average age 28. 157 applicants, 37% accepted, 23 enrolled. In 2010, 3 master's, 20 doctorates awarded. *Degree requirements:* For master's, thesis optional; for doctorate, one foreign language, thesis/dissertation, qualifying exam. *Entrance requirements:* For master's and doctorate, GRE General Test, GRE Subject Test. Additional exam requirements/recommendations for international students: Required—TOEFL (minimum score 570 paper-based; 230 computer-based; 89 iBT); Recommended—IELTS (minimum score 8). *Application deadline:* For fall admission, 12/15 for domestic and international students. Application fee: $70 ($90 for international students). Electronic applications accepted. *Financial support:* Fellowships, research assistantships, teaching assistantships, institutionally sponsored loans and tuition waivers available. Financial award applicants required to submit FAFSA. *Faculty research:* Marine chemistry; biochemistry; inorganic, organic, and physical chemistry. *Unit head:* Janet Jones, Graduate Program Coordinator, 831-459-2023, E-mail: jajones@ucsc.edu. *Application contact:* Janet Jones, Graduate Program Coordinator, 831-459-2023, E-mail: jajones@ucsc.edu.

University of Central Florida, College of Sciences, Department of Chemistry, Orlando, FL 32816. Offers chemistry (MS, PhD); computer forensics (Certificate). Part-time and evening/weekend programs available. *Faculty:* 24 full-time (1 woman), 7 part-time/adjunct (1 woman). *Students:* 75 full-time (32 women), 22 part-time (3 women); includes 20 minority (4 Black or African American, non-Hispanic/Latino; 1 American Indian or Alaska Native, non-Hispanic/Latino; 6 Asian, non-Hispanic/Latino; 9 Hispanic/Latino), 32 international. Average age 31. 103 applicants, 56% accepted, 28 enrolled. In 2010, 4 master's, 9 doctorates, 7 other advanced degrees awarded. *Degree requirements:* For master's, thesis, final exam. *Entrance requirements:* For master's, GRE General Test, minimum GPA of 3.0 in last 60 hours. Additional exam requirements/recommendations for international students: Required—TOEFL. *Application deadline:* For fall admission, 7/15 for domestic students; for spring admission, 12/1 for domestic students. Application fee: $30. Electronic applications accepted. *Expenses:* Tuition, state resident: part-time $256.56 per credit hour. Tuition, nonresident: part-time $1011.52 per credit hour. Part-time tuition and fees vary according to program. *Financial support:* In 2010–11, 65 students received support, including 7 fellowships with partial tuition reimbursements available (averaging $3,100 per year), 41 research assistantships with partial tuition reimbursements available (averaging $7,000 per year), 51 teaching assistantships with partial tuition reimbursements available (averaging $10,300 per year); career-related internships or fieldwork, Federal Work-Study, institutionally sponsored loans, tuition waivers (partial), and unspecified assistantships also available. Financial award application deadline: 3/1; financial award applicants required to submit FAFSA. *Faculty research:* Physical and synthetic organic chemistry, lasers, polymers, biochemical action of pesticides, environmental analysis. *Unit head:* Dr. Kevin D. Belfield, Chair, 407-823-2246, Fax: 407-823-2252, E-mail: kbelfield@mail.ucf.edu. *Application contact:* Dr. Kevin D. Belfield, Chair, 407-823-2246, Fax: 407-823-2252, E-mail: kbelfield@mail.ucf.edu.

University of Central Oklahoma, College of Graduate Studies and Research, College of Mathematics and Science, Department of Chemistry, Edmond, OK 73034-5209. Offers MS. Part-time programs available. *Entrance requirements:* For master's, GRE General Test. Electronic applications accepted.

University of Chicago, Division of the Physical Sciences, Department of Chemistry, Chicago, IL 60637-1513. Offers PhD. *Faculty:* 24 full-time (2 women). *Students:* 188 full-time (55 women); includes 1 Black or African American, non-Hispanic/Latino; 10 Asian, non-Hispanic/Latino; 6 Hispanic/Latino, 96 international. Average age 24. 383 applicants, 40% accepted, 57 enrolled. In 2010, 26 doctorates awarded. *Degree requirements:* For doctorate, comprehensive exam, thesis/dissertation. *Entrance requirements:* For doctorate, GRE General Test, GRE Subject Test. Additional exam requirements/recommendations for international students: Required—TOEFL (minimum score 600 paper-based; 205 computer-based; 104 iBT), IELTS (minimum score 7). *Application deadline:* For fall admission, 12/31 for domestic and international students. Applications are processed on a rolling basis. Application fee: $55. Electronic applications accepted. *Expenses:* Contact institution. *Financial support:* In 2010–11, 16 fellowships with full tuition reimbursements (averaging $28,113 per year), 117 research assistantships with full tuition reimbursements (averaging $25,544 per year), 55 teaching assistantships with full tuition reimbursements (averaging $30,768 per year) were awarded; institutionally sponsored loans, scholarships/grants, traineeships, health care benefits, and unspecified assistantships also available. Financial award application deadline: 12/31; financial award applicants required to submit FAFSA. *Faculty research:* Organic, inorganic, physical, biological chemistry. Total annual research expenditures: $12.8 million. *Unit head:* Dr. Richard F. Jordan, Chairman, 773-702-8639, Fax: 773-702-6594, E-mail: chem-chair@uchicago.edu. *Application*

contact: Dr. Vera Dragisich, Executive Officer, 773-702-7250, Fax: 773-702-6594, E-mail: v-dragisich@uchicago.edu.

University of Cincinnati, Graduate School, McMicken College of Arts and Sciences, Department of Chemistry, Cincinnati, OH 45221. Offers analytical chemistry (MS, PhD); biochemistry (MS, PhD); inorganic chemistry (MS, PhD); organic chemistry (MS, PhD); physical chemistry (MS, PhD); polymer chemistry (MS, PhD); sensors (PhD). Part-time and evening/weekend programs available. Terminal master's awarded for partial completion of doctoral program. *Degree requirements:* For master's, thesis optional; for doctorate, comprehensive exam, thesis/dissertation. *Entrance requirements:* For master's and doctorate, GRE General Test. Additional exam requirements/recommendations for international students: Required—TOEFL (minimum score 580 paper-based; 237 computer-based). Electronic applications accepted. *Faculty research:* Biomedical chemistry, laser chemistry, surface science, chemical sensors, synthesis.

University of Colorado at Colorado Springs, College of Letters, Arts and Sciences, Master of Sciences Program, Colorado Springs, CO 80933-7150. Offers applied science—bioscience (M Sc); applied science—physics (M Sc); biology (M Sc); chemistry (M Sc); health promotion (M Sc); mathematics (M Sc); physics (M Sc); sports medicine (M Sc); sports nutrition (M Sc). Part-time programs available. *Students:* 19 full-time (10 women), 11 part-time (4 women); includes 2 Asian, non-Hispanic/Latino; 3 Hispanic/Latino. Average age 34. 20 applicants, 55% accepted, 7 enrolled. In 2010, 14 master's awarded. *Degree requirements:* For master's, thesis or alternative. *Entrance requirements:* For master's, minimum GPA of 2.75. *Application deadline:* For fall admission, 6/1 priority date for domestic students; for spring admission, 12/1 for domestic students. Application fee: $60 ($75 for international students). *Expenses:* Contact institution. *Financial support:* Fellowships, research assistantships, teaching assistantships, career-related internships or fieldwork, Federal Work-Study, and scholarships/grants available. Support available to part-time students. Financial award application deadline: 3/1; financial award applicants required to submit FAFSA. *Faculty research:* Biomechanics and physiology of elite athletic training, genetic engineering in yeast and bacteria including phage display and DNA repair, immunology and cell biology, synthetic organic chemistry. *Application contact:* Michael Sanderson, Information Contact, 719-255-3417, Fax: 719-255-3037, E-mail: gradschl@uccs.edu.

University of Colorado Boulder, Graduate School, College of Arts and Sciences, Department of Chemistry and Biochemistry, Boulder, CO 80309. Offers biochemistry (PhD); chemistry (MS). *Faculty:* 41 full-time (7 women). *Students:* 197 full-time (82 women), 3 part-time (1 woman); includes 21 minority (3 Black or African American, non-Hispanic/Latino; 2 American Indian or Alaska Native, non-Hispanic/Latino; 8 Asian, non-Hispanic/Latino; 6 Hispanic/Latino; 2 Two or more races, non-Hispanic/Latino), 31 international. Average age 27. 639 applicants, 42 enrolled. In 2010, 9 master's, 23 doctorates awarded. *Degree requirements:* For master's, comprehensive exam or thesis; for doctorate, comprehensive exam, thesis/dissertation, cumulative exam. *Entrance requirements:* For master's, GRE General Test, GRE Subject Test, minimum undergraduate GPA of 2.75; for doctorate, GRE General Test, GRE Subject Test, minimum GPA of 3.0. *Application deadline:* For fall admission, 1/15 priority date for domestic students, 1/15 for international students. Applications are processed on a rolling basis. Application fee: $50 ($60 for international students). *Financial support:* In 2010–11, 48 fellowships with full tuition reimbursements (averaging $12,195 per year), 110 research assistantships with full tuition reimbursements (averaging $16,014 per year) were awarded; institutionally sponsored loans, traineeships, and tuition waivers (full) also available. Support available to part-time students. *Faculty research:* Analytical, atmospheric, biochemistry, biophysical, chemical physics, environmental, inorganic, organic and physical chemistry. Total annual research expenditures: $20.6 million.

University of Colorado Denver, College of Liberal Arts and Sciences, Department of Chemistry, Denver, CO 80217-3364. Offers MS. Part-time programs available. *Faculty:* 12 full-time (3 women). *Students:* 9 full-time (2 women), 7 part-time (3 women); includes 1 Black or African American, non-Hispanic/Latino; 2 Asian, non-Hispanic/Latino; 1 Hispanic/Latino, 1 international. Average age 28. 15 applicants, 40% accepted, 4 enrolled. In 2010, 5 master's awarded. *Degree requirements:* For master's, comprehensive exam, thesis or alternative, 30-33 credit hours. *Entrance requirements:* For master's, GRE General Test and GRE Subject Test in chemistry (recommended), undergraduate degree in chemistry, including two semesters of organic, analytical and physical chemistry, with laboratories, and one semester of inorganic chemistry; minimum undergraduate GPA of 3.0. Additional exam requirements/recommendations for international students: Required—TOEFL (minimum score 525 paper-based; 197 computer-based). *Application deadline:* For fall admission, 1/15 priority date for domestic students; for spring admission, 12/23 priority date for domestic students. Applications are processed on a rolling basis. Application fee: $50 ($75 for international students). Electronic applications accepted. *Expenses:* Tuition, state resident: full-time $7332; part-time $355 per credit hour. Tuition, nonresident: full-time $18,990; part-time $1055 per credit hour. Required fees: $998. Tuition and fees vary according to course level, course load, degree level, campus/location, program, reciprocity agreements and student level. *Financial support:* Research assistantships, teaching assistantships, Federal Work-Study available. Financial award application deadline: 4/1; financial award applicants required to submit FAFSA. *Faculty research:* Enzymology of proteinases, computational chemistry, metal-organic coordination and materials chemistry, environmental chemistry, materials chemistry. *Unit head:* Dr. Mark Anderson, Professor and Chair, 303-352-3530, Fax: 303-556-4776, E-mail: mark.anderson@ucdenver.edu. *Application contact:* Laura Cuellar, Program Assistant, 303-556-3259, Fax: 303-556-4776, E-mail: laura.cuellar@ucdenver.edu.

University of Connecticut, Graduate School, College of Liberal Arts and Sciences, Department of Chemistry, Storrs, CT 06269. Offers MS, PhD. Terminal master's awarded for partial completion of doctoral program. *Degree requirements:* For master's, comprehensive exam; for doctorate, thesis/dissertation. *Entrance requirements:* For master's and doctorate, GRE General Test, GRE Subject Test. Additional exam requirements/recommendations for international students: Required—TOEFL (minimum score 550 paper-based; 213 computer-based). Electronic applications accepted.

University of Dayton, Graduate School, College of Arts and Sciences, Department of Chemistry, Dayton, OH 45469-1300. Offers MS. *Faculty:* 9 full-time (0 women). *Students:* 4 full-time (2 women), 1 (woman) part-time, all international. Average age 25. 16 applicants, 31% accepted, 1 enrolled. In 2010, 4 master's awarded. *Degree requirements:* For master's, thesis, 30 credit hours (21 course and 9 research). *Entrance requirements:* For master's, GRE, American Chemical Society standardized exams. Additional exam requirements/recommendations for international students: Required—TOEFL (minimum score 550 paper-based; 213 computer-based; 80 iBT), TWE. *Application deadline:* For fall admission, 3/1 priority date for domestic and international students; for winter admission, 7/1 priority date for international students; for spring admission, 1/1 priority date for international students. Applications are processed on a rolling basis. Application fee: $0. Electronic applications accepted. *Expenses:* Tuition: Full-time $7800; part-time $650 per credit hour. *Financial support:* In 2010–11, 5 teaching assistantships with full tuition reimbursements (averaging $11,694 per year) were awarded; institutionally sponsored loans, health care benefits, and unspecified assistantships also available. Financial award applicants required to submit FAFSA. *Faculty research:* Organic synthesis, medicinal chemistry, enzyme purification, physical organic, materials chemistry and nanotechnology. Total annual research expenditures: $4. *Unit head:* Dr. Mark Masthay, Chair, Chemistry Department, 937-229-2631, E-mail: mark.masthay@notes.udayton.edu. *Application contact:* Alexander Popovski, Associate Director of Graduate and International Admissions, 937-229-2357, Fax: 937-229-4729, E-mail: alex.popovski@notes.udayton.edu.

University of Delaware, College of Arts and Sciences, Department of Chemistry and Biochemistry, Newark, DE 19716. Offers biochemistry (MA, MS, PhD); chemistry (MA, MS,

PhD). Part-time programs available. Terminal master's awarded for partial completion of doctoral program. *Degree requirements:* For master's, one foreign language, thesis (for some programs); for doctorate, one foreign language, thesis/dissertation, cumulative exam. *Entrance requirements:* For master's and doctorate, GRE General Test. Additional exam requirements/recommendations for international students: Required—TOEFL (minimum score 600 paper-based; 260 computer-based). Electronic applications accepted. *Faculty research:* Micro-organisms, bone, cancer metastosis, developmental biology, cell biology, molecular biology.

University of Denver, Faculty of Natural Sciences and Mathematics, Department of Chemistry, Denver, CO 80208. Offers MA, MS, PhD. Part-time programs available. *Faculty:* 13 full-time (2 women), 19 part-time/adjunct (14 women). *Students:* 11 full-time (5 women), 13 part-time (8 women); includes 1 minority (American Indian or Alaska Native, non-Hispanic/Latino), 8 international. Average age 28. 41 applicants, 39% accepted, 7 enrolled. In 2010, 3 doctorates awarded. Terminal master's awarded for partial completion of doctoral program. *Degree requirements:* For master's, comprehensive exam (for some programs), thesis; for doctorate, comprehensive exam, thesis/dissertation. *Entrance requirements:* For master's, GRE General Test (for MS). Additional exam requirements/recommendations for international students: Required—TOEFL (minimum score 550 paper-based; 80 iBT). *Application deadline:* For fall admission, 3/1 priority date for domestic students. Applications are processed on a rolling basis. Application fee: $60. Electronic applications accepted. *Expenses:* Tuition: Full-time $35,604; part-time $29,670 per year. Required fees: $687 per year. Tuition and fees vary according to program. *Financial support:* In 2010–11, 5 research assistantships with full and partial tuition reimbursements (averaging $19,299 per year), 15 teaching assistantships with full and partial tuition reimbursements (averaging $19,084 per year) were awarded; career-related internships or fieldwork, Federal Work-Study, institutionally sponsored loans, and scholarships/grants also available. Support available to part-time students. Financial award application deadline: 3/1; financial award applicants required to submit FAFSA. *Faculty research:* Atmospheric chemistry, magnetic resonance, molecular spectroscopy, laser photolysis, biophysical chemistry. Total annual research expenditures: $1.6 million. *Unit head:* Dr. Joseph M. Hornback, Chair, 303-871-2981, Fax: 303-871-2254, E-mail: jhornbac@du.edu. *Application contact:* Information Contact, 303-871-2435, Fax: 303-871-2254, E-mail: chem-info@du.edu.

University of Detroit Mercy, College of Engineering and Science, Department of Chemistry and Biochemistry, Detroit, MI 48221. Offers chemistry (MS). Evening/weekend programs available. *Degree requirements:* For master's, thesis. *Entrance requirements:* For master's, GRE General Test, minimum GPA of 3.0. *Faculty research:* Polymer and physical chemistry, industrial aspects of chemistry.

University of Florida, Graduate School, College of Liberal Arts and Sciences, Department of Chemistry, Gainesville, FL 32611. Offers MS, MST, PhD. *Faculty:* 43 full-time (7 women), 2 part-time/adjunct (0 women). *Students:* 279 full-time (109 women), 10 part-time (5 women); includes 9 Black or African American, non-Hispanic/Latino; 11 Asian, non-Hispanic/Latino; 4 Hispanic/Latino, 162 international. Average age 27. 711 applicants, 9% accepted, 61 enrolled. In 2010, 18 master's, 44 doctorates awarded. Terminal master's awarded for partial completion of doctoral program. *Degree requirements:* For master's, thesis; for doctorate, comprehensive exam, thesis/dissertation. *Entrance requirements:* For master's and doctorate, GRE General Test, minimum GPA of 3.0. Additional exam requirements/recommendations for international students: Required—TOEFL (minimum score 550 paper-based; 213 computer-based; 80 iBT), IELTS (minimum score 6). *Application deadline:* For fall admission, 1/1 priority date for domestic students, 1/1 for international students; for spring admission, 9/1 for domestic and international students. Applications are processed on a rolling basis. Application fee: $30. Electronic applications accepted. *Expenses:* Tuition, state resident: full-time $10,915.92. Tuition, nonresident: full-time $28,309. *Financial support:* In 2010–11, 277 students received support, including 37 fellowships, 88 research assistantships (averaging $19,815 per year), 152 teaching assistantships (averaging $19,907 per year); institutionally sponsored loans and unspecified assistantships also available. Financial award applicants required to submit FAFSA. *Faculty research:* Organic, analytical, physical, inorganic, and biological chemistry. *Unit head:* Dr. Daniel R. Talham, Chair, 352-392-5266, Fax: 352-392-3255, E-mail: chair@chem.ufl.edu. *Application contact:* Dr. Ben Smith, Graduate Coordinator, 352-392-0256, Fax: 352-392-8758, E-mail: bwsmith@chem.ufl.edu.

University of Georgia, College of Arts and Sciences, Department of Chemistry, Athens, GA 30602. Offers analytical chemistry (MS, PhD); inorganic chemistry (MS, PhD); organic chemistry (MS, PhD); physical chemistry (MS, PhD). *Faculty:* 27 full-time (3 women). *Students:* 149 full-time (46 women), 3 part-time (1 woman); includes 5 Black or African American, non-Hispanic/Latino; 8 Asian, non-Hispanic/Latino; 1 Hispanic/Latino; 1 Two or more races, non-Hispanic/Latino, 58 international. 176 applicants, 38% accepted, 27 enrolled. In 2010, 6 master's, 20 doctorates awarded. Terminal master's awarded for partial completion of doctoral program. *Degree requirements:* For master's, thesis; for doctorate, one foreign language, thesis/dissertation. *Entrance requirements:* For master's and doctorate, GRE General Test. Additional exam requirements/recommendations for international students: Required—TOEFL (minimum score 213 computer-based). *Application deadline:* For fall admission, 7/1 priority date for domestic students; for spring admission, 11/15 for domestic students. Application fee: $50. Electronic applications accepted. *Expenses:* Tuition, state resident: full-time $7200; part-time $344 per credit hour. Tuition, nonresident: full-time $21,900; part-time $944 per credit hour. Tuition and fees vary according to course load and program. *Financial support:* Fellowships, research assistantships, teaching assistantships, unspecified assistantships available. *Unit head:* Dr. Jon Amster, Head, 706-542-2726, E-mail: jamster@uga.edu. *Application contact:* Dr. George F. Majetich, Graduate Coordinator, 706-542-1966, Fax: 706-542-9454, E-mail: majetich@chem.uga.edu.

University of Guelph, Graduate Studies, College of Physical and Engineering Science, Guelph-Waterloo Centre for Graduate Work in Chemistry and Biochemistry, Guelph, ON N1G 2W1, Canada. Offers M Sc, PhD. M Sc, PhD offered jointly with University of Waterloo. Part-time programs available. *Degree requirements:* For master's, thesis; for doctorate, thesis/dissertation. *Faculty research:* Inorganic, analytical, biological, physical/theoretical, polymer, and organic chemistry.

University of Hawaii at Manoa, Graduate Division, College of Natural Sciences, Department of Chemistry, Honolulu, HI 96822. Offers MS, PhD. Part-time programs available. *Faculty:* 14 full-time (1 woman). *Students:* 36 full-time (6 women), 1 part-time (0 women); includes 9 minority (1 American Indian or Alaska Native, non-Hispanic/Latino; 3 Asian, non-Hispanic/Latino; 2 Hispanic/Latino; 1 Native Hawaiian or other Pacific Islander, non-Hispanic/Latino; 2 Two or more races, non-Hispanic/Latino), 14 international. Average age 29. 62 applicants, 47% accepted, 17 enrolled. In 2010, 5 master's, 2 doctorates awarded. *Degree requirements:* For master's, comprehensive exam, thesis; for doctorate, comprehensive exam, thesis/dissertation. *Entrance requirements:* For master's and doctorate, GRE General Test, GRE Subject Test. Additional exam requirements/recommendations for international students: Required—TOEFL (minimum score 500 paper-based; 173 computer-based; 61 iBT), IELTS (minimum score 5). *Application deadline:* For fall admission, 5/1 for domestic students, 3/1 for international students; for spring admission, 9/1 for domestic students, 8/1 for international students. Applications are processed on a rolling basis. Application fee: $60. *Financial support:* In 2010–11, 3 fellowships (averaging $1,667 per year), 8 research assistantships (averaging $18,438 per year), 25 teaching assistantships (averaging $15,811 per year) were awarded. Support available to part-time students. *Faculty research:* Marine natural products, biophysical spectroscopy, zeolites, organometallic hydrides, new visual pigments, theory of surfaces. Total annual research expenditures: $2.3 million. *Application contact:* Thomas Hemscheidt, Graduate Chair, 808-956-7480, Fax: 808-956-5908, E-mail: hemschei@hawaii.edu.

University of Houston, College of Natural Sciences and Mathematics, Department of Chemistry, Houston, TX 77204. Offers MA, PhD. Part-time programs available. *Faculty:* 21 full-time (1 woman), 4 part-time/adjunct (1 woman). *Students:* 110 full-time (40 women), 3 part-time (1 woman); includes 3 Black or African American, non-Hispanic/Latino; 5 Asian, non-Hispanic/Latino; 5 Hispanic/Latino; 2 Two or more races, non-Hispanic/Latino, 87 international. Average age 28. 161 applicants, 33% accepted, 34 enrolled. In 2010, 4 master's, 15 doctorates awarded. Terminal master's awarded for partial completion of doctoral program. *Degree requirements:* For master's, thesis; for doctorate, thesis/dissertation, oral presentation. *Entrance requirements:* For master's and doctorate, GRE General Test. Additional exam requirements/recommendations for international students: Required—TOEFL (minimum score 79 iBT), IELTS (minimum score 6.5). *Application deadline:* For fall admission, 4/1 for domestic and international students. Applications are processed on a rolling basis. Application fee: $0 ($75 for international students). Electronic applications accepted. *Expenses:* Tuition, state resident: full-time $8592; part-time $358 per credit hour. Tuition, nonresident: full-time $16,032; part-time $668 per credit hour. Required fees: $2889. Tuition and fees vary according to course load and program. *Financial support:* In 2010–11, 1 fellowship with partial tuition reimbursement (averaging $3,000 per year), 39 research assistantships with partial tuition reimbursements (averaging $12,704 per year), 58 teaching assistantships with partial tuition reimbursements (averaging $14,000 per year) were awarded; career-related internships or fieldwork, Federal Work-Study, institutionally sponsored loans, scholarships/grants, health care benefits, and unspecified assistantships also available. Support available to part-time students. Financial award application deadline: 2/1. *Faculty research:* Materials, molecular design, surface science, structural chemistry, synthesis. *Unit head:* Dr. David Hoffman, Chairperson, 713-743-2701, Fax: 713-743-2709, E-mail: hoffman@uh.edu. *Application contact:* Dr. David Hoffman, Chairperson, 713-743-2701, Fax: 713-743-2709, E-mail: hoffman@uh.edu.

University of Houston–Clear Lake, School of Science and Computer Engineering, Program in Chemistry, Houston, TX 77058-1098. Offers MS. Part-time and evening/weekend programs available. *Entrance requirements:* For master's, GRE General Test. Additional exam requirements/recommendations for international students: Required—TOEFL (minimum score 550 paper-based; 213 computer-based).

University of Idaho, College of Graduate Studies, College of Science, Department of Chemistry, Moscow, ID 83844-2282. Offers MS, PhD. *Faculty:* 9 full-time, 2 part-time/adjunct. *Students:* 35 full-time, 5 part-time. Average age 30. In 2010, 2 master's, 1 doctorate awarded. *Degree requirements:* For master's, thesis or alternative; for doctorate, one foreign language, thesis/dissertation. *Entrance requirements:* For master's, minimum GPA of 2.8; for doctorate, minimum undergraduate GPA of 2.8, 3.0 graduate. *Application deadline:* For fall admission, 8/1 for domestic students; for spring admission, 12/15 for domestic students. Applications are processed on a rolling basis. Application fee: $60. Electronic applications accepted. *Expenses:* Tuition, nonresident: part-time $580 per credit. Required fees: $306 per credit. *Financial support:* Fellowships, research assistantships, teaching assistantships available. Financial award applicants required to submit FAFSA. *Faculty research:* Analytical chemistry, inorganic chemistry, organic chemistry, physical chemistry. *Unit head:* Dr. Ray von Wandruska, Chair, 208-885-6552, E-mail: chemoff@uidaho.edu. *Application contact:* Dr. Ray von Wandruska, Chair, 208-885-6552, E-mail: chemoff@uidaho.edu.

University of Illinois at Chicago, College of Pharmacy and Graduate College, Graduate Programs in Pharmacy, Chicago, IL 60607-7128. Offers biopharmaceutical sciences (PhD); forensic science (MS); medicinal chemistry (MS, PhD); pharmacognosy (MS, PhD); pharmacy administration (MS, PhD). Terminal master's awarded for partial completion of doctoral program. *Degree requirements:* For master's, variable foreign language requirement, thesis; for doctorate, variable foreign language requirement, thesis/dissertation. *Entrance requirements:* For master's and doctorate, GRE General Test. Additional exam requirements/recommendations for international students: Required—TOEFL. Electronic applications accepted. *Expenses:* Contact institution.

University of Illinois at Chicago, Graduate College, College of Liberal Arts and Sciences, Department of Chemistry, Chicago, IL 60607-7128. Offers MS, PhD. Part-time programs available. Terminal master's awarded for partial completion of doctoral program. *Degree requirements:* For master's, thesis or cumulative exam; for doctorate, one foreign language, thesis/dissertation, cumulative exams. *Entrance requirements:* For master's and doctorate, GRE Subject Test, minimum GPA of 3.0. Additional exam requirements/recommendations for international students: Required—TOEFL. Electronic applications accepted.

University of Illinois at Urbana–Champaign, Graduate College, College of Liberal Arts and Sciences, School of Chemical Sciences, Department of Chemistry, Champaign, IL 61820. Offers astrochemistry (PhD); chemical physics (PhD); chemistry (MA, MS, PhD); teaching of chemistry (MS); MS/JD; MS/MBA. *Faculty:* 33 full-time (6 women). *Students:* 277 full-time (84 women), 5 part-time (0 women); includes 5 Black or African American, non-Hispanic/Latino; 1 American Indian or Alaska Native, non-Hispanic/Latino; 15 Asian, non-Hispanic/Latino; 9 Hispanic/Latino; 8 Two or more races, non-Hispanic/Latino, 59 international. 549 applicants, 9% accepted, 42 enrolled. In 2010, 13 master's, 40 doctorates awarded. *Entrance requirements:* For master's and doctorate, GRE General Test, GRE Subject Test, minimum GPA of 3.0. Additional exam requirements/recommendations for international students: Required—TOEFL (minimum score 580 paper-based; 237 computer-based). *Application deadline:* Applications are processed on a rolling basis. Application fee: $75 ($90 for international students). Electronic applications accepted. *Financial support:* In 2010–11, 115 fellowships, 186 research assistantships, 124 teaching assistantships were awarded; tuition waivers (full and partial) also available. *Unit head:* Steven C. Zimmerman, Head, 217-333-6655, Fax: 217-244-5943, E-mail: sczimmer@illinois.edu. *Application contact:* Krista Smith, Office Support Specialist, 217-244-4844, Fax: 217-244-5943, E-mail: kristasm@illinois.edu.

The University of Iowa, Graduate College, College of Liberal Arts and Sciences, Department of Chemistry, Iowa City, IA 52242-1316. Offers MS, PhD. *Degree requirements:* For master's, thesis optional, exam; for doctorate, comprehensive exam, thesis/dissertation. *Entrance requirements:* For master's and doctorate, GRE General Test, minimum GPA of 3.0. Additional exam requirements/recommendations for international students: Required—TOEFL (minimum score 550 paper-based; 213 computer-based; 81 iBT). Electronic applications accepted.

The University of Kansas, Graduate Studies, College of Liberal Arts and Sciences, Department of Chemistry, Lawrence, KS 66045. Offers MS, PhD. *Faculty:* 29. *Students:* 108 full-time (49 women), 2 part-time (0 women); includes 8 minority (1 Black or African American, non-Hispanic/Latino; 3 Asian, non-Hispanic/Latino; 3 Hispanic/Latino; 1 Two or more races, non-Hispanic/Latino), 30 international. Average age 27. 199 applicants, 27% accepted, 33 enrolled. In 2010, 3 master's, 14 doctorates awarded. *Degree requirements:* For master's, thesis; for doctorate, comprehensive exam, thesis/dissertation. *Entrance requirements:* For master's and doctorate, GRE General Test. Additional exam requirements/recommendations for international students: Required—TOEFL. *Application deadline:* For fall admission, 2/1 priority date for domestic and international students; for spring admission, 9/1 priority date for domestic students, 7/1 priority date for international students. Applications are processed on a rolling basis. Application fee: $55 ($65 for international students). Electronic applications accepted. *Expenses:* Tuition, state resident: full-time $7092; part-time $295.50 per credit hour. Tuition, nonresident: full-time $16,590; part-time $691.25 per credit hour. Required fees: $858; $71.49 per credit hour. Tuition and fees vary according to course load, campus/location and program. *Financial support:* Fellowships with full tuition reimbursements, research assistantships with full and partial tuition reimbursements, teaching assistantships with full and partial tuition reimbursements, scholarships/grants, traineeships, tuition waivers (full), and unspecified assistantships available. Financial award application deadline: 4/15. *Faculty research:* Organometallic and inorganic synthetic methodology, bioanalytical chemistry, computational materials science,

Peterson's Graduate Programs in the Physical Sciences, Mathematics, Agricultural Sciences, the Environment & Natural Resources 2012

www.facebook.com/petersonspublishing 69

Chemistry

The University of Kansas (continued)
proteomics, biophysical chemistry. *Unit head:* Prof. Craig E. Lunte, Chair, 785-864-4670, Fax: 785-864-5396, E-mail: clunte@ku.edu. *Application contact:* Prof. Brian B. Laird, Associate Chair for Graduate Studies, 785-864-4632, Fax: 785-864-5396, E-mail: blaird@ku.edu.

University of Kentucky, Graduate School, College of Arts and Sciences, Program in Chemistry, Lexington, KY 40506-0032. Offers MS, PhD. Part-time programs available. Terminal master's awarded for partial completion of doctoral program. *Degree requirements:* For master's, comprehensive exam, thesis optional; for doctorate, comprehensive exam, thesis/dissertation. *Entrance requirements:* For master's, GRE General Test, minimum undergraduate GPA of 2.75; for doctorate, GRE General Test, minimum graduate GPA of 3.0. Additional exam requirements/recommendations for international students: Required—TOEFL (minimum score 550 paper-based; 213 computer-based). Electronic applications accepted. *Faculty research:* Analytical, inorganic, organic, and physical chemistry; biological chemistry; nuclear chemistry; radiochemistry; materials chemistry.

University of Lethbridge, School of Graduate Studies, Lethbridge, AB T1K 3M4, Canada. Offers accounting (MScM); addictions counseling (M Sc); agricultural biotechnology (M Sc); agricultural studies (M Sc, MA); anthropology (MA); archaeology (MA); art (MA, MFA); biochemistry (M Sc); biological sciences (M Sc); biomolecular science (PhD); biosystems and biodiversity (PhD); Canadian studies (MA); chemistry (M Sc); computer science (M Sc); computer science and geographical information science (M Sc); counseling psychology (M Ed); dramatic arts (MA); earth, space, and physical science (PhD); economics (MA); educational leadership (M Ed); English (MA); environmental science (M Sc); evolution and behavior (PhD); exercise science (M Sc); finance (MScM); French (MA); French/German (MA); French/Spanish (MA); general education (M Ed); general management (MScM); geography (M Sc, MA); German (MA); health science (M Sc); history (MA); human resource management and labour relations (MScM); individualized multidisciplinary (M Sc, MA); information systems (MScM); international management (MScM); kinesiology (M Sc, MA); management (M Sc, MA); marketing (MScM); mathematics (M Sc); music (M Mus, MA); Native American studies (MA); neuroscience (M Sc, PhD); new media (MA); nursing (M Sc); philosophy (MA); physics (M Sc); policy and strategy (MScM); political science (MA); psychology (M Sc, MA); religious studies (MA); social sciences (MA); sociology (MA); theatre and dramatic arts (MFA); theoretical and computational science (PhD); urban and regional studies (MA); women's studies (MA). Part-time and evening/weekend programs available. *Degree requirements:* For doctorate, comprehensive exam, thesis/dissertation. *Entrance requirements:* For master's, GMAT (M Sc in management), bachelor's degree in related field, minimum GPA of 3.0 during previous 20 graded semester courses, 2 years teaching or related experience (M Ed); for doctorate, master's degree, minimum graduate GPA of 3.5. Additional exam requirements/recommendations for international students: Required—TOEFL. *Faculty research:* Movement and brain plasticity, gibberellin physiology, photosynthesis, carbon cycling, molecular properties of main-group ring components.

University of Louisville, Graduate School, College of Arts and Sciences, Department of Chemistry, Louisville, KY 40292-0001. Offers analytical chemistry (MS, PhD); biochemistry (MS, PhD); chemical physics (PhD); inorganic chemistry (MS, PhD); organic chemistry (MS, PhD); physical chemistry (MS, PhD). *Faculty:* 21 full-time (4 women). *Students:* 55 full-time (24 women), 4 part-time (0 women); includes 1 Black or African American, non-Hispanic/Latino; 1 Asian, non-Hispanic/Latino, 42 international. Average age 29. 79 applicants, 27% accepted, 7 enrolled. In 2010, 7 master's, 5 doctorates awarded. Terminal master's awarded for partial completion of doctoral program. *Degree requirements:* For master's, variable foreign language requirement, comprehensive exam, thesis optional; for doctorate, variable foreign language requirement, comprehensive exam, thesis/dissertation. *Entrance requirements:* For master's, BA or BS courseowork; for doctorate, none, BA or BS coursework. Additional exam requirements/recommendations for international students: Required—TOEFL. *Application deadline:* For fall admission, 3/15 for domestic and international students; for winter admission, 9/15 for domestic and international students. Applications are processed on a rolling basis. Application fee: $50. Electronic applications accepted. *Expenses:* Tuition, state resident: full-time $9144; part-time $508 per credit hour. Tuition, nonresident: full-time $19,026; part-time $1057 per credit hour. Tuition and fees vary according to program and reciprocity agreements. *Financial support:* In 2010–11, 33 teaching assistantships with full tuition reimbursements (averaging $22,000 per year) were awarded; fellowships with full tuition reimbursements, research assistantships with full tuition reimbursements, career-related internships or fieldwork, scholarships/grants, traineeships, health care benefits, and unspecified assistantships also available. Support available to part-time students. Financial award application deadline: 3/15. *Faculty research:* Computational chemistry, biophysics nuclear magnetic resonance, synthetic organic chemistry, synthetic inorganic chemistry, medicinal chemistry, protein chemistry, enzymology, nanochemistry, electrochemistry, analytical chemistry, synthetic biology, bioinformatics. Total annual research expenditures: $2.5 million. *Unit head:* Dr. Richard J. Wittebort, Professor and Chair. *Application contact:* Sherry Nalley, Administrator, 502-852-6798.

University of Maine, Graduate School, College of Liberal Arts and Sciences, Department of Chemistry, Orono, ME 04469. Offers MS, PhD. *Faculty:* 13 full-time (4 women). *Students:* 19 full-time (6 women), 5 part-time (2 women); includes 3 minority (1 American Indian or Alaska Native, non-Hispanic/Latino; 2 Asian, non-Hispanic/Latino), 16 international. Average age 31. 23 applicants, 35% accepted, 4 enrolled. In 2010, 4 master's awarded. Terminal master's awarded for partial completion of doctoral program. *Degree requirements:* For master's, thesis; for doctorate, thesis/dissertation, oral exam. *Entrance requirements:* For master's and doctorate, GRE General Test. Additional exam requirements/recommendations for international students: Required—TOEFL. *Application deadline:* For fall admission, 2/1 priority date for domestic students. Applications are processed on a rolling basis. Application fee: $65. Electronic applications accepted. *Expenses:* Tuition, state resident: full-time $400. Tuition, nonresident: full-time $1050. *Financial support:* In 2010–11, 2 research assistantships with tuition reimbursements (averaging $17,550 per year), 15 teaching assistantships with tuition reimbursements (averaging $16,000 per year) were awarded; tuition waivers (full and partial) also available. Financial award application deadline: 3/1. *Faculty research:* Quantum mechanics, insect chemistry, organic synthesis. *Unit head:* Dr. Alice Bruce, Chair, 207-581-1168. *Application contact:* Scott G. Delcourt, Associate Dean of the Graduate School, 207-581-3291, Fax: 207-581-3232, E-mail: graduate@maine.edu.

The University of Manchester, School of Chemical Engineering and Analytical Science, Manchester, United Kingdom. Offers biocatalysis (M Phil, PhD); chemical engineering (M Phil, PhD); chemical engineering and analytical science (M Phil, D Eng, PhD); colloids, crystals, interfaces and materials (M Phil, PhD); environment and sustainable technology (M Phil, PhD); instrumentation (M Phil, PhD); multi-scale modeling (M Phil, PhD); process integration (M Phil, PhD); systems biology (M Phil, PhD).

The University of Manchester, School of Chemistry, Manchester, United Kingdom. Offers biological chemistry (PhD); chemistry (M Ent, M Phil, M Sc, D Ent, PhD); inorganic chemistry (PhD); materials chemistry (PhD); nanoscience (PhD); nuclear fission (PhD); organic chemistry (PhD); physical chemistry (PhD); theoretical chemistry (PhD).

The University of Manchester, School of Earth, Atmospheric and Environmental Sciences, Manchester, United Kingdom. Offers atmospheric sciences (M Phil, M Sc, PhD); basin studies and petroleum geosciences (M Phil, M Sc, PhD); earth, atmospheric and environmental sciences (M Phil, M Sc, PhD); environmental geochemistry and cosmochemistry (M Phil, M Sc, PhD); isotope geochemistry and cosmochemistry (M Phil, M Sc, PhD); paleontology (M Phil, M Sc, PhD); physics and chemistry of minerals and fluids (M Phil, M Sc, PhD); structural and petrological geosciences (M Phil, M Sc, PhD).

University of Manitoba, Faculty of Graduate Studies, Faculty of Science, Department of Chemistry, Winnipeg, MB R3T 2N2, Canada. Offers M Sc, PhD. *Degree requirements:* For master's, thesis; for doctorate, one foreign language, thesis/dissertation.

University of Maryland, Baltimore County, Graduate School, College of Arts, Humanities and Social Sciences, Department of Education, Program in Teaching, Baltimore, MD 21250. Offers early childhood education (MAT); elementary education (MAT); secondary education (MAT), including art, biology, chemistry, dance, earth/space science, English, foreign language, mathematics, music, physics, theatre; secondary science (MAT), including social studies. Part-time and evening/weekend programs available. *Faculty:* 24 full-time (18 women), 25 part-time/adjunct (19 women). *Students:* 59 full-time (46 women), 56 part-time (42 women); includes 1 Black or African American, non-Hispanic/Latino; 8 Asian, non-Hispanic/Latino; 3 Hispanic/Latino, 3 international. Average age 31. 88 applicants, 57% accepted, 39 enrolled. In 2010, 106 master's awarded. *Degree requirements:* For master's, comprehensive exam (for some programs), thesis (for some programs). *Entrance requirements:* For master's, PRAXIS I and II, minimum GPA of 3.0. Additional exam requirements/recommendations for international students: Required—TOEFL. *Application deadline:* For fall admission, 6/1 for domestic students; for spring admission, 11/1 for domestic students. Applications are processed on a rolling basis. Application fee: $50. Electronic applications accepted. *Financial support:* In 2010–11, 6 students received support, including research assistantships with full tuition reimbursements available (averaging $12,000 per year); career-related internships or fieldwork, Federal Work-Study, scholarships/grants, tuition waivers, and unspecified assistantships also available. Financial award application deadline: 3/1. *Faculty research:* STEM teacher education, culturally sensitive pedagogy, ESOL/bilingual education, early childhood education, language, literacy and culture. *Unit head:* Dr. Susan M. Blunck, Director, 410-455-2869, Fax: 410-455-3986, E-mail: blunck@umbc.edu. *Application contact:* Cheryl Johnson, 410-455-3388, E-mail: blackwel@umbc.edu.

University of Maryland, Baltimore County, Graduate School, College of Natural and Mathematical Sciences, Department of Chemistry and Biochemistry, Program in Chemistry, Baltimore, MD 21250. Offers MS, PhD. Part-time programs available. *Faculty:* 18 full-time (5 women), 3 part-time/adjunct (0 women). *Students:* 47 full-time (27 women), 5 part-time (2 women); includes 5 Black or African American, non-Hispanic/Latino; 2 Asian, non-Hispanic/Latino; 1 Two or more races, non-Hispanic/Latino, 22 international. Average age 27. 81 applicants, 33% accepted, 11 enrolled. In 2010, 5 master's, 9 doctorates awarded. Terminal master's awarded for partial completion of doctoral program. *Degree requirements:* For master's, thesis optional; for doctorate, comprehensive exam, thesis/dissertation. *Entrance requirements:* For master's, GRE General Test, minimum GPA of 3.0; for doctorate, GRE General Test, GRE Subject Test (recommended), minimum GPA of 3.0. Additional exam requirements/recommendations for international students: Required—TOEFL (minimum score 550 paper-based; 213 computer-based; 80 iBT). *Application deadline:* For fall admission, 6/1 for domestic students, 1/1 for international students; for spring admission, 11/1 for domestic students, 5/1 for international students. Applications are processed on a rolling basis. Application fee: $50. Electronic applications accepted. *Financial support:* In 2010–11, 44 students received support, including 3 fellowships with full tuition reimbursements available (averaging $24,000 per year), 16 research assistantships with full tuition reimbursements available (averaging $21,000 per year), 25 teaching assistantships with full tuition reimbursements available (averaging $21,000 per year); health care benefits also available. *Faculty research:* Bio-organic chemistry, enzyme catalysis, protein-nucleic acid interactions. Total annual research expenditures: $5 million. *Unit head:* Dr. William R. LaCourse, Director, Graduate Program, 410-455-2491, Fax: 410-455-2608, E-mail: chemgrad@umbc.edu. *Application contact:* Patricia Gagne, Graduate Program Management Specialist, 866-PHD-UMBC, Fax: 410-455-2608, E-mail: pgagne1@umbc.edu.

University of Maryland, College Park, Academic Affairs, College of Computer, Mathematical and Natural Sciences, Department of Chemistry and Biochemistry, Chemistry Program, College Park, MD 20742. Offers analytical chemistry (MS, PhD); inorganic chemistry (MS, PhD); organic chemistry (MS, PhD); physical chemistry (MS, PhD). Part-time and evening/weekend programs available. *Students:* 128 full-time (65 women), 5 part-time (1 woman); includes 14 Black or African American, non-Hispanic/Latino; 3 Asian, non-Hispanic/Latino; 3 Hispanic/Latino; 2 Two or more races, non-Hispanic/Latino, 62 international. 398 applicants, 16% accepted, 22 enrolled. In 2010, 3 master's, 16 doctorates awarded. Terminal master's awarded for partial completion of doctoral program. *Degree requirements:* For master's, thesis optional; for doctorate, thesis/dissertation, 2 seminar presentations, oral exam. *Entrance requirements:* For master's and doctorate, GRE General Test, GRE Subject Test (recommended), minimum GPA of 3.0, 3 letters of recommendation. Additional exam requirements/recommendations for international students: Required—TOEFL. *Application deadline:* For fall admission, 2/1 for domestic and international students. Applications are processed on a rolling basis. Application fee: $75. Electronic applications accepted. *Expenses:* Tuition, area resident: Part-time $471 per credit hour. Tuition, state resident: part-time $471 per credit hour. Tuition, nonresident: part-time $1016 per credit hour. Required fees: $337 per term. *Financial support:* In 2010–11, 9 fellowships with full tuition reimbursements (averaging $24,410 per year), 48 research assistantships (averaging $19,514 per year), 64 teaching assistantships (averaging $19,155 per year) were awarded. Financial award applicants required to submit FAFSA. *Faculty research:* Environmental chemistry, nuclear chemistry, lunar and environmental analysis, x-ray crystallography. *Unit head:* Dr. Michael Doyle, Chairperson, 301-405-1795, Fax: 301-314-2779, E-mail: mdoyle3@umd.edu. *Application contact:* Dean of Graduate School, 301-405-0358, Fax: 301-314-9305.

University of Massachusetts Amherst, Graduate School, College of Natural Sciences, Department of Chemistry, Amherst, MA 01003. Offers MS, PhD. Part-time programs available. *Faculty:* 30 full-time (5 women). *Students:* 140 full-time (60 women); includes 16 minority (9 Black or African American, non-Hispanic/Latino; 2 Asian, non-Hispanic/Latino; 5 Hispanic/Latino), 85 international. Average age 27. 310 applicants, 27% accepted, 29 enrolled. In 2010, 10 master's, 17 doctorates awarded. Terminal master's awarded for partial completion of doctoral program. *Degree requirements:* For master's, thesis (for some programs); for doctorate, comprehensive exam, thesis/dissertation. *Entrance requirements:* For master's and doctorate, GRE General Test. Additional exam requirements/recommendations for international students: Required—TOEFL (minimum score 550 paper-based; 213 computer-based; 80 iBT), IELTS (minimum score 6.5). *Application deadline:* For fall admission, 1/15 for domestic and international students. Applications are processed on a rolling basis. Application fee: $50 ($65 for international students). Electronic applications accepted. *Expenses:* Tuition, state resident: full-time $2640. Required fees: $8282. One-time fee: $357 full-time. *Financial support:* In 2010–11, 24 fellowships with full tuition reimbursements (averaging $4,404 per year), 107 research assistantships with full tuition reimbursements (averaging $15,068 per year), 52 teaching assistantships with full tuition reimbursements (averaging $13,726 per year) were awarded; career-related internships or fieldwork, Federal Work-Study, scholarships/grants, traineeships, health care benefits, tuition waivers (full), and unspecified assistantships also available. Support available to part-time students. Financial award application deadline: 1/15; financial award applicants required to submit FAFSA. *Unit head:* Dr. Igor Kaltashov, Graduate Program Director, 413-545-2664, Fax: 413-545-4490. *Application contact:* Jean M. Ames, Supervisor of Admissions, 413-545-0722, Fax: 413-577-0010, E-mail: gradadm@grad.umass.edu.

University of Massachusetts Boston, Office of Graduate Studies, College of Science and Mathematics, Program in Chemistry, Boston, MA 02125-3393. Offers MS. Part-time and evening/weekend programs available. *Degree requirements:* For master's, comprehensive exam, thesis, oral exams. *Entrance requirements:* For master's, GRE General Test, GRE Subject Test, minimum GPA of 2.75. *Faculty research:* Synthesis and mechanisms of organic nitrogen compounds, application of spin resonance in the study of structure and dynamics,

chemical education and teacher training, new synthetic reagents, structural study of inorganic solids by infrared and Raman spectroscopy.

University of Massachusetts Dartmouth, Graduate School, College of Arts and Sciences, Department of Chemistry, North Dartmouth, MA 02747-2300. Offers MS, PhD. Part-time programs available. *Faculty:* 17 full-time (3 women), 2 part-time/adjunct (1 woman). *Students:* 19 full-time (10 women), 8 part-time (2 women); includes 1 Asian, non-Hispanic/Latino, 16 international. Average age 27. 20 applicants, 75% accepted, 7 enrolled. In 2010, 5 master's awarded. *Degree requirements:* For master's, comprehensive exam (for some programs), thesis or alternative; for doctorate, thesis/dissertation (for some programs). *Entrance requirements:* For master's, GRE (recommended), 2 letters of recommendation; for doctorate, GRE. Additional exam requirements/recommendations for international students: Required—TOEFL (minimum score 550 paper-based). *Application deadline:* For fall admission, 5/1 for domestic students, 3/1 for international students; for spring admission, 11/1 for domestic students, 9/1 for international students. Application fee: $40 ($60 for international students). Electronic applications accepted. *Expenses:* Tuition, state resident: full-time $2071; part-time $86 per credit. Tuition, nonresident: full-time $8099; part-time $337 per credit. Required fees: $9446; $394 per credit. One-time fee: $75. Part-time tuition and fees vary according to class time, course load, degree level and reciprocity agreements. *Financial support:* In 2010–11, 6 research assistantships with full tuition reimbursements (averaging $7,969 per year), 10 teaching assistantships with full tuition reimbursements (averaging $13,000 per year) were awarded; Federal Work-Study also available. Support available to part-time students. Financial award application deadline: 3/1; financial award applicants required to submit FAFSA. *Faculty research:* Inorganic chemistry, biochemical kinetics, photochemistry, ion-molecule reactions, atmosphere chemistry. Total annual research expenditures: $1.3 million. *Unit head:* Dr. Timothy Su, Director, 508-999-8238, Fax: 508-999-9167, E-mail: tsu@umassd.edu. *Application contact:* Elan Turcotte-Shamski, Graduate Admissions Officer, 508-999-8604, Fax: 508-999-8183, E-mail: graduate@umassd.edu.

University of Massachusetts Lowell, College of Arts and Sciences, Department of Chemistry, Lowell, MA 01854-2881. Offers analytical chemistry (PhD); biochemistry (PhD); chemistry (MS, PhD); environmental studies (PhD); green chemistry (PhD); inorganic chemistry (PhD); organic chemistry (PhD); polymer science (MS). Terminal master's awarded for partial completion of doctoral program. *Degree requirements:* For master's, thesis; for doctorate, 2 foreign languages, thesis/dissertation. *Entrance requirements:* For master's and doctorate, GRE General Test. Electronic applications accepted.

University of Memphis, Graduate School, College of Arts and Sciences, Department of Chemistry, Memphis, TN 38152. Offers analytical chemistry (MS, PhD); computational chemistry (MS, PhD); inorganic chemistry (MS, PhD); organic chemistry (MS, PhD); physical chemistry (MS, PhD). Part-time programs available. *Faculty:* 6 full-time (1 woman). *Students:* 39 full-time (16 women), 5 part-time (3 women); includes 8 minority (6 Black or African American, non-Hispanic/Latino; 2 Asian, non-Hispanic/Latino), 6 international. Average age 28. 37 applicants, 30% accepted, 8 enrolled. In 2010, 3 master's, 5 doctorates awarded. Terminal master's awarded for partial completion of doctoral program. *Degree requirements:* For master's, comprehensive exam, thesis or alternative; for doctorate, comprehensive exam, thesis/dissertation. *Entrance requirements:* For master's and doctorate, GRE General Test, admission to Graduate School plus 32 undergraduate hours in chemistry. Additional exam requirements/recommendations for international students: Required—TOEFL. *Application deadline:* For fall admission, 7/1 for domestic students, 5/1 for international students; for winter admission, 9/15 for international students; for spring admission, 12/1 for domestic students. Applications are processed on a rolling basis. Application fee: $35 ($60 for international students). Electronic applications accepted. *Financial support:* In 2010–11, 12 students received support; research assistantships with full tuition reimbursements available, teaching assistantships with full tuition reimbursements available, Federal Work-Study, scholarships/grants, and unspecified assistantships available. Financial award application deadline: 2/15; financial award applicants required to submit FAFSA. *Faculty research:* Computational chemistry, materials chemistry, organic/polymer synthesis, drug design/delivery, water chemistry. *Unit head:* Dr. Abby L. Parrill, Professor and Chair, 901-678-2638, Fax: 901-678-3447, E-mail: aparrill@memphis.edu. *Application contact:* Dr. Gary Emmert, Associate Professor and Graduate Coordinator, 901-678-2636, Fax: 901-678-3447, E-mail: gemmert@memphis.edu.

University of Miami, Graduate School, College of Arts and Sciences, Department of Chemistry, Coral Gables, FL 33124. Offers chemistry (MS); inorganic chemistry (PhD); organic chemistry (PhD); physical chemistry (PhD). Terminal master's awarded for partial completion of doctoral program. *Degree requirements:* For master's, comprehensive exam; for doctorate, comprehensive exam, thesis/dissertation. *Entrance requirements:* For master's and doctorate, GRE General Test. Additional exam requirements/recommendations for international students: Required—TOEFL (minimum score 550 paper-based; 213 computer-based). Electronic applications accepted. *Faculty research:* Supramolecular chemistry, electrochemistry, surface chemistry, catalysis, organometalic.

University of Michigan, Horace H. Rackham School of Graduate Studies, College of Literature, Science, and the Arts, Department of Chemistry, Ann Arbor, MI 48109-1055. Offers analytical chemistry (PhD); chemical biology (PhD); inorganic chemistry (PhD); material chemistry (PhD); organic chemistry (PhD); physical chemistry (PhD). *Faculty:* 39 full-time (8 women). *Students:* 201 full-time (106 women); includes 19 minority (1 Black or African American, non-Hispanic/Latino; 12 Asian, non-Hispanic/Latino; 4 Hispanic/Latino; 2 Two or more races, non-Hispanic/Latino), 60 international. Average age 26. 565 applicants, 38% accepted, 39 enrolled. In 2010, 58 doctorates awarded. *Degree requirements:* For doctorate, thesis/dissertation, oral defense of dissertation, organic cumulative proficiency exams. *Entrance requirements:* For doctorate, GRE General Test, GRE Subject Test (recommended), 3 letters of recommendation. Additional exam requirements/recommendations for international students: Required—TOEFL (minimum score 560 paper-based; 220 computer-based; 84 iBT). *Application deadline:* For fall admission, 1/15 for domestic students, 12/15 for international students. Applications are processed on a rolling basis. Application fee: $0 ($75 for international students). Electronic applications accepted. *Expenses:* Tuition, state resident: full-time $17,784; part-time $1116 per credit hour. Tuition, nonresident: full-time $35,944; part-time $2125 per credit hour. International tuition: $35,994 full-time. Required fees: $95 per semester. Tuition and fees vary according to course load, degree level and program. *Financial support:* In 2010–11, 201 students received support, including 23 fellowships with full tuition reimbursements available (averaging $25,905 per year), 54 research assistantships with full tuition reimbursements available (averaging $25,905 per year), 118 teaching assistantships with full tuition reimbursements available (averaging $25,905 per year); career-related internships or fieldwork, scholarships/grants, traineeships, health care benefits, and unspecified assistantships also available. *Faculty research:* Biological catalysis, protein engineering, chemical sensors, de novo metalloprotein design, supramolecular architecture. *Unit head:* Dr. Carol A. Fierke, Chair, 734-763-9681, Fax: 734-647-4847. *Application contact:* Margarita Bekiares, Graduate Program Coordinator, 734-764-7278, Fax: 734-647-4865, E-mail: chemadmissions@umich.edu.

University of Minnesota, Duluth, Graduate School, Swenson College of Science and Engineering, Department of Chemistry and Biochemistry, Duluth, MN 55812-2496. Offers MS. Part-time programs available. *Degree requirements:* For master's, thesis. *Entrance requirements:* For master's, bachelor's degree in chemistry, minimum GPA of 3.0. Additional exam requirements/recommendations for international students: Required—TOEFL (minimum score 550 paper-based; 213 computer-based; 79 iBT), IELTS (minimum score 6.5). *Faculty research:* Physical, inorganic, organic, and analytical chemistry; biochemistry and molecular biology.

University of Minnesota, Twin Cities Campus, Institute of Technology, Department of Chemistry, Minneapolis, MN 55455-0213. Offers MS, PhD. Part-time programs available.

Terminal master's awarded for partial completion of doctoral program. *Degree requirements:* For master's, thesis or alternative; for doctorate, thesis/dissertation, preliminary candidacy exams. *Entrance requirements:* For master's and doctorate, GRE General Test. Additional exam requirements/recommendations for international students: Required—TOEFL. *Faculty research:* Analytical, biological, inorganic, organic, and physical chemistry.

University of Minnesota, Twin Cities Campus, School of Public Health, Division of Environmental Health Sciences, Area in Environmental Chemistry, Minneapolis, MN 55455-0213. Offers MS, PhD. *Degree requirements:* For doctorate, thesis/dissertation. *Entrance requirements:* For master's and doctorate, GRE General Test. Electronic applications accepted.

University of Mississippi, Graduate School, College of Liberal Arts, Department of Chemistry and Biochemistry, Oxford, University, MS 38677. Offers MS, DA, PhD. *Students:* 39 full-time (21 women), 2 part-time (0 women); includes 26 minority (6 Black or African American, non-Hispanic/Latino; 15 Asian, non-Hispanic/Latino; 2 Hispanic/Latino; 1 Native Hawaiian or other Pacific Islander, non-Hispanic/Latino; 2 Two or more races, non-Hispanic/Latino). In 2010, 3 master's, 1 doctorate awarded. *Degree requirements:* For master's, thesis; for doctorate, one foreign language, thesis/dissertation. *Entrance requirements:* For master's, GRE General Test, minimum GPA of 3.0; for doctorate, GRE General Test. Additional exam requirements/recommendations for international students: Required—TOEFL. *Application deadline:* For fall admission, 4/1 for domestic students; for spring admission, 10/1 for domestic students. Applications are processed on a rolling basis. Application fee: $25. Electronic applications accepted. *Financial support:* Scholarships/grants available. Financial award application deadline: 3/1; financial award applicants required to submit FAFSA. *Unit head:* Dr. Charles Hussey, Chairman, 662-915-7301, Fax: 662-915-7300, E-mail: chemistry@olemiss.edu. *Application contact:* Dr. Christy M. Wyandt, Associate Dean, 662-915-7474, Fax: 662-915-7577, E-mail: cwyandt@olemiss.edu.

University of Missouri, Graduate School, College of Arts and Sciences, Department of Chemistry, Columbia, MO 65211. Offers analytical chemistry (MS, PhD); inorganic chemistry (MS, PhD); organic chemistry (MS, PhD); physical chemistry (MS, PhD). *Faculty:* 30 full-time (6 women), 2 part-time/adjunct (0 women). *Students:* 92 full-time (35 women), 5 part-time (1 woman); includes 5 minority (2 Black or African American, non-Hispanic/Latino; 2 Asian, non-Hispanic/Latino; 1 Hispanic/Latino), 46 international. Average age 27. 99 applicants, 21% accepted, 19 enrolled. In 2010, 3 master's, 16 doctorates awarded. *Degree requirements:* For master's, thesis; for doctorate, one foreign language, comprehensive exam, thesis/dissertation. *Entrance requirements:* For master's, GRE General Test, minimum GPA of 3.0; for doctorate, GRE General Test (minimum score: Verbal 450, Quantitative 600, Analytical 3), minimum GPA of 3.0. Additional exam requirements/recommendations for international students: Required—TOEFL (minimum score 600 paper-based; 250 computer-based; 100 iBT). *Application deadline:* For fall admission, 4/1 priority date for domestic students; for winter admission, 10/15 for domestic students. Applications are processed on a rolling basis. Application fee: $45 ($60 for international students). Electronic applications accepted. *Financial support:* In 2010–11, 9 fellowships with full tuition reimbursements, 15 research assistantships with full tuition reimbursements, 78 teaching assistantships with full tuition reimbursements were awarded; institutionally sponsored loans, traineeships, health care benefits, and unspecified assistantships also available. *Faculty research:* Analytical, organic, biological, physical, inorganic and radiochemistry. *Unit head:* Dr. Jerry Atwood, Department Chair, 573-882-8374, E-mail: atwoodj@missouri.edu. *Application contact:* Jerry Brightwell, Administrative Assistant, 573-884-6832, E-mail: brightwellj@missouri.edu.

University of Missouri–Kansas City, College of Arts and Sciences, Department of Chemistry, Kansas City, MO 64110-2499. Offers analytical chemistry (MS, PhD); inorganic chemistry (MS, PhD); organic chemistry (MS, PhD); physical chemistry (MS, PhD); polymer chemistry (MS, PhD). PhD (interdisciplinary) offered through the School of Graduate Studies. Part-time and evening/weekend programs available. *Faculty:* 17 full-time (3 women). *Students:* 5 part-time (2 women); includes 1 minority (Black or African American, non-Hispanic/Latino). Average age 37. 19 applicants, 37% accepted, 1 enrolled. In 2010, 4 master's awarded. *Degree requirements:* For master's, thesis (for some programs); for doctorate, thesis/dissertation. *Entrance requirements:* For master's, equivalent of American Chemical Society approved bachelor's degree in chemistry; for doctorate, GRE General Test, equivalent of American Chemical Society approved bachelor's degree in chemistry. Additional exam requirements/recommendations for international students: Required—TOEFL (minimum score 550 paper-based; 213 computer-based; 80 iBT), TWE. *Application deadline:* For fall admission, 4/15 for domestic and international students; for spring admission, 10/15 for domestic and international students. Applications are processed on a rolling basis. Application fee: $45 ($50 for international students). Electronic applications accepted. *Expenses:* Tuition, state resident: full-time $5522.40; part-time $306.80 per credit hour. Tuition, nonresident: full-time $7128; part-time $792 per credit hour. Required fees: $261.15 per term. *Financial support:* In 2010–11, 7 research assistantships with partial tuition reimbursements (averaging $18,311 per year), 16 teaching assistantships with partial tuition reimbursements (averaging $16,906 per year) were awarded; Federal Work-Study, institutionally sponsored loans, and scholarships/grants also available. Support available to part-time students. Financial award application deadline: 3/1; financial award applicants required to submit FAFSA. *Faculty research:* Molecular spectroscopy, characterization and synthesis of materials and compounds, computational chemistry, natural products, drug delivery systems and anti-tumor agents. Total annual research expenditures: $729,815. *Unit head:* Dr. Kathleen V. Kilway, Chair, 816-235-2289, Fax: 816-235-5502. *Application contact:* Graduate Recruiting Committee, 816-235-2272, Fax: 816-235-5502, E-mail: umkc-chemdept@umkc.edu.

University of Missouri–St. Louis, College of Arts and Sciences, Department of Chemistry and Biochemistry, St. Louis, MO 63121. Offers chemistry (MS, PhD), including biochemistry, inorganic chemistry, organic chemistry, physical chemistry. Part-time and evening/weekend programs available. *Faculty:* 19 full-time (3 women), 7 part-time/adjunct (1 woman). *Students:* 24 full-time (11 women), 37 part-time (13 women); includes 1 Black or African American, non-Hispanic/Latino; 2 Asian, non-Hispanic/Latino; 1 Hispanic/Latino, 24 international. Average age 30. 75 applicants, 29% accepted, 7 enrolled. In 2010, 13 master's, 7 doctorates awarded. Terminal master's awarded for partial completion of doctoral program. *Degree requirements:* For master's, thesis optional; for doctorate, thesis/dissertation. *Entrance requirements:* For master's, 2 letters of recommendation; for doctorate, GRE General Test, 3 letters of recommendation. Additional exam requirements/recommendations for international students: Required—TOEFL (minimum score 550 paper-based; 213 computer-based). *Application deadline:* For fall admission, 7/1 priority date for domestic and international students; for spring admission, 12/1 priority date for domestic and international students. Applications are processed on a rolling basis. Application fee: $35 ($40 for international students). Electronic applications accepted. *Expenses:* Tuition, state resident: full-time $5522; part-time $306.80 per credit hour. Tuition, nonresident: full-time $14,253; part-time $792.10 per credit hour. Required fees: $658; $49 per credit hour. One-time fee: $12. Tuition and fees vary according to program. *Financial support:* In 2010–11, 18 research assistantships with full and partial tuition reimbursements (averaging $13,104 per year), 18 teaching assistantships with full and partial tuition reimbursements (averaging $13,270 per year) were awarded; fellowships with full and partial tuition reimbursements also available. *Faculty research:* Metallaborane chemistry, serum transferrin chemistry, natural products chemistry, organic synthesis. *Unit head:* Dr. Cynthia Dupureur, Director of Graduate Studies, 314-516-5311, Fax: 314-516-5342, E-mail: gradchem@umsl.edu. *Application contact:* 314-516-5458, Fax: 314-516-6996, E-mail: gradadm@umsl.edu.

The University of Montana, Graduate School, College of Arts and Sciences, Department of Chemistry, Missoula, MT 59812-0002. Offers chemistry (MS, PhD), including environmental/analytical chemistry, inorganic chemistry, organic chemistry, physical chemistry. Terminal master's

Peterson's Graduate Programs in the Physical Sciences, Mathematics, Agricultural Sciences, the Environment & Natural Resources 2012

www.facebook.com/petersonspublishing　　**71**

Chemistry

The University of Montana (continued)

awarded for partial completion of doctoral program. *Degree requirements:* For master's, thesis (for some programs); for doctorate, thesis/dissertation. *Entrance requirements:* For master's and doctorate, GRE General Test. Additional exam requirements/recommendations for international students: Required—TOEFL (minimum score 575 paper-based; 230 computer-based). *Faculty research:* Reaction mechanisms and kinetics, inorganic and organic synthesis, analytical chemistry, natural products.

University of Nebraska–Lincoln, Graduate College, College of Arts and Sciences, Department of Chemistry, Lincoln, NE 68588. Offers analytical chemistry (PhD); biochemistry (PhD); chemistry (MS); inorganic chemistry (PhD); materials chemistry (PhD); organic chemistry (PhD); physical chemistry (PhD). *Degree requirements:* For master's, one foreign language, thesis optional, departmental qualifying exam; for doctorate, one foreign language, comprehensive exam, thesis/dissertation, departmental qualifying exams. *Entrance requirements:* For master's and doctorate, GRE. Additional exam requirements/recommendations for international students: Required—TOEFL (minimum score 550 paper-based; 213 computer-based). Electronic applications accepted. *Faculty research:* Bioorganic and bioinorganic chemistry, biophysical and bioanalytical chemistry, structure-function of DNA and proteins, organometallics, mass spectrometry.

University of Nevada, Las Vegas, Graduate College, College of Science, Department of Chemistry, Las Vegas, NV 89154-4003. Offers biochemistry (MS); chemistry (MS, PhD); radiochemistry (PhD). Part-time programs available. *Faculty:* 18 full-time (3 women), 1 part-time/adjunct (0 women). *Students:* 41 full-time (21 women), 8 part-time (3 women); includes 21 minority (2 Black or African American, non-Hispanic/Latino; 2 Asian, non-Hispanic/Latino; 2 Hispanic/Latino; 1 Native Hawaiian or other Pacific Islander, non-Hispanic/Latino; 14 Two or more races, non-Hispanic/Latino), 13 international. Average age 30. 39 applicants, 49% accepted, 9 enrolled. In 2010, 3 master's, 4 doctorates awarded. *Degree requirements:* For master's, thesis. *Entrance requirements:* For master's and doctorate, GRE General Test. Additional exam requirements/recommendations for international students: Required—TOEFL (minimum score 550 paper-based; 213 computer-based; 80 iBT), IELTS (minimum score 7). *Application deadline:* For fall admission, 2/1 priority date for domestic and international students; for spring admission, 10/1 priority date for domestic and international students. Applications are processed on a rolling basis. Application fee: $60 ($95 for international students). Electronic applications accepted. *Expenses:* Tuition, area resident: Part-time $239.50 per credit. Tuition, state resident: part-time $239.50 per credit. Tuition, nonresident: part-time $503 per credit. Required fees: $108 per semester. Tuition and fees vary according to course load, program and reciprocity agreements. *Financial support:* In 2010–11, 23 students received support, including 7 research assistantships with partial tuition reimbursements available (averaging $17,957 per year), 16 teaching assistantships with partial tuition reimbursements available (averaging $11,250 per year); institutionally sponsored loans, scholarships/grants, health care benefits, and unspecified assistantships also available. Financial award application deadline: 3/1. *Faculty research:* Material science, biochemistry, chemical education, physical chemistry and theoretical computation, analytical and organic chemistry. Total annual research expenditures: $1.8 million. *Unit head:* Dr. Dennis Lindle, Chair/Professor, 702-895-4426, Fax: 702-895-4072, E-mail: lindle@unlv.nevada.edu. *Application contact:* Graduate Coordinator, 702-895-3320, Fax: 702-895-4180, E-mail: gradcollege@unlv.edu.

University of Nevada, Reno, Graduate School, College of Science, Department of Chemistry, Reno, NV 89557. Offers MS, PhD. Terminal master's awarded for partial completion of doctoral program. *Degree requirements:* For master's, thesis; for doctorate, one foreign language, thesis/dissertation. *Entrance requirements:* For master's, GRE, minimum GPA of 2.75; for doctorate, GRE, minimum GPA of 3.0. Additional exam requirements/recommendations for international students: Required—TOEFL (minimum score 500 paper-based; 173 computer-based; 61 iBT), IELTS (minimum score 6). Electronic applications accepted. *Expenses:* Tuition, state resident: full-time $2219; part-time $246 per credit. Tuition, nonresident: part-time $510 per credit. International tuition: $9009 full-time. Required fees: $59 per term. One-time fee: $101. Tuition and fees vary according to course load. *Faculty research:* Organic/inorganic chemistry, physical chemistry, chemical chemistry, physics, organometallic chemistry.

University of New Brunswick Fredericton, School of Graduate Studies, Faculty of Science, Department of Chemistry, Fredericton, NB E3B 5A3, Canada. Offers M Sc, PhD. *Faculty:* 14 full-time (1 woman). *Students:* 32 full-time (13 women), 2 part-time (1 woman); includes 1 Black or African American, non-Hispanic/Latino; 9 Asian, non-Hispanic/Latino. In 2010, 5 master's, 2 doctorates awarded. Terminal master's awarded for partial completion of doctoral program. *Degree requirements:* For master's, thesis; for doctorate, comprehensive exam, thesis/dissertation. *Entrance requirements:* For master's and doctorate, minimum GPA of 3.0. Additional exam requirements/recommendations for international students: Required—TOEFL, IELTS. *Application deadline:* For fall admission, 3/1 priority date for domestic students. Application fee: $50 Canadian dollars. *Expenses:* Tuition, area resident: Full-time $3708; part-time $927 per term. International tuition: $6300 full-time. Required fees: $50 per term. *Financial support:* In 2010–11, 8 fellowships (averaging $18,000 per year), 46 research assistantships (averaging $1,595 per year), 45 teaching assistantships (averaging $3,800 per year) were awarded; scholarships/grants also available. *Faculty research:* Electrochemistry, synthetic inorganic and organic chemistry, molecular spectroscopy, computational and theoretical chemistry, catalytic processes, materials chemistry, supramolecular chemistry, chemical energy storage and conversion. Total annual research expenditures: $1.1 million. *Unit head:* Dr. Sean McGrady, Director of Graduate Studies, 506-452-6340, Fax: 506-453-4981, E-mail: smcgrady@unb.ca. *Application contact:* Krista Coy, Graduate Secretary, 506-453-4781, Fax: 506-453-4981, E-mail: coyy@unb.ca.

University of New Hampshire, Graduate School, College of Engineering and Physical Sciences, Department of Chemistry, Durham, NH 03824. Offers chemistry (MS, MST, PhD); chemistry education (PhD). *Faculty:* 28 full-time (17 women). *Students:* 33 full-time (14 women), 13 part-time (5 women); includes 2 minority (1 Hispanic/Latino; 1 Two or more races, non-Hispanic/Latino), 18 international. Average age 29. 57 applicants, 54% accepted, 9 enrolled. In 2010, 6 master's, 8 doctorates awarded. Terminal master's awarded for partial completion of doctoral program. *Degree requirements:* For master's, thesis; for doctorate, one foreign language, thesis/dissertation. *Entrance requirements:* Additional exam requirements/recommendations for international students: Required—TOEFL (minimum score 550 paper-based; 213 computer-based; 80 iBT). *Application deadline:* For fall admission, 4/1 priority date for domestic students, 4/1 for international students; for spring admission, 12/1 for domestic students. Applications are processed on a rolling basis. Application fee: $65. *Financial support:* In 2010–11, 41 students received support, including 5 research assistantships, 32 teaching assistantships; fellowships, Federal Work-Study, scholarships/grants, and tuition waivers (full and partial) also available. Support available to part-time students. Financial award application deadline: 2/15. *Faculty research:* Analytical, physical, organic, and inorganic chemistry. *Unit head:* Dr. Chuck Zercher, Chairperson, 603-862-1550. *Application contact:* Cindi Rohwer, Coordinator, 603-862-1550, E-mail: chem.dept@unh.edu.

University of New Mexico, Graduate School, College of Arts and Sciences, Department of Chemistry and Chemical Biology, Albuquerque, NM 87131-2039. Offers MS, PhD. *Faculty:* 24 full-time (7 women), 7 part-time/adjunct (3 women). *Students:* 42 full-time (11 women), 4 part-time (3 women); includes 2 minority (1 American Indian or Alaska Native, non-Hispanic/Latino; 1 Hispanic/Latino), 29 international. Average age 30. 27 applicants, 22% accepted, 4 enrolled. In 2010, 3 master's, 8 doctorates awarded. Terminal master's awarded for partial completion of doctoral program. *Degree requirements:* For master's, comprehensive exam, thesis (for some programs); for doctorate, comprehensive exam, thesis/dissertation. *Entrance requirements:* For master's and doctorate, department exams. Additional exam requirements/recommendations for international students: Required—TOEFL (minimum score 550 paper-based; 213 computer-based). *Application deadline:* For fall admission, 2/1 for domestic and international students. Application fee: $50. Electronic applications accepted. *Expenses:* Tuition, state resident: full-time $5991; part-time $251 per credit hour. Tuition, nonresident: full-time $14,405; part-time $800.20 per credit hour. Tuition and fees vary according to course level, course load, program and reciprocity agreements. *Financial support:* In 2010–11, 45 students received support, including 11 fellowships (averaging $986 per year), 33 research assistantships with tuition reimbursements available (averaging $11,215 per year), 30 teaching assistantships (averaging $15,341 per year); scholarships/grants, health care benefits, and unspecified assistantships also available. Financial award application deadline: 2/1; financial award applicants required to submit FAFSA. *Faculty research:* Analytical, inorganic, organic, and physical chemistry; biological chemistry. Total annual research expenditures: $1.8 million. *Unit head:* Dr. David G. Bear, Chair, 505-277-6655, Fax: 505-277-2609, E-mail: dbear@salud.unm.edu. *Application contact:* Karen McElveny, Coordinator, Program Advisement, 505-277-1779, Fax: 505-277-2609, E-mail: kamc@unm.edu.

University of New Orleans, Graduate School, College of Sciences, Department of Chemistry, New Orleans, LA 70148. Offers MS, PhD. *Degree requirements:* For master's, variable foreign language requirement, thesis, departmental qualifying exam; for doctorate, variable foreign language requirement, thesis/dissertation, departmental qualifying exam. *Entrance requirements:* For master's and doctorate, GRE General Test. Additional exam requirements/recommendations for international students: Required—TOEFL (minimum score 550 paper-based; 213 computer-based; 79 iBT). Electronic applications accepted. *Faculty research:* Synthesis and reactions of novel compounds, high-temperature kinetics, calculations of molecular electrostatic potentials, structures and reactions of metal complexes.

The University of North Carolina at Chapel Hill, Graduate School, College of Arts and Sciences, Department of Chemistry, Chapel Hill, NC 27599. Offers MA, MS, PhD. *Degree requirements:* For master's, comprehensive exam, thesis (for some programs); for doctorate, comprehensive exam, thesis/dissertation. *Entrance requirements:* For master's and doctorate, GRE General Test, GRE Subject Test, minimum GPA of 3.0.

The University of North Carolina at Charlotte, Graduate School, College of Arts and Sciences, Department of Chemistry, Charlotte, NC 28223-0001. Offers chemistry (MS); nanoscale science (PhD). Part-time programs available. *Faculty:* 16 full-time (3 women). *Students:* 16 full-time (3 women), 19 part-time (8 women); includes 4 minority (all Black or African American, non-Hispanic/Latino), 4 international. Average age 25. 31 applicants, 45% accepted, 10 enrolled. In 2010, 8 master's awarded. Terminal master's awarded for partial completion of doctoral program. *Degree requirements:* For master's, thesis; for doctorate, thesis/dissertation. *Entrance requirements:* For master's, GRE General Test or MAT, minimum GPA of 3.0 in undergraduate major, 2.75 overall. Additional exam requirements/recommendations for international students: Required—TOEFL (minimum score 557 paper-based; 220 computer-based; 83 iBT). *Application deadline:* For fall admission, 7/1 for domestic students, 5/1 for international students; for spring admission, 11/1 for domestic students, 10/1 for international students. Applications are processed on a rolling basis. Application fee: $55. Electronic applications accepted. *Expenses:* Tuition, state resident: full-time $3464. Tuition, nonresident: full-time $14,297. Required fees: $2094. Tuition and fees vary according to course load. *Financial support:* In 2010–11, 29 students received support, including 2 fellowships (averaging $25,507 per year), 5 research assistantships (averaging $14,200 per year), 22 teaching assistantships (averaging $15,663 per year); career-related internships or fieldwork, Federal Work-Study, institutionally sponsored loans, scholarships/grants, and unspecified assistantships also available. Support available to part-time students. Financial award application deadline: 4/1; financial award applicants required to submit FAFSA. *Faculty research:* Biophysical organic chemistry and biochemistry; polymers, biomaterials and nanostructures; materials chemistry; synthetic organic and inorganic chemistry; bioanalytical chemistry. Total annual research expenditures: $498,986. *Unit head:* Dr. Bernadette T. Donovan-Merkert, Chair, 704-687-4436, Fax: 704-687-3151, E-mail: bdonovan@uncc.edu. *Application contact:* Kathy B. Giddings, Director of Graduate Admissions, 704-687-5503, Fax: 704-687-3279, E-mail: gradadm@uncc.edu.

The University of North Carolina at Greensboro, Graduate School, College of Arts and Sciences, Department of Chemistry and Biochemistry, Greensboro, NC 27412-5001. Offers biochemistry (MS); chemistry (MS). *Degree requirements:* For master's, one foreign language, thesis. *Entrance requirements:* For master's, GRE General Test. Additional exam requirements/recommendations for international students: Required—TOEFL. Electronic applications accepted. *Faculty research:* Synthesis of novel cyclopentadienes, molybdenum hydroxylase-cata ladder polymers, vinyl silicones.

The University of North Carolina Wilmington, College of Arts and Sciences, Department of Chemistry and Biochemistry, Wilmington, NC 28403-3297. Offers MS. Part-time programs available. *Faculty:* 17 full-time (2 women). *Students:* 21 full-time (14 women), 22 part-time (9 women); includes 2 Black or African American, non-Hispanic/Latino; 1 American Indian or Alaska Native, non-Hispanic/Latino; 2 Asian, non-Hispanic/Latino; 2 Hispanic/Latino; 1 Two or more races, non-Hispanic/Latino. Average age 26. 40 applicants, 78% accepted, 28 enrolled. In 2010, 11 master's awarded. *Degree requirements:* For master's, comprehensive exam, thesis. *Entrance requirements:* For master's, GRE General Test, minimum B average in undergraduate major. Additional exam requirements/recommendations for international students: Required—TOEFL (minimum score 550 paper-based; 217 computer-based; 79 iBT), IELTS (minimum score 6.5). *Application deadline:* For fall admission, 6/1 for domestic students. Applications are processed on a rolling basis. Application fee: $60. *Financial support:* In 2010–11, 12 teaching assistantships were awarded; career-related internships or fieldwork and Federal Work-Study also available. Support available to part-time students. Financial award application deadline: 3/15. *Unit head:* Dr. James H. Reeves, Chairman, 910-962-3450, E-mail: reeves@uncw.edu. *Application contact:* Dr. James H. Reeves, Chairman, 910-962-3450, E-mail: reeves@uncw.edu.

University of North Dakota, Graduate School, College of Arts and Sciences, Department of Chemistry, Grand Forks, ND 58202. Offers MS, PhD. *Faculty:* 11 full-time (4 women), 4 part-time/adjunct (1 woman). *Students:* 25 full-time (9 women), 8 part-time (4 women); includes 3 minority (1 Black or African American, non-Hispanic/Latino; 2 Asian, non-Hispanic/Latino), 17 international. Average age 28. 31 applicants, 35% accepted, 6 enrolled. In 2010, 1 master's, 6 doctorates awarded. Terminal master's awarded for partial completion of doctoral program. *Degree requirements:* For master's, thesis, final exam; for doctorate, comprehensive exam, thesis/dissertation, final exam. *Entrance requirements:* For master's and doctorate, GRE General Test, GRE Subject Test, minimum GPA of 3.0. Additional exam requirements/recommendations for international students: Required—TOEFL (minimum score 550 paper-based; 213 computer-based; 79 iBT), IELTS (minimum score 6.5). *Application deadline:* For fall admission, 8/1 priority date for domestic students, 5/1 priority date for international students; for spring admission, 12/1 priority date for domestic students, 9/1 priority date for international students. Applications are processed on a rolling basis. Application fee: $35. Electronic applications accepted. *Expenses:* Tuition, state resident: full-time $5857; part-time $306.74 per credit. Tuition, nonresident: full-time $15,666; part-time $729.77 per credit. Required fees: $53.42 per credit. Tuition and fees vary according to course load, program and reciprocity agreements. *Financial support:* In 2010–11, 20 research assistantships with full and partial tuition reimbursements (averaging $11,822 per year), 14 teaching assistantships with full and partial tuition reimbursements (averaging $9,800 per year) were awarded; fellowships with full and partial tuition reimbursements, Federal Work-Study, institutionally sponsored loans, scholarships/grants, health care benefits, tuition waivers (full and partial), and unspecified assistantships also available. Support available to part-time students. Financial award application deadline: 3/15; financial award applicants required to submit FAFSA. *Faculty research:* Synthetic and

72 www.facebook.com/petersonspublishing

Peterson's Graduate Programs in the Physical Sciences, Mathematics, Agricultural Sciences, the Environment & Natural Resources 2012

structural organometallic chemistry, photochemistry, theoretical chemistry, chromatographic chemistry, x-ray crystallography. Total annual research expenditures: $1.5 million. *Unit head:* Dr. Kathryn Thomasson, Graduate Director, 701-777-3199, Fax: 701-777-2331, E-mail: kthomasson@chem.und.edu. *Application contact:* Matt Anderson, Admissions Specialist, 701-777-2947, Fax: 701-777-3619, E-mail: matthew.anderson@gradschool.und.edu.

University of Northern Colorado, Graduate School, College of Natural and Health Sciences, Department of Chemistry and Biochemistry, Greeley, CO 80639. Offers chemical education (MS, PhD); chemistry (MS). Part-time programs available. *Faculty:* 9 full-time (3 women). *Students:* 16 full-time (7 women), 2 part-time (both women); includes 1 Black or African American, non-Hispanic/Latino; 3 Asian, non-Hispanic/Latino, 1 international. Average age 31. 14 applicants, 57% accepted, 5 enrolled. In 2010, 2 master's, 3 doctorates awarded. *Degree requirements:* For master's, comprehensive exam, thesis or alternative; for doctorate, comprehensive exam, thesis/dissertation. *Entrance requirements:* For master's, 3 letters of reference; for doctorate, GRE General Test, 3 letters of reference. *Application deadline:* Applications are processed on a rolling basis. Application fee: $50 ($60 for international students). Electronic applications accepted. *Expenses:* Tuition, state resident: full-time $6199; part-time $344 per credit hour. Tuition, nonresident: full-time $14,834; part-time $824 per credit hour. Required fees: $1091; $60.60 per credit hour. Tuition and fees vary according to course load, degree level and program. *Financial support:* In 2010–11, 8 research assistantships (averaging $10,682 per year), 6 teaching assistantships (averaging $16,385 per year) were awarded; fellowships, unspecified assistantships also available. Financial award application deadline: 3/1; financial award applicants required to submit FAFSA. *Unit head:* Dr. Richard Hyslop, Program Coordinator, 970-351-2559. *Application contact:* Linda Sisson, Graduate Student Admission Coordinator, 970-351-1807, Fax: 970-351-2371, E-mail: linda.sisson@unco.edu.

University of Northern Iowa, Graduate College, College of Natural Sciences, Department of Chemistry, Cedar Falls, IA 50614. Offers applied chemistry and biochemistry (PSM); chemistry (MA, MS). Part-time programs available. *Students:* 4 full-time (1 woman), 3 part-time (all women), 2 international. 14 applicants, 21% accepted, 3 enrolled. In 2010, 3 master's awarded. *Degree requirements:* For master's, comprehensive exam (for some programs), thesis (for some programs). *Entrance requirements:* For master's, minimum GPA of 3.0, 3 letters of recommendation. Additional exam requirements/recommendations for international students: Required—TOEFL (minimum score 500 paper-based; 180 computer-based; 61 iBT). *Application deadline:* For fall admission, 8/1 priority date for domestic students. Applications are processed on a rolling basis. Application fee: $50 ($70 for international students). Electronic applications accepted. *Financial support:* Career-related internships or fieldwork, Federal Work-Study, scholarships/grants, and tuition waivers (full and partial) available. Support available to part-time students. Financial award application deadline: 2/1. *Unit head:* Dr. William S. Harwood, Head, 319-273-2437, Fax: 319-273-7127, E-mail: bill.harwood@uni.edu. *Application contact:* Laurie S. Russell, Record Analyst, 319-273-2623, Fax: 319-273-2885, E-mail: laurie.russell@uni.edu.

University of North Texas, Toulouse Graduate School, College of Arts and Sciences, Department of Chemistry, Denton, TX 76203. Offers MS, PhD. Part-time and evening/weekend programs available. Terminal master's awarded for partial completion of doctoral program. *Degree requirements:* For master's, comprehensive exam, thesis (for some programs); for doctorate, one foreign language, comprehensive exam, thesis/dissertation. *Entrance requirements:* For master's, GRE General Test, 2 letters of recommendation; for doctorate, GRE General Test, 2 letters of recommendation, transcripts, statement of purpose. Additional exam requirements/recommendations for international students: Recommended—TOEFL (minimum score 550 paper-based; 213 computer-based). *Application deadline:* For fall admission, 7/15 for domestic students; for spring admission, 11/15 for domestic students. *Expenses:* Tuition, state resident: full-time $4298; part-time $239 per credit hour. Tuition, nonresident: full-time $10,782; part-time $549 per credit hour. Required fees: $1292; $270 per credit hour. *Financial support:* Fellowships with full tuition reimbursements, research assistantships with partial tuition reimbursements, teaching assistantships with partial tuition reimbursements, career-related internships or fieldwork, Federal Work-Study, and institutionally sponsored loans available. Financial award application deadline: 4/1. *Faculty research:* Analytical, inorganic, physical, and organic chemistry and materials. *Application contact:* Graduate Coordinator, 940-565-3554, Fax: 940-565-4318.

University of Notre Dame, Graduate School, College of Science, Department of Chemistry and Biochemistry, Notre Dame, IN 46556. Offers biochemistry (MS, PhD); inorganic chemistry (MS, PhD); organic chemistry (MS, PhD); physical chemistry (MS, PhD). Terminal master's awarded for partial completion of doctoral program. *Degree requirements:* For master's, comprehensive exam, thesis; for doctorate, thesis/dissertation, qualifying exam. *Entrance requirements:* For master's and doctorate, GRE General Test, GRE Subject Test (strongly recommended). Additional exam requirements/recommendations for international students: Required—TOEFL (minimum score 600 paper-based; 250 computer-based; 80 iBT). Electronic applications accepted. *Faculty research:* Reaction design and mechanistic studies; reactive intermediates; synthesis, structure and reactivity of organometallic cluster complexes and biologically active natural products; bioorganic chemistry; enzymology.

University of Oklahoma, College of Arts and Sciences, Department of Chemistry and Biochemistry, Norman, OK 73019. Offers chemistry and biochemistry (MS, PhD), including bioinformatics, cellular and behavioral neurobiology (PhD), chemistry. Part-time programs available. *Faculty:* 27 full-time (6 women). *Students:* 72 full-time (27 women), 26 part-time (11 women); includes 12 minority (6 Black or African American, non-Hispanic/Latino; 1 American Indian or Alaska Native, non-Hispanic/Latino; 2 Asian, non-Hispanic/Latino; 1 Hispanic/Latino; 2 Two or more races, non-Hispanic/Latino), 50 international. Average age 28. 31 applicants, 61% accepted, 16 enrolled. In 2010, 17 master's, 17 doctorates awarded. Terminal master's awarded for partial completion of doctoral program. *Degree requirements:* For master's, thesis optional; for doctorate, thesis/dissertation. *Entrance requirements:* For master's, GRE, BS in chemistry; for doctorate, GRE. Additional exam requirements/recommendations for international students: Required—TOEFL (minimum score 550 paper-based; 213 computer-based; 79 iBT). *Application deadline:* For fall admission, 4/1 priority date for domestic students, 4/1 for international students; for spring admission, 9/1 priority date for domestic students, 9/1 for international students. Applications are processed on a rolling basis. Application fee: $40 ($90 for international students). Electronic applications accepted. *Expenses:* Tuition, state resident: full-time $3892.80; part-time $162.20 per credit hour. Tuition, nonresident: full-time $14,167; part-time $590.30 per credit hour. Required fees: $2523.40; $94.60 per credit hour. Tuition and fees vary according to course load and degree level. *Financial support:* In 2010–11, 1 fellowship with full tuition reimbursement (averaging $5,000 per year), 24 research assistantships with partial tuition reimbursements (averaging $14,788 per year), 62 teaching assistantships with partial tuition reimbursements (averaging $16,444 per year) were awarded; scholarships/grants and unspecified assistantships also available. Financial award application deadline: 4/1; financial award applicants required to submit FAFSA. *Faculty research:* Structural biology, synthesis and catalysis, biomaterials, membrane biochemistry, genomics. Total annual research expenditures: $6.8 million. *Unit head:* Dr. George Richter-Addo, Chair, 405-325-4811, Fax: 405-325-6111, E-mail: grichteraddo@ou.edu. *Application contact:* Angela Link-Perez, Graduate Program Assistant, 405-325-4811 Ext. 62946, Fax: 405-325-6111, E-mail: alperez@ou.edu.

University of Oregon, Graduate School, College of Arts and Sciences, Department of Chemistry, Eugene, OR 97403. Offers biochemistry (MA, MS, PhD); chemistry (MA, MS, PhD). Terminal master's awarded for partial completion of doctoral program. *Degree requirements:* For doctorate, thesis/dissertation. *Entrance requirements:* For master's and doctorate, GRE General Test, minimum GPA of 3.0. Additional exam requirements/recommendations for international students: Required—TOEFL. *Faculty research:* Organic chemistry, organometallic chemistry, inorganic chemistry, physical chemistry, materials science, biochemistry, chemical physics, molecular or cell biology.

University of Ottawa, Faculty of Graduate and Postdoctoral Studies, Faculty of Science, Ottawa-Carleton Chemistry Institute, Ottawa, ON K1N 6N5, Canada. Offers M Sc, PhD. M Sc, PhD offered jointly with Carleton University. *Degree requirements:* For master's, thesis, seminar; for doctorate, comprehensive exam, thesis/dissertation, 2 seminars. *Entrance requirements:* For master's, honors B Sc degree or equivalent, minimum B average; for doctorate, honors B Sc with minimum B average or M Sc in chemistry with minimum B+ average. Electronic applications accepted. *Faculty research:* Organic chemistry, physical chemistry, inorganic chemistry.

University of Pennsylvania, School of Arts and Sciences, Graduate Group in Chemistry, Philadelphia, PA 19104. Offers MS, PhD. *Faculty:* 28 full-time (4 women), 11 part-time/adjunct (1 woman). *Students:* 181 full-time (81 women), 1 (woman) part-time; includes 3 Black or African American, non-Hispanic/Latino; 10 Asian, non-Hispanic/Latino; 6 Hispanic/Latino, 88 international. 453 applicants, 27% accepted, 35 enrolled. In 2010, 23 master's, 25 doctorates awarded. *Degree requirements:* For doctorate, thesis/dissertation. *Entrance requirements:* For doctorate, GRE General Test, GRE Subject Test, previous graduate course work in organic, inorganic, and physical chemistry, and general physics, each with a lab, as well as differential and integral calculus. Additional exam requirements/recommendations for international students: Required—TOEFL. *Application deadline:* For fall admission, 12/1 priority date for domestic students. Application fee: $70. Electronic applications accepted. *Expenses:* Tuition: Full-time $25,660; part-time $4758 per course. Required fees: $2152; $270 per course. Tuition and fees vary according to course load, degree level and program. *Financial support:* Fellowships, research assistantships, teaching assistantships, institutionally sponsored loans, scholarships/grants, traineeships, health care benefits, and unspecified assistantships available. Financial award application deadline: 12/15. *Unit head:* Gary A. Molander, Department Chair, Chemistry, 215-573-8604, E-mail: gmolandr@sas.upenn.edu. *Application contact:* Gary A. Molander, Department Chair, Chemistry, 215-573-8604, E-mail: gmolandr@sas.upenn.edu.

University of Pittsburgh, School of Arts and Sciences, Department of Chemistry, Pittsburgh, PA 15260. Offers MS, PhD. Part-time and evening/weekend programs available. *Faculty:* 31 full-time (4 women), 15 part-time/adjunct (3 women). *Students:* 205 full-time (62 women), 3 part-time (2 women); includes 1 Black or African American, non-Hispanic/Latino; 2 Asian, non-Hispanic/Latino; 2 Hispanic/Latino, 93 international. Average age 24. 382 applicants, 41% accepted, 51 enrolled. In 2010, 11 master's, 21 doctorates awarded. Terminal master's awarded for partial completion of doctoral program. *Degree requirements:* For master's, comprehensive exam, thesis; for doctorate, comprehensive exam, thesis/dissertation. *Entrance requirements:* For master's and doctorate, GRE General Test, GRE Subject Test. Additional exam requirements/recommendations for international students: Required—TOEFL (minimum score 600 paper-based; 250 computer-based; 100 iBT). *Application deadline:* For fall admission, 2/1 priority date for domestic and international students. Applications are processed on a rolling basis. Application fee: $50. Electronic applications accepted. *Expenses:* Tuition, state resident: full-time $17,304; part-time $701 per credit. Tuition, nonresident: full-time $29,554; part-time $1210 per credit. Required fees: $740; $214 per term. Tuition and fees vary according to program. *Financial support:* In 2010–11, 205 students received support, including 10 fellowships with tuition reimbursements available (averaging $25,354 per year), 125 research assistantships with tuition reimbursements available (averaging $22,845 per year), 70 teaching assistantships with tuition reimbursements available (averaging $23,280 per year); Federal Work-Study, scholarships/grants, health care benefits, and unspecified assistantships also available. Financial award application deadline: 2/1. *Faculty research:* Analytical, biological, inorganic and materials including nanostructured materials, organic, physical and theoretical. Total annual research expenditures: $10.1 million. *Unit head:* Dr. David H. Waldeck, Chairman, 412-624-0415, Fax: 412-624-1649, E-mail: chemchr@pitt.edu. *Application contact:* Fran Nagy, Graduate Program Administrator, 412-624-8501, Fax: 412-624-8611, E-mail: fnagy@pitt.edu.

See Display on next page and Close-Up on page 109.

University of Prince Edward Island, Faculty of Science, Charlottetown, PE C1A 4P3, Canada. Offers biology (M Sc); chemistry (M Sc). *Degree requirements:* For master's, thesis. *Entrance requirements:* Additional exam requirements/recommendations for international students: Required—TOEFL (minimum score 550 paper-based; 213 computer-based; 80 iBT), Canadian Academic English Language Assessment, Michigan English Language Assessment Battery, Canadian Test of English for Scholars and Trainees. *Faculty research:* Ecology and wildlife biology, molecular, genetics and biotechnology, organametallic, bio-organic, supramolecular and synthetic organic chemistry, neurobiology and stoke materials science.

University of Puerto Rico, Mayagüez Campus, Graduate Studies, College of Arts and Sciences, Department of Chemistry, Mayagüez, PR 00681-9000. Offers chemistry (MS, PhD). Part-time programs available. *Students:* 76 full-time (41 women), 2 part-time (1 woman); includes 54 Hispanic/Latino, 24 international. 16 applicants, 75% accepted, 11 enrolled. In 2010, 6 master's, 2 doctorates awarded. *Degree requirements:* For master's, one foreign language, comprehensive exam, thesis; for doctorate, comprehensive exam, thesis/dissertation. *Entrance requirements:* For master's, GRE, BS in chemistry or the equivalent. *Application deadline:* For fall admission, 2/15 for domestic and international students; for spring admission, 9/15 for domestic and international students. Applications are processed on a rolling basis. Application fee: $25. *Expenses:* Tuition, state resident: full-time $1188. Tuition, nonresident: full-time $1188. International tuition: $6126 full-time. Tuition and fees vary according to course level and course load. *Financial support:* In 2010–11, 45 research assistantships (averaging $15,000 per year), 87 teaching assistantships (averaging $8,500 per year) were awarded; Federal Work-Study and institutionally sponsored loans also available. *Faculty research:* Biochemistry, spectroscopy, food chemistry, physical chemistry, electrochemistry. Total annual research expenditures: $2.6 million. *Unit head:* Dr. Francis A. Patron, Director, 787-265-5458, Fax: 787-265-3849, E-mail: francisb.patron@upr.edu. *Application contact:* Dr. Rodolfo Romanach, Graduate Program Coordinator, 787-832-4040 Ext. 3122, Fax: 787-265-3849, E-mail: rodolfoj.romanach@upr.edu.

University of Puerto Rico, Río Piedras, College of Natural Sciences, Department of Chemistry, San Juan, PR 00931-3300. Offers MS, PhD. Part-time programs available. *Degree requirements:* For master's, one foreign language, comprehensive exam, thesis; for doctorate, one foreign language, comprehensive exam, thesis/dissertation. *Entrance requirements:* For master's, GRE General Test, GRE Subject Test, interview, minimum GPA of 3.0, letter of recommendation; for doctorate, GRE General Test, GRE Subject Test, minimum GPA of 3.0, letter of recommendation. Additional exam requirements/recommendations for international students: Required—TOEFL.

University of Regina, Faculty of Graduate Studies and Research, Faculty of Science, Department of Chemistry and Biochemistry, Regina, SK S4S 0A2, Canada. Offers analytical/environmental chemistry (M Sc, PhD); biophysics of biological interfaces (M Sc, PhD); enzymology/chemical biology (M Sc, PhD); inorganic/organometallic chemistry (M Sc, PhD); signal transduction and mechanisms of cancer cell regulation (M Sc, PhD); supramolecular organic photochemistry and photophysics (M Sc, PhD); synthetic organic chemistry (M Sc, PhD); theoretical/computational chemistry (M Sc, PhD). *Faculty:* 10 full-time (2 women). *Students:* 19 full-time (9 women), 2 part-time (1 woman). 20 applicants, 40% accepted. In 2010, 2 master's, 1 doctorate awarded. *Degree requirements:* For master's, thesis; for doctorate, thesis/dissertation. *Entrance requirements:* Additional exam requirements/recommendations for international students: Required—TOEFL (minimum score 580 paper-based; 80 iBT). *Application deadline:* Applications are processed on a rolling basis. Application fee: $100.

Peterson's Graduate Programs in the Physical Sciences, Mathematics, Agricultural Sciences, the Environment & Natural Resources 2012

www.facebook.com/petersonspublishing 73

Chemistry

Electronic applications accepted. Tuition and fees charges are reported in Canadian dollars. *Expenses:* Tuition, area resident: Full-time $3244.50 Canadian dollars; part-time $180.25 Canadian dollars per credit hour. International tuition: $4744.50 Canadian dollars full-time. Required fees: $494 Canadian dollars; $115.25 Canadian dollars per credit hour. $115.25 Canadian dollars per semester. Tuition and fees vary according to program. *Financial support:* In 2010–11, 3 fellowships (averaging $20,000 per year), 2 research assistantships (averaging $17,250 per year), 8 teaching assistantships (averaging $6,965 per year) were awarded; scholarships/grants also available. Financial award application deadline: 6/15. *Faculty research:* Asymmetric synthesis and methodology, theoretical and computational chemistry, biophysical biochemistry, analytical and environmental chemistry, chemical biology. *Unit head:* Dr. Lynn Mihichuk, Head, 306-585-4793, Fax: 306-337-2409, E-mail: lynn.mihichuk@uregina.ca. *Application contact:* Dr. Tanya Dahms, Graduate Program Coordinator, 306-585-4246, Fax: 306-337-2409, E-mail: tanya.dahms@uregina.ca.

University of Rhode Island, Graduate School, College of Arts and Sciences, Department of Chemistry, Kingston, RI 02881. Offers MS, PhD. Part-time and evening/weekend programs available. *Faculty:* 16 full-time (4 women), 1 (woman) part-time/adjunct. *Students:* 42 full-time (18 women), 14 part-time (5 women); includes 6 minority (2 Black or African American, non-Hispanic/Latino; 3 Asian, non-Hispanic/Latino; 1 Hispanic/Latino), 13 international. In 2010, 3 master's, 5 doctorates awarded. *Degree requirements:* For master's, comprehensive exam (for some programs), thesis optional; for doctorate, comprehensive exam, thesis/dissertation. *Entrance requirements:* For master's, GRE (for graduates of non-US universities), 2 letters of recommendation; for doctorate, GRE (for graduates of non-U. S. universities), 2 letters of recommendation. Additional exam requirements/recommendations for international students: Required—TOEFL (minimum score 550 paper-based; 213 computer-based). *Application deadline:* For fall admission, 7/15 for domestic students, 1/15 for international students; for spring admission, 11/15 for domestic students, 9/15 for international students. Application fee: $65. Electronic applications accepted. *Expenses:* Tuition, state resident: full-time $9588; part-time $533 per credit hour. Tuition, nonresident: full-time $22,968; part-time $1276 per credit hour. Required fees: $1282; $68 per semester. Tuition and fees vary according to program. *Financial support:* In 2010–11, 4 research assistantships with full and partial tuition reimbursements (averaging $7,175 per year), 32 teaching assistantships with full and partial tuition reimbursements (averaging $12,509 per year) were awarded. Financial award applicants required to submit FAFSA. *Faculty research:* Analytical chemistry, biochemistry, analytical/nanoscience, materials/analytical, theoretical chemistry. Total annual research expenditures: $2.5 million. *Unit head:* Dr. William Euler, Chairperson, 401-874-5090, Fax: 401-874-5072, E-mail: weuler@chm.uri.edu. *Application contact:* Dr. William Euler, Chairperson, 401-874-5090, Fax: 401-874-5072, E-mail: weuler@chm.uri.edu.

University of Rochester, School of Arts and Sciences, Department of Chemistry, Rochester, NY 14627. Offers MS, PhD. Terminal master's awarded for partial completion of doctoral program. *Degree requirements:* For doctorate, thesis/dissertation, qualifying exam. *Entrance requirements:* For master's and doctorate, GRE General Test. Additional exam requirements/recommendations for international students: Required—TOEFL.

University of San Francisco, College of Arts and Sciences, Department of Chemistry, San Francisco, CA 94117-1080. Offers MS. Part-time and evening/weekend programs available. *Faculty:* 2 full-time (0 women). *Students:* 13 full-time (6 women); includes 3 minority (2 Asian, non-Hispanic/Latino; 1 Native Hawaiian or other Pacific Islander, non-Hispanic/Latino), 6 international. Average age 25. 42 applicants, 14% accepted, 4 enrolled. In 2010, 2 master's awarded. *Degree requirements:* For master's, thesis. *Entrance requirements:* For master's, GRE General Test, GRE Subject Test, BS in chemistry or related field. *Application deadline:* Applications are processed on a rolling basis. Application fee: $55 ($65 for international students). *Expenses:* Tuition: Full-time $20,070; part-time $1115 per credit hour. Tuition and fees vary according to course load, degree level and program. *Financial support:* In 2010–11, 13 students received support; fellowships, research assistantships, teaching assistantships, career-related internships or fieldwork, Federal Work-Study, institutionally sponsored loans, and tuition waivers (partial) available. Support available to part-time students. Financial award application deadline: 3/2; financial award applicants required to submit FAFSA. *Faculty research:* Organic photochemistry, genetics of chromatic adaptation, electron transfer processes in solution, metabolism of protein hormones. Total annual research expenditures: $75,000. *Unit head:* Dr. Jeff Curtis, Chair, 415-422-6157, Fax: 415-422-5157. *Application contact:* Information Contact, 415-422-5135, Fax: 415-422-2217, E-mail: asgraduate@usfca.edu.

University of Saskatchewan, College of Graduate Studies and Research, College of Arts and Sciences, Department of Chemistry, Saskatoon, SK S7N 5A2, Canada. Offers M Sc, PhD. *Degree requirements:* For master's, thesis; for doctorate, comprehensive exam (for some programs), thesis/dissertation. *Entrance requirements:* Additional exam requirements/recommendations for international students: Required—TOEFL (minimum score 80 iBT); Recommended—IELTS (minimum score 6.5). Electronic applications accepted.

The University of Scranton, College of Graduate and Continuing Education, Department of Chemistry, Program in Chemistry, Scranton, PA 18510. Offers MA, MS. Part-time and evening/weekend programs available. *Faculty:* 10 full-time (3 women), 1 part-time/adjunct (0 women). *Students:* 7 full-time (5 women), 4 part-time (3 women); includes 1 Hispanic/Latino, 2 international. Average age 28. 32 applicants, 25% accepted. In 2010, 3 master's awarded. *Degree requirements:* For master's, comprehensive exam (for some programs), thesis (for some programs), capstone experience. *Entrance requirements:* For master's, minimum GPA of 2.75. Additional exam requirements/recommendations for international students: Required—TOEFL (minimum score 500 paper-based; 173 computer-based), IELTS (minimum score 5.5). *Application deadline:* Applications are processed on a rolling basis. Application fee: $0. *Financial support:* Fellowships, teaching assistantships, career-related internships or fieldwork, Federal Work-Study, and unspecified assistantships available. Support available to part-time students. Financial award application deadline: 3/1. *Unit head:* Dr. Christopher A. Baumann, Director, 570-941-6389, Fax: 570-941-7510, E-mail: cab@scranton.edu. *Application contact:* Dr. Christopher A. Baumann, Director, 570-941-6389, Fax: 570-941-7510, E-mail: cab@scranton.edu.

The University of Scranton, College of Graduate and Continuing Education, Department of Chemistry, Program in Clinical Chemistry, Scranton, PA 18510. Offers MA, MS. Part-time and evening/weekend programs available. *Faculty:* 10 full-time (3 women), 1 part-time/adjunct (0 women). *Students:* 8 full-time (5 women), 3 part-time (2 women), 5 international. Average age 25. 8 applicants, 50% accepted. In 2010, 4 master's awarded. *Degree requirements:* For master's, comprehensive exam (for some programs), thesis (for some programs), capstone experience. *Entrance requirements:* For master's, minimum GPA of 2.75. Additional exam requirements/recommendations for international students: Required—TOEFL (minimum score 500 paper-based; 173 computer-based), IELTS (minimum score 5.5). *Application deadline:* Applications are processed on a rolling basis. Application fee: $0. *Financial support:* Fellowships, teaching assistantships, career-related internships or fieldwork, Federal Work-Study, and unspecified assistantships available. Support available to part-time students. Financial award application deadline: 3/1. *Unit head:* Dr. Christopher A. Baumann, Director, 570-941-6389, Fax: 570-941-7510, E-mail: cab@scranton.edu. *Application contact:* Dr. Christopher A. Baumann, Director, 570-941-6389, Fax: 570-941-7510, E-mail: cab@scranton.edu.

University of South Carolina, The Graduate School, College of Arts and Sciences, Department of Chemistry and Biochemistry, Columbia, SC 29208. Offers IMA, MAT, MS, PhD. IMA and MAT offered in cooperation with the College of Education. Part-time programs available. Terminal master's awarded for partial completion of doctoral program. *Degree requirements:* For master's, comprehensive exam, thesis; for doctorate, comprehensive exam, thesis/dissertation. *Entrance requirements:* For master's and doctorate, GRE General Test. Additional

74   www.facebook.com/petersonspublishing

Peterson's Graduate Programs in the Physical Sciences, Mathematics, Agricultural Sciences, the Environment & Natural Resources 2012

exam requirements/recommendations for international students: Required—TOEFL. Electronic applications accepted. *Faculty research:* Spectroscopy, crystallography, organic and organometallic synthesis, analytical chemistry, materials.

The University of South Dakota, Graduate School, College of Arts and Sciences, Department of Chemistry, Vermillion, SD 57069-2390. Offers MNS, MS, PhD. *Degree requirements:* For master's, comprehensive exam, thesis. *Entrance requirements:* For master's, minimum GPA of 2.7; for doctorate, GRE, minimum GPA of 2.7. Additional exam requirements/recommendations for international students: Required—TOEFL (minimum score 550 paper-based; 213 computer-based; 79 iBT), GRE. Electronic applications accepted. *Faculty research:* Electrochemistry, photochemistry, inorganic synthesis, environmental and solid-state chemistry.

University of Southern California, Graduate School, Dana and David Dornsife College of Letters, Arts and Sciences, Department of Chemistry, Los Angeles, CA 90089. Offers chemistry (PhD); physical chemistry (PhD). *Faculty:* 27 full-time (2 women), 7 part-time/adjunct (0 women). *Students:* 126 full-time (42 women); includes 3 Asian, non-Hispanic/Latino; 2 Hispanic/Latino, 66 international. Average age 26. 406 applicants, 21% accepted, 39 enrolled. In 2010, 16 doctorates awarded. Terminal master's awarded for partial completion of doctoral program. *Degree requirements:* For doctorate, thesis/dissertation. *Entrance requirements:* For doctorate, GRE General Test and TOEFL. Additional exam requirements/recommendations for international students: Required—TOEFL. *Application deadline:* For fall admission, 1/15 for domestic and international students; for spring admission, 11/1 for domestic and international students. Applications are processed on a rolling basis. Application fee: $0. Electronic applications accepted. *Expenses:* Tuition: Full-time $31,240; part-time $1420 per unit. Required fees: $600. One-time fee: $35 full-time. Full-time tuition and fees vary according to degree level and program. *Financial support:* In 2010–11, 3 fellowships with full tuition reimbursements (averaging $30,000 per year), 30 research assistantships with full tuition reimbursements (averaging $25,667 per year), 101 teaching assistantships with full tuition reimbursements (averaging $25,667 per year) were awarded. Financial award application deadline: 1/15. *Faculty research:* Biological chemistry, inorganic chemistry, organic chemistry, physical chemistry, theoretical chemistry. *Unit head:* Dr. Charles McKenna, Chair. *Application contact:* Katherine McKissick, Graduate Advisor, 213-740-7036, E-mail: mckissic@usc.edu.

University of Southern Mississippi, Graduate School, College of Science and Technology, Department of Chemistry and Biochemistry, Hattiesburg, MS 39406-0001. Offers analytical chemistry (MS, PhD); biochemistry (MS, PhD); inorganic chemistry (MS, PhD); organic chemistry (MS, PhD); physical chemistry (MS, PhD). *Faculty:* 16 full-time (4 women). *Students:* 23 full-time (11 women), 1 part-time (0 women); includes 1 Black or African American, non-Hispanic/Latino, 11 international. Average age 29. 35 applicants, 20% accepted, 5 enrolled. In 2010, 3 master's, 8 doctorates awarded. *Degree requirements:* For master's, comprehensive exam, thesis; for doctorate, comprehensive exam, thesis/dissertation. *Entrance requirements:* For master's, GRE General Test, minimum GPA of 2.75 in last 60 hours; for doctorate, GRE General Test, minimum GPA of 3.5. Additional exam requirements/recommendations for international students: Required—TOEFL, IELTS. *Application deadline:* For fall admission, 3/1 priority date for domestic students, 3/1 for international students. Applications are processed on a rolling basis. Application fee: $50. *Financial support:* In 2010–11, 3 research assistantships with full tuition reimbursements (averaging $17,000 per year), 19 teaching assistantships with full tuition reimbursements (averaging $20,700 per year) were awarded; fellowships, Federal Work-Study, institutionally sponsored loans, scholarships/grants, health care benefits, and unspecified assistantships also available. Support available to part-time students. Financial award application deadline: 3/15; financial award applicants required to submit FAFSA. *Faculty research:* Plant biochemistry, photo chemistry, polymer chemistry, x-ray analysis, enzyme chemistry. *Unit head:* Dr. Sabine Heinhorst, Chair, 601-266-4701, Fax: 601-266-6075. *Application contact:* Dr. Sabine Heinhorst, Graduate Coordinator, 601-266-4702, Fax: 601-266-6075.

University of South Florida, Graduate School, College of Arts and Sciences, Department of Chemistry, Tampa, FL 33620-9951. Offers analytical chemistry (MS, PhD); biochemistry (MS, PhD); computational chemistry (MS, PhD); environmental chemistry (MS, PhD); inorganic chemistry (MS, PhD); organic chemistry (MS); physical chemistry (MS, PhD); polymer chemistry (PhD). Part-time programs available. *Faculty:* 15 full-time (1 woman). *Students:* 120 full-time (42 women), 9 part-time (2 women); includes 7 Black or African American, non-Hispanic/Latino; 8 Asian, non-Hispanic/Latino; 8 Hispanic/Latino, 62 international. Average age 29. 1,118 applicants, 4% accepted, 20 enrolled. In 2010, 4 master's, 14 doctorates awarded. Terminal master's awarded for partial completion of doctoral program. *Degree requirements:* For master's, comprehensive exam, thesis (for some programs); for doctorate, 2 foreign languages, comprehensive exam, thesis/dissertation. *Entrance requirements:* For master's, GRE General Test or GMAT, minimum GPA of 3.0. Additional exam requirements/recommendations for international students: Required—TOEFL (minimum score 550 paper-based; 213 computer-based). *Application deadline:* For fall admission, 2/15 priority date for domestic students, 1/2 priority date for international students; for spring admission, 10/1 priority date for domestic students, 6/1 priority date for international students. Applications are processed on a rolling basis. Application fee: $30. Electronic applications accepted. *Financial support:* In 2010–11, 39 research assistantships (averaging $14,359 per year), 99 teaching assistantships with tuition reimbursements (averaging $15,094 per year) were awarded; unspecified assistantships also available. Financial award application deadline: 6/30. *Faculty research:* Synthesis, bio-organic chemistry, bioinorganic chemistry, environmental chemistry, NMR. Total annual research expenditures: $3.9 million. *Unit head:* Dr. Randy Larsen, Chairperson, 813-974-4129, Fax: 813-974-3203, E-mail: rlarsen@cas.usf.edu. *Application contact:* Patricia Muisener, Director, 813-974-1730, Fax: 813-974-3203, E-mail: muisener@cas.usf.edu.

The University of Tennessee, Graduate School, College of Arts and Sciences, Department of Chemistry, Knoxville, TN 37996. Offers analytical chemistry (MS, PhD); chemical physics (PhD); environmental chemistry (MS, PhD); inorganic chemistry (MS, PhD); organic chemistry (MS, PhD); physical chemistry (MS, PhD); polymer chemistry (MS, PhD); theoretical chemistry (PhD). Part-time programs available. Terminal master's awarded for partial completion of doctoral program. *Degree requirements:* For master's, thesis; for doctorate, thesis/dissertation. *Entrance requirements:* For master's and doctorate, GRE General Test, minimum GPA of 2.7. Additional exam requirements/recommendations for international students: Required—TOEFL. Electronic applications accepted. *Expenses:* Tuition, state resident: full-time $7440; part-time $414 per credit hour. Tuition, nonresident: full-time $22,478; part-time $1250 per credit hour. Required fees: $922; $43 per credit hour. Tuition and fees vary according to program.

The University of Texas at Arlington, Graduate School, College of Science, Department of Chemistry and Biochemistry, Arlington, TX 76019. Offers chemistry (MS, PhD). Part-time programs available. *Faculty:* 15 full-time (0 women), 4 part-time/adjunct (0 women). *Students:* 69 full-time (28 women), 8 part-time (4 women); includes 7 Asian, non-Hispanic/Latino; 1 Hispanic/Latino, 48 international. 48 applicants, 100% accepted, 21 enrolled. In 2010, 5 master's, 7 doctorates awarded. Terminal master's awarded for partial completion of doctoral program. *Degree requirements:* For master's, comprehensive exam (for some programs), thesis optional; for doctorate, comprehensive exam, thesis/dissertation, internship, oral defense of dissertation. *Entrance requirements:* For master's, GRE General Test, minimum GPA of 3.0 in last 60 hours of course work; for doctorate, GRE General Test, minimum GPA of 3.0 in last 60 hours of coursework. Additional exam requirements/recommendations for international students: Required—TOEFL (minimum score 550 paper-based; 213 computer-based; 80 iBT). *Application deadline:* For fall admission, 6/1 for domestic students, 3/1 for international students; for spring admission, 10/15 for domestic students, 9/15 for international students. Applications are processed on a rolling basis. Application fee: $40 ($70 for international students). Electronic applications accepted. *Expenses:* Tuition, state resident: full-time $7500. Tuition, nonresident: full-time $13,080. International tuition: $13,250 full-time. *Financial support:* In 2010–11, 4 fellowships (averaging $1,000 per year), 25 research assistantships with partial tuition reimbursements (averaging $21,000 per year), 31 teaching assistantships with partial tuition reimbursements (averaging $20,000 per year) were awarded; career-related internships or fieldwork, Federal Work-Study, institutionally sponsored loans, scholarships/grants, health care benefits, tuition waivers (partial), and unspecified assistantships also available. Financial award application deadline: 6/1; financial award applicants required to submit FAFSA. *Unit head:* Dr. Rasika Dias, Chairman, 817-272-3171, Fax: 817-272-3808, E-mail: dias@uta.edu. *Application contact:* Dr. Peter Kroll, Graduate Adviser, 817-272-3814, Fax: 817-272-3808, E-mail: pkroll@uta.edu.

The University of Texas at Austin, Graduate School, College of Natural Sciences, Department of Chemistry and Biochemistry, Austin, TX 78712-1111. Offers analytical chemistry (MA, PhD); biochemistry (MA, PhD); inorganic chemistry (MA, PhD); organic chemistry (MA, PhD); physical chemistry (MA, PhD). *Entrance requirements:* For master's and doctorate, GRE General Test.

The University of Texas at Dallas, School of Natural Sciences and Mathematics, Programs in Chemistry, Richardson, TX 75080. Offers MS, PhD. Part-time and evening/weekend programs available. *Faculty:* 17 full-time (2 women), 2 part-time/adjunct (0 women). *Students:* 55 full-time (25 women), 5 part-time (4 women); includes 8 minority (4 Asian, non-Hispanic/Latino; 4 Hispanic/Latino), 43 international. Average age 28. 103 applicants, 31% accepted, 4 enrolled. In 2010, 7 master's, 9 doctorates awarded. *Degree requirements:* For master's, thesis optional, thesis or internship; for doctorate, comprehensive exam, thesis/dissertation, research practica. *Entrance requirements:* For master's and doctorate, GRE General Test, minimum GPA of 3.0 in upper-level course work in field. Additional exam requirements/recommendations for international students: Required—TOEFL (minimum score 600 paper-based; 250 computer-based). *Application deadline:* For fall admission, 7/15 for domestic students, 5/1 priority date for international students; for spring admission, 11/15 for domestic students, 9/1 priority date for international students. Applications are processed on a rolling basis. Application fee: $50 ($100 for international students). Electronic applications accepted. *Expenses:* Tuition, state resident: full-time $10,248; part-time $569 per credit hour. Tuition, nonresident: full-time $18,544; part-time $1030 per credit hour. Tuition and fees vary according to course load. *Financial support:* In 2010–11, 52 students received support, including 26 research assistantships with partial tuition reimbursements available (averaging $14,425 per year), 25 teaching assistantships with partial tuition reimbursements available (averaging $14,472 per year); career-related internships or fieldwork, Federal Work-Study, institutionally sponsored loans, scholarships/grants, and unspecified assistantships also available. Support available to part-time students. Financial award application deadline: 4/30; financial award applicants required to submit FAFSA. *Faculty research:* Advanced nano-materials; novel MR imaging agents; peptidomimetics to treat diabetes; semiconducting polymers for organic electronics; macrocyclic receptors for catalysis, medicine, materials science; electroactive polymers. *Unit head:* Dr. John P. Ferraris, Department Head, 972-883-2905, Fax: 972-883-2925, E-mail: chemistry@utdallas.edu. *Application contact:* Dr. Inga H. Musselman, Associate Department Head, 972-883-2706, Fax: 972-883-2925, E-mail: imusselm@utdallas.edu.

The University of Texas at El Paso, Graduate School, College of Science, Department of Chemistry, El Paso, TX 79968-0001. Offers MS, PhD. Part-time and evening/weekend programs available. *Students:* 42 (15 women); includes 1 Asian, non-Hispanic/Latino; 22 Hispanic/Latino, 16 international. Average age 34. In 2010, 8 master's, 1 doctorate awarded. *Degree requirements:* For master's, thesis; for doctorate, thesis/dissertation. *Entrance requirements:* For master's, GRE, minimum GPA of 3.0; for doctorate, GRE, letters of recommendation. Additional exam requirements/recommendations for international students: Required—TOEFL; Recommended—IELTS. *Application deadline:* For fall admission, 8/1 priority date for domestic students, 3/1 for international students; for spring admission, 11/1 priority date for domestic students, 9/1 for international students. Applications are processed on a rolling basis. Application fee: $45 ($80 for international students). Electronic applications accepted. *Financial support:* In 2010–11, research assistantships with partial tuition reimbursements (averaging $20,250 per year), teaching assistantships with partial tuition reimbursements (averaging $16,200 per year) were awarded; fellowships with partial tuition reimbursements, institutionally sponsored loans, scholarships/grants, health care benefits, tuition waivers (partial), and unspecified assistantships also available. Support available to part-time students. Financial award application deadline: 3/15; financial award applicants required to submit FAFSA. *Unit head:* Dr. Jorge Gardea-Torresdey, Chairperson, 915-747-5359, Fax: 915-747-5748, E-mail: jgardea@utep.edu. *Application contact:* Dr. Patricia D. Witherspoon, Dean of the Graduate School, 915-747-5491, Fax: 915-747-5788, E-mail: withersp@utep.edu.

The University of Texas at San Antonio, College of Sciences, Department of Chemistry, San Antonio, TX 78249-0617. Offers MS, PhD. Part-time programs available. *Faculty:* 13 full-time (1 woman), 1 part-time/adjunct (0 women). *Students:* 25 full-time (11 women), 10 part-time (3 women); includes 9 minority (1 Black or African American, non-Hispanic/Latino; 5 Hispanic/Latino; 3 Two or more races, non-Hispanic/Latino), 12 international. Average age 29. 39 applicants, 28% accepted, 6 enrolled. In 2010, 2 master's, 2 doctorates awarded. *Degree requirements:* For master's, comprehensive exam (for some programs), thesis (for some programs). *Entrance requirements:* For master's, GRE General Test, minimum GPA of 3.0 in all undergraduate chemistry courses, 2 letters of recommendation. Additional exam requirements/recommendations for international students: Required—TOEFL (minimum score 500 paper-based; 173 computer-based; 61 iBT), IELTS (minimum score 5). *Application deadline:* For fall admission, 7/1 for domestic students, 4/1 for international students; for spring admission, 11/1 for domestic students, 9/1 for international students. Applications are processed on a rolling basis. Application fee: $45 ($80 for international students). Electronic applications accepted. *Expenses:* Tuition, state resident: full-time $4172; part-time $231.75 per credit hour. Tuition, nonresident: full-time $15,332; part-time $851.75 per credit hour. *Financial support:* In 2010–11, 27 students received support, including 25 fellowships (averaging $27,617 per year), 15 research assistantships (averaging $18,700 per year), 23 teaching assistantships (averaging $13,184 per year); career-related internships or fieldwork, scholarships/grants, tuition waivers, and unspecified assistantships also available. Support available to part-time students. *Faculty research:* Sensors and micro fluidics; signal transduction and transcription factor purification; metals in medicine and nanomaterials; asymmetric and catalytic synthesis; experimental, theoretical and computational techniques. Total annual research expenditures: $1 million. *Unit head:* Dr. Waldemar Gorski, Interim Chair, 210-458-5469, Fax: 210-458-7428, E-mail: waldemar.gorski@utsa.edu. *Application contact:* Veronica Ramirez, Assistant Dean of the Graduate School, 210-458-4330, Fax: 210-458-4332, E-mail: graduatestudies@utsa.edu.

See Display on next page and Close-Up on page 111.

The University of Texas–Pan American, College of Science and Engineering, Department of Chemistry, Edinburg, TX 78539. Offers MS.

University of the Sciences in Philadelphia, College of Graduate Studies, Program in Chemistry, Biochemistry and Pharmacognosy, Philadelphia, PA 19104-4495. Offers biochemistry (MS, PhD); chemistry (MS, PhD); pharmacognosy (MS, PhD). Part-time programs available. *Degree requirements:* For master's, thesis, qualifying exams; for doctorate, comprehensive exam, thesis/dissertation, qualifying exams. *Entrance requirements:* For master's and doctorate, GRE General Test, GRE Subject Test. Additional exam requirements/recommendations for international students: Required—TOEFL, TWE. *Expenses:* Contact institution. *Faculty research:* Organic and medicinal synthesis, mass spectroscopy use in protein analysis, study of analogues of taxol, cholesteryl esters.

The University of Toledo, College of Graduate Studies, College of Natural Sciences and Mathematics, Department of Chemistry, Toledo, OH 43606-3390. Offers analytical chemistry (MS, PhD); biological chemistry (MS, PhD); inorganic chemistry (MS, PhD); organic chemistry

Chemistry

(MS, PhD); physical chemistry (MS, PhD). Part-time programs available. *Faculty:* 24. *Students:* 63 full-time (22 women), 4 part-time (2 women); includes 2 minority (1 Asian, non-Hispanic/Latino; 1 Hispanic/Latino), 45 international. Average age 27. 111 applicants, 17% accepted, 16 enrolled. In 2010, 4 master's, 6 doctorates awarded. *Degree requirements:* For master's, thesis; for doctorate, thesis/dissertation. *Entrance requirements:* For master's and doctorate, GRE General Test, GRE Subject Test, A minimum 2.7 cumulative point-hour ratio (on a 4.0 scale) for all previous academic work. Three letters of recommendation, a statement of purpose, and transcripts from all prior institutions attended. Additional exam requirements/recommendations for international students: Required—TOEFL (minimum score 550 paper-based; 213 computer-based; 80 iBT), IELTS (minimum score 6.5). *Application deadline:* For fall admission, 1/15 priority date for domestic and international students. Applications are processed on a rolling basis. Application fee: $45 ($75 for international students). Electronic applications accepted. *Expenses:* Tuition, state resident: full-time $11,426; part-time $476 per credit hour. Tuition, nonresident: full-time $21,660; part-time $903 per credit hour. One-time fee: $62. *Financial support:* Fellowships with tuition reimbursements, research assistantships with full tuition reimbursements, teaching assistantships with full tuition reimbursements, Federal Work-Study, institutionally sponsored loans, scholarships/grants, tuition waivers (full), and unspecified assistantships available. Support available to part-time students. *Faculty research:* Enzymology, materials chemistry, crystallography, theoretical chemistry. *Unit head:* Dr. Alan Pinkerton, Chair, 419-530-7902, Fax: 419-530-4033, E-mail: alan.pinkerton@utoledo.edu. *Application contact:* Graduate School Office, 419-530-4723, Fax: 419-530-4724, E-mail: grdsch@utnet.utoledo.edu.

University of Toronto, School of Graduate Studies, Physical Sciences Division, Department of Chemistry, Toronto, ON M5S 1A1, Canada. Offers M Sc, PhD. *Degree requirements:* For master's, thesis; for doctorate, thesis/dissertation, oral exam, thesis defense. *Entrance requirements:* For master's, bachelor's degree in chemistry or a related field; for doctorate, master's degree in chemistry or a related field.

University of Tulsa, Graduate School, College of Engineering and Natural Sciences, Department of Chemistry and Biochemistry, Program in Chemistry, Tulsa, OK 74104-3189. Offers MS, PhD. Part-time programs available. *Faculty:* 9 full-time (0 women). *Students:* 9 full-time (1 woman), 1 part-time (0 women), 2 international. Average age 30. 19 applicants, 53% accepted, 1 enrolled. In 2010, 1 master's awarded. Terminal master's awarded for partial completion of doctoral program. *Degree requirements:* For master's, thesis (for some programs). *Entrance requirements:* For master's, GRE General Test. Additional exam requirements/recommendations for international students: Required—TOEFL (minimum score 550 paper-based; 213 computer-based; 80 iBT), IELTS (minimum score 6). *Application deadline:* Applications are processed on a rolling basis. Application fee: $40. Electronic applications accepted. *Expenses:* Tuition: Full-time $16,902; part-time $939 per credit hour. Required fees: $1020; $4 per credit hour. Tuition and fees vary according to course load. *Financial support:* In 2010–11, 10 students received support, including 2 fellowships (averaging $1,000 per year), 4 research assistantships with full tuition reimbursements available (averaging $13,051 per year), 7 teaching assistantships with full tuition reimbursements available (averaging $11,434 per year); career-related internships or fieldwork, Federal Work-Study, scholarships/grants, health care benefits, tuition waivers (full and partial), and unspecified assistantships also available. Support available to part-time students. Financial award application deadline: 2/1; financial award applicants required to submit FAFSA. *Unit head:* Dr. Dale C. Teeters, Chairperson, 918-631-2515, Fax: 918-631-3404, E-mail: dale-teeters@utulsa.edu. *Application contact:* Dr. Kenneth Roberts, Advisor, 918-631-3090, Fax: 918-631-3404, E-mail: kproberts@utulsa.edu.

University of Utah, Graduate School, College of Science, Department of Chemistry, Salt Lake City, UT 84112-0850. Offers chemical physics (PhD); chemistry (M Phil, MA, MS, PhD); science teacher education (MS). Part-time programs available. Postbaccalaureate distance learning degree programs offered. *Faculty:* 31 full-time (5 women), 3 part-time/adjunct (0 women). *Students:* 157 full-time (52 women), 29 part-time (10 women); includes 11 minority (1 Black or African American, non-Hispanic/Latino; 6 Asian, non-Hispanic/Latino; 2 Hispanic/Latino; 2 Two or more races, non-Hispanic/Latino), 67 international. Average age 27. 271 applicants, 30% accepted, 46 enrolled. In 2010, 4 master's, 17 doctorates awarded. Terminal master's awarded for partial completion of doctoral program. *Degree requirements:* For master's, thesis optional, 20 hours course work, 10 hours research; for doctorate, thesis/dissertation, 18 hours course work, 14 hours research. *Entrance requirements:* For master's and doctorate, GRE General Test, minimum GPA of 3.0. Additional exam requirements/recommendations for international students: Required—TOEFL (minimum score 620 paper-based; 260 computer-based; 105 iBT). *Application deadline:* For fall admission, 4/1 for domestic and international students; for spring admission, 11/1 for domestic and international students. Application fee: $55 ($65 for international students). Electronic applications accepted. *Expenses:* Tuition, area resident: Part-time $179.19 per credit hour. Tuition, state resident: full-time $4384. Tuition, nonresident: full-time $16,684; part-time $630.67 per credit hour. Required fees: $350 per semester. Tuition and fees vary according to course load, degree level and program. *Financial support:* In 2010–11, 1 fellowship with tuition reimbursement (averaging $22,000 per year), 128 research assistantships with tuition reimbursements (averaging $22,500 per year), 55 teaching assistantships with tuition reimbursements (averaging $22,000 per year) were awarded; scholarships/grants and tuition waivers (full) also available. Financial award application deadline: 4/1; financial award applicants required to submit FAFSA. *Faculty research:* Biological, theoretical, inorganic, organic, and physical-analytical chemistry. Total annual research expenditures: $14.4 million. *Unit head:* Dr. Henry S. White, Chair, 801-585-6256, Fax: 801-581-8433, E-mail: chair@chemistry.utah.edu. *Application contact:* Jo Hoovey, Graduate Coordinator, 801-581-4393, Fax: 801-581-5408, E-mail: jhoovey@chem.utah.edu.

University of Vermont, Graduate College, College of Arts and Sciences, Department of Chemistry, Burlington, VT 05405. Offers chemistry (MS, PhD). *Students:* 41 (16 women); includes 1 American Indian or Alaska Native, non-Hispanic/Latino; 2 Asian, non-Hispanic/Latino; 1 Hispanic/Latino, 14 international. 66 applicants, 42% accepted, 10 enrolled. In 2010, 5 master's, 3 doctorates awarded. *Degree requirements:* For master's, one foreign language, thesis; for doctorate, 2 foreign languages, thesis/dissertation. *Entrance requirements:* For master's and doctorate, GRE General Test. Additional exam requirements/recommendations for international students: Required—TOEFL (minimum score 550 paper-based; 213 computer-based; 80 iBT). *Application deadline:* For fall admission, 4/1 priority date for domestic students. Applications are processed on a rolling basis. Application fee: $40. Electronic applications accepted. *Expenses:* Tuition, state resident: part-time $537 per credit hour. Tuition, nonresident: part-time $1355 per credit hour. *Financial support:* Fellowships, research assistantships, teaching assistantships available. Financial award application deadline: 3/1. *Unit head:* Dr. D. Matthews, Chairperson, 802-656-2594. *Application contact:* Dr. Rory Waterman, Coordinator, 802-656-2594.

University of Victoria, Faculty of Graduate Studies, Faculty of Science, Department of Chemistry, Victoria, BC V8W 2Y2, Canada. Offers M Sc, PhD. *Degree requirements:* For master's, thesis; for doctorate, thesis/dissertation, candidacy exam. *Entrance requirements:* For master's and doctorate, GRE Subject Test. Additional exam requirements/recommendations for international students: Required—TOEFL (minimum score 575 paper-based; 233 computer-based), IELTS (minimum score 7). Electronic applications accepted. *Faculty research:* Laser spectroscopy and dynamics; inorganic, organic, and organometallic synthesis; electro and surface chemistry.

University of Virginia, College and Graduate School of Arts and Sciences, Department of Chemistry, Charlottesville, VA 22903. Offers MA, MS, PhD. *Faculty:* 25 full-time (2 women). *Students:* 102 full-time (42 women), 1 part-time (0 women); includes 1 Black or African American, non-Hispanic/Latino; 7 Asian, non-Hispanic/Latino; 1 Hispanic/Latino; 1 Two or

more races, non-Hispanic/Latino, 27 international. Average age 26. 272 applicants, 19% accepted, 15 enrolled. In 2010, 4 master's, 9 doctorates awarded. *Degree requirements:* For master's, comprehensive exam, thesis; for doctorate, comprehensive exam, thesis/dissertation. *Entrance requirements:* For master's and doctorate, GRE General Test; GRE Subject Test (recommended). Additional exam requirements/recommendations for international students: Required—TOEFL (minimum score 600 paper-based; 250 computer-based; 90 iBT), IELTS (minimum score 7). *Application deadline:* For fall admission, 2/1 for domestic and international students. Application fee: $60. Electronic applications accepted. *Financial support:* Fellowships, teaching assistantships available. Financial award applicants required to submit FAFSA. *Unit head:* David Cafiso, Chairman, 434-924-3344, Fax: 434-924-3710, E-mail: chem@virginia.edu. *Application contact:* David Cafiso, Chairman, 434-924-3344, Fax: 434-924-3710, E-mail: chem@virginia.edu.

University of Washington, Graduate School, College of Arts and Sciences, Department of Chemistry, Seattle, WA 98195. Offers MS, PhD. Terminal master's awarded for partial completion of doctoral program. *Degree requirements:* For master's, thesis (for some programs); for doctorate, thesis/dissertation. *Entrance requirements:* For master's and doctorate, GRE Subject Test, minimum GPA of 3.0. Additional exam requirements/recommendations for international students: Required—TOEFL. *Faculty research:* Biopolymers, material science and nanotechnology, organometallic chemistry, analytical chemistry, bioorganic chemistry.

University of Waterloo, Graduate Studies, Faculty of Science, Guelph-Waterloo Centre for Graduate Work in Chemistry and Biochemistry, Waterloo, ON N2L 3G1, Canada. Offers M Sc, PhD. M Sc, PhD offered jointly with University of Guelph. Part-time programs available. *Degree requirements:* For master's and doctorate, project or thesis. *Entrance requirements:* For master's, GRE, honors degree, minimum B average; for doctorate, GRE, master's degree, minimum B average. Additional exam requirements/recommendations for international students: Required—TOEFL, TWE. Electronic applications accepted. *Faculty research:* Polymer, physical, inorganic, organic, and theoretical chemistry.

The University of Western Ontario, Faculty of Graduate Studies, Physical Sciences Division, Department of Chemistry, London, ON N6A 5B8, Canada. Offers M Sc, PhD. *Degree requirements:* For master's, thesis; for doctorate, thesis/dissertation. *Entrance requirements:* For master's, minimum B+ average, honors B Sc in chemistry; for doctorate, M Sc or equivalent in chemistry. Additional exam requirements/recommendations for international students: Required—TOEFL (paper-based 570; computer-based 230) or IELTS (paper-based 6). *Faculty research:* Materials, inorganic, organic, physical and theoretical chemistry.

University of Windsor, Faculty of Graduate Studies, Faculty of Science, Department of Chemistry and Biochemistry, Windsor, ON N9B 3P4, Canada. Offers M Sc, PhD. Part-time programs available. *Degree requirements:* For master's, thesis; for doctorate, comprehensive exam, thesis/dissertation. *Entrance requirements:* For master's and doctorate, minimum B average. Additional exam requirements/recommendations for international students: Required—TOEFL (minimum score 560 paper-based; 220 computer-based), GRE. Electronic applications accepted. *Faculty research:* Molecular biology/recombinant DNA techniques (PCR, cloning mutagenesis), No/02 detectors, western immunoblotting and detection, CD/NMR protein/peptide structure determination, confocal/electron microscopes.

University of Wisconsin–Madison, Graduate School, College of Engineering, Program in Environmental Chemistry and Technology, Madison, WI 53706. Offers MS, PhD. Part-time programs available. *Faculty:* 13 full-time (2 women). *Students:* 11 full-time (5 women); includes 1 Hispanic/Latino, 2 international. 62 applicants, 2% accepted, 1 enrolled. In 2010, 2 doctorates awarded. Terminal master's awarded for partial completion of doctoral program. *Degree requirements:* For master's, thesis or alternative; for doctorate, thesis/dissertation. *Entrance requirements:* For master's and doctorate, GRE General Test. Additional exam requirements/recommendations for international students: Required—TOEFL. *Application deadline:* For fall admission, 1/1 priority date for domestic students, 1/1 for international students. Application fee: $45. Electronic applications accepted. *Expenses:* Tuition, state resident: full-time $9887.36; part-time $617.96 per credit. Tuition, nonresident: full-time $24,054; part-time $1503.40 per credit. Required fees: $67.63 per credit. Tuition and fees vary according to reciprocity agreements. *Financial support:* In 2010–11, fellowships with full tuition reimbursements (averaging $19,032 per year), 10 research assistantships with full tuition reimbursements (averaging $19,032 per year) were awarded; Federal Work-Study and institutionally sponsored loans also available. Financial award application deadline: 1/1. *Faculty research:* Chemical limnology, chemical remediation, geochemistry, photocatalysis, water quality. Total annual research expenditures: $1 million. *Unit head:* Dr. Marc A. Anderson, Chair, 608-263-3264, E-mail: nanopor@wisc.edu. *Application contact:* Mary Possin, Student Services Coordinator, 608-263-3264, Fax: 608-265-2340, E-mail: mcpossin@wisc.edu.

University of Wisconsin–Madison, Graduate School, College of Letters and Science, Department of Chemistry, Madison, WI 53706-1380. Offers MS, PhD. Part-time programs available. Terminal master's awarded for partial completion of doctoral program. *Degree requirements:* For master's, thesis (for some programs); for doctorate, thesis/dissertation, cumulative exams, research proposal, seminar. *Entrance requirements:* For master's and doctorate, GRE, minimum GPA of 3.0. Additional exam requirements/recommendations for international students: Required—TOEFL. Electronic applications accepted. *Expenses:* Tuition, state resident: full-time $9887.36; part-time $617.96 per credit. Tuition, nonresident: full-time $24,054; part-time $1503.40 per credit. Required fees: $67.63 per credit. Tuition and fees vary according to reciprocity agreements. *Faculty research:* Analytical, inorganic, organic, physical, and macromolecular chemistry.

University of Wisconsin–Milwaukee, Graduate School, College of Letters and Sciences, Department of Chemistry, Milwaukee, WI 53201-0413. Offers biogeochemistry (PhD); chemistry (MS, PhD). *Faculty:* 22 full-time (4 women). *Students:* 58 full-time (20 women), 16 part-time (10 women); includes 3 Black or African American, non-Hispanic/Latino; 3 Asian, non-Hispanic/Latino, 27 international. Average age 30. 52 applicants, 33% accepted, 5 enrolled. In 2010, 5 master's, 10 doctorates awarded. *Degree requirements:* For master's, thesis or alternative; for doctorate, thesis/dissertation. *Entrance requirements:* For doctorate, GRE General Test. Additional exam requirements/recommendations for international students: Required—TOEFL (minimum score 600 paper-based; 79 iBT), IELTS (minimum score 6.5). *Application deadline:* For fall admission, 1/1 priority date for domestic students; for spring admission, 9/1 for domestic students. Applications are processed on a rolling basis. Application fee: $56 ($96 for international students). *Financial support:* In 2010–11, 3 fellowships, 30 research assistantships, 46 teaching assistantships were awarded; career-related internships or fieldwork, unspecified assistantships, and project assistantships also available. Support available to part-time students. Financial award application deadline: 4/15; financial award applicants required to submit FAFSA. *Faculty research:* Analytical chemistry, biochemistry, inorganic chemistry, organic chemistry, physical chemistry. Total annual research expenditures: $3 million. *Unit head:* Peter Geissinger, Representative, 414-229-5230, Fax: 414-229-5530, E-mail: geissing@uwm.edu. *Application contact:* General Information Contact, 414-229-4982, Fax: 414-229-6967, E-mail: gradschool@uwm.edu.

University of Wyoming, College of Arts and Sciences, Department of Chemistry, Laramie, WY 82070. Offers MS, PhD. *Degree requirements:* For master's, thesis; for doctorate, thesis/dissertation. *Entrance requirements:* For master's and doctorate, GRE General Test, minimum GPA of 3.0. Additional exam requirements/recommendations for international students: Required—TOEFL (minimum score 600 paper-based). Electronic applications accepted. *Faculty research:* Organic chemistry, inorganic chemistry, analytical chemistry, physical chemistry.

Utah State University, School of Graduate Studies, College of Science, Department of Chemistry and Biochemistry, Logan, UT 84322. Offers biochemistry (MS, PhD); chemistry (MS, PhD). Part-time programs available. Terminal master's awarded for partial completion of doctoral program. *Degree requirements:* For master's, thesis, oral and written exams; for doctorate, thesis/dissertation, oral and written exams. *Entrance requirements:* For master's and doctorate, GRE General Test, minimum GPA of 3.0. Additional exam requirements/recommendations for international students: Required—TOEFL. *Faculty research:* Analytical, inorganic, organic, and physical chemistry; iron in asbestos chemistry and carcinogenicity; dicopper complexes; photothermal spectrometry; metal molecule clusters.

Vanderbilt University, Graduate School, Department of Chemistry, Nashville, TN 37240-1001. Offers analytical chemistry (MAT, MS, PhD); inorganic chemistry (MAT, MS, PhD); organic chemistry (MAT, MS, PhD); physical chemistry (MAT, MS, PhD); theoretical chemistry (MAT, MS, PhD). *Faculty:* 21 full-time (3 women). *Students:* 121 full-time (43 women); includes 18 minority (8 Black or African American, non-Hispanic/Latino; 1 American Indian or Alaska Native, non-Hispanic/Latino; 3 Asian, non-Hispanic/Latino; 1 Hispanic/Latino; 5 Two or more races, non-Hispanic/Latino). Average age 26. 373 applicants, 23% accepted, 39 enrolled. In 2010, 4 master's, 17 doctorates awarded. Terminal master's awarded for partial completion of doctoral program. *Degree requirements:* For master's, thesis; for doctorate, thesis/dissertation, area, qualifying, and final exams. *Entrance requirements:* For master's and doctorate, GRE General Test, GRE Subject Test (recommended). Additional exam requirements/recommendations for international students: Required—TOEFL (minimum score 570 paper-based; 230 computer-based; 88 iBT). *Application deadline:* For fall admission, 1/15 for domestic and international students. Application fee: $0. Electronic applications accepted. *Financial support:* Fellowships with full and partial tuition reimbursements, research assistantships with full tuition reimbursements, teaching assistantships with full tuition reimbursements, Federal Work-Study, institutionally sponsored loans, scholarships/grants, traineeships, and health care benefits available. Financial award application deadline: 1/15; financial award applicants required to submit CSS PROFILE or FAFSA. *Faculty research:* Chemical synthesis; mechanistic, theoretical, bioorganic, analytical, and spectroscopic chemistry. *Unit head:* Mike P. Stone, PhD, Chair, 615-322-2589, Fax: 615-343-1234, E-mail: michael.p.stone@vanderbilt.edu. *Application contact:* Charles M. Lukehart, PhD, Director of Graduate Studies, 615-322-2861, Fax: 615-343-1234, E-mail: charles.m.lukehart@vanderbilt.edu.

Villanova University, Graduate School of Liberal Arts and Sciences, Department of Chemistry, Villanova, PA 19085-1699. Offers MS. Part-time and evening/weekend programs available. *Faculty:* 6 full-time (1 woman). *Students:* 20 full-time (9 women), 14 part-time (7 women); includes 6 minority (1 Black or African American, non-Hispanic/Latino; 2 Asian, non-Hispanic/Latino; 1 Hispanic/Latino; 1 Native Hawaiian or other Pacific Islander, non-Hispanic/Latino; 1 Two or more races, non-Hispanic/Latino), 3 international. Average age 26. 25 applicants, 64% accepted, 8 enrolled. In 2010, 20 master's awarded. *Degree requirements:* For master's, thesis (for some programs). *Entrance requirements:* For master's, GRE General Test, minimum GPA of 2.5. Additional exam requirements/recommendations for international students: Required—TOEFL. *Application deadline:* For fall admission, 3/1 priority date for domestic and international students; for spring admission, 11/15 priority date for domestic and international students. Applications are processed on a rolling basis. Application fee: $50. Electronic applications accepted. *Expenses:* Contact institution. *Financial support:* Research assistantships, Federal Work-Study and unspecified assistantships available. Financial award applicants required to submit FAFSA. *Unit head:* Dr. Barry Selinsky, Chair, 610-519-4840. *Application contact:* Dr. Barry Selinsky, Chair, 610-519-4840.

Virginia Commonwealth University, Graduate School, College of Humanities and Sciences, Department of Chemistry, Richmond, VA 23284-9005. Offers analytical chemistry (MS, PhD); chemical physics (PhD); inorganic chemistry (MS, PhD); organic chemistry (MS, PhD); physical chemistry (MS, PhD). Part-time programs available. *Students:* 51 full-time (23 women), 14 part-time (6 women); includes 7 minority (3 Black or African American, non-Hispanic/Latino; 2 Asian, non-Hispanic/Latino; 1 Hispanic/Latino; 1 Two or more races, non-Hispanic/Latino), 26 international. 76 applicants, 33% accepted, 10 enrolled. In 2010, 6 master's, 5 doctorates awarded. Terminal master's awarded for partial completion of doctoral program. *Degree requirements:* For master's, thesis; for doctorate, thesis/dissertation, comprehensive cumulative exams, research proposal. *Entrance requirements:* For master's, GRE General Test, 30 undergraduate credits in chemistry; for doctorate, GRE General Test. Additional exam requirements/recommendations for international students: Required—Either TOEFL (minimum score: paper-based 600, computer-based 250) or IELTS (6.5). *Application deadline:* For fall admission, 3/15 for domestic students; for spring admission, 11/15 for domestic students. Applications are processed on a rolling basis. Application fee: $50. Electronic applications accepted. *Expenses:* Tuition, state resident: full-time $4308; part-time $479 per credit hour. Tuition, nonresident: full-time $8942; part-time $994 per credit hour. Required fees: $2000; $85 per credit hour. Tuition and fees vary according to course level, course load, degree level, campus/location and program. *Financial support:* Fellowships, research assistantships, teaching assistantships, career-related internships or fieldwork and institutionally sponsored loans available. Support available to part-time students. Financial award application deadline: 7/1; financial award applicants required to submit FAFSA. *Faculty research:* Physical, organic, inorganic, analytical, and polymer chemistry; chemical physics. *Unit head:* Dr. Scott Gronert, Chair, 804-828-1298, Fax: 804-828-8599, E-mail: sgronert@vcu.edu. *Application contact:* Dr. Maryanne M. Collinson, Chair, Graduate Recruiting and Admissions Committee, 804-828-7509, E-mail: mselshal@vcu.edu.

Virginia Polytechnic Institute and State University, Graduate School, College of Science, Department of Chemistry, Blacksburg, VA 24061. Offers MS, PhD. *Faculty:* 36 full-time (9 women). *Students:* 148 full-time (64 women), 6 part-time (3 women); includes 2 Black or African American, non-Hispanic/Latino; 1 American Indian or Alaska Native, non-Hispanic/Latino; 4 Asian, non-Hispanic/Latino; 1 Hispanic/Latino, 72 international. Average age 27. 212 applicants, 33% accepted, 32 enrolled. In 2010, 10 master's, 14 doctorates awarded. *Degree requirements:* For master's, comprehensive exam (for some programs), thesis (for some programs); for doctorate, comprehensive exam (for some programs), thesis/dissertation (for some programs). *Entrance requirements:* For master's and doctorate, GRE. Additional exam requirements/recommendations for international students: Required—TOEFL (minimum score 550 paper-based; 213 computer-based). *Application deadline:* For fall admission, 7/1 for domestic and international students; for spring admission, 12/1 for domestic and international students. Applications are processed on a rolling basis. Application fee: $65. Electronic applications accepted. *Expenses:* Tuition, area resident: Full-time $9399; part-time $488 per credit hour. Tuition, state resident: full-time $9399; part-time $488 per credit hour. Tuition, nonresident: full-time $17,854; part-time $957.75 per credit hour. International tuition: $17,854 full-time. Required fees: $1534. Full-time tuition and fees vary according to program. *Financial support:* In 2010–11, 2 fellowships with full tuition reimbursements (averaging $4,500 per year), 42 research assistantships with full tuition reimbursements (averaging $19,128 per year), 86 teaching assistantships with full tuition reimbursements (averaging $17,227 per year) were awarded; career-related internships or fieldwork, Federal Work-Study, scholarships/grants, health care benefits, and unspecified assistantships also available. Financial award application deadline: 1/15. *Faculty research:* Analytical, inorganic, organic, physical, and polymer chemistry. Total annual research expenditures: $10.4 million. *Unit head:* Dr. James M. Tanko, UNIT HEAD, 540-231-6687, Fax: 540-231-3255, E-mail: jtanko@vt.edu. *Application contact:* Paul Deck, Contact, 540-231-3493, Fax: 540-231-3255, E-mail: pdeck@vt.edu.

Wake Forest University, Graduate School of Arts and Sciences, Department of Chemistry, Winston-Salem, NC 27109. Offers analytical chemistry (MS, PhD); inorganic chemistry (MS, PhD); organic chemistry (MS, PhD); physical chemistry (MS, PhD). Part-time programs available. *Degree requirements:* For master's, one foreign language, comprehensive exam, thesis; for

Peterson's Graduate Programs in the Physical Sciences, Mathematics, Agricultural Sciences, the Environment & Natural Resources 2012

www.facebook.com/petersonspublishing   **77**

Chemistry

Wake Forest University (continued)

doctorate, 2 foreign languages, comprehensive exam, thesis/dissertation. *Entrance requirements:* For master's and doctorate, GRE General Test. Additional exam requirements/recommendations for international students: Required—TOEFL (minimum score 213 computer-based). Electronic applications accepted.

Washington State University, Graduate School, College of Sciences, Department of Chemistry, Pullman, WA 99164. Offers MS, PhD. *Faculty:* 25. *Students:* 74 full-time (27 women), 12 part-time (5 women); includes 1 Black or African American, non-Hispanic/Latino; 5 Asian, non-Hispanic/Latino; 2 Hispanic/Latino, 19 international. Average age 29. 186 applicants, 20% accepted, 18 enrolled. In 2010, 6 master's, 4 doctorates awarded. Terminal master's awarded for partial completion of doctoral program. *Degree requirements:* For master's, comprehensive exam (for some programs), thesis (for some programs), oral exam, teaching experience; for doctorate, comprehensive exam, thesis/dissertation, oral exam, written exam. *Entrance requirements:* For master's and doctorate, GRE General Test, GRE Subject Test (recommended), transcripts from each post-secondary school attended (photocopies acceptable); three letters of recommendation. Additional exam requirements/recommendations for international students: Required—TOEFL. *Application deadline:* For fall admission, 3/1 priority date for domestic students, 3/1 for international students; for spring admission, 10/1 priority date for domestic students, 7/1 for international students. Applications are processed on a rolling basis. Application fee: $50. *Expenses:* Tuition, state resident: full-time $8552; part-time $443 per credit. Tuition, nonresident: full-time $21,650; part-time $1083 per credit. Required fees: $846. *Financial support:* In 2010–11, 3 fellowships (averaging $8,977 per year), 12 research assistantships with full and partial tuition reimbursements (averaging $13,917 per year), 23 teaching assistantships with full and partial tuition reimbursements (averaging $13,056 per year) were awarded; career-related internships or fieldwork, Federal Work-Study, institutionally sponsored loans, scholarships/grants, health care benefits, and unspecified assistantships also available. Financial award application deadline: 2/15; financial award applicants required to submit FAFSA. *Faculty research:* Environmental chemistry, materials chemistry, radio chemistry, bio-organic, computational chemistry. *Unit head:* Kerry W. Hipps, Chair, 509-335-8866, Fax: 509-335-8867, E-mail: chemistry@wsu.edu. *Application contact:* Graduate School Admissions, 800-GRADWSU, Fax: 509-335-1949, E-mail: gradsch@wsu.edu.

Washington State University Tri-Cities, Graduate Programs, Program in Chemistry, Richland, WA 99354. Offers MS, PhD. *Faculty:* 25. *Students:* 2 full-time (0 women), 8 part-time (3 women). Average age 35. 186 applicants, 20% accepted.Terminal master's awarded for partial completion of doctoral program. *Degree requirements:* For master's, comprehensive exam (for some programs), thesis; for doctorate, comprehensive exam, thesis/dissertation. *Entrance requirements:* For master's and doctorate, GRE, minimum GPA of 3.0, 3 letters of recommendation. Additional exam requirements/recommendations for international students: Required—TOEFL. *Application deadline:* For fall admission, 3/1 priority date for domestic students, 3/1 for international students; for spring admission, 10/1 priority date for domestic students, 7/1 for international students. Applications are processed on a rolling basis. Application fee: $50. *Financial support:* In 2010–11, 1 student received support. Career-related internships or fieldwork, Federal Work-Study, institutionally sponsored loans, scholarships/grants, health care benefits, and unspecified assistantships available. Financial award application deadline: 2/15; financial award applicants required to submit FAFSA. *Unit head:* Dr. Kerry Hipps, Chair, 509-335-3442. *Application contact:* Bonnie Bates, Academic Coordinator, 509-372-7171, Fax: 509-335-1949, E-mail: bbates@tricity.wsu.edu.

Washington University in St. Louis, Graduate School of Arts and Sciences, Department of Chemistry, St. Louis, MO 63130-4899. Offers PhD. Terminal master's awarded for partial completion of doctoral program. *Degree requirements:* For doctorate, thesis/dissertation. *Entrance requirements:* For doctorate, GRE General Test, GRE Subject Test. Electronic applications accepted.

Wayne State University, College of Liberal Arts and Sciences, Department of Chemistry, Detroit, MI 48202. Offers MA, MS, PhD. *Faculty:* 14 full-time (4 women). *Students:* 141 full-time (64 women), 4 part-time (3 women); includes 11 minority (4 Black or African American, non-Hispanic/Latino; 5 Asian, non-Hispanic/Latino; 2 Hispanic/Latino), 101 international. Average age 28. 433 applicants, 14% accepted, 20 enrolled. In 2010, 6 master's, 19 doctorates awarded. *Degree requirements:* For master's, thesis (for some programs); for doctorate, thesis/dissertation. *Entrance requirements:* For master's, BA with minimum GPA of 3.0, letters of recommendation. Additional exam requirements/recommendations for international students: Required—TOEFL (minimum score 550 paper-based; 213 computer-based); Recommended—TWE (minimum score 6). *Application deadline:* For fall admission, 7/1 for domestic students, 6/1 for international students; for winter admission, 10/1 for international students; for spring admission, 2/1 for international students. Applications are processed on a rolling basis. Application fee: $30 ($50 for international students). Electronic applications accepted. *Expenses:* Tuition, state resident: full-time $7662; part-time $478.85 per credit hour. Tuition, nonresident: full-time $16,920; part-time $1057.55 per credit hour. Required fees: $571.20; $35.70 per credit hour. $188.05 per semester. Tuition and fees vary according to course load and program. *Financial support:* In 2010–11, 3 fellowships (averaging $20,000 per year), 47 research assistantships (averaging $19,481 per year), 83 teaching assistantships (averaging $19,516 per year) were awarded. Financial award application deadline: 7/1. *Faculty research:* Natural products synthesis, molecular biology, molecular mechanics calculations, organometallic chemistry, experimental physical chemistry. *Unit head:* James Rigby, Chair, 313-577-3472, Fax: 313-577-8822, E-mail: aa392@wayne.edu. *Application contact:* Charles Winter, Graduate Director, 313-577-5224, E-mail: chw@chem.wayne.edu.

Wesleyan University, Graduate Programs, Department of Chemistry, Middletown, CT 06459. Offers biochemistry (MA, PhD); chemical physics (MA, PhD); inorganic chemistry (MA, PhD); organic chemistry (MA, PhD); physical chemistry (MA, PhD); theoretical chemistry (MA, PhD). *Faculty:* 12 full-time (2 women). *Students:* 29 full-time (9 women); includes 3 Black or African American, non-Hispanic/Latino; 7 Asian, non-Hispanic/Latino; 2 Hispanic/Latino, 12 international. Average age 26. 48 applicants, 23% accepted, 5 enrolled. In 2010, 6 master's, 6 doctorates awarded. Terminal master's awarded for partial completion of doctoral program. *Degree requirements:* For master's, thesis, proposal; for doctorate, thesis/dissertation, proposal. *Entrance requirements:* For doctorate, GRE General Test, 3 recommendations. Additional exam requirements/recommendations for international students: Required—TOEFL. *Application deadline:* Applications are processed on a rolling basis. Application fee: $0. Electronic applications accepted. *Expenses:* Tuition: Full-time $43,404. Required fees: $830. *Financial support:* In 2010–11, 9 research assistantships with full tuition reimbursements, 18 teaching assistantships with full tuition reimbursements were awarded; institutionally sponsored loans also available. Financial award application deadline: 4/15; financial award applicants required to submit FAFSA. *Unit head:* Dr. Joseph Knee, Chair, 860-685-2210. *Application contact:* Cait Zinser, Information Contact, 860-685-2573, Fax: 860-685-2211, E-mail: czinser@wesleyan.edu.

West Chester University of Pennsylvania, Office of Graduate Studies, College of Arts and Sciences, Department of Chemistry, West Chester, PA 19383. Offers Teaching Certificate. Part-time and evening/weekend programs available. *Students:* 3 applicants, 67% accepted, 0 enrolled. *Degree requirements:* For Teaching Certificate, minimum overall GPA of 3.0, PRAXIS I and Chemistry PRAXIS. *Entrance requirements:* For degree, minimum GPA of 2.8 in most recent 48 credits. Additional exam requirements/recommendations for international students: Required—TOEFL (minimum score 550 paper-based; 213 computer-based; 80 iBT). *Application deadline:* For fall admission, 4/15 priority date for domestic students, 3/15 for international students; for spring admission, 10/15 for domestic students, 9/1 for international students. Applications are processed on a rolling basis. Application fee: $35. Electronic applications accepted. *Expenses:* Tuition, state resident: full-time $6966; part-time $387 per credit. Tuition, nonresident: full-time $11,146; part-time $619 per credit. Required fees: $1614.40; $133.24 per credit. Part-time tuition and fees vary according to campus/location. *Financial support:* Unspecified assistantships available. Support available to part-time students. Financial award application deadline: 2/15; financial award applicants required to submit FAFSA. *Unit head:* Dr. Blaise Frost, Chair, 610-436-2526, E-mail: bfrost@wcupa.edu. *Application contact:* Dr. John Townsend, Secondary Education Advisor, 610-436-1063, E-mail: jtownsend@wcupa.edu.

Western Carolina University, Graduate School, College of Arts and Sciences, Department of Chemistry and Physics, Cullowhee, NC 28723. Offers chemistry (MS). *Degree requirements:* For master's, thesis. *Entrance requirements:* For master's, GRE General Test, undergraduate science degree with minimum GPA of 3.0, 3 letters of recommendation. Additional exam requirements/recommendations for international students: Required—TOEFL (minimum score 550 paper-based; 270 computer-based; 79 iBT). *Faculty research:* Trace metal analysis, metal waste reduction, supramolecular chemistry, free radical biophysical chemistry.

Western Illinois University, School of Graduate Studies, College of Arts and Sciences, Department of Chemistry, Macomb, IL 61455-1390. Offers MS. Part-time programs available. *Students:* 39 full-time (16 women); includes 1 minority (Asian, non-Hispanic/Latino), 30 international. Average age 24. 105 applicants, 34% accepted. In 2010, 19 master's awarded. *Degree requirements:* For master's, thesis or alternative. *Entrance requirements:* Additional exam requirements/recommendations for international students: Required—TOEFL (minimum score 530 paper-based; 71 iBT). *Application deadline:* Applications are processed on a rolling basis. Application fee: $30. Electronic applications accepted. *Expenses:* Tuition, state resident: full-time $6370; part-time $265.40 per credit hour. Tuition, nonresident: full-time $12,740; part-time $530.80 per credit hour. Required fees: $75.67 per credit hour. *Financial support:* In 2010–11, 21 students received support, including 9 research assistantships with full tuition reimbursements available (averaging $7,280 per year), 12 teaching assistantships with full tuition reimbursements available (averaging $8,400 per year). Financial award applicants required to submit FAFSA. *Unit head:* Dr. Rose McConnell, Chairperson, 309-298-1538. *Application contact:* Evelyn Hoing, Assistant Director of Graduate Studies, 309-298-1806, Fax: 309-298-2345, E-mail: grad-office@wiu.edu.

Western Kentucky University, Graduate Studies, Ogden College of Science and Engineering, Department of Chemistry, Bowling Green, KY 42101. Offers MA Ed, MS. *Degree requirements:* For master's, comprehensive exam, thesis. *Entrance requirements:* For master's, GRE General Test, minimum GPA of 2.75. Additional exam requirements/recommendations for international students: Required—TOEFL (minimum score 555 paper-based; 213 computer-based). *Faculty research:* Catatonic surfactants, directed orthometalation reactions, thermal stability and degradation mechanisms, co-firing refused derived fuels, laser fluorescence.

Western Michigan University, Graduate College, College of Arts and Sciences, Department of Chemistry, Kalamazoo, MI 49008. Offers MS, PhD. *Degree requirements:* For master's, thesis, departmental qualifying and oral exams; for doctorate, thesis/dissertation.

Western Washington University, Graduate School, College of Sciences and Technology, Department of Chemistry, Bellingham, WA 98225-5996. Offers MS. Part-time programs available. *Degree requirements:* For master's, thesis (for some programs). *Entrance requirements:* For master's, GRE General Test, minimum GPA of 3.0 in last 60 semester hours or last 90 quarter hours. Additional exam requirements/recommendations for international students: Required—TOEFL (minimum score 567 paper-based; 227 computer-based). Electronic applications accepted. *Faculty research:* Bio-, organic, inorganic, physical, analytical chemistry.

West Texas A&M University, College of Agriculture, Nursing, and Natural Sciences, Department of Mathematics, Physical Sciences and Engineering Technology, Program in Chemistry, Canyon, TX 79016-0001. Offers MS. Part-time programs available. *Degree requirements:* For master's, comprehensive exam, thesis optional. *Entrance requirements:* For master's, GRE General Test. Additional exam requirements/recommendations for international students: Required—TOEFL (minimum score 550 paper-based). Electronic applications accepted. *Faculty research:* Biochemistry; inorganic, organic, and physical chemistry; vibrational spectroscopy; magnetic susceptibilities; carbene chemistry.

West Virginia University, Eberly College of Arts and Sciences, Department of Chemistry, Morgantown, WV 26506. Offers analytical chemistry (MS, PhD); inorganic chemistry (MS, PhD); organic chemistry (MS, PhD); physical chemistry (MS, PhD); theoretical chemistry (MS, PhD). Part-time programs available. Postbaccalaureate distance learning degree programs offered (no on-campus study). Terminal master's awarded for partial completion of doctoral program. *Degree requirements:* For master's, thesis; for doctorate, thesis/dissertation. *Entrance requirements:* For master's, GRE General Test, GRE Subject Test (recommended), minimum GPA of 2.5; for doctorate, GRE General Test, GRE Subject Test (recommended), minimum GPA of 2.75. Additional exam requirements/recommendations for international students: Required—TOEFL. Electronic applications accepted. *Faculty research:* Analysis of proteins, drug interactions, solids and effluents by advanced separation methods; new synthetic strategies for complex organic molecules; synthesis and structural characterization of metal complexes for polymerization catalysis, nonlinear science, spectroscopy.

Wichita State University, Graduate School, Fairmount College of Liberal Arts and Sciences, Department of Chemistry, Wichita, KS 67260. Offers MS, PhD. *Unit head:* Dr. David Eichhorn, Chair, 316-978-3120, Fax: 316-978-3431, E-mail: david.eichhorn@wichita.edu. *Application contact:* Dr. Dennis Burns, Graduate Coordinator, 316-978-3120, E-mail: dennis.burns@wichita.edu.

Wilfrid Laurier University, Faculty of Graduate and Postdoctoral Studies, Faculty of Science, Department of Chemistry, Waterloo, ON N2L 3C5, Canada. Offers M Sc. *Faculty:* 10 full-time (2 women), 1 part-time/adjunct (0 women). *Students:* 11 full-time (6 women), 1 part-time, 1 international. 5 applicants, 80% accepted, 4 enrolled. In 2010, 1 master's awarded. *Degree requirements:* For master's, thesis. *Entrance requirements:* For master's, honors degree or equivalent in chemistry, biochemistry or a related discipline; minimum B average in last two full-time undergraduate years. Additional exam requirements/recommendations for international students: Required—TOEFL (minimum score 89 iBT). *Application deadline:* For fall admission, 2/1 priority date for domestic and international students. Application fee: $100. Electronic applications accepted. Tuition and fees charges are reported in Canadian dollars. *Expenses:* Tuition, area resident: Full-time $15,300 Canadian dollars; part-time $1200 Canadian dollars per credit. International tuition: $21,300 Canadian dollars full-time. Required fees: $650 Canadian dollars; $100 Canadian dollars per credit. Tuition and fees vary according to course load, degree level, campus/location and program. *Financial support:* In 2010–11, 20 fellowships, 20 teaching assistantships were awarded; career-related internships or fieldwork, scholarships/grants, health care benefits, and unspecified assistantships also available. *Faculty research:* Cold regions water science, biophysical methods, biochemistry, nanochemistry. *Unit head:* Dr. Masoud Jelokhani, Graduate Coordinator, 519-884-0710 Ext. 2284, Fax: 519-746-0677, E-mail: mjelokhani@wlu.ca. *Application contact:* Rosemary Spingett, Graduate Admissions and Records Officer, 519-884-0710 Ext. 3078, Fax: 519-884-1020, E-mail: gradstudies@wlu.ca.

Worcester Polytechnic Institute, Graduate Studies and Research, Department of Chemistry and Biochemistry, Worcester, MA 01609-2280. Offers biochemistry (MS, PhD); chemistry (MS, PhD). Evening/weekend programs available. *Faculty:* 6 full-time (0 women). *Students:* 15 full-time (8 women); includes 1 Native Hawaiian or other Pacific Islander, non-Hispanic/Latino, 7 international. 80 applicants, 6% accepted, 4 enrolled. In 2010, 1 master's, 2 doctorates awarded. *Degree requirements:* For master's, thesis; for doctorate, comprehensive exam, thesis/dissertation. *Entrance requirements:* For master's, GRE General Test, 3 letters of recommendation; for doctorate, GRE General Test, 3 letters of recommendation, statement of

purpose. Additional exam requirements/recommendations for international students: Required—TOEFL (minimum score 550 paper-based; 213 computer-based; 79 iBT), IELTS (minimum score 6.5). *Application deadline:* For fall admission, 1/1 priority date for domestic and international students; for spring admission, 10/1 priority date for domestic and international students. Applications are processed on a rolling basis. Application fee: $70. Electronic applications accepted. *Expenses:* Tuition: Full-time $20,862; part-time $1159 per term. One-time fee: $15. *Financial support:* Career-related internships or fieldwork, institutionally sponsored loans, scholarships/grants, and unspecified assistantships available. Financial award application deadline: 1/1; financial award applicants required to submit FAFSA. *Faculty research:* Catalysis experimental and computational protein biophysics, biological metals,synthetic methods, surface chemistry, computational chemistry. *Unit head:* Dr. Kristin K. Wobbe, Interim Head, 508-831-5371, Fax: 508-831-5933, E-mail: kwobbe@wpi.edu. *Application contact:* Dr. James Dittami, Graduate Coordinator, 508-831-5371, Fax: 508-831-5933, E-mail: jdittami@wpi.edu.

Wright State University, School of Graduate Studies, College of Science and Mathematics, Department of Chemistry, Dayton, OH 45435. Offers chemistry (MS); environmental sciences (MS). Part-time and evening/weekend programs available. *Degree requirements:* For master's, oral defense of thesis, seminar. *Entrance requirements:* Additional exam requirements/recommendations for international students: Required—TOEFL. *Faculty research:* Polymer synthesis and characterization, laser kinetics, organic and inorganic synthesis, analytical and environmental chemistry.

Yale University, Graduate School of Arts and Sciences, Department of Chemistry, New Haven, CT 06520. Offers biophysical chemistry (PhD); inorganic chemistry (PhD); organic chemistry (PhD); physical and theoretical chemistry (PhD). *Degree requirements:* For doctorate, thesis/dissertation. *Entrance requirements:* For doctorate, GRE General Test, GRE Subject Test. Additional exam requirements/recommendations for international students: Required—TOEFL.

York University, Faculty of Graduate Studies, Faculty of Science and Engineering, Program in Chemistry, Toronto, ON M3J 1P3, Canada. Offers M Sc, PhD. Part-time and evening/weekend programs available. *Degree requirements:* For master's, thesis or alternative; for doctorate, thesis/dissertation. Electronic applications accepted.

Youngstown State University, Graduate School, College of Science, Technology, Engineering and Mathematics, Department of Chemistry, Youngstown, OH 44555-0001. Offers analytical chemistry (MS); biochemistry (MS); chemistry education (MS); inorganic chemistry (MS); organic chemistry (MS); physical chemistry (MS). Part-time programs available. *Degree requirements:* For master's, thesis. *Entrance requirements:* For master's, bachelor's degree in chemistry, minimum GPA of 2.7. Additional exam requirements/recommendations for international students: Required—TOEFL. *Faculty research:* Analysis of antioxidants, chromatography, defects and disorder in crystalline oxides, hydrogen bonding, novel organic and organometallic materials.

Inorganic Chemistry

Auburn University, Graduate School, College of Sciences and Mathematics, Department of Chemistry and Biochemistry, Auburn University, AL 36849. Offers analytical chemistry (MS, PhD); biochemistry (MS, PhD); inorganic chemistry (MS, PhD); organic chemistry (MS, PhD); physical chemistry (MS, PhD). Part-time programs available. *Faculty:* 27 full-time (6 women). *Students:* 39 full-time (20 women), 21 part-time (8 women); includes 4 Black or African American, non-Hispanic/Latino; 1 Asian, non-Hispanic/Latino; 1 Hispanic/Latino, 41 international. Average age 28. 54 applicants, 11% accepted, 3 enrolled. In 2010, 1 master's, 13 doctorates awarded. *Degree requirements:* For master's, thesis (for some programs); for doctorate, thesis/dissertation, oral and written exams. *Entrance requirements:* For master's and doctorate, GRE General Test. *Application deadline:* For fall admission, 7/7 for domestic students; for spring admission, 11/24 for domestic students. Applications are processed on a rolling basis. Application fee: $50 ($60 for international students). Electronic applications accepted. *Expenses:* Tuition, state resident: full-time $7002. Tuition, nonresident: full-time $21,898. International tuition: $22,116 full-time. Required fees: $892. Tuition and fees vary according to course load and program. *Financial support:* Fellowships, research assistantships, teaching assistantships available. Financial award application deadline: 3/15; financial award applicants required to submit FAFSA. *Unit head:* Dr. J. V. Ortiz, Chair, 334-844-4043, Fax: 334-844-4043. *Application contact:* Dr. George Flowers, Dean of the Graduate School, 334-844-2125.

Boston College, Graduate School of Arts and Sciences, Department of Chemistry, Chestnut Hill, MA 02467-3800. Offers biochemistry (PhD); inorganic chemistry (PhD); organic chemistry (PhD); physical chemistry (PhD); science education (MST). Part-time programs available. *Degree requirements:* For doctorate, thesis/dissertation, qualifying exam. *Entrance requirements:* For doctorate, GRE General Test, GRE Subject Test. Additional exam requirements/recommendations for international students: Required—TOEFL (minimum score 600 paper-based; 250 computer-based; 100 iBT). Electronic applications accepted.

Brandeis University, Graduate School of Arts and Sciences, Department of Chemistry, Waltham, MA 02454. Offers inorganic chemistry (MS, PhD); organic chemistry (MS, PhD); physical chemistry (MS, PhD). *Faculty:* 26 full-time (14 women). *Students:* 43 full-time (14 women); includes 1 Black or African American, non-Hispanic/Latino, 27 international. 115 applicants, 25% accepted, 14 enrolled. In 2010, 9 master's, 8 doctorates awarded. Terminal master's awarded for partial completion of doctoral program. *Degree requirements:* For master's, thesis, 1 year of residency; for doctorate, one foreign language, thesis/dissertation, 3 years of residency, 2 seminars, qualifying exams. *Entrance requirements:* For master's and doctorate, GRE General Test, resume, letters of recommendation. Additional exam requirements/recommendations for international students: Required—TOEFL (minimum score 600 paper-based; 250 computer-based; 100 iBT); Recommended—IELTS (minimum score 7). *Application deadline:* For fall admission, 1/15 priority date for domestic students. Applications are processed on a rolling basis. Application fee: $75. Electronic applications accepted. *Financial support:* In 2010–11, 23 fellowships with full tuition reimbursements (averaging $24,500 per year), 14 research assistantships with full tuition reimbursements (averaging $24,500 per year), teaching assistantships with partial tuition reimbursements (averaging $3,200 per year) were awarded; scholarships/grants and health care benefits also available. Financial award application deadline: 4/15; financial award applicants required to submit FAFSA. *Faculty research:* Oscillating chemical reactions, molecular recognition systems, protein crystallography, synthesis of natural product spectroscopy and magnetic resonance. *Unit head:* Dr. Judith Herzfeld, Chair, Graduate Program in Chemistry, 781-736-2540, Fax: 781-736-2516, E-mail: herzfeld@brandeis.edu. *Application contact:* Charlotte Haygazian, Graduate Department Coordinator, 781-736-2500, Fax: 781-736-2516, E-mail: chemadm@brandeis.edu.

California State University, Los Angeles, Graduate Studies, College of Natural and Social Sciences, Department of Chemistry and Biochemistry, Los Angeles, CA 90032-8530. Offers analytical chemistry (MS); biochemistry (MS); chemistry (MS); inorganic chemistry (MS); organic chemistry (MS); physical chemistry (MS). Part-time and evening/weekend programs available. *Faculty:* 5 part-time/adjunct (1 woman). *Students:* 19 full-time (15 women), 24 part-time (12 women); includes 21 minority (3 Black or African American, non-Hispanic/Latino; 8 Asian, non-Hispanic/Latino; 10 Hispanic/Latino), 9 international. Average age 30. 22 applicants, 100% accepted, 10 enrolled. In 2010, 7 master's awarded. *Degree requirements:* For master's, one foreign language, comprehensive exam or thesis. *Entrance requirements:* Additional exam requirements/recommendations for international students: Required—TOEFL. *Application deadline:* For fall admission, 5/1 for domestic and international students. Applications are processed on a rolling basis. Application fee: $55. *Financial support:* Federal Work-Study available. Support available to part-time students. Financial award application deadline: 3/1. *Faculty research:* Intercalation of heavy metal, carborane chemistry, conductive polymers and fabrics, titanium reagents, computer modeling and synthesis. *Unit head:* Dr. Robert L. Vellanoweth, Chair, 323-343-2300, Fax: 323-343-6490, E-mail: rvellan@calstatela.edu. *Application contact:* Dr. Allan Muchlinski, Dean of Graduate Studies, 323-343-3820 Ext. 3827, Fax: 323-343-5653, E-mail: amuchli@exchange.calstatela.edu.

Carnegie Mellon University, Mellon College of Science, Department of Chemistry, Pittsburgh, PA 15213-3891. Offers biotechnology and management (MS); chemistry (PhD), including bioinorganic, bioorganic, organic and materials, biophysics and spectroscopy, computational and theoretical, polymer; colloids, polymers and surfaces (MS). Part-time programs available. Terminal master's awarded for partial completion of doctoral program. *Degree requirements:* For doctorate, thesis/dissertation, departmental qualifying and oral exams, teaching experience. *Entrance requirements:* For master's, GRE General Test; for doctorate, GRE General Test, GRE Subject Test. Additional exam requirements/recommendations for international students: Required—TOEFL. Electronic applications accepted. *Faculty research:* Physical and theoretical chemistry, chemical synthesis, biophysical/bioinorganic chemistry.

Cleveland State University, College of Graduate Studies, College of Sciences and Health Professions, Department of Chemistry, Cleveland, OH 44115. Offers analytical chemistry (MS); clinical chemistry (MS); clinical/bioanalytical chemistry (PhD), including cellular and molecular medicine, clinical chemistry, clinical/bioanalytical chemistry; environmental chemistry (MS); inorganic chemistry (MS); pharmaceutical/organic chemistry (MS); physical chemistry (MS). Part-time and evening/weekend programs available. *Faculty:* 13 full-time (0 women), 1 (woman) part-time/adjunct. *Students:* 58 full-time (29 women), 42 part-time (17 women); includes 4 Black or African American, non-Hispanic/Latino; 3 Asian, non-Hispanic/Latino; 1 Hispanic/Latino, 70 international. Average age 28. 76 applicants, 74% accepted, 16 enrolled. In 2010, 4 master's, 15 doctorates awarded. *Degree requirements:* For master's, thesis optional; for doctorate, comprehensive exam, thesis/dissertation. *Entrance requirements:* For master's and doctorate, GRE General Test. Additional exam requirements/recommendations for international students: Required—TOEFL (minimum score 525 paper-based; 197 computer-based; 65 iBT). *Application deadline:* For fall admission, 1/15 priority date for domestic and international students. Applications are processed on a rolling basis. Application fee: $30. Electronic applications accepted. *Expenses:* Tuition, state resident: full-time $8447; part-time $469 per credit hour. Tuition, nonresident: full-time $16,020; part-time $890 per credit hour. Required fees: $50. *Financial support:* In 2010–11, 44 students received support, including 5 fellowships with full tuition reimbursements available (averaging $30,000 per year), 13 research assistantships with full tuition reimbursements available (averaging $20,000 per year), 24 teaching assistantships with full tuition reimbursements available (averaging $18,500 per year); scholarships/grants and unspecified assistantships also available. Financial award application deadline: 1/15. *Faculty research:* Bioanalytical techniques and molecular diagnostics, glycoproteomics and antithrombotic agents, drug discovery and innovation, analytical pharmacology, inflammatory disease research. Total annual research expenditures: $3 million. *Unit head:* Dr. David J. Anderson, Interim Chair, 216-687-2467, Fax: 216-687-9298, E-mail: d.anderson@csuohio.edu. *Application contact:* Richelle P. Emery, Administrative Coordinator, 216-687-2457, Fax: 216-687-9298, E-mail: r.emery@csuohio.edu.

Columbia University, Graduate School of Arts and Sciences, Division of Natural Sciences, Department of Chemistry, New York, NY 10027. Offers chemical physics (M Phil, PhD); inorganic chemistry (M Phil, MA, PhD); organic chemistry (M Phil, MA, PhD); MD/PhD. *Degree requirements:* For master's, one foreign language, teaching experience, oral/written exams (M Phil); for doctorate, one foreign language, thesis/dissertation. *Entrance requirements:* For master's and doctorate, GRE General Test, GRE Subject Test. Additional exam requirements/recommendations for international students: Required—TOEFL. *Faculty research:* Biophysics.

Cornell University, Graduate School, Graduate Fields of Arts and Sciences, Field of Chemistry and Chemical Biology, Ithaca, NY 14853-0001. Offers analytical chemistry (PhD); bio-organic chemistry (PhD); biophysical chemistry (PhD); chemical biology (PhD); chemical physics (PhD); inorganic chemistry (PhD); materials chemistry (PhD); organic chemistry (PhD); organometallic chemistry (PhD); physical chemistry (PhD); polymer chemistry (PhD); theoretical chemistry (PhD). *Faculty:* 46 full-time (3 women). *Students:* 163 full-time (63 women); includes 10 Asian, non-Hispanic/Latino; 3 Hispanic/Latino, 49 international. Average age 24. 340 applicants, 36% accepted, 48 enrolled. In 2010, 31 doctorates awarded. *Degree requirements:* For doctorate, comprehensive exam, thesis/dissertation. *Entrance requirements:* For doctorate, GRE General Test, GRE Subject Test (chemistry), 3 letters of recommendation. Additional exam requirements/recommendations for international students: Required—TOEFL (minimum score 600 paper-based; 250 computer-based; 77 iBT). *Application deadline:* For fall admission, 1/10 for domestic students. Application fee: $80. Electronic applications accepted. *Expenses:* Tuition: Full-time $29,500. Required fees: $76. Tuition and fees vary according to degree level and program. *Financial support:* In 2010–11, 19 fellowships with full tuition reimbursements, 69 research assistantships with full tuition reimbursements, 68 teaching assistantships with full tuition reimbursements were awarded; institutionally sponsored loans, scholarships/grants, health care benefits, tuition waivers (full and partial), and unspecified assistantships also available. Financial award applicants required to submit FAFSA. *Faculty research:* Analytical, organic, inorganic, physical, materials, chemical biology. *Unit head:* Director of Graduate Studies, 607-255-4139, Fax: 607-255-4137. *Application contact:* Graduate Field Assistant, 607-255-4139, Fax: 607-255-4137, E-mail: chemgrad@cornell.edu.

Eastern New Mexico University, Graduate School, College of Liberal Arts and Sciences, Department of Physical Sciences, Portales, NM 88130. Offers chemistry (MS), including analytical, biochemistry, inorganic, organic, physical. Part-time programs available. *Faculty:* 3 full-time (0 women). *Students:* 7 full-time (2 women), 2 part-time (1 woman), 6 international. Average age 32. 10 applicants, 40% accepted, 4 enrolled. In 2010, 3 master's awarded. *Degree requirements:* For master's, thesis optional, seminar, oral and written comprehensive exams. *Entrance requirements:* For master's, ACS placement examination, minimum GPA of 3.0; 2 letters of recommendation; personal statement of career goals; bachelor's degree with one year minimum each of general, organic, and analytical chemistry. Additional exam requirements/recommendations for international students: Required—TOEFL (minimum score 550 paper-based; 213 computer-based; 79 iBT), IELTS (minimum score 6). *Application deadline:* For fall admission, 7/20 priority date for domestic students, 6/20 priority date for international students; for spring admission, 12/15 priority date for domestic students, 11/15 priority date for

Inorganic Chemistry

Eastern New Mexico University (continued)
international students. Applications are processed on a rolling basis. Application fee: $10. Electronic applications accepted. *Expenses:* Tuition, state resident: full-time $3210; part-time $130 per credit hour. Tuition, nonresident: full-time $8652; part-time $360.50 per credit hour. Required fees: $1212; $50.50 per credit hour. Tuition and fees vary according to course load. *Financial support:* In 2010–11, 1 research assistantship with partial tuition reimbursement (averaging $8,500 per year), 9 teaching assistantships with partial tuition reimbursements (averaging $8,500 per year) were awarded; career-related internships or fieldwork and unspecified assistantships also available. Support available to part-time students. Financial award application deadline: 3/1; financial award applicants required to submit FAFSA. *Faculty research:* Synfuel, electrochemistry, protein chemistry. *Unit head:* Dr. Juacho Yan, Graduate Coordinator, 575-562-2174, Fax: 575-562-2192, E-mail: juacho.yan@enmu.edu. *Application contact:* Sharon Potter, Department Secretary, Chemistry/Physical Sciences, 575-562-2174, Fax: 575-562-2192, E-mail: sharon.potter@enmu.edu.

Florida State University, The Graduate School, College of Arts and Sciences, Department of Chemistry and Biochemistry, Tallahassee, FL 32306-4390. Offers analytical chemistry (MS, PhD); biochemistry (MS, PhD); inorganic chemistry (MS, PhD); materials chemistry (PhD); organic chemistry (MS, PhD); physical chemistry (MS, PhD). *Faculty:* 38 full-time (5 women), 3 part-time/adjunct (0 women). *Students:* 142 full-time (46 women), 8 part-time (4 women); includes 12 minority (6 Black or African American, non-Hispanic/Latino; 3 Asian, non-Hispanic/Latino; 3 Hispanic/Latino), 68 international. Average age 25. 299 applicants, 17% accepted, 19 enrolled. In 2010, 10 master's, 20 doctorates awarded. Terminal master's awarded for partial completion of doctoral program. *Degree requirements:* For master's, comprehensive exam (for some programs), thesis (for some programs), cumulative exams; for doctorate, comprehensive exam (for some programs), thesis/dissertation, cumulative exams. *Entrance requirements:* For master's and doctorate, GRE General Test, minimum B average in undergraduate course work. Additional exam requirements/recommendations for international students: Required—TOEFL (minimum score 550 paper-based; 213 computer-based; 80 iBT). *Application deadline:* For fall admission, 12/15 priority date for domestic and international students; for spring admission, 9/15 for domestic and international students. Applications are processed on a rolling basis. Application fee: $30. Electronic applications accepted. *Expenses:* Tuition, state resident: full-time $8238.24. *Financial support:* In 2010–11, 150 students received support, including fellowships with full tuition reimbursements available (averaging $20,000 per year), 50 research assistantships with full tuition reimbursements available (averaging $20,000 per year), 100 teaching assistantships with full tuition reimbursements available (averaging $20,000 per year). Financial award application deadline: 12/15; financial award applicants required to submit FAFSA. *Faculty research:* Materials synthesis including polymers, natural products; catalysis, NMR; mass spectrometry; optical spectroscopy, scattering techniques, computational chemistry, separation technology; nanostructured materials including metallic, semiconducting and magnetic nanocrystals; nanoscience interfaced with biology; supramolecular materials for solar energy conversion. Total annual research expenditures: $5.6 million. *Unit head:* Dr. Timothy Logan, Chairman, 850-644-1244, Fax: 850-644-8281, E-mail: gradinfo@chem.fsu.edu. *Application contact:* Dr. Tyler McQuade, Chair, Graduate Admissions Committee, 888-525-9286, Fax: 850-644-0465, E-mail: gradinfo@chem.fsu.edu.

Georgetown University, Graduate School of Arts and Sciences, Department of Chemistry, Washington, DC 20057. Offers analytical chemistry (PhD); biochemistry (PhD); computational chemistry (PhD); inorganic chemistry (PhD); materials chemistry (PhD); organic chemistry (PhD); physical chemistry (PhD); theoretical chemistry (PhD). Terminal master's awarded for partial completion of doctoral program. *Degree requirements:* For doctorate, comprehensive exam, thesis/dissertation. *Entrance requirements:* For doctorate, GRE General Test. Additional exam requirements/recommendations for international students: Required—TOEFL.

The George Washington University, Columbian College of Arts and Sciences, Department of Chemistry, Washington, DC 20052. Offers analytical chemistry (MS, PhD); inorganic chemistry (MS, PhD); materials science (MS, PhD); organic chemistry (MS, PhD); physical chemistry (MS, PhD). Part-time and evening/weekend programs available. *Faculty:* 15 full-time (4 women), 5 part-time/adjunct (2 women). *Students:* 21 full-time (10 women), 10 part-time (5 women); includes 3 Asian, non-Hispanic/Latino; 1 Hispanic/Latino, 9 international. Average age 28. 33 applicants, 45% accepted, 7 enrolled. In 2010, 4 master's, 2 doctorates awarded. Terminal master's awarded for partial completion of doctoral program. *Degree requirements:* For master's, comprehensive exam, thesis or alternative; for doctorate, thesis/dissertation, general exam. *Entrance requirements:* For master's and doctorate, GRE General Test, interview, minimum GPA of 3.0. Additional exam requirements/recommendations for international students: Required—TOEFL (minimum score 550 paper-based; 213 computer-based; 80 iBT). *Application deadline:* For fall admission, 1/15 priority date for domestic and international students; for spring admission, 9/1 priority date for domestic and international students. Applications are processed on a rolling basis. Application fee: $75. Electronic applications accepted. *Financial support:* In 2010–11, 27 students received support; fellowships with tuition reimbursements available, research assistantships, teaching assistantships with tuition reimbursements available, Federal Work-Study and tuition waivers available. Financial award application deadline: 1/15. *Unit head:* Dr. Michael King, Chair, 202-994-6488. *Application contact:* Information Contact, 202-994-6121, E-mail: gwchem@gwu.edu.

Harvard University, Graduate School of Arts and Sciences, Department of Chemistry and Chemical Biology, Cambridge, MA 02138. Offers biochemical chemistry (PhD); inorganic chemistry (PhD); organic chemistry (PhD); physical chemistry (PhD). *Degree requirements:* For doctorate, thesis/dissertation, cumulative exams. *Entrance requirements:* For doctorate, GRE General Test, GRE Subject Test. Additional exam requirements/recommendations for international students: Required—TOEFL. *Expenses:* Tuition: Full-time $34,976. Required fees: $1166. Full-time tuition and fees vary according to program.

See Close-Up on page 99.

Howard University, Graduate School, Department of Chemistry, Washington, DC 20059-0002. Offers analytical chemistry (MS, PhD); atmospheric (MS, PhD); biochemistry (MS, PhD); environmental (MS, PhD); inorganic chemistry (MS, PhD); organic chemistry (MS, PhD); physical chemistry (MS, PhD). Terminal master's awarded for partial completion of doctoral program. *Degree requirements:* For master's, comprehensive exam, thesis, teaching experience; for doctorate, comprehensive exam, thesis/dissertation, teaching experience. *Entrance requirements:* For master's, GRE General Test, minimum GPA of 2.7; for doctorate, GRE General Test, minimum GPA of 3.0. Additional exam requirements/recommendations for international students: Required—TOEFL. Electronic applications accepted. *Faculty research:* Synthetic organics, materials, natural products, mass spectrometry.

Indiana University Bloomington, University Graduate School, College of Arts and Sciences, Department of Chemistry, Bloomington, IN 47405. Offers analytical chemistry (PhD); chemical biology chemistry (PhD); chemistry (MAT); inorganic chemistry (PhD); materials chemistry (PhD); organic chemistry (PhD); physical chemistry (PhD). *Faculty:* 42 full-time (4 women). *Students:* 224 full-time (77 women); includes 19 minority (7 Black or African American, non-Hispanic/Latino; 1 American Indian or Alaska Native, non-Hispanic/Latino; 8 Asian, non-Hispanic/Latino; 3 Hispanic/Latino), 68 international. Average age 27. 270 applicants, 39% accepted, 31 enrolled. In 2010, 1 master's, 20 doctorates awarded. Terminal master's awarded for partial completion of doctoral program. *Degree requirements:* For master's, thesis; for doctorate, thesis/dissertation. *Entrance requirements:* For master's and doctorate, GRE General Test, GRE Subject Test. Additional exam requirements/recommendations for international students: Required—TOEFL. *Application deadline:* For fall admission, 1/15 priority date for domestic students, 12/15 for international students. Applications are processed on a rolling basis. Application fee: $55 ($65 for international students). *Financial support:* In 2010–11, 200 students received support, including 10 fellowships with full tuition reimbursements available, 76 research assistantships with full tuition reimbursements available, 111 teaching assistantships with full tuition reimbursements available; Federal Work-Study and institutionally sponsored loans also available. *Faculty research:* Synthesis of complex natural products, organic reaction mechanisms, organic electrochemistry, transitive-metal chemistry, solid-state and surface chemistry. Total annual research expenditures: $7.7 million. *Unit head:* David Giedroc, Chairperson, 812-855-6239, E-mail: chemchair@indiana.edu. *Application contact:* Daneil Mindiola, Director of Graduate Admissions, 812-855-2069, Fax: 812-855-8385, E-mail: mindiola@indiana.edu.

Kansas State University, Graduate School, College of Arts and Sciences, Department of Chemistry, Manhattan, KS 66506. Offers analytical chemistry (MS); biological chemistry (MS); chemistry (PhD); inorganic chemistry (MS); materials chemistry (MS); organic chemistry (MS); physical chemistry (MS). Terminal master's awarded for partial completion of doctoral program. *Degree requirements:* For master's, thesis; for doctorate, thesis/dissertation. *Entrance requirements:* For master's and doctorate, GRE, minimum GPA of 3.0. Additional exam requirements/recommendations for international students: Required—TOEFL (minimum score 550 paper-based; 213 computer-based). Electronic applications accepted. *Faculty research:* Inorganic chemistry, organic and biological chemistry, analytical chemistry, physical chemistry, materials chemistry and nanotechnology.

Kent State University, College of Arts and Sciences, Department of Chemistry and Biochemistry, Kent, OH 44242-0001. Offers analytical chemistry (MS, PhD); biochemistry (MS, PhD); chemistry (MA); inorganic chemistry (MS, PhD); organic chemistry (MS, PhD); physical chemistry (MS, PhD). Terminal master's awarded for partial completion of doctoral program. *Degree requirements:* For master's, comprehensive exam, thesis; for doctorate, comprehensive exam, thesis/dissertation. *Entrance requirements:* For master's and doctorate, placement exam, GRE General Test, GRE Subject Test (recommended), minimum GPA of 2.75. Additional exam requirements/recommendations for international students: Required—TOEFL (minimum score 525 paper-based; 71 iBT). Electronic applications accepted. *Expenses:* Tuition, state resident: full-time $7866; part-time $437 per credit hour. Tuition, nonresident: full-time $14,022; part-time $779 per credit hour. *Faculty research:* Biological chemistry, materials chemistry, molecular spectroscopy.

See Display on page 57 and Close-Up on page 101.

Marquette University, Graduate School, College of Arts and Sciences, Department of Chemistry, Milwaukee, WI 53201-1881. Offers analytical chemistry (MS, PhD); bioanalytical chemistry (MS, PhD); biophysical chemistry (MS, PhD); chemical physics (MS, PhD); inorganic chemistry (MS, PhD); organic chemistry (MS, PhD); physical chemistry (MS, PhD). Part-time programs available. *Faculty:* 27 full-time (3 women), 1 part-time/adjunct (0 women). *Students:* 33 full-time (12 women), 16 part-time (3 women); includes 4 minority (2 Black or African American, non-Hispanic/Latino; 2 Asian, non-Hispanic/Latino), 37 international. Average age 29. 25 applicants, 92% accepted, 10 enrolled. In 2010, 2 master's, 1 doctorate awarded. Terminal master's awarded for partial completion of doctoral program. *Degree requirements:* For master's, comprehensive exam; for doctorate, thesis/dissertation, cumulative exams. *Entrance requirements:* For master's and doctorate, GRE Subject Test (optional), official transcripts from all current and previous colleges/universities except Marquette, three letters of recommendation from individuals familiar with the applicant's academic work. Additional exam requirements/recommendations for international students: Required—TOEFL (minimum score 530 paper-based; 78 computer-based). *Application deadline:* Applications are processed on a rolling basis. Application fee: $50. Electronic applications accepted. *Expenses:* Tuition: Full-time $16,290; part-time $905 per credit hour. Tuition and fees vary according to program. *Financial support:* In 2010–11, 2 fellowships, 4 research assistantships, 27 teaching assistantships were awarded; Federal Work-Study, institutionally sponsored loans, scholarships/grants, and tuition waivers (full and partial) also available. Support available to part-time students. Financial award application deadline: 2/15. *Faculty research:* Inorganic complexes, laser Raman spectroscopy, organic synthesis, synthetic bioinorganic chemistry, electro-active organic molecules. Total annual research expenditures: $1.2 million. *Unit head:* Dr. Michael Ryan, Chair, 414-288-3537, Fax: 414-288-7066. *Application contact:* Dr. Mark Steinmetz, Director of Graduate Studies, 414-288-7374, Fax: 414-288-7066.

Massachusetts Institute of Technology, School of Science, Department of Chemistry, Cambridge, MA 02139. Offers biological chemistry (PhD, Sc D); inorganic chemistry (PhD, Sc D); organic chemistry (PhD, Sc D); physical chemistry (PhD, Sc D). *Faculty:* 29 full-time (7 women). *Students:* 227 full-time (78 women); includes 44 minority (5 Black or African American, non-Hispanic/Latino; 1 American Indian or Alaska Native, non-Hispanic/Latino; 27 Asian, non-Hispanic/Latino; 9 Hispanic/Latino; 2 Two or more races, non-Hispanic/Latino), 65 international. Average age 25. 516 applicants, 25% accepted, 55 enrolled. In 2010, 34 doctorates awarded. *Degree requirements:* For doctorate, comprehensive exam, thesis/dissertation, 2 terms as a teaching assistant. *Entrance requirements:* For doctorate, GRE General Test. Additional exam requirements/recommendations for international students: Required—IELTS (minimum score 7); Recommended—TOEFL (minimum score 600 paper-based; 250 computer-based). *Application deadline:* For fall admission, 12/15 for domestic and international students. Application fee: $75. Electronic applications accepted. *Expenses:* Tuition: Full-time $38,940; part-time $605 per unit. Required fees: $272. *Financial support:* In 2010–11, 213 students received support, including 66 fellowships with tuition reimbursements available (averaging $33,072 per year), 123 research assistantships with tuition reimbursements available (averaging $29,440 per year), 38 teaching assistantships with tuition reimbursements available (averaging $31,275 per year); Federal Work-Study, institutionally sponsored loans, scholarships/grants, health care benefits, and unspecified assistantships also available. *Faculty research:* Synthetic organic and inorganic chemistry; biomolecular reactions and structure; multidimensional spectroscopy and chemical dynamics; inorganic, organometallic, and organic chemical catalysis; materials chemistry including surface science, nanoscience and polymers. Total annual research expenditures: $32.1 million. *Unit head:* Prof. Sylvia T. Ceyer, Department Head, 617-253-1803, Fax: 617-258-7500. *Application contact:* Graduate Administrator, 617-253-1845, Fax: 617-258-0241, E-mail: chemgradeducation@mit.edu.

McMaster University, School of Graduate Studies, Faculty of Science, Department of Chemistry, Hamilton, ON L8S 4M2, Canada. Offers analytical chemistry (M Sc, PhD); chemical physics (M Sc, PhD); chemistry (M Sc, PhD); inorganic chemistry (M Sc, PhD); organic chemistry (M Sc, PhD); physical chemistry (M Sc, PhD); polymer chemistry (M Sc, PhD). Part-time programs available. Terminal master's awarded for partial completion of doctoral program. *Degree requirements:* For master's, thesis; for doctorate, comprehensive exam, thesis/dissertation. *Entrance requirements:* For master's, minimum B+ average. Additional exam requirements/recommendations for international students: Required—TOEFL (minimum score 550 paper-based; 213 computer-based).

Northeastern University, College of Science, Department of Chemistry and Chemical Biology, Boston, MA 02115-5096. Offers analytical chemistry (PhD); chemistry (MS, PhD); inorganic chemistry (PhD); organic chemistry (PhD); physical chemistry (PhD). Part-time and evening/weekend programs available. *Faculty:* 24 full-time (5 women), 7 part-time/adjunct (0 women). *Students:* 98 full-time (58 women), 31 part-time (15 women). 190 applicants, 32% accepted, 34 enrolled. In 2010, 16 master's, 6 doctorates awarded. Terminal master's awarded for partial completion of doctoral program. *Degree requirements:* For master's, thesis (for some programs); for doctorate, thesis/dissertation, qualifying exam in specialty area. *Entrance requirements:* Additional exam requirements/recommendations for international students: Required—TOEFL. *Application deadline:* For fall admission, 2/1 priority date for domestic and international students. Applications are processed on a rolling basis. Application fee: $50. Electronic applications accepted. *Financial support:* In 2010–11, 41 research assistantships with tuition reimburse-

80 www.facebook.com/petersonspublishing

Peterson's Graduate Programs in the Physical Sciences, Mathematics, Agricultural Sciences, the Environment & Natural Resources 2012

ments (averaging $18,285 per year), 38 teaching assistantships with tuition reimbursements (averaging $18,285 per year) were awarded; fellowships with tuition reimbursements, career-related internships or fieldwork, Federal Work-Study, scholarships/grants, tuition waivers (partial), and unspecified assistantships also available. Financial award application deadline: 3/1; financial award applicants required to submit FAFSA. *Faculty research:* Bioanalysis, biorganic and medicinal chemistry, biophysical chemistry, nanomaterials, proteonics. *Unit head:* Dr. Robert Hanson, Graduate Coordinator, 617-373-3313, Fax: 617-373-8795, E-mail: chemistry-grad-info@neu.edu. *Application contact:* Jo-Anne Dickinson, Admissions Contact, 617-373-5990, Fax: 617-373-7281, E-mail: gsas@neu.edu.

Oregon State University, Graduate School, College of Science, Department of Chemistry, Corvallis, OR 97331. Offers analytical chemistry (MS, PhD); chemistry (MA, MAIS); inorganic chemistry (MS, PhD); nuclear and radiation chemistry (MS, PhD); organic chemistry (MS, PhD); physical chemistry (MS, PhD). Part-time programs available. Terminal master's awarded for partial completion of doctoral program. *Degree requirements:* For master's, one foreign language, thesis; for doctorate, one foreign language, thesis/dissertation. *Entrance requirements:* For master's and doctorate, minimum GPA of 3.0 in last 90 hours of course work. Additional exam requirements/recommendations for international students: Required—TOEFL. *Faculty research:* Solid state chemistry, enzyme reaction mechanisms, structure and dynamics of gas molecules, chemiluminescence, nonlinear optical spectroscopy.

Purdue University, Graduate School, College of Science, Department of Chemistry, West Lafayette, IN 47907. Offers analytical chemistry (MS, PhD); biochemistry (MS, PhD); chemical education (MS, PhD); inorganic chemistry (MS, PhD); organic chemistry (MS, PhD); physical chemistry (MS, PhD). Terminal master's awarded for partial completion of doctoral program. *Degree requirements:* For master's, thesis; for doctorate, thesis/dissertation. *Entrance requirements:* Additional exam requirements/recommendations for international students: Required—TOEFL. Electronic applications accepted.

Rensselaer Polytechnic Institute, Graduate School, School of Science, Program in Chemistry, Troy, NY 12180-3590. Offers analytical chemistry (MS, PhD); biochemistry (MS, PhD); inorganic chemistry (MS, PhD); organic chemistry (MS, PhD); physical chemistry (MS, PhD); polymer chemistry (MS, PhD). Part-time and evening/weekend programs available. *Faculty:* 16 full-time (2 women). *Students:* 42 full-time (18 women), 3 part-time (1 woman); includes 1 Black or African American, non-Hispanic/Latino; 4 Asian, non-Hispanic/Latino, 16 international. Average age 24. 139 applicants, 16% accepted, 6 enrolled. In 2010, 5 master's, 8 doctorates awarded. Terminal master's awarded for partial completion of doctoral program. *Degree requirements:* For master's, thesis (for some programs); for doctorate, comprehensive exam, thesis/dissertation. *Entrance requirements:* For master's, GRE General Test, GRE Subject Test (strongly recommended); for doctorate, GRE General Test, GRE Subject Test (chemistry or biochemistry strongly recommended). Additional exam requirements/recommendations for international students: Required—TOEFL (minimum score 570 paper-based; 230 computer-based; 88 iBT). *Application deadline:* For fall admission, 2/1 priority date for domestic students; for spring admission, 11/15 for domestic students. Applications are processed on a rolling basis. Application fee: $75. Electronic applications accepted. *Expenses:* Tuition: Full-time $39,600; part-time $1650 per credit. Required fees: $1896. *Financial support:* In 2010–11, 1 fellowship with full tuition reimbursement (averaging $23,000 per year), 12 research assistantships with full tuition reimbursements (averaging $23,000 per year), 23 teaching assistantships with full tuition reimbursements (averaging $23,000 per year) were awarded; institutionally sponsored loans and tuition waivers (full and partial) also available. Financial award application deadline: 2/1. *Faculty research:* Synthetic polymer and biopolymer chemistry, physical chemistry of polymeric systems, bioanalytical chemistry, synthetic and computational drug design, protein folding and protein design. Total annual research expenditures: $1.1 million. *Unit head:* Dr. Curtis M. Breneman, Chair, 518-276-3264, Fax: 518-276-4887, E-mail: brenoc@rpi.edu. *Application contact:* Sharon E. Gardner, Graduate Program Administrator, 518-276-2140, Fax: 518-276-4887, E-mail: derris@rpi.edu.

Rice University, Graduate Programs, Wiess School of Natural Sciences, Department of Chemistry, Houston, TX 77251-1892. Offers chemistry (MA); inorganic chemistry (PhD); organic chemistry (PhD); physical chemistry (PhD). Terminal master's awarded for partial completion of doctoral program. *Degree requirements:* For master's, thesis; for doctorate, thesis/dissertation. *Entrance requirements:* For master's and doctorate, GRE General Test, minimum GPA of 3.0. Additional exam requirements/recommendations for international students: Required—TOEFL (minimum score 600 paper-based; 250 computer-based; 90 iBT). Electronic applications accepted. *Faculty research:* Nanoscience, biomaterials, nanobioinformatics, fullerene pharmaceuticals.

Rutgers, The State University of New Jersey, Newark, Graduate School, Program in Chemistry, Newark, NJ 07102. Offers analytical chemistry (MS, PhD); biochemistry (MS, PhD); inorganic chemistry (MS, PhD); organic chemistry (MS, PhD); physical chemistry (MS, PhD). Part-time and evening/weekend programs available. *Faculty:* 13 full-time (3 women). *Students:* 29 full-time (14 women), 32 part-time (19 women); includes 2 Black or African American, non-Hispanic/Latino; 30 Asian, non-Hispanic/Latino; 3 Hispanic/Latino. 153 applicants, 45% accepted, 17 enrolled. In 2010, 4 master's, 9 doctorates awarded. Terminal master's awarded for partial completion of doctoral program. *Degree requirements:* For master's, thesis optional, cumulative exams; for doctorate, thesis/dissertation, exams, research proposal. *Entrance requirements:* For master's and doctorate, GRE General Test, minimum undergraduate B average. Additional exam requirements/recommendations for international students: Required—TOEFL. *Application deadline:* For fall admission, 7/1 priority date for domestic students; for spring admission, 12/1 for domestic students. Applications are processed on a rolling basis. Application fee: $60. Electronic applications accepted. *Expenses:* Tuition, state resident: part-time $600 per credit. Tuition, nonresident: full-time $10,694. *Financial support:* In 2010–11, 35 students received support, including 5 fellowships (averaging $18,000 per year), 6 research assistantships with full and partial tuition reimbursements available (averaging $23,112 per year), 20 teaching assistantships with full and partial tuition reimbursements available (averaging $23,112 per year); Federal Work-Study and institutionally sponsored loans also available. Financial award application deadline: 3/1. *Faculty research:* Medicinal chemistry, natural products, isotope effects, biophysics and biorganic approaches to enzyme mechanisms, organic and organometallic synthesis. *Unit head:* Prof. Frank Jordan, Chairman and Program Director, 973-353-5741, Fax: 973-353-1264, E-mail: frjordan@andromeda.rutgers.edu. *Application contact:* Jason Hand, Director of Admissions, 973-353-5205, Fax: 973-353-1440.

Rutgers, The State University of New Jersey, New Brunswick, Graduate School-New Brunswick, Department of Chemistry and Chemical Biology, Piscataway, NJ 08854-8097. Offers biological chemistry (MS, PhD); inorganic chemistry (MS, PhD); organic chemistry (MS, PhD); physical chemistry (MS, PhD). Part-time and evening/weekend programs available. Terminal master's awarded for partial completion of doctoral program. *Degree requirements:* For master's, thesis or alternative, exam; for doctorate, thesis/dissertation, 1 year residency. *Entrance requirements:* For master's and doctorate, GRE General Test, GRE Subject Test. Additional exam requirements/recommendations for international students: Required—TOEFL. Electronic applications accepted. *Expenses:* Tuition, state resident: full-time $7200; part-time $600 per credit. Tuition, nonresident: full-time $11,124; part-time $927 per credit. *Faculty research:* Biophysical organic/bioorganic, inorganic/bioinorganic, theoretical, and solid-state/surface chemistry.

Seton Hall University, College of Arts and Sciences, Department of Chemistry and Biochemistry, South Orange, NJ 07079-2697. Offers analytical chemistry (MS, PhD); biochemistry (MS, PhD); chemistry (MS); inorganic chemistry (MS, PhD); organic chemistry (MS, PhD); physical chemistry (MS, PhD). Part-time and evening/weekend programs available. Terminal master's awarded for partial completion of doctoral program. *Degree requirements:* For master's, thesis optional; for doctorate, comprehensive exam, thesis/dissertation. *Entrance requirements:* Additional exam requirements/recommendations for international students: Required—TOEFL. Electronic applications accepted. *Faculty research:* DNA metal reactions; chromatography; bioinorganic, biophysical, organometallic, polymer chemistry; heterogeneous catalyst; synthetic organic and carbohydrate chemistry.

Southern University and Agricultural and Mechanical College, Graduate School, College of Sciences, Department of Chemistry, Baton Rouge, LA 70813. Offers analytical chemistry (MS); biochemistry (MS); environmental sciences (MS); inorganic chemistry (MS); organic chemistry (MS); physical chemistry (MS). *Degree requirements:* For master's, thesis. *Entrance requirements:* For master's, GMAT or GRE General Test. Additional exam requirements/recommendations for international students: Required—TOEFL (minimum score 525 paper-based; 193 computer-based). *Faculty research:* Synthesis of macrocyclic ligands, latex accelerators, anticancer drugs, biosensors, absorption isotheums, isolation of specific enzymes from plants.

State University of New York at Binghamton, Graduate School, School of Arts and Sciences, Department of Chemistry, Binghamton, NY 13902-6000. Offers analytical chemistry (PhD); chemistry (MA, MS); inorganic chemistry (PhD); organic chemistry (PhD); physical chemistry (PhD). Part-time programs available. *Faculty:* 15 full-time (4 women), 3 part-time/adjunct (2 women). *Students:* 28 full-time (8 women), 29 part-time (17 women); includes 2 Black or African American, non-Hispanic/Latino; 4 Asian, non-Hispanic/Latino; 2 Hispanic/Latino, 34 international. Average age 29. 35 applicants, 40% accepted, 9 enrolled. In 2010, 5 master's, 8 doctorates awarded. Terminal master's awarded for partial completion of doctoral program. *Degree requirements:* For master's, thesis or alternative, oral exam, seminar presentation; for doctorate, thesis/dissertation, cumulative exams. *Entrance requirements:* For master's and doctorate, GRE General Test, GRE Subject Test. Additional exam requirements/recommendations for international students: Required—TOEFL (minimum score 550 paper-based; 213 computer-based; 80 iBT). *Application deadline:* For fall admission, 1/15 priority date for domestic and international students; for spring admission, 10/15 priority date for domestic and international students. Applications are processed on a rolling basis. Application fee: $60. Electronic applications accepted. *Financial support:* In 2010–11, 51 students received support, including 5 fellowships with full tuition reimbursements available (averaging $18,000 per year), 9 research assistantships with full tuition reimbursements available (averaging $18,000 per year), 35 teaching assistantships with full tuition reimbursements available (averaging $18,000 per year); career-related internships or fieldwork, Federal Work-Study, institutionally sponsored loans, scholarships/grants, health care benefits, tuition waivers (full), and unspecified assistantships also available. Financial award application deadline: 2/15; financial award applicants required to submit FAFSA. *Unit head:* Dr. Wayne E. Jones, Chairperson, 607-777-2421, E-mail: wjones@binghamton.edu. *Application contact:* Catherin Smith, Recruiting and Admissions Coordinator, 607-777-2151, Fax: 607-777-2501, E-mail: cmsmith@binghamton.edu.

Texas Christian University, College of Science and Engineering, Department of Chemistry, Fort Worth, TX 76129-0002. Offers biochemistry (MS, PhD); chemistry (MA); inorganic (MS, PhD); organic (MS, PhD); physical (MS, PhD). Part-time and evening/weekend programs available. *Faculty:* 11 full-time (2 women), 1 (woman) part-time/adjunct. *Students:* 19 full-time (9 women), 2 part-time (both women); includes 1 American Indian or Alaska Native, non-Hispanic/Latino; 3 Asian, non-Hispanic/Latino; 4 Hispanic/Latino, 9 international. Average age 24. 23 applicants, 26% accepted, 5 enrolled. In 2010, 3 doctorates awarded. *Degree requirements:* For master's, thesis; for doctorate, thesis/dissertation, literature seminar, cumulative exams, research progress report, original proposal. *Entrance requirements:* For master's and doctorate, GRE General Test. Additional exam requirements/recommendations for international students: Required—TOEFL. *Application deadline:* For fall admission, 3/1 priority date for domestic and international students; for spring admission, 9/1 priority date for domestic and international students. Applications are processed on a rolling basis. Application fee: $50. Electronic applications accepted. *Expenses:* Tuition: Full-time $18,720; part-time $1040 per credit hour. Tuition and fees vary according to course load and program. *Financial support:* Fellowships, teaching assistantships, unspecified assistantships available. Financial award application deadline: 3/1. *Faculty research:* Phase transitions and transport properties of bio/macromolecular solutions, nanoscale biomaterials, electronic structure theory, synthetic methodology and total synthesis of natural products, chemistry and biology of (bio)polymers. *Unit head:* Dr. Robert Neilson, Chairperson; Professor, 817-257-7345, Fax: 817-257-5851, E-mail: r.neilson@tcu.edu. *Application contact:* Dr. Sergei V. Rzyuba, Director of Graduate Studies; Assistant Professor, 817-257-6218, Fax: 817-257-5851, E-mail: s.dzyuba@tcu.edu.

Tufts University, Graduate School of Arts and Sciences, Department of Chemistry, Medford, MA 02155. Offers analytical chemistry (MS, PhD); bioorganic chemistry (MS, PhD); environmental chemistry (MS, PhD); inorganic chemistry (MS, PhD); organic chemistry (MS, PhD); physical chemistry (MS, PhD). Terminal master's awarded for partial completion of doctoral program. *Degree requirements:* For master's, thesis optional; for doctorate, thesis/dissertation. *Entrance requirements:* For master's and doctorate, GRE General Test, GRE Subject Test. Additional exam requirements/recommendations for international students: Required—TOEFL (minimum score 600 paper-based; 250 computer-based; 80 iBT). Electronic applications accepted. *Expenses:* Tuition: Full-time $39,624; part-time $3962 per course. Required fees: $40 per year. Full-time tuition and fees vary according to degree level, program and student level. Part-time tuition and fees vary according to course load.

University of Calgary, Faculty of Graduate Studies, Faculty of Science, Department of Chemistry, Calgary, AB T2N 1N4, Canada. Offers analytical chemistry (M Sc, PhD); applied chemistry (M Sc, PhD); inorganic chemistry (M Sc, PhD); organic chemistry (M Sc, PhD); physical chemistry (M Sc, PhD); polymer chemistry (M Sc, PhD); theoretical chemistry (M Sc, PhD). *Degree requirements:* For master's, thesis; for doctorate, thesis/dissertation, candidacy exam. *Entrance requirements:* For master's, minimum GPA of 3.0; for doctorate, honors B Sc degree with minimum GPA of 3.7 or M Sc with minimum GPA of 3.3. Additional exam requirements/recommendations for international students: Required—TOEFL (minimum score 580 paper-based; 237 computer-based). Electronic applications accepted. *Faculty research:* Chemical analysis, chemical dynamics, synthesis theory.

University of Cincinnati, Graduate School, McMicken College of Arts and Sciences, Department of Chemistry, Cincinnati, OH 45221. Offers analytical chemistry (MS, PhD); biochemistry (MS, PhD); inorganic chemistry (MS, PhD); organic chemistry (MS, PhD); physical chemistry (MS, PhD); polymer chemistry (MS, PhD); sensors (PhD). Part-time and evening/weekend programs available. Terminal master's awarded for partial completion of doctoral program. *Degree requirements:* For master's, thesis optional; for doctorate, comprehensive exam, thesis/dissertation. *Entrance requirements:* For master's and doctorate, GRE General Test. Additional exam requirements/recommendations for international students: Required—TOEFL (minimum score 580 paper-based; 237 computer-based). Electronic applications accepted. *Faculty research:* Biomedical chemistry, laser chemistry, surface science, chemical sensors, synthesis.

University of Georgia, College of Arts and Sciences, Department of Chemistry, Athens, GA 30602. Offers analytical chemistry (MS, PhD); inorganic chemistry (MS, PhD); organic chemistry (MS, PhD); physical chemistry (MS, PhD). *Faculty:* 27 full-time (3 women). *Students:* 149 full-time (46 women), 3 part-time (1 woman); includes 5 Black or African American, non-Hispanic/Latino; 8 Asian, non-Hispanic/Latino; 1 Hispanic/Latino; 1 Two or more races, non-Hispanic/Latino, 58 international. 176 applicants, 38% accepted, 27 enrolled. In 2010, 6 master's, 20 doctorates awarded. Terminal master's awarded for partial completion of doctoral program. *Degree requirements:* For master's, thesis; for doctorate, one foreign language, thesis/dissertation. *Entrance requirements:* For master's and doctorate, GRE General Test. Additional exam requirements/recommendations for international students: Required—TOEFL (minimum

Inorganic Chemistry

University of Georgia (continued)
score 213 computer-based). *Application deadline:* For fall admission, 7/1 priority date for domestic students; for spring admission, 11/15 for domestic students. Application fee: $50. Electronic applications accepted. *Expenses:* Tuition, state resident: full-time $7200; part-time $344 per credit hour. Tuition, nonresident: full-time $21,900; part-time $944 per credit hour. Tuition and fees vary according to course load and program. *Financial support:* Fellowships, research assistantships, teaching assistantships, unspecified assistantships available. *Unit head:* Dr. Jon Amster, Head, 706-542-2726, E-mail: jamster@uga.edu. *Application contact:* Dr. George F. Majetich, Graduate Coordinator, 706-542-1966, Fax: 706-542-9454, E-mail: majetich@chem.uga.edu.

University of Louisville, Graduate School, College of Arts and Sciences, Department of Chemistry, Louisville, KY 40292-0001. Offers analytical chemistry (MS, PhD); biochemistry (MS, PhD); chemical physics (PhD); inorganic chemistry (MS, PhD); organic chemistry (MS, PhD); physical chemistry (MS, PhD). *Faculty:* 21 full-time (4 women). *Students:* 55 full-time (24 women), 4 part-time (0 women); includes 1 Black or African American, non-Hispanic/Latino; 1 Asian, non-Hispanic/Latino, 42 international. Average age 29. 79 applicants, 27% accepted, 7 enrolled. In 2010, 7 master's, 5 doctorates awarded. Terminal master's awarded for partial completion of doctoral program. *Degree requirements:* For master's, variable foreign language requirement, comprehensive exam, thesis optional; for doctorate, variable foreign language requirement, comprehensive exam, thesis/dissertation. *Entrance requirements:* For master's, BA or BS courseowork; for doctorate, none, BA or BS coursework. Additional exam requirements/recommendations for international students: Required—TOEFL. *Application deadline:* For fall admission, 3/15 for domestic and international students; for winter admission, 9/15 for domestic and international students. Applications are processed on a rolling basis. Application fee: $50. Electronic applications accepted. *Expenses:* Tuition, state resident: full-time $9144; part-time $508 per credit hour. Tuition, nonresident: full-time $19,026; part-time $1057 per credit hour. Tuition and fees vary according to program and reciprocity agreements. *Financial support:* In 2010–11, 33 teaching assistantships with full tuition reimbursements (averaging $22,000 per year) were awarded; fellowships with full tuition reimbursements, research assistantships with full tuition reimbursements, career-related internships or fieldwork, scholarships/grants, traineeships, health care benefits, and unspecified assistantships also available. Support available to part-time students. Financial award application deadline: 3/15. *Faculty research:* Computational chemistry, biophysics nuclear magnetic resonance, synthetic organic chemistry, synthetic inorganic chemistry, medicinal chemistry, protein chemistry, enzymology, nanochemistry, electrochemistry, analytical chemistry, synthetic biology, bioinformatics. Total annual research expenditures: $2.5 million. *Unit head:* Dr. Richard J. Wittebort, Professor and Chair. *Application contact:* Sherry Nalley, Administrator, 502-852-6798.

The University of Manchester, School of Chemistry, Manchester, United Kingdom. Offers biological chemistry (PhD); chemistry (M Ent, M Phil, M Sc, D Ent, PhD); inorganic chemistry (PhD); materials chemistry (PhD); nanoscience (PhD); nuclear fission (PhD); organic chemistry (PhD); physical chemistry (PhD); theoretical chemistry (PhD).

University of Maryland, College Park, Academic Affairs, College of Computer, Mathematical and Natural Sciences, Department of Chemistry and Biochemistry, Chemistry Program, College Park, MD 20742. Offers analytical chemistry (MS, PhD); inorganic chemistry (MS, PhD); organic chemistry (MS, PhD); physical chemistry (MS, PhD). Part-time and evening/weekend programs available. *Students:* 128 full-time (65 women), 5 part-time (1 woman); includes 14 Black or African American, non-Hispanic/Latino; 3 Asian, non-Hispanic/Latino; 3 Hispanic/Latino; 2 Two or more races, non-Hispanic/Latino, 62 international. 398 applicants, 16% accepted, 22 enrolled. In 2010, 3 master's, 16 doctorates awarded. Terminal master's awarded for partial completion of doctoral program. *Degree requirements:* For master's, thesis optional; for doctorate, thesis/dissertation, 2 seminar presentations, oral exam. *Entrance requirements:* For master's and doctorate, GRE General Test, GRE Subject Test (recommended), minimum GPA of 3.0, 3 letters of recommendation. Additional exam requirements/recommendations for international students: Required—TOEFL. *Application deadline:* For fall admission, 2/1 for domestic and international students. Applications are processed on a rolling basis. Application fee: $75. Electronic applications accepted. *Expenses:* Tuition, area resident: Part-time $471 per credit hour. Tuition, state resident: part-time $471 per credit hour. Tuition, nonresident: part-time $1016 per credit hour. Required fees: $337 per term. *Financial support:* In 2010–11, 9 fellowships with full tuition reimbursements (averaging $24,410 per year), 48 research assistantships (averaging $19,514 per year), 64 teaching assistantships (averaging $19,155 per year) were awarded. Financial award applicants required to submit FAFSA. *Faculty research:* Environmental chemistry, nuclear chemistry, lunar and environmental analysis, x-ray crystallography. *Unit head:* Dr. Michael Doyle, Chairperson, 301-405-1795, Fax: 301-314-2779, E-mail: mdoyle3@umd.edu. *Application contact:* Dean of Graduate School, 301-405-0358, Fax: 301-314-9305.

University of Massachusetts Lowell, College of Arts and Sciences, Department of Chemistry, Lowell, MA 01854-2881. Offers analytical chemistry (PhD); biochemistry (PhD); chemistry (MS, PhD); environmental studies (PhD); green chemistry (PhD); inorganic chemistry (PhD); organic chemistry (PhD); polymer science (MS). Terminal master's awarded for partial completion of doctoral program. *Degree requirements:* For master's, thesis; for doctorate, 2 foreign languages, thesis/dissertation. *Entrance requirements:* For master's and doctorate, GRE General Test. Electronic applications accepted.

University of Memphis, Graduate School, College of Arts and Sciences, Department of Chemistry, Memphis, TN 38152. Offers analytical chemistry (MS, PhD); computational chemistry (MS, PhD); inorganic chemistry (MS, PhD); organic chemistry (MS, PhD); physical chemistry (MS, PhD). Part-time programs available. *Faculty:* 6 full-time (1 woman). *Students:* 39 full-time (16 women), 5 part-time (3 women); includes 8 minority (6 Black or African American, non-Hispanic/Latino; 2 Asian, non-Hispanic/Latino), 6 international. Average age 28. 37 applicants, 30% accepted, 8 enrolled. In 2010, 3 master's, 5 doctorates awarded. Terminal master's awarded for partial completion of doctoral program. *Degree requirements:* For master's, comprehensive exam, thesis or alternative; for doctorate, comprehensive exam, thesis/dissertation. *Entrance requirements:* For master's and doctorate, GRE General Test, admission to Graduate School plus 32 undergraduate hours in chemistry. Additional exam requirements/recommendations for international students: Required—TOEFL. *Application deadline:* For fall admission, 7/1 for domestic students, 5/1 for international students; for winter admission, 9/15 for international students; for spring admission, 12/1 for domestic students. Applications are processed on a rolling basis. Application fee: $35 ($60 for international students). Electronic applications accepted. *Financial support:* In 2010–11, 12 students received support; research assistantships with full tuition reimbursements available, teaching assistantships with full tuition reimbursements available, Federal Work-Study, scholarships/grants, and unspecified assistantships available. Financial award application deadline: 2/15; financial award applicants required to submit FAFSA. *Faculty research:* Computational chemistry, materials chemistry, organic/polymer synthesis, drug design/delivery, water chemistry. *Unit head:* Dr. Abby L. Parrill, Professor and Chair, 901-678-2638, Fax: 901-678-3447, E-mail: aparrill@memphis.edu. *Application contact:* Dr. Gary Emmert, Associate Professor and Graduate Coordinator, 901-678-2636, Fax: 901-678-3447, E-mail: gemmert@memphis.edu.

University of Miami, Graduate School, College of Arts and Sciences, Department of Chemistry, Coral Gables, FL 33124. Offers chemistry (MS); inorganic chemistry (PhD); organic chemistry (PhD); physical chemistry (PhD). Terminal master's awarded for partial completion of doctoral program. *Degree requirements:* For master's, comprehensive exam; for doctorate, comprehensive exam, thesis/dissertation. *Entrance requirements:* For master's and doctorate, GRE General Test. Additional exam requirements/recommendations for international students: Required—TOEFL (minimum score 550 paper-based; 213 computer-based). Electronic applications accepted. *Faculty research:* Supramolecular chemistry, electrochemistry, surface chemistry, catalysis, organometalic.

University of Michigan, Horace H. Rackham School of Graduate Studies, College of Literature, Science, and the Arts, Department of Chemistry, Ann Arbor, MI 48109-1055. Offers analytical chemistry (PhD); chemical biology (PhD); inorganic chemistry (PhD); material chemistry (PhD); organic chemistry (PhD); physical chemistry (PhD). *Faculty:* 39 full-time (8 women). *Students:* 201 full-time (106 women); includes 19 minority (1 Black or African American, non-Hispanic/Latino; 12 Asian, non-Hispanic/Latino; 4 Hispanic/Latino; 2 Two or more races, non-Hispanic/Latino), 60 international. Average age 26. 565 applicants, 38% accepted, 39 enrolled. In 2010, 58 doctorates awarded. *Degree requirements:* For doctorate, thesis/dissertation, oral defense of dissertation, organic cumulative proficiency exams. *Entrance requirements:* For doctorate, GRE General Test, GRE Subject Test (recommended), 3 letters of recommendation. Additional exam requirements/recommendations for international students: Required—TOEFL (minimum score 560 paper-based; 220 computer-based; 84 iBT). *Application deadline:* For fall admission, 1/15 for domestic students, 12/15 for international students. Applications are processed on a rolling basis. Application fee: $0 ($75 for international students). Electronic applications accepted. *Expenses:* Tuition, state resident: full-time $17,784; part-time $1116 per credit hour. Tuition, nonresident: full-time $35,944; part-time $2125 per credit hour. International tuition: $35,994 full-time. Required fees: $95 per semester. Tuition and fees vary according to course load, degree level and program. *Financial support:* In 2010–11, 201 students received support, including 23 fellowships with full tuition reimbursements available (averaging $25,905 per year), 54 research assistantships with full tuition reimbursements available (averaging $25,905 per year), 118 teaching assistantships with full tuition reimbursements available (averaging $25,905 per year); career-related internships or fieldwork, scholarships/grants, traineeships, health care benefits, and unspecified assistantships also available. *Faculty research:* Biological catalysis, protein engineering, chemical sensors, de novo metalloprotein design, supramolecular architecture. *Unit head:* Dr. Carol A. Fierke, Chair, 734-763-9681, Fax: 734-647-4847. *Application contact:* Margarita Bekiares, Graduate Program Coordinator, 734-764-7278, Fax: 734-647-4865, E-mail: chemadmissions@umich.edu.

University of Missouri, Graduate School, College of Arts and Sciences, Department of Chemistry, Columbia, MO 65211. Offers analytical chemistry (MS, PhD); inorganic chemistry (MS, PhD); organic chemistry (MS, PhD); physical chemistry (MS, PhD). *Faculty:* 30 full-time (6 women), 2 part-time/adjunct (0 women). *Students:* 92 full-time (35 women), 5 part-time (1 woman); includes 5 minority (2 Black or African American, non-Hispanic/Latino; 2 Asian, non-Hispanic/Latino; 1 Hispanic/Latino), 46 international. Average age 27. 99 applicants, 21% accepted, 19 enrolled. In 2010, 3 master's, 16 doctorates awarded. *Degree requirements:* For master's, thesis; for doctorate, one foreign language, comprehensive exam, thesis/dissertation. *Entrance requirements:* For master's, GRE General Test, minimum GPA of 3.0; for doctorate, GRE General Test (minimum score: Verbal 450, Quantitative 600, Analytical 3), minimum GPA of 3.0. Additional exam requirements/recommendations for international students: Required—TOEFL (minimum score 600 paper-based; 250 computer-based; 100 iBT). *Application deadline:* For fall admission, 4/1 priority date for domestic students; for winter admission, 10/15 for domestic students. Applications are processed on a rolling basis. Application fee: $45 ($60 for international students). Electronic applications accepted. *Financial support:* In 2010–11, 9 fellowships with full tuition reimbursements, 15 research assistantships with full tuition reimbursements, 78 teaching assistantships with full tuition reimbursements were awarded; institutionally sponsored loans, traineeships, health care benefits, and unspecified assistantships also available. *Faculty research:* Analytical, organic, biological, physical, inorganic and radiochemistry. *Unit head:* Dr. Jerry Atwood, Department Chair, 573-882-8374, E-mail: atwoodj@missouri.edu. *Application contact:* Jerry Brightwell, Administrative Assistant, 573-884-6832, E-mail: brightwellj@missouri.edu.

University of Missouri–Kansas City, College of Arts and Sciences, Department of Chemistry, Kansas City, MO 64110-2499. Offers analytical chemistry (MS, PhD); inorganic chemistry (MS, PhD); organic chemistry (MS, PhD); physical chemistry (MS, PhD); polymer chemistry (MS, PhD). PhD (interdisciplinary) offered through the School of Graduate Studies. Part-time and evening/weekend programs available. *Faculty:* 17 full-time (3 women). *Students:* 5 part-time (2 women); includes 1 minority (Black or African American, non-Hispanic/Latino). Average age 37. 19 applicants, 37% accepted, 1 enrolled. In 2010, 4 master's awarded. *Degree requirements:* For master's, thesis (for some programs); for doctorate, thesis/dissertation. *Entrance requirements:* For master's, equivalent of American Chemical Society approved bachelor's degree in chemistry; for doctorate, GRE General Test, equivalent of American Chemical Society approved bachelor's degree in chemistry. Additional exam requirements/recommendations for international students: Required—TOEFL (minimum score 550 paper-based; 213 computer-based; 80 iBT), TWE. *Application deadline:* For fall admission, 4/15 for domestic and international students; for spring admission, 10/15 for domestic and international students. Applications are processed on a rolling basis. Application fee: $45 ($50 for international students). Electronic applications accepted. *Expenses:* Tuition, state resident: full-time $5522.40; part-time $306.80 per credit hour. Tuition, nonresident: full-time $7128; part-time $792 per credit hour. Required fees: $261.15 per term. *Financial support:* In 2010–11, 7 research assistantships with partial tuition reimbursements (averaging $18,311 per year), 16 teaching assistantships with partial tuition reimbursements (averaging $16,906 per year) were awarded; Federal Work-Study, institutionally sponsored loans, and scholarships/grants also available. Support available to part-time students. Financial award application deadline: 3/1; financial award applicants required to submit FAFSA. *Faculty research:* Molecular spectroscopy, characterization and synthesis of materials and compounds, computational chemistry, natural products, drug delivery systems and anti-tumor agents. Total annual research expenditures: $729,815. *Unit head:* Dr. Kathleen V. Kilway, Chair, 816-235-2289, Fax: 816-235-5502. *Application contact:* Graduate Recruiting Committee, 816-235-2272, Fax: 816-235-5502, E-mail: umkc-chemdept@umkc.edu.

University of Missouri–St. Louis, College of Arts and Sciences, Department of Chemistry and Biochemistry, St. Louis, MO 63121. Offers chemistry (MS, PhD), including biochemistry, inorganic chemistry, organic chemistry, physical chemistry. Part-time and evening/weekend programs available. *Faculty:* 19 full-time (3 women), 7 part-time/adjunct (1 woman). *Students:* 24 full-time (11 women), 37 part-time (13 women); includes 1 Black or African American, non-Hispanic/Latino; 2 Asian, non-Hispanic/Latino; 1 Hispanic/Latino, 24 international. Average age 30. 75 applicants, 29% accepted, 7 enrolled. In 2010, 13 master's, 7 doctorates awarded. Terminal master's awarded for partial completion of doctoral program. *Degree requirements:* For master's, thesis optional; for doctorate, thesis/dissertation. *Entrance requirements:* For master's, 2 letters of recommendation; for doctorate, GRE General Test, 3 letters of recommendation. Additional exam requirements/recommendations for international students: Required—TOEFL (minimum score 550 paper-based; 213 computer-based). *Application deadline:* For fall admission, 7/1 priority date for domestic and international students; for spring admission, 12/1 priority date for domestic and international students. Applications are processed on a rolling basis. Application fee: $35 ($40 for international students). Electronic applications accepted. *Expenses:* Tuition, state resident: full-time $5522; part-time $306.80 per credit hour. Tuition, nonresident: full-time $14,253; part-time $792.10 per credit hour. Required fees: $658; $49 per credit hour. One-time fee: $12. Tuition and fees vary according to program. *Financial support:* In 2010–11, 18 research assistantships with full and partial tuition reimbursements (averaging $13,104 per year), 18 teaching assistantships with full and partial tuition reimbursements (averaging $13,270 per year) were awarded; fellowships with full and partial tuition reimbursements also available. *Faculty research:* Metalloborane chemistry, serum transferrin chemistry, natural products chemistry, organic synthesis. *Unit head:* Dr. Cynthia Dupureur, Director of Graduate Studies, 314-516-5311, Fax: 314-516-5342, E-mail: gradchem@umsl.edu. *Application contact:* 314-516-5458, Fax: 314-516-6996, E-mail: gradadm@umsl.edu.

The University of Montana, Graduate School, College of Arts and Sciences, Department of Chemistry, Missoula, MT 59812-0002. Offers chemistry (MS, PhD), including environmental/analytical chemistry, inorganic chemistry, organic chemistry, physical chemistry. Terminal master's awarded for partial completion of doctoral program. *Degree requirements:* For master's, thesis (for some programs); for doctorate, thesis/dissertation. *Entrance requirements:* For master's and doctorate, GRE General Test. Additional exam requirements/recommendations for international students: Required—TOEFL (minimum score 575 paper-based; 230 computer-based). *Faculty research:* Reaction mechanisms and kinetics, inorganic and organic synthesis, analytical chemistry, natural products.

University of Nebraska–Lincoln, Graduate College, College of Arts and Sciences, Department of Chemistry, Lincoln, NE 68588. Offers analytical chemistry (PhD); biochemistry (PhD); chemistry (MS); inorganic chemistry (PhD); materials chemistry (PhD); organic chemistry (PhD); physical chemistry (PhD). *Degree requirements:* For master's, one foreign language, thesis optional, departmental qualifying exam; for doctorate, one foreign language, comprehensive exam, thesis/dissertation, departmental qualifying exams. *Entrance requirements:* For master's and doctorate, GRE. Additional exam requirements/recommendations for international students: Required—TOEFL (minimum score 550 paper-based; 213 computer-based). Electronic applications accepted. *Faculty research:* Bioorganic and bioinorganic chemistry, biophysical and bioanalytical chemistry, structure-function of DNA and proteins, organometallics, mass spectrometry.

University of Notre Dame, Graduate School, College of Science, Department of Chemistry and Biochemistry, Notre Dame, IN 46556. Offers biochemistry (MS, PhD); inorganic chemistry (MS, PhD); organic chemistry (MS, PhD); physical chemistry (MS, PhD). Terminal master's awarded for partial completion of doctoral program. *Degree requirements:* For master's, comprehensive exam, thesis; for doctorate, thesis/dissertation, qualifying exam. *Entrance requirements:* For master's and doctorate, GRE General Test, GRE Subject Test (strongly recommended). Additional exam requirements/recommendations for international students: Required—TOEFL (minimum score 600 paper-based; 250 computer-based; 80 iBT). Electronic applications accepted. *Faculty research:* Reaction design and mechanistic studies; reactive intermediates; synthesis, structure and reactivity of organometallic cluster complexes and biologically active natural products; bioorganic chemistry; enzymology.

University of Regina, Faculty of Graduate Studies and Research, Faculty of Science, Department of Chemistry and Biochemistry, Regina, SK S4S 0A2, Canada. Offers analytical/environmental chemistry (M Sc, PhD); biophysics of biological interfaces (M Sc, PhD); enzymology/chemical biology (M Sc, PhD); inorganic/organometallic chemistry (M Sc, PhD); signal transduction and mechanisms of cancer cell regulation (M Sc, PhD); supramolecular organic photochemistry and photophysics (M Sc, PhD); synthetic organic chemistry (M Sc, PhD); theoretical/computational chemistry (M Sc, PhD). *Faculty:* 10 full-time (2 women). *Students:* 19 full-time (9 women), 2 part-time (1 woman). 20 applicants, 40% accepted. In 2010, 2 master's, 1 doctorate awarded. *Degree requirements:* For master's, thesis; for doctorate, thesis/dissertation. *Entrance requirements:* Additional exam requirements/recommendations for international students: Required—TOEFL (minimum score 580 paper-based; 80 iBT). *Application deadline:* Applications are processed on a rolling basis. Application fee: $100. Electronic applications accepted. Tuition and fees charges are reported in Canadian dollars. *Expenses:* Tuition, area resident: Full-time $3244.50 Canadian dollars; part-time $180.25 Canadian dollars per credit hour. International tuition: $4744.50 Canadian dollars full-time. Required fees: $494 Canadian dollars; $115.25 Canadian dollars per credit hour. $115.25 Canadian dollars per semester. Tuition and fees vary according to program. *Financial support:* In 2010–11, 3 fellowships (averaging $20,000 per year), 2 research assistantships (averaging $17,250 per year), 8 teaching assistantships (averaging $6,965 per year) were awarded; scholarships/grants also available. Financial award application deadline: 6/15. *Faculty research:* Asymmetric synthesis and methodology, theoretical and computational chemistry, biophysical biochemistry, analytical and environmental chemistry, chemical biology. *Unit head:* Dr. Lynn Mihichuk, Head, 306-585-4793, Fax: 306-337-2409, E-mail: lynn.mihichuk@uregina.ca. *Application contact:* Dr. Tanya Dahms, Graduate Program Coordinator, 306-585-4246, Fax: 306-337-2409, E-mail: tanya.dahms@uregina.ca.

University of Southern Mississippi, Graduate School, College of Science and Technology, Department of Chemistry and Biochemistry, Hattiesburg, MS 39406-0001. Offers analytical chemistry (MS, PhD); biochemistry (MS, PhD); inorganic chemistry (MS, PhD); organic chemistry (MS, PhD); physical chemistry (MS, PhD). *Faculty:* 16 full-time (4 women). *Students:* 23 full-time (11 women), 1 part-time (0 women); includes 1 Black or African American, non-Hispanic/Latino, 11 international. Average age 29. 35 applicants, 20% accepted, 5 enrolled. In 2010, 3 master's, 8 doctorates awarded. *Degree requirements:* For master's, comprehensive exam, thesis; for doctorate, comprehensive exam, thesis/dissertation. *Entrance requirements:* For master's, GRE General Test, minimum GPA of 2.75 in last 60 hours; for doctorate, GRE General Test, minimum GPA of 3.5. Additional exam requirements/recommendations for international students: Required—TOEFL, IELTS. *Application deadline:* For fall admission, 3/1 priority date for domestic students, 3/1 for international students. Applications are processed on a rolling basis. Application fee: $50. *Financial support:* In 2010–11, 3 research assistantships with full tuition reimbursements (averaging $17,000 per year), 19 teaching assistantships with full tuition reimbursements (averaging $20,700 per year) were awarded; fellowships, Federal Work-Study, institutionally sponsored loans, scholarships/grants, health care benefits, and unspecified assistantships also available. Support available to part-time students. Financial award application deadline: 3/15; financial award applicants required to submit FAFSA. *Faculty research:* Plant biochemistry, photo chemistry, polymer chemistry, x-ray analysis, enzyme chemistry. *Unit head:* Dr. Sabine Heinhorst, Chair, 601-266-4701, Fax: 601-266-6075. *Application contact:* Dr. Sabine Heinhorst, Graduate Coordinator, 601-266-4702, Fax: 601-266-6075.

University of South Florida, Graduate School, College of Arts and Sciences, Department of Chemistry, Tampa, FL 33620-9951. Offers analytical chemistry (MS, PhD); biochemistry (MS, PhD); computational chemistry (MS, PhD); environmental chemistry (MS, PhD); inorganic chemistry (MS, PhD); organic chemistry (MS); physical chemistry (MS, PhD); polymer chemistry (PhD). Part-time programs available. *Faculty:* 15 full-time (1 woman). *Students:* 120 full-time (42 women), 9 part-time (2 women); includes 7 Black or African American, non-Hispanic/Latino, 8 Asian, non-Hispanic/Latino, 8 Hispanic/Latino, 62 international. Average age 29. 1,118 applicants, 4% accepted, 20 enrolled. In 2010, 4 master's, 14 doctorates awarded. Terminal master's awarded for partial completion of doctoral program. *Degree requirements:* For master's, comprehensive exam, thesis (for some programs); for doctorate, 2 foreign languages, comprehensive exam, thesis/dissertation. *Entrance requirements:* For master's, GRE General Test or GMAT, minimum GPA of 3.0. Additional exam requirements/recommendations for international students: Required—TOEFL (minimum score 550 paper-based; 213 computer-based). *Application deadline:* For fall admission, 2/15 priority date for domestic students, 1/2 priority date for international students; for spring admission, 10/1 priority date for domestic students, 6/1 priority date for international students. Applications are processed on a rolling basis. Application fee: $30. Electronic applications accepted. *Financial support:* In 2010–11, 39 research assistantships (averaging $14,359 per year), 39 teaching assistantships with tuition reimbursements (averaging $15,094 per year) were awarded; unspecified assistantships also available. Financial award application deadline: 6/30. *Faculty research:* Synthesis, bio-organic chemistry, bioinorganic chemistry, environmental chemistry, NMR. Total annual research expenditures: $3.9 million. *Unit head:* Dr. Randy Larsen, Chairperson, 813-974-4129, Fax: 813-974-3203, E-mail: rlarsen@cas.usf.edu. *Application contact:* Patricia Muisener, Director, 813-974-1730, Fax: 813-974-3203, E-mail: muisener@cas.usf.edu.

The University of Tennessee, Graduate School, College of Arts and Sciences, Department of Chemistry, Knoxville, TN 37996. Offers analytical chemistry (MS, PhD); chemical physics (PhD); environmental chemistry (MS, PhD); inorganic chemistry (MS, PhD); organic chemistry (MS, PhD); physical chemistry (MS, PhD); polymer chemistry (MS, PhD); theoretical chemistry (PhD). Part-time programs available. Terminal master's awarded for partial completion of doctoral program. *Degree requirements:* For master's, thesis; for doctorate, thesis/dissertation. *Entrance requirements:* For master's and doctorate, GRE General Test, minimum GPA of 2.7. Additional exam requirements/recommendations for international students: Required—TOEFL. Electronic applications accepted. *Expenses:* Tuition, state resident: full-time $7440; part-time $414 per credit hour. Tuition, nonresident: full-time $22,478; part-time $1250 per credit hour. Required fees: $922; $43 per credit hour. Tuition and fees vary according to program.

The University of Texas at Austin, Graduate School, College of Natural Sciences, Department of Chemistry and Biochemistry, Austin, TX 78712-1111. Offers analytical chemistry (MA, PhD); biochemistry (MA, PhD); inorganic chemistry (MA, PhD); organic chemistry (MA, PhD); physical chemistry (MA, PhD). *Entrance requirements:* For master's and doctorate, GRE General Test.

The University of Toledo, College of Graduate Studies, College of Natural Sciences and Mathematics, Department of Chemistry, Toledo, OH 43606-3390. Offers analytical chemistry (MS, PhD); biological chemistry (MS, PhD); inorganic chemistry (MS, PhD); organic chemistry (MS, PhD); physical chemistry (MS, PhD). Part-time programs available. *Faculty:* 24. *Students:* 63 full-time (22 women), 4 part-time (2 women); includes 2 minority (1 Asian, non-Hispanic/Latino; 1 Hispanic/Latino), 45 international. Average age 27. 111 applicants, 17% accepted, 16 enrolled. In 2010, 4 master's, 6 doctorates awarded. *Degree requirements:* For master's, thesis; for doctorate, thesis/dissertation. *Entrance requirements:* For master's and doctorate, GRE General Test, GRE Subject Test, A minimum 2.7 cumulative point-hour ratio (on a 4.0 scale) for all previous academic work. Three letters of recommendation, a statement of purpose, and transcripts from all prior institutions attended. Additional exam requirements/recommendations for international students: Required—TOEFL (minimum score 550 paper-based; 213 computer-based; 80 iBT), IELTS (minimum score 6.5). *Application deadline:* For fall admission, 1/15 priority date for domestic and international students. Applications are processed on a rolling basis. Application fee: $45 ($75 for international students). Electronic applications accepted. *Expenses:* Tuition, state resident: full-time $11,426; part-time $476 per credit hour. Tuition, nonresident: full-time $21,660; part-time $903 per credit hour. One-time fee: $62. *Financial support:* Fellowships with tuition reimbursements, research assistantships with full tuition reimbursements, teaching assistantships with full tuition reimbursements, Federal Work-Study, institutionally sponsored loans, scholarships/grants, tuition waivers (full), and unspecified assistantships available. Support available to part-time students. *Faculty research:* Enzymology, materials chemistry, crystallography, theoretical chemistry. *Unit head:* Dr. Alan Pinkerton, Chair, 419-530-7902, Fax: 419-530-4033, E-mail: alan.pinkerton@utoledo.edu. *Application contact:* Graduate School Office, 419-530-4723, Fax: 419-530-4724, E-mail: grdsch@utnet.utoledo.edu.

Vanderbilt University, Graduate School, Department of Chemistry, Nashville, TN 37240-1001. Offers analytical chemistry (MAT, MS, PhD); inorganic chemistry (MAT, MS, PhD); organic chemistry (MAT, MS, PhD); physical chemistry (MAT, MS, PhD); theoretical chemistry (MAT, MS, PhD). *Faculty:* 21 full-time (3 women). *Students:* 121 full-time (43 women); includes 18 minority (8 Black or African American, non-Hispanic/Latino; 1 American Indian or Alaska Native, non-Hispanic/Latino; 3 Asian, non-Hispanic/Latino; 1 Hispanic/Latino; 5 Two or more races, non-Hispanic/Latino). Average age 26. 373 applicants, 23% accepted, 39 enrolled. In 2010, 4 master's, 17 doctorates awarded. Terminal master's awarded for partial completion of doctoral program. *Degree requirements:* For master's, thesis; for doctorate, thesis/dissertation, area, qualifying, and final exams. *Entrance requirements:* For master's and doctorate, GRE General Test, GRE Subject Test (recommended). Additional exam requirements/recommendations for international students: Required—TOEFL (minimum score 570 paper-based; 230 computer-based; 88 iBT). *Application deadline:* For fall admission, 1/15 for domestic and international students. Application fee: $0. Electronic applications accepted. *Financial support:* Fellowships with full and partial tuition reimbursements, research assistantships with full tuition reimbursements, teaching assistantships with full tuition reimbursements, Federal Work-Study, institutionally sponsored loans, scholarships/grants, traineeships, and health care benefits available. Financial award application deadline: 1/15; financial award applicants required to submit CSS PROFILE or FAFSA. *Faculty research:* Chemical synthesis; mechanistic, theoretical, bioorganic, analytical, and spectroscopic chemistry. *Unit head:* Mike P. Stone, PhD, Chair, 615-322-2589, Fax: 615-343-1234, E-mail: michael.p.stone@vanderbilt.edu. *Application contact:* Charles M. Lukehart, PhD, Director of Graduate Studies, 615-322-2861, Fax: 615-343-1234, E-mail: charles.m.lukehart@vanderbilt.edu.

Virginia Commonwealth University, Graduate School, College of Humanities and Sciences, Department of Chemistry, Richmond, VA 23284-9005. Offers analytical chemistry (MS, PhD); chemical physics (PhD); inorganic chemistry (MS, PhD); organic chemistry (MS, PhD); physical chemistry (MS, PhD). Part-time programs available. *Students:* 51 full-time (23 women), 14 part-time (6 women); includes 7 minority (3 Black or African American, non-Hispanic/Latino; 2 Asian, non-Hispanic/Latino; 1 Hispanic/Latino; 1 Two or more races, non-Hispanic/Latino), 26 international. 76 applicants, 33% accepted, 10 enrolled. In 2010, 6 master's, 5 doctorates awarded. Terminal master's awarded for partial completion of doctoral program. *Degree requirements:* For master's, thesis; for doctorate, thesis/dissertation, comprehensive cumulative exams, research proposal. *Entrance requirements:* For master's, GRE General Test, 30 undergraduate credits in chemistry; for doctorate, GRE General Test. Additional exam requirements/recommendations for international students: Required—Either TOEFL (minimum score: paper-based 600, computer-based 250) or IELTS (6.5). *Application deadline:* For fall admission, 3/15 for domestic students; for spring admission, 11/15 for domestic students. Applications are processed on a rolling basis. Application fee: $50. Electronic applications accepted. *Expenses:* Tuition, state resident: full-time $4308; part-time $479 per credit hour. Tuition, nonresident: full-time $8942; part-time $994 per credit hour. Required fees: $2000; $85 per credit hour. Tuition and fees vary according to course level, course load, degree level, campus/location and program. *Financial support:* Fellowships, research assistantships, teaching assistantships, career-related internships or fieldwork and institutionally sponsored loans available. Support available to part-time students. Financial award application deadline: 7/1; financial award applicants required to submit FAFSA. *Faculty research:* Physical, organic, inorganic, analytical, and polymer chemistry; chemical physics. *Unit head:* Dr. Scott Gronert, Chair, 804-828-1298, Fax: 804-828-8599, E-mail: sgronert@vcu.edu. *Application contact:* Dr. Maryanne M. Collinson, Chair, Graduate Recruiting and Admissions Committee, 804-828-7509, E-mail: mselshal@vcu.edu.

Wake Forest University, Graduate School of Arts and Sciences, Department of Chemistry, Winston-Salem, NC 27109. Offers analytical chemistry (MS, PhD); inorganic chemistry (MS, PhD); organic chemistry (MS, PhD); physical chemistry (MS, PhD). Part-time programs available. *Degree requirements:* For master's, one foreign language, comprehensive exam, thesis; for doctorate, 2 foreign languages, comprehensive exam, thesis/dissertation. *Entrance requirements:* For master's and doctorate, GRE General Test. Additional exam requirements/recommendations for international students: Required—TOEFL (minimum score 213 computer-based). Electronic applications accepted.

Wesleyan University, Graduate Programs, Department of Chemistry, Middletown, CT 06459. Offers biochemistry (MA, PhD); chemical physics (MA, PhD); inorganic chemistry (MA, PhD); organic chemistry (MA, PhD); physical chemistry (MA, PhD); theoretical chemistry (MA, PhD). *Faculty:* 12 full-time (2 women). *Students:* 29 full-time (9 women); includes 3 Black or African American, non-Hispanic/Latino; 7 Asian, non-Hispanic/Latino; 2 Hispanic/Latino, 12 international. Average age 26. 48 applicants, 23% accepted, 5 enrolled. In 2010, 6 master's, 6 doctorates awarded. Terminal master's awarded for partial completion of doctoral program. *Degree requirements:* For master's, thesis, proposal; for doctorate, thesis/dissertation, proposal. *Entrance*

Inorganic Chemistry

Wesleyan University (continued)

requirements: For doctorate, GRE General Test, 3 recommendations. Additional exam requirements/recommendations for international students: Required—TOEFL. *Application deadline:* Applications are processed on a rolling basis. Application fee: $0. Electronic applications accepted. *Expenses:* Tuition: Full-time $43,404. Required fees: $830. *Financial support:* In 2010–11, 9 research assistantships with full tuition reimbursements, 18 teaching assistantships with full tuition reimbursements were awarded; institutionally sponsored loans also available. Financial award application deadline: 4/15; financial award applicants required to submit FAFSA. *Unit head:* Dr. Joseph Knee, Chair, 860-685-2210. *Application contact:* Cait Zinser, Information Contact, 860-685-2573, Fax: 860-685-2211, E-mail: czinser@wesleyan.edu.

West Virginia University, Eberly College of Arts and Sciences, Department of Chemistry, Morgantown, WV 26506. Offers analytical chemistry (MS, PhD); inorganic chemistry (MS, PhD); organic chemistry (MS, PhD); physical chemistry (MS, PhD); theoretical chemistry (MS, PhD). Part-time programs available. Postbaccalaureate distance learning degree programs offered (no on-campus study). Terminal master's awarded for partial completion of doctoral program. *Degree requirements:* For master's, thesis; for doctorate, thesis/dissertation. *Entrance requirements:* For master's, GRE General Test, GRE Subject Test (recommended), minimum GPA of 2.5; for doctorate, GRE General Test, GRE Subject Test (recommended), minimum GPA of 2.75. Additional exam requirements/recommendations for international students: Required—TOEFL. Electronic applications accepted. *Faculty research:* Analysis of proteins, drug interactions, solids and effluents by advanced separation methods; new synthetic strategies for complex organic molecules; synthesis and structural characterization of metal complexes for polymerization catalysis, nonlinear science, spectroscopy.

Yale University, Graduate School of Arts and Sciences, Department of Chemistry, New Haven, CT 06520. Offers biophysical chemistry (PhD); inorganic chemistry (PhD); organic chemistry (PhD); physical and theoretical chemistry (PhD). *Degree requirements:* For doctorate, thesis/dissertation. *Entrance requirements:* For doctorate, GRE General Test, GRE Subject Test. Additional exam requirements/recommendations for international students: Required—TOEFL.

Youngstown State University, Graduate School, College of Science, Technology, Engineering and Mathematics, Department of Chemistry, Youngstown, OH 44555-0001. Offers analytical chemistry (MS); biochemistry (MS); chemistry education (MS); inorganic chemistry (MS); organic chemistry (MS); physical chemistry (MS). Part-time programs available. *Degree requirements:* For master's, thesis. *Entrance requirements:* For master's, bachelor's degree in chemistry, minimum GPA of 2.7. Additional exam requirements/recommendations for international students: Required—TOEFL. *Faculty research:* Analysis of antioxidants, chromatography, defects and disorder in crystalline oxides, hydrogen bonding, novel organic and organometallic materials.

Organic Chemistry

Auburn University, Graduate School, College of Sciences and Mathematics, Department of Chemistry and Biochemistry, Auburn University, AL 36849. Offers analytical chemistry (MS, PhD); biochemistry (MS, PhD); inorganic chemistry (MS, PhD); organic chemistry (MS, PhD); physical chemistry (MS, PhD). Part-time programs available. *Faculty:* 27 full-time (6 women). *Students:* 39 full-time (20 women), 21 part-time (8 women); includes 4 Black or African American, non-Hispanic/Latino; 1 Asian, non-Hispanic/Latino; 1 Hispanic/Latino, 41 international. Average age 28. 54 applicants, 11% accepted, 3 enrolled. In 2010, 1 master's, 13 doctorates awarded. *Degree requirements:* For master's, thesis (for some programs); for doctorate, thesis/dissertation, oral and written exams. *Entrance requirements:* For master's and doctorate, GRE General Test. *Application deadline:* For fall admission, 7/7 for domestic students; for spring admission, 11/24 for domestic students. Applications are processed on a rolling basis. Application fee: $50 ($60 for international students). Electronic applications accepted. *Expenses:* Tuition, state resident: full-time $7002. Tuition, nonresident: full-time $21,898. International tuition: $22,116 full-time. Required fees: $892. Tuition and fees vary according to course load and program. *Financial support:* Fellowships, research assistantships, teaching assistantships available. Financial award application deadline: 3/15; financial award applicants required to submit FAFSA. *Unit head:* Dr. J. V. Ortiz, Chair, 334-844-4043, Fax: 334-844-4043. *Application contact:* Dr. George Flowers, Dean of the Graduate School, 334-844-2125.

Boston College, Graduate School of Arts and Sciences, Department of Chemistry, Chestnut Hill, MA 02467-3800. Offers biochemistry (PhD); inorganic chemistry (PhD); organic chemistry (PhD); physical chemistry (PhD); science education (MST). Part-time programs available. *Degree requirements:* For doctorate, thesis/dissertation, qualifying exam. *Entrance requirements:* For doctorate, GRE General Test, GRE Subject Test. Additional exam requirements/recommendations for international students: Required—TOEFL (minimum score 600 paper-based; 250 computer-based; 100 iBT). Electronic applications accepted.

Brandeis University, Graduate School of Arts and Sciences, Department of Chemistry, Waltham, MA 02454. Offers inorganic chemistry (MS, PhD); organic chemistry (MS, PhD); physical chemistry (MS, PhD). *Faculty:* 26 full-time (14 women). *Students:* 43 full-time (14 women); includes 1 Black or African American, non-Hispanic/Latino, 27 international. 115 applicants, 25% accepted, 14 enrolled. In 2010, 9 master's, 8 doctorates awarded. Terminal master's awarded for partial completion of doctoral program. *Degree requirements:* For master's, thesis, 1 year of residency; for doctorate, one foreign language, thesis/dissertation, 3 years of residency, 2 seminars, qualifying exams. *Entrance requirements:* For master's and doctorate, GRE General Test, resume, letters of recommendation. Additional exam requirements/recommendations for international students: Required—TOEFL (minimum score 600 paper-based; 250 computer-based; 100 iBT); Recommended—IELTS (minimum score 7). *Application deadline:* For fall admission, 1/15 priority date for domestic students. Applications are processed on a rolling basis. Application fee: $75. Electronic applications accepted. *Financial support:* In 2010–11, 23 fellowships with full tuition reimbursements (averaging $24,500 per year), 14 research assistantships with full tuition reimbursements (averaging $24,500 per year), teaching assistantships with partial tuition reimbursements (averaging $3,200 per year) were awarded; scholarships/grants and health care benefits also available. Financial award application deadline: 4/15; financial award applicants required to submit FAFSA. *Faculty research:* Oscillating chemical reactions, molecular recognition systems, protein crystallography, synthesis of natural product spectroscopy and magnetic resonance. *Unit head:* Dr. Judith Herzfeld, Chair, Graduate Program in Chemistry, 781-736-2540, Fax: 781-736-2516, E-mail: herzfeld@brandeis.edu. *Application contact:* Charlotte Haygazian, Graduate Department Coordinator, 781-736-2500, Fax: 781-736-2516, E-mail: chemadm@brandeis.edu.

California State University, Los Angeles, Graduate Studies, College of Natural and Social Sciences, Department of Chemistry and Biochemistry, Los Angeles, CA 90032-8530. Offers analytical chemistry (MS); biochemistry (MS); chemistry (MS); inorganic chemistry (MS); organic chemistry (MS); physical chemistry (MS). Part-time and evening/weekend programs available. *Faculty:* 5 part-time/adjunct (1 woman). *Students:* 19 full-time (15 women), 24 part-time (12 women); includes 21 minority (3 Black or African American, non-Hispanic/Latino; 8 Asian, non-Hispanic/Latino; 10 Hispanic/Latino), 9 international. Average age 30. 22 applicants, 100% accepted, 10 enrolled. In 2010, 7 master's awarded. *Degree requirements:* For master's, one foreign language, comprehensive exam or thesis. *Entrance requirements:* Additional exam requirements/recommendations for international students: Required—TOEFL. *Application deadline:* For fall admission, 5/1 for domestic and international students. Applications are processed on a rolling basis. Application fee: $55. *Financial support:* Federal Work-Study available. Support available to part-time students. Financial award application deadline: 3/1. *Faculty research:* Intercalation of heavy metal, carborane chemistry, conductive polymers and fabrics, titanium reagents, computer modeling and synthesis. *Unit head:* Dr. Robert L. Vellanoweth, Chair, 323-343-2300, Fax: 323-343-6490, E-mail: rvellan@calstatela.edu. *Application contact:* Dr. Allan Muchlinski, Dean of Graduate Studies, 323-343-3820 Ext. 3827, Fax: 323-343-5653, E-mail: amuchli@exchange.calstatela.edu.

Carnegie Mellon University, Mellon College of Science, Department of Chemistry, Pittsburgh, PA 15213-3891. Offers biotechnology and management (MS); chemistry (PhD), including bioinorganic, bioorganic, organic and materials, biophysics and spectroscopy, computational and theoretical, polymer; colloids, polymers and surfaces (MS). Part-time programs available. Terminal master's awarded for partial completion of doctoral program. *Degree requirements:* For doctorate, thesis/dissertation, departmental qualifying and oral exams, teaching experience. *Entrance requirements:* For master's, GRE General Test; for doctorate, GRE General Test, GRE Subject Test. Additional exam requirements/recommendations for international students: Required—TOEFL. Electronic applications accepted. *Faculty research:* Physical and theoretical chemistry, chemical synthesis, biophysical/bioinorganic chemistry.

Cleveland State University, College of Graduate Studies, College of Sciences and Health Professions, Department of Chemistry, Cleveland, OH 44115. Offers analytical chemistry (MS); clinical chemistry (MS); clinical/bioanalytical chemistry (PhD), including cellular and molecular medicine, clinical chemistry, clinical/bioanalytical chemistry; environmental chemistry (MS); inorganic chemistry (MS); pharmaceutical/organic chemistry (MS); physical chemistry (MS). Part-time and evening/weekend programs available. *Faculty:* 13 full-time (0 women), 1 (woman) part-time/adjunct. *Students:* 58 full-time (29 women), 42 part-time (17 women); includes 4 Black or African American, non-Hispanic/Latino; 3 Asian, non-Hispanic/Latino; 1 Hispanic/Latino, 70 international. Average age 28. 76 applicants, 74% accepted, 16 enrolled. In 2010, 4 master's, 15 doctorates awarded. *Degree requirements:* For master's, thesis optional; for doctorate, comprehensive exam, thesis/dissertation. *Entrance requirements:* For master's and doctorate, GRE General Test. Additional exam requirements/recommendations for international students: Required—TOEFL (minimum score 525 paper-based; 197 computer-based; 65 iBT). *Application deadline:* For fall admission, 1/15 priority date for domestic and international students. Applications are processed on a rolling basis. Application fee: $30. Electronic applications accepted. *Expenses:* Tuition, state resident: full-time $8447; part-time $469 per credit hour. Tuition, nonresident: full-time $16,020; part-time $890 per credit hour. Required fees: $50. *Financial support:* In 2010–11, 44 students received support, including 5 fellowships with full tuition reimbursements available (averaging $30,000 per year), 13 research assistantships with full tuition reimbursements available (averaging $20,000 per year), 24 teaching assistantships with full tuition reimbursements available (averaging $18,500 per year); scholarships/grants and unspecified assistantships also available. Financial award application deadline: 1/15. *Faculty research:* Bioanalytical techniques and molecular diagnostics, glycoproteomics and antithrombotic agents, drug discovery and innovation, analytical pharmacology, inflammatory disease research. Total annual research expenditures: $3 million. *Unit head:* Dr. David J. Anderson, Interim Chair, 216-687-2467, Fax: 216-687-9298, E-mail: d.anderson@csuohio.edu. *Application contact:* Richelle P. Emery, Administrative Coordinator, 216-687-2457, Fax: 216-687-9298, E-mail: r.emery@csuohio.edu.

Columbia University, Graduate School of Arts and Sciences, Division of Natural Sciences, Department of Chemistry, New York, NY 10027. Offers chemical physics (M Phil, PhD); inorganic chemistry (M Phil, MA, PhD); organic chemistry (M Phil, MA, PhD); MD/PhD. *Degree requirements:* For master's, one foreign language, teaching experience, oral/written exams (M Phil); for doctorate, one foreign language, thesis/dissertation. *Entrance requirements:* For master's and doctorate, GRE General Test, GRE Subject Test. Additional exam requirements/recommendations for international students: Required—TOEFL. *Faculty research:* Biophysics.

Cornell University, Graduate School, Graduate Fields of Arts and Sciences, Field of Chemistry and Chemical Biology, Ithaca, NY 14853-0001. Offers analytical chemistry (PhD); bio-organic chemistry (PhD); biophysical chemistry (PhD); chemical biology (PhD); chemical physics (PhD); inorganic chemistry (PhD); materials chemistry (PhD); organic chemistry (PhD); organometallic chemistry (PhD); physical chemistry (PhD); polymer chemistry (PhD); theoretical chemistry (PhD). *Faculty:* 46 full-time (3 women). *Students:* 163 full-time (63 women); includes 10 Asian, non-Hispanic/Latino; 3 Hispanic/Latino, 49 international. Average age 24. 340 applicants, 36% accepted, 48 enrolled. In 2010, 31 doctorates awarded. *Degree requirements:* For doctorate, comprehensive exam, thesis/dissertation. *Entrance requirements:* For doctorate, GRE General Test, GRE Subject Test (chemistry), 3 letters of recommendation. Additional exam requirements/recommendations for international students: Required—TOEFL (minimum score 600 paper-based; 250 computer-based; 77 iBT). *Application deadline:* For fall admission, 1/10 for domestic students. Application fee: $80. Electronic applications accepted. *Expenses:* Tuition: Full-time $29,500. Required fees: $76. Tuition and fees vary according to degree level and program. *Financial support:* In 2010–11, 19 fellowships with full tuition reimbursements, 69 research assistantships with full tuition reimbursements, 68 teaching assistantships with full tuition reimbursements were awarded; institutionally sponsored loans, scholarships/grants, health care benefits, tuition waivers (full and partial), and unspecified assistantships also available. Financial award applicants required to submit FAFSA. *Faculty research:* Analytical, organic, inorganic, physical, materials, chemical biology. *Unit head:* Director of Graduate Studies, 607-255-4139, Fax: 607-255-4137. *Application contact:* Graduate Field Assistant, 607-255-4139, Fax: 607-255-4137, E-mail: chemgrad@cornell.edu.

Eastern New Mexico University, Graduate School, College of Liberal Arts and Sciences, Department of Physical Sciences, Portales, NM 88130. Offers chemistry (MS), including analytical, biochemistry, inorganic, organic, physical. Part-time programs available. *Faculty:* 3 full-time (0 women). *Students:* 7 full-time (2 women), 2 part-time (1 woman), 6 international. Average age 32. 10 applicants, 40% accepted, 4 enrolled. In 2010, 3 master's awarded. *Degree requirements:* For master's, thesis optional, seminar, oral and written comprehensive exams. *Entrance requirements:* For master's, ACS placement examination, minimum GPA of 3.0; 2 letters of recommendation; personal statement of career goals; bachelor's degree with one year minimum each of general, organic, and analytical chemistry. Additional exam requirements/recommendations for international students: Required—TOEFL (minimum score 550 paper-based; 213 computer-based; 79 iBT), IELTS (minimum score 6). *Application deadline:* For fall admission, 7/20 priority date for domestic students, 6/20 priority date for international students; for spring admission, 12/15 priority date for domestic students, 11/15 priority date for international students. Applications are processed on a rolling basis. Application fee: $10. Electronic applications accepted. *Expenses:* Tuition, state resident: full-time $3210; part-time

$130 per credit hour. Tuition, nonresident: full-time $8652; part-time $360.50 per credit hour. Required fees: $1212; $50.50 per credit hour. Tuition and fees vary according to course load. *Financial support:* In 2010–11, 1 research assistantship with partial tuition reimbursement (averaging $8,500 per year), 9 teaching assistantships with partial tuition reimbursements (averaging $8,500 per year) were awarded; career-related internships or fieldwork and unspecified assistantships also available. Support available to part-time students. Financial award application deadline: 3/1; financial award applicants required to submit FAFSA. *Faculty research:* Synfuel, electrochemistry, protein chemistry. *Unit head:* Dr. Juacho Yan, Graduate Coordinator, 575-562-2174, Fax: 575-562-2192, E-mail: juacho.yan@enmu.edu. *Application contact:* Sharon Potter, Department Secretary, Chemistry/Physical Sciences, 575-562-2174, Fax: 575-562-2192, E-mail: sharon.potter@enmu.edu.

Florida State University, The Graduate School, College of Arts and Sciences, Department of Chemistry and Biochemistry, Tallahassee, FL 32306-4390. Offers analytical chemistry (MS, PhD); biochemistry (MS, PhD); inorganic chemistry (MS, PhD); materials chemistry (PhD); organic chemistry (MS, PhD); physical chemistry (MS, PhD). *Faculty:* 38 full-time (5 women), 3 part-time/adjunct (0 women). *Students:* 142 full-time (46 women), 8 part-time (4 women); includes 12 minority (6 Black or African American, non-Hispanic/Latino; 3 Asian, non-Hispanic/Latino; 3 Hispanic/Latino), 68 international. Average age 25. 299 applicants, 17% accepted, 19 enrolled. In 2010, 10 master's, 20 doctorates awarded. Terminal master's awarded for partial completion of doctoral program. *Degree requirements:* For master's, comprehensive exam (for some programs), thesis (for some programs), cumulative exams; for doctorate, comprehensive exam (for some programs), thesis/dissertation, cumulative exams. *Entrance requirements:* For master's and doctorate, GRE General Test, minimum B average in undergraduate course work. Additional exam requirements/recommendations for international students: Required—TOEFL (minimum score 550 paper-based; 213 computer-based; 80 iBT). *Application deadline:* For fall admission, 12/15 priority date for domestic and international students; for spring admission, 9/15 for domestic and international students. Applications are processed on a rolling basis. Application fee: $30. Electronic applications accepted. *Expenses:* Tuition, state resident: full-time $8238.24. *Financial support:* In 2010–11, 150 students received support, including fellowships with full tuition reimbursements available (averaging $20,000 per year), 50 research assistantships with full tuition reimbursements available (averaging $20,000 per year), 100 teaching assistantships with full tuition reimbursements available (averaging $20,000 per year). Financial award application deadline: 12/15; financial award applicants required to submit FAFSA. *Faculty research:* Materials synthesis including polymers, natural products; catalysis, NMR; mass spectrometry; optical spectroscopy, scattering techniques, computational chemistry, separation technology; nanostructured materials including metallic, semiconducting and magnetic nanocrystals; nanoscience interfaced with biology; supramolecular materials for solar energy conversion. Total annual research expenditures: $5.6 million. *Unit head:* Dr. Timothy Logan, Chairman, 850-644-1244, Fax: 850-644-8281, E-mail: gradinfo@chem.fsu.edu. *Application contact:* Dr. Tyler McQuade, Chair, Graduate Admissions Committee, 888-525-9286, Fax: 850-644-0465, E-mail: gradinfo@chem.fsu.edu.

Georgetown University, Graduate School of Arts and Sciences, Department of Chemistry, Washington, DC 20057. Offers analytical chemistry (PhD); biochemistry (PhD); computational chemistry (PhD); inorganic chemistry (PhD); materials chemistry (PhD); organic chemistry (PhD); physical chemistry (PhD); theoretical chemistry (PhD). Terminal master's awarded for partial completion of doctoral program. *Degree requirements:* For doctorate, comprehensive exam, thesis/dissertation. *Entrance requirements:* For doctorate, GRE General Test. Additional exam requirements/recommendations for international students: Required—TOEFL.

The George Washington University, Columbian College of Arts and Sciences, Department of Chemistry, Washington, DC 20052. Offers analytical chemistry (MS, PhD); inorganic chemistry (MS, PhD); materials science (MS, PhD); organic chemistry (MS, PhD); physical chemistry (MS, PhD). Part-time and evening/weekend programs available. *Faculty:* 15 full-time (4 women), 5 part-time/adjunct (2 women). *Students:* 21 full-time (10 women), 10 part-time (5 women); includes 3 Asian, non-Hispanic/Latino; 1 Hispanic/Latino, 9 international. Average age 28. 33 applicants, 45% accepted, 7 enrolled. In 2010, 4 master's, 2 doctorates awarded. Terminal master's awarded for partial completion of doctoral program. *Degree requirements:* For master's, comprehensive exam, thesis or alternative; for doctorate, thesis/dissertation, general exam. *Entrance requirements:* For master's and doctorate, GRE General Test, interview, minimum GPA of 3.0. Additional exam requirements/recommendations for international students: Required—TOEFL (minimum score 550 paper-based; 213 computer-based; 80 iBT). *Application deadline:* For fall admission, 1/15 priority date for domestic and international students; for spring admission, 9/1 priority date for domestic and international students. Applications are processed on a rolling basis. Application fee: $75. Electronic applications accepted. *Financial support:* In 2010–11, 27 students received support; fellowships with tuition reimbursements available, research assistantships, teaching assistantships with tuition reimbursements available, Federal Work-Study and tuition waivers available. Financial award application deadline: 1/15. *Unit head:* Dr. Michael King, Chair, 202-994-6488. *Application contact:* Information Contact, 202-994-6121, E-mail: gwchem@gwu.edu.

Harvard University, Graduate School of Arts and Sciences, Department of Chemistry and Chemical Biology, Cambridge, MA 02138. Offers biochemical chemistry (PhD); inorganic chemistry (PhD); organic chemistry (PhD); physical chemistry (PhD). *Degree requirements:* For doctorate, thesis/dissertation, cumulative exams. *Entrance requirements:* For doctorate, GRE General Test, GRE Subject Test. Additional exam requirements/recommendations for international students: Required—TOEFL. *Expenses:* Tuition: Full-time $34,976. Required fees: $1166. Full-time tuition and fees vary according to program.

See Close-Up on page 99.

Howard University, Graduate School, Department of Chemistry, Washington, DC 20059-0002. Offers analytical chemistry (MS, PhD); atmospheric (MS, PhD); biochemistry (MS, PhD); environmental (MS, PhD); inorganic chemistry (MS, PhD); organic chemistry (MS, PhD); physical chemistry (MS, PhD). Terminal master's awarded for partial completion of doctoral program. *Degree requirements:* For master's, comprehensive exam, thesis, teaching experience; for doctorate, comprehensive exam, thesis/dissertation, teaching experience. *Entrance requirements:* For master's, GRE General Test, minimum GPA of 2.7; for doctorate, GRE General Test, minimum GPA of 3.0. Additional exam requirements/recommendations for international students: Required—TOEFL. Electronic applications accepted. *Faculty research:* Synthetic organics, materials, natural products, mass spectrometry.

Indiana University Bloomington, University Graduate School, College of Arts and Sciences, Department of Chemistry, Bloomington, IN 47405. Offers analytical chemistry (PhD); chemical biology chemistry (PhD); chemistry (MAT); inorganic chemistry (PhD); materials chemistry (PhD); organic chemistry (PhD); physical chemistry (PhD). *Faculty:* 42 full-time (4 women). *Students:* 224 full-time (77 women); includes 19 minority (7 Black or African American, non-Hispanic/Latino; 1 American Indian or Alaska Native, non-Hispanic/Latino; 8 Asian, non-Hispanic/Latino; 3 Hispanic/Latino), 68 international. Average age 27. 270 applicants, 39% accepted, 31 enrolled. In 2010, 1 master's, 20 doctorates awarded. Terminal master's awarded for partial completion of doctoral program. *Degree requirements:* For master's, thesis; for doctorate, thesis/dissertation. *Entrance requirements:* For master's and doctorate, GRE General Test, GRE Subject Test. Additional exam requirements/recommendations for international students: Required—TOEFL. *Application deadline:* For fall admission, 1/15 priority date for domestic students, 12/15 for international students. Applications are processed on a rolling basis. Application fee: $55 ($65 for international students). *Financial support:* In 2010–11, 200 students received support, including 10 fellowships with full tuition reimbursements available, 76 research assistantships with full tuition reimbursements available, 111 teaching assistantships with full tuition reimbursements available; Federal Work-Study and institutionally sponsored loans also available. *Faculty research:* Synthesis of complex natural products, organic reaction mechanisms, organic electrochemistry, transitive-metal chemistry, solid-state and surface chemistry. Total annual research expenditures: $7.7 million. *Unit head:* David Giedroc, Chairperson, 812-855-6239, E-mail: chemchair@indiana.edu. *Application contact:* Daneil Mindiola, Director of Graduate Admissions, 812-855-2069, Fax: 812-855-8385, E-mail: mindiola@indiana.edu.

Instituto Tecnológico y de Estudios Superiores de Monterrey, Campus Monterrey, Graduate and Research Division, Program in Natural and Social Sciences, Monterrey, Mexico. Offers biotechnology (MS); chemistry (MS, PhD); communications (MS); education (MA). Part-time programs available. *Degree requirements:* For master's, one foreign language, thesis; for doctorate, one foreign language, thesis/dissertation. *Entrance requirements:* For master's, EXADEP; for doctorate, EXADEP, master's degree in related field. Additional exam requirements/recommendations for international students: Required—TOEFL. *Faculty research:* Cultural industries, mineral substances, bioremediation, food processing, CQ in industrial chemical processing.

Kansas State University, Graduate School, College of Arts and Sciences, Department of Chemistry, Manhattan, KS 66506. Offers analytical chemistry (MS); biological chemistry (MS); chemistry (PhD); inorganic chemistry (MS); materials chemistry (MS); organic chemistry (MS); physical chemistry (MS). Terminal master's awarded for partial completion of doctoral program. *Degree requirements:* For master's, thesis; for doctorate, thesis/dissertation. *Entrance requirements:* For master's and doctorate, GRE, minimum GPA of 3.0. Additional exam requirements/recommendations for international students: Required—TOEFL (minimum score 550 paper-based; 213 computer-based). Electronic applications accepted. *Faculty research:* Inorganic chemistry, organic and biological chemistry, analytical chemistry, physical chemistry, materials chemistry and nanotechnology.

Kent State University, College of Arts and Sciences, Department of Chemistry and Biochemistry, Kent, OH 44242-0001. Offers analytical chemistry (MS, PhD); biochemistry (MS, PhD); chemistry (MA); inorganic chemistry (MS, PhD); organic chemistry (MS, PhD); physical chemistry (MS, PhD). Terminal master's awarded for partial completion of doctoral program. *Degree requirements:* For master's, comprehensive exam, thesis; for doctorate, comprehensive exam, thesis/dissertation. *Entrance requirements:* For master's and doctorate, placement exam, GRE General Test, GRE Subject Test (recommended), minimum GPA of 2.75. Additional exam requirements/recommendations for international students: Required—TOEFL (minimum score 525 paper-based; 71 iBT). Electronic applications accepted. *Expenses:* Tuition, state resident: full-time $7866; part-time $437 per credit hour. Tuition, nonresident: full-time $14,022; part-time $779 per credit hour. *Faculty research:* Biological chemistry, materials chemistry, molecular spectroscopy.

See Display on page 57 and Close-Up on page 101.

Laurentian University, School of Graduate Studies and Research, Programme in Chemistry and Biochemistry, Sudbury, ON P3E 2C6, Canada. Offers analytical chemistry (M Sc); biochemistry (M Sc); environmental chemistry (M Sc); organic chemistry (M Sc); physical/theoretical chemistry (M Sc). Part-time programs available. *Degree requirements:* For master's, thesis or alternative. *Entrance requirements:* For master's, honors degree with minimum second class. *Faculty research:* Cell cycle checkpoints, kinetic modeling, toxicology to metal stress, quantum chemistry, biogeochemistry metal speciation.

Marquette University, Graduate School, College of Arts and Sciences, Department of Chemistry, Milwaukee, WI 53201-1881. Offers analytical chemistry (MS, PhD); bioanalytical chemistry (MS, PhD); biophysical chemistry (MS, PhD); chemical physics (MS, PhD); inorganic chemistry (MS, PhD); organic chemistry (MS, PhD); physical chemistry (MS, PhD). Part-time programs available. *Faculty:* 27 full-time (3 women), 1 part-time/adjunct (0 women). *Students:* 33 full-time (12 women), 16 part-time (3 women); includes 4 minority (2 Black or African American, non-Hispanic/Latino; 2 Asian, non-Hispanic/Latino), 37 international. Average age 29. 25 applicants, 92% accepted, 10 enrolled. In 2010, 2 master's, 1 doctorate awarded. Terminal master's awarded for partial completion of doctoral program. *Degree requirements:* For master's, comprehensive exam; for doctorate, thesis/dissertation, cumulative exams. *Entrance requirements:* For master's and doctorate, GRE Subject Test (optional), official transcripts from all current and previous colleges/universities except Marquette, three letters of recommendation from individuals familiar with the applicant's academic work. Additional exam requirements/recommendations for international students: Required—TOEFL (minimum score 530 paper-based; 78 computer-based). *Application deadline:* Applications are processed on a rolling basis. Application fee: $50. Electronic applications accepted. *Expenses:* Tuition: Full-time $16,290; part-time $905 per credit hour. Tuition and fees vary according to program. *Financial support:* In 2010–11, 2 fellowships, 4 research assistantships, 27 teaching assistantships were awarded; Federal Work-Study, institutionally sponsored loans, scholarships/grants, and tuition waivers (full and partial) also available. Support available to part-time students. Financial award application deadline: 2/15. *Faculty research:* Inorganic complexes, laser Raman spectroscopy, organic synthesis, synthetic bioinorganic chemistry, electro-active organic molecules. Total annual research expenditures: $1.2 million. *Unit head:* Dr. Michael Ryan, Chair, 414-288-3537, Fax: 414-288-7066. *Application contact:* Dr. Mark Steinmetz, Director of Graduate Studies, 414-288-7374, Fax: 414-288-7066.

Massachusetts College of Pharmacy and Health Sciences, Graduate Studies, Program in Applied Natural Products, Boston, MA 02115-5896. Offers MANP. *Students:* 4 part-time (3 women). Average age 40. 5 applicants, 80% accepted, 4 enrolled. *Application deadline:* For fall admission, 7/1 priority date for domestic students, 7/1 for international students. Application fee: $70. *Financial support:* Application deadline: 3/15. *Unit head:* Lana Dvorkin-Camiel, Director of Master of Applied Natural Products Program, 617-732-2939, E-mail: lana.dvorkin-camiel@mcphs.edu. *Application contact:* Brian Barilone, Assistant Director of Transfer and Graduate Admission, 617-879-5032, E-mail: admissions@mcphs.edu.

Massachusetts Institute of Technology, School of Engineering, Department of Civil and Environmental Engineering, Cambridge, MA 02139. Offers biological oceanography (PhD, Sc D); chemical oceanography (PhD, Sc D); civil and environmental engineering (M Eng, SM, PhD, Sc D); civil and environmental systems (PhD, Sc D); civil engineering (PhD, Sc D, CE); coastal engineering (PhD, Sc D); construction engineering and management (PhD, Sc D); environmental biology (PhD, Sc D); environmental chemistry (PhD, Sc D); environmental engineering (PhD, Sc D); environmental fluid mechanics (PhD, Sc D); geotechnical and geoenvironmental engineering (PhD, Sc D); hydrology (PhD, Sc D); information technology (PhD, Sc D); oceanographic engineering (PhD, Sc D); structures and materials (PhD, Sc D); transportation (PhD, Sc D); SM/MBA. *Faculty:* 36 full-time (6 women). *Students:* 181 full-time (56 women); includes 27 minority (3 Black or African American, non-Hispanic/Latino; 10 Asian, non-Hispanic/Latino; 10 Hispanic/Latino; 4 Two or more races, non-Hispanic/Latino), 93 international. Average age 26. 525 applicants, 29% accepted, 74 enrolled. In 2010, 85 master's, 18 doctorates, 2 other advanced degrees awarded. *Degree requirements:* For master's and CE, thesis; for doctorate, comprehensive exam, thesis/dissertation. *Entrance requirements:* For master's and doctorate, GRE General Test. Additional exam requirements/recommendations for international students: Required—TOEFL (minimum score 577 paper-based; 233 computer-based; 90 iBT), IELTS (minimum score 7). *Application deadline:* For fall admission, 1/2 for domestic and international students. Application fee: $75. Electronic applications accepted. *Expenses:* Tuition: Full-time $38,940; part-time $605 per unit. Required fees: $272. *Financial support:* In 2010–11, 146 students received support, including 50 fellowships with tuition reimbursements available (averaging $21,808 per year), 90 research assistantships with tuition reimbursements available (averaging $28,452 per year), 20 teaching assistantships with tuition reimbursements available (averaging $27,842 per year); career-related internships

Organic Chemistry

Massachusetts Institute of Technology (continued)
or fieldwork, Federal Work-Study, institutionally sponsored loans, scholarships/grants, health care benefits, and unspecified assistantships also available. *Faculty research:* Environmental chemistry; environmental microbiology; environmental fluid mechanics and coastal engineering; geotechnical engineering and geomechanics; hydrology and hydroclimatology; mechanics of materials and structures; operations research/supply chain; transportation. Total annual research expenditures: $19.5 million. *Unit head:* Prof. Andrew Whittle, Department Head, 617-253-7101. *Application contact:* Patricia Glidden, Graduate Admissions Coordinator, 617-253-7119, Fax: 617-258-6775, E-mail: cee-admissions@mit.edu.

Massachusetts Institute of Technology, School of Science, Department of Chemistry, Cambridge, MA 02139. Offers biological chemistry (PhD, Sc D); inorganic chemistry (PhD, Sc D); organic chemistry (PhD, Sc D); physical chemistry (PhD, Sc D). *Faculty:* 29 full-time (7 women). *Students:* 227 full-time (78 women); includes 44 minority (5 Black or African American, non-Hispanic/Latino; 1 American Indian or Alaska Native, non-Hispanic/Latino; 27 Asian, non-Hispanic/Latino; 9 Hispanic/Latino; 2 Two or more races, non-Hispanic/Latino), 65 international. Average age 25. 516 applicants, 25% accepted, 55 enrolled. In 2010, 34 doctorates awarded. *Degree requirements:* For doctorate, comprehensive exam, thesis/dissertation, 2 terms as a teaching assistant. *Entrance requirements:* For doctorate, GRE General Test. Additional exam requirements/recommendations for international students: Required—IELTS (minimum score 7); Recommended—TOEFL (minimum score 600 paper-based; 250 computer-based). *Application deadline:* For fall admission, 12/15 for domestic and international students. Application fee: $75. Electronic applications accepted. *Expenses:* Tuition: Full-time $38,940; part-time $605 per unit. Required fees: $272. *Financial support:* In 2010–11, 213 students received support, including 66 fellowships with tuition reimbursements available (averaging $33,072 per year), 123 research assistantships with tuition reimbursements available (averaging $29,440 per year), 38 teaching assistantships with tuition reimbursements available (averaging $31,275 per year); Federal Work-Study, institutionally sponsored loans, scholarships/grants, health care benefits, and unspecified assistantships also available. *Faculty research:* Synthetic organic and inorganic chemistry; biomolecular reactions and structure; multidimensional spectroscopy and chemical dynamics; inorganic, organometallic, and organic chemical catalysis; materials chemistry including surface science, nanoscience and polymers. Total annual research expenditures: $32.1 million. *Unit head:* Prof. Sylvia T. Ceyer, Department Head, 617-253-1803, Fax: 617-258-7500. *Application contact:* Graduate Administrator, 617-253-1845, Fax: 617-258-0241, E-mail: chemgradeducation@mit.edu.

McMaster University, School of Graduate Studies, Faculty of Science, Department of Chemistry, Hamilton, ON L8S 4M2, Canada. Offers analytical chemistry (M Sc, PhD); chemical physics (M Sc, PhD); chemistry (M Sc, PhD); inorganic chemistry (M Sc, PhD); organic chemistry (M Sc, PhD); physical chemistry (M Sc, PhD); polymer chemistry (M Sc, PhD). Part-time programs available. Terminal master's awarded for partial completion of doctoral program. *Degree requirements:* For master's, thesis; for doctorate, comprehensive exam, thesis/dissertation. *Entrance requirements:* For master's, minimum B+ average. Additional exam requirements/recommendations for international students: Required—TOEFL (minimum score 550 paper-based; 213 computer-based).

Northeastern University, College of Science, Department of Chemistry and Chemical Biology, Boston, MA 02115-5096. Offers analytical chemistry (PhD); chemistry (MS, PhD); inorganic chemistry (PhD); organic chemistry (PhD); physical chemistry (PhD). Part-time and evening/weekend programs available. *Faculty:* 24 full-time (5 women), 7 part-time/adjunct (0 women). *Students:* 98 full-time (58 women), 31 part-time (15 women). 190 applicants, 32% accepted, 34 enrolled. In 2010, 16 master's, 6 doctorates awarded. Terminal master's awarded for partial completion of doctoral program. *Degree requirements:* For master's, thesis (for some programs); for doctorate, thesis/dissertation, qualifying exam in specialty area. *Entrance requirements:* Additional exam requirements/recommendations for international students: Required—TOEFL. *Application deadline:* For fall admission, 2/1 priority date for domestic and international students. Applications are processed on a rolling basis. Application fee: $50. Electronic applications accepted. *Financial support:* In 2010–11, 41 research assistantships with tuition reimbursements (averaging $18,285 per year), 38 teaching assistantships with tuition reimbursements (averaging $18,285 per year) were awarded; fellowships with tuition reimbursements, career-related internships or fieldwork, Federal Work-Study, scholarships/grants, tuition waivers (partial), and unspecified assistantships also available. Financial award application deadline: 3/1; financial award applicants required to submit FAFSA. *Faculty research:* Bioanalysis, biorganic and medicinal chemistry, biophysical chemistry, nanomaterials, proteomics. *Unit head:* Dr. Robert Hanson, Graduate Coordinator, 617-373-3313, Fax: 617-373-8795, E-mail: chemistry-grad-info@neu.edu. *Application contact:* Jo-Anne Dickinson, Admissions Contact, 617-373-5990, Fax: 617-373-7281, E-mail: gsas@neu.edu.

Old Dominion University, College of Sciences, Program in Chemistry, Norfolk, VA 23529. Offers analytical chemistry (MS); biochemistry (MS); chemistry (PhD); environmental chemistry (MS); organic chemistry (MS); physical chemistry (MS). Part-time and evening/weekend programs available. *Faculty:* 14 full-time (5 women), 2 part-time/adjunct (0 women). *Students:* 36 full-time (22 women), 1 part-time (0 women); includes 3 minority (1 Black or African American, non-Hispanic/Latino; 1 Asian, non-Hispanic/Latino; 1 Hispanic/Latino), 16 international. Average age 29. 35 applicants, 60% accepted, 8 enrolled. In 2010, 6 master's, 2 doctorates awarded. *Degree requirements:* For master's, comprehensive exam, thesis. *Entrance requirements:* For master's, GRE General Test, minimum GPA of 3.0 in major, 2.5 overall; for doctorate, GRE General Test. Additional exam requirements/recommendations for international students: Required—TOEFL. *Application deadline:* For fall admission, 7/1 for domestic students, 1/15 for international students; for spring admission, 11/1 for domestic students, 8/15 for international students. Applications are processed on a rolling basis. Application fee: $30. Electronic applications accepted. *Expenses:* Tuition, state resident: full-time $8592; part-time $358 per credit. Tuition, nonresident: full-time $21,672; part-time $903 per credit. Required fees: $119 per semester. One-time fee: $50. *Financial support:* In 2010–11, 6 students received support, including fellowships (averaging $18,000 per year), research assistantships with tuition reimbursements available (averaging $21,000 per year), teaching assistantships with tuition reimbursements available (averaging $18,000 per year); career-related internships or fieldwork, scholarships/grants, and unspecified assistantships also available. Financial award application deadline: 2/15; financial award applicants required to submit FAFSA. *Faculty research:* Biogeochemistry, materials chemistry, bioanalytical chemistry, computational chemistry, organic chemistry. Total annual research expenditures: $2.6 million. *Unit head:* Dr. Craig A. Bayse, Graduate Program Director, 757-683-4097, Fax: 757-683-4628, E-mail: chemgpd@odu.edu. *Application contact:* Valerie DeCosta, Grants and Graduate Program Assistant, 757-683-6979, Fax: 757-683-4628, E-mail: chemgpd@odu.edu.

Oregon State University, Graduate School, College of Science, Department of Chemistry, Corvallis, OR 97331. Offers analytical chemistry (MS, PhD); chemistry (MA, MAIS); inorganic chemistry (MS, PhD); nuclear and radiation chemistry (MS, PhD); organic chemistry (MS, PhD); physical chemistry (MS, PhD). Part-time programs available. Terminal master's awarded for partial completion of doctoral program. *Degree requirements:* For master's, one foreign language, thesis; for doctorate, one foreign language, thesis/dissertation. *Entrance requirements:* For master's and doctorate, minimum GPA of 3.0 in last 90 hours of course work. Additional exam requirements/recommendations for international students: Required—TOEFL. *Faculty research:* Solid state chemistry, enzyme reaction mechanisms, structure and dynamics of gas molecules, chemiluminescence, nonlinear optical spectroscopy.

Purdue University, Graduate School, College of Science, Department of Chemistry, West Lafayette, IN 47907. Offers analytical chemistry (MS, PhD); biochemistry (MS, PhD); chemical education (MS, PhD); inorganic chemistry (MS, PhD); organic chemistry (MS, PhD); physical chemistry (MS, PhD). Terminal master's awarded for partial completion of doctoral program. *Degree requirements:* For master's, thesis; for doctorate, thesis/dissertation. *Entrance requirements:* Additional exam requirements/recommendations for international students: Required—TOEFL. Electronic applications accepted.

Rensselaer Polytechnic Institute, Graduate School, School of Science, Program in Chemistry, Troy, NY 12180-3590. Offers analytical chemistry (MS, PhD); biochemistry (MS, PhD); inorganic chemistry (MS, PhD); organic chemistry (MS, PhD); physical chemistry (MS, PhD); polymer chemistry (MS, PhD). Part-time and evening/weekend programs available. *Faculty:* 16 full-time (2 women). *Students:* 42 full-time (18 women), 3 part-time (1 woman); includes 1 Black or African American, non-Hispanic/Latino; 4 Asian, non-Hispanic/Latino, 16 international. Average age 24. 139 applicants, 16% accepted, 6 enrolled. In 2010, 5 master's, 8 doctorates awarded. Terminal master's awarded for partial completion of doctoral program. *Degree requirements:* For master's, thesis (for some programs); for doctorate, comprehensive exam, thesis/dissertation. *Entrance requirements:* For master's, GRE General Test, GRE Subject Test (strongly recommended); for doctorate, GRE General Test, GRE Subject Test (chemistry or biochemistry strongly recommended). Additional exam requirements/recommendations for international students: Required—TOEFL (minimum score 570 paper-based; 230 computer-based; 88 iBT). *Application deadline:* For fall admission, 2/1 priority date for domestic students; for spring admission, 11/15 for domestic students. Applications are processed on a rolling basis. Application fee: $75. Electronic applications accepted. *Expenses:* Tuition: Full-time $39,600; part-time $1650 per credit. Required fees: $1896. *Financial support:* In 2010–11, 1 fellowship with full tuition reimbursement (averaging $23,000 per year), 12 research assistantships with full tuition reimbursements (averaging $23,000 per year), 23 teaching assistantships with full tuition reimbursements (averaging $23,000 per year) were awarded; institutionally sponsored loans and tuition waivers (full and partial) also available. Financial award application deadline: 2/1. *Faculty research:* Synthetic polymer and biopolymer chemistry, physical chemistry of polymeric systems, bioanalytical chemistry, synthetic and computational drug design, protein folding and protein design. Total annual research expenditures: $1.1 million. *Unit head:* Dr. Curtis M. Breneman, Chair, 518-276-3264, Fax: 518-276-4887, E-mail: brenec@rpi.edu. *Application contact:* Sharon E. Gardner, Graduate Program Administrator, 518-276-2140, Fax: 518-276-4887, E-mail: derris@rpi.edu.

Rice University, Graduate Programs, Wiess School of Natural Sciences, Department of Chemistry, Houston, TX 77251-1892. Offers chemistry (MA); inorganic chemistry (PhD); organic chemistry (PhD); physical chemistry (PhD). Terminal master's awarded for partial completion of doctoral program. *Degree requirements:* For master's, thesis; for doctorate, thesis/dissertation. *Entrance requirements:* For master's and doctorate, GRE General Test, minimum GPA of 3.0. Additional exam requirements/recommendations for international students: Required—TOEFL (minimum score 600 paper-based; 250 computer-based; 90 iBT). Electronic applications accepted. *Faculty research:* Nanoscience, biomaterials, nanobioinformatics, fullerene pharmaceuticals.

Rutgers, The State University of New Jersey, Newark, Graduate School, Program in Chemistry, Newark, NJ 07102. Offers analytical chemistry (MS, PhD); biochemistry (MS, PhD); inorganic chemistry (MS, PhD); organic chemistry (MS, PhD); physical chemistry (MS, PhD). Part-time and evening/weekend programs available. *Faculty:* 13 full-time (3 women). *Students:* 29 full-time (14 women), 32 part-time (19 women); includes 2 Black or African American, non-Hispanic/Latino; 30 Asian, non-Hispanic/Latino; 3 Hispanic/Latino. 153 applicants, 45% accepted, 17 enrolled. In 2010, 4 master's, 9 doctorates awarded. Terminal master's awarded for partial completion of doctoral program. *Degree requirements:* For master's, thesis optional, cumulative exams; for doctorate, thesis/dissertation, exams, research proposal. *Entrance requirements:* For master's and doctorate, GRE General Test, minimum undergraduate B average. Additional exam requirements/recommendations for international students: Required—TOEFL. *Application deadline:* For fall admission, 7/1 priority date for domestic students; for spring admission, 12/1 for domestic students. Applications are processed on a rolling basis. Application fee: $60. Electronic applications accepted. *Expenses:* Tuition, state resident: part-time $600 per credit. Tuition, nonresident: full-time $10,694. *Financial support:* In 2010–11, 35 students received support, including 5 fellowships (averaging $18,000 per year), 6 research assistantships with full and partial tuition reimbursements available (averaging $23,112 per year), 20 teaching assistantships with full and partial tuition reimbursements available (averaging $23,112 per year); Federal Work-Study and institutionally sponsored loans also available. Financial award application deadline: 3/1. *Faculty research:* Medicinal chemistry, natural products, isotope effects, biophysics and biorganic approaches to enzyme mechanisms, organic and organometallic synthesis. *Unit head:* Prof. Frank Jordan, Chairman and Program Director, 973-353-5741, Fax: 973-353-1264, E-mail: frjordan@andromeda.rutgers.edu. *Application contact:* Jason Hand, Director of Admissions, 973-353-5205, Fax: 973-353-1440.

Rutgers, The State University of New Jersey, New Brunswick, Graduate School-New Brunswick, Department of Chemistry and Chemical Biology, Piscataway, NJ 08854-8097. Offers biological chemistry (MS, PhD); inorganic chemistry (MS, PhD); organic chemistry (MS, PhD); physical chemistry (MS, PhD). Part-time and evening/weekend programs available. Terminal master's awarded for partial completion of doctoral program. *Degree requirements:* For master's, thesis or alternative, exam; for doctorate, thesis/dissertation, 1 year residency. *Entrance requirements:* For master's and doctorate, GRE General Test, GRE Subject Test. Additional exam requirements/recommendations for international students: Required—TOEFL. Electronic applications accepted. *Expenses:* Tuition, state resident: full-time $7200; part-time $600 per credit. Tuition, nonresident: full-time $11,124; part-time $927 per credit. *Faculty research:* Biophysical organic/bioorganic, inorganic/bioinorganic, theoretical, and solid-state/surface chemistry.

Seton Hall University, College of Arts and Sciences, Department of Chemistry and Biochemistry, South Orange, NJ 07079-2697. Offers analytical chemistry (MS, PhD); biochemistry (MS, PhD); chemistry (MS); inorganic chemistry (MS, PhD); organic chemistry (MS, PhD); physical chemistry (MS, PhD). Part-time and evening/weekend programs available. Terminal master's awarded for partial completion of doctoral program. *Degree requirements:* For master's, thesis optional; for doctorate, comprehensive exam, thesis/dissertation. *Entrance requirements:* Additional exam requirements/recommendations for international students: Required—TOEFL. Electronic applications accepted. *Faculty research:* DNA metal reactions; chromatography; bioinorganic, biophysical, organometallic, polymer chemistry; heterogeneous catalyst; synthetic organic and carbohydrate chemistry.

Southern University and Agricultural and Mechanical College, Graduate School, College of Sciences, Department of Chemistry, Baton Rouge, LA 70813. Offers analytical chemistry (MS); biochemistry (MS); environmental sciences (MS); inorganic chemistry (MS); organic chemistry (MS); physical chemistry (MS). *Degree requirements:* For master's, thesis. *Entrance requirements:* For master's, GMAT or GRE General Test. Additional exam requirements/recommendations for international students: Required—TOEFL (minimum score 525 paper-based; 193 computer-based). *Faculty research:* Synthesis of macrocyclic ligands, latex accelerators, anticancer drugs, biosensors, absorption isotheums, isolation of specific enzymes from plants.

State University of New York at Binghamton, Graduate School, School of Arts and Sciences, Department of Chemistry, Binghamton, NY 13902-6000. Offers analytical chemistry (PhD); chemistry (MA, MS); inorganic chemistry (PhD); organic chemistry (PhD); physical chemistry (PhD). Part-time programs available. *Faculty:* 15 full-time (4 women), 3 part-time/adjunct (2 women). *Students:* 28 full-time (8 women), 29 part-time (17 women); includes 2 Black or African American, non-Hispanic/Latino; 4 Asian, non-Hispanic/Latino; 2 Hispanic/Latino, 34 international. Average age 29. 35 applicants, 40% accepted, 9 enrolled. In 2010, 5 master's, 8 doctorates awarded. Terminal master's awarded for partial completion of doctoral

program. *Degree requirements:* For master's, thesis or alternative, oral exam, seminar presentation; for doctorate, thesis/dissertation, cumulative exams. *Entrance requirements:* For master's and doctorate, GRE General Test, GRE Subject Test. Additional exam requirements/recommendations for international students: Required—TOEFL (minimum score 550 paper-based; 213 computer-based; 80 iBT). *Application deadline:* For fall admission, 1/15 priority date for domestic and international students; for spring admission, 10/15 priority date for domestic and international students. Applications are processed on a rolling basis. Application fee: $60. Electronic applications accepted. *Financial support:* In 2010–11, 51 students received support, including 5 fellowships with full tuition reimbursements available (averaging $18,000 per year), 9 research assistantships with full tuition reimbursements available (averaging $18,000 per year), 35 teaching assistantships with full tuition reimbursements available (averaging $18,000 per year); career-related internships or fieldwork, Federal Work-Study, institutionally sponsored loans, scholarships/grants, health care benefits, tuition waivers (full), and unspecified assistantships also available. Financial award application deadline: 2/15; financial award applicants required to submit FAFSA. *Unit head:* Dr. Wayne E. Jones, Chairperson, 607-777-2421, E-mail: wjones@binghamton.edu. *Application contact:* Catherin Smith, Recruiting and Admissions Coordinator, 607-777-2151, Fax: 607-777-2501, E-mail: cmsmith@binghamton.edu.

State University of New York College of Environmental Science and Forestry, Department of Chemistry, Syracuse, NY 13210-2779. Offers biochemistry (MPS, MS, PhD); environmental and forest chemistry (MPS, MS, PhD); organic chemistry (MPS); organic chemistry of natural products (MS, PhD); polymer chemistry (MPS, MS, PhD). *Degree requirements:* For master's, thesis; for doctorate, comprehensive exam, thesis/dissertation. *Entrance requirements:* For master's and doctorate, GRE General Test, GRE Subject Test, minimum GPA of 3.0. Additional exam requirements/recommendations for international students: Required—TOEFL (minimum score 550 paper-based; 213 computer-based; 80 iBT), IELTS (minimum score 6). Electronic applications accepted. *Expenses:* Tuition, state resident: full-time $8370; part-time $349 per credit hour. Tuition, nonresident: full-time $13,780. Required fees: $30.30 per credit hour. $20 per year. *Faculty research:* Polymer chemistry, biochemistry.

Stevens Institute of Technology, Graduate School, Charles V. Schaefer Jr. School of Engineering, Department of Chemistry, Chemical Biology and Biomedical Engineering, Hoboken, NJ 07030. Offers analytical chemistry (PhD, Certificate); bioinformatics (PhD, Certificate); biomedical chemistry (Certificate); biomedical engineering (M Eng, Certificate); chemical biology (MS, PhD, Certificate); chemical physiology (Certificate); chemistry (MS, PhD); organic chemistry (PhD); physical chemistry (PhD); polymer chemistry (PhD, Certificate). Part-time and evening/weekend programs available. Postbaccalaureate distance learning degree programs offered (no on-campus study). *Students:* 66 full-time (35 women), 25 part-time (7 women); includes 2 Black or African American, non-Hispanic/Latino; 14 Asian, non-Hispanic/Latino; 8 Hispanic/Latino, 31 international. Average age 26. 109 applicants, 68% accepted.Terminal master's awarded for partial completion of doctoral program. *Degree requirements:* For master's, thesis or alternative; for doctorate, one foreign language, thesis/dissertation; for Certificate, project or thesis. *Entrance requirements:* Additional exam requirements/recommendations for international students: Required—TOEFL. *Application deadline:* Applications are processed on a rolling basis. Application fee: $50. Electronic applications accepted. *Financial support:* Fellowships, research assistantships, teaching assistantships available. Financial award application deadline: 4/1. *Faculty research:* Biochemical reaction engineering, polymerization engineering, reactor design, biochemical process control and synthesis. *Unit head:* Philip Leopold, Director, 201-216-8957, Fax: 201-216-8196, E-mail: pleopold@stevens.edu. *Application contact:* Graduate Admissions, 800-496-4935, Fax: 201-216-8044, E-mail: gradadmissions@stevens.edu.

Texas Christian University, College of Science and Engineering, Department of Chemistry, Fort Worth, TX 76129-0002. Offers biochemistry (MS, PhD); chemistry (MA); inorganic (MS, PhD); organic (MS, PhD); physical (MS, PhD). Part-time and evening/weekend programs available. *Faculty:* 11 full-time (2 women), 1 (woman) part-time/adjunct. *Students:* 19 full-time (9 women), 2 part-time (both women); includes 1 American Indian or Alaska Native, non-Hispanic/Latino; 3 Asian, non-Hispanic/Latino; 4 Hispanic/Latino, 9 international. Average age 24. 23 applicants, 26% accepted, 5 enrolled. In 2010, 3 doctorates awarded. *Degree requirements:* For master's, thesis; for doctorate, thesis/dissertation, literature seminar, cumulative exams, research progress report, original proposal. *Entrance requirements:* For master's and doctorate, GRE General Test. Additional exam requirements/recommendations for international students: Required—TOEFL. *Application deadline:* For fall admission, 3/1 priority date for domestic and international students; for spring admission, 9/1 priority date for domestic and international students. Applications are processed on a rolling basis. Application fee: $50. Electronic applications accepted. *Expenses:* Tuition: Full-time $18,720; part-time $1040 per credit hour. Tuition and fees vary according to course load and program. *Financial support:* Fellowships, teaching assistantships, unspecified assistantships available. Financial award application deadline: 3/1. *Faculty research:* Phase transitions and transport properties of bio/macromolecular solutions, nanoscale biomaterials, electronic structure theory, synthetic methodology and total synthesis of natural products, chemistry and biology of (bio)polymers. *Unit head:* Dr. Robert Neilson, Chairperson; Professor, 817-257-7345, Fax: 817-257-5851, E-mail: r.neilson@tcu.edu. *Application contact:* Dr. Sergei V. Rzyuba, Director of Graduate Studies; Assistant Professor, 817-257-6218, Fax: 817-257-5851, E-mail: s.dzyuba@tcu.edu.

Tufts University, Graduate School of Arts and Sciences, Department of Chemistry, Medford, MA 02155. Offers analytical chemistry (MS, PhD); bioorganic chemistry (MS, PhD); environmental chemistry (MS, PhD); inorganic chemistry (MS, PhD); organic chemistry (MS, PhD); physical chemistry (MS, PhD). Terminal master's awarded for partial completion of doctoral program. *Degree requirements:* For master's, thesis optional; for doctorate, thesis/dissertation. *Entrance requirements:* For master's and doctorate, GRE General Test, GRE Subject Test. Additional exam requirements/recommendations for international students: Required—TOEFL (minimum score 600 paper-based; 250 computer-based; 80 iBT). Electronic applications accepted. *Expenses:* Tuition: Full-time $39,624; part-time $3962 per course. Required fees: $40 per year. Full-time tuition and fees vary according to degree level, program and student level. Part-time tuition and fees vary according to course load.

University of Calgary, Faculty of Graduate Studies, Faculty of Science, Department of Chemistry, Calgary, AB T2N 1N4, Canada. Offers analytical chemistry (M Sc, PhD); applied chemistry (M Sc, PhD); inorganic chemistry (M Sc, PhD); organic chemistry (M Sc, PhD); physical chemistry (M Sc, PhD); polymer chemistry (M Sc, PhD); theoretical chemistry (M Sc, PhD). *Degree requirements:* For master's, thesis; for doctorate, thesis/dissertation, candidacy exam. *Entrance requirements:* For master's, minimum GPA of 3.0; for doctorate, honors B Sc degree with minimum GPA of 3.7 or M Sc with minimum GPA of 3.3. Additional exam requirements/recommendations for international students: Required—TOEFL (minimum score 580 paper-based; 237 computer-based). Electronic applications accepted. *Faculty research:* Chemical analysis, chemical dynamics, synthesis theory.

University of Cincinnati, Graduate School, McMicken College of Arts and Sciences, Department of Chemistry, Cincinnati, OH 45221. Offers analytical chemistry (MS, PhD); biochemistry (MS, PhD); inorganic chemistry (MS, PhD); organic chemistry (MS, PhD); physical chemistry (MS, PhD); polymer chemistry (MS, PhD); sensors (PhD). Part-time and evening/weekend programs available. Terminal master's awarded for partial completion of doctoral program. *Degree requirements:* For master's, thesis optional; for doctorate, comprehensive exam, thesis/dissertation. *Entrance requirements:* For master's and doctorate, GRE General Test. Additional exam requirements/recommendations for international students: Required—TOEFL (minimum score 580 paper-based; 237 computer-based). Electronic applications accepted. *Faculty research:* Biomedical chemistry, laser chemistry, surface science, chemical sensors, synthesis.

University of Georgia, College of Arts and Sciences, Department of Chemistry, Athens, GA 30602. Offers analytical chemistry (MS, PhD); inorganic chemistry (MS, PhD); organic chemistry (MS, PhD); physical chemistry (MS, PhD). *Faculty:* 27 full-time (3 women). *Students:* 149 full-time (46 women), 3 part-time (1 woman); includes 5 Black or African American, non-Hispanic/Latino; 8 Asian, non-Hispanic/Latino; 1 Hispanic/Latino; 1 Two or more races, non-Hispanic/Latino, 58 international. 176 applicants, 38% accepted, 27 enrolled. In 2010, 6 master's, 20 doctorates awarded. Terminal master's awarded for partial completion of doctoral program. *Degree requirements:* For master's, thesis; for doctorate, one foreign language, thesis/dissertation. *Entrance requirements:* For master's and doctorate, GRE General Test. Additional exam requirements/recommendations for international students: Required—TOEFL (minimum score 213 computer-based). *Application deadline:* For fall admission, 7/1 priority date for domestic students; for spring admission, 11/15 for domestic students. Application fee: $50. Electronic applications accepted. *Expenses:* Tuition, state resident: full-time $7200; part-time $344 per credit hour. Tuition, nonresident: full-time $21,900; part-time $944 per credit hour. Tuition and fees vary according to course load and program. *Financial support:* Fellowships, research assistantships, teaching assistantships, unspecified assistantships available. *Unit head:* Dr. Jon Amster, Head, 706-542-2726, E-mail: jamster@uga.edu. *Application contact:* Dr. George F. Majetich, Graduate Coordinator, 706-542-1966, Fax: 706-542-9454, E-mail: majetich@chem.uga.edu.

University of Louisville, Graduate School, College of Arts and Sciences, Department of Chemistry, Louisville, KY 40292-0001. Offers analytical chemistry (MS, PhD); biochemistry (MS, PhD); chemical physics (PhD); inorganic chemistry (MS, PhD); organic chemistry (MS, PhD); physical chemistry (MS, PhD). *Faculty:* 21 full-time (4 women). *Students:* 55 full-time (24 women), 4 part-time (0 women); includes 1 Black or African American, non-Hispanic/Latino; 1 Asian, non-Hispanic/Latino, 42 international. Average age 29. 79 applicants, 27% accepted, 7 enrolled. In 2010, 7 master's, 5 doctorates awarded. Terminal master's awarded for partial completion of doctoral program. *Degree requirements:* For master's, variable foreign language requirement, comprehensive exam, thesis optional; for doctorate, variable foreign language requirement, comprehensive exam, thesis/dissertation. *Entrance requirements:* For master's, BA or BS courseowork; for doctorate, none, BA or BS coursework. Additional exam requirements/recommendations for international students: Required—TOEFL. *Application deadline:* For fall admission, 3/15 for domestic and international students; for winter admission, 9/15 for domestic and international students. Applications are processed on a rolling basis. Application fee: $50. Electronic applications accepted. *Expenses:* Tuition, state resident: full-time $9144; part-time $508 per credit hour. Tuition, nonresident: full-time $19,026; part-time $1057 per credit hour. Tuition and fees vary according to program and reciprocity agreements. *Financial support:* In 2010–11, 33 teaching assistantships with full tuition reimbursements (averaging $22,000 per year) were awarded; fellowships with full tuition reimbursements, research assistantships with full tuition reimbursements, career-related internships or fieldwork, scholarships/grants, traineeships, health care benefits, and unspecified assistantships also available. Support available to part-time students. Financial award application deadline: 3/15. *Faculty research:* Computational chemistry, biophysics nuclear magnetic resonance, synthetic organic chemistry, synthetic inorganic chemistry, medicinal chemistry, protein chemistry, enzymology, nanochemistry, electrochemistry, analytical chemistry, synthetic biology, bioinformatics. Total annual research expenditures: $2.5 million. *Unit head:* Dr. Richard J. Wittebort, Professor and Chair. *Application contact:* Sherry Nalley, Administrator, 502-852-6798.

The University of Manchester, School of Chemistry, Manchester, United Kingdom. Offers biological chemistry (PhD); chemistry (M Ent, M Phil, M Sc, D Ent, PhD); inorganic chemistry (PhD); materials chemistry (PhD); nanoscience (PhD); nuclear fission (PhD); organic chemistry (PhD); physical chemistry (PhD); theoretical chemistry (PhD).

University of Maryland, College Park, Academic Affairs, College of Computer, Mathematical and Natural Sciences, Department of Chemistry and Biochemistry, Chemistry Program, College Park, MD 20742. Offers analytical chemistry (MS, PhD); inorganic chemistry (MS, PhD); organic chemistry (MS, PhD); physical chemistry (MS, PhD). Part-time and evening/weekend programs available. *Students:* 128 full-time (65 women), 5 part-time (1 woman); includes 14 Black or African American, non-Hispanic/Latino; 3 Asian, non-Hispanic/Latino; 3 Hispanic/Latino; 2 Two or more races, non-Hispanic/Latino, 62 international. 398 applicants, 16% accepted, 22 enrolled. In 2010, 3 master's, 16 doctorates awarded. Terminal master's awarded for partial completion of doctoral program. *Degree requirements:* For master's, thesis optional; for doctorate, thesis/dissertation, 2 seminar presentations, oral exam. *Entrance requirements:* For master's and doctorate, GRE General Test, GRE Subject Test (recommended), minimum GPA of 3.0, 3 letters of recommendation. Additional exam requirements/recommendations for international students: Required—TOEFL. *Application deadline:* For fall admission, 2/1 for domestic and international students. Applications are processed on a rolling basis. Application fee: $75. Electronic applications accepted. *Expenses:* Tuition, area resident: Part-time $471 per credit hour. Tuition, state resident: part-time $471 per credit hour. Tuition, nonresident: part-time $1016 per credit hour. Required fees: $337 per term. *Financial support:* In 2010–11, 9 fellowships with full tuition reimbursements (averaging $24,410 per year), 48 research assistantships (averaging $19,514 per year), 64 teaching assistantships (averaging $19,155 per year) were awarded. Financial award applicants required to submit FAFSA. *Faculty research:* Environmental chemistry, nuclear chemistry, lunar and environmental analysis, x-ray crystallography. *Unit head:* Dr. Michael Doyle, Chairperson, 301-405-1795, Fax: 301-314-2779, E-mail: mdoyle3@umd.edu. *Application contact:* Dean of Graduate School, 301-405-0358, Fax: 301-314-9305.

University of Massachusetts Lowell, College of Arts and Sciences, Department of Chemistry, Lowell, MA 01854-2881. Offers analytical chemistry (PhD); biochemistry (PhD); chemistry (MS, PhD); environmental studies (PhD); green chemistry (PhD); inorganic chemistry (PhD); organic chemistry (PhD); polymer science (MS). Terminal master's awarded for partial completion of doctoral program. *Degree requirements:* For master's, thesis; for doctorate, 2 foreign languages, thesis/dissertation. *Entrance requirements:* For master's and doctorate, GRE General Test. Electronic applications accepted.

University of Memphis, Graduate School, College of Arts and Sciences, Department of Chemistry, Memphis, TN 38152. Offers analytical chemistry (MS, PhD); computational chemistry (MS, PhD); inorganic chemistry (MS, PhD); organic chemistry (MS, PhD); physical chemistry (MS, PhD). Part-time programs available. *Faculty:* 6 full-time (1 woman). *Students:* 39 full-time (16 women), 5 part-time (3 women); includes 8 minority (6 Black or African American, non-Hispanic/Latino; 2 Asian, non-Hispanic/Latino), 6 international. Average age 28. 37 applicants, 30% accepted, 8 enrolled. In 2010, 3 master's, 5 doctorates awarded. Terminal master's awarded for partial completion of doctoral program. *Degree requirements:* For master's, comprehensive exam, thesis or alternative; for doctorate, comprehensive exam, thesis/dissertation. *Entrance requirements:* For master's and doctorate, GRE General Test, admission to Graduate School plus 32 undergraduate hours in chemistry. Additional exam requirements/recommendations for international students: Required—TOEFL. *Application deadline:* For fall admission, 7/1 for domestic students, 5/1 for international students; for winter admission, 9/15 for international students; for spring admission, 12/1 for domestic students. Applications are processed on a rolling basis. Application fee: $35 ($60 for international students). Electronic applications accepted. *Financial support:* In 2010–11, 12 students received support; research assistantships with full tuition reimbursements available, teaching assistantships with full tuition reimbursements available, Federal Work-Study, scholarships/grants, and unspecified assistantships available. Financial award application deadline: 2/15; financial award applicants required to submit FAFSA. *Faculty research:* Computational chemistry, materials chemistry, organic/polymer synthesis, drug design/delivery, water chemistry. *Unit head:* Dr. Abby L. Parrill, Professor and Chair, 901-678-2638, Fax: 901-678-3447, E-mail: aparrill@memphis.edu.

Organic Chemistry

University of Memphis (continued)

Application contact: Dr. Gary Emmert, Associate Professor and Graduate Coordinator, 901-678-2636, Fax: 901-678-3447, E-mail: gemmert@memphis.edu.

University of Miami, Graduate School, College of Arts and Sciences, Department of Chemistry, Coral Gables, FL 33124. Offers chemistry (MS); inorganic chemistry (PhD); organic chemistry (PhD); physical chemistry (PhD). Terminal master's awarded for partial completion of doctoral program. *Degree requirements:* For master's, comprehensive exam; for doctorate, comprehensive exam, thesis/dissertation. *Entrance requirements:* For master's and doctorate, GRE General Test. Additional exam requirements/recommendations for international students: Required—TOEFL (minimum score 550 paper-based; 213 computer-based). Electronic applications accepted. *Faculty research:* Supramolecular chemistry, electrochemistry, surface chemistry, catalysis, organometalic.

University of Michigan, Horace H. Rackham School of Graduate Studies, College of Literature, Science, and the Arts, Department of Chemistry, Ann Arbor, MI 48109-1055. Offers analytical chemistry (PhD); chemical biology (PhD); inorganic chemistry (PhD); material chemistry (PhD); organic chemistry (PhD); physical chemistry (PhD). *Faculty:* 39 full-time (8 women). *Students:* 201 full-time (106 women); includes 19 minority (1 Black or African American, non-Hispanic/Latino; 12 Asian, non-Hispanic/Latino; 4 Hispanic/Latino; 2 Two or more races, non-Hispanic/Latino), 60 international. Average age 26. 565 applicants, 38% accepted, 39 enrolled. In 2010, 58 doctorates awarded. *Degree requirements:* For doctorate, thesis/dissertation, oral defense of dissertation, organic cumulative proficiency exams. *Entrance requirements:* For doctorate, GRE General Test, GRE Subject Test (recommended), 3 letters of recommendation. Additional exam requirements/recommendations for international students: Required—TOEFL (minimum score 560 paper-based; 220 computer-based; 84 iBT). *Application deadline:* For fall admission, 1/15 for domestic students, 12/15 for international students. Applications are processed on a rolling basis. Application fee: $0 ($75 for international students). Electronic applications accepted. *Expenses:* Tuition, state resident: full-time $17,784; part-time $1116 per credit hour. Tuition, nonresident: full-time $35,944; part-time $2125 per credit hour. International tuition: $35,994 full-time. Required fees: $95 per semester. Tuition and fees vary according to course load, degree level and program. *Financial support:* In 2010–11, 201 students received support, including 23 fellowships with full tuition reimbursements available (averaging $25,905 per year), 54 research assistantships with full tuition reimbursements available (averaging $25,905 per year), 118 teaching assistantships with full tuition reimbursements available (averaging $25,905 per year); career-related internships or fieldwork, scholarships/grants, traineeships, health care benefits, and unspecified assistantships also available. *Faculty research:* Biological catalysis, protein engineering, chemical sensors, de novo metalloprotein design, supramolecular architecture. *Unit head:* Dr. Carol A. Fierke, Chair, 734-763-9681, Fax: 734-647-4847. *Application contact:* Margarita Bekiares, Graduate Program Coordinator, 734-764-7278, Fax: 734-647-4865, E-mail: chemadmissions@umich.edu.

University of Missouri, Graduate School, College of Arts and Sciences, Department of Chemistry, Columbia, MO 65211. Offers analytical chemistry (MS, PhD); inorganic chemistry (MS, PhD); organic chemistry (MS, PhD); physical chemistry (MS, PhD). *Faculty:* 30 full-time (6 women), 2 part-time/adjunct (0 women). *Students:* 92 full-time (35 women), 5 part-time (1 woman); includes 5 minority (2 Black or African American, non-Hispanic/Latino; 2 Asian, non-Hispanic/Latino; 1 Hispanic/Latino), 46 international. Average age 27. 99 applicants, 21% accepted, 19 enrolled. In 2010, 3 master's, 16 doctorates awarded. *Degree requirements:* For master's, thesis; for doctorate, one foreign language, comprehensive exam, thesis/dissertation. *Entrance requirements:* For master's, GRE General Test, minimum GPA of 3.0; for doctorate, GRE General Test (minimum score: Verbal 450, Quantitative 600, Analytical 3), minimum GPA of 3.0. Additional exam requirements/recommendations for international students: Required—TOEFL (minimum score 600 paper-based; 250 computer-based; 100 iBT). *Application deadline:* For fall admission, 4/1 priority date for domestic students; for winter admission, 10/15 for domestic students. Applications are processed on a rolling basis. Application fee: $45 ($60 for international students). Electronic applications accepted. *Financial support:* In 2010–11, 9 fellowships with full tuition reimbursements, 15 research assistantships with full tuition reimbursements, 78 teaching assistantships with full tuition reimbursements were awarded; institutionally sponsored loans, traineeships, health care benefits, and unspecified assistantships also available. *Faculty research:* Analytical, organic, biological, physical, inorganic and radiochemistry. *Unit head:* Dr. Jerry Atwood, Department Chair, 573-882-8374, E-mail: atwoodj@missouri.edu. *Application contact:* Jerry Brightwell, Administrative Assistant, 573-884-6832, E-mail: brightwellj@missouri.edu.

University of Missouri–Kansas City, College of Arts and Sciences, Department of Chemistry, Kansas City, MO 64110-2499. Offers analytical chemistry (MS, PhD); inorganic chemistry (MS, PhD); organic chemistry (MS, PhD); physical chemistry (MS, PhD); polymer chemistry (MS, PhD). PhD (interdisciplinary) offered through the School of Graduate Studies. Part-time and evening/weekend programs available. *Faculty:* 17 full-time (3 women). *Students:* 5 part-time (2 women); includes 1 minority (Black or African American, non-Hispanic/Latino). Average age 37. 19 applicants, 37% accepted, 1 enrolled. In 2010, 4 master's awarded. *Degree requirements:* For master's, thesis (for some programs); for doctorate, thesis/dissertation. *Entrance requirements:* For master's, equivalent of American Chemical Society approved bachelor's degree in chemistry; for doctorate, GRE General Test, equivalent of American Chemical Society approved bachelor's degree in chemistry. Additional exam requirements/recommendations for international students: Required—TOEFL (minimum score 550 paper-based; 213 computer-based; 80 iBT), TWE. *Application deadline:* For fall admission, 4/15 for domestic and international students; for spring admission, 10/15 for domestic and international students. Applications are processed on a rolling basis. Application fee: $45 ($50 for international students). Electronic applications accepted. *Expenses:* Tuition, state resident: full-time $5522.40; part-time $306.80 per credit hour. Tuition, nonresident: full-time $7128; part-time $792 per credit hour. Required fees: $261.15 per term. *Financial support:* In 2010–11, 7 research assistantships with partial tuition reimbursements (averaging $18,311 per year), 16 teaching assistantships with partial tuition reimbursements (averaging $16,906 per year) were awarded; Federal Work-Study, institutionally sponsored loans, and scholarships/grants also available. Support available to part-time students. Financial award application deadline: 3/1; financial award applicants required to submit FAFSA. *Faculty research:* Molecular spectroscopy, characterization and synthesis of materials and compounds, computational chemistry, natural products, drug delivery systems and anti-tumor agents. Total annual research expenditures: $729,815. *Unit head:* Dr. Kathleen V. Kilway, Chair, 816-235-2289, Fax: 816-235-5502. *Application contact:* Graduate Recruiting Committee, 816-235-2272, Fax: 816-235-5502, E-mail: umkc-chemdept@umkc.edu.

University of Missouri–St. Louis, College of Arts and Sciences, Department of Chemistry and Biochemistry, St. Louis, MO 63121. Offers chemistry (MS, PhD), including biochemistry, inorganic chemistry, organic chemistry, physical chemistry. Part-time and evening/weekend programs available. *Faculty:* 19 full-time (3 women), 7 part-time/adjunct (1 woman). *Students:* 24 full-time (11 women), 37 part-time (13 women); includes 1 Black or African American, non-Hispanic/Latino; 2 Asian, non-Hispanic/Latino; 1 Hispanic/Latino, 24 international. Average age 30. 75 applicants, 29% accepted, 7 enrolled. In 2010, 13 master's, 7 doctorates awarded. Terminal master's awarded for partial completion of doctoral program. *Degree requirements:* For master's, thesis optional; for doctorate, thesis/dissertation. *Entrance requirements:* For master's, 2 letters of recommendation; for doctorate, GRE General Test, 3 letters of recommendation. Additional exam requirements/recommendations for international students: Required—TOEFL (minimum score 550 paper-based; 213 computer-based). *Application deadline:* For fall admission, 7/1 priority date for domestic and international students; for spring admission, 12/1 priority date for domestic and international students. Applications are processed on a rolling basis. Application fee: $35 ($40 for international students). Electronic applications accepted. *Expenses:* Tuition, state resident: full-time $5522; part-time $306.80 per credit hour. Tuition, nonresident: full-time $14,253; part-time $792.10 per credit hour. Required fees: $658; $49 per credit hour. One-time fee: $12. Tuition and fees vary according to program. *Financial support:* In 2010–11, 18 research assistantships with full and partial tuition reimbursements (averaging $13,104 per year), 18 teaching assistantships with full and partial tuition reimbursements (averaging $13,270 per year) were awarded; fellowships with full and partial tuition reimbursements also available. *Faculty research:* Metallaborane chemistry, serum transferrin chemistry, natural products chemistry, organic synthesis. *Unit head:* Dr. Cynthia Dupureur, Director of Graduate Studies, 314-516-5311, Fax: 314-516-5342, E-mail: gradchem@umsl.edu. *Application contact:* 314-516-5458, Fax: 314-516-6996, E-mail: gradadm@umsl.edu.

The University of Montana, Graduate School, College of Arts and Sciences, Department of Chemistry, Missoula, MT 59812-0002. Offers chemistry (MS, PhD), including environmental/analytical chemistry, inorganic chemistry, organic chemistry, physical chemistry. Terminal master's awarded for partial completion of doctoral program. *Degree requirements:* For master's, thesis (for some programs); for doctorate, thesis/dissertation. *Entrance requirements:* For master's and doctorate, GRE General Test. Additional exam requirements/recommendations for international students: Required—TOEFL (minimum score 575 paper-based; 230 computer-based). *Faculty research:* Reaction mechanisms and kinetics, inorganic and organic synthesis, analytical chemistry, natural products.

University of Nebraska–Lincoln, Graduate College, College of Arts and Sciences, Department of Chemistry, Lincoln, NE 68588. Offers analytical chemistry (PhD); biochemistry (PhD); chemistry (MS); inorganic chemistry (PhD); materials chemistry (PhD); organic chemistry (PhD); physical chemistry (PhD). *Degree requirements:* For master's, one foreign language, thesis optional, departmental qualifying exam; for doctorate, one foreign language, comprehensive exam, thesis/dissertation, departmental qualifying exams. *Entrance requirements:* For master's and doctorate, GRE. Additional exam requirements/recommendations for international students: Required—TOEFL (minimum score 550 paper-based; 213 computer-based). Electronic applications accepted. *Faculty research:* Bioorganic and bioinorganic chemistry, biophysical and bioanalytical chemistry, structure-function of DNA and proteins, organometallics, mass spectrometry.

University of Notre Dame, Graduate School, College of Science, Department of Chemistry and Biochemistry, Notre Dame, IN 46556. Offers biochemistry (MS, PhD); inorganic chemistry (MS, PhD); organic chemistry (MS, PhD); physical chemistry (MS, PhD). Terminal master's awarded for partial completion of doctoral program. *Degree requirements:* For master's, comprehensive exam, thesis; for doctorate, thesis/dissertation, qualifying exam. *Entrance requirements:* For master's and doctorate, GRE General Test, GRE Subject Test (strongly recommended). Additional exam requirements/recommendations for international students: Required—TOEFL (minimum score 600 paper-based; 250 computer-based; 80 iBT). Electronic applications accepted. *Faculty research:* Reaction design and mechanistic studies; reactive intermediates; synthesis, structure and reactivity of organometallic cluster complexes and biologically active natural products; bioorganic chemistry; enzymology.

University of Regina, Faculty of Graduate Studies and Research, Faculty of Science, Department of Chemistry and Biochemistry, Regina, SK S4S 0A2, Canada. Offers analytical/environmental chemistry (M Sc, PhD); biophysics of biological interfaces (M Sc, PhD); enzymology/chemical biology (M Sc, PhD); inorganic/organometallic chemistry (M Sc, PhD); signal transduction and mechanisms of cancer cell regulation (M Sc, PhD); supramolecular organic photochemistry and photophysics (M Sc, PhD); synthetic organic chemistry (M Sc, PhD); theoretical/computational chemistry (M Sc, PhD). *Faculty:* 10 full-time (2 women). *Students:* 19 full-time (9 women), 2 part-time (1 woman). 20 applicants, 40% accepted. In 2010, 2 master's, 1 doctorate awarded. *Degree requirements:* For master's, thesis; for doctorate, thesis/dissertation. *Entrance requirements:* Additional exam requirements/recommendations for international students: Required—TOEFL (minimum score 580 paper-based; 80 iBT). *Application deadline:* Applications are processed on a rolling basis. Application fee: $100. Electronic applications accepted. Tuition and fees charges are reported in Canadian dollars. *Expenses:* Tuition, area resident: Full-time $3244.50 Canadian dollars; part-time $180.25 Canadian dollars per credit hour. International tuition: $4744.50 Canadian dollars full-time. Required fees: $494 Canadian dollars; $115.25 Canadian dollars per credit hour. $115.25 Canadian dollars per semester. Tuition and fees vary according to program. *Financial support:* In 2010–11, 3 fellowships (averaging $20,000 per year), 2 research assistantships (averaging $17,250 per year), 8 teaching assistantships (averaging $6,965 per year) were awarded; scholarships/grants also available. Financial award application deadline: 6/15. *Faculty research:* Asymmetric synthesis and methodology, theoretical and computational chemistry, biophysical biochemistry, analytical and environmental chemistry, chemical biology. *Unit head:* Dr. Lynn Mihichuk, Head, 306-585-4793, Fax: 306-337-2409, E-mail: lynn.mihichuk@uregina.ca. *Application contact:* Dr. Tanya Dahms, Graduate Program Coordinator, 306-585-4246, Fax: 306-337-2409, E-mail: tanya.dahms@uregina.ca.

University of Southern Mississippi, Graduate School, College of Science and Technology, Department of Chemistry and Biochemistry, Hattiesburg, MS 39406-0001. Offers analytical chemistry (MS, PhD); biochemistry (MS, PhD); inorganic chemistry (MS, PhD); organic chemistry (MS, PhD); physical chemistry (MS, PhD). *Faculty:* 16 full-time (4 women). *Students:* 23 full-time (11 women), 1 part-time (0 women); includes 1 Black or African American, non-Hispanic/Latino, 11 international. Average age 29. 35 applicants, 20% accepted, 5 enrolled. In 2010, 3 master's, 8 doctorates awarded. *Degree requirements:* For master's, comprehensive exam, thesis; for doctorate, comprehensive exam, thesis/dissertation. *Entrance requirements:* For master's, GRE General Test, minimum GPA of 2.75 in last 60 hours; for doctorate, GRE General Test, minimum GPA of 3.5. Additional exam requirements/recommendations for international students: Required—TOEFL, IELTS. *Application deadline:* For fall admission, 3/1 priority date for domestic students, 3/1 for international students. Applications are processed on a rolling basis. Application fee: $50. *Financial support:* In 2010–11, 3 research assistantships with full tuition reimbursements (averaging $17,000 per year), 19 teaching assistantships with full tuition reimbursements (averaging $20,700 per year) were awarded; fellowships, Federal Work-Study, institutionally sponsored loans, scholarships/grants, health care benefits, and unspecified assistantships also available. Support available to part-time students. Financial award application deadline: 3/15; financial award applicants required to submit FAFSA. *Faculty research:* Plant biochemistry, photo chemistry, polymer chemistry, x-ray analysis, enzyme chemistry. *Unit head:* Dr. Sabine Heinhorst, Chair, 601-266-4701, Fax: 601-266-6075. *Application contact:* Dr. Sabine Heinhorst, Graduate Coordinator, 601-266-4702, Fax: 601-266-6075.

University of South Florida, Graduate School, College of Arts and Sciences, Department of Chemistry, Tampa, FL 33620-9951. Offers analytical chemistry (MS, PhD); biochemistry (MS, PhD); computational chemistry (MS, PhD); environmental chemistry (MS, PhD); inorganic chemistry (MS, PhD); organic chemistry (MS); physical chemistry (MS, PhD); polymer chemistry (PhD). Part-time programs available. *Faculty:* 15 full-time (1 woman). *Students:* 120 full-time (42 women), 9 part-time (2 women); includes 7 Black or African American, non-Hispanic/Latino; 8 Asian, non-Hispanic/Latino; 8 Hispanic/Latino, 62 international. Average age 29. 1,118 applicants, 4% accepted, 20 enrolled. In 2010, 4 master's, 14 doctorates awarded. Terminal master's awarded for partial completion of doctoral program. *Degree requirements:* For master's, comprehensive exam, thesis (for some programs); for doctorate, 2 foreign languages, comprehensive exam, thesis/dissertation. *Entrance requirements:* For master's, GRE General Test or GMAT, minimum GPA of 3.0. Additional exam requirements/recommendations for international students: Required—TOEFL (minimum score 550 paper-based; 213 computer-based). *Application deadline:* For fall admission, 2/15 priority date for domestic students, 1/2 priority date for international students; for spring admission, 10/1 priority date for domestic students, 6/1 priority date for international students. Applications are

processed on a rolling basis. Application fee: $30. Electronic applications accepted. *Financial support:* In 2010–11, 39 research assistantships (averaging $14,359 per year), 99 teaching assistantships with tuition reimbursements (averaging $15,094 per year) were awarded; unspecified assistantships also available. Financial award application deadline: 6/30. *Faculty research:* Synthesis, bio-organic chemistry, bioinorganic chemistry, environmental chemistry, NMR. Total annual research expenditures: $3.9 million. *Unit head:* Dr. Randy Larsen, Chairperson, 813-974-4129, Fax: 813-974-3203, E-mail: rlarsen@cas.usf.edu. *Application contact:* Patricia Muisener, Director, 813-974-1730, Fax: 813-974-3203, E-mail: muisener@cas.usf.edu.

The University of Tennessee, Graduate School, College of Arts and Sciences, Department of Chemistry, Knoxville, TN 37996. Offers analytical chemistry (MS, PhD); chemical physics (PhD); environmental chemistry (MS, PhD); inorganic chemistry (MS, PhD); organic chemistry (MS, PhD); physical chemistry (MS, PhD); polymer chemistry (MS, PhD); theoretical chemistry (PhD). Part-time programs available. Terminal master's awarded for partial completion of doctoral program. *Degree requirements:* For master's, thesis; for doctorate, thesis/dissertation. *Entrance requirements:* For master's and doctorate, GRE General Test, minimum GPA of 2.7. Additional exam requirements/recommendations for international students: Required—TOEFL. Electronic applications accepted. *Expenses:* Tuition, state resident: full-time $7440; part-time $414 per credit hour. Tuition, nonresident: full-time $22,478; part-time $1250 per credit hour. Required fees: $922; $43 per credit hour. Tuition and fees vary according to program.

The University of Texas at Austin, Graduate School, College of Natural Sciences, Department of Chemistry and Biochemistry, Austin, TX 78712-1111. Offers analytical chemistry (MA, PhD); biochemistry (MA, PhD); inorganic chemistry (MA, PhD); organic chemistry (MA, PhD); physical chemistry (MA, PhD). *Entrance requirements:* For master's and doctorate, GRE General Test.

The University of Toledo, College of Graduate Studies, College of Natural Sciences and Mathematics, Department of Chemistry, Toledo, OH 43606-3390. Offers analytical chemistry (MS, PhD); biological chemistry (MS, PhD); inorganic chemistry (MS, PhD); organic chemistry (MS, PhD); physical chemistry (MS, PhD). Part-time programs available. *Faculty:* 24. *Students:* 63 full-time (22 women), 4 part-time (2 women); includes 2 minority (1 Asian, non-Hispanic/Latino; 1 Hispanic/Latino), 45 international. Average age 27. 111 applicants, 17% accepted, 16 enrolled. In 2010, 4 master's, 6 doctorates awarded. *Degree requirements:* For master's, thesis; for doctorate, thesis/dissertation. *Entrance requirements:* For master's and doctorate, GRE General Test, GRE Subject Test, A minimum 2.7 cumulative point-hour ratio (on a 4.0 scale) for all previous academic work. Three letters of recommendation, a statement of purpose, and transcripts from all prior institutions attended. Additional exam requirements/recommendations for international students: Required—TOEFL (minimum score 550 paper-based; 213 computer-based; 80 iBT), IELTS (minimum score 6.5). *Application deadline:* For fall admission, 1/15 priority date for domestic and international students. Applications are processed on a rolling basis. Application fee: $45 ($75 for international students). Electronic applications accepted. *Expenses:* Tuition, state resident: full-time $11,426; part-time $476 per credit hour. Tuition, nonresident: full-time $21,660; part-time $903 per credit hour. One-time fee: $62. *Financial support:* Fellowships with tuition reimbursements, research assistantships with full tuition reimbursements, teaching assistantships with full tuition reimbursements, Federal Work-Study, institutionally sponsored loans, scholarships/grants, tuition waivers (full), and unspecified assistantships available. Support available to part-time students. *Faculty research:* Enzymology, materials chemistry, crystallography, theoretical chemistry. *Unit head:* Dr. Alan Pinkerton, Chair, 419-530-7902, Fax: 419-530-4033, E-mail: alan.pinkerton@utoledo.edu. *Application contact:* Graduate School Office, 419-530-4723, Fax: 419-530-4724, E-mail: grdsch@utnet.utoledo.edu.

Vanderbilt University, Graduate School, Department of Chemistry, Nashville, TN 37240-1001. Offers analytical chemistry (MAT, MS, PhD); inorganic chemistry (MAT, MS, PhD); organic chemistry (MAT, MS, PhD); physical chemistry (MAT, MS, PhD); theoretical chemistry (MAT, MS, PhD). *Faculty:* 21 full-time (3 women). *Students:* 121 full-time (43 women); includes 18 minority (8 Black or African American, non-Hispanic/Latino; 1 American Indian or Alaska Native, non-Hispanic/Latino; 3 Asian, non-Hispanic/Latino; 1 Hispanic/Latino; 5 Two or more races, non-Hispanic/Latino). Average age 26. 373 applicants, 23% accepted, 39 enrolled. In 2010, 4 master's, 17 doctorates awarded. Terminal master's awarded for partial completion of doctoral program. *Degree requirements:* For master's, thesis; for doctorate, thesis/dissertation, area, qualifying, and final exams. *Entrance requirements:* For master's and doctorate, GRE General Test, GRE Subject Test (recommended). Additional exam requirements/recommendations for international students: Required—TOEFL (minimum score 570 paper-based; 230 computer-based; 88 iBT). *Application deadline:* For fall admission, 1/15 for domestic and international students. Application fee: $0. Electronic applications accepted. *Financial support:* Fellowships with full and partial tuition reimbursements, research assistantships with full tuition reimbursements, teaching assistantships with full tuition reimbursements, Federal Work-Study, institutionally sponsored loans, scholarships/grants, traineeships, and health care benefits available. Financial award application deadline: 1/15; financial award applicants required to submit CSS PROFILE or FAFSA. *Faculty research:* Chemical synthesis; mechanistic, theoretical, bioorganic, analytical, and spectroscopic chemistry. *Unit head:* Mike P. Stone, PhD, Chair, 615-322-2589, Fax: 615-343-1234, E-mail: michael.p.stone@vanderbilt.edu. *Application contact:* Charles M. Lukehart, PhD, Director of Graduate Studies, 615-322-2861, Fax: 615-343-1234, E-mail: charles.m.lukehart@vanderbilt.edu.

Virginia Commonwealth University, Graduate School, College of Humanities and Sciences, Department of Chemistry, Richmond, VA 23284-9005. Offers analytical chemistry (MS, PhD); chemical physics (PhD); inorganic chemistry (MS, PhD); organic chemistry (MS, PhD); physical chemistry (MS, PhD). Part-time programs available. *Students:* 51 full-time (23 women), 14 part-time (6 women); includes 7 minority (3 Black or African American, non-Hispanic/Latino; 2 Asian, non-Hispanic/Latino; 1 Hispanic/Latino; 1 Two or more races, non-Hispanic/Latino), 26 international. 76 applicants, 33% accepted, 10 enrolled. In 2010, 6 master's, 5 doctorates awarded. Terminal master's awarded for partial completion of doctoral program. *Degree requirements:* For master's, thesis; for doctorate, thesis/dissertation, comprehensive cumulative exams, research proposal. *Entrance requirements:* For master's, GRE General Test, 30 undergraduate credits in chemistry; for doctorate, GRE General Test. Additional exam requirements/recommendations for international students: Required—Either TOEFL (minimum score: paper-based 600, computer-based 250) or IELTS (6.5). *Application deadline:* For fall admission, 3/15 for domestic students; for spring admission, 11/15 for domestic students. Applications are processed on a rolling basis. Application fee: $50. Electronic applications accepted. *Expenses:* Tuition, state resident: full-time $4308; part-time $479 per credit hour. Tuition, nonresident: full-time $8942; part-time $994 per credit hour. Required fees: $2000; $85 per credit hour. Tuition and fees vary according to course level, course load, degree level, campus/location and program. *Financial support:* Fellowships, research assistantships, teaching assistantships, career-related internships or fieldwork and institutionally sponsored loans available. Support available to part-time students. Financial award application deadline: 7/1; financial award applicants required to submit FAFSA. *Faculty research:* Physical, organic, inorganic, analytical, and polymer chemistry; chemical physics. *Unit head:* Dr. Scott Gronert, Chair, 804-828-1298, Fax: 804-828-8599, E-mail: sgronert@vcu.edu. *Application contact:* Dr. Maryanne M. Collinson, Chair, Graduate Recruiting and Admissions Committee, 804-828-7509, E-mail: mselshal@vcu.edu.

Wake Forest University, Graduate School of Arts and Sciences, Department of Chemistry, Winston-Salem, NC 27109. Offers analytical chemistry (MS, PhD); inorganic chemistry (MS, PhD); organic chemistry (MS, PhD); physical chemistry (MS, PhD). Part-time programs available. *Degree requirements:* For master's, one foreign language, comprehensive exam, thesis; for doctorate, 2 foreign languages, comprehensive exam, thesis/dissertation. *Entrance requirements:* For master's and doctorate, GRE General Test. Additional exam requirements/recommendations for international students: Required—TOEFL (minimum score 213 computer-based). Electronic applications accepted.

Wesleyan University, Graduate Programs, Department of Chemistry, Middletown, CT 06459. Offers biochemistry (MA, PhD); chemical physics (MA, PhD); inorganic chemistry (MA, PhD); organic chemistry (MA, PhD); physical chemistry (MA, PhD); theoretical chemistry (MA, PhD). *Faculty:* 12 full-time (2 women). *Students:* 29 full-time (9 women); includes 3 Black or African American, non-Hispanic/Latino; 7 Asian, non-Hispanic/Latino; 2 Hispanic/Latino, 12 international. Average age 26. 48 applicants, 23% accepted, 5 enrolled. In 2010, 6 master's, 6 doctorates awarded. Terminal master's awarded for partial completion of doctoral program. *Degree requirements:* For master's, thesis, proposal; for doctorate, thesis/dissertation, proposal. *Entrance requirements:* For doctorate, GRE General Test, 3 recommendations. Additional exam requirements/recommendations for international students: Required—TOEFL. *Application deadline:* Applications are processed on a rolling basis. Application fee: $0. Electronic applications accepted. *Expenses:* Tuition: Full-time $43,404. Required fees: $830. *Financial support:* In 2010–11, 9 research assistantships with full tuition reimbursements, 18 teaching assistantships with full tuition reimbursements were awarded; institutionally sponsored loans also available. Financial award application deadline: 4/15; financial award applicants required to submit FAFSA. *Unit head:* Dr. Joseph Knee, Chair, 860-685-2210. *Application contact:* Cait Zinser, Information Contact, 860-685-2573, Fax: 860-685-2211, E-mail: czinser@wesleyan.edu.

West Virginia University, Eberly College of Arts and Sciences, Department of Chemistry, Morgantown, WV 26506. Offers analytical chemistry (MS, PhD); inorganic chemistry (MS, PhD); organic chemistry (MS, PhD); physical chemistry (MS, PhD); theoretical chemistry (MS, PhD). Part-time programs available. Postbaccalaureate distance learning degree programs offered (no on-campus study). Terminal master's awarded for partial completion of doctoral program. *Degree requirements:* For master's, thesis; for doctorate, thesis/dissertation. *Entrance requirements:* For master's, GRE General Test, GRE Subject Test (recommended), minimum GPA of 2.5; for doctorate, GRE General Test, GRE Subject Test (recommended), minimum GPA of 2.75. Additional exam requirements/recommendations for international students: Required—TOEFL. Electronic applications accepted. *Faculty research:* Analysis of proteins, drug interactions, solids and effluents by advanced separation methods; new synthetic strategies for complex organic molecules; synthesis and structural characterization of metal complexes for polymerization catalysis, nonlinear science, spectroscopy.

Yale University, Graduate School of Arts and Sciences, Department of Chemistry, New Haven, CT 06520. Offers biophysical chemistry (PhD); inorganic chemistry (PhD); organic chemistry (PhD); physical and theoretical chemistry (PhD). *Degree requirements:* For doctorate, thesis/dissertation. *Entrance requirements:* For doctorate, GRE General Test, GRE Subject Test. Additional exam requirements/recommendations for international students: Required—TOEFL.

Youngstown State University, Graduate School, College of Science, Technology, Engineering and Mathematics, Department of Chemistry, Youngstown, OH 44555-0001. Offers analytical chemistry (MS); biochemistry (MS); chemistry education (MS); inorganic chemistry (MS); organic chemistry (MS); physical chemistry (MS). Part-time programs available. *Degree requirements:* For master's, thesis. *Entrance requirements:* For master's, bachelor's degree in chemistry, minimum GPA of 2.7. Additional exam requirements/recommendations for international students: Required—TOEFL. *Faculty research:* Analysis of antioxidants, chromatography, defects and disorder in crystalline oxides, hydrogen bonding, novel organic and organometallic materials.

Physical Chemistry

Auburn University, Graduate School, College of Sciences and Mathematics, Department of Chemistry and Biochemistry, Auburn University, AL 36849. Offers analytical chemistry (MS, PhD); biochemistry (MS, PhD); inorganic chemistry (MS, PhD); organic chemistry (MS, PhD); physical chemistry (MS, PhD). Part-time programs available. *Faculty:* 27 full-time (6 women). *Students:* 39 full-time (20 women), 21 part-time (8 women); includes 4 Black or African American, non-Hispanic/Latino; 1 Asian, non-Hispanic/Latino; 1 Hispanic/Latino, 41 international. Average age 28. 54 applicants, 11% accepted, 3 enrolled. In 2010, 1 master's, 13 doctorates awarded. *Degree requirements:* For master's, thesis (for some programs); for doctorate, thesis/dissertation, oral and written exams. *Entrance requirements:* For master's and doctorate, GRE General Test. *Application deadline:* For fall admission, 7/7 for domestic students; for spring admission, 11/24 for domestic students. Applications are processed on a rolling basis. Application fee: $50 ($60 for international students). Electronic applications accepted. *Expenses:* Tuition, state resident: full-time $7002. Tuition, nonresident: full-time $21,898. International tuition: $22,116 full-time. Required fees: $892. Tuition and fees vary according to course load and program. *Financial support:* Fellowships, research assistantships, teaching assistantships available. Financial award application deadline: 3/15; financial award applicants required to submit FAFSA. *Unit head:* Dr. J. V. Ortiz, Chair, 334-844-4043, Fax: 334-844-4043. *Application contact:* Dr. George Flowers, Dean of the Graduate School, 334-844-2125.

Boston College, Graduate School of Arts and Sciences, Department of Chemistry, Chestnut Hill, MA 02467-3800. Offers biochemistry (PhD); inorganic chemistry (PhD); organic chemistry (PhD); physical chemistry (PhD); science education (MST). Part-time programs available. *Degree requirements:* For doctorate, thesis/dissertation, qualifying exam. *Entrance requirements:* For doctorate, GRE General Test, GRE Subject Test. Additional exam requirements/recommendations for international students: Required—TOEFL (minimum score 600 paper-based; 250 computer-based; 100 iBT). Electronic applications accepted.

Brandeis University, Graduate School of Arts and Sciences, Department of Chemistry, Waltham, MA 02454. Offers inorganic chemistry (MS, PhD); organic chemistry (MS, PhD); physical chemistry (MS, PhD). *Faculty:* 26 full-time (14 women). *Students:* 43 full-time (14 women); includes 1 Black or African American, non-Hispanic/Latino, 27 international. 115 applicants, 25% accepted, 14 enrolled. In 2010, 9 master's, 8 doctorates awarded. Terminal master's awarded for partial completion of doctoral program. *Degree requirements:* For master's, thesis, 1 year of residency; for doctorate, one foreign language, thesis/dissertation, 3 years of residency, 2 seminars, qualifying exams. *Entrance requirements:* For master's and doctorate, GRE General Test, resume, letters of recommendation. Additional exam requirements/recommendations for international students: Required—TOEFL (minimum score 600 paper-based; 250 computer-based; 100 iBT); Recommended—IELTS (minimum score 7). *Application*

Physical Chemistry

Brandeis University (continued)

deadline: For fall admission, 1/15 priority date for domestic students. Applications are processed on a rolling basis. Application fee: $75. Electronic applications accepted. *Financial support:* In 2010–11, 23 fellowships with full tuition reimbursements (averaging $24,500 per year), 14 research assistantships with full tuition reimbursements (averaging $24,500 per year), teaching assistantships with partial tuition reimbursements (averaging $3,200 per year) were awarded; scholarships/grants and health care benefits also available. Financial award application deadline: 4/15; financial award applicants required to submit FAFSA. *Faculty research:* Oscillating chemical reactions, molecular recognition systems, protein crystallography, synthesis of natural product spectroscopy and magnetic resonance. *Unit head:* Dr. Judith Herzfeld, Chair, Graduate Program in Chemistry, 781-736-2540, Fax: 781-736-2516, E-mail: herzfeld@brandeis.edu. *Application contact:* Charlotte Haygazian, Graduate Department Coordinator, 781-736-2500, Fax: 781-736-2516, E-mail: chemadm@brandeis.edu.

California State University, Los Angeles, Graduate Studies, College of Natural and Social Sciences, Department of Chemistry and Biochemistry, Los Angeles, CA 90032-8530. Offers analytical chemistry (MS); biochemistry (MS); chemistry (MS); inorganic chemistry (MS); organic chemistry (MS); physical chemistry (MS). Part-time and evening/weekend programs available. *Faculty:* 5 part-time/adjunct (1 woman). *Students:* 19 full-time (15 women), 24 part-time (12 women); includes 21 minority (3 Black or African American, non-Hispanic/Latino; 8 Asian, non-Hispanic/Latino; 10 Hispanic/Latino), 9 international. Average age 30. 22 applicants, 100% accepted, 10 enrolled. In 2010, 7 master's awarded. *Degree requirements:* For master's, one foreign language, comprehensive exam or thesis. *Entrance requirements:* Additional exam requirements/recommendations for international students: Required—TOEFL. *Application deadline:* For fall admission, 5/1 for domestic and international students. Applications are processed on a rolling basis. Application fee: $55. *Financial support:* Federal Work-Study available. Support available to part-time students. Financial award application deadline: 3/1. *Faculty research:* Intercalation of heavy metal, carborane chemistry, conductive polymers and fabrics, titanium reagents, computer modeling and synthesis. *Unit head:* Dr. Robert L. Vellanoweth, Chair, 323-343-2300, Fax: 323-343-6490, E-mail: rvellan@calstatela.edu. *Application contact:* Dr. Allan Muchlinski, Dean of Graduate Studies, 323-343-3820 Ext. 3827, Fax: 323-343-5653, E-mail: amuchli@exchange.calstatela.edu.

Cleveland State University, College of Graduate Studies, College of Sciences and Health Professions, Department of Chemistry, Cleveland, OH 44115. Offers analytical chemistry (MS); clinical chemistry (MS); clinical/bioanalytical chemistry (PhD), including cellular and molecular medicine, clinical chemistry, clinical/bioanalytical chemistry; environmental chemistry (MS); inorganic chemistry (MS); pharmaceutical/organic chemistry (MS); physical chemistry (MS). Part-time and evening/weekend programs available. *Faculty:* 13 full-time (0 women), 1 (woman) part-time/adjunct. *Students:* 58 full-time (29 women), 42 part-time (17 women); includes 4 Black or African American, non-Hispanic/Latino; 3 Asian, non-Hispanic/Latino; 1 Hispanic/Latino, 70 international. Average age 28. 76 applicants, 74% accepted, 16 enrolled. In 2010, 4 master's, 15 doctorates awarded. *Degree requirements:* For master's, thesis optional; for doctorate, comprehensive exam, thesis/dissertation. *Entrance requirements:* For master's and doctorate, GRE General Test. Additional exam requirements/recommendations for international students: Required—TOEFL (minimum score 525 paper-based; 197 computer-based; 65 iBT). *Application deadline:* For fall admission, 1/15 priority date for domestic and international students. Applications are processed on a rolling basis. Application fee: $30. Electronic applications accepted. *Expenses:* Tuition, state resident: full-time $8447; part-time $469 per credit hour. Tuition, nonresident: full-time $16,020; part-time $890 per credit hour. Required fees: $50. *Financial support:* In 2010–11, 44 students received support, including 5 fellowships with full tuition reimbursements available (averaging $30,000 per year), 13 research assistantships with full tuition reimbursements available (averaging $20,000 per year), 24 teaching assistantships with full tuition reimbursements available (averaging $18,500 per year); scholarships/grants and unspecified assistantships also available. Financial award application deadline: 1/15. *Faculty research:* Bioanalytical techniques and molecular diagnostics, glycoproteomics and antithrombotic agents, drug discovery and innovation, analytical pharmacology, inflammatory disease research. Total annual research expenditures: $3 million. *Unit head:* Dr. David J. Anderson, Interim Chair, 216-687-2467, Fax: 216-687-9298, E-mail: d.anderson@csuohio.edu. *Application contact:* Richelle P. Emery, Administrative Coordinator, 216-687-2457, Fax: 216-687-9298, E-mail: r.emery@csuohio.edu.

Cornell University, Graduate School, Graduate Fields of Arts and Sciences, Field of Chemistry and Chemical Biology, Ithaca, NY 14853-0001. Offers analytical chemistry (PhD); bio-organic chemistry (PhD); biophysical chemistry (PhD); chemical biology (PhD); chemical physics (PhD); inorganic chemistry (PhD); materials chemistry (PhD); organic chemistry (PhD); organometallic chemistry (PhD); physical chemistry (PhD); polymer chemistry (PhD); theoretical chemistry (PhD). *Faculty:* 46 full-time (3 women). *Students:* 163 full-time (63 women); includes 10 Asian, non-Hispanic/Latino; 3 Hispanic/Latino, 49 international. Average age 24. 340 applicants, 36% accepted, 48 enrolled. In 2010, 31 doctorates awarded. *Degree requirements:* For doctorate, comprehensive exam, thesis/dissertation. *Entrance requirements:* For doctorate, GRE General Test, GRE Subject Test (chemistry), 3 letters of recommendation. Additional exam requirements/recommendations for international students: Required—TOEFL (minimum score 600 paper-based; 250 computer-based; 77 iBT). *Application deadline:* For fall admission, 1/10 for domestic students. Application fee: $80. Electronic applications accepted. *Expenses:* Tuition: Full-time $29,500. Required fees: $76. Tuition and fees vary according to degree level and program. *Financial support:* In 2010–11, 19 fellowships with full tuition reimbursements, 69 research assistantships with full tuition reimbursements, 68 teaching assistantships with full tuition reimbursements were awarded; institutionally sponsored loans, scholarships/grants, health care benefits, tuition waivers (full and partial), and unspecified assistantships also available. Financial award applicants required to submit FAFSA. *Faculty research:* Analytical, organic, inorganic, physical, materials, chemical biology. *Unit head:* Director of Graduate Studies, 607-255-4139, Fax: 607-255-4137. *Application contact:* Graduate Field Assistant, 607-255-4139, Fax: 607-255-4137, E-mail: chemgrad@cornell.edu.

Eastern New Mexico University, Graduate School, College of Liberal Arts and Sciences, Department of Physical Sciences, Portales, NM 88130. Offers chemistry (MS), including analytical, biochemistry, inorganic, organic, physical. Part-time programs available. *Faculty:* 3 full-time (0 women). *Students:* 7 full-time (2 women), 2 part-time (1 woman), 6 international. Average age 32. 10 applicants, 40% accepted, 4 enrolled. In 2010, 3 master's awarded. *Degree requirements:* For master's, thesis optional, seminar, oral and written comprehensive exams. *Entrance requirements:* For master's, ACS placement examination, minimum GPA of 3.0; 2 letters of recommendation; personal statement of career goals; bachelor's degree with one year minimum each of general, organic, and analytical chemistry. Additional exam requirements/recommendations for international students: Required—TOEFL (minimum score 550 paper-based; 213 computer-based; 79 iBT), IELTS (minimum score 6). *Application deadline:* For fall admission, 7/20 priority date for domestic students, 6/20 priority date for international students; for spring admission, 12/15 priority date for domestic students, 11/15 priority date for international students. Applications are processed on a rolling basis. Application fee: $10. Electronic applications accepted. *Expenses:* Tuition, state resident: full-time $3210; part-time $130 per credit hour. Tuition, nonresident: full-time $8652; part-time $360.50 per credit hour. Required fees: $1212; $50.50 per credit hour. Tuition and fees vary according to course load. *Financial support:* In 2010–11, 1 research assistantship with partial tuition reimbursement (averaging $8,500 per year), 9 teaching assistantships with partial tuition reimbursements (averaging $8,500 per year) were awarded; career-related internships or fieldwork and unspecified assistantships also available. Support available to part-time students. Financial award application deadline: 3/1; financial award applicants required to submit FAFSA. *Faculty research:* Synfuel, electrochemistry, protein chemistry. *Unit head:* Dr. Juacho Yan, Graduate Coordinator, 575-562-2174, Fax: 575-562-2192, E-mail: juacho.yan@enmu.edu. *Application contact:* Sharon Potter, Department Secretary, Chemistry/Physical Sciences, 575-562-2174, Fax: 575-562-2192, E-mail: sharon.potter@enmu.edu.

Florida State University, The Graduate School, College of Arts and Sciences, Department of Chemistry and Biochemistry, Tallahassee, FL 32306-4390. Offers analytical chemistry (MS, PhD); biochemistry (MS, PhD); inorganic chemistry (MS, PhD); materials chemistry (PhD); organic chemistry (MS, PhD); physical chemistry (MS, PhD). *Faculty:* 38 full-time (5 women), 3 part-time/adjunct (0 women). *Students:* 142 full-time (46 women), 8 part-time (4 women); includes 12 minority (6 Black or African American, non-Hispanic/Latino; 3 Asian, non-Hispanic/Latino; 3 Hispanic/Latino), 68 international. Average age 25. 299 applicants, 17% accepted, 19 enrolled. In 2010, 10 master's, 20 doctorates awarded. Terminal master's awarded for partial completion of doctoral program. *Degree requirements:* For master's, comprehensive exam (for some programs), thesis (for some programs), cumulative exams; for doctorate, comprehensive exam (for some programs), thesis/dissertation, cumulative exams. *Entrance requirements:* For master's and doctorate, GRE General Test, minimum B average in undergraduate course work. Additional exam requirements/recommendations for international students: Required—TOEFL (minimum score 550 paper-based; 213 computer-based; 80 iBT). *Application deadline:* For fall admission, 12/15 priority date for domestic and international students; for spring admission, 9/15 for domestic and international students. Applications are processed on a rolling basis. Application fee: $30. Electronic applications accepted. *Expenses:* Tuition, state resident: full-time $8238.24. *Financial support:* In 2010–11, 150 students received support, including fellowships with full tuition reimbursements available (averaging $20,000 per year), 50 research assistantships with full tuition reimbursements available (averaging $20,000 per year), 100 teaching assistantships with full tuition reimbursements available (averaging $20,000 per year). Financial award application deadline: 12/15; financial award applicants required to submit FAFSA. *Faculty research:* Materials synthesis including polymers, natural products; catalysis, NMR; mass spectrometry; optical spectroscopy, scattering techniques, computational chemistry, separation technology; nanostructured materials including metallic, semiconducting and magnetic nanocrystals; nanoscience interfaced with biology; supramolecular materials for solar energy conversion. Total annual research expenditures: $5.6 million. *Unit head:* Dr. Timothy Logan, Chairman, 850-644-1244, Fax: 850-644-8281, E-mail: gradinfo@chem.fsu.edu. *Application contact:* Dr. Tyler McQuade, Chair, Graduate Admissions Committee, 888-525-9286, Fax: 850-644-0465, E-mail: gradinfo@chem.fsu.edu.

Georgetown University, Graduate School of Arts and Sciences, Department of Chemistry, Washington, DC 20057. Offers analytical chemistry (PhD); biochemistry (PhD); computational chemistry (PhD); inorganic chemistry (PhD); materials chemistry (PhD); organic chemistry (PhD); physical chemistry (PhD); theoretical chemistry (PhD). Terminal master's awarded for partial completion of doctoral program. *Degree requirements:* For doctorate, comprehensive exam, thesis/dissertation. *Entrance requirements:* For doctorate, GRE General Test. Additional exam requirements/recommendations for international students: Required—TOEFL.

The George Washington University, Columbian College of Arts and Sciences, Department of Chemistry, Washington, DC 20052. Offers analytical chemistry (MS, PhD); inorganic chemistry (MS, PhD); materials science (MS, PhD); organic chemistry (MS, PhD); physical chemistry (MS, PhD). Part-time and evening/weekend programs available. *Faculty:* 15 full-time (4 women), 5 part-time/adjunct (2 women). *Students:* 21 full-time (10 women), 10 part-time (5 women); includes 3 Asian, non-Hispanic/Latino; 1 Hispanic/Latino, 9 international. Average age 28. 33 applicants, 45% accepted, 7 enrolled. In 2010, 4 master's, 2 doctorates awarded. Terminal master's awarded for partial completion of doctoral program. *Degree requirements:* For master's, comprehensive exam, thesis or alternative; for doctorate, thesis/dissertation, general exam. *Entrance requirements:* For master's and doctorate, GRE General Test, interview, minimum GPA of 3.0. Additional exam requirements/recommendations for international students: Required—TOEFL (minimum score 550 paper-based; 213 computer-based; 80 iBT). *Application deadline:* For fall admission, 1/15 priority date for domestic and international students; for spring admission, 9/1 priority date for domestic and international students. Applications are processed on a rolling basis. Application fee: $75. Electronic applications accepted. *Financial support:* In 2010–11, 27 students received support; fellowships with tuition reimbursements available, research assistantships, teaching assistantships with tuition reimbursements available, Federal Work-Study and tuition waivers available. Financial award application deadline: 1/15. *Unit head:* Dr. Michael King, Chair, 202-994-6488. *Application contact:* Information Contact, 202-994-6121, E-mail: gwchem@gwu.edu.

Harvard University, Graduate School of Arts and Sciences, Department of Chemistry and Chemical Biology, Cambridge, MA 02138. Offers biochemical chemistry (PhD); inorganic chemistry (PhD); organic chemistry (PhD); physical chemistry (PhD). *Degree requirements:* For doctorate, thesis/dissertation, cumulative exams. *Entrance requirements:* For doctorate, GRE General Test, GRE Subject Test. Additional exam requirements/recommendations for international students: Required—TOEFL. *Expenses:* Tuition: Full-time $34,976. Required fees: $1166. Full-time tuition and fees vary according to program.

See Close-Up on page 99.

Howard University, Graduate School, Department of Chemistry, Washington, DC 20059-0002. Offers analytical chemistry (MS, PhD); atmospheric (MS, PhD); biochemistry (MS, PhD); environmental (MS, PhD); inorganic chemistry (MS, PhD); organic chemistry (MS, PhD); physical chemistry (MS, PhD). Terminal master's awarded for partial completion of doctoral program. *Degree requirements:* For master's, comprehensive exam, thesis, teaching experience; for doctorate, comprehensive exam, thesis/dissertation, teaching experience. *Entrance requirements:* For master's, GRE General Test, minimum GPA of 2.7; for doctorate, GRE General Test, minimum GPA of 3.0. Additional exam requirements/recommendations for international students: Required—TOEFL. Electronic applications accepted. *Faculty research:* Synthetic organics, materials, natural products, mass spectrometry.

Indiana University Bloomington, University Graduate School, College of Arts and Sciences, Department of Chemistry, Bloomington, IN 47405. Offers analytical chemistry (PhD); chemical biology chemistry (PhD); chemistry (MAT); inorganic chemistry (PhD); materials chemistry (PhD); organic chemistry (PhD); physical chemistry (PhD). *Faculty:* 42 full-time (4 women). *Students:* 224 full-time (77 women); includes 19 minority (7 Black or African American, non-Hispanic/Latino; 1 American Indian or Alaska Native, non-Hispanic/Latino; 8 Asian, non-Hispanic/Latino; 3 Hispanic/Latino), 68 international. Average age 27. 270 applicants, 39% accepted, 31 enrolled. In 2010, 1 master's, 20 doctorates awarded. Terminal master's awarded for partial completion of doctoral program. *Degree requirements:* For master's, thesis; for doctorate, thesis/dissertation. *Entrance requirements:* For master's and doctorate, GRE General Test, GRE Subject Test. Additional exam requirements/recommendations for international students: Required—TOEFL. *Application deadline:* For fall admission, 1/15 priority date for domestic students, 12/15 for international students. Applications are processed on a rolling basis. Application fee: $55 ($65 for international students). *Financial support:* In 2010–11, 200 students received support, including 10 fellowships with full tuition reimbursements available, 76 research assistantships with full tuition reimbursements available, 111 teaching assistantships with full tuition reimbursements available; Federal Work-Study and institutionally sponsored loans also available. *Faculty research:* Synthesis of complex natural products, organic reaction mechanisms, organic electrochemistry, transitive-metal chemistry, solid-state and surface chemistry. Total annual research expenditures: $7.7 million. *Unit head:* David Giedroc, Chairperson, 812-855-6239, E-mail: chemchair@indiana.edu. *Application contact:* Daneil Mindiola, Director of Graduate Admissions, 812-855-2069, Fax: 812-855-8385, E-mail: mindiola@indiana.edu.

Kansas State University, Graduate School, College of Arts and Sciences, Department of Chemistry, Manhattan, KS 66506. Offers analytical chemistry (MS); biological chemistry (MS);

90 www.facebook.com/petersonspublishing

Peterson's Graduate Programs in the Physical Sciences, Mathematics, Agricultural Sciences, the Environment & Natural Resources 2012

chemistry (PhD); inorganic chemistry (MS); materials chemistry (MS); organic chemistry (MS); physical chemistry (MS). Terminal master's awarded for partial completion of doctoral program. *Degree requirements:* For master's, thesis; for doctorate, thesis/dissertation. *Entrance requirements:* For master's and doctorate, GRE, minimum GPA of 3.0. Additional exam requirements/recommendations for international students: Required—TOEFL (minimum score 550 paper-based; 213 computer-based). Electronic applications accepted. *Faculty research:* Inorganic chemistry, organic and biological chemistry, analytical chemistry, physical chemistry, materials chemistry and nanotechnology.

Kent State University, College of Arts and Sciences, Department of Chemistry and Biochemistry, Kent, OH 44242-0001. Offers analytical chemistry (MS, PhD); biochemistry (MS, PhD); chemistry (MA); inorganic chemistry (MS, PhD); organic chemistry (MS, PhD); physical chemistry (MS, PhD). Terminal master's awarded for partial completion of doctoral program. *Degree requirements:* For master's, comprehensive exam, thesis; for doctorate, comprehensive exam, thesis/dissertation. *Entrance requirements:* For master's and doctorate, placement exam, GRE General Test, GRE Subject Test (recommended), minimum GPA of 2.75. Additional exam requirements/recommendations for international students: Required—TOEFL (minimum score 525 paper-based; 71 iBT). Electronic applications accepted. *Expenses:* Tuition, state resident: full-time $7866; part-time $437 per credit hour. Tuition, nonresident: full-time $14,022; part-time $779 per credit hour. *Faculty research:* Biological chemistry, materials chemistry, molecular spectroscopy.

See Display on page 57 and Close-Up on page 101.

Laurentian University, School of Graduate Studies and Research, Programme in Chemistry and Biochemistry, Sudbury, ON P3E 2C6, Canada. Offers analytical chemistry (M Sc); biochemistry (M Sc); environmental chemistry (M Sc); organic chemistry (M Sc); physical/theoretical chemistry (M Sc). Part-time programs available. *Degree requirements:* For master's, thesis or alternative. *Entrance requirements:* For master's, honors degree with minimum second class. *Faculty research:* Cell cycle checkpoints, kinetic modeling, toxicology to metal stress, quantum chemistry, biogeochemistry metal speciation.

Marquette University, Graduate School, College of Arts and Sciences, Department of Chemistry, Milwaukee, WI 53201-1881. Offers analytical chemistry (MS, PhD); bioanalytical chemistry (MS, PhD); biophysical chemistry (MS, PhD); chemical physics (MS, PhD); inorganic chemistry (MS, PhD); organic chemistry (MS, PhD); physical chemistry (MS, PhD). Part-time programs available. *Faculty:* 27 full-time (3 women), 1 part-time/adjunct (0 women). *Students:* 33 full-time (12 women), 16 part-time (3 women); includes 4 minority (2 Black or African American, non-Hispanic/Latino; 2 Asian, non-Hispanic/Latino), 37 international. Average age 29. 25 applicants, 92% accepted, 10 enrolled. In 2010, 2 master's, 1 doctorate awarded. Terminal master's awarded for partial completion of doctoral program. *Degree requirements:* For master's, comprehensive exam; for doctorate, thesis/dissertation, cumulative exams. *Entrance requirements:* For master's and doctorate, GRE Subject Test (optional), official transcripts from all current and previous colleges/universities except Marquette, three letters of recommendation from individuals familiar with the applicant's academic work. Additional exam requirements/recommendations for international students: Required—TOEFL (minimum score 530 paper-based; 78 computer-based). *Application deadline:* Applications are processed on a rolling basis. Application fee: $50. Electronic applications accepted. *Expenses:* Tuition: Full-time $16,290; part-time $905 per credit hour. Tuition and fees vary according to program. *Financial support:* In 2010–11, 2 fellowships, 4 research assistantships, 27 teaching assistantships were awarded; Federal Work-Study, institutionally sponsored loans, scholarships/grants, and tuition waivers (full and partial) also available. Support available to part-time students. Financial award application deadline: 2/15. *Faculty research:* Inorganic complexes, laser Raman spectroscopy, organic synthesis, synthetic bioinorganic chemistry, electro-active organic molecules. Total annual research expenditures: $1.2 million. *Unit head:* Dr. Michael Ryan, Chair, 414-288-3537, Fax: 414-288-7066. *Application contact:* Dr. Mark Steinmetz, Director of Graduate Studies, 414-288-7374, Fax: 414-288-7066.

Massachusetts Institute of Technology, School of Science, Department of Chemistry, Cambridge, MA 02139. Offers biological chemistry (PhD, Sc D); inorganic chemistry (PhD, Sc D); organic chemistry (PhD, Sc D); physical chemistry (PhD, Sc D). *Faculty:* 29 full-time (7 women). *Students:* 227 full-time (78 women); includes 44 minority (5 Black or African American, non-Hispanic/Latino; 1 American Indian or Alaska Native, non-Hispanic/Latino; 27 Asian, non-Hispanic/Latino; 9 Hispanic/Latino; 2 Two or more races, non-Hispanic/Latino), 65 international. Average age 25. 516 applicants, 25% accepted, 55 enrolled. In 2010, 34 doctorates awarded. *Degree requirements:* For doctorate, comprehensive exam, thesis/dissertation, 2 terms as a teaching assistant. *Entrance requirements:* For doctorate, GRE General Test. Additional exam requirements/recommendations for international students: Required—IELTS (minimum score 7); Recommended—TOEFL (minimum score 600 paper-based; 250 computer-based). *Application deadline:* For fall admission, 12/15 for domestic and international students. Application fee: $75. Electronic applications accepted. *Expenses:* Tuition: Full-time $38,940; part-time $605 per unit. Required fees: $272. *Financial support:* In 2010–11, 213 students received support, including 66 fellowships with tuition reimbursements available (averaging $33,072 per year), 123 research assistantships with tuition reimbursements available (averaging $29,440 per year), 38 teaching assistantships with tuition reimbursements available (averaging $31,275 per year); Federal Work-Study, institutionally sponsored loans, scholarships/grants, health care benefits, and unspecified assistantships also available. *Faculty research:* Synthetic organic and inorganic chemistry; biomolecular reactions and structure; multidimensional spectroscopy and chemical dynamics; inorganic, organometallic, and organic chemical catalysis; materials chemistry including surface science, nanoscience and polymers. Total annual research expenditures: $32.1 million. *Unit head:* Prof. Sylvia T. Ceyer, Department Head, 617-253-1803, Fax: 617-258-7500. *Application contact:* Graduate Administrator, 617-253-1845, Fax: 617-258-0241, E-mail: chemgradeducation@mit.edu.

McMaster University, School of Graduate Studies, Faculty of Science, Department of Chemistry, Hamilton, ON L8S 4M2, Canada. Offers analytical chemistry (M Sc, PhD); chemical physics (M Sc, PhD); chemistry (M Sc, PhD); inorganic chemistry (M Sc, PhD); organic chemistry (M Sc, PhD); physical chemistry (M Sc, PhD); polymer chemistry (M Sc, PhD). Part-time programs available. Terminal master's awarded for partial completion of doctoral program. *Degree requirements:* For master's, thesis; for doctorate, comprehensive exam, thesis/dissertation. *Entrance requirements:* For master's, minimum B+ average. Additional exam requirements/recommendations for international students: Required—TOEFL (minimum score 550 paper-based; 213 computer-based).

Northeastern University, College of Science, Department of Chemistry and Chemical Biology, Boston, MA 02115-5096. Offers analytical chemistry (PhD); chemistry (MS, PhD); inorganic chemistry (PhD); organic chemistry (PhD); physical chemistry (PhD). Part-time and evening/weekend programs available. *Faculty:* 24 full-time (5 women), 7 part-time/adjunct (0 women). *Students:* 98 full-time (58 women), 31 part-time (15 women). 190 applicants, 32% accepted, 34 enrolled. In 2010, 16 master's, 6 doctorates awarded. Terminal master's awarded for partial completion of doctoral program. *Degree requirements:* For master's, thesis (for some programs); for doctorate, thesis/dissertation, qualifying exam in specialty area. *Entrance requirements:* Additional exam requirements/recommendations for international students: Required—TOEFL. *Application deadline:* For fall admission, 2/1 priority date for domestic and international students. Applications are processed on a rolling basis. Application fee: $50. Electronic applications accepted. *Financial support:* In 2010–11, 41 research assistantships with tuition reimbursements (averaging $18,285 per year), 38 teaching assistantships with tuition reimbursements (averaging $18,285 per year) were awarded; fellowships with tuition reimbursements, career-related internships or fieldwork, Federal Work-Study, scholarships/grants, tuition waivers (partial), and unspecified assistantships also available. Financial award application deadline: 3/1; financial award applicants required to submit FAFSA. *Faculty research:* Bioanalysis, biorganic and medicinal chemistry, biophysical chemistry, nanomaterials, proteonics. *Unit head:* Dr. Robert Hanson, Graduate Coordinator, 617-373-3313, Fax: 617-373-8795, E-mail: chemistry-grad-info@neu.edu. *Application contact:* Jo-Anne Dickinson, Admissions Contact, 617-373-5990, Fax: 617-373-7281, E-mail: gsas@neu.edu.

Old Dominion University, College of Sciences, Program in Chemistry, Norfolk, VA 23529. Offers analytical chemistry (MS); biochemistry (MS); chemistry (PhD); environmental chemistry (MS); organic chemistry (MS); physical chemistry (MS). Part-time and evening/weekend programs available. *Faculty:* 14 full-time (5 women), 2 part-time/adjunct (0 women). *Students:* 36 full-time (22 women), 1 part-time (0 women); includes 3 minority (1 Black or African American, non-Hispanic/Latino; 1 Asian, non-Hispanic/Latino; 1 Hispanic/Latino), 16 international. Average age 29. 35 applicants, 60% accepted, 8 enrolled. In 2010, 6 master's, 2 doctorates awarded. *Degree requirements:* For master's, comprehensive exam, thesis. *Entrance requirements:* For master's, GRE General Test, minimum GPA of 3.0 in major, 2.5 overall; for doctorate, GRE General Test. Additional exam requirements/recommendations for international students: Required—TOEFL. *Application deadline:* For fall admission, 7/1 for domestic students, 1/15 for international students; for spring admission, 11/1 for domestic students, 8/15 for international students. Applications are processed on a rolling basis. Application fee: $30. Electronic applications accepted. *Expenses:* Tuition, state resident: full-time $8592; part-time $358 per credit. Tuition, nonresident: full-time $21,672; part-time $903 per credit. Required fees: $119 per semester. One-time fee: $50. *Financial support:* In 2010–11, 6 students received support, including fellowships (averaging $18,000 per year), research assistantships with tuition reimbursements available (averaging $21,000 per year), teaching assistantships with tuition reimbursements available (averaging $18,000 per year); career-related internships or fieldwork, scholarships/grants, and unspecified assistantships also available. Financial award application deadline: 2/15; financial award applicants required to submit FAFSA. *Faculty research:* Biogeochemistry, materials chemistry, bioanalytical chemistry, computational chemistry, organic chemistry. Total annual research expenditures: $2.6 million. *Unit head:* Dr. Craig A. Bayse, Graduate Program Director, 757-683-4097, Fax: 757-683-4628, E-mail: chemgpd@odu.edu. *Application contact:* Valerie DeCosta, Grants and Graduate Program Assistant, 757-683-6979, Fax: 757-683-4628, E-mail: chemgpd@odu.edu.

Oregon State University, Graduate School, College of Science, Department of Chemistry, Corvallis, OR 97331. Offers analytical chemistry (MS, PhD); chemistry (MA, MAIS); inorganic chemistry (MS, PhD); nuclear and radiation chemistry (MS, PhD); organic chemistry (MS, PhD); physical chemistry (MS, PhD). Part-time programs available. Terminal master's awarded for partial completion of doctoral program. *Degree requirements:* For master's, one foreign language, thesis; for doctorate, one foreign language, thesis/dissertation. *Entrance requirements:* For master's and doctorate, minimum GPA of 3.0 in last 90 hours of course work. Additional exam requirements/recommendations for international students: Required—TOEFL. *Faculty research:* Solid state chemistry, enzyme reaction mechanisms, structure and dynamics of gas molecules, chemiluminescence, nonlinear optical spectroscopy.

Purdue University, Graduate School, College of Science, Department of Chemistry, West Lafayette, IN 47907. Offers analytical chemistry (MS, PhD); biochemistry (MS, PhD); chemical education (MS, PhD); inorganic chemistry (MS, PhD); organic chemistry (MS, PhD); physical chemistry (MS, PhD). Terminal master's awarded for partial completion of doctoral program. *Degree requirements:* For master's, thesis; for doctorate, thesis/dissertation. *Entrance requirements:* Additional exam requirements/recommendations for international students: Required—TOEFL. Electronic applications accepted.

Rensselaer Polytechnic Institute, Graduate School, School of Science, Program in Chemistry, Troy, NY 12180-3590. Offers analytical chemistry (MS, PhD); biochemistry (MS, PhD); inorganic chemistry (MS, PhD); organic chemistry (MS, PhD); physical chemistry (MS, PhD); polymer chemistry (MS, PhD). Part-time and evening/weekend programs available. *Faculty:* 16 full-time (2 women). *Students:* 42 full-time (18 women), 3 part-time (1 woman); includes 1 Black or African American, non-Hispanic/Latino; 4 Asian, non-Hispanic/Latino, 16 international. Average age 24. 139 applicants, 16% accepted, 6 enrolled. In 2010, 5 master's, 8 doctorates awarded. Terminal master's awarded for partial completion of doctoral program. *Degree requirements:* For master's, thesis (for some programs); for doctorate, comprehensive exam, thesis/dissertation. *Entrance requirements:* For master's, GRE General Test, GRE Subject Test (strongly recommended); for doctorate, GRE General Test, GRE Subject Test (chemistry or biochemistry strongly recommended). Additional exam requirements/recommendations for international students: Required—TOEFL (minimum score 570 paper-based; 230 computer-based; 88 iBT). *Application deadline:* For fall admission, 2/1 priority date for domestic students; for spring admission, 11/15 for domestic students. Applications are processed on a rolling basis. Application fee: $75. Electronic applications accepted. *Expenses:* Tuition: Full-time $39,600; part-time $1650 per credit. Required fees: $1896. *Financial support:* In 2010–11, 1 fellowship with full tuition reimbursement (averaging $23,000 per year), 12 research assistantships with full tuition reimbursements (averaging $23,000 per year), 23 teaching assistantships with full tuition reimbursements (averaging $23,000 per year) were awarded; institutionally sponsored loans and tuition waivers (full and partial) also available. Financial award application deadline: 2/1. *Faculty research:* Synthetic polymer and biopolymer chemistry, physical chemistry of polymeric systems, bioanalytical chemistry, synthetic and computational drug design, protein folding and protein design. Total annual research expenditures: $1.1 million. *Unit head:* Dr. Curtis M. Breneman, Chair, 518-276-3264, Fax: 518-276-4887, E-mail: brenec@rpi.edu. *Application contact:* Sharon E. Gardner, Graduate Program Administrator, 518-276-2140, Fax: 518-276-4887, E-mail: derris@rpi.edu.

Rice University, Graduate Programs, Wiess School of Natural Sciences, Department of Chemistry, Houston, TX 77251-1892. Offers chemistry (MA); inorganic chemistry (PhD); organic chemistry (PhD); physical chemistry (PhD). Terminal master's awarded for partial completion of doctoral program. *Degree requirements:* For master's, thesis; for doctorate, thesis/dissertation. *Entrance requirements:* For master's and doctorate, GRE General Test, minimum GPA of 3.0. Additional exam requirements/recommendations for international students: Required—TOEFL (minimum score 600 paper-based; 250 computer-based; 90 iBT). Electronic applications accepted. *Faculty research:* Nanoscience, biomaterials, nanobioinformatics, fullerene pharmaceuticals.

Rutgers, The State University of New Jersey, Newark, Graduate School, Program in Chemistry, Newark, NJ 07102. Offers analytical chemistry (MS, PhD); biochemistry (MS, PhD); inorganic chemistry (MS, PhD); organic chemistry (MS, PhD); physical chemistry (MS, PhD). Part-time and evening/weekend programs available. *Faculty:* 13 full-time (3 women). *Students:* 29 full-time (14 women), 32 part-time (19 women); includes 2 Black or African American, non-Hispanic/Latino; 30 Asian, non-Hispanic/Latino; 3 Hispanic/Latino. 153 applicants, 45% accepted, 17 enrolled. In 2010, 4 master's, 9 doctorates awarded. Terminal master's awarded for partial completion of doctoral program. *Degree requirements:* For master's, thesis optional, cumulative exams; for doctorate, thesis/dissertation, exams, research proposal. *Entrance requirements:* For master's and doctorate, GRE General Test, minimum undergraduate B average. Additional exam requirements/recommendations for international students: Required—TOEFL. *Application deadline:* For fall admission, 7/1 priority date for domestic students; for spring admission, 12/1 for domestic students. Applications are processed on a rolling basis. Application fee: $60. Electronic applications accepted. *Expenses:* Tuition, state resident: part-time $600 per credit. Tuition, nonresident: full-time $10,694. *Financial support:* In 2010–11, 35 students received support, including 5 fellowships (averaging $18,000 per year), 6 research assistantships with full and partial tuition reimbursements available (averaging $23,112 per year), 20 teaching assistantships with full and partial tuition reimbursements available (averaging $23,112 per year); Federal Work-Study and institutionally sponsored loans also available.

Peterson's Graduate Programs in the Physical Sciences, Mathematics, Agricultural Sciences, the Environment & Natural Resources 2012

www.facebook.com/petersonspublishing 91

Physical Chemistry

Rutgers, The State University of New Jersey, Newark (continued)
Financial award application deadline: 3/1. *Faculty research:* Medicinal chemistry, natural products, isotope effects, biophysics and biorganic approaches to enzyme mechanisms, organic and organometallic synthesis. *Unit head:* Prof. Frank Jordan, Chairman and Program Director, 973-353-5741, Fax: 973-353-1264, E-mail: frjordan@andromeda.rutgers.edu. *Application contact:* Jason Hand, Director of Admissions, 973-353-5205, Fax: 973-353-1440.

Rutgers, The State University of New Jersey, New Brunswick, Graduate School-New Brunswick, Department of Chemistry and Chemical Biology, Piscataway, NJ 08854-8097. Offers biological chemistry (MS, PhD); inorganic chemistry (MS, PhD); organic chemistry (MS, PhD); physical chemistry (MS, PhD). Part-time and evening/weekend programs available. Terminal master's awarded for partial completion of doctoral program. *Degree requirements:* For master's, thesis or alternative, exam; for doctorate, thesis/dissertation, 1 year residency. *Entrance requirements:* For master's and doctorate, GRE General Test, GRE Subject Test. Additional exam requirements/recommendations for international students: Required—TOEFL. Electronic applications accepted. *Expenses:* Tuition, state resident: full-time $7200; part-time $600 per credit. Tuition, nonresident: full-time $11,124; part-time $927 per credit. *Faculty research:* Biophysical organic/bioorganic, inorganic/bioinorganic, theoretical, and solid-state/surface chemistry.

Seton Hall University, College of Arts and Sciences, Department of Chemistry and Biochemistry, South Orange, NJ 07079-2697. Offers analytical chemistry (MS, PhD); biochemistry (MS, PhD); chemistry (MS); inorganic chemistry (MS, PhD); organic chemistry (MS, PhD); physical chemistry (MS, PhD). Part-time and evening/weekend programs available. Terminal master's awarded for partial completion of doctoral program. *Degree requirements:* For master's, thesis optional; for doctorate, comprehensive exam, thesis/dissertation. *Entrance requirements:* Additional exam requirements/recommendations for international students: Required—TOEFL. Electronic applications accepted. *Faculty research:* DNA metal reactions; chromatography; bioinorganic, biophysical, organometallic, polymer chemistry; heterogeneous catalyst; synthetic organic and carbohydrate chemistry.

Southern University and Agricultural and Mechanical College, Graduate School, College of Sciences, Department of Chemistry, Baton Rouge, LA 70813. Offers analytical chemistry (MS); biochemistry (MS); environmental sciences (MS); inorganic chemistry (MS); organic chemistry (MS); physical chemistry (MS). *Degree requirements:* For master's, thesis. *Entrance requirements:* For master's, GMAT or GRE General Test. Additional exam requirements/recommendations for international students: Required—TOEFL (minimum score 525 paper-based; 193 computer-based). *Faculty research:* Synthesis of macrocyclic ligands, latex accelerators, anticancer drugs, biosensors, absorption isotheums, isolation of specific enzymes from plants.

State University of New York at Binghamton, Graduate School, School of Arts and Sciences, Department of Chemistry, Binghamton, NY 13902-6000. Offers analytical chemistry (PhD); chemistry (MA, MS); inorganic chemistry (PhD); organic chemistry (PhD); physical chemistry (PhD). Part-time programs available. *Faculty:* 15 full-time (4 women), 3 part-time/adjunct (2 women). *Students:* 28 full-time (8 women), 29 part-time (17 women); includes 2 Black or African American, non-Hispanic/Latino; 4 Asian, non-Hispanic/Latino; 2 Hispanic/Latino, 34 international. Average age 29. 35 applicants, 40% accepted, 9 enrolled. In 2010, 5 master's, 8 doctorates awarded. Terminal master's awarded for partial completion of doctoral program. *Degree requirements:* For master's, thesis or alternative, oral exam, seminar presentation; for doctorate, thesis/dissertation, cumulative exams. *Entrance requirements:* For master's and doctorate, GRE General Test, GRE Subject Test. Additional exam requirements/recommendations for international students: Required—TOEFL (minimum score 550 paper-based; 213 computer-based; 80 iBT). *Application deadline:* For fall admission, 1/15 priority date for domestic and international students; for spring admission, 10/15 priority date for domestic and international students. Applications are processed on a rolling basis. Application fee: $60. Electronic applications accepted. *Financial support:* In 2010–11, 51 students received support, including 5 fellowships with full tuition reimbursements available (averaging $18,000 per year), 9 research assistantships with full tuition reimbursements available (averaging $18,000 per year), 35 teaching assistantships with full tuition reimbursements available (averaging $18,000 per year); career-related internships or fieldwork, Federal Work-Study, institutionally sponsored loans, scholarships/grants, health care benefits, tuition waivers (full), and unspecified assistantships also available. Financial award application deadline: 2/15; financial award applicants required to submit FAFSA. *Unit head:* Dr. Wayne E. Jones, Chairperson, 607-777-2421, E-mail: wjones@binghamton.edu. *Application contact:* Catherin Smith, Recruiting and Admissions Coordinator, 607-777-2151, Fax: 607-777-2501, E-mail: cmsmith@binghamton.edu.

Stevens Institute of Technology, Graduate School, Charles V. Schaefer Jr. School of Engineering, Department of Chemistry, Chemical Biology and Biomedical Engineering, Hoboken, NJ 07030. Offers analytical chemistry (PhD, Certificate); bioinformatics (PhD, Certificate); biomedical chemistry (Certificate); biomedical engineering (M Eng, Certificate); chemical biology (MS, PhD, Certificate); chemical physiology (Certificate); chemistry (MS, PhD); organic chemistry (PhD); physical chemistry (PhD); polymer chemistry (PhD, Certificate). Part-time and evening/weekend programs available. Postbaccalaureate distance learning degree programs offered (no on-campus study). *Students:* 66 full-time (35 women), 25 part-time (7 women); includes 2 Black or African American, non-Hispanic/Latino; 14 Asian, non-Hispanic/Latino; 8 Hispanic/Latino, 31 international. Average age 26. 109 applicants, 68% accepted. Terminal master's awarded for partial completion of doctoral program. *Degree requirements:* For master's, thesis or alternative; for doctorate, one foreign language, thesis/dissertation; for Certificate, project or thesis. *Entrance requirements:* Additional exam requirements/recommendations for international students: Required—TOEFL. *Application deadline:* Applications are processed on a rolling basis. Application fee: $50. Electronic applications accepted. *Financial support:* Fellowships, research assistantships, teaching assistantships available. Financial award application deadline: 4/1. *Faculty research:* Biochemical reaction engineering, polymerization engineering, reactor design, biochemical process control and synthesis. *Unit head:* Philip Leopold, Director, 201-216-8957, Fax: 201-216-8196, E-mail: pleopold@stevens.edu. *Application contact:* Graduate Admissions, 800-496-4935, Fax: 201-216-8044, E-mail: gradadmissions@stevens.edu.

Texas Christian University, College of Science and Engineering, Department of Chemistry, Fort Worth, TX 76129-0002. Offers biochemistry (MS, PhD); chemistry (MA); inorganic (MS, PhD); organic (MS, PhD); physical (MS, PhD). Part-time and evening/weekend programs available. *Faculty:* 11 full-time (2 women), 1 (woman) part-time/adjunct. *Students:* 19 full-time (9 women), 2 part-time (both women); includes 1 American Indian or Alaska Native, non-Hispanic/Latino; 3 Asian, non-Hispanic/Latino; 4 Hispanic/Latino, 9 international. Average age 24. 23 applicants, 26% accepted, 5 enrolled. In 2010, 3 doctorates awarded. *Degree requirements:* For master's, thesis; for doctorate, thesis/dissertation, literature seminar, cumulative exams, research progress report, original proposal. *Entrance requirements:* For master's and doctorate, GRE General Test. Additional exam requirements/recommendations for international students: Required—TOEFL. *Application deadline:* For fall admission, 3/1 priority date for domestic and international students; for spring admission, 9/1 priority date for domestic and international students. Applications are processed on a rolling basis. Application fee: $50. Electronic applications accepted. *Expenses:* Tuition: Full-time $18,720; part-time $1040 per credit hour. Tuition and fees vary according to course load and program. *Financial support:* Fellowships, teaching assistantships, unspecified assistantships available. Financial award application deadline: 3/1. *Faculty research:* Phase transitions and transport properties of bio/macromolecular solutions, nanoscale biomaterials, electronic structure theory, synthetic methodology and total synthesis of natural products, chemistry and biology of (bio)polymers. *Unit head:* Dr. Robert Neilson, Chairperson; Professor, 817-257-7345, Fax: 817-257-5851, E-mail: r.neilson@tcu.edu. *Application contact:* Dr. Sergei V. Rzyuba, Director of Graduate Studies; Assistant Professor, 817-257-6218, Fax: 817-257-5851, E-mail: s.dzyuba@tcu.edu.

Tufts University, Graduate School of Arts and Sciences, Department of Chemistry, Medford, MA 02155. Offers analytical chemistry (MS, PhD); bioorganic chemistry (MS, PhD); environmental chemistry (MS, PhD); inorganic chemistry (MS, PhD); organic chemistry (MS, PhD); physical chemistry (MS, PhD). Terminal master's awarded for partial completion of doctoral program. *Degree requirements:* For master's, thesis optional; for doctorate, thesis/dissertation. *Entrance requirements:* For master's and doctorate, GRE General Test, GRE Subject Test. Additional exam requirements/recommendations for international students: Required—TOEFL (minimum score 600 paper-based; 250 computer-based; 80 iBT). Electronic applications accepted. *Expenses:* Tuition: Full-time $39,624; part-time $3962 per course. Required fees: $40 per year. Full-time tuition and fees vary according to degree level, program and student level. Part-time tuition and fees vary according to course load.

University of Calgary, Faculty of Graduate Studies, Faculty of Science, Department of Chemistry, Calgary, AB T2N 1N4, Canada. Offers analytical chemistry (M Sc, PhD); applied chemistry (M Sc, PhD); inorganic chemistry (M Sc, PhD); organic chemistry (M Sc, PhD); physical chemistry (M Sc, PhD); polymer chemistry (M Sc, PhD); theoretical chemistry (M Sc, PhD). *Degree requirements:* For master's, thesis; for doctorate, thesis/dissertation, candidacy exam. *Entrance requirements:* For master's, minimum GPA of 3.0; for doctorate, honors B Sc degree with minimum GPA of 3.7 or M Sc with minimum GPA of 3.3. Additional exam requirements/recommendations for international students: Required—TOEFL (minimum score 580 paper-based; 237 computer-based). Electronic applications accepted. *Faculty research:* Chemical analysis, chemical dynamics, synthesis theory.

University of Cincinnati, Graduate School, McMicken College of Arts and Sciences, Department of Chemistry, Cincinnati, OH 45221. Offers analytical chemistry (MS, PhD); biochemistry (MS, PhD); inorganic chemistry (MS, PhD); organic chemistry (MS, PhD); physical chemistry (MS, PhD); polymer chemistry (MS, PhD); sensors (PhD). Part-time and evening/weekend programs available. Terminal master's awarded for partial completion of doctoral program. *Degree requirements:* For master's, thesis optional; for doctorate, comprehensive exam, thesis/dissertation. *Entrance requirements:* For master's and doctorate, GRE General Test. Additional exam requirements/recommendations for international students: Required—TOEFL (minimum score 580 paper-based; 237 computer-based). Electronic applications accepted. *Faculty research:* Biomedical chemistry, laser chemistry, surface science, chemical sensors, synthesis.

University of Georgia, College of Arts and Sciences, Department of Chemistry, Athens, GA 30602. Offers analytical chemistry (MS, PhD); inorganic chemistry (MS, PhD); organic chemistry (MS, PhD); physical chemistry (MS, PhD). *Faculty:* 27 full-time (3 women). *Students:* 149 full-time (46 women), 3 part-time (1 woman); includes 5 Black or African American, non-Hispanic/Latino; 8 Asian, non-Hispanic/Latino; 1 Hispanic/Latino; 1 Two or more races, non-Hispanic/Latino, 58 international. 176 applicants, 38% accepted, 27 enrolled. In 2010, 6 master's, 20 doctorates awarded. Terminal master's awarded for partial completion of doctoral program. *Degree requirements:* For master's, thesis; for doctorate, one foreign language, thesis/dissertation. *Entrance requirements:* For master's and doctorate, GRE General Test. Additional exam requirements/recommendations for international students: Required—TOEFL (minimum score 213 computer-based). *Application deadline:* For fall admission, 7/1 priority date for domestic students; for spring admission, 11/15 for domestic students. Application fee: $50. Electronic applications accepted. *Expenses:* Tuition, state resident: full-time $7200; part-time $344 per credit hour. Tuition, nonresident: full-time $21,900; part-time $944 per credit hour. Tuition and fees vary according to course load and program. *Financial support:* Fellowships, research assistantships, teaching assistantships, unspecified assistantships available. *Unit head:* Dr. Jon Amster, Head, 706-542-2726, E-mail: jamster@uga.edu. *Application contact:* Dr. George F. Majetich, Graduate Coordinator, 706-542-1966, Fax: 706-542-9454, E-mail: majetich@chem.uga.edu.

University of Louisville, Graduate School, College of Arts and Sciences, Department of Chemistry, Louisville, KY 40292-0001. Offers analytical chemistry (MS, PhD); biochemistry (MS, PhD); chemical physics (PhD); inorganic chemistry (MS, PhD); organic chemistry (MS, PhD); physical chemistry (MS, PhD). *Faculty:* 21 full-time (4 women). *Students:* 55 full-time (24 women), 4 part-time (0 women); includes 1 Black or African American, non-Hispanic/Latino; 1 Asian, non-Hispanic/Latino, 42 international. Average age 29. 79 applicants, 27% accepted, 7 enrolled. In 2010, 7 master's, 5 doctorates awarded. Terminal master's awarded for partial completion of doctoral program. *Degree requirements:* For master's, variable foreign language requirement, comprehensive exam, thesis optional; for doctorate, variable foreign language requirement, comprehensive exam, thesis/dissertation. *Entrance requirements:* For master's, BA or BS courseowork; for doctorate, none, BA or BS coursework. Additional exam requirements/recommendations for international students: Required—TOEFL. *Application deadline:* For fall admission, 3/15 for domestic and international students; for winter admission, 9/15 for domestic and international students. Applications are processed on a rolling basis. Application fee: $50. Electronic applications accepted. *Expenses:* Tuition, state resident: full-time $9144; part-time $508 per credit hour. Tuition, nonresident: full-time $19,026; part-time $1057 per credit hour. Tuition and fees vary according to program and reciprocity agreements. *Financial support:* In 2010–11, 33 teaching assistantships with full tuition reimbursements (averaging $22,000 per year) were awarded; fellowships with full tuition reimbursements, research assistantships with full tuition reimbursements, career-related internships or fieldwork, scholarships/grants, traineeships, health care benefits, and unspecified assistantships also available. Support available to part-time students. Financial award application deadline: 3/15. *Faculty research:* Computational chemistry, biophysics nuclear magnetic resonance, synthetic organic chemistry, synthetic inorganic chemistry, medicinal chemistry, protein chemistry, enzymology, nanochemistry, electrochemistry, analytical chemistry, synthetic biology, bioinformatics. Total annual research expenditures: $2.5 million. *Unit head:* Dr. Richard J. Wittebort, Professor and Chair. *Application contact:* Sherry Nalley, Administrator, 502-852-6798.

The University of Manchester, School of Chemistry, Manchester, United Kingdom. Offers biological chemistry (PhD); chemistry (M Ent, M Phil, M Sc, D Ent, PhD); inorganic chemistry (PhD); materials chemistry (PhD); nanoscience (PhD); nuclear fission (PhD); organic chemistry (PhD); physical chemistry (PhD); theoretical chemistry (PhD).

University of Maryland, College Park, Academic Affairs, College of Computer, Mathematical and Natural Sciences, Department of Chemistry and Biochemistry, Chemistry Program, College Park, MD 20742. Offers analytical chemistry (MS, PhD); inorganic chemistry (MS, PhD); organic chemistry (MS, PhD); physical chemistry (MS, PhD). Part-time and evening/weekend programs available. *Students:* 128 full-time (65 women), 5 part-time (1 woman); includes 14 Black or African American, non-Hispanic/Latino; 3 Asian, non-Hispanic/Latino; 3 Hispanic/Latino; 2 Two or more races, non-Hispanic/Latino, 62 international. 398 applicants, 16% accepted, 22 enrolled. In 2010, 3 master's, 16 doctorates awarded. Terminal master's awarded for partial completion of doctoral program. *Degree requirements:* For master's, thesis optional; for doctorate, thesis/dissertation, 2 seminar presentations, oral exam. *Entrance requirements:* For master's and doctorate, GRE General Test, GRE Subject Test (recommended), minimum GPA of 3.0, 3 letters of recommendation. Additional exam requirements/recommendations for international students: Required—TOEFL. *Application deadline:* For fall admission, 2/1 for domestic and international students. Applications are processed on a rolling basis. Application fee: $75. Electronic applications accepted. *Expenses:* Tuition, area resident: Part-time $471 per credit hour. Tuition, state resident: part-time $471 per credit hour. Tuition, nonresident: part-time $1016 per credit hour. Required fees: $337 per term. *Financial support:* In 2010–11, 9 fellowships with full tuition reimbursements (averaging $24,410 per year), 48 research assistantships (averaging $19,514 per year), 64 teaching assistantships (averaging $19,155 per year) were awarded. Financial award applicants required to submit FAFSA. *Faculty*

research: Environmental chemistry, nuclear chemistry, lunar and environmental analysis, x-ray crystallography. *Unit head:* Dr. Michael Doyle, Chairperson, 301-405-1795, Fax: 301-314-2779, E-mail: mdoyle3@umd.edu. *Application contact:* Dean of Graduate School, 301-405-0358, Fax: 301-314-9305.

University of Memphis, Graduate School, College of Arts and Sciences, Department of Chemistry, Memphis, TN 38152. Offers analytical chemistry (MS, PhD); computational chemistry (MS, PhD); inorganic chemistry (MS, PhD); organic chemistry (MS, PhD); physical chemistry (MS, PhD). Part-time programs available. *Faculty:* 6 full-time (1 woman). *Students:* 39 full-time (16 women), 5 part-time (3 women); includes 8 minority (6 Black or African American, non-Hispanic/Latino; 2 Asian, non-Hispanic/Latino), 6 international. Average age 28. 37 applicants, 30% accepted, 8 enrolled. In 2010, 3 master's, 5 doctorates awarded. Terminal master's awarded for partial completion of doctoral program. *Degree requirements:* For master's, comprehensive exam, thesis or alternative; for doctorate, comprehensive exam, thesis/dissertation. *Entrance requirements:* For master's and doctorate, GRE General Test, admission to Graduate School plus 32 undergraduate hours in chemistry. Additional exam requirements/recommendations for international students: Required—TOEFL. *Application deadline:* For fall admission, 7/1 for domestic students, 5/1 for international students; for winter admission, 9/15 for international students; for spring admission, 12/1 for domestic students. Applications are processed on a rolling basis. Application fee: $35 ($60 for international students). Electronic applications accepted. *Financial support:* In 2010–11, 12 students received support; research assistantships with full tuition reimbursements available, teaching assistantships with full tuition reimbursements available, Federal Work-Study, scholarships/grants, and unspecified assistantships available. Financial award application deadline: 2/15; financial award applicants required to submit FAFSA. *Faculty research:* Computational chemistry, materials chemistry, organic/polymer synthesis, drug design/delivery, water chemistry. *Unit head:* Dr. Abby L. Parrill, Professor and Chair, 901-678-2638, Fax: 901-678-3447, E-mail: aparrill@memphis.edu. *Application contact:* Dr. Gary Emmert, Associate Professor and Graduate Coordinator, 901-678-2636, Fax: 901-678-3447, E-mail: gemmert@memphis.edu.

University of Miami, Graduate School, College of Arts and Sciences, Department of Chemistry, Coral Gables, FL 33124. Offers chemistry (MS); inorganic chemistry (PhD); organic chemistry (PhD); physical chemistry (PhD). Terminal master's awarded for partial completion of doctoral program. *Degree requirements:* For master's, comprehensive exam; for doctorate, comprehensive exam, thesis/dissertation. *Entrance requirements:* For master's and doctorate, GRE General Test. Additional exam requirements/recommendations for international students: Required—TOEFL (minimum score 550 paper-based; 213 computer-based). Electronic applications accepted. *Faculty research:* Supramolecular chemistry, electrochemistry, surface chemistry, catalysis, organometalic.

University of Michigan, Horace H. Rackham School of Graduate Studies, College of Literature, Science, and the Arts, Department of Chemistry, Ann Arbor, MI 48109-1055. Offers analytical chemistry (PhD); chemical biology (PhD); inorganic chemistry (PhD); material chemistry (PhD); organic chemistry (PhD); physical chemistry (PhD). *Faculty:* 39 full-time (8 women). *Students:* 201 full-time (106 women); includes 19 minority (1 Black or African American, non-Hispanic/Latino; 12 Asian, non-Hispanic/Latino; 4 Hispanic/Latino; 2 Two or more races, non-Hispanic/Latino), 60 international. Average age 26. 565 applicants, 38% accepted, 39 enrolled. In 2010, 58 doctorates awarded. *Degree requirements:* For doctorate, thesis/dissertation, oral defense of dissertation, organic cumulative proficiency exams. *Entrance requirements:* For doctorate, GRE General Test, GRE Subject Test (recommended), 3 letters of recommendation. Additional exam requirements/recommendations for international students: Required—TOEFL (minimum score 560 paper-based; 220 computer-based; 84 iBT). *Application deadline:* For fall admission, 1/15 for domestic students, 12/15 for international students. Applications are processed on a rolling basis. Application fee: $0 ($75 for international students). Electronic applications accepted. *Expenses:* Tuition, state resident: full-time $17,784; part-time $1116 per credit hour. Tuition, nonresident: full-time $35,944; part-time $2125 per credit hour. International tuition: $35,994 full-time. Required fees: $95 per semester. Tuition and fees vary according to course load, degree level and program. *Financial support:* In 2010–11, 201 students received support, including 23 fellowships with full tuition reimbursements available (averaging $25,905 per year), 54 research assistantships with full tuition reimbursements available (averaging $25,905 per year), 118 teaching assistantships with full tuition reimbursements available (averaging $25,905 per year); career-related internships or fieldwork, scholarships/grants, traineeships, health care benefits, and unspecified assistantships also available. *Faculty research:* Biological catalysis, protein engineering, chemical sensors, de novo metalloprotein design, supramolecular architecture. *Unit head:* Dr. Carol A. Fierke, Chair, 734-763-9681, Fax: 734-647-4847. *Application contact:* Margarita Bekiares, Graduate Program Coordinator, 734-764-7278, Fax: 734-647-4865, E-mail: chemadmissions@umich.edu.

University of Missouri, Graduate School, College of Arts and Sciences, Department of Chemistry, Columbia, MO 65211. Offers analytical chemistry (MS, PhD); inorganic chemistry (MS, PhD); organic chemistry (MS, PhD); physical chemistry (MS, PhD). *Faculty:* 30 full-time (6 women), 2 part-time/adjunct (0 women). *Students:* 92 full-time (35 women), 5 part-time (1 woman); includes 5 minority (2 Black or African American, non-Hispanic/Latino; 2 Asian, non-Hispanic/Latino; 1 Hispanic/Latino), 46 international. Average age 27. 99 applicants, 21% accepted, 19 enrolled. In 2010, 3 master's, 16 doctorates awarded. *Degree requirements:* For master's, thesis; for doctorate, one foreign language, comprehensive exam, thesis/dissertation. *Entrance requirements:* For master's, GRE General Test, minimum GPA of 3.0; for doctorate, GRE General Test (minimum score: Verbal 450, Quantitative 600, Analytical 3), minimum GPA of 3.0. Additional exam requirements/recommendations for international students: Required—TOEFL (minimum score 600 paper-based; 250 computer-based; 100 iBT). *Application deadline:* For fall admission, 4/1 priority date for domestic students; for winter admission, 10/15 for domestic students. Applications are processed on a rolling basis. Application fee: $45 ($60 for international students). Electronic applications accepted. *Financial support:* In 2010–11, 9 fellowships with full tuition reimbursements, 15 research assistantships with full tuition reimbursements, 78 teaching assistantships with full tuition reimbursements were awarded; institutionally sponsored loans, traineeships, health care benefits, and unspecified assistantships also available. *Faculty research:* Analytical, organic, biological, physical, inorganic and radiochemistry. *Unit head:* Dr. Jerry Atwood, Department Chair, 573-882-8374, E-mail: atwoodj@missouri.edu. *Application contact:* Jerry Brightwell, Administrative Assistant, 573-884-6832, E-mail: brightwellj@missouri.edu.

University of Missouri–Kansas City, College of Arts and Sciences, Department of Chemistry, Kansas City, MO 64110-2499. Offers analytical chemistry (MS, PhD); inorganic chemistry (MS, PhD); organic chemistry (MS, PhD); physical chemistry (MS, PhD); polymer chemistry (MS, PhD). PhD (interdisciplinary) offered through the School of Graduate Studies. Part-time and evening/weekend programs available. *Faculty:* 17 full-time (3 women). *Students:* 5 part-time (2 women); includes 1 minority (Black or African American, non-Hispanic/Latino). Average age 37. 19 applicants, 37% accepted, 1 enrolled. In 2010, 4 master's awarded. *Degree requirements:* For master's, thesis (for some programs); for doctorate, thesis/dissertation. *Entrance requirements:* For master's, equivalent of American Chemical Society approved bachelor's degree in chemistry; for doctorate, GRE General Test, equivalent of American Chemical Society approved bachelor's degree in chemistry. Additional exam requirements/recommendations for international students: Required—TOEFL (minimum score 550 paper-based; 213 computer-based; 80 iBT), TWE. *Application deadline:* For fall admission, 4/15 for domestic and international students; for spring admission, 10/15 for domestic and international students. Applications are processed on a rolling basis. Application fee: $45 ($50 for international students). Electronic applications accepted. *Expenses:* Tuition, state resident: full-time $5522.40; part-time $306.80 per credit hour. Tuition, nonresident: full-time $7128; part-time $792 per credit hour. Required fees: $261.15 per term. *Financial support:* In 2010–11, 7 research assistantships with partial tuition reimbursements (averaging $18,311 per year), 16 teaching assistantships with partial tuition reimbursements (averaging $16,906 per year) were awarded; Federal Work-Study, institutionally sponsored loans, and scholarships/grants also available. Support available to part-time students. Financial award application deadline: 3/1; financial award applicants required to submit FAFSA. *Faculty research:* Molecular spectroscopy, characterization and synthesis of materials and compounds, computational chemistry, natural products, drug delivery systems and anti-tumor agents. Total annual research expenditures: $729,815. *Unit head:* Dr. Kathleen V. Kilway, Chair, 816-235-2289, Fax: 816-235-5502. *Application contact:* Graduate Recruiting Committee, 816-235-2272, Fax: 816-235-5502, E-mail: umkc-chemdept@umkc.edu.

University of Missouri–St. Louis, College of Arts and Sciences, Department of Chemistry and Biochemistry, St. Louis, MO 63121. Offers chemistry (MS, PhD), including biochemistry, inorganic chemistry, organic chemistry, physical chemistry. Part-time and evening/weekend programs available. *Faculty:* 19 full-time (3 women), 7 part-time/adjunct (1 woman). *Students:* 24 full-time (11 women), 37 part-time (13 women); includes 1 Black or African American, non-Hispanic/Latino; 2 Asian, non-Hispanic/Latino; 1 Hispanic/Latino, 24 international. Average age 30. 75 applicants, 29% accepted, 7 enrolled. In 2010, 13 master's, 7 doctorates awarded. Terminal master's awarded for partial completion of doctoral program. *Degree requirements:* For master's, thesis optional; for doctorate, thesis/dissertation. *Entrance requirements:* For master's, 2 letters of recommendation; for doctorate, GRE General Test, 3 letters of recommendation. Additional exam requirements/recommendations for international students: Required—TOEFL (minimum score 550 paper-based; 213 computer-based). *Application deadline:* For fall admission, 7/1 priority date for domestic and international students; for spring admission, 12/1 priority date for domestic and international students. Applications are processed on a rolling basis. Application fee: $35 ($40 for international students). Electronic applications accepted. *Expenses:* Tuition, state resident: full-time $5522; part-time $306.80 per credit hour. Tuition, nonresident: full-time $14,253; part-time $792.10 per credit hour. Required fees: $658; $49 per credit hour. One-time fee: $12. Tuition and fees vary according to program. *Financial support:* In 2010–11, 18 research assistantships with full and partial tuition reimbursements (averaging $13,104 per year), 18 teaching assistantships with full and partial tuition reimbursements (averaging $13,270 per year) were awarded; fellowships with full and partial tuition reimbursements also available. *Faculty research:* Metallaborane chemistry, serum transferrin chemistry, natural products chemistry, organic synthesis. *Unit head:* Dr. Cynthia Dupureur, Director of Graduate Studies, 314-516-5311, Fax: 314-516-5342, E-mail: gradchem@umsl.edu. *Application contact:* 314-516-5458, Fax: 314-516-6996, E-mail: gradadm@umsl.edu.

The University of Montana, Graduate School, College of Arts and Sciences, Department of Chemistry, Missoula, MT 59812-0002. Offers chemistry (MS, PhD), including environmental/analytical chemistry, inorganic chemistry, organic chemistry, physical chemistry. Terminal master's awarded for partial completion of doctoral program. *Degree requirements:* For master's, thesis (for some programs); for doctorate, thesis/dissertation. *Entrance requirements:* For master's and doctorate, GRE General Test. Additional exam requirements/recommendations for international students: Required—TOEFL (minimum score 575 paper-based; 230 computer-based). *Faculty research:* Reaction mechanisms and kinetics, inorganic and organic synthesis, analytical chemistry, natural products.

University of Nebraska–Lincoln, Graduate College, College of Arts and Sciences, Department of Chemistry, Lincoln, NE 68588. Offers analytical chemistry (PhD); biochemistry (PhD); chemistry (MS); inorganic chemistry (PhD); materials chemistry (PhD); organic chemistry (PhD); physical chemistry (PhD). *Degree requirements:* For master's, one foreign language, thesis optional, departmental qualifying exam; for doctorate, one foreign language, comprehensive exam, thesis/dissertation, departmental qualifying exams. *Entrance requirements:* For master's and doctorate, GRE. Additional exam requirements/recommendations for international students: Required—TOEFL (minimum score 550 paper-based; 213 computer-based). Electronic applications accepted. *Faculty research:* Bioorganic and bioinorganic chemistry, biophysical and bioanalytical chemistry, structure-function of DNA and proteins, organometallics, mass spectrometry.

University of Notre Dame, Graduate School, College of Science, Department of Chemistry and Biochemistry, Notre Dame, IN 46556. Offers biochemistry (MS, PhD); inorganic chemistry (MS, PhD); organic chemistry (MS, PhD); physical chemistry (MS, PhD). Terminal master's awarded for partial completion of doctoral program. *Degree requirements:* For master's, comprehensive exam, thesis; for doctorate, thesis/dissertation, qualifying exam. *Entrance requirements:* For master's and doctorate, GRE General Test, GRE Subject Test (strongly recommended). Additional exam requirements/recommendations for international students: Required—TOEFL (minimum score 600 paper-based; 250 computer-based; 80 iBT). Electronic applications accepted. *Faculty research:* Reaction design and mechanistic studies; reactive intermediates; synthesis, structure and reactivity of organometallic cluster complexes and biologically active natural products; bioorganic chemistry; enzymology.

University of Southern California, Graduate School, Dana and David Dornsife College of Letters, Arts and Sciences, Department of Chemistry, Los Angeles, CA 90089. Offers chemistry (PhD); physical chemistry (PhD). *Faculty:* 27 full-time (2 women), 7 part-time/adjunct (0 women). *Students:* 126 full-time (42 women); includes 3 Asian, non-Hispanic/Latino; 2 Hispanic/Latino, 66 international. Average age 26. 406 applicants, 21% accepted, 39 enrolled. In 2010, 16 doctorates awarded. Terminal master's awarded for partial completion of doctoral program. *Degree requirements:* For doctorate, thesis/dissertation. *Entrance requirements:* For doctorate, GRE General Test and TOEFL. Additional exam requirements/recommendations for international students: Required—TOEFL. *Application deadline:* For fall admission, 1/15 for domestic and international students; for spring admission, 11/1 for domestic and international students. Applications are processed on a rolling basis. Application fee: $0. Electronic applications accepted. *Expenses:* Tuition: Full-time $31,240; part-time $1420 per unit. Required fees: $600. One-time fee: $35 full-time. Full-time tuition and fees vary according to degree level and program. *Financial support:* In 2010–11, 3 fellowships with full tuition reimbursements (averaging $30,000 per year), 30 research assistantships with full tuition reimbursements (averaging $25,667 per year), 101 teaching assistantships with full tuition reimbursements (averaging $25,667 per year) were awarded. Financial award application deadline: 1/15. *Faculty research:* Biological chemistry, inorganic chemistry, organic chemistry, physical chemistry, theoretical chemistry. *Unit head:* Dr. Charles McKenna, Chair. *Application contact:* Katherine McKissick, Graduate Advisor, 213-740-7036, E-mail: mckissic@usc.edu.

University of Southern Mississippi, Graduate School, College of Science and Technology, Department of Chemistry and Biochemistry, Hattiesburg, MS 39406-0001. Offers analytical chemistry (MS, PhD); biochemistry (MS, PhD); inorganic chemistry (MS, PhD); organic chemistry (MS, PhD); physical chemistry (MS, PhD). *Faculty:* 16 full-time (4 women). *Students:* 23 full-time (11 women), 1 part-time (0 women); includes 1 Black or African American, non-Hispanic/Latino, 11 international. Average age 29. 35 applicants, 20% accepted, 5 enrolled. In 2010, 3 master's, 8 doctorates awarded. *Degree requirements:* For master's, comprehensive exam, thesis; for doctorate, comprehensive exam, thesis/dissertation. *Entrance requirements:* For master's, GRE General Test, minimum GPA of 2.75 in last 60 hours; for doctorate, GRE General Test, minimum GPA of 3.5. Additional exam requirements/recommendations for international students: Required—TOEFL, IELTS. *Application deadline:* For fall admission, 3/1 priority date for domestic students, 3/1 for international students. Applications are processed on a rolling basis. Application fee: $50. *Financial support:* In 2010–11, 3 research assistantships with full tuition reimbursements (averaging $17,000 per year), 19 teaching assistantships with full tuition reimbursements (averaging $20,700 per year) were awarded; fellowships, Federal Work-Study, institutionally sponsored loans, scholarships/grants, health care benefits, and unspecified assistantships also available. Support available to part-time students. Financial

Peterson's Graduate Programs in the Physical Sciences, Mathematics, Agricultural Sciences, the Environment & Natural Resources 2012

www.facebook.com/petersonspublishing 93

Physical Chemistry

University of Southern Mississippi (continued)
award application deadline: 3/15; financial award applicants required to submit FAFSA. *Faculty research:* Plant biochemistry, photo chemistry, polymer chemistry, x-ray analysis, enzyme chemistry. *Unit head:* Dr. Sabine Heinhorst, Chair, 601-266-4701, Fax: 601-266-6075. *Application contact:* Dr. Sabine Heinhorst, Graduate Coordinator, 601-266-4702, Fax: 601-266-6075.

University of South Florida, Graduate School, College of Arts and Sciences, Department of Chemistry, Tampa, FL 33620-9951. Offers analytical chemistry (MS, PhD); biochemistry (MS, PhD); computational chemistry (MS, PhD); environmental chemistry (MS, PhD); inorganic chemistry (MS, PhD); organic chemistry (MS); physical chemistry (MS, PhD); polymer chemistry (PhD). Part-time programs available. *Faculty:* 15 full-time (1 woman). *Students:* 120 full-time (42 women), 9 part-time (2 women); includes 7 Black or African American, non-Hispanic/Latino; 8 Asian, non-Hispanic/Latino; 8 Hispanic/Latino, 62 international. Average age 29. 1,118 applicants, 4% accepted, 20 enrolled. In 2010, 4 master's, 14 doctorates awarded. Terminal master's awarded for partial completion of doctoral program. *Degree requirements:* For master's, comprehensive exam, thesis (for some programs); for doctorate, 2 foreign languages, comprehensive exam, thesis/dissertation. *Entrance requirements:* For master's, GRE General Test or GMAT, minimum GPA of 3.0. Additional exam requirements/recommendations for international students: Required—TOEFL (minimum score 550 paper-based; 213 computer-based). *Application deadline:* For fall admission, 2/15 priority date for domestic students, 1/2 priority date for international students; for spring admission, 10/1 priority date for domestic students, 6/1 priority date for international students. Applications are processed on a rolling basis. Application fee: $30. Electronic applications accepted. *Financial support:* In 2010–11, 39 research assistantships (averaging $14,359 per year), 99 teaching assistantships with tuition reimbursements (averaging $15,094 per year) were awarded; unspecified assistantships also available. Financial award application deadline: 6/30. *Faculty research:* Synthesis, bio-organic chemistry, bioinorganic chemistry, environmental chemistry, NMR. Total annual research expenditures: $3.9 million. *Unit head:* Dr. Randy Larsen, Chairperson, 813-974-4129, Fax: 813-974-3203, E-mail: rlarsen@cas.usf.edu. *Application contact:* Patricia Muisener, Director, 813-974-1730, Fax: 813-974-3203, E-mail: muisener@cas.usf.edu.

The University of Tennessee, Graduate School, College of Arts and Sciences, Department of Chemistry, Knoxville, TN 37996. Offers analytical chemistry (MS, PhD); chemical physics (PhD); environmental chemistry (MS, PhD); inorganic chemistry (MS, PhD); organic chemistry (MS, PhD); physical chemistry (MS, PhD); polymer chemistry (MS, PhD); theoretical chemistry (PhD). Part-time programs available. Terminal master's awarded for partial completion of doctoral program. *Degree requirements:* For master's, thesis; for doctorate, thesis/dissertation. *Entrance requirements:* For master's and doctorate, GRE General Test, minimum GPA of 2.7. Additional exam requirements/recommendations for international students: Required—TOEFL. Electronic applications accepted. *Expenses:* Tuition, state resident: full-time $7440; part-time $414 per credit hour. Tuition, nonresident: full-time $22,478; part-time $1250 per credit hour. Required fees: $922; $43 per credit hour. Tuition and fees vary according to program.

The University of Texas at Austin, Graduate School, College of Natural Sciences, Department of Chemistry and Biochemistry, Austin, TX 78712-1111. Offers analytical chemistry (MA, PhD); biochemistry (MA, PhD); inorganic chemistry (MA, PhD); organic chemistry (MA, PhD); physical chemistry (MA, PhD). *Entrance requirements:* For master's and doctorate, GRE General Test.

The University of Toledo, College of Graduate Studies, College of Natural Sciences and Mathematics, Department of Chemistry, Toledo, OH 43606-3390. Offers analytical chemistry (MS, PhD); biological chemistry (MS, PhD); inorganic chemistry (MS, PhD); organic chemistry (MS, PhD); physical chemistry (MS, PhD). Part-time programs available. *Faculty:* 24. *Students:* 63 full-time (22 women), 4 part-time (2 women); includes 2 minority (1 Asian, non-Hispanic/Latino; 1 Hispanic/Latino), 45 international. Average age 27. 111 applicants, 17% accepted, 16 enrolled. In 2010, 4 master's, 6 doctorates awarded. *Degree requirements:* For master's, thesis; for doctorate, thesis/dissertation. *Entrance requirements:* For master's and doctorate, GRE General Test, GRE Subject Test, A minimum 2.7 cumulative point-hour ratio (on a 4.0 scale) for all previous academic work. Three letters of recommendation, a statement of purpose, and transcripts from all prior institutions attended. Additional exam requirements/recommendations for international students: Required—TOEFL (minimum score 550 paper-based; 213 computer-based; 80 iBT), IELTS (minimum score 6.5). *Application deadline:* For fall admission, 1/15 priority date for domestic and international students. Applications are processed on a rolling basis. Application fee: $45 ($75 for international students). Electronic applications accepted. *Expenses:* Tuition, state resident: full-time $11,426; part-time $476 per credit hour. Tuition, nonresident: full-time $21,660; part-time $903 per credit hour. One-time fee: $62. *Financial support:* Fellowships with tuition reimbursements, research assistantships with full tuition reimbursements, teaching assistantships with full tuition reimbursements, Federal Work-Study, institutionally sponsored loans, scholarships/grants, tuition waivers (full), and unspecified assistantships available. Support available to part-time students. *Faculty research:* Enzymology, materials chemistry, crystallography, theoretical chemistry. *Unit head:* Dr. Alan Pinkerton, Chair, 419-530-7902, Fax: 419-530-4033, E-mail: alan.pinkerton@utoledo.edu. *Application contact:* Graduate School Office, 419-530-4723, Fax: 419-530-4724, E-mail: grdsch@utnet.utoledo.edu.

Vanderbilt University, Graduate School, Department of Chemistry, Nashville, TN 37240-1001. Offers analytical chemistry (MAT, MS, PhD); inorganic chemistry (MAT, MS, PhD); organic chemistry (MAT, MS, PhD); physical chemistry (MAT, MS, PhD); theoretical chemistry (MAT, MS, PhD). *Faculty:* 21 full-time (3 women). *Students:* 121 full-time (43 women); includes 18 minority (8 Black or African American, non-Hispanic/Latino; 1 American Indian or Alaska Native, non-Hispanic/Latino; 3 Asian, non-Hispanic/Latino; 1 Hispanic/Latino; 5 Two or more races, non-Hispanic/Latino). Average age 26. 373 applicants, 23% accepted, 39 enrolled. In 2010, 4 master's, 17 doctorates awarded. Terminal master's awarded for partial completion of doctoral program. *Degree requirements:* For master's, thesis; for doctorate, thesis/dissertation, area, qualifying, and final exams. *Entrance requirements:* For master's and doctorate, GRE General Test, GRE Subject Test (recommended). Additional exam requirements/recommendations for international students: Required—TOEFL (minimum score 570 paper-based; 230 computer-based; 88 iBT). *Application deadline:* For fall admission, 1/15 for domestic and international students. Application fee: $0. Electronic applications accepted. *Financial support:* Fellowships with full and partial tuition reimbursements, research assistantships with full tuition reimbursements, teaching assistantships with full tuition reimbursements, Federal Work-Study, institutionally sponsored loans, scholarships/grants, traineeships, and health care benefits available. Financial award application deadline: 1/15; financial award applicants required to submit CSS PROFILE or FAFSA. *Faculty research:* Chemical synthesis; mechanistic, theoretical, bioorganic, analytical, and spectroscopic chemistry. *Unit head:* Mike P. Stone, PhD, Chair, 615-322-2589, Fax: 615-343-1234, E-mail: michael.p.stone@vanderbilt.edu. *Application contact:* Charles M. Lukehart, PhD, Director of Graduate Studies, 615-322-2861, Fax: 615-343-1234, E-mail: charles.m.lukehart@vanderbilt.edu.

Virginia Commonwealth University, Graduate School, College of Humanities and Sciences, Department of Chemistry, Richmond, VA 23284-9005. Offers analytical chemistry (MS, PhD); chemical physics (PhD); inorganic chemistry (MS, PhD); organic chemistry (MS, PhD); physical chemistry (MS, PhD). Part-time programs available. *Students:* 51 full-time (23 women), 14 part-time (6 women); includes 7 minority (3 Black or African American, non-Hispanic/Latino; 2 Asian, non-Hispanic/Latino; 1 Hispanic/Latino; 1 Two or more races, non-Hispanic/Latino), 26 international. 76 applicants, 33% accepted, 10 enrolled. In 2010, 6 master's, 5 doctorates awarded. Terminal master's awarded for partial completion of doctoral program. *Degree requirements:* For master's, thesis; for doctorate, thesis/dissertation, comprehensive cumulative exams, research proposal. *Entrance requirements:* For master's, GRE General Test, 30 undergraduate credits in chemistry; for doctorate, GRE General Test. Additional exam requirements/recommendations for international students: Required—Either TOEFL (minimum score: paper-based 600, computer-based 250) or IELTS (6.5). *Application deadline:* For fall admission, 3/15 for domestic students; for spring admission, 11/15 for domestic students. Applications are processed on a rolling basis. Application fee: $50. Electronic applications accepted. *Expenses:* Tuition, state resident: full-time $4308; part-time $479 per credit hour. Tuition, nonresident: full-time $8942; part-time $994 per credit hour. Required fees: $2000; $85 per credit hour. Tuition and fees vary according to course level, course load, degree level, campus/location and program. *Financial support:* Fellowships, research assistantships, teaching assistantships, career-related internships or fieldwork and institutionally sponsored loans available. Support available to part-time students. Financial award application deadline: 7/1; financial award applicants required to submit FAFSA. *Faculty research:* Physical, organic, inorganic, analytical, and polymer chemistry; chemical physics. *Unit head:* Dr. Scott Gronert, Chair, 804-828-1298, Fax: 804-828-8599, E-mail: sgronert@vcu.edu. *Application contact:* Dr. Maryanne M. Collinson, Chair, Graduate Recruiting and Admissions Committee, 804-828-7509, E-mail: mselshal@vcu.edu.

Wake Forest University, Graduate School of Arts and Sciences, Department of Chemistry, Winston-Salem, NC 27109. Offers analytical chemistry (MS, PhD); inorganic chemistry (MS, PhD); organic chemistry (MS, PhD); physical chemistry (MS, PhD). Part-time programs available. *Degree requirements:* For master's, one foreign language, comprehensive exam, thesis; for doctorate, 2 foreign languages, comprehensive exam, thesis/dissertation. *Entrance requirements:* For master's and doctorate, GRE General Test. Additional exam requirements/recommendations for international students: Required—TOEFL (minimum score 213 computer-based). Electronic applications accepted.

West Virginia University, Eberly College of Arts and Sciences, Department of Chemistry, Morgantown, WV 26506. Offers analytical chemistry (MS, PhD); inorganic chemistry (MS, PhD); organic chemistry (MS, PhD); physical chemistry (MS, PhD); theoretical chemistry (MS, PhD). Part-time programs available. Postbaccalaureate distance learning degree programs offered (no on-campus study). Terminal master's awarded for partial completion of doctoral program. *Degree requirements:* For master's, thesis; for doctorate, thesis/dissertation. *Entrance requirements:* For master's, GRE General Test, GRE Subject Test (recommended), minimum GPA of 2.5; for doctorate, GRE General Test, GRE Subject Test (recommended), minimum GPA of 2.75. Additional exam requirements/recommendations for international students: Required—TOEFL. Electronic applications accepted. *Faculty research:* Analysis of proteins, drug interactions, solids and effluents by advanced separation methods; new synthetic strategies for complex organic molecules; synthesis and structural characterization of metal complexes for polymerization catalysis, nonlinear science, spectroscopy.

Yale University, Graduate School of Arts and Sciences, Department of Chemistry, New Haven, CT 06520. Offers biophysical chemistry (PhD); inorganic chemistry (PhD); organic chemistry (PhD); physical and theoretical chemistry (PhD). *Degree requirements:* For doctorate, thesis/dissertation. *Entrance requirements:* For doctorate, GRE General Test, GRE Subject Test. Additional exam requirements/recommendations for international students: Required—TOEFL.

Youngstown State University, Graduate School, College of Science, Technology, Engineering and Mathematics, Department of Chemistry, Youngstown, OH 44555-0001. Offers analytical chemistry (MS); biochemistry (MS); chemistry education (MS); inorganic chemistry (MS); organic chemistry (MS); physical chemistry (MS). Part-time programs available. *Degree requirements:* For master's, thesis. *Entrance requirements:* For master's, bachelor's degree in chemistry, minimum GPA of 2.7. Additional exam requirements/recommendations for international students: Required—TOEFL. *Faculty research:* Analysis of antioxidants, chromatography, defects and disorder in crystalline oxides, hydrogen bonding, novel organic and organometallic materials.

Theoretical Chemistry

Carnegie Mellon University, Mellon College of Science, Department of Chemistry, Pittsburgh, PA 15213-3891. Offers biotechnology and management (MS); chemistry (PhD), including bioinorganic, bioorganic, organic and materials, biophysics and spectroscopy, computational and theoretical, polymer; colloids, polymers and surfaces (MS). Part-time programs available. Terminal master's awarded for partial completion of doctoral program. *Degree requirements:* For doctorate, thesis/dissertation, departmental qualifying and oral exams, teaching experience. *Entrance requirements:* For master's, GRE General Test; for doctorate, GRE General Test, GRE Subject Test. Additional exam requirements/recommendations for international students: Required—TOEFL. Electronic applications accepted. *Faculty research:* Physical and theoretical chemistry, chemical synthesis, biophysical/bioinorganic chemistry.

Cornell University, Graduate School, Graduate Fields of Arts and Sciences, Field of Chemistry and Chemical Biology, Ithaca, NY 14853-0001. Offers analytical chemistry (PhD); bio-organic chemistry (PhD); biophysical chemistry (PhD); chemical biology (PhD); chemical physics (PhD); inorganic chemistry (PhD); materials chemistry (PhD); organic chemistry (PhD); organometallic chemistry (PhD); physical chemistry (PhD); polymer chemistry (PhD); theoretical chemistry (PhD). *Faculty:* 46 full-time (3 women). *Students:* 163 full-time (63 women); includes 10 Asian, non-Hispanic/Latino; 3 Hispanic/Latino, 49 international. Average age 24. 340 applicants, 36% accepted, 48 enrolled. In 2010, 31 doctorates awarded. *Degree requirements:* For doctorate, comprehensive exam, thesis/dissertation. *Entrance requirements:* For doctorate, GRE General Test, GRE Subject Test (chemistry), 3 letters of recommendation. Additional exam requirements/recommendations for international students: Required—TOEFL (minimum score 600 paper-based; 250 computer-based; 77 iBT). *Application deadline:* For fall admission, 1/10 for domestic students. Application fee: $80. Electronic applications accepted. *Expenses:* Tuition: Full-time $29,500. Required fees: $76. Tuition and fees vary according to degree level and program. *Financial support:* In 2010–11, 19 fellowships with full tuition reimbursements, 69 research assistantships with full tuition reimbursements, 68 teaching assistantships with full tuition reimbursements were awarded; institutionally sponsored loans, scholarships/grants, health care benefits, tuition waivers (full and partial), and unspecified assistantships also available. Financial award applicants required to submit FAFSA. *Faculty research:* Analytical, organic, inorganic, physical, materials, chemical biology. *Unit head:* Director of Graduate

Studies, 607-255-4139, Fax: 607-255-4137. *Application contact:* Graduate Field Assistant, 607-255-4139, Fax: 607-255-4137, E-mail: chemgrad@cornell.edu.

Georgetown University, Graduate School of Arts and Sciences, Department of Chemistry, Washington, DC 20057. Offers analytical chemistry (PhD); biochemistry (PhD); computational chemistry (PhD); inorganic chemistry (PhD); materials chemistry (PhD); organic chemistry (PhD); physical chemistry (PhD); theoretical chemistry (PhD). Terminal master's awarded for partial completion of doctoral program. *Degree requirements:* For doctorate, comprehensive exam, thesis/dissertation. *Entrance requirements:* For doctorate, GRE General Test. Additional exam requirements/recommendations for international students: Required—TOEFL.

Laurentian University, School of Graduate Studies and Research, Programme in Chemistry and Biochemistry, Sudbury, ON P3E 2C6, Canada. Offers analytical chemistry (M Sc); biochemistry (M Sc); environmental chemistry (M Sc); organic chemistry (M Sc); physical/ theoretical chemistry (M Sc). Part-time programs available. *Degree requirements:* For master's, thesis or alternative. *Entrance requirements:* For master's, honors degree with minimum second class. *Faculty research:* Cell cycle checkpoints, kinetic modeling, toxicology to metal stress, quantum chemistry, biogeochemistry metal speciation.

University of Calgary, Faculty of Graduate Studies, Faculty of Science, Department of Chemistry, Calgary, AB T2N 1N4, Canada. Offers analytical chemistry (M Sc, PhD); applied chemistry (M Sc, PhD); inorganic chemistry (M Sc, PhD); organic chemistry (M Sc, PhD); physical chemistry (M Sc, PhD); polymer chemistry (M Sc, PhD); theoretical chemistry (M Sc, PhD). *Degree requirements:* For master's, thesis; for doctorate, thesis/dissertation, candidacy exam. *Entrance requirements:* For master's, minimum GPA of 3.0; for doctorate, honors B Sc degree with minimum GPA of 3.7 or M Sc with minimum GPA of 3.3. Additional exam requirements/recommendations for international students: Required—TOEFL (minimum score 580 paper-based; 237 computer-based). Electronic applications accepted. *Faculty research:* Chemical analysis, chemical dynamics, synthesis theory.

The University of Manchester, School of Chemistry, Manchester, United Kingdom. Offers biological chemistry (PhD); chemistry (M Ent, M Phil, M Sc, D Ent, PhD); inorganic chemistry (PhD); materials chemistry (PhD); nanoscience (PhD); nuclear fission (PhD); organic chemistry (PhD); physical chemistry (PhD); theoretical chemistry (PhD).

University of Regina, Faculty of Graduate Studies and Research, Faculty of Science, Department of Chemistry and Biochemistry, Regina, SK S4S 0A2, Canada. Offers analytical/ environmental chemistry (M Sc, PhD); biophysics of biological interfaces (M Sc, PhD); enzymology/chemical biology (M Sc, PhD); inorganic/organometallic chemistry (M Sc, PhD); signal transduction and mechanisms of cancer cell regulation (M Sc, PhD); supramolecular organic photochemistry and photophysics (M Sc, PhD); synthetic organic chemistry (M Sc, PhD); theoretical/computational chemistry (M Sc, PhD). *Faculty:* 10 full-time (2 women). *Students:* 19 full-time (9 women), 2 part-time (1 woman). 20 applicants, 40% accepted. In 2010, 2 master's, 1 doctorate awarded. *Degree requirements:* For master's, thesis; for doctorate, thesis/dissertation. *Entrance requirements:* Additional exam requirements/recommendations for international students: Required—TOEFL (minimum score 580 paper-based; 80 iBT). *Application deadline:* Applications are processed on a rolling basis. Application fee: $100. Electronic applications accepted. Tuition and fees charges are reported in Canadian dollars. *Expenses:* Tuition, area resident: Full-time $3244.50 Canadian dollars; part-time $180.25 Canadian dollars per credit hour. International tuition: $4744.50 Canadian dollars full-time. Required fees: $494 Canadian dollars; $115.25 Canadian dollars per credit hour. $115.25 Canadian dollars per semester. Tuition and fees vary according to program. *Financial support:* In 2010–11, 3 fellowships (averaging $20,000 per year), 2 research assistantships (averaging $17,250 per year), 8 teaching assistantships (averaging $6,965 per year) were awarded; scholarships/grants also available. Financial award application deadline: 6/15. *Faculty research:* Asymmetric synthesis and methodology, theoretical and computational chemistry, biophysical biochemistry, analytical and environmental chemistry, chemical biology. *Unit head:* Dr. Lynn Mihichuk, Head, 306-585-4793, Fax: 306-337-2409, E-mail: lynn.mihichuk@uregina.ca. *Application contact:* Dr. Tanya Dahms, Graduate Program Coordinator, 306-585-4246, Fax: 306-337-2409, E-mail: tanya.dahms@uregina.ca.

The University of Tennessee, Graduate School, College of Arts and Sciences, Department of Chemistry, Knoxville, TN 37996. Offers analytical chemistry (MS, PhD); chemical physics (PhD); environmental chemistry (MS, PhD); inorganic chemistry (MS, PhD); organic chemistry (MS, PhD); physical chemistry (MS, PhD); polymer chemistry (MS, PhD); theoretical chemistry (PhD). Part-time programs available. Terminal master's awarded for partial completion of doctoral program. *Degree requirements:* For master's, thesis; for doctorate, thesis/dissertation. *Entrance requirements:* For master's and doctorate, GRE General Test, minimum GPA of 2.7.

Additional exam requirements/recommendations for international students: Required—TOEFL. Electronic applications accepted. *Expenses:* Tuition, state resident: full-time $7440; part-time $414 per credit hour. Tuition, nonresident: full-time $22,478; part-time $1250 per credit hour. Required fees: $922; $43 per credit hour. Tuition and fees vary according to program.

Vanderbilt University, Graduate School, Department of Chemistry, Nashville, TN 37240-1001. Offers analytical chemistry (MAT, MS, PhD); inorganic chemistry (MAT, MS, PhD); organic chemistry (MAT, MS, PhD); physical chemistry (MAT, MS, PhD); theoretical chemistry (MAT, MS, PhD). *Faculty:* 21 full-time (3 women). *Students:* 121 full-time (43 women); includes 18 minority (8 Black or African American, non-Hispanic/Latino; 1 American Indian or Alaska Native, non-Hispanic/Latino; 3 Asian, non-Hispanic/Latino; 1 Hispanic/Latino; 5 Two or more races, non-Hispanic/Latino). Average age 26. 373 applicants, 23% accepted, 39 enrolled. In 2010, 4 master's, 17 doctorates awarded. Terminal master's awarded for partial completion of doctoral program. *Degree requirements:* For master's, thesis; for doctorate, thesis/dissertation, area, qualifying, and final exams. *Entrance requirements:* For master's and doctorate, GRE General Test, GRE Subject Test (recommended). Additional exam requirements/ recommendations for international students: Required—TOEFL (minimum score 570 paper-based; 230 computer-based; 88 iBT). *Application deadline:* For fall admission, 1/15 for domestic and international students. Application fee: $0. Electronic applications accepted. *Financial support:* Fellowships with full and partial tuition reimbursements, research assistantships with full tuition reimbursements, teaching assistantships with full tuition reimbursements, Federal Work-Study, institutionally sponsored loans, scholarships/grants, traineeships, and health care benefits available. Financial award application deadline: 1/15; financial award applicants required to submit CSS PROFILE or FAFSA. *Faculty research:* Chemical synthesis; mechanistic, theoretical, bioorganic, analytical, and spectroscopic chemistry. *Unit head:* Mike P. Stone, PhD, Chair, 615-322-2589, Fax: 615-343-1234, E-mail: michael.p.stone@vanderbilt.edu. *Application contact:* Charles M. Lukehart, PhD, Director of Graduate Studies, 615-322-2861, Fax: 615-343-1234, E-mail: charles.m.lukehart@vanderbilt.edu.

Wesleyan University, Graduate Programs, Department of Chemistry, Middletown, CT 06459. Offers biochemistry (MA, PhD); chemical physics (MA, PhD); inorganic chemistry (MA, PhD); organic chemistry (MA, PhD); physical chemistry (MA, PhD); theoretical chemistry (MA, PhD). *Faculty:* 12 full-time (2 women). *Students:* 29 full-time (9 women); includes 3 Black or African American, non-Hispanic/Latino; 7 Asian, non-Hispanic/Latino; 2 Hispanic/Latino, 12 international. Average age 26. 48 applicants, 23% accepted, 5 enrolled. In 2010, 6 master's, 6 doctorates awarded. Terminal master's awarded for partial completion of doctoral program. *Degree requirements:* For master's, thesis, proposal; for doctorate, thesis/dissertation, proposal. *Entrance requirements:* For doctorate, GRE General Test, 3 recommendations. Additional exam requirements/recommendations for international students: Required—TOEFL. *Application deadline:* Applications are processed on a rolling basis. Application fee: $0. Electronic applications accepted. *Expenses:* Tuition: Full-time $43,404. Required fees: $830. *Financial support:* In 2010–11, 9 research assistantships with full tuition reimbursements, 18 teaching assistantships with full tuition reimbursements were awarded; institutionally sponsored loans also available. Financial award application deadline: 4/15; financial award applicants required to submit FAFSA. *Unit head:* Dr. Joseph Knee, Chair, 860-685-2210. *Application contact:* Cait Zinser, Information Contact, 860-685-2573, Fax: 860-685-2211, E-mail: czinser@wesleyan.edu.

West Virginia University, Eberly College of Arts and Sciences, Department of Chemistry, Morgantown, WV 26506. Offers analytical chemistry (MS, PhD); inorganic chemistry (MS, PhD); organic chemistry (MS, PhD); physical chemistry (MS, PhD); theoretical chemistry (MS, PhD). Part-time programs available. Postbaccalaureate distance learning degree programs offered (no on-campus study). Terminal master's awarded for partial completion of doctoral program. *Degree requirements:* For master's, thesis; for doctorate, thesis/dissertation. *Entrance requirements:* For master's, GRE General Test, GRE Subject Test (recommended), minimum GPA of 2.5; for doctorate, GRE General Test, GRE Subject Test (recommended), minimum GPA of 2.75. Additional exam requirements/recommendations for international students: Required—TOEFL. Electronic applications accepted. *Faculty research:* Analysis of proteins, drug interactions, solids and effluents by advanced separation methods; new synthetic strategies for complex organic molecules; synthesis and structural characterization of metal complexes for polymerization catalysis, nonlinear science, spectroscopy.

Yale University, Graduate School of Arts and Sciences, Department of Chemistry, New Haven, CT 06520. Offers biophysical chemistry (PhD); inorganic chemistry (PhD); organic chemistry (PhD); physical and theoretical chemistry (PhD). *Degree requirements:* For doctorate, thesis/dissertation. *Entrance requirements:* For doctorate, GRE General Test, GRE Subject Test. Additional exam requirements/recommendations for international students: Required—TOEFL.

Peterson's Graduate Programs in the Physical Sciences, Mathematics, Agricultural Sciences, the Environment & Natural Resources 2012

www.facebook.com/petersonspublishing   **95**

BRYN MAWR

BRYN MAWR COLLEGE

Graduate Program in Chemistry

Programs of Study

Since the founding of Bryn Mawr in 1885, the Department of Chemistry has offered programs leading to either the M.A. or Ph.D. degrees. The graduate program in chemistry is designed to prepare men and women for professional careers in research and teaching by providing them with a sound background in modern chemistry.

Students have the opportunity to learn chemistry through exceptionally close interactions with faculty members who have a special interest in teaching as well as research. The number of students participating in a graduate seminar typically ranges between 3 and 8. Students are kept aware of the latest developments in chemistry through the departmental colloquium, where faculty, postdoctoral researchers, and students gather to hear chemists from other institutions present their latest research, and many other opportunities on campus and in the Philadelphia area.

Research Facilities

Students in the Department of Chemistry have access to outstanding laboratory facilities, including a 400-MHz NMR spectrometer; atomic force microscope; gas chromatograph–mass spectrometer (GC/MS); liquid chromatograph–mass spectrometer (LC-MS); liquid scintillation counter; cold rooms; four computational servers with Gaussian 03 and Sybyl 6.92; Fourier-transform infrared spectrometers FT-IR); potentiostats for voltammetry, electrodeposition, and electroanalytical chemistry; biopotentiostat; ultraviolet visible (UV-Vis) spectrometers; fluorescence spectrophotometer; and a machine shop.

Students also have access to first-class library resources, including SciFinder Scholar; a campus collection comprised of over one million volumes, including books, documents, microform, and multimedia material; a tri-college collection with Haverford and Swarthmore of one million-plus titles; and over 550 journal subscriptions in the sciences with Internet access to the most recent issues.

Financial Aid

Bryn Mawr offers full-time graduate students in good standing teaching and research assistantships with a stipend of $18,000, and tuition coverage and health insurance subsidy in the amount of $24,000, for a total financial package of $42,000 annually.

Cost of Study

Full-time tuition is $34,110 per year; part-time tuition is $5685 for one unit, $11,370 for two units. Units of supervised work cost $910 and the fee for maintaining matriculation (continuing enrollment) is $460 per semester.

Living and Housing Costs

Students live locally or in Philadelphia. Shared apartments can be rented for $600 to $900 per month and studio apartments begin at $800 per month. Other expenses include transportation (about $165 per month if commuting from Philadelphia) and health insurance (approximately $2500 per year for domestic students and approximately $1500 for international students). Complete information about Bryn Mawr's cost of attendance may be found at http://www.brynmawr.edu/sfs/cost/cost_index.html.

Student Group

Typically about 85 percent of the graduate students in the Department of Chemistry are women, and 15 percent are men. Students in the program have the opportunity to be part of Bryn Mawr's Graduate Group in Science and Mathematics, an interdisciplinary group including graduate programs in chemistry, mathematics, and physics. The group facilitates scholarly and social interactions among graduate students, promotes interdisciplinary research projects, and provides a mentoring program by graduate students.

Student Outcomes

After completing the program at Bryn Mawr, graduate students have gone on to postdoctoral appointments at Stanford University, Thomas Jefferson University, University of Pennsylvania, University of Pittsburgh; and University of California, Santa Cruz; academic positions at Chestnut Hill College, Delaware Valley College, Drexel University, Eastern College, Haverford College, James Madison University, Rosemont College, and University of New Haven; and positions in industry with firms including Bristol-Myers Squibb, GlaxoSmithKline, Merck, Roche Bioscience, and Wyeth.

Location

Bryn Mawr is a suburb of Philadelphia, the fifth-largest city in the United States. It is well served by rail lines (the Main Line) and by bus. Philadelphia is renowned for music, museums, and sports, and it is also a culinary mecca with restaurants serving many cuisines. The metropolitan area has more than 100 museums and fifty colleges and universities, with a total population of 220,000 students.

The College

Bryn Mawr is a liberal arts college for women with two coeducational graduate schools: the Graduate School of Arts and Sciences and the Graduate School of Social Work and Social Research. Founded in 1885, Bryn Mawr was the first institution in the United States to offer the Ph.D. to women, and graduate education continues to be a significant part of its mission. Graduate students number approximately 400, out of a total enrollment of approximately 1,750 including undergraduates.

Applying

Students may apply to the Graduate Program in Chemistry online at: https://app.applyyourself.com/?id=brynmawrg.

Students who have questions and are interested in applying to the Department of Chemistry are encouraged to complete the contact form at http://www.brynmawr.edu/admissions/graduate/GSAS_REQUEST_CONTACT_CHEM.shtml.

Correspondence and Information

Department of Chemistry
Bryn Mawr College
101 North Merion Avenue
Bryn Mawr, Pennsylvania 19010-2899

Phone: 610-526-7392
E-mail: admissions@brynmawr.edu
Web site: http://www.brynmawr.edu/chemistry/graduate

Peterson's Graduate Programs in the Physical Sciences, Mathematics, Agricultural Sciences, the Environment & Natural Resources 2012

www.facebook.com/petersonspublishing   **97**

Bryn Mawr College

THE FACULTY AND THEIR RESEARCH

Sharon J. Nieter Burgmayer, Professor; Ph.D., North Carolina, 1984. Inorganic and bioinorganic chemistry: the role of transition metals in enzymes.

Michelle M. Francl, Professor; Ph.D., California, Irvine, 1983. Physical chemistry, computational chemistry and molecular architecture.

Jonas Goldsmith, Assistant Professor; Ph.D., Cornell, 2002. Electrochemistry, development and characterization of functional nanomaterials.

William Malachowski, Professor and Chair; Ph.D., Michigan, 1993. Synthetic organic chemistry, peptidomimetic synthesis, development of new asymmetric synthetic methods.

Frank B. Mallory, Professor Emeritus; Ph.D., Caltech, 1958. Organic chemistry, photochemistry and clear magnetic resonance spectroscopy.

Susan A. White, Professor; Ph.D., Johns Hopkins, 1988. Biochemistry, biochemical studies of RNA and RNA-protein interactions.

98   www.facebook.com/petersonspublishing

Peterson's Graduate Programs in the Physical Sciences, Mathematics, Agricultural Sciences, the Environment & Natural Resources 2012

HARVARD UNIVERSITY

Department of Chemistry and Chemical Biology

Programs of Study

The Department of Chemistry and Chemical Biology offers a program of study that leads to the degree of Doctor of Philosophy (Ph.D.) in chemistry in the special fields of biological, inorganic, organic, and physical chemistry. An interdepartmental Ph.D. program in chemical physics is also available. Upon entering the program, students formulate a plan of study in consultation with a Curriculum Advising Committee. Students must obtain honor grades in four advanced half courses (five for chemical physics). The course work is usually expected to be completed by the end of the second term of residence. Students are expected to present and defend an independent research proposal anytime from the first semester of their second year through the end of their fourth year (June 30). Although the curriculum for the Ph.D. degree includes the course, research proposal, and oral defense requirements, the majority of the graduate student's time and energy is devoted to original investigations in a chosen field of research. Students are expected to join a research group in their second term of residence, but no later than the third. The Ph.D. dissertation is based on independent scholarly research, which, upon conclusion, is defended in an oral examination before a Ph.D. committee. The preparation of a satisfactory thesis normally requires at least four years of full-time research.

Research Facilities

Departmental research facilities are located in six buildings on the historic main Harvard campus: Mallinckrodt, Conant, Converse, Naito, Bauer, and the Mallinckrodt/Hoffman "Link." These laboratories are adjacent to the Departments of Stem Cell and Regenerative Biology, Molecular and Cellular Biology, Organismic and Evolutionary Biology, Physics, Earth and Planetary Sciences, the Centers for Systems Biology and Brain Science, and the School of Engineering and Applied Sciences. Also nearby is the Science Center, which houses Mathematics, Statistics, and History of Science but is devoted primarily to undergraduate teaching facilities. In addition to the faculty research labs, the Chemistry and Chemical Biology complex contains facilities for analytical instrumentation (NMR, X-ray Crystallography, and X-ray Diffractometry), a library, and computer workstations for molecular modeling and chemical information retrieval. A machine shop, electronics shop, and facilities for mass spectrometry, protein structure determination, materials synthesis, nanofabrication, and imaging are available in adjacent departments. Nearly all CCB faculty members are affiliated with multiple cross-departmental programs and research centers at Harvard.

Financial Aid

The Department of Chemistry and Chemical Biology meets the financial needs of its graduate students through Departmental scholarships, Departmental fellowships, teaching fellowships, research assistantships, and independent outside fellowships. Financial support is awarded on a twelve-month basis, enabling students to pursue their research throughout the year. Tuition is afforded to all graduate students in good standing for the tenure of the Ph.D. program.

Cost of Study

As stated in the Financial Aid section, tuition is waived for all Ph.D. students in good standing.

Living and Housing Costs

Dormitory rooms for single students are available, with costs (excluding meals) that ranged from $5674 for a single room to $8910 for a two-room suite in 2010–11. Married and single students may apply for apartments managed by Harvard Planning and Real Estate. The monthly costs are studio apartment, $956–$1656; one-bedroom apartment, $1376–$2090; two-bedroom apartment, $1730–$3082; and three-bedroom apartment, $2070–$4064. There are also many privately owned apartments nearby and within commuting distance.

Student Group

The Graduate School of Arts and Sciences (GSAS) has an enrollment of approximately 4,000 graduate students. There are approximately 170 students in the Department of Chemistry and Chemical Biology, 43 percent of whom are international students.

Student Outcomes

In 2010, 9 percent of the Ph.D. recipients entered positions in academia, 9 percent accepted permanent positions in industry, 70 percent conducted postdoctoral research before accepting permanent positions in academia or industry, and 12 percent pursued other directions.

Location

Cambridge, a city of over 100,000, is just minutes from Boston. It is a scientific and intellectual center, teeming with activities in all areas of creativity and study. The Cambridge/Boston area is a major cultural center, with its many public and university museums, theaters, symphony, and numerous private, special interest, and historical collections and performances. New England abounds in possibilities for recreational pursuits, from camping, hiking, and skiing in the mountains of New Hampshire and Vermont to swimming and sailing on the seashores of Cape Cod and Maine.

The University

Harvard College was established in 1636, and its charter, which still guides the University, was granted in 1650. An early brochure, published in 1643, justified the College's existence: "To advance Learning and perpetuate it to Posterity...." Today, Harvard University, with its network of graduate and professional schools, occupies a noteworthy position in the academic world, and the Department of Chemistry and Chemical Biology offers an educational program in keeping with the University's long-standing record of achievement.

Applying

Applications for admission to study for the Ph.D. degree in chemistry may be accessed at the GSAS Web site at http://www.gsas.harvard.edu/apply/apply.php. Applications are accepted online from students who have received a bachelor's degree or equivalent.

The application process should begin during the summer or fall of the year preceding desired entrance. Completed online applications and any paper supporting materials should be submitted to the GSAS Admissions Office by December 1, though this date may vary slightly from year to year.

Correspondence and Information

Graduate Admissions Office
Department of Chemistry and Chemical Biology
Harvard University
12 Oxford Street
Cambridge, Massachusetts 02138

Phone: 617-496-3208
E-mail: admissions@chemistry.harvard.edu
Web site: http://www.chem.harvard.edu

Peterson's Graduate Programs in the Physical Sciences, Mathematics, Agricultural Sciences, the Environment & Natural Resources 2012

www.facebook.com/petersonspublishing   **99**

Harvard University

THE FACULTY AND THEIR RESEARCH

Joanna Aizenberg, Gordon McKay Professor of Materials Science, Susan S. and Kenneth L. Wallach Professor at the Radcliffe Institute for Advanced Study, and Professor of Chemistry and Chemical Biology; Ph.D., Weizmann (Israel), 1996. Biomimetic inorganic materials synthesis, self-assembly, crystal engineering, surface chemistry, nanofabrication, biomaterials, biomechanics, biooptics.

James G. Anderson, Philip S. Weld Professor of Atmospheric Chemistry; Ph.D., Colorado, 1970. Chemical reactivity of radical and radical-molecule systems; chemical catalysis sustained by free radical chain reactions in the earth's stratosphere and troposphere; mechanistic links between chemistry, radiation, and dynamics in the atmosphere that control climate; high-accuracy satellite observations for testing and systematic improvement of climate forecasts.

Alan Aspuru-Guzik, Assistant Professor of Chemistry and Chemical Biology; Ph.D., Berkeley, 2004. Theoretical physical chemistry; quantum computation and its application to chemistry problems; development of electronic structure methods for atoms and molecules: density functional theory and quantum Monte Carlo; theoretical understanding and design of renewable energy materials.

Theodore A. Betley, Assistant Professor of Chemistry and Chemical Biology; Ph.D., Caltech, 2005. Synthetic inorganic chemistry targeting chemical energy conversion, structure and reactivity of polymetallic and organometallic compounds.

Adam E. Cohen, Assistant Professor of Chemistry and Chemical Biology and of Physics; Ph.D., Cambridge, 2003; Ph.D., Stanford, 2007. Single-molecule spectroscopy and biophysics; Brownian motion and feedback control; electrokinetics, polymer physics, fluctuation-induced forces; nonequilibrium van der Waals/Casimir forces; instrumentation.

Cynthia M. Friend, Theodore William Richards Professor of Chemistry and Professor of Materials Science; Ph.D., Berkeley, 1981. Surface chemistry: heterogeneous catalysis, nanostructure growth, environmental chemistry, laser-assisted materials processing, heterogeneous chemistry relevant to origins of life, chemical sensor technology.

Roy Gerald Gordon, Thomas Dudley Cabot Professor of Chemistry; Ph.D., Harvard, 1964. Intermolecular forces, transport processes, and molecular motion; theory of crystal structures and phase transitions, kinetics of crystal growth; solar energy, chemical vapor deposition; synthesis of inorganic precursors to new materials, thin films and their applications to microelectronics and solar cells.

Eric J. Heller, Professor of Chemistry and Physics; Ph.D., Harvard, 1973. Few-body quantum mechanics, scattering theory, and quantum chaos; physics of semiconductor devices, ultracold molecular collisions, and nonadiabatic interactions in molecules and gases.

Eric N. Jacobsen, Sheldon Emery Professor of Chemistry; Ph.D., Berkeley, 1986. Mechanistic and synthetic organic chemistry; development of new synthetic methods with emphasis on asymmetric catalysis; physical-organic studies of reactivity and recognition phenomena in homogeneous catalysis; stereoselective synthesis of natural products.

Daniel Kahne, Professor of Chemistry and Chemical Biology and Professor of Biological Chemistry and Molecular Pharmacology; Ph.D., Columbia, 1986. Synthetic organic chemistry and its applications to problems in chemistry and biology.

Charles M. Lieber, Mark Hyman Jr. Professor of Chemistry; Ph.D., Stanford, 1985. Chemistry and physics of materials with an emphasis on nanoscale systems; rational synthesis of new nanoscale building blocks and nanostructured solids; development of methodologies for hierarchical assembly of nanoscale building blocks into complex and functional systems; investigation of fundamental electronic, optical, and optoelectronic properties of nanoscale materials; design and development of nanoelectronics and nanophotonic systems, with emphasis on electrically based biological detection, digital and quantum computing, and photonic systems.

David R. Liu, Professor of Chemistry and Chemical Biology and Howard Hughes Medical Institute Investigator; Ph.D., Berkeley, 1999. Organic chemistry and chemical biology of molecular evolution, nucleic acid–templated organic synthesis, reaction discovery, protein and nucleic acid evolution and engineering, synthetic polymer evolution; generally, effective molarity-based approaches to controlling reactivity and evolution-based approaches to the discovery of functional synthetic and biological molecules.

Andrew G. Myers, Professor of Chemistry and Chemical Biology and Amory Houghton Professor of Chemistry; Ph.D., Harvard, 1985. Synthesis and study of complex natural products; development of synthetic methodology.

Erin O'Shea, Professor of Molecular and Cellular Biology and of Chemistry and Chemical Biology, Howard Hughes Medical Institute Investigator, and Director of the Center for Systems Biology; Ph.D., MIT, 1992. Systems-level and molecular analysis of signaling pathways; transcriptional regulatory network architecture, function, and evolution; regulation and mechanism of oscillation of a circadian clock.

Hongkun Park, Professor of Chemistry and Chemical Biology and Professor of Physics; Ph.D., Stanford, 1996. Physics and chemistry of nanostructured materials; development of neuro-electronic interface; electron transport through individual molecules, nanowires, and nanotubes; single-molecule optoelectronics; synthesis and characterization of transition-metal-oxide and chalcogenide nanostructures; interrogation of complex neural networks using optical and electronic techniques.

Tobias Ritter, Assistant Professor of Chemistry and Chemical Biology; Ph.D., Swiss Federal Institute of Technology, 2004. Synthetic organic and organometallic chemistry, development of new synthetic methods based on transition-metal catalysis, stereoselective synthesis of biologically active natural and unnatural products.

Alan Saghatelian, Assistant Professor of Chemistry and Chemical Biology; Ph.D., California, San Diego (Scripps), 2002. Development and application of global metabolite profiling (metabolomics) as a general discovery tool for chemical biology, elucidation of molecules and metabolic pathways that control phenotype at the cellular and physiological level.

Stuart L. Schreiber, Morris Loeb Professor of Chemistry and Chemical Biology and Howard Hughes Medical Institute Investigator; Ph.D., Harvard, 1981. Development of diversity-oriented synthesis, chemical genetics, and ChemBank; application to an understanding of cell circuitry and disease biology.

Matthew D. Shair, Professor of Chemistry and Chemical Biology; Ph.D., Columbia, 1995. Synthesis of small molecules that have interesting biological functions and elucidation of their cellular mechanisms; development of organic synthesis.

Eugene I. Shakhnovich, Professor of Chemistry and Chemical Biology; Ph.D., Moscow, 1984. Theoretical biomolecular science, including protein folding, theory of molecular evolution, structural bioinformatics, rational drug design, populational genomics, other complex systems including complex polymers and spin glasses.

Gregory L. Verdine, Erving Professor of Chemistry; Ph.D., Columbia, 1986. Protein-nucleic acid interactions, transcriptional regulation, X-ray crystallography, structure and function of DNA-processing enzymes, discovery of novel ligands to peptide receptors.

George M. Whitesides, Woodford L. and Ann A. Flowers University Professor; Ph.D., Caltech, 1964. Physical organic chemistry, materials science, biophysics, complexity, surface science, microfluidics, self-assembly, microtechnology and nanotechnology, cell-surface biochemistry.

Xiaoliang Sunney Xie, Professor; Ph.D., California, San Diego, 1990. Single-molecule spectroscopy and dynamics, molecular interaction and chemical dynamics in biological systems, live cell imaging.

Xiaowei Zhuang, Professor of Chemistry and Chemical Biology and of Physics and Howard Hughes Medical Institute Investigator; Ph.D., Berkeley, 1996. Investigating complex biological processes at the single-molecule level, live cell imaging, development of new techniques for single-molecule sensing and imaging.

Affiliate Members of the Department of Chemistry and Chemical Biology

Jon Clardy, Professor of Biological Chemistry and Molecular Pharmacology (Medical School); Ph.D., Harvard, 1969. Discovery of biologically active small molecules using DNA-based approaches or high-throughput screening and chemical analysis, protein structure and enzymology, functioning of small molecules as carriers of biological information, new biosynthetic pathways, new microbial biology.

Efthimios Kaxiras, Gordon McKay Professor of Applied Physics and Professor of Physics (SEAS); Ph.D., MIT, 1987. Development of computational methodologies for coupling spatial and temporal scales; optical and electronic properties for nucleic acids, melanin, and flavonoids; structure and properties of carbon and other nanotubes, surface nanowires and nanodots, and graphene nanoflakes; effect of chemical impurities on the large-scale mechanical behavior of solids.

Suzanne Walker, Professor of Microbiology and Molecular Genetics (Medical School); Ph.D., Princeton, 1992. Chemical biology: synthetic organic chemistry applied to the study of biochemical molecules, enzymology, mechanism of action of antibiotics.

Christopher Walsh, Hamilton Kuhn Professor of Biological Chemistry and Molecular Pharmacology (Medical School); Ph.D., Rockefeller, 1970. Molecular basis of biological catalysis, with focus on the structure and function of enzymes; biosynthesis and mechanism of action of antibiotics and bacterial siderophores.

100   www.facebook.com/petersonspublishing

*Peterson's Graduate Programs in the Physical Sciences, Mathematics,
Agricultural Sciences, the Environment & Natural Resources 2012*

KENT STATE UNIVERSITY

Department of Chemistry and Biochemistry

Programs of Study

The Department of Chemistry and Biochemistry offers programs leading to the Master of Science (M.S.) and Doctor of Philosophy (Ph.D.) degrees in the traditional divisions of analytical, inorganic, organic, and physical chemistry and biochemistry. A variety of interdisciplinary areas are covered in bioanalytical chemistry, bioinorganic chemistry, biophysics, and molecular/cell biology. Faculty members also have research interests in the specialty areas of liquid crystals, photonic materials, spectroscopy, nanomaterials, separations, and surface science.

Graduate students are required to complete a program of core courses in their area of specialization and at least one (for M.S. candidates) or two (for Ph.D. candidates) elective courses in other areas of chemistry. The extraordinary breadth of the program gives students considerable flexibility in curriculum design, ensuring a modern and dynamic graduate education. At the end of the second year, doctoral students must pass a written examination in their field of specialization and defend an original research proposal for their dissertation. Students typically complete their doctoral program with their thesis defense after 4.5 years.

Research Facilities

Kent State University is home to excellent research facilities. The chemistry department has advanced NMR, X-ray, mass spectrometry, and proteomics core facilities. Research laboratories are located primarily in Williams Hall and the attached Science Research Laboratory. In addition, excellent materials' characterization facilities and one of the largest academic clean room facilities in the nation are housed in the nearby Liquid Crystal Institute. A confocal microscopy core facility located in the biology department is also available to chemistry students. Williams Hall houses two large lecture halls, classrooms, undergraduate and research laboratories, the Chemistry-Physics Library, chemical stockrooms, and glass and electronics shops. A machine shop, which is jointly operated with the physics department, is located in adjoining Smith Hall. Spectrometers include 500-MHz, 400-MHz (solids), and 300-MHz high-resolution NMR instruments; electrospray, MALDI-TOF, LC/ESI, protein chip SELDI mass spectrometers; various high-end FT-IR spectrometers, including a focal plane array FT-IR microscope for spectroscopic imaging; photon-counting fluorometer; circular dichroism; ESR, FPLC, UV/visible spectrometers; AA/AE equipment; and an EDX-700 energy dispersive X-ray spectrometer. An X-ray facility includes a Siemens D5000 Powder diffractometer and a Bruker AXS CCD instrument for single-crystal structural elucidation. Equipment available in specialty areas includes a microwave spectrometer, an LCQ electrospray mass spectrometer with MS/MS capability, a phosphorimager, Microcal VP DSC and ITC calorimeters, Bruker Vector 33 FTIR-NIR, Jobin Yvon Raman spectrometer with inverted microscope, laser tweezer instrumentation, particle sizer, Cary Eclipse fluorescence spectrophotometer, MF^2 Jobin Yvon fluorescence lifetime spectrometer, fluorescence correlation spectrometer, ThermoFinnigan Polaris Q115W GC-MS, a BAS electrochemical analyzer, various preparative centrifuges, a molecular dynamic Typhoon 8600 imaging system, and PCR and DNA sequencing and cell culture facilities. Individual research groups in the Department of Chemistry and Biochemistry maintain a variety of computer systems, including PCs and workstations. High-performance computing is made possible with access to the Ohio Supercomputer Center, which maintains Cray T94, Cray T3E, IBM SP2, and SGI Origin 2000 supercomputers. The Department has advanced molecular modeling facilities, including Cerius, Felix, Hyperchem, InsightII/Discover, Macromodel, and Spartan packages for modeling surfaces and interfaces, polymers, proteins, and nucleic acids, as well as facilities for performing ab initio calculations of molecular properties and molecular dynamics. A 3-D immersive classroom equipped with a rear projection system that generates 6' x 7' three-dimensional images when viewed with shutter glasses is available in Williams Hall and is frequently used for a variety of graduate classes. The chemistry/physics library in Williams Hall provides online access to virtually all chemical/biochemical journals as well as a broad variety of chemical databases, including the Chemical Abstracts SciFinder Service.

Financial Aid

Graduate students are generously supported through teaching and research assistantships as well as University fellowships. Students in good academic standing are guaranteed appointments for periods of at least 4½ years (Ph.D. candidates) or 2½ years (M.S. candidates). Stipends for 2011–12 range from $18,000 (M.S.) to $20,000 (Ph.D.) for a twelve-month appointment. A $1010 credit is made toward the University's health insurance plan. First-year bonuses and renewable merit fellowships providing an additional $2500 per year are available to outstanding doctoral applicants. In addition, first-year bonuses of $1250 are available for highly talented students pursuing their Ph.D. in physical chemistry. Advanced Ph.D. students are typically funded through research assistantships ($20,000 or higher) provided by their respective advisors.

Cost of Study

Graduate tuition and fees for the 2011–12 academic year are $7232, for which a tuition scholarship is provided.

Living and Housing Costs

Rooms in the graduate hall of residence are $2515 to $3360 per semester; married students' apartments may be rented for $669 to $699 per month (all utilities included). Information concerning off-campus housing may be obtained from the University housing office. Costs vary widely, but apartments typically rent for $500 to $600 per month.

Student Group

The ethnically diverse and highly talented chemistry graduate student population currently numbers about 45. There are approximately 23,000 students enrolled at the main campus of Kent State University; 12,000 additional students attend the seven regional campuses.

Location

Kent, a college town of about 28,000, is located 35 miles southeast of Cleveland and 12 miles east of Akron in a peaceful suburban setting. Kent offers the cultural advantages of a major metropolitan complex as well as the relaxed pace of semirural living. There are a number of music (e.g., Kent State's folk festival and free chamber music concerts in the summer), theater, and visual art groups at the University and in the community. Blossom Music Center, the summer home of the Cleveland Orchestra and the site of Kent State's cooperative programs in art, music, and theater, is only 15 miles from the main campus. This beautiful outdoor concert venue is also the site for many critically acclaimed rock concerts throughout the summer months. The newly expanded Akron and Cleveland art museums are within easy reach of the campus. Cleveland is also the home of the world-renowned Rock and Roll Hall of Fame and several professional sport teams. There are a wide variety of recreational facilities available on the campus and within the local area, including West Branch State Park and the Cuyahoga Valley National Park. Nearby Lake Erie and its beaches offer a broad range of water recreational activities. Winter activities include ice skating as well as downhill and cross-country skiing. Kent State's state-of-the-art recreation and wellness center is available for graduate students free of charge.

The University

Established in 1910, Kent State University is one of Ohio's largest and oldest state universities. The campus contains 820 acres of wooded hillsides plus an airport and an eighteen-hole golf course. There are approximately 100 buildings on the main campus. Bachelor's, master's, and doctoral degrees are offered in more than thirty subject areas. The full-time faculty numbers approximately 1,200.

Applying

The online application system for the graduate program is located at: http://www.kent.edu/admissions/apply/. To ensure full consideration, candidates for admission for the upcoming fall semester should make certain that all their application material is received by the University no later than January 10. However, applications will be accepted until all positions are filled. In the case that late applications cannot be considered for fall admission, they will be automatically considered for admission the following spring semester. A limited number of positions are available for spring admission. Candidates should ensure that their application package is complete no later than September 1.

Application material must include all pertinent transcripts, general GRE exam, personal statement, three letters of recommendation, and a CV/resume. Domestic applicants can send all application materials to: Research and Graduate Studies, Office of Graduate Services, 16 Cartwright Hall, Kent State University, P. O. Box 5190, Kent, Ohio 44242-0001.

Foreign students must also provide TOEFL or IELTS exam scores. The minimum cutoff for the TOEFL is 525 on the paper-based exam, and 71 on the Internet-based test. The minimum cutoff for the IELTS is a score of six. Although the subject GRE is not required, candidates are encouraged to provide a subject GRE to strengthen their file. International applicants can send all application materials to: Office of International Affairs, Kent State University, 106 Van Campen Hall, 21 Loop Road, Kent, Ohio 44242, U.S.A.

Correspondence and Information

General Correspondence:

Graduate Coordinator
Department of Chemistry and Biochemistry
Kent State University
Kent, Ohio 44242

Phone: 330-672-2032
Fax: 330-672-3816
E-mail: chemgc@kent.edu
Web site: http://www.kent.edu/chemistry

Kent State University

THE FACULTY AND THEIR RESEARCH

Research groups are supported through grants awarded by the National Science Foundation, the National Institutes of Health, the Department of Energy, the Department of Defense, and other federal and state funding agencies.

Soumitra Basu, Assistant Professor; Ph.D., Thomas Jefferson, 1996. Biochemistry: molecular modulation of RNA function, anticancer therapeutics using RNAi, alternative translation modes with implications for tumor angiogenesis, chemical modification of RNA, toxicoribonomics.

Nicola E. Brasch, Associate Professor; Ph.D., Otago (New Zealand), 1994. Bioinorganic and medicinal chemistry; vitamin B_{12} and the B_{12}-dependent enzyme reactions; vanadium chemistry; inorganic drug delivery systems; synthesis, kinetics, and mechanism.

Scott D. Bunge, Assistant Professor; Ph.D., Georgia Tech, 2001. Inorganic chemistry: molecular design, organometallics, coordination chemistry, air-sensitive synthesis, catalysis, X-ray crystallography, thin films, nanomaterials.

Bansidhar Datta, Associate Professor; Ph.D., Nebraska–Lincoln, 1989. Biochemistry and molecular biology: mechanism of protein synthesis initiation in mammals; studies of posttranslational modifications, such as O-glycosylation and phosphorylation of translational regulator, p67; molecular cloning of translational regulatory proteins; studies of the evolutionary origins of the regulatory/structural domains in p67.

Edwin S. Gould, University Professor; Ph.D., UCLA, 1950. Inorganic chemistry: mechanisms of inorganic redox reactions; catalysis of redox reactions by organic species; electron-transfer reactions of flavin-related systems; reactions of cobalt, chromium, vanadium, titanium, europium, uranium, ruthenium, indium, peroxynitrous acid, and trioxodinitrate; reactions of water-soluble radical species.

Roger B. Gregory, Professor; Ph.D., Sheffield (England), 1980. Biochemistry: protein conformational dynamics; the characterization of dynamic substructures in proteins; protein hydration and glass transition behavior; proteomics: development and application of high-sensitivity methods for protein characterization, including protein-protein interactions and protein chemical modifications.

Songping D. Huang, Associate Professor; Ph.D., Michigan State, 1993. Inorganic chemistry: molecule-based magnetic and nonlinear optical materials, organic conductors and superconductors, novel microporous and mesoporous materials, synthesis and crystal growth of metal oxides and chalcogenides.

Mietek Jaroniec, Professor; Ph.D., Lublin (Poland), 1976. Physical/analytical/materials chemistry: adsorption and chromatography at the gas/solid and liquid/solid interface; synthesis and modification of adsorbents, catalysts, and chromatographic packings with tailored surface and structural properties; self-assembled organic-inorganic nanomaterials; ordered mesoporous carbons synthesized via templating and imprinting methods; characterization of nanoporous materials.

Anatoly K. Khitrin, Associate Professor; Ph.D., Institute of Chemical Physics, Russian Academy of Sciences, 1985. Physical chemistry: NMR techniques, theory of magnetic resonance, material science, quantum computing and microimaging.

Hanbin Mao, Assistant Professor; Ph.D., Texas A&M, 2003. Bioanalytical and biophysical chemistry: micro total analysis systems ("lab-on-a-chip"), laser and magnetic tweezers, single-molecule DNA and DNA-protein interactions, drug-screening.

Paul Sampson, Professor; Ph.D., Birmingham (England), 1983. Synthetic organic chemistry: development of new synthetic methods; synthetic (stereoselective) organofluorine chemistry, with applications to the synthesis of fluorinated liquid crystals and carbohydrate analogs; development of new organometallic synthons as building blocks for organic synthesis.

Alexander J. Seed, Associate Professor; Ph.D., Hull (England), 1995. Organic chemistry, design, synthesis, and physical characterization of liquid crystals; ferroelectric, antiferroelectric, and high-twisting power materials for optical applications; new heterocyclic synthetic methodology.

Diane Stroup, Associate Professor; Ph.D., Ohio State, 1992. Biochemistry: control of mammalian gene expression by regulation of transcriptional and posttranscriptional processes, study of nuclear hormone receptors and signal transduction events.

Chun-che Tsai, Professor; Ph.D., Indiana, 1968. Biochemistry: interaction of drugs with nucleic acids; structure and activity of anticancer drugs, antiviral agents, antibiotic drugs, and interferon inducers; structure and biological function relationships; X-ray diffraction; quantitative structure-activity relationships (QSAR); molecular and drug design.

Michael J. Tubergen, Associate Professor; Ph.D., Chicago, 1991. Physical chemistry: high-resolution microwave spectroscopy for molecular structure determination of hydrogen-bonded complexes and biological molecules.

Robert J. Twieg, Distinguished Professor; Ph.D., Berkeley, 1976. Organic chemistry and materials science: development of organic and polymeric materials with novel electronic and optoelectronic properties, including nonlinear optical chromophores, photorefractive chromophores, organic semiconductors, fluorescent tags, and liquid crystals, with emphasis on applications and durability issues.

John L. West, Professor; Ph.D., Carnegie Mellon, 1980. Physical chemistry: materials science; liquid crystal polymer formulations for display applications, basic studies of liquid crystal alignment.

102   www.facebook.com/petersonspublishing

Peterson's Graduate Programs in the Physical Sciences, Mathematics, Agricultural Sciences, the Environment & Natural Resources 2012

SELECTED PUBLICATIONS

Basu, S., and S. A. Strobel. Identification of specific monovalent metal ion binding sites within RNA. *Methods* 122:264–75, 2001.

Basu, S., A. Szewczak, M. Cocco, and S. A. Strobel. Direct detection of specific monovalent metal ion binding to a DNA G-quartet by ^{205}T1 NMR. *J. Am. Chem. Soc.* 122:3240–1, 2000.

Basu, S., and S. A. Strobel. Thiophilic metal ion rescue of phosphorothioate interference within the Tetrahymena ribozyme P4-P6 domain. *RNA* 5:1399–407, 1999.

Hannibal, L., C. A. Smith, D. W. Jacobsen, and **N. E. Brasch.** Nitroxylcob(III)alamin: Synthesis and X-ray structural characterization. *Angew. Chem.* 46:5140, 2007.

Hannibal, L., et al. **(N. E. Brasch).** X-ray structural characterization of imidazolylcobalamin and histidinylcobalamin: Cobalamin models for aquacobalamin bound to the B_{12} transporter protein transcobalamin. *Inorg. Chem.* 46:3613, 2007.

Mukherjee, R., et al. **(N. E. Brasch).** Structural and spectroscopic evidence for the formation of trinuclear and tetranuclear V(III)/carboxylate complexes of acetate and related derivatives in aqueous solution. *Inorg. Chem.* 46:1575, 2007.

Bunge, S. D., J. A. Bertke, and T. L. Cleland. Synthesis, structure, and reactivity of low-coordinate 1,1,3,3-tetraethylguanidinate complexes. *Inorg. Chem.* 48(16):8037–43, 2009.

Bunge, S. D., J. A. Ocana, T. L. Cleland, and J. L. Steele. Synthetic, structural, and theoretical investigation of guanidinate complexes containing planar Cu_6 cores. *Inorg. Chem.* 48(11):4619–21, 2009.

Monegan, J. D., and **S. D. Bunge.** Structurally characterized 1,1,3,3-tetramethylguanidine solvated magnesium aryloxide complexes: [Mg(μ-OEt)(DBP)(H-TMG)]$_2$, [Mg(μ -OBc)(DBP)(H-IMG)]$_2$, [Mg(μ -TMBA)(DBP)(H-TMG)]$_2$, [Mg(μ -DPP)(DBP)(H-TMG)]$_2$, [Mg(BMP)$_2$(H-TMG)$_2$], [Mg(O-2,6-Ph$_2$C$_6$H$_3$)$_2$ (H-TMG)$_2$]. *Inorg. Chem.* 48(7):3248–56, 2009.

Datta, B., et al. Autoproteolysis of rat p67 generates several peptide fragments: The N-terminal fragment, p26, is required for the protection of eIF2 alpha from phosphorylation. *Biochemistry* 46(11):3465, 2007.

Ghosh A., et al. **(B. Datta).** The N-terminal lysine residue-rich domain II and the 340-430 amino acid segment of eukaryotic initiation factor 2-associated glycoprotein p67 are the binding sites for the gamma subunit of eIF2. *Exp. Cell Res.* 312(16):3184, 2006.

Datta, B., et al. The binding between p67 and eukaryotic initiation factor 2 plays important roles in the protection of eIF2 alpha from phosphorylation by kinases. *Arch. Biochem. Biophys.* 452(2):138, 2006.

Mukherjee, R., Z. Y. Yang, and **E. S. Gould.** Reductions by titanium(II) as catalyzed by titanium(IV). *Dalton Trans.* 6:772, 2006.

Yang, Z. Y., and **E. S. Gould.** Reactions of molybdenum(VI) with metal ion reductants. *Dalt. Trans.* 28:3427, 2006.

Yang, Z., and **E. S. Gould.** Electron transfer. 160. Reductions by aquatitanium(II). *Dalton Trans.* 1781, 2005.

Roh, J. H., et al. **(R. B. Gregory).** Influence of hydration on the dynamics of lysozyme. *Biophys. J.* 91(7):2573, 2006.

Roh, J. H., et al. **(R. B. Gregory).** Onsets of anharmonicity in protein dynamics. *Phys. Rev. Lett.* 95(3): 038101, 2005.

Gregory, R. B. Protein hydration and glass transitions. In *The Properties of Water in Foods*, pp. 55–99, ed. D. Reid. New York: Chapman-Hall, 1997.

Fu, D. W., et al. **(S. D. Huang).** Dielectric anisotropy of a homochiral trinuclear nickel(II) complex. *J. Am. Chem. Soc.* 129(17):5346, 2007.

Ye, Q., et al. **(S. D. Huang).** Ferroelectric metal-organic framework with a high dielectric constant. *J. Am. Chem. Soc.* 128(20):6554, 2006.

Vanchura, B. A., et al. **(S. D. Huang).** Direct synthesis of mesostructured lamellar molybdenum disulfides using a molten neutral n-alkylamine as the solvent and template. *J. Am. Chem. Soc.* 124(41):12090, 2002.

Celer, E. B., and **M. Jaroniec.** Temperature-programmed microwave-assisted synthesis of SBA-15 ordered mesoporous silica. *J. Am. Chem. Soc.* 128(44):14408, 2006.

Gierszal, K. P., and **M. Jaroniec.** Carbons with extremely large volume of uniform mesopores synthesized by carbonization of phenolic resin film formed on colloidal silica template. *J. Am. Chem. Soc.* 128(31):10026, 2006.

Jaroniec, M. Materials science: Organosilica the conciliator. *Nature* 442(7103):638, 2006.

Lee, J. S., T. Adams, and **A. K. Khitrin.** Experimental demonstration of a stimulated polarization wave in a chain of nuclear spins. *New J. Phys.* 9(4): 83, 2007.

Lee, J. S., and **A. K. Khitrin.** Constant-time method for measuring inter-nuclear distances in static powders. *J. Magn. Reson.* 186:327, 2007.

Lee, J. S., and **A. K. Khitrin.** NMR quantum toys. *Concepts Magn. Reson.* 30A:194, 2007.

Luchette, P., N. Abiy, and **H. Mao.** Microanalysis of clouding process at the single droplet level. *Sensor. Actuator B Chem.* 128:154–60, 2007.

Mao, H., et al. Temperature control methods in a laser-tweezers system. *Biophys. J.* 89:1308, 2005.

Mao, H., P. Cremer, and M. Manson. A versatile, sensitive microfluidic assay for bacterial chemotaxis. *Proc. Natl. Acad. Sci. U.S.A.* 100:5449, 2003.

Chumachenko, N., and **P. Sampson.** Synthesis of beta-hydroxy sulfones via opening of hydrophilic epoxides with zinc sulfinates in aqueous media. *Tetrahedron* 62(18):4540, 2006.

Novikov, Y. Y., and **P. Sampson.** 1-bromo-1-lithioethene: A practical reagent in organic synthesis. *J. Org. Chem.* 70(25):10247, 2005.

Chumachenko, N., **P. Sampson,** A. D. Hunter, and M. Zeller. β-acyloxysulfonyl tethers for intramolecular Diels-Alder cycloaddition reactions. *Org. Lett.* 7:3203, 2005.

Sybo, B., et al. **(P. Sampson** and **A. J. Seed).** 1,3,4-Thiadiazole-2-carboxylate esters: New synthetic methodology for the preparation of an elusive family of self-organizing materials. *J. Mater. Chem.* 17(32):3406–11, 2007.

Seed, A. J. Synthesis of self-organizing mesogenic materials containing a sulfur-based five-membered heterocyclic core. *Chem. Soc. Rev.* 36(12):2046–69, 2007.

McCoy, B. K., et al. **(A. J. Seed).** Smectic-C^*_α phase with two coexistent helical pitch values and a first-order smectic-C^*_α to smectic-C^* transition. *Phys. Rev. E* 75(5-1): 051706, 2007.

Docherty, J., et al. **(C. C. Tsai).** In vivo anti-herpes simplex virus activity of resveratrol, a cyclin dependent kinase gene inhibitor. *Antivir. Res.* 57(3):86, 2003.

Tsai, C. C., et al. In vivo and in vitro antiherpetic effects of hydroxytolans. *Antivir. Res.* 57(3):87, 2003.

Peterson's Graduate Programs in the Physical Sciences, Mathematics, Agricultural Sciences, the Environment & Natural Resources 2012

www.facebook.com/petersonspublishing   **103**

Kent State University

Nassiri, M. R., et al. **(C. C. Tsai).** The activity of Mg2+ and poly r(A-U) against HIV-I. *Antivir. Res.* 46(1):32, 2000.

Tubergen, M. J., et al. Rotational spectra and conformational structures of 1-phenyl-2-propanol, methamphetamine, and 1-phenyl-2-propanone. *J. Phys. Chem. A* 110(49):13188, 2006.

Tubergen, M. J., et al. Rotational spectra, nuclear quadrupole hyperfine tensors, and conformational structures of the mustard gas simulent 2-chloroethyl ethyl sulfide. *J. Mol. Spectros.* 233(2):180, 2005.

Tubergen, M. J., C. R. Torok, and R. J. Lavrich. Effect of solvent on molecular conformation: Microwave spectra and structures of 2-aminoethanol van der Waals complexes. *J. Chem. Phys.* 119:8397–403, 2003.

Wang, H., et al. **(R. J. Twieg).** The influence of tetrahydroquinoline rings in dicyanomethylenedihydrofuran (DCDHF) single-molecule fluorophores. *Tetrahedron* 63(1):103, 2007.

Lu, Z. K.; et al. **(R. J. Twieg).** Long-wavelength analogue of PRODAN: Synthesis and properties of Anthradan, a fluorophore with a 2,6-donor-acceptor anthracene structure. *J. Org. Chem.* 71(26):9651, 2006.

Ellman, B., et al. **(R. J. Twieg).** High mobility, low dispersion hole transport in 1,4-diiodobenzene. *Adv. Mater.* 18(17):2284, 2006.

Li, F. H., et al. **(J. West).** Orientational coupling amplification in ferroelectric nematic colloids. *Phys. Rev. Lett.* 97(14): 147801, 2006.

Buyuktanir, E. A., et al. **(J. L. West).** Field-induced polymer wall formation in a bistable smectic-A liquid crystal display. *Appl. Phys. Lett.* 89(3): 031101, 2006.

West, J. L., et al. Colloidal particles at a nematic-isotropic interface: Effects of confinement. *Eur. Phys. J. E* 20(2):237, 2006.

104 www.facebook.com/petersonspublishing

Peterson's Graduate Programs in the Physical Sciences, Mathematics, Agricultural Sciences, the Environment & Natural Resources 2012

PRINCETON UNIVERSITY

Department of Chemistry

Programs of Study	The Department of Chemistry offers a program of study leading to the degree of Doctor of Philosophy. The graduate program emphasizes research, and students enter a research group by the end of the first semester. Students are required to take six graduate courses in chemistry and allied areas, satisfying at least four of ten areas of distribution, and are expected to participate in the active lecture and seminar programs throughout their graduate careers.
	Early in the second year, students take a general examination that consists of an oral defense of a thesis-related subject. Presentation of an original research proposal, unrelated to the thesis research, is also required. Upon satisfactory completion of these steps, students advance to candidacy for the degree of Doctor of Philosophy in chemistry. The degree is awarded primarily on the basis of a thesis describing original research in one of the areas of chemistry. The normal length of the entire Ph.D. program is four to five years.
	Programs of graduate study in materials and neuroscience are also offered, in cooperation with other science departments at Princeton University.
Research Facilities	In fall 2010, the department moved to a new, state-of-the-art chemistry building designed by Hopkins Architects, a London-based firm that has earned numerous awards for its work in the United Kingdom. The new building is adjacent to the physics, molecular biology, and mathematics departments as well as the Lewis-Siegler Genomics Institute. A wide variety of research instrumentation is available, both in the departmental instrument facility and in individual faculty members' laboratories. This instrumentation includes NMR; ESR; mass spectrometry (high-resolution and gas chromatograph integrated); and visible, ultraviolet, and infrared spectrometers. Recent instrument acquisitions include three 500 MHz NMRs with cryoprobes and autosamplers, a high resolution ESI-TOF mass spectrometer, an LC-interfaced Q-TOF mass spectrometer for proteomics studies, a fast LC-triple quadrupole mass spectrometer, and a suite of bench-top FT-IR spectrometers for routine analysis. There is research equipment for ultrahigh vacuum surface studies, including electron diffraction and electron spectroscopy equipment. Tunable and fixed wavelength laser sources, gas and liquid chromatographic equipment, X-ray diffraction facilities, and controlled atmosphere dry boxes also are available to students.
Financial Aid	All admitted students receive funding during the normal period of study, usually five years. This funding covers tuition, health insurance, and a maintenance allowance, typically in the form of assistantships in instruction or research. In 2011–12, students earn $22,290 to $26,550 during the ten-month academic year, plus a summer stipend of $5000. First-year graduate students are not required to teach, as they receive fellowship funds that allow them to concentrate on course work.
Cost of Study	See the Financial Aid section.
Living and Housing Costs	Rooms at the Graduate College cost from $4212 to $7278 for the 2011–12 academic year of thirty-five weeks. Several meal plans are available, priced from $3305 to $5498. University apartments for both single and married students currently rent for $704 to $2020 per month. Accommodations are also available in the surrounding community.
Student Group	The total number of graduate students in chemistry is currently about 150. Postdoctoral students number about 80. A wide variety of academic, ethnic, and national backgrounds is represented among these students.
Location	Princeton University and the surrounding community together provide an ideal environment for learning and research. From the point of view of a chemist at the University, the engineering, physics, mathematics, and molecular biology departments, as well as the plasma physics lab on the Forrestal campus, provide valuable associates, supplementary facilities, and sources of special knowledge. Many corporations have research laboratories near Princeton, leading to fruitful collaborations, seminars and lecture series, and employment opportunities after graduation.
	Because of the nature of the institutions located here, the small community of Princeton has a very high proportion of professional people. To satisfy the needs of this unusual community, the intellectual and cultural activities approach the number and variety ordinarily found only in large cities, but with the advantage that everything is within walking distance. There are many film series, a resident repertory theater, orchestras, ballet, and chamber music and choral groups. Scientific seminars and other symposia bring prominent visitors from every field of endeavor.
	Princeton's picturesque countryside provides a pleasant area for work and recreation, yet New York City and Philadelphia are each only about an hour away.
The University	Princeton University was founded in 1746 as the College of New Jersey. At its 150th anniversary in 1896, the trustees changed the name to Princeton University. The Graduate School was organized in 1901 and has since won international recognition in mathematics, the natural sciences, philosophy, and the humanities.
Applying	Application instructions, including the online application, are available at http://www.princeton.edu/gradschool/admission/. The application deadline for the Department of Chemistry is December 15 for all applicants. All applications must be done online and accompanied by an application fee, which is $90 for applications in fall of 2011 for admission in fall of 2012. There is no spring admission period.
	Admission consideration is given to all candidates without regard to race, color, national origin, religion, sex, or handicap.
Correspondence and Information	Sallie Dunner Graduate Administrator Department of Chemistry Frick Chemistry Laboratory Princeton University Princeton, New Jersey 08544 Phone: 609-258-4116 E-mail: sdunner@princeton.edu Web site: http://www.princeton.edu/chemistry

Peterson's Graduate Programs in the Physical Sciences, Mathematics, Agricultural Sciences, the Environment & Natural Resources 2012

www.facebook.com/petersonspublishing **105**

Princeton University

THE FACULTY AND THEIR RESEARCH

The faculty members represent all major areas of chemistry, and there is much interdisciplinary and collaborative research both within the Department and with other departments and programs in the University. The following list briefly indicates the areas of interest of each professor.

S. L. Bernasek. Chemical physics of surfaces: basic studies of chemisorption on well-characterized transition-metal surfaces using electron diffraction and electron spectroscopy, surface reaction dynamics, heterogeneous catalysis.

A. B. Bocarsly. Inorganic materials chemistry, chemistry of alternate energy systems, chemical mitigation of carbon dioxide, electrochemistry, photochemistry, semiconductor photoelectrochemistry, coordination chemistry.

R. Car. Chemical physics and materials science; electronic structure theory and ab initio molecular dynamics; computer modeling and simulation of solids, liquids, disordered systems, and molecular structures; structural phase transitions and chemical reactions.

J. Carey. Biophysical chemistry: protein and nucleic acid structure, function, and interactions; protein folding and stability.

R. J. Cava. Materials chemistry; synthesis of new oxide, intermetallic, pnictide, and chalcogenide compounds, and characterization of their crystal structures and electronic and magnetic properties.

P. J. Chirik. Inorganic, organometallic, and organic chemistry: Base metal catalysis directed toward commodity and fine chemical synthesis, energy-efficient methods for N_2 functionalization and understanding electronic structure of redox-active metal-ligand complexes.

A. G. Doyle. Organic and organometallic chemistry: discovery and development of new catalytic routes to chiral building blocks of importance in the enantioselective synthesis of natural products, pharmaceuticals, materials.

D. Fiedler. Chemical biology, bioinorganic chemistry: signaling functions of small molecule second messengers.

J. T. Groves. Bioorganic and bioinorganic chemistry, synthetic and mechanistic studies of reactions of biological interest, transition metal redox catalysis, models and mimics of metalloenzymes, biochemical mechanisms of protein nitration, the chemical biology of iron acquisition by siderophores and models of biological membranes.

M. Hecht. Biochemistry and chemical biology, protein folding and misfolding, protein design, synthetic biology, Alzheimer's disease.

R. Knowles. Synthetic organic chemistry, with an emphasis on stereoselective catalysis, unconventional redox processes, molecular recognition, and complex target.

D. W. C. MacMillan. Organic synthesis and catalysis: new concepts in synthetic organic chemistry involving organocatalysis, organo-cascade catalysis, metal-mediated catalysis, and total synthesis of natural products and pharmaceuticals.

T. W. Muir. Organic chemistry, biochemistry, and cell biology: investigating the physiochemical basis of protein function in complex systems of biomedical interest with new chemical biology technologies.

J. Rabinowitz. Biochemical kinetics, cellular metabolism, chemical basis of complex biological processes.

H. Rabitz. Physical chemistry, biomolecular modeling, laser control of molecular processes, molecular collisions, theory of chemical reactions, time- and space-dependent molecular manipulation.

C. E. Schutt. Structural biology, structure and function of proteins and cellular organelles, X-ray crystallography.

J. Schwartz. Organometallic chemistry, surface and interface organic and inorganic chemistry and their applications to biomaterials and electronic materials.

A. Selloni. Computational physics and chemistry and modeling of materials; structural, electronic, and dynamic properties of semiconductor and oxide surfaces; chemisorption and surface reactions.

M. F. Semmelhack. Organometallic and electrogenerated intermediates in organic synthesis, synthesis of unusual ring systems in natural and unnatural molecules.

Z. G. Soos. Chemical physics, electronic states of conjugated polymers and ion-radical solids, paramagnetic and charge transfer excitons, one-dimensional models.

E. J. Sorensen. Organic chemistry: chemical synthesis of bioactive natural products and molecular probes for biological research, bioinspired strategies for chemical synthesis, architectural self-constructions and novel methods for synthesis.

S. Torquato. Statistical mechanics and materials science; theory and computer simulations of disordered heterogeneous materials, liquids, amorphous solids, and biological materials; optimization in materials science; simulations of peptide binding; modeling the growth of tumors.

H. Yang. Physical chemistry, reaction dynamics in complex systems, development and application of single-molecule spectroscopy and methods to elucidate functional consequences in protein conformational dynamics in vitro and in living cells, self assembly of biological macromolecules and nanostructures, biofuels and basic sciences in sustainable energy solutions.

Associated Faculty

E. A. Carter, Department of Mechanical and Aerospace Engineering and of Applied and Computational Mathematics. Development of quantum mechanics-based methods to predict behavior of molecules and materials, with applications to combustion chemistry, nanoscale physics, and materials science, with a new emphasis on alternative energy research.

B. Bassler, Department of Molecular Biology. Cell-to-cell communication in bacteria.

B. Garcia. Department of Molecular Biology. Quantitative biochemistry applied to the analysis of chromatin and nuclear signaling proteins.

F. M. Hughson, Department of Molecular Biology. Biochemical and X-ray crystallographic studies of intracellular trafficking and bacterial quorum sensing.

B. Koel, Department of Chemical and Biological Engineering. Surface chemistry and interfacial processes: heterogeneous catalysis of hydrocarbon conversion, solar photochemistry, electrocatalytic processes, fuel cells, plasma-surface interactions, environmental remediation by iron nanoparticles.

M. Llinas, Department of Molecular Biology. Cellular metabolism, biochemistry, genomics, microbiology, parasitology.

M. C. McAlpine. Department of Mechanical and Aerospace Engineering. Materials science: nanotechnology and biomaterials-enabled approaches to addressing fundamental problems in medicine, energy, and flexible electronics.

F. M. M. Morel, Department of Geosciences. Environmental chemistry, trace metal geochemistry, metals-biota interactions.

S. M. Myneni, Department of Geosciences. Environmental chemistry, ion hydration and complexation, interfacial chemistry, X-ray spectroscopy.

J. Stock, Department of Molecular Biology. Protein chemistry, cell biology, pharmacology.

New Frick Chemistry Laboratory.

106 www.facebook.com/petersonspublishing

Peterson's Graduate Programs in the Physical Sciences, Mathematics, Agricultural Sciences, the Environment & Natural Resources 2012

SELECTED PUBLICATIONS

Tao, F., G.-Q. Xu, and **(S. L. Bernasek).** Electronic and structural factors in modification and functionalization of clean and passivated semiconductor surfaces with aromatic systems. *Chem. Rev.* 109(9):3991–4024, 2009.

Peng, T. L., and **S. L. Bernasek.** The internal energy of CO_2 produced by the catalytic oxidation of CH_3OH by O_2 on polycrystalline platinum. *J. Chem. Phys.* 131(15):154701–10, 2009.

Oncel, N. and **S. L. Bernasek.** Ni(II)- and vanadyloctaethylporphyrin self-assembled layers formed on bare and 5-(octadecyloxy)isophthalic acid covered graphite. *Langmuir* 25(16):9290–5, 2009.

Bhargava, G., T. A. Ramanarayanan, and **S. L. Bernasek.** Imidazole-Fe interaction in an aqueous chloride medium: Effect of cathodic reduction of the native oxide. *Langmuir* 26(1):215–9, 2009.

McDermott, J. E., et al. **(S. L. Bernasek** and **J. Schwartz).** Organophosphonate self-assembled monolayers for gate dielectric surface modification of pentacene-based organic thin-film transistors: A comparative study. *J. Phys. Chem.* 111(49):12333–8, 2007.

Burgess, C. M., N. Yao, and **A. B. Bocarsly.** Stabilizing cyanosols: Amorphous cyanide bridged transition metal polymer nanoparticles. *J. Mat. Chem.* 19(46):8846–55, 2009.

Barton, E. E., D. M. Rampulla, and **A. B. Bocarsly.** Selective solar-driven reduction of CO_2 to methanol using a catalyzed p-GaP based photoelectrochemical cell. *J. Am. Chem. Soc.* 130(20):6342–4, 2008.

Majsztrik, P., **A. B. Bocarsly,** and J. Benziger. Water permeation through nafion membranes: The role of water activity. *J. Phys. Chem. B* 112(51):16280–9, 2008.

Vondrova, M., et al. **(A. B. Bocarsly).** Autoreduction of Pd-Co and Pt-Co cyanogels: Exploration of cyanometalate coordination chemistry at elevated temperatures. *J. Am. Chem. Soc.* 130(16):5563–72, 2008.

Melichercik, S. R., et al. **(J. Carey).** Symmetric allosteric mechanism of hexameric *Escherichia coli* arginine repressor exploits competition between L-arginine ligands and resident arginine residues. *PLoS Computational Biology* 6(6):e1000801, 2010.

Lapkouski, M., et al. **(J. Carey).** Structure of the motor subunit of type I restriction-modification complex EcoR124I. *Nat. Struct. Mol. Biol.* 16:94–5, 2008.

Carey, J., et al. WrbA bridges bacterial flavodoxins and eukaryotic NAD(P)H:quinone oxidoreductases. *Protein Sci.* 16(10):2301–5, 2007.

Chwee, T. S., and **E. A. Carter.** Cholesky decomposition within local multireference singles and doubles configuration interaction. *J. Chem. Phys.* 132(7):074104–14, 2010.

Huang, C., and **E. A. Carter.** Nonlocal orbital-free kinetic energy density functional for semiconductors. *Phys. Rev. B* 81(4):045206–21, 2010.

Sharifzadeh, S., P. Huang, and **E. A. Carter.** Origin of tunneling lineshape trends for Kondo states of Co adatoms on coinage metal surfaces. *J. Phys. Condens. Matter* 21(35):355501, 2009.

McQueen, T.M., et. al. **(R. J. Cava).** Tetragonal-to-orthorhombic structural phase transition at 90K in the superconductor $Fe_{1.01}Se$. *Phys. Rev. Lett.* 103(5):057002, 2009.

McQueen, T. M., et al. **(R. J. Cava, R. A. Pascal, Jr.,** and **Z. G. Soos).** Realization of the bond order wave (BOW) phase of extended Hubbard models in Rb-TCNQ(II). *Chem. Phys. Lett.* 475(1–3):44–8, 2009.

West, D.V. et. al. **(R. J. Cava).** The $A^{2+}Mn_5(SO_4)_6$ family of triangular lattice, ferrimagnetic sulfates. *J. Solid State Chem.* 182(6):1343–50, 2009.

Klimczuk, T., et. al. **(R. J. Cava).** Superconductivity at 2.2 K in the layered oxypnictide $La_3Ni_4P_4O_2$. *Phys. Rev. B* 79(1):012505, 2009.

Kalow, J. A., and **Doyle, A. G.** Enantioselective ring opening of epoxides by fluoride anion promoted by a cooperative dual-catalyst system. *J. Am. Chem. Soc.* 132(10):3268–9, 2010.

Zee, B. M., et al. **(B. A. Garcia).** In vivo residue-specific histone methylation dynamics. *J. Biol. Chem.* 285(5):3341–50, 2010.

Zee, B. M., and **B. A. Garcia.** Electron transfer dissociation facilitates sequencing of adenosine diphosphate-ribosylated peptides. *Anal. Chem.* 82(1):28–31, 2010.

Young, N. L., et al. **(B. A. Garcia).** High throughput characterization of combinatorial histone codes. *Mol. Cell. Proteomics* 8(10):2266–84, 2009.

LeRoy, G., et al. **(B. A. Garcia).** Heterochromatin protein 1 is extensively decorated with histone code-like post-translational modifications. *Mol. Cell. Proteomics* 8(11):2432–42, 2009.

Bell, S. R., and **J. T. Groves.** A highly reactive P450 model compound I. *J. Am. Chem. Soc.* 131(28):9640–1, 2009.

Su, J., and **J. T. Groves.** Direct detection of the oxygen rebound intermediates, ferryl Mb and NO_2, in the reaction of metMyoglobin with peroxynitrite. *J. Am. Chem. Soc.* 131(36):12979–88, 2009.

Austin, R. N., et al. **(J. T. Groves).** Cage escape competes with geminate recombination during alkane hydroxylation by the diiron oxygenase AlkB. *Angew. Chem.* 47(28):5232–4, 2008, doi:10.1002/anie.200801184.

Jin, N., M. Ibrahim, T. G. Spiro, and **J. T. Groves.** Trans-dioxo manganese(V) porphyrins. *J. Am. Chem. Soc.* 129(41):12416–7, 2007.

Patel, S., L. H. Bradley, S. Jinadasa, and **M. H. Hecht.** Cofactor binding and enzymatic activity in an unevolved superfamily of de novo designed 4-helix bundle proteins. *Protein Sci.* 18(7):1388–1400, 2009.

Kim, W., and **M. H. Hecht.** Mutations enhance the aggregation propensity of the Alzheimer's Aβ peptide. *J. Mol. Biol.* 377(2):565–74, 2008.

Go, A., S. Kim, J. Baum, and **M. H. Hecht.** Structure and dynamics of de novo proteins from a designed superfamily of 4-helix bundles. *Protein Sci.* 17(5):821–32, 2008.

Kim, W., et al. **(M. H. Hecht.)** A high throughput screen for compounds that inhibit aggregation of the Alzheimer's peptide. *ACS Chemical Biology* 1(7):461–9, 2006.

Hecht, M. H., et al. De novo proteins from designed combinatorial libraries. *Protein Sci.* 13(7):1711–23, 2004.

Richardson, B. C., et al. **(F. M. Hughson).** Structural basis for a human glycosylation disorder caused by mutation of the COG_4 gene. *Proc. Natl. Acad. Sci. Unit. States Am.* 106(32):13329–34, 2009.

Ren, Y., et al. **(F. M. Hughson).** A structure-based mechanism for vesicle capture by the multisubunit tethering complex Dsl1. *Cell* 139(6):1119–29, 2009.

Boer, V. M., et al. **(J. D. Rabinowitz).** Growth-limiting intracellular metabolites in yeast growing under diverse nutrient limitations. *Mol. Biol. Cell* 21(1):198–211, 2010.

Peterson's Graduate Programs in the Physical Sciences, Mathematics, Agricultural Sciences, the Environment & Natural Resources 2012

www.facebook.com/petersonspublishing   **107**

Princeton University

Lu, W., et al. **(J. D. Rabinowitz).** Metabolomic analysis via reversed-phase ion-pairing liquid chromatography coupled to a stand alone orbitrap mass spectrometer. *Anal. Chem.* 82(8):3212–21, 2010.

DiMaggio Jr., P. A., et al. **(J. D. Rabinowitz** and **H. A. Rabitz).** Enhancing molecular discovery using descriptor-free rearrangement clustering techniques for sparse data sets. *AIChE Journal* 56(2):405–18, 2010.

Kelly, R. C., et al. **(J. D. Rabinowitz, M. F. Semmelhack,** and **F. M. Hughson).** The *Vibrio cholerae* quorum-sensing autoinducer CAI-1: Analysis of the biosynthetic enzyme CqsA. *Nat. Chem. Biol.* 5:891–5, 2009.

Dang, L., et al. **(J. D. Rabinowitz).** Cancer-associated IDH1 mutations produce 2-hydroxyglutarate. *Nature* 462:739–44, 2009.

Bennett, B. D., et al. **(J. D. Rabinowitz).** Absolute metabolite concentrations and implied enzyme active site occupancy in *Escherichia coli. Nat. Chem. Biol.* 5:593–9, 2009.

Roth, M., et al. **(H. Rabitz).** Quantum control of tightly competitive product channels. *Phys. Rev. Lett.* 102(25):253001, 2009.

Yuan, J., et al. **(H. Rabitz** and **J. Rabinowitz).** Metabolomics-driven quantitative analysis of ammonia assimilation in *E. coli. Mol. Syst. Biol.* 5:302, 2009.

Hillberg, L., et al. **(C. E. Schutt).** Tropomyosins are present in lamellipodia of motile cells. *Eur. J. Cell Biol.* 85:399–409, 2006.

Schuler, H., R. Karlsson, **C. E. Schutt,** and U. Lindberg. The connection between actin ATPase and polymerization. *Adv. Mol. Cell Biol.* 37:49–66, 2006.

Traina, C. A., T. J. Dennes, and **J. Schwartz.** A modular monolayer coating enables cell targeting by luminescent yttria nanoparticles. *Bioconjugate Chem.* 20(3):437–9, 2009.

Dennes, T. J., and **J. Schwartz.** A nanoscale adhesion layer to promote cell attachment on PEEK. *J. Am. Chem. Soc.* 131(10):3456–7, 2009.

Liang, J., Q. Sun, **A. Selloni,** and **G. Scoles.** Side-by-side characterization of electron tunneling through monolayers of isomeric molecules: A combined experimental and theoretical study. *J. Phys. Chem. B* 110:24797, 2006.

Sun, Q., and **A. Selloni.** Interface and molecular electronic structure vs tunneling characteristics of CH3- and CF3-terminated thiol monolayers on Au(111). *J. Phys. Chem. A* 110:11396–400, 2006.

Gong, X., **A. Selloni,** M. Batzill, and U. Diebold. Steps on anatase TiO2(101). *Nat. Mater.* 5:665–70, 2006.

Miller, S. T., et al. **(M. F. Semmelhack** and **F. M. Hughson).** Salmonella typhimurium recognizes a chemically distinct form of the bacterial quorum sensing signal AI-2. *Mol. Cell* 15:677–87, 2004.

Semmelhack, **M. F.,** and R. J. Hooley. Palladium-catalyzed hydrostannylations of highly hindered acetyolenes in hexane. *Tetrahedron Lett.* 44:5737–9, 2003.

Semmelhack, **M. F.,** L. Wu, **R. A. Pascal Jr.,** and D. M. Ho. Conformational control in activation of an enediyne. *J. Am. Chem. Soc.* 125:10496–7, 2003.

D'Avino, G., et al. **(Z. G. Soos).** Anomalous dispersion of optical phonons at the neutral-ionic transition: Evidence from diffuse X-ray scattering. *Phys. Rev. Lett.* 99(15):156407, 2007.

Bewick, S. A., and **Z. G. Soos.** Peierls transitions in ionic organic charge-transfer crystals with spin and charge degrees of freedom. *J. Phys. Chem. B* 110(38):18748–57, 2006.

Anderson, E. A., E. J. Alexanian, and **E. J. Sorensen.** A synthesis of the furanosteroidal antibiotic viridian. *Angew. Chem. Int. Ed.* 43:1998–2001, 2004.

Adam, G. C., C. D. Vanderwal, **E. J. Sorensen,** and B. F. Cravatt. (-)-FR182877 is a potent and selective inhibitor of carboxylesterase-1. *Angew. Chem. Int. Ed.* 42:5480–4, 2003.

Vosburg, D. A., S. Weiler, and **E. J. Sorensen.** Concise stereocontrolled routes to fumagillol, fumagillin, and TNP-470. *Chirality* 15:156–66, 2003.

Vanderwal, C. D., D. A. Vosburg, S. Weiler, and **E. J. Sorensen.** An enantioselective synthesis of FR182877 provides a chemical rationalization of its structure and affords multigram quantities of its direct precursor. *J. Am. Chem. Soc.* 125:5393–407, 2003.

Li, Z., and **J. B. Stock.** Protein carboxyl methylation and the biochemistry of memory. *Biol. Chem.* 390(11):1087–96, 2009.

Xing, Y., et al. **(J. B. Stock).** Structural mechanism of demethylation and inactivation of protein phosphatase 2A. *Cell* 133(1):154–63, 2008.

Gordon, J. S., et al. **(J. B. Stock).** Topical N-acetyl-S-farnesyl-L-cysteine inhibits mouse skin inflammation, and unlike dexamethasone, its effects are restricted to the application site. *J. Invest. Dermatol.* 128(3):643–54, 2008.

Torquato, S., and Y. Jiao. Dense packings of the Platonic and Archimedean solids. *Nature* 460:876–9, 2009.

Batten, R. D., F. H. Stillinger, and **S. Torquato.** Interactions leading to disordered ground states and unusual low-temperature behavior. *Phys. Rev. E* 80(3):031105–29, 2009.

Torquato, S., and Y. Jiao. Dense packings of polyhedra: Platonic and Archimedean solids. *Phys. Rev. E* 80:041104–35, 2009.

Florescu, M., **S. Torquato,** and P. J. Steinhardt. Complete band gaps in two-dimensional photonic quasicrystals. *Phys. Rev. B* 80(15):155112–9, 2009.

Y. Jiaoa, F. H. Stillinger, and **S. Torquato.** A superior descriptor of random textures and its predictive capacity. *Proc. Natl. Acad. Sci. Unit. States Am.* 106(42):17634–9, 2009.

108 www.facebook.com/petersonspublishing

Peterson's Graduate Programs in the Physical Sciences, Mathematics, Agricultural Sciences, the Environment & Natural Resources 2012

UNIVERSITY OF PITTSBURGH

Department of Chemistry

Programs of Study

The Department offers programs of study leading to the M.S. and Ph.D. degrees in analytical, biological, inorganic, organic, and physical chemistry and in chemical physics. Interdisciplinary research is currently conducted in the areas of surface science, natural product synthesis, biological chemistry, bioanalytical chemistry, combinatorial chemistry, laser spectroscopy, materials science, electrochemistry, nanoscience, organometallic chemistry, and computational and theoretical chemistry. Both advanced degree programs involve original research and course work. Other requirements include a comprehensive examination, a thesis, a seminar, and, for the Ph.D. candidate, a proposal. For the typical Ph.D. candidate, this process takes four to five years. Representative of current research activities in the Department in analytical chemistry are techniques in electroanalytical chemistry, in vivo electrochemistry, UV resonance Raman spectroscopy, microseparations and nanoseparations, sensors and selective extraction, NMR, EPR, mass spectrometry, and vibrational circular dichroism. Fields of research in biological chemistry include structural dynamics of biological systems, design of soluble membrane proteins, neurochemistry, and molecular design and recognition. In inorganic chemistry, studies are being conducted on organo–transition-metal complexes, redox reactions, complexes of biological interest, transition-metal polymers, and optoelectronic materials; in organic chemistry, on reaction mechanisms, ion transport, total synthesis, drug design, natural products synthesis, bioorganic chemistry, synthetic methodology, organometallics, enzyme mechanisms, and physical-organic chemistry. Research areas in physical chemistry include Raman, photoelectron, Auger, NMR, EPR, infrared, and mass spectroscopy; electron-stimulated desorption ion angular distribution (ESDIAD); condensed-phase spectroscopy; high-resolution laser spectroscopy; molecular spectroscopy; electron and molecular beam scattering; electronic emission spectroscopy; and catalysis. Theoretical fields of research include electronic structure, reaction mechanisms, electron transfer theory, quantum mechanics, and new material design. Research on computer applications to chemistry is under way in a variety of areas.

Research Facilities

The Department of Chemistry is housed in two buildings, a fifteen-story and a three-story complex, containing a vast array of modern research instruments and in-house machine, electronics, and glassblowing shops. The Chemistry Library has access to more than 30,000 monographs and bound periodicals and more than 200 chemistry journal subscriptions. Online access is provided for full-text journals and important chemistry-related databases. In 2002, the Department of Chemistry received a five-year, $9.6-million grant from the National Institute of General Medical Sciences (NIGMS, a subdivision of NIH) to build one of the nation's first Centers for Excellence in Chemical Methods and Library Development. Shared Departmental instrumentation includes four 300-MHz NMRs, one 500-MHz NMR, and one 600-MHz NMR with LC-NMR and MAS capabilities; three high-resolution mass spectrometers; an LC/MS, a triple quadrupole MS, and four low-resolution mass spectrometers; a light-scattering instrument; a circular dichroism spectrophotometer; a spectropolarimeter; X-ray systems—single crystal, powder, small-angle scattering, and fluorescence; a scanning electron microscope; a vibrating sample magnetometer; several FT-IR and UV-VIS spectrophotometers; and computer and workstation clusters.

Financial Aid

Seventy teaching assistantships and teaching fellowships are available. The former provided $22,280 in 2010–11 for the three trimesters of the year; the fellowships (awarded to superior students after their first year) carried an annual stipend of $26,847. Most advanced students are supported by research assistantships and fellowships, which paid up to $2219 per month. All teaching assistantships, fellowships, and research assistantships include a full scholarship that covers all tuition, fees, and medical insurance. Special Arts and Sciences Fellowships are offered to qualified entering students to assist them in career development throughout their graduate studies. These fellowships consist of the following: (1) a stipend ($25,732) for the first year, during which the student receives two semesters of fellowship support and teaching experience through a one-semester TA appointment; (2) an academic spending account totaling $1500 for the purchase of books, software, or other items intended to advance the student's research endeavors; and funding for travel (up to $500) to a scientific meeting of the student's choosing; (3) up to $2000 for the purchase of a personal computer (Mac or PC, desktop or portable, including software); upon successful completion of the Ph.D. program at Pitt, the title of the computer will be transferred from the University to the student; and (4) a stipend of $1550 per month (up to $6200) for the summer term prior to enrollment in classes, allowing the student to conduct research in any Chemistry Department faculty member's laboratory (with mutual consent). Additional fellowships are partially provided through funds from Bayer BMS, Sunoco, and the Ashe Fund (University of Pittsburgh).

Cost of Study

All graduate assistants and fellows receive full-tuition scholarships. Tuition and fees for full-time study in 2010 were $15,127 per term for out-of-state students and $9002 for state residents.

Living and Housing Costs

Most graduate students prefer private housing, which is available in a wide range of apartments and rooms in areas of Pittsburgh near the campus. The University maintains a housing office to assist students seeking off-campus housing. Living costs compare favorably with other urban areas.

Student Group

The University enrolls about 17,000 students, including about 9,500 graduate and professional school students. Most parts of the United States and many other countries are represented. Almost 200 full-time graduate chemistry students are supported by the various sources listed under Financial Aid. The University is coeducational in all schools and divisions; more than one third of the graduate chemistry students are women. An honorary chemistry society promotes a social program for all faculty members and graduate students in the Department.

Location

Deservedly, Pittsburgh is currently ranked "among the most livable cities in the United States" by Rand McNally. It is recognized for its outstanding blend of cultural, educational, and technological resources. Pittsburgh's famous Golden Triangle is enclosed by the Allegheny and Monongahela Rivers, which meet at the Point in downtown Pittsburgh to form the Ohio River. Pittsburgh has enjoyed a dynamic renaissance in the last few years. The city's cultural resources include the Pittsburgh Ballet, Opera Company, Symphony Orchestra, Civic Light Opera, and Public Theatre and the Three Rivers Shakespeare Festival. Many outdoor activities, such as rock climbing, rafting, sailing, skiing, and hunting, are also available within a 50-mile radius.

The University

The University of Pittsburgh, founded in 1787, is the oldest school west of the Allegheny Mountains. Although privately endowed and controlled, the University is state related to permit lower tuition rates for Pennsylvania residents and to provide a steady source of funds for all of its programs. Attracting more than $310 million in sponsored research annually, the University has continued to increase in stature.

Applying

Applications for September admission and assistantships should be made prior to February 1. However, special cases may be considered throughout the year. A background that includes a B.S. degree in chemistry, with courses in mathematics through integral calculus, is preferred. GRE scores, including the chemistry Subject Test, are required for fellowship consideration (see the Financial Aid section). For admission, the General Test of the GRE is required, and the Subject Test in chemistry is suggested. International applicants must submit TOEFL, GRE Subject, and GRE test scores.

Correspondence and Information

Graduate Admissions
Department of Chemistry
University of Pittsburgh
Pittsburgh, Pennsylvania 15260

Phone: 412-624-8501
E-mail: gradadm@pitt.edu
Web site: http://www.chem.pitt.edu

Peterson's Graduate Programs in the Physical Sciences, Mathematics, Agricultural Sciences, the Environment & Natural Resources 2012

www.facebook.com/petersonspublishing   **109**

University of Pittsburgh

THE FACULTY AND THEIR RESEARCH

S. Amemiya, Associate Professor; Ph.D., Tokyo, 1998. Analytical chemistry: electrochemical sensors, scanning electrochemical microscopy, chemical imaging, nanostructures, ion and electron transfer at interfaces, liquid-liquid interfaces, biomembranes, molecular recognition, ion channel.

S. A. Asher, Professor; Ph.D., Berkeley, 1977. Analytical and physical chemistry: resonance Raman spectroscopy, biophysical chemistry, material science, protein folding, nanoscale and mesoscale smart materials, heme proteins, photonic crystals.

K. Brummond, Professor; Ph.D., Penn State, 1991. Organic chemistry: organometallic chemistry, synthesis of natural products, diversity-oriented synthesis.

T. M. Chapman, Associate Professor; Ph.D., Polytechnic of Brooklyn, 1965. Organic chemistry: new polymers of uncommon architecture, dendritic polymers, polymer surfactants and emulsifiers, tissue engineering, controlled drug delivery, gene transfer, electron transfer in dendritic polymers, polymers for CO_2 sequestration.

L. T. Chong, Assistant Professor; Ph.D., California, San Francisco, 2002. Computational biophysics: protein binding and switching, intrinsically disordered proteins, molecular simulations.

R. D. Coalson, Professor of Chemistry and Physics; Ph.D., Harvard, 1984. Physical chemistry: quantum theory of rate processes, optical spectroscopy, computational techniques for quantum dynamics, structure and energetics of macroions in solution; design of optical waveguides and photonic bandgap structures; laser control of condensed-phase electron transfer; theoretical/computational approaches to the transport of ions and polymers through biological (protein) pores.

T. Cohen, Professor Emeritus; Ph.D., USC, 1955. Organic chemistry: new synthetic methods, particularly those involving organometallics, most often of main group elements; synthesis of natural products using the new synthetic methods; mechanistic studies.

N. J. Cooper, Bettye J. and Ralph E. Bailey Dean of Arts and Sciences and Dean of the College of General Studies; D.Phil., Oxford, 1976. Inorganic chemistry: synthetic and mechanistic inorganic and organometallic chemistry.

D. P. Curran, Bayer Professor and Distinguished Service Professor; Ph.D., Rochester, 1979. Organic chemistry: natural products total synthesis and new synthetic methodology, synthesis via free-radical reactions, fluorous chemistry, carbene boranes.

P. Floreancig, Professor; Ph.D., Stanford, 1997. Organic chemistry: total synthesis of natural products and bioactive analogs, methodology development, electron transfer chemistry.

S. Garrett-Roe, Assistant Professor; Ph.D., Berkeley, 2005. Ultrafast dynamics: the hydrogen bond network of water, solvation dynamics, peptide dynamics, ion selectivity in potassium ion channels, ionic liquids, multidimensional femtosecond spectroscopies.

M. F. Golde, Associate Professor; Ph.D., Cambridge, 1972. Physical chemistry: kinetic and spectroscopic studies of mechanisms of formation and removal of electronically excited atoms and small molecules, ion-electron recombination and similar species.

J. J. Grabowski, Associate Professor; Ph.D., Colorado, 1983. Physical-organic chemistry: reactive intermediates; reaction mechanisms; novel uses of mass spectrometry and photochemistry for organic, analytical, or environmental chemistry; novel uses of modern technology for chemical education.

W. S. Horne, Assistant Professor; Ph.D., Scripps Research Institute, 2005. Bioorganic chemistry: design, synthesis, and study of synthetic analogues of polypeptides and proteins for biomedical and materials applications.

G. R. Hutchison, Assistant Professor; Ph.D., Northwestern, 2004. Molecular materials: design and characterization of electronic materials, computational and theoretical modeling, charge transport, mechanical dynamics of smart materials, reversible self-assembly, organic photovoltaics.

K. D. Jordan, Professor; Ph.D., MIT, 1974. Physical chemistry: theoretical studies of the electronic structure of molecules, electron-induced chemistry, computer simulations, hydrogen-bonded clusters, chemical reactions at semiconductor and carbon nanotube surfaces, properties of hydrates, parallel computational methods.

K. Koide, Associate Professor; Ph.D., California, San Diego, 1997. Organic chemistry and chemical biology: natural product synthesis, automated synthesis, fluorescent sensors for RNA and ion imaging, synthetic methodology.

H. Liu, Assistant Professor; Ph.D., Berkeley, 2007. Physical chemistry and nanomaterials: reaction chemistry of graphene, DNA-based nanolithography, semiconductor quantum dots.

X. Liu, Assistant Professor; Ph.D., ETH Zurich, 2007. Total and combinatorial (bio)synthesis of natural product, novel synthetic method and platform development, carbohydrate chemistry, glycobiology, drug discovery, biomaterial, synthetic biology.

T. Y. Meyer, Associate Professor; Ph.D., Iowa, 1991. Polymer and inorganic chemistry: polymer synthesis, structure-function correlations in repeating sequence copolymers, stimuli-sensitive materials, preparation of materials for biomedical applications, sensors.

A. C. Michael, Professor; Ph.D., Emory, 1987. Analytical chemistry: new microsensor technologies for neurochemical monitoring in the central nervous system; investigations of the chemical aspects of brain disorders such as Parkinson's disease, schizophrenia, and substance abuse; quantitative aspects of in vivo chemical measurements.

J. E. Millstone, Assistant Professor; Ph.D., Northwestern, 2008. Inorganic and materials chemistry: nanoscale interfacial phenomena, nanomaterial synthesis, mechanochemistry, electroactive organic-inorganic composites, bioelectromechanical devices, catalysis.

S. G. Nelson, Professor; Ph.D., Rochester, 1991. Organic chemistry: natural products total synthesis, new synthetic methods, asymmetric catalysis and organometallic chemistry.

R. A. S. Robinson, Assistant Professor; Ph.D., Indiana Bloomington, 2007. Analytical and biological chemistry: proteomics of aging, immunosenescence, and neurodegenerative diseases; multidimensional separations involving liquid chromatography, mass spectrometry, and ion mobility spectrometry; instrumentation development; bioinformatics.

N. L. Rosi, Assistant Professor; Ph.D., Michigan, 2003. Materials chemistry: hybrid organic and inorganic solid-state materials; biomaterials; bioinspired design and assembly of new materials; nanoparticle synthesis and assembly; porous materials; gas storage (hydrogen, methane); drug delivery.

S. K. Saxena, Associate Professor; Ph.D., Cornell, 1997. Analytical, biophysical, and physical chemistry: spectroscopy; pulsed electron spin resonance; structure, folding, and dynamics of nanostructured materials; protein-DNA complexes and membrane proteins; metals in biology.

M. M. Spence, Assistant Professor; Ph.D., Berkeley, 2002. Physical chemistry: membrane proteins, antimicrobial peptides, peptide neurotoxins, lipid structure and dynamics, liquid- and solid-state NMR.

A. Star, Assistant Professor; Ph.D., Tel Aviv, 2000. Analytical and materials chemistry; nanotechnology-enabled chemical sensing and energy conversion.

M. A. Trakselis, Assistant Professor; Ph.D., Penn State, 2002. Biological chemistry: enzymatic mechanisms of proteins alone and in complexes involved in DNA replication and repair, biophysical and biochemical characterization of enzyme complexes, design of novel biohybrid polymeric catalysts.

D. H. Waldeck, Professor and Department Chair; Ph.D., Chicago, 1983. Analytical and physical chemistry: bioelectrochemistry, biophysics, electrochemistry, electron tunneling, homogenous and heterogenous electron transfer, nanoscience, molecular electronics, plasmonics, solar energy conversion, nanophotonics.

S. G. Weber, Professor; Ph.D., McGill, 1979. Analytical chemistry: capillary separations and sensitive detection for bioanalysis; sampling, sensors and selective extraction; microreactors; electrochemistry.

C. S. Wilcox, Professor; Ph.D., Caltech, 1979. Organic chemistry: diffusion-reaction processes, precipitons and separation methods for parallel synthesis and combinatorial chemistry, chemical synthesis, molecular recognition and the molecular torsion balance, self-assembling materials.

P. Wipf, Distinguished University Professor of Chemistry, Professor of Pharmaceutical Sciences, and Director, Center for Chemical Methodologies and Library Development; Ph.D., Zurich, 1987. Organic chemistry: total synthesis of natural products; organometallic, heterocyclic, and medicinal chemistry.

110 www.facebook.com/petersonspublishing

Peterson's Graduate Programs in the Physical Sciences, Mathematics, Agricultural Sciences, the Environment & Natural Resources 2012

THE UNIVERSITY OF TEXAS AT SAN ANTONIO

Ph.D. Program in Chemistry

Programs of Study

The Ph.D. degree in chemistry is offered by the Department of Chemistry at the University of Texas at San Antonio (UTSA) (http://www.utsa.edu/chem). The primary objective of the program is to educate students in a broad range of chemistry subdisciplines and to focus on one or two specialized areas. This training ensures that graduates are well prepared to participate and contribute to the chemistry profession in all its facets.

The curriculum is designed to provide an overview of contemporary chemistry through the core and elective courses, participation in research seminars and colloquia, teaching opportunities, and interactions with faculty. All students are required to take courses in analytical chemistry, biochemistry, inorganic or organic chemistry, and physical chemistry, as well as a course on ethics in research and teaching. Additional required elective courses are normally taken in fields close to the student's area of specialization.

The department is committed to conduct advanced chemical research to increase the fundamental knowledge base; train the next generation of chemists for industrial/academic careers, as well as scientifically literate citizens; and to assist in educational, technological, and economic outreach to San Antonio and South Texas.

Research Facilities

The Department of Chemistry's research programs occupy space in the Biotechnology, Sciences, and Engineering building of the main campus. The Department of Chemistry, individual faculty members, and College of Sciences maintain a range of state-of-the-art facilities and provide staff support for their care and technical assistance. These facilities include an NMR facility, X-ray diffraction facility, Mass Spectrometry facility, X-band EPR facility, Electronic Instrumentation Shop, and Machine shop. These facilities provide the graduate students and research personnel with instrumentation capabilities and training that are among the best in the region.

The University of Texas library system provides readily available electronic and physical access to a wealth of information resources and services to students. The library collections include over 1,152,000 books and 2,300 periodical subscriptions; electronic access to over 39,000 electronic periodical and serial titles, including 20,000 full text journals; and a variety of databases for searching primary and patent literature. New graduate students receive training on the availability, use of databases, and other library resources.

Financial Aid

All students accepted into the graduate program in chemistry who maintain a good academic standing are provided with financial support in the form of fellowships, teaching assistantships, or research assistantships. For first-year students, financial support is typically in the form of a teaching assistantship during the academic year and a research assistantship during the summer. Outstanding first-year students are supported by fellowships or traineeship assistance. Students beyond their first year are typically supported by research assistantships from faculty research grants.

Cost of Study

For the 2011–12 academic year, tuition and fees for a full-time graduate degree student (9 semester hours) are approximately $3149 per semester for Texas residents and $8783 per semester for nonresidents. Some courses and programs have additional fees. Please view the following Web sites for more information: http://www.utsa.edu/fiscalservices/tuition.html and http://www.graduateschool.utsa.edu/prospective_students/detail/graduate_tuition_and_fees.

Living and Housing Costs

On-campus University housing is available and includes apartment-style living at four complexes—Chisholm Hall, University Oaks, Laurel Village, and Chaparral Village. Off-campus housing is also available and includes many apartments adjacent to the University as well as many located within a 5-mile drive. The rate for a one-bedroom apartment is approximately $500 per month.

Student Group

In the 2010 fall semester, the University enrolled more than 30,000 students; more than 4,000 of those were graduate students.

Location

San Antonio, with a population of 1.5 million, is one of the nation's major metropolitan areas. As the home of the Alamo and numerous other missions built by the Franciscans, the city is historically and culturally diverse. The Guadalupe Cultural Arts Center, McNay Art Museum, the San Antonio Museum of Art, and the Witte Museum enrich the city. The performing arts are represented by the San Antonio Symphony, the annual Tejano Music Festival and Tejano Music Awards, and performances by opera and ballet companies. Also notable are Sea World, Six Flags Fiesta Texas, Brackenridge Park, the San Antonio Botanical Garden, and the downtown Riverwalk. The San Antonio Zoo has the third-largest collection in North America. A city landmark is the Tower of the Americas, which was built for the 1968 World's Fair. San Antonio is home to the National Basketball Association's Spurs, league champions in 2000, 2003, 2005, and 2007. Numerous nearby lakes allow almost year-round outdoor activity, and the beaches of the Texas Gulf coast are within a 2-hour drive. San Antonio is home to numerous festivals throughout the year, including the Fiesta San Antonio and the Rodeo with activities such as parades, fairs, and concerts.

The University

The University was founded in 1969 and has since become a comprehensive metropolitan institution. Its research expenditures place it in the top 25 percent of public universities in Texas. The University has entered a new building and recruitment phase with a goal of greatly expanding the research effort in the sciences. UTSA Roadrunners football is slated to compete as an NCAA Division I FCS independent in August 2011 and is expected to transition to the Division I FSB subdivision by 2013.

Applying

Prospective graduate students can apply online via the Graduate School Web site, www.graduateschool.utsa.edu. All application deadlines are located on this site. The application fee is $30 for UTSA alumni or current students, $45 for domestic students, and $80 for international students. For a listing of grad program requirements, students should go to the pull-down menu of programs. For a checklist of Graduate Admissions items, visit www.graduateschool.utsa.edu/prospective_students/detail/utsa_checklist/. Since requirements and deadlines vary by program, students should consult the Graduate Catalog for official documentation on requirements, policies, and procedures.

Correspondence and Information

For application information:
The Graduate School
The University of Texas at San Antonio
One UTSA Circle
San Antonio, Texas 78249

Phone: 210-458-4330
Web site: http://www.graduateschool.utsa.edu

For program information:
Department of Chemistry
The University of Texas at San Antonio
One UTSA Circle
San Antonio, Texas 78249

Phone: 210-458-5469
E-mail: chemistry@utsa.edu
Web site: http://www.utsa.edu/chem

Peterson's Graduate Programs in the Physical Sciences, Mathematics, Agricultural Sciences, the Environment & Natural Resources 2012

www.facebook.com/petersonspublishing   **111**

The University of Texas at San Antonio

THE FACULTY AND THEIR RESEARCH

Stephan B. H. Bach, Associate Professor; Ph.D., Florida. Environmental chemistry, molecular recognition.

Banglan Chen, Professor; Ph.D., Singapore. Inorganic chemistry, materials chemistry, nanomaterials, molecular recognition.

Orkid Coskuner-Weber, Assistant Professor; Ph.D., Cologne (Germany). Identification of active sites of biocomplexes, structure-function relationships of biomolecules and biometallic species, reaction mechanism description between ligands and receptors.

Walter C. Ermler, Professor; Ph.D., Ohio State. Theoretical physical chemistry, relativistic quantum chemistry, bonding and spectra of heavy-element compounds.

Doug E. Frantz, Assistant Professor; Ph.D., Texas A&M. Synthetic methodology, transition metal catalysis, asymmetric catalysis heterocyclic synthesis, medicinal chemistry and drug discovery, anticancer agents, stem cell differentiation, regenerative medicine.

Carlos D. Garcia, Associate Professor; Ph.D., Córdoba (Argentina). Adsorption of proteins on CNT, capillary electrophoresis and microfluidics, electrochemical detection.

Waldmar Gorski, Professor and Department Chair; Ph.D., Warsaw. Electrochemical (bio)sensors, modified electrodes, electrocatalysts.

Hyunsoo Han, Associate Professor; Ph.D., Princeton. Asymmetric catalysis, organic synthesis, polymer and combinatorial chemistry.

Harry W. Jarret, Lutcher Brown Distinguished Professor; Ph.D., North Carolina at Chapel Hill. Biochemistry, proteomics, cell signaling, transcription.

Donald M. Kurtz, Lutcher Brown Distinguished Professor; Ph.D., Northwestern. Inorganic chemistry, nonheme iron enzymes

Oleg Larionov, Assistant Professor; Ph.D., Göttingen (Germany). Medicinal chemistry, synthesis of natural products, enantioselective catalysis.

Ghezai T. Musie, Associate Professor; Ph.D., Texas A&M. Inorganic chemistry, bioinorganic chemistry, catalysis and materials, green chemistry.

George R. Negrete, Professor; Ph.D., California, Santa Cruz. Novel fatty amino acids in liposomal delivery of medicinal agents, asymmetric synthesis via stoicheometric and organocatalytic methods, polycyclic aromatic hydrocarbon, medicinal chemistry.

Zachary J. Tonzetich, Assistant Professor; Ph.D., MIT. Synthetic inorganic and organometallic chemistry, bioinorganic chemistry, catalysis, odd-electron organometallics.

Cong-Gui Zhao, Professor; Ph.D., Würzburg (Germany). Asymmetric reaction and catalysis, medicinal chemistry, green chemistry, organophosphorus and small-ring compounds.

112   www.facebook.com/petersonspublishing

*Peterson's Graduate Programs in the Physical Sciences, Mathematics,
Agricultural Sciences, the Environment & Natural Resources 2012*

Section 3
Geosciences

This section contains a directory of institutions offering graduate work in geosciences, followed by in-depth entries submitted by institutions that chose to prepare detailed program descriptions. Additional information about programs listed in the directory but not augmented by an in-depth entry may be obtained by writing directly to the dean of a graduate school or chair of a department at the address given in the directory.

For programs offering related work, see all other areas in this book. In the other guides in this series:

Graduate Programs in the Humanities, Arts & Social Sciences
See *Geography*

Graduate Programs in the Biological Sciences
See *Biological and Biomedical Sciences, Biophysics,* and *Botany and Plant Biology*

Graduate Programs in Engineering & Applied Sciences
See *Aerospace/Aeronautical Engineering; Agricultural Engineering and Bioengineering; Civil and Environmental Engineering; Energy and Power Engineering (Nuclear Engineering); Engineering and Applied Sciences; Geological, Mineral/Mining, and Petroleum Engineering;* and *Mechanical Engineering and Mechanics*

CONTENTS

Program Directories

Close-Up and Display

Geochemistry

California Institute of Technology, Division of Geological and Planetary Sciences, Pasadena, CA 91125-0001. Offers geobiology (MS, PhD); geochemistry (MS, PhD); geology (MS, PhD); geophysics (MS, PhD); planetary science (MS, PhD). *Faculty:* 38 full-time (6 women). *Students:* 76 full-time (39 women); includes 1 Black or African American, non-Hispanic/Latino; 4 Asian, non-Hispanic/Latino; 1 Hispanic/Latino, 28 international. Average age 26. 102 applicants, 28% accepted, 9 enrolled. In 2010, 12 master's, 14 doctorates awarded. *Degree requirements:* For doctorate, thesis/dissertation. *Entrance requirements:* For doctorate, GRE General Test. Additional exam requirements/recommendations for international students: Required—TOEFL; Recommended—IELTS, TWE. *Application deadline:* For fall admission, 1/1 for domestic and international students. Application fee: $80. Electronic applications accepted. *Financial support:* In 2010–11, 75 students received support, including 14 fellowships with full tuition reimbursements available (averaging $27,000 per year), 62 research assistantships with full tuition reimbursements available (averaging $27,000 per year); teaching assistantships with full tuition reimbursements available, institutionally sponsored loans, scholarships/grants, health care benefits, and unspecified assistantships also available. Financial award applicants required to submit FAFSA. *Faculty research:* Planetary surfaces, evolution of anaerobic respiratory processes, structural geology and tectonics, theoretical and numerical seismology, global biogeochemical cycles. *Unit head:* Dr. Kenneth A. Farley, Chairman, 626-395-6111, Fax: 626-795-6028, E-mail: dianb@gps.caltech.edu. *Application contact:* Dr. Robert W. Clayton, Academic Officer, 626-395-6909, Fax: 626-795-6028, E-mail: dianb@gps.caltech.edu.

California State University, Fullerton, Graduate Studies, College of Natural Science and Mathematics, Department of Chemistry and Biochemistry, Fullerton, CA 92834-9480. Offers chemistry (MS); geochemistry (MS). Part-time programs available. *Students:* 7 full-time (3 women), 21 part-time (13 women); includes 8 Asian, non-Hispanic/Latino; 3 Hispanic/Latino, 5 international. Average age 27. 52 applicants, 44% accepted, 8 enrolled. In 2010, 10 master's awarded. *Degree requirements:* For master's, thesis, departmental qualifying exam. *Entrance requirements:* For master's, minimum GPA of 2.5 in last 60 units of course work, major in chemistry or related field. Application fee: $55. *Financial support:* Research assistantships, teaching assistantships, career-related internships or fieldwork, Federal Work-Study, institutionally sponsored loans, and scholarships/grants available. Support available to part-time students. Financial award application deadline: 3/1; financial award applicants required to submit FAFSA. *Unit head:* Dr. Christopher Meyer, Chair, 657-278-3621. *Application contact:* Admissions/Applications, 657-278-2371.

Colorado School of Mines, Graduate School, Department of Chemistry and Geochemistry and Department of Geology and Geological Engineering, Program in Geochemistry, Golden, CO 80401. Offers MS, PhD. Part-time programs available. *Students:* 7 full-time (4 women). Average age 30. 15 applicants, 60% accepted, 3 enrolled. In 2010, 2 doctorates awarded. *Degree requirements:* For master's, thesis (for some programs); for doctorate, comprehensive exam, thesis/dissertation. *Entrance requirements:* For master's and doctorate, GRE General Test. Additional exam requirements/recommendations for international students: Required—TOEFL (minimum score 550 paper-based; 213 computer-based; 80 iBT). *Application deadline:* For fall admission, 1/15 for domestic students, 1/15 priority date for international students; for spring admission, 10/15 priority date for domestic and international students. Application fee: $50 ($70 for international students). Electronic applications accepted. *Expenses:* Tuition, state resident: full-time $11,550; part-time $641 per credit. Tuition, nonresident: full-time $25,980; part-time $1444 per credit. Required fees: $1874; $937 per semester. *Financial support:* In 2010–11, fellowships with full tuition reimbursements (averaging $20,000 per year), research assistantships with full tuition reimbursements (averaging $20,000 per year), teaching assistantships with full tuition reimbursements (averaging $20,000 per year) were awarded; scholarships/grants, health care benefits, and unspecified assistantships also available. Financial award application deadline: 1/15; financial award applicants required to submit FAFSA. *Faculty research:* Geochemical analysis, organic geochemistry, hydrochemical systems, environmental microbiology, process control programming. *Unit head:* Dr. Dan Knauss, Department Head, 303-273-3625, Fax: 303-273-3629, E-mail: dknauss@mines.edu. *Application contact:* Tina Voelker, Associate Professor, 303-273-3152, Fax: 303-273-3629, E-mail: tvoelker@mines.edu.

Colorado School of Mines, Graduate School, Department of Geology and Geological Engineering, Golden, CO 80401. Offers geochemistry (MS, PMS, PhD); geological engineering (ME, MS, PhD); geology (MS, PhD). Part-time programs available. *Faculty:* 23 full-time (7 women), 4 part-time/adjunct (2 women). *Students:* 122 full-time (49 women), 24 part-time (9 women); includes 2 Black or African American, non-Hispanic/Latino; 3 American Indian or Alaska Native, non-Hispanic/Latino; 1 Asian, non-Hispanic/Latino; 3 Hispanic/Latino, 20 international. Average age 29. 206 applicants, 48% accepted, 44 enrolled. In 2010, 40 master's, 3 doctorates awarded. *Degree requirements:* For master's, thesis (for some programs); for doctorate, comprehensive exam, thesis/dissertation. *Entrance requirements:* For master's and doctorate, GRE General Test. Additional exam requirements/recommendations for international students: Required—TOEFL (minimum score 550 paper-based; 213 computer-based; 80 iBT). *Application deadline:* For fall admission, 1/15 for domestic and international students; for spring admission, 10/15 for domestic and international students. Application fee: $50 ($70 for international students). Electronic applications accepted. *Expenses:* Tuition, state resident: full-time $11,550; part-time $641 per credit. Tuition, nonresident: full-time $25,980; part-time $1444 per credit. Required fees: $1874; $937 per semester. *Financial support:* In 2010–11, 74 students received support, including 14 fellowships with full tuition reimbursements available (averaging $20,000 per year), 44 research assistantships with full tuition reimbursements available (averaging $20,000 per year), 16 teaching assistantships with full tuition reimbursements available (averaging $20,000 per year); scholarships/grants, health care benefits, and unspecified assistantships also available. Financial award application deadline: 1/15; financial award applicants required to submit FAFSA. *Faculty research:* Predictive sediment modeling, petrophysics, aquifer-contaminant flow modeling, water-rock interactions, geotechnical engineering. Total annual research expenditures: $3 million. *Unit head:* Dr. John Humphrey, Department Head, 303-273-3819, Fax: 303-273-3859, E-mail: jhumphre@mines.edu. *Application contact:* Dr. Christian Shorey, Lecturer, 303-273-3556, Fax: 303-273-3859, E-mail: cshorey@mines.edu.

Columbia University, Graduate School of Arts and Sciences, Division of Natural Sciences, Department of Earth and Environmental Sciences, New York, NY 10027. Offers geochemistry (M Phil, MA, PhD); geodetic sciences (M Phil, MA, PhD); geophysics (M Phil, MA, PhD); oceanography (M Phil, MA, PhD). *Degree requirements:* For master's, thesis or alternative, fieldwork, written exam; for doctorate, one foreign language, thesis/dissertation. *Entrance requirements:* For master's and doctorate, GRE General Test, GRE Subject Test, major in natural or physical science. Additional exam requirements/recommendations for international students: Required—TOEFL. *Faculty research:* Structural geology and stratigraphy, petrology, paleontology, rare gas, isotope and aqueous geochemistry.

Cornell University, Graduate School, Graduate Fields of Engineering, Field of Geological Sciences, Ithaca, NY 14853. Offers economic geology (M Eng, MS, PhD); engineering geology (M Eng, MS, PhD); environmental geophysics (M Eng, MS, PhD); general geology (M Eng, MS, PhD); geobiology (M Eng, MS, PhD); geochemistry and isotope geology (M Eng, MS, PhD); geohydrology (M Eng, MS, PhD); geomorphology (M Eng, MS, PhD); geophysics (M Eng, MS, PhD); geotectonics (M Eng, MS, PhD); marine geology (MS, PhD); mineralogy (M Eng, MS, PhD); paleontology (M Eng, MS, PhD); petroleum geology (M Eng, MS, PhD); petrology (M Eng, MS, PhD); planetary geology (M Eng, MS, PhD); Precambrian geology (M Eng, MS, PhD); Quaternary geology (M Eng, MS, PhD); rock mechanics (M Eng, MS, PhD); sedimentology (M Eng, MS, PhD); seismology (M Eng, MS, PhD); stratigraphy (M Eng, MS, PhD); structural geology (M Eng, MS, PhD). *Faculty:* 36 full-time (5 women). *Students:* 38 full-time (15 women); includes 2 Asian, non-Hispanic/Latino; 2 Hispanic/Latino, 9 international. Average age 27. 84 applicants, 25% accepted, 17 enrolled. In 2010, 3 master's, 5 doctorates awarded. *Degree requirements:* For master's, thesis (MS); for doctorate, comprehensive exam, thesis/dissertation. *Entrance requirements:* For master's and doctorate, GRE General Test, 3 letters of recommendation. Additional exam requirements/recommendations for international students: Required—TOEFL (minimum score 550 paper-based; 213 computer-based; 77 iBT). *Application deadline:* For fall admission, 1/15 priority date for domestic students. Applications are processed on a rolling basis. Application fee: $70. Electronic applications accepted. *Expenses:* Tuition: Full-time $29,500. Required fees: $76. Tuition and fees vary according to degree level and program. *Financial support:* In 2010–11, 25 students received support, including 10 fellowships with full tuition reimbursements available, 14 research assistantships with full tuition reimbursements available, 10 teaching assistantships with full tuition reimbursements available; institutionally sponsored loans, scholarships/grants, health care benefits, tuition waivers (full and partial), and unspecified assistantships also available. Financial award applicants required to submit FAFSA. *Faculty research:* Geophysics, structural geology, petrology, geochemistry, geodynamics. *Unit head:* Director of Graduate Studies, 607-255-5466, Fax: 607-254-4780. *Application contact:* Graduate Field Assistant, 607-255-5466, Fax: 607-254-4780, E-mail: gradprog@geology.cornell.edu.

Georgia Institute of Technology, Graduate Studies and Research, College of Sciences, School of Earth and Atmospheric Sciences, Atlanta, GA 30332-0340. Offers atmospheric chemistry, aerosols and clouds (MS, PhD); dynamics of weather and climate (MS, PhD); geochemistry (MS, PhD); geophysics (MS, PhD); oceanography (MS, PhD); paleoclimate (MS, PhD); planetary science (MS, PhD); remote sensing (MS, PhD). Part-time programs available. Terminal master's awarded for partial completion of doctoral program. *Degree requirements:* For master's, thesis or alternative; for doctorate, comprehensive exam, thesis/dissertation. *Entrance requirements:* For master's, GRE, letters of recommendation; for doctorate, GRE, academic transcripts, letters of recommendation, personal statement. Additional exam requirements/recommendations for international students: Required—TOEFL (minimum score 550 paper-based; 213 computer-based; 79 iBT). *Faculty research:* Geophysics; atmospheric chemistry, aerosols and clouds; dynamics of weather and climate; geochemistry; oceanography; paleoclimate; planetary science; remote sensing.

Indiana University Bloomington, University Graduate School, College of Arts and Sciences, Department of Geological Sciences, Bloomington, IN 47405-7000. Offers biogeochemistry (MS, PhD); economic geology (MS, PhD); geobiology (MS, PhD); geophysics, structural geology and tectonics (MS, PhD); hydrogeology (MS, PhD); mineralogy (MS, PhD); stratigraphy and sedimentology (MS, PhD). *Faculty:* 17 full-time (1 woman). *Students:* 48 full-time (24 women), 5 part-time (1 woman); includes 4 minority (2 Black or African American, non-Hispanic/Latino; 1 Hispanic/Latino; 1 Two or more races, non-Hispanic/Latino), 20 international. Average age 29. 70 applicants, 24% accepted, 16 enrolled. In 2010, 3 master's, 4 doctorates awarded. Terminal master's awarded for partial completion of doctoral program. *Degree requirements:* For master's, thesis or alternative; for doctorate, comprehensive exam, thesis/dissertation. *Entrance requirements:* For master's and doctorate, GRE General Test. Additional exam requirements/recommendations for international students: Required—TOEFL. *Application deadline:* For fall admission, 1/15 priority date for domestic students, 12/15 for international students; for spring admission, 9/1 priority date for domestic students, 9/1 for international students. Applications are processed on a rolling basis. Application fee: $55 ($65 for international students). *Financial support:* In 2010–11, 10 fellowships with full tuition reimbursements (averaging $17,300 per year), 6 research assistantships with full tuition reimbursements (averaging $16,370 per year), 12 teaching assistantships with full tuition reimbursements (averaging $15,150 per year) were awarded; career-related internships or fieldwork, Federal Work-Study, and institutionally sponsored loans also available. *Faculty research:* Geophysics, geochemistry, hydrogeology, geobiology, planetary science. Total annual research expenditures: $644,299. *Unit head:* Simon Brassell, Chair, 812-855-5581, Fax: 812-855-7899, E-mail: geochair@indiana.edu. *Application contact:* Mary Iverson, Graduate Secretary, 812-855-7214, Fax: 812-855-7899, E-mail: miverson@indiana.edu.

Massachusetts Institute of Technology, School of Science, Department of Earth, Atmospheric, and Planetary Sciences, Cambridge, MA 02139. Offers atmospheric chemistry (PhD, Sc D); atmospheric science (SM, PhD, Sc D); chemical oceanography (SM, PhD, Sc D); climate physics and chemistry (SM, PhD, Sc D); earth and planetary sciences (SM); geochemistry (PhD, Sc D); geology (PhD, Sc D); geophysics (PhD, Sc D); marine geology and geophysics (SM, PhD, Sc D); physical oceanography (SM, PhD, Sc D); planetary sciences (PhD, Sc D). *Faculty:* 36 full-time (7 women). *Students:* 165 full-time (86 women); includes 17 minority (2 Black or African American, non-Hispanic/Latino; 2 American Indian or Alaska Native, non-Hispanic/Latino; 5 Asian, non-Hispanic/Latino; 5 Hispanic/Latino; 3 Two or more races, non-Hispanic/Latino), 50 international. Average age 27. 227 applicants, 33% accepted, 38 enrolled. In 2010, 12 master's, 26 doctorates awarded. Terminal master's awarded for partial completion of doctoral program. *Degree requirements:* For master's, thesis; for doctorate, comprehensive exam, thesis/dissertation. *Entrance requirements:* For master's, GRE General Test; for doctorate, GRE General Test, GRE Subject Test (chemistry or physics for planetary science area). Additional exam requirements/recommendations for international students: Required—TOEFL (minimum score 577 paper-based; 233 computer-based; 91 iBT), IELTS (minimum score 7). *Application deadline:* For fall admission, 1/5 for domestic and international students; for spring admission, 11/1 for domestic and international students. Application fee: $75. Electronic applications accepted. *Expenses:* Tuition: Full-time $38,940; part-time $605 per unit. Required fees: $272. *Financial support:* In 2010–11, 123 students received support, including 62 fellowships with tuition reimbursements available (averaging $30,852 per year), 88 research assistantships with tuition reimbursements available (averaging $30,258 per year), 13 teaching assistantships with tuition reimbursements available (averaging $30,323 per year); Federal Work-Study, institutionally sponsored loans, scholarships/grants, health care benefits, and unspecified assistantships also available. *Faculty research:* Formation, dynamics and evolution of planetary systems; origin, composition, structure and dynamics of the atmospheres, oceans, surfaces and interiors of the Earth and other planets; evolution and interaction of the physical, chemical, geological and biological components of the Earth system; characterization of past, present and potential future climates and the causes and consequences of climate change; interplay of energy and the environment. Total annual research expenditures: $24.8 million. *Unit head:* Prof. Maria Zuber, Department Head, 617-253-2127, Fax: 617-253-8298, E-mail: eapsinfo@mit.edu. *Application contact:* EAPS Education Office, 617-253-3381, Fax: 617-253-8298, E-mail: eapsinfo@mit.edu.

McMaster University, School of Graduate Studies, Faculty of Science, School of Geography and Earth Sciences, Hamilton, ON L8S 4M2, Canada. Offers geochemistry (PhD); geology (M Sc, PhD); human geography (MA, PhD); physical geography (M Sc, PhD). Part-time programs available. Terminal master's awarded for partial completion of doctoral program. *Degree requirements:* For master's, thesis; for doctorate, comprehensive exam, thesis/dissertation. *Entrance requirements:* For master's, minimum B+ average. Additional exam requirements/recommendations for international students: Required—TOEFL (minimum score 550 paper-based; 213 computer-based).

Missouri University of Science and Technology, Graduate School, Department of Geological Sciences and Engineering, Rolla, MO 65409. Offers geological engineering (MS, DE, PhD); geology and geophysics (MS, PhD), including geochemistry, geology, geophysics, groundwater

and environmental geology; petroleum engineering (MS, DE, PhD). Part-time programs available. *Degree requirements:* For master's, thesis optional; for doctorate, comprehensive exam, thesis/dissertation. *Entrance requirements:* For master's, GRE General Test (minimum score 600 quantitative, writing 3.5), minimum GPA of 3.0 in last 4 semesters; for doctorate, GRE General Test (minimum: Q 600, GRE WR 3.5). Additional exam requirements/recommendations for international students: Required—TOEFL. Electronic applications accepted. *Faculty research:* Digital image processing and geographic information systems, mineralogy, igneous and sedimentary petrology-geochemistry, sedimentology groundwater hydrology and contaminant transport.

Montana Tech of The University of Montana, Graduate School, Geosciences Programs, Butte, MT 59701-8997. Offers geochemistry (MS); geological engineering (MS); geology (MS); geophysical engineering (MS); hydrogeological engineering (MS); hydrogeology (MS). Part-time programs available. *Faculty:* 16 full-time (4 women), 4 part-time/adjunct (0 women). *Students:* 15 full-time (6 women), 10 part-time (5 women); includes 1 Black or African American, non-Hispanic/Latino; 1 American Indian or Alaska Native, non-Hispanic/Latino, 2 international. 9 applicants, 89% accepted, 8 enrolled. In 2010, 4 master's awarded. *Degree requirements:* For master's, comprehensive exam (for some programs), thesis (for some programs). *Entrance requirements:* For master's, GRE General Test, minimum GPA of 3.0. Additional exam requirements/recommendations for international students: Required—TOEFL (minimum score 525 paper-based; 195 computer-based; 71 iBT). *Application deadline:* For fall admission, 4/1 priority date for domestic students, 3/1 priority date for international students; for spring admission, 10/1 priority date for domestic students, 7/1 priority date for international students. Applications are processed on a rolling basis. Application fee: $30. Electronic applications accepted. *Expenses:* Tuition, state resident: full-time $5084. Tuition, nonresident: full-time $15,104. *Financial support:* In 2010–11, 17 students received support, including 10 teaching assistantships with partial tuition reimbursements available (averaging $5,200 per year); research assistantships with partial tuition reimbursements available, career-related internships or fieldwork, tuition waivers (full and partial), and unspecified assistantships also available. Financial award application deadline: 4/1; financial award applicants required to submit FAFSA. *Faculty research:* Water resource development, seismic processing, petroleum reservoir characterization, environmental geochemistry, geologic mapping. *Unit head:* Dr. Mary MacLaughlin, Department Head, 406-496-4655, Fax: 406-496-4260, E-mail: mmaclaughlin@mtech.edu. *Application contact:* Fred Sullivan, Administrator, Graduate School, 406-496-4304, Fax: 406-496-4710, E-mail: fsullivan@mtech.edu.

New Mexico Institute of Mining and Technology, Graduate Studies, Department of Earth and Environmental Science, Program in Geology and Geochemistry, Socorro, NM 87801. Offers geochemistry (MS, PhD); geology (MS, PhD). *Degree requirements:* For master's, thesis optional; for doctorate, thesis/dissertation. *Entrance requirements:* For master's, GRE General Test; for doctorate, GRE General Test, GRE Subject Test. Additional exam requirements/recommendations for international students: Required—TOEFL (minimum score 540 paper-based; 207 computer-based). Electronic applications accepted. *Faculty research:* Care and karst topography, soil/water chemistry and properties, geochemistry of ore deposits.

Ohio University, Graduate College, College of Arts and Sciences, Department of Geological Sciences, Athens, OH 45701-2979. Offers environmental geochemistry (MS); environmental geology (MS); environmental/hydrology (MS); geology (MS); geology education (MS); geomorphology/surficial processes (MS); geophysics (MS); hydrogeology (MS); sedimentology (MS); structure/tectonics (MS). Part-time programs available. *Students:* 14 full-time (8 women), 1 (woman) part-time. 15 applicants, 60% accepted, 8 enrolled. In 2010, 7 master's awarded. *Degree requirements:* For master's, thesis. *Entrance requirements:* Additional exam requirements/recommendations for international students: Required—TOEFL (minimum score 550 paper-based; 80 iBT) or IELTS (minimum score 6.5). *Application deadline:* For fall admission, 2/1 priority date for domestic and international students. Application fee: $50 ($55 for international students). Electronic applications accepted. *Financial support:* Research assistantships with full tuition reimbursements, teaching assistantships with full tuition reimbursements, Federal Work-Study, institutionally sponsored loans, scholarships/grants, tuition waivers (partial), and unspecified assistantships available. Financial award application deadline: 2/1. *Faculty research:* Geoscience education, tectonics, fluvial geomorphology, invertebrate paleontology, mine/hydrology. Total annual research expenditures: $649,020. *Unit head:* Dr. Gregory Nadon, Chair, 740-593-4212, Fax: 740-593-0486, E-mail: nadon@ohio.edu. *Application contact:* Dr. Douglas Green, Graduate Chair, 740-593-1843, Fax: 740-593-0486, E-mail: green@ohio.edu.

University of California, Los Angeles, Graduate Division, College of Letters and Science, Department of Earth and Space Sciences, Program in Geochemistry, Los Angeles, CA 90095. Offers MS, PhD. *Students:* 13 full-time (8 women); includes 2 minority (1 Black or African American, non-Hispanic/Latino; 1 American Indian or Alaska Native, non-Hispanic/Latino). Average age 30. 13 applicants, 23% accepted, 1 enrolled. In 2010, 1 master's, 2 doctorates awarded. Terminal master's awarded for partial completion of doctoral program. *Degree requirements:* For master's, comprehensive exams or thesis; for doctorate, thesis/dissertation, oral and written qualifying exams. *Entrance requirements:* For master's, GRE General Test, minimum GPA of 3.0, bachelor's degree in related field; for doctorate, GRE General Test, minimum undergraduate GPA of 3.0, bachelor's degree in related field. *Application deadline:* For fall admission, 1/15 for domestic and international students. Application fee: $70 ($90 for international students). Electronic applications accepted. *Financial support:* In 2010–11, 13 fellowships with full and partial tuition reimbursements, 13 research assistantships with full and partial tuition reimbursements, 10 teaching assistantships with full and partial tuition reimbursements were awarded; Federal Work-Study, institutionally sponsored loans, scholarships/grants, health care benefits, tuition waivers (full and partial), and unspecified assistantships also available. Financial award application deadline: 3/1; financial award applicants required to submit FAFSA. *Unit head:* Dr. Craig E. Manning, 310-825-1475, E-mail: manning@ess.ucla.edu. *Application contact:* Department Office, 310-825-3917, E-mail: holbrook@ess.ucla.edu.

University of Hawaii at Manoa, Graduate Division, School of Ocean and Earth Science and Technology, Department of Geology and Geophysics, Honolulu, HI 96822. Offers high-pressure geophysics and geochemistry (MS, PhD); hydrogeology and engineering geology (MS, PhD); marine geology and geophysics (MS, PhD); planetary geosciences and remote sensing (MS, PhD); seismology and solid-earth geophysics (MS, PhD); volcanology, petrology, and geochemistry (MS, PhD). Part-time programs available. *Faculty:* 72 full-time (15 women), 6 part-time/adjunct (3 women). *Students:* 38 full-time (20 women), 5 part-time (3 women); includes 8 minority (1 Black or African American, non-Hispanic/Latino; 2 Asian, non-Hispanic/Latino; 1 Hispanic/Latino; 1 Native Hawaiian or other Pacific Islander, non-Hispanic/Latino; 3 Two or more races, non-Hispanic/Latino), 6 international. Average age 31. 64 applicants, 23% accepted, 7 enrolled. In 2010, 7 master's, 8 doctorates awarded. Terminal master's awarded for partial completion of doctoral program. *Degree requirements:* For master's, thesis optional; for doctorate, comprehensive exam, thesis/dissertation. *Entrance requirements:* For master's and doctorate, GRE General Test, minimum GPA of 3.0. Additional exam requirements/recommendations for international students: Required—TOEFL (minimum score 580 paper-based; 237 computer-based; 92 iBT), IELTS (minimum score 5). *Application deadline:* For fall admission, 1/15 for domestic students, 1/1 for international students; for spring admission, 9/1 for domestic students, 8/15 for international students. Application fee: $60. *Financial support:* In 2010–11, 7 fellowships (averaging $1,359 per year), 30 research assistantships (averaging $23,988 per year), 4 teaching assistantships (averaging $15,350 per year) were awarded. Total annual research expenditures: $3.8 million. *Application contact:* Dr. Gregory Moore, Chair, 808-956-7640, Fax: 808-956-5512, E-mail: gg-dept@soest.hawaii.edu.

The University of Manchester, School of Earth, Atmospheric and Environmental Sciences, Manchester, United Kingdom. Offers atmospheric sciences (M Phil, M Sc, PhD); basin studies and petroleum geosciences (M Phil, M Sc, PhD); earth, atmospheric and environmental sciences (M Phil, M Sc, PhD); environmental geochemistry and cosmochemistry (M Phil, M Sc, PhD); isotope geochemistry and cosmochemistry (M Phil, M Sc, PhD); paleontology (M Phil, M Sc, PhD); physics and chemistry of minerals and fluids (M Phil, M Sc, PhD); structural and petrological geosciences (M Phil, M Sc, PhD).

University of Nevada, Reno, Graduate School, College of Science, Mackay School of Earth Sciences and Engineering, Department of Geological Sciences, Program in Geochemistry, Reno, NV 89557. Offers MS, PhD. Terminal master's awarded for partial completion of doctoral program. *Degree requirements:* For master's, thesis optional; for doctorate, thesis/dissertation. *Entrance requirements:* For master's, GRE General Test, minimum GPA of 2.75; for doctorate, GRE General Test, minimum GPA of 3.0. Additional exam requirements/recommendations for international students: Required—TOEFL (minimum score 500 paper-based; 173 computer-based; 61 iBT), IELTS (minimum score 6). Electronic applications accepted. *Expenses:* Tuition, state resident: full-time $2219; part-time $246 per credit. Tuition, nonresident: part-time $510 per credit. International tuition: $9009 full-time. Required fees: $59 per term. One-time fee: $101. Tuition and fees vary according to course load.

University of New Hampshire, Graduate School, College of Engineering and Physical Sciences, Department of Earth Sciences, Durham, NH 03824. Offers earth sciences (MS), including geochemical systems, geology, ocean mapping, oceanography; hydrology (MS). *Faculty:* 17 full-time (5 women). *Students:* 21 full-time (13 women), 8 part-time (4 women); includes 2 minority (1 Black or African American, non-Hispanic/Latino; 1 Asian, non-Hispanic/Latino), 4 international. Average age 27. 55 applicants, 65% accepted, 16 enrolled. In 2010, 8 master's awarded. *Degree requirements:* For master's, thesis. *Entrance requirements:* For master's, GRE General Test. Additional exam requirements/recommendations for international students: Required—TOEFL (minimum score 550 paper-based; 213 computer-based; 80 iBT). *Application deadline:* For fall admission, 4/1 priority date for domestic students, 4/1 for international students; for spring admission, 12/1 for domestic students. Applications are processed on a rolling basis. Application fee: $65. Electronic applications accepted. *Financial support:* In 2010–11, 24 students received support, including 13 research assistantships, 7 teaching assistantships; fellowships, career-related internships or fieldwork, Federal Work-Study, scholarships/grants, and tuition waivers (full and partial) also available. Support available to part-time students. Financial award application deadline: 2/15. *Unit head:* Dr. Will Clyde, Chairperson, 603-862-1718, E-mail: earth.sciences@unh.edu. *Application contact:* Sue Clark, Administrative Assistant, 603-862-1718, E-mail: earth.sciences@unh.edu.

The University of Texas at Dallas, School of Natural Sciences and Mathematics, Program in Geosciences, Richardson, TX 75080. Offers geochemistry (MS, PhD); geophysics (MS, PhD); geospatial information sciences (MS, PhD); hydrogeology (MS, PhD); sedimentary, stratigraphy, paleontology (PhD); stratigraphy, paleontology (MS); structural geology and tectonics (MS, PhD). Part-time and evening/weekend programs available. *Faculty:* 11 full-time (1 woman). *Students:* 38 full-time (13 women), 25 part-time (8 women); includes 11 minority (4 Black or African American, non-Hispanic/Latino; 4 Asian, non-Hispanic/Latino; 3 Hispanic/Latino), 19 international. Average age 32. 48 applicants, 46% accepted, 12 enrolled. In 2010, 9 master's, 1 doctorate awarded. *Degree requirements:* For master's, thesis optional; for doctorate, thesis/dissertation. *Entrance requirements:* For master's and doctorate, GRE General Test, minimum GPA of 3.0 in upper-level course work in field. Additional exam requirements/recommendations for international students: Required—TOEFL (minimum score 550 paper-based; 215 computer-based). *Application deadline:* For fall admission, 7/15 for domestic students, 5/1 priority date for international students; for spring admission, 11/15 for domestic students, 9/1 priority date for international students. Applications are processed on a rolling basis. Application fee: $50 ($100 for international students). Electronic applications accepted. *Expenses:* Tuition, state resident: full-time $10,248; part-time $569 per credit hour. Tuition, nonresident: full-time $18,544; part-time $1030 per credit hour. Tuition and fees vary according to course load. *Financial support:* In 2010–11, 38 students received support, including 15 research assistantships with partial tuition reimbursements available (averaging $14,400 per year), 14 teaching assistantships with partial tuition reimbursements available (averaging $13,905 per year); career-related internships or fieldwork, Federal Work-Study, institutionally sponsored loans, scholarships/grants, and unspecified assistantships also available. Support available to part-time students. Financial award application deadline: 4/30; financial award applicants required to submit FAFSA. *Faculty research:* Cybermapping, GPS applications for geophysics and geology, seismology and ground-penetrating radar, numerical modeling, signal processing and inverse modeling techniques in seismology. *Unit head:* Dr. John Oldow, Department Head, 972-883-2403, Fax: 972-883-2537, E-mail: geosciences@utdallas.edu. *Application contact:* Dr. Robert J. Stern, Graduate Advisor, 972-883-2442, Fax: 972-883-2537, E-mail: rjstern@utdallas.edu.

University of Wisconsin–Milwaukee, Graduate School, College of Letters and Sciences, Department of Chemistry, Milwaukee, WI 53201-0413. Offers biogeochemistry (PhD); chemistry (MS, PhD). *Faculty:* 22 full-time (4 women). *Students:* 58 full-time (20 women), 16 part-time (10 women); includes 3 Black or African American, non-Hispanic/Latino; 3 Asian, non-Hispanic/Latino, 27 international. Average age 30. 52 applicants, 33% accepted, 5 enrolled. In 2010, 5 master's, 10 doctorates awarded. *Degree requirements:* For master's, thesis or alternative; for doctorate, thesis/dissertation. *Entrance requirements:* For doctorate, GRE General Test. Additional exam requirements/recommendations for international students: Required—TOEFL (minimum score 600 paper-based; 79 iBT), IELTS (minimum score 6.5). *Application deadline:* For fall admission, 1/1 priority date for domestic students; for spring admission, 9/1 for domestic students. Applications are processed on a rolling basis. Application fee: $56 ($96 for international students). *Financial support:* In 2010–11, 3 fellowships, 30 research assistantships, 46 teaching assistantships were awarded; career-related internships or fieldwork, unspecified assistantships, and project assistantships also available. Support available to part-time students. Financial award application deadline: 4/15; financial award applicants required to submit FAFSA. *Faculty research:* Analytical chemistry, biochemistry, inorganic chemistry, organic chemistry, physical chemistry. Total annual research expenditures: $3 million. *Unit head:* Peter Geissinger, Representative, 414-229-5230, Fax: 414-229-5530, E-mail: geissing@uwm.edu. *Application contact:* General Information Contact, 414-229-4982, Fax: 414-229-6967, E-mail: gradschool@uwm.edu.

Woods Hole Oceanographic Institution, MIT/WHOI Joint Program in Oceanography/Applied Ocean Science and Engineering, Woods Hole, MA 02543-1541. Offers applied ocean sciences (PhD); biological oceanography (PhD, Sc D); chemical oceanography (PhD, Sc D); civil and environmental and oceanographic engineering (PhD); electrical and oceanographic engineering (PhD); geochemistry (PhD); geophysics (PhD); marine biology (PhD); marine geochemistry (PhD, Sc D); marine geology (PhD, Sc D); marine geophysics (PhD); mechanical and oceanographic engineering (PhD); ocean engineering (PhD); oceanographic engineering (M Eng, MS, PhD, Sc D, Eng); paleoceanography (PhD); physical oceanography (PhD, Sc D). MS, PhD, Sc D offered jointly with Massachusetts Institute of Technology. Terminal master's awarded for partial completion of doctoral program. *Degree requirements:* For master's and Eng, thesis (for some programs); for doctorate, thesis/dissertation. *Entrance requirements:* For master's, GRE General Test; for doctorate, GRE General Test, GRE Subject Test. Additional exam requirements/recommendations for international students: Required—TOEFL. Electronic applications accepted.

Yale University, Graduate School of Arts and Sciences, Department of Geology and Geophysics, New Haven, CT 06520. Offers biogeochemistry (PhD); climate dynamics (PhD); geochemistry (PhD); geophysics (PhD); meteorology (PhD); oceanography (PhD); paleontology (PhD); paleooceanography (PhD); petrology (PhD); tectonics (PhD). *Degree requirements:* For doctorate, thesis/dissertation. *Entrance requirements:* For doctorate, GRE General Test. Additional exam requirements/recommendations for international students: Required—TOEFL.

Geodetic Sciences

Columbia University, Graduate School of Arts and Sciences, Division of Natural Sciences, Department of Earth and Environmental Sciences, New York, NY 10027. Offers geochemistry (M Phil, MA, PhD); geodetic sciences (M Phil, MA, PhD); geophysics (M Phil, MA, PhD); oceanography (M Phil, MA, PhD). *Degree requirements:* For master's, thesis or alternative, fieldwork, written exam; for doctorate, one foreign language, thesis/dissertation. *Entrance requirements:* For master's and doctorate, GRE General Test, GRE Subject Test, major in natural or physical science. Additional exam requirements/recommendations for international students: Required—TOEFL. *Faculty research:* Structural geology and stratigraphy, petrology, paleontology, rare gas, isotope and aqueous geochemistry.

The Ohio State University, Graduate School, College of Arts and Sciences, Division of Natural and Mathematical Sciences, School of Earth Sciences, Columbus, OH 43210. Offers geodetic science (MS); geological sciences (MS, PhD). *Faculty:* 30. *Students:* 32 full-time (17 women), 15 part-time (6 women); includes 1 Black or African American, non-Hispanic/Latino; 3 Hispanic/Latino; 1 Two or more races, non-Hispanic/Latino, 4 international. Average age 29. In 2010, 3 master's, 9 doctorates awarded. *Degree requirements:* For master's, thesis; for doctorate, thesis/dissertation. *Entrance requirements:* For master's and doctorate, GRE. Additional exam requirements/recommendations for international students: Required—TOEFL (minimum score 600 paper-based; 250 computer-based). *Application deadline:* For fall admission, 8/15 priority date for domestic students, 7/1 priority date for international students; for winter admission, 12/1 priority date for domestic students, 11/1 priority date for international students; for spring admission, 3/1 priority date for domestic students, 2/1 priority date for international students. Applications are processed on a rolling basis. Application fee: $40 ($50 for international students). Electronic applications accepted. *Expenses:* Tuition, state resident: full-time $10,605. Tuition, nonresident: full-time $26,535. Tuition and fees vary according to course load and program. *Unit head:* W. Berry Lyons, Director, 614-688-3241, Fax: 614-292-7688, E-mail: lyons.142@osu.edu. *Application contact:* Graduate Admissions, 614-292-9444, Fax: 614-292-3895, E-mail: domestic.grad@osu.edu.

The Ohio State University, Graduate School, College of Engineering, Department of Civil and Environmental Engineering and Geodetic Science, Columbus, OH 43210. Offers civil engineering (MS, PhD); geodetic science and surveying (MS, PhD). *Students:* 78 full-time (18 women), 38 part-time (3 women); includes 2 Black or African American, non-Hispanic/Latino; 1 Asian, non-Hispanic/Latino; 1 Hispanic/Latino; 2 Two or more races, non-Hispanic/Latino, 66 international. Average age 28. In 2010, 29 master's, 8 doctorates awarded. *Expenses:* Tuition, state resident: full-time $10,605. Tuition, nonresident: full-time $26,535. Tuition and fees vary according to course load and program. *Unit head:* Dr. Carolyn J. Merry, Chair, 614-292-2771, Fax: 614-292-9379, E-mail: merry.1@osu.edu. *Application contact:* Dr. Carolyn J. Merry, Chair, 614-292-2771, Fax: 614-292-9379, E-mail: merry.1@osu.edu.

State University of New York College of Environmental Science and Forestry, Department of Environmental Resources Engineering, Syracuse, NY 13210-2779. Offers ecological engineering (MS, PhD); environmental and resources engineering (MPS, MS, PhD); environmental management (MPS); geospatial information science and engineering (MS, PhD); mapping sciences (MPS); water resources engineering (MS, PhD). *Degree requirements:* For master's, thesis (for some programs); for doctorate, comprehensive exam, thesis/dissertation. *Entrance requirements:* For master's and doctorate, GRE General Test, minimum GPA of 3.0. Additional exam requirements/recommendations for international students: Required—TOEFL (minimum score 550 paper-based; 213 computer-based; 80 iBT), IELTS (minimum score 6). *Expenses:* Tuition, state resident: full-time $8370; part-time $349 per credit hour. Tuition, nonresident: full-time $13,780. Required fees: $30.30 per credit hour. $20 per year. *Faculty research:* Forest engineering, paper science and engineering, wood products engineering.

Université Laval, Faculty of Forestry and Geomatics, Department of Geomatics Sciences, Programs in Geomatics Sciences, Québec, QC G1K 7P4, Canada. Offers M Sc, PhD. Terminal master's awarded for partial completion of doctoral program. *Degree requirements:* For master's, thesis (for some programs); for doctorate, comprehensive exam, thesis/dissertation. *Entrance requirements:* For master's and doctorate, knowledge of French and English. Electronic applications accepted.

University of New Brunswick Fredericton, School of Graduate Studies, Faculty of Engineering, Department of Geodesy and Geomatics, Fredericton, NB E3B 5A3, Canada. Offers land information management (Diploma); mapping, charting and geodesy (Diploma); surveying engineering (M Eng, M Sc E, PhD). *Faculty:* 9 full-time (1 woman), 13 part-time/adjunct (1 woman). *Students:* 37 full-time (5 women), 4 part-time (0 women). In 2010, 9 master's, 3 doctorates awarded. *Degree requirements:* For master's, thesis; for doctorate, comprehensive exam, thesis/dissertation, qualifying exam. *Entrance requirements:* For master's and doctorate, minimum GPA of 3.0. Additional exam requirements/recommendations for international students: Required—TOEFL (minimum score 580 paper-based), TWE (minimum score 4). *Application deadline:* For fall admission, 3/1 priority date for domestic students. Applications are processed on a rolling basis. Application fee: $50 Canadian dollars. *Expenses:* Tuition, area resident: Full-time $3708; part-time $927 per term. International tuition: $6300 full-time. Required fees: $50 per term. *Financial support:* In 2010–11, 23 research assistantships, 22 teaching assistantships were awarded; fellowships also available. *Faculty research:* Remote sensing, ocean mapping, land administration. *Unit head:* Dr. Sue Nichols, Director of Graduate Studies, 506-453-5141, Fax: 506-453-4943, E-mail: nichols@unb.ca. *Application contact:* Sylvia Whitaker, Graduate Secretary, 506-458-7085, Fax: 506-453-4943, E-mail: swhitake@unb.ca.

Geology

Acadia University, Faculty of Pure and Applied Science, Department of Earth and Environmental Science, Wolfville, NS B4P 2R6, Canada. Offers M Sc. *Faculty:* 8 full-time (2 women), 5 part-time/adjunct (0 women). *Students:* 9 full-time (3 women), 2 part-time (1 woman). Average age 24. 9 applicants, 67% accepted, 5 enrolled. In 2010, 4 master's awarded. *Degree requirements:* For master's, thesis. *Entrance requirements:* For master's, BSC (honours) in geology or equivalent. Additional exam requirements/recommendations for international students: Required—TOEFL (minimum score 580 paper-based; 237 computer-based; 93 iBT), IELTS (minimum score 6.5). *Application deadline:* For fall admission, 2/1 priority date for domestic and international students. Applications are processed on a rolling basis. Application fee: $50. *Financial support:* Research assistantships, teaching assistantships, scholarships/grants and unspecified assistantships available. Financial award application deadline: 2/1. *Faculty research:* Igneous, metamorphic, and Quaternary geology; stratigraphy; remote sensing; tectonics, carbonate sedimentology. *Unit head:* Dr. Robert Raeside, Head, 902-585-1323, Fax: 902-585-1816, E-mail: rob.raeside@acadiau.ca. *Application contact:* Dr. Robert Raeside, Head, 902-585-1323, Fax: 902-585-1816, E-mail: rob.raeside@acadiau.ca.

Alabama State University, Department of Earth and Environmental Sciences, Montgomery, AL 36101-0271. Offers MS, PhD. *Degree requirements:* For master's, one foreign language, thesis or alternative; for doctorate, one foreign language, thesis/dissertation. *Entrance requirements:* For master's, GRE General Test, minimum B average in undergraduate course work; for doctorate, GRE General Test. Additional exam requirements/recommendations for international students: Required—TOEFL. Electronic applications accepted. *Faculty research:* Sedimentation, isotopes, biogeochemistry, marine geology, structural geology.

American University of Beirut, Graduate Programs, Faculty of Arts and Sciences, Beirut, Lebanon. Offers anthropology (MA); Arabic language and literature (MA); archaeology (MA); biology (MS); chemistry (MS); computational science (MS); computer science (MS); economics (MA); education (MA); English language (MA); English literature (MA); environmental policy planning (MSES); financial economics (MAFE); geology (MS); history (MA); mathematics (MA, MS); Middle Eastern studies (MA); philosophy (MA); physics (MS); political studies (MA); psychology (MA); public administration (MA); sociology (MA); statistics (MA, MS). Part-time programs available. *Faculty:* 229 full-time (98 women), 136 part-time/adjunct (79 women). *Students:* 158 full-time (104 women), 263 part-time (171 women). Average age 25. 356 applicants, 59% accepted, 127 enrolled. In 2010, 57 master's awarded. *Degree requirements:* For master's, one foreign language, comprehensive exam, thesis (for some programs). *Entrance requirements:* For master's, GRE, letter of recommendation. Additional exam requirements/recommendations for international students: Required—TOEFL (minimum score 600 paper-based; 250 computer-based; 97 iBT), IELTS (minimum score 7). *Application deadline:* For fall admission, 4/30 for domestic and international students; for spring admission, 11/1 for domestic and international students. Application fee: $50. *Expenses:* Tuition: Full-time $12,294; part-time $683 per credit. Required fees: $499; $499 per credit. Tuition and fees vary according to course load and program. *Financial support:* In 2010–11, 33 students received support. Career-related internships or fieldwork, institutionally sponsored loans, scholarships/grants, health care benefits, and unspecified assistantships available. Financial award application deadline: 2/4; financial award applicants required to submit FAFSA. *Faculty research:* Modern and contemporary world theatre; mineralogy, petrology, and geochemistry; cell differentiation and transformation; combinatorial technologies; philosophy of action; continental philosophy; Phoenician epigraphy; nascent complex societies and urbanism; the economies of the Arab world; environmental economics; tectonophysics; host-parasite interactions; innate immunity; insect-plant interactions; history of the Ottoman archives; decentralization; transparency and corruption. Total annual research expenditures: $622,243. *Unit head:* Dr. Patrick McGreevy, Dean, 961-137-4374 Ext. 3800, Fax: 961-174-4461, E-mail: pm07@aub.edu.lb. *Application contact:* Dr. Salim Kanaan, Director, Admissions Office, 961-135-0000 Ext. 2594, Fax: 961-175-0775, E-mail: sk00@aub.edu.lb.

Arizona State University, College of Liberal Arts and Sciences, School of Earth and Space Exploration, Tempe, AZ 85287-1404. Offers astrophysics (MS, PhD); exploration systems design (PhD); geological sciences (MS, PhD). PhD in exploration systems design is offered in collaboration with the Fulton Schools of Engineering. *Faculty:* 43 full-time (4 women), 2 part-time/adjunct (1 woman). *Students:* 89 full-time (32 women), 16 part-time (8 women); includes 12 minority (2 American Indian or Alaska Native, non-Hispanic/Latino; 4 Asian, non-Hispanic/Latino; 6 Hispanic/Latino), 18 international. Average age 30. 181 applicants, 28% accepted, 28 enrolled. In 2010, 6 master's, 7 doctorates awarded. Terminal master's awarded for partial completion of doctoral program. *Degree requirements:* For master's, thesis, interactive Program of Study (iPOS) submitted before completing 50 percent of required credit hours; for doctorate, thesis/dissertation, interactive Program of Study (iPOS) submitted before completing 50 percent of required credit hours. *Entrance requirements:* For master's and doctorate, GRE, minimum GPA of 3.0 or equivalent in last 2 years of work leading to bachelor's degree. Additional exam requirements/recommendations for international students: Required—TOEFL, IELTS, or Pearson Test of English. *Application deadline:* For fall admission, 1/15 for domestic and international students; for spring admission, 10/1 for domestic and international students. Applications are processed on a rolling basis. Application fee: $70 ($90 for international students). Electronic applications accepted. *Expenses:* Tuition, state resident: full-time $8510; part-time $608 per credit. Tuition, nonresident: full-time $16,542; part-time $919 per credit. Required fees: $339; $110 per credit. Part-time tuition and fees vary according to course load. *Financial support:* In 2010–11, 52 research assistantships with full and partial tuition reimbursements (averaging $15,804 per year), 42 teaching assistantships with full and partial tuition reimbursements (averaging $15,169 per year) were awarded; fellowships with full tuition reimbursements, career-related internships or fieldwork, Federal Work-Study, institutionally sponsored loans, scholarships/grants, and tuition waivers (full and partial) also available. Financial award application deadline: 3/1; financial award applicants required to submit FAFSA. Total annual research expenditures: $18.8 million. *Unit head:* Dr. Kip Hodges, Director, 480-965-5331, Fax: 480-965-8102, E-mail: kvhodges@asu.edu. *Application contact:* Graduate Admissions, 480-965-6113.

Auburn University, Graduate School, College of Sciences and Mathematics, Department of Geology and Geography, Auburn University, AL 36849. Offers geography (MS); geology (MS). Part-time programs available. *Faculty:* 14 full-time (2 women), 1 part-time/adjunct (0 women). *Students:* 13 full-time (3 women), 8 part-time (3 women), 4 international. Average age 28. 25 applicants, 56% accepted, 7 enrolled. In 2010, 5 master's awarded. *Degree requirements:* For master's, computer language or geographic information systems, field camp. *Entrance requirements:* For master's, GRE General Test. *Application deadline:* For fall admission, 7/7 for domestic students; for spring admission, 11/24 for domestic students. Applications are processed on a rolling basis. Application fee: $50 ($60 for international students). Electronic applications accepted. *Expenses:* Tuition, state resident: full-time $7002. Tuition, nonresident: full-time $21,898. International tuition: $22,116 full-time. Required fees: $892. Tuition and fees vary according to course load and program. *Financial support:* Research assistantships, teaching assistantships, Federal Work-Study available. Support available to part-time students. Financial award application deadline: 3/15; financial award applicants required to submit FAFSA. *Faculty research:* Empirical magma dynamics and melt migration, ore mineralogy, role of terrestrial plant biomass in deposition, metamorphic petrology and isotope geochemistry, reef development, crinoid topology. *Unit head:* Dr. Charles E. Savrda, Professor/Interim Dean, 334-844-4282. *Application contact:* Dr. George Flowers, Dean of the Graduate School, 334-844-2125.

Ball State University, Graduate School, College of Sciences and Humanities, Department of Geology, Muncie, IN 47306-1099. Offers MA, MS. *Faculty:* 6. *Students:* 3 full-time (all women), 6 part-time (2 women); includes 1 Hispanic/Latino, 1 international. Average age 39. 4 applicants, 25% accepted, 0 enrolled. In 2010, 2 master's awarded. *Degree requirements:* For master's, thesis (for some programs). *Entrance requirements:* For master's, GRE General Test. Application fee: $50. *Expenses:* Tuition, state resident: full-time $6160; part-time $299 per credit hour. Tuition, nonresident: full-time $16,020; part-time $783 per credit hour. Required fees: $2278; $95 per credit hour. *Financial support:* In 2010–11, 1 research assistantship (averaging $10,000 per year), 5 teaching assistantships with full tuition reimbursements

(averaging $10,226 per year) were awarded; career-related internships or fieldwork also available. Financial award application deadline: 3/1. *Faculty research:* Environmental geology, geophysics, stratigraphy. *Unit head:* Scott Rice-Snow, Interim Chairman. *Application contact:* Dr. Kirsten Nicholson.

Baylor University, Graduate School, College of Arts and Sciences, Department of Geology, Waco, TX 76798. Offers earth science (MA); geology (MS, PhD). *Faculty:* 12 full-time (1 woman). *Students:* 24 full-time (9 women), 4 part-time (2 women); includes 1 American Indian or Alaska Native, non-Hispanic/Latino, 4 international. In 2010, 1 master's awarded. *Degree requirements:* For master's, thesis; for doctorate, thesis/dissertation. *Entrance requirements:* For master's and doctorate, GRE General Test. *Application deadline:* For fall admission, 3/15 priority date for domestic students. Applications are processed on a rolling basis. Application fee: $25. *Financial support:* In 2010–11, 18 teaching assistantships were awarded; Federal Work-Study and institutionally sponsored loans also available. *Faculty research:* Petroleum geology, geophysics, engineering geology, hydrogeology. *Unit head:* Dr. Steve Dworkin, Graduate Program Director, 254-710-2186, Fax: 254-710-2673, E-mail: steve_dworkin@baylor.edu. *Application contact:* Paulette Penney, Administrative Assistant, 254-710-2361, Fax: 254-710-3870, E-mail: paulette_penney@baylor.edu.

Boise State University, Graduate College, College of Arts and Sciences, Department of Geosciences, Program in Geology, Boise, ID 83725-0399. Offers MS, PhD. Part-time programs available. *Degree requirements:* For master's, thesis. *Entrance requirements:* For master's, GRE General Test, BS in related field, minimum GPA of 3.0. Electronic applications accepted.

Boston College, Graduate School of Arts and Sciences, Department of Geology and Geophysics, Chestnut Hill, MA 02467-3800. Offers MS, MBA/MS. *Degree requirements:* For master's, thesis. *Entrance requirements:* For master's, GRE General Test, GRE Subject Test. Additional exam requirements/recommendations for international students: Required—TOEFL (minimum score 600 paper-based; 250 computer-based; 100 iBT). Electronic applications accepted. *Faculty research:* Coastal and marine geology, experimental sedimentology, geomagnetism, igneous petrology, paleontology.

Bowling Green State University, Graduate College, College of Arts and Sciences, Department of Geology, Bowling Green, OH 43403. Offers MS. Part-time programs available. *Degree requirements:* For master's, thesis. *Entrance requirements:* For master's, GRE General Test. Additional exam requirements/recommendations for international students: Required—TOEFL. Electronic applications accepted. *Faculty research:* Remote sensing, environmental geology, geological information systems, structural geology, geochemistry.

Brigham Young University, Graduate Studies, College of Physical and Mathematical Sciences, Department of Geological Sciences, Provo, UT 84602-1001. Offers MS. *Faculty:* 16 full-time (2 women), 2 part-time/adjunct (0 women). *Students:* 27 full-time (6 women); includes 1 American Indian or Alaska Native, non-Hispanic/Latino; 1 Asian, non-Hispanic/Latino. Average age 23. 20 applicants, 60% accepted, 7 enrolled. In 2010, 5 master's awarded. *Degree requirements:* For master's, thesis. *Entrance requirements:* For master's, GRE General Test, minimum GPA of 3.0 in last 60 hours of course work. Additional exam requirements/recommendations for international students: Required—TOEFL. *Application deadline:* For fall admission, 2/1 priority date for domestic students, 2/1 for international students; for winter admission, 9/15 priority date for domestic students, 9/15 for international students. Applications are processed on a rolling basis. Application fee: $50. *Expenses:* Tuition: Full-time $5580; part-time $310 per credit hour. Tuition and fees vary according to program and student's religious affiliation. *Financial support:* In 2010–11, 25 students received support, including 2 research assistantships with partial tuition reimbursements available (averaging $17,000 per year), 16 teaching assistantships with partial tuition reimbursements available (averaging $15,383 per year); career-related internships or fieldwork, institutionally sponsored loans, scholarships/grants, and tuition waivers (partial) also available. Financial award application deadline: 2/1. *Faculty research:* Regional tectonics, hydrogeochemistry, crystal chemistry and crystallography, stratigraphy, environmental geophysics, petrology. Total annual research expenditures: $112,000. *Unit head:* Dr. Scott Ritter, Chairman, 801-422-4239, Fax: 801-422-0267, E-mail: scott_ritter@byu.edu. *Application contact:* Dr. Michael J. Dorais, Graduate Coordinator, 801-422-1347, Fax: 801-422-0267, E-mail: michael_dorais@byu.edu.

Brooklyn College of the City University of New York, Division of Graduate Studies, Department of Earth and Environmental Sciences, Brooklyn, NY 11210-2889. Offers MA, PhD. Evening/weekend programs available. *Students:* 1 (woman) full-time, 18 part-time (8 women); includes 11 minority (4 Black or African American, non-Hispanic/Latino; 3 Asian, non-Hispanic/Latino; 4 Hispanic/Latino), 2 international. Average age 31. 10 applicants, 100% accepted, 8 enrolled. In 2010, 3 master's awarded. Terminal master's awarded for partial completion of doctoral program. *Degree requirements:* For master's, comprehensive exam, thesis or alternative, qualifying exams, 30 credits. *Entrance requirements:* For master's, bachelor's degree in geology or equivalent, fieldwork, 2 letters of recommendation; for doctorate, GRE. Additional exam requirements/recommendations for international students: Required—TOEFL (minimum score 550 paper-based; 213 computer-based; 79 iBT). *Application deadline:* For fall admission, 8/20 for domestic students, 6/15 priority date for international students; for spring admission, 1/15 for domestic students, 11/15 priority date for international students. Applications are processed on a rolling basis. Application fee: $125. Electronic applications accepted. *Expenses:* Tuition, state resident: full-time $7360; part-time $310 per credit hour. Tuition, nonresident: full-time $13,800; part-time $575 per credit hour. Required fees: $190 per semester. *Financial support:* Career-related internships or fieldwork, Federal Work-Study, institutionally sponsored loans, and scholarships/grants available. Support available to part-time students. Financial award application deadline: 5/1; financial award applicants required to submit FAFSA. *Faculty research:* Geochemistry, petrology, tectonophysics, hydrogeology, sedimentary geology, environmental geology. *Unit head:* Dr. Wayne Powell, Chairperson, 718-951-5416, Fax: 718-951-4753, E-mail: wpowell@brooklyn.cuny.edu. *Application contact:* Hernan Sierra, Graduate Admissions Coordinator, 718-951-4536, Fax: 718-951-4506, E-mail: grads@brooklyn.cuny.edu.

California Institute of Technology, Division of Geological and Planetary Sciences, Pasadena, CA 91125-0001. Offers geobiology (MS, PhD); geochemistry (MS, PhD); geology (MS, PhD); geophysics (MS, PhD); planetary science (MS, PhD). *Faculty:* 38 full-time (6 women). *Students:* 76 full-time (39 women); includes 1 Black or African American, non-Hispanic/Latino; 4 Asian, non-Hispanic/Latino; 1 Hispanic/Latino, 28 international. Average age 26. 102 applicants, 28% accepted, 9 enrolled. In 2010, 12 master's, 14 doctorates awarded. *Degree requirements:* For doctorate, thesis/dissertation. *Entrance requirements:* For doctorate, GRE General Test. Additional exam requirements/recommendations for international students: Required—TOEFL; Recommended—IELTS, TWE. *Application deadline:* For fall admission, 1/1 for domestic and international students. Application fee: $80. Electronic applications accepted. *Financial support:* In 2010–11, 75 students received support, including 14 fellowships with full tuition reimbursements available (averaging $27,000 per year), 62 research assistantships with full tuition reimbursements available (averaging $27,000 per year); teaching assistantships with full tuition reimbursements available, institutionally sponsored loans, scholarships/grants, health care benefits, and unspecified assistantships also available. Financial award applicants required to submit FAFSA. *Faculty research:* Planetary surfaces, evolution of anaerobic respiratory processes, structural geology and tectonics, theoretical and numerical seismology, global biogeochemical cycles. *Unit head:* Dr. Kenneth A. Farley, Chairman, 626-395-6111, Fax: 626-795-6028, E-mail: dianb@gps.caltech.edu. *Application contact:* Dr. Robert W. Clayton, Academic Officer, 626-395-6909, Fax: 626-795-6028, E-mail: dianb@gps.caltech.edu.

California State University, Bakersfield, Division of Graduate Studies, School of Natural Sciences and Mathematics, Program in Geology, Bakersfield, CA 93311. Offers geology (MS); hydrogeology (MS); petroleum geology (MS). Part-time and evening/weekend programs available. *Degree requirements:* For master's, thesis. *Entrance requirements:* For master's, GRE General Test, BS in geology.

California State University, Chico, Graduate School, College of Natural Sciences, Department of Geological and Environmental Sciences, Chico, CA 95929-0722. Offers environmental science (MS); geosciences (MS), including hydrology/hydrogeology. Part-time programs available. *Students:* 13 full-time (4 women), 10 part-time (5 women); includes 2 Hispanic/Latino, 1 international. Average age 34. 24 applicants, 54% accepted, 8 enrolled. In 2010, 2 master's awarded. *Entrance requirements:* For master's, GRE General Test. Additional exam requirements/recommendations for international students: Required—TOEFL (minimum score 550 paper-based; 213 computer-based; 80 iBT), IELTS (minimum score 6.5). *Application deadline:* For fall admission, 3/1 priority date for domestic students, 3/1 for international students; for spring admission, 9/15 priority date for domestic students, 9/15 for international students. Applications are processed on a rolling basis. Application fee: $55. Electronic applications accepted. *Financial support:* Fellowships, teaching assistantships available. *Unit head:* Dr. Karolyn Johnston, Chair, 530-898-5262. *Application contact:* Dr. Karolyn Johnston, Chair, 530-898-5262.

California State University, East Bay, Office of Academic Programs and Graduate Studies, College of Science, Department of Earth and Environmental Sciences, Hayward, CA 94542-3000. Offers geology (MS). Evening/weekend programs available. *Faculty:* 3 full-time (0 women), 2 part-time/adjunct (1 woman). *Students:* 4 full-time (3 women), 10 part-time (4 women); includes 1 Hispanic/Latino, 2 international. Average age 34. 11 applicants, 45% accepted, 2 enrolled. In 2010, 1 master's awarded. *Degree requirements:* For master's, thesis. *Entrance requirements:* For master's, GRE, minimum GPA of 2.75 in field, 2.5 overall. Additional exam requirements/recommendations for international students: Required—TOEFL (minimum score 550 paper-based; 213 computer-based). *Application deadline:* For fall admission, 6/30 for domestic and international students. Application fee: $55. Electronic applications accepted. *Financial support:* Career-related internships or fieldwork, Federal Work-Study, and institutionally sponsored loans available. Support available to part-time students. Financial award application deadline: 3/2; financial award applicants required to submit FAFSA. *Unit head:* Dr. Jeffrey Seitz, Chair/Graduate Coordinator, 510-885-3486, Fax: 510-885-2526, E-mail: jeffrey.seitz@csueastbay.edu. *Application contact:* Dr. Donna Wiley, Interim Associate Director, 510-885-2928, Fax: 510-885-4777, E-mail: donna.wiley@csueastbay.edu.

California State University, Fresno, Division of Graduate Studies, College of Science and Mathematics, Department of Earth and Environmental Sciences, Fresno, CA 93740-8027. Offers geology (MS). Part-time programs available. *Degree requirements:* For master's, thesis. *Entrance requirements:* For master's, GRE General Test, undergraduate geology degree, minimum GPA of 2.7. Additional exam requirements/recommendations for international students: Required—TOEFL. Electronic applications accepted. *Faculty research:* Water drainage, pollution, cartography, creek restoration, nitrate contamination.

California State University, Fullerton, Graduate Studies, College of Natural Science and Mathematics, Department of Geological Sciences, Fullerton, CA 92834-9480. Offers MS. Part-time programs available. *Students:* 2 full-time (both women), 12 part-time (7 women); includes 2 Hispanic/Latino; 1 Two or more races, non-Hispanic/Latino, 1 international. Average age 32. 22 applicants, 27% accepted, 5 enrolled. In 2010, 5 master's awarded. *Degree requirements:* For master's, thesis. *Entrance requirements:* For master's, bachelor's degree in geology, minimum GPA of 3.0 in geology courses. Application fee: $55. *Financial support:* Research assistantships, teaching assistantships, career-related internships or fieldwork, Federal Work-Study, institutionally sponsored loans, and scholarships/grants available. Support available to part-time students. Financial award application deadline: 3/1; financial award applicants required to submit FAFSA. *Unit head:* Dr. David Bowman, Chair, 657-278-3882. *Application contact:* Admissions/Applications, 657-278-2371.

California State University, Long Beach, Graduate Studies, College of Natural Sciences and Mathematics, Department of Geological Sciences, Long Beach, CA 90840. Offers geology (MS); geophysics (MS). Part-time programs available. *Faculty:* 6 full-time (0 women). *Students:* 11 full-time (6 women), 23 part-time (9 women); includes 1 Black or African American, non-Hispanic/Latino; 1 American Indian or Alaska Native, non-Hispanic/Latino; 3 Asian, non-Hispanic/Latino; 6 Hispanic/Latino, 1 international. Average age 32. 33 applicants, 67% accepted, 14 enrolled. *Degree requirements:* For master's, thesis. *Entrance requirements:* For master's, GRE General Test. *Application deadline:* For fall admission, 7/1 for domestic students. Applications are processed on a rolling basis. Application fee: $55. Electronic applications accepted. *Financial support:* Research assistantships, teaching assistantships, Federal Work-Study, institutionally sponsored loans, and scholarships/grants available. Financial award application deadline: 3/2. *Faculty research:* Paleontology, geophysics, structural geology, organic geochemistry, sedimentary geology. *Unit head:* Robert D. Francis, Chair, 562-985-4929, Fax: 562-985-8638, E-mail: rfrancis@csulb.edu. *Application contact:* Gregory Holk, Graduate Advisor, 562-985-5006, Fax: 562-985-8638, E-mail: gholk@csulb.edu.

California State University, Los Angeles, Graduate Studies, College of Natural and Social Sciences, Department of Geological Sciences, Los Angeles, CA 90032-8530. Offers MS. Program offered jointly with California State University, Northridge. Part-time and evening/weekend programs available. *Faculty:* 3 full-time (1 woman), 2 part-time/adjunct (0 women). *Students:* 17 full-time (12 women), 18 part-time (8 women); includes 16 minority (1 Black or African American, non-Hispanic/Latino; 9 Asian, non-Hispanic/Latino; 5 Hispanic/Latino; 1 Two or more races, non-Hispanic/Latino), 1 international. Average age 31. 22 applicants, 95% accepted, 15 enrolled. In 2010, 6 master's awarded. *Degree requirements:* For master's, comprehensive exam or thesis. *Entrance requirements:* Additional exam requirements/recommendations for international students: Required—TOEFL (minimum score 500 paper-based; 173 computer-based). *Application deadline:* For fall admission, 5/1 for domestic and international students. Applications are processed on a rolling basis. Application fee: $55. Electronic applications accepted. *Financial support:* Federal Work-Study available. Support available to part-time students. Financial award application deadline: 3/1. *Unit head:* Dr. Kim Bishop, Chair, 323-343-2435, Fax: 323-343-5609, E-mail: kbishop@calstatela.edu. *Application contact:* Dr. Alan Muchlinski, Dean of Graduate Studies, 323-343-3820, Fax: 323-343-5653, E-mail: amuchli@exchange.calstatela.edu.

California State University, Northridge, Graduate Studies, College of Science and Mathematics, Department of Geological Sciences, Northridge, CA 91330. Offers geology (MS). Part-time and evening/weekend programs available. *Degree requirements:* For master's, thesis. *Entrance requirements:* For master's, GRE General Test, minimum GPA of 2.75. Additional exam requirements/recommendations for international students: Required—TOEFL. *Faculty research:* Petrology of California Miocene volcanics, sedimentology of California Miocene formations, Eocene gastropods, structure of White/Inyo Mountains, seismology of Californian and Mexican earthquakes.

Case Western Reserve University, School of Graduate Studies, Department of Geological Sciences, Cleveland, OH 44106. Offers MS, PhD. Part-time programs available. *Faculty:* 7 full-time (1 woman), 7 part-time/adjunct (0 women). *Students:* 7 full-time (4 women), 3 international. Average age 31. 21 applicants, 19% accepted, 1 enrolled.Terminal master's awarded for partial completion of doctoral program. *Degree requirements:* For master's, thesis or alternative; for doctorate, thesis/dissertation. *Entrance requirements:* For master's and doctorate, GRE General Test, GRE Subject Test. Additional exam requirements/recommendations for international students: Required—TOEFL (minimum score 550 paper-based; 213 computer-based; 79 iBT). *Application deadline:* For fall admission, 2/1 priority date for domestic students; for spring admission, 11/15 for domestic students. Applications are processed on a rolling basis. Application fee: $50. Electronic applications accepted. *Financial*

Geology

Case Western Reserve University (continued)

support: Research assistantships, teaching assistantships, Federal Work-Study and tuition waivers (partial) available. Support available to part-time students. Financial award application deadline: 2/1; financial award applicants required to submit FAFSA. *Faculty research:* Geochemistry, hydrology, ecology, geomorphology, planetary science, stratigraphy and basin analysis, igneous petrology. *Unit head:* Gerald Matisoff, Chairman, 216-368-3677, Fax: 216-368-3691, E-mail: gerald.matisoff@case.edu. *Application contact:* James Van Orman, Chair, Graduate Admission Committee, 216-368-3690, Fax: 216-368-3691, E-mail: james.vanorman@case.edu.

Central Washington University, Graduate Studies and Research, College of the Sciences, Department of Geological Sciences, Ellensburg, WA 98926. Offers MS. Part-time programs available. *Degree requirements:* For master's, thesis. *Entrance requirements:* For master's, GRE General Test, minimum GPA of 3.0. Additional exam requirements/recommendations for international students: Required—TOEFL (minimum score 550 paper-based; 213 computer-based; 79 iBT).

Colorado School of Mines, Graduate School, Department of Geology and Geological Engineering, Golden, CO 80401. Offers geochemistry (MS, PMS, PhD); geological engineering (ME, MS, PhD); geology (MS, PhD). Part-time programs available. *Faculty:* 23 full-time (7 women), 4 part-time/adjunct (2 women). *Students:* 122 full-time (49 women), 24 part-time (9 women); includes 2 Black or African American, non-Hispanic/Latino; 3 American Indian or Alaska Native, non-Hispanic/Latino; 1 Asian, non-Hispanic/Latino; 3 Hispanic/Latino, 20 international. Average age 29. 206 applicants, 48% accepted, 44 enrolled. In 2010, 40 master's, 3 doctorates awarded. *Degree requirements:* For master's, thesis (for some programs); for doctorate, comprehensive exam, thesis/dissertation. *Entrance requirements:* For master's and doctorate, GRE General Test. Additional exam requirements/recommendations for international students: Required—TOEFL (minimum score 550 paper-based; 213 computer-based; 80 iBT). *Application deadline:* For fall admission, 1/15 for domestic and international students; for spring admission, 10/15 for domestic and international students. Application fee: $50 ($70 for international students). Electronic applications accepted. *Expenses:* Tuition, state resident: full-time $11,550; part-time $641 per credit. Tuition, nonresident: full-time $25,980; part-time $1444 per credit. Required fees: $1874; $937 per semester. *Financial support:* In 2010–11, 74 students received support, including 14 fellowships with full tuition reimbursements available (averaging $20,000 per year), 44 research assistantships with full tuition reimbursements available (averaging $20,000 per year), 16 teaching assistantships with full tuition reimbursements available (averaging $20,000 per year); scholarships/grants, health care benefits, and unspecified assistantships also available. Financial award application deadline: 1/15; financial award applicants required to submit FAFSA. *Faculty research:* Predictive sediment modeling, petrophysics, aquifer-contaminant flow modeling, water-rock interactions, geotechnical engineering. Total annual research expenditures: $3 million. *Unit head:* Dr. John Humphrey, Department Head, 303-273-3819, Fax: 303-273-3859, E-mail: jhumphre@mines.edu. *Application contact:* Dr. Christian Shorey, Lecturer, 303-273-3556, Fax: 303-273-3859, E-mail: cshorey@mines.edu.

Cornell University, Graduate School, Graduate Fields of Engineering, Field of Geological Sciences, Ithaca, NY 14853. Offers economic geology (M Eng, MS, PhD); engineering geology (M Eng, MS, PhD); environmental geophysics (M Eng, MS, PhD); general geology (M Eng, MS, PhD); geobiology (M Eng, MS, PhD); geochemistry and isotope geology (M Eng, MS, PhD); geohydrology (M Eng, MS, PhD); geomorphology (M Eng, MS, PhD); geophysics (M Eng, MS, PhD); geotectonics (M Eng, MS, PhD); marine geology (MS, PhD); mineralogy (M Eng, MS, PhD); paleontology (M Eng, MS, PhD); petroleum geology (M Eng, MS, PhD); petrology (M Eng, MS, PhD); planetary geology (M Eng, MS, PhD); Precambrian geology (M Eng, MS, PhD); Quaternary geology (M Eng, MS, PhD); rock mechanics (M Eng, MS, PhD); sedimentology (M Eng, MS, PhD); seismology (M Eng, MS, PhD); stratigraphy (M Eng, MS, PhD); structural geology (M Eng, MS, PhD). *Faculty:* 36 full-time (5 women). *Students:* 38 full-time (15 women); includes 2 Asian, non-Hispanic/Latino; 2 Hispanic/Latino, 9 international. Average age 27. 84 applicants, 25% accepted, 17 enrolled. In 2010, 3 master's, 5 doctorates awarded. *Degree requirements:* For master's, thesis (MS); for doctorate, comprehensive exam, thesis/dissertation. *Entrance requirements:* For master's and doctorate, GRE General Test, 3 letters of recommendation. Additional exam requirements/recommendations for international students: Required—TOEFL (minimum score 550 paper-based; 213 computer-based; 77 iBT). *Application deadline:* For fall admission, 1/15 priority date for domestic students. Applications are processed on a rolling basis. Application fee: $70. Electronic applications accepted. *Expenses:* Tuition: Full-time $29,500. Required fees: $76. Tuition and fees vary according to degree level and program. *Financial support:* In 2010–11, 25 students received support, including 10 fellowships with full tuition reimbursements available, 14 research assistantships with full tuition reimbursements available, 10 teaching assistantships with full tuition reimbursements available; institutionally sponsored loans, scholarships/grants, health care benefits, tuition waivers (full and partial), and unspecified assistantships also available. Financial award applicants required to submit FAFSA. *Faculty research:* Geophysics, structural geology, petrology, geochemistry, geodynamics. *Unit head:* Director of Graduate Studies, 607-255-5466, Fax: 607-254-4780. *Application contact:* Graduate Field Assistant, 607-255-5466, Fax: 607-254-4780, E-mail: gradprog@geology.cornell.edu.

Duke University, Graduate School, Division of Earth and Ocean Sciences, Durham, NC 27708. Offers MS, PhD. Part-time programs available. *Faculty:* 11 full-time. *Students:* 23 full-time (12 women); includes 1 Asian, non-Hispanic/Latino, 5 international. 35 applicants, 17% accepted, 4 enrolled. In 2010, 1 doctorate awarded. Terminal master's awarded for partial completion of doctoral program. *Degree requirements:* For master's, thesis; for doctorate, thesis/dissertation. *Entrance requirements:* For master's and doctorate, GRE General Test. Additional exam requirements/recommendations for international students: Required—TOEFL (minimum score 550 paper-based; 213 computer-based; 83 iBT), IELTS (minimum score 7). *Application deadline:* For fall admission, 12/8 priority date for domestic and international students; for spring admission, 10/15 for domestic and international students. Application fee: $75. Electronic applications accepted. *Financial support:* Fellowships, research assistantships, teaching assistantships, Federal Work-Study available. Financial award application deadline: 12/8. *Unit head:* Alan Boudreau, Director of Graduate Studies, 919-681-4426, Fax: 919-684-5833, E-mail: cabrera@duke.edu. *Application contact:* Elizabeth Hutton, Director of Admissions, 919-684-3913, Fax: 919-684-2277, E-mail: grad-admissions@duke.edu.

East Carolina University, Graduate School, Thomas Harriot College of Arts and Sciences, Department of Geology, Greenville, NC 27858-4353. Offers MS. Part-time programs available. *Degree requirements:* For master's, one foreign language, comprehensive exam, thesis. *Entrance requirements:* For master's, GRE General Test. Additional exam requirements/recommendations for international students: Required—TOEFL. *Expenses:* Tuition, state resident: full-time $3130; part-time $391.25 per credit hour. Tuition, nonresident: full-time $13,817; part-time $1727.13 per credit hour. Required fees: $1916; $239.50 per credit hour. Tuition and fees vary according to campus/location and program.

Eastern Kentucky University, The Graduate School, College of Arts and Sciences, Department of Earth Sciences, Richmond, KY 40475-3102. Offers geology (MS, PhD). PhD program offered jointly with University of Kentucky. Part-time programs available. *Degree requirements:* For master's, thesis. *Entrance requirements:* For master's, GRE General Test, minimum GPA of 2.5. *Faculty research:* Hydrogeology, sedimentary geology, geochemistry, environmental geology, tectonics.

Florida Atlantic University, Charles E. Schmidt College of Science, Department of Geosciences, Boca Raton, FL 33431-0991. Offers geography (MA); geology (MS); geosciences (PhD). Part-time programs available. *Faculty:* 14 full-time (3 women), 1 part-time/adjunct (0 women). *Students:* 24 full-time (14 women), 12 part-time (5 women); includes 5 minority (1 Asian, non-Hispanic/Latino; 4 Hispanic/Latino), 3 international. Average age 34. 25 applicants, 52% accepted, 11 enrolled. In 2010, 6 master's awarded. *Degree requirements:* For master's, thesis (for some programs). *Entrance requirements:* For master's, GRE General Test, minimum GPA of 3.0. *Application deadline:* For fall admission, 3/15 for domestic and international students; for spring admission, 10/15 for domestic and international students. Applications are processed on a rolling basis. Application fee: $30. Electronic applications accepted. *Expenses:* Tuition, area resident: Part-time $319.96 per credit. Tuition, state resident: part-time $319.96 per credit. Tuition, nonresident: part-time $926.42 per credit. *Financial support:* Research assistantships with partial tuition reimbursements, teaching assistantships with partial tuition reimbursements, career-related internships or fieldwork, Federal Work-Study, institutionally sponsored loans, and unspecified assistantships available. *Faculty research:* GIS applications, paleontology, hydrogeology, economic development. *Unit head:* Dr. Russell Ivy, Chair, 561-297-3295, Fax: 561-297-2745, E-mail: ivy@fau.edu. *Application contact:* Dr. David Warburton, Graduate Coordinator, 561-297-3312, Fax: 561-297-2745, E-mail: warburto@fau.edu.

Florida State University, The Graduate School, College of Arts and Sciences, Department of Earth, Ocean and Atmospheric Science, Program in Geological Sciences, Tallahassee, FL 32306. Offers MS, PhD. *Faculty:* 13 full-time (1 woman), 1 part-time/adjunct (0 women). *Students:* 34 full-time (19 women), 4 part-time (2 women). Average age 27. *Degree requirements:* For master's, thesis; for doctorate, thesis/dissertation. *Entrance requirements:* For master's and doctorate, GRE General Test, minimum GPA of 3.0. Additional exam requirements/recommendations for international students: Required—TOEFL (minimum score 550 paper-based; 80 iBT). *Application deadline:* For fall admission, 3/1 priority date for domestic and international students; for spring admission, 8/1 priority date for domestic and international students. Applications are processed on a rolling basis. Application fee: $30. Electronic applications accepted. *Expenses:* Tuition, state resident: full-time $8238.24. *Financial support:* In 2010–11, 18 students received support; fellowships, research assistantships, teaching assistantships, career-related internships or fieldwork and Federal Work-Study available. Financial award application deadline: 2/7; financial award applicants required to submit FAFSA. *Faculty research:* Appalachian and collisional tectonics, surface and groundwater hydrogeology, micropaleontology, isotope and trace element geochemistry, coastal and estuarine studies. Total annual research expenditures: $2.3 million. *Unit head:* Dr. Lynn Dudley, Chairman, 850-644-3864, Fax: 850-644-4214, E-mail: ldudley@fsu.edu. *Application contact:* Sharon R. Wynn, Student Coordinator, 850-644-5860, Fax: 850-644-4214, E-mail: srwynn@fsu.edu.

Fort Hays State University, Graduate School, College of Arts and Sciences, Department of Geosciences, Program in Geosciences, Hays, KS 67601-4099. Offers geography (MS); geology (MS). *Degree requirements:* For master's, comprehensive exam, thesis. *Entrance requirements:* For master's, GRE General Test. Additional exam requirements/recommendations for international students: Required—TOEFL (minimum score 550 paper-based; 213 computer-based). Electronic applications accepted. *Faculty research:* Cretaceous and late Cenozoic stratigraphy, sedimentation, paleontology.

Georgia State University, College of Arts and Sciences, Department of Geosciences, Program in Geology, Atlanta, GA 30302-3083. Offers MA. *Degree requirements:* For master's, one foreign language, comprehensive exam (for some programs), thesis or alternative. *Entrance requirements:* For master's, GRE General Test, minimum GPA of 2.75. Additional exam requirements/recommendations for international students: Required—TOEFL.

Hofstra University, School of Education, Health, and Human Services, Programs in Teaching—Secondary Education, Hempstead, NY 11549. Offers business education (MS Ed); English education (MA, MS Ed); foreign language and TESOL (MS Ed); foreign language education (MA, MS Ed), including French, German, Russian, Spanish; mathematics education (MA, MS Ed); science education (MA, MS Ed), including biology, chemistry, earth science, geology, physics; secondary education (Advanced Certificate); social studies education (MA, MS Ed). Part-time and evening/weekend programs available. Postbaccalaureate distance learning degree programs offered (minimal on-campus study). *Students:* 114 full-time (74 women), 61 part-time (36 women); includes 7 Black or African American, non-Hispanic/Latino; 1 American Indian or Alaska Native, non-Hispanic/Latino; 8 Asian, non-Hispanic/Latino; 10 Hispanic/Latino; 1 Native Hawaiian or other Pacific Islander, non-Hispanic/Latino. Average age 27. 153 applicants, 90% accepted, 59 enrolled. In 2010, 102 master's, 11 other advanced degrees awarded. *Degree requirements:* For master's, one foreign language, comprehensive exam (for some programs), thesis (for some programs), exit project, electronic portfolio, student teaching, fieldwork, curriculum project; for Advanced Certificate, 3 foreign languages, comprehensive exam (for some programs), thesis project. *Entrance requirements:* For master's, 2 letters of recommendation, teacher certification (MA), essay; for Advanced Certificate, 2 letters of recommendation, essay, interview and/or portfolio. Additional exam requirements/recommendations for international students: Required—TOEFL (minimum score 550 paper-based; 213 computer-based; 80 iBT). *Application deadline:* Applications are processed on a rolling basis. Application fee: $70 ($75 for international students). Electronic applications accepted. *Expenses:* Tuition: Full-time $18,000; part-time $1000 per credit hour. Required fees: $970; $145 per term. Tuition and fees vary according to program. *Financial support:* In 2010–11, 108 students received support, including 14 fellowships with full and partial tuition reimbursements available (averaging $3,943 per year), 1 research assistantship with full and partial tuition reimbursement available (averaging $6,574 per year); career-related internships or fieldwork, Federal Work-Study, institutionally sponsored loans, scholarships/grants, tuition waivers (full and partial), unspecified assistantships, and scholarships also available. Support available to part-time students. Financial award applicants required to submit FAFSA. *Faculty research:* Appropriate content and pedagogy in secondary school disciplines, adolescent development, secondary school organization, alternative secondary school programs. *Unit head:* Dr. Esther Fusco, Chairperson, 516-463-7704, Fax: 516-463-6196, E-mail: catezf@hofstra.edu. *Application contact:* Carol Drummer, Dean of Graduate Admissions, 516-463-4876, Fax: 516-463-4664, E-mail: gradstudent@hofstra.edu.

Humboldt State University, Academic Programs, College of Natural Resources and Sciences, Programs in Environmental Systems, Arcata, CA 95521-8299. Offers environmental systems (MS), including energy, environment and society, environmental resources engineering, geology, math modeling. *Students:* 35 full-time (12 women), 6 part-time (0 women); includes 4 minority (1 Asian, non-Hispanic/Latino; 3 Hispanic/Latino), 2 international. Average age 28. 72 applicants, 29% accepted, 15 enrolled. In 2010, 21 master's awarded. *Degree requirements:* For master's, thesis. *Entrance requirements:* For master's, GRE, appropriate bachelor's degree, minimum GPA of 2.5, 3 letters of recommendation. Additional exam requirements/recommendations for international students: Required—TOEFL. *Application deadline:* For fall admission, 2/15 for domestic students; for spring admission, 10/15 for domestic students. Applications are processed on a rolling basis. Application fee: $55. Tuition and fees vary according to program. *Financial support:* Application deadline: 3/1. *Faculty research:* Mathematical modeling, international development technology, geology, environmental resources engineering. *Unit head:* Dr. Chris Dugaw, Chair, 707-826-4251, Fax: 707-826-4145, E-mail: dugaw@humboldt.edu. *Application contact:* Julie Tucker, Administrative Support, 707-826-3256, Fax: 707-826-3140, E-mail: jlt7002@humboldt.edu.

ICR Graduate School, Graduate Programs, Santee, CA 92071. Offers astro/geophysics (MS); biology (MS); geology (MS); science education (MS). Part-time programs available. *Degree requirements:* For master's, comprehensive exam (for some programs), thesis (for some programs). *Entrance requirements:* For master's, minimum undergraduate GPA of 3.0, bachelor's degree in science or science education. *Faculty research:* Age of the earth, limits of variation, catastrophe, optimum methods for teaching.

Idaho State University, Office of Graduate Studies, College of Arts and Sciences, Department of Geosciences, Pocatello, ID 83209-8072. Offers geographic information science (MS); geology (MNS, MS); geology with emphasis in environmental geoscience (MS); geophysics/hydrology/geology (MS); geotechnology (Postbaccalaureate Certificate). Part-time programs available. *Degree requirements:* For master's, comprehensive exam, thesis, oral colloquium; for Postbaccalaureate Certificate, thesis optional, minimum 19 credits. *Entrance requirements:* For master's, GRE General Test (minimum 50th percentile in 2 sections), 3 letters of recommendation; for Postbaccalaureate Certificate, GRE General Test, 3 letters of recommendation, bachelor's degree, statement of goals. Additional exam requirements/recommendations for international students: Required—TOEFL (minimum score 550 paper-based; 213 computer-based; 80 iBT). Electronic applications accepted. *Faculty research:* Quantitative field mapping and sampling: microscopic, geochemical, and isotopic analysis of rocks, minerals and water; remote sensing, geographic information systems, and global positioning systems: environmental and watershed management; surficial and fluvial processes: landscape change; regional tectonics, structural geology; planetary geology.

Indiana University Bloomington, University Graduate School, College of Arts and Sciences, Department of Geological Sciences, Bloomington, IN 47405-7000. Offers biogeochemistry (MS, PhD); economic geology (MS, PhD); geobiology (MS, PhD); geophysics, structural geology and tectonics (MS, PhD); hydrogeology (MS, PhD); mineralogy (MS, PhD); stratigraphy and sedimentology (MS, PhD). *Faculty:* 17 full-time (1 woman). *Students:* 48 full-time (24 women), 5 part-time (1 woman); includes 4 minority (2 Black or African American, non-Hispanic/Latino; 1 Hispanic/Latino; 1 Two or more races, non-Hispanic/Latino), 20 international. Average age 29. 70 applicants, 24% accepted, 16 enrolled. In 2010, 3 master's, 4 doctorates awarded. Terminal master's awarded for partial completion of doctoral program. *Degree requirements:* For master's, thesis or alternative; for doctorate, comprehensive exam, thesis/dissertation. *Entrance requirements:* For master's and doctorate, GRE General Test. Additional exam requirements/recommendations for international students: Required—TOEFL. *Application deadline:* For fall admission, 1/15 priority date for domestic students, 12/15 for international students; for spring admission, 9/1 priority date for domestic students, 9/1 for international students. Applications are processed on a rolling basis. Application fee: $55 ($65 for international students). *Financial support:* In 2010–11, 10 fellowships with full tuition reimbursements (averaging $17,300 per year), 6 research assistantships with full tuition reimbursements (averaging $16,370 per year), 12 teaching assistantships with full tuition reimbursements (averaging $15,150 per year) were awarded; career-related internships or fieldwork, Federal Work-Study, and institutionally sponsored loans also available. *Faculty research:* Geophysics, geochemistry, hydrogeology, geobiology, planetary science. Total annual research expenditures: $644,299. *Unit head:* Simon Brassell, Chair, 812-855-5581, Fax: 812-855-7899, E-mail: geochair@indiana.edu. *Application contact:* Mary Iverson, Graduate Secretary, 812-855-7214, Fax: 812-855-7899, E-mail: miverson@indiana.edu.

Indiana University–Purdue University Indianapolis, School of Science, Department of Earth Sciences, Indianapolis, IN 46202-3272. Offers applied earth sciences (PhD); geology (MS). Part-time and evening/weekend programs available. *Faculty:* 8 full-time (2 women). *Students:* 10 full-time (8 women), 8 part-time (3 women), 8 international. Average age 29. 12 applicants, 58% accepted, 5 enrolled. In 2010, 7 master's awarded. *Degree requirements:* For master's, thesis (for some programs). *Entrance requirements:* For master's, GRE General Test, minimum GPA of 3.0. Application fee: $55 ($65 for international students). *Financial support:* In 2010–11, 2 fellowships with full tuition reimbursements (averaging $12,000 per year), 7 teaching assistantships with full tuition reimbursements (averaging $12,103 per year) were awarded; research assistantships with full tuition reimbursements, scholarships/grants also available. Financial award application deadline: 3/1. *Faculty research:* Wetland hydrology, groundwater contamination, soils, sedimentology, sediment chemistry. *Unit head:* Gabriel Filippelli, Chair, 317-274-7484, Fax: 317-274-7966. *Application contact:* Lenore P. Tedesco, Associate Professor, 317-274-7484, Fax: 317-274-7966, E-mail: ltedesco@iupui.edu.

Iowa State University of Science and Technology, Graduate College, College of Liberal Arts and Sciences, Department of Geological and Atmospheric Sciences, Ames, IA 50011. Offers earth science (MS, PhD); environmental science (MS, PhD); geology (MS, PhD); meteorology (MS, PhD). *Faculty:* 20 full-time (2 women). *Students:* 33 full-time (8 women), 8 part-time (3 women); includes 1 Asian, non-Hispanic/Latino, 3 international. 45 applicants, 49% accepted, 9 enrolled. In 2010, 9 master's, 5 doctorates awarded. *Degree requirements:* For master's, thesis (for some programs); for doctorate, thesis/dissertation. *Entrance requirements:* For master's and doctorate, GRE General Test. Additional exam requirements/recommendations for international students: Required—TOEFL (minimum score 550 paper-based; 79 iBT), IELTS (minimum score 6.5). *Application deadline:* For fall admission, 1/1 priority date for domestic students. Applications are processed on a rolling basis. Application fee: $40 ($90 for international students). Electronic applications accepted. *Financial support:* In 2010–11, 23 research assistantships with full and partial tuition reimbursements (averaging $12,780 per year), 8 teaching assistantships with full and partial tuition reimbursements (averaging $6,806 per year) were awarded; fellowships, scholarships/grants, health care benefits, and unspecified assistantships also available. *Unit head:* Dr. Carl E. Jacobson, Chair, 515-294-4477. *Application contact:* Dr. Carl E. Jacobson, Chair, 515-294-4477.

Kansas State University, Graduate School, College of Arts and Sciences, Department of Geology, Manhattan, KS 66506. Offers MS. *Degree requirements:* For master's, thesis. *Entrance requirements:* For master's, GRE General Test, GRE Subject Test. Additional exam requirements/recommendations for international students: Required—TOEFL. Electronic applications accepted. *Faculty research:* Seismology/tectonics, sedimentology and paleobiology, quaternary geology, orogenesis, earth science education, igneous petrology.

Kent State University, College of Arts and Sciences, Department of Geology, Kent, OH 44242-0001. Offers applied geology (PhD); geology (MS). *Degree requirements:* For master's, thesis; for doctorate, one foreign language, thesis/dissertation. *Entrance requirements:* For master's, minimum GPA of 2.75; for doctorate, GRE General Test, GRE Subject Test, minimum GPA of 3.0. Additional exam requirements/recommendations for international students: Required—TOEFL (minimum score 575 paper-based; 232 computer-based). Electronic applications accepted. *Expenses:* Tuition, state resident: full-time $7866; part-time $437 per credit hour. Tuition, nonresident: full-time $14,022; part-time $779 per credit hour. *Faculty research:* Groundwater, surface water, engineering geology, paleontology, structural geology.

Lakehead University, Graduate Studies, Department of Geology, Thunder Bay, ON P7B 5E1, Canada. Offers M Sc. Part-time and evening/weekend programs available. *Degree requirements:* For master's, thesis, department seminar, oral exam. *Entrance requirements:* For master's, minimum B average, honours bachelors degree in geology. Additional exam requirements/recommendations for international students: Required—TOEFL. *Faculty research:* Rock physics, sedimentology, mineralogy and economic geology, geochemistry, petrology of alkaline rocks.

Laurentian University, School of Graduate Studies and Research, Programme in Geology (Earth Sciences), Sudbury, ON P3E 2C6, Canada. Offers geology (M Sc); mineral deposits and precambrian geology (PhD); mineral exploration (M Sc). Part-time programs available. *Degree requirements:* For master's, thesis. *Entrance requirements:* For master's, honors degree with second class or better. *Faculty research:* Localization and metallogenesis of Ni-Cu-(PGE) sulfide mineralization in the Thompson Nickel Belt, mapping lithology and ore-grade and monitoring dissolved organic carbon in lakes using remote sensing, global reefs, volcanic effects on VMS deposits.

Lehigh University, College of Arts and Sciences, Department of Earth and Environmental Sciences, Bethlehem, PA 18015. Offers MS, PhD. *Faculty:* 14 full-time (1 woman), 1 (woman) part-time/adjunct. *Students:* 26 full-time (10 women), 2 part-time (1 woman), 4 international. Average age 27. 57 applicants, 23% accepted, 10 enrolled. In 2010, 10 master's, 1 doctorate awarded. Terminal master's awarded for partial completion of doctoral program. *Degree requirements:* For master's, thesis; for doctorate, thesis/dissertation. *Entrance requirements:* For master's and doctorate, GRE General Test, transcripts, recommendation letters, research statement, faculty advocates. Additional exam requirements/recommendations for international students: Required—TOEFL (minimum score 85 iBT). *Application deadline:* For fall admission, 1/15 for domestic and international students. Applications are processed on a rolling basis. Application fee: $75. Electronic applications accepted. *Financial support:* In 2010–11, 13 students received support, including 3 fellowships with full tuition reimbursements available (averaging $15,400 per year), 12 research assistantships with full tuition reimbursements available (averaging $15,400 per year), 10 teaching assistantships with full tuition reimbursements available (averaging $15,400 per year); career-related internships or fieldwork, Federal Work-Study, institutionally sponsored loans, scholarships/grants, tuition waivers (full and partial), and unspecified assistantships also available. Support available to part-time students. Financial award application deadline: 1/15. *Faculty research:* Tectonics, surficial processes, ecology, environmental change. Total annual research expenditures: $1.1 million. *Unit head:* Dr. Frank J. Pazzaglia, Chairman, 610-758-3667, Fax: 610-758-3677, E-mail: fjp3@lehigh.edu. *Application contact:* Dr. Zicheng Yu, Graduate Coordinator, 610-758-6751, Fax: 610-758-3677, E-mail: ziy2@lehigh.edu.

Louisiana State University and Agricultural and Mechanical College, Graduate School, College of Basic Sciences, Department of Geology and Geophysics, Baton Rouge, LA 70803. Offers MS, PhD. *Faculty:* 16 full-time (6 women), 1 (woman) part-time/adjunct. *Students:* 43 full-time (14 women), 13 part-time (2 women); includes 3 Black or African American, non-Hispanic/Latino; 1 Asian, non-Hispanic/Latino; 1 Hispanic/Latino; 1 Two or more races, non-Hispanic/Latino, 10 international. Average age 27. 62 applicants, 53% accepted, 11 enrolled. In 2010, 20 master's, 1 doctorate awarded. Terminal master's awarded for partial completion of doctoral program. *Degree requirements:* For master's, thesis; for doctorate, thesis/dissertation. *Entrance requirements:* For master's and doctorate, GRE General Test, minimum GPA of 3.0. Additional exam requirements/recommendations for international students: Required—TOEFL (minimum score 550 paper-based; 213 computer-based; 79 iBT) or IELTS (minimum score 6.5). *Application deadline:* For fall admission, 1/25 priority date for domestic students, 5/15 for international students; for spring admission, 10/15 for international students. Applications are processed on a rolling basis. Application fee: $50 ($70 for international students). Electronic applications accepted. *Financial support:* In 2010–11, 42 students received support, including 2 fellowships with full tuition reimbursements available (averaging $14,917 per year), 19 research assistantships with full and partial tuition reimbursements available (averaging $19,302 per year), 15 teaching assistantships with full and partial tuition reimbursements available (averaging $14,258 per year); career-related internships or fieldwork, Federal Work-Study, institutionally sponsored loans, health care benefits, tuition waivers (full and partial), and unspecified assistantships also available. Financial award application deadline: 3/15; financial award applicants required to submit FAFSA. *Faculty research:* Geophysics, sedimentology, geochemistry, geomicrobiology, tectonics. Total annual research expenditures: $917,832. *Unit head:* Dr. Carol Wicks, Chair, 225-578-3353, Fax: 225-578-2302, E-mail: glande@lsu.edu. *Application contact:* Jeffrey Nunn, Graduate Coordinator, 225-578-6657, E-mail: gljeff@lsu.edu.

Massachusetts Institute of Technology, School of Science, Department of Earth, Atmospheric, and Planetary Sciences, Cambridge, MA 02139. Offers atmospheric chemistry (PhD, Sc D); atmospheric science (SM, PhD, Sc D); chemical oceanography (SM, PhD, Sc D); climate physics and chemistry (SM, PhD, Sc D); earth and planetary sciences (SM); geochemistry (PhD, Sc D); geology (PhD, Sc D); geophysics (PhD, Sc D); marine geology and geophysics (SM, PhD, Sc D); physical oceanography (SM, PhD, Sc D); planetary sciences (PhD, Sc D). *Faculty:* 36 full-time (7 women). *Students:* 165 full-time (86 women); includes 17 minority (2 Black or African American, non-Hispanic/Latino; 2 American Indian or Alaska Native, non-Hispanic/Latino; 5 Asian, non-Hispanic/Latino; 5 Hispanic/Latino; 3 Two or more races, non-Hispanic/Latino), 50 international. Average age 27. 227 applicants, 33% accepted, 38 enrolled. In 2010, 12 master's, 26 doctorates awarded. Terminal master's awarded for partial completion of doctoral program. *Degree requirements:* For master's, thesis; for doctorate, comprehensive exam, thesis/dissertation. *Entrance requirements:* For master's, GRE General Test; for doctorate, GRE General Test, GRE Subject Test (chemistry or physics for planetary science area). Additional exam requirements/recommendations for international students: Required—TOEFL (minimum score 577 paper-based; 233 computer-based; 91 iBT), IELTS (minimum score 7). *Application deadline:* For fall admission, 1/5 for domestic and international students; for spring admission, 11/1 for domestic and international students. Application fee: $75. Electronic applications accepted. *Expenses:* Tuition: Full-time $38,940; part-time $605 per unit. Required fees: $272. *Financial support:* In 2010–11, 123 students received support, including 62 fellowships with tuition reimbursements available (averaging $30,852 per year), 88 research assistantships with tuition reimbursements available (averaging $30,258 per year), 13 teaching assistantships with tuition reimbursements available (averaging $30,323 per year); Federal Work-Study, institutionally sponsored loans, scholarships/grants, health care benefits, and unspecified assistantships also available. *Faculty research:* Formation, dynamics and evolution of planetary systems; origin, composition, structure and dynamics of the atmospheres, oceans, surfaces and interiors of the Earth and other planets; evolution and interaction of the physical, chemical, geological and biological components of the Earth system; characterization of past, present and potential future climates and the causes and consequences of climate change; interplay of energy and the environment. Total annual research expenditures: $24.8 million. *Unit head:* Prof. Maria Zuber, Department Head, 617-253-2127, Fax: 617-253-8298, E-mail: eapsinfo@mit.edu. *Application contact:* EAPS Education Office, 617-253-3381, Fax: 617-253-8298, E-mail: eapsinfo@mit.edu.

McMaster University, School of Graduate Studies, Faculty of Science, School of Geography and Earth Sciences, Hamilton, ON L8S 4M2, Canada. Offers geochemistry (PhD); geology (M Sc, PhD); human geography (MA, PhD); physical geography (M Sc, PhD). Part-time programs available. Terminal master's awarded for partial completion of doctoral program. *Degree requirements:* For master's, thesis; for doctorate, comprehensive exam, thesis/dissertation. *Entrance requirements:* For master's, minimum B+ average. Additional exam requirements/recommendations for international students: Required—TOEFL (minimum score 550 paper-based; 213 computer-based).

Memorial University of Newfoundland, School of Graduate Studies, Department of Earth Sciences, St. John's, NL A1C 5S7, Canada. Offers geology (M Sc, PhD); geophysics (M Sc, PhD). Part-time programs available. *Degree requirements:* For master's, thesis; for doctorate, comprehensive exam, thesis/dissertation, oral thesis defense, entry evaluation. *Entrance requirements:* For master's, honors B Sc; for doctorate, M Sc. Electronic applications accepted. *Faculty research:* Geochemistry, sedimentology, paleoceanography and global change, mineral deposits, petroleum geology, hydrology.

Miami University, Graduate School, College of Arts and Science, Department of Geology, Oxford, OH 45056. Offers MA, MS, PhD. Part-time programs available. *Students:* 30 full-time (16 women); includes 4 minority (1 Black or African American, non-Hispanic/Latino; 2 Asian, non-Hispanic/Latino; 1 Two or more races, non-Hispanic/Latino), 12 international. Average age 28. In 2010, 8 master's, 2 doctorates awarded. *Entrance requirements:* For master's, GRE General Test, GRE Subject Test, minimum undergraduate GPA of 3.0 during previous 2 years or 2.75 overall; for doctorate, GRE General Test, GRE Subject Test, minimum GPA of 2.75 (undergraduate) or 3.0 (graduate). Additional exam requirements/recommendations for international students: Required—TOEFL. *Application deadline:* For fall admission, 2/1 for domestic and international students. Application fee: $35. *Expenses:* Tuition, state resident: full-time $11,616; part-time $484 per credit hour. Tuition, nonresident: full-time $25,656; part-time

Geology

Miami University (continued)

$1069 per credit hour. Required fees: $528. *Financial support:* Fellowships with full tuition reimbursements, research assistantships with full tuition reimbursements, teaching assistantships with full tuition reimbursements, Federal Work-Study, institutionally sponsored loans, health care benefits, tuition waivers (full), and unspecified assistantships available. Financial award application deadline: 3/1; financial award applicants required to submit FAFSA. *Unit head:* Dr. William Hart, Department Chair and Professor, 513-529-3216, Fax: 513-529-1542, E-mail: hartwk@muohio.edu. *Application contact:* Dr. Elisabeth Widom, Director of Graduate Studies, 513-529-5048, E-mail: widome@muohio.edu.

Michigan Technological University, Graduate School, College of Engineering, Department of Geological and Mining Engineering and Sciences, Program in Geology, Houghton, MI 49931. Offers MS, PhD. Part-time programs available. Terminal master's awarded for partial completion of doctoral program. *Degree requirements:* For master's, comprehensive exam; for doctorate, comprehensive exam, thesis/dissertation. *Entrance requirements:* Additional exam requirements/recommendations for international students: Required—TOEFL (minimum score 550 paper-based; 213 computer-based). Electronic applications accepted.

Missouri State University, Graduate College, College of Natural and Applied Sciences, Department of Geography, Geology, and Planning, Springfield, MO 65897. Offers geospatial sciences (MS); natural and applied science (MNAS), including geography, geology and planning; secondary education (MS Ed), including earth science, geography. Part-time and evening/weekend programs available. *Degree requirements:* For master's, comprehensive exam, thesis (for some programs). *Entrance requirements:* For master's, GRE General Test (MS, MNAS), minimum undergraduate GPA of 3.0 (MS, MNAS), 9-12 teacher certification (MS Ed). Additional exam requirements/recommendations for international students: Required—TOEFL (minimum score 550 paper-based; 213 computer-based; 79 iBT). Electronic applications accepted. *Expenses:* Tuition, state resident: full-time $3348; part-time $186 per credit hour. Tuition, nonresident: full-time $6696; part-time $372 per credit hour. Required fees: $238 per semester. Tuition and fees vary according to course level, course load and program. *Faculty research:* Stratigraphy and ancient meteorite impacts, environmental geochemistry of karst, hyperspectral image processing, water quality, small town planning.

Missouri University of Science and Technology, Graduate School, Department of Geological Sciences and Engineering, Rolla, MO 65409. Offers geological engineering (MS, DE, PhD); geology and geophysics (MS, PhD), including geochemistry, geology, geophysics, groundwater and environmental geology; petroleum engineering (MS, DE, PhD). Part-time programs available. *Degree requirements:* For master's, thesis optional; for doctorate, comprehensive exam, thesis/dissertation. *Entrance requirements:* For master's, GRE General Test (minimum score 600 quantitative, writing 3.5), minimum GPA of 3.0 in last 4 semesters; for doctorate, GRE General Test (minimum: Q 600, GRE WR 3.5). Additional exam requirements/recommendations for international students: Required—TOEFL. Electronic applications accepted. *Faculty research:* Digital image processing and geographic information systems, mineralogy, igneous and sedimentary petrology-geochemistry, sedimentology groundwater hydrology and contaminant transport.

Montana Tech of The University of Montana, Graduate School, Geosciences Programs, Butte, MT 59701-8997. Offers geochemistry (MS); geological engineering (MS); geology (MS); geophysical engineering (MS); hydrogeological engineering (MS); hydrogeology (MS). Part-time programs available. *Faculty:* 16 full-time (4 women), 4 part-time/adjunct (0 women). *Students:* 15 full-time (6 women), 10 part-time (5 women); includes 1 Black or African American, non-Hispanic/Latino; 1 American Indian or Alaska Native, non-Hispanic/Latino, 2 international. 9 applicants, 89% accepted, 8 enrolled. In 2010, 4 master's awarded. *Degree requirements:* For master's, comprehensive exam (for some programs), thesis (for some programs). *Entrance requirements:* For master's, GRE General Test, minimum GPA of 3.0. Additional exam requirements/recommendations for international students: Required—TOEFL (minimum score 525 paper-based; 195 computer-based; 71 iBT). *Application deadline:* For fall admission, 4/1 priority date for domestic students, 3/1 priority date for international students; for spring admission, 10/1 priority date for domestic students, 7/1 priority date for international students. Applications are processed on a rolling basis. Application fee: $30. Electronic applications accepted. *Expenses:* Tuition, state resident: full-time $5084. Tuition, nonresident: full-time $15,104. *Financial support:* In 2010–11, 17 students received support, including 10 teaching assistantships with partial tuition reimbursements available (averaging $5,200 per year); research assistantships with partial tuition reimbursements available, career-related internships or fieldwork, tuition waivers (full and partial), and unspecified assistantships also available. Financial award application deadline: 4/1; financial award applicants required to submit FAFSA. *Faculty research:* Water resource development, seismic processing, petroleum reservoir characterization, environmental geochemistry, geologic mapping. *Unit head:* Dr. Mary MacLaughlin, Department Head, 406-496-4655, Fax: 406-496-4260, E-mail: mmaclaughlin@mtech.edu. *Application contact:* Fred Sullivan, Administrator, Graduate School, 406-496-4304, Fax: 406-496-4710, E-mail: fsullivan@mtech.edu.

New Mexico Institute of Mining and Technology, Graduate Studies, Department of Earth and Environmental Science, Program in Geology and Geochemistry, Socorro, NM 87801. Offers geochemistry (MS, PhD); geology (MS, PhD). *Degree requirements:* For master's, thesis optional; for doctorate, thesis/dissertation. *Entrance requirements:* For master's, GRE General Test; for doctorate, GRE General Test, GRE Subject Test. Additional exam requirements/recommendations for international students: Required—TOEFL (minimum score 540 paper-based; 207 computer-based). Electronic applications accepted. *Faculty research:* Cave and karst topography, soil/water chemistry and properties, geochemistry of ore deposits.

New Mexico State University, Graduate School, College of Arts and Sciences, Department of Geological Sciences, Las Cruces, NM 88003-8001. Offers MS. Part-time programs available. *Faculty:* 6 full-time (2 women). *Students:* 14 full-time (4 women), 7 part-time (2 women). Average age 27. 22 applicants, 100% accepted, 6 enrolled. In 2010, 3 master's awarded. *Degree requirements:* For master's, thesis. *Entrance requirements:* For master's, GRE General Test, BS in geology or the equivalent. Additional exam requirements/recommendations for international students: Required—TOEFL. *Application deadline:* For fall admission, 7/1 priority date for domestic and international students; for spring admission, 11/1 priority date for domestic and international students. Applications are processed on a rolling basis. Application fee: $30 ($50 for international students). Electronic applications accepted. *Expenses:* Tuition, state resident: full-time $4536; part-time $242 per credit. Tuition, nonresident: full-time $15,816; part-time $712 per credit. Required fees: $636 per term. *Financial support:* In 2010–11, 2 research assistantships with full tuition reimbursements (averaging $9,616 per year), 11 teaching assistantships with partial tuition reimbursements (averaging $16,450 per year) were awarded; career-related internships or fieldwork, Federal Work-Study, institutionally sponsored loans, scholarships/grants, health care benefits, and unspecified assistantships also available. Support available to part-time students. Financial award application deadline: 2/15; financial award applicants required to submit FAFSA. *Faculty research:* Geochemistry, tectonics, sedimentology, stratigraphy, igneous petrology. *Unit head:* Dr. Nancy J. McMillan, Head, 575-646-2708, Fax: 575-646-1056, E-mail: nmcmille@nmsu.edu. *Application contact:* Dr. Jeff Amato, Professor, 575-646-3017, Fax: 575-646-1056, E-mail: amato@nmsu.edu.

Northern Arizona University, Graduate College, College of Engineering, Forestry and Natural Sciences, School of Earth Sciences and Environmental Sustainability, Flagstaff, AZ 86011. Offers climate science and solutions (MS); earth science (MS); environmental sciences and policy (MS); geology (MS). *Faculty:* 27 full-time (7 women). *Students:* 50 full-time (22 women), 18 part-time (9 women); includes 4 minority (1 American Indian or Alaska Native, non-Hispanic/Latino; 1 Asian, non-Hispanic/Latino; 2 Hispanic/Latino), 2 international. 113 applicants, 31% accepted, 27 enrolled. In 2010, 21 master's awarded. *Degree requirements:* For master's, comprehensive exam (for some programs), thesis (for some programs). *Entrance requirements:* Additional exam requirements/recommendations for international students: Required—TOEFL (minimum score 550 paper-based; 213 computer-based; 80 iBT), IELTS (minimum score 7). *Application deadline:* For fall admission, 2/1 priority date for domestic and international students. Applications are processed on a rolling basis. Application fee: $65. Electronic applications accepted. *Financial support:* In 2010–11, 6 fellowships, 7 research assistantships with partial tuition reimbursements (averaging $12,866 per year), 28 teaching assistantships with partial tuition reimbursements (averaging $12,477 per year) were awarded; career-related internships or fieldwork, Federal Work-Study, scholarships/grants, health care benefits, tuition waivers (full and partial), and unspecified assistantships also available. Financial award applicants required to submit FAFSA. *Unit head:* Dr. Abe Springer, Director, 928-523-7198. *Application contact:* Dr. Abe Springer, Director, 928-523-7198.

Northern Illinois University, Graduate School, College of Liberal Arts and Sciences, Department of Geology and Environmental Geosciences, De Kalb, IL 60115-2854. Offers geology (MS, PhD). Part-time programs available. *Faculty:* 11 full-time (1 woman), 1 (woman) part-time/adjunct. *Students:* 16 full-time (5 women), 26 part-time (13 women); includes 1 Black or African American, non-Hispanic/Latino; 1 Asian, non-Hispanic/Latino, 6 international. Average age 30. 25 applicants, 72% accepted, 12 enrolled. In 2010, 11 master's, 1 doctorate awarded. Terminal master's awarded for partial completion of doctoral program. *Degree requirements:* For master's, comprehensive exam, thesis optional, research seminar; for doctorate, thesis/dissertation, candidacy exam, dissertation defense, internship, research seminar. *Entrance requirements:* For master's, GRE General Test, bachelor's degree in engineering or science, minimum GPA of 2.75; for doctorate, GRE General Test, bachelor's or master's degree in engineering or science, minimum graduate GPA of 3.2. Additional exam requirements/recommendations for international students: Required—TOEFL (minimum score 550 paper-based; 213 computer-based). *Application deadline:* For fall admission, 6/1 for domestic students, 5/1 for international students; for spring admission, 11/1 for domestic students, 10/1 for international students. Applications are processed on a rolling basis. Application fee: $30. Electronic applications accepted. *Expenses:* Tuition, state resident: full-time $7200; part-time $300 per credit hour. Tuition, nonresident: full-time $14,400; part-time $600 per credit hour. Required fees: $79 per credit hour. *Financial support:* In 2010–11, 1 research assistantship with full tuition reimbursement, 23 teaching assistantships with full tuition reimbursements were awarded; fellowships with full tuition reimbursements, career-related internships or fieldwork, Federal Work-Study, scholarships/grants, tuition waivers (full), and unspecified assistantships also available. Support available to part-time students. Financial award applicants required to submit FAFSA. *Faculty research:* Micropaleontology, environmental geochemistry, glacial geology, igneous petrology, statistical analyses of fracture networks. *Unit head:* Dr. Colin Booth, Chair, 815-753-0523, Fax: 815-753-1945, E-mail: cbooth@niu.edu. *Application contact:* Dr. James Walker, Director of Graduate Studies, 815-753-7936, E-mail: jim@geol.niu.edu.

Northwestern University, The Graduate School, Judd A. and Marjorie Weinberg College of Arts and Sciences, Department of Geological Sciences, Evanston, IL 60208. Offers MS, PhD. Admissions and degrees offered through The Graduate School. Part-time programs available. *Degree requirements:* For doctorate, thesis/dissertation. *Entrance requirements:* For master's and doctorate, GRE General Test. Additional exam requirements/recommendations for international students: Required—TOEFL. Electronic applications accepted.

The Ohio State University, Graduate School, College of Arts and Sciences, Division of Natural and Mathematical Sciences, School of Earth Sciences, Columbus, OH 43210. Offers geodetic science (MS); geological sciences (MS, PhD). *Faculty:* 30. *Students:* 32 full-time (17 women), 15 part-time (6 women); includes 1 Black or African American, non-Hispanic/Latino; 3 Hispanic/Latino; 1 Two or more races, non-Hispanic/Latino, 4 international. Average age 29. In 2010, 3 master's, 9 doctorates awarded. *Degree requirements:* For master's, thesis; for doctorate, thesis/dissertation. *Entrance requirements:* For master's and doctorate, GRE. Additional exam requirements/recommendations for international students: Required—TOEFL (minimum score 600 paper-based; 250 computer-based). *Application deadline:* For fall admission, 8/15 priority date for domestic students, 7/1 priority date for international students; for winter admission, 12/1 priority date for domestic students, 11/1 priority date for international students; for spring admission, 3/1 priority date for domestic students, 2/1 priority date for international students. Applications are processed on a rolling basis. Application fee: $40 ($50 for international students). Electronic applications accepted. *Expenses:* Tuition, state resident: full-time $10,605. Tuition, nonresident: full-time $26,535. Tuition and fees vary according to course load and program. *Unit head:* W. Berry Lyons, Director, 614-688-3241, Fax: 614-292-7688, E-mail: lyons.142@osu.edu. *Application contact:* Graduate Admissions, 614-292-9444, Fax: 614-292-3895, E-mail: domestic.grad@osu.edu.

Ohio University, Graduate College, College of Arts and Sciences, Department of Geological Sciences, Athens, OH 45701-2979. Offers environmental geochemistry (MS); environmental geology (MS); environmental/hydrology (MS); geology (MS); geology education (MS); geomorphology/surficial processes (MS); geophysics (MS); hydrogeology (MS); sedimentology (MS); structure/tectonics (MS). Part-time programs available. *Students:* 14 full-time (8 women), 1 (woman) part-time. 15 applicants, 60% accepted, 8 enrolled. In 2010, 7 master's awarded. *Degree requirements:* For master's, thesis. *Entrance requirements:* Additional exam requirements/recommendations for international students: Required—TOEFL (minimum score 550 paper-based; 80 iBT) or IELTS (minimum score 6.5). *Application deadline:* For fall admission, 2/1 priority date for domestic and international students. Application fee: $50 ($55 for international students). Electronic applications accepted. *Financial support:* Research assistantships with full tuition reimbursements, teaching assistantships with full tuition reimbursements, Federal Work-Study, institutionally sponsored loans, scholarships/grants, tuition waivers (partial), and unspecified assistantships available. Financial award application deadline: 2/1. *Faculty research:* Geoscience education, tectonics, fluvial geomorphology, invertebrate paleontology, mine/hydrology. Total annual research expenditures: $649,020. *Unit head:* Dr. Gregory Nadon, Chair, 740-593-4212, Fax: 740-593-0486, E-mail: nadon@ohio.edu. *Application contact:* Dr. Douglas Green, Graduate Chair, 740-593-1843, Fax: 740-593-0486, E-mail: green@ohio.edu.

Oklahoma State University, College of Arts and Sciences, School of Geology, Stillwater, OK 74078. Offers MS, PhD. *Faculty:* 11 full-time (3 women), 2 part-time/adjunct (1 woman). *Students:* 35 full-time (8 women), 23 part-time (9 women); includes 1 American Indian or Alaska Native, non-Hispanic/Latino; 1 Hispanic/Latino, 14 international. Average age 29. 73 applicants, 40% accepted, 16 enrolled. In 2010, 9 master's, 2 doctorates awarded. *Degree requirements:* For master's, thesis; for doctorate, comprehensive exam, thesis/dissertation. *Entrance requirements:* For master's, GRE; for doctorate, GRE. Additional exam requirements/recommendations for international students: Required—TOEFL (minimum score 550 paper-based; 79 iBT). *Application deadline:* For fall admission, 3/1 priority date for international students; for spring admission, 8/1 priority date for international students. Applications are processed on a rolling basis. Application fee: $40 ($75 for international students). Electronic applications accepted. *Expenses:* Tuition, state resident: full-time $3716; part-time $154.85 per credit hour. Tuition, nonresident: full-time $14,892; part-time $621 per credit hour. Required fees: $2044; $85.20 per credit hour. One-time fee: $50. Tuition and fees vary according to course load and campus/location. *Financial support:* In 2010–11, 8 research assistantships (averaging $10,418 per year), 20 teaching assistantships (averaging $8,053 per year) were awarded; career-related internships or fieldwork, Federal Work-Study, scholarships/grants, health care benefits, tuition waivers (partial), and unspecified assistantships also available. Support available to part-time students. Financial award application deadline: 3/1; financial award applicants required to submit FAFSA. *Faculty research:* Groundwater hydrology, petroleum geology. *Unit head:* Dr. Jay Gregg, Head, 405-744-6358, Fax: 405-744-7841. *Application contact:* Dr. Gordon Emslie, Dean, 405-744-6368, Fax: 405-744-0355, E-mail: grad-i@okstate.edu.

120 www.facebook.com/petersonspublishing

Peterson's Graduate Programs in the Physical Sciences, Mathematics, Agricultural Sciences, the Environment & Natural Resources 2012

Oregon State University, Graduate School, College of Science, Department of Geosciences, Program in Geology, Corvallis, OR 97331. Offers MA, MAIS, MS, PhD. Part-time programs available. Terminal master's awarded for partial completion of doctoral program. *Degree requirements:* For master's, variable foreign language requirement, thesis; for doctorate, one foreign language, thesis/dissertation. *Entrance requirements:* For master's and doctorate, GRE General Test, GRE Subject Test, minimum GPA of 3.0 in last 90 hours. Additional exam requirements/recommendations for international students: Required—TOEFL. *Faculty research:* Hydrogeology, geomorphology, ocean geology, geochemistry, earthquake geology.

Portland State University, Graduate Studies, College of Liberal Arts and Sciences, Department of Geology, Portland, OR 97207-0751. Offers environmental sciences and resources (PhD); geology (MA, MS); science/geology (MAT, MST). Part-time programs available. *Faculty:* 10 full-time (2 women), 3 part-time/adjunct (2 women). *Students:* 15 full-time (6 women), 26 part-time (5 women); includes 1 American Indian or Alaska Native, non-Hispanic/Latino. Average age 30. 20 applicants, 90% accepted, 8 enrolled. In 2010, 4 master's awarded. *Degree requirements:* For master's, comprehensive exam, thesis, field comprehensive; for doctorate, thesis/dissertation, 2 years of residency. *Entrance requirements:* For master's, GRE General Test, GRE Subject Test, BA/BS in geology, minimum GPA of 3.0 in upper-division course work or 2.75 overall. Additional exam requirements/recommendations for international students: Required—TOEFL (minimum score 550 paper-based; 213 computer-based). *Application deadline:* 1/31 priority date for domestic and international students. Applications are processed on a rolling basis. Application fee: $50. *Expenses:* Tuition, state resident: full-time $8505; part-time $315 per credit. Tuition, nonresident: full-time $13,284; part-time $492 per credit. Required fees: $1482; $21 per credit. $99 per term. One-time fee: $120. Part-time tuition and fees vary according to course load and program. *Financial support:* In 2010–11, 8 teaching assistantships with full tuition reimbursements (averaging $11,702 per year) were awarded; research assistantships with full tuition reimbursements, career-related internships or fieldwork, Federal Work-Study, scholarships/grants, and unspecified assistantships also available. Support available to part-time students. Financial award application deadline: 3/1; financial award applicants required to submit FAFSA. *Faculty research:* Sediment transport, volcanic environmental geology, coastal and fluvial processes. Total annual research expenditures: $1.8 million. *Unit head:* Dr. Andrew Fountain, Chair, 503-725-3386, Fax: 503-725-3025, E-mail: andrew@pdx.edu. *Application contact:* Nancy Eriksson, Office Coordinator, 503-725-3022, Fax: 503-725-3025, E-mail: nancye@pdx.edu.

Queens College of the City University of New York, Division of Graduate Studies, Mathematics and Natural Sciences Division, School of Earth and Environmental Sciences, Flushing, NY 11367-1597. Offers MA. Part-time and evening/weekend programs available. *Faculty:* 14 full-time (4 women). *Students:* 1 (woman) full-time, 17 part-time (11 women); includes 2 Asian, non-Hispanic/Latino; 3 Hispanic/Latino, 2 international. 13 applicants, 38% accepted, 3 enrolled. *Degree requirements:* For master's, comprehensive exam, thesis. *Entrance requirements:* For master's, GRE, previous course work in calculus, physics, and chemistry; minimum GPA of 3.0. Additional exam requirements/recommendations for international students: Required—TOEFL. *Application deadline:* For fall admission, 4/1 for domestic students; for spring admission, 11/1 for domestic students. Applications are processed on a rolling basis. Application fee: $125. *Financial support:* Career-related internships or fieldwork, Federal Work-Study, institutionally sponsored loans, tuition waivers (partial), and unspecified assistantships available. Support available to part-time students. Financial award application deadline: 4/1; financial award applicants required to submit FAFSA. *Faculty research:* Sedimentology/stratigraphy, paleontology, field petrology. *Unit head:* Dr. Yan Zheng, Chairperson, 718-997-3300. *Application contact:* Dr. Hannes Brueckner, Graduate Adviser, 718-997-3300, E-mail: hannes_brueckner@qc.edu.

Queen's University at Kingston, School of Graduate Studies and Research, Faculty of Arts and Sciences, Department of Geological Sciences and Geological Engineering, Kingston, ON K7L 3N6, Canada. Offers M Sc, M Sc Eng, PhD. Part-time programs available. *Degree requirements:* For master's, thesis (for some programs); for doctorate, comprehensive exam, thesis/dissertation. *Entrance requirements:* Additional exam requirements/recommendations for international students: Required—TOEFL. *Faculty research:* Geochemistry, sedimentology, geophysics, economic geology, structural geology.

Rensselaer Polytechnic Institute, Graduate School, School of Science, Program in Geology, Troy, NY 12180-3590. Offers MS, PhD. Part-time programs available. *Faculty:* 8 full-time (1 woman), 1 part-time/adjunct (0 women). *Students:* 11 full-time (3 women), 1 (woman) part-time; includes 1 Hispanic/Latino, 3 international. Average age 27. 36 applicants, 31% accepted, 6 enrolled. In 2010, 2 master's, 1 doctorate awarded. Terminal master's awarded for partial completion of doctoral program. *Degree requirements:* For master's, comprehensive exam, thesis (for some programs); for doctorate, comprehensive exam, thesis/dissertation. *Entrance requirements:* For master's and doctorate, GRE General Test. Additional exam requirements/recommendations for international students: Required—TOEFL. *Application deadline:* For fall admission, 1/15 priority date for domestic students. Applications are processed on a rolling basis. Application fee: $75. Electronic applications accepted. *Expenses:* Tuition: Full-time $39,600; part-time $1650 per credit. Required fees: $1896. *Financial support:* In 2010–11, 7 research assistantships with full tuition reimbursements (averaging $17,972 per year), 4 teaching assistantships with full tuition reimbursements (averaging $8,750 per year) were awarded; fellowships with full tuition reimbursements, career-related internships or fieldwork and scholarships/grants also available. Financial award application deadline: 2/1; financial award applicants required to submit FAFSA. *Faculty research:* Geochemistry, petrology, geophysics, environmental geochemistry, planetary geology. Total annual research expenditures: $2.3 million. *Unit head:* Dr. Frank Spear, Chair, 518-276-6474, Fax: 518-276-2012, E-mail: ees@rpi.edu. *Application contact:* Dr. Steven Roecker, Professor, 518-276-6773, Fax: 518-276-2012, E-mail: ees@rpi.edu.

Rutgers, The State University of New Jersey, Newark, Graduate School, Program in Environmental Geology, Newark, NJ 07102. Offers MS. Part-time and evening/weekend programs available. *Faculty:* 7 full-time (3 women). *Students:* 3 full-time (2 women), 8 part-time (3 women); includes 1 Hispanic/Latino. 10 applicants, 50% accepted, 3 enrolled. *Degree requirements:* For master's, comprehensive exam, thesis optional. *Entrance requirements:* For master's, GRE General Test, minimum B average. *Application deadline:* For fall admission, 6/1 for domestic students; for spring admission, 12/1 for domestic students. Application fee: $60. Electronic applications accepted. *Expenses:* Tuition, state resident: part-time $600 per credit. Tuition, nonresident: full-time $10,694. *Faculty research:* Environmental geology, plate tectonics, geoarchaeology, geophysics, mineralogy-petrology. Total annual research expenditures: $124,000. *Unit head:* Dr. Alex Gates, Program Coordinator and Adviser, 973-353-5034, Fax: 973-353-5100, E-mail: agates@andromeda.rutgers.edu. *Application contact:* Jason Hand, Director of Admissions, 973-353-5205, Fax: 973-353-1440.

Rutgers, The State University of New Jersey, New Brunswick, Graduate School-New Brunswick, Department of Earth and Planetary Sciences, Piscataway, NJ 08854-8097. Offers geological sciences (MS, PhD). Part-time programs available. *Degree requirements:* For master's, thesis; for doctorate, comprehensive exam, thesis/dissertation. *Entrance requirements:* For master's and doctorate, GRE General Test, GRE Subject Test (recommended). Electronic applications accepted. *Expenses:* Tuition, state resident: full-time $7200; part-time $600 per credit. Tuition, nonresident: full-time $11,124; part-time $927 per credit. *Faculty research:* Basin analysis, volcanology, quaternary studies, engineering geophysics, marine geology, biogeochemistry and paleoceanography.

St. Francis Xavier University, Graduate Studies, Department of Earth Sciences, Antigonish, NS B2G 2W5, Canada. Offers M Sc. *Degree requirements:* For master's, thesis. *Entrance requirements:* Additional exam requirements/recommendations for international students: Required—TOEFL (minimum score 580 paper-based; 236 computer-based). *Faculty research:* Environmental earth sciences, global change tectonics, paleoclimatology, crustal fluids.

San Diego State University, Graduate and Research Affairs, College of Sciences, Department of Geological Sciences, San Diego, CA 92182. Offers MS. Part-time programs available. *Degree requirements:* For master's, thesis. *Entrance requirements:* For master's, GRE General Test, bachelor's degree in related field, 2 letters of reference. Additional exam requirements/recommendations for international students: Required—TOEFL. Electronic applications accepted. *Faculty research:* Earthquakes, hydrology, meteorological analysis and tomography studies.

San Jose State University, Graduate Studies and Research, College of Science, Department of Geology, San Jose, CA 95192-0001. Offers MS. *Degree requirements:* For master's, thesis. *Entrance requirements:* For master's, GRE. Electronic applications accepted.

South Dakota School of Mines and Technology, Graduate Division, Department of Geology and Geological Engineering, Rapid City, SD 57701-3995. Offers geology and geological engineering (MS, PhD); paleontology (MS). Part-time programs available. *Degree requirements:* For master's, thesis; for doctorate, thesis/dissertation. *Entrance requirements:* For master's and doctorate, GRE General Test, GRE Subject Test. Additional exam requirements/recommendations for international students: Required—TOEFL, TWE. Electronic applications accepted. *Faculty research:* Contaminants in soil, nitrate leaching, environmental changes, fracture formations, greenhouse effect.

Southern Illinois University Carbondale, Graduate School, College of Science, Department of Geology, Carbondale, IL 62901-4701. Offers environmental resources and policy (PhD); geology (MS, PhD). *Degree requirements:* For master's, thesis; for doctorate, one foreign language, thesis/dissertation. *Entrance requirements:* For master's, GRE, minimum GPA of 2.7; for doctorate, GRE General Test, minimum GPA of 3.25. Additional exam requirements/recommendations for international students: Required—TOEFL.

Southern Methodist University, Dedman College, Department of Earth Sciences, Program in Geology, Dallas, TX 75275. Offers MS, PhD. Part-time programs available. *Faculty:* 7 full-time (0 women), 6 part-time/adjunct (2 women). *Students:* 25 applicants, 16% accepted. In 2010, 3 master's, 3 doctorates awarded. *Degree requirements:* For master's, thesis, qualifying exam; for doctorate, thesis/dissertation, qualifying exam. *Entrance requirements:* For master's and doctorate, GRE General Test, minimum GPA of 3.0, letters of recommendation. Additional exam requirements/recommendations for international students: Required—TOEFL. *Application deadline:* For fall admission, 2/1 priority date for domestic and international students; for spring admission, 11/30 for domestic students. Applications are processed on a rolling basis. Application fee: $50. *Financial support:* In 2010–11, fellowships with full tuition reimbursements (averaging $15,000 per year), research assistantships with full tuition reimbursements (averaging $15,000 per year), teaching assistantships with full tuition reimbursements (averaging $15,000 per year) were awarded; scholarships/grants and unspecified assistantships also available. Financial award application deadline: 2/1; financial award applicants required to submit FAFSA. *Faculty research:* Geothermal, paleontology, environmental, stable isotope geochemistry. Total annual research expenditures: $400,000. *Unit head:* Dr. Robert T. Gregory, Chair, 214-768-3075, Fax: 214-768-2701, E-mail: bgregory@smu.edu. *Application contact:* Dr. John V. Walther, Graduate Advisor, 214-768-3174, Fax: 214-768-2701, E-mail: walther@smu.edu.

State University of New York at Binghamton, Graduate School, School of Arts and Sciences, Department of Geological Sciences, Binghamton, NY 13902-6000. Offers MA, PhD. Part-time programs available. *Faculty:* 10 full-time (1 woman), 2 part-time/adjunct (both women). *Students:* 15 full-time (3 women), 18 part-time (10 women); includes 2 Asian, non-Hispanic/Latino; 3 Hispanic/Latino, 3 international. Average age 30. 25 applicants, 36% accepted, 5 enrolled. In 2010, 4 master's, 1 doctorate awarded. Terminal master's awarded for partial completion of doctoral program. *Degree requirements:* For master's, thesis or alternative; for doctorate, variable foreign language requirement, thesis/dissertation, departmental qualifying exam. *Entrance requirements:* For master's and doctorate, GRE General Test, GRE Subject Test. Additional exam requirements/recommendations for international students: Required—TOEFL (minimum score 550 paper-based; 213 computer-based; 80 iBT). *Application deadline:* For fall admission, 2/15 priority date for domestic and international students; for spring admission, 9/15 priority date for domestic and international students. Applications are processed on a rolling basis. Application fee: $60. Electronic applications accepted. *Financial support:* In 2010–11, 12 students received support, including 2 research assistantships with full tuition reimbursements available (averaging $10,000 per year), 10 teaching assistantships with full tuition reimbursements available (averaging $15,500 per year); career-related internships or fieldwork, Federal Work-Study, institutionally sponsored loans, scholarships/grants, health care benefits, tuition waivers (full and partial), and unspecified assistantships also available. Financial award application deadline: 2/15; financial award applicants required to submit FAFSA. *Unit head:* Dr. Robert Demicco, Chairperson, 607-777-2604, E-mail: demicco@binghamton.edu. *Application contact:* Catherine Smith, Recruiting and Admissions Coordinator, 607-777-2151, Fax: 607-777-2501, E-mail: cmsmith@binghamton.edu.

Stephen F. Austin State University, Graduate School, College of Sciences and Mathematics, Department of Geology, Nacogdoches, TX 75962. Offers MS, MSNS. *Degree requirements:* For master's, comprehensive exam. *Entrance requirements:* For master's, GRE General Test, minimum GPA of 2.8 in last 60 hours, 2.5 overall. Additional exam requirements/recommendations for international students: Required—TOEFL. *Faculty research:* Stratigraphy of Kaibab limestone, Utah; structure of Ouachita Mountains, Arkansas; groundwater chemistry of Carrizo Sand, Texas.

Sul Ross State University, School of Arts and Sciences, Department of Earth and Physical Sciences, Alpine, TX 79832. Offers MS. Part-time programs available. *Degree requirements:* For master's, thesis optional. *Entrance requirements:* For master's, GRE General Test, minimum GPA of 2.5 in last 60 hours of undergraduate work.

Syracuse University, College of Arts and Sciences, Program in Earth Sciences, Syracuse, NY 13244. Offers MA, MS, PhD. Part-time programs available. *Students:* 25 full-time (7 women), 4 part-time (3 women); includes 3 minority (1 Black or African American, non-Hispanic/Latino; 1 Asian, non-Hispanic/Latino; 1 Hispanic/Latino), 4 international. Average age 27. 28 applicants, 21% accepted, 6 enrolled. In 2010, 2 master's, 3 doctorates awarded. *Degree requirements:* For master's, thesis (for some programs), research tool; for doctorate, thesis/dissertation, 2 research tools. *Entrance requirements:* For master's and doctorate, GRE General Test, GRE Subject Test. Additional exam requirements/recommendations for international students: Required—TOEFL (minimum score 100 iBT). *Application deadline:* For fall admission, 1/15 priority date for domestic and international students. Application fee: $75. Electronic applications accepted. *Expenses:* Tuition: Part-time $1162 per credit. *Financial support:* Fellowships with full tuition reimbursements, research assistantships with full tuition reimbursements, teaching assistantships with full and partial tuition reimbursements, tuition waivers (partial) available. Financial award application deadline: 1/1; financial award applicants required to submit FAFSA. *Unit head:* Dr. Jeff Karson, Chair, 315-443-7976, Fax: 315-443-3363, E-mail: jakarson@syr.edu. *Application contact:* Jolene Fitch, Information Contact, 315-443-2672, E-mail: jofitch@syr.edu.

Temple University, College of Science and Technology, Department of Earth and Environmental Science, Philadelphia, PA 19122-6096. Offers MS. *Faculty:* 9 full-time (3 women). *Students:* 14 full-time (5 women), 2 part-time (0 women); includes 1 Black or African American, non-Hispanic/Latino. 20 applicants, 60% accepted, 8 enrolled. In 2010, 5 master's awarded. *Degree requirements:* For master's, thesis, qualifying exam. *Entrance requirements:* For master's, GRE General Test, minimum GPA of 3.0. Additional exam requirements/recommendations for international students: Required—TOEFL (minimum score 550 paper-

Geology

Temple University (continued)

based; 213 computer-based; 79 iBT). *Application deadline:* For fall admission, 2/1 for domestic students, 12/15 for international students; for spring admission, 10/1 for domestic students, 8/1 for international students. Application fee: $50. Electronic applications accepted. *Financial support:* Fellowships, research assistantships with full tuition reimbursements, teaching assistantships with full tuition reimbursements, scholarships/grants available. Financial award application deadline: 1/15; financial award applicants required to submit FAFSA. *Faculty research:* Hydraulic modeling, environmental geochemistry and geophysics, paleosas, cyclic stratigraphy, materials research. Total annual research expenditures: $50,000. *Unit head:* Dr. David Grandstaff, Chair, 215-204-8227, Fax: 215-204-3496, E-mail: ees@temple.edu. *Application contact:* Dr. David Grandstaff, Chair, 215-204-8227, Fax: 215-204-3496, E-mail: ees@temple.edu.

Texas A&M University, College of Geosciences, Department of Geology and Geophysics, College Station, TX 77843. Offers geology (MS, PhD); geophysics (MS, PhD). *Faculty:* 34. *Students:* 113 full-time (50 women), 13 part-time (3 women); includes 11 minority (5 Asian, non-Hispanic/Latino; 6 Hispanic/Latino), 46 international. Average age 31. In 2010, 14 master's, 7 doctorates awarded. *Degree requirements:* For master's, thesis; for doctorate, thesis/dissertation. *Entrance requirements:* For master's and doctorate, GRE General Test. Additional exam requirements/recommendations for international students: Required—TOEFL. *Application deadline:* For fall admission, 3/1 priority date for domestic students, 1/15 for international students; for spring admission, 10/1 priority date for domestic students, 8/15 for international students. Applications are processed on a rolling basis. Application fee: $50 ($75 for international students). Electronic applications accepted. *Financial support:* In 2010–11, fellowships with partial tuition reimbursements (averaging $1,000 per year), research assistantships with partial tuition reimbursements (averaging $11,925 per year), teaching assistantships with partial tuition reimbursements (averaging $11,925 per year) were awarded; Federal Work-Study, institutionally sponsored loans, scholarships/grants, tuition waivers (partial), and unspecified assistantships also available. Financial award application deadline: 3/1; financial award applicants required to submit FAFSA. *Faculty research:* Environmental and engineering geology and geophysics, petroleum geology, tectonophysics, geochemistry. *Unit head:* Dr. Andreas Kronenberg, Head, 979-845-0132, E-mail: kronenberg@geo.tamu.edu. *Application contact:* Dr. Andreas Kronenberg, Head, 979-845-0132, E-mail: kronenberg@geo.tamu.edu.

Texas A&M University–Kingsville, College of Graduate Studies, College of Arts and Sciences, Department of Geosciences, Kingsville, TX 78363. Offers applied geology (MS). Part-time and evening/weekend programs available. *Degree requirements:* For master's, comprehensive exam, thesis. *Entrance requirements:* For master's, GRE General Test, minimum GPA of 3.0. Additional exam requirements/recommendations for international students: Required—TOEFL. *Faculty research:* Stratigraphy and sedimentology of modern coastal sediments, sandstone diagnosis, vertebrate paleontology, structural geology.

Texas Christian University, College of Science and Engineering, Department of Geology, Fort Worth, TX 76129-0002. Offers MS. Part-time programs available. *Degree requirements:* For master's, thesis, preliminary exam. *Entrance requirements:* For master's, GRE General Test. Additional exam requirements/recommendations for international students: Required—TOEFL (minimum score 550 paper-based; 213 computer-based; 80 iBT). *Application deadline:* For fall admission, 2/28 for domestic and international students. Applications are processed on a rolling basis. Application fee: $50. *Expenses:* Tuition: Full-time $18,720; part-time $1040 per credit hour. Tuition and fees vary according to course load and program. *Financial support:* In 2010–11, 7 teaching assistantships with full and partial tuition reimbursements (averaging $14,000 per year) were awarded; unspecified assistantships also available. Financial award application deadline: 2/28. *Unit head:* Dr. Ken Morgan, Director, 817-257-7270, E-mail: k.morgan@tcu.edu. *Application contact:* Dr. Helge Alsleben, Asst. Professor, 817-257-7270, E-mail: h.alsleben@tcu.edu.

Texas Christian University, College of Science and Engineering, School of Geology, Energy and the Environment, Fort Worth, TX 76129-0002. Offers environmental science (MS); geology (MS); MBA/MEM. *Expenses:* Tuition: Full-time $18,720; part-time $1040 per credit hour. Tuition and fees vary according to course load and program. *Unit head:* Dr. Demitris Kouris, Dean, 817-257-7727, E-mail: d.kouris@tcu.edu. *Application contact:* Dr. Magnus Rittby, Associate Dean for Administration and Graduate Programs, 817-257-7729, Fax: 817-257-7736, E-mail: m.rittby@tcu.edu.

Université du Québec à Montréal, Graduate Programs, Program in Earth Sciences, Montreal, QC H3C 3P8, Canada. Offers earth sciences (M Sc); mineral resources (PhD); non-renewable resources (DESS). Part-time programs available. Terminal master's awarded for partial completion of doctoral program. *Degree requirements:* For master's, thesis (for some programs); for doctorate, thesis/dissertation. *Entrance requirements:* For master's, appropriate bachelor's degree or equivalent, proficiency in French. *Faculty research:* Economic geology, structural geology, geochemistry, Quaternary geology, isotopic geochemistry.

Université Laval, Faculty of Sciences and Engineering, Department of Geology and Geological Engineering, Québec, QC G1K 7P4, Canada. Offers earth sciences (M Sc, PhD), including earth sciences, environmental technologies (M Sc); geology (M Sc, PhD). Terminal master's awarded for partial completion of doctoral program. *Degree requirements:* For master's, thesis (for some programs); for doctorate, comprehensive exam, thesis/dissertation. *Entrance requirements:* For master's and doctorate, knowledge of French. Electronic applications accepted. *Faculty research:* Engineering, economics, regional geology.

University at Albany, State University of New York, College of Arts and Sciences, Department of Earth and Atmospheric Sciences, Albany, NY 12222-0001. Offers atmospheric science (MS, PhD); geology (MS, PhD). *Degree requirements:* For master's, one foreign language, comprehensive exam, thesis; for doctorate, 2 foreign languages, comprehensive exam, thesis/dissertation, oral exams. *Entrance requirements:* For master's and doctorate, GRE General Test. Additional exam requirements/recommendations for international students: Required—TOEFL (minimum score 550 paper-based; 213 computer-based). Electronic applications accepted. *Faculty research:* Environmental geochemistry, tectonics, mesoscale meteorology, atmospheric chemistry.

University at Buffalo, the State University of New York, Graduate School, College of Arts and Sciences, Department of Geology, Buffalo, NY 14260. Offers MA, MS, PhD. Part-time programs available. *Faculty:* 14 full-time (6 women), 1 part-time/adjunct (0 women). *Students:* 53 full-time (18 women), 1 (woman) part-time; includes 1 American Indian or Alaska Native, non-Hispanic/Latino; 1 Hispanic/Latino, 5 international. Average age 26. 86 applicants, 40% accepted, 18 enrolled. In 2010, 11 master's, 2 doctorates awarded. *Degree requirements:* For master's, project or thesis; for doctorate, thesis/dissertation, dissertation defense. *Entrance requirements:* For master's and doctorate, GRE General Test. Additional exam requirements/recommendations for international students: Required—TOEFL (minimum score 550 paper-based; 213 computer-based; 79 iBT). *Application deadline:* For fall admission, 2/1 priority date for domestic and international students; for spring admission, 10/1 priority date for domestic and international students. Applications are processed on a rolling basis. Application fee: $75. Electronic applications accepted. *Financial support:* In 2010–11, 31 students received support, including 5 fellowships with full tuition reimbursements available (averaging $6,000 per year), 12 research assistantships with full tuition reimbursements available (averaging $15,500 per year), 14 teaching assistantships with full tuition reimbursements available (averaging $15,500 per year); Federal Work-Study, scholarships/grants, health care benefits, and unspecified assistantships also available. Financial award application deadline: 2/1; financial award applicants required to submit FAFSA. *Faculty research:* Environmental geology, hydrogeology, geochemistry, fractured rocks, volcanology. Total annual research expenditures: $2.1 million. *Unit head:* Dr. Richelle M. Allen-King, Professor and Chair, 716-645-3489, Fax: 716-645-3999, E-mail: geology@buffalo.edu. *Application contact:* Dr. Charles E. Mitchell, Director of Graduate Studies, 716-645-4290, Fax: 716-645-3999, E-mail: cem@buffalo.edu.

The University of Akron, Graduate School, Buchtel College of Arts and Sciences, Department of Geology, Akron, OH 44325. Offers earth science (MS); environmental geology (MS); geology (MS); geophysics (MS). Part-time programs available. *Faculty:* 10 full-time (1 woman), 5 part-time/adjunct (1 woman). *Students:* 11 full-time (2 women), 1 part-time (0 women). Average age 29. 13 applicants, 85% accepted, 6 enrolled. In 2010, 5 master's awarded. *Degree requirements:* For master's, comprehensive exam, thesis, seminar, proficiency exam. *Entrance requirements:* For master's, minimum GPA of 2.75, three letters of recommendation, statement of purpose. Additional exam requirements/recommendations for international students: Required—TOEFL (minimum score 550 paper-based; 213 computer-based; 79 iBT). *Application deadline:* Applications are processed on a rolling basis. Application fee: $30 ($40 for international students). Electronic applications accepted. *Expenses:* Tuition, state resident: full-time $6800; part-time $378 per credit hour. Tuition, nonresident: full-time $11,644; part-time $647 per credit hour. Required fees: $1265. One-time fee: $30 full-time. *Financial support:* In 2010–11, 1 research assistantship with full tuition reimbursement, 11 teaching assistantships with full tuition reimbursements were awarded. *Faculty research:* Terrestrial environmental change, Karst hydrogeology, lacustrine paleoenvironments, environmental magnetism and geophysics. Total annual research expenditures: $168,874. *Unit head:* Dr. John Szabo, Chair, 330-972-8039, E-mail: jszabo@uakron.edu. *Application contact:* Dr. LaVerne Friberg, Director of Graduate Studies, 330-972-8046, E-mail: lfribe1@uakron.edu.

The University of Alabama, Graduate School, College of Arts and Sciences, Department of Geological Sciences, Tuscaloosa, AL 35487. Offers MS, PhD. *Faculty:* 14 full-time (4 women). *Students:* 18 full-time (8 women), 29 part-time (7 women); includes 4 minority (1 Black or African American, non-Hispanic/Latino; 1 American Indian or Alaska Native, non-Hispanic/Latino; 1 Asian, non-Hispanic/Latino; 1 Hispanic/Latino), 11 international. Average age 30. 38 applicants, 55% accepted, 7 enrolled. In 2010, 7 master's, 6 doctorates awarded. Terminal master's awarded for partial completion of doctoral program. *Degree requirements:* For master's, comprehensive exam, thesis; for doctorate, comprehensive exam, thesis/dissertation. *Entrance requirements:* For master's and doctorate, GRE. Additional exam requirements/recommendations for international students: Required—TOEFL (minimum score 550 paper-based; 213 computer-based; 79 iBT). *Application deadline:* For fall admission, 3/1 priority date for domestic and international students; for spring admission, 10/1 priority date for domestic and international students. Applications are processed on a rolling basis. Application fee: $50 ($60 for international students). Electronic applications accepted. *Expenses:* Tuition, state resident: full-time $7900. Tuition, nonresident: full-time $20,500. *Financial support:* In 2010–11, 11 research assistantships with full tuition reimbursements (averaging $13,595 per year), 29 teaching assistantships with full tuition reimbursements (averaging $13,365 per year) were awarded; career-related internships or fieldwork, Federal Work-Study, and institutionally sponsored loans also available. *Faculty research:* Structure, petrology, stratigraphy, geochemistry, hydrogeology, geophysics. Total annual research expenditures: $903,814. *Unit head:* Dr. Harold H. Stowell, Chairperson and Professor, 205-348-5095, E-mail: hstowell@wgs.geo.ua.edu. *Application contact:* Dr. Andrew Mark Goodliffe, Graduate Program Director, 205-348-7167, E-mail: amg@ua.edu.

University of Alaska Fairbanks, College of Natural Sciences and Mathematics, Department of Geology and Geophysics, Fairbanks, AK 99775-5780. Offers geology (MS, PhD), including economic geology (PhD), petroleum geology (MS), quaternary geology (PhD), remote sensing, volcanology (PhD); geophysics (MS, PhD), including remote sensing, snow, ice, and permafrost geophysics (MS), solid-earth geophysics (MS). Part-time programs available. *Faculty:* 10 full-time (4 women). *Students:* 61 full-time (28 women), 12 part-time (6 women); includes 6 minority (1 Black or African American, non-Hispanic/Latino; 1 Hispanic/Latino; 4 Two or more races, non-Hispanic/Latino), 17 international. Average age 30. 68 applicants, 25% accepted, 17 enrolled. In 2010, 9 master's, 6 doctorates awarded. Terminal master's awarded for partial completion of doctoral program. *Degree requirements:* For master's, comprehensive exam, thesis, oral exam, oral defense; for doctorate, comprehensive exam, thesis/dissertation, oral exam, oral defense. *Entrance requirements:* For master's and doctorate, GRE General Test. Additional exam requirements/recommendations for international students: Required—TOEFL (minimum score 550 paper-based; 213 computer-based). *Application deadline:* For fall admission, 6/1 for domestic students, 3/1 for international students; for spring admission, 10/15 for domestic students, 9/1 for international students. Applications are processed on a rolling basis. Application fee: $60. Electronic applications accepted. *Expenses:* Tuition, state resident: full-time $5688; part-time $316 per credit. Tuition, nonresident: full-time $11,628; part-time $646 per credit. Required fees: $289 per semester. Tuition and fees vary according to course load and reciprocity agreements. *Financial support:* In 2010–11, 43 research assistantships with tuition reimbursements (averaging $12,026 per year), 7 teaching assistantships with tuition reimbursements (averaging $13,030 per year) were awarded; fellowships with tuition reimbursements, Federal Work-Study, scholarships/grants, health care benefits, and unspecified assistantships also available. Support available to part-time students. Financial award application deadline: 2/15; financial award applicants required to submit FAFSA. *Faculty research:* Glacial surging, volcanology, geochronology, impact cratering, permafrost geophysics. *Unit head:* Dr. Benard Coakley, Department Chair, 907-474-7565, Fax: 907-474-5163, E-mail: geology@uaf.edu. *Application contact:* Dr. Benard Coakley, Department Chair, 907-474-7565, Fax: 907-474-5163, E-mail: geology@uaf.edu.

University of Arkansas, Graduate School, J. William Fulbright College of Arts and Sciences, Department of Geosciences, Program in Geology, Fayetteville, AR 72701-1201. Offers MS. Part-time programs available. *Students:* 14 full-time (4 women), 9 part-time (2 women), 1 international. 19 applicants, 74% accepted. In 2010, 8 master's awarded. *Degree requirements:* For master's, thesis. *Application deadline:* For fall admission, 4/1 for international students; for spring admission, 10/1 for international students. Applications are processed on a rolling basis. Application fee: $40 ($50 for international students). Electronic applications accepted. *Financial support:* In 2010–11, 11 teaching assistantships were awarded; fellowships, research assistantships, career-related internships or fieldwork and Federal Work-Study also available. Support available to part-time students. Financial award application deadline: 4/1; financial award applicants required to submit FAFSA. *Unit head:* Dr. Ralph Davis, Graduate Coordinator, 479-575-3355, Fax: 479-575-3469, E-mail: ralphd@uark.edu. *Application contact:* Dr. Doy Zachry, Graduate Admissions, 479-575-2785, E-mail: dzachry@uark.edu.

The University of British Columbia, Faculty of Science, Department of Earth and Ocean Sciences, Vancouver, BC V6T 1Z4, Canada. Offers atmospheric science (M Sc, PhD); geological engineering (M Eng, MA Sc, PhD); geological sciences (M Sc, PhD); geophysics (M Sc, MA Sc, PhD); oceanography (M Sc, PhD). *Degree requirements:* For master's, thesis (for some programs); for doctorate, comprehensive exam, thesis/dissertation. *Entrance requirements:* Additional exam requirements/recommendations for international students: Required—TOEFL (minimum score 600 paper-based; 250 computer-based; 100 iBT). Electronic applications accepted. Tuition charges are reported in Canadian dollars. *Expenses:* Tuition, area resident: Full-time $4179 Canadian dollars. International tuition: $7344 Canadian dollars full-time. *Faculty research:* Oceans and atmosphere, environmental earth science, hydro geology, mineral deposits, geophysics.

University of Calgary, Faculty of Graduate Studies, Faculty of Science, Department of Geology and Geophysics, Calgary, AB T2N 1N4, Canada. Offers geology (M Sc, PhD); geophysics (M Sc, PhD). Part-time programs available. Terminal master's awarded for partial completion of doctoral program. *Degree requirements:* For master's, thesis; for doctorate, thesis/dissertation, candidacy exam. *Entrance requirements:* For master's, B Sc; for doctorate, honors B Sc or M Sc. Additional exam requirements/recommendations for international students:

Required—TOEFL. Electronic applications accepted. *Faculty research:* Geochemistry, petrology, paleontology, stratigraphy, exploration and solid-earth geophysics.

University of California, Berkeley, Graduate Division, College of Letters and Science, Department of Earth and Planetary Science, Berkeley, CA 94720-1500. Offers geology (MA, MS, PhD); geophysics (MA, MS, PhD). Terminal master's awarded for partial completion of doctoral program. *Degree requirements:* For master's, oral exam (MA), thesis (MS); for doctorate, comprehensive exam, thesis/dissertation, candidacy exams. *Entrance requirements:* For master's and doctorate, GRE General Test, minimum GPA of 3.0, 3 letters of recommendation. Additional exam requirements/recommendations for international students: Required—TOEFL. *Faculty research:* Tectonics, environmental geology, high-pressure geophysics and seismology, economic geology, geochemistry.

University of California, Davis, Graduate Studies, Program in Geology, Davis, CA 95616. Offers MS, PhD. Terminal master's awarded for partial completion of doctoral program. *Degree requirements:* For master's, thesis; for doctorate, thesis/dissertation. *Entrance requirements:* For master's and doctorate, GRE General Test, GRE Subject Test, minimum GPA of 3.0. Additional exam requirements/recommendations for international students: Required—TOEFL (minimum score 550 paper-based; 213 computer-based). Electronic applications accepted. *Faculty research:* Petrology, paleontology, geophysics, sedimentology, structure/tectonics.

University of California, Los Angeles, Graduate Division, College of Letters and Science, Department of Earth and Space Sciences, Program in Geology, Los Angeles, CA 90095. Offers MS, PhD. *Students:* 17 full-time (8 women); includes 4 minority (1 Black or African American, non-Hispanic/Latino; 2 Asian, non-Hispanic/Latino; 1 Two or more races, non-Hispanic/Latino), 2 international. Average age 26. 48 applicants, 27% accepted, 8 enrolled. In 2010, 1 master's awarded. Terminal master's awarded for partial completion of doctoral program. *Degree requirements:* For master's, comprehensive exams or thesis; for doctorate, thesis/dissertation, oral and written qualifying exams. *Entrance requirements:* For master's, GRE General Test, minimum GPA of 3.0, bachelor's degree in related field; for doctorate, GRE General Test, minimum undergraduate GPA of 3.0, bachelor's degree in related field. *Application deadline:* For fall admission, 1/15 for domestic and international students. Application fee: $70 ($90 for international students). Electronic applications accepted. *Financial support:* In 2010–11, 11 fellowships with full and partial tuition reimbursements, 6 research assistantships with full and partial tuition reimbursements, 10 teaching assistantships with full and partial tuition reimbursements were awarded; Federal Work-Study, institutionally sponsored loans, scholarships/grants, health care benefits, tuition waivers (full and partial), and unspecified assistantships also available. Financial award application deadline: 3/1; financial award applicants required to submit FAFSA. *Unit head:* Dr. Craig E. Manning, Chair, 310-206-3290, E-mail: manning@ess.ucla.edu. *Application contact:* Department Office, 310-825-3917, E-mail: holbrook@ess.ucla.edu.

University of California, Riverside, Graduate Division, Department of Earth Sciences, Riverside, CA 92521-0102. Offers geological sciences (MS, PhD). *Faculty:* 13 full-time (1 woman). *Students:* 31 full-time (10 women); includes 2 Hispanic/Latino, 2 international. Average age 30. In 2010, 2 doctorates awarded. Terminal master's awarded for partial completion of doctoral program. *Degree requirements:* For master's, thesis, final oral exam; for doctorate, thesis/dissertation, qualifying exams, final oral exam. *Entrance requirements:* For master's and doctorate, GRE General Test, minimum GPA of 3.2. Additional exam requirements/recommendations for international students: Required—TOEFL (minimum score 550 paper-based; 213 computer-based; 80 iBT). *Application deadline:* For fall admission, 5/1 for domestic students, 2/1 for international students; for winter admission, 9/1 for domestic students, 7/1 for international students; for spring admission, 12/1 for domestic students, 10/1 for international students. Applications are processed on a rolling basis. Application fee: $60 ($75 for international students). Electronic applications accepted. *Financial support:* In 2010–11, fellowships with full and partial tuition reimbursements (averaging $12,000 per year), research assistantships with full and partial tuition reimbursements (averaging $16,000 per year), teaching assistantships with full and partial tuition reimbursements (averaging $16,500 per year) were awarded; career-related internships or fieldwork, Federal Work-Study, institutionally sponsored loans, health care benefits, tuition waivers (full and partial), and unspecified assistantships also available. Financial award application deadline: 1/5; financial award applicants required to submit FAFSA. *Faculty research:* Applied and solid earth geophysics, tectonic geomorphology, fluid-rock interaction, paleobiology-ecology, sedimentary-geochemistry. *Unit head:* Dr. Mary Droser, Chair, 951-827-3797, Fax: 951-827-4324, E-mail: mary.droser@ucr.edu. *Application contact:* John Herring, Graduate Program Assistant, 951-827-3435, Fax: 951-827-4324, E-mail: geology@ucr.edu.

University of California, Santa Barbara, Graduate Division, College of Letters and Sciences, Division of Mathematics, Life, and Physical Sciences, Department of Earth Science, Santa Barbara, CA 93106-9620. Offers geological sciences (PhD); geophysics (MS). *Faculty:* 16 full-time (2 women), 3 part-time/adjunct (1 woman). *Students:* 47 full-time (22 women); includes 1 American Indian or Alaska Native, non-Hispanic/Latino; 4 Asian, non-Hispanic/Latino; 7 Hispanic/Latino. Average age 27. 93 applicants, 31% accepted, 16 enrolled. In 2010, 5 master's, 3 doctorates awarded. Terminal master's awarded for partial completion of doctoral program. *Degree requirements:* For master's, comprehensive exam, thesis, 30 units; for doctorate, comprehensive exam, thesis/dissertation, 30 units, oral qualifying exam. *Entrance requirements:* For master's and doctorate, GRE General Test. Additional exam requirements/recommendations for international students: Required—TOEFL (minimum score 550 paper-based; 80 iBT), IELTS (minimum score 7). *Application deadline:* For fall admission, 1/1 for domestic and international students. Application fee: $70 ($90 for international students). Electronic applications accepted. *Financial support:* In 2010–11, 38 students received support, including 24 fellowships with full and partial tuition reimbursements available (averaging $9,407 per year), 19 research assistantships with full and partial tuition reimbursements available (averaging $6,722 per year), 25 teaching assistantships with full and partial tuition reimbursements available (averaging $9,978 per year); tuition waivers (full and partial) also available. Financial award application deadline: 1/1; financial award applicants required to submit CSS PROFILE or FAFSA. *Faculty research:* Geology, geomaterials and earth's structure; geomorphology, tectonics; geophysics, seismology; paleoclimate, paleoceanography and geochemistry; paleobiology, evolution and paleontology. *Unit head:* Giulia Brofferio, Business Officer, 805-893-4604, Fax: 805-893-2314, E-mail: brofferio@geol.ucsb.edu. *Application contact:* Hannah Ocampo, Graduate Program Assistant, 805-893-3329, Fax: 805-893-2314, E-mail: ocampo@geol.ucsb.edu.

University of Cincinnati, Graduate School, McMicken College of Arts and Sciences, Department of Geology, Cincinnati, OH 45221. Offers MS, PhD. Part-time programs available. *Degree requirements:* For master's, thesis; for doctorate, comprehensive exam, thesis/dissertation. *Entrance requirements:* For master's and doctorate, GRE General Test, 1 year of course work in physics, chemistry, and calculus. Additional exam requirements/recommendations for international students: Required—TOEFL. Electronic applications accepted. *Faculty research:* Paleobiology, sequence stratigraphy, earth systems history, quaternary, groundwater.

University of Colorado Boulder, Graduate School, College of Arts and Sciences, Department of Geological Sciences, Boulder, CO 80309. Offers geology (MS, PhD); geophysics (PhD). *Faculty:* 29 full-time (8 women). *Students:* 73 full-time (37 women), 17 part-time (14 women); includes 7 minority (2 American Indian or Alaska Native, non-Hispanic/Latino; 1 Asian, non-Hispanic/Latino; 2 Hispanic/Latino; 2 Two or more races, non-Hispanic/Latino), 6 international. Average age 30. 251 applicants, 21 enrolled. In 2010, 9 master's, 14 doctorates awarded. Terminal master's awarded for partial completion of doctoral program. *Degree requirements:* For master's, comprehensive exam, thesis; for doctorate, comprehensive exam, thesis/dissertation. *Entrance requirements:* For master's, GRE General Test, minimum undergraduate GPA of 3.0; for doctorate, GRE General Test, minimum GPA of 2.75. *Application deadline:* For fall admission, 12/15 priority date for domestic students, 12/1 for international students. Application fee: $50 ($60 for international students). *Financial support:* In 2010–11, 28 fellowships with full tuition reimbursements (averaging $13,580 per year), 45 research assistantships with full tuition reimbursements (averaging $15,474 per year) were awarded; Federal Work-Study, institutionally sponsored loans, scholarships/grants, and tuition waivers (full) also available. Financial award application deadline: 1/15. *Faculty research:* Sedimentology, stratigraphy, economic geology of mineral deposits, fossil fuels, hydrogeology and water resources, geophysics, isotope geology, paleobiology, mineralogy, remote sensing. Total annual research expenditures: $9.4 million.

University of Connecticut, Graduate School, College of Liberal Arts and Sciences, Center for Integrative Geosciences, Storrs, CT 06269. Offers geological sciences (MS, PhD). *Degree requirements:* For doctorate, thesis/dissertation. *Entrance requirements:* For master's and doctorate, GRE General Test. Additional exam requirements/recommendations for international students: Required—TOEFL (minimum score 550 paper-based; 213 computer-based). Electronic applications accepted.

University of Delaware, College of Earth, Ocean, and Environment, Department of Geological Sciences, Newark, DE 19716. Offers MA, PhD.

University of Florida, Graduate School, College of Liberal Arts and Sciences, Department of Geological Sciences, Gainesville, FL 32611. Offers geology (MS, MST, PhD). *Faculty:* 17 full-time (3 women). *Students:* 35 full-time (16 women), 4 part-time (2 women); includes 1 Asian, non-Hispanic/Latino; 2 Hispanic/Latino, 8 international. Average age 29. 55 applicants, 40% accepted, 10 enrolled. In 2010, 6 master's, 5 doctorates awarded. Terminal master's awarded for partial completion of doctoral program. *Degree requirements:* For master's, thesis (for some programs), Thesis and non-thesis M.S. options; for doctorate, one foreign language, thesis/dissertation. *Entrance requirements:* For master's, GRE General Test score greater than 1000, minimum GPA of 3.0; for doctorate, GRE General Test score greater than 1100, minimum GPA of 3.0. Additional exam requirements/recommendations for international students: Required—TOEFL (minimum score 550 paper-based; 213 computer-based; 80 iBT), IELTS (minimum score 6). *Application deadline:* For fall admission, 1/15 for domestic students; for spring admission, 10/1 for domestic students. Applications are processed on a rolling basis. Application fee: $30. Electronic applications accepted. *Expenses:* Tuition, state resident: full-time $10,915.92. Tuition, nonresident: full-time $28,309. *Financial support:* In 2010–11, 39 students received support, including 4 fellowships with full tuition reimbursements available, 19 research assistantships with full tuition reimbursements available (averaging $16,810 per year), 16 teaching assistantships with full tuition reimbursements available (averaging $15,290 per year); career-related internships or fieldwork, Federal Work-Study, institutionally sponsored loans, and scholarships/grants also available. Support available to part-time students. Financial award application deadline: 3/1; financial award applicants required to submit FAFSA. *Faculty research:* Paleoclimatology, tectonophysics, petrochemistry, marine geology, geochemistry, hydrology. *Unit head:* Michael R. Perfit, PhD, Chair, 352-392-2231, Fax: 352-392-9294, E-mail: mperfit@ufl.edu. *Application contact:* John Jaeger, PhD, Graduate Coordinator, 352-392-2231, Fax: 352-392-9294, E-mail: jmjaeger@ufl.edu.

University of Georgia, College of Arts and Sciences, Department of Geology, Athens, GA 30602. Offers MS, PhD. *Faculty:* 14 full-time (3 women), 1 part-time/adjunct (0 women). *Students:* 25 full-time (14 women), 11 part-time (5 women); includes 1 Black or African American, non-Hispanic/Latino, 1 international. 43 applicants, 35% accepted, 12 enrolled. In 2010, 9 master's, 2 doctorates awarded. *Degree requirements:* For master's, thesis; for doctorate, one foreign language, thesis/dissertation. *Entrance requirements:* For master's and doctorate, GRE General Test. *Application deadline:* For fall admission, 7/1 priority date for domestic students; for spring admission, 11/15 for domestic students. Application fee: $50. Electronic applications accepted. *Expenses:* Tuition, state resident: full-time $7200; part-time $344 per credit hour. Tuition, nonresident: full-time $21,900; part-time $944 per credit hour. Tuition and fees vary according to course load and program. *Financial support:* Fellowships, research assistantships, teaching assistantships, unspecified assistantships available. *Unit head:* Dr. Michael F. Roden, Head, 706-542-2652, Fax: 706-542-2425, E-mail: mroden@uga.edu. *Application contact:* Dr. Steven M. Holland, Graduate Coordinator, 706-542-0424, Fax: 706-542-2425, E-mail: stratum@uga.edu.

University of Hawaii at Manoa, Graduate Division, School of Ocean and Earth Science and Technology, Department of Geology and Geophysics, Honolulu, HI 96822. Offers high-pressure geophysics and geochemistry (MS, PhD); hydrogeology and engineering geology (MS, PhD); marine geology and geophysics (MS, PhD); planetary geosciences and remote sensing (MS, PhD); seismology and solid-earth geophysics (MS, PhD); volcanology, petrology, and geochemistry (MS, PhD). Part-time programs available. *Faculty:* 72 full-time (15 women), 6 part-time/adjunct (3 women). *Students:* 38 full-time (20 women), 5 part-time (3 women); includes 8 minority (1 Black or African American, non-Hispanic/Latino; 2 Asian, non-Hispanic/Latino; 1 Hispanic/Latino; 1 Native Hawaiian or other Pacific Islander, non-Hispanic/Latino; 3 Two or more races, non-Hispanic/Latino), 6 international. Average age 31. 64 applicants, 23% accepted, 7 enrolled. In 2010, 7 master's, 8 doctorates awarded. Terminal master's awarded for partial completion of doctoral program. *Degree requirements:* For master's, thesis optional; for doctorate, comprehensive exam, thesis/dissertation. *Entrance requirements:* For master's and doctorate, GRE General Test, minimum GPA of 3.0. Additional exam requirements/recommendations for international students: Required—TOEFL (minimum score 580 paper-based; 237 computer-based; 92 iBT), IELTS (minimum score 5). *Application deadline:* For fall admission, 1/15 for domestic students, 1/1 for international students; for spring admission, 9/1 for domestic students, 8/15 for international students. Application fee: $60. *Financial support:* In 2010–11, 7 fellowships (averaging $1,359 per year), 30 research assistantships (averaging $23,988 per year), 4 teaching assistantships (averaging $15,350 per year) were awarded. Total annual research expenditures: $3.8 million. *Application contact:* Dr. Gregory Moore, Chair, 808-956-7640, Fax: 808-956-5512, E-mail: gg-dept@soest.hawaii.edu.

University of Houston, College of Natural Sciences and Mathematics, Department of Earth and Atmospheric Sciences, Houston, TX 77204. Offers atmospheric science (PhD); geology (MA, PhD); geophysics (PhD). Part-time programs available. *Faculty:* 23 full-time (4 women), 5 part-time/adjunct (1 woman). *Students:* 149 full-time (44 women), 88 part-time (27 women); includes 10 Black or African American, non-Hispanic/Latino; 9 Asian, non-Hispanic/Latino; 15 Hispanic/Latino, 97 international. Average age 31. 198 applicants, 71% accepted, 69 enrolled. In 2010, 33 master's, 6 doctorates awarded. *Degree requirements:* For master's, thesis; for doctorate, comprehensive exam, thesis/dissertation. *Entrance requirements:* For master's and doctorate, GRE General Test . Additional exam requirements/recommendations for international students: Required—TOEFL (minimum score 550 paper-based; 213 computer-based; 79 iBT), IELTS (minimum score 6.5). *Application deadline:* For fall admission, 7/1 for domestic students, 4/1 for international students; for spring admission, 12/1 for domestic students, 10/1 for international students. Applications are processed on a rolling basis. Application fee: $0 ($75 for international students). Electronic applications accepted. *Expenses:* Tuition, state resident: full-time $8592; part-time $358 per credit hour. Tuition, nonresident: full-time $16,032; part-time $668 per credit hour. Required fees: $2889. Tuition and fees vary according to course load and program. *Financial support:* In 2010–11, 6 fellowships with partial tuition reimbursements (averaging $11,668 per year), 19 research assistantships with partial tuition reimbursements (averaging $13,600 per year), 9 teaching assistantships with partial tuition reimbursements (averaging $13,736 per year) were awarded; career-related internships or fieldwork, Federal Work-Study, institutionally sponsored loans, scholarships/grants, health care benefits, and unspecified assistantships also available. Support available to part-time students. Financial award application deadline: 2/1. *Faculty research:* Atmospherics sciences,

Geology

University of Houston (continued)
seismic and solid earth geophysics, tectonics, environmental hydrochemistry, carbonates, micropaleontology, structure and tectonics, petroleum geology. *Unit head:* Dr. John Casey, Chairman, 713-743-3399, Fax: 713-748-7906, E-mail: jfcasey@uh.edu. *Application contact:* Sylvia Marshall, Advising Assistant, 713-743-3401, Fax: 713-748-7906, E-mail: smarshall@uh.edu.

University of Idaho, College of Graduate Studies, College of Science, Department of Geological Sciences, Program in Geology, Moscow, ID 83844-2282. Offers MS, PhD. *Students:* 19 full-time, 4 part-time. Average age 31. In 2010, 6 master's, 2 doctorates awarded. *Entrance requirements:* For master's, minimum GPA of 2.8. *Application deadline:* For fall admission, 8/1 for domestic students; for spring admission, 12/15 for domestic students. Applications are processed on a rolling basis. Application fee: $60. Electronic applications accepted. *Expenses:* Tuition, nonresident: part-time $580 per credit. Required fees: $306 per credit. *Financial support:* Applicants required to submit FAFSA. *Unit head:* Dr. Mickey Gunter, Head, 208-885-6491, E-mail: geology@uidaho.edu. *Application contact:* Dr. Mickey Gunter, Head, 208-885-6491, E-mail: geology@uidaho.edu.

University of Illinois at Chicago, Graduate College, College of Liberal Arts and Sciences, Department of Earth and Environmental Sciences, Chicago, IL 60607-7128. Offers MS, PhD. *Degree requirements:* For master's, thesis; for doctorate, thesis/dissertation. *Entrance requirements:* For master's and doctorate, GRE General Test, minimum GPA of 2.75. Additional exam requirements/recommendations for international students: Required—TOEFL. Electronic applications accepted.

University of Illinois at Urbana–Champaign, Graduate College, College of Liberal Arts and Sciences, School of Earth, Society and Environment, Department of Geology, Champaign, IL 61820. Offers geology (MS, PhD); teaching of earth sciences (MS). *Faculty:* 13 full-time (3 women). *Students:* 27 full-time (10 women), 4 part-time (3 women); includes 1 minority (Asian, non-Hispanic/Latino), 11 international. 52 applicants, 17% accepted, 9 enrolled. In 2010, 8 master's awarded. Terminal master's awarded for partial completion of doctoral program. *Entrance requirements:* For master's and doctorate, GRE General Test, minimum GPA of 3.0. Additional exam requirements/recommendations for international students: Required—TOEFL. *Application deadline:* Applications are processed on a rolling basis. Application fee: $75 ($90 for international students). Electronic applications accepted. *Financial support:* In 2010–11, 3 fellowships, 19 research assistantships, 13 teaching assistantships were awarded; Federal Work-Study and tuition waivers (full and partial) also available. *Faculty research:* Hydrogeology, structure/tectonics, mineral science. *Unit head:* Wang-Ping Chen, Head, 217-333-2744, Fax: 217-244-4996, E-mail: wpchen@illinois.edu. *Application contact:* Marilyn K. Whalen, Office Administrator, 217-333-3542, Fax: 217-244-4996, E-mail: mkt@illinois.edu.

The University of Kansas, Graduate Studies, College of Liberal Arts and Sciences, Department of Geology, Lawrence, KS 66045. Offers MS, PhD. PhD offered jointly with Kansas State University. *Students:* 83 full-time (29 women), 25 part-time (11 women); includes 2 American Indian or Alaska Native, non-Hispanic/Latino; 7 Hispanic/Latino; 1 Two or more races, non-Hispanic/Latino, 16 international. Average age 27. 117 applicants, 44% accepted, 29 enrolled. In 2010, 5 master's, 1 doctorate awarded. *Degree requirements:* For master's, thesis or alternative; for doctorate, comprehensive exam, thesis/dissertation. *Entrance requirements:* For master's and doctorate, GRE General Test, 3 letters of recommendation. Additional exam requirements/recommendations for international students: Required—TOEFL. *Application deadline:* For fall admission, 2/1 priority date for domestic and international students; for spring admission, 10/31 priority date for domestic and international students. Applications are processed on a rolling basis. Application fee: $45 ($55 for international students). Electronic applications accepted. *Expenses:* Tuition, state resident: full-time $7092; part-time $295.50 per credit hour. Tuition, nonresident: full-time $16,590; part-time $691.25 per credit hour. Required fees: $858; $71.49 per credit hour. Tuition and fees vary according to course load, campus/location and program. *Financial support:* Fellowships with full and partial tuition reimbursements, research assistantships with full and partial tuition reimbursements, teaching assistantships with full and partial tuition reimbursements, unspecified assistantships available. Financial award application deadline: 2/1. *Faculty research:* Sedimentology, paleontology, tectonics, geophysics, hyrdogeology. *Unit head:* Robert H. Goldstein, Chair, 785-864-4974, Fax: 785-864-5276, E-mail: gold@ku.edu. *Application contact:* Yolanda G. Davis, Graduate Coordinator, 785-864-4975, Fax: 785-864-5276, E-mail: yolanda@ku.edu.

University of Kentucky, Graduate School, College of Arts and Sciences, Program in Geology, Lexington, KY 40506-0032. Offers MS, PhD. *Degree requirements:* For master's, comprehensive exam, thesis; for doctorate, comprehensive exam, thesis/dissertation. *Entrance requirements:* For master's, GRE General Test, minimum undergraduate GPA of 2.75; for doctorate, GRE General Test, minimum graduate GPA of 3.0. Additional exam requirements/recommendations for international students: Required—TOEFL (minimum score 550 paper-based; 213 computer-based). Electronic applications accepted. *Faculty research:* Structure tectonics, geophysics, stratigraphy, hydrogeology, coal geology.

University of Louisiana at Lafayette, College of Sciences, Department of Geology, Lafayette, LA 70504. Offers MS. Part-time programs available. *Degree requirements:* For master's, comprehensive exam, thesis. *Entrance requirements:* For master's, GRE General Test, minimum GPA of 2.75. Additional exam requirements/recommendations for international students: Required—TOEFL (minimum score 550 paper-based; 213 computer-based). Electronic applications accepted. *Faculty research:* Aquifer contamination, coastal erosion, geochemistry of peat, petroleum geology and geophysics, remote sensing and geographic information systems applications.

University of Maine, Graduate School, Climate Change Institute, Orono, ME 04469. Offers MS. Part-time programs available. *Students:* 9 full-time (5 women), 1 (woman) part-time, 1 international. Average age 27. 14 applicants, 29% accepted, 2 enrolled. *Degree requirements:* For master's, thesis. *Entrance requirements:* For master's, GRE General Test. Additional exam requirements/recommendations for international students: Required—TOEFL. *Application deadline:* For fall admission, 2/1 priority date for domestic students. Applications are processed on a rolling basis. Application fee: $65. Electronic applications accepted. *Expenses:* Tuition, state resident: full-time $400. Tuition, nonresident: full-time $1050. *Financial support:* In 2010–11, 8 research assistantships with tuition reimbursements (averaging $17,425 per year), 2 teaching assistantships (averaging $12,790 per year) were awarded. Financial award application deadline: 3/1. *Faculty research:* Geology, glacial geology, anthropology. *Unit head:* Dr. Paul Mayewski, Director, 207-581-3019, Fax: 207-581-1203. *Application contact:* Scott G. Delcourt, Associate Dean of the Graduate School, 207-581-3291, Fax: 207-581-3232, E-mail: graduate@maine.edu.

University of Maine, Graduate School, College of Natural Sciences, Forestry, and Agriculture, Department of Earth Sciences, Orono, ME 04469. Offers water resources (MS, PhD). Part-time programs available. *Faculty:* 10 full-time (2 women), 4 part-time/adjunct (1 woman). *Students:* 21 full-time (11 women), 10 part-time (4 women), 6 international. Average age 29. 37 applicants, 51% accepted, 11 enrolled. In 2010, 3 master's, 4 doctorates awarded. *Degree requirements:* For master's, thesis; for doctorate, one foreign language, thesis/dissertation. *Entrance requirements:* For master's and doctorate, GRE General Test. Additional exam requirements/recommendations for international students: Required—TOEFL. *Application deadline:* For fall admission, 2/1 priority date for domestic students. Applications are processed on a rolling basis. Application fee: $65. Electronic applications accepted. *Expenses:* Tuition, state resident: full-time $400. Tuition, nonresident: full-time $1050. *Financial support:* In 2010–11, 5 research assistantships with tuition reimbursements (averaging $16,130 per year), 6 teaching assistantships with tuition reimbursements (averaging $12,790 per year) were awarded; Federal Work-Study, institutionally sponsored loans, and tuition waivers (full and partial) also available. Financial award application deadline: 3/1. *Faculty research:* Appalachian bedrock geology, Quaternary studies, marine geology. *Unit head:* Dr. Joseph Kelley, Chair, 207-581-2162, Fax: 207-581-2202. *Application contact:* Scott G. Delcourt, Associate Dean of the Graduate School, 207-581-3291, Fax: 207-581-3232, E-mail: graduate@maine.edu.

University of Manitoba, Faculty of Graduate Studies, Clayton H. Riddell Faculty of Environment, Earth, and Resources, Department of Geological Sciences, Winnipeg, MB R3T 2N2, Canada. Offers geology (M Sc, PhD); geophysics (M Sc, PhD). *Degree requirements:* For master's, thesis; for doctorate, thesis/dissertation. *Entrance requirements:* For master's and doctorate, GRE General Test, GRE Subject Test (geology), minimum GPA of 3.0. Additional exam requirements/recommendations for international students: Required—TOEFL.

University of Maryland, College Park, Academic Affairs, College of Computer, Mathematical and Natural Sciences, Department of Geology, College Park, MD 20742. Offers MS, PhD. *Faculty:* 26 full-time (6 women), 6 part-time/adjunct (4 women). *Students:* 34 full-time (13 women); includes 3 minority (1 Black or African American, non-Hispanic/Latino; 1 Asian, non-Hispanic/Latino; 1 Hispanic/Latino), 7 international. 74 applicants, 26% accepted, 10 enrolled. In 2010, 5 master's, 4 doctorates awarded. *Degree requirements:* For master's, thesis, oral defense; for doctorate, thesis/dissertation. *Entrance requirements:* For master's, GRE General Test, minimum GPA of 3.0, 3 letters of recommendation; for doctorate, GRE General Test, 3 letters of recommendation. Additional exam requirements/recommendations for international students: Required—TOEFL. *Application deadline:* For fall admission, 3/15 for domestic students, 2/1 for international students; for spring admission, 10/1 for domestic students, 6/1 for international students. Applications are processed on a rolling basis. Application fee: $75. Electronic applications accepted. *Expenses:* Tuition, area resident: Part-time $471 per credit hour. Tuition, state resident: part-time $471 per credit hour. Tuition, nonresident: part-time $1016 per credit hour. Required fees: $337 per term. *Financial support:* In 2010–11, 2 fellowships with partial tuition reimbursements (averaging $10,800 per year), 6 research assistantships (averaging $19,635 per year), 26 teaching assistantships (averaging $20,060 per year) were awarded; Federal Work-Study and scholarships/grants also available. Support available to part-time students. Financial award application deadline: 2/15; financial award applicants required to submit FAFSA. Total annual research expenditures: $2.7 million. *Unit head:* Dr. Michael Brown, Chairman, 301-405-4065, Fax: 301-314-9661, E-mail: mbrown@umd.edu. *Application contact:* Dr. Charles A. Caramello, Dean of Graduate School, 301-405-0358, Fax: 301-314-9305, E-mail: ccaramel@umd.edu.

University of Memphis, Graduate School, College of Arts and Sciences, Department of Earth Sciences, Memphis, TN 38152. Offers archaeology (MS); earth sciences (PhD); geographic information systems (Graduate Certificate); geography (MA, MS); geology (MS); geophysics (MS); interdisciplinary (MS). Part-time and evening/weekend programs available. *Faculty:* 15 full-time (3 women), 6 part-time/adjunct (2 women). *Students:* 35 full-time (7 women), 28 part-time (13 women); includes 5 Black or African American, non-Hispanic/Latino; 1 Asian, non-Hispanic/Latino, 15 international. Average age 33. 48 applicants, 69% accepted, 18 enrolled. In 2010, 2 master's, 2 doctorates, 1 other advanced degree awarded. Terminal master's awarded for partial completion of doctoral program. *Degree requirements:* For master's, comprehensive exam, thesis, seminar presentation; for doctorate, thesis/dissertation. *Entrance requirements:* For master's, GRE General Test, 3 letters of recommendation, statement of research interests; for doctorate, GRE General Test, 2 letters of recommendation, resume, personal statement. Additional exam requirements/recommendations for international students: Required—TOEFL (minimum score 550 paper-based; 210 computer-based). *Application deadline:* For fall admission, 1/31 for domestic students; for spring admission, 11/1 for domestic students. Applications are processed on a rolling basis. Application fee: $35 ($60 for international students). Electronic applications accepted. *Financial support:* In 2010–11, 18 students received support; fellowships with full tuition reimbursements available, research assistantships with full tuition reimbursements available, teaching assistantships with full tuition reimbursements available, Federal Work-Study, scholarships/grants, and unspecified assistantships available. Financial award application deadline: 2/15; financial award applicants required to submit FAFSA. *Faculty research:* Hazards, active tectonics, geophysics, hydrology and water resources, spatial analysis. *Unit head:* Dr. M. Jerry Bartholomew, Chair, 901-678-4536, Fax: 901-678-4467, E-mail: jbrthlm1@memphis.edu. *Application contact:* Dr. Arlene Hill, Associate Professor and Graduate Program Coordinator, 901-678-4358, Fax: 901-678-2178, E-mail: dlarsen@memphis.edu.

University of Michigan, Horace H. Rackham School of Graduate Studies, College of Literature, Science, and the Arts, Department of Geological Sciences, Ann Arbor, MI 48109-1005. Offers geology (MS, PhD). *Faculty:* 27 full-time (6 women), 9 part-time/adjunct (4 women). *Students:* 60 full-time (30 women), 2 part-time (0 women); includes 9 minority (1 American Indian or Alaska Native, non-Hispanic/Latino; 3 Asian, non-Hispanic/Latino; 3 Hispanic/Latino; 2 Two or more races, non-Hispanic/Latino), 21 international. Average age 28. 113 applicants, 28% accepted, 23 enrolled. In 2010, 5 master's, 8 doctorates awarded. Terminal master's awarded for partial completion of doctoral program. *Degree requirements:* For master's, thesis; for doctorate, comprehensive exam, thesis/dissertation, oral defense of dissertation. *Entrance requirements:* For master's and doctorate, GRE General Test. Additional exam requirements/recommendations for international students: Required—TOEFL (minimum score 560 paper-based; 220 computer-based; 84 iBT). *Application deadline:* For fall admission, 1/5 for domestic and international students; for winter admission, 11/1 for domestic and international students. Application fee: $65 ($75 for international students). Electronic applications accepted. *Expenses:* Tuition, state resident: full-time $17,784; part-time $1116 per credit hour. Tuition, nonresident: full-time $35,944; part-time $2125 per credit hour. International tuition: $35,994 full-time. Required fees: $95 per semester. Tuition and fees vary according to course load, degree level and program. *Financial support:* Fellowships with full tuition reimbursements, research assistantships with full tuition reimbursements, teaching assistantships with full tuition reimbursements, career-related internships or fieldwork, scholarships/grants, health care benefits, and unspecified assistantships available. Financial award application deadline: 1/5; financial award applicants required to submit FAFSA. *Faculty research:* Isotope geochemistry, paleoclimatology, mineral physics, tectonics, paleontology. *Unit head:* Dr. Rebecca Lange, Chair, 734-764-1435, Fax: 734-763-4690, E-mail: geosci@umich.edu. *Application contact:* Anne Hudon, Graduate Program Coordinator, 734-615-3034, Fax: 734-763-4690, E-mail: geosci@umich.edu.

University of Minnesota, Duluth, Graduate School, Swenson College of Science and Engineering, Department of Geological Sciences, Duluth, MN 55812-2496. Offers MS, PhD. PhD offered jointly with University of Minnesota, Twin Cities Campus. Part-time programs available. *Degree requirements:* For master's, thesis, final oral exam, written and oral research proposal. *Entrance requirements:* For master's, GRE General Test, minimum GPA of 3.0. Additional exam requirements/recommendations for international students: Required—TOEFL (minimum score 550 paper-based; 213 computer-based). Electronic applications accepted. *Faculty research:* Surface processes, tectonics, planetary geology, paleoclimate, petrology.

University of Minnesota, Twin Cities Campus, Institute of Technology, Department of Geology and Geophysics, Minneapolis, MN 55455-0213. Offers geology (MS, PhD); geophysics (MS, PhD). Terminal master's awarded for partial completion of doctoral program. *Degree requirements:* For master's, thesis; for doctorate, thesis/dissertation. *Entrance requirements:* For master's and doctorate, GRE General Test, 3 letters of recommendation. Additional exam requirements/recommendations for international students: Required—TOEFL (minimum score 550 paper-based; 213 computer-based). Electronic applications accepted. *Faculty research:* Geochemistry, paleoclimate studies, structure/tectonics, geofluids.

University of Missouri, Graduate School, College of Arts and Sciences, Department of Geological Sciences, Columbia, MO 65211. Offers MS, PhD. *Faculty:* 13 full-time (4 women), 2 part-time/adjunct (0 women). *Students:* 31 full-time (11 women), 5 part-time (1 woman), 14

international. Average age 28. 48 applicants, 42% accepted, 12 enrolled. In 2010, 5 master's, 4 doctorates awarded. *Degree requirements:* For master's, thesis; for doctorate, variable foreign language requirement, thesis/dissertation. *Entrance requirements:* For master's and doctorate, GRE General Test, minimum GPA of 3.0. Additional exam requirements/ recommendations for international students: Required—TOEFL (minimum score 530 paper-based; 197 computer-based; 71 iBT). *Application deadline:* For fall admission, 2/15 priority date for domestic students. Applications are processed on a rolling basis. Application fee: $45 ($60 for international students). Electronic applications accepted. *Financial support:* In 2010–11, 2 fellowships with full tuition reimbursements, 17 research assistantships with full tuition reimbursements, 13 teaching assistantships with full tuition reimbursements were awarded; institutionally sponsored loans, health care benefits, and unspecified assistantships also available. *Faculty research:* Geochemistry, tectonics, economic geology, biogeochemistry, geophysics. *Unit head:* Dr. Kevin L. Shelton, Department Chair, 573-882-6568, E-mail: sheltonkl@missouri.edu. *Application contact:* Alice Thompson, Administrative Assistant, 573-882-6785, E-mail: thompsonae@missouri.edu.

University of Missouri–Kansas City, College of Arts and Sciences, Department of Geosciences, Kansas City, MO 64110-2499. Offers environmental and urban geosciences (MS); geosciences (PhD). PhD (interdisciplinary) offered through the School of Graduate Studies. Part-time programs available. *Faculty:* 10 full-time (3 women), 2 part-time/adjunct (0 women). *Students:* 3 full-time (1 woman), 25 part-time (11 women); includes 2 minority (both Hispanic/ Latino), 3 international. Average age 34. 17 applicants, 76% accepted, 7 enrolled. *Degree requirements:* For master's, thesis; for doctorate, thesis/dissertation, qualifying exam. *Entrance requirements:* For master's, GRE General Test, minimum GPA of 3.0. Additional exam requirements/recommendations for international students: Required—TOEFL (minimum score 550 paper-based; 213 computer-based; 80 iBT). *Application deadline:* For fall admission, 3/15 priority date for domestic and international students. Applications are processed on a rolling basis. Application fee: $45 ($50 for international students). Electronic applications accepted. *Expenses:* Tuition, state resident: full-time $5522.40; part-time $306.80 per credit hour. Tuition, nonresident: full-time $7128; part-time $792 per credit hour. Required fees: $261.15 per term. *Financial support:* In 2010–11, 2 research assistantships with partial tuition reimbursements (averaging $12,600 per year), 20 teaching assistantships with partial tuition reimbursements (averaging $11,211 per year) were awarded; Federal Work-Study, institutionally sponsored loans, and tuition waivers (full and partial) also available. Support available to part-time students. Financial award application deadline: 3/1; financial award applicants required to submit FAFSA. *Faculty research:* Neotectonics and applied geophysics, environmental geosciences, urban geoscience, geoinformatics–remote sensing, atmospheric research. Total annual research expenditures: $310,535. *Unit head:* Dr. Jimmy Adegoke, Chair, 816-235-1334, Fax: 816-235-5535, E-mail: adegokej@umkc.edu. *Application contact:* Dr. Ray Coveney, Associate Professor, 816-235-1334, Fax: 816-235-5535, E-mail: coveneyr@umkc.edu.

The University of Montana, Graduate School, College of Arts and Sciences, Department of Geology, Missoula, MT 59812-0002. Offers applied geoscience (PhD); geology (MS, PhD). *Degree requirements:* For doctorate, thesis/dissertation. *Entrance requirements:* For master's and doctorate, GRE General Test. Additional exam requirements/recommendations for international students: Required—TOEFL (minimum score 525 paper-based; 197 computer-based). *Faculty research:* Environmental geoscience, regional structure and tectonics, groundwater geology, petrology, mineral deposits.

University of Nevada, Reno, Graduate School, College of Science, Mackay School of Earth Sciences and Engineering, Department of Geological Sciences, Program in Geology, Reno, NV 89557. Offers MS, PhD. Terminal master's awarded for partial completion of doctoral program. *Degree requirements:* For master's, thesis optional; for doctorate, thesis/dissertation. *Entrance requirements:* For master's, GRE General Test, minimum GPA of 2.75; for doctorate, GRE General Test, minimum GPA of 3.0. Additional exam requirements/recommendations for international students: Required—TOEFL (minimum score 500 paper-based; 173 computer-based; 61 iBT), IELTS (minimum score 6). Electronic applications accepted. *Expenses:* Tuition, state resident: full-time $2219; part-time $246 per credit. Tuition, nonresident: part-time $510 per credit. International tuition: $9009 full-time. Required fees: $59 per term. One-time fee: $101. Tuition and fees vary according to course load. *Faculty research:* Mineral exploration, geochemistry, hydrology.

University of New Brunswick Fredericton, School of Graduate Studies, Faculty of Science, Department of Geology, Fredericton, NB E3B 5A3, Canada. Offers M Sc, PhD. Part-time programs available. *Faculty:* 10 full-time (0 women). *Students:* 32 full-time (15 women), 3 part-time (0 women). In 2010, 2 master's awarded. *Degree requirements:* For master's, thesis; for doctorate, thesis/dissertation. *Entrance requirements:* For master's, minimum GPA of 3.0, B Sc in earth sciences or related subject; for doctorate, minimum GPA of 3.0; M Sc in earth science or related subject. Additional exam requirements/recommendations for international students: Required—TOEFL, IELTS, TWE. *Application deadline:* For fall admission, 3/1 priority date for domestic students. Applications are processed on a rolling basis. Application fee: $50 Canadian dollars. *Expenses:* Tuition, area resident: Full-time $3708; part-time $927 per term. International tuition: $6300 full-time. Required fees: $50 per term. *Financial support:* In 2010–11, research assistantships (averaging $1,160 per year), teaching assistantships (averaging $2,016 per year) were awarded. *Faculty research:* Hydrogeology, glacial geology, petrology, paleontology, aqueous and hydrothermal geochemistry. Total annual research expenditures: $133,936. *Unit head:* Dr. David Keighley, Director of Graduate Studies, 506-453-5196, Fax: 506-453-5055, E-mail: keig@unb.ca. *Application contact:* Christine Lodge, 506-453-4803, Fax: 506-453-5055, E-mail: lodge@unb.ca.

University of New Hampshire, Graduate School, College of Engineering and Physical Sciences, Department of Earth Sciences, Durham, NH 03824. Offers earth sciences (MS), including geochemical systems, geology, ocean mapping, oceanography; hydrology (MS). *Faculty:* 17 full-time (5 women). *Students:* 21 full-time (13 women), 8 part-time (4 women); includes 2 minority (1 Black or African American, non-Hispanic/Latino; 1 Asian, non-Hispanic/ Latino), 4 international. Average age 27. 55 applicants, 65% accepted, 16 enrolled. In 2010, 8 master's awarded. *Degree requirements:* For master's, thesis. *Entrance requirements:* For master's, GRE General Test. Additional exam requirements/recommendations for international students: Required—TOEFL (minimum score 550 paper-based; 213 computer-based; 80 iBT). *Application deadline:* For fall admission, 4/1 priority date for domestic students, 4/1 for international students; for spring admission, 12/1 for domestic students. Applications are processed on a rolling basis. Application fee: $65. Electronic applications accepted. *Financial support:* In 2010–11, 24 students received support, including 13 research assistantships, 7 teaching assistantships; fellowships, career-related internships or fieldwork, Federal Work-Study, scholarships/grants, and tuition waivers (full and partial) also available. Support available to part-time students. Financial award application deadline: 2/15. *Unit head:* Dr. Will Clyde, Chairperson, 603-862-1718, E-mail: earth.sciences@unh.edu. *Application contact:* Sue Clark, Administrative Assistant, 603-862-1718, E-mail: earth.sciences@unh.edu.

The University of North Carolina at Chapel Hill, Graduate School, College of Arts and Sciences, Department of Geological Sciences, Chapel Hill, NC 27599. Offers MS, PhD. *Degree requirements:* For master's, comprehensive exam, thesis; for doctorate, one foreign language, comprehensive exam, thesis/dissertation. *Entrance requirements:* For master's and doctorate, GRE General Test, minimum GPA of 3.0. Electronic applications accepted. *Faculty research:* Paleoceanography, igneous petrology, paleontology, geophysics, structural geology.

The University of North Carolina Wilmington, College of Arts and Sciences, Department of Geography and Geology, Wilmington, NC 28403-3297. Offers geology (MS); marine science (MS). *Faculty:* 19 full-time (5 women). *Students:* 3 full-time (1 woman), 15 part-time (7 women), 1 international. Average age 30. 46 applicants, 65% accepted, 19 enrolled. In 2010, 2 master's awarded. *Degree requirements:* For master's, comprehensive exam, thesis. *Entrance requirements:* For master's, GRE General Test, GRE Subject Test, minimum B average in undergraduate major and basic courses for prerequisite to geology. *Application deadline:* For fall admission, 2/15 for domestic students. Applications are processed on a rolling basis. Application fee: $45. *Financial support:* In 2010–11, 21 teaching assistantships were awarded; career-related internships or fieldwork and Federal Work-Study also available. Support available to part-time students. Financial award application deadline: 3/15. *Unit head:* Dr. Lynn Leonard, Chair, 910-962-2338, Fax: 910-962-7077, E-mail: lynnl@uncw.edu. *Application contact:* Dr. Michael Smith, Graduate Coordinator, 910-962-3496, Fax: 910-962-7077, E-mail: smithms@uncw.edu.

University of North Dakota, Graduate School, School of Engineering and Mines, Department of Geology, Grand Forks, ND 58202. Offers MA, MS, PhD. *Faculty:* 7 full-time (0 women), 1 part-time/adjunct (0 women). *Students:* 10 full-time (3 women), 11 part-time (2 women), 4 international. Average age 31. 11 applicants, 45% accepted, 5 enrolled. In 2010, 2 master's awarded. *Degree requirements:* For master's, thesis, final exam; for doctorate, one foreign language, comprehensive exam, thesis/dissertation, final exam. *Entrance requirements:* For master's and doctorate, GRE General Test, minimum GPA of 3.0. Additional exam requirements/ recommendations for international students: Required—TOEFL (minimum score 550 paper-based; 213 computer-based; 79 iBT), IELTS (minimum score 6.5). *Application deadline:* For fall admission, 8/1 priority date for domestic students, 5/1 priority date for international students; for spring admission, 12/1 priority date for domestic students, 9/1 priority date for international students. Applications are processed on a rolling basis. Application fee: $35. Electronic applications accepted. *Expenses:* Tuition, state resident: full-time $5857; part-time $306.74 per credit. Tuition, nonresident: full-time $15,666; part-time $729.77 per credit. Required fees: $53.42 per credit. Tuition and fees vary according to course load, program and reciprocity agreements. *Financial support:* In 2010–11, 12 students received support, including 7 research assistantships with full and partial tuition reimbursements available (averaging $11,921 per year), 5 teaching assistantships with full and partial tuition reimbursements available (averaging $9,979 per year); fellowships with full and partial tuition reimbursements available, career-related internships or fieldwork, Federal Work-Study, institutionally sponsored loans, scholarships/ grants, health care benefits, tuition waivers (full and partial), and unspecified assistantships also available. Support available to part-time students. Financial award application deadline: 3/15; financial award applicants required to submit FAFSA. *Faculty research:* Hydrogeology, environmental geology, geological engineering, sedimentology, geomorphology. Total annual research expenditures: $32,217. *Unit head:* Dr. Philip J. Gerla, Graduate Director, 701-777-3305, Fax: 701-777-4449, E-mail: phil.gerla@mail.und.nodak.edu. *Application contact:* Staci Wells, Admissions Associate, 701-777-2945, Fax: 701-777-3619, E-mail: staci.wells@gradschool.und.edu.

University of Oklahoma, College of Earth and Energy, ConocoPhillips School of Geology and Geophysics, Program in Geology, Norman, OK 73019. Offers MS, PhD. Part-time programs available. *Students:* 49 full-time (17 women), 21 part-time (7 women); includes 4 minority (2 American Indian or Alaska Native, non-Hispanic/Latino; 1 Hispanic/Latino; 1 Two or more races, non-Hispanic/Latino), 22 international. Average age 28. 70 applicants, 26% accepted, 14 enrolled. In 2010, 12 master's, 4 doctorates awarded. *Degree requirements:* For master's, comprehensive exam, thesis; for doctorate, one foreign language, thesis/dissertation, general exam. *Entrance requirements:* For master's, GRE General Test, bachelor's degree in geology; for doctorate, GRE General Test. Additional exam requirements/recommendations for international students: Required—TOEFL (minimum score 550 paper-based; 213 computer-based; 79 iBT). *Application deadline:* For fall admission, 2/1 priority date for domestic students, 4/1 for international students; for spring admission, 9/1 for domestic and international students. Applications are processed on a rolling basis. Application fee: $40 ($90 for international students). Electronic applications accepted. *Expenses:* Tuition, state resident: full-time $3892.80; part-time $162.20 per credit hour. Tuition, nonresident: full-time $14,167; part-time $590.30 per credit hour. Required fees: $2523.40; $94.60 per credit hour. Tuition and fees vary according to course load and degree level. *Financial support:* In 2010–11, 59 students received support. Scholarships/grants and unspecified assistantships available. Financial award application deadline: 2/1; financial award applicants required to submit FAFSA. *Faculty research:* Earth systems, lithospheric dynamics, energy, geochemistry, and geophysics. *Unit head:* Dr. Douglas Elmore, Director and Associate Provost, 405-325-3253, Fax: 405-325-3140, E-mail: delmore@ou.edu. *Application contact:* Donna S. Mullins, Coordinator for Administrative Student Services and Corporate Recruiting, 405-325-3255, Fax: 405-325-3140, E-mail: dsmullins@ou.edu.

University of Oregon, Graduate School, College of Arts and Sciences, Department of Geological Sciences, Eugene, OR 97403. Offers MA, MS, PhD. *Degree requirements:* For master's, foreign language (MA). *Entrance requirements:* For master's and doctorate, GRE General Test, GRE Subject Test.

University of Pittsburgh, School of Arts and Sciences, Department of Geology and Planetary Science, Pittsburgh, PA 15260-3332. Offers geographical information systems (PM Sc); geology and planetary science (MS, PhD). Part-time programs available. *Faculty:* 9 full-time (1 woman), 4 part-time/adjunct (1 woman). *Students:* 26 full-time (13 women), 9 part-time (4 women); includes 1 Asian, non-Hispanic/Latino, 1 international. Average age 30. 56 applicants, 36% accepted, 8 enrolled. In 2010, 3 master's, 2 doctorates awarded. *Degree requirements:* For master's, thesis, oral thesis defense; for doctorate, comprehensive exam, thesis/dissertation, oral dissertation defense. *Entrance requirements:* For master's and doctorate, GRE General Test. Additional exam requirements/recommendations for international students: Required—TOEFL (minimum score 550 paper-based; 213 computer-based; 80 iBT). *Application deadline:* For fall admission, 2/1 priority date for domestic students, 2/1 for international students. Application fee: $50. Electronic applications accepted. *Expenses:* Tuition, state resident: full-time $17,304; part-time $701 per credit. Tuition, nonresident: full-time $29,554; part-time $1210 per credit. Required fees: $740; $214 per term. Tuition and fees vary according to program. *Financial support:* In 2010–11, 25 students received support, including 3 fellowships with full tuition reimbursements available (averaging $16,140 per year), 10 research assistantships with full and partial tuition reimbursements available (averaging $14,400 per year), 9 teaching assistantships with full and partial tuition reimbursements available (averaging $15,830 per year); career-related internships or fieldwork, Federal Work-Study, institutionally sponsored loans, scholarships/grants, and tuition waivers (full and partial) also available. Support available to part-time students. Financial award application deadline: 2/1; financial award applicants required to submit FAFSA. *Faculty research:* Geographical information systems, hydrology, low temperature geochemistry, volcanology, paleoclimatology. Total annual research expenditures: $1.5 million. *Unit head:* Dr. William Harbert, Chair, 412-624-8783, Fax: 412-624-3914, E-mail: harbert@pitt.edu. *Application contact:* Dr. Michael Ramsey, Director of Graduate Studies, 412-624-8772, Fax: 412-624-3914, E-mail: mramsey@pitt.edu.

University of Puerto Rico, Mayagüez Campus, Graduate Studies, College of Arts and Sciences, Department of Geology, Mayagüez, PR 00681-9000. Offers MS. Part-time programs available. *Students:* 17 full-time (9 women); includes 16 Hispanic/Latino, 1 international. 4 applicants, 50% accepted, 2 enrolled. In 2010, 2 master's awarded. *Degree requirements:* For master's, comprehensive exam, thesis. *Entrance requirements:* For master's, GRE General Test, BS in geology or the equivalent; minimum GPA of 2.8. *Application deadline:* For fall admission, 2/15 for domestic and international students; for spring admission, 9/15 for domestic and international students. Applications are processed on a rolling basis. Application fee: $25. *Expenses:* Tuition, state resident: full-time $1188. Tuition, nonresident: full-time $1188. International tuition: $6126 full-time. Tuition and fees vary according to course level and course load. *Financial support:* In 2010–11, 8 students received support, including fellowships (averaging $12,000 per year), 8 research assistantships (averaging $15,000 per year), 8 teaching assistant-

Peterson's Graduate Programs in the Physical Sciences, Mathematics, Agricultural Sciences, the Environment & Natural Resources 2012

www.facebook.com/petersonspublishing 125

Geology

University of Puerto Rico, Mayagüez Campus (continued)
ships (averaging $8,500 per year). *Faculty research:* Seismology, applied geophysics, geographic information systems, environmental remote sensing, petrology. Total annual research expenditures: $363,164. *Unit head:* Dr. Fernando Gilbes, 787-832-4040 Ext. 3000, E-mail: fernando.gilbes@upr.edu. *Application contact:* Marsha Irizarry, 787-832-4040 Ext. 2414, Fax: 787-265-3845, E-mail: irizarrym@uprm.edu.

University of Regina, Faculty of Graduate Studies and Research, Faculty of Science, Department of Geology, Regina, SK S4S 0A2, Canada. Offers M Sc, PhD. PhD program offered on a special case basis. *Faculty:* 7 full-time (3 women). *Students:* 10 full-time (6 women), 4 part-time (0 women). 7 applicants, 86% accepted. In 2010, 4 master's, 1 doctorate awarded. *Degree requirements:* For master's, thesis; for doctorate, thesis/dissertation. *Entrance requirements:* Additional exam requirements/recommendations for international students: Required—TOEFL (minimum score 580 paper-based; 80 iBT). *Application deadline:* Applications are processed on a rolling basis. Application fee: $100. Electronic applications accepted. Tuition and fees charges are reported in Canadian dollars. *Expenses:* Tuition, area resident: Full-time $3244.50 Canadian dollars; part-time $180.25 Canadian dollars per credit hour. International tuition: $4744.50 Canadian dollars full-time. Required fees: $494 Canadian dollars; $115.25 Canadian dollars per credit hour. $115.25 Canadian dollars per semester. Tuition and fees vary according to program. *Financial support:* In 2010–11, 1 fellowship (averaging $18,000 per year), 1 research assistantship (averaging $16,500 per year), 3 teaching assistantships (averaging $6,759 per year) were awarded; scholarships/grants also available. Financial award application deadline: 6/15. *Faculty research:* Quaternary and economic geology; volcanology; organic, igneous, and metamorphic petrology; carbonate sedimentology and basin analysis; mineralogy. *Unit head:* Dr. Hairuo Qing, Head, 306-585-4677, Fax: 306-585-5433, E-mail: hairuo.qing@uregina.ca. *Application contact:* Dr. Kathryn Bethune, Graduate Program Coordinator, 306-585-4270, Fax: 306-585-5433, E-mail: kathryn.bethune@uregina.ca.

University of Rochester, School of Arts and Sciences, Department of Earth and Environmental Sciences, Rochester, NY 14627. Offers geological sciences (MS, PhD). *Degree requirements:* For doctorate, thesis/dissertation, qualifying exam. *Entrance requirements:* For master's and doctorate, GRE General Test. Additional exam requirements/recommendations for international students: Required—TOEFL.

University of Saskatchewan, College of Graduate Studies and Research, College of Arts and Sciences and College of Engineering, Department of Geological Sciences, Saskatoon, SK S7N 5A2, Canada. Offers M Sc, PhD, Diploma. *Degree requirements:* For master's, thesis; for doctorate, comprehensive exam (for some programs), thesis/dissertation. *Entrance requirements:* Additional exam requirements/recommendations for international students: Required—TOEFL (minimum score 80 iBT); Recommended—IELTS (minimum score 6.5). Electronic applications accepted.

University of South Carolina, The Graduate School, College of Arts and Sciences, Department of Geological Sciences, Columbia, SC 29208. Offers MS, PhD. Terminal master's awarded for partial completion of doctoral program. *Degree requirements:* For master's, thesis; for doctorate, comprehensive exam, thesis/dissertation, published paper. *Entrance requirements:* For master's and doctorate, GRE General Test. Additional exam requirements/recommendations for international students: Required—TOEFL (minimum score 570 paper-based; 230 computer-based; 75 iBT). Electronic applications accepted. *Faculty research:* Environmental geology, tectonics, petrology, coastal processes, paleoclimatology.

University of Southern Mississippi, Graduate School, College of Science and Technology, Department of Geography and Geology, Hattiesburg, MS 39406-0001. Offers geography (MS, PhD); geology (MS). Part-time programs available. *Faculty:* 11 full-time (2 women), 1 part-time/adjunct (0 women). *Students:* 20 full-time (3 women), 11 part-time (5 women). Average age 34. 18 applicants, 44% accepted, 7 enrolled. In 2010, 7 master's awarded. *Degree requirements:* For master's, comprehensive exam, thesis (for some programs), internships; for doctorate, comprehensive exam, thesis/dissertation. *Entrance requirements:* For master's, GMAT, GRE General Test, minimum GPA of 3.0 for last 60 hours; for doctorate, GRE, minimum GPA of 3.5. Additional exam requirements/recommendations for international students: Required—TOEFL, IELTS. *Application deadline:* For fall admission, 3/15 for domestic and international students; for spring admission, 1/3 for domestic students. Applications are processed on a rolling basis. Application fee: $50. Electronic applications accepted. *Financial support:* In 2010–11, 1 research assistantship with tuition reimbursement (averaging $18,000 per year), 8 teaching assistantships with full tuition reimbursements (averaging $8,700 per year) were awarded; fellowships with full tuition reimbursements, career-related internships or fieldwork, Federal Work-Study, scholarships/grants, health care benefits, and unspecified assistantships also available. Financial award application deadline: 3/15; financial award applicants required to submit FAFSA. *Faculty research:* City and regional planning, geographic techniques, physical geography, human geography. *Unit head:* Dr. Clifton Dixon, Chair, 601-266-4729, Fax: 601-266-6219, E-mail: c.dixon@usm.edu. *Application contact:* Dr. Clifton Dixon, Director, Graduate Studies, 601-266-4729, Fax: 601-266-6219.

University of South Florida, Graduate School, College of Arts and Sciences, Department of Geology, Tampa, FL 33620-9951. Offers MS, PhD. Part-time programs available. *Faculty:* 10 full-time (1 woman). *Students:* 40 full-time (13 women), 23 part-time (9 women); includes 2 Black or African American, non-Hispanic/Latino; 1 Asian, non-Hispanic/Latino; 1 Two or more races, non-Hispanic/Latino, 11 international. Average age 34. 62 applicants, 42% accepted, 19 enrolled. In 2010, 12 master's awarded. *Degree requirements:* For master's, comprehensive exam, thesis (for some programs); for doctorate, comprehensive exam, thesis/dissertation. *Entrance requirements:* For master's, GRE General Test, minimum GPA of 3.0 in last 60 hours of course work; for doctorate, GRE General Test. Additional exam requirements/recommendations for international students: Required—TOEFL (minimum score 550 paper-based; 213 computer-based). *Application deadline:* For fall admission, 2/15 for domestic students, 1/2 for international students; for spring admission, 10/15 for domestic students, 6/1 for international students. Application fee: $30. Electronic applications accepted. *Financial support:* In 2010–11, 6 research assistantships (averaging $17,235 per year), 30 teaching assistantships with tuition reimbursements (averaging $15,979 per year) were awarded; unspecified assistantships also available. Financial award application deadline: 6/30; financial award applicants required to submit FAFSA. Total annual research expenditures: $1.5 million. *Unit head:* Chuck Connor, Chairperson, 813-974-0325, Fax: 813-974-2654, E-mail: cconnor@cas.usf.edu. *Application contact:* Ping Wang, Director, 813-974-9170, Fax: 813-974-2654, E-mail: pwang@cas.usf.edu.

The University of Tennessee, Graduate School, College of Arts and Sciences, Department of Geological Sciences, Knoxville, TN 37996. Offers geology (MS, PhD). Part-time programs available. *Degree requirements:* For master's, thesis; for doctorate, one foreign language, thesis/dissertation. *Entrance requirements:* For master's and doctorate, GRE General Test, minimum GPA of 2.7. Additional exam requirements/recommendations for international students: Required—TOEFL. Electronic applications accepted. *Expenses:* Tuition, state resident: full-time $7440; part-time $414 per credit hour. Tuition, nonresident: full-time $22,478; part-time $1250 per credit hour. Required fees: $922; $43 per credit hour. Tuition and fees vary according to program.

The University of Texas at Arlington, Graduate School, College of Science, Department of Earth and Environmental Sciences, Program in Environmental and Earth Sciences, Arlington, TX 76019. Offers environmental science (MS, PhD); geology (MS, PhD). Part-time and evening/weekend programs available. *Faculty:* 5 full-time (0 women), 1 part-time/adjunct (0 women). *Students:* 22 full-time (13 women), 25 part-time (12 women); includes 2 Black or African American, non-Hispanic/Latino; 1 American Indian or Alaska Native, non-Hispanic/Latino; 2 Asian, non-Hispanic/Latino; 4 Hispanic/Latino, 11 international. 23 applicants, 74% accepted, 10 enrolled. In 2010, 11 master's, 1 doctorate awarded. Terminal master's awarded for partial completion of doctoral program. *Degree requirements:* For master's, thesis optional; for doctorate, comprehensive exam, thesis/dissertation. *Entrance requirements:* For master's, GRE General Test. Additional exam requirements/recommendations for international students: Required—TOEFL (minimum score 550 paper-based; 213 computer-based). *Application deadline:* Applications are processed on a rolling basis. Application fee: $35 ($50 for international students). Electronic applications accepted. *Expenses:* Tuition, state resident: full-time $7500. Tuition, nonresident: full-time $13,080. International tuition: $13,250 full-time. *Financial support:* In 2010–11, 4 fellowships (averaging $1,000 per year), 7 teaching assistantships (averaging $14,700 per year) were awarded; career-related internships or fieldwork, Federal Work-Study, institutionally sponsored loans, scholarships/grants, health care benefits, and unspecified assistantships also available. Financial award applicants required to submit FAFSA. *Unit head:* Dr. John S. Wickham, Chair, 817-272-2987, Fax: 817-272-2628, E-mail: wickham@uta.edu. *Application contact:* Dr. Andrew Hunt, Graduate Advisor, 817-272-2987, Fax: 817-272-2628, E-mail: hunt@uta.edu.

The University of Texas at Austin, Graduate School, Jackson School of Geosciences, Austin, TX 78712-1111. Offers MA, MS, PhD. Part-time programs available. *Degree requirements:* For master's, report (MA), thesis (MS); for doctorate, thesis/dissertation. *Entrance requirements:* For master's and doctorate, GRE General Test. Electronic applications accepted. *Faculty research:* Sedimentary geology, geophysics, hydrogeology, structure/tectonics, vertebrate paleontology.

The University of Texas at El Paso, Graduate School, College of Science, Department of Geological Sciences, El Paso, TX 79968-0001. Offers geological sciences (MS, PhD); geophysics (MS). Part-time and evening/weekend programs available. *Students:* 52 (18 women); includes 1 Black or African American, non-Hispanic/Latino; 14 Hispanic/Latino, 16 international. Average age 34. 21 applicants, 67% accepted. In 2010, 8 master's, 2 doctorates awarded. *Degree requirements:* For master's, thesis; for doctorate, one foreign language, thesis/dissertation. *Entrance requirements:* For master's, GRE, minimum GPA of 3.0, BS in geology or equivalent; for doctorate, GRE, minimum GPA of 3.0, MS in geology or equivalent. Additional exam requirements/recommendations for international students: Required—TOEFL. *Application deadline:* For fall admission, 7/1 priority date for domestic students, 3/1 for international students; for spring admission, 11/1 priority date for domestic students, 9/1 for international students. Applications are processed on a rolling basis. Application fee: $15 ($65 for international students). Electronic applications accepted. *Financial support:* In 2010–11, 36 students received support, including research assistantships with partial tuition reimbursements available (averaging $21,812 per year), teaching assistantships with partial tuition reimbursements available (averaging $17,450 per year); fellowships with partial tuition reimbursements available, career-related internships or fieldwork, institutionally sponsored loans, scholarships/grants, and tuition waivers (partial) also available. Support available to part-time students. Financial award application deadline: 3/15; financial award applicants required to submit FAFSA. *Unit head:* Aaron A. Velasco, Chair, 915-747-5501, Fax: 915-747-5073, E-mail: velasco@geo.utep.edu. *Application contact:* Dr. Charles H. Ambler, Dean of the Graduate School, 915-747-5491 Ext. 7886, Fax: 915-747-5788, E-mail: cambler@utep.edu.

The University of Texas at San Antonio, College of Sciences, Department of Geological Sciences, San Antonio, TX 78249-0617. Offers MS. Part-time programs available. *Faculty:* 7 full-time (2 women), 1 part-time/adjunct (0 women). *Students:* 8 full-time (4 women), 7 part-time (1 woman); includes 3 minority (2 Hispanic/Latino; 1 Two or more races, non-Hispanic/Latino), 2 international. Average age 29. 16 applicants, 75% accepted, 7 enrolled. In 2010, 2 master's awarded. *Degree requirements:* For master's, comprehensive exam (for some programs), thesis (for some programs). *Entrance requirements:* For master's, GRE General Test, minimum GPA of 3.0 in last 60 hours. Additional exam requirements/recommendations for international students: Required—TOEFL (minimum score 500 paper-based; 173 computer-based; 61 iBT), IELTS (minimum score 5). *Application deadline:* For fall admission, 7/1 for domestic students, 4/1 for international students; for spring admission, 11/1 for domestic students, 9/1 for international students. Applications are processed on a rolling basis. Application fee: $45 ($80 for international students). Electronic applications accepted. *Expenses:* Tuition, state resident: full-time $4172; part-time $231.75 per credit hour. Tuition, nonresident: full-time $15,332; part-time $851.75 per credit hour. *Financial support:* In 2010–11, 7 students received support, including 2 fellowships (averaging $38,000 per year), 8 teaching assistantships (averaging $11,125 per year); scholarships/grants, tuition waivers, and unspecified assistantships also available. Support available to part-time students. *Faculty research:* Water resources/hydrogeology, low-temperature geochemistry, petrology and tectonics, energy resources, paleoclimatology, landscape dynamics. Total annual research expenditures: $396,687. *Unit head:* Dr. Allan R. Dutton, Interim Department Chair, 210-458-4455, Fax: 210-458-4469, E-mail: allan.dutton@utsa.edu. *Application contact:* Veronica Ramirez, Assistant Dean of the Graduate School, 210-458-4330, Fax: 210-458-4332, E-mail: graduatestudies@utsa.edu.

See Display on page 389 and Close-Up on page 399.

The University of Texas of the Permian Basin, Office of Graduate Studies, College of Arts and Sciences, Department of Physical Sciences, Program in Geology, Odessa, TX 79762-0001. Offers MS. *Degree requirements:* For master's, comprehensive exam, thesis or alternative. *Entrance requirements:* For master's, GRE General Test. Additional exam requirements/recommendations for international students: Required—TOEFL (minimum score 550 paper-based; 213 computer-based).

The University of Toledo, College of Graduate Studies, College of Natural Sciences and Mathematics, Department of Environmental Sciences, Toledo, OH 43606-3390. Offers geology (MS), including earth surface processes, general geology. Part-time programs available. *Faculty:* 30. *Students:* 9 full-time (5 women), 1 (woman) part-time; includes 1 minority (Black or African American, non-Hispanic/Latino), 1 international. Average age 30. 9 applicants, 56% accepted, 5 enrolled. In 2010, 2 master's awarded. *Degree requirements:* For master's, thesis. *Entrance requirements:* For master's, GRE General Test, A minimum 2.7 cumulative point-hour ratio (on a 4.0 scale) for all previous academic work. Three letters of recommendation, a statement of purpose, and transcripts from all prior institutions attended. Additional exam requirements/recommendations for international students: Required—TOEFL (minimum score 550 paper-based; 213 computer-based; 80 iBT), IELTS (minimum score 6.5). *Application deadline:* For fall admission, 1/15 priority date for domestic and international students. Applications are processed on a rolling basis. Application fee: $45 ($75 for international students). Electronic applications accepted. *Expenses:* Tuition, state resident: full-time $11,426; part-time $476 per credit hour. Tuition, nonresident: full-time $21,660; part-time $903 per credit hour. One-time fee: $62. *Financial support:* Research assistantships with tuition reimbursements, teaching assistantships with tuition reimbursements, Federal Work-Study, institutionally sponsored loans, scholarships/grants, tuition waivers (full), and unspecified assistantships available. Support available to part-time students. *Faculty research:* Environmental geochemistry, geophysics, petrology and mineralogy, paleontology, geohydrology. *Unit head:* Dr. Timothy G. Fisher, Chair, 419-530-2883, E-mail: timothy.fisher@utoledo.edu. *Application contact:* Graduate School Office, 419-530-4723, Fax: 419-530-4724, E-mail: grdsch@utnet.utoledo.edu.

University of Toronto, School of Graduate Studies, Physical Sciences Division, Department of Geology, Toronto, ON M5S 1A1, Canada. Offers M Sc, MA Sc, PhD. Part-time programs available. *Degree requirements:* For master's, thesis (for some programs); for doctorate, thesis/dissertation. *Entrance requirements:* For master's, B Sc or BA Sc, or equivalent; letters of reference; for doctorate, M Sc or equivalent, minimum B+ average, letters of reference.

University of Utah, Graduate School, College of Mines and Earth Sciences, Department of Geology and Geophysics, Salt Lake City, UT 84112. Offers environmental engineering (ME,

MS, PhD); geological engineering (ME, MS, PhD); geology (MS, PhD); geophysics (MS, PhD). *Faculty:* 21 full-time (4 women), 4 part-time/adjunct (1 woman). *Students:* 51 full-time (13 women), 19 part-time (6 women); includes 1 minority (Hispanic/Latino), 15 international. Average age 30. 128 applicants, 27% accepted, 23 enrolled. In 2010, 10 master's, 8 doctorates awarded. Terminal master's awarded for partial completion of doctoral program. *Degree requirements:* For master's, comprehensive exam, thesis; for doctorate, thesis/dissertation, qualifying exam (written and oral). *Entrance requirements:* For master's and doctorate, GRE General Test, minimum GPA of 3.25. Additional exam requirements/recommendations for international students: Required—TOEFL (minimum score 500 paper-based; 173 computer-based). *Application deadline:* For fall admission, 1/15 priority date for domestic and international students. Applications are processed on a rolling basis. Application fee: $55 ($65 for international students). Electronic applications accepted. *Expenses:* Tuition, area resident: Part-time $179.19 per credit hour. Tuition, state resident: full-time $4384. Tuition, nonresident: full-time $16,684; part-time $630.67 per credit hour. Required fees: $350 per semester. Tuition and fees vary according to course load, degree level and program. *Financial support:* In 2010–11, 22 students received support, including 11 fellowships with full tuition reimbursements available (averaging $13,450 per year), 45 research assistantships with full tuition reimbursements available (averaging $21,858 per year), 11 teaching assistantships with full tuition reimbursements available (averaging $13,450 per year); career-related internships or fieldwork, institutionally sponsored loans, scholarships/grants, unspecified assistantships, and stipends also available. Financial award application deadline: 1/15; financial award applicants required to submit FAFSA. *Faculty research:* Igneous, metamorphic, and sedimentary petrology; ore deposits; aqueous geochemistry; isotope geochemistry; heat flow. Total annual research expenditures: $2.2 million. *Unit head:* Dr. Kip Solomon, Chair, 801-581-7231, Fax: 801-581-7065, E-mail: kip.solomon@utah.edu. *Application contact:* Dr. Allan A. Ekdale, Director of Graduate Studies, 801-581-7266, Fax: 801-581-7065, E-mail: a.ekdale@utah.edu.

University of Vermont, Graduate College, College of Arts and Sciences, Department of Geology, Burlington, VT 05405. Offers MS. *Students:* 13 (7 women); includes 1 Hispanic/Latino. 31 applicants, 23% accepted, 5 enrolled. In 2010, 2 master's awarded. *Degree requirements:* For master's, thesis. *Entrance requirements:* For master's, GRE General Test. Additional exam requirements/recommendations for international students: Required—TOEFL (minimum score 550 paper-based; 213 computer-based; 80 iBT). *Application deadline:* For fall admission, 2/15 priority date for domestic students. Applications are processed on a rolling basis. Application fee: $40. Electronic applications accepted. *Expenses:* Tuition, state resident: part-time $537 per credit hour. Tuition, nonresident: part-time $1355 per credit hour. *Financial support:* Research assistantships, teaching assistantships available. Financial award application deadline: 3/1. *Faculty research:* Mineralogy, lake sediments, structural geology. *Unit head:* Dr. Char Mehrtens, Chairperson, 802-656-3396. *Application contact:* Dr. A. Lini, Coordinator, 802-656-3396.

University of Washington, Graduate School, College of Arts and Sciences, Department of Earth and Space Sciences, Seattle, WA 98195. Offers geology (MS, PhD); geophysics (MS, PhD). *Degree requirements:* For master's, thesis or alternative, departmental qualifying exam, final exam; for doctorate, thesis/dissertation, departmental qualifying exam, general and final exams. *Entrance requirements:* For master's and doctorate, GRE General Test, minimum GPA of 3.0. Additional exam requirements/recommendations for international students: Required—TOEFL (minimum score 580 paper-based). Electronic applications accepted.

The University of Western Ontario, Faculty of Graduate Studies, Physical Sciences Division, Department of Earth Sciences, London, ON N6A 5B8, Canada. Offers environment and sustainability (MES); geology (M Sc, PhD); geology and environmental science (M Sc, PhD); geophysics (M Sc, PhD); geophysics and environmental science (M Sc, PhD). *Degree requirements:* For master's, thesis; for doctorate, thesis/dissertation, qualifying exam. *Entrance requirements:* For master's, honors in B Sc; for doctorate, M Sc. Additional exam requirements/recommendations for international students: Required—TOEFL. *Faculty research:* Geophysics, geochemistry, paleontology, sedimentology/stratigraphy, glaciology/quaternary.

University of Wisconsin–Madison, Graduate School, College of Letters and Science, Department of Geology and Geophysics, Program in Geology, Madison, WI 53706-1380. Offers MS, PhD. *Degree requirements:* For master's, thesis; for doctorate, one foreign language, thesis/dissertation. *Entrance requirements:* For master's and doctorate, GRE General Test. *Expenses:* Tuition, state resident: full-time $9887.36; part-time $617.96 per credit. Tuition, nonresident: full-time $24,054; part-time $1503.40 per credit. Required fees: $67.63 per credit. Tuition and fees vary according to reciprocity agreements.

University of Wisconsin–Milwaukee, Graduate School, College of Letters and Sciences, Department of Geosciences, Milwaukee, WI 53201-0413. Offers geological sciences (MS, PhD). *Faculty:* 12 full-time (3 women). *Students:* 15 full-time (9 women), 10 part-time (3 women), 1 international. Average age 31. 28 applicants, 43% accepted, 4 enrolled. In 2010, 4 master's awarded. *Degree requirements:* For master's, thesis; for doctorate, one foreign language, thesis/dissertation. *Entrance requirements:* For master's, GRE General Test, minimum GPA of 3.0; for doctorate, GRE General Test, master's degree. Additional exam requirements/recommendations for international students: Required—TOEFL (minimum score 550 paper-based; 79 iBT), IELTS (minimum score 6.5). *Application deadline:* For fall admission, 1/1 priority date for domestic students; for spring admission, 9/1 for domestic students. Applications are processed on a rolling basis. Application fee: $56 ($96 for international students). Electronic applications accepted. *Financial support:* In 2010–11, 4 research assistantships, 11 teaching assistantships were awarded; career-related internships or fieldwork and unspecified assistantships also available. Support available to part-time students. Financial award application deadline: 4/15; financial award applicants required to submit FAFSA. *Faculty research:* Geology, geosciences, geophysics, hydrogeology, paleontology. Total annual research expenditures: $419,000. *Unit head:* Barry Cameron, Representative, 414-229-3136, Fax: 414-229-5452, E-mail: bcameron@uwm.edu. *Application contact:* General Information Contact, 414-229-4982, Fax: 414-229-6967, E-mail: gradschool@uwm.edu.

University of Wyoming, College of Arts and Sciences, Department of Geology and Geophysics, Laramie, WY 82070. Offers geology (MS, PhD); geophysics (MS, PhD). Part-time programs available. *Degree requirements:* For master's, comprehensive exam, thesis; for doctorate, comprehensive exam, thesis/dissertation. *Entrance requirements:* For master's and doctorate, GRE General Test, minimum GPA of 3.0. *Faculty research:* Low-temp geochemistry, geohydrology, paleontology, structure/tectonics, sedimentation and petroleum geology, petrology, geophysics/seismology.

Utah State University, School of Graduate Studies, College of Science, Department of Geology, Logan, UT 84322. Offers MS. *Degree requirements:* For master's, thesis. *Entrance requirements:* For master's, GRE General Test, minimum GPA of 3.0. Additional exam requirements/recommendations for international students: Required—TOEFL. *Faculty research:* Sedimentary geology, structural geology, regional tectonics, hydrogeology petrology.

Washington State University, Graduate School, College of Sciences, School of Earth and Environmental Sciences, Department of Geology, Pullman, WA 99164. Offers MS, PhD. *Faculty:* 9. *Students:* 20 full-time (7 women), 5 part-time (2 women); includes 1 American Indian or Alaska Native, non-Hispanic/Latino. Average age 29. 31 applicants, 19% accepted, 6 enrolled. In 2010, 3 master's, 1 doctorate awarded. *Degree requirements:* For master's, comprehensive exam (for some programs), thesis, oral exam; for doctorate, one foreign language, comprehensive exam, thesis/dissertation, oral exam, written exam. *Entrance requirements:* For master's and doctorate, GRE General Test, official copies of college transcripts, minimum GPA of 3.0, 3 letters of recommendation. Additional exam requirements/recommendations for international students: Required—TOEFL (minimum score 560 paper-based; 220 computer-based). *Application deadline:* For fall admission, 1/10 priority date for domestic students, 1/10 for international students; for spring admission, 7/1 priority date for domestic students, 7/1 for international students. Applications are processed on a rolling basis. Application fee: $50. Electronic applications accepted. *Expenses:* Tuition, state resident: full-time $8552; part-time $443 per credit. Tuition, nonresident: full-time $21,650; part-time $1083 per credit. Required fees: $846. *Financial support:* In 2010–11, 4 fellowships (averaging $2,700 per year), 5 research assistantships with full and partial tuition reimbursements (averaging $13,917 per year), 18 teaching assistantships with full and partial tuition reimbursements (averaging $13,056 per year) were awarded; career-related internships or fieldwork, Federal Work-Study, institutionally sponsored loans, and scholarships/grants also available. Financial award application deadline: 2/1; financial award applicants required to submit FAFSA. *Faculty research:* Genesis of ore deposits, geohydrology of the Pacific Northwest, geochemistry and petrology of plateau basalts. Total annual research expenditures: $358,000. *Unit head:* Dr. John A. Wolff, Acting Director, 509-335-2825, Fax: 509-335-7816, E-mail: jawolff@mail.wsu.edu. *Application contact:* Graduate School Admissions, 800-GRADWSU, Fax: 509-335-1949, E-mail: gradsch@wsu.edu.

Wayne State University, College of Liberal Arts and Sciences, Department of Geology, Detroit, MI 48202. Offers MA, MS. *Faculty:* 2 full-time (0 women). *Students:* 2 full-time (1 woman), 3 part-time (2 women); includes 1 American Indian or Alaska Native, non-Hispanic/Latino. Average age 29. 2 applicants, 50% accepted, 1 enrolled. *Degree requirements:* For master's, thesis. *Entrance requirements:* For master's, GRE General Test. Additional exam requirements/recommendations for international students: Required—TOEFL (minimum score 550 paper-based; 213 computer-based); Recommended—TWE (minimum score 6). *Application deadline:* For fall admission, 7/1 for domestic students, 6/1 for international students; for winter admission, 10/1 for international students; for spring admission, 2/1 for international students. Applications are processed on a rolling basis. Application fee: $30 ($50 for international students). Electronic applications accepted. *Expenses:* Tuition, state resident: full-time $7662; part-time $478.85 per credit hour. Tuition, nonresident: full-time $16,920; part-time $1057.55 per credit hour. Required fees: $571.20; $35.70 per credit hour. $188.05 per semester. Tuition and fees vary according to course load and program. *Financial support:* In 2010–11, 2 research assistantships (averaging $19,492 per year) were awarded; teaching assistantships with tuition reimbursements. *Faculty research:* Glacial geology of Southeastern Michigan; applications of U-Th-series, cosmogenic and anthrogenic radionuclides as tracers and chronometers in the environment; geochemical exploration of ore deposits using trace-elemental and stable isotopic (light-elemental) analytical tools; fate and transport of groundwater contaminants in glacial sediments; environmental radioactivity and geochronology. *Unit head:* James D. Tucker, Chair, 313-577-2783, Fax: 313-577-6891, E-mail: ao1754@wayne.edu. *Application contact:* Jeffrey Howard, Graduate Director, 313-577-3258, E-mail: aa2675@wayne.edu.

West Chester University of Pennsylvania, Office of Graduate Studies, College of Arts and Sciences, Department of Geology and Astronomy, West Chester, PA 19383. Offers earth-space science (Teaching Certificate); general science (Teaching Certificate); geoscience (MA). Part-time and evening/weekend programs available. *Students:* 7 full-time (2 women), 20 part-time (11 women); includes 1 minority (Black or African American, non-Hispanic/Latino). Average age 33. 14 applicants, 86% accepted, 6 enrolled. In 2010, 7 master's awarded. *Degree requirements:* For master's, comprehensive exam (for some programs), thesis optional. *Entrance requirements:* For master's, minimum GPA of 2.5. Additional exam requirements/recommendations for international students: Required—TOEFL (minimum score 550 paper-based; 213 computer-based; 80 iBT). *Application deadline:* For fall admission, 4/15 priority date for domestic students, 3/15 for international students; for spring admission, 10/15 for domestic students, 9/1 for international students. Applications are processed on a rolling basis. Application fee: $35. Electronic applications accepted. *Expenses:* Tuition, state resident: full-time $6966; part-time $387 per credit. Tuition, nonresident: full-time $11,146; part-time $619 per credit. Required fees: $1614.40; $133.24 per credit. Part-time tuition and fees vary according to campus/location. *Financial support:* Unspecified assistantships available. Support available to part-time students. Financial award application deadline: 2/15; financial award applicants required to submit FAFSA. *Faculty research:* Developing and using a meteorological data station. *Unit head:* Dr. Marc Gagne, Chair, 610-436-2727, E-mail: mgagne@wcupa.edu. *Application contact:* Dr. Steven Good, Graduate Coordinator, 610-436-2203, E-mail: sgood@wcupa.edu.

Western Kentucky University, Graduate Studies, Ogden College of Science and Engineering, Department of Geography and Geology, Bowling Green, KY 42101. Offers geoscience (MS). *Degree requirements:* For master's, comprehensive exam, thesis or alternative. *Entrance requirements:* For master's, GRE General Test, minimum GPA of 2.75. Additional exam requirements/recommendations for international students: Required—TOEFL (minimum score 555 paper-based; 213 computer-based; 79 iBT). *Faculty research:* Hydroclimatology, electronic data sets, groundwater, sinkhole liquification potential, meteorological analysis.

Western Washington University, Graduate School, College of Sciences and Technology, Department of Geology, Bellingham, WA 98225-5996. Offers MS. Part-time programs available. *Degree requirements:* For master's, thesis. *Entrance requirements:* For master's, GRE General Test, minimum GPA of 3.0 in last 60 semester hours or last 90 quarter hours. Additional exam requirements/recommendations for international students: Required—TOEFL (minimum score 567 paper-based; 227 computer-based). Electronic applications accepted. *Faculty research:* Structure/tectonics; sedimentary, glacial and quaternary geomorphology; igneous and metamorphic petrology; hydrology, geophysics.

West Virginia University, Eberly College of Arts and Sciences, Department of Geology and Geography, Program in Geology, Morgantown, WV 26506. Offers geomorphology (MS, PhD); geophysics (MS, PhD); hydrogeology (MS, PhD); paleontology (MS, PhD); petroleum geology (PhD); petrology (MS, PhD); stratigraphy (MS, PhD); structure (MS, PhD). Part-time programs available. Terminal master's awarded for partial completion of doctoral program. *Degree requirements:* For master's, thesis (for some programs); for doctorate, comprehensive exam, thesis/dissertation. *Entrance requirements:* For master's, GRE General Test, minimum GPA of 2.5; for doctorate, GRE General Test, minimum GPA of 3.3. Additional exam requirements/recommendations for international students: Required—TOEFL.

Wichita State University, Graduate School, Fairmount College of Liberal Arts and Sciences, Department of Geology, Wichita, KS 67260. Offers earth, environmental, and physical sciences (MS). Part-time programs available. *Unit head:* Dr. William Parcell, Chair, 316-978-3140, E-mail: william.parcell@wichita.edu. *Application contact:* Dr. Collette Burke, Graduate Coordinator, 316-978-3140, E-mail: collette.burke@wichita.edu.

Wright State University, School of Graduate Studies, College of Science and Mathematics, Department of Earth and Environmental Sciences, Program in Geological Sciences, Dayton, OH 45435. Offers MS. Part-time programs available. *Degree requirements:* For master's, thesis. *Entrance requirements:* Additional exam requirements/recommendations for international students: Required—TOEFL.

Yale University, Graduate School of Arts and Sciences, Department of Geology and Geophysics, New Haven, CT 06520. Offers biogeochemistry (PhD); climate dynamics (PhD); geochemistry (PhD); geophysics (PhD); meteorology (PhD); oceanography (PhD); paleontology (PhD); paleooceanography (PhD); petrology (PhD); tectonics (PhD). *Degree requirements:* For doctorate, thesis/dissertation. *Entrance requirements:* For doctorate, GRE General Test. Additional exam requirements/recommendations for international students: Required—TOEFL.

Geophysics

Boise State University, Graduate College, College of Arts and Sciences, Department of Geosciences, Master's Program in Geophysics, Boise, ID 83725-0399. Offers MS. Part-time programs available. *Degree requirements:* For master's, thesis. *Entrance requirements:* For master's, GRE General Test, minimum GPA of 3.0, BS in related field. Additional exam requirements/recommendations for international students: Required—TOEFL. Electronic applications accepted. *Faculty research:* Shallow seismic profile, seismic hazard, tectonics, hazardous waste disposal.

Boise State University, Graduate College, College of Arts and Sciences, Department of Geosciences, Program in Geophysics, Boise, ID 83725-0399. Offers PhD. Part-time programs available. *Degree requirements:* For doctorate, comprehensive exam, thesis/dissertation. *Entrance requirements:* For doctorate, GRE General Test. Electronic applications accepted.

Boston College, Graduate School of Arts and Sciences, Department of Geology and Geophysics, Chestnut Hill, MA 02467-3800. Offers MS, MBA/MS. *Degree requirements:* For master's, thesis. *Entrance requirements:* For master's, GRE General Test, GRE Subject Test. Additional exam requirements/recommendations for international students: Required—TOEFL (minimum score 600 paper-based; 250 computer-based; 100 iBT). Electronic applications accepted. *Faculty research:* Coastal and marine geology, experimental sedimentology, geomagnetism, igneous petrology, paleontology.

Bowling Green State University, Graduate College, College of Arts and Sciences, Department of Physics and Astronomy, Bowling Green, OH 43403. Offers geophysics (MS); physics (MAT, MS). *Degree requirements:* For master's, thesis or alternative. *Entrance requirements:* For master's, GRE General Test. Additional exam requirements/recommendations for international students: Required—TOEFL. Electronic applications accepted. *Faculty research:* Computational physics, solid-state physics, materials science, theoretical physics.

California Institute of Technology, Division of Geological and Planetary Sciences, Pasadena, CA 91125-0001. Offers geobiology (MS, PhD); geochemistry (MS, PhD); geology (MS, PhD); geophysics (MS, PhD); planetary science (MS, PhD). *Faculty:* 38 full-time (6 women). *Students:* 76 full-time (39 women); includes 1 Black or African American, non-Hispanic/Latino; 4 Asian, non-Hispanic/Latino; 1 Hispanic/Latino, 28 international. Average age 26. 102 applicants, 28% accepted, 9 enrolled. In 2010, 12 master's, 14 doctorates awarded. *Degree requirements:* For doctorate, thesis/dissertation. *Entrance requirements:* For doctorate, GRE General Test. Additional exam requirements/recommendations for international students: Required—TOEFL; Recommended—IELTS, TWE. *Application deadline:* For fall admission, 1/1 for domestic and international students. Application fee: $80. Electronic applications accepted. *Financial support:* In 2010–11, 75 students received support, including 14 fellowships with full tuition reimbursements available (averaging $27,000 per year), 62 research assistantships with full tuition reimbursements available (averaging $27,000 per year); teaching assistantships with full tuition reimbursements available, institutionally sponsored loans, scholarships/grants, health care benefits, and unspecified assistantships also available. Financial award applicants required to submit FAFSA. *Faculty research:* Planetary surfaces, evolution of anaerobic respiratory processes, structural geology and tectonics, theoretical and numerical seismology, global biogeochemical cycles. *Unit head:* Dr. Kenneth A. Farley, Chairman, 626-395-6111, Fax: 626-795-6028, E-mail: dianb@gps.caltech.edu. *Application contact:* Dr. Robert W. Clayton, Academic Officer, 626-395-6909, Fax: 626-795-6028, E-mail: dianb@gps.caltech.edu.

California State University, Long Beach, Graduate Studies, College of Natural Sciences and Mathematics, Department of Geological Sciences, Long Beach, CA 90840. Offers geology (MS); geophysics (MS). Part-time programs available. *Faculty:* 6 full-time (0 women). *Students:* 11 full-time (6 women), 23 part-time (9 women); includes 1 Black or African American, non-Hispanic/Latino; 1 American Indian or Alaska Native, non-Hispanic/Latino; 3 Asian, non-Hispanic/Latino; 6 Hispanic/Latino, 1 international. Average age 32. 33 applicants, 67% accepted, 14 enrolled. *Degree requirements:* For master's, thesis. *Entrance requirements:* For master's, GRE General Test. *Application deadline:* For fall admission, 7/1 for domestic students. Applications are processed on a rolling basis. Application fee: $55. Electronic applications accepted. *Financial support:* Research assistantships, teaching assistantships, Federal Work-Study, institutionally sponsored loans, and scholarships/grants available. Financial award application deadline: 3/2. *Faculty research:* Paleontology, geophysics, structural geology, organic geochemistry, sedimentary geology. *Unit head:* Robert D. Francis, Chair, 562-985-4929, Fax: 562-985-8638, E-mail: rfrancis@csulb.edu. *Application contact:* Gregory Holk, Graduate Advisor, 562-985-5006, Fax: 562-985-8638, E-mail: gholk@csulb.edu.

Colorado School of Mines, Graduate School, Department of Geophysics, Golden, CO 80401. Offers geophysical engineering (ME, MS, PhD); geophysics (MS, PhD); mineral exploration and mining geosciences (PMS). Part-time programs available. *Faculty:* 16 full-time (1 woman), 4 part-time/adjunct (0 women). *Students:* 79 full-time (20 women), 5 part-time (3 women); includes 1 American Indian or Alaska Native, non-Hispanic/Latino; 2 Asian, non-Hispanic/Latino; 3 Hispanic/Latino, 48 international. Average age 30. 127 applicants, 33% accepted, 24 enrolled. In 2010, 13 master's, 6 doctorates awarded. *Degree requirements:* For master's, thesis (for some programs); for doctorate, one foreign language, comprehensive exam, thesis/dissertation, oral exams. *Entrance requirements:* For master's and doctorate, GRE General Test. Additional exam requirements/recommendations for international students: Required—TOEFL (minimum score 550 paper-based; 213 computer-based; 80 iBT). *Application deadline:* For fall admission, 1/15 for domestic and international students; for spring admission, 10/15 for domestic and international students. Application fee: $50 ($70 for international students). Electronic applications accepted. *Expenses:* Tuition, state resident: full-time $11,550; part-time $641 per credit. Tuition, nonresident: full-time $25,980; part-time $1444 per credit. Required fees: $1874; $937 per semester. *Financial support:* In 2010–11, 50 students received support, including 6 fellowships with full tuition reimbursements available (averaging $20,000 per year), 42 research assistantships with full tuition reimbursements available (averaging $20,000 per year), 2 teaching assistantships with full tuition reimbursements available (averaging $20,000 per year); scholarships/grants, health care benefits, and unspecified assistantships also available. Financial award application deadline: 1/15; financial award applicants required to submit FAFSA. *Faculty research:* Seismic exploration, gravity and geomagnetic fields, electrical mapping and sounding, bore hole measurements, environmental physics. Total annual research expenditures: $4.5 million. *Unit head:* Dr. Terence K. Young, Department Head, 303-273-3454, Fax: 303-273-3478, E-mail: tkyoung@mines.edu. *Application contact:* Michelle Szobody, Office Manager, 303-273-3935, Fax: 303-273-3478, E-mail: mszobody@mines.edu.

Columbia University, Graduate School of Arts and Sciences, Division of Natural Sciences, Department of Earth and Environmental Sciences, New York, NY 10027. Offers geochemistry (M Phil, MA, PhD); geodetic sciences (M Phil, MA, PhD); geophysics (M Phil, MA, PhD); oceanography (M Phil, MA, PhD). *Degree requirements:* For master's, thesis or alternative, fieldwork, written exam; for doctorate, one foreign language, thesis/dissertation. *Entrance requirements:* For master's and doctorate, GRE General Test, GRE Subject Test, major in natural or physical science. Additional exam requirements/recommendations for international students: Required—TOEFL. *Faculty research:* Structural geology and stratigraphy, petrology, paleontology, rare gas, isotope and aqueous geochemistry.

Cornell University, Graduate School, Graduate Fields of Engineering, Field of Geological Sciences, Ithaca, NY 14853. Offers economic geology (M Eng, MS, PhD); engineering geology (M Eng, MS, PhD); environmental geophysics (M Eng, MS, PhD); general geology (M Eng, MS, PhD); geobiology (M Eng, MS, PhD); geochemistry and isotope geology (M Eng, MS, PhD); geohydrology (M Eng, MS, PhD); geomorphology (M Eng, MS, PhD); geophysics (M Eng, MS, PhD); geotectonics (M Eng, MS, PhD); marine geology (MS, PhD); mineralogy (M Eng, MS, PhD); paleontology (M Eng, MS, PhD); petroleum geology (M Eng, MS, PhD); petrology (M Eng, MS, PhD); planetary geology (M Eng, MS, PhD); Precambrian geology (M Eng, MS, PhD); Quaternary geology (M Eng, MS, PhD); rock mechanics (M Eng, MS, PhD); sedimentology (M Eng, MS, PhD); seismology (M Eng, MS, PhD); stratigraphy (M Eng, MS, PhD); structural geology (M Eng, MS, PhD). *Faculty:* 36 full-time (5 women). *Students:* 38 full-time (15 women); includes 2 Asian, non-Hispanic/Latino; 2 Hispanic/Latino, 9 international. Average age 27. 84 applicants, 25% accepted, 17 enrolled. In 2010, 3 master's, 5 doctorates awarded. *Degree requirements:* For master's, thesis (MS); for doctorate, comprehensive exam, thesis/dissertation. *Entrance requirements:* For master's and doctorate, GRE General Test, 3 letters of recommendation. Additional exam requirements/recommendations for international students: Required—TOEFL (minimum score 550 paper-based; 213 computer-based; 77 iBT). *Application deadline:* For fall admission, 1/15 priority date for domestic students. Applications are processed on a rolling basis. Application fee: $70. Electronic applications accepted. *Expenses:* Tuition: Full-time $29,500. Required fees: $76. Tuition and fees vary according to degree level and program. *Financial support:* In 2010–11, 25 students received support, including 10 fellowships with full tuition reimbursements available, 14 research assistantships with full tuition reimbursements available, 10 teaching assistantships with full tuition reimbursements available; institutionally sponsored loans, scholarships/grants, health care benefits, tuition waivers (full and partial), and unspecified assistantships also available. Financial award applicants required to submit FAFSA. *Faculty research:* Geophysics, structural geology, petrology, geochemistry, geodynamics. *Unit head:* Director of Graduate Studies, 607-255-5466, Fax: 607-254-4780. *Application contact:* Graduate Field Assistant, 607-255-5466, Fax: 607-254-4780, E-mail: gradprog@geology.cornell.edu.

Florida State University, The Graduate School, College of Arts and Sciences, Interdisciplinary Program in Geophysical Fluid Dynamics, Tallahassee, FL 32306. Offers PhD. *Faculty:* 16 full-time (2 women). *Students:* 5 full-time (0 women), 1 part-time (0 women), 2 international. Average age 30. 4 applicants, 25% accepted, 0 enrolled. *Degree requirements:* For doctorate, thesis/dissertation, departmental qualifying exam. *Entrance requirements:* For doctorate, GRE General Test, GRE Subject Test, minimum GPA of 3.0. Additional exam requirements/recommendations for international students: Required—TOEFL (minimum score 550 paper-based; 80 iBT). *Application deadline:* For fall admission, 3/30 for domestic and international students. Application fee: $30. Electronic applications accepted. *Expenses:* Tuition, state resident: full-time $8238.24. *Financial support:* In 2010–11, 1 research assistantship (averaging $19,305 per year) was awarded; fellowships, unspecified assistantships also available. Financial award applicants required to submit FAFSA. *Faculty research:* Hurricane dynamics, convection, air-sea interaction, wave-mean flow interaction, numerical models. Total annual research expenditures: $369,802. *Unit head:* Dr. Carol A. Clayson, Director, 850-644-2488, Fax: 850-644-8972, E-mail: clayson@met.fsu.edu. *Application contact:* Vijaya Challa, Academic Coordinator, 850-644-5594, Fax: 850-644-8972, E-mail: vijaya@gfdi.fsu.edu.

Georgia Institute of Technology, Graduate Studies and Research, College of Sciences, School of Earth and Atmospheric Sciences, Atlanta, GA 30332-0340. Offers atmospheric chemistry, aerosols and clouds (MS, PhD); dynamics of weather and climate (MS, PhD); geochemistry (MS, PhD); geophysics (MS, PhD); oceanography (MS, PhD); paleoclimate (MS, PhD); planetary science (MS, PhD); remote sensing (MS, PhD). Part-time programs available. Terminal master's awarded for partial completion of doctoral program. *Degree requirements:* For master's, thesis or alternative; for doctorate, comprehensive exam, thesis/dissertation. *Entrance requirements:* For master's, GRE, letters of recommendation; for doctorate, GRE, academic transcripts, letters of recommendation, personal statement. Additional exam requirements/recommendations for international students: Required—TOEFL (minimum score 550 paper-based; 213 computer-based; 79 iBT). *Faculty research:* Geophysics; atmospheric chemistry, aerosols and clouds; dynamics of weather and climate; geochemistry; oceanography; paleoclimate; planetary science; remote sensing.

ICR Graduate School, Graduate Programs, Santee, CA 92071. Offers astro/geophysics (MS); biology (MS); geology (MS); science education (MS). Part-time programs available. *Degree requirements:* For master's, comprehensive exam (for some programs), thesis (for some programs). *Entrance requirements:* For master's, minimum undergraduate GPA of 3.0, bachelor's degree in science or science education. *Faculty research:* Age of the earth, limits of variation, catastrophe, optimum methods for teaching.

Idaho State University, Office of Graduate Studies, College of Arts and Sciences, Department of Geosciences, Pocatello, ID 83209-8072. Offers geographic information science (MS); geology (MNS, MS); geology with emphasis in environmental geoscience (MS); geophysics/hydrology/geology (MS); geotechnology (Postbaccalaureate Certificate). Part-time programs available. *Degree requirements:* For master's, comprehensive exam, thesis, oral colloquium; for Postbaccalaureate Certificate, thesis optional, minimum 19 credits. *Entrance requirements:* For master's, GRE General Test (minimum 50th percentile in 2 sections), 3 letters of recommendation; for Postbaccalaureate Certificate, GRE General Test, 3 letters of recommendation, bachelor's degree, statement of goals. Additional exam requirements/recommendations for international students: Required—TOEFL (minimum score 550 paper-based; 213 computer-based; 80 iBT). Electronic applications accepted. *Faculty research:* Quantitative field mapping and sampling: microscopic, geochemical, and isotopic analysis of rocks, minerals and water; remote sensing, geographic information systems, and global positioning systems: environmental and watershed management; surficial and fluvial processes: landscape change; regional tectonics, structural geology; planetary geology.

Indiana University Bloomington, University Graduate School, College of Arts and Sciences, Department of Geological Sciences, Bloomington, IN 47405-7000. Offers biogeochemistry (MS, PhD); economic geology (MS, PhD); geobiology (MS, PhD); geophysics, structural geology and tectonics (MS, PhD); hydrogeology (MS, PhD); mineralogy (MS, PhD); stratigraphy and sedimentology (MS, PhD). *Faculty:* 17 full-time (1 woman). *Students:* 48 full-time (24 women), 5 part-time (1 woman); includes 4 minority (2 Black or African American, non-Hispanic/Latino; 1 Hispanic/Latino; 1 Two or more races, non-Hispanic/Latino), 20 international. Average age 29. 70 applicants, 24% accepted, 16 enrolled. In 2010, 3 master's, 4 doctorates awarded. Terminal master's awarded for partial completion of doctoral program. *Degree requirements:* For master's, thesis or alternative; for doctorate, comprehensive exam, thesis/dissertation. *Entrance requirements:* For master's and doctorate, GRE General Test. Additional exam requirements/recommendations for international students: Required—TOEFL. *Application deadline:* For fall admission, 1/15 priority date for domestic students, 12/15 for international students; for spring admission, 9/1 priority date for domestic students, 9/1 for international students. Applications are processed on a rolling basis. Application fee: $55 ($65 for international students). *Financial support:* In 2010–11, 10 fellowships with full tuition reimbursements (averaging $17,300 per year), 6 research assistantships with full tuition reimbursements (averaging $16,370 per year), 12 teaching assistantships with full tuition reimbursements (averaging $15,150 per year) were awarded; career-related internships or fieldwork, Federal Work-Study, and institutionally sponsored loans also available. *Faculty research:* Geophysics, geochemistry, hydrogeology, geobiology, planetary science. Total annual research expenditures: $644,299. *Unit head:* Simon Brassell, Chair, 812-855-5581, Fax: 812-855-7899, E-mail: geochair@indiana.edu. *Application contact:* Mary Iverson, Graduate Secretary, 812-855-7214, Fax: 812-855-7899, E-mail: miverson@indiana.edu.

Louisiana State University and Agricultural and Mechanical College, Graduate School, College of Basic Sciences, Department of Geology and Geophysics, Baton Rouge, LA 70803. Offers MS, PhD. *Faculty:* 16 full-time (6 women), 1 (woman) part-time/adjunct. *Students:* 43

full-time (14 women), 13 part-time (2 women); includes 3 Black or African American, non-Hispanic/Latino; 1 Asian, non-Hispanic/Latino; 1 Hispanic/Latino; 1 Two or more races, non-Hispanic/Latino, 10 international. Average age 27. 62 applicants, 53% accepted, 11 enrolled. In 2010, 20 master's, 1 doctorate awarded. Terminal master's awarded for partial completion of doctoral program. *Degree requirements:* For master's, thesis; for doctorate, thesis/dissertation. *Entrance requirements:* For master's and doctorate, GRE General Test, minimum GPA of 3.0. Additional exam requirements/recommendations for international students: Required—TOEFL (minimum score 550 paper-based; 213 computer-based; 79 iBT) or IELTS (minimum score 6.5). *Application deadline:* For fall admission, 1/25 priority date for domestic students, 5/15 for international students; for spring admission, 10/15 for international students. Applications are processed on a rolling basis. Application fee: $50 ($70 for international students). Electronic applications accepted. *Financial support:* In 2010–11, 42 students received support, including 2 fellowships with full tuition reimbursements available (averaging $14,917 per year), 19 research assistantships with full and partial tuition reimbursements available (averaging $19,302 per year), 15 teaching assistantships with full and partial tuition reimbursements available (averaging $14,258 per year); career-related internships or fieldwork, Federal Work-Study, institutionally sponsored loans, health care benefits, tuition waivers (full and partial), and unspecified assistantships also available. Financial award application deadline: 3/15; financial award applicants required to submit FAFSA. *Faculty research:* Geophysics, sedimentology, geochemistry, geomicrobiology, tectonics. Total annual research expenditures: $917,832. *Unit head:* Dr. Carol Wicks, Chair, 225-578-3353, Fax: 225-578-2302, E-mail: glande@lsu.edu. *Application contact:* Jeffrey Nunn, Graduate Coordinator, 225-578-6657, E-mail: gljeff@lsu.edu.

Massachusetts Institute of Technology, School of Science, Department of Earth, Atmospheric, and Planetary Sciences, Cambridge, MA 02139. Offers atmospheric chemistry (PhD, Sc D); atmospheric science (SM, PhD, Sc D); chemical oceanography (SM, PhD, Sc D); climate physics and chemistry (SM, PhD, Sc D); earth and planetary sciences (SM); geochemistry (PhD, Sc D); geology (PhD, Sc D); geophysics (PhD, Sc D); marine geology and geophysics (SM, PhD, Sc D); physical oceanography (SM, PhD, Sc D); planetary sciences (PhD, Sc D). *Faculty:* 36 full-time (7 women). *Students:* 165 full-time (86 women); includes 17 minority (2 Black or African American, non-Hispanic/Latino; 2 American Indian or Alaska Native, non-Hispanic/Latino; 5 Asian, non-Hispanic/Latino; 5 Hispanic/Latino; 3 Two or more races, non-Hispanic/Latino), 50 international. Average age 27. 227 applicants, 33% accepted, 38 enrolled. In 2010, 12 master's, 26 doctorates awarded. Terminal master's awarded for partial completion of doctoral program. *Degree requirements:* For master's, thesis; for doctorate, comprehensive exam, thesis/dissertation. *Entrance requirements:* For master's, GRE General Test; for doctorate, GRE General Test, GRE Subject Test (chemistry or physics for planetary science area). Additional exam requirements/recommendations for international students: Required—TOEFL (minimum score 577 paper-based; 233 computer-based; 91 iBT), IELTS (minimum score 7). *Application deadline:* For fall admission, 1/5 for domestic and international students; for spring admission, 11/1 for domestic and international students. Application fee: $75. Electronic applications accepted. *Expenses:* Tuition: Full-time $38,940; part-time $605 per unit. Required fees: $272. *Financial support:* In 2010–11, 123 students received support, including 62 fellowships with tuition reimbursements available (averaging $30,852 per year), 88 research assistantships with tuition reimbursements available (averaging $30,258 per year), 13 teaching assistantships with tuition reimbursements available (averaging $30,323 per year); Federal Work-Study, institutionally sponsored loans, scholarships/grants, health care benefits, and unspecified assistantships also available. *Faculty research:* Formation, dynamics and evolution of planetary systems; origin, composition, structure and dynamics of the atmospheres, oceans, surfaces and interiors of the Earth and other planets; evolution and interaction of the physical, chemical, geological and biological components of the Earth system; characterization of past, present and potential future climates and the causes and consequences of climate change; interplay of energy and the environment. Total annual research expenditures: $24.8 million. *Unit head:* Prof. Maria Zuber, Department Head, 617-253-2127, Fax: 617-253-8298, E-mail: eapsinfo@mit.edu. *Application contact:* EAPS Education Office, 617-253-3381, Fax: 617-253-8298, E-mail: eapsinfo@mit.edu.

Memorial University of Newfoundland, School of Graduate Studies, Department of Earth Sciences, St. John's, NL A1C 5S7, Canada. Offers geology (M Sc, PhD); geophysics (M Sc, PhD). Part-time programs available. *Degree requirements:* For master's, thesis; for doctorate, comprehensive exam, thesis/dissertation, oral thesis defense, entry evaluation. *Entrance requirements:* For master's, honors B Sc; for doctorate, M Sc. Electronic applications accepted. *Faculty research:* Geochemistry, sedimentology, paleoceanography and global change, mineral deposits, petroleum geology, hydrology.

Michigan Technological University, Graduate School, College of Engineering, Department of Geological and Mining Engineering and Sciences, Program in Geophysics, Houghton, MI 49931. Offers MS. Part-time programs available. *Degree requirements:* For master's, comprehensive exam. *Entrance requirements:* Additional exam requirements/recommendations for international students: Required—TOEFL (minimum score 550 paper-based; 213 computer-based). Electronic applications accepted.

Missouri University of Science and Technology, Graduate School, Department of Geological Sciences and Engineering, Rolla, MO 65409. Offers geological engineering (MS, DE, PhD); geology and geophysics (MS, PhD), including geochemistry, geology, geophysics, groundwater and environmental geology; petroleum engineering (MS, DE, PhD). Part-time programs available. *Degree requirements:* For master's, thesis optional; for doctorate, comprehensive exam, thesis/dissertation. *Entrance requirements:* For master's, GRE General Test (minimum score 600 quantitative, writing 3.5), minimum GPA of 3.0 in last 4 semesters; for doctorate, GRE General Test (minimum: Q 600, GRE WR 3.5). Additional exam requirements/recommendations for international students: Required—TOEFL. Electronic applications accepted. *Faculty research:* Digital image processing and geographic information systems, mineralogy, igneous and sedimentary petrology-geochemistry, sedimentology groundwater hydrology and contaminant transport.

New Mexico Institute of Mining and Technology, Graduate Studies, Department of Earth and Environmental Science, Program in Geophysics, Socorro, NM 87801. Offers MS, PhD. *Degree requirements:* For master's, thesis optional; for doctorate, thesis/dissertation. *Entrance requirements:* For master's, GRE General Test; for doctorate, GRE General Test, GRE Subject Test. Additional exam requirements/recommendations for international students: Required—TOEFL (minimum score 540 paper-based; 207 computer-based). *Faculty research:* Earthquake and volcanic seismology, subduction zone tectonics, network seismology, physical properties of sediments in fault zones.

Ohio University, Graduate College, College of Arts and Sciences, Department of Geological Sciences, Athens, OH 45701-2979. Offers environmental geochemistry (MS); environmental geology (MS); environmental/hydrology (MS); geology (MS); geology education (MS); geomorphology/surficial processes (MS); geophysics (MS); hydrogeology (MS); sedimentology (MS); structure/tectonics (MS). Part-time programs available. *Students:* 14 full-time (8 women), 1 (woman) part-time. 15 applicants, 60% accepted, 8 enrolled. In 2010, 7 master's awarded. *Degree requirements:* For master's, thesis. *Entrance requirements:* Additional exam requirements/recommendations for international students: Required—TOEFL (minimum score 550 paper-based; 80 iBT) or IELTS (minimum score 6.5). *Application deadline:* For fall admission, 2/1 priority date for domestic and international students. Application fee: $50 ($55 for international students). Electronic applications accepted. *Financial support:* Research assistantships with full tuition reimbursements, teaching assistantships with full tuition reimbursements, Federal Work-Study, institutionally sponsored loans, scholarships/grants, tuition waivers (partial), and unspecified assistantships available. Financial award application deadline: 2/1. *Faculty research:* Geoscience education, tectonics, fluvial geomorphology, invertebrate paleontology, mine/hydrology. Total annual research expenditures: $649,020. *Unit head:* Dr. Gregory Nadon, Chair, 740-593-4212, Fax: 740-593-0486, E-mail: nadon@ohio.edu. *Application contact:* Dr. Douglas Green, Graduate Chair, 740-593-1843, Fax: 740-593-0486, E-mail: green@ohio.edu.

Oregon State University, Graduate School, College of Oceanic and Atmospheric Sciences, Program in Geophysics, Corvallis, OR 97331. Offers MA, MS, PhD. Terminal master's awarded for partial completion of doctoral program. *Degree requirements:* For master's, thesis optional; for doctorate, thesis/dissertation. *Entrance requirements:* For master's and doctorate, GRE General Test, minimum GPA of 3.0 in last 90 hours. Additional exam requirements/recommendations for international students: Required—TOEFL. *Faculty research:* Seismic waves; gravitational, geothermal, and electromagnetic fields; rock magnetism; paleomagnetism.

Rice University, Graduate Programs, Wiess School–Professional Science Master's Programs, Professional Master's Program in Subsurface Geosciences, Houston, TX 77251-1892. Offers geophysics (MS). Part-time programs available. *Degree requirements:* For master's, internship. *Entrance requirements:* For master's, GRE, letters of recommendation (4). Additional exam requirements/recommendations for international students: Required—TOEFL (minimum score 600 paper-based; 250 computer-based; 90 iBT). Electronic applications accepted. *Faculty research:* Seismology, geodynamics, wave propagation, bio-geochemistry, remote sensing.

Saint Louis University, Graduate Education, College of Arts and Sciences and Graduate Education, Department of Earth and Atmospheric Sciences, St. Louis, MO 63103-2097. Offers geophysics (PhD); geoscience (MS); meteorology (M Pr Met, MS-R, PhD). Part-time programs available. *Degree requirements:* For master's, thesis (for some programs), comprehensive oral exam; for doctorate, thesis/dissertation, preliminary exams. *Entrance requirements:* For master's, GRE General Test, letters of recommendation, resume; for doctorate, GRE General Test, letters of recommendation, resumé, goal statement, transcripts. Additional exam requirements/recommendations for international students: Required—TOEFL (minimum score 525 paper-based; 194 computer-based). Electronic applications accepted. *Faculty research:* Structural geology, mesoscale meteorology and severe storms, weather and climate change prediction.

Southern Methodist University, Dedman College, Department of Earth Sciences, Program in Applied Geophysics, Dallas, TX 75275. Offers MS. Part-time programs available. *Faculty:* 3 full-time (0 women), 2 part-time/adjunct (0 women). *Degree requirements:* For master's, thesis optional, qualifying exam. *Entrance requirements:* For master's, GRE General Test, minimum GPA of 3.0, letters of recommendation. Additional exam requirements/recommendations for international students: Required—TOEFL. *Application deadline:* For fall admission, 2/1 priority date for domestic and international students; for spring admission, 11/30 for domestic students. Applications are processed on a rolling basis. Application fee: $50. *Financial support:* Tuition waivers (full and partial) available. Financial award application deadline: 2/1; financial award applicants required to submit FAFSA. *Faculty research:* Geothermal energy, seismology. Total annual research expenditures: $800,000. *Unit head:* Dr. Robert T. Gregory, Chair, 214-768-3075, Fax: 214-768-2701, E-mail: bgregory@smu.edu. *Application contact:* Dr. John V. Walther, Graduate Advisor, 214-768-3174, Fax: 214-768-2701, E-mail: walther@smu.edu.

Southern Methodist University, Dedman College, Department of Earth Sciences, Program in Geophysics, Dallas, TX 75275. Offers MS, PhD. Part-time programs available. *Faculty:* 3 full-time (0 women), 2 part-time/adjunct (0 women). *Students:* 12 applicants, 42% accepted. In 2010, 2 master's, 2 doctorates awarded. *Degree requirements:* For master's, thesis (for some programs), qualifying exam; for doctorate, thesis/dissertation, qualifying exam. *Entrance requirements:* For master's and doctorate, GRE General Test, minimum GPA of 3.0, letters of recommendation. Additional exam requirements/recommendations for international students: Required—TOEFL. *Application deadline:* For fall admission, 2/1 priority date for domestic and international students; for spring admission, 11/30 for domestic students. Applications are processed on a rolling basis. Application fee: $50. *Financial support:* In 2010–11, fellowships with full tuition reimbursements (averaging $15,000 per year), research assistantships with full tuition reimbursements (averaging $15,000 per year), teaching assistantships with full tuition reimbursements (averaging $15,000 per year) were awarded; scholarships/grants, tuition waivers (full and partial), and unspecified assistantships also available. Financial award application deadline: 2/1; financial award applicants required to submit FAFSA. *Faculty research:* Seismology, heat flow, tectonics. Total annual research expenditures: $800,000. *Unit head:* Dr. Robert T. Gregory, Chair, 214-768-3075, Fax: 214-768-2701, E-mail: bgregory@smu.edu. *Application contact:* Dr. John V. Walther, Graduate Advisor, 214-768-3174, Fax: 214-768-2701, E-mail: walther@smu.edu.

Stanford University, School of Earth Sciences, Department of Geophysics, Stanford, CA 94305-9991. Offers MS, PhD. Terminal master's awarded for partial completion of doctoral program. *Degree requirements:* For master's, thesis; for doctorate, thesis/dissertation. *Entrance requirements:* For master's and doctorate, GRE General Test. Additional exam requirements/recommendations for international students: Required—TOEFL. Electronic applications accepted. *Expenses:* Tuition: Full-time $38,700; part-time $860 per unit. One-time fee: $200 full-time.

Texas A&M University, College of Geosciences, Department of Geology and Geophysics, College Station, TX 77843. Offers geology (MS, PhD); geophysics (MS, PhD). *Faculty:* 34. *Students:* 113 full-time (50 women), 13 part-time (3 women); includes 11 minority (5 Asian, non-Hispanic/Latino; 6 Hispanic/Latino), 46 international. Average age 31. In 2010, 14 master's, 7 doctorates awarded. *Degree requirements:* For master's, thesis; for doctorate, thesis/dissertation. *Entrance requirements:* For master's and doctorate, GRE General Test. Additional exam requirements/recommendations for international students: Required—TOEFL. *Application deadline:* For fall admission, 3/1 priority date for domestic students, 1/15 for international students; for spring admission, 10/1 priority date for domestic students, 8/15 for international students. Applications are processed on a rolling basis. Application fee: $50 ($75 for international students). Electronic applications accepted. *Financial support:* In 2010–11, fellowships with partial tuition reimbursements (averaging $1,000 per year), research assistantships with partial tuition reimbursements (averaging $11,925 per year), teaching assistantships with partial tuition reimbursements (averaging $11,925 per year) were awarded; Federal Work-Study, institutionally sponsored loans, scholarships/grants, tuition waivers (partial), and unspecified assistantships also available. Financial award application deadline: 3/1; financial award applicants required to submit FAFSA. *Faculty research:* Environmental and engineering geology and geophysics, petroleum geology, tectonophysics, geochemistry. *Unit head:* Dr. Andreas Kronenberg, Head, 979-845-0132, E-mail: kronenberg@geo.tamu.edu. *Application contact:* Dr. Andreas Kronenberg, Head, 979-845-0132, E-mail: kronenberg@geo.tamu.edu.

The University of Akron, Graduate School, Buchtel College of Arts and Sciences, Department of Geology, Program in Geophysics, Akron, OH 44325. Offers MS. *Students:* 1 (woman) full-time. Average age 48. 3 applicants, 67% accepted, 0 enrolled. *Degree requirements:* For master's, comprehensive exam, thesis, seminar, proficiency exam. *Entrance requirements:* For master's, minimum GPA of 2.75, letters of recommendation, statement of purpose. Additional exam requirements/recommendations for international students: Required—TOEFL (minimum score 550 paper-based; 213 computer-based; 79 iBT). *Application deadline:* Applications are processed on a rolling basis. Application fee: $30 ($40 for international students). Electronic applications accepted. *Expenses:* Tuition, state resident: full-time $6800; part-time $378 per credit hour. Tuition, nonresident: full-time $11,644; part-time $647 per credit hour. Required fees: $1265. One-time fee: $30 full-time. *Unit head:* Dr. LaVerne Friberg, Director of Graduate Studies, 330-972-8046, E-mail: lfribe1@uakron.edu. *Application contact:* Dr. LaVerne Friberg, Director of Graduate Studies, 330-972-8046, E-mail: lfribe1@uakron.edu.

University of Alaska Fairbanks, College of Natural Sciences and Mathematics, Department of Geology and Geophysics, Fairbanks, AK 99775-5780. Offers geology (MS, PhD), including

Geophysics

University of Alaska Fairbanks (continued)
economic geology (PhD), petroleum geology (MS), quaternary geology (PhD), remote sensing, volcanology (PhD); geophysics (MS, PhD), including remote sensing, snow, ice, and permafrost geophysics (MS), solid-earth geophysics (MS). Part-time programs available. *Faculty:* 10 full-time (4 women). *Students:* 61 full-time (28 women), 12 part-time (6 women); includes 6 minority (1 Black or African American, non-Hispanic/Latino; 1 Hispanic/Latino; 4 Two or more races, non-Hispanic/Latino), 17 international. Average age 30. 68 applicants, 25% accepted, 17 enrolled. In 2010, 9 master's, 6 doctorates awarded. Terminal master's awarded for partial completion of doctoral program. *Degree requirements:* For master's, comprehensive exam, thesis, oral exam, oral defense; for doctorate, comprehensive exam, thesis/dissertation, oral exam, oral defense. *Entrance requirements:* For master's and doctorate, GRE General Test. Additional exam requirements/recommendations for international students: Required—TOEFL (minimum score 550 paper-based; 213 computer-based). *Application deadline:* For fall admission, 6/1 for domestic students, 3/1 for international students; for spring admission, 10/15 for domestic students, 9/1 for international students. Applications are processed on a rolling basis. Application fee: $60. Electronic applications accepted. *Expenses:* Tuition, state resident: full-time $5688; part-time $316 per credit. Tuition, nonresident: full-time $11,628; part-time $646 per credit. Required fees: $289 per semester. Tuition and fees vary according to course load and reciprocity agreements. *Financial support:* In 2010–11, 43 research assistantships with tuition reimbursements (averaging $12,026 per year), 7 teaching assistantships with tuition reimbursements (averaging $13,030 per year) were awarded; fellowships with tuition reimbursements, Federal Work-Study, scholarships/grants, health care benefits, and unspecified assistantships also available. Support available to part-time students. Financial award application deadline: 2/15; financial award applicants required to submit FAFSA. *Faculty research:* Glacial surging, volcanology, geochronology, impact cratering, permafrost geophysics. *Unit head:* Dr. Benard Coakley, Department Chair, 907-474-7565, Fax: 907-474-5163, E-mail: geology@uaf.edu. *Application contact:* Dr. Benard Coakley, Department Chair, 907-474-7565, Fax: 907-474-5163, E-mail: geology@uaf.edu.

University of Alberta, Faculty of Graduate Studies and Research, Department of Physics, Edmonton, AB T6G 2E1, Canada. Offers astrophysics (M Sc, PhD); condensed matter (M Sc, PhD); geophysics (M Sc, PhD); medical physics (M Sc, PhD); subatomic physics (M Sc, PhD). *Degree requirements:* For master's, thesis; for doctorate, thesis/dissertation. *Entrance requirements:* For master's and doctorate, minimum GPA of 7.0 on a 9.0 scale. Additional exam requirements/recommendations for international students: Required—TOEFL. *Faculty research:* Cosmology, astroparticle physics, high-intermediate energy, magnetism, superconductivity.

The University of British Columbia, Faculty of Science, Department of Earth and Ocean Sciences, Vancouver, BC V6T 1Z4, Canada. Offers atmospheric science (M Sc, PhD); geological engineering (M Eng, MA Sc, PhD); geological sciences (M Sc, PhD); geophysics (M Sc, MA Sc, PhD); oceanography (M Sc, PhD). *Degree requirements:* For master's, thesis (for some programs); for doctorate, comprehensive exam, thesis/dissertation. *Entrance requirements:* Additional exam requirements/recommendations for international students: Required—TOEFL (minimum score 600 paper-based; 250 computer-based; 100 iBT). Electronic applications accepted. Tuition charges are reported in Canadian dollars. *Expenses:* Tuition, area resident: Full-time $4179 Canadian dollars. International tuition: $7344 Canadian dollars full-time. *Faculty research:* Oceans and atmosphere, environmental earth science, hydro geology, mineral deposits, geophysics.

University of Calgary, Faculty of Graduate Studies, Faculty of Science, Department of Geology and Geophysics, Calgary, AB T2N 1N4, Canada. Offers geology (M Sc, PhD); geophysics (M Sc, PhD). Part-time programs available. Terminal master's awarded for partial completion of doctoral program. *Degree requirements:* For master's, thesis; for doctorate, thesis/dissertation, candidacy exam. *Entrance requirements:* For master's, B Sc; for doctorate, honors B Sc or M Sc. Additional exam requirements/recommendations for international students: Required—TOEFL. Electronic applications accepted. *Faculty research:* Geochemistry, petrology, paleontology, stratigraphy, exploration and solid-earth geophysics.

University of California, Berkeley, Graduate Division, College of Letters and Science, Department of Earth and Planetary Science, Berkeley, CA 94720-1500. Offers geology (MA, MS, PhD); geophysics (MA, MS, PhD). Terminal master's awarded for partial completion of doctoral program. *Degree requirements:* For master's, oral exam (MA), thesis (MS); for doctorate, comprehensive exam, thesis/dissertation, candidacy exams. *Entrance requirements:* For master's and doctorate, GRE General Test, minimum GPA of 3.0, 3 letters of recommendation. Additional exam requirements/recommendations for international students: Required—TOEFL. *Faculty research:* Tectonics, environmental geology, high-pressure geophysics and seismology, economic geology, geochemistry.

University of California, Los Angeles, Graduate Division, College of Letters and Science, Department of Earth and Space Sciences, Program in Geophysics and Space Physics, Los Angeles, CA 90095. Offers MS, PhD. *Students:* 30 full-time (17 women); includes 2 minority (both Asian, non-Hispanic/Latino), 14 international. Average age 26. 51 applicants, 24% accepted, 4 enrolled. In 2010, 4 master's, 6 doctorates awarded. Terminal master's awarded for partial completion of doctoral program. *Degree requirements:* For master's, comprehensive exams or thesis; for doctorate, thesis/dissertation, oral and written qualifying exams. *Entrance requirements:* For master's, GRE General Test, minimum GPA of 3.0, bachelor's degree in related field; for doctorate, GRE General Test, minimum undergraduate GPA of 3.0, bachelor's degree in related field. *Application deadline:* For fall admission, 1/15 for domestic and international students. Application fee: $70 ($90 for international students). Electronic applications accepted. *Financial support:* In 2010–11, 31 fellowships with full and partial tuition reimbursements, 29 research assistantships with full and partial tuition reimbursements, 7 teaching assistantships with full and partial tuition reimbursements were awarded; Federal Work-Study, institutionally sponsored loans, scholarships/grants, health care benefits, tuition waivers (full and partial), and unspecified assistantships also available. Financial award application deadline: 3/1; financial award applicants required to submit FAFSA. *Unit head:* Dr. Craig E. Manning, Chair, 310-206-3290, E-mail: manning@ess.ucla.edu. *Application contact:* Departmental Office, 310-825-3917, E-mail: holbrook@ess.ucla.edu.

University of California, Santa Barbara, Graduate Division, College of Letters and Sciences, Division of Mathematics, Life, and Physical Sciences, Department of Earth Science, Santa Barbara, CA 93106-9620. Offers geological sciences (PhD); geophysics (MS). *Faculty:* 16 full-time (2 women), 3 part-time/adjunct (1 woman). *Students:* 47 full-time (22 women); includes 1 American Indian or Alaska Native, non-Hispanic/Latino; 4 Asian, non-Hispanic/Latino; 7 Hispanic/Latino. Average age 27. 93 applicants, 31% accepted, 16 enrolled. In 2010, 5 master's, 3 doctorates awarded. Terminal master's awarded for partial completion of doctoral program. *Degree requirements:* For master's, comprehensive exam, thesis, 30 units; for doctorate, comprehensive exam, thesis/dissertation, 30 units, oral qualifying exam. *Entrance requirements:* For master's and doctorate, GRE General Test. Additional exam requirements/recommendations for international students: Required—TOEFL (minimum score 550 paper-based; 80 iBT), IELTS (minimum score 7). *Application deadline:* For fall admission, 1/1 for domestic and international students. Application fee: $70 ($90 for international students). Electronic applications accepted. *Financial support:* In 2010–11, 38 students received support, including 24 fellowships with full and partial tuition reimbursements available (averaging $9,407 per year), 19 research assistantships with full and partial tuition reimbursements available (averaging $6,722 per year), 25 teaching assistantships with full and partial tuition reimbursements available (averaging $9,978 per year); tuition waivers (full and partial) also available. Financial award application deadline: 1/1; financial award applicants required to submit CSS PROFILE or FAFSA. *Faculty research:* Geology, geomaterials and earth's structure; geomorphology, tectonics; geophysics, seismology; paleoclimate, paleoceanography and geochemistry; paleobiology, evolution and paleontology. *Unit head:* Giulia Brofferio, Business Officer, 805-893-4604, Fax: 805-893-2314, E-mail: brofferio@geol.ucsb.edu. *Application contact:* Hannah Ocampo, Graduate Program Assistant, 805-893-3329, Fax: 805-893-2314, E-mail: ocampo@geol.ucsb.edu.

University of Chicago, Division of the Physical Sciences, Department of the Geophysical Sciences, Chicago, IL 60637-1513. Offers atmospheric sciences (SM, PhD); earth sciences (SM, PhD); paleobiology (PhD); planetary and space sciences (SM, PhD). *Faculty:* 21 full-time (3 women). *Students:* 37 full-time (23 women); includes 1 Hispanic/Latino, 14 international. Average age 27. 63 applicants, 35% accepted, 9 enrolled. In 2010, 2 master's, 7 doctorates awarded. Terminal master's awarded for partial completion of doctoral program. *Degree requirements:* For master's, thesis, seminar; for doctorate, variable foreign language requirement, comprehensive exam, thesis/dissertation. *Entrance requirements:* For doctorate, GRE General Test. Additional exam requirements/recommendations for international students: Required—TOEFL (minimum score 600 paper-based; 250 computer-based; 96 iBT), IELTS (minimum score 7). *Application deadline:* For fall admission, 1/10 for domestic and international students. Application fee: $55. Electronic applications accepted. *Financial support:* In 2010–11, research assistantships with full tuition reimbursements (averaging $20,511 per year), teaching assistantships with full tuition reimbursements (averaging $21,915 per year) were awarded; fellowships, Federal Work-Study, institutionally sponsored loans, scholarships/grants, tuition waivers (partial), and unspecified assistantships also available. Financial award application deadline: 1/9. *Faculty research:* Climatology, evolutionary paleontology, petrology, geochemistry, oceanic sciences. *Unit head:* Dr. Michael Foote, Chairman, 773-702-8102, Fax: 773-702-9505. *Application contact:* David J. Taylor, Graduate Student Services Coordinator, 773-702-8180, Fax: 773-702-9505, E-mail: info@geosci.uchicago.edu.

University of Colorado Boulder, Graduate School, College of Arts and Sciences, Department of Geological Sciences, Boulder, CO 80309. Offers geology (MS, PhD); geophysics (PhD). *Faculty:* 29 full-time (8 women). *Students:* 73 full-time (37 women), 17 part-time (14 women); includes 7 minority (2 American Indian or Alaska Native, non-Hispanic/Latino; 1 Asian, non-Hispanic/Latino; 2 Hispanic/Latino; 2 Two or more races, non-Hispanic/Latino), 6 international. Average age 30. 251 applicants, 21 enrolled. In 2010, 9 master's, 14 doctorates awarded. Terminal master's awarded for partial completion of doctoral program. *Degree requirements:* For master's, comprehensive exam, thesis; for doctorate, comprehensive exam, thesis/dissertation. *Entrance requirements:* For master's, GRE General Test, minimum undergraduate GPA of 3.0; for doctorate, GRE General Test, minimum GPA of 2.75. *Application deadline:* For fall admission, 12/15 priority date for domestic students, 12/1 for international students. Application fee: $50 ($60 for international students). *Financial support:* In 2010–11, 28 fellowships with full tuition reimbursements (averaging $13,580 per year), 45 research assistantships with full tuition reimbursements (averaging $15,474 per year) were awarded; Federal Work-Study, institutionally sponsored loans, scholarships/grants, and tuition waivers (full) also available. Financial award application deadline: 1/15. *Faculty research:* Sedimentology, stratigraphy, economic geology of mineral deposits, fossil fuels, hydrogeology and water resources, geophysics, isotope geology, paleobiology, mineralogy, remote sensing. Total annual research expenditures: $9.4 million.

University of Colorado Boulder, Graduate School, College of Arts and Sciences, Department of Physics, Boulder, CO 80309. Offers chemical physics (PhD); geophysics (PhD); liquid crystal science and technology (PhD); mathematical physics (PhD); medical physics (PhD); optical sciences and engineering (PhD); physics (MS, PhD). *Faculty:* 50 full-time (7 women). *Students:* 147 full-time (28 women), 72 part-time (10 women); includes 12 minority (6 Asian, non-Hispanic/Latino; 6 Hispanic/Latino), 75 international. Average age 27. 503 applicants, 37 enrolled. In 2010, 16 master's, 31 doctorates awarded. Terminal master's awarded for partial completion of doctoral program. *Degree requirements:* For master's, comprehensive exam, thesis or alternative; for doctorate, comprehensive exam, thesis/dissertation. *Entrance requirements:* For master's and doctorate, GRE General Test, GRE Subject Test, minimum undergraduate GPA of 3.0. Additional exam requirements/recommendations for international students: Required—TOEFL. *Application deadline:* For fall admission, 1/15 priority date for domestic students, 1/15 for international students. Applications are processed on a rolling basis. Application fee: $50 ($60 for international students). Electronic applications accepted. *Financial support:* In 2010–11, 21 fellowships with full tuition reimbursements (averaging $15,999 per year), 146 research assistantships with full tuition reimbursements (averaging $16,586 per year) were awarded; scholarships/grants also available. Financial award application deadline: 1/15. *Faculty research:* Atomic and molecular physics, nuclear physics, condensed matter, elementary particle physics, laser or optical physics, plasma physics, geophysics, astrophysics and chemical physics. Total annual research expenditures: $16.8 million.

University of Hawaii at Manoa, Graduate Division, School of Ocean and Earth Science and Technology, Department of Geology and Geophysics, Honolulu, HI 96822. Offers high-pressure geophysics and geochemistry (MS, PhD); hydrogeology and engineering geology (MS, PhD); marine geology and geophysics (MS, PhD); planetary geosciences and remote sensing (MS, PhD); seismology and solid-earth geophysics (MS, PhD); volcanology, petrology, and geochemistry (MS, PhD). Part-time programs available. *Faculty:* 72 full-time (15 women), 6 part-time/adjunct (3 women). *Students:* 38 full-time (20 women), 5 part-time (3 women); includes 8 minority (1 Black or African American, non-Hispanic/Latino; 2 Asian, non-Hispanic/Latino; 1 Hispanic/Latino; 1 Native Hawaiian or other Pacific Islander, non-Hispanic/Latino; 3 Two or more races, non-Hispanic/Latino), 6 international. Average age 31. 64 applicants, 23% accepted, 7 enrolled. In 2010, 7 master's, 8 doctorates awarded. Terminal master's awarded for partial completion of doctoral program. *Degree requirements:* For master's, thesis optional; for doctorate, comprehensive exam, thesis/dissertation. *Entrance requirements:* For master's and doctorate, GRE General Test, minimum GPA of 3.0. Additional exam requirements/recommendations for international students: Required—TOEFL (minimum score 580 paper-based; 237 computer-based; 92 iBT), IELTS (minimum score 5). *Application deadline:* For fall admission, 1/15 for domestic students, 1/1 for international students; for spring admission, 9/1 for domestic students, 8/15 for international students. Application fee: $60. *Financial support:* In 2010–11, 7 fellowships (averaging $1,359 per year), 30 research assistantships (averaging $23,988 per year), 4 teaching assistantships (averaging $15,350 per year) were awarded. Total annual research expenditures: $3.8 million. *Application contact:* Dr. Gregory Moore, Chair, 808-956-7640, Fax: 808-956-5512, E-mail: gg-dept@soest.hawaii.edu.

University of Houston, College of Natural Sciences and Mathematics, Department of Earth and Atmospheric Sciences, Houston, TX 77204. Offers atmospheric science (PhD); geology (MA, PhD); geophysics (PhD). Part-time programs available. *Faculty:* 23 full-time (4 women), 5 part-time/adjunct (1 woman). *Students:* 149 full-time (44 women), 88 part-time (27 women); includes 10 Black or African American, non-Hispanic/Latino; 9 Asian, non-Hispanic/Latino; 15 Hispanic/Latino, 97 international. Average age 31. 198 applicants, 71% accepted, 69 enrolled. In 2010, 33 master's, 6 doctorates awarded. *Degree requirements:* For master's, thesis; for doctorate, comprehensive exam, thesis/dissertation. *Entrance requirements:* For master's and doctorate, GRE General Test . Additional exam requirements/recommendations for international students: Required—TOEFL (minimum score 550 paper-based; 213 computer-based; 79 iBT), IELTS (minimum score 6.5). *Application deadline:* For fall admission, 7/1 for domestic students, 4/1 for international students; for spring admission, 12/1 for domestic students, 10/1 for international students. Applications are processed on a rolling basis. Application fee: $0 ($75 for international students). Electronic applications accepted. *Expenses:* Tuition, state resident: full-time $8592; part-time $358 per credit hour. Tuition, nonresident: full-time $16,032; part-time $668 per credit hour. Required fees: $2889. Tuition and fees vary according to course load and program. *Financial support:* In 2010–11, 6 fellowships with partial tuition reimbursements (averaging $11,668 per year), 19 research assistantships with partial tuition reimbursements (averaging $13,600 per year), 9 teaching assistantships with partial tuition

reimbursements (averaging $13,736 per year) were awarded; career-related internships or fieldwork, Federal Work-Study, institutionally sponsored loans, scholarships/grants, health care benefits, and unspecified assistantships also available. Support available to part-time students. Financial award application deadline: 2/1. *Faculty research:* Atmospherics sciences, seismic and solid earth geophysics, tectonics, environmental hydrochemistry, carbonates, micropaleontology, structure and tectonics, petroleum geology. *Unit head:* Dr. John Casey, Chairman, 713-743-3399, Fax: 713-748-7906, E-mail: jfcasey@uh.edu. *Application contact:* Sylvia Marshall, Advising Assistant, 713-743-3401, Fax: 713-748-7906, E-mail: smarshall@uh.edu.

University of Manitoba, Faculty of Graduate Studies, Clayton H. Riddell Faculty of Environment, Earth, and Resources, Department of Geological Sciences, Winnipeg, MB R3T 2N2, Canada. Offers geology (M Sc, PhD); geophysics (M Sc, PhD). *Degree requirements:* For master's, thesis; for doctorate, thesis/dissertation. *Entrance requirements:* For master's and doctorate, GRE General Test, GRE Subject Test (geology), minimum GPA of 3.0. Additional exam requirements/recommendations for international students: Required—TOEFL.

University of Memphis, Graduate School, College of Arts and Sciences, Department of Earth Sciences, Memphis, TN 38152. Offers archaeology (MS); earth sciences (PhD); geographic information systems (Graduate Certificate); geography (MA, MS); geology (MS); geophysics (MS); interdisciplinary (MS). Part-time and evening/weekend programs available. *Faculty:* 15 full-time (3 women), 6 part-time/adjunct (2 women). *Students:* 35 full-time (7 women), 28 part-time (13 women); includes 5 Black or African American, non-Hispanic/Latino; 1 Asian, non-Hispanic/Latino, 15 international. Average age 33. 48 applicants, 69% accepted, 18 enrolled. In 2010, 2 master's, 2 doctorates, 1 other advanced degree awarded. Terminal master's awarded for partial completion of doctoral program. *Degree requirements:* For master's, comprehensive exam, thesis, seminar presentation; for doctorate, thesis/dissertation. *Entrance requirements:* For master's, GRE General Test, 3 letters of recommendation, statement of research interests; for doctorate, GRE General Test, 2 letters of recommendation, resume, personal statement. Additional exam requirements/recommendations for international students: Required—TOEFL (minimum score 550 paper-based; 210 computer-based). *Application deadline:* For fall admission, 1/31 for domestic students; for spring admission, 11/1 for domestic students. Applications are processed on a rolling basis. Application fee: $35 ($60 for international students). Electronic applications accepted. *Financial support:* In 2010–11, 18 students received support; fellowships with full tuition reimbursements available, research assistantships with full tuition reimbursements available, teaching assistantships with full tuition reimbursements available, Federal Work-Study, scholarships/grants, and unspecified assistantships available. Financial award application deadline: 2/15; financial award applicants required to submit FAFSA. *Faculty research:* Hazards, active tectonics, geophysics, hydrology and water resources, spatial analysis. *Unit head:* Dr. M. Jerry Bartholomew, Chair, 901-678-4536, Fax: 901-678-4467, E-mail: jbrthlm1@memphis.edu. *Application contact:* Dr. Arlene Hill, Associate Professor and Graduate Program Coordinator, 901-678-4358, Fax: 901-678-2178, E-mail: dlarsen@memphis.edu.

University of Miami, Graduate School, Rosenstiel School of Marine and Atmospheric Science, Division of Marine Geology and Geophysics, Coral Gables, FL 33124. Offers MS, PhD. Terminal master's awarded for partial completion of doctoral program. *Degree requirements:* For master's, comprehensive exam, thesis; for doctorate, comprehensive exam, thesis/dissertation. *Entrance requirements:* For master's and doctorate, GRE General Test. Additional exam requirements/recommendations for international students: Required—TOEFL (minimum score 550 paper-based; 213 computer-based). Electronic applications accepted. *Faculty research:* Carbonate sedimentology, low-temperature geochemistry, paleoceanography, geodesy and tectonics.

University of Minnesota, Twin Cities Campus, Institute of Technology, Department of Geology and Geophysics, Minneapolis, MN 55455-0213. Offers geology (MS, PhD); geophysics (MS, PhD). Terminal master's awarded for partial completion of doctoral program. *Degree requirements:* For master's, thesis; for doctorate, thesis/dissertation. *Entrance requirements:* For master's and doctorate, GRE General Test, 3 letters of recommendation. Additional exam requirements/recommendations for international students: Required—TOEFL (minimum score 550 paper-based; 213 computer-based). Electronic applications accepted. *Faculty research:* Geochemistry, paleoclimate studies, structure/tectonics, geofluids.

University of Nevada, Reno, Graduate School, College of Science, Mackay School of Earth Sciences and Engineering, Department of Geological Sciences, Program in Geophysics, Reno, NV 89557. Offers MS, PhD. Terminal master's awarded for partial completion of doctoral program. *Degree requirements:* For master's, thesis optional; for doctorate, thesis/dissertation. *Entrance requirements:* For master's, GRE General Test, minimum GPA of 2.75; for doctorate, GRE General Test, minimum GPA of 3.0. Additional exam requirements/recommendations for international students: Required—TOEFL (minimum score 500 paper-based; 173 computer-based; 61 iBT), IELTS (minimum score 6). Electronic applications accepted. *Expenses:* Tuition, state resident: full-time $2219; part-time $246 per credit. Tuition, nonresident: part-time $510 per credit. International tuition: $9009 full-time. Required fees: $59 per term. One-time fee: $101. Tuition and fees vary according to course load. *Faculty research:* Geophysics exploration, seismology, remote sensing.

University of Oklahoma, College of Earth and Energy, ConocoPhillips School of Geology and Geophysics, Program in Geophysics, Norman, OK 73019. Offers MS, PhD. Part-time programs available. *Students:* 24 full-time (7 women), 9 part-time (3 women); includes 3 minority (1 American Indian or Alaska Native, non-Hispanic/Latino; 2 Asian, non-Hispanic/Latino), 22 international. Average age 28. 31 applicants, 32% accepted, 7 enrolled. In 2010, 5 master's, 3 doctorates awarded. *Degree requirements:* For master's, comprehensive exam, thesis. *Entrance requirements:* For master's, GRE General Test. Additional exam requirements/recommendations for international students: Required—TOEFL (minimum score 550 paper-based; 213 computer-based; 79 iBT). *Application deadline:* For fall admission, 2/1 priority date for domestic students, 4/1 for international students; for spring admission, 9/1 for domestic and international students. Applications are processed on a rolling basis. Application fee: $40 ($90 for international students). Electronic applications accepted. *Expenses:* Tuition, state resident: full-time $3892.80; part-time $162.20 per credit hour. Tuition, nonresident: full-time $14,167; part-time $590.30 per credit hour. Required fees: $2523.40; $94.60 per credit hour. Tuition and fees vary according to course load and degree level. *Financial support:* In 2010–11, 31 students received support. Scholarships/grants and unspecified assistantships available. Financial award application deadline: 2/1; financial award applicants required to submit FAFSA. *Faculty research:* Lithospheric structure and evolution, basin studies, outcrop-scale investigations of sandbodies in Turbidite channels. *Unit head:* Doug Elmore, Associate Provost/ Director, 405-325-3253, Fax: 405-325-3140, E-mail: delmore@ou.edu. *Application contact:* Donna S. Mullins, Coordinator of Administrative Student Services and Corporate Recruiting, 405-325-3255, Fax: 405-325-3140, E-mail: dsmullins@ou.edu.

The University of Texas at Dallas, School of Natural Sciences and Mathematics, Program in Geosciences, Richardson, TX 75080. Offers geochemistry (MS, PhD); geophysics (MS, PhD); geospatial information sciences (MS, PhD); hydrogeology (MS, PhD); sedimentary, stratigraphy, paleontology (PhD); stratigraphy, paleontology (MS); structural geology and tectonics (MS, PhD). Part-time and evening/weekend programs available. *Faculty:* 11 full-time (1 woman). *Students:* 38 full-time (13 women), 25 part-time (8 women); includes 11 minority (4 Black or African American, non-Hispanic/Latino; 4 Asian, non-Hispanic/Latino; 3 Hispanic/Latino), 19 international. Average age 32. 48 applicants, 46% accepted, 12 enrolled. In 2010, 9 master's, 1 doctorate awarded. *Degree requirements:* For master's, thesis optional; for doctorate, thesis/dissertation. *Entrance requirements:* For master's and doctorate, GRE General Test, minimum GPA of 3.0 in upper-level course work in field. Additional exam requirements/recommendations for international students: Required—TOEFL (minimum score 550 paper-based; 215 computer-based). *Application deadline:* For fall admission, 7/15 for domestic students, 5/1 priority date for international students; for spring admission, 11/15 for domestic students, 9/1 priority date for international students. Applications are processed on a rolling basis. Application fee: $50 ($100 for international students). Electronic applications accepted. *Expenses:* Tuition, state resident: full-time $10,248; part-time $569 per credit hour. Tuition, nonresident: full-time $18,544; part-time $1030 per credit hour. Tuition and fees vary according to course load. *Financial support:* In 2010–11, 38 students received support, including 15 research assistantships with partial tuition reimbursements available (averaging $14,400 per year), 14 teaching assistantships with partial tuition reimbursements available (averaging $13,905 per year); career-related internships or fieldwork, Federal Work-Study, institutionally sponsored loans, scholarships/grants, and unspecified assistantships also available. Support available to part-time students. Financial award application deadline: 4/30; financial award applicants required to submit FAFSA. *Faculty research:* Cybermapping, GPS applications for geophysics and geology, seismology and ground-penetrating radar, numerical modeling, signal processing and inverse modeling techniques in seismology. *Unit head:* Dr. John Oldow, Department Head, 972-883-2403, Fax: 972-883-2537, E-mail: geosciences@utdallas.edu. *Application contact:* Dr. Robert J. Stem, Graduate Advisor, 972-883-2442, Fax: 972-883-2537, E-mail: rjstern@utdallas.edu.

The University of Texas at El Paso, Graduate School, College of Science, Department of Geological Sciences, Program in Geophysics, El Paso, TX 79968-0001. Offers MS. Part-time and evening/weekend programs available. *Students:* 8 (2 women); includes 1 Black or African American, non-Hispanic/Latino; 4 Hispanic/Latino, 1 international. Average age 34. In 2010, 3 master's awarded. *Degree requirements:* For master's, thesis. *Entrance requirements:* For master's, minimum GPA of 3.0, letters of recommendation. Additional exam requirements/recommendations for international students: Required—TOEFL; Recommended—IELTS. *Application deadline:* For fall admission, 8/1 priority date for domestic students, 3/1 for international students; for spring admission, 11/1 priority date for domestic students, 9/1 for international students. Applications are processed on a rolling basis. Application fee: $45 ($80 for international students). Electronic applications accepted. *Financial support:* In 2010–11, research assistantships with partial tuition reimbursements (averaging $21,812 per year), teaching assistantships with partial tuition reimbursements (averaging $17,450 per year) were awarded; fellowships with partial tuition reimbursements, institutionally sponsored loans, scholarships/grants, health care benefits, tuition waivers (partial), and unspecified assistantships also available. Support available to part-time students. Financial award application deadline: 3/15; financial award applicants required to submit FAFSA. *Unit head:* Dr. Diane Doser, Coordinator, 915-747-5501, Fax: 915-747-5073, E-mail: doser@utep.edu. *Application contact:* Dr. Patricia D. Witherspoon, Dean of the Graduate School, 915-747-5491, Fax: 915-747-5788, E-mail: withersp@utep.edu.

University of Utah, Graduate School, College of Mines and Earth Sciences, Department of Geology and Geophysics, Salt Lake City, UT 84112. Offers environmental engineering (ME, MS, PhD); geological engineering (ME, MS, PhD); geology (MS, PhD); geophysics (MS, PhD). *Faculty:* 21 full-time (4 women), 4 part-time/adjunct (1 woman). *Students:* 51 full-time (13 women), 19 part-time (6 women); includes 1 minority (Hispanic/Latino), 15 international. Average age 30. 128 applicants, 27% accepted, 23 enrolled. In 2010, 10 master's, 8 doctorates awarded. Terminal master's awarded for partial completion of doctoral program. *Degree requirements:* For master's, comprehensive exam, thesis; for doctorate, thesis/dissertation, qualifying exam (written and oral). *Entrance requirements:* For master's and doctorate, GRE General Test, minimum GPA of 3.25. Additional exam requirements/recommendations for international students: Required—TOEFL (minimum score 500 paper-based; 173 computer-based). *Application deadline:* For fall admission, 1/15 priority date for domestic and international students. Applications are processed on a rolling basis. Application fee: $55 ($65 for international students). Electronic applications accepted. *Expenses:* Tuition, area resident: Part-time $179.19 per credit hour. Tuition, state resident: full-time $4384. Tuition, nonresident: full-time $16,684; part-time $630.67 per credit hour. Required fees: $350 per semester. Tuition and fees vary according to course load, degree level and program. *Financial support:* In 2010–11, 22 students received support, including 11 fellowships with full tuition reimbursements available (averaging $13,450 per year), 45 research assistantships with full tuition reimbursements available (averaging $21,858 per year), 11 teaching assistantships with full tuition reimbursements available (averaging $13,450 per year); career-related internships or fieldwork, institutionally sponsored loans, scholarships/grants, unspecified assistantships, and stipends also available. Financial award application deadline: 1/15; financial award applicants required to submit FAFSA. *Faculty research:* Igneous, metamorphic, and sedimentary petrology; ore deposits; aqueous geochemistry; isotope geochemistry; heat flow. Total annual research expenditures: $2.2 million. *Unit head:* Dr. Kip Solomon, Chair, 801-581-7231, Fax: 801-581-7065, E-mail: kip.solomon@utah.edu. *Application contact:* Dr. Allan A. Ekdale, Director of Graduate Studies, 801-581-7266, Fax: 801-581-7065, E-mail: a.ekdale@utah.edu.

University of Victoria, Faculty of Graduate Studies, Faculty of Science, Department of Physics and Astronomy, Victoria, BC V8W 2Y2, Canada. Offers astronomy and astrophysics (M Sc, PhD); condensed matter physics (M Sc, PhD); experimental particle physics (M Sc, PhD); medical physics (M Sc, PhD); ocean physics (M Sc, PhD); theoretical physics (M Sc, PhD). *Degree requirements:* For master's, thesis; for doctorate, comprehensive exam, thesis/dissertation, candidacy exam. *Entrance requirements:* For master's and doctorate, GRE. Additional exam requirements/recommendations for international students: Required—TOEFL (minimum score 575 paper-based; 233 computer-based), IELTS (minimum score 7). Electronic applications accepted. *Faculty research:* Old stellar populations; observational cosmology and large scale structure; cp violation; atlas.

University of Washington, Graduate School, College of Arts and Sciences, Department of Earth and Space Sciences, Seattle, WA 98195. Offers geology (MS, PhD); geophysics (MS, PhD). *Degree requirements:* For master's, thesis or alternative, departmental qualifying exam, final exam; for doctorate, thesis/dissertation, departmental qualifying exam, general and final exams. *Entrance requirements:* For master's and doctorate, GRE General Test, minimum GPA of 3.0. Additional exam requirements/recommendations for international students: Required—TOEFL (minimum score 580 paper-based). Electronic applications accepted.

The University of Western Ontario, Faculty of Graduate Studies, Physical Sciences Division, Department of Earth Sciences, London, ON N6A 5B8, Canada. Offers environment and sustainability (MES); geology (M Sc, PhD); geology and environmental science (M Sc, PhD); geophysics (M Sc, PhD); geophysics and environmental science (M Sc, PhD). *Degree requirements:* For master's, thesis; for doctorate, thesis/dissertation, qualifying exam. *Entrance requirements:* For master's, honors in B Sc; for doctorate, M Sc. Additional exam requirements/recommendations for international students: Required—TOEFL. *Faculty research:* Geophysics, geochemistry, paleontology, sedimentology/stratigraphy, glaciology/quaternary.

University of Wisconsin–Madison, Graduate School, College of Letters and Science, Department of Geology and Geophysics, Program in Geophysics, Madison, WI 53706-1380. Offers MS, PhD. *Degree requirements:* For master's, thesis; for doctorate, one foreign language, thesis/dissertation. *Entrance requirements:* For master's and doctorate, GRE General Test. *Expenses:* Tuition, state resident: full-time $9887.36; part-time $617.96 per credit. Tuition, nonresident: full-time $24,054; part-time $1503.40 per credit. Required fees: $67.63 per credit. Tuition and fees vary according to reciprocity agreements.

University of Wyoming, College of Arts and Sciences, Department of Geology and Geophysics, Laramie, WY 82070. Offers geology (MS, PhD); geophysics (MS, PhD). Part-time programs available. *Degree requirements:* For master's, comprehensive exam, thesis; for doctorate, comprehensive exam, thesis/dissertation. *Entrance requirements:* For master's and doctorate, GRE General Test, minimum GPA of 3.0. *Faculty research:* Low-temp geochemistry,

Geophysics

University of Wyoming (continued)
geohydrology, paleontology, structure/tectonics, sedimentation and petroleum geology, petrology, geophysics/seismology.

West Virginia University, Eberly College of Arts and Sciences, Department of Geology and Geography, Program in Geology, Morgantown, WV 26506. Offers geomorphology (MS, PhD); geophysics (MS, PhD); hydrogeology (MS, PhD); paleontology (MS, PhD); petroleum geology (PhD); petrology (MS, PhD); stratigraphy (MS, PhD); structure (MS, PhD). Part-time programs available. Terminal master's awarded for partial completion of doctoral program. *Degree requirements:* For master's, thesis (for some programs); for doctorate, comprehensive exam, thesis/dissertation. *Entrance requirements:* For master's, GRE General Test, minimum GPA of 2.5; for doctorate, GRE General Test, minimum GPA of 3.3. Additional exam requirements/recommendations for international students: Required—TOEFL.

Woods Hole Oceanographic Institution, MIT/WHOI Joint Program in Oceanography/Applied Ocean Science and Engineering, Woods Hole, MA 02543-1541. Offers applied ocean sciences (PhD); biological oceanography (PhD, Sc D); chemical oceanography (PhD, Sc D); civil and environmental and oceanographic engineering (PhD); electrical and oceanographic engineering (PhD); geochemistry (PhD); geophysics (PhD); marine biology (PhD); marine geochemistry (PhD, Sc D); marine geology (PhD, Sc D); marine geophysics (PhD); mechanical and oceanographic engineering (PhD); ocean engineering (PhD); oceanographic engineering (M Eng, MS, PhD, Sc D, Eng); paleoceanography (PhD); physical oceanography (PhD, Sc D). MS, PhD, Sc D offered jointly with Massachusetts Institute of Technology. Terminal master's awarded for partial completion of doctoral program. *Degree requirements:* For master's and Eng, thesis (for some programs); for doctorate, thesis/dissertation. *Entrance requirements:* For master's, GRE General Test; for doctorate, GRE General Test, GRE Subject Test. Additional exam requirements/recommendations for international students: Required—TOEFL. Electronic applications accepted.

Wright State University, School of Graduate Studies, College of Science and Mathematics, Department of Physics, Program in Physics, Dayton, OH 45435. Offers geophysics (MS); medical physics (MS). Part-time and evening/weekend programs available. *Degree requirements:* For master's, thesis. *Entrance requirements:* Additional exam requirements/recommendations for international students: Required—TOEFL. *Faculty research:* Solid-state physics, optics, geophysics.

Yale University, Graduate School of Arts and Sciences, Department of Geology and Geophysics, New Haven, CT 06520. Offers biogeochemistry (PhD); climate dynamics (PhD); geochemistry (PhD); geophysics (PhD); meteorology (PhD); oceanography (PhD); paleontology (PhD); paleooceanography (PhD); petrology (PhD); tectonics (PhD). *Degree requirements:* For doctorate, thesis/dissertation. *Entrance requirements:* For doctorate, GRE General Test. Additional exam requirements/recommendations for international students: Required—TOEFL.

Geosciences

Alabama State University, Department of Earth and Environmental Sciences, Montgomery, AL 36101-0271. Offers MS, PhD. *Degree requirements:* For master's, one foreign language, thesis or alternative; for doctorate, one foreign language, thesis/dissertation. *Entrance requirements:* For master's, GRE General Test, minimum B average in undergraduate course work; for doctorate, GRE General Test. Additional exam requirements/recommendations for international students: Required—TOEFL. Electronic applications accepted. *Faculty research:* Sedimentation, isotopes, biogeochemistry, marine geology, structural geology.

Arizona State University, College of Liberal Arts and Sciences, School of Earth and Space Exploration, Tempe, AZ 85287-1404. Offers astrophysics (MS, PhD); exploration systems design (PhD); geological sciences (MS, PhD). PhD in exploration systems design is offered in collaboration with the Fulton Schools of Engineering. *Faculty:* 43 full-time (4 women), 2 part-time/adjunct (1 woman). *Students:* 89 full-time (32 women), 16 part-time (8 women); includes 12 minority (2 American Indian or Alaska Native, non-Hispanic/Latino; 4 Asian, non-Hispanic/Latino; 6 Hispanic/Latino), 18 international. Average age 30. 181 applicants, 28% accepted, 28 enrolled. In 2010, 6 master's, 7 doctorates awarded. Terminal master's awarded for partial completion of doctoral program. *Degree requirements:* For master's, thesis, interactive Program of Study (iPOS) submitted before completing 50 percent of required credit hours; for doctorate, thesis/dissertation, interactive Program of Study (iPOS) submitted before completing 50 percent of required credit hours. *Entrance requirements:* For master's and doctorate, GRE, minimum GPA of 3.0 or equivalent in last 2 years of work leading to bachelor's degree. Additional exam requirements/recommendations for international students: Required—TOEFL, IELTS, or Pearson Test of English. *Application deadline:* For fall admission, 1/15 for domestic and international students; for spring admission, 10/1 for domestic and international students. Applications are processed on a rolling basis. Application fee: $70 ($90 for international students). Electronic applications accepted. *Expenses:* Tuition, state resident: full-time $8510; part-time $608 per credit. Tuition, nonresident: full-time $16,542; part-time $919 per credit. Required fees: $339; $110 per credit. Part-time tuition and fees vary according to course load. *Financial support:* In 2010–11, 52 research assistantships with full and partial tuition reimbursements (averaging $15,804 per year), 42 teaching assistantships with full and partial tuition reimbursements (averaging $15,169 per year) were awarded; fellowships with full tuition reimbursements, career-related internships or fieldwork, Federal Work-Study, institutionally sponsored loans, scholarships/grants, and tuition waivers (full and partial) also available. Financial award application deadline: 3/1; financial award applicants required to submit FAFSA. Total annual research expenditures: $18.8 million. *Unit head:* Dr. Kip Hodges, Director, 480-965-5331, Fax: 480-965-8102, E-mail: kvhodges@asu.edu. *Application contact:* Graduate Admissions, 480-965-6113.

Baylor University, Graduate School, College of Arts and Sciences, Department of Geology, Waco, TX 76798. Offers earth science (MA); geology (MS, PhD). *Faculty:* 12 full-time (1 woman). *Students:* 24 full-time (9 women), 4 part-time (2 women); includes 1 American Indian or Alaska Native, non-Hispanic/Latino, 4 international. In 2010, 1 master's awarded. *Degree requirements:* For master's, thesis; for doctorate, thesis/dissertation. *Entrance requirements:* For master's and doctorate, GRE General Test. *Application deadline:* For fall admission, 3/15 priority date for domestic students. Applications are processed on a rolling basis. Application fee: $25. *Financial support:* In 2010–11, 18 teaching assistantships were awarded; Federal Work-Study and institutionally sponsored loans also available. *Faculty research:* Petroleum geology, geophysics, engineering geology, hydrogeology. *Unit head:* Dr. Steve Dworkin, Graduate Program Director, 254-710-2186, Fax: 254-710-2673, E-mail: steve_dworkin@baylor.edu. *Application contact:* Paulette Penney, Administrative Assistant, 254-710-2361, Fax: 254-710-3870, E-mail: paulette_penney@baylor.edu.

Baylor University, Graduate School, College of Arts and Sciences, The Institute of Ecological, Earth and Environmental Sciences, Waco, TX 76798. Offers PhD. *Students:* 7 full-time (3 women); includes 1 minority (Two or more races, non-Hispanic/Latino), 5 international. In 2010, 1 doctorate awarded. *Unit head:* Dr. Joseph D. White, Director, 254-710-2911, E-mail: joseph_d_white@baylor.edu. *Application contact:* Suzanne Keener, Administrative Assistant, 254-710-3588, Fax: 254-710-3870.

Boise State University, Graduate College, College of Arts and Sciences, Department of Geosciences, Program in Earth Science, Boise, ID 83725-0399. Offers MS. Part-time programs available. *Degree requirements:* For master's, thesis. *Entrance requirements:* For master's, GRE General Test, minimum GPA of 3.0, BS in related field. Electronic applications accepted.

Boston University, Graduate School of Arts and Sciences, Department of Earth Sciences, Boston, MA 02215. Offers MA, PhD. *Students:* 24 full-time (14 women), 1 (woman) part-time; includes 1 minority (Asian, non-Hispanic/Latino), 4 international. Average age 27. 58 applicants, 31% accepted, 6 enrolled. In 2010, 3 master's, 3 doctorates awarded. Terminal master's awarded for partial completion of doctoral program. *Degree requirements:* For master's, one foreign language, comprehensive exam, thesis; for doctorate, one foreign language, comprehensive exam, thesis/dissertation. *Entrance requirements:* For master's and doctorate, GRE General Test, 3 letters of recommendation. Additional exam requirements/recommendations for international students: Required—TOEFL (minimum score 550 paper-based; 213 computer-based). *Application deadline:* For fall admission, 1/15 for domestic and international students; for spring admission, 10/15 for domestic and international students. Application fee: $70. Electronic applications accepted. *Expenses:* Tuition: Full-time $39,314; part-time $1228 per credit. Required fees: $40 per semester. *Financial support:* In 2010–11, 1 fellowship with full tuition reimbursement (averaging $19,300 per year), 10 research assistantships with full tuition reimbursements (averaging $18,800 per year), 8 teaching assistantships with full tuition reimbursements (averaging $18,800 per year) were awarded; Federal Work-Study and unspecified assistantships also available. Support available to part-time students. Financial award application deadline: 1/15; financial award applicants required to submit FAFSA. *Unit head:* Mark Friedl, Chairman, 617-353-5745, Fax: 617-353-3290, E-mail: friedl@bu.edu. *Application contact:* Christine Jeudy, Department Administrator, 617-353-2529, Fax: 617-353-3290, E-mail: cjeudy@bu.edu.

Boston University, School of Education, Boston, MA 02215. Offers counseling (Ed M, CAGS), including community, school, sport psychology; counseling psychology (Ed D); curriculum and teaching (Ed M, Ed D, CAGS), including early childhood (Ed D), educational media and technology (Ed D), English and language arts (Ed D), mathematics (Ed D), physical education and coaching (Ed D), science (Ed D), social studies education (Ed D), special education (Ed D); developmental studies (Ed D), including literacy and language, reading education; developmental studies in literacy and language education (Ed M, CAGS); early childhood education (Ed M, CAGS); education of the deaf (Ed M, CAGS); educational leadership and development (Ed D), including educational administration (Ed M, Ed D, CAGS), higher education administration (Ed M, Ed D, CAGS); educational media and technology (Ed M, CAGS); elementary education (Ed M); English and language arts (Ed M, CAGS); English education (MAT); health education (Ed M, CAGS); Latin and classical studies (MAT); mathematics education (Ed M, MAT, CAGS); mathematics for teaching (MMT); modern foreign language education (MAT), including French, Spanish; physical education and coaching (Ed M, CAGS); policy, planning, and administration (Ed M, CAGS), including community education leadership, educational administration (Ed M, Ed D, CAGS), higher education administration (Ed M, Ed D, CAGS); reading education (Ed M, CAGS); science education (Ed M, MAT, CAGS), including biology (MAT), chemistry (MAT), earth science (MAT), general science (MAT), physics (MAT); social studies education (Ed M, MAT, CAGS), including history (MAT), political science (MAT); special education (Ed M, Ed D, CAGS), including disability studies (Ed M), moderate disabilities (Ed M), severe disabilities (Ed M), special education administration (Ed M); teaching English as a second language (Ed M, CAGS). Part-time programs available. *Faculty:* 57 full-time, 39 part-time/adjunct. *Students:* 245 full-time (191 women), 376 part-time (274 women); includes 83 minority (14 Black or African American, non-Hispanic/Latino; 2 American Indian or Alaska Native, non-Hispanic/Latino; 28 Asian, non-Hispanic/Latino; 31 Hispanic/Latino; 2 Native Hawaiian or other Pacific Islander, non-Hispanic/Latino; 6 Two or more races, non-Hispanic/Latino), 79 international. Average age 30. 1,270 applicants, 66% accepted, 292 enrolled. In 2010, 273 master's, 15 doctorates, 7 other advanced degrees awarded. Terminal master's awarded for partial completion of doctoral program. *Degree requirements:* For master's, thesis (for some programs); for doctorate, comprehensive exam, thesis/dissertation; for CAGS, comprehensive exam. *Entrance requirements:* For master's and CAGS, GRE General Test or Miller Analogies Test (MAT); for doctorate, GRE General Test. Additional exam requirements/recommendations for international students: Required—TOEFL, IELTS. *Application deadline:* For fall admission, 1/15 priority date for domestic and international students; for spring admission, 9/15 priority date for domestic and international students. Applications are processed on a rolling basis. Application fee: $70. Electronic applications accepted. *Expenses:* Tuition: Full-time $39,314; part-time $1228 per credit. Required fees: $40 per semester. *Financial support:* In 2010–11, 276 students received support, including 31 fellowships with full tuition reimbursements available, 16 research assistantships, 26 teaching assistantships with partial tuition reimbursements available; career-related internships or fieldwork, Federal Work-Study, and scholarships/grants also available. Support available to part-time students. Financial award applicants required to submit FAFSA. *Faculty research:* Deaf studies, social emotional learning, civic engagement and education, STEM education, pre-college educational pipelines. Total annual research expenditures: $2.6 million. *Unit head:* Dr. Hardin Coleman, Dean, 617-353-3213. *Application contact:* Dana Fernandez, Director of Enrollment, 617-353-4237, Fax: 617-353-8937, E-mail: sedgrad@bu.edu.

Brock University, Faculty of Graduate Studies, Faculty of Mathematics and Science, Program in Earth Sciences, St. Catharines, ON L2S 3A1, Canada. Offers M Sc. Part-time programs available. *Degree requirements:* For master's, thesis. *Entrance requirements:* For master's, honors B Sc in earth sciences. Additional exam requirements/recommendations for international students: Required—TOEFL (minimum score 550 paper-based; 213 computer-based; 80 iBT), IELTS (minimum score 6.5), TWE (minimum score 4). Electronic applications accepted. *Faculty research:* Clastic sedimentology, environmental geology, geochemistry, micropaleontology, structural geology.

Brooklyn College of the City University of New York, Division of Graduate Studies, School of Education, Program in Adolescence Education and Special Subjects, Brooklyn, NY 11210-2889. Offers adolescence science education (MAT); art teacher (MA); biology teacher (MA); chemistry teacher (MA); earth science teacher (MAT); English teacher (MA); French teacher (MA); health and nutrition sciences: health teacher (MS Ed); mathematics teacher (MA); music education (CAS); music teacher (MA); physical education teacher (MS Ed); physics teacher (MA); social studies teacher (MA); Spanish teacher (MA). Part-time and evening/weekend programs available. *Students:* 26 full-time (15 women), 418 part-time (241 women); includes 133 minority (72 Black or African American, non-Hispanic/Latino; 22 Asian, non-Hispanic/Latino; 39 Hispanic/Latino), 9 international. Average age 31. 221 applicants, 76% accepted, 107 enrolled. In 2010, 149 master's, 12 other advanced degrees awarded. *Degree requirements:* For master's, comprehensive exam (for some programs), thesis (for some programs). *Entrance requirements:* For master's, LAST, previous course work in education, resume, 2 letters of

recommendation, essay. Additional exam requirements/recommendations for international students: Required—TOEFL (minimum score 500 paper-based; 173 computer-based; 61 iBT). *Application deadline:* For fall admission, 7/15 for domestic students, 7/1 for international students; for spring admission, 11/15 for domestic students, 10/1 for international students. Applications are processed on a rolling basis. Application fee: $125. Electronic applications accepted. *Expenses:* Tuition, state resident: full-time $7360; part-time $310 per credit hour. Tuition, nonresident: full-time $13,800; part-time $575 per credit hour. Required fees: $190 per semester. *Financial support:* Career-related internships or fieldwork, Federal Work-Study, institutionally sponsored loans, and scholarships/grants available. Support available to part-time students. Financial award application deadline: 5/1; financial award applicants required to submit FAFSA. *Faculty research:* Interdisciplinary education, semiotics, discourse analysis, autobiography, teacher identity. *Unit head:* Prof. Stephen Phillips, Program Head, 718-951-5214, E-mail: phillips@brooklyn.cuny.edu. *Application contact:* Hernan Sierra, Graduate Admissions Coordinator, 718-951-4536, Fax: 718-951-4506, E-mail: grads@brooklyn.cuny.edu.

Brooklyn College of the City University of New York, Division of Graduate Studies, School of Education, Program in Middle Childhood Education (Science), Brooklyn, NY 11210-2889. Offers biology (MA); chemistry (MA); earth science (MA); general science (MA); physics (MA). Part-time and evening/weekend programs available. *Students:* 3 full-time (1 woman), 74 part-time (46 women); includes 29 minority (12 Black or African American, non-Hispanic/Latino; 8 Asian, non-Hispanic/Latino; 9 Hispanic/Latino), 4 international. Average age 32. 29 applicants, 97% accepted, 21 enrolled. In 2010, 24 master's awarded. *Entrance requirements:* For master's, LAST, interview, previous course work in education and mathematics, resume, 2 letters of recommendation, essay. Additional exam requirements/recommendations for international students: Required—TOEFL (minimum score 500 paper-based; 173 computer-based; 61 iBT). *Application deadline:* For fall admission, 7/15 priority date for domestic students, 6/1 priority date for international students; for spring admission, 11/15 priority date for domestic students, 10/1 priority date for international students. Applications are processed on a rolling basis. Application fee: $125. Electronic applications accepted. *Expenses:* Tuition, state resident: full-time $7360; part-time $310 per credit hour. Tuition, nonresident: full-time $13,800; part-time $575 per credit hour. Required fees: $190 per semester. *Financial support:* Federal Work-Study, institutionally sponsored loans, and scholarships/grants available. Support available to part-time students. Financial award application deadline: 5/1; financial award applicants required to submit FAFSA. *Faculty research:* Geometric thinking, mastery of basic facts, problem-solving strategies, history of mathematics. *Unit head:* Dr. Jennifer Adams, Program Head, 718-951-5214, E-mail: jadams@brooklyn.cuny.edu. *Application contact:* Hernan Sierra, Graduate Admissions Coordinator, 718-951-4536, Fax: 718-951-4506, E-mail: grads@brooklyn.cuny.edu.

Brown University, Graduate School, Department of Geological Sciences, Providence, RI 02912. Offers MA, Sc M, PhD. *Degree requirements:* For doctorate, thesis/dissertation, 1 semester of teaching experience, preliminary exam. *Faculty research:* Geochemistry, mineral kinetics, igneous and metamorphic petrology, tectonophysics including geophysics and structural geology, paleoclimatology, paleoceanography, sedimentation, planetary geology.

California State University, Chico, Graduate School, College of Natural Sciences, Department of Geological and Environmental Sciences, Program in Geosciences, Chico, CA 95929-0722. Offers hydrology/hydrogeology (MS). Part-time programs available. *Students:* 5 full-time (1 woman), 4 part-time (2 women); includes 1 Hispanic/Latino. Average age 36. 9 applicants, 44% accepted, 3 enrolled. In 2010, 1 master's awarded. *Degree requirements:* For master's, thesis, oral exam. *Entrance requirements:* For master's, GRE General Test. Additional exam requirements/recommendations for international students: Required—TOEFL (minimum score 550 paper-based; 213 computer-based; 80 iBT), IELTS (minimum score 6.5). *Application deadline:* For fall admission, 3/1 priority date for domestic students, 3/1 for international students; for spring admission, 9/15 priority date for domestic students, 9/15 for international students. Applications are processed on a rolling basis. Application fee: $55. Electronic applications accepted. *Financial support:* Fellowships available. *Unit head:* Dr. William Murphy, Graduate Coordinator, 530-898-5163. *Application contact:* Dr. William Murphy, Graduate Coordinator, 530-898-5163.

Carleton University, Faculty of Graduate Studies, Faculty of Science, Department of Earth Sciences, Ottawa, ON K1S 5B6, Canada. Offers M Sc, PhD. Programs offered jointly with University of Ottawa. *Degree requirements:* For master's, thesis, seminar; for doctorate, comprehensive exam, thesis/dissertation, seminar. *Entrance requirements:* For master's, honors degree in science; for doctorate, M Sc. Additional exam requirements/recommendations for international students: Required—TOEFL. *Faculty research:* Resource geology, geophysics, basin analysis, lithosphere dynamics.

Case Western Reserve University, School of Graduate Studies, Department of Geological Sciences, Cleveland, OH 44106. Offers MS, PhD. Part-time programs available. *Faculty:* 7 full-time (1 woman), 7 part-time/adjunct (0 women). *Students:* 7 full-time (4 women), 3 international. Average age 31. 21 applicants, 19% accepted, 1 enrolled.Terminal master's awarded for partial completion of doctoral program. *Degree requirements:* For master's, thesis or alternative; for doctorate, thesis/dissertation. *Entrance requirements:* For master's and doctorate, GRE General Test, GRE Subject Test. Additional exam requirements/recommendations for international students: Required—TOEFL (minimum score 550 paper-based; 213 computer-based; 79 iBT). *Application deadline:* For fall admission, 2/1 priority date for domestic students; for spring admission, 11/15 for domestic students. Applications are processed on a rolling basis. Application fee: $50. Electronic applications accepted. *Financial support:* Research assistantships, teaching assistantships, Federal Work-Study and tuition waivers (partial) available. Support available to part-time students. Financial award application deadline: 2/1; financial award applicants required to submit FAFSA. *Faculty research:* Geochemistry, hydrology, ecology, geomorphology, planetary science, stratigraphy and basin analysis, igneous petrology. *Unit head:* Gerald Matisoff, Chairman, 216-368-3677, Fax: 216-368-3691, E-mail: gerald.matisoff@case.edu. *Application contact:* James Van Orman, Chair, Graduate Admission Committee, 216-368-3690, Fax: 216-368-3691, E-mail: james.vanorman@case.edu.

Central Connecticut State University, School of Graduate Studies, School of Arts and Sciences, Department of Physics and Earth Science, New Britain, CT 06050-4010. Offers natural sciences (MS); science education (Certificate). Part-time and evening/weekend programs available. *Faculty:* 12 full-time (4 women), 17 part-time/adjunct (4 women). *Students:* 11 part-time (7 women); includes 1 minority (Asian, non-Hispanic/Latino). Average age 38. 3 applicants, 100% accepted, 2 enrolled. In 2010, 9 master's, 1 other advanced degree awarded. *Degree requirements:* For master's, comprehensive exam, thesis or alternative; for Certificate, qualifying exam. *Entrance requirements:* For master's, minimum undergraduate GPA of 2.7. Additional exam requirements/recommendations for international students: Required—TOEFL. *Application deadline:* For fall admission, 7/1 for domestic students; for spring admission, 12/1 for domestic students. Applications are processed on a rolling basis. Application fee: $50. Electronic applications accepted. *Expenses:* Tuition, area resident: Full-time $5012; part-time $470 per credit. Tuition, state resident: full-time $7518; part-time $482 per credit. Tuition, nonresident: full-time $13,962; part-time $482 per credit. Required fees: $3772. One-time fee: $62 part-time. *Financial support:* In 2010–11, 1 student received support. Career-related internships or fieldwork, Federal Work-Study, scholarships/grants, and unspecified assistantships available. Support available to part-time students. Financial award application deadline: 2/15; financial award applicants required to submit FAFSA. *Faculty research:* Elementary/secondary science education, particle and solid states, weather patterns, planetary studies. *Unit head:* Dr. Ali Antar, Chair, 860-832-2930. *Application contact:* Dr. Ali Antar, Chair, 860-832-2930.

City College of the City University of New York, Graduate School, College of Liberal Arts and Science, Division of Science, Department of Earth and Atmospheric Sciences, New York, NY 10031-9198. Offers earth and environmental science (PhD); earth systems science (MA). PhD program offered jointly with Graduate School and University Center of the City University of New York. *Degree requirements:* For master's, comprehensive exam, thesis. *Entrance requirements:* Additional exam requirements/recommendations for international students: Required—TOEFL (minimum score 500 paper-based; 61 iBT). Electronic applications accepted. *Faculty research:* Water resources, high-temperature geochemistry, sedimentary basin analysis, tectonics.

Colorado State University, Graduate School, Warner College of Natural Resources, Department of Geosciences, Fort Collins, CO 80523-1482. Offers earth sciences (PhD); geosciences (MS). Part-time programs available. *Faculty:* 11 full-time (4 women). *Students:* 24 full-time (10 women), 28 part-time (14 women); includes 1 Asian, non-Hispanic/Latino; 2 Hispanic/Latino, 5 international. Average age 31. 88 applicants, 40% accepted, 15 enrolled. In 2010, 7 master's, 4 doctorates awarded. *Degree requirements:* For master's, thesis; for doctorate, comprehensive exam, thesis/dissertation. *Entrance requirements:* For master's and doctorate, GRE General Test, minimum GPA of 3.0, letters of recommendation. Additional exam requirements/recommendations for international students: Required—TOEFL (minimum score 550 paper-based; 213 computer-based; 80 iBT); Recommended—IELTS (minimum score 6). *Application deadline:* For fall admission, 2/15 priority date for domestic and international students; for spring admission, 7/15 priority date for domestic and international students. Applications are processed on a rolling basis. Application fee: $50. Electronic applications accepted. *Expenses:* Tuition, state resident: full-time $7434; part-time $413 per credit. Tuition, nonresident: full-time $19,022; part-time $1057 per credit. Required fees: $1729; $88 per credit. *Financial support:* In 2010–11, 27 students received support, including 1 fellowship (averaging $44,500 per year), 19 research assistantships with full tuition reimbursements available (averaging $12,888 per year), 7 teaching assistantships with full tuition reimbursements available (averaging $6,430 per year); scholarships/grants also available. Financial award application deadline: 2/15; financial award applicants required to submit FAFSA. *Faculty research:* Snow, surface, and groundwater hydrology; fluvial geomorphology; geographic information systems; geochemistry; chemical weathering. Total annual research expenditures: $1.4 million. *Unit head:* Dr. Sally J. Sutton, Head, 970-491-5995, Fax: 970-491-6307, E-mail: sally.sutton@colostate.edu. *Application contact:* Sharyl Pierson, Administrative Assistant, 970-491-5661, Fax: 970-491-6307, E-mail: sharyl@cnr.colostate.edu.

Columbia University, Graduate School of Arts and Sciences, Division of Natural Sciences, Department of Earth and Environmental Sciences, New York, NY 10027. Offers geochemistry (M Phil, MA, PhD); geodetic sciences (M Phil, MA, PhD); geophysics (M Phil, MA, PhD); oceanography (M Phil, MA, PhD). *Degree requirements:* For master's, thesis or alternative, fieldwork, written exam; for doctorate, one foreign language, thesis/dissertation. *Entrance requirements:* For master's and doctorate, GRE General Test, GRE Subject Test, major in natural or physical science. Additional exam requirements/recommendations for international students: Required—TOEFL. *Faculty research:* Structural geology and stratigraphy, petrology, paleontology, rare gas, isotope and aqueous geochemistry.

Cornell University, Graduate School, Graduate Fields of Engineering, Field of Geological Sciences, Ithaca, NY 14853. Offers economic geology (M Eng, MS, PhD); engineering geology (M Eng, MS, PhD); environmental geophysics (M Eng, MS, PhD); general geology (M Eng, MS, PhD); geobiology (M Eng, MS, PhD); geochemistry and isotope geology (M Eng, MS, PhD); geohydrology (M Eng, MS, PhD); geomorphology (M Eng, MS, PhD); geophysics (M Eng, MS, PhD); geotectonics (M Eng, MS, PhD); marine geology (MS, PhD); mineralogy (M Eng, MS, PhD); paleontology (M Eng, MS, PhD); petroleum geology (M Eng, MS, PhD); petrology (M Eng, MS, PhD); planetary geology (M Eng, MS, PhD); Precambrian geology (M Eng, MS, PhD); Quaternary geology (M Eng, MS, PhD); rock mechanics (M Eng, MS, PhD); sedimentology (M Eng, MS, PhD); seismology (M Eng, MS, PhD); stratigraphy (M Eng, MS, PhD); structural geology (M Eng, MS, PhD). *Faculty:* 36 full-time (5 women). *Students:* 38 full-time (15 women); includes 2 Asian, non-Hispanic/Latino; 2 Hispanic/Latino, 9 international. Average age 27. 84 applicants, 25% accepted, 17 enrolled. In 2010, 3 master's, 5 doctorates awarded. *Degree requirements:* For master's, thesis (MS); for doctorate, comprehensive exam, thesis/dissertation. *Entrance requirements:* For master's and doctorate, GRE General Test, 3 letters of recommendation. Additional exam requirements/recommendations for international students: Required—TOEFL (minimum score 550 paper-based; 213 computer-based; 77 iBT). *Application deadline:* For fall admission, 1/15 priority date for domestic students. Applications are processed on a rolling basis. Application fee: $70. Electronic applications accepted. *Expenses:* Tuition: Full-time $29,500. Required fees: $76. Tuition and fees vary according to degree level and program. *Financial support:* In 2010–11, 25 students received support, including 10 fellowships with full tuition reimbursements available, 14 research assistantships with full tuition reimbursements available, 10 teaching assistantships with full tuition reimbursements available; institutionally sponsored loans, scholarships/grants, health care benefits, tuition waivers (full and partial), and unspecified assistantships also available. Financial award applicants required to submit FAFSA. *Faculty research:* Geophysics, structural geology, petrology, geochemistry, geodynamics. *Unit head:* Director of Graduate Studies, 607-255-5466, Fax: 607-254-4780. *Application contact:* Graduate Field Assistant, 607-255-5466, Fax: 607-254-4780, E-mail: gradprog@geology.cornell.edu.

Dalhousie University, Faculty of Science, Department of Earth Sciences, Halifax, NS B3H 4R2, Canada. Offers M Sc, PhD. *Degree requirements:* For master's, one foreign language, thesis; for doctorate, one foreign language, thesis/dissertation. *Entrance requirements:* Additional exam requirements/recommendations for international students: Required—TOEFL, IELTS, CANTEST, CAEL, or Michigan English Language Assessment Battery. *Faculty research:* Marine geology and geophysics, Appalachian and Grenville geology, micropaleontology, geodynamics and structural geology, geochronology.

Dartmouth College, Arts and Sciences Graduate Programs, Department of Earth Sciences, Hanover, NH 03755. Offers MS, PhD. Terminal master's awarded for partial completion of doctoral program. *Degree requirements:* For master's, thesis; for doctorate, thesis/dissertation. *Entrance requirements:* For master's and doctorate, GRE General Test, GRE Subject Test. Additional exam requirements/recommendations for international students: Required—TOEFL. *Faculty research:* Geochemistry, remote sensing, geophysics, hydrology, economic geology.

Eastern Michigan University, Graduate School, College of Arts and Sciences, Department of Geography and Geology, Program in Earth Science Education, Ypsilanti, MI 48197. Offers MS. *Students:* 1 (woman) full-time, 10 part-time (8 women). Average age 36. In 2010, 3 master's awarded. Application fee: $35. *Application contact:* Dr. Sandra Rutherford, Program Advisor, 734-487-8588, Fax: 734-487-6979, E-mail: srutherf@emich.edu.

Emporia State University, Graduate School, College of Liberal Arts and Sciences, Department of Physical Sciences, Emporia, KS 66801-5087. Offers earth science (MS); geospatial analysis (Postbaccalaureate Certificate); physical science (MS). Part-time programs available. Postbaccalaureate distance learning degree programs offered (minimal on-campus study). *Faculty:* 15 full-time (2 women), 1 (woman) part-time/adjunct. *Students:* 6 full-time (2 women), 23 part-time (8 women); includes 2 minority (1 American Indian or Alaska Native, non-Hispanic/Latino; 1 Native Hawaiian or other Pacific Islander, non-Hispanic/Latino), 6 international. 3 applicants, 100% accepted, 1 enrolled. In 2010, 7 master's, 3 other advanced degrees awarded. *Degree requirements:* For master's, comprehensive exam or thesis. *Entrance requirements:* For master's, physical science qualifying exam, appropriate undergraduate degree. Additional exam requirements/recommendations for international students: Required—TOEFL (minimum score 520 paper-based; 133 computer-based; 68 iBT). *Application deadline:* For fall admission, 8/15 priority date for domestic students. Applications are processed on a rolling basis. Application fee: $30 ($75 for international students). Electronic applications accepted. *Expenses:* Tuition, state resident: full-time $4382; part-time $183 per credit hour.

Geosciences

Emporia State University (continued)

Tuition, nonresident: full-time $13,572; part-time $566 per credit hour. Required fees: $1022; $62 per credit hour. Tuition and fees vary according to course level, course load and campus/location. *Financial support:* In 2010–11, 2 research assistantships with full tuition reimbursements (averaging $7,059 per year), 8 teaching assistantships with full tuition reimbursements (averaging $7,857 per year) were awarded; Federal Work-Study, institutionally sponsored loans, health care benefits, and unspecified assistantships also available. Financial award application deadline: 3/15; financial award applicants required to submit FAFSA. *Faculty research:* Bredigite, larnite, and dicalcium silicates–Marble Canyon. *Unit head:* Dr. DeWayne Backhus, Chair, 620-341-5330, Fax: 620-341-6055, E-mail: dbackhus@emporia.edu. *Application contact:* Dr. DeWayne Backhus, Chair, 620-341-5330, Fax: 620-341-6055, E-mail: dbackhus@emporia.edu.

Florida Atlantic University, Charles E. Schmidt College of Science, Department of Geosciences, Boca Raton, FL 33431-0991. Offers geography (MA); geology (MS); geosciences (PhD). Part-time programs available. *Faculty:* 14 full-time (3 women), 1 part-time/adjunct (0 women). *Students:* 24 full-time (14 women), 12 part-time (5 women); includes 5 minority (1 Asian, non-Hispanic/Latino; 4 Hispanic/Latino), 3 international. Average age 34. 25 applicants, 52% accepted, 11 enrolled. In 2010, 6 master's awarded. *Degree requirements:* For master's, thesis (for some programs). *Entrance requirements:* For master's, GRE General Test, minimum GPA of 3.0. *Application deadline:* For fall admission, 3/15 for domestic and international students; for spring admission, 10/15 for domestic and international students. Applications are processed on a rolling basis. Application fee: $30. Electronic applications accepted. *Expenses:* Tuition, area resident: Part-time $319.96 per credit. Tuition, state resident: part-time $319.96 per credit. Tuition, nonresident: part-time $926.42 per credit. *Financial support:* Research assistantships with partial tuition reimbursements, teaching assistantships with partial tuition reimbursements, career-related internships or fieldwork, Federal Work-Study, institutionally sponsored loans, and unspecified assistantships available. *Faculty research:* GIS applications, paleontology, hydrogeology, economic development. *Unit head:* Dr. Russell Ivy, Chair, 561-297-3295, Fax: 561-297-2745, E-mail: ivy@fau.edu. *Application contact:* Dr. David Warburton, Graduate Coordinator, 561-297-3312, Fax: 561-297-2745, E-mail: warburto@fau.edu.

Florida International University, College of Arts and Sciences, Department of Earth and Environment, Program in Geosciences, Miami, FL 33199. Offers MS, PhD. Part-time and evening/weekend programs available. *Students:* 31 full-time (14 women), 6 part-time (4 women); includes 4 Black or African American, non-Hispanic/Latino; 8 Hispanic/Latino, 10 international. Average age 28. 43 applicants, 23% accepted, 10 enrolled. In 2010, 5 master's, 1 doctorate awarded. *Degree requirements:* For master's, thesis optional; for doctorate, comprehensive exam, thesis/dissertation. *Entrance requirements:* For master's, GRE (minimum score of 1000), minimum GPA of 3.0 during last two years of undergraduate study, letter of intent, 3 letters of recommendation, resume; for doctorate, GRE (minimum score of 1120), minimum GPA of 3.0 during last two years of undergraduate study, letter of intent, 3 letters of recommendation, resume. Additional exam requirements/recommendations for international students: Required—TOEFL (minimum score 550 paper-based; 80 iBT). *Application deadline:* For fall admission, 2/15 for domestic and international students; for spring admission, 9/1 for domestic and international students. Application fee: $30. Electronic applications accepted. *Financial support:* Institutionally sponsored loans and scholarships/grants available. Financial award application deadline: 3/1; financial award applicants required to submit FAFSA. *Unit head:* Dr. Rosemary Hickey-Vargas, Chair, Earth and Environment Department, 305-348-2365, Fax: 305-348-3877. *Application contact:* Dr. Andrew Macfarlane, Earth Sciences, Graduate Program Director, 305-348-2365, Fax: 305-348-3877, E-mail: macfarla@fiu.edu.

Fort Hays State University, Graduate School, College of Arts and Sciences, Department of Geosciences, Program in Geosciences, Hays, KS 67601-4099. Offers geography (MS); geology (MS). *Degree requirements:* For master's, comprehensive exam, thesis. *Entrance requirements:* For master's, GRE General Test. Additional exam requirements/recommendations for international students: Required—TOEFL (minimum score 550 paper-based; 213 computer-based). Electronic applications accepted. *Faculty research:* Cretaceous and late Cenozoic stratigraphy, sedimentation, paleontology.

George Mason University, College of Science, Department of Geography and Geoinformation Science, Fairfax, VA 22030. Offers earth system science (MS); earth systems and geoinformation sciences (PhD); geographic and cartographic sciences (MS); geographic information sciences (Certificate); geoinformatics and geospatial intelligence (MS); geospatial intelligence (Certificate); remote sensing (Certificate). *Faculty:* 31 full-time (7 women), 7 part-time/adjunct (0 women). *Students:* 32 full-time (8 women), 194 part-time (69 women); includes 23 minority (4 Black or African American, non-Hispanic/Latino; 1 American Indian or Alaska Native, non-Hispanic/Latino; 6 Asian, non-Hispanic/Latino; 8 Hispanic/Latino; 1 Native Hawaiian or other Pacific Islander, non-Hispanic/Latino; 3 Two or more races, non-Hispanic/Latino), 27 international. Average age 35. 156 applicants, 74% accepted, 82 enrolled. In 2010, 23 master's, 1 doctorate, 24 other advanced degrees awarded. *Degree requirements:* For master's, thesis optional. *Entrance requirements:* For master's, GRE General Test, minimum GPA of 3.0 in last 60 hours; BS or BA in geography, cartography, or related field. Additional exam requirements/recommendations for international students: Required—TOEFL (minimum score 570 paper-based; 230 computer-based; 88 iBT). *Application deadline:* For fall admission, 5/1 for domestic students; for spring admission, 11/1 for domestic students. Application fee: $100. Electronic applications accepted. *Expenses:* Tuition, state resident: full-time $8192; part-time $440 per credit hour. Tuition, nonresident: full-time $22,952; part-time $1055 per credit hour. Required fees: $2364; $99 per credit hour. *Financial support:* In 2010–11, 23 students received support, including 2 fellowships with full tuition reimbursements available (averaging $18,000 per year), 17 research assistantships with full and partial tuition reimbursements available (averaging $16,244 per year), 4 teaching assistantships with full and partial tuition reimbursements available (averaging $10,345 per year); career-related internships or fieldwork, Federal Work-Study, scholarships/grants, unspecified assistantships, and health care benefits (full-time research or teaching assistantship recipients) also available. Support available to part-time students. Financial award application deadline: 3/1; financial award applicants required to submit FAFSA. *Faculty research:* Gender and earth science, earth science education, remote sensing, planetary geology, hydrology. Total annual research expenditures: $912,752. *Unit head:* Agouris Peggy, Chair, 703-993-9265, Fax: 703-993-9230, E-mail: pagouris@gmu.edu. *Application contact:* Tim Born, Associate Dean of Academic and Student Affairs, 703-993-4171, Fax: 703-993-9034, E-mail: tborn@gmu.edu.

Georgia Institute of Technology, Graduate Studies and Research, College of Sciences, School of Earth and Atmospheric Sciences, Atlanta, GA 30332-0340. Offers atmospheric chemistry, aerosols and clouds (MS, PhD); dynamics of weather and climate (MS, PhD); geochemistry (MS, PhD); geophysics (MS, PhD); oceanography (MS, PhD); paleoclimate (MS, PhD); planetary science (MS, PhD); remote sensing (MS, PhD). Part-time programs available. Terminal master's awarded for partial completion of doctoral program. *Degree requirements:* For master's, thesis or alternative; for doctorate, comprehensive exam, thesis/dissertation. *Entrance requirements:* For master's, GRE, letters of recommendation; for doctorate, GRE, academic transcripts, letters of recommendation, personal statement. Additional exam requirements/recommendations for international students: Required—TOEFL (minimum score 550 paper-based; 213 computer-based; 79 iBT). *Faculty research:* Geophysics; atmospheric chemistry, aerosols and clouds; dynamics of weather and climate; geochemistry; oceanography; paleoclimate; planetary science; remote sensing.

Georgia State University, College of Arts and Sciences, Department of Geosciences, Atlanta, GA 30302-3083. Offers geographic information systems (Certificate); geography (MA); geology (MA); hydrogeology (Certificate). Part-time and evening/weekend programs available. *Degree requirements:* For master's, one foreign language, comprehensive exam (for some programs), thesis or alternative. *Entrance requirements:* For master's, GRE General Test, minimum GPA of 2.75. Additional exam requirements/recommendations for international students: Required—TOEFL. Electronic applications accepted. *Faculty research:* Clay mineralogy, geoinformatics, fracture analysis, sedimentology, groundwater.

Graduate School and University Center of the City University of New York, Graduate Studies, Program in Earth and Environmental Sciences, New York, NY 10016-4039. Offers PhD. *Degree requirements:* For doctorate, one foreign language, comprehensive exam, thesis/dissertation. *Entrance requirements:* For doctorate, GRE General Test. Additional exam requirements/recommendations for international students: Required—TOEFL. Electronic applications accepted.

Harvard University, Graduate School of Arts and Sciences, Department of Earth and Planetary Sciences, Cambridge, MA 02138. Offers AM, PhD. Terminal master's awarded for partial completion of doctoral program. *Degree requirements:* For doctorate, comprehensive exam, thesis/dissertation. *Entrance requirements:* For doctorate, GRE General Test. Additional exam requirements/recommendations for international students: Required—TOEFL. Electronic applications accepted. *Expenses:* Tuition: Full-time $34,976. Required fees: $1166. Full-time tuition and fees vary according to program. *Faculty research:* Economic geography, geochemistry, geophysics, mineralogy, crystallography.

Hofstra University, School of Education, Health, and Human Services, Programs in Teaching—Secondary Education, Hempstead, NY 11549. Offers business education (MS Ed); English education (MA, MS Ed); foreign language and TESOL (MS Ed); foreign language education (MA, MS Ed), including French, German, Russian, Spanish; mathematics education (MA, MS Ed); science education (MA, MS Ed), including biology, chemistry, earth science, geology, physics; secondary education (Advanced Certificate); social studies education (MA, MS Ed). Part-time and evening/weekend programs available. Postbaccalaureate distance learning degree programs offered (minimal on-campus study). *Students:* 114 full-time (74 women), 61 part-time (36 women); includes 7 Black or African American, non-Hispanic/Latino; 1 American Indian or Alaska Native, non-Hispanic/Latino; 8 Asian, non-Hispanic/Latino; 10 Hispanic/Latino; 1 Native Hawaiian or other Pacific Islander, non-Hispanic/Latino. Average age 27. 153 applicants, 90% accepted, 59 enrolled. In 2010, 102 master's, 11 other advanced degrees awarded. *Degree requirements:* For master's, one foreign language, comprehensive exam (for some programs), thesis (for some programs), exit project, electronic portfolio, student teaching, fieldwork, curriculum project; for Advanced Certificate, 3 foreign languages, comprehensive exam (for some programs), thesis project. *Entrance requirements:* For master's, 2 letters of recommendation, teacher certification (MA), essay; for Advanced Certificate, 2 letters of recommendation, essay, interview and/or portfolio. Additional exam requirements/recommendations for international students: Required—TOEFL (minimum score 550 paper-based; 213 computer-based; 80 iBT). *Application deadline:* Applications are processed on a rolling basis. Application fee: $70 ($75 for international students). Electronic applications accepted. *Expenses:* Tuition: Full-time $18,000; part-time $1000 per credit hour. Required fees: $970; $145 per term. Tuition and fees vary according to program. *Financial support:* In 2010–11, 108 students received support, including 14 fellowships with full and partial tuition reimbursements available (averaging $3,943 per year), 1 research assistantship with full and partial tuition reimbursement available (averaging $6,574 per year); career-related internships or fieldwork, Federal Work-Study, institutionally sponsored loans, scholarships/grants, tuition waivers (full and partial), unspecified assistantships, and scholarships also available. Support available to part-time students. Financial award applicants required to submit FAFSA. *Faculty research:* Appropriate content and pedagogy in secondary school disciplines, adolescent development, secondary school organization, alternative secondary school programs. *Unit head:* Dr. Esther Fusco, Chairperson, 516-463-7704, Fax: 516-463-6196, E-mail: catezf@hofstra.edu. *Application contact:* Carol Drummer, Dean of Graduate Admissions, 516-463-4876, Fax: 516-463-4664, E-mail: gradstudent@hofstra.edu.

Hunter College of the City University of New York, Graduate School, School of Arts and Sciences, Department of Geography, New York, NY 10021-5085. Offers analytical geography (MA); earth system science (MA); environmental and social issues (MA); geographic information science (Certificate); geographic information systems (MA); teaching earth science (MA). Part-time and evening/weekend programs available. *Faculty:* 13 full-time (7 women), 8 part-time/adjunct (1 woman). *Students:* 2 full-time (both women), 50 part-time (23 women); includes 5 Black or African American, non-Hispanic/Latino; 4 Asian, non-Hispanic/Latino; 5 Hispanic/Latino. Average age 31. 22 applicants, 82% accepted, 12 enrolled. In 2010, 15 master's, 3 other advanced degrees awarded. *Degree requirements:* For master's, comprehensive exam or thesis. *Entrance requirements:* For master's, GRE General Test, minimum B average in major, B- overall; 18 credits of course work in geography; 2 letters of recommendation; for Certificate, minimum B average in major, B- overall. Additional exam requirements/recommendations for international students: Required—TOEFL. *Application deadline:* For fall admission, 4/1 for domestic students; for spring admission, 11/1 for domestic students. Applications are processed on a rolling basis. Application fee: $125. *Financial support:* In 2010–11, 1 fellowship (averaging $3,000 per year), 2 research assistantships (averaging $10,000 per year), 10 teaching assistantships (averaging $6,000 per year) were awarded; career-related internships or fieldwork, Federal Work-Study, institutionally sponsored loans, and unspecified assistantships also available. Financial award application deadline: 3/1. *Faculty research:* Urban geography, economic geography, geographic information science, demographic methods, climate change. *Unit head:* Prof. William Solecki, Chair, 212-772-4536, Fax: 212-772-5268, E-mail: wsolecki@hunter.cuny.edu. *Application contact:* Prof. Marianna Pavlovskaya, Graduate Adviser, 212-772-5320, Fax: 212-772-5268, E-mail: mpavlov@geo.hunter.cuny.edu.

Hunter College of the City University of New York, Graduate School, School of Education, Programs in Secondary Education, New York, NY 10021-5085. Offers biology education (MA); chemistry education (MA); earth science (MA); English education (MA); French education (MA); Italian education (MA); mathematics education (MA); physics education (MA); social studies education (MA); Spanish education (MA). *Accreditation:* NCATE. *Faculty:* 59 full-time (25 women), 39 part-time/adjunct (29 women). *Students:* 30 full-time (19 women), 224 part-time (136 women); includes 16 Black or African American, non-Hispanic/Latino; 1 American Indian or Alaska Native, non-Hispanic/Latino; 23 Asian, non-Hispanic/Latino; 30 Hispanic/Latino, 6 international. Average age 31. 788 applicants, 45% accepted, 233 enrolled. In 2010, 113 master's awarded. *Degree requirements:* For master's, thesis. *Entrance requirements:* Additional exam requirements/recommendations for international students: Required—TOEFL. *Application deadline:* For fall admission, 4/1 for domestic students, 2/1 for international students; for spring admission, 11/1 for domestic students, 9/1 for international students. Applications are processed on a rolling basis. Application fee: $125. *Financial support:* Fellowships, tuition waivers (full and partial) available. Support available to part-time students. *Unit head:* Dr. Kate Garret, Coordinator, 212-772-4700, E-mail: kgarret@hunter.cuny.edu. *Application contact:* Milena Solo, Director for Graduate Admissions, 212-772-4482, Fax: 212-650-3336, E-mail: milena.solo@hunter.cuny.edu.

Idaho State University, Office of Graduate Studies, College of Arts and Sciences, Department of Geosciences, Pocatello, ID 83209-8072. Offers geographic information science (MS); geology (MNS, MS); geology with emphasis in environmental geoscience (MS); geophysics/hydrology/geology (MS); geotechnology (Postbaccalaureate Certificate). Part-time programs available. *Degree requirements:* For master's, comprehensive exam, thesis, oral colloquium; for Postbaccalaureate Certificate, thesis optional, minimum 19 credits. *Entrance requirements:* For master's, GRE General Test (minimum 50th percentile in 2 sections), 3 letters of recommendation; for Postbaccalaureate Certificate, GRE General Test, 3 letters of recommendation, bachelor's degree, statement of goals. Additional exam requirements/recommendations for

international students: Required—TOEFL (minimum score 550 paper-based; 213 computer-based; 80 iBT). Electronic applications accepted. *Faculty research:* Quantitative field mapping and sampling: microscopic, geochemical, and isotopic analysis of rocks, minerals and water; remote sensing, geographic information systems, and global positioning systems: environmental and watershed management; surficial and fluvial processes: landscape change; regional tectonics, structural geology; planetary geology.

Indiana University Bloomington, University Graduate School, College of Arts and Sciences, Department of Geological Sciences, Bloomington, IN 47405-7000. Offers biogeochemistry (MS, PhD); economic geology (MS, PhD); geobiology (MS, PhD); geophysics, structural geology and tectonics (MS, PhD); hydrogeology (MS, PhD); mineralogy (MS, PhD); stratigraphy and sedimentology (MS, PhD). *Faculty:* 17 full-time (1 woman). *Students:* 48 full-time (24 women), 5 part-time (1 woman); includes 4 minority (2 Black or African American, non-Hispanic/Latino; 1 Hispanic/Latino; 1 Two or more races, non-Hispanic/Latino), 20 international. Average age 29. 70 applicants, 24% accepted, 16 enrolled. In 2010, 3 master's, 4 doctorates awarded. Terminal master's awarded for partial completion of doctoral program. *Degree requirements:* For master's, thesis or alternative; for doctorate, comprehensive exam, thesis/dissertation. *Entrance requirements:* For master's and doctorate, GRE General Test. Additional exam requirements/recommendations for international students: Required—TOEFL. *Application deadline:* For fall admission, 1/15 priority date for domestic students, 12/15 for international students; for spring admission, 9/1 priority date for domestic students, 9/1 for international students. Applications are processed on a rolling basis. Application fee: $55 ($65 for international students). *Financial support:* In 2010–11, 10 fellowships with full tuition reimbursements (averaging $17,300 per year), 6 research assistantships with full tuition reimbursements (averaging $16,370 per year), 12 teaching assistantships with full tuition reimbursements (averaging $15,150 per year) were awarded; career-related internships or fieldwork, Federal Work-Study, and institutionally sponsored loans also available. *Faculty research:* Geophysics, geochemistry, hydrogeology, geobiology, planetary science. Total annual research expenditures: $644,299. *Unit head:* Simon Brassell, Chair, 812-855-5581, Fax: 812-855-7899, E-mail: geochair@indiana.edu. *Application contact:* Mary Iverson, Graduate Secretary, 812-855-7214, Fax: 812-855-7899, E-mail: miverson@indiana.edu.

Indiana University–Purdue University Indianapolis, School of Science, Department of Earth Sciences, Indianapolis, IN 46202-3272. Offers applied earth sciences (PhD); geology (MS). Part-time and evening/weekend programs available. *Faculty:* 8 full-time (2 women). *Students:* 10 full-time (8 women), 8 part-time (3 women), 8 international. Average age 29. 12 applicants, 58% accepted, 5 enrolled. In 2010, 7 master's awarded. *Degree requirements:* For master's, thesis (for some programs). *Entrance requirements:* For master's, GRE General Test, minimum GPA of 3.0. Application fee: $55 ($65 for international students). *Financial support:* In 2010–11, 2 fellowships with full tuition reimbursements (averaging $12,000 per year), 7 teaching assistantships with full tuition reimbursements (averaging $12,103 per year) were awarded; research assistantships with full tuition reimbursements, scholarships/grants also available. Financial award application deadline: 3/1. *Faculty research:* Wetland hydrology, groundwater contamination, soils, sedimentology, sediment chemistry. *Unit head:* Gabriel Filippelli, Chair, 317-274-7484, Fax: 317-274-7966. *Application contact:* Lenore P. Tedesco, Associate Professor, 317-274-7484, Fax: 317-274-7966, E-mail: ltedesco@iupui.edu.

Iowa State University of Science and Technology, Graduate College, College of Liberal Arts and Sciences, Department of Geological and Atmospheric Sciences, Ames, IA 50011. Offers earth science (MS, PhD); environmental science (MS, PhD); geology (MS, PhD); meteorology (MS, PhD). *Faculty:* 20 full-time (2 women). *Students:* 33 full-time (8 women), 8 part-time (3 women); includes 1 Asian, non-Hispanic/Latino, 3 international. 45 applicants, 49% accepted, 9 enrolled. In 2010, 9 master's, 5 doctorates awarded. *Degree requirements:* For master's, thesis (for some programs); for doctorate, thesis/dissertation. *Entrance requirements:* For master's and doctorate, GRE General Test. Additional exam requirements/recommendations for international students: Required—TOEFL (minimum score 550 paper-based; 79 iBT), IELTS (minimum score 6.5). *Application deadline:* For fall admission, 1/1 priority date for domestic students. Applications are processed on a rolling basis. Application fee: $40 ($90 for international students). Electronic applications accepted. *Financial support:* In 2010–11, 23 research assistantships with full and partial tuition reimbursements (averaging $12,780 per year), 8 teaching assistantships with full and partial tuition reimbursements (averaging $6,806 per year) were awarded; fellowships, scholarships/grants, health care benefits, and unspecified assistantships also available. *Unit head:* Dr. Carl E. Jacobson, Chair, 515-294-4477. *Application contact:* Dr. Carl E. Jacobson, Chair, 515-294-4477.

The Johns Hopkins University, Zanvyl Krieger School of Arts and Sciences, The Morton K. Blaustein Department of Earth and Planetary Sciences, Baltimore, MD 21218-2699. Offers MA, PhD. *Faculty:* 12 full-time (2 women), 1 (woman) part-time/adjunct. *Students:* 24 full-time (12 women); includes 3 minority (2 Hispanic/Latino; 1 Two or more races, non-Hispanic/Latino), 8 international. Average age 28. 32 applicants, 44% accepted, 12 enrolled. In 2010, 3 master's, 6 doctorates awarded. *Degree requirements:* For doctorate, comprehensive exam, thesis/dissertation. *Entrance requirements:* For master's and doctorate, GRE General Test. Additional exam requirements/recommendations for international students: Required—TOEFL (minimum score 600 paper-based; 250 computer-based; 100 iBT), IELTS. *Application deadline:* For fall admission, 1/15 for domestic and international students. Application fee: $75. Electronic applications accepted. *Financial support:* In 2010–11, 23 students received support, including 14 fellowships with full tuition reimbursements available (averaging $24,666 per year), 7 research assistantships with full tuition reimbursements available (averaging $24,666 per year), 5 teaching assistantships with full tuition reimbursements available (averaging $24,666 per year); institutionally sponsored loans, scholarships/grants, traineeships, health care benefits, tuition waivers (full), and unspecified assistantships also available. Financial award application deadline: 4/15; financial award applicants required to submit FAFSA. *Faculty research:* Oceanography, atmospheric sciences, geophysics, geology, geochemistry. Total annual research expenditures: $2.2 million. *Unit head:* Dr. Darryn Waugh, Chair, 410-516-8344, Fax: 410-516-7933, E-mail: waugh@jhu.edu. *Application contact:* Kristen L. Gaines, Academic Program Coordinator, 410-516-7034, Fax: 410-516-7933, E-mail: kgaines@jhu.edu.

Lehigh University, College of Arts and Sciences, Department of Earth and Environmental Sciences, Bethlehem, PA 18015. Offers MS, PhD. *Faculty:* 14 full-time (1 woman), 1 (woman) part-time/adjunct. *Students:* 26 full-time (10 women), 2 part-time (1 woman), 4 international. Average age 27. 57 applicants, 23% accepted, 10 enrolled. In 2010, 10 master's, 1 doctorate awarded. Terminal master's awarded for partial completion of doctoral program. *Degree requirements:* For master's, thesis; for doctorate, thesis/dissertation. *Entrance requirements:* For master's and doctorate, GRE General Test, transcripts, recommendation letters, research statement, faculty advocates. Additional exam requirements/recommendations for international students: Required—TOEFL (minimum score 85 iBT). *Application deadline:* For fall admission, 1/15 for domestic and international students. Applications are processed on a rolling basis. Application fee: $75. Electronic applications accepted. *Financial support:* In 2010–11, 13 students received support, including 3 fellowships with full tuition reimbursements available (averaging $15,400 per year), 12 research assistantships with full tuition reimbursements available (averaging $15,400 per year), 10 teaching assistantships with full tuition reimbursements available (averaging $15,400 per year); career-related internships or fieldwork, Federal Work-Study, institutionally sponsored loans, scholarships/grants, tuition waivers (full and partial), and unspecified assistantships also available. Support available to part-time students. Financial award application deadline: 1/15. *Faculty research:* Tectonics, surficial processes, ecology, environmental change. Total annual research expenditures: $1.1 million. *Unit head:* Dr. Frank J. Pazzaglia, Chairman, 610-758-3667, Fax: 610-758-3677, E-mail: fjp3@lehigh.edu. *Application contact:* Dr. Zicheng Yu, Graduate Coordinator, 610-758-6751, Fax: 610-758-3677, E-mail: ziy2@lehigh.edu.

Loma Linda University, School of Science and Technology, Department of Biological and Earth Sciences, Loma Linda, CA 92350. Offers MS, PhD. *Degree requirements:* For master's, comprehensive exam, thesis; for doctorate, comprehensive exam, thesis/dissertation. *Entrance requirements:* For master's, minimum GPA of 3.0. Additional exam requirements/recommendations for international students: Required—TOEFL (minimum score 550 paper-based; 213 computer-based).

Long Island University, C.W. Post Campus, College of Liberal Arts and Sciences, Department of Earth and Environmental Science, Brookville, NY 11548-1300. Offers earth science (MS); earth science education (MS); environmental studies (MS).

Massachusetts Institute of Technology, School of Science, Department of Earth, Atmospheric, and Planetary Sciences, Cambridge, MA 02139. Offers atmospheric chemistry (PhD, Sc D); atmospheric science (SM, PhD, Sc D); chemical oceanography (SM, PhD, Sc D); climate physics and chemistry (SM, PhD, Sc D); earth and planetary sciences (SM); geochemistry (PhD, Sc D); geology (PhD, Sc D); geophysics (PhD, Sc D); marine geology and geophysics (SM, PhD, Sc D); physical oceanography (SM, PhD, Sc D); planetary sciences (PhD, Sc D). *Faculty:* 36 full-time (7 women). *Students:* 165 full-time (86 women); includes 17 minority (2 Black or African American, non-Hispanic/Latino; 2 American Indian or Alaska Native, non-Hispanic/Latino; 5 Asian, non-Hispanic/Latino; 5 Hispanic/Latino; 3 Two or more races, non-Hispanic/Latino), 50 international. Average age 27. 227 applicants, 33% accepted, 38 enrolled. In 2010, 12 master's, 26 doctorates awarded. Terminal master's awarded for partial completion of doctoral program. *Degree requirements:* For master's, thesis; for doctorate, comprehensive exam, thesis/dissertation. *Entrance requirements:* For master's, GRE General Test; for doctorate, GRE General Test, GRE Subject Test (chemistry or physics for planetary science area). Additional exam requirements/recommendations for international students: Required—TOEFL (minimum score 577 paper-based; 233 computer-based; 91 iBT), IELTS (minimum score 7). *Application deadline:* For fall admission, 1/5 for domestic and international students; for spring admission, 11/1 for domestic and international students. Application fee: $75. Electronic applications accepted. *Expenses:* Tuition: Full-time $38,940; part-time $605 per unit. Required fees: $272. *Financial support:* In 2010–11, 123 students received support, including 62 fellowships with tuition reimbursements available (averaging $30,852 per year), 88 research assistantships with tuition reimbursements available (averaging $30,258 per year), 13 teaching assistantships with tuition reimbursements available (averaging $30,323 per year); Federal Work-Study, institutionally sponsored loans, scholarships/grants, health care benefits, and unspecified assistantships also available. *Faculty research:* Formation, dynamics and evolution of planetary systems; origin, composition, structure and dynamics of the atmospheres, oceans, surfaces and interiors of the Earth and other planets; evolution and interaction of the physical, chemical, geological and biological components of the Earth system; characterization of past, present and potential future climates and the causes and consequences of climate change; interplay of energy and the environment. Total annual research expenditures: $24.8 million. *Unit head:* Prof. Maria Zuber, Department Head, 617-253-2127, Fax: 617-253-8298, E-mail: eapsinfo@mit.edu. *Application contact:* EAPS Education Office, 617-253-3381, Fax: 617-253-8298, E-mail: eapsinfo@mit.edu.

McGill University, Faculty of Graduate and Postdoctoral Studies, Faculty of Science, Department of Earth and Planetary Sciences, Montréal, QC H3A 2T5, Canada. Offers M Sc, PhD.

McMaster University, School of Graduate Studies, Faculty of Science, School of Geography and Earth Sciences, Hamilton, ON L8S 4M2, Canada. Offers geochemistry (PhD); geology (M Sc, PhD); human geography (MA, PhD); physical geography (M Sc, PhD). Part-time programs available. Terminal master's awarded for partial completion of doctoral program. *Degree requirements:* For master's, thesis; for doctorate, comprehensive exam, thesis/dissertation. *Entrance requirements:* For master's, minimum B+ average. Additional exam requirements/recommendations for international students: Required—TOEFL (minimum score 550 paper-based; 213 computer-based).

Memorial University of Newfoundland, School of Graduate Studies, Department of Earth Sciences, St. John's, NL A1C 5S7, Canada. Offers geology (M Sc, PhD); geophysics (M Sc, PhD). Part-time programs available. *Degree requirements:* For master's, thesis; for doctorate, comprehensive exam, thesis/dissertation, oral thesis defense, entry evaluation. *Entrance requirements:* For master's, honors B Sc; for doctorate, M Sc. Electronic applications accepted. *Faculty research:* Geochemistry, sedimentology, paleoceanography and global change, mineral deposits, petroleum geology, hydrology.

Michigan State University, The Graduate School, College of Natural Science, Department of Geological Sciences, East Lansing, MI 48824. Offers environmental geosciences (MS, PhD); environmental geosciences-environmental toxicology (PhD); geological sciences (MS, PhD). *Degree requirements:* For master's, thesis (for those without prior thesis work); for doctorate, thesis/dissertation. *Entrance requirements:* For master's, GRE General Test, minimum GPA of 3.0, course work in geoscience, 3 letters of recommendation; for doctorate, GRE General Test, 3 letters of recommendation. Additional exam requirements/recommendations for international students: Required—TOEFL (minimum score 550 paper-based; 213 computer-based), Michigan State University ELT (minimum score 85), Michigan English Language Assessment Battery (minimum score 83). Electronic applications accepted. *Faculty research:* Water in the environment, global and biological change, crystal dynamics.

Middle Tennessee State University, College of Graduate Studies, College of Liberal Arts, Department of Geosciences, Murfreesboro, TN 37132. Offers Graduate Certificate. Part-time and evening/weekend programs available. Postbaccalaureate distance learning degree programs offered. *Entrance requirements:* Additional exam requirements/recommendations for international students: Required—TOEFL (minimum score 525 paper-based; 195 computer-based; 71 iBT) or IELTS (minimum score 6). *Expenses:* Tuition, state resident: full-time $4632. Tuition, nonresident: full-time $11,520. *Financial support:* Application deadline: 5/1. *Unit head:* Dr. Ronald L. Zawislak, Chair, 615-898-2726, Fax: 615-898-5592, E-mail: rlz1@mtsu.edu. *Application contact:* Dr. Michael Allen, Dean and Vice Provost for Research, 615-898-2840, Fax: 615-904-8020, E-mail: mallen@mtsu.edu.

Mississippi State University, College of Arts and Sciences, Department of Geosciences, Mississippi State, MS 39762. Offers earth and atmospheric science (PhD); geoscience (MS). MA program is only available online. Postbaccalaureate distance learning degree programs offered (no on-campus study). *Faculty:* 20 full-time (3 women), 1 part-time/adjunct (0 women). *Students:* 65 full-time (16 women), 258 part-time (142 women); includes 35 minority (12 Black or African American, non-Hispanic/Latino; 6 American Indian or Alaska Native, non-Hispanic/Latino; 4 Asian, non-Hispanic/Latino; 12 Hispanic/Latino; 1 Two or more races, non-Hispanic/Latino), 8 international. Average age 36. 204 applicants, 88% accepted, 146 enrolled. In 2010, 107 master's awarded. *Degree requirements:* For master's, thesis (for some programs), comprehensive oral or written exam. *Entrance requirements:* For master's, GRE (for on-campus applicants), minimum undergraduate GPA of 2.75. Additional exam requirements/recommendations for international students: Required—TOEFL (minimum score 475 paper-based; 153 computer-based; 53 iBT); Recommended—IELTS (minimum score 4.5). *Application deadline:* For fall admission, 7/1 for domestic students, 5/1 for international students; for spring admission, 11/1 for domestic students, 9/1 for international students. Applications are processed on a rolling basis. Application fee: $40. Electronic applications accepted. *Expenses:* Tuition, state resident: full-time $2730.50; part-time $304 per credit hour. Tuition, nonresident: full-time $6901; part-time $767 per credit hour. *Financial support:* In 2010–11, 13 research assistantships with full tuition reimbursements (averaging $21,646 per year), 24 teaching assistantships with full tuition reimbursements (averaging $13,140 per year) were awarded; Federal Work-Study, institutionally sponsored loans, scholarships/grants, tuition waivers (partial), and

Geosciences

Mississippi State University (continued)

unspecified assistantships also available. Financial award application deadline: 4/1; financial award applicants required to submit FAFSA. *Faculty research:* Climatology, hydrogeology, sedimentology, meteorology. Total annual research expenditures: $5.2 million. *Unit head:* Dr. Darrel Schmitz, Professor and Head, 662-325-3915, Fax: 662-325-9423, E-mail: schmitz@geosci.msstate.edu. *Application contact:* Dr. Christopher P. Dewey, Associate Professor/Graduate Coordinator, 662-325-2909, Fax: 662-325-9423, E-mail: cpd4@msstate.edu.

Missouri State University, Graduate College, College of Natural and Applied Sciences, Department of Geography, Geology, and Planning, Springfield, MO 65897. Offers geospatial sciences (MS); natural and applied science (MNAS), including geography, geology and planning; secondary education (MS Ed), including earth science, geography. Part-time and evening/weekend programs available. *Degree requirements:* For master's, comprehensive exam, thesis (for some programs). *Entrance requirements:* For master's, GRE General Test (MS, MNAS), minimum undergraduate GPA of 3.0 (MS, MNAS), 9-12 teacher certification (MS Ed). Additional exam requirements/recommendations for international students: Required—TOEFL (minimum score 550 paper-based; 213 computer-based; 79 iBT). Electronic applications accepted. *Expenses:* Tuition, state resident: full-time $3348; part-time $186 per credit hour. Tuition, nonresident: full-time $6696; part-time $372 per credit hour. Required fees: $238 per semester. Tuition and fees vary according to course level, course load and program. *Faculty research:* Stratigraphy and ancient meteorite impacts, environmental geochemistry of karst, hyperspectral image processing, water quality, small town planning.

Montana State University, College of Graduate Studies, College of Letters and Science, Department of Earth Sciences, Bozeman, MT 59717. Offers MS, PhD. Part-time programs available. *Faculty:* 12 full-time (2 women), 3 part-time/adjunct (1 woman). *Students:* 13 full-time (6 women), 40 part-time (18 women); includes 4 minority (1 American Indian or Alaska Native, non-Hispanic/Latino; 2 Hispanic/Latino; 1 Two or more races, non-Hispanic/Latino), 8 international. Average age 30. 56 applicants, 25% accepted, 11 enrolled. In 2010, 5 master's, 1 doctorate awarded. *Degree requirements:* For master's, comprehensive exam, thesis (for some programs); for doctorate, comprehensive exam, thesis/dissertation. *Entrance requirements:* For master's and doctorate, GRE General Test, minimum GPA of 3.0. Additional exam requirements/recommendations for international students: Required—TOEFL (minimum score 550 paper-based; 213 computer-based). *Application deadline:* For fall admission, 7/15 priority date for domestic students, 5/15 priority date for international students; for spring admission, 12/1 priority date for domestic students, 10/1 priority date for international students. Applications are processed on a rolling basis. Application fee: $30. Electronic applications accepted. *Expenses:* Tuition, state resident: full-time $5553.90. Tuition, nonresident: full-time $14,646. Required fees: $1233. *Financial support:* In 2010–11, 21 students received support, including 7 research assistantships with full tuition reimbursements available (averaging $13,000 per year), 15 teaching assistantships with full tuition reimbursements available (averaging $10,485 per year); career-related internships or fieldwork, institutionally sponsored loans, scholarships/grants, and traineeships also available. Financial award application deadline: 3/1; financial award applicants required to submit FAFSA. *Faculty research:* Dinosaur paleontology, climate history/geomicrobiology, stratigraphy/sedimentology/structure/carbon sequestration, igneous petrology South America, historical/urban economic geography western U. S. and China. Total annual research expenditures: $961,613. *Unit head:* Dr. Stephan Custer, Head, 406-994-6906, Fax: 406-994-6923, E-mail: scuster@montana.edu. *Application contact:* Dr. Carl A. Fox, Vice Provost for Graduate Education, 406-994-4145, Fax: 406-994-7433, E-mail: gradstudy@montana.edu.

Montana Tech of The University of Montana, Graduate School, Geosciences Programs, Butte, MT 59701-8997. Offers geochemistry (MS); geological engineering (MS); geology (MS); geophysical engineering (MS); hydrogeological engineering (MS); hydrogeology (MS). Part-time programs available. *Faculty:* 16 full-time (4 women), 4 part-time/adjunct (0 women). *Students:* 15 full-time (6 women), 10 part-time (5 women); includes 1 Black or African American, non-Hispanic/Latino; 1 American Indian or Alaska Native, non-Hispanic/Latino, 2 international. 9 applicants, 89% accepted, 8 enrolled. In 2010, 4 master's awarded. *Degree requirements:* For master's, comprehensive exam (for some programs), thesis (for some programs). *Entrance requirements:* For master's, GRE General Test, minimum GPA of 3.0. Additional exam requirements/recommendations for international students: Required—TOEFL (minimum score 525 paper-based; 195 computer-based; 71 iBT). *Application deadline:* For fall admission, 4/1 priority date for domestic students, 3/1 priority date for international students; for spring admission, 10/1 priority date for domestic students, 7/1 priority date for international students. Applications are processed on a rolling basis. Application fee: $30. Electronic applications accepted. *Expenses:* Tuition, state resident: full-time $5084. Tuition, nonresident: full-time $15,104. *Financial support:* In 2010–11, 17 students received support, including 10 teaching assistantships with partial tuition reimbursements available (averaging $5,200 per year); research assistantships with partial tuition reimbursements available, career-related internships or fieldwork, tuition waivers (full and partial), and unspecified assistantships also available. Financial award application deadline: 4/1; financial award applicants required to submit FAFSA. *Faculty research:* Water resource development, seismic processing, petroleum reservoir characterization, environmental geochemistry, geologic mapping. *Unit head:* Dr. Mary MacLaughlin, Department Head, 406-496-4655, Fax: 406-496-4260, E-mail: mmaclaughlin@mtech.edu. *Application contact:* Fred Sullivan, Administrator, Graduate School, 406-496-4304, Fax: 406-496-4710, E-mail: fsullivan@mtech.edu.

Montclair State University, The Graduate School, College of Science and Mathematics, Department of Earth and Environmental Studies, Montclair, NJ 07043-1624. Offers earth science (Certificate); environmental management (MA, PhD); environmental studies (MS), including environmental education, environmental management, environmental science; geographic information science (Certificate); geoscience (MS), including geoscience. Part-time and evening/weekend programs available. *Faculty:* 16 full-time (2 women), 20 part-time/adjunct (7 women). *Students:* 39 full-time (19 women), 59 part-time (29 women); includes 3 Black or African American, non-Hispanic/Latino; 1 Asian, non-Hispanic/Latino; 4 Hispanic/Latino, 17 international. Average age 34. 43 applicants, 65% accepted, 21 enrolled. In 2010, 23 master's, 1 doctorate, 2 other advanced degrees awarded. *Degree requirements:* For master's, comprehensive exam, thesis or alternative; for doctorate, thesis/dissertation. *Entrance requirements:* For master's, GRE General Test, 2 letters of recommendation; for doctorate, GRE General Test, 3 letters of recommendation. Additional exam requirements/recommendations for international students: Required—TOEFL (minimum score: 83 iBT) or IELTS. *Application deadline:* For fall admission, 6/1 for international students; for spring admission, 10/1 for international students. Applications are processed on a rolling basis. Application fee: $60. Electronic applications accepted. *Expenses:* Tuition, state resident: part-time $501.34 per credit. Tuition, nonresident: part-time $773.88 per credit. Required fees: $71.15 per credit. *Financial support:* In 2010–11, 3 fellowships (averaging $15,000 per year); 9 research assistantships with full tuition reimbursements (averaging $7,000 per year), 13 teaching assistantships with full tuition reimbursements (averaging $15,000 per year) were awarded; Federal Work-Study, scholarships/grants, and unspecified assistantships also available. Support available to part-time students. Financial award application deadline: 3/1; financial award applicants required to submit FAFSA. *Faculty research:* Antarctica, carbon pools, contaminated sediments, wetlands. Total annual research expenditures: $712,648. *Unit head:* Dr. Matthew Goring, Chairperson, 973-655-5409. *Application contact:* Amy Aiello, Director of Graduate Admissions and Operations, 973-655-5147, Fax: 973-655-7869, E-mail: graduate.school@montclair.edu.

Murray State University, College of Science, Engineering and Technology, Program in Geosciences, Murray, KY 42071. Offers MS. Part-time programs available. *Degree requirements:* For master's, comprehensive exam, thesis optional. *Entrance requirements:* Additional exam requirements/recommendations for international students: Required—TOEFL, IELTS.

New Mexico Institute of Mining and Technology, Graduate Studies, Department of Earth and Environmental Science, Socorro, NM 87801. Offers geology and geochemistry (MS, PhD), including geochemistry, geology; geophysics (MS, PhD); hydrology (MS, PhD). *Degree requirements:* For master's, thesis optional; for doctorate, thesis/dissertation. *Entrance requirements:* For master's, GRE General Test; for doctorate, GRE General Test, GRE Subject Test. Additional exam requirements/recommendations for international students: Required—TOEFL. *Faculty research:* Seismology, geochemistry, caves and karst topography, hydrology, volcanology.

North Carolina Central University, Division of Academic Affairs, College of Science and Technology, Department of Environmental, Earth and Geospatial Sciences, Durham, NC 27707-3129. Offers earth sciences (MS). *Degree requirements:* For master's, one foreign language, comprehensive exam. *Entrance requirements:* For master's, GRE, minimum GPA of 3.0 in major, 2.5 overall. Additional exam requirements/recommendations for international students: Required—TOEFL.

North Carolina State University, Graduate School, College of Physical and Mathematical Sciences, Department of Marine, Earth, and Atmospheric Sciences, Raleigh, NC 27695. Offers marine, earth, and atmospheric sciences (MS, PhD); meteorology (MS, PhD); oceanography (MS, PhD). PhD offered jointly with The University of North Carolina Wilmington. Terminal master's awarded for partial completion of doctoral program. *Degree requirements:* For master's, thesis (for some programs), final oral exam; for doctorate, comprehensive exam, thesis/dissertation, final oral exam, preliminary oral and written exams. *Entrance requirements:* For master's, GRE General Test, minimum GPA of 3.0; for doctorate, GRE General Test, GRE Subject Test (for disciplines in biological oceanography and geology), minimum GPA of 3.0. Additional exam requirements/recommendations for international students: Required—TOEFL (minimum score 550 paper-based). Electronic applications accepted. *Faculty research:* Boundary layer and air quality meteorology; climate and mesoscale dynamics; biological, chemical, geological, and physical oceanography; hard rock, soft rock, environmental, and paleogeology.

Northwestern University, The Graduate School, Judd A. and Marjorie Weinberg College of Arts and Sciences, Department of Geological Sciences, Evanston, IL 60208. Offers MS, PhD. Admissions and degrees offered through The Graduate School. Part-time programs available. *Degree requirements:* For doctorate, thesis/dissertation. *Entrance requirements:* For master's and doctorate, GRE General Test. Additional exam requirements/recommendations for international students: Required—TOEFL. Electronic applications accepted.

Oregon State University, Graduate School, College of Science, Department of Geosciences, Corvallis, OR 97331. Offers geography (MA, MAIS, MS, PhD); geology (MA, MAIS, MS, PhD). Part-time programs available. Terminal master's awarded for partial completion of doctoral program. *Degree requirements:* For doctorate, one foreign language, thesis/dissertation. *Entrance requirements:* For master's and doctorate, GRE General Test, GRE Subject Test, minimum GPA of 3.0 in last 90 hours. Additional exam requirements/recommendations for international students: Required—TOEFL.

Penn State University Park, Graduate School, College of Earth and Mineral Sciences, Department of Geosciences, State College, University Park, PA 16802-1503. Offers MS, PhD.

Princeton University, Graduate School, Department of Geosciences, Princeton, NJ 08544-1019. Offers atmospheric and oceanic sciences (PhD); geosciences (PhD); ocean sciences and marine biology (PhD). *Degree requirements:* For doctorate, one foreign language, thesis/dissertation. *Entrance requirements:* For doctorate, GRE General Test. Additional exam requirements/recommendations for international students: Required—TOEFL (minimum score 600 paper-based; 250 computer-based). Electronic applications accepted. *Faculty research:* Biogeochemistry, climate science, earth history, regional geology and tectonics, solid-earth geophysics.

Purdue University, Graduate School, College of Science, Department of Earth and Atmospheric Sciences, West Lafayette, IN 47907. Offers MS, PhD. *Degree requirements:* For master's, thesis; for doctorate, one foreign language, thesis/dissertation. *Entrance requirements:* For master's and doctorate, GRE General Test. Additional exam requirements/recommendations for international students: Required—TOEFL. Electronic applications accepted. *Faculty research:* Geology, geophysics, hydrogeology, paleoclimatology, environmental science.

Rice University, Graduate Programs, Wiess School of Natural Sciences, Department of Earth Science, Houston, TX 77251-1892. Offers MS, PhD. Terminal master's awarded for partial completion of doctoral program. *Degree requirements:* For master's, comprehensive exam, thesis, annual department report and presentation, qualifying exam, orals, 2 publications; for doctorate, comprehensive exam, thesis/dissertation, annual department report and presentation, qualifying exam, orals, 3 publications. *Entrance requirements:* For master's and doctorate, GRE. Additional exam requirements/recommendations for international students: Required—TOEFL (minimum score 600 paper-based; 90 iBT), IELTS. Electronic applications accepted. *Faculty research:* Seismology, structural geology, tectonics and paleomagnetism, geodynamics, high temperature geochemistry, volcanic processes.

Rice University, Graduate Programs, Wiess School–Professional Science Master's Programs, Professional Master's Program in Subsurface Geosciences, Houston, TX 77251-1892. Offers geophysics (MS). Part-time programs available. *Degree requirements:* For master's, internship. *Entrance requirements:* For master's, GRE, letters of recommendation (4). Additional exam requirements/recommendations for international students: Required—TOEFL (minimum score 600 paper-based; 250 computer-based; 90 iBT). Electronic applications accepted. *Faculty research:* Seismology, geodynamics, wave propagation, bio-geochemistry, remote sensing.

St. Francis Xavier University, Graduate Studies, Department of Earth Sciences, Antigonish, NS B2G 2W5, Canada. Offers M Sc. *Degree requirements:* For master's, thesis. *Entrance requirements:* Additional exam requirements/recommendations for international students: Required—TOEFL (minimum score 580 paper-based; 236 computer-based). *Faculty research:* Environmental earth sciences, global change tectonics, paleoclimatology, crustal fluids.

Saint Louis University, Graduate Education, College of Arts and Sciences and Graduate Education, Department of Earth and Atmospheric Sciences, St. Louis, MO 63103-2097. Offers geophysics (PhD); geoscience (MS); meteorology (M Pr Met, MS-R, PhD). Part-time programs available. *Degree requirements:* For master's, thesis (for some programs), comprehensive oral exam; for doctorate, thesis/dissertation, preliminary exams. *Entrance requirements:* For master's, GRE General Test, letters of recommendation, resume; for doctorate, GRE General Test, letters of recommendation, resumé, goal statement, transcripts. Additional exam requirements/recommendations for international students: Required—TOEFL (minimum score 525 paper-based; 194 computer-based). Electronic applications accepted. *Faculty research:* Structural geology, mesoscale meteorology and severe storms, weather and climate change prediction.

St. Thomas University, School of Leadership Studies, Institute for Education, Miami Gardens, FL 33054-6459. Offers earth/space science (Certificate); educational administration (MS, Certificate); educational leadership (Ed D); elementary education (MS); ESOL (Certificate); gifted education (Certificate); instructional technology (MS, Certificate); professional/studies (Certificate); reading (MS, Certificate); special education (MS). Part-time and evening/weekend programs available. *Degree requirements:* For master's, comprehensive exam; for doctorate, comprehensive exam, thesis/dissertation. *Entrance requirements:* For master's, interview, minimum GPA of 3.0 or GRE; for doctorate, GRE or MAT. Additional exam requirements/recommendations for international students: Required—TOEFL (minimum score 550 paper-based; 213 computer-based; 79 iBT). Electronic applications accepted.

San Francisco State University, Division of Graduate Studies, College of Science and Engineering, Department of Geosciences, San Francisco, CA 94132-1722. Offers MS. *Application deadline:* Applications are processed on a rolling basis. *Unit head:* Dr. Oswaldo Garcia, Chair, 415-338-2061. *Application contact:* Dr. Karen Grove, Graduate Coordinator, 415-338-2061, E-mail: kgrove@sfsu.edu.

Simon Fraser University, Graduate Studies, Faculty of Science, Department of Earth Sciences, Burnaby, BC V5A 1S6, Canada. Offers M Sc, PhD. Part-time programs available. *Degree requirements:* For master's, thesis. *Entrance requirements:* For master's, minimum GPA of 3.0. Additional exam requirements/recommendations for international students: Required—TOEFL or IELTS. Electronic applications accepted. *Faculty research:* Earth surface processes, environmental geoscience, surficial and Quaternary geology, sedimentology.

South Dakota State University, Graduate School, College of Engineering, Geospatial Science and Engineering Program, Brookings, SD 57007. Offers PhD. Part-time programs available. *Degree requirements:* For doctorate, comprehensive exam, thesis/dissertation. *Entrance requirements:* For doctorate, GRE. Additional exam requirements/recommendations for international students: Required—TOEFL (minimum score 525 paper-based; 197 computer-based; 71 iBT). *Faculty research:* Deforestation, land use/cover change, GIS spatial modeling.

Stanford University, School of Earth Sciences, Department of Geological and Environmental Sciences, Stanford, CA 94305-9991. Offers MS, PhD, Eng. Terminal master's awarded for partial completion of doctoral program. *Degree requirements:* For master's and Eng, thesis; for doctorate, thesis/dissertation. *Entrance requirements:* For master's, doctorate, and Eng, GRE General Test. Additional exam requirements/recommendations for international students: Required—TOEFL. Electronic applications accepted. *Expenses:* Tuition: Full-time $38,700; part-time $860 per unit. One-time fee: $200 full-time.

Stanford University, School of Earth Sciences, Earth Systems Program, Stanford, CA 94305-9991. Offers MS. Students admitted at the undergraduate level. Electronic applications accepted. *Expenses:* Tuition: Full-time $38,700; part-time $860 per unit. One-time fee: $200 full-time.

State University of New York at New Paltz, Graduate School, School of Education, Department of Secondary Education, New Paltz, NY 12561. Offers adolescence education: biology (MAT, MS Ed); adolescence education: chemistry (MAT, MS Ed); adolescence education: earth science (MAT, MS Ed); adolescence education: English (MAT, MS Ed); adolescence education: French (MAT, MS Ed); adolescence education: social studies (MAT, MS Ed); adolescence education: Spanish (MAT, MS Ed); second language education (MS Ed). *Accreditation:* NCATE. Part-time and evening/weekend programs available. *Faculty:* 7 full-time (5 women), 7 part-time/adjunct (5 women). *Students:* 84 full-time (49 women), 78 part-time (52 women); includes 1 Black or African American, non-Hispanic/Latino; 4 Asian, non-Hispanic/Latino; 20 Hispanic/Latino; 2 Two or more races, non-Hispanic/Latino, 1 international. Average age 30. 122 applicants, 75% accepted, 68 enrolled. In 2010, 88 master's awarded. *Degree requirements:* For master's, comprehensive exam (for some programs), portfolio. *Entrance requirements:* For master's, minimum GPA of 3.0, New York state teaching certificate (MS Ed). Additional exam requirements/recommendations for international students: Required—TOEFL (minimum score 550 paper-based; 213 computer-based; 80 iBT), IELTS (minimum score 6.5). *Application deadline:* For fall admission, 3/1 priority date for domestic students, 3/1 for international students; for spring admission, 10/1 priority date for domestic students, 10/1 for international students. Application fee: $50. Electronic applications accepted. *Expenses:* Tuition, state resident: full-time $8370; part-time $349 per credit hour. Tuition, nonresident: full-time $13,780; part-time $574 per credit hour. Required fees: $1165; $33.80 per credit hour. $175 per term. Tuition and fees vary according to program. *Financial support:* In 2010–11, 13 students received support, including 5 fellowships (averaging $5,000 per year), 3 research assistantships with partial tuition reimbursements available (averaging $5,000 per year); Federal Work-Study, institutionally sponsored loans, and tuition waivers (full) also available. Financial award application deadline: 8/1; financial award applicants required to submit FAFSA. *Unit head:* Dr. Devon Duhaney, Chair, 845-257-2850, E-mail: duhaneyd@newpaltz.edu. *Application contact:* Caroline Murphy, Graduate Admissions Advisor, 845-257-3285, Fax: 845-257-3284, E-mail: gradschool@newpaltz.edu.

State University of New York College at Oneonta, Graduate Education, Department of Earth Sciences, Oneonta, NY 13820-4015. Offers MA. Part-time and evening/weekend programs available. *Students:* 2 full-time (1 woman). Average age 26. 1 applicant, 100% accepted, 1 enrolled. In 2010, 1 master's awarded. *Degree requirements:* For master's, thesis. *Entrance requirements:* For master's, GRE General Test. *Application deadline:* For fall admission, 3/25 priority date for domestic students; for spring admission, 10/1 priority date for domestic students. Applications are processed on a rolling basis. Application fee: $50. *Expenses:* Tuition, state resident: full-time $8370; part-time $349 per credit hour. Tuition, nonresident: full-time $13,780; part-time $558 per credit hour. Required fees: $899; $22 per credit hour. *Financial support:* Fellowships available. *Unit head:* Dr. James Ebert, Chair, 607-436-3707, E-mail: ebertjr@oneonta.edu. *Application contact:* Patrick J. Mente, Director of Graduate Studies, 607-436-2523, Fax: 607-436-3084, E-mail: gradstudies@oneonta.edu.

Stony Brook University, State University of New York, Graduate School, College of Arts and Sciences, Department of Geosciences, Stony Brook, NY 11794. Offers earth science (MAT); geosciences (MS, PhD). MAT offered through the School of Professional Development. *Faculty:* 16 full-time (3 women), 2 part-time/adjunct (1 woman). *Students:* 29 full-time (21 women), 5 part-time (1 woman); includes 2 Black or African American, non-Hispanic/Latino; 1 American Indian or Alaska Native, non-Hispanic/Latino, 14 international. Average age 29. 54 applicants, 35% accepted, 7 enrolled. In 2010, 6 master's, 6 doctorates awarded. Terminal master's awarded for partial completion of doctoral program. *Degree requirements:* For master's, thesis or alternative; for doctorate, thesis/dissertation. *Entrance requirements:* For master's and doctorate, GRE General Test, minimum GPA of 3.0. Additional exam requirements/recommendations for international students: Required—TOEFL. *Application deadline:* For fall admission, 1/15 for domestic students. Application fee: $100. *Expenses:* Tuition, state resident: full-time $8370; part-time $349 per credit. Tuition, nonresident: full-time $13,780; part-time $574 per credit. Required fees: $994. *Financial support:* In 2010–11, 18 research assistantships, 9 teaching assistantships were awarded; fellowships also available. *Faculty research:* Astronomy, theoretical and observational astrophysics, paleontology, petrology, crystallography. Total annual research expenditures: $6.6 million. *Unit head:* Dr. Richard Reeder, Chair, 631-632-8139, Fax: 631-632-8240, E-mail: rjreeder@stonybrook.edu. *Application contact:* Dr. Daniel Davis, Director, 631-632-8200, Fax: 631-632-8240, E-mail: daniel.davis@notes.cc.sunysb.edu.

Texas A&M University–Commerce, Graduate School, College of Arts and Sciences, Department of Biological and Earth Sciences, Commerce, TX 75429-3011. Offers M Ed, MS. *Degree requirements:* For master's, comprehensive exam, thesis (for some programs). *Entrance requirements:* For master's, GRE General Test. Electronic applications accepted. *Faculty research:* Microbiology, botany, environmental science, birds.

Texas Tech University, Graduate School, College of Arts and Sciences, Department of Geosciences, Lubbock, TX 79409. Offers atmospheric science (MS); geosciences (MS, PhD). Part-time programs available. *Faculty:* 17 full-time (2 women), 1 part-time/adjunct (0 women). *Students:* 41 full-time (11 women), 18 part-time (6 women); includes 1 Black or African American, non-Hispanic/Latino; 5 Hispanic/Latino, 9 international. Average age 27. 81 applicants, 22% accepted, 15 enrolled. In 2010, 14 master's, 2 doctorates awarded. *Degree requirements:* For master's, thesis or alternative; for doctorate, comprehensive exam, thesis/dissertation. *Entrance requirements:* For master's and doctorate, GRE General Test. Additional exam requirements/recommendations for international students: Required—TOEFL (minimum score 550 paper-based; 213 computer-based; 79 iBT). *Application deadline:* For fall admission, 6/1 priority date for domestic students, 1/15 priority date for international students; for spring admission, 9/1 priority date for domestic students, 6/15 priority date for international students. Applications are processed on a rolling basis. Application fee: $50 ($75 for international students). Electronic applications accepted. *Expenses:* Tuition, state resident: full-time $5495.76; part-time $228.99 per credit hour. Tuition, nonresident: full-time $12,936; part-time $538.99 per credit hour. Required fees: $2674; $36 per credit hour. $905 per semester. *Financial support:* In 2010–11, 30 students received support, including 4 research assistantships with partial tuition reimbursements available (averaging $5,780 per year), 5 teaching assistantships with partial tuition reimbursements available (averaging $2,352 per year). Financial award application deadline: 4/15; financial award applicants required to submit FAFSA. *Faculty research:* Sedimentology and paleontology, geophysics, geochemistry, geospatial technology, hurricanes and severe storms. Total annual research expenditures: $955,317. *Unit head:* Dr. Calvin Barnes, Chairman, 806-742-3102, Fax: 806-742-0100, E-mail: cal.barnes@ttu.edu. *Application contact:* Dr. Seiichi Nagihara, Associate Professor, 806-742-3102, Fax: 806-724-0100, E-mail: seiichi.nagihara@ttu.edu.

Université du Québec à Chicoutimi, Graduate Programs, Program in Earth Sciences, Chicoutimi, QC G7H 2B1, Canada. Offers M Sc A. Part-time programs available. *Degree requirements:* For master's, thesis. *Entrance requirements:* For master's, appropriate bachelor's degree, proficiency in French.

Université du Québec à Montréal, Graduate Programs, Program in Earth and Atmospheric Sciences, Montréal, QC H3C 3P8, Canada. Offers atmospheric sciences (M Sc); Earth and atmospheric sciences (PhD); Earth science (M Sc); meteorology (PhD, Diploma). PhD programs offered jointly with McGill University. Part-time programs available. *Degree requirements:* For master's, thesis. *Entrance requirements:* For master's and Diploma, appropriate bachelor's degree or equivalent, proficiency in French; for doctorate, appropriate master's degree or equivalent, proficiency in French.

Université du Québec à Montréal, Graduate Programs, Program in Earth Sciences, Montreal, QC H3C 3P8, Canada. Offers earth sciences (M Sc); mineral resources (PhD); non-renewable resources (DESS). Part-time programs available. Terminal master's awarded for partial completion of doctoral program. *Degree requirements:* For master's, thesis (for some programs); for doctorate, thesis/dissertation. *Entrance requirements:* For master's, appropriate bachelor's degree or equivalent, proficiency in French. *Faculty research:* Economic geology, structural geology, geochemistry, Quaternary geology, isotopic geochemistry.

Université du Québec, Institut National de la Recherche Scientifique, Graduate Programs, Research Center—Water, Earth and Environment, Québec, QC G1K 9A9, Canada. Offers earth sciences (M Sc, PhD); earth sciences-environmental technologies (M Sc); water sciences (M Sc, PhD). Part-time programs available. *Faculty:* 41. *Students:* 196 full-time (79 women), 17 part-time (5 women), 94 international. Average age 30. In 2010, 19 master's, 17 doctorates awarded. *Degree requirements:* For master's, thesis optional; for doctorate, thesis/dissertation. *Entrance requirements:* For master's, appropriate bachelor's degree, proficiency in French; for doctorate, appropriate master's degree, proficiency in French. *Application deadline:* For fall admission, 3/30 for domestic and international students; for winter admission, 11/1 for domestic and international students; for spring admission, 3/1 for domestic and international students. Application fee: $30. *Financial support:* Fellowships, research assistantships, teaching assistantships available. *Faculty research:* Land use, impacts of climate change, adaptation to climate change, integrated management of resources (mineral and water). *Unit head:* Yves Begin, Director, 418-654-2524, Fax: 418-654-2600, E-mail: info@ete.inrs.ca. *Application contact:* Yvonne Boisvert, Registrar, 418-654-3861, Fax: 418-654-3858, E-mail: registrariat@adm.inrs.ca.

Université Laval, Faculty of Sciences and Engineering, Department of Geology and Geological Engineering, Programs in Earth Sciences, Québec, QC G1K 7P4, Canada. Offers earth sciences (M Sc, PhD); environmental technologies (M Sc). Offered jointly with INRS-Géressources. Terminal master's awarded for partial completion of doctoral program. *Degree requirements:* For master's, thesis (for some programs); for doctorate, comprehensive exam, thesis/dissertation. *Entrance requirements:* For master's and doctorate, knowledge of French. Electronic applications accepted.

University at Albany, State University of New York, College of Arts and Sciences, Department of Earth and Atmospheric Sciences, Albany, NY 12222-0001. Offers atmospheric science (MS, PhD); geology (MS, PhD). *Degree requirements:* For master's, one foreign language, comprehensive exam, thesis; for doctorate, 2 foreign languages, comprehensive exam, thesis/dissertation, oral exams. *Entrance requirements:* For master's and doctorate, GRE General Test. Additional exam requirements/recommendations for international students: Required—TOEFL (minimum score 550 paper-based; 213 computer-based). Electronic applications accepted. *Faculty research:* Environmental geochemistry, tectonics, mesoscale meteorology, atmospheric chemistry.

University at Buffalo, the State University of New York, Graduate School, College of Arts and Sciences, Department of Geography, Buffalo, NY 14260. Offers earth systems science (MA); economic geography and international business and world trade (MA); environmental and earth systems science (MS); environmental modeling and analysis (MA); geographic information science (MA, Certificate); geographic information systems and science (MS); geography (MA, PhD); urban and regional geography (MA); MA/MBA. *Faculty:* 14 full-time (6 women), 1 part-time/adjunct (0 women). *Students:* 60 full-time (24 women), 49 part-time (13 women); includes 1 Black or African American, non-Hispanic/Latino; 46 Asian, non-Hispanic/Latino; 4 Hispanic/Latino, 1 international. 162 applicants, 46% accepted, 38 enrolled. In 2010, 21 master's, 5 doctorates awarded. Terminal master's awarded for partial completion of doctoral program. *Degree requirements:* For master's, thesis (for some programs), project; for doctorate, thesis/dissertation. *Entrance requirements:* For master's, GRE General Test, minimum GPA of 2.9; for doctorate, GRE General Test, minimum GPA of 3.0. Additional exam requirements/recommendations for international students: Required—TOEFL (minimum score 550 paper-based; 213 computer-based; 79 iBT). *Application deadline:* For fall admission, 7/1 priority date for domestic students, 1/10 priority date for international students; for spring admission, 12/1 priority date for domestic students, 10/1 priority date for international students. Applications are processed on a rolling basis. Application fee: $75. Electronic applications accepted. *Financial support:* In 2010–11, 19 students received support, including 7 fellowships with full tuition reimbursements available (averaging $5,714 per year), 14 teaching assistantships with full tuition reimbursements available (averaging $13,520 per year); research assistantships with full tuition reimbursements available, career-related internships or fieldwork, Federal Work-Study, institutionally sponsored loans, traineeships, health care benefits, and unspecified assistantships also available. Financial award application deadline: 1/10. *Faculty research:* International business and world trade, geographic information systems and cartography, transportation, urban and regional analysis, physical and environmental geography. Total annual research expenditures: $944,614. *Unit head:* Dr. Sharmistha Bagchi-Sen, Chairman, 716-645-0473, Fax: 716-645-2329, E-mail: geosbs@buffalo.edu. *Application contact:* Betsy Abraham, Graduate Secretary, 716-645-0471, Fax: 716-645-2329, E-mail: babraham@buffalo.edu.

The University of Akron, Graduate School, Buchtel College of Arts and Sciences, Department of Geology, Program in Earth Science, Akron, OH 44325. Offers MS. *Students:* 1 (woman) full-time. Average age 24. 1 applicant, 100% accepted, 0 enrolled. In 2010, 1 master's awarded. *Degree requirements:* For master's, comprehensive exam, thesis, seminar, proficiency exam. *Entrance requirements:* For master's, minimum GPA of 2.75, letters of recommendation, statement of purpose. Additional exam requirements/recommendations for international students: Required—TOEFL (minimum score 550 paper-based; 213 computer-based; 79 iBT). *Application deadline:* Applications are processed on a rolling basis. Application fee:

Geosciences

The University of Akron (continued)

$30 ($40 for international students). Electronic applications accepted. *Expenses:* Tuition, state resident: full-time $6800; part-time $378 per credit hour. Tuition, nonresident: full-time $11,644; part-time $647 per credit hour. Required fees: $1265. One-time fee: $30 full-time. *Unit head:* Dr. LaVerne Friberg, Director of Graduate Studies, 330-972-8046, E-mail: lfribe1@uakron.edu. *Application contact:* Dr. LaVerne Friberg, Director of Graduate Studies, 330-972-8046, E-mail: lfribe1@uakron.edu.

University of Alberta, Faculty of Graduate Studies and Research, Department of Earth and Atmospheric Sciences, Edmonton, AB T6G 2E1, Canada. Offers M Sc, MA, PhD. *Degree requirements:* For master's, thesis, residency; for doctorate, thesis/dissertation, residency. *Entrance requirements:* For master's, B Sc, minimum GPA of 6.5 on a 9.0 scale; for doctorate, M Sc. Additional exam requirements/recommendations for international students: Required—TOEFL or Michigan English Language Assessment Battery. Electronic applications accepted. *Faculty research:* Geology, human geography, physical geography, meteorology.

The University of Arizona, College of Science, Department of Geosciences, Tucson, AZ 85721. Offers MS, PhD. Part-time programs available. *Faculty:* 21 full-time (4 women), 4 part-time/adjunct (0 women). *Students:* 67 full-time (31 women), 10 part-time (3 women); includes 2 Black or African American, non-Hispanic/Latino; 3 Hispanic/Latino; 1 Two or more races, non-Hispanic/Latino, 8 international. Average age 30. 171 applicants, 15% accepted, 13 enrolled. In 2010, 14 master's, 12 doctorates awarded. Terminal master's awarded for partial completion of doctoral program. *Degree requirements:* For master's, thesis or prepublication; for doctorate, comprehensive exam, thesis/dissertation. *Entrance requirements:* For master's, GRE General Test, 3 letters of recommendation, curriculum vitae; for doctorate, GRE General Test, statement of purpose, 3 letters of recommendation, curriculum vitae. Additional exam requirements/recommendations for international students: Required—TOEFL (minimum score 550 paper-based; 213 computer-based; 79 iBT). *Application deadline:* For fall admission, 1/15 for domestic and international students. Applications are processed on a rolling basis. Application fee: $75. Electronic applications accepted. *Expenses:* Tuition, state resident: full-time $7692. *Financial support:* In 2010–11, 36 research assistantships with full tuition reimbursements (averaging $23,134 per year), 24 teaching assistantships with full tuition reimbursements (averaging $22,822 per year) were awarded; career-related internships or fieldwork, institutionally sponsored loans, scholarships/grants, health care benefits, tuition waivers (partial), and unspecified assistantships also available. Financial award application deadline: 1/15. *Faculty research:* Tectonics, geophysics, geochemistry/petrology, economic geology, Quaternary studies, stratigraphy/paleontology. Total annual research expenditures: $4.9 million. *Unit head:* Dr. Karl Flessa, Head, 520-621-7336, Fax: 520-621-2672, E-mail: kflessa@geo.arizona.edu. *Application contact:* Anne Chase, Graduate Program Office, 520-621-6004, Fax: 520-621-2672, E-mail: gradapps@geo.arizona.edu.

University of Arkansas at Little Rock, Graduate School, College of Science and Mathematics, Program in Geospatial Technology, Little Rock, AR 72204-1099. Offers Graduate Certificate.

University of California, Irvine, School of Physical Sciences, Department of Earth System Science, Irvine, CA 92697. Offers MS, PhD. *Students:* 40 full-time (27 women); includes 2 minority (1 Black or African American, non-Hispanic/Latino; 1 Hispanic/Latino), 17 international. Average age 28. 36 applicants, 39% accepted, 7 enrolled. In 2010, 14 master's, 5 doctorates awarded. *Degree requirements:* For doctorate, thesis/dissertation. *Entrance requirements:* For master's and doctorate, GRE General Test, GRE Subject Test, minimum GPA of 3.0. Additional exam requirements/recommendations for international students: Required—TOEFL (minimum score 550 paper-based; 213 computer-based). *Application deadline:* For fall admission, 1/15 priority date for domestic students, 1/15 for international students. Applications are processed on a rolling basis. Application fee: $80 ($100 for international students). Electronic applications accepted. *Financial support:* Fellowships, research assistantships with full tuition reimbursements, teaching assistantships, career-related internships or fieldwork, institutionally sponsored loans, traineeships, health care benefits, and unspecified assistantships available. Financial award application deadline: 3/1; financial award applicants required to submit FAFSA. *Faculty research:* Atmospheric chemistry, climate change, isotope biogeochemistry, global environmental chemistry. *Unit head:* Michael L. Goulden, Chair, 949-824-1983, Fax: 949-824-3874, E-mail: mgoulden@uci.edu. *Application contact:* Cynthia A. Dennis, Department Assistant, 949-824-3876, Fax: 949-824-3874, E-mail: cadennis@uci.edu.

University of California, Los Angeles, Graduate Division, College of Letters and Science, Department of Earth and Space Sciences, Los Angeles, CA 90095. Offers geochemistry (MS, PhD); geology (MS, PhD); geophysics and space physics (MS, PhD). *Faculty:* 22 full-time (2 women). *Students:* 60 full-time (33 women); includes 8 minority (2 Black or African American, non-Hispanic/Latino; 1 American Indian or Alaska Native, non-Hispanic/Latino; 4 Asian, non-Hispanic/Latino; 1 Two or more races, non-Hispanic/Latino), 16 international. Average age 27. 112 applicants, 25% accepted, 13 enrolled. In 2010, 6 master's, 8 doctorates awarded. Terminal master's awarded for partial completion of doctoral program. *Degree requirements:* For master's, comprehensive exams or thesis; for doctorate, thesis/dissertation, oral and written qualifying exams. *Entrance requirements:* For master's, GRE General Test, minimum GPA of 3.0; for doctorate, GRE General Test, minimum undergraduate GPA of 3.0. *Application deadline:* For fall admission, 1/15 for domestic and international students. Application fee: $70 ($90 for international students). Electronic applications accepted. *Financial support:* In 2010–11, 55 fellowships with full and partial tuition reimbursements, 48 research assistantships with full and partial tuition reimbursements, 27 teaching assistantships with full and partial tuition reimbursements were awarded; Federal Work-Study, institutionally sponsored loans, scholarships/grants, traineeships, health care benefits, tuition waivers (full and partial), and unspecified assistantships also available. Financial award application deadline: 3/1; financial award applicants required to submit FAFSA. *Unit head:* Dr. Craig E. Manning, Chair, 310-825-1475, E-mail: manning@ess.ucla.edu. *Application contact:* Departmental Office, 310-825-3917, E-mail: holbrook@ess.ucla.edu.

University of California, San Diego, Office of Graduate Studies, Scripps Institution of Oceanography, La Jolla, CA 92093. Offers earth sciences (PhD); marine biology (PhD); oceanography (PhD). *Faculty:* 98. *Students:* 241 (115 women); includes 3 Black or African American, non-Hispanic/Latino; 4 American Indian or Alaska Native, non-Hispanic/Latino; 13 Asian, non-Hispanic/Latino, 52 international. 392 applicants, 19% accepted, 35 enrolled. *Degree requirements:* For doctorate, comprehensive exam, thesis/dissertation. *Entrance requirements:* For doctorate, GRE General Test, Suggested for Ocean Biosciences Program: GRE Subject Test, See: http://scrippseducation.ucsd.edu/Graduate_Students/Prospective_Students/. Additional exam requirements/recommendations for international students: Required—TOEFL (minimum score 550 paper-based; 213 computer-based; 80 iBT). *Application deadline:* For fall admission, 1/2 for domestic and international students. Application fee: $80 ($100 for international students). Electronic applications accepted. *Financial support:* Fellowships with full and partial tuition reimbursements, research assistantships with tuition reimbursements, teaching assistantships with tuition reimbursements, health care benefits available. *Unit head:* Dr. Douglas H. Bartlett, Chair, 858-534-3206, E-mail: siodept@sio.ucsd.edu. *Application contact:* Krystle Shertz, Graduate Coordinator, 858-534-3206, E-mail: kshertz@ucsd.edu.

University of California, Santa Barbara, Graduate Division, College of Letters and Sciences, Division of Mathematics, Life, and Physical Sciences, Department of Earth Science, Santa Barbara, CA 93106-9620. Offers geological sciences (PhD); geophysics (MS). *Faculty:* 16 full-time (2 women), 3 part-time/adjunct (1 woman). *Students:* 47 full-time (22 women); includes 1 American Indian or Alaska Native, non-Hispanic/Latino; 4 Asian, non-Hispanic/Latino; 7 Hispanic/Latino. Average age 27. 93 applicants, 31% accepted, 16 enrolled. In 2010, 5 master's, 3 doctorates awarded. Terminal master's awarded for partial completion of doctoral program. *Degree requirements:* For master's, comprehensive exam, thesis, 30 units; for doctorate, comprehensive exam, thesis/dissertation, 30 units, oral qualifying exam. *Entrance requirements:* For master's and doctorate, GRE General Test. Additional exam requirements/recommendations for international students: Required—TOEFL (minimum score 550 paper-based; 80 iBT), IELTS (minimum score 7). *Application deadline:* For fall admission, 1/1 for domestic and international students. Application fee: $70 ($90 for international students). Electronic applications accepted. *Financial support:* In 2010–11, 38 students received support, including 24 fellowships with full and partial tuition reimbursements available (averaging $9,407 per year), 19 research assistantships with full and partial tuition reimbursements available (averaging $6,722 per year), 25 teaching assistantships with full and partial tuition reimbursements available (averaging $9,978 per year); tuition waivers (full and partial) also available. Financial award application deadline: 1/1; financial award applicants required to submit CSS PROFILE or FAFSA. *Faculty research:* Geology, geomaterials and earth's structure; geomorphology, tectonics; geophysics, seismology; paleoclimate, paleoceanography and geochemistry; paleobiology, evolution and paleontology. *Unit head:* Giulia Brofferio, Business Officer, 805-893-4604, Fax: 805-893-2314, E-mail: brofferio@geol.ucsb.edu. *Application contact:* Hannah Ocampo, Graduate Program Assistant, 805-893-3329, Fax: 805-893-2314, E-mail: ocampo@geol.ucsb.edu.

University of California, Santa Cruz, Division of Graduate Studies, Division of Physical and Biological Sciences, Department of Earth and Planetary Sciences, Santa Cruz, CA 95064. Offers MS, PhD. *Students:* 59 full-time (31 women); includes 6 minority (2 Asian, non-Hispanic/Latino; 3 Hispanic/Latino; 1 Two or more races, non-Hispanic/Latino), 7 international. Average age 28. 132 applicants, 23% accepted, 12 enrolled. In 2010, 4 master's, 7 doctorates awarded. Terminal master's awarded for partial completion of doctoral program. *Degree requirements:* For master's, thesis; for doctorate, one foreign language, thesis/dissertation, qualifying exam. *Entrance requirements:* For master's and doctorate, GRE General Test. Additional exam requirements/recommendations for international students: Required—TOEFL (minimum score 550 paper-based; 220 computer-based; 83 iBT); Recommended—IELTS (minimum score 8). *Application deadline:* For fall admission, 1/5 for domestic and international students. Application fee: $70 ($90 for international students). Electronic applications accepted. *Financial support:* Fellowships, research assistantships, teaching assistantships, institutionally sponsored loans and tuition waivers available. Financial award applicants required to submit FAFSA. *Faculty research:* Evolution of continental margins and orogenic belts, geologic processes occurring at plate boundaries, deep-sea sediment diagenesis, paleoecology, hydrogeology. *Unit head:* Cathy Smith, Graduate Program Coordinator, 831-459-2504, E-mail: cdsmith@ucsc.edu. *Application contact:* Cathy Smith, Graduate Program Coordinator, 831-459-2504, E-mail: cdsmith@ucsc.edu.

University of Chicago, Division of the Physical Sciences, Department of the Geophysical Sciences, Chicago, IL 60637-1513. Offers atmospheric sciences (SM, PhD); earth sciences (SM, PhD); paleobiology (PhD); planetary and space sciences (SM, PhD). *Faculty:* 21 full-time (3 women). *Students:* 37 full-time (23 women); includes 1 Hispanic/Latino, 14 international. Average age 27. 63 applicants, 35% accepted, 9 enrolled. In 2010, 2 master's, 7 doctorates awarded. Terminal master's awarded for partial completion of doctoral program. *Degree requirements:* For master's, thesis, seminar; for doctorate, variable foreign language requirement, comprehensive exam, thesis/dissertation. *Entrance requirements:* For doctorate, GRE General Test. Additional exam requirements/recommendations for international students: Required—TOEFL (minimum score 600 paper-based; 250 computer-based; 96 iBT), IELTS (minimum score 7). *Application deadline:* For fall admission, 1/10 for domestic and international students. Application fee: $55. Electronic applications accepted. *Financial support:* In 2010–11, research assistantships with full tuition reimbursements (averaging $20,511 per year), teaching assistantships with full tuition reimbursements (averaging $21,915 per year) were awarded; fellowships, Federal Work-Study, institutionally sponsored loans, scholarships/grants, tuition waivers (partial), and unspecified assistantships also available. Financial award application deadline: 1/9. *Faculty research:* Climatology, evolutionary paleontology, petrology, geochemistry, oceanic sciences. *Unit head:* Dr. Michael Foote, Chairman, 773-702-8102, Fax: 773-702-9505. *Application contact:* David J. Taylor, Graduate Student Services Coordinator, 773-702-8180, Fax: 773-702-9505, E-mail: info@geosci.uchicago.edu.

University of Florida, Graduate School, College of Liberal Arts and Sciences, Department of Geological Sciences, Gainesville, FL 32611. Offers geology (MS, MST, PhD). *Faculty:* 17 full-time (3 women). *Students:* 35 full-time (16 women), 4 part-time (2 women); includes 1 Asian, non-Hispanic/Latino; 2 Hispanic/Latino, 8 international. Average age 29. 55 applicants, 40% accepted, 10 enrolled. In 2010, 6 master's, 5 doctorates awarded. Terminal master's awarded for partial completion of doctoral program. *Degree requirements:* For master's, thesis (for some programs), Thesis and non-thesis M.S. options; for doctorate, one foreign language, thesis/dissertation. *Entrance requirements:* For master's, GRE General Test score greater than 1000, minimum GPA of 3.0; for doctorate, GRE General Test score greater than 1100, minimum GPA of 3.0. Additional exam requirements/recommendations for international students: Required—TOEFL (minimum score 550 paper-based; 213 computer-based; 80 iBT), IELTS (minimum score 6). *Application deadline:* For fall admission, 1/15 for domestic students; for spring admission, 10/1 for domestic students. Applications are processed on a rolling basis. Application fee: $30. Electronic applications accepted. *Expenses:* Tuition, state resident: full-time $10,915.92. Tuition, nonresident: full-time $28,309. *Financial support:* In 2010–11, 39 students received support, including 4 fellowships with full tuition reimbursements available, 19 research assistantships with full tuition reimbursements available (averaging $16,810 per year), 16 teaching assistantships with full tuition reimbursements available (averaging $15,290 per year); career-related internships or fieldwork, Federal Work-Study, institutionally sponsored loans, and scholarships/grants also available. Support available to part-time students. Financial award application deadline: 3/1; financial award applicants required to submit FAFSA. *Faculty research:* Paleoclimatology, tectonophysics, petrochemistry, marine geology, geochemistry, hydrology. *Unit head:* Michael R. Perfit, PhD, Chair, 352-392-2231, Fax: 352-392-9294, E-mail: mperfit@ufl.edu. *Application contact:* John Jaeger, PhD, Graduate Coordinator, 352-392-2231, Fax: 352-392-9294, E-mail: jmjaeger@ufl.edu.

University of Illinois at Chicago, Graduate College, College of Liberal Arts and Sciences, Department of Earth and Environmental Sciences, Chicago, IL 60607-7128. Offers MS, PhD. *Degree requirements:* For master's, thesis; for doctorate, thesis/dissertation. *Entrance requirements:* For master's and doctorate, GRE General Test, minimum GPA of 2.75. Additional exam requirements/recommendations for international students: Required—TOEFL. Electronic applications accepted.

University of Illinois at Urbana–Champaign, Graduate College, College of Liberal Arts and Sciences, School of Earth, Society and Environment, Department of Geology, Champaign, IL 61820. Offers geology (MS, PhD); teaching of earth sciences (MS). *Faculty:* 13 full-time (3 women). *Students:* 27 full-time (10 women), 4 part-time (3 women); includes 1 minority (Asian, non-Hispanic/Latino), 11 international. 52 applicants, 17% accepted, 9 enrolled. In 2010, 8 master's awarded. Terminal master's awarded for partial completion of doctoral program. *Entrance requirements:* For master's and doctorate, GRE General Test, minimum GPA of 3.0. Additional exam requirements/recommendations for international students: Required—TOEFL. *Application deadline:* Applications are processed on a rolling basis. Application fee: $75 ($90 for international students). Electronic applications accepted. *Financial support:* In 2010–11, 3 fellowships, 19 research assistantships, 13 teaching assistantships were awarded; Federal Work-Study and tuition waivers (full and partial) also available. *Faculty research:* Hydrogeology, structure/tectonics, mineral science. *Unit head:* Wang-Ping Chen, Head, 217-333-2744, Fax: 217-244-4996, E-mail: wpchen@illinois.edu. *Application contact:* Marilyn K. Whalen, Office Administrator, 217-333-3542, Fax: 217-244-4996, E-mail: mkt@illinois.edu.

The University of Iowa, Graduate College, College of Liberal Arts and Sciences, Department of Geoscience, Iowa City, IA 52242-1316. Offers MS, PhD. *Degree requirements:* For master's, thesis optional, exam; for doctorate, comprehensive exam, thesis/dissertation. *Entrance requirements:* For master's and doctorate, GRE General Test, minimum GPA of 3.0. Additional exam requirements/recommendations for international students: Required—TOEFL (minimum score 550 paper-based; 213 computer-based; 81 iBT). Electronic applications accepted.

University of Maine, Graduate School, College of Education and Human Development, Interdisciplinary Program in Teaching, Orono, ME 04469. Offers earth sciences (MST); generalist (MST); mathematics (MST); physics and astronomy (MST). *Students:* 10 full-time (7 women), 20 part-time (17 women); includes 1 minority (Black or African American, non-Hispanic/Latino). Average age 40. 13 applicants, 46% accepted, 6 enrolled. In 2010, 17 master's awarded. *Entrance requirements:* For master's, GRE General Test, MAT. Application fee: $65. *Expenses:* Tuition, state resident: full-time $400. Tuition, nonresident: full-time $1050. *Unit head:* Dr. Susan McKay, Director, 207-581-1016. *Application contact:* Scott G. Delcourt, Associate Dean of the Graduate School, 207-581-3219, Fax: 207-581-3232, E-mail: graduate@maine.edu.

University of Maine, Graduate School, College of Natural Sciences, Forestry, and Agriculture, Department of Earth Sciences, Orono, ME 04469. Offers water resources (MS, PhD). Part-time programs available. *Faculty:* 10 full-time (2 women), 4 part-time/adjunct (1 woman). *Students:* 21 full-time (11 women), 10 part-time (4 women), 6 international. Average age 29. 37 applicants, 51% accepted, 11 enrolled. In 2010, 3 master's, 4 doctorates awarded. *Degree requirements:* For master's, thesis; for doctorate, one foreign language, thesis/dissertation. *Entrance requirements:* For master's and doctorate, GRE General Test. Additional exam requirements/recommendations for international students: Required—TOEFL. *Application deadline:* For fall admission, 2/1 priority date for domestic students. Applications are processed on a rolling basis. Application fee: $65. Electronic applications accepted. *Expenses:* Tuition, state resident: full-time $400. Tuition, nonresident: full-time $1050. *Financial support:* In 2010–11, 5 research assistantships with tuition reimbursements (averaging $16,130 per year), 6 teaching assistantships with tuition reimbursements (averaging $12,790 per year) were awarded; Federal Work-Study, institutionally sponsored loans, and tuition waivers (full and partial) also available. Financial award application deadline: 3/1. *Faculty research:* Appalachian bedrock geology, Quaternary studies, marine geology. *Unit head:* Dr. Joseph Kelley, Chair, 207-581-2162, Fax: 207-581-2202. *Application contact:* Scott G. Delcourt, Associate Dean of the Graduate School, 207-581-3291, Fax: 207-581-3232, E-mail: graduate@maine.edu.

The University of Manchester, School of Earth, Atmospheric and Environmental Sciences, Manchester, United Kingdom. Offers atmospheric sciences (M Phil, M Sc, PhD); basin studies and petroleum geosciences (M Phil, M Sc, PhD); earth, atmospheric and environmental sciences (M Phil, M Sc, PhD); environmental geochemistry and cosmochemistry (M Phil, M Sc, PhD); isotope geochemistry and cosmochemistry (M Phil, M Sc, PhD); paleontology (M Phil, M Sc, PhD); physics and chemistry of minerals and fluids (M Phil, M Sc, PhD); structural and petrological geosciences (M Phil, M Sc, PhD).

University of Massachusetts Amherst, Graduate School, College of Natural Sciences, Department of Geosciences, Program in Geosciences, Amherst, MA 01003. Offers MS, PhD. Part-time programs available. *Students:* 24 full-time (9 women), 28 part-time (17 women); includes 3 minority (1 Asian, non-Hispanic/Latino; 2 Two or more races, non-Hispanic/Latino), 10 international. Average age 35. 72 applicants, 53% accepted, 11 enrolled. In 2010, 6 master's, 4 doctorates awarded. Terminal master's awarded for partial completion of doctoral program. *Degree requirements:* For master's, thesis or alternative; for doctorate, one foreign language, comprehensive exam, thesis/dissertation. *Entrance requirements:* For master's and doctorate, GRE General Test. Additional exam requirements/recommendations for international students: Required—TOEFL (minimum score 550 paper-based; 213 computer-based; 80 iBT), IELTS (minimum score 6.5). *Application deadline:* For fall admission, 1/15 for domestic and international students; for spring admission, 10/1 for domestic and international students. Applications are processed on a rolling basis. Application fee: $50 ($65 for international students). Electronic applications accepted. *Expenses:* Tuition, state resident: full-time $2640. Required fees: $8282. One-time fee: $357 full-time. *Financial support:* Fellowships, research assistantships, teaching assistantships, career-related internships or fieldwork, Federal Work-Study, scholarships/grants, traineeships, health care benefits, tuition waivers (full), and unspecified assistantships available. Support available to part-time students. Financial award application deadline: 1/15; financial award applicants required to submit FAFSA. *Unit head:* Dr. Laurie Brown, Graduate Program Director, 413-545-2286, Fax: 413-545-1200. *Application contact:* Jean M. Ames, Supervisor of Admissions, 413-545-0722, Fax: 413-577-0010, E-mail: gradadm@grad.umass.edu.

University of Missouri–Kansas City, College of Arts and Sciences, Department of Geosciences, Kansas City, MO 64110-2499. Offers environmental and urban geosciences (MS); geosciences (PhD). PhD (interdisciplinary) offered through the School of Graduate Studies. Part-time programs available. *Faculty:* 10 full-time (3 women), 2 part-time/adjunct (0 women). *Students:* 3 full-time (1 woman), 25 part-time (11 women); includes 2 minority (both Hispanic/Latino), 3 international. Average age 34. 17 applicants, 76% accepted, 7 enrolled. *Degree requirements:* For master's, thesis; for doctorate, thesis/dissertation, qualifying exam. *Entrance requirements:* For master's, GRE General Test, minimum GPA of 3.0. Additional exam requirements/recommendations for international students: Required—TOEFL (minimum score 550 paper-based; 213 computer-based; 80 iBT). *Application deadline:* For fall admission, 3/15 priority date for domestic and international students. Applications are processed on a rolling basis. Application fee: $45 ($50 for international students). Electronic applications accepted. *Expenses:* Tuition, state resident: full-time $5522.40; part-time $306.80 per credit hour. Tuition, nonresident: full-time $7128; part-time $792 per credit hour. Required fees: $261.15 per term. *Financial support:* In 2010–11, 2 research assistantships with partial tuition reimbursements (averaging $12,600 per year), 20 teaching assistantships with partial tuition reimbursements (averaging $11,211 per year) were awarded; Federal Work-Study, institutionally sponsored loans, and tuition waivers (full and partial) also available. Support available to part-time students. Financial award application deadline: 3/1; financial award applicants required to submit FAFSA. *Faculty research:* Neotectonics and applied geophysics, environmental geosciences, urban geoscience, geoinformatics–remote sensing, atmospheric research. Total annual research expenditures: $310,535. *Unit head:* Dr. Jimmy Adegoke, Chair, 816-235-1334, Fax: 816-235-5535, E-mail: adegokej@umkc.edu. *Application contact:* Dr. Ray Coveney, Associate Professor, 816-235-1334, Fax: 816-235-5535, E-mail: coveneyr@umkc.edu.

The University of Montana, Graduate School, College of Arts and Sciences, Department of Geology, Missoula, MT 59812-0002. Offers applied geoscience (PhD); geology (MS, PhD). *Degree requirements:* For doctorate, thesis/dissertation. *Entrance requirements:* For master's and doctorate, GRE General Test. Additional exam requirements/recommendations for international students: Required—TOEFL (minimum score 525 paper-based; 197 computer-based). *Faculty research:* Environmental geoscience, regional structure and tectonics, groundwater geology, petrology, mineral deposits.

University of Nebraska–Lincoln, Graduate College, College of Arts and Sciences, Department of Geosciences, Lincoln, NE 68588. Offers MS, PhD. *Degree requirements:* For master's, thesis optional, departmental qualifying exam; for doctorate, comprehensive exam, thesis/dissertation, departmental qualifying exams. *Entrance requirements:* For master's and doctorate, GRE General Test. Additional exam requirements/recommendations for international students: Required—TOEFL (minimum score 550 paper-based; 213 computer-based). Electronic applications accepted. *Faculty research:* Hydrogeology, sedimentology, environmental geology, vertebrate paleontology.

University of Nevada, Las Vegas, Graduate College, College of Science, Department of Geoscience, Las Vegas, NV 89154-4010. Offers MS, PhD. Part-time programs available. *Faculty:* 16 full-time (3 women), 1 (woman) part-time/adjunct. *Students:* 38 full-time (17 women), 18 part-time (9 women); includes 14 minority (1 Black or African American, non-Hispanic/Latino; 1 American Indian or Alaska Native, non-Hispanic/Latino; 2 Hispanic/Latino; 10 Two or more races, non-Hispanic/Latino), 14 international. Average age 31. 40 applicants, 40% accepted, 8 enrolled. In 2010, 8 master's, 5 doctorates awarded. *Degree requirements:* For master's, comprehensive exam, thesis; for doctorate, comprehensive exam, thesis/dissertation. *Entrance requirements:* For master's and doctorate, GRE General Test. Additional exam requirements/recommendations for international students: Required—TOEFL (minimum score 550 paper-based; 213 computer-based; 80 iBT), IELTS (minimum score 7). *Application deadline:* For fall admission, 2/1 priority date for domestic and international students; for spring admission, 10/1 priority date for domestic and international students. Applications are processed on a rolling basis. Application fee: $60 ($95 for international students). Electronic applications accepted. *Expenses:* Tuition, area resident: Part-time $239.50 per credit. Tuition, state resident: part-time $239.50 per credit. Tuition, nonresident: part-time $503 per credit. Required fees: $108 per semester. Tuition and fees vary according to course load, program and reciprocity agreements. *Financial support:* In 2010–11, 37 students received support, including 14 research assistantships with partial tuition reimbursements available (averaging $16,706 per year), 22 teaching assistantships with partial tuition reimbursements available (averaging $12,318 per year); institutionally sponsored loans, scholarships/grants, health care benefits, and unspecified assistantships also available. Financial award application deadline: 3/1. *Faculty research:* Petrology, geochemistry and economic geology; climate and earth surface processes; structural geology and tectonics; sedimentary geology and paleontology; hydrogeologic and environmental science. Total annual research expenditures: $1.3 million. *Unit head:* Dr. Michael Wells, Chair/Professor, 702-895-0828, Fax: 702-895-4064, E-mail: michael.wells@unlv.edu. *Application contact:* Graduate College Admissions Evaluator, 702-895-3320, Fax: 702-895-4180, E-mail: gradcollege@unlv.edu.

University of New Hampshire, Graduate School, College of Engineering and Physical Sciences, Department of Earth Sciences, Durham, NH 03824. Offers earth sciences (MS), including geochemical systems, geology, ocean mapping, oceanography; hydrology (MS). *Faculty:* 17 full-time (5 women). *Students:* 21 full-time (13 women), 8 part-time (4 women); includes 2 minority (1 Black or African American, non-Hispanic/Latino; 1 Asian, non-Hispanic/Latino), 4 international. Average age 27. 55 applicants, 65% accepted, 16 enrolled. In 2010, 8 master's awarded. *Degree requirements:* For master's, thesis. *Entrance requirements:* For master's, GRE General Test. Additional exam requirements/recommendations for international students: Required—TOEFL (minimum score 550 paper-based; 213 computer-based; 80 iBT). *Application deadline:* For fall admission, 4/1 priority date for domestic students, 4/1 for international students; for spring admission, 12/1 for domestic students. Applications are processed on a rolling basis. Application fee: $65. Electronic applications accepted. *Financial support:* In 2010–11, 24 students received support, including 13 research assistantships, 7 teaching assistantships; fellowships, career-related internships or fieldwork, Federal Work-Study, scholarships/grants, and tuition waivers (full and partial) also available. Support available to part-time students. Financial award application deadline: 2/15. *Unit head:* Dr. Will Clyde, Chairperson, 603-862-1718, E-mail: earth.sciences@unh.edu. *Application contact:* Sue Clark, Administrative Assistant, 603-862-1718, E-mail: earth.sciences@unh.edu.

University of New Haven, Graduate School, College of Arts and Sciences, Program in Environmental Sciences, West Haven, CT 06516-1916. Offers environmental ecology (Certificate); environmental geoscience (MS); environmental health and management (MS); environmental science (MS); geographical information systems (Certificate). Part-time and evening/weekend programs available. *Students:* 13 full-time (5 women), 24 part-time (10 women); includes 2 Black or African American, non-Hispanic/Latino; 1 American Indian or Alaska Native, non-Hispanic/Latino; 1 Asian, non-Hispanic/Latino; 1 Hispanic/Latino, 4 international. Average age 27. 29 applicants, 100% accepted, 14 enrolled. In 2010, 13 master's, 1 other advanced degree awarded. *Degree requirements:* For master's, thesis or alternative. *Application deadline:* For fall admission, 5/31 for international students; for winter admission, 10/15 for international students; for spring admission, 1/15 for international students. Applications are processed on a rolling basis. Application fee: $50. Electronic applications accepted. *Financial support:* Research assistantships with partial tuition reimbursements, teaching assistantships with partial tuition reimbursements, career-related internships or fieldwork, Federal Work-Study, scholarships/grants, tuition waivers, and unspecified assistantships available. Support available to part-time students. Financial award applicants required to submit FAFSA. *Faculty research:* Mapping and assessing geological and living resources in Long Island Sound, geology, San Salvador Island, Bahamas. *Unit head:* Dr. Roman Zajac, Coordinator, 203-932-7108. *Application contact:* Eloise Gormley, Director of Graduate Admissions, 203-932-7449, Fax: 203-932-7137, E-mail: gradinfo@newhaven.edu.

University of New Mexico, Graduate School, College of Arts and Sciences, Department of Earth and Planetary Sciences, Albuquerque, NM 87131-2039. Offers MS, PhD. Part-time programs available. *Faculty:* 32 full-time (5 women), 18 part-time/adjunct (8 women). *Students:* 50 full-time (31 women), 7 part-time (5 women); includes 5 minority (1 American Indian or Alaska Native, non-Hispanic/Latino; 3 Hispanic/Latino; 1 Two or more races, non-Hispanic/Latino), 4 international. Average age 30. 97 applicants, 14% accepted, 13 enrolled. In 2010, 9 master's, 2 doctorates awarded. Terminal master's awarded for partial completion of doctoral program. *Degree requirements:* For master's, comprehensive exam, thesis; for doctorate, comprehensive exam, thesis/dissertation. *Entrance requirements:* For master's and doctorate, GRE General Test. Additional exam requirements/recommendations for international students: Required—TOEFL. *Application deadline:* For fall admission, 1/31 priority date for domestic students, 1/31 for international students; for spring admission, 11/1 priority date for domestic and international students. Application fee: $50. Electronic applications accepted. *Expenses:* Tuition, state resident: full-time $5991; part-time $251 per credit hour. Tuition, nonresident: full-time $14,405; part-time $800.20 per credit hour. Tuition and fees vary according to course level, course load, program and reciprocity agreements. *Financial support:* In 2010–11, 54 students received support, including 23 fellowships with full tuition reimbursements available (averaging $2,714 per year), 46 research assistantships with full tuition reimbursements available (averaging $14,363 per year), 27 teaching assistantships with full tuition reimbursements available (averaging $1,982 per year); scholarships/grants and health care benefits also available. Financial award application deadline: 1/31; financial award applicants required to submit FAFSA. *Faculty research:* Climatology, experimental petrology, geochemistry, geographic information technologies, geomorphology, geophysics, hydrogeology, ingeneous petrology, metamorphic petrology, meteoritics, meteorology, micrometeorites, mineralogy, paleoclimatology, paleonology, pedology, petrology, physical volcanology, planetary sciences, precambrian geology, quantenary geology, sedimentary geochemistry, sedimentology, stable isotope geochemistry, stratigraphy, structural geology, tectonics, volcanology. Total annual research expenditures: $2.5 million. *Unit head:* Dr. John W. Geissman, Chair, 505-277-4204, Fax: 505-277-8843, E-mail: jgeiss@unm.edu. *Application contact:* Cindy Jaramillo, Administrative Assistant II, 505-277-1635, Fax: 505-277-8843, E-mail: epsdept@unm.edu.

University of New Orleans, Graduate School, College of Sciences, Department of Earth and Environmental Sciences, New Orleans, LA 70148. Offers MS. Evening/weekend programs available. *Degree requirements:* For master's, thesis. *Entrance requirements:* For master's, GRE General Test. Additional exam requirements/recommendations for international students: Required—TOEFL (minimum score 550 paper-based; 213 computer-based; 79 iBT). Electronic applications accepted. *Faculty research:* Continental margin structure and seismology, burial diagenesis of siliclastic sediments, tectonics at convergent plate margins, continental shelf sediment stability, early diagenesis of carbonates.

Geosciences

The University of North Carolina at Charlotte, Graduate School, College of Arts and Sciences, Department of Geography and Earth Sciences, Charlotte, NC 28223-0001. Offers earth sciences (MS); geography (MA), including community planning, geographic location science and technologies, location analysis, transportation studies, urban regional analysis; geography and urban regional analysis (PhD). Part-time and evening/weekend programs available. *Faculty:* 27 full-time (9 women), 2 part-time/adjunct (1 woman). *Students:* 57 full-time (26 women), 38 part-time (12 women); includes 5 minority (3 Black or African American, non-Hispanic/Latino; 1 Hispanic/Latino; 1 Native Hawaiian or other Pacific Islander, non-Hispanic/Latino), 17 international. Average age 30. 46 applicants, 72% accepted, 17 enrolled. In 2010, 18 master's awarded. *Degree requirements:* For master's, comprehensive exam, thesis or alternative, project. *Entrance requirements:* For master's, GRE General Test or MAT, Doppelt Mathematical Reasoning Test, minimum GPA of 3.0 in undergraduate major, 2.75 overall. Additional exam requirements/recommendations for international students: Required—TOEFL (minimum score 557 paper-based; 220 computer-based; 83 iBT). *Application deadline:* For fall admission, 7/1 for domestic students, 5/1 for international students; for spring admission, 11/1 for domestic students, 10/1 for international students. Applications are processed on a rolling basis. Application fee: $55. Electronic applications accepted. *Expenses:* Tuition, state resident: full-time $3464. Tuition, nonresident: full-time $14,297. Required fees: $2094. Tuition and fees vary according to course load. *Financial support:* In 2010–11, 48 students received support, including 2 fellowships (averaging $17,876 per year), 23 research assistantships (averaging $10,760 per year), 23 teaching assistantships (averaging $9,449 per year); career-related internships or fieldwork, institutionally sponsored loans, scholarships/grants, and unspecified assistantships also available. Support available to part-time students. Financial award application deadline: 4/1; financial award applicants required to submit FAFSA. *Faculty research:* Location analysis, applications of GIS technology, community planning and development, regional economic modeling, retail geography. Total annual research expenditures: $755,074. *Unit head:* Dr. Harrison Campbell, Graduate Coordinator, 704-687-5997, Fax: 704-687-3182, E-mail: hscampbe@uncc.edu. *Application contact:* Kathy B. Giddings, Director of Graduate Admissions, 704-687-5503, Fax: 704-687-3279, E-mail: gradadm@uncc.edu.

The University of North Carolina Wilmington, College of Arts and Sciences, Department of Geography and Geology, Wilmington, NC 28403-3297. Offers geology (MS); marine science (MS). *Faculty:* 19 full-time (5 women). *Students:* 3 full-time (1 woman), 15 part-time (7 women), 1 international. Average age 30. 46 applicants, 65% accepted, 19 enrolled. In 2010, 2 master's awarded. *Degree requirements:* For master's, comprehensive exam, thesis. *Entrance requirements:* For master's, GRE General Test, GRE Subject Test, minimum B average in undergraduate major and basic courses for prerequisite to geology. *Application deadline:* For fall admission, 2/15 for domestic students. Applications are processed on a rolling basis. Application fee: $45. *Financial support:* In 2010–11, 21 teaching assistantships were awarded; career-related internships or fieldwork and Federal Work-Study also available. Support available to part-time students. Financial award application deadline: 3/15. *Unit head:* Dr. Lynn Leonard, Chair, 910-962-2338, Fax: 910-962-7077, E-mail: lynnl@uncw.edu. *Application contact:* Dr. Michael Smith, Graduate Coordinator, 910-962-3496, Fax: 910-962-7077, E-mail: smithms@uncw.edu.

University of North Dakota, Graduate School, John D. Odegard School of Aerospace Sciences, Program in Earth System Science and Policy, Grand Forks, ND 58202. Offers MEM, MS, PhD. Part-time programs available. *Faculty:* 7 full-time (3 women), 2 part-time/adjunct (both women). *Students:* 14 full-time (8 women), 5 part-time (2 women); includes 2 minority (both Asian, non-Hispanic/Latino), 5 international. Average age 27. 14 applicants, 43% accepted, 6 enrolled. In 2010, 6 master's, 1 doctorate awarded. *Degree requirements:* For master's, thesis (for some programs); for doctorate, thesis/dissertation (for some programs). *Entrance requirements:* For master's and doctorate, GRE General Test, minimum GPA of 3.0. Additional exam requirements/recommendations for international students: Required—TOEFL (minimum score 550 paper-based; 213 computer-based; 79 iBT), IELTS (minimum score 6.5). *Application deadline:* For fall admission, 8/1 priority date for domestic and international students; for spring admission, 9/1 priority date for domestic and international students. Applications are processed on a rolling basis. Application fee: $35. Electronic applications accepted. *Expenses:* Tuition, state resident: full-time $5857; part-time $306.74 per credit. Tuition, nonresident: full-time $15,666; part-time $729.77 per credit. Required fees: $53.42 per credit. Tuition and fees vary according to course load, program and reciprocity agreements. *Financial support:* In 2010–11, 11 students received support, including 11 research assistantships with full and partial tuition reimbursements available (averaging $11,715 per year); fellowships with full and partial tuition reimbursements available, teaching assistantships with full and partial tuition reimbursements available, Federal Work-Study, scholarships/grants, traineeships, health care benefits, and unspecified assistantships also available. Support available to part-time students. Financial award applicants required to submit FAFSA. Total annual research expenditures: $5.3 million. *Unit head:* Dr. Rebecca Romsdahl, Graduate Director, 701-777-2648, E-mail: rebecca.romsdahl@und.nodak.edu. *Application contact:* Staci Wells, Admissions Specialist, 701-777-0748, Fax: 701-777-3619, E-mail: staci.wells@gradschool.und.edu.

University of Northern Colorado, Graduate School, College of Natural and Health Sciences, School of Chemistry, Earth Sciences and Physics, Program in Earth Sciences, Greeley, CO 80639. Offers MA. Part-time programs available. *Faculty:* 8 full-time (2 women). *Students:* 6 full-time (2 women), 4 part-time (1 woman). Average age 37. 2 applicants, 50% accepted, 1 enrolled. In 2010, 3 master's awarded. *Degree requirements:* For master's, comprehensive exam. *Entrance requirements:* For master's, GRE General Test, 3 letters of recommendation. *Application deadline:* Applications are processed on a rolling basis. Application fee: $50 ($60 for international students). Electronic applications accepted. *Expenses:* Tuition, state resident: full-time $6199; part-time $344 per credit hour. Tuition, nonresident: full-time $14,834; part-time $824 per credit hour. Required fees: $1091; $60.60 per credit hour. Tuition and fees vary according to course load, degree level and program. *Financial support:* In 2010–11, 1 research assistantship (averaging $3,011 per year), 1 teaching assistantship (averaging $6,755 per year) were awarded; fellowships, unspecified assistantships also available. Financial award application deadline: 3/1; financial award applicants required to submit FAFSA. *Unit head:* Dr. Emmett Evanoff, Program Coordinator, 970-351-2647. *Application contact:* Linda Sisson, Graduate Student Admission Coordinator, 970-351-1807, Fax: 970-351-2371, E-mail: linda.sisson@unco.edu.

University of Northern Iowa, Graduate College, College of Natural Sciences, Program in Science Education, Cedar Falls, IA 50614. Offers earth science education (MA); physics education (MA); science education (MA). *Students:* 3 full-time (2 women), 24 part-time (16 women); includes 1 minority (Asian, non-Hispanic/Latino). 5 applicants, 80% accepted, 1 enrolled. In 2010, 12 master's awarded. *Degree requirements:* For master's, comprehensive exam (for some programs), thesis or alternative. *Entrance requirements:* For master's, minimum GPA of 3.0. Additional exam requirements/recommendations for international students: Required—TOEFL (minimum score 500 paper-based; 180 computer-based; 61 iBT). *Application deadline:* For fall admission, 8/1 priority date for domestic students. Applications are processed on a rolling basis. Application fee: $50 ($70 for international students). Electronic applications accepted. *Financial support:* Application deadline: 2/1. *Unit head:* Dr. Cherin A. Lee, Director, 319-273-7357, Fax: 319-273-3051, E-mail: cherin.lee@uni.edu. *Application contact:* Laurie S. Russell, Record Analyst, 319-273-2623, Fax: 319-273-2885, E-mail: laurie.russell@uni.edu.

University of Notre Dame, Graduate School, College of Engineering, Department of Civil Engineering and Geological Sciences, Notre Dame, IN 46556. Offers bioengineering (MS Bio E); civil engineering (MSCE); civil engineering and geological sciences (PhD); environmental engineering (MS Env E); geological sciences (MS). Terminal master's awarded for partial completion of doctoral program. *Degree requirements:* For master's, comprehensive exam; for doctorate, thesis/dissertation, candidacy exam. *Entrance requirements:* For master's and doctorate, GRE General Test. Additional exam requirements/recommendations for international students: Required—TOEFL (minimum score 600 paper-based; 250 computer-based; 80 iBT). Electronic applications accepted. *Faculty research:* Environmental modeling, biological-waste treatment, petrology, environmental geology, geochemistry.

University of Ottawa, Faculty of Graduate and Postdoctoral Studies, Faculty of Science, Ottawa-Carleton Geoscience Centre, Ottawa, ON K1N 6N5, Canada. Offers earth sciences (M Sc, PhD). M Sc, PhD offered jointly with Carleton University. *Degree requirements:* For master's, thesis, seminar; for doctorate, comprehensive exam, thesis/dissertation, seminar. *Entrance requirements:* For master's, honors B Sc degree or equivalent, minimum B average; for doctorate, honors B Sc with minimum B average or M Sc with minimum B+ average. Electronic applications accepted. *Faculty research:* Environmental geoscience, geochemistry/petrology, geomatics/geomathematics, mineral resource studies.

University of Pennsylvania, School of Arts and Sciences, Graduate Group in Earth and Environmental Science, Philadelphia, PA 19104. Offers MS, PhD. Part-time programs available. *Faculty:* 8 full-time (1 woman), 4 part-time/adjunct (0 women). *Students:* 18 full-time (11 women), 4 international. 36 applicants, 17% accepted, 6 enrolled. In 2010, 2 doctorates awarded. *Degree requirements:* For master's, one foreign language, thesis; for doctorate, one foreign language, thesis/dissertation. *Entrance requirements:* For master's and doctorate, GRE General Test. Additional exam requirements/recommendations for international students: Required—TOEFL. *Application deadline:* For fall admission, 12/1 priority date for domestic students. Application fee: $70. Electronic applications accepted. *Expenses:* Tuition: Full-time $25,660; part-time $4758 per course. Required fees: $2152; $270 per course. Tuition and fees vary according to course load, degree level and program. *Financial support:* Fellowships, research assistantships, teaching assistantships, institutionally sponsored loans, scholarships/grants, traineeships, health care benefits, and unspecified assistantships available. Financial award application deadline: 12/15. *Faculty research:* Isotope geochemistry, regional tectonics, environmental geology, metamorphic and igneous petrology, paleontology.

University of Rhode Island, Graduate School, College of the Environment and Life Sciences, Department of Geosciences, Kingston, RI 02881. Offers environmental science and management (MESM); environmental sciences (MS, PhD). Part-time programs available. *Faculty:* 6 full-time (2 women), 1 (woman) part-time/adjunct. *Students:* 4 full-time (1 woman), 5 part-time (3 women). *Degree requirements:* For master's, comprehensive exam (for some programs), thesis optional; for doctorate, comprehensive exam, thesis/dissertation. *Entrance requirements:* For master's and doctorate, GRE, 2 letters of recommendation. Additional exam requirements/recommendations for international students: Required—TOEFL (minimum score 550 paper-based; 213 computer-based). *Application deadline:* For fall admission, 7/15 for domestic students, 2/1 for international students; for spring admission, 11/15 for domestic students, 7/15 for international students. Application fee: $65. Electronic applications accepted. *Expenses:* Tuition, state resident: full-time $9588; part-time $533 per credit hour. Tuition, nonresident: full-time $22,968; part-time $1276 per credit hour. Required fees: $1282; $68 per semester. Tuition and fees vary according to program. *Financial support:* In 2010–11, 2 research assistantships with partial tuition reimbursements (averaging $10,412 per year), 4 teaching assistantships with full tuition reimbursements (averaging $13,894 per year) were awarded. Financial award application deadline: 7/15; financial award applicants required to submit FAFSA. *Faculty research:* Hydrology and water resources, interior of the earth, quaternary and modern depositional environments, geobiology of Mesozoic terrestrial ecosystems. Total annual research expenditures: $2.2 million. *Unit head:* Dr. Anne Veeger, Chair, 401-874-2187, Fax: 401-874-2190, E-mail: veeger@uri.edu. *Application contact:* Dr. Thomas Boving, Director of Graduate Studies, 401-874-7053, Fax: 401-874-2190, E-mail: boving@uri.edu.

University of Rochester, School of Arts and Sciences, Department of Earth and Environmental Sciences, Rochester, NY 14627. Offers geological sciences (MS, PhD). *Degree requirements:* For doctorate, thesis/dissertation, qualifying exam. *Entrance requirements:* For master's and doctorate, GRE General Test. Additional exam requirements/recommendations for international students: Required—TOEFL.

University of South Carolina, The Graduate School, College of Arts and Sciences, Department of Geological Sciences, Columbia, SC 29208. Offers MS, PhD. Terminal master's awarded for partial completion of doctoral program. *Degree requirements:* For master's, thesis; for doctorate, comprehensive exam, thesis/dissertation, published paper. *Entrance requirements:* For master's and doctorate, GRE General Test. Additional exam requirements/recommendations for international students: Required—TOEFL (minimum score 570 paper-based; 230 computer-based; 75 iBT). Electronic applications accepted. *Faculty research:* Environmental geology, tectonics, petrology, coastal processes, paleoclimatology.

University of Southern California, Graduate School, Dana and David Dornsife College of Letters, Arts and Sciences, Department of Earth Sciences, Los Angeles, CA 90089. Offers geological sciences (MS, PhD). Only Ph.D. and M.S./Ph.D. students are funded. Part-time programs available. *Faculty:* 18 full-time (2 women), 4 part-time/adjunct (1 woman). *Students:* 53 full-time (29 women), 2 part-time (0 women); includes 9 minority (1 Black or African American, non-Hispanic/Latino; 3 Asian, non-Hispanic/Latino; 4 Hispanic/Latino; 1 Two or more races, non-Hispanic/Latino), 18 international. 57 applicants, 39% accepted, 12 enrolled. In 2010, 12 doctorates awarded. Terminal master's awarded for partial completion of doctoral program. *Degree requirements:* For master's, thesis; for doctorate, comprehensive exam, thesis/dissertation. *Entrance requirements:* For master's and doctorate, GRE. Additional exam requirements/recommendations for international students: Required—TOEFL. *Application deadline:* For fall admission, 1/1 for domestic students, 1/1 priority date for international students. Applications are processed on a rolling basis. Application fee: $85. Electronic applications accepted. *Expenses:* Tuition: Full-time $31,240; part-time $1420 per unit. Required fees: $600. One-time fee: $35 full-time. Full-time tuition and fees vary according to degree level and program. *Financial support:* In 2010–11, 49 students received support, including 15 fellowships with full tuition reimbursements available (averaging $21,200 per year), 10 research assistantships with full tuition reimbursements available (averaging $20,000 per year), 24 teaching assistantships with full tuition reimbursements available (averaging $20,000 per year); institutionally sponsored loans, scholarships/grants, health care benefits, unspecified assistantships, and summer support, research and travel funds also available. *Faculty research:* Geophysics, paleoceanography, geochemistry, geobiology, structure, tectonics. Total annual research expenditures: $12 million. *Unit head:* Dr. David J. Bottjer, Chair, 213-740-6100, Fax: 213-740-8801, E-mail: dbottjer@usc.edu. *Application contact:* Cynthia Waite, Academic Advisor, 213-740-6109, Fax: 213-740-8801, E-mail: waite@usc.edu.

The University of Texas at Austin, Graduate School, Jackson School of Geosciences, Austin, TX 78712-1111. Offers MA, MS, PhD. Part-time programs available. *Degree requirements:* For master's, report (MA), thesis (MS); for doctorate, thesis/dissertation. *Entrance requirements:* For master's and doctorate, GRE General Test. Electronic applications accepted. *Faculty research:* Sedimentary geology, geophysics, hydrogeology, structure/tectonics, vertebrate paleontology.

The University of Texas at Dallas, School of Natural Sciences and Mathematics, Program in Geosciences, Richardson, TX 75080. Offers geochemistry (MS, PhD); geophysics (MS, PhD); geospatial information sciences (MS, PhD); hydrogeology (MS, PhD); sedimentary, stratigraphy, paleontology (PhD); stratigraphy, paleontology (MS); structural geology and tectonics (MS, PhD). Part-time and evening/weekend programs available. *Faculty:* 11 full-time (1 woman). *Students:* 38 full-time (13 women), 25 part-time (8 women); includes 11 minority (4 Black or African American, non-Hispanic/Latino; 4 Asian, non-Hispanic/Latino; 3 Hispanic/Latino), 19 international. Average age 32. 48 applicants, 46% accepted, 12 enrolled. In 2010, 9 master's, 1 doctorate awarded. *Degree requirements:* For master's, thesis optional; for doctorate, thesis/

dissertation. *Entrance requirements:* For master's and doctorate, GRE General Test, minimum GPA of 3.0 in upper-level course work in field. Additional exam requirements/recommendations for international students: Required—TOEFL (minimum score 550 paper-based; 215 computer-based). *Application deadline:* For fall admission, 7/15 for domestic students, 5/1 priority date for international students; for spring admission, 11/15 for domestic students, 9/1 priority date for international students. Applications are processed on a rolling basis. Application fee: $50 ($100 for international students). Electronic applications accepted. *Expenses:* Tuition, state resident: full-time $10,248; part-time $569 per credit hour. Tuition, nonresident: full-time $18,544; part-time $1030 per credit hour. Tuition and fees vary according to course load. *Financial support:* In 2010–11, 38 students received support, including 15 research assistantships with partial tuition reimbursements available (averaging $14,400 per year), 14 teaching assistantships with partial tuition reimbursements available (averaging $13,905 per year); career-related internships or fieldwork, Federal Work-Study, institutionally sponsored loans, scholarships/grants, and unspecified assistantships also available. Support available to part-time students. Financial award application deadline: 4/30; financial award applicants required to submit FAFSA. *Faculty research:* Cybermapping, GPS applications for geophysics and geology, seismology and ground-penetrating radar, numerical modeling, signal processing and inverse modeling techniques in seismology. *Unit head:* Dr. John Oldow, Department Head, 972-883-2403, Fax: 972-883-2537, E-mail: geosciences@utdallas.edu. *Application contact:* Dr. Robert J. Stern, Graduate Advisor, 972-883-2442, Fax: 972-883-2537, E-mail: rjstern@utdallas.edu.

The University of Toledo, College of Graduate Studies, College of Natural Sciences and Mathematics, Department of Environmental Sciences, Toledo, OH 43606-3390. Offers geology (MS), including earth surface processes, general geology. Part-time programs available. *Faculty:* 30. *Students:* 9 full-time (5 women), 1 (woman) part-time; includes 1 minority (Black or African American, non-Hispanic/Latino), 1 international. Average age 30. 9 applicants, 56% accepted, 5 enrolled. In 2010, 2 master's awarded. *Degree requirements:* For master's, thesis. *Entrance requirements:* For master's, GRE General Test, A minimum 2.7 cumulative point-hour ratio (on a 4.0 scale) for all previous academic work. Three letters of recommendation, a statement of purpose, and transcripts from all prior institutions attended. Additional exam requirements/recommendations for international students: Required—TOEFL (minimum score 550 paper-based; 213 computer-based; 80 iBT), IELTS (minimum score 6.5). *Application deadline:* For fall admission, 1/15 priority date for domestic and international students. Applications are processed on a rolling basis. Application fee: $45 ($75 for international students). Electronic applications accepted. *Expenses:* Tuition, state resident: full-time $11,426; part-time $476 per credit hour. Tuition, nonresident: full-time $21,660; part-time $903 per credit hour. One-time fee: $62. *Financial support:* Research assistantships with tuition reimbursements, teaching assistantships with tuition reimbursements, Federal Work-Study, institutionally sponsored loans, scholarships/grants, tuition waivers (full), and unspecified assistantships available. Support available to part-time students. *Faculty research:* Environmental geochemistry, geophysics, petrology and mineralogy, paleontology, geohydrology. *Unit head:* Dr. Timothy G. Fisher, Chair, 419-530-2883, E-mail: timothy.fisher@utoledo.edu. *Application contact:* Graduate School Office, 419-530-4723, Fax: 419-530-4724, E-mail: grdsch@utnet.utoledo.edu.

University of Tulsa, Graduate School, College of Engineering and Natural Sciences, Department of Geosciences, Tulsa, OK 74104-3189. Offers MS, PhD, JD/MS. Part-time programs available. *Faculty:* 10 full-time (1 woman), 2 part-time/adjunct (1 woman). *Students:* 16 full-time (10 women), 4 part-time (2 women); includes 1 minority (Black or African American, non-Hispanic/Latino), 10 international. Average age 27. 59 applicants, 53% accepted, 8 enrolled. In 2010, 10 master's awarded. Terminal master's awarded for partial completion of doctoral program. *Degree requirements:* For master's, thesis (for some programs); for doctorate, comprehensive exam, thesis/dissertation. *Entrance requirements:* For master's and doctorate, GRE General Test. Additional exam requirements/recommendations for international students. Required—TOEFL (minimum score 550 paper-based; 213 computer-based; 80 iBT), IELTS (minimum score 6). *Application deadline:* Applications are processed on a rolling basis. Application fee: $40. Electronic applications accepted. *Expenses:* Tuition: Full-time $16,902; part-time $939 per credit hour. Required fees: $1020; $4 per credit hour. Tuition and fees vary according to course load. *Financial support:* In 2010–11, 10 students received support, including 1 fellowship with full and partial tuition reimbursement available (averaging $1,550 per year), 2 research assistantships with full and partial tuition reimbursements available (averaging $9,176 per year), 8 teaching assistantships with full and partial tuition reimbursements available (averaging $8,845 per year); career-related internships or fieldwork, scholarships/grants, health care benefits, and unspecified assistantships also available. Support available to part-time students. Financial award application deadline: 2/1; financial award applicants required to submit FAFSA. *Faculty research:* Petroleum exploration/production and environmental science, including clastic sedimentology, petroleum seismology, seismic stratigraphy, structural geology, geochemistry, and biogeoscience. Total annual research expenditures: $404,606. *Unit head:* Dr. Bryan Tapp, Chairperson, 918-631-3018, Fax: 918-631-2091, E-mail: jbt@utulsa.edu. *Application contact:* Dr. Peter J. Michael, Adviser, 918-631-3017, Fax: 918-631-2156, E-mail: pjm@utulsa.edu.

University of Victoria, Faculty of Graduate Studies, Faculty of Science, School of Earth and Ocean Sciences, Victoria, BC V8W 2Y2, Canada. Offers M Sc, PhD. Part-time programs available. *Degree requirements:* For master's, thesis; for doctorate, thesis/dissertation, candidacy exam. *Entrance requirements:* For master's and doctorate, GRE. Additional exam requirements/recommendations for international students: Required—TOEFL (minimum score 575 paper-based; 233 computer-based), IELTS (minimum score 7). Electronic applications accepted. *Faculty research:* Climate modeling, geology.

University of Waterloo, Graduate Studies, Faculty of Science, Department of Earth Sciences, Waterloo, ON N2L 3G1, Canada. Offers M Sc, PhD. Part-time programs available. *Degree requirements:* For master's, research paper or thesis; for doctorate, comprehensive exam, thesis/dissertation. *Entrance requirements:* For master's, GRE, honors degree, minimum B average; for doctorate, GRE, master's degree, minimum B average. Additional exam requirements/recommendations for international students: Required—TOEFL, TWE. Electronic applications accepted. *Faculty research:* Environmental geology, soil physics.

The University of Western Ontario, Faculty of Graduate Studies, Physical Sciences Division, Department of Earth Sciences, London, ON N6A 5B8, Canada. Offers environment and sustainability (MES); geology (M Sc, PhD); geology and environmental science (M Sc, PhD); geophysics (M Sc, PhD); geophysics and environmental science (M Sc, PhD). *Degree requirements:* For master's, thesis; for doctorate, thesis/dissertation, qualifying exam. *Entrance requirements:* For master's, honors in B Sc; for doctorate, M Sc. Additional exam requirements/recommendations for international students: Required—TOEFL. *Faculty research:* Geophysics, geochemistry, paleontology, sedimentology/stratigraphy, glaciology/quaternary.

University of Windsor, Faculty of Graduate Studies, Faculty of Science, Department of Earth Sciences, Windsor, ON N9B 3P4, Canada. Offers M Sc, PhD. Part-time programs available. *Degree requirements:* For master's, thesis; for doctorate, comprehensive exam, thesis/dissertation. *Entrance requirements:* For master's, minimum B average; for doctorate, minimum B average, copies of publication abstract. Additional exam requirements/recommendations for international students: Required—TOEFL (minimum score 560 paper-based; 220 computer-based). *Faculty research:* Aqueous geochemistry and hydrothermal processes, igneous petrochemistry, radiogenic isotopes, radiometric age-dating, diagenetic and sedimentary geochemistry.

Virginia Polytechnic Institute and State University, Graduate School, College of Science, Department of Geosciences, Blacksburg, VA 24061. Offers MS, PhD. *Faculty:* 16 full-time (3 women), 1 (woman) part-time/adjunct. *Students:* 58 full-time (28 women), 1 part-time (0 women); includes 2 Asian, non-Hispanic/Latino; 1 Hispanic/Latino, 21 international. Average age 28. 61 applicants, 23% accepted, 13 enrolled. In 2010, 9 master's, 4 doctorates awarded. *Degree requirements:* For master's, comprehensive exam (for some programs), thesis (for some programs); for doctorate, comprehensive exam (for some programs), thesis/dissertation (for some programs). *Entrance requirements:* For master's and doctorate, GRE. Additional exam requirements/recommendations for international students: Required—TOEFL (minimum score 550 paper-based; 213 computer-based). *Application deadline:* For fall admission, 7/1 for domestic and international students; for spring admission, 12/1 for domestic and international students. Applications are processed on a rolling basis. Application fee: $65. Electronic applications accepted. *Expenses:* Tuition, area resident: Full-time $9399; part-time $488 per credit hour. Tuition, state resident: full-time $9399; part-time $488 per credit hour. Tuition, nonresident: full-time $17,854; part-time $957.75 per credit hour. International tuition: $17,854 full-time. Required fees: $1534. Full-time tuition and fees vary according to program. *Financial support:* In 2010–11, 8 fellowships with full tuition reimbursements (averaging $16,920 per year), 21 research assistantships with full tuition reimbursements (averaging $15,991 per year), 22 teaching assistantships with full tuition reimbursements (averaging $12,837 per year) were awarded; career-related internships or fieldwork, Federal Work-Study, scholarships/grants, health care benefits, and unspecified assistantships also available. Financial award application deadline: 1/15. *Faculty research:* Paleontology/geobiology, active tectonics, geomorphology, mineralogy/crystallography, mineral physics. Total annual research expenditures: $2.6 million. *Unit head:* Dr. Kenneth A. Eriksson, UNIT HEAD, 540-231-6521, Fax: 540-231-3386, E-mail: kaeson@vt.edu. *Application contact:* Madeline Schreiber, Contact, 540-231-3377, Fax: 540-231-3386, E-mail: mschreib@vt.edu.

Washington State University, Graduate School, College of Sciences, School of Earth and Environmental Sciences, Pullman, WA 99164. Offers MS, PhD. Application fee: $50. *Expenses:* Tuition, state resident: full-time $8552; part-time $443 per credit. Tuition, nonresident: full-time $21,650; part-time $1083 per credit. Required fees: $846. *Unit head:* Dr. Steve Bollens, Director, 509-335-3009, E-mail: bollens@vancouver.wsu.edu. *Application contact:* Graduate School Admissions, 800-GRADWSU, Fax: 509-335-1949, E-mail: gradsch@wsu.edu.

Washington University in St. Louis, Graduate School of Arts and Sciences, Department of Earth and Planetary Sciences, St. Louis, MO 63130-4899. Offers earth and planetary sciences (MA); planetary sciences (PhD). Terminal master's awarded for partial completion of doctoral program. *Degree requirements:* For master's, thesis; for doctorate, thesis/dissertation. *Entrance requirements:* For master's and doctorate, GRE General Test. Electronic applications accepted.

Wesleyan University, Graduate Programs, Department of Earth and Environmental Sciences, Middletown, CT 06459. Offers MA. *Faculty:* 3 full-time (1 woman), 1 (woman) part-time/adjunct. *Students:* 6 full-time (1 woman); includes 1 American Indian or Alaska Native, non-Hispanic/Latino; 1 Hispanic/Latino. Average age 25. 5 applicants, 60% accepted, 2 enrolled. In 2010, 4 master's awarded. *Degree requirements:* For master's, thesis. *Entrance requirements:* For master's, GRE General Test, GRE Subject Test. Additional exam requirements/recommendations for international students: Required—TOEFL. *Application deadline:* For fall admission, 1/15 for domestic and international students. Applications are processed on a rolling basis. Application fee: $0. Electronic applications accepted. *Expenses:* Tuition: Full-time $43,404. Required fees: $830. *Financial support:* In 2010–11, 4 teaching assistantships with full tuition reimbursements were awarded; tuition waivers (full and partial) also available. Financial award application deadline: 4/15; financial award applicants required to submit FAFSA. *Faculty research:* Tectonics, volcanology, stratigraphy, coastal processes, geochemistry. *Unit head:* Dr. Peter Patton, Chair, 860-685-2268, E-mail: ppatton@wesleyan.edu. *Application contact:* Ginny Harris, Administrative Assistant, 860-685-2244, E-mail: vharris@wesleyan.edu.

West Chester University of Pennsylvania, Office of Graduate Studies, College of Arts and Sciences, Department of Geology and Astronomy, West Chester, PA 19383. Offers earth-space science (Teaching Certificate); general science (Teaching Certificate); geoscience (MA). Part-time and evening/weekend programs available. *Students:* 7 full-time (2 women), 20 part-time (11 women); includes 1 minority (Black or African American, non-Hispanic/Latino). Average age 33. 14 applicants, 86% accepted, 6 enrolled. In 2010, 7 master's awarded. *Degree requirements:* For master's, comprehensive exam (for some programs), thesis optional. *Entrance requirements:* For master's, minimum GPA of 2.5. Additional exam requirements/recommendations for international students: Required—TOEFL (minimum score 550 paper-based; 213 computer-based; 80 iBT). *Application deadline:* For fall admission, 4/15 priority date for domestic students, 3/15 for international students; for spring admission, 10/15 for domestic students, 9/1 for international students. Applications are processed on a rolling basis. Application fee: $35. Electronic applications accepted. *Expenses:* Tuition, state resident: full-time $6966; part-time $387 per credit. Tuition, nonresident: full-time $11,146; part-time $619 per credit. Required fees: $1614.40; $133.24 per credit. Part-time tuition and fees vary according to campus/location. *Financial support:* Unspecified assistantships available. Support available to part-time students. Financial award application deadline: 2/15; financial award applicants required to submit FAFSA. *Faculty research:* Developing and using a meteorological data station. *Unit head:* Dr. Marc Gagne, Chair, 610-436-2727, E-mail: mgagne@wcupa.edu. *Application contact:* Dr. Steven Good, Graduate Coordinator, 610-436-2203, E-mail: sgood@wcupa.edu.

Western Connecticut State University, Division of Graduate Studies and External Programs, School of Arts and Sciences, Department of Physics, Astronomy and Meteorology, Danbury, CT 06810-6885. Offers earth and planetary sciences (MA). Part-time programs available. *Students:* 4 full-time (0 women), 8 part-time (2 women); includes 2 minority (both Hispanic/Latino). Average age 28. *Degree requirements:* For master's, thesis, completion of program in 6 years. *Entrance requirements:* For master's, minimum GPA of 2.5 or GRE; one year each of calculus-based physics and calculus; semester course in differential equations. Additional exam requirements/recommendations for international students: Recommended—TOEFL (minimum score 550 paper-based; 213 computer-based; 79 iBT), IELTS (minimum score 6). *Application deadline:* For fall admission, 8/5 priority date for domestic students; for spring admission, 1/5 priority date for domestic students. Applications are processed on a rolling basis. Application fee: $50. *Expenses:* Tuition, state resident: full-time $5012; part-time $417 per credit hour. Tuition, nonresident: full-time $13,962; part-time $423 per credit hour. Required fees: $3886. Full-time tuition and fees vary according to course load, degree level and program. *Financial support:* Application deadline: 5/1. *Unit head:* Dr. James Boyle, Graduate Coordinator, 203-837-8856. *Application contact:* Chris Shankle, Associate Director of Graduate Admissions, 203-837-9005, Fax: 203-837-8326, E-mail: shanklec@wcsu.edu.

Western Kentucky University, Graduate Studies, Ogden College of Science and Engineering, Department of Geography and Geology, Bowling Green, KY 42101. Offers geoscience (MS). *Degree requirements:* For master's, comprehensive exam, thesis or alternative. *Entrance requirements:* For master's, GRE General Test, minimum GPA of 2.75. Additional exam requirements/recommendations for international students: Required—TOEFL (minimum score 555 paper-based; 213 computer-based; 79 iBT). *Faculty research:* Hydroclimatology, electronic data sets, groundwater, sinkhole liquification potential, meteorological analysis.

Western Michigan University, Graduate College, College of Arts and Sciences, Department of Geosciences, Program in Earth Science, Kalamazoo, MI 49008. Offers MA. *Degree requirements:* For master's, thesis or alternative, oral exam. *Entrance requirements:* For master's, GRE General Test.

Western Michigan University, Graduate College, College of Arts and Sciences, Department of Geosciences, Program in Geosciences, Kalamazoo, MI 49008. Offers MS, PhD. *Degree requirements:* For master's, oral exam; for doctorate, thesis/dissertation, oral exam. *Entrance requirements:* For master's and doctorate, GRE General Test.

Geosciences

Yale University, Graduate School of Arts and Sciences, Department of Geology and Geophysics, New Haven, CT 06520. Offers biogeochemistry (PhD); climate dynamics (PhD); geochemistry (PhD); geophysics (PhD); meteorology (PhD); oceanography (PhD); paleontology (PhD); paleooceanography (PhD); petrology (PhD); tectonics (PhD). *Degree requirements:* For doctorate, thesis/dissertation. *Entrance requirements:* For doctorate, GRE General Test. Additional exam requirements/recommendations for international students: Required—TOEFL.

York University, Faculty of Graduate Studies, Faculty of Science and Engineering, Program in Earth and Space Science, Toronto, ON M3J 1P3, Canada. Offers M Sc, PhD. Part-time and evening/weekend programs available. *Degree requirements:* For master's, thesis or alternative; for doctorate, thesis/dissertation. Electronic applications accepted.

Hydrogeology

California State University, Chico, Graduate School, College of Natural Sciences, Department of Geological and Environmental Sciences, Program in Geosciences, Chico, CA 95929-0722. Offers hydrology/hydrogeology (MS). Part-time programs available. *Students:* 5 full-time (1 woman), 4 part-time (2 women); includes 1 Hispanic/Latino. Average age 36. 9 applicants, 44% accepted, 3 enrolled. In 2010, 1 master's awarded. *Degree requirements:* For master's, thesis, oral exam. *Entrance requirements:* For master's, GRE General Test. Additional exam requirements/recommendations for international students: Required—TOEFL (minimum score 550 paper-based; 213 computer-based; 80 iBT), IELTS (minimum score 6.5). *Application deadline:* For fall admission, 3/1 priority date for domestic students, 3/1 for international students; for spring admission, 9/15 priority date for domestic students, 9/15 for international students. Applications are processed on a rolling basis. Application fee: $55. Electronic applications accepted. *Financial support:* Fellowships available. *Unit head:* Dr. William Murphy, Graduate Coordinator, 530-898-5163. *Application contact:* Dr. William Murphy, Graduate Coordinator, 530-898-5163.

Clemson University, Graduate School, College of Engineering and Science, Department of Environmental Engineering and Earth Sciences, Program in Hydrogeology, Clemson, SC 29634. Offers MS. *Students:* 18 full-time (6 women), 7 part-time (3 women); includes 1 Two or more races, non-Hispanic/Latino, 3 international. Average age 28. 13 applicants, 77% accepted, 7 enrolled. In 2010, 3 master's awarded. *Degree requirements:* For master's, thesis optional. *Entrance requirements:* For master's, GRE General Test, minimum GPA of 3.0 during previous 2 years. Additional exam requirements/recommendations for international students: Required—TOEFL. *Application deadline:* Applications are processed on a rolling basis. Application fee: $70 ($80 for international students). Electronic applications accepted. *Expenses:* Tuition, state resident: full-time $6492; part-time $400 per credit hour. Tuition, nonresident: full-time $13,634; part-time $800 per credit hour. Required fees: $262 per semester. Part-time tuition and fees vary according to course load and program. *Financial support:* In 2010–11, 17 students received support, including 1 fellowship with full and partial tuition reimbursement available (averaging $2,000 per year), 9 research assistantships with partial tuition reimbursements available (averaging $17,784 per year), 7 teaching assistantships with partial tuition reimbursements available (averaging $17,784 per year); career-related internships or fieldwork, institutionally sponsored loans, scholarships/grants, health care benefits, and unspecified assistantships also available. Support available to part-time students. Financial award application deadline: 6/1; financial award applicants required to submit FAFSA. *Faculty research:* Groundwater, geology, environmental geology, geochemistry, remediation, stratigraphy. Total annual research expenditures: $670,000. *Unit head:* Dr. Tanju Karanfil, Chair, 864-653-1005, Fax: 864-656-5973, E-mail: tkaranf@clemson.edu. *Application contact:* Dr. James W. Castle, Graduate Program Coordinator, 864-656-5015, Fax: 864-656-5973, E-mail: jcastle@clemson.edu.

Georgia State University, College of Arts and Sciences, Department of Geosciences, Atlanta, GA 30302-3083. Offers geographic information systems (Certificate); geography (MA); geology (MA); hydrogeology (Certificate). Part-time and evening/weekend programs available. *Degree requirements:* For master's, one foreign language, comprehensive exam (for some programs), thesis or alternative. *Entrance requirements:* For master's, GRE General Test, minimum GPA of 2.75. Additional exam requirements/recommendations for international students: Required—TOEFL. Electronic applications accepted. *Faculty research:* Clay mineralogy, geoinformatics, fracture analysis, sedimentology, groundwater.

Illinois State University, Graduate School, College of Arts and Sciences, Department of Geography-Geology, Normal, IL 61790-2200. Offers hydrogeology (MS). *Degree requirements:* For master's, thesis optional. *Entrance requirements:* For master's, GRE General Test. *Faculty research:* Thermal transport within the hyporheic zone, nutrient cycling in watersheds, water quality in karst systems, ground water dating using dissolved helium.

Indiana University Bloomington, University Graduate School, College of Arts and Sciences, Department of Geological Sciences, Bloomington, IN 47405-7000. Offers biogeochemistry (MS, PhD); economic geology (MS, PhD); geobiology (MS, PhD); geophysics, structural geology and tectonics (MS, PhD); hydrogeology (MS, PhD); mineralogy (MS, PhD); stratigraphy and sedimentology (MS, PhD). *Faculty:* 17 full-time (1 woman). *Students:* 48 full-time (24 women), 5 part-time (1 woman); includes 4 minority (2 Black or African American, non-Hispanic/Latino; 1 Hispanic/Latino; 1 Two or more races, non-Hispanic/Latino), 20 international. Average age 29. 70 applicants, 24% accepted, 16 enrolled. In 2010, 3 master's, 4 doctorates awarded. Terminal master's awarded for partial completion of doctoral program. *Degree requirements:* For master's, thesis or alternative; for doctorate, comprehensive exam, thesis/dissertation. *Entrance requirements:* For master's and doctorate, GRE General Test. Additional exam requirements/recommendations for international students: Required—TOEFL. *Application deadline:* For fall admission, 1/15 priority date for domestic students, 12/15 for international students; for spring admission, 9/1 priority date for domestic students, 9/1 for international students. Applications are processed on a rolling basis. Application fee: $55 ($65 for international students). *Financial support:* In 2010–11, 10 fellowships with full tuition reimbursements (averaging $17,300 per year), 6 research assistantships with full tuition reimbursements (averaging $16,370 per year), 12 teaching assistantships with full tuition reimbursements (averaging $15,150 per year) were awarded; career-related internships or fieldwork, Federal Work-Study, and institutionally sponsored loans also available. *Faculty research:* Geophysics, geochemistry, hydrogeology, geobiology, planetary science. Total annual research expenditures: $644,299. *Unit head:* Simon Brassell, Chair, 812-855-5581, Fax: 812-855-7899, E-mail: geochair@indiana.edu. *Application contact:* Mary Iverson, Graduate Secretary, 812-855-7214, Fax: 812-855-7899, E-mail: miverson@indiana.edu.

Montana Tech of The University of Montana, Graduate School, Geosciences Programs, Butte, MT 59701-8997. Offers geochemistry (MS); geological engineering (MS); geology (MS); geophysical engineering (MS); hydrogeological engineering (MS); hydrogeology (MS). Part-time programs available. *Faculty:* 16 full-time (4 women), 4 part-time/adjunct (0 women). *Students:* 15 full-time (6 women), 10 part-time (5 women); includes 1 Black or African American, non-Hispanic/Latino; 1 American Indian or Alaska Native, non-Hispanic/Latino, 2 international. 9 applicants, 89% accepted, 8 enrolled. In 2010, 4 master's awarded. *Degree requirements:* For master's, comprehensive exam (for some programs), thesis (for some programs). *Entrance requirements:* For master's, GRE General Test, minimum GPA of 3.0. Additional exam requirements/recommendations for international students: Required—TOEFL (minimum score 525 paper-based; 195 computer-based; 71 iBT). *Application deadline:* For fall admission, 4/1 priority date for domestic students, 3/1 priority date for international students; for spring admission, 10/1 priority date for domestic students, 7/1 priority date for international students. Applications are processed on a rolling basis. Application fee: $30. Electronic applications accepted. *Expenses:* Tuition, state resident: full-time $5084. Tuition, nonresident: full-time $15,104. *Financial support:* In 2010–11, 17 students received support, including 10 teaching assistantships with partial tuition reimbursements available (averaging $5,200 per year); research assistantships with partial tuition reimbursements available, career-related internships or fieldwork, tuition waivers (full and partial), and unspecified assistantships also available. Financial award application deadline: 4/1; financial award applicants required to submit FAFSA. *Faculty research:* Water resource development, seismic processing, petroleum reservoir characterization, environmental geochemistry, geologic mapping. *Unit head:* Dr. Mary MacLaughlin, Department Head, 406-496-4655, Fax: 406-496-4260, E-mail: mmaclaughlin@mtech.edu. *Application contact:* Fred Sullivan, Administrator, Graduate School, 406-496-4304, Fax: 406-496-4710, E-mail: fsullivan@mtech.edu.

Ohio University, Graduate College, College of Arts and Sciences, Department of Geological Sciences, Athens, OH 45701-2979. Offers environmental geochemistry (MS); environmental geology (MS); environmental/hydrology (MS); geology (MS); geology education (MS); geomorphology/surficial processes (MS); geophysics (MS); hydrogeology (MS); sedimentology (MS); structure/tectonics (MS). Part-time programs available. *Students:* 14 full-time (8 women), 1 (woman) part-time. 15 applicants, 60% accepted, 8 enrolled. In 2010, 7 master's awarded. *Degree requirements:* For master's, thesis. *Entrance requirements:* Additional exam requirements/recommendations for international students: Required—TOEFL (minimum score 550 paper-based; 80 iBT) or IELTS (minimum score 6.5). *Application deadline:* For fall admission, 2/1 priority date for domestic and international students. Application fee: $50 ($55 for international students). Electronic applications accepted. *Financial support:* Research assistantships with full tuition reimbursements, teaching assistantships with full tuition reimbursements, Federal Work-Study, institutionally sponsored loans, scholarships/grants, tuition waivers (partial), and unspecified assistantships available. Financial award application deadline: 2/1. *Faculty research:* Geoscience education, tectonics, fluvial geomorphology, invertebrate paleontology, mine/hydrology. Total annual research expenditures: $649,020. *Unit head:* Dr. Gregory Nadon, Chair, 740-593-4212, Fax: 740-593-0486, E-mail: nadon@ohio.edu. *Application contact:* Dr. Douglas Green, Graduate Chair, 740-593-1843, Fax: 740-593-0486, E-mail: green@ohio.edu.

University of Hawaii at Manoa, Graduate Division, School of Ocean and Earth Science and Technology, Department of Geology and Geophysics, Honolulu, HI 96822. Offers high-pressure geophysics and geochemistry (MS, PhD); hydrogeology and engineering geology (MS, PhD); marine geology and geophysics (MS, PhD); planetary geosciences and remote sensing (MS, PhD); seismology and solid-earth geophysics (MS, PhD); volcanology, petrology, and geochemistry (MS, PhD). Part-time programs available. *Faculty:* 72 full-time (15 women), 6 part-time/adjunct (3 women). *Students:* 38 full-time (20 women), 5 part-time (3 women); includes 8 minority (1 Black or African American, non-Hispanic/Latino; 2 Asian, non-Hispanic/Latino; 1 Hispanic/Latino; 1 Native Hawaiian or other Pacific Islander, non-Hispanic/Latino; 3 Two or more races, non-Hispanic/Latino), 6 international. Average age 31. 64 applicants, 23% accepted, 7 enrolled. In 2010, 7 master's, 8 doctorates awarded. Terminal master's awarded for partial completion of doctoral program. *Degree requirements:* For master's, thesis optional; for doctorate, comprehensive exam, thesis/dissertation. *Entrance requirements:* For master's and doctorate, GRE General Test, minimum GPA of 3.0. Additional exam requirements/recommendations for international students: Required—TOEFL (minimum score 580 paper-based; 237 computer-based; 92 iBT), IELTS (minimum score 5). *Application deadline:* For fall admission, 1/15 for domestic students, 1/1 for international students; for spring admission, 9/1 for domestic students, 8/15 for international students. Application fee: $60. *Financial support:* In 2010–11, 7 fellowships (averaging $1,359 per year), 30 research assistantships (averaging $23,988 per year), 4 teaching assistantships (averaging $15,350 per year) were awarded. Total annual research expenditures: $3.8 million. *Application contact:* Dr. Gregory Moore, Chair, 808-956-7640, Fax: 808-956-5512, E-mail: gg-dept@soest.hawaii.edu.

University of Nevada, Reno, Graduate School, Interdisciplinary Program in Hydrologic Sciences, Reno, NV 89557. Offers hydrogeology (MS, PhD); hydrology (MS, PhD). Offered through the M. C. Fleischmann College of Agriculture, the College of Engineering, the Mackay School of Mines, and the Desert Research Institute. Terminal master's awarded for partial completion of doctoral program. *Degree requirements:* For master's, thesis optional; for doctorate, thesis/dissertation. *Entrance requirements:* For master's and doctorate, GRE General Test, minimum GPA of 3.0. Additional exam requirements/recommendations for international students: Required—TOEFL (minimum score 500 paper-based; 173 computer-based; 61 iBT), IELTS (minimum score 6). Electronic applications accepted. *Expenses:* Tuition, state resident: full-time $2219; part-time $246 per credit. Tuition, nonresident: part-time $510 per credit. International tuition: $9009 full-time. Required fees: $59 per term. One-time fee: $101. Tuition and fees vary according to course load. *Faculty research:* Groundwater, water resources, surface water, soil science.

The University of Texas at Dallas, School of Natural Sciences and Mathematics, Program in Geosciences, Richardson, TX 75080. Offers geochemistry (MS, PhD); geophysics (MS, PhD); geospatial information sciences (MS, PhD); hydrogeology (MS, PhD); sedimentary, stratigraphy, paleontology (PhD); stratigraphy, paleontology (MS); structural geology and tectonics (MS, PhD). Part-time and evening/weekend programs available. *Faculty:* 11 full-time (1 woman). *Students:* 38 full-time (13 women), 25 part-time (8 women); includes 11 minority (4 Black or African American, non-Hispanic/Latino; 4 Asian, non-Hispanic/Latino; 3 Hispanic/Latino), 19 international. Average age 32. 48 applicants, 46% accepted, 12 enrolled. In 2010, 9 master's, 1 doctorate awarded. *Degree requirements:* For master's, thesis optional; for doctorate, thesis/dissertation. *Entrance requirements:* For master's and doctorate, GRE General Test, minimum GPA of 3.0 in upper-level course work in field. Additional exam requirements/recommendations for international students: Required—TOEFL (minimum score 550 paper-based; 215 computer-based). *Application deadline:* For fall admission, 7/15 for domestic students, 5/1 priority date for international students; for spring admission, 11/15 for domestic students, 9/1 priority date for international students. Applications are processed on a rolling basis. Application fee: $50 ($100 for international students). Electronic applications accepted. *Expenses:* Tuition, state resident: full-time $10,248; part-time $569 per credit hour. Tuition, nonresident: full-time $18,544; part-time $1030 per credit hour. Tuition and fees vary according to course load. *Financial support:* In 2010–11, 38 students received support, including 15 research assistantships with partial tuition reimbursements available (averaging $14,400 per year), 14 teaching assistantships with partial tuition reimbursements available (averaging $13,905 per year); career-related internships or fieldwork, Federal Work-Study, institutionally sponsored loans, scholarships/

grants, and unspecified assistantships also available. Support available to part-time students. Financial award application deadline: 4/30; financial award applicants required to submit FAFSA. *Faculty research:* Cybermapping, GPS applications for geophysics and geology, seismology and ground-penetrating radar, numerical modeling, signal processing and inverse modeling techniques in seismology. *Unit head:* Dr. John Oldow, Department Head, 972-883-2403, Fax: 972-883-2537, E-mail: geosciences@utdallas.edu. *Application contact:* Dr. Robert J. Stern, Graduate Advisor, 972-883-2442, Fax: 972-883-2537, E-mail: rjstern@utdallas.edu.

West Virginia University, Eberly College of Arts and Sciences, Department of Geology and Geography, Program in Geology, Morgantown, WV 26506. Offers geomorphology (MS, PhD); geophysics (MS, PhD); hydrogeology (MS, PhD); paleontology (MS, PhD); petroleum geology (PhD); petrology (MS, PhD); stratigraphy (MS, PhD); structure (MS, PhD). Part-time programs available. Terminal master's awarded for partial completion of doctoral program. *Degree requirements:* For master's, thesis (for some programs); for doctorate, comprehensive exam, thesis/dissertation. *Entrance requirements:* For master's, GRE General Test, minimum GPA of 2.5; for doctorate, GRE General Test, minimum GPA of 3.3. Additional exam requirements/recommendations for international students: Required—TOEFL.

Hydrology

Auburn University, Graduate School, Ginn College of Engineering, Department of Civil Engineering, Auburn University, AL 36849. Offers construction engineering and management (MCE, MS, PhD); environmental engineering (MCE, MS, PhD); geotechnical/materials engineering (MCE, MS, PhD); hydraulics/hydrology (MCE, MS, PhD); structural engineering (MCE, MS, PhD); transportation engineering (MCE, MS, PhD). Part-time programs available. *Faculty:* 21 full-time (1 woman), 3 part-time/adjunct (1 woman). *Students:* 46 full-time (15 women), 39 part-time (5 women); includes 3 Black or African American, non-Hispanic/Latino; 1 Asian, non-Hispanic/Latino, 29 international. Average age 26. 136 applicants, 43% accepted, 26 enrolled. In 2010, 19 master's, 4 doctorates awarded. *Degree requirements:* For master's, project (MCE), thesis (MS); for doctorate, comprehensive exam, thesis/dissertation. *Entrance requirements:* For master's and doctorate, GRE General Test. *Application deadline:* For fall admission, 7/7 for domestic students; for spring admission, 11/24 for domestic students. Applications are processed on a rolling basis. Application fee: $50 ($60 for international students). Electronic applications accepted. *Expenses:* Tuition, state resident: full-time $7002. Tuition, nonresident: full-time $21,898. International tuition: $22,116 full-time. Required fees: $892. Tuition and fees vary according to course load and program. *Financial support:* Fellowships, research assistantships, teaching assistantships, Federal Work-Study available. Support available to part-time students. Financial award application deadline: 3/15; financial award applicants required to submit FAFSA. *Unit head:* Dr. J. Michael Stallings, Head, 334-844-4320. *Application contact:* Dr. George Flowers, Dean of the Graduate School, 334-844-2125.

California State University, Bakersfield, Division of Graduate Studies, School of Natural Sciences and Mathematics, Program in Geology, Bakersfield, CA 93311. Offers geology (MS); hydrogeology (MS); petroleum geology (MS). Part-time and evening/weekend programs available. *Degree requirements:* For master's, thesis. *Entrance requirements:* For master's, GRE General Test, BS in geology.

California State University, Chico, Graduate School, College of Natural Sciences, Department of Geological and Environmental Sciences, Program in Geosciences, Chico, CA 95929-0722. Offers hydrology/hydrogeology (MS). Part-time programs available. *Students:* 5 full-time (1 woman), 4 part-time (2 women); includes 1 Hispanic/Latino. Average age 36. 9 applicants, 44% accepted, 3 enrolled. In 2010, 1 master's awarded. *Degree requirements:* For master's, thesis, oral exam. *Entrance requirements:* For master's, GRE General Test. Additional exam requirements/recommendations for international students: Required—TOEFL (minimum score 550 paper-based; 213 computer-based; 80 iBT), IELTS (minimum score 6.5). *Application deadline:* For fall admission, 3/1 priority date for domestic students, 3/1 for international students; for spring admission, 9/15 priority date for domestic students, 9/15 for international students. Applications are processed on a rolling basis. Application fee: $55. Electronic applications accepted. *Financial support:* Fellowships available. *Unit head:* Dr. William Murphy, Graduate Coordinator, 530-898-5163. *Application contact:* Dr. William Murphy, Graduate Coordinator, 530-898-5163.

Colorado State University, Graduate School, Warner College of Natural Resources, Department of Forest, Rangeland, and Watershed Stewardship, Fort Collins, CO 80523-1472. Offers forest sciences (MS, PhD); natural resources stewardship (MNRS); rangeland ecosystem science (MS, PhD); watershed science (MS). Part-time programs available. Postbaccalaureate distance learning degree programs offered (no on-campus study). *Faculty:* 18 full-time (5 women), 2 part-time/adjunct (0 women). *Students:* 45 full-time (21 women), 90 part-time (31 women); includes 9 minority (3 American Indian or Alaska Native, non-Hispanic/Latino; 1 Asian, non-Hispanic/Latino; 5 Hispanic/Latino), 9 international. Average age 34. 59 applicants, 76% accepted, 28 enrolled. In 2010, 27 master's, 2 doctorates awarded. *Degree requirements:* For master's, thesis (for some programs); for doctorate, comprehensive exam, thesis/dissertation. *Entrance requirements:* For master's, GRE General Test (minimum score 1000 verbal and quantitative), minimum GPA of 3.0, 3 letters of recommendation; for doctorate, GRE General Test (combined minimum score of 1100 on the Verbal and Quantitative sections), minimum GPA of 3.0, 3 letters of recommendation, statement of research interest. Additional exam requirements/recommendations for international students: Required—TOEFL (minimum score 550 paper-based; 213 computer-based; 80 iBT), IELTS (minimum score 6.5). *Application deadline:* For fall admission, 2/15 priority date for domestic and international students; for spring admission, 7/15 priority date for domestic and international students. Applications are processed on a rolling basis. Application fee: $50. Electronic applications accepted. *Expenses:* Tuition, state resident: full-time $7434; part-time $413 per credit. Tuition, nonresident: full-time $19,022; part-time $1057 per credit. Required fees: $1729; $88 per credit. *Financial support:* In 2010–11, 46 students received support, including 1 fellowship (averaging $23,971 per year), 32 research assistantships with full and partial tuition reimbursements available (averaging $15,871 per year), 13 teaching assistantships with full and partial tuition reimbursements available (averaging $7,106 per year); Federal Work-Study, scholarships/grants, and unspecified assistantships also available. Financial award application deadline: 2/15; financial award applicants required to submit FAFSA. *Faculty research:* Ecology, natural resource management, hydrology, restoration, human dimensions. Total annual research expenditures: $2.4 million. *Unit head:* Dr. Frederick Smith, Interim Department Head, 970-491-7505, Fax: 970-491-6754, E-mail: fwsmith@colostate.edu. *Application contact:* Sonya LeFebre, Coordinator, 970-491-1907, Fax: 970-491-6754, E-mail: sonya.lefebre@colostate.edu.

Cornell University, Graduate School, Graduate Fields of Engineering, Field of Civil and Environmental Engineering, Ithaca, NY 14853-0001. Offers engineering management (M Eng, MS, PhD); environmental engineering (M Eng, MS, PhD); environmental fluid mechanics and hydrology (M Eng, MS, PhD); environmental systems engineering (M Eng, MS, PhD); geotechnical engineering (M Eng, MS, PhD); remote sensing (M Eng, MS, PhD); structural engineering (M Eng, MS, PhD); structural mechanics (M Eng, MS); transportation engineering (MS, PhD); transportation systems engineering (M Eng); water resource systems (M Eng, MS, PhD). *Faculty:* 36 full-time (4 women). *Students:* 148 full-time (48 women); includes 3 Black or African American, non-Hispanic/Latino; 1 American Indian or Alaska Native, non-Hispanic/Latino; 16 Asian, non-Hispanic/Latino; 16 Hispanic/Latino, 60 international. Average age 24. 390 applicants, 56% accepted, 76 enrolled. In 2010, 93 master's, 5 doctorates awarded. Terminal master's awarded for partial completion of doctoral program. *Degree requirements:* For master's, thesis (MS); for doctorate, comprehensive exam, thesis/dissertation. *Entrance requirements:* For master's and doctorate, GRE General Test (recommended), 2 letters of recommendation. Additional exam requirements/recommendations for international students: Required—TOEFL (minimum score 600 paper-based; 250 computer-based; 77 iBT). *Application deadline:* For fall admission, 1/15 priority date for domestic students; for spring admission, 10/15 for domestic students. Application fee: $70. Electronic applications accepted. *Expenses:* Tuition: Full-time $29,500. Required fees: $76. Tuition and fees vary according to degree level and program. *Financial support:* In 2010–11, 50 students received support, including 17 fellowships with full tuition reimbursements available, 33 research assistantships with full tuition reimbursements available, 15 teaching assistantships with full tuition reimbursements available; institutionally sponsored loans, scholarships/grants, health care benefits, tuition waivers (full and partial), and unspecified assistantships also available. Financial award applicants required to submit FAFSA. *Faculty research:* Environmental engineering, geotechnical engineering, remote sensing, environmental fluid mechanics and hydrology, structural engineering. *Unit head:* Director of Graduate Studies, 607-255-7560, Fax: 607-255-9004. *Application contact:* Graduate Field Assistant, 607-255-7560, Fax: 607-255-9004, E-mail: cee_grad@cornell.edu.

Cornell University, Graduate School, Graduate Fields of Engineering, Field of Geological Sciences, Ithaca, NY 14853. Offers economic geology (M Eng, MS, PhD); engineering geology (M Eng, MS, PhD); environmental geophysics (M Eng, MS, PhD); general geology (M Eng, MS, PhD); geobiology (M Eng, MS, PhD); geochemistry and isotope geology (M Eng, MS, PhD); geohydrology (M Eng, MS, PhD); geomorphology (M Eng, MS, PhD); geophysics (M Eng, MS, PhD); geotectonics (M Eng, MS, PhD); marine geology (MS, PhD); mineralogy (M Eng, MS, PhD); paleontology (M Eng, MS, PhD); petroleum geology (M Eng, MS, PhD); petrology (M Eng, MS, PhD); planetary geology (M Eng, MS, PhD); Precambrian geology (M Eng, MS, PhD); Quaternary geology (M Eng, MS, PhD); rock mechanics (M Eng, MS, PhD); sedimentology (M Eng, MS, PhD); seismology (M Eng, MS, PhD); stratigraphy (M Eng, MS, PhD); structural geology (M Eng, MS, PhD). *Faculty:* 36 full-time (5 women). *Students:* 38 full-time (15 women); includes 2 Asian, non-Hispanic/Latino; 2 Hispanic/Latino, 9 international. Average age 27. 84 applicants, 25% accepted, 17 enrolled. In 2010, 3 master's, 5 doctorates awarded. *Degree requirements:* For master's, thesis (MS); for doctorate, comprehensive exam, thesis/dissertation. *Entrance requirements:* For master's and doctorate, GRE General Test, 3 letters of recommendation. Additional exam requirements/recommendations for international students: Required—TOEFL (minimum score 550 paper-based; 213 computer-based; 77 iBT). *Application deadline:* For fall admission, 1/15 priority date for domestic students. Applications are processed on a rolling basis. Application fee: $70. Electronic applications accepted. *Expenses:* Tuition: Full-time $29,500. Required fees: $76. Tuition and fees vary according to degree level and program. *Financial support:* In 2010–11, 25 students received support, including 10 fellowships with full tuition reimbursements available, 14 research assistantships with full tuition reimbursements available, 10 teaching assistantships with full tuition reimbursements available; institutionally sponsored loans, scholarships/grants, health care benefits, tuition waivers (full and partial), and unspecified assistantships also available. Financial award applicants required to submit FAFSA. *Faculty research:* Geophysics, structural geology, petrology, geochemistry, geodynamics. *Unit head:* Director of Graduate Studies, 607-255-5466, Fax: 607-254-4780. *Application contact:* Graduate Field Assistant, 607-255-5466, Fax: 607-254-4780, E-mail: gradprog@geology.cornell.edu.

Drexel University, College of Engineering, Department of Civil, Architectural, and Environmental Engineering, Philadelphia, PA 19104-2875. Offers architectural / building systems engineering (MS, PhD); civil engineering (MS, PhD); environmental engineering (MS, PhD); geotechnical, geoenvironmental and geosynthetics engineering (MS, PhD); hydraulics, hydrology and water resources engineering (MS, PhD); structures (MS). Part-time and evening/weekend programs available. *Degree requirements:* For master's, thesis optional; for doctorate, thesis/dissertation. *Entrance requirements:* For master's, minimum GPA of 3.0; for doctorate, minimum GPA of 3.5, MS in civil engineering. Additional exam requirements/recommendations for international students: Required—TOEFL. Electronic applications accepted. *Faculty research:* Structural dynamics, hazardous wastes, water resources, pavement materials, groundwater.

Idaho State University, Office of Graduate Studies, College of Arts and Sciences, Department of Geosciences, Pocatello, ID 83209-8072. Offers geographic information science (MS); geology (MNS, MS); geology with emphasis in environmental geoscience (MS); geophysics/hydrology/geology (MS); geotechnology (Postbaccalaureate Certificate). Part-time programs available. *Degree requirements:* For master's, comprehensive exam, thesis, oral colloquium; for Postbaccalaureate Certificate, thesis optional, minimum 19 credits. *Entrance requirements:* For master's, GRE General Test (minimum 50th percentile in 2 sections), 3 letters of recommendation; for Postbaccalaureate Certificate, GRE General Test, 3 letters of recommendation, bachelor's degree, statement of goals. Additional exam requirements/recommendations for international students: Required—TOEFL (minimum score 550 paper-based; 213 computer-based; 80 iBT). Electronic applications accepted. *Faculty research:* Quantitative field mapping and sampling: microscopic, geochemical, and isotopic analysis of rocks, minerals and water; remote sensing, geographic information systems, and global positioning systems: environmental and watershed management; surficial and fluvial processes: landscape change; regional tectonics, structural geology; planetary geology.

Illinois State University, Graduate School, College of Arts and Sciences, Department of Geography-Geology, Normal, IL 61790-2200. Offers hydrogeology (MS). *Degree requirements:* For master's, thesis optional. *Entrance requirements:* For master's, GRE General Test. *Faculty research:* Thermal transport within the hyporheic zone, nutrient cycling in watersheds, water quality in karst systems, ground water dating using dissolved helium.

Massachusetts Institute of Technology, School of Engineering, Department of Civil and Environmental Engineering, Cambridge, MA 02139. Offers biological oceanography (PhD, Sc D); chemical oceanography (PhD, Sc D); civil and environmental engineering (M Eng, SM, PhD, Sc D); civil and environmental systems (PhD, Sc D); civil engineering (PhD, Sc D, CE); coastal engineering (PhD, Sc D); construction engineering and management (PhD, Sc D); environmental biology (PhD, Sc D); environmental chemistry (PhD, Sc D); environmental engineering (PhD, Sc D); environmental fluid mechanics (PhD, Sc D); geotechnical and geoenvironmental engineering (PhD, Sc D); hydrology (PhD, Sc D); information technology (PhD, Sc D); oceanographic engineering (PhD, Sc D); structures and materials (PhD, Sc D); transportation (PhD, Sc D); SM/MBA. *Faculty:* 36 full-time (6 women). *Students:* 181 full-time

Hydrology

Massachusetts Institute of Technology (continued)

(56 women); includes 27 minority (3 Black or African American, non-Hispanic/Latino; 10 Asian, non-Hispanic/Latino; 10 Hispanic/Latino; 4 Two or more races, non-Hispanic/Latino), 93 international. Average age 26. 525 applicants, 29% accepted, 74 enrolled. In 2010, 85 master's, 18 doctorates, 2 other advanced degrees awarded. *Degree requirements:* For master's and CE, thesis; for doctorate, comprehensive exam, thesis/dissertation. *Entrance requirements:* For master's and doctorate, GRE General Test. Additional exam requirements/recommendations for international students: Required—TOEFL (minimum score 577 paper-based; 233 computer-based; 90 iBT), IELTS (minimum score 7). *Application deadline:* For fall admission, 1/2 for domestic and international students. Application fee: $75. Electronic applications accepted. *Expenses:* Tuition: Full-time $38,940; part-time $605 per unit. Required fees: $272. *Financial support:* In 2010–11, 146 students received support, including 50 fellowships with tuition reimbursements available (averaging $21,808 per year), 90 research assistantships with tuition reimbursements available (averaging $28,452 per year), 20 teaching assistantships with tuition reimbursements available (averaging $27,842 per year); career-related internships or fieldwork, Federal Work-Study, institutionally sponsored loans, scholarships/grants, health care benefits, and unspecified assistantships also available. *Faculty research:* Environmental chemistry; environmental microbiology; environmental fluid mechanics and coastal engineering; geotechnical engineering and geomechanics; hydrology and hydroclimatology; mechanics of materials and structures; operations research/supply chain; transportation. Total annual research expenditures: $19.5 million. *Unit head:* Prof. Andrew Whittle, Department Head, 617-253-7101. *Application contact:* Patricia Glidden, Graduate Admissions Coordinator, 617-253-7119, Fax: 617-258-6775, E-mail: cee-admissions@mit.edu.

Missouri University of Science and Technology, Graduate School, Department of Civil, Architectural, and Environmental Engineering, Rolla, MO 65409. Offers civil engineering (MS, DE, PhD); construction engineering (MS, DE, PhD); environmental engineering (MS); fluid mechanics (MS, DE, PhD); geotechnical engineering (MS, DE, PhD); hydrology and hydraulic engineering (MS, DE, PhD). Part-time and evening/weekend programs available. Terminal master's awarded for partial completion of doctoral program. *Degree requirements:* For master's, thesis optional; for doctorate, comprehensive exam, thesis/dissertation. *Entrance requirements:* For master's, GRE General Test (minimum combined score 1100), minimum GPA of 3.0; for doctorate, GRE General Test (minimum score: verbal and quantitative 400, writing 3.5), minimum GPA of 3.0. Additional exam requirements/recommendations for international students: Required—TOEFL. Electronic applications accepted. *Faculty research:* Earthquake engineering, structural optimization and control systems, structural health monitoring/damage detection, soil-structure interaction, soil mechanics and foundation engineering.

Murray State University, College of Science, Engineering and Technology, Program in Water Science, Murray, KY 42071. Offers MS. Part-time programs available. *Degree requirements:* For master's, comprehensive exam, thesis. *Entrance requirements:* For master's, GRE General Test. Electronic applications accepted. *Faculty research:* Water chemistry, GIS, amphibian biology, nutrient chemistry, limnology.

New Mexico Institute of Mining and Technology, Graduate Studies, Department of Earth and Environmental Science, Program in Hydrology, Socorro, NM 87801. Offers MS, PhD. *Degree requirements:* For master's, thesis; for doctorate, thesis/dissertation. *Entrance requirements:* For master's, GRE General Test; for doctorate, GRE General Test, GRE Subject Test. Additional exam requirements/recommendations for international students: Required—TOEFL (minimum score 540 paper-based; 207 computer-based). *Faculty research:* Surface and subsurface hydrology, numerical simulation, stochastic hydrology, water quality, modeling.

Stevens Institute of Technology, Graduate School, Charles V. Schaefer Jr. School of Engineering, Department of Civil, Environmental, and Ocean Engineering, Program in Civil Engineering, Hoboken, NJ 07030. Offers civil engineering (PhD); geotechnical engineering (Certificate); geotechnical/geoenvironmental engineering (M Eng, Engr); hydrologic modeling (M Eng); stormwater management (M Eng); structural engineering (M Eng, Engr); water resources engineering (M Eng). *Students:* 22 full-time (6 women), 36 part-time (11 women); includes 10 Asian, non-Hispanic/Latino; 3 Hispanic/Latino, 16 international. Average age 28. 37 applicants, 86% accepted. *Degree requirements:* For master's, thesis optional; for doctorate, variable foreign language requirement, thesis/dissertation; for other advanced degree, project or thesis. *Entrance requirements:* For doctorate, GRE. Additional exam requirements/recommendations for international students: Required—TOEFL. *Application deadline:* Applications are processed on a rolling basis. Application fee: $50. Electronic applications accepted. *Financial support:* Application deadline: 4/15. *Unit head:* Dr. David A. Vaccari, Director, 201-216-5570, Fax: 201-216-5352, E-mail: dvaccari@stevens.edu. *Application contact:* Dr. David A. Vaccari, Director, 201-216-5570, Fax: 201-216-5352, E-mail: dvaccari@stevens.edu.

Université du Québec, Institut National de la Recherche Scientifique, Graduate Programs, Research Center—Water, Earth and Environment, Québec, QC G1K 9A9, Canada. Offers earth sciences (M Sc, PhD); earth sciences-environmental technologies (M Sc); water sciences (M Sc, PhD). Part-time programs available. *Faculty:* 41. *Students:* 196 full-time (79 women), 17 part-time (5 women), 94 international. Average age 30. In 2010, 19 master's, 17 doctorates awarded. *Degree requirements:* For master's, thesis optional; for doctorate, thesis/dissertation. *Entrance requirements:* For master's, appropriate bachelor's degree, proficiency in French; for doctorate, appropriate master's degree, proficiency in French. *Application deadline:* For fall admission, 3/30 for domestic and international students; for winter admission, 11/1 for domestic and international students; for spring admission, 3/1 for domestic and international students. Application fee: $30. *Financial support:* Fellowships, research assistantships, teaching assistantships available. *Faculty research:* Land use, impacts of climate change, adaptation to climate change, integrated management of resources (mineral and water). *Unit head:* Yves Begin, Director, 418-654-2524, Fax: 418-654-2600, E-mail: info@ete.inrs.ca. *Application contact:* Yvonne Boisvert, Registrar, 418-654-3861, Fax: 418-654-3858, E-mail: registrariat@adm.inrs.ca.

The University of Arizona, College of Science, Department of Hydrology and Water Resources, Tucson, AZ 85721. Offers MS, PhD. Part-time programs available. *Faculty:* 15 full-time (2 women). *Students:* 37 full-time (10 women), 11 part-time (4 women); includes 5 Hispanic/Latino; 3 Two or more races, non-Hispanic/Latino, 10 international. Average age 33. 66 applicants, 14% accepted, 9 enrolled. In 2010, 6 master's, 4 doctorates awarded. *Degree requirements:* For master's, thesis; for doctorate, thesis/dissertation. *Entrance requirements:* For master's, GRE General Test, 3 letters of recommendation, bachelor's degree in related field; for doctorate, GRE General Test, minimum undergraduate GPA of 3.2, graduate 3.4; 3 letters of recommendation; master's degree in related field; master's thesis abstract. Additional exam requirements/recommendations for international students: Required—TOEFL (minimum score 550 paper-based; 213 computer-based; 79 iBT). *Application deadline:* For fall admission, 5/1 for domestic students, 12/1 for international students; for spring admission, 10/1 for domestic students, 6/1 for international students. Applications are processed on a rolling basis. Application fee: $75. Electronic applications accepted. *Expenses:* Tuition, state resident: full-time $7692. *Financial support:* In 2010–11, 20 research assistantships with full tuition reimbursements (averaging $23,223 per year), 4 teaching assistantships with full tuition reimbursements (averaging $23,586 per year) were awarded; institutionally sponsored loans, scholarships/grants, health care benefits, and unspecified assistantships also available. Financial award application deadline: 1/31. *Faculty research:* Subsurface and surface hydrology, hydrometeorology/climatology, applied remote sensing, water resource systems, environmental hydrology and water quality. Total annual research expenditures: $5.5 million. *Unit head:* Thomas Maddock, Department Head, 520-621-7120, E-mail: maddock@hwr.arizona.edu. *Application contact:* Terrie Thompson, Academic Advising Coordinator, 520-621-3131, Fax: 520-621-1422, E-mail: programs@hwr.arizona.edu.

University of California, Davis, Graduate Studies, Graduate Group in Hydrologic Sciences, Davis, CA 95616. Offers MS, PhD. Terminal master's awarded for partial completion of doctoral program. *Degree requirements:* For master's, comprehensive exam (for some programs), thesis (for some programs); for doctorate, thesis/dissertation. *Entrance requirements:* For master's, GRE General Test, minimum GPA of 3.0; for doctorate, GRE. Additional exam requirements/recommendations for international students: Required—TOEFL (minimum score 550 paper-based; 213 computer-based). Electronic applications accepted. *Faculty research:* Pollutant transport in surface and subsurface waters, subsurface heterogeneity, micrometeorology evaporation, biodegradation.

University of Colorado Boulder, Graduate School, College of Engineering and Applied Science, Department of Civil, Environmental, and Architectural Engineering, Boulder, CO 80309. Offers building systems (MS, PhD); construction engineering management (MS, PhD); environmental engineering (MS, PhD); geotechnical engineering and geomechanics (MS, PhD); hydrology, water resources and environmental fluid mechanics (MS, PhD); structural engineering and structural mechanics (MS, PhD). *Faculty:* 38 full-time (6 women). *Students:* 255 full-time (86 women), 40 part-time (11 women); includes 40 minority (1 Black or African American, non-Hispanic/Latino; 2 American Indian or Alaska Native, non-Hispanic/Latino; 15 Asian, non-Hispanic/Latino; 20 Hispanic/Latino; 2 Two or more races, non-Hispanic/Latino), 61 international. Average age 28. 420 applicants, 95 enrolled. In 2010, 56 master's, 18 doctorates awarded. *Degree requirements:* For master's, comprehensive exam, thesis or alternative; for doctorate, thesis/dissertation. *Entrance requirements:* For master's, GRE General Test, minimum undergraduate GPA of 3.0. *Application deadline:* For fall admission, 3/1 for domestic students, 12/1 for international students; for spring admission, 10/31 for domestic students, 10/1 for international students. Application fee: $50 ($60 for international students). *Financial support:* In 2010–11, 45 fellowships (averaging $7,876 per year), 68 research assistantships (averaging $15,204 per year) were awarded. Financial award application deadline: 1/15. *Faculty research:* Building systems engineering, construction engineering and management, environmental engineering, geoenvironmental engineering, geotechnical engineering, materials and mechanics, structural engineering, water resources engineering, life-cycle engineering. Total annual research expenditures: $8 million.

University of Colorado Denver, College of Engineering and Applied Science, Department of Civil Engineering, Denver, CO 80217-3364. Offers civil engineering (PhD); environmental and sustainability engineering (MS); geographic information systems (MS); geotechnical engineering (MS); hydrology and hydraulics (MS); structural engineering (MS); transportation engineering (MS). Part-time and evening/weekend programs available. *Faculty:* 14 full-time (1 woman), 6 part-time/adjunct (0 women). *Students:* 66 full-time (13 women), 72 part-time (16 women); includes 9 Black or African American, non-Hispanic/Latino; 8 Asian, non-Hispanic/Latino; 11 Hispanic/Latino, 15 international. Average age 32. 72 applicants, 54% accepted, 29 enrolled. In 2010, 14 master's, 3 doctorates awarded. *Degree requirements:* For master's, comprehensive exam, thesis or alternative; for doctorate, comprehensive exam, thesis/dissertation. *Entrance requirements:* For master's, GRE, statement of purpose, transcripts, references; for doctorate, GRE, statement of purpose, transcripts, references, letter of support from faculty stating willingness to serve as dissertation advisor and outlining plan for financial support. Additional exam requirements/recommendations for international students: Required—TOEFL (minimum score 525 paper-based; 197 computer-based). *Application deadline:* For fall admission, 7/15 for domestic students, 6/15 for international students; for spring admission, 12/1 for domestic students, 11/1 for international students. Applications are processed on a rolling basis. Application fee: $50 ($75 for international students). Electronic applications accepted. *Expenses:* Contact institution. *Financial support:* Research assistantships, teaching assistantships, career-related internships or fieldwork and Federal Work-Study available. Financial award application deadline: 4/1; financial award applicants required to submit FAFSA. *Faculty research:* Environmental engineering and sustainable systems, geosynthetics, hydrologic andhydraulic engineering, structural engineering, transportation, transportation energy use and greenhouse gas emissions. *Unit head:* Dr. Nien-Yin Chang, Acting Chair, 303-556-2810, Fax: 303-556-2368, E-mail: nien.chang@ucdenver.edu. *Application contact:* Mindy Gewuerz, Program Assistant, 303-556-6712, Fax: 303-556-2368, E-mail: mindy.gewuerz@ucdenver.edu.

University of Idaho, College of Graduate Studies, College of Science, Department of Geological Sciences, Program in Hydrology, Moscow, ID 83844-2282. Offers MS. *Students:* 3 full-time, 2 part-time. Average age 26. In 2010, 1 master's awarded. *Entrance requirements:* For master's, minimum GPA of 2.8. *Application deadline:* For fall admission, 8/1 for domestic students; for spring admission, 12/15 for domestic students. Applications are processed on a rolling basis. Application fee: $60. Electronic applications accepted. *Expenses:* Tuition, nonresident: part-time $580 per credit. Required fees: $306 per credit. *Financial support:* Applicants required to submit FAFSA. *Unit head:* Dr. Mickey Gunter, Head, 208-885-6491. *Application contact:* Dr. Mickey Gunter, Head, 208-885-6491.

University of Nevada, Reno, Graduate School, Interdisciplinary Program in Hydrologic Sciences, Reno, NV 89557. Offers hydrogeology (MS, PhD); hydrology (MS, PhD). Offered through the M. C. Fleischmann College of Agriculture, the College of Engineering, the Mackay School of Mines, and the Desert Research Institute. Terminal master's awarded for partial completion of doctoral program. *Degree requirements:* For master's, thesis optional; for doctorate, thesis/dissertation. *Entrance requirements:* For master's and doctorate, GRE General Test, minimum GPA of 3.0. Additional exam requirements/recommendations for international students: Required—TOEFL (minimum score 500 paper-based; 173 computer-based; 61 iBT), IELTS (minimum score 6). Electronic applications accepted. *Expenses:* Tuition, state resident: full-time $2219; part-time $246 per credit. Tuition, nonresident: part-time $510 per credit. International tuition: $9009 full-time. Required fees: $59 per term. One-time fee: $101. Tuition and fees vary according to course load. *Faculty research:* Groundwater, water resources, surface water, soil science.

University of New Brunswick Fredericton, School of Graduate Studies, Faculty of Engineering, Department of Civil Engineering, Fredericton, NB E3B 5A3, Canada. Offers construction engineering and management (M Eng, M Sc E, PhD); environmental engineering (M Eng, M Sc E, PhD); environmental studies (M Eng); geotechnical engineering (M Eng, M Sc E, PhD); groundwater/hydrology (M Eng, M Sc E, PhD); materials (M Eng, M Sc E, PhD); pavements (M Eng, M Sc E, PhD); structures (M Eng, M Sc E, PhD); transportation (M Eng, M Sc E, PhD). Part-time programs available. *Faculty:* 13 full-time (1 woman), 7 part-time/adjunct (1 woman). *Students:* 34 full-time (8 women), 16 part-time (2 women). In 2010, 16 master's, 6 doctorates awarded. *Degree requirements:* For master's, thesis, proposal; for doctorate, comprehensive exam, thesis/dissertation, qualifying exam; proposal; 27 credit hours of courses. *Entrance requirements:* For master's, minimum GPA of 3.0; B Sc E in civil engineering or related engineering degree; for doctorate, minimum GPA of 3.0; graduate degree in engineering or applied science. Additional exam requirements/recommendations for international students: Required—TWE (minimum score 4), TOEFL (minimum score 580 paper-based; 237 computer-based) or IELTS (minimum score 7.5). *Application deadline:* For fall admission, 5/1 priority date for domestic students; for winter admission, 11/1 priority date for domestic students. Applications are processed on a rolling basis. Application fee: $50 Canadian dollars. *Expenses:* Tuition, area resident: Full-time $3708; part-time $927 per term. International tuition: $6300 full-time. Required fees: $50 per term. *Financial support:* In 2010–11, 52 research assistantships (averaging $7,000 per year), 46 teaching assistantships (averaging $2,000 per year) were awarded; career-related internships or fieldwork and scholarships/grants also available. *Faculty research:* Construction engineering and management; materials and infrastructure renewal; highway and pavement research; structures and solid mechanics; geotechnical, soil; structure interaction; transportation and planning; environment, solid waste management. *Unit head:* Dr. Eric Hildebrand, Director of Graduate Studies, 506-453-5113, Fax: 506-453-3568,

E-mail: edh@unb.ca. *Application contact:* Joyce Moore, Graduate Secretary, 506-452-6127, Fax: 506-453-3568, E-mail: civil-grad@unb.ca.

University of New Hampshire, Graduate School, College of Engineering and Physical Sciences, Department of Earth Sciences, Durham, NH 03824. Offers earth sciences (MS), including geochemical systems, geology, ocean mapping, oceanography; hydrology (MS). *Faculty:* 17 full-time (5 women). *Students:* 21 full-time (13 women), 8 part-time (4 women); includes 2 minority (1 Black or African American, non-Hispanic/Latino; 1 Asian, non-Hispanic/Latino), 4 international. Average age 27. 55 applicants, 65% accepted, 16 enrolled. In 2010, 8 master's awarded. *Degree requirements:* For master's, thesis. *Entrance requirements:* For master's, GRE General Test. Additional exam requirements/recommendations for international students: Required—TOEFL (minimum score 550 paper-based; 213 computer-based; 80 iBT). *Application deadline:* For fall admission, 4/1 priority date for domestic students, 4/1 for international students; for spring admission, 12/1 for domestic students. Applications are processed on a rolling basis. Application fee: $65. Electronic applications accepted. *Financial support:* In 2010–11, 24 students received support, including 13 research assistantships, 7 teaching assistantships; fellowships, career-related internships or fieldwork, Federal Work-Study, scholarships/grants, and tuition waivers (full and partial) also available. Support available to part-time students. Financial award application deadline: 2/15. *Unit head:* Dr. Will Clyde, Chairperson, 603-862-1718, E-mail: earth.sciences@unh.edu. *Application contact:* Sue Clark, Administrative Assistant, 603-862-1718, E-mail: earth.sciences@unh.edu.

University of Southern Mississippi, Graduate School, College of Science and Technology, Department of Marine Science, Stennis Space Center, MS 39529. Offers hydrographic science (MS); marine science (MS, PhD). Part-time programs available. *Faculty:* 17 full-time (2 women), 1 part-time/adjunct (0 women). *Students:* 36 full-time (13 women), 11 part-time (5 women); includes 11 Asian, non-Hispanic/Latino; 3 Hispanic/Latino. Average age 31. 35 applicants, 54% accepted, 16 enrolled. In 2010, 15 master's, 2 doctorates awarded. *Degree requirements:* For master's, comprehensive exam, thesis, oral qualifying exam (marine science); for doctorate, 2 foreign languages, comprehensive exam, thesis/dissertation, oral qualifying exam. *Entrance requirements:* For master's, GRE General Test, minimum GPA of 3.0; for doctorate, GRE General Test, minimum GPA of 3.0 (undergraduate), 3.5 (graduate). Additional exam requirements/recommendations for international students: Required—TOEFL. *Application deadline:* For fall admission, 3/1 priority date for domestic and international students. Applications are processed on a rolling basis. Application fee: $50. Electronic applications accepted. *Financial support:* In 2010–11, 4 students received support, including 26 research assistantships with full tuition reimbursements available (averaging $20,400 per year), 4 teaching assistantships with full tuition reimbursements available (averaging $20,400 per year); Federal Work-Study and institutionally sponsored loans also available. Financial award application deadline: 3/15. *Faculty research:* Chemical, biological, physical, and geological marine science; remote sensing; bio-optics; numerical modeling; hydrography. Total annual research expenditures: $5.8 million. *Unit head:* Dr. Steven E. Lohrenz, Chair, 228-688-3177, Fax: 228-688-1121, E-mail: marine.science@usm.edu. *Application contact:* Linda Downs, Senior Office Support Specialist, 228-688-3177, Fax: 228-688-1121, E-mail: marine.science@usm.edu.

University of Washington, Graduate School, College of Engineering, Department of Civil and Environmental Engineering, Seattle, WA 98195-2700. Offers construction engineering (MSCE); environmental engineering (MS, MSCE, MSE, PhD); hydrology, water resources, and environmental fluid mechanics (MS, MSCE, MSE, PhD); structural and geotechnical engineering and mechanics (MS, MSCE, MSE, PhD); transportation and construction engineering (MS, MSE, PhD); transportation engineering (MSCE). Part-time programs available. Postbaccalaureate distance learning degree programs offered (no on-campus study). *Faculty:* 44 full-time (10 women), 12 part-time/adjunct (1 woman). *Students:* 197 full-time (65 women), 65 part-time (15 women); includes 5 Black or African American, non-Hispanic/Latino; 28 Asian, non-Hispanic/Latino; 5 Hispanic/Latino, 55 international. 522 applicants, 51% accepted, 101 enrolled. In 2010, 68 master's, 5 doctorates awarded. Terminal master's awarded for partial completion of doctoral program. *Degree requirements:* For master's, thesis (for some programs); for doctorate, comprehensive exam, thesis/dissertation, General, qualifying, and final exams. Completion of doctoral degree within 10 years. *Entrance requirements:* For master's, GRE General Test, Minimum GPA of 3.0, statement of purpose, letters of recommendation, transcripts; for doctorate, GRE General Test, minimum GPA of 3.5, statement of purpose, letters of recommendation, transcripts. Additional exam requirements/recommendations for international students: Required—TOEFL (minimum score 580 paper-based; 237 computer-based; 92 iBT); Recommended—IELTS (minimum score 7). *Application deadline:* For fall admission, 1/10 priority date for domestic and international students. Application fee: $75. Electronic applications accepted. *Financial support:* In 2010–11, 2 students received support, including 25 fellowships with full and partial tuition reimbursements available (averaging $16,173 per year), 75 research assistantships with full tuition reimbursements available (averaging $16,515 per year), 11 teaching assistantships with full tuition reimbursements available (averaging $16,263 per year); scholarships/grants also available. Financial award application deadline: 1/10; financial award applicants required to submit FAFSA. *Faculty research:* Environmental/water resources, hydrology; construction/transportation; structures/ geotechnical. Total annual research expenditures: $14.4 million. *Unit head:* Dr. Gregory R. Miller, Professor and Chair, 206-543-0350, Fax: 206-543-1543, E-mail: gmiller@uw.edu. *Application contact:* Lorna Latal, Graduate Adviser, 206-543-2574, Fax: 206-543-1543, E-mail: llatal@u.washington.edu.

Virginia Polytechnic Institute and State University, Graduate School, College of Engineering, Department of Civil and Environmental Engineering, Blacksburg, VA 24061. Offers civil engineering (M Eng, MS, PhD); civil infrastructure systems (Certificate); environmental engineering (MS); environmental sciences and engineering (MS); transportation systems engineering (Certificate); treatment process engineering (Certificate); urban hydrology and stormwater management (Certificate); water quality management (Certificate). *Accreditation:* ABET (one or more programs are accredited). *Faculty:* 44 full-time (8 women), 1 part-time/adjunct (0 women). *Students:* 320 full-time (108 women), 70 part-time (20 women); includes 9 Black or African American, non-Hispanic/Latino; 15 Asian, non-Hispanic/Latino; 13 Hispanic/Latino, 126 international. Average age 27. 639 applicants, 44% accepted, 121 enrolled. In 2010, 97 master's, 18 doctorates awarded. *Degree requirements:* For master's, comprehensive exam (for some programs), thesis (for some programs); for doctorate, comprehensive exam (for some programs), thesis/dissertation (for some programs). *Entrance requirements:* For master's and doctorate, GRE. Additional exam requirements/recommendations for international students: Required—TOEFL (minimum score 550 paper-based; 213 computer-based). *Application deadline:* For fall admission, 7/1 for domestic and international students; for spring admission, 12/1 for domestic and international students. Applications are processed on a rolling basis. Application fee: $65. Electronic applications accepted. *Expenses:* Tuition, area resident: Full-time $9399; part-time $488 per credit hour. Tuition, state resident: full-time $9399; part-time $488 per credit hour. Tuition, nonresident: full-time $17,854; part-time $957.75 per credit hour. International tuition: $17,854 full-time. Required fees: $1534. Full-time tuition and fees vary according to program. *Financial support:* In 2010–11, 35 fellowships with full tuition reimbursements (averaging $5,861 per year), 82 research assistantships with full tuition reimbursements (averaging $20,397 per year), 33 teaching assistantships with full tuition reimbursements (averaging $14,542 per year) were awarded; career-related internships or fieldwork, Federal Work-Study, scholarships/grants, health care benefits, and unspecified assistantships also available. Financial award application deadline: 1/15. *Faculty research:* Construction, environmental geotechnical hydrosystems, structures and transportation engineering. Total annual research expenditures: $12.2 million. *Unit head:* Dr. Sam Easterling, UNIT HEAD, 540-231-5143, Fax: 540-231-7532, E-mail: seaster@vt.edu. *Application contact:* Marc Widdowson, Contact, 540-231-7153, Fax: 540-231-7532, E-mail: mwiddows@vt.edu.

Limnology

Baylor University, Graduate School, College of Arts and Sciences, Department of Biology, Waco, TX 76798. Offers biology (MA, MS, PhD); environmental biology (MS); limnology (MS). Part-time programs available. *Faculty:* 13 full-time (3 women). *Students:* 34 full-time (14 women), 2 part-time (both women); includes 4 minority (2 Hispanic/Latino; 2 Two or more races, non-Hispanic/Latino), 13 international. In 2010, 6 master's, 1 doctorate awarded. *Degree requirements:* For master's, thesis (for some programs); for doctorate, thesis/dissertation. *Entrance requirements:* For master's and doctorate, GRE General Test. *Application deadline:* For fall admission, 1/31 priority date for domestic students. Applications are processed on a rolling basis. Application fee: $25. *Financial support:* Teaching assistantships, career-related internships or fieldwork, Federal Work-Study, institutionally sponsored loans, and tuition waivers (full and partial) available. Support available to part-time students. Financial award application deadline: 2/28. *Faculty research:* Terrestrial ecology, aquatic ecology, genetics. *Unit head:* Dr. Myeongwoo Lee, Graduate Program Director, 254-710-2141, Fax: 254-710-2969, E-mail: myeongwoo_lee@baylor.edu. *Application contact:* Tamara Lehmann, Administrative Assistant, 254-710-2911, Fax: 254-710-2969, E-mail: tamara_lehmann@baylor.edu.

Cornell University, Graduate School, Graduate Fields of Agriculture and Life Sciences, Field of Ecology and Evolutionary Biology, Ithaca, NY 14853-0001. Offers ecology (PhD), including animal ecology, applied ecology, biogeochemistry, community and ecosystem ecology, limnology, oceanography, physiological ecology, plant ecology, population ecology, theoretical ecology, vertebrate zoology; evolutionary biology (PhD), including ecological genetics, paleobiology, population biology, systematics. *Faculty:* 48 full-time (13 women). *Students:* 51 full-time (37 women); includes 1 Asian, non-Hispanic/Latino; 3 Hispanic/Latino, 8 international. Average age 27. 108 applicants, 12% accepted, 10 enrolled. In 2010, 16 doctorates awarded. *Degree requirements:* For doctorate, comprehensive exam, thesis/dissertation, 2 semesters of teaching experience. *Entrance requirements:* For doctorate, GRE General Test, GRE Subject Test (biology), 2 letters of recommendation. Additional exam requirements/recommendations for international students: Required—TOEFL (minimum score 550 paper-based; 213 computer-based; 77 iBT). *Application deadline:* For fall admission, 12/15 for domestic students. Application fee: $70. Electronic applications accepted. *Expenses:* Tuition: Full-time $29,500. Required fees: $76. Tuition and fees vary according to degree level and program. *Financial support:* In 2010–11, 23 fellowships with full tuition reimbursements, 5 research assistantships with full tuition reimbursements, 21 teaching assistantships with full tuition reimbursements were awarded; institutionally sponsored loans, scholarships/grants, health care benefits, tuition waivers (full and partial), and unspecified assistantships also available. Financial award applicants required to submit FAFSA. *Faculty research:* Population and organismal biology, population and evolutionary genetics, systematics and macroevolution, biochemistry, conservation biology. *Unit head:* Director of Graduate Studies, 607-254-4230. *Application contact:* Graduate Field Assistant, 607-254-4230, E-mail: eeb_grad_req@cornell.edu.

University of Alaska Fairbanks, School of Fisheries and Ocean Sciences, Program in Marine Sciences and Limnology, Fairbanks, AK 99775-7220. Offers marine biology (MS, PhD); oceanography (PhD), including biological oceanography, chemical oceanography, fisheries, geological oceanography, physical oceanography. Part-time programs available. *Faculty:* 8 full-time (4 women). *Students:* 40 full-time (26 women), 12 part-time (7 women); includes 3 minority (2 Asian, non-Hispanic/Latino; 1 Hispanic/Latino), 3 international. Average age 31. 54 applicants, 26% accepted, 14 enrolled. In 2010, 6 master's, 1 doctorate awarded. *Degree requirements:* For master's, comprehensive exam, thesis, oral defense; for doctorate, comprehensive exam, thesis/dissertation, oral defense. *Entrance requirements:* For master's and doctorate, GRE General Test. Additional exam requirements/recommendations for international students: Required—TOEFL (minimum score 550 paper-based; 213 computer-based; 80 iBT). *Application deadline:* For fall admission, 6/1 for domestic students, 3/1 for international students; for spring admission, 10/15 for domestic students, 8/1 for international students. Applications are processed on a rolling basis. Application fee: $60. Electronic applications accepted. *Expenses:* Tuition, state resident: full-time $5688; part-time $316 per credit. Tuition, nonresident: full-time $11,628; part-time $646 per credit. Required fees: $289 per semester. Tuition and fees vary according to course load and reciprocity agreements. *Financial support:* In 2010–11, 24 research assistantships with tuition reimbursements (averaging $11,704 per year), 9 teaching assistantships with tuition reimbursements (averaging $11,008 per year) were awarded; fellowships with tuition reimbursements, career-related internships or fieldwork, Federal Work-Study, scholarships/grants, health care benefits, and unspecified assistantships also available. Support available to part-time students. Financial award application deadline: 7/1; financial award applicants required to submit FAFSA. *Unit head:* Katrin Iken, Co-Chair, 907-474-7289, Fax: 907-474-5863, E-mail: academics@sfos.uaf.edu. *Application contact:* Christina Neumann, Academic Manager, 907-474-7289, Fax: 907-474-5863, E-mail: clneumann@alaska.edu.

University of Florida, Graduate School, College of Agricultural and Life Sciences, Department of Fisheries and Aquatic Sciences, Gainesville, FL 32611. Offers MFAS, MS, PhD. Part-time programs available. *Students:* 5 full-time (2 women), 2 part-time (1 woman), 1 international. Average age 29. 34 applicants, 26% accepted, 8 enrolled. In 2010, 1 master's awarded. *Degree requirements:* For master's, thesis (for some programs), Thesis required for Masters of Science. Technical paper required for MFAS degree; for doctorate, comprehensive exam, thesis/dissertation. *Entrance requirements:* For master's and doctorate, GRE General Test, minimum GPA of 3.0. Additional exam requirements/recommendations for international students: Required—TOEFL (minimum score 550 paper-based; 213 computer-based; 80 iBT), IELTS (minimum score 6). *Application deadline:* For fall admission, 6/1 for domestic students, 3/1 for international students; for spring admission, 10/1 for domestic students, 8/1 for international students. Applications are processed on a rolling basis. Application fee: $30. Electronic applications accepted. *Expenses:* Tuition, state resident: full-time $10,915.92. Tuition, nonresident: full-time $28,309. *Financial support:* In 2010–11, 4 students received support, including 1 fellowship, 3 research assistantships (averaging $20,141 per year); unspecified assistantships also available. Financial award application deadline: 1/31; financial award applicants required to submit FAFSA. *Faculty research:* Conservation and management of aquatic ecosystems; aquatic animal health; water quality, nutrients, and eutrophication; sustainable and quantitative fisheries; aquaculture or ornamental fish, marine baitfish, and shellfish. Total annual research expenditures: $10 million. *Unit head:* Nancy J. Peterson, PhD, Associate Director, 352-846-0848, Fax: 352-846-1277, E-mail: njp@ufl.edu. *Application contact:* Charles Cichra, PhD, Graduate Coordinator, 352-273-3621, Fax: 352-392-3672, E-mail: cecichra@ufl.edu.

Limnology

University of Wisconsin–Madison, Graduate School, College of Engineering, Program in Limnology and Marine Science, Madison, WI 53706. Offers MS, PhD. *Faculty:* 21 full-time (7 women). *Students:* 14 full-time (3 women); includes 1 Hispanic/Latino. 36 applicants, 11% accepted, 3 enrolled. In 2010, 1 doctorate awarded. Terminal master's awarded for partial completion of doctoral program. *Degree requirements:* For master's, thesis; for doctorate, thesis/dissertation. *Entrance requirements:* For master's and doctorate, GRE General Test. Additional exam requirements/recommendations for international students: Required—TOEFL. *Application deadline:* For fall admission, 1/1 priority date for domestic students, 1/1 for international students. Application fee: $45. Electronic applications accepted. *Expenses:* Tuition, state resident: full-time $9887.36; part-time $617.96 per credit. Tuition, nonresident: full-time $24,054; part-time $1503.40 per credit. Required fees: $67.63 per credit. Tuition and fees vary according to reciprocity agreements. *Financial support:* In 2010–11, fellowships with full tuition reimbursements (averaging $19,032 per year), 16 research assistantships with full tuition reimbursements (averaging $19,032 per year), 4 teaching assistantships with full tuition reimbursements (averaging $19,032 per year) were awarded; Federal Work-Study and institutionally sponsored loans also available. Financial award application deadline: 1/1. *Faculty research:* Lake ecosystems, ecosystem modeling, geochemistry, physiological ecology, chemical limnology. *Unit head:* Jake K. Vander Zanden, Chair. *Application contact:* Mary Possin, Student Services Coordinator, 608-263-3264, Fax: 608-265-2340, E-mail: mcpossin@wisc.edu.

Marine Geology

Cornell University, Graduate School, Graduate Fields of Engineering, Field of Geological Sciences, Ithaca, NY 14853. Offers economic geology (M Eng, MS, PhD); engineering geology (M Eng, MS, PhD); environmental geophysics (M Eng, MS, PhD); general geology (M Eng, MS, PhD); geobiology (M Eng, MS, PhD); geochemistry and isotope geology (M Eng, MS, PhD); geohydrology (M Eng, MS, PhD); geomorphology (M Eng, MS, PhD); geophysics (M Eng, MS, PhD); geotectonics (M Eng, MS, PhD); marine geology (MS, PhD); mineralogy (M Eng, MS, PhD); paleontology (M Eng, MS, PhD); petroleum geology (M Eng, MS, PhD); petrology (M Eng, MS, PhD); planetary geology (M Eng, MS, PhD); Precambrian geology (M Eng, MS, PhD); Quaternary geology (M Eng, MS, PhD); rock mechanics (M Eng, MS, PhD); sedimentology (M Eng, MS, PhD); seismology (M Eng, MS, PhD); stratigraphy (M Eng, MS, PhD); structural geology (M Eng, MS, PhD). *Faculty:* 36 full-time (5 women). *Students:* 38 full-time (15 women); includes 2 Asian, non-Hispanic/Latino; 2 Hispanic/Latino, 9 international. Average age 27. 84 applicants, 25% accepted, 17 enrolled. In 2010, 3 master's, 5 doctorates awarded. *Degree requirements:* For master's, thesis (MS); for doctorate, comprehensive exam, thesis/dissertation. *Entrance requirements:* For master's and doctorate, GRE General Test, 3 letters of recommendation. Additional exam requirements/recommendations for international students: Required—TOEFL (minimum score 550 paper-based; 213 computer-based; 77 iBT). *Application deadline:* For fall admission, 1/15 priority date for domestic students. Applications are processed on a rolling basis. Application fee: $70. Electronic applications accepted. *Expenses:* Tuition: Full-time $29,500. Required fees: $76. Tuition and fees vary according to degree level and program. *Financial support:* In 2010–11, 25 students received support, including 10 fellowships with full tuition reimbursements available, 14 research assistantships with full tuition reimbursements available, 10 teaching assistantships with full tuition reimbursements available; institutionally sponsored loans, scholarships/grants, health care benefits, tuition waivers (full and partial), and unspecified assistantships also available. Financial award applicants required to submit FAFSA. *Faculty research:* Geophysics, structural geology, petrology, geochemistry, geodynamics. *Unit head:* Director of Graduate Studies, 607-255-5466, Fax: 607-254-4780. *Application contact:* Graduate Field Assistant, 607-255-5466, Fax: 607-254-4780, E-mail: gradprog@geology.cornell.edu.

Massachusetts Institute of Technology, School of Science, Department of Earth, Atmospheric, and Planetary Sciences, Cambridge, MA 02139. Offers atmospheric chemistry (PhD, Sc D); atmospheric science (SM, PhD, Sc D); chemical oceanography (SM, PhD, Sc D); climate physics and chemistry (SM, PhD, Sc D); earth and planetary sciences (SM); geochemistry (PhD, Sc D); geology (PhD, Sc D); geophysics (PhD, Sc D); marine geology and geophysics (SM, PhD, Sc D); physical oceanography (SM, PhD, Sc D); planetary sciences (PhD, Sc D). *Faculty:* 36 full-time (7 women). *Students:* 165 full-time (86 women); includes 17 minority (2 Black or African American, non-Hispanic/Latino; 2 American Indian or Alaska Native, non-Hispanic/Latino; 5 Asian, non-Hispanic/Latino; 5 Hispanic/Latino; 3 Two or more races, non-Hispanic/Latino), 50 international. Average age 27. 227 applicants, 33% accepted, 38 enrolled. In 2010, 12 master's, 26 doctorates awarded. Terminal master's awarded for partial completion of doctoral program. *Degree requirements:* For master's, thesis; for doctorate, comprehensive exam, thesis/dissertation. *Entrance requirements:* For master's, GRE General Test; for doctorate, GRE General Test, GRE Subject Test (chemistry or physics for planetary science area). Additional exam requirements/recommendations for international students: Required—TOEFL (minimum score 577 paper-based; 233 computer-based; 91 iBT), IELTS (minimum score 7). *Application deadline:* For fall admission, 1/5 for domestic and international students; for spring admission, 11/1 for domestic and international students. Application fee: $75. Electronic applications accepted. *Expenses:* Tuition: Full-time $38,940; part-time $605 per unit. Required fees: $272. *Financial support:* In 2010–11, 123 students received support, including 62 fellowships with tuition reimbursements available (averaging $30,852 per year), 88 research assistantships with tuition reimbursements available (averaging $30,258 per year), 13 teaching assistantships with tuition reimbursements available (averaging $30,323 per year); Federal Work-Study, institutionally sponsored loans, scholarships/grants, health care benefits, and unspecified assistantships also available. *Faculty research:* Formation, dynamics and evolution of planetary systems; origin, composition, structure and dynamics of the atmospheres, oceans, surfaces and interiors of the Earth and other planets; evolution and interaction of the physical, chemical, geological and biological components of the Earth system; characterization of past, present and potential future climates and the causes and consequences of climate change; interplay of energy and the environment. Total annual research expenditures: $24.8 million. *Unit head:* Prof. Maria Zuber, Department Head, 617-253-2127, Fax: 617-253-8298, E-mail: eapsinfo@mit.edu. *Application contact:* EAPS Education Office, 617-253-3381, Fax: 617-253-8298, E-mail: eapsinfo@mit.edu.

University of Delaware, College of Earth, Ocean, and Environment, Newark, DE 19716. Offers geography (MA, MS, PhD); geology (MS, PhD); marine science and policy (MMP, MS, PhD), including marine policy (MMP), marine studies (MS, PhD), oceanography (PhD); ocean engineering (MS, PhD). *Degree requirements:* For master's, thesis; for doctorate, thesis/dissertation. *Entrance requirements:* For master's and doctorate, GRE General Test. Additional exam requirements/recommendations for international students: Required—TOEFL. Electronic applications accepted. *Faculty research:* Marine biology and biochemistry, oceanography, marine policy, physical ocean science and engineering, ocean engineering.

University of Hawaii at Manoa, Graduate Division, School of Ocean and Earth Science and Technology, Department of Geology and Geophysics, Honolulu, HI 96822. Offers high-pressure geophysics and geochemistry (MS, PhD); hydrogeology and engineering geology (MS, PhD); marine geology and geophysics (MS, PhD); planetary geosciences and remote sensing (MS, PhD); seismology and solid-earth geophysics (MS, PhD); volcanology, petrology, and geochemistry (MS, PhD). Part-time programs available. *Faculty:* 72 full-time (15 women), 6 part-time/adjunct (3 women). *Students:* 38 full-time (20 women), 5 part-time (3 women); includes 8 minority (1 Black or African American, non-Hispanic/Latino; 2 Asian, non-Hispanic/Latino; 1 Hispanic/Latino; 1 Native Hawaiian or other Pacific Islander, non-Hispanic/Latino; 3 Two or more races, non-Hispanic/Latino), 6 international. Average age 31. 64 applicants, 23% accepted, 7 enrolled. In 2010, 7 master's, 8 doctorates awarded. Terminal master's awarded for partial completion of doctoral program. *Degree requirements:* For master's, thesis optional; for doctorate, comprehensive exam, thesis/dissertation. *Entrance requirements:* For master's and doctorate, GRE General Test, minimum GPA of 3.0. Additional exam requirements/recommendations for international students: Required—TOEFL (minimum score 580 paper-based; 237 computer-based; 92 iBT), IELTS (minimum score 5). *Application deadline:* For fall admission, 1/15 for domestic students, 1/1 for international students; for spring admission, 9/1 for domestic students, 8/15 for international students. Application fee: $60. *Financial support:* In 2010–11, 7 fellowships (averaging $1,359 per year), 30 research assistantships (averaging $23,988 per year), 4 teaching assistantships (averaging $15,350 per year) were awarded. Total annual research expenditures: $3.8 million. *Application contact:* Dr. Gregory Moore, Chair, 808-956-7640, Fax: 808-956-5512, E-mail: gg-dept@soest.hawaii.edu.

University of Miami, Graduate School, Rosenstiel School of Marine and Atmospheric Science, Division of Marine Geology and Geophysics, Coral Gables, FL 33124. Offers MS, PhD. Terminal master's awarded for partial completion of doctoral program. *Degree requirements:* For master's, comprehensive exam, thesis; for doctorate, comprehensive exam, thesis/dissertation. *Entrance requirements:* For master's and doctorate, GRE General Test. Additional exam requirements/recommendations for international students: Required—TOEFL (minimum score 550 paper-based; 213 computer-based). Electronic applications accepted. *Faculty research:* Carbonate sedimentology, low-temperature geochemistry, paleoceanography, geodesy and tectonics.

University of Washington, Graduate School, College of Ocean and Fishery Sciences, School of Oceanography, Seattle, WA 98195. Offers biological oceanography (MS, PhD); chemical oceanography (MS, PhD); marine geology and geophysics (MS, PhD); physical oceanography (MS, PhD). Terminal master's awarded for partial completion of doctoral program. *Degree requirements:* For master's, research project; for doctorate, thesis/dissertation. *Entrance requirements:* For master's and doctorate, GRE General Test, minimum GPA of 3.0. Additional exam requirements/recommendations for international students: Required—TOEFL. Electronic applications accepted. *Faculty research:* Global climate change, hydrothermal vent systems, marine microbiology, marine and freshwater biogeochemistry, biological-physical interactions.

Woods Hole Oceanographic Institution, MIT/WHOI Joint Program in Oceanography/Applied Ocean Science and Engineering, Woods Hole, MA 02543-1541. Offers applied ocean sciences (PhD); biological oceanography (PhD, Sc D); chemical oceanography (PhD, Sc D); civil and environmental and oceanographic engineering (PhD); electrical and oceanographic engineering (PhD); geochemistry (PhD); geophysics (PhD); marine biology (PhD); marine geochemistry (PhD, Sc D); marine geology (PhD, Sc D); marine geophysics (PhD); mechanical and oceanographic engineering (PhD); ocean engineering (PhD); oceanographic engineering (M Eng, MS, PhD, Sc D, Eng); paleoceanography (PhD); physical oceanography (PhD, Sc D). MS, PhD, Sc D offered jointly with Massachusetts Institute of Technology. Terminal master's awarded for partial completion of doctoral program. *Degree requirements:* For master's and Eng, thesis (for some programs); for doctorate, thesis/dissertation. *Entrance requirements:* For master's, GRE General Test; for doctorate, GRE General Test, GRE Subject Test. Additional exam requirements/recommendations for international students: Required—TOEFL. Electronic applications accepted.

Mineralogy

Cornell University, Graduate School, Graduate Fields of Engineering, Field of Geological Sciences, Ithaca, NY 14853. Offers economic geology (M Eng, MS, PhD); engineering geology (M Eng, MS, PhD); environmental geophysics (M Eng, MS, PhD); general geology (M Eng, MS, PhD); geobiology (M Eng, MS, PhD); geochemistry and isotope geology (M Eng, MS, PhD); geohydrology (M Eng, MS, PhD); geomorphology (M Eng, MS, PhD); geophysics (M Eng, MS, PhD); geotectonics (M Eng, MS, PhD); marine geology (MS, PhD); mineralogy (M Eng, MS, PhD); paleontology (M Eng, MS, PhD); petroleum geology (M Eng, MS, PhD); petrology (M Eng, MS, PhD); planetary geology (M Eng, MS, PhD); Precambrian geology (M Eng, MS, PhD); Quaternary geology (M Eng, MS, PhD); rock mechanics (M Eng, MS, PhD); sedimentology (M Eng, MS, PhD); seismology (M Eng, MS, PhD); stratigraphy (M Eng, MS, PhD); structural geology (M Eng, MS, PhD). *Faculty:* 36 full-time (5 women). *Students:* 38 full-time (15 women); includes 2 Asian, non-Hispanic/Latino; 2 Hispanic/Latino, 9 international. Average age 27. 84 applicants, 25% accepted, 17 enrolled. In 2010, 3 master's, 5 doctorates awarded. *Degree requirements:* For master's, thesis (MS); for doctorate, comprehensive exam, thesis/dissertation. *Entrance requirements:* For master's and doctorate, GRE General Test, 3 letters of recommendation. Additional exam requirements/recommendations for international students: Required—TOEFL (minimum score 550 paper-based; 213 computer-based; 77 iBT). *Application deadline:* For fall admission, 1/15 priority date for domestic students. Applications are processed on a rolling basis. Application fee: $70. Electronic applications accepted. *Expenses:* Tuition: Full-time $29,500. Required fees: $76. Tuition and fees vary according to degree level and program. *Financial support:* In 2010–11, 25 students received support, including 10 fellowships with full tuition reimbursements available, 14 research assistantships with full tuition reimbursements available, 10 teaching assistantships with full tuition reimbursements available; institutionally sponsored loans, scholarships/grants, health care benefits, tuition waivers (full

146 www.facebook.com/petersonspublishing

Peterson's Graduate Programs in the Physical Sciences, Mathematics, Agricultural Sciences, the Environment & Natural Resources 2012

and partial), and unspecified assistantships also available. Financial award applicants required to submit FAFSA. *Faculty research:* Geophysics, structural geology, petrology, geochemistry, geodynamics. *Unit head:* Director of Graduate Studies, 607-255-5466, Fax: 607-254-4780. *Application contact:* Graduate Field Assistant, 607-255-5466, Fax: 607-254-4780, E-mail: gradprog@geology.cornell.edu.

Indiana University Bloomington, University Graduate School, College of Arts and Sciences, Department of Geological Sciences, Bloomington, IN 47405-7000. Offers biogeochemistry (MS, PhD); economic geology (MS, PhD); geobiology (MS, PhD); geophysics, structural geology and tectonics (MS, PhD); hydrogeology (MS, PhD); mineralogy (MS, PhD); stratigraphy and sedimentology (MS, PhD). *Faculty:* 17 full-time (1 woman). *Students:* 48 full-time (24 women), 5 part-time (1 woman); includes 4 minority (2 Black or African American, non-Hispanic/Latino; 1 Hispanic/Latino; 1 Two or more races, non-Hispanic/Latino), 20 international. Average age 29. 70 applicants, 24% accepted, 16 enrolled. In 2010, 3 master's, 4 doctorates awarded. Terminal master's awarded for partial completion of doctoral program. *Degree requirements:* For master's, thesis or alternative; for doctorate, comprehensive exam, thesis/dissertation. *Entrance requirements:* For master's and doctorate, GRE General Test. Additional exam requirements/recommendations for international students: Required—TOEFL. *Application deadline:* For fall admission, 1/15 priority date for domestic students, 12/15 for international students; for spring admission, 9/1 priority date for domestic students, 9/1 for international students. Applications are processed on a rolling basis. Application fee: $55 ($65 for international students). *Financial support:* In 2010–11, 10 fellowships with full tuition reimbursements (averaging $17,300 per year), 6 research assistantships with full tuition reimbursements (averaging $16,370 per year), 12 teaching assistantships with full tuition reimbursements (averaging $15,150 per year) were awarded; career-related internships or fieldwork, Federal Work-Study, and institutionally sponsored loans also available. *Faculty research:* Geophysics, geochemistry, hydrogeology, geobiology, planetary science. Total annual research expenditures: $644,299. *Unit head:* Simon Brassell, Chair, 812-855-5581, Fax: 812-855-7899, E-mail: geochair@indiana.edu. *Application contact:* Mary Iverson, Graduate Secretary, 812-855-7214, Fax: 812-855-7899, E-mail: miverson@indiana.edu.

Université du Québec à Chicoutimi, Graduate Programs, Program in Mineral Resources, Chicoutimi, QC G7H 2B1, Canada. Offers PhD. Program offered jointly with Université du Québec à Montréal. Part-time programs available. *Degree requirements:* For doctorate, thesis/dissertation. *Entrance requirements:* For doctorate, appropriate master's degree, proficiency in French.

Université du Québec à Montréal, Graduate Programs, Program in Earth Sciences, Montreal, QC H3C 3P8, Canada. Offers earth sciences (M Sc); mineral resources (PhD); non-renewable resources (DESS). Part-time programs available. Terminal master's awarded for partial completion of doctoral program. *Degree requirements:* For master's, thesis (for some programs); for doctorate, thesis/dissertation. *Entrance requirements:* For master's, appropriate bachelor's degree or equivalent, proficiency in French. *Faculty research:* Economic geology, structural geology, geochemistry, Quaternary geology, isotopic geochemistry.

Université du Québec à Montréal, Graduate Programs, Program in Mineral Resources, Montréal, QC H3C 3P8, Canada. Offers PhD. Program offered jointly with Université du Québec à Chicoutimi. Part-time programs available. *Degree requirements:* For doctorate, thesis/dissertation. *Entrance requirements:* For doctorate, appropriate master's degree or equivalent, proficiency in French.

Paleontology

Cornell University, Graduate School, Graduate Fields of Engineering, Field of Geological Sciences, Ithaca, NY 14853. Offers economic geology (M Eng, MS, PhD); engineering geology (M Eng, MS, PhD); environmental geophysics (M Eng, MS, PhD); general geology (M Eng, MS, PhD); geobiology (M Eng, MS, PhD); geochemistry and isotope geology (M Eng, MS, PhD); geohydrology (M Eng, MS, PhD); geomorphology (M Eng, MS, PhD); geophysics (M Eng, MS, PhD); geotectonics (M Eng, MS, PhD); marine geology (MS, PhD); mineralogy (M Eng, MS, PhD); paleontology (M Eng, MS, PhD); petroleum geology (M Eng, MS, PhD); petrology (M Eng, MS, PhD); planetary geology (M Eng, MS, PhD); Precambrian geology (M Eng, MS, PhD); Quaternary geology (M Eng, MS, PhD); rock mechanics (M Eng, MS, PhD); sedimentology (M Eng, MS, PhD); seismology (M Eng, MS, PhD); stratigraphy (M Eng, MS, PhD); structural geology (M Eng, MS, PhD). *Faculty:* 36 full-time (5 women). *Students:* 38 full-time (15 women); includes 2 Asian, non-Hispanic/Latino; 2 Hispanic/Latino, 9 international. Average age 27. 84 applicants, 25% accepted, 17 enrolled. In 2010, 3 master's, 5 doctorates awarded. *Degree requirements:* For master's, thesis (MS); for doctorate, comprehensive exam, thesis/dissertation. *Entrance requirements:* For master's and doctorate, GRE General Test, 3 letters of recommendation. Additional exam requirements/recommendations for international students: Required—TOEFL (minimum score 550 paper-based; 213 computer-based; 77 iBT). *Application deadline:* For fall admission, 1/15 priority date for domestic students. Applications are processed on a rolling basis. Application fee: $70. Electronic applications accepted. *Expenses:* Tuition: Full-time $29,500. Required fees: $76. Tuition and fees vary according to degree level and program. *Financial support:* In 2010–11, 25 students received support, including 10 fellowships with full tuition reimbursements available, 14 research assistantships with full tuition reimbursements available, 10 teaching assistantships with full tuition reimbursements available; institutionally sponsored loans, scholarships/grants, health care benefits, tuition waivers (full and partial), and unspecified assistantships also available. Financial award applicants required to submit FAFSA. *Faculty research:* Geophysics, structural geology, petrology, geochemistry, geodynamics. *Unit head:* Director of Graduate Studies, 607-255-5466, Fax: 607-254-4780. *Application contact:* Graduate Field Assistant, 607-255-5466, Fax: 607-254-4780, E-mail: gradprog@geology.cornell.edu.

Duke University, Graduate School, Department of Biological Anthropology and Anatomy, Durham, NC 27710. Offers cellular and molecular biology (PhD); gross anatomy and physical anthropology (PhD), including comparative morphology of human and non-human primates, primate social behavior, vertebrate paleontology; neuroanatomy (PhD). *Faculty:* 9 full-time. *Students:* 13 full-time (9 women); includes 1 Black or African American, non-Hispanic/Latino; 2 Hispanic/Latino, 1 international. 54 applicants, 9% accepted, 2 enrolled. In 2010, 2 doctorates awarded. *Degree requirements:* For doctorate, one foreign language, thesis/dissertation. *Entrance requirements:* For doctorate, GRE General Test. Additional exam requirements/recommendations for international students: Required—TOEFL (minimum score 550 paper-based; 213 computer-based; 83 iBT), IELTS (minimum score 7). *Application deadline:* For fall admission, 12/8 priority date for domestic and international students. Application fee: $75. Electronic applications accepted. *Financial support:* Fellowships, teaching assistantships, Federal Work-Study available. Financial award application deadline: 12/31. *Unit head:* Daniel Schmitt, Director of Graduate Studies, 919-684-4124, Fax: 919-684-8542, E-mail: mlsquire@duke.edu. *Application contact:* Elizabeth Hutton, Director of Admissions, 919-684-3913, Fax: 919-684-2277, E-mail: grad-admissions@duke.edu.

East Tennessee State University, School of Graduate Studies, College of Arts and Sciences, Department of Biological Sciences, Johnson City, TN 37614. Offers biology (MS); microbiology (MS); paleontology (MS). *Faculty:* 12 full-time (0 women). *Students:* 43 full-time (20 women), 9 part-time (5 women); includes 3 minority (2 Hispanic/Latino; 1 Two or more races, non-Hispanic/Latino), 17 international. Average age 26. 53 applicants, 43% accepted, 19 enrolled. In 2010, 20 master's awarded. *Degree requirements:* For master's, comprehensive exam, thesis optional. *Entrance requirements:* For master's, GRE General Test or GRE Subject Test, minimum GPA of 3.0. Additional exam requirements/recommendations for international students: Required—TOEFL (minimum score 550 paper-based; 213 computer-based; 79 iBT). *Application deadline:* For fall admission, 4/1 priority date for domestic students, 2/1 for international students; for spring admission, 9/1 for domestic students, 7/1 for international students. Application fee: $25 ($35 for international students). Electronic applications accepted. *Financial support:* In 2010–11, 1 research assistantship with full tuition reimbursement (averaging $6,000 per year), 15 teaching assistantships with full tuition reimbursements (averaging $6,000 per year) were awarded; institutionally sponsored loans, scholarships/grants, and unspecified assistantships also available. Financial award application deadline: 7/1; financial award applicants required to submit FAFSA. *Faculty research:* Vertebrate natural history, mutation rates in fruit flies, regulation of plant secondary metabolism, plant biochemistry, timekeeping in honeybees, gene expression in diapausing flies. Total annual research expenditures: $226,807. *Unit head:* Dr. Dan M. Johnson, Chair, 423-439-4329, Fax: 423-439-5958, E-mail: johnsodm@etsu.edu. *Application contact:* Admissions and Records Clerk, 423-439-4221, Fax: 423-439-5624, E-mail: gradsch@etsu.edu.

South Dakota School of Mines and Technology, Graduate Division, Department of Geology and Geological Engineering, Rapid City, SD 57701-3995. Offers geology and geological engineering (MS, PhD); paleontology (MS). Part-time programs available. *Degree requirements:* For master's, thesis; for doctorate, thesis/dissertation. *Entrance requirements:* For master's and doctorate, GRE General Test, GRE Subject Test. Additional exam requirements/recommendations for international students: Required—TOEFL, TWE. Electronic applications accepted. *Faculty research:* Contaminants in soil, nitrate leaching, environmental changes, fracture formations, greenhouse effect.

South Dakota School of Mines and Technology, Graduate Division, Program in Paleontology, Rapid City, SD 57701-3995. Offers MS. Part-time programs available. *Degree requirements:* For master's, thesis. *Entrance requirements:* For master's, GRE General Test, GRE Subject Test. Additional exam requirements/recommendations for international students: Required—TOEFL, TWE. Electronic applications accepted. *Faculty research:* Cretaceous vertebrates, Miocene vertebrates, Oligocene vertebrates.

University of Chicago, Division of the Physical Sciences, Department of the Geophysical Sciences, Chicago, IL 60637-1513. Offers atmospheric sciences (SM, PhD); earth sciences (SM, PhD); paleobiology (PhD); planetary and space sciences (SM, PhD). *Faculty:* 21 full-time (3 women). *Students:* 37 full-time (23 women); includes 1 Hispanic/Latino, 14 international. Average age 27. 63 applicants, 35% accepted, 9 enrolled. In 2010, 2 master's, 7 doctorates awarded. Terminal master's awarded for partial completion of doctoral program. *Degree requirements:* For master's, thesis, seminar; for doctorate, variable foreign language requirement, comprehensive exam, thesis/dissertation. *Entrance requirements:* For doctorate, GRE General Test. Additional exam requirements/recommendations for international students: Required—TOEFL (minimum score 600 paper-based; 250 computer-based; 96 iBT), IELTS (minimum score 7). *Application deadline:* For fall admission, 1/10 for domestic and international students. Application fee: $55. Electronic applications accepted. *Financial support:* In 2010–11, research assistantships with full tuition reimbursements (averaging $20,511 per year), teaching assistantships with full tuition reimbursements (averaging $21,915 per year) were awarded; fellowships, Federal Work-Study, institutionally sponsored loans, scholarships/grants, tuition waivers (partial), and unspecified assistantships also available. Financial award application deadline: 1/9. *Faculty research:* Climatology, evolutionary paleontology, petrology, geochemistry, oceanic sciences. *Unit head:* Dr. Michael Foote, Chairman, 773-702-8102, Fax: 773-702-9505. *Application contact:* David J. Taylor, Graduate Student Services Coordinator, 773-702-8180, Fax: 773-702-9505, E-mail: info@geosci.uchicago.edu.

The University of Manchester, School of Earth, Atmospheric and Environmental Sciences, Manchester, United Kingdom. Offers atmospheric sciences (M Phil, M Sc, PhD); basin studies and petroleum geosciences (M Phil, M Sc, PhD); earth, atmospheric and environmental sciences (M Phil, M Sc, PhD); environmental geochemistry and cosmochemistry (M Phil, M Sc, PhD); isotope geochemistry and cosmochemistry (M Phil, M Sc, PhD); paleontology (M Phil, M Sc, PhD); physics and chemistry of minerals and fluids (M Phil, M Sc, PhD); structural and petrological geosciences (M Phil, M Sc, PhD).

The University of Texas at Dallas, School of Natural Sciences and Mathematics, Program in Geosciences, Richardson, TX 75080. Offers geochemistry (MS, PhD); geophysics (MS, PhD); geospatial information sciences (MS, PhD); hydrogeology (MS, PhD); sedimentary, stratigraphy, paleontology (PhD); stratigraphy, paleontology (MS); structural geology and tectonics (MS, PhD). Part-time and evening/weekend programs available. *Faculty:* 11 full-time (1 woman). *Students:* 38 full-time (13 women), 25 part-time (8 women); includes 11 minority (4 Black or African American, non-Hispanic/Latino; 4 Asian, non-Hispanic/Latino; 3 Hispanic/Latino), 19 international. Average age 32. 48 applicants, 46% accepted, 12 enrolled. In 2010, 9 master's, 1 doctorate awarded. *Degree requirements:* For master's, thesis optional; for doctorate, thesis/dissertation. *Entrance requirements:* For master's and doctorate, GRE General Test, minimum GPA of 3.0 in upper-level course work in field. Additional exam requirements/recommendations for international students: Required—TOEFL (minimum score 550 paper-based; 215 computer-based). *Application deadline:* For fall admission, 7/15 for domestic students, 5/1 priority date for international students; for spring admission, 11/15 for domestic students, 9/1 priority date for international students. Applications are processed on a rolling basis. Application fee: $50 ($100 for international students). Electronic applications accepted. *Expenses:* Tuition, state resident: full-time $10,248; part-time $569 per credit hour. Tuition, nonresident: full-time $18,544; part-time $1030 per credit hour. Tuition and fees vary according to course load. *Financial support:* In 2010–11, 38 students received support, including 15 research assistantships with partial tuition reimbursements available (averaging $14,400 per year), 14 teaching assistantships with partial tuition reimbursements available (averaging $13,905 per year); career-related internships or fieldwork, Federal Work-Study, institutionally sponsored loans, scholarships/grants, and unspecified assistantships also available. Support available to part-time students. Financial award application deadline: 4/30; financial award applicants required to submit FAFSA. *Faculty research:* Cybermapping, GPS applications for geophysics and geology, seismology and ground-penetrating radar, numerical modeling, signal processing and inverse modeling techniques in seismology. *Unit head:* Dr. John Oldow, Department Head, 972-883-2403, Fax: 972-883-2537, E-mail: geosciences@utdallas.edu. *Application contact:* Dr. Robert J. Stern, Graduate Advisor, 972-883-2442, Fax: 972-883-2537, E-mail: rjstern@utdallas.edu.

West Virginia University, Eberly College of Arts and Sciences, Department of Geology and Geography, Program in Geology, Morgantown, WV 26506. Offers geomorphology (MS, PhD);

West Virginia University (continued)
geophysics (MS, PhD); hydrogeology (MS, PhD); paleontology (MS, PhD); petroleum geology (PhD); petrology (MS, PhD); stratigraphy (MS, PhD); structure (MS, PhD). Part-time programs available. Terminal master's awarded for partial completion of doctoral program. *Degree requirements:* For master's, thesis (for some programs); for doctorate, comprehensive exam, thesis/dissertation. *Entrance requirements:* For master's, GRE General Test, minimum GPA of 2.5; for doctorate, GRE General Test, minimum GPA of 3.3. Additional exam requirements/ recommendations for international students: Required—TOEFL.

Yale University, Graduate School of Arts and Sciences, Department of Geology and Geophysics, New Haven, CT 06520. Offers biogeochemistry (PhD); climate dynamics (PhD); geochemistry (PhD); geophysics (PhD); meteorology (PhD); oceanography (PhD); paleontology (PhD); paleooceanography (PhD); petrology (PhD); tectonics (PhD). *Degree requirements:* For doctorate, thesis/dissertation. *Entrance requirements:* For doctorate, GRE General Test. Additional exam requirements/recommendations for international students: Required—TOEFL.

Planetary and Space Sciences

Air Force Institute of Technology, Graduate School of Engineering and Management, Department of Operational Sciences, Dayton, OH 45433-7765. Offers logistics management (MS); operations research (MS, PhD); space operations (MS). Part-time programs available. *Degree requirements:* For master's, thesis; for doctorate, thesis/dissertation. *Entrance requirements:* For doctorate, GRE General Test, minimum GPA of 3.0, U.S. citizenship. *Faculty research:* Optimization, simulation, combat modeling and analysis, reliability and maintainability, resource scheduling.

Arizona State University, College of Liberal Arts and Sciences, School of Earth and Space Exploration, Tempe, AZ 85287-1404. Offers astrophysics (MS, PhD); exploration systems design (PhD); geological sciences (MS, PhD). PhD in exploration systems design is offered in collaboration with the Fulton Schools of Engineering. *Faculty:* 43 full-time (4 women), 2 part-time/adjunct (1 woman). *Students:* 89 full-time (32 women), 16 part-time (8 women); includes 12 minority (2 American Indian or Alaska Native, non-Hispanic/Latino; 4 Asian, non-Hispanic/Latino; 6 Hispanic/Latino), 18 international. Average age 30. 181 applicants, 28% accepted, 28 enrolled. In 2010, 6 master's, 7 doctorates awarded. Terminal master's awarded for partial completion of doctoral program. *Degree requirements:* For master's, thesis, interactive Program of Study (iPOS) submitted before completing 50 percent of required credit hours; for doctorate, thesis/dissertation, interactive Program of Study (iPOS) submitted before completing 50 percent of required credit hours. *Entrance requirements:* For master's and doctorate, GRE, minimum GPA of 3.0 or equivalent in last 2 years of work leading to bachelor's degree. Additional exam requirements/recommendations for international students: Required—TOEFL, IELTS, or Pearson Test of English. *Application deadline:* For fall admission, 1/15 for domestic and international students; for spring admission, 10/1 for domestic and international students. Applications are processed on a rolling basis. Application fee: $70 ($90 for international students). Electronic applications accepted. *Expenses:* Tuition, state resident: full-time $8510; part-time $608 per credit. Tuition, nonresident: full-time $16,542; part-time $919 per credit. Required fees: $339; $110 per credit. Part-time tuition and fees vary according to course load. *Financial support:* In 2010–11, 52 research assistantships with full and partial tuition reimbursements (averaging $15,804 per year), 42 teaching assistantships with full and partial tuition reimbursements (averaging $15,169 per year) were awarded; fellowships with full tuition reimbursements, career-related internships or fieldwork, Federal Work-Study, institutionally sponsored loans, scholarships/grants, and tuition waivers (full and partial) also available. Financial award application deadline: 3/1; financial award applicants required to submit FAFSA. Total annual research expenditures: $18.8 million. *Unit head:* Dr. Kip Hodges, Director, 480-965-5331, Fax: 480-965-8102, E-mail: kvhodges@asu.edu. *Application contact:* Graduate Admissions, 480-965-6113.

California Institute of Technology, Division of Geological and Planetary Sciences, Pasadena, CA 91125-0001. Offers geobiology (MS, PhD); geochemistry (MS, PhD); geology (MS, PhD); geophysics (MS, PhD); planetary science (MS, PhD). *Faculty:* 38 full-time (6 women). *Students:* 76 full-time (39 women); includes 1 Black or African American, non-Hispanic/Latino; 4 Asian, non-Hispanic/Latino; 1 Hispanic/Latino, 28 international. Average age 26. 102 applicants, 28% accepted, 9 enrolled. In 2010, 12 master's, 14 doctorates awarded. *Degree requirements:* For doctorate, thesis/dissertation. *Entrance requirements:* For doctorate, GRE General Test. Additional exam requirements/recommendations for international students: Required—TOEFL; Recommended—IELTS, TWE. *Application deadline:* For fall admission, 1/1 for domestic and international students. Application fee: $80. Electronic applications accepted. *Financial support:* In 2010–11, 75 students received support, including 14 fellowships with full tuition reimbursements available (averaging $27,000 per year), 62 research assistantships with full tuition reimbursements available (averaging $27,000 per year); teaching assistantships with full tuition reimbursements available, institutionally sponsored loans, scholarships/grants, health care benefits, and unspecified assistantships also available. Financial award applicants required to submit FAFSA. *Faculty research:* Planetary surfaces, evolution of anaerobic respiratory processes, structural geology and tectonics, theoretical and numerical seismology, global biogeochemical cycles. *Unit head:* Dr. Kenneth A. Farley, Chairman, 626-395-6111, Fax: 626-795-6028, E-mail: dianb@gps.caltech.edu. *Application contact:* Dr. Robert W. Clayton, Academic Officer, 626-395-6909, Fax: 626-795-6028, E-mail: dianb@gps.caltech.edu.

Columbia University, Graduate School of Arts and Sciences, Division of Natural Sciences, Program in Atmospheric and Planetary Science, New York, NY 10027. Offers M Phil, PhD. Offered jointly through the Departments of Geological Sciences, Astronomy, and Physics and in cooperation with NASA Goddard Space Flight Center's Institute for Space Studies. *Degree requirements:* For doctorate, variable foreign language requirement, thesis/dissertation. *Entrance requirements:* For doctorate, GRE General Test, GRE Subject Test, previous course work in mathematics and physics. Additional exam requirements/recommendations for international students: Required—TOEFL. *Faculty research:* Climate, weather prediction.

Cornell University, Graduate School, Graduate Fields of Arts and Sciences, Field of Astronomy and Space Sciences, Ithaca, NY 14853-0001. Offers astronomy (PhD); astrophysics (PhD); general space sciences (PhD); infrared astronomy (PhD); planetary studies (PhD); radio astronomy (PhD); radiophysics (PhD); theoretical astrophysics (PhD). *Faculty:* 25 full-time (2 women). *Students:* 28 full-time (11 women); includes 3 Asian, non-Hispanic/Latino; 1 Hispanic/Latino, 7 international. Average age 26. 88 applicants, 24% accepted, 2 enrolled. In 2010, 3 doctorates awarded. *Degree requirements:* For doctorate, comprehensive exam, thesis/ dissertation. *Entrance requirements:* For doctorate, GRE General Test, GRE Subject Test (physics), 3 letters of recommendation. Additional exam requirements/recommendations for international students: Required—TOEFL (minimum score 600 paper-based; 250 computer-based; 77 iBT). *Application deadline:* For fall admission, 1/15 for domestic students. Application fee: $80. Electronic applications accepted. *Expenses:* Tuition: Full-time $29,500. Required fees: $76. Tuition and fees vary according to degree level and program. *Financial support:* In 2010–11, 2 fellowships with full tuition reimbursements, 17 research assistantships with full tuition reimbursements, 9 teaching assistantships with full tuition reimbursements were awarded; institutionally sponsored loans, scholarships/grants, health care benefits, tuition waivers (full and partial), and unspecified assistantships also available. Financial award applicants required to submit FAFSA. *Faculty research:* Observational astrophysics, planetary sciences, cosmology, instrumentation, gravitational astrophysics. *Unit head:* Director of Graduate Studies, 607-255-4341. *Application contact:* Graduate Field Assistant, 607-255-4341, E-mail: oconnor@astro.cornell.edu.

Florida Institute of Technology, Graduate Programs, College of Science, Department of Physics and Space Sciences, Melbourne, FL 32901-6975. Offers interdisciplinary science (MS); physics (MS, PhD); space sciences (MS, PhD). Part-time programs available. *Faculty:* 12 full-time (1 woman). *Students:* 33 full-time (12 women), 10 part-time (2 women); includes 4 minority (2 Asian, non-Hispanic/Latino; 2 Hispanic/Latino), 12 international. Average age 29. 75 applicants, 44% accepted, 7 enrolled. In 2010, 7 master's, 4 doctorates awarded. Terminal master's awarded for partial completion of doctoral program. *Degree requirements:* For master's, comprehensive exam, thesis optional, oral exam, 6 credits math method; for doctorate, one foreign language, comprehensive exam, thesis/dissertation, publication in referred journal, seminar on dissertation research, dissertation published in a major journal. *Entrance requirements:* For master's, minimum GPA of 3.0, resume, 3 letters of recommendation, vector analysis, statement of objectives; for doctorate, GRE General and Subject Tests (recommended), minimum GPA of 3.2, resume, 3 letters of recommendation, statement of objectives. Additional exam requirements/recommendations for international students: Required—TOEFL (minimum score 550 paper-based; 213 computer-based; 79 iBT). *Application deadline:* For fall admission, 4/1 for international students; for spring admission, 9/30 for international students. Applications are processed on a rolling basis. Application fee: $50. Electronic applications accepted. *Expenses:* Tuition: Part-time $1040 per credit hour. Tuition and fees vary according to campus/location. *Financial support:* In 2010–11, 13 research assistantships with full and partial tuition reimbursements (averaging $13,018 per year), 16 teaching assistantships with full and partial tuition reimbursements (averaging $12,769 per year) were awarded; career-related internships or fieldwork, institutionally sponsored loans, tuition waivers (partial), unspecified assistantships, and tuition remissions also available. Support available to part-time students. Financial award application deadline: 3/1; financial award applicants required to submit FAFSA. *Faculty research:* Lasers, semiconductors, magnetism, quantum devices, high energy physics. Total annual research expenditures: $2.9 million. *Unit head:* Dr. Terry D. Oswalt, Department Head, 321-674-7325, Fax: 321-674-7482, E-mail: toswalt@fit.edu. *Application contact:* Cheryl A. Brown, Associate Director of Graduate Admissions, 321-674-7581, Fax: 321-723-9468, E-mail: cbrown@fit.edu.

Georgia Institute of Technology, Graduate Studies and Research, College of Sciences, School of Earth and Atmospheric Sciences, Atlanta, GA 30332-0340. Offers atmospheric chemistry, aerosols and clouds (MS, PhD); dynamics of weather and climate (MS, PhD); geochemistry (MS, PhD); geophysics (MS, PhD); oceanography (MS, PhD); paleoclimate (MS, PhD); planetary science (MS, PhD); remote sensing (MS, PhD). Part-time programs available. Terminal master's awarded for partial completion of doctoral program. *Degree requirements:* For master's, thesis or alternative; for doctorate, comprehensive exam, thesis/dissertation. *Entrance requirements:* For master's, GRE, letters of recommendation; for doctorate, GRE, academic transcripts, letters of recommendation, personal statement. Additional exam requirements/recommendations for international students: Required—TOEFL (minimum score 550 paper-based; 213 computer-based; 79 iBT). *Faculty research:* Geophysics; atmospheric chemistry, aerosols and clouds; dynamics of weather and climate; geochemistry; oceanography; paleoclimate; planetary science; remote sensing.

Hampton University, Graduate College, Department of Atmospheric and Planetary Sciences, Hampton, VA 23668. Offers atmospheric sciences (MS, PhD); planetary sciences (MS, PhD).

Harvard University, Graduate School of Arts and Sciences, Department of Earth and Planetary Sciences, Cambridge, MA 02138. Offers AM, PhD. Terminal master's awarded for partial completion of doctoral program. *Degree requirements:* For doctorate, comprehensive exam, thesis/dissertation. *Entrance requirements:* For doctorate, GRE General Test. Additional exam requirements/recommendations for international students: Required—TOEFL. Electronic applications accepted. *Expenses:* Tuition: Full-time $34,976. Required fees: $1166. Full-time tuition and fees vary according to program. *Faculty research:* Economic geography, geochemistry, geophysics, mineralogy, crystallography.

Massachusetts Institute of Technology, School of Science, Department of Earth, Atmospheric, and Planetary Sciences, Cambridge, MA 02139. Offers atmospheric chemistry (PhD, Sc D); atmospheric science (SM, PhD, Sc D); chemical oceanography (SM, PhD, Sc D); climate physics and chemistry (SM, PhD, Sc D); earth and planetary sciences (SM); geochemistry (PhD, Sc D); geology (PhD, Sc D); geophysics (PhD, Sc D); marine geology and geophysics (SM, PhD, Sc D); physical oceanography (SM, PhD, Sc D); planetary sciences (PhD, Sc D). *Faculty:* 36 full-time (7 women). *Students:* 165 full-time (86 women); includes 17 minority (2 Black or African American, non-Hispanic/Latino; 2 American Indian or Alaska Native, non-Hispanic/Latino; 5 Asian, non-Hispanic/Latino; 5 Hispanic/Latino; 3 Two or more races, non-Hispanic/Latino), 50 international. Average age 27. 227 applicants, 33% accepted, 38 enrolled. In 2010, 12 master's, 26 doctorates awarded. Terminal master's awarded for partial completion of doctoral program. *Degree requirements:* For master's, thesis; for doctorate, comprehensive exam, thesis/dissertation. *Entrance requirements:* For master's, GRE General Test; for doctorate, GRE General Test, GRE Subject Test (chemistry or physics for planetary science area). Additional exam requirements/recommendations for international students: Required—TOEFL (minimum score 577 paper-based; 233 computer-based; 91 iBT), IELTS (minimum score 7). *Application deadline:* For fall admission, 1/5 for domestic and international students; for spring admission, 11/1 for domestic and international students. Application fee: $75. Electronic applications accepted. *Expenses:* Tuition: Full-time $38,940; part-time $605 per unit. Required fees: $272. *Financial support:* In 2010–11, 123 students received support, including 62 fellowships with tuition reimbursements available (averaging $30,852 per year), 88 research assistantships with tuition reimbursements available (averaging $30,258 per year), 13 teaching assistantships with tuition reimbursements available (averaging $30,323 per year); Federal Work-Study, institutionally sponsored loans, scholarships/grants, health care benefits, and unspecified assistantships also available. *Faculty research:* Formation, dynamics and evolution of planetary systems; origin, composition, structure and dynamics of the atmospheres, oceans, surfaces and interiors of the Earth and other planets; evolution and interaction of the physical, chemical, geological and biological components of the Earth system; characterization of past, present and potential future climates and the causes and consequences of climate change; interplay of energy and the environment. Total annual research expenditures: $24.8 million. *Unit head:* Prof. Maria Zuber, Department Head, 617-253-2127, Fax: 617-253-8298, E-mail: eapsinfo@mit.edu. *Application contact:* EAPS Education Office, 617-253-3381, Fax: 617-253-8298, E-mail: eapsinfo@mit.edu.

McGill University, Faculty of Graduate and Postdoctoral Studies, Faculty of Science, Department of Earth and Planetary Sciences, Montréal, QC H3A 2T5, Canada. Offers M Sc, PhD.

St. Thomas University, School of Leadership Studies, Institute for Education, Miami Gardens, FL 33054-6459. Offers earth/space science (Certificate); educational administration (MS, Certificate); educational leadership (Ed D); elementary education (MS); ESOL (Certificate); gifted education (Certificate); instructional technology (MS, Certificate); professional/studies (Certificate); reading (MS, Certificate); special education (MS). Part-time and evening/weekend programs available. *Degree requirements:* For master's, comprehensive exam; for doctorate, comprehensive exam, thesis/dissertation. *Entrance requirements:* For master's, interview, minimum GPA of 3.0 or GRE; for doctorate, GRE or MAT. Additional exam requirements/recommendations for international students: Required—TOEFL (minimum score 550 paper-based; 213 computer-based; 79 iBT). Electronic applications accepted.

The University of Arizona, College of Science, Department of Planetary Sciences, Tucson, AZ 85721. Offers MS, PhD. *Faculty:* 14 full-time (3 women), 5 part-time/adjunct (1 woman). *Students:* 23 full-time (15 women), 5 part-time (1 woman); includes 1 Hispanic/Latino; 4 Two or more races, non-Hispanic/Latino, 8 international. Average age 28. 51 applicants, 14% accepted, 7 enrolled. In 2010, 9 doctorates awarded. *Degree requirements:* For master's, thesis (for some programs); for doctorate, one foreign language, thesis/dissertation. *Entrance requirements:* For master's and doctorate, 3 letters of recommendation. Additional exam requirements/recommendations for international students: Required—TOEFL (minimum score 550 paper-based; 213 computer-based; 79 iBT). *Application deadline:* For fall admission, 1/15 for domestic and international students. Applications are processed on a rolling basis. Application fee: $75. Electronic applications accepted. *Expenses:* Tuition, state resident: full-time $7692. *Financial support:* In 2010–11, 10 research assistantships with full tuition reimbursements (averaging $21,652 per year), 19 teaching assistantships with full tuition reimbursements (averaging $20,954 per year) were awarded; scholarships/grants, health care benefits, tuition waivers (partial), and unspecified assistantships also available. Financial award application deadline: 2/15. *Faculty research:* Cosmochemistry, planetary geology, astronomy, space physics, planetary physics. Total annual research expenditures: $20.6 million. *Unit head:* Dr. Michael Drake, Regents Professor, Head and Director, 520-621-6962, Fax: 520-621-4933, E-mail: drake@lpl.arizona.edu. *Application contact:* Pam Streett, Information Contact, 520-621-6954, Fax: 520-621-4933, E-mail: admissions@lpl.arizona.edu.

University of Arkansas, Graduate School, Interdisciplinary Program in Space and Planetary Sciences, Fayetteville, AR 72701-1201. Offers MS, PhD. *Students:* 9 full-time (5 women), 18 part-time (8 women); includes 1 minority (Hispanic/Latino), 7 international. 8 applicants, 100% accepted. In 2010, 5 doctorates awarded. *Application deadline:* For fall admission, 4/1 for international students; for spring admission, 10/1 for international students. Applications are processed on a rolling basis. Application fee: $40 ($50 for international students). Electronic applications accepted. *Financial support:* In 2010–11, 6 fellowships, 20 research assistantships, 4 teaching assistantships were awarded. *Unit head:* Dr. Lin Oliver, Director, 479-575-6571, E-mail: woliver@uark.edu. *Application contact:* Graduate Admissions, 479-575-6246, Fax: 479-575-5908, E-mail: gradinfo@uark.edu.

University of California, Los Angeles, Graduate Division, College of Letters and Science, Department of Earth and Space Sciences, Los Angeles, CA 90095. Offers geochemistry (MS, PhD); geology (MS, PhD); geophysics and space physics (MS, PhD). *Faculty:* 22 full-time (2 women). *Students:* 60 full-time (33 women); includes 8 minority (2 Black or African American, non-Hispanic/Latino; 1 American Indian or Alaska Native, non-Hispanic/Latino; 4 Asian, non-Hispanic/Latino; 1 Two or more races, non-Hispanic/Latino), 16 international. Average age 27. 112 applicants, 25% accepted, 13 enrolled. In 2010, 6 master's, 8 doctorates awarded. Terminal master's awarded for partial completion of doctoral program. *Degree requirements:* For master's, comprehensive exams or thesis; for doctorate, thesis/dissertation, oral and written qualifying exams. *Entrance requirements:* For master's, GRE General Test, minimum GPA of 3.0; for doctorate, GRE General Test, minimum undergraduate GPA of 3.0. *Application deadline:* For fall admission, 1/15 for domestic and international students. Application fee: $70 ($90 for international students). Electronic applications accepted. *Financial support:* In 2010–11, 55 fellowships with full and partial tuition reimbursements, 48 research assistantships with full and partial tuition reimbursements, 27 teaching assistantships with full and partial tuition reimbursements were awarded; Federal Work-Study, institutionally sponsored loans, scholarships/grants, traineeships, health care benefits, tuition waivers (full and partial), and unspecified assistantships also available. Financial award application deadline: 3/1; financial award applicants required to submit FAFSA. *Unit head:* Dr. Craig E. Manning, Chair, 310-825-1475, E-mail: manning@ess.ucla.edu. *Application contact:* Departmental Office, 310-825-3917, E-mail: holbrook@ess.ucla.edu.

University of California, Santa Cruz, Division of Graduate Studies, Division of Physical and Biological Sciences, Department of Earth and Planetary Sciences, Santa Cruz, CA 95064. Offers MS, PhD. *Students:* 59 full-time (31 women); includes 6 minority (2 Asian, non-Hispanic/Latino; 3 Hispanic/Latino; 1 Two or more races, non-Hispanic/Latino), 7 international. Average age 28. 132 applicants, 23% accepted, 12 enrolled. In 2010, 4 master's, 7 doctorates awarded. Terminal master's awarded for partial completion of doctoral program. *Degree requirements:* For master's, thesis; for doctorate, one foreign language, thesis/dissertation, qualifying exam. *Entrance requirements:* For master's and doctorate, GRE General Test. Additional exam requirements/recommendations for international students: Required—TOEFL (minimum score 550 paper-based; 220 computer-based; 83 iBT); Recommended—IELTS (minimum score 8). *Application deadline:* For fall admission, 1/5 for domestic and international students. Application fee: $70 ($90 for international students). Electronic applications accepted. *Financial support:* Fellowships, research assistantships, teaching assistantships, institutionally sponsored loans and tuition waivers available. Financial award applicants required to submit FAFSA. *Faculty research:* Evolution of continental margins and orogenic belts, geologic processes occurring at plate boundaries, deep-sea sediment diagenesis, paleoecology, hydrogeology. *Unit head:* Cathy Smith, Graduate Program Coordinator, 831-459-2504, E-mail: cdsmith@ucsc.edu. *Application contact:* Cathy Smith, Graduate Program Coordinator, 831-459-2504, E-mail: cdsmith@ucsc.edu.

University of Chicago, Division of the Physical Sciences, Department of the Geophysical Sciences, Chicago, IL 60637-1513. Offers atmospheric sciences (SM, PhD); earth sciences (SM, PhD); paleobiology (PhD); planetary and space sciences (SM, PhD). *Faculty:* 21 full-time (3 women). *Students:* 37 full-time (23 women); includes 1 Hispanic/Latino, 14 international. Average age 27. 63 applicants, 35% accepted, 9 enrolled. In 2010, 2 master's, 7 doctorates awarded. Terminal master's awarded for partial completion of doctoral program. *Degree requirements:* For master's, thesis, seminar; for doctorate, variable foreign language requirement, comprehensive exam, thesis/dissertation. *Entrance requirements:* For doctorate, GRE General Test. Additional exam requirements/recommendations for international students: Required—TOEFL (minimum score 600 paper-based; 250 computer-based; 96 iBT), IELTS (minimum score 7). *Application deadline:* For fall admission, 1/10 for domestic and international students. Application fee: $55. Electronic applications accepted. *Financial support:* In 2010–11, research assistantships with full tuition reimbursements (averaging $20,511 per year), teaching assistantships with full tuition reimbursements (averaging $21,915 per year) were awarded; fellowships, Federal Work-Study, institutionally sponsored loans, scholarships/grants, tuition waivers (partial), and unspecified assistantships also available. Financial award application deadline: 1/9. *Faculty research:* Climatology, evolutionary paleontology, petrology, geochemistry, oceanic sciences. *Unit head:* Dr. Michael Foote, Chairman, 773-702-8102, Fax: 773-702-9505. *Application contact:* David J. Taylor, Graduate Student Services Coordinator, 773-702-8180, Fax: 773-702-9505, E-mail: info@geosci.uchicago.edu.

University of Hawaii at Manoa, Graduate Division, School of Ocean and Earth Science and Technology, Department of Geology and Geophysics, Honolulu, HI 96822. Offers high-pressure geophysics and geochemistry (MS, PhD); hydrogeology and engineering geology (MS, PhD); marine geology and geophysics (MS, PhD); planetary geosciences and remote sensing (MS, PhD); seismology and solid-earth geophysics (MS, PhD); volcanology, petrology, and geochemistry (MS, PhD). Part-time programs available. *Faculty:* 72 full-time (15 women), 6 part-time/adjunct (3 women). *Students:* 38 full-time (20 women), 5 part-time (3 women); includes 8 minority (1 Black or African American, non-Hispanic/Latino; 2 Asian, non-Hispanic/Latino; 1 Hispanic/Latino; 1 Native Hawaiian or other Pacific Islander, non-Hispanic/Latino; 3 Two or more races, non-Hispanic/Latino), 6 international. Average age 31. 64 applicants, 23% accepted, 7 enrolled. In 2010, 7 master's, 8 doctorates awarded. Terminal master's awarded for partial completion of doctoral program. *Degree requirements:* For master's, thesis optional; for doctorate, comprehensive exam, thesis/dissertation. *Entrance requirements:* For master's and doctorate, GRE General Test, minimum GPA of 3.0. Additional exam requirements/recommendations for international students: Required—TOEFL (minimum score 580 paper-based; 237 computer-based; 92 iBT), IELTS (minimum score 5). *Application deadline:* For fall admission, 1/15 for domestic students, 1/1 for international students; for spring admission, 9/1 for domestic students, 8/15 for international students. Application fee: $60. *Financial support:* In 2010–11, 7 fellowships (averaging $1,359 per year), 30 research assistantships (averaging $23,988 per year), 4 teaching assistantships (averaging $15,350 per year) were awarded. Total annual research expenditures: $3.8 million. *Application contact:* Dr. Gregory Moore, Chair, 808-956-7640, Fax: 808-956-5512, E-mail: gg-dept@soest.hawaii.edu.

University of Houston, College of Liberal Arts and Social Sciences, Department of Health and Human Performance, Houston, TX 77204. Offers exercise science (MS); human nutrition (MS); human space exploration sciences (MS); kinesiology (PhD); physical education (M Ed). *Accreditation:* NCATE (one or more programs are accredited). Part-time and evening/weekend programs available. *Faculty:* 14 full-time (4 women), 4 part-time/adjunct (1 woman). *Students:* 47 full-time (25 women), 28 part-time (9 women); includes 9 Black or African American, non-Hispanic/Latino; 2 Asian, non-Hispanic/Latino; 5 Hispanic/Latino; 1 Two or more races, non-Hispanic/Latino, 9 international. Average age 27. 87 applicants, 49% accepted, 22 enrolled. In 2010, 32 master's, 2 doctorates awarded. *Degree requirements:* For master's, comprehensive exam (for some programs), thesis (for some programs); for doctorate, comprehensive exam, thesis/dissertation, qualifying exam, candidacy paper. *Entrance requirements:* For master's, GRE (minimum 35th percentile on each section), minimum cumulative GPA of 3.0; for doctorate, GRE (minimum 35th percentile on each section), minimum cumulative GPA of 3.3. Additional exam requirements/recommendations for international students: Required—TOEFL (minimum score 550 paper-based; 79 iBT). *Application deadline:* For fall admission, 4/1 for domestic and international students; for spring admission, 10/1 for domestic and international students. Applications are processed on a rolling basis. Application fee: $45 ($75 for international students). Electronic applications accepted. *Expenses:* Tuition, state resident: full-time $8592; part-time $358 per credit hour. Tuition, nonresident: full-time $16,032; part-time $668 per credit hour. Required fees: $2889. Tuition and fees vary according to course load and program. *Financial support:* In 2010–11, 4 research assistantships with full tuition reimbursements (averaging $8,640 per year), 29 teaching assistantships with full tuition reimbursements (averaging $8,518 per year) were awarded; career-related internships or fieldwork, Federal Work-Study, institutionally sponsored loans, scholarships/grants, health care benefits, and unspecified assistantships also available. Support available to part-time students. Financial award application deadline: 2/1. *Faculty research:* Biomechanics, exercise physiology, obesity, nutrition, space exploration science. *Unit head:* Dr. Charles Layne, Chairperson, 713-743-9868, Fax: 713-743-9860, E-mail: clayne2@uh.edu. *Application contact:* Todd Boutte, Graduate Admission Counselor, 713-743-0571, Fax: 713-743-0123, E-mail: tboutte@mail.coe.uh.edu.

University of Maryland, Baltimore County, Graduate School, College of Arts, Humanities and Social Sciences, Department of Education, Program in Teaching, Baltimore, MD 21250. Offers early childhood education (MAT); elementary education (MAT); secondary education (MAT), including art, biology, chemistry, dance, earth/space science, English, foreign language, mathematics, music, physics, theatre; secondary science (MAT), including social studies. Part-time and evening/weekend programs available. *Faculty:* 24 full-time (18 women), 25 part-time/adjunct (19 women). *Students:* 59 full-time (46 women), 56 part-time (42 women); includes 1 Black or African American, non-Hispanic/Latino; 8 Asian, non-Hispanic/Latino; 3 Hispanic/Latino, 3 international. Average age 31. 88 applicants, 57% accepted, 39 enrolled. In 2010, 106 master's awarded. *Degree requirements:* For master's, comprehensive exam (for some programs), thesis (for some programs). *Entrance requirements:* For master's, PRAXIS I and II, minimum GPA of 3.0. Additional exam requirements/recommendations for international students: Required—TOEFL. *Application deadline:* For fall admission, 6/1 for domestic students; for spring admission, 11/1 for domestic students. Applications are processed on a rolling basis. Application fee: $50. Electronic applications accepted. *Financial support:* In 2010–11, 6 students received support, including research assistantships with full tuition reimbursements available (averaging $12,000 per year); career-related internships or fieldwork, Federal Work-Study, scholarships/grants, tuition waivers, and unspecified assistantships also available. Financial award application deadline: 3/1. *Faculty research:* STEM teacher education, culturally sensitive pedagogy, ESOL/bilingual education, early childhood education, language, literacy and culture. *Unit head:* Dr. Susan M. Blunck, Director, 410-455-2869, Fax: 410-455-3986, E-mail: blunck@umbc.edu. *Application contact:* Cheryl Johnson, 410-455-3388, E-mail: blackwel@umbc.edu.

University of Michigan, Horace H. Rackham School of Graduate Studies, College of Engineering, Department of Atmospheric, Oceanic, and Space Sciences, Ann Arbor, MI 48109. Offers atmospheric and space sciences (MS, PhD); geoscience and remote sensing (PhD); space and planetary sciences (PhD); space engineering (M Eng). Part-time programs available. *Students:* 92 full-time (31 women), 1 part-time (0 women). 179 applicants, 60% accepted, 52 enrolled. In 2010, 29 master's, 6 doctorates awarded. Terminal master's awarded for partial completion of doctoral program. *Degree requirements:* For master's, thesis (for some programs); for doctorate, thesis/dissertation, oral defense of dissertation, preliminary exams. *Entrance requirements:* For master's and doctorate, GRE General Test. Additional exam requirements/recommendations for international students: Required—TOEFL. *Application deadline:* Applications are processed on a rolling basis. Application fee: $65 ($75 for international students). Electronic applications accepted. *Expenses:* Tuition, state resident: full-time $17,784; part-time $1116 per credit hour. Tuition, nonresident: full-time $35,944; part-time $2125 per credit hour. International tuition: $35,994 full-time. Required fees: $95 per semester. Tuition and fees vary according to course load, degree level and program. *Financial support:* Fellowships, research assistantships, teaching assistantships, career-related internships or fieldwork, Federal Work-Study, institutionally sponsored loans, and health care benefits available. Support available to part-time students. Financial award applicants required to submit FAFSA. *Faculty research:* Planetary environments, space instrumentation, air pollution meteorology, global climate change, sun-earth connection, space weather. *Unit head:* Tamas Gombosi, Chair, 734-764-7222, Fax: 734-615-4645, E-mail: tamas@umich.edu. *Application contact:* Margaret Reid, Student Services Associate, 734-936-0482, Fax: 734-763-0437, E-mail: aoss.um@umich.edu.

University of New Mexico, Graduate School, College of Arts and Sciences, Department of Earth and Planetary Sciences, Albuquerque, NM 87131-2039. Offers MS, PhD. Part-time programs available. *Faculty:* 32 full-time (5 women), 18 part-time/adjunct (8 women). *Students:* 50 full-time (31 women), 7 part-time (5 women); includes 5 minority (1 American Indian or Alaska Native, non-Hispanic/Latino; 3 Hispanic/Latino; 1 Two or more races, non-Hispanic/Latino), 4 international. Average age 30. 97 applicants, 14% accepted, 13 enrolled. In 2010, 9 master's, 2 doctorates awarded. Terminal master's awarded for partial completion of doctoral program. *Degree requirements:* For master's, comprehensive exam, thesis; for doctorate, comprehensive exam, thesis/dissertation. *Entrance requirements:* For master's and doctorate, GRE General Test. Additional exam requirements/recommendations for international students:

Planetary and Space Sciences

University of New Mexico (continued)

Required—TOEFL. *Application deadline:* For fall admission, 1/31 priority date for domestic students, 1/31 for international students; for spring admission, 11/1 priority date for domestic and international students. Application fee: $50. Electronic applications accepted. *Expenses:* Tuition, state resident: full-time $5991; part-time $251 per credit hour. Tuition, nonresident: full-time $14,405; part-time $800.20 per credit hour. Tuition and fees vary according to course level, course load, program and reciprocity agreements. *Financial support:* In 2010–11, 54 students received support, including 23 fellowships with full tuition reimbursements available (averaging $2,714 per year), 46 research assistantships with full tuition reimbursements available (averaging $14,363 per year), 27 teaching assistantships with full tuition reimbursements available (averaging $1,982 per year); scholarships/grants and health care benefits also available. Financial award application deadline: 1/31; financial award applicants required to submit FAFSA. *Faculty research:* Climatology, experimental petrology, geochemistry, geographic information technologies, geomorphology, geophysics, hydrogeology, igneneous petrology, metamorphic petrology, meteoritics, meteorology, micrometeorites, mineralogy, paleoclimatology, paleonology, pedology, petrology, physical volcanology, planetary sciences, precambrian geology, quanternary geology, sedimentary geochemistry, sedimentology, stable isotope geochemistry, stratigraphy, structural geology, tectonics, volcanology. Total annual research expenditures: $2.5 million. *Unit head:* Dr. John W. Geissman, Chair, 505-277-4204, Fax: 505-277-8843, E-mail: jgeiss@unm.edu. *Application contact:* Cindy Jaramillo, Administrative Assistant II, 505-277-1635, Fax: 505-277-8843, E-mail: epsdept@unm.edu.

University of North Dakota, Graduate School, John D. Odegard School of Aerospace Sciences, Space Studies Program, Grand Forks, ND 58202. Offers MS. Part-time programs available. Postbaccalaureate distance learning degree programs offered (minimal on-campus study). *Faculty:* 8 full-time (0 women), 1 part-time/adjunct (0 women). *Students:* 17 full-time (6 women), 60 part-time (16 women); includes 7 minority (2 Black or African American, non-Hispanic/Latino; 2 American Indian or Alaska Native, non-Hispanic/Latino; 1 Asian, non-Hispanic/Latino; 2 Hispanic/Latino), 8 international. Average age 34. 39 applicants, 79% accepted, 26 enrolled. In 2010, 26 master's awarded. *Degree requirements:* For master's, comprehensive exam, thesis or alternative. *Entrance requirements:* For master's, minimum GPA of 3.0. Additional exam requirements/recommendations for international students: Required—TOEFL (minimum score 550 paper-based; 213 computer-based; 79 iBT), IELTS (minimum score 6.5). *Application deadline:* For fall admission, 8/1 priority date for domestic students, 5/1 priority date for international students; for spring admission, 12/1 priority date for domestic students, 9/1 priority date for international students. Applications are processed on a rolling basis. Application fee: $35. Electronic applications accepted. *Expenses:* Tuition, state resident: full-time $5857; part-time $306.74 per credit. Tuition, nonresident: full-time $15,666; part-time $729.77 per credit. Required fees: $53.42 per credit. Tuition and fees vary according to course load, program and reciprocity agreements. *Financial support:* In 2010–11, 9 students received support, including 8 research assistantships with full and partial tuition reimbursements available (averaging $7,151 per year), 1 teaching assistantship with full and partial tuition reimbursement available (averaging $5,206 per year); fellowships with full and partial tuition reimbursements available, career-related internships or fieldwork, Federal Work-Study, institutionally sponsored loans, scholarships/grants, health care benefits, tuition waivers (full and partial), and unspecified assistantships also available. Support available to part-time students. Financial award application deadline: 3/15; financial award applicants required to submit FAFSA. *Faculty research:* Earth-approaching asteroids, international remote sensing statutes, Mercury fly-by design, origin of meteorites, craters on Venus. Total annual research expenditures: $786,679. *Unit head:* Dr. Ron Fevig, Graduate Director, 701-777-6790, Fax: 701-777-3711, E-mail: rfevig@space.edu. *Application contact:* Staci Wells, Admissions Specialist, 701-777-0748, Fax: 701-777-3619, E-mail: staci.wells@gradschool.und.edu.

University of Pittsburgh, School of Arts and Sciences, Department of Geology and Planetary Science, Pittsburgh, PA 15260-3332. Offers geographical information systems (PM Sc); geology and planetary science (MS, PhD). Part-time programs available. *Faculty:* 9 full-time (1 woman), 4 part-time/adjunct (1 woman). *Students:* 26 full-time (13 women), 9 part-time (4 women); includes 1 Asian, non-Hispanic/Latino, 1 international. Average age 30. 56 applicants, 36% accepted, 8 enrolled. In 2010, 3 master's, 2 doctorates awarded. *Degree requirements:* For master's, thesis, oral thesis defense; for doctorate, comprehensive exam, thesis/dissertation, oral dissertation defense. *Entrance requirements:* For master's and doctorate, GRE General Test. Additional exam requirements/recommendations for international students: Required—TOEFL (minimum score 550 paper-based; 213 computer-based; 80 iBT). *Application deadline:* For fall admission, 2/1 priority date for domestic students, 2/1 for international students. Application fee: $50. Electronic applications accepted. *Expenses:* Tuition, state resident: full-time $17,304; part-time $701 per credit. Tuition, nonresident: full-time $29,554; part-time $1210 per credit. Required fees: $740; $214 per term. Tuition and fees vary according to program. *Financial support:* In 2010–11, 25 students received support, including 3 fellowships with full tuition reimbursements available (averaging $16,140 per year), 10 research assistantships with full and partial tuition reimbursements available (averaging $14,400 per year), 9 teaching assistantships with full and partial tuition reimbursements available (averaging $15,830 per year); career-related internships or fieldwork, Federal Work-Study, institutionally sponsored loans, scholarships/grants, and tuition waivers (full and partial) also available. Support available to part-time students. Financial award application deadline: 2/1; financial award applicants required to submit FAFSA. *Faculty research:* Geographical information systems, hydrology, low temperature geochemistry, volcanology, paleoclimatology. Total annual research expenditures: $1.5 million. *Unit head:* Dr. William Harbert, Chair, 412-624-8783, Fax: 412-624-3914, E-mail: harbert@pitt.edu. *Application contact:* Dr. Michael Ramsey, Director of Graduate Studies, 412-624-8772, Fax: 412-624-3914, E-mail: mramsey@pitt.edu.

Washington University in St. Louis, Graduate School of Arts and Sciences, Department of Earth and Planetary Sciences, St. Louis, MO 63130-4899. Offers earth and planetary sciences (MA); planetary sciences (PhD). Terminal master's awarded for partial completion of doctoral program. *Degree requirements:* For master's, thesis; for doctorate, thesis/dissertation. *Entrance requirements:* For master's and doctorate, GRE General Test. Electronic applications accepted.

West Chester University of Pennsylvania, Office of Graduate Studies, College of Arts and Sciences, Department of Geology and Astronomy, West Chester, PA 19383. Offers earth-space science (Teaching Certificate); general science (Teaching Certificate); geoscience (MA). Part-time and evening/weekend programs available. *Students:* 7 full-time (2 women), 20 part-time (11 women); includes 1 minority (Black or African American, non-Hispanic/Latino). Average age 33. 14 applicants, 86% accepted, 6 enrolled. In 2010, 7 master's awarded. *Degree requirements:* For master's, comprehensive exam (for some programs), thesis optional. *Entrance requirements:* For master's, minimum GPA of 2.5. Additional exam requirements/recommendations for international students: Required—TOEFL (minimum score 550 paper-based; 213 computer-based; 79 iBT). *Application deadline:* For fall admission, 4/15 priority date for domestic students, 3/15 for international students; for spring admission, 10/15 for domestic students, 9/1 for international students. Applications are processed on a rolling basis. Application fee: $35. Electronic applications accepted. *Expenses:* Tuition, state resident: full-time $6966; part-time $387 per credit. Tuition, nonresident: full-time $11,146; part-time $619 per credit. Required fees: $1614.40; $133.24 per credit. Part-time tuition and fees vary according to campus/location. *Financial support:* Unspecified assistantships available. Support available to part-time students. Financial award application deadline: 2/15; financial award applicants required to submit FAFSA. *Faculty research:* Developing and using a meteorological data station. *Unit head:* Dr. Marc Gagne, Chair, 610-436-2727, E-mail: mgagne@wcupa.edu. *Application contact:* Dr. Steven Good, Graduate Coordinator, 610-436-2203, E-mail: sgood@wcupa.edu.

Western Connecticut State University, Division of Graduate Studies and External Programs, School of Arts and Sciences, Department of Physics, Astronomy and Meteorology, Danbury, CT 06810-6885. Offers earth and planetary sciences (MA). Part-time programs available. *Students:* 4 full-time (0 women), 8 part-time (2 women); includes 2 minority (both Hispanic/Latino). Average age 28. *Degree requirements:* For master's, thesis, completion of program in 6 years. *Entrance requirements:* For master's, minimum GPA of 2.5 or GRE; one year each of calculus-based physics and calculus; semester course in differential equations. Additional exam requirements/recommendations for international students: Recommended—TOEFL (minimum score 550 paper-based; 213 computer-based; 79 iBT), IELTS (minimum score 6). *Application deadline:* For fall admission, 8/5 priority date for domestic students; for spring admission, 1/5 priority date for domestic students. Applications are processed on a rolling basis. Application fee: $50. *Expenses:* Tuition, state resident: full-time $5012; part-time $417 per credit hour. Tuition, nonresident: full-time $13,962; part-time $423 per credit hour. Required fees: $3886. Full-time tuition and fees vary according to course load, degree level and program. *Financial support:* Application deadline: 5/1. *Unit head:* Dr. James Boyle, Graduate Coordinator, 203-837-8856. *Application contact:* Chris Shankle, Associate Director of Graduate Admissions, 203-837-9005, Fax: 203-837-8326, E-mail: shanklec@wcsu.edu.

Yale University, Graduate School of Arts and Sciences, Department of Astronomy, New Haven, CT 06520. Offers astronomy (PhD); solar and terrestrial physics (PhD). *Degree requirements:* For doctorate, thesis/dissertation. *Entrance requirements:* For doctorate, GRE General Test, GRE Subject Test (physics).

York University, Faculty of Graduate Studies, Faculty of Science and Engineering, Program in Earth and Space Science, Toronto, ON M3J 1P3, Canada. Offers M Sc, PhD. Part-time and evening/weekend programs available. *Degree requirements:* For master's, thesis or alternative; for doctorate, thesis/dissertation. Electronic applications accepted.

150 www.facebook.com/petersonspublishing

Peterson's Graduate Programs in the Physical Sciences, Mathematics, Agricultural Sciences, the Environment & Natural Resources 2012

Section 4
Marine Sciences and Oceanography

This section contains a directory of institutions offering graduate work in marine sciences and oceanography, followed by in-depth entries submitted by institutions that chose to prepare detailed program descriptions. Additional information about programs listed in the directory but not augmented by an in-depth entry may be obtained by writing directly to the dean of a graduate school or chair of a department at the address given in the directory.

For programs offering related work, see also in this book *Chemistry, Geosciences, Meteorology and Atmospheric Sciences,* and *Physics.* In the other guides in this series:

Graduate Programs in the Biological Sciences

See *Biological and Biomedical Sciences; Ecology, Environmental Biology, and Evolutionary Biology;* and *Marine Biology*

Graduate Programs in Engineering & Applied Sciences

See *Civil and Environmental Engineering, Engineering and Applied Sciences,* and *Ocean Engineering*

CONTENTS

Marine Sciences

American University, College of Arts and Sciences, Department of Biology, Washington, DC 20016-8007. Offers applied science (MS); biology (MA, MS); environmental science (MS), including environmental science, marine science. Part-time programs available. *Faculty:* 9 full-time (3 women), 3 part-time/adjunct (0 women). *Students:* 8 full-time (2 women), 8 part-time (6 women); includes 3 minority (1 Black or African American, non-Hispanic/Latino; 2 Asian, non-Hispanic/Latino), 2 international. Average age 25. 40 applicants, 53% accepted, 3 enrolled. In 2010, 10 master's awarded. *Degree requirements:* For master's, comprehensive exam, thesis (for some programs). *Entrance requirements:* For master's, GRE General Test, GRE Subject Test. Additional exam requirements/recommendations for international students: Required—TOEFL. *Application deadline:* For fall admission, 2/1 for domestic students; for spring admission, 10/1 for domestic students. Application fee: $80. *Financial support:* Fellowships, research assistantships with tuition reimbursements, teaching assistantships with tuition reimbursements, career-related internships or fieldwork, Federal Work-Study, and institutionally sponsored loans available. Financial award application deadline: 2/1. *Faculty research:* Neurobiology, cave biology, population genetics, vertebrate physiology. *Unit head:* Dr. David Carlini, Chair, 202-885-2194, Fax: 202-885-2182, E-mail: carlini@american.edu. *Application contact:* Kathleen Clowery, Director, Graduate Admissions, 202-885-3621, Fax: 202-885-1505.

California State University, East Bay, Office of Academic Programs and Graduate Studies, College of Science, Department of Biological Sciences, Marine Science Program, Moss Landing, CA 95039. Offers MS. *Degree requirements:* For master's, thesis. *Entrance requirements:* For master's, GRE Subject Test, minimum GPA of 3.0 in field, 2.75 overall. Additional exam requirements/recommendations for international students: Required—TOEFL. *Application deadline:* For fall admission, 3/15 for domestic students; for spring admission, 10/15 for domestic students. Application fee: $55. *Financial support:* Federal Work-Study, institutionally sponsored loans, and scholarships/grants available. Support available to part-time students. Financial award application deadline: 3/1; financial award applicants required to submit FAFSA. *Unit head:* Dr. Kenneth H. Coale, Director, 831-771-4400, Fax: 831-632-4403, E-mail: coale@mlml.calstate.edu. *Application contact:* Donna Wiley, Administrative Support Coordinator, 510-885-2928, Fax: 510-885-4777, E-mail: donna.wiley@csueastbay.edu.

California State University, Fresno, Division of Graduate Studies, College of Science and Mathematics, Program in Marine Sciences, Fresno, CA 93740-8027. Offers MS. Part-time programs available. Postbaccalaureate distance learning degree programs offered. *Degree requirements:* For master's, thesis. *Entrance requirements:* For master's, GRE General Test, minimum GPA of 3.0. Additional exam requirements/recommendations for international students: Required—TOEFL. Electronic applications accepted. *Faculty research:* Wetlands ecology, land/water conservation, water irrigation.

California State University, Monterey Bay, College of Science, Media Arts and Technology, Moss Landing Marine Laboratories, Seaside, CA 93955-8001. Offers MS. Part-time programs available. *Degree requirements:* For master's, thesis, thesis defense. *Entrance requirements:* For master's, selected MLML faculty member to serve as potential thesis advisor and selected consortium institution to serve as home campus. Additional exam requirements/recommendations for international students: Required—TOEFL (minimum score 525 paper-based; 213 computer-based; 71 iBT). Electronic applications accepted. *Faculty research:* Remote sensing microbiology trace elements, chemistry ecology of birds, mammals, turtles and fish, invasive species, marine phycology.

California State University, Sacramento, Graduate Studies, College of Natural Sciences and Mathematics, Department of Biological Sciences, Sacramento, CA 95819. Offers biological sciences (MA, MS); immunohematology (MS); marine science (MS). Part-time programs available. *Degree requirements:* For master's, thesis, writing proficiency exam. *Entrance requirements:* For master's, bachelor's degree in biology or equivalent, minimum GPA of 3.0 in biology, minimum overall GPA of 2.75 during last 2 years of course work. Additional exam requirements/recommendations for international students: Required—TOEFL. Electronic applications accepted.

Coastal Carolina University, College of Natural and Applied Sciences, Conway, SC 29528-6054. Offers coastal marine and wetland studies (MS). Part-time and evening/weekend programs available. *Faculty:* 16 full-time (2 women). *Students:* 16 full-time (11 women), 18 part-time (11 women); includes 1 minority (Hispanic/Latino). Average age 25. 39 applicants, 49% accepted, 13 enrolled. In 2010, 10 master's awarded. *Degree requirements:* For master's, thesis. *Entrance requirements:* For master's, GRE, 2 letters of recommendation, resume. Additional exam requirements/recommendations for international students: Required—TOEFL (minimum score 550 paper-based; 213 computer-based; 79 iBT). *Application deadline:* For fall admission, 3/1 priority date for domestic and international students; for spring admission, 11/1 priority date for domestic and international students. Applications are processed on a rolling basis. Application fee: $45. Electronic applications accepted. *Expenses:* Tuition, state resident: full-time $10,080; part-time $420 per credit hour. Tuition, nonresident: full-time $12,840; part-time $535 per credit hour. Required fees: $80; $40 per semester. Tuition and fees vary according to program. *Financial support:* Fellowships, research assistantships, unspecified assistantships available. Support available to part-time students. Financial award application deadline: 3/1; financial award applicants required to submit FAFSA. *Unit head:* Dr. Michael H. Roberts, Dean, 843-349-2282, Fax: 843-349-2545, E-mail: mroberts@coastal.edu. *Application contact:* Dr. Deborah A. Vrooman, Interim Director of Graduate Studies, 843-349-2783, Fax: 843-349-6444, E-mail: vroomand@coastal.edu.

College of Charleston, Graduate School, School of Sciences and Mathematics, Program in Marine Biology, Charleston, SC 29412. Offers MS. *Faculty:* 38 full-time (13 women), 8 part-time/adjunct (4 women). *Students:* 17 full-time (12 women), 28 part-time (14 women); includes 1 minority (Hispanic/Latino). Average age 25. 86 applicants, 24% accepted, 16 enrolled. In 2010, 18 master's awarded. *Degree requirements:* For master's, comprehensive exam, thesis. *Entrance requirements:* For master's, GRE General Test, 3 letters of recommendation. Additional exam requirements/recommendations for international students: Required—TOEFL (minimum score 81 iBT). *Application deadline:* For fall admission, 2/1 for domestic and international students; for spring admission, 11/1 for domestic and international students. Application fee: $45. Electronic applications accepted. *Financial support:* In 2010–11, 4 fellowships (averaging $22,000 per year), 22 research assistantships (averaging $19,000 per year), 19 teaching assistantships (averaging $16,000 per year) were awarded; career-related internships or fieldwork, Federal Work-Study, institutionally sponsored loans, scholarships/grants, and unspecified assistantships also available. Support available to part-time students. Financial award application deadline: 4/1; financial award applicants required to submit FAFSA. *Faculty research:* Ecology, environmental physiology, marine genomics, bioinformatics, toxicology, cell biology, population biology, fisheries science, animal physiology, biodiversity, estuarine ecology, evolution and systematics, microbial processes, plant physiology, immunology. *Unit head:* Dr. Craig J. Plante, Director, 843-953-9187, Fax: 843-953-9199, E-mail: plantec@cofc.edu. *Application contact:* Susan Hallatt, Director of Graduate Admissions, 843-953-5614, Fax: 843-953-1434, E-mail: hallatts@cofc.edu.

The College of William and Mary, Virginia Institute of Marine Science, Gloucester Point, VA 23062. Offers MS, PhD. *Faculty:* 53 full-time (14 women), 8 part-time/adjunct (0 women). *Students:* 100 full-time (66 women), 6 part-time (4 women); includes 11 minority (3 Black or African American, non-Hispanic/Latino; 1 American Indian or Alaska Native, non-Hispanic/Latino; 2 Asian, non-Hispanic/Latino; 2 Hispanic/Latino; 2 Native Hawaiian or other Pacific Islander, non-Hispanic/Latino; 1 Two or more races, non-Hispanic/Latino), 13 international. Average age 28. 118 applicants, 29% accepted, 27 enrolled. In 2010, 10 master's, 15 doctorates awarded. *Median time to degree:* Of those who began their doctoral program in fall 2002, 100% received their degree in 8 years or less. *Degree requirements:* For master's, thesis, qualifying exam; for doctorate, comprehensive exam, thesis/dissertation, qualifying exam. *Entrance requirements:* For master's, GRE, appropriate bachelor's degree; for doctorate, GRE, appropriate bachelor's and master's degrees. Additional exam requirements/recommendations for international students: Required—TOEFL. *Application deadline:* For fall admission, 1/15 for domestic and international students. Application fee: $50. Electronic applications accepted. *Expenses:* Tuition, state resident: full-time $6400; part-time $345 per credit hour. Tuition, nonresident: full-time $19,720; part-time $920 per credit hour. Required fees: $4368. *Financial support:* In 2010–11, 97 students received support, including 16 fellowships with full tuition reimbursements available (averaging $19,005 per year), 73 research assistantships with full tuition reimbursements available (averaging $19,005 per year), 8 teaching assistantships with partial tuition reimbursements available (averaging $6,500 per year); career-related internships or fieldwork, Federal Work-Study, scholarships/grants, health care benefits, and unspecified assistantships also available. Support available to part-time students. Financial award application deadline: 6/15; financial award applicants required to submit FAFSA. *Faculty research:* Marine science, oceanography, marine ecology, fisheries, environmental science and ecotoxicology. Total annual research expenditures: $19.8 million. *Unit head:* Dr. John T. Wells, Dean/Director, 804-684-7102, Fax: 804-684-7009, E-mail: wells@vims.edu. *Application contact:* Fonda J. Powell, Admissions Coordinator, 804-684-7105, Fax: 804-684-7881, E-mail: fonda@vims.edu.

Cornell University, Graduate School, Graduate Fields of Agriculture and Life Sciences, Field of Natural Resources, Ithaca, NY 14853-0001. Offers aquatic science (MPS, MS, PhD); environmental management (MPS); fishery science (MPS, MS, PhD); forest science (MPS, MS, PhD); resource policy and management (MPS, MS, PhD); wildlife science (MPS, MS, PhD). *Faculty:* 36 full-time (7 women). *Students:* 48 full-time (21 women); includes 1 Asian, non-Hispanic/Latino; 1 Hispanic/Latino, 11 international. Average age 30. 52 applicants, 27% accepted, 11 enrolled. In 2010, 8 master's, 6 doctorates awarded. *Degree requirements:* For master's, thesis (MS), project paper (MPS); for doctorate, comprehensive exam, thesis/dissertation. *Entrance requirements:* For master's and doctorate, GRE General Test, 2 letters of recommendation. Additional exam requirements/recommendations for international students: Required—TOEFL (minimum score 550 paper-based; 213 computer-based; 77 iBT). *Application deadline:* For spring admission, 10/30 for domestic students. Applications are processed on a rolling basis. Application fee: $70. Electronic applications accepted. *Expenses:* Tuition: Full-time $29,500. Required fees: $76. Tuition and fees vary according to degree level and program. *Financial support:* In 2010–11, 9 fellowships with full tuition reimbursements, 16 research assistantships with full tuition reimbursements, 15 teaching assistantships with full tuition reimbursements were awarded; institutionally sponsored loans, scholarships/grants, health care benefits, tuition waivers (full and partial), and unspecified assistantships also available. Financial award applicants required to submit FAFSA. *Faculty research:* Ecosystem-level dynamics, systems modeling, conservation biology/management, resource management's human dimensions, biogeochemistry. *Unit head:* Director of Graduate Studies, 607-255-2807, Fax: 607-255-0349. *Application contact:* Graduate Field Assistant, 607-255-2807, Fax: 607-255-0349, E-mail: nrgrad@cornell.edu.

Duke University, Graduate School, Program in Marine Science and Conservation, Beaufort, NC 28516. Offers MS. *Faculty:* 18 full-time. *Students:* 26 full-time (20 women); includes 1 American Indian or Alaska Native, non-Hispanic/Latino; 1 Asian, non-Hispanic/Latino, 5 international. 54 applicants, 30% accepted, 10 enrolled. In 2010, 1 master's awarded. *Entrance requirements:* Additional exam requirements/recommendations for international students: Required—TOEFL (minimum score 550 paper-based; 213 computer-based; 83 iBT), IELTS. *Application deadline:* For fall admission, 12/8 priority date for domestic students. Application fee: $75. *Financial support:* Fellowships, research assistantships, teaching assistantships available. *Unit head:* Lisa Campbell, Director of Graduate Studies, 252-504-7585, Fax: 252-504-7648. *Application contact:* Elizabeth Hutton, Director of Admissions, 919-684-3913, Fax: 919-684-2277, E-mail: grad-admissions@duke.edu.

Duke University, Nicholas School of the Environment, Durham, NC 27708-0328. Offers coastal environmental management (MEM); DEL-environmental leadership (MEM); energy and environment (MEM); environmental economics and policy (MEM); environmental health and security (MEM); forest resource management (MF); global environmental change (MEM); resource ecology (MEM); water and air resources (MEM); JD/AM; JD/MEM; JD/MF; MAT/MEM; MBA/MEM; MBA/MF; MEM/MPP; MF/MPP. *Accreditation:* SAF (one or more programs are accredited). Part-time programs available. *Degree requirements:* For master's, thesis. *Entrance requirements:* For master's, GRE General Test, previous course work in biology or ecology, calculus, statistics, and microeconomics; computer familiarity with word processing and data analysis. Additional exam requirements/recommendations for international students: Required—TOEFL (minimum score 550 paper-based; 213 computer-based). Electronic applications accepted. *Expenses:* Contact institution. *Faculty research:* Ecosystem management, conservation ecology, earth systems, risk assessment.

Florida State University, The Graduate School, College of Arts and Sciences, Department of Earth, Ocean and Atmospheric Science, Program in Oceanography, Tallahassee, FL 32306-4320. Offers aquatic environmental science (MS); oceanography (MS, PhD). *Faculty:* 15 full-time (1 woman). *Students:* 48 full-time (24 women); includes 1 Black or African American, non-Hispanic/Latino; 3 Asian, non-Hispanic/Latino, 9 international. Average age 27. 61 applicants, 36% accepted, 10 enrolled. In 2010, 8 master's, 4 doctorates awarded. *Median time to degree:* Of those who began their doctoral program in fall 2002, 100% received their degree in 8 years or less. *Degree requirements:* For master's, thesis; for doctorate, comprehensive exam, thesis/dissertation. *Entrance requirements:* For master's and doctorate, GRE General Test. Additional exam requirements/recommendations for international students: Required—TOEFL (minimum score 550 paper-based; 213 computer-based; 80 iBT). *Application deadline:* For fall admission, 2/15 priority date for domestic and international students; for spring admission, 7/15 priority date for domestic and international students. Applications are processed on a rolling basis. Application fee: $35. Electronic applications accepted. *Expenses:* Tuition, state resident: full-time $8238.24. *Financial support:* In 2010–11, 41 students received support, including 1 fellowship with full tuition reimbursement available, 26 research assistantships with full tuition reimbursements available, 14 teaching assistantships with full tuition reimbursements available. Financial award application deadline: 2/15; financial award applicants required to submit FAFSA. *Faculty research:* Trace metals in seawater, currents and waves, modeling, benthic ecology, marine biogeochemistry. *Unit head:* Dr. Jeffrey Chanton, Area Coordinator, 850-644-6700, Fax: 850-644-2581, E-mail: chanton@ocean.fsu.edu. *Application contact:* Michaela Lupiani, Academic Coordinator, 850-644-6700, Fax: 850-644-2581, E-mail: admissions@ocean.fsu.edu.

Georgia Institute of Technology, Graduate Studies and Research, College of Sciences, School of Earth and Atmospheric Sciences, Atlanta, GA 30332-0340. Offers atmospheric chemistry, aerosols and clouds (MS, PhD); dynamics of weather and climate (MS, PhD); geochemistry (MS, PhD); geophysics (MS, PhD); oceanography (MS, PhD); paleoclimate (MS, PhD); planetary science (MS, PhD); remote sensing (MS, PhD). Part-time programs available. Terminal master's awarded for partial completion of doctoral program. *Degree requirements:* For master's, thesis or alternative; for doctorate, comprehensive exam, thesis/dissertation. *Entrance requirements:* For master's, GRE, letters of recommendation; for doctorate, GRE, academic transcripts, letters of recommendation, personal statement. Additional exam requirements/recommendations for international students: Required—TOEFL (minimum score

550 paper-based; 213 computer-based; 79 iBT). *Faculty research:* Geophysics; atmospheric chemistry, aerosols and clouds; dynamics of weather and climate; geochemistry; oceanography; paleoclimate; planetary science; remote sensing.

Hawai'i Pacific University, College of Natural and Computational Sciences, Honolulu, HI 96813. Offers global leadership and sustainable development (MA); marine science (MS). *Degree requirements:* For master's, thesis. *Entrance requirements:* For master's, GRE, bachelor's degree in science or marine science, minimum GPA of 3.0. Additional exam requirements/recommendations for international students: Recommended—TOEFL (minimum score 550 paper-based; 213 computer-based; 80 iBT), TWE (minimum score 5). Electronic applications accepted.

See Close-Up on page 161.

Instituto Tecnologico de Santo Domingo, Graduate School, Area of Basic And Environmental Sciences, Santo Domingo, Dominican Republic. Offers environmental science (M En S), including environmental education, environmental management, marine resources, natural resources management; mathematics (MS, PhD); renewable energy technology (MS, Certificate).

Medical University of South Carolina, College of Graduate Studies, Program in Molecular and Cellular Biology and Pathobiology, Charleston, SC 29425. Offers cancer biology (PhD); cardiovascular biology (PhD); cardiovascular imaging (PhD); cell regulation (PhD); craniofacial biology (PhD); genetics and development (PhD); marine biomedicine (PhD); DMD/PhD; MD/PhD. *Faculty:* 137 full-time (33 women). *Students:* 27 full-time (20 women); includes 3 Black or African American, non-Hispanic/Latino; 1 Hispanic/Latino, 6 international. Average age 30. In 2010, 16 doctorates awarded. *Degree requirements:* For doctorate, thesis/dissertation, oral and written exams. *Entrance requirements:* For doctorate, GRE General Test, interview, minimum GPA of 3.0. Additional exam requirements/recommendations for international students: Required—TOEFL (minimum score 600 paper-based; 250 computer-based; 100 iBT). *Application deadline:* For fall admission, 1/15 priority date for domestic and international students. Applications are processed on a rolling basis. Application fee: $0 ($85 for international students). Electronic applications accepted. *Financial support:* In 2010–11, 39 research assistantships with partial tuition reimbursements (averaging $23,000 per year) were awarded; Federal Work-Study and scholarships/grants also available. Support available to part-time students. Financial award application deadline: 3/10; financial award applicants required to submit FAFSA. *Unit head:* Dr. Donald R. Menick, Director, 843-876-5045, Fax: 843-792-6590, E-mail: menickd@musc.edu. *Application contact:* Dr. Cynthia F. Wright, Associate Dean for Admissions and Career Development, 843-792-2564, Fax: 843-792-6590, E-mail: wrightcf@musc.edu.

Memorial University of Newfoundland, School of Graduate Studies, Interdisciplinary Program in Marine Studies, St. John's, NL A1C 5S7, Canada. Offers fisheries resource management (MMS, Advanced Diploma). Part-time programs available. *Degree requirements:* For master's, report. *Entrance requirements:* For master's and Advanced Diploma, high 2nd class degree from a recognized university. *Faculty research:* Biological, ecological and oceanographic aspects of world fisheries; economics; political science; sociology.

North Carolina State University, Graduate School, College of Physical and Mathematical Sciences, Department of Marine, Earth, and Atmospheric Sciences, Raleigh, NC 27695. Offers marine, earth, and atmospheric sciences (MS, PhD); meteorology (MS, PhD); oceanography (MS, PhD). PhD offered jointly with The University of North Carolina Wilmington. Terminal master's awarded for partial completion of doctoral program. *Degree requirements:* For master's, thesis (for some programs), final oral exam; for doctorate, comprehensive exam, thesis/dissertation, final oral exam, preliminary oral and written exams. *Entrance requirements:* For master's, GRE General Test, minimum GPA of 3.0; for doctorate, GRE General Test, GRE Subject Test (for disciplines in biological oceanography and geology), minimum GPA of 3.0. Additional exam requirements/recommendations for international students: Required—TOEFL (minimum score 550 paper-based). Electronic applications accepted. *Faculty research:* Boundary layer and air quality meteorology; climate and mesoscale dynamics; biological, chemical, geological, and physical oceanography; hard rock, soft rock, environmental, and paleogeology.

Nova Southeastern University, Oceanographic Center, Program in Coastal Zone Management, Dania Beach, FL 33004. Offers MS. *Faculty:* 15 full-time (1 woman), 5 part-time/adjunct (0 women). *Students:* 21 full-time (14 women), 20 part-time (14 women); includes 1 American Indian or Alaska Native, non-Hispanic/Latino; 4 Hispanic/Latino, 1 international. Average age 30. 44 applicants, 52% accepted, 2 enrolled. In 2010, 12 master's awarded. *Degree requirements:* For master's, thesis. *Entrance requirements:* For master's, GRE. Additional exam requirements/recommendations for international students: Required—TOEFL (minimum score 550 paper-based). *Application deadline:* Applications are processed on a rolling basis. Application fee: $50. *Financial support:* Career-related internships or fieldwork, Federal Work-Study, scholarships/grants, and unspecified assistantships available. Financial award applicants required to submit FAFSA. *Unit head:* Dr. Richard Spieler, Director of Academic Programs, 954-262-3600, Fax: 954-262-4020, E-mail: spieler@nova.edu. *Application contact:* Dr. Richard Spieler, Director of Academic Programs, 954-262-3600, Fax: 954-262-4020, E-mail: spieler@nova.edu.

Nova Southeastern University, Oceanographic Center, Program in Marine Environmental Science, Fort Lauderdale, FL 33314-7796. Offers MS. *Faculty:* 15 full-time (1 woman), 5 part-time/adjunct (0 women). *Students:* 4 full-time (all women), 5 part-time (3 women); includes 2 Hispanic/Latino. Average age 25. 14 applicants, 64% accepted, 6 enrolled. In 2010, 2 master's awarded. *Degree requirements:* For master's, thesis. *Entrance requirements:* For master's, GRE. Additional exam requirements/recommendations for international students: Required—TOEFL (minimum score 550 paper-based). *Application deadline:* Applications are processed on a rolling basis. Application fee: $50. *Unit head:* Dr. Richard Dodge, Dean, 954-262-3600, Fax: 954-262-4020, E-mail: dodge@nsu.nova.edu. *Application contact:* Dr. Richard Spieler, Director of Academic Programs, 954-262-3600, Fax: 954-262-4020, E-mail: spieler@nova.edu.

Oregon State University, Graduate School, College of Oceanic and Atmospheric Sciences, Program in Marine Resource Management, Corvallis, OR 97331. Offers MA, MS. *Degree requirements:* For master's, thesis optional. *Entrance requirements:* For master's, GRE General Test, minimum GPA of 3.0 in last 90 hours of course work. Additional exam requirements/recommendations for international students: Required—TOEFL. *Faculty research:* Ocean and coastal resources, fisheries resources, marine pollution, marine recreation and tourism.

San Francisco State University, Division of Graduate Studies, College of Science and Engineering, Department of Biology, Program in Marine Science, San Francisco, CA 94132-1722. Offers MS. Program offered through the Moss Landing Marine Laboratories. *Application deadline:* Applications are processed on a rolling basis. *Unit head:* Drew Seals, Coordinator, 831-771-4401, E-mail: dseals@mlml.calstate.edu. *Application contact:* Drew Seals, Coordinator, 831-771-4401, E-mail: dseals@mlml.calstate.edu.

San Jose State University, Graduate Studies and Research, College of Science, Moss Landing Marine Laboratories, San Jose, CA 95192-0001. Offers MS. *Degree requirements:* For master's, thesis, qualifying exam. *Entrance requirements:* For master's, GRE. Electronic applications accepted. *Faculty research:* Physical oceanography, marine geology, ecology, ichthyology, invertebrate zoology.

Savannah State University, Master of Science in Marine Sciences Program, Savannah, GA 31404. Offers MS. Part-time programs available. *Students:* 12 full-time (5 women), 9 part-time (7 women); includes 7 Black or African American, non-Hispanic/Latino; 2 Asian, non-Hispanic/Latino. Average age 29. In 2010, 8 master's awarded. *Degree requirements:* For master's, comprehensive exam. *Entrance requirements:* For master's, GRE General Test, 3 letters of recommendation, minimum GPA of 3.0, essay. Additional exam requirements/recommendations for international students: Required—TOEFL. *Application deadline:* For fall admission, 7/1 for domestic students, 5/15 for international students; for spring admission, 10/31 for domestic students, 10/1 for international students. Applications are processed on a rolling basis. Application fee: $20. Electronic applications accepted. *Expenses:* Tuition, state resident: full-time $4042. Tuition, nonresident: full-time $15,028. Required fees: $1350. *Financial support:* Career-related internships or fieldwork, Federal Work-Study, institutionally sponsored loans, scholarships/grants, and unspecified assistantships available. Financial award applicants required to submit FAFSA. *Unit head:* Dr. Matthew Gilligan, Coordinator, 912-358-4098, E-mail: gilliganm@savannahstate.edu. *Application contact:* Emily Crawford, Interim Dean of Graduate Studies, 912-358-4182, Fax: 912-356-2299, E-mail: crawford@savnnahstate.edu.

Stony Brook University, State University of New York, Graduate School, School of Marine and Atmospheric Sciences, Institute for Terrestrial and Planetary Atmospheres, Program in Marine Sciences, Stony Brook, NY 11794. Offers MS, PhD. Evening/weekend programs available. *Degree requirements:* For doctorate, one foreign language, comprehensive exam, thesis/dissertation. *Entrance requirements:* For master's, GRE General Test, official transcripts, minimum GPA of 3.0, 3 letters of recommendation; for doctorate, GRE General Test, minimum GPA of 3.0, 3 letters of recommendation. Additional exam requirements/recommendations for international students: Required—TOEFL (minimum score 600 paper-based; 213 computer-based). *Application deadline:* For fall admission, 1/15 priority date for domestic students; for spring admission, 10/1 priority date for domestic students. Application fee: $100. Electronic applications accepted. *Expenses:* Tuition, state resident: full-time $8370; part-time $349 per credit. Tuition, nonresident: full-time $13,780; part-time $574 per credit. Required fees: $994. *Financial support:* Fellowships, research assistantships, teaching assistantships, career-related internships or fieldwork available. *Unit head:* Minghua Zhang, Director, 631-632-8318. *Application contact:* Dr. Glenn R. Lopez, Assistant Director, 631-632-8660, Fax: 631-632-8200, E-mail: glopez@notes.cc.sunysb.edu.

Texas A&M University at Galveston, Department of Marine Sciences, Galveston, TX 77553-1675. Offers marine resources management (MMRM). *Faculty:* 33 full-time (7 women). *Students:* 20 full-time (11 women), 11 part-time (8 women); includes 2 minority (1 Asian, non-Hispanic/Latino; 1 Hispanic/Latino), 1 international. Average age 23. 17 applicants, 82% accepted, 12 enrolled. In 2010, 12 master's awarded. *Degree requirements:* For master's, thesis (for some programs). *Entrance requirements:* For master's, GRE, course work in economics. Additional exam requirements/recommendations for international students: Required—TOEFL (minimum score 550 paper-based; 213 computer-based). *Application deadline:* Applications are processed on a rolling basis. Application fee: $50 ($75 for international students). Electronic applications accepted. *Financial support:* In 2010–11, 10 students received support, including 10 teaching assistantships; research assistantships, scholarships/grants, health care benefits, and unspecified assistantships also available. Financial award application deadline: 4/1; financial award applicants required to submit FAFSA. *Faculty research:* Biogeochemistry, physical oceanography, theoretical chemistry, marine policy. *Unit head:* Dr. Patrick Louchouarn, Professor/Head, 409-740-4710. *Application contact:* Dr. Frederick C. Schlemmer, Associate Professor/Graduate Advisor, 409-740-4518, Fax: 409-740-4429, E-mail: schlemme@tamug.edu.

Texas A&M University–Corpus Christi, Graduate Studies and Research, College of Science and Technology, Program in Coastal and Marine System Science, Corpus Christi, TX 78412-5503. Offers PhD.

University of Alaska Fairbanks, School of Fisheries and Ocean Sciences, Program in Marine Sciences and Limnology, Fairbanks, AK 99775-7220. Offers marine biology (MS, PhD); oceanography (PhD), including biological oceanography, chemical oceanography, fisheries, geological oceanography, physical oceanography. Part-time programs available. *Faculty:* 8 full-time (4 women). *Students:* 40 full-time (26 women), 12 part-time (7 women); includes 3 minority (2 Asian, non-Hispanic/Latino; 1 Hispanic/Latino), 3 international. Average age 31. 54 applicants, 26% accepted, 14 enrolled. In 2010, 6 master's, 1 doctorate awarded. *Degree requirements:* For master's, comprehensive exam, thesis, oral defense; for doctorate, comprehensive exam, thesis/dissertation, oral defense. *Entrance requirements:* For master's and doctorate, GRE General Test. Additional exam requirements/recommendations for international students: Required—TOEFL (minimum score 550 paper-based; 213 computer-based; 80 iBT). *Application deadline:* For fall admission, 6/1 for domestic students, 3/1 for international students; for spring admission, 10/15 for domestic students, 8/1 for international students. Applications are processed on a rolling basis. Application fee: $60. Electronic applications accepted. *Expenses:* Tuition, state resident: full-time $5688; part-time $316 per credit. Tuition, nonresident: full-time $11,628; part-time $646 per credit. Required fees: $289 per semester. Tuition and fees vary according to course load and reciprocity agreements. *Financial support:* In 2010–11, 24 research assistantships with tuition reimbursements (averaging $11,704 per year), 9 teaching assistantships with tuition reimbursements (averaging $11,008 per year) were awarded; fellowships with tuition reimbursements, career-related internships or fieldwork, Federal Work-Study, scholarships/grants, health care benefits, and unspecified assistantships also available. Support available to part-time students. Financial award application deadline: 7/1; financial award applicants required to submit FAFSA. *Unit head:* Katrin Iken, Co-Chair, 907-474-7289, Fax: 907-474-5863, E-mail: academics@sfos.uaf.edu. *Application contact:* Christina Neumann, Academic Manager, 907-474-7289, Fax: 907-474-5863, E-mail: clneumann@alaska.edu.

The University of British Columbia, Faculty of Science, Department of Earth and Ocean Sciences, Vancouver, BC V6T 1Z4, Canada. Offers atmospheric science (M Sc, PhD); geological engineering (M Eng, MA Sc, PhD); geological sciences (M Sc, PhD); geophysics (M Sc, MA Sc, PhD); oceanography (M Sc, PhD). *Degree requirements:* For master's, thesis (for some programs); for doctorate, comprehensive exam, thesis/dissertation. *Entrance requirements:* Additional exam requirements/recommendations for international students: Required—TOEFL (minimum score 600 paper-based; 250 computer-based; 100 iBT). Electronic applications accepted. Tuition charges are reported in Canadian dollars. *Expenses:* Tuition, area resident: Full-time $4179 Canadian dollars. International tuition: $7344 Canadian dollars full-time. *Faculty research:* Oceans and atmosphere, environmental earth science, hydro geology, mineral deposits, geophysics.

University of California, San Diego, Office of Graduate Studies, Scripps Institution of Oceanography, Program in Marine Biodiversity and Conservation, La Jolla, CA 92093. Offers MAS. *Entrance requirements:* For master's, minimum 3 years post-baccalaureate work experience. Additional exam requirements/recommendations for international students: Required—TOEFL. Electronic applications accepted.

University of California, Santa Barbara, Graduate Division, College of Letters and Sciences, Division of Mathematics, Life, and Physical Sciences, Interdepartmental Program in Marine Science, Santa Barbara, CA 93106-9620. Offers MS, PhD. *Faculty:* 43 full-time (10 women). *Students:* 22 full-time (13 women); includes 1 American Indian or Alaska Native, non-Hispanic/Latino; 1 Asian, non-Hispanic/Latino. Average age 31. 49 applicants, 10% accepted, 0 enrolled. In 2010, 6 master's, 4 doctorates awarded. *Degree requirements:* For master's, thesis, 39 units; for doctorate, comprehensive exam, thesis/dissertation, 31 units. *Entrance requirements:* For master's and doctorate, GRE. Additional exam requirements/recommendations for international students: Required—TOEFL (minimum score 550 paper-based; 80 iBT), IELTS (minimum score 7). *Application deadline:* For fall admission, 12/15 for domestic and international students. Application fee: $70 ($90 for international students). Electronic applications accepted. *Financial support:* In 2010–11, 22 students received support, including 19 fellowships with full tuition reimbursements available (averaging $11,468 per year), 17 research assistantships with full tuition reimbursements available (averaging $10,895 per year), 10

Marine Sciences

University of California, Santa Barbara (continued)
teaching assistantships with full tuition reimbursements available (averaging $7,908 per year); career-related internships or fieldwork, Federal Work-Study, institutionally sponsored loans, scholarships/grants, health care benefits, tuition waivers (full and partial), and unspecified assistantships also available. Support available to part-time students. Financial award application deadline: 12/15; financial award applicants required to submit FAFSA. *Faculty research:* Ocean carbon cycling, paleooceanography, physiology of marine organisms, bio-optical oceanography, biological oceanography. *Unit head:* Prof. Libe Washburn, Chair/Professor of Geography, 805-893-7367, Fax: 805-893-2578, E-mail: washburn@eri.ucsb.edu. *Application contact:* Melanie Fujii, Graduate Program Assistant, 805-893-8162, Fax: 805-893-5885, E-mail: fujii@lifesci.ucsb.edu.

University of California, Santa Cruz, Division of Graduate Studies, Division of Physical and Biological Sciences, Department of Ocean Sciences, Santa Cruz, CA 95064. Offers MS, PhD. *Students:* 40 full-time (26 women); includes 3 minority (all Hispanic/Latino), 6 international. Average age 30. 55 applicants, 13% accepted, 4 enrolled. In 2010, 1 master's, 4 doctorates awarded. Terminal master's awarded for partial completion of doctoral program. *Degree requirements:* For master's, thesis; for doctorate, comprehensive exam, thesis/dissertation, seminar, qualifying exam. *Entrance requirements:* For master's and doctorate, GRE General Test, GRE Subject Test, 3 letters of recommendation. Additional exam requirements/recommendations for international students: Required—TOEFL (minimum score 550 paper-based; 220 computer-based; 83 iBT); Recommended—IELTS (minimum score 8). *Application deadline:* For fall admission, 1/15 for domestic and international students. Application fee: $70 ($90 for international students). Electronic applications accepted. *Financial support:* Fellowships, research assistantships, teaching assistantships, institutionally sponsored loans and tuition waivers available. Financial award applicants required to submit FAFSA. *Faculty research:* Sediment, marine organic and trace metal biogeochemistry; paleoceanography; remote sensing (satellite oceanography); coastal circulation processes; the development of software applications for real-time data acquisition and data visualization; climatology. *Unit head:* Diana Austin, Graduate Program Coordinator, 831-459-2563, E-mail: djaustin@ucsc.edu. *Application contact:* Diana Austin, Graduate Program Coordinator, 831-459-2563, E-mail: djaustin@ucsc.edu.

University of Connecticut, Graduate School, College of Liberal Arts and Sciences, Department of Marine Sciences, Storrs, CT 06269. Offers MS, PhD. Terminal master's awarded for partial completion of doctoral program. *Degree requirements:* For master's, comprehensive exam; for doctorate, thesis/dissertation. *Entrance requirements:* Additional exam requirements/recommendations for international students: Required—TOEFL (minimum score 550 paper-based; 213 computer-based). Electronic applications accepted.

University of Delaware, College of Earth, Ocean, and Environment, School of Marine Science and Policy, Newark, DE 19716. Offers marine policy (MMP); marine studies (MS, PhD), including marine biosciences, oceanography, physical ocean science and engineering; oceanography (PhD).

University of Florida, Graduate School, College of Agricultural and Life Sciences, Department of Fisheries and Aquatic Sciences, Gainesville, FL 32611. Offers MFAS, MS, PhD. Part-time programs available. *Students:* 5 full-time (2 women), 2 part-time (1 woman), 1 international. Average age 29. 34 applicants, 26% accepted, 8 enrolled. In 2010, 1 master's awarded. *Degree requirements:* For master's, thesis (for some programs), Thesis required for Masters of Science. Technical paper required for MFAS degree; for doctorate, comprehensive exam, thesis/dissertation. *Entrance requirements:* For master's and doctorate, GRE General Test, minimum GPA of 3.0. Additional exam requirements/recommendations for international students: Required—TOEFL (minimum score 550 paper-based; 213 computer-based; 80 iBT), IELTS (minimum score 6). *Application deadline:* For fall admission, 6/1 for domestic students, 3/1 for international students; for spring admission, 10/1 for domestic students, 8/1 for international students. Applications are processed on a rolling basis. Application fee: $30. Electronic applications accepted. *Expenses:* Tuition, state resident: full-time $10,915.92. Tuition, nonresident: full-time $28,309. *Financial support:* In 2010–11, 4 students received support, including 1 fellowship, 3 research assistantships (averaging $20,141 per year); unspecified assistantships also available. Financial award application deadline: 1/31; financial award applicants required to submit FAFSA. *Faculty research:* Conservation and management of aquatic ecosystems; aquatic animal health; water quality, nutrients, and eutrophication; sustainable and quantitative fisheries; aquaculture or ornamental fish, marine baitfish, and shellfish. Total annual research expenditures: $10 million. *Unit head:* Nancy J. Peterson, PhD, Associate Director, 352-846-0848, Fax: 352-846-1277, E-mail: njp@ufl.edu. *Application contact:* Charles Cichra, PhD, Graduate Coordinator, 352-273-3621, Fax: 352-392-3672, E-mail: cecichra@ufl.edu.

University of Georgia, College of Arts and Sciences, Department of Marine Sciences, Athens, GA 30602. Offers MS, PhD. *Faculty:* 15 full-time (5 women), 2 part-time/adjunct (0 women). *Students:* 28 full-time (15 women), 1 (woman) part-time; includes 2 Hispanic/Latino, 10 international. Average age 28. 28 applicants, 29% accepted, 4 enrolled. In 2010, 2 master's awarded. *Degree requirements:* For master's, thesis; for doctorate, comprehensive exam, thesis/dissertation, teaching experience, field research experience. *Entrance requirements:* For master's and doctorate, GRE General Test. Additional exam requirements/recommendations for international students: Required—TOEFL. *Application deadline:* For fall admission, 2/1 priority date for domestic and international students; for spring admission, 10/15 priority date for domestic students, 9/1 priority date for international students. Applications are processed on a rolling basis. Application fee: $50. Electronic applications accepted. *Expenses:* Tuition, state resident: full-time $7200; part-time $344 per credit hour. Tuition, nonresident: full-time $21,900; part-time $944 per credit hour. Tuition and fees vary according to course load and program. *Financial support:* In 2010–11, 9 fellowships with full tuition reimbursements (averaging $20,000 per year), 21 research assistantships with full tuition reimbursements (averaging $18,000 per year), 11 teaching assistantships with full tuition reimbursements (averaging $18,000 per year) were awarded. *Faculty research:* Microbial ecology, biogeochemistry, polar biology, coastal ecology, coastal circulation. *Unit head:* Dr. Brian Binder, Director, 706-542-6408, Fax: 706-542-5888, E-mail: bbinder@uga.edu. *Application contact:* Dr. Ming-yi Sun, Graduate Coordinator, 706-542-5709, E-mail: mysun@uga.edu.

University of Hawaii at Manoa, Graduate Division, College of Social Sciences, Department of Geography, Graduate Ocean Policy Certificate Program, Honolulu, HI 96822. Offers Graduate Certificate. Part-time programs available. *Students:* 3 full-time (2 women), 2 part-time (1 woman). Average age 36. 4 applicants, 100% accepted, 4 enrolled. In 2010, 2 Graduate Certificates awarded. *Entrance requirements:* Additional exam requirements/recommendations for international students: Required—TOEFL (minimum score 500 paper-based; 173 computer-based; 61 iBT), IELTS (minimum score 5). *Application deadline:* For fall admission, 3/1 for domestic students, 2/1 for international students; for spring admission, 9/1 for domestic students, 8/1 for international students. Application fee: $60. *Financial support:* In 2010–11, 1 fellowship (averaging $500 per year), 1 research assistantship (averaging $25,902 per year), 1 teaching assistantship (averaging $15,558 per year) were awarded. Total annual research expenditures: $21.4 million. *Application contact:* Alison Rieser, Program Director, 808-956-8467, Fax: 808-956-3512, E-mail: rieser@hawaii.edu.

University of Maine, Graduate School, College of Natural Sciences, Forestry, and Agriculture, School of Marine Sciences, Orono, ME 04469. Offers marine biology (MS, PhD); marine policy (MS); oceanography (MS, PhD). Part-time programs available. *Faculty:* 30 full-time (9 women), 2 part-time/adjunct (1 woman). *Students:* 46 full-time (22 women), 12 part-time (3 women), 8 international. Average age 29. 107 applicants, 12% accepted, 13 enrolled. In 2010, 9 master's, 2 doctorates awarded. *Degree requirements:* For master's, thesis; for doctorate, thesis/dissertation. *Entrance requirements:* For master's and doctorate, GRE General Test. Additional exam requirements/recommendations for international students: Required—TOEFL. *Application deadline:* For fall admission, 2/1 priority date for domestic students. Applications are processed on a rolling basis. Application fee: $65. Electronic applications accepted. *Expenses:* Tuition, state resident: full-time $400. Tuition, nonresident: full-time $1050. *Financial support:* In 2010–11, 1 fellowship with tuition reimbursement (averaging $20,000 per year), 42 research assistantships with tuition reimbursements (averaging $19,170 per year), 3 teaching assistantships with tuition reimbursements (averaging $12,790 per year) were awarded; career-related internships or fieldwork, Federal Work-Study, and tuition waivers (full and partial) also available. Support available to part-time students. Financial award application deadline: 3/1. *Faculty research:* Coastal processes, microbial ecology, crustacean systematics. *Unit head:* Dr. Peter Jumars, Director, 207-581-3321, Fax: 207-581-4388. *Application contact:* Scott G. Delcourt, Associate Dean of the Graduate School, 207-581-3291, Fax: 207-581-3232, E-mail: graduate@maine.edu.

University of Maryland, Baltimore, Graduate School, Program in Marine-Estuarine-Environmental Sciences, Baltimore, MD 21201. Offers MS, PhD. Part-time programs available. *Faculty:* 7. *Students:* 1 (woman) full-time, all international. 1 applicant, 0% accepted, 0 enrolled.Terminal master's awarded for partial completion of doctoral program. *Degree requirements:* For master's, thesis, oral defense; for doctorate, comprehensive exam, thesis/dissertation, proposal defense, oral defense. *Entrance requirements:* For master's and doctorate, GRE General Test, minimum GPA of 3.0. Additional exam requirements/recommendations for international students: Required—TOEFL. *Application deadline:* For fall admission, 2/1 for domestic students, 1/1 for international students; for spring admission, 9/1 for domestic students. Applications are processed on a rolling basis. Application fee: $50. Electronic applications accepted. Part-time tuition and fees vary according to course load, degree level and program. *Financial support:* In 2010–11, 1 research assistantship with tuition reimbursement was awarded; fellowships with tuition reimbursements, teaching assistantships with tuition reimbursements, scholarships/grants and unspecified assistantships also available. *Unit head:* Dr. Kennedy T. Paynter, Director, Marine-Estuarine-Environmental Science Graduate Program, 301-405-6938, Fax: 301-314-4139, E-mail: mees@umd.edu. *Application contact:* Dr. Kennedy T. Paynter, Director, Marine-Estuarine-Environmental Science Graduate Program, 301-405-6938, Fax: 301-314-4139, E-mail: mees@umd.edu.

University of Maryland, Baltimore County, Graduate School, Marine-Estuarine-Environmental Sciences Graduate Program, Baltimore, MD 21250. Offers MS, PhD. Part-time programs available. *Faculty:* 14. *Students:* 5 full-time (3 women), 1 part-time (0 women); includes 1 Black or African American, non-Hispanic/Latino; 1 Hispanic/Latino. 8 applicants, 0% accepted, 0 enrolled. In 2010, 1 master's, 1 doctorate awarded. *Degree requirements:* For master's, thesis, oral defense; for doctorate, comprehensive exam, thesis/dissertation, proposal defense, oral defense. *Entrance requirements:* For master's and doctorate, GRE General Test, minimum GPA of 3.0. Additional exam requirements/recommendations for international students: Required—TOEFL. *Application deadline:* For fall admission, 2/1 for domestic students, 1/1 for international students; for spring admission, 9/1 for domestic students. Applications are processed on a rolling basis. Application fee: $50. Electronic applications accepted. *Financial support:* In 2010–11, 2 fellowships with tuition reimbursements (averaging $22,500 per year), 1 research assistantship with tuition reimbursement (averaging $21,000 per year), 1 teaching assistantship with tuition reimbursement (averaging $20,000 per year) were awarded; career-related internships or fieldwork, scholarships/grants, and unspecified assistantships also available. Financial award application deadline: 12/1. *Unit head:* Dr. Kennedy T. Paynter, Director, 301-405-6938, Fax: 301-314-4139, E-mail: mees@umd.edu. *Application contact:* Dr. Kennedy T. Paynter, Director, 301-405-6938, Fax: 301-314-4139, E-mail: mees@umd.edu.

University of Maryland, College Park, Academic Affairs, College of Computer, Mathematical and Natural Sciences, Program in Marine-Estuarine-Environmental Sciences, College Park, MD 20742. Offers MS, PhD. Intercampus, interdisciplinary program. Part-time programs available. *Faculty:* 132. *Students:* 122 (78 women); includes 4 Black or African American, non-Hispanic/Latino; 2 Asian, non-Hispanic/Latino; 4 Hispanic/Latino, 27 international. 131 applicants, 32% accepted, 32 enrolled. In 2010, 11 master's, 7 doctorates awarded. Terminal master's awarded for partial completion of doctoral program. *Degree requirements:* For master's, thesis, oral defense; for doctorate, comprehensive exam, thesis/dissertation, proposal defense, oral defense. *Entrance requirements:* For master's and doctorate, GRE General Test, minimum GPA of 3.0. Additional exam requirements/recommendations for international students: Required—TOEFL. *Application deadline:* For fall admission, 2/1 for domestic and international students; for spring admission, 9/1 for domestic students, 6/1 for international students. Applications are processed on a rolling basis. Application fee: $60. Electronic applications accepted. *Expenses:* Tuition, area resident: Part-time $471 per credit hour. Tuition, state resident: part-time $471 per credit hour. Tuition, nonresident: part-time $1016 per credit hour. Required fees: $337 per term. *Financial support:* In 2010–11, 9 teaching assistantships with full tuition reimbursements were awarded; fellowships with full tuition reimbursements, research assistantships with full tuition reimbursements, Federal Work-Study, scholarships/grants, traineeships, health care benefits, and unspecified assistantships also available. Financial award application deadline: 1/1; financial award applicants required to submit FAFSA. *Faculty research:* Marine and estuarine organisms, terrestrial and freshwater ecology, remote environmental sensing, fisheries science, oceanography, environmental chemistry. *Unit head:* Dr. Kennedy T. Paynter, Director, 301-405-6938, Fax: 301-314-4139, E-mail: mees@umd.edu. *Application contact:* Dr. Kennedy T. Paynter, Director, 301-405-6938, Fax: 301-314-4139, E-mail: mees@umd.edu.

University of Maryland Eastern Shore, Graduate Programs, Department of Natural Sciences, Program in Marine-Estuarine-Environmental Sciences, Princess Anne, MD 21853-1299. Offers MS, PhD. Part-time programs available. *Faculty:* 26. *Students:* 29 (17 women); includes 13 Black or African American, non-Hispanic/Latino; 1 Asian, non-Hispanic/Latino, 10 international. 16 applicants, 25% accepted, 4 enrolled. In 2010, 2 master's, 2 doctorates awarded. *Degree requirements:* For master's, thesis; for doctorate, comprehensive exam, thesis/dissertation, proposal defense. *Entrance requirements:* For master's and doctorate, GRE General Test, minimum GPA of 3.0. Additional exam requirements/recommendations for international students: Required—TOEFL. *Application deadline:* For fall admission, 2/1 for domestic and international students; for spring admission, 9/1 for domestic students, 8/1 for international students. Applications are processed on a rolling basis. Application fee: $30. Electronic applications accepted. *Financial support:* In 2010–11, 30 students received support; fellowships with tuition reimbursements available, research assistantships with tuition reimbursements available, teaching assistantships with tuition reimbursements available, career-related internships or fieldwork, scholarships/grants, and unspecified assistantships available. Support available to part-time students. Financial award application deadline: 1/1. *Unit head:* Dr. Kennedy T. Paynter, Director, 301-405-6938, Fax: 301-314-4139, E-mail: mees@umd.edu. *Application contact:* Dr. Kennedy T. Paynter, Director, 301-405-6938, Fax: 301-314-4139, E-mail: mees@umd.edu.

University of Massachusetts Amherst, Graduate School, Interdisciplinary Programs, Program in Marine Science and Technology, Amherst, MA 01003. Offers MS, PhD. Part-time programs available. *Students:* 3 full-time (all women). Average age 27. In 2010, 1 doctorate awarded. Terminal master's awarded for partial completion of doctoral program. *Degree requirements:* For master's, thesis or alternative; for doctorate, comprehensive exam, thesis/dissertation. *Entrance requirements:* For master's and doctorate, GRE General Test, 3 letters of recommendation. Additional exam requirements/recommendations for international students: Required—TOEFL (minimum score 550 paper-based; 213 computer-based; 80 iBT), IELTS (minimum score 6.5). *Application deadline:* For fall admission, 12/15 for domestic and international students; for spring admission, 10/1 for domestic and international students. Applications are processed on a rolling basis. Application fee: $50 ($65 for international students). Electronic applications accepted. *Expenses:* Tuition, state resident: full-time $2640. Required

fees: $8282. One-time fee: $357 full-time. *Financial support:* Fellowships, research assistantships, teaching assistantships, career-related internships or fieldwork, Federal Work-Study, scholarships/grants, traineeships, health care benefits, tuition waivers (full), and unspecified assistantships available. Support available to part-time students. Financial award application deadline: 12/15; financial award applicants required to submit FAFSA. *Unit head:* Dr. Francis Juanes, Graduate Program Director, 413-545-2666, Fax: 413-545-4358. *Application contact:* Jean M. Ames, Supervisor of Admissions, 413-545-0722, Fax: 413-577-0010, E-mail: gradadm@grad.umass.edu.

University of Massachusetts Boston, Office of Graduate Studies, College of Science and Mathematics, Department of Environmental, Earth and Ocean Sciences, Track in Environmental, Earth and Ocean Sciences, Boston, MA 02125-3393. Offers PhD. Part-time and evening/weekend programs available. *Degree requirements:* For doctorate, comprehensive exam, thesis/dissertation, oral exams. *Entrance requirements:* For doctorate, GRE General Test, minimum GPA of 2.75. *Faculty research:* Conservation genetics, anthropogenic and natural influences on community structures of coral reef factors, geographical variation in mitochondrial DNA, protein chemistry and enzymology pertaining to insect cuticle.

University of Massachusetts Dartmouth, Graduate School, School of Marine Science and Technology, Program in Marine Science and Technology, North Dartmouth, MA 02747-2300. Offers MS, PhD. Terminal master's awarded for partial completion of doctoral program. *Degree requirements:* For master's, thesis or alternative; for doctorate, comprehensive exam, thesis/dissertation. *Entrance requirements:* For master's and doctorate, GRE, minimum GPA of 3.0, 3 letters of recommendation. Additional exam requirements/recommendations for international students: Required—TOEFL (minimum score 600 paper-based; 213 computer-based). Electronic applications accepted. *Expenses:* Tuition, state resident: full-time $2071; part-time $86 per credit. Tuition, nonresident: full-time $8099; part-time $337 per credit. Required fees: $9446; $394 per credit. One-time fee: $75. Part-time tuition and fees vary according to class time, course load, degree level and reciprocity agreements. *Faculty research:* Storm-forced and internal wave dynamics, estuarine circulation, marine biogeochemical cycles, spatial distributions of marine fishes and invertebrates, plankton communities.

University of Miami, Graduate School, Rosenstiel School of Marine and Atmospheric Science, Division of Applied Marine Physics, Coral Gables, FL 33124. Offers applied marine physics (MS, PhD), including coastal ocean dynamics, underwater acoustics and geoacoustics (PhD), wave surface dynamics and air-sea interaction (PhD). Part-time programs available. Terminal master's awarded for partial completion of doctoral program. *Degree requirements:* For master's, comprehensive exam, thesis; for doctorate, comprehensive exam, thesis/dissertation. *Entrance requirements:* For master's and doctorate, GRE General Test. Additional exam requirements/recommendations for international students: Required—TOEFL (minimum score 550 paper-based; 213 computer-based). Electronic applications accepted.

University of Miami, Graduate School, Rosenstiel School of Marine and Atmospheric Science, Division of Marine and Atmospheric Chemistry, Coral Gables, FL 33124. Offers MS, PhD. Terminal master's awarded for partial completion of doctoral program. *Degree requirements:* For master's, comprehensive exam, thesis; for doctorate, comprehensive exam, thesis/dissertation. *Entrance requirements:* For master's and doctorate, GRE General Test. Additional exam requirements/recommendations for international students: Required—TOEFL (minimum score 550 paper-based; 213 computer-based). Electronic applications accepted. *Faculty research:* Global change issues, chemistry of marine waters and marine atmosphere.

University of Michigan, School of Natural Resources and Environment, Program in Natural Resources and Environment, Ann Arbor, MI 48109. Offers aquatic sciences: research and management (MS); behavior, education and communication (MS); conservation biology (MS); conservation ecology (MS); environmental informatics (MS); environmental justice (MS); environmental policy and planning (MS); natural resources and environment (PhD); sustainable systems (MS); terrestrial ecosystems (MS); MS/AM; MS/JD; MS/MBA. *Faculty:* 42 full-time, 23 part-time/adjunct. *Students:* 450 full-time (254 women); includes 7 Black or African American, non-Hispanic/Latino; 2 American Indian or Alaska Native, non-Hispanic/Latino; 35 Asian, non-Hispanic/Latino; 13 Hispanic/Latino; 6 Two or more races, non-Hispanic/Latino, 50 international. Average age 27. 692 applicants. In 2010, 133 master's, 11 doctorates awarded. Terminal master's awarded for partial completion of doctoral program. *Degree requirements:* For master's, practicum or group project; for doctorate, comprehensive exam, thesis/dissertation, oral defense of dissertation, preliminary exam. *Entrance requirements:* For master's, GRE General Test; for doctorate, GRE General Test, master's degree. Additional exam requirements/recommendations for international students: Required—TOEFL (minimum score 560 paper-based; 220 computer-based; 84 iBT). *Application deadline:* For fall admission, 1/5 priority date for domestic and international students. Applications are processed on a rolling basis. Application fee: $65 ($75 for international students). Electronic applications accepted. *Expenses:* Tuition, state resident: full-time $17,784; part-time $1116 per credit hour. Tuition, nonresident: full-time $35,944; part-time $2125 per credit hour. International tuition: $35,994 full-time. Required fees: $95 per semester. Tuition and fees vary according to course load, degree level and program. *Financial support:* Fellowships with tuition reimbursements, research assistantships with tuition reimbursements, teaching assistantships with tuition reimbursements, career-related internships or fieldwork, Federal Work-Study, institutionally sponsored loans, scholarships/grants, health care benefits, and unspecified assistantships available. Support available to part-time students. Financial award application deadline: 1/5; financial award applicants required to submit FAFSA. *Faculty research:* Stream ecology, plant-insect interactions, fish biology, resource control and reproductive success, remote sensing, conservation ecology. *Application contact:* Graduate Admissions Team, 734-764-6453, Fax: 734-936-2195, E-mail: snre.admissions@umich.edu.

University of New England, College of Arts and Sciences, Program in Marine Sciences, Biddeford, ME 04005-9526. Offers MS. *Students:* 17 full-time (16 women); includes 1 Asian, non-Hispanic/Latino. 35 applicants, 40% accepted, 8 enrolled. In 2010, 5 master's awarded. *Degree requirements:* For master's, thesis. *Application deadline:* For fall admission, 2/15 for domestic students. *Unit head:* Stephan I. Zeeman, Chair, Department of Marine Sciences, 207-602-2410, E-mail: szeeman@une.edu. *Application contact:* Stacy Gato, Assistant Director of Graduate Admissions, 207-221-4225, Fax: 207-221-4898, E-mail: gradadmissions@une.edu.

University of New Hampshire, Graduate School, College of Life Sciences and Agriculture, Department of Natural Resources, Durham, NH 03824. Offers environmental conservation (MS); forestry (MS); integrated coastal ecosystem science, policy, management (MS); natural resources (MS); water resources (MS); wildlife (MS). Part-time programs available. *Faculty:* 40 full-time. *Students:* 22 full-time (8 women), 27 part-time (15 women); includes 1 Asian, non-Hispanic/Latino; 1 Hispanic/Latino, 1 international. Average age 30. 54 applicants, 39% accepted, 14 enrolled. In 2010, 13 master's awarded. *Degree requirements:* For master's, thesis or alternative. *Entrance requirements:* For master's, GRE General Test. Additional exam requirements/recommendations for international students: Required—TOEFL (minimum score 550 paper-based; 213 computer-based; 80 iBT). *Application deadline:* For fall admission, 6/1 for domestic students, 4/1 for international students; for spring admission, 12/1 for domestic students. Applications are processed on a rolling basis. Application fee: $65. Electronic applications accepted. *Financial support:* In 2010–11, 23 students received support, including 3 fellowships, 6 research assistantships, 14 teaching assistantships; career-related internships or fieldwork, Federal Work-Study, scholarships/grants, and tuition waivers (full and partial) also available. Support available to part-time students. Financial award application deadline: 2/15. *Unit head:* Dr. John Halstead, Chairperson, 603-862-3950, E-mail: natural.resources@unh.edu. *Application contact:* Linda Scogin, Administrative Assistant, 603-862-3932, E-mail: natural.resources@unh.edu.

The University of North Carolina at Chapel Hill, Graduate School, College of Arts and Sciences, Department of Marine Sciences, Chapel Hill, NC 27599. Offers MS, PhD. *Degree requirements:* For master's, comprehensive exam, thesis; for doctorate, comprehensive exam, thesis/dissertation. *Entrance requirements:* For master's and doctorate, GRE General Test, GRE Subject Test, minimum GPA of 3.0.

The University of North Carolina at Chapel Hill, Graduate School, School of Public Health, Department of Environmental Sciences and Engineering, Chapel Hill, NC 27599. Offers air, radiation and industrial hygiene (MPH, MS, MSEE, MSPH, PhD); aquatic and atmospheric sciences (MPH, MS, MSPH, PhD); environmental engineering (MPH, MS, MSEE, MSPH, PhD); environmental health sciences (MPH, MS, MSPH, PhD); environmental management and policy (MPH, MS, MSPH, PhD). Terminal master's awarded for partial completion of doctoral program. *Degree requirements:* For master's, comprehensive exam, thesis (for some programs), research paper; for doctorate, comprehensive exam, thesis/dissertation. *Entrance requirements:* For master's and doctorate, GRE General Test, minimum GPA of 3.0. Additional exam requirements/recommendations for international students: Required—TOEFL. Electronic applications accepted. *Faculty research:* Air, radiation and industrial hygiene, aquatic and atmospheric sciences, environmental health sciences, environmental management and policy, water resources engineering.

The University of North Carolina Wilmington, College of Arts and Sciences, Department of Biology and Marine Biology, Wilmington, NC 28403-3297. Offers biology (MS); marine biology (MS, PhD). Part-time programs available. *Faculty:* 34 full-time (7 women). *Students:* 39 part-time (21 women); includes 1 minority (Hispanic/Latino), 1 international. Average age 28. 96 applicants, 27% accepted, 21 enrolled. In 2010, 15 master's awarded. *Degree requirements:* For master's, comprehensive exam, thesis; for doctorate, comprehensive exam, thesis/dissertation. *Entrance requirements:* For master's, GRE General Test, GRE Subject Test, minimum B average in undergraduate major; for doctorate, GRE General Test, minimum B average in undergraduate major and graduate courses. Additional exam requirements/recommendations for international students: Required—TOEFL (minimum score 550 paper-based; 217 computer-based; 79 iBT), IELTS (minimum score 6.5). *Application deadline:* For fall admission, 3/15 for domestic students. Applications are processed on a rolling basis. Application fee: $60. Electronic applications accepted. *Financial support:* In 2010–11, 24 research assistantships with full and partial tuition reimbursements (averaging $14,000 per year), 36 teaching assistantships with full and partial tuition reimbursements (averaging $14,000 per year) were awarded; career-related internships or fieldwork and Federal Work-Study also available. Support available to part-time students. Financial award application deadline: 3/15. *Faculty research:* Ecology, physiology, cell and molecular biology, systematics, biomechanics. Total annual research expenditures: $3.1 million. *Unit head:* Dr. Martin H. Posey, Chairman, 910-962-3487, E-mail: poseym@uncw.edu. *Application contact:* Dr. D. Ann Pabst, Graduate Coordinator, 910-962-7266, Fax: 910-962-4066, E-mail: pabsta@uncw.edu.

University of Puerto Rico, Mayagüez Campus, Graduate Studies, College of Arts and Sciences, Department of Marine Sciences, Mayagüez, PR 00681-9000. Offers MS, PhD. Part-time programs available. *Students:* 53 full-time (25 women); includes 43 Hispanic/Latino, 10 international. 6 applicants, 50% accepted, 3 enrolled. In 2010, 5 master's, 3 doctorates awarded. *Degree requirements:* For master's, one foreign language, thesis, departmental and comprehensive final exams; for doctorate, one foreign language, thesis/dissertation, qualifying, comprehensive, and final exams. *Entrance requirements:* For master's, GRE, minimum GPA of 3.0; for doctorate, GRE, minimum GPA of 3.5. *Application deadline:* For fall admission, 2/15 for domestic and international students; for spring admission, 9/15 for domestic and international students. Applications are processed on a rolling basis. Application fee: $25. *Expenses:* Tuition, state resident: full-time $1188. Tuition, nonresident: full-time $1188. International tuition: $6126 full-time. Tuition and fees vary according to course level and course load. *Financial support:* In 2010–11, 20 students received support, including fellowships (averaging $12,000 per year), 20 research assistantships (averaging $15,000 per year), teaching assistantships (averaging $8,500 per year); Federal Work-Study and institutionally sponsored loans also available. *Faculty research:* Marine botany, ecology, chemistry, and parasitology; fisheries; ichthyology; aquaculture. Total annual research expenditures: $2 million. *Unit head:* Dr. Nilda Aponte, Director, 787-265-3838, Fax: 787-265-3838, E-mail: nilda.aponte2@upr.edu. *Application contact:* Monserrate Casiano, Secretary, 787-832-4040 Ext. 3447, Fax: 787-265-3838, E-mail: monserrate.casiano@upr.edu.

University of Rhode Island, Graduate School, College of the Environment and Life Sciences, Department of Fisheries, Animal and Veterinary Science, Kingston, RI 02881. Offers animal health and disease (MS); animal science (MS); aquaculture (MS); aquatic pathology (MS); environmental sciences (PhD), including animal science, aquacultural science, aquatic pathology, fisheries science; fisheries (MS). *Faculty:* 10 full-time (4 women). *Students:* 14 full-time (7 women), 6 part-time (1 woman); includes 4 minority (2 Black or African American, non-Hispanic/Latino; 2 Hispanic/Latino), 3 international. In 2010, 3 master's, 2 doctorates awarded. *Degree requirements:* For master's, comprehensive exam (for some programs), thesis optional; for doctorate, comprehensive exam, thesis/dissertation. *Entrance requirements:* For master's and doctorate, GRE, 2 letters of recommendation. Additional exam requirements/recommendations for international students: Required—TOEFL (minimum score 550 paper-based; 213 computer-based). *Application deadline:* For fall admission, 7/15 for domestic students, 2/1 for international students; for spring admission, 11/15 for domestic students, 7/15 for international students. Application fee: $65. Electronic applications accepted. *Expenses:* Tuition, state resident: full-time $9588; part-time $533 per credit hour. Tuition, nonresident: full-time $22,968; part-time $1276 per credit hour. Required fees: $1282; $68 per semester. Tuition and fees vary according to program. *Financial support:* In 2010–11, 9 research assistantships with full and partial tuition reimbursements (averaging $11,492 per year), 3 teaching assistantships with full and partial tuition reimbursements (averaging $12,894 per year) were awarded. Financial award application deadline: 7/15; financial award applicants required to submit FAFSA. Total annual research expenditures: $1.8 million. *Unit head:* Dr. David Bengtson, Chair, 401-874-2668, Fax: 401-874-7575, E-mail: bengtson@uri.edu. *Application contact:* Dr. Marta Gomez-Chiarri, Director of Graduate Studies, 401-874-2917, Fax: 401-874-7575, E-mail: gomezchi@uri.edu.

University of San Diego, College of Arts and Sciences, Department of Marine Science and Environmental Studies, San Diego, CA 92110-2492. Offers marine science (MS). Part-time programs available. *Faculty:* 3 full-time (1 woman). *Students:* 9 full-time (7 women), 8 part-time (5 women); includes 1 Black or African American, non-Hispanic/Latino; 2 Hispanic/Latino; 2 Two or more races, non-Hispanic/Latino. Average age 25. 23 applicants, 52% accepted, 8 enrolled. In 2010, 7 master's awarded. *Degree requirements:* For master's, thesis. *Entrance requirements:* For master's, GRE General Test, minimum GPA of 3.0, undergraduate major in science. Additional exam requirements/recommendations for international students: Required—TOEFL (minimum score 580 paper-based; 237 computer-based; 83 iBT), TWE. *Application deadline:* For fall admission, 4/1 for domestic and international students. Applications are processed on a rolling basis. Application fee: $45. Electronic applications accepted. *Expenses:* Tuition: Full-time $21,744; part-time $1208 per unit. Required fees: $224. Full-time tuition and fees vary according to course load and degree level. *Financial support:* In 2010–11, 11 students received support. Career-related internships or fieldwork, Federal Work-Study, institutionally sponsored loans, and unspecified assistantships available. Support available to part-time students. Financial award application deadline: 4/1; financial award applicants required to submit FAFSA. *Faculty research:* Marine ecology, environmental geology and geochemistry, climatology, physiological ecology, fisheries and aquaculture. *Unit head:* Dr. Ronald S. Kaufmann, Director, 619-260-5904, Fax: 619-260-6874, E-mail: kaufmann@sandiego.edu. *Application contact:* Stephen Pultz, Director of Admissions and Enrollment, 619-260-4506, Fax: 619-260-6836, E-mail: admissions@sandiego.edu.

Marine Sciences

University of South Alabama, Graduate School, College of Arts and Sciences, Department of Marine Sciences, Mobile, AL 36688-0002. Offers MS, PhD. *Faculty:* 5 full-time (1 woman). *Students:* 30 full-time (21 women), 13 part-time (6 women); includes 2 minority (1 Hispanic/Latino; 1 Native Hawaiian or other Pacific Islander, non-Hispanic/Latino), 7 international. 36 applicants, 33% accepted, 9 enrolled. In 2010, 4 master's, 4 doctorates awarded. *Degree requirements:* For master's, comprehensive exam, thesis optional; for doctorate, one foreign language, comprehensive exam, thesis/dissertation, research project. *Entrance requirements:* For master's, GRE, minimum GPA of 3.0, BS in marine sciences or related discipline; for doctorate, GRE, BS or MS in marine sciences or related discipline; minimum undergraduate GPA of 3.0, graduate 3.25. Additional exam requirements/recommendations for international students: Required—TOEFL. *Application deadline:* For fall admission, 4/1 priority date for domestic students, 3/1 priority date for international students. Applications are processed on a rolling basis. Application fee: $35. *Expenses:* Tuition, state resident: part-time $300 per credit hour. Tuition, nonresident: part-time $600 per credit hour. Required fees: $150 per semester. *Financial support:* In 2010–11, fellowships with tuition reimbursements (averaging $13,600 per year), research assistantships (averaging $16,000 per year) were awarded. Financial award application deadline: 4/1. *Unit head:* Dr. Robert Shipp, Chair, 251-460-7136, Fax: 251-460-7136. *Application contact:* Dr. Robert Shipp, Chair, 251-460-7136, Fax: 251-460-7136.

University of South Carolina, The Graduate School, College of Arts and Sciences, Marine Science Program, Columbia, SC 29208. Offers MS, PhD. *Degree requirements:* For master's, thesis; for doctorate, comprehensive exam, thesis/dissertation. *Entrance requirements:* For master's and doctorate, GRE General Test. Additional exam requirements/recommendations for international students: Required—TOEFL (minimum score 570 paper-based; 230 computer-based). Electronic applications accepted. *Faculty research:* Biological, chemical, geological, and physical oceanography; policy.

University of Southern California, Graduate School, Dana and David Dornsife College of Letters, Arts and Sciences, Graduate Program in Ocean Sciences, Los Angeles, CA 90089. Offers MS, PhD. Only Ph.D. and M.S./Ph.D. students are funded. Part-time programs available. *Faculty:* 20 full-time (6 women), 1 (woman) part-time/adjunct. *Students:* 6 full-time (3 women), 1 (woman) part-time, 4 international. 4 applicants, 50% accepted, 2 enrolled. In 2010, 1 doctorate awarded. Terminal master's awarded for partial completion of doctoral program. *Degree requirements:* For master's, thesis; for doctorate, comprehensive exam, thesis/dissertation. *Entrance requirements:* For master's and doctorate, GRE. Additional exam requirements/recommendations for international students: Required—TOEFL. *Application deadline:* For fall admission, 1/1 for domestic and international students. Applications are processed on a rolling basis. Application fee: $85. Electronic applications accepted. *Expenses:* Tuition: Full-time $31,240; part-time $1420 per unit. Required fees: $600. One-time fee: $35 full-time. Full-time tuition and fees vary according to degree level and program. *Financial support:* In 2010–11, 7 students received support, including 2 fellowships with full tuition reimbursements available (averaging $21,200 per year), 2 research assistantships with full tuition reimbursements available (averaging $20,000 per year), 3 teaching assistantships with full tuition reimbursements available (averaging $20,000 per year); scholarships/grants, health care benefits, unspecified assistantships, and summer support also available. *Faculty research:* Microbial ecology, biogeochemical cycles, marine chemistry, marine biology, global change. *Unit head:* Prof. Douglas E. Hammond, Director, 213-740-5837, Fax: 213-740-8801, E-mail: dhammond@usc.edu. *Application contact:* Cynthia Waite, Academic Advisor, 213-740-6109, Fax: 213-740-8801, E-mail: waite@usc.edu.

University of Southern Mississippi, Graduate School, College of Science and Technology, Department of Coastal Sciences, Ocean Springs, MS 39566-7000. Offers MS, PhD. Part-time programs available. *Faculty:* 17 full-time (4 women), 2 part-time/adjunct (0 women). *Students:* 38 full-time (22 women), 10 part-time (4 women); includes 1 Black or African American, non-Hispanic/Latino; 1 Hispanic/Latino, 8 international. Average age 31. 21 applicants, 52% accepted, 10 enrolled. In 2010, 8 master's, 2 doctorates awarded. Terminal master's awarded for partial completion of doctoral program. *Degree requirements:* For master's, comprehensive exam, thesis; for doctorate, comprehensive exam, thesis/dissertation. *Entrance requirements:* For master's, GRE General Test, minimum GPA of 3.0 for last 60 hours; for doctorate, GRE General Test, minimum undergraduate GPA of 3.0, graduate 3.5. Additional exam requirements/recommendations for international students: Required—TOEFL, IELTS. *Application deadline:* For fall admission, 3/1 priority date for domestic students, 3/1 for international students. Applications are processed on a rolling basis. Application fee: $50. Electronic applications accepted. *Financial support:* In 2010–11, 1 fellowship with full tuition reimbursement (averaging $10,000 per year), 34 research assistantships with full tuition reimbursements (averaging $16,232 per year) were awarded; Federal Work-Study, scholarships/grants, health care benefits, and unspecified assistantships also available. Financial award application deadline: 3/15; financial award applicants required to submit FAFSA. *Unit head:* Dr. Jeffrey Lotz, Chair, 228-872-4215, Fax: 228-872-4295. *Application contact:* Kalin Buttrich, Administrative Assistant, 228-872-4201, Fax: 228-872-4295.

University of Southern Mississippi, Graduate School, College of Science and Technology, Department of Marine Science, Stennis Space Center, MS 39529. Offers hydrographic science (MS); marine science (MS, PhD). Part-time programs available. *Faculty:* 17 full-time (2 women), 1 part-time/adjunct (0 women). *Students:* 36 full-time (13 women), 11 part-time (5 women); includes 11 Asian, non-Hispanic/Latino; 3 Hispanic/Latino. Average age 31. 35 applicants, 54% accepted, 16 enrolled. In 2010, 15 master's, 2 doctorates awarded. *Degree requirements:* For master's, comprehensive exam, thesis, oral qualifying exam (marine science); for doctorate, 2 foreign languages, comprehensive exam, thesis/dissertation, oral qualifying exam. *Entrance requirements:* For master's, GRE General Test, minimum GPA of 3.0; for doctorate, GRE General Test, minimum GPA of 3.0 (undergraduate), 3.5 (graduate). Additional exam requirements/recommendations for international students: Required—TOEFL. *Application deadline:* For fall admission, 3/1 priority date for domestic and international students. Applications are processed on a rolling basis. Application fee: $50. Electronic applications accepted. *Financial support:* In 2010–11, 4 students received support, including 26 research assistantships with full tuition reimbursements available (averaging $20,400 per year), 4 teaching assistantships with full tuition reimbursements available (averaging $20,400 per year); Federal Work-Study and institutionally sponsored loans also available. Financial award application deadline: 3/15. *Faculty research:* Chemical, biological, physical, and geological marine science; remote sensing; bio-optics; numerical modeling; hydrography. Total annual research expenditures: $5.8 million. *Unit head:* Dr. Steven E. Lohrenz, Chair, 228-688-3177, Fax: 228-688-1121, E-mail: marine.science@usm.edu. *Application contact:* Linda Downs, Senior Office Support Specialist, 228-688-3177, Fax: 228-688-1121, E-mail: marine.science@usm.edu.

University of South Florida, Graduate School, College of Marine Science, Saint Petersburg, FL 33701. Offers biological oceanography (MS, PhD); chemical oceanography (MS, PhD); geological oceanography (MS, PhD); interdisciplinary (MS, PhD); marine resource assessment (MS, PhD); physical oceanography (MS, PhD). Part-time programs available. *Faculty:* 24 full-time (6 women). *Students:* 69 full-time (41 women), 35 part-time (20 women); includes 6 Black or African American, non-Hispanic/Latino; 11 Hispanic/Latino; 1 Two or more races, non-Hispanic/Latino, 11 international. Average age 31. 98 applicants, 29% accepted, 15 enrolled. In 2010, 7 master's, 7 doctorates awarded. Terminal master's awarded for partial completion of doctoral program. *Degree requirements:* For master's, thesis, successful oral defense; for doctorate, comprehensive exam, thesis/dissertation, successful oral defense. *Entrance requirements:* For master's, GRE General Test; for doctorate, GRE General Test, bachelor's degree or equivalent from regionally-accredited university, minimum B average or GPA of 3.0 in all upper-division work attempted. Additional exam requirements/recommendations for international students: Required—TOEFL (minimum score 550 paper-based; 213 computer-based; 79 iBT). *Application deadline:* For fall admission, 1/15 for domestic students, 1/2 for international students; for spring admission, 10/1 for domestic students, 7/1 for international students. Applications are processed on a rolling basis. Application fee: $30. *Financial support:* In 2010–11, 73 students received support. Health care benefits and unspecified assistantships available. Financial award application deadline: 1/15. *Faculty research:* Trace metal chemistry, water quality, organic and isotopic geochemistry, physical chemistry, nutrient chemistry. Total annual research expenditures: $9.2 million. *Unit head:* Dr. Edward S. Van Vleet, Professor and Director of Academic Programs and Student Affairs, 727-553-1165, Fax: 727-553-1189, E-mail: vanvleet@marine.usf.edu. *Application contact:* Dawna L. Ishler, Academic Services Administrator, 727-553-3944, Fax: 727-553-1189, E-mail: dishler@usf.edu.

The University of Texas at Austin, Graduate School, College of Natural Sciences, Department of Marine Science, Austin, TX 78712-1111. Offers MS, PhD. *Degree requirements:* For master's, thesis; for doctorate, thesis/dissertation. *Entrance requirements:* For master's and doctorate, GRE General Test. Additional exam requirements/recommendations for international students: Required—TOEFL.

University of the Virgin Islands, Graduate Programs, Division of Science and Mathematics, Program in Environmental and Marine Science, Saint Thomas, VI 00802-9990. Offers MS. *Entrance requirements:* For master's, GRE. Additional exam requirements/recommendations for international students: Required—TOEFL (minimum score 550 paper-based; 213 computer-based).

University of Wisconsin–La Crosse, Office of University Graduate Studies, College of Science and Health, Department of Biology, La Crosse, WI 54601-3742. Offers aquatic sciences (MS); biology (MS); cellular and molecular biology (MS); clinical microbiology (MS); microbiology (MS); nurse anesthesia (MS); physiology (MS). Part-time programs available. *Faculty:* 31. *Students:* 23 full-time (14 women), 42 part-time (25 women); includes 4 minority (1 Asian, non-Hispanic/Latino; 3 Hispanic/Latino), 1 international. Average age 28. 100 applicants, 34% accepted, 29 enrolled. In 2010, 20 master's awarded. *Degree requirements:* For master's, comprehensive exam, thesis. *Entrance requirements:* For master's, GRE General Test, minimum GPA of 2.85. Additional exam requirements/recommendations for international students: Required—TOEFL (minimum score 550 paper-based; 213 computer-based; 79 iBT). *Application deadline:* For fall admission, 2/1 priority date for domestic and international students; for spring admission, 1/4 priority date for domestic and international students. Applications are processed on a rolling basis. Application fee: $56. Electronic applications accepted. *Expenses:* Tuition, state resident: full-time $7121; part-time $395.61 per credit. Tuition, nonresident: full-time $16,891; part-time $938.41 per credit. Part-time tuition and fees vary according to course load, program and reciprocity agreements. *Financial support:* In 2010–11, 14 research assistantships with partial tuition reimbursements (averaging $10,124 per year) were awarded; Federal Work-Study, scholarships/grants, health care benefits, and tuition waivers (partial) also available. Support available to part-time students. Financial award application deadline: 3/15; financial award applicants required to submit FAFSA. *Unit head:* Dr. Thomas Volk, Coordinator of Graduate Studies, 608-785-6972, Fax: 608-785-6959, E-mail: volk.thom@uwlax.edu. *Application contact:* Kathryn Kiefer, Director of Admissions, 608-785-8939, E-mail: admissions@uwlax.edu.

University of Wisconsin–Madison, Graduate School, College of Letters and Science, Department of Atmospheric and Oceanic Sciences, Madison, WI 53706-1380. Offers MS, PhD. Part-time programs available. *Degree requirements:* For master's, thesis (for some programs); for doctorate, thesis/dissertation. *Entrance requirements:* For master's and doctorate, GRE General Test, minimum GPA of 3.0; previous course work in chemistry, mathematics, and physics. Electronic applications accepted. *Expenses:* Tuition, state resident: full-time $9887.36; part-time $617.96 per credit. Tuition, nonresident: full-time $24,054; part-time $1503.40 per credit. Required fees: $67.63 per credit. Tuition and fees vary according to reciprocity agreements. *Faculty research:* Satellite meteorology, weather systems, global climate change, numerical modeling, atmosphere-ocean interaction.

Western Washington University, Graduate School, Huxley College of the Environment, Department of Environmental Sciences, Bellingham, WA 98225-5996. Offers environmental science (MS); marine and estuarine science (MS). Part-time programs available. *Degree requirements:* For master's, thesis. *Entrance requirements:* For master's, GRE General Test, minimum GPA of 3.0 in last 60 semester hours or last 90 quarter hours. Additional exam requirements/recommendations for international students: Required—TOEFL (minimum score 567 paper-based; 227 computer-based). Electronic applications accepted. *Faculty research:* Landscape ecology, climate change, watershed studies, environmental toxicology and risk assessment, aquatic toxicology, toxic algae, invasive species.

Oceanography

Columbia University, Graduate School of Arts and Sciences, Division of Natural Sciences, Department of Earth and Environmental Sciences, New York, NY 10027. Offers geochemistry (M Phil, MA, PhD); geodetic sciences (M Phil, MA, PhD); geophysics (M Phil, MA, PhD); oceanography (M Phil, MA, PhD). *Degree requirements:* For master's, thesis or alternative, fieldwork, written exam; for doctorate, one foreign language, thesis/dissertation. *Entrance requirements:* For master's and doctorate, GRE General Test, GRE Subject Test, major in natural or physical science. Additional exam requirements/recommendations for international students: Required—TOEFL. *Faculty research:* Structural geology and stratigraphy, petrology, paleontology, rare gas, isotope and aqueous geochemistry.

Cornell University, Graduate School, Graduate Fields of Agriculture and Life Sciences, Field of Ecology and Evolutionary Biology, Ithaca, NY 14853-0001. Offers ecology (PhD), including animal ecology, applied ecology, biogeochemistry, community and ecosystem ecology, limnology, oceanography, physiological ecology, plant ecology, population ecology, theoretical ecology, vertebrate zoology; evolutionary biology (PhD), including ecological genetics, paleobiology, population biology, systematics. *Faculty:* 48 full-time (13 women). *Students:* 51 full-time (37 women); includes 1 Asian, non-Hispanic/Latino; 3 Hispanic/Latino, 8 international. Average age 27. 108 applicants, 12% accepted, 10 enrolled. In 2010, 16 doctorates awarded. *Degree requirements:* For doctorate, comprehensive exam, thesis/dissertation, 2 semesters of teaching experience. *Entrance requirements:* For doctorate, GRE General Test, GRE Subject Test (biology), 2 letters of recommendation. Additional exam requirements/recommendations for international students: Required—TOEFL (minimum score 550 paper-based; 213 computer-based; 77 iBT). *Application deadline:* For fall admission, 12/15 for domestic students. Application

fee: $70. Electronic applications accepted. *Expenses:* Tuition: Full-time $29,500. Required fees: $76. Tuition and fees vary according to degree level and program. *Financial support:* In 2010–11, 23 fellowships with full tuition reimbursements, 5 research assistantships with full tuition reimbursements, 21 teaching assistantships with full tuition reimbursements were awarded; institutionally sponsored loans, scholarships/grants, health care benefits, tuition waivers (full and partial), and unspecified assistantships also available. Financial award applicants required to submit FAFSA. *Faculty research:* Population and organismal biology, population and evolutionary genetics, systematics and macroevolution, biochemistry, conservation biology. *Unit head:* Director of Graduate Studies, 607-254-4230. *Application contact:* Graduate Field Assistant, 607-254-4230, E-mail: eeb_grad_req@cornell.edu.

Dalhousie University, Faculty of Science, Department of Oceanography, Halifax, NS B3H 4R2, Canada. Offers M Sc, PhD. *Degree requirements:* For master's, thesis; for doctorate, thesis/dissertation. *Entrance requirements:* Additional exam requirements/recommendations for international students: Required—TOEFL, IELTS, CANTEST, CAEL, or Michigan English Language Assessment Battery. Electronic applications accepted. *Faculty research:* Biological and physical oceanography, chemical and geological oceanography, atmospheric sciences.

Florida Institute of Technology, Graduate Programs, College of Engineering, Department of Marine and Environmental Systems, Program in Oceanography, Melbourne, FL 32901-6975. Offers MS, PhD. Part-time programs available. *Faculty:* 11 full-time (0 women), 3 part-time/adjunct (0 women). *Students:* 12 full-time (6 women), 2 part-time (both women), 3 international. Average age 28. 16 applicants, 56% accepted, 5 enrolled. In 2010, 4 master's, 1 doctorate awarded. *Degree requirements:* For master's, comprehensive exam (for some programs), thesis (for some programs), seminar, field project, written final exam, internship, technical paper, oral presentation; for doctorate, comprehensive exam, thesis/dissertation, seminar, internships, publications. *Entrance requirements:* For master's, GRE General Test, minimum GPA of 3.0, 3 letters of recommendation, resume, transcripts, statement of objectives; for doctorate, GRE General Test, minimum GPA of 3.3, resume, 3 letters of recommendation, statement of objectives, on-campus interview (highly recommended). Additional exam requirements/recommendations for international students: Required—TOEFL (minimum score 550 paper-based; 213 computer-based; 79 iBT). *Application deadline:* Applications are processed on a rolling basis. Application fee: $50. Electronic applications accepted. *Expenses:* Tuition: Part-time $1040 per credit hour. Tuition and fees vary according to campus/location. *Financial support:* In 2010–11, 5 fellowships with full and partial tuition reimbursements (averaging $7,240 per year), 5 research assistantships with full and partial tuition reimbursements (averaging $3,664 per year), 10 teaching assistantships with full and partial tuition reimbursements (averaging $6,670 per year) were awarded; career-related internships or fieldwork, institutionally sponsored loans, tuition waivers (partial), unspecified assistantships, and tuition remissions also available. Support available to part-time students. Financial award application deadline: 3/1; financial award applicants required to submit FAFSA. *Faculty research:* Marine geochemistry, ecosystem dynamics, coastal processes, marine pollution, environmental modeling. Total annual research expenditures: $1.7 million. *Unit head:* Dr. George Maul, Department Head, 321-674-7453, Fax: 321-674-7212, E-mail: gmaul@fit.edu. *Application contact:* Cheryl A. Brown, Assocxiate Director of Graduate Admission, 321-674-7581, Fax: 321-723-9468, E-mail: cbrown@fit.edu.

Florida State University, The Graduate School, College of Arts and Sciences, Department of Earth, Ocean and Atmospheric Science, Program in Oceanography, Tallahassee, FL 32306-4320. Offers aquatic environmental science (MS); oceanography (MS, PhD). *Faculty:* 15 full-time (1 woman). *Students:* 48 full-time (24 women); includes 1 Black or African American, non-Hispanic/Latino; 3 Asian, non-Hispanic/Latino, 9 international. Average age 27. 61 applicants, 36% accepted, 10 enrolled. In 2010, 8 master's, 4 doctorates awarded. *Median time to degree:* Of those who began their doctoral program in fall 2002, 100% received their degree in 8 years or less. *Degree requirements:* For master's, thesis; for doctorate, comprehensive exam, thesis/dissertation. *Entrance requirements:* For master's and doctorate, GRE General Test. Additional exam requirements/recommendations for international students: Required—TOEFL (minimum score 550 paper-based; 213 computer-based; 80 iBT). *Application deadline:* For fall admission, 2/15 priority date for domestic and international students; for spring admission, 7/15 priority date for domestic and international students. Applications are processed on a rolling basis. Application fee: $35. Electronic applications accepted. *Expenses:* Tuition, state resident: full-time $8238.24. *Financial support:* In 2010–11, 41 students received support, including 1 fellowship with full tuition reimbursement available, 26 research assistantships with full tuition reimbursements available, 14 teaching assistantships with full tuition reimbursements available. Financial award application deadline: 2/15; financial award applicants required to submit FAFSA. *Faculty research:* Trace metals in seawater, currents and waves, modeling, benthic ecology, marine biogeochemistry. *Unit head:* Dr. Jeffrey Chanton, Area Coordinator, 850-644-6700, Fax: 850-644-2581, E-mail: chanton@ocean.fsu.edu. *Application contact:* Michaela Lupiani, Academic Coordinator, 850-644-6700, Fax: 850-644-2581, E-mail: admissions@ocean.fsu.edu.

Georgia Institute of Technology, Graduate Studies and Research, College of Sciences, School of Earth and Atmospheric Sciences, Atlanta, GA 30332-0340. Offers atmospheric chemistry, aerosols and clouds (MS, PhD); dynamics of weather and climate (MS, PhD); geochemistry (MS, PhD); geophysics (MS, PhD); oceanography (MS, PhD); paleoclimate (MS, PhD); planetary science (MS, PhD); remote sensing (MS, PhD). Part-time programs available. Terminal master's awarded for partial completion of doctoral program. *Degree requirements:* For master's, thesis or alternative; for doctorate, comprehensive exam, thesis/dissertation. *Entrance requirements:* For master's, GRE, letters of recommendation; for doctorate, GRE, academic transcripts, letters of recommendation, personal statement. Additional exam requirements/recommendations for international students: Required—TOEFL (minimum score 550 paper-based; 213 computer-based; 79 iBT). *Faculty research:* Geophysics; atmospheric chemistry, aerosols and clouds; dynamics of weather and climate; geochemistry; oceanography; paleoclimate; planetary science; remote sensing.

Louisiana State University and Agricultural and Mechanical College, Graduate School, School of the Coast and Environment, Department of Oceanography and Coastal Sciences, Baton Rouge, LA 70803. Offers MS, PhD. *Faculty:* 29 full-time (4 women), 2 part-time/adjunct (0 women). *Students:* 51 full-time (30 women), 4 part-time (2 women); includes 1 Hispanic/Latino, 12 international. Average age 29. 37 applicants, 22% accepted, 7 enrolled. In 2010, 7 master's, 7 doctorates awarded. *Degree requirements:* For master's, thesis (for some programs); for doctorate, one foreign language, thesis/dissertation. *Entrance requirements:* For master's, GRE General Test, minimum GPA of 3.0; for doctorate, GRE General Test, MA or MS, minimum GPA of 3.0. Additional exam requirements/recommendations for international students: Required—TOEFL (minimum score 550 paper-based; 213 computer-based; 79 iBT) or IELTS (minimum score 6.5). *Application deadline:* For fall admission, 1/25 priority date for domestic students, 5/15 for international students; for spring admission, 10/15 for international students. Applications are processed on a rolling basis. Application fee: $50 ($70 for international students). *Financial support:* In 2010–11, 54 students received support, including 8 fellowships (averaging $17,589 per year), 44 research assistantships with full and partial tuition reimbursements available (averaging $19,606 per year); teaching assistantships with full and partial tuition reimbursements available, Federal Work-Study, institutionally sponsored loans, scholarships/grants, health care benefits, tuition waivers (full and partial), and unspecified assistantships also available. Support available to part-time students. Financial award applicants required to submit FAFSA. *Faculty research:* Physical and geological oceanography, wetland sustainability and restoration fisheries, coastal ecology and biogeochemistry. Total annual research expenditures: $8.1 million. *Unit head:* Dr. Donald Baltz, Chair, 225-578-6308, Fax: 225-578-6307, E-mail: dbaltz@lsu.edu. *Application contact:* Dr. Charles Lindau, Graduate Adviser, 225-578-8766, Fax: 225-578-6423, E-mail: clinda1@lsu.edu.

Massachusetts Institute of Technology, School of Engineering, Department of Civil and Environmental Engineering, Cambridge, MA 02139. Offers biological oceanography (PhD, Sc D); chemical oceanography (PhD, Sc D); civil and environmental engineering (M Eng, SM, PhD, Sc D); civil and environmental systems (PhD, Sc D); civil engineering (PhD, Sc D, CE); coastal engineering (PhD, Sc D); construction engineering and management (PhD, Sc D); environmental biology (PhD, Sc D); environmental chemistry (PhD, Sc D); environmental engineering (PhD, Sc D); environmental fluid mechanics (PhD, Sc D); geotechnical and geoenvironmental engineering (PhD, Sc D); hydrology (PhD, Sc D); information technology (PhD, Sc D); oceanographic engineering (PhD, Sc D); structures and materials (PhD, Sc D); transportation (PhD, Sc D); SM/MBA. *Faculty:* 36 full-time (6 women). *Students:* 181 full-time (56 women); includes 27 minority (3 Black or African American, non-Hispanic/Latino; 10 Asian, non-Hispanic/Latino; 10 Hispanic/Latino; 4 Two or more races, non-Hispanic/Latino), 93 international. Average age 26. 525 applicants, 29% accepted, 74 enrolled. In 2010, 85 master's, 18 doctorates, 2 other advanced degrees awarded. *Degree requirements:* For master's and CE, thesis; for doctorate, comprehensive exam, thesis/dissertation. *Entrance requirements:* For master's and doctorate, GRE General Test. Additional exam requirements/recommendations for international students: Required—TOEFL (minimum score 577 paper-based; 233 computer-based; 90 iBT), IELTS (minimum score 7). *Application deadline:* For fall admission, 1/2 for domestic and international students. Application fee: $75. Electronic applications accepted. *Expenses:* Tuition: Full-time $38,940; part-time $605 per unit. Required fees: $272. *Financial support:* In 2010–11, 146 students received support, including 50 fellowships with tuition reimbursements available (averaging $21,808 per year), 90 research assistantships with tuition reimbursements available (averaging $28,452 per year), 20 teaching assistantships with tuition reimbursements available (averaging $27,842 per year); career-related internships or fieldwork, Federal Work-Study, institutionally sponsored loans, scholarships/grants, health care benefits, and unspecified assistantships also available. *Faculty research:* Environmental chemistry; environmental microbiology; environmental fluid mechanics and coastal engineering; geotechnical engineering and geomechanics; hydrology and hydroclimatology; mechanics of materials and structures; operations research/supply chain; transportation. Total annual research expenditures: $19.5 million. *Unit head:* Prof. Andrew Whittle, Department Head, 617-253-7101. *Application contact:* Patricia Glidden, Graduate Admissions Coordinator, 617-253-7119, Fax: 617-258-6775, E-mail: cee-admissions@mit.edu.

Massachusetts Institute of Technology, School of Science, Department of Biology, Cambridge, MA 02139-4307. Offers biochemistry (PhD); biological oceanography (PhD); biology (PhD); biophysical chemistry and molecular structure (PhD); cell biology (PhD); computational and systems biology (PhD); developmental biology (PhD); genetics (PhD); immunology (PhD); microbiology (PhD); molecular biology (PhD); neurobiology (PhD). *Faculty:* 56 full-time (14 women). *Students:* 251 full-time (135 women); includes 74 minority (4 Black or African American, non-Hispanic/Latino; 1 American Indian or Alaska Native, non-Hispanic/Latino; 29 Asian, non-Hispanic/Latino; 33 Hispanic/Latino; 7 Two or more races, non-Hispanic/Latino), 29 international. Average age 26. 652 applicants, 18% accepted, 58 enrolled. In 2010, 41 doctorates awarded. *Degree requirements:* For doctorate, comprehensive exam, thesis/dissertation. *Entrance requirements:* For doctorate, GRE General Test. Additional exam requirements/recommendations for international students: Required—TOEFL (minimum score 577 paper-based; 233 computer-based), IELTS (minimum score 6.5). *Application deadline:* For fall admission, 12/1 for domestic and international students. Application fee: $75. Electronic applications accepted. *Expenses:* Tuition: Full-time $38,940; part-time $605 per unit. Required fees: $272. *Financial support:* In 2010–11, 215 students received support, including 115 fellowships with tuition reimbursements available (averaging $33,090 per year), 132 research assistantships with tuition reimbursements available (averaging $31,846 per year); teaching assistantships with tuition reimbursements available, Federal Work-Study, institutionally sponsored loans, scholarships/grants, traineeships, health care benefits, and unspecified assistantships also available. *Faculty research:* DNA recombination, replication and repair; transcription and gene regulation; signal transduction; cell cycle; neuronal cell fate. Total annual research expenditures: $60.6 million. *Unit head:* Prof. Chris Kaiser, Department Head, 617-253-4701, E-mail: mitbio@mit.edu. *Application contact:* Biology Education Office, 617-253-3717, Fax: 617-258-9329, E-mail: gradbio@mit.edu.

Massachusetts Institute of Technology, School of Science, Department of Earth, Atmospheric, and Planetary Sciences, Cambridge, MA 02139. Offers atmospheric chemistry (PhD, Sc D); atmospheric science (SM, PhD, Sc D); chemical oceanography (SM, PhD, Sc D); climate physics and chemistry (SM, PhD, Sc D); earth and planetary sciences (SM); geochemistry (PhD, Sc D); geology (PhD, Sc D); geophysics (PhD, Sc D); marine geology and geophysics (SM, PhD, Sc D); physical oceanography (SM, PhD, Sc D); planetary sciences (PhD, Sc D). *Faculty:* 36 full-time (7 women). *Students:* 165 full-time (86 women); includes 17 minority (2 Black or African American, non-Hispanic/Latino; 2 American Indian or Alaska Native, non-Hispanic/Latino; 5 Asian, non-Hispanic/Latino; 5 Hispanic/Latino; 3 Two or more races, non-Hispanic/Latino), 50 international. Average age 27. 227 applicants, 33% accepted, 38 enrolled. In 2010, 12 master's, 26 doctorates awarded. Terminal master's awarded for partial completion of doctoral program. *Degree requirements:* For master's, thesis; for doctorate, comprehensive exam, thesis/dissertation. *Entrance requirements:* For master's, GRE General Test; for doctorate, GRE General Test, GRE Subject Test (chemistry or physics for planetary science area). Additional exam requirements/recommendations for international students: Required—TOEFL (minimum score 577 paper-based; 233 computer-based; 91 iBT), IELTS (minimum score 7). *Application deadline:* For fall admission, 1/5 for domestic and international students; for spring admission, 11/1 for domestic and international students. Application fee: $75. Electronic applications accepted. *Expenses:* Tuition: Full-time $38,940; part-time $605 per unit. Required fees: $272. *Financial support:* In 2010–11, 123 students received support, including 62 fellowships with tuition reimbursements available (averaging $30,852 per year), 88 research assistantships with tuition reimbursements available (averaging $30,258 per year), 13 teaching assistantships with tuition reimbursements available (averaging $30,323 per year); Federal Work-Study, institutionally sponsored loans, scholarships/grants, health care benefits, and unspecified assistantships also available. *Faculty research:* Formation, dynamics and evolution of planetary systems; origin, composition, structure and dynamics of the atmospheres, oceans, surfaces and interiors of the Earth and other planets; evolution and interaction of the physical, chemical, geological and biological components of the Earth system; characterization of past, present and potential future climates and the causes and consequences of climate change; interplay of energy and the environment. Total annual research expenditures: $24.8 million. *Unit head:* Prof. Maria Zuber, Department Head, 617-253-2127, Fax: 617-253-8298, E-mail: eapsinfo@mit.edu. *Application contact:* EAPS Education Office, 617-253-3381, Fax: 617-253-8298, E-mail: eapsinfo@mit.edu.

McGill University, Faculty of Graduate and Postdoctoral Studies, Faculty of Science, Department of Atmospheric and Oceanic Sciences, Montréal, QC H3A 2T5, Canada. Offers atmospheric science (M Sc, PhD); physical oceanography (M Sc, PhD). PhD program in physical oceanography offered jointly with Université Laval.

Memorial University of Newfoundland, School of Graduate Studies, Department of Physics and Physical Oceanography, St. John's, NL A1C 5S7, Canada. Offers atomic and molecular physics (M Sc, PhD); condensed matter physics (M Sc, PhD); physical oceanography (M Sc, PhD); physics (M Sc). Part-time programs available. *Degree requirements:* For master's, thesis, seminar presentation on thesis topic; for doctorate, comprehensive exam, thesis/dissertation, oral defense of thesis. *Entrance requirements:* For master's, honors B Sc or equivalent; for doctorate, M Sc or equivalent. Electronic applications accepted. *Faculty research:* Experiment and theory in atomic and molecular physics, condensed matter physics, physical oceanography, theoretical geophysics and applied nuclear physics.

Naval Postgraduate School, Graduate Programs, Department of Oceanography, Monterey, CA 93943. Offers MS, PhD. Program only open to commissioned officers of the United States

Oceanography

Naval Postgraduate School (continued)
and friendly nations and selected United States federal civilian employees. Part-time programs available. *Degree requirements:* For master's, thesis; for doctorate, one foreign language, thesis/dissertation.

Naval Postgraduate School, Graduate Programs, Program in Undersea Warfare, Monterey, CA 93943. Offers applied science (MS); electrical engineering (MS); engineering acoustics (MS); operations research (MS); physical oceanography (MS). Program only open to commissioned officers of the United States and friendly nations and selected United States federal civilian employees. Part-time programs available. *Degree requirements:* For master's, thesis.

North Carolina State University, Graduate School, College of Physical and Mathematical Sciences, Department of Marine, Earth, and Atmospheric Sciences, Raleigh, NC 27695. Offers marine, earth, and atmospheric sciences (MS, PhD); meteorology (MS, PhD); oceanography (MS, PhD). PhD offered jointly with The University of North Carolina Wilmington. Terminal master's awarded for partial completion of doctoral program. *Degree requirements:* For master's, thesis (for some programs), final oral exam; for doctorate, comprehensive exam, thesis/dissertation, final oral exam, preliminary oral and written exams. *Entrance requirements:* For master's, GRE General Test, minimum GPA of 3.0; for doctorate, GRE General Test, GRE Subject Test (for disciplines in biological oceanography and geology), minimum GPA of 3.0. Additional exam requirements/recommendations for international students: Required—TOEFL (minimum score 550 paper-based). Electronic applications accepted. *Faculty research:* Boundary layer and air quality meteorology; climate and mesoscale dynamics; biological, chemical, geological, and physical oceanography; hard rock, soft rock, environmental, and paleogeology.

Nova Southeastern University, Oceanographic Center, Program in Marine Biology and Oceanography, Fort Lauderdale, FL 33314-7796. Offers marine biology (PhD); oceanography (PhD). *Faculty:* 15 full-time (1 woman), 5 part-time/adjunct (0 women). *Students:* 10 full-time (6 women), 3 part-time (2 women); includes 1 Black or African American, non-Hispanic/Latino, 1 international. Average age 37. 3 applicants, 67% accepted, 1 enrolled. In 2010, 3 doctorates awarded. *Degree requirements:* For doctorate, comprehensive exam, thesis/dissertation. *Entrance requirements:* For doctorate, GRE, master's degree. Additional exam requirements/recommendations for international students: Required—TOEFL (minimum score 550 paper-based). Application fee: $50. *Financial support:* In 2010–11, 3 research assistantships (averaging $20,000 per year) were awarded; Federal Work-Study, scholarships/grants, tuition waivers (partial), and unspecified assistantships also available. Support available to part-time students. *Unit head:* Dr. Richard Dodge, Dean, 954-262-3600, Fax: 954-262-4020, E-mail: dodge@nsu.nova.edu. *Application contact:* Dr. Richard Spieler, Director of Academic Programs, 954-262-3600, Fax: 954-262-4020, E-mail: spieler@nova.edu.

Nova Southeastern University, Oceanographic Center, Program in Physical Oceanography, Fort Lauderdale, FL 33314-7796. Offers MS. *Faculty:* 15 full-time (1 woman), 5 part-time/adjunct (0 women). *Students:* 1 full-time (0 women), 3 part-time (2 women); includes 1 Black or African American, non-Hispanic/Latino; 1 Hispanic/Latino, 1 international. 7 applicants, 14% accepted, 0 enrolled. *Degree requirements:* For master's, thesis. *Entrance requirements:* For master's, GRE, 1 year course work in calculus. Additional exam requirements/recommendations for international students: Required—TOEFL (minimum score 550 paper-based). *Application deadline:* Applications are processed on a rolling basis. Application fee: $50. *Unit head:* Dr. Richard Dodge, Dean, 954-262-3600, Fax: 954-262-4020, E-mail: dodge@nsu.nova.edu. *Application contact:* Dr. Richard Spieler, Director of Academic Programs, 954-262-3600, Fax: 954-262-4020, E-mail: spieler@nova.edu.

Old Dominion University, College of Sciences, Department of Ocean, Earth and Atmospheric Sciences, Norfolk, VA 23529. Offers ocean and earth sciences (MS); oceanography (PhD). Part-time programs available. *Faculty:* 25 full-time (6 women), 1 part-time/adjunct (0 women). *Students:* 32 full-time (18 women), 15 part-time (4 women); includes 2 minority (1 Black or African American, non-Hispanic/Latino; 1 Asian, non-Hispanic/Latino), 11 international. Average age 31. 32 applicants, 44% accepted, 6 enrolled. In 2010, 4 master's, 4 doctorates awarded. Terminal master's awarded for partial completion of doctoral program. *Degree requirements:* For master's, comprehensive exam (for some programs), thesis (for some programs), 10 days of ship time or fieldwork; for doctorate, comprehensive exam, thesis/dissertation, 10 days of ship time or fieldwork. *Entrance requirements:* For master's, GRE General Test, minimum GPA of 3.0 in major, 2.8 overall; for doctorate, GRE General Test. Additional exam requirements/recommendations for international students: Required—TOEFL (minimum score 550 paper-based; 213 computer-based). *Application deadline:* For fall admission, 2/1 priority date for domestic and international students. Applications are processed on a rolling basis. Application fee: $40. Electronic applications accepted. *Expenses:* Tuition, state resident: full-time $8592; part-time $358 per credit. Tuition, nonresident: full-time $21,672; part-time $903 per credit. Required fees: $119 per semester. One-time fee: $50. *Financial support:* In 2010–11, 16 students received support, including 3 fellowships with full tuition reimbursements available (averaging $22,000 per year), 25 research assistantships with full tuition reimbursements available (averaging $22,000 per year), 14 teaching assistantships with full tuition reimbursements available (averaging $15,500 per year); career-related internships or fieldwork, scholarships/grants, and unspecified assistantships also available. Support available to part-time students. Financial award application deadline: 2/1; financial award applicants required to submit FAFSA. *Faculty research:* Biological, chemical, geological and physical oceanography. *Unit head:* Dr. Fred Dobbs, Graduate Program Director, 757-683-5329, Fax: 757-683-5303, E-mail: oceangpd@odu.edu. *Application contact:* Dr. Fred Dobbs, Graduate Program Director, 757-683-5329, Fax: 757-683-5303, E-mail: oceangpd@odu.edu.

Oregon State University, Graduate School, College of Oceanic and Atmospheric Sciences, Program in Oceanography, Corvallis, OR 97331. Offers MA, MS, PhD. Terminal master's awarded for partial completion of doctoral program. *Degree requirements:* For master's, thesis optional; for doctorate, thesis/dissertation. *Entrance requirements:* For master's and doctorate, GRE General Test, minimum GPA of 3.0 in last 90 hours of course work. Additional exam requirements/recommendations for international students: Required—TOEFL. *Faculty research:* Biological, chemical, geological, and physical oceanography.

Princeton University, Graduate School, Department of Geosciences, Program in Atmospheric and Oceanic Sciences, Princeton, NJ 08544-1019. Offers PhD. *Degree requirements:* For doctorate, one foreign language, thesis/dissertation. *Entrance requirements:* For doctorate, GRE General Test, GRE Subject Test. Additional exam requirements/recommendations for international students: Required—TOEFL (minimum score 600 paper-based; 250 computer-based). Electronic applications accepted. *Faculty research:* Climate dynamics, middle atmosphere dynamics and chemistry, oceanic circulation, marine geochemistry, numerical modeling.

Rutgers, The State University of New Jersey, New Brunswick, Graduate School-New Brunswick, Program in Oceanography, Piscataway, NJ 08854-8097. Offers MS, PhD. Terminal master's awarded for partial completion of doctoral program. *Degree requirements:* For master's, thesis; for doctorate, comprehensive exam, thesis/dissertation. *Entrance requirements:* For master's and doctorate, GRE General Test, 1 year course work in calculus, physics, chemistry. Additional exam requirements/recommendations for international students: Required—TOEFL. Electronic applications accepted. *Expenses:* Tuition, state resident: full-time $7200; part-time $600 per credit. Tuition, nonresident: full-time $11,124; part-time $927 per credit. *Faculty research:* Coastal observations and modeling, estuarine ecology/fish/benthos, geochemistry, deep sea ecology/hydrothermal vents, molecular biology applications.

Texas A&M University, College of Geosciences, Department of Oceanography, College Station, TX 77843. Offers MS, PhD. *Faculty:* 26. *Students:* 74 full-time (45 women), 13 part-time (2 women); includes 7 minority (1 Black or African American, non-Hispanic/Latino; 3 Asian, non-Hispanic/Latino; 3 Hispanic/Latino), 33 international. Average age 28. In 2010, 5 master's, 3 doctorates awarded. *Degree requirements:* For master's, thesis; for doctorate, thesis/dissertation. *Entrance requirements:* For master's and doctorate, GRE General Test. Additional exam requirements/recommendations for international students: Required—TOEFL. *Application deadline:* For fall admission, 1/15 priority date for domestic students; for spring admission, 10/1 for domestic students. Applications are processed on a rolling basis. Application fee: $50 ($75 for international students). Electronic applications accepted. *Financial support:* In 2010–11, fellowships with partial tuition reimbursements (averaging $18,000 per year), research assistantships with partial tuition reimbursements (averaging $18,000 per year), teaching assistantships with partial tuition reimbursements (averaging $18,000 per year) were awarded; Federal Work-Study, scholarships/grants, and tuition waivers (partial) also available. Financial award application deadline: 1/15. *Faculty research:* Ocean circulation, climate studies, coastal and shelf dynamics, marine phytoplankton, stable isotope geochemistry. *Unit head:* Piers Chapman, Head, 979-845-7211, Fax: 979-845-6331. *Application contact:* Christine Arnold, Academic Advisor II, 979-845-7688, Fax: 979-845-6331, E-mail: chrisarnold@tamu.edu.

Université du Québec à Rimouski, Graduate Programs, Program in Oceanography, Rimouski, QC G5L 3A1, Canada. Offers M Sc, PhD. Part-time programs available. *Degree requirements:* For master's, thesis; for doctorate, thesis/dissertation. *Entrance requirements:* For master's, appropriate bachelor's degree, proficiency in French; for doctorate, appropriate master's degree, proficiency in French.

Université Laval, Faculty of Sciences and Engineering, Program in Oceanography, Québec, QC G1K 7P4, Canada. Offers PhD. Program offered jointly with McGill University and Université du Québec à Rimouski. *Degree requirements:* For doctorate, comprehensive exam, thesis/dissertation. *Entrance requirements:* For doctorate, knowledge of French, knowledge of English. Additional exam requirements/recommendations for international students: Required—TOEFL. Electronic applications accepted.

University of Alaska Fairbanks, School of Fisheries and Ocean Sciences, Program in Marine Sciences and Limnology, Fairbanks, AK 99775-7220. Offers marine biology (MS, PhD); oceanography (PhD), including biological oceanography, chemical oceanography, fisheries, geological oceanography, physical oceanography. Part-time programs available. *Faculty:* 8 full-time (4 women). *Students:* 40 full-time (26 women), 12 part-time (7 women); includes 3 minority (2 Asian, non-Hispanic/Latino; 1 Hispanic/Latino), 3 international. Average age 31. 54 applicants, 26% accepted, 14 enrolled. In 2010, 6 master's, 1 doctorate awarded. *Degree requirements:* For master's, comprehensive exam, thesis, oral defense; for doctorate, comprehensive exam, thesis/dissertation, oral defense. *Entrance requirements:* For master's and doctorate, GRE General Test. Additional exam requirements/recommendations for international students: Required—TOEFL (minimum score 550 paper-based; 213 computer-based; 80 iBT). *Application deadline:* For fall admission, 6/1 for domestic students, 3/1 for international students; for spring admission, 10/15 for domestic students, 8/1 for international students. Applications are processed on a rolling basis. Application fee: $60. Electronic applications accepted. *Expenses:* Tuition, state resident: full-time $5688; part-time $316 per credit. Tuition, nonresident: full-time $11,628; part-time $646 per credit. Required fees: $289 per semester. Tuition and fees vary according to course load and reciprocity agreements. *Financial support:* In 2010–11, 24 research assistantships with tuition reimbursements (averaging $11,704 per year), 9 teaching assistantships with tuition reimbursements (averaging $11,008 per year) were awarded; fellowships with tuition reimbursements, career-related internships or fieldwork, Federal Work-Study, scholarships/grants, health care benefits, and unspecified assistantships also available. Support available to part-time students. Financial award application deadline: 7/1; financial award applicants required to submit FAFSA. *Unit head:* Katrin Iken, Co-Chair, 907-474-7289, Fax: 907-474-5863, E-mail: academics@sfos.uaf.edu. *Application contact:* Christina Neumann, Academic Manager, 907-474-7289, Fax: 907-474-5863, E-mail: clneumann@alaska.edu.

The University of British Columbia, Faculty of Science, Department of Earth and Ocean Sciences, Vancouver, BC V6T 1Z4, Canada. Offers atmospheric science (M Sc, PhD); geological engineering (M Eng, MA Sc, PhD); geological sciences (M Sc, PhD); geophysics (M Sc, MA Sc, PhD); oceanography (M Sc, PhD). *Degree requirements:* For master's, thesis (for some programs); for doctorate, comprehensive exam, thesis/dissertation. *Entrance requirements:* Additional exam requirements/recommendations for international students: Required—TOEFL (minimum score 600 paper-based; 250 computer-based; 100 iBT). Electronic applications accepted. Tuition charges are reported in Canadian dollars. *Expenses:* Tuition, area resident: Full-time $4179 Canadian dollars. International tuition: $7344 Canadian dollars full-time. *Faculty research:* Oceans and atmosphere, environmental earth science, hydro geology, mineral deposits, geophysics.

University of California, San Diego, Office of Graduate Studies, Scripps Institution of Oceanography, La Jolla, CA 92093. Offers earth sciences (PhD); marine biology (PhD); oceanography (PhD). *Faculty:* 98. *Students:* 241 (115 women); includes 3 Black or African American, non-Hispanic/Latino; 4 American Indian or Alaska Native, non-Hispanic/Latino; 13 Asian, non-Hispanic/Latino, 52 international. 392 applicants, 19% accepted, 35 enrolled. *Degree requirements:* For doctorate, comprehensive exam, thesis/dissertation. *Entrance requirements:* For doctorate, GRE General Test, Suggested for Ocean Biosciences Program: GRE Subject Test, See: http://scrippseducation.ucsd.edu/Graduate_Students/Prospective_Students/. Additional exam requirements/recommendations for international students: Required—TOEFL (minimum score 550 paper-based; 213 computer-based; 80 iBT). *Application deadline:* For fall admission, 1/2 for domestic and international students. Application fee: $80 ($100 for international students). Electronic applications accepted. *Financial support:* Fellowships with full and partial tuition reimbursements, research assistantships with tuition reimbursements, teaching assistantships with tuition reimbursements, health care benefits available. *Unit head:* Dr. Douglas H. Bartlett, Chair, 858-534-3206, E-mail: siodept@sio.ucsd.edu. *Application contact:* Krystle Shertz, Graduate Coordinator, 858-534-3206, E-mail: kshertz@ucsd.edu.

University of Colorado Boulder, Graduate School, College of Arts and Sciences, Department of Atmospheric and Oceanic Sciences, Boulder, CO 80309. Offers MS, PhD. *Faculty:* 13 full-time (6 women). *Students:* 65 full-time (30 women), 2 part-time (1 woman); includes 8 minority (1 Black or African American, non-Hispanic/Latino; 1 American Indian or Alaska Native, non-Hispanic/Latino; 3 Asian, non-Hispanic/Latino; 3 Hispanic/Latino), 14 international. Average age 29. 82 applicants, 11 enrolled. In 2010, 9 master's, 7 doctorates awarded. *Entrance requirements:* For master's, minimum undergraduate GPA of 3.0. *Application deadline:* For fall admission, 2/1 for domestic students, 12/1 for international students; for spring admission, 10/1 for domestic and international students. *Financial support:* In 2010–11, 11 fellowships (averaging $2,321 per year), 40 research assistantships (averaging $16,795 per year) were awarded. *Faculty research:* Large-scale dynamics of the ocean and the atmosphere, air-sea interaction, radiative transfer and remote sensing of the ocean and the atmosphere, sea ice and its role in climate. Total annual research expenditures: $19.4 million.

University of Connecticut, Graduate School, College of Liberal Arts and Sciences, Department of Marine Sciences, Storrs, CT 06269. Offers MS, PhD. Terminal master's awarded for partial completion of doctoral program. *Degree requirements:* For master's, comprehensive exam; for doctorate, thesis/dissertation. *Entrance requirements:* Additional exam requirements/recommendations for international students: Required—TOEFL (minimum score 550 paper-based; 213 computer-based). Electronic applications accepted.

University of Delaware, College of Earth, Ocean, and Environment, School of Marine Science and Policy, Newark, DE 19716. Offers marine policy (MMP); marine studies (MS, PhD), including marine biosciences, oceanography, physical ocean science and engineering; oceanography (PhD).

University of Hawaii at Manoa, Graduate Division, School of Ocean and Earth Science and Technology, Department of Oceanography, Honolulu, HI 96822. Offers MS, PhD. Part-time programs available. *Faculty:* 60 full-time (10 women), 8 part-time/adjunct (0 women). *Students:* 73 full-time (42 women), 4 part-time (3 women); includes 17 minority (1 Black or African American, non-Hispanic/Latino; 7 Asian, non-Hispanic/Latino; 3 Hispanic/Latino; 1 Native Hawaiian or other Pacific Islander, non-Hispanic/Latino; 5 Two or more races, non-Hispanic/Latino), 22 international. Average age 29. 117 applicants, 19% accepted, 21 enrolled. In 2010, 10 master's, 7 doctorates awarded. Terminal master's awarded for partial completion of doctoral program. *Degree requirements:* For master's, one foreign language, comprehensive exam, thesis, field experience; for doctorate, one foreign language, comprehensive exam, thesis/dissertation, field experience. *Entrance requirements:* For master's and doctorate, GRE General Test. Additional exam requirements/recommendations for international students: Required—TOEFL (minimum score 560 paper-based; 220 computer-based; 83 iBT), IELTS (minimum score 5). *Application deadline:* For fall admission, 1/15 for domestic and international students; for spring admission, 9/1 for domestic students, 8/15 for international students. Application fee: $60. *Financial support:* In 2010–11, 4 students received support, including 8 fellowships (averaging $1,666 per year), 63 research assistantships (averaging $23,738 per year), 8 teaching assistantships (averaging $21,931 per year); career-related internships or fieldwork, institutionally sponsored loans, and tuition waivers (full and partial) also available. Financial award applicants required to submit FAFSA. *Faculty research:* Physical oceanography, marine chemistry, biological oceanography, atmospheric chemistry, marine geology. *Application contact:* Kelvin Richards, Graduate Chair, 808-956-2913, Fax: 808-956-5035, E-mail: rkelvin@hawaii.edu.

University of Maine, Graduate School, College of Natural Sciences, Forestry, and Agriculture, School of Marine Sciences, Program in Oceanography, Orono, ME 04469. Offers MS, PhD. Part-time programs available. *Students:* 15 full-time (5 women), 6 part-time (1 woman), 4 international. Average age 29. 25 applicants, 20% accepted, 5 enrolled. In 2010, 3 master's awarded. *Degree requirements:* For master's, thesis; for doctorate, thesis/dissertation. *Entrance requirements:* For master's and doctorate, GRE General Test. Additional exam requirements/recommendations for international students: Required—TOEFL. *Application deadline:* For fall admission, 2/1 priority date for domestic students. Applications are processed on a rolling basis. Application fee: $65. Electronic applications accepted. *Expenses:* Tuition, state resident: full-time $400. Tuition, nonresident: full-time $1050. *Financial support:* Fellowships with tuition reimbursements, research assistantships with tuition reimbursements, teaching assistantships with tuition reimbursements, career-related internships or fieldwork, Federal Work-Study, and tuition waivers (full and partial) available. Support available to part-time students. Financial award application deadline: 3/1. *Faculty research:* Coastal processes, microbial ecology, crustacean systematics. *Unit head:* Dr. Larry Mayer, Coordinator, 207-581-3321. *Application contact:* Scott G. Delcourt, Associate Dean of the Graduate School, 207-581-3291, Fax: 207-581-3232, E-mail: graduate@maine.edu.

University of Maryland, College Park, Academic Affairs, College of Computer, Mathematical and Natural Sciences, Department of Atmospheric and Oceanic Science, College Park, MD 20742. Offers MS, PMS, PhD. Part-time and evening/weekend programs available. Postbaccalaureate distance learning degree programs offered. *Faculty:* 28 full-time (7 women), 6 part-time/adjunct (0 women). *Students:* 48 full-time (23 women), 12 part-time (8 women); includes 4 minority (2 Asian, non-Hispanic/Latino; 1 Hispanic/Latino; 1 Two or more races, non-Hispanic/Latino), 21 international. 102 applicants, 25% accepted, 16 enrolled. In 2010, 4 master's, 9 doctorates awarded. Terminal master's awarded for partial completion of doctoral program. *Degree requirements:* For master's, comprehensive exam, scholarly paper, written and oral exams; for doctorate, thesis/dissertation, exam. *Entrance requirements:* For master's, GRE General Test, background in mathematics, experience in scientific computer languages, 3 letters of recommendation; for doctorate, GRE General Test. *Application deadline:* For fall admission, 1/15 for domestic and international students; for spring admission, 11/1 for domestic students, 6/1 for international students. Applications are processed on a rolling basis. Application fee: $75. Electronic applications accepted. *Expenses:* Tuition, area resident: Part-time $471 per credit hour. Tuition, state resident: part-time $471 per credit hour. Tuition, nonresident: part-time $1016 per credit hour. Required fees: $337 per term. *Financial support:* In 2010–11, 3 fellowships with full and partial tuition reimbursements (averaging $9,698 per year), 18 research assistantships (averaging $20,707 per year), 20 teaching assistantships (averaging $19,890 per year) were awarded; Federal Work-Study and scholarships/grants also available. Support available to part-time students. Financial award applicants required to submit FAFSA. *Faculty research:* Weather, atmospheric chemistry, air pollution, global change, radiation. Total annual research expenditures: $4 million. *Unit head:* James A. Carton, Chair, 301-405-5365, Fax: 301-314-9482, E-mail: carton@umd.edu. *Application contact:* Dr. Charles A. Caramello, Dean of Graduate School, 301-405-0358, Fax: 301-314-9305, E-mail: ccaramel@umd.edu.

University of Miami, Graduate School, Rosenstiel School of Marine and Atmospheric Science, Division of Meteorology and Physical Oceanography, Coral Gables, FL 33124. Offers meteorology (MS, PhD); physical oceanography (MS, PhD). Terminal master's awarded for partial completion of doctoral program. *Degree requirements:* For master's, comprehensive exam, thesis; for doctorate, comprehensive exam, thesis/dissertation. *Entrance requirements:* For master's and doctorate, GRE General Test. Additional exam requirements/recommendations for international students: Required—TOEFL (minimum score 550 paper-based; 213 computer-based). Electronic applications accepted.

University of New Hampshire, Graduate School, College of Engineering and Physical Sciences, Department of Earth Sciences, Durham, NH 03824. Offers earth sciences (MS), including geochemical systems, geology, ocean mapping, oceanography; hydrology (MS). *Faculty:* 17 full-time (5 women). *Students:* 21 full-time (13 women), 8 part-time (4 women); includes 2 minority (1 Black or African American, non-Hispanic/Latino; 1 Asian, non-Hispanic/Latino), 4 international. Average age 27. 55 applicants, 65% accepted, 16 enrolled. In 2010, 8 master's awarded. *Degree requirements:* For master's, thesis. *Entrance requirements:* For master's, GRE General Test. Additional exam requirements/recommendations for international students: Required—TOEFL (minimum score 550 paper-based; 213 computer-based; 80 iBT). *Application deadline:* For fall admission, 4/1 priority date for domestic students, 4/1 for international students; for spring admission, 12/1 for domestic students. Applications are processed on a rolling basis. Application fee: $65. Electronic applications accepted. *Financial support:* In 2010–11, 24 students received support, including 13 research assistantships, 7 teaching assistantships; fellowships, career-related internships or fieldwork, Federal Work-Study, scholarships/grants, and tuition waivers (full and partial) also available. Support available to part-time students. Financial award application deadline: 2/15. *Unit head:* Dr. Will Clyde, Chairperson, 603-862-1718, E-mail: earth.sciences@unh.edu. *Application contact:* Sue Clark, Administrative Assistant, 603-862-1718, E-mail: earth.sciences@unh.edu.

University of New Hampshire, Graduate School, College of Engineering and Physical Sciences, Program in Ocean Engineering, Durham, NH 03824. Offers ocean engineering (MS, PhD); ocean mapping (MS, Postbaccalaureate Certificate). *Faculty:* 13 full-time (1 woman). *Students:* 18 full-time (4 women), 5 part-time (0 women); includes 1 minority (Hispanic/Latino), 14 international. Average age 30. 25 applicants, 88% accepted, 12 enrolled. In 2010, 2 master's, 5 other advanced degrees awarded. *Degree requirements:* For master's, thesis. *Entrance requirements:* Additional exam requirements/recommendations for international students: Required—TOEFL (minimum score 550 paper-based; 213 computer-based; 80 iBT). *Application deadline:* For fall admission, 4/1 priority date for domestic students; for spring admission, 12/1 for domestic students. Applications are processed on a rolling basis. Application fee: $65. Electronic applications accepted. *Financial support:* In 2010–11, 11 students received support, including 10 research assistantships, 1 teaching assistantship; fellowships, Federal Work-Study, scholarships/grants, and tuition waivers (full and partial) also available. Support available to part-time students. Financial award application deadline: 2/15. *Unit head:* Dr. Kenneth Baldwin, Chairperson, 603-862-1898. *Application contact:* Jennifer Bedsole, Information Contact, 603-862-0672, E-mail: ocean.engineering@unh.edu.

University of Rhode Island, Graduate School, Graduate School of Oceanography, Narragansett, RI 02882. Offers MO, MS, PhD, MBA/MO, PhD/MMA, PhD/MA. Part-time programs available. *Faculty:* 25 full-time (7 women), 5 part-time/adjunct (1 woman). *Students:* 64 full-time (35 women), 18 part-time (12 women); includes 3 minority (all Asian, non-Hispanic/Latino), 7 international. In 2010, 10 master's, 10 doctorates awarded. *Degree requirements:* For master's, comprehensive exam (for some programs), thesis optional; for doctorate, comprehensive exam, thesis/dissertation. *Entrance requirements:* For master's, GRE, 2 letters of recommendation; for doctorate, GRE, 3 letters of recommendation. Additional exam requirements/recommendations for international students: Required—TOEFL (minimum score 600 paper-based; 250 computer-based; 100 iBT). *Application deadline:* For fall admission, 1/15 for domestic and international students; for spring admission, 11/15 for domestic students, 7/15 for international students. Application fee: $65. Electronic applications accepted. *Expenses:* Tuition, state resident: full-time $9588; part-time $533 per credit hour. Tuition, nonresident: full-time $22,968; part-time $1276 per credit hour. Required fees: $1282; $68 per semester. Tuition and fees vary according to program. *Financial support:* In 2010–11, 29 research assistantships with full and partial tuition reimbursements (averaging $9,617 per year), 9 teaching assistantships with full and partial tuition reimbursements (averaging $9,724 per year) were awarded. Financial award application deadline: 1/15; financial award applicants required to submit FAFSA. *Faculty research:* The Subduction Factory, life in extreme environments, the marine nitrogen cycle, hurricane prediction, Antarctic ocean circulation. Total annual research expenditures: $27.9 million. *Unit head:* Dr. David M. Farmer, Dean, 401-874-6222, Fax: 401-874-6889, E-mail: thedean@gso.uri.edu. *Application contact:* Dr. David M. Farmer, Dean, 401-874-6222, Fax: 401-874-6889, E-mail: thedean@gso.uri.edu.

University of Southern California, Graduate School, Dana and David Dornsife College of Letters, Arts and Sciences, Department of Biological Sciences, Program in Marine Biology and Biological Oceanography, Los Angeles, CA 90089. Offers marine and environmental biology (MS); marine biology and biological oceanography (PhD). *Faculty:* 21 full-time (6 women), 11 part-time/adjunct (4 women). *Students:* 10 full-time (7 women); includes 6 minority (1 Black or African American, non-Hispanic/Latino; 3 Asian, non-Hispanic/Latino; 1 Hispanic/Latino; 1 Two or more races, non-Hispanic/Latino), 1 international. 35 applicants, 37% accepted, 10 enrolled. In 2010, 1 master's awarded. Terminal master's awarded for partial completion of doctoral program. *Degree requirements:* For master's, research paper, course work; for doctorate, comprehensive exam, thesis/dissertation, course work, qualifying examination, dissertation defense. *Entrance requirements:* For master's and doctorate, GRE, 3 letters of recommendation, personal statement, resume, minimum GPA of 3.0. Additional exam requirements/recommendations for international students: Required—TOEFL (minimum score 600 paper-based; 250 computer-based; 100 iBT). *Application deadline:* For fall admission, 12/1 priority date for domestic and international students. Application fee: $85. Electronic applications accepted. *Expenses:* Tuition: Full-time $31,240; part-time $1420 per unit. Required fees: $600. One-time fee: $35 full-time. Full-time tuition and fees vary according to degree level and program. *Financial support:* In 2010–11, 49 students received support, including 15 fellowships with full tuition reimbursements available (averaging $28,500 per year), 14 research assistantships with full tuition reimbursements available (averaging $26,700 per year), 13 teaching assistantships with full tuition reimbursements available (averaging $26,700 per year); scholarships/grants, traineeships, health care benefits, and tuition waivers also available. *Faculty research:* Microbial ecology, biogeochemistry, and geobiology; biodiversity and molecular ecology; integrative organismal biology; conservation biology; marine genomics. *Unit head:* Dr. David A. Caron, Professor of Biological Sciences, Director of the MBBO Graduate Program, 213-740-0203, E-mail: dcaron@usc.edu. *Application contact:* Adolfo dela Rosa, Student Services Advisor I, 213-821-3164, Fax: 213-740-1380, E-mail: adolfode@usc.edu.

University of South Florida, Graduate School, College of Marine Science, Saint Petersburg, FL 33701. Offers biological oceanography (MS, PhD); chemical oceanography (MS, PhD); geological oceanography (MS, PhD); interdisciplinary (MS, PhD); marine resource assessment (MS, PhD); physical oceanography (MS, PhD). Part-time programs available. *Faculty:* 24 full-time (6 women). *Students:* 69 full-time (41 women), 35 part-time (20 women); includes 6 Black or African American, non-Hispanic/Latino; 11 Hispanic/Latino; 1 Two or more races, non-Hispanic/Latino, 11 international. Average age 31. 98 applicants, 29% accepted, 15 enrolled. In 2010, 7 master's, 7 doctorates awarded. Terminal master's awarded for partial completion of doctoral program. *Degree requirements:* For master's, thesis, successful oral defense; for doctorate, comprehensive exam, thesis/dissertation, successful oral defense. *Entrance requirements:* For master's, GRE General Test; for doctorate, GRE General Test, bachelor's degree or equivalent from regionally-accredited university, minimum B average or GPA of 3.0 in all upper-division work attempted. Additional exam requirements/recommendations for international students: Required—TOEFL (minimum score 550 paper-based; 213 computer-based; 79 iBT). *Application deadline:* For fall admission, 1/15 for domestic students, 1/2 for international students; for spring admission, 10/1 for domestic students, 7/1 for international students. Applications are processed on a rolling basis. Application fee: $30. *Financial support:* In 2010–11, 73 students received support. Health care benefits and unspecified assistantships available. Financial award application deadline: 1/15. *Faculty research:* Trace metal chemistry, water quality, organic and isotopic geochemistry, physical chemistry, nutrient chemistry. Total annual research expenditures: $9.2 million. *Unit head:* Dr. Edward S. Van Vleet, Professor and Director of Academic Programs and Student Affairs, 727-553-1165, Fax: 727-553-1189, E-mail: vanvleet@marine.usf.edu. *Application contact:* Dawna L. Ishler, Academic Services Administrator, 727-553-3944, Fax: 727-553-1189, E-mail: dishler@usf.edu.

University of Victoria, Faculty of Graduate Studies, Faculty of Science, School of Earth and Ocean Sciences, Victoria, BC V8W 2Y2, Canada. Offers M Sc, PhD. Part-time programs available. *Degree requirements:* For master's, thesis; for doctorate, thesis/dissertation, candidacy exam. *Entrance requirements:* For master's and doctorate, GRE. Additional exam requirements/recommendations for international students: Required—TOEFL (minimum score 575 paper-based; 233 computer-based), IELTS (minimum score 7). Electronic applications accepted. *Faculty research:* Climate modeling, geology.

University of Washington, Graduate School, College of Ocean and Fishery Sciences, School of Oceanography, Seattle, WA 98195. Offers biological oceanography (MS, PhD); chemical oceanography (MS, PhD); marine geology and geophysics (MS, PhD); physical oceanography (MS, PhD). Terminal master's awarded for partial completion of doctoral program. *Degree requirements:* For master's, research project; for doctorate, thesis/dissertation. *Entrance requirements:* For master's and doctorate, GRE General Test, minimum GPA of 3.0. Additional exam requirements/recommendations for international students: Required—TOEFL. Electronic applications accepted. *Faculty research:* Global climate change, hydrothermal vent systems, marine microbiology, marine and freshwater biogeochemistry, biological-physical interactions.

University of Wisconsin–Madison, Graduate School, College of Engineering, Program in Limnology and Marine Science, Madison, WI 53706. Offers MS, PhD. *Faculty:* 21 full-time (7 women). *Students:* 14 full-time (3 women); includes 1 Hispanic/Latino. 36 applicants, 11% accepted, 3 enrolled. In 2010, 1 doctorate awarded. Terminal master's awarded for partial completion of doctoral program. *Degree requirements:* For master's, thesis; for doctorate,

Oceanography

University of Wisconsin–Madison (continued)
thesis/dissertation. *Entrance requirements:* For master's and doctorate, GRE General Test. Additional exam requirements/recommendations for international students: Required—TOEFL. *Application deadline:* For fall admission, 1/1 priority date for domestic students, 1/1 for international students. Application fee: $45. Electronic applications accepted. *Expenses:* Tuition, state resident: full-time $9887.36; part-time $617.96 per credit. Tuition, nonresident: full-time $24,054; part-time $1503.40 per credit. Required fees: $67.63 per credit. Tuition and fees vary according to reciprocity agreements. *Financial support:* In 2010–11, fellowships with full tuition reimbursements (averaging $19,032 per year), 16 research assistantships with full tuition reimbursements (averaging $19,032 per year), 4 teaching assistantships with full tuition reimbursements (averaging $19,032 per year) were awarded; Federal Work-Study and institutionally sponsored loans also available. Financial award application deadline: 1/1. *Faculty research:* Lake ecosystems, ecosystem modeling, geochemistry, physiological ecology, chemical limnology. *Unit head:* Jake K. Vander Zanden, Chair. *Application contact:* Mary Possin, Student Services Coordinator, 608-263-3264, Fax: 608-265-2340, E-mail: mcpossin@wisc.edu.

University of Wisconsin–Madison, Graduate School, College of Letters and Science, Department of Atmospheric and Oceanic Sciences, Madison, WI 53706-1380. Offers MS, PhD. Part-time programs available. *Degree requirements:* For master's, thesis (for some programs); for doctorate, thesis/dissertation. *Entrance requirements:* For master's and doctorate, GRE General Test, minimum GPA of 3.0; previous course work in chemistry, mathematics, and physics. Electronic applications accepted. *Expenses:* Tuition, state resident: full-time $9887.36; part-time $617.96 per credit. Tuition, nonresident: full-time $24,054; part-time $1503.40 per credit. Required fees: $67.63 per credit. Tuition and fees vary according to reciprocity

agreements. *Faculty research:* Satellite meteorology, weather systems, global climate change, numerical modeling, atmosphere-ocean interaction.

Woods Hole Oceanographic Institution, MIT/WHOI Joint Program in Oceanography/Applied Ocean Science and Engineering, Woods Hole, MA 02543-1541. Offers applied ocean sciences (PhD); biological oceanography (PhD, Sc D); chemical oceanography (PhD, Sc D); civil and environmental and oceanographic engineering (PhD); electrical and oceanographic engineering (PhD); geochemistry (PhD); geophysics (PhD); marine biology (PhD); marine geochemistry (PhD, Sc D); marine geology (PhD, Sc D); marine geophysics (PhD); mechanical and oceanographic engineering (PhD); ocean engineering (PhD); oceanographic engineering (M Eng, MS, PhD, Sc D, Eng); paleoceanography (PhD); physical oceanography (PhD, Sc D). MS, PhD, Sc D offered jointly with Massachusetts Institute of Technology. Terminal master's awarded for partial completion of doctoral program. *Degree requirements:* For master's and Eng, thesis (for some programs); for doctorate, thesis/dissertation. *Entrance requirements:* For master's, GRE General Test; for doctorate, GRE General Test, GRE Subject Test. Additional exam requirements/recommendations for international students: Required—TOEFL. Electronic applications accepted.

Yale University, Graduate School of Arts and Sciences, Department of Geology and Geophysics, New Haven, CT 06520. Offers biogeochemistry (PhD); climate dynamics (PhD); geochemistry (PhD); geophysics (PhD); meteorology (PhD); oceanography (PhD); paleontology (PhD); paleoceanography (PhD); petrology (PhD); tectonics (PhD). *Degree requirements:* For doctorate, thesis/dissertation. *Entrance requirements:* For doctorate, GRE General Test. Additional exam requirements/recommendations for international students: Required—TOEFL.

160 www.facebook.com/petersonspublishing

Peterson's Graduate Programs in the Physical Sciences, Mathematics, Agricultural Sciences, the Environment & Natural Resources 2012

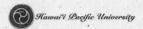

HAWAI'I PACIFIC UNIVERSITY

Master of Science in Marine Science

Program of Study	Hawai'i Pacific University's (HPU) Master of Science in marine science is a research-based degree program that emphasizes a hands-on approach to learning through the completion of an original thesis project under the mentorship of an experienced marine science researcher. Individualized programs of study ensure that the students have the best possible preparation based on their individual interests, background, and abilities.
	Marine science faculty members and researchers in the College of Natural and Computational Sciences work in many fields critical to the understanding and sustainable use of marine resources and systems, including aquaculture, marine biogeochemistry, marine natural product chemistry, benthic ecology, spatial ecology, coral reef ecology, inorganic carbon cycle dynamics, phycology, environmental microbiology, toxicology, marine mammal physiology, and ichthyology.
	The program is designed to be completed in two years of full-time study. In the first year students take a core course sequence and complete a proposal for their thesis research topic. Thesis research is conducted through the next year, culminating in oral and written presentation of a thesis. Full-time students will take the equivalent of three classes per semester. Graduates have the knowledge and skills to be successful in marine-related technical positions in industry, government, and education or for entry into doctoral marine science programs.
Research Facilities	Research facilities include state-of-the-art laboratories at the Windward Oahu Hawai'i Loa campus and the Oceanic Institute; classes are held at both locations.
	Located on the windward shores of O'ahu just steps from the Pacific Ocean, the Oceanic Institute is a gateway to the latest science and innovation in marine biology, marine aquaculture, biotechnology, and ocean resource management. Learning and research opportunities abound in this hands-on environment, ranging from new tactics in shrimp production and marine nutrition to fisheries restoration and ecological interactions between cultured fish and wild populations.
	On the Hawai'i Loa campus are classroom facilities, including wet labs and computer access; indoor and outdoor aquaculture laboratories; maturation and hatchery facilities; biosecure facilities for shrimp and finfish production; large-scale algae, copepod, rotifer, and brine shrimp live-feed production facilities; and analytical laboratories for water quality, physical parameters, and biochemical analyses.
	Students in marine science also gain field and research experience aboard the *Kaholo,* HPU's 45-foot, double-hulled research boat.
Financial Aid	Hawai'i Pacific University offers several types of graduate scholarships to new, full-time, degree-seeking students. U.S. citizens, permanent residents, and international students who have a demonstrated financial need may apply.
	HPU's graduate scholarships include the Trustee ($6000 per year), the Dean ($4000 per year), and the Graduate Kokua ($2000 per year). New, full-time, degree-seeking students who believe they have a financial need may apply for these graduate scholarships. Other factors that may be considered when evaluating requests are previous academic record, community involvement and service, and professional work experience and achievement.
	Priority consideration is given to those students who apply by the deadline. Applications received after the priority deadline will be awarded on a funds-available basis. Applicants will be notified by mail as decisions are made. The type and value of the scholarship will be explained in the award letter.
Cost of Study	In 2011–12, graduate tuition for the marine science program is $1030 per credit. Full-time tuition (9 credits per semester) is $18,540. Other costs include books, personal expenses, fees, and a student bus pass, for a total of $3190.
Living and Housing Costs	The University has residence halls, off-campus housing for graduate students, and an apartment referral service. For the 2011–12 academic year, housing expenses are approximately $12,230. Off-campus housing is available for a comparable price. For further graduate housing information, students should visit www.hpu.edu/housing.
Student Group	Students in the program hold undergraduate degrees in marine science, marine biology, environmental science, or other relevant fields, or they have completed sufficient course work in these areas. As the largest private university in Hawai'i, HPU students come from every state in the U.S. and more than other 100 countries. The diversity of the student body stimulates learning about other cultures firsthand, both in and out of the classroom. There is no majority population at HPU. Students are encouraged to examine the values, customs, traditions, and principles of others to gain a clearer understanding of their own perspectives. HPU students develop friendships with students throughout the United States and the world and establish important connections for success in the global economy of the twenty-first century.
Location	Hawai'i Pacific combines the excitement of an urban, downtown campus with the serenity of the windward side of the island. The main campus is located in downtown Honolulu, the business and financial center of the Pacific, within walking distance of shopping and dining. Iolani Palace, the only palace in the U.S., is a few blocks away, as are the State Capitol, City Hall, and the Blaisdell Concert Hall. The Honolulu Academy of Arts, Museum of Contemporary Art, Waikiki Aquarium, Honolulu Zoo, and many other cultural attractions are located nearby.
	The Hawai'i Loa campus is 8 miles away in Kaneohe, at the base of the Ko'olau Mountains; it is the site of the School of Nursing, the marine science program, and a variety of other course offerings. HPU is also affiliated with the Oceanic Institute, an applied aquaculture research facility located on a 56-acre site at Makapu'u Point on the windward coast. All three sites are conveniently linked by shuttle.
The University	Hawai'i Pacific University, a coeducational, nonsectarian, career-oriented university founded in 1965, is the largest private institution for higher learning in Hawai'i, offering more than fifty undergraduate programs and thirteen graduate programs to 8,200 students. HPU's innovative programs anticipate the changing needs of the community and prepare graduates to live and work as active members of a global society. Students come from all fifty states and from more than 100 countries, making HPU one of the most culturally diverse universities in the world.
Applying	When reviewing an application for admittance into the graduate program, the Graduate Admission Committee considers several factors, including completion of a science or marine science baccalaureate degree from an accredited institution, undergraduate grade point average (GPA) of 3.0 or higher, the results of the Graduate Record Examinations (GRE) General Test, and the outcome of an interview with a graduate program faculty member either in person or by telephone. Applicants whose native language is not English must either complete the English Foundations Program (EFP) requirements or have an exemption from EFP through a TOEFL with a score of 550 or above (including a TWE of 5) to demonstrate proficiency in English as a second language.
	Applicants are accepted into the program only if the Graduate Admissions Committee has identified a suitable mentor and the faculty member has agreed to mentor the student. In addition to the graduate application form, each applicant should submit a statement on their desired research area and include a preliminary projection of resources or other considerations to determine if the potential research activity can be supported by the college.
	A holistic approach is used, and no one factor will exclude an applicant from consideration. The University is seeking students who have demonstrated the ability and motivation to do graduate level work.
	Applicants who have not completed a science or marine science baccalaureate may still apply to the graduate program. However, students may be required to complete the required prerequisite courses.
	The University has a rolling admission process and reviews applications throughout the year. In order to ensure adequate time for evaluation and correspondence, it is strongly recommended that applications be submitted early.
Correspondence and Information	Graduate Admissions Hawai'i Pacific University 1164 Bishop Street, #911 Honolulu, Hawai'i 96813
	Phone: 808-544-1135 866-GRAD-HPU (toll-free) Fax: 808-544-0280 E-mail: graduate@hpu.edu Web site: www.hpu.edu/hpumsms

*Peterson's Graduate Programs in the Physical Sciences, Mathematics,
Agricultural Sciences, the Environment & Natural Resources 2011*

www.twitter.com/usgradschools **161**

Hawai'i Pacific University

THE FACULTY AND THEIR RESEARCH

Brian Bozlee, Associate Professor of Chemistry, Premedical Studies, Biochemistry, and Marine/Environmental Science; Ph.D. (physical chemistry), Oregon State. Applications of surface-enhanced Raman spectroscopy. (bbozlee@hpu.edu)
A simplified model to predict the effect of increasing atmospheric CO_2 on carbonate chemistry in the ocean. *J. Chem. Ed.* 85(2): 213–17, 2008. With Janebo and Jahn.
Reformulation of the Michaelis-Menten Equation: How enzyme-catalyzed reactions depend on free energy. *J. Chem. Ed.* 84(1):106–7, 2007.

Andrew Marsh Brittain, Associate Professor of Microbiology; Ph. D. (microbiology), Hawaii at Manoa. Marine and environmental microbiology. (abrittain@hpu.edu)
Genetic algorithm application. *Biosystems* 39:2, 1997. With Noever and Matsos.
Self organized criticality in closed ecosystems: Carbon dioxide fluctuations in Biosphere II. *Int. J. Climatology* 16:1–6, 1996. With Cronise and Noever.

Susan M. Carstenn, Assistant Professor of Environmental Science and Marine and Environmental Science; Ph.D. (systems ecology/environmental science), Florida. Finding better ways interface humanity and the environment, with particular emphasis on wetland and coastal ecosystem processes. (scarstenn@hpu.edu)
A new direction for large-scale experimental design and analysis. *Front. Ecol. Environ.* 4(5):227, 2006. With Miao.
Ecological implications of natural recovery and fire on phosphorus storages, cattail expansion and native vegetation recovery. Final Research Plan to South Florida Water Management District, West Palm Beach, Florida, 2006. With Miao.

Yongli Chen, Assistant Professor of Chemistry; Ph.D. (biophysics), Tsinghua (Beijing). How abusive drugs like cocaine affect the mammalian central nervous system, finding and designing small organic molecules that can alleviate the drug's effect, screening interesting marine natural products using glutamate receptors as molecular targets, understanding of the biochemistry behind the action of marine pharmaceuticals to facilitate drug development and modification for optimization.
Coumarin-caged glycine that can be photolyzed within 3 μs by visible light. *Biochemistry* 46:5479–84, 2007. With Shembekar, Carpenter, and Hess.
A protecting group for carboxylic acids that can be photolyzed by visible light. *Biochemistry* 44:7107–14, 2005. With Shembekar, Carpenter, and Hess.

John L. Culliney, Professor of Biology and Marine Biology; Ph.D. (zoology), Duke. Philosophy and ecology of cooperation in nature, environmental histories of tropical islands, propagation of native Hawaiian plants, marine invertebrate larval biology. (jculliney@hpu.edu)
Islands in a Far Sea: The Fate of Nature in Hawai'i. 420 pp. Honolulu: University of Hawai'i Press, 2006 (revised edition).

Valerie Franck, Assistant Professor of Biology and Marine and Environmental Science; Ph.D. (marine biology), California, Santa Barbara. Understanding the complex factors that regulate primary production and phytoplankton species composition, role of iron limitation in regulating the phytoplankton species composition and biogeochemical cycling of silicon and nitrogen. (vfranck@hpu.edu)
Comparison of size-dependent carbon, nitrate, and silicic acid uptake rates in high- and low-iron waters. *Limnology Oceanography* 50:825–38, 2005. With Smith, Bruland, and Brzezinski.
Iron and zinc effects on silicic acid and nitrate uptake kinetics in three high-nutrient, low-chlorophyll (HNLC) regions. *Marine Ecology Progress Series* 252:15–33, 2003. With Smith, Bruland, and Brzezinski.

Varis Grundmanis, Associate Professor of Oceanography and Marine and Environmental Sciences; Ph.D. (chemical oceanography), Washington (Seattle). Photographic documentation of marine life in Oahu Marine Life Conservation Districts; physical/chemical oceanography of Kaneohe Bay, Oahu, Hawaii; photographic documentation of marine life in Oahu Marine Life Conservation Districts; physical/chemical oceanography of Kaneohe Bay, Oahu, Hawaii. (vgrundmanis@hpu.edu)

John Gutrich, Associate Professor of Environmental Studies; Ph.D., Ohio State. Ecological economics, ecosystem modeling, wetland ecology and mitigation, invasive species management, risk assessment, sustainable development. (jgutrich@hpu.edu)

Warren Hays, Associate Professor of Biology; Ph.D. (zoology), Hawaii at Manoa. Behavioral ecology of small mammals, especially the social systems of mongooses and shrews; cryptic social systems; evolution of sociality; mammalian scent marking and pheromone systems. (whays@hpu.edu)
Impact of the small Indian mongoose (*Herpestes javanicus*) (Carnivora: Herpestidae) on native vertebrate populations in areas of introduction. *Pacific Science* 61:3–16, 2007. With Conant.
A morphometric trend linked to male sociality in the small Indian mongoose, *Herpestes javanicus*, in Hawaii. *Acta Theriologica* 51:303–10, 2006. With Simberloff.

F. David Horgen, Associate Professor of Chemistry, Marine and Environmental Sciences, Biochemistry, and Premedical Studies and Coordinator of the Shared Instrumentation Facility; Ph.D. (pharmacognosy), Illinois at Chicago. Discovery of biologically active secondary metabolites from marine organisms; screening marine bacteria, fungi, algae, and invertebrates for their ability to modulate the function of transient receptor potential (TRP) cation channels; investigating marine cyanobacteria for novel non-ribosomally biosynthesized peptides. (dhorgen@hpu.edu)
Determination of microbial community structures of shrimp floc cultures by biomarkers and analysis of floc amino acid profiles. *Aquaculture Res.* 39(2): 118–33, 2008. With Ju et al.
Lehualides A-D, new metabolites from a Hawaiian sponge of the genus *Plakortis* (Homosclerophorida: Plakinidae). *J. Natural Products* 68:1400–3, 2005. With Sata et al.

David Hyrenbach, Assistant Professor of Oceanography; Ph.D. (biological oceanography), California, San Diego (Scripps). Oceanic habitats of far-ranging pelagic vertebrates (seabirds, turtles, cetaceans, tunas) and the physical mechanisms (upwelling, convergence) that define predictable areas of enhanced biological activity in pelagic systems.
Do the largest reserves protect whales or whalers? *Science* 307:525–26, 2005. With Gerber and Zacharias.
Marine bird and cetacean associations with bathymetric habitats and shallow-water topographies: Implications for trophic transfer and conservation. In *The Role of Biophysical Coupling in Concentrating Marine Organisms Around Shallow Topographies*, J. F. Dower and R. D. Brodeur, eds. *J. Marine Systems* 50(1-2):79–99, 2004. With Yen and Sydeman.

Brenda A. Jensen, Assistant Professor of Biology and Marine and Environmental Sciences; Ph.D. (biological oceanography), MIT/Woods Hole Oceanographic Institution. Molecular responses to environmental stress, evaluating species-specific susceptibility within tropical marine communities, and developing in vitro and ex vivo (e.g. cell culture) methods to assess susceptibility to environmental contaminants in rare and protected species such as marine mammals, particularly responses of the immune system and those mediated by members of the PER-ARNT-SIM (PAS) family of proteins, which control certain biochemical responses caused by environmental contaminants and hypoxia. (bjensen@hpu.edu)
Aryl hydrocarbon receptor (AhR) agonists suppress interleukin-6 expression by bone marrow stromal cells: An immunotoxicology study. *Environmental Health: A Global Access Science Source* 2:16, 2003. With Leeman et al.
Environmental chemical-induced pro/pre-B cell apoptosis: Analysis of c-Myc, p27Kip1, and p21WAF1 reveals a death pathway distinct from clonal deletion. *J. Immunol.* 170(10):4897–904, 2003. With Ryu et al.

Samuel Kahng, Assistant Professor of Oceanography; Ph.D. (biological oceanography), Hawai'i. Ecological impacts of *Carijoa riisei* on Black Coral Habitat.
Impact of an alien octocoral (*Carijoa riisei*) on black corals in Hawai'i. *Coral Reefs* 24(4):556–62, 2005. With Grigg.

Keith E. Korsmeyer, Associate Professor of Biology and Marine Sciences and Biology; Ph.D. (marine biology), California, San Diego (Scripps). Comparative and ecological physiology of fishes, in particular, the metabolic, energetic, and cardio-respiratory specializations of fishes, and the influence of environment on physiological function: cardiac function and oxygen transport to tissues, metabolic compensations to changes in habitat, such as temperature and hypoxia, and bioenergetics of swimming. (kkorsmeyer@hpu.edu)
Swimming alters responses to hypoxia in the Adriatic sturgeon *Acipenser naccarii*. *J. Fish Biol.* 70(2):651–8, 2007. With McKenzie et al.
Energetics of median and paired fin swimming, body and caudal fin swimming, and gait transition in parrotfish (*Scarus schlegeli*) and triggerfish (*Rhinecanthus aculeatus*). *J. Experimental Biol.* 205(9):1253–63, 2002. With Steffensen and Herskin.

Martha Sykes, Associate Professor of Geology and Environmental Science and Assistant Dean of the College of Natural Sciences; Ph.D. (geology), Arizona State. Reform of science education to better meet needs of undergraduates, especially non-science majors and pre-service teachers. (msykes@hpu.edu)
A carbon-13 method for evaluating degradation of starch-based polymers. *J. Environmental Polymer Degradation* 6:23–34, 1994. With Yeh and Gauldie.

Catherine Unabia, Assistant Professor of Biology; Ph.D. (zoology, marine invertebrates), Hawaii at Manoa. Larval biology, chemical ecology, seagrass communities, marine microbiology and biotechnology, molluscan evolution and systematics. (cunabia@hpu.edu)
The snail *Smaragdia bryanae* (Neritopsina, Neritidae) is a specialist herbivore of the seagrass *Halophila hawaiiana (Alismatidae, Hydrocharitaceae). Invertebrate Biol.* 130(2):100–14, 2011.
The role of bacteria in the settlement and metamorphosis of the polychaete *Hydroides elegans. Marine Biol.* 133:55–64, 1999. With Hadfield.

Eric W. Vetter, Associate Professor of Oceanography, Marine Sciences, and Biology; Ph.D. (oceanography), California, San Diego (Scripps). Effects of macrophyte detritus on communities in deep submarine canyons, carbon sources for infauna in submarine canyons, impact of submarine canyons on nearshore fisheries, effects of CO_2 sequestration on benthic communities, scavenger communities on the Hawaiian Slope, influences of hydrothermal venting on benthic animals on Loihi Seamount. (vetter@hpu.edu)
Leptostraca. In The Light and Smith Manual: Intertidal Invertebrates from Central California to Oregon, 4th edition, pp. 484–89, ed. J. T. Carlton. Berkeley: University of California Press, 2007. With Haney and Martin.
Ecological effects of deep-ocean CO_2 enrichment: Insights from natural high-CO_2 habitats. *J. Geophysical Res., Oceans* 110:C09S13–23, 2005. With Smith.

Kristi West, Assistant Professor of Biology and Marine Sciences; Ph.D. (biomedical science), Hawaii at Manoa; Ph.D. (marine ecology), L'Universite de la Polynesie Francaise. Physiology of cetaceans, especially from a nutritional and reproductive perspective; describing life-history traits in cetaceans, in particular those for poorly known species; marine mammal stranding events and information that can be gained by performing thorough necropsies; disease prevalence and environmental influences on Hawaiian cetaceans. (kwest@hpu.edu)
Effect of lactation stage and concurrent pregnancy on milk composition in the bottlenose dolphin. *J. Zoology* 273(2):148–60, 2007. With Oftedal et al.
Distribution of the rough-toothed dolphin (*Steno bredanensis*) around the Windward Islands, French Polynesia. *Pacific Sci.* 59(1):17–24, 2005. With Gannier.

Christopher D. Winn, Associate Professor of Oceanography and Director of Marine and Environmental Science; Ph.D. (oceanography), Hawai'i. Marine biogeochemistry and the oceanic carbon cycle. (cwinn@hpu.edu)
Consistency and synthesis of Pacific Ocean CO_2 survey data. *Deep-Sea Res. II* 49:21–58, 2002. With Lamb et al.
Remineralization ratios in the subtropical North Pacific Gyre. *Aquatic Chemistry* 6:65–86, 2000. With Yuan-Huli et al.

Section 5
Meteorology and Atmospheric Sciences

This section contains a directory of institutions offering graduate work in meteorology and atmospheric sciences, followed by in-depth entries submitted by institutions that chose to prepare detailed program descriptions. Additional information about programs listed in the directory may be obtained by writing directly to the dean of a graduate school or chair of a department at the address given in the directory.

For programs offering related work, see also in this book *Astronomy and Astrophysics, Geosciences, Marine Sciences and Oceanography,* and *Physics.* In the other guides in this series:

Graduate Programs in the Biological Sciences
See *Biological and Biomedical Sciences* and *Biophysics*
Graduate Programs in Engineering & Applied Sciences
See *Aerospace/Aeronautical Engineering, Civil and Environmental Engineering, Engineering and Applied Sciences,* and *Mechanical Engineering and Mechanics*

CONTENTS

Program Directories

Atmospheric Sciences

Arizona State University, College of Liberal Arts and Sciences, School of Geographical Sciences, Tempe, AZ 85287-5302. Offers atmospheric science (Graduate Certificate); geographic education (MAS); geographic information systems (MAS); geographical information science (Graduate Certificate); geography (MA, PhD); transportation systems (Graduate Certificate); urban and environmental planning (MUEP). *Faculty:* 34 full-time (9 women), 2 part-time/adjunct (both women). *Students:* 125 full-time (40 women), 47 part-time (25 women); includes 24 minority (4 Black or African American, non-Hispanic/Latino; 1 American Indian or Alaska Native, non-Hispanic/Latino; 1 Asian, non-Hispanic/Latino; 16 Hispanic/Latino; 2 Two or more races, non-Hispanic/Latino), 34 international. Average age 30. 261 applicants, 56% accepted, 79 enrolled. In 2010, 76 master's, 3 doctorates, 13 other advanced degrees awarded. Terminal master's awarded for partial completion of doctoral program. *Degree requirements:* For master's, thesis, interactive Program of Study (iPOS) submitted before completing 50 percent of required credit hours; for doctorate, comprehensive exam, thesis/dissertation, interactive Program of Study (iPOS) submitted before completing 50 percent of required credit hours. *Entrance requirements:* For master's and doctorate, GRE, minimum GPA of 3.0 or equivalent in last 2 years of work leading to bachelor's degree. Additional exam requirements/recommendations for international students: Required—TOEFL, IELTS, or Pearson Test of English. *Application deadline:* For fall admission, 1/15 for domestic and international students. Applications are processed on a rolling basis. Application fee: $70 ($90 for international students). Electronic applications accepted. *Expenses:* Contact institution. *Financial support:* In 2010–11, 25 research assistantships with full and partial tuition reimbursements (averaging $15,546 per year), 50 teaching assistantships with full and partial tuition reimbursements (averaging $10,686 per year) were awarded; fellowships with full tuition reimbursements, career-related internships or fieldwork, Federal Work-Study, institutionally sponsored loans, scholarships/grants, and tuition waivers (full and partial) also available. Financial award application deadline: 3/1; financial award applicants required to submit FAFSA. Total annual research expenditures: $2.6 million. *Unit head:* Dr. Luc Anselin, Chair and Director, 480-965-7533, E-mail: luc.anselin@asu.edu. *Application contact:* Graduate Admissions, 480-965-6113.

Bard College, Bard Center for Environmental Policy, Annandale-on-Hudson, NY 12504. Offers climate science and policy (MS, Professional Certificate), including agriculture (MS), ecosystems (MS); environmental policy (MS, Professional Certificate); sustainability (MBA); MS/JD; MS/MAT. Part-time programs available. *Faculty:* 10 full-time (5 women), 6 part-time/adjunct (3 women). *Students:* 58 full-time (41 women). Average age 26. 75 applicants, 77% accepted, 28 enrolled. In 2010, 13 master's awarded. *Degree requirements:* For master's, thesis, 4-month, full-time internship. *Entrance requirements:* For master's, GRE, coursework in statistics, chemistry and one other semester of college science; personal statement; curriculum vitae; 3 letters of recommendation; sample of written work. Additional exam requirements/recommendations for international students: Required—TOEFL (minimum score 600 paper-based; 250 computer-based; 100 iBT). *Application deadline:* For winter admission, 1/15 priority date for domestic and international students; for spring admission, 5/15 for domestic and international students. Applications are processed on a rolling basis. Application fee: $65. Electronic applications accepted. *Expenses:* Contact institution. *Financial support:* In 2010–11, 58 students received support, including 58 fellowships (averaging $7,000 per year), 6 research assistantships (averaging $6,000 per year), 1 teaching assistantship (averaging $6,000 per year); career-related internships or fieldwork, scholarships/grants, tuition waivers (full), and unspecified assistantships also available. Support available to part-time students. Financial award application deadline: 2/15; financial award applicants required to submit FAFSA. *Faculty research:* Climate and agriculture, alternative energy, environmental economics, environmental toxicology, EPA law, sustainable development, international relations, literature and composition, human rights, agronomy, advocacy, leadership. *Unit head:* Dr. Eban Goodstein, Director, 845-758-7067, Fax: 845-758-7636, E-mail: ebangood@bard.edu. *Application contact:* Molly Williams, Admissions Coordinator, 845-758-7071, Fax: 845-758-7636, E-mail: mwilliam@bard.edu.

City College of the City University of New York, Graduate School, College of Liberal Arts and Science, Division of Science, Department of Earth and Atmospheric Sciences, New York, NY 10031-9198. Offers earth and environmental science (PhD); earth systems science (MA). PhD program offered jointly with Graduate School and University Center of the City University of New York. *Degree requirements:* For master's, comprehensive exam, thesis. *Entrance requirements:* Additional exam requirements/recommendations for international students: Required—TOEFL (minimum score 500 paper-based; 61 iBT). Electronic applications accepted. *Faculty research:* Water resources, high-temperature geochemistry, sedimentary basin analysis, tectonics.

Clemson University, Graduate School, College of Engineering and Science, Department of Physics and Astronomy, Clemson, SC 29634. Offers physics (MS, PhD), including astronomy and astrophysics, atmospheric physics, biophysics. Part-time programs available. *Faculty:* 25 full-time (4 women), 2 part-time/adjunct (0 women). *Students:* 63 full-time (19 women); includes 3 Black or African American, non-Hispanic/Latino, 26 international. Average age 27. 66 applicants, 92% accepted, 21 enrolled. In 2010, 2 master's, 6 doctorates awarded. Terminal master's awarded for partial completion of doctoral program. *Degree requirements:* For master's, thesis or alternative; for doctorate, thesis/dissertation. *Entrance requirements:* For master's and doctorate, GRE General Test. Additional exam requirements/recommendations for international students: Required—TOEFL. *Application deadline:* For fall admission, 1/15 priority date for domestic students; for spring admission, 9/15 priority date for domestic students. Applications are processed on a rolling basis. Application fee: $70 ($80 for international students). Electronic applications accepted. *Expenses:* Tuition, state resident: full-time $6492; part-time $400 per credit hour. Tuition, nonresident: full-time $13,634; part-time $800 per credit hour. Required fees: $262 per semester. Part-time tuition and fees vary according to course load and program. *Financial support:* In 2010–11, 58 students received support, including 1 fellowship with full and partial tuition reimbursement available (averaging $16,000 per year), 26 research assistantships with partial tuition reimbursements available (averaging $13,559 per year), 43 teaching assistantships with partial tuition reimbursements available (averaging $14,097 per year); career-related internships or fieldwork, institutionally sponsored loans, scholarships/grants, health care benefits, and unspecified assistantships also available. Support available to part-time students. Financial award application deadline: 6/1; financial award applicants required to submit FAFSA. *Faculty research:* Radiation physics, solid-state physics, nuclear physics, radar and lidar studies of atmosphere. Total annual research expenditures: $2.4 million. *Unit head:* Dr. Peter Barnes, Chair, 864-656-3419, Fax: 864-656-0805, E-mail: peterb@clemson.edu. *Application contact:* Dr. Murray Daw, Graduate Coordinator, 864-656-6702, Fax: 864-656-0805, E-mail: physgradinfo-l@clemson.edu.

Colorado State University, Graduate School, College of Engineering, Department of Atmospheric Science, Fort Collins, CO 80523-1371. Offers MS, PhD. Part-time programs available. *Faculty:* 15 full-time (3 women), 1 part-time/adjunct (0 women). *Students:* 64 full-time (25 women), 26 part-time (11 women); includes 9 minority (1 Black or African American, non-Hispanic/Latino; 5 Hispanic/Latino; 3 Two or more races, non-Hispanic/Latino), 7 international. Average age 27. 110 applicants, 26% accepted, 20 enrolled. In 2010, 13 master's, 4 doctorates awarded. *Degree requirements:* For master's, thesis optional; for doctorate, comprehensive exam, thesis/dissertation. *Entrance requirements:* For master's, GRE General Test, minimum GPA of 3.0; BS in physics, math, atmospheric science, engineering, chemistry or related major; calculus-based math and differential equations; calculus-based physics; letters of recommendation; for doctorate, GRE General Test, minimum GPA of 3.0; MS with thesis in atmospheric science or related field; statement with interests; curriculum vitae; letters of recommendation. Additional exam requirements/recommendations for international students: Required—TOEFL (minimum score 550 paper-based; 213 computer-based; 80 iBT), IELTS (minimum score 6). *Application deadline:* For fall admission, 1/15 priority date for domestic and international students; for spring admission, 9/15 priority date for domestic and international students. Applications are processed on a rolling basis. Application fee: $50. Electronic applications accepted. *Expenses:* Contact institution. *Financial support:* In 2010–11, 63 students received support, including 7 fellowships with full tuition reimbursements available (averaging $39,076 per year), 56 research assistantships with full tuition reimbursements available (averaging $24,238 per year); teaching assistantships with partial tuition reimbursements available, scholarships/grants, health care benefits, and unspecified assistantships also available. Support available to part-time students. Financial award application deadline: 4/15; financial award applicants required to submit FAFSA. *Faculty research:* Global circulation and climate, atmospheric chemistry, radiation and remote sensing, marine meteorology, mesoscale meteorology. Total annual research expenditures: $14.3 million. *Unit head:* Dr. Richard Johnson, Head, 970-491-8321, Fax: 970-491-8449, E-mail: richard.johnson@colostate.edu. *Application contact:* Dr. Sonia Kreidenweis, Student Counselor, 970-491-8350, Fax: 970-491-8483, E-mail: sonia@atmos.colostate.edu.

Columbia University, Graduate School of Arts and Sciences, Division of Natural Sciences, Program in Atmospheric and Planetary Science, New York, NY 10027. Offers M Phil, PhD. Offered jointly through the Departments of Geological Sciences, Astronomy, and Physics and in cooperation with NASA Goddard Space Flight Center's Institute for Space Studies. *Degree requirements:* For doctorate, variable foreign language requirement, thesis/dissertation. *Entrance requirements:* For doctorate, GRE General Test, GRE Subject Test, previous course work in mathematics and physics. Additional exam requirements/recommendations for international students: Required—TOEFL. *Faculty research:* Climate, weather prediction.

Columbia University, Graduate School of Arts and Sciences, Program in Climate and Society, New York, NY 10027. Offers MA.

Cornell University, Graduate School, Graduate Fields of Agriculture and Life Sciences, Field of Atmospheric Science, Ithaca, NY 14853-0001. Offers MS, PhD. *Faculty:* 14 full-time (1 woman). *Students:* 9 full-time (4 women); includes 1 Asian, non-Hispanic/Latino, 3 international. Average age 26. 49 applicants, 12% accepted, 3 enrolled. In 2010, 1 master's, 1 doctorate awarded. *Degree requirements:* For master's, thesis; for doctorate, comprehensive exam, thesis/dissertation. *Entrance requirements:* For master's and doctorate, GRE General Test, 2 letters of recommendation. Additional exam requirements/recommendations for international students: Required—TOEFL (minimum score 550 paper-based; 213 computer-based; 77 iBT). *Application deadline:* For fall admission, 2/1 for domestic students; for spring admission, 8/1 priority date for domestic students. Application fee: $70. Electronic applications accepted. *Expenses:* Tuition: Full-time $29,500. Required fees: $76. Tuition and fees vary according to degree level and program. *Financial support:* In 2010–11, 5 research assistantships with full tuition reimbursements, 1 teaching assistantship with full tuition reimbursement were awarded; fellowships with full tuition reimbursements, institutionally sponsored loans, traineeships, health care benefits, tuition waivers (full and partial), and unspecified assistantships also available. Financial award applicants required to submit FAFSA. *Faculty research:* Applied climatology, climate dynamics, statistical meteorology/climatology, synoptic meteorology, upper atmospheric science. *Unit head:* Director of Graduate Studies, 607-255-3034, Fax: 607-255-2106, E-mail: atmscigradfield@cornell.edu. *Application contact:* Graduate Field Assistant, 607-255-3034, Fax: 607-255-2106, E-mail: pmv2@cornell.edu.

Creighton University, Graduate School, College of Arts and Sciences, Program in Atmospheric Sciences, Omaha, NE 68178-0001. Offers MS. Part-time programs available. *Faculty:* 4 full-time (0 women). *Students:* 4 full-time (0 women), 2 part-time (0 women); includes 1 minority (Asian, non-Hispanic/Latino). Average age 25. 6 applicants, 100% accepted, 2 enrolled. In 2010, 4 master's awarded. *Degree requirements:* For master's, thesis optional. *Entrance requirements:* For master's, GRE General Test, 3 letters of recommendation. Additional exam requirements/recommendations for international students: Required—TOEFL (minimum score 550 paper-based; 213 computer-based; 80 iBT). *Application deadline:* For fall admission, 3/1 for domestic and international students. Application fee: $50. Electronic applications accepted. *Expenses:* Tuition: Full-time $12,168; part-time $676 per credit hour. Required fees: $131 per semester. Tuition and fees vary according to program. *Financial support:* In 2010–11, 1 research assistantship with full tuition reimbursement (averaging $14,000 per year), 3 teaching assistantships with full tuition reimbursements (averaging $10,698 per year) were awarded. Support available to part-time students. Financial award applicants required to submit FAFSA. *Unit head:* Dr. Joseph Zehnder, Chair, 402-280-2448, E-mail: zehnder@creighton.edu. *Application contact:* Taunya Plater, Senior Program Coordinator, 402-280-2870, Fax: 402-280-2899, E-mail: taunyaplater@creighton.edu.

George Mason University, College of Science, Department of Climate Dynamics, Fairfax, VA 22030. Offers PhD. *Faculty:* 14 full-time (4 women), 11 part-time/adjunct (4 women). *Students:* 11 full-time (4 women), 11 part-time (7 women); includes 1 minority (Hispanic/Latino), 15 international. Average age 32. 18 applicants, 61% accepted, 4 enrolled. *Entrance requirements:* Additional exam requirements/recommendations for international students: Required—TOEFL (minimum score 570 paper-based; 230 computer-based; 88 iBT). Application fee: $100. *Expenses:* Tuition, state resident: full-time $8192; part-time $440 per credit hour. Tuition, nonresident: full-time $22,952; part-time $1055 per credit hour. Required fees: $2364; $99 per credit hour. *Financial support:* In 2010–11, 20 students received support, including 3 fellowships (averaging $18,000 per year), 17 research assistantships (averaging $14,824 per year), 2 teaching assistantships (averaging $7,800 per year); career-related internships or fieldwork, Federal Work-Study, scholarships/grants, unspecified assistantships, and health care benefits (full-time research or teaching assistantship recipients) also available. Financial award applicants required to submit FAFSA. Total annual research expenditures: $1.6 million. *Unit head:* Dr. Jagadisn Shukla, Chairman, 703-993-1983. *Application contact:* Dr. Tim Born, Associate Dean for Graduate Programs, 703-993-4171, Fax: 703-993-9034, E-mail: tborn@gmu.edu.

Georgia Institute of Technology, Graduate Studies and Research, College of Sciences, School of Earth and Atmospheric Sciences, Atlanta, GA 30332-0340. Offers atmospheric chemistry, aerosols and clouds (MS, PhD); dynamics of weather and climate (MS, PhD); geochemistry (MS, PhD); geophysics (MS, PhD); oceanography (MS, PhD); paleoclimate (MS, PhD); planetary science (MS, PhD); remote sensing (MS, PhD). Part-time programs available. Terminal master's awarded for partial completion of doctoral program. *Degree requirements:* For master's, thesis or alternative; for doctorate, comprehensive exam, thesis/dissertation. *Entrance requirements:* For master's, GRE, letters of recommendation; for doctorate, GRE, academic transcripts, letters of recommendation, personal statement. Additional exam requirements/recommendations for international students: Required—TOEFL (minimum score 550 paper-based; 213 computer-based; 79 iBT). *Faculty research:* Geophysics; atmospheric chemistry, aerosols and clouds; dynamics of weather and climate; geochemistry; oceanography; paleoclimate; planetary science; remote sensing.

Hampton University, Graduate College, Department of Atmospheric and Planetary Sciences, Hampton, VA 23668. Offers atmospheric sciences (MS, PhD); planetary sciences (MS, PhD).

Hampton University, Graduate College, Department of Physics, Hampton, VA 23668. Offers atmospheric physics (MS, PhD); medical physics (MS, PhD); nuclear physics (MS, PhD); optical physics (MS, PhD). Part-time and evening/weekend programs available. Terminal master's awarded for partial completion of doctoral program. *Degree requirements:* For master's, thesis optional; for doctorate, thesis/dissertation, oral defense, qualifying exam. *Entrance*

requirements: For master's, GRE General Test; for doctorate, GRE General Test, minimum GPA of 3.0 or master's degree in physics or related field. *Faculty research:* Laser optics, remote sensing.

Howard University, Graduate School and School of Engineering and Computer Science, Department of Atmospheric Sciences, Washington, DC 20059-0002. Offers MS, PhD. Part-time programs available. Terminal master's awarded for partial completion of doctoral program. *Degree requirements:* For master's, thesis; for doctorate, one foreign language, comprehensive exam, thesis/dissertation. *Entrance requirements:* For master's, GRE General Test, minimum GPA of 3.0; for doctorate, GRE General Test, minimum GPA of 3.2. Additional exam requirements/recommendations for international students: Required—TOEFL (minimum score 550 paper-based; 213 computer-based). *Faculty research:* Atmospheric chemistry, climate, atmospheric radiation, gravity waves, aerosols, extraterrestrial atmospheres, turbulence.

Howard University, Graduate School, Department of Chemistry, Washington, DC 20059-0002. Offers analytical chemistry (MS, PhD); atmospheric (MS, PhD); biochemistry (MS, PhD); environmental (MS, PhD); inorganic chemistry (MS, PhD); organic chemistry (MS, PhD); physical chemistry (MS, PhD). Terminal master's awarded for partial completion of doctoral program. *Degree requirements:* For master's, comprehensive exam, thesis, teaching experience; for doctorate, comprehensive exam, thesis/dissertation, teaching experience. *Entrance requirements:* For master's, GRE General Test, minimum GPA of 2.7; for doctorate, GRE General Test, minimum GPA of 3.0. Additional exam requirements/recommendations for international students: Required—TOEFL. Electronic applications accepted. *Faculty research:* Synthetic organics, materials, natural products, mass spectrometry.

Massachusetts Institute of Technology, School of Science, Department of Earth, Atmospheric, and Planetary Sciences, Cambridge, MA 02139. Offers atmospheric chemistry (PhD, Sc D); atmospheric science (SM, PhD, Sc D); chemical oceanography (SM, PhD, Sc D); climate physics and chemistry (SM, PhD, Sc D); earth and planetary sciences (SM); geochemistry (PhD, Sc D); geology (PhD, Sc D); geophysics (PhD, Sc D); marine geology and geophysics (SM, PhD, Sc D); physical oceanography (SM, PhD, Sc D); planetary sciences (PhD, Sc D). *Faculty:* 36 full-time (7 women). *Students:* 165 full-time (86 women); includes 17 minority (2 Black or African American, non-Hispanic/Latino; 2 American Indian or Alaska Native, non-Hispanic/Latino; 5 Asian, non-Hispanic/Latino; 5 Hispanic/Latino; 3 Two or more races, non-Hispanic/Latino), 50 international. Average age 27. 227 applicants, 33% accepted, 38 enrolled. In 2010, 12 master's, 26 doctorates awarded. Terminal master's awarded for partial completion of doctoral program. *Degree requirements:* For master's, thesis; for doctorate, comprehensive exam, thesis/dissertation. *Entrance requirements:* For master's, GRE General Test; for doctorate, GRE General Test, GRE Subject Test (chemistry or physics for planetary science area). Additional exam requirements/recommendations for international students: Required—TOEFL (minimum score 577 paper-based; 233 computer-based; 91 iBT), IELTS (minimum score 7). *Application deadline:* For fall admission, 1/5 for domestic and international students; for spring admission, 11/1 for domestic and international students. Application fee: $75. Electronic applications accepted. *Expenses:* Tuition: Full-time $38,940; part-time $605 per unit. Required fees: $272. *Financial support:* In 2010–11, 123 students received support, including 62 fellowships with tuition reimbursements available (averaging $30,852 per year), 88 research assistantships with tuition reimbursements available (averaging $30,258 per year), 13 teaching assistantships with tuition reimbursements available (averaging $30,323 per year); Federal Work-Study, institutionally sponsored loans, scholarships/grants, health care benefits, and unspecified assistantships also available. *Faculty research:* Formation, dynamics and evolution of planetary systems; origin, composition, structure and dynamics of the atmospheres, oceans, surfaces and interiors of the Earth and other planets; evolution and interaction of the physical, chemical, geological and biological components of the Earth system; characterization of past, present and potential future climates and the causes and consequences of climate change; interplay of energy and the environment. Total annual research expenditures: $24.8 million. *Unit head:* Prof. Maria Zuber, Department Head, 617-253-2127, Fax: 617-253-8298, E-mail: eapsinfo@mit.edu. *Application contact:* EAPS Education Office, 617-253-3381, Fax: 617-253-8298, E-mail: eapsinfo@mit.edu.

McGill University, Faculty of Graduate and Postdoctoral Studies, Faculty of Science, Department of Atmospheric and Oceanic Sciences, Montréal, QC H3A 2T5, Canada. Offers atmospheric science (M Sc, PhD); physical oceanography (M Sc, PhD). PhD program in physical oceanography offered jointly with Université Laval.

Michigan Technological University, Graduate School, College of Sciences and Arts, Atmospheric Sciences Program, Houghton, MI 49931. Offers PhD. *Degree requirements:* For doctorate, comprehensive exam, thesis/dissertation. *Entrance requirements:* For doctorate, GRE, minimum GPA of 3.0. Additional exam requirements/recommendations for international students: Required—TOEFL (minimum score 600 paper-based). *Faculty research:* Volcano/atmospheric interactions, atmospheric chemistry, atmospheric physics, atmosphere-biosphere interactions.

Mississippi State University, College of Arts and Sciences, Department of Geosciences, Mississippi State, MS 39762. Offers earth and atmospheric science (PhD); geoscience (MS). MA program is only available online. Postbaccalaureate distance learning degree programs offered (no on-campus study). *Faculty:* 20 full-time (3 women), 1 part-time/adjunct (0 women). *Students:* 65 full-time (16 women), 258 part-time (142 women); includes 35 minority (12 Black or African American, non-Hispanic/Latino; 6 American Indian or Alaska Native, non-Hispanic/Latino; 4 Asian, non-Hispanic/Latino; 12 Hispanic/Latino; 1 Two or more races, non-Hispanic/Latino), 8 international. Average age 36. 204 applicants, 88% accepted, 146 enrolled. In 2010, 107 master's awarded. *Degree requirements:* For master's, thesis (for some programs), comprehensive oral or written exam. *Entrance requirements:* For master's, GRE (for on-campus applicants), minimum undergraduate GPA of 2.75. Additional exam requirements/recommendations for international students: Required—TOEFL (minimum score 475 paper-based; 153 computer-based; 53 iBT); Recommended—IELTS (minimum score 4.5). *Application deadline:* For fall admission, 7/1 for domestic students, 5/1 for international students; for spring admission, 11/1 for domestic students, 9/1 for international students. Applications are processed on a rolling basis. Application fee: $40. Electronic applications accepted. *Expenses:* Tuition, state resident: full-time $2730.50; part-time $304 per credit hour. Tuition, nonresident: full-time $6901; part-time $767 per credit hour. *Financial support:* In 2010–11, 13 research assistantships with full tuition reimbursements (averaging $21,646 per year), 24 teaching assistantships with full tuition reimbursements (averaging $13,140 per year) were awarded; Federal Work-Study, institutionally sponsored loans, scholarships/grants, tuition waivers (partial), and unspecified assistantships also available. Financial award application deadline: 4/1; financial award applicants required to submit FAFSA. *Faculty research:* Climatology, hydrogeology, sedimentology, meteorology. Total annual research expenditures: $5.2 million. *Unit head:* Dr. Darrel Schmitz, Professor and Head, 662-325-3915, Fax: 662-325-9423, E-mail: schmitz@geosci.msstate.edu. *Application contact:* Dr. Christopher P. Dewey, Associate Professor/Graduate Coordinator, 662-325-2909, Fax: 662-325-9423, E-mail: cpd4@msstate.edu.

New Mexico Institute of Mining and Technology, Graduate Studies, Department of Physics, Socorro, NM 87801. Offers astrophysics (MS, PhD); atmospheric physics (MS, PhD); instrumentation (MS); mathematical physics (PhD). *Degree requirements:* For master's, thesis optional; for doctorate, thesis/dissertation. *Entrance requirements:* For master's, GRE General Test; for doctorate, GRE General Test, GRE Subject Test. Additional exam requirements/recommendations for international students: Required—TOEFL (minimum score 540 paper-based; 207 computer-based). *Faculty research:* Cloud physics, stellar and extragalactic processes.

North Carolina State University, Graduate School, College of Physical and Mathematical Sciences, Department of Marine, Earth, and Atmospheric Sciences, Raleigh, NC 27695. Offers marine, earth, and atmospheric sciences (MS, PhD); meteorology (MS, PhD); oceanography (MS, PhD). PhD offered jointly with The University of North Carolina Wilmington. Terminal master's awarded for partial completion of doctoral program. *Degree requirements:* For master's, thesis (for some programs), final oral exam; for doctorate, comprehensive exam, thesis/dissertation, final oral exam, preliminary oral and written exams. *Entrance requirements:* For master's, GRE General Test, minimum GPA of 3.0; for doctorate, GRE General Test, GRE Subject Test (for disciplines in biological oceanography and geology), minimum GPA of 3.0. Additional exam requirements/recommendations for international students: Required—TOEFL (minimum score 550 paper-based). Electronic applications accepted. *Faculty research:* Boundary layer and air quality meteorology; climate and mesoscale dynamics; biological, chemical, geological, and physical oceanography; hard rock, soft rock, environmental, and paleo-geology.

Northern Arizona University, Graduate College, College of Engineering, Forestry and Natural Sciences, School of Earth Sciences and Environmental Sustainability, Flagstaff, AZ 86011. Offers climate science and solutions (MS); earth science (MS); environmental sciences and policy (MS); geology (MS). *Faculty:* 27 full-time (7 women). *Students:* 50 full-time (22 women), 18 part-time (9 women); includes 4 minority (1 American Indian or Alaska Native, non-Hispanic/Latino; 1 Asian, non-Hispanic/Latino; 2 Hispanic/Latino), 2 international. 113 applicants, 31% accepted, 27 enrolled. In 2010, 21 master's awarded. *Degree requirements:* For master's, comprehensive exam (for some programs), thesis (for some programs). *Entrance requirements:* Additional exam requirements/recommendations for international students: Required—TOEFL (minimum score 550 paper-based; 213 computer-based; 80 iBT), IELTS (minimum score 7). *Application deadline:* For fall admission, 2/1 priority date for domestic and international students. Applications are processed on a rolling basis. Application fee: $65. Electronic applications accepted. *Financial support:* In 2010–11, 6 fellowships, 7 research assistantships with partial tuition reimbursements (averaging $12,866 per year), 28 teaching assistantships with partial tuition reimbursements (averaging $12,477 per year) were awarded; career-related internships or fieldwork, Federal Work-Study, scholarships/grants, health care benefits, tuition waivers (full and partial), and unspecified assistantships also available. Financial award applicants required to submit FAFSA. *Unit head:* Dr. Abe Springer, Director, 928-523-7198. *Application contact:* Dr. Abe Springer, Director, 928-523-7198.

The Ohio State University, Graduate School, College of Arts and Sciences, Division of Social and Behavioral Sciences, Department of Geography, Columbus, OH 43210. Offers atmospheric sciences (MS, PhD); geography (MA, PhD). *Faculty:* 24. *Students:* 47 full-time (17 women), 26 part-time (9 women); includes 1 Asian, non-Hispanic/Latino, 21 international. Average age 29. In 2010, 14 master's, 10 doctorates awarded. *Degree requirements:* For doctorate, variable foreign language requirement, thesis/dissertation. *Entrance requirements:* Additional exam requirements/recommendations for international students: Recommended—TOEFL (minimum score 600 paper-based; 250 computer-based). *Application deadline:* For fall admission, 8/15 priority date for domestic students, 7/1 priority date for international students; for winter admission, 12/1 priority date for domestic students, 11/1 priority date for international students; for spring admission, 3/1 priority date for domestic students, 2/1 priority date for international students. Applications are processed on a rolling basis. Application fee: $40 ($50 for international students). Electronic applications accepted. *Expenses:* Tuition, state resident: full-time $10,605. Tuition, nonresident: full-time $26,535. Tuition and fees vary according to course load and program. *Financial support:* Fellowships, research assistantships, teaching assistantships, Federal Work-Study and institutionally sponsored loans available. Support available to part-time students. *Unit head:* Morton O'Kelly, Chair, 614-292-8744, Fax: 614-292-6213, E-mail: okelly.1@osu.edu. *Application contact:* 614-292-9444, Fax: 614-292-3895, E-mail: domestic.grad@osu.edu.

Oregon State University, Graduate School, College of Oceanic and Atmospheric Sciences, Program in Atmospheric Sciences, Corvallis, OR 97331. Offers MA, MS, PhD. Terminal master's awarded for partial completion of doctoral program. *Degree requirements:* For master's, variable foreign language requirement, thesis, qualifying exams; for doctorate, thesis/dissertation, qualifying exams. *Entrance requirements:* For master's and doctorate, GRE General Test, minimum GPA of 3.0 in last 90 hours of course work. Additional exam requirements/recommendations for international students: Required—TOEFL. *Faculty research:* Planetary atmospheres, boundary layer dynamics, climate, statistical meteorology, satellite meteorology, atmospheric chemistry.

Princeton University, Graduate School, Department of Geosciences, Program in Atmospheric and Oceanic Sciences, Princeton, NJ 08544-1019. Offers PhD. *Degree requirements:* For doctorate, one foreign language, thesis/dissertation. *Entrance requirements:* For doctorate, GRE General Test, GRE Subject Test. Additional exam requirements/recommendations for international students: Required—TOEFL (minimum score 600 paper-based; 250 computer-based). Electronic applications accepted. *Faculty research:* Climate dynamics, middle atmosphere dynamics and chemistry, oceanic circulation, marine geochemistry, numerical modeling.

Purdue University, Graduate School, College of Science, Department of Earth and Atmospheric Sciences, West Lafayette, IN 47907. Offers MS, PhD. *Degree requirements:* For master's, thesis; for doctorate, one foreign language, thesis/dissertation. *Entrance requirements:* For master's and doctorate, GRE General Test. Additional exam requirements/recommendations for international students: Required—TOEFL. Electronic applications accepted. *Faculty research:* Geology, geophysics, hydrogeology, paleoclimatology, environmental science.

Rutgers, The State University of New Jersey, New Brunswick, Graduate School-New Brunswick, Department of Environmental Sciences, Piscataway, NJ 08854-8097. Offers air pollution and resources (MS, PhD); aquatic biology (MS, PhD); aquatic chemistry (MS, PhD); atmospheric science (MS, PhD); chemistry and physics of aerosol and hydrosol systems (MS, PhD); environmental chemistry (MS, PhD); environmental microbiology (MS, PhD); environmental toxicology (PhD); exposure assessment (PhD); fate and effects of pollutants (MS, PhD); pollution prevention and control (MS, PhD); water and wastewater treatment (MS, PhD); water resources (MS, PhD). Terminal master's awarded for partial completion of doctoral program. *Degree requirements:* For master's, comprehensive exam, thesis or alternative, oral final exam; for doctorate, comprehensive exam, thesis/dissertation, thesis defense, qualifying exam. *Entrance requirements:* For master's and doctorate, GRE General Test. Additional exam requirements/recommendations for international students: Required—TOEFL. Electronic applications accepted. *Expenses:* Tuition, state resident: full-time $7200; part-time $600 per credit. Tuition, nonresident: full-time $11,124; part-time $927 per credit. *Faculty research:* Biological waste treatment; contaminant fate and transport; air, soil and water quality.

South Dakota School of Mines and Technology, Graduate Division, PhD Program in Atmospheric and Environmental Sciences, Rapid City, SD 57701-3995. Offers PhD. Program offered jointly with South Dakota State University. *Degree requirements:* For doctorate, comprehensive exam, thesis/dissertation. *Entrance requirements:* For doctorate, GRE General Test, GRE Subject Test. Additional exam requirements/recommendations for international students: Required—TOEFL, TWE. Electronic applications accepted.

South Dakota School of Mines and Technology, Graduate Division, Program in Atmospheric Sciences, Rapid City, SD 57701-3995. Offers MS. Part-time programs available. *Degree requirements:* For master's, thesis. *Entrance requirements:* Additional exam requirements/recommendations for international students: Required—TOEFL, TWE. Electronic applications accepted. *Faculty research:* Hailstorm observations and numerical modeling, microbursts and lightning, radiative transfer, remote sensing.

Atmospheric Sciences

Stony Brook University, State University of New York, Graduate School, School of Marine and Atmospheric Sciences, Institute for Terrestrial and Planetary Atmospheres, Program in Atmospheric Sciences, Stony Brook, NY 11794. Offers MS, PhD. Evening/weekend programs available. *Students:* 106 full-time (62 women), 12 part-time (7 women); includes 1 Black or African American, non-Hispanic/Latino; 2 Asian, non-Hispanic/Latino; 6 Hispanic/Latino, 37 international. 156 applicants, 35% accepted, 21 enrolled. In 2010, 15 master's, 11 doctorates awarded. *Degree requirements:* For doctorate, one foreign language, comprehensive exam, thesis/dissertation. *Entrance requirements:* For master's, GRE, minimum GPA of 3.0, 3 letters of recommendation; for doctorate, GRE, official transcripts, minimum GPA of 3.0, 3 letters of recommendation. Additional exam requirements/recommendations for international students: Required—TOEFL (minimum score 600 paper-based; 213 computer-based). *Application deadline:* For fall admission, 1/15 priority date for domestic students; for spring admission, 10/1 priority date for domestic students. Application fee: $100. Electronic applications accepted. *Expenses:* Tuition, state resident: full-time $8370; part-time $349 per credit. Tuition, nonresident: full-time $13,780; part-time $574 per credit. Required fees: $994. *Financial support:* In 2010–11, 45 research assistantships, 16 teaching assistantships were awarded; fellowships, career-related internships or fieldwork also available. *Unit head:* Minghua Zhang, Director, 631-632-8318. *Application contact:* Dr. Glenn R. Lopez, Assistant Director, 631-632-8660, Fax: 631-632-8200, E-mail: glopez@notes.cc.sunysb.edu.

Texas Tech University, Graduate School, College of Arts and Sciences, Department of Geosciences, Lubbock, TX 79409. Offers atmospheric science (MS); geosciences (MS, PhD). Part-time programs available. *Faculty:* 17 full-time (2 women), 1 part-time/adjunct (0 women). *Students:* 41 full-time (11 women), 18 part-time (6 women); includes 1 Black or African American, non-Hispanic/Latino; 5 Hispanic/Latino, 9 international. Average age 27. 81 applicants, 22% accepted, 15 enrolled. In 2010, 14 master's, 2 doctorates awarded. *Degree requirements:* For master's, thesis or alternative; for doctorate, comprehensive exam, thesis/dissertation. *Entrance requirements:* For master's and doctorate, GRE General Test. Additional exam requirements/recommendations for international students: Required—TOEFL (minimum score 550 paper-based; 213 computer-based; 79 iBT). *Application deadline:* For fall admission, 6/1 priority date for domestic students, 1/15 priority date for international students; for spring admission, 9/1 priority date for domestic students, 6/15 priority date for international students. Applications are processed on a rolling basis. Application fee: $50 ($75 for international students). Electronic applications accepted. *Expenses:* Tuition, state resident: full-time $5495.76; part-time $228.99 per credit hour. Tuition, nonresident: full-time $12,936; part-time $538.99 per credit hour. Required fees: $2674; $36 per credit hour. $905 per semester. *Financial support:* In 2010–11, 30 students received support, including 4 research assistantships with partial tuition reimbursements available (averaging $5,780 per year), 5 teaching assistantships with partial tuition reimbursements available (averaging $2,352 per year). Financial award application deadline: 4/15; financial award applicants required to submit FAFSA. *Faculty research:* Sedimentology and paleontology, geophysics, geochemistry, geospatial technology, hurricanes and severe storms. Total annual research expenditures: $955,317. *Unit head:* Dr. Calvin Barnes, Chairman, 806-742-3102, Fax: 806-742-0100, E-mail: cal.barnes@ttu.edu. *Application contact:* Dr. Seiichi Nagihara, Associate Professor, 806-742-3102, Fax: 806-724-0100, E-mail: seiichi.nagihara@ttu.edu.

Université du Québec à Montréal, Graduate Programs, Program in Earth and Atmospheric Sciences, Montréal, QC H3C 3P8, Canada. Offers atmospheric sciences (M Sc); Earth and atmospheric sciences (PhD); Earth science (M Sc); meteorology (PhD, Diploma). PhD programs offered jointly with McGill University. Part-time programs available. *Degree requirements:* For master's, thesis. *Entrance requirements:* For master's and Diploma, appropriate bachelor's degree or equivalent, proficiency in French; for doctorate, appropriate master's degree or equivalent, proficiency in French.

University at Albany, State University of New York, College of Arts and Sciences, Department of Earth and Atmospheric Sciences, Albany, NY 12222-0001. Offers atmospheric science (MS, PhD); geology (MS, PhD). *Degree requirements:* For master's, one foreign language, comprehensive exam, thesis; for doctorate, 2 foreign languages, comprehensive exam, thesis/dissertation, oral exams. *Entrance requirements:* For master's and doctorate, GRE General Test. Additional exam requirements/recommendations for international students: Required—TOEFL (minimum score 550 paper-based; 213 computer-based). Electronic applications accepted. *Faculty research:* Environmental geochemistry, tectonics, mesoscale meteorology, atmospheric chemistry.

The University of Alabama in Huntsville, School of Graduate Studies, College of Science, Department of Atmospheric and Environmental Science, Huntsville, AL 35899. Offers MS, PhD. Part-time and evening/weekend programs available. *Faculty:* 9 full-time (0 women), 3 part-time/adjunct (2 women). *Students:* 26 full-time (12 women), 7 part-time (3 women); includes 1 minority (Black or African American, non-Hispanic/Latino), 7 international. Average age 27. 30 applicants, 53% accepted, 10 enrolled. In 2010, 11 master's, 5 doctorates awarded. *Degree requirements:* For master's, comprehensive exam, thesis or alternative, oral and written exams; for doctorate, comprehensive exam, thesis/dissertation, oral and written exams. *Entrance requirements:* For master's, GRE General Test, minimum GPA of 3.0; sequence of courses in calculus (including the calculus of vector-valued functions); courses in linear algebra and ordinary differential equations; two semesters each of chemistry and calculus-based physics; proficiency in at least one high-level computer programming language; for doctorate, GRE General Test, minimum GPA of 3.0. Additional exam requirements/recommendations for international students: Required—TOEFL (minimum score 550 paper-based; 213 computer-based; 62 iBT). *Application deadline:* For fall admission, 7/15 for domestic students, 4/1 for international students; for spring admission, 11/30 for domestic students, 9/1 for international students. Applications are processed on a rolling basis. Application fee: $40 ($50 for international students). Electronic applications accepted. *Expenses:* Tuition, state resident: full-time $7250; part-time $407.75 per credit hour. Tuition, nonresident: full-time $17,358; part-time $970.05 per credit hour. Required fees: $246.80 per semester. Tuition and fees vary according to course load and program. *Financial support:* In 2010–11, 25 students received support, including 24 research assistantships with full and partial tuition reimbursements available (averaging $14,325 per year), 1 teaching assistantship with full and partial tuition reimbursement available (averaging $13,500 per year); career-related internships or fieldwork, Federal Work-Study, institutionally sponsored loans, scholarships/grants, health care benefits, tuition waivers, and unspecified assistantships also available. Support available to part-time students. Financial award application deadline: 4/1; financial award applicants required to submit FAFSA. *Faculty research:* Satellite remote sensing, severe weather, mesoscale modeling, atmospheric chemistry, data assimilation. Total annual research expenditures: $9.8 million. *Unit head:* Dr. Sundar Christopher, Chair, 256-922-7872, Fax: 256-922-7755, E-mail: sundar@nsstc.uah.edu. *Application contact:* Kathy Biggs, Graduate Studies Admissions Manager, 256-824-6199, Fax: 256-824-6405, E-mail: deangrad@uah.edu.

University of Alaska Fairbanks, College of Natural Sciences and Mathematics, Program in Atmospheric Science, Fairbanks, AK 99775-7320. Offers MS, PhD. Part-time programs available. *Faculty:* 10 full-time (3 women), 1 part-time/adjunct (0 women). *Students:* 13 full-time (7 women), 3 part-time (1 woman); includes 2 minority (1 Asian, non-Hispanic/Latino; 1 Native Hawaiian or other Pacific Islander, non-Hispanic/Latino), 7 international. Average age 32. 20 applicants, 10% accepted, 2 enrolled. In 2010, 1 master's, 2 doctorates awarded. *Degree requirements:* For master's, comprehensive exam, thesis, oral defense; for doctorate, comprehensive exam, thesis/dissertation, oral defense. *Entrance requirements:* Additional exam requirements/recommendations for international students: Required—TOEFL (minimum score 550 paper-based; 213 computer-based; 80 iBT). *Application deadline:* For fall admission, 6/1 for domestic students, 3/1 for international students; for spring admission, 10/15 for domestic students, 9/1 for international students. Applications are processed on a rolling basis. Application fee: $60. Electronic applications accepted. *Expenses:* Tuition, state resident: full-time $5688; part-time $316 per credit. Tuition, nonresident: full-time $11,628; part-time $646 per credit. Required fees: $289 per semester. Tuition and fees vary according to course load and reciprocity agreements. *Financial support:* In 2010–11, 13 research assistantships with tuition reimbursements (averaging $15,229 per year) were awarded; fellowships with tuition reimbursements, teaching assistantships with tuition reimbursements, Federal Work-Study, scholarships/grants, health care benefits, and unspecified assistantships also available. Support available to part-time students. Financial award application deadline: 2/15; financial award applicants required to submit FAFSA. *Faculty research:* Sea ice, climate modeling, atmospheric chemistry, global change, cloud and aerosol physics. *Unit head:* Dr. Nicole Moelders, Program Chair, 907-474-7368, Fax: 907-474-7379, E-mail: atmos@gi.alaska.edu. *Application contact:* Dr. Nicole Moelders, Program Chair, 907-474-7368, Fax: 907-474-7379, E-mail: atmos@gi.alaska.edu.

The University of Arizona, College of Science, Department of Atmospheric Sciences, Tucson, AZ 85721. Offers MS, PhD. *Faculty:* 7 full-time (2 women). *Students:* 18 full-time (6 women), 10 part-time (5 women); includes 2 Hispanic/Latino; 1 Two or more races, non-Hispanic/Latino, 8 international. Average age 29. 34 applicants, 18% accepted, 6 enrolled. In 2010, 5 master's, 1 doctorate awarded. *Degree requirements:* For master's, thesis or alternative; for doctorate, comprehensive exam, thesis/dissertation. *Entrance requirements:* For master's, GRE General Test, 3 letters of recommendation; for doctorate, GRE General Test, 3 letters of recommendation, statement of purpose. Additional exam requirements/recommendations for international students: Required—TOEFL (minimum score 550 paper-based; 213 computer-based; 79 iBT). *Application deadline:* For fall admission, 2/1 for domestic students, 12/1 for international students. Applications are processed on a rolling basis. Application fee: $75. Electronic applications accepted. *Expenses:* Tuition, state resident: full-time $7692. *Financial support:* In 2010–11, 12 research assistantships with full tuition reimbursements (averaging $20,979 per year), 11 teaching assistantships with full tuition reimbursements (averaging $20,979 per year) were awarded; scholarships/grants, health care benefits, tuition waivers (full), and unspecified assistantships also available. *Faculty research:* Climate dynamics, radiative transfer and remote sensing, atmospheric chemistry, atmosphere dynamics, atmospheric electricity. Total annual research expenditures: $2.4 million. *Unit head:* Eric A. Betterton, Head, 520-621-6831, E-mail: betterton@atmo.arizona.edu. *Application contact:* Sonya Flores-Basurto, Information Contact, 520-621-6831, Fax: 520-621-6833, E-mail: sfloresb@email.arizona.edu.

The University of British Columbia, Faculty of Science, Department of Earth and Ocean Sciences, Vancouver, BC V6T 1Z4, Canada. Offers atmospheric science (M Sc, PhD); geological engineering (M Eng, MA Sc, PhD); geological sciences (M Sc, PhD); geophysics (M Sc, MA Sc, PhD); oceanography (M Sc, PhD). *Degree requirements:* For master's, thesis (for some programs); for doctorate, comprehensive exam, thesis/dissertation. *Entrance requirements:* Additional exam requirements/recommendations for international students: Required—TOEFL (minimum score 600 paper-based; 250 computer-based; 100 iBT). Electronic applications accepted. Tuition charges are reported in Canadian dollars. *Expenses:* Tuition, area resident: Full-time $4179 Canadian dollars. International tuition: $7344 Canadian dollars full-time. *Faculty research:* Oceans and atmosphere, environmental earth science, hydro geology, mineral deposits, geophysics.

University of California, Davis, Graduate Studies, Graduate Group in Atmospheric Sciences, Davis, CA 95616. Offers MS, PhD. *Degree requirements:* For master's, comprehensive exam or thesis; for doctorate, thesis/dissertation, 3 part qualifying exam. *Entrance requirements:* For master's and doctorate, GRE General Test, minimum GPA of 3.0. Additional exam requirements/recommendations for international students: Required—TOEFL (minimum score 550 paper-based; 213 computer-based). Electronic applications accepted. *Faculty research:* Air quality, biometeorology, climate dynamics, boundary layer large-scale dynamics.

University of California, Los Angeles, Graduate Division, College of Letters and Science, Department of Atmospheric Sciences, Los Angeles, CA 90095. Offers MS, PhD. *Faculty:* 16 full-time (3 women). *Students:* 47 full-time (23 women); includes 10 minority (8 Asian, non-Hispanic/Latino; 2 Hispanic/Latino), 21 international. Average age 26. 68 applicants, 59% accepted, 16 enrolled. In 2010, 3 master's, 3 doctorates awarded. Terminal master's awarded for partial completion of doctoral program. *Degree requirements:* For master's, comprehensive exam or thesis; for doctorate, thesis/dissertation, oral and written qualifying exams. *Entrance requirements:* For master's, GRE General Test, minimum GPA of 3.0; for doctorate, GRE General Test, minimum undergraduate GPA of 3.0. *Application deadline:* For fall admission, 12/15 for domestic and international students. Application fee: $70 ($90 for international students). Electronic applications accepted. *Financial support:* In 2010–11, 31 fellowships with full and partial tuition reimbursements, 35 research assistantships with full and partial tuition reimbursements, 16 teaching assistantships with full and partial tuition reimbursements were awarded; Federal Work-Study, institutionally sponsored loans, scholarships/grants, health care benefits, tuition waivers (full and partial), and unspecified assistantships also available. Financial award application deadline: 3/1; financial award applicants required to submit FAFSA. *Unit head:* Dr. David C. Neelin, Chair, 310-206-3734, E-mail: neelin@atmos.ucla.edu. *Application contact:* Departmental Office, 310-825-1217, E-mail: studentinfo@atmos.ucla.edu.

University of Chicago, Division of the Physical Sciences, Department of the Geophysical Sciences, Chicago, IL 60637-1513. Offers atmospheric sciences (SM, PhD); earth sciences (SM, PhD); paleobiology (PhD); planetary and space sciences (SM, PhD). *Faculty:* 21 full-time (3 women). *Students:* 37 full-time (23 women); includes 1 Hispanic/Latino, 14 international. Average age 27. 63 applicants, 35% accepted, 9 enrolled. In 2010, 2 master's, 7 doctorates awarded. Terminal master's awarded for partial completion of doctoral program. *Degree requirements:* For master's, thesis, seminar; for doctorate, variable foreign language requirement, comprehensive exam, thesis/dissertation. *Entrance requirements:* For doctorate, GRE General Test. Additional exam requirements/recommendations for international students: Required—TOEFL (minimum score 600 paper-based; 250 computer-based; 96 iBT), IELTS (minimum score 7). *Application deadline:* For fall admission, 1/10 for domestic and international students. Application fee: $55. Electronic applications accepted. *Financial support:* In 2010–11, research assistantships with full tuition reimbursements (averaging $20,511 per year), teaching assistantships with full tuition reimbursements (averaging $21,915 per year) were awarded; fellowships, Federal Work-Study, institutionally sponsored loans, scholarships/grants, tuition waivers (partial), and unspecified assistantships also available. Financial award application deadline: 1/9. *Faculty research:* Climatology, evolutionary paleontology, petrology, geochemistry, oceanic sciences. *Unit head:* Dr. Michael Foote, Chairman, 773-702-8102, Fax: 773-702-9505. *Application contact:* David J. Taylor, Graduate Student Services Coordinator, 773-702-8180, Fax: 773-702-9505, E-mail: info@geosci.uchicago.edu.

University of Colorado Boulder, Graduate School, College of Arts and Sciences, Department of Atmospheric and Oceanic Sciences, Boulder, CO 80309. Offers MS, PhD. *Faculty:* 13 full-time (6 women). *Students:* 65 full-time (30 women), 2 part-time (1 woman); includes 8 minority (1 Black or African American, non-Hispanic/Latino; 1 American Indian or Alaska Native, non-Hispanic/Latino; 3 Asian, non-Hispanic/Latino; 3 Hispanic/Latino), 14 international. Average age 29. 82 applicants, 11 enrolled. In 2010, 9 master's, 7 doctorates awarded. *Entrance requirements:* For master's, minimum undergraduate GPA of 3.0. *Application deadline:* For fall admission, 2/1 for domestic students, 12/1 for international students; for spring admission, 10/1 for domestic and international students. *Financial support:* In 2010–11, 11 fellowships (averaging $2,321 per year), 40 research assistantships (averaging $16,795 per year) were awarded. *Faculty research:* Large-scale dynamics of the ocean and the atmosphere, air-sea interaction, radiative transfer and remote sensing of the ocean and the atmosphere, sea ice and its role in climate. Total annual research expenditures: $19.4 million.

University of Guelph, Graduate Studies, Ontario Agricultural College, Department of Land Resource Science, Guelph, ON N1G 2W1, Canada. Offers atmospheric science (M Sc, PhD); environmental and agricultural earth sciences (M Sc, PhD); land resources management (M Sc, PhD); soil science (M Sc, PhD). Part-time programs available. *Degree requirements:* For master's, thesis (for some programs), research project (non-thesis track); for doctorate, comprehensive exam, thesis/dissertation. *Entrance requirements:* For master's, minimum B-average during previous 2 years of course work; for doctorate, minimum B average during previous 2 years of course work. Additional exam requirements/recommendations for international students: Required—TOEFL (minimum score 550 paper-based; 213 computer-based). Electronic applications accepted. *Faculty research:* Soil science, environmental earth science, land resource management.

University of Houston, College of Natural Sciences and Mathematics, Department of Earth and Atmospheric Sciences, Houston, TX 77204. Offers atmospheric science (PhD); geology (MA, PhD); geophysics (PhD). Part-time programs available. *Faculty:* 23 full-time (4 women), 5 part-time/adjunct (1 woman). *Students:* 149 full-time (44 women), 88 part-time (27 women); includes 10 Black or African American, non-Hispanic/Latino; 9 Asian, non-Hispanic/Latino; 15 Hispanic/Latino, 97 international. Average age 31. 198 applicants, 71% accepted, 69 enrolled. In 2010, 33 master's, 6 doctorates awarded. *Degree requirements:* For master's, thesis; for doctorate, comprehensive exam, thesis/dissertation. *Entrance requirements:* For master's and doctorate, GRE General Test . Additional exam requirements/recommendations for international students: Required—TOEFL (minimum score 550 paper-based; 213 computer-based; 79 iBT), IELTS (minimum score 6.5). *Application deadline:* For fall admission, 7/1 for domestic students, 4/1 for international students; for spring admission, 12/1 for domestic students, 10/1 for international students. Applications are processed on a rolling basis. Application fee: $0 ($75 for international students). Electronic applications accepted. *Expenses:* Tuition, state resident: full-time $8592; part-time $358 per credit hour. Tuition, nonresident: full-time $16,032; part-time $668 per credit hour. Required fees: $2889. Tuition and fees vary according to course load and program. *Financial support:* In 2010–11, 6 fellowships with partial tuition reimbursements (averaging $11,668 per year), 19 research assistantships with partial tuition reimbursements (averaging $13,600 per year), 9 teaching assistantships with partial tuition reimbursements (averaging $13,736 per year) were awarded; career-related internships or fieldwork, Federal Work-Study, institutionally sponsored loans, scholarships/grants, health care benefits, and unspecified assistantships also available. Support available to part-time students. Financial award application deadline: 2/1. *Faculty research:* Atmospherics sciences, seismic and solid earth geophysics, tectonics, environmental hydrochemistry, carbonates, micropaleontology, structure and tectonics, petroleum geology. *Unit head:* Dr. John Casey, Chairman, 713-743-3399, Fax: 713-748-7906, E-mail: jfcasey@uh.edu. *Application contact:* Sylvia Marshall, Advising Assistant, 713-743-3401, Fax: 713-748-7906, E-mail: smarshall@uh.edu.

University of Illinois at Urbana–Champaign, Graduate College, College of Liberal Arts and Sciences, School of Earth, Society and Environment, Department of Atmospheric Sciences, Champaign, IL 61820. Offers MS, PhD. *Faculty:* 11 full-time (2 women). *Students:* 38 full-time (23 women), 12 part-time (2 women); includes 1 Hispanic/Latino; 1 Two or more races, non-Hispanic/Latino, 17 international. 80 applicants, 15% accepted, 9 enrolled. In 2010, 12 master's, 4 doctorates awarded. *Entrance requirements:* For master's and doctorate, GRE General Test, minimum GPA of 3.0. Additional exam requirements/recommendations for international students: Required—TOEFL. *Application deadline:* Applications are processed on a rolling basis. Application fee: $75 ($90 for international students). Electronic applications accepted. *Financial support:* In 2010–11, 1 fellowship, 44 research assistantships, 20 teaching assistantships were awarded; tuition waivers (full and partial) also available. *Unit head:* Robert Rauber, Head, 217-333-2835, Fax: 217-244-4393, E-mail: r-rauber@illinois.edu. *Application contact:* Nena L. Richards, Office Administrator, 217-333-2046, Fax: 217-244-4393, E-mail: nenar@illinois.edu.

The University of Kansas, Graduate Studies, College of Liberal Arts and Sciences, Department of Geography, Lawrence, KS 66045-7613. Offers atmospheric science (MS); geography (MA, PhD); MUP/MA. Part-time programs available. *Faculty:* 23 full-time (4 women). *Students:* 75 full-time (28 women), 12 part-time (3 women); includes 5 minority (1 Black or African American, non-Hispanic/Latino; 3 American Indian or Alaska Native, non-Hispanic/Latino; 1 Hispanic/Latino), 12 international. Average age 32. 71 applicants, 49% accepted, 20 enrolled. In 2010, 9 master's, 9 doctorates awarded. *Degree requirements:* For master's, comprehensive exam, thesis, thesis defense; for doctorate, one foreign language, comprehensive exam, thesis/dissertation, dissertation defense. *Entrance requirements:* For master's and doctorate, GRE General Test, 3 letters of reference, transcripts, statement of interests. Additional exam requirements/recommendations for international students: Required—TOEFL. *Application deadline:* For fall admission, 1/15 priority date for domestic and international students; for spring admission, 11/1 for domestic students, 10/1 for international students. Applications are processed on a rolling basis. Application fee: $55 ($65 for international students). Electronic applications accepted. *Expenses:* Tuition, state resident: full-time $7092; part-time $295.50 per credit hour. Tuition, nonresident: full-time $16,590; part-time $691.25 per credit hour. Required fees: $858; $71.49 per credit hour. Tuition and fees vary according to course load, campus/location and program. *Financial support:* Fellowships with full tuition reimbursements, research assistantships with full tuition reimbursements, teaching assistantships with full and partial tuition reimbursements, unspecified assistantships available. Financial award application deadline: 1/15. *Faculty research:* Physical geography, techniques (cartography, GIS, remote sensing), cultural/regional geography, atmospheric science. *Unit head:* Terry Slocum, Chair, 785-864-5146, Fax: 785-864-5378, E-mail: t-slocum@ku.edu. *Application contact:* Stephen Egbert, Graduate Director, 785-864-4252, Fax: 785-864-5378, E-mail: s-egbert@ku.edu.

The University of Manchester, School of Earth, Atmospheric and Environmental Sciences, Manchester, United Kingdom. Offers atmospheric sciences (M Phil, M Sc, PhD); basin studies and petroleum geosciences (M Phil, M Sc, PhD); earth, atmospheric and environmental sciences (M Phil, M Sc, PhD); environmental geochemistry and cosmochemistry (M Phil, M Sc, PhD); isotope geochemistry and cosmochemistry (M Phil, M Sc, PhD); paleontology (M Phil, M Sc, PhD); physics and chemistry of minerals and fluids (M Phil, M Sc, PhD); structural and petrological geosciences (M Phil, M Sc, PhD).

University of Maryland, Baltimore County, Graduate School, College of Natural and Mathematical Sciences, Department of Physics, Program in Atmospheric Physics, Baltimore, MD 21250. Offers MS, PhD. *Faculty:* 25 full-time (4 women), 20 part-time/adjunct (1 woman). *Students:* 13 full-time (5 women), 8 international. Average age 25. 5 applicants, 80% accepted, 3 enrolled. In 2010, 1 doctorate awarded. *Degree requirements:* For master's, thesis optional; for doctorate, comprehensive exam, thesis/dissertation. *Entrance requirements:* For master's and doctorate, GRE General Test, minimum GPA of 3.0. Additional exam requirements/recommendations for international students: Required—TOEFL (minimum score 587 paper-based; 240 computer-based; 95 iBT). *Application deadline:* For fall admission, 6/1 for domestic students, 5/1 for international students; for spring admission, 1/1 for domestic students, 11/1 for international students. Applications are processed on a rolling basis. Application fee: $50. Electronic applications accepted. *Financial support:* In 2010–11, 11 students received support, including 1 fellowship with full tuition reimbursement available (averaging $30,000 per year), 7 research assistantships with full tuition reimbursements available (averaging $25,000 per year), 4 teaching assistantships with full tuition reimbursements available (averaging $22,000 per year); career-related internships or fieldwork, scholarships/grants, health care benefits, unspecified assistantships, and NASA Student Fellowship also available. Support available to part-time students. Financial award application deadline: 5/31. *Faculty research:* Lidar, remote sensing, aerosols, satellite remote sensing. Total annual research expenditures: $2.7 million. *Unit head:* Dr. Vanderlei Martins, Graduate Program Director, 410-455-2513, Fax: 410-455-1072, E-mail: martins@umbc.edu. *Application contact:* Dr. Vanderlei Martins, 410-455-2513, Fax: 410-455-1072, E-mail: martins@umbc.edu.

University of Massachusetts Lowell, College of Arts and Sciences, Department of Environmental, Earth and Atmospheric Sciences, Lowell, MA 01854-2881. Offers atmospheric science (MS, PhD).

University of Michigan, Horace H. Rackham School of Graduate Studies, College of Engineering, Department of Atmospheric, Oceanic, and Space Sciences, Ann Arbor, MI 48109. Offers atmospheric and space sciences (MS, PhD); geoscience and remote sensing (PhD); space and planetary sciences (PhD); space engineering (M Eng). Part-time programs available. *Students:* 92 full-time (31 women), 1 part-time (0 women). 179 applicants, 60% accepted, 52 enrolled. In 2010, 29 master's, 6 doctorates awarded. Terminal master's awarded for partial completion of doctoral program. *Degree requirements:* For master's, thesis (for some programs); for doctorate, thesis/dissertation, oral defense of dissertation, preliminary exams. *Entrance requirements:* For master's and doctorate, GRE General Test. Additional exam requirements/recommendations for international students: Required—TOEFL. *Application deadline:* Applications are processed on a rolling basis. Application fee: $65 ($75 for international students). Electronic applications accepted. *Expenses:* Tuition, state resident: full-time $17,784; part-time $1116 per credit hour. Tuition, nonresident: full-time $35,944; part-time $2125 per credit hour. International tuition: $35,994 full-time. Required fees: $95 per semester. Tuition and fees vary according to course load, degree level and program. *Financial support:* Fellowships, research assistantships, teaching assistantships, career-related internships or fieldwork, Federal Work-Study, institutionally sponsored loans, and health care benefits available. Support available to part-time students. Financial award applicants required to submit FAFSA. *Faculty research:* Planetary environments, space instrumentation, air pollution meteorology, global climate change, sun-earth connection, space weather. *Unit head:* Tamas Gombosi, Chair, 734-764-7222, Fax: 734-615-4645, E-mail: tamas@umich.edu. *Application contact:* Margaret Reid, Student Services Associate, 734-936-0482, Fax: 734-763-0437, E-mail: aoss.um@umich.edu.

University of Missouri, Graduate School, School of Natural Resources, Department of Soil, Environmental, and Atmospheric Sciences, Columbia, MO 65211. Offers atmospheric science (MS, PhD); soil science (MS, PhD). *Degree requirements:* For doctorate, thesis/dissertation. *Entrance requirements:* For master's and doctorate, GRE General Test, minimum GPA of 3.0. Additional exam requirements/recommendations for international students: Required—TOEFL (minimum score 530 paper-based; 197 computer-based; 71 iBT).

University of Nevada, Reno, Graduate School, Interdisciplinary Program in Atmospheric Sciences, Reno, NV 89557. Offers MS, PhD. Terminal master's awarded for partial completion of doctoral program. *Degree requirements:* For master's, thesis optional; for doctorate, thesis/dissertation. *Entrance requirements:* For master's, GRE (recommended), minimum GPA of 2.75; for doctorate, GRE (recommended), minimum GPA of 3.0. Additional exam requirements/recommendations for international students: Required—TOEFL (minimum score 500 paper-based; 173 computer-based; 61 iBT), IELTS (minimum score 6). Electronic applications accepted. *Expenses:* Tuition, state resident: full-time $2219; part-time $246 per credit. Tuition, nonresident: part-time $510 per credit. International tuition: $9009 full-time. Required fees: $59 per term. One-time fee: $101. Tuition and fees vary according to course load. *Faculty research:* Atmospheric chemistry, cloud and aerosol physics, atmospheric optics, mesoscale meterology.

The University of North Carolina at Chapel Hill, Graduate School, School of Public Health, Department of Environmental Sciences and Engineering, Chapel Hill, NC 27599. Offers air, radiation and industrial hygiene (MPH, MS, MSEE, MSPH, PhD); aquatic and atmospheric sciences (MPH, MS, MSPH, PhD); environmental engineering (MPH, MS, MSEE, MSPH, PhD); environmental health sciences (MPH, MS, MSPH, PhD); environmental management and policy (MPH, MS, MSPH, PhD). Terminal master's awarded for partial completion of doctoral program. *Degree requirements:* For master's, comprehensive exam, thesis (for some programs), research paper; for doctorate, comprehensive exam, thesis/dissertation. *Entrance requirements:* For master's and doctorate, GRE General Test, minimum GPA of 3.0. Additional exam requirements/recommendations for international students: Required—TOEFL. Electronic applications accepted. *Faculty research:* Air, radiation and industrial hygiene, aquatic and atmospheric sciences, environmental health sciences, environmental management and policy, water resources engineering.

University of North Dakota, Graduate School, John D. Odegard School of Aerospace Sciences, Department of Atmospheric Sciences, Grand Forks, ND 58202. Offers MS, PhD. Part-time programs available. *Faculty:* 11 full-time (2 women), 5 part-time/adjunct (1 woman). *Students:* 18 full-time (5 women), 9 part-time (1 woman); includes 1 minority (Black or African American, non-Hispanic/Latino), 3 international. Average age 25. 17 applicants, 82% accepted, 7 enrolled. In 2010, 6 master's awarded. *Degree requirements:* For master's, comprehensive exam, thesis or alternative. *Entrance requirements:* For master's and doctorate, GRE General Test, minimum GPA of 3.0. Additional exam requirements/recommendations for international students: Required—TOEFL (minimum score 550 paper-based; 213 computer-based; 79 iBT), IELTS (minimum score 6.5). *Application deadline:* For fall admission, 8/1 priority date for domestic students, 5/1 priority date for international students; for spring admission, 11/1 priority date for domestic students, 9/1 priority date for international students. Applications are processed on a rolling basis. Application fee: $35. Electronic applications accepted. *Expenses:* Tuition, state resident: full-time $5857; part-time $306.74 per credit. Tuition, nonresident: full-time $15,666; part-time $729.77 per credit. Required fees: $53.42 per credit. Tuition and fees vary according to course load, program and reciprocity agreements. *Financial support:* In 2010–11, 21 students received support, including 15 research assistantships with full and partial tuition reimbursements available (averaging $9,945 per year), 6 teaching assistantships with full and partial tuition reimbursements available (averaging $10,413 per year); fellowships with full and partial tuition reimbursements available, Federal Work-Study, institutionally sponsored loans, scholarships/grants, health care benefits, tuition waivers (full and partial), and unspecified assistantships also available. Support available to part-time students. Financial award application deadline: 3/15; financial award applicants required to submit FAFSA. Total annual research expenditures: $1 million. *Unit head:* Dr. Leon F. Osborne, Graduate Director, 701-777-2184, Fax: 701-777-5032. *Application contact:* Staci Wells, Admissions Specialist, 701-777-0748, Fax: 701-777-3619, E-mail: staci.wells@gradschool.und.edu.

University of Utah, Graduate School, College of Mines and Earth Sciences, Department of Atmospheric Sciences, Salt Lake City, UT 84112. Offers MS, PhD. Part-time programs available. *Faculty:* 10 full-time (1 woman), 2 part-time/adjunct (0 women). *Students:* 26 full-time (7 women), 15 part-time (6 women); includes 3 minority (all Hispanic/Latino), 7 international. Average age 27. 50 applicants, 34% accepted, 14 enrolled. In 2010, 9 master's awarded. Terminal master's awarded for partial completion of doctoral program. *Degree requirements:* For master's, comprehensive exam, thesis optional; for doctorate, comprehensive exam, thesis/dissertation. *Entrance requirements:* For master's and doctorate, GRE General Test, minimum GPA of 3.0, 3 letters of reference. Additional exam requirements/recommendations for international students: Required—TOEFL (minimum score 500 paper-based; 173 computer-based; 61 iBT). *Application deadline:* For fall admission, 1/7 priority date for domestic and international students. Applications are processed on a rolling basis. Application fee: $55 ($65 for international students). Electronic applications accepted. *Expenses:* Tuition, area resident: Part-time $179.19 per credit hour. Tuition, state resident: full-time $4384. Tuition, nonresident: full-time $16,684; part-time $630.67 per credit hour. Required fees: $350 per semester. Tuition and fees vary according to course load, degree level and program. *Financial support:* In 2010–11, 30 students received support, including 4 fellowships (averaging $30,000 per year), 26 research assistantships (averaging $21,000 per year). Financial award application deadline: 2/15; financial award applicants required to submit FAFSA. *Faculty research:* Clouds, aerosols, and climate; numerical weather prediction; mountain weather and climate; tropical convection

University of Utah (continued)
and storms; climate variability and change. Total annual research expenditures: $2.4 million. *Unit head:* Dr. Kevin D. Perry, Chair, 801-585-9482, Fax: 801-585-3681, E-mail: kevin.perry@utah.edu. *Application contact:* Kathy Roberts, Executive Secretary, 801-581-6136, Fax: 801-585-3681, E-mail: kathy.roberts@utah.edu.

University of Washington, Graduate School, College of Arts and Sciences, Department of Atmospheric Sciences, Seattle, WA 98195. Offers MS, PhD. *Degree requirements:* For master's, thesis; for doctorate, thesis/dissertation, qualifying exam. *Entrance requirements:* For master's and doctorate, GRE General Test, minimum GPA of 3.0. Additional exam requirements/recommendations for international students: Required—TOEFL. *Faculty research:* Climate change, synoptic and mesoscale meteorology, atmospheric chemistry, cloud physics, dynamics of the atmosphere.

University of Wisconsin–Madison, Graduate School, College of Letters and Science, Department of Atmospheric and Oceanic Sciences, Madison, WI 53706-1380. Offers MS, PhD. Part-time programs available. *Degree requirements:* For master's, thesis (for some programs); for doctorate, thesis/dissertation. *Entrance requirements:* For master's and doctorate, GRE General Test, minimum GPA of 3.0; previous course work in chemistry, mathematics, and physics. Electronic applications accepted. *Expenses:* Tuition, state resident: full-time $9887.36; part-time $617.96 per credit. Tuition, nonresident: full-time $24,054; part-time $1503.40 per credit. Required fees: $67.63 per credit. Tuition and fees vary according to reciprocity agreements. *Faculty research:* Satellite meteorology, weather systems, global climate change, numerical modeling, atmosphere-ocean interaction.

University of Wyoming, College of Engineering and Applied Sciences, Department of Atmospheric Science, Laramie, WY 82070. Offers MS, PhD. Postbaccalaureate distance learning degree programs offered (minimal on-campus study). Terminal master's awarded for partial completion of doctoral program. *Degree requirements:* For master's, thesis; for doctorate, comprehensive exam, thesis/dissertation. *Entrance requirements:* For master's and doctorate, GRE General Test, minimum GPA of 3.0. Additional exam requirements/recommendations for international students: Required—TOEFL (minimum score 525 paper-based; 250 computer-based). Electronic applications accepted. *Expenses:* Contact institution. *Faculty research:* Cloud physics; aerosols, boundary layer processes; airborne observations; stratospheric aerosols and gases.

Yale University, Graduate School of Arts and Sciences, Department of Geology and Geophysics, New Haven, CT 06520. Offers biogeochemistry (PhD); climate dynamics (PhD); geochemistry (PhD); geophysics (PhD); meteorology (PhD); oceanography (PhD); paleontology (PhD); paleooceanography (PhD); petrology (PhD); tectonics (PhD). *Degree requirements:* For doctorate, thesis/dissertation. *Entrance requirements:* For doctorate, GRE General Test. Additional exam requirements/recommendations for international students: Required—TOEFL.

Meteorology

Columbia University, Graduate School of Arts and Sciences, Program in Climate and Society, New York, NY 10027. Offers MA.

Florida Institute of Technology, Graduate Programs, College of Engineering, Department of Marine and Environmental Systems, Melbourne, FL 32901-6975. Offers earth remote sensing (MS); environmental resource management (MS); environmental science (MS, PhD); meteorology (MS); ocean engineering (MS, PhD); oceanography (MS, PhD). Part-time programs available. *Faculty:* 11 full-time (0 women), 3 part-time/adjunct (0 women). *Students:* 47 full-time (16 women), 15 part-time (5 women); includes 4 minority (1 Black or African American, non-Hispanic/Latino; 1 Asian, non-Hispanic/Latino; 1 Hispanic/Latino; 1 Two or more races, non-Hispanic/Latino), 10 international. Average age 27. 118 applicants, 49% accepted, 19 enrolled. In 2010, 21 master's, 1 doctorate awarded. *Degree requirements:* For master's, comprehensive exam (for some programs), thesis (for some programs), seminar, field project, written final exam, internship, technical paper, oral presentation or internship; for doctorate, comprehensive exam, thesis/dissertation, seminar, internships (oceanography and environmental science), publications. *Entrance requirements:* For master's, GRE General Test (environmental science, oceanography, environmental resource management, meteorology, earth remote sensing), 3 letters of recommendation, minimum GPA of 3.0, resume, transcripts, statement of objectives; for doctorate, GRE General Test (oceanography, environmental science), resume, 3 letters of recommendation, minimum GPA of 3.3, statement of objectives, on campus interview (highly recommended). Additional exam requirements/recommendations for international students: Required—TOEFL (minimum score 550 paper-based; 213 computer-based; 79 iBT). *Application deadline:* For fall admission, 4/1 for international students; for spring admission, 9/30 for international students. Applications are processed on a rolling basis. Application fee: $50. Electronic applications accepted. *Expenses:* Tuition: Part-time $1040 per credit hour. Tuition and fees vary according to campus/location. *Financial support:* In 2010–11, 5 fellowships with full and partial tuition reimbursements (averaging $7,240 per year), 5 research assistantships with full and partial tuition reimbursements (averaging $3,664 per year), 10 teaching assistantships with full and partial tuition reimbursements (averaging $6,670 per year) were awarded; career-related internships or fieldwork, institutionally sponsored loans, tuition waivers (partial), unspecified assistantships, and tuition remissions also available. Support available to part-time students. Financial award application deadline: 3/1; financial award applicants required to submit FAFSA. Total annual research expenditures: $1.7 million. *Unit head:* Dr. George Maul, Department Head, 321-674-7453, Fax: 321-674-7212, E-mail: gmaul@fit.edu. *Application contact:* Cheryl A. Brown, Associate Director of Graduate Admissions, 321-674-7581, Fax: 321-723-9468, E-mail: cbrown@fit.edu.

Florida State University, The Graduate School, College of Arts and Sciences, Department of Earth, Ocean and Atmospheric Science, Program in Meteorology, Tallahassee, FL 32306-4520. Offers MS, PhD. *Faculty:* 15 full-time (3 women). *Students:* 71 full-time (22 women), 15 part-time (5 women); includes 7 minority (2 Black or African American, non-Hispanic/Latino; 4 Hispanic/Latino; 1 Native Hawaiian or other Pacific Islander, non-Hispanic/Latino), 9 international. Average age 25. 92 applicants, 61% accepted, 28 enrolled. In 2010, 15 master's, 6 doctorates awarded. Terminal master's awarded for partial completion of doctoral program. *Degree requirements:* For master's, thesis optional; for doctorate, comprehensive exam, thesis/dissertation. *Entrance requirements:* For master's, GRE General Test (minimum score 1100 verbal and quantitative), minimum GPA of 3.0 in upper-division work; for doctorate, GRE General Test (minimum combined Verbal and Quantitative score: 1100), minimum GPA of 3.0, faculty sponsor. Additional exam requirements/recommendations for international students: Required—TOEFL (minimum score 550 paper-based; 213 computer-based; 80 iBT). *Application deadline:* For fall admission, 2/15 priority date for domestic students, 2/1 for international students; for spring admission, 11/1 for domestic students, 6/30 for international students. Applications are processed on a rolling basis. Application fee: $30. *Expenses:* Tuition, state resident: full-time $8238.24. *Financial support:* In 2010–11, 56 students received support, including 2 fellowships with partial tuition reimbursements available (averaging $19,000 per year), 39 research assistantships with partial tuition reimbursements available (averaging $21,500 per year), 15 teaching assistantships with partial tuition reimbursements available (averaging $21,500 per year); career-related internships or fieldwork, scholarships/grants, and unspecified assistantships also available. *Faculty research:* Physical, dynamic, and synoptic meteorology; climatology. Total annual research expenditures: $600,000. *Unit head:* Dr. Lynn Dudley, Chairman, 850-644-3864, Fax: 850-644-9642, E-mail: bobe@met.fsu.edu. *Application contact:* Marc Unger, Academic Program Specialist, 850-644-8580, Fax: 850-644-9642, E-mail: munger@fsu.edu.

Georgia Institute of Technology, Graduate Studies and Research, College of Sciences, School of Earth and Atmospheric Sciences, Atlanta, GA 30332-0340. Offers atmospheric chemistry, aerosols and clouds (MS, PhD); dynamics of weather and climate (MS, PhD); geochemistry (MS, PhD); geophysics (MS, PhD); oceanography (MS, PhD); paleoclimate (MS, PhD); planetary science (MS, PhD); remote sensing (MS, PhD). Part-time programs available. Terminal master's awarded for partial completion of doctoral program. *Degree requirements:* For master's, thesis or alternative; for doctorate, comprehensive exam, thesis/dissertation. *Entrance requirements:* For master's, GRE, letters of recommendation; for doctorate, GRE, academic transcripts, letters of recommendation, personal statement. Additional exam requirements/recommendations for international students: Required—TOEFL (minimum score 550 paper-based; 213 computer-based; 79 iBT). *Faculty research:* Geophysics; atmospheric chemistry, aerosols and clouds; dynamics of weather and climate; geochemistry; oceanography; paleoclimate; planetary science; remote sensing.

Iowa State University of Science and Technology, Graduate College, College of Liberal Arts and Sciences, Department of Geological and Atmospheric Sciences, Ames, IA 50011. Offers earth science (MS, PhD); environmental science (MS, PhD); geology (MS, PhD); meteorology (MS, PhD). *Faculty:* 20 full-time (2 women). *Students:* 33 full-time (8 women), 8 part-time (3 women); includes 1 Asian, non-Hispanic/Latino, 3 international. 45 applicants, 49% accepted, 9 enrolled. In 2010, 9 master's, 5 doctorates awarded. *Degree requirements:* For master's, thesis (for some programs); for doctorate, thesis/dissertation. *Entrance requirements:* For master's and doctorate, GRE General Test. Additional exam requirements/recommendations for international students: Required—TOEFL (minimum score 550 paper-based; 79 iBT), IELTS (minimum score 6.5). *Application deadline:* For fall admission, 1/1 priority date for domestic students. Applications are processed on a rolling basis. Application fee: $40 ($90 for international students). Electronic applications accepted. *Financial support:* In 2010–11, 23 research assistantships with full and partial tuition reimbursements (averaging $12,780 per year), 8 teaching assistantships with full and partial tuition reimbursements (averaging $6,806 per year) were awarded; fellowships, scholarships/grants, health care benefits, and unspecified assistantships also available. *Unit head:* Dr. Carl E. Jacobson, Chair, 515-294-4477. *Application contact:* Dr. Carl E. Jacobson, Chair, 515-294-4477.

McGill University, Faculty of Graduate and Postdoctoral Studies, Faculty of Agricultural and Environmental Sciences, Department of Natural Resource Sciences, Montréal, QC H3A 2T5, Canada. Offers entomology (M Sc, PhD); environmental assessment (M Sc); forest science (M Sc, PhD); microbiology (M Sc, PhD); micrometeorology (M Sc, PhD); neotropical environment (M Sc, PhD); soil science (M Sc, PhD); wildlife biology (M Sc, PhD).

Naval Postgraduate School, Graduate Programs, Department of Meteorology, Monterey, CA 93943. Offers MS, PhD. Program only open to commissioned officers of the United States and friendly nations and selected United States federal civilian employees. Part-time programs available. *Degree requirements:* For master's, thesis; for doctorate, one foreign language, thesis/dissertation.

North Carolina State University, Graduate School, College of Physical and Mathematical Sciences, Department of Marine, Earth, and Atmospheric Sciences, Raleigh, NC 27695. Offers marine, earth, and atmospheric sciences (MS, PhD); meteorology (MS, PhD); oceanography (MS, PhD). PhD offered jointly with The University of North Carolina Wilmington. Terminal master's awarded for partial completion of doctoral program. *Degree requirements:* For master's, thesis (for some programs), final oral exam; for doctorate, comprehensive exam, thesis/dissertation, final oral exam, preliminary oral and written exams. *Entrance requirements:* For master's, GRE General Test, minimum GPA of 3.0; for doctorate, GRE General Test, GRE Subject Test (for disciplines in biological oceanography and geology), minimum GPA of 3.0. Additional exam requirements/recommendations for international students: Required—TOEFL (minimum score 550 paper-based). Electronic applications accepted. *Faculty research:* Boundary layer and air quality meteorology; climate and mesoscale dynamics; biological, chemical, geological, and physical oceanography; hard rock, soft rock, environmental, and paleogeology.

Northern Arizona University, Graduate College, College of Engineering, Forestry and Natural Sciences, School of Earth Sciences and Environmental Sustainability, Flagstaff, AZ 86011. Offers climate science and solutions (MS); earth science (MS); environmental sciences and policy (MS); geology (MS). *Faculty:* 27 full-time (7 women). *Students:* 50 full-time (22 women), 18 part-time (9 women); includes 4 minority (1 American Indian or Alaska Native, non-Hispanic/Latino; 1 Asian, non-Hispanic/Latino; 2 Hispanic/Latino), 2 international. 113 applicants, 31% accepted, 27 enrolled. In 2010, 21 master's awarded. *Degree requirements:* For master's, comprehensive exam (for some programs), thesis (for some programs). *Entrance requirements:* Additional exam requirements/recommendations for international students: Required—TOEFL (minimum score 550 paper-based; 213 computer-based; 80 iBT), IELTS (minimum score 7). *Application deadline:* For fall admission, 2/1 priority date for domestic and international students. Applications are processed on a rolling basis. Application fee: $65. Electronic applications accepted. *Financial support:* In 2010–11, 6 fellowships, 7 research assistantships with partial tuition reimbursements (averaging $12,866 per year), 28 teaching assistantships with partial tuition reimbursements (averaging $12,477 per year) were awarded; career-related internships or fieldwork, Federal Work-Study, scholarships/grants, health care benefits, tuition waivers (full and partial), and unspecified assistantships also available. Financial award applicants required to submit FAFSA. *Unit head:* Dr. Abe Springer, Director, 928-523-7198. *Application contact:* Dr. Abe Springer, Director, 928-523-7198.

Penn State University Park, Graduate School, College of Earth and Mineral Sciences, Department of Meteorology, State College, University Park, PA 16802-1503. Offers MS, PhD.

Plymouth State University, College of Graduate Studies, Graduate Studies in Education, Program in Science, Plymouth, NH 03264-1595. Offers applied meteorology (MS); environmental science and policy (MS); science education (MS).

Saint Louis University, Graduate Education, College of Arts and Sciences and Graduate Education, Department of Earth and Atmospheric Sciences, St. Louis, MO 63103-2097. Offers geophysics (PhD); geoscience (MS); meteorology (M Pr Met, MS-R, PhD). Part-time programs available. *Degree requirements:* For master's, thesis (for some programs), comprehensive oral exam; for doctorate, thesis/dissertation, preliminary exams. *Entrance requirements:* For master's, GRE General Test, letters of recommendation, resume; for doctorate, GRE General Test,

letters of recommendation, resumé, goal statement, transcripts. Additional exam requirements/recommendations for international students: Required—TOEFL (minimum score 525 paper-based; 194 computer-based). Electronic applications accepted. *Faculty research:* Structural geology, mesoscale meteorology and severe storms, weather and climate change prediction.

San Jose State University, Graduate Studies and Research, College of Science, Department of Meteorology and Climate Science, San Jose, CA 95192-0001. Offers meteorology (MS). *Degree requirements:* For master's, thesis or alternative. *Entrance requirements:* For master's, GRE. Electronic applications accepted.

Texas A&M University, College of Geosciences, Department of Atmospheric Sciences, College Station, TX 77843. Offers MS, PhD. *Faculty:* 16. *Students:* 54 full-time (15 women), 4 part-time (1 woman); includes 2 minority (1 Asian, non-Hispanic/Latino; 1 Hispanic/Latino), 21 international. Average age 28. In 2010, 8 master's, 8 doctorates awarded. *Degree requirements:* For master's, thesis; for doctorate, thesis/dissertation. *Entrance requirements:* For master's and doctorate, GRE General Test. Additional exam requirements/recommendations for international students: Required—TOEFL. *Application deadline:* For fall admission, 3/1 for domestic students; for spring admission, 10/1 for domestic students. Applications are processed on a rolling basis. Application fee: $50 ($75 for international students). Electronic applications accepted. *Financial support:* In 2010–11, fellowships (averaging $16,500 per year), research assistantships with tuition reimbursements (averaging $15,000 per year), teaching assistantships (averaging $15,000 per year) were awarded; career-related internships or fieldwork, institutionally sponsored loans, scholarships/grants, and tuition waivers (partial) also available. Financial award application deadline: 3/1; financial award applicants required to submit FAFSA. *Faculty research:* Radar and satellite rainfall relationships, mesoscale dynamics and numerical modeling, climatology. *Unit head:* Kenneth Bowman, Head, 979-862-7671, E-mail: k-bowman@tamu.edu. *Application contact:* Christine Arnold, Academic Advisor II, 979-845-7688, Fax: 979-862-4466, E-mail: chrisarnold@tamu.edu.

Université du Québec à Montréal, Graduate Programs, Program in Earth and Atmospheric Sciences, Montréal, QC H3C 3P8, Canada. Offers atmospheric sciences (M Sc); Earth and atmospheric sciences (PhD); Earth science (M Sc); meteorology (PhD, Diploma). PhD programs offered jointly with McGill University. Part-time programs available. *Degree requirements:* For master's, thesis. *Entrance requirements:* For master's and Diploma, appropriate bachelor's degree or equivalent, proficiency in French; for doctorate, appropriate master's degree or equivalent, proficiency in French.

University of Hawaii at Manoa, Graduate Division, School of Ocean and Earth Science and Technology, Department of Meteorology, Honolulu, HI 96822. Offers MS, PhD. Part-time programs available. *Faculty:* 17 full-time (1 woman), 6 part-time/adjunct (0 women). *Students:* 27 full-time (7 women), 5 part-time (2 women); includes 2 minority (1 Asian, non-Hispanic/Latino; 1 Hispanic/Latino), 15 international. Average age 30. 38 applicants, 53% accepted, 9 enrolled. In 2010, 3 master's, 2 doctorates awarded. *Degree requirements:* For master's, comprehensive exam, thesis; for doctorate, comprehensive exam, thesis/dissertation. *Entrance requirements:* For master's and doctorate, GRE General Test. Additional exam requirements/recommendations for international students: Required—TOEFL (minimum score 560 paper-based; 220 computer-based; 83 iBT), IELTS (minimum score 5). *Application deadline:* For fall admission, 3/1 for domestic students, 1/15 for international students; for spring admission, 9/1 for domestic students, 8/1 for international students. Application fee: $60. *Financial support:* In 2010–11, 25 students received support, including 2 fellowships (averaging $133 per year), 22 research assistantships (averaging $20,783 per year), 3 teaching assistantships (averaging $18,568 per year); Federal Work-Study and tuition waivers (full) also available. *Faculty research:* Tropical cyclones, air-sea interactions, mesoscale meteorology, intraseasonal oscillations, tropical climate. Total annual research expenditures: $6 million. *Application contact:* Fei-Fei Jin, Graduate Chairperson, 808-956-2567, Fax: 808-956-2877, E-mail: jff@hawaii.edu.

University of Maryland, College Park, Academic Affairs, College of Computer, Mathematical and Natural Sciences, Department of Atmospheric and Oceanic Science, College Park, MD 20742. Offers MS, PMS, PhD. Part-time and evening/weekend programs available. Post-baccalaureate distance learning degree programs offered. *Faculty:* 28 full-time (7 women), 6 part-time/adjunct (0 women). *Students:* 48 full-time (23 women), 12 part-time (8 women); includes 4 minority (2 Asian, non-Hispanic/Latino; 1 Hispanic/Latino; 1 Two or more races, non-Hispanic/Latino), 21 international. 102 applicants, 25% accepted, 16 enrolled. In 2010, 4 master's, 9 doctorates awarded. Terminal master's awarded for partial completion of doctoral program. *Degree requirements:* For master's, comprehensive exam, scholarly paper, written and oral exam; for doctorate, thesis/dissertation, exam. *Entrance requirements:* For master's, GRE General Test, background in mathematics, experience in scientific computer languages, 3 letters of recommendation; for doctorate, GRE General Test. *Application deadline:* For fall admission, 1/15 for domestic and international students; for spring admission, 11/1 for domestic students, 6/1 for international students. Applications are processed on a rolling basis. Application

fee: $75. Electronic applications accepted. *Expenses:* Tuition, area resident: Part-time $471 per credit hour. Tuition, state resident: part-time $471 per credit hour. Tuition, nonresident: part-time $1016 per credit hour. Required fees: $337 per term. *Financial support:* In 2010–11, 3 fellowships with full and partial tuition reimbursements (averaging $9,698 per year), 18 research assistantships (averaging $20,707 per year), 20 teaching assistantships (averaging $19,890 per year) were awarded; Federal Work-Study and scholarships/grants also available. Support available to part-time students. Financial award applicants required to submit FAFSA. *Faculty research:* Weather, atmospheric chemistry, air pollution, global change, radiation. Total annual research expenditures: $4 million. *Unit head:* James A. Carton, Chair, 301-405-5365, Fax: 301-314-9482, E-mail: carton@umd.edu. *Application contact:* Dr. Charles A. Caramello, Dean of Graduate School, 301-405-0358, Fax: 301-314-9305, E-mail: ccaramel@umd.edu.

University of Miami, Graduate School, Rosenstiel School of Marine and Atmospheric Science, Division of Meteorology and Physical Oceanography, Coral Gables, FL 33124. Offers meteorology (MS, PhD); physical oceanography (MS, PhD). Terminal master's awarded for partial completion of doctoral program. *Degree requirements:* For master's, comprehensive exam, thesis; for doctorate, comprehensive exam, thesis/dissertation. *Entrance requirements:* For master's and doctorate, GRE General Test. Additional exam requirements/recommendations for international students: Required—TOEFL (minimum score 550 paper-based; 213 computer-based). Electronic applications accepted.

University of Oklahoma, College of Atmospheric and Geographic Sciences, School of Meteorology, Norman, OK 73072. Offers meteorology (MS, PhD); professional meteorology (MS). *Faculty:* 37 full-time (4 women), 6 part-time/adjunct (1 woman). *Students:* 85 full-time (23 women), 15 part-time (3 women); includes 5 minority (1 Black or African American, non-Hispanic/Latino; 1 American Indian or Alaska Native, non-Hispanic/Latino; 3 Asian, non-Hispanic/Latino), 15 international. Average age 27. 78 applicants, 14% accepted, 11 enrolled. In 2010, 14 master's, 3 doctorates awarded. Terminal master's awarded for partial completion of doctoral program. *Degree requirements:* For master's, comprehensive exam, thesis or alternative; for doctorate, one foreign language, thesis/dissertation, departmental qualifying exam. *Entrance requirements:* For master's, GRE, bachelor's degree in related area; for doctorate, GRE. Additional exam requirements/recommendations for international students: Required—TOEFL (minimum score 600 paper-based; 213 computer-based; 79 iBT). *Application deadline:* For fall admission, 2/1 priority date for domestic students, 4/1 for international students; for spring admission, 11/1 for domestic students, 9/1 for international students. Applications are processed on a rolling basis. Application fee: $40 ($90 for international students). Electronic applications accepted. *Expenses:* Tuition, state resident: full-time $3892.80; part-time $162.20 per credit hour. Tuition, nonresident: full-time $14,167; part-time $590.30 per credit hour. Required fees: $2523.40; $94.60 per credit hour. Tuition and fees vary according to course load and degree level. *Financial support:* In 2010–11, 10 fellowships with full tuition reimbursements (averaging $5,000 per year), 75 research assistantships (averaging $17,281 per year), 17 teaching assistantships with partial tuition reimbursements (averaging $17,885 per year) were awarded; health care benefits and unspecified assistantships also available. Financial award application deadline: 2/1; financial award applicants required to submit FAFSA. *Faculty research:* Numerical weather prediction and data assimilation; mesoscale dynamics and severe weather; tropical convection; climate issues and renewable energy. Total annual research expenditures: $7.9 million. *Unit head:* David Parsons, Director, 405-325-8565, Fax: 405-325-7689, E-mail: dparsons@ou.edu. *Application contact:* Celia Jones, Coordinator, Academic Student Services, 405-325-6571, Fax: 405-325-7689, E-mail: cjones@ou.edu.

Utah State University, School of Graduate Studies, College of Agriculture, Department of Plants, Soils, and Biometeorology, Logan, UT 84322. Offers biometeorology (MS, PhD); ecology (MS, PhD); plant science (MS, PhD); soil science (MS, PhD). Part-time programs available. Terminal master's awarded for partial completion of doctoral program. *Degree requirements:* For master's, thesis; for doctorate, thesis/dissertation. *Entrance requirements:* For master's, GRE General Test, BS in plant, soil, atmospheric science, or related field; minimum GPA of 3.0; for doctorate, GRE General Test, minimum GPA of 3.0. Additional exam requirements/recommendations for international students: Required—TOEFL. Electronic applications accepted. *Faculty research:* Biotechnology and genomics, plant physiology and biology, nutrient and water efficient landscapes, physical-chemical-biological processes in soil, environmental biophysics and climate.

Yale University, Graduate School of Arts and Sciences, Department of Geology and Geophysics, New Haven, CT 06520. Offers biogeochemistry (PhD); climate dynamics (PhD); geochemistry (PhD); geophysics (PhD); meteorology (PhD); oceanography (PhD); paleontology (PhD); paleooceanography (PhD); petrology (PhD); tectonics (PhD). *Degree requirements:* For doctorate, thesis/dissertation. *Entrance requirements:* For doctorate, GRE General Test. Additional exam requirements/recommendations for international students: Required—TOEFL.

Peterson's Graduate Programs in the Physical Sciences, Mathematics, Agricultural Sciences, the Environment & Natural Resources 2012

www.facebook.com/petersonspublishing   **169**

Section 6
Physics

This section contains a directory of institutions offering graduate work in physics, followed by in-depth entries submitted by institutions that chose to prepare detailed program descriptions. Additional information about programs listed in the directory but not augmented by an in-depth entry may be obtained by writing directly to the dean of a graduate school or chair of a department at the address given in the directory.

For programs offering related work, see all other areas in this book. In the other guides in this series:

Graduate Programs in the Biological Sciences
See *Biological and Biomedical Sciences* and *Biophysics*

Graduate Programs in Engineering & Applied Sciences
See *Aerospace/Aeronautical Engineering, Electrical and Computer Engineering, Energy and Power Engineering (Nuclear Engineering), Engineering and Applied Sciences, Engineering Physics, Materials Sciences and Engineering,* and *Mechanical Engineering and Mechanics*

Graduate Programs in Business, Education, Health, Information Studies, Law & Social Work
See *Allied Health and Optometry* and *Vision Sciences*

CONTENTS

Acoustics

Penn State University Park, Graduate School, Intercollege Graduate Programs and College of Engineering, Intercollege Graduate Program in Acoustics, State College, University Park, PA 16802-1503. Offers M Eng, MS, PhD. *Unit head:* Dr. Anthony Atchley, Project Chair, 814-865-6364, Fax: 814-865-7595, E-mail: atchley@psu.edu. *Application contact:* Cynthia E. Nicosia, Director, Graduate Enrollment Services, 814-865-1795, Fax: 814-865-4627, E-mail: cey1@psu.edu.

Rensselaer Polytechnic Institute, Graduate School, School of Architecture, PhD Program in Architectural Sciences, Troy, NY 12180-3590. Offers acoustics (PhD); built ecologies (PhD); lighting (PhD). *Faculty:* 12 full-time (4 women), 7 part-time/adjunct (3 women). *Students:* 25 full-time (7 women), 4 part-time (1 woman); includes 2 Black or African American, non-Hispanic/Latino; 1 Hispanic/Latino; 1 Two or more races, non-Hispanic/Latino, 9 international. Average age 31. 50 applicants, 28% accepted, 7 enrolled. In 2010, 4 doctorates awarded. *Degree requirements:* For doctorate, comprehensive exam (for some programs), thesis/dissertation. *Entrance requirements:* For doctorate, GRE General Test, resume, portfolio, research writing sample. Additional exam requirements/recommendations for international students: Required—TOEFL (minimum score 570 paper-based; 230 computer-based; 89 iBT), IELTS (minimum score 6.5). *Application deadline:* For fall admission, 1/1 priority date for domestic students, 1/1 for international students. Applications are processed on a rolling basis. Application fee: $75. Electronic applications accepted. *Expenses:* Tuition: Full-time $39,600; part-time $1650 per credit. Required fees: $1896. *Financial support:* In 2010–11, 23 students received support, including 5 fellowships with full tuition reimbursements available (averaging $23,000 per year), 17 research assistantships with tuition reimbursements available (averaging $17,500 per year), 1 teaching assistantship with full tuition reimbursement available (averaging $17,500 per year); career-related internships or fieldwork, institutionally sponsored loans, scholarships/grants, and unspecified assistantships also available. Financial award application deadline: 1/1. *Faculty research:* Lighting, acoustics, computation, building systems. *Unit head:* Prof. Ted Krueger, Head, Graduate Programs, 518-276-2562, Fax: 518-276-3034, E-mail: krueger@rpi.edu. *Application contact:* Erin Bermingham, Senior Graduate Programs Administrator, 518-276-3986, Fax: 518-276-3034, E-mail: bermie@rpi.edu.

Rensselaer Polytechnic Institute, Graduate School, School of Architecture, Program in Architectural Acoustics, Troy, NY 12180-3590. Offers MS. *Faculty:* 2 full-time (0 women), 1 part-time/adjunct (0 women). *Students:* 14 full-time (5 women), 6 part-time (0 women); includes 1 Black or African American, non-Hispanic/Latino; 1 Asian, non-Hispanic/Latino; 1 Hispanic/Latino, 3 international. Average age 26. 32 applicants, 47% accepted, 10 enrolled. In 2010, 6 master's awarded. *Degree requirements:* For master's, thesis. *Entrance requirements:* For master's, GRE General Test. Additional exam requirements/recommendations for international students: Required—TOEFL (minimum score 570 paper-based; 230 computer-based; 89 iBT), IELTS (minimum score 6.5). *Application deadline:* For fall admission, 1/1 priority date for domestic and international students. Applications are processed on a rolling basis. Application fee: $75. Electronic applications accepted. *Expenses:* Tuition: Full-time $39,600; part-time $1650 per credit. Required fees: $1896. *Financial support:* In 2010–11, 8 students received support, including 1 fellowship with full tuition reimbursement available (averaging $23,500 per year), 6 research assistantships with full tuition reimbursements available (averaging $17,500 per year), 1 teaching assistantship with full tuition reimbursement available (averaging $17,500 per year); institutionally sponsored loans, scholarships/grants, and unspecified assistantships also available. Financial award application deadline: 1/1. *Faculty research:* Acoustics: modeling, auralization, signal processing. Total annual research expenditures: $94,000. *Unit head:* Prof. Ted Krueger, Head, Graduate Programs, 518-276-6466, E-mail: krueger@rpi.edu. *Application contact:* Erin Bermingham, Senior Program Administrator, 518-276-3986, Fax: 518-276-3034, E-mail: bermie@rpi.edu.

University of Massachusetts Dartmouth, Graduate School, College of Engineering, Department of Electrical and Computer Engineering, North Dartmouth, MA 02747-2300. Offers acoustics (Postbaccalaureate Certificate); communications (Postbaccalaureate Certificate); computer engineering (MS, PhD); computer systems engineering (Postbaccalaureate Certificate); digital signal processing (Postbaccalaureate Certificate); electrical engineering (MS, PhD); electrical engineering systems (Postbaccalaureate Certificate). Part-time programs available. *Faculty:* 17 full-time (3 women), 3 part-time/adjunct (0 women). *Students:* 32 full-time (6 women), 48 part-time (13 women); includes 2 Black or African American, non-Hispanic/Latino; 1 American Indian or Alaska Native, non-Hispanic/Latino; 4 Asian, non-Hispanic/Latino, 47 international. Average age 29. 97 applicants, 84% accepted, 19 enrolled. In 2010, 17 master's, 1 other advanced degree awarded. *Degree requirements:* For master's, culminating project or thesis; for doctorate, comprehensive exam, thesis/dissertation. *Entrance requirements:* For master's, GRE, minimum undergraduate GPA of 3.0, 3 letters of recommendation; for doctorate, GRE. Additional exam requirements/recommendations for international students: Required—TOEFL (minimum score 550 paper-based; 213 computer-based). *Application deadline:* For fall admission, 2/1 priority date for domestic students, 12/1 for international students; for spring admission, 11/1 priority date for domestic students, 9/1 for international students. Applications are processed on a rolling basis. Application fee: $40 ($60 for international students). Electronic applications accepted. *Expenses:* Tuition, state resident: full-time $2071; part-time $86 per credit. Tuition, nonresident: full-time $8099; part-time $337 per credit. Required fees: $9446; $394 per credit. One-time fee: $75. Part-time tuition and fees vary according to class time, course load, degree level and reciprocity agreements. *Financial support:* In 2010–11, 2 fellowships with full tuition reimbursements (averaging $16,000 per year), 14 research assistantships with full tuition reimbursements (averaging $11,096 per year), 9 teaching assistantships with full tuition reimbursements (averaging $12,500 per year) were awarded; Federal Work-Study and unspecified assistantships also available. Support available to part-time students. Financial award application deadline: 3/1; financial award applicants required to submit FAFSA. *Faculty research:* Speech acoustics, marine applications, signals and systems, applied electromagnetics, intelligent agency. Total annual research expenditures: $1.1 million. *Unit head:* Dr. Karen Payton, Director, 508-999-8434, Fax: 508-999-8489, E-mail: kpayton@umassd.edu. *Application contact:* Elan Turcotte-Shamski, Graduate Admissions Officer, 508-999-8604, Fax: 508-999-8183, E-mail: graduate@umassd.edu.

Applied Physics

Air Force Institute of Technology, Graduate School of Engineering and Management, Department of Engineering Physics, Dayton, OH 45433-7765. Offers applied physics (MS, PhD); electro-optics (MS, PhD); materials science (PhD); nuclear engineering (MS, PhD); space physics (MS). Part-time programs available. *Degree requirements:* For master's, thesis; for doctorate, thesis/dissertation. *Entrance requirements:* For master's and doctorate, GRE General Test, minimum GPA of 3.0, U.S. citizenship. *Faculty research:* High-energy lasers, space physics, nuclear weapon effects, semiconductor physics.

Alabama Agricultural and Mechanical University, School of Graduate Studies, School of Arts and Sciences, Department of Physics, Huntsville, AL 35811. Offers physics (MS, PhD), including applied physics (PhD), materials science (PhD), optics/lasers (PhD). Part-time and evening/weekend programs available. *Degree requirements:* For doctorate, thesis/dissertation. *Entrance requirements:* For master's and doctorate, GRE General Test. Additional exam requirements/recommendations for international students: Required—TOEFL (minimum score 500 paper-based; 173 computer-based; 61 iBT). Electronic applications accepted.

California Institute of Technology, Division of Engineering and Applied Science, Option in Applied Physics, Pasadena, CA 91125-0001. Offers MS, PhD. *Faculty:* 8 full-time (1 woman). *Students:* 40 full-time (7 women). 144 applicants, 17% accepted, 2 enrolled. In 2010, 5 master's, 4 doctorates awarded. *Degree requirements:* For doctorate, thesis/dissertation. *Application deadline:* For fall admission, 1/1 for domestic students. Application fee: $0. Electronic applications accepted. *Financial support:* In 2010–11, 3 fellowships, 30 research assistantships, 10 teaching assistantships were awarded. *Faculty research:* Solid-state electronics, quantum electronics, plasmas, linear and nonlinear laser optics, electromagnetic theory. *Unit head:* Dr. Sandra M. Troian, Academic Officer, 626-395-3362, E-mail: stroian@caltech.edu. *Application contact:* Natalie Gilmore, Assistant Dean of Graduate Studies, 626-395-3812, Fax: 626-577-9246, E-mail: ngilmore@caltech.edu.

Carnegie Mellon University, Mellon College of Science, Department of Physics, Pittsburgh, PA 15213-3891. Offers applied physics (PhD); physics (MS, PhD). *Degree requirements:* For doctorate, thesis/dissertation, qualifying exam. *Entrance requirements:* For doctorate, GRE General Test, GRE Subject Test. Additional exam requirements/recommendations for international students: Required—TOEFL. Electronic applications accepted. *Faculty research:* Astrophysics, condensed matter physics, biological physics, medium energy and nuclear physics, high-energy physics.

Christopher Newport University, Graduate Studies, Department of Physics, Computer Science, and Engineering, Newport News, VA 23606-2998. Offers applied physics and computer science (MS). Part-time and evening/weekend programs available. *Faculty:* 6 full-time (0 women), 2 part-time/adjunct (0 women). *Students:* 4 full-time (0 women), 15 part-time (2 women); includes 3 minority (2 Black or African American, non-Hispanic/Latino; 1 Two or more races, non-Hispanic/Latino). Average age 29. 10 applicants, 100% accepted, 2 enrolled. In 2010, 8 master's awarded. *Degree requirements:* For master's, comprehensive exam (for some programs), thesis optional. *Entrance requirements:* For master's, GRE General Test, minimum GPA of 3.0. Additional exam requirements/recommendations for international students: Required—TOEFL (minimum score 580 paper-based; 237 computer-based; 92 iBT). *Application deadline:* For fall admission, 8/15 priority date for domestic students, 4/1 for international students; for spring admission, 10/15 for domestic students, 10/1 for international students. Applications are processed on a rolling basis. Application fee: $50. Electronic applications accepted. *Expenses:* Tuition, state resident: part-time $418 per credit hour. Tuition, nonresident: part-time $769 per credit hour. *Financial support:* In 2010–11, 3 research assistantships with full and partial tuition reimbursements (averaging $2,000 per year) were awarded; fellowships with full tuition reimbursements, career-related internships or fieldwork, Federal Work-Study, and unspecified assistantships also available. Support available to part-time students. Financial award application deadline: 3/1; financial award applicants required to submit FAFSA. *Faculty research:* Advanced programming methodologies, experimental nuclear physics, computer architecture, semiconductor nanophysics, laser and optical fiber sensors. *Unit head:* Dr. Antonio Siochi, Coordinator, 757-594-7569, Fax: 757-594-7919, E-mail: siochi@cnu.edu. *Application contact:* Lyn Sawyer, Associate Director, Graduate Admissions and Records, 757-594-7544, Fax: 757-594-7649, E-mail: gradstdy@cnu.edu.

Colorado School of Mines, Graduate School, Department of Physics, Golden, CO 80401. Offers applied physics (MS, PhD). Part-time programs available. *Faculty:* 32 full-time (5 women), 7 part-time/adjunct (0 women). *Students:* 57 full-time (12 women), 2 part-time (0 women); includes 1 Hispanic/Latino, 10 international. Average age 30. 85 applicants, 29% accepted, 19 enrolled. In 2010, 3 master's, 6 doctorates awarded. *Degree requirements:* For master's, thesis (for some programs); for doctorate, comprehensive exam, thesis/dissertation. *Entrance requirements:* For master's and doctorate, GRE General Test, GRE Subject Test. Additional exam requirements/recommendations for international students: Required—TOEFL (minimum score 550 paper-based; 213 computer-based; 80 iBT). *Application deadline:* For fall admission, 1/15 priority date for domestic and international students; for spring admission, 10/15 priority date for domestic and international students. Application fee: $50 ($70 for international students). Electronic applications accepted. *Expenses:* Tuition, state resident: full-time $11,550; part-time $641 per credit. Tuition, nonresident: full-time $25,980; part-time $1444 per credit. Required fees: $1874; $937 per semester. *Financial support:* In 2010–11, 53 students received support, including 1 fellowship with full tuition reimbursement available (averaging $20,000 per year), 34 research assistantships with full tuition reimbursements available (averaging $20,000 per year), 18 teaching assistantships with full tuition reimbursements available (averaging $20,000 per year); scholarships/grants, health care benefits, and unspecified assistantships also available. Financial award application deadline: 1/15; financial award applicants required to submit FAFSA. *Faculty research:* Light scattering, low-energy nuclear physics, high fusion plasma diagnostics, laser operations, mathematical physics. Total annual research expenditures: $2 million. *Unit head:* Dr. Thomas Furtak, Department Head, 303-273-3843, Fax: 303-273-3919, E-mail: tfurtak@mines.edu. *Application contact:* Dr. Tim Ohno, Professor, 303-273-3847, Fax: 303-273-3919, E-mail: tohno@mines.edu.

Columbia University, Fu Foundation School of Engineering and Applied Science, Department of Applied Physics and Applied Mathematics, New York, NY 10027. Offers applied physics (Eng Sc D); applied physics and applied mathematics (MS, PhD, Engr); materials science and engineering (MS, Eng Sc D, PhD); medical physics (MS). Part-time programs available. Postbaccalaureate distance learning degree programs offered (no on-campus study). *Faculty:* 32 full-time (2 women), 23 part-time/adjunct (2 women). *Students:* 126 full-time (28 women), 23 part-time (5 women); includes 14 minority (2 Black or African American, non-Hispanic/Latino; 8 Asian, non-Hispanic/Latino; 1 Hispanic/Latino; 3 Two or more races, non-Hispanic/Latino), 60 international. Average age 28. 344 applicants, 22% accepted, 36 enrolled. In 2010, 56 master's, 13 doctorates awarded. Terminal master's awarded for partial completion of doctoral program. *Degree requirements:* For master's, comprehensive exam; for doctorate, thesis/dissertation, qualifying exam. *Entrance requirements:* For master's, GRE General Test, GRE Subject Test (strongly recommended); for doctorate, GRE General Test, GRE Subject Test (applied physics); for Engr, GRE General Test. Additional exam requirements/recommendations for international students: Required—TOEFL, IELTS. *Application deadline:* For fall admission, 12/1 priority date for domestic and international students; for spring admission, 10/1 priority date for domestic and international students. Application fee: $95. Electronic applications accepted. *Financial support:* In 2010–11, 73 students received support, including 3 fellowships with full tuition reimbursements available (averaging $30,000 per year), 53 research assistantships with full tuition reimbursements available (averaging $30,667 per year), 17 teaching assistantships

172 www.facebook.com/petersonspublishing

Peterson's Graduate Programs in the Physical Sciences, Mathematics, Agricultural Sciences, the Environment & Natural Resources 2012

The Fu Foundation School of Engineering and Applied Science

Department of Applied Physics and Applied Mathematics

The Department of Applied Physics and Applied Mathematics includes graduate studies in the fields of applied physics, applied mathematics, and materials science and engineering.

The graduate program in applied physics includes plasma physics and controlled fusion; solid state physics; optical and laser physics; medical physics; atmospheric, oceanic, and earth physics, and applied mathematics.

The graduate program in materials science and engineering focuses on understanding, designing, and producing technology-enabling materials by analyzing the relationships amongst the synthesis and processing of materials, their properties, and their detailed structure.

Questions: **seasgradmit@columbia.edu**
Financial Aid Questions: **engradfinaid@columbia.edu**

http://www.engineering.columbia.edu/graduate-2

---

with full tuition reimbursements available (averaging $30,667 per year). Financial award application deadline: 12/1; financial award applicants required to submit FAFSA. *Faculty research:* Plasma, solid state, optical and laser physics; atmospheric, oceanic and earth physics; computational math and applied mathematics; materials science and engineering. *Unit head:* Dr. Irving P. Herman, Professor and Department Chairman, 212-854-4457, E-mail: seasinfo.apam@columbia.edu. *Application contact:* Montserrat Fernandez-Pinkley, Student Services Coordinator, 212-854-4457, Fax: 212-854-8257, E-mail: mf2157@columbia.edu.

See Close-Up on page 211.

Cornell University, Graduate School, Graduate Fields of Engineering, Field of Applied Physics, Ithaca, NY 14853-0001. Offers applied physics (PhD); engineering physics (M Eng). *Faculty:* 39 full-time (4 women). *Students:* 83 full-time (15 women); includes 8 Asian, non-Hispanic/Latino; 3 Hispanic/Latino, 39 international. Average age 25. 170 applicants, 35% accepted, 30 enrolled. In 2010, 11 master's, 16 doctorates awarded. *Degree requirements:* For doctorate, comprehensive exam, thesis/dissertation, written exams. *Entrance requirements:* For master's, GRE General Test, 3 letters of recommendation; for doctorate, GRE General Test, GRE Subject Test (physics), GRE Writing Assessment, 3 letters of recommendation. Additional exam requirements/recommendations for international students: Required—TOEFL (minimum score 600 paper-based; 250 computer-based; 77 iBT). *Application deadline:* For fall admission, 1/15 for domestic students. Application fee: $70. Electronic applications accepted. *Expenses:* Tuition: Full-time $29,500. Required fees: $76. Tuition and fees vary according to degree level and program. *Financial support:* In 2010–11, 70 students received support, including 7 fellowships with full tuition reimbursements available, 48 research assistantships with full tuition reimbursements available, 9 teaching assistantships with full tuition reimbursements available; institutionally sponsored loans, scholarships/grants, health care benefits, tuition waivers (full and partial), and unspecified assistantships also available. *Faculty research:* Quantum and nonlinear optics, plasma physics, solid state physics, condensed matter physics and nanotechnology, electron and x-ray spectroscopy. *Unit head:* Graduate Faculty Representative, 607-255-0638. *Application contact:* Graduate Field Assistant, 607-255-0638, E-mail: aep_info@cornell.edu.

DePaul University, College of Liberal Arts and Sciences, Department of Physics, Chicago, IL 60604-2287. Offers applied physics (MS). Part-time and evening/weekend programs available. *Faculty:* 6 full-time (2 women), 3 part-time/adjunct (0 women). *Students:* 8 full-time (2 women), 6 part-time (4 women); includes 1 Black or African American, non-Hispanic/Latino; 1 Hispanic/Latino, 3 international. Average age 23. 12 applicants, 42% accepted, 3 enrolled. In 2010, 3 master's awarded. *Degree requirements:* For master's, thesis, oral exams. *Entrance requirements:* For master's, 2 letters of recommendation, BA in physics or closely related field. Additional exam requirements/recommendations for international students: Required—TOEFL. *Application deadline:* For fall admission, 5/1 priority date for domestic students, 4/1 priority date for international students. Applications are processed on a rolling basis. Application fee: $25. Electronic applications accepted. *Financial support:* In 2010–11, teaching assistantships with full tuition reimbursements available (averaging $9,000 per year); tuition waivers (full) also available. *Faculty research:* Optics, solid-state physics, cosmology, atomic physics, nuclear physics. Total annual research expenditures: $54,000. *Unit head:* Dr. Christopher G. Goedde, Chairman, 773-325-7330, Fax: 773-325-7334, E-mail: egoedde@condor.depaul.edu. *Application contact:* Dr. Jesus Pando, Associate Professor, 773-325-7330, Fax: 773-325-7334.

George Mason University, College of Science, Department of Physics and Astronomy, Fairfax, VA 22030. Offers applied and engineering physics (MS); physics (PhD). *Faculty:* 30 full-time (9 women), 6 part-time/adjunct (1 woman). *Students:* 11 full-time (0 women), 48 part-time (16 women); includes 12 minority (1 Black or African American, non-Hispanic/Latino; 7 Asian, non-Hispanic/Latino; 4 Hispanic/Latino), 9 international. Average age 33. 41 applicants, 68% accepted, 15 enrolled. In 2010, 5 master's, 3 doctorates awarded. *Degree requirements:* For master's, thesis optional. *Entrance requirements:* For master's, minimum GPA of 2.75 in last 60 hours of course work. Additional exam requirements/recommendations for international students: Required—TOEFL (minimum score 570 paper-based; 230 computer-based; 88 iBT). *Application deadline:* For fall admission, 5/1 for domestic students; for spring admission, 11/1 for domestic students. Application fee: $100. Electronic applications accepted. *Expenses:* Tuition, state resident: full-time $8192; part-time $440 per credit hour. Tuition, nonresident: full-time $22,952; part-time $1055 per credit hour. Required fees: $2364; $99 per credit hour. *Financial support:* In 2010–11, 25 students received support, including 3 fellowships with full tuition reimbursements available (averaging $18,000 per year), 12 research assistantships with full and partial tuition reimbursements available (averaging $15,945 per year), 11 teaching assistantships with full and partial tuition reimbursements available (averaging $11,298 per year); career-related internships or fieldwork, Federal Work-Study, scholarships/grants, unspecified assistantships, and health care benefits (full-time research or teaching assistantship recipients) also available. Support available to part-time students. Financial award application deadline: 3/1; financial award applicants required to submit FAFSA. *Faculty research:* Astronomy, astrophysics, and space and planetary science; astronomy and physics education; atomic physics; biophysics and neuroscience. Total annual research expenditures: $2.4 million. *Unit head:* Dr. Michael Summers, Chairman, 703-993-3971, Fax: 703-993-1269, E-mail: msummers@gmu.edu. *Application contact:* Dr. Paul So, Information Contact, 703-993-4377, E-mail: paso@gmu.edu.

Harvard University, Graduate School of Arts and Sciences, Department of Physics, Cambridge, MA 02138. Offers experimental physics (PhD); medical engineering/medical physics (PhD), including applied physics, engineering sciences, physics; theoretical physics (PhD). *Degree requirements:* For doctorate, thesis/dissertation, final exams, laboratory experience. *Entrance requirements:* For doctorate, GRE General Test, GRE Subject Test. Additional exam requirements/recommendations for international students: Required—TOEFL. *Expenses:* Tuition: Full-time $34,976. Required fees: $1166. Full-time tuition and fees vary according to program. *Faculty research:* Particle physics, condensed matter physics, atomic physics.

Harvard University, Graduate School of Arts and Sciences, School of Engineering and Applied Sciences, Cambridge, MA 02138. Offers applied mathematics (ME, SM, PhD); applied physics (ME, SM, PhD); computer science (ME, SM, PhD); engineering science (ME); engineering sciences (SM, PhD). Part-time programs available. Terminal master's awarded for partial completion of doctoral program. *Degree requirements:* For master's, thesis optional; for doctorate, comprehensive exam, thesis/dissertation. *Entrance requirements:* For master's and doctorate, GRE General Test, GRE Subject Test (recommended), 3 letters of recommendation. Additional exam requirements/recommendations for international students: Required—TOEFL (minimum score 80 iBT). Electronic applications accepted. *Expenses:* Tuition: Full-time $34,976. Required fees: $1166. Full-time tuition and fees vary according to program. *Faculty research:* Applied mathematics, applied physics, computer science and electrical engineering, environmental engineering, mechanical and biomedical engineering.

Idaho State University, Office of Graduate Studies, College of Arts and Sciences, Department of Physics, Pocatello, ID 83209-8106. Offers applied physics (PhD); health physics (MS); physics (MNS). Part-time programs available. *Degree requirements:* For master's, comprehensive

Peterson's Graduate Programs in the Physical Sciences, Mathematics, Agricultural Sciences, the Environment & Natural Resources 2012

www.facebook.com/petersonspublishing **173**

Applied Physics

Idaho State University (continued)

exam, thesis (for some programs), oral exam (for some programs); for doctorate, comprehensive exam, thesis/dissertation (for some programs), oral exam, written qualifying exam in physics or health physics after 1st year. *Entrance requirements:* For master's, GRE General Test, 3 letters of recommendation, BS or BA in physics, teaching certificate (MNS); for doctorate, GRE General Test (minimum 50th percentile), 3 letters of recommendation, statement of career goals. Additional exam requirements/recommendations for international students: Required—TOEFL (minimum score 550 paper-based; 213 computer-based; 80 iBT). Electronic applications accepted. *Faculty research:* Ion beam applications, low-energy nuclear physics, relativity and cosmology, observational astronomy.

Iowa State University of Science and Technology, Graduate College, College of Liberal Arts and Sciences, Department of Physics and Astronomy, Ames, IA 50011. Offers applied physics (MS, PhD); astrophysics (MS, PhD); condensed matter physics (MS, PhD); high energy physics (MS, PhD); nuclear physics (MS, PhD); physics (MS, PhD). Part-time programs available. *Faculty:* 48 full-time (4 women), 4 part-time/adjunct (0 women). *Students:* 97 full-time (19 women), 6 part-time (0 women); includes 3 Asian, non-Hispanic/Latino, 53 international. 179 applicants, 32% accepted, 18 enrolled. In 2010, 4 master's, 11 doctorates awarded. Terminal master's awarded for partial completion of doctoral program. *Degree requirements:* For master's, thesis (for some programs); for doctorate, thesis/dissertation. *Entrance requirements:* For master's and doctorate, GRE General Test, GRE Subject Test (physics). Additional exam requirements/recommendations for international students: Required—TOEFL (minimum score 550 paper-based; 79 iBT), IELTS (minimum score 6.5). *Application deadline:* For fall admission, 2/15 priority date for domestic and international students; for spring admission, 10/15 for domestic and international students. Applications are processed on a rolling basis. Application fee: $40 ($90 for international students). Electronic applications accepted. *Financial support:* In 2010–11, 54 research assistantships with full and partial tuition reimbursements (averaging $12,890 per year), 34 teaching assistantships with full and partial tuition reimbursements (averaging $13,928 per year) were awarded; fellowships, Federal Work-Study, institutionally sponsored loans, scholarships/grants, health care benefits, and unspecified assistantships also available. Support available to part-time students. Financial award application deadline: 2/15. *Faculty research:* Condensed-matter physics, including superconductivity and new materials; high-energy and nuclear physics; astronomy and astrophysics; atmospheric and environmental physics. Total annual research expenditures: $8.8 million. *Unit head:* Dr. Joseph Shinar, Chair, 515-294-3455, Fax: 515-294-6027, E-mail: phys_astro@iastate.edu. *Application contact:* Dr. Steven Kawaler, Director of Graduate Education, 515-294-9728, E-mail: phys_astro@iastate.edu.

The Johns Hopkins University, Engineering for Professionals, Part-time Program in Applied Physics, Baltimore, MD 21218-2699. Offers MS, Post-Master's Certificate. Part-time and evening/weekend programs available. *Faculty:* 10 part-time/adjunct (0 women). *Students:* 4 full-time (0 women), 69 part-time (21 women); includes 20 minority (4 Black or African American, non-Hispanic/Latino; 7 Asian, non-Hispanic/Latino; 6 Hispanic/Latino; 1 Native Hawaiian or other Pacific Islander, non-Hispanic/Latino; 2 Two or more races, non-Hispanic/Latino). Average age 29. 34 applicants, 79% accepted, 21 enrolled. In 2010, 19 master's awarded. *Application deadline:* Applications are processed on a rolling basis. Application fee: $75. Electronic applications accepted. *Financial support:* Institutionally sponsored loans available. *Unit head:* Dr. Harry K. Charles, Chair, 443-778-8050, E-mail: harry.charles@jhuapl.edu. *Application contact:* Priyanka Dwivedi, Admissions Manager, 410-516-2300, Fax: 410-579-8049, E-mail: pdwived1@jhu.edu.

Laurentian University, School of Graduate Studies and Research, Programme in Physics, Sudbury, ON P3E 2C6, Canada. Offers M Sc. Part-time programs available. *Degree requirements:* For master's, thesis or alternative. *Entrance requirements:* For master's, honors degree with second class or better. *Faculty research:* Solar neutrino physics and astrophysics, applied acoustics and ultrasonics, powder science and technology, solid state physics, theoretical physics.

Mississippi State University, College of Arts and Sciences, Department of Physics and Astronomy, Mississippi State, MS 39762. Offers engineering (PhD), including applied physics; physics (MS). PhD is interdisciplinary. Part-time programs available. *Faculty:* 11 full-time (0 women). *Students:* 38 full-time (8 women), 3 part-time (0 women); includes 3 minority (1 Black or African American, non-Hispanic/Latino; 2 Hispanic/Latino), 32 international. Average age 29. 38 applicants, 45% accepted, 10 enrolled. In 2010, 6 master's, 4 doctorates awarded. *Degree requirements:* For master's, thesis optional, comprehensive oral or written exam; for doctorate, thesis/dissertation, comprehensive oral or written exam. *Entrance requirements:* For master's, GRE, minimum GPA of 2.75 on last two years of undergraduate courses; for doctorate, GRE. Additional exam requirements/recommendations for international students: Required—TOEFL (minimum score 475 paper-based; 153 computer-based; 53 iBT); Recommended—IELTS (minimum score 4.5). *Application deadline:* For fall admission, 7/1 priority date for domestic students, 5/1 for international students; for spring admission, 11/1 priority date for domestic students, 9/1 for international students. Applications are processed on a rolling basis. Application fee: $40. Electronic applications accepted. *Expenses:* Tuition, state resident: full-time $2730.50; part-time $304 per credit hour. Tuition, nonresident: full-time $6901; part-time $767 per credit hour. *Financial support:* In 2010–11, 5 research assistantships with full tuition reimbursements (averaging $14,310 per year), 22 teaching assistantships with full tuition reimbursements (averaging $13,023 per year) were awarded; Federal Work-Study, institutionally sponsored loans, and unspecified assistantships also available. Financial award application deadline: 3/15; financial award applicants required to submit FAFSA. *Faculty research:* Atomic/molecular spectroscopy, theoretical optics, gamma-ray astronomy, experimental nuclear physics, computational physics. Total annual research expenditures: $2 million. *Unit head:* Dr. Mark A. Novotny, Department Head and Professor, 662-325-2806, Fax: 662-325-8898, E-mail: man40@ra.msstate.edu. *Application contact:* Dr. David Monts, Professor and Graduate Coordinator, 662-325-2931, Fax: 662-325-8898, E-mail: physics@msstate.edu.

Naval Postgraduate School, Graduate Programs, Department of Physics, Monterey, CA 93943. Offers applied physics (MS); engineering acoustics (MS); physics (MS, PhD). Program only open to commissioned officers of the United States and friendly nations and selected United States federal civilian employees. Part-time programs available. *Degree requirements:* For master's, thesis; for doctorate, one foreign language, thesis/dissertation.

New Jersey Institute of Technology, Office of Graduate Studies, College of Science and Liberal Arts, Department of Physics, Program in Applied Physics, Newark, NJ 07102. Offers MS, PhD. Part-time and evening/weekend programs available. *Students:* 28 full-time (4 women), 6 part-time (0 women); includes 3 Asian, non-Hispanic/Latino; 1 Hispanic/Latino, 24 international. Average age 32. 58 applicants, 33% accepted, 7 enrolled. In 2010, 1 master's, 5 doctorates awarded. Terminal master's awarded for partial completion of doctoral program. *Degree requirements:* For master's, thesis optional; for doctorate, thesis/dissertation, residency. *Entrance requirements:* For master's, GRE General Test; for doctorate, GRE General Test, minimum graduate GPA of 3.5. Additional exam requirements/recommendations for international students: Required—TOEFL (minimum score 550 paper-based; 213 computer-based; 79 iBT). *Application deadline:* For fall admission, 6/5 priority date for domestic students, 4/1 for international students; for spring admission, 11/15 for domestic and international students. Applications are processed on a rolling basis. Application fee: $65. Electronic applications accepted. *Expenses:* Tuition, state resident: full-time $14,724; part-time $818 per credit. Tuition, nonresident: full-time $20,304; part-time $1128 per credit. Required fees: $2272; $209 per credit. $103 per semester. One-time fee: $312 full-time; $212 part-time. *Financial support:* Fellowships with full and partial tuition reimbursements, research assistantships with full and partial tuition reimbursements, teaching assistantships with full and partial tuition reimbursements, career-related internships or fieldwork, Federal Work-Study, institutionally sponsored loans, and unspecified assistantships available. Financial award application deadline: 3/15. *Unit head:* Dr. N.M. Ravindra, Chair, 973-596-3278, E-mail: n.m.ravindra@njit.edu. *Application contact:* Kathryn Kelly, Director of Admissions, 973-596-3300, Fax: 973-596-3461, E-mail: admissions@njit.edu.

Northern Arizona University, Graduate College, College of Engineering, Forestry and Natural Sciences, Department of Physics and Astronomy, Flagstaff, AZ 86011. Offers applied physics (MS). Part-time programs available. *Faculty:* 13 full-time (2 women). *Students:* 16 full-time (8 women), 1 part-time (0 women); includes 1 minority (Hispanic/Latino), 3 international. Average age 37. 22 applicants, 55% accepted, 7 enrolled. In 2010, 3 master's awarded. *Degree requirements:* For master's, thesis optional. *Entrance requirements:* Additional exam requirements/recommendations for international students: Required—TOEFL (minimum score 550 paper-based; 213 computer-based; 80 iBT), IELTS (minimum score 7). *Application deadline:* For fall admission, 1/15 priority date for domestic and international students. Applications are processed on a rolling basis. Application fee: $65. Electronic applications accepted. *Financial support:* In 2010–11, 4 research assistantships with partial tuition reimbursements (averaging $12,390 per year), 11 teaching assistantships with partial tuition reimbursements (averaging $12,390 per year) were awarded; Federal Work-Study, scholarships/grants, health care benefits, tuition waivers (full and partial), and unspecified assistantships also available. Financial award applicants required to submit FAFSA. *Unit head:* Dr. Kathy Eastwood, Chair, 928-523-7159, Fax: 928-523-1371, E-mail: kathy.eastwood@nau.edu. *Application contact:* Jamie Housholder, Administrative Assistant, 928-523-8170, Fax: 928-523-1371, E-mail: astro.physics@nau.edu.

Oregon State University, Graduate School, College of Science, Department of Physics, Corvallis, OR 97331. Offers applied physics (MS); physics (MA, MS, PhD). Part-time programs available. Terminal master's awarded for partial completion of doctoral program. *Degree requirements:* For master's, thesis optional, qualifying exam; for doctorate, thesis/dissertation, qualifying exam. *Entrance requirements:* For master's and doctorate, minimum GPA of 3.0 in last 90 hours. Additional exam requirements/recommendations for international students: Required—TOEFL.

Pittsburg State University, Graduate School, College of Arts and Sciences, Department of Physics, Pittsburg, KS 66762. Offers applied physics (MS); physics (MS); professional physics (MS). *Degree requirements:* For master's, thesis or alternative.

Polytechnic Institute of NYU, Department of Applied Physics, Brooklyn, NY 11201-2990. Offers MS, PhD. Part-time and evening/weekend programs available. *Faculty:* 3 full-time (0 women). *Students:* 1 full-time (0 women), all international. Average age 29. *Degree requirements:* For master's, comprehensive exam (for some programs), thesis (for some programs); for doctorate, comprehensive exam, thesis/dissertation. *Entrance requirements:* For master's, BA in physics; for doctorate, departmental qualifying exam, BS in physics. Additional exam requirements/recommendations for international students: Required—TOEFL (minimum score 550 paper-based; 213 computer-based; 80 iBT); Recommended—IELTS (minimum score 6.5). *Application deadline:* For fall admission, 7/31 priority date for domestic students, 4/30 priority date for international students; for spring admission, 12/31 priority date for domestic students, 11/30 priority date for international students. Applications are processed on a rolling basis. Application fee: $75. Electronic applications accepted. *Expenses:* Tuition: Full-time $21,492; part-time $1194 per credit. Required fees: $385 per semester. Tuition and fees vary according to course load. *Financial support:* Fellowships, research assistantships, teaching assistantships, institutionally sponsored loans available. Support available to part-time students. Financial award applicants required to submit FAFSA. *Faculty research:* Combining microdroplets, UHV cryogenic scanning, tunneling, surface spectroscopy of a single aerosol particle. Total annual research expenditures: $517,982. *Unit head:* Dr. Lorcan M. Folan, Head, 718-260-3072, E-mail: lfolan@poly.edu. *Application contact:* JeanCarlo Bonilla, Director of Graduate Enrollment Management, 718-260-3182, Fax: 718-260-3624, E-mail: gradinfo@poly.edu.

Rice University, Rice Quantum Institute, Houston, TX 77251-1892. Offers MS, PhD. *Degree requirements:* For master's, thesis; for doctorate, thesis/dissertation. *Entrance requirements:* For master's and doctorate, GRE General Test, GRE Subject Test (physics), minimum GPA of 3.0. Additional exam requirements/recommendations for international students: Required—TOEFL (minimum score 600 paper-based; 250 computer-based; 90 iBT). Electronic applications accepted. *Faculty research:* Nanotechnology, solid state materials, atomic physics, thin films.

Rutgers, The State University of New Jersey, Newark, Graduate School, Program in Applied Physics, Newark, NJ 07102. Offers MS, PhD. MS, PhD offered jointly with New Jersey Institute of Technology. *Faculty:* 25 full-time (0 women), 1 part-time/adjunct (0 women). *Students:* 3 full-time (1 woman), 1 (woman) part-time; includes 2 Asian, non-Hispanic/Latino. 8 applicants, 25% accepted, 0 enrolled. *Entrance requirements:* For master's and doctorate, GRE. Additional exam requirements/recommendations for international students: Required—TOEFL. *Application deadline:* For fall admission, 7/1 for domestic students; for spring admission, 12/1 for domestic students. Application fee: $60. *Expenses:* Tuition, state resident: part-time $600 per credit. Tuition, nonresident: full-time $10,694. *Financial support:* In 2010–11, 3 teaching assistantships with full and partial tuition reimbursements (averaging $23,112 per year) were awarded. *Unit head:* Zhen Wu, Program Coordinator, 973-353-1311, E-mail: zwu@andromeda.rutgers.edu. *Application contact:* Elizabeth Wheeler, Administrative Assistant, 201-973-1312, E-mail: ewheeler@andromeda.rutgers.edu.

Southern Illinois University Carbondale, Graduate School, College of Science, Department of Physics, Carbondale, IL 62901-4701. Offers MS, PhD. *Degree requirements:* For master's, one foreign language, thesis. *Entrance requirements:* For master's, minimum GPA of 2.7. Additional exam requirements/recommendations for international students: Required—TOEFL. *Faculty research:* Atomic, molecular, nuclear, and mathematical physics; statistical mechanics; solid-state and low-temperature physics; rheology; material science.

Stanford University, School of Humanities and Sciences, Department of Applied Physics, Stanford, CA 94305-9991. Offers MS, PhD. Terminal master's awarded for partial completion of doctoral program. *Degree requirements:* For doctorate, thesis/dissertation. *Entrance requirements:* For master's and doctorate, GRE General Test, GRE Subject Test. Additional exam requirements/recommendations for international students: Required—TOEFL. Electronic applications accepted. *Expenses:* Tuition: Full-time $38,700; part-time $860 per unit. One-time fee: $200 full-time.

State University of New York at Binghamton, Graduate School, School of Arts and Sciences, Department of Physics, Applied Physics, and Astronomy, Binghamton, NY 13902-6000. Offers applied physics (MS); physics (MA, MS, PhD). *Faculty:* 12 full-time (1 woman), 8 part-time/adjunct (4 women). *Students:* 14 full-time (0 women); includes 1 Black or African American, non-Hispanic/Latino, 2 international. Average age 26. 20 applicants, 75% accepted, 7 enrolled. In 2010, 3 master's awarded. *Degree requirements:* For master's, thesis or alternative. *Entrance requirements:* For master's, GRE General Test, GRE Subject Test. Additional exam requirements/recommendations for international students: Required—TOEFL (minimum score 550 paper-based; 213 computer-based; 80 iBT). *Application deadline:* For fall admission, 2/15 priority date for domestic and international students; for spring admission, 10/15 priority date for domestic and international students. Applications are processed on a rolling basis. Application fee: $60. Electronic applications accepted. *Financial support:* In 2010–11, 14 students received support, including 1 research assistantship with full tuition reimbursement available (averaging $11,000 per year), 13 teaching assistantships with full tuition reimbursements available (averaging $11,000 per year); career-related internships or fieldwork, Federal Work-Study, institutionally sponsored loans, scholarships/grants, health care benefits, and unspecified assistantships also available. Financial award application deadline: 2/15; financial award

applicants required to submit FAFSA. *Unit head:* Dr. Eric Cotts, Chairperson, 607-777-4371, E-mail: ecotts@binghamton.edu. *Application contact:* Catherine Smith, Recruiting and Admissions Coordinator, 607-777-2151, Fax: 607-777-2501, E-mail: cmsmith@binghamton.edu.

Texas A&M University, College of Science, Department of Physics and Astronomy, College Station, TX 77843. Offers applied physics (PhD); physics (MS, PhD). *Faculty:* 50. *Students:* 176 full-time (26 women), 2 part-time (1 woman); includes 2 Black or African American, non-Hispanic/Latino; 2 American Indian or Alaska Native, non-Hispanic/Latino; 8 Asian, non-Hispanic/Latino; 11 Hispanic/Latino, 89 international. In 2010, 9 master's, 11 doctorates awarded. Terminal master's awarded for partial completion of doctoral program. *Degree requirements:* For master's, thesis (for some programs); for doctorate, thesis/dissertation. *Entrance requirements:* For master's and doctorate, GRE General Test, GRE Subject Test. Additional exam requirements/recommendations for international students: Required—TOEFL. *Application deadline:* For fall admission, 3/1 priority date for domestic students; for spring admission, 8/1 for domestic students. Application fee: $50 ($75 for international students). Electronic applications accepted. *Financial support:* In 2010–11, research assistantships (averaging $16,200 per year), teaching assistantships (averaging $16,200 per year) were awarded; fellowships also available. Financial award application deadline: 3/1; financial award applicants required to submit FAFSA. *Faculty research:* Condensed-matter, atomic/molecular, high-energy, and nuclear physics; quantum optics. *Unit head:* Dr. Edward S. Fry, Head, 979-845-7717, E-mail: fry@physics.tamu.edu. *Application contact:* Dr. George W. Kattawar, Professor, 979-845-1180, Fax: 979-845-2590, E-mail: kattawar@tamu.edu.

Texas Tech University, Graduate School, College of Arts and Sciences, Department of Physics, Lubbock, TX 79409. Offers applied physics (MS); physics (MS, PhD). Part-time programs available. *Faculty:* 14 full-time (1 woman), 1 part-time/adjunct (0 women). *Students:* 52 full-time (10 women), 2 part-time (0 women); includes 1 Black or African American, non-Hispanic/Latino; 2 Hispanic/Latino; 1 Two or more races, non-Hispanic/Latino, 35 international. Average age 28. 46 applicants, 52% accepted, 13 enrolled. In 2010, 6 master's, 3 doctorates awarded. *Degree requirements:* For master's, variable foreign language requirement, thesis or alternative; for doctorate, variable foreign language requirement, thesis/dissertation. *Entrance requirements:* For master's and doctorate, GRE General Test. Additional exam requirements/recommendations for international students: Required—TOEFL (minimum score 550 paper-based; 213 computer-based; 79 iBT). *Application deadline:* For fall admission, 6/1 priority date for domestic students, 1/15 priority date for international students; for spring admission, 9/1 priority date for domestic students, 6/15 priority date for international students. Applications are processed on a rolling basis. Application fee: $50 ($75 for international students). Electronic applications accepted. *Expenses:* Tuition, state resident: full-time $5495.76; part-time $228.99 per credit hour. Tuition, nonresident: full-time $12,936; part-time $538.99 per credit hour. Required fees: $2674; $36 per credit hour. $905 per semester. *Financial support:* In 2010–11, 49 students received support, including 10 research assistantships with partial tuition reimbursements available (averaging $4,740 per year), 12 teaching assistantships with partial tuition reimbursements available (averaging $5,946 per year). Financial award application deadline: 4/15; financial award applicants required to submit FAFSA. *Faculty research:* Biophysics, high energy and nuclear physics, condensed matter physics, atomic and molecular physics, physics education. Total annual research expenditures: $1.5 million. *Unit head:* Dr. Roger Lichti, Chair, 806-742-3767, Fax: 806-742-1182, E-mail: roger.lichti@ttu.edu. *Application contact:* Dr. Mahdi Sanati, Graduate Recruiter, 806-742-3767, Fax: 806-742-1182, E-mail: m.sanati@ttu.edu.

Towson University, Program in Applied Physics, Towson, MD 21252-0001. Offers MS. *Students:* 2 full-time (0 women), 3 part-time (2 women), 3 international. *Expenses:* Tuition, state resident: part-time $324 per credit. Tuition, nonresident: part-time $681 per credit. Required fees: $95 per term. *Unit head:* Dr. Raj Kolagani, Dean, 410-704-3134, E-mail: rkolagani@towson.edu. *Application contact:* Dr. Raj Kolagani, Dean, 410-704-3134, E-mail: rkolagani@towson.edu.

The University of Arizona, College of Science, Department of Physics, Program in Applied and Industrial Physics, Tucson, AZ 85721. Offers PMS. Part-time programs available. *Students:* 5 full-time (1 woman), 1 part-time (0 women), 2 international. Average age 30. 13 applicants, 38% accepted, 5 enrolled. In 2010, 4 master's awarded. *Degree requirements:* For master's, thesis or alternative, internship, colloquium, business courses. *Entrance requirements:* Additional exam requirements/recommendations for international students: Required—TOEFL (minimum score 550 paper-based; 213 computer-based; 79 iBT). Application fee: $75. Electronic applications accepted. *Expenses:* Tuition, state resident: full-time $7692. *Financial support:* Career-related internships or fieldwork, Federal Work-Study, and scholarships/grants available. *Faculty research:* Nanotechnology, optics, medical imaging, high energy physics, biophysics. *Unit head:* Dr. Michael Shupe, Department Head, 520-621-2679, E-mail: shupe@physics.arizona.edu. *Application contact:* Lisa Shapouri, Graduate Coordinator, 520-621-2290, Fax: 520-621-4721, E-mail: lisas@physics.arizona.edu.

University of Arkansas, Graduate School, J. William Fulbright College of Arts and Sciences, Department of Physics, Fayetteville, AR 72701-1201. Offers applied physics (MS); physics (MS, PhD); physics education (MA). *Students:* 7 full-time (2 women), 39 part-time (8 women); includes 1 minority (Asian, non-Hispanic/Latino), 26 international. 15 applicants, 100% accepted. In 2010, 6 master's, 3 doctorates awarded. *Degree requirements:* For master's, thesis; for doctorate, thesis/dissertation. *Application deadline:* For fall admission, 4/1 for international students; for spring admission, 10/1 for international students. Applications are processed on a rolling basis. Application fee: $40 ($50 for international students). Electronic applications accepted. *Financial support:* In 2010–11, 9 fellowships with tuition reimbursements, 21 research assistantships, 22 teaching assistantships were awarded; career-related internships or fieldwork and Federal Work-Study also available. Support available to part-time students. Financial award application deadline: 4/1; financial award applicants required to submit FAFSA. *Unit head:* Dr. Surendra Singh, Departmental Chairperson, 479-575-2506, Fax: 479-575-4580, E-mail: ssingh@uark.edu. *Application contact:* Dr. Huaxiang Fu, Graduate Coordinator, 479-575-8606, E-mail: hfu@uark.edu.

University of California, San Diego, Office of Graduate Studies, Department of Electrical and Computer Engineering, La Jolla, CA 92093. Offers applied ocean science (MS, PhD); applied physics (MS, PhD); communication theory and systems (MS, PhD); computer engineering (MS, PhD); electrical engineering (M Eng); electronic circuits and systems (MS, PhD); intelligent systems, robotics and control (MS, PhD); photonics (MS, PhD); signal and image processing (MS, PhD). MS only offered to students who have been admitted to the PhD program. *Entrance requirements:* For master's and doctorate, GRE General Test. Electronic applications accepted.

University of Denver, Faculty of Natural Sciences and Mathematics, Department of Physics and Astronomy, Denver, CO 80208. Offers MS, PhD. Part-time programs available. *Faculty:* 10 full-time (2 women), 1 part-time/adjunct (0 women). *Students:* 7 full-time (2 women), 10 part-time (3 women); includes 2 minority (1 Asian, non-Hispanic/Latino; 1 Hispanic/Latino), 2 international. Average age 28. 28 applicants, 36% accepted, 5 enrolled. In 2010, 1 doctorate awarded. Terminal master's awarded for partial completion of doctoral program. *Degree requirements:* For master's, thesis optional; for doctorate, thesis/dissertation. *Entrance requirements:* For master's and doctorate, GRE General Test; GRE Subject Test in physics (strongly preferred). Additional exam requirements/recommendations for international students: Required—TOEFL (minimum score 550 paper-based; 80 iBT). *Application deadline:* For fall admission, 3/1 priority date for domestic students. Applications are processed on a rolling basis. Application fee: $60. Electronic applications accepted. *Expenses:* Tuition: Full-time $35,604; part-time $29,670 per year. Required fees: $687 per year. Tuition and fees vary according to program. *Financial support:* In 2010–11, 11 research assistantships with full and partial tuition reimbursements (averaging $19,299 per year), 7 teaching assistantships with full and partial tuition reimbursements (averaging $19,299 per year) were awarded; career-related internships or fieldwork, Federal Work-Study, institutionally sponsored loans, scholarships/grants, and unspecified assistantships also available. Support available to part-time students. Financial award application deadline: 3/1; financial award applicants required to submit FAFSA. *Faculty research:* Atomic and molecular beams and collisions, infrared astronomy, acoustic emission from stressed solids, nano materials. *Unit head:* Dr. Davor Balzar, Chair, 303-871-2238, E-mail: davor.balzar@du.edu. *Application contact:* Barbara Stephen, Assistant to the Chair, 303-871-2238, E-mail: barbara.stephen@du.edu.

University of Maryland, Baltimore County, Graduate School, College of Natural and Mathematical Sciences, Department of Physics, Program in Applied Physics, Baltimore, MD 21250. Offers astrophysics (PhD); optics (MS, PhD); quantum optics (PhD); solid state physics (MS, PhD). Part-time programs available. *Faculty:* 24 full-time (3 women), 18 part-time/adjunct (2 women). *Students:* 31 full-time (10 women), 3 part-time (0 women); includes 3 Black or African American, non-Hispanic/Latino, 15 international. Average age 24. 28 applicants, 43% accepted, 7 enrolled. In 2010, 4 master's, 4 doctorates awarded. Terminal master's awarded for partial completion of doctoral program. *Degree requirements:* For master's, thesis optional; for doctorate, comprehensive exam, thesis/dissertation. *Entrance requirements:* For master's, GRE General Test, minimum GPA of 3.0; for doctorate, GRE General Test, GRE Subject Test, minimum GPA of 3.0. Additional exam requirements/recommendations for international students: Required—TOEFL. *Application deadline:* For fall admission, 5/31 for domestic and international students; for spring admission, 11/30 for domestic students. Applications are processed on a rolling basis. Application fee: $50. Electronic applications accepted. *Financial support:* In 2010–11, 30 students received support, including 4 fellowships with full tuition reimbursements available (averaging $27,000 per year), 14 research assistantships with full tuition reimbursements available (averaging $24,000 per year), 12 teaching assistantships with full tuition reimbursements available (averaging $22,000 per year); career-related internships or fieldwork, scholarships/grants, health care benefits, and unspecified assistantships also available. Support available to part-time students. Financial award application deadline: 5/31. *Faculty research:* Astrophysics, atmospheric physics, nanophysics, optics, quantum optics and quantum information. Total annual research expenditures: $4.8 million. *Unit head:* Dr. Todd Pittman, EdD, Graduate Program Director, 410-455-2513, Fax: 410-455-1072, E-mail: todd.pittman@umbc.edu. *Application contact:* Dr. Lazlo L. Takacs, Director, 410-455-2524, Fax: 410-455-1072, E-mail: takacs@umbc.edu.

University of Massachusetts Boston, Office of Graduate Studies, College of Science and Mathematics, Program in Applied Physics, Boston, MA 02125-3393. Offers MS. Part-time and evening/weekend programs available. *Degree requirements:* For master's, thesis optional. *Entrance requirements:* For master's, minimum GPA of 2.75. *Faculty research:* Experimental laser research, nonlinear optics, experimental and theoretical solid state physics, semiconductor devices, opto-electronics.

University of Massachusetts Lowell, College of Arts and Sciences, Department of Physics and Applied Physics, Program in Applied Physics, Lowell, MA 01854-2881. Offers applied mechanics (PhD); applied physics (MS, PhD), including optical sciences (MS). Terminal master's awarded for partial completion of doctoral program. *Degree requirements:* For master's, thesis; for doctorate, 2 foreign languages, thesis/dissertation. *Entrance requirements:* For master's, GRE General Test, 3 letters of reference; for doctorate, GRE General Test, transcripts, 3 letters of reference. Additional exam requirements/recommendations for international students: Required—TOEFL.

University of Michigan, Horace H. Rackham School of Graduate Studies, College of Literature, Science, and the Arts, Applied Physics Program, Ann Arbor, MI 48198. Offers PhD. *Faculty:* 120 full-time (18 women). *Students:* 69 full-time (18 women); includes 18 minority (10 Black or African American, non-Hispanic/Latino; 2 American Indian or Alaska Native, non-Hispanic/Latino; 3 Asian, non-Hispanic/Latino; 3 Hispanic/Latino), 12 international. Average age 23. 105 applicants, 20% accepted, 12 enrolled. In 2010, 11 doctorates awarded. *Degree requirements:* For doctorate, oral defense of dissertation, preliminary and qualifying exams. *Entrance requirements:* For doctorate, GRE General Test. Additional exam requirements/recommendations for international students: Required—TOEFL. *Application deadline:* For fall admission, 1/15 for domestic and international students. Applications are processed on a rolling basis. Application fee: $60 ($75 for international students). Electronic applications accepted. *Expenses:* Tuition, state resident: full-time $17,784; part-time $1116 per credit hour. Tuition, nonresident: full-time $35,944; part-time $2125 per credit hour. International tuition: $35,994 full-time. Required fees: $95 per semester. Tuition and fees vary according to course load, degree level and program. *Financial support:* In 2010–11, 22 students received support, including 31 fellowships with full tuition reimbursements available (averaging $26,000 per year), 34 research assistantships with full tuition reimbursements available (averaging $26,000 per year), 4 teaching assistantships with full tuition reimbursements available; traineeships, health care benefits, and unspecified assistantships also available. Financial award application deadline: 1/15; financial award applicants required to submit FAFSA. *Faculty research:* Optical sciences, materials research, quantum structures, medical imaging, environment and science policy. Total annual research expenditures: $1.1 million. *Unit head:* Dr. Cagliyan Kurdak, Director, 734-647-4650, Fax: 734-764-2193, E-mail: kurdak@umich.edu. *Application contact:* Charles N. Sutton, Program Assistant, 734-764-4595, Fax: 734-764-2193, E-mail: csutton@umich.edu.

University of Missouri–St. Louis, College of Arts and Sciences, Department of Physics and Astronomy, St. Louis, MO 63121. Offers physics (MS, PhD), including applied physics (MS), astrophysics (MS). Part-time and evening/weekend programs available. *Faculty:* 12 full-time (2 women), 4 part-time/adjunct (1 woman). *Students:* 10 full-time (2 women), 13 part-time (4 women), 2 international. Average age 34. 17 applicants, 29% accepted, 4 enrolled. In 2010, 3 master's, 3 doctorates awarded. Terminal master's awarded for partial completion of doctoral program. *Degree requirements:* For master's, thesis optional; for doctorate, thesis/dissertation. *Entrance requirements:* For master's, GRE General Test; for doctorate, GRE General Test, 2 letters of recommendation. Additional exam requirements/recommendations for international students: Required—TOEFL (minimum score 550 paper-based; 213 computer-based). *Application deadline:* For fall admission, 7/1 for domestic and international students; for spring admission, 12/1 for domestic students, 11/1 for international students. Application fee: $35 ($40 for international students). Electronic applications accepted. *Expenses:* Tuition, state resident: full-time $5522; part-time $306.80 per credit hour. Tuition, nonresident: full-time $14,253; part-time $792.10 per credit hour. Required fees: $658; $49 per credit hour. One-time fee: $12. Tuition and fees vary according to program. *Financial support:* In 2010–11, 4 research assistantships with full and partial tuition reimbursements (averaging $16,125 per year), 10 teaching assistantships with full and partial tuition reimbursements (averaging $14,815 per year) were awarded; fellowships with full tuition reimbursements, career-related internships or fieldwork also available. Financial award applicants required to submit FAFSA. *Faculty research:* Biophysics, atomic physics, nonlinear dynamics, materials science. *Unit head:* Dr. Phil Fraundorf, Director of Graduate Studies, 314-516-5931, Fax: 314-516-6152, E-mail: fraundorfp@msx.umsl.edu. *Application contact:* 314-516-5458, Fax: 314-516-6996, E-mail: gradadm@umsl.edu.

The University of North Carolina at Charlotte, Graduate School, College of Arts and Sciences, Department of Physics and Optical Science, Charlotte, NC 28223-0001. Offers applied physics (MS); optical science and engineering (MS, PhD). *Faculty:* 21 full-time (4 women). *Students:* 39 full-time (7 women), 13 part-time (4 women); includes 1 minority (Asian, non-Hispanic/Latino), 29 international. Average age 27. 42 applicants, 79% accepted, 15 enrolled. In 2010, 8 master's, 9 doctorates awarded. Terminal master's awarded for partial completion of doctoral program. *Degree requirements:* For master's, thesis optional; for doctorate, thesis/dissertation optional. *Entrance requirements:* For master's, GRE General Test, minimum

Applied Physics

The University of North Carolina at Charlotte (continued)

GPA of 3.0 during previous 2 years, 2.75 overall. Additional exam requirements/recommendations for international students: Required—TOEFL (minimum score 557 paper-based; 220 computer-based; 83 iBT). *Application deadline:* For fall admission, 7/15 for domestic students, 5/1 for international students; for spring admission, 11/15 for domestic students, 10/1 for international students. Applications are processed on a rolling basis. Application fee: $55. Electronic applications accepted. *Expenses:* Tuition, state resident: full-time $3464. Tuition, nonresident: full-time $14,297. Required fees: $2094. Tuition and fees vary according to course load. *Financial support:* In 2010–11, 35 students received support, including 6 fellowships (averaging $40,536 per year), 9 research assistantships (averaging $9,718 per year), 18 teaching assistantships (averaging $13,041 per year); career-related internships or fieldwork, institutionally sponsored loans, scholarships/grants, and unspecified assistantships also available. Support available to part-time students. Financial award application deadline: 4/1; financial award applicants required to submit FAFSA. *Faculty research:* Optics, lasers, microscopy, fibers, astrophysics. Total annual research expenditures: $1.3 million. *Unit head:* Dr. Patrick Moyer, Interim Chair, 704-687-8148, Fax: 704-687-3160, E-mail: pjmoyer@uncc.edu. *Application contact:* Kathy B. Giddings, Director of Graduate Admissions, 704-687-5503, Fax: 704-687-3279, E-mail: gradadm@uncc.edu.

University of Northern Iowa, Graduate College, College of Natural Sciences, Department of Physics, Cedar Falls, IA 50614. Offers applied physics (PSM). *Students:* 3 full-time (0 women), 3 part-time (0 women), 1 international. 9 applicants, 67% accepted, 3 enrolled. In 2010, 5 master's awarded. *Degree requirements:* For master's, comprehensive exam (for some programs), thesis or alternative. *Entrance requirements:* For master's, minimum GPA of 3.0. Additional exam requirements/recommendations for international students: Required—TOEFL (minimum score 500 paper-based; 180 computer-based; 61 IBT). *Application deadline:* For fall admission, 8/1 priority date for domestic students. Applications are processed on a rolling basis. Application fee: $50 ($70 for international students). Electronic applications accepted. *Financial support:* Career-related internships or fieldwork, Federal Work-Study, scholarships/grants, and tuition waivers (full and partial) available. Support available to part-time students. Financial award application deadline: 2/1. *Unit head:* Dr. C. Clifton Chancey, Head, 319-273-2420, E-mail: c.chancey@uni.edu. *Application contact:* Laurie S. Russell, Record Analyst, 319-273-2623, Fax: 319-273-2885, E-mail: laurie.russell@uni.edu.

University of South Florida, Graduate School, College of Arts and Sciences, Department of Physics, Tampa, FL 33620-9951. Offers applied physics (PhD); physics (MS). Part-time programs available. *Faculty:* 19 full-time (2 women). *Students:* 67 full-time (11 women), 4 part-time (0 women); includes 1 Black or African American, non-Hispanic/Latino; 1 Asian, non-Hispanic/Latino; 1 Hispanic/Latino, 31 international. Average age 29. 89 applicants, 47% accepted, 20 enrolled. In 2010, 6 master's, 9 doctorates awarded. *Degree requirements:* For master's, comprehensive exam, thesis optional; for doctorate, 2 foreign languages, comprehensive exam, thesis/dissertation. *Entrance requirements:* For master's, GRE General Test, minimum GPA of 3.0 in last 60 hours of course work; for doctorate, GRE General Test, minimum graduate GPA of 3.2. Additional exam requirements/recommendations for international students: Required—TOEFL (minimum score 550 paper-based). *Application deadline:* For fall admission, 2/15 priority date for domestic students, 1/2 for international students; for spring admission, 9/1 for domestic students, 7/1 for international students. Applications are processed on a rolling basis. Application fee: $30. Electronic applications accepted. *Financial support:* In 2010–11, 23 research assistantships (averaging $14,450 per year), 39 teaching assistantships with tuition reimbursements (averaging $14,081 per year) were awarded; unspecified assistantships also available. *Faculty research:* Biophysics and biomedical physics, atomic molecular and optical physics, solid state and materials physics, physics education. Total annual research expenditures: $2.3 million. *Unit head:* Dr. Pritish Mukherjee, Director of Graduate Studies, 813-974-2871, Fax: 813-974-5813, E-mail: pritish@cas.usf.edu. *Application contact:* Dale Johnson, Program Director, 813-974-5125, Fax: 813-974-5813, E-mail: dejohnso@cas.usf.edu.

The University of Texas at Austin, Graduate School, College of Natural Sciences, Department of Physics, Austin, TX 78712-1111. Offers MA, MS, PhD. *Degree requirements:* For master's, thesis; for doctorate, thesis/dissertation. *Entrance requirements:* For master's and doctorate, GRE General Test, GRE Subject Test (physics). Electronic applications accepted.

University of Washington, Graduate School, College of Arts and Sciences, Department of Physics, Seattle, WA 98195. Offers MS, PhD. Part-time and evening/weekend programs available. Terminal master's awarded for partial completion of doctoral program. *Degree requirements:* For doctorate, thesis/dissertation. *Entrance requirements:* For master's, GRE; for doctorate, GRE General Test, GRE Subject Test. Additional exam requirements/recommendations for international students: Required—TOEFL. Electronic applications accepted. *Faculty research:* Astro-, atomic, condensed-matter, nuclear, and particle physics; physics education.

Virginia Commonwealth University, Graduate School, College of Humanities and Sciences, Department of Physics, Program in Physics and Applied Physics, Richmond, VA 23284-9005. Offers MS. *Students:* 12 full-time (5 women); includes 1 Black or African American, non-Hispanic/Latino; 2 Asian, non-Hispanic/Latino. 12 applicants, 83% accepted, 7 enrolled. In 2010, 4 master's awarded. *Entrance requirements:* For master's, GRE or MAT. Additional exam requirements/recommendations for international students: Required—TOEFL (minimum score 600 paper-based; 250 computer-based; 100 iBT); Recommended—IELTS (minimum score 6.5). *Application deadline:* For fall admission, 8/1 for domestic students; for spring admission, 12/1 for domestic students. Applications are processed on a rolling basis. Application fee: $50. Electronic applications accepted. *Expenses:* Tuition, state resident: full-time $4308; part-time $479 per credit hour. Tuition, nonresident: full-time $8942; part-time $994 per credit hour. Required fees: $2000; $85 per credit hour. Tuition and fees vary according to course level, course load, degree level, campus/location and program. *Financial support:* Federal Work-Study and institutionally sponsored loans available. Support available to part-time students. *Faculty research:* Theoretical and experimental condensed matter physics, general relativity and cosmology, physics education. *Unit head:* Dr. Alison A. Baski, Chair, 804-828-1821, Fax: 804-828-7073, E-mail: aabaski@vcu.edu. *Application contact:* Dr. Shiv N. Khanna, Graduate Program Director, 804-828-1820, Fax: 804-828-7073, E-mail: snkhanna@vcu.edu.

West Virginia University, Eberly College of Arts and Sciences, Department of Physics, Morgantown, WV 26506. Offers applied physics (MS, PhD); astrophysics (MS, PhD); chemical physics (MS, PhD); condensed matter physics (MS, PhD); elementary particle physics (MS, PhD); materials physics (MS, PhD); plasma physics (MS, PhD); solid state physics (MS, PhD); statistical physics (MS, PhD); theoretical physics (MS, PhD). Terminal master's awarded for partial completion of doctoral program. *Degree requirements:* For master's, thesis or alternative, qualifying exam; for doctorate, thesis/dissertation, qualifying exam. *Entrance requirements:* For master's and doctorate, GRE General Test, minimum GPA of 3.0. Additional exam requirements/recommendations for international students: Required—TOEFL. *Faculty research:* Experimental and theoretical condensed-matter, plasma, high-energy theory, nonlinear dynamics, space physics.

Yale University, Graduate School of Arts and Sciences, School of Engineering and Applied Science, Department of Applied Physics, New Haven, CT 06520. Offers MS, PhD. Terminal master's awarded for partial completion of doctoral program. *Degree requirements:* For doctorate, thesis/dissertation, area exam. *Entrance requirements:* For master's and doctorate, GRE General Test. Additional exam requirements/recommendations for international students: Required—TOEFL. *Faculty research:* Condensed-matter physics, optical physics, materials science.

Chemical Physics

Columbia University, Graduate School of Arts and Sciences, Division of Natural Sciences, Department of Chemistry, Program in Chemical Physics, New York, NY 10027. Offers M Phil, PhD. *Entrance requirements:* For master's, GRE General Test, GRE Subject Test. Additional exam requirements/recommendations for international students: Required—TOEFL.

Cornell University, Graduate School, Graduate Fields of Arts and Sciences, Field of Chemistry and Chemical Biology, Ithaca, NY 14853-0001. Offers analytical chemistry (PhD); bio-organic chemistry (PhD); biophysical chemistry (PhD); chemical biology (PhD); chemical physics (PhD); inorganic chemistry (PhD); materials chemistry (PhD); organic chemistry (PhD); organometallic chemistry (PhD); physical chemistry (PhD); polymer chemistry (PhD); theoretical chemistry (PhD). *Faculty:* 46 full-time (3 women). *Students:* 163 full-time (63 women); includes 10 Asian, non-Hispanic/Latino; 3 Hispanic/Latino, 49 international. Average age 24. 340 applicants, 36% accepted, 48 enrolled. In 2010, 31 doctorates awarded. *Degree requirements:* For doctorate, comprehensive exam, thesis/dissertation. *Entrance requirements:* For doctorate, GRE General Test, GRE Subject Test (chemistry), 3 letters of recommendation. Additional exam requirements/recommendations for international students: Required—TOEFL (minimum score 600 paper-based; 250 computer-based; 77 iBT). *Application deadline:* For fall admission, 1/10 for domestic students. Application fee: $80. Electronic applications accepted. *Expenses:* Tuition: Full-time $29,500. Required fees: $76. Tuition and fees vary according to degree level and program. *Financial support:* In 2010–11, 19 fellowships with full tuition reimbursements, 69 research assistantships with full tuition reimbursements, 68 teaching assistantships with full tuition reimbursements were awarded; institutionally sponsored loans, scholarships/grants, health care benefits, tuition waivers (full and partial), and unspecified assistantships also available. Financial award applicants required to submit FAFSA. *Faculty research:* Analytical, organic, inorganic, physical, materials, chemical biology. *Unit head:* Director of Graduate Studies, 607-255-4139, Fax: 607-255-4137. *Application contact:* Graduate Field Assistant, 607-255-4139, Fax: 607-255-4137, E-mail: chemgrad@cornell.edu.

Harvard University, Graduate School of Arts and Sciences, Committee on Chemical Physics, Cambridge, MA 02138. Offers PhD. *Degree requirements:* For doctorate, one foreign language, thesis/dissertation, cumulative exams. *Entrance requirements:* For doctorate, GRE General Test, GRE Subject Test. Additional exam requirements/recommendations for international students: Required—TOEFL. *Expenses:* Tuition: Full-time $34,976. Required fees: $1166. Full-time tuition and fees vary according to program.

Kent State University, College of Arts and Sciences, Chemical Physics Interdisciplinary Program, Kent, OH 44242-0001. Offers MS, PhD. Offered in cooperation with the Departments of Chemistry, Mathematics and Computer Science, and Physics and the Liquid Crystal Institute. Terminal master's awarded for partial completion of doctoral program. *Degree requirements:* For master's, thesis; for doctorate, thesis/dissertation, candidacy exam. *Entrance requirements:* For master's and doctorate, GRE. Additional exam requirements/recommendations for international students: Required—TOEFL (minimum score 525 paper-based; 197 computer-based). Electronic applications accepted. *Expenses:* Tuition, state resident: full-time $7866; part-time $437 per credit hour. Tuition, nonresident: full-time $14,022; part-time $779 per credit hour.

Marquette University, Graduate School, College of Arts and Sciences, Department of Chemistry, Milwaukee, WI 53201-1881. Offers analytical chemistry (MS, PhD); bioanalytical chemistry (MS, PhD); biophysical chemistry (MS, PhD); chemical physics (MS, PhD); inorganic chemistry (MS, PhD); organic chemistry (MS, PhD); physical chemistry (MS, PhD). Part-time programs available. *Faculty:* 27 full-time (3 women), 1 part-time/adjunct (0 women). *Students:* 33 full-time (12 women), 16 part-time (3 women); includes 4 minority (2 Black or African American, non-Hispanic/Latino; 2 Asian, non-Hispanic/Latino), 37 international. Average age 29. 25 applicants, 92% accepted, 10 enrolled. In 2010, 2 master's, 1 doctorate awarded. Terminal master's awarded for partial completion of doctoral program. *Degree requirements:* For master's, comprehensive exam; for doctorate, thesis/dissertation, cumulative exams. *Entrance requirements:* For master's and doctorate, GRE Subject Test (optional), official transcripts from all current and previous colleges/universities except Marquette, three letters of recommendation from individuals familiar with the applicant's academic work. Additional exam requirements/recommendations for international students: Required—TOEFL (minimum score 530 paper-based; 78 computer-based). *Application deadline:* Applications are processed on a rolling basis. Application fee: $50. Electronic applications accepted. *Expenses:* Tuition: Full-time $16,290; part-time $905 per credit hour. Tuition and fees vary according to program. *Financial support:* In 2010–11, 2 fellowships, 4 research assistantships, 27 teaching assistantships were awarded; Federal Work-Study, institutionally sponsored loans, scholarships/grants, and tuition waivers (full and partial) also available. Support available to part-time students. Financial award application deadline: 2/15. *Faculty research:* Inorganic complexes, laser Raman spectroscopy, organic synthesis, synthetic bioinorganic chemistry, electro-active organic molecules. Total annual research expenditures: $1.2 million. *Unit head:* Dr. Michael Ryan, Chair, 414-288-3537, Fax: 414-288-7066. *Application contact:* Dr. Mark Steinmetz, Director of Graduate Studies, 414-288-7374, Fax: 414-288-7066.

McMaster University, School of Graduate Studies, Faculty of Science, Department of Chemistry, Hamilton, ON L8S 4M2, Canada. Offers analytical chemistry (M Sc, PhD); chemical physics (M Sc, PhD); chemistry (M Sc, PhD); inorganic chemistry (M Sc, PhD); organic chemistry (M Sc, PhD); physical chemistry (M Sc, PhD); polymer chemistry (M Sc, PhD). Part-time programs available. Terminal master's awarded for partial completion of doctoral program. *Degree requirements:* For master's, thesis; for doctorate, comprehensive exam, thesis/dissertation. *Entrance requirements:* For master's, minimum B+ average. Additional exam requirements/recommendations for international students: Required—TOEFL (minimum score 550 paper-based; 213 computer-based).

Michigan State University, The Graduate School, College of Natural Science, Department of Chemistry, East Lansing, MI 48824. Offers chemical physics (PhD); chemistry (MS, PhD); chemistry-environmental toxicology (PhD); computational chemistry (MS). *Entrance requirements:* Additional exam requirements/recommendations for international students: Required—TOEFL. Electronic applications accepted. *Faculty research:* Analytical chemistry, inorganic and organic chemistry, nuclear chemistry, physical chemistry, theoretical and computational chemistry.

The Ohio State University, Graduate School, College of Arts and Sciences, Division of Natural and Mathematical Sciences, Program in Chemical Physics, Columbus, OH 43210.

Offers MS, PhD. *Faculty:* 34. *Students:* 3 full-time (0 women), 9 part-time (3 women); includes 1 Asian, non-Hispanic/Latino, 4 international. Average age 28. In 2010, 5 doctorates awarded. *Degree requirements:* For master's, thesis optional; for doctorate, thesis/dissertation. *Entrance requirements:* For master's and doctorate, GRE General Test, GRE Subject Test (chemistry or physics). Additional exam requirements/recommendations for international students: Recommended—TOEFL (minimum score 600 paper-based; 250 computer-based). *Application deadline:* For fall admission, 8/15 priority date for domestic students, 7/1 priority date for international students; for winter admission, 12/1 priority date for domestic students, 11/1 priority date for international students; for spring admission, 3/1 priority date for domestic students, 2/1 priority date for international students. Applications are processed on a rolling basis. Application fee: $40 ($50 for international students). Electronic applications accepted. *Expenses:* Tuition, state resident: full-time $10,605. Tuition, nonresident: full-time $26,535. Tuition and fees vary according to course load and program. *Financial support:* Fellowships, research assistantships, teaching assistantships, Federal Work-Study and institutionally sponsored loans available. Support available to part-time students. *Unit head:* Dr. Terry A. Miller, Director, 614-292-2569, Fax: 614-292-1948, E-mail: miller.104@osu.edu. *Application contact:* 614-292-9444, Fax: 614-292-3895, E-mail: domestic.grad@osu.edu.

Simon Fraser University, Graduate Studies, Faculty of Science, Department of Chemistry, Burnaby, BC V5A 1S6, Canada. Offers chemical physics (PhD); chemistry (PhD). *Degree requirements:* For master's, thesis; for doctorate, thesis/dissertation. *Entrance requirements:* For master's, minimum GPA of 3.0. Additional exam requirements/recommendations for international students: Required—TOEFL (minimum score 600 paper-based; 250 computer-based; 100 iBT). Electronic applications accepted. *Faculty research:* Organic chemistry, nuclear chemistry, physical chemistry, inorganic chemistry, theoretical chemistry.

Simon Fraser University, Graduate Studies, Faculty of Science, Department of Physics, Burnaby, BC V5A 1S6, Canada. Offers biophysics (M Sc, PhD); chemical physics (M Sc, PhD); physics (M Sc, PhD). *Degree requirements:* For master's, thesis; for doctorate, thesis/dissertation. *Entrance requirements:* For master's, minimum GPA of 3.0; for doctorate, minimum GPA of 3.5. Additional exam requirements/recommendations for international students: Required—TOEFL or IELTS. *Faculty research:* Solid-state physics, magnetism, energy research, superconductivity, nuclear physics.

University of Colorado Boulder, Graduate School, College of Arts and Sciences, Department of Physics, Boulder, CO 80309. Offers chemical physics (PhD); geophysics (PhD); liquid crystal science and technology (PhD); mathematical physics (PhD); medical physics (PhD); optical sciences and engineering (PhD); physics (MS, PhD). *Faculty:* 50 full-time (7 women). *Students:* 147 full-time (28 women), 72 part-time (10 women); includes 12 minority (6 Asian, non-Hispanic/Latino; 6 Hispanic/Latino), 75 international. Average age 27. 503 applicants, 37 enrolled. In 2010, 16 master's, 31 doctorates awarded. Terminal master's awarded for partial completion of doctoral program. *Degree requirements:* For master's, comprehensive exam, thesis or alternative; for doctorate, comprehensive exam, thesis/dissertation. *Entrance requirements:* For master's and doctorate, GRE General Test, GRE Subject Test, minimum undergraduate GPA of 3.0. Additional exam requirements/recommendations for international students: Required—TOEFL. *Application deadline:* For fall admission, 1/15 priority date for domestic students, 1/15 for international students. Applications are processed on a rolling basis. Application fee: $50 ($60 for international students). Electronic applications accepted. *Financial support:* In 2010–11, 21 fellowships with full tuition reimbursements (averaging $15,999 per year), 146 research assistantships with full tuition reimbursements (averaging $16,586 per year) were awarded; scholarships/grants also available. Financial award application deadline: 1/15. *Faculty research:* Atomic and molecular physics, nuclear physics, condensed matter, elementary particle physics, laser or optical physics, plasma physics, geophysics, astrophysics and chemical physics. Total annual research expenditures: $16.8 million.

University of Illinois at Urbana–Champaign, Graduate College, College of Liberal Arts and Sciences, School of Chemical Sciences, Department of Chemistry, Champaign, IL 61820. Offers astrochemistry (PhD); chemical physics (PhD); chemistry (MA, MS, PhD); teaching of chemistry (MS); MS/JD; MS/MBA. *Faculty:* 33 full-time (6 women). *Students:* 277 full-time (84 women), 5 part-time (0 women); includes 5 Black or African American, non-Hispanic/Latino; 1 American Indian or Alaska Native, non-Hispanic/Latino; 15 Asian, non-Hispanic/Latino; 9 Hispanic/Latino; 8 Two or more races, non-Hispanic/Latino, 59 international. 549 applicants, 9% accepted, 42 enrolled. In 2010, 13 master's, 40 doctorates awarded. *Entrance requirements:* For master's and doctorate, GRE General Test, GRE Subject Test, minimum GPA of 3.0. Additional exam requirements/recommendations for international students: Required—TOEFL (minimum score 580 paper-based; 237 computer-based). *Application deadline:* Applications are processed on a rolling basis. Application fee: $75 ($90 for international students). Electronic applications accepted. *Financial support:* In 2010–11, 115 fellowships, 186 research assistantships, 124 teaching assistantships were awarded; tuition waivers (full and partial) also available. *Unit head:* Steven C. Zimmerman, Head, 217-333-6655, Fax: 217-244-5943, E-mail: sczimmer@illinois.edu. *Application contact:* Krista Smith, Office Support Specialist, 217-244-4844, Fax: 217-244-5943, E-mail: kristasm@illinois.edu.

University of Louisville, Graduate School, College of Arts and Sciences, Department of Chemistry, Louisville, KY 40292-0001. Offers analytical chemistry (MS, PhD); biochemistry (MS, PhD); chemical physics (PhD); inorganic chemistry (MS, PhD); organic chemistry (MS, PhD); physical chemistry (MS, PhD). *Faculty:* 21 full-time (4 women). *Students:* 55 full-time (24 women), 4 part-time (0 women); includes 1 Black or African American, non-Hispanic/Latino; 1 Asian, non-Hispanic/Latino, 42 international. Average age 29. 79 applicants, 27% accepted, 7 enrolled. In 2010, 7 master's, 5 doctorates awarded. Terminal master's awarded for partial completion of doctoral program. *Degree requirements:* For master's, variable foreign language requirement, comprehensive exam, thesis optional; for doctorate, variable foreign language requirement, comprehensive exam, thesis/dissertation. *Entrance requirements:* For master's, BA or BS courseowork; for doctorate, none, BA or BS coursework. Additional exam requirements/recommendations for international students: Required—TOEFL. *Application deadline:* For fall admission, 3/15 for domestic and international students; for winter admission, 9/15 for domestic and international students. Applications are processed on a rolling basis. Application fee: $50. Electronic applications accepted. *Expenses:* Tuition, state resident: full-time $9144; part-time $508 per credit hour. Tuition, nonresident: full-time $19,026; part-time $1057 per credit hour. Tuition and fees vary according to program and reciprocity agreements. *Financial support:* In 2010–11, 33 teaching assistantships with full tuition reimbursements (averaging $22,000 per year) were awarded; fellowships with full tuition reimbursements, research assistantships with full tuition reimbursements, career-related internships or fieldwork, scholarships/grants, traineeships, health care benefits, and unspecified assistantships also available. Support available to part-time students. Financial award application deadline: 3/15. *Faculty research:* Computational chemistry, biophysics nuclear magnetic resonance, synthetic organic chemistry, synthetic inorganic chemistry, medicinal chemistry, protein chemistry, enzymology, nanochemistry, electrochemistry, analytical chemistry, synthetic biology, bioinformatics. Total annual research expenditures: $2.5 million. *Unit head:* Dr. Richard J. Wittebort, Professor and Chair. *Application contact:* Sherry Nalley, Administrator, 502-852-6798.

University of Maryland, College Park, Academic Affairs, College of Computer, Mathematical and Natural Sciences, Institute for Physical Science and Technology, Program in Chemical Physics, College Park, MD 20742. Offers MS, PhD. Part-time and evening/weekend programs available. *Students:* 33 full-time (8 women), 2 part-time (both women); includes 4 minority (3 Asian, non-Hispanic/Latino; 1 Hispanic/Latino), 16 international. 28 applicants, 39% accepted, 5 enrolled. In 2010, 7 doctorates awarded. Terminal master's awarded for partial completion of doctoral program. *Degree requirements:* For master's, thesis optional, paper, qualifying exam; for doctorate, thesis/dissertation, seminars. *Entrance requirements:* For master's, GRE General Test, GRE Subject Test (chemistry, math or physics), minimum GPA of 3.3, 3 letters of recommendation; for doctorate, GRE Subject Test (chemistry, math, or physics), GRE General Test, minimum GPA of 3.3, 3 letters of recommendation. *Application deadline:* For fall admission, 2/1 for domestic and international students; for spring admission, 6/1 for domestic and international students. Applications are processed on a rolling basis. Application fee: $75. Electronic applications accepted. *Expenses:* Tuition, area resident: Part-time $471 per credit hour. Tuition, state resident: part-time $471 per credit hour. Tuition, nonresident: part-time $1016 per credit hour. Required fees: $337 per term. *Financial support:* In 2010–11, 3 fellowships with full and partial tuition reimbursements (averaging $20,700 per year), 26 research assistantships (averaging $20,116 per year), 4 teaching assistantships (averaging $17,893 per year) were awarded; Federal Work-Study and scholarships/grants also available. Financial award applicants required to submit FAFSA. *Faculty research:* Discrete molecules and gases; dynamic phenomena; thermodynamics, statistical mechanical theory and quantum mechanical theory; atmospheric physics; biophysics. *Unit head:* Dr. Michael A. Coplan, Director, 301-405-4858, Fax: 301-314-9396, E-mail: coplan@umd.edu. *Application contact:* Dean of Graduate School, 301-405-0358, Fax: 301-314-9305.

University of Nevada, Reno, Graduate School, Interdisciplinary Program in Chemical Physics, Reno, NV 89557. Offers PhD. *Degree requirements:* For doctorate, thesis/dissertation. *Entrance requirements:* For doctorate, GRE, minimum GPA of 3.0. Additional exam requirements/recommendations for international students: Required—TOEFL (minimum score 500 paper-based; 173 computer-based; 61 iBT). Electronic applications accepted. *Expenses:* Tuition, state resident: full-time $2219; part-time $246 per credit. Tuition, nonresident: part-time $510 per credit. International tuition: $9009 full-time. Required fees: $59 per term. One-time fee: $101. Tuition and fees vary according to course load. *Faculty research:* Atomic and molecular physics, physical chemistry.

The University of Tennessee, Graduate School, College of Arts and Sciences, Department of Chemistry, Knoxville, TN 37996. Offers analytical chemistry (MS, PhD); chemical physics (PhD); environmental chemistry (MS, PhD); inorganic chemistry (MS, PhD); organic chemistry (MS, PhD); physical chemistry (MS, PhD); polymer chemistry (MS, PhD); theoretical chemistry (PhD). Part-time programs available. Terminal master's awarded for partial completion of doctoral program. *Degree requirements:* For master's, thesis; for doctorate, thesis/dissertation. *Entrance requirements:* For master's and doctorate, GRE General Test, minimum GPA of 2.7. Additional exam requirements/recommendations for international students: Required—TOEFL. Electronic applications accepted. *Expenses:* Tuition, state resident: full-time $7440; part-time $414 per credit hour. Tuition, nonresident: full-time $22,478; part-time $1250 per credit hour. Required fees: $922; $43 per credit hour. Tuition and fees vary according to program.

University of Utah, Graduate School, College of Science, Department of Chemistry, Salt Lake City, UT 84112-0850. Offers chemical physics (PhD); chemistry (M Phil, MA, MS, PhD); science teacher education (MS). Part-time programs available. Postbaccalaureate distance learning degree programs offered. *Faculty:* 31 full-time (5 women), 3 part-time/adjunct (0 women). *Students:* 157 full-time (52 women), 29 part-time (10 women); includes 11 minority (1 Black or African American, non-Hispanic/Latino; 6 Asian, non-Hispanic/Latino; 2 Hispanic/Latino; 2 Two or more races, non-Hispanic/Latino), 67 international. Average age 27. 271 applicants, 30% accepted, 46 enrolled. In 2010, 4 master's, 17 doctorates awarded. Terminal master's awarded for partial completion of doctoral program. *Degree requirements:* For master's, thesis optional, 20 hours course work, 10 hours research; for doctorate, thesis/dissertation, 18 hours course work, 14 hours research. *Entrance requirements:* For master's and doctorate, GRE General Test, minimum GPA of 3.0. Additional exam requirements/recommendations for international students: Required—TOEFL (minimum score 620 paper-based; 260 computer-based; 105 iBT). *Application deadline:* For fall admission, 4/1 for domestic and international students; for spring admission, 11/1 for domestic and international students. Application fee: $55 ($65 for international students). Electronic applications accepted. *Expenses:* Tuition, area resident: Part-time $179.19 per credit hour. Tuition, state resident: full-time $4384. Tuition, nonresident: full-time $16,684; part-time $630.67 per credit hour. Required fees: $350 per semester. Tuition and fees vary according to course load, degree level and program. *Financial support:* In 2010–11, 1 fellowship with tuition reimbursement (averaging $22,000 per year), 128 research assistantships with tuition reimbursements (averaging $22,500 per year), 55 teaching assistantships with tuition reimbursements (averaging $22,000 per year) were awarded; scholarships/grants and tuition waivers (full) also available. Financial award application deadline: 4/1; financial award applicants required to submit FAFSA. *Faculty research:* Biological, theoretical, inorganic, organic, and physical-analytical chemistry. Total annual research expenditures: $14.4 million. *Unit head:* Dr. Henry S. White, Chair, 801-585-6256, Fax: 801-581-8433, E-mail: chair@chemistry.utah.edu. *Application contact:* Jo Hoovey, Graduate Coordinator, 801-581-4393, Fax: 801-581-5408, E-mail: jhoovey@chem.utah.edu.

University of Utah, Graduate School, College of Science, Department of Physics and Astronomy, Salt Lake City, UT 84112. Offers chemical physics (PhD); medical physics (MS, PhD); physics (MA, MS, PhD); physics teaching (PhD). Part-time programs available. *Faculty:* 34 full-time (2 women), 2 part-time/adjunct (0 women). *Students:* 69 full-time (15 women), 18 part-time (5 women); includes 3 minority (1 Asian, non-Hispanic/Latino; 2 Hispanic/Latino), 38 international. Average age 30. 35 applicants, 74% accepted, 12 enrolled. In 2010, 12 master's, 11 doctorates awarded. Terminal master's awarded for partial completion of doctoral program. *Degree requirements:* For master's, comprehensive exam (for some programs), thesis or alternative, teaching experience, departmental exam; for doctorate, comprehensive exam, thesis/dissertation, departmental qualifying exam. *Entrance requirements:* For master's and doctorate, GRE General Test, GRE Subject Test, minimum GPA of 3.0. Additional exam requirements/recommendations for international students: Required—TOEFL (minimum score 500 paper-based; 173 computer-based; 69 iBT). *Application deadline:* For fall admission, 4/1 priority date for domestic and international students. Applications are processed on a rolling basis. Application fee: $55 ($65 for international students). Electronic applications accepted. *Expenses:* Tuition, area resident: Part-time $179.19 per credit hour. Tuition, state resident: full-time $4384. Tuition, nonresident: full-time $16,684; part-time $630.67 per credit hour. Required fees: $350 per semester. Tuition and fees vary according to course load, degree level and program. *Financial support:* In 2010–11, 61 teaching assistantships with full and partial tuition reimbursements (averaging $14,626 per year) were awarded; Federal Work-Study, institutionally sponsored loans, and scholarships/grants also available. Financial award application deadline: 2/15; financial award applicants required to submit FAFSA. *Faculty research:* High-energy, cosmic-ray, astrophysics, medical physics, condensed matter, relativity applied physics. Total annual research expenditures: $6.5 million. *Unit head:* Dr. David Kieda, Chair, 801-581-6901, Fax: 801-581-4801, E-mail: kieda@physics.utah.edu. *Application contact:* Jackie Hadley, Graduate Secretary, 801-581-6861, Fax: 801-581-4801, E-mail: jackie@physics.utah.edu.

University of Utah, Graduate School, College of Science, Interdepartmental Program in Chemical Physics, Salt Lake City, UT 84112-1107. Offers PhD. *Students:* 1 applicant, 100% accepted, 0 enrolled. *Degree requirements:* For doctorate, comprehensive exam, thesis/dissertation. *Entrance requirements:* For doctorate, GRE General Test, GRE Subject Test (physics), minimum undergraduate GPA of 3.0. Additional exam requirements/recommendations for international students: Required—TOEFL (minimum score 500 paper-based; 173 computer-based). *Application deadline:* For fall admission, 4/1 for domestic and international students; for spring admission, 11/1 for domestic and international students. Application fee: $55 ($65 for international students). *Expenses:* Tuition, area resident: Part-time $179.19 per credit hour. Tuition, state resident: full-time $4384. Tuition, nonresident: full-time $16,684; part-time $630.67 per credit hour. Required fees: $350 per semester. Tuition and fees vary according to course load, degree level and program. *Financial support:* Applicants required to submit FAFSA. *Unit*

Chemical Physics

University of Utah *(continued)*
head: Dr. Charles A. Wight, Coordinator of Medical Physics, 801-581-8796, E-mail: wight@chemistry.utah.edu. *Application contact:* Information Contact, 801-581-6958, E-mail: office@science.utah.edu.

Virginia Commonwealth University, Graduate School, College of Humanities and Sciences, Department of Chemistry, Richmond, VA 23284-9005. Offers analytical chemistry (MS, PhD); chemical physics (PhD); inorganic chemistry (MS, PhD); organic chemistry (MS, PhD); physical chemistry (MS, PhD). Part-time programs available. *Students:* 51 full-time (23 women), 14 part-time (6 women); includes 7 minority (3 Black or African American, non-Hispanic/Latino; 2 Asian, non-Hispanic/Latino; 1 Hispanic/Latino; 1 Two or more races, non-Hispanic/Latino), 26 international. 76 applicants, 33% accepted, 10 enrolled. In 2010, 6 master's, 5 doctorates awarded. Terminal master's awarded for partial completion of doctoral program. *Degree requirements:* For master's, thesis; for doctorate, thesis/dissertation, comprehensive cumulative exams, research proposal. *Entrance requirements:* For master's, GRE General Test, 30 undergraduate credits in chemistry; for doctorate, GRE General Test. Additional exam requirements/recommendations for international students: Required—Either TOEFL (minimum score: paper-based 600, computer-based 250) or IELTS (6.5). *Application deadline:* For fall admission, 3/15 for domestic students; for spring admission, 11/15 for domestic students. Applications are processed on a rolling basis. Application fee: $50. Electronic applications accepted. *Expenses:* Tuition, state resident: full-time $4308; part-time $479 per credit hour. Tuition, nonresident: full-time $8942; part-time $994 per credit hour. Required fees: $2000; $85 per credit hour. Tuition and fees vary according to course level, course load, degree level, campus/location and program. *Financial support:* Fellowships, research assistantships, teaching assistantships, career-related internships or fieldwork and institutionally sponsored loans available. Support available to part-time students. Financial award application deadline: 7/1;

financial award applicants required to submit FAFSA. *Faculty research:* Physical, organic, inorganic, analytical, and polymer chemistry; chemical physics. *Unit head:* Dr. Scott Gronert, Chair, 804-828-1298, Fax: 804-828-8599, E-mail: sgronert@vcu.edu. *Application contact:* Dr. Maryanne M. Collinson, Chair, Graduate Recruiting and Admissions Committee, 804-828-7509, E-mail: mselshal@vcu.edu.

Wesleyan University, Graduate Programs, Department of Chemistry and Department of Physics, Program in Chemical Physics, Middletown, CT 06459. Offers MA, PhD. Terminal master's awarded for partial completion of doctoral program. *Degree requirements:* For master's, one foreign language, thesis; for doctorate, one foreign language, thesis/dissertation. *Entrance requirements:* For master's, GRE General Test, GRE Subject Test; for doctorate, GRE Subject Test, BA or BS in chemistry or physics. Additional exam requirements/recommendations for international students: Required—TOEFL. Electronic applications accepted. *Expenses:* Tuition: Full-time $43,404. Required fees: $830. *Faculty research:* Spectroscopy, photochemistry, reactive collisions, surface physics, quantum theory.

West Virginia University, Eberly College of Arts and Sciences, Department of Physics, Morgantown, WV 26506. Offers applied physics (MS, PhD); astrophysics (MS, PhD); chemical physics (MS, PhD); condensed matter physics (MS, PhD); elementary particle physics (MS, PhD); materials physics (MS, PhD); plasma physics (MS, PhD); solid state physics (MS, PhD); statistical physics (MS, PhD); theoretical physics (MS, PhD). Terminal master's awarded for partial completion of doctoral program. *Degree requirements:* For master's, thesis or alternative, qualifying exam; for doctorate, thesis/dissertation, qualifying exam. *Entrance requirements:* For master's and doctorate, GRE General Test, minimum GPA of 3.0. Additional exam requirements/recommendations for international students: Required—TOEFL. *Faculty research:* Experimental and theoretical condensed-matter, plasma, high-energy theory, nonlinear dynamics, space physics.

Condensed Matter Physics

Cleveland State University, College of Graduate Studies, College of Sciences and Health Professions, Department of Physics, Cleveland, OH 44115. Offers applied optics (MS); condensed matter physics (MS); medical physics (MS); optics and materials (MS); optics and medical imaging (MS). Part-time and evening/weekend programs available. *Faculty:* 10 full-time (1 woman), 4 part-time/adjunct (1 woman). *Students:* 3 full-time (0 women), 10 part-time (4 women); includes 1 Asian, non-Hispanic/Latino; 1 Two or more races, non-Hispanic/Latino, 1 international. Average age 29. 28 applicants, 39% accepted, 5 enrolled. In 2010, 3 master's awarded. *Entrance requirements:* For master's, undergraduate degree in engineering, physics, chemistry or mathematics. Additional exam requirements/recommendations for international students: Required—TOEFL (minimum score 525 paper-based; 197 computer-based). *Application deadline:* For fall admission, 7/15 priority date for domestic and international students. Applications are processed on a rolling basis. Application fee: $30. Electronic applications accepted. *Expenses:* Tuition, state resident: full-time $8447; part-time $469 per credit hour. Tuition, nonresident: full-time $16,020; part-time $890 per credit hour. Required fees: $50. *Financial support:* In 2010–11, 1 research assistantship with full and partial tuition reimbursement (averaging $5,666 per year) was awarded; fellowships with tuition reimbursements, teaching assistantships, tuition waivers (full) also available. *Faculty research:* Statistical physics, experimental solid-state physics, theoretical optics, experimental biological physics (macromolecular crystallography), experimental optics. Total annual research expenditures: $350,000. *Unit head:* Dr. Miron Kaufman, Chairperson, 216-687-2436, Fax: 216-523-7268, E-mail: m.kaufman@csuohio.edu. *Application contact:* Dr. James A. Lock, Director, 216-687-2420, Fax: 216-523-7268, E-mail: j.lock@csuohio.edu.

Emory University, Laney Graduate School, Department of Physics, Atlanta, GA 30322-1100. Offers biophysics (PhD); condensed matter physics (PhD); non-linear physics (PhD); radiological physics (PhD); soft condensed matter physics (PhD); solid-state physics (PhD); statistical physics (PhD); MS/PhD. *Degree requirements:* For doctorate, thesis/dissertation, qualifier proposal (PhD). *Entrance requirements:* For doctorate, GRE General Test, minimum GPA of 3.0. Additional exam requirements/recommendations for international students: Required—TOEFL (minimum score 600 paper-based). Electronic applications accepted. *Expenses:* Tuition: Full-time $33,800. Required fees: $1300. *Faculty research:* Experimental studies of the structure and function of metalloproteins, soft condensed matter, granular materials, biophotonics and fluorescence correlation spectroscopy, single molecule studies of DNA-protein systems.

Iowa State University of Science and Technology, Graduate College, College of Liberal Arts and Sciences, Department of Physics and Astronomy, Ames, IA 50011. Offers applied physics (MS, PhD); astrophysics (MS, PhD); condensed matter physics (MS, PhD); high energy physics (MS, PhD); nuclear physics (MS, PhD); physics (MS, PhD). Part-time programs available. *Faculty:* 48 full-time (4 women), 4 part-time/adjunct (0 women). *Students:* 97 full-time (19 women), 6 part-time (0 women); includes 3 Asian, non-Hispanic/Latino, 53 international. 179 applicants, 32% accepted, 18 enrolled. In 2010, 4 master's, 11 doctorates awarded. Terminal master's awarded for partial completion of doctoral program. *Degree requirements:* For master's, thesis (for some programs); for doctorate, thesis/dissertation. *Entrance requirements:* For master's and doctorate, GRE General Test, GRE Subject Test (physics). Additional exam requirements/recommendations for international students: Required—TOEFL (minimum score 550 paper-based; 79 iBT), IELTS (minimum score 6.5). *Application deadline:* For fall admission, 2/15 priority date for domestic and international students; for spring admission, 10/15 for domestic and international students. Applications are processed on a rolling basis. Application fee: $40 ($90 for international students). Electronic applications accepted. *Financial support:* In 2010–11, 54 research assistantships with full and partial tuition reimbursements (averaging $12,890 per year), 34 teaching assistantships with full and partial tuition reimbursements (averaging $13,928 per year) were awarded; fellowships, Federal Work-Study, institutionally sponsored loans, scholarships/grants, health care benefits, and unspecified assistantships also available. Support available to part-time students. Financial award application deadline: 2/15. *Faculty research:* Condensed-matter physics, including superconductivity and new materials; high-energy and nuclear physics; astronomy and astrophysics; atmospheric and environmental physics. Total annual research expenditures: $8.8 million. *Unit head:* Dr. Joseph Shinar, Chair, 515-294-3455, Fax: 515-294-6027, E-mail: phys_astro@iastate.edu. *Application contact:* Dr. Steven Kawaler, Director of Graduate Education, 515-294-9728, E-mail: phys_astro@iastate.edu.

Memorial University of Newfoundland, School of Graduate Studies, Department of Physics and Physical Oceanography, St. John's, NL A1C 5S7, Canada. Offers atomic and molecular physics (M Sc, PhD); condensed matter physics (M Sc, PhD); physical oceanography (M Sc, PhD); physics (M Sc). Part-time programs available. *Degree requirements:* For master's, thesis, seminar presentation on thesis topic; for doctorate, comprehensive exam, thesis/dissertation, oral defense of thesis. *Entrance requirements:* For master's, honors B Sc or equivalent; for doctorate, M Sc or equivalent. Electronic applications accepted. *Faculty research:* Experiment and theory in atomic and molecular physics, condensed matter physics, physical oceanography, theoretical geophysics and applied nuclear physics.

Rutgers, The State University of New Jersey, New Brunswick, Graduate School-New Brunswick, Department of Physics and Astronomy, Piscataway, NJ 08854-8097. Offers astronomy (MS, PhD); biophysics (PhD); condensed matter physics (MS, PhD); elementary particle physics (MS, PhD); intermediate energy nuclear physics (MS); nuclear physics (MS, PhD); physics (MST); surface science (PhD); theoretical physics (MS, PhD). Part-time programs available. Terminal master's awarded for partial completion of doctoral program. *Degree requirements:* For master's, comprehensive exam, thesis or alternative; for doctorate, comprehensive exam, thesis/dissertation. *Entrance requirements:* For master's and doctorate, GRE General Test, GRE Subject Test. Additional exam requirements/recommendations for international students: Required—TOEFL (minimum score 560 paper-based). Electronic applications accepted. *Expenses:* Tuition, state resident: full-time $7200; part-time $600 per credit. Tuition, nonresident: full-time $11,124; part-time $927 per credit. *Faculty research:* Astronomy, high energy, condensed matter, surface, nuclear physics.

University of Alberta, Faculty of Graduate Studies and Research, Department of Physics, Edmonton, AB T6G 2E1, Canada. Offers astrophysics (M Sc, PhD); condensed matter (M Sc, PhD); geophysics (M Sc, PhD); medical physics (M Sc, PhD); subatomic physics (M Sc, PhD). *Degree requirements:* For master's, thesis; for doctorate, thesis/dissertation. *Entrance requirements:* For master's and doctorate, minimum GPA of 7.0 on a 9.0 scale. Additional exam requirements/recommendations for international students: Required—TOEFL. *Faculty research:* Cosmology, astroparticle physics, high-intermediate energy, magnetism, superconductivity.

The University of Manchester, School of Physics and Astronomy, Manchester, United Kingdom. Offers astronomy and astrophysics (M Sc, PhD); biological physics (M Sc, PhD); condensed matter physics (M Sc, PhD); nonlinear and liquid crystals physics (M Sc, PhD); nuclear physics (M Sc, PhD); particle physics (M Sc, PhD); photon physics (M Sc, PhD); physics (M Sc, PhD); theoretical physics (M Sc, PhD).

University of Victoria, Faculty of Graduate Studies, Faculty of Science, Department of Physics and Astronomy, Victoria, BC V8W 2Y2, Canada. Offers astronomy and astrophysics (M Sc, PhD); condensed matter physics (M Sc, PhD); experimental particle physics (M Sc, PhD); medical physics (M Sc, PhD); ocean physics (M Sc, PhD); theoretical physics (M Sc, PhD). *Degree requirements:* For master's, thesis; for doctorate, comprehensive exam, thesis/dissertation, candidacy exam. *Entrance requirements:* For master's and doctorate, GRE. Additional exam requirements/recommendations for international students: Required—TOEFL (minimum score 575 paper-based; 233 computer-based), IELTS (minimum score 7). Electronic applications accepted. *Faculty research:* Old stellar populations; observational cosmology and large scale structure; cp violation; atlas.

West Virginia University, Eberly College of Arts and Sciences, Department of Physics, Morgantown, WV 26506. Offers applied physics (MS, PhD); astrophysics (MS, PhD); chemical physics (MS, PhD); condensed matter physics (MS, PhD); elementary particle physics (MS, PhD); materials physics (MS, PhD); plasma physics (MS, PhD); solid state physics (MS, PhD); statistical physics (MS, PhD); theoretical physics (MS, PhD). Terminal master's awarded for partial completion of doctoral program. *Degree requirements:* For master's, thesis or alternative, qualifying exam; for doctorate, thesis/dissertation, qualifying exam. *Entrance requirements:* For master's and doctorate, GRE General Test, minimum GPA of 3.0. Additional exam requirements/recommendations for international students: Required—TOEFL. *Faculty research:* Experimental and theoretical condensed-matter, plasma, high-energy theory, nonlinear dynamics, space physics.

178 www.facebook.com/petersonspublishing

Peterson's Graduate Programs in the Physical Sciences, Mathematics, Agricultural Sciences, the Environment & Natural Resources 2012

Mathematical Physics

New Mexico Institute of Mining and Technology, Graduate Studies, Department of Physics, Socorro, NM 87801. Offers astrophysics (MS, PhD); atmospheric physics (MS, PhD); instrumentation (MS); mathematical physics (PhD). *Degree requirements:* For master's, thesis optional; for doctorate, thesis/dissertation. *Entrance requirements:* For master's, GRE General Test; for doctorate, GRE General Test, GRE Subject Test. Additional exam requirements/recommendations for international students: Required—TOEFL (minimum score 540 paper-based; 207 computer-based). *Faculty research:* Cloud physics, stellar and extragalactic processes.

University of Alberta, Faculty of Graduate Studies and Research, Department of Mathematical and Statistical Sciences, Edmonton, AB T6G 2E1, Canada. Offers applied mathematics (M Sc, PhD); biostatistics (M Sc); mathematical finance (M Sc, PhD); mathematical physics (M Sc, PhD); mathematics (M Sc, PhD); statistics (M Sc, PhD, Postgraduate Diploma). Part-time programs available. Terminal master's awarded for partial completion of doctoral program. *Degree requirements:* For master's, thesis (for some programs); for doctorate, comprehensive exam, thesis/dissertation. *Entrance requirements:* Additional exam requirements/recommendations for international students: Required—TOEFL (minimum score 580 paper-based; 237 computer-based). Electronic applications accepted. *Faculty research:* Classical and functional analysis, algebra, differential equations, geometry.

University of Colorado Boulder, Graduate School, College of Arts and Sciences, Department of Physics, Boulder, CO 80309. Offers chemical physics (PhD); geophysics (PhD); liquid crystal science and technology (PhD); mathematical physics (PhD); medical physics (PhD); optical sciences and engineering (PhD); physics (MS, PhD). *Faculty:* 50 full-time (7 women). *Students:* 147 full-time (28 women), 72 part-time (10 women); includes 12 minority (6 Asian, non-Hispanic/Latino; 6 Hispanic/Latino), 75 international. Average age 27. 503 applicants, 37 enrolled. In 2010, 16 master's, 31 doctorates awarded. Terminal master's awarded for partial completion of doctoral program. *Degree requirements:* For master's, comprehensive exam, thesis or alternative; for doctorate, comprehensive exam, thesis/dissertation. *Entrance requirements:* For master's and doctorate, GRE General Test, GRE Subject Test, minimum undergraduate GPA of 3.0. Additional exam requirements/recommendations for international students: Required—TOEFL. *Application deadline:* For fall admission, 1/15 priority date for domestic students, 1/15 for international students. Applications are processed on a rolling basis. Application fee: $50 ($60 for international students). Electronic applications accepted. *Financial support:* In 2010–11, 21 fellowships with full tuition reimbursements (averaging $15,999 per year), 146 research assistantships with full tuition reimbursements (averaging $16,586 per year) were awarded; scholarships/grants also available. Financial award application deadline: 1/15. *Faculty research:* Atomic and molecular physics, nuclear physics, condensed matter, elementary particle physics, laser or optical physics, plasma physics, geophysics, astrophysics and chemical physics. Total annual research expenditures: $16.8 million.

Optical Sciences

Air Force Institute of Technology, Graduate School of Engineering and Management, Department of Electrical and Computer Engineering, Dayton, OH 45433-7765. Offers computer engineering (MS, PhD); computer systems/science (MS); electrical engineering (MS, PhD); electro-optics (MS, PhD). *Accreditation:* ABET (one or more programs are accredited). Part-time programs available. *Degree requirements:* For master's, thesis; for doctorate, thesis/dissertation. *Entrance requirements:* For master's and doctorate, GRE General Test, minimum GPA of 3.0, U.S. citizenship. *Faculty research:* Remote sensing, information survivability, microelectronics, computer networks, artificial intelligence.

Air Force Institute of Technology, Graduate School of Engineering and Management, Department of Engineering Physics, Dayton, OH 45433-7765. Offers applied physics (MS, PhD); electro-optics (MS, PhD); materials science (PhD); nuclear engineering (MS, PhD); space physics (MS). Part-time programs available. *Degree requirements:* For master's, thesis; for doctorate, thesis/dissertation. *Entrance requirements:* For master's and doctorate, GRE General Test, minimum GPA of 3.0, U.S. citizenship. *Faculty research:* High-energy lasers, space physics, nuclear weapon effects, semiconductor physics.

Alabama Agricultural and Mechanical University, School of Graduate Studies, School of Arts and Sciences, Department of Physics, Huntsville, AL 35811. Offers physics (MS, PhD), including applied physics (PhD), materials science (PhD), optics/lasers (PhD). Part-time and evening/weekend programs available. *Degree requirements:* For doctorate, thesis/dissertation. *Entrance requirements:* For master's and doctorate, GRE General Test. Additional exam requirements/recommendations for international students: Required—TOEFL (minimum score 500 paper-based; 173 computer-based; 61 iBT). Electronic applications accepted.

Cleveland State University, College of Graduate Studies, College of Sciences and Health Professions, Department of Physics, Cleveland, OH 44115. Offers applied optics (MS); condensed matter physics (MS); medical physics (MS); optics and materials (MS); optics and medical imaging (MS). Part-time and evening/weekend programs available. *Faculty:* 10 full-time (1 woman), 4 part-time/adjunct (1 woman). *Students:* 3 full-time (0 women), 10 part-time (4 women); includes 1 Asian, non-Hispanic/Latino; 1 Two or more races, non-Hispanic/Latino, 1 international. Average age 29. 28 applicants, 39% accepted, 5 enrolled. In 2010, 3 master's awarded. *Entrance requirements:* For master's, undergraduate degree in engineering, physics, chemistry or mathematics. Additional exam requirements/recommendations for international students: Required—TOEFL (minimum score 525 paper-based; 197 computer-based). *Application deadline:* For fall admission, 7/15 priority date for domestic and international students. Applications are processed on a rolling basis. Application fee: $30. Electronic applications accepted. *Expenses:* Tuition, state resident: full-time $8447; part-time $469 per credit hour. Tuition, nonresident: full-time $16,020; part-time $890 per credit hour. Required fees: $50. *Financial support:* In 2010–11, 1 research assistantship with full and partial tuition reimbursement (averaging $5,666 per year) was awarded; fellowships with tuition reimbursements, teaching assistantships, tuition waivers (full) also available. *Faculty research:* Statistical physics, experimental solid-state physics, theoretical optics, experimental biological physics (macromolecular crystallography), experimental optics. Total annual research expenditures: $350,000. *Unit head:* Dr. Miron Kaufman, Chairperson, 216-687-2436, Fax: 216-523-7268, E-mail: m.kaufman@csuohio.edu. *Application contact:* Dr. James A. Lock, Director, 216-687-2420, Fax: 216-523-7268, E-mail: j.lock@csuohio.edu.

Delaware State University, Graduate Programs, Department of Physics, Dover, DE 19901-2277. Offers applied optics (MS); optics (PhD); physics (MS); physics teaching (MS). Part-time and evening/weekend programs available. *Entrance requirements:* For master's, minimum GPA of 3.0 in major, 2.75 overall. Additional exam requirements/recommendations for international students: Required—TOEFL. Electronic applications accepted. *Faculty research:* Thermal properties of solids, nuclear physics, radiation damage in solids.

Duke University, Graduate School, Pratt School of Engineering, Master of Engineering Program, Durham, NC 27708-0271. Offers biomedical engineering (M Eng); civil engineering (M Eng); electrical and computer engineering (M Eng); environmental engineering (M Eng); materials science and engineering (M Eng); mechanical engineering (M Eng); photonics and optical sciences (M Eng). Part-time programs available. *Faculty:* 123 full-time, 1 part-time/adjunct. *Students:* 9 full-time (4 women); includes 2 minority (both Asian, non-Hispanic/Latino), 3 international. Average age 24. *Entrance requirements:* For master's, GRE General Test, resume, 3 letters of recommendation, statement of purpose. Additional exam requirements/recommendations for international students: Required—TOEFL. *Application deadline:* For fall admission, 6/15 for domestic students, 2/15 for international students; for spring admission, 11/1 for domestic students, 9/1 for international students. Application fee: $75. *Financial support:* Merit scholarships/grants available. *Unit head:* Dr. Bradley A. Fox, Executive Director, 919-660-5455, Fax: 919-660-5456. *Application contact:* Erin Degerman, Admissions Coordinator, 919-668-6789, Fax: 919-660-5456, E-mail: erin.degerman@duke.edu.

École Polytechnique de Montréal, Graduate Programs, Department of Engineering Physics, Montréal, QC H3C 3A7, Canada. Offers optical engineering (M Eng, M Sc A, PhD); solid-state physics and engineering (M Eng, M Sc A, PhD). Part-time programs available. *Degree requirements:* For master's, one foreign language, thesis; for doctorate, one foreign language, thesis/dissertation. *Entrance requirements:* For master's, minimum GPA of 2.75; for doctorate, minimum GPA of 3.0. *Faculty research:* Optics, thin-film physics, laser spectroscopy, plasmas, photonic devices.

Norfolk State University, School of Graduate Studies, School of Science and Technology, Program in Optical Engineering, Norfolk, VA 23504. Offers MS.

North Carolina Agricultural and Technical State University, Graduate School, College of Engineering, Department of Electrical and Computer Engineering, Greensboro, NC 27411. Offers electrical engineering (MSEE, PhD), including communications and signal processing (MSEE), computer engineering (MSEE), electronic and optical materials and devices (MSEE), power systems and controls (MSEE). Part-time programs available. *Degree requirements:* For master's, project, thesis defense; for doctorate, thesis/dissertation. *Entrance requirements:* For master's, GRE General Test, GRE Subject Test, minimum GPA of 2.8; for doctorate, GRE General Test, minimum GPA of 3.0. *Faculty research:* Semiconductor compounds, VLSI design, image processing, optical systems and devices, fault-tolerant computing.

The Ohio State University, College of Optometry, Columbus, OH 43210. Offers optometry (OD); vision science (MS, PhD); OD/MS. *Accreditation:* AOA (one or more programs are accredited). *Students:* 259 full-time (138 women), 5 part-time (2 women); includes 2 Black or African American, non-Hispanic/Latino; 1 American Indian or Alaska Native, non-Hispanic/Latino; 16 Asian, non-Hispanic/Latino; 4 Hispanic/Latino, 4 international. Average age 27. In 2010, 62 first professional degrees, 12 master's, 1 doctorate awarded. *Degree requirements:* For master's, thesis; for doctorate, thesis/dissertation. *Entrance requirements:* Additional exam requirements/recommendations for international students: Required—TOEFL (minimum score 600 paper-based; 250 computer-based). *Application deadline:* For fall admission, 8/15 priority date for domestic students, 7/1 priority date for international students; for winter admission, 12/1 priority date for domestic students, 11/1 priority date for international students; for spring admission, 3/1 priority date for domestic students, 2/1 priority date for international students. Applications are processed on a rolling basis. Electronic applications accepted. *Expenses:* Contact institution. *Financial support:* Research assistantships with full tuition reimbursements, teaching assistantships with full tuition reimbursements, Federal Work-Study, institutionally sponsored loans, and scholarships/grants available. Financial award application deadline: 2/1; financial award applicants required to submit FAFSA. *Unit head:* Dr. Melvin Shipp, Dean, 614-292-3246, Fax: 614-292-7493, E-mail: shipp.25@osu.edu. *Application contact:* 614-292-9444, Fax: 614-292-3895, E-mail: domestic.grad@osu.edu.

Rochester Institute of Technology, Graduate Enrollment Services, College of Science, Health Sciences and Sustainability, Center for Imaging Science, Rochester, NY 14623-5603. Offers MS, PhD. Part-time programs available. Postbaccalaureate distance learning degree programs offered (no on-campus study). *Students:* 74 full-time (24 women), 31 part-time (10 women); includes 1 Black or African American, non-Hispanic/Latino; 1 Hispanic/Latino, 47 international. Average age 29. 82 applicants, 63% accepted, 41 enrolled. In 2010, 11 master's, 11 doctorates awarded. Terminal master's awarded for partial completion of doctoral program. *Degree requirements:* For master's, thesis; for doctorate, thesis/dissertation. *Entrance requirements:* For master's, GRE, minimum GPA of 3.0. Additional exam requirements/recommendations for international students: Required—TOEFL (minimum score 600 paper-based; 250 computer-based; 100 iBT) or IELTS (minimum score 6.5). *Application deadline:* For fall admission, 1/15 priority date for domestic and international students. Applications are processed on a rolling basis. Application fee: $50. Electronic applications accepted. *Expenses:* Tuition: Full-time $33,234; part-time $924 per credit hour. Required fees: $219. *Financial support:* In 2010–11, 70 students received support; fellowships with full and partial tuition reimbursements available, research assistantships, teaching assistantships, career-related internships or fieldwork, scholarships/grants, unspecified assistantships, and merit-based fellowships covering full tuition and stipends available. Support available to part-time students. Financial award applicants required to submit FAFSA. *Faculty research:* Biomedical imaging, nano-imaging, remote sensing, sensor development, vision and visual perception, astronomy and space weather alert technologies, computational photography, graphical display, emergency response, environmental forecasting, cultural heritage and the application of imaging science to green energy initiatives. *Unit head:* Dr. Stefi Baum, Director, 585-475-6220, Fax: 585-475-5988, E-mail: baum@cis.rit.edu. *Application contact:* Diane Ellison, Assistant Vice President, Graduate Enrollment Services, 585-475-2229, Fax: 585-475-7164, E-mail: gradinfo@rit.edu.

Rose-Hulman Institute of Technology, Faculty of Engineering and Applied Sciences, Department of Physics and Optical Engineering, Terre Haute, IN 47803-3999. Offers optical engineering (MS). Part-time programs available. *Faculty:* 15 full-time (3 women), 1 part-time/adjunct (0 women). *Students:* 7 full-time (3 women), 3 part-time (0 women), 1 international. Average age 25. 10 applicants, 100% accepted, 3 enrolled. In 2010, 2 master's awarded. *Degree requirements:* For master's, thesis. *Entrance requirements:* For master's, GRE, minimum GPA of 3.0. Additional exam requirements/recommendations for international students: Required—TOEFL (minimum score 580 paper-based; 237 computer-based; 92 iBT). *Application deadline:* For fall admission, 2/1 priority date for domestic students. Applications are processed on a rolling basis. Application fee: $0. *Expenses:* Tuition: Full-time $35,595; part-time $1038 per credit hour. *Financial support:* In 2010–11, 8 students received support; fellowships with full and partial tuition reimbursements available, research assistantships with full and partial tuition reimbursements available, teaching assistantships, institutionally sponsored loans, scholarships/grants, and tuition waivers (full and partial) available. Financial award application

Optical Sciences

Rose-Hulman Institute of Technology (continued)
deadline: 2/1. *Faculty research:* Optical design, laser systems, non-linear optics, metrology, optical MEMs, bio-photonics. Total annual research expenditures: $895,905. *Unit head:* Dr. Charles Joenathan, Chairman, 812-877-8494, Fax: 812-877-8023, E-mail: charles.joenathan@rose-hulman.edu. *Application contact:* Dr. Daniel J. Moore, Associate Dean of the Faculty, 812-877-8110, Fax: 812-877-8061, E-mail: daniel.j.moore@rose-hulman.edu.

The University of Alabama in Huntsville, School of Graduate Studies, College of Engineering, Department of Electrical and Computer Engineering, Huntsville, AL 35899. Offers computer engineering (MSE, PhD); electrical engineering (MSE, PhD); optical science and engineering (PhD); optics and photonics (MSE); software engineering (MSSE). Part-time and evening/weekend programs available. *Faculty:* 25 full-time (3 women), 4 part-time/adjunct (0 women). *Students:* 47 full-time (10 women), 145 part-time (21 women); includes 20 minority (7 Black or African American, non-Hispanic/Latino; 1 American Indian or Alaska Native, non-Hispanic/Latino; 9 Asian, non-Hispanic/Latino; 2 Hispanic/Latino; 1 Two or more races, non-Hispanic/Latino), 32 international. Average age 32. 190 applicants, 56% accepted, 57 enrolled. In 2010, 58 master's, 6 doctorates awarded. *Degree requirements:* For master's, comprehensive exam, thesis or alternative, oral and written exams; for doctorate, comprehensive exam, thesis/dissertation, oral and written exams. *Entrance requirements:* For master's, GRE General Test, appropriate bachelor's degree, minimum GPA of 3.0; for doctorate, GRE General Test, minimum GPA of 3.0. Additional exam requirements/recommendations for international students: Required—TOEFL (minimum score 500 paper-based; 173 computer-based; 62 iBT). *Application deadline:* For fall admission, 7/15 for domestic students, 4/1 for international students; for spring admission, 11/30 for domestic students, 9/1 for international students. Applications are processed on a rolling basis. Application fee: $40 ($50 for international students). Electronic applications accepted. *Expenses:* Tuition, state resident: full-time $7250; part-time $407.75 per credit hour. Tuition, nonresident: full-time $17,358; part-time $970.05 per credit hour. Required fees: $246.80 per semester. Tuition and fees vary according to course load and program. *Financial support:* In 2010–11, 42 students received support, including 16 research assistantships with full and partial tuition reimbursements available (averaging $10,649 per year), 21 teaching assistantships with full and partial tuition reimbursements available (averaging $10,593 per year); career-related internships or fieldwork, Federal Work-Study, institutionally sponsored loans, scholarships/grants, health care benefits, tuition waivers, and unspecified assistantships also available. Support available to part-time students. Financial award application deadline: 4/1; financial award applicants required to submit FAFSA. *Faculty research:* Optical signal processing, electromagnetics, photonics, nonlinear waves, computer architecture. Total annual research expenditures: $13.5 million. *Unit head:* Dr. Robert Lindquist, Chair, 256-824-6316, Fax: 256-824-6803, E-mail: lindquis@ece.uah.edu. *Application contact:* Kathy Biggs, Graduate Studies Admissions Manager, 256-824-6199, Fax: 256-824-6405, E-mail: deangrad@uah.edu.

The University of Alabama in Huntsville, School of Graduate Studies, Interdisciplinary Studies, Interdisciplinary Program in Optical Science and Engineering, Huntsville, AL 35899. Offers PhD. Part-time and evening/weekend programs available. *Faculty:* 12 full-time (0 women), 2 part-time/adjunct (0 women). *Students:* 7 full-time (1 woman), 2 part-time (0 women), 6 international. Average age 28. 23 applicants, 22% accepted, 2 enrolled. In 2010, 1 doctorate awarded. *Degree requirements:* For doctorate, comprehensive exam, thesis/dissertation, written and oral exams. *Entrance requirements:* For doctorate, GRE General Test, minimum GPA of 3.0, BS in physical science or engineering. Additional exam requirements/recommendations for international students: Required—TOEFL (minimum score 550 paper-based; 213 computer-based; 62 iBT). *Application deadline:* For fall admission, 7/15 for domestic students, 4/1 for international students; for spring admission, 11/30 for domestic students, 9/1 for international students. Applications are processed on a rolling basis. Application fee: $40 ($50 for international students). Electronic applications accepted. *Expenses:* Tuition, state resident: full-time $7250; part-time $407.75 per credit hour. Tuition, nonresident: full-time $17,358; part-time $970.05 per credit hour. Required fees: $246.80 per semester. Tuition and fees vary according to course load and program. *Financial support:* In 2010–11, 7 students received support, including 7 research assistantships with full and partial tuition reimbursements available (averaging $12,842 per year); career-related internships or fieldwork, Federal Work-Study, institutionally sponsored loans, scholarships/grants, health care benefits, and unspecified assistantships also available. Support available to part-time students. Financial award application deadline: 4/1; financial award applicants required to submit FAFSA. *Faculty research:* Laser technology, holography, optical communications, medical image processing, computer design. Total annual research expenditures: $3.4 million. *Unit head:* Dr. Robert G. Lindquist, Program Director, 256-824-2882, Fax: 256-824-6618, E-mail: lindquist@ece.uah.edu. *Application contact:* Kathy Biggs, Graduate Studies Admissions Manager, 256-824-6199, Fax: 256-824-6405, E-mail: deangrad@uah.edu.

The University of Arizona, College of Optical Sciences, Tucson, AZ 85721. Offers MS, PhD. Part-time programs available. *Faculty:* 26 full-time (3 women), 2 part-time/adjunct (0 women). *Students:* 141 full-time (30 women), 121 part-time (22 women); includes 43 minority (6 Black or African American, non-Hispanic/Latino; 1 American Indian or Alaska Native, non-Hispanic/Latino; 16 Asian, non-Hispanic/Latino; 11 Hispanic/Latino; 1 Native Hawaiian or other Pacific Islander, non-Hispanic/Latino; 8 Two or more races, non-Hispanic/Latino), 73 international. Average age 32. 261 applicants, 29% accepted, 53 enrolled. In 2010, 44 master's, 23 doctorates awarded. *Degree requirements:* For master's, thesis (for some programs), exam; for doctorate, thesis/dissertation, oral and written exams. *Entrance requirements:* For master's, GRE General Test, GRE Subject Test (recommended), minimum GPA of 3.0, 2 letters of recommendation, resume; for doctorate, GRE General Test, GRE Subject Test (recommended), minimum GPA of 3.0, 2 letters of recommendation, statement of purpose, resume. Additional exam requirements/recommendations for international students: Required—TOEFL. *Application deadline:* For fall admission, 1/1 for domestic students, 12/1 for international students. Applications are processed on a rolling basis. Application fee: $75. Electronic applications accepted. *Expenses:* Tuition, state resident: full-time $7692. *Financial support:* In 2010–11, 105 research assistantships with full tuition reimbursements (averaging $22,192 per year), 29 teaching assistantships with full tuition reimbursements (averaging $20,978 per year) were awarded; fellowships, scholarships/grants also available. Financial award application deadline: 1/1. *Faculty research:* Medical optics, medical imaging, optical data storage, optical bistability, nonlinear optical effects. Total annual research expenditures: $17.8 million. *Unit head:* Dr. James Wyant, Dean, 520-621-6997, Fax: 520-621-9613, E-mail: jcwyant@optics.arizona.edu. *Application contact:* Gail Varin, Coordinator, Graduate Academic Progress, 520-626-0888, E-mail: gail@optics.arizona.edu.

University of Central Florida, College of Optics and Photonics, Orlando, FL 32816. Offers optics (MS, PhD). Part-time and evening/weekend programs available. *Faculty:* 20 full-time (0 women). *Students:* 119 full-time (17 women), 19 part-time (1 woman); includes 2 Black or African American, non-Hispanic/Latino; 3 Asian, non-Hispanic/Latino; 5 Hispanic/Latino, 72 international. Average age 28. 232 applicants, 28% accepted, 33 enrolled. In 2010, 21 master's, 17 doctorates awarded. *Degree requirements:* For master's, thesis or alternative; for doctorate, thesis/dissertation, departmental qualifying exam, candidacy exam. *Entrance requirements:* For master's, GRE General Test, minimum GPA of 3.0 in last 60 hours; for doctorate, GRE General Test, minimum GPA of 3.5 in last 60 hours. Additional exam requirements/recommendations for international students: Required—TOEFL. *Application deadline:* For fall admission, 2/1 priority date for domestic students; for spring admission, 12/1 for domestic students. Application fee: $30. Electronic applications accepted. *Expenses:* Tuition, state resident: part-time $256.56 per credit hour. Tuition, nonresident: part-time $1011.52 per credit hour. Part-time tuition and fees vary according to program. *Financial support:* In 2010–11, 85 students received support, including 5 fellowships with partial tuition reimbursements available (averaging $8,700 per year), 116 research assistantships with partial tuition reimbursements available (averaging $11,700 per year); career-related internships or fieldwork, Federal Work-Study, institutionally sponsored loans, tuition waivers (partial), and unspecified assistantships also available. Financial award application deadline: 3/1; financial award applicants required to submit FAFSA. *Unit head:* Dr. Bahaa E. Saleh, Dean and Director, 407-882-3326, E-mail: besaleh@creol.ucf.edu. *Application contact:* Dr. Bahaa E. Saleh, Dean and Director, 407-882-3326, E-mail: besaleh@creol.ucf.edu.

University of Colorado Boulder, Graduate School, College of Arts and Sciences, Department of Physics, Boulder, CO 80309. Offers chemical physics (PhD); geophysics (PhD); liquid crystal science and technology (PhD); mathematical physics (PhD); medical physics (PhD); optical sciences and engineering (PhD); physics (MS, PhD). *Faculty:* 50 full-time (7 women). *Students:* 147 full-time (28 women), 72 part-time (10 women); includes 12 minority (6 Asian, non-Hispanic/Latino; 6 Hispanic/Latino), 75 international. Average age 27. 503 applicants, 37 enrolled. In 2010, 16 master's, 31 doctorates awarded. Terminal master's awarded for partial completion of doctoral program. *Degree requirements:* For master's, comprehensive exam, thesis or alternative; for doctorate, comprehensive exam, thesis/dissertation. *Entrance requirements:* For master's and doctorate, GRE General Test, GRE Subject Test, minimum undergraduate GPA of 3.0. Additional exam requirements/recommendations for international students: Required—TOEFL. *Application deadline:* For fall admission, 1/15 priority date for domestic students, 1/15 for international students. Applications are processed on a rolling basis. Application fee: $50 ($60 for international students). Electronic applications accepted. *Financial support:* In 2010–11, 21 fellowships with full tuition reimbursements (averaging $15,999 per year), 146 research assistantships with full tuition reimbursements (averaging $16,586 per year) were awarded; scholarships/grants also available. Financial award application deadline: 1/15. *Faculty research:* Atomic and molecular physics, nuclear physics, condensed matter, elementary particle physics, laser or optical physics, plasma physics, geophysics, astrophysics and chemical physics. Total annual research expenditures: $16.8 million.

University of Dayton, Graduate School, School of Engineering, Program in Electro-Optics, Dayton, OH 45469-1300. Offers MSEO, PhD. Part-time and evening/weekend programs available. *Faculty:* 6 full-time (0 women), 2 part-time/adjunct (0 women). *Students:* 32 full-time (6 women), 3 part-time (1 woman); includes 2 minority (1 Black or African American, non-Hispanic/Latino; 1 Asian, non-Hispanic/Latino), 11 international. Average age 26. 38 applicants, 47% accepted, 9 enrolled. In 2010, 9 master's, 5 doctorates awarded. *Degree requirements:* For master's, comprehensive exam (for some programs), thesis (for some programs); for doctorate, comprehensive exam, thesis/dissertation, departmental qualifying exam. *Entrance requirements:* For master's, BS; for doctorate, MS. Additional exam requirements/recommendations for international students: Required—TOEFL (minimum score 550 paper-based; 213 computer-based; 80 iBT). *Application deadline:* For fall admission, 8/1 for domestic students, 3/1 priority date for international students; for winter admission, 11/1 for domestic students, 9/1 priority date for international students; for spring admission, 11/1 for domestic students, 9/1 priority date for international students. Applications are processed on a rolling basis. Application fee: $0 ($50 for international students). Electronic applications accepted. *Expenses:* Tuition: Full-time $7800; part-time $650 per credit hour. *Financial support:* In 2010–11, 3 fellowships with full tuition reimbursements (averaging $30,000 per year), 23 research assistantships with full tuition reimbursements (averaging $18,000 per year), 4 teaching assistantships with full tuition reimbursements (averaging $14,000 per year) were awarded; institutionally sponsored loans, health care benefits, and unspecified assistantships also available. Financial award applicants required to submit FAFSA. *Faculty research:* Spatial and spatiotemporal solitary waves and their stabilization in nonlinear negative index materials, stimulated photorefractive backscatter leading to six-wave mixing and phase conjugation in iron doped lithium niobate, modeling and characterization of PLZT adaptive microlenses, experimental investigation of self-starting operation in a F8L based on a symmetrical NOLM, negative refraction and sub-wavelength focusing in the visible range using transparent metallo-dielectric stacks. Total annual research expenditures: $1.8 million. *Unit head:* Dr. Joseph W. Haus, Director, 937-229-2797, Fax: 937-229-2097, E-mail: jhaus@notes.udayton.edu. *Application contact:* Alexander Popovski, Associate Director of International and Graduate Admissions, 937-229-2357, Fax: 937-229-4729, E-mail: alex.popovski@notes.udayton.edu.

University of Maryland, Baltimore County, Graduate School, College of Natural and Mathematical Sciences, Department of Physics, Program in Applied Physics, Baltimore, MD 21250. Offers astrophysics (PhD); optics (MS, PhD); quantum optics (PhD); solid state physics (MS, PhD). Part-time programs available. *Faculty:* 24 full-time (3 women), 18 part-time/adjunct (2 women). *Students:* 31 full-time (10 women), 3 part-time (0 women); includes 3 Black or African American, non-Hispanic/Latino, 15 international. Average age 24. 28 applicants, 43% accepted, 7 enrolled. In 2010, 4 master's, 4 doctorates awarded. Terminal master's awarded for partial completion of doctoral program. *Degree requirements:* For master's, thesis optional; for doctorate, comprehensive exam, thesis/dissertation. *Entrance requirements:* For master's, GRE General Test, minimum GPA of 3.0; for doctorate, GRE General Test, GRE Subject Test, minimum GPA of 3.0. Additional exam requirements/recommendations for international students: Required—TOEFL. *Application deadline:* For fall admission, 5/31 for domestic and international students; for spring admission, 11/30 for domestic students. Applications are processed on a rolling basis. Application fee: $50. Electronic applications accepted. *Financial support:* In 2010–11, 30 students received support, including 4 fellowships with full tuition reimbursements available (averaging $27,000 per year), 14 research assistantships with full tuition reimbursements available (averaging $24,000 per year), 12 teaching assistantships with full tuition reimbursements available (averaging $22,000 per year); career-related internships or fieldwork, scholarships/grants, health care benefits, and unspecified assistantships also available. Support available to part-time students. Financial award application deadline: 5/31. *Faculty research:* Astrophysics, atmospheric physics, nanophysics, optics, quantum optics and quantum information. Total annual research expenditures: $4.8 million. *Unit head:* Dr. Todd Pittman, EdD, Graduate Program Director, 410-455-2513, Fax: 410-455-1072, E-mail: todd.pittman@umbc.edu. *Application contact:* Dr. Lazlo L. Takacs, Director, 410-455-2524, Fax: 410-455-1072, E-mail: takacs@umbc.edu.

University of Massachusetts Lowell, College of Arts and Sciences, Department of Physics and Applied Physics, Program in Applied Physics, Lowell, MA 01854-2881. Offers applied mechanics (PhD); applied physics (MS, PhD), including optical sciences (MS). Terminal master's awarded for partial completion of doctoral program. *Degree requirements:* For master's, thesis; for doctorate, 2 foreign languages, thesis/dissertation. *Entrance requirements:* For master's, GRE General Test, 3 letters of reference; for doctorate, GRE General Test, transcripts, 3 letters of reference. Additional exam requirements/recommendations for international students: Required—TOEFL.

University of New Mexico, Graduate School, College of Arts and Sciences, Program in Optical Science and Engineering, Albuquerque, NM 87131-2039. Offers MS, PhD. Part-time programs available. *Students:* 38 full-time (9 women), 12 part-time (0 women); includes 1 Asian, non-Hispanic/Latino; 1 Hispanic/Latino, 32 international. Average age 29. 73 applicants, 16% accepted, 9 enrolled. In 2010, 11 master's, 7 doctorates awarded. Terminal master's awarded for partial completion of doctoral program. *Degree requirements:* For master's, comprehensive exam (for some programs), thesis (for some programs); for doctorate, comprehensive exam, thesis/dissertation. *Entrance requirements:* For master's and doctorate, GRE, relevant undergraduate coursework, curriculum vitae, letters of recommendation. Additional exam requirements/recommendations for international students: Required—TOEFL (minimum score 575 paper-based; 213 computer-based; 79 iBT), IELTS (minimum score 7). *Application deadline:* For fall admission, 1/15 for domestic students; for spring admission, 8/1 for domestic students. Application fee: $50. Electronic applications accepted. *Expenses:* Tuition, state resident: full-time $5991; part-time $251 per credit hour. Tuition, nonresident: full-time $14,405;

part-time $800.20 per credit hour. Tuition and fees vary according to course level, course load, program and reciprocity agreements. *Financial support:* In 2010–11, 34 students received support, including 3 research assistantships with full tuition reimbursements available (averaging $16,097 per year), 13 teaching assistantships with full tuition reimbursements available (averaging $7,148 per year); fellowships with full tuition reimbursements available, career-related internships or fieldwork, scholarships/grants, health care benefits, and unspecified assistantships also available. Support available to part-time students. Financial award application deadline: 2/1. *Faculty research:* Advanced materials, atom optics, biomedical optics, fiber optics, laser cooling, high intensity interactions, lithography, nano photonics, nonlinear optics, optical imaging, optical sensors, optoelectronics, quantum optics, spectroscopy, ultrafast phenomena. *Unit head:* Dr. Luke Lester, General Chair, 505-277-7805, Fax: 505-277-7801, E-mail: luke@chtm.unm.edu. *Application contact:* Doris Williams, Program Advisor, 505-277-7764, Fax: 505-277-7801, E-mail: dorisw@chtm.unm.edu.

The University of North Carolina at Charlotte, Graduate School, College of Arts and Sciences, Department of Physics and Optical Science, Charlotte, NC 28223-0001. Offers applied physics (MS); optical science and engineering (MS, PhD). *Faculty:* 21 full-time (4 women). *Students:* 39 full-time (7 women), 13 part-time (4 women); includes 1 minority (Asian, non-Hispanic/Latino), 29 international. Average age 27. 42 applicants, 79% accepted, 15 enrolled. In 2010, 8 master's, 9 doctorates awarded. Terminal master's awarded for partial completion of doctoral program. *Degree requirements:* For master's, thesis optional; for doctorate, thesis/dissertation optional. *Entrance requirements:* For master's, GRE General Test, minimum GPA of 3.0 during previous 2 years, 2.75 overall. Additional exam requirements/recommendations for international students: Required—TOEFL (minimum score 557 paper-based; 220 computer-based; 83 iBT). *Application deadline:* For fall admission, 7/15 for domestic students, 5/1 for international students; for spring admission, 11/15 for domestic students, 10/1 for international students. Applications are processed on a rolling basis. Application fee: $55. Electronic applications accepted. *Expenses:* Tuition, state resident: full-time $3464. Tuition, nonresident: full-time $14,297. Required fees: $2094. Tuition and fees vary according to course load. *Financial support:* In 2010–11, 35 students received support, including 6 fellowships (averaging $40,536 per year), 9 research assistantships (averaging $9,718 per year), 18 teaching assistantships (averaging $13,041 per year); career-related internships or fieldwork, institutionally sponsored loans, scholarships/grants, and unspecified assistantships also available. Support available to part-time students. Financial award application deadline: 4/1; financial award applicants required to submit FAFSA. *Faculty research:* Optics, lasers, microscopy, fibers, astrophysics. Total annual research expenditures: $1.3 million. *Unit head:* Dr. Patrick Moyer, Interim Chair, 704-687-8148, Fax: 704-687-3160, E-mail: pjmoyer@uncc.edu. *Application contact:* Kathy B. Giddings, Director of Graduate Admissions, 704-687-5503, Fax: 704-687-3279, E-mail: gradadm@uncc.edu.

University of Rochester, Hajim School of Engineering and Applied Sciences, Institute of Optics, Rochester, NY 14627. Offers MS, PhD. Terminal master's awarded for partial completion of doctoral program. *Degree requirements:* For master's, comprehensive exam; for doctorate, thesis/dissertation, preliminary and qualifying exams. *Entrance requirements:* For master's and doctorate, GRE. Additional exam requirements/recommendations for international students: Required—TOEFL.

University of Rochester, School of Nursing, Rochester, NY 14642. Offers acute care nurse practitioner (MS); adult nurse practitioner (MS); adult psychiatric mental health nurse practitioner (MS); adult/geriatric nurse practitioner (MS); care of children and families/pediatric nurse practitioner (MS); care of children and families/pediatric nurse practitioner with pediatric behavioral health (MS); care of children and families/pediatric nurse practitioner/neonatal nurse practitioner (MS); child and adolescent psychiatric mental health nurse practitioner (MS); clinical nurse leader (MS); disaster response and emergency preparedness (MS); family nurse practitioner (MS); health care organization management and leadership (MS); health practice research (PhD); health promotion, education and technology (MS); nursing (Certificate). *Accreditation:* AACN; NLN (one or more programs are accredited). Part-time programs available. Postbaccalaureate distance learning degree programs offered (minimal on-campus study). Terminal master's awarded for partial completion of doctoral program. *Degree requirements:* For master's, comprehensive exam or thesis; for doctorate, thesis/dissertation. *Entrance requirements:* For master's, BS in nursing, minimum GPA of 3.0, course work in statistics; for doctorate, GRE General Test, MS in nursing, minimum GPA of 3.5; for Certificate, MS in nursing. Additional exam requirements/recommendations for international students: Recommended—TOEFL (minimum score 560 paper-based; 230 computer-based; 88 iBT). *Faculty research:* Clinical research in aging, managing asthma in children, interventions to improve outcomes in critically ill children and their mothers, nurse home visitation studies, medical device evaluation, critical care clinical studies, high risk behavior and prevention, palliative care, pregnancy-related weight gain.

Photonics

Boston University, College of Engineering, Department of Electrical and Computer Engineering, Boston, MA 02215. Offers computer engineering (M Eng, MS, PhD); electrical engineering (M Eng, MS, PhD); photonics (M Eng, MS). Part-time programs available. *Faculty:* 40 full-time (3 women), 5 part-time/adjunct (0 women). *Students:* 205 full-time (34 women), 15 part-time (1 woman); includes 21 minority (1 Black or African American, non-Hispanic/Latino; 16 Asian, non-Hispanic/Latino; 4 Hispanic/Latino), 141 international. Average age 25. 810 applicants, 25% accepted, 112 enrolled. In 2010, 62 master's, 15 doctorates awarded. Terminal master's awarded for partial completion of doctoral program. *Degree requirements:* For master's, thesis (for some programs); for doctorate, comprehensive exam, thesis/dissertation. *Entrance requirements:* For master's and doctorate, GRE General Test. Additional exam requirements/recommendations for international students: Required—TOEFL (minimum score 550 paper-based; 213 computer-based; 84 iBT), IELTS (minimum score 6). *Application deadline:* For fall admission, 4/1 for domestic and international students; for spring admission, 10/1 for domestic and international students. Applications are processed on a rolling basis. Application fee: $70. Electronic applications accepted. *Expenses:* Tuition: Full-time $39,314; part-time $1228 per credit. Required fees: $40 per semester. *Financial support:* In 2010–11, 126 students received support, including 8 fellowships with full tuition reimbursements available (averaging $28,200 per year), 82 research assistantships with full tuition reimbursements available (averaging $18,800 per year), 18 teaching assistantships with full tuition reimbursements available (averaging $18,800 per year); career-related internships or fieldwork, Federal Work-Study, institutionally sponsored loans, scholarships/grants, traineeships, and health care benefits also available. Financial award application deadline: 1/15; financial award applicants required to submit FAFSA. *Faculty research:* Communications and computer networks; signal, image, video, and multimedia processing; solid-state materials, devices, and photonics; systems, control, and reliable computing; VLSI, computer engineering and high-performance computing. *Unit head:* Dr. David Castanon, Chairman, ad Interim, 617-353-9880, Fax: 617-353-6440, E-mail: dac@bu.edu. *Application contact:* Stephen Doherty, Director of Graduate Programs, 617-353-9760, Fax: 617-353-0259, E-mail: enggrad@bu.edu.

Duke University, Graduate School, Pratt School of Engineering, Master of Engineering Program, Durham, NC 27708-0271. Offers biomedical engineering (M Eng); civil engineering (M Eng); electrical and computer engineering (M Eng); environmental engineering (M Eng); materials science and engineering (M Eng); mechanical engineering (M Eng); photonics and optical sciences (M Eng). Part-time programs available. *Faculty:* 123 full-time, 1 part-time/adjunct. *Students:* 9 full-time (4 women); includes 2 minority (both Asian, non-Hispanic/Latino), 3 international. Average age 24. *Entrance requirements:* For master's, GRE General Test, resume, 3 letters of recommendation, statement of purpose. Additional exam requirements/recommendations for international students: Required—TOEFL. *Application deadline:* For fall admission, 6/15 for domestic students, 2/15 for international students; for spring admission, 11/1 for domestic students, 9/1 for international students. Application fee: $75. *Financial support:* Merit scholarships/grants available. *Unit head:* Dr. Bradley A. Fox, Executive Director, 919-660-5455, Fax: 919-660-5456. *Application contact:* Erin Degerman, Admissions Coordinator, 919-668-6789, Fax: 919-660-5456, E-mail: erin.degerman@duke.edu.

Lehigh University, College of Arts and Sciences, Department of Physics, Bethlehem, PA 18015. Offers photonics (MS); physics (MS, PhD); polymer science (MS, PhD). Part-time programs available. *Faculty:* 17 full-time (1 woman). *Students:* 42 full-time (14 women), 2 part-time (0 women); includes 1 minority (Black or African American, non-Hispanic/Latino), 17 international. Average age 26. 73 applicants, 15% accepted, 8 enrolled. In 2010, 19 master's, 5 doctorates awarded. *Degree requirements:* For doctorate, comprehensive exam, thesis/dissertation. *Entrance requirements:* Additional exam requirements/recommendations for international students: Required—TOEFL (minimum score 213 computer-based; 85 iBT). *Application deadline:* For fall admission, 2/15 priority date for domestic and international students. Applications are processed on a rolling basis. Application fee: $75. Electronic applications accepted. *Financial support:* In 2010–11, 44 students received support, including 5 fellowships with full tuition reimbursements available (averaging $23,000 per year), 19 research assistantships with full tuition reimbursements available (averaging $22,180 per year), 20 teaching assistantships with full tuition reimbursements available (averaging $22,180 per year); career-related internships or fieldwork, Federal Work-Study, institutionally sponsored loans, scholarships/grants, tuition waivers (full and partial), and unspecified assistantships also available. Support available to part-time students. Financial award application deadline: 1/15. *Faculty research:* Condensed matter physics; atomic, molecular and optical physics; plasma physics; nonlinear optics and photonics; astronomy and astrophysics. Total annual research expenditures: $3.5 million. *Unit head:* Dr. Volkmar Dierolf, Chair, 610-758-3915, Fax: 610-758-5730, E-mail: vod2@lehigh.edu. *Application contact:* Dr. Ivan Biaggio, Graduate Admissions Officer, 610-758-4916, Fax: 610-758-5730, E-mail: ivb2@lehigh.edu.

Lehigh University, P.C. Rossin College of Engineering and Applied Science, Department of Electrical and Computer Engineering, Bethlehem, PA 18015. Offers electrical engineering (M Eng, MS, PhD); photonics (MS); wireless network engineering (MS). Part-time programs available. *Faculty:* 20 full-time (3 women). *Students:* 58 full-time (12 women), 7 part-time (1 woman), 52 international. Average age 27. 258 applicants, 11% accepted, 20 enrolled. In 2010, 18 master's, 17 doctorates awarded. Terminal master's awarded for partial completion of doctoral program. *Degree requirements:* For master's, thesis optional; for doctorate, thesis/dissertation, qualifying or comprehensive exam for all 1st year PhD's; general exam 7 months or more prior to completion/dissertation defense. *Entrance requirements:* For master's and doctorate, GRE General Test, BS in field or related field. Additional exam requirements/recommendations for international students: Required—TOEFL (minimum score 79 iBT). *Application deadline:* For fall admission, 1/15 priority date for domestic and international students; for spring admission, 11/1 for domestic and international students. Application fee: $75. Electronic applications accepted. *Financial support:* In 2010–11, 4 fellowships with full tuition reimbursements (averaging $18,360 per year), 42 research assistantships with full tuition reimbursements (averaging $21,600 per year), 5 teaching assistantships with full tuition reimbursements (averaging $18,819 per year) were awarded; career-related internships or fieldwork, Federal Work-Study, institutionally sponsored loans, scholarships/grants, tuition waivers (full and partial), and unspecified assistantships also available. Support available to part-time students. Financial award application deadline: 1/15. *Faculty research:* Nanostructures/nanodevices, terahertz generation, analog devices, mixed mode design and signal circuits, optoelectronic sensors, micro-fabrication technology and design, packaging/reliability of microsensors, coding and networking information theory, radio frequency, wireless and optical wireless communication, wireless networks. Total annual research expenditures: $4.3 million. *Unit head:* Dr. Filbert J. Bartoli, Chair, 610-758-4069, Fax: 610-758-6279, E-mail: fjb205@lehigh.edu. *Application contact:* Coley B. Burke, Graduate Coordinator, 610-758-4072, Fax: 610-758-6279, E-mail: cbb310@lehigh.edu.

Lehigh University, P.C. Rossin College of Engineering and Applied Science, Department of Materials Science and Engineering, Bethlehem, PA 18015. Offers materials science and engineering (M Eng, MS, PhD); photonics (MS); polymer science/engineering (M Eng, MS, PhD); MBA/E. Part-time programs available. *Faculty:* 13 full-time (3 women), 1 part-time/adjunct (0 women). *Students:* 27 full-time (4 women), 4 part-time (1 woman); includes 1 minority (Asian, non-Hispanic/Latino), 14 international. Average age 26. 411 applicants, 2% accepted, 7 enrolled. In 2010, 8 master's, 2 doctorates awarded. *Degree requirements:* For master's, thesis; for doctorate, comprehensive exam, thesis/dissertation. *Entrance requirements:* For master's and doctorate, GRE General Test, minimum GPA of 3.0. Additional exam requirements/recommendations for international students: Required—TOEFL (minimum score 487 paper-based; 216 computer-based; 85 iBT). *Application deadline:* For fall admission, 1/15 priority date for domestic students, 1/15 for international students; for spring admission, 12/1 priority date for domestic students, 12/1 for international students. Applications are processed on a rolling basis. Application fee: $75. Electronic applications accepted. *Financial support:* In 2010–11, 7 fellowships with full and partial tuition reimbursements (averaging $22,400 per year), 21 research assistantships with full tuition reimbursements (averaging $22,449 per year), 5 teaching assistantships with partial tuition reimbursements (averaging $17,512 per year) were awarded; career-related internships or fieldwork, Federal Work-Study, institutionally sponsored loans, scholarships/grants, and unspecified assistantships also available. Support available to part-time students. Financial award application deadline: 1/15. *Faculty research:* Metals, ceramics, crystals, polymers, fatigue crack propagation. Total annual research expenditures: $4.3 million. *Unit head:* Dr. Helen Chan, Chairperson, 610-758-5554, Fax: 610-758-4244, E-mail: hmc0@lehigh.edu. *Application contact:* Anne Marie Lobley, Graduate Administrative Coordinator, 610-758-4222, Fax: 610-758-4244, E-mail: amme@lehigh.edu.

Oklahoma State University, College of Arts and Sciences, Department of Physics, Stillwater, OK 74078. Offers photonics (MS, PhD); physics (MS, PhD). *Faculty:* 30 full-time (8 women), 2 part-time/adjunct (0 women). *Students:* 5 full-time (0 women), 33 part-time (6 women); includes 1 American Indian or Alaska Native, non-Hispanic/Latino; 1 Hispanic/Latino, 26 international. Average age 29. 46 applicants, 22% accepted, 3 enrolled. In 2010, 2 master's, 7 doctorates awarded. *Degree requirements:* For master's, thesis; for doctorate, comprehensive exam, thesis/dissertation, oral defense of dissertation, preliminary exam, qualifying exam. *Entrance requirements:* For master's and doctorate, GRE. Additional exam requirements/recommendations

Peterson's Graduate Programs in the Physical Sciences, Mathematics, Agricultural Sciences, the Environment & Natural Resources 2012

www.facebook.com/petersonspublishing **181**

Photonics

Oklahoma State University (continued)

for international students: Required—TOEFL (minimum score 550 paper-based; 79 iBT). *Application deadline:* For fall admission, 3/1 priority date for international students; for spring admission, 8/1 priority date for international students. Applications are processed on a rolling basis. Application fee: $40 ($75 for international students). Electronic applications accepted. *Expenses:* Tuition, state resident: full-time $3716; part-time $154.85 per credit hour. Tuition, nonresident: full-time $14,892; part-time $621 per credit hour. Required fees: $2044; $85.20 per credit hour. One-time fee: $50. Tuition and fees vary according to course load and campus/location. *Financial support:* In 2010–11, 23 research assistantships (averaging $18,637 per year), 38 teaching assistantships (averaging $16,985 per year) were awarded; career-related internships or fieldwork, Federal Work-Study, scholarships/grants, health care benefits, tuition waivers (partial), and unspecified assistantships also available. Support available to part-time students. Financial award application deadline: 3/1; financial award applicants required to submit FAFSA. *Faculty research:* Lasers and photonics, non-linear optical materials, turbulence, structure and function of biological membranes, particle theory. *Unit head:* Dr. James Wicksted, Head, 405-744-5796, Fax: 405-744-6811. *Application contact:* Dr. Gordon Emslie, Dean, 405-744-6368, Fax: 405-744-0355, E-mail: grad-i@okstate.edu.

Oklahoma State University, Graduate College, Stillwater, OK 74078. Offers environmental science (MS); international studies (MS); natural and applied science (MS); photonics (PhD); plant science (PhD). Programs are interdisciplinary. *Faculty:* 2 full-time (1 woman). *Students:* 69 full-time (40 women), 131 part-time (68 women); includes 13 Black or African American, non-Hispanic/Latino; 15 American Indian or Alaska Native, non-Hispanic/Latino; 8 Asian, non-Hispanic/Latino; 8 Hispanic/Latino, 70 international. Average age 30. 690 applicants, 74% accepted, 75 enrolled. In 2010, 66 master's, 7 doctorates awarded. *Degree requirements:* For master's, thesis (for some programs); for doctorate, comprehensive exam, thesis/dissertation. *Entrance requirements:* For master's and doctorate, GRE or GMAT. Additional exam requirements/recommendations for international students: Required—TOEFL (minimum score 550 paper-based; 79 iBT). *Application deadline:* For fall admission, 3/1 priority date for international students; for spring admission, 8/1 priority date for international students. Applications are processed on a rolling basis. Application fee: $40 ($75 for international students). Electronic applications accepted. *Expenses:* Tuition, state resident: full-time $3716; part-time $154.85 per credit hour. Tuition, nonresident: full-time $14,892; part-time $621 per credit hour. Required fees: $2044; $85.20 per credit hour. One-time fee: $50. Tuition and fees vary according to course load and campus/location. *Financial support:* In 2010–11, 2 research assistantships (averaging $12,900 per year) were awarded; career-related internships or fieldwork, Federal Work-Study, scholarships/grants, health care benefits, tuition waivers (partial), and unspecified assistantships also available. Support available to part-time students. Financial award application deadline: 3/1; financial award applicants required to submit FAFSA. *Unit head:* Dr. Gordon Emslie, Dean, 405-744-6368, Fax: 405-744-0355, E-mail: grad-i@okstate.edu. *Application contact:* Dr. Susan Mathew, Coordinator of Admissions, 405-744-6368, Fax: 405-744-0355, E-mail: grad-i@okstate.edu.

Princeton University, Princeton Institute for the Science and Technology of Materials (PRISM), Princeton, NJ 08544-1019. Offers materials (PhD).

Stevens Institute of Technology, Graduate School, Charles V. Schaefer Jr. School of Engineering, Department of Electrical and Computer Engineering, Program in Electrical Engineering, Hoboken, NJ 07030. Offers computer architecture and digital systems (M Eng); electrical engineering (PhD); microelectronics and photonics science and technology (M Eng); signal processing for communications (M Eng); telecommunications systems engineering (M Eng); wireless communications (M Eng, Certificate). *Students:* 161 full-time (20 women), 54 part-time (4 women); includes 1 Black or African American, non-Hispanic/Latino; 28 Asian, non-Hispanic/Latino; 2 Hispanic/Latino, 140 international. Average age 26. 177 applicants, 80% accepted. *Degree requirements:* For master's, thesis optional; for doctorate, variable foreign language requirement, thesis/dissertation. *Entrance requirements:* For master's, doctorate, and Certificate, GRE. Additional exam requirements/recommendations for international students: Required—TOEFL. *Application deadline:* Applications are processed on a rolling basis. Application fee: $50. Electronic applications accepted. *Unit head:* Prof. Yu-Dong Yao, Head, 201-216-5264. *Application contact:* Graduate Admissions, 800-496-4935, Fax: 201-216-8044, E-mail: gradadmissions@stevens.edu.

Stevens Institute of Technology, Graduate School, Charles V. Schaefer Jr. School of Engineering, Interdisciplinary Program in Microelectronics and Photonics, Hoboken, NJ 07030. Offers Certificate. *Unit head:* Dr. George Korfiatis, Dean, 201-216-5263. *Application contact:* Graduate Admissions, 800-496-4935, Fax: 201-216-8044, E-mail: gradadmissions@stevens.edu.

The University of Alabama in Huntsville, School of Graduate Studies, College of Engineering, Department of Electrical and Computer Engineering, Huntsville, AL 35899. Offers computer engineering (MSE, PhD); electrical engineering (MSE, PhD); optical science and engineering (PhD); optics and photonics (MSE); software engineering (MSSE). Part-time and evening/weekend programs available. *Faculty:* 25 full-time (3 women), 4 part-time/adjunct (0 women). *Students:* 47 full-time (10 women), 145 part-time (21 women); includes 20 minority (7 Black or African American, non-Hispanic/Latino; 1 American Indian or Alaska Native, non-Hispanic/Latino; 9 Asian, non-Hispanic/Latino; 2 Hispanic/Latino; 1 Two or more races, non-Hispanic/Latino), 32 international. Average age 32. 190 applicants, 56% accepted, 57 enrolled. In 2010, 58 master's, 6 doctorates awarded. *Degree requirements:* For master's, comprehensive exam, thesis or alternative, oral and written exams; for doctorate, comprehensive exam, thesis/dissertation, oral and written exams. *Entrance requirements:* For master's, GRE General Test, appropriate bachelor's degree, minimum GPA of 3.0; for doctorate, GRE General Test, minimum GPA of 3.0. Additional exam requirements/recommendations for international students: Required—TOEFL (minimum score 500 paper-based; 173 computer-based; 62 iBT). *Application deadline:* For fall admission, 7/15 for domestic students, 4/1 for international students; for spring admission, 11/30 for domestic students, 9/1 for international students. Applications are processed on a rolling basis. Application fee: $40 ($50 for international students). Electronic applications accepted. *Expenses:* Tuition, state resident: full-time $7250; part-time $407.75 per credit hour. Tuition, nonresident: full-time $17,358; part-time $970.05 per credit hour. Required fees: $246.80 per semester. Tuition and fees vary according to course load and program. *Financial support:* In 2010–11, 42 students received support, including 16 research assistantships with full and partial tuition reimbursements available (averaging $10,649 per year), 21 teaching assistantships with full and partial tuition reimbursements available (averaging $10,593 per year); career-related internships or fieldwork, Federal Work-Study, institutionally sponsored loans, scholarships/grants, health care benefits, tuition waivers, and unspecified assistantships also available. Support available to part-time students. Financial award application deadline: 4/1; financial award applicants required to submit FAFSA. *Faculty research:* Optical signal processing, electromagnetics, photonics, nonlinear waves, computer architecture. Total annual research expenditures: $13.5 million. *Unit head:* Dr. Robert Lindquist, Chair, 256-824-6316, Fax: 256-824-6803, E-mail: lindquis@ece.uah.edu. *Application contact:* Kathy Biggs, Graduate Studies Admissions Manager, 256-824-6199, Fax: 256-824-6405, E-mail: deangrad@uah.edu.

The University of Alabama in Huntsville, School of Graduate Studies, College of Science, Department of Physics, Huntsville, AL 35899. Offers optics and photonics technology (MS); physics (MS, PhD). Part-time and evening/weekend programs available. *Faculty:* 19 full-time (0 women), 1 part-time/adjunct (0 women). *Students:* 35 full-time (9 women), 20 part-time (8 women); includes 2 minority (both Asian, non-Hispanic/Latino), 13 international. Average age 30. 50 applicants, 58% accepted, 17 enrolled. In 2010, 7 master's awarded. *Degree requirements:* For master's, comprehensive exam, thesis or alternative, oral and written exams; for doctorate, comprehensive exam, thesis/dissertation, oral and written exams. *Entrance requirements:* For master's and doctorate, GRE General Test, minimum GPA of 3.0. Additional exam requirements/recommendations for international students: Required—TOEFL (minimum score 550 paper-based; 213 computer-based; 62 iBT). *Application deadline:* For fall admission, 7/15 for domestic students, 4/1 for international students; for spring admission, 11/30 for domestic students, 9/1 for international students. Applications are processed on a rolling basis. Application fee: $40 ($50 for international students). Electronic applications accepted. *Expenses:* Tuition, state resident: full-time $7250; part-time $407.75 per credit hour. Tuition, nonresident: full-time $17,358; part-time $970.05 per credit hour. Required fees: $246.80 per semester. Tuition and fees vary according to course load and program. *Financial support:* In 2010–11, 31 students received support, including 19 research assistantships with full and partial tuition reimbursements available (averaging $14,278 per year), 11 teaching assistantships with full and partial tuition reimbursements available (averaging $14,000 per year); career-related internships or fieldwork, Federal Work-Study, institutionally sponsored loans, scholarships/grants, health care benefits, and unspecified assistantships also available. Support available to part-time students. Financial award application deadline: 4/1; financial award applicants required to submit FAFSA. *Faculty research:* Space physics, cosmology/general relativity, optics/quantum optics, astrophysics/gamma-ray astronomy, strophysical instrumentation. Total annual research expenditures: $6.1 million. *Unit head:* Dr. Gary Zank, Chair, 256-824-2481, Fax: 256-824-6873, E-mail: gary.zank@uah.edu. *Application contact:* Kathy Biggs, Graduate Studies Admissions Manager, 256-824-6199, Fax: 256-824-6405, E-mail: deangrad@uah.edu.

University of Arkansas, Graduate School, Interdisciplinary Program in Microelectronics and Photonics, Fayetteville, AR 72701-1201. Offers MS, PhD. *Students:* 7 full-time (2 women), 44 part-time (4 women); includes 8 minority (6 Black or African American, non-Hispanic/Latino; 2 Asian, non-Hispanic/Latino), 17 international. 10 applicants, 100% accepted. In 2010, 4 master's, 2 doctorates awarded. *Degree requirements:* For doctorate, thesis/dissertation. *Application deadline:* For fall admission, 4/1 for international students; for spring admission, 10/1 for international students. Applications are processed on a rolling basis. Application fee: $40 ($50 for international students). Electronic applications accepted. *Financial support:* In 2010–11, 5 fellowships with tuition reimbursements, 17 research assistantships, 3 teaching assistantships were awarded. Financial award application deadline: 4/1; financial award applicants required to submit FAFSA. *Unit head:* Dr. Ken Vickers, Head, 479-575-2875, Fax: 479-575-4580, E-mail: vickers@uark.edu. *Application contact:* Graduate Admissions, 479-575-6246, Fax: 479-575-5908, E-mail: gradinfo@uark.edu.

University of California, San Diego, Office of Graduate Studies, Department of Electrical and Computer Engineering, La Jolla, CA 92093. Offers applied ocean science (MS, PhD); applied physics (MS, PhD); communication theory and systems (MS, PhD); computer engineering (MS, PhD); electrical engineering (M Eng); electronic circuits and systems (MS, PhD); intelligent systems, robotics and control (MS, PhD); photonics (MS, PhD); signal and image processing (MS, PhD). MS only offered to students who have been admitted to the PhD program. *Entrance requirements:* For master's and doctorate, GRE General Test. Electronic applications accepted.

University of California, Santa Barbara, Graduate Division, College of Engineering, Department of Electrical and Computer Engineering, Santa Barbara, CA 93106-2014. Offers communications, control and signal processing (PhD); computer engineering (MS); electronics and photonics (MS); MS/PhD. *Faculty:* 37 full-time (3 women), 1 part-time/adjunct (0 women). *Students:* 251 full-time (45 women); includes 2 Black or African American, non-Hispanic/Latino; 2 American Indian or Alaska Native, non-Hispanic/Latino; 123 Asian, non-Hispanic/Latino; 10 Hispanic/Latino; 1 Native Hawaiian or other Pacific Islander, non-Hispanic/Latino. Average age 26. 1,040 applicants, 27% accepted, 79 enrolled. In 2010, 47 master's, 31 doctorates awarded. Terminal master's awarded for partial completion of doctoral program. *Degree requirements:* For master's, comprehensive exam, thesis; for doctorate, thesis/dissertation. *Entrance requirements:* For master's and doctorate, GRE General Test. Additional exam requirements/recommendations for international students: Required—TOEFL (minimum score 550 paper-based; 80 iBT), IELTS (minimum score 7). *Application deadline:* For fall admission, 12/15 for domestic and international students; for winter admission, 11/1 for domestic and international students; for spring admission, 1/1 for domestic and international students. Application fee: $70 ($90 for international students). Electronic applications accepted. *Financial support:* In 2010–11, 196 students received support, including 70 fellowships with full and partial tuition reimbursements available (averaging $7,181 per year), 155 research assistantships with full and partial tuition reimbursements available (averaging $15,235 per year), 54 teaching assistantships with full and partial tuition reimbursements available (averaging $9,910 per year); tuition waivers (full and partial) also available. Financial award application deadline: 12/15; financial award applicants required to submit FAFSA. *Faculty research:* Communications, signal processing, computer engineering, control, electronics and photonics. Total annual research expenditures: $25.5 million. *Unit head:* Prof. Jerry Gibson, Chair, 805-893-3821, Fax: 805-893-6262, E-mail: gibson@ece.ucsb.edu. *Application contact:* Erika Raquel Klukovich, Graduate Admissions Coordinator, 805-893-3114, Fax: 805-893-5402, E-mail: erika@ece.ucsb.edu.

University of Central Florida, College of Optics and Photonics, Orlando, FL 32816. Offers optics (MS, PhD). Part-time and evening/weekend programs available. *Faculty:* 20 full-time (0 women). *Students:* 119 full-time (17 women), 19 part-time (1 woman); includes 2 Black or African American, non-Hispanic/Latino; 3 Asian, non-Hispanic/Latino; 5 Hispanic/Latino, 72 international. Average age 28. 232 applicants, 28% accepted, 33 enrolled. In 2010, 21 master's, 17 doctorates awarded. *Degree requirements:* For master's, thesis or alternative; for doctorate, thesis/dissertation, departmental qualifying exam, candidacy exam. *Entrance requirements:* For master's, GRE General Test, minimum GPA of 3.0 in last 60 hours; for doctorate, GRE General Test, minimum GPA of 3.5 in last 60 hours. Additional exam requirements/recommendations for international students: Required—TOEFL. *Application deadline:* For fall admission, 2/1 priority date for domestic students; for spring admission, 12/1 for domestic students. Application fee: $30. Electronic applications accepted. *Expenses:* Tuition, state resident: part-time $256.56 per credit hour. Tuition, nonresident: part-time $1011.52 per credit hour. Part-time tuition and fees vary according to program. *Financial support:* In 2010–11, 85 students received support, including 5 fellowships with partial tuition reimbursements available (averaging $8,700 per year), 116 research assistantships with partial tuition reimbursements available (averaging $11,700 per year); career-related internships or fieldwork, Federal Work-Study, institutionally sponsored loans, tuition waivers (partial), and unspecified assistantships also available. Financial award application deadline: 3/1; financial award applicants required to submit FAFSA. *Unit head:* Dr. Bahaa E. Saleh, Dean and Director, 407-882-3326, E-mail: besaleh@creol.ucf.edu. *Application contact:* Dr. Bahaa E. Saleh, Dean and Director, 407-882-3326, E-mail: besaleh@creol.ucf.edu.

182 www.facebook.com/petersonspublishing

Peterson's Graduate Programs in the Physical Sciences, Mathematics, Agricultural Sciences, the Environment & Natural Resources 2012

Physics

Alabama Agricultural and Mechanical University, School of Graduate Studies, School of Arts and Sciences, Department of Physics, Huntsville, AL 35811. Offers physics (MS, PhD), including applied physics (PhD), materials science (PhD), optics/lasers (PhD). Part-time and evening/weekend programs available. *Degree requirements:* For doctorate, thesis/dissertation. *Entrance requirements:* For master's and doctorate, GRE General Test. Additional exam requirements/recommendations for international students: Required—TOEFL (minimum score 500 paper-based; 173 computer-based; 61 iBT). Electronic applications accepted.

American University of Beirut, Graduate Programs, Faculty of Arts and Sciences, Beirut, Lebanon. Offers anthropology (MA); Arabic language and literature (MA); archaeology (MA); biology (MS); chemistry (MS); computational science (MS); computer science (MS); economics (MA); education (MA); English language (MA); English literature (MA); environmental policy planning (MSES); financial economics (MAFE); geology (MS); history (MA); mathematics (MA, MS); Middle Eastern studies (MA); philosophy (MA); physics (MS); political studies (MA); psychology (MA); public administration (MA); sociology (MA); statistics (MA, MS). Part-time programs available. *Faculty:* 229 full-time (98 women), 136 part-time/adjunct (79 women). *Students:* 158 full-time (104 women), 263 part-time (171 women). Average age 25. 356 applicants, 59% accepted, 127 enrolled. In 2010, 57 master's awarded. *Degree requirements:* For master's, one foreign language, comprehensive exam, thesis (for some programs). *Entrance requirements:* For master's, GRE, letter of recommendation. Additional exam requirements/recommendations for international students: Required—TOEFL (minimum score 600 paper-based; 250 computer-based; 97 iBT), IELTS (minimum score 7). *Application deadline:* For fall admission, 4/30 for domestic and international students; for spring admission, 11/1 for domestic and international students. Application fee: $50. *Expenses:* Tuition: Full-time $12,294; part-time $683 per credit. Required fees: $499; $499 per credit. Tuition and fees vary according to course load and program. *Financial support:* In 2010–11, 33 students received support. Career-related internships or fieldwork, institutionally sponsored loans, scholarships/grants, health care benefits, and unspecified assistantships available. Financial award application deadline: 2/4; financial award applicants required to submit FAFSA. *Faculty research:* Modern and contemporary world theatre; mineralogy, petrology, and geochemistry; cell differentiation and transformation; combinatorial technologies; philosophy of action; continental philosophy; Phoenician epigraphy; nascent complex societies and urbanism; the economies of the Arab world; environmental economics; tectonophysics; host-parasite interactions; innate immunity; insect-plant interactions; history of the Ottoman archives; decentralization; transparency and corruption. Total annual research expenditures: $622,243. *Unit head:* Dr. Patrick McGreevy, Dean, 961-137-4374 Ext. 3800, Fax: 961-174-4461, E-mail: pm07@aub.edu.lb. *Application contact:* Dr. Salim Kanaan, Director, Admissions Office, 961-135-0000 Ext. 2594, Fax: 961-175-0775, E-mail: sk00@aub.edu.lb.

Arizona State University, College of Liberal Arts and Sciences, Department of Physics, Tempe, AZ 85287-1504. Offers nanoscience (PSM); physics (MNS, PhD). Part-time programs available. *Faculty:* 38 full-time (5 women), 1 part-time/adjunct (0 women). *Students:* 109 full-time (24 women), 21 part-time (9 women); includes 9 minority (5 Asian, non-Hispanic/Latino; 2 Hispanic/Latino; 2 Two or more races, non-Hispanic/Latino), 69 international. Average age 28. 166 applicants, 43% accepted, 29 enrolled. In 2010, 12 master's, 8 doctorates awarded. Terminal master's awarded for partial completion of doctoral program. *Degree requirements:* For master's, comprehensive exam, thesis or alternative, interactive Program of Study (iPOS) submitted before completing 50 percent of required credit hours; for doctorate, comprehensive exam, thesis/dissertation, interactive Program of Study (iPOS) submitted before completing 50 percent of required credit hours. *Entrance requirements:* For master's and doctorate, GRE, minimum GPA of 3.0 or equivalent in last 2 years of work leading to bachelor's degree. Additional exam requirements/recommendations for international students: Required—TOEFL, IELTS, or Pearson Test of English. *Application deadline:* For fall admission, 3/1 for domestic and international students; for spring admission, 9/1 for domestic and international students. Applications are processed on a rolling basis. Application fee: $70 ($90 for international students). Electronic applications accepted. *Expenses:* Contact institution. *Financial support:* In 2010–11, 49 research assistantships with tuition reimbursements (averaging $15,550 per year), 54 teaching assistantships with tuition reimbursements (averaging $15,486 per year) were awarded; fellowships with full tuition reimbursements, career-related internships or fieldwork, Federal Work-Study, institutionally sponsored loans, scholarships/grants, and tuition waivers (full and partial) also available. Financial award application deadline: 3/1; financial award applicants required to submit FAFSA. Total annual research expenditures: $5.5 million. *Unit head:* Dr. Robert J. Nemanich, Chair, 480-965-3561, E-mail: robert.nemanich@asu.edu. *Application contact:* Graduate Admissions, 480-965-6113.

Auburn University, Graduate School, College of Sciences and Mathematics, Department of Physics, Auburn University, AL 36849. Offers MS, PhD. Part-time programs available. *Faculty:* 23 full-time (1 woman). *Students:* 21 full-time (3 women), 25 part-time (6 women); includes 1 Asian, non-Hispanic/Latino; 3 Hispanic/Latino, 16 international. Average age 28. 32 applicants, 31% accepted, 9 enrolled. In 2010, 5 master's, 4 doctorates awarded. *Degree requirements:* For doctorate, thesis/dissertation, oral and written exams. *Entrance requirements:* For master's and doctorate, GRE General Test. *Application deadline:* For fall admission, 7/7 for domestic students; for spring admission, 11/24 for domestic students. Applications are processed on a rolling basis. Application fee: $50 ($60 for international students). Electronic applications accepted. *Expenses:* Tuition, state resident: full-time $7002. Tuition, nonresident: full-time $21,898. International tuition: $22,116 full-time. Required fees: $892. Tuition and fees vary according to course load and program. *Financial support:* Research assistantships, teaching assistantships, career-related internships or fieldwork and Federal Work-Study available. Support available to part-time students. Financial award application deadline: 3/15; financial award applicants required to submit FAFSA. *Faculty research:* Atomic/radiative physics, plasma physics, condensed matter physics, space physics, nonlinear dynamics. *Unit head:* Dr. Joe D. Perez, Head, 334-844-4264. *Application contact:* Dr. George Flowers, Dean of the Graduate School, 334-844-2125.

Ball State University, Graduate School, College of Sciences and Humanities, Department of Physics and Astronomy, Program in Physics, Muncie, IN 47306-1099. Offers MA, MAE, MS. *Faculty:* 14. *Students:* 16 full-time (8 women), 10 part-time (1 woman); includes 1 Hispanic/Latino, 5 international. Average age 26. 26 applicants, 73% accepted, 10 enrolled. In 2010, 8 master's awarded. *Entrance requirements:* For master's, GRE General Test. Application fee: $50. *Expenses:* Tuition, state resident: full-time $6160; part-time $299 per credit hour. Tuition, nonresident: full-time $16,020; part-time $783 per credit hour. Required fees: $2278; $95 per credit hour. *Financial support:* In 2010–11, 2 research assistantships with full tuition reimbursements (averaging $12,405 per year), 11 teaching assistantships with full tuition reimbursements (averaging $12,655 per year) were awarded. Financial award application deadline: 3/1. *Faculty research:* Solar energy, particle physics, atomic spectroscopy. *Unit head:* Dr. Thomas Robertson. *Application contact:* Dr. Robert Morris, Associate Provost for Research and Dean of the Graduate School, 765-285-1300, E-mail: rmorris@bsu.edu.

Baylor University, Graduate School, College of Arts and Sciences, Department of Physics, Waco, TX 76798. Offers MA, MS, PhD. *Students:* 32 full-time (7 women); includes 2 minority (both Hispanic/Latino), 17 international. In 2010, 4 master's awarded. *Degree requirements:* For master's, thesis or alternative; for doctorate, one foreign language, thesis/dissertation. *Entrance requirements:* For master's and doctorate, GRE General Test. *Application deadline:* Applications are processed on a rolling basis. Application fee: $25. *Financial support:* Fellowships, teaching assistantships, Federal Work-Study and institutionally sponsored loans available. *Unit head:* Dr. Walter Wilcox, Graduate Program Director, 254-710-2510, Fax: 254-710-5083, E-mail: walter_wilcox@baylor.edu. *Application contact:* Marian Nunn-Graves, Administrative Assistant, 254-710-2511, Fax: 254-710-3870, E-mail: marian_nunn-graves@baylor.edu.

Boston College, Graduate School of Arts and Sciences, Department of Physics, Chestnut Hill, MA 02467-3800. Offers MS, PhD. Terminal master's awarded for partial completion of doctoral program. *Degree requirements:* For master's, thesis (for some programs); for doctorate, thesis/dissertation. *Entrance requirements:* For master's and doctorate, GRE General Test, GRE Subject Test. Additional exam requirements/recommendations for international students: Required—TOEFL (minimum score 600 paper-based; 250 computer-based; 100 iBT). Electronic applications accepted. *Faculty research:* Atmospheric/space physics, astrophysics, atomic and molecular physics, fusion and plasmas, solid-state physics.

Boston University, Graduate School of Arts and Sciences, Department of Physics, Boston, MA 02215. Offers MA, PhD. *Students:* 108 full-time (16 women); includes 7 minority (3 Asian, non-Hispanic/Latino; 4 Hispanic/Latino), 50 international. Average age 26. 318 applicants, 20% accepted, 17 enrolled. In 2010, 4 master's, 13 doctorates awarded. Terminal master's awarded for partial completion of doctoral program. *Degree requirements:* For master's, one foreign language, comprehensive exam, thesis or alternative; for doctorate, one foreign language, comprehensive exam, thesis/dissertation. *Entrance requirements:* For master's and doctorate, GRE General Test, GRE Subject Test. Additional exam requirements/recommendations for international students: Required—TOEFL (minimum score 600 paper-based; 250 computer-based). *Application deadline:* For fall admission, 1/15 for domestic and international students. Application fee: $70. Electronic applications accepted. *Expenses:* Tuition: Full-time $39,314; part-time $1228 per credit. Required fees: $40 per semester. *Financial support:* In 2010–11, 2 fellowships with full tuition reimbursements (averaging $19,300 per year), 71 research assistantships (averaging $18,800 per year), 29 teaching assistantships with full tuition reimbursements (averaging $18,800 per year) were awarded; Federal Work-Study and scholarships/grants also available. Support available to part-time students. Financial award application deadline: 1/15; financial award applicants required to submit FAFSA. *Unit head:* Dr. Claudio Rebbi, Chairman, 617-353-9058, Fax: 617-353-9393, E-mail: rebbi@bu.edu. *Application contact:* Mirtha M. Cabello, Administrative Coordinator, 617-353-2623, Fax: 617-353-9393, E-mail: cabello@bu.edu.

See Close-Up on page 207.

Boston University, School of Education, Boston, MA 02215. Offers counseling (Ed M, CAGS), including community, school, sport psychology; counseling psychology (Ed D); curriculum and teaching (Ed M, Ed D, CAGS), including early childhood (Ed D), educational media and technology (Ed D), English and language arts (Ed D), mathematics (Ed D), physical education and coaching (Ed D), science (Ed D), social studies education (Ed D), special education (Ed D); developmental studies (Ed D), including literacy and language, reading education; developmental studies in literacy and language education (Ed M, CAGS); early childhood education (Ed M, CAGS); education of the deaf (Ed M, CAGS); educational leadership and development (Ed D), including educational administration (Ed M, Ed D, CAGS), higher education administration (Ed M, Ed D, CAGS); educational media and technology (Ed M, CAGS); elementary education (Ed M); English and language arts (Ed M, CAGS); English education (MAT); health education (Ed M, CAGS); Latin and classical studies (MAT); mathematics education (Ed M, MAT, CAGS); mathematics for teaching (MMT); modern foreign language education (MAT), including French, Spanish; physical education and coaching (Ed M, CAGS); policy, planning, and administration (Ed M, CAGS), including community education leadership, educational administration (Ed M, Ed D, CAGS), higher education administration (Ed M, Ed D, CAGS); reading education (Ed M, CAGS); science education (Ed M, MAT, CAGS), including biology (MAT), chemistry (MAT), earth science (MAT), general science (MAT), physics (MAT); social studies education (Ed M, MAT, CAGS), including history (MAT), political science (MAT); special education (Ed M, Ed D, CAGS), including disability studies (Ed M), moderate disabilities (Ed M), severe disabilities (Ed M), special education administration (Ed M); teaching English as a second language (Ed M, CAGS). Part-time programs available. *Faculty:* 57 full-time, 39 part-time/adjunct. *Students:* 245 full-time (191 women), 376 part-time (274 women); includes 83 minority (14 Black or African American, non-Hispanic/Latino; 2 American Indian or Alaska Native, non-Hispanic/Latino; 28 Asian, non-Hispanic/Latino; 31 Hispanic/Latino; 2 Native Hawaiian or other Pacific Islander, non-Hispanic/Latino; 6 Two or more races, non-Hispanic/Latino), 79 international. Average age 30. 1,270 applicants, 66% accepted, 292 enrolled. In 2010, 273 master's, 15 doctorates, 7 other advanced degrees awarded. Terminal master's awarded for partial completion of doctoral program. *Degree requirements:* For master's, thesis (for some programs); for doctorate, comprehensive exam, thesis/dissertation; for CAGS, comprehensive exam. *Entrance requirements:* For master's and CAGS, GRE General Test or Miller Analogies Test (MAT); for doctorate, GRE General Test. Additional exam requirements/recommendations for international students: Required—TOEFL, IELTS. *Application deadline:* For fall admission, 1/15 priority date for domestic and international students; for spring admission, 9/15 priority date for domestic and international students. Applications are processed on a rolling basis. Application fee: $70. Electronic applications accepted. *Expenses:* Tuition: Full-time $39,314; part-time $1228 per credit. Required fees: $40 per semester. *Financial support:* In 2010–11, 276 students received support, including 31 fellowships with full tuition reimbursements available, 16 research assistantships, 26 teaching assistantships with partial tuition reimbursements available; career-related internships or fieldwork, Federal Work-Study, and scholarships/grants also available. Support available to part-time students. Financial award applicants required to submit FAFSA. *Faculty research:* Deaf studies, social emotional learning, civic engagement and education, STEM education, pre-college educational pipelines. Total annual research expenditures: $2.6 million. *Unit head:* Dr. Hardin Coleman, Dean, 617-353-3213. *Application contact:* Dana Fernandez, Director of Enrollment, 617-353-4237, Fax: 617-353-8937, E-mail: sedgrad@bu.edu.

Bowling Green State University, Graduate College, College of Arts and Sciences, Department of Physics and Astronomy, Bowling Green, OH 43403. Offers geophysics (MS); physics (MAT, MS). *Degree requirements:* For master's, thesis or alternative. *Entrance requirements:* For master's, GRE General Test. Additional exam requirements/recommendations for international students: Required—TOEFL. Electronic applications accepted. *Faculty research:* Computational physics, solid-state physics, materials science, theoretical physics.

Brandeis University, Graduate School of Arts and Sciences, Department of Physics, Waltham, MA 02454-9110. Offers MS, PhD. Part-time programs available. *Faculty:* 18 full-time (3 women), 1 part-time/adjunct (0 women). *Students:* 46 full-time (7 women); includes 1 Hispanic/Latino, 20 international. 73 applicants, 29% accepted, 13 enrolled. In 2010, 3 master's, 4 doctorates awarded. Terminal master's awarded for partial completion of doctoral program. *Degree requirements:* For master's, qualifying exam, 1 year residency; for doctorate, thesis/dissertation, advanced exam. *Entrance requirements:* For master's, GRE General Test, GRE Subject Test, resume, letters of recommendation; for doctorate, GRE General Test, GRE Subject Test, resume, 2 letters of recommendation (3rd suggested). Additional exam requirements/recommendations for international students: Required—TOEFL (minimum score 600 paper-based; 250 computer-based; 100 iBT); Recommended—IELTS (minimum score 7). *Application deadline:* For fall admission, 1/15 priority date for domestic students. Application fee: $75. Electronic applications accepted. *Financial support:* In 2010–11, 16 fellowships with full tuition reimbursements (averaging $23,100 per year), 26 research assistantships with full tuition reimbursements (averaging $23,100 per year), 10 teaching assistantships with partial tuition reimbursements (averaging $1,250 per year) were awarded; scholarships/grants, health care benefits, and tuition waivers (full) also available. Financial award application deadline: 1/15; financial award applicants required to submit FAFSA. *Faculty research:* Astrophysics, condensed-

Physics

Brandeis University (continued)
matter and biophysics, high energy and gravitational theory, particle physics, microfluidics, radio astronomy, string theory. *Unit head:* Dr. Howard Schnitzer, Chair, 781-736-2882, Fax: 781-736-2915, E-mail: schnitzer@brandeis.edu. *Application contact:* Catherine Broderick, Department Administrator, 781-736-2802, Fax: 781-736-3412, E-mail: cbroderi@brandeis.edu.

Brigham Young University, Graduate Studies, College of Physical and Mathematical Sciences, Department of Physics and Astronomy, Provo, UT 84602-1001. Offers physics (MS, PhD); physics and astronomy (PhD). Part-time programs available. *Faculty:* 29 full-time (2 women). *Students:* 34 full-time (4 women); includes 2 Asian, non-Hispanic/Latino; 1 Hispanic/Latino. Average age 29. 20 applicants, 50% accepted, 9 enrolled. In 2010, 8 master's, 4 doctorates awarded. Terminal master's awarded for partial completion of doctoral program. *Degree requirements:* For master's, thesis; for doctorate, thesis/dissertation, qualifying exam. *Entrance requirements:* For master's and doctorate, GRE Subject Test (physics) General GRE Required, minimum GPA of 3.0 in last 60 hours, ecclesiastical endorsement. Additional exam requirements/recommendations for international students: Required—TOEFL (minimum score 580 paper-based; 85 iBT), IELTS (minimum score 7). *Application deadline:* For fall admission, 1/15 priority date for domestic and international students. Application fee: $50. Electronic applications accepted. *Expenses:* Tuition: Full-time $5580; part-time $310 per credit hour. Tuition and fees vary according to program and student's religious affiliation. *Financial support:* In 2010–11, 37 students received support, including 27 research assistantships with full tuition reimbursements available (averaging $19,730 per year), 15 teaching assistantships with full tuition reimbursements available (averaging $18,780 per year); fellowships with full tuition reimbursements available, institutionally sponsored loans and tuition waivers (full) also available. Support available to part-time students. Financial award application deadline: 1/15. *Faculty research:* Acoustics; atomic, molecular, and optical physics; theoretical and mathematical physics; condensed matter; astrophysics and plasma. Total annual research expenditures: $2 million. *Unit head:* Dr. Ross L. Spencer, Chair, 801-422-2341, Fax: 801-422-0553, E-mail: ross_spencer@byu.edu. *Application contact:* Dr. J. Ward Moody, Graduate Coordinator, 801-422-4347, Fax: 801-422-0553, E-mail: jmoody@byu.edu.

Brock University, Faculty of Graduate Studies, Faculty of Mathematics and Science, Program in Physics, St. Catharines, ON L2S 3A1, Canada. Offers M Sc. Part-time programs available. *Degree requirements:* For master's, thesis. *Entrance requirements:* For master's, honors B Sc in physics. Additional exam requirements/recommendations for international students: Required—TOEFL (minimum score 550 paper-based; 213 computer-based; 80 iBT), IELTS (minimum score 6.5), TWE (minimum score 4). Electronic applications accepted. *Faculty research:* Quantum physics, optical properties, non-crystalline materials, condensed matter physics, biophysics.

Brooklyn College of the City University of New York, Division of Graduate Studies, Department of Physics, Brooklyn, NY 11210-2889. Offers MA, PhD. Part-time programs available. *Students:* 2 part-time (1 woman); includes 1 minority (Black or African American, non-Hispanic/Latino). Average age 38. 3 applicants, 67% accepted, 2 enrolled.Terminal master's awarded for partial completion of doctoral program. *Degree requirements:* For master's, comprehensive exam, thesis or alternative, 30 credits. *Entrance requirements:* For master's, 2 letters of recommendation, 12 credits in advanced physics; for doctorate, GRE. Additional exam requirements/recommendations for international students: Required—TOEFL (minimum score 500 paper-based; 173 computer-based; 61 iBT). *Application deadline:* For fall admission, 3/1 priority date for domestic students, 2/1 priority date for international students; for spring admission, 11/1 priority date for domestic students, 10/1 priority date for international students. Applications are processed on a rolling basis. Application fee: $125. Electronic applications accepted. *Expenses:* Tuition, state resident: full-time $7360; part-time $310 per credit hour. Tuition, nonresident: full-time $13,800; part-time $575 per credit hour. Required fees: $190 per semester. *Financial support:* Federal Work-Study, institutionally sponsored loans, and scholarships/grants available. Support available to part-time students. Financial award application deadline: 5/1; financial award applicants required to submit FAFSA. *Unit head:* Dr. Ken Miyano, Chairperson, 718-951-5418, Fax: 718-951-4407, E-mail: kemiyano@brooklyn.cuny.edu. *Application contact:* Hernan Sierra, Graduate Admissions Coordinator, 718-951-4536, Fax: 718-951-4506, E-mail: grads@brooklyn.cuny.edu.

Brooklyn College of the City University of New York, Division of Graduate Studies, School of Education, Program in Middle Childhood Education (Science), Brooklyn, NY 11210-2889. Offers biology (MA); chemistry (MA); earth science (MA); general science (MA); physics (MA). Part-time and evening/weekend programs available. *Students:* 3 full-time (1 woman), 74 part-time (46 women); includes 29 minority (12 Black or African American, non-Hispanic/Latino; 8 Asian, non-Hispanic/Latino; 9 Hispanic/Latino), 4 international. Average age 32. 29 applicants, 97% accepted, 21 enrolled. In 2010, 24 master's awarded. *Entrance requirements:* For master's, LAST, interview, previous course work in education and mathematics, resume, 2 letters of recommendation, essay. Additional exam requirements/recommendations for international students: Required—TOEFL (minimum score 500 paper-based; 173 computer-based; 61 iBT). *Application deadline:* For fall admission, 7/15 priority date for domestic students, 6/1 priority date for international students; for spring admission, 11/15 priority date for domestic students, 10/1 priority date for international students. Applications are processed on a rolling basis. Application fee: $125. Electronic applications accepted. *Expenses:* Tuition, state resident: full-time $7360; part-time $310 per credit hour. Tuition, nonresident: full-time $13,800; part-time $575 per credit hour. Required fees: $190 per semester. *Financial support:* Federal Work-Study, institutionally sponsored loans, and scholarships/grants available. Support available to part-time students. Financial award application deadline: 5/1; financial award applicants required to submit FAFSA. *Faculty research:* Geometric thinking, mastery of basic facts, problem-solving strategies, history of mathematics. *Unit head:* Dr. Jennifer Adams, Program Head, 718-951-5214, E-mail: jadams@brooklyn.cuny.edu. *Application contact:* Hernan Sierra, Graduate Admissions Coordinator, 718-951-4536, Fax: 718-951-4506, E-mail: grads@brooklyn.cuny.edu.

Brown University, Graduate School, Department of Physics, Providence, RI 02912. Offers Sc M, PhD. *Degree requirements:* For doctorate, thesis/dissertation, qualifying and oral exams.

Bryn Mawr College, Graduate School of Arts and Sciences, Department of Physics, Bryn Mawr, PA 19010-2899. Offers MA, PhD. *Faculty:* 3. *Students:* 1 full-time (0 women), 2 part-time (1 woman). Average age 26. 3 applicants, 0% accepted, 0 enrolled. In 2010, 1 master's awarded. *Degree requirements:* For master's, one foreign language, thesis; for doctorate, one foreign language, thesis/dissertation. *Entrance requirements:* For master's and doctorate, GRE General Test, GRE Subject Test. Additional exam requirements/recommendations for international students: Required—TOEFL (minimum score 600 paper-based; 250 computer-based). *Application deadline:* For fall admission, 1/3 for domestic and international students. Application fee: $50. *Financial support:* In 2010–11, 1 research assistantship with full tuition reimbursement (averaging $4,750 per year), 2 teaching assistantships with partial tuition reimbursements (averaging $14,000 per year) were awarded; Federal Work-Study, scholarships/grants, tuition waivers (partial), and tuition awards also available. Support available to part-time students. Financial award application deadline: 1/3. *Unit head:* Dr. Liz McCormack, Dean of Graduate Studies, 610-526-5358. *Application contact:* Teri Lobo, Administrative Assistant to the Graduate School of Arts and Sciences Dean, 610-526-5074.

See Display on next page and Close-Up on page 209.

California Institute of Technology, Division of Physics, Mathematics and Astronomy, Department of Physics, Pasadena, CA 91125-0001. Offers PhD. *Degree requirements:* For doctorate, thesis/dissertation, candidacy and final exams. *Entrance requirements:* For doctorate, GRE General Test, GRE Subject Test. Additional exam requirements/recommendations for international students: Required—TOEFL. *Faculty research:* High-energy physics, nuclear physics, condensed-matter physics, theoretical physics and astrophysics, gravity physics.

California State University, Fresno, Division of Graduate Studies, College of Science and Mathematics, Department of Physics, Fresno, CA 93740-8027. Offers MS. Part-time programs available. *Degree requirements:* For master's, thesis or alternative. *Entrance requirements:* For master's, GRE General Test, minimum GPA of 2.5. Additional exam requirements/recommendations for international students: Required—TOEFL. Electronic applications accepted. *Faculty research:* Energy, astronomy, silicon vertex detector, neuroimaging, particle physics.

California State University, Fullerton, Graduate Studies, College of Natural Science and Mathematics, Department of Physics, Fullerton, CA 92834-9480. Offers MA. Part-time programs available. *Students:* 3 full-time (1 woman), 11 part-time (1 woman); includes 1 Asian, non-Hispanic/Latino, 2 international. Average age 26. 19 applicants, 63% accepted, 9 enrolled. In 2010, 6 master's awarded. Application fee: $55. *Financial support:* Research assistantships, teaching assistantships, career-related internships or fieldwork, Federal Work-Study, institutionally sponsored loans, and scholarships/grants available. Support available to part-time students. Financial award application deadline: 3/1; financial award applicants required to submit FAFSA. *Unit head:* Dr. Morty Khakoo, Chair, 657-278-3366. *Application contact:* Admissions/Applications, 657-278-2371.

California State University, Long Beach, Graduate Studies, College of Natural Sciences and Mathematics, Department of Physics and Astronomy, Long Beach, CA 90840. Offers physics (MS). Part-time programs available. *Faculty:* 9 full-time (2 women). *Students:* 10 full-time (2 women), 25 part-time (2 women); includes 6 Asian, non-Hispanic/Latino; 1 Hispanic/Latino, 2 international. Average age 31. 31 applicants, 81% accepted, 15 enrolled. In 2010, 15 master's awarded. *Degree requirements:* For master's, comprehensive exam or thesis. *Application deadline:* For fall admission, 7/1 for domestic students. Applications are processed on a rolling basis. Application fee: $55. Electronic applications accepted. *Financial support:* Federal Work-Study, institutionally sponsored loans, and scholarships/grants available. Financial award application deadline: 3/2. *Faculty research:* Musical acoustics, modern optics, neutrino physics, quantum gravity, atomic physics. *Unit head:* Dr. Patrick Kenealy, Chair, 562-985-8745, Fax: 562-985-7924, E-mail: kenealyp@csulb.edu. *Application contact:* Dr. Chuhee Kwon, Graduate Advisor, 562-985-4855, Fax: 562-985-7924, E-mail: ckwon@csulb.edu.

California State University, Los Angeles, Graduate Studies, College of Natural and Social Sciences, Department of Physics and Astronomy, Los Angeles, CA 90032-8530. Offers physics (MS). Part-time and evening/weekend programs available. *Faculty:* 2 full-time (1 woman), 4 part-time/adjunct (0 women). *Students:* 4 full-time (2 women), 10 part-time (1 woman); includes 10 minority (1 Black or African American, non-Hispanic/Latino; 4 Asian, non-Hispanic/Latino; 5 Hispanic/Latino), 1 international. Average age 30. 13 applicants, 85% accepted, 3 enrolled. In 2010, 4 master's awarded. *Degree requirements:* For master's, comprehensive exam or thesis. *Entrance requirements:* Additional exam requirements/recommendations for international students: Required—TOEFL (minimum score 500 paper-based; 173 computer-based). *Application deadline:* For fall admission, 5/1 for domestic and international students. Applications are processed on a rolling basis. Application fee: $55. Electronic applications accepted. *Financial support:* Federal Work-Study available. Support available to part-time students. Financial award application deadline: 3/1. *Faculty research:* Intermediate energy, nuclear physics, condensed-matter physics, biophysics. *Unit head:* Dr. Edward Rezayi, Chair, 323-343-2100, Fax: 323-343-2497, E-mail: erizayi@calstatela.edu. *Application contact:* Dr. Alan Muchlinski, Dean of Graduate Studies, 323-343-3820, Fax: 323-343-5653, E-mail: amuchli@exchange.calstatela.edu.

California State University, Northridge, Graduate Studies, College of Science and Mathematics, Department of Physics and Astronomy, Northridge, CA 91330. Offers physics (MS). Part-time and evening/weekend programs available. *Degree requirements:* For master's, thesis or comprehensive exam. *Entrance requirements:* For master's, GRE General Test or minimum GPA of 3.0. Additional exam requirements/recommendations for international students: Required—TOEFL.

Carleton University, Faculty of Graduate Studies, Faculty of Science, Department of Physics, Ottawa, ON K1S 5B6, Canada. Offers M Sc, PhD. Programs offered jointly with University of Ottawa. *Degree requirements:* For master's, thesis optional, seminar; for doctorate, comprehensive exam, thesis/dissertation, seminar. *Entrance requirements:* For master's, honors degree in science; for doctorate, M Sc. Additional exam requirements/recommendations for international students: Required—TOEFL. *Faculty research:* Experimental and theoretical elementary particle physics, medical physics.

Carnegie Mellon University, Mellon College of Science, Department of Physics, Pittsburgh, PA 15213-3891. Offers applied physics (PhD); physics (MS, PhD). *Degree requirements:* For doctorate, thesis/dissertation, qualifying exam. *Entrance requirements:* For doctorate, GRE General Test, GRE Subject Test. Additional exam requirements/recommendations for international students: Required—TOEFL. Electronic applications accepted. *Faculty research:* Astrophysics, condensed matter physics, biological physics, medium energy and nuclear physics, high-energy physics.

Case Western Reserve University, School of Graduate Studies, Department of Physics, Cleveland, OH 44106. Offers MS, PhD. Part-time programs available. *Faculty:* 19 full-time (3 women), 4 part-time/adjunct (0 women). *Students:* 49 full-time (8 women); includes 1 Hispanic/Latino, 23 international. Average age 26. 191 applicants, 24% accepted, 13 enrolled. In 2010, 4 master's, 8 doctorates awarded. Terminal master's awarded for partial completion of doctoral program. *Degree requirements:* For master's, exam; for doctorate, thesis/dissertation, qualifying exam, topical exam. *Entrance requirements:* For master's and doctorate, GRE General Test, GRE Subject Test (physics). Additional exam requirements/recommendations for international students: Required—TOEFL (minimum score 550 paper-based; 213 computer-based; 79 iBT). *Application deadline:* For fall admission, 1/15 priority date for domestic students. Applications are processed on a rolling basis. Application fee: $8. Electronic applications accepted. *Financial support:* Fellowships, research assistantships, teaching assistantships available. Financial award application deadline: 2/15. *Faculty research:* Condensed-matter physics, imaging physics, nonlinear optics, high-energy physics, cosmology and astrophysics. *Unit head:* Daniel Akerib, Chairman, 216-368-4000, E-mail: daniel.akerib@case.edu. *Application contact:* Patricia Bacevice, Admissions, 216-368-4000, Fax: 216-368-4671, E-mail: pab6@case.edu.

The Catholic University of America, School of Arts and Sciences, Department of Physics, Washington, DC 20064. Offers MS, PhD. Part-time programs available. *Faculty:* 12 full-time (2 women). *Students:* 13 full-time (4 women), 18 part-time (8 women); includes 1 Asian, non-Hispanic/Latino; 1 Hispanic/Latino, 8 international. Average age 29. 33 applicants, 52% accepted, 12 enrolled. In 2010, 4 master's, 2 doctorates awarded. *Degree requirements:* For master's, comprehensive exam, thesis or alternative; for doctorate, comprehensive exam, thesis/dissertation, oral exam. *Entrance requirements:* For master's and doctorate, GRE General Test, statement of purpose, official copies of academic transcripts, three letters of recommendation. Additional exam requirements/recommendations for international students: Required—TOEFL (minimum score 580 paper-based; 237 computer-based). *Application deadline:* For fall admission, 8/1 priority date for domestic students, 7/15 for international students; for spring admission, 12/1 priority date for domestic students, 10/15 for international students. Applications are processed on a rolling basis. Application fee: $55. Electronic applications accepted. *Expenses:* Tuition: Full-time $33,580; part-time $1315 per credit hour. Required fees: $80; $40 per semester hour. One-time fee: $425. *Financial support:* Fellowships, research assistantships, teaching assistantships, Federal Work-Study, scholarships/grants, tuition waivers (full and partial), and unspecified assistantships available. Financial award application deadline: 2/1;

184 www.facebook.com/petersonspublishing

Peterson's Graduate Programs in the Physical Sciences, Mathematics, Agricultural Sciences, the Environment & Natural Resources 2012

Physics

BRYN MAWR
COLLEGE

Graduate Program in Physics

Why Bryn Mawr Physics?

Small, student-oriented classes

Exciting cutting-edge research

Opportunities for collaborative and interdisciplinary work

A liberal-arts-college setting near the City of Philadelphia

Diverse and progressive teaching experiences

Discover for yourself what Bryn Mawr has to offer!

plan your visit at:

www.brynmawr.edu/physics/graduate

financial award applicants required to submit FAFSA. *Faculty research:* Glass and ceramics technologies, astrophysics and computational sciences, the role of evolution in galaxy properties, nuclear physics, biophysics. Total annual research expenditures: $11.6 million. *Unit head:* Dr. Daniel I. Sober, Chair, 202-319-5856, Fax: 202-319-4448, E-mail: sober@cua.edu. *Application contact:* Andrew Woodall, Director of Graduate Admissions, 202-319-5057, Fax: 202-319-6533, E-mail: cua-admissions@cua.edu.

Central Connecticut State University, School of Graduate Studies, School of Arts and Sciences, Department of Physics and Earth Science, New Britain, CT 06050-4010. Offers natural sciences (MS); science education (Certificate). Part-time and evening/weekend programs available. *Faculty:* 12 full-time (4 women), 17 part-time/adjunct (4 women). *Students:* 11 part-time (7 women); includes 1 minority (Asian, non-Hispanic/Latino). Average age 38. 3 applicants, 100% accepted, 2 enrolled. In 2010, 9 master's, 1 other advanced degree awarded. *Degree requirements:* For master's, comprehensive exam, thesis or alternative; for Certificate, qualifying exam. *Entrance requirements:* For master's, minimum undergraduate GPA of 2.7. Additional exam requirements/recommendations for international students: Required—TOEFL. *Application deadline:* For fall admission, 7/1 for domestic students; for spring admission, 12/1 for domestic students. Applications are processed on a rolling basis. Application fee: $50. Electronic applications accepted. *Expenses:* Tuition, area resident: Full-time $5012; part-time $470 per credit. Tuition, state resident: full-time $7518; part-time $482 per credit. Tuition, nonresident: full-time $13,962; part-time $482 per credit. Required fees: $3772. One-time fee: $62 part-time. *Financial support:* In 2010–11, 1 student received support. Career-related internships or fieldwork, Federal Work-Study, scholarships/grants, and unspecified assistantships available. Support available to part-time students. Financial award application deadline: 2/15; financial award applicants required to submit FAFSA. *Faculty research:* Elementary/secondary science education, particle and solid states, weather patterns, planetary studies. *Unit head:* Dr. Ali Antar, Chair, 860-832-2930. *Application contact:* Dr. Ali Antar, Chair, 860-832-2930.

Central Michigan University, College of Graduate Studies, College of Science and Technology, Department of Physics, Mount Pleasant, MI 48859. Offers physics (MS); science of advanced materials (PhD). PhD is an interdisciplinary program. Part-time programs available. *Faculty:* 5 full-time (0 women), 1 part-time/adjunct (0 women). *Students:* 4 full-time (1 woman), 12 part-time (2 women), 9 international. Average age 28. *Degree requirements:* For master's, thesis or alternative; for doctorate, comprehensive exam, thesis/dissertation. *Entrance requirements:* For doctorate, GRE, bachelor's degree in physics, chemistry, biochemistry, biology, geology, engineering, mathematics, or other relevant area. *Application deadline:* For fall admission, 6/1 for international students; for spring admission, 10/1 for international students. Applications are processed on a rolling basis. Application fee: $35 ($45 for international students). Electronic applications accepted. *Expenses:* Tuition, state resident: full-time $8208; part-time $456 per credit hour. Tuition, nonresident: full-time $13,788; part-time $766 per credit hour. One-time fee: $25. *Financial support:* In 2010–11, 5 teaching assistantships with tuition reimbursements were awarded; fellowships with tuition reimbursements, research assistantships with tuition reimbursements, career-related internships or fieldwork, Federal Work-Study, unspecified assistantships, and out-of-state merit awards, non-resident graduate awards also available. *Faculty research:* Science of advanced materials, polymer physics, laser spectroscopy, observational astronomy, nuclear physics. *Unit head:* Dr. Koblar Alan Jackson, Chairperson, 989-774-3321, Fax: 989-774-2697, E-mail: jacks1ka@cmich.edu. *Application contact:* Jessica Lapp, Coordinator, Science of Advanced Materials Program, 989-774-2221, Fax: 989-774-2657, E-mail: lapp1jw@cmich.edu.

Christopher Newport University, Graduate Studies, Department of Physics, Computer Science, and Engineering, Newport News, VA 23606-2998. Offers applied physics and computer science (MS). Part-time and evening/weekend programs available. *Faculty:* 6 full-time (0 women), 2 part-time/adjunct (0 women). *Students:* 4 full-time (0 women), 15 part-time (2 women); includes 3 minority (2 Black or African American, non-Hispanic/Latino; 1 Two or more races, non-Hispanic/Latino). Average age 29. 10 applicants, 100% accepted, 2 enrolled. In 2010, 8 master's awarded. *Degree requirements:* For master's, comprehensive exam (for some programs), thesis optional. *Entrance requirements:* For master's, GRE General Test, minimum GPA of 3.0. Additional exam requirements/recommendations for international students: Required—TOEFL (minimum score 580 paper-based; 237 computer-based; 92 iBT). *Application deadline:* For fall admission, 8/15 priority date for domestic students, 4/1 for international students; for spring admission, 10/15 for domestic students, 10/1 for international students. Applications are processed on a rolling basis. Application fee: $50. Electronic applications accepted. *Expenses:* Tuition, state resident: part-time $418 per credit hour. Tuition, nonresident: part-time $769 per credit hour. *Financial support:* In 2010–11, 3 research assistantships with full and partial tuition reimbursements (averaging $2,000 per year) were awarded; fellowships with full tuition reimbursements, career-related internships or fieldwork, Federal Work-Study, and unspecified assistantships also available. Support available to part-time students. Financial award application deadline: 3/1; financial award applicants required to submit FAFSA. *Faculty research:* Advanced programming methodologies, experimental nuclear physics, computer architecture, semiconductor nanophysics, laser and optical fiber sensors. *Unit head:* Dr. Antonio Siochi, Coordinator, 757-594-7569, Fax: 757-594-7919, E-mail: siochi@cnu.edu. *Application contact:* Lyn Sawyer, Associate Director, Graduate Admissions and Records, 757-594-7544, Fax: 757-594-7649, E-mail: gradstdy@cnu.edu.

City College of the City University of New York, Graduate School, College of Liberal Arts and Science, Division of Science, Department of Physics, New York, NY 10031-9198. Offers MA, PhD. PhD program offered jointly with Graduate School and University Center of the City University of New York. Terminal master's awarded for partial completion of doctoral program. *Degree requirements:* For master's, comprehensive exam; for doctorate, thesis/dissertation. *Entrance requirements:* For doctorate, GRE. Additional exam requirements/recommendations for international students: Required—TOEFL (minimum score 500 paper-based; 61 iBT). Electronic applications accepted.

Clark Atlanta University, School of Arts and Sciences, Department of Physics, Atlanta, GA 30314. Offers MS. Part-time programs available. *Faculty:* 4 full-time (0 women), 1 part-time/adjunct (0 women). *Students:* 3 full-time (1 woman), 1 part-time (0 women); includes 2 Black or African American, non-Hispanic/Latino, 2 international. Average age 31. 3 applicants, 100% accepted, 2 enrolled. *Degree requirements:* For master's, one foreign language, comprehensive exam, thesis optional. *Entrance requirements:* For master's, GRE General Test, minimum GPA of 2.5. Additional exam requirements/recommendations for international students: Required—TOEFL (minimum score 500 paper-based; 173 computer-based; 61 iBT). *Application deadline:* For fall admission, 4/1 for domestic and international students; for spring admission, 11/1 for domestic and international students. Applications are processed on a rolling basis. Application fee: $40 ($55 for international students). *Expenses:* Tuition: Full-time $12,942; part-time $719 per credit hour. Required fees: $710; $355 per semester. *Financial support:* Scholarships/grants and unspecified assistantships available. Financial award application deadline: 4/30; financial award applicants required to submit FAFSA. *Faculty research:* Fusion energy, investigations of nonlinear differential equations, difference schemes, collisions in dense plasma. *Unit head:* Dr. Swaraj Tayal, Chairperson, 404-880-6877, E-mail: stayal@cau.edu. *Application contact:* Michelle Clark-Davis, Graduate Program Admissions, 404-880-6605, E-mail: cauadmissions@cau.edu.

Clarkson University, Graduate School, School of Arts and Sciences, Department of Physics, Potsdam, NY 13699. Offers MS, PhD. Part-time programs available. *Faculty:* 11 full-time (1 woman), 1 part-time/adjunct (0 women). *Students:* 13 full-time (1 woman), 7 international. Average age 26. 26 applicants, 65% accepted, 4 enrolled. In 2010, 2 master's, 2 doctorates awarded. Terminal master's awarded for partial completion of doctoral program. *Degree*

Peterson's Graduate Programs in the Physical Sciences, Mathematics, Agricultural Sciences, the Environment & Natural Resources 2012

www.facebook.com/petersonspublishing **185**

Physics

Clarkson University (continued)

requirements: For doctorate, thesis/dissertation, departmental qualifying exam. *Entrance requirements:* For master's and doctorate, GRE, transcripts of all college coursework, three letters of recommendation; resume and personal statement (recommended). Additional exam requirements/recommendations for international students: Required—TOEFL, TSE recommended. *Application deadline:* For fall admission, 1/30 priority date for domestic and international students; for spring admission, 9/1 priority date for domestic and international students. Applications are processed on a rolling basis. Application fee: $25 ($35 for international students). Electronic applications accepted. *Expenses:* Tuition: Part-time $1136 per credit hour. *Financial support:* In 2010–11, 13 students received support, including 2 fellowships with full tuition reimbursements available (averaging $21,580 per year), 1 research assistantship with full tuition reimbursement available (averaging $21,580 per year), 11 teaching assistantships with full tuition reimbursements available (averaging $21,580 per year); scholarships/grants, tuition waivers (partial), and unspecified assistantships also available. *Faculty research:* Diffusion and kinetics, biochemical computing, microthermometers, nanosize particles. Total annual research expenditures: $549,007. *Unit head:* Dr. Dipankar Roy, Division Head, 315-268-2396, Fax: 315-268-7754, E-mail: samoy@clarkson.edu. *Application contact:* Jennifer Reed, Graduate School Coordinator, School of Arts and Sciences, 315-268-3802, Fax: 315-268-3989, E-mail: sciencegrad@clarkson.edu.

Clark University, Graduate School, Department of Physics, Worcester, MA 01610-1477. Offers MA, PhD. Part-time programs available. *Faculty:* 5 full-time (0 women). *Students:* 9 full-time (3 women), 6 international. Average age 28. 16 applicants, 31% accepted, 2 enrolled. In 2010, 3 master's, 1 doctorate awarded. Terminal master's awarded for partial completion of doctoral program. *Degree requirements:* For master's, thesis or alternative; for doctorate, one foreign language, thesis/dissertation. *Entrance requirements:* Additional exam requirements/recommendations for international students: Required—TOEFL. *Application deadline:* For fall admission, 2/1 for domestic students. Application fee: $50. *Expenses:* Tuition: Full-time $37,000; part-time $1156 per credit hour. Required fees: $30; $1156 per credit hour. *Financial support:* In 2010–11, 3 research assistantships with full tuition reimbursements (averaging $18,280 per year), 5 teaching assistantships with full tuition reimbursements (averaging $18,280 per year) were awarded; fellowships with full and partial tuition reimbursements, Federal Work-Study and tuition waivers (full and partial) also available. Financial award application deadline: 4/1. *Faculty research:* Statistical and thermal physics, magnetic properties of materials, computer simulation, particle diffusion. Total annual research expenditures: $740,000. *Unit head:* Dr. Clark Agosta, Chair, 508-793-7169. *Application contact:* Sujata Davis, Department Secretary, 508-793-7169, Fax: 508-793-8861, E-mail: sdavis1@clarku.edu.

Clemson University, Graduate School, College of Engineering and Science, Department of Physics and Astronomy, Clemson, SC 29634. Offers physics (MS, PhD), including astronomy and astrophysics, atmospheric physics, biophysics. Part-time programs available. *Faculty:* 25 full-time (4 women), 2 part-time/adjunct (0 women). *Students:* 63 full-time (19 women); includes 3 Black or African American, non-Hispanic/Latino, 26 international. Average age 27. 66 applicants, 92% accepted, 21 enrolled. In 2010, 2 master's, 6 doctorates awarded. Terminal master's awarded for partial completion of doctoral program. *Degree requirements:* For master's, thesis or alternative; for doctorate, thesis/dissertation. *Entrance requirements:* For master's and doctorate, GRE General Test. Additional exam requirements/recommendations for international students: Required—TOEFL. *Application deadline:* For fall admission, 1/15 priority date for domestic students; for spring admission, 9/15 priority date for domestic students. Applications are processed on a rolling basis. Application fee: $70 ($80 for international students). Electronic applications accepted. *Expenses:* Tuition, state resident: full-time $6492; part-time $400 per credit hour. Tuition, nonresident: full-time $13,634; part-time $800 per credit hour. Required fees: $262 per semester. Part-time tuition and fees vary according to course load and program. *Financial support:* In 2010–11, 58 students received support, including 1 fellowship with full and partial tuition reimbursement available (averaging $16,000 per year), 26 research assistantships with partial tuition reimbursements available (averaging $13,559 per year), 43 teaching assistantships with partial tuition reimbursements available (averaging $14,097 per year); career-related internships or fieldwork, institutionally sponsored loans, scholarships/grants, health care benefits, and unspecified assistantships also available. Support available to part-time students. Financial award application deadline: 6/1; financial award applicants required to submit FAFSA. *Faculty research:* Radiation physics, solid-state physics, nuclear physics, radar and lidar studies of atmosphere. Total annual research expenditures: $2.4 million. *Unit head:* Dr. Peter Barnes, Chair, 864-656-3419, Fax: 864-656-0805, E-mail: peterb@clemson.edu. *Application contact:* Dr. Murray Daw, Graduate Coordinator, 864-656-6702, Fax: 864-656-0805, E-mail: physgradinfo-l@clemson.edu.

Cleveland State University, College of Graduate Studies, College of Sciences and Health Professions, Department of Physics, Cleveland, OH 44115. Offers applied optics (MS); condensed matter physics (MS); medical physics (MS); optics and materials (MS); optics and medical imaging (MS). Part-time and evening/weekend programs available. *Faculty:* 10 full-time (1 woman), 4 part-time/adjunct (1 woman). *Students:* 3 full-time (0 women), 10 part-time (4 women); includes 1 Asian, non-Hispanic/Latino; 1 Two or more races, non-Hispanic/Latino, 1 international. Average age 29. 28 applicants, 39% accepted, 5 enrolled. In 2010, 3 master's awarded. *Entrance requirements:* For master's, undergraduate degree in engineering, physics, chemistry or mathematics. Additional exam requirements/recommendations for international students: Required—TOEFL (minimum score 525 paper-based; 197 computer-based). *Application deadline:* For fall admission, 7/15 priority date for domestic and international students. Applications are processed on a rolling basis. Application fee: $30. Electronic applications accepted. *Expenses:* Tuition, state resident: full-time $8447; part-time $469 per credit hour. Tuition, nonresident: full-time $16,020; part-time $890 per credit hour. Required fees: $50. *Financial support:* In 2010–11, 1 research assistantship with full and partial tuition reimbursement (averaging $5,666 per year) was awarded; fellowships with tuition reimbursements, teaching assistantships, tuition waivers (full) also available. *Faculty research:* Statistical physics, experimental solid-state physics, theoretical optics, experimental biological physics (macromolecular crystallography), experimental optics. Total annual research expenditures: $350,000. *Unit head:* Dr. Miron Kaufman, Chairperson, 216-687-2436, Fax: 216-523-7268, E-mail: m.kaufman@csuohio.edu. *Application contact:* Dr. James A. Lock, Director, 216-687-2420, Fax: 216-523-7268, E-mail: j.lock@csuohio.edu.

The College of William and Mary, Faculty of Arts and Sciences, Department of Physics, Williamsburg, VA 23187-8795. Offers MS, PhD. *Faculty:* 26 full-time (4 women), 13 part-time/adjunct (3 women). *Students:* 59 full-time (18 women), 1 part-time (0 women); includes 2 minority (1 Hispanic/Latino; 1 Two or more races, non-Hispanic/Latino), 23 international. Average age 26. 133 applicants, 22% accepted, 8 enrolled. In 2010, 16 master's, 10 doctorates awarded. Terminal master's awarded for partial completion of doctoral program. *Degree requirements:* For master's, minimum GPA of 3.0, 32 credit hours; for doctorate, comprehensive exam, thesis/dissertation, 1 year residency, 2 semesters of physics teaching. *Entrance requirements:* For doctorate, GRE General Test, GRE Subject Test, minimum GPA of 2.5. Additional exam requirements/recommendations for international students: Required—TOEFL. *Application deadline:* For fall admission, 2/1 priority date for domestic and international students. Applications are processed on a rolling basis. Application fee: $45. Electronic applications accepted. *Expenses:* Tuition, state resident: full-time $6400; part-time $345 per credit hour. Tuition, nonresident: full-time $19,720; part-time $920 per credit hour. Required fees: $4368. *Financial support:* Research assistantships with full tuition reimbursements, teaching assistantships with full tuition reimbursements, career-related internships or fieldwork, health care benefits, tuition waivers (full), and unspecified assistantships available. *Faculty research:* Nuclear/particle, condensed-matter, atomic, and plasma physics; accelerator physics; molecular/optical physics; computational/nonlinear physics. Total annual research expenditures: $4 million. *Unit head:* Dr. Keith Griffioen, Chair, 757-221-3500, Fax: 757-221-3540, E-mail: chair@physics.wm.edu. *Application contact:* Dr. Marc Sher, Chair of Admissions, 757-221-3538, Fax: 757-221-3540, E-mail: grad@physics.wm.edu.

Colorado School of Mines, Graduate School, Department of Physics, Golden, CO 80401. Offers applied physics (MS, PhD). Part-time programs available. *Faculty:* 32 full-time (5 women), 7 part-time/adjunct (0 women). *Students:* 57 full-time (12 women), 2 part-time (0 women); includes 1 Hispanic/Latino, 10 international. Average age 30. 85 applicants, 29% accepted, 19 enrolled. In 2010, 3 master's, 6 doctorates awarded. *Degree requirements:* For master's, thesis (for some programs); for doctorate, comprehensive exam, thesis/dissertation. *Entrance requirements:* For master's and doctorate, GRE General Test, GRE Subject Test. Additional exam requirements/recommendations for international students: Required—TOEFL (minimum score 550 paper-based; 213 computer-based; 80 iBT). *Application deadline:* For fall admission, 1/15 priority date for domestic and international students; for spring admission, 10/15 priority date for domestic and international students. Application fee: $50 ($70 for international students). Electronic applications accepted. *Expenses:* Tuition, state resident: full-time $11,550; part-time $641 per credit. Tuition, nonresident: full-time $25,980; part-time $1444 per credit. Required fees: $1874; $937 per semester. *Financial support:* In 2010–11, 53 students received support, including 1 fellowship with full tuition reimbursement available (averaging $20,000 per year), 34 research assistantships with full tuition reimbursements available (averaging $20,000 per year), 18 teaching assistantships with full tuition reimbursements available (averaging $20,000 per year); scholarships/grants, health care benefits, and unspecified assistantships also available. Financial award application deadline: 1/15; financial award applicants required to submit FAFSA. *Faculty research:* Light scattering, low-energy nuclear physics, high fusion plasma diagnostics, laser operations, mathematical physics. Total annual research expenditures: $2 million. *Unit head:* Dr. Thomas Furtak, Department Head, 303-273-3843, Fax: 303-273-3919, E-mail: tfurtak@mines.edu. *Application contact:* Dr. Tim Ohno, Professor, 303-273-3847, Fax: 303-273-3919, E-mail: tohno@mines.edu.

Colorado State University, Graduate School, College of Natural Sciences, Department of Physics, Fort Collins, CO 80523-1875. Offers MS, PhD. Postbaccalaureate distance learning degree programs offered (no on-campus study). *Faculty:* 19 full-time (2 women), 1 part-time/adjunct (0 women). *Students:* 26 full-time (3 women), 31 part-time (7 women); includes 6 minority (1 Black or African American, non-Hispanic/Latino; 1 American Indian or Alaska Native, non-Hispanic/Latino; 2 Asian, non-Hispanic/Latino; 2 Two or more races, non-Hispanic/Latino), 12 international. Average age 26. 34 applicants, 68% accepted, 10 enrolled. In 2010, 20 master's, 4 doctorates awarded. Terminal master's awarded for partial completion of doctoral program. *Degree requirements:* For master's, comprehensive exam (for some programs), thesis (for some programs); for doctorate, comprehensive exam, thesis/dissertation. *Entrance requirements:* For master's, GRE General Test or GRE Subject Test (physics), minimum GPA of 3.0; 3 letters of recommendation; for doctorate, GRE General Test or GRE Subject Test (physics), minimum GPA of 3.0; transcripts; 3 letters of recommendation; BA (for domestic students); statement of purpose. Additional exam requirements/recommendations for international students: Required—TOEFL (minimum score 550 paper-based; 213 computer-based; 80 iBT). *Application deadline:* For fall admission, 2/15 priority date for domestic and international students; for spring admission, 7/15 priority date for domestic and international students. Applications are processed on a rolling basis. Application fee: $50. Electronic applications accepted. *Expenses:* Tuition, state resident: full-time $7434; part-time $413 per credit. Tuition, nonresident: full-time $19,022; part-time $1057 per credit. Required fees: $1729; $88 per credit. *Financial support:* In 2010–11, 56 students received support, including 7 fellowships (averaging $27,601 per year), 25 research assistantships with full tuition reimbursements available (averaging $14,635 per year), 24 teaching assistantships with full tuition reimbursements available (averaging $13,908 per year); health care benefits also available. Financial award application deadline: 1/15; financial award applicants required to submit FAFSA. *Faculty research:* Experimental condensed-matter physics, laser spectroscopy, optics, theoretical condensed-matter physics, particle physics. Total annual research expenditures: $2.5 million. *Unit head:* Dr. John Harton, Chair, 970-491-6246, Fax: 970-491-7947, E-mail: john.harton@colostate.edu. *Application contact:* Wendy Gleason, Secretary, Graduate Admissions Committee, 970-491-6207, Fax: 970-491-7947, E-mail: wendy.gleason@colostate.edu.

Columbia University, Graduate School of Arts and Sciences, Division of Natural Sciences, Department of Physics, New York, NY 10027. Offers philosophical foundations of physics (MA); physics (M Phil, PhD). *Degree requirements:* For doctorate, thesis/dissertation. *Entrance requirements:* For master's and doctorate, GRE General Test, GRE Subject Test, 3 years of course work in physics. Additional exam requirements/recommendations for international students: Required—TOEFL. *Faculty research:* Theoretical physics; astrophysics; low-, medium-, and high-energy physics.

Concordia University, School of Graduate Studies, Faculty of Arts and Science, Department of Physics, Montréal, QC H3G 1M8, Canada. Offers M Sc, PhD.

Cornell University, Graduate School, Graduate Fields of Arts and Sciences, Field of Physics, Ithaca, NY 14853-0001. Offers experimental physics (MS, PhD); physics (MS, PhD); theoretical physics (MS, PhD). *Faculty:* 54 full-time (5 women). *Students:* 154 full-time (25 women); includes 1 Black or African American, non-Hispanic/Latino; 4 Asian, non-Hispanic/Latino; 3 Hispanic/Latino, 75 international. Average age 25. 409 applicants, 21% accepted, 31 enrolled. In 2010, 38 master's, 25 doctorates awarded. *Degree requirements:* For doctorate, comprehensive exam, thesis/dissertation. *Entrance requirements:* For doctorate, GRE General Test, GRE Subject Test (physics), 3 letters of recommendation. Additional exam requirements/recommendations for international students: Required—TOEFL (minimum score 620 paper-based; 260 computer-based; 105 iBT). *Application deadline:* For fall admission, 1/3 for domestic students. Application fee: $80. Electronic applications accepted. *Expenses:* Tuition: Full-time $29,500. Required fees: $76. Tuition and fees vary according to degree level and program. *Financial support:* In 2010–11, 24 fellowships with full tuition reimbursements, 67 research assistantships with full tuition reimbursements, 52 teaching assistantships with full tuition reimbursements were awarded; institutionally sponsored loans, scholarships/grants, health care benefits, tuition waivers (full and partial), and unspecified assistantships also available. Financial award applicants required to submit FAFSA. *Faculty research:* Experimental condensed matter physics, theoretical condensed matter physics, experimental high energy particle physics, theoretical particle physics and field theory, theoretical astrophysics. *Unit head:* Director of Graduate Studies, 607-255-7561. *Application contact:* Graduate Field Assistant, 607-255-7561, E-mail: physics-grad-adm@cornell.edu.

Creighton University, Graduate School, College of Arts and Sciences, Program in Physics, Omaha, NE 68178-0001. Offers MS. Part-time programs available. *Faculty:* 11 full-time (2 women). *Students:* 13 full-time (3 women), 1 part-time (0 women); includes 1 minority (Hispanic/Latino), 4 international. Average age 26. 17 applicants, 35% accepted, 6 enrolled. In 2010, 6 master's awarded. *Degree requirements:* For master's, comprehensive exam, thesis (for some programs). *Entrance requirements:* For master's, GRE General Test, 3 letters of recommendation. Additional exam requirements/recommendations for international students: Required—TOEFL (minimum score 550 paper-based; 213 computer-based; 80 iBT). *Application deadline:* For fall admission, 3/1 for domestic and international students. Applications are processed on a rolling basis. Application fee: $50. Electronic applications accepted. *Expenses:* Tuition: Full-time $12,168; part-time $676 per credit hour. Required fees: $131 per semester. Tuition and fees vary according to program. *Financial support:* In 2010–11, 8 students received support, including 8 teaching assistantships with full tuition reimbursements available (averaging $11,073 per year). Financial award applicants required to submit FAFSA. *Unit head:* Dr. Sam Cipolla, Chair, 402-280-2133, E-mail: samcip@creighton.edu. *Application contact:* Taunya Plater, Senior Program Coordinator, 402-280-2870, Fax: 402-280-2899, E-mail: taunyaplater@creighton.edu.

186 www.facebook.com/petersonspublishing

Peterson's Graduate Programs in the Physical Sciences, Mathematics, Agricultural Sciences, the Environment & Natural Resources 2012

Dalhousie University, Faculty of Science, Department of Physics and Atmospheric Science, Halifax, NS B3H 3J5, Canada. Offers M Sc, PhD. *Degree requirements:* For master's, thesis; for doctorate, thesis/dissertation. *Entrance requirements:* Additional exam requirements/recommendations for international students: Required—TOEFL, IELTS, CANTEST, CAEL, or Michigan English Language Assessment Battery. Electronic applications accepted. *Faculty research:* Applied, experimental, and solid-state physics.

Dartmouth College, Arts and Sciences Graduate Programs, Department of Physics and Astronomy, Hanover, NH 03755. Offers MS, PhD. Terminal master's awarded for partial completion of doctoral program. *Degree requirements:* For master's, thesis; for doctorate, thesis/dissertation. *Entrance requirements:* For master's and doctorate, GRE General Test, GRE Subject Test. Additional exam requirements/recommendations for international students: Required—TOEFL. *Faculty research:* Matter physics, plasma and beam physics, space physics, astronomy, cosmology.

Delaware State University, Graduate Programs, Department of Physics, Dover, DE 19901-2277. Offers applied optics (MS); optics (PhD); physics (MS); physics teaching (MS). Part-time and evening/weekend programs available. *Entrance requirements:* For master's, minimum GPA of 3.0 in major, 2.75 overall. Additional exam requirements/recommendations for international students: Required—TOEFL. Electronic applications accepted. *Faculty research:* Thermal properties of solids, nuclear physics, radiation damage in solids.

DePaul University, College of Liberal Arts and Sciences, Department of Physics, Chicago, IL 60604-2287. Offers applied physics (MS). Part-time and evening/weekend programs available. *Faculty:* 6 full-time (2 women), 3 part-time/adjunct (0 women). *Students:* 8 full-time (2 women), 6 part-time (4 women); includes 1 Black or African American, non-Hispanic/Latino; 1 Hispanic/Latino, 3 international. Average age 23. 12 applicants, 42% accepted, 3 enrolled. In 2010, 3 master's awarded. *Degree requirements:* For master's, thesis, oral exams. *Entrance requirements:* For master's, 2 letters of recommendation, BA in physics or closely related field. Additional exam requirements/recommendations for international students: Required—TOEFL. *Application deadline:* For fall admission, 5/1 priority date for domestic students, 4/1 priority date for international students. Applications are processed on a rolling basis. Application fee: $25. Electronic applications accepted. *Financial support:* In 2010–11, teaching assistantships with full tuition reimbursements (averaging $9,000 per year); tuition waivers (full) also available. *Faculty research:* Optics, solid-state physics, cosmology, atomic physics, nuclear physics. Total annual research expenditures: $54,000. *Unit head:* Dr. Christopher G. Goedde, Chairman, 773-325-7330, Fax: 773-325-7334, E-mail: egoedde@condor.depaul.edu. *Application contact:* Dr. Jesus Pando, Associate Professor, 773-325-7330, Fax: 773-325-7334.

Drew University, Caspersen School of Graduate Studies, Program in Education, Madison, NJ 07940-1493. Offers biology (MAT); chemistry (MAT); English (MAT); French (MAT); Italian (MAT); math (MAT); physics (MAT); social studies (MAT); Spanish (MAT); theatre arts (MAT). Part-time programs available. *Entrance requirements:* For master's, transcripts, personal statement, recommendations. Additional exam requirements/recommendations for international students: Required—TOEFL, TWE. *Expenses:* Contact institution.

Drexel University, College of Arts and Sciences, Department of Physics, Philadelphia, PA 19104-2875. Offers MS, PhD. Terminal master's awarded for partial completion of doctoral program. *Degree requirements:* For doctorate, thesis/dissertation. *Entrance requirements:* For master's and doctorate, GRE. Additional exam requirements/recommendations for international students: Required—TOEFL. Electronic applications accepted. *Faculty research:* Nuclear structure, mesoscale meteorology, numerical astrophysics, numerical weather prediction, earth energy radiation budget.

Duke University, Graduate School, Department of Medical Physics, Durham, NC 27708-0586. Offers MS, PhD. *Faculty:* 54 full-time. *Students:* 58 full-time (22 women); includes 2 Black or African American, non-Hispanic/Latino; 5 Asian, non-Hispanic/Latino; 1 Hispanic/Latino, 18 international. 165 applicants, 37% accepted, 33 enrolled. In 2010, 13 master's awarded. *Entrance requirements:* For master's and doctorate, GRE General. Additional exam requirements/recommendations for international students: Required—TOEFL (minimum score 550 paper-based; 213 computer-based; 83 iBT), IELTS (minimum score 7). *Application deadline:* For fall admission, 12/8 priority date for domestic and international students. Application fee: $75. Electronic applications accepted. *Financial support:* Fellowships, research assistantships, teaching assistantships available. Financial award application deadline: 12/15. *Unit head:* Ehsan Samei, Director, 919-684-1400, Fax: 919-684-1490, E-mail: olga.baranova@duke.edu. *Application contact:* Elizabeth Hutton, Director of Admissions, 919-684-3913, Fax: 919-684-2277, E-mail: grad-admissions@duke.edu.

Duke University, Graduate School, Department of Physics, Durham, NC 27708. Offers PhD. *Faculty:* 36 full-time. *Students:* 75 full-time (16 women); includes 1 American Indian or Alaska Native, non-Hispanic/Latino; 3 Asian, non-Hispanic/Latino, 51 international. 194 applicants, 28% accepted, 16 enrolled. In 2010, 11 doctorates awarded. *Degree requirements:* For doctorate, thesis/dissertation. *Entrance requirements:* For doctorate, GRE General Test, GRE Subject Test. Additional exam requirements/recommendations for international students: Required—TOEFL (minimum score 550 paper-based; 213 computer-based; 83 iBT), IELTS (minimum score 7). *Application deadline:* For fall admission, 12/8 priority date for domestic and international students. Application fee: $75. *Financial support:* Fellowships, research assistantships, teaching assistantships, Federal Work-Study available. Financial award application deadline: 12/8. *Unit head:* Dr. Richard G. Palmer, Director of Graduate Studies, 919-660-2502, Fax: 919-606-2525, E-mail: donna@phy.duke.edu. *Application contact:* Elizabeth Hutton, Director of Admissions, 919-684-3913, Fax: 919-684-2277, E-mail: grad-admissions@duke.edu.

East Carolina University, Graduate School, Thomas Harriot College of Arts and Sciences, Department of Physics, Greenville, NC 27858-4353. Offers applied and biomedical physics (MS); medical physics (MS); physics (PhD). Part-time programs available. *Degree requirements:* For master's, one foreign language, comprehensive exam. *Entrance requirements:* For master's, GRE General Test. Additional exam requirements/recommendations for international students: Required—TOEFL. *Expenses:* Tuition, state resident: full-time $3130; part-time $391.25 per credit hour. Tuition, nonresident: full-time $13,817; part-time $1727.13 per credit hour. Required fees: $1916; $239.50 per credit hour. Tuition and fees vary according to campus/location and program.

Eastern Michigan University, Graduate School, College of Arts and Sciences, Department of Physics and Astronomy, Ypsilanti, MI 48197. Offers general science (MS); physics (MS); physics education (MS). Part-time and evening/weekend programs available. Postbaccalaureate distance learning degree programs offered (minimal on-campus study). *Faculty:* 11 full-time (4 women). *Students:* 7 full-time (1 woman), 11 part-time (4 women); includes 2 minority (both Black or African American, non-Hispanic/Latino), 1 international. Average age 30. 17 applicants, 47% accepted, 6 enrolled. In 2010, 5 master's awarded. *Entrance requirements:* Additional exam requirements/recommendations for international students: Required—TOEFL. *Application deadline:* Applications are processed on a rolling basis. Application fee: $35. *Financial support:* Fellowships, research assistantships with full tuition reimbursements, teaching assistantships with full tuition reimbursements, career-related internships or fieldwork, Federal Work-Study, institutionally sponsored loans, scholarships/grants, tuition waivers, and unspecified assistantships available. Support available to part-time students. Financial award applicants required to submit FAFSA. *Unit head:* James Carroll, Department Head, 734-487-4144, Fax: 734-487-0989, E-mail: jcarroll@emich.edu. *Application contact:* James Carroll, Department Head, 734-487-4144, Fax: 734-487-0989, E-mail: jcarroll@emich.edu.

Emory University, Laney Graduate School, Department of Physics, Atlanta, GA 30322-1100. Offers biophysics (PhD); condensed matter physics (PhD); non-linear physics (PhD); radiological physics (PhD); soft condensed matter physics (PhD); solid-state physics (PhD); statistical physics (PhD); MS/PhD. *Degree requirements:* For doctorate, thesis/dissertation, qualifier proposal (PhD). *Entrance requirements:* For doctorate, GRE General Test, minimum GPA of 3.0. Additional exam requirements/recommendations for international students: Required—TOEFL (minimum score 600 paper-based). Electronic applications accepted. *Expenses:* Tuition: Full-time $33,800. Required fees: $1300. *Faculty research:* Experimental studies of the structure and function of metalloproteins, soft condensed matter, granular materials, biophotonics and fluorescence correlation spectroscopy, single molecule studies of DNA-protein systems.

Fisk University, Division of Graduate Studies, Department of Physics, Nashville, TN 37208-3051. Offers MA. *Degree requirements:* For master's, thesis. *Entrance requirements:* For master's, GRE General Test, GRE Subject Test, minimum GPA of 3.0. Electronic applications accepted. *Faculty research:* Molecular physics, astrophysics, surface physics, nanobase materials, optical processing.

Florida Agricultural and Mechanical University, Division of Graduate Studies, Research, and Continuing Education, College of Arts and Sciences, Department of Physics, Tallahassee, FL 32307-3200. Offers MS, PhD. *Degree requirements:* For master's, comprehensive exam, thesis optional; for doctorate, comprehensive exam, thesis/dissertation. *Entrance requirements:* For master's, GRE General Test, minimum GPA of 3.0; for doctorate, GRE General Test, minimum GPA of 3.0, letters of recommendation (2). Additional exam requirements/recommendations for international students: Required—TOEFL (minimum score 550 paper-based). *Faculty research:* Plasma physics, quantum mechanics, condensed matter physics, astrophysics, laser ablation.

Florida Atlantic University, Charles E. Schmidt College of Science, Department of Physics, Boca Raton, FL 33431-0991. Offers MS, PhD. Part-time programs available. *Faculty:* 18 full-time (3 women), 3 part-time/adjunct (0 women). *Students:* 34 full-time (6 women); includes 3 minority (1 Black or African American, non-Hispanic/Latino; 2 Hispanic/Latino), 20 international. Average age 32. 19 applicants, 53% accepted, 7 enrolled. In 2010, 1 master's, 3 doctorates awarded. *Degree requirements:* For master's, thesis; for doctorate, thesis/dissertation. *Entrance requirements:* For master's, GRE General Test, minimum GPA of 3.0; for doctorate, GRE General Test. Additional exam requirements/recommendations for international students: Required—TOEFL (minimum score 500 paper-based; 173 computer-based). *Application deadline:* For fall admission, 7/1 for domestic students, 2/15 for international students; for spring admission, 11/1 for domestic students, 7/15 for international students. Applications are processed on a rolling basis. Application fee: $30. *Expenses:* Tuition, area resident: Part-time $319.96 per credit. Tuition, state resident: part-time $319.96 per credit. Tuition, nonresident: part-time $926.42 per credit. *Financial support:* Fellowships, research assistantships with tuition reimbursements, teaching assistantships with tuition reimbursements, Federal Work-Study and unspecified assistantships available. *Faculty research:* Astrophysics, spectroscopy, mathematical physics, theory of metals, superconductivity. *Unit head:* Dr. Warner A. Miller, Chair, 561-297-3382, Fax: 561-297-2662, E-mail: wam@physics.fau.edu. *Application contact:* Dr. Warner A. Miller, Chair, 561-297-3382, Fax: 561-297-2662, E-mail: wam@physics.fau.edu.

Florida Institute of Technology, Graduate Programs, College of Science, Department of Physics and Space Sciences, Melbourne, FL 32901-6975. Offers interdisciplinary science (MS); physics (MS, PhD); space sciences (MS, PhD). Part-time programs available. *Faculty:* 12 full-time (1 woman). *Students:* 33 full-time (12 women), 10 part-time (2 women); includes 4 minority (2 Asian, non-Hispanic/Latino; 2 Hispanic/Latino), 12 international. Average age 29. 75 applicants, 44% accepted, 7 enrolled. In 2010, 7 master's, 4 doctorates awarded. Terminal master's awarded for partial completion of doctoral program. *Degree requirements:* For master's, comprehensive exam, thesis optional, oral exam, 6 credits math method; for doctorate, one foreign language, comprehensive exam, thesis/dissertation, publication in referred journal, seminar on dissertation research, dissertation published in a major journal. *Entrance requirements:* For master's, minimum GPA of 3.0, resume, 3 letters of recommendation, vector analysis, statement of objectives; for doctorate, GRE General and Subject Tests (recommended), minimum GPA of 3.2, resume, 3 letters of recommendation, statement of objectives. Additional exam requirements/recommendations for international students: Required—TOEFL (minimum score 550 paper-based; 213 computer-based; 79 iBT). *Application deadline:* For fall admission, 4/1 for international students; for spring admission, 9/30 for international students. Applications are processed on a rolling basis. Application fee: $50. Electronic applications accepted. *Expenses:* Tuition: Part-time $1040 per credit hour. Tuition and fees vary according to campus/location. *Financial support:* In 2010–11, 13 research assistantships with full and partial tuition reimbursements (averaging $13,018 per year), 16 teaching assistantships with full and partial tuition reimbursements (averaging $12,769 per year) were awarded; career-related internships or fieldwork, institutionally sponsored loans, tuition waivers (partial), unspecified assistantships, and tuition remissions also available. Support available to part-time students. Financial award application deadline: 3/1; financial award applicants required to submit FAFSA. *Faculty research:* Lasers, semiconductors, magnetism, quantum devices, high energy physics. Total annual research expenditures: $2.9 million. *Unit head:* Dr. Terry D. Oswalt, Department Head, 321-674-7325, Fax: 321-674-7482, E-mail: toswalt@fit.edu. *Application contact:* Cheryl A. Brown, Associate Director of Graduate Admissions, 321-674-7581, Fax: 321-723-9468, E-mail: cbrown@fit.edu.

Florida International University, College of Arts and Sciences, Department of Physics, Miami, FL 33199. Offers MS, PhD. Part-time and evening/weekend programs available. *Faculty:* 7 full-time (3 women), 4 part-time/adjunct (1 woman). *Students:* 33 full-time (7 women), 6 part-time (1 woman); includes 2 Asian, non-Hispanic/Latino; 13 Hispanic/Latino, 15 international. Average age 25. 43 applicants, 21% accepted, 9 enrolled. In 2010, 3 master's, 1 doctorate awarded. *Degree requirements:* For master's, one foreign language, thesis; for doctorate, one foreign language, comprehensive exam, thesis/dissertation. *Entrance requirements:* For master's and doctorate, GRE General Test, 2 letters of recommendation. Additional exam requirements/recommendations for international students: Required—TOEFL (minimum score 550 paper-based; 80 iBT). *Application deadline:* For fall admission, 6/1 for domestic students, 4/1 for international students; for spring admission, 10/1 for domestic students, 9/1 for international students. Applications are processed on a rolling basis. Application fee: $30. Electronic applications accepted. *Financial support:* Institutionally sponsored loans and scholarships/grants available. Financial award application deadline: 3/1; financial award applicants required to submit FAFSA. *Faculty research:* Molecular collision processes (molecular beams), biophysical optics. *Unit head:* Dr. Walter Van Hamme, Chair, Physics Department, 305-348-2605, Fax: 305-348-3053, E-mail: walter.vanhamme@fiu.edu. *Application contact:* Dr. Brain Raue, Graduate Program Director, 305-348-3958, Fax: 305-348-3053, E-mail: brian.raue@fiu.edu.

Florida State University, The Graduate School, College of Arts and Sciences, Department of Physics, Tallahassee, FL 32306. Offers MS, PhD. *Faculty:* 45 full-time (2 women), 4 part-time/adjunct (1 woman). *Students:* 130 full-time (19 women); includes 2 Black or African American, non-Hispanic/Latino; 1 American Indian or Alaska Native, non-Hispanic/Latino; 50 Asian, non-Hispanic/Latino; 4 Hispanic/Latino. Average age 28. 221 applicants, 33% accepted, 29 enrolled. In 2010, 3 master's, 13 doctorates awarded. *Degree requirements:* For doctorate, comprehensive exam, thesis/dissertation. *Entrance requirements:* For master's and doctorate, GRE General Test, minimum GPA of 3.0. Additional exam requirements/recommendations for international students: Required—TOEFL (minimum score 550 paper-based; 213 computer-based; 80 iBT). *Application deadline:* For fall admission, 4/15 for domestic and international students. Application fee: $30. Electronic applications accepted. *Expenses:* Tuition, state resident: full-time $8238.24. *Financial support:* In 2010–11, 112 students received support, including 86 research assistantships with full tuition reimbursements available (averaging $18,000 per year), 44 teaching assistantships with full tuition reimbursements available (averaging $18,000 per year); fellowships, career-related internships or fieldwork and Federal

Physics

Florida State University
Physics Department

FSU Physics department has large research programs in theoretical, experimental, and computational—condensed matter, nuclear, and high-energy—physics. There are also opportunities for biophysics and astrophysics related research.

The presence of the National High Magnetic Field Laboratory at FSU adds to the many research tools available to us, both on campus and at the many other national and international facilities where we have research partnerships.

For more information, contact:
Graduate Coordinator
Physics Department
Tallahassee, FL 32303
madams@physics.fsu.edu
http://www.physics.fsu.edu/

Florida State University (continued)
Work-Study also available. Financial award application deadline: 2/15; financial award applicants required to submit FAFSA. *Faculty research:* High energy physics, computational physics, biophysics, condensed matter physics, nuclear physics, astrophysics. Total annual research expenditures: $3.5 million. *Unit head:* Dr. Mark A. Riley, Chairman, 850-644-2867, Fax: 850-644-8630, E-mail: chair@physics.fsu.edu. *Application contact:* Melissa W. Adams, Academic Support Assistant, 850-644-3245, Fax: 850-644-8630, E-mail: graduate@phy.fsu.edu.

See Close-Up on page 215.

George Mason University, College of Science, Department of Physics and Astronomy, Fairfax, VA 22030. Offers applied and engineering physics (MS); physics (PhD). *Faculty:* 30 full-time (9 women), 6 part-time/adjunct (1 woman). *Students:* 11 full-time (0 women), 48 part-time (16 women); includes 12 minority (1 Black or African American, non-Hispanic/Latino; 7 Asian, non-Hispanic/Latino; 4 Hispanic/Latino), 9 international. Average age 33. 41 applicants, 68% accepted, 15 enrolled. In 2010, 5 master's, 3 doctorates awarded. *Degree requirements:* For master's, thesis optional. *Entrance requirements:* For master's, minimum GPA of 2.75 in last 60 hours of course work. Additional exam requirements/recommendations for international students: Required—TOEFL (minimum score 570 paper-based; 230 computer-based; 88 iBT). *Application deadline:* For fall admission, 5/1 for domestic students; for spring admission, 11/1 for domestic students. Application fee: $100. Electronic applications accepted. *Expenses:* Tuition, state resident: full-time $8192; part-time $440 per credit hour. Tuition, nonresident: full-time $22,952; part-time $1055 per credit hour. Required fees: $2364; $99 per credit hour. *Financial support:* In 2010–11, 25 students received support, including 3 fellowships with full tuition reimbursements available (averaging $18,000 per year), 12 research assistantships with full and partial tuition reimbursements available (averaging $15,945 per year), 11 teaching assistantships with full and partial tuition reimbursements available (averaging $11,298 per year); career-related internships or fieldwork, Federal Work-Study, scholarships/grants, unspecified assistantships, and health care benefits (full-time research or teaching assistantship recipients) also available. Support available to part-time students. Financial award application deadline: 3/1; financial award applicants required to submit FAFSA. *Faculty research:* Astronomy, astrophysics, and space and planetary science; astronomy and physics education; atomic physics; biophysics and neuroscience. Total annual research expenditures: $2.4 million. *Unit head:* Dr. Michael Summers, Chairman, 703-993-3971, Fax: 703-993-1269, E-mail: msummers@gmu.edu. *Application contact:* Dr. Paul So, Information Contact, 703-993-4377, E-mail: paso@gmu.edu.

The George Washington University, Columbian College of Arts and Sciences, Department of Physics, Washington, DC 20052. Offers MA, PhD. Part-time and evening/weekend programs available. *Faculty:* 20 full-time (3 women), 10 part-time/adjunct (3 women). *Students:* 16 full-time (2 women), 17 part-time (6 women); includes 1 Black or African American, non-Hispanic/Latino; 2 Asian, non-Hispanic/Latino; 1 Native Hawaiian or other Pacific Islander, non-Hispanic/Latino, 19 international. Average age 29. 37 applicants, 95% accepted, 6 enrolled. In 2010, 8 master's, 4 doctorates awarded. *Degree requirements:* For doctorate, thesis/dissertation, general exam. *Entrance requirements:* For master's and doctorate, GRE General Test, minimum GPA of 3.0. Additional exam requirements/recommendations for international students: Required—TOEFL (minimum score 550 paper-based; 213 computer-based; 80 iBT). *Application deadline:* For fall admission, 1/15 priority date for domestic and international students; for spring admission, 10/1 priority date for domestic students, 9/1 priority date for international students. Applications are processed on a rolling basis. Application fee: $75. Electronic applica-

tions accepted. *Financial support:* In 2010–11, 24 students received support; fellowships with full tuition reimbursements available, research assistantships, teaching assistantships with tuition reimbursements available, Federal Work-Study and tuition waivers available. Financial award application deadline: 1/15. *Unit head:* Dr. Cornelius Bennhold, Chair, 202-994-6274. *Application contact:* Dr. Mark Reeves, Director, 202-994-6279, Fax: 202-994-3001, E-mail: reevesme@gwu.edu.

Georgia Institute of Technology, Graduate Studies and Research, College of Sciences, School of Physics, Atlanta, GA 30332-0001. Offers MS, PhD. Part-time programs available. Terminal master's awarded for partial completion of doctoral program. *Degree requirements:* For doctorate, comprehensive exam, thesis/dissertation. *Entrance requirements:* For master's, GRE General Test, GRE Subject Test, minimum GPA of 3.0; for doctorate, GRE General Test, GRE Subject Test, minimum GPA of 3.4. Additional exam requirements/recommendations for international students: Required—TOEFL. Electronic applications accepted. *Faculty research:* Atomic and molecular physics, chemical physics, condensed matter, optics, nonlinear physics and chaos.

Georgia State University, College of Arts and Sciences, Department of Physics and Astronomy, Program in Physics, Atlanta, GA 30302-3083. Offers MS, PhD. Part-time and evening/weekend programs available. Terminal master's awarded for partial completion of doctoral program. *Degree requirements:* For master's, one foreign language, thesis or alternative, exam; for doctorate, 2 foreign languages, thesis/dissertation, exam. *Entrance requirements:* For master's, GRE General Test; for doctorate, GRE General Test, GRE Subject Test. Additional exam requirements/recommendations for international students: Required—TOEFL. Electronic applications accepted. *Faculty research:* Biophysics; nuclear, condensed-matter, and atomic physics; astrophysics.

Graduate School and University Center of the City University of New York, Graduate Studies, Program in Physics, New York, NY 10016-4039. Offers PhD. *Degree requirements:* For doctorate, thesis/dissertation. *Entrance requirements:* For doctorate, GRE General Test. Additional exam requirements/recommendations for international students: Required—TOEFL. Electronic applications accepted. *Faculty research:* Condensed-matter, particle, nuclear, and atomic physics.

Hampton University, Graduate College, Department of Physics, Hampton, VA 23668. Offers atmospheric physics (MS, PhD); medical physics (MS, PhD); nuclear physics (MS, PhD); optical physics (MS, PhD). Part-time and evening/weekend programs available. Terminal master's awarded for partial completion of doctoral program. *Degree requirements:* For master's, thesis optional; for doctorate, thesis/dissertation, oral defense, qualifying exam. *Entrance requirements:* For master's, GRE General Test; for doctorate, GRE General Test, minimum GPA of 3.0 or master's degree in physics or related field. *Faculty research:* Laser optics, remote sensing.

Harvard University, Graduate School of Arts and Sciences, Department of Physics, Cambridge, MA 02138. Offers experimental physics (PhD); medical engineering/medical physics (PhD), including applied physics, engineering sciences, physics; theoretical physics (PhD). *Degree requirements:* For doctorate, thesis/dissertation, final exams, laboratory experience. *Entrance requirements:* For doctorate, GRE General Test, GRE Subject Test. Additional exam requirements/recommendations for international students: Required—TOEFL. *Expenses:* Tuition: Full-time $34,976. Required fees: $1166. Full-time tuition and fees vary according to program. *Faculty research:* Particle physics, condensed matter physics, atomic physics.

---

188 www.facebook.com/petersonspublishing

Peterson's Graduate Programs in the Physical Sciences, Mathematics, Agricultural Sciences, the Environment & Natural Resources 2012

Hofstra University, School of Education, Health, and Human Services, Programs in Teaching—Secondary Education, Hempstead, NY 11549. Offers business education (MS Ed); English education (MA, MS Ed); foreign language and TESOL (MS Ed); foreign language education (MA, MS Ed), including French, German, Russian, Spanish; mathematics education (MA, MS Ed); science education (MA, MS Ed), including biology, chemistry, earth science, geology, physics; secondary education (Advanced Certificate); social studies education (MA, MS Ed). Part-time and evening/weekend programs available. Postbaccalaureate distance learning degree programs offered (minimal on-campus study). *Students:* 114 full-time (74 women), 61 part-time (36 women); includes 7 Black or African American, non-Hispanic/Latino; 1 American Indian or Alaska Native, non-Hispanic/Latino; 8 Asian, non-Hispanic/Latino; 10 Hispanic/Latino; 1 Native Hawaiian or other Pacific Islander, non-Hispanic/Latino. Average age 27. 153 applicants, 90% accepted, 59 enrolled. In 2010, 102 master's, 11 other advanced degrees awarded. *Degree requirements:* For master's, one foreign language, comprehensive exam (for some programs), thesis (for some programs), exit project, electronic portfolio, student teaching, fieldwork, curriculum project; for Advanced Certificate, 3 foreign languages, comprehensive exam (for some programs), thesis project. *Entrance requirements:* For master's, 2 letters of recommendation, teacher certification (MA), essay; for Advanced Certificate, 2 letters of recommendation, essay, interview and/or portfolio. Additional exam requirements/recommendations for international students: Required—TOEFL (minimum score 550 paper-based; 213 computer-based; 80 iBT). *Application deadline:* Applications are processed on a rolling basis. Application fee: $70 ($75 for international students). Electronic applications accepted. *Expenses:* Tuition: Full-time $18,000; part-time $1000 per credit hour. Required fees: $970; $145 per term. Tuition and fees vary according to program. *Financial support:* In 2010–11, 108 students received support, including 14 fellowships with full and partial tuition reimbursements available (averaging $3,943 per year), 1 research assistantship with full and partial tuition reimbursement available (averaging $6,574 per year); career-related internships or fieldwork, Federal Work-Study, institutionally sponsored loans, scholarships/grants, tuition waivers (full and partial), unspecified assistantships, and scholarships also available. Support available to part-time students. Financial award applicants required to submit FAFSA. *Faculty research:* Appropriate content and pedagogy in secondary school disciplines, adolescent development, secondary school organization, alternative secondary school programs. *Unit head:* Dr. Esther Fusco, Chairperson, 516-463-7704, Fax: 516-463-6196, E-mail: catezf@hofstra.edu. *Application contact:* Carol Drummer, Dean of Graduate Admissions, 516-463-4876, Fax: 516-463-4664, E-mail: gradstudent@hofstra.edu.

Howard University, Graduate School, Department of Physics and Astronomy, Washington, DC 20059-0002. Offers physics (MS, PhD). *Degree requirements:* For master's, comprehensive exam (for some programs), thesis (for some programs); for doctorate, comprehensive exam, thesis/dissertation, departmental qualifying exam. *Entrance requirements:* For master's, GRE General Test, bachelor's degree in physics or related field, minimum GPA of 3.0; for doctorate, GRE General Test, bachelor's or master's degree in physics or related field, minimum GPA of 3.0. Additional exam requirements/recommendations for international students: Required—TOEFL (minimum score 550 paper-based; 213 computer-based). Electronic applications accepted. *Faculty research:* Atmospheric physics, spectroscopy and optical physics, high energy physics, condensed matter.

Hunter College of the City University of New York, Graduate School, School of Arts and Sciences, Department of Physics, New York, NY 10021-5085. Offers MA, PhD. PhD offered jointly with Graduate School and University Center of the City University of New York. Part-time programs available. *Faculty:* 3 full-time (2 women). *Students:* 4 full-time (0 women), 12 part-time (2 women); includes 4 Black or African American, non-Hispanic/Latino; 2 Asian, non-Hispanic/Latino; 2 Hispanic/Latino. Average age 26. 13 applicants, 69% accepted, 4 enrolled. In 2010, 5 master's awarded. Terminal master's awarded for partial completion of doctoral program. *Degree requirements:* For master's, comprehensive exam or thesis. *Entrance requirements:* For master's, minimum 36 credits of course work in mathematics and physics. Additional exam requirements/recommendations for international students: Required—TOEFL. *Application deadline:* For fall admission, 4/1 for domestic students, 2/1 for international students; for spring admission, 11/1 for domestic students, 9/1 for international students. Application fee: $125. *Financial support:* In 2010–11, research assistantships (averaging $20,000 per year), teaching assistantships (averaging $9,000 per year) were awarded; Federal Work-Study, scholarships/grants, and tuition waivers (partial) also available. Support available to part-time students. *Faculty research:* Experimental and theoretical quantum optics, experimental and theoretical condensed matter, mathematical physics. *Unit head:* Ying-Chin Chen, Chairperson, 212-772-5248, Fax: 212-772-5390, E-mail: y.c.chen@hunter.cuny.edu. *Application contact:* William Zlata, Director for Graduate Admissions, 212-772-4482, Fax: 212-650-3336, E-mail: admissions@hunter.cuny.edu.

Idaho State University, Office of Graduate Studies, College of Arts and Sciences, Department of Physics, Pocatello, ID 83209-8106. Offers applied physics (PhD); health physics (MS); physics (MNS). Part-time programs available. *Degree requirements:* For master's, comprehensive exam, thesis (for some programs), oral exam (for some programs); for doctorate, comprehensive exam, thesis/dissertation (for some programs), oral exam, written qualifying exam in physics or health physics after 1st year. *Entrance requirements:* For master's, GRE General Test, 3 letters of recommendation, BS or BA in physics, teaching certificate (MNS); for doctorate, GRE General Test (minimum 50th percentile), 3 letters of recommendation, statement of career goals. Additional exam requirements/recommendations for international students: Required—TOEFL (minimum score 550 paper-based; 213 computer-based; 80 iBT). Electronic applications accepted. *Faculty research:* Ion beam applications, low-energy nuclear physics, relativity and cosmology, observational astronomy.

Illinois Institute of Technology, Graduate College, College of Science and Letters, Department of Biological, Chemical and Physical Sciences, Physics Division, Chicago, IL 60616. Offers health physics (MHP); physics (MS, PhD). Part-time and evening/weekend programs available. Postbaccalaureate distance learning degree programs offered (minimal on-campus study). *Faculty:* 22 full-time (2 women), 4 part-time/adjunct (1 woman). *Students:* 34 full-time (9 women), 42 part-time (10 women); includes 12 minority (4 Black or African American, non-Hispanic/Latino; 6 Asian, non-Hispanic/Latino; 2 Two or more races, non-Hispanic/Latino), 23 international. Average age 32. 111 applicants, 71% accepted, 42 enrolled. In 2010, 14 master's, 3 doctorates awarded. Terminal master's awarded for partial completion of doctoral program. *Degree requirements:* For master's, comprehensive exam (for some programs), thesis (for some programs); for doctorate, comprehensive exam, thesis/dissertation. *Entrance requirements:* For master's, GRE General Test (minimum score 1000 Quantitative and Verbal, 2.5 Analytical Writing), minimum undergraduate GPA of 3.0; for doctorate, GRE General Test (minimum score 1100 Quantitative and Verbal, 3.0 Analytical Writing), minimum undergraduate GPA of 3.0. Additional exam requirements/recommendations for international students: Required—TOEFL (minimum score 523 paper-based; 213 computer-based; 70 iBT); Recommended—IELTS (minimum score 5.5). *Application deadline:* For fall admission, 5/1 for domestic and international students; for spring admission, 10/15 for domestic and international students. Applications are processed on a rolling basis. Application fee: $40. Electronic applications accepted. *Expenses:* Tuition: Full-time $18,576; part-time $1032 per credit hour. Required fees: $583 per semester. One-time fee: $150. Tuition and fees vary according to program and student level. *Financial support:* In 2010–11, 5 fellowships with full and partial tuition reimbursements (averaging $17,347 per year), 9 research assistantships with full and partial tuition reimbursements (averaging $9,704 per year), 9 teaching assistantships with full and partial tuition reimbursements (averaging $7,750 per year) were awarded; Federal Work-Study, institutionally sponsored loans, scholarships/grants, health care benefits, and unspecified assistantships also available. Support available to part-time students. Financial award applicants required to submit FAFSA. *Faculty research:* Experimental, condensed-matter physics; experimental elementary particle physics; membrane biophysics; synchroton radiation techniques; experimental high energy physics, especially symmetry violation and rare decays of hyperons and charm and beauty hadrons. Total annual research expenditures: $2.6 million. *Unit head:* Dr. Grant Bunker, Associate Chair and Professor, 312-567-3385, Fax: 312-567-3576, E-mail: bunker@iit.edu. *Application contact:* Deborah Gibson, Director, Graduate Admission, 866-472-3448, Fax: 312-567-3138, E-mail: inquiry.grad@iit.edu.

Indiana University Bloomington, University Graduate School, College of Arts and Sciences, Department of Physics, Bloomington, IN 47405-7000. Offers MAT, MS, PhD. Part-time programs available. Postbaccalaureate distance learning degree programs offered (no on-campus study). *Faculty:* 36 full-time (5 women), 11 part-time/adjunct (0 women). *Students:* 102 full-time (20 women), 2 part-time (0 women); includes 8 minority (1 Black or African American, non-Hispanic/Latino; 3 Asian, non-Hispanic/Latino; 4 Hispanic/Latino), 55 international. Average age 27. 195 applicants, 48% accepted, 30 enrolled. In 2010, 10 master's, 11 doctorates awarded. Terminal master's awarded for partial completion of doctoral program. *Degree requirements:* For master's, comprehensive exam (for some programs), thesis (for some programs), qualifying exam; for doctorate, comprehensive exam, thesis/dissertation, qualifying exam. *Entrance requirements:* For master's and doctorate, GRE General Test, GRE Subject Test (physics), minimum GPA of 3.0. Additional exam requirements/recommendations for international students: Required—TOEFL (minimum score 550 paper-based; 213 computer-based; 80 iBT). *Application deadline:* For fall admission, 1/15 priority date for domestic students, 12/1 priority date for international students; for spring admission, 10/1 priority date for domestic students, 9/1 priority date for international students. Applications are processed on a rolling basis. Application fee: $55 ($65 for international students). Electronic applications accepted. *Financial support:* In 2010–11, 1 fellowship with full and partial tuition reimbursement (averaging $18,000 per year), 48 research assistantships with partial tuition reimbursements (averaging $18,800 per year), 30 teaching assistantships with partial tuition reimbursements (averaging $15,530 per year) were awarded; health care benefits also available. *Unit head:* Dr. Rick Van Kooten, Chair, 812-855-1247, Fax: 812-855-5533, E-mail: gradphys@indiana.edu. *Application contact:* Tracey McGookey, Student Services Assistant, 812-856-7059, E-mail: tmcgooke@indiana.edu.

Indiana University of Pennsylvania, School of Graduate Studies and Research, College of Natural Sciences and Mathematics, Department of Physics, Program in Physics, Indiana, PA 15705-1087. Offers MA, MS. Part-time programs available. *Faculty:* 6 full-time (0 women). *Students:* 10 full-time (1 woman), 1 part-time (0 women), 2 international. Average age 25. 7 applicants, 86% accepted, 5 enrolled. In 2010, 4 master's awarded. *Degree requirements:* For master's, comprehensive exam (for some programs), thesis (for some programs). *Application deadline:* For fall admission, 7/1 priority date for domestic students; for spring admission, 11/1 for domestic students. Applications are processed on a rolling basis. Application fee: $40. *Financial support:* In 2010–11, 8 research assistantships with full and partial tuition reimbursements (averaging $4,417 per year) were awarded; Federal Work-Study also available. Support available to part-time students. Financial award application deadline: 3/15; financial award applicants required to submit FAFSA. *Unit head:* Dr. Greg Kenning, Graduate Coordinator, 724-357-2318, E-mail: greg.kenning@iup.edu. *Application contact:* Dr. Muhammad Numan, Graduate Coordinator, 724-357-2318, E-mail: mznuman@iup.edu.

Indiana University–Purdue University Indianapolis, School of Science, Department of Physics, Indianapolis, IN 46202-2896. Offers MS, PhD. PhD offered jointly with Purdue University. Part-time programs available. *Faculty:* 4 full-time (0 women). *Students:* 15 full-time (1 woman), 6 part-time (1 woman); includes 3 minority (2 Black or African American, non-Hispanic/Latino; 1 Hispanic/Latino), 7 international. Average age 31. 18 applicants, 11% accepted, 2 enrolled. In 2010, 4 master's awarded. Terminal master's awarded for partial completion of doctoral program. *Degree requirements:* For master's, thesis optional; for doctorate, thesis/dissertation. *Entrance requirements:* Additional exam requirements/recommendations for international students: Required—TOEFL. *Application deadline:* For fall admission, 3/1 priority date for domestic students. Applications are processed on a rolling basis. Application fee: $55 ($65 for international students). *Financial support:* In 2010–11, 6 fellowships with full tuition reimbursements (averaging $14,204 per year), 6 teaching assistantships with full tuition reimbursements (averaging $6,245 per year) were awarded; research assistantships with full tuition reimbursements, Federal Work-Study, institutionally sponsored loans, and tuition waivers (full and partial) also available. Support available to part-time students. Financial award application deadline: 3/1. *Faculty research:* Magnetic resonance, photosynthesis, optical physics, biophysics, physics of materials. *Unit head:* Guantam Vemuri, Chair, 317-274-6900, E-mail: gvemuri@iupui.edu. *Application contact:* Guantam Vemuri, Chair, 317-274-6900, E-mail: gvemuri@iupui.edu.

Iowa State University of Science and Technology, Graduate College, College of Liberal Arts and Sciences, Department of Physics and Astronomy, Ames, IA 50011. Offers applied physics (MS, PhD); astrophysics (MS, PhD); condensed matter physics (MS, PhD); high energy physics (MS, PhD); nuclear physics (MS, PhD); physics (MS, PhD). Part-time programs available. *Faculty:* 48 full-time (4 women), 4 part-time/adjunct (0 women). *Students:* 97 full-time (19 women), 6 part-time (0 women); includes 3 Asian, non-Hispanic/Latino, 53 international. 179 applicants, 32% accepted, 18 enrolled. In 2010, 4 master's, 11 doctorates awarded. Terminal master's awarded for partial completion of doctoral program. *Degree requirements:* For master's, thesis (for some programs); for doctorate, thesis/dissertation. *Entrance requirements:* For master's and doctorate, GRE General Test, GRE Subject Test (physics). Additional exam requirements/recommendations for international students: Required—TOEFL (minimum score 550 paper-based; 79 iBT), IELTS (minimum score 6.5). *Application deadline:* For fall admission, 2/15 priority date for domestic and international students; for spring admission, 10/15 for domestic and international students. Applications are processed on a rolling basis. Application fee: $40 ($90 for international students). Electronic applications accepted. *Financial support:* In 2010–11, 54 research assistantships with full and partial tuition reimbursements (averaging $12,890 per year), 34 teaching assistantships with full and partial tuition reimbursements (averaging $13,928 per year) were awarded; fellowships, Federal Work-Study, institutionally sponsored loans, scholarships/grants, health care benefits, and unspecified assistantships also available. Support available to part-time students. Financial award application deadline: 2/15. *Faculty research:* Condensed-matter physics, including superconductivity and new materials; high-energy and nuclear physics; astronomy and astrophysics; atmospheric and environmental physics. Total annual research expenditures: $8.8 million. *Unit head:* Dr. Joseph Shinar, Chair, 515-294-3455, Fax: 515-294-6027, E-mail: phys_astro@iastate.edu. *Application contact:* Dr. Steven Kawaler, Director of Graduate Education, 515-294-9728, E-mail: phys_astro@iastate.edu.

The Johns Hopkins University, Zanvyl Krieger School of Arts and Sciences, Henry A. Rowland Department of Physics and Astronomy, Baltimore, MD 21218-2699. Offers astronomy (PhD); physics (PhD). *Faculty:* 30 full-time (2 women), 14 part-time/adjunct (3 women). *Students:* 105 full-time (18 women); includes 6 minority (3 Asian, non-Hispanic/Latino; 1 Hispanic/Latino; 2 Two or more races, non-Hispanic/Latino), 48 international. Average age 26. 258 applicants, 19% accepted, 49 enrolled. In 2010, 8 doctorates awarded. *Degree requirements:* For doctorate, comprehensive exam, thesis/dissertation, minimum B- average on required coursework. *Entrance requirements:* For doctorate, GRE General Test, GRE Subject Test. Additional exam requirements/recommendations for international students: Required—TOEFL (minimum score 600 paper-based; 250 computer-based; 100 iBT), IELTS. *Application deadline:* For fall admission, 1/15 for domestic and international students. Application fee: $75. Electronic applications accepted. *Financial support:* In 2010–11, 107 students received support, including 4 fellowships with full tuition reimbursements available (averaging $26,000 per year), 55 research assistantships with full tuition reimbursements available (averaging $26,000 per year), 48 teaching assistantships with full tuition reimbursements available (averaging $19,500 per year); career-related internships or fieldwork, Federal Work-Study, institutionally sponsored loans, tuition waivers (partial), and unspecified assistantships also available. Financial award

Physics

The Johns Hopkins University (continued)
application deadline: 4/15; financial award applicants required to submit FAFSA. *Faculty research:* High-energy physics, condensed-matter, astrophysics, particle and experimental physics, plasma physics. Total annual research expenditures: $24.9 million. *Unit head:* Dr. Daniel H. Reich, Chair, 410-516-7346, Fax: 410-516-7239, E-mail: dhr@pha.jhu.edu. *Application contact:* Carmelita D. King, Academic Affairs Administrator, 410-516-7344, Fax: 410-516-7239, E-mail: jazzy@pha.jhu.edu.

Kent State University, College of Arts and Sciences, Department of Physics, Kent, OH 44242-0001. Offers MA, MS, PhD. Terminal master's awarded for partial completion of doctoral program. *Degree requirements:* For master's, thesis; for doctorate, comprehensive exam, thesis/dissertation. *Entrance requirements:* For master's and doctorate, GRE, minimum GPA of 3.0. Additional exam requirements/recommendations for international students: Required—TOEFL. Electronic applications accepted. *Expenses:* Tuition, state resident: full-time $7866; part-time $437 per credit hour. Tuition, nonresident: full-time $14,022; part-time $779 per credit hour. *Faculty research:* Correlated electron materials physics, liquid crystals, complex fluids, computational biophysics, QCD-Hadranphysics.

Lakehead University, Graduate Studies, Department of Physics, Thunder Bay, ON P7B 5E1, Canada. Offers M Sc. *Degree requirements:* For master's, thesis or alternative. *Entrance requirements:* For master's, minimum B average. Additional exam requirements/recommendations for international students: Required—TOEFL. *Faculty research:* Absorbed water, radiation reaction, superlattices and quantum well structures, polaron interactions.

Lehigh University, College of Arts and Sciences, Department of Physics, Bethlehem, PA 18015. Offers photonics (MS); physics (MS, PhD); polymer science (MS, PhD). Part-time programs available. *Faculty:* 17 full-time (1 woman). *Students:* 42 full-time (14 women), 2 part-time (0 women); includes 1 minority (Black or African American, non-Hispanic/Latino), 17 international. Average age 26. 73 applicants, 15% accepted, 8 enrolled. In 2010, 19 master's, 5 doctorates awarded. *Degree requirements:* For doctorate, comprehensive exam, thesis/dissertation. *Entrance requirements:* Additional exam requirements/recommendations for international students: Required—TOEFL (minimum score 213 computer-based; 85 iBT). *Application deadline:* For fall admission, 2/15 priority date for domestic and international students. Applications are processed on a rolling basis. Application fee: $75. Electronic applications accepted. *Financial support:* In 2010–11, 44 students received support, including 5 fellowships with full tuition reimbursements available (averaging $23,000 per year), 19 research assistantships with full tuition reimbursements available (averaging $22,180 per year), 20 teaching assistantships with full tuition reimbursements available (averaging $22,180 per year); career-related internships or fieldwork, Federal Work-Study, institutionally sponsored loans, scholarships/grants, tuition waivers (full and partial), and unspecified assistantships also available. Support available to part-time students. Financial award application deadline: 1/15. *Faculty research:* Condensed matter physics; atomic, molecular and optical physics; plasma physics; nonlinear optics and photonics; astronomy and astrophysics. Total annual research expenditures: $3.5 million. *Unit head:* Dr. Volkmar Dierolf, Chair, 610-758-3915, Fax: 610-758-5730, E-mail: vod2@lehigh.edu. *Application contact:* Dr. Ivan Biaggio, Graduate Admissions Officer, 610-758-4916, Fax: 610-758-5730, E-mail: ivb2@lehigh.edu.

Louisiana State University and Agricultural and Mechanical College, Graduate School, College of Basic Sciences, Department of Physics and Astronomy, Baton Rouge, LA 70803. Offers astronomy (PhD); astrophysics (PhD); medical physics (MS); physics (MS, PhD). *Faculty:* 47 full-time (5 women), 1 part-time/adjunct (0 women). *Students:* 99 full-time (24 women), 4 part-time (0 women); includes 1 Black or African American, non-Hispanic/Latino; 1 Asian, non-Hispanic/Latino; 3 Hispanic/Latino, 43 international. Average age 27. 103 applicants, 17% accepted, 14 enrolled. In 2010, 9 master's, 12 doctorates awarded. Terminal master's awarded for partial completion of doctoral program. *Degree requirements:* For master's, thesis or alternative; for doctorate, thesis/dissertation. *Entrance requirements:* For master's and doctorate, GRE General Test, minimum GPA of 3.0. Additional exam requirements/recommendations for international students: Required—TOEFL (minimum score 550 paper-based; 213 computer-based; 79 iBT) or IELTS (minimum score 6.5). *Application deadline:* For fall admission, 1/25 priority date for domestic students, 5/15 for international students; for spring admission, 10/15 for international students. Applications are processed on a rolling basis. Application fee: $50 ($70 for international students). Electronic applications accepted. *Financial support:* In 2010–11, 103 students received support, including 15 fellowships with full tuition reimbursements available (averaging $16,537 per year), 48 research assistantships with full and partial tuition reimbursements available (averaging $20,677 per year), 40 teaching assistantships with full and partial tuition reimbursements available (averaging $18,525 per year); Federal Work-Study, institutionally sponsored loans, health care benefits, tuition waivers (full and partial), and unspecified assistantships also available. Financial award application deadline: 3/15; financial award applicants required to submit FAFSA. *Faculty research:* Experimentation and numerical relativity, condensed matter astrophysics, quantum computing, medical physics. Total annual research expenditures: $8.8 million. *Unit head:* Dr. Michael Cherry, Chair, 225-578-2261, Fax: 225-578-5855, E-mail: cherry@phys.lsu.edu. *Application contact:* Arnell Dangerfield, Administrative Coordinator, 225-578-1193, Fax: 225-578-5855, E-mail: adanger@lsu.edu.

Louisiana Tech University, Graduate School, College of Engineering and Science, Department of Physics, Ruston, LA 71272. Offers applied computational analysis and modeling (PhD); physics (MS). Part-time programs available. *Degree requirements:* For master's, thesis or alternative; for doctorate, thesis/dissertation. *Entrance requirements:* For master's, GRE General Test, minimum GPA of 3.0 in last 60 hours. Additional exam requirements/recommendations for international students: Required—TOEFL. *Faculty research:* Experimental high energy physics, laser/optics, computational physics, quantum gravity.

Marshall University, Academic Affairs Division, College of Science, Department of Physical Science and Physics, Huntington, WV 25755. Offers physical science (MS). *Faculty:* 11 full-time (3 women). *Students:* 12 full-time (5 women), 7 part-time (2 women); includes 3 Black or African American, non-Hispanic/Latino; 2 American Indian or Alaska Native, non-Hispanic/Latino; 1 Asian, non-Hispanic/Latino, 2 international. Average age 32. In 2010, 2 master's awarded. *Degree requirements:* For master's, thesis optional. *Entrance requirements:* For master's, GRE General Test. Application fee: $40. *Unit head:* Dr. Nicola Orsini, Chairperson, 304-696-2756, E-mail: orsini@marshall.edu. *Application contact:* Information Contact, 304-746-1900, Fax: 304-746-1902, E-mail: services@marshall.edu.

Massachusetts Institute of Technology, School of Science, Department of Physics, Cambridge, MA 02139. Offers SM, PhD. *Faculty:* 71 full-time (6 women). *Students:* 234 full-time (43 women); includes 26 minority (2 Black or African American, non-Hispanic/Latino; 12 Asian, non-Hispanic/Latino; 11 Hispanic/Latino; 1 Two or more races, non-Hispanic/Latino), 120 international. Average age 26. 624 applicants, 14% accepted, 37 enrolled. In 2010, 2 master's, 44 doctorates awarded. Terminal master's awarded for partial completion of doctoral program. *Degree requirements:* For master's, thesis; for doctorate, comprehensive exam, thesis/dissertation. *Entrance requirements:* For master's and doctorate, GRE General Test, GRE Subject Test (physics). Additional exam requirements/recommendations for international students: Required—IELTS (minimum score 6.5). *Application deadline:* For fall admission, 12/15 for domestic and international students; for spring admission, 11/1 for domestic and international students. Application fee: $75. Electronic applications accepted. *Expenses:* Tuition: Full-time $38,940; part-time $605 per unit. Required fees: $272. *Financial support:* In 2010–11, 229 students received support, including 60 fellowships with tuition reimbursements available (averaging $31,582 per year), 134 research assistantships with tuition reimbursements available (averaging $31,290 per year), 35 teaching assistantships with tuition reimbursements available (averaging $31,574 per year); career-related internships or fieldwork, Federal Work-Study, institutionally sponsored loans, scholarships/grants, health care benefits, and unspecified assistantships also available. *Faculty research:* High-energy and nuclear physics; condensed matter physics; astrophysics; atomic physics; biophysics; plasma physics. Total annual research expenditures: $99.8 million. *Unit head:* Prof. Edmund Bertschinger, Department Head, 617-253-4800, Fax: 617-253-8554, E-mail: physics@mit.edu. *Application contact:* Graduate Admissions, 617-253-4841, Fax: 617-258-8319, E-mail: physics-grad@mit.edu.

McGill University, Faculty of Graduate and Postdoctoral Studies, Faculty of Science, Department of Physics, Montréal, QC H3A 2T5, Canada. Offers M Sc, PhD.

McMaster University, School of Graduate Studies, Faculty of Science, Department of Physics and Astronomy, Hamilton, ON L8S 4M2, Canada. Offers astrophysics (PhD); physics (PhD). Part-time programs available. *Degree requirements:* For doctorate, comprehensive exam, thesis/dissertation. *Entrance requirements:* For doctorate, minimum B+ average. Additional exam requirements/recommendations for international students: Required—TOEFL (minimum score 550 paper-based; 213 computer-based). *Faculty research:* Condensed matter, astrophysics, nuclear, medical, nonlinear dynamics.

Memorial University of Newfoundland, School of Graduate Studies, Department of Physics and Physical Oceanography, St. John's, NL A1C 5S7, Canada. Offers atomic and molecular physics (M Sc, PhD); condensed matter physics (M Sc, PhD); physical oceanography (M Sc, PhD); physics (M Sc). Part-time programs available. *Degree requirements:* For master's, thesis, seminar presentation on thesis topic; for doctorate, comprehensive exam, thesis/dissertation, oral defense of thesis. *Entrance requirements:* For master's, honors B Sc or equivalent; for doctorate, M Sc or equivalent. Electronic applications accepted. *Faculty research:* Experiment and theory in atomic and molecular physics, condensed matter physics, physical oceanography, theoretical geophysics and applied nuclear physics.

Miami University, Graduate School, College of Arts and Science, Department of Physics, Oxford, OH 45056. Offers MAT. Part-time programs available. *Students:* 18 full-time (2 women), 1 part-time (0 women); includes 2 minority (1 Asian, non-Hispanic/Latino; 1 Two or more races, non-Hispanic/Latino), 6 international. Average age 25. In 2010, 12 master's awarded. *Entrance requirements:* For master's, GRE (recommended), minimum undergraduate cumulative GPA of 2.75. Additional exam requirements/recommendations for international students: Required—TOEFL. Application fee: $50. *Expenses:* Tuition, state resident: full-time $11,616; part-time $484 per credit hour. Tuition, nonresident: full-time $25,656; part-time $1069 per credit hour. Required fees: $528. *Financial support:* Fellowships with full tuition reimbursements, research assistantships, teaching assistantships, Federal Work-Study, institutionally sponsored loans, health care benefits, tuition waivers (full), and unspecified assistantships available. Financial award application deadline: 3/1; financial award applicants required to submit FAFSA. *Unit head:* Dr. Michael Pechan, Chair, 513-529-4518, Fax: 513-529-5629, E-mail: pechanmj@muohio.edu. *Application contact:* Dr. Samir Bali, Graduate Director, 513-529-5635, E-mail: balis@muohio.edu.

Michigan State University, The Graduate School, College of Natural Science, Department of Physics and Astronomy, East Lansing, MI 48824. Offers astrophysics and astronomy (MS, PhD); physics (MS, PhD). *Entrance requirements:* Additional exam requirements/recommendations for international students: Required—TOEFL (minimum score 550 paper-based; 213 computer-based), Michigan State University ELT (minimum score 85), Michigan English Language Assessment Battery (minimum score 83). Electronic applications accepted. *Faculty research:* Nuclear and accelerator physics, high energy physics, condensed matter physics, biophysics, astrophysics and astronomy.

Michigan State University, National Superconducting Cyclotron Laboratory, East Lansing, MI 48824. Offers chemistry (PhD); physics (PhD).

Michigan Technological University, Graduate School, College of Sciences and Arts, Department of Physics, Program in Physics, Houghton, MI 49931. Offers MS, PhD. Part-time programs available. Terminal master's awarded for partial completion of doctoral program. *Degree requirements:* For master's, comprehensive exam (for some programs), thesis (for some programs); for doctorate, comprehensive exam, thesis/dissertation. *Entrance requirements:* For master's and doctorate, GRE, BS in physics or related discipline. Additional exam requirements/recommendations for international students: Required—TOEFL (minimum score 570 paper-based; 230 computer-based). Electronic applications accepted.

Minnesota State University Mankato, College of Graduate Studies, College of Science, Engineering and Technology, Department of Physics and Astronomy, Mankato, MN 56001. Offers MS. *Students:* 2 full-time (0 women), 4 part-time (1 woman). *Degree requirements:* For master's, one foreign language, comprehensive exam, thesis or alternative. *Entrance requirements:* For master's, minimum GPA of 3.0 during previous 2 years, recommendation letters. Additional exam requirements/recommendations for international students: Required—TOEFL. *Application deadline:* For fall admission, 7/1 priority date for domestic students; for spring admission, 11/1 for domestic students. Applications are processed on a rolling basis. Application fee: $40. Electronic applications accepted. *Financial support:* Research assistantships, teaching assistantships with full tuition reimbursements, Federal Work-Study and unspecified assistantships available. Support available to part-time students. Financial award application deadline: 3/15; financial award applicants required to submit FAFSA. *Unit head:* Dr. Youwen Xu, Chairperson, 507-389-5742. *Application contact:* 507-389-2321, E-mail: grad@mnsu.edu.

Mississippi State University, College of Arts and Sciences, Department of Physics and Astronomy, Mississippi State, MS 39762. Offers engineering (PhD), including applied physics; physics (MS). PhD is interdisciplinary. Part-time programs available. *Faculty:* 11 full-time (0 women). *Students:* 38 full-time (8 women), 3 part-time (0 women); includes 3 minority (1 Black or African American, non-Hispanic/Latino; 2 Hispanic/Latino), 32 international. Average age 29. 38 applicants, 45% accepted, 10 enrolled. In 2010, 6 master's, 4 doctorates awarded. *Degree requirements:* For master's, thesis optional, comprehensive oral or written exam; for doctorate, thesis/dissertation, comprehensive oral or written exam. *Entrance requirements:* For master's, GRE, minimum GPA of 2.75 on last two years of undergraduate courses; for doctorate, GRE. Additional exam requirements/recommendations for international students: Required—TOEFL (minimum score 475 paper-based; 153 computer-based; 53 iBT); Recommended—IELTS (minimum score 4.5). *Application deadline:* For fall admission, 7/1 priority date for domestic students, 5/1 for international students; for spring admission, 11/1 priority date for domestic students, 9/1 for international students. Applications are processed on a rolling basis. Application fee: $40. Electronic applications accepted. *Expenses:* Tuition, state resident: full-time $2730.50; part-time $304 per credit hour. Tuition, nonresident: full-time $6901; part-time $767 per credit hour. *Financial support:* In 2010–11, 5 research assistantships with full tuition reimbursements (averaging $14,310 per year), 22 teaching assistantships with full tuition reimbursements (averaging $13,023 per year) were awarded; Federal Work-Study, institutionally sponsored loans, and unspecified assistantships also available. Financial award application deadline: 3/15; financial award applicants required to submit FAFSA. *Faculty research:* Atomic/molecular spectroscopy, theoretical optics, gamma-ray astronomy, experimental nuclear physics, computational physics. Total annual research expenditures: $2 million. *Unit head:* Dr. Mark A. Novotny, Department Head and Professor, 662-325-2806, Fax: 662-325-8898, E-mail: man40@ra.msstate.edu. *Application contact:* Dr. David Monts, Professor and Graduate Coordinator, 662-325-2931, Fax: 662-325-8898, E-mail: physics@msstate.edu.

Missouri University of Science and Technology, Graduate School, Department of Physics, Rolla, MO 65409. Offers MS, MST, PhD. *Entrance requirements:* For master's, GRE (minimum score 600 quantitative, 3 writing); for doctorate, GRE (minimum score: 600 quantitative, 3.5

writing). Additional exam requirements/recommendations for international students: Required—TOEFL (minimum score 550 paper-based; 213 computer-based).

Montana State University, College of Graduate Studies, College of Letters and Science, Department of Physics, Bozeman, MT 59717. Offers MS, PhD. Part-time programs available. *Faculty:* 16 full-time (3 women), 5 part-time/adjunct (2 women). *Students:* 16 full-time (5 women), 36 part-time (5 women); includes 2 minority (1 Black or African American, non-Hispanic/Latino; 1 Two or more races, non-Hispanic/Latino), 10 international. Average age 29. 59 applicants, 15% accepted, 7 enrolled. In 2010, 8 master's, 2 doctorates awarded. *Degree requirements:* For master's, comprehensive exam, thesis (for some programs); for doctorate, comprehensive exam, thesis/dissertation. *Entrance requirements:* For master's and doctorate, GRE General Test, GRE Subject Test (physics). Additional exam requirements/recommendations for international students: Required—TOEFL (minimum score 550 paper-based; 213 computer-based). *Application deadline:* For fall admission, 7/15 priority date for domestic students, 5/15 priority date for international students; for spring admission, 12/1 priority date for domestic students, 10/1 priority date for international students. Applications are processed on a rolling basis. Application fee: $30. Electronic applications accepted. *Expenses:* Tuition, state resident: full-time $5553.90. Tuition, nonresident: full-time $14,646. Required fees: $1233. *Financial support:* In 2010–11, 47 students received support, including 1 fellowship with full tuition reimbursement available (averaging $19,320 per year), 25 research assistantships with full tuition reimbursements available (averaging $19,320 per year), 21 teaching assistantships with full tuition reimbursements available (averaging $17,520 per year); career-related internships or fieldwork, scholarships/grants, traineeships, health care benefits, and unspecified assistantships also available. Financial award application deadline: 3/1; financial award applicants required to submit FAFSA. *Faculty research:* Nanotechnology, gravitational wave, astronomy, photodynamic theory, diode laser development, solar radiation transfer. Total annual research expenditures: $6.7 million. *Unit head:* Dr. Richard Smith, Head, 406-994-6152, Fax: 406-994-4452, E-mail: smith@physics.montana.edu. *Application contact:* Dr. Carl A. Fox, Vice Provost for Graduate Education, 406-994-4145, Fax: 406-994-7433, E-mail: gradstudy@montana.edu.

Naval Postgraduate School, Graduate Programs, Department of Physics, Monterey, CA 93943. Offers applied physics (MS); engineering acoustics (MS); physics (MS, PhD). Program only open to commissioned officers of the United States and friendly nations and selected United States federal civilian employees. Part-time programs available. *Degree requirements:* For master's, thesis; for doctorate, one foreign language, thesis/dissertation.

New Mexico Institute of Mining and Technology, Graduate Studies, Department of Physics, Socorro, NM 87801. Offers astrophysics (MS, PhD); atmospheric physics (MS, PhD); instrumentation (MS); mathematical physics (PhD). *Degree requirements:* For master's, thesis optional; for doctorate, thesis/dissertation. *Entrance requirements:* For master's, GRE General Test; for doctorate, GRE General Test, GRE Subject Test. Additional exam requirements/recommendations for international students: Required—TOEFL (minimum score 540 paper-based; 207 computer-based). *Faculty research:* Cloud physics, stellar and extragalactic processes.

New Mexico State University, Graduate School, College of Arts and Sciences, Department of Physics, Las Cruces, NM 88003-8001. Offers MS, PhD. Part-time programs available. *Faculty:* 11 full-time (0 women). *Students:* 28 full-time (6 women), 5 part-time (1 woman); includes 4 minority (1 Black or African American, non-Hispanic/Latino; 1 American Indian or Alaska Native, non-Hispanic/Latino; 2 Hispanic/Latino), 25 international. Average age 32. 36 applicants, 92% accepted, 4 enrolled. In 2010, 6 master's awarded. Terminal master's awarded for partial completion of doctoral program. *Degree requirements:* For master's, thesis optional; for doctorate, comprehensive exam, thesis/dissertation. *Entrance requirements:* For master's and doctorate, GRE General Test, GRE Subject Test. Additional exam requirements/recommendations for international students: Required—TOEFL (minimum score 550 paper-based; 79 iBT). *Application deadline:* For fall admission, 3/1 priority date for domestic and international students; for spring admission, 10/1 priority date for domestic and international students. Applications are processed on a rolling basis. Application fee: $30 ($50 for international students). Electronic applications accepted. *Expenses:* Tuition, state resident: full-time $4536; part-time $242 per credit. Tuition, nonresident: full-time $15,816; part-time $712 per credit. Required fees: $636 per term. *Financial support:* In 2010–11, 11 research assistantships (averaging $12,210 per year), 18 teaching assistantships (averaging $15,332 per year) were awarded; fellowships, health care benefits and unspecified assistantships also available. Financial award application deadline: 3/15. *Faculty research:* Nuclear and particle physics, optics, materials science, geophysics, physics education, atmospheric physics. *Unit head:* Dr. Stefan Zollner, Head, 575-646-7627, Fax: 575-646-1934, E-mail: zollner@nmsu.edu. *Application contact:* Dr. Vassilios Papavassiliou, 575-646-3831, Fax: 575-646-1934, E-mail: graduate_advisor@physics.nmsu.edu.

New York University, Graduate School of Arts and Science, Department of Physics, New York, NY 10012-1019. Offers MS, PhD. Part-time programs available. *Faculty:* 25 full-time (1 woman), 5 part-time/adjunct (0 women). *Students:* 68 full-time (6 women), 8 part-time (3 women); includes 1 Hispanic/Latino, 47 international. Average age 27. 238 applicants, 20% accepted, 13 enrolled. In 2010, 4 master's, 8 doctorates awarded. Terminal master's awarded for partial completion of doctoral program. *Degree requirements:* For master's, thesis (for some programs); for doctorate, one foreign language, thesis/dissertation, research seminar, teaching experience. *Entrance requirements:* For master's, GRE General Test, GRE Subject Test, bachelor's degree in physics; for doctorate, GRE General Test, GRE Subject Test. Additional exam requirements/recommendations for international students: Required—TOEFL. *Application deadline:* For fall admission, 12/15 for domestic students. Application fee: $90. *Financial support:* Fellowships with tuition reimbursements, research assistantships with tuition reimbursements, teaching assistantships with tuition reimbursements, Federal Work-Study, institutionally sponsored loans, scholarships/grants, health care benefits, and unspecified assistantships available. Financial award application deadline: 12/15; financial award applicants required to submit FAFSA. *Faculty research:* Atomic physics, elementary particles and fields, astrophysics, condensed-matter physics, neuromagnetism. *Unit head:* David Grier, Chairman, 212-998-7700, Fax: 212-995-4016, E-mail: dgphys@nyu.edu. *Application contact:* Evette Ma, Graduate Department Contact, 212-998-7700, Fax: 212-995-4016, E-mail: dgsphys@nyu.edu.

North Carolina Central University, Division of Academic Affairs, College of Science and Technology, Department of Physics, Durham, NC 27707-3129. Offers MS.

North Carolina State University, Graduate School, College of Physical and Mathematical Sciences, Department of Physics, Raleigh, NC 27695. Offers MS, PhD. Part-time programs available. Terminal master's awarded for partial completion of doctoral program. *Degree requirements:* For master's, thesis (for some programs); for doctorate, thesis/dissertation. *Entrance requirements:* For master's and doctorate, GRE General Test, GRE Subject Test. Electronic applications accepted. *Faculty research:* Astrophysics, optics, physics education, biophysics, geophysics.

North Dakota State University, College of Graduate and Interdisciplinary Studies, College of Science and Mathematics, Department of Physics, Fargo, ND 58108. Offers MS, PhD. Part-time programs available. *Faculty:* 4 full-time. *Students:* 7 full-time (0 women), 1 part-time (0 women), 6 international. Average age 25. 1 applicant, 100% accepted, 1 enrolled. Terminal master's awarded for partial completion of doctoral program. *Degree requirements:* For master's, thesis; for doctorate, comprehensive exam, thesis/dissertation. *Entrance requirements:* Additional exam requirements/recommendations for international students: Required—TOEFL (minimum score 550 paper-based; 215 computer-based; 79 iBT). *Application deadline:* For fall admission, 3/1 priority date for domestic students, 5/1 priority date for international students; for spring admission, 9/1 priority date for domestic and international students. Applications are processed on a rolling basis. Application fee: $45 ($60 for international students). *Financial support:* In

2010–11, 2 students received support, including 2 research assistantships with tuition reimbursements available (averaging $16,000 per year), teaching assistantships with tuition reimbursements available (averaging $12,000 per year); career-related internships or fieldwork, scholarships/grants, and unspecified assistantships also available. Support available to part-time students. Financial award application deadline: 4/15; financial award applicants required to submit FAFSA. *Faculty research:* Biophysics; condensed matter; surface physics; general relativity, gravitation, and space physics; nonlinear physics. Total annual research expenditures: $105,500. *Unit head:* Dr. Daniel Kroll, Director, 701-231-8968, Fax: 701-231-7088, E-mail: daniel.kroll@ndsu.edu. *Application contact:* Dr. Alexander Wagner, Graduate Advisory Committee Chair, 701-231-9582, Fax: 701-231-7088, E-mail: alexander.wagner@ndsu.edu.

Northeastern University, College of Science, Department of Physics, Boston, MA 02115-5096. Offers MS, PhD. Part-time programs available. *Faculty:* 27 full-time (3 women), 9 part-time/adjunct (4 women). *Students:* 52 full-time (10 women). Average age 30. 143 applicants, 41% accepted, 14 enrolled. In 2010, 9 master's, 5 doctorates awarded. Terminal master's awarded for partial completion of doctoral program. *Degree requirements:* For master's, thesis optional; for doctorate, thesis/dissertation, qualifying exam. *Entrance requirements:* For master's and doctorate, GRE General Test, GRE Subject Test. *Application deadline:* For fall admission, 2/1 priority date for domestic and international students. Application fee: $50. *Financial support:* In 2010–11, 20 research assistantships with tuition reimbursements (averaging $18,285 per year), 34 teaching assistantships with tuition reimbursements (averaging $18,285 per year) were awarded; Federal Work-Study, tuition waivers (full and partial), and unspecified assistantships also available. Financial award application deadline: 3/1; financial award applicants required to submit FAFSA. *Faculty research:* Elementary particles and astroparticle physics, nanophysics and condensed matter physics, biological and biomedical physics. *Unit head:* Dr. George Alverson, Graduate Coordinator, 617-373-2938, Fax: 617-373-2943, E-mail: gradphysics@neu.edu. *Application contact:* Jo-Anne Dickinson, Admissions Contact, 617-363-5990, Fax: 617-373-7281, E-mail: gsas@neu.edu.

Northern Arizona University, Graduate College, College of Engineering, Forestry and Natural Sciences, Department of Physics and Astronomy, Flagstaff, AZ 86011. Offers applied physics (MS). Part-time programs available. *Faculty:* 13 full-time (2 women). *Students:* 16 full-time (8 women), 1 part-time (0 women); includes 1 minority (Hispanic/Latino), 3 international. Average age 37. 22 applicants, 55% accepted, 7 enrolled. In 2010, 3 master's awarded. *Degree requirements:* For master's, thesis optional. *Entrance requirements:* Additional exam requirements/recommendations for international students: Required—TOEFL (minimum score 550 paper-based; 213 computer-based; 80 iBT), IELTS (minimum score 7). *Application deadline:* For fall admission, 1/15 priority date for domestic and international students. Applications are processed on a rolling basis. Application fee: $65. Electronic applications accepted. *Financial support:* In 2010–11, 4 research assistantships with partial tuition reimbursements (averaging $12,390 per year), 11 teaching assistantships with partial tuition reimbursements (averaging $12,390 per year) were awarded; Federal Work-Study, scholarships/grants, health care benefits, tuition waivers (full and partial), and unspecified assistantships also available. Financial award applicants required to submit FAFSA. *Unit head:* Dr. Kathy Eastwood, Chair, 928-523-7159, Fax: 928-523-1371, E-mail: kathy.eastwood@nau.edu. *Application contact:* Jamie Housholder, Administrative Assistant, 928-523-8170, Fax: 928-523-1371, E-mail: astro.physics@nau.edu.

Northern Illinois University, Graduate School, College of Liberal Arts and Sciences, Department of Physics, De Kalb, IL 60115-2854. Offers MS, PhD. Part-time programs available. *Faculty:* 18 full-time (3 women), 3 part-time/adjunct (0 women). *Students:* 28 full-time (4 women), 20 part-time (0 women); includes 1 Black or African American, non-Hispanic/Latino; 1 Asian, non-Hispanic/Latino; 3 Hispanic/Latino; 1 Two or more races, non-Hispanic/Latino, 13 international. Average age 30. 51 applicants, 63% accepted, 12 enrolled. In 2010, 8 master's, 3 doctorates awarded. Terminal master's awarded for partial completion of doctoral program. *Degree requirements:* For master's, comprehensive exam, thesis or alternative, research seminar; for doctorate, thesis/dissertation, candidacy exam, dissertation defense, research seminar. *Entrance requirements:* For master's, GRE General Test, minimum GPA of 2.75; for doctorate, GRE General Test, GRE Subject Test (physics), bachelor's degree in physics or related field; minimum undergraduate GPA of 2.75, graduate 3.2. Additional exam requirements/recommendations for international students: Required—TOEFL (minimum score 550 paper-based; 213 computer-based). *Application deadline:* For fall admission, 6/1 for domestic students, 5/1 for international students; for spring admission, 11/1 for domestic students, 10/1 for international students. Applications are processed on a rolling basis. Application fee: $30. Electronic applications accepted. *Expenses:* Tuition, state resident: full-time $7200; part-time $300 per credit hour. Tuition, nonresident: full-time $14,400; part-time $600 per credit hour. Required fees: $79 per credit hour. *Financial support:* In 2010–11, 18 research assistantships with full tuition reimbursements, 18 teaching assistantships with full tuition reimbursements were awarded; fellowships with full tuition reimbursements, career-related internships or fieldwork, Federal Work-Study, scholarships/grants, and unspecified assistantships also available. Support available to part-time students. Financial award applicants required to submit FAFSA. *Faculty research:* Band-structure interpolation schemes, nonlinear procession beams, Mossbauer spectroscopy, beam physics. *Unit head:* Dr. Suzanne Willis, Chair, 815-753-6470, Fax: 815-753-8565, E-mail: swillis@niu.edu. *Application contact:* Dr. David Hedin, Director of Graduate Studies, 815-753-6483, E-mail: hedin@niu.edu.

Northwestern University, The Graduate School, Judd A. and Marjorie Weinberg College of Arts and Sciences, Department of Physics and Astronomy, Evanston, IL 60208. Offers astrophysics (PhD); physics (MS, PhD). Admissions and degrees offered through The Graduate School. *Degree requirements:* For doctorate, thesis/dissertation, qualifying exam. *Entrance requirements:* For doctorate, GRE General Test, GRE Subject Test. Additional exam requirements/recommendations for international students: Required—TOEFL. *Faculty research:* Nuclear and particle physics, condensed-matter physics, nonlinear physics, astrophysics.

Oakland University, Graduate Study and Lifelong Learning, College of Arts and Sciences, Department of Physics, Rochester, MI 48309-4401. Offers medical physics (PhD); physics (MS). *Degree requirements:* For doctorate, thesis/dissertation. *Entrance requirements:* For master's, minimum GPA of 3.0 for unconditional admission; for doctorate, GRE Subject Test, GRE General Test, minimum GPA of 3.0 for unconditional admission. Additional exam requirements/recommendations for international students: Required—TOEFL (minimum score 550 paper-based; 213 computer-based). Electronic applications accepted. *Expenses:* Contact institution. *Faculty research:* Quantitative molecular imagings of articular cartilage, multifunctional ferrite-ferroelectric layered structures for microwave and millimeter wave devices, magnoelectric materials for antenna structures.

The Ohio State University, Graduate School, College of Arts and Sciences, Division of Natural and Mathematical Sciences, Department of Physics, Columbus, OH 43210. Offers MS, PhD. *Faculty:* 61. *Students:* 62 full-time (14 women), 107 part-time (16 women); includes 1 American Indian or Alaska Native, non-Hispanic/Latino; 6 Asian, non-Hispanic/Latino; 3 Hispanic/Latino; 1 Two or more races, non-Hispanic/Latino, 39 international. Average age 26. In 2010, 21 master's, 28 doctorates awarded. *Degree requirements:* For master's, thesis optional; for doctorate, thesis/dissertation. *Entrance requirements:* For master's and doctorate, GRE General Test, GRE Subject Test (physics). Additional exam requirements/recommendations for international students: Required—TOEFL (minimum score 600 paper-based; 250 computer-based). *Application deadline:* For fall admission, 8/15 priority date for domestic students, 7/1 priority date for international students; for winter admission, 12/1 priority date for domestic students, 11/1 priority date for international students; for spring admission, 3/1 priority date for domestic students, 2/1 priority date for international students. Applications are processed on a rolling basis. Application fee: $40 ($50 for international students). Electronic applications accepted. *Expenses:* Tuition, state resident: full-time $10,605. Tuition, nonresident: full-time

Peterson's Graduate Programs in the Physical Sciences, Mathematics, Agricultural Sciences, the Environment & Natural Resources 2012

www.facebook.com/petersonspublishing   **191**

Physics

The Ohio State University (continued)
$26,535. Tuition and fees vary according to course load and program. *Financial support:* Fellowships, research assistantships, teaching assistantships, Federal Work-Study and institutionally sponsored loans available. Support available to part-time students. *Unit head:* James J. Beatty, Chair, 614-292-2653, E-mail: beatty@mps.ohio-state.edu. *Application contact:* 614-292-9444, Fax: 614-292-3895, E-mail: domestic.grad@osu.edu.

Ohio University, Graduate College, College of Arts and Sciences, Department of Physics and Astronomy, Athens, OH 45701. Offers astronomy (MS, PhD); physics (MS, PhD). Part-time programs available. *Faculty:* 27 full-time (3 women), 5 part-time/adjunct (1 woman). *Students:* 85 full-time (29 women); includes 1 Hispanic/Latino, 66 international. Average age 27. 125 applicants, 38% accepted, 21 enrolled. In 2010, 7 master's, 9 doctorates awarded. Terminal master's awarded for partial completion of doctoral program. *Degree requirements:* For master's, thesis or alternative; for doctorate, comprehensive exam, thesis/dissertation. *Entrance requirements:* For master's and doctorate, minimum GPA of 3.0. Additional exam requirements/recommendations for international students: Required—TOEFL (minimum score 600 paper-based; 250 computer-based; 100 iBT), IELTS (minimum score 7), TWE (minimum score 4). *Application deadline:* For fall admission, 2/1 priority date for domestic and international students. Applications are processed on a rolling basis. Application fee: $0. Electronic applications accepted. *Financial support:* In 2010–11, 1 fellowship with tuition reimbursement (averaging $22,205 per year), 42 research assistantships with full tuition reimbursements (averaging $23,908 per year), 31 teaching assistantships with full tuition reimbursements (averaging $21,726 per year) were awarded; scholarships/grants and unspecified assistantships also available. Financial award application deadline: 4/1. *Faculty research:* Nuclear physics, condensed-matter physics, nonlinear systems, astrophysics, biophysics. Total annual research expenditures: $4.3 million. *Unit head:* Dr. Joseph Shields, Chair, 740-593-0336, Fax: 740-593-0433, E-mail: shields@helios.phy.ohiou.edu. *Application contact:* Dr. Marcus Boettcher, Graduate Admissions Chair, 740-593-1714, Fax: 740-593-0433, E-mail: gradapp@phy.ohiou.edu.

See Display on next page and Close-Up on page 217.

Oklahoma State University, College of Arts and Sciences, Department of Physics, Stillwater, OK 74078. Offers photonics (MS, PhD); physics (MS, PhD). *Faculty:* 30 full-time (8 women), 2 part-time/adjunct (0 women). *Students:* 5 full-time (0 women), 33 part-time (6 women); includes 1 American Indian or Alaska Native, non-Hispanic/Latino; 1 Hispanic/Latino, 26 international. Average age 29. 46 applicants, 22% accepted, 3 enrolled. In 2010, 2 master's, 7 doctorates awarded. *Degree requirements:* For master's, thesis; for doctorate, comprehensive exam, thesis/dissertation, oral defense of dissertation, preliminary exam, qualifying exam. *Entrance requirements:* For master's and doctorate, GRE. Additional exam requirements/recommendations for international students: Required—TOEFL (minimum score 550 paper-based; 79 iBT). *Application deadline:* For fall admission, 3/1 priority date for international students; for spring admission, 8/1 priority date for international students. Applications are processed on a rolling basis. Application fee: $40 ($75 for international students). Electronic applications accepted. *Expenses:* Tuition, state resident: full-time $3716; part-time $154.85 per credit hour. Tuition, nonresident: full-time $14,892; part-time $621 per credit hour. Required fees: $2044; $85.20 per credit hour. One-time fee: $50. Tuition and fees vary according to course load and campus/location. *Financial support:* In 2010–11, 23 research assistantships (averaging $18,637 per year), 38 teaching assistantships (averaging $16,985 per year) were awarded; career-related internships or fieldwork, Federal Work-Study, scholarships/grants, health care benefits, tuition waivers (partial), and unspecified assistantships also available. Support available to part-time students. Financial award application deadline: 3/1; financial award applicants required to submit FAFSA. *Faculty research:* Lasers and photonics, non-linear optical materials, turbulence, structure and function of biological membranes, particle theory. *Unit head:* Dr. James Wicksted, Head, 405-744-5796, Fax: 405-744-6811. *Application contact:* Dr. Gordon Emslie, Dean, 405-744-6368, Fax: 405-744-0355, E-mail: grad-i@okstate.edu.

Old Dominion University, College of Sciences, Program in Physics, Norfolk, VA 23529. Offers MS, PhD. *Faculty:* 22 full-time (2 women), 14 part-time/adjunct (1 woman). *Students:* 37 full-time (5 women), 5 part-time (3 women), 28 international. Average age 31. 53 applicants, 38% accepted, 10 enrolled. In 2010, 9 master's, 6 doctorates awarded. Terminal master's awarded for partial completion of doctoral program. *Degree requirements:* For master's, comprehensive exam, thesis optional; for doctorate, comprehensive exam, thesis/dissertation. *Entrance requirements:* For master's, BS in physics or related field, minimum GPA of 3.0 in major; for doctorate, GRE General Test; GRE Subject Test (strongly recommended), minimum GPA of 3.0; two reference letters. Additional exam requirements/recommendations for international students: Required—TOEFL (minimum score 550 paper-based; 213 computer-based; 79 iBT). *Application deadline:* For fall admission, 2/15 for domestic and international students. Applications are processed on a rolling basis. Application fee: $40. Electronic applications accepted. *Expenses:* Tuition, state resident: full-time $8592; part-time $358 per credit. Tuition, nonresident: full-time $21,672; part-time $903 per credit. Required fees: $119 per semester. One-time fee: $50. *Financial support:* In 2010–11, 42 students received support, including 3 fellowships (averaging $15,000 per year), 32 research assistantships with full and partial tuition reimbursements available (averaging $24,000 per year), 14 teaching assistantships with full tuition reimbursements available (averaging $22,000 per year); career-related internships or fieldwork, scholarships/grants, tuition waivers (full), and unspecified assistantships also available. Support available to part-time students. Financial award application deadline: 2/15; financial award applicants required to submit FAFSA. *Faculty research:* Nuclear and particle physics, atomic physics, condensed-matter physics, plasma physics, accelerator physics. *Unit head:* Dr. Lepsha Vuskovic, Graduate Program Director, 757-683-4611, Fax: 757-683-3038, E-mail: vuskovic@odu.edu. *Application contact:* Dr. Mark Havey, Graduate Recruitment & Admissions Director, 757-683-4612, Fax: 757-683-3038, E-mail: mhavey@odu.edu.

Oregon State University, Graduate School, College of Science, Department of Physics, Corvallis, OR 97331. Offers applied physics (MS); physics (MA, MS, PhD). Part-time programs available. Terminal master's awarded for partial completion of doctoral program. *Degree requirements:* For master's, thesis optional, qualifying exam; for doctorate, thesis/dissertation, qualifying exam. *Entrance requirements:* For master's and doctorate, minimum GPA of 3.0 in last 90 hours. Additional exam requirements/recommendations for international students: Required—TOEFL.

Penn State University Park, Graduate School, Eberly College of Science, Department of Physics, State College, University Park, PA 16802-1503. Offers M Ed, MS, PhD. *Unit head:* Dr. Jayanth R. Banavar, Head, 814-865-7533, Fax: 814-865-0978, E-mail: jrb16@psu.edu. *Application contact:* Rick Robinett, Director of Graduate Studies, 814-863-0965, E-mail: rq9@psu.edu.

Pittsburg State University, Graduate School, College of Arts and Sciences, Department of Physics, Pittsburg, KS 66762. Offers applied physics (MS); physics (MS); professional physics (MS). *Degree requirements:* For master's, thesis or alternative.

Portland State University, Graduate Studies, College of Liberal Arts and Sciences, Department of Physics, Portland, OR 97207-0751. Offers MA, MS, PhD. Part-time programs available. *Faculty:* 16 full-time (1 woman), 1 part-time/adjunct (0 women). *Students:* 28 full-time (9 women), 16 part-time (1 woman); includes 3 Hispanic/Latino, 9 international. Average age 31. 21 applicants, 71% accepted, 12 enrolled. In 2010, 9 master's awarded. *Degree requirements:* For master's, variable foreign language requirement, thesis, oral exam, written report; for doctorate, thesis/dissertation. *Entrance requirements:* For master's, GRE General Test, minimum GPA of 3.0 in upper-division course work or 2.75 overall, 2 letters of recommendation. Additional exam requirements/recommendations for international students: Required—TOEFL (minimum score 550 paper-based; 213 computer-based). *Application deadline:* For fall admission, 4/1 priority date for domestic students, 3/1 for international students; for winter admission, 9/1 for domestic students, 8/1 for international students; for spring admission, 11/1 for domestic and international students. Applications are processed on a rolling basis. Application fee: $50. *Expenses:* Tuition, state resident: full-time $8505; part-time $315 per credit. Tuition, nonresident: full-time $13,284; part-time $492 per credit. Required fees: $1482; $21 per credit. $99 per term. One-time fee: $120. Part-time tuition and fees vary according to course load and program. *Financial support:* In 2010–11, 5 research assistantships with full tuition reimbursements (averaging $19,987 per year), 16 teaching assistantships with full tuition reimbursements (averaging $15,000 per year) were awarded; career-related internships or fieldwork, Federal Work-Study, and unspecified assistantships also available. Support available to part-time students. Financial award application deadline: 3/1; financial award applicants required to submit FAFSA. *Faculty research:* Statistical physics, membrane biophysics, low-temperature physics, electron microscopy, atmospheric physics. Total annual research expenditures: $2.1 million. *Unit head:* Dr. Drake Mitchell, Interim Department Chair, 503-725-3812, Fax: 503-725-3888. *Application contact:* Peter Leung, Coordinator, 503-725-3812, Fax: 503-725-3888.

Princeton University, Graduate School, Department of Physics, Princeton, NJ 08544-1019. Offers PhD. *Degree requirements:* For doctorate, thesis/dissertation, qualifying exam. *Entrance requirements:* For doctorate, GRE General Test, GRE Subject Test. Additional exam requirements/recommendations for international students: Required—TOEFL (minimum score 600 paper-based; 250 computer-based). Electronic applications accepted.

Purdue University, Graduate School, College of Science, Department of Physics, West Lafayette, IN 47907. Offers MS, PhD. Part-time programs available. Terminal master's awarded for partial completion of doctoral program. *Degree requirements:* For master's, qualifying exam; for doctorate, thesis/dissertation, qualifying exam. *Entrance requirements:* For master's and doctorate, GRE General Test, GRE Subject Test (physics). Additional exam requirements/recommendations for international students: Required—TOEFL. Electronic applications accepted. *Faculty research:* Solid-state, elementary particle, and nuclear physics; biological physics; acoustics; astrophysics.

Queens College of the City University of New York, Division of Graduate Studies, Mathematics and Natural Sciences Division, Department of Physics, Flushing, NY 11367-1597. Offers MA, PhD. Part-time and evening/weekend programs available. *Faculty:* 11 full-time (1 woman). *Students:* 4 part-time (2 women); includes 1 Asian, non-Hispanic/Latino; 1 Hispanic/Latino, 1 international. 11 applicants, 36% accepted, 2 enrolled. In 2010, 2 master's awarded. *Degree requirements:* For master's, comprehensive exam. *Entrance requirements:* For master's, previous course work in calculus, minimum GPA of 3.0. Additional exam requirements/recommendations for international students: Required—TOEFL. *Application deadline:* For fall admission, 4/1 for domestic students; for spring admission, 11/1 for domestic students. Applications are processed on a rolling basis. Application fee: $125. *Financial support:* Career-related internships or fieldwork, Federal Work-Study, institutionally sponsored loans, and tuition waivers (partial) available. Support available to part-time students. Financial award application deadline: 4/1; financial award applicants required to submit FAFSA. *Faculty research:* Solid-state physics, low temperature physics, elementary particles and fields. *Unit head:* Dr. Alexander Lisyansky, Chairperson, 718-997-3350, E-mail: alexander_lisyansky@qc.edu. *Application contact:* Dr. J. Marion Dickey, Graduate Adviser, 718-997-3350.

Queen's University at Kingston, School of Graduate Studies and Research, Faculty of Arts and Sciences, Department of Physics, Kingston, ON K7L 3N6, Canada. Offers M Sc, M Sc Eng, PhD. Part-time programs available. *Degree requirements:* For master's, thesis; for doctorate, comprehensive exam, thesis/dissertation. *Entrance requirements:* For master's, first or upper second class honours in Physics; for doctorate, M Sc or M Sc Eng. Additional exam requirements/recommendations for international students: Required—TOEFL (minimum score 550 paper-based; 213 computer-based). *Faculty research:* Theoretical physics, astronomy and astrophysics, subatomic, condensed matter, applied and engineering.

Rensselaer Polytechnic Institute, Graduate School, School of Science, Department of Physics, Applied Physics and Astronomy, Troy, NY 12180-3590. Offers MS, PhD. Part-time programs available. *Faculty:* 25 full-time (4 women), 3 part-time/adjunct. *Students:* 59 full-time (12 women), 2 part-time; includes 1 Black or African American, non-Hispanic/Latino; 22 Asian, non-Hispanic/Latino. Average age 25. 145 applicants, 40% accepted, 12 enrolled. In 2010, 10 master's, 13 doctorates awarded. *Degree requirements:* For doctorate, thesis/dissertation. *Entrance requirements:* For master's and doctorate, GRE General Test, GRE Subject Test. Additional exam requirements/recommendations for international students: Required—TOEFL (minimum score 600 paper-based; 250 computer-based; 100 iBT). *Application deadline:* For fall admission, 1/1 for domestic and international students; for spring admission, 8/15 for domestic and international students. Applications are processed on a rolling basis. Application fee: $75. Electronic applications accepted. *Expenses:* Tuition: Full-time $39,600; part-time $1650 per credit. Required fees: $1896. *Financial support:* In 2010–11, 47 students received support, including 7 fellowships with full tuition reimbursements available (averaging $30,000 per year), 22 research assistantships with full tuition reimbursements available (averaging $23,000 per year), 18 teaching assistantships with full tuition reimbursements available (averaging $23,000 per year). Financial award application deadline: 2/1. *Faculty research:* Astrophysics, condensed matter, particle physics, optical and biological physics. Total annual research expenditures: $8.5 million. *Unit head:* Dr. Xi-Cheng Zhang, Acting Chair, 518-276-8391, Fax: 518-276-6680, E-mail: mcquade@rpi.edu. *Application contact:* Shengbai Zhang, Chair, Graduate Recruiting Committee, 518-276-8391, Fax: 518-276-6680, E-mail: mcquade@rpi.edu.

Rice University, Graduate Programs, Wiess School of Natural Sciences, Department of Physics and Astronomy, Houston, TX 77251-1892. Offers nanoscale physics (MS); physics and astronomy (PhD); science teaching (MST). Part-time programs available. *Degree requirements:* For master's, thesis (for some programs); for doctorate, thesis/dissertation, minimum B average. *Entrance requirements:* For master's, GRE General Test; for doctorate, GRE General Test, GRE Subject Test. Additional exam requirements/recommendations for international students: Required—TOEFL (minimum score 600 paper-based; 250 computer-based; 90 iBT). Electronic applications accepted. *Faculty research:* Optical physics; ultra cold atoms; membrane electr-statics, peptides, proteins and lipids; solar astrophysics; stellar activity; magnetic fields; young stars.

Rice University, Graduate Programs, Wiess School–Professional Science Master's Programs, Professional Master's Program in Nanoscale Physics, Houston, TX 77251-1892. Offers MS. *Degree requirements:* For master's, internship. *Entrance requirements:* For master's, GRE General Test, bachelor's degree in physics and related field, 4 letters of recommendation. Additional exam requirements/recommendations for international students: Required—TOEFL (minimum score 600 paper-based; 250 computer-based; 90 iBT). Electronic applications accepted. *Faculty research:* Atomic, molecular, and applied physics, surface and condensed matter physics.

Royal Military College of Canada, Division of Graduate Studies and Research, Science Division, Department of Physics, Kingston, ON K7K 7B4, Canada. Offers M Sc. *Degree requirements:* For master's, thesis. *Entrance requirements:* For master's, honour's degree with second-class standing. Electronic applications accepted.

Rutgers, The State University of New Jersey, New Brunswick, Graduate School-New Brunswick, Department of Physics and Astronomy, Piscataway, NJ 08854-8097. Offers astronomy (MS, PhD); biophysics (PhD); condensed matter physics (MS, PhD); elementary particle physics (MS, PhD); intermediate energy nuclear physics (MS); nuclear physics (MS, PhD); physics (MST); surface science (PhD); theoretical physics (MS, PhD). Part-time programs

available. Terminal master's awarded for partial completion of doctoral program. *Degree requirements:* For master's, comprehensive exam, thesis or alternative; for doctorate, comprehensive exam, thesis/dissertation. *Entrance requirements:* For master's and doctorate, GRE General Test, GRE Subject Test. Additional exam requirements/recommendations for international students: Required—TOEFL (minimum score 560 paper-based). Electronic applications accepted. *Expenses:* Tuition, state resident: full-time $7200; part-time $600 per credit. Tuition, nonresident: full-time $11,124; part-time $927 per credit. *Faculty research:* Astronomy, high energy, condensed matter, surface, nuclear physics.

St. Francis Xavier University, Graduate Studies, Department of Physics, Antigonish, NS B2G 2W5, Canada. Offers M Sc. *Degree requirements:* For master's, thesis. *Entrance requirements:* For master's, minimum B average in undergraduate course work, honors degree in physics or related area. Additional exam requirements/recommendations for international students: Required—TOEFL (minimum score 580 paper-based; 236 computer-based). *Faculty research:* Atomic and molecular spectroscopy, quantum theory, many body theory, mathematical physics, phase transitions.

San Diego State University, Graduate and Research Affairs, College of Sciences, Department of Physics, Program in Physics, San Diego, CA 92182. Offers MA, MS. Part-time programs available. *Degree requirements:* For master's, thesis, oral exam. *Entrance requirements:* For master's, GRE General Test, GRE Subject Test (physics), 2 letters of recommendation. Additional exam requirements/recommendations for international students: Required—TOEFL. Electronic applications accepted.

San Francisco State University, Division of Graduate Studies, College of Science and Engineering, Department of Physics and Astronomy, San Francisco, CA 94132-1722. Offers physics (MS). Part-time programs available. *Application deadline:* Applications are processed on a rolling basis. Electronic applications accepted. *Unit head:* Dr. Susan Lea, Graduate Coordinator, 415-338-1659, E-mail: physics@stars.sfsu.edu. *Application contact:* Maarten Golterman, Graduate Coordinator, 415-338-1659, E-mail: maarten@stars.sfsu.edu.

San Jose State University, Graduate Studies and Research, College of Science, Department of Physics and Astronomy, San Jose, CA 95192-0001. Offers computational physics (MS); physics (MS). Part-time and evening/weekend programs available. *Degree requirements:* For master's, thesis optional. *Entrance requirements:* For master's, GRE. Electronic applications accepted. *Faculty research:* Astrophysics, atmospheric physics, elementary particles, dislocation theory, general relativity.

Simon Fraser University, Graduate Studies, Faculty of Science, Department of Physics, Burnaby, BC V5A 1S6, Canada. Offers biophysics (M Sc, PhD); chemical physics (M Sc, PhD); physics (M Sc, PhD). *Degree requirements:* For master's, thesis; for doctorate, thesis/dissertation. *Entrance requirements:* For master's, minimum GPA of 3.0; for doctorate, minimum GPA of 3.5. Additional exam requirements/recommendations for international students: Required—TOEFL or IELTS. *Faculty research:* Solid-state physics, magnetism, energy research, superconductivity, nuclear physics.

South Dakota School of Mines and Technology, Graduate Division, Program in Physics, Rapid City, SD 57701-3995. Offers MS, PhD.

South Dakota State University, Graduate School, College of Engineering, Department of Physics, Brookings, SD 57007. Offers engineering (MS). Part-time programs available. *Degree requirements:* For master's, comprehensive exam (for some programs), thesis (for some programs), oral exam. *Entrance requirements:* Additional exam requirements/recommendations for international students: Required—TOEFL (minimum score 580 paper-based; 237 computer-based). *Faculty research:* Materials science, astrophysics, remote sensing and atmospheric corrections, theoretical and computational physics, applied physics.

Southeastern Louisiana University, College of Science and Technology, Program in Integrated Science and Technology, Hammond, LA 70402. Offers chemistry (MS); computer science (MS); information technology (MS); mathematics (MS); physics (MS). Part-time and evening/weekend programs available. *Faculty:* 11 full-time (3 women). *Students:* 13 full-time (5 women), 11 part-time (2 women); includes 1 minority (Asian, non-Hispanic/Latino), 8 international. Average age 32. 13 applicants, 46% accepted, 4 enrolled. In 2010, 5 master's awarded. *Degree requirements:* For master's, thesis (for some programs), 33-36 hours. *Entrance requirements:* For master's, GRE (minimum combined score 850), 2 letters of reference; minimum GPA of 2.75; 30 hours of course work including chemistry, physics, industrial technology, or mathematics. Additional exam requirements/recommendations for international students: Required—TOEFL (minimum score 500 paper-based; 173 computer-based; 61 iBT). *Application deadline:* For fall admission, 7/15 priority date for domestic students, 6/1 priority date for international students; for spring admission, 12/1 priority date for domestic students, 10/1 priority date for international students. Applications are processed on a rolling basis. Application fee: $20 ($30 for international students). Electronic applications accepted. *Expenses:* Tuition, state resident: full-time $3533. Tuition, nonresident: full-time $12,002. Required fees: $907. Tuition and fees vary according to degree level. *Financial support:* In 2010–11, 7 students received support, including 7 research assistantships (averaging $10,100 per year); career-related internships or fieldwork, Federal Work-Study, institutionally sponsored loans, and unspecified assistantships also available. Support available to part-time students. Financial award application deadline: 5/1; financial award applicants required to submit FAFSA. *Faculty research:* Computational statistics, medicinal chemistry, machine learning, optical interferometry, strength of materials and structure. *Unit head:* Dr. Ken Li, Coordinator, 985-549-3822, Fax: 985-549-2099, E-mail: kli@selu.edu. *Application contact:* Sandra Meyers, Graduate Admissions Analyst, 985-549-5620, Fax: 985-549-5632, E-mail: admissions@selu.edu.

Southern Illinois University Carbondale, Graduate School, College of Science, Department of Physics, Carbondale, IL 62901-4701. Offers MS, PhD. *Degree requirements:* For master's, one foreign language, thesis. *Entrance requirements:* For master's, minimum GPA of 2.7. Additional exam requirements/recommendations for international students: Required—TOEFL. *Faculty research:* Atomic, molecular, nuclear, and mathematical physics; statistical mechanics; solid-state and low-temperature physics; rheology; material science.

Southern Methodist University, Dedman College, Department of Physics, Dallas, TX 75275. Offers MS, PhD. Part-time programs available. *Faculty:* 13 full-time (1 woman), 1 part-time/adjunct (0 women). *Students:* 9 full-time (4 women), 7 part-time (1 woman); includes 1 Hispanic/Latino, 12 international. Average age 27. 30 applicants, 27% accepted, 6 enrolled. In 2010, 1 doctorate awarded. Terminal master's awarded for partial completion of doctoral program. *Degree requirements:* For master's, thesis optional, oral exam; for doctorate, thesis/dissertation, written exam. *Entrance requirements:* For master's and doctorate, GRE General Test, GRE Subject Test (physics), minimum GPA of 3.0. Additional exam requirements/recommendations for international students: Required—TOEFL. *Application deadline:* For fall admission, 2/1 priority date for domestic and international students. Application fee: $60. Electronic applications accepted. *Financial support:* In 2010–11, 4 research assistantships with full tuition reimbursements (averaging $21,000 per year), 6 teaching assistantships with full tuition reimbursements (averaging $19,500 per year) were awarded; health care benefits and tuition waivers (partial) also available. Financial award application deadline: 2/1; financial award applicants required to submit FAFSA. *Faculty research:* Particle physics, cosmology, astrophysics, mathematics physics, computational physics. Total annual research expenditures: $1 million. *Unit head:* Prof. Fredrick Olness, Head, 214-768-2495, Fax: 214-768-4095, E-mail: olness@smu.edu. *Application contact:* Prof. Jingbo Ye, Director of Graduate Recruitment, Fax: 214-768-4095.

Peterson's Graduate Programs in the Physical Sciences, Mathematics, Agricultural Sciences, the Environment & Natural Resources 2012

www.facebook.com/petersonspublishing   **193**

College of Science and Technology

TEMPLE UNIVERSITY®

DEPARTMENT OF PHYSICS

- **Graduate program leads to Master of Arts (M.A.) and Doctor of Philosophy (Ph.D.) degrees.**

- **Program's objective: to assist the student in gaining an understanding of physics sufficiently broad to form a basis for independent research, as well as to give the student the experience of doing significant research under the guidance of a mature scientist.**

- **Both theoretical and experimental approaches are included in the program.**

- **Areas of specialization: particle physics; condensed matter physics; and atomic, molecular, and optical physics.**

For more information, contact:
Graduate Administrator
Temple University
Department of Physics
College of Science and Technology
1900 N. 13th Street, Barton Hall, Room 116A
Philadelphia, PA 19122
Physics@temple.edu

www.temple.edu/physics

Southern University and Agricultural and Mechanical College, Graduate School, College of Sciences, Department of Physics, Baton Rouge, LA 70813. Offers MS. *Degree requirements:* For master's, thesis. *Entrance requirements:* For master's, GMAT or GRE General Test. Additional exam requirements/recommendations for international students: Required—TOEFL (minimum score 525 paper-based; 193 computer-based). *Faculty research:* Piezoelectric materials and devices, predictive ab-instio calculations, high energy physics, surface growth studies, semiconductor and intermetallics.

Stanford University, School of Humanities and Sciences, Department of Physics, Stanford, CA 94305-9991. Offers PhD. *Degree requirements:* For doctorate, thesis/dissertation, oral exam, qualifying exam. *Entrance requirements:* For doctorate, GRE General Test, GRE Subject Test. Additional exam requirements/recommendations for international students: Required—TOEFL. Electronic applications accepted. *Expenses:* Tuition: Full-time $38,700; part-time $860 per unit. One-time fee: $200 full-time.

State University of New York at Binghamton, Graduate School, School of Arts and Sciences, Department of Physics, Applied Physics, and Astronomy, Binghamton, NY 13902-6000. Offers applied physics (MS); physics (MA, MS, PhD). *Faculty:* 12 full-time (1 woman), 8 part-time/adjunct (4 women). *Students:* 14 full-time (0 women); includes 1 Black or African American, non-Hispanic/Latino, 2 international. Average age 26. 20 applicants, 75% accepted, 7 enrolled. In 2010, 3 master's awarded. *Degree requirements:* For master's, thesis or alternative. *Entrance requirements:* For master's, GRE General Test, GRE Subject Test. Additional exam requirements/recommendations for international students: Required—TOEFL (minimum score 550 paper-based; 213 computer-based; 80 iBT). *Application deadline:* For fall admission, 2/15 priority date for domestic and international students; for spring admission, 10/15 priority date for domestic and international students. Applications are processed on a rolling basis. Application fee: $60. Electronic applications accepted. *Financial support:* In 2010–11, 14 students received support, including 1 research assistantship with full tuition reimbursement available (averaging $11,000 per year), 13 teaching assistantships with full tuition reimbursements available (averaging $11,000 per year); career-related internships or fieldwork, Federal Work-Study, institutionally sponsored loans, scholarships/grants, health care benefits, and unspecified assistantships also available. Financial award application deadline: 2/15; financial award applicants required to submit FAFSA. *Unit head:* Dr. Eric Cotts, Chairperson, 607-777-4371, E-mail: ecotts@binghamton.edu. *Application contact:* Catherine Smith, Recruiting and Admissions Coordinator, 607-777-2151, Fax: 607-777-2501, E-mail: cmsmith@binghamton.edu.

Stephen F. Austin State University, Graduate School, College of Sciences and Mathematics, Department of Physics and Astronomy, Nacogdoches, TX 75962. Offers physics (MS). Part-time programs available. *Degree requirements:* For master's, comprehensive exam. *Entrance requirements:* For master's, GRE General Test, minimum GPA of 2.8 in last 60 hours, 2.5 overall. Additional exam requirements/recommendations for international students: Required—TOEFL. *Faculty research:* Low-temperature physics, x-ray spectroscopy and metallic glasses, infrared spectroscopy.

Stevens Institute of Technology, Graduate School, Charles V. Schaefer Jr. School of Engineering, Department of Physics and Engineering Physics, Hoboken, NJ 07030. Offers applied optics (Certificate); engineering physics (M Eng); microdevices and microsystems (Certificate); physics (MS, PhD); plasma and surface physics (Certificate). Part-time and evening/weekend programs available. *Students:* 46 full-time (6 women), 8 part-time (0 women); includes 1 Black or African American, non-Hispanic/Latino; 4 Asian, non-Hispanic/Latino; 4 Hispanic/Latino, 23 international. Average age 30. 44 applicants, 100% accepted. Terminal

master's awarded for partial completion of doctoral program. *Degree requirements:* For master's, thesis optional; for doctorate, thesis/dissertation. *Entrance requirements:* For master's and doctorate, GRE. Additional exam requirements/recommendations for international students: Required—TOEFL. *Application deadline:* Applications are processed on a rolling basis. Application fee: $50. Electronic applications accepted. *Financial support:* Fellowships, research assistantships, teaching assistantships, Federal Work-Study and institutionally sponsored loans available. *Faculty research:* Laser spectroscopy, physical kinetics, semiconductor-device physics, condensed-matter theory. *Unit head:* Knut Stamnes, Director, 201-216-8194, Fax: 201-216-5638, E-mail: kstamnes@stevens.edu. *Application contact:* H. L. Cui, Chairman, Graduate Committee, 201-216-5637, Fax: 201-216-5638, E-mail: hcui@stevens-tech.edu.

Stony Brook University, State University of New York, Graduate School, College of Arts and Sciences, Department of Physics and Astronomy, Program in Physics, Stony Brook, NY 11794. Offers modern research instrumentation (MS); physics (MA, PhD); physics education (MAT). *Students:* 177 full-time (35 women), 2 part-time (0 women); includes 3 Black or African American, non-Hispanic/Latino; 5 Asian, non-Hispanic/Latino; 4 Hispanic/Latino; 2 Two or more races, non-Hispanic/Latino, 109 international. *Degree requirements:* For doctorate, one foreign language, thesis/dissertation. *Entrance requirements:* For master's and doctorate, GRE General Test. Additional exam requirements/recommendations for international students: Required—TOEFL. *Application deadline:* For fall admission, 1/15 for domestic students. Application fee: $100. *Expenses:* Tuition, state resident: full-time $8370; part-time $349 per credit. Tuition, nonresident: full-time $13,780; part-time $574 per credit. Required fees: $994. *Financial support:* Fellowships, research assistantships, teaching assistantships available. Financial award application deadline: 2/1. *Unit head:* Dr. Lazlo Mihaly, Chair, 631-632-8100, Fax: 631-632-8176, E-mail: lazlo.mihaly@stonybrook.edu. *Application contact:* Director, 631-632-8100, Fax: 631-632-8176.

Syracuse University, College of Arts and Sciences, Program in Physics, Syracuse, NY 13244. Offers MS, PhD. Part-time programs available. *Students:* 69 full-time (12 women), 2 part-time (1 woman); includes 2 minority (both Hispanic/Latino), 46 international. Average age 28. 163 applicants, 29% accepted, 11 enrolled. In 2010, 1 master's, 6 doctorates awarded. Terminal master's awarded for partial completion of doctoral program. *Degree requirements:* For master's, thesis or alternative; for doctorate, thesis/dissertation. *Entrance requirements:* For master's and doctorate, GRE General Test, GRE Subject Test. Additional exam requirements/recommendations for international students: Required—TOEFL (minimum score 100 iBT). *Application deadline:* For fall admission, 2/1 priority date for domestic and international students. Application fee: $75. Electronic applications accepted. *Expenses:* Tuition: Part-time $1162 per credit. *Financial support:* Fellowships with full tuition reimbursements, research assistantships with full and partial tuition reimbursements, teaching assistantships with full and partial tuition reimbursements, tuition waivers (partial) available. Financial award application deadline: 1/1; financial award applicants required to submit FAFSA. *Unit head:* Dr. Simon Catterall, Director, Graduate Studies, 315-443-5978, E-mail: smc@phy.syr.edu. *Application contact:* Dr. Simon Catterall, Director, Graduate Studies, 315-443-5978, E-mail: smc@phy.syr.edu.

Temple University, College of Science and Technology, Department of Physics, Philadelphia, PA 19122-6096. Offers MA, PhD. *Faculty:* 15 full-time (4 women). *Students:* 38 full-time (8 women), 3 part-time (0 women); includes 1 Black or African American, non-Hispanic/Latino; 3 Asian, non-Hispanic/Latino; 1 Hispanic/Latino; 1 Two or more races, non-Hispanic/Latino, 16 international. 38 applicants, 37% accepted, 10 enrolled. In 2010, 8 master's, 7 doctorates awarded. Terminal master's awarded for partial completion of doctoral program. *Degree*

194 www.facebook.com/petersonspublishing

Peterson's Graduate Programs in the Physical Sciences, Mathematics, Agricultural Sciences, the Environment & Natural Resources 2012

requirements: For master's, comprehensive exam, thesis or alternative; for doctorate, thesis/dissertation, 2 comprehensive exams. *Entrance requirements:* For master's and doctorate, GRE General Test, minimum GPA of 3.0. Additional exam requirements/recommendations for international students: Required—TOEFL (minimum score 550 paper-based; 213 computer-based; 79 iBT). *Application deadline:* For fall admission, 7/15 for domestic students, 12/15 for international students; for spring admission, 11/15 for domestic students, 8/1 for international students. Applications are processed on a rolling basis. Application fee: $50. Electronic applications accepted. *Financial support:* Fellowships, research assistantships, teaching assistantships, tuition waivers (full and partial) available. Financial award application deadline: 1/15; financial award applicants required to submit FAFSA. *Faculty research:* Laser-based molecular spectroscopy, elementary particle physics, statistical mechanics, solid-state physics. *Unit head:* Dr. Rongjia Tao, Chair, 215-204-7634, Fax: 215-204-5652, E-mail: physics@temple.edu. *Application contact:* Dr. Rongjia Tao, Chair, 215-204-7634, Fax: 215-204-5652, E-mail: physics@temple.edu.

See Display on page 194 and Close-Up on page 221.

Texas A&M International University, Office of Graduate Studies and Research, College of Arts and Sciences, Department of Mathematical and Physical Science, Laredo, TX 78041-1900. Offers MA. *Faculty:* 3 full-time (0 women). *Students:* 9 full-time (1 woman), 5 part-time (1 woman); includes 34 Hispanic/Latino, 1 international. Average age 33. 22 applicants, 77% accepted, 13 enrolled. *Entrance requirements:* For master's, GRE General Test. Additional exam requirements/recommendations for international students: Required—TOEFL (minimum score 550 paper-based; 213 computer-based). *Application deadline:* For fall admission, 4/30 priority date for domestic students; for spring admission, 11/30 for domestic students, 10/1 for international students. Applications are processed on a rolling basis. Application fee: $25. *Financial support:* In 2010–11, 1 student received support, including 4 research assistantships (averaging $9,100 per year). Financial award application deadline: 11/1. *Unit head:* Dr. Rafic Bachnak, Chair, 956-326-2408, Fax: 956-326-2439, E-mail: rbachnak@tamiu.edu. *Application contact:* Suzanne Hansen-Alford, Director of Graduate Recruiting, 956-326-3023, Fax: 956-326-3021, E-mail: graduateschool@tamiu.edu.

Texas A&M University, College of Science, Department of Physics and Astronomy, College Station, TX 77843. Offers applied physics (PhD); physics (MS, PhD). *Faculty:* 50. *Students:* 176 full-time (26 women), 2 part-time (1 woman); includes 2 Black or African American, non-Hispanic/Latino; 2 American Indian or Alaska Native, non-Hispanic/Latino; 8 Asian, non-Hispanic/Latino; 11 Hispanic/Latino, 89 international. In 2010, 9 master's, 11 doctorates awarded. Terminal master's awarded for partial completion of doctoral program. *Degree requirements:* For master's, thesis (for some programs); for doctorate, thesis/dissertation. *Entrance requirements:* For master's and doctorate, GRE General Test, GRE Subject Test. Additional exam requirements/recommendations for international students: Required—TOEFL. *Application deadline:* For fall admission, 3/1 priority date for domestic students; for spring admission, 8/1 for domestic students. Application fee: $50 ($75 for international students). Electronic applications accepted. *Financial support:* In 2010–11, research assistantships (averaging $16,200 per year), teaching assistantships (averaging $16,200 per year) were awarded; fellowships also available. Financial award application deadline: 3/1; financial award applicants required to submit FAFSA. *Faculty research:* Condensed-matter, atomic/molecular, high-energy, and nuclear physics; quantum optics. *Unit head:* Dr. Edward S. Fry, Head, 979-845-7717, E-mail: fry@physics.tamu.edu. *Application contact:* Dr. George W. Kattawar, Professor, 979-845-1180, Fax: 979-845-2590, E-mail: kattawar@tamu.edu.

Texas A&M University–Commerce, Graduate School, College of Arts and Sciences, Department of Physics, Commerce, TX 75429-3011. Offers M Ed, MS. Part-time programs available. *Degree requirements:* For master's, comprehensive exam, thesis (for some programs). *Entrance requirements:* For master's, GRE General Test. Electronic applications accepted.

Texas Christian University, College of Science and Engineering, Department of Physics and Astronomy, Fort Worth, TX 76129-0002. Offers physics (MA, MS, PhD), including astrophysics (PhD), business (PhD), physics (PhD); PhD/MBA. Terminal master's awarded for partial completion of doctoral program. *Degree requirements:* For master's, comprehensive exam, thesis; for doctorate, comprehensive exam, thesis/dissertation, paper submitted to scientific journal. *Entrance requirements:* For master's and doctorate, GRE General Test, minimum GPA of 3.0. Additional exam requirements/recommendations for international students: Required—TOEFL (minimum score 600 paper-based). *Application deadline:* For fall admission, 2/1 for domestic and international students; for spring admission, 10/1 for domestic and international students. Applications are processed on a rolling basis. Application fee: $50. Electronic applications accepted. *Expenses:* Tuition: Full-time $18,720; part-time $1040 per credit hour. Tuition and fees vary according to course load and program. *Financial support:* In 2010–11, 11 teaching assistantships (averaging $18,000 per year) were awarded; tuition waivers also available. Financial award application deadline: 2/1. *Unit head:* Dr. T. W. Zerda, Chairperson, 817-257-7375 Ext. 7124, Fax: 817-257-7742, E-mail: t.zerda@tcu.edu. *Application contact:* Dr. Yuri Strzhemechny, Assistant Professor, 817-257-7375 Ext. 5793, Fax: 817-257-7742, E-mail: y.strzhemechny@tcu.edu.

Texas State University–San Marcos, Graduate School, College of Science, Department of Physics, San Marcos, TX 78666. Offers material physics (MS); physics (MS). Part-time programs available. *Faculty:* 6 full-time (2 women), 1 part-time/adjunct (0 women). *Students:* 9 full-time (0 women), 3 part-time (1 woman); includes 1 minority (Hispanic/Latino), 1 international. Average age 27. 9 applicants, 89% accepted, 4 enrolled. In 2010, 6 master's awarded. *Degree requirements:* For master's, comprehensive exam, thesis (for some programs). *Entrance requirements:* For master's, minimum GPA of 2.75 in junior- and senior-level physics courses or 2.5 with GRE (minimum combined score of 900 Verbal and Quantitative). Additional exam requirements/recommendations for international students: Required—TOEFL (minimum score 550 paper-based; 213 computer-based; 78 iBT). *Application deadline:* For fall admission, 6/15 priority date for domestic students, 6/1 priority date for international students; for spring admission, 10/15 priority date for domestic students, 10/1 priority date for international students. Applications are processed on a rolling basis. Application fee: $40 ($90 for international students). Electronic applications accepted. *Expenses:* Tuition, state resident: full-time $6024; part-time $251 per credit hour. Tuition, nonresident: full-time $13,536; part-time $564 per credit hour. Required fees: $1776; $50 per credit hour. $306 per semester. *Financial support:* In 2010–11, 3 students received support, including 2 research assistantships (averaging $5,076 per year), 6 teaching assistantships (averaging $5,076 per year); career-related internships or fieldwork, Federal Work-Study, and institutionally sponsored loans also available. Support available to part-time students. Financial award application deadline: 4/1; financial award applicants required to submit FAFSA. *Faculty research:* High-temperature superconductors, historical astronomy, general relativity. Total annual research expenditures: $794,240. *Unit head:* Dr. David Donnelly, Chair, 512-245-2131, Fax: 512-245-2131, E-mail: dd14@txstate.edu. *Application contact:* Dr. J. Michael Willoughby, Dean of Graduate School, 512-245-2581, Fax: 512-245-8365, E-mail: gradcollege@txstate.edu.

Texas Tech University, Graduate School, College of Arts and Sciences, Department of Physics, Lubbock, TX 79409. Offers applied physics (MS); physics (MS, PhD). Part-time programs available. *Faculty:* 14 full-time (1 woman), 1 part-time/adjunct (0 women). *Students:* 52 full-time (10 women), 2 part-time (0 women); includes 1 Black or African American, non-Hispanic/Latino; 2 Hispanic/Latino; 1 Two or more races, non-Hispanic/Latino, 35 international. Average age 28. 46 applicants, 52% accepted, 13 enrolled. In 2010, 6 master's, 3 doctorates awarded. *Degree requirements:* For master's, variable foreign language requirement, thesis or alternative; for doctorate, variable foreign language requirement, thesis/dissertation. *Entrance requirements:* For master's and doctorate, GRE General Test. Additional exam requirements/recommendations for international students: Required—TOEFL (minimum

score 550 paper-based; 213 computer-based; 79 iBT). *Application deadline:* For fall admission, 6/1 priority date for domestic students, 1/15 priority date for international students; for spring admission, 9/1 priority date for domestic students, 6/15 priority date for international students. Applications are processed on a rolling basis. Application fee: $50 ($75 for international students). Electronic applications accepted. *Expenses:* Tuition, state resident: full-time $5495.76; part-time $228.99 per credit hour. Tuition, nonresident: full-time $12,936; part-time $538.99 per credit hour. Required fees: $2674; $36 per credit hour. $905 per semester. *Financial support:* In 2010–11, 49 students received support, including 10 research assistantships with partial tuition reimbursements available (averaging $4,740 per year), 12 teaching assistantships with partial tuition reimbursements available (averaging $5,946 per year). Financial award application deadline: 4/15; financial award applicants required to submit FAFSA. *Faculty research:* Biophysics, high energy and nuclear physics, condensed matter physics, atomic and molecular physics, physics education. Total annual research expenditures: $1.5 million. *Unit head:* Dr. Roger Lichti, Chair, 806-742-3767, Fax: 806-742-1182, E-mail: roger.lichti@ttu.edu. *Application contact:* Dr. Mahdi Sanati, Graduate Recruiter, 806-742-3767, Fax: 806-742-1182, E-mail: m.sanati@ttu.edu.

Trent University, Graduate Studies, Program in Applications of Modeling in the Natural and Social Sciences, Department of Physics, Peterborough, ON K9J 7B8, Canada. Offers M Sc. Part-time programs available. *Degree requirements:* For master's, thesis. *Entrance requirements:* For master's, honours degree. *Faculty research:* Radiation physics, chemical physics.

Tufts University, Graduate School of Arts and Sciences, Department of Physics and Astronomy, Medford, MA 02155. Offers physics (MS, PhD). Terminal master's awarded for partial completion of doctoral program. *Degree requirements:* For master's, thesis optional; for doctorate, thesis/dissertation. *Entrance requirements:* For master's and doctorate, GRE General Test. Additional exam requirements/recommendations for international students: Required—TOEFL (minimum score 550 paper-based; 213 computer-based; 80 iBT). Electronic applications accepted. *Expenses:* Tuition: Full-time $39,624; part-time $3962 per course. Required fees: $40 per year. Full-time tuition and fees vary according to degree level, program and student level. Part-time tuition and fees vary according to course load.

Tulane University, School of Science and Engineering, Department of Physics and Engineering Physics, New Orleans, LA 70118-5669. Offers physics (PhD). *Degree requirements:* For doctorate, thesis/dissertation. *Entrance requirements:* For doctorate, GRE General Test. Additional exam requirements/recommendations for international students: Required—TOEFL. Electronic applications accepted. *Faculty research:* Surface physics, condensed-matter experiment, condensed-matter theory, nuclear theory, polymers.

Université de Moncton, Faculty of Science, Department of Physics and Astronomy, Moncton, NB E1A 3E9, Canada. Offers M Sc. Part-time programs available. *Degree requirements:* For master's, thesis. *Entrance requirements:* For master's, proficiency in French. Electronic applications accepted. *Faculty research:* Thin films, optical properties, solar selective surfaces, microgravity and photonic materials.

Université de Montréal, Faculty of Arts and Sciences, Department of Physics, Montréal, QC H3C 3J7, Canada. Offers M Sc, PhD. *Degree requirements:* For doctorate, thesis/dissertation, general exam. Electronic applications accepted. *Faculty research:* Astronomy; biophysics; solid-state, plasma, and nuclear physics.

Université de Sherbrooke, Faculty of Sciences, Department of Physics, Sherbrooke, QC J1K 2R1, Canada. Offers M Sc, PhD. *Degree requirements:* For master's, thesis; for doctorate, comprehensive exam, thesis/dissertation. *Entrance requirements:* For doctorate, master's degree. Electronic applications accepted. *Faculty research:* Solid-state physics, quantum computing.

Université du Québec à Trois-Rivières, Graduate Programs, Program in Physics, Trois-Rivières, QC G9A 5H7, Canada. Offers matter and energy (MS, PhD).

Université Laval, Faculty of Sciences and Engineering, Department of Physics, Physical Engineering, and Optics, Programs in Physics, Québec, QC G1K 7P4, Canada. Offers M Sc, PhD. Terminal master's awarded for partial completion of doctoral program. *Degree requirements:* For master's, thesis; for doctorate, comprehensive exam, thesis/dissertation. *Entrance requirements:* For master's and doctorate, knowledge of French, comprehension of written English. Electronic applications accepted.

University at Albany, State University of New York, College of Arts and Sciences, Department of Physics, Albany, NY 12222-0001. Offers MS, PhD. *Degree requirements:* For master's, one foreign language; for doctorate, one foreign language, thesis/dissertation. *Entrance requirements:* Additional exam requirements/recommendations for international students: Required—TOEFL (minimum score 550 paper-based; 213 computer-based). Electronic applications accepted. *Faculty research:* Condensed-matter physics, high-energy physics, applied physics, electronic materials, theoretical particle physics.

University at Buffalo, the State University of New York, Graduate School, College of Arts and Sciences, Department of Physics, Buffalo, NY 14260. Offers MS, PhD. Part-time programs available. *Faculty:* 27 full-time (3 women), 5 part-time/adjunct (0 women). *Students:* 90 full-time (15 women); includes 1 minority (Hispanic/Latino), 53 international. Average age 29. 190 applicants, 20% accepted, 30 enrolled. In 2010, 9 master's, 10 doctorates awarded. Terminal master's awarded for partial completion of doctoral program. *Degree requirements:* For master's, thesis optional; for doctorate, comprehensive exam, thesis/dissertation. *Entrance requirements:* For master's, letters of recommendation; for doctorate, GRE General Test, letters of recommendation. Additional exam requirements/recommendations for international students: Required—TOEFL (minimum score 550 paper-based; 213 computer-based; 79 iBT). *Application deadline:* For fall admission, 2/1 priority date for domestic and international students. Application fee: $75. Electronic applications accepted. *Financial support:* In 2010–11, 6 fellowships with full tuition reimbursements (averaging $7,750 per year), 30 research assistantships with full tuition reimbursements (averaging $17,000 per year), 39 teaching assistantships with full tuition reimbursements (averaging $16,500 per year) were awarded; Federal Work-Study, institutionally sponsored loans, scholarships/grants, health care benefits, and unspecified assistantships also available. Financial award application deadline: 3/1; financial award applicants required to submit FAFSA. *Faculty research:* Condensed-matter physics (experimental and theoretical), cosmology (theoretical), high energy and particle physics (experimental and theoretical), computational physics, biophysics (experimental and theoretical), materials physics. Total annual research expenditures: $2.6 million. *Unit head:* Dr. Hong Luo, Chairman, 716-645-3421, Fax: 716-645-2507, E-mail: luo@buffalo.edu. *Application contact:* Dr. Xuedong Hu, Director of Graduate Studies, 716-645-5444, Fax: 716-645-2507, E-mail: xhu@buffalo.edu.

The University of Akron, Graduate School, Buchtel College of Arts and Sciences, Department of Physics, Akron, OH 44325. Offers MS. Part-time and evening/weekend programs available. *Faculty:* 8 full-time (1 woman), 2 part-time/adjunct (0 women). *Students:* 11 full-time (3 women), 1 part-time (0 women), 8 international. Average age 26. 13 applicants, 54% accepted, 6 enrolled. In 2010, 4 master's awarded. *Degree requirements:* For master's, thesis, written exam or formal report. *Entrance requirements:* For master's, hold a baccalaureate degree in Physics or a related field, letters of recommendation, resume, statement of purpose. Additional exam requirements/recommendations for international students: Required—TOEFL (minimum score 550 paper-based; 213 computer-based; 79 iBT). *Application deadline:* For fall admission, 3/15 for domestic students. Applications are processed on a rolling basis. Application fee: $30 ($40 for international students). Electronic applications accepted. *Expenses:* Tuition, state resident: full-time $6800; part-time $378 per credit hour. Tuition, nonresident: full-time $11,644; part-time $647 per credit hour. Required fees: $1265. One-time fee: $30 full-time. *Financial*

Peterson's Graduate Programs in the Physical Sciences, Mathematics, Agricultural Sciences, the Environment & Natural Resources 2012

www.facebook.com/petersonspublishing **195**

Physics

The University of Akron (continued)

support: In 2010–11, 1 research assistantship, 12 teaching assistantships with full tuition reimbursements were awarded. *Faculty research:* Materials physics, surface physics, nanotechnology, polymer physics, condensed matter physics. Total annual research expenditures: $36,260. *Unit head:* Dr. Robert Mallik, Chair, 330-972-7145, E-mail: rmallik@uakron.edu. *Application contact:* Dr. Ben Hu, Graduate Director, 330-972-8093, E-mail: byhu@uakron.edu.

The University of Alabama, Graduate School, College of Arts and Sciences, Department of Physics and Astronomy, Tuscaloosa, AL 35487-0324. Offers physics (MS, PhD). *Faculty:* 21 full-time (1 woman). *Students:* 14 full-time (5 women), 30 part-time (6 women), 28 international. Average age 27. 36 applicants, 56% accepted, 11 enrolled. In 2010, 7 master's, 3 doctorates awarded. Terminal master's awarded for partial completion of doctoral program. *Degree requirements:* For master's, thesis optional, oral exam; for doctorate, thesis/dissertation, oral and written exams. *Entrance requirements:* For master's and doctorate, GRE General or Subject Test, minimum GPA of 3.0. Additional exam requirements/recommendations for international students: Required—TOEFL (minimum score 550 paper-based; 213 computer-based; 79 iBT). *Application deadline:* For fall admission, 7/6 priority date for domestic students, 2/1 for international students; for spring admission, 11/22 for domestic students. Applications are processed on a rolling basis. Application fee: $50 ($60 for international students). Electronic applications accepted. *Expenses:* Tuition, state resident: full-time $7900. Tuition, nonresident: full-time $20,500. *Financial support:* In 2010–11, 39 students received support, including 1 fellowship with full tuition reimbursement available (averaging $18,000 per year), 13 research assistantships with full tuition reimbursements available (averaging $14,000 per year), 25 teaching assistantships with full tuition reimbursements available (averaging $13,900 per year); career-related internships or fieldwork and institutionally sponsored loans also available. Financial award application deadline: 4/1. *Faculty research:* Condensed-matter, high-energy physics; molecular spectroscopy; astrophysics; particle astrophysics. Total annual research expenditures: $2.1 million. *Unit head:* Dr. Raymond E. White, Chairman and Professor, 205-348-5050, Fax: 205-348-5051, E-mail: rwhite@ua.edu. *Application contact:* Louise F. Labosier, Admissions Officer, 205-348-5921, Fax: 205-348-0400, E-mail: labosier@aalan.ua.edu.

The University of Alabama at Birmingham, College of Arts and Sciences, Program in Physics, Birmingham, AL 35294. Offers MS, PhD. *Students:* 36 full-time (9 women), 1 part-time (0 women); includes 4 minority (1 Black or African American, non-Hispanic/Latino; 3 Hispanic/Latino), 13 international. Average age 28. 23 applicants, 70% accepted, 7 enrolled. In 2010, 3 master's, 2 doctorates awarded. Terminal master's awarded for partial completion of doctoral program. *Degree requirements:* For master's, thesis optional; for doctorate, thesis/dissertation. *Entrance requirements:* For master's and doctorate, GRE General Test, minimum GPA of 3.0. Additional exam requirements/recommendations for international students: Required—TOEFL. *Application deadline:* Applications are processed on a rolling basis. Electronic applications accepted. *Expenses:* Tuition, state resident: full-time $5482. Tuition, nonresident: full-time $12,430. Tuition and fees vary according to program. *Financial support:* In 2010–11, 6 fellowships with full tuition reimbursements (averaging $15,741 per year), 11 research assistantships with full tuition reimbursements (averaging $17,344 per year), 11 teaching assistantships with full tuition reimbursements (averaging $16,000 per year) were awarded; career-related internships or fieldwork, Federal Work-Study, institutionally sponsored loans, scholarships/grants, traineeships, health care benefits, and unspecified assistantships also available. Support available to part-time students. Financial award application deadline: 4/15; financial award applicants required to submit FAFSA. *Faculty research:* Laser physics, space physics, optics, biophysics, material physics. *Unit head:* Dr. David L. Shealy, Chair, 205-934-4736, Fax: 205-934-8042. *Application contact:* Jerrie Delynn McCurry, Administrative Support Specialist, 205-975-8094, Fax: 205-934-8042, E-mail: jerried@uab.edu.

The University of Alabama in Huntsville, School of Graduate Studies, College of Science, Department of Physics, Huntsville, AL 35899. Offers optics and photonics technology (MS); physics (MS, PhD). Part-time and evening/weekend programs available. *Faculty:* 19 full-time (0 women), 1 part-time/adjunct (0 women). *Students:* 35 full-time (9 women), 20 part-time (8 women); includes 2 minority (both Asian, non-Hispanic/Latino), 13 international. Average age 30. 50 applicants, 58% accepted, 17 enrolled. In 2010, 7 master's awarded. *Degree requirements:* For master's, comprehensive exam, thesis or alternative, oral and written exams; for doctorate, comprehensive exam, thesis/dissertation, oral and written exams. *Entrance requirements:* For master's and doctorate, GRE General Test, minimum GPA of 3.0. Additional exam requirements/recommendations for international students: Required—TOEFL (minimum score 550 paper-based; 213 computer-based; 62 iBT). *Application deadline:* For fall admission, 7/15 for domestic students, 4/1 for international students; for spring admission, 11/30 for domestic students, 9/1 for international students. Applications are processed on a rolling basis. Application fee: $40 ($50 for international students). Electronic applications accepted. *Expenses:* Tuition, state resident: full-time $7250; part-time $407.75 per credit hour. Tuition, nonresident: full-time $17,358; part-time $970.05 per credit hour. Required fees: $246.80 per semester. Tuition and fees vary according to course load and program. *Financial support:* In 2010–11, 31 students received support, including 19 research assistantships with full and partial tuition reimbursements available (averaging $14,278 per year), 11 teaching assistantships with full and partial tuition reimbursements available (averaging $14,000 per year); career-related internships or fieldwork, Federal Work-Study, institutionally sponsored loans, scholarships/grants, health care benefits, and unspecified assistantships also available. Support available to part-time students. Financial award application deadline: 4/1; financial award applicants required to submit FAFSA. *Faculty research:* Space physics, cosmology/general relativity, optics/quantum optics, astrophysics/gamma-ray astronomy, strophysical instrumentation. Total annual research expenditures: $6.1 million. *Unit head:* Dr. Gary Zank, Chair, 256-824-2481, Fax: 256-824-6873, E-mail: gary.zank@uah.edu. *Application contact:* Kathy Biggs, Graduate Studies Admissions Manager, 256-824-6199, Fax: 256-824-6405, E-mail: deangrad@uah.edu.

University of Alaska Fairbanks, College of Natural Sciences and Mathematics, Department of Physics, Fairbanks, AK 99775-5920. Offers computational physics (MS); physics (MAT, MS, PhD); space physics (MS, PhD). Part-time programs available. *Faculty:* 5 full-time (1 woman). *Students:* 28 full-time (6 women); includes 2 minority (1 Black or African American, non-Hispanic/Latino; 1 American Indian or Alaska Native, non-Hispanic/Latino), 8 international. Average age 29. 28 applicants, 36% accepted, 10 enrolled. In 2010, 1 master's, 2 doctorates awarded. Terminal master's awarded for partial completion of doctoral program. *Degree requirements:* For master's, comprehensive exam, thesis or alternative; for doctorate, comprehensive exam, thesis/dissertation, oral defense. *Entrance requirements:* Additional exam requirements/recommendations for international students: Required—TOEFL (minimum score 550 paper-based; 213 computer-based; 80 iBT). *Application deadline:* For fall admission, 6/1 for domestic students, 3/1 for international students; for spring admission, 10/15 for domestic students, 9/1 for international students. Applications are processed on a rolling basis. Application fee: $60. Electronic applications accepted. *Expenses:* Tuition, state resident: full-time $5688; part-time $316 per credit. Tuition, nonresident: full-time $11,628; part-time $646 per credit. Required fees: $289 per semester. Tuition and fees vary according to course load and reciprocity agreements. *Financial support:* In 2010–11, 18 research assistantships with tuition reimbursements (averaging $12,399 per year), 9 teaching assistantships with tuition reimbursements (averaging $18,259 per year) were awarded; fellowships with tuition reimbursements, Federal Work-Study, scholarships/grants, health care benefits, and unspecified assistantships also available. Support available to part-time students. Financial award application deadline: 2/15; financial award applicants required to submit FAFSA. *Faculty research:* Atmospheric and ionospheric radar studies, space plasma theory, magnetospheric dynamics, space weather and auroral studies, turbulence and complex systems. *Unit head:* Ataur Chowdhury, Chair, 907-474-7339, Fax: 907-474-6130, E-mail: physics@uaf.edu. *Application contact:* Ataur Chowdhury, Chair, 907-474-7339, Fax: 907-474-6130, E-mail: physics@uaf.edu.

University of Alberta, Faculty of Graduate Studies and Research, Department of Physics, Edmonton, AB T6G 2E1, Canada. Offers astrophysics (M Sc, PhD); condensed matter (M Sc, PhD); geophysics (M Sc, PhD); medical physics (M Sc, PhD); subatomic physics (M Sc, PhD). *Degree requirements:* For master's, thesis; for doctorate, thesis/dissertation. *Entrance requirements:* For master's and doctorate, minimum GPA of 7.0 on a 9.0 scale. Additional exam requirements/recommendations for international students: Required—TOEFL. *Faculty research:* Cosmology, astroparticle physics, high-intermediate energy, magnetism, superconductivity.

The University of Arizona, College of Science, Department of Physics, Tucson, AZ 85721. Offers applied and industrial physics (PMS); physics (MS, PhD). Part-time programs available. *Faculty:* 24 full-time (1 woman), 3 part-time/adjunct (1 woman). *Students:* 63 full-time (12 women), 12 part-time (0 women); includes 1 Asian, non-Hispanic/Latino; 1 Hispanic/Latino; 2 Two or more races, non-Hispanic/Latino, 31 international. Average age 28. 154 applicants. In 2010, 1 master's, 8 doctorates awarded. Terminal master's awarded for partial completion of doctoral program. *Degree requirements:* For master's, comprehensive exam (for some programs), thesis optional; for doctorate, comprehensive exam, thesis/dissertation. *Entrance requirements:* For master's and doctorate, GRE General Test, GRE Subject Test, minimum GPA of 3.2, 3 letters of recommendation. Additional exam requirements/recommendations for international students: Required—TOEFL (minimum score 550 paper-based; 213 computer-based; 79 iBT). *Application deadline:* For fall admission, 2/1 for domestic students, 12/1 for international students. Applications are processed on a rolling basis. Application fee: $75. Electronic applications accepted. *Expenses:* Tuition, state resident: full-time $7692. *Financial support:* In 2010–11, 21 research assistantships with full tuition reimbursements (averaging $21,408 per year), 35 teaching assistantships with full tuition reimbursements (averaging $20,108 per year) were awarded; career-related internships or fieldwork, scholarships/grants, health care benefits, tuition waivers (full and partial), and unspecified assistantships also available. Financial award application deadline: 5/1. *Faculty research:* Astrophysics; high-energy, condensed-matter, atomic and molecular physics; optics. Total annual research expenditures: $3.8 million. *Unit head:* Dr. Michael Shupe, Head, 520-621-2679, E-mail: shupe@physics.arizona.edu. *Application contact:* Lisa Shapouri, Graduate Coordinator, 520-621-2290, Fax: 520-621-4721, E-mail: lisas@physics.arizona.edu.

University of Arkansas, Graduate School, J. William Fulbright College of Arts and Sciences, Department of Physics, Fayetteville, AR 72701-1201. Offers applied physics (MS); physics (MS, PhD); physics education (MA). *Students:* 7 full-time (2 women), 39 part-time (8 women); includes 1 minority (Asian, non-Hispanic/Latino), 26 international. 15 applicants, 100% accepted. In 2010, 6 master's, 3 doctorates awarded. *Degree requirements:* For master's, thesis; for doctorate, thesis/dissertation. *Application deadline:* For fall admission, 4/1 for international students; for spring admission, 10/1 for international students. Applications are processed on a rolling basis. Application fee: $40 ($50 for international students). Electronic applications accepted. *Financial support:* In 2010–11, 9 fellowships with tuition reimbursements, 21 research assistantships, 22 teaching assistantships were awarded; career-related internships or fieldwork and Federal Work-Study also available. Support available to part-time students. Financial award application deadline: 4/1; financial award applicants required to submit FAFSA. *Unit head:* Dr. Surendra Singh, Departmental Chairperson, 479-575-2506, Fax: 479-575-4580, E-mail: ssingh@uark.edu. *Application contact:* Dr. Huaxiang Fu, Graduate Coordinator, 479-575-8606, E-mail: hfu@uark.edu.

The University of British Columbia, Faculty of Science, Program in Physics, Vancouver, BC V6T 1Z1, Canada. Offers engineering physics (MA Sc); physics (M Sc, PhD). *Degree requirements:* For master's, thesis; for doctorate, comprehensive exam, thesis/dissertation. *Entrance requirements:* For master's, GRE General Test, honors degree; for doctorate, GRE General Test, master's degree. Additional exam requirements/recommendations for international students: Required—TOEFL. Tuition charges are reported in Canadian dollars. *Expenses:* Tuition, area resident: Full-time $4179 Canadian dollars. International tuition: $7344 Canadian dollars full-time. *Faculty research:* Applied physics, astrophysics, condensed matter, plasma physics, subatomic physics, astronomy.

University of Calgary, Faculty of Graduate Studies, Faculty of Science, Department of Physics and Astronomy, Calgary, AB T2N 1N4, Canada. Offers M Sc, PhD. Part-time programs available. *Degree requirements:* For master's, thesis; for doctorate, thesis/dissertation, oral candidacy exam, written qualifying exam. *Entrance requirements:* For master's and doctorate, GRE General Test, GRE Subject Test. Additional exam requirements/recommendations for international students: Required—TOEFL (minimum score 550 paper-based; 213 computer-based). Electronic applications accepted. *Faculty research:* Astronomy and astrophysics, mass spectrometry, atmospheric physics, space physics, medical physics.

University of California, Berkeley, Graduate Division, College of Letters and Science, Department of Physics, Berkeley, CA 94720-1500. Offers PhD. *Degree requirements:* For doctorate, thesis/dissertation, qualifying exam. *Entrance requirements:* For doctorate, GRE General Test, GRE Subject Test, minimum GPA of 3.0, 3 letters of recommendation. Additional exam requirements/recommendations for international students: Required—TOEFL (minimum score 570 paper-based; 230 computer-based). *Faculty research:* Astrophysics (experimental and theoretical), condensed matter physics (experimental and theoretical), particle physics (experimental and theoretical), atomic/molecular physics, biophysics and complex systems.

University of California, Davis, Graduate Studies, Program in Physics, Davis, CA 95616. Offers MS, PhD. Terminal master's awarded for partial completion of doctoral program. *Degree requirements:* For master's, comprehensive exam (for some programs), thesis (for some programs); for doctorate, thesis/dissertation. *Entrance requirements:* For master's and doctorate, GRE General Test, GRE Subject Test, minimum GPA of 3.0. Additional exam requirements/recommendations for international students: Required—TOEFL (minimum score 550 paper-based; 213 computer-based). Electronic applications accepted. *Faculty research:* Astrophysics, condensed-matter physics, nuclear physics, particle physics, quantum optics.

University of California, Irvine, School of Physical Sciences, Department of Physics and Astronomy, Irvine, CA 92697. Offers physics (MS, PhD); MD/PhD. *Students:* 115 full-time (18 women), 1 (woman) part-time; includes 23 minority (2 Black or African American, non-Hispanic/Latino; 18 Asian, non-Hispanic/Latino; 2 Hispanic/Latino; 1 Two or more races, non-Hispanic/Latino), 25 international. Average age 28. 268 applicants, 25% accepted, 26 enrolled. In 2010, 12 master's, 8 doctorates awarded. Terminal master's awarded for partial completion of doctoral program. *Degree requirements:* For doctorate, thesis/dissertation. *Entrance requirements:* For master's and doctorate, GRE General Test, GRE Subject Test, minimum GPA of 3.0. Additional exam requirements/recommendations for international students: Required—TOEFL (minimum score 550 paper-based; 213 computer-based). *Application deadline:* For fall admission, 1/15 priority date for domestic and international students. Application fee: $80 ($100 for international students). Electronic applications accepted. *Financial support:* Fellowships with full tuition reimbursements, research assistantships with full tuition reimbursements, teaching assistantships with partial tuition reimbursements, institutionally sponsored loans, traineeships, health care benefits, and unspecified assistantships available. Financial award application deadline: 3/1; financial award applicants required to submit FAFSA. *Faculty research:* Condensed-matter physics, plasma physics, astrophysics, particle physics, chemical and materials physics, biophysics. *Unit head:* William H. Parker, Chair, 949-824-5948, Fax: 949-824-2174, E-mail: william.parker@uci.edu. *Application contact:* Michelle Fay Welch, Graduate Student Affairs Officer, 949-824-3496, Fax: 949-824-7988, E-mail: marons@uci.edu.

University of California, Los Angeles, Graduate Division, College of Letters and Science, Department of Physics and Astronomy, Program in Physics, Los Angeles, CA 90095. Offers physics (MS, PhD); physics education (MAT). MAT admits only applicants whose objective is Ph D. *Students:* 133 full-time (17 women); includes 19 minority (2 Black or African American,

non-Hispanic/Latino; 13 Asian, non-Hispanic/Latino; 3 Hispanic/Latino; 1 Two or more races, non-Hispanic/Latino), 30 international. Average age 26. 257 applicants, 23% accepted, 19 enrolled. In 2010, 10 master's, 20 doctorates awarded. Terminal master's awarded for partial completion of doctoral program. *Degree requirements:* For master's, comprehensive exam; for doctorate, thesis/dissertation, oral and written qualifying exams. *Entrance requirements:* For master's, GRE General Test, GRE Subject Test (physics), minimum GPA of 3.0, BS in related field; for doctorate, GRE General Test, GRE Subject Test (physics), minimum undergraduate GPA of 3.0, BS in related field. *Application deadline:* For fall admission, 12/15 for domestic and international students. Application fee: $70 ($90 for international students). Electronic applications accepted. *Financial support:* In 2010–11, 104 fellowships with full and partial tuition reimbursements, 105 research assistantships with full and partial tuition reimbursements, 84 teaching assistantships with full and partial tuition reimbursements were awarded; Federal Work-Study, institutionally sponsored loans, scholarships/grants, health care benefits, tuition waivers (full and partial), and unspecified assistantships also available. Financial award application deadline: 3/1; financial award applicants required to submit FAFSA. *Unit head:* Dr. James Rosenzweig, Chair, 310-825-3440, E-mail: rosenzweig@physics.ucla.edu. *Application contact:* Carol Finn, Graduate Counselor, 310-825-2307, E-mail: apply@physics.ucla.edu.

University of California, Merced, Division of Graduate Studies, School of Natural Sciences, Merced, CA 95343. Offers applied mathematics (MS, PhD); biological engineering and small-scale technologies (MS, PhD); environmental systems (MS, PhD); mechanical engineering and applied mechanics (MS, PhD); physics and chemistry (PhD); quantitative and systems biology (MS, PhD).

University of California, Riverside, Graduate Division, Department of Physics and Astronomy, Riverside, CA 92521-0102. Offers physics (MS, PhD). Part-time programs available. Terminal master's awarded for partial completion of doctoral program. *Degree requirements:* For master's, comprehensive exams or thesis; for doctorate, thesis/dissertation, qualifying exams. *Entrance requirements:* For master's and doctorate, GRE General Test, GRE Subject Test, minimum GPA of 3.2. Additional exam requirements/recommendations for international students: Required—TOEFL (minimum score 550 paper-based; 213 computer-based; 80 iBT). Electronic applications accepted. *Faculty research:* Laser physics and surface science, elementary particle and heavy ion physics, plasma physics, optical physics, astrophysics.

University of California, San Diego, Office of Graduate Studies, Department of Physics, La Jolla, CA 92093. Offers biophysics (MS, PhD); physics (MS, PhD); physics/materials physics (MS). *Degree requirements:* For doctorate, thesis/dissertation. *Entrance requirements:* For master's and doctorate, GRE General Test, GRE Subject Test. Additional exam requirements/recommendations for international students: Required—TOEFL. Electronic applications accepted.

University of California, Santa Barbara, Graduate Division, College of Letters and Sciences, Division of Mathematics, Life, and Physical Sciences, Department of Physics, Santa Barbara, CA 93106-9530. Offers PhD. *Faculty:* 51 full-time (7 women), 3 part-time/adjunct (0 women). *Students:* 136 full-time (22 women); includes 16 Asian, non-Hispanic/Latino; 4 Hispanic/Latino. Average age 26. 501 applicants, 18% accepted, 25 enrolled. In 2010, 20 doctorates awarded. Terminal master's awarded for partial completion of doctoral program. *Degree requirements:* For doctorate, comprehensive exam, thesis/dissertation. *Entrance requirements:* For doctorate, GRE General Test, GRE Subject Test (physics). Additional exam requirements/recommendations for international students: Required—TOEFL (minimum score 550 paper-based; 80 iBT), IELTS (minimum score 7). *Application deadline:* For fall admission, 12/15 priority date for domestic students, 12/15 for international students. Application fee: $70 ($90 for international students). Electronic applications accepted. *Financial support:* In 2010–11, 128 students received support, including 36 fellowships with full tuition reimbursements available (averaging $15,988 per year), 90 research assistantships with full tuition reimbursements available (averaging $14,230 per year), 54 teaching assistantships with partial tuition reimbursements available (averaging $9,690 per year); Federal Work-Study also available. Financial award application deadline: 12/15; financial award applicants required to submit FAFSA. *Faculty research:* High energy theory/experimental physics, condensed matter theory/experimental physics, astrophysics and cosmology, biophysics, gravity and relativity. Total annual research expenditures: $12.9 million. *Unit head:* Prof. Omar Blaes, Chair/Professor, 805-893-7239, Fax: 805-893-7239, E-mail: blaes@physics.ucsb.edu. *Application contact:* Prof. Leon Balents, Admissions Chair, 805-893-6381, Fax: 805-893-6381, E-mail: balents@physics.ucsb.edu.

University of California, Santa Cruz, Division of Graduate Studies, Division of Physical and Biological Sciences, Department of Physics, Santa Cruz, CA 95064. Offers MS, PhD. *Students:* 57 full-time (12 women); includes 15 minority (1 Black or African American, non-Hispanic/Latino; 4 Asian, non-Hispanic/Latino; 9 Hispanic/Latino; 1 Native Hawaiian or other Pacific Islander, non-Hispanic/Latino), 3 international. Average age 27. 149 applicants, 15% accepted, 9 enrolled. In 2010, 4 master's, 3 doctorates awarded. Terminal master's awarded for partial completion of doctoral program. *Degree requirements:* For master's, thesis; for doctorate, one foreign language, thesis/dissertation, qualifying exam. *Entrance requirements:* For master's and doctorate, GRE General Test, GRE Subject Test. Additional exam requirements/recommendations for international students: Required—TOEFL (minimum score 550 paper-based; 220 computer-based; 83 iBT); Recommended—IELTS (minimum score 8). *Application deadline:* For fall admission, 1/15 for domestic and international students. Application fee: $70 ($90 for international students). Electronic applications accepted. *Financial support:* Fellowships, research assistantships, teaching assistantships, institutionally sponsored loans and tuition waivers available. Financial award applicants required to submit FAFSA. *Faculty research:* Theoretical and experimental particle physics, astrophysics and cosmology, condensed matter physics. *Unit head:* Jennifer Raab, Graduate Program Coordinator, 831-459-4122, E-mail: jhild@ucsc.edu. *Application contact:* Jennifer Raab, Graduate Program Coordinator, 831-459-4122, E-mail: jhild@ucsc.edu.

University of Central Florida, College of Sciences, Department of Physics, Orlando, FL 32816. Offers MS, PhD. Part-time and evening/weekend programs available. *Faculty:* 33 full-time (7 women), 1 (woman) part-time/adjunct. *Students:* 82 full-time (17 women), 3 part-time (1 woman); includes 1 Black or African American, non-Hispanic/Latino; 4 Hispanic/Latino, 55 international. Average age 29. 101 applicants, 55% accepted, 16 enrolled. In 2010, 4 master's, 11 doctorates awarded. *Degree requirements:* For master's, thesis or alternative; for doctorate, thesis/dissertation, candidacy and qualifying exams. *Entrance requirements:* For master's, GRE General Test, minimum GPA of 3.0 in last 60 hours of course work; for doctorate, GRE General Test, GRE Subject Test, minimum GPA of 3.0 in last 60 hours or master's qualifying exam. Additional exam requirements/recommendations for international students: Required—TOEFL. *Application deadline:* For fall admission, 2/15 priority date for domestic students. Application fee: $30. Electronic applications accepted. *Expenses:* Tuition, state resident: part-time $256.56 per credit hour. Tuition, nonresident: part-time $1011.52 per credit hour. Part-time tuition and fees vary according to program. *Financial support:* In 2010–11, 67 students received support, including 7 fellowships with partial tuition reimbursements available (averaging $3,200 per year), 61 research assistantships with partial tuition reimbursements available (averaging $10,300 per year), 41 teaching assistantships with partial tuition reimbursements available (averaging $10,200 per year); career-related internships or fieldwork, Federal Work-Study, institutionally sponsored loans, tuition waivers (partial), and unspecified assistantships also available. Financial award application deadline: 3/1; financial award applicants required to submit FAFSA. *Faculty research:* Atomic-molecular physics, condensed-matter physics, biophysics of proteins, laser physics. *Unit head:* Dr. Talat Rahman, Chair, 407-823-5785, E-mail: trahman@mail.ucf.edu. *Application contact:* Dr. Talat Rahman, Chair, 407-823-5785, E-mail: trahman@mail.ucf.edu.

University of Central Oklahoma, College of Graduate Studies and Research, College of Mathematics and Science, Department of Physics and Engineering, Edmond, OK 73034-5209. Offers MS. Part-time programs available. *Degree requirements:* For master's, thesis optional. *Entrance requirements:* For master's, 24 hours of course work in physics. Additional exam requirements/recommendations for international students: Required—TOEFL (minimum score 550 paper-based; 213 computer-based). Electronic applications accepted. *Faculty research:* Acoustics, solid-state physics/optical properties, molecular dynamics, nuclear physics, crystallography.

University of Chicago, Division of the Physical Sciences, Department of Physics, Chicago, IL 60637-1513. Offers PhD. *Degree requirements:* For doctorate, comprehensive exam, thesis/dissertation. *Entrance requirements:* For doctorate, bachelor's degree in physics or related area. Additional exam requirements/recommendations for international students: Required—TOEFL (minimum score 102 iBT).

University of Chicago, Division of the Physical Sciences, Program in the Physical Sciences, Chicago, IL 60637-1513. Offers MS. Part-time programs available. *Degree requirements:* For master's, thesis. *Entrance requirements:* For master's, GRE. Additional exam requirements/recommendations for international students: Required—TOEFL.

University of Cincinnati, Graduate School, McMicken College of Arts and Sciences, Department of Physics, Cincinnati, OH 45221. Offers MS, PhD. Terminal master's awarded for partial completion of doctoral program. *Degree requirements:* For master's, thesis optional; for doctorate, thesis/dissertation. *Entrance requirements:* For master's and doctorate, GRE General Test, GRE Subject Test. Additional exam requirements/recommendations for international students: Required—TOEFL (minimum score 540 paper-based; 207 computer-based). Electronic applications accepted. *Faculty research:* Condensed matter physics, experimental particle physics, theoretical high energy physics, astronomy and astrophysics, computational physics.

University of Colorado at Colorado Springs, College of Letters, Arts and Sciences, Master of Sciences Program, Colorado Springs, CO 80933-7150. Offers applied science—bioscience (M Sc); applied science—physics (M Sc); biology (M Sc); chemistry (M Sc); health promotion (M Sc); mathematics (M Sc); physics (M Sc); sports medicine (M Sc); sports nutrition (M Sc). Part-time programs available. *Students:* 19 full-time (10 women), 11 part-time (4 women); includes 2 Asian, non-Hispanic/Latino; 3 Hispanic/Latino. Average age 34. 20 applicants, 55% accepted, 7 enrolled. In 2010, 14 master's awarded. *Degree requirements:* For master's, thesis or alternative. *Entrance requirements:* For master's, minimum GPA of 2.75. *Application deadline:* For fall admission, 6/1 priority date for domestic students; for spring admission, 12/1 for domestic students. Application fee: $60 ($75 for international students). *Expenses:* Contact institution. *Financial support:* Fellowships, research assistantships, teaching assistantships, career-related internships or fieldwork, Federal Work-Study, and scholarships/grants available. Support available to part-time students. Financial award application deadline: 3/1; financial award applicants required to submit FAFSA. *Faculty research:* Biomechanics and physiology of elite athletic training, genetic engineering in yeast and bacteria including phage display and DNA repair, immunology and cell biology, synthetic organic chemistry. *Application contact:* Michael Sanderson, Information Contact, 719-255-3417, Fax: 719-255-3037, E-mail: gradschl@uccs.edu.

University of Colorado Boulder, Graduate School, College of Arts and Sciences, Department of Physics, Boulder, CO 80309. Offers chemical physics (PhD); geophysics (PhD); liquid crystal science and technology (PhD); mathematical physics (PhD); medical physics (PhD); optical sciences and engineering (PhD); physics (MS, PhD). *Faculty:* 50 full-time (7 women). *Students:* 147 full-time (28 women), 72 part-time (10 women); includes 12 minority (6 Asian, non-Hispanic/Latino; 6 Hispanic/Latino), 75 international. Average age 27. 503 applicants, 37 enrolled. In 2010, 16 master's, 31 doctorates awarded. Terminal master's awarded for partial completion of doctoral program. *Degree requirements:* For master's, comprehensive exam, thesis or alternative; for doctorate, comprehensive exam, thesis/dissertation. *Entrance requirements:* For master's and doctorate, GRE General Test, GRE Subject Test, minimum undergraduate GPA of 3.0. Additional exam requirements/recommendations for international students: Required—TOEFL. *Application deadline:* For fall admission, 1/15 priority date for domestic students, 1/15 for international students. Applications are processed on a rolling basis. Application fee: $50 ($60 for international students). Electronic applications accepted. *Financial support:* In 2010–11, 21 fellowships with full tuition reimbursements (averaging $15,999 per year), 146 research assistantships with full tuition reimbursements (averaging $16,586 per year) were awarded; scholarships/grants also available. Financial award application deadline: 1/15. *Faculty research:* Atomic and molecular physics, nuclear physics, condensed matter, elementary particle physics, laser or optical physics, plasma physics, geophysics, astrophysics and chemical physics. Total annual research expenditures: $16.8 million.

University of Connecticut, Graduate School, College of Liberal Arts and Sciences, Department of Physics, Storrs, CT 06269. Offers MS, PhD. *Degree requirements:* For master's, comprehensive exam; for doctorate, thesis/dissertation. *Entrance requirements:* For master's and doctorate, GRE General Test, GRE Subject Test. Additional exam requirements/recommendations for international students: Required—TOEFL (minimum score 550 paper-based; 213 computer-based). Electronic applications accepted.

University of Delaware, College of Arts and Sciences, Department of Physics and Astronomy, Newark, DE 19716. Offers MS, PhD. Part-time programs available. Terminal master's awarded for partial completion of doctoral program. *Degree requirements:* For master's, thesis; for doctorate, thesis/dissertation. *Entrance requirements:* For master's and doctorate, GRE General Test, GRE Subject Test. Additional exam requirements/recommendations for international students: Required—TOEFL (minimum score 600 paper-based; 250 computer-based). Electronic applications accepted. *Faculty research:* Magnetoresistance and magnetic materials, ultrafast optical phenomena, superfluidity, elementary particle physics, stellar atmospheres and interiors.

University of Denver, Faculty of Natural Sciences and Mathematics, Department of Physics and Astronomy, Denver, CO 80208. Offers MS, PhD. Part-time programs available. *Faculty:* 10 full-time (2 women), 1 part-time/adjunct (0 women). *Students:* 7 full-time (2 women), 10 part-time (3 women); includes 2 minority (1 Asian, non-Hispanic/Latino; 1 Hispanic/Latino), 2 international. Average age 28. 28 applicants, 36% accepted, 5 enrolled. In 2010, 1 doctorate awarded. Terminal master's awarded for partial completion of doctoral program. *Degree requirements:* For master's, thesis optional; for doctorate, thesis/dissertation. *Entrance requirements:* For master's and doctorate, GRE General Test; GRE Subject Test in physics (strongly preferred). Additional exam requirements/recommendations for international students: Required—TOEFL (minimum score 550 paper-based; 80 iBT). *Application deadline:* For fall admission, 3/1 priority date for domestic students. Applications are processed on a rolling basis. Application fee: $60. Electronic applications accepted. *Expenses:* Tuition: Full-time $35,604; part-time $29,670 per year. Required fees: $687 per year. Tuition and fees vary according to program. *Financial support:* In 2010–11, 11 research assistantships with full and partial tuition reimbursements (averaging $19,299 per year), 7 teaching assistantships with full and partial tuition reimbursements (averaging $19,299 per year) were awarded; career-related internships or fieldwork, Federal Work-Study, institutionally sponsored loans, scholarships/grants, and unspecified assistantships also available. Support available to part-time students. Financial award application deadline: 3/1; financial award applicants required to submit FAFSA. *Faculty research:* Atomic and molecular beams and collisions, infrared astronomy, acoustic emission from stressed solids, nano materials. *Unit head:* Dr. Davor Balzar, Chair, 303-871-2238, E-mail: davor.balzar@du.edu. *Application contact:* Barbara Stephen, Assistant to the Chair, 303-871-2238, E-mail: barbara.stephen@du.edu.

University of Florida, Graduate School, College of Liberal Arts and Sciences, Department of Physics, Gainesville, FL 32611. Offers MS, MST, PhD. *Faculty:* 45 full-time (4 women), 2 part-time/adjunct (0 women). *Students:* 154 full-time (22 women), 1 part-time (0 women);

Physics

University of Florida (continued)

includes 5 Asian, non-Hispanic/Latino; 7 Hispanic/Latino, 82 international. Average age 27. 313 applicants, 22% accepted, 24 enrolled. In 2010, 5 master's, 15 doctorates awarded. Terminal master's awarded for partial completion of doctoral program. *Degree requirements:* For doctorate, comprehensive exam, thesis/dissertation. *Entrance requirements:* For master's and doctorate, GRE General Test, minimum GPA of 3.0. Additional exam requirements/recommendations for international students: Required—TOEFL (minimum score 550 paper-based; 213 computer-based; 80 iBT), IELTS (minimum score 6). *Application deadline:* For spring admission, 2/1 for domestic students, 1/1 for international students. Applications are processed on a rolling basis. Application fee: $30. Electronic applications accepted. *Expenses:* Tuition, state resident: full-time $10,915.92. Tuition, nonresident: full-time $28,309. *Financial support:* In 2010–11, 199 students received support, including 34 fellowships with tuition reimbursements available, 80 research assistantships with tuition reimbursements available (averaging $17,799 per year), 85 teaching assistantships with tuition reimbursements available (averaging $18,920 per year); unspecified assistantships also available. Financial award applicants required to submit FAFSA. *Faculty research:* Astrophysics, biological physics (molecular, magnetic resonance imaging, spectroscopy, biomagnetism), chemical physics (molecular, nano-scale physics, solid state, surface physics, quantum chemistry, quantum electron dynamics, molecular biology), experimental and theory condensed matter physics, low temperature physics (theory and experimental, mathematical physics. Total annual research expenditures: $8.4 million. *Unit head:* John M. Yelton, PhD, Chair, 352-392-8475, Fax: 352-392-0524, E-mail: yelton@phys.ufl.edu. *Application contact:* Dr. James N. Fry, Graduate Coordinator, 352-392-6692, Fax: 352-392-0524, E-mail: fry@ufl.edu.

University of Georgia, College of Arts and Sciences, Department of Physics and Astronomy, Athens, GA 30602. Offers physics (MS, PhD). *Faculty:* 21 full-time (2 women). *Students:* 47 full-time (14 women), 2 part-time (1 woman), 27 international. 84 applicants, 26% accepted, 11 enrolled. In 2010, 1 master's, 12 doctorates awarded. *Degree requirements:* For master's, thesis; for doctorate, one foreign language, thesis/dissertation. *Entrance requirements:* For master's and doctorate, GRE General Test. *Application deadline:* For fall admission, 7/1 priority date for domestic students; for spring admission, 11/15 for domestic students. Application fee: $50. Electronic applications accepted. *Expenses:* Tuition, state resident: full-time $7200; part-time $344 per credit hour. Tuition, nonresident: full-time $21,900; part-time $944 per credit hour. Tuition and fees vary according to course load and program. *Financial support:* Fellowships, research assistantships, teaching assistantships, unspecified assistantships available. *Unit head:* Dr. William M. Dennis, Head, 706-542-2882, Fax: 706-542-2492, E-mail: bill@physast.uga.edu. *Application contact:* Dr. Loris Magnani, Graduate Coordinator, 706-542-2476, Fax: 706-542-2492, E-mail: loris@physast.uga.edu.

University of Guelph, Graduate Studies, College of Physical and Engineering Science, Guelph-Waterloo Physics Institute, Guelph, ON N1G 2W1, Canada. Offers M Sc, PhD. M Sc, PhD offered jointly with University of Waterloo. Part-time programs available. *Degree requirements:* For master's, project or thesis; for doctorate, comprehensive exam, thesis/dissertation. *Entrance requirements:* For master's, GRE Subject Test, minimum B average for honors degree; for doctorate, GRE Subject Test, minimum B average. Additional exam requirements/recommendations for international students: Required—TOEFL (minimum score 550 paper-based; 213 computer-based), TWE (minimum score 4). *Faculty research:* Condensed matter and material physics, quantum computing, astrophysics and gravitation, industrial and applied physics, subatomic physics.

University of Hawaii at Manoa, Graduate Division, College of Natural Sciences, Department of Physics and Astronomy, Program in Physics, Honolulu, HI 96822. Offers MS, PhD. Part-time programs available. *Faculty:* 23 full-time (0 women), 5 part-time/adjunct (0 women). *Students:* 27 full-time (5 women); includes 7 minority (1 Black or African American, non-Hispanic/Latino; 3 Asian, non-Hispanic/Latino; 2 Hispanic/Latino; 1 Two or more races, non-Hispanic/Latino), 3 international. Average age 30. 43 applicants, 42% accepted, 3 enrolled. In 2010, 5 master's, 1 doctorate awarded. *Degree requirements:* For master's, thesis optional; for doctorate, comprehensive exam, thesis/dissertation. *Entrance requirements:* For master's and doctorate, GRE General Test. Additional exam requirements/recommendations for international students: Required—TOEFL (minimum score 560 paper-based; 220 computer-based; 83 iBT), IELTS (minimum score 5). *Application deadline:* For fall admission, 1/15 for domestic and international students; for spring admission, 8/1 for domestic and international students. Application fee: $60. *Financial support:* In 2010–11, 1 student received support, including 9 fellowships (averaging $989 per year), 15 research assistantships (averaging $19,034 per year), 9 teaching assistantships (averaging $15,767 per year). Total annual research expenditures: $2.5 million. *Application contact:* Pui K. Lam, Graduate Chairperson, 808-956-7087, Fax: 808-956-7107, E-mail: plam@hawaii.edu.

University of Houston, College of Natural Sciences and Mathematics, Department of Physics, Houston, TX 77204. Offers MA, PhD. Part-time programs available. *Faculty:* 20 full-time (1 woman), 4 part-time/adjunct (1 woman). *Students:* 83 full-time (25 women), 12 part-time (2 women); includes 4 Asian, non-Hispanic/Latino; 2 Hispanic/Latino, 65 international. Average age 30. 101 applicants, 53% accepted, 24 enrolled. In 2010, 14 master's, 13 doctorates awarded. Terminal master's awarded for partial completion of doctoral program. *Entrance requirements:* For master's and doctorate, GRE General Test. *Application deadline:* For fall admission, 7/1 for domestic students; for spring admission, 11/1 for domestic students. Applications are processed on a rolling basis. Application fee: $0 ($75 for international students). Electronic applications accepted. *Expenses:* Tuition, state resident: full-time $8592; part-time $358 per credit hour. Tuition, nonresident: full-time $16,032; part-time $668 per credit hour. Required fees: $2889. Tuition and fees vary according to course load and program. *Financial support:* In 2010–11, 34 research assistantships with partial tuition reimbursements (averaging $11,136 per year), 24 teaching assistantships with partial tuition reimbursements (averaging $13,104 per year) were awarded; career-related internships or fieldwork, Federal Work-Study, institutionally sponsored loans, scholarships/grants, health care benefits, and unspecified assistantships also available. Support available to part-time students. Financial award application deadline: 2/1. *Faculty research:* Condensed-matter, particle physics; high-temperature superconductivity; material/space physics; chaos. *Unit head:* Dr. Lawrence Pinsky, Chairperson, 713-743-3550, Fax: 713-743-3589, E-mail: pinsky@uh.edu. *Application contact:* Dr. Lawrence Pinsky, Chairperson, 713-743-3550, Fax: 713-743-3589, E-mail: pinsky@uh.edu.

University of Houston–Clear Lake, School of Science and Computer Engineering, Program in Physics, Houston, TX 77058-1098. Offers MS. Part-time and evening/weekend programs available. *Entrance requirements:* For master's, GRE General Test. Additional exam requirements/recommendations for international students: Required—TOEFL (minimum score 550 paper-based; 213 computer-based).

University of Idaho, College of Graduate Studies, College of Science, Department of Physics, Moscow, ID 83844-2282. Offers MS, PhD. *Faculty:* 5 full-time. *Students:* 26 full-time, 2 part-time. Average age 31. In 2010, 8 master's, 1 doctorate awarded. *Degree requirements:* For master's, thesis; for doctorate, thesis/dissertation. *Entrance requirements:* For master's, GRE, minimum GPA of 2.8; for doctorate, GRE, minimum undergraduate GPA of 2.8, 3.0 graduate. *Application deadline:* For fall admission, 8/1 for domestic students; for spring admission, 12/15 for domestic students. Applications are processed on a rolling basis. Application fee: $60. Electronic applications accepted. *Expenses:* Tuition, nonresident: part-time $580 per credit. Required fees: $306 per credit. *Financial support:* Research assistantships, teaching assistantships available. Financial award applicants required to submit FAFSA. *Faculty research:* Condensed matter physics, nuclear physics, biological physics, astronomy/planetary science. *Unit head:* Dr. David McIlroy, Chair, 208-885-6380, E-mail: physics@uidaho.edu. *Application contact:* Dr. David McIlroy, Chair, 208-885-6380, E-mail: physics@uidaho.edu.

University of Illinois at Chicago, Graduate College, College of Liberal Arts and Sciences, Department of Physics, Chicago, IL 60607-7128. Offers MS, PhD. Terminal master's awarded for partial completion of doctoral program. *Degree requirements:* For doctorate, thesis/dissertation. *Entrance requirements:* For master's and doctorate, GRE General Test, minimum GPA of 3.0. Additional exam requirements/recommendations for international students: Required—TOEFL. Electronic applications accepted. *Faculty research:* High-energy, laser, and solid-state physics.

University of Illinois at Urbana–Champaign, Graduate College, College of Engineering, Department of Physics, Champaign, IL 61820. Offers physics (MS, PhD); teaching of physics (MS). *Faculty:* 52 full-time (6 women), 1 part-time/adjunct (0 women). *Students:* 180 full-time (25 women), 81 part-time (9 women); includes 3 Black or African American, non-Hispanic/Latino; 16 Asian, non-Hispanic/Latino; 4 Hispanic/Latino; 2 Two or more races, non-Hispanic/Latino, 127 international. 479 applicants, 10% accepted, 44 enrolled. In 2010, 15 master's, 51 doctorates awarded. *Entrance requirements:* For master's, GRE, minimum GPA of 3.0; for doctorate, GRE, minimum GPA of 3.5. Additional exam requirements/recommendations for international students: Required—TOEFL (minimum score 550 paper-based; 213 computer-based; 79 iBT) or IELTS (minimum score 6.5). *Application deadline:* Applications are processed on a rolling basis. Application fee: $75 ($90 for international students). Electronic applications accepted. *Financial support:* In 2010–11, 23 fellowships, 180 research assistantships, 128 teaching assistantships were awarded; tuition waivers (full and partial) also available. *Unit head:* Dale J. VanHarlingen, Head, 217-333-3760, Fax: 217-244-4293, E-mail: dvh@illinois.edu. *Application contact:* Melodee Jo Schweighart, Office Manager, 217-333-3645, Fax: 217-244-5073, E-mail: mschweig@illinois.edu.

The University of Iowa, Graduate College, College of Liberal Arts and Sciences, Department of Physics and Astronomy, Program in Physics, Iowa City, IA 52242-1316. Offers MS, PhD. *Degree requirements:* For master's, thesis optional, exam; for doctorate, comprehensive exam, thesis/dissertation. *Entrance requirements:* For master's and doctorate, GRE General Test, minimum GPA of 3.0. Additional exam requirements/recommendations for international students: Required—TOEFL (minimum score 550 paper-based; 213 computer-based; 81 iBT). Electronic applications accepted.

The University of Kansas, Graduate Studies, College of Liberal Arts and Sciences, Department of Physics and Astronomy, Lawrence, KS 66045. Offers computational physics and astronomy (MS); physics (MS, PhD). *Students:* 39 full-time (9 women), 4 part-time (1 woman); includes 2 minority (1 Black or African American, non-Hispanic/Latino; 1 Hispanic/Latino), 13 international. Average age 28. 41 applicants, 29% accepted, 5 enrolled. In 2010, 2 master's, 2 doctorates awarded. Terminal master's awarded for partial completion of doctoral program. *Degree requirements:* For master's, thesis (for some programs); for doctorate, comprehensive exam, thesis/dissertation, computer skills, communication skills. *Entrance requirements:* For master's and doctorate, GRE Subject Test (physics), undergraduate degree. Additional exam requirements/recommendations for international students: Required—TOEFL. *Application deadline:* For fall admission, 5/1 priority date for domestic and international students; for spring admission, 11/15 for domestic and international students. Applications are processed on a rolling basis. Application fee: $55 ($65 for international students). Electronic applications accepted. *Expenses:* Tuition, state resident: full-time $7092; part-time $295.50 per credit hour. Tuition, nonresident: full-time $16,590; part-time $691.25 per credit hour. Required fees: $858; $71.49 per credit hour. Tuition and fees vary according to course load, campus/location and program. *Financial support:* Fellowships with full and partial tuition reimbursements, research assistantships with full and partial tuition reimbursements, teaching assistantships with full and partial tuition reimbursements, health care benefits and unspecified assistantships available. Financial award application deadline: 5/1. *Faculty research:* Condensed-matter, cosmology, elementary particles, nuclear physics, space physics, astrophysics, astrobiology, biophysics, high energy. *Unit head:* Dr. Stephen J. Sanders, Chair, 785-864-4626, Fax: 785-864-5262. *Application contact:* Tess Gratton, Graduate Admission Specialist, 785-864-4626, Fax: 785-864-5262, E-mail: physics@ku.edu.

University of Kentucky, Graduate School, College of Arts and Sciences, Program in Physics and Astronomy, Lexington, KY 40506-0032. Offers physics (MS, PhD). *Degree requirements:* For master's, comprehensive exam, thesis optional; for doctorate, comprehensive exam, thesis/dissertation. *Entrance requirements:* For master's, GRE General Test, minimum undergraduate GPA of 2.75; for doctorate, GRE General Test, minimum graduate GPA of 3.0. Additional exam requirements/recommendations for international students: Required—TOEFL (minimum score 550 paper-based; 213 computer-based). Electronic applications accepted. *Faculty research:* Astrophysics, active galactic nuclei, and radio astronomy; Rydbert atoms, and electron scattering; TOF spectroscopy, hyperon interactions and muons; particle theory, lattice gauge theory, quark, and skyrmion models.

University of Lethbridge, School of Graduate Studies, Lethbridge, AB T1K 3M4, Canada. Offers accounting (MScM); addictions counseling (M Sc); agricultural biotechnology (M Sc); agricultural studies (M Sc, MA); anthropology (MA); archaeology (MA); art (MA, MFA); biochemistry (M Sc); biological sciences (M Sc); biomolecular science (PhD); biosystems and biodiversity (PhD); Canadian studies (MA); chemistry (M Sc); computer science (M Sc); computer science and geographical information science (M Sc); counseling psychology (M Ed); dramatic arts (MA); earth, space, and physical science (PhD); economics (MA); educational leadership (M Ed); English (MA); environmental science (M Sc); evolution and behavior (PhD); exercise science (M Sc); finance (MScM); French (MA); French/German (MA); French/Spanish (MA); general education (M Ed); general management (MScM); geography (M Sc, MA); German (MA); health science (M Sc); history (MA); human resource management and labour relations (MScM); individualized multidisciplinary (M Sc, MA); information systems (MScM); international management (MScM); kinesiology (M Sc, MA); management (M Sc, MA); marketing (MScM); mathematics (M Sc); music (M Mus, MA); Native American studies (MA); neuroscience (M Sc, PhD); new media (MA); nursing (M Sc); philosophy (MA); physics (M Sc); policy and strategy (MScM); political science (MA); psychology (M Sc, MA); religious studies (MA); social sciences (MA); sociology (MA); theatre and dramatic arts (MFA); theoretical and computational science (PhD); urban and regional studies (MA); women's studies (MA). Part-time and evening/weekend programs available. *Degree requirements:* For doctorate, comprehensive exam, thesis/dissertation. *Entrance requirements:* For master's, GMAT (M Sc in management), bachelor's degree in related field, minimum GPA of 3.0 during previous 20 graded semester courses, 2 years teaching or related experience (M Ed); for doctorate, master's degree, minimum graduate GPA of 3.5. Additional exam requirements/recommendations for international students: Required—TOEFL. *Faculty research:* Movement and brain plasticity, gibberellin physiology, photosynthesis, carbon cycling, molecular properties of main-group ring components.

University of Louisiana at Lafayette, College of Sciences, Department of Physics, Lafayette, LA 70504. Offers MS. Part-time programs available. *Degree requirements:* For master's, thesis. *Entrance requirements:* For master's, GRE General Test, minimum GPA of 2.75. Additional exam requirements/recommendations for international students: Required—TOEFL (minimum score 550 paper-based; 213 computer-based). Electronic applications accepted. *Faculty research:* Environmental physics, geophysics, astrophysics, acoustics, atomic physics.

University of Louisville, Graduate School, College of Arts and Sciences, Department of Physics and Astronomy, Louisville, KY 40292. Offers physics (MS, PhD). Part-time programs available. *Faculty:* 17 full-time (2 women), 8 part-time/adjunct (0 women). *Students:* 25 full-time (6 women), 3 part-time; includes 1 Black or African American, non-Hispanic/Latino, 10 international. Average age 33. 35 applicants, 43% accepted, 12 enrolled. In 2010, 5 master's awarded. Terminal master's awarded for partial completion of doctoral program. *Degree requirements:* For master's, thesis optional; for doctorate, comprehensive exam, thesis/dissertation. *Entrance requirements:* For master's, GRE General Test. Additional exam

requirements/recommendations for international students: Required—TOEFL (minimum score 550 paper-based; 213 computer-based; 80 iBT). *Application deadline:* For fall admission, 3/1 priority date for domestic and international students. Applications are processed on a rolling basis. Application fee: $50. Electronic applications accepted. *Expenses:* Tuition, state resident: full-time $9144; part-time $508 per credit hour. Tuition, nonresident: full-time $19,026; part-time $1057 per credit hour. Tuition and fees vary according to program and reciprocity agreements. *Financial support:* In 2010–11, 17 students received support; fellowships, research assistantships, teaching assistantships available. *Faculty research:* Condensed matter physics; atmospheric science; high energy physics; astrophysics; atomic, molecular, and optical physics. *Unit head:* Dr. Chakram S. Jayanthi, Professor and Chair of Physics and Astronomy, 502-852-6790, Fax: 502-852-0742, E-mail: csjaya01@louisville.edu. *Application contact:* Dr. Chris L. Davis, Professor of Physics, 502-852-0852, Fax: 502-852-0742, E-mail: c.l.davis@louisville.edu.

University of Maine, Graduate School, College of Education and Human Development, Interdisciplinary Program in Teaching, Orono, ME 04469. Offers earth sciences (MST); generalist (MST); mathematics (MST); physics and astronomy (MST). *Students:* 10 full-time (7 women), 20 part-time (17 women); includes 1 minority (Black or African American, non-Hispanic/Latino). Average age 40. 13 applicants, 46% accepted, 6 enrolled. In 2010, 17 master's awarded. *Entrance requirements:* For master's, GRE General Test, MAT. Application fee: $65. *Expenses:* Tuition, state resident: full-time $400. Tuition, nonresident: full-time $1050. *Unit head:* Dr. Susan McKay, Director, 207-581-1016. *Application contact:* Scott G. Delcourt, Associate Dean of the Graduate School, 207-581-3219, Fax: 207-581-3232, E-mail: graduate@maine.edu.

University of Maine, Graduate School, College of Liberal Arts and Sciences, Department of Physics and Astronomy, Orono, ME 04469. Offers engineering physics (M Eng); physics (MS, PhD). *Faculty:* 14 full-time (1 woman), 4 part-time/adjunct (2 women). *Students:* 18 full-time (4 women), 21 part-time (3 women), 7 international. Average age 29. 19 applicants, 37% accepted, 7 enrolled. In 2010, 1 master's, 5 doctorates awarded. Terminal master's awarded for partial completion of doctoral program. *Degree requirements:* For doctorate, thesis/dissertation. *Entrance requirements:* For master's, GRE General Test, GRE Subject Test; for doctorate, GRE General Test. Additional exam requirements/recommendations for international students: Required—TOEFL. *Application deadline:* For fall admission, 2/1 priority date for domestic students. Applications are processed on a rolling basis. Application fee: $65. Electronic applications accepted. *Expenses:* Tuition, state resident: full-time $400. Tuition, nonresident: full-time $1050. *Financial support:* In 2010–11, 5 research assistantships with tuition reimbursements (averaging $14,842 per year), 15 teaching assistantships with tuition reimbursements (averaging $13,815 per year) were awarded; tuition waivers (full and partial) also available. Financial award application deadline: 3/1. *Faculty research:* Solid-state physics, fluids, biophysics, plasma physics, surface physics. *Unit head:* Dr. Susan McKay, Chair, 207-581-1015, Fax: 207-581-3410. *Application contact:* Scott G. Delcourt, Associate Dean of the Graduate School, 207-581-3291, Fax: 207-581-3232, E-mail: graduate@maine.edu.

The University of Manchester, School of Earth, Atmospheric and Environmental Sciences, Manchester, United Kingdom. Offers atmospheric sciences (M Phil, M Sc, PhD); basin studies and petroleum geosciences (M Phil, M Sc, PhD); earth, atmospheric and environmental sciences (M Phil, M Sc, PhD); environmental geochemistry and cosmochemistry (M Phil, M Sc, PhD); isotope geochemistry and cosmochemistry (M Phil, M Sc, PhD); paleontology (M Phil, M Sc, PhD); physics and chemistry of minerals and fluids (M Phil, M Sc, PhD); structural and petrological geosciences (M Phil, M Sc, PhD).

The University of Manchester, School of Physics and Astronomy, Manchester, United Kingdom. Offers astronomy and astrophysics (M Sc, PhD); biological physics (M Sc, PhD); condensed matter physics (M Sc, PhD); nonlinear and liquid crystals physics (M Sc, PhD); nuclear physics (M Sc, PhD); particle physics (M Sc, PhD); photon physics (M Sc, PhD); physics (M Sc, PhD); theoretical physics (M Sc, PhD).

University of Manitoba, Faculty of Graduate Studies, Faculty of Science, Department of Physics and Astronomy, Winnipeg, MB R3T 2N2, Canada. Offers M Sc, PhD. *Degree requirements:* For master's, thesis; for doctorate, one foreign language, thesis/dissertation.

University of Maryland, Baltimore County, Graduate School, College of Arts, Humanities and Social Sciences, Department of Education, Program in Teaching, Baltimore, MD 21250. Offers early childhood education (MAT); elementary education (MAT); secondary education (MAT), including art, biology, chemistry, dance, earth/space science, English, foreign language, mathematics, music, physics, theatre; secondary science (MAT), including social studies. Part-time and evening/weekend programs available. *Faculty:* 24 full-time (18 women), 25 part-time/adjunct (19 women). *Students:* 59 full-time (46 women), 56 part-time (42 women); includes 1 Black or African American, non-Hispanic/Latino; 8 Asian, non-Hispanic/Latino; 3 Hispanic/Latino, 3 international. Average age 31. 88 applicants, 57% accepted, 39 enrolled. In 2010, 106 master's awarded. *Degree requirements:* For master's, comprehensive exam (for some programs), thesis (for some programs). *Entrance requirements:* For master's, PRAXIS I and II, minimum GPA of 3.0. Additional exam requirements/recommendations for international students: Required—TOEFL. *Application deadline:* For fall admission, 6/1 for domestic students; for spring admission, 11/1 for domestic students. Applications are processed on a rolling basis. Application fee: $50. Electronic applications accepted. *Financial support:* In 2010–11, 6 students received support, including research assistantships with full tuition reimbursements available (averaging $12,000 per year); career-related internships or fieldwork, Federal Work-Study, scholarships/grants, tuition waivers, and unspecified assistantships also available. Financial award application deadline: 3/1. *Faculty research:* STEM teacher education, culturally sensitive pedagogy, ESOL/bilingual education, early childhood education, language, literacy and culture. *Unit head:* Dr. Susan M. Blunck, Director, 410-455-2869, Fax: 410-455-3986, E-mail: blunck@umbc.edu. *Application contact:* Cheryl Johnson, 410-455-3388, E-mail: blackwel@umbc.edu.

University of Maryland, Baltimore County, Graduate School, College of Natural and Mathematical Sciences, Department of Physics, Baltimore, MD 21250. Offers applied physics (MS, PhD), including astrophysics (PhD), optics, quantum optics (PhD), solid state physics; atmospheric physics (MS, PhD). Part-time programs available. *Faculty:* 24 full-time (3 women), 18 part-time/adjunct (2 women). *Students:* 43 full-time (14 women), 3 part-time (0 women); includes 4 Black or African American, non-Hispanic/Latino, 26 international. Average age 24. 33 applicants, 48% accepted, 10 enrolled. In 2010, 6 master's, 5 doctorates awarded. Terminal master's awarded for partial completion of doctoral program. *Degree requirements:* For master's, thesis optional; for doctorate, comprehensive exam, thesis/dissertation. *Entrance requirements:* For master's and doctorate, GRE General Test, GRE Subject Test (may be waived), minimum GPA of 3.0. Additional exam requirements/recommendations for international students: Required—TOEFL. *Application deadline:* For fall admission, 5/31 for domestic and international students; for spring admission, 11/30 for domestic students. Applications are processed on a rolling basis. Application fee: $50. Electronic applications accepted. *Financial support:* In 2010–11, 42 students received support, including 5 fellowships with full tuition reimbursements available (averaging $30,000 per year), 21 research assistantships with full tuition reimbursements available (averaging $26,000 per year), 16 teaching assistantships with full tuition reimbursements available (averaging $22,000 per year); career-related internships or fieldwork, scholarships/grants, health care benefits, and unspecified assistantships also available. Support available to part-time students. Financial award application deadline: 5/31. *Faculty research:* Quantum optics and computing, optics, astrophysics, atmospheric physics, nanophysics. Total annual research expenditures: $7.5 million. *Unit head:* Dr. L. Michael Hayden, Chairman, 410-455-2513, Fax: 410-455-1072, E-mail: hayden@umbc.edu. *Application contact:* Dr. Lazlo Takacs, Graduate Admissions Director, 410-455-2524, Fax: 410-455-1072, E-mail: takacs@umbc.edu.

University of Maryland, College Park, Academic Affairs, College of Computer, Mathematical and Natural Sciences, Department of Physics, College Park, MD 20742. Offers MS, PhD. Part-time and evening/weekend programs available. *Faculty:* 176 full-time (25 women), 33 part-time/adjunct (2 women). *Students:* 230 full-time (28 women), 7 part-time (2 women); includes 15 minority (3 Black or African American, non-Hispanic/Latino; 8 Asian, non-Hispanic/Latino; 3 Hispanic/Latino; 1 Two or more races, non-Hispanic/Latino), 81 international. 700 applicants, 18% accepted, 40 enrolled. In 2010, 12 master's, 34 doctorates awarded. Terminal master's awarded for partial completion of doctoral program. *Degree requirements:* For master's, thesis optional; for doctorate, thesis/dissertation. *Entrance requirements:* For master's, GRE General Test, GRE Subject Test (physics), minimum GPA of 3.0, 3 letters of recommendation; for doctorate, GRE General Test, GRE Subject Test (physics), 3 letters of recommendation. *Application deadline:* For fall admission, 1/15 for domestic and international students. Applications are processed on a rolling basis. Application fee: $75. Electronic applications accepted. *Expenses:* Tuition, area resident: Part-time $471 per credit hour. Tuition, state resident: part-time $471 per credit hour. Tuition, nonresident: part-time $1016 per credit hour. Required fees: $337 per term. *Financial support:* In 2010–11, 13 fellowships with full and partial tuition reimbursements (averaging $18,056 per year), 176 research assistantships (averaging $19,403 per year), 52 teaching assistantships (averaging $17,947 per year) were awarded; Federal Work-Study and scholarships/grants also available. Support available to part-time students. Financial award applicants required to submit FAFSA. *Faculty research:* Astrometeorology, superconductivity, particle astrophysics, plasma physics, elementary particle theory. Total annual research expenditures: $26.5 million. *Unit head:* Dr. Drew Baden, Chair, 301-405-5946, Fax: 301-405-0327, E-mail: drew@umd.edu. *Application contact:* Dean of the Graduate School, 301-401-0358.

University of Massachusetts Amherst, Graduate School, College of Natural Sciences, Department of Physics, Amherst, MA 01003. Offers MS, PhD. Part-time programs available. *Faculty:* 40 full-time (5 women). *Students:* 82 full-time (19 women), 1 part-time (0 women); includes 4 minority (3 Hispanic/Latino; 1 Two or more races, non-Hispanic/Latino), 46 international. Average age 28. 180 applicants, 25% accepted, 12 enrolled. In 2010, 10 master's, 9 doctorates awarded. Terminal master's awarded for partial completion of doctoral program. *Degree requirements:* For master's, thesis or alternative; for doctorate, comprehensive exam, thesis/dissertation. *Entrance requirements:* For master's and doctorate, GRE General Test, GRE Subject Test (physics). Additional exam requirements/recommendations for international students: Required—TOEFL (minimum score 550 paper-based; 213 computer-based; 80 iBT), IELTS (minimum score 6.5). *Application deadline:* For fall admission, 2/1 for domestic and international students. Applications are processed on a rolling basis. Application fee: $50 ($65 for international students). Electronic applications accepted. *Expenses:* Tuition, state resident: full-time $2640. Required fees: $8282. One-time fee: $357 full-time. *Financial support:* In 2010–11, 4 fellowships with full tuition reimbursements (averaging $1,267 per year), 61 research assistantships with full tuition reimbursements (averaging $14,194 per year), 47 teaching assistantships with full tuition reimbursements (averaging $9,313 per year) were awarded; career-related internships or fieldwork, Federal Work-Study, scholarships/grants, traineeships, health care benefits, tuition waivers (full), and unspecified assistantships also available. Support available to part-time students. Financial award application deadline: 2/1; financial award applicants required to submit FAFSA. *Unit head:* Dr. Krishna S. Kumar, Graduate Program Director, 413-545-2548, Fax: 413-545-0648. *Application contact:* Jean M. Ames, Supervisor of Admissions, 413-545-0722, Fax: 413-577-0010, E-mail: gradadm@grad.umass.edu.

University of Massachusetts Dartmouth, Graduate School, College of Engineering, Department of Physics, North Dartmouth, MA 02747-2300. Offers MS. Part-time programs available. *Faculty:* 10 full-time (1 woman), 1 part-time/adjunct (0 women). *Students:* 12 full-time (2 women), 7 part-time (2 women); includes 2 Two or more races, non-Hispanic/Latino, 7 international. Average age 25. 18 applicants, 89% accepted, 6 enrolled. In 2010, 7 master's awarded. *Degree requirements:* For master's, thesis or alternative. *Entrance requirements:* For master's, GRE (for financial consideration), 3 letters of recommendation. Additional exam requirements/recommendations for international students: Required—TOEFL (minimum score 500 paper-based). *Application deadline:* For fall admission, 4/20 priority date for domestic students, 2/20 priority date for international students; for spring admission, 11/15 priority date for domestic students, 9/15 priority date for international students. Applications are processed on a rolling basis. Application fee: $40 ($60 for international students). Electronic applications accepted. *Expenses:* Tuition, state resident: full-time $2071; part-time $86 per credit. Tuition, nonresident: full-time $8099; part-time $337 per credit. Required fees: $9446; $394 per credit. One-time fee: $75. Part-time tuition and fees vary according to class time, course load, degree level and reciprocity agreements. *Financial support:* In 2010–11, 7 research assistantships with full tuition reimbursements (averaging $8,154 per year), 8 teaching assistantships with full tuition reimbursements (averaging $12,500 per year) were awarded; Federal Work-Study also available. Support available to part-time students. Financial award application deadline: 3/1; financial award applicants required to submit FAFSA. *Faculty research:* AMO physics, ocean physics, experimental nuclear physics, theoretical particle physics, astrophysics. Total annual research expenditures: $353,413. *Unit head:* Dr. Gaurav Khanna, Director, 508-910-6605, Fax: 508-999-9115, E-mail: gkhanna@umassd.edu. *Application contact:* Elan Turcotte-Shamski, Graduate Admissions Officer, 508-999-8604, Fax: 508-999-8183, E-mail: graduate@umassd.edu.

University of Massachusetts Lowell, College of Arts and Sciences, Department of Physics and Applied Physics, Program in Physics, Lowell, MA 01854-2881. Offers MS, PhD. *Degree requirements:* For master's, thesis; for doctorate, 2 foreign languages, thesis/dissertation. *Entrance requirements:* For master's, GRE General Test, 3 letters of reference; for doctorate, GRE General Test, transcripts, 3 letters of reference. Additional exam requirements/recommendations for international students: Required—TOEFL.

University of Memphis, Graduate School, College of Arts and Sciences, Department of Physics, Memphis, TN 38152. Offers MS. Part-time programs available. *Faculty:* 4 full-time (0 women). *Students:* 8 full-time (2 women), 2 part-time (1 woman), 2 international. Average age 32. 9 applicants, 78% accepted, 2 enrolled. In 2010, 6 master's awarded. *Degree requirements:* For master's, comprehensive exam, thesis or alternative. *Entrance requirements:* For master's, GRE General Test or MAT, 20 undergraduate hours of course work in physics. *Application deadline:* For fall admission, 8/1 for domestic students; for spring admission, 12/1 for domestic students. Applications are processed on a rolling basis. Application fee: $35 ($60 for international students). Electronic applications accepted. *Financial support:* In 2010–11, 5 students received support; research assistantships with full tuition reimbursements available, teaching assistantships with full tuition reimbursements available, Federal Work-Study, institutionally sponsored loans, scholarships/grants, and unspecified assistantships available. Financial award application deadline: 2/15; financial award applicants required to submit FAFSA. *Faculty research:* Solid-state physics, materials science, biophysics, astrophysics, physics education. *Unit head:* Dr. M. Shah Jahan, Chair, 901-678-2620, Fax: 901-678-4733, E-mail: mjahan@memphis.edu. *Application contact:* Dr. Sanjay Mishra, Coordinator of Graduate Studies, 901-678-3115, Fax: 901-678-4733, E-mail: srmishra@memphis.edu.

University of Miami, Graduate School, College of Arts and Sciences, Department of Physics, Coral Gables, FL 33124. Offers MS, PhD. Terminal master's awarded for partial completion of doctoral program. *Degree requirements:* For master's, comprehensive exam; for doctorate, comprehensive exam, thesis/dissertation. *Entrance requirements:* For master's and doctorate, GRE General Test, GRE Subject Test. Additional exam requirements/recommendations for international students: Required—TOEFL (minimum score 550 paper-based; 213 computer-based; 80 iBT). Electronic applications accepted. *Faculty research:* High-energy theory, marine and atmospheric optics, plasma physics, solid-state physics.

Physics

University of Michigan, Horace H. Rackham School of Graduate Studies, College of Literature, Science, and the Arts, Department of Physics, Ann Arbor, MI 48109. Offers MS, PhD. *Faculty:* 62 full-time (13 women). *Students:* 114 full-time (25 women); includes 3 Black or African American, non-Hispanic/Latino; 1 American Indian or Alaska Native, non-Hispanic/Latino; 2 Asian, non-Hispanic/Latino; 4 Hispanic/Latino; 49 international. Average age 27. 378 applicants, 30% accepted, 28 enrolled. In 2010, 12 master's, 17 doctorates awarded. Terminal master's awarded for partial completion of doctoral program. *Degree requirements:* For doctorate, thesis/dissertation, oral defense of dissertation, preliminary exam. *Entrance requirements:* For master's and doctorate, GRE General Test. Additional exam requirements/recommendations for international students: Required—TOEFL (minimum score 600 paper-based; 250 computer-based; 100 iBT). *Application deadline:* For fall admission, 12/15 for domestic and international students. Application fee: $60 ($75 for international students). Electronic applications accepted. *Expenses:* Tuition, state resident: full-time $17,784; part-time $1116 per credit hour. Tuition, nonresident: full-time $35,944; part-time $2125 per credit hour. International tuition: $35,994 full-time. Required fees: $95 per semester. Tuition and fees vary according to course load, degree level and program. *Financial support:* In 2010–11, 25,041 fellowships with full tuition reimbursements (averaging $24,600 per year), research assistantships with full tuition reimbursements (averaging $22,797 per year), 20,867 teaching assistantships with full tuition reimbursements (averaging $22,797 per year) were awarded. *Faculty research:* Elementary particle, solid-state, atomic, and molecular physics (theoretical and experimental). Total annual research expenditures: $14 million. *Unit head:* Dr. Bradford Orr, Chair, 734-764-4437. *Application contact:* Christina A. Zigulis, Graduate Coordinator, 734-936-0658, Fax: 734-763-9694, E-mail: physics.inquiries@umich.edu.

University of Minnesota, Duluth, Graduate School, Swenson College of Science and Engineering, Department of Physics, Duluth, MN 55812-2496. Offers MS. Part-time programs available. *Degree requirements:* For master's, thesis optional, final oral exam. *Entrance requirements:* For master's, minimum GPA of 3.0 (preferred). Additional exam requirements/recommendations for international students: Required—TOEFL (minimum score 550 paper-based; 213 computer-based; 79 iBT), IELTS (minimum score 6.5), or Michigan English Language Assessment Battery (minimum score 80). Electronic applications accepted. *Faculty research:* Computational physics, neutrino physics, oceanography, computational particle physics, optics, condensed matter.

University of Minnesota, Twin Cities Campus, Institute of Technology, School of Physics and Astronomy, Department of Physics, Minneapolis, MN 55455-0213. Offers MS, PhD. Part-time programs available. *Degree requirements:* For master's, thesis; for doctorate, thesis/dissertation. *Entrance requirements:* For master's and doctorate, GRE General Test, GRE Subject Test. *Faculty research:* Condensed matter, elementary particle, space, nuclear and atomic physics.

University of Mississippi, Graduate School, College of Liberal Arts, Department of Physics and Astronomy, Oxford, University, MS 38677. Offers physics (MA, MS, PhD). *Students:* 32 full-time (6 women); includes 1 Black or African American, non-Hispanic/Latino; 12 Asian, non-Hispanic/Latino; 2 Hispanic/Latino; 1 Native Hawaiian or other Pacific Islander, non-Hispanic/Latino, 15 international. In 2010, 4 master's, 5 doctorates awarded. *Degree requirements:* For master's, thesis (for some programs); for doctorate, thesis/dissertation. *Entrance requirements:* For master's, GRE General Test, minimum GPA of 3.0; for doctorate, GRE General Test. Additional exam requirements/recommendations for international students: Required—TOEFL. *Application deadline:* For fall admission, 4/1 for domestic students; for spring admission, 10/1 for domestic students. Applications are processed on a rolling basis. Application fee: $25. Electronic applications accepted. *Financial support:* Scholarships/grants available. Financial award application deadline: 3/1; financial award applicants required to submit FAFSA. *Unit head:* Dr. Lucien M. Cremaldi, Chairman, 662-915-7046, Fax: 662-915-5045, E-mail: physics@phy.olemiss.edu. *Application contact:* Dr. Christy M. Wyandt, Associate Dean, 662-915-7474, Fax: 662-915-7577, E-mail: cwyandt@olemiss.edu.

University of Missouri, Graduate School, College of Arts and Sciences, Department of Physics and Astronomy, Columbia, MO 65211. Offers MS, PhD. *Faculty:* 34 full-time (9 women), 1 (woman) part-time/adjunct. *Students:* 31 full-time (7 women), 17 part-time (3 women); includes 2 minority (1 Asian, non-Hispanic/Latino; 1 Two or more races, non-Hispanic/Latino), 27 international. Average age 29. 66 applicants, 17% accepted, 11 enrolled. In 2010, 5 master's, 5 doctorates awarded. Terminal master's awarded for partial completion of doctoral program. *Degree requirements:* For doctorate, one foreign language, comprehensive exam, thesis/dissertation. *Entrance requirements:* For master's and doctorate, GRE General Test, minimum GPA of 3.0. Additional exam requirements/recommendations for international students: Required—TOEFL (minimum score 550 paper-based; 213 computer-based; 80 iBT). *Application deadline:* For fall admission, 3/15 priority date for domestic students. Applications are processed on a rolling basis. Application fee: $45 ($60 for international students). Electronic applications accepted. *Financial support:* In 2010–11, 35 research assistantships with full tuition reimbursements, 10 teaching assistantships with full tuition reimbursements were awarded; institutionally sponsored loans, health care benefits, and unspecified assistantships also available. *Faculty research:* Experimental and theoretical condensed-matter physics, biological physics, astronomy/astrophysics. *Unit head:* Dr. Peter Pfeifer, Department Chair, 573-882-2335, E-mail: pfeiferp@missouri.edu. *Application contact:* Dr. Carsten Ullrich, Director of Graduate Studies, 573-882-3335, E-mail: ullrichc@missouri.edu.

University of Missouri–Kansas City, College of Arts and Sciences, Department of Physics, Kansas City, MO 64110-2499. Offers MS, PhD. PhD (interdisciplinary) offered through the School of Graduate Studies. Part-time and evening/weekend programs available. *Faculty:* 12 full-time (1 woman). *Students:* 9 full-time (1 woman), 10 part-time (1 woman), 5 international. Average age 30. 17 applicants, 71% accepted, 9 enrolled. In 2010, 7 master's awarded. Terminal master's awarded for partial completion of doctoral program. *Degree requirements:* For master's, comprehensive exam, thesis optional; for doctorate, comprehensive exam, thesis/dissertation. *Entrance requirements:* For master's and doctorate, GRE General Test. Additional exam requirements/recommendations for international students: Required—TOEFL (minimum score 550 paper-based; 213 computer-based; 80 iBT). *Application deadline:* For fall admission, 4/1 priority date for domestic and international students; for spring admission, 11/1 priority date for domestic and international students. Applications are processed on a rolling basis. Application fee: $45 ($50 for international students). Electronic applications accepted. *Expenses:* Tuition, state resident: full-time $5522.40; part-time $306.80 per credit hour. Tuition, nonresident: full-time $7128; part-time $792 per credit hour. Required fees: $261.15 per term. *Financial support:* In 2010–11, 6 research assistantships with full and partial tuition reimbursements (averaging $14,133 per year), 15 teaching assistantships with full and partial tuition reimbursements (averaging $14,440 per year) were awarded; Federal Work-Study, institutionally sponsored loans, and tuition waivers (full and partial) also available. Support available to part-time students. Financial award application deadline: 3/1; financial award applicants required to submit FAFSA. *Faculty research:* Surface physics, material science, statistical mechanics, computational physics, relativity and quantum theory. Total annual research expenditures: $862,018. *Unit head:* Dr. Michael Kruger, Chair, 816-235-5441, E-mail: krugerm@umkc.edu. *Application contact:* Dr. Da Ming Zhu, Principal Graduate Advisor, 816-235-5326, Fax: 816-235-5221, E-mail: zhud@umkc.edu.

University of Missouri–St. Louis, College of Arts and Sciences, Department of Physics and Astronomy, St. Louis, MO 63121. Offers physics (MS, PhD), including applied physics (MS), astrophysics (MS). Part-time and evening/weekend programs available. *Faculty:* 12 full-time (2 women), 4 part-time/adjunct (1 woman). *Students:* 10 full-time (2 women), 13 part-time (4 women), 2 international. Average age 34. 17 applicants, 29% accepted, 4 enrolled. In 2010, 3 master's, 3 doctorates awarded. Terminal master's awarded for partial completion of doctoral

program. *Degree requirements:* For master's, thesis optional; for doctorate, thesis/dissertation. *Entrance requirements:* For master's, GRE General Test; for doctorate, GRE General Test, 2 letters of recommendation. Additional exam requirements/recommendations for international students: Required—TOEFL (minimum score 550 paper-based; 213 computer-based). *Application deadline:* For fall admission, 7/1 for domestic and international students; for spring admission, 12/1 for domestic students, 11/1 for international students. Application fee: $35 ($40 for international students). Electronic applications accepted. *Expenses:* Tuition, state resident: full-time $5522; part-time $306.80 per credit hour. Tuition, nonresident: full-time $14,253; part-time $792.10 per credit hour. Required fees: $658; $49 per credit hour. One-time fee: $12. Tuition and fees vary according to program. *Financial support:* In 2010–11, 4 research assistantships with full and partial tuition reimbursements (averaging $16,125 per year), 10 teaching assistantships with full and partial tuition reimbursements (averaging $14,815 per year) were awarded; fellowships with full tuition reimbursements, career-related internships or fieldwork also available. Financial award applicants required to submit FAFSA. *Faculty research:* Biophysics, atomic physics, nonlinear dynamics, materials science. *Unit head:* Dr. Phil Fraundorf, Director of Graduate Studies, 314-516-5931, Fax: 314-516-6152, E-mail: fraundorfp@msx.umsl.edu. *Application contact:* 314-516-5458, Fax: 314-516-6996, E-mail: gradadm@umsl.edu.

University of Nebraska–Lincoln, Graduate College, College of Arts and Sciences, Department of Physics and Astronomy, Lincoln, NE 68588. Offers astronomy (MS, PhD); physics (MS, PhD). *Degree requirements:* For master's, thesis optional; for doctorate, comprehensive exam, thesis/dissertation. *Entrance requirements:* For master's and doctorate, GRE General Test. Additional exam requirements/recommendations for international students: Required—TOEFL (minimum score 550 paper-based; 213 computer-based). Electronic applications accepted. *Faculty research:* Electromagnetics of solids and thin films, photoionization, ion collisions with atoms, molecules and surfaces, nanostructures.

University of Nevada, Las Vegas, Graduate College, College of Science, Department of Physics, Las Vegas, NV 89154-4002. Offers astronomy (MS, PhD); physics (MS, PhD). Part-time programs available. *Faculty:* 16 full-time (0 women), 6 part-time/adjunct (2 women). *Students:* 22 full-time (3 women), 1 part-time (0 women); includes 11 minority (1 Hispanic/Latino; 10 Two or more races, non-Hispanic/Latino), 9 international. Average age 29. 12 applicants, 42% accepted, 5 enrolled. In 2010, 7 master's, 2 doctorates awarded. *Degree requirements:* For master's, thesis, oral exam; for doctorate, comprehensive exam, thesis/dissertation. *Entrance requirements:* For master's and doctorate, GRE General Test. Additional exam requirements/recommendations for international students: Required—TOEFL (minimum score 550 paper-based; 213 computer-based; 80 iBT), IELTS (minimum score 7). *Application deadline:* For fall admission, 8/1 priority date for domestic and international students; for spring admission, 10/1 priority date for domestic and international students. Applications are processed on a rolling basis. Application fee: $60 ($95 for international students). Electronic applications accepted. *Expenses:* Tuition, area resident: Part-time $239.50 per credit. Tuition, state resident: part-time $239.50 per credit. Tuition, nonresident: part-time $503 per credit. Required fees: $108 per semester. Tuition and fees vary according to course load, program and reciprocity agreements. *Financial support:* In 2010–11, 13 research assistantships with partial tuition reimbursements (averaging $16,395 per year), 15 teaching assistantships with partial tuition reimbursements (averaging $12,856 per year) were awarded; institutionally sponsored loans, scholarships/grants, health care benefits, and unspecified assistantships also available. Financial award application deadline: 3/1. *Faculty research:* Gamma-ray bursters astrophysics, cosmology and dark matter astrophysics, experimental high pressure physics, theoretical condensed matter physics, laser-plasma atomic physics. Total annual research expenditures: $5 million. *Unit head:* Dr. Tao Pang, Chair/Professor, 702-895-4454, Fax: 702-895-0804, E-mail: pang@physics.unlv.edu. *Application contact:* Graduate College Admissions Evaluator, 702-895-3320, Fax: 702-895-4180, E-mail: gradcollege@unlv.edu.

University of Nevada, Reno, Graduate School, College of Science, Department of Physics, Reno, NV 89557. Offers MS, PhD. Terminal master's awarded for partial completion of doctoral program. *Degree requirements:* For master's, thesis optional; for doctorate, thesis/dissertation. *Entrance requirements:* For master's, GRE General Test, GRE Subject Test, minimum GPA of 2.75; for doctorate, GRE General Test, GRE Subject Test, minimum GPA of 3.0. Additional exam requirements/recommendations for international students: Required—TOEFL (minimum score 500 paper-based; 173 computer-based; 61 iBT), IELTS (minimum score 6). Electronic applications accepted. *Expenses:* Tuition, state resident: full-time $2219; part-time $246 per credit. Tuition, nonresident: part-time $510 per credit. International tuition: $9009 full-time. Required fees: $59 per term. One-time fee: $101. Tuition and fees vary according to course load. *Faculty research:* Atomic and molecular physics.

University of New Brunswick Fredericton, School of Graduate Studies, Faculty of Science, Department of Physics, Fredericton, NB E3B 5A3, Canada. Offers M Sc, PhD. Part-time programs available. *Faculty:* 8 full-time (0 women), 1 (woman) part-time/adjunct. *Students:* 18 full-time (4 women). In 2010, 4 master's, 1 doctorate awarded. *Degree requirements:* For master's, thesis; for doctorate, comprehensive exam, thesis/dissertation. *Entrance requirements:* For master's, B Sc with minimum B average; for doctorate, M Sc, minimum GPA of 3.0. Additional exam requirements/recommendations for international students: Required—TOEFL, TWE. *Application deadline:* For fall admission, 3/1 priority date for domestic students. Applications are processed on a rolling basis. Application fee: $50 Canadian dollars. Electronic applications accepted. *Expenses:* Tuition, area resident: Full-time $3708; part-time $927 per term. International tuition: $6300 full-time. Required fees: $50 per term. *Financial support:* In 2010–11, 2 fellowships with tuition reimbursements (averaging $17,500 per year), 11 research assistantships (averaging $12,000 per year), 25 teaching assistantships (averaging $4,200 per year) were awarded. *Faculty research:* Optical and laser spectroscopy, infrared and microwave spectroscopy, magnetic resonance and magnetic resonance imaging, space and atmospheric physics, theoretical atomic and molecular physics, space plasma theory, theoretical molecular spectroscopy. *Unit head:* Dr. Igor Mastikhin, Director of Graduate Studies, 506-458-7927, Fax: 506-453-4581, E-mail: mast@unb.ca. *Application contact:* Elinor MacFarlane, Graduate Secretary, 506-453-4723, Fax: 506-453-4581, E-mail: elinor@unb.ca.

University of New Hampshire, Graduate School, College of Engineering and Physical Sciences, Department of Physics, Durham, NH 03824. Offers MS, PhD. *Faculty:* 32 full-time (4 women). *Students:* 32 full-time (8 women), 27 part-time (7 women); includes 5 minority (2 American Indian or Alaska Native, non-Hispanic/Latino; 3 Asian, non-Hispanic/Latino), 26 international. Average age 28. 107 applicants, 39% accepted, 16 enrolled. In 2010, 6 master's, 7 doctorates awarded. Terminal master's awarded for partial completion of doctoral program. *Degree requirements:* For master's, thesis or alternative; for doctorate, thesis/dissertation. *Entrance requirements:* For master's and doctorate, GRE General Test. Additional exam requirements/recommendations for international students: Required—TOEFL (minimum score 550 paper-based; 213 computer-based; 80 iBT). *Application deadline:* For fall admission, 4/1 priority date for domestic students, 4/1 for international students; for spring admission, 12/1 for domestic students. Applications are processed on a rolling basis. Application fee: $65. Electronic applications accepted. *Financial support:* In 2010–11, 57 students received support, including 1 fellowship, 36 research assistantships, 20 teaching assistantships; Federal Work-Study, scholarships/grants, and tuition waivers (full and partial) also available. Support available to part-time students. Financial award application deadline: 2/15. *Faculty research:* Astrophysics and space physics, nuclear physics, atomic and molecular physics, nonlinear dynamical systems. *Unit head:* Dr. Eberhard Moebius, Chairperson, 603-862-1951. *Application contact:* Katie Makem-Boucher, Administrative Assistant, 603-862-2669, E-mail: physics.grad.info@unh.edu.

University of New Mexico, Graduate School, College of Arts and Sciences, Department of Physics and Astronomy, Albuquerque, NM 87131-2039. Offers biomedical physics (MS, PhD);

physics (MS, PhD). Part-time programs available. *Faculty:* 48 full-time (5 women), 9 part-time/adjunct (1 woman). *Students:* 78 full-time (16 women), 9 part-time (2 women); includes 2 Black or African American, non-Hispanic/Latino; 1 American Indian or Alaska Native, non-Hispanic/Latino; 4 Asian, non-Hispanic/Latino; 4 Hispanic/Latino; 1 Native Hawaiian or other Pacific Islander, non-Hispanic/Latino, 25 international. Average age 29. 97 applicants, 24% accepted, 19 enrolled. In 2010, 6 master's, 2 doctorates awarded. Terminal master's awarded for partial completion of doctoral program. *Degree requirements:* For master's, comprehensive exam (for some programs), thesis optional, for MS non-thesis, must pass dept preliminary exams as MS level; for doctorate, comprehensive exam, thesis/dissertation. *Entrance requirements:* For master's, GRE; for doctorate, GRE General Test; GRE Physics Subject Test. Additional exam requirements/recommendations for international students: Required—TOEFL (minimum score 550 paper-based; 213 computer-based; 80 iBT), IELTS (minimum score 7). *Application deadline:* For fall admission, 1/15 for domestic students, 1/15 priority date for international students; for spring admission, 8/1 for domestic students, 8/1 priority date for international students. Application fee: $50. Electronic applications accepted. *Expenses:* Tuition, state resident: full-time $5991; part-time $251 per credit hour. Tuition, nonresident: full-time $14,405; part-time $800.20 per credit hour. Tuition and fees vary according to course level, course load, program and reciprocity agreements. *Financial support:* In 2010–11, 82 students received support, including 3 fellowships with full tuition reimbursements available (averaging $8,333 per year), 64 research assistantships with full tuition reimbursements available (averaging $16,189 per year), 41 teaching assistantships with full tuition reimbursements available (averaging $7,637 per year); career-related internships or fieldwork, scholarships/grants, traineeships, health care benefits, and unspecified assistantships also available. Support available to part-time students. Financial award application deadline: 2/1; financial award applicants required to submit FAFSA. *Faculty research:* Astronomy and astrophysics, biological physics, condensed-matter physics, nonlinear science and complexity, optics and photonics, quantum information, subatomic physics. Total annual research expenditures: $6 million. *Unit head:* Dr. Bernd Bassalleck, Chair, 505-277-1517, Fax: 505-277-1520, E-mail: bossek@unm.edu. *Application contact:* Alisa Gibson, Program Advisement Coordinator, 505-277-1514, Fax: 505-277-1520, E-mail: agibson@unm.edu.

University of New Orleans, Graduate School, College of Sciences, Department of Physics, New Orleans, LA 70148. Offers MS, PhD. Part-time and evening/weekend programs available. *Degree requirements:* For master's, thesis (for some programs). *Entrance requirements:* For master's, GRE General Test. Additional exam requirements/recommendations for international students: Required—TOEFL (minimum score 550 paper-based; 213 computer-based; 79 iBT). Electronic applications accepted. *Faculty research:* Underwater acoustics, applied electromagnetics, experimental atomic beams, digital signal processing, astrophysics.

The University of North Carolina at Chapel Hill, Graduate School, College of Arts and Sciences, Department of Physics and Astronomy, Chapel Hill, NC 27599. Offers physics (MS, PhD). Terminal master's awarded for partial completion of doctoral program. *Degree requirements:* For master's, comprehensive exam; for doctorate, comprehensive exam, thesis/dissertation. *Entrance requirements:* For master's and doctorate, GRE General Test, minimum GPA of 3.0. Electronic applications accepted. *Faculty research:* Observational astronomy, fullerenes, polarized beams, nanotubes, nucleosynthesis in stars and supernovae, superstring theory, ballistic transport in semiconductors, gravitation.

University of North Dakota, Graduate School, College of Arts and Sciences, Department of Physics, Grand Forks, ND 58202. Offers MS, PhD. *Faculty:* 7 full-time (0 women), 1 part-time/adjunct (0 women). *Students:* 8 full-time (2 women), 5 part-time (1 woman); includes 1 minority (Asian, non-Hispanic/Latino), 5 international. Average age 31. 18 applicants, 17% accepted, 3 enrolled. In 2010, 1 master's, 1 doctorate awarded. *Degree requirements:* For master's, thesis, final exam; for doctorate, comprehensive exam, thesis/dissertation, final exam. *Entrance requirements:* For master's, minimum GPA of 3.0; for doctorate, minimum GPA of 3.5. Additional exam requirements/recommendations for international students: Required—TOEFL (minimum score 550 paper-based; 213 computer-based; 79 iBT), IELTS (minimum score 6.5). *Application deadline:* For fall admission, 3/1 for domestic students, 3/1 priority date for international students. Application fee: $35. Electronic applications accepted. *Expenses:* Tuition, state resident: full-time $5857; part-time $306.74 per credit. Tuition, nonresident: full-time $15,666; part-time $729.77 per credit. Required fees: $53.42 per credit. Tuition and fees vary according to course load, program and reciprocity agreements. *Financial support:* In 2010–11, 11 students received support, including 4 research assistantships with full tuition reimbursements available (averaging $11,648 per year), 7 teaching assistantships with full tuition reimbursements available (averaging $9,946 per year); fellowships with full and partial tuition reimbursements available, Federal Work-Study, institutionally sponsored loans, scholarships/grants, health care benefits, tuition waivers (full and partial), and unspecified assistantships also available. Support available to part-time students. Financial award application deadline: 3/15; financial award applicants required to submit FAFSA. *Faculty research:* Solid state physics, atomic and molecular physics, astrophysics, health physics. Total annual research expenditures: $104,110. *Unit head:* Dr. Kanishka Marasinghe, Graduate Director, 701-777-3560, Fax: 701-777-3523, E-mail: k.marasinghe@und.nodak.edu. *Application contact:* Matt Anderson, Admissions Specialist, 701-777-2947, Fax: 701-777-3619, E-mail: matthew.anderson@gradschool.und.edu.

University of Northern Iowa, Graduate College, College of Natural Sciences, Department of Physics, Cedar Falls, IA 50614. Offers applied physics (PSM). *Students:* 3 full-time (0 women), 3 part-time (0 women), 1 international. 9 applicants, 67% accepted, 3 enrolled. In 2010, 5 master's awarded. *Degree requirements:* For master's, comprehensive exam (for some programs), thesis or alternative. *Entrance requirements:* For master's, minimum GPA of 3.0. Additional exam requirements/recommendations for international students: Required—TOEFL (minimum score 500 paper-based; 180 computer-based; 61 iBT). *Application deadline:* For fall admission, 8/1 priority date for domestic students. Applications are processed on a rolling basis. Application fee: $50 ($70 for international students). Electronic applications accepted. *Financial support:* Career-related internships or fieldwork, Federal Work-Study, scholarships/grants, and tuition waivers (full and partial) available. Support available to part-time students. Financial award application deadline: 2/1. *Unit head:* Dr. C. Clifton Chancey, Head, 319-273-2420, E-mail: c.chancey@uni.edu. *Application contact:* Laurie S. Russell, Record Analyst, 319-273-2623, Fax: 319-273-2885, E-mail: laurie.russell@uni.edu.

University of Northern Iowa, Graduate College, College of Natural Sciences, Program in Science Education, Cedar Falls, IA 50614. Offers earth science education (MA); physics education (MA); science education (MA). *Students:* 3 full-time (2 women), 24 part-time (16 women); includes 1 minority (Asian, non-Hispanic/Latino). 5 applicants, 80% accepted, 1 enrolled. In 2010, 12 master's awarded. *Degree requirements:* For master's, comprehensive exam (for some programs), thesis or alternative. *Entrance requirements:* For master's, minimum GPA of 3.0. Additional exam requirements/recommendations for international students: Required—TOEFL (minimum score 500 paper-based; 180 computer-based; 61 iBT). *Application deadline:* For fall admission, 8/1 priority date for domestic students. Applications are processed on a rolling basis. Application fee: $50 ($70 for international students). Electronic applications accepted. *Financial support:* Application deadline: 2/1. *Unit head:* Dr. Cherin A. Lee, Director, 319-273-7357, Fax: 319-273-3051, E-mail: cherin.lee@uni.edu. *Application contact:* Laurie S. Russell, Record Analyst, 319-273-2623, Fax: 319-273-2885, E-mail: laurie.russell@uni.edu.

University of North Texas, Toulouse Graduate School, College of Arts and Sciences, Department of Physics, Denton, TX 76203. Offers MA, MS, PhD. Terminal master's awarded for partial completion of doctoral program. *Degree requirements:* For master's, comprehensive exam (for some programs), thesis or problems; for doctorate, one foreign language, comprehensive exam (for some programs), thesis/dissertation. *Entrance requirements:* For master's and doctorate, GRE General Test, 2 letters of recommendation. Additional exam requirements/recommendations for international students: Recommended—TOEFL (minimum score 550 paper-based; 213 computer-based; 79 iBT). *Application deadline:* Applications are processed on a rolling basis. Electronic applications accepted. *Expenses:* Tuition, state resident: full-time $4298; part-time $239 per credit hour. Tuition, nonresident: full-time $10,782; part-time $549 per credit hour. Required fees: $1292; $270 per credit hour. *Financial support:* Fellowships with tuition reimbursements, research assistantships with tuition reimbursements, teaching assistantships, scholarships/grants, health care benefits, and unspecified assistantships available. Financial award applicants required to submit FAFSA. *Faculty research:* Atomic, molecular optical; condensed matter, experimental microwave, theoretical, semiconductor. *Application contact:* Graduate Adviser, 940-565-2630, Fax: 940-565-2515.

University of Notre Dame, Graduate School, College of Science, Department of Physics, Notre Dame, IN 46556. Offers MS, PhD. *Degree requirements:* For doctorate, thesis/dissertation, candidacy exam. *Entrance requirements:* For doctorate, GRE General Test, GRE Subject Test. Additional exam requirements/recommendations for international students: Required—TOEFL (minimum score 600 paper-based; 250 computer-based; 80 iBT). Electronic applications accepted. *Faculty research:* High energy, nuclear, atomic, condensed-matter physics; astrophysics; biophysics.

University of Oklahoma, College of Arts and Sciences, Department of Physics and Astronomy, Norman, OK 73019. Offers physics (MS, PhD). Part-time programs available. *Faculty:* 29 full-time (4 women). *Students:* 57 full-time (13 women), 8 part-time (4 women); includes 1 minority (Asian, non-Hispanic/Latino), 26 international. Average age 29. 14 applicants, 79% accepted, 11 enrolled. In 2010, 6 master's, 10 doctorates awarded. Terminal master's awarded for partial completion of doctoral program. *Degree requirements:* For master's, thesis or alternative, departmental qualifying exam; for doctorate, thesis/dissertation, comprehensive, departmental qualifying, oral, and written exams. *Entrance requirements:* For master's and doctorate, GRE General Test, GRE Subject Test, 3 letters of recommendation. Additional exam requirements/recommendations for international students: Required—TOEFL (minimum score 600 paper-based; 250 computer-based; 79 iBT). *Application deadline:* For fall admission, 3/1 for domestic students, 4/1 for international students; for spring admission, 11/1 for domestic students, 9/1 for international students. Application fee: $40 ($90 for international students). Electronic applications accepted. *Expenses:* Tuition, state resident: full-time $3892.80; part-time $162.20 per credit hour. Tuition, nonresident: full-time $14,167; part-time $590.30 per credit hour. Required fees: $2523.40; $94.60 per credit hour. Tuition and fees vary according to course load and degree level. *Financial support:* In 2010–11, 28 research assistantships with partial tuition reimbursements (averaging $16,202 per year), 31 teaching assistantships with partial tuition reimbursements (averaging $15,051 per year) were awarded; health care benefits and unspecified assistantships also available. Financial award application deadline: 3/1; financial award applicants required to submit FAFSA. *Faculty research:* Astronomy and astrophysics, condensed matter physics, atomic molecular and optical physics, high energy physics. Total annual research expenditures: $4.4 million. *Unit head:* Greg Parker, Chair, 405-325-3961, Fax: 405-325-7557, E-mail: parker@nhn.ou.edu. *Application contact:* Debbie Barnhill, University Student Services Assistant, 405-325-3961 Ext. 36101, Fax: 405-325-7557, E-mail: dbarnhill@ou.edu.

University of Oregon, Graduate School, College of Arts and Sciences, Department of Physics, Eugene, OR 97403. Offers MA, MS, PhD. Terminal master's awarded for partial completion of doctoral program. *Degree requirements:* For doctorate, thesis/dissertation. *Entrance requirements:* For master's and doctorate, GRE General Test, GRE Subject Test, minimum GPA of 3.0. Additional exam requirements/recommendations for international students: Required—TOEFL. *Faculty research:* Solid-state and chemical physics, optical physics, elementary particle physics, astrophysics, atomic and molecular physics.

University of Ottawa, Faculty of Graduate and Postdoctoral Studies, Faculty of Science, Ottawa-Carleton Institute for Physics, Ottawa, ON K1N 6N5, Canada. Offers M Sc, PhD. M Sc, PhD offered jointly with Carleton University. *Degree requirements:* For master's, thesis or alternative; for doctorate, comprehensive exam, thesis/dissertation, seminar. *Entrance requirements:* For master's, honors B Sc degree or equivalent, minimum B average; for doctorate, M Sc, minimum B+ average. Electronic applications accepted. *Faculty research:* Condensed matter physics and statistical physics (CMS), subatomic physics (SAP), medical physics (Med).

University of Pennsylvania, School of Arts and Sciences, Graduate Group in Physics and Astronomy, Philadelphia, PA 19104. Offers medical physics (MS); physics (PhD). Part-time programs available. *Faculty:* 44 full-time (5 women), 17 part-time/adjunct (1 woman). *Students:* 109 full-time (27 women), 1 part-time (0 women); includes 10 Asian, non-Hispanic/Latino; 2 Hispanic/Latino, 22 international. 373 applicants, 13% accepted, 20 enrolled. In 2010, 22 master's, 14 doctorates awarded. *Degree requirements:* For doctorate, thesis/dissertation, oral, preliminary, and final exams. *Entrance requirements:* For doctorate, GRE General Test, GRE Subject Test (recommended). Additional exam requirements/recommendations for international students: Required—TOEFL. *Application deadline:* For fall admission, 12/1 priority date for domestic students. Application fee: $70. Electronic applications accepted. *Expenses:* Tuition: Full-time $25,660; part-time $4758 per course. Required fees: $2152; $270 per course. Tuition and fees vary according to course load, degree level and program. *Financial support:* Fellowships, research assistantships, teaching assistantships, institutionally sponsored loans, scholarships/grants, traineeships, health care benefits, and unspecified assistantships available. Financial award application deadline: 12/15. *Faculty research:* Astrophysics, condensed matter experiment, condensed matter theory, particle experiment, particle theory. Total annual research expenditures: $7.3 million. *Unit head:* Larry Gladney, Department Chair, Physics and Astronomy, 215-898-8152, E-mail: gladney@sas.upenn.edu. *Application contact:* Millicent Minnick, Academic Coordinator, 215-898-3125, E-mail: admiss@physics.upenn.edu.

University of Pittsburgh, School of Arts and Sciences, Department of Physics and Astronomy, Pittsburgh, PA 15260. Offers physics (MS, PhD). *Faculty:* 39 full-time (7 women). *Students:* 92 full-time (19 women); includes 1 Asian, non-Hispanic/Latino, 60 international. Average age 25. 323 applicants, 28% accepted, 27 enrolled. In 2010, 12 master's, 8 doctorates awarded. Terminal master's awarded for partial completion of doctoral program. *Degree requirements:* For master's, comprehensive exam, thesis optional; for doctorate, comprehensive exam, thesis/dissertation, preliminary and comprehensive exams, 2 terms of student teaching, seminar and/or professional talk presentations, annual committee review meeting, oral/written dissertation. *Entrance requirements:* For master's and doctorate, GRE General Test, GRE Subject Test, minimum GPA of 3.0. Additional exam requirements/recommendations for international students: Required—TOEFL (minimum score 577 paper-based; 233 computer-based; 90 iBT) or IELTS (minimum score 6.5). *Application deadline:* For fall admission, 1/31 priority date for domestic and international students. Applications are processed on a rolling basis. Application fee: $0 ($50 for international students). Electronic applications accepted. *Expenses:* Tuition, state resident: full-time $17,304; part-time $701 per credit. Tuition, nonresident: full-time $29,554; part-time $1210 per credit. Required fees: $740; $214 per term. Tuition and fees vary according to program. *Financial support:* In 2010–11, 9 fellowships with full tuition reimbursements (averaging $27,819 per year), 52 research assistantships with full tuition reimbursements (averaging $23,280 per year), 30 teaching assistantships with full tuition reimbursements (averaging $23,280 per year) were awarded; scholarships/grants, health care benefits, tuition waivers, and unspecified assistantships also available. Financial award application deadline: 1/31. *Faculty research:* Astrophysics and cosmology, particle and astroparticle physics, condensed matter and solid-state physics, quantum information, biological physics, nanoscience. Total annual research expenditures: $5.9 million. *Unit head:* Dr. David Turnshek, Chairman, 412-624-6381, Fax: 412-624-9163, E-mail: davidt@pitt.edu. *Application contact:* Dr. Andrew Zentner, Admissions, 412-624-9000, Fax: 412-624-9163, E-mail: zentner@pitt.edu.

Peterson's Graduate Programs in the Physical Sciences, Mathematics, Agricultural Sciences, the Environment & Natural Resources 2012

www.facebook.com/petersonspublishing **201**

Physics

University of Puerto Rico, Mayagüez Campus, Graduate Studies, College of Arts and Sciences, Department of Physics, Mayagüez, PR 00681-9000. Offers MS. Part-time programs available. *Students:* 28 full-time (8 women); includes 8 Hispanic/Latino, 20 international. 20 applicants, 40% accepted, 1 enrolled. In 2010, 9 master's awarded. *Degree requirements:* For master's, comprehensive exam, thesis. *Entrance requirements:* For master's, bachelor's degree in physics or its equivalent. *Application deadline:* For fall admission, 2/15 for domestic and international students; for spring admission, 9/15 for domestic and international students. Applications are processed on a rolling basis. Application fee: $25. *Expenses:* Tuition, state resident: full-time $1188. Tuition, nonresident: full-time $1188. International tuition: $6126 full-time. Tuition and fees vary according to course level and course load. *Financial support:* In 2010–11, 16 students received support, including fellowships (averaging $12,000 per year), research assistantships (averaging $15,000 per year), 16 teaching assistantships (averaging $8,500 per year); Federal Work-Study and institutionally sponsored loans also available. *Faculty research:* Atomic and molecular physics, nuclear physics, nonlinear thermostatics, fluid dynamics, molecular spectroscopy. Total annual research expenditures: $1.8 million. *Unit head:* Dr. Dorial Castellanos, Interim Director, 787-265-3844, Fax: 787-832-1135, E-mail: dorial.castellanos@upr.edu. *Application contact:* Vanessa Gonzalez, Secretary, 787-832-4040 Ext. 3073, Fax: 787-832-1135, E-mail: vanessa@uprm.edu.

University of Puerto Rico, Río Piedras, College of Natural Sciences, Department of Physics, San Juan, PR 00931-3300. Offers chemical physics (PhD); physics (MS). Part-time programs available. *Degree requirements:* For master's, comprehensive exam, thesis; for doctorate, comprehensive exam, thesis/dissertation. *Entrance requirements:* For master's, GRE General Test, GRE Subject Test, interview, minimum GPA of 3.0, letter of recommendation (3); for doctorate, GRE, master's degree, minimum GPA of 3.0, letter of recommendation (3). Additional exam requirements/recommendations for international students: Required—TOEFL. *Faculty research:* Energy transfer process through Van der Vacqs interactions, study of the photodissociation of ketene.

University of Regina, Faculty of Graduate Studies and Research, Faculty of Science, Department of Physics, Regina, SK S4S 0A2, Canada. Offers M Sc, PhD. *Faculty:* 8 full-time (0 women). *Students:* 7 full-time (1 woman). 3 applicants, 100% accepted. In 2010, 2 master's awarded. *Degree requirements:* For master's, thesis; for doctorate, thesis/dissertation. *Entrance requirements:* For master's, honors degree in physics or engineering physics; overall average of 70 per cent or better; for doctorate, MSc or equivalent. Additional exam requirements/recommendations for international students: Required—TOEFL (minimum score 580 paper-based; 80 iBT). *Application deadline:* For fall admission, 5/15 for domestic and international students; for winter admission, 8/15 for domestic and international students. Application fee: $100. Electronic applications accepted. Tuition and fees charges are reported in Canadian dollars. *Expenses:* Tuition, area resident: Full-time $3244.50 Canadian dollars; part-time $180.25 Canadian dollars per credit hour. International tuition: $4744.50 Canadian dollars full-time. Required fees: $494 Canadian dollars; $115.25 Canadian dollars per credit hour. $115.25 Canadian dollars per semester. Tuition and fees vary according to program. *Financial support:* In 2010–11, 3 fellowships (averaging $20,000 per year), 1 research assistantship (averaging $18,000 per year), 2 teaching assistantships (averaging $7,088 per year) were awarded; career-related internships or fieldwork and scholarships/grants also available. Financial award application deadline: 6/15. *Faculty research:* Quantum mechanics, theoretical nuclear physics, quantum field theory, relativistic astrophysics and cosmology, classical electrodynamics. *Unit head:* Dr. Neil Ashton, Head, 306-585-4252, Fax: 306-585-5659, E-mail: neil.ashton@uregina.ca. *Application contact:* Dr. Zisis Papandreau, Graduate Program Coordinator, 306-585-5379, Fax: 306-585-5659, E-mail: grad@phys.uregina.ca.

University of Rhode Island, Graduate School, College of Arts and Sciences, Department of Physics, Kingston, RI 02881. Offers MS, PhD. Part-time and evening/weekend programs available. *Faculty:* 16 full-time (2 women), 3 part-time/adjunct (1 woman). *Students:* 14 full-time (4 women), 2 part-time (0 women); includes 2 minority (both Asian, non-Hispanic/Latino), 9 international. In 2010, 1 master's awarded. *Degree requirements:* For master's, comprehensive exam (for some programs), thesis optional; for doctorate, comprehensive exam, thesis/dissertation. *Entrance requirements:* For master's and doctorate, 2 letters of recommendation. Additional exam requirements/recommendations for international students: Required—TOEFL (minimum score 550 paper-based; 213 computer-based). *Application deadline:* For fall admission, 4/15 for domestic students, 2/1 for international students. Application fee: $65. Electronic applications accepted. *Expenses:* Tuition, state resident: full-time $9588; part-time $533 per credit hour. Tuition, nonresident: full-time $22,968; part-time $1276 per credit hour. Required fees: $1282; $68 per semester. Tuition and fees vary according to program. *Financial support:* In 2010–11, 16 teaching assistantships with full and partial tuition reimbursements (averaging $14,256 per year) were awarded. Financial award application deadline: 3/1; financial award applicants required to submit FAFSA. Total annual research expenditures: $910,861. *Unit head:* Dr. Jan Northby, Chair, 401-874-2042, Fax: 401-874-2380, E-mail: jnorthby@uri.edu. *Application contact:* Dr. Jan Northby, Chair, 401-874-2042, Fax: 401-874-2380, E-mail: jnorthby@uri.edu.

University of Rochester, School of Arts and Sciences, Department of Physics and Astronomy, Program in Physics and Astronomy, Rochester, NY 14627.

University of Rochester, School of Arts and Sciences, Department of Physics and Astronomy, Programs in Physics, Rochester, NY 14627.

University of Saskatchewan, College of Graduate Studies and Research, College of Arts and Sciences, Department of Physics and Engineering Physics, Saskatoon, SK S7N 5A2, Canada. Offers M Sc, PhD. *Degree requirements:* For master's, thesis; for doctorate, comprehensive exam (for some programs), thesis/dissertation. *Entrance requirements:* Additional exam requirements/recommendations for international students: Required—TOEFL (minimum score 80 iBT); Recommended—IELTS (minimum score 6.5). Electronic applications accepted.

University of South Carolina, The Graduate School, College of Arts and Sciences, Department of Physics and Astronomy, Columbia, SC 29208. Offers IMA, MAT, MS, PSM, PhD. IMA and MAT offered in cooperation with the College of Education. Part-time programs available. Terminal master's awarded for partial completion of doctoral program. *Degree requirements:* For master's, comprehensive exam, thesis; for doctorate, one foreign language, comprehensive exam, thesis/dissertation. *Entrance requirements:* For master's and doctorate, GRE General Test, GRE Subject Test. Additional exam requirements/recommendations for international students: Required—TOEFL (minimum score 570 paper-based; 230 computer-based; 75 iBT). Electronic applications accepted. *Faculty research:* Condensed matter, intermediate-energy nuclear physics, foundations of quantum mechanics, astronomy/astrophysics.

The University of South Dakota, Graduate School, College of Arts and Sciences, Department of Earth Sciences and Physics, Vermillion, SD 57069-2390. Offers physics (MS, PhD). PhD program offered jointly with South Dakota School of Mines and Technology and South Dakota State University. *Entrance requirements:* For master's and doctorate, GRE.

University of Southern California, Graduate School, Dana and David Dornsife College of Letters, Arts and Sciences, Department of Physics and Astronomy, Los Angeles, CA 90089. Offers physics (MA, MS, PhD). Part-time programs available. *Faculty:* 25 full-time (2 women). *Students:* 66 full-time (12 women), 3 part-time (0 women); includes 9 minority (5 Asian, non-Hispanic/Latino; 3 Hispanic/Latino; 1 Two or more races, non-Hispanic/Latino), 45 international. 118 applicants, 20% accepted, 15 enrolled. In 2010, 9 doctorates awarded. Terminal master's awarded for partial completion of doctoral program. *Degree requirements:* For master's, comprehensive exam, thesis (for some programs); for doctorate, comprehensive exam, thesis/dissertation. *Entrance requirements:* For doctorate, GRE General Test, GRE Physics Test, TOEFL for International Students, 3 letters of recommendation, statement of purpose. Additional exam requirements/recommendations for international students: Required—TOEFL (minimum score 550 paper-based; 213 computer-based; 80 iBT). *Application deadline:* For fall admission, 12/1 priority date for domestic and international students. Application fee: $85. Electronic applications accepted. *Expenses:* Tuition: Full-time $31,240; part-time $1420 per unit. Required fees: $600. One-time fee: $35 full-time. Full-time tuition and fees vary according to degree level and program. *Financial support:* In 2010–11, 100 students received support, including 5 fellowships with full tuition reimbursements available (averaging $28,000 per year), 2 research assistantships with full tuition reimbursements available (averaging $25,656 per year), 50 teaching assistantships with full tuition reimbursements available (averaging $24,612 per year). Financial award application deadline: 12/1. *Faculty research:* High-energy particle theory, condensed matter physics, astrophysics, solar and cosmology, biophysics, computational physics. Total annual research expenditures: $4 million. *Unit head:* Dr. Werner Dappen, Chair, 213-740-0848, Fax: 213-740-8094, E-mail: physics@college.usc.edu. *Application contact:* Dr. Elena Pierpaoli, Graduate Admission Committee Chair, 213-740-1117, Fax: 213-740-8094, E-mail: physicsgradadmis@college.usc.edu.

University of Southern Mississippi, Graduate School, College of Science and Technology, Department of Physics and Astronomy, Hattiesburg, MS 39406-0001. Offers computational science (PhD); physics (MS). *Faculty:* 10 full-time (1 woman). *Students:* 9 full-time (2 women), 1 part-time (0 women), 5 international. Average age 31. 12 applicants, 83% accepted, 3 enrolled. In 2010, 4 master's awarded. *Degree requirements:* For master's, comprehensive exam, thesis; for doctorate, comprehensive exam, thesis/dissertation. *Entrance requirements:* For master's, GRE General Test, minimum GPA of 2.75 in last 60 hours; for doctorate, GRE General Test, minimum GPA of 3.5. Additional exam requirements/recommendations for international students: Required—TOEFL, IELTS. *Application deadline:* For fall admission, 3/1 priority date for domestic students, 3/1 for international students; for spring admission, 1/10 priority date for domestic and international students. Applications are processed on a rolling basis. Application fee: $50. *Financial support:* In 2010–11, research assistantships with full tuition reimbursements (averaging $11,800 per year), 15 teaching assistantships with full tuition reimbursements (averaging $11,800 per year) were awarded; Federal Work-Study, scholarships/grants, health care benefits, and unspecified assistantships also available. Financial award application deadline: 3/15; financial award applicants required to submit FAFSA. *Faculty research:* Polymers, atomic physics, fluid mechanics, liquid crystals, refractory materials. *Unit head:* Dr. Khin Maung, Chair, 601-266-4934, Fax: 601-266-5149. *Application contact:* Dr. Khin Maung, Chair, 601-266-4934, Fax: 601-266-5149.

University of South Florida, Graduate School, College of Arts and Sciences, Department of Physics, Tampa, FL 33620-9951. Offers applied physics (PhD); physics (MS). Part-time programs available. *Faculty:* 19 full-time (2 women). *Students:* 67 full-time (11 women), 4 part-time (0 women); includes 1 Black or African American, non-Hispanic/Latino; 1 Asian, non-Hispanic/Latino; 1 Hispanic/Latino, 31 international. Average age 29. 89 applicants, 47% accepted, 20 enrolled. In 2010, 6 master's, 9 doctorates awarded. *Degree requirements:* For master's, comprehensive exam, thesis optional; for doctorate, 2 foreign languages, comprehensive exam, thesis/dissertation. *Entrance requirements:* For master's, GRE General Test, minimum GPA of 3.0 in last 60 hours of course work; for doctorate, GRE General Test, minimum graduate GPA of 3.2. Additional exam requirements/recommendations for international students: Required—TOEFL (minimum score 550 paper-based). *Application deadline:* For fall admission, 2/15 priority date for domestic students, 1/2 for international students; for spring admission, 9/1 for domestic students, 7/1 for international students. Applications are processed on a rolling basis. Application fee: $30. Electronic applications accepted. *Financial support:* In 2010–11, 23 research assistantships (averaging $14,450 per year), 39 teaching assistantships with tuition reimbursements (averaging $14,081 per year) were awarded; unspecified assistantships also available. *Faculty research:* Biophysics and biomedical physics, atomic molecular and optical physics, solid state and materials physics, physics education. Total annual research expenditures: $2.3 million. *Unit head:* Dr. Pritish Mukherjee, Director of Graduate Studies, 813-974-2871, Fax: 813-974-5813, E-mail: pritish@cas.usf.edu. *Application contact:* Dale Johnson, Program Director, 813-974-5125, Fax: 813-974-5813, E-mail: dejohnso@cas.usf.edu.

The University of Tennessee, Graduate School, College of Arts and Sciences, Department of Physics and Astronomy, Knoxville, TN 37996. Offers physics (MS, PhD). Part-time programs available. *Degree requirements:* For master's, thesis or alternative; for doctorate, thesis/dissertation. *Entrance requirements:* For master's and doctorate, minimum GPA of 2.7. Additional exam requirements/recommendations for international students: Required—TOEFL. Electronic applications accepted. *Expenses:* Tuition, state resident: full-time $7440; part-time $414 per credit hour. Tuition, nonresident: full-time $22,478; part-time $1250 per credit hour. Required fees: $922; $43 per credit hour. Tuition and fees vary according to program.

The University of Tennessee Space Institute, Graduate Programs, Program in Physics, Tullahoma, TN 37388-9700. Offers MS, PhD. *Faculty:* 4 full-time (1 woman), 2 part-time/adjunct (0 women). *Students:* 7 full-time (0 women), 3 part-time (0 women); includes 1 minority (Native Hawaiian or other Pacific Islander, non-Hispanic/Latino), 1 international. 3 applicants, 100% accepted, 1 enrolled. In 2010, 5 master's, 1 doctorate awarded. *Degree requirements:* For master's, thesis (for some programs); for doctorate, one foreign language, thesis/dissertation. *Entrance requirements:* For master's and doctorate, GRE General Test, GRE Subject Test. Additional exam requirements/recommendations for international students: Required—TOEFL (minimum score 550 paper-based; 213 computer-based; 80 iBT), IELTS (minimum score 6.5). *Application deadline:* For fall admission, 2/1 for international students; for spring admission, 6/15 for international students. Applications are processed on a rolling basis. Application fee: $35. Electronic applications accepted. *Financial support:* In 2010–11, 1 fellowship (averaging $2,500 per year), 7 research assistantships with full tuition reimbursements (averaging $17,791 per year) were awarded; career-related internships or fieldwork, Federal Work-Study, institutionally sponsored loans, health care benefits, tuition waivers (full and partial), and unspecified assistantships also available. Financial award applicants required to submit FAFSA. *Unit head:* Dr. Horace Crater, Degree Program Chairman, 931-393-7469, Fax: 931-393-7444, E-mail: hcrater@utsi.edu. *Application contact:* Dee Merriman, Coordinator III, 931-393-7213, Fax: 931-393-7211, E-mail: dmerrima@utsi.edu.

The University of Texas at Arlington, Graduate School, College of Science, Department of Physics, Arlington, TX 76019. Offers physics (MS); physics and applied physics (PhD). Part-time programs available. Terminal master's awarded for partial completion of doctoral program. *Degree requirements:* For master's, thesis optional; for doctorate, comprehensive exam, thesis/dissertation, internship or substitute. *Entrance requirements:* For master's, GRE General Test, minimum GPA of 3.0 in last 60 hours of course work; for doctorate, GRE General Test, minimum GPA of 3.0 in last 60 hours of course work, 30 hours graduate course work in physics. Additional exam requirements/recommendations for international students: Required—TOEFL (minimum score 550 paper-based; 213 computer-based). *Application deadline:* For fall admission, 6/15 for domestic students. Applications are processed on a rolling basis. Application fee: $35 ($50 for international students). *Expenses:* Tuition, state resident: full-time $7500. Tuition, nonresident: full-time $13,080. International tuition: $13,250 full-time. *Financial support:* Fellowships with partial tuition reimbursements, research assistantships, teaching assistantships, career-related internships or fieldwork, Federal Work-Study, institutionally sponsored loans, scholarships/grants, health care benefits, tuition waivers, and unspecified assistantships available. Support available to part-time students. Financial award application deadline: 6/1; financial award applicants required to submit FAFSA. *Faculty research:* Particle physics, astrophysics, condensed matter theory and experiment. *Unit head:* Dr. Alex Weiss, Chair, 817-272-2266, Fax: 817-272-3637, E-mail: weiss@uta.edu. *Application contact:* Dr. Qiming Zhang, Graduate Advisor, 817-272-2266, Fax: 817-272-3637, E-mail: zhang@uta.edu.

The University of Texas at Austin, Graduate School, College of Natural Sciences, Department of Physics, Austin, TX 78712-1111. Offers MA, MS, PhD. *Degree requirements:* For master's, thesis; for doctorate, thesis/dissertation. *Entrance requirements:* For master's and doctorate, GRE General Test, GRE Subject Test (physics). Electronic applications accepted.

The University of Texas at Brownsville, Graduate Studies, College of Science, Mathematics and Technology, Brownsville, TX 78520-4991. Offers biological sciences (MS, MSIS); mathematics (MS); physics (MS). Part-time and evening/weekend programs available. *Degree requirements:* For master's, comprehensive exam, thesis optional. *Entrance requirements:* For master's, GRE General Test. Additional exam requirements/recommendations for international students: Required—TOEFL. *Faculty research:* Fish, insects, barrier islands, algae, curlits.

The University of Texas at Dallas, School of Natural Sciences and Mathematics, Program in Physics, Richardson, TX 75080. Offers applied physics (MS); physics (MS, PhD). Part-time and evening/weekend programs available. *Faculty:* 22 full-time (0 women), 1 (woman) part-time/adjunct. *Students:* 53 full-time (6 women), 20 part-time (3 women); includes 6 minority (1 Black or African American, non-Hispanic/Latino; 1 Asian, non-Hispanic/Latino; 2 Hispanic/Latino; 1 Native Hawaiian or other Pacific Islander, non-Hispanic/Latino; 1 Two or more races, non-Hispanic/Latino), 22 international. Average age 29. 67 applicants, 34% accepted, 11 enrolled. In 2010, 13 master's, 5 doctorates awarded. *Degree requirements:* For master's, thesis optional, industrial internship; for doctorate, thesis/dissertation, publishable paper. *Entrance requirements:* For master's and doctorate, GRE General Test, minimum GPA of 3.0 in upper-level coursework in field. Additional exam requirements/recommendations for international students: Required—TOEFL (minimum score 550 paper-based; 215 computer-based). *Application deadline:* For fall admission, 7/15 for domestic students, 5/1 priority date for international students; for spring admission, 11/15 for domestic students, 9/1 priority date for international students. Applications are processed on a rolling basis. Application fee: $50 ($100 for international students). Electronic applications accepted. *Expenses:* Tuition, state resident: full-time $10,248; part-time $569 per credit hour. Tuition, nonresident: full-time $18,544; part-time $1030 per credit hour. Tuition and fees vary according to course load. *Financial support:* In 2010–11, 48 students received support, including 23 research assistantships with partial tuition reimbursements available (averaging $14,067 per year), 20 teaching assistantships with partial tuition reimbursements available (averaging $14,310 per year); career-related internships or fieldwork, Federal Work-Study, institutionally sponsored loans, scholarships/grants, and unspecified assistantships also available. Support available to part-time students. Financial award application deadline: 4/30; financial award applicants required to submit FAFSA. *Faculty research:* Ionospheric and magnetospheric electrodynamics; high-energy proton collisions and muon detector design and construction (CERN Research); condensed matter physics with emphasis on nanoscience; optical properties of solids including semiconductors, thermoelectric materials and nanomaterials; gravitational lensing and applications to cosmology. *Unit head:* Dr. Robert Glosser, Department Head, 972-883-2876, Fax: 972-883-2848, E-mail: physweb@utdallas.edu. *Application contact:* Dr. Gregory D. Earle, Graduate Advisor, 972-883-6828, Fax: 972-883-2848, E-mail: physweb@utdallas.edu.

The University of Texas at El Paso, Graduate School, College of Science, Department of Physics, El Paso, TX 79968-0001. Offers MS. Part-time and evening/weekend programs available. *Students:* 14 (4 women); includes 4 Hispanic/Latino, 10 international. Average age 34. In 2010, 8 master's awarded. *Degree requirements:* For master's, thesis optional. *Entrance requirements:* For master's, GRE, minimum GPA of 3.0. Additional exam requirements/recommendations for international students: Required—TOEFL; Recommended—IELTS. *Application deadline:* For fall admission, 8/1 priority date for domestic students, 3/1 for international students; for spring admission, 11/1 priority date for domestic students, 9/1 for international students. Applications are processed on a rolling basis. Application fee: $45 ($80 for international students). Electronic applications accepted. *Financial support:* In 2010–11, research assistantships with partial tuition reimbursements (averaging $20,250 per year), teaching assistantships (averaging $16,200 per year) were awarded; fellowships with partial tuition reimbursements, institutionally sponsored loans, scholarships/grants, health care benefits, tuition waivers (partial), and unspecified assistantships also available. Support available to part-time students. Financial award application deadline: 3/15; financial award applicants required to submit FAFSA. *Unit head:* Dr. Vivian Incera, Chair, 915-747-5715, Fax: 915-747-5447, E-mail: vincera@utep.edu. *Application contact:* Dr. Patricia D. Witherspoon, Dean of the Graduate School, 915-747-5491, Fax: 915-747-5788, E-mail: withersp@utep.edu.

The University of Texas at San Antonio, College of Sciences, Department of Physics and Astronomy, San Antonio, TX 78249-0617. Offers physics (MS, PhD). *Faculty:* 11 full-time (1 woman), 7 part-time/adjunct (0 women). *Students:* 46 full-time (7 women), 14 part-time (3 women); includes 10 minority (1 Black or African American, non-Hispanic/Latino; 3 Asian, non-Hispanic/Latino; 5 Hispanic/Latino; 1 Two or more races, non-Hispanic/Latino), 19 international. Average age 31. 44 applicants, 95% accepted, 24 enrolled. In 2010, 4 master's, 3 doctorates awarded. *Degree requirements:* For master's, comprehensive exam (for some programs), thesis (for some programs); for doctorate, comprehensive exam, thesis/dissertation (for some programs). *Entrance requirements:* For master's and doctorate, GRE, minimum GPA of 3.0. Additional exam requirements/recommendations for international students: Required—TOEFL (minimum score 500 paper-based; 173 computer-based; 61 iBT), IELTS (minimum score 5). *Application deadline:* For fall admission, 7/1 for domestic students, 4/1 for international students; for spring admission, 11/1 for domestic students, 9/1 for international students. Applications are processed on a rolling basis. Application fee: $45 ($80 for international students). Electronic applications accepted. *Expenses:* Tuition, state resident: full-time $4172; part-time $231.75 per credit hour. Tuition, nonresident: full-time $15,332; part-time $851.75 per credit hour. *Financial support:* In 2010–11, 25 students received support, including 3 fellowships (averaging $43,541 per year), 9 research assistantships (averaging $19,556 per year), 24 teaching assistantships (averaging $13,046 per year); career-related internships or fieldwork, scholarships/grants, tuition waivers, and unspecified assistantships also available. Support available to part-time students. *Faculty research:* Nanotechnology, experimental physics, astrophysics, theoretical physics. Total annual research expenditures: $1.8 million. *Unit head:* Dr. Miguel Yacaman, Chair, 210-458-5451, Fax: 210-458-4919, E-mail: miguel.yacaman@utsa.edu. *Application contact:* Veronica Ramirez, Assistant Dean of the Graduate School, 210-458-4330, Fax: 210-458-4332, E-mail: graduatestudies@utsa.edu.

The University of Toledo, College of Graduate Studies, College of Natural Sciences and Mathematics, Department of Physics and Astronomy, Toledo, OH 43606-3390. Offers physics (MS, PhD). *Faculty:* 29. *Students:* 56 full-time (9 women), 4 part-time (2 women), 25 international. Average age 28. 94 applicants, 15% accepted, 13 enrolled. In 2010, 1 master's, 4 doctorates awarded. *Degree requirements:* For master's, thesis; for doctorate, thesis/dissertation, departmental qualifying exam. *Entrance requirements:* For master's and doctorate, GRE General Test, GRE Subject Test, A minimum 2.7 cumulative point-hour ratio (on a 4.0 scale) for all previous academic work. Three letters of recommendation, a statement of purpose, and transcripts from all prior institutions attended. Additional exam requirements/recommendations for international students: Required—TOEFL (minimum score 550 paper-based; 213 computer-based; 80 iBT), IELTS (minimum score 6.5). *Application deadline:* For fall admission, 1/15 priority date for domestic and international students. Applications are processed on a rolling basis. Application fee: $45 ($75 for international students). Electronic applications accepted. *Expenses:* Tuition, state resident: full-time $11,426; part-time $476 per credit hour. Tuition, nonresident: full-time $21,660; part-time $903 per credit hour. One-time fee: $62. *Financial support:* Research assistantships with tuition reimbursements, teaching assistantships with tuition reimbursements, Federal Work-Study, institutionally sponsored loans, scholarships/grants, tuition waivers (full), and unspecified assistantships available. Support available to part-time students. *Faculty research:* Atomic physics, solid-state physics, materials science, astrophysics. *Unit head:* Dr. Lawrence Anderson-Huang, Chair, 419-530-7257, E-mail: lawrence.anderson@utoledo.edu. *Application contact:* Graduate School Office, 419-530-4723, Fax: 419-537-4724, E-mail: grdsch@utnet.utoledo.edu.

University of Toronto, School of Graduate Studies, Physical Sciences Division, Department of Physics, Toronto, ON M5S 1A1, Canada. Offers M Sc, PhD. *Degree requirements:* For master's, thesis optional; for doctorate, thesis/dissertation. *Entrance requirements:* For master's, minimum B+ average in an honors physics program or equivalent, 2 letters of reference; for doctorate, M Sc degree in physics or a related field, 2 letters of reference.

University of Tulsa, Graduate School, College of Engineering and Natural Sciences, Department of Physics and Engineering Physics, Program in Physics, Tulsa, OK 74104-3189. Offers MS. Part-time programs available. *Faculty:* 7 full-time (0 women). *Students:* 5 full-time (1 woman); includes 1 minority (American Indian or Alaska Native, non-Hispanic/Latino), 3 international. Average age 24. 171 applicants, 5% accepted, 2 enrolled. In 2010, 2 master's awarded. *Degree requirements:* For master's, thesis. *Entrance requirements:* For master's, GRE General Test. Additional exam requirements/recommendations for international students: Required—TOEFL (minimum score 550 paper-based; 213 computer-based; 80 iBT), IELTS (minimum score 6). *Application deadline:* Applications are processed on a rolling basis. Application fee: $40. Electronic applications accepted. *Expenses:* Tuition: Full-time $16,902; part-time $939 per credit hour. Required fees: $1020; $4 per credit hour. Tuition and fees vary according to course load. *Financial support:* In 2010–11, 5 students received support, including 2 research assistantships (averaging $12,000 per year), 3 teaching assistantships (averaging $9,951 per year); fellowships, career-related internships or fieldwork, Federal Work-Study, scholarships/grants, health care benefits, tuition waivers, and unspecified assistantships also available. Support available to part-time students. Financial award application deadline: 2/1. *Faculty research:* Nanotechnology, theoretical plasma physics, theoretical and experimental condensed matter, optics, applications of laser spectroscopy to environmental applications. Total annual research expenditures: $2.3 million. *Unit head:* Dr. George Miller, Advisor and Program Chair, 918-631-3021, Fax: 918-631-2995, E-mail: george-miller@utulsa.edu. *Application contact:* Dr. George Miller, Advisor and Program Chair, 918-631-3021, Fax: 918-631-2995, E-mail: george-miller@utulsa.edu.

University of Utah, Graduate School, College of Science, Department of Physics and Astronomy, Salt Lake City, UT 84112. Offers chemical physics (PhD); medical physics (MS, PhD); physics (MA, MS, PhD); physics teaching (PhD). Part-time programs available. *Faculty:* 34 full-time (2 women), 2 part-time/adjunct (0 women). *Students:* 69 full-time (15 women), 18 part-time (5 women); includes 3 minority (1 Asian, non-Hispanic/Latino; 2 Hispanic/Latino), 38 international. Average age 30. 35 applicants, 74% accepted, 12 enrolled. In 2010, 12 master's, 11 doctorates awarded. Terminal master's awarded for partial completion of doctoral program. *Degree requirements:* For master's, comprehensive exam (for some programs), thesis or alternative, teaching experience, departmental exam; for doctorate, comprehensive exam, thesis/dissertation, departmental qualifying exam. *Entrance requirements:* For master's and doctorate, GRE General Test, GRE Subject Test, minimum GPA of 3.0. Additional exam requirements/recommendations for international students: Required—TOEFL (minimum score 500 paper-based; 173 computer-based; 69 iBT). *Application deadline:* For fall admission, 4/1 priority date for domestic and international students. Applications are processed on a rolling basis. Application fee: $55 ($65 for international students). Electronic applications accepted. *Expenses:* Tuition, area resident: Part-time $179.19 per credit hour. Tuition, state resident: full-time $4384. Tuition, nonresident: full-time $16,684; part-time $630.67 per credit hour. Required fees: $350 per semester. Tuition and fees vary according to course load, degree level and program. *Financial support:* In 2010–11, 61 teaching assistantships with full and partial tuition reimbursements (averaging $14,626 per year) were awarded; Federal Work-Study, institutionally sponsored loans, and scholarships/grants also available. Financial award application deadline: 2/15; financial award applicants required to submit FAFSA. *Faculty research:* High-energy, cosmic-ray, astrophysics, medical physics, condensed matter, relativity applied physics. Total annual research expenditures: $6.5 million. *Unit head:* Dr. David Kieda, Chair, 801-581-6901, Fax: 801-581-4801, E-mail: kieda@physics.utah.edu. *Application contact:* Jackie Hadley, Graduate Secretary, 801-581-6861, Fax: 801-581-4801, E-mail: jackie@physics.utah.edu.

University of Vermont, Graduate College, College of Arts and Sciences, Department of Physics, Burlington, VT 05405. Offers MS. *Students:* 4 (1 woman). 4 applicants, 25% accepted, 0 enrolled. *Entrance requirements:* For master's, GRE General Test. Additional exam requirements/recommendations for international students: Required—TOEFL (minimum score 550 paper-based; 213 computer-based; 80 iBT). *Application deadline:* For fall admission, 4/1 priority date for domestic students. Applications are processed on a rolling basis. Application fee: $40. Electronic applications accepted. *Expenses:* Tuition, state resident: part-time $537 per credit hour. Tuition, nonresident: part-time $1355 per credit hour. *Financial support:* Fellowships, research assistantships, teaching assistantships available. Financial award application deadline: 3/1. *Unit head:* Dr. D. Clougherty, Chairperson, 802-656-2644. *Application contact:* Prof. Kevork Spartalian, Coordinator, 802-656-2644.

University of Victoria, Faculty of Graduate Studies, Faculty of Science, Department of Physics and Astronomy, Victoria, BC V8W 2Y2, Canada. Offers astronomy and astrophysics (M Sc, PhD); condensed matter physics (M Sc, PhD); experimental particle physics (M Sc, PhD); medical physics (M Sc, PhD); ocean physics (M Sc, PhD); theoretical physics (M Sc, PhD). *Degree requirements:* For master's, thesis; for doctorate, comprehensive exam, thesis/dissertation, candidacy exam. *Entrance requirements:* For master's and doctorate, GRE. Additional exam requirements/recommendations for international students: Required—TOEFL (minimum score 575 paper-based; 233 computer-based), IELTS (minimum score 7). Electronic applications accepted. *Faculty research:* Old stellar populations; observational cosmology and large scale structure; cp violation; atlas.

University of Virginia, College and Graduate School of Arts and Sciences, Department of Physics, Charlottesville, VA 22903. Offers physics (MA, MS, PhD); physics education (MA). *Faculty:* 31 full-time (4 women). *Students:* 87 full-time (20 women); includes 2 Asian, non-Hispanic/Latino; 1 Hispanic/Latino, 58 international. Average age 26. 194 applicants, 20% accepted, 10 enrolled. In 2010, 30 master's, 7 doctorates awarded. *Degree requirements:* For master's, thesis (for some programs); for doctorate, comprehensive exam, thesis/dissertation. *Entrance requirements:* For master's and doctorate, GRE General Test, GRE Subject Test, 2 or more letters of recommendation. Additional exam requirements/recommendations for international students: Required—TOEFL (minimum score 600 paper-based; 250 computer-based; 90 iBT), IELTS. *Application deadline:* For fall admission, 1/7 for domestic and international students. Applications are processed on a rolling basis. Application fee: $60. Electronic applications accepted. *Financial support:* Fellowships, research assistantships, teaching assistantships available. Financial award applicants required to submit FAFSA. *Unit head:* Joe Poon, Chair, 434-924-3781, Fax: 434-924-4576, E-mail: phys-chair@physics.virginia.edu. *Application contact:* Despina Louca, Associate Chair for Graduate Studies, 434-924-3781, Fax: 434-924-4576, E-mail: grad-info-request@physics.virginia.edu.

University of Washington, Graduate School, College of Arts and Sciences, Department of Physics, Seattle, WA 98195. Offers MS, PhD. Part-time and evening/weekend programs available. Terminal master's awarded for partial completion of doctoral program. *Degree requirements:* For doctorate, thesis/dissertation. *Entrance requirements:* For master's, GRE; for doctorate, GRE General Test, GRE Subject Test. Additional exam requirements/recommendations for international students: Required—TOEFL. Electronic applications accepted. *Faculty research:* Astro-, atomic, condensed-matter, nuclear, and particle physics; physics education.

Physics

University of Waterloo, Graduate Studies, Faculty of Science, Guelph-Waterloo Physics Institute, Waterloo, ON N2L 3G1, Canada. Offers M Sc, PhD. M Sc, PhD offered jointly with University of Guelph. Part-time programs available. *Degree requirements:* For master's, project or thesis; for doctorate, thesis/dissertation. *Entrance requirements:* For master's, GRE Subject Test, honors degree, minimum B average; for doctorate, GRE Subject Test, master's degree, minimum B average. Additional exam requirements/recommendations for international students: Required—TOEFL; TWE. Electronic applications accepted. *Faculty research:* Condensed-matter and materials physics; industrial and applied physics; subatomic physics; astrophysics and gravitation; atomic, molecular, and optical physics.

The University of Western Ontario, Faculty of Graduate Studies, Physical Sciences Division, Department of Applied Mathematics, London, ON N6A 5B8, Canada. Offers applied mathematics (M Sc, PhD); theoretical physics (PhD). *Degree requirements:* For master's, thesis or alternative; for doctorate, comprehensive exam, thesis/dissertation. *Entrance requirements:* For master's and doctorate, minimum B average. Additional exam requirements/recommendations for international students: Required—TOEFL. *Faculty research:* Fluid dynamics, mathematical and computational methods, theoretical physics.

The University of Western Ontario, Faculty of Graduate Studies, Physical Sciences Division, Department of Physics and Astronomy, Program in Physics, London, ON N6A 5B8, Canada. Offers M Sc, PhD. Terminal master's awarded for partial completion of doctoral program. *Degree requirements:* For master's, thesis; for doctorate, comprehensive exam, thesis/dissertation. *Entrance requirements:* For master's, GRE Subject Test (physics), honors B Sc degree, minimum B average (Canadian), A- (international); for doctorate, minimum B average (Canadian), A- (international). Additional exam requirements/recommendations for international students: Required—TOEFL (minimum score 580 paper-based; 237 computer-based). *Faculty research:* Condensed-matter and surface science, space and atmospheric physics, atomic and molecular physics, medical physics, theoretical physics.

University of Windsor, Faculty of Graduate Studies, Faculty of Science, Department of Physics, Windsor, ON N9B 3P4, Canada. Offers M Sc, PhD. Part-time programs available. *Degree requirements:* For master's, thesis or alternative; for doctorate, thesis/dissertation. *Entrance requirements:* For master's, GRE General Test, minimum B average; for doctorate, GRE General Test, master's degree. Additional exam requirements/recommendations for international students: Required—TOEFL (minimum score 560 paper-based; 220 computer-based), GRE Subject Test in physics. Electronic applications accepted. *Faculty research:* Electrodynamics, plasma physics, atomic structure/particles, spectroscopy, quantum mechanics.

University of Wisconsin–Madison, Graduate School, College of Letters and Science, Department of Physics, Madison, WI 53706-1380. Offers MA, MS, PhD. Terminal master's awarded for partial completion of doctoral program. *Degree requirements:* For master's, qualifying exam, thesis (MS); for doctorate, thesis/dissertation, preliminary and qualifying exams. *Entrance requirements:* For master's and doctorate, GRE, minimum GPA of 3.0. Additional exam requirements/recommendations for international students: Required—TOEFL. Electronic applications accepted. *Expenses:* Tuition, state resident: full-time $9887.36; part-time $617.96 per credit. Tuition, nonresident: full-time $24,054; part-time $1503.40 per credit. Required fees: $67.63 per credit. Tuition and fees vary according to reciprocity agreements. *Faculty research:* Atomic, physics, condensed matter, astrophysics, particles and fields.

University of Wisconsin–Milwaukee, Graduate School, College of Letters and Sciences, Department of Physics, Milwaukee, WI 53201-0413. Offers MS, PhD. *Faculty:* 22 full-time (4 women). *Students:* 26 full-time (8 women), 10 part-time (4 women); includes 2 Asian, non-Hispanic/Latino, 22 international. Average age 29. 60 applicants, 37% accepted, 8 enrolled. In 2010, 1 master's, 4 doctorates awarded. *Degree requirements:* For master's, thesis or alternative; for doctorate, one foreign language, thesis/dissertation. *Entrance requirements:* For master's, GRE General Test, curriculum vitae; for doctorate, GRE General Test. Additional exam requirements/recommendations for international students: Required—TOEFL (minimum score 550 paper-based; 79 iBT), IELTS (minimum score 6.5). *Application deadline:* For fall admission, 1/1 priority date for domestic students; for spring admission, 9/1 for domestic students. Applications are processed on a rolling basis. Application fee: $56 ($96 for international students). Electronic applications accepted. *Financial support:* In 2010–11, 1 fellowship, 14 research assistantships, 20 teaching assistantships were awarded; career-related internships or fieldwork and unspecified assistantships also available. Support available to part-time students. Financial award application deadline: 4/15; financial award applicants required to submit FAFSA. *Faculty research:* Gravitation, biophysics, condensed matter, optics, medical. Total annual research expenditures: $4.7 million. *Unit head:* Paul Lyman, Representative, 414-229-4626, Fax: 414-229-4474, E-mail: plyman@uwm.edu. *Application contact:* General Information Contact, 414-229-4982, Fax: 414-229-6967, E-mail: gradschool@uwm.edu.

Utah State University, School of Graduate Studies, College of Science, Department of Physics, Logan, UT 84322. Offers MS, PhD. Part-time programs available. Terminal master's awarded for partial completion of doctoral program. *Degree requirements:* For master's, thesis; for doctorate, comprehensive exam, thesis/dissertation. *Entrance requirements:* For master's and doctorate, GRE General Test, minimum GPA of 3.0. Additional exam requirements/recommendations for international students: Required—TOEFL (minimum score 550 paper-based; 213 computer-based). Electronic applications accepted. *Faculty research:* Upper-atmosphere physics, relativity, gravitational magnetism, particle physics, nanotechnology.

Vanderbilt University, Graduate School, Department of Physics and Astronomy, Nashville, TN 37240-1001. Offers astronomy (MS); physics (MA, MAT, MS, PhD). *Faculty:* 33 full-time (3 women). *Students:* 71 full-time (19 women), 1 part-time (0 women); includes 6 Black or African American, non-Hispanic/Latino; 2 Asian, non-Hispanic/Latino; 4 Hispanic/Latino. Average age 28. 179 applicants, 18% accepted, 15 enrolled. In 2010, 6 master's, 9 doctorates awarded. *Degree requirements:* For master's, thesis; for doctorate, comprehensive exam, thesis/dissertation, final and qualifying exams. *Entrance requirements:* For master's, GRE General Test; for doctorate, GRE General Test, GRE Subject Test. Additional exam requirements/recommendations for international students: Required—TOEFL (minimum score 570 paper-based; 230 computer-based; 88 iBT). *Application deadline:* For fall admission, 1/15 for domestic and international students. Application fee: $0. Electronic applications accepted. *Financial support:* Fellowships with full and partial tuition reimbursements, research assistantships with full tuition reimbursements, teaching assistantships with full tuition reimbursements, career-related internships or fieldwork, Federal Work-Study, and institutionally sponsored loans available. Financial award application deadline: 1/15; financial award applicants required to submit CSS PROFILE or FAFSA. *Faculty research:* Experimental and theoretical physics, free electron laser, living-state physics, heavy-ion physics, nuclear structure. *Unit head:* Robert J. Scherrer, PhD, Chair, 615-322-2828, Fax: 615-343-7263, E-mail: robert.scherrer@vanderbilt.edu. *Application contact:* Julia Velkovska, PhD, Director of Graduate Studies, 615-322-0656, Fax: 615-343-7263, E-mail: julia.velkovska@vanderbilt.edu.

Virginia Commonwealth University, Graduate School, College of Humanities and Sciences, Department of Physics, Program in Physics and Applied Physics, Richmond, VA 23284-9005. Offers MS. *Students:* 12 full-time (5 women); includes 1 Black or African American, non-Hispanic/Latino; 2 Asian, non-Hispanic/Latino. 12 applicants, 83% accepted, 7 enrolled. In 2010, 4 master's awarded. *Entrance requirements:* For master's, GRE or MAT. Additional exam requirements/recommendations for international students: Required—TOEFL (minimum score 600 paper-based; 250 computer-based; 100 iBT); Recommended—IELTS (minimum score 6.5). *Application deadline:* For fall admission, 8/1 for domestic students; for spring admission, 12/1 for domestic students. Applications are processed on a rolling basis. Application fee: $50. Electronic applications accepted. *Expenses:* Tuition, state resident: full-time $4308; part-time $479 per credit hour. Tuition, nonresident: full-time $8942; part-time $994 per credit hour. Required fees: $2000; $85 per credit hour. Tuition and fees vary according to course level, course load, degree level, campus/location and program. *Financial support:* Federal Work-Study and institutionally sponsored loans available. Support available to part-time students. *Faculty research:* Theoretical and experimental condensed matter physics, general relativity and cosmology, physics education. *Unit head:* Dr. Alison A. Baski, Chair, 804-828-1821, Fax: 804-828-7073, E-mail: aabaski@vcu.edu. *Application contact:* Dr. Shiv N. Khanna, Graduate Program Director, 804-828-1820, Fax: 804-828-7073, E-mail: snkhanna@vcu.edu.

Virginia Polytechnic Institute and State University, Graduate School, College of Science, Department of Physics, Blacksburg, VA 24061. Offers MS, PhD. *Faculty:* 25 full-time (4 women). *Students:* 71 full-time (16 women), 1 part-time (0 women), 43 international. Average age 27. 81 applicants, 52% accepted, 17 enrolled. In 2010, 6 master's, 9 doctorates awarded. *Degree requirements:* For master's, comprehensive exam (for some programs), thesis (for some programs); for doctorate, comprehensive exam (for some programs), thesis/dissertation (for some programs). *Entrance requirements:* For master's and doctorate, GRE. Additional exam requirements/recommendations for international students: Required—TOEFL (minimum score 550 paper-based; 213 computer-based). *Application deadline:* For fall admission, 7/1 for domestic and international students; for spring admission, 12/1 for domestic and international students. Applications are processed on a rolling basis. Application fee: $65. Electronic applications accepted. *Expenses:* Tuition, area resident: Full-time $9399; part-time $488 per credit hour. Tuition, state resident: full-time $9399; part-time $488 per credit hour. Tuition, nonresident: full-time $17,854; part-time $957.75 per credit hour. International tuition: $17,854 full-time. Required fees: $1534. Full-time tuition and fees vary according to program. *Financial support:* In 2010–11, 17 research assistantships with full tuition reimbursements (averaging $17,272 per year), 38 teaching assistantships with full tuition reimbursements (averaging $15,846 per year) were awarded; career-related internships or fieldwork, Federal Work-Study, scholarships/grants, health care benefits, and unspecified assistantships also available. Financial award application deadline: 1/15. *Faculty research:* Condensed matter, particle physics, theoretical and experimental astrophysics, biophysics, mathematical physics. Total annual research expenditures: $3.7 million. *Unit head:* Dr. Beate Schmittmann, UNIT HEAD, 540-231-7472, Fax: 540-231-7511, E-mail: physics.chair@vt.edu. *Application contact:* Uwe Tauber, Contact, 540-231-8998, Fax: 540-231-7511, E-mail: tauber@vt.edu.

Virginia State University, School of Graduate Studies, Research, and Outreach, School of Engineering, Science and Technology, Department of Chemistry and Physics, Petersburg, VA 23806-0001. Offers physics (MS). *Degree requirements:* For master's, one foreign language, thesis. *Entrance requirements:* For master's, GRE General Test. *Expenses:* Tuition, state resident: full-time $5576; part-time $335 per credit hour. Tuition, nonresident: full-time $13,402; part-time $670 per credit hour.

Wake Forest University, Graduate School of Arts and Sciences, Department of Physics, Winston-Salem, NC 27109. Offers MS, PhD. Part-time programs available. *Degree requirements:* For master's, thesis; for doctorate, comprehensive exam, thesis/dissertation. *Entrance requirements:* For master's and doctorate, GRE General Test. Additional exam requirements/recommendations for international students: Required—TOEFL (minimum score 213 computer-based; 79 iBT). Electronic applications accepted.

Washington State University, Graduate School, College of Sciences, Department of Physics and Astronomy, Pullman, WA 99164. Offers physics (MS, PhD). *Faculty:* 20. *Students:* 64 full-time (12 women); includes 1 Hispanic/Latino, 34 international. Average age 28. 127 applicants, 39% accepted, 12 enrolled. In 2010, 6 master's, 2 doctorates awarded. Terminal master's awarded for partial completion of doctoral program. *Degree requirements:* For master's, comprehensive exam (for some programs), thesis (for some programs), oral exam; for doctorate, comprehensive exam, thesis/dissertation, oral exam, written exam. *Entrance requirements:* For master's and doctorate, GRE General Test, GRE Subject Test, minimum GPA of 3.0 in last half of undergraduate work completed. Additional exam requirements/recommendations for international students: Required—TOEFL (minimum score 550 paper-based; 214 computer-based; 80 iBT), IELTS. *Application deadline:* For fall admission, 1/10 priority date for domestic students, 1/10 for international students; for spring admission, 7/1 priority date for domestic students, 7/1 for international students. Applications are processed on a rolling basis. Application fee: $50. Electronic applications accepted. *Expenses:* Tuition, state resident: full-time $8552; part-time $443 per credit. Tuition, nonresident: full-time $21,650; part-time $1083 per credit. Required fees: $846. *Financial support:* In 2010–11, 41 students received support, including 1 fellowship with full and partial tuition reimbursement available (averaging $5,000 per year), 15 research assistantships with full and partial tuition reimbursements available (averaging $13,917 per year), 25 teaching assistantships with full and partial tuition reimbursements available (averaging $13,056 per year); Federal Work-Study and institutionally sponsored loans also available. Financial award application deadline: 3/1; financial award applicants required to submit FAFSA. *Faculty research:* Linear and nonlinear acoustics and optics, shock wave dynamics, solid-state physics, surface physics, high-pressure and semiconductor physics. Total annual research expenditures: $2.5 million. *Unit head:* Steve L. Tomsovic, Chair, 509-335-7207, Fax: 509-335-7816, E-mail: tomsovic@wsu.edu. *Application contact:* Graduate School Admissions, 800-GRADWSU, Fax: 509-335-1949, E-mail: gradsch@wsu.edu.

Washington University in St. Louis, Graduate School of Arts and Sciences, Department of Physics, St. Louis, MO 63130-4899. Offers PhD. Terminal master's awarded for partial completion of doctoral program. *Degree requirements:* For doctorate, thesis/dissertation. *Entrance requirements:* For doctorate, GRE General Test. Electronic applications accepted.

Wayne State University, College of Liberal Arts and Sciences, Department of Physics and Astronomy, Detroit, MI 48202. Offers physics (MA, MS, PhD). *Faculty:* 15 full-time (1 woman). *Students:* 54 full-time (12 women), 6 part-time (3 women); includes 5 minority (2 Black or African American, non-Hispanic/Latino; 1 American Indian or Alaska Native, non-Hispanic/Latino; 2 Asian, non-Hispanic/Latino), 35 international. Average age 30. 61 applicants, 28% accepted, 11 enrolled. In 2010, 11 master's, 6 doctorates awarded. *Degree requirements:* For doctorate, thesis/dissertation. *Entrance requirements:* For master's, GRE, 3 letters of recommendation; for doctorate, GRE, 3 letters of recommendation; personal statement. Additional exam requirements/recommendations for international students: Required—TOEFL (minimum score 550 paper-based; 213 computer-based); Recommended—TWE (minimum score 6). *Application deadline:* For fall admission, 7/1 for domestic students, 6/1 for international students; for winter admission, 10/1 for international students; for spring admission, 2/1 for international students. Applications are processed on a rolling basis. Application fee: $30 ($50 for international students). Electronic applications accepted. *Expenses:* Tuition, state resident: full-time $7662; part-time $478.85 per credit hour. Tuition, nonresident: full-time $16,920; part-time $1057.55 per credit hour. Required fees: $571.20; $35.70 per credit hour. $188.05 per semester. Tuition and fees vary according to course load and program. *Financial support:* In 2010–11, 3 fellowships with tuition reimbursements (averaging $18,328 per year), 22 research assistantships with tuition reimbursements (averaging $17,284 per year), 25 teaching assistantships with tuition reimbursements (averaging $16,984 per year) were awarded; Federal Work-Study also available. Financial award application deadline: 7/1. *Faculty research:* High energy particle physics, relativistic heavy ion physics, theoretical physics, positron and atomic physics, condensed matter and nano-scale physics. *Unit head:* Ratna Naik, Chair, 313-577-2756, Fax: 313-577-3932, E-mail: naik@physics.wayne.edu. *Application contact:* Jogindra Wadehra, Graduate Director, 313-577-2740, E-mail: wadehra@physics.wayne.edu.

Wesleyan University, Graduate Programs, Department of Physics, Middletown, CT 06459. Offers MA, PhD. *Faculty:* 9 full-time (1 woman). *Students:* 17 full-time (6 women); includes 7 Asian, non-Hispanic/Latino; 2 Hispanic/Latino, 12 international. Average age 25. 58 applicants, 3% accepted, 2 enrolled. In 2010, 2 master's awarded. Terminal master's awarded for partial completion of doctoral program. *Degree requirements:* For master's, thesis; for doctorate,

thesis/dissertation. *Entrance requirements:* For master's, GRE General Test, GRE Subject Test; for doctorate, GRE Subject Test. Additional exam requirements/recommendations for international students: Required—TOEFL. *Application deadline:* Applications are processed on a rolling basis. Application fee: $0. Electronic applications accepted. *Expenses:* Tuition: Full-time $43,404. Required fees: $830. *Financial support:* In 2010–11, 2 research assistantships with full tuition reimbursements, 11 teaching assistantships with full tuition reimbursements were awarded; institutionally sponsored loans and tuition waivers (full) also available. Financial award application deadline: 4/15; financial award applicants required to submit FAFSA. *Faculty research:* Biophysics, computational soft matter physics, mesoscopic transport, semiclassical methods and quantum chaos, disordered systems, theoretical atomic physics, low-temperature physics, magnetic resonance, atomic collisions, laser spectroscopy, surface physics, turbulence, granular media. *Unit head:* Dr. Reinhold Blumel, Chairman, 860-685-2032, E-mail: rblumel@wesleyan.edu. *Application contact:* Erinn Savage, Information Contact, 860-685-2030, Fax: 860-685-2031, E-mail: esavage@wesleyan.edu.

Western Illinois University, School of Graduate Studies, College of Arts and Sciences, Department of Physics, Macomb, IL 61455-1390. Offers MS. Part-time programs available. *Students:* 15 full-time (3 women); includes 1 minority (Asian, non-Hispanic/Latino), 11 international. Average age 27. 5 applicants, 100% accepted. In 2010, 2 master's awarded. *Degree requirements:* For master's, thesis or alternative. *Entrance requirements:* Additional exam requirements/recommendations for international students: Required—TOEFL (minimum score 550 paper-based; 213 computer-based; 80 iBT). *Application deadline:* Applications are processed on a rolling basis. Application fee: $30. Electronic applications accepted. *Expenses:* Tuition, state resident: full-time $6370; part-time $265.40 per credit hour. Tuition, nonresident: full-time $12,740; part-time $530.80 per credit hour. Required fees: $75.67 per credit hour. *Financial support:* In 2010–11, 12 students received support, including 12 research assistantships with full tuition reimbursements available (averaging $7,280 per year); health care benefits also available. Financial award applicants required to submit FAFSA. *Unit head:* Dr. Mark Boley, Interim Chairperson, 309-298-1538. *Application contact:* Evelyn Hoing, Assistant Director of Graduate Studies, 309-298-1806, Fax: 309-298-2345, E-mail: grad-office@wiu.edu.

Western Kentucky University, Graduate Studies, Ogden College of Science and Engineering, Department of Physics and Astronomy, Bowling Green, KY 42101. Offers homeland security sciences (MS); physics (MA Ed).

Western Michigan University, Graduate College, College of Arts and Sciences, Department of Physics, Kalamazoo, MI 49008. Offers MA, PhD. *Degree requirements:* For master's, thesis; for doctorate, thesis/dissertation, oral exam. *Entrance requirements:* For doctorate, GRE General Test.

West Virginia University, Eberly College of Arts and Sciences, Department of Physics, Morgantown, WV 26506. Offers applied physics (MS, PhD); astrophysics (MS, PhD); chemical physics (MS, PhD); condensed matter physics (MS, PhD); elementary particle physics (MS, PhD); materials physics (MS, PhD); plasma physics (MS, PhD); solid state physics (MS, PhD);

statistical physics (MS, PhD); theoretical physics (MS, PhD). Terminal master's awarded for partial completion of doctoral program. *Degree requirements:* For master's, thesis or alternative, qualifying exam; for doctorate, thesis/dissertation, qualifying exam. *Entrance requirements:* For master's and doctorate, GRE General Test, minimum GPA of 3.0. Additional exam requirements/recommendations for international students: Required—TOEFL. *Faculty research:* Experimental and theoretical condensed-matter, plasma, high-energy theory, nonlinear dynamics, space physics.

Worcester Polytechnic Institute, Graduate Studies and Research, Department of Physics, Worcester, MA 01609-2280. Offers MS, PhD. *Faculty:* 7 full-time (2 women), 1 (woman) part-time/adjunct. *Students:* 13 full-time (2 women), 1 (woman) part-time; includes 1 Black or African American, non-Hispanic/Latino; 1 Native Hawaiian or other Pacific Islander, non-Hispanic/Latino, 6 international. 43 applicants, 28% accepted, 2 enrolled. In 2010, 3 master's, 2 doctorates awarded. *Degree requirements:* For master's, thesis; for doctorate, comprehensive exam, thesis/dissertation. *Entrance requirements:* For master's, GRE (recommended), 3 letters of recommendation; for doctorate, GRE (recommended), 3 letters of recommendation, statement of purpose (recommended). Additional exam requirements/recommendations for international students: Required—TOEFL (minimum score 550 paper-based; 213 computer-based; 79 iBT), IELTS (minimum score 6.5). *Application deadline:* For fall admission, 1/1 priority date for domestic students, 1/1 for international students; for spring admission, 10/1 priority date for domestic students, 10/1 for international students. Applications are processed on a rolling basis. Application fee: $70. Electronic applications accepted. *Expenses:* Tuition: Full-time $20,862; part-time $1159 per term. One-time fee: $15. *Financial support:* Career-related internships or fieldwork, institutionally sponsored loans, scholarships/grants, and unspecified assistantships available. Financial award application deadline: 1/1; financial award applicants required to submit FAFSA. *Faculty research:* Soft-condensed matter, complex fluids, biophysics, quantum and atom optics, wave function engineering. *Unit head:* Dr. Germano S. Iannacchione, Head, 508-831-5258, Fax: 508-831-5886, E-mail: gsiannac@wpi.edu. *Application contact:* Dr. A.K. Paravind, Graduate Coordinator, 508-831-5258, Fax: 508-831-5886, E-mail: paravind@wpi.edu.

Wright State University, School of Graduate Studies, College of Science and Mathematics, Department of Physics, Program in Physics, Dayton, OH 45435. Offers geophysics (MS); medical physics (MS). Part-time and evening/weekend programs available. *Degree requirements:* For master's, thesis. *Entrance requirements:* Additional exam requirements/recommendations for international students: Required—TOEFL. *Faculty research:* Solid-state physics, optics, geophysics.

Yale University, Graduate School of Arts and Sciences, Department of Physics, New Haven, CT 06520. Offers PhD. *Degree requirements:* For doctorate, thesis/dissertation. *Entrance requirements:* For doctorate, GRE General Test, GRE Subject Test.

York University, Faculty of Graduate Studies, Faculty of Science and Engineering, Program in Physics and Astronomy, Toronto, ON M3J 1P3, Canada. Offers M Sc, PhD. Part-time and evening/weekend programs available. *Degree requirements:* For master's, thesis or alternative; for doctorate, comprehensive exam, thesis/dissertation. Electronic applications accepted.

Plasma Physics

Princeton University, Graduate School, Department of Astrophysical Sciences, Program in Plasma Physics, Princeton, NJ 08544-1019. Offers PhD. *Degree requirements:* For doctorate, thesis/dissertation. *Entrance requirements:* For doctorate, GRE General Test, GRE Subject Test. Additional exam requirements/recommendations for international students: Required—TOEFL (minimum score 600 paper-based; 250 computer-based). *Faculty research:* Magnetic fusion energy research, plasma physics, x-ray laser studies.

University of Colorado Boulder, Graduate School, College of Arts and Sciences, Department of Astrophysical and Planetary Sciences, Boulder, CO 80309. Offers astrophysics (MS, PhD); planetary science (MS, PhD). *Faculty:* 20 full-time (3 women). *Students:* 48 full-time (14 women); includes 3 minority (1 American Indian or Alaska Native, non-Hispanic/Latino; 2 Asian, non-Hispanic/Latino), 4 international. Average age 26. 140 applicants, 9 enrolled. In 2010, 10 master's, 7 doctorates awarded. Terminal master's awarded for partial completion of doctoral program. *Degree requirements:* For master's, comprehensive exam, thesis or alternative; for doctorate, one foreign language, thesis/dissertation. *Entrance requirements:* For master's, GRE General Test, GRE Subject Test, minimum undergraduate GPA of 3.0; for doctorate, GRE General Test, GRE Subject Test. *Application deadline:* For fall admission, 1/15 priority date for domestic students, 12/1 for international students. Applications are processed on a rolling

basis. Application fee: $50 ($60 for international students). *Financial support:* In 2010–11, 13 fellowships (averaging $22,199 per year), 33 research assistantships (averaging $17,541 per year) were awarded; tuition waivers (full) also available. Support available to part-time students. Financial award application deadline: 1/15. *Faculty research:* Stellar and extragalactic astrophysics cosmology, space astronomy, planetary science. Total annual research expenditures: $31.2 million.

West Virginia University, Eberly College of Arts and Sciences, Department of Physics, Morgantown, WV 26506. Offers applied physics (MS, PhD); astrophysics (MS, PhD); chemical physics (MS, PhD); condensed matter physics (MS, PhD); elementary particle physics (MS, PhD); materials physics (MS, PhD); plasma physics (MS, PhD); solid state physics (MS, PhD); statistical physics (MS, PhD); theoretical physics (MS, PhD). Terminal master's awarded for partial completion of doctoral program. *Degree requirements:* For master's, thesis or alternative, qualifying exam; for doctorate, thesis/dissertation, qualifying exam. *Entrance requirements:* For master's and doctorate, GRE General Test, minimum GPA of 3.0. Additional exam requirements/recommendations for international students: Required—TOEFL. *Faculty research:* Experimental and theoretical condensed-matter, plasma, high-energy theory, nonlinear dynamics, space physics.

Theoretical Physics

Cornell University, Graduate School, Graduate Fields of Arts and Sciences, Field of Physics, Ithaca, NY 14853-0001. Offers experimental physics (MS, PhD); physics (MS, PhD); theoretical physics (MS, PhD). *Faculty:* 54 full-time (5 women). *Students:* 154 full-time (25 women); includes 1 Black or African American, non-Hispanic/Latino; 4 Asian, non-Hispanic/Latino; 3 Hispanic/Latino, 75 international. Average age 25. 409 applicants, 21% accepted, 31 enrolled. In 2010, 38 master's, 25 doctorates awarded. *Degree requirements:* For doctorate, comprehensive exam, thesis/dissertation. *Entrance requirements:* For doctorate, GRE General Test, GRE Subject Test (physics), 3 letters of recommendation. Additional exam requirements/recommendations for international students: Required—TOEFL (minimum score 620 paper-based; 260 computer-based; 105 iBT). *Application deadline:* For fall admission, 1/3 for domestic students. Application fee: $80. Electronic applications accepted. *Expenses:* Tuition: Full-time $29,500. Required fees: $76. Tuition and fees vary according to degree level and program. *Financial support:* In 2010–11, 24 fellowships with full tuition reimbursements, 67 research assistantships with full tuition reimbursements, 52 teaching assistantships with full tuition reimbursements were awarded; institutionally sponsored loans, scholarships/grants, health care benefits, tuition waivers (full and partial), and unspecified assistantships also available. Financial award applicants required to submit FAFSA. *Faculty research:* Experimental condensed matter physics, theoretical condensed matter physics, experimental high energy particle physics, theoretical particle physics and field theory, theoretical astrophysics. *Unit head:* Director of Graduate Studies, 607-255-7561. *Application contact:* Graduate Field Assistant, 607-255-7561, E-mail: physics-grad-adm@cornell.edu.

Delaware State University, Graduate Programs, Department of Applied Mathematics and Theoretical Physics, Interdisciplinary Program in Applied Mathematics and Theoretical Physics, Dover, DE 19901-2277. Offers PhD. *Degree requirements:* For doctorate, one foreign language,

thesis defense. *Entrance requirements:* For doctorate, GRE General Test, MS degree in physics or mathematics. Additional exam requirements/recommendations for international students: Required—TOEFL (minimum score 550 paper-based).

Harvard University, Graduate School of Arts and Sciences, Department of Physics, Cambridge, MA 02138. Offers experimental physics (PhD); medical engineering/medical physics (PhD), including applied physics, engineering sciences, physics; theoretical physics (PhD). *Degree requirements:* For doctorate, thesis/dissertation, final exams, laboratory experience. *Entrance requirements:* For doctorate, GRE General Test, GRE Subject Test. Additional exam requirements/recommendations for international students: Required—TOEFL. *Expenses:* Tuition: Full-time $34,976. Required fees: $1166. Full-time tuition and fees vary according to program. *Faculty research:* Particle physics, condensed matter physics, atomic physics.

Rutgers, The State University of New Jersey, New Brunswick, Graduate School-New Brunswick, Department of Physics and Astronomy, Piscataway, NJ 08854-8097. Offers astronomy (MS, PhD); biophysics (PhD); condensed matter physics (MS, PhD); elementary particle physics (MS, PhD); intermediate energy nuclear physics (MS); nuclear physics (MS, PhD); physics (MST); surface science (PhD); theoretical physics (MS, PhD). Part-time programs available. Terminal master's awarded for partial completion of doctoral program. *Degree requirements:* For master's, comprehensive exam, thesis or alternative; for doctorate, comprehensive exam, thesis/dissertation. *Entrance requirements:* For master's and doctorate, GRE General Test, GRE Subject Test. Additional exam requirements/recommendations for international students: Required—TOEFL (minimum score 560 paper-based). Electronic applications accepted. *Expenses:* Tuition, state resident: full-time $7200; part-time $600 per credit. Tuition, nonresident: full-time $11,124; part-time $927 per credit. *Faculty research:* Astronomy, high energy, condensed matter, surface, nuclear physics.

Peterson's Graduate Programs in the Physical Sciences, Mathematics, Agricultural Sciences, the Environment & Natural Resources 2012

www.facebook.com/petersonspublishing   **205**

Theoretical Physics

The University of Manchester, School of Physics and Astronomy, Manchester, United Kingdom. Offers astronomy and astrophysics (M Sc, PhD); biological physics (M Sc, PhD); condensed matter physics (M Sc, PhD); nonlinear and liquid crystals physics (M Sc, PhD); nuclear physics (M Sc, PhD); particle physics (M Sc, PhD); photon physics (M Sc, PhD); physics (M Sc, PhD); theoretical physics (M Sc, PhD).

University of Victoria, Faculty of Graduate Studies, Faculty of Science, Department of Physics and Astronomy, Victoria, BC V8W 2Y2, Canada. Offers astronomy and astrophysics (M Sc, PhD); condensed matter physics (M Sc, PhD); experimental particle physics (M Sc, PhD); medical physics (M Sc, PhD); ocean physics (M Sc, PhD); theoretical physics (M Sc, PhD). *Degree requirements:* For master's, thesis; for doctorate, comprehensive exam, thesis/dissertation, candidacy exam. *Entrance requirements:* For master's and doctorate, GRE. Additional exam requirements/recommendations for international students: Required—TOEFL (minimum score 575 paper-based; 233 computer-based), IELTS (minimum score 7). Electronic applications accepted. *Faculty research:* Old stellar populations; observational cosmology and large scale structure; cp violation; atlas.

West Virginia University, Eberly College of Arts and Sciences, Department of Physics, Morgantown, WV 26506. Offers applied physics (MS, PhD); astrophysics (MS, PhD); chemical physics (MS, PhD); condensed matter physics (MS, PhD); elementary particle physics (MS, PhD); materials physics (MS, PhD); plasma physics (MS, PhD); solid state physics (MS, PhD); statistical physics (MS, PhD); theoretical physics (MS, PhD). Terminal master's awarded for partial completion of doctoral program. *Degree requirements:* For master's, thesis or alternative, qualifying exam; for doctorate, thesis/dissertation, qualifying exam. *Entrance requirements:* For master's and doctorate, GRE General Test, minimum GPA of 3.0. Additional exam requirements/recommendations for international students: Required—TOEFL. *Faculty research:* Experimental and theoretical condensed-matter, plasma, high-energy theory, nonlinear dynamics, space physics.

206   www.facebook.com/petersonspublishing

Peterson's Graduate Programs in the Physical Sciences, Mathematics, Agricultural Sciences, the Environment & Natural Resources 2012

BOSTON UNIVERSITY

Department of Physics

Programs of Study	The Department of Physics offers multiple programs leading to the Ph.D. in physics with an optional M.A. degree. Research opportunities are offered in experimental high-energy particle physics, particle astrophysics, theoretical particle physics and cosmology, biological physics, experimental and theoretical condensed-matter physics, polymer physics, econophysics, and statistical physics.
	The Ph.D. degree requires the completion of 64 credit hours (equivalent to sixteen semester courses), an honors grade on the written comprehensive exam, an oral comprehensive exam, a departmental seminar, completion of a dissertation, and a dissertation oral defense. The dissertation must exhibit an original contribution to the field. Each student must satisfy a residency requirement of a minimum of two consecutive semesters of full-time graduate study at Boston University. The average time to complete a Ph.D. degree is about six years.
	The M.A. degree requires the completion of 32 credit hours (equivalent to eight semester courses) and a passing grade on the written comprehensive exam or the completion of a master's thesis. The requirements for a master's degree may be satisfied as part of the Ph.D. degree program. Each student must satisfy a residency requirement of a minimum of two consecutive semesters of full-time graduate study at Boston University.
Research Facilities	The Department of Physics is part of Boston University's Science and Engineering Complex, centrally located on the main Charles River Campus. Condensed-matter physics facilities include electronic and mechanical nanostructure fabrication and measurement, metastable-helium-atom probes of surface spin order and dynamics, photoemission and soft X-ray fluorescence probes of electronic structure in novel materials, X-ray diffractometers, and the optics and transport of electrons at high fields and low temperatures. Biological physics and polymer physics labs include dynamical light scattering, Raman and Brillouin scattering, and infrared and far-infrared absorption spectroscopy as well as modern facilities for genetically manipulating biomolecules. Physicists at the Center for Photonics develop and use near-field scanning optical and infrared microscopy, ultrafast infrared spectroscopy, entangled photons for quantum information processing and entangled photon microscopy, and a full complement of molecular beam epitaxy and device processing facilities, the latter primarily with InGaAl-nitride wide-band-gap semiconductor materials and devices. The high-energy physics labs include facilities for the design, production, and testing of key components of various particle detectors. Collaborations include the D0 experiment at Fermilab; the ATLAS and CMS experiments at the CERN Large Hadron Collider; the MuLan experiment at PSI, Switzerland; the Super-Kamiokande experiment in Kamioka, Japan, including the KEK/K2K and T2K/JPARC neutrino accelerator projects; the CLEAN/DEAP dark matter experiments; and the neutron EDM experiment at ORNL. For computation, workstations are networked to two major Departmental SGI servers as well as computer clusters provided by the University for student use. In addition, students have access to the University's high-end computational resources, which include IBM p690 servers with 112 processors (580 Gflops), an IBM p655 system with forty-eight processors (210 Gflops), an IBM Linux cluster with fifty-two dual-processor compute nodes and twenty-four display nodes, and advanced visualization facilities.
Financial Aid	Through a combination of teaching fellowships, research assistantships, and University fellowships, physics graduate students are supported full-time and receive full-tuition scholarships for the duration of their studies based on satisfactory academic standing. The standard stipend for teaching fellows and research assistants is currently $29,300 per calendar year plus the basic student medical insurance.
Cost of Study	Tuition and fees are provided for as described above. Books and supplies are estimated to cost an additional $600 per year.
Living and Housing Costs	A limited amount of graduate student housing is available on the Boston University campus at approximately $7800 per year for a single room. However, most graduate students generally rent apartments, which are widely available from private sources in the Boston area.
Student Group	Currently, the Department has about 114 graduate students engaged in work toward the Ph.D. and M.A. degrees, and it prides itself on the close contact maintained between students and faculty members.
Student Outcomes	Recent Ph.D. recipients from the Department of Physics have been awarded the Wigner Fellowship at Oak Ridge, National Research Council Postdoctoral Fellowships, and the IBM Supercomputer Research Award, among others. Other graduates have gone on to permanent positions at Bell Laboratories, NEC Corporation, NASA, and NIST and to tenure-track faculty positions at major research universities.
Location	Boston University is located in Boston, Massachusetts, which is a major metropolitan center of cultural, scholarly, scientific, and technological activity. Besides Boston University, there are many major academic institutions in the area. Seminars and colloquia are announced in a Boston Area Physics Calendar.
The University and The Department	Boston University is a private urban university with a faculty of 3,936 members and a student population of 33,480. The University consists of fifteen schools and colleges. The Department of Physics is part of the College of Arts and Sciences and the Graduate School. The Department has an active faculty of 38 full-time members and has experienced significant growth in recent years.
Applying	The application deadline is December 15 for admission in September for the fall semester. Spring semester admission is possible but is uncommon; interested applicants should send an inquiry to the Department of Physics Director of Graduate Studies before applying. Application information and forms are available online at http://physics.bu.edu/grad.html. For admission to the graduate programs, a bachelor's degree in physics or astronomy is required. Exceptional candidates from other fields are considered. Official test results of the Graduate Record Examinations (GRE) (General Test and Subject Test in physics) are required. The minimum acceptable score for admission is dependent on the applicant's overall record. Official results of the Test of English as a Foreign Language (TOEFL) are required of all applicants whose native language is not English. The minimum score requirements are 600 for the paper-based test; or for the Internet-based test, reading section 21, listening section 18, speaking section 23, and writing section 22.
Correspondence and Information	Chair, Graduate Admissions Committee Department of Physics Boston University 590 Commonwealth Avenue Boston, Massachusetts 02215 Phone: 617-353-2623 E-mail: cabello@physics.bu.edu Web site: http://physics.bu.edu/

Peterson's Graduate Programs in the Physical Sciences, Mathematics, Agricultural Sciences, the Environment & Natural Resources 2012

www.facebook.com/petersonspublishing   **207**

Boston University

THE FACULTY AND THEIR RESEARCH

Steven Ahlen, Ph.D., Berkeley, 1976. Experimental particle physics and astrophysics.
Richard Averitt, Ph.D., Rice, 1998. Experimental condensed-matter physics.
Rama Bansil, Ph.D., Rochester, 1974. Experimental condensed-matter physics, biological physics.
Kevin Black Ph.D., Boston University, 2005. Experimental particle physics and astrophysics.
Tulika Bose, Ph.D., Columbia, 2006. Experimental particle physics and astrophysics.
John Butler, Ph.D., Stanford, 1986. Experimental particle physics and astrophysics.
Robert Carey, Ph.D., Harvard, 1989. Experimental particle physics and astrophysics, experimental medium-energy physics.
David Campbell, Ph.D., Cambridge, 1970. Quantum condensed-matter physics.
Antonio H. Castro Neto, Ph.D., Illinois, 1994. Quantum condensed-matter theory.
Claudio Chamon, Ph.D., MIT, 1996. Quantum condensed-matter theory.
Andrew G. Cohen, Ph.D., Harvard, 1986. Theoretical particle physics.
Andrew G. Duffy, Ph.D., Queen's at Kingston, 1995. Physics education research.
Maged El-Batanouny, Ph.D., California, Davis, 1978. Experimental condensed-matter physics.
Shyamsunder Erramilli, Ph.D., Illinois, 1986. Biological physics.
Sheldon Glashow, Ph.D., Harvard, 1958. Theoretical particle physics.
Bennett B. Goldberg, Ph.D., Brown, 1987. Experimental condensed-matter physics.
Emanuel Katz, Ph.D., MIT, 2001. Theoretical particle theory.
Edward Kearns, Ph.D., Harvard, 1990. Experimental particle physics and astrophysics.
William Klein, Ph.D., Temple, 1972. Statistical physics.
Kenneth D. Lane, Ph.D., Johns Hopkins, 1970. Theoretical particle physics.
Karl Ludwig, Ph.D., Stanford, 1986. Experimental condensed-matter physics.
Pankaj Mehta, Ph.D., Rutgers, 2006. Biological physics, statistical physics.
James Miller, Ph.D., Carnegie Mellon, 1974. Experimental medium-energy physics, experimental particle physics and astrophysics.
Pritiraj Mohanty, Ph.D., Maryland, College Park, 1998. Experimental condensed-matter physics.
So-Young Pi, Ph.D., SUNY at Stony Brook, 1974. Theoretical particle physics.
Anatoli Polkovnikov, Ph.D., Yale, 2003. Quantum condensed-matter physics.
Claudio Rebbi, Ph.D., Turin (Italy), 1967. Director, Center for Computational Science; theoretical particle physics.
Sidney Redner, Ph.D., MIT, 1977. Statistical physics.
B. Lee Roberts, Ph.D., William and Mary, 1974. Experimental medium-energy physics, experimental particle physics and astrophysics.
James Rohlf, Ph.D., Caltech, 1980. Experimental particle physics and astrophysics.
Kenneth Rothschild, Ph.D., MIT, 1973. Biological physics.
Anders Sandvik, Ph.D., California, Santa Barbara, 1993. Quantum condensed-matter physics.
Martin Schmaltz, Ph.D., California, San Diego, 1995. Theoretical particle physics.
William J. Skocpol, Ph.D., Harvard, 1974. Experimental condensed-matter physics.
Kevin E. Smith, Ph.D., Yale, 1988. Experimental condensed-matter physics.
H. Eugene Stanley, Ph.D., Harvard, 1967. Director, Center for Polymer Studies; statistical physics.
James L. Stone, Ph.D., Michigan, 1976. Experimental particle physics and astrophysics.
Lawrence R. Sulak, Ph.D., Princeton, 1970. Experimental particle physics and astrophysics.
Ophelia Tsui, Ph.D., Princeton, 1996. Biological physics, experimental condensed-matter physics.
J. Scott Whitaker, Ph.D., Berkeley, 1976. Experimental particle physics and astrophysics.

Research Faculty and Staff
Mi Kyung Hong, Ph.D., Illinois, 1988. Experimental biophysics.
Plamen Ivanov, Ph.D., Boston University, 1998. Polymer physics.
Paul Krapivsky, Ph.D., Moscow Physical Technical Institute, 1991. Theoretical condensed-matter physics.
James Shank, Ph.D., Berkeley, 1988. High-energy physics.
Saul Youseff, Ph.D., Carnegie Mellon, 1992. High-energy physics.

Affiliated Faculty
Irving Bigio, joint appointment with the College of Engineering; Ph.D., Michigan, 1974. Biomedical and biological physics.
Kenneth Brecher, joint appointment with the Department of Astronomy; Ph.D., MIT, 1969. Theoretical astrophysics.
Richard Brower, joint appointment with the College of Engineering; Ph.D., Berkeley, 1969. Theoretical particle physics.
Charles Delisi, joint appointment with the College of Engineering; Ph.D., NYU, 1969. Elementary particle theory.
Alvaro DeRújula, joint appointment with CERN; Ph.D., Madrid, 1968. Theoretical particle physics.
Evan Evans, joint appointment with the College of Engineering; Ph.D., California, San Diego, 1970. Biological physics.
Amit Meller, Ph.D., Weizmann Institute of Science, 1998. Biological physics.
Jerome Mertz, joint appointment with the College of Engineering; Ph.D., Paris VI (joint with California, Santa Barbara), 1991. Biological physics.
Theodore Moustakas, joint appointment with the College of Engineering; Ph.D., Columbia, 1974. Synthetic novel materials.
Alexander Sergienko, joint appointment with the College of Engineering; Ph.D., Moscow, 1987. Correlation spectroscopy.
Anna Swan, joint appointment with the College of Engineering; Ph.D., 1993, Boston University. Experimental condensed-matter physics.
Malvin Teich, joint appointment with the College of Engineering; Ph.D., Cornell, 1966. Quantum optics and imaging.
M. Selim Unlu, joint appointment with the College of Engineering; Ph.D., Illinois, 1997. Nearfield optical microscopy and spectroscopy.

Emeriti
Ed Booth, Emeritus; Ph.D., Johns Hopkins, 1955. Biological physics.
Bernard Chasan, Emeritus; Ph.D., Cornell, 1961. Biological physics.
Robert Cohen, Director Emeritus; Ph.D., Yale, 1948.
Ernesto Corinaldesi, Emeritus; Ph.D., Manchester, 1951. Quantum mechanics.
Dean S. Edmonds Jr., Emeritus; Ph.D., MIT, 1958. Electronics and instrumentation.
Wolfgang Franzen, Emeritus; Ph.D., Pennsylvania, 1949. Atomic physics, surface physics.
Bill Hellman, Emeritus; Ph.D., Syracuse, 1961. Elementary particle theory.
Abner Shimony, Emeritus; Ph.D. Princeton, 1962. Foundations of physics.
John Stachel, Emeritus, Curator of Einstein papers in the United States; Ph.D., Stevens, 1952. General relativity, foundations of relativistic space-time theories.
Charles R. Willis, Emeritus; Ph.D., Syracuse, 1957. Biophysics, nonlinear physics, statistical physics.
George O. Zimmerman, Emeritus; Ph.D., Yale, 1963. Low-temperature physics, magnetism.

208 www.facebook.com/petersonspublishing

Peterson's Graduate Programs in the Physical Sciences, Mathematics, Agricultural Sciences, the Environment & Natural Resources 2012

BRYN MAWR COLLEGE

Graduate Program in Physics

Programs of Study	Bryn Mawr's graduate program in physics is designed to give students both a broad background in physics and a high degree of expertise in a chosen field of research. While the department is small, it provides a breadth of coverage in physics, which includes the different specialties of the faculty members, covering a variety of topics and research interests. Students may select from Ph.D. and master's programs in experimental, theoretical, and computational research specialties including atomic and optical physics, molecular spectroscopy and dynamics, condensed matter physics using nuclear magnetic resonance techniques, and topics in fundamental theoretical physics.
	Formal graduate course work is handled in small tutorials, which can be tailored to the needs of the students, and contributes to the supportive and stimulating campus environment. Students may also take introductory or advanced graduate courses at the University of Pennsylvania or at Drexel University in nearby Philadelphia (about 30 minutes by car or train). Research projects can also be interdisciplinary in nature, involving two or more groups in Bryn Mawr's physics, mathematics, and chemistry departments.
	Research in the department has been recognized and sponsored by funding from agencies such as the National Science Foundation, the National Institutes of Health, the American Chemical Society, Research Corporation for Science Advancement, and the North Atlantic Treaty Organization. The Physics Department's research programs have also been supported by a variety of generous grants to Bryn Mawr College from many corporations, foundations, and private individuals. The facilities and equipment available for experimental research are of high quality and enable each research group to remain competitive in its area.
Research Facilities	Students in the Department of Physics have access to outstanding laboratory facilities, including an atomic force microscope, electrochemical deposition system, class 1000 soft-curtain clean room, vibrating sample magnetometer, x-ray diffractometer, solid-state nuclear magnetic resonance (NMR) spectrometer, various tunable pulsed and CW laser systems, molecular beam apparatus, two ultra-high vacuum systems for laser cooling and trapping, access to the Advanced Photon Source (APS) of Argonne National Laboratory and the Center for Functional Nanomaterials (CFN) at Brookhaven National Laboratory, and a machine and Instrument shop.
	Students also have access to first-class library resources, including SciFinder Scholar; a campus collection comprised of over one million volumes, including books, documents, microform, and multimedia material; a tri-college collection with Haverford and Swarthmore of one million-plus titles; and over 550 journal subscriptions in the sciences with Internet access to the most recent issues.
Financial Aid	Bryn Mawr offers full-time graduate students in good standing teaching and research assistantships with a stipend of $22,750, and tuition coverage and health insurance subsidy in the amount of $24,000, for a total financial package of $46,750 annually.
Cost of Study	Full-time tuition is $34,110 per year; part-time tuition is $5685 for one unit, $11,370 for two units. Units of supervised work cost $910 and the fee for maintaining matriculation (continuing enrollment) is $460 per semester.
Living and Housing Costs	Students live locally or in Philadelphia. Shared apartments can be rented for $600 to $900 per month; studio apartments begin at $800 per month. Other expenses include transportation (about $165 per month if commuting from Philadelphia) and health insurance (approximately $2500 per year for domestic students and approximately $1500 for international students). Complete information about Bryn Mawr's Cost of Attendance, may be found at: http://www.brynmawr.edu/sfs/cost/cost_index.html.
Student Group	Students in graduate program in physics have the opportunity to be part of Bryn Mawr's Graduate Group in Science and Mathematics, an interdisciplinary group including graduate programs in chemistry, mathematics, and physics. The group facilitates scholarly and social interactions among graduate students, promotes interdisciplinary research projects, and provides a mentoring program by graduate students.
Student Outcomes	After completing the program at Bryn Mawr, graduate students have gone on to postdoctoral appointments at the University of Pennsylvania, Vanderbilt University, and the Lawrence Livermore National Laboratory; academic positions at Bates College, University of Connecticut, Dickinson College, Drew University, University of Michigan, Middlebury College, Mount Union College, Rice University, Stony Brook University (SUNY), and Ursinus College; and positions in industry with firms including IBM, Alcatel-Lucent, the U.S. Naval Research Laboratory, and AT&T Labs.
Location	Bryn Mawr is a suburb of Philadelphia, the fifth-largest city in the United States. It is well served by rail lines (the Main Line) and by bus. Philadelphia is renowned for music, museums, and sports, and it is also a culinary mecca with restaurants serving many cuisines. The metropolitan area has more than 100 museums and fifty colleges and universities, with a total population of 220,000 students.
The College	Bryn Mawr is a liberal arts college for women with two coeducational graduate schools: the Graduate School of Arts and Sciences and the Graduate School of Social Work and Social Research. Founded in 1885, Bryn Mawr was the first institution in the United States to offer the Ph.D. to women, and graduate education continues to be a significant part of its mission. Graduate students number approximately 400, out of a total enrollment of approximately 1,750 including undergraduates.
Applying	Students may apply to the Graduate Program in Physics online at: https://app.applyyourself.com/?id=brynmawrg.
	Students who have questions and are interested in applying to the Department of Physics are encouraged to complete the contact form at http://www.brynmawr.edu/admissions/graduate/GSAS_REQUEST_CONTACT_PHYSICS.shtml.
Correspondence and Information	Department of Physics Bryn Mawr College 101 North Merion Avenue Bryn Mawr, Pennsylvania 19010-2899 Phone: 610-526-5152 E-mail: admissions@brynmawr.edu Web site: http://www.brynmawr.edu/physics/graduate

Peterson's Graduate Programs in the Physical Sciences, Mathematics, Agricultural Sciences, the Environment & Natural Resources 2012

www.facebook.com/petersonspublishing　　**209**

Bryn Mawr College

THE FACULTY AND THEIR RESEARCH

James Battat, Assistant Professor; Ph.D., Harvard, 2008. The intersection of experimental particle physics and astronomy.
Peter A. Beckmann, Professor; Ph.D., British Columbia, 1975. Solid-state nuclear magnetic resonance.
Xuemei May Cheng, Assistant Professor; Ph.D., Johns Hopkins, 2006. Nanomaterials and spintronics.
Elizabeth F. McCormack, Professor; Ph.D., Yale, 1989. Molecular spectroscopy and dynamics.
Michael W. Noel, Associate Professor; Ph.D., Rochester, 1996. Ultracold Rydberg atoms.
Michael B. Schulz, Assistant Professor; Ph.D. Stanford, 2002. High-energy physics, quantum field theory, string theory.

210 www.facebook.com/petersonspublishing

Peterson's Graduate Programs in the Physical Sciences, Mathematics,
Agricultural Sciences, the Environment & Natural Resources 2012

COLUMBIA UNIVERSITY

Department of Applied Physics and Applied Mathematics

Programs of Study

The Department of Applied Physics and Applied Mathematics offers graduate study leading to the degrees of Master of Science (M.S.), Doctor of Engineering Science (Eng.Sc.D.), and Doctor of Philosophy (Ph.D.).

The following fields of research (topics of emphasis in parentheses) are available for doctoral study: theoretical and experimental plasma physics (fusion and space plasmas), applied mathematics (analysis of partial differential equations, large-scale scientific computing, nonlinear dynamics, inverse problems, medical imaging, geophysical/geological fluid dynamics, and biomathematics), solid-state physics (semiconductor, surface, low-dimensional physics, and molecular electronics), optical and laser physics (laser interactions with matter and quantum optics), nuclear science (medical applications), earth science (atmosphere, ocean, and climate science and geophysics), and materials science and engineering (thin films; nanomaterials; electronic, optical, and magnetic materials; and mechanical response of materials). Successful completion of 30 points (semester hours) or more of approved graduate course work beyond the master's degree is required for the doctoral degree. In addition, all doctoral candidates must pass written and oral qualifying exams and successfully defend an approved dissertation based on original research. For the M.S. degree, candidates must successfully complete a minimum of 30 points of credit of approved graduate course work at Columbia. A 36-point CAMPEP-approved M.S. degree in medical physics is offered in collaboration with faculty members from the College of Physicians and Surgeons and the Mailman School of Public Health. It prepares students for professional careers in medical physics and provides preparation for the ABR certification exam.

Research Facilities

Research equipment in the Plasma Physics Laboratory includes a toroidal high-beta tokamak for basic and applied research, a steady-state plasma experiment using a linear magnetic mirror, a large laboratory collisionless terrella used to investigate space plasma physics, and the CNT stellarator for nonneutral and antimatter plasma research. The plasma physics group is jointly operating a plasma confinement experiment, LDX, with MIT, incorporating a levitated superconducting ring. The plasma physics group is also actively involved in the NSTX experiment at the Princeton Plasma Physics Laboratory and on the DIII-D Tokamak at General Atomics in San Diego and is part of the U.S. national effort on the ITER project. Research equipment in the solid-state physics and laser physics laboratories includes extensive laser and spectroscopy facilities, a clean room that includes photolithography and thin-film fabrication systems, ultrahigh-vacuum surface preparation and analysis chambers, direct laser writing stations, a molecular-beam epitaxy machine, picosecond and femtosecond lasers, and diamond anvil cells. Research is also conducted in the shared characterization laboratories operated by the NSF Nanoscale Science and Engineering Center, and the DOE Energy Frontier Research Center, which focuses on conversion of sunlight into electricity in nanometer-sized thin films. Materials science and engineering facilities include transmission and scanning electron microscopes, scanning tunneling microscopes and atomic-force microscopes, X-ray diffractometers, an ellipsometer, an X-ray photoelectron spectrometer, laser processing equipment, and mechanical testing equipment. Magnetic and electrical measurement characterization equipment is also available.

There are research opportunities in medical physics at the Columbia–Presbyterian Medical Center, as well as at other medical institutes, employing state-of-the-art medical diagnostic imaging and treatment equipment.

The Applied Mathematics Division is closely linked with the Lamont Doherty Earth Observatory (LDEO), with 5 faculty members sharing appointments in the Department of Earth and Environmental Sciences and with the NASA Goddard Institute for Space Studies (GISS). There are also close ties with Columbia's Center for Computational Biology and Bioinformatics (C2B2) and Columbia's Center for the Multiscale Analysis of Genomic and Cellular Networks (MAGNet).

The Department maintains an extensive network of workstations and desktop computers. It has recently acquired a SiCortex supercomputer with 1,458 cores, which is used for a wide range of departmental computational activities. The research of the plasma physics group is supported by a dedicated data acquisition/data analysis system. Computational researchers have local access to Columbia's 256-processor Linux cluster and to supercomputer systems at the National Center for Atmospheric Research and the Lawrence Berkeley, Brookhaven, and Oak Ridge National Laboratories.

Financial Aid

Financial support is awarded to doctoral candidates only on a competitive basis in the form of assistantships that provide a stipend, a tuition allowance, and medical fees. For 2011–12, the stipend for teaching assistants is $23,350 for nine months; for research assistants, the stipend is $31,133 for twelve months.

Cost of Study

For 2011–12, full-time tuition (RU) for the academic year is $37,552; for master's degree and for part-time study, the cost is $1472 per credit. In addition to medical fees (approximately $1400 for basic coverage), annual fees range from $698–$1000.

Living and Housing Costs

The cost of on-campus, single-student housing (dormitories, suites, and apartments) ranges from $3000 to $6700 per term; married student accommodations range from $1300 to $2250 per month. For the single student, a minimum of $23,000 should be allowed for board, room, and personal expenses for the academic year.

Student Group

Approximately 27,600 students attend the fifteen schools and colleges of Columbia University; more than half are graduate students. On average, the Department has 120 graduate and 110 undergraduate students. The student population has a diverse and international character. Admission is highly competitive; in 2010–11, 47 master's- and Ph.D.-track students matriculated out of 343 applicants, with all doctoral program students being fully supported.

Student Outcomes

Recent Ph.D. recipients have found employment as postdoctoral research scientists at universities in the United States and abroad and as staff members in advanced technology industries and at national laboratories. Some have secured college-level faculty positions. Most M.S. graduates continue studying for the doctorate; a few go on to medical school or law school. M.S. graduates from the program in medical physics have secured positions in hospital departments of radiology and nuclear medicine or have entered doctoral programs.

Location

The 32-acre campus is situated in Morningside Heights on the Upper West Side of Manhattan. This location, 15 minutes from the heart of New York City, allows Columbia to be an integral part of the city while maintaining the character of a unique neighborhood. Cultural, recreational, and athletic opportunities abound at city museums, libraries, concert halls, theaters, restaurants, stadiums, parks, and beaches.

The University and The Department

With extensive resources and an outstanding faculty, Columbia University has played an eminent role in American education since its founding in 1754. The Department of Applied Physics and Applied Mathematics, a department at the forefront of interdisciplinary research and teaching, was established in 1978 as part of the Graduate School of Arts and Sciences and the Fu Foundation School of Engineering and Applied Sciences. The Graduate Program in Materials Science and Engineering joined the Department in fall 2000.

Applying

For fall admission, applications should be submitted online as follows: December 1 for doctoral, doctoral-track, and all financial aid applicants; applications for Master of Science, part-time, and nondegree candidates are reviewed on a rolling basis. Scores from the GRE General Test are required. The GRE Subject Test is required for applicants to the applied physics doctoral program. The GRE Subject Test is strongly urged for doctoral applicants in applied mathematics and materials science and engineering. TOEFL scores are required for students from non-English-speaking countries.

Admissions information and application forms can be found online at http://www.engineering.columbia.edu/graduate-2.

Correspondence and Information

Chairman, Graduate Admissions Committee
Department of Applied Physics and Applied Mathematics
200 S. W. Mudd Building, MC 4701
Columbia University
New York, New York 10027
Phone: 212-854-4457
            212-854-6438 (admissions)
E-mail: seasinfo.apam@columbia.edu
            seasgradmit@columbia.edu (admissions)
Web site: http://www.apam.columbia.edu
            http://www.engineering.columbia.edu/

Peterson's Graduate Programs in the Physical Sciences, Mathematics, Agricultural Sciences, the Environment & Natural Resources 2012

www.facebook.com/petersonspublishing   **211**

Columbia University

THE FACULTY AND THEIR RESEARCH

In the Department of Applied Physics and Applied Mathematics, theoretical and experimental research is conducted by 34 full-time faculty members, 18 adjunct professors, and 53 research scientists. Areas of research include applied mathematics, earth/atmosphere/ocean/climate science, biomathematics, biophysics, numerical analysis, inverse problems, medical imaging, space physics, surface physics, condensed-matter physics, electromagnetism, materials science, nanoscience, medical physics, optical and laser physics, plasma physics, and fusion energy science.

William E. Bailey, Associate Professor; Ph.D., Stanford, 1999. Nanoscale magnetic films and heterostructures, materials issues in spin-polarized transport, materials engineering of magnetic dynamics.

Guillaume Bal, Professor; Ph.D., Paris, 1997. Applied mathematics, partial differential equations with random coefficients, high-frequency waves in random media and application to time reversal, inverse problems and imaging with applications to medical imaging and geophysical imaging.

Katayun Barmak, Professor; Ph.D., MIT, 1989. Processing and structure (crystal structure and microstructure) relationships to electrical and magnetic properties of metal films, developing transmission electron microscopy automated orientation imaging techniques that can be applied to the study of nanostructured materials, use of differential scanning calorimetry for the study solid-state reactions and phase transformations in thin films.

Daniel Bienstock, Professor (joint with Industrial Engineering and Operations Research); Ph.D., MIT, 1985. Applied mathematics, methodology and high-performance implementation of optimization algorithms, applications of optimization: preventing national-scale blackouts, emergency management, approximate solution of massively large optimization problems, higher-dimensional reformulation techniques for integer programming, robust optimization.

Simon J. L. Billinge, Professor; Ph.D., Pennsylvania, 1992. Nanoscale structure-property relationships in functional nanomaterials studied using novel X-ray and neutron scattering techniques coupled with advanced computing, solving the nanostructure problem.

Allen H. Boozer, Professor; Ph.D., Cornell, 1970. Plasma theory, theory of magnetic confinement for fusion energy, nonlinear dynamics.

Mark A. Cane, Professor (joint with Earth and Environmental Sciences); Ph.D., MIT, 1975. Climate dynamics, impacts of climate on society, climate forecasting, physical oceanography, geophysical fluid dynamics, computational fluid dynamics.

Siu-Wai Chan, Professor; Sc.D., MIT, 1985. Nanoparticles, electronic ceramics, grain boundaries and interfaces, oxide thin films.

C. K. Chu, Professor Emeritus; Ph.D., NYU (Courant), 1959. Applied mathematics.

Vincent Duchene, Assistant Professor, Ph.D., Paris, 2011. Partial differential equations, fluid mechanics, hyperbolic equations, Schrödinger operator, mathematical physics, numerical simulations.

Dirk R. Englund, Assistant Professor (joint with Electrical Engineering); Ph.D., Stanford, 2008. Quantum optics in photonic nanostructures, photonic crystal optoelectronic devices and networks, quantum information and metrology, nonlinear optics, electron and nuclear spin-dynamics in solid state systems.

Morton B. Friedman, Professor (joint with Civil Engineering); D.Sc., NYU, 1953. Applied mathematics and mechanics, numerical analysis, parallel computing.

Irving P. Herman, Professor; Ph.D., MIT, 1977. Nanocrystals, optical spectroscopy of nanostructured materials, laser diagnostics of thin-film processing, mechanical properties of nanomaterials.

James Im, Professor; Ph.D., MIT, 1985. Laser-induced crystallization of thin films, phase transformations and nucleation in condensed systems.

Philip Kim, Professor (joint with Physics); Harvard, 1999. Experimental condensed matter physics, physical properties and applications of nanoscale low-dimensional materials, quantum thermal transport phenomena in 1-dimensional nanoscaled materials, mesoscopic thermoelectricity and thermoelectric applications of nanoscale materials, quantum transport in novel 2-dimensional materials, mesoscopic electron transport, thermodynamic processes for sensors and electric devices.

Chris A. Marianetti, Assistant Professor; Ph.D., MIT, 2004. Predicting materials properties from first-principles computations, density-functional theory, dynamical mean-field theory, transition-metal oxides, actinides, energy storage and conversion materials.

Thomas C. Marshall, Professor Emeritus; Ph.D., Illinois, 1960. Accelerator concepts, relativistic beams and radiation, free-electron lasers.

Michael E. Mauel, Professor; Sc.D., MIT, 1983. Plasma physics, waves and instabilities, fusion and equilibrium control, space physics, plasma processing, international energy policy.

Gerald A. Navratil, Professor; Ph.D., Wisconsin–Madison, 1976. Plasma physics, plasma diagnostics, fusion energy science.

I. Cevdet Noyan, Professor; Ph.D., Northwestern, 1984. Characterization and modeling of mechanical and micromechanical deformation, residual stress analysis and nondestructive testing, X-ray and neutron diffraction, microdiffrication analysis.

Richard M. Osgood, Professor (joint with Electrical Engineering); Ph.D., MIT, 1973. Nanoscale optical and electronic phenomena (experimental and computational), femtosecond lasers and laser probing, low-dimensional physics, integrated optics, nanofabrication and materials growth.

Aron Pinczuk, Professor; Ph.D., Pennsylvania, 1969. Spectroscopy of semiconductors and insulators, quantum structures, systems of reduced dimensions, atomic layers of graphene, electron quantum fluids.

Lorenzo M. Polvani, Professor; Ph.D., MIT, 1988. Atmospheric and climate dynamics, geophysical fluid dynamics, numerical methods for weather and climate modeling, planetary atmospheres.

Malvin A. Ruderman, Professor (joint with Physics); Ph.D., Caltech, 1951. Theoretical astrophysics, neutron stars, pulsars, early universe, cosmic gamma rays.

Christopher H. Scholz, Professor (joint with Earth and Environmental Sciences); Ph.D., MIT, 1967. Experimental and theoretical rock mechanics, especially friction, fracture, and hydraulic transport properties; nonlinear systems; mechanics of earthquakes and faulting.

Tiffany A. Shaw, Assistant Professor (joint with Earth and Environmental Sciences), Ph.D., Toronto, 2009. Atmospheric science, advection-diffusion of a passive scalar, Hamiltonian geophysical fluid dynamics, multiple scale asymptotics, wave-mean flow interaction.

Amiya K. Sen, Professor (joint with Electrical Engineering); Ph.D., Columbia, 1963. Plasma physics, fluctuations and anomalous transport in plasmas, control of plasma instabilities, plasma transport.

Adam H. Sobel, Professor; Ph.D., MIT, 1998. Atmospheric science, geophysical fluid dynamics, tropical meteorology, climate dynamics.

Marc W. Spiegelman, Professor; Ph.D., Cambridge, 1989. Coupled fluid/solid mechanics, reactive fluid flow, solid earth and magma dynamics, scientific computation/modeling.

Horst L. Stormer, Professor Emeritus; Ph.D., Stuttgart, 1977. Semiconductors, electronic transport, low-dimensional physics, transport in nanostructures.

Latha Venkataraman, Associate Professor; Ph.D., Harvard, 1999. Single-molecule transport, single-molecule-force spectroscopy, electron transport in nanowires, scanning tunneling microscopy and spectroscopy.

Wen I. Wang, Professor (joint with Electrical Engineering); Ph.D., Cornell, 1981. Heterostructure devices and physics, materials properties, molecular-beam epitaxy.

Michael I. Weinstein, Professor; Ph.D., NYU (Courant), 1982. Applied mathematics; partial differential equations and analysis; waves in nonlinear, inhomogeneous, and random media; dynamical systems; multiscale phenomena; applications to nonlinear optics; mathematical physics; fluid dynamics; geosciences.

Chris H. Wiggins, Associate Professor; Ph.D., Princeton, 1998. Applied mathematics, mathematical biology, biopolymer dynamics, soft condensed matter, genetic networks and network inference, machine learning.

Cheng-Shie Wuu, Professor (Public Health, Environmental Health Sciences, and Applied Physics); Ph.D., Kansas, 1985. Microdosimetry, biophysical modeling, dosimetry of brachytherapy, gel dosimetry, second cancers induced by radiotherapy, medical physics.

The Schapiro Center for Engineering and Physical Science Research; to the right, the Seeley W. Mudd Building, home of the Fu Foundation School of Engineering and Applied Science.

Faculty and research staff members and students of the Plasma Physics Laboratory in front of the Tokamak, HBT-EP.

Low Memorial Library and grounds.

212   www.facebook.com/petersonspublishing

Peterson's Graduate Programs in the Physical Sciences, Mathematics, Agricultural Sciences, the Environment & Natural Resources 2012

SELECTED PUBLICATIONS

William E. Bailey

Interface-related damping in polycrystalline Ni81Fe19/Cu/Co93Zr7 tri-layers. *J. Appl. Phys.* 105:07D309, 2009.

Weakly coupled motion of individual layers in ferromagnetic resonance. *Phys. Rev. B: Condens. Matter* 74(6):064409, 2006.

Low relaxation rate in epitaxial vanadium-doped ultrathin iron films. *Phys. Rev. Lett.* 98(11):117601, 2007.

Dopants for independent control of precessional frequency and damping in Ni0.8Fe 0.2(50 nm) thin films. *Appl. Phys. Lett.* 77(6), 2006.

Guillaume Bal

Inverse of transport theory and applications. *Inverse Probl.* 25:053001, 2009.

Convergence to SPDEs Stratonovich form. *Comm. Math. Phys.* 292(2):457–77, 2009.

Time reversal and refocusing in random media. *SIAM J. Appl. Math.* 63(5):1475–98, 2003.

Radiative transport limit for the random Schroedinger equation. *Nonlinearity* 15:513–29, 2002.

Daniel Bienstock

The $N-k$ problem in power grids: New models, formulations and computation. *SIAM J. Optim.* 20(5):2352–80, 2010.

Faster approximation algorithms for covering and packing problems. *SIAM J. Comput.* 35:825–54, 2006.

Subset algebra lift operators for 0-1 integer programming. *SIAM J. Optim.* 15:63–95, 2004.

Potential function methods for approximately solving linear programming problems, theory and practice. *Kluwer Academic Publishers.* Boston, 2002.

Simon J. L. Billinge

The problem with determining atomic structure at the nanoscale. *Science* 316:561–5, 2007.

Ab initio determination of solid-state nanostructure. *Nature* 440:655–8, 2006.

Underneath the Bragg Peaks: Structural Analysis of Complex Materials. Elsevier Science: Oxford, 2004.

Beyond crystallography: The study of disorder nanocrystallinity and crystallographically challenged materials. *Chem. Commun.* 7:749–60, 2004.

Allen H. Boozer

Use of non-axisymmetric shaping in magnetic fusion. *Phys. Plasmas* 16:058102, 2009.

Stellarators and the path from ITER to DEMO. *Plasma Phys. Contr. Fusion* 50:124005, 2008.

Control of asymmetric magnetic perturbations in tokamaks. *Phys. Rev. Lett.* 99:195003, 2007.

Physics of magnetically confined plasmas. *Rev. Modern Phys.* 76:1071–141, 2004.

Mark A. Cane

The El Niño–Southern Oscillation Phenomenon. London: Cambridge University Press, 2010.

The evolution of El Niño, past and future. *Earth Planet. Sci. Lett.* 104:1–10, 2005.

Mapping tropical Pacific sea level: Data assimilation via a reduced state space Kalman filter. *J. Geophys. Res.* 101:22,599–617, 1996.

Experimental forecasts of El Niño. *Nature* 322:827–32, 1986.

Siu-Wai Chan

Controlled synthesis of Co_3O_4 nanopolyhedrons and nanosheets at low temperature. *Chem. Comm.* 48:7569–71, 2009.

In situ ultra-small-angle X-ray scattering study of solution-mediated formation and growth of nanocrystalline ceria. *J. Appl. Crystallogr.* 41(5):918–29, 2008.

Cubic phase stabilization in nanoparticles of hafnia-zirconia oxides: Particle-size and annealing environment effects. *J. Appl. Phys.* 103(12):124303–7, 2008.

Synthesis and redox behavior of nanocrystalline hausmannite. *Chem. Mater.* 19:5609–16, 2007.

C. K. Chu

Domain decomposition for shallow water equations. In *Contemporary Mathematics, Proceedings of the 7th International Conference on Domain Decomposition Methods in Science and Engineering,* October 1993.

Equilibrium response of ocean deep-water circulation to variations in Ekman pumping and deep-water sources. *J. Phys. Oceanogr.* 22:1129, 1992.

Lagrangian turbulence in Stokes flow. *Phys. Fluids* 30:687, 1987.

Solitary waves generated by boundary motion. *Comm. Pure Appl. Math.* 36:495, 1983.

Dirk R. Englund

Resonant excitation of a quantum dot strongly coupled to a photonic crystal nanocavity. *Phys. Rev. Lett.* 104(7):073904, 2010.

Controlled phase shifts with a single quantum dot. *Science* 320(5877):769–72, 2008.

Controlling cavity reflectivity with a single quantum dot. *Nature* 450(7171):857–61, 2007.

Controlling the spontaneous emission rate of single quantum dots in a 2D photonic crystal. *Phys. Rev. Lett.* 95(1):013904, 2005.

Irving P. Herman

Formation of thick, large-area nanoparticle superlattices in lithographically defined geometries. *Nano Lett.* 10(4):1517–21, 2010.

Viscoplastic and granular behavior in films of colloidal nanocrystals. *Phys. Rev. Lett.* 98:026103, 2007.

Physics of the Human Body. Berlin/Heidelberg/New York: Springer, 2007.

Raman microprobe analysis of elastic strain and fracture in electrophoretically deposited CdSe nanocrystal films. *Nano Lett.* 6:175–80, 2006.

James Im

Stochastic modeling of solid nucleation in supercooled liquids. *Appl. Phys. Lett.* 78:3454–6, 2001.

On determining the relevance of athermal nucleation in rapidly quenched liquids. *Appl. Phys. Lett.* 72:662, 1998.

Sequential lateral solidification of thin silicon films on SiO_2. *Appl. Phys. Lett.* 69:2864, 1996.

Phase transformation mechanisms involved in excimer laser crystallization of amorphous silicon films. *Appl. Phys. Lett.* 63:1969–71, 1993.

Philip Kim

Symmetry breaking of the zero energy Landau level in bilayer graphene. *Phys. Rev. Lett.* 104(6):066801, 2010.

Observation of the fractional quantum hall effect in graphene. *Nature* 462(7270):196–9, 2009.

Thermoelectric and magnetothermoelectric transport measurements of graphene. *Phys. Rev. Lett.* 102(9):096807, 2009.

Quantum interference and carrier collimation in grapheneheterojunctions. *Nat. Phys.* 5:222–6, 2009.

Chris A. Marianetti

Electronic coherence in delta-Pu: A DMFT study. *Phys. Rev. Lett.* 101:056403, 2008.

Quasiparticle dispersion and heat capacity of Na0.3CoO2: A DMFT study. *Phys. Rev. Lett.* 99:246404, 2007.

Na induced correlations in the cobaltates. *Phys. Rev. Lett.* 98:176405, 2007.

Electronic structure calculations with dynamical mean-field theory. *Rev. Mod. Phys.* 78:865, 2006.

Thomas C. Marshall

Experimental observation of constructive superposition of wake fields generated by electron bunches in a dielectric-lined waveguide. *Phys. Rev. Sci. Tech.* 9:011301, 2006.

Rectangular dielectric-lined two-beam accelerator structure. In *Particle Accelerator Conference Proceedings,* May 2005.

Nondestructive diagnostic for electron bunch length in accelerators using the wake field radiation spectrum. *Phys. Rev. Sci. Tech.* 8:062801, 2005.

Strong wake fields generated by a train of femtosecond bunches in a planar dielectric microstructure. *Phys. Rev. Special Top.–Accelerators Beams* 7:05130, 2004.

Michael E. Mauel

Turbulent inward pinch of plasma confined by a levitated dipole magnet. *Nat. Phys.* 6:207–12, 2010.

Global and local characterization of turbulent and chaotic structures in a dipole-confined plasma. *Phys. Plasmas* 16:055902, 2009.

Confinement improvement with magnetic levitation of a superconducting dipole. *Nucl. Fusion* 49:055023, 2009.

A Kalman filter for feedback control of rotating external kink instabilities in the presence of noise. *Phys. Plasmas* 16:056112, 2009.

Helium-catalyzed D-D fusion in a levitated dipole. *Nucl. Fusion* 44:193–203, 2004.

Gerald A. Navratil

Measurement of resistive wall mode stability in rotating high-beta DIII-D plasmas. *Nucl. Fusion* 45:368, 2005.

Scaling of the critical plasma rotation for stabilization of the n+1 RWM in DIII-D. *Nucl. Fusion* 44:1197, 2004.

Sustained rotational stabilization of DIII-D plasmas above the no-wall beta limit. *Phys. Plasmas* 9:1997, 2002.

Modeling of active control of external MHD instabilities. *Phys. Plasmas* 8:2170, 2001.

I. Cevdet Noyan.

Measurement of strain/load transfer in parallel seven-wire strands with neutron diffraction. *Exp. Mech.* 50(2):265–72, 2010.

A rigorous comparison of X-ray diffraction thickness measurement techniques using silicon-on-insulator thin films. *J. Appl. Cryst.* 42(3):401–10, 2009.

Peterson's Graduate Programs in the Physical Sciences, Mathematics, Agricultural Sciences, the Environment & Natural Resources 2012

www.facebook.com/petersonspublishing   **213**

Columbia University

Strain measured in a silicon-on-insulator, complementary metal-oxide-semiconductor device channel induced by embedded silicon-carbon source/drain regions. *Appl. Phys. Lett.* 94(6):063502, 2009.

Applicability of real-space methods to diffraction strain measurements in single crystals. *J. Appl. Cryst.* 41(5):944–9, 2008.

Richard M. Osgood Jr.

Spectro-microscopy of single- and multi-layer graphene supported by a weakly interacting substrate. *Phys. Rev. B (Rapid Comms)* 78:201408.

Engineering nonlinearities in nanoscale optical systems: physics and applications in dispersion-engineered Si nanophotonic wires. *Adv. Opt. Photon.* 1:162–235, 2009.

Experimental demonstration of near-infrared negative-index metamaterials. *Phys. Rev. Lett.* 95:137404, 2005.

Image-state electron scattering on flat Ag/Pt(111) and stepped Ag/Pt(997) surfaces. *Phys. Rev. B* 71:165424, 2004.

Aron Pinczuk

Electric field effect tuning of electron-phonon coupling in graphene. *Phys. Rev. Lett.* 98(16):166802, 2007.

Transition from free to interacting composite fermions away from nu=1/3. *Phys. Rev. Lett.* 97:036804, 2006.

Extrinsic optical recombination in pentacene single crystals: Evidence of gap states. *Appl. Phys. Lett.* 87(21):211117, 2005.

Splitting of long-wavelength modes of the fractional quantum hall liquid at nu=1/3. *Phys. Rev. Lett.* 95(6):066803, 2005.

Lorenzo M. Polvani

The impact of stratospheric ozone recovery on the Southern Hemisphere westerly jet. *Science* 320(5882):1486–9, 2008.

Transport and mixing of chemical airmasses in idealized baroclinic life cycles. *J. Geophys. Res. Atmos.* 112:D23102, 2007.

Numerically converged solutions of the global primitive equations for testing the dynamical core of atmospheric GCMs. *Monthly Weather Rev.* 11:2539–52, 2004.

Tropospheric response to stratospheric perturbations in a relatively simple general circulation model. *Geophys. Res. Lett.* 29(7):1114, 2002.

The morphogenesis of bands and zonal winds with the atmospheres of the giant outer planets. *Science* 273:335–7, 1996.

Malvin A. Ruderman

A central engine for cosmic gamma-ray burst sources. *Astrophys. J.* 542:243, 2000.

Millisecond pulsar alignment: PSR 0437–47. *Astrophys. J.* 493:397, 1998.

Neutron star magnetic field evolution, crust movement and glitches. *Astrophys. J.* 492:267, 1998.

Models for X-ray emission from isolated pulsars. *Astrophys. J.* 498:373, 1998.

Christopher H. Scholz.

Transition regimes for growing crack populations. *Phys. Rev. E* 65:056105, 2002.

Slip-length scaling for earthquakes: Observations and theory and implications for earthquake physics. *Geophys. Res. Lett.* 28:2995–8, 2001.

Evidence of a strong San Andreas fault. *Geology* 28:163–6, 2000.

Experimental evidence for different strain regimes of crack populations in a clay model. *Geophys. Res. Lett.* 26:1081–4, 1999.

Amiya K. Sen

Radial plasma transport in axisymmetricmagneticfields. *Trans. Fusion & Technology* 48:51111, 2006.

Observation and identification of zonal flows in a basic experiment. *Plasma Phys. Controlled Fusion* 48:51111, 2006.

A new paradigm of plasma transport. *Phys. Plasmas* 13, 2006.

Adaptive optimal stochastic state feedback control of resistive wall modes in tokamaks. *Phys. Plasmas* 13:012512, 2006.

Adam H. Sobel

Poleward-propagating intraseasonal monsoon disturbances in an intermediate-complexity axisymmetric model. *J. Atmos. Sci.* 65:470–89, 2008.

Instability of the axisymmetric monsoon flow and intraseasonal oscillation. *J. Geophys. Res.* 113: D07108, 2008. doi:10.1029/2007JD009291

On the wavelength of the Rossby waves radiated by tropical cyclones. *J. Atmos. Sci.* 65:644–54, 2008.

The role of surface fluxes in tropical intraseasonal oscillations. *Nature Geoscience* 1:653–7, 2008.

Marc W. Spiegelman

A semi-Lagrangian Crank-Nicolson algorithm for the numerical solution of advection-diffusion problems. *Geochem. Geophys. Geosyst.* 7(4):Q04014, 2006.

Linear analysis of melt band formation by simple shear. *Geochem. Geophys. Geosyst.* 4(9):8615, 2003.

Extreme chemical variability as a consequence of channelized melt transport. *Geochem. Geophys. Geosyst.* 4(7):1055, 2003.

Causes and consequences of flow organization during melt transport: The reaction infiltration instability in compactible media. *J. Geophys. Res.* 106(B2):2061–77, 2001.

Horst L. Stormer

High frequency magneto oscillations in GaAs/AlGaAs quantum wells. *Phys. Rev. Lett.* 98:036804, 2007.

Experimental observation of the quantum Hall effect and Berry's phase in graphene. *Nature* 438:201, 2005.

Quantization of the diagonal resistance: Density gradients and the empirical resistance rule in a 2D system. *Phys. Rev. Lett.* 95:066808, 2005.

Evidence for skyrmion crystallization from NMR relaxation experiments. *Phys. Rev. Lett.* 94:196803, 2005.

Latha Venkataraman

Mechanically-controlled binary conductance switching of a single-molecule junction. *Nature Nanotechnology* 4:230, 2009.

Formation and evolution of single molecule junctions. *Phys. Rev. Lett.* 102:126803, 2009.

Single molecule conductance and link chemistry: A comparison of phosphines, methyl thiols and amines. *J. Am. Chem. Soc.* 129:15768–9, 2007.

Single molecule conductance and link chemistry: A comparison of phosphines, methyl thiols and amines. *J. Am. Chem. Soc.* 129:15768–9, 2007.

Electronics and chemistry: Varying single molecule junction conductance with chemical substituent. *Nano Letters* 7:502–6, 2007.

Dependence of single molecule junction conductance on molecular conformation. *Nature* 442:904–7, 2006.

Single-molecule circuits with well-defined molecular conductance. *Nano Letters* 6:458–62, 2006.

Wen I. Wang

Normal incidence intervalence subband absorption in GaSb quantum well enhanced by coupling to InAs conduction band. *Appl. Phys. Lett.* 62:609–11, 1993.

Normal incidence infrared absorption in AlAs/AlGaAs x-valley multiquantum wells. *Appl. Phys. Lett.* 61:1697–9, 1992.

High breakdown voltage AlSbAs/InAs n-channel field effect transistors. *IEEE Electron Device Lett.* 13:192–4, 1992.

Michael I. Weinstein

Cloaking via change of variables for the Helmholtz equation. *Comm. Pure Appl. Math.* 63(8):973–1016, 2010.

A multiscale model of partial melts: 1. Effective equations. *J. Geophys. Res.* 115:B04410, 2010.

A multiscale model of partial melts: 2. Computational studies. *J. Geophys. Res.* 115:B04411, 2010.

Band-edge solitons, nonlinear Schrodinger/Gross–Pitaevskii equations, and effective media. *SIAM J. Multiscale Modeling and Simulation* 8(4):1055–101, 2010.

Chris H. Wiggins

A stochastic spectral analysis of transcriptional regulatory cascades. *Proc. Natl. Acad. Sci. U.S.A.* 106:6529–34, 2009. http://www.ncbi.nlm.nih.gov/pubmed/19351901?dopt=Abstract

A Bayesian approach to network modularity. *Phys. Rev. Lett.* 100:258701, 2008. http://link.aps.org/doi/10.1103/PhysRevLett.100.258701

Multiple events on single molecules: Unbiased estimation in single-molecule biophysics. *Proc. Natl. Acad. Sci. U.S.A.* 104:1750–5, 2006.

Information-theoretic approach to network modularity. *Physical Review E* 71:046117, 2005.

Inferring network mechanisms: The *Drosophila melanogaster* protein interaction network. *Proc. Natl. Acad. Sci. U.S.A.* 102(9):3192–7, 2005.

Cheng-Shie Wuu

3-D dose verification for IMRT using optical CT based polymer gel dosimetry. *Med. Phys.* 33(5):1412–9, 2006.

Radiation-induced second cancers: The impact of 3D-CRT and IMRT. *Int. J. Radiat. Oncol. Biol. Phys.* 56(1):83–8, 2003.

Dosimetry study of Re-188 liquid balloon for intravascular brachytherapy using polymer gel dosimeters and laser-beam optical CT scanner. *Med. Phys.* 30(2):132–7, 2003.

Dosimetric and volumetric criteria for selecting a source activity and/or a source type (I-125 or Pd-103) in the presence of irregular seed placement in permanent prostate implants. *Int. J. Radiat. Oncol. Biol. Phys.* 47:815–20, 2000.

214 www.facebook.com/petersonspublishing

Peterson's Graduate Programs in the Physical Sciences, Mathematics, Agricultural Sciences, the Environment & Natural Resources 2012

FLORIDA STATE UNIVERSITY

Department of Physics

Programs of Study	The Department of Physics at Florida State University (FSU) offers programs of study that lead to the M.S. and Ph.D. degrees. The Department has approximately 45 teaching faculty members and another 40 Ph.D. physicists engaged in a variety of research programs. The graduate program has 130 students, and almost all hold research or teaching assistantships. The programs of study include experimental and theoretical atomic, condensed-matter, high-energy, materials science, and nuclear physics. Two University institutes have major physics research components—the Material Science and Technology Center (MARTECH) for condensed-matter physics and the National High Magnetic Field Laboratory (NHMFL) for research on materials using very high magnetic fields.
	The National High Magnetic Field Laboratory is the only user facility of its kind in the Western Hemisphere. The laboratory develops and provides a variety of research magnets at the highest fields available in the world. The laboratory hosts roughly 1,000 scientists annually to perform experiments in scientific disciplines as diverse as biology, chemistry, engineering, geochemistry, materials science, medicine, and physics. This unique facility supports an extensive in-house research program that advances its scientific and technical capabilities. The in-house research program is built around leading scientists and engineers who concentrate on the study of strongly correlated electron systems, molecular conductors, magnetic materials, magnetic resonance, cryogenics, and new approaches to measuring materials' properties in high magnetic fields. Research at the laboratory is opening new frontiers of science at high magnetic fields, which have enormous potential for commercial and industrial applications. The laboratory also has one of the world's foremost magnet and science technology groups, which designs and builds this new generation of magnets. In 1999, the lab brought online a new 45-Tesla hybrid magnet, the most powerful magnet of its kind in the world. In 2004, the laboratory commissioned the world's first ultrawide-bore 900-MHz NMR magnet for chemical and biomedical research. The National High Magnetic Field Laboratory has many exciting research opportunities for graduate students who wish to pursue research at the edge of parameter space in any area of science utilizing these world-class resources and instruments.
	The Department offers both course work–only and thesis-type M.S. degrees. Five-year B.S./M.S. programs in computational physics and physics education have been introduced. Students studying for the Ph.D. degree are also required to pass a written qualifying examination on classical mechanics, electricity magnetism, quantum mechanics, thermodynamics and statistical mechanics, and modern physics. Within six months of passing the written qualifying examination, students should pass an oral examination on the subject of their prospective research. The only formal course requirement is to take three advanced-topics courses and a course in field theory.
Research Facilities	The Department occupies three adjacent buildings: the eight-story Physics Research Building, the Leroy Collins Research Laboratory Building, and an undergraduate physics classroom and laboratory building. Extensive experimental facilities include a 9.5-MV Super FN Tandem Van de Graaff accelerator with superconducting post-accelerator, a precision Penning trap mass spectrometer, a detector development laboratory for high-energy particle detectors, high-resolution Fourier-transform IR spectrometers, an ion implantation facility, instrumentation for research at liquid helium temperature and thin-film preparation, UHV (including surface analysis, molecular-beam epitaxy, and atomic cluster facilities), facilities for high- and low-temperature superconductivity, small-angle and standard X-ray diffractometry, crystal-growth facilities, scanning electron and tunneling microscopy, image analysis, quasielastic light scattering, polarized electron energy-loss spectroscopy, a helium atom–beam crystal surface-scattering apparatus, and a unique aerosol physics–electron irradiation system.
	In addition to in-house facilities, ongoing experiments use accelerator and other research equipment at Fermilab, Bates, Brookhaven, Oak Ridge, Thomas Jefferson National Accelerator Facility (TJNAF), and CERN. Computational facilities at FSU include an IBM multiprocessor supercomputer, a state-of-the-art visualization lab, and a 120-CPU Beowulf cluster in the Department. Extensive networking facilities provide access to computers on and off campus. More information on individual faculty member research can be found on the Department's Web site at http://www.physics.fsu.edu.
Financial Aid	The Department offers teaching and research assistantships and fellowships. The fellowships include several that are designed to help develop promising young minority physicists. The assistantship stipend is $18,000 for twelve months, with a workload equivalent to 6 contact hours in an elementary laboratory. In general, summer assistantships are provided for all students. Students are teaching assistants during the first academic year, but most are supported by research assistantships during and after their first summer.
Cost of Study	All tuition and fees for physics graduate students are covered by the Department in 2011–12.
Living and Housing Costs	Apartments and houses are readily available in Tallahassee. A typical one-bedroom unfurnished apartment within walking distance of the physics building rents for $450 per month. The University has married-student housing with rents that in range from $376 to $642 per month for a one-bedroom apartment to $402 to $642 per month for a two- or three-bedroom apartment. National surveys show that the cost of living in Tallahassee is 10 to 15 percent lower than that in most areas of the United States.
Student Group	Florida State University is a comprehensive university with a total of 39,136 students, of whom 8,370 are graduate or professional students. The Department of Physics has 130 graduate students. Students entering with a B.S. degree in physics typically attain the Ph.D. within 5½ years.
Location	Tallahassee is the capital city of the state of Florida. Its population is about 185,000. Many employment opportunities exist for students' spouses in Tallahassee. Students can live in relatively rural surroundings and still be only 20 minutes from the University. Extensive sports facilities and active city leagues exist in the city. Graduate students' fees cover membership in a state-of-the-art, on-campus recreation center. Because of the mild winter climate, people in this region tend to be outdoor-oriented. The Gulf of Mexico is about 30 miles from the campus.
The University and The Department	The presentations of the Schools of Fine Arts and Music provide cultural opportunities that are usually available only in much larger cities. The University Symphony, the Flying High Circus, and other theater and music groups give students the opportunity to participate in many activities in addition to their physics studies. FSU has active programs in intercollegiate and intramural sports.
	Recent major additions in the FSU Science Center include an interdisciplinary Materials Sciences and Technology Center and the National High Magnetic Field Laboratory. The NHMFL houses the world's highest field DC magnets, making FSU one of the principal centers for magnetic research. In addition to the teaching faculty at the Department of Physics, there are 8 research faculty members at the NHMFL.
Applying	Assistantship decisions are based on a student's transcript, GRE General Test scores, TOEFL scores, statement of purpose, and three letters of recommendation. The deadline for completed applications to be on file with the physics department is January 15 for international students and February 15 for U.S. citizens. To apply to the Department of Physics at Florida State University, students should go to the University's Admissions Office Web site (http://admissions.fsu.edu/).
Correspondence and Information	Professor Simon Capstick Graduate Physics Program Department of Physics Florida State University Tallahassee, Florida 32306-4350 Phone: 850-644-4473 Fax: 850-644-8630 E-mail: graduate@phy.fsu.edu Web site: http://www.physics.fsu.edu

Peterson's Graduate Programs in the Physical Sciences, Mathematics, Agricultural Sciences, the Environment & Natural Resources 2012

www.facebook.com/petersonspublishing

215

Florida State University

THE FACULTY AND THEIR RESEARCH

Todd Adams, Associate Professor; Ph.D., Notre Dame, 1997. Experimental high-energy physics, particle physics, supersymmetry.
Andrew Askew, Assistant Professor; Ph.D., Rice, 2004. High energy experimental particle physics.
Bernd Berg, Professor; Ph.D., Free University of Berlin, 1977. Theoretical physics: lattice gauge theory, computational physics.
Susan K. Blessing, Professor; Ph.D., Indiana, 1989. Experimental high-energy physics: elementary particle physics.
Gregory S. Boebinger, Professor and Director, National High Magnetic Field Laboratory; Ph.D., MIT, 1986. Magnetism, experimental condensed-matter physics, correlated electron systems.
Nicholas Bonesteel, Professor; Ph.D., Cornell, 1991. Theoretical physics: condensed-matter physics, many-body theory, magnetism, quantum Hall effect.
James S. Brooks, Professor; Ph.D., Oregon, 1973. Experimental physics: low temperature, high–magnetic field condensed matter, organic conductor, quantum fluid physics.
Jianming Cao, Associate Professor; Ph.D., Rochester, 1996. Experimental condensed-matter physics, ultrafast dynamics probed by lasers.
Simon C. Capstick, Professor; Ph.D., Toronto, 1986. Theoretical nuclear and particle physics: computational physics.
Irinel Chiorescu, Assistant Professor; Ph.D., CNRS Grenoble (France), 2000. Experimental condensed-matter physics, magnetic flux qubits.
Paul Cottle, Professor; Ph.D., Yale, 1986. Experimental heavy-ion nuclear physics, teacher preparation.
Volker Crede, Assistant Professor; Ph.D., Bonn (Germany), 2000. Experimental nuclear physics, quark matter.
Vladimir Dobrosavljevic, Professor; Ph.D., Brown, 1988. Theoretical condensed-matter physics, disordered systems and glasses, metal-insulator transitions.
Dennis Duke, Professor; Ph.D., Iowa State, 1974. Theoretical physics, elementary particle physics, computational physics.
Paul M. Eugenio, Associate Professor; Ph.D., Massachusetts Amherst, 1998. Experimental nuclear physics, quark-gluon structure of matter and hadron spectroscopy.
Marcia Fenley, Assistant Professor; Ph.D., Rutgers, 1991. Computational biophysics, electrostatics in macromolecules.
Christopher Gerardy, Assistant Professor; Ph.D., Dartmouth, 2002. Observational astronomy, stellar explosions.
Stephen Hill, Professor; Ph.D., Oxford, 1994. Experimental condensed matter physics.
Peter Hoeflich, Associate Professor; Ph.D., Heidelberg, 1986. Theoretical astrophysics; dark energy, dark matter, and dark ages.
Kirby Kemper, Professor; Ph.D., Indiana, 1968. Experimental physics: polarization studies in heavy-ion reactions.
David M. Lind, Associate Professor; Ph.D., Rice, 1986. Experimental condensed-matter physics, magnetic superlattices.
Efstratios Manousakis, Professor; Ph.D., Illinois at Urbana-Champaign, 1985. Theoretical physics: condensed-matter physics, many-body theory, superconductivity.
Hon Kie Ng, Associate Professor; Ph.D., McMaster, 1984. Experimental physics: far-infrared spectroscopy, superconductivity, highly correlated electron systems, spectroscopy in high magnetic fields.
Takemichi Okui, Assistant Professor; Ph.D., Berkeley, 2003. Theoretical high energy particle physics.
Joseph F. Owens, Professor; Ph.D., Tufts, 1973. Theoretical physics: elementary particles.
Jorge Piekarewicz, Professor; Ph.D., Pennsylvania, 1985. Theoretical nuclear physics, collective nuclear modes, equation of state of dense matter, neutron stars.
Harrison B. Prosper, Professor; Ph.D., Manchester (England), 1980. Experimental high-energy physics: particle physics.
Laura Reina, Professor; Ph.D., Trieste, 1992. Theoretical high-energy physics: elementary particle physics.
Per Arne Rikvold, Professor; Ph.D., Temple, 1983. Theoretical condensed-matter physics: statistical physics, surface and interface science.
Mark A. Riley, Professor and Chair of the Department; Ph.D., Liverpool, 1985. Experimental physics: nuclear structure physics.
Winston Roberts, Professor; Ph.D., Guelph, 1988. Theoretical hadron physics.
Grigory Rogachev, Assistant Professor; Ph.D., Kurchatov Institute (Moscow), 1999. Experimental nuclear physics: nucleosynthesis.
Pedro Schlottmann, Professor; Ph.D., Munich Technical, 1973. Theoretical physics, high-T_c superconductors, heavy fermions, magnetism.
Shahid A. Shaheen, Associate Professor; Ph.D., Ruhr-Bochum, 1985. Experimental condensed-matter physics: permanent magnets, magnet materials and materials science.
Samuel L. Tabor, Professor; Ph.D., Stanford, 1972. Experimental physics: high-spin states in nuclei, nuclei far from stability.
Oskar Vafek, Assistant Professor; Ph.D., Johns Hopkins, 2003. Theoretical condensed-matter physics: quantum phase transitions, superconductivity.
David Van Winkle, Professor; Ph.D., Colorado, 1984. Experimental condensed-matter physics: liquid crystal gels.
Alexander Volya, Assistant Professor; Ph.D., Michigan State, 2000. Theoretical nuclear physics, nuclear structure models.
Stephan von Molnár, Professor; Ph.D., California, Riverside, 1965. Experimental physics: correlation effects in electronic systems, magnetic semiconductors, magnetic nanostructures.
Horst Wahl, Professor; Ph.D., Vienna, 1969. Experimental physics: elementary particle physics.
Maitri Warusawithana, Assistant Professor; Ph.D., Illinois at Urbana-Champaign, 2005. Materials science and engineering.
Christopher Wiebe, Assistant Professor; Ph.D., McMaster, 2002. Experimental condensed-matter physics: highly correlated electron systems, geometrically frustrated materials, superconductivity.
Ingo Wiedenhöver, Associate Professor; Ph.D., Cologne (Germany), 1995. Experimental nuclear physics, radioactive beams.
Peng Xiong, Professor; Ph.D., Brown, 1995. Experimental condensed-matter physics: nanobiophysics systems.
Kun Yang, Professor; Ph.D., Indiana, 1994. Theoretical physics: condensed matter, computational physics.
Huan-Xiang Zhou, Professor; Ph.D., Drexel, 1988. Computational and experimental biophysics, protein stability folding, protein-protein interactions.

RESEARCH ACTIVITIES

Theoretical

Astrophysics. Advanced stages of stellar evolution, core-collapse and thermonuclear supernovae, compact stellar remnants, thermonuclear astrophysical combustion, radiative transfer (Hoeflich).
Computational Biophysics. Electrostatics and dynamics of biomolecules in aqueous environments (Zhou, Fenley).
Condensed Matter. Many-body theory of magnetism, magnetic properties of solids, high-temperature superconductivity, heavy fermions, adsorption, phase transitions (Bonesteel, Dobrosavljevic, Manousakis, Rikvold, Schlottmann, Vafek, Yang).
Elementary Particles and Fields. Strong and electroweak interaction phenomenology in high-energy particle physics (Owens, Reina). Lattice gauge theory and numerical simulations of various physical systems (Berg, Duke).
Hadron Physics (Roberts).
Nuclear Theory. Nuclear structure and studies, emphasizing transitions; collective nuclear modes; structure and electromagnetic interactions of baryons and nuclei; structure and phases of neutron stars (Capstick, Piekarewicz, Volya).

Experimental

Astrophysics. Multiwavelength studies of supernova explosions using new observing technology (Gerardy).
Atomic and Molecular Physics. Precision atomic measurements using Penning trap (Myers).
Condensed Matter. Biomolecular ordering, nanophysics/biophysics, liquid crystals, gels, spintronics, hard magnetic materials, surface physics, subpicosecond spectroscopy, low- and high-temperature superconductivity, highly correlated electron systems, organic crystals, quantum qubits (Balicas, Boebinger, Brooks, Brunel, Cao, Chiorescu, Choi, Engel, Jaroszynski, Kuhns, Lind, McGill, Ng, Popovic, Reyes, Shaheen, Smirnov, Suslov, Tozer, von Molnár, Van Winkle, Wang, Xiong).
Elementary Particles and Fields. Collider physics, strong and electroweak interactions in high-energy particle physics (Adams, Blessing, S. Hagopian, Prosper, Wahl).
Nuclear Physics. Hadron spectroscopy; heavy-ion reactions and radioactive beams; photoproduction of baryons and mesons; search for exotic and hybrid mesons; search for new strangeonia states; search for missing baryons; particle detector development and computational physics; heavy-ion fusion and fragmentation studies; properties of nuclear systems at high angular momentum and far from stability; laser-induced polarization; octupole structure in nuclei; light-ion nuclear spectroscopy; alpha, beta, and gamma spectroscopy; relativistic heavy-ion reactions (Cottle, Crede, Eugenio, Frawley, Kemper, Riley, Rogachev, Tabor, Wiedenhöver).

216 www.facebook.com/petersonspublishing

Peterson's Graduate Programs in the Physical Sciences, Mathematics, Agricultural Sciences, the Environment & Natural Resources 2012

OHIO UNIVERSITY

Department of Physics and Astronomy

Programs of Study

The Department of Physics and Astronomy offers graduate study and research programs leading to the Master of Arts, Master of Science, and Doctor of Philosophy degrees. The program of study emphasizes individual needs and interests in addition to essential general requirements of the discipline. Major areas of current research are experimental and theoretical condensed-matter and surface physics, nanoscience, mathematical and computational physics, biological physics, astronomy and astrophysics.

At the end of a student's first year of graduate study, his or her suitability to continue toward the Ph.D. is evaluated by the full faculty. This evaluation is based primarily on the student's GPA in the core courses. The courses in the second year cover more advanced topics. Master's degrees require completion of 45 graduate credits in physics and have both thesis and nonthesis options.

Prospective student can listen to what current students have to say about the program on the Department of Physics and Astronomy's YouTube page at http://www.youtube.com/OhioUPhysics.

Research Facilities

The physics department occupies two wings of Clippinger Laboratories, a modern, well-equipped research building; the Edwards Accelerator Building, which contains Ohio University's 4.5-MV high-intensity tandem Van de Graaff accelerator; and the Surface Science Research Laboratory, which is isolated from mechanical and electrical disturbances. Specialized facilities for measuring structural, thermal, transport, optical, and magnetic properties of condensed matter are available. In addition to research computers in laboratories, students have access to a Beowulf cluster and the Ohio Supercomputer Center, where massively parallel systems are located. Ohio University is a partner in the MDM Observatory at Kitt Peak, Arizona, which provides guaranteed access to major research telescopes.

Financial Aid

Financial aid is available in the form of teaching assistantships (TAs) and research assistantships (RAs). All cover the full cost of tuition plus a stipend from which a quarterly fee of $572 must be paid by the student. The current stipend level for TAs and RAs is $21,726 per year. TAs require approximately 15 to 20 hours per week of laboratory and/or teaching duties.

Cost of Study

Tuition and fees are $3126 per quarter for Ohio residents and $5790 per quarter for out-of-state students. Students on TA or RA support receive tuition waivers. Students not otherwise covered by health insurance must pay a $1245 annual premium for student health insurance.

Living and Housing Costs

On-campus rooms for single students are $1265 per quarter, while married student apartments cost from $650 to $950 per month. A number of off-campus apartments and rooms are available at various costs.

Student Group

About 20,042 students study on the main campus of the University, and 3,353 of these are graduate students. The graduate student enrollment in the physics department ranges from 70 to 80.

Location

Athens is a city of about 25,000, situated in the rolling Appalachian foothills of southeastern Ohio. The surrounding landscape consists of wooded hills rising about the Hocking River valley, and the area offers many outdoor recreational opportunities. Eight state parks lie within easy driving distance of the campus and are popular spots for relaxation. The outstanding intellectual and cultural activities sponsored by this diverse university community are pleasantly blended in Athens with a vibrant tradition in the visual and performing arts.

The University and The Department

Ohio University, founded in 1804 and the oldest institution of higher education in the Northwest Territory, is a comprehensive university with a wide range of graduate and undergraduate programs. The Ph.D. program in physics began in 1959, and more than 250 doctoral degrees have been awarded. Currently, the Department has 27 regular faculty members and additional part-time faculty and postdoctoral fellows. Sponsored research in the Department amounts to approximately $4.1 million per year and comes from NSF, DOE, DOD, NASA, and the state of Ohio. Further information can be found at the Department's home page (http://www.phy.ohiou.edu).

Applying

Online application procedures and downloadable forms can be found at http://www.ohio.edu/graduate/apply.cfm. Information can also be obtained by e-mailing the Department of Physics and Astronomy at gradapp@helios.phy.ohiou.edu.

Correspondence and Information

Graduate Admissions Chair
Department of Physics and Astronomy
Ohio University
Athens, Ohio 45701

Phone: 740-593-1718
E-mail: gradapp@helios.phy.ohio.edu
Web site: http://www.phy.ohiou.edu

Peterson's Graduate Programs in the Physical Sciences, Mathematics, Agricultural Sciences, the Environment & Natural Resources 2012

www.facebook.com/petersonspublishing   **217**

Ohio University

THE FACULTY AND THEIR RESEARCH

Professors

Carl R. Brune, Ph.D., Caltech, 1994. Experimental nuclear astrophysics.

David A. Drabold, Distinguished Professor; Ph.D., Washington (St. Louis), 1989. Theoretical condensed matter, computational methodology for electronic structure, theory of topologically disordered materials.

Charlotte Elster, Dr.rer.nat., Bonn, 1986. Nuclear and intermediate-energy theory.

Alexander O. Govorov, Ph.D., Novosibirsk (Russia), 1991. Theoretical condensed-matter physics, nanoscience.

Steven M. Grimes, Distinguished Professor, Emeritus; Ph.D., Wisconsin–Madison, 1968. Nuclear physics.

Kenneth H. Hicks, Ph.D., Colorado, 1984. Nuclear and intermediate-energy physics.

Saw-Wai Hla, Ph.D., Ljubljana (Slovenia), 1997. Experimental condensed-matter and surface physics, nanoscience.

David C. Ingram, Ph.D., Salford (England), 1980. Atomic collisions in solids, thin films, deposition and analysis, surface physics.

Peter Jung, Distinguished Professor; Ph.D., Ulm (Germany), 1985. Nonequilibrium statistical physics, nonlinear stochastic processes, pattern formation, biophysics.

Martin E. Kordesch, Ph.D., Case Western Reserve, 1984. Surface physics, wide-gap materials.

Daniel Phillips, Ph.D., Flinders (Australia), 1995. Theoretical nuclear and particle physics.

Prakash Madappa, Ph.D., Bombay, 1979. Theoretical nuclear and particle astrophysics.

Joseph C. Shields, Chair of the Department; Ph.D., Berkeley, 1991. Astrophysics, interstellar medium, active galactic nuclei.

Arthur Smith, Ph.D., Texas at Austin, 1995. Experimental semiconductors, thin film.

Thomas S. Statler, Ph.D., Princeton, 1986. Astrophysics, galactic structure and dynamics.

Sergio E. Ulloa, Ph.D., SUNY at Buffalo, 1984. Theoretical condensed-matter physics.

Associate Professors

Markus Böttcher, Ph.D., Bonn, 1997. High-energy astrophysics.

Ido Braslavsky, Ph.D., Israel Institute of Technology, 1998. Biophysics.

Horacio E. Castillo, Ph.D., Illinois, 1998. Theoretical condensed-matter physics.

Douglas Clowe, Ph.D., Hawaii, 1998. Observational astrophysics.

Mark Lucas, Ph.D., Illinois, 1994. Experimental nuclear physics., physics education.

Alexander Neiman, Ph.D., Saratov State (Russia), 1991. Biophysics, nonlinear dynamics, stochastic processes.

Nancy Sandler, Ph.D., Illinois, 1998. Theoretical condensed-matter physics.

David F. J. Tees, Ph.D., McGill, 1996. Experimental biophysics, nanoscience.

Assistant Professors

Gang Chen, Ph.D., Lehigh, 2004. Experimental condensed-matter physics.

Justin Frantz, Ph.D., Columbia, 2004. Experimental Nuclear Physics.

Julie Roche, Ph.D., Un. B. Pascal (France), 1998. Nuclear and intermediate-energy physics.

Andreas Schiller, Ph.D., Oslo, 2000. Experimental nuclear physics.

Eric Stinaff, Ph.D., Iowa State, 2002. Experimental nanoscience.

THEORETICAL RESEARCH ACTIVITIES

Astrophysics. Studies of galaxies and galaxy clusters, with emphasis on galaxy structure, dynamics, and interactions; dark matter and dark energy; quasars and supermassive black holes in galaxy nuclei; high-energy astrophysics related to accretion onto compact objects, relativistic jets, and gamma-ray bursts; asteroids and solar system dynamics. Investigations into these topics employ multiwavelength observations with major facilities (Hubble Space Telescope, Chandra X-ray Observatory, MDM Observatory at Kitt Peak, Arizona) as well as theoretical efforts, including analytic calculations and large-scale numerical simulations.

Biophysics. Computational modeling of complex cellular signaling networks, especially intracellular and intercellular calcium signaling, modeling of neural and glial functions in healthy and epileptic tissue, stochastic modeling of electroreceptors in paddle fish, modeling of the neuronal circuitry of the cat's retina, stochastic and coherence resonance in excitable biologic systems, nanoscale ion channel and receptor clusters, and modeling slow axonal transport.

Condensed-Matter Theory. Statistical mechanics and nonequilibrium dynamics of disordered systems and glassy materials. Some areas of interest include nanoscale-sized dynamical heterogeneities in glassy materials, slow activation-controlled motion of topological defects (e.g., vortices, dislocations), and disordered electronic systems; methodology of first principles simulation: development of local basis density functional methods, time-dependent density functional theory and efficient computation of Wannier functions, and the single-particle-density matrix; theory of disordered insulators: Anderson transition, photo-structural response, novel schemes for structural modeling of glasses, and studies of pressure-induced polyamorphism; and optical and transport phenomena in nanoscale systems, including quantum dots, rings, and channels. Recent activity covers excitons in quantum rings, spin transport in nanocrystals, and quantum acoustoelectric interactions on nanoscale. Other nanoscience problems of interest include electronic transport in complex molecule systems, the role of controlled disorder on the metallic or insulating nature of one- and two-dimensional systems, and the role of collective effects on the optical and transport properties of quantum dot arrays and studies of low-dimensional strongly correlated electron systems, disordered electronic systems, and quantum-Hall-effect physics.

Mathematical and Computational Physics. Quantum simulation, ab initio calculations, and visualization of many-body and few-body systems in condensed-matter and nuclear physics; numerical methods and algorithmic development for high-performance vector and parallel computers; analytical and algorithmic studies in differential and integral equations, probability theory, and series expansions.

Nuclear/Particle Physics and Astrophysics. Research in theoretical nuclear/particle physics at Ohio University focuses on the dynamics of the matter that makes up the atomic nucleus, and examines manifestations of these dynamics in systems ranging in size from a single proton to a neutron star. Researchers combine data from laboratory experiments, astronomical observations, and theoretical studies in order to examine the role of the fundamental forces of nature within these systems. Current topics of interest include models of the nucleon-nucleon force; structure of light nuclei, especially as probed in proton, electron, and photon scattering; proton and neutron structure; reactions on exotic nuclei; relativistic heavy-ion collisions; physics and astrophysics of neutron stars and supernovae; and gravitational waves.

EXPERIMENTAL RESEARCH ACTIVITIES

Astrophysics. Spectroscopic observations of stellar motions and stellar populations in elliptical galaxies and evidence for dark matter, ionized gas in galaxies, gravitational lensing studies of galaxy clusters, nuclear physics applied to astrophysics.

Biological Physics. Stochastic resonance in psychophysics and animal behavior, studies of stochastic nonlinear dynamics in paddlefish electroreceptors, experimental determination of the response of single-cell-adhesion molecules to applied forces using a microcantilever device, lipid bilayer tether pulling on leukocytes and platelets using micropipette aspiration, studies of cell adhesion in pressure gradients in micropipettes, determination of cell membrane mechanical properties, optical studies of biomolecules at the single-molecule level using total internal reflection fluorescence microscopy and fluorescence resonance energy transfer, biomineralization, studies of ice-modifying antifreeze proteins, studies of DNA-protein interactions using optical methods.

Condensed-Matter and Surface Science. Current projects encompass various areas in nanoscale science; scanning-probe techniques; and synthesis and characterization of photonic, composite, and electronic materials. Relevant projects are illustrated by the following list: thin-film growth (by molecular-beam epitaxy) and characterization (using scanning-probe microscopy techniques, including spin-polarized) of the structural, electronic, and magnetic properties of transition-metal nitride layers and magnetic-doped nitride semiconductors; single-atom/molecule manipulation using ultrahigh-vacuum, low-temperature scanning-tunneling microscopy; development of single-molecule electronics; molecular and metal thin films; surface science; electron microscopy of nanoscale structures; amorphous semiconductors and their photonics and electronic properties; MeV ion-beam analysis of materials and measurement of relevant cross-sections; ion-beam and plasma deposition of materials and their characterization; effect of hydrogen and nitrogen to the properties of amorphous carbon; optical spectroscopy and ultrafast laser studies of semiconductor nanostructures and nanostructure-based devices; optical spin manipulation and nanophotonics of individual and coupled nanostructures; growth of semiconducting chalcogenide nanowires for nonvolatile electric memory; synthesis of periodic mesoporous materials through a self-assembly approach; atomic and nanoscale structure characterization by X-ray absorption, fine structure, and small/wide angle X-ray scattering; and study of transparent conductive oxides, low work function surfaces, and thermionic cathodes.

Nuclear and Intermediate-Energy Physics. Contemporary research in experimental nuclear physics involves collaboration with scientists from many different institutions and heavy use of specialized accelerator facilities around the world. Ohio University nuclear physicists are recognized leaders in a variety of experimental programs spanning a broad energy domain. At higher energies, Ohio University's faculty members are leading research programs at Jefferson Laboratory in Virginia. These include the study of electromagnetic production of strange baryons and the search for new exotic baryons in Hall B, precision measurements of the weak charge of the proton in Hall C, and the study of the nature of the gluonic flux tube in Hall D; an active program studying the photoexcitation of the nucleon is also ongoing at the SPring-8 experiment in Japan. At lower energies, faculty members are directing research programs in several distinct areas, including fundamental symmetries in nuclear reactions via precision tests of charge symmetry breaking at TRIUMF in Canada, exotic nuclei far from the line of stability at GANIL and the Hahn-Meitner Institute in Europe, measurements of neutron cross sections at Los Alamos in New Mexico, studies of nuclear level densities at the Holifield Radioactive Ion Beam Facility in Tennessee, and studies of pion photoproduction and QCD sum rules with the LEGS facility at Brookhaven National Laboratory in New York. The Department also operates the high-intensity Ohio University Tandem Van de Graaff accelerator with its unique beam swinger magnet and long flight path for high-precision measurements of various nuclear cross sections and projects in medical physics. The research program is supported by the Ohio University Institute for Nuclear and Particle Physics. Grants are provided by the U.S. National Science Foundation and the U.S. Department of Energy.

218 www.facebook.com/petersonspublishing

Peterson's Graduate Programs in the Physical Sciences, Mathematics, Agricultural Sciences, the Environment & Natural Resources 2012

SELECTED PUBLICATIONS

Abdo, A. A., et al. **(M. Böttcher).** The first Fermi multifrequency campaign on BL Lacertae: Characterizing the low-activity state of the eponymous blazar. *Astrophys. J.* 730(2):101, 2011.

Joshi, M., and **Böttcher, M.** Time-dependent radiation transfer in the internal shock model scenario for blazar jets. *Astrophys. J.* 727(1):21, 2011.

Roustazadeh, P., and **M. Böttcher.** Very high energy gamma-ray-induced pair cascades in the radiation fields of dust tori of active galactic nuclei: Application to Cen A. *Astrophys. J.* 728(2):134, 2011.

Azuma, R. E., et al. **(C. R. Brune).** AZURE: An *R*-matrix code for nuclear astrophysics. *Phys. Rev. C* 81(4):045805, 2010.

Tang, X. D., et al. **(C. R. Brune).** Determination of the $E1$ component of the low-energy $^{12}C(\alpha,\gamma)^{16}O$ cross section. *Phys. Rev. C* 81(4):045809, 2010.

Boyd, Richard, Lee Bernstein, and **C. R. Brune.** Studying nuclear astrophysics at NIF. *Phys. Today* 62(6):60–61, 2009.

Parsaeian, A., and **H. E. Castillo.** Equilibrium and nonequilibrium fluctuations in a glass-forming liquid. *Phys. Rev. Lett.* 102(5):055704, 2009.

Castillo, H. E. Time reparametrization symmetry in spin-glass models. *Phys. Rev. B.* 78(21):214430, 2008.

Castillo, H. E., and A. Parsaeian. Local fluctuations in the ageing of a simple structural glass. *Nat. Phys.* 3(1):26–28, 2007.

Chen, G., F. Inam, and **D. A. Drabold.** Structural origin of the intermediate phase in Ge–Se glasses. *Appl. Phys. Lett.* 97(13):131901, 2010.

Chen G., and C. Wan. Residual strain in thermally annealed periodic mesopourous silica revealed by X-ray scattering. *Appl. Phys. Lett.* 96(14):141906, 2010.

Krumpelt, M., et al. **(G. Chen).** The effect of chromium oxyhydroxide on solid oxide fuel cells. *J. Electrochem. Soc.* 157(2):B228–33.

Chung, Sun Mi, et al. **(D. Clowe).** Star formation in the Bullet Cluster. I. The infrared luminosity function and star formation rate. *Astrophys. J.* 725(2): 1536–49, 2010.

Sanglia, R. P., et al. **(D. Clowe).** The fundamental plane of EDisCS galaxies. The effect of size evolution. *Astron. Astrophys* 524: id.A6, 2010.

Guennou, L., et al. **(D. Clowe).** The DAFT/FADA survey. I. Photometric redshifts along lines of sight to clusters in the z = [0.4, 0.9] interval. *Astron. Astrophys* 523: id.A21, 2010.

Cai, B., X. Zhang, and **D. A. Drabold.** Building block modeling technique: Application to ternary chalcogenide glasses g-$Ge_2As_4Se_4$ and g-$AsGe_{0.8}Se_{0.8}$. *Phys. Rev. B* 83(9):092202, 2011.

Prasai, B., and **D. A. Drabold.** Ab initio simulation of solid electrolyte materials in liquid and glassy phases. *Phys. Rev. B* 83(9):094202, 2011.

Zhang, M., and **D. A. Drabold.** Comparison of the Kubo formula, the microscopic response method, and the Greenwood formula. *Phys. Rev. E* 83(1):012103, 2011.

Polyzou, W. N. and **Ch. Elster** et al. Mini review of Poincaré invariant quantum theory. *Few Body Syst.* 49:129–147, 2011.

Khaldi, K., **Ch. Elster,** and W. Glöckle. The $n+n+a$ system in a continuum Faddeev formulation. *Phys. Rev. C* 82(5):054002, 2010.

J. Golak, et al. **(Ch. Elster).** Two nucleon systems in three dimensions. *Phys. Rev. C* 81(3):034006, 2010.

Govorov, A. O., et al. Theory of circular dichroism of nanomaterials comprising chiral molecules and nanocrystals: Plasmon enhancement, dipole interactions, and dielectric effects. *Nano Letters* 10(4):1374–82, 2010.

Carmeli, I., et al. **(A. O. Govorov).** Broad band enhancement of light absorption in photosytem I by metal nanoparticle antennas. *Nano Letters* 10(6):2069–74, 2010.

Kleemans, N. A. J. M., et al. **(A. O. Govorov).** Many-body exciton states in self-assembled quantum dots coupled to a Fermi sea. *Nat. Phys.* 6(7):534–8, 2010.

Kohri, H., et al. **(K. H. Hicks)** (the LEPS Collaboration). Near-threshold Lambda(1520) production by the gamma p -> K+Lambda(1520) reaction at forward K+ angles. *Phys. Rev. Lett.* 104(17):172001, 2010.

Anefalos-Pereira, S., et al. **(K. H. Hicks)** (the CLAS Collaboration). Differential cross section of $\gamma n \to K+\Sigma-$ on bound neutrons with incident photons from 1.1 to 3.6 GeV. *Phys. Lett. B* 688(4–5):289–93, 2010.

Chang, W. C., et al. **(K. H. Hicks)** (the CLAS Collaboration). Measurement of the incoherent $\gamma d \to \phi pn$ photoproduction near threshold. *Phys. Lett. B* 684(1):6–10, 2010.

Perera, U. G. E., et al. **(S.-W. Hla** and **S. E. Ulloa).** Spatially extended Kondo state in magnetic molecules induced by interfacial charge transfer. *Phys. Rev.Lett.* 105(10): 106601, 2010.

Serrate, D., et al. **(S.-W. Hla).** Imaging and manipulating the spin direction of individual atoms. *Nature Nanotechnology* 5(5):350–3, 2010.

Clark, K., et al. **(S.-W. Hla).** Superconductivity in just four pairs of $(BETS)_2$-$GaCl_4$ molecules. *Nature Nanotechnology* 5(4):261–5, 2010.

Nandasiri, M. I., et al. **(D. C. Ingram).** Ion beam analysis of the thermal stability of hydrogenated diamond-like carbon thin films on Si substrate. *Twentieth International Conference on the Application of Accelerators in Research and Industry: Twentieth International Conferencing,* 2009.

Khoshman, J. M., **(D. C. Ingram,** and **M. E. Kordesch).** Growth and optical properties of amorphous $Be_{0.13}Zn_{0.38}O_{0.49}$ thin films prepared by radio frequency magnetron sputtering. *Journal of Non-Crystalline Solids* 354(19–25) 2783–6, 2008.

Khoshman, J. M., **(D. C. Ingram,** and **M. E. Kordesch).** Bandgap engineering in amorphous Be_xZn_yO thin films. *Appl .Phys. Lett.* 92(9):091902, 2008.

Shuai, J., R. Sheng, and **P. Jung.** Entropically modified spiking ability and periodicity in clustered channels. *Phys. Rev. E* 81(5):051913, 2010.

Jung, P., and P. Talkner. Ticks of a random clock. *Eur. Phys. J. Spec. Top.* 187(1):223–30, 2010.

Jung, P., D. Swaminathan, and A. Ullah. Calcium spikes: Chance or necessity? *Chem. Phys.* 375(2–3):625–9, 2010.

Vaughn, J. M., K. D. Jamison, and **M. E. Kordesch.** In situ emission microscopy of scandium/scandium-oxide and barium/barium-oxide thin films on tungsten. *IEEE Trans. Electron. Dev.* 56(5):794–8, 2009.

Khoshman, J. M., W. D. Jennings, and **M. E. Kordesch.** Ellipsometric study of a-Be3N2 thin films prepared by radio frequency magnetron sputtering. *Appl. Surf. Sci.* 255:12, 6190–4, 2009.

Blanpied, G., et al. **(M. Lucas).** The N $\to$. Δ transition from simultaneous measurements of p(γ,π^+) and p(γ,γ). *Phys. Rev. Lett.* 79:4337, 1997.

Peterson's Graduate Programs in the Physical Sciences, Mathematics, Agricultural Sciences, the Environment & Natural Resources 2012

www.facebook.com/petersonspublishing   **219**

Ohio University

Feldman, G., et al. **(M. Lucas).** Compton scattering, meson-exchange, and the polarizabilities of bound nucleons. *Phys. Rev. C: Nucl. Phys.* 54:2124, 1996.

Han, L., and **A. B. Neiman.** Spontaneous oscillations, signal amplification, and synchronization in a model of active hair bundle mechanics. *Phys. Rev. E* 81(4):041913, 2010.

Nguyen, H., **A. B. Neiman.** Spontaneous dynamics and response properties of a Hodgkin-Huxley-type neuron model driven by harmonic synaptic noise. *Eur. Phys. J. Spec. Top.* 187(1):179–87, 2010.

Prager, T., **A. B. Neiman,** and L. Schimansky-Geier. Periodic renewal processes: Application to periodically driven FitzHugh-Nagumo system. *Eur. Phys. J. B* 69(1):119–26, 2009.

Baru, V., et al. **(D. R. Phillips).** Precision calculation of the $\pi-d$ scattering length and its impact on threshold πN scattering. *Phys. Lett. B* 694(4–5):473–7, 2011.

Ji, C., **D. R. Phillips,** and L. Platter. Beyond universality in three-body recombination: An effective field theory treatment. *Europhys. Lett.* 92(1):13003, 2010.

Yang, C.-J., **Ch. Elster,** and **D. R. Phillips.** Subtractive renormalization of the NN interaction in chiral effective theory up to next-to-next–to-leading order: S waves. Phys. Rev. C 80(4):044002, 2009.

Androic, D., et al. **(J. Roche)** (G0 Collaboration). Strange quark contributions to parity-violating asymmetries in the backward angle G0 electron scattering experiment. *Phys. Rev. Lett.* 104(1):012001, 2010.

Fuchey, E., et al. **(J. Roche)** Exclusive neutral pion electroproduction in the deeply virtual regime. *Phys. Rev. C* 83(2):025201, 2011.

Androic, D., et al. **(J. Roche)** (G0 Collaboration). The G0 experiment: Apparatus for parity-violating electron scattering measurements at forward and backward angles. *Nuclear Instruments and Methods in Physics Research Section A: Accelerators, Spectrometers, Detectors and Associated Equipment* 646(1):59–86, 2011.

Zarea, M., and **N. Sandler.** Rashba spin-orbit interaction in graphene and zigzag nanoribbons. *Phys. Rev. B* 79:165442, 2009.

Dias da Silva, L. G. G. V., et al. **(N. Sandler** and **S. E. Ulloa).** Tunable pseudogap Kondo effect and quantum phase transitions in Aharonov-Bohm interferometers. *Phys. Rev. Lett.* 102:166806, 2009.

Zarea, M., Carlos Büsser, and **N. Sandler.** Unscreened Coulomb interactions and the quantum spin hall phase in neutral zigzag graphene ribbons *Phys. Rev. Lett.* 101:196802, 2008.

Schiller, A., et al. Selective population and neutron decay of an excited state of $_{23}$O. *Phys. Rev. Lett.* 99:112501, 2007.

Schiller, A., and M. Thoennessen. Compilation of giant electric dipole resonances built on excited states. *At. Data Nucl. Data Tables* 93:549, 2007.

Schiller, A., et al. Low-energy M1 excitation mode in $_{172}$Yb. *Phys. Lett. B* 633:225, 2006.

Watson, C. R., et al. **(J. C. Shields).** The star formation and nuclear accretion histories of normal galaxies in the AGES survey. *Astrophys. J.* 696(2):2206–19, 2009.

Schlesinger, K., et al. **(J. C. Shields).** The nuclear outflows and feedback in the Seyfert 2 galaxy Markarian 573. *Astrophys. J.* 699(1):857–70, 2009.

Sarzi, M., and **J. C. Shields** et al. The SAURON Project – XVI: On the sources of ionisation for the gas in elliptical and lenticular galaxies. *Mon. Not. Roy. Astron. Soc.* 402(4):2187–210, 2010.

Wang, Kangkang, et al. **(A. R. Smith).** A modular designed ultra-high-vacuum spin-polarized scanning tunneling microscope with controllable magnetic fields for investigating epitaxial thin films. *Rev. Sci. Instrum.* 82(5):053703, 2011.

Wang, Kangkang, et al. **(A. R. Smith).** Structural controlled magnetic anisotropy in Heusler L10–MnGa epitaxial thin films. *Appl. Phys. Lett.* 98(16):162507, 2011.

Wang, Kangkang, et al. **(A. R. Smith).** Two-dimensional Mn structure on the GaN growth surface and evidence for room-temperature spin ordering. *Phys. Rev. B* 83(16):165407, 2011.

Statler, T. S. Extreme sensitivity of the YORP effect to small-scale topography. *Icarus* 202(2):502–13, 2009.

Diehl, S., and **T. S. Statler.** The hot interstellar medium in normal elliptical galaxies. III. The thermal structure of the gas. *Astrophys. J.* 687(2):986–96, 2008.

Diehl, S., and **T. S. Statler.** The hot interstellar medium in normal elliptical galaxies. II. Morphological evidence for AGN feedback. *Astrophys. J.* 680(2):897–910, 2008.

Bracker, A. S., et al. **(E. A. Stinaff).** Engineering electron and hole tunneling with asymmetric InAs quantum dot molecules. *Appl. Phys. Lett.* 89(23):233110, 2006.

Ponomarev, I. V., et al. **(E. A. Stinaff).** Theory of spin states in coupled quantum dots. *Phys. Status Solidi B* 243(15):3869–73, 2006.

Pai, A., P. Sundd, and **D. F. J. Tees.** In situ microrheological determination of neutrophil stiffening following adhesion in a model capillary. *Ann. Biomed. Eng.* 36:596–603, 2008.

Sundd, P., X. Zou, D.J. Goetz, and **D. F. J. Tees.** Leukocyte adhesion in capillary-sized, P-selectin-coated micropipettes. *Microcirculation* 15:109–22, 2008.

Tees, D. F. J., R. E. Waugh, and D. A. Hammer. A microcantilever device to assess the effect of force on the lifetime of selectin-carbohydrate bonds. *Biophys. J.* 80:668–82, 2001.

Vernek, E., P. A. Orellana, and **S. E. Ulloa.** Suppression of Kondo screening by the Dicke effect in multiple quantum dots. *Phys. Rev. B* 82(16):165304, 2010.

Rolon, J. E., and **S. E. Ulloa.** Coherent control of indirect excitonic qubits in optically driven quantum dot molecules. *Phys. Rev. B* 82(11):115307, 2010.

Zhang, W., et al. **(S. E. Ulloa).** Interchain coupling induced localization/delocalization in coupled one-dimensional ordered and disordered chains. *Phys. Rev. B* 81(21):214201, 2010.

Peterson's Graduate Programs in the Physical Sciences, Mathematics, Agricultural Sciences, the Environment & Natural Resources 2012

TEMPLE UNIVERSITY
of the Commonwealth System of Higher Education

Department of Physics

Programs of Study

The Department of Physics at the Temple University offers the M.A. and Ph.D. degrees. The M.A. program requires 24 semester hours of credit. Normally, required courses for the M.A. degree encompass 18 hours; the other 6 semester hours are used for thesis research or for additional courses. The student must also pass the M.A. comprehensive examination in physics. No specific number of graduate credits is required for the Ph.D. degree, but an approved program of graduate courses must be satisfactorily completed. A dissertation and dissertation examination are required. An M.A. degree is not necessary for the Ph.D. degree. The Ph.D. qualifying examination in physics is taken after completion of two years of graduate study. There is a one-year residence requirement for the Ph.D. degree. Students whose native language is not English must pass an examination in spoken and written English. There is no other language requirement for either the M.A. or the Ph.D. degree. Each full-time graduate student is given a desk in one of the several student offices. Lecturers from other institutions describe their research activities at a weekly colloquium. Informal discussions with members of the faculty are frequent.

Research Facilities

The Department is housed in Barton Hall, which has "smart" lecture theaters, offices, classrooms, and laboratories. Temple's library provides online access to frequently used journals, and contains several thousand volumes of books. A student shop and a materials preparation facility are available. The University computer facilities are based on a UNIX-cluster-composed Digital Equipment Corporation Alphas, including a high-performance numerical compute-server. The Departmental computer facilities include a local area network (LAN) of five Windows XP workstations, and eight host LAN of Linux workstations. The Departmental local area networks are connected to a fiber-optic campus backbone through which all University mainframe computer facilities can be reached. High-speed access to the Internet is readily available from all Departmental computers. Electronic information retrieval is provided by the Temple University library's Scholars Information System, which subscribes to a wide range of online databases. The research laboratories are conducting a variety of studies on optical hole-burning and multiple quantum well structures; laser-based molecular spectroscopy; low-temperature properties of alloys and intermetallics, including valence fluctuations and heavy fermion behavior; high-temperature superconductivity; Mössbauer spectroscopy; nucleon structure; dark-matter detection; and electrorheology and magnetorheology. The Department also uses outside facilities, including the Los Alamos Meson Physics Facility, the Brookhaven National Laboratory, the Stanford Linear Accelerator Center, the Thomas Jefferson National Accelerator Facility, and the National High Magnetic Laboratory. Theoretical work is being conducted in such areas as elementary particles and their interactions, statistical mechanics, biophysics, general relativity, and condensed-matter theory.

Financial Aid

Aid is available to qualified full-time students in the form of assistantships and fellowships funded by the University and various extramural agencies. All forms of financial aid include a stipend plus tuition. The specific type of aid offered to a particular student depends on the student's qualifications and program of study. Summer support for qualified students is also normally available. Currently, the minimum stipend for the academic year is $16,204, but it can be supplemented up to $18,535. In addition, academic year stipends can be supplemented by summer stipends. For students with grant-supported research assistantships, the stipend is much higher.

Cost of Study

The annual tuition for full-time graduate study in 2011–12 is $731 per credit hour for residents of Pennsylvania and $1004 per credit hour for nonresidents. Minimal fees are charged for various services, such as microfilming theses.

Living and Housing Costs

Room and board costs for students living on campus are $9992 per year in 2011–12. University-sponsored apartments, both furnished and unfurnished, are available.

Student Group

The Department has 40 full-time graduate students; nearly all are supported by assistantships or fellowships.

Location

Philadelphia is the fifth-largest city in the country, with a metropolitan population of more than 2 million. The city has a world-renowned symphony orchestra, a ballet company, two professional opera companies, and a chamber music society. Besides attracting touring plays, Philadelphia has a professional repertory theater, and many amateur troupes. All sports and forms of recreation are easily accessible. The city is world famous for its historic sites and parks, and for the eighteenth-century charm that is carefully maintained in the oldest section. The climate is temperate, with an average winter temperature of 33 degrees, and an average summer temperature of 75 degrees.

The University

The development of Temple University has been in line with the ideal of "educational opportunity for the able and deserving student of limited means." With a rich heritage of social purpose, Temple seeks to provide the opportunity for high-quality education without regard to a student's race, creed, or station in life. Affiliation with the Commonwealth System of Higher Education underpins Temple's character as a public institution.

Applying

All application material, both for admission and for financial awards, should be received by early March for admission in the fall semester. Notification regarding admission and the awarding of an assistantship is made as soon as the application has been screened.

Correspondence and Information

For program information and all applications:
Graduate Chairman
Department of Physics 009-00
Barton Hall
Temple University
Philadelphia, Pennsylvania 19122-6052

Phone: 215-204-7736
Fax: 215-204-5652
E-mail: physics@temple.edu
Web site: http://www.temple.edu/physics

For general information on graduate programs:
Dean
Graduate School
Temple University
Philadelphia, Pennsylvania 19122

Temple University

THE FACULTY AND THEIR RESEARCH

Atomic, Molecular and Optical Physics

Z. Hasan, Professor; Ph.D., Australian National, 1979. Laser materials, laser spectroscopy of solids.
R. L. Intemann, Professor Emeritus; Ph.D., Stevens, 1964. Theoretical atomic physics, inner-shell processes.
S. Kotochigova, Research Associate Professor; Ph.D., St. Petersburg. Relativistic quantum theory: atomic and molecular applications.
M. Lyyra, Professor; Ph.D., Stockholm, 1984. Laser spectroscopy, molecular coherence effects, laser-atom interactions.
M. Mackie, Research Assistant Professor; Ph.D., Connecticut, 1999. Bose-Einstein condensates.
R. Tao, Professor and Chairman; Ph.D., Columbia, 1982. Photonic crystals, nonlinear optics.

Condensed-Matter Physics

K. Chen, Professor; Ph.D., Chinese Academy of Sciences, 2001. Superconductivity, thin film.
Z. Hasan, Professor; Ph.D., Australian National, 1979. Optical and magnetooptical properties of solids.
M. Ivarone, Associate Professor; Ph.D., Napoli (Italy), 1996. Experimental condensed-matter physics.
C. L. Lin, Associate Professor; Ph.D., Temple, 1985. Heavy fermions, crystal fields, valence fluctuations, the Kondo effect, high-temperature superconductivity.
T. Mihalisin, Professor; Ph.D., Rochester, 1967. Crystal fields, valence fluctuations and the Kondo effect in magnetic systems.
P. S. Riseborough, Professor; Ph.D., Imperial College (London), 1977. Theoretical condensed-matter physics and statistical mechanics.
D. Santamore, Assistant Professor; Ph.D., Caltech, 2003. Theoretical condensed-matter physics and atomic physics, solid-state implantations of a quantum computer exploration of many-body physics in ultracold atom systems.
R. Tahir-Kheli, Professor; D.Phil., Oxford, 1962. Theory of magnetism, randomly disordered systems.
R. Tao, Professor and Chairman; Ph.D., Columbia, 1982. Electrorheological and magnetorheological fluids, self-aggregation of superconducting particles.
X. Xi, Professor, Ph.D. Beijing University, 1987. Materials physics of oxide and boride thin films at the nanoscale level.
T. Yuen, Associate Professor; Ph.D., Temple, 1990. Experimental condensed-matter physics, Mössbauer spectroscopy.

Educational Development Physics

L. Dubeck, Professor; Ph.D., Rutgers, 1965. Development, publication, and testing of precollege science materials.
Z. Dziembowski, Associate Professor; Ph.D., Warsaw, 1975. In-service elementary and secondary teacher training, inquiry-based instruction.
R. B. Weinberg, Professor Emeritus; Ph.D., Columbia, 1963. Teaching physicist.

Elementary Particle Physics and Cosmology

Z. Dziembowski, Associate Professor; Ph.D., Warsaw, 1975. Theoretical particle physics.
J. Franklin, Professor Emeritus; Ph.D., Illinois, 1956. Theoretical particle physics, quark and parton theory, S-matrix theory.
C. J. Martoff, Professor; Ph.D., Berkeley, 1980. Experimental particle physics: investigation of weak interactions and development of particle detectors for the study of dark matter, using negative ion drift.
A. Metz, Assistant Professor; Ph.D., Mainz, 1997. Theoretical nuclear and particle physics: investigation of the quark and gluon structure of strongly interacting particles (most notably the nucleon) through the electroweak and strong interaction.
Z. E. Meziani, Professor; Ph.D., Paris, 1984. Experimental high-energy nuclear physics: investigation of the flavor and spin structure of the nucleon at the Stanford Linear Accelerator Center, search for transition region between nucleon-meson to quark-gluon description of few-body nuclear systems at the Continuous Electron Beam Accelerator Facility.
D. E. Neville, Professor Emeritus; Ph.D., Chicago, 1962. Theoretical particle physics, symmetries and quark models, quantum gravity.

Statistical Physics

T. Burkhardt, Professor; Ph.D., Stanford, 1967. Statistical mechanics and many-body theory.
E. Gawlinski, Associate Professor; Ph.D., Boston University, 1983. Statistical mechanics and computational physics.
P. S. Riseborough, Professor; Ph.D., Imperial College (London), 1977. Theoretical condensed-matter physics and statistical mechanics.

Barton Hall, the physics building.

The Elementary Particle Physics Laboratory.

222   www.facebook.com/petersonspublishing

Peterson's Graduate Programs in the Physical Sciences, Mathematics, Agricultural Sciences, the Environment & Natural Resources 2012

ACADEMIC AND PROFESSIONAL PROGRAMS IN MATHEMATICS

Section 7
Mathematical Sciences

This section contains a directory of institutions offering graduate work in mathematical sciences, followed by in-depth entries submitted by institutions that chose to prepare detailed program descriptions. Additional information about programs listed in the directory but not augmented by an in-depth entry may be obtained by writing directly to the dean of a graduate school or chair of a department at the address given in the directory.

For programs offering work in related fields, see all other areas in this book. In the other guides in this series:

Graduate Programs in the Humanities, Arts & Social Sciences
See *Economics* and *Psychology* and *Counseling*

Graduate Programs in the Biological Sciences
See *Biological and Biomedical Sciences; Biophysics; Genetics, Developmental Biology, and Reproductive Biology;* and *Pharmacology and Toxicology*

Graduate Programs in Engineering & Applied Sciences
See *Biomedical Engineering and Biotechnology; Chemical Engineering (Biochemical Engineering); Computer Science and Information Technology; Electrical and Computer Engineering; Engineering and Applied Sciences;* and *Industrial Engineering*

Graduate Programs in Business, Education, Health, Information Studies, Law & Social Work
See *Business Administration and Management, Library and Information Studies,* and *Public Health*

CONTENTS

Applied Mathematics

Acadia University, Faculty of Pure and Applied Science, Department of Mathematics and Statistics, Wolfville, NS B4P 2R6, Canada. Offers applied mathematics and statistics (M Sc). *Faculty:* 12 full-time (3 women), 2 part-time/adjunct (0 women). *Students:* 5 full-time (2 women), 2 part-time (1 woman). 8 applicants, 63% accepted, 3 enrolled. *Degree requirements:* For master's, thesis. *Entrance requirements:* For master's, honors degree in mathematics, statistics or equivalent. Additional exam requirements/recommendations for international students: Required—TOEFL (minimum score 580 paper-based; 237 computer-based; 93 iBT), IELTS (minimum score 6.5). *Application deadline:* For fall admission, 2/1 priority date for domestic and international students. Applications are processed on a rolling basis. Application fee: $50. *Financial support:* Fellowships, research assistantships, teaching assistantships, career-related internships or fieldwork and unspecified assistantships available. Financial award application deadline: 2/1. *Faculty research:* Geophysical fluid dynamics, machine scheduling problems, control theory, stochastic optimization, survival analysis. *Unit head:* Dr. Jeff Hooper, Head, 902-585-1382, Fax: 902-585-1074, E-mail: jeff.hooper@acadiau.ca. *Application contact:* Dr. Richard Karsten, Graduate Coordinator, 902-585-1608, Fax: 902-585-1074, E-mail: richard.karsten@acadiau.ca.

Air Force Institute of Technology, Graduate School of Engineering and Management, Department of Mathematics and Statistics, Dayton, OH 45433-7765. Offers applied mathematics (MS, PhD). Part-time programs available. *Degree requirements:* For master's, thesis; for doctorate, thesis/dissertation. *Entrance requirements:* For master's, GRE General Test, minimum GPA of 3.0, U.S. citizenship or permanent U.S. residency; for doctorate, GRE General Test, minimum GPA of 3.5, U.S. citizenship or permanent U.S. residency. *Faculty research:* Electromagnetics, groundwater modeling, nonlinear diffusion, goodness of fit, finite element analysis.

Arizona State University, College of Liberal Arts and Sciences, Department of Mathematics and Statistics, Tempe, AZ 85287-1804. Offers applied mathematics (PhD); computational biosciences (PhD); mathematics (MA, MNS, PhD); mathematics education (PhD); statistics (PhD). Part-time programs available. *Faculty:* 94 full-time (32 women), 4 part-time/adjunct (1 woman). *Students:* 72 full-time (21 women), 23 part-time (10 women); includes 9 minority (2 Black or African American, non-Hispanic/Latino; 3 Asian, non-Hispanic/Latino; 4 Hispanic/Latino), 24 international. Average age 30. 168 applicants, 48% accepted, 26 enrolled. In 2010, 17 master's, 19 doctorates awarded. Terminal master's awarded for partial completion of doctoral program. *Median time to degree:* Of those who began their doctoral program in fall 2002, 69% received their degree in 8 years or less. *Degree requirements:* For master's, thesis or alternative, interactive Program of Study (iPOS) submitted before completing 50 percent of required credit hours; for doctorate, comprehensive exam, thesis/dissertation, interactive Program of Study (iPOS) submitted before completing 50 percent of required credit hours. *Entrance requirements:* For master's and doctorate, GRE General Test, minimum GPA of 3.0 or equivalent in last 2 years of work leading to bachelor's degree. Additional exam requirements/recommendations for international students: Required—TOEFL, IELTS, or Pearson Test of English. *Application deadline:* For fall admission, 1/1 for domestic and international students. Applications are processed on a rolling basis. Application fee: $70 ($90 for international students). Electronic applications accepted. *Expenses:* Contact institution. *Financial support:* In 2010–11, 12 research assistantships with full and partial tuition reimbursements (averaging $18,559 per year), 55 teaching assistantships with full and partial tuition reimbursements (averaging $17,743 per year) were awarded; fellowships with full tuition reimbursements, career-related internships or fieldwork, Federal Work-Study, institutionally sponsored loans, scholarships/grants, and tuition waivers (partial) also available. Financial award application deadline: 3/1; financial award applicants required to submit FAFSA. Total annual research expenditures: $4.5 million. *Unit head:* Dr. Wayne Raskind, Director, 480-965-3951, E-mail: raskind@asu.edu. *Application contact:* Graduate Admissions, 480-965-6113.

Arizona State University, College of Liberal Arts and Sciences, School of Human Evolution and Social Change, Tempe, AZ 85287-2402. Offers anthropology (PhD); anthropology (archaeology) (PhD); anthropology (bioarchaeology) (PhD); anthropology (museum studies) (MA); anthropology (physical) (PhD); applied mathematics for the life and social sciences (PhD); environmental social science (PhD); environmental social science (urbanism) (PhD); global health (MA); global health (health and culture) (PhD); global health (urbanism) (PhD); immigration studies (Graduate Certificate). *Faculty:* 52 full-time (19 women), 4 part-time/adjunct (2 women). *Students:* 127 full-time (77 women), 52 part-time (37 women); includes 43 minority (8 Black or African American, non-Hispanic/Latino; 4 American Indian or Alaska Native, non-Hispanic/Latino; 4 Asian, non-Hispanic/Latino; 26 Hispanic/Latino; 1 Two or more races, non-Hispanic/Latino), 19 international. Average age 32. 250 applicants, 24% accepted, 25 enrolled. In 2010, 8 master's, 18 doctorates, 7 other advanced degrees awarded. Terminal master's awarded for partial completion of doctoral program. *Degree requirements:* For master's, thesis or alternative, interactive Program of Study (iPOS) submitted before completing 50 percent of required credit hours; for doctorate, comprehensive exam, thesis/dissertation, interactive Program of Study (iPOS) submitted before completing 50 percent of required credit hours. *Entrance requirements:* For master's and doctorate, GRE, minimum GPA of 3.0 or equivalent in last 2 years of work leading to bachelor's degree. Additional exam requirements/recommendations for international students: Required—TOEFL, IELTS, or Pearson Test of English. *Application deadline:* For fall admission, 12/15 for domestic students, 12/1 for international students. Applications are processed on a rolling basis. Application fee: $70 ($90 for international students). Electronic applications accepted. *Expenses:* Tuition, state resident: full-time $8510; part-time $608 per credit. Tuition, nonresident: full-time $16,542; part-time $919 per credit. Required fees: $339; $110 per credit. Part-time tuition and fees vary according to course load. *Financial support:* In 2010–11, 30 research assistantships with full and partial tuition reimbursements (averaging $14,993 per year), 63 teaching assistantships with full and partial tuition reimbursements (averaging $15,266 per year) were awarded; fellowships with full tuition reimbursements, career-related internships or fieldwork, Federal Work-Study, institutionally sponsored loans, scholarships/grants, and tuition waivers (full and partial) also available. Financial award application deadline: 3/1; financial award applicants required to submit FAFSA. Total annual research expenditures: $3.8 million. *Unit head:* Dr. Sander van der Leeuw, Director, 480-965-6214, E-mail: vanderle@asu.edu. *Application contact:* Graduate Admissions, 480-965-6113.

Auburn University, Graduate School, College of Sciences and Mathematics, Department of Mathematics and Statistics, Auburn University, AL 36849. Offers applied mathematics (MAM, MS); mathematics (MS, PhD); probability and statistics (M Prob S); statistics (MS). *Faculty:* 54 full-time (8 women), 4 part-time/adjunct (1 woman). *Students:* 50 full-time (8 women), 44 part-time (17 women); includes 2 Black or African American, non-Hispanic/Latino; 1 Asian, non-Hispanic/Latino; 1 Hispanic/Latino, 46 international. Average age 28. 212 applicants, 52% accepted, 20 enrolled. In 2010, 16 master's, 10 doctorates awarded. *Degree requirements:* For doctorate, thesis/dissertation. *Entrance requirements:* For master's, GRE General Test, undergraduate mathematics background; for doctorate, GRE General Test, GRE Subject Test. *Application deadline:* For fall admission, 7/7 priority date for domestic students; for spring admission, 11/24 for domestic students. Applications are processed on a rolling basis. Application fee: $50 ($60 for international students). Electronic applications accepted. *Expenses:* Tuition, state resident: full-time $7002. Tuition, nonresident: full-time $21,898. International tuition: $22,116 full-time. Required fees: $892. Tuition and fees vary according to course load and program. *Financial support:* Fellowships, teaching assistantships available. Financial award applicants required to submit FAFSA. *Faculty research:* Pure and applied mathematics. *Unit head:* Dr. Michel Smith, Chair, 334-844-4290, Fax: 334-844-6655. *Application contact:* Dr. George Flowers, Dean of the Graduate School, 334-844-2125.

Bowie State University, Graduate Programs, Program in Applied and Computational Mathematics, Bowie, MD 20715-9465. Offers MS. Part-time and evening/weekend programs available. *Degree requirements:* For master's, comprehensive exam. *Entrance requirements:* For master's, calculus sequence, differential equations, linear algebra, CORTT, mathematical probability and statistics. Electronic applications accepted. *Expenses:* Tuition, state resident: full-time $4080; part-time $340 per credit. Tuition, nonresident: full-time $7752; part-time $646 per credit. Required fees: $2128; $340 per credit.

Brown University, Graduate School, Division of Applied Mathematics, Providence, RI 02912. Offers Sc M, PhD. *Degree requirements:* For master's, thesis or alternative; for doctorate, one foreign language, thesis/dissertation, oral exam. *Entrance requirements:* For master's and doctorate, GRE General Test.

California Institute of Technology, Division of Engineering and Applied Science, Option in Applied and Computational Mathematics, Pasadena, CA 91125-0001. Offers MS, PhD. *Faculty:* 5 full-time (0 women). *Students:* 21 full-time (3 women). 86 applicants, 5% accepted, 0 enrolled. In 2010, 1 master's, 1 doctorate awarded. *Degree requirements:* For doctorate, thesis/dissertation. *Entrance requirements:* For doctorate, GRE Subject Test. *Application deadline:* For fall admission, 1/1 for domestic students. Application fee: $0. Electronic applications accepted. *Financial support:* In 2010–11, 2 fellowships, 4 research assistantships, 15 teaching assistantships were awarded. *Faculty research:* Theoretical and computational fluid mechanics, numerical analysis, ordinary and partial differential equations, linear and nonlinear wave propagation, perturbation and asymptotic methods. *Unit head:* Dr. Houman Owhadi, Academic Officer, 626-395-4547, E-mail: owhadi@caltech.edu. *Application contact:* Natalie Gilmore, Assistant Dean of Graduate Studies, 626-395-3812, Fax: 626-577-9246, E-mail: ngilmore@caltech.edu.

California State Polytechnic University, Pomona, Academic Affairs, College of Science, Program in Mathematics, Pomona, CA 91768-2557. Offers applied mathematics (MS); pure mathematics (MS). Part-time programs available. *Students:* 16 full-time (7 women), 38 part-time (21 women); includes 22 minority (2 Black or African American, non-Hispanic/Latino; 13 Asian, non-Hispanic/Latino; 7 Hispanic/Latino), 4 international. Average age 32. 76 applicants, 51% accepted, 11 enrolled. In 2010, 16 master's awarded. *Degree requirements:* For master's, thesis or alternative. *Entrance requirements:* For master's, GRE General Test. *Application deadline:* For fall admission, 5/1 priority date for domestic students; for winter admission, 10/15 priority date for domestic students; for spring admission, 1/20 priority date for domestic students. Applications are processed on a rolling basis. Application fee: $55. Electronic applications accepted. *Expenses:* Tuition, state resident: full-time $5386; part-time $2850 per year. Tuition, nonresident: full-time $12,082; part-time $248 per credit. Required fees: $577; $248 per credit. $577 per year. Tuition and fees vary according to course load and program. *Financial support:* Career-related internships or fieldwork, Federal Work-Study, and institutionally sponsored loans available. Support available to part-time students. Financial award application deadline: 3/2; financial award applicants required to submit FAFSA. *Unit head:* Dr. Amber Rosin, Graduate Coordinator, 909-869-2426, Fax: 909-869-4904, E-mail: arrosin@csupomona.edu. *Application contact:* Scott J. Duncan, Director, Admissions, 909-869-3258, Fax: 909-869-4529, E-mail: sjduncan@csupomona.edu.

California State University, East Bay, Office of Academic Programs and Graduate Studies, College of Science, Department of Mathematics and Computer Science, Mathematics Program, Hayward, CA 94542-3000. Offers applied math (MS); mathematics (MS); mathematics teaching (MS). Part-time and evening/weekend programs available. *Faculty:* 6 full-time (4 women). *Students:* 19 full-time (7 women), 60 part-time (27 women); includes 28 minority (3 Black or African American, non-Hispanic/Latino; 1 American Indian or Alaska Native, non-Hispanic/Latino; 19 Asian, non-Hispanic/Latino; 2 Hispanic/Latino; 1 Native Hawaiian or other Pacific Islander, non-Hispanic/Latino; 2 Two or more races, non-Hispanic/Latino), 3 international. Average age 36. 115 applicants, 22% accepted, 14 enrolled. In 2010, 16 master's awarded. *Degree requirements:* For master's, comprehensive exam or thesis. *Entrance requirements:* For master's, minimum GPA of 3.0 in field. Additional exam requirements/recommendations for international students: Required—TOEFL (minimum score 550 paper-based; 213 computer-based). *Application deadline:* For fall admission, 6/30 for domestic and international students. Application fee: $55. Electronic applications accepted. *Financial support:* Fellowships, teaching assistantships, Federal Work-Study, institutionally sponsored loans, and scholarships/grants available. Support available to part-time students. Financial award application deadline: 3/1; financial award applicants required to submit FAFSA. *Unit head:* Prof. Edna Reiter, Chair, 510-885-3414, Fax: 510-885-4169, E-mail: edna.reiter@csueastbay.edu. *Application contact:* Dr. Donna Wiley, Interim Associate Director, 510-885-2928, Fax: 510-885-4777, E-mail: donna.wiley@csueastbay.edu.

California State University, Fullerton, Graduate Studies, College of Natural Science and Mathematics, Department of Mathematics, Fullerton, CA 92834-9480. Offers applied mathematics (MA); mathematics (MA); mathematics for secondary school teachers (MA). Part-time programs available. *Students:* 17 full-time (4 women), 64 part-time (32 women); includes 1 Black or African American, non-Hispanic/Latino; 24 Asian, non-Hispanic/Latino; 9 Hispanic/Latino; 2 Two or more races, non-Hispanic/Latino, 1 international. Average age 30. 104 applicants, 62% accepted, 38 enrolled. In 2010, 28 master's awarded. *Degree requirements:* For master's, comprehensive exam or project. *Entrance requirements:* For master's, minimum GPA of 2.5 in last 60 units of course work, major in mathematics or related field. Application fee: $55. *Financial support:* Research assistantships, teaching assistantships, career-related internships or fieldwork, Federal Work-Study, institutionally sponsored loans, and scholarships/grants available. Support available to part-time students. Financial award application deadline: 3/1; financial award applicants required to submit FAFSA. *Unit head:* Dr. Paul Deland, Chair, 657-278-3631. *Application contact:* Admissions/Applications, 657-278-2371.

California State University, Long Beach, Graduate Studies, College of Engineering, Department of Mechanical and Aerospace Engineering, Long Beach, CA 90840. Offers aerospace engineering (MSAE); engineering and industrial applied mathematics (PhD); interdisciplinary engineering (MSE); management engineering (MSE); mechanical engineering (MSME). Part-time programs available. *Faculty:* 14 full-time (3 women), 6 part-time/adjunct (0 women). *Students:* 44 full-time (1 woman), 56 part-time (8 women); includes 1 Black or African American, non-Hispanic/Latino; 1 American Indian or Alaska Native, non-Hispanic/Latino; 30 Asian, non-Hispanic/Latino; 15 Hispanic/Latino, 15 international. Average age 28. 169 applicants, 41% accepted, 25 enrolled. In 2010, 32 master's awarded. *Entrance requirements:* Additional exam requirements/recommendations for international students: Required—TOEFL. *Application deadline:* For fall admission, 7/1 for domestic students. Application fee: $55. Electronic applications accepted. *Financial support:* Career-related internships or fieldwork, Federal Work-Study, institutionally sponsored loans, scholarships/grants, and unspecified assistantships available. Financial award application deadline: 3/2. *Faculty research:* Unsteady turbulent flows, solar energy, energy conversion, CAD/CAM, computer-assisted instruction. *Unit head:* Dr. Hamid Hefazi, Chair, 562-985-1502, Fax: 562-985-1564, E-mail: hefazi@csulb.edu. *Application contact:* Dr. Hamid Rahai, Graduate Advisor, 562-985-5132, Fax: 562-985-4408, E-mail: rahai@csulb.edu.

California State University, Long Beach, Graduate Studies, College of Natural Sciences and Mathematics, Department of Mathematics and Statistics, Long Beach, CA 90840. Offers mathematics (MS), including applied mathematics, applied statistics, mathematics education for secondary school teachers. Part-time programs available. *Faculty:* 18 full-time (7 women), 3 part-time/adjunct (2 women). *Students:* 53 full-time (19 women), 107 part-time (35 women);

includes 4 Black or African American, non-Hispanic/Latino; 52 Asian, non-Hispanic/Latino; 24 Hispanic/Latino, 13 international. Average age 30. 175 applicants, 71% accepted, 80 enrolled. In 2010, 28 master's awarded. *Degree requirements:* For master's, comprehensive exam or thesis. *Application deadline:* For fall admission, 7/1 for domestic students; for spring admission, 12/1 for domestic students. Applications are processed on a rolling basis. Application fee: $55. Electronic applications accepted. *Financial support:* Teaching assistantships, Federal Work-Study, institutionally sponsored loans, scholarships/grants, and traineeships available. Financial award application deadline: 3/2. *Faculty research:* Algebra, functional analysis, partial differential equations, operator theory, numerical analysis. *Unit head:* Dr. Robert Mena, Chair, 562-985-4721, Fax: 562-985-8227, E-mail: rmena@csulb.edu. *Application contact:* Dr. Ngo Viet, Graduate Associate Chair, 562-985-4721, Fax: 562-985-8227, E-mail: viet@csulb.edu.

California State University, Los Angeles, Graduate Studies, College of Natural and Social Sciences, Department of Mathematics, Los Angeles, CA 90032-8530. Offers mathematics (MS), including applied mathematics, mathematics. Part-time and evening/weekend programs available. *Faculty:* 4 full-time (1 woman). *Students:* 31 full-time (15 women), 29 part-time (9 women); includes 31 minority (1 Black or African American, non-Hispanic/Latino; 17 Asian, non-Hispanic/Latino; 9 Hispanic/Latino; 4 Two or more races, non-Hispanic/Latino), 9 international. Average age 34. 41 applicants, 100% accepted, 23 enrolled. In 2010, 25 master's awarded. *Degree requirements:* For master's, comprehensive exam or thesis. *Entrance requirements:* For master's, previous course work in mathematics. Additional exam requirements/recommendations for international students: Required—TOEFL (minimum score 500 paper-based; 173 computer-based). *Application deadline:* For fall admission, 5/1 for domestic and international students. Applications are processed on a rolling basis. Application fee: $55. Electronic applications accepted. *Financial support:* Teaching assistantships, Federal Work-Study available. Support available to part-time students. Financial award application deadline: 3/1. *Faculty research:* Group theory, functional analysis, convexity theory, ordered geometry. *Unit head:* Dr. Silva Heubach, Chair, 323-343-2150, Fax: 323-343-5071, E-mail: sheubac@calstatela.edu. *Application contact:* Dr. Alan Muchlinski, Dean of Graduate Studies, 323-343-3820, Fax: 323-343-5653, E-mail: amuchli@exchange.calstatela.edu.

California State University, Northridge, Graduate Studies, College of Science and Mathematics, Department of Mathematics, Northridge, CA 91330. Offers applied mathematics (MS); mathematics (MS); mathematics for educational careers (MS). Part-time and evening/weekend programs available. *Degree requirements:* For master's, thesis (for some programs). *Entrance requirements:* For master's, GRE (if cumulative undergraduate GPA less than 3.0). Additional exam requirements/recommendations for international students: Required—TOEFL.

Carnegie Mellon University, Mellon College of Science, Department of Mathematical Sciences, Pittsburgh, PA 15213-3891. Offers algorithms, combinatorics, and optimization (PhD); applied mathematics (PhD); computational finance (MS); mathematical finance (PhD); mathematical sciences (MS, DA, PhD); pure and applied logic (PhD). Part-time programs available. Terminal master's awarded for partial completion of doctoral program. *Degree requirements:* For doctorate, thesis/dissertation. *Entrance requirements:* For master's and doctorate, GRE General Test, GRE Subject Test. Additional exam requirements/recommendations for international students: Required—TOEFL. Electronic applications accepted. *Faculty research:* Continuum mechanics, discrete mathematics, applied and computational mathematics.

Case Western Reserve University, School of Graduate Studies, Department of Mathematics, Cleveland, OH 44106. Offers applied mathematics (MS, PhD); mathematics (MS, PhD). Part-time programs available. *Faculty:* 18 full-time (5 women), 1 part-time/adjunct (0 women). *Students:* 16 full-time (7 women), 4 part-time (3 women), 9 international. Average age 27. 84 applicants, 14% accepted, 4 enrolled. In 2010, 3 master's, 2 doctorates awarded. Terminal master's awarded for partial completion of doctoral program. *Degree requirements:* For master's, thesis or alternative, thesis (applied mathematics); for doctorate, thesis/dissertation. *Entrance requirements:* For master's and doctorate, GRE General Test. Additional exam requirements/recommendations for international students: Required—TOEFL (minimum score 550 paper-based; 213 computer-based; 79 iBT). *Application deadline:* For fall admission, 1/15 priority date for domestic students; for spring admission, 11/12 for domestic students. Applications are processed on a rolling basis. Application fee: $50. Electronic applications accepted. *Financial support:* Research assistantships, teaching assistantships available. Financial award application deadline: 1/15. *Faculty research:* Probability theory, convexity and high-dimensional phenomena, imaging, geometric evaluation of curves, dynamical systems, large scale scientific computing, life sciences. *Unit head:* Daniela Calvetti, Chair, 216-368-2880, Fax: 216-368-5163, E-mail: daniela.calvetti@case.edu. *Application contact:* Gaythresa Lewis, Admissions, 216-368-5014, Fax: 216-368-5163, E-mail: gxl34@case.edu.

Central European University, Graduate Studies, School of Social Sciences and Humanities, Budapest, Hungary. Offers economics (MA, PhD); gender studies (MA, PhD); international relations and European studies (MA, PhD); mathematics and its applications (MS, PhD); medieval studies (MA, PhD); nationalism studies (MA, PhD); philosophy (MA, PhD); political science (MA, PhD); public policy (MA, PhD); sociology and social anthropology (MA, PhD). *Faculty:* 90 full-time (29 women), 13 part-time/adjunct (7 women). *Students:* 732 full-time (404 women). Average age 28. 3,639 applicants, 22% accepted, 416 enrolled. In 2010, 278 master's, 16 doctorates awarded. Terminal master's awarded for partial completion of doctoral program. *Degree requirements:* For master's, one foreign language, thesis; for doctorate, one foreign language, comprehensive exam, thesis/dissertation. *Entrance requirements:* For master's, interview; for doctorate, GRE, CEU subject test, interview. Additional exam requirements/recommendations for international students: Required—TOEFL (minimum score 570 paper-based; 230 computer-based); Recommended—IELTS (minimum score 6.5). *Application deadline:* For fall admission, 1/15 priority date for domestic and international students. Application fee: $0. Electronic applications accepted. Tuition and fees charges are reported in euros. *Expenses:* Tuition: Full-time 11,000 euros. Required fees: 250 euros. One-time fee: 200 euros full-time. Tuition and fees vary according to degree level, program, reciprocity agreements and student level. *Financial support:* In 2010–11, 402 students received support, including 416 fellowships with full and partial tuition reimbursements available (averaging $6,200 per year); career-related internships or fieldwork, institutionally sponsored loans, and scholarships/grants also available. Financial award application deadline: 1/5. *Faculty research:* Civil society, fiscal decentralization, party politics, political philosophy (especially liberalism, theory of democracy). Total annual research expenditures: $35,000. *Unit head:* Dr. Katalin Farkas, Provost/Academic Pro Rector, 361-327-3000 Ext. 2227, E-mail: farkask@ceu.hu. *Application contact:* Zsuzsanna Jaszberenyi, Admissions Officer, 361-327-3009, Fax: 361-327-3211, E-mail: admissions@ceu.hu.

Claremont Graduate University, Graduate Programs, School of Mathematical Sciences, Claremont, CA 91711-6160. Offers computational and systems biology (PhD); computational mathematics and numerical analysis (MA, MS); computational science (PhD); engineering and industrial applied mathematics (PhD); mathematics (PhD); operations research and statistics (MA, MS); physical applied mathematics (MA, MS); pure mathematics (MA, MS); scientific computing (MA, MS); systems and control theory (MA, MS). Part-time programs available. *Faculty:* 6 full-time (0 women). *Students:* 50 full-time (15 women), 11 part-time (1 woman); includes 2 Black or African American, non-Hispanic/Latino; 9 Asian, non-Hispanic/Latino; 7 Hispanic/Latino; 3 Two or more races, non-Hispanic/Latino, 13 international. Average age 36. In 2010, 17 master's, 11 doctorates awarded. Terminal master's awarded for partial completion of doctoral program. *Entrance requirements:* For master's and doctorate, GRE General Test. Additional exam requirements/recommendations for international students: Required—TOEFL (minimum score 550 paper-based; 213 computer-based; 80 iBT). *Application deadline:* For fall admission, 2/1 priority date for domestic students. Applications are processed on a rolling

basis. Application fee: $60. Electronic applications accepted. *Expenses:* Tuition: Full-time $35,748; part-time $1554 per unit. Required fees: $215 per semester. *Financial support:* Fellowships, research assistantships, Federal Work-Study, institutionally sponsored loans, scholarships/grants, and tuition waivers (full and partial) available. Support available to part-time students. Financial award application deadline: 2/15; financial award applicants required to submit FAFSA. *Unit head:* John Angus, Dean, 909-621-8080, Fax: 909-607-8261, E-mail: john.angus@cgu.edu. *Application contact:* Susan Townzen, Program Coordinator, 909-621-8080, Fax: 909-607-8261, E-mail: susan.n.townzen@cgu.edu.

Clemson University, Graduate School, College of Engineering and Science, Department of Mathematical Sciences, Clemson, SC 29634. Offers applied and pure mathematics (MS, PhD); computational mathematics (MS, PhD); operations research (MS, PhD); statistics (MS, PhD). Part-time programs available. *Faculty:* 48 full-time (13 women), 12 part-time/adjunct (4 women). *Students:* 127 full-time (51 women), 5 part-time (2 women); includes 2 Black or African American, non-Hispanic/Latino; 1 American Indian or Alaska Native, non-Hispanic/Latino; 1 Two or more races, non-Hispanic/Latino, 36 international. Average age 26. 163 applicants, 79% accepted, 51 enrolled. In 2010, 27 master's, 5 doctorates awarded. *Degree requirements:* For master's, thesis optional, final project; for doctorate, thesis/dissertation, qualifying exams. *Entrance requirements:* For master's and doctorate, GRE General Test. Additional exam requirements/recommendations for international students: Required—TOEFL. *Application deadline:* For fall admission, 1/15 priority date for domestic and international students; for spring admission, 10/1 priority date for domestic students, 9/15 priority date for international students. Applications are processed on a rolling basis. Application fee: $70 ($80 for international students). Electronic applications accepted. *Expenses:* Tuition, state resident: full-time $6492; part-time $400 per credit hour. Tuition, nonresident: full-time $13,634; part-time $800 per credit hour. Required fees: $262 per semester. Part-time tuition and fees vary according to course load and program. *Financial support:* In 2010–11, 110 students received support, including 2 fellowships with full and partial tuition reimbursements available (averaging $6,000 per year), 8 research assistantships with partial tuition reimbursements available (averaging $19,823 per year), 101 teaching assistantships with partial tuition reimbursements available (averaging $17,582 per year); career-related internships or fieldwork, institutionally sponsored loans, scholarships/grants, health care benefits, and unspecified assistantships also available. Support available to part-time students. Financial award application deadline: 4/15. *Faculty research:* Applied and computational analysis, cryptography, discrete mathematics, optimization, statistics. Total annual research expenditures: $823,404. *Unit head:* Dr. Robert L. Taylor, Chair, 864-656-5240, Fax: 864-656-5230, E-mail: rtaylo2@clemson.edu. *Application contact:* Dr. K.B. Kulasekera, Graduate Coordinator, 864-656-5231, Fax: 864-656-5230, E-mail: kk@clemson.edu.

Columbia University, Fu Foundation School of Engineering and Applied Science, Department of Applied Physics and Applied Mathematics, New York, NY 10027. Offers applied physics (Eng Sc D); applied physics and applied mathematics (MS, PhD, Engr); materials science and engineering (MS, Eng Sc D, PhD); medical physics (MS). Part-time programs available. Post-baccalaureate distance learning degree programs offered (no on-campus study). *Faculty:* 32 full-time (2 women), 23 part-time/adjunct (2 women). *Students:* 126 full-time (28 women), 23 part-time (5 women); includes 14 minority (2 Black or African American, non-Hispanic/Latino; 8 Asian, non-Hispanic/Latino; 1 Hispanic/Latino; 3 Two or more races, non-Hispanic/Latino), 60 international. Average age 28. 344 applicants, 22% accepted, 36 enrolled. In 2010, 56 master's, 13 doctorates awarded. Terminal master's awarded for partial completion of doctoral program. *Degree requirements:* For master's, comprehensive exam; for doctorate, thesis/dissertation, qualifying exam. *Entrance requirements:* For master's, GRE General Test, GRE Subject Test (strongly recommended); for doctorate, GRE General Test, GRE Subject Test (applied physics); for Engr, GRE General Test. Additional exam requirements/recommendations for international students: Required—TOEFL, IELTS. *Application deadline:* For fall admission, 12/1 priority date for domestic and international students; for spring admission, 10/1 priority date for domestic and international students. Application fee: $95. Electronic applications accepted. *Financial support:* In 2010–11, 73 students received support, including 3 fellowships with full tuition reimbursements available (averaging $30,000 per year), 53 research assistantships with full tuition reimbursements available (averaging $30,667 per year), 17 teaching assistantships with full tuition reimbursements available (averaging $30,667 per year). Financial award application deadline: 12/1; financial award applicants required to submit FAFSA. *Faculty research:* Plasma, solid state, optical and laser physics; atmospheric, oceanic and earth physics; computational math and applied mathematics; materials science and engineering. *Unit head:* Dr. Irving P. Herman, Professor and Department Chairman, 212-854-4457, E-mail: seasinfo.apam@columbia.edu. *Application contact:* Montserrat Fernandez-Pinkley, Student Services Coordinator, 212-854-4457, Fax: 212-854-8257, E-mail: mf2157@columbia.edu.

See Display on page 173 and Close-Up on page 211.

Cornell University, Graduate School, Graduate Fields of Arts and Sciences, Center for Applied Mathematics, Ithaca, NY 14853-0001. Offers PhD. *Faculty:* 92 full-time (6 women). *Students:* 37 full-time (14 women); includes 2 Asian, non-Hispanic/Latino; 4 Hispanic/Latino, 9 international. Average age 25. 167 applicants, 9% accepted, 7 enrolled. In 2010, 7 doctorates awarded. *Degree requirements:* For doctorate, one foreign language, comprehensive exam, thesis/dissertation. *Entrance requirements:* For doctorate, GRE General Test, GRE Subject Test (mathematics recommended), 3 letters of recommendation. Additional exam requirements/recommendations for international students: Required—TOEFL (minimum score 550 paper-based; 213 computer-based; 77 iBT). *Application deadline:* For fall admission, 1/15 for domestic students. Application fee: $80. Electronic applications accepted. *Expenses:* Tuition: Full-time $29,500. Required fees: $76. Tuition and fees vary according to degree level and program. *Financial support:* In 2010–11, 7 fellowships with full tuition reimbursements, 13 research assistantships with full tuition reimbursements, 13 teaching assistantships with full tuition reimbursements were awarded; institutionally sponsored loans, scholarships/grants, health care benefits, tuition waivers (full and partial), and unspecified assistantships also available. Financial award applicants required to submit FAFSA. *Faculty research:* Nonlinear systems and PDEs, numerical methods, signal and image processing, mathematical biology, discrete mathematics and optimization. *Unit head:* Director of Graduate Studies, 607-255-4756, Fax: 607-255-9860. *Application contact:* Graduate Field Assistant, 607-255-4756, Fax: 607-255-9860, E-mail: appliedmath@cornell.edu.

Cornell University, Graduate School, Graduate Fields of Engineering, Field of Chemical Engineering, Ithaca, NY 14853-0001. Offers advanced materials processing (M Eng, MS, PhD); applied mathematics and computational methods (M Eng, MS, PhD); biochemical engineering (M Eng, MS, PhD); chemical reaction engineering (M Eng, MS, PhD); classical and statistical thermodynamics (M Eng, MS, PhD); fluid dynamics, rheology and biorheology (M Eng, MS, PhD); heat and mass transfer (M Eng, MS, PhD); kinetics and catalysis (M Eng, MS, PhD); polymers (M Eng, MS, PhD); surface science (M Eng, MS, PhD). *Faculty:* 29 full-time (2 women). *Students:* 116 full-time (34 women); includes 1 Black or African American, non-Hispanic/Latino; 17 Asian, non-Hispanic/Latino; 5 Hispanic/Latino, 45 international. Average age 24. 392 applicants, 35% accepted, 70 enrolled. In 2010, 35 master's, 17 doctorates awarded. *Degree requirements:* For master's, thesis (MS); for doctorate, comprehensive exam, thesis/dissertation. *Entrance requirements:* For master's and doctorate, GRE General Test, 2 letters of recommendation. Additional exam requirements/recommendations for international students: Required—TOEFL (minimum score 600 paper-based; 237 computer-based; 77 iBT). *Application deadline:* For fall admission, 1/15 priority date for domestic students. Application fee: $70. Electronic applications accepted. *Expenses:* Tuition: Full-time $29,500. Required fees: $76. Tuition and fees vary according to degree level and program. *Financial support:* In 2010–11, 67 students received support, including 20 fellowships with full tuition reimbursements available, 40 research assistantships with full tuition reimbursements available,

Peterson's Graduate Programs in the Physical Sciences, Mathematics, Agricultural Sciences, the Environment & Natural Resources 2012

www.facebook.com/petersonspublishing   **227**

Applied Mathematics

Cornell University (continued)
13 teaching assistantships with full tuition reimbursements available; institutionally sponsored loans, scholarships/grants, health care benefits, tuition waivers (full and partial), and unspecified assistantships also available. Financial award applicants required to submit FAFSA. *Faculty research:* Biochemical, biomedical and metabolic engineering; fluid and polymer dynamics; surface science and chemical kinetics; electronics materials; microchemical systems and nanotechnology. *Unit head:* Director of Graduate Studies, 607-255-4550. *Application contact:* Graduate Field Assistant, 607-255-4550, E-mail: dgs@cheme.cornell.edu.

Cornell University, Graduate School, Graduate Fields of Engineering, Field of Operations Research and Information Engineering, Ithaca, NY 14853. Offers applied probability and statistics (PhD); manufacturing systems engineering (PhD); mathematical programming (PhD); operations research and industrial engineering (M Eng). *Faculty:* 35 full-time (5 women). *Students:* 162 full-time (46 women); includes 3 Black or African American, non-Hispanic/Latino; 14 Asian, non-Hispanic/Latino; 3 Hispanic/Latino, 117 international. Average age 23. 1,076 applicants, 34% accepted, 139 enrolled. In 2010, 85 master's, 6 doctorates awarded. *Degree requirements:* For doctorate, comprehensive exam, thesis/dissertation. *Entrance requirements:* For master's and doctorate, GRE General Test, 3 letters of recommendation. Additional exam requirements/recommendations for international students: Required—TOEFL (minimum score 600 paper-based; 250 computer-based; 100 iBT). *Application deadline:* For fall admission, 12/15 for domestic students. Application fee: $70. Electronic applications accepted. *Expenses:* Tuition: Full-time $29,500. Required fees: $76. Tuition and fees vary according to degree level and program. *Financial support:* In 2010–11, 44 students received support, including 12 fellowships with full tuition reimbursements available, 9 research assistantships with full tuition reimbursements available, 24 teaching assistantships with full tuition reimbursements available; institutionally sponsored loans, scholarships/grants, health care benefits, tuition waivers (full and partial), and unspecified assistantships also available. Financial award applicants required to submit FAFSA. *Faculty research:* Mathematical programming and combinatorial optimization, statistics, stochastic processes, mathematical finance, simulation, manufacturing, e-commerce. *Unit head:* Director of Graduate Studies, 607-255-9128, Fax: 607-255-9129. *Application contact:* Graduate Field Assistant, 607-255-9128, Fax: 607-255-9129, E-mail: orie@cornell.edu.

Dalhousie University, Faculty of Engineering, Department of Engineering Mathematics, Halifax, NS B3J 2X4, Canada. Offers M Sc, PhD. *Degree requirements:* For master's, thesis; for doctorate, thesis/dissertation. *Entrance requirements:* Additional exam requirements/recommendations for international students: Required—TOEFL, IELTS, CANTEST, CAEL, or Michigan English Language Assessment Battery. Electronic applications accepted. *Faculty research:* Piecewise regression and robust statistics, random field theory, dynamical systems, wave loads on offshore structures, digital signal processing.

Delaware State University, Graduate Programs, Department of Applied Mathematics and Theoretical Physics, Interdisciplinary Program in Applied Mathematics and Theoretical Physics, Dover, DE 19901-2277. Offers PhD. *Degree requirements:* For doctorate, one foreign language, thesis defense. *Entrance requirements:* For doctorate, GRE General Test, MS degree in physics or mathematics. Additional exam requirements/recommendations for international students: Required—TOEFL (minimum score 550 paper-based).

Delaware State University, Graduate Programs, Department of Mathematics, Program in Applied Mathematics, Dover, DE 19901-2277. Offers MS. *Entrance requirements:* Additional exam requirements/recommendations for international students: Required—TOEFL (minimum score 550 paper-based). Electronic applications accepted.

DePaul University, College of Liberal Arts and Sciences, Department of Mathematical Sciences, Chicago, IL 60614. Offers applied mathematics (MS), including actuarial science or statistics; applied statistics (MS, Certificate); mathematics education (MA). Part-time and evening/weekend programs available. *Faculty:* 23 full-time (6 women), 18 part-time/adjunct (5 women). *Students:* 111 full-time (60 women), 66 part-time (30 women); includes 16 Black or African American, non-Hispanic/Latino; 17 Asian, non-Hispanic/Latino; 16 Hispanic/Latino; 2 Two or more races, non-Hispanic/Latino, 10 international. Average age 30. 40 applicants, 100% accepted. In 2010, 30 master's awarded. *Degree requirements:* For master's, comprehensive exam. *Entrance requirements:* Additional exam requirements/recommendations for international students: Required—TOEFL. *Application deadline:* For fall admission, 7/30 for domestic students, 6/30 for international students; for winter admission, 11/30 for domestic students, 10/31 for international students; for spring admission, 2/15 for domestic students. Applications are processed on a rolling basis. Application fee: $25. *Financial support:* In 2010–11, 12 students received support, including research assistantships with partial tuition reimbursements available (averaging $6,000 per year); teaching assistantships, tuition waivers (full) also available. Financial award application deadline: 4/30. *Faculty research:* Verbally prime algebras, enveloping algebras of Lie, superalgebras and related rings, harmonic analysis, estimation theory. *Unit head:* Dr. Ahmed I. Zayed, Chairperson, 773-325-7806, Fax: 773-325-7807, E-mail: azayed@depaul.edu. *Application contact:* Ann Spittle, Director of Graduate Admissions, 312-362-8300, Fax: 312-362-5749, E-mail: admitdpu@depaul.edu.

East Carolina University, Graduate School, Thomas Harriot College of Arts and Sciences, Department of Mathematics, Greenville, NC 27858-4353. Offers applied mathematics (MA); mathematics (MA). Part-time and evening/weekend programs available. *Degree requirements:* For master's, comprehensive exam. *Entrance requirements:* For master's, GRE General Test, MAT. Additional exam requirements/recommendations for international students: Required—TOEFL. *Expenses:* Tuition, state resident: full-time $3130; part-time $391.25 per credit hour. Tuition, nonresident: full-time $13,817; part-time $1727.13 per credit hour. Required fees: $1916; $239.50 per credit hour. Tuition and fees vary according to campus/location and program.

École Polytechnique de Montréal, Graduate Programs, Department of Mathematics and Industrial Engineering, Montréal, QC H3C 3A7, Canada. Offers ergonomy (M Eng, M Sc A, DESS); mathematical method in CA engineering (M Eng, M Sc A, PhD); operational research (M Eng, M Sc A, PhD); production (M Eng, M Sc A); technology management (M Eng, M Sc A). DESS program offered jointly with HEC Montreal and Université de Montréal. Part-time programs available. *Degree requirements:* For master's, one foreign language, thesis. *Entrance requirements:* For master's, minimum GPA of 2.75. *Faculty research:* Use of computers in organizations.

Florida Atlantic University, Charles E. Schmidt College of Science, Department of Mathematical Sciences, Boca Raton, FL 33431-0991. Offers applied mathematics and statistics (MS); mathematical sciences (MS, MST, PhD). Part-time programs available. *Faculty:* 37 full-time (5 women), 4 part-time/adjunct (0 women). *Students:* 49 full-time (7 women), 25 part-time (15 women); includes 17 minority (6 Black or African American, non-Hispanic/Latino; 9 Asian, non-Hispanic/Latino; 2 Hispanic/Latino), 29 international. Average age 31. 73 applicants, 41% accepted, 22 enrolled. In 2010, 26 master's, 8 doctorates awarded. Terminal master's awarded for partial completion of doctoral program. *Degree requirements:* For master's, comprehensive exam (for some programs), thesis (for some programs); for doctorate, comprehensive exam, thesis/dissertation. *Entrance requirements:* For master's and doctorate, GRE General Test, minimum GPA of 3.0. Additional exam requirements/recommendations for international students: Required—TOEFL (minimum score 500 paper-based; 173 computer-based). *Application deadline:* For fall admission, 7/1 priority date for domestic students, 2/15 priority date for international students; for spring admission, 11/1 priority date for domestic students, 7/15 priority date for international students. Applications are processed on a rolling basis. Application fee: $30. Electronic applications accepted. *Expenses:* Tuition, area resident: Part-time $319.96 per credit. Tuition, state resident: part-time $319.96 per credit. Tuition, nonresident: part-time $926.42 per credit. *Financial support:* In 2010–11, fellowships with partial tuition reimbursements (averaging $20,000 per year), teaching assistantships with partial tuition reimbursements (averaging $20,000 per year) were awarded; Federal Work-Study also available. Financial award application deadline: 4/1. *Faculty research:* Cryptography, statistics, algebra, analysis, combinatorics. *Unit head:* Dr. Lee Klingler, Chair, 561-297-0274, Fax: 561-297-2436, E-mail: klingler@fau.edu. *Application contact:* Dr. Heinrich Niederhausen, Graduate Director, 561-297-3237, Fax: 561-297-2436, E-mail: niederha@fau.edu.

Florida Institute of Technology, Graduate Programs, College of Science, Department of Mathematical Sciences, Melbourne, FL 32901-6975. Offers applied mathematics (MS, PhD); operations research (MS, PhD). Part-time and evening/weekend programs available. *Faculty:* 8 full-time (1 woman). *Students:* 29 full-time (9 women), 17 part-time (2 women); includes 5 minority (3 Black or African American, non-Hispanic/Latino; 1 Asian, non-Hispanic/Latino; 1 Hispanic/Latino), 21 international. Average age 32. 70 applicants, 69% accepted, 12 enrolled. In 2010, 5 master's, 3 doctorates awarded. *Degree requirements:* For master's, comprehensive exam (for some programs), thesis optional; for doctorate, comprehensive exam, thesis/dissertation, Preliminary Exam. *Entrance requirements:* For master's, minimum GPA of 3.0, computer programming literacy; for doctorate, minimum GPA of 3.2, resume, 3 letters of recommendation, statement of objectives. Additional exam requirements/recommendations for international students: Required—TOEFL (minimum score 550 paper-based; 213 computer-based; 79 iBT). *Application deadline:* For fall admission, 4/1 for international students; for spring admission, 9/30 for international students. Applications are processed on a rolling basis. Application fee: $50. Electronic applications accepted. *Expenses:* Tuition: Part-time $1040 per credit hour. Tuition and fees vary according to campus/location. *Financial support:* In 2010–11, 16 teaching assistantships with full and partial tuition reimbursements (averaging $8,933 per year) were awarded; research assistantships, career-related internships or fieldwork, institutionally sponsored loans, tuition waivers (partial), unspecified assistantships, and tuition remissions also available. Support available to part-time students. Financial award application deadline: 3/1; financial award applicants required to submit FAFSA. *Faculty research:* Real analysis, numerical analysis, statistics, data analysis, combinatorics, artificial intelligence, simulation. Total annual research expenditures: $78,876. *Unit head:* Dr. Semen Koksal, Department Head, 321-674-8765, Fax: 321-674-7412, E-mail: skoksal@fit.edu. *Application contact:* Cheryl A. Brown, Associate Director of Graduate Admissions, 321-674-7581, Fax: 321-723-9468, E-mail: cbrown@fit.edu.

Florida State University, The Graduate School, College of Arts and Sciences, Department of Mathematics, Tallahassee, FL 32306-4510. Offers applied computational mathematics (MS, PhD); biomedical mathematics (MS, PhD); financial mathematics (MS, PhD); pure mathematics (MS, PhD). Part-time programs available. *Faculty:* 46 full-time (11 women), 2 part-time/adjunct (both women). *Students:* 139 full-time (35 women), 7 part-time (0 women); includes 3 Black or African American, non-Hispanic/Latino; 3 Asian, non-Hispanic/Latino; 4 Hispanic/Latino, 92 international. Average age 26. 342 applicants, 40% accepted, 39 enrolled. In 2010, 42 master's, 8 doctorates awarded. Terminal master's awarded for partial completion of doctoral program. *Degree requirements:* For master's, comprehensive exam (for some programs), thesis optional; for doctorate, comprehensive exam (for some programs), thesis/dissertation, candidacy exam including written qualifying examinations which differ by degree concentrations. *Entrance requirements:* For master's and doctorate, GRE General Test, minimum upper-division GPA of 3.0, 4-year bachelor's degree. Additional exam requirements/recommendations for international students: Required—TOEFL (minimum score 213 computer-based; 80 iBT), IELTS (minimum score 6.5). *Application deadline:* For fall admission, 1/3 priority date for domestic students, 12/15 priority date for international students; for spring admission, 11/1 for domestic and international students. Applications are processed on a rolling basis. Application fee: $30. Electronic applications accepted. *Expenses:* Tuition, state resident: full-time $8238.24. *Financial support:* In 2010–11, 102 students received support, including 6 fellowships with full tuition reimbursements available (averaging $19,000 per year), 15 research assistantships with full tuition reimbursements available (averaging $20,000 per year), 75 teaching assistantships with full tuition reimbursements available (averaging $18,000 per year); career-related internships or fieldwork, institutionally sponsored loans, scholarships/grants, health care benefits, tuition waivers (full and partial), and unspecified assistantships also available. *Faculty research:* Geometric topology, algebraic geometry, fluid dynamics, financial mathematics, biomedical mathematics. *Unit head:* Dr. Philip L. Bowers, Chairperson, 850-645-3338, Fax: 850-644-4053, E-mail: bowers@math.fsu.edu. *Application contact:* Dr. Bettye Anne Case, Associate Chair for Graduate Studies, 850-644-1586, Fax: 850-644-4053, E-mail: case@math.fsu.edu.

The George Washington University, Columbian College of Arts and Sciences, Department of Mathematics, Washington, DC 20052. Offers applied mathematics (MA, MS, PhD); pure mathematics (MA, MS, PhD). Part-time and evening/weekend programs available. *Faculty:* 18 full-time (3 women), 6 part-time/adjunct (2 women). *Students:* 17 full-time (5 women), 6 part-time (2 women); includes 1 Black or African American, non-Hispanic/Latino; 1 Asian, non-Hispanic/Latino; 1 Hispanic/Latino, 8 international. Average age 27. 73 applicants, 79% accepted, 9 enrolled. In 2010, 7 master's, 4 doctorates awarded. Terminal master's awarded for partial completion of doctoral program. *Degree requirements:* For master's, comprehensive exam; for doctorate, one foreign language, thesis/dissertation, general exam. *Entrance requirements:* For master's and doctorate, GRE General Test, minimum GPA of 3.0, interview. Additional exam requirements/recommendations for international students: Required—TOEFL (minimum score 550 paper-based; 213 computer-based; 80 iBT). *Application deadline:* For fall admission, 1/15 priority date for domestic and international students; for spring admission, 10/1 priority date for domestic students, 9/1 priority date for international students. Applications are processed on a rolling basis. Application fee: $75. Electronic applications accepted. *Financial support:* In 2010–11, 17 students received support; fellowships with full tuition reimbursements available, teaching assistantships with tuition reimbursements available, Federal Work-Study and tuition waivers available. Financial award application deadline: 1/15. *Unit head:* John B. Conway, Chair, 202-994-0553, E-mail: conway@gwu.edu. *Application contact:* John B. Conway, Chair, 202-994-0553, E-mail: conway@gwu.edu.

Georgia Institute of Technology, Graduate Studies and Research, College of Sciences, School of Mathematics, Atlanta, GA 30332-0001. Offers algorithms, combinatorics, and optimization (PhD); applied mathematics (MS); bioinformatics (PhD); mathematics (PhD); quantitative and computational finance (MS); statistics (MS Stat). Terminal master's awarded for partial completion of doctoral program. *Degree requirements:* For master's, thesis or alternative; for doctorate, one foreign language, thesis/dissertation. *Entrance requirements:* For master's, GRE General Test, minimum GPA of 3.0; for doctorate, GRE General Test, GRE Subject Test, minimum GPA of 3.0. Additional exam requirements/recommendations for international students: Required—TOEFL. Electronic applications accepted. *Faculty research:* Dynamical systems, discrete mathematics, probability and statistics, mathematical physics.

Hampton University, Graduate College, Program in Applied Mathematics, Hampton, VA 23668. Offers computational mathematics (MS); nonlinear science (MS); statistics and probability (MS). *Degree requirements:* For master's, thesis optional. *Entrance requirements:* For master's, GRE General Test.

Harvard University, Graduate School of Arts and Sciences, School of Engineering and Applied Sciences, Cambridge, MA 02138. Offers applied mathematics (ME, SM, PhD); applied physics (ME, SM, PhD); computer science (ME, SM, PhD); engineering science (ME); engineering sciences (SM, PhD). Part-time programs available. Terminal master's awarded for partial completion of doctoral program. *Degree requirements:* For master's, thesis optional; for doctorate, comprehensive exam, thesis/dissertation. *Entrance requirements:* For master's and doctorate, GRE General Test, GRE Subject Test (recommended), 3 letters of recommendation. Additional exam requirements/recommendations for international students: Required—TOEFL

(minimum score 80 iBT). Electronic applications accepted. *Expenses:* Tuition: Full-time $34,976. Required fees: $1166. Full-time tuition and fees vary according to program. *Faculty research:* Applied mathematics, applied physics, computer science and electrical engineering, environmental engineering, mechanical and biomedical engineering.

Howard University, Graduate School, Department of Mathematics, Washington, DC 20059-0002. Offers applied mathematics (MS, PhD); mathematics (MS, PhD). Part-time programs available. Terminal master's awarded for partial completion of doctoral program. *Degree requirements:* For master's, comprehensive exam, thesis or alternative, qualifying exam; for doctorate, 2 foreign languages, comprehensive exam, thesis/dissertation, qualifying exams. *Entrance requirements:* For master's, GRE General Test, minimum GPA of 3.0; for doctorate, GRE General Test. Additional exam requirements/recommendations for international students: Required—TOEFL. Electronic applications accepted.

Hunter College of the City University of New York, Graduate School, School of Arts and Sciences, Department of Mathematics and Statistics, New York, NY 10021-5085. Offers applied mathematics (MA); mathematics for secondary education (MA); pure mathematics (MA). Part-time and evening/weekend programs available. *Faculty:* 5 full-time (0 women), 2 part-time/adjunct (1 woman). *Students:* 8 full-time (4 women), 82 part-time (31 women); includes 2 Black or African American, non-Hispanic/Latino; 23 Asian, non-Hispanic/Latino; 5 Hispanic/Latino, 9 international. Average age 31. 58 applicants, 52% accepted, 21 enrolled. In 2010, 15 master's awarded. *Degree requirements:* For master's, one foreign language, comprehensive exam, thesis (for some programs). *Entrance requirements:* For master's, GRE General Test, 24 credits in mathematics. Additional exam requirements/recommendations for international students: Required—TOEFL. *Application deadline:* For fall admission, 4/1 for domestic students, 2/1 for international students; for spring admission, 11/1 for domestic students, 9/1 for international students. Application fee: $125. *Financial support:* Federal Work-Study, institutionally sponsored loans, scholarships/grants, and tuition waivers (partial) available. Support available to part-time students. *Faculty research:* Data analysis, dynamical systems, computer graphics, topology, statistical decision theory. *Unit head:* Ada Peluso, Chairperson, 212-772-5300, Fax: 212-772-4858, E-mail: peluso@math.hunter.cuny.edu. *Application contact:* William Zlata, Director for Graduate Admissions, 212-772-4482, Fax: 212-650-3336, E-mail: admissions@hunter.cuny.edu.

Illinois Institute of Technology, Graduate College, College of Science and Letters, Department of Applied Mathematics, Chicago, IL 60616-3793. Offers applied mathematics (MS, PhD); collegiate mathematics (PhD); mathematical finance (MMF). MMF program held jointly with Stuart School of Business, PhD (collegiate mathematics) with Department of Math and Science Education. *Faculty:* 16 full-time (1 woman), 8 part-time/adjunct (0 women). *Students:* 32 full-time (10 women), 5 part-time (3 women); includes 3 minority (2 Hispanic/Latino; 1 Two or more races, non-Hispanic/Latino), 24 international. Average age 26. 88 applicants, 85% accepted, 15 enrolled. In 2010, 8 master's, 1 doctorate awarded. Terminal master's awarded for partial completion of doctoral program. *Degree requirements:* For master's, comprehensive exam, thesis; for doctorate, comprehensive exam, thesis/dissertation. *Entrance requirements:* For master's, GRE General Test (minimum scores: 1100 Quantitative and Verbal, 2.5 Analytical Writing), minimum undergraduate GPA of 3.0; for doctorate, GRE General Test (minimum scores: 1100 Quantitative and Verbal, 3.0 Analytical Writing), minimum undergraduate GPA of 3.5. Additional exam requirements/recommendations for international students: Required—TOEFL (minimum score 523 paper-based; 70 iBT); Recommended—IELTS (minimum score 5.5). *Application deadline:* For fall admission, 5/1 for domestic and international students; for spring admission, 10/15 for domestic and international students. Applications are processed on a rolling basis. Application fee: $50. Electronic applications accepted. *Expenses:* Tuition: Full-time $18,576; part-time $1032 per credit hour. Required fees: $583 per semester. One time fee: $150. Tuition and fees vary according to program and student level. *Financial support:* In 2010–11, 5 research assistantships with full and partial tuition reimbursements (averaging $8,536 per year), 12 teaching assistantships with full and partial tuition reimbursements (averaging $7,734 per year) were awarded; fellowships with full and partial tuition reimbursements, career-related internships or fieldwork, Federal Work-Study, institutionally sponsored loans, scholarships/grants, health care benefits, tuition waivers (partial), and unspecified assistantships also available. Support available to part-time students. Financial award applicants required to submit FAFSA. *Faculty research:* Applied analysis, computational mathematics, discrete applied mathematics, stochastics, mathematical finance. Total annual research expenditures: $442,291. *Unit head:* Fred J. Hickernell, Chairman/Professor, 312-567-8983, Fax: 312-567-3135, E-mail: hickernell@iit.edu. *Application contact:* Deborah Gibson, Director, Graduate Admission, 866-472-3448, Fax: 312-567-3138, E-mail: inquiry.grad@iit.edu.

Indiana University Bloomington, University Graduate School, College of Arts and Sciences, Department of Mathematics, Bloomington, IN 47405-7000. Offers applied mathematics-numerical analysis (MA, PhD); mathematics education (MAT); probability-statistics (MA, PhD); pure mathematics (MA). *Faculty:* 46 full-time (3 women). *Students:* 130 full-time (25 women), 1 part-time (0 women); includes 11 minority (1 Black or African American, non-Hispanic/Latino; 1 American Indian or Alaska Native, non-Hispanic/Latino; 8 Asian, non-Hispanic/Latino; 1 Hispanic/Latino), 72 international. Average age 27. 223 applicants, 25% accepted, 27 enrolled. In 2010, 12 master's, 13 doctorates awarded. Terminal master's awarded for partial completion of doctoral program. *Degree requirements:* For doctorate, one foreign language, thesis/dissertation. *Entrance requirements:* For master's and doctorate, GRE General Test, GRE Subject Test. Additional exam requirements/recommendations for international students: Required—TOEFL. *Application deadline:* For fall admission, 1/15 priority date for domestic and international students. Applications are processed on a rolling basis. Application fee: $55 ($65 for international students). Electronic applications accepted. *Financial support:* In 2010–11, 2 students received support, including 9 fellowships with full tuition reimbursements available (averaging $21,450 per year), 11 research assistantships with full tuition reimbursements available (averaging $16,045 per year), 96 teaching assistantships with full tuition reimbursements available (averaging $15,870 per year); scholarships/grants, health care benefits, and unspecified assistantships also available. Financial award application deadline: 1/15. *Faculty research:* Topology, geometry, algebra, applied, analysis. *Unit head:* Kevin Zumbrun, Chair, 812-855-2200. *Application contact:* Kate Bowman, Graduate Secretary, 812-855-2645, Fax: 812-855-0046, E-mail: gradmath@indiana.edu.

Indiana University of Pennsylvania, School of Graduate Studies and Research, College of Natural Sciences and Mathematics, Department of Mathematics, Program in Applied Mathematics, Indiana, PA 15705-1087. Offers MS. *Faculty:* 9 full-time (4 women). *Students:* 16 full-time (3 women), 3 part-time (0 women); includes 4 minority (2 Black or African American, non-Hispanic/Latino; 1 Asian, non-Hispanic/Latino; 1 Two or more races, non-Hispanic/Latino), 4 international. Average age 26. 24 applicants, 58% accepted, 5 enrolled. In 2010, 6 master's awarded. *Degree requirements:* For master's, thesis optional. *Entrance requirements:* For master's, 2 letters of recommendation. Additional exam requirements/recommendations for international students: Required—TOEFL. *Application deadline:* For fall admission, 7/1 priority date for domestic students; for spring admission, 11/1 for domestic students. Applications are processed on a rolling basis. Application fee: $40. *Financial support:* In 2010–11, 12 research assistantships with full and partial tuition reimbursements (averaging $2,657 per year) were awarded; Federal Work-Study also available. Support available to part-time students. Financial award application deadline: 3/15; financial award applicants required to submit FAFSA. *Unit head:* Dr. Yu-Ju Kuo, Graduate Coordinator, 724-357-4765, E-mail: yuju.kuo@iup.edu. *Application contact:* Dr. Jacqueline Gorman, Dean's Associate, 724-357-2609, E-mail: jgorman@iup.edu.

Indiana University–Purdue University Fort Wayne, College of Arts and Sciences, Department of Mathematical Sciences, Fort Wayne, IN 46805-1499. Offers applied mathematics (MS); applied statistics (Certificate); mathematics (MS); operations research (MS); teaching (MAT). Part-time and evening/weekend programs available. *Faculty:* 18 full-time (4 women), 1 (woman) part-time/adjunct. *Students:* 3 full-time (0 women), 17 part-time (6 women). Average age 33. 12 applicants, 100% accepted, 12 enrolled. In 2010, 4 master's, 3 other advanced degrees awarded. *Entrance requirements:* For master's, minimum GPA of 3.0, major or minor in mathematics, three letters of recommendation. Additional exam requirements/recommendations for international students: Required—TOEFL (minimum score 550 paper-based; 213 computer-based; 77 iBT); Recommended—TWE. *Application deadline:* For fall admission, 8/1 priority date for domestic students, 7/1 priority date for international students; for spring admission, 12/1 for domestic students, 10/1 for international students. Applications are processed on a rolling basis. Application fee: $55 ($60 for international students). Electronic applications accepted. *Expenses:* Tuition, state resident: full-time $4824; part-time $268 per credit. Tuition, nonresident: full-time $11,625; part-time $646 per credit. Required fees: $555; $30.85 per credit. Tuition and fees vary according to course load. *Financial support:* In 2010–11, 9 teaching assistantships with partial tuition reimbursements (averaging $12,740 per year) were awarded; scholarships/grants and unspecified assistantships also available. Support available to part-time students. Financial award application deadline: 3/1; financial award applicants required to submit FAFSA. *Faculty research:* Axis-supported external fields, discipline of doubt, t-design graphs. *Unit head:* Dr. David A. Legg, Chair, 260-481-6222, Fax: 260-481-0155, E-mail: legg@ipfw.edu. *Application contact:* Dr. W. Douglas Weakley, Director of Graduate Studies, 260-481-6233, Fax: 260-481-0155, E-mail: weakley@ipfw.edu.

Indiana University–Purdue University Indianapolis, School of Science, Department of Mathematical Sciences, Doctoral Program in Mathematics, Indianapolis, IN 46202-2896. Offers applied mathematics (PhD); mathematics (PhD). *Students:* 13 full-time (6 women), 6 part-time; includes 2 minority (1 Black or African American, non-Hispanic/Latino; 1 Hispanic/Latino), 8 international. Average age 29. 13 applicants, 62% accepted, 7 enrolled.Application fee: $55 ($65 for international students). *Unit head:* Slawomir Klimek, Director of Graduate Programs, 317-274-6918, E-mail: grad-program@math.iupui.edu. *Application contact:* Slawomir Klimek, Director of Graduate Programs, 317-274-6918, E-mail: grad-program@math.iupui.edu.

Indiana University–Purdue University Indianapolis, School of Science, Department of Mathematical Sciences, Master's Program in Mathematics, Indianapolis, IN 46202-2896. Offers applied mathematics (MS); applied statistics (MS); mathematics (MS). *Students:* 6 full-time (1 woman), 18 part-time (7 women); includes 5 minority (1 Black or African American, non-Hispanic/Latino; 3 Asian, non-Hispanic/Latino; 1 Hispanic/Latino), 3 international. Average age 36. 4 applicants, 75% accepted, 3 enrolled. In 2010, 10 master's awarded. Application fee: $55 ($65 for international students). *Unit head:* Slawomir Klimek, Director of Graduate Programs, 317-274-6918, E-mail: grad-program@math.iupui.edu. *Application contact:* Slawomir Klimek, Director of Graduate Programs, 317-274-6918, E-mail: grad-program@math.iupui.edu.

Indiana University South Bend, College of Liberal Arts and Sciences, South Bend, IN 46634-7111. Offers applied mathematics and computer science (MS); applied psychology (MA); English (MA); liberal studies (MLS). Part-time and evening/weekend programs available. *Faculty:* 79 full-time (33 women). *Students:* 34 full-time (18 women), 100 part-time (69 women); includes 23 minority (15 Black or African American, non-Hispanic/Latino; 2 American Indian or Alaska Native, non-Hispanic/Latino; 3 Asian, non-Hispanic/Latino; 2 Hispanic/Latino; 1 Two or more races, non-Hispanic/Latino), 16 international. Average age 37. 44 applicants, 84% accepted, 27 enrolled. In 2010, 21 master's awarded. *Degree requirements:* For master's, thesis (for some programs). *Entrance requirements:* For master's, minimum GPA of 3.0. Additional exam requirements/recommendations for international students: Required—TOEFL. *Application deadline:* For fall admission, 7/31 priority date for domestic students, 7/1 priority date for international students; for spring admission, 3/31 priority date for domestic students, 11/1 priority date for international students. Applications are processed on a rolling basis. Application fee: $50 ($60 for international students). *Financial support:* In 2010–11, 5 students received support, including 5 teaching assistantships; Federal Work-Study also available. Support available to part-time students. *Faculty research:* Artificial intelligence, bioinformatics, English language and literature, creative writing, computer networks. Total annual research expenditures: $127,000. *Unit head:* Dr. Lynn R. Williams, Dean, 574-520-4322, Fax: 574-520-4528, E-mail: lwilliam@iusb.edu. *Application contact:* Dr. Lynn R. Williams, Dean, 574-520-4322, Fax: 574-520-4528, E-mail: lwilliam@iusb.edu.

Inter American University of Puerto Rico, San Germán Campus, Graduate Studies Center, Program in Applied Mathematics, San Germán, PR 00683-5008. Offers MA. Part-time and evening/weekend programs available. *Degree requirements:* For master's, comprehensive exam. *Entrance requirements:* For master's, EXADEP or GRE General Test, minimum GPA of 3.0. *Expenses:* Tuition: Part-time $202 per credit. Required fees: $258 per semester.

Iowa State University of Science and Technology, Graduate College, College of Liberal Arts and Sciences, Department of Mathematics, Ames, IA 50011. Offers applied mathematics (MS, PhD); mathematics (MS, PhD); school mathematics (MSM). *Faculty:* 43 full-time (6 women), 2 part-time/adjunct (1 woman). *Students:* 82 full-time (24 women), 14 part-time (4 women); includes 3 Black or African American, non-Hispanic/Latino; 3 Asian, non-Hispanic/Latino; 5 Hispanic/Latino, 38 international. 150 applicants, 21% accepted, 15 enrolled. In 2010, 9 master's, 7 doctorates awarded. *Degree requirements:* For master's, thesis or alternative; for doctorate, thesis/dissertation. *Entrance requirements:* For master's and doctorate, GRE General Test. Additional exam requirements/recommendations for international students: Required—TOEFL (minimum score 550 paper-based; 79 iBT), IELTS (minimum score 6.5). *Application deadline:* For fall admission, 2/1 priority date for domestic and international students; for spring admission, 10/1 priority date for domestic and international students. Application fee: $40 ($90 for international students). Electronic applications accepted. *Financial support:* In 2010–11, 7 research assistantships with full and partial tuition reimbursements (averaging $7,827 per year), 67 teaching assistantships with full and partial tuition reimbursements (averaging $11,732 per year) were awarded; fellowships, scholarships/grants, health care benefits, and unspecified assistantships also available. *Unit head:* Dr. Wolfgang Kliemann, Chair, 515-294-1752, Fax: 515-294-5454, E-mail: gradmath@iastate.edu. *Application contact:* Dr. Paul Sacks, Director of Graduate Education, 515-294-0393, E-mail: gradmath@iastate.edu.

The Johns Hopkins University, Engineering for Professionals, Part-time Program in Applied and Computational Mathematics, Baltimore, MD 21218-2699. Offers MS, Post-Master's Certificate. Part-time and evening/weekend programs available. *Faculty:* 13 part-time/adjunct (2 women). *Students:* 4 full-time (2 women), 100 part-time (24 women); includes 21 minority (6 Black or African American, non-Hispanic/Latino; 8 Asian, non-Hispanic/Latino; 6 Hispanic/Latino; 1 Two or more races, non-Hispanic/Latino), 2 international. Average age 29. 21 applicants, 95% accepted, 19 enrolled. In 2010, 23 master's awarded. *Application deadline:* Applications are processed on a rolling basis. Application fee: $75. Electronic applications accepted. *Financial support:* Institutionally sponsored loans available. Financial award applicants required to submit FAFSA. Total annual research expenditures: $606,210. *Unit head:* Dr. Jim Spall, Program Chair, 443-778-4960, E-mail: james.spall@jhuapl.edu. *Application contact:* Priyanka Dwivedi, Admissions Manager, 410-516-2300, Fax: 410-579-8049, E-mail: pdwived1@jhu.edu.

The Johns Hopkins University, G. W. C. Whiting School of Engineering, Department of Applied Mathematics and Statistics, Baltimore, MD 21218-2699. Offers computational medicine (PhD); discrete mathematics (MA, MSE, PhD); financial mathematics (MSE); operations research/optimization/decision science (MA, MSE, PhD); statistics/probability/stochastic processes (MA, MSE, PhD). *Faculty:* 17 full-time (3 women), 4 part-time/adjunct (0 women). *Students:* 72 full-time (27 women), 3 part-time (0 women); includes 10 minority (1 Black or African American, non-Hispanic/Latino; 7 Asian, non-Hispanic/Latino; 2 Two or more races, non-Hispanic/Latino), 51 international. Average age 25. 306 applicants, 47% accepted, 36

Applied Mathematics

The Johns Hopkins University (continued)

enrolled. In 2010, 26 master's, 7 doctorates awarded. Terminal master's awarded for partial completion of doctoral program. *Degree requirements:* For master's, thesis (for some programs); for doctorate, thesis/dissertation, oral exam, introductory exam. *Entrance requirements:* For master's and doctorate, GRE General Test, GRE Subject Test. Additional exam requirements/recommendations for international students: Required—TOEFL (minimum score 600 paper-based; 250 computer-based; 100 iBT). *Application deadline:* For fall admission, 1/15 for domestic and international students; for spring admission, 9/15 for domestic and international students. Application fee: $75. Electronic applications accepted. *Financial support:* In 2010–11, 40 students received support, including 9 fellowships with full tuition reimbursements available (averaging $19,800 per year), 19 research assistantships with full tuition reimbursements available (averaging $1,800 per year), 9 teaching assistantships with full tuition reimbursements available (averaging $1,800 per year); Federal Work-Study, institutionally sponsored loans, scholarships/grants, health care benefits, tuition waivers (partial), and unspecified assistantships also available. Financial award application deadline: 1/15. *Faculty research:* Discrete mathematics, probability, statistics, optimization and operations research, scientific computation, financial mathematics. Total annual research expenditures: $1.3 million. *Unit head:* Dr. Daniel Q. Naiman, Chair, 410-516-7203, Fax: 410-516-7459, E-mail: daniel.naiman@jhu.edu. *Application contact:* Kristin Bechtel, Academic Program Coordinator, 410-516-7198, Fax: 410-516-7459, E-mail: kbechtel@jhu.edu.

Kent State University, College of Arts and Sciences, Department of Mathematical Sciences, Kent, OH 44242-0001. Offers applied mathematics (MA, MS, PhD); pure mathematics (MA, MS, PhD). Part-time programs available. *Degree requirements:* For master's, thesis optional; for doctorate, one foreign language, thesis/dissertation. Electronic applications accepted. *Expenses:* Tuition, state resident: full-time $7866; part-time $437 per credit hour. Tuition, nonresident: full-time $14,022; part-time $779 per credit hour. *Faculty research:* Approximation theory, measure theory, ring theory, functional analysis, complex analysis.

Lehigh University, College of Arts and Sciences, Department of Mathematics, Bethlehem, PA 18015. Offers applied mathematics (MS, PhD); mathematics (MS, PhD); statistics (MS). Part-time programs available. *Faculty:* 21 full-time (1 woman). *Students:* 37 full-time (20 women), 3 part-time (0 women); includes 2 minority (1 Asian, non-Hispanic/Latino; 1 Hispanic/Latino), 17 international. Average age 25. 105 applicants, 50% accepted, 11 enrolled. In 2010, 6 master's, 5 doctorates awarded. Terminal master's awarded for partial completion of doctoral program. *Degree requirements:* For master's, comprehensive exam, thesis optional; for doctorate, comprehensive exam, thesis/dissertation, qualifying exams, general exam. *Entrance requirements:* For master's and doctorate, minimum undergraduate GPA of 2.75, 3.0 for last two semesters; adequate background in math. Additional exam requirements/recommendations for international students: Required—TOEFL (minimum score 550 paper-based; 213 computer-based; 85 iBT). *Application deadline:* For fall admission, 1/15 priority date for domestic and international students; for spring admission, 12/1 priority date for domestic and international students. Applications are processed on a rolling basis. Application fee: $75. Electronic applications accepted. *Financial support:* In 2010–11, 35 students received support, including 2 fellowships with full tuition reimbursements available (averaging $25,000 per year), 23 teaching assistantships with full tuition reimbursements available (averaging $17,500 per year); research assistantships with full tuition reimbursements available, scholarships/grants and tuition waivers (partial) also available. Financial award application deadline: 1/15. *Faculty research:* Probability and statistics, geometry and topology, number theory, algebra, differential equations. Total annual research expenditures: $192,998. *Unit head:* Dr. Wei-Min Huang, Chairman, 610-758-3730, Fax: 610-758-3767, E-mail: wh02@lehigh.edu. *Application contact:* Dr. Terry Napier, Graduate Coordinator, 610-758-3755, E-mail: mathgrad@lehigh.edu.

Long Island University, C.W. Post Campus, College of Liberal Arts and Sciences, Department of Mathematics, Brookville, NY 11548-1300. Offers applied mathematics (MS); mathematics education (MS); mathematics for secondary school teachers (MS). Part-time and evening/weekend programs available. *Degree requirements:* For master's, thesis or alternative, oral presentation. *Entrance requirements:* Additional exam requirements/recommendations for international students: Required—TOEFL. Electronic applications accepted. *Faculty research:* Differential geometry, topological groups, general topology, number theory, analysis and statistics, numerical analysis.

McGill University, Faculty of Graduate and Postdoctoral Studies, Faculty of Science, Department of Mathematics and Statistics, Montréal, QC H3A 2T5, Canada. Offers computational science and engineering (M Sc); mathematics and statistics (M Sc, MA, PhD), including applied mathematics (M Sc, MA), pure mathematics (M Sc, MA), statistics (M Sc, MA).

Michigan State University, The Graduate School, College of Natural Science, Department of Mathematics, East Lansing, MI 48824. Offers applied mathematics (MS, PhD); industrial mathematics (MS); mathematics (MAT, MS, PhD). *Entrance requirements:* Additional exam requirements/recommendations for international students: Required—TOEFL. Electronic applications accepted.

Missouri University of Science and Technology, Graduate School, Department of Mathematics and Statistics, Rolla, MO 65409. Offers applied mathematics (MS); mathematics (MST, PhD), including mathematics (PhD), mathematics education (MST), statistics (PhD). Terminal master's awarded for partial completion of doctoral program. *Degree requirements:* For master's, thesis or alternative; for doctorate, one foreign language, thesis/dissertation. *Entrance requirements:* For master's and doctorate, GRE General Test, GRE Subject Test. Electronic applications accepted. *Faculty research:* Analysis, differential equations, topology, statistics.

Montclair State University, The Graduate School, College of Science and Mathematics, Department of Mathematics, Montclair, NJ 07043-1624. Offers math education (Ed D); mathematics (Certificate); physical science (Certificate); statistics (MS), including mathematics education, pure and applied mathematics; teaching middle grades math (MA, Certificate). Part-time and evening/weekend programs available. *Faculty:* 32 full-time (10 women), 30 part-time/adjunct (14 women). *Students:* 21 full-time (9 women), 109 part-time (81 women); includes 9 Black or African American, non-Hispanic/Latino; 5 Asian, non-Hispanic/Latino; 9 Hispanic/Latino; 2 Two or more races, non-Hispanic/Latino, 1 international. Average age 34. 36 applicants, 81% accepted, 20 enrolled. In 2010, 28 master's, 2 doctorates, 7 other advanced degrees awarded. *Degree requirements:* For master's, comprehensive exam. *Entrance requirements:* For master's, GRE General Test, 2 letters of recommendation. Additional exam requirements/recommendations for international students: Required—TOEFL (minimum iBT score of 83) or IELTS. *Application deadline:* For fall admission, 6/1 for international students; for spring admission, 10/1 for international students. Applications are processed on a rolling basis. Application fee: $60. *Expenses:* Tuition, state resident: part-time $501.34 per credit. Tuition, nonresident: part-time $773.88 per credit. Required fees: $71.15 per credit. *Financial support:* In 2010–11, 8 research assistantships with full tuition reimbursements (averaging $7,000 per year), 1 teaching assistantship with full tuition reimbursement (averaging $15,000 per year) were awarded; Federal Work-Study, scholarships/grants, and unspecified assistantships also available. Support available to part-time students. Financial award application deadline: 3/1; financial award applicants required to submit FAFSA. *Faculty research:* Mathematical sciences, math education. Total annual research expenditures: $1.2 million. *Unit head:* Dr. Helen Roberts, Chairperson, 973-655-5132. *Application contact:* Amy Aiello, Director of Graduate Admissions and Operations, 973-655-5147, Fax: 973-655-7869, E-mail: graduate.school@montclair.edu.

Naval Postgraduate School, Graduate Programs, Department of Mathematics, Monterey, CA 93943. Offers applied mathematics (MS, PhD). Program only open to commissioned officers of the United States and friendly nations and selected United States federal civilian employees. Part-time programs available. *Degree requirements:* For master's, thesis; for doctorate, one foreign language, thesis/dissertation.

New Jersey Institute of Technology, Office of Graduate Studies, College of Science and Liberal Arts, Department of Mathematical Science, Program in Applied Mathematics, Newark, NJ 07102. Offers MS. Part-time and evening/weekend programs available. *Students:* 16 full-time (5 women), 5 part-time (2 women); includes 4 Black or African American, non-Hispanic/Latino; 2 Asian, non-Hispanic/Latino; 3 Hispanic/Latino, 2 international. Average age 27. 30 applicants, 33% accepted, 5 enrolled. In 2010, 6 master's awarded. *Entrance requirements:* For master's, GRE General Test. Additional exam requirements/recommendations for international students: Required—TOEFL (minimum score 550 paper-based; 213 computer-based; 79 iBT). *Application deadline:* For fall admission, 6/5 priority date for domestic students, 4/1 for international students; for spring admission, 11/15 for domestic and international students. Applications are processed on a rolling basis. Application fee: $65. Electronic applications accepted. *Expenses:* Tuition, state resident: full-time $14,724; part-time $818 per credit. Tuition, nonresident: full-time $20,304; part-time $1128 per credit. Required fees: $2272; $209 per credit. $103 per semester. One-time fee: $312 full-time; $212 part-time. *Financial support:* Fellowships with full and partial tuition reimbursements, research assistantships with full and partial tuition reimbursements, teaching assistantships with full and partial tuition reimbursements, career-related internships or fieldwork, Federal Work-Study, institutionally sponsored loans, and unspecified assistantships available. Financial award application deadline: 3/15. *Unit head:* Dr. Daljit S. Ahluwalia, Chair, 973-596-8465, E-mail: daljit.ahluwalia@njit.edu. *Application contact:* Kathryn Kelly, Director of Admissions, 973-596-3300, Fax: 973-596-3461, E-mail: admissions@njit.edu.

New Mexico Institute of Mining and Technology, Graduate Studies, Department of Mathematics, Socorro, NM 87801. Offers applied math (PhD); mathematics (MS); operations research (MS). *Degree requirements:* For master's, thesis optional; for doctorate, thesis/dissertation. *Entrance requirements:* For master's, GRE General Test. Additional exam requirements/recommendations for international students: Required—TOEFL (minimum score 540 paper-based; 207 computer-based). *Faculty research:* Applied mathematics, differential equations, industrial mathematics, numerical analysis, stochastic processes.

North Carolina Central University, Division of Academic Affairs, College of Science and Technology, Department of Mathematics and Computer Science, Durham, NC 27707-3129. Offers applied mathematics (MS); mathematics education (MS); pure mathematics (MS). Part-time and evening/weekend programs available. *Degree requirements:* For master's, one foreign language, comprehensive exam, thesis. *Entrance requirements:* For master's, minimum GPA of 3.0 in major, 2.5 overall. Additional exam requirements/recommendations for international students: Required—TOEFL. *Faculty research:* Structure theorems for Lie algebra, Kleene monoids and semi-groups, theoretical computer science, mathematics education.

North Carolina State University, Graduate School, College of Physical and Mathematical Sciences, Department of Mathematics, Program in Applied Mathematics, Raleigh, NC 27695. Offers MS, PhD. *Degree requirements:* For master's, thesis (for some programs); for doctorate, thesis/dissertation. *Entrance requirements:* For master's and doctorate, GRE, GRE Subject Test. Electronic applications accepted. *Faculty research:* Biological and physical modeling, numerical analysis, control, stochastic processes, industrial mathematics.

North Dakota State University, College of Graduate and Interdisciplinary Studies, College of Science and Mathematics, Department of Mathematics, Fargo, ND 58108. Offers applied mathematics (MS, PhD); mathematics (MS, PhD). *Faculty:* 15 full-time, 4 part-time/adjunct. *Students:* 24 full-time (7 women), 2 part-time (1 woman); includes 1 Two or more races, non-Hispanic/Latino, 6 international. Average age 28. 26 applicants, 35% accepted, 5 enrolled. In 2010, 3 master's, 2 doctorates awarded. *Degree requirements:* For master's, comprehensive exam, thesis; for doctorate, one foreign language, comprehensive exam, thesis/dissertation, computer proficiency. *Entrance requirements:* For master's and doctorate, GRE General Test. Additional exam requirements/recommendations for international students: Required—TOEFL (minimum score 525 paper-based; 197 computer-based; 71 iBT), IELTS. *Application deadline:* For fall admission, 5/1 priority date for domestic and international students; for spring admission, 8/1 for domestic students, 8/1 priority date for international students. Applications are processed on a rolling basis. Application fee: $45 ($60 for international students). Electronic applications accepted. *Financial support:* In 2010–11, 5 fellowships with full tuition reimbursements (averaging $18,000 per year), 1 research assistantship with tuition reimbursement (averaging $14,000 per year), 17 teaching assistantships with full tuition reimbursements (averaging $9,300 per year) were awarded; Federal Work-Study, institutionally sponsored loans, and tuition waivers (full) also available. Support available to part-time students. Financial award application deadline: 3/31. *Faculty research:* Discrete mathematics, number theory, analysis theory, algebra, applied math. Total annual research expenditures: $33,227. *Unit head:* Dr. Warren Shreve, Chair, 701-231-8171, Fax: 701-231-7598, E-mail: warren.shreve@ndsu.edu. *Application contact:* Dr. Jim Coykendall, Graduate Program Director, 701-231-8079, Fax: 701-231-7598, E-mail: jim.coykendall@ndsu.edu.

Northeastern University, College of Science, Department of Mathematics, Boston, MA 02115-5096. Offers applied mathematics (MS); mathematics (MS, PhD); operations research (MSOR). Part-time and evening/weekend programs available. *Faculty:* 39 full-time (5 women), 15 part-time/adjunct (7 women). *Students:* 52 full-time (16 women), 3 part-time (2 women). 164 applicants, 58% accepted, 14 enrolled. In 2010, 6 master's, 7 doctorates awarded. *Degree requirements:* For master's, thesis (for some programs); for doctorate, thesis/dissertation, qualifying exams. *Entrance requirements:* For master's and doctorate, GRE Subject Test, GRE General Test. Additional exam requirements/recommendations for international students: Required—TOEFL. *Application deadline:* For fall admission, 2/1 priority date for domestic and international students. Applications are processed on a rolling basis. Application fee: $50. Electronic applications accepted. *Financial support:* In 2010–11, 26 teaching assistantships with tuition reimbursements (averaging $17,345 per year) were awarded; research assistantships with tuition reimbursements, Federal Work-Study, institutionally sponsored loans, tuition waivers (full and partial), and unspecified assistantships also available. Financial award application deadline: 3/1; financial award applicants required to submit FAFSA. *Faculty research:* Algebra and singularities, combinatorics, topology, probability and statistics, geometric analysis and partial differential equations. *Unit head:* Dr. Jerzy Weyman, Graduate Coordinator, 617-373-5513, Fax: 617-373-5658, E-mail: j.weyman@neu.edu. *Application contact:* Jo-Anne Dickinson, Admissions Contact, 617-373-5990, Fax: 617-373-7281, E-mail: gsas@neu.edu.

Northwestern University, The Graduate School, Interdepartmental Programs, Program in Mathematical Methods in Social Science, Evanston, IL 60208. Offers MS.

Northwestern University, McCormick School of Engineering and Applied Science, Department of Engineering Sciences and Applied Mathematics, Evanston, IL 60208. Offers MS, PhD. Admissions and degrees offered through The Graduate School. Part-time programs available. *Faculty:* 12 full-time (1 woman). *Students:* 43 full-time (9 women), 2 part-time (0 women); includes 7 minority (1 Black or African American, non-Hispanic/Latino; 1 American Indian or Alaska Native, non-Hispanic/Latino; 2 Asian, non-Hispanic/Latino; 2 Hispanic/Latino; 1 Two or more races, non-Hispanic/Latino), 7 international. Average age 26. 97 applicants, 14% accepted, 9 enrolled. In 2010, 17 master's, 4 doctorates awarded. Terminal master's awarded for partial completion of doctoral program. *Degree requirements:* For master's, comprehensive exam; for doctorate, comprehensive exam, thesis/dissertation. *Entrance requirements:* For master's, General Exam of GRE; for doctorate, GRE. Additional exam requirements/recommendations for international students: Required—TOEFL (minimum score 577 paper-based, 233 computer-based, 90 iBT) or IELTS (7). *Application deadline:* For fall admission, 1/15 for domestic and

international students. Application fee: $75. Electronic applications accepted. *Financial support:* Fellowships with full tuition reimbursements, research assistantships with full tuition reimbursements, teaching assistantships with full tuition reimbursements, career-related internships or fieldwork, institutionally sponsored loans, health care benefits, and unspecified assistantships available. Financial award application deadline: 1/15; financial award applicants required to submit FAFSA. *Faculty research:* Acoustics, asymptotic analysis, bifurcation theory, combustion theory, fluid dynamics, information technology, math biology, microfluidics, moving boundary problems, nonlinear dynamics, pattern formation, waves. Total annual research expenditures: $1.9 million. *Unit head:* Dr. Vladimir Volpert, Chair, 847-491-8095, Fax: 847-491-2178, E-mail: v-volpert@northwestern.edu. *Application contact:* Dr. David Chopp, Admission Officer, 847-491-8391, Fax: 847-491-2178, E-mail: chopp@northwestern.edu.

Oakland University, Graduate Study and Lifelong Learning, College of Arts and Sciences, Department of Mathematics and Statistics, Program in Applied Mathematical Sciences, Rochester, MI 48309-4401. Offers PhD.

Oakland University, Graduate Study and Lifelong Learning, College of Arts and Sciences, Department of Mathematics and Statistics, Program in Industrial Applied Mathematics, Rochester, MI 48309-4401. Offers MS. Part-time and evening/weekend programs available. *Entrance requirements:* For master's, minimum GPA of 3.0 for unconditional admission. Additional exam requirements/recommendations for international students: Required—TOEFL (minimum score 550 paper-based; 213 computer-based). Electronic applications accepted. *Expenses:* Contact institution.

Oklahoma State University, College of Arts and Sciences, Department of Mathematics, Stillwater, OK 74078. Offers applied mathematics (MS, PhD); mathematics education (MS, PhD); pure mathematics (MS, PhD). *Faculty:* 37 full-time (7 women), 5 part-time/adjunct (4 women). *Students:* 4 full-time (1 woman), 26 part-time (6 women); includes 1 Asian, non-Hispanic/Latino, 20 international. Average age 31. 69 applicants, 16% accepted, 6 enrolled. In 2010, 2 doctorates awarded. *Degree requirements:* For master's, thesis, creative component, or report; for doctorate, comprehensive exam, thesis/dissertation. *Entrance requirements:* For master's and doctorate, GRE (recommended). Additional exam requirements/recommendations for international students: Required—TOEFL (minimum score 550 paper-based; 79 iBT). *Application deadline:* For fall admission, 3/1 for domestic and international students; for spring admission, 10/15 for domestic students, 10/15 priority date for international students. Applications are processed on a rolling basis. Application fee: $40 ($75 for international students). Electronic applications accepted. *Expenses:* Tuition, state resident: full-time $3716; part-time $154.85 per credit hour. Tuition, nonresident: full-time $14,892; part-time $621 per credit hour. Required fees: $2044; $85.20 per credit hour. One-time fee: $50. Tuition and fees vary according to course load and campus/location. *Financial support:* In 2010–11, 29 teaching assistantships (averaging $18,431 per year) were awarded; health care benefits and tuition waivers (partial) also available. Financial award application deadline: 3/1; financial award applicants required to submit FAFSA. *Unit head:* Dr. Dale Alspach, Head, 405-744-5688, Fax: 405-744-8275. *Application contact:* Dr. Mark Payton, Dean, 405-744-6368, Fax: 405-744-0355, E-mail: grad-i@okstate.edu.

Penn State University Park, Graduate School, Eberly College of Science, Department of Mathematics, State College, University Park, PA 16802-1503. Offers mathematics (MA), including applied mathematics. *Unit head:* Dr. John Roe, Head, 814-865-7527, Fax: 814-865-3735, E-mail: roe@math.psu.edu. *Application contact:* Dr. Dimitri Burago, Associate Head of Graduate Studies, 814-865-7741, E-mail: burago@math.psu.edu.

Princeton University, Graduate School, Program in Applied and Computational Mathematics, Princeton, NJ 08544-1019. Offers PhD. *Degree requirements:* For doctorate, thesis/dissertation. *Entrance requirements:* For doctorate, GRE General Test, GRE Subject Test. Additional exam requirements/recommendations for international students: Required—TOEFL (minimum score 600 paper-based; 250 computer-based). Electronic applications accepted.

Rensselaer Polytechnic Institute, Graduate School, School of Science, Program in Applied Mathematics, Troy, NY 12180-3590. Offers MS. Part-time programs available. *Faculty:* 23 full-time (3 women), 4 part-time/adjunct (1 woman). *Students:* 45 full-time (18 women), 3 part-time (2 women); includes 3 Black or African American, non-Hispanic/Latino; 5 Asian, non-Hispanic/Latino; 1 Hispanic/Latino. Average age 22. 87 applicants, 52% accepted, 15 enrolled. In 2010, 9 master's awarded. *Entrance requirements:* For master's, GRE General Test. Additional exam requirements/recommendations for international students: Required—TOEFL. *Application deadline:* For fall admission, 1/15 priority date for domestic students. Applications are processed on a rolling basis. Application fee: $75. Electronic applications accepted. *Expenses:* Tuition: Full-time $39,600; part-time $1650 per credit. Required fees: $1896. *Financial support:* In 2010–11, 3 students received support. Career-related internships or fieldwork and institutionally sponsored loans available. Financial award application deadline: 1/15. *Faculty research:* Mathematical modeling, differential equations, applications of mathematics in science and engineering, operations research, analysis. Total annual research expenditures: $3.2 million. *Application contact:* Dawnmarie Robens, Graduate Student Coordinator, 518-276-6414, Fax: 518-276-4824, E-mail: robensd@rpi.edu.

Rice University, Graduate Programs, George R. Brown School of Engineering, Department of Computational and Applied Mathematics, Houston, TX 77251-1892. Offers computational and applied mathematics (MA, MCAM, PhD); computational science and engineering (PhD). *Degree requirements:* For master's, comprehensive exam (for some programs), thesis (for some programs); for doctorate, comprehensive exam, thesis/dissertation. *Entrance requirements:* For master's and doctorate, GRE General Test, minimum GPA of 3.0. Additional exam requirements/recommendations for international students: Required—TOEFL (minimum score 600 paper-based; 250 computer-based; 90 iBT). Electronic applications accepted. *Faculty research:* Inverse problems, partial differential equations, computer algorithms, computational modeling, optimization theory.

Rochester Institute of Technology, Graduate Enrollment Services, College of Science, Health Sciences and Sustainability, School of Mathematical Sciences, Rochester, NY 14623-5603. Offers industrial and applied mathematics (MS). Part-time and evening/weekend programs available. *Students:* 15 full-time (6 women), 4 part-time (3 women); includes 1 Hispanic/Latino, 5 international. Average age 25. 27 applicants, 63% accepted, 5 enrolled. In 2010, 4 master's awarded. *Degree requirements:* For master's, thesis. *Entrance requirements:* For master's, GRE General Test (recommended), minimum GPA of 3.0. Additional exam requirements/recommendations for international students: Required—TOEFL (minimum score 550 paper-based; 213 computer-based; 79 iBT) or IELTS (minimum score 6.5). *Application deadline:* For fall admission, 2/15 priority date for domestic and international students. Applications are processed on a rolling basis. Application fee: $50. Electronic applications accepted. *Expenses:* Tuition: Full-time $33,234; part-time $924 per credit hour. Required fees: $219. *Financial support:* In 2010–11, 13 students received support; research assistantships with partial tuition reimbursements available, teaching assistantships with partial tuition reimbursements available, career-related internships or fieldwork, scholarships/grants, and unspecified assistantships available. Support available to part-time students. Financial award applicants required to submit FAFSA. *Faculty research:* Abstract algebra, bioinformatics, combinatorics and graph theory, complex variables, cryptography, dynamical systems and chaos, statistics, topology. *Unit head:* Dr. Douglas Meadows, Head of SMS, 585-475-5129, E-mail: dsmsma@rit.edu. *Application contact:* Diane Ellison, Assistant Vice President, Graduate Enrollment Services, 585-475-2229, Fax: 585-475-7164, E-mail: gradinfo@rit.edu.

Rutgers, The State University of New Jersey, New Brunswick, Graduate School-New Brunswick, Department of Mathematics, Piscataway, NJ 08854-8097. Offers applied mathematics (MS, PhD); mathematics (MS, PhD). Part-time programs available. *Degree requirements:* For doctorate, one foreign language, comprehensive exam, thesis/dissertation. *Entrance requirements:* For master's and doctorate, GRE General Test, GRE Subject Test. Additional exam requirements/recommendations for international students: Required—TOEFL. *Expenses:* Tuition, state resident: full-time $7200; part-time $600 per credit. Tuition, nonresident: full-time $11,124; part-time $927 per credit. *Faculty research:* Logic and set theory, number theory, mathematical physics, control theory, partial differential equations.

St. John's University, St. John's College of Liberal Arts and Sciences, Department of Mathematics and Computer Science, Queens, NY 11439. Offers algebra (MA); analysis (MA); applied mathematics (MA); computer science (MA); geometry-topology (MA); logic and foundations (MA); probability and statistics (MA). Part-time and evening/weekend programs available. *Students:* 4 full-time (1 woman), 3 part-time (1 woman); includes 3 minority (1 Black or African American, non-Hispanic/Latino; 1 Asian, non-Hispanic/Latino; 1 Hispanic/Latino). Average age 25. 19 applicants, 42% accepted, 5 enrolled. In 2010, 3 master's awarded. *Degree requirements:* For master's, comprehensive exam, thesis optional. *Entrance requirements:* For master's, minimum GPA of 3.0. Additional exam requirements/recommendations for international students: Required—TOEFL (minimum score 600 paper-based; 250 computer-based; 100 iBT), IELTS (minimum score 5.5). *Application deadline:* For fall admission, 5/1 priority date for domestic and international students; for spring admission, 11/1 priority date for domestic and international students. Applications are processed on a rolling basis. Application fee: $70. Electronic applications accepted. *Expenses:* Tuition: Full-time $17,100; part-time $950 per credit. Required fees: $340; $170 per semester. Tuition and fees vary according to program. *Financial support:* Research assistantships, scholarships/grants available. Support available to part-time students. Financial award application deadline: 3/1; financial award applicants required to submit FAFSA. *Faculty research:* Functional analysis and operator theory, algebraic K-theory, applied mathematics, measure theory, differential geometry and mathematics education. *Unit head:* Dr. Charles Traina, Chair, 718-990-6166, E-mail: trainac@stjohns.edu. *Application contact:* Kathleen Davis, Director of Graduate Admission, 718-990-1601, Fax: 718-990-5686, E-mail: gradhelp@stjohns.edu.

San Diego State University, Graduate and Research Affairs, College of Sciences, Department of Mathematics and Statistics, Program in Applied Mathematics, San Diego, CA 92182. Offers MS. Part-time programs available. *Degree requirements:* For master's, comprehensive exam. *Entrance requirements:* For master's, GRE General Test. Additional exam requirements/recommendations for international students: Required—TOEFL. Electronic applications accepted. *Faculty research:* Modeling, computational fluid dynamics, biomathematics, thermodynamics.

San Jose State University, Graduate Studies and Research, College of Science, Department of Mathematics, San Jose, CA 95192-0001. Offers applied mathematics (MS); mathematics (MA, MS); mathematics education (MA); statistics (MA). Part-time and evening/weekend programs available. *Degree requirements:* For master's, comprehensive exam, thesis (for some programs). *Entrance requirements:* For master's, GRE Subject Test. Electronic applications accepted. *Faculty research:* Artificial intelligence, algorithms, numerical analysis, software database, number theory.

Santa Clara University, School of Engineering, Program in Applied Mathematics, Santa Clara, CA 95053. Offers applied mathematics (MS); mathematical finance (MS). Part-time and evening/weekend programs available. *Students:* 8 full-time (2 women), 17 part-time (7 women); includes 6 minority (all Asian, non-Hispanic/Latino), 2 international. Average age 30. 8 applicants, 75% accepted, 3 enrolled. In 2010, 1 master's awarded. *Degree requirements:* For master's, thesis (for some programs). *Entrance requirements:* For master's, GRE (waiver may be available), transcript. Additional exam requirements/recommendations for international students: Required—TOEFL (minimum score 550 paper-based; 213 computer-based; 79 iBT). *Application deadline:* For fall admission, 8/12 for domestic students, 7/15 for international students; for winter admission, 10/28 for domestic students, 9/23 for international students; for spring admission, 2/25 for domestic students, 1/21 for international students. Applications are processed on a rolling basis. Application fee: $60. Electronic applications accepted. *Expenses:* Contact institution. *Financial support:* Research assistantships, teaching assistantships available. Financial award application deadline: 3/2; financial award applicants required to submit FAFSA. *Unit head:* Dr. Alex Zecevic, Associate Dean for Graduate Studies, 408-554-2394, E-mail: azecevic@scu.edu. *Application contact:* Stacey Tinker, Director of Admissions, Graduate Engineering, 408-554-4748, Fax: 408-554-4323, E-mail: stinker@scu.edu.

Simon Fraser University, Graduate Studies, Faculty of Science, Department of Mathematics, Burnaby, BC V5A 1S6, Canada. Offers applied and computational mathematics (M Sc, PhD); mathematics (M Sc, PhD). *Degree requirements:* For master's, thesis; for doctorate, thesis/dissertation. *Entrance requirements:* For master's, GRE General Test, minimum GPA of 3.0, 3 letters of reference; for doctorate, GRE General Test, minimum GPA of 3.5, 3 letters of reference. Additional exam requirements/recommendations for international students: Required—TWE or IELTS. Electronic applications accepted. *Faculty research:* Semi-groups, number theory, optimization, combinations.

Southern Methodist University, Dedman College, Department of Mathematics, Dallas, TX 75275. Offers computational and applied mathematics (MS, PhD). *Faculty:* 17 full-time (2 women), 3 part-time/adjunct (2 women). *Students:* 18 full-time (7 women); includes 1 Black or African American, non-Hispanic/Latino; 1 Asian, non-Hispanic/Latino; 2 Hispanic/Latino, 7 international. Average age 27. 25 applicants, 28% accepted, 6 enrolled. In 2010, 4 master's, 3 doctorates awarded. *Degree requirements:* For master's, oral exams; for doctorate, thesis/dissertation, oral and written exams. *Entrance requirements:* For master's and doctorate, GRE General Test, minimum GPA of 3.0, 18 undergraduate hours in mathematics beyond first and second year calculus. Additional exam requirements/recommendations for international students: Required—TOEFL. *Application deadline:* For fall admission, 2/1 priority date for domestic students, 2/1 for international students; for spring admission, 11/30 for domestic students. Applications are processed on a rolling basis. Application fee: $75. Electronic applications accepted. *Financial support:* In 2010–11, 18 students received support, including 5 research assistantships with full tuition reimbursements available (averaging $18,000 per year), 13 teaching assistantships with full tuition reimbursements available (averaging $16,500 per year); career-related internships or fieldwork, scholarships/grants, health care benefits, tuition waivers, and unspecified assistantships also available. Support available to part-time students. Financial award application deadline: 2/1; financial award applicants required to submit FAFSA. *Faculty research:* Numerical analysis and scientific computation, fluid dynamics, optics, wave propagation, mathematical biology. Total annual research expenditures: $369,480. *Unit head:* Dr. Douglas A. Reinelt, Chairman, 214-768-2506, Fax: 214-768-2355, E-mail: mathchair@mail.smu.edu. *Application contact:* Dr. Thomas W. Carr, Director of Graduate Studies, 214-768-3460, E-mail: math@mail.smu.edu.

Stevens Institute of Technology, Graduate School, Charles V. Schaefer Jr. School of Engineering, Department of Mathematical Sciences, Program in Applied Mathematics, Hoboken, NJ 07030. Offers MS. *Students:* 8 full-time (2 women), 2 part-time (0 women); includes 1 Asian, non-Hispanic/Latino, 6 international. Average age 24. 3 applicants, 33% accepted. *Degree requirements:* For master's, thesis optional. *Entrance requirements:* For master's, GRE. Additional exam requirements/recommendations for international students: Required—TOEFL. *Application deadline:* Applications are processed on a rolling basis. Application fee: $50. Electronic applications accepted. *Unit head:* Dr. Robert Gilman, Director, 201-216-5449, Fax: 201-216-8321. *Application contact:* Dr. Milos Dostal, Professor, 201-216-5426.

Stony Brook University, State University of New York, Graduate School, College of Engineering and Applied Sciences, Department of Applied Mathematics and Statistics, Stony Brook, NY 11794. Offers MS, PhD. *Faculty:* 20 full-time (3 women), 3 part-time/adjunct (1

Peterson's Graduate Programs in the Physical Sciences, Mathematics, Agricultural Sciences, the Environment & Natural Resources 2012

www.facebook.com/petersonspublishing 231

Applied Mathematics

Stony Brook University, State University of New York (continued)

woman). *Students:* 271 full-time (108 women), 13 part-time (3 women); includes 3 Black or African American, non-Hispanic/Latino; 21 Asian, non-Hispanic/Latino; 8 Hispanic/Latino; 1 Two or more races, non-Hispanic/Latino, 208 international. Average age 28. 483 applicants, 79% accepted, 116 enrolled. In 2010, 46 master's, 16 doctorates awarded. *Degree requirements:* For master's, thesis or alternative; for doctorate, one foreign language, comprehensive exam, thesis/dissertation. *Entrance requirements:* For master's and doctorate, GRE General Test. Additional exam requirements/recommendations for international students: Required—TOEFL. *Application deadline:* For fall admission, 1/15 for domestic students. Application fee: $100. *Expenses:* Tuition, state resident: full-time $8370; part-time $349 per credit. Tuition, nonresident: full-time $13,780; part-time $574 per credit. Required fees: $994. *Financial support:* In 2010–11, 44 research assistantships, 47 teaching assistantships were awarded; fellowships also available. *Faculty research:* Biostatistics, combinatorial analysis, differential equations, modeling. Total annual research expenditures: $3.7 million. *Unit head:* Dr. Jim Glimm, Chairman, 631-632-8360. *Application contact:* Dr. Xiaolin Li, Graduate Director, 631-632-8354, Fax: 631-632-8490, E-mail: linli@ams.sunysb.edu.

Temple University, College of Science and Technology, Department of Mathematics, Philadelphia, PA 19122-6096. Offers applied mathematics (MA); mathematics (PhD); pure mathematics (MA). Part-time and evening/weekend programs available. *Faculty:* 16 full-time (1 woman). *Students:* 20 full-time (2 women), 7 part-time (3 women), 5 international. 59 applicants, 24% accepted, 6 enrolled. In 2010, 7 master's, 3 doctorates awarded. Terminal master's awarded for partial completion of doctoral program. *Degree requirements:* For master's, thesis optional, written exam; for doctorate, 2 foreign languages, thesis/dissertation, oral and written exams. *Entrance requirements:* For master's, GRE General Test, minimum GPA of 3.0; for doctorate, GRE General Test, GRE Subject Test, minimum GPA of 3.0. Additional exam requirements/recommendations for international students: Required—TOEFL (minimum score 550 paper-based; 213 computer-based; 79 iBT). *Application deadline:* For fall admission, 2/15 priority date for domestic students, 12/15 for international students; for spring admission, 11/15 priority date for domestic students, 8/1 for international students. Applications are processed on a rolling basis. Application fee: $50. Electronic applications accepted. *Financial support:* Fellowships, research assistantships, teaching assistantships, Federal Work-Study and institutionally sponsored loans available. Financial award application deadline: 1/15; financial award applicants required to submit FAFSA. *Faculty research:* Differential geometry, numerical analysis. *Unit head:* Dr. Edward Letzter, Chair, 215-204-4650, Fax: 215-204-6433, E-mail: mathematics@temple.edu. *Application contact:* Dr. Edward Letzter, Chair, 215-204-4650, Fax: 215-204-6433, E-mail: mathematics@temple.edu.

Texas A&M University–Corpus Christi, Graduate Studies and Research, College of Science and Technology, Program in Mathematics, Corpus Christi, TX 78412-5503. Offers applied and computational mathematics (MS); curriculum content (MS). Part-time programs available. *Degree requirements:* For master's, thesis (for some programs). *Entrance requirements:* For master's, 2 letters of recommendation.

Texas State University–San Marcos, Graduate School, College of Science, Department of Mathematics, Program in Industrial Mathematics, San Marcos, TX 78666. Offers MS. Part-time programs available. *Students:* 5 applicants, 80% accepted, 0 enrolled. In 2010, 1 master's awarded. *Degree requirements:* For master's, comprehensive exam, thesis. *Entrance requirements:* For master's, GRE, minimum GPA of 2.75 in last 60 hours of undergraduate work. Additional exam requirements/recommendations for international students: Required—TOEFL (minimum score 550 paper-based; 213 computer-based; 78 iBT). *Application deadline:* For fall admission, 6/15 priority date for domestic students, 6/1 priority date for international students; for spring admission, 10/15 priority date for domestic students, 10/1 priority date for international students. Applications are processed on a rolling basis. Application fee: $40 ($90 for international students). Electronic applications accepted. *Expenses:* Tuition, state resident: full-time $6024; part-time $251 per credit hour. Tuition, nonresident: full-time $13,536; part-time $564 per credit hour. Required fees: $1776; $50 per credit hour. $306 per semester. *Financial support:* Research assistantships, teaching assistantships, Federal Work-Study, institutionally sponsored loans, scholarships/grants, health care benefits, and unspecified assistantships available. Support available to part-time students. Financial award application deadline: 4/1; financial award applicants required to submit FAFSA. *Unit head:* Dr. Stanley Wayment, Graduate Advisor, 512-245-2551, Fax: 512-245-3425, E-mail: sw05@txstate.edu. *Application contact:* Dr. Gregory Passty, Graduate Adviser, 512-245-3446, Fax: 512-245-3425, E-mail: gp02@txstate.edu.

Texas State University–San Marcos, Graduate School, College of Science, Department of Mathematics, Program in Mathematics, San Marcos, TX 78666. Offers MS. *Faculty:* 16 full-time (7 women), 1 part-time/adjunct (0 women). *Students:* 11 full-time (4 women), 13 part-time (5 women); includes 9 minority (2 Black or African American, non-Hispanic/Latino; 2 Asian, non-Hispanic/Latino; 4 Hispanic/Latino; 1 Two or more races, non-Hispanic/Latino). Average age 32. 11 applicants, 82% accepted, 6 enrolled. In 2010, 7 master's awarded. *Degree requirements:* For master's, comprehensive exam, thesis (for some programs). *Entrance requirements:* For master's, GRE, minimum GPA of 2.75 in last 60 hours of undergraduate course work. Additional exam requirements/recommendations for international students: Required—TOEFL (minimum score 550 paper-based; 213 computer-based; 78 iBT). *Application deadline:* For fall admission, 6/15 priority date for domestic students, 6/1 priority date for international students; for spring admission, 10/15 priority date for domestic students, 10/1 priority date for international students. Applications are processed on a rolling basis. Application fee: $40 ($90 for international students). Electronic applications accepted. *Expenses:* Tuition, state resident: full-time $6024; part-time $251 per credit hour. Tuition, nonresident: full-time $13,536; part-time $564 per credit hour. Required fees: $1776; $50 per credit hour. $306 per semester. *Financial support:* In 2010–11, 8 students received support, including 2 research assistantships (averaging $2,613 per year), 7 teaching assistantships (averaging $6,257 per year); Federal Work-Study, institutionally sponsored loans, scholarships/grants, health care benefits, and unspecified assistantships also available. Support available to part-time students. Financial award application deadline: 4/1; financial award applicants required to submit FAFSA. *Faculty research:* Dynamic geometry, research in groups, route protocal. Total annual research expenditures: $728,080. *Unit head:* Dr. Stanley Wayment, Graduate Advisor, 512-245-3555, Fax: 512-245-3425, E-mail: sw05@txstate.edu. *Application contact:* Dr. Gregory Passty, Graduate Adviser, 512-245-3446, Fax: 512-245-3425, E-mail: gp02@txstate.edu.

Towson University, Program in Applied and Industrial Mathematics, Towson, MD 21252-0001. Offers MS. Part-time and evening/weekend programs available. *Students:* 12 full-time (4 women), 22 part-time (8 women); includes 2 minority (1 Asian, non-Hispanic/Latino; 1 Hispanic/Latino), 10 international. Average age 30. In 2010, 4 master's awarded. *Degree requirements:* For master's, internships. *Entrance requirements:* For master's, bachelor's degree in mathematics or related field, minimum GPA of 3.0, including (3) terms of calculus, (1) differential equivalent one in linear algebra. Additional exam requirements/recommendations for international students: Required—TOEFL (minimum score 550 paper-based). *Application deadline:* Applications are processed on a rolling basis. Application fee: $50. Electronic applications accepted. *Expenses:* Tuition, state resident: part-time $324 per credit. Tuition, nonresident: part-time $681 per credit. Required fees: $95 per term. *Financial support:* Teaching assistantships with full tuition reimbursements, unspecified assistantships available. Financial award application deadline: 4/1; financial award applicants required to submit FAFSA. *Faculty research:* Partial differential equations, numerical computations, statistics, probability, game theory. *Unit head:* Xuezhang Hou, Graduate Program Director, 410-704-2578, Fax: 410-704-4149, E-mail: xhou@towson.edu. *Application contact:* 410-704-2501, Fax: 410-704-4675, E-mail: grads@towson.edu.

Tulane University, School of Science and Engineering, Department of Mathematics, New Orleans, LA 70118-5669. Offers applied mathematics (MS); mathematics (MS, PhD); statistics (MS). *Degree requirements:* For master's, thesis (for some programs); for doctorate, thesis/dissertation. *Entrance requirements:* For master's, GRE General Test, minimum B average in undergraduate course work; for doctorate, GRE General Test. Additional exam requirements/recommendations for international students: Required—TOEFL. Electronic applications accepted.

The University of Akron, Graduate School, Buchtel College of Arts and Sciences, Department of Theoretical and Applied Mathematics, Program in Applied Mathematics, Akron, OH 44325. Offers MS. *Students:* 23 full-time (6 women), 1 part-time (0 women); includes 1 Asian, non-Hispanic/Latino; 1 Hispanic/Latino, 3 international. Average age 23. 21 applicants, 86% accepted, 7 enrolled. In 2010, 6 master's awarded. *Degree requirements:* For master's, thesis optional, seminar and comprehensive exam or thesis. *Entrance requirements:* For master's, minimum GPA of 2.75, three letters of recommendation, statement of purpose. Additional exam requirements/recommendations for international students: Required—TOEFL (minimum score 550 paper-based; 213 computer-based; 79 iBT). *Application deadline:* Applications are processed on a rolling basis. Application fee: $30 ($40 for international students). Electronic applications accepted. *Expenses:* Tuition, state resident: full-time $6800; part-time $378 per credit hour. Tuition, nonresident: full-time $11,644; part-time $647 per credit hour. Required fees: $1265. One-time fee: $30 full-time. *Faculty research:* Analysis of nonlinear partial differential equations, finite groups and character theory, mathematics education, modeling and simulation of continuum and nanoscale systems, numerical analysis and scientific computation. *Unit head:* Dr. Gerald Young, Coordinator, 330-972-5731, Fax: 330-972-8630, E-mail: gyoung1@uakron.edu. *Application contact:* Dr. Gerald Young, Coordinator, 330-972-5731, Fax: 330-972-8630, E-mail: gyoung1@uakron.edu.

The University of Akron, Graduate School, College of Engineering, Program in Engineering Applied Mathematics, Akron, OH 44325. Offers PhD. *Students:* 2 full-time (both women), 1 (woman) part-time, 1 international. Average age 30. In 2010, 1 doctorate awarded. *Degree requirements:* For doctorate, one foreign language, thesis/dissertation, candidacy exam, qualifying exam. *Entrance requirements:* For doctorate, GRE, minimum GPA of 3.0 with bachelor's or master's degree; two letters of recommendation, statement of purpose. Additional exam requirements/recommendations for international students: Required—TOEFL (minimum score 550 paper-based; 213 computer-based; 79 iBT). *Application deadline:* Applications are processed on a rolling basis. Application fee: $30 ($40 for international students). Electronic applications accepted. *Expenses:* Tuition, state resident: full-time $6800; part-time $378 per credit hour. Tuition, nonresident: full-time $11,644; part-time $647 per credit hour. Required fees: $1265. One-time fee: $30 full-time. *Unit head:* Dr. Gerald Young, Coordinator, 330-972-5731, E-mail: jerry@math.uakron.edu. *Application contact:* Dr. Craig Menzemer, Director of Graduate Studies, College of Engineering, 330-972-5536, E-mail: ccmenze@uakron.edu.

The University of Alabama, Graduate School, College of Arts and Sciences, Department of Mathematics, Tuscaloosa, AL 35487. Offers applied mathematics (PhD); mathematics (MA, PhD); pure mathematics (PhD). *Faculty:* 26 full-time (0 women). *Students:* 31 full-time (13 women), 21 part-time (3 women); includes 4 minority (3 Black or African American, non-Hispanic/Latino; 1 Two or more races, non-Hispanic/Latino), 26 international. Average age 28. 51 applicants, 59% accepted, 14 enrolled. In 2010, 8 master's, 1 doctorate awarded. Terminal master's awarded for partial completion of doctoral program. *Degree requirements:* For master's, thesis or alternative; for doctorate, thesis/dissertation. *Entrance requirements:* For master's and doctorate, GRE General Test, minimum GPA of 3.0. Additional exam requirements/recommendations for international students: Required—TOEFL (minimum score 550 paper-based; 79 iBT). *Application deadline:* For fall admission, 7/1 for domestic students, 5/31 for international students; for spring admission, 11/30 for domestic students, 10/31 for international students. Applications are processed on a rolling basis. Application fee: $50 ($60 for international students). Electronic applications accepted. *Expenses:* Tuition, state resident: full-time $7900. Tuition, nonresident: full-time $20,500. *Financial support:* In 2010–11, 1 fellowship with full tuition reimbursement (averaging $30,000 per year), 35 teaching assistantships with full tuition reimbursements (averaging $12,258 per year) were awarded; research assistantships with full tuition reimbursements, Federal Work-Study, institutionally sponsored loans, scholarships/grants, and unspecified assistantships also available. Support available to part-time students. Financial award application deadline: 7/1. *Faculty research:* Analysis, topology, algebra, fluid mechanics and system control theory, optimization, stochastic processes, numerical analysis. Total annual research expenditures: $13,950. *Unit head:* Dr. Zhijian Wu, Chairperson and Professor, 205-348-5080, Fax: 205-348-7067, E-mail: zwu@as.ua.edu. *Application contact:* Dr. Vo Liem, Director, 205-348-4898, Fax: 205-348-7067, E-mail: vliem@as.ua.edu.

The University of Alabama at Birmingham, College of Arts and Sciences, Program in Applied Mathematics, Birmingham, AL 35294. Offers PhD. *Students:* 19 full-time (6 women), 4 part-time (1 woman); includes 4 minority (2 Black or African American, non-Hispanic/Latino; 1 Asian, non-Hispanic/Latino; 1 Two or more races, non-Hispanic/Latino), 11 international. Average age 32. 12 applicants, 92% accepted, 6 enrolled. In 2010, 1 doctorate awarded. *Expenses:* Tuition, state resident: full-time $5482. Tuition, nonresident: full-time $12,430. Tuition and fees vary according to program. *Unit head:* Dr. Rudi Weikard, 205-934-2154. *Application contact:* Julie Bryant, Director of Graduate Admissions, 205-934-8227, Fax: 205-934-8413, E-mail: jbryant@uab.edu.

The University of Alabama in Huntsville, School of Graduate Studies, College of Science, Department of Mathematical Sciences, Huntsville, AL 35899. Offers applied mathematics (PhD); mathematics (MA, MS). PhD offered jointly with The University of Alabama (Tuscaloosa), The University of Alabama at Birmingham. Part-time and evening/weekend programs available. *Faculty:* 13 full-time (0 women). *Students:* 16 full-time (9 women), 16 part-time (6 women); includes 7 minority (4 Black or African American, non-Hispanic/Latino; 3 Asian, non-Hispanic/Latino), 6 international. Average age 29. 28 applicants, 50% accepted, 10 enrolled. In 2010, 4 master's, 1 doctorate awarded. *Degree requirements:* For master's, comprehensive exam, thesis or alternative, oral and written exams; for doctorate, comprehensive exam, thesis/dissertation, oral and written exams. *Entrance requirements:* For master's and doctorate, GRE General Test, minimum GPA of 3.0. Additional exam requirements/recommendations for international students: Required—TOEFL (minimum score 550 paper-based; 213 computer-based; 62 iBT). *Application deadline:* For fall admission, 7/15 for domestic students, 4/1 for international students; for spring admission, 11/30 for domestic students, 9/1 for international students. Applications are processed on a rolling basis. Application fee: $40 ($50 for international students). Electronic applications accepted. *Expenses:* Tuition, state resident: full-time $7250; part-time $407.75 per credit hour. Tuition, nonresident: full-time $17,358; part-time $970.05 per credit hour. Required fees: $246.80 per semester. Tuition and fees vary according to course load and program. *Financial support:* In 2010–11, 13 students received support, including 16 teaching assistantships with full and partial tuition reimbursements available (averaging $10,575 per year); career-related internships or fieldwork, Federal Work-Study, institutionally sponsored loans, scholarships/grants, health care benefits, and unspecified assistantships also available. Support available to part-time students. Financial award application deadline: 4/1; financial award applicants required to submit FAFSA. *Faculty research:* Dynamical systems, mathematical biology, stochastic processes, numerical analysis, combinatorics. Total annual research expenditures: $277,636. *Unit head:* Dr. Jia Li, Chair, 256-824-6470, Fax: 256-824-6173, E-mail: li@math.uah.edu. *Application contact:* Kathy Biggs, Graduate Studies Admissions Manager, 256-824-6199, Fax: 256-824-6405, E-mail: deangrad@uah.edu.

University of Alberta, Faculty of Graduate Studies and Research, Department of Mathematical and Statistical Sciences, Edmonton, AB T6G 2E1, Canada. Offers applied mathematics (M Sc, PhD); biostatistics (M Sc); mathematical finance (M Sc, PhD); mathematical physics (M Sc,

PhD); mathematics (M Sc, PhD); statistics (M Sc, PhD, Postgraduate Diploma). Part-time programs available. Terminal master's awarded for partial completion of doctoral program. *Degree requirements:* For master's, thesis (for some programs); for doctorate, comprehensive exam, thesis/dissertation. *Entrance requirements:* Additional exam requirements/recommendations for international students: Required—TOEFL (minimum score 580 paper-based; 237 computer-based). Electronic applications accepted. *Faculty research:* Classical and functional analysis, algebra, differential equations, geometry.

The University of Arizona, College of Science, Department of Mathematics, Program in Mathematical Sciences, Tucson, AZ 85721. Offers applied science and business (PMS). Part-time programs available. *Students:* 51 full-time (13 women), 46 part-time (31 women); includes 2 Black or African American, non-Hispanic/Latino; 1 American Indian or Alaska Native, non-Hispanic/Latino; 2 Asian, non-Hispanic/Latino; 2 Hispanic/Latino, 15 international. Average age 33. *Degree requirements:* For master's, thesis, internships, colloquium, business courses. *Entrance requirements:* For master's, GRE, minimum GPA of 3.0, statement of purpose. Additional exam requirements/recommendations for international students: Required—TOEFL (minimum score 550 paper-based). Application fee: $75. *Expenses:* Tuition, state resident: full-time $7692. *Financial support:* Research assistantships, teaching assistantships, career-related internships or fieldwork, Federal Work-Study, scholarships/grants, health care benefits, and unspecified assistantships available. *Faculty research:* Algebra, coding theory, graph theory, combinatorics, probability. *Unit head:* Dr. Michael Tabor, Head, 520-621-4664, Fax: 520-626-5048, E-mail: tabor@math.arizona.edu. *Application contact:* Alaina G. Levine, Director of Special Projects, College of Science, 520-621-3374, Fax: 520-621-8389, E-mail: alaina@u.arizona.edu.

The University of Arizona, Graduate Interdisciplinary Programs, Graduate Interdisciplinary Program in Applied Mathematics, Tucson, AZ 85721. Offers applied mathematics (MS, PhD); mathematical sciences (PMS). *Faculty:* 1. *Students:* 39 full-time (10 women); includes 1 Asian, non-Hispanic/Latino; 4 Hispanic/Latino; 1 Two or more races, non-Hispanic/Latino, 4 international. Average age 28. 108 applicants, 10% accepted, 11 enrolled. In 2010, 9 master's, 7 doctorates awarded. Terminal master's awarded for partial completion of doctoral program. *Degree requirements:* For master's, thesis (for some programs); for doctorate, comprehensive exam, thesis/dissertation. *Entrance requirements:* For master's, GRE, 3 letters of recommendation; for doctorate, GRE, 3 letters of recommendation, statement of purpose. Additional exam requirements/recommendations for international students: Required—TOEFL (minimum score 575 paper-based; 230 computer-based; 80 iBT). *Application deadline:* For fall admission, 1/15 for domestic students, 1/30 for international students. Applications are processed on a rolling basis. Application fee: $65. Electronic applications accepted. *Expenses:* Tuition, state resident: full-time $7692. *Financial support:* In 2010–11, 1 research assistantship with full tuition reimbursement (averaging $17,120 per year) was awarded; institutionally sponsored loans, scholarships/grants, health care benefits, tuition waivers (full), and unspecified assistantships also available. Financial award application deadline: 3/1; financial award applicants required to submit FAFSA. *Faculty research:* Dynamical systems and chaos, partial differential equations, pattern formation, fluid dynamics and turbulence, scientific computation, mathematical physics, mathematical biology, medical imaging, applied probability and stochastic processes. Total annual research expenditures: $22,526. *Unit head:* Dr. Michael Tabor, Head, 520-621-4664, Fax: 520-626-5048, E-mail: tabor@math.arizona.edu. *Application contact:* Graduate Coordinator, 520-621-2016, Fax: 520-626-5048, E-mail: applmath@u.arizona.edu.

University of Arkansas at Little Rock, Graduate School, College of Science and Mathematics, Department of Mathematics and Statistics, Little Rock, AR 72204-1099. Offers applied statistics (Graduate Certificate); mathematical sciences (MS). Part-time and evening/weekend programs available. *Degree requirements:* For master's, comprehensive exam. *Entrance requirements:* For master's, GRE General Test, GRE Subject Test, minimum GPA of 2.7, previous course work in advanced mathematics.

The University of British Columbia, Institute of Applied Mathematics, Vancouver, BC V6T 1Z1, Canada. Offers M Sc, PhD. *Degree requirements:* For master's, thesis (for some programs); for doctorate, comprehensive exam, thesis/dissertation. *Entrance requirements:* For doctorate, master's degree. Additional exam requirements/recommendations for international students: Required—TOEFL. Tuition charges are reported in Canadian dollars. *Expenses:* Tuition, area resident: Full-time $4179 Canadian dollars. International tuition: $7344 Canadian dollars full-time. *Faculty research:* Applied analysis, optimization, mathematical biology, numerical analysis, fluid mechanics.

University of California, Berkeley, Graduate Division, College of Letters and Science, Department of Mathematics, Program in Applied Mathematics, Berkeley, CA 94720-1500. Offers PhD. *Degree requirements:* For doctorate, 2 foreign languages, thesis/dissertation, qualifying exam. *Entrance requirements:* For doctorate, GRE General Test, GRE Subject Test, minimum GPA of 3.0, 3 letters of recommendation.

University of California, Davis, Graduate Studies, Graduate Group in Applied Mathematics, Davis, CA 95616. Offers MS, PhD. Terminal master's awarded for partial completion of doctoral program. *Degree requirements:* For master's, thesis; for doctorate, one foreign language, thesis/dissertation. *Entrance requirements:* For master's, GRE General Test, GRE Subject Test, minimum GPA of 3.0; for doctorate, GRE General Test, GRE Subject Test, master's degree, minimum GPA of 3.0. Additional exam requirements/recommendations for international students: Required—TOEFL (minimum score 550 paper-based; 213 computer-based). Electronic applications accepted. *Faculty research:* Mathematical biology, control and optimization, atmospheric sciences, theoretical chemistry, mathematical physics.

University of California, Merced, Division of Graduate Studies, School of Natural Sciences, Merced, CA 95343. Offers applied mathematics (MS, PhD); biological engineering and small-scale technologies (MS, PhD); environmental systems (MS, PhD); mechanical engineering and applied mechanics (MS, PhD); physics and chemistry (PhD); quantitative and systems biology (MS, PhD).

University of California, San Diego, Office of Graduate Studies, Department of Mathematics, La Jolla, CA 92093. Offers applied mathematics (MA); mathematics (MA, PhD); statistics (MS). *Degree requirements:* For doctorate, thesis/dissertation. *Entrance requirements:* For master's and doctorate, GRE General Test, GRE Subject Test. Electronic applications accepted.

University of California, Santa Barbara, Graduate Division, College of Letters and Sciences, Division of Mathematics, Life, and Physical Sciences, Department of Mathematics, Santa Barbara, CA 93106-3080. Offers applied mathematics (MA), including computational science and engineering; mathematics (MA, PhD), including computational science and engineering; MA/PhD. *Faculty:* 29 full-time (3 women). *Students:* 50 full-time (11 women); includes 2 Black or African American, non-Hispanic/Latino; 6 Asian, non-Hispanic/Latino; 6 Hispanic/Latino. Average age 26. 151 applicants, 21% accepted, 9 enrolled. In 2010, 7 master's, 10 doctorates awarded. Terminal master's awarded for partial completion of doctoral program. *Degree requirements:* For master's, comprehensive exam (for some programs), thesis (for some programs); for doctorate, comprehensive exam, thesis/dissertation. *Entrance requirements:* For master's and doctorate, GRE General Test, GRE Subject Test (math). Additional exam requirements/recommendations for international students: Required—TOEFL (minimum score 575 paper-based; 80 iBT), IELTS (minimum score 7). *Application deadline:* For fall admission, 1/1 priority date for domestic and international students. Application fee: $70 ($90 for international students). Electronic applications accepted. *Financial support:* In 2010–11, 50 students received support, including 15 fellowships with full tuition reimbursements available (averaging $11,684 per year), 11 research assistantships with full tuition reimbursements available (averaging $7,984 per year), 42 teaching assistantships with partial tuition reimbursements available (averaging $16,637 per year); Federal Work-Study, institutionally sponsored loans, health care benefits, and tuition waivers (full and partial) also available. Financial award application deadline: 3/2; financial award applicants required to submit FAFSA. *Faculty research:* Topology, differential geometry, algebra, applied mathematics, partial differential equations. Total annual research expenditures: $205,000. *Unit head:* Prof. Martin Scharlemann, Chair, 805-893-8340, Fax: 805-893-2385, E-mail: mgscharl@math.ucsb.edu. *Application contact:* Medina Price, Graduate Advisor, 805-893-8192, Fax: 805-893-2385, E-mail: price@math.ucsb.edu.

University of California, Santa Cruz, Division of Graduate Studies, Jack Baskin School of Engineering, Program in Statistics and Applied Mathematics, Santa Cruz, CA 95064. Offers MS, PhD. *Students:* 38 full-time (22 women), 7 part-time (0 women); includes 8 minority (2 Asian, non-Hispanic/Latino; 6 Hispanic/Latino), 11 international. Average age 30. 64 applicants, 44% accepted, 12 enrolled. In 2010, 2 doctorates awarded. Terminal master's awarded for partial completion of doctoral program. *Degree requirements:* For master's, seminar, qualifying exam, capstone project; for doctorate, thesis/dissertation, seminar, qualifying exam. *Entrance requirements:* For master's and doctorate, GRE General Test; GRE Subject Test in math (recommended). Additional exam requirements/recommendations for international students: Required—TOEFL (minimum score 570 paper-based; 230 computer-based; 89 iBT); Recommended—IELTS (minimum score 8). *Application deadline:* For fall admission, 1/3 for domestic and international students. Application fee: $70 ($90 for international students). Electronic applications accepted. *Financial support:* Fellowships, research assistantships, teaching assistantships, institutionally sponsored loans and tuition waivers available. Financial award applicants required to submit FAFSA. *Faculty research:* Bayesian nonparametric methods; computationally intensive Bayesian inference, prediction, and decision-making; envirometrics; fluid mechanics; mathematical biology. *Unit head:* Tracie Tucker, Graduate Program Coordinator, 831-459-5737, E-mail: ttucker@soe.ucsc.edu. *Application contact:* Tracie Tucker, Graduate Program Coordinator, 831-459-5737, E-mail: ttucker@soe.ucsc.edu.

University of Central Arkansas, Graduate School, College of Natural Sciences and Math, Department of Mathematics, Conway, AR 72035-0001. Offers applied mathematics (MS); math education (MA). Part-time programs available. *Faculty:* 16 full-time (4 women). *Students:* 10 full-time (4 women), 3 part-time (2 women); includes 1 minority (Asian, non-Hispanic/Latino), 3 international. Average age 29. 8 applicants, 100% accepted, 4 enrolled. In 2010, 7 master's awarded. *Degree requirements:* For master's, comprehensive exam, thesis optional. *Entrance requirements:* For master's, GRE General Test, minimum GPA of 2.7. Additional exam requirements/recommendations for international students: Required—TOEFL (minimum score 550 paper-based; 213 computer-based). *Application deadline:* For fall admission, 3/1 priority date for domestic students; for spring admission, 10/1 priority date for domestic students. Applications are processed on a rolling basis. Application fee: $25 ($50 for international students). *Financial support:* In 2010–11, 11 teaching assistantships with partial tuition reimbursements (averaging $8,500 per year) were awarded; Federal Work-Study, scholarships/grants, and unspecified assistantships also available. Financial award application deadline: 2/15; financial award applicants required to submit FAFSA. *Unit head:* Dr. Ramesh Garimella, Chair, 501-450-3147, Fax: 501-450-5662, E-mail: rameshg@uca.edu. *Application contact:* Susan Wood, Admissions Assistant, 501-450-3124, Fax: 501-450-5678, E-mail: swood@uca.edu.

University of Central Florida, College of Sciences, Department of Mathematics, Orlando, FL 32816. Offers applied mathematics (Certificate); mathematical science (MS); mathematics (PhD). Part-time and evening/weekend programs available. *Faculty:* 46 full-time (10 women), 8 part-time/adjunct (0 women). *Students:* 45 full-time (15 women), 22 part-time (10 women); includes 6 Black or African American, non-Hispanic/Latino; 3 Asian, non-Hispanic/Latino; 5 Hispanic/Latino, 13 International. Average age 32. 77 applicants, 71% accepted, 24 enrolled. In 2010, 3 master's, 2 doctorates awarded. *Degree requirements:* For master's, thesis or alternative; for doctorate, thesis/dissertation, candidacy exam. *Entrance requirements:* For master's, GRE General Test, minimum GPA of 3.0 in last 60 hours; for doctorate, GRE Subject Test, minimum GPA of 3.0 in last 60 hours or master's qualifying exam. Additional exam requirements/recommendations for international students: Required—TOEFL. *Application deadline:* For fall admission, 7/15 for domestic students; for spring admission, 12/1 for domestic students. Application fee: $30. Electronic applications accepted. *Expenses:* Tuition, state resident: part-time $256.56 per credit hour. Tuition, nonresident: part-time $1011.52 per credit hour. Part-time tuition and fees vary according to program. *Financial support:* In 2010–11, 36 students received support, including 7 fellowships with partial tuition reimbursements available (averaging $8,200 per year), 4 research assistantships with partial tuition reimbursements available (averaging $4,400 per year), 38 teaching assistantships with partial tuition reimbursements available (averaging $12,400 per year); career-related internships or fieldwork, Federal Work-Study, institutionally sponsored loans, tuition waivers (partial), and unspecified assistantships also available. Financial award application deadline: 3/1; financial award applicants required to submit FAFSA. *Faculty research:* Applied mathematics, analysis, approximation theory, graph theory, mathematical statistics. *Unit head:* Dr. Piotr Mikusinski, Chair, 407-823-0445, Fax: 407-823-6253, E-mail: piotrm@mail.ucf.edu. *Application contact:* Dr. Piotr Mikusinski, Chair, 407-823-0445, Fax: 407-823-6253, E-mail: piotrm@mail.ucf.edu.

University of Central Missouri, The Graduate School, College of Science and Technology, Warrensburg, MO 64093. Offers applied mathematics (MS); aviation safety (MS); biology (MS); computer science (MS); environmental studies (MA); industrial management (MS); mathematics (MS); technology (MS); technology management (PhD). PhD is offered jointly with Indiana State University. Part-time programs available. Postbaccalaureate distance learning degree programs offered. *Entrance requirements:* Additional exam requirements/recommendations for international students: Required—TOEFL (minimum score 550 paper-based; 79 computer-based). Electronic applications accepted.

University of Central Oklahoma, College of Graduate Studies and Research, College of Mathematics and Science, Department of Mathematics and Statistics, Edmond, OK 73034-5209. Offers applied mathematical sciences (MS), including computer science, mathematics, mathematics/computer science teaching, statistics. Part-time programs available. *Degree requirements:* For master's, thesis. *Entrance requirements:* Additional exam requirements/recommendations for international students: Required—TOEFL (minimum score 550 paper-based; 213 computer-based). Electronic applications accepted. *Faculty research:* Curvature, FAA, math education.

University of Chicago, Division of the Physical Sciences, Department of Mathematics, Program in Applied Mathematics, Chicago, IL 60637-1513. Offers SM, PhD. *Degree requirements:* For master's, one foreign language, oral exams; for doctorate, one foreign language, thesis/dissertation, 2 qualifying exams. *Entrance requirements:* For master's and doctorate, GRE General Test, GRE Subject Test. Additional exam requirements/recommendations for international students: Required—TOEFL (minimum score 600 paper-based; 250 computer-based). *Application deadline:* For fall admission, 1/5 for domestic students. Application fee: $55. Electronic applications accepted. *Financial support:* Fellowships, research assistantships, teaching assistantships available. Financial award application deadline: 1/5. *Faculty research:* Applied analysis, dynamical systems, theoretical biology, math-physics. *Application contact:* Laurie Wail, Graduate Studies Assistant, 773-702-7358, Fax: 773-702-9787, E-mail: lwail@math.uchicago.edu.

University of Cincinnati, Graduate School, McMicken College of Arts and Sciences, Department of Mathematical Sciences, Cincinnati, OH 45221. Offers applied mathematics (MS, PhD); mathematics education (MAT); pure mathematics (MS, PhD); statistics (MS, PhD). Part-time programs available. Terminal master's awarded for partial completion of doctoral program. *Degree requirements:* For master's, comprehensive exam, thesis or alternative; for doctorate,

Applied Mathematics

University of Cincinnati (continued)
one foreign language, comprehensive exam, thesis/dissertation. *Entrance requirements:* For master's, GRE, teacher certification (MAT); for doctorate, GRE. Additional exam requirements/recommendations for international students: Required—TOEFL. Electronic applications accepted. *Faculty research:* Algebra, analysis, differential equations, numerical analysis, statistics.

University of Colorado at Colorado Springs, College of Letters, Arts and Sciences, Department of Mathematics, Colorado Springs, CO 80933-7150. Offers applied mathematics (MS); applied science (PhD); mathematics (M Sc). Part-time and evening/weekend programs available. *Faculty:* 11 full-time (1 woman), 1 (woman) part-time/adjunct. *Students:* 10 full-time (3 women), 10 part-time (6 women), 2 international. Average age 34. 9 applicants, 78% accepted, 6 enrolled. In 2010, 2 master's awarded. *Degree requirements:* For master's, thesis, qualifying exam. *Entrance requirements:* For master's, GRE General Test, minimum GPA of 3.0. Additional exam requirements/recommendations for international students: Required—TOEFL. *Application deadline:* For fall admission, 6/15 for domestic students. Applications are processed on a rolling basis. Application fee: $60 ($75 for international students). *Expenses:* Tuition, state resident: full-time $7916. Tuition, nonresident: full-time $16,610. Tuition and fees vary according to course load, degree level, program, reciprocity agreements and student level. *Financial support:* Teaching assistantships, Federal Work-Study and scholarships/grants available. Support available to part-time students. Financial award application deadline: 3/1; financial award applicants required to submit FAFSA. *Faculty research:* Abelian groups and noncommutative rings, hormone analysis and computer vision, probability and mathematical physics, stochastic dynamics, probability models. *Unit head:* Dr. Sarbarish Chakravarty, Chair, 719-255-3549, Fax: 719-255-3605, E-mail: schakrav@uccs.edu. *Application contact:* Elizabeth Buzo, Graduate Liaison, 719-255-3554, Fax: 719-255-3605, E-mail: ebuzo@uccs.edu.

University of Colorado Boulder, Graduate School, College of Arts and Sciences, Department of Applied Mathematics, Boulder, CO 80309. Offers MS, PhD. Part-time programs available. *Faculty:* 16 full-time (2 women). *Students:* 70 full-time (13 women), 6 part-time (0 women); includes 10 minority (1 Black or African American, non-Hispanic/Latino; 5 Asian, non-Hispanic/Latino; 4 Hispanic/Latino), 10 international. Average age 27. 106 applicants, 16 enrolled. In 2010, 25 master's, 7 doctorates awarded. Terminal master's awarded for partial completion of doctoral program. *Degree requirements:* For master's, comprehensive exam, thesis or alternative; for doctorate, one foreign language, comprehensive exam, thesis/dissertation. *Entrance requirements:* For master's, GRE General Test, minimum undergraduate GPA of 2.75; for doctorate, GRE General Test. Additional exam requirements/recommendations for international students: Required—TOEFL. *Application deadline:* For fall admission, 2/1 priority date for domestic students, 12/1 for international students. Applications are processed on a rolling basis. Application fee: $50 ($60 for international students). *Financial support:* In 2010–11, 24 fellowships (averaging $7,649 per year), 25 research assistantships (averaging $14,920 per year) were awarded; scholarships/grants and traineeships also available. Support available to part-time students. *Faculty research:* Non-linear phenomena, computational mathematics, physical applied mathematics, statistics. Total annual research expenditures: $2.8 million.

University of Colorado Denver, College of Liberal Arts and Sciences, Department of Mathematical and Statistical Sciences, Denver, CO 80217. Offers applied mathematics (MS, PhD). Part-time programs available. *Faculty:* 26 full-time (4 women), 2 part-time/adjunct (1 woman). *Students:* 29 full-time (8 women), 23 part-time (11 women); includes 3 Asian, non-Hispanic/Latino, 10 international. Average age 33. 61 applicants, 56% accepted, 12 enrolled. In 2010, 9 master's, 4 doctorates awarded. *Degree requirements:* For master's, comprehensive exam, thesis optional, 30 hours of course work with minimum GPA of 3.0; for doctorate, comprehensive exam, thesis/dissertation. *Entrance requirements:* For master's and doctorate, GRE General Test; GRE Subject Test in math (recommended), 30 hours of course work in mathematics (24 of which must be upper-division mathematics), minimum GPA of 3.0. Additional exam requirements/recommendations for international students: Required—TOEFL (minimum score 525 paper-based; 192 computer-based; 71 iBT). *Application deadline:* For fall admission, 4/1 for domestic students; for spring admission, 11/1 for domestic students. Applications are processed on a rolling basis. Application fee: $50 ($75 for international students). Electronic applications accepted. *Expenses:* Tuition, state resident: full-time $7332; part-time $355 per credit hour. Tuition, nonresident: full-time $18,990; part-time $1055 per credit hour. Required fees: $998. Tuition and fees vary according to course level, course load, degree level, campus/location, program, reciprocity agreements and student level. *Financial support:* Fellowships with partial tuition reimbursements, research assistantships with full tuition reimbursements, teaching assistantships with full tuition reimbursements, Federal Work-Study, scholarships/grants, and unspecified assistantships available. Financial award application deadline: 4/1; financial award applicants required to submit FAFSA. *Faculty research:* Computational mathematics, computational biology, discrete mathematics and geometry probability and statistics, optimization. *Unit head:* Dr. Stephanie Santorico, Graduate Program Director, 303-556-2547, E-mail: stephanie.santorico@ucdenver.edu. *Application contact:* Lindsay Hiatt, Graduate Program Assistant, 303-556-2341, E-mail: lindsay.hiatt@ucdenver.edu.

University of Connecticut, Graduate School, College of Liberal Arts and Sciences, Department of Mathematics, Field of Applied Financial Mathematics, Storrs, CT 06269. Offers MS. *Degree requirements:* For master's, comprehensive exam. *Entrance requirements:* Additional exam requirements/recommendations for international students: Required—TOEFL (minimum score 550 paper-based; 213 computer-based). Electronic applications accepted.

University of Dayton, Graduate School, College of Arts and Sciences, Department of Mathematics, Dayton, OH 45469-1300. Offers applied mathematics (MAS); financial mathematics (MFM); mathematics education (MME). Part-time and evening/weekend programs available. *Faculty:* 15 full-time (5 women). *Students:* 17 full-time (10 women), 8 part-time (1 woman); includes 2 minority (1 Black or African American, non-Hispanic/Latino; 1 Two or more races, non-Hispanic/Latino), 13 international. Average age 27. 42 applicants, 88% accepted, 11 enrolled. In 2010, 8 master's awarded. *Entrance requirements:* For master's, minimum undergraduate GPA of 2.8 (MAS), 3.0 (MFM, MME). Additional exam requirements/recommendations for international students: Required—TOEFL (minimum score 550 paper-based; 213 computer-based; 80 iBT). *Application deadline:* For fall admission, 3/1 priority date for domestic students, 7/1 priority date for international students; for winter admission, 7/1 priority date for international students; for spring admission, 1/1 priority date for international students. Application fee: $0 ($50 for international students). Electronic applications accepted. *Expenses:* Tuition: Full-time $7800; part-time $650 per credit hour. *Financial support:* In 2010–11, 6 teaching assistantships with full tuition reimbursements (averaging $13,400 per year) were awarded; institutionally sponsored loans, health care benefits, and unspecified assistantships also available. Financial award applicants required to submit FAFSA. *Faculty research:* Differential equations, integral equations, general topology, measure theory, graph theory, financial math, math education, numerical analysis. *Unit head:* Dr. Joe D. Mashburn, Chair, 937-229-2511, Fax: 937-229-2566, E-mail: joe.mashburn@notes.udayton.edu. *Application contact:* Alexander Popovski, Associate Director of Graduate and International Admissions, 937-229-2357, Fax: 937-229-4729, E-mail: alex.popovski@notes.udayton.edu.

University of Delaware, College of Arts and Sciences, Department of Mathematical Sciences, Newark, DE 19716. Offers applied mathematics (MS, PhD); mathematics (MS, PhD). Part-time programs available. Terminal master's awarded for partial completion of doctoral program. *Degree requirements:* For master's, thesis (for some programs); for doctorate, one foreign language, thesis/dissertation, qualifying exam. *Entrance requirements:* For master's and doctorate, GRE General Test. Additional exam requirements/recommendations for international students: Required—TOEFL. Electronic applications accepted. *Faculty research:* Scattering theory, inverse problems, fluid dynamics, numerical analysis, combinatorics.

University of Georgia, College of Arts and Sciences, Department of Mathematics, Athens, GA 30602. Offers applied mathematical science (MAMS); mathematics (MA, PhD). *Faculty:* 31 full-time (4 women). *Students:* 48 full-time (14 women); includes 1 Black or African American, non-Hispanic/Latino; 1 Asian, non-Hispanic/Latino; 2 Hispanic/Latino, 12 international. 117 applicants, 14% accepted, 7 enrolled. In 2010, 4 master's, 3 doctorates awarded. *Degree requirements:* For master's, one foreign language, thesis (for some programs); for doctorate, 2 foreign languages, thesis/dissertation. *Entrance requirements:* For master's and doctorate, GRE General Test. *Application deadline:* For fall admission, 7/1 priority date for domestic students; for spring admission, 11/15 for domestic students. Application fee: $50. Electronic applications accepted. *Expenses:* Tuition, state resident: full-time $7200; part-time $344 per credit hour. Tuition, nonresident: full-time $21,900; part-time $944 per credit hour. Tuition and fees vary according to course load and program. *Financial support:* Fellowships, research assistantships, teaching assistantships, unspecified assistantships available. *Unit head:* Dr. Malcolm Adams, Head, 706-542-2564, E-mail: fu@math.uga.edu. *Application contact:* Dr. Brian D. Boe, Graduate Coordinator, 706-542-2547, Fax: 706-542-2573, E-mail: grad@math.uga.edu.

University of Guelph, Graduate Studies, College of Physical and Engineering Science, Department of Mathematics and Statistics, Guelph, ON N1G 2W1, Canada. Offers applied mathematics (PhD); applied statistics (PhD); mathematics and statistics (M Sc). Part-time programs available. *Degree requirements:* For master's, thesis (for some programs); for doctorate, thesis/dissertation. *Entrance requirements:* For master's, minimum B- average during previous 2 years of course work; for doctorate, minimum B average. Additional exam requirements/recommendations for international students: Required—TOEFL (minimum score 550 paper-based; 213 computer-based; 89 iBT), IELTS (minimum score 6.5). *Faculty research:* Dynamical systems, mathematical biology, numerical analysis, linear and nonlinear models, reliability and bioassay.

University of Houston, College of Natural Sciences and Mathematics, Department of Mathematics, Houston, TX 77204. Offers applied mathematics (MS); mathematics (MA, PhD). Part-time programs available. *Faculty:* 29 full-time (2 women), 1 (woman) part-time/adjunct. *Students:* 87 full-time (37 women), 41 part-time (21 women); includes 3 Black or African American, non-Hispanic/Latino; 12 Asian, non-Hispanic/Latino; 9 Hispanic/Latino; 1 Two or more races, non-Hispanic/Latino, 55 international. Average age 31. 42 applicants, 83% accepted, 18 enrolled. In 2010, 23 master's, 12 doctorates awarded. *Degree requirements:* For master's, thesis optional. *Entrance requirements:* For master's and doctorate, GRE V-Q . Additional exam requirements/recommendations for international students: Required—TOEFL (minimum score 550 paper-based; 79 iBT), IELTS (minimum score 6.5). *Application deadline:* For fall admission, 7/3 for domestic students, 5/1 for international students; for spring admission, 12/4 for domestic students, 10/1 for international students. Applications are processed on a rolling basis. Application fee: $0 ($75 for international students). Electronic applications accepted. *Expenses:* Tuition, state resident: full-time $8592; part-time $358 per credit hour. Tuition, nonresident: full-time $16,032; part-time $668 per credit hour. Required fees: $2889. Tuition and fees vary according to course load and program. *Financial support:* In 2010–11, 14 research assistantships with partial tuition reimbursements (averaging $8,720 per year), 23 teaching assistantships with partial tuition reimbursements (averaging $13,184 per year) were awarded; career-related internships or fieldwork, Federal Work-Study, institutionally sponsored loans, scholarships/grants, health care benefits, and unspecified assistantships also available. Support available to part-time students. Financial award application deadline: 2/1. *Faculty research:* Applied mathematics, modern analysis, computational science, geometry, dynamical systems. *Unit head:* Dr. Jeffery E. Morgan, Chairperson, 713-743-3500, Fax: 713-743-3505, E-mail: jmorgan@math.uh.edu. *Application contact:* Dr. Jeffery E. Morgan, Chairperson, 713-743-3500, Fax: 713-743-3505, E-mail: jmorgan@math.uh.edu.

University of Illinois at Chicago, Graduate College, College of Liberal Arts and Sciences, Department of Mathematics, Statistics, and Computer Science, Chicago, IL 60607-7128. Offers applied mathematics (MS, PhD); computational finance (MS, PhD); computer science (MS, PhD); mathematics (DA); mathematics and information sciences for industry (MS); probability and statistics (PhD); pure mathematics (MS, PhD); statistics (MS); teaching of mathematics (MST), including elementary, secondary. Part-time programs available. *Faculty:* 36 full-time (3 women). *Students:* 150 full-time (54 women), 31 part-time (18 women); includes 3 Black or African American, non-Hispanic/Latino; 1 Asian, non-Hispanic/Latino; 8 Hispanic/Latino, 62 international. Average age 26. 224 applicants, 56% accepted, 43 enrolled. In 2010, 34 master's, 17 doctorates awarded. *Degree requirements:* For master's, comprehensive exam; for doctorate, one foreign language, thesis/dissertation. *Entrance requirements:* For master's and doctorate, GRE General Test, minimum GPA of 3.0. Additional exam requirements/recommendations for international students: Required—TOEFL (minimum score 100 iBT). *Application deadline:* For fall admission, 1/1 for domestic and international students; for spring admission, 10/1 for domestic students, 7/15 for international students. Applications are processed on a rolling basis. Application fee: $60. Electronic applications accepted. *Financial support:* In 2010–11, 109 students received support, including 2 fellowships with full tuition reimbursements available (averaging $20,000 per year), 8 research assistantships with full tuition reimbursements available (averaging $17,000 per year), 87 teaching assistantships with full tuition reimbursements available (averaging $17,000 per year); Federal Work-Study, scholarships/grants, and tuition waivers (full) also available. Financial award application deadline: 1/1. *Unit head:* Lawrence Ein, Head, 312-996-3044, E-mail: ein@math.uic.edu. *Application contact:* Brooke Shipley, Director of Graduate Studies, 312-996-5119, E-mail: dgs@math.uic.edu.

University of Illinois at Urbana–Champaign, Graduate College, College of Liberal Arts and Sciences, Department of Mathematics, Champaign, IL 61820. Offers applied mathematics (MS); applied mathematics: actuarial science (MS); mathematics (MA, MS, PhD); teaching of mathematics (MS). *Faculty:* 65 full-time (5 women), 4 part-time/adjunct (0 women). *Students:* 159 full-time (45 women), 35 part-time (10 women); includes 13 minority (7 Asian, non-Hispanic/Latino; 4 Hispanic/Latino; 2 Two or more races, non-Hispanic/Latino), 105 international. 454 applicants, 22% accepted, 50 enrolled. In 2010, 48 master's, 19 doctorates awarded. *Entrance requirements:* For master's, GRE General Test, GRE Subject Test (mathematics), minimum GPA of 3.0; for doctorate, GRE General Test, GRE Subject Test (math), minimum GPA of 3.0. Additional exam requirements/recommendations for international students: Required—TOEFL (minimum score 550 paper-based; 213 computer-based). *Application deadline:* Applications are processed on a rolling basis. Application fee: $75 ($90 for international students). Electronic applications accepted. *Financial support:* In 2010–11, 26 fellowships, 40 research assistantships, 146 teaching assistantships were awarded; tuition waivers (full and partial) also available. *Unit head:* Sheldon Katz, Chair, 217-265-6258, Fax: 217-333-9576, E-mail: katzs@illinois.edu. *Application contact:* Marci Blocher, Office Support Specialist, 217-333-3350, Fax: 217-333-9576, E-mail: mblocher@illinois.edu.

The University of Iowa, Graduate College, Program in Applied Mathematical and Computational Sciences, Iowa City, IA 52242-1316. Offers PhD. *Degree requirements:* For doctorate, comprehensive exam, thesis/dissertation. *Entrance requirements:* For doctorate, GRE General Test, minimum GPA of 3.0. Additional exam requirements/recommendations for international students: Required—TOEFL (minimum score 620 paper-based; 260 computer-based; 105 iBT). Electronic applications accepted.

University of Kentucky, Graduate School, College of Arts and Sciences, Program in Mathematics, Lexington, KY 40506-0032. Offers applied mathematics (MS); mathematics (MA, MS, PhD). *Degree requirements:* For master's, comprehensive exam, thesis optional; for doctorate, one foreign language, comprehensive exam, thesis/dissertation. *Entrance requirements:* For master's, GRE General Test, minimum undergraduate GPA of 2.75; for doctorate, GRE General Test, minimum graduate GPA of 3.0. Additional exam requirements/recommendations

234 www.facebook.com/petersonspublishing

Peterson's Graduate Programs in the Physical Sciences, Mathematics, Agricultural Sciences, the Environment & Natural Resources 2012

for international students: Required—TOEFL (minimum score 550 paper-based; 213 computer-based). Electronic applications accepted. *Faculty research:* Numerical analysis, combinatorics, partial differential equations, algebra and number theory, real and complex analysis.

University of Louisville, Graduate School, College of Arts and Sciences, Department of Mathematics, Louisville, KY 40292. Offers applied and industrial mathematics (PhD); mathematics (MA). Part-time programs available. *Faculty:* 30 full-time (8 women), 3 part-time/adjunct (1 woman). *Students:* 34 full-time (13 women), 6 part-time (2 women); includes 2 Black or African American, non-Hispanic/Latino; 1 Hispanic/Latino, 9 international. Average age 29. 31 applicants, 77% accepted, 10 enrolled. In 2010, 3 master's, 1 doctorate awarded. Terminal master's awarded for partial completion of doctoral program. *Degree requirements:* For master's, comprehensive exam (for some programs), thesis optional; for doctorate, comprehensive exam, thesis/dissertation, internship, project. *Entrance requirements:* For master's and doctorate, GRE General Test. Additional exam requirements/recommendations for international students: Required—TOEFL (minimum score 550 paper-based; 215 computer-based; 79 iBT). *Application deadline:* For fall admission, 3/15 priority date for domestic and international students; for winter admission, 8/15 priority date for domestic and international students. Applications are processed on a rolling basis. Application fee: $50. Electronic applications accepted. *Expenses:* Tuition, state resident: full-time $9144; part-time $508 per credit hour. Tuition, nonresident: full-time $19,026; part-time $1057 per credit hour. Tuition and fees vary according to program and reciprocity agreements. *Financial support:* In 2010–11, 25 students received support, including 2 fellowships with full tuition reimbursements available (averaging $20,000 per year), 1 research assistantship (averaging $20,000 per year), 25 teaching assistantships with full tuition reimbursements available (averaging $20,000 per year); health care benefits and unspecified assistantships also available. Financial award application deadline: 3/15. *Faculty research:* Algebra, analysis, bio-mathematics, combinatorics and graph theory, coding theory, consesus theory, financial mathematics, functional equations, partial differential equations. Total annual research expenditures: $77,000. *Unit head:* Dr. Thomas Riedel, Chair, 502-852-6826, Fax: 502-852-7132, E-mail: thomas.riedel@louisville.edu. *Application contact:* Dr. Bingtuan Li, Graduate Studies Director, 502-852-6826, Fax: 502-852-7132, E-mail: bing.li@louisville.edu.

The University of Manchester, School of Mathematics, Manchester, United Kingdom. Offers actuarial science (PhD); applied mathematics (M Phil, PhD); applied numerical computing (M Phil, PhD); financial mathematics (M Phil, PhD); mathematical logic (M Phil); probability (M Phil, PhD); pure mathematics (M Phil, PhD); statistics (M Phil, PhD).

University of Maryland, Baltimore County, Graduate School, College of Natural and Mathematical Sciences, Department of Mathematics and Statistics, Program in Applied Mathematics, Baltimore, MD 21250. Offers MS, PhD. Part-time and evening/weekend programs available. *Faculty:* 23 full-time (4 women). *Students:* 18 full-time (7 women), 7 part-time (2 women); includes 3 minority (1 Black or African American, non-Hispanic/Latino; 1 Asian, non-Hispanic/Latino; 1 Two or more races, non-Hispanic/Latino), 7 international. Average age 28. 26 applicants, 65% accepted, 7 enrolled. In 2010, 3 master's, 3 doctorates awarded. Terminal master's awarded for partial completion of doctoral program. *Degree requirements:* For master's, comprehensive exam (for some programs), thesis (for some programs); for doctorate, comprehensive exam, thesis/dissertation. *Entrance requirements:* For master's and doctorate, GRE General Test, minimum GPA of 3.0. Additional exam requirements/recommendations for international students: Required—TOEFL (minimum score 600 paper-based; 250 computer-based; 100 iBT). *Application deadline:* For fall admission, 2/15 priority date for domestic students, 1/1 priority date for international students; for spring admission, 10/15 priority date for domestic students, 5/1 priority date for international students. Applications are processed on a rolling basis. Application fee: $50. Electronic applications accepted. *Financial support:* In 2010–11, 15 students received support, including 3 research assistantships with full tuition reimbursements available (averaging $15,500 per year), 12 teaching assistantships with full tuition reimbursements available (averaging $15,500 per year); fellowships with full tuition reimbursements available, career-related internships or fieldwork, scholarships/grants, health care benefits, tuition waivers (full and partial), and unspecified assistantships also available. Support available to part-time students. Financial award application deadline: 2/15. *Faculty research:* Numerical analysis and scientific computation, optimization theory and algorithms, differential equations and mathematical modeling, mathematical biology and bioinformatics. Total annual research expenditures: $552,206. *Unit head:* Dr. Kathleen Hoffman, Director, 410-455-2434, Fax: 410-455-1066, E-mail: khoffman@math.umbc.edu. *Application contact:* Dr. Kathleen Hoffman, Director, 410-455-2434, Fax: 410-455-1066, E-mail: khoffman@math.umbc.edu.

University of Maryland, College Park, Academic Affairs, College of Computer, Mathematical and Natural Sciences, Department of Mathematics, Applied Mathematics Program, College Park, MD 20742. Offers MS, PhD. Part-time and evening/weekend programs available. *Students:* 82 full-time (29 women), 14 part-time (2 women); includes 16 minority (4 Black or African American, non-Hispanic/Latino; 1 American Indian or Alaska Native, non-Hispanic/Latino; 7 Asian, non-Hispanic/Latino; 2 Hispanic/Latino; 2 Two or more races, non-Hispanic/Latino), 34 international. 282 applicants, 12% accepted, 20 enrolled. In 2010, 13 master's, 15 doctorates awarded. Terminal master's awarded for partial completion of doctoral program. *Degree requirements:* For master's, thesis optional, seminar, scholarly paper; for doctorate, comprehensive exam, thesis/dissertation, exams, seminars. *Entrance requirements:* For master's and doctorate, GRE General Test, GRE Subject Test, minimum GPA of 3.0, 3 letters of recommendation. *Application deadline:* For fall admission, 1/10 for domestic and international students; for spring admission, 9/15 for domestic students, 6/1 for international students. Applications are processed on a rolling basis. Application fee: $75. Electronic applications accepted. *Expenses:* Tuition, area resident: Part-time $471 per credit hour. Tuition, state resident: part-time $471 per credit hour. Tuition, nonresident: part-time $1016 per credit hour. Required fees: $337 per term. *Financial support:* In 2010–11, 6 fellowships with full and partial tuition reimbursements (averaging $14,500 per year), 23 research assistantships (averaging $19,767 per year), 44 teaching assistantships (averaging $17,308 per year) were awarded. Financial award applicants required to submit FAFSA. *Unit head:* Konstantina Travisa, Director, 301-405-4489, Fax: 301-314-8027, E-mail: trivisa@umd.edu. *Application contact:* Dr. Charles A. Caramello, Dean of Graduate School, 301-405-0358, Fax: 301-314-9305, E-mail: ccaramel@umd.edu.

University of Massachusetts Amherst, Graduate School, College of Natural Sciences, Department of Mathematics and Statistics, Program in Applied Mathematics, Amherst, MA 01003. Offers MS. *Students:* 8 full-time (2 women), 3 international. Average age 28. 34 applicants, 24% accepted, 5 enrolled. In 2010, 4 master's awarded. *Entrance requirements:* Additional exam requirements/recommendations for international students: Required—TOEFL (minimum score 550 paper-based; 213 computer-based; 80 iBT), IELTS (minimum score 6.5). *Application deadline:* For fall admission, 2/1 for domestic and international students. Applications are processed on a rolling basis. Application fee: $50 ($65 for international students). Electronic applications accepted. *Expenses:* Tuition, state resident: full-time $2640. Required fees: $8282. One-time fee: $357 full-time. *Financial support:* Fellowships, research assistantships, teaching assistantships, career-related internships or fieldwork, Federal Work-Study, scholarships/grants, traineeships, health care benefits, tuition waivers (full), and unspecified assistantships available. Support available to part-time students. Financial award application deadline: 2/1; financial award applicants required to submit FAFSA. *Unit head:* Dr. Siman Wong, Graduate Program Director, 413-545-2282, Fax: 413-545-1801. *Application contact:* Jean M. Ames, Chair, Admissions Committee, 413-545-0722, Fax: 413-577-0010, E-mail: gradadm@grad.umass.edu.

University of Massachusetts Lowell, College of Arts and Sciences, Department of Mathematical Sciences, Lowell, MA 01854-2881. Offers applied mathematics (MS); computational mathematics (PhD); mathematics (MS). Part-time programs available. *Entrance requirements:* For master's, GRE General Test.

University of Memphis, Graduate School, College of Arts and Sciences, Department of Mathematical Sciences, Memphis, TN 38152. Offers applied mathematics (MS); applied statistics (PhD); bioinformatics (MS); computer science (PhD); computer sciences (MS); mathematics (MS, PhD); statistics (MS, PhD). Part-time programs available. *Faculty:* 19 full-time (4 women), 3 part-time/adjunct (0 women). *Students:* 38 full-time (12 women), 21 part-time (12 women); includes 8 minority (5 Black or African American, non-Hispanic/Latino; 2 Asian, non-Hispanic/Latino; 1 Hispanic/Latino), 25 international. Average age 34. 49 applicants, 55% accepted, 9 enrolled. In 2010, 6 master's, 5 doctorates awarded. Terminal master's awarded for partial completion of doctoral program. *Degree requirements:* For master's, comprehensive exam; for doctorate, one foreign language, thesis/dissertation, oral exams. *Entrance requirements:* For master's and doctorate, GRE General Test, minimum GPA of 2.5. Additional exam requirements/recommendations for international students: Required—TOEFL (minimum score 550 paper-based; 210 computer-based). *Application deadline:* For fall admission, 8/1 for domestic students, 5/1 priority date for international students; for spring admission, 12/1 for domestic students, 9/1 priority date for international students. Applications are processed on a rolling basis. Application fee: $35 ($60 for international students). Electronic applications accepted. *Financial support:* In 2010–11, 22 students received support; fellowships with full tuition reimbursements available, research assistantships with full tuition reimbursements available, teaching assistantships with full tuition reimbursements available, career-related internships or fieldwork, Federal Work-Study, scholarships/grants, and unspecified assistantships available. Financial award application deadline: 2/15; financial award applicants required to submit FAFSA. *Faculty research:* Combinatorics, ergodic theory, graph theory, Ramsey theory, applied statistics. *Unit head:* Dr. James E. Jamison, Chairman, 901-678-2482, Fax: 901-678-2480, E-mail: jjamison@memphis.edu. *Application contact:* Dr. Anna Kaminska, Coordinator of Graduate Studies, 901-678-2494, Fax: 901-678-2480.

University of Michigan–Dearborn, College of Arts, Sciences, and Letters, Master of Science in Applied and Computational Mathematics Program, Dearborn, MI 48128. Offers MS. Part-time and evening/weekend programs available. *Faculty:* 8 full-time (2 women). *Students:* 2 full-time (1 woman), 18 part-time (8 women); includes 2 Black or African American, non-Hispanic/Latino; 2 Asian, non-Hispanic/Latino. Average age 40. 2 applicants, 50% accepted, 1 enrolled. In 2010, 2 master's awarded. *Degree requirements:* For master's, thesis or alternative, project. *Entrance requirements:* For master's, 3 letters of recommendation, minimum GPA of 3.0, 2 years course work in math. Additional exam requirements/recommendations for international students: Required—TOEFL (minimum score 560 paper-based; 220 computer-based). *Application deadline:* For fall admission, 8/1 priority date for domestic students, 4/1 for international students; for winter admission, 12/1 priority date for domestic students, 11/1 for international students; for spring admission, 4/1 for domestic students, 3/1 for international students. Applications are processed on a rolling basis. Application fee: $60 ($75 for international students). Electronic applications accepted. *Financial support:* Federal Work-Study and scholarships/grants available. Support available to part-time students. Financial award application deadline: 4/1; financial award applicants required to submit FAFSA. *Faculty research:* Partial differential equations, statistics, discrete optimization, approximation theory, stochastic processes. *Unit head:* Dr. Joan Remski, Director, 313-593-4994, E-mail: remski@umd.umich.edu. *Application contact:* Carol Ligienza, Coordinator, CASL Graduate Programs, 313-593-1183, Fax: 313-583-6700, E-mail: caslgrad@umd.umich.edu.

University of Minnesota, Duluth, Graduate School, Swenson College of Science and Engineering, Department of Mathematics and Statistics, Duluth, MN 55812-2496. Offers applied and computational mathematics (MS). Part-time programs available. *Degree requirements:* For master's, thesis or alternative. *Entrance requirements:* For master's, GRE General Test, minimum GPA of 3.0. Additional exam requirements/recommendations for international students: Required—TOEFL (minimum score 550 paper-based; 213 computer-based; 79 iBT); Recommended—TWE. Electronic applications accepted. *Faculty research:* Discrete mathematics, diagnostic markers, combinatorics, biostatistics, mathematical modeling and scientific computation.

University of Missouri, Graduate School, College of Arts and Sciences, Department of Mathematics, Program in Applied Mathematics, Columbia, MO 65211. Offers MS. *Students:* 7 full-time (3 women); includes 1 minority (Hispanic/Latino). Average age 23. 10 applicants, 10% accepted, 1 enrolled. In 2010, 3 master's awarded. *Degree requirements:* For master's, thesis. *Entrance requirements:* For master's, GRE General Test, minimum GPA of 3.0. Additional exam requirements/recommendations for international students: Required—TOEFL (minimum score 500 paper-based; 173 computer-based; 61 iBT). *Application deadline:* For fall admission, 1/15 for domestic and international students. Applications are processed on a rolling basis. Application fee: $45 ($60 for international students). Electronic applications accepted. *Financial support:* Fellowships, research assistantships, teaching assistantships, institutionally sponsored loans, health care benefits, and unspecified assistantships available. *Faculty research:* areas of mathematics used frequently in applications. *Unit head:* Dr. Glen Himmelberg, Department Chair, 573-882-6222, E-mail: himmelbergg@missouri.edu. *Application contact:* Amy Crews, Administrative Assistant, 573-882-6222, E-mail: crewsae@missouri.edu.

University of Missouri–St. Louis, College of Arts and Sciences, Department of Mathematics and Computer Science, St. Louis, MO 63121. Offers applied mathematics (PhD), including computer science, mathematics; computer science (MS); mathematics (MA). Part-time and evening/weekend programs available. *Faculty:* 16 full-time (2 women), 1 part-time/adjunct (0 women). *Students:* 21 full-time (8 women), 43 part-time (13 women); includes 9 minority (5 Black or African American, non-Hispanic/Latino; 2 American Indian or Alaska Native, non-Hispanic/Latino; 2 Asian, non-Hispanic/Latino), 17 international. Average age 32. 98 applicants, 49% accepted, 12 enrolled. In 2010, 18 master's awarded. *Degree requirements:* For master's, thesis optional; for doctorate, thesis/dissertation. *Entrance requirements:* For master's, GRE (for TA assistantships), 2 letters of recommendation; C programming, C++ or Java (for computer science); for doctorate, GRE General Test, 3 letters of recommendation. Additional exam requirements/recommendations for international students: Required—TOEFL (minimum score 550 paper-based; 213 computer-based). *Application deadline:* For fall admission, 7/1 priority date for domestic and international students; for spring admission, 12/1 priority date for domestic and international students. Applications are processed on a rolling basis. Application fee: $35 ($40 for international students). Electronic applications accepted. *Expenses:* Tuition, state resident: full-time $5522; part-time $306.80 per credit hour. Tuition, nonresident: full-time $14,253; part-time $792.10 per credit hour. Required fees: $658; $49 per credit hour. One-time fee: $12. Tuition and fees vary according to program. *Financial support:* In 2010–11, 5 research assistantships with full and partial tuition reimbursements (averaging $10,845 per year), 7 teaching assistantships with full and partial tuition reimbursements (averaging $13,285 per year) were awarded; fellowships with full tuition reimbursements also available. Financial award applicants required to submit FAFSA. *Faculty research:* Statistics, algebra, analysis. *Unit head:* Dr. Shiying Zhao, Director of Graduate Studies, 314-516-5741, Fax: 314-516-5400, E-mail: zhao@arch.cs.umsl.edu. *Application contact:* 314-516-5458, Fax: 314-516-6996, E-mail: gradadm@umsl.edu.

University of New Hampshire, Graduate School, College of Engineering and Physical Sciences, Department of Mathematics and Statistics, Durham, NH 03824. Offers applied mathematics (MS); industrial statistics (Postbaccalaureate Certificate); mathematics (MS, MST, PhD); mathematics education (PhD); statistics (MS). *Faculty:* 21 full-time (5 women). *Students:* 31 full-time (13 women), 25 part-time (10 women); includes 2 minority (both Two or more races, non-Hispanic/Latino), 17 international. Average age 31. 71 applicants, 49% accepted, 19 enrolled. In 2010, 17 master's, 6 doctorates, 3 other advanced degrees awarded. Terminal

Peterson's Graduate Programs in the Physical Sciences, Mathematics, Agricultural Sciences, the Environment & Natural Resources 2012

www.facebook.com/petersonspublishing 235

Applied Mathematics

University of New Hampshire (continued)
master's awarded for partial completion of doctoral program. *Degree requirements:* For doctorate, 2 foreign languages, thesis/dissertation. *Entrance requirements:* Additional exam requirements/ recommendations for international students: Required—TOEFL (minimum score 550 paper-based; 213 computer-based; 80 iBT). *Application deadline:* For fall admission, 4/1 priority date for domestic students, 4/1 for international students; for spring admission, 12/1 for domestic students. Applications are processed on a rolling basis. Application fee: $65. Electronic applications accepted. *Financial support:* In 2010–11, 40 students received support, including 3 fellowships, 2 research assistantships, 34 teaching assistantships; Federal Work-Study, scholarships/grants, and tuition waivers (full and partial) also available. Support available to part-time students. Financial award application deadline: 2/15. *Faculty research:* Operator theory, complex analysis, algebra, nonlinear dynamics, statistics. *Unit head:* Dr. Edward Hindon, Chairperson, 603-862-2320. *Application contact:* Jan Jankowski, Administrative Assistant, 603-862-2320, E-mail: jan.jankowski@unh.edu.

The University of North Carolina at Charlotte, Graduate School, College of Arts and Sciences, Department of Mathematics and Statistics, Charlotte, NC 28223-0001. Offers applied mathematics (MS, PhD); mathematics (MS); mathematics education (MA). Part-time and evening/weekend programs available. *Faculty:* 43 full-time (5 women). *Students:* 51 full-time (16 women), 30 part-time (14 women); includes 13 minority (9 Black or African American, non-Hispanic/Latino; 3 Asian, non-Hispanic/Latino; 1 Hispanic/Latino), 38 international. Average age 29. 63 applicants, 95% accepted, 23 enrolled. In 2010, 16 master's, 4 doctorates awarded. *Degree requirements:* For master's, comprehensive exam, thesis or alternative; for doctorate, thesis/dissertation. *Entrance requirements:* For master's, GRE General Test, minimum GPA of 3.0 in undergraduate major, 2.75 overall; for doctorate, GRE General Test, minimum overall GPA of 3.0. Additional exam requirements/recommendations for international students: Required—TOEFL (minimum score: 557 paper-based; 220 computer-based; or 83 iBT), Michigan English Language Assessment Battery (minimum score 78), IELTS (minimum score 6.5), or post-secondary degree earned in a country or province where English is the primary spoken language. *Application deadline:* For fall admission, 7/1 for domestic students, 5/1 for international students; for spring admission, 11/1 for domestic students, 10/1 for international students. Applications are processed on a rolling basis. Application fee: $55. Electronic applications accepted. *Expenses:* Tuition, state resident: full-time $3464. Tuition, nonresident: full-time $14,297. Required fees: $2094. Tuition and fees vary according to course load. *Financial support:* In 2010–11, 50 students received support, including 6 fellowships (averaging $37,414 per year), 8 research assistantships (averaging $14,738 per year), 36 teaching assistantships (averaging $13,340 per year); career-related internships or fieldwork, Federal Work-Study, institutionally sponsored loans, scholarships/grants, and unspecified assistantships also available. Support available to part-time students. Financial award application deadline: 4/1; financial award applicants required to submit FAFSA. *Faculty research:* Numerical analysis, differential equations, probability, algebra, analysis, mathematics education, statistics. Total annual research expenditures: $1.3 million. *Unit head:* Dr. Alan S. Dow, Chair, 704-687-4560, Fax: 704-687-6415, E-mail: adow@uncc.edu. *Application contact:* Kathy B. Giddings, Director of Graduate Admissions, 704-687-5503, Fax: 704-687-3279, E-mail: gradadm@uncc.edu.

University of Northern Iowa, Graduate College, College of Natural Sciences, Department of Mathematics, Cedar Falls, IA 50614. Offers industrial mathematics (PSM), including actuarial science, continuous quality improvement, mathematical computing and modeling; mathematics (MA), including mathematics, secondary; mathematics for middle grades 4-8 (MA). Part-time programs available. *Students:* 19 full-time (13 women), 22 part-time (17 women); includes 2 minority (1 Asian, non-Hispanic/Latino; 1 Two or more races, non-Hispanic/Latino), 5 international. 20 applicants, 40% accepted, 6 enrolled. In 2010, 18 master's awarded. *Degree requirements:* For master's, comprehensive exam (for some programs), thesis or alternative. *Entrance requirements:* For master's, minimum GPA of 3.0. Additional exam requirements/ recommendations for international students: Required—TOEFL (minimum score 600 paper-based; 250 computer-based; 100 iBT). *Application deadline:* For fall admission, 8/1 priority date for domestic students. Applications are processed on a rolling basis. Application fee: $50 ($70 for international students). Electronic applications accepted. *Financial support:* Career-related internships or fieldwork, Federal Work-Study, scholarships/grants, and tuition waivers (full and partial) available. Support available to part-time students. Financial award application deadline: 2/1. *Unit head:* Dr. Douglas Mupasiri, Interim Head, 319-273-2012, Fax: 319-273-2546, E-mail: douglas.mupasiri@uni.edu. *Application contact:* Laurie S. Russell, Record Analyst, 319-273-2623, Fax: 319-273-2885, E-mail: laurie.russell@uni.edu.

University of Notre Dame, Graduate School, College of Science, Department of Mathematics, Notre Dame, IN 46556. Offers algebra (PhD); algebraic geometry (PhD); applied mathematics (MSAM); complex analysis (PhD); differential geometry (PhD); logic (PhD); partial differential equations (PhD); topology (PhD). Terminal master's awarded for partial completion of doctoral program. *Degree requirements:* For doctorate, one foreign language, thesis/dissertation, qualifying exam. *Entrance requirements:* For master's and doctorate, GRE General Test, GRE Subject Test. Additional exam requirements/recommendations for international students: Required—TOEFL (minimum score 600 paper-based; 250 computer-based; 80 iBT). Electronic applications accepted. *Faculty research:* Algebra, analysis, geometry/topology, logic, applied math.

University of Pennsylvania, School of Arts and Sciences, Graduate Group in Applied Mathematics and Computational Science, Philadelphia, PA 19104. Offers PhD. *Faculty:* 26 full-time (2 women). *Students:* 17 full-time (6 women), 1 part-time (0 women), 17 international. 93 applicants, 14% accepted, 5 enrolled. *Application deadline:* For fall admission, 1/15 for domestic students. *Expenses:* Tuition: Full-time $25,660; part-time $4758 per course. Required fees: $2152; $270 per course. Tuition and fees vary according to course load, degree level and program. *Financial support:* Institutionally sponsored loans, scholarships/grants, traineeships, health care benefits, and unspecified assistantships available. *Unit head:* Dr. C.L. Epstein, Graduate Chair, 215-898-8476, E-mail: cle@math.upenn.edu. *Application contact:* Dr. C.L. Epstein, Graduate Chair, 215-898-8476, E-mail: cle@math.upenn.edu.

University of Pittsburgh, School of Arts and Sciences, Department of Mathematics, Pittsburgh, PA 15260. Offers applied mathematics (MA, MS); mathematics (MA, MS, PhD). Part-time programs available. *Faculty:* 33 full-time (5 women), 16 part-time/adjunct (2 women). *Students:* 79 full-time (24 women), 4 part-time (2 women); includes 2 Black or African American, non-Hispanic/Latino; 1 Native Hawaiian or other Pacific Islander, non-Hispanic/Latino, 42 international. 266 applicants, 15% accepted, 21 enrolled. In 2010, 17 master's, 12 doctorates awarded. Terminal master's awarded for partial completion of doctoral program. *Degree requirements:* For master's, comprehensive exam, thesis (for some programs); for doctorate, comprehensive exam, thesis/dissertation, preliminary exams, defense of dissertation. *Entrance requirements:* For master's, GRE General Test, GRE Subject Test (recommended), minimum GPA of 3.0; for doctorate, GRE General Test, GRE Subject Test (recommended), minimum GPA of 3.0, minimum QPA of 3.25 in math curriculum. Additional exam requirements/ recommendations for international students: Required—TOEFL (minimum score 550 paper-based; 213 computer-based; 80 iBT), IELTS (minimum score 6.5). *Application deadline:* For fall admission, 1/15 priority date for domestic and international students; for spring admission, 9/1 priority date for domestic students, 9/1 for international students. Applications are processed on a rolling basis. Application fee: $50. Electronic applications accepted. *Expenses:* Tuition, state resident: full-time $17,304; part-time $701 per credit. Tuition, nonresident: full-time $29,554; part-time $1210 per credit. Required fees: $740; $214 per term. Tuition and fees vary according to program. *Financial support:* In 2010–11, 84 students received support, including 8 fellowships with full and partial tuition reimbursements available (averaging $18,350 per year), 11 research assistantships with full and partial tuition reimbursements available (averaging $16,000 per year), 53 teaching assistantships with full and partial tuition reimbursements available (averaging $15,830 per year); institutionally sponsored loans, scholarships/grants, traineeships, health care benefits, tuition waivers (partial), and unspecified assistantships also available. Financial award application deadline: 1/15. *Faculty research:* Algebra, analysis, computational math, geometry/topology, math biology. Total annual research expenditures: $1.8 million. *Unit head:* Ivan Yotov, Chair, 412-624-8361, Fax: 412-624-8397, E-mail: yotov@math.pitt.edu. *Application contact:* Molly Williams, Administrator, 412-624-1175, Fax: 412-624-8397, E-mail: mollyw@pitt.edu.

University of Puerto Rico, Mayagüez Campus, Graduate Studies, College of Arts and Sciences, Department of Mathematical Sciences, Mayagüez, PR 00681-9000. Offers applied mathematics (MS); pure mathematics (MS); scientific computation (MS); statistics (MS). Part-time programs available. *Students:* 40 full-time (11 women), 1 part-time (0 women); includes 7 Hispanic/Latino, 34 international. 19 applicants, 26% accepted, 3 enrolled. In 2010, 7 master's awarded. *Degree requirements:* For master's, one foreign language, comprehensive exam, thesis optional. *Entrance requirements:* For master's, undergraduate degree in mathematics or its equivalent. *Application deadline:* For fall admission, 2/15 for domestic and international students; for spring admission, 9/15 for domestic and international students. Applications are processed on a rolling basis. Application fee: $25. *Expenses:* Tuition, state resident: full-time $1188. Tuition, nonresident: full-time $1188. International tuition: $6126 full-time. Tuition and fees vary according to course level and course load. *Financial support:* In 2010–11, 39 students received support, including fellowships (averaging $12,000 per year), 20 research assistantships (averaging $15,000 per year), 39 teaching assistantships (averaging $8,500 per year); Federal Work-Study and institutionally sponsored loans also available. *Faculty research:* Automata theory, linear algebra, logic. Total annual research expenditures: $2.7 million. *Unit head:* Prof. Silvestre Col??n, Director, 787-832-4040 Ext. 3848, Fax: 787-265-5454, E-mail: silvestre.colon@upr.edu. *Application contact:* Prof. Silvestre Col??n, Director, 787-832-4040 Ext. 3848, Fax: 787-265-5454, E-mail: silvestre.colon@upr.edu.

University of Rhode Island, Graduate School, College of Arts and Sciences, Department of Computer Science and Statistics, Kingston, RI 02881. Offers applied mathematics (PhD), including computer science, statistics; computer science (MS, PhD); digital forensics (Graduate Certificate); statistics (MS). Part-time programs available. *Faculty:* 10 full-time (3 women), 2 part-time/adjunct (0 women). *Students:* 39 full-time (10 women), 44 part-time (11 women); includes 16 minority (2 Black or African American, non-Hispanic/Latino; 2 American Indian or Alaska Native, non-Hispanic/Latino; 2 Asian, non-Hispanic/Latino; 2 Hispanic/Latino; 8 Native Hawaiian or other Pacific Islander, non-Hispanic/Latino), 8 international. In 2010, 5 master's awarded. *Degree requirements:* For master's, comprehensive exam (for some programs), thesis optional; for doctorate, comprehensive exam, thesis/dissertation. *Entrance requirements:* For master's and doctorate, GRE, 2 letters of recommendation. Additional exam requirements/ recommendations for international students: Required—TOEFL (minimum score 550 paper-based; 213 computer-based). *Application deadline:* For fall admission, 7/15 for domestic students, 2/1 for international students; for spring admission, 11/15 for domestic students, 7/15 for international students. Application fee: $65. Electronic applications accepted. *Expenses:* Tuition, state resident: full-time $9588; part-time $533 per credit hour. Tuition, nonresident: full-time $22,968; part-time $1276 per credit hour. Required fees: $1282; $68 per semester. Tuition and fees vary according to program. *Financial support:* In 2010–11, 1 research assistantship (averaging $5,210 per year), 10 teaching assistantships with full and partial tuition reimbursements (averaging $10,456 per year) were awarded. Financial award application deadline: 2/1; financial award applicants required to submit FAFSA. *Faculty research:* Bioinformatics, computer and digital forensics, behavioral model of pedestrian dynamics, real-time distributed object computing, cryptography. Total annual research expenditures: $962,948. *Unit head:* Dr. James G. Kowalski, Chair, 401-874-2510, Fax: 401-874-4617, E-mail: kowalski@cs.uri.edu. *Application contact:* Dr. Victor Fay-Wolfe, Director of Graduate Studies, 401-874-2701, Fax: 401-874-4617, E-mail: wolfe@cs.uri.edu.

University of Rhode Island, Graduate School, College of Arts and Sciences, Department of Mathematics, Kingston, RI 02881. Offers applied mathematical sciences (MS, PhD); mathematics (MS, PhD). Part-time programs available. *Faculty:* 19 full-time (4 women), 1 part-time/adjunct (0 women). *Students:* 23 full-time (10 women), 10 part-time (1 woman), 2 international. In 2010, 7 master's, 2 doctorates awarded. *Degree requirements:* For master's, comprehensive exam (for some programs), thesis optional; for doctorate, one foreign language, comprehensive exam, thesis/dissertation optional. *Entrance requirements:* For master's and doctorate, 2 letters of recommendation. Additional exam requirements/recommendations for international students: Required—TOEFL (minimum score 550 paper-based; 213 computer-based). *Application deadline:* For fall admission, 7/15 for domestic students, 2/1 for international students; for spring admission, 11/15 for domestic students, 7/15 for international students. Application fee: $65. Electronic applications accepted. *Expenses:* Tuition, state resident: full-time $9588; part-time $533 per credit hour. Tuition, nonresident: full-time $22,968; part-time $1276 per credit hour. Required fees: $1282; $68 per semester. Tuition and fees vary according to program. *Financial support:* In 2010–11, 2 research assistantships with full tuition reimbursements (averaging $13,894 per year), 13 teaching assistantships with full and partial tuition reimbursements (averaging $13,560 per year) were awarded. Financial award application deadline: 7/15; financial award applicants required to submit FAFSA. *Unit head:* Dr. Nancy Eaton, Chairman, 401-874-2709, Fax: 401-874-4454, E-mail: eaton@math.uri.edu. *Application contact:* Dr. Woong Kook, Director of Graduate Studies, 401-874-4421, Fax: 401-874-4454, E-mail: andrewk@math.uri.edu.

University of Rochester, School of Arts and Sciences, Department of Mathematics, Program in Applied Mathematics, Rochester, NY 14627.

University of Southern California, Graduate School, Dana and David Dornsife College of Letters, Arts and Sciences, Department of Mathematics, Los Angeles, CA 90089. Offers applied mathematics (MA, MS, PhD); mathematical finance (MS); mathematics (MA, PhD); statistics (MS). Part-time programs available. *Faculty:* 48 full-time (6 women). *Students:* 103 full-time (33 women), 14 part-time (6 women); includes 11 minority (8 Asian, non-Hispanic/Latino; 1 Hispanic/Latino; 2 Two or more races, non-Hispanic/Latino), 85 international. 559 applicants, 20% accepted, 32 enrolled. In 2010, 37 master's, 7 doctorates awarded. Terminal master's awarded for partial completion of doctoral program. *Degree requirements:* For master's, comprehensive exam (for some programs), thesis (for some programs); for doctorate, one foreign language, comprehensive exam, thesis/dissertation. *Entrance requirements:* For master's, GRE General Test, GMAT; for doctorate, GRE—General and Subject in Mathematics. Additional exam requirements/recommendations for international students: Required—TOEFL (minimum score 100 iBT). *Application deadline:* For fall and spring admission, 12/1 for domestic and international students. Applications are processed on a rolling basis. Application fee: $85. Electronic applications accepted. *Expenses:* Tuition: Full-time $31,240; part-time $1420 per unit. Required fees: $600. One-time fee: $35 full-time. Full-time tuition and fees vary according to degree level and program. *Financial support:* In 2010–11, 68 students received support, including 5 fellowships with full tuition reimbursements available (averaging $19,250 per year), 3 research assistantships with full tuition reimbursements available (averaging $19,250 per year), 58 teaching assistantships with full tuition reimbursements available (averaging $19,250 per year). Financial award application deadline: 12/1. *Faculty research:* Algebra, algebraic geometry and number theory, analysis/partial differential equations, applied mathematics, financial mathematics, probability, combinatorics and statistics. Total annual research expenditures: $1.7 million. *Unit head:* Prof. Gary Rosen, Chair, 213-740-1717, Fax: 213-740-2424, E-mail: grosen@usc.edu. *Application contact:* Amy Yung, Department Coordinator, 213-740-8168, Fax: 213-740-2424, E-mail: amy@usc.edu.

The University of Tennessee, Graduate School, College of Arts and Sciences, Department of Mathematics, Knoxville, TN 37996. Offers applied mathematics (MS); mathematical ecology

(PhD); mathematics (M Math, MS, PhD). Part-time programs available. *Degree requirements:* For master's, thesis or alternative; for doctorate, one foreign language, thesis/dissertation. *Entrance requirements:* For master's and doctorate, minimum GPA of 2.7. Additional exam requirements/recommendations for international students: Required—TOEFL. Electronic applications accepted. *Expenses:* Tuition, state resident: full-time $7440; part-time $414 per credit hour. Tuition, nonresident: full-time $22,478; part-time $1250 per credit hour. Required fees: $922; $43 per credit hour. Tuition and fees vary according to program.

The University of Tennessee Space Institute, Graduate Programs, Program in Applied Mathematics, Tullahoma, TN 37388-9700. Offers MS. Part-time programs available. *Faculty:* 3 part-time/adjunct (0 women). *Students:* 1 (woman) full-time, all international. *Degree requirements:* For master's, thesis (for some programs). *Entrance requirements:* Additional exam requirements/recommendations for international students: Required—TOEFL (minimum score 550 paper-based; 213 computer-based; 80 iBT), IELTS (minimum score 6.5). *Application deadline:* For fall admission, 2/1 for international students; for spring admission, 6/15 for international students. Applications are processed on a rolling basis. Application fee: $35. *Financial support:* Fellowships, research assistantships with full tuition reimbursements, career-related internships or fieldwork, Federal Work-Study, institutionally sponsored loans, health care benefits, tuition waivers (partial), and unspecified assistantships available. Financial award applicants required to submit FAFSA. *Application contact:* Dee Merriman, Coordinator III, 931-393-7213, Fax: 931-393-7211, E-mail: dmerrima@utsi.edu.

The University of Texas at Arlington, Graduate School, College of Science, Department of Mathematics, Arlington, TX 76019. Offers applied math (MS); mathematics (PhD); mathematics education (MA). Part-time and evening/weekend programs available. *Faculty:* 26 full-time (7 women). *Students:* 54 full-time (19 women), 75 part-time (32 women); includes 13 Black or African American, non-Hispanic/Latino; 7 Asian, non-Hispanic/Latino; 12 Hispanic/Latino, 31 international. 86 applicants, 99% accepted, 63 enrolled. In 2010, 11 master's, 9 doctorates awarded. *Degree requirements:* For master's, comprehensive exam, thesis or alternative; for doctorate, comprehensive exam, thesis/dissertation, preliminary examinations. *Entrance requirements:* For master's, GRE General Test (minimum score 350 verbal, 650 quantitative); for doctorate, GRE General Test (minimum score: 350 verbal, 700 quantitative), 30 hours of graduate course work in mathematics, minimum GPA of 3.0 in last 60 hours of course work. Additional exam requirements/recommendations for international students: Required—TOEFL (minimum score 550 paper-based; 213 computer-based; 79 iBT). *Application deadline:* For fall admission, 6/1 priority date for domestic students, 4/1 for international students; for winter admission, 10/15 priority date for domestic students, 9/15 for international students. Applications are processed on a rolling basis. Application fee: $35 ($50 for international students). Electronic applications accepted. *Expenses:* Tuition, state resident: full-time $7500. Tuition, nonresident: full-time $13,080. International tuition: $13,250 full-time. *Financial support:* In 2010–11, 36 students received support, including 17 fellowships with full tuition reimbursements available (averaging $27,500 per year), 2 research assistantships with partial tuition reimbursements available, 23 teaching assistantships with partial tuition reimbursements available (averaging $20,750 per year); Federal Work-Study, institutionally sponsored loans, scholarships/grants, health care benefits, and unspecified assistantships also available. Financial award application deadline: 6/1; financial award applicants required to submit FAFSA. *Faculty research:* Algebra, combinatorics and geometry, applied mathematics and mathematical biology, computational mathematics, mathematics education, probability and statistics. *Unit head:* Dr. Zhu Jiaping, Chair, 817-272-1114, E-mail: jpzhu@uta.edu. *Application contact:* Dr. Jianzhong Su, Graduate Advisor, 817-272-5684, Fax: 817-272-5802, E-mail: su@uta.edu.

The University of Texas at Austin, Graduate School, Program in Computational and Applied Mathematics, Austin, TX 78712-1111. Offers MA, PhD. Terminal master's awarded for partial completion of doctoral program. *Degree requirements:* For master's, thesis optional; for doctorate, thesis/dissertation, 3 area qualifying exams. Electronic applications accepted.

The University of Texas at Dallas, School of Natural Sciences and Mathematics, Department of Mathematical Sciences, Richardson, TX 75080. Offers applied mathematics (MS, PhD); engineering mathematics (MS); mathematical science (MS); statistics (MS, PhD). Part-time and evening/weekend programs available. *Faculty:* 15 full-time (2 women). *Students:* 43 full-time (16 women), 22 part-time (6 women); includes 20 minority (6 Black or African American, non-Hispanic/Latino; 11 Asian, non-Hispanic/Latino; 3 Hispanic/Latino), 23 international. Average age 32. 147 applicants, 32% accepted, 9 enrolled. In 2010, 18 master's, 6 doctorates awarded. *Degree requirements:* For master's, thesis optional; for doctorate, thesis/dissertation. *Entrance requirements:* For master's, GRE General Test, minimum GPA of 3.0 in upper-level course work in field; for doctorate, GRE General Test, minimum GPA of 3.5 in upper-level course work in field. Additional exam requirements/recommendations for international students: Required—TOEFL (minimum score 550 paper-based; 215 computer-based). *Application deadline:* For fall admission, 7/15 for domestic students, 5/1 priority date for international students; for spring admission, 11/15 for domestic students, 9/1 priority date for international students. Applications are processed on a rolling basis. Application fee: $50 ($100 for international students). Electronic applications accepted. *Expenses:* Tuition, state resident: full-time $10,248; part-time $569 per credit hour. Tuition, nonresident: full-time $18,544; part-time $1030 per credit hour. Tuition and fees vary according to course load. *Financial support:* In 2010–11, 39 students received support, including 2 research assistantships (averaging $15,750 per year), 31 teaching assistantships with partial tuition reimbursements available (averaging $13,933 per year); career-related internships or fieldwork, Federal Work-Study, institutionally sponsored loans, scholarships/grants, and unspecified assistantships also available. Support available to part-time students. Financial award application deadline: 4/30; financial award applicants required to submit FAFSA. *Faculty research:* Sequential analysis, applications in semiconductor manufacturing, medical image analysis, computational anatomy, information theory, probability theory. *Unit head:* Dr. Wieslaw Z. Krawcewicz, Department Head, 972-883-6820, Fax: 972-883-6622, E-mail: wieslaw@utdallas.edu. *Application contact:* Dr. Wieslaw Z. Krawcewicz, Department Head, 972-883-6820, Fax: 972-883-6622, E-mail: wieslaw@utdallas.edu.

The University of Texas at San Antonio, College of Sciences, Department of Mathematics, San Antonio, TX 78249-0617. Offers applied mathematics-industrial mathematics (MS); mathematics (MS); mathematics education (MS). Part-time and evening/weekend programs available. *Faculty:* 9 full-time (1 woman). *Students:* 22 full-time (8 women), 45 part-time (20 women); includes 30 minority (2 Black or African American, non-Hispanic/Latino; 4 Asian, non-Hispanic/Latino; 22 Hispanic/Latino; 2 Two or more races, non-Hispanic/Latino), 9 international. Average age 30. 41 applicants, 76% accepted, 23 enrolled. In 2010, 11 master's awarded. *Degree requirements:* For master's, comprehensive exam (for some programs), thesis (for some programs). *Entrance requirements:* For master's, GRE General Test, minimum GPA of 3.0 in last 60 hours. Additional exam requirements/recommendations for international students: Required—TOEFL (minimum score 500 paper-based; 173 computer-based; 61 iBT), IELTS (minimum score 5). *Application deadline:* For fall admission, 7/1 for domestic students, 4/1 for international students; for spring admission, 11/1 for domestic students, 9/1 for international students. Applications are processed on a rolling basis. Application fee: $45 ($80 for international students). Electronic applications accepted. *Expenses:* Tuition, state resident: full-time $4172; part-time $231.75 per credit hour. Tuition, nonresident: full-time $15,332; part-time $851.75 per credit hour. *Financial support:* In 2010–11, 9 students received support, including 1 research assistantship (averaging $22,800 per year), 25 teaching assistantships (averaging $11,536 per year); scholarships/grants, tuition waivers, and unspecified assistantships also available. Support available to part-time students. *Faculty research:* Computational statistics, deterministic and stochastic differential equations, applications of mathematics to architecture and urbanism, mathematical biology, numerical analysis. Total annual research expenditures: $117,596. *Unit head:* Dr. Francis A. Norman, Department Chair, 210-458-5735, Fax: 210-458-4439, E-mail: sandy.norman@utsa.edu. *Application contact:* Veronica Ramirez,

Assistant Dean of the Graduate School, 210-458-4330, Fax: 210-458-4332, E-mail: graduatestudies@utsa.edu.

The University of Toledo, College of Graduate Studies, College of Natural Sciences and Mathematics, Department of Mathematics, Toledo, OH 43606-3390. Offers applied mathematics (MS, PhD); mathematics (MA, PhD); statistics (MS, PhD). Part-time programs available. *Faculty:* 25. *Students:* 44 full-time (12 women), 13 part-time (7 women), 44 international. Average age 30. 84 applicants, 43% accepted, 19 enrolled. In 2010, 15 master's, 2 doctorates awarded. *Degree requirements:* For master's, thesis; for doctorate, 2 foreign languages, thesis/dissertation. *Entrance requirements:* For master's and doctorate, GRE General Test, GRE Subject Test, A minimum 2.7 cumulative point-hour ratio (on a 4.0 scale) for all previous academic work. Three letters of recommendation, a statement of purpose, and transcripts from all prior institutions attended. Additional exam requirements/recommendations for international students: Required—TOEFL (minimum score 550 paper-based; 213 computer-based; 80 iBT), IELTS (minimum score 6.5). *Application deadline:* For fall admission, 1/15 priority date for domestic and international students. Applications are processed on a rolling basis. Application fee: $45 ($75 for international students). Electronic applications accepted. *Expenses:* Tuition, state resident: full-time $11,426; part-time $476 per credit hour. Tuition, nonresident: full-time $21,660; part-time $903 per credit hour. One-time fee: $62. *Financial support:* Research assistantships with full tuition reimbursements, teaching assistantships with full tuition reimbursements, Federal Work-Study, institutionally sponsored loans, scholarships/grants, and unspecified assistantships available. Support available to part-time students. *Faculty research:* Topology. *Unit head:* Dr. Paul Hewitt, Chair, 419-530-2568, E-mail: paul.hewitt@utoledo.edu. *Application contact:* Graduate School Office, 419-530-4723, Fax: 419-530-4723, E-mail: grdsch@utnet.utoledo.edu.

University of Tulsa, Graduate School, Collins College of Business, Finance/Applied Mathematics Program, Tulsa, OK 74104-3189. Offers MS/MS. Part-time and evening/weekend programs available. *Students:* 2 full-time (both women). Average age 24. 11 applicants, 73% accepted, 1 enrolled. *Entrance requirements:* Additional exam requirements/recommendations for international students: Required—TOEFL (minimum score 575 paper-based; 231 computer-based), IELTS (minimum score 6.5). *Application deadline:* Applications are processed on a rolling basis. Application fee: $40. Electronic applications accepted. *Expenses:* Tuition: Full-time $16,902; part-time $939 per credit hour. Required fees: $1020; $4 per credit hour. Tuition and fees vary according to course load. *Financial support:* In 2010–11, 2 students received support, including 2 teaching assistantships (averaging $7,961 per year); fellowships, career-related internships or fieldwork, Federal Work-Study, institutionally sponsored loans, scholarships/grants, health care benefits, tuition waivers (full and partial), and unspecified assistantships also available. Support available to part-time students. Financial award application deadline: 2/1; financial award applicants required to submit FAFSA. *Unit head:* Linda Nichols, Associate Dean, 918-631-2242, Fax: 918-631-2142, E-mail: linda-nichols@utulsa.edu. *Application contact:* Linda Nichols, Associate Dean, 918-631-2242, Fax: 918-631-2142, E-mail: linda-nichols@utulsa.edu.

University of Washington, Graduate School, College of Arts and Sciences, Department of Applied Mathematics, Seattle, WA 98195. Offers MS, PhD. Terminal master's awarded for partial completion of doctoral program. *Degree requirements:* For master's, thesis optional; for doctorate, thesis/dissertation. *Entrance requirements:* For master's and doctorate, GRE, minimum GPA of 3.0. Additional exam requirements/recommendations for international students: Required—TOEFL. Electronic applications accepted. *Faculty research:* Mathematical modeling for physical, biological, social, and engineering sciences; development of mathematical methods for analysis, including perturbation, asymptotic, transform, vocational, and numerical methods.

University of Washington, Graduate School, College of Arts and Sciences, Department of Mathematics, Seattle, WA 98195. Offers mathematics (MA, MS, PhD); numerical analysis (MS); optimization (MS). Part-time programs available. Terminal master's awarded for partial completion of doctoral program. *Degree requirements:* For master's, thesis optional; for doctorate, 2 foreign languages, thesis/dissertation. *Entrance requirements:* For master's, GRE, minimum GPA of 3.0; for doctorate, GRE General Test, GRE Subject Test (mathematics), minimum GPA of 3.0. Additional exam requirements/recommendations for international students: Required—TOEFL. Electronic applications accepted. *Faculty research:* Algebra, analysis, probability, combinatorics and geometry.

University of Waterloo, Graduate Studies, Faculty of Mathematics, Department of Applied Mathematics, Waterloo, ON N2L 3G1, Canada. Offers M Math, PhD. Part-time programs available. *Degree requirements:* For master's, research paper or thesis; for doctorate, thesis/dissertation. *Entrance requirements:* For master's, honors degree in field, minimum B+ average; for doctorate, master's degree, minimum B+ average. Additional exam requirements/recommendations for international students: Required—TOEFL (minimum score 600 paper-based; 250 computer-based; 100 iBT), TWE (minimum score 4). Electronic applications accepted. *Faculty research:* Differential equations, quantum theory, statistical mechanics, fluid mechanics, relativity, control theory.

The University of Western Ontario, Faculty of Graduate Studies, Physical Sciences Division, Department of Applied Mathematics, London, ON N6A 5B8, Canada. Offers applied mathematics (M Sc, PhD); theoretical physics (PhD). *Degree requirements:* For master's, thesis or alternative; for doctorate, comprehensive exam, thesis/dissertation. *Entrance requirements:* For master's and doctorate, minimum B average. Additional exam requirements/recommendations for international students: Required—TOEFL. *Faculty research:* Fluid dynamics, mathematical and computational methods, theoretical physics.

University of West Georgia, College of Arts and Sciences, Department of Mathematics, Carrollton, GA 30118. Offers mathematics (MSM); teaching and applied mathematics (MS). *Faculty:* 13 full-time (2 women). *Students:* 5 part-time (2 women). Average age 26. 8 applicants, 50% accepted, 0 enrolled. *Degree requirements:* For master's, comprehensive exam, thesis optional, 36 credit hours. *Entrance requirements:* For master's, GRE. Additional exam requirements/recommendations for international students: Required—TOEFL (minimum score 523 paper-based; 193 computer-based; 69 iBT). *Application deadline:* For fall admission, 7/17 for domestic students, 6/6 for international students; for spring admission, 11/20 for domestic students, 10/3 for international students. Applications are processed on a rolling basis. Application fee: $30. Electronic applications accepted. *Expenses:* Tuition, state resident: full-time $4130; part-time $173 per semester hour. Tuition, nonresident: full-time $16,524; part-time $689 per semester hour. Required fees: $1586; $44.01 per semester hour. $397 per semester. Tuition and fees vary according to program. *Financial support:* In 2010–11, 3 students received support, including 3 teaching assistantships (averaging $6,800 per year); unspecified assistantships also available. *Unit head:* Dr. Minh Nguyen, Interim Chair, 678-839-6489, E-mail: vnguyen@westga.edu. *Application contact:* Dr. Charles W. Clark, Dean, 678-839-6508, E-mail: cclark@westga.edu.

Utah State University, School of Graduate Studies, College of Science, Department of Mathematics and Statistics, Logan, UT 84322. Offers industrial mathematics (MS); mathematical sciences (PhD); mathematics (M Math, MS); statistics (MS). Part-time programs available. Terminal master's awarded for partial completion of doctoral program. *Degree requirements:* For master's, thesis optional, qualifying exam; for doctorate, one foreign language, comprehensive exam, thesis/dissertation. *Entrance requirements:* For master's and doctorate, GRE General Test, minimum GPA of 3.0. Additional exam requirements/recommendations for international students: Required—TOEFL. *Faculty research:* Differential equations, computational mathematics, dynamical systems, probability and statistics, pure mathematics.

Peterson's Graduate Programs in the Physical Sciences, Mathematics, Agricultural Sciences, the Environment & Natural Resources 2012

www.facebook.com/petersonspublishing   **237**

Applied Mathematics

Virginia Commonwealth University, Graduate School, College of Humanities and Sciences, Department of Mathematics and Applied Mathematics, Richmond, VA 23284-9005. Offers applied mathematics (MS); mathematics (MS); operations research (MS); statistical sciences and operations research (MS). *Students:* 21 full-time (11 women), 23 part-time (9 women); includes 6 minority (3 Black or African American, non-Hispanic/Latino; 2 Asian, non-Hispanic/Latino; 1 Two or more races, non-Hispanic/Latino), 6 international. 29 applicants, 72% accepted, 17 enrolled. In 2010, 14 master's awarded. *Degree requirements:* For master's, thesis optional. *Entrance requirements:* For master's, GRE General Test, GRE Subject Test, 30 undergraduate semester credits in the mathematical sciences or closely-related fields. Additional exam requirements/recommendations for international students: Required—TOEFL (minimum score 600 paper-based; 250 computer-based; 100 iBT); Recommended—IELTS (minimum score 6.5). *Application deadline:* For fall admission, 3/1 for domestic students; for spring admission, 10/1 for domestic students. Applications are processed on a rolling basis. Application fee: $50. Electronic applications accepted. *Expenses:* Tuition, state resident: full-time $4308; part-time $479 per credit hour. Tuition, nonresident: full-time $8942; part-time $994 per credit hour. Required fees: $2000; $85 per credit hour. Tuition and fees vary according to course level, course load, degree level, campus/location and program. *Financial support:* Fellowships, research assistantships, teaching assistantships, Federal Work-Study and institutionally sponsored loans available. Support available to part-time students. Financial award applicants required to submit FAFSA. *Faculty research:* Mathematics, applied mathematics. *Unit head:* Dr. Andrew M. Lewis, Chair, 804-828-1301 Ext. 128, Fax: 804-828-8785, E-mail: amlewis@vcu.edu. *Application contact:* Dr. John F. Berglund, Graduate Program Director, 804-828-1301, E-mail: jfberglu@vcu.edu.

Washington State University, Graduate School, College of Sciences, Department of Mathematics, Pullman, WA 99164. Offers applied mathematics (MS, PhD); mathematics teaching (MS, PhD). Part-time programs available. *Faculty:* 26. *Students:* 33 full-time (11 women), 5 part-time (3 women); includes 1 Black or African American, non-Hispanic/Latino; 2 Asian, non-Hispanic/Latino, 10 international. Average age 29. 84 applicants, 29% accepted, 9 enrolled. In 2010, 7 master's, 1 doctorate awarded. *Degree requirements:* For master's, comprehensive exam (for some programs), thesis (for some programs), oral exam, project; for doctorate, 2 foreign languages, comprehensive exam, thesis/dissertation, oral exam, written exam. *Entrance requirements:* For master's and doctorate, minimum GPA of 3.0, 3 letters of recommendation. Additional exam requirements/recommendations for international students: Required—TOEFL (minimum score 600 paper-based; 250 computer-based), IELTS. *Application deadline:* For fall admission, 1/10 for domestic and international students; for spring admission, 7/1 for domestic and international students. Applications are processed on a rolling basis. Application fee: $50. Electronic applications accepted. *Expenses:* Tuition, state resident: full-time $8552; part-time $443 per credit. Tuition, nonresident: full-time $21,650; part-time $1083 per credit. Required fees: $846. *Financial support:* In 2010–11, 33 students received support, including 2 fellowships with tuition reimbursements available (averaging $2,500 per year), 3 research assistantships with full and partial tuition reimbursements available (averaging $14,634 per year), 27 teaching assistantships with full and partial tuition reimbursements available (averaging $13,383 per year); career-related internships or fieldwork, Federal Work-Study, institutionally sponsored loans, health care benefits, and tuition waivers (partial) also available. Financial award application deadline: 2/15; financial award applicants required to submit FAFSA. *Faculty research:* Computational mathematics, operations research, modeling in the natural sciences, applied statistics. *Unit head:* Dr. K.A. Ariyawansa, Chair, 509-335-4918, Fax: 509-335-1188, E-mail: ari@wsu.edu. *Application contact:* Graduate School Admissions, 800-GRADWSU, Fax: 509-335-1949, E-mail: gradsch@wsu.edu.

Wayne State University, College of Liberal Arts and Sciences, Department of Mathematics, Program in Applied Mathematics, Detroit, MI 48202. Offers MA, PhD. *Faculty:* 20 full-time (2 women). *Students:* 2 full-time (both women), 12 part-time (3 women); includes 3 Black or African American, non-Hispanic/Latino; 1 Asian, non-Hispanic/Latino, 1 international. Average age 35. 12 applicants, 50% accepted, 4 enrolled. In 2010, 3 master's awarded. *Degree requirements:* For doctorate, thesis/dissertation. *Entrance requirements:* Additional exam requirements/recommendations for international students: Required—TOEFL (minimum score 550 paper-based; 213 computer-based); Recommended—TWE (minimum score 6). *Application deadline:* For fall admission, 7/1 for domestic students, 6/1 for international students; for winter admission, 10/1 for international students; for spring admission, 2/1 for international students. Applications are processed on a rolling basis. Application fee: $30 ($50 for international students). Electronic applications accepted. *Expenses:* Tuition, state resident: full-time $7662; part-time $478.85 per credit hour. Tuition, nonresident: full-time $16,920; part-time $1057.55 per credit hour. Required fees: $571.20; $35.70 per credit hour. $188.05 per semester. Tuition and fees vary according to course load and program. *Unit head:* Lowell Hansen, Chair, 313-577-7596, E-mail: lowell@math.wayne.edu. *Application contact:* Bert Schreiber, Professor, 313-577-8838, E-mail: bschreiber@wayne.edu.

Western Illinois University, School of Graduate Studies, College of Arts and Sciences, Department of Mathematics, Macomb, IL 61455-1390. Offers applied math (Certificate); mathematics (MS). Part-time programs available. *Students:* 10 full-time (3 women), 2 part-time (both women), 4 international. Average age 30. 9 applicants, 67% accepted. In 2010, 8 master's, 3 other advanced degrees awarded. *Degree requirements:* For master's, thesis or alternative. *Entrance requirements:* Additional exam requirements/recommendations for international students: Required—TOEFL (minimum score 500 paper-based; 173 computer-based; 61 iBT). *Application deadline:* Applications are processed on a rolling basis. Application fee: $30. Electronic applications accepted. *Expenses:* Tuition, state resident: full-time $6370; part-time $265.40 per credit hour. Tuition, nonresident: full-time $12,740; part-time $530.80 per credit hour. Required fees: $75.67 per credit hour. *Financial support:* In 2010–11, 10 students received support, including 6 research assistantships with full tuition reimbursements available (averaging $7,280 per year), 4 teaching assistantships with full tuition reimbursements available (averaging $8,400 per year). Financial award applicants required to submit FAFSA. *Unit head:* Dr. Iraj Kalantari, Chairperson, 309-298-1054. *Application contact:* Evelyn Hoing, Assistant Director of Graduate Studies, 309-298-1806, Fax: 309-298-2345, E-mail: grad-office@wiu.edu.

Western Michigan University, Graduate College, College of Arts and Sciences, Department of Mathematics, Program in Applied and Computational Mathematics, Kalamazoo, MI 49008. Offers MS.

West Virginia University, Eberly College of Arts and Sciences, Department of Mathematics, Morgantown, WV 26506. Offers applied mathematics (MS, PhD); discrete mathematics (PhD); interdisciplinary mathematics (MS); mathematics for secondary education (MS); pure mathematics (MS). Part-time programs available. Terminal master's awarded for partial completion of doctoral program. *Degree requirements:* For master's, comprehensive exam (for some programs), thesis optional; for doctorate, one foreign language, comprehensive exam, thesis/dissertation. *Entrance requirements:* For master's, GRE Subject Test (recommended), minimum GPA of 2.5; for doctorate, GRE Subject Test (recommended), master's degree in mathematics. Additional exam requirements/recommendations for international students: Required—TOEFL (paper-based 550; computer-based 213) or IELTS (paper-based 6). *Faculty research:* Combinatorics and graph theory, differential equations, applied and computational mathematics.

Wichita State University, Graduate School, Fairmount College of Liberal Arts and Sciences, Department of Mathematics and Statistics, Wichita, KS 67260. Offers applied mathematics (PhD); mathematics (MS). Part-time programs available. *Unit head:* Dr. Buma Fridman, Chair, 316-978-3160, Fax: 316-978-3748, E-mail: buma.fridman@wichita.edu. *Application contact:* Dr. Kenneth Miller, Graduate Coordinator, 316-978-3160, Fax: 316-978-3748, E-mail: kenneth.miller@wichita.edu.

Worcester Polytechnic Institute, Graduate Studies and Research, Department of Mathematical Sciences, Worcester, MA 01609-2280. Offers applied mathematics (MS); applied statistics (MS); financial mathematics (MS); industrial mathematics (MS); mathematical sciences (PhD, Graduate Certificate); mathematics (MME). Part-time and evening/weekend programs available. *Faculty:* 17 full-time (1 woman), 6 part-time/adjunct (2 women). *Students:* 48 full-time (20 women), 27 part-time (11 women); includes 3 Black or African American, non-Hispanic/Latino; 2 Hispanic/Latino; 2 Native Hawaiian or other Pacific Islander, non-Hispanic/Latino, 38 international. 230 applicants, 56% accepted, 26 enrolled. In 2010, 21 master's, 2 doctorates awarded. *Degree requirements:* For master's, thesis (for some programs); for doctorate, comprehensive exam, thesis/dissertation. *Entrance requirements:* For master's and doctorate, GRE General Test, GRE Subject Test in math (recommended), 3 letters of recommendation. Additional exam requirements/recommendations for international students: Required—TOEFL (minimum score 550 paper-based; 213 computer-based; 79 iBT), IELTS (minimum score 6.5). *Application deadline:* For fall admission, 1/1 priority date for domestic students, 1/1 for international students; for spring admission, 10/1 priority date for domestic students, 10/1 for international students. Applications are processed on a rolling basis. Application fee: $70. Electronic applications accepted. *Expenses:* Tuition: Full-time $20,862; part-time $1159 per term. One-time fee: $15. *Financial support:* Career-related internships or fieldwork, institutionally sponsored loans, scholarships/grants, and unspecified assistantships available. Financial award application deadline: 1/1; financial award applicants required to submit FAFSA. *Faculty research:* Applied analysis and differential equations, computational mathematics, discrete mathematics, applied and computational statistics, industrial and financial mathematics, mathematical biology. *Unit head:* Dr. Bogdan Vernescu, Head, 508-831-5241, Fax: 508-831-5824, E-mail: vernescu@wpi.edu. *Application contact:* Dr. Joseph Petruccelli, Graduate Coordinator, 508-831-5241, Fax: 508-831-5824, E-mail: jdp@wpi.edu.

Wright State University, School of Graduate Studies, College of Science and Mathematics, Department of Mathematics and Statistics, Program in Applied Mathematics, Dayton, OH 45435. Offers MS. *Degree requirements:* For master's, comprehensive exam. *Entrance requirements:* For master's, bachelor's degree in mathematics or related field. Additional exam requirements/recommendations for international students: Required—TOEFL. *Faculty research:* Control theory, ordinary differential equations, partial differential equations, numerical analysis, mathematical modeling.

Yale University, Graduate School of Arts and Sciences, Program in Applied Mathematics, New Haven, CT 06520. Offers M Phil, MS, PhD. *Entrance requirements:* For doctorate, GRE General Test.

York University, Faculty of Graduate Studies, Faculty of Science and Engineering, Program in Mathematics and Statistics, Toronto, ON M3J 1P3, Canada. Offers industrial and applied mathematics (M Sc); mathematics and statistics (MA, PhD). Part-time programs available. *Degree requirements:* For master's, thesis optional; for doctorate, one foreign language, comprehensive exam, thesis/dissertation. Electronic applications accepted.

Youngstown State University, Graduate School, College of Science, Technology, Engineering and Mathematics, Department of Mathematics and Statistics, Youngstown, OH 44555-0001. Offers applied mathematics (MS); computer science (MS); secondary mathematics (MS); statistics (MS). Part-time programs available. *Degree requirements:* For master's, comprehensive exam, thesis optional. *Entrance requirements:* For master's, minimum GPA of 2.7 in computer science and mathematics. Additional exam requirements/recommendations for international students: Required—TOEFL. *Faculty research:* Regression analysis, numerical analysis, statistics, Markov chain, topology and fuzzy sets.

Applied Statistics

American University, College of Arts and Sciences, Department of Mathematics and Statistics, Washington, DC 22016-8050. Offers applied statistics (Certificate); mathematics (MA); statistics (MS). Part-time and evening/weekend programs available. *Faculty:* 25 full-time (7 women), 12 part-time/adjunct (0 women). *Students:* 9 full-time (2 women), 12 part-time (7 women); includes 2 minority (1 Black or African American, non-Hispanic/Latino; 1 Asian, non-Hispanic/Latino), 3 international. Average age 29. 38 applicants, 68% accepted, 7 enrolled. In 2010, 6 master's awarded. *Degree requirements:* For master's, comprehensive exam, thesis or alternative, tools of research in foreign language or computer language. *Entrance requirements:* For master's, GRE; for Certificate, bachelor's degree. Additional exam requirements/recommendations for international students: Required—TOEFL. *Application deadline:* For fall admission, 2/1 for domestic students; for spring admission, 10/1 for domestic students. Application fee: $80. *Financial support:* Fellowships, research assistantships, teaching assistantships, career-related internships or fieldwork, Federal Work-Study, institutionally sponsored loans, and unspecified assistantships available. Support available to part-time students. Financial award application deadline: 2/1. *Faculty research:* Logic, random processes, probability analysis, biostatistics, statistical computing. *Unit head:* Dr. Mary W. Gray, Chair, 202-885-3171, Fax: 202-885-3155, E-mail: mgray@american.edu. *Application contact:* Kathleen Clowery, Director, Graduate Admissions, 202-885-3621, Fax: 202-885-1505.

Bowling Green State University, Graduate College, College of Arts and Sciences, Department of Mathematics and Statistics, Bowling Green, OH 43403. Offers applied statistics (MS); mathematics (MA, MAT, PhD); statistics (PhD). Part-time programs available. *Degree requirements:* For master's, thesis or alternative; for doctorate, comprehensive exam, thesis/dissertation. *Entrance requirements:* For master's and doctorate, GRE General Test. Additional exam requirements/recommendations for international students: Required—TOEFL. Electronic applications accepted. *Faculty research:* Statistics and probability, algebra, analysis.

Bowling Green State University, Graduate College, College of Business Administration, Department of Applied Statistics and Operations Research, Bowling Green, OH 43403. Offers applied statistics (MS). Part-time programs available. *Degree requirements:* For master's, thesis or alternative. *Entrance requirements:* For master's, GRE General Test. Additional exam requirements/recommendations for international students: Required—TOEFL. Electronic applications accepted. *Faculty research:* Reliability, linear models, time series, statistical quality control.

238   www.facebook.com/petersonspublishing

Peterson's Graduate Programs in the Physical Sciences, Mathematics, Agricultural Sciences, the Environment & Natural Resources 2012

Brigham Young University, Graduate Studies, College of Physical and Mathematical Sciences, Department of Statistics, Provo, UT 84602-1001. Offers applied statistics (MS). *Faculty:* 16 full-time (3 women). *Students:* 26 full-time (8 women); includes 1 minority (Asian, non-Hispanic/Latino). Average age 26. 26 applicants, 69% accepted, 14 enrolled. In 2010, 6 master's awarded. *Degree requirements:* For master's, comprehensive exam, thesis (for some programs). *Entrance requirements:* For master's, GRE General Test, minimum undergraduate GPA of 3.3; course work in statistical methods, theory, multivariable calculus and linear algebra with minimum B- average. Additional exam requirements/recommendations for international students: Required—TOEFL (minimum score 580 paper-based; 237 computer-based; 85 iBT). *Application deadline:* For fall admission, 2/1 for domestic and international students. Application fee: $50. Electronic applications accepted. *Expenses:* Tuition: Full-time $5580; part-time $310 per credit hour. Tuition and fees vary according to program and student's religious affiliation. *Financial support:* In 2010–11, 20 students received support, including 8 research assistantships with full and partial tuition reimbursements available (averaging $10,000 per year), 18 teaching assistantships with full and partial tuition reimbursements available (averaging $10,000 per year); scholarships/grants and unspecified assistantships also available. Financial award application deadline: 2/1. *Faculty research:* Statistical genetics, reliability and pollution monitoring, Bayesian methods. Total annual research expenditures: $42,000. *Unit head:* Dr. Del T. Scott, Chair, 801-422-7054, Fax: 801-422-0635, E-mail: scottd@byu.edu. *Application contact:* Dr. Christopher Shane Reese, Graduate Coordinator, 801-422-9250, Fax: 801-422-0635, E-mail: reese@stat.byu.edu.

California State University, Long Beach, Graduate Studies, College of Natural Sciences and Mathematics, Department of Mathematics and Statistics, Long Beach, CA 90840. Offers mathematics (MS), including applied mathematics, applied statistics, mathematics education for secondary school teachers. Part-time programs available. *Faculty:* 18 full-time (7 women), 3 part-time/adjunct (2 women). *Students:* 53 full-time (19 women), 107 part-time (35 women); includes 4 Black or African American, non-Hispanic/Latino; 52 Asian, non-Hispanic/Latino; 24 Hispanic/Latino, 13 international. Average age 30. 175 applicants, 71% accepted, 80 enrolled. In 2010, 28 master's awarded. *Degree requirements:* For master's, comprehensive exam or thesis. *Application deadline:* For fall admission, 7/1 for domestic students; for spring admission, 12/1 for domestic students. Applications are processed on a rolling basis. Application fee: $55. Electronic applications accepted. *Financial support:* Teaching assistantships, Federal Work-Study, institutionally sponsored loans, scholarships/grants, and traineeships available. Financial award application deadline: 3/2. *Faculty research:* Algebra, functional analysis, partial differential equations, operator theory, numerical analysis. *Unit head:* Dr. Robert Mena, Chair, 562-985-4721, Fax: 562-985-8227, E-mail: rmena@csulb.edu. *Application contact:* Dr. Ngo Viet, Graduate Associate Chair, 562-985-4721, Fax: 562-985-8227, E-mail: viet@csulb.edu.

Cornell University, Graduate School, Graduate Fields of Engineering, Field of Statistics, Ithaca, NY 14853-0001. Offers applied statistics (MPS); biometry (MS, PhD); decision theory (MS, PhD); economic and social statistics (MS, PhD); engineering statistics (MS, PhD); experimental design (MS, PhD); mathematical statistics (MS, PhD); probability (MS, PhD); sampling (MS, PhD); statistical computing (MS, PhD); stochastic processes (MS, PhD). *Faculty:* 21 full-time (2 women). *Students:* 76 full-time (37 women); includes 4 Asian, non-Hispanic/Latino; 2 Hispanic/Latino, 53 international. Average age 24. 429 applicants, 27% accepted, 50 enrolled. In 2010, 36 master's, 3 doctorates awarded. Terminal master's awarded for partial completion of doctoral program. *Degree requirements:* For master's, project (MPS), thesis (MS); for doctorate, one foreign language, thesis/dissertation. *Entrance requirements:* For master's, GRE General Test (MS), 2 letters of recommendation (MS, MPS); for doctorate, GRE General Test, 2 letters of recommendation. Additional exam requirements/recommendations for international students: Required—TOEFL (minimum score 550 paper-based; 213 computer-based; 77 iBT). *Application deadline:* For fall admission, 1/15 for domestic students. Applications are processed on a rolling basis. Application fee: $70. Electronic applications accepted. *Expenses:* Tuition: Full-time $29,500. Required fees: $76. Tuition and fees vary according to degree level and program. *Financial support:* In 2010–11, 26 students received support, including 3 fellowships with full tuition reimbursements available, 9 research assistantships with full tuition reimbursements available, 17 teaching assistantships with full tuition reimbursements available; institutionally sponsored loans, scholarships/grants, tuition waivers (full and partial), and unspecified assistantships also available. Financial award applicants required to submit FAFSA. *Faculty research:* Bayesian analysis, survival analysis, nonparametric statistics, stochastic processes, mathematical statistics. *Unit head:* Director of Graduate Studies, 607-255-8066. *Application contact:* Graduate Field Assistant, 607-255-8066, E-mail: csc@cornell.edu.

DePaul University, College of Liberal Arts and Sciences, Department of Mathematical Sciences, Chicago, IL 60614. Offers applied mathematics (MS), including actuarial science or statistics; applied statistics (MS, Certificate); mathematics education (MA). Part-time and evening/weekend programs available. *Faculty:* 23 full-time (6 women), 18 part-time/adjunct (5 women). *Students:* 111 full-time (60 women), 66 part-time (30 women); includes 16 Black or African American, non-Hispanic/Latino; 17 Asian, non-Hispanic/Latino; 16 Hispanic/Latino; 2 Two or more races, non-Hispanic/Latino, 10 international. Average age 30. 40 applicants, 100% accepted. In 2010, 30 master's awarded. *Degree requirements:* For master's, comprehensive exam. *Entrance requirements:* Additional exam requirements/recommendations for international students: Required—TOEFL. *Application deadline:* For fall admission, 7/30 for domestic students, 6/30 for international students; for winter admission, 11/30 for domestic students, 10/31 for international students; for spring admission, 2/15 for domestic students. Applications are processed on a rolling basis. Application fee: $25. *Financial support:* In 2010–11, 12 students received support, including research assistantships with partial tuition reimbursements available (averaging $6,000 per year); teaching assistantships, tuition waivers (full) also available. Financial award application deadline: 4/30. *Faculty research:* Verbally prime algebras, enveloping algebras of Lie, superalgebras and related rings, harmonic analysis, estimation theory. *Unit head:* Dr. Ahmed I. Zayed, Chairperson, 773-325-7806, Fax: 773-325-7807, E-mail: azayed@depaul.edu. *Application contact:* Ann Spittle, Director of Graduate Admissions, 312-362-8300, Fax: 312-362-5749, E-mail: admitdpu@depaul.edu.

Eastern Michigan University, Graduate School, College of Arts and Sciences, Department of Mathematics, Ypsilanti, MI 48197. Offers applied statistics (MA); computer science (MA); mathematics (MA); mathematics education (MA). Part-time and evening/weekend programs available. Postbaccalaureate distance learning degree programs offered (minimal on-campus study). *Faculty:* 22 full-time (7 women). *Students:* 5 full-time (3 women), 50 part-time (26 women); includes 7 minority (4 Black or African American, non-Hispanic/Latino; 2 Asian, non-Hispanic/Latino; 1 Hispanic/Latino), 10 international. Average age 35. 35 applicants, 54% accepted, 15 enrolled. In 2010, 19 master's awarded. *Degree requirements:* For master's, thesis optional. *Entrance requirements:* Additional exam requirements/recommendations for international students: Required—TOEFL. *Application deadline:* Applications are processed on a rolling basis. Application fee: $35. *Financial support:* Fellowships, research assistantships with full tuition reimbursements, teaching assistantships with full tuition reimbursements, career-related internships or fieldwork, Federal Work-Study, institutionally sponsored loans, scholarships/grants, tuition waivers (partial), and unspecified assistantships available. Support available to part-time students. Financial award applicants required to submit FAFSA. *Unit head:* Dr. Christopher Gardiner, Department Head, 734-487-1444, Fax: 734-487-2489, E-mail: cgardiner@emich.edu. *Application contact:* Dr. Bingwu Wang, Graduate Coordinator, 734-487-5044, Fax: 734-487-2489, E-mail: bwang@emich.edu.

Florida State University, The Graduate School, College of Arts and Sciences, Department of Statistics, Tallahassee, FL 32306-4330. Offers applied statistics (MS); biostatistics (MS, PhD); mathematical statistics (MS, PhD). Part-time programs available. *Faculty:* 15 full-time (2 women). *Students:* 52 full-time (21 women), 20 part-time (8 women); includes 10 Black or African American, non-Hispanic/Latino; 5 Asian, non-Hispanic/Latino; 8 Hispanic/Latino, 27 international. Average age 29. 182 applicants, 15% accepted, 18 enrolled. In 2010, 4 master's, 10 doctorates awarded. Terminal master's awarded for partial completion of doctoral program. *Degree requirements:* For doctorate, thesis/dissertation, departmental qualifying exam. *Entrance requirements:* For master's, GRE General Test, previous course work in calculus, minimum GPA of 3.0; for doctorate, GRE General Test, minimum GPA of 3.0, 1 course in linear algebra (preferred), calculus I-III, real analysis. Additional exam requirements/recommendations for international students: Required—TOEFL (minimum score 600 paper-based; 250 computer-based; 100 iBT). *Application deadline:* For fall admission, 7/1 for domestic and international students; for spring admission, 11/1 for domestic and international students. Applications are processed on a rolling basis. Application fee: $30. Electronic applications accepted. *Expenses:* Tuition, state resident: full-time $8238.24. *Financial support:* In 2010–11, 49 students received support, including 1 fellowship with full tuition reimbursement available (averaging $19,000 per year), 10 research assistantships with full tuition reimbursements available (averaging $22,185 per year), 41 teaching assistantships with full tuition reimbursements available (averaging $19,653 per year); Federal Work-Study, institutionally sponsored loans, scholarships/grants, health care benefits, and unspecified assistantships also available. Support available to part-time students. Financial award application deadline: 2/15; financial award applicants required to submit FAFSA. *Faculty research:* Statistical inference, probability theory, biostatistics, nonparametric estimation, automatic target recognition. *Unit head:* Dr. Dan McGee, Chairman, 850-644-3218, Fax: 850-644-5271, E-mail: info@stat.fsu.edu. *Application contact:* Chauncey Richburg, Academic Support Assistant, 850-644-3514, Fax: 850-644-5271, E-mail: richburg@stat.fsu.edu.

Indiana University–Purdue University Fort Wayne, College of Arts and Sciences, Department of Mathematical Sciences, Fort Wayne, IN 46805-1499. Offers applied mathematics (MS); applied statistics (Certificate); mathematics (MS); operations research (MS); teaching (MAT). Part-time and evening/weekend programs available. *Faculty:* 18 full-time (4 women), 1 (woman) part-time/adjunct. *Students:* 3 full-time (0 women), 17 part-time (6 women). Average age 33. 12 applicants, 100% accepted, 12 enrolled. In 2010, 4 master's, 3 other advanced degrees awarded. *Entrance requirements:* For master's, minimum GPA of 3.0, major or minor in mathematics, three letters of recommendation. Additional exam requirements/recommendations for international students: Required—TOEFL (minimum score 550 paper-based; 213 computer-based; 77 iBT); Recommended—TWE. *Application deadline:* For fall admission, 8/1 priority date for domestic students, 7/1 priority date for international students; for spring admission, 12/1 for domestic students, 10/1 for international students. Applications are processed on a rolling basis. Application fee: $55 ($60 for international students). Electronic applications accepted. *Expenses:* Tuition, state resident: full-time $4824; part-time $268 per credit. Tuition, nonresident: full-time $11,625; part-time $646 per credit. Required fees: $555; $30.85 per credit. Tuition and fees vary according to course load. *Financial support:* In 2010–11, 9 teaching assistantships with partial tuition reimbursements (averaging $12,740 per year) were awarded; scholarships/grants and unspecified assistantships also available. Support available to part-time students. Financial award application deadline: 3/1; financial award applicants required to submit FAFSA. *Faculty research:* Axis-supported external fields, discipline of doubt, t-design graphs. *Unit head:* Dr. David A. Legg, Chair, 260-481-6222, Fax: 260-481-0155, E-mail: legg@ipfw.edu. *Application contact:* Dr. W. Douglas Weakley, Director of Graduate Studies, 260-481-6233, Fax: 260-481-0155, E-mail: weakley@ipfw.edu.

Indiana University–Purdue University Indianapolis, School of Science, Department of Mathematical Sciences, Master's Program in Mathematics, Indianapolis, IN 46202-2896. Offers applied mathematics (MS); applied statistics (MS); mathematics (MS). *Students:* 6 full-time (1 woman), 18 part-time (7 women); includes 5 minority (1 Black or African American, non-Hispanic/Latino; 3 Asian, non-Hispanic/Latino; 1 Hispanic/Latino), 3 international. Average age 36. 4 applicants, 75% accepted, 3 enrolled. In 2010, 10 master's awarded. Application fee: $55 ($65 for international students). *Unit head:* Slawomir Klimek, Director of Graduate Programs, 317-274-6918, E-mail: grad-program@math.iupui.edu. *Application contact:* Slawomir Klimek, Director of Graduate Programs, 317-274-6918, E-mail: grad-program@math.iupui.edu.

Instituto Tecnológico y de Estudios Superiores de Monterrey, Campus Monterrey, Graduate and Research Division, Programs in Engineering, Monterrey, Mexico. Offers applied statistics (M Eng); artificial intelligence (PhD); automation engineering (M Eng); chemical engineering (M Eng); civil engineering (M Eng); electrical engineering (M Eng); electronic engineering (M Eng); environmental engineering (M Eng); industrial engineering (M Eng, PhD); manufacturing engineering (M Eng); mechanical engineering (M Eng); systems and quality engineering (M Eng). M Eng program offered jointly with University of Waterloo; PhD in industrial engineering with Texas A&M University. Part-time and evening/weekend programs available. Terminal master's awarded for partial completion of doctoral program. *Degree requirements:* For master's, one foreign language, thesis; for doctorate, one foreign language, thesis/dissertation. *Entrance requirements:* For master's, EXADEP; for doctorate, GRE, master's degree in related field. Additional exam requirements/recommendations for international students: Required—TOEFL. *Faculty research:* Flexible manufacturing cells, materials, statistical methods, environmental prevention, control and evaluation.

Kennesaw State University, College of Science and Mathematics, Program in Applied Statistics, Kennesaw, GA 30144-5591. Offers MSAS. Part-time and evening/weekend programs available. *Students:* 28 full-time (10 women), 42 part-time (18 women); includes 25 minority (15 Black or African American, non-Hispanic/Latino; 1 American Indian or Alaska Native, non-Hispanic/Latino; 5 Asian, non-Hispanic/Latino; 3 Hispanic/Latino; 1 Two or more races, non-Hispanic/Latino), 7 international. Average age 33. 24 applicants, 83% accepted, 16 enrolled. In 2010, 32 master's awarded. *Entrance requirements:* For master's, GRE, minimum GPA of 2.75, resume. Additional exam requirements/recommendations for international students: Required—TOEFL (minimum score 550 paper-based; 213 computer-based; 80 iBT), IELTS (minimum score 6). *Application deadline:* For fall admission, 6/1 for domestic and international students; for spring admission, 11/1 for domestic and international students. Applications are processed on a rolling basis. Application fee: $60. Electronic applications accepted. *Expenses:* Tuition, state resident: full-time $5500; part-time $225 per credit hour. Tuition, nonresident: full-time $16,100; part-time $813 per credit hour. Required fees: $673 per semester. *Financial support:* In 2010–11, 2 research assistantships (averaging $4,000 per year) were awarded; unspecified assistantships also available. Financial award application deadline: 4/1; financial award applicants required to submit FAFSA. *Unit head:* Dr. Lewis Van Brackle, Director, 678-797-2409, E-mail: lvanbrac@kennesaw.edu. *Application contact:* Tamara Hutto, Admissions Counselor, 770-420-4377, Fax: 770-423-6885, E-mail: vmarquez@kennesaw.edu.

Louisiana State University and Agricultural and Mechanical College, Graduate School, College of Agriculture, Department of Experimental Statistics, Baton Rouge, LA 70803. Offers applied statistics (M App St). Part-time programs available. *Faculty:* 9 full-time (1 woman). *Students:* 15 full-time (12 women), 4 part-time (2 women); includes 2 Asian, non-Hispanic/Latino, 11 international. Average age 29. 23 applicants, 57% accepted, 4 enrolled. In 2010, 8 master's awarded. *Degree requirements:* For master's, project. *Entrance requirements:* For master's, GRE General Test, minimum GPA of 3.0. Additional exam requirements/recommendations for international students: Required—TOEFL (minimum score 550 paper-based; 213 computer-based; 79 iBT) or IELTS (minimum score 6.5). *Application deadline:* For fall admission, 1/25 priority date for domestic students, 5/15 for international students; for spring admission, 10/15 priority date for domestic students, 10/15 for international students. Applications are processed on a rolling basis. Application fee: $50 ($70 for international students). Electronic applications accepted. *Financial support:* In 2010–11, 14 students received support, including 2 research assistantships with partial tuition reimbursements available (averaging $14,700 per year), 10 teaching assistantships with partial tuition reimbursements available (averaging $10,085 per year); fellowships, career-related internships or fieldwork, Federal Work-Study, institutionally sponsored loans, tuition waivers (full and partial), and

Applied Statistics

Louisiana State University and Agricultural and Mechanical College (continued)

unspecified assistantships also available. Financial award application deadline: 4/1; financial award applicants required to submit FAFSA. *Faculty research:* Linear models, statistical computing, ecological statistics. *Unit head:* Dr. James Geaghan, Head, 225-578-8303, Fax: 225-578-8344, E-mail: head@stat.lsu.edu. *Application contact:* Dr. James Geaghan, Graduate Adviser, 225-578-8303, E-mail: jgeaghan@lsu.edu.

Loyola University Chicago, Graduate School, Department of Mathematical Sciences and Statistics, Chicago, IL 60660. Offers applied statistics (MS); mathematics and statistics (MS), including pure mathematics. Part-time programs available. *Faculty:* 19 full-time (4 women). *Students:* 29 full-time (20 women), 6 part-time (2 women); includes 11 minority (1 Black or African American, non-Hispanic/Latino; 6 Asian, non-Hispanic/Latino; 3 Hispanic/Latino; 1 Two or more races, non-Hispanic/Latino), 6 international. Average age 28. 64 applicants, 75% accepted, 23 enrolled. In 2010, 21 master's awarded. *Entrance requirements:* For master's, GRE General Test. Additional exam requirements/recommendations for international students: Required—TOEFL. *Application deadline:* For fall admission, 8/1 for domestic students; for spring admission, 12/1 for domestic students. Applications are processed on a rolling basis. Application fee: $0. Electronic applications accepted. *Expenses:* Tuition: Full-time $14,940; part-time $830 per credit hour. Required fees: $87 per semester. Part-time tuition and fees vary according to course load and program. *Financial support:* In 2010–11, 13 students received support, including 6 teaching assistantships with tuition reimbursements available (averaging $10,000 per year); career-related internships or fieldwork, Federal Work-Study, institutionally sponsored loans, and tuition waivers (partial) also available. Financial award application deadline: 3/15. *Faculty research:* Probability and statistics, differential equations, algebra, combinations. Total annual research expenditures: $10,000. *Unit head:* Dr. Robert Jensen, Chair, 773-508-3578, Fax: 773-508-2123, E-mail: rjensen@luc.edu. *Application contact:* Dr. W. Cary Huffman, Graduate Program Director, Mathematics, 773-508-3563, Fax: 773-508-2123, E-mail: whuffma@luc.edu.

McMaster University, School of Graduate Studies, Faculty of Science, Department of Mathematics and Statistics, Program in Statistics, Hamilton, ON L8S 4M2, Canada. Offers applied statistics (M Sc); medical statistics (M Sc); statistical theory (M Sc). *Degree requirements:* For master's, thesis or alternative. *Entrance requirements:* For master's, honors degree background in mathematics and statistics. Additional exam requirements/recommendations for international students: Required—TOEFL (minimum score 550 paper-based; 213 computer-based). *Faculty research:* Development of polymer production technology, quality of life in patients who use pharmaceutical agents, mathematical modeling, order statistics from progressively censored samples, nonlinear stochastic model in genetics.

Michigan State University, The Graduate School, College of Natural Science, Department of Statistics and Probability, East Lansing, MI 48824. Offers applied statistics (MS); statistics (MS, PhD). *Entrance requirements:* Additional exam requirements/recommendations for international students: Required—TOEFL. Electronic applications accepted.

New Jersey Institute of Technology, Office of Graduate Studies, College of Science and Liberal Arts, Department of Mathematical Science, Program in Applied Statistics, Newark, NJ 07102. Offers MS. Part-time and evening/weekend programs available. *Students:* 14 full-time (4 women), 14 part-time (4 women); includes 8 Asian, non-Hispanic/Latino; 2 Hispanic/Latino, 8 international. Average age 32. 68 applicants, 32% accepted, 9 enrolled. In 2010, 13 master's awarded. *Entrance requirements:* For master's, GRE General Test. Additional exam requirements/recommendations for international students: Required—TOEFL (minimum score 550 paper-based; 213 computer-based; 79 iBT). *Application deadline:* For fall admission, 6/5 priority date for domestic students, 4/1 for international students; for spring admission, 11/15 for domestic and international students. Applications are processed on a rolling basis. Application fee: $65. Electronic applications accepted. *Expenses:* Tuition, state resident: full-time $14,724; part-time $818 per credit. Tuition, nonresident: full-time $20,304; part-time $1128 per credit. Required fees: $2272; $209 per credit. $103 per semester. One-time fee: $312 full-time; $212 part-time. *Financial support:* Fellowships with full and partial tuition reimbursements, research assistantships with full and partial tuition reimbursements, teaching assistantships with full and partial tuition reimbursements, career-related internships or fieldwork, Federal Work-Study, institutionally sponsored loans, and unspecified assistantships available. Financial award application deadline: 3/15. *Unit head:* Dr. Manish Bhattacharjee, Director, 973-596-2949, Fax: 973-596-5591, E-mail: manish.bhattacharjee@njit.edu. *Application contact:* Kathryn Kelly, Director of Admissions, 973-596-3300, Fax: 973-596-3461, E-mail: admissions@njit.edu.

New Mexico State University, Graduate School, College of Business, Department of Economics, Applied Statistics and International Business, Las Cruces, NM 88003. Offers applied statistics (MS); economic development (DED); economics (MA). Part-time programs available. *Faculty:* 12 full-time (2 women), 2 part-time/adjunct (1 woman). *Students:* 64 full-time (21 women), 16 part-time (5 women); includes 22 minority (3 Black or African American, non-Hispanic/Latino; 2 Asian, non-Hispanic/Latino; 17 Hispanic/Latino), 37 international. Average age 31. 84 applicants, 83% accepted, 34 enrolled. In 2010, 16 master's awarded. Terminal master's awarded for partial completion of doctoral program. *Degree requirements:* For master's, comprehensive exam, thesis or alternative; for doctorate, comprehensive exam, thesis/dissertation, internship, written project. *Entrance requirements:* For master's, minimum GPA of 3.0; for doctorate, appropriate master's degree, minimum GPA of 3.0. Additional exam requirements/recommendations for international students: Required—TOEFL (minimum score 530 paper-based; 71 computer-based), IELTS. *Application deadline:* Applications are processed on a rolling basis. Application fee: $30 ($50 for international students). Electronic applications accepted. *Expenses:* Tuition, state resident: full-time $4536; part-time $242 per credit. Tuition, nonresident: full-time $15,816; part-time $712 per credit. Required fees: $636 per term. *Financial support:* In 2010–11, 34 students received support, including 14 research assistantships (averaging $11,225 per year), 29 teaching assistantships (averaging $6,846 per year); fellowships, career-related internships or fieldwork, Federal Work-Study, and health care benefits also available. Support available to part-time students. Financial award application deadline: 3/1. *Faculty research:* Public utilities, environment, linear models, biological sampling, public policy, economic development, energy. *Unit head:* Dr. Richard V. Adkisson, Head, 575-646-4988, Fax: 575-646-1915, E-mail: radkisso@nmsu.edu. *Application contact:* Dr. Richard V. Adkisson, Head, 575-646-4988, Fax: 575-646-1915, E-mail: radkisso@nmsu.edu.

North Dakota State University, College of Graduate and Interdisciplinary Studies, College of Science and Mathematics, Department of Statistics, Fargo, ND 58108. Offers applied statistics (MS, Certificate); statistics (PhD); MS/MS. *Faculty:* 4 full-time (2 women), 1 part-time/adjunct (0 women). *Students:* 1 (woman) full-time, 3 part-time (2 women), 1 international. Average age 24. 8 applicants, 100% accepted, 1 enrolled. In 2010, 2 doctorates awarded. *Degree requirements:* For master's, comprehensive exam, thesis; for doctorate, comprehensive exam, thesis/dissertation. *Entrance requirements:* For master's and doctorate, minimum GPA of 3.0. Additional exam requirements/recommendations for international students: Required—TOEFL (minimum score 550 paper-based; 213 computer-based; 79 iBT). *Application deadline:* Applications are processed on a rolling basis. Application fee: $45 ($60 for international students). *Financial support:* In 2010–11, 2 fellowships with full tuition reimbursements, 7 research assistantships with full tuition reimbursements, 9 teaching assistantships with full tuition reimbursements were awarded; career-related internships or fieldwork, Federal Work-Study, institutionally sponsored loans, and tuition waivers (full) also available. Financial award application deadline: 4/15. *Faculty research:* Nonparametric statistics, survival analysis, multivariate analysis, distribution theory, inference modeling, biostatistics. *Unit head:* Dr. Rhonda Magel, Chair, 701-231-7532, Fax: 701-231-8734, E-mail: ndsu.stats@ndsu.edu. *Application contact:* Judy Normann, Academic Assistant, 701-231-7532, Fax: 702-231-8734, E-mail: ndsu.stats@ndsu.edu.

Northern Arizona University, Graduate College, College of Engineering, Forestry and Natural Sciences, Department of Mathematics and Statistics, Flagstaff, AZ 86011. Offers applied statistics (Certificate); mathematics (MAT, MS); statistics (MS). Part-time programs available. *Faculty:* 42 full-time (12 women). *Students:* 23 full-time (10 women), 18 part-time (11 women); includes 8 minority (3 Black or African American, non-Hispanic/Latino; 1 Asian, non-Hispanic/Latino; 4 Hispanic/Latino), 1 international. Average age 28. 33 applicants, 61% accepted, 12 enrolled. In 2010, 15 master's, 1 other advanced degree awarded. *Degree requirements:* For master's, comprehensive exam (for some programs), thesis (for some programs). *Entrance requirements:* For master's, minimum GPA of 3.0. Additional exam requirements/recommendations for international students: Required—TOEFL (minimum score 550 paper-based; 213 computer-based; 80 iBT), IELTS (minimum score 7). *Application deadline:* For fall admission, 3/15 priority date for domestic and international students; for spring admission, 10/15 priority date for domestic and international students. Applications are processed on a rolling basis. Application fee: $65. Electronic applications accepted. *Financial support:* In 2010–11, 22 teaching assistantships with partial tuition reimbursements (averaging $14,051 per year) were awarded; Federal Work-Study, scholarships/grants, health care benefits, tuition waivers (full and partial), and unspecified assistantships also available. Financial award applicants required to submit FAFSA. *Faculty research:* Topology, statistics, groups, ring theory, number theory. *Unit head:* Dr. Janet M. McShane, Chair, 928-523-1252, Fax: 928-523-5847, E-mail: janet.mcshane@nau.edu. *Application contact:* Sharon O'Connor, Chair, 928-523-3481, Fax: 928-523-5847, E-mail: math.grad@nau.edu.

Oakland University, Graduate Study and Lifelong Learning, College of Arts and Sciences, Department of Mathematics and Statistics, Program in Applied Statistics, Rochester, MI 48309-4401. Offers MS. Part-time and evening/weekend programs available. *Entrance requirements:* For master's, minimum GPA of 3.0 for unconditional admission. Additional exam requirements/recommendations for international students: Required—TOEFL (minimum score 550 paper-based; 213 computer-based). Electronic applications accepted. *Expenses:* Contact institution.

Rochester Institute of Technology, Graduate Enrollment Services, Kate Gleason College of Engineering, Center of Quality and Applied Statistics, Rochester, NY 14623-5603. Offers applied statistics (MS); statistical quality (AC). Part-time and evening/weekend programs available. Postbaccalaureate distance learning degree programs offered (no on-campus study). *Students:* 19 full-time (12 women), 39 part-time (12 women); includes 5 Asian, non-Hispanic/Latino; 3 Hispanic/Latino, 11 international. Average age 34. 38 applicants, 61% accepted, 15 enrolled. In 2010, 18 master's, 1 other advanced degree awarded. *Degree requirements:* For master's, oral exam. *Entrance requirements:* For master's, course work in calculus, minimum GPA of 3.0. Additional exam requirements/recommendations for international students: Required—TOEFL (minimum score 570 paper-based; 230 computer-based; 88 iBT) or IELTS (minimum score 6.5). *Application deadline:* For fall admission, 2/15 priority date for domestic and international students; for winter admission, 10/15 for domestic students; for spring admission, 2/1 for domestic students. Applications are processed on a rolling basis. Application fee: $50. *Expenses:* Tuition: Full-time $33,234; part-time $924 per credit hour. Required fees: $219. *Financial support:* In 2010–11, 33 students received support; research assistantships with partial tuition reimbursements available, career-related internships or fieldwork, institutionally sponsored loans, scholarships/grants, and unspecified assistantships available. Support available to part-time students. Financial award applicants required to submit FAFSA. *Faculty research:* Industrial statistics, quality control. *Unit head:* Dr. Donald Baker, Director, 585-475-6990, Fax: 585-475-5959, E-mail: cqas@rit.edu. *Application contact:* Diane Ellison, Assistant Vice President, Graduate Enrollment Services, 585-475-2229, Fax: 585-475-7164, E-mail: gradinfo@rit.edu.

Rutgers, The State University of New Jersey, New Brunswick, Graduate School-New Brunswick, Program in Statistics, Piscataway, NJ 08854-8097. Offers applied statistics (MS); biostatistics (MS); data mining (MS); quality and productivity management (MS); statistics (MS, PhD). Part-time programs available. Terminal master's awarded for partial completion of doctoral program. *Degree requirements:* For master's, comprehensive exam, essay, exam, non-thesis essay paper; for doctorate, one foreign language, thesis/dissertation, qualifying oral and written exams. *Entrance requirements:* For master's, GRE General Test; for doctorate, GRE General Test, GRE Subject Test (recommended). Additional exam requirements/recommendations for international students: Required—TOEFL (minimum score 550 paper-based; 213 computer-based). Electronic applications accepted. *Expenses:* Tuition, state resident: full-time $7200; part-time $600 per credit. Tuition, nonresident: full-time $11,124; part-time $927 per credit. *Faculty research:* Probability, decision theory, linear models, multivariate statistics, statistical computing.

St. Cloud State University, School of Graduate Studies, College of Science and Engineering, Program in Applied Statistics, St. Cloud, MN 56301-4498. Offers MS.

Stevens Institute of Technology, Graduate School, Charles V. Schaefer Jr. School of Engineering, Department of Mathematical Sciences, Program in Applied Statistics, Hoboken, NJ 07030. Offers Certificate. *Students:* 5 applicants, 80% accepted. *Entrance requirements:* Additional exam requirements/recommendations for international students: Required—TOEFL. *Application deadline:* Applications are processed on a rolling basis. Application fee: $50. Electronic applications accepted. *Unit head:* Dr. Robert Gilman, Director, 201-216-5449, Fax: 201-216-8321. *Application contact:* Dr. Milos Dostal, Professor, 201-216-5426.

Syracuse University, College of Arts and Sciences, Program in Applied Statistics, Syracuse, NY 13244. Offers MS. Part-time programs available. *Students:* 6 full-time (5 women), 2 part-time (1 woman), 7 international. Average age 24. 46 applicants, 63% accepted, 5 enrolled. In 2010, 8 master's awarded. *Entrance requirements:* For master's, GRE General Test. Additional exam requirements/recommendations for international students: Required—TOEFL (minimum score 100 iBT). *Application deadline:* For fall admission, 2/1 priority date for domestic and international students. Application fee: $75. Electronic applications accepted. *Expenses:* Tuition: Part-time $1162 per credit. *Financial support:* Fellowships with full and partial tuition reimbursements, teaching assistantships with full and partial tuition reimbursements, tuition waivers available. Financial award application deadline: 1/1; financial award applicants required to submit FAFSA. *Unit head:* Dr. Pinyuen Chen, Graduate Contact, 315-443-1577, E-mail: pinchen@syr.edu. *Application contact:* Dr. Pinyuen Chen, Graduate Contact, 315-443-1577, E-mail: pinchen@syr.edu.

The University of Alabama, Graduate School, Manderson Graduate School of Business, Department of Information Systems, Statistics, and Management Science, Program of Information Systems, Statistics, and Management Science—Applied Statistics, Tuscaloosa, AL 35487. Offers applied statistics (MS, PhD). *Faculty:* 22 full-time (4 women). *Students:* 14 full-time (6 women), 7 part-time (2 women); includes 3 minority (1 Black or African American, non-Hispanic/Latino; 2 Asian, non-Hispanic/Latino), 12 international. Average age 30. 13 applicants, 46% accepted, 3 enrolled. In 2010, 12 master's, 4 doctorates awarded. Terminal master's awarded for partial completion of doctoral program. *Degree requirements:* For master's, comprehensive exam; for doctorate, comprehensive exam, thesis/dissertation. *Entrance requirements:* For master's and doctorate, GMAT or GRE, 3 semesters of calculus and linear algebra. Additional exam requirements/recommendations for international students: Required—TOEFL (minimum score 550 paper-based; 213 computer-based), IELTS (minimum score 6.5). *Application deadline:* For spring admission, 3/1 priority date for domestic and international students. Applications are processed on a rolling basis. Application fee: $50 ($60 for international students). Electronic applications accepted. *Expenses:* Tuition, state resident: full-time $7900. Tuition, nonresident: full-time $20,500. *Financial support:* In 2010–11, 9 students received support, including 7 teaching assistantships with tuition reimbursements available

(averaging $13,500 per year); scholarships/grants and health care benefits also available. Financial award application deadline: 3/1. *Faculty research:* Data mining, regression analysis, statistical quality control, nonparametric statistics, design of experiments. *Unit head:* Dr. Michael D. Conerly, Professor and Department Head, 205-348-8902, E-mail: mconerly@cba.ua.edu. *Application contact:* Dana Merchant, Administrative Secretary, 205-348-8904, E-mail: dmerchan@cba.ua.edu.

University of Arkansas at Little Rock, Graduate School, College of Science and Mathematics, Department of Mathematics and Statistics, Little Rock, AR 72204-1099. Offers applied statistics (Graduate Certificate); mathematical sciences (MS). Part-time and evening/weekend programs available. *Degree requirements:* For master's, comprehensive exam. *Entrance requirements:* For master's, GRE General Test, GRE Subject Test, minimum GPA of 2.7, previous course work in advanced mathematics.

University of California, Riverside, Graduate Division, Department of Statistics, Riverside, CA 92521-0102. Offers applied statistics (PhD); statistics (MS). Terminal master's awarded for partial completion of doctoral program. *Degree requirements:* For master's, comprehensive exam; for doctorate, comprehensive exam, thesis/dissertation. *Entrance requirements:* For master's and doctorate, GRE General Test. Additional exam requirements/recommendations for international students: Required—TOEFL (minimum score 550 paper-based; 213 computer-based; 80 iBT). Electronic applications accepted. *Faculty research:* Design and analysis of gene expression experiments using DNA microarrays, statistical design and analysis of experiments, linear models, probability models and statistical inference, SNP/SFP discovery using DNA microarray, genetic mapping.

University of California, Santa Barbara, Graduate Division, College of Letters and Sciences, Division of Mathematics, Life, and Physical Sciences, Department of Statistics and Applied Probability, Santa Barbara, CA 93106-3110. Offers financial mathematics and statistics (PhD); quantitative methods in the social sciences (PhD); statistics (MA), including applied statistics, mathematical statistics; statistics and applied probability (PhD); MA/PhD. *Faculty:* 11 full-time (3 women). *Students:* 49 full-time (17 women); includes 30 Asian, non-Hispanic/Latino; 2 Hispanic/Latino. Average age 29. 195 applicants, 20% accepted, 14 enrolled. In 2010, 16 master's, 2 doctorates awarded. Terminal master's awarded for partial completion of doctoral program. *Degree requirements:* For master's, comprehensive exam, thesis (for some programs); for doctorate, comprehensive exam, thesis/dissertation. *Entrance requirements:* For master's and doctorate, GRE General Test. Additional exam requirements/recommendations for international students: Required—TOEFL (minimum score 550 paper-based; 80 iBT), IELTS (minimum score 7). *Application deadline:* For fall admission, 1/1 priority date for domestic and international students; for winter admission, 11/1 priority date for domestic and international students; for spring admission, 2/1 priority date for domestic and international students. Application fee: $70 ($90 for international students). Electronic applications accepted. *Financial support:* In 2010–11, 23 students received support, including 6 fellowships with full tuition reimbursements available (averaging $11,285 per year), 1 research assistantship with full and partial tuition reimbursement available (averaging $2,790 per year), 28 teaching assistantships with partial tuition reimbursements available (averaging $14,557 per year). Financial award application deadline: 1/1; financial award applicants required to submit FAFSA. *Faculty research:* Bayesian inference, financial mathematics, stochastic processes, environmental statistics, biostatistical modeling. Total annual research expenditures: $139,480. *Unit head:* Dr. Yuedong Wang, Chair, 805-893-4870, E-mail: yeudong@pstat.ucsb.edu. *Application contact:* Rickie R. Smith, Graduate Program Assistant, 805-893-2129, Fax: 805-893-2334, E-mail: smith@pstat.ucsb.edu.

University of Guelph, Graduate Studies, College of Physical and Engineering Science, Department of Mathematics and Statistics, Guelph, ON N1G 2W1, Canada. Offers applied mathematics (PhD); applied statistics (PhD); mathematics and statistics (M Sc). Part-time programs available. *Degree requirements:* For master's, thesis (for some programs); for doctorate, thesis/dissertation. *Entrance requirements:* For master's, minimum B- average during previous 2 years of course work; for doctorate, minimum B average. Additional exam requirements/recommendations for international students: Required—TOEFL (minimum score 550 paper-based; 213 computer-based; 89 iBT), IELTS (minimum score 6.5). *Faculty research:* Dynamical systems, mathematical biology, numerical analysis, linear and nonlinear models, reliability and bioassay.

University of Illinois at Urbana–Champaign, Graduate College, College of Liberal Arts and Sciences, Department of Statistics, Champaign, IL 61820. Offers applied statistics (MS); statistics (PhD). *Faculty:* 11 full-time (4 women). *Students:* 50 full-time (26 women), 12 part-time (5 women); includes 5 minority (1 Black or African American, non-Hispanic/Latino; 4 Asian, non-Hispanic/Latino), 44 international. 299 applicants, 14% accepted, 18 enrolled. In 2010, 41 master's, 3 doctorates awarded. *Entrance requirements:* For master's and doctorate, GRE, minimum GPA of 3.0. Additional exam requirements/recommendations for international students: Required—TOEFL (minimum score 590 paper-based; 243 computer-based). *Application deadline:* Applications are processed on a rolling basis. Application fee: $75 ($90 for international students). Electronic applications accepted. *Financial support:* In 2010–11, 1 fellowship, 29 research assistantships, 33 teaching assistantships were awarded; tuition waivers (full and partial) also available. *Faculty research:* Statistical decision theory, sequential analysis, computer-aided stochastic modeling. *Unit head:* Douglas G. Simpson, Chair, 217-244-0885, Fax: 217-244-7190, E-mail: dgs@illinois.edu. *Application contact:* Melissa Banks, Office Support Specialist, 217-333-2167, Fax: 217-244-7190, E-mail: mdbanks@illinois.edu.

University of Memphis, Graduate School, College of Arts and Sciences, Department of Mathematical Sciences, Memphis, TN 38152. Offers applied mathematics (MS); applied statistics (PhD); bioinformatics (MS); computer science (PhD); computer sciences (MS); mathematics (MS, PhD); statistics (MS, PhD). Part-time programs available. *Faculty:* 19 full-time (4 women), 3 part-time/adjunct (0 women). *Students:* 38 full-time (12 women), 21 part-time (12 women); includes 8 minority (5 Black or African American, non-Hispanic/Latino; 2 Asian, non-Hispanic/Latino; 1 Hispanic/Latino), 25 international. Average age 34. 49 applicants, 55% accepted, 9 enrolled. In 2010, 6 master's, 5 doctorates awarded. Terminal master's awarded for partial completion of doctoral program. *Degree requirements:* For master's, comprehensive exam; for doctorate, one foreign language, thesis/dissertation, oral exams. *Entrance requirements:* For master's and doctorate, GRE General Test, minimum GPA of 2.5. Additional exam requirements/recommendations for international students: Required—TOEFL (minimum score 550 paper-based; 210 computer-based). *Application deadline:* For fall admission, 8/1 for domestic students, 5/1 priority date for international students; for spring admission, 12/1 for domestic students, 9/1 priority date for international students. Applications are processed on a rolling basis. Application fee: $35 ($60 for international students). Electronic applications accepted. *Financial support:* In 2010–11, 22 students received support; fellowships with full tuition reimbursements available, research assistantships with full tuition reimbursements available, teaching assistantships with full tuition reimbursements available, career-related internships or fieldwork, Federal Work-Study, scholarships/grants, and unspecified assistantships available. Financial award application deadline: 2/15; financial award applicants required to submit FAFSA. *Faculty research:* Combinatorics, ergodic theory, graph theory, Ramsey theory, applied statistics. *Unit head:* Dr. James E. Jamison, Chairman, 901-678-2482, Fax: 901-678-2480, E-mail: jjamison@memphis.edu. *Application contact:* Dr. Anna Kaminska, Coordinator of Graduate Studies, 901-678-2494, Fax: 901-678-2480.

University of Michigan, Horace H. Rackham School of Graduate Studies, College of Literature, Science, and the Arts, Department of Statistics, Ann Arbor, MI 48109. Offers applied statistics (AM); statistics (AM, PhD). *Faculty:* 33 full-time (8 women), 1 part-time/adjunct (0 women). *Students:* 113 full-time (49 women); includes 1 American Indian or Alaska Native, non-Hispanic/Latino; 3 Asian, non-Hispanic/Latino; 1 Hispanic/Latino, 76 international. Average age 27. 413

applicants, 20% accepted, 38 enrolled. In 2010, 37 master's, 6 doctorates awarded. Terminal master's awarded for partial completion of doctoral program. *Degree requirements:* For master's, thesis; for doctorate, thesis/dissertation, oral defense of dissertation, preliminary exam. *Entrance requirements:* For master's and doctorate, GRE General Test. Additional exam requirements/recommendations for international students: Required—TOEFL (minimum score 560 paper-based; 220 computer-based; 84 iBT), IELTS (minimum score 6.5). *Application deadline:* For fall admission, 1/31 priority date for domestic students, 1/15 priority date for international students. Applications are processed on a rolling basis. Application fee: $65 ($75 for international students). Electronic applications accepted. *Expenses:* Tuition, state resident: full-time $17,784; part-time $1116 per credit hour. Tuition, nonresident: full-time $35,944; part-time $2125 per credit hour. International tuition: $35,994 full-time. Required fees: $95 per semester. Tuition and fees vary according to course load, degree level and program. *Financial support:* In 2010–11, 62 students received support, including 3 fellowships with full and partial tuition reimbursements available (averaging $25,000 per year), 17 research assistantships with full and partial tuition reimbursements available (averaging $17,270 per year), 42 teaching assistantships with full and partial tuition reimbursements available (averaging $17,270 per year); career-related internships or fieldwork, Federal Work-Study, institutionally sponsored loans, scholarships/grants, health care benefits, and unspecified assistantships also available. Financial award application deadline: 1/31. *Faculty research:* Reliability and degradation modeling, biological and legal applications, bioinformatics, statistical computing, covariance estimation. *Unit head:* Prof. Tailen Hsing, Chair, 734-763-3519, Fax: 734-763-4676, E-mail: statchair@umich.edu. *Application contact:* Lu Ann Custer, Graduate Secretary, 734-763-3520, Fax: 734-763-4676, E-mail: stat-admiss-ques@umich.edu.

University of Northern Colorado, Graduate School, College of Education and Behavioral Sciences, Program in Applied Statistics and Research Methods, Greeley, CO 80639. Offers MS, PhD. Part-time programs available. *Faculty:* 9 full-time (5 women). *Students:* 27 full-time (16 women), 17 part-time (3 women); includes 1 Black or African American, non-Hispanic/Latino; 5 Asian, non-Hispanic/Latino; 2 Hispanic/Latino, 4 international. Average age 38. 20 applicants, 70% accepted, 9 enrolled. In 2010, 12 master's, 13 doctorates awarded. *Degree requirements:* For master's, comprehensive exam; for doctorate, comprehensive exam, thesis/dissertation. *Entrance requirements:* For master's, 3 letters of reference; for doctorate, GRE General Test, 3 letters of reference. *Application deadline:* Applications are processed on a rolling basis. Application fee: $50 ($60 for international students). Electronic applications accepted. *Expenses:* Tuition, state resident: full-time $6199; part-time $344 per credit hour. Tuition, nonresident: full-time $14,834; part-time $824 per credit hour. Required fees: $1091; $60.60 per credit hour. Tuition and fees vary according to course load, degree level and program. *Financial support:* In 2010–11, 24 research assistantships (averaging $4,257 per year), 9 teaching assistantships (averaging $4,244 per year) were awarded; fellowships also available. Financial award application deadline: 3/1. *Unit head:* Dr. Susan Hutchinson, Program Coordinator, 970-351-2807, Fax: 970-351-1669. *Application contact:* Linda Sisson, Graduate Student Admission Coordinator, 970-351-1807, Fax: 970-351-2371, E-mail: linda.sisson@unco.edu.

University of Pittsburgh, School of Arts and Sciences, Department of Statistics, Pittsburgh, PA 15260. Offers applied statistics (MA, MS); statistics (MA, MS, PhD). Part-time programs available. *Faculty:* 7 full-time (1 woman). *Students:* 34 full-time (19 women), 4 part-time (0 women); includes 1 Black or African American, non-Hispanic/Latino, 30 international. Average age 23. 309 applicants, 19% accepted, 16 enrolled. In 2010, 7 master's, 2 doctorates awarded. Terminal master's awarded for partial completion of doctoral program. *Degree requirements:* For master's, comprehensive exam, thesis (for some programs); for doctorate, comprehensive exam, thesis/dissertation. *Entrance requirements:* For master's, 3 semesters of calculus, 1 semester of linear algebra, 1 year of mathematical statistics; for doctorate, 3 semesters of calculus, 1 semester of linear algebra, 1 year of mathematical statistics, 1 semester of advanced calculus. Additional exam requirements/recommendations for international students: Required—TOEFL (minimum score 550 paper-based; 213 computer-based; 80 iBT). *Application deadline:* For fall admission, 1/15 priority date for domestic and international students; for spring admission, 10/1 priority date for domestic students, 9/1 priority date for international students. Application fee: $50. Electronic applications accepted. *Expenses:* Tuition, state resident: full-time $17,304; part-time $701 per credit. Tuition, nonresident: full-time $29,554; part-time $1210 per credit. Required fees: $740; $214 per term. Tuition and fees vary according to program. *Financial support:* In 2010–11, 1 fellowship with full tuition reimbursement (averaging $18,546 per year), 7 research assistantships with full tuition reimbursements (averaging $16,140 per year), 13 teaching assistantships with full tuition reimbursements (averaging $15,520 per year) were awarded; career-related internships or fieldwork, Federal Work-Study, institutionally sponsored loans, scholarships/grants, health care benefits, and unspecified assistantships also available. Financial award application deadline: 1/15. *Faculty research:* Multivariate statistics, time series, reliability, meta-analysis, linear and nonlinear regression modeling. *Unit head:* Satish Iyengar, Chair, 412-624-8341, Fax: 412-648-8814, E-mail: sii@pitt.edu. *Application contact:* Leon J. Gleser, Director of Graduate Studies, 412-624-3925, Fax: 412-648-8814, E-mail: gleser@pitt.edu.

University of South Carolina, The Graduate School, College of Arts and Sciences, Department of Statistics, Columbia, SC 29208. Offers applied statistics (CAS); industrial statistics (MIS); statistics (MS, PhD). Part-time and evening/weekend programs available. Postbaccalaureate distance learning degree programs offered (minimal on-campus study). Terminal master's awarded for partial completion of doctoral program. *Degree requirements:* For master's, thesis; for doctorate, comprehensive exam, thesis/dissertation. *Entrance requirements:* For master's, GRE General Test or GMAT, 2 years of work experience (MIS); for doctorate, GRE General Test; for CAS, GRE General Test or GMAT. Additional exam requirements/recommendations for international students: Required—TOEFL (minimum score 600 paper-based; 250 computer-based; 100 iBT). Electronic applications accepted. *Expenses:* Contact institution. *Faculty research:* Reliability, environmentrics, statistics computing, psychometrics, bioinformatics.

The University of Texas at San Antonio, College of Business, Department of Management Science and Statistics, San Antonio, TX 78249-0617. Offers applied statistics (MS, PhD); management science (MBA). *Accreditation:* AACSB. Part-time and evening/weekend programs available. *Faculty:* 15 full-time (4 women), 1 part-time/adjunct (0 women). *Students:* 34 full-time (12 women), 23 part-time (6 women); includes 13 minority (2 Black or African American, non-Hispanic/Latino; 5 Asian, non-Hispanic/Latino; 5 Hispanic/Latino; 1 Native Hawaiian or other Pacific Islander, non-Hispanic/Latino), 16 international. Average age 31. 51 applicants, 67% accepted, 25 enrolled. In 2010, 15 master's, 1 doctorate awarded. *Degree requirements:* For master's, comprehensive exam (for some programs), thesis (for some programs). *Entrance requirements:* For master's, GMAT, minimum GPA of 3.0. Additional exam requirements/recommendations for international students: Required—TOEFL (minimum score 500 paper-based; 173 computer-based; 61 iBT). *Application deadline:* For fall admission, 7/1 for domestic students, 4/1 for international students; for spring admission, 11/1 for domestic students, 9/1 for international students. Applications are processed on a rolling basis. Application fee: $45 ($80 for international students). Electronic applications accepted. *Expenses:* Tuition, state resident: full-time $4172; part-time $231.75 per credit hour. Tuition, nonresident: full-time $15,332; part-time $851.75 per credit hour. *Financial support:* In 2010–11, 13 students received support, including 1 fellowship (averaging $45,000 per year), 79 research assistantships (averaging $13,264 per year), 8 teaching assistantships (averaging $8,000 per year). *Faculty research:* Applied statistics, biostatistics, supply chain management. Total annual research expenditures: $23,518. *Unit head:* Dr. Raydel Tullous, PhD, Department Chair, 210-458-6345, Fax: 210-458-6350, E-mail: raydel.tullous@utsa.edu. *Application contact:* Veronica Ramirez, Assistant Dean of the Graduate School, 210-458-7841, Fax: 210-458-4332, E-mail: graduatestudies@utsa.edu.

Peterson's Graduate Programs in the Physical Sciences, Mathematics, Agricultural Sciences, the Environment & Natural Resources 2012

www.facebook.com/petersonspublishing   **241**

Applied Statistics

University of the District of Columbia, College of Arts and Sciences, Department of Mathematics, Program in Applied Statistics, Washington, DC 20008-1175. Offers MS. *Degree requirements:* For master's, internship or thesis. *Expenses:* Tuition, state resident: full-time $7580; part-time $421 per credit. Tuition, nonresident: full-time $14,580; part-time $810 per credit. Required fees: $620; $30 per credit. One-time fee: $100 part-time.

University of West Florida, College of Arts and Sciences: Sciences, Department of Mathematics and Statistics, Pensacola, FL 32514-5750. Offers applied statistics (MS); mathematical sciences (MS). Part-time and evening/weekend programs available. *Faculty:* 8 full-time (1 woman). *Students:* 17 full-time (6 women), 47 part-time (29 women); includes 5 Black or African American, non-Hispanic/Latino; 2 Asian, non-Hispanic/Latino; 3 Hispanic/Latino; 1 Two or more races, non-Hispanic/Latino, 1 international. Average age 33. 41 applicants, 95% accepted, 32 enrolled. In 2010, 13 master's awarded. *Degree requirements:* For master's, thesis optional. *Entrance requirements:* For master's, GRE General Test, minimum GPA of 3.0. Additional exam requirements/recommendations for international students: Required—TOEFL (minimum score 550 paper-based; 213 computer-based). *Application deadline:* For fall admission, 6/1 for domestic students, 5/15 for international students; for spring admission, 10/1 for domestic and international students. Applications are processed on a rolling basis. Application fee: $30. *Expenses:* Tuition, state resident: full-time $4982; part-time $208 per credit hour. Tuition, nonresident: full-time $20,059; part-time $836 per credit hour. Required fees: $1365; $57 per credit hour. *Financial support:* In 2010–11, 25 fellowships with partial tuition reimbursements (averaging $421 per year), 4 research assistantships with partial tuition reimbursements (averaging $3,280 per year), 7 teaching assistantships with partial tuition reimbursements (averaging $5,141 per year) were awarded; unspecified assistantships also available. Financial award application deadline: 4/15; financial award applicants required to submit FAFSA. *Unit head:* Dr. Kuiyuan Li, Chairperson, 850-474-2287, E-mail: mathstat@uwf.edu. *Application contact:* Terry McCray, Assistant Director of Graduate Admissions, 850-473-7718, Fax: 850-473-7714, E-mail: gradadmissions@uwf.edu.

Villanova University, Graduate School of Liberal Arts and Sciences, Department of Mathematical Sciences, Program in Applied Statistics, Villanova, PA 19085-1699. Offers MS. Part-time and evening/weekend programs available. *Students:* 16 full-time (9 women), 13 part-time (5 women); includes 3 minority (all Asian, non-Hispanic/Latino), 1 international. Average age 29. 21 applicants, 95% accepted, 11 enrolled. In 2010, 15 master's awarded. *Degree requirements:* For master's, comprehensive exam. *Entrance requirements:* For master's, GRE, minimum GPA of 3.0. Additional exam requirements/recommendations for international students: Required—TOEFL. *Application deadline:* For fall admission, 3/1 priority date for domestic and international students; for spring admission, 11/15 priority date for domestic and international students. Applications are processed on a rolling basis. Application fee: $50. Electronic applications accepted. *Expenses:* Tuition: Part-time $700 per credit. Part-time tuition and fees vary according to degree level and program. *Financial support:* Research assistantships, Federal Work-Study available. Financial award applicants required to submit FAFSA. *Unit head:* Dr. Michael Levitan, Director, 610-519-4818. *Application contact:* Dr. Adele Lindenmeyr, Dean, Graduate School of Liberal Arts and Sciences, 610-519-7093, Fax: 610-519-7096.

Washington State University, Graduate School, College of Agricultural, Human, and Natural Resource Sciences, Department of Statistics, Pullman, WA 99164. Offers applied statistics (MS); theoretical statistics (MS). *Faculty:* 7. *Students:* 12 full-time (7 women), 1 part-time (0 women), 12 international. Average age 29. 35 applicants, 26% accepted, 3 enrolled. In 2010, 12 master's awarded. *Degree requirements:* For master's, comprehensive exam (for some programs), thesis (for some programs), project. *Entrance requirements:* For master's, GRE, three letters of reference; official copies of all college transcripts. Additional exam requirements/recommendations for international students: Required—TOEFL (minimum score 560 paper-based; 220 computer-based), IELTS. *Application deadline:* For fall admission, 1/10 for domestic and international students; for spring admission, 7/1 for domestic and international students. Application fee: $50. *Expenses:* Tuition, state resident: full-time $8552; part-time $443 per credit. Tuition, nonresident: full-time $21,650; part-time $1083 per credit. Required fees: $846. *Financial support:* In 2010–11, 10 students received support, including 4 teaching assistantships with tuition reimbursements available (averaging $18,204 per year). *Faculty research:* Environmental statistics, logistic regression, statistical methods for ecology and wildlife, spatial data analysis, linear and non-linear models. Total annual research expenditures: $9,000. *Unit head:* Dr. Michael A. Jacroux, Professor/Chair, 509-335-8645, Fax: 509-335-8369, E-mail: jacroux@wsu.edu. *Application contact:* Graduate School Admissions, 800-GRADWSU, Fax: 509-335-1949, E-mail: gradsch@wsu.edu.

West Chester University of Pennsylvania, Office of Graduate Studies, College of Arts and Sciences, Department of Mathematics, West Chester, PA 19383. Offers applied statistics (MS, Certificate); mathematics (MA, Teaching Certificate). Part-time and evening/weekend programs available. *Students:* 17 full-time (7 women), 61 part-time (25 women); includes 22 minority (10 Black or African American, non-Hispanic/Latino; 10 Asian, non-Hispanic/Latino; 2 Hispanic/Latino), 9 international. Average age 31. 50 applicants, 80% accepted, 15 enrolled. In 2010, 31 master's, 1 other advanced degree awarded. *Degree requirements:* For master's, thesis optional. *Entrance requirements:* For master's, GMAT, GRE General Test, or MAT are required for Mathematics MA, optional for Applied Statistics Program, interview; for other advanced degree, GMAT, GRE General Test, or MAT are required for Mathematics Teaching Certificate, optional for Applied Statistics Program. Additional exam requirements/recommendations for international students: Required—TOEFL (minimum score 550 paper-based; 213 computer-based; 80 iBT). *Application deadline:* For fall admission, 4/15 priority date for domestic students, 3/15 for international students; for spring admission, 10/15 for domestic students, 9/1 for international students. Applications are processed on a rolling basis. Application fee: $35. Electronic applications accepted. *Expenses:* Tuition, state resident: full-time $6966; part-time $387 per credit. Tuition, nonresident: full-time $11,146; part-time $619 per credit. Required fees: $1614.40; $133.24 per credit. Part-time tuition and fees vary according to campus/location. *Financial support:* Unspecified assistantships available. Support available to part-time students. Financial award application deadline: 2/15; financial award applicants required to submit FAFSA. *Faculty research:* Teachers teaching with technology in service training program, biostatistics, hierarchial linear models, clustered bionary outcome date. *Unit head:* Dr. Kathleen Jackson, Chair, 610-436-2537, E-mail: kjackson@wcupa.edu. *Application contact:* Dr. Gail Gallitano, Graduate Coordinator for Mathematics, 610-436-2452, E-mail: ggallitano@wcupa.edu.

Worcester Polytechnic Institute, Graduate Studies and Research, Department of Mathematical Sciences, Worcester, MA 01609-2280. Offers applied mathematics (MS); applied statistics (MS); financial mathematics (MS); industrial mathematics (MS); mathematical sciences (PhD, Graduate Certificate); mathematics (MME). Part-time and evening/weekend programs available. *Faculty:* 17 full-time (1 woman), 6 part-time/adjunct (2 women). *Students:* 48 full-time (20 women), 27 part-time (11 women); includes 3 Black or African American, non-Hispanic/Latino; 2 Hispanic/Latino; 2 Native Hawaiian or other Pacific Islander, non-Hispanic/Latino, 38 international. 230 applicants, 56% accepted, 26 enrolled. In 2010, 21 master's, 2 doctorates awarded. *Degree requirements:* For master's, thesis (for some programs); for doctorate, comprehensive exam, thesis/dissertation. *Entrance requirements:* For master's and doctorate, GRE General Test, GRE Subject Test in math (recommended), 3 letters of recommendation. Additional exam requirements/recommendations for international students: Required—TOEFL (minimum score 550 paper-based; 213 computer-based; 79 iBT), IELTS (minimum score 6.5). *Application deadline:* For fall admission, 1/1 priority date for domestic students, 1/1 for international students; for spring admission, 10/1 priority date for domestic students, 10/1 for international students. Applications are processed on a rolling basis. Application fee: $70. Electronic applications accepted. *Expenses:* Tuition: Full-time $20,862; part-time $1159 per term. One-time fee: $15. *Financial support:* Career-related internships or fieldwork, institutionally sponsored loans, scholarships/grants, and unspecified assistantships available. Financial award application deadline: 1/1; financial award applicants required to submit FAFSA. *Faculty research:* Applied analysis and differential equations, computational mathematics, discrete mathematics, applied and computational statistics, industrial and financial mathematics, mathematical biology. *Unit head:* Dr. Bogdan Vernescu, Head, 508-831-5241, Fax: 508-831-5824, E-mail: vernescu@wpi.edu. *Application contact:* Dr. Joseph Petruccelli, Graduate Coordinator, 508-831-5241, Fax: 508-831-5824, E-mail: jdp@wpi.edu.

Wright State University, School of Graduate Studies, College of Science and Mathematics, Department of Mathematics and Statistics, Program in Applied Statistics, Dayton, OH 45435. Offers MS. *Degree requirements:* For master's, comprehensive exam. *Entrance requirements:* For master's, 1 year of course work in calculus and matrix algebra, previous course work in computer programming and statistics. Additional exam requirements/recommendations for international students: Required—TOEFL. *Faculty research:* Reliability theory, stochastic process, nonparametric statistics, design of experiments, multivariate statistics.

Biomathematics

North Carolina State University, Graduate School, College of Physical and Mathematical Sciences, Program in Biomathematics, Raleigh, NC 27695. Offers M Biomath, MS, PhD. Part-time programs available. Terminal master's awarded for partial completion of doctoral program. *Degree requirements:* For master's, thesis (for some programs); for doctorate, thesis/dissertation. *Entrance requirements:* For master's and doctorate, GRE General Test. Additional exam requirements/recommendations for international students: Required—TOEFL. Electronic applications accepted. *Faculty research:* Theory and methods of biological modeling, theoretical biology (genetics, ecology, neurobiology), applied biology (wildlife).

University of California, Los Angeles, David Geffen School of Medicine and Graduate Division, Graduate Programs in Medicine, Department of Biomathematics, Program in Biomathematics, Los Angeles, CA 90095. Offers MS, PhD. *Faculty:* 5 full-time (0 women). *Students:* 9 full-time (2 women); includes 3 minority (all Asian, non-Hispanic/Latino), 2 international. Average age 29. 16 applicants, 38% accepted, 2 enrolled. In 2010, 3 master's, 3 doctorates awarded. Application fee: $70 ($90 for international students). Electronic applications accepted. *Financial support:* In 2010–11, 10 fellowships, 7 research assistantships were awarded; teaching assistantships. *Unit head:* Dr. Elliot Landaw, Chair, 310-825-6743, E-mail: elandaw@biomath.ucla.edu. *Application contact:* Departmental Office, 310-825-5554, E-mail: gradprog@biomath.ucla.edu.

The University of Texas Health Science Center at Houston, Graduate School of Biomedical Sciences, Program in Biomathematics and Biostatistics, Houston, TX 77225-0036. Offers MS, PhD, MD/PhD. Terminal master's awarded for partial completion of doctoral program. *Degree requirements:* For master's, thesis; for doctorate, thesis/dissertation. *Entrance requirements:* For master's and doctorate, GRE General Test. Additional exam requirements/recommendations for international students: Required—TOEFL. Electronic applications accepted. *Faculty research:* Biostatistics, biomarkers, epidemiology, bioinformatics, computational biology.

Biometry

Cornell University, Graduate School, Graduate Fields of Agriculture and Life Sciences, Field of Biometry, Ithaca, NY 14853-0001. Offers MS, PhD. *Faculty:* 11 full-time (0 women). *Students:* 1 full-time (0 women); includes Asian, non-Hispanic/Latino. Average age 39. 8 applicants, 0% accepted, 0 enrolled.Terminal master's awarded for partial completion of doctoral program. *Degree requirements:* For master's, thesis; for doctorate, comprehensive exam, thesis/dissertation. *Entrance requirements:* For master's and doctorate, GRE General Test, 2 letters of recommendation. Additional exam requirements/recommendations for international students: Required—TOEFL (minimum score 550 paper-based; 213 computer-based; 77 iBT). *Application deadline:* For fall admission, 1/15 for domestic students. Application fee: $70. Electronic applications accepted. *Expenses:* Tuition: Full-time $29,500. Required fees: $76. Tuition and fees vary according to degree level and program. *Financial support:* In 2010–11, 1 fellowship with full tuition reimbursement was awarded; research assistantships with full tuition reimbursements, teaching assistantships with full tuition reimbursements, institutionally sponsored loans, scholarships/grants, health care benefits, tuition waivers (full and partial), and unspecified assistantships also available. Financial award applicants required to submit FAFSA. *Faculty research:* Environmental, agricultural, and biological statistics; biomathematics; modern nonparametric statistics; statistical genetics; computational statistics. *Unit head:* Director of Graduate Studies, 607-255-8066. *Application contact:* Graduate Field Assistant, 607-255-8066, E-mail: bscb@cornell.edu.

Cornell University, Graduate School, Graduate Fields of Engineering, Field of Statistics, Ithaca, NY 14853-0001. Offers applied statistics (MPS); biometry (MS, PhD); decision theory (MS, PhD); economic and social statistics (MS, PhD); engineering statistics (MS, PhD); experimental design (MS, PhD); mathematical statistics (MS, PhD); probability (MS, PhD); sampling (MS, PhD); statistical computing (MS, PhD); stochastic processes (MS, PhD). *Faculty:*

21 full-time (2 women). *Students:* 76 full-time (37 women); includes 4 Asian, non-Hispanic/Latino; 2 Hispanic/Latino, 53 international. Average age 24. 429 applicants, 27% accepted, 50 enrolled. In 2010, 36 master's, 3 doctorates awarded. Terminal master's awarded for partial completion of doctoral program. *Degree requirements:* For master's, project (MPS), thesis (MS); for doctorate, one foreign language, thesis/dissertation. *Entrance requirements:* For master's, GRE General Test (MS), 2 letters of recommendation (MS, MPS); for doctorate, GRE General Test, 2 letters of recommendation. Additional exam requirements/recommendations for international students: Required—TOEFL (minimum score 550 paper-based; 213 computer-based; 77 iBT). *Application deadline:* For fall admission, 1/15 for domestic students. Applications are processed on a rolling basis. Application fee: $70. Electronic applications accepted. *Expenses:* Tuition: Full-time $29,500. Required fees: $76. Tuition and fees vary according to degree level and program. *Financial support:* In 2010–11, 26 students received support, including 3 fellowships with full tuition reimbursements available, 9 research assistantships with full tuition reimbursements available, 17 teaching assistantships with full tuition reimbursements available; institutionally sponsored loans, scholarships/grants, tuition waivers (full and partial), and unspecified assistantships also available. Financial award applicants required to submit FAFSA. *Faculty research:* Bayesian analysis, survival analysis, nonparametric statistics, stochastic processes, mathematical statistics. *Unit head:* Director of Graduate Studies, 607-255-8066. *Application contact:* Graduate Field Assistant, 607-255-8066, E-mail: csc@cornell.edu.

San Diego State University, Graduate and Research Affairs, College of Health and Human Services, Program in Biostatistics and Biometry, San Diego, CA 92182. Offers biometry (MPH). Electronic applications accepted.

University of California, Los Angeles, David Geffen School of Medicine and Graduate Division, Graduate Programs in Medicine, Department of Biomathematics, Los Angeles, CA 90095. Offers biomathematics (MS, PhD); clinical research (MS). *Faculty:* 5 full-time (0 women). *Students:* 23 full-time (11 women); includes 8 minority (all Asian, non-Hispanic/Latino), 2 international. Average age 32. 19 applicants, 47% accepted, 5 enrolled. In 2010, 8 master's, 3 doctorates awarded. *Degree requirements:* For master's, comprehensive exam or thesis; for doctorate, thesis/dissertation, oral and written qualifying exams. *Entrance requirements:* For master's and doctorate, GRE General Test, GRE Subject Test. *Application deadline:* For fall admission, 1/15 for domestic students. Application fee: $70 ($90 for international students). Electronic applications accepted. *Financial support:* In 2010–11, 7 fellowships, 18 teaching assistantships were awarded; research assistantships, Federal Work-Study, institutionally sponsored loans, scholarships/grants, and tuition waivers (full and partial) also available. Financial award application deadline: 3/1. *Unit head:* Dr. Elliot Landaw, Chair, 310-825-6743, Fax: 310-825-8685, E-mail: elandaw@biomath.ucla.edu. *Application contact:* Departmental Office, 310-825-5554, Fax: 310-825-8685, E-mail: gradprog@biomath.ucla.edu.

See Display on next page and Close-Up on page 307.

University of Wisconsin–Madison, Graduate School, College of Letters and Science, Department of Statistics, Biometry Program, Madison, WI 53706-1380. Offers MS. *Expenses:* Tuition, state resident: full-time $9887.36; part-time $617.96 per credit. Tuition, nonresident: full-time $24,054; part-time $1503.40 per credit. Required fees: $67.63 per credit. Tuition and fees vary according to reciprocity agreements.

Biostatistics

American University of Beirut, Graduate Programs, Faculty of Health Sciences, Beirut, Lebanon. Offers environmental sciences (MSES), including environmental health; epidemiology (MS); epidemiology and biostatistics (MPH); health management and policy (MPH); health promotion and community health (MPH); population health (MS). Part-time programs available. *Faculty:* 33 full-time (23 women), 8 part-time/adjunct (3 women). *Students:* 64 full-time (55 women), 111 part-time (85 women). Average age 26. 209 applicants, 67% accepted, 75 enrolled. In 2010, 54 master's awarded. *Degree requirements:* For master's, one foreign language, comprehensive exam, thesis (for some programs). *Entrance requirements:* For master's, 2 letters of recommendation, personal statement, transcripts. Additional exam requirements/recommendations for international students: Required—TOEFL (minimum score 600 paper-based; 250 computer-based; 97 iBT), IELTS (minimum score 7). *Application deadline:* For fall admission, 2/20 for domestic and international students; for spring admission, 11/1 for domestic and international students. Application fee: $50. Electronic applications accepted. *Expenses:* Tuition: Full-time $12,294; part-time $683 per credit. Required fees: $499; $499 per credit. Tuition and fees vary according to course load and program. *Financial support:* In 2010–11, 65 students received support. Scholarships/grants, health care benefits, and unspecified assistantships available. Financial award application deadline: 2/20. *Faculty research:* Tobacco control; health of the elderly; youth health; mental health; women's health; reproductive and sexual health, including HIV/AIDS; water quality; health systems; quality in health care delivery; health human resources; health policy; occupational and environmental health; social inequality; social determinants of health; chronic diseases. Total annual research expenditures: $1.5 million. *Unit head:* Iman Adel Nuwayhid, Dean, 961-134-0119, Fax: 961-174-4470, E-mail: nuwayhid@aub.edu.lb. *Application contact:* Mitra Tauk, Assistant for Graduate Student Affairs, 961-135-0000 Ext. 4687, Fax: 961-174-4470, E-mail: mt12@aub.edu.lb.

Boston University, Graduate School of Arts and Sciences, Intercollegiate Program in Biostatistics, Boston, MA 02215. Offers MA, PhD. *Students:* 56 full-time (35 women), 39 part-time (27 women); includes 19 minority (4 Black or African American, non-Hispanic/Latino; 13 Asian, non-Hispanic/Latino; 1 Hispanic/Latino; 1 Two or more races, non-Hispanic/Latino), 24 international. Average age 30. 114 applicants, 36% accepted, 11 enrolled. In 2010, 24 master's, 8 doctorates awarded. Terminal master's awarded for partial completion of doctoral program. *Degree requirements:* For master's, one foreign language, comprehensive exam; for doctorate, one foreign language, comprehensive exam, thesis/dissertation. *Entrance requirements:* For master's and doctorate, GRE General Test, 2 letters of recommendation. Additional exam requirements/recommendations for international students: Required—TOEFL (minimum score 550 paper-based; 213 computer-based). *Application deadline:* For fall admission, 3/1 for domestic and international students; for spring admission, 10/15 for domestic and international students. Application fee: $70. Electronic applications accepted. *Expenses:* Tuition: Full-time $39,314; part-time $1228 per credit. Required fees: $40 per semester. *Financial support:* In 2010–11, 40 students received support, including 40 research assistantships with full tuition reimbursements available (averaging $18,400 per year); fellowships, teaching assistantships also available. Support available to part-time students. Financial award application deadline: 1/15; financial award applicants required to submit FAFSA. *Unit head:* Lisa Sullivan, Chairman, 617-638-5047, Fax: 617-638-4458, E-mail: lsull@bu.edu. *Application contact:* MyHanh SloatTran, Curriculum Coordinator, 617-638-5207, Fax: 617-638-6484, E-mail: msloat@bu.edu.

Boston University, School of Public Health, Biostatistics Department, Boston, MA 02215. Offers MA, MPH, PhD. Part-time and evening/weekend programs available. *Faculty:* 26 full-time, 18 part-time/adjunct. *Students:* 10 full-time (8 women), 16 part-time (13 women); includes 2 Black or African American, non-Hispanic/Latino; 3 Asian, non-Hispanic/Latino, 2 international. Average age 27. 79 applicants, 46% accepted, 14 enrolled. In 2010, 16 master's, 5 doctorates awarded. *Entrance requirements:* For master's, GRE, GMAT, LSAT, DAT, or MCAT; for doctorate, GRE. Additional exam requirements/recommendations for international students: Required—TOEFL (minimum score 600 paper-based; 250 computer-based; 100 iBT), IELTS (minimum score 6). *Application deadline:* For fall admission, 2/1 priority date for domestic and international students; for spring admission, 10/15 priority date for domestic and international students. Applications are processed on a rolling basis. Application fee: $115. Electronic applications accepted. *Expenses:* Tuition: Full-time $39,314; part-time $1228 per credit. Required fees: $40 per semester. *Financial support:* Career-related internships or fieldwork, Federal Work-Study, institutionally sponsored loans, scholarships/grants, traineeships, health care benefits, and unspecified assistantships available. Support available to part-time students. Financial award application deadline: 3/1; financial award applicants required to submit FAFSA. *Unit head:* Dr. Lisa Sullivan, PhD, Chair, 617-638-5176, Fax: 617-638-4458, E-mail: biostat@bu.edu. *Application contact:* LePhan Quan, Associate Director of Admissions, 617-638-4640, Fax: 617-638-5299, E-mail: asksph@bu.edu.

Brown University, Graduate School, Division of Biology and Medicine, Department of Community Health, Providence, RI 02912. Offers health services research (MS, PhD); public health (MPH); statistical science (MS, PhD), including biostatistics, epidemiology; MD/PhD. *Accreditation:* CEPH. *Degree requirements:* For doctorate, thesis/dissertation, preliminary exam. *Entrance requirements:* For master's and doctorate, GRE General Test. Additional exam requirements/recommendations for international students: Required—TOEFL.

Brown University, Graduate School, Division of Biology and Medicine, Department of Community Health, Center for Statistical Science, Program in Biostatistics, Providence, RI 02912. Offers MS, PhD, MD/PhD. *Degree requirements:* For doctorate, thesis/dissertation, preliminary exam. *Entrance requirements:* For master's and doctorate, GRE General Test.

California State University, East Bay, Office of Academic Programs and Graduate Studies, College of Science, Department of Statistics and Biostatistics, Biostatistics Program, Hayward, CA 94542-3000. Offers MS. Part-time and evening/weekend programs available. *Faculty:* 7 full-time (3 women). *Students:* 4 full-time (all women), 34 part-time (21 women); includes 1 Black or African American, non-Hispanic/Latino; 17 Asian, non-Hispanic/Latino; 1 Hispanic/Latino, 7 international. Average age 31. 41 applicants, 56% accepted, 15 enrolled. In 2010, 8 master's awarded. *Degree requirements:* For master's, comprehensive exam. *Entrance requirements:* For master's, minimum GPA of 3.0; math through lower-division calculus. Additional exam requirements/recommendations for international students: Required—TOEFL (minimum score 550 paper-based; 213 computer-based). *Application deadline:* For fall admission, 6/30 for domestic and international students. Application fee: $55. Electronic applications accepted. *Financial support:* Fellowships, career-related internships or fieldwork, Federal Work-Study, scholarships/grants, and unspecified assistantships available. Support available to part-time students. Financial award application deadline: 3/1; financial award applicants required to submit FAFSA. *Unit head:* Dr. Eric Suess, Chair, 510-885-3435, Fax: 510-885-4714, E-mail: eric.suess@csueastbay.edu. *Application contact:* Donna Wiley, Interim Associate Director, 510-885-2928, Fax: 510-885-4777, E-mail: donna.wiley@csueastbay.edu.

Case Western Reserve University, School of Medicine and School of Graduate Studies, Graduate Programs in Medicine, Department of Epidemiology and Biostatistics, Program in Biostatistics, Cleveland, OH 44106. Offers MS, PhD. Part-time programs available. Terminal master's awarded for partial completion of doctoral program. *Degree requirements:* For master's, comprehensive exam, thesis, exam/practicum; for doctorate, comprehensive exam, thesis/dissertation. *Entrance requirements:* For master's, GRE General Test or MCAT, 3 recommendations; for doctorate, GRE General Test, 3 recommendations. Additional exam requirements/recommendations for international students: Required—TOEFL (minimum score 550 paper-based; 213 computer-based). Electronic applications accepted. *Faculty research:* Survey sampling and statistical computing, generalized linear models, statistical modeling, models in breast cancer survival.

Columbia University, Columbia University Mailman School of Public Health, Division of Biostatistics, New York, NY 10032. Offers MPH, MS, Dr PH, PhD. PhD offered in cooperation with the Graduate School of Arts and Sciences. Part-time programs available. *Students:* 15 full-time (11 women), 74 part-time (36 women); includes 1 Black or African American, non-Hispanic/Latino; 10 Asian, non-Hispanic/Latino; 4 Hispanic/Latino, 31 international. Average age 32. 147 applicants, 48% accepted, 18 enrolled. In 2010, 30 master's, 4 doctorates awarded. *Degree requirements:* For doctorate, thesis/dissertation. *Entrance requirements:* For master's, GRE General Test; for doctorate, GRE General Test, MPH or equivalent (Dr PH). Additional exam requirements/recommendations for international students: Required—TOEFL (minimum score 600 paper-based; 250 computer-based; 100 iBT). *Application deadline:* For fall admission, 1/5 for domestic students. Applications are processed on a rolling basis. Application fee: $60. Electronic applications accepted. *Financial support:* Research assistantships, teaching assistantships, career-related internships or fieldwork and Federal Work-Study available. Financial award application deadline: 2/1; financial award applicants required to submit FAFSA. *Faculty research:* Statistical methods and public health implications of: biomedical experiments, clinical trials, functional data analysis, statistical genetics, and observational studies. *Unit head:* Dr. Roger Vaughan, Department Chairperson, 212-342-2271, Fax: 212-305-9408. *Application contact:* Dr. Roger Vaughan, Department Chairperson, 212-342-2271, Fax: 212-305-9408.

Drexel University, School of Biomedical Engineering, Science and Health Systems, Philadelphia, PA 19104-2875. Offers biomedical engineering (MS, PhD); biomedical science (MS, PhD); biostatistics (MS); clinical/rehabilitation engineering (MS); MD/PhD. *Degree requirements:* For doctorate, thesis/dissertation, 1 year of residency, qualifying exam. *Entrance requirements:* For master's, minimum GPA of 3.0; for doctorate, minimum GPA of 3.0, MS. Additional exam requirements/recommendations for international students: Required—TOEFL. Electronic applications accepted. *Faculty research:* Cardiovascular dynamics, diagnostic and therapeutic ultrasound.

Drexel University, School of Public Health, Department of Epidemiology and Biostatistics, Philadelphia, PA 19104-2875. Offers biostatistics (MS); epidemiology (PhD); epidemiology and biostatistics (Certificate).

Duke University, School of Medicine, Program in Biostatistics, Durham, NC 27708-0586. Offers MS. *Unit head:* Dr. Edward G. Buckley, Vice Dean, Medical Education, 919-668-3381, Fax: 919-660-7040, E-mail: buckl002@mc.duke.edu. *Application contact:* Dr. Brenda E. Armstrong, Director of Admissions, 919-684-2985, Fax: 919-684-8893, E-mail: mcdadm@mc.duke.edu.

East Tennessee State University, School of Graduate Studies, College of Public Health, Department of Public Health, Johnson City, TN 37614. Offers biostatistics (MPH); community health (MPH, DPH); environmental health sciences (MPH); epidemiology (MPH, Certificate); gerontology (Certificate); health care management (Certificate); health services administration

Biostatistics

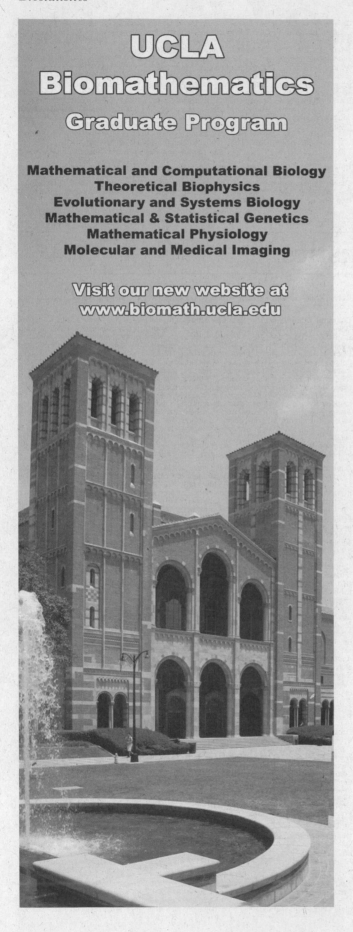

UCLA Biomathematics Graduate Program

Mathematical and Computational Biology
Theoretical Biophysics
Evolutionary and Systems Biology
Mathematical & Statistical Genetics
Mathematical Physiology
Molecular and Medical Imaging

Visit our new website at
www.biomath.ucla.edu

(MPH); rural health (Certificate). *Accreditation:* CEPH. Part-time programs available. Post-baccalaureate distance learning degree programs offered (no on-campus study). *Faculty:* 9 full-time (3 women). *Students:* 49 full-time (29 women), 32 part-time (22 women); includes 15 minority (10 Black or African American, non-Hispanic/Latino; 4 Asian, non-Hispanic/Latino; 1 Hispanic/Latino), 17 international. Average age 32. 151 applicants, 38% accepted, 32 enrolled. In 2010, 38 master's, 6 other advanced degrees awarded. Terminal master's awarded for partial completion of doctoral program. *Degree requirements:* For master's, comprehensive exam, thesis optional, field experience; for doctorate, comprehensive exam, thesis/dissertation, culminating experience/practicum. *Entrance requirements:* For master's, GRE General Test, minimum GPA of 2.75; for doctorate, GRE General Test, MPH or equivalent. Additional exam requirements/recommendations for international students: Required—TOEFL (minimum score 550 paper-based; 213 computer-based; 79 iBT). *Application deadline:* For fall admission, 3/1 for domestic and international students. Application fee: $25 ($35 for international students). Electronic applications accepted. *Financial support:* In 2010–11, 6 research assistantships with full tuition reimbursements (averaging $6,000 per year), 4 teaching assistantships with full tuition reimbursements (averaging $6,000 per year) were awarded; career-related internships or fieldwork, institutionally sponsored loans, scholarships/grants, tuition waivers (full), and unspecified assistantships also available. Financial award application deadline: 7/1; financial award applicants required to submit FAFSA. *Faculty research:* Rural health issues, youth and adolescent health, health of the elderly, environmental epidemiology, spatial analysis of data. Total annual research expenditures: $616,124. *Unit head:* Dr. Rob Pack, Assistant Dean, 423-439-4243, Fax: 423-439-5238, E-mail: packr@etsu.edu. *Application contact:* Admissions and Records Clerk, 423-439-4221, Fax: 423-439-5624, E-mail: gradsch@etsu.edu.

Emory University, Laney Graduate School, Department of Biostatistics, Atlanta, GA 30322-1100. Offers biostatistics (MPH, MSPH, PhD); public health informatics (MSPH). *Degree requirements:* For doctorate, comprehensive exam, thesis/dissertation. *Entrance requirements:* For doctorate, GRE General Test. Additional exam requirements/recommendations for international students: Required—TOEFL (minimum score 550 paper-based; 220 computer-based). Electronic applications accepted. *Expenses:* Tuition: Full-time $33,800. Required fees: $1300. *Faculty research:* Vaccine efficacy, clinical trials, spatial statistics, statistical genetics, neuroimaging.

Emory University, Rollins School of Public Health, Department of Biostatistics and Bioinformatics, Atlanta, GA 30322-1100. Offers MPH, MSPH. Part-time programs available. *Degree requirements:* For master's, thesis, practicum. *Entrance requirements:* For master's, GRE General Test. Additional exam requirements/recommendations for international students: Required—TOEFL (minimum score 550 paper-based; 213 computer-based; 80 iBT). Electronic applications accepted. *Expenses:* Tuition: Full-time $33,800. Required fees: $1300.

Florida International University, Stempel College of Public Health and Social Work, Programs in Public Health, Miami, FL 33199. Offers biostatistics (MPH); environmental and occupational health (MPH, PhD); epidemiology (MPH, PhD); health policy and management (MPH); health promotion and disease prevention (PhD); health promotion and diseases prevention (MPH). Ph D is fall admission only; MPH offered jointly with University of Miami. *Accreditation:* CEPH. Part-time and evening/weekend programs available. Postbaccalaureate distance learning degree programs offered (no on-campus study). *Faculty:* 9 full-time (4 women), 5 part-time/adjunct (2 women). *Students:* 260 full-time (180 women), 194 part-time (153 women); includes 160 Black or African American, non-Hispanic/Latino; 1 American Indian or Alaska Native, non-Hispanic/Latino; 27 Asian, non-Hispanic/Latino; 133 Hispanic/Latino, 56 international. Average age 36. 697 applicants, 31% accepted, 197 enrolled. In 2010, 97 master's, 2 doctorates awarded. *Degree requirements:* For master's, thesis optional; for doctorate, comprehensive exam, thesis/dissertation. *Entrance requirements:* For master's, minimum GPA of 3.0, letters of recommendation; for doctorate, GRE, resume, minimum GPA of 3.0, letters of recommendation, letter of intent. Additional exam requirements/recommendations for international students: Required—TOEFL (minimum score 550 paper-based; 80 iBT). *Application deadline:* For fall admission, 6/1 for domestic students, 4/1 for international students; for spring admission, 10/1 for domestic students, 9/1 for international students. Applications are processed on a rolling basis. Application fee: $30. Electronic applications accepted. *Expenses:* Contact institution. *Financial support:* Institutionally sponsored loans, scholarships/grants, and tuition waivers (full) available. Financial award application deadline: 3/1; financial award applicants required to submit FAFSA. *Faculty research:* Drugs/AIDS intervention among migrant workers, provision of services for active/recovering drug users with HIV. *Unit head:* Dr. Gilbert Ramirez, Associate Dean for Academic and Student Affairs, 305-348-7774, E-mail: ph@fiu.edu. *Application contact:* Nanett Rojas, Assistant Director of Graduate Admissions, 305-348-7442, Fax: 305-348-7441, E-mail: gradadm@fiu.edu.

Florida State University, The Graduate School, College of Arts and Sciences, Department of Statistics, Tallahassee, FL 32306-4330. Offers applied statistics (MS); biostatistics (MS, PhD); mathematical statistics (MS, PhD). Part-time programs available. *Faculty:* 15 full-time (2 women). *Students:* 52 full-time (21 women), 20 part-time (8 women); includes 10 Black or African American, non-Hispanic/Latino; 5 Asian, non-Hispanic/Latino; 8 Hispanic/Latino, 27 international. Average age 29. 182 applicants, 15% accepted, 18 enrolled. In 2010, 4 master's, 10 doctorates awarded. Terminal master's awarded for partial completion of doctoral program. *Degree requirements:* For doctorate, thesis/dissertation, departmental qualifying exam. *Entrance requirements:* For master's, GRE General Test, previous course work in calculus, minimum GPA of 3.0; for doctorate, GRE General Test, minimum GPA of 3.0, 1 course in linear algebra (preferred), calculus I-III, real analysis. Additional exam requirements/recommendations for international students: Required—TOEFL (minimum score 600 paper-based; 250 computer-based; 100 iBT). *Application deadline:* For fall admission, 7/1 for domestic and international students; for spring admission, 11/1 for domestic and international students. Applications are processed on a rolling basis. Application fee: $30. Electronic applications accepted. *Expenses:* Tuition, state resident: full-time $8238.24. *Financial support:* In 2010–11, 49 students received support, including 1 fellowship with full tuition reimbursement available (averaging $19,000 per year), 10 research assistantships with full tuition reimbursements available (averaging $22,185 per year), 41 teaching assistantships with full tuition reimbursements available (averaging $19,653 per year); Federal Work-Study, institutionally sponsored loans, scholarships/grants, health care benefits, and unspecified assistantships also available. Support available to part-time students. Financial award application deadline: 2/15; financial award applicants required to submit FAFSA. *Faculty research:* Statistical inference, probability theory, biostatistics, nonparametric estimation, automatic target recognition. *Unit head:* Dr. Dan McGee, Chairman, 850-644-3218, Fax: 850-644-5271, E-mail: info@stat.fsu.edu. *Application contact:* Chauncey Richburg, Academic Support Assistant, 850-644-3514, Fax: 850-644-5271, E-mail: richburg@stat.fsu.edu.

George Mason University, College of Health and Human Services, Department of Global and Community Health, Fairfax, VA 22030. Offers biostatistics (Certificate); epidemiology (Certificate); epidemiology and biostatistics (MS); gerontology (Certificate); global health (MS, Certificate); nutrition (Certificate); public health (MPH, Certificate); rehabilitation science (Certificate). *Faculty:* 15 full-time (10 women), 21 part-time/adjunct (17 women). *Students:* 99 full-time (80 women), 158 part-time (126 women); includes 110 minority (66 Black or African American, non-Hispanic/Latino; 1 American Indian or Alaska Native, non-Hispanic/Latino; 30 Asian, non-Hispanic/Latino; 11 Hispanic/Latino; 2 Two or more races, non-Hispanic/Latino), 23 international. Average age 32. 202 applicants, 41% accepted, 41 enrolled. In 2010, 29 master's, 11 other advanced degrees awarded. *Degree requirements:* For master's, comprehensive exam (for some programs), thesis or practicum. *Entrance requirements:* For master's, GRE, BA with minimum GPA of 3.0, 2 letters of recommendation. Additional exam requirements/recommendations for international students: Required—TOEFL (minimum score 570 paper-based; 230 computer-based; 88 iBT). *Application deadline:* For fall admission, 4/1 priority date for domestic students,

244   www.facebook.com/petersonspublishing

Peterson's Graduate Programs in the Physical Sciences, Mathematics, Agricultural Sciences, the Environment & Natural Resources 2012

4/1 for international students; for spring admission, 11/1 for domestic and international students. Applications are processed on a rolling basis. Application fee: $100. Electronic applications accepted. *Expenses:* Tuition, state resident: full-time $8192; part-time $440 per credit hour. Tuition, nonresident: full-time $22,952; part-time $1055 per credit hour. Required fees: $2364; $99 per credit hour. *Financial support:* In 2010–11, 15 students received support, including 13 research assistantships with full and partial tuition reimbursements available (averaging $13,006 per year), 3 teaching assistantships with full and partial tuition reimbursements available (averaging $15,000 per year); career-related internships or fieldwork, Federal Work-Study, scholarships/grants, unspecified assistantships, and research awards, health care benefits health care benefits (full-time research or teaching assistantship recipients) also available. Financial award application deadline: 3/1; financial award applicants required to submit FAFSA. *Faculty research:* Providing introductory and advanced degrees in health-related disciplines centered in global and community issues, health issues and the needs of affected populations at the regional and global level. Total annual research expenditures: $13,285. *Unit head:* Dr. Shirley S. Travis, Dean, 703-993-1918. *Application contact:* Allan Weiss, Office Manager, 703-993-3126, E-mail: aweiss2@gmu.edu.

George Mason University, Volgenau School of Engineering, Department of Statistics, Fairfax, VA 22030. Offers biostatistics (Certificate); federal statistics (Certificate); statistical science (MS, PhD). Part-time and evening/weekend programs available. *Faculty:* 11 full-time (2 women), 5 part-time/adjunct (0 women). *Students:* 14 full-time (9 women), 55 part-time (23 women); includes 2 Black or African American, non-Hispanic/Latino; 11 Asian, non-Hispanic/Latino; 3 Hispanic/Latino, 17 international. Average age 32. 61 applicants, 77% accepted, 19 enrolled. In 2010, 17 master's, 2 doctorates, 1 other advanced degree awarded. Terminal master's awarded for partial completion of doctoral program. *Degree requirements:* For master's, comprehensive exam, thesis optional, qualifying exams; for doctorate, comprehensive exam, thesis/dissertation, qualifying exams. *Entrance requirements:* For master's, GRE (recommended), letters of recommendation, resume; for doctorate, GRE (recommended), personal goal statement, resume, 2 transcripts, letters of recommendation. Additional exam requirements/recommendations for international students: Required—TOEFL (minimum score 570 paper-based; 230 computer-based; 88 iBT), IELTS (minimum score 6.5). *Application deadline:* For fall admission, 3/15 priority date for domestic students, 12/15 priority date for international students; for spring admission, 10/1 for domestic and international students. Applications are processed on a rolling basis. Application fee: $100. Electronic applications accepted. *Expenses:* Tuition, state resident: full-time $8192; part-time $440 per credit hour. Tuition, nonresident: full-time $22,952; part-time $1055 per credit hour. Required fees: $2364; $99 per credit hour. *Financial support:* In 2010–11, 22 students received support, including 2 fellowships with full tuition reimbursements available (averaging $18,000 per year), 5 research assistantships with full and partial tuition reimbursements available (averaging $15,170 per year), 15 teaching assistantships with full and partial tuition reimbursements available (averaging $11,180 per year); Federal Work-Study, scholarships/grants, unspecified assistantships, and health care benefits (full-time research or teaching assistantship recipients) also available. Financial award application deadline: 3/1; financial award applicants required to submit FAFSA. *Faculty research:* Computational statistics, nonparametric function estimation, scientific and statistical visualization, statistical applications to engineering, survey research. Total annual research expenditures: $179,978. *Unit head:* Dr. William Rosenberger, Chair, 703-993-3645, Fax: 703-993-1700, E-mail: satistics@gmu.edu. *Application contact:* Elizabeth Quigley, Administrative Assistant, 703-993-9107, E-mail: equigley@gmu.edu.

Georgetown University, Graduate School of Arts and Sciences, Programs in Biomedical Sciences, Department of Biostatistics, Bioinformatics and Biomathematics, Washington, DC 20057-1484. Offers biostatistics (MS), including bioinformatics, epidemiology. *Entrance requirements:* For master's, GRE General Test. Additional exam requirements/recommendations for international students: Required—TOEFL. *Faculty research:* Occupation epidemiology, cancer.

The George Washington University, Columbian College of Arts and Sciences, Program in Biostatistics, Washington, DC 20052. Offers MS, PhD. *Students:* 4 full-time (3 women), 11 part-time (8 women); includes 1 Black or African American, non-Hispanic/Latino; 3 Asian, non-Hispanic/Latino, 5 international. Average age 32. 55 applicants, 53% accepted, 2 enrolled. In 2010, 2 master's, 3 doctorates awarded. *Degree requirements:* For master's, comprehensive exam; for doctorate, thesis/dissertation, general exam. *Entrance requirements:* For master's and doctorate, GRE General Test, minimum GPA of 3.0. Additional exam requirements/recommendations for international students: Required—TOEFL (minimum score 550 paper-based; 213 computer-based; 80 iBT). *Application deadline:* For fall admission, 1/15 priority date for domestic and international students; for spring admission, 10/1 priority date for domestic students, 9/1 priority date for international students. Applications are processed on a rolling basis. Application fee: $75. Electronic applications accepted. *Financial support:* In 2010–11, 1 student received support; fellowships with full tuition reimbursements available, teaching assistantships, tuition waivers available. *Unit head:* Dr. Zhaohai Li, Director, 202-994-7844, Fax: 202-994-6917, E-mail: zli@gwu.edu. *Application contact:* Dr. Zhaohai Li, Director, 202-994-7844, Fax: 202-994-6917, E-mail: zli@gwu.edu.

The George Washington University, School of Public Health and Health Services, Department of Epidemiology and Biostatistics, Washington, DC 20052. Offers biostatistics (MPH); epidemiology (MPH); microbiology and emerging infectious diseases (MSPH). *Faculty:* 19 full-time (11 women), 28 part-time/adjunct (17 women). *Students:* 59 full-time (51 women), 49 part-time (34 women); includes 16 Black or African American, non-Hispanic/Latino; 1 American Indian or Alaska Native, non-Hispanic/Latino; 25 Asian, non-Hispanic/Latino; 6 Hispanic/Latino; 3 Two or more races, non-Hispanic/Latino, 9 international. Average age 28. 193 applicants, 74% accepted, 39 enrolled. In 2010, 43 master's awarded. *Degree requirements:* For master's, case study or special project. *Entrance requirements:* For master's, GMAT, GRE General Test, or MCAT. Additional exam requirements/recommendations for international students: Required—TOEFL. *Application deadline:* For fall admission, 4/15 priority date for domestic students, 4/15 for international students; for spring admission, 11/1 for domestic and international students. Applications are processed on a rolling basis. Application fee: $75. *Financial support:* In 2010–11, 6 students received support. Tuition waivers available. Financial award application deadline: 2/15. *Unit head:* Dr. Alan E. Greenberg, Chair, 202-994-0612, E-mail: aeg1@gwu.edu. *Application contact:* Jane Smith, Director of Admissions, 202-994-0248, Fax: 202-994-1860, E-mail: sphhsinfo@gwumc.edu.

Georgia Health Sciences University, College of Graduate Studies, Program in Biostatistics, Augusta, GA 30912. Offers MS, PhD. *Faculty:* 10 full-time (3 women). *Students:* 9 full-time (5 women); includes 1 Black or African American, non-Hispanic/Latino; 3 Asian, non-Hispanic/Latino, 1 international. Average age 28. 15 applicants, 53% accepted, 2 enrolled. In 2010, 3 master's awarded. *Degree requirements:* For master's, thesis or alternative. *Entrance requirements:* For master's, GRE General Test, substantial mathematics background, computer literacy. Additional exam requirements/recommendations for international students: Required—TOEFL (minimum score 550 paper-based; 213 computer-based; 79 iBT). *Application deadline:* For fall admission, 2/1 for domestic students. Application fee: $30. Electronic applications accepted. *Expenses:* Tuition, state resident: full-time $7500; part-time $313 per semester hour. Tuition, nonresident: full-time $24,772; part-time $1033 per semester hour. Required fees: $1112. *Financial support:* In 2010–11, 10 research assistantships with full tuition reimbursements (averaging $14,000 per year) were awarded; unspecified assistantships also available. *Faculty research:* Computational biology, clinical trials, statistical genetics, statistical epidemiology, survival analysis. Total annual research expenditures: $315,059. *Unit head:* Dr. Varghese George, Chair, 706-721-3785, E-mail: vgeorge@georgiahealth.edu. *Application contact:* Dr. Jennifer Waller, Graduate Program Director and Associate Professor, 706-721-0814, E-mail: jwaller@georgiahealth.edu.

Georgia Southern University, Jack N. Averitt College of Graduate Studies, Jiann-Ping Hsu College of Public Health, Program in Public Health, Statesboro, GA 30460. Offers biostatistics (MPH, Dr PH); community health behavior and education (Dr PH); community health education (MPH); environmental health sciences (MPH); epidemiology (MPH); health services policy management (MPH); public health leadership (Dr PH). Part-time programs available. *Students:* 69 full-time (46 women), 28 part-time (22 women); includes 41 Black or African American, non-Hispanic/Latino; 4 Asian, non-Hispanic/Latino, 20 international. Average age 31. 60 applicants, 72% accepted, 20 enrolled. In 2010, 23 master's, 1 doctorate awarded. *Degree requirements:* For master's, thesis optional, practicum; for doctorate, comprehensive exam, thesis/dissertation, practicum. *Entrance requirements:* For master's, GRE General Test, minimum GPA of 2.75, resume, 3 letters of reference; for doctorate, GRE, GMAT, MCAT, LSAT, 3 letters of reference, statement of purpose, resume or curriculum vitae. Additional exam requirements/recommendations for international students: Required—TOEFL (minimum score 550 paper-based; 213 computer-based; 80 iBT). *Application deadline:* For fall admission, 3/1 priority date for domestic and international students; for spring admission, 10/1 priority date for domestic students, 10/1 for international students. Applications are processed on a rolling basis. Application fee: $50. Electronic applications accepted. *Expenses:* Contact institution. *Financial support:* In 2010–11, 75 students received support, including research assistantships with partial tuition reimbursements available (averaging $7,200 per year), teaching assistantships with partial tuition reimbursements available (averaging $7,200 per year); career-related internships or fieldwork, Federal Work-Study, scholarships/grants, tuition waivers (partial), and unspecified assistantships also available. Support available to part-time students. Financial award application deadline: 4/15; financial award applicants required to submit FAFSA. *Faculty research:* Rural public health best practices, health disparity elimination, community initiatives to enhance public health, cost effectiveness analysis, epidemiology of rural public health, environmental health issues, health care system assessment, rural health care, health policy and healthcare financing. *Unit head:* Dr. Charles Hardy, Dean, 912-478-2674, Fax: 912-478-5811, E-mail: chardy@georgiasouthern.edu. *Application contact:* Dr. Sarah Peterson, Coordinator for Graduate Student Recruitment, 912-478-2413, Fax: 912-478-5811, E-mail: speterson@georgiasouthern.edu.

Grand Valley State University, College of Liberal Arts and Sciences, Program in Biostatistics, Allendale, MI 49401-9403. Offers MS. *Entrance requirements:* For master's, minimum GPA of 3.0. *Faculty research:* Biometrical models, spatial methods, medical statistics, design of experiments.

Harvard University, Graduate School of Arts and Sciences, Department of Biostatistics, Cambridge, MA 02138. Offers PhD. *Expenses:* Tuition: Full-time $34,976. Required fees: $1166. Full-time tuition and fees vary according to program.

Harvard University, Harvard School of Public Health, Department of Biostatistics, Boston, MA 02115-6096. Offers SM, PhD. Part-time programs available. *Faculty:* 51 full-time (17 women), 7 part-time/adjunct (3 women). *Students:* 82 full-time; includes 4 Black or African American, non-Hispanic/Latino; 13 Asian, non-Hispanic/Latino; 2 Hispanic/Latino; 1 Two or more races, non-Hispanic/Latino, 25 international. Average age 26. 176 applicants, 27% accepted, 27 enrolled. In 2010, 11 master's, 1 doctorate awarded. *Degree requirements:* For doctorate, thesis/dissertation, oral and written qualifying exams. *Entrance requirements:* For master's and doctorate, GRE, prior training in mathematics and/or statistics. Additional exam requirements/recommendations for international students: Required—TOEFL (minimum score 590 paper-based; 240 computer-based; 95 iBT); Recommended—IELTS (minimum score 7). *Application deadline:* For fall admission, 12/15 for domestic and international students. Application fee: $115. Electronic applications accepted. *Expenses:* Tuition: Full-time $34,976. Required fees: $1166. Full-time tuition and fees vary according to program. *Financial support:* Fellowships, research assistantships, teaching assistantships, Federal Work-Study, scholarships/grants, traineeships, tuition waivers (partial), and unspecified assistantships available. Support available to part-time students. Financial award application deadline: 2/8; financial award applicants required to submit FAFSA. *Faculty research:* Statistical genetics, clinical trials, cancer and AIDS research, environmental and mental health, dose response modeling. *Unit head:* Dr. Victor DeGruttola, Chair, 617-432-1056, Fax: 617-432-5619, E-mail: degrut@hsph.harvard.edu. *Application contact:* Vincent W. James, Director of Admissions, 617-432-1031, Fax: 617-432-7080, E-mail: admissions@hsph.harvard.edu.

Hunter College of the City University of New York, Graduate School, Schools of the Health Professions, School of Health Sciences, Programs in Urban Public Health, Program in Epidemiology and Biostatistics, New York, NY 10021-5085. Offers MPH. Part-time and evening/weekend programs available. *Faculty:* 26 full-time (17 women), 21 part-time/adjunct (16 women). *Students:* 10 full-time (8 women), 27 part-time (25 women); includes 5 Black or African American, non-Hispanic/Latino; 3 Asian, non-Hispanic/Latino; 2 Hispanic/Latino. Average age 30. 48 applicants, 44% accepted, 11 enrolled. *Degree requirements:* For master's, comprehensive exam, thesis optional, internship. *Entrance requirements:* For master's, GRE General Test, previous course work in calculus and statistics. Additional exam requirements/recommendations for international students: Required—TOEFL. *Application deadline:* For fall admission, 4/1 for domestic students; for spring admission, 11/1 for domestic students. Application fee: $125. *Financial support:* In 2010–11, 6 fellowships were awarded; career-related internships or fieldwork, Federal Work-Study, institutionally sponsored loans, and tuition waivers (partial) also available. Support available to part-time students. Financial award application deadline: 3/1. *Unit head:* Victoria Frye, Coordinator, 212-481-7580, Fax: 212-481-5260, E-mail: vfrye@hunter.cuny.edu. *Application contact:* Milena Solo, Director for Graduate Admissions, 212-772-4288, Fax: 212-650-3336, E-mail: milena.solo@hunter.cuny.edu.

Iowa State University of Science and Technology, Graduate College, Interdisciplinary Programs, Bioinformatics and Computational Biology Program, Ames, IA 50011. Offers MS, PhD. *Students:* 54 full-time (22 women), 34 international. In 2010, 1 master's, 5 doctorates awarded. *Degree requirements:* For doctorate, thesis/dissertation. *Entrance requirements:* For master's and doctorate, GRE General Test. Additional exam requirements/recommendations for international students: Recommended—IELTS. *Application deadline:* For fall admission, 1/15 priority date for domestic students, 1/15 for international students; for spring admission, 10/15 for domestic and international students. Application fee: $40 ($90 for international students). Electronic applications accepted. *Financial support:* In 2010–11, 47 research assistantships with full and partial tuition reimbursements (averaging $22,000 per year), 3 teaching assistantships (averaging $20,000 per year) were awarded; fellowships with full tuition reimbursements, scholarships/grants, traineeships, health care benefits, and unspecified assistantships also available. *Faculty research:* Functional and structural genomics, genome evolution, macromolecular structure and function, mathematical biology and biological statistics, metabolic and developmental networks. *Unit head:* Dr. Julie Dickerson, Chair, Supervising Committee, 515-294-5122, Fax: 515-294-6790, E-mail: bcb@iastate.edu. *Application contact:* Dr. Julie Dickerson, Chair, Supervising Committee, 515-294-5122, Fax: 515-294-6790, E-mail: bcb@iastate.edu.

The Johns Hopkins University, Bloomberg School of Public Health, Department of Biostatistics, Baltimore, MD 21205-2179. Offers bioinformatics (MHS); biostatistics (MHS, Sc M, PhD). Part-time programs available. *Faculty:* 34 full-time (11 women), 16 part-time/adjunct (3 women). *Students:* 47 full-time (25 women), 3 part-time (0 women); includes 6 minority (1 Black or African American, non-Hispanic/Latino; 3 Asian, non-Hispanic/Latino; 1 Hispanic/Latino; 1 Two or more races, non-Hispanic/Latino), 25 international. Average age 26. 197 applicants, 22% accepted, 22 enrolled. In 2010, 15 master's, 6 doctorates awarded. *Degree requirements:* For master's, comprehensive exam (for some programs), thesis (for some programs), written exam, final project; for doctorate, comprehensive exam, thesis/dissertation, 1 year full-time residency, oral and written exams. *Entrance requirements:* For master's and doctorate, GRE General Test, course work in calculus and matrix algebra, 3 letters of recommendation, curriculum vitae. Additional exam requirements/recommendations for international

Biostatistics

The Medical College of Wisconsin
Graduate School of Biomedical Sciences
Division of Biostatistics

PhD in Biostatistics— A mix of theory and practical experience for students in a medical college setting.

Visit our website today— www.mcw.edu/biostatistics

8701 Watertown Plank Road • Milwaukee, WI 53226

Graduate School: 414.955.8218 • Recruitment Office: 414.955.4402

Email: gradschool@mcw.edu

MEDICAL COLLEGE OF WISCONSIN

The Johns Hopkins University *(continued)*
students: Required—TOEFL (minimum score 600 paper-based; 250 computer-based). *Application deadline:* For fall admission, 1/15 for domestic and international students. Applications are processed on a rolling basis. Application fee: $45. Electronic applications accepted. *Financial support:* In 2010–11, 49 students received support, including 33 research assistantships (averaging $22,000 per year); fellowships, Federal Work-Study, institutionally sponsored loans, scholarships/grants, traineeships, health care benefits, and unspecified assistantships also available. Financial award application deadline: 3/15; financial award applicants required to submit FAFSA. *Faculty research:* Statistical genetics, bioinformatics, statistical computing, statistical methods, environmental statistics. Total annual research expenditures: $4.2 million. *Unit head:* Dr. Karen Bandeen-Roche, Chair, 410-955-3067, Fax: 410-955-0958, E-mail: kbandeen@jhsph.edu. *Application contact:* Mary Joy Argo, Academic Administrator, 410-614-4454, Fax: 410-955-0958, E-mail: margo@jhsph.edu.

Loma Linda University, School of Public Health, Programs in Epidemiology and Biostatistics, Loma Linda, CA 92350. Offers MPH, MSPH, Dr PH, Postbaccalaureate Certificate. *Entrance requirements:* Additional exam requirements/recommendations for international students: Required—Michigan English Language Assessment Battery or TOEFL.

Louisiana State University Health Sciences Center, School of Graduate Studies in New Orleans, Department of Biostatistics, New Orleans, LA 70112-2223. Offers MPH, MS, PhD. Terminal master's awarded for partial completion of doctoral program. *Degree requirements:* For master's, comprehensive exam, thesis; for doctorate, comprehensive exam, thesis/dissertation. *Entrance requirements:* For master's and doctorate, GRE General Test. Additional exam requirements/recommendations for international students: Required—TOEFL. *Faculty research:* Longitudinal data, repeated measures, missing data, generalized estimating equations, multivariate methods.

Louisiana State University Health Sciences Center, School of Public Health, New Orleans, LA 70112. Offers behavioral and community health sciences (MPH); biostatistics (MPH, MS, PhD); community health sciences (PhD); environmental and occupational health sciences (MPH); epidemiology (MPH, PhD); health policy and systems management (MPH). Part-time programs available. *Entrance requirements:* For master's, GRE General Test.

McGill University, Faculty of Graduate and Postdoctoral Studies, Faculty of Medicine, Department of Epidemiology and Biostatistics, Montréal, QC H3A 2T5, Canada. Offers community health (M Sc); environmental health (M Sc); epidemiology and biostatistics (M Sc, PhD, Diploma); health care evaluation (M Sc); medical statistics (M Sc). *Accreditation:* CEPH (one or more programs are accredited).

Medical College of Wisconsin, Graduate School of Biomedical Sciences, Department of Population Health, Division of Biostatistics, Milwaukee, WI 53226-0509. Offers PhD. Part-time programs available. *Degree requirements:* For doctorate, comprehensive exam, thesis/dissertation. *Entrance requirements:* For doctorate, GRE General Test. Additional exam requirements/recommendations for international students: Required—TOEFL. Electronic applications accepted. *Expenses:* Tuition: Full-time $30,000; part-time $710 per credit. Required fees: $150. *Faculty research:* Survival analysis, spatial statistics, time series, genetic statistics, Bayesian statistics.

See Close-Up on page 305.

Medical University of South Carolina, College of Graduate Studies, Division of Biostatistics and Epidemiology, Charleston, SC 29425. Offers biostatistics (MS, PhD); epidemiology (MS, PhD); DMD/PhD; MD/PhD. *Faculty:* 21 full-time (14 women), 1 part-time/adjunct (0 women). *Students:* 21 full-time (16 women); includes 3 Black or African American, non-Hispanic/Latino; 1 Hispanic/Latino, 4 international. Average age 29. 36 applicants, 31% accepted, 5 enrolled. In 2010, 4 doctorates awarded. Terminal master's awarded for partial completion of doctoral program. *Degree requirements:* For master's, comprehensive exam, thesis (for some programs); for doctorate, comprehensive exam, oral and written exams. *Entrance requirements:* For master's, GRE General Test, two semesters of college-level calculus; for doctorate, GRE General Test, interview, minimum GPA of 3.0, two semesters of college-level calculus. Additional exam requirements/recommendations for international students: Required—TOEFL (minimum score 600 paper-based; 250 computer-based; 100 iBT). *Application deadline:* For fall admission, 1/15 priority date for domestic and international students. Applications are processed on a rolling basis. Application fee: $0 ($85 for international students). Electronic applications accepted. *Financial support:* In 2010–11, 18 students received support, including 18 research assistantships with partial tuition reimbursements available (averaging $23,000 per year); Federal Work-Study and scholarships/grants also available. Support available to part-time students. Financial award application deadline: 3/10; financial award applicants required to submit FAFSA. *Faculty research:* Health disparities, central nervous system injuries, radiation exposure, analysis of clinical trial data, biomedical information. *Unit head:* Dr. Yuko Y. Palesch, Professor/Director, 843-876-1917, Fax: 843-792-6590, E-mail: paleschy@musc.edu. *Application contact:* Dr. Ramesh Ramakrishnan, Associate Professor, 843-876-1140, Fax: 843-876-1126, E-mail: ramakris@musc.edu.

Middle Tennessee State University, College of Graduate Studies, College of Basic and Applied Sciences, Program in Professional Science, Murfreesboro, TN 37132. Offers biostatistics (MS); health care informatics (MS). Part-time and evening/weekend programs available. Postbaccalaureate distance learning degree programs offered. *Students:* 8 full-time (4 women), 65 part-time (44 women); includes 15 Black or African American, non-Hispanic/Latino; 17 Asian, non-Hispanic/Latino; 2 Hispanic/Latino; 1 Two or more races, non-Hispanic/Latino. Average age 28. 40 applicants, 55% accepted, 22 enrolled. In 2010, 25 master's awarded. *Degree requirements:* For master's, comprehensive exam. *Entrance requirements:* For master's, GRE. Additional exam requirements/recommendations for international students: Required—TOEFL (minimum score 525 paper-based; 195 computer-based; 71 iBT) or IELTS (minimum score 6). *Application deadline:* For fall admission, 6/1 for domestic and international students. Applications are processed on a rolling basis. Application fee: $25 ($30 for international students). *Expenses:* Tuition, state resident: full-time $4632. Tuition, nonresident: full-time $11,520. *Financial support:* In 2010–11, 7 students received support. Institutionally sponsored loans available. Support available to part-time students. Financial award application deadline: 5/1. *Unit head:* Dr. Thomas Cheatham, Dean, 615-898-5508, Fax: 615-898-2615. *Application contact:* Dr. Michael Allen, Dean and Vice Provost for Research, 615-898-2840, Fax: 615-904-8020, E-mail: mallen@mtsu.edu.

New Jersey Institute of Technology, Office of Graduate Studies, College of Science and Liberal Arts, Department of Mathematical Science, Program in Biostatistics, Newark, NJ 07102. Offers MS. Part-time and evening/weekend programs available. Postbaccalaureate distance learning degree programs offered. *Students:* 6 full-time (4 women), 12 part-time (6 women); includes 1 Black or African American, non-Hispanic/Latino; 9 Asian, non-Hispanic/Latino, 4 international. Average age 31. 24 applicants, 29% accepted, 6 enrolled. In 2010, 1 master's awarded. Terminal master's awarded for partial completion of doctoral program. *Degree requirements:* For master's, thesis optional. *Entrance requirements:* For master's, GRE General Test. Additional exam requirements/recommendations for international students: Required—TOEFL (minimum score 550 paper-based; 213 computer-based; 79 iBT). *Application deadline:* For fall admission, 6/5 for domestic students; 4/1 for international students; for spring admission, 11/15 for domestic and international students. Applications are processed on a rolling basis. Application fee: $65. Electronic applications accepted. *Expenses:* Tuition, state resident: full-time $14,724; part-time $818 per credit. Tuition, nonresident: full-time $20,304; part-time $1128 per credit. Required fees: $2272; $209 per credit. $103 per semester. One-time fee: $312 full-time; $212 part-time. *Financial support:* Career-related internships or fieldwork, Federal Work-Study, institutionally sponsored loans, and unspecified assistantships available. Financial award application deadline: 3/15. *Unit head:* Dr. Daljit S. Ahluwalia, Chair, 973-596-8465, Fax: 973-596-5591, E-mail: daljit.ahluwalia@njit.edu. *Application contact:* Kathryn Kelly, Director of Admissions, 973-596-3300, Fax: 973-596-3461, E-mail: admissions@njit.edu.

246 www.facebook.com/petersonspublishing

Peterson's Graduate Programs in the Physical Sciences, Mathematics, Agricultural Sciences, the Environment & Natural Resources 2012

The Ohio State University, Graduate School, College of Arts and Sciences, Division of Natural and Mathematical Sciences, Department of Statistics, Columbus, OH 43210. Offers biostatistics (PhD); statistics (M Appl Stat, MS, PhD). *Faculty:* 29. *Students:* 77 full-time (32 women), 40 part-time (18 women); includes 2 Black or African American, non-Hispanic/Latino; 5 Asian, non-Hispanic/Latino, 55 international. Average age 27. In 2010, 44 master's, 11 doctorates awarded. *Degree requirements:* For master's, thesis optional; for doctorate, thesis/dissertation. *Entrance requirements:* For master's and doctorate, GRE General Test. Additional exam requirements/recommendations for international students: Required—TOEFL (minimum score 600 paper-based; 250 computer-based). *Application deadline:* For fall admission, 8/15 priority date for domestic students, 7/1 priority date for international students; for winter admission, 12/1 priority date for domestic students, 11/1 priority date for international students; for spring admission, 3/1 priority date for domestic students, 2/1 priority date for international students. Applications are processed on a rolling basis. Application fee: $40 ($50 for international students). Electronic applications accepted. *Expenses:* Tuition, state resident: full-time $10,605. Tuition, nonresident: full-time $26,535. Tuition and fees vary according to course load and program. *Financial support:* Fellowships, research assistantships, teaching assistantships, Federal Work-Study and institutionally sponsored loans available. Support available to part-time students. *Unit head:* Doug Wolfe, Chair, 614-292-0293, Fax: 614-292-2096, E-mail: wolfe.9@osu.edu. *Application contact:* 614-292-9444, Fax: 614-292-3895, E-mail: domestic.grad@osu.edu.

Oregon Health & Science University, School of Medicine, Graduate Programs in Medicine, Department of Public Health and Preventive Medicine, Portland, OR 97239-3098. Offers epidemiology and biostatistics (MPH). *Accreditation:* CEPH. Part-time programs available. *Faculty:* 7 full-time (3 women), 39 part-time/adjunct (17 women). *Students:* 82 full-time (56 women); includes 2 Black or African American, non-Hispanic/Latino; 2 American Indian or Alaska Native, non-Hispanic/Latino; 7 Asian, non-Hispanic/Latino; 1 Hispanic/Latino; 1 Native Hawaiian or other Pacific Islander, non-Hispanic/Latino, 4 international. Average age 30. 61 applicants, 64% accepted, 22 enrolled. In 2010, 22 master's awarded. *Degree requirements:* For master's, thesis, fieldwork/internship. *Entrance requirements:* For master's, GRE General Test (minimum scores: 500 Verbal/600 Quantitative/4.5 Analytical), previous undergraduate course work in statistics. Additional exam requirements/recommendations for international students: Required—TOEFL (minimum score 550 paper-based; 213 computer-based; 87 iBT). *Application deadline:* For fall admission, 2/1 for domestic students. Application fee: $65. Electronic applications accepted. *Financial support:* Health care benefits available. *Faculty research:* Health services, health care access, health policy, environmental and occupational health. *Unit head:* Thomas M. Becker, MD, Professor/Chair, 503-494-8257, Fax: 503-494-4981, E-mail: pmph@ohsu.edu. *Application contact:* Tree Triano, Education Manager, 503-494-2012, Fax: 503-494-4981, E-mail: pmph@ohsu.edu.

Rice University, Graduate Programs, George R. Brown School of Engineering, Department of Statistics, Houston, TX 77251-1892. Offers bioinformatics (PhD); biostatistics (PhD); computational finance (PhD); general statistics (PhD); statistics (M Stat, MA); MBA/M Stat. Part-time programs available. *Degree requirements:* For master's, comprehensive exam; for doctorate, comprehensive exam, thesis/dissertation. *Entrance requirements:* For master's and doctorate, GRE General Test, minimum GPA of 3.0. Additional exam requirements/recommendations for international students: Required—TOEFL (minimum score 630 paper-based; 250 computer-based; 90 iBT). Electronic applications accepted. *Faculty research:* Statistical genetics, non parametric function estimation, computational statistics and visualization, stochastic processes.

Rutgers, The State University of New Jersey, New Brunswick, Graduate School-New Brunswick, BioMaPS Institute for Quantitative Biology, Piscataway, NJ 08854-8097. Offers computational biology and molecular biophysics (PhD). *Degree requirements:* For doctorate, comprehensive exam, thesis/dissertation. *Entrance requirements:* For doctorate, GRE. Additional exam requirements/recommendations for international students: Required—TOEFL. Electronic applications accepted. *Expenses:* Tuition, state resident: full-time $7200; part-time $600 per credit. Tuition, nonresident: full-time $11,124; part-time $927 per credit. *Faculty research:* Structural biology, systems biology, bioinformatics, translational medicine, genomics.

Rutgers, The State University of New Jersey, New Brunswick, Graduate School-New Brunswick, Program in Statistics, Piscataway, NJ 08854-8097. Offers applied statistics (MS); biostatistics (MS); data mining (MS); quality and productivity management (MS); statistics (MS, PhD). Part-time programs available. Terminal master's awarded for partial completion of doctoral program. *Degree requirements:* For master's, comprehensive exam, essay, exam, non-thesis essay paper; for doctorate, one foreign language, thesis/dissertation, qualifying oral and written exams. *Entrance requirements:* For master's, GRE General Test; for doctorate, GRE General Test, GRE Subject Test (recommended). Additional exam requirements/recommendations for international students: Required—TOEFL (minimum score 550 paper-based; 213 computer-based). Electronic applications accepted. *Expenses:* Tuition, state resident: full-time $7200; part-time $600 per credit. Tuition, nonresident: full-time $11,124; part-time $927 per credit. *Faculty research:* Probability, decision theory, linear models, multivariate statistics, statistical computing.

San Diego State University, Graduate and Research Affairs, College of Health and Human Services, Graduate School of Public Health, San Diego, CA 92182. Offers environmental health (MPH); epidemiology (MPH, PhD), including biostatistics (MPH); global emergency preparedness and response (MS); global health (PhD); health behavior (PhD); health promotion (MPH); health services administration (MPH); toxicology (MS); MPH/MA; MSW/MPH. *Accreditation:* ABET (one or more programs are accredited); CAHME (one or more programs are accredited); CEPH (one or more programs are accredited). Part-time programs available. *Degree requirements:* For master's, comprehensive exam (for some programs), thesis (for some programs); for doctorate, thesis/dissertation. *Entrance requirements:* For master's, GMAT (MPH in health services administration), GRE General Test; for doctorate, GRE General Test. Additional exam requirements/recommendations for international students: Required—TOEFL. *Faculty research:* Evaluation of tobacco, AIDS prevalence and prevention, mammography, infant death project, Alzheimer's in elderly Chinese.

Tufts University, Sackler School of Graduate Biomedical Sciences, Division of Clinical Care Research, Medford, MA 02155. Offers MS, PhD. *Faculty:* 37 full-time (11 women). *Students:* 23 full-time (15 women), 1 part-time (0 women); includes 1 Black or African American, non-Hispanic/Latino; 4 Asian, non-Hispanic/Latino, 10 international. Average age 33. 32 applicants, 41% accepted, 13 enrolled. In 2010, 7 master's awarded. Terminal master's awarded for partial completion of doctoral program. *Degree requirements:* For master's, thesis; for doctorate, thesis/dissertation. *Entrance requirements:* For master's and doctorate, MD or PhD, strong clinical research background. Additional exam requirements/recommendations for international students: Required—TOEFL. *Application deadline:* For fall admission, 12/15 for domestic and international students. Applications are processed on a rolling basis. Application fee: $70. Electronic applications accepted. *Expenses:* Tuition: Full-time $39,624; part-time $3962 per course. Required fees: $40 per year. Full-time tuition and fees vary according to degree level, program and student level. Part-time tuition and fees vary according to course load. *Financial support:* In 2010–11, 27 fellowships with full tuition reimbursements were awarded. Financial award application deadline: 12/15. *Faculty research:* Clinical study design, mathematical modeling, meta analysis, epidemiologic research, coronary heart disease. *Unit head:* Dr. Harry P. Selker, Program Director, 617-636-5009, Fax: 617-636-8023, E-mail: hselker@lifespan.org. *Application contact:* Kellie Johnston, Associate Director of Admissions, 617-636-6767, Fax: 617-636-0375, E-mail: sackler-school@tufts.edu.

Tulane University, School of Public Health and Tropical Medicine, Department of Biostatistics, New Orleans, LA 70118-5669. Offers MS, MSPH, PhD, Sc D. MS and PhD offered through the Graduate School. Part-time programs available. *Degree requirements:* For doctorate, comprehensive exam, thesis/dissertation. *Entrance requirements:* For master's and doctorate, GRE General Test. Additional exam requirements/recommendations for international students: Required—TOEFL. Electronic applications accepted. *Faculty research:* Clinical trials, measurement, longitudinal analyses.

University at Albany, State University of New York, School of Public Health, Department of Epidemiology and Biostatistics, Albany, NY 12222-0001. Offers MS, PhD. *Degree requirements:* For master's, thesis; for doctorate, thesis/dissertation. *Entrance requirements:* For master's and doctorate, GRE General Test. Additional exam requirements/recommendations for international students: Required—TOEFL (minimum score 550 paper-based; 213 computer-based). Electronic applications accepted.

University at Buffalo, the State University of New York, Graduate School, School of Public Health and Health Professions, Department of Biostatistics, Buffalo, NY 14260. Offers MA, PhD. *Faculty:* 10 full-time (3 women), 2 part-time/adjunct (0 women). *Students:* 30 full-time (13 women), 10 part-time (4 women); includes 1 Black or African American, non-Hispanic/Latino; 7 Asian, non-Hispanic/Latino, 19 international. Average age 31. 61 applicants, 61% accepted, 12 enrolled. In 2010, 9 master's, 1 doctorate awarded. Terminal master's awarded for partial completion of doctoral program. *Degree requirements:* For master's, comprehensive exam, thesis optional, final oral exam, practical data analysis experience; for doctorate, comprehensive exam, thesis/dissertation, final oral exam. *Entrance requirements:* For master's, GRE, 3 semesters of course work in calculus (mathematics), course work in real analysis (preferred), course work in linear algebra; for doctorate, GRE, master's degree in statistics, biostatistics or equivalent. Additional exam requirements/recommendations for international students: Required—TOEFL (minimum score 640 paper-based; 250 computer-based; 79 iBT). *Application deadline:* For fall admission, 4/1 priority date for domestic and international students. Application fee: $50. Electronic applications accepted. *Financial support:* In 2010–11, 12 students received support, including 1 fellowship (averaging $4,000 per year), 6 research assistantships with full tuition reimbursements available (averaging $15,000 per year), 5 teaching assistantships with full tuition reimbursements available (averaging $12,000 per year); institutionally sponsored loans, scholarships/grants, and tuition waivers (partial) also available. Financial award application deadline: 2/1; financial award applicants required to submit FAFSA. *Faculty research:* Biostatistics, longitudinal data analysis, nonparametrics, statistical genetics, epidemiology. *Unit head:* Dr. Alan D. Hutson, Chair and Associate Professor, 716-829-2594, Fax: 716-829-2200, E-mail: ahutson@buffalo.edu. *Application contact:* Dr. Lili Tian, Director of Graduate Studies and Professor, 716-829-2715, Fax: 716-829-2200, E-mail: ltian@buffalo.edu.

The University of Alabama at Birmingham, School of Public Health, Program in Biostatistics, Birmingham, AL 35294. Offers MS, PhD. *Students:* 28 full-time (10 women), 14 part-time (3 women); includes 6 minority (1 Black or African American, non-Hispanic/Latino; 5 Asian, non-Hispanic/Latino), 17 international. Average age 33. 42 applicants, 48% accepted, 9 enrolled. In 2010, 2 master's, 3 doctorates awarded. *Degree requirements:* For master's, variable foreign language requirement, thesis, fieldwork, research project; for doctorate, variable foreign language requirement, comprehensive exam, thesis/dissertation. *Entrance requirements:* For master's, GRE General Test or MAT, minimum GPA of 3.0; for doctorate, GRE General Test or MAT, MPH or MSPH, minimum GPA of 3.0, interview. *Expenses:* Contact institution. *Financial support:* Fellowships, career-related internships or fieldwork available. *Unit head:* Dr. George Howard, Chair, 205-934-4905, Fax: 205-975-2540, E-mail: ghoward@uab.edu. *Application contact:* Nancy O. Pinson, Coordinator of Student Admissions, 205-934-4993, Fax: 205-975-5484.

University of Alberta, Faculty of Graduate Studies and Research, Department of Mathematical and Statistical Sciences, Edmonton, AB T6G 2E1, Canada. Offers applied mathematics (M Sc, PhD); biostatistics (M Sc); mathematical finance (M Sc, PhD); mathematical physics (M Sc, PhD); mathematics (M Sc, PhD); statistics (M Sc, PhD, Postgraduate Diploma). Part-time programs available. Terminal master's awarded for partial completion of doctoral program. *Degree requirements:* For master's, thesis (for some programs); for doctorate, comprehensive exam, thesis/dissertation. *Entrance requirements:* Additional exam requirements/recommendations for international students: Required—TOEFL (minimum score 580 paper-based; 237 computer-based). Electronic applications accepted. *Faculty research:* Classical and functional analysis, algebra, differential equations, geometry.

The University of Arizona, Mel and Enid Zuckerman College of Public Health, Program in Biostatistics, Tucson, AZ 85721. Offers PhD. *Faculty:* 8 full-time (5 women), 1 (woman) part-time/adjunct. *Students:* 8 full-time (5 women), 5 part-time (3 women); includes 1 Black or African American, non-Hispanic/Latino; 2 Hispanic/Latino; 1 Two or more races, non-Hispanic/Latino, 4 international. Average age 31. 29 applicants, 34% accepted, 3 enrolled. *Entrance requirements:* Additional exam requirements/recommendations for international students: Required—TOEFL (minimum score 550 paper-based; 213 computer-based; 79 iBT). *Application deadline:* For fall admission, 1/1 for domestic and international students. Applications are processed on a rolling basis. Application fee: $75. Electronic applications accepted. *Expenses:* Tuition, state resident: full-time $7692. *Financial support:* In 2010–11, 6 research assistantships (averaging $18,151 per year), 10 teaching assistantships (averaging $18,469 per year) were awarded. *Unit head:* Dr. Iman Hakim, Interim Dean, 520-626-7083, E-mail: ihakim@email.arizona.edu. *Application contact:* Lorraine Varela, Special Assistant to the Dean, 520-626-3201, E-mail: varelal@coph.arizona.edu.

University of California, Berkeley, Graduate Division, School of Public Health, Group in Biostatistics, Berkeley, CA 94720-1500. Offers MA, PhD. *Accreditation:* CEPH (one or more programs are accredited). *Degree requirements:* For master's, oral exam; for doctorate, thesis/dissertation, oral exam. *Entrance requirements:* For master's and doctorate, GRE General Test, minimum GPA of 3.0, 3 letters of recommendation. Additional exam requirements/recommendations for international students: Required—TOEFL.

University of California, Davis, Graduate Studies, Graduate Group in Biostatistics, Davis, CA 95616. Offers MS, PhD. *Degree requirements:* For master's, comprehensive exam; for doctorate, thesis/dissertation. *Entrance requirements:* Additional exam requirements/recommendations for international students: Required—TOEFL (minimum score 550 paper-based; 213 computer-based). Electronic applications accepted.

University of California, Los Angeles, Graduate Division, School of Public Health, Department of Biostatistics, Los Angeles, CA 90095. Offers MPH, MS, Dr PH, PhD. *Degree requirements:* For master's, comprehensive exam; for doctorate, thesis/dissertation, oral and written qualifying exams. *Entrance requirements:* For master's, GRE General Test, minimum GPA of 3.0; for doctorate, GRE General Test, minimum undergraduate GPA of 3.0. Electronic applications accepted.

University of Cincinnati, Graduate School, College of Medicine, Graduate Programs in Biomedical Sciences, Department of Environmental Health, Cincinnati, OH 45221. Offers environmental and industrial hygiene (MS, PhD); environmental and occupational medicine (MS); environmental genetics and molecular toxicology (MS, PhD); epidemiology and biostatistics (MS, PhD); occupational safety and ergonomics (MS, PhD). *Accreditation:* ABET (one or more programs are accredited). Terminal master's awarded for partial completion of doctoral program. *Degree requirements:* For master's, thesis; for doctorate, thesis/dissertation, qualifying exam. *Entrance requirements:* For master's, GRE General Test, bachelor's degree in science; for doctorate, GRE General Test. Additional exam requirements/recommendations for international students: Required—TOEFL (minimum score 600 paper-based; 250 computer-based; 100 iBT). Electronic applications accepted. *Faculty research:* Carcinogens and mutagenesis, pulmonary studies, reproduction and development.

Biostatistics

University of Colorado Denver, Colorado School of Public Health, Department of Biostatistics and Informatics, Aurora, CO 80045. Offers MS, PhD. Part-time programs available. *Students:* 14 full-time (7 women), 14 part-time (8 women); includes 1 American Indian or Alaska Native, non-Hispanic/Latino; 2 Asian, non-Hispanic/Latino; 2 Hispanic/Latino, 2 international. Average age 32. 15 applicants, 53% accepted, 7 enrolled. In 2010, 5 master's, 3 doctorates awarded. Terminal master's awarded for partial completion of doctoral program. *Degree requirements:* For master's, thesis or alternative, 34 credit hours; for doctorate, comprehensive exam, thesis/dissertation, 78 credit hours. *Entrance requirements:* For master's, GRE General Test, baccalaureate degree in scientific field, minimum GPA of 3.0, math course work through integral calculus, two official copies of all academic transcripts, four letters of recommendation/reference, essays describing the applicant's career goals and reasons for applying to the program, resume; for doctorate, GRE General Test, baccalaureate degree in scientific field; master's degree in biostatistics, statistics or equivalent; minimum GPA of 3.0; math course work through integral calculus; two official copies of all academic transcripts; four letters of recommendation/reference; essays; resume. Additional exam requirements/recommendations for international students: Required—TOEFL (minimum score 550 paper-based; 213 computer-based; 80 iBT). *Application deadline:* For fall admission, 2/1 for domestic students. Application fee: $65. Electronic applications accepted. *Expenses:* Contact institution. *Financial support:* Fellowships, research assistantships, Federal Work-Study, scholarships/grants, and unspecified assistantships available. Financial award application deadline: 3/1; financial award applicants required to submit FAFSA. *Faculty research:* Health policy research, nonlinear mixed effects models for longitudinal data, statistical methods in nutrition, clinical trials. *Unit head:* Dr. Gary Grunwald, Director, 303-724-4360, Fax: 303-724-4620, E-mail: gary.grunwald@ucdenver.edu. *Application contact:* Fayette Augillard, Program Coordinator, 303-724-4442, Fax: 303-724-4620, E-mail: fayette.augillard@ucdenver.edu.

University of Florida, Graduate School, College of Public Health and Health Professions and College of Medicine, Programs in Public Health, Gainesville, FL 32611. Offers biostatistics (MPH); environmental health (MPH); epidemiology (MPH); public health management and policy (MPH); public health practice (MPH); social and behavioral sciences (MPH). Postbaccalaureate distance learning degree programs offered. *Students:* 127 full-time (85 women), 38 part-time (22 women); includes 21 Black or African American, non-Hispanic/Latino; 19 Asian, non-Hispanic/Latino; 16 Hispanic/Latino, 11 international. Average age 28. 263 applicants, 29% accepted, 48 enrolled. In 2010, 54 master's awarded. *Degree requirements:* For master's, internship. *Entrance requirements:* For master's, GRE General Test, minimum GPA of 3.0. Additional exam requirements/recommendations for international students: Required—TOEFL (minimum score 550 paper-based; 213 computer-based; 80 iBT), IELTS (minimum score 6). Application fee: $30. *Expenses:* Tuition, state resident: full-time $10,915.92. Tuition, nonresident: full-time $28,309. *Financial support:* In 2010–11, 12 students received support, including 4 fellowships, 5 research assistantships (averaging $14,122 per year), 3 teaching assistantships (averaging $12,501 per year). Financial award applicants required to submit FAFSA. *Unit head:* Prof. Mary Peoples-Sheps, Associate Dean for Public Health, 352-273-6084, Fax: 352-273-6448, E-mail: mpeoplessheps@phhp.ufl.edu. *Application contact:* Prof. Mary Peoples-Sheps, Associate Dean for Public Health, 352-273-6084, Fax: 352-273-6448, E-mail: mpeoplessheps@phhp.ufl.edu.

University of Georgia, College of Public Health, Program in Biostatistics, Athens, GA 30602. Offers MPH. *Expenses:* Tuition, state resident: full-time $7200; part-time $344 per credit hour. Tuition, nonresident: full-time $21,900; part-time $944 per credit hour. Tuition and fees vary according to course load and program. *Unit head:* Dr. Joel M. Lee, Dean, 706-542-3709, E-mail: joellee@uga.edu. *Application contact:* Mitchela Salum, Graduate Coordinator, 706-583-0885, E-mail: msalum@uga.edu.

University of Illinois at Chicago, Graduate College, School of Public Health, Biostatistics Section, Chicago, IL 60607-7128. Offers biostatistics (MS, PhD); quantitative methods (MPH). Part-time programs available. Terminal master's awarded for partial completion of doctoral program. *Degree requirements:* For master's, thesis, field practicum; for doctorate, thesis/dissertation, independent research, internship. *Entrance requirements:* For master's and doctorate, GRE General Test, minimum GPA of 2.75. Additional exam requirements/recommendations for international students: Required—TOEFL. Electronic applications accepted.

The University of Iowa, Graduate College, College of Public Health, Department of Biostatistics, Iowa City, IA 52242-1316. Offers MS, PhD. *Degree requirements:* For master's, thesis optional, exam; for doctorate, comprehensive exam, thesis/dissertation. *Entrance requirements:* For master's and doctorate, GRE General Test, minimum GPA of 3.0. Additional exam requirements/recommendations for international students: Required—TOEFL (minimum score 600 paper-based; 250 computer-based; 100 iBT). Electronic applications accepted.

The University of Kansas, University of Kansas Medical Center, School of Medicine, Department of Biostatistics, Kansas City, KS 66160. Offers MS, PhD. *Faculty:* 10 full-time (3 women). *Students:* 3 full-time (all women), all international. Average age 29. 9 applicants, 33% accepted, 3 enrolled. *Degree requirements:* For master's, comprehensive exam; for doctorate, comprehensive exam, thesis/dissertation. *Entrance requirements:* For master's, GRE, coursework in calculus, computer programming, linear algebra, differential equations, and numerical analysis; for doctorate, master's degree. Additional exam requirements/recommendations for international students: Required—TOEFL. *Application deadline:* For fall admission, 3/31 for domestic and international students. Application fee: $60. Electronic applications accepted. *Expenses:* Tuition, state resident: full-time $7092; part-time $295.50 per credit hour. Tuition, nonresident: full-time $16,590; part-time $691.25 per credit hour. Required fees: $858; $71.49 per credit hour. Tuition and fees vary according to course load, campus/location and program. *Financial support:* Research assistantships with full tuition reimbursements, scholarships/grants, traineeships, and unspecified assistantships available. Financial award application deadline: 2/14; financial award applicants required to submit FAFSA. *Faculty research:* Biostatistics, clinical trials. Total annual research expenditures: $184,000. *Unit head:* Dr. Matthew Mayo, PhD, Chair and Professor, 913-588-4735 Ext. 913, Fax: 913-588-0252, E-mail: mmayo@kumc.edu. *Application contact:* Tami Walz, Marketing, Recruitment and Graduate Education Coordinator, 913-588-2757, Fax: 913-588-0252, E-mail: twalz@kumc.edu.

University of Louisville, Graduate School, School of Public Health and Information Sciences, Department of Bioinformatics and Biostatistics, Louisville, KY 40292-0001. Offers biostatistics (MS, PhD); decision science (MS). Part-time programs available. *Faculty:* 9 full-time (3 women), 2 part-time/adjunct (1 woman). *Students:* 15 full-time (6 women), 5 part-time (3 women); includes 2 Asian, non-Hispanic/Latino, 10 international. Average age 32. 25 applicants, 64% accepted, 4 enrolled. In 2010, 7 master's, 2 doctorates awarded. *Degree requirements:* For master's, thesis; for doctorate, comprehensive exam, thesis/dissertation. *Entrance requirements:* For master's and doctorate, GRE, official transcripts, undergraduate GPA, statement of purpose, resume/CV, letters of recommendation, foreign transcript evaluation. Additional exam requirements/recommendations for international students: Required—TOEFL (minimum score 600 paper-based; 250 computer-based; 100 iBT). *Application deadline:* For fall admission, 3/1 for domestic and international students. Application fee: $50. Electronic applications accepted. *Expenses:* Tuition, state resident: full-time $9144; part-time $508 per credit hour. Tuition, nonresident: full-time $19,026; part-time $1057 per credit hour. Tuition and fees vary according to program and reciprocity agreements. *Financial support:* In 2010–11, 9 students received support, including 3 research assistantships with full tuition reimbursements available (averaging $20,000 per year); health care benefits and unspecified assistantships also available. Financial award applicants required to submit FAFSA. *Faculty research:* Bioinformatics, compound decision problems, infectious disease modeling, inference, statistical genetics, genomics, clinical trials, information theory, utility theory and measurement. Total annual research expenditures: $173,590. *Unit head:* Dr. Robert Esterhay, Interim Department Chair, 502-852-6135, Fax: 502-852-3294, E-mail: robert.esterhay@louisville.edu. *Application contact:* Lynne Dosker, Administrative Assistant, 502-852-1827, Fax: 502-852-3294, E-mail: lcdosk01@louisville.edu.

University of Maryland, Baltimore, School of Medicine, Department of Epidemiology and Preventive Medicine, Baltimore, MD 21201. Offers biostatistics (MS); clinical research (MS); epidemiology and preventative medicine (PhD); epidemiology and preventive medicine (MPH, MS); gerontology (PhD); human genetics and genomic (PhD); human genetics and genomic medicine (MS); molecular epidemiology (MS, PhD); toxicology (MS, PhD); JD/MS; MD/PhD; MS/PhD. *Accreditation:* CEPH. Part-time programs available. *Students:* 84 full-time (57 women), 64 part-time (46 women); includes 17 Black or African American, non-Hispanic/Latino; 23 Asian, non-Hispanic/Latino; 4 Hispanic/Latino, 18 international. Average age 32. In 2010, 21 master's, 10 doctorates awarded. *Entrance requirements:* For master's and doctorate, GRE General Test. Additional exam requirements/recommendations for international students: Required—TOEFL (minimum score 550 paper-based; 213 computer-based; 80 iBT); Recommended—IELTS. *Application deadline:* For fall admission, 1/15 for domestic and international students. Electronic applications accepted. *Expenses:* Contact institution. *Financial support:* In 2010–11, research assistantships with partial tuition reimbursements (averaging $25,000 per year); fellowships, Federal Work-Study, scholarships/grants, and unspecified assistantships also available. Financial award application deadline: 3/1; financial award applicants required to submit FAFSA. *Unit head:* Dr. Patricia Langenberg, Program Director, 410-706-3251, Fax: 410-706-8013. *Application contact:* Danielle Fitzpatrick, Program Coordinator, 410-706-8492, Fax: 410-706-4225, E-mail: dfitzpatrick@epi.umaryland.edu.

University of Maryland, Baltimore County, Graduate School, College of Natural and Mathematical Sciences, Department of Mathematics and Statistics, Program in Statistics, Baltimore, MD 21250. Offers biostatistics (PhD); environmental statistics (MS); statistics (MS, PhD). Part-time and evening/weekend programs available. *Faculty:* 8 full-time (3 women). *Students:* 31 full-time (14 women), 24 part-time (14 women); includes 14 minority (5 Black or African American, non-Hispanic/Latino; 9 Asian, non-Hispanic/Latino), 17 international. Average age 30. 54 applicants, 80% accepted, 15 enrolled. In 2010, 9 master's, 2 doctorates awarded. Terminal master's awarded for partial completion of doctoral program. *Degree requirements:* For master's, comprehensive exam (for some programs), thesis (for some programs); for doctorate, comprehensive exam, thesis/dissertation. *Entrance requirements:* For master's and doctorate, GRE General Test, minimum GPA of 3.0. Additional exam requirements/recommendations for international students: Required—TOEFL (minimum score 600 paper-based; 250 computer-based; 100 iBT). *Application deadline:* For fall admission, 2/15 priority date for domestic students, 1/1 priority date for international students; for spring admission, 10/15 priority date for domestic students, 5/1 priority date for international students. Applications are processed on a rolling basis. Application fee: $50. Electronic applications accepted. *Financial support:* In 2010–11, 22 students received support, including 6 research assistantships with full tuition reimbursements available (averaging $15,500 per year), 16 teaching assistantships with full tuition reimbursements available (averaging $15,878 per year); fellowships with full tuition reimbursements available, career-related internships or fieldwork, scholarships/grants, health care benefits, tuition waivers (full and partial), and unspecified assistantships also available. Support available to part-time students. Financial award application deadline: 2/15. *Faculty research:* Design of experiments, statistical decision theory and inference, time series analysis, biostatistics and environmental statistics, bioinformatics. Total annual research expenditures: $2.8 million. *Unit head:* Dr. Anindya Roy, Director, 410-455-2435, Fax: 410-455-1066, E-mail: anindya@math.umbc.edu. *Application contact:* Dr. Anindya Roy, Director, 410-455-2435, Fax: 410-455-1066, E-mail: anindya@math.umbc.edu.

University of Maryland, College Park, Academic Affairs, School of Public Health, Department of Epidemiology and Biostatistics, College Park, MD 20742. Offers biostatistics (MPH); epidemiology (MPH, PhD). *Faculty:* 12 full-time (9 women), 3 part-time/adjunct (all women). *Students:* 19 full-time (14 women), 11 part-time (10 women); includes 6 minority (1 Black or African American, non-Hispanic/Latino; 4 Asian, non-Hispanic/Latino; 1 Hispanic/Latino), 7 international. 131 applicants, 8% accepted, 7 enrolled. In 2010, 8 master's awarded. *Application deadline:* For fall admission, 1/15 for domestic and international students. Application fee: $75. *Expenses:* Tuition, area resident: Part-time $471 per credit hour. Tuition, state resident: part-time $471 per credit hour. Tuition, nonresident: part-time $1016 per credit hour. Required fees: $337 per term. *Financial support:* In 2010–11, 4 fellowships with full and partial tuition reimbursements (averaging $21,845 per year), 2 research assistantships (averaging $15,878 per year), 2 teaching assistantships (averaging $15,878 per year) were awarded. Total annual research expenditures: $1.2 million. *Unit head:* Dr. Deborah Young, Chair, 301-405-2496, E-mail: dryoung@umd.edu. *Application contact:* Dr. Charles A. Caramello, Dean of Graduate School, 301-405-0358, Fax: 301-314-9305.

University of Maryland, College Park, Academic Affairs, School of Public Health, Department of Public and Community Health, College Park, MD 20742. Offers biostatistics (MPH); community health education (MPH); environmental health sciences (MPH); epidemiology (MPH); public/community health (PhD). *Accreditation:* CEPH. Part-time and evening/weekend programs available. *Faculty:* 28 full-time (17 women), 9 part-time/adjunct (7 women). *Students:* 26 full-time (23 women), 21 part-time (20 women); includes 22 minority (16 Black or African American, non-Hispanic/Latino; 5 Asian, non-Hispanic/Latino; 1 Hispanic/Latino), 1 international. 160 applicants, 14% accepted, 11 enrolled. In 2010, 7 master's, 4 doctorates awarded. *Degree requirements:* For master's, thesis optional; for doctorate, comprehensive exam, thesis/dissertation. *Entrance requirements:* For master's, GRE General Test, minimum GPA of 3.0, 3 letters of recommendation; for doctorate, GRE General Test, minimum GPA of 3.5, 3 letters of recommendation. Additional exam requirements/recommendations for international students: Required—TOEFL. *Application deadline:* For fall admission, 1/15 for domestic and international students; for spring admission, 6/1 for international students. Applications are processed on a rolling basis. Application fee: $75. Electronic applications accepted. *Expenses:* Tuition, area resident: Part-time $471 per credit hour. Tuition, state resident: part-time $471 per credit hour. Tuition, nonresident: part-time $1016 per credit hour. Required fees: $337 per term. *Financial support:* In 2010–11, 6 research assistantships (averaging $15,775 per year), 19 teaching assistantships (averaging $15,855 per year) were awarded; fellowships, career-related internships or fieldwork, Federal Work-Study, and scholarships/grants also available. Support available to part-time students. Financial award applicants required to submit FAFSA. *Faculty research:* Controlling stress and tension, women's health, aging and public policy, adolescent health, long-term care. Total annual research expenditures: $3.7 million. *Unit head:* Dr. Elbert Glover, Chair, 301-405-2467, Fax: 301-314-9167, E-mail: eglover1@umd.edu. *Application contact:* Dean of Graduate School, 301-405-0358.

University of Massachusetts Amherst, Graduate School, School of Public Health and Health Sciences, Department of Public Health, Amherst, MA 01003. Offers biostatistics (MPH, MS, PhD); community health education (MPH, MS, PhD); environmental health sciences (MPH, MS, PhD); epidemiology (MPH, MS, PhD); health policy and management (MPH, MS, PhD); nutrition (PhD); public health practice (MPH). *Accreditation:* CEPH (one or more programs are accredited). Part-time and evening/weekend programs available. Postbaccalaureate distance learning degree programs offered (no on-campus study). *Faculty:* 38 full-time (23 women). *Students:* 116 full-time (92 women), 215 part-time (153 women); includes 58 minority (19 Black or African American, non-Hispanic/Latino; 15 Asian, non-Hispanic/Latino; 16 Hispanic/Latino; 1 Native Hawaiian or other Pacific Islander, non-Hispanic/Latino; 7 Two or more races, non-Hispanic/Latino), 58 international. Average age 36. 311 applicants, 58% accepted, 85 enrolled. In 2010, 99 master's, 2 doctorates awarded. Terminal master's awarded for partial completion of doctoral program. *Degree requirements:* For master's, thesis (for some programs); for doctorate, comprehensive exam, thesis/dissertation. *Entrance requirements:* For master's and

doctorate, GRE General Test. Additional exam requirements/recommendations for international students: Required—TOEFL (minimum score 550 paper-based; 213 computer-based; 80 iBT), IELTS (minimum score 6.5). *Application deadline:* For fall admission, 2/1 for domestic and international students. Applications are processed on a rolling basis. Application fee: $40 ($65 for international students). Electronic applications accepted. *Expenses:* Tuition, state resident: full-time $2640. Required fees: $8282. One-time fee: $357 full-time. *Financial support:* In 2010–11, 35 research assistantships with full tuition reimbursements (averaging $7,080 per year), 25 teaching assistantships with full tuition reimbursements (averaging $5,902 per year) were awarded; fellowships, career-related internships or fieldwork, Federal Work-Study, scholarships/grants, traineeships, health care benefits, tuition waivers (full), and unspecified assistantships also available. Support available to part-time students. Financial award application deadline: 2/1. *Unit head:* Dr. Paula Stamps, Graduate Program Director, 413-545-2861, Fax: 413-545-0964. *Application contact:* Jean M. Ames, Supervisor of Admissions, 413-545-0722, Fax: 413-577-0010, E-mail: gradadm@grad.umass.edu.

University of Medicine and Dentistry of New Jersey, UMDNJ–School of Public Health (UMDNJ, Rutgers, NJIT) Piscataway/New Brunswick Campus, Piscataway, NJ 08854. Offers biostatistics (MPH, MS, Dr PH, PhD); clinical epidemiology (Certificate); environmental and occupational health (MPH, Dr PH, PhD, Certificate); epidemiology (MPH, Dr PH, PhD); general public health (Certificate); health education and behavioral science (MPH, Dr PH, PhD); health systems and policy (MPH, PhD); public health preparedness (Certificate); DO/MPH; JD/MPH; MD/MPH; MPH/MBA; MPH/MSPA; MS/MPH; Psy D/MPH. Part-time and evening/weekend programs available. *Degree requirements:* For master's, thesis, internship; for doctorate, comprehensive exam, thesis/dissertation. *Entrance requirements:* For master's, GRE General Test; for doctorate, GRE General Test, MPH (Dr PH); MA, MPH, or MS (PhD). Additional exam requirements/recommendations for international students: Required—TOEFL. *Application deadline:* For fall admission, 5/1 for domestic students; for spring admission, 10/1 for domestic students. Application fee: $115. Electronic applications accepted. *Unit head:* Tina Greco, Program Coordinator, 732-235-4646, Fax: 732-235-5476, E-mail: grecotm@umdnj.edu. *Application contact:* Janet Zamorski, Staff Assistant, 732-235-4646, E-mail: zamorsja@umdnj.edu.

University of Memphis, Graduate School, School of Public Health, Memphis, TN 38152. Offers biostatistics (MPH); environmental health (MPH); epidemiology (MPH); health systems management (MPH); public health (MHA); social and behavioral sciences (MPH). Part-time and evening/weekend programs available. Postbaccalaureate distance learning degree programs offered. *Faculty:* 5 full-time (2 women), 4 part-time/adjunct (2 women). *Students:* 45 full-time (23 women), 29 part-time (14 women); includes 19 Black or African American, non-Hispanic/Latino; 6 Asian, non-Hispanic/Latino; 2 Hispanic/Latino, 7 international. Average age 32. 57 applicants, 70% accepted, 22 enrolled. In 2010, 17 master's awarded. *Degree requirements:* For master's, comprehensive exam, thesis. *Entrance requirements:* For master's, GRE, letters of recommendation. Additional exam requirements/recommendations for international students: Required—TOEFL. *Application deadline:* For fall admission, 4/1 for domestic students; for spring admission, 11/1 for domestic students. Application fee: $35 ($60 for international students). Electronic applications accepted. *Financial support:* In 2010–11, 46 students received support; research assistantships with full tuition reimbursements available, Federal Work-Study, scholarships/grants, and unspecified assistantships available. Financial award application deadline: 2/15; financial award applicants required to submit FAFSA. *Faculty research:* Health and medical savings accounts, adoption rates, health informatics, Telehealth technologies, biostatistics, environmental health, epidemiology, health systems management, social and behavioral sciences. *Unit head:* Dr. Lisa M. Klesges, Director, 901-678-4637, E-mail: lmklsges@memphis.edu. *Application contact:* Dr. Lisa M. Klesges, Director, 901-678-4637, E-mail: lmklsges@memphis.edu.

University of Michigan, School of Public Health, Department of Biostatistics, Ann Arbor, MI 48109. Offers MPH, MS, PhD. MS and PhD offered through the Horace H. Rackham School of Graduate Studies. *Faculty:* 27 full-time (11 women), 10 part-time/adjunct (3 women). *Students:* 89 full-time (46 women), 66 part-time (28 women); includes 21 minority (1 Black or African American, non-Hispanic/Latino; 18 Asian, non-Hispanic/Latino; 2 Two or more races, non-Hispanic/Latino), 87 international. Average age 27. 277 applicants, 42% accepted, 45 enrolled. In 2010, 30 master's, 7 doctorates awarded. Terminal master's awarded for partial completion of doctoral program. *Degree requirements:* For doctorate, oral defense of dissertation, qualifying exam. *Entrance requirements:* For master's, GRE General Test; for doctorate, GRE General Test, master's degree. Additional exam requirements/recommendations for international students: Required—TOEFL (minimum score 560 paper-based; 220 computer-based; 100 iBT). *Application deadline:* For fall admission, 1/15 priority date for domestic and international students. Applications are processed on a rolling basis. Application fee: $65 ($75 for international students). Electronic applications accepted. *Expenses:* Tuition, state resident: full-time $17,784; part-time $1116 per credit hour. Tuition, nonresident: full-time $35,944; part-time $2125 per credit hour. International tuition: $35,994 full-time. Required fees: $95 per semester. Tuition and fees vary according to course load, degree level and program. *Financial support:* In 2010–11, 103 students received support, including 13 fellowships with full tuition reimbursements available (averaging $20,976 per year), 65 research assistantships with full tuition reimbursements available (averaging $25,041 per year), 10 teaching assistantships with partial tuition reimbursements available (averaging $16,694 per year); scholarships/grants, traineeships, and tuition waivers (full) also available. Financial award application deadline: 1/15. *Faculty research:* Statistical genetics, categorical data analysis, incomplete data, survival analysis, modeling. Total annual research expenditures: $14.4 million. *Unit head:* Dr. Trivellore Raghunathan, Chair, 734-615-9832, Fax: 734-763-2215, E-mail: teraghu@umich.edu. *Application contact:* Nicole Fenech, Student Services Coordinator, 734-615-9817, Fax: 734-763-2215, E-mail: sph.bio.inquiries@umich.edu.

University of Michigan, School of Public Health, Program in Clinical Research Design and Statistical Analysis, Ann Arbor, MI 48109. Offers MS. Offered through the Horace H. Rackham School of Graduate Studies; program admits applicants in odd-numbered calendar years only. Evening/weekend programs available. *Faculty:* 11 full-time (4 women), 1 part-time/adjunct (0 women). *Students:* 26 full-time (12 women); includes 6 minority (all Asian, non-Hispanic/Latino), 6 international. Average age 35. *Degree requirements:* For master's, comprehensive exam. *Entrance requirements:* For master's, GRE General Test or MCAT. Additional exam requirements/recommendations for international students: Recommended—TOEFL (minimum score 560 paper-based; 220 computer-based; 100 iBT). *Application deadline:* For fall admission, 1/15 priority date for domestic and international students. Applications are processed on a rolling basis. Application fee: $65 ($75 for international students). Electronic applications accepted. *Expenses:* Contact institution. *Financial support:* Institutionally sponsored loans and scholarships/grants available. Financial award application deadline: 3/15; financial award applicants required to submit FAFSA. *Faculty research:* Survival analysis, missing data, Bayesian inference, health economics, quality of life. Total annual research expenditures: $14.4 million. *Unit head:* Dr. Trivellore Raghunathan, Director, 734-615-9832, E-mail: teraghu@umich.edu. *Application contact:* Fatma Nedjari, Information Contact, 734-615-9812, Fax: 734-763-2215, E-mail: sph.bio.inquiries@umich.edu.

University of Minnesota, Twin Cities Campus, School of Public Health, Major in Biostatistics, Minneapolis, MN 55455-0213. Offers MPH, MS, PhD. Part-time programs available. Terminal master's awarded for partial completion of doctoral program. *Degree requirements:* For master's, comprehensive exam; for doctorate, comprehensive exam, thesis/dissertation. *Entrance requirements:* For master's, GRE General Test, course work in applied statistics, computer programming, multivariable calculus, linear algebra; for doctorate, GRE General Test, bachelor's or master's degree in statistics, biostatistics or mathematics. Additional exam requirements/recommendations for international students: Required—TOEFL (minimum score 600 paper-based; 250 computer-based; 90 iBT). Electronic applications accepted. *Faculty research:* Analysis of spatial and longitudinal data, Bayes/Empirical Bayes methods, survival analysis, longitudinal models, generalized linear models.

The University of North Carolina at Chapel Hill, Graduate School, School of Public Health, Department of Biostatistics, Chapel Hill, NC 27599. Offers MPH, MS, Dr PH, PhD. Part-time programs available. *Degree requirements:* For master's, comprehensive exam, thesis, major paper; for doctorate, comprehensive exam, thesis/dissertation. *Entrance requirements:* For master's and doctorate, GRE General Test, minimum GPA of 3.0. Additional exam requirements/recommendations for international students: Required—TOEFL. Electronic applications accepted. *Faculty research:* Cancer, cardiovascular, environmental biostatistics; AIDS and other infectious diseases; statistical genetics; demography and population studies.

University of North Texas Health Science Center at Fort Worth, School of Public Health, Fort Worth, TX 76107-2699. Offers biostatistics (MPH); community health (MPH); disease control and prevention (Dr PH); environmental and occupational health sciences (MPH); epidemiology (MPH); health administration (MHA); health policy and management (MPH, Dr PH); DO/MPH; MS/MPH; MSN/MPH. MPH offered jointly with University of North Texas; DO/MPH with Texas College of Osteopathic Medicine. *Accreditation:* CEPH. Part-time and evening/weekend programs available. *Degree requirements:* For master's, thesis or alternative, supervised internship; for doctorate, thesis/dissertation, supervised internship. *Entrance requirements:* For master's, GRE General Test. Additional exam requirements/recommendations for international students: Required—TOEFL. Electronic applications accepted.

University of Oklahoma Health Sciences Center, Graduate College, College of Public Health, Program in Biostatistics and Epidemiology, Oklahoma City, OK 73190. Offers biostatistics (MPH, MS, Dr PH, PhD); epidemiology (MPH, MS, Dr PH, PhD). *Accreditation:* CEPH (one or more programs are accredited). Part-time programs available. *Degree requirements:* For master's, comprehensive exam, thesis (for some programs); for doctorate, comprehensive exam, thesis/dissertation. *Entrance requirements:* For master's, 3 letters of recommendation, resume; for doctorate, GRE General Test, letters of recommendation. Additional exam requirements/recommendations for international students: Required—TOEFL (minimum score 570 paper-based; 230 computer-based), TWE. *Faculty research:* Statistical methodology, applied statistics, acute and chronic disease epidemiology.

University of Pennsylvania, Perelman School of Medicine, Biomedical Graduate Studies, Graduate Group in Epidemiology and Biostatistics, Philadelphia, PA 19104. Offers biostatistics (MS, PhD). Part-time programs available. *Faculty:* 108 full-time (40 women). *Students:* 23 full-time (14 women), 7 part-time (3 women); includes 18 Asian, non-Hispanic/Latino. Average age 25. 65 applicants, 28% accepted, 10 enrolled. In 2010, 5 master's, 5 doctorates awarded. Terminal master's awarded for partial completion of doctoral program. *Degree requirements:* For master's, thesis, evaluations examination; for doctorate, thesis/dissertation, evaluations exam, preliminary exam. *Entrance requirements:* For master's and doctorate, GRE, 1 year of course work in calculus, 1 semester of course work in linear algebra, working knowledge of programming language. Additional exam requirements/recommendations for international students: Required—TOEFL. *Application deadline:* For fall admission, 12/1 for domestic and international students. Application fee: $70. *Expenses:* Tuition: Full-time $25,660; part-time $4758 per course. Required fees: $2152; $270 per course. Tuition and fees vary according to course load, degree level and program. *Financial support:* In 2010–11, 21 students received support, including 12 fellowships with full and partial tuition reimbursements available (averaging $21,500 per year), 9 research assistantships with full and partial tuition reimbursements available (averaging $21,500 per year), 1 teaching assistantship with full and partial tuition reimbursement available (averaging $21,500 per year); career-related internships or fieldwork, institutionally sponsored loans, scholarships/grants, traineeships, health care benefits, and unspecified assistantships also available. Financial award application deadline: 12/1. *Faculty research:* Randomized clinical trials, data coordinating centers, methodological approaches to non-experimental epidemiologic studies, theoretical research in biostatistics. Total annual research expenditures: $43 million. *Unit head:* Dr. Daniel F. Heitjan, Chair, 215-573-7328, Fax: 215-573-4865, E-mail: dheitjan@mail.med.upenn.edu. *Application contact:* Ann R. Facciolo, Program Manager, 215-573-3881, Fax: 215-573-4865, E-mail: facciolo@mail.med.upenn.edu.

University of Pittsburgh, Graduate School of Public Health, Department of Biostatistics, Pittsburgh, PA 15260. Offers MPH, MS, Dr PH, PhD. Part-time programs available. *Faculty:* 25 full-time (8 women), 20 part-time/adjunct (8 women). *Students:* 81 full-time (50 women), 13 part-time (5 women); includes 2 Black or African American, non-Hispanic/Latino; 11 Asian, non-Hispanic/Latino; 1 Hispanic/Latino, 59 international. Average age 32. 194 applicants, 72% accepted, 22 enrolled. In 2010, 13 master's, 5 doctorates awarded. Terminal master's awarded for partial completion of doctoral program. *Degree requirements:* For master's, thesis; for doctorate, one foreign language, thesis/dissertation. *Entrance requirements:* For master's and doctorate, GRE General Test, previous course work in biology, calculus, and Fortran. Additional exam requirements/recommendations for international students: Required—TOEFL (minimum score 550 paper-based; 213 computer-based; 80 iBT). *Application deadline:* For fall admission, 3/30 priority date for domestic students, 3/1 priority date for international students; for spring admission, 11/30 for domestic students, 4/5 priority date for international students. Applications are processed on a rolling basis. Application fee: $115. Electronic applications accepted. *Expenses:* Tuition, state resident: full-time $17,304; part-time $701 per credit. Tuition, nonresident: full-time $29,554; part-time $1210 per credit. Required fees: $740; $214 per term. Tuition and fees vary according to program. *Financial support:* In 2010–11, 62 students received support, including 56 research assistantships with full tuition reimbursements available (averaging $23,032 per year), 6 teaching assistantships with full tuition reimbursements available (averaging $25,612 per year); traineeships and tuition waivers (full and partial) also available. Financial award application deadline: 4/15. *Faculty research:* Survival analysis, environmental risk assessment, statistical computing, longitudinal data analysis, experimental design. Total annual research expenditures: $3 million. *Unit head:* Dr. Gary M. Marsh, Interim Chair, 412-624-3022, Fax: 412-624-9969, E-mail: gmarsh@pitt.edu. *Application contact:* Dr. Lisa Weissfeld, Professor, 412-624-3023, Fax: 412-624-2183, E-mail: lweis@pitt.edu.

University of Puerto Rico, Medical Sciences Campus, Graduate School of Public Health, Department of Social Sciences, Program in Biostatistics, San Juan, PR 00936-5067. Offers MPH. Part-time programs available. *Entrance requirements:* For master's, GRE, previous course work in algebra. *Expenses:* Contact institution.

University of Rochester, School of Medicine and Dentistry, Graduate Programs in Medicine and Dentistry, Department of Biostatistics and Computational Biology, Program in Medical Statistics, Rochester, NY 14627. Offers medical statistics (MS).

University of Rochester, School of Medicine and Dentistry, Graduate Programs in Medicine and Dentistry, Department of Biostatistics and Computational Biology, Programs in Statistics, Rochester, NY 14627. Offers MA, PhD.

University of South Carolina, The Graduate School, Arnold School of Public Health, Department of Epidemiology and Biostatistics, Program in Biostatistics, Columbia, SC 29208. Offers MPH, MSPH, Dr PH, PhD. Part-time programs available. *Degree requirements:* For master's, comprehensive exam, thesis (for some programs), practicum (MPH); for doctorate, comprehensive exam, thesis/dissertation (for some programs), practicum (Dr PH). *Entrance requirements:* For master's, GRE General Test; for doctorate, GRE General Test, master's degree. Additional exam requirements/recommendations for international students: Required—TOEFL (minimum score 570 paper-based; 230 computer-based; 88 iBT). Electronic applications accepted. *Faculty research:* Bayesian methods, biometric modeling, nonlinear regression, health survey methodology, measurement of health status.

Biostatistics

University of Southern California, Keck School of Medicine and Graduate School, Graduate Programs in Medicine, Department of Preventive Medicine, Division of Biostatistics, Los Angeles, CA 90089. Offers applied biostatistics/epidemiology (MS); biostatistics (MS, PhD); epidemiology (PhD); genetic epidemiology and statistical genetics (PhD); molecular epidemiology (MS, PhD). *Faculty:* 71 full-time (30 women). *Students:* 103 full-time (63 women); includes 21 Asian, non-Hispanic/Latino; 4 Hispanic/Latino, 55 international. Average age 29. 79 applicants, 52% accepted, 18 enrolled. In 2010, 6 master's, 4 doctorates awarded. Terminal master's awarded for partial completion of doctoral program. *Degree requirements:* For master's, thesis; for doctorate, thesis/dissertation. *Entrance requirements:* For master's and doctorate, GRE General Test, GRE Subject Test, minimum GPA of 3.0. Additional exam requirements/recommendations for international students: Required—TOEFL (minimum score 600 paper-based; 250 computer-based; 100 iBT). *Application deadline:* For fall admission, 12/1 priority date for domestic students, 12/1 for international students. Application fee: $85. Electronic applications accepted. *Expenses:* Tuition: Full-time $31,240; part-time $1420 per unit. Required fees: $600. One-time fee: $35 full-time. Full-time tuition and fees vary according to degree level and program. *Financial support:* In 2010–11, 3 fellowships with full tuition reimbursements (averaging $27,600 per year), 50 research assistantships with full tuition reimbursements (averaging $27,600 per year), 24 teaching assistantships with full and partial tuition reimbursements (averaging $15,525 per year) were awarded; career-related internships or fieldwork, Federal Work-Study, institutionally sponsored loans, scholarships/grants, health care benefits, and unspecified assistantships also available. Financial award application deadline: 5/3. *Faculty research:* Clinical trials in ophthalmology and cancer research, methods of analysis for epidemiological studies, genetic epidemiology. Total annual research expenditures: $1.3 million. *Unit head:* Dr. Stanley P. Azen, Co-Director, 323-442-1810, Fax: 323-442-2993, E-mail: mtrujill@usc.edu. *Application contact:* Mary L. Trujillo, Student Adviser, 323-442-1810, Fax: 323-442-2993, E-mail: mtrujill@usc.edu.

University of Southern California, Keck School of Medicine and Graduate School, Graduate Programs in Medicine, Department of Preventive Medicine, Master of Public Health Program, Alhambra, CA 91803. Offers biostatistics/epidemiology (MPH); child and family health (MPH); global health leadership (MPH); health communication (MPH); health promotion (MPH). *Accreditation:* CEPH. Part-time programs available. *Faculty:* 22 full-time (12 women), 3 part-time/adjunct (0 women). *Students:* 208 full-time (152 women), 3 part-time (2 women); includes 15 Black or African American, non-Hispanic/Latino; 78 Asian, non-Hispanic/Latino; 14 Hispanic/Latino, 38 international. Average age 24. 218 applicants, 73% accepted, 88 enrolled. In 2010, 80 master's awarded. *Degree requirements:* For master's, practicum, final report, oral presentation. *Entrance requirements:* For master's, GRE General Test, MCAT, GMAT, minimum GPA of 3.0. Additional exam requirements/recommendations for international students: Required—TOEFL (minimum score 600 paper-based; 250 computer-based; 100 iBT). *Application deadline:* For fall admission, 6/1 priority date for domestic and international students; for spring admission, 11/1 priority date for domestic students, 10/1 priority date for international students. Applications are processed on a rolling basis. Application fee: $85. Electronic applications accepted. *Expenses:* Tuition: Full-time $31,240; part-time $1420 per unit. Required fees: $600. One-time fee: $35 full-time. Full-time tuition and fees vary according to degree level and program. *Financial support:* In 2010–11, 185 students received support. Career-related internships or fieldwork, Federal Work-Study, institutionally sponsored loans, and scholarships/grants available. Support available to part-time students. Financial award application deadline: 5/3; financial award applicants required to submit CSS PROFILE or FAFSA. *Faculty research:* Substance abuse prevention, cancer and heart disease prevention, mass media and health communication research, health promotion, treatment compliance. *Unit head:* Dr. Thomas W. Valente, Director, 626-457-4139, Fax: 626-457-6699, E-mail: tvalente@usc.edu. *Application contact:* Chrystal Romero, Admissions Counselor, 626-457-6676, Fax: 626-457-6699, E-mail: ccromero@usc.edu.

University of Southern Mississippi, Graduate School, College of Health, Department of Community Health Sciences, Hattiesburg, MS 39406-0001. Offers epidemiology and biostatistics (MPH); health education (MPH); health policy/administration (MPH); occupational/environmental health (MPH); public health nutrition (MPH). *Accreditation:* CEPH. Part-time and evening/weekend programs available. *Faculty:* 8 full-time (4 women), 1 part-time/adjunct (0 women). *Students:* 74 full-time (52 women), 19 part-time (15 women); includes 37 Black or African American, non-Hispanic/Latino; 2 Hispanic/Latino; 3 Two or more races, non-Hispanic/Latino, 6 international. Average age 32. 71 applicants, 63% accepted, 35 enrolled. In 2010, 46 master's awarded. *Degree requirements:* For master's, comprehensive exam, thesis (for some programs). *Entrance requirements:* For master's, GRE General Test, minimum GPA of 2.75 in last 60 hours. Additional exam requirements/recommendations for international students: Required—TOEFL, IELTS. *Application deadline:* For fall admission, 3/1 priority date for domestic and international students; for spring admission, 1/10 priority date for domestic and international students. Applications are processed on a rolling basis. Application fee: $50. Electronic applications accepted. *Financial support:* In 2010–11, 5 research assistantships with full tuition reimbursements (averaging $7,000 per year), 1 teaching assistantship with full tuition reimbursement (averaging $8,263 per year) were awarded; career-related internships or fieldwork, Federal Work-Study, institutionally sponsored loans, scholarships/grants, health care benefits, and unspecified assistantships also available. Financial award application deadline: 3/15; financial award applicants required to submit FAFSA. *Faculty research:* Rural health care delivery, school health, nutrition of pregnant teens, risk factor reduction, sexually transmitted diseases. *Unit head:* Dr. Emanual Ahua, Interim Chair, 601-266-5437, Fax: 601-266-5043. *Application contact:* Dr. Emanual Ahua, Interim Chair, 601-266-5437, Fax: 601-266-5043.

University of South Florida, Graduate School, College of Public Health, Department of Epidemiology and Biostatistics, Tampa, FL 33620-9951. Offers MPH, MSPH, PhD. *Accreditation:* CEPH (one or more programs are accredited). Part-time and evening/weekend programs available. *Degree requirements:* For master's, comprehensive exam, thesis (for some programs); for doctorate, comprehensive exam, thesis/dissertation. *Entrance requirements:* For master's, GRE General Test, minimum GPA of 3.0 in upper-level course work, goal statement letter, two professional letters of recommendation, resume/curriculum vitae; for doctorate, GRE General Test, minimum GPA of 3.0 in upper-level course work, 3 professional letters of recommendation, resume/curriculum vitae, writing sample. Additional exam requirements/recommendations for international students: Required—TOEFL (minimum score 550 paper-based; 213 computer-based; 79 iBT). Electronic applications accepted. *Faculty research:* Dementia, mental illness, mental health preventative trails, rural health outreach, clinical and administrative studies.

The University of Texas Health Science Center at Houston, Graduate School of Biomedical Sciences, Program in Biomathematics and Biostatistics, Houston, TX 77225-0036. Offers MS, PhD, MD/PhD. Terminal master's awarded for partial completion of doctoral program. *Degree requirements:* For master's, thesis; for doctorate, thesis/dissertation. *Entrance requirements:* For master's and doctorate, GRE General Test. Additional exam requirements/recommendations for international students: Required—TOEFL. Electronic applications accepted. *Faculty research:* Biostatistics, biomarkers, epidemiology, bioinformatics, computational biology.

The University of Toledo, College of Graduate Studies, College of Medicine and Life Sciences, Department of Public Health and Preventative Medicine, Toledo, OH 43606-3390. Offers biostatistics and epidemiology (Certificate); contemporary gerontological practice (Certificate); environmental and occupational health and safety (MPH), including public health; epidemiology (MPH, Certificate); health administration (MPH); health promotion (MPH); nutrition (MPH); occupational health (MSOH, Certificate); MD/MPH. Part-time programs available. *Faculty:* 5. *Students:* 98 full-time (69 women), 42 part-time (28 women); includes 20 Black or African American, non-Hispanic/Latino; 8 Asian, non-Hispanic/Latino; 4 Hispanic/Latino, 3 international. Average age 29. 132 applicants, 75% accepted, 70 enrolled. In 2010, 44 master's, 28 other advanced degrees awarded. *Degree requirements:* For master's, thesis or alternative. *Entrance requirements:* For master's, GRE (international applicants only), Minimum undergraduate GPA of 3.0. Three letters of recommendation, a statement of purpose and transcripts from all prior institutions attended; for Certificate, GRE, Minimum undergraduate GPA of 3.0. Three letters of recommendation, a statement of purpose and transcripts from all prior institutions attended. Additional exam requirements/recommendations for international students: Required—TOEFL (minimum score 550 paper-based; 213 computer-based; 80 iBT), IELTS (minimum score 6.5). *Application deadline:* For fall admission, 6/15 for domestic students, 3/15 for international students; for spring admission, 10/15 for domestic students, 2/15 for international students. Applications are processed on a rolling basis. Application fee: $45 ($75 for international students). Electronic applications accepted. *Expenses:* Tuition, state resident: full-time $11,426; part-time $476 per credit hour. Tuition, nonresident: full-time $21,660; part-time $903 per credit hour. One-time fee: $62. *Financial support:* In 2010–11, 14 research assistantships with full tuition reimbursements (averaging $10,000 per year) were awarded; Federal Work-Study, institutionally sponsored loans, scholarships/grants, tuition waivers (full and partial), and unspecified assistantships also available. *Unit head:* Dr. Sheryl A. Milz, Chair, 419-383-3976, Fax: 419-383-6140, E-mail: sheryl.milz@utoledo.edu. *Application contact:* Joan Mulligan, Admissions Analyst, 419-383-4186, Fax: 419-383-6140, E-mail: joan.mulligan@utoledo.edu.

University of Utah, Graduate School, Interdepartmental Program in Statistics, Salt Lake City, UT 84112-1107. Offers biostatistics (M Stat); econometrics (M Stat); educational psychology (M Stat); mathematics (M Stat); sociology (M Stat); statistics (M Stat). Part-time programs available. *Students:* 28 full-time (11 women), 17 part-time (9 women); includes 2 Black or African American, non-Hispanic/Latino; 2 Asian, non-Hispanic/Latino; 2 Hispanic/Latino, 10 international. Average age 30. 59 applicants, 44% accepted, 12 enrolled. In 2010, 15 master's awarded. *Degree requirements:* For master's, comprehensive exam, projects. *Entrance requirements:* For master's, GRE General Test (sociology and educational psychology), minimum GPA of 3.0; course work in calculus, matrix theory, statistics. Additional exam requirements/recommendations for international students: Required—TOEFL (minimum score 500 paper-based; 173 computer-based). *Application deadline:* For fall admission, 7/1 for domestic students, 4/1 for international students. Applications are processed on a rolling basis. Application fee: $55 ($65 for international students). *Expenses:* Tuition, area resident: Part-time $179.19 per credit hour. Tuition, state resident: full-time $4384. Tuition, nonresident: full-time $16,684; part-time $630.67 per credit hour. Required fees: $350 per semester. Tuition and fees vary according to course load, degree level and program. *Financial support:* Career-related internships or fieldwork available. *Faculty research:* Biostatistics, management, economics, educational psychology, mathematics. *Unit head:* Tariq Mughal, Chair, University Statistics Committee, 801-585-9547, E-mail: tariaq.mughal@business.utah.edu. *Application contact:* Laura Egbert, MSTAT Program Coordinator, 801-585-6853, E-mail: laura.demattia@utah.edu.

University of Utah, School of Medicine and Graduate School, Graduate Programs in Medicine, Programs in Public Health, Salt Lake City, UT 84112-1107. Offers biostatistics (M Stat); public health (MPH, MSPH, PhD). *Accreditation:* CEPH (one or more programs are accredited). Part-time programs available. *Degree requirements:* For master's, comprehensive exam, thesis or project (MSPH); for doctorate, comprehensive exam, thesis/dissertation. *Entrance requirements:* For master's and doctorate, GRE General Test, 3 letters of reference, in-person interviews, minimum GPA of 3.0. Additional exam requirements/recommendations for international students: Required—TOEFL (minimum score 550 paper-based; 175 computer-based). Electronic applications accepted. *Expenses:* Tuition, area resident: Part-time $179.19 per credit hour. Tuition, state resident: full-time $4384. Tuition, nonresident: full-time $16,684; part-time $630.67 per credit hour. Required fees: $350 per semester. Tuition and fees vary according to course load, degree level and program. *Faculty research:* Health services, health policy, epidemiology of chronic disease, infectious disease epidemiology, cancer epidemiology.

University of Vermont, Graduate College, College of Engineering and Mathematics, Department of Mathematics and Statistics, Program in Biostatistics, Burlington, VT 05405. Offers MS. *Students:* 4 (2 women). 13 applicants, 38% accepted, 3 enrolled. In 2010, 4 master's awarded. *Degree requirements:* For master's, thesis or alternative. *Entrance requirements:* Additional exam requirements/recommendations for international students: Required—TOEFL (minimum score 550 paper-based; 213 computer-based; 80 iBT). *Application deadline:* For fall admission, 4/1 priority date for domestic students. Applications are processed on a rolling basis. Application fee: $40. Electronic applications accepted. *Expenses:* Tuition, state resident: part-time $537 per credit hour. Tuition, nonresident: part-time $1355 per credit hour. *Financial support:* Fellowships, research assistantships, teaching assistantships available. Financial award application deadline: 3/1. *Unit head:* Dr. Jeff Buzas, Coordinator, 802-656-2940. *Application contact:* Dr. Jeff Buzas, Coordinator, 802-656-2940.

University of Washington, Graduate School, Interdisciplinary Graduate Program in Quantitative Ecology and Resource Management, Seattle, WA 98195. Offers MS, PhD. *Degree requirements:* For master's, thesis; for doctorate, thesis/dissertation. *Entrance requirements:* For master's and doctorate, GRE General Test, minimum GPA of 3.0. Additional exam requirements/recommendations for international students: Required—TOEFL. Electronic applications accepted. *Faculty research:* Population dynamics, statistical analysis, ecological modeling and systems analysis of aquatic and terrestrial ecosystems.

University of Washington, Graduate School, School of Public Health, Department of Biostatistics, Seattle, WA 98195. Offers biostatistics (MPH, MS, PhD); clinical research (MS), including biostatistics; statistical genetics (PhD). *Faculty:* 46 full-time (22 women), 6 part-time/adjunct (1 woman). *Students:* 74 full-time (39 women), 6 part-time (5 women); includes 7 Asian, non-Hispanic/Latino; 1 Hispanic/Latino, 27 international. Average age 28. 202 applicants, 14% accepted, 15 enrolled. In 2010, 14 master's, 8 doctorates awarded. Terminal master's awarded for partial completion of doctoral program. *Degree requirements:* For master's, comprehensive exam, thesis, computer proficiency, consulting, departmental qualifying exams; for doctorate, comprehensive exam, thesis/dissertation, computer proficiency, consulting, departmental qualifying exams. *Entrance requirements:* For master's, GRE General Test; for doctorate, GRE General Test, Master's degree. Additional exam requirements/recommendations for international students: Required—TOEFL. *Application deadline:* For fall admission, 1/2 for domestic students. Application fee: $75. Electronic applications accepted. *Financial support:* In 2010–11, 80 research assistantships with full and partial tuition reimbursements (averaging $21,000 per year), 12 teaching assistantships with full and partial tuition reimbursements (averaging $21,000 per year) were awarded; scholarships/grants, traineeships, and health care benefits also available. *Faculty research:* Statistical methods for survival data analysis, clinical trials, epidemiological case control and cohort studies, statistical genetics. *Unit head:* Dr. Bruce Weir, Department Chair, 206-543-1044. *Application contact:* Alex Mackenzie, Counseling Services Coordinator, 206-543-1044, Fax: 206-543-3286, E-mail: alexam@u.washington.edu.

University of Waterloo, Graduate Studies, Faculty of Mathematics, Department of Statistics and Actuarial Science, Waterloo, ON N2L 3G1, Canada. Offers actuarial science (M Math, PhD); biostatistics (PhD); statistics (M Math, PhD); statistics-biostatistics (M Math); statistics-computing (M Math); statistics-finance (M Math). *Degree requirements:* For master's, research paper or thesis; for doctorate, comprehensive exam, thesis/dissertation. *Entrance requirements:* For master's, honors degree in field, minimum B+ average; for doctorate, master's degree, minimum B+ average. Additional exam requirements/recommendations for international students: Required—TOEFL (minimum score 600 paper-based; 250 computer-based; 90 iBT), TWE (minimum score 4.5). Electronic applications accepted. *Faculty research:* Data analysis, risk theory, inference, stochastic processes, quantitative finance.

The University of Western Ontario, Faculty of Graduate Studies, Biosciences Division, Department of Epidemiology and Biostatistics, London, ON N6A 5B8, Canada. Offers M Sc,

PhD. *Accreditation:* CEPH (one or more programs are accredited). Part-time programs available. *Degree requirements:* For master's, thesis; for doctorate, comprehensive exam, thesis proposal defense. *Entrance requirements:* For master's, BA or B Sc honors degree, minimum B+ average in last 10 courses; for doctorate, M Sc or equivalent, minimum B+ average in last 10 courses. *Faculty research:* Chronic disease epidemiology, clinical epidemiology.

Virginia Commonwealth University, Medical College of Virginia-Professional Programs, School of Medicine, School of Medicine Graduate Programs, Department of Biostatistics, Richmond, VA 23284-9005. Offers MS, PhD, MD/PhD. Part-time programs available. *Faculty:* 11 full-time (3 women). *Students:* 25 full-time (18 women), 8 part-time (4 women); includes 6 minority (5 Asian, non-Hispanic/Latino; 1 Two or more races, non-Hispanic/Latino), 10 international. 41 applicants, 63% accepted, 11 enrolled. In 2010, 6 master's, 6 doctorates awarded. Terminal master's awarded for partial completion of doctoral program. *Degree requirements:* For master's, thesis; for doctorate, thesis/dissertation, comprehensive oral and written exams. *Entrance requirements:* For master's and doctorate, GRE, MCAT or DAT. Additional exam requirements/recommendations for international students: Required—TOEFL (minimum score 600 paper-based; 250 computer-based; 100 iBT). *Application deadline:* For fall admission, 1/7 priority date for domestic students. Application fee: $50. Electronic applications accepted. *Expenses:* Tuition, state resident: full-time $4308; part-time $479 per credit hour. Tuition, nonresident: full-time $8942; part-time $994 per credit hour. Required fees: $2000; $85 per credit hour. Tuition and fees vary according to course level, course load, degree level, campus/location and program. *Financial support:* Fellowships, teaching assistantships, career-related internships or fieldwork available. *Faculty research:* Health services, linear models, response surfaces, design and analysis of drug/chemical combinations, clinical trials. *Unit head:* Dr. Donna K. McClish, Director, Graduate Programs in Biostatistics, 804-827-2050, Fax: 804-828-8900, E-mail: mcclish@vcu.edu. *Application contact:* Russell M. Boyle, Associate Director, Graduate Programs in Biostatistics, 804-827-2049, E-mail: boyle@vcu.edu.

Yale University, School of Medicine, Yale School of Public Health, New Haven, CT 06520. Offers applied biostatistics and epidemiology (APMPH); biostatistics (MPH, MS, PhD), including global health (MPH); chronic disease epidemiology (MPH, PhD), including global health (MPH); environmental health sciences (MPH, PhD), including global health (MPH); epidemiology of microbial diseases (MPH, PhD), including global health (MPH); global health (APMPH); health management (MPH), including global health; health policy (MPH), including global health; health policy and administration (APMPH, PhD); occupational and environmental medicine (APMPH); preventive medicine (APMPH); social and behavioral sciences (APMPH, MPH), including global health (MPH); JD/MPH; M Div/MPH; MBA/MPH; MD/MPH; MEM/MPH; MFS/MPH; MPH/MA; MSN/MPH. MS and PhD offered through the Graduate School. Part-time programs available. *Faculty:* 67 full-time (37 women), 53 part-time/adjunct (18 women). *Students:* 209 full-time (169 women), 8 part-time (4 women); includes 24 Black or African American, non-Hispanic/Latino; 44 Asian, non-Hispanic/Latino; 9 Hispanic/Latino, 21 international. Average age 26. 1,100 applicants, 117 enrolled. In 2010, 124 master's, 8 doctorates awarded. Terminal master's awarded for partial completion of doctoral program. *Degree requirements:* For master's, thesis, summer internship; for doctorate, comprehensive exam, thesis/dissertation, residency. *Entrance requirements:* For master's, GMAT, GRE, or MCAT, two years of undergraduate coursework in math and science; for doctorate, GRE General Test. Additional exam requirements/recommendations for international students: Required—TOEFL (minimum score 100 iBT). *Application deadline:* For fall admission, 1/15 priority date for domestic and international students. Applications are processed on a rolling basis. Application fee: $115. Electronic applications accepted. *Expenses:* Contact institution. *Financial support:* In 2010–11, 21 fellowships with full tuition reimbursements (averaging $12,560 per year), 4 research assistantships with full tuition reimbursements (averaging $24,910 per year) were awarded; teaching assistantships with full tuition reimbursements, career-related internships or fieldwork, Federal Work-Study, institutionally sponsored loans, scholarships/grants, and tuition waivers (full and partial) also available. Support available to part-time students. Financial award application deadline: 3/1; financial award applicants required to submit FAFSA. *Faculty research:* Genetic and emerging infections epidemiology, virology, cost/quality, vector biology, quantitative methods, aging, asthma, cancer. *Unit head:* Dr. Paul D. Cleary, Dean and Chairman, 203-785-2867, Fax: 203-785-6103, E-mail: paul.cleary@yale.edu. *Application contact:* Jacqui R. Comshaw, Director of Admissions, 203-785-2844, Fax: 203-785-4845, E-mail: ysph.admissions@yale.edu.

Computational Sciences

American University of Beirut, Graduate Programs, Faculty of Arts and Sciences, Beirut, Lebanon. Offers anthropology (MA); Arabic language and literature (MA); archaeology (MA); biology (MS); chemistry (MS); computational science (MS); computer science (MS); economics (MA); education (MA); English language (MA); English literature (MA); environmental policy planning (MSES); financial economics (MAFE); geology (MS); history (MA); mathematics (MA, MS); Middle Eastern studies (MA); philosophy (MA); physics (MS); political studies (MA); psychology (MA); public administration (MA); sociology (MA); statistics (MA, MS). Part-time programs available. *Faculty:* 229 full-time (98 women), 136 part-time/adjunct (79 women). *Students:* 158 full-time (104 women), 263 part-time (171 women). Average age 25. 356 applicants, 59% accepted, 127 enrolled. In 2010, 57 master's awarded. *Degree requirements:* For master's, one foreign language, comprehensive exam, thesis (for some programs). *Entrance requirements:* For master's, GRE, letter of recommendation. Additional exam requirements/recommendations for international students: Required—TOEFL (minimum score 600 paper-based; 250 computer-based; 97 iBT), IELTS (minimum score 7). *Application deadline:* For fall admission, 4/30 for domestic and international students; for spring admission, 11/1 for domestic and international students. Application fee: $50. *Expenses:* Tuition: Full-time $12,294; part-time $683 per credit. Required fees: $499; $499 per credit. Tuition and fees vary according to course load and program. *Financial support:* In 2010–11, 33 students received support. Career-related internships or fieldwork, institutionally sponsored loans, scholarships/grants, health care benefits, and unspecified assistantships available. Financial award application deadline: 2/4; financial award applicants required to submit FAFSA. *Faculty research:* Modern and contemporary world theatre; mineralogy, petrology, and geochemistry; cell differentiation and transformation; combinatorial technologies; philosophy of action; continental philosophy; Phoenician epigraphy; nascent complex societies and urbanism; the economies of the Arab world; environmental economics; tectonophysics; host-parasite interactions; innate immunity; insect-plant interactions; history of the Ottoman archives; decentralization; transparency and corruption. Total annual research expenditures: $622,243. *Unit head:* Dr. Patrick McGreevy, Dean, 961-137-4374 Ext. 3800, Fax: 961-174-4461, E-mail: pm07@aub.edu.lb. *Application contact:* Dr. Salim Kanaan, Director, Admissions Office, 961-135-0000 Ext. 2594, Fax: 961-175-0775, E-mail: sk00@aub.edu.lb.

California Institute of Technology, Division of Engineering and Applied Science, Option in Computation and Neural Systems, Pasadena, CA 91125-0001. Offers MS, PhD. *Faculty:* 3 full-time (0 women). *Students:* 41 full-time (12 women). 122 applicants, 11% accepted, 5 enrolled. In 2010, 6 doctorates awarded. Terminal master's awarded for partial completion of doctoral program. *Degree requirements:* For doctorate, thesis/dissertation, qualifying exam. *Entrance requirements:* For doctorate, GRE General Test. *Application deadline:* For fall admission, 1/1 for domestic students. Application fee: $0. *Financial support:* In 2010–11, 3 fellowships, 34 research assistantships, 5 teaching assistantships were awarded; Federal Work-Study and institutionally sponsored loans also available. Financial award application deadline: 1/15. *Faculty research:* Biological and artificial computational devices, modeling of sensory processes and learning, theory of collective computation. *Unit head:* Dr. Ali Hajimiri, Academic Officer, 626-395-2312, E-mail: hajimiri@caltech.edu. *Application contact:* Natalie Gilmore, Assistant Dean of Graduate Studies, 626-395-3812, Fax: 626-577-9246, E-mail: ngilmore@caltech.edu.

Carnegie Mellon University, Carnegie Institute of Technology, Department of Civil and Environmental Engineering, Pittsburgh, PA 15213. Offers advanced infrastructure systems (MS, PhD); civil and environmental engineering (MS, PhD); civil and environmental engineering/engineering and public policy (PhD); civil engineering (MS, PhD); computational mechanics (MS, PhD); computational science and engineering (MS, PhD); environmental engineering (MS, PhD); environmental management and science (MS, PhD). Part-time programs available. *Faculty:* 20 full-time (3 women), 15 part-time/adjunct (5 women). *Students:* 144 full-time (67 women), 8 part-time (2 women); includes 4 Black or African American, non-Hispanic/Latino; 1 American Indian or Alaska Native, non-Hispanic/Latino; 9 Asian, non-Hispanic/Latino, 99 international. Average age 26. 388 applicants, 66% accepted, 80 enrolled. In 2010, 62 master's, 8 doctorates awarded. Terminal master's awarded for partial completion of doctoral program. *Degree requirements:* For master's, thesis optional; for doctorate, comprehensive exam, thesis/dissertation, qualifying exam, public defense of dissertation. *Entrance requirements:* For master's and doctorate, GRE General Test. Additional exam requirements/recommendations for international students: Required—TOEFL (minimum score 84 iBT). *Application deadline:* For fall admission, 1/15 priority date for domestic and international students; for spring admission, 9/30 priority date for domestic and international students. Application fee: $65. Electronic applications accepted. *Financial support:* In 2010–11, 134 students received support, including 27 fellowships with full and partial tuition reimbursements available (averaging $21,708 per year), 42 research assistantships with full and partial tuition reimbursements available (averaging $24,474 per year); tuition waivers (partial) and unspecified assistantships also available. Financial award application deadline: 1/15. *Faculty research:* Advanced infrastructure systems; environmental engineering science and management; mechanics, materials, and computing; green design; global sustainable construction. Total annual research expenditures: $4.7 million. *Unit head:* Dr. James H. Garrett, Head, 412-268-2941, Fax: 412-268-7813, E-mail: garrett@cmu.edu. *Application contact:* Maxine A. Leffard, Director of the Graduate Program, 412-268-5673, Fax: 412-268-7813, E-mail: ce-admissions@andrew.cmu.edu.

Carnegie Mellon University, Tepper School of Business, Program in Algorithms, Combinatorics, and Optimization, Pittsburgh, PA 15213-3891. Offers PhD. *Degree requirements:* For doctorate, thesis/dissertation. *Entrance requirements:* For doctorate, GRE General Test.

Claremont Graduate University, Graduate Programs, School of Mathematical Sciences, Claremont, CA 91711-6160. Offers computational and systems biology (PhD); computational mathematics and numerical analysis (MA, MS); computational science (PhD); engineering and industrial applied mathematics (PhD); mathematics (PhD); operations research and statistics (MA, MS); physical applied mathematics (MA, MS); pure mathematics (MA, MS); scientific computing (MA, MS); systems and control theory (MA, MS). Part-time programs available. *Faculty:* 6 full-time (0 women). *Students:* 50 full-time (15 women), 11 part-time (1 woman); includes 2 Black or African American, non-Hispanic/Latino; 9 Asian, non-Hispanic/Latino; 7 Hispanic/Latino; 3 Two or more races, non-Hispanic/Latino, 13 international. Average age 36. In 2010, 17 master's, 11 doctorates awarded. Terminal master's awarded for partial completion of doctoral program. *Entrance requirements:* For master's and doctorate, GRE General Test. Additional exam requirements/recommendations for international students: Required—TOEFL (minimum score 550 paper-based; 213 computer-based; 80 iBT). *Application deadline:* For fall admission, 2/1 priority date for domestic students. Applications are processed on a rolling basis. Application fee: $60. Electronic applications accepted. *Expenses:* Tuition: Full-time $35,748; part-time $1554 per unit. Required fees: $215 per semester. *Financial support:* Fellowships, research assistantships, Federal Work-Study, institutionally sponsored loans, scholarships/grants, and tuition waivers (full and partial) available. Support available to part-time students. Financial award application deadline: 2/15; financial award applicants required to submit FAFSA. *Unit head:* John Angus, Dean, 909-621-8080, Fax: 909-607-8261, E-mail: john.angus@cgu.edu. *Application contact:* Susan Townzen, Program Coordinator, 909-621-8080, Fax: 909-607-8261, E-mail: susan.n.townzen@cgu.edu.

Clemson University, Graduate School, College of Engineering and Science, Department of Mathematical Sciences, Clemson, SC 29634. Offers applied and pure mathematics (MS, PhD); computational mathematics (MS, PhD); operations research (MS, PhD); statistics (MS, PhD). Part-time programs available. *Faculty:* 48 full-time (13 women), 12 part-time/adjunct (4 women). *Students:* 127 full-time (51 women), 5 part-time (2 women); includes 2 Black or African American, non-Hispanic/Latino; 1 American Indian or Alaska Native, non-Hispanic/Latino; 1 Two or more races, non-Hispanic/Latino, 36 international. Average age 26. 163 applicants, 79% accepted, 51 enrolled. In 2010, 27 master's, 5 doctorates awarded. *Degree requirements:* For master's, thesis optional, final project; for doctorate, thesis/dissertation, qualifying exams. *Entrance requirements:* For master's and doctorate, GRE General Test. Additional exam requirements/recommendations for international students: Required—TOEFL. *Application deadline:* For fall admission, 1/15 priority date for domestic and international students; for spring admission, 10/1 priority date for domestic students, 9/15 priority date for international students. Applications are processed on a rolling basis. Application fee: $70 ($80 for international students). Electronic applications accepted. *Expenses:* Tuition, state resident: full-time $6492; part-time $400 per credit hour. Tuition, nonresident: full-time $13,634; part-time $800 per credit hour. Required fees: $262 per semester. Part-time tuition and fees vary according to course load and program. *Financial support:* In 2010–11, 110 students received support, including 2 fellowships with full and partial tuition reimbursements available (averaging $6,000 per year), 8 research assistantships with partial tuition reimbursements available (averaging $19,823 per year), 101 teaching assistantships with partial tuition reimbursements available (averaging $17,582 per year); career-related internships or fieldwork, institutionally sponsored loans, scholarships/grants, health care benefits, and unspecified assistantships also available. Support available to part-time students. Financial award application deadline: 4/15. *Faculty research:* Applied and computational analysis, cryptography, discrete mathematics, optimization, statistics. Total annual research expenditures: $823,404. *Unit head:* Dr. Robert L. Taylor, Chair, 864-656-5240, Fax: 864-656-5230, E-mail: rtaylo2@clemson.edu. *Application contact:* Dr. K.B. Kulasekera, Graduate Coordinator, 864-656-5231, Fax: 864-656-5230, E-mail: kk@clemson.edu.

The College at Brockport, State University of New York, School of Science and Mathematics, Department of Computational Science, Brockport, NY 14420-2997. Offers MS. Part-time programs available. *Students:* 1 full-time (0 women), 2 part-time (0 women). 4 applicants, 100% accepted, 2 enrolled. In 2010, 3 master's awarded. *Degree requirements:* For master's,

Computational Sciences

The College at Brockport, State University of New York (continued)
thesis. *Entrance requirements:* For master's, minimum GPA of 3.0, letters of recommendation; statement of objectives. Additional exam requirements/recommendations for international students: Required—TOEFL (minimum score 550 paper-based; 213 computer-based; 79 iBT). *Application deadline:* For fall admission, 7/15 priority date for domestic and international students; for spring admission, 11/15 priority date for domestic and international students. Application fee: $50. Electronic applications accepted. *Financial support:* Federal Work-Study, scholarships/grants, and unspecified assistantships available. Support available to part-time students. Financial award application deadline: 3/15; financial award applicants required to submit FAFSA. *Faculty research:* Parallel computing; fluid and particle dynamics; molecular simulation; engine combustion; computational mathematics, science, and technology education. *Unit head:* Dr. Robert Tuzun, Chairperson, 585-395-5368, Fax: 585-395-5020, E-mail: rtuzun@brockport.edu.

The College of William and Mary, Faculty of Arts and Sciences, Department of Computer Science, Program in Computational Operations Research, Williamsburg, VA 23187-8795. Offers computer science (MS), including operations research. Part-time programs available. *Faculty:* 9 full-time (2 women), 2 part-time/adjunct (1 woman). *Students:* 19 full-time (6 women), 7 international. Average age 26. 25 applicants, 80% accepted, 10 enrolled. In 2010, 9 master's awarded. *Degree requirements:* For master's, research project. *Entrance requirements:* For master's, GRE General Test, minimum GPA of 2.5. Additional exam requirements/recommendations for international students: Required—TOEFL. *Application deadline:* For fall admission, 3/1 priority date for domestic students, 3/15 priority date for international students; for spring admission, 11/1 for domestic and international students. Applications are processed on a rolling basis. Application fee: $45. Electronic applications accepted. *Expenses:* Tuition, state resident: full-time $6400; part-time $345 per credit hour. Tuition, nonresident: full-time $19,720; part-time $920 per credit hour. Required fees: $4368. *Financial support:* In 2010–11, 13 students received support, including 6 fellowships (averaging $9,000 per year), 7 teaching assistantships with full tuition reimbursements available (averaging $11,500 per year); scholarships/grants, tuition waivers (full), and unspecified assistantships also available. Financial award application deadline: 3/1; financial award applicants required to submit FAFSA. *Faculty research:* Metaheuristics, reliability, optimization, statistics, networks. *Unit head:* Dr. Rex Kincaid, Professor, 757-221-2038, Fax: 757-221-1717, E-mail: rrkinc@math.wm.edu. *Application contact:* Vanessa Godwin, Administrative Director, 757-221-3455, Fax: 757-221-1717, E-mail: cor@cs.wm.edu.

Cornell University, Graduate School, Graduate Fields of Engineering, Field of Chemical Engineering, Ithaca, NY 14853-0001. Offers advanced materials processing (M Eng, MS, PhD); applied mathematics and computational methods (M Eng, MS, PhD); biochemical engineering (M Eng, MS, PhD); chemical reaction engineering (M Eng, MS, PhD); classical and statistical thermodynamics (M Eng, MS, PhD); fluid dynamics, rheology and biorheology (M Eng, MS, PhD); heat and mass transfer (M Eng, MS, PhD); kinetics and catalysis (M Eng, MS, PhD); polymers (M Eng, MS, PhD); surface science (M Eng, MS, PhD). *Faculty:* 29 full-time (2 women). *Students:* 116 full-time (34 women); includes 1 Black or African American, non-Hispanic/Latino; 17 Asian, non-Hispanic/Latino; 5 Hispanic/Latino, 45 international. Average age 24. 392 applicants, 35% accepted, 70 enrolled. In 2010, 35 master's, 17 doctorates awarded. *Degree requirements:* For master's, thesis (MS); for doctorate, comprehensive exam, thesis/dissertation. *Entrance requirements:* For master's and doctorate, GRE General Test, 2 letters of recommendation. Additional exam requirements/recommendations for international students: Required—TOEFL (minimum score 600 paper-based; 237 computer-based; 77 iBT). *Application deadline:* For fall admission, 1/15 priority date for domestic students. Application fee: $70. Electronic applications accepted. *Expenses:* Tuition: Full-time $29,500. Required fees: $76. Tuition and fees vary according to degree level and program. *Financial support:* In 2010–11, 67 students received support, including 20 fellowships with full tuition reimbursements available, 40 research assistantships with full tuition reimbursements available, 13 teaching assistantships with full tuition reimbursements available; institutionally sponsored loans, scholarships/grants, health care benefits, tuition waivers (full and partial), and unspecified assistantships also available. Financial award applicants required to submit FAFSA. *Faculty research:* Biochemical, biomedical and metabolic engineering; fluid and polymer dynamics; surface science and chemical kinetics; electronics materials; microchemical systems and nanotechnology. *Unit head:* Director of Graduate Studies, 607-255-4550. *Application contact:* Graduate Field Assistant, 607-255-4550, E-mail: dgs@cheme.cornell.edu.

Florida State University, The Graduate School, College of Arts and Sciences, Department of Scientific Computing, Tallahassee, FL 32306-4120. Offers computational science (MS, PhD). Part-time programs available. *Faculty:* 14 full-time (2 women). *Students:* 37 full-time (7 women), 2 part-time (0 women); includes 1 Black or African American, non-Hispanic/Latino; 1 Asian, non-Hispanic/Latino; 4 Hispanic/Latino; 1 Native Hawaiian or other Pacific Islander, non-Hispanic/Latino, 12 international. Average age 24. 42 applicants, 29% accepted, 8 enrolled. In 2010, 4 master's, 1 doctorate awarded. Terminal master's awarded for partial completion of doctoral program. *Degree requirements:* For master's, thesis (for some programs); for doctorate, comprehensive exam, thesis/dissertation. *Entrance requirements:* For master's and doctorate, GRE General Test, knowledge of at least one object-oriented computing language. Additional exam requirements/recommendations for international students: Required—TOEFL (minimum score 550 paper-based; 80 iBT). *Application deadline:* For fall admission, 1/15 for domestic and international students. Application fee: $30. Electronic applications accepted. *Expenses:* Tuition, state resident: full-time $8238.24. *Financial support:* In 2010–11, 38 students received support, including 2 fellowships with full tuition reimbursements available (averaging $21,000 per year), 15 research assistantships with full tuition reimbursements available (averaging $20,000 per year), 21 teaching assistantships with full tuition reimbursements available (averaging $20,000 per year); unspecified assistantships also available. Financial award application deadline: 1/15. *Unit head:* Dr. Joseph Travis, Dean, 850-644-1081. *Application contact:* Maribel Amwake, Graduate Academic Coordinator, 850-644-0143, Fax: 850-644-0098, E-mail: mamwake@fsu.edu.

George Mason University, College of Science, Department of Computational and Data Sciences, Fairfax, VA 22030. Offers computational sciences (MS); computational sciences and informatics (PhD); computational techniques and applications (Certificate). *Faculty:* 21 full-time (2 women), 3 part-time/adjunct (0 women). *Students:* 15 full-time (3 women), 86 part-time (21 women); includes 2 Black or African American, non-Hispanic/Latino; 9 Asian, non-Hispanic/Latino; 3 Hispanic/Latino, 19 international. Average age 36. 58 applicants, 52% accepted, 20 enrolled. In 2010, 4 master's, 7 doctorates, 2 other advanced degrees awarded. *Entrance requirements:* Additional exam requirements/recommendations for international students: Required—TOEFL (minimum score 570 paper-based; 230 computer-based; 88 iBT). Application fee: $100. *Expenses:* Tuition, state resident: full-time $8192; part-time $440 per credit hour. Tuition, nonresident: full-time $22,952; part-time $1055 per credit hour. Required fees: $2364; $99 per credit hour. *Financial support:* In 2010–11, 21 students received support, including 3 fellowships with full tuition reimbursements available (averaging $18,000 per year), 15 research assistantships with full and partial tuition reimbursements available (averaging $14,724 per year), 4 teaching assistantships with full and partial tuition reimbursements available (averaging $9,360 per year); career-related internships or fieldwork, Federal Work-Study, scholarships/grants, unspecified assistantships, and health care benefits (full-time research or teaching assistantship recipients) also available. Total annual research expenditures: $1.5 million. *Unit head:* Dr. Dimitrius Papaconstantopoulos, Chairman, 703-993-3807. *Application contact:* Dr. Tim Born, Associate Dean for Graduate Programs, 703-993-4171, Fax: 703-993-9034, E-mail: tborn@gmu.edu.

Hampton University, Graduate College, Program in Applied Mathematics, Hampton, VA 23668. Offers computational mathematics (MS); nonlinear science (MS); statistics and probability (MS). *Degree requirements:* For master's, thesis optional. *Entrance requirements:* For master's, GRE General Test.

Lehigh University, P.C. Rossin College of Engineering and Applied Science, Department of Mechanical Engineering and Mechanics, Bethlehem, PA 18015. Offers computational engineering and mechanics (MS, PhD); mechanical engineering (M Eng, MS, PhD, MBA/E); polymer science/engineering (M Eng, MS, PhD, MBA/E); MBA/E. Part-time and evening/weekend programs available. Postbaccalaureate distance learning degree programs offered. *Faculty:* 24 full-time (0 women). *Students:* 106 full-time (12 women), 34 part-time (2 women); includes 7 minority (3 Black or African American, non-Hispanic/Latino; 3 Asian, non-Hispanic/Latino; 1 Hispanic/Latino), 71 international. Average age 26. 408 applicants, 29% accepted, 59 enrolled. In 2010, 23 master's, 7 doctorates awarded. Terminal master's awarded for partial completion of doctoral program. *Degree requirements:* For master's, thesis; for doctorate, thesis/dissertation, general exam. *Entrance requirements:* Additional exam requirements/recommendations for international students: Required—TOEFL (minimum score 550 paper-based; 213 computer-based; 79 iBT). *Application deadline:* For fall admission, 7/15 for domestic and international students; for spring admission, 12/1 for domestic and international students. Applications are processed on a rolling basis. Application fee: $75. Electronic applications accepted. *Financial support:* In 2010–11, 74 students received support, including 9 fellowships with full and partial tuition reimbursements available (averaging $23,280 per year), 23 research assistantships with full and partial tuition reimbursements available (averaging $20,700 per year), 24 teaching assistantships with full and partial tuition reimbursements available (averaging $24,480 per year); unspecified assistantships and Dean's doctoral assistantships also available. Financial award application deadline: 1/15. *Faculty research:* Thermofluids, dynamic systems, CAD/CAM, computational mechanics, solid mechanics. Total annual research expenditures: $3.3 million. *Unit head:* Dr. D. Gary Harlow, Chairman, 610-758-4102, Fax: 610-758-6224, E-mail: dgh0@lehigh.edu. *Application contact:* Jo Ann M. Casciano, Graduate Coordinator, 610-758-4107, Fax: 610-758-6224, E-mail: jmc4@lehigh.edu.

Marquette University, Graduate School, College of Arts and Sciences, Department of Mathematics, Statistics, and Computer Science, Milwaukee, WI 53201-1881. Offers bioinformatics (MS); computational sciences (MS, PhD); computing (MS); mathematics education (MS). Part-time and evening/weekend programs available. Postbaccalaureate distance learning degree programs offered (minimal on-campus study). *Faculty:* 27 full-time (9 women), 8 part-time/adjunct (3 women). *Students:* 13 full-time (2 women), 26 part-time (7 women); includes 2 minority (1 Black or African American, non-Hispanic/Latino; 1 Asian, non-Hispanic/Latino), 15 international. Average age 31. 57 applicants, 42% accepted, 10 enrolled. In 2010, 9 master's awarded. Terminal master's awarded for partial completion of doctoral program. *Degree requirements:* For master's, thesis or alternative, Master's essay with oral presentation; for doctorate, comprehensive exam, thesis/dissertation, Qualifying Examination. *Entrance requirements:* For master's, official transcripts from all current and previous colleges/universities except Marquette, three letters of recommendation; for doctorate, GRE General Test, official transcripts from all current and previous colleges/universities except Marquette, three letters of recommendation, English-language publications authored by applicant (if applicable, strongly recommended). Additional exam requirements/recommendations for international students: Required—TOEFL (minimum score 530 paper-based; 78 computer-based). *Application deadline:* For fall admission, 1/15 for domestic and international students. Applications are processed on a rolling basis. Application fee: $50. Electronic applications accepted. *Expenses:* Tuition: Full-time $16,290; part-time $905 per credit hour. Tuition and fees vary according to program. *Financial support:* In 2010–11, 4 fellowships, 6 research assistantships, 15 teaching assistantships were awarded; Federal Work-Study, institutionally sponsored loans, scholarships/grants, and tuition waivers (full and partial) also available. Support available to part-time students. Financial award application deadline: 2/15. *Faculty research:* Models of physiological systems, mathematical immunology, computational group theory, mathematical logic, computational science. Total annual research expenditures: $696,366. *Unit head:* Dr. Gary Krenz, Chair, 414-288-7573, Fax: 414-288-1578. *Application contact:* Dr. Francis Pastijn, Director of Graduate Studies, 414-288-5229.

Massachusetts Institute of Technology, School of Engineering and School of Science and MIT Sloan School of Management, Program in Computation for Design and Optimization, Cambridge, MA 02139. Offers SM. *Faculty:* 39 full-time (5 women). *Students:* 13 full-time (1 woman), 6 international. Average age 26. 49 applicants, 24% accepted, 6 enrolled. In 2010, 22 master's awarded. *Degree requirements:* For master's, thesis. *Entrance requirements:* For master's, GRE General Test, 3 letters of recommendation. Additional exam requirements/recommendations for international students: Required—IELTS. *Application deadline:* For fall admission, 1/10 for domestic and international students. Application fee: $75. Electronic applications accepted. *Expenses:* Tuition: Full-time $38,940; part-time $605 per unit. Required fees: $272. *Financial support:* In 2010–11, 8 students received support, including 1 fellowship with tuition reimbursement available, 10 research assistantships with tuition reimbursements available (averaging $27,324 per year); teaching assistantships with tuition reimbursements available, institutionally sponsored loans, scholarships/grants, health care benefits, and unspecified assistantships also available. *Faculty research:* Finite element methods; partial differential equations; applied optimization; computational mechanics; optimization theory. *Unit head:* Prof. Nicolas Hadjiconstantinou, Director, 617-253-3725, E-mail: cdo_info@mit.edu. *Application contact:* Laura F. Koller, Academic Administrator, 617-253-3725, E-mail: cdo_info@mit.edu.

McGill University, Faculty of Graduate and Postdoctoral Studies, Faculty of Science, Department of Mathematics and Statistics, Montréal, QC H3A 2T5, Canada. Offers computational science and engineering (M Sc); mathematics and statistics (M Sc, MA, PhD), including applied mathematics (M Sc, MA), pure mathematics (M Sc, MA), statistics (M Sc, MA).

Memorial University of Newfoundland, School of Graduate Studies, Interdisciplinary Program in Computational Science, St. John's, NL A1C 5S7, Canada. Offers computational science (M Sc); computational science (cooperative) (M Sc). *Degree requirements:* For master's, thesis optional. *Entrance requirements:* For master's, honors B Sc or significant background in the field. Electronic applications accepted. *Faculty research:* Scientific computing, modeling and simulation, computational fluid dynamics, polymer physics, computational chemistry.

Miami University, Graduate School, School of Engineering and Applied Science, Computational Science and Engineering Program, Oxford, OH 45056. Offers MS. *Students:* 13 full-time (2 women), 1 part-time (0 women); includes 1 minority (Hispanic/Latino), 6 international. Average age 24. *Entrance requirements:* For master's, GRE. Additional exam requirements/recommendations for international students: Required—TOEFL. *Application deadline:* For fall admission, 2/1 for domestic and international students. Application fee: $50. *Expenses:* Tuition, state resident: full-time $11,616; part-time $484 per credit hour. Tuition, nonresident: full-time $25,656; part-time $1069 per credit hour. Required fees: $528. *Financial support:* Fellowships, research assistantships, teaching assistantships, health care benefits and unspecified assistantships available. Financial award application deadline: 3/1; financial award applicants required to submit FAFSA. *Unit head:* Dr. Marek Dollar, Dean, 513-529-0700, E-mail: seasfyi@muohio.edu. *Application contact:* School of Engineering and Applied Science, 513-529-0700, E-mail: seasfyi@muohio.edu.

Michigan Technological University, Graduate School, College of Engineering, Program in Computational Science and Engineering, Houghton, MI 49931. Offers PhD. Part-time programs available. *Degree requirements:* For doctorate, comprehensive exam, thesis/dissertation. *Entrance requirements:* For doctorate, MS in relevant discipline. Additional exam requirements/recommendations for international students: Required—TOEFL (minimum score 550 paper-based; 213 computer-based). Electronic applications accepted. *Expenses:* Contact institution.

Princeton University, Graduate School, Program in Applied and Computational Mathematics, Princeton, NJ 08544-1019. Offers PhD. *Degree requirements:* For doctorate, thesis/dissertation. *Entrance requirements:* For doctorate, GRE General Test, GRE Subject Test. Additional exam requirements/recommendations for international students: Required—TOEFL (minimum score 600 paper-based; 250 computer-based). Electronic applications accepted.

Rice University, Graduate Programs, George R. Brown School of Engineering, Department of Computational and Applied Mathematics, Houston, TX 77251-1892. Offers computational and applied mathematics (MA, MCAM, PhD); computational science and engineering (PhD). *Degree requirements:* For master's, comprehensive exam (for some programs), thesis (for some programs); for doctorate, comprehensive exam, thesis/dissertation. *Entrance requirements:* For master's and doctorate, GRE General Test, minimum GPA of 3.0. Additional exam requirements/recommendations for international students: Required—TOEFL (minimum score 600 paper-based; 250 computer-based; 90 iBT). Electronic applications accepted. *Faculty research:* Inverse problems, partial differential equations, computer algorithms, computational modeling, optimization theory.

Rice University, Graduate Programs, George R. Brown School of Engineering, Program in Computational Science and Engineering, Houston, TX 77251-1892. Offers MCSE.

The Richard Stockton College of New Jersey, School of Graduate and Continuing Studies, Program in Computational Science, Pomona, NJ 08240-0195. Offers MS. Part-time and evening/weekend programs available. *Faculty:* 4 full-time (1 woman), 4 part-time/adjunct (3 women). *Students:* 2 full-time (0 women), 15 part-time (8 women); includes 4 minority (1 American Indian or Alaska Native, non-Hispanic/Latino; 2 Asian, non-Hispanic/Latino; 1 Hispanic/Latino). Average age 29. 17 applicants, 47% accepted, 7 enrolled. *Degree requirements:* For master's, thesis optional. *Entrance requirements:* For master's, GRE. Additional exam requirements/recommendations for international students: Required—TOEFL. *Application deadline:* For fall admission, 7/1 for domestic and international students; for spring admission, 12/1 for domestic and international students. Applications are processed on a rolling basis. Application fee: $50. Electronic applications accepted. *Expenses:* Tuition, state resident: full-time $9310; part-time $517.25 per credit. Tuition, nonresident: full-time $14,332; part-time $796.23 per credit. Required fees: $2600; $144 per credit. $70 per semester. Tuition and fees vary according to degree level. *Financial support:* In 2010–11, 3 students received support, including 3 research assistantships; Federal Work-Study, scholarships/grants, and unspecified assistantships also available. Financial award application deadline: 3/1; financial award applicants required to submit FAFSA. *Unit head:* Dr. J. Russell Manson, Program Director, 609-652-4354, E-mail: russell.manson@stockton.edu. *Application contact:* Tara Williams, Assistant Director of Enrollment Management, 609-626-3640, Fax: 609-626-6050, E-mail: gradschool@stockton.edu.

Sam Houston State University, College of Arts and Sciences, Department of Computer Science, Huntsville, TX 77341. Offers computing and information science (MS). Part-time programs available. *Faculty:* 8 full-time (3 women). *Students:* 22 full-time (3 women), 30 part-time (9 women); includes 2 Black or African American, non-Hispanic/Latino; 1 Hispanic/Latino, 27 international. Average age 29. 29 applicants, 83% accepted, 15 enrolled. In 2010, 9 master's awarded. *Entrance requirements:* For master's, GRE General Test. Additional exam requirements/recommendations for international students: Required—TOEFL (minimum score 550 paper-based; 213 computer-based; 79 iBT). *Application deadline:* For fall admission, 8/1 for domestic and international students; for spring admission, 12/1 for domestic and international students. Application fee: $20. *Expenses:* Tuition, state resident: full-time $1363; part-time $163 per credit hour. Tuition, nonresident: full-time $3856; part-time $473 per credit hour. *Financial support:* Research assistantships, teaching assistantships, Federal Work-Study, institutionally sponsored loans, and tuition waivers (partial) available. Support available to part-time students. Financial award application deadline: 5/31; financial award applicants required to submit FAFSA. *Unit head:* Dr. Peter Cooper, Chair, 936-294-1569, Fax: 936-294-4312, E-mail: css_pac@shsu.edu. *Application contact:* Dr. Jiuhung Ji, Advisor, 936-294-1579, E-mail: csc_jxj@shsu.edu.

San Diego State University, Graduate and Research Affairs, College of Sciences, Program in Computational Science, San Diego, CA 92182. Offers MS, PhD. *Degree requirements:* For master's, thesis; for doctorate, thesis/dissertation. *Entrance requirements:* For master's, GRE General Test, 3 letters of recommendation; for doctorate, GRE, 3 letters of recommendation. Additional exam requirements/recommendations for international students: Required—TOEFL. Electronic applications accepted.

Simon Fraser University, Graduate Studies, Faculty of Science, Department of Mathematics, Burnaby, BC V5A 1S6, Canada. Offers applied and computational mathematics (M Sc, PhD); mathematics (M Sc, PhD). *Degree requirements:* For master's, thesis; for doctorate, thesis/dissertation. *Entrance requirements:* For master's, GRE General Test, minimum GPA of 3.0, 3 letters of reference; for doctorate, GRE General Test, minimum GPA of 3.5, 3 letters of reference. Additional exam requirements/recommendations for international students: Required—TWE or IELTS. Electronic applications accepted. *Faculty research:* Semi-groups, number theory, optimization, combinations.

South Dakota State University, Graduate School, College of Engineering, Department of Mathematics and Statistics, Brookings, SD 57007. Offers computational science and statistics (PhD); mathematics (MS); statistics (MS). Part-time programs available. *Faculty:* 12 full-time (1 woman). *Students:* 30 full-time (10 women), 12 part-time (4 women); includes 14 minority (all Asian, non-Hispanic/Latino). 25 applicants, 72% accepted, 12 enrolled. In 2010, 12 master's, 3 doctorates awarded. Terminal master's awarded for partial completion of doctoral program. *Degree requirements:* For master's, thesis (for some programs), oral exam; for doctorate, comprehensive exam, thesis/dissertation, oral and written exams. *Entrance requirements:* Additional exam requirements/recommendations for international students: Required—TOEFL (minimum score 550 paper-based; 213 computer-based; 80 iBT); Recommended—IELTS. *Application deadline:* For fall admission, 4/1 for domestic and international students. Applications are processed on a rolling basis. Application fee: $35. *Financial support:* In 2010–11, 5 fellowships with partial tuition reimbursements (averaging $22,847 per year), 9 research assistantships with partial tuition reimbursements (averaging $20,580 per year), 16 teaching assistantships with partial tuition reimbursements (averaging $17,135 per year) were awarded; unspecified assistantships also available. *Faculty research:* Financial mathematics, predictive analytics, operations research, bioinformatics, biostatistics, computational science, statistics, number theory, abstract algebra. Total annual research expenditures: $310,000. *Unit head:* Dr. Kurt Cogswell, Head, 605-688-6196, Fax: 605-688-5880, E-mail: kurt.cogswell@sdstate.edu. *Application contact:* Dr. Don Vestal, Graduate Coordinator, 605-688-6196, Fax: 605-688-5880, E-mail: don.vestal@sdstate.edu.

Southern Methodist University, Dedman College, Department of Mathematics, Dallas, TX 75275. Offers computational and applied mathematics (MS, PhD). *Faculty:* 17 full-time (2 women), 3 part-time/adjunct (2 women). *Students:* 18 full-time (7 women); includes 1 Black or African American, non-Hispanic/Latino; 1 Asian, non-Hispanic/Latino; 2 Hispanic/Latino, 7 international. Average age 27. 25 applicants, 28% accepted, 6 enrolled. In 2010, 4 master's, 3 doctorates awarded. *Degree requirements:* For master's, oral exams; for doctorate, thesis/dissertation, oral and written exams. *Entrance requirements:* For master's and doctorate, GRE General Test, minimum GPA of 3.0, 18 undergraduate hours in mathematics beyond first and second year calculus. Additional exam requirements/recommendations for international students: Required—TOEFL. *Application deadline:* For fall admission, 2/1 priority date for domestic students, 2/1 for international students; for spring admission, 11/30 for domestic students. Applications are processed on a rolling basis. Application fee: $75. Electronic applications accepted. *Financial support:* In 2010–11, 18 students received support, including 5 research assistantships with full tuition reimbursements available (averaging $18,000 per year), 13 teaching assistantships with full tuition reimbursements available (averaging $16,500 per year); career-related internships or fieldwork, scholarships/grants, health care benefits, tuition waivers, and unspecified assistantships also available. Support available to part-time students. Financial award application deadline: 2/1; financial award applicants required to submit FAFSA. *Faculty research:* Numerical analysis and scientific computation, fluid dynamics, optics, wave propagation, mathematical biology. Total annual research expenditures: $369,480. *Unit head:* Dr. Douglas A. Reinelt, Chairman, 214-768-2506, Fax: 214-768-2355, E-mail: mathchair@mail.smu.edu. *Application contact:* Dr. Thomas W. Carr, Director of Graduate Studies, 214-768-3460, E-mail: math@mail.smu.edu.

Stanford University, School of Engineering, Program in Scientific Computing and Computational Mathematics, Stanford, CA 94305-9991. Offers MS, PhD. Terminal master's awarded for partial completion of doctoral program. *Degree requirements:* For doctorate, thesis/dissertation, qualifying exam. *Entrance requirements:* For master's, GRE General Test; for doctorate, GRE General Test, GRE Subject Test. Additional exam requirements/recommendations for international students: Required—TOEFL. Electronic applications accepted. *Expenses:* Tuition: Full-time $38,700; part-time $860 per unit. One-time fee: $200 full-time.

Temple University, College of Science and Technology, Department of Mathematics, Philadelphia, PA 19122-6096. Offers applied mathematics (MA); mathematics (PhD); pure mathematics (MA). Part-time and evening/weekend programs available. *Faculty:* 16 full-time (1 woman). *Students:* 20 full-time (2 women), 7 part-time (3 women), 5 international. 59 applicants, 24% accepted, 6 enrolled. In 2010, 7 master's, 3 doctorates awarded. Terminal master's awarded for partial completion of doctoral program. *Degree requirements:* For master's, thesis optional, written exam; for doctorate, 2 foreign languages, thesis/dissertation, oral and written exams. *Entrance requirements:* For master's, GRE General Test, minimum GPA of 3.0; for doctorate, GRE General Test, GRE Subject Test, minimum GPA of 3.0. Additional exam requirements/recommendations for international students: Required—TOEFL (minimum score 550 paper-based; 213 computer-based; 79 iBT). *Application deadline:* For fall admission, 2/15 priority date for domestic students, 12/15 for international students; for spring admission, 11/15 priority date for domestic students, 8/1 for international students. Applications are processed on a rolling basis. Application fee: $50. Electronic applications accepted. *Financial support:* Fellowships, research assistantships, teaching assistantships, Federal Work-Study and institutionally sponsored loans available. Financial award application deadline: 1/15; financial award applicants required to submit FAFSA. *Faculty research:* Differential geometry, numerical analysis. *Unit head:* Dr. Edward Letzter, Chair, 215-204-4650, Fax: 215-204-6433, E-mail: mathematics@temple.edu. *Application contact:* Dr. Edward Letzter, Chair, 215-204-4650, Fax: 215-204-6433, E-mail: mathematics@temple.edu.

University of Alaska Fairbanks, College of Natural Sciences and Mathematics, Department of Physics, Fairbanks, AK 99775-5920. Offers computational physics (MS); physics (MAT, MS, PhD); space physics (MS, PhD). Part-time programs available. *Faculty:* 5 full-time (1 woman). *Students:* 28 full-time (6 women); includes 2 minority (1 Black or African American, non-Hispanic/Latino; 1 American Indian or Alaska Native, non-Hispanic/Latino), 8 international. Average age 29. 28 applicants, 36% accepted, 10 enrolled. In 2010, 1 master's, 2 doctorates awarded. Terminal master's awarded for partial completion of doctoral program. *Degree requirements:* For master's, comprehensive exam, thesis or alternative; for doctorate, comprehensive exam, thesis/dissertation, oral defense. *Entrance requirements:* Additional exam requirements/recommendations for international students: Required—TOEFL (minimum score 550 paper-based; 213 computer-based; 80 iBT). *Application deadline:* For fall admission, 6/1 for domestic students, 3/1 for international students; for spring admission, 10/15 for domestic students, 9/1 for international students. Applications are processed on a rolling basis. Application fee: $60. Electronic applications accepted. *Expenses:* Tuition, state resident: full-time $5688; part-time $316 per credit. Tuition, nonresident: full-time $11,628; part-time $646 per credit. Required fees: $289 per semester. Tuition and fees vary according to course load and reciprocity agreements. *Financial support:* In 2010–11, 18 research assistantships with tuition reimbursements (averaging $12,399 per year), 9 teaching assistantships with tuition reimbursements (averaging $18,259 per year) were awarded; fellowships with tuition reimbursements, Federal Work-Study, scholarships/grants, health care benefits, and unspecified assistantships also available. Support available to part-time students. Financial award application deadline: 2/15; financial award applicants required to submit FAFSA. *Faculty research:* Atmospheric and ionospheric radar studies, space plasma theory, magnetospheric dynamics, space weather and auroral studies, turbulence and complex systems. *Unit head:* Ataur Chowdhury, Chair, 907-474-7339, Fax: 907-474-6130, E-mail: physics@uaf.edu. *Application contact:* Ataur Chowdhury, Chair, 907-474-7339, Fax: 907-474-6130, E-mail: physics@uaf.edu.

University of California, Santa Barbara, Graduate Division, College of Engineering, Department of Computer Science, Santa Barbara, CA 93106-5110. Offers cognitive science (PhD); computational science and engineering (PhD); computer science (MS, PhD); technology and society (PhD). *Faculty:* 33 full-time (5 women), 5 part-time/adjunct (0 women). *Students:* 135 full-time (31 women); includes 51 Asian, non-Hispanic/Latino; 4 Hispanic/Latino. Average age 27. 481 applicants, 20% accepted, 30 enrolled. In 2010, 33 master's, 12 doctorates awarded. Terminal master's awarded for partial completion of doctoral program. *Degree requirements:* For master's, comprehensive exam (for some programs), thesis (for some programs), project (for some programs); for doctorate, thesis/dissertation. *Entrance requirements:* For master's and doctorate, GRE. Additional exam requirements/recommendations for international students: Required—TOEFL (minimum score 600 paper-based; 100 iBT), IELTS (minimum score 7). *Application deadline:* For fall admission, 12/15 for domestic and international students. Application fee: $70 ($90 for international students). Electronic applications accepted. *Financial support:* In 2010–11, 117 students received support, including 36 fellowships with full and partial tuition reimbursements available (averaging $10,486 per year), 77 research assistantships with full and partial tuition reimbursements available (averaging $12,464 per year), 47 teaching assistantships with partial tuition reimbursements available (averaging $10,383 per year); career-related internships or fieldwork, Federal Work-Study, institutionally sponsored loans, scholarships/grants, health care benefits, tuition waivers (full and partial), and unspecified assistantships also available. Financial award application deadline: 12/15; financial award applicants required to submit FAFSA. *Faculty research:* Networking and security, database systems, computational science and engineering, programming languages and software engineering, human computer interaction. Total annual research expenditures: $8 million. *Unit head:* Subhash Suri, Chair, 805-893-5334, Fax: 805-893-8553, E-mail: suri@cs.ucsb.edu. *Application contact:* Morgan Marcos, Graduate Program Assistant, 805-893-4322, Fax: 805-893-8553, E-mail: mmarcos@cs.ucsb.edu.

University of California, Santa Barbara, Graduate Division, College of Engineering, Department of Mechanical Engineering, Santa Barbara, CA 93106-5070. Offers computational science and engineering (MS, PhD); mechanical engineering (MS, PhD); MS/PhD. *Faculty:* 27 full-time (4 women), 7 part-time/adjunct (3 women). *Students:* 76 full-time (11 women); includes 1 Black or African American, non-Hispanic/Latino; 18 Asian, non-Hispanic/Latino; 2 Hispanic/Latino. Average age 27. 270 applicants, 11% accepted, 15 enrolled. In 2010, 7 master's, 8 doctorates awarded. *Degree requirements:* For master's, thesis; for doctorate, comprehensive exam, thesis/dissertation. *Entrance requirements:* For master's and doctorate, GRE. Additional exam requirements/recommendations for international students: Required—TOEFL (minimum score 550 paper-based; 80 iBT), IELTS (minimum score 7). *Application deadline:* For fall admission, 1/1 for domestic and international students. Application fee: $70 ($90 for international students). Electronic applications accepted. *Financial support:* In 2010–11, 72 students received support, including 18 fellowships with full and partial tuition reimbursements available (averaging $11,139 per year), 57 research assistantships with full and partial tuition reimbursements available (averaging $13,711 per year), 45 teaching assistantships with full and partial tuition reimbursements available (averaging $9,120 per year); scholarships/grants, health care

Peterson's Graduate Programs in the Physical Sciences, Mathematics, Agricultural Sciences, the Environment & Natural Resources 2012

www.facebook.com/petersonspublishing 253

Computational Sciences

University of California, Santa Barbara (continued)

benefits, tuition waivers (full and partial), and unspecified assistantships also available. Financial award application deadline: 1/1; financial award applicants required to submit FAFSA. *Faculty research:* Micro/nanoscale technology; computational science and engineering; dynamics systems, controls and robotics; thermofluid sciences, solid mechanics, materials, and structures. *Unit head:* Dr. Kimberly Turner, Chair, 805-893-8080, Fax: 805-893-8651, E-mail: turner@engineering.ucsb.edu. *Application contact:* Laura L. Reynolds, Staff Graduate Program Advisor, 805-893-2239, Fax: 805-893-8651, E-mail: megrad@engineering.ucsb.edu.

University of California, Santa Barbara, Graduate Division, College of Letters and Sciences, Division of Mathematics, Life, and Physical Sciences, Department of Ecology, Evolution, and Marine Biology, Santa Barbara, CA 93106-9620. Offers computational science and engineering (MA); computational sciences and engineering (PhD); ecology, evolution, and marine biology (MA, PhD); MA/PhD. *Faculty:* 27 full-time (7 women). *Students:* 59 full-time (38 women); includes 2 Black or African American, non-Hispanic/Latino; 5 Asian, non-Hispanic/Latino; 2 Hispanic/Latino. Average age 29. 119 applicants, 11% accepted, 8 enrolled. In 2010, 5 master's, 3 doctorates awarded. *Degree requirements:* For master's, comprehensive exam (for some programs), thesis (for some programs); for doctorate, comprehensive exam, thesis/dissertation. *Entrance requirements:* For master's and doctorate, GRE General Test. Additional exam requirements/recommendations for international students: Required—TOEFL (minimum score 550 paper-based; 80 iBT), IELTS. *Application deadline:* For fall admission, 12/15 for domestic and international students. Application fee: $70 ($90 for international students). Electronic applications accepted. *Financial support:* In 2010–11, 54 students received support, including 35 fellowships with full and partial tuition reimbursements available (averaging $10,812 per year), 21 research assistantships with full and partial tuition reimbursements available (averaging $8,441 per year), 43 teaching assistantships with partial tuition reimbursements available (averaging $9,346 per year); Federal Work-Study, scholarships/grants, traineeships, health care benefits, and tuition waivers (full and partial) also available. Financial award application deadline: 12/15; financial award applicants required to submit FAFSA. *Faculty research:* Community ecology, evolution, marine biology, population genetics, stream ecology. *Unit head:* Dr. Cheryl Briggs, Chair, 805-893-2415, Fax: 805-893-5885. *Application contact:* Melanie Fujii, Staff Graduate Advisor, 805-893-2979, Fax: 805-893-5885, E-mail: eemb-info@lifesci.ucsb.edu.

University of California, Santa Barbara, Graduate Division, College of Letters and Sciences, Division of Mathematics, Life, and Physical Sciences, Department of Mathematics, Santa Barbara, CA 93106-3080. Offers applied mathematics (MA), including computational science and engineering; mathematics (MA, PhD), including computational science and engineering; MA/PhD. *Faculty:* 29 full-time (3 women). *Students:* 50 full-time (11 women); includes 2 Black or African American, non-Hispanic/Latino; 6 Asian, non-Hispanic/Latino; 6 Hispanic/Latino. Average age 26. 151 applicants, 21% accepted, 9 enrolled. In 2010, 7 master's, 10 doctorates awarded. Terminal master's awarded for partial completion of doctoral program. *Degree requirements:* For master's, comprehensive exam (for some programs), thesis (for some programs); for doctorate, comprehensive exam, thesis/dissertation. *Entrance requirements:* For master's and doctorate, GRE General Test, GRE Subject Test (math). Additional exam requirements/recommendations for international students: Required—TOEFL (minimum score 575 paper-based; 80 iBT), IELTS (minimum score 7). *Application deadline:* For fall admission, 1/1 priority date for domestic and international students. Application fee: $70 ($90 for international students). Electronic applications accepted. *Financial support:* In 2010–11, 50 students received support, including 15 fellowships with full tuition reimbursements available (averaging $11,684 per year), 11 research assistantships with full tuition reimbursements available (averaging $7,984 per year), 42 teaching assistantships with partial tuition reimbursements available (averaging $16,637 per year); Federal Work-Study, institutionally sponsored loans, health care benefits, and tuition waivers (full and partial) also available. Financial award application deadline: 3/2; financial award applicants required to submit FAFSA. *Faculty research:* Topology, differential geometry, algebra, applied mathematics, partial differential equations. Total annual research expenditures: $205,000. *Unit head:* Prof. Martin Scharlemann, Chair, 805-893-8340, Fax: 805-893-2385, E-mail: mgscharl@math.ucsb.edu. *Application contact:* Medina Price, Graduate Advisor, 805-893-8192, Fax: 805-893-2385, E-mail: price@math.ucsb.edu.

The University of Iowa, Graduate College, Program in Applied Mathematical and Computational Sciences, Iowa City, IA 52242-1316. Offers PhD. *Degree requirements:* For doctorate, comprehensive exam, thesis/dissertation. *Entrance requirements:* For doctorate, GRE General Test, minimum GPA of 3.0. Additional exam requirements/recommendations for international students: Required—TOEFL (minimum score 620 paper-based; 260 computer-based; 105 iBT). Electronic applications accepted.

The University of Kansas, Graduate Studies, College of Liberal Arts and Sciences, Department of Physics and Astronomy, Lawrence, KS 66045. Offers computational physics and astronomy (MS); physics (MS, PhD). *Students:* 39 full-time (9 women), 4 part-time (1 woman); includes 2 minority (1 Black or African American, non-Hispanic/Latino; 1 Hispanic/Latino), 13 international. Average age 28. 41 applicants, 29% accepted, 5 enrolled. In 2010, 2 master's, 2 doctorates awarded. Terminal master's awarded for partial completion of doctoral program. *Degree requirements:* For master's, thesis (for some programs); for doctorate, comprehensive exam, thesis/dissertation, computer skills, communication skills. *Entrance requirements:* For master's and doctorate, GRE Subject Test (physics), undergraduate degree. Additional exam requirements/recommendations for international students: Required—TOEFL. *Application deadline:* For fall admission, 5/1 priority date for domestic and international students; for spring admission, 11/15 for domestic and international students. Applications are processed on a rolling basis. Application fee: $55 ($65 for international students). Electronic applications accepted. *Expenses:* Tuition, state resident: full-time $7092; part-time $295.50 per credit hour. Tuition, nonresident: full-time $16,590; part-time $691.25 per credit hour. Required fees: $858; $71.49 per credit hour. Tuition and fees vary according to course load, campus/location and program. *Financial support:* Fellowships with full and partial tuition reimbursements, research assistantships with full and partial tuition reimbursements, teaching assistantships with full and partial tuition reimbursements, health care benefits and unspecified assistantships available. Financial award application deadline: 5/1. *Faculty research:* Condensed-matter, cosmology, elementary particles, nuclear physics, space physics, astrophysics, astrobiology, biophysics, high energy. *Unit head:* Dr. Stephen J. Sanders, Chair, 785-864-4626, Fax: 785-864-5262. *Application contact:* Tess Gratton, Graduate Admission Specialist, 785-864-4626, Fax: 785-864-5262, E-mail: physics@ku.edu.

University of Lethbridge, School of Graduate Studies, Lethbridge, AB T1K 3M4, Canada. Offers accounting (MScM); addictions counseling (M Sc); agricultural biotechnology (M Sc); agricultural studies (M Sc, MA); anthropology (MA); archaeology (MA); art (MA, MFA); biochemistry (M Sc); biological sciences (M Sc); biomolecular science (PhD); biosystems and biodiversity (PhD); Canadian studies (MA); chemistry (M Sc); computer science (M Sc); computer science and geographical information science (M Sc); counseling psychology (M Ed); dramatic arts (MA); earth, space, and physical science (PhD); economics (MA); educational leadership (M Ed); English (MA); environmental science (M Sc); evolution and behavior (PhD); exercise science (M Sc); finance (MScM); French (MA); French/German (MA); French/Spanish (MA); general education (M Ed); general management (MScM); geography (M Sc, MA); German (MA); health science (M Sc); history (MA); human resource management and labour relations (MScM); individualized multidisciplinary (M Sc, MA); information systems (MScM); international management (MScM); kinesiology (M Sc, MA); management (M Sc, MA); marketing (MScM); mathematics (M Sc); music (M Mus, MA); Native American studies (MA); neuroscience (M Sc, PhD); new media (MA); nursing (M Sc); philosophy (MA); physics (M Sc); policy and strategy (MScM); political science (MA); psychology (M Sc, MA); religious studies (MA); social sciences (MA); sociology (MA); theatre and dramatic arts (MFA); theoretical and computational science (PhD); urban and regional studies (MA); women's studies (MA). Part-time and evening/weekend programs available. *Degree requirements:* For doctorate, comprehensive exam, thesis/dissertation. *Entrance requirements:* For master's, GMAT (M Sc in management), bachelor's degree in related field, minimum GPA of 3.0 during previous 20 graded semester courses, 2 years teaching or related experience (M Ed); for doctorate, master's degree, minimum graduate GPA of 3.5. Additional exam requirements/recommendations for international students: Required—TOEFL. *Faculty research:* Movement and brain plasticity, gibberellin physiology, photosynthesis, carbon cycling, molecular properties of main-group ring components.

University of Manitoba, Faculty of Graduate Studies, Faculty of Science, Program in Mathematical, Computational and Statistical Sciences, Winnipeg, MB R3T 2N2, Canada. Offers MMCSS.

University of Massachusetts Lowell, College of Arts and Sciences, Department of Mathematical Sciences, Lowell, MA 01854-2881. Offers applied mathematics (MS); computational mathematics (PhD); mathematics (MS). Part-time programs available. *Entrance requirements:* For master's, GRE General Test.

University of Michigan–Dearborn, College of Arts, Sciences, and Letters, Master of Science in Applied and Computational Mathematics Program, Dearborn, MI 48128. Offers MS. Part-time and evening/weekend programs available. *Faculty:* 8 full-time (2 women). *Students:* 2 full-time (1 woman), 18 part-time (8 women); includes 2 Black or African American, non-Hispanic/Latino; 2 Asian, non-Hispanic/Latino. Average age 40. 2 applicants, 50% accepted, 1 enrolled. In 2010, 2 master's awarded. *Degree requirements:* For master's, thesis or alternative, project. *Entrance requirements:* For master's, 3 letters of recommendation, minimum GPA of 3.0, 2 years course work in math. Additional exam requirements/recommendations for international students: Required—TOEFL (minimum score 560 paper-based; 220 computer-based). *Application deadline:* For fall admission, 8/1 priority date for domestic students, 4/1 for international students; for winter admission, 12/1 priority date for domestic students, 11/1 for international students; for spring admission, 4/1 for domestic students, 3/1 for international students. Applications are processed on a rolling basis. Application fee: $60 ($75 for international students). Electronic applications accepted. *Financial support:* Federal Work-Study and scholarships/grants available. Support available to part-time students. Financial award application deadline: 4/1; financial award applicants required to submit FAFSA. *Faculty research:* Partial differential equations, statistics, discrete optimization, approximation theory, stochastic processes. *Unit head:* Dr. Joan Remski, Director, 313-593-4994, E-mail: remski@umd.umich.edu. *Application contact:* Carol Ligienza, Coordinator, CASL Graduate Programs, 313-593-1183, Fax: 313-583-6700, E-mail: caslgrad@umd.umich.edu.

University of Minnesota, Duluth, Graduate School, Swenson College of Science and Engineering, Department of Mathematics and Statistics, Duluth, MN 55812-2496. Offers applied and computational mathematics (MS). Part-time programs available. *Degree requirements:* For master's, thesis or alternative. *Entrance requirements:* For master's, GRE General Test, minimum GPA of 3.0. Additional exam requirements/recommendations for international students: Required—TOEFL (minimum score 550 paper-based; 213 computer-based; 79 iBT); Recommended—TWE. Electronic applications accepted. *Faculty research:* Discrete mathematics, diagnostic markers, combinatorics, biostatistics, mathematical modeling and scientific computation.

University of Minnesota, Twin Cities Campus, Graduate School, Scientific Computation Program, Minneapolis, MN 55455-0213. Offers MS, PhD. Part-time programs available. *Degree requirements:* For master's, thesis; for doctorate, thesis/dissertation. *Entrance requirements:* For doctorate, GRE General Test. Additional exam requirements/recommendations for international students: Required—TOEFL (minimum score 550 paper-based; 213 computer-based; 79 iBT), IELTS (minimum score 6.5). Electronic applications accepted. *Faculty research:* Parallel computations, quantum mechanical dynamics, computational materials science, computational fluid dynamics, computational neuroscience.

University of New Haven, Graduate School, Tagliatela College of Engineering, Program in Computer and Information Science, West Haven, CT 06516-1916. Offers computer science (MS, Certificate), including advanced applications (MS), computer applications (Certificate), computer programming (Certificate), computer systems (MS), computing (Certificate), database and information systems (MS), network administration (Certificate), network systems (MS), software engineering and development (MS). Part-time and evening/weekend programs available. *Students:* 54 full-time (12 women), 25 part-time (4 women); includes 1 Black or African American, non-Hispanic/Latino; 3 Asian, non-Hispanic/Latino, 51 international. Average age 28. 204 applicants, 100% accepted, 40 enrolled. In 2010, 19 master's, 1 other advanced degree awarded. *Degree requirements:* For master's, thesis or alternative. *Entrance requirements:* Additional exam requirements/recommendations for international students: Required—TOEFL (minimum score 520 paper-based; 190 computer-based; 70 iBT); Recommended—IELTS (minimum score 5.5). *Application deadline:* For fall admission, 5/31 for international students; for winter admission, 10/15 for international students; for spring admission, 1/15 for international students. Applications are processed on a rolling basis. Application fee: $50. Electronic applications accepted. *Financial support:* Research assistantships with partial tuition reimbursements, teaching assistantships with partial tuition reimbursements, career-related internships or fieldwork, Federal Work-Study, scholarships/grants, tuition waivers, and unspecified assistantships available. Support available to part-time students. Financial award applicants required to submit FAFSA. *Unit head:* Dr. Tahany Fergany, Coordinator, 203-932-7067. *Application contact:* Eloise Gormley, Director of Graduate Admissions, 203-932-7449, Fax: 203-932-7137, E-mail: gradinfo@newhaven.edu.

University of New Mexico, Graduate School, Program in Computational Science and Engineering, Albuquerque, NM 87131-2039. Offers Post-Doctoral Certificate. *Application deadline:* For fall admission, 6/30 for domestic students; for spring admission, 11/15 for domestic students. Application fee: $50. Electronic applications accepted. *Expenses:* Tuition, state resident: full-time $5991; part-time $251 per credit hour. Tuition, nonresident: full-time $14,405; part-time $800.20 per credit hour. Tuition and fees vary according to course level, course load, program and reciprocity agreements. *Financial support:* Application deadline: 3/1. *Faculty research:* Arts technology, biophysics and nanoscale systems, chemistry and chemical biology, civil engineering, climate and weather modeling, computational biology and bioinformatics, cyberinfrastructure, digital arts and humanities, electromagnetics, energy grid modeling, high performance computing and scalable systems, image processing, materials physics, visualization and virtual environments, observational astronomy, open science grid, particle physics, quantum materials and devices, systems biology. *Unit head:* Dr. Susan Rachel Atlas, Unit Administrator, 505-277-0727, Fax: 505-277-8235, E-mail: director@hpc.unm.edu. *Application contact:* Stephanie Grant, Associate Director, Admissions, 505-277-0727, Fax: 505-277-8235, E-mail: slgrant@unm.edu.

University of Pennsylvania, School of Arts and Sciences, Graduate Group in Applied Mathematics and Computational Science, Philadelphia, PA 19104. Offers PhD. *Faculty:* 26 full-time (2 women). *Students:* 17 full-time (6 women), 1 part-time (0 women), 17 international. 93 applicants, 14% accepted, 5 enrolled. *Application deadline:* For fall admission, 1/15 for domestic students. *Expenses:* Tuition: Full-time $25,660; part-time $4758 per course. Required fees: $2152; $270 per course. Tuition and fees vary according to course load, degree level and program. *Financial support:* Institutionally sponsored loans, scholarships/grants, traineeships, health care benefits, and unspecified assistantships available. *Unit head:* Dr. C.L. Epstein, Graduate Chair, 215-898-8476, E-mail: cle@math.upenn.edu. *Application contact:* Dr. C.L. Epstein, Graduate Chair, 215-898-8476, E-mail: cle@math.upenn.edu.

University of Puerto Rico, Mayagüez Campus, Graduate Studies, College of Arts and Sciences, Department of Mathematical Sciences, Mayagüez, PR 00681-9000. Offers applied mathematics (MS); pure mathematics (MS); scientific computation (MS); statistics (MS). Part-time programs available. *Students:* 40 full-time (11 women), 1 part-time (0 women); includes 7 Hispanic/Latino, 34 international. 19 applicants, 26% accepted, 3 enrolled. In 2010, 7 master's awarded. *Degree requirements:* For master's, one foreign language, comprehensive exam, thesis optional. *Entrance requirements:* For master's, undergraduate degree in mathematics or its equivalent. *Application deadline:* For fall admission, 2/15 for domestic and international students; for spring admission, 9/15 for domestic and international students. Applications are processed on a rolling basis. Application fee: $25. *Expenses:* Tuition, state resident: full-time $1188. Tuition, nonresident: full-time $1188. International tuition: $6126 full-time. Tuition and fees vary according to course level and course load. *Financial support:* In 2010–11, 39 students received support, including fellowships (averaging $12,000 per year), 20 research assistantships (averaging $15,000 per year), 39 teaching assistantships (averaging $8,500 per year); Federal Work-Study and institutionally sponsored loans also available. *Faculty research:* Automata theory, linear algebra, logic. Total annual research expenditures: $2.7 million. *Unit head:* Prof. Silvestre Col??n, Director, 787-832-4040 Ext. 3848, Fax: 787-265-5454, E-mail: silvestre.colon@upr.edu. *Application contact:* Prof. Silvestre Col??n, Director, 787-832-4040 Ext. 3848, Fax: 787-265-5454, E-mail: silvestre.colon@upr.edu.

The University of South Dakota, Graduate School, College of Arts and Sciences, Department of Computer Science, Vermillion, SD 57069-2390. Offers computational sciences and statistics (PhD); computer science (MS). Part-time programs available. *Degree requirements:* For master's, thesis optional. *Entrance requirements:* For master's, GRE General Test, GRE Subject Test (recommended), minimum GPA of 2.7. Additional exam requirements/recommendations for international students: Required—TOEFL (minimum score 550 paper-based; 213 computer-based; 79 iBT). Electronic applications accepted.

University of Southern Mississippi, Graduate School, College of Science and Technology, Department of Mathematics, Hattiesburg, MS 39406-0001. Offers computational science (PhD); mathematics (MS). Part-time programs available. *Faculty:* 11 full-time (3 women), 1 part-time/adjunct (0 women). *Students:* 11 full-time (8 women), 2 part-time (0 women); includes 3 Black or African American, non-Hispanic/Latino; 1 Asian, non-Hispanic/Latino, 3 international. Average age 29. 12 applicants, 83% accepted, 5 enrolled. In 2010, 1 master's awarded. *Degree requirements:* For master's, comprehensive exam, thesis or alternative; for doctorate, comprehensive exam, thesis/dissertation. *Entrance requirements:* For master's, GRE General Test, minimum GPA of 2.75 in last 60 hours; for doctorate, GRE General Test, minimum GPA of 3.5. Additional exam requirements/recommendations for international students: Required—TOEFL, IELTS. *Application deadline:* For fall admission, 3/15 priority date for domestic and international students; for spring admission, 1/10 priority date for domestic and international students. Applications are processed on a rolling basis. Application fee: $50. Electronic applications accepted. *Financial support:* In 2010–11, 1 fellowship (averaging $18,000 per year), research assistantships with full tuition reimbursements (averaging $11,500 per year), 11,500 teaching assistantships with full tuition reimbursements (averaging $11,408 per year) were awarded; Federal Work-Study, scholarships/grants, health care benefits, and unspecified assistantships also available. Financial award application deadline: 3/15; financial award applicants required to submit FAFSA. *Faculty research:* Dynamical systems, numerical analysis and multigrid methods, random number generation, matrix theory, group theory. *Unit head:* Dr. Joseph Kolibal, Interim Chair, 601-266-4289, Fax: 601-266-5818. *Application contact:* Dr. James Lambers, Director, Graduate Admissions, 601-266-4289, Fax: 601-266-5818.

University of Southern Mississippi, Graduate School, College of Science and Technology, Department of Physics and Astronomy, Hattiesburg, MS 39406-0001. Offers computational science (PhD); physics (MS). *Faculty:* 10 full-time (1 woman). *Students:* 9 full-time (2 women), 1 part-time (0 women), 5 international. Average age 31. 12 applicants, 83% accepted, 3 enrolled. In 2010, 4 master's awarded. *Degree requirements:* For master's, comprehensive exam, thesis; for doctorate, comprehensive exam, thesis/dissertation. *Entrance requirements:* For master's, GRE General Test, minimum GPA of 2.75 in last 60 hours; for doctorate, GRE General Test, minimum GPA of 3.5. Additional exam requirements/recommendations for international students: Required—TOEFL, IELTS. *Application deadline:* For fall admission, 3/1 priority date for domestic students, 3/1 for international students; for spring admission, 1/10 priority date for domestic and international students. Applications are processed on a rolling basis. Application fee: $50. *Financial support:* In 2010–11, research assistantships with full tuition reimbursements (averaging $11,800 per year), 15 teaching assistantships with full tuition reimbursements (averaging $11,800 per year) were awarded; Federal Work-Study, scholarships/grants, health care benefits, and unspecified assistantships also available. Financial award application deadline: 3/15; financial award applicants required to submit FAFSA. *Faculty research:* Polymers, atomic physics, fluid mechanics, liquid crystals, refractory materials. *Unit head:* Dr. Khin Maung, Chair, 601-266-4934, Fax: 601-266-5149. *Application contact:* Dr. Khin Maung, Chair, 601-266-4934, Fax: 601-266-5149.

University of Southern Mississippi, Graduate School, College of Science and Technology, School of Computing, Hattiesburg, MS 39406-0001. Offers computational science (MS, PhD); computer science (MS). *Faculty:* 18 full-time (3 women), 1 (woman) part-time/adjunct. *Students:* 58 full-time (11 women), 19 part-time (4 women); includes 5 Black or African American, non-Hispanic/Latino; 1 Asian, non-Hispanic/Latino; 1 Hispanic/Latino, 44 international. Average age 29. 66 applicants, 80% accepted, 16 enrolled. In 2010, 22 master's, 2 doctorates awarded. *Degree requirements:* For master's, comprehensive exam, thesis; for doctorate, comprehensive exam, thesis/dissertation. *Entrance requirements:* For master's, GRE General Test, minimum GPA of 2.75 in last 60 hours; for doctorate, GRE General Test, minimum GPA of 3.5. Additional exam requirements/recommendations for international students: Required—TOEFL, IELTS. *Application deadline:* For fall admission, 3/15 priority date for domestic students, 3/15 for international students; for spring admission, 1/10 priority date for domestic and international students. Applications are processed on a rolling basis. Application fee: $50. Electronic applications accepted. *Financial support:* In 2010–11, 29 research assistantships with full tuition reimbursements (averaging $8,800 per year), 7 teaching assistantships with full tuition reimbursements (averaging $10,000 per year) were awarded; Federal Work-Study, institutionally sponsored loans, scholarships/grants, health care benefits, and unspecified assistantships also available. Financial award application deadline: 3/15; financial award applicants required to submit FAFSA. *Faculty research:* Satellite telecommunications, advanced life-support systems, artificial intelligence. *Unit head:* Dr. Chaoyang Zhang, Chair, 601-266-4949, Fax: 601-266-6452. *Application contact:* Dr. Chaoyang Zhang, Manager of Graduate Admissions, 601-266-4949, Fax: 601-266-6452.

The University of Tennessee at Chattanooga, Graduate School, College of Engineering and Computer Science, Program in Computational Engineering, Chattanooga, TN 37403. Offers PhD. *Faculty:* 6 full-time (0 women). *Students:* 8 full-time (1 woman), 9 part-time (1 woman); includes 1 minority (Asian, non-Hispanic/Latino), 6 international. Average age 30. 7 applicants, 43% accepted, 2 enrolled. In 2010, 1 doctorate awarded. *Degree requirements:* For doctorate, comprehensive exam, thesis/dissertation. *Entrance requirements:* For doctorate, GRE General Test. Additional exam requirements/recommendations for international students: Required—TOEFL (minimum score 550 paper-based; 213 computer-based; 79 iBT), IELTS (minimum score 6). *Application deadline:* For fall admission, 8/1 priority date for domestic students, 6/1 for international students; for spring admission, 12/1 priority date for domestic students, 10/1 for international students. Applications are processed on a rolling basis. Application fee: $35. Electronic applications accepted. *Financial support:* In 2010–11, 8 research assistantships with full and partial tuition reimbursements (averaging $5,500 per year) were awarded; career-related internships or fieldwork, scholarships/grants, and unspecified assistantships also available. Support available to part-time students. *Faculty research:* Computational fluid dynamics, design optimization, solution algorithms, hydronamics and propulsion. Total annual research expenditures: $4 million. *Unit head:* Dr. Tim Swafford, Director, 423-425-5497, Fax: 423-425-5517, E-mail: tim-swafford@utc.edu. *Application contact:* Dr. Jerald Ainsworth, Dean of Graduate Studies, 423-425-4478, Fax: 423-425-5223, E-mail: jerald-ainsworth@utc.edu.

The University of Tennessee at Chattanooga, Graduate School, College of Engineering and Computer Science, Program in Engineering, Chattanooga, TN 37403. Offers chemical engineering (MS Engr); civil engineering (MS Engr); computational engineering (MS Engr); electrical engineering (MS Engr); industrial engineering (MS Engr); mechanical engineering (MS Engr). Part-time and evening/weekend programs available. *Faculty:* 8 full-time (0 women). *Students:* 27 full-time (5 women), 31 part-time (6 women); includes 12 minority (7 Black or African American, non-Hispanic/Latino; 1 Asian, non-Hispanic/Latino; 4 Hispanic/Latino), 10 international. Average age 29. 43 applicants, 100% accepted, 26 enrolled. In 2010, 16 master's awarded. *Degree requirements:* For master's, comprehensive exam, thesis or alternative, engineering project. *Entrance requirements:* For master's, GRE General Test, minimum undergraduate GPA of 2.5 or 3.0 in last 30 hours of coursework. Additional exam requirements/recommendations for international students: Required—TOEFL (minimum score 550 paper-based; 213 computer-based; 79 iBT), IELTS (minimum score 6). *Application deadline:* For fall admission, 8/1 priority date for domestic students, 6/1 for international students; for spring admission, 12/1 priority date for domestic students, 10/1 for international students. Applications are processed on a rolling basis. Application fee: $35. Electronic applications accepted. *Financial support:* In 2010–11, 23 research assistantships with full and partial tuition reimbursements (averaging $5,500 per year) were awarded; career-related internships or fieldwork, scholarships/grants, and unspecified assistantships also available. Support available to part-time students. *Faculty research:* Quality control and reliability engineering, financial management, thermal science, energy conservation, structural analysis. Total annual research expenditures: $2.6 million. *Unit head:* Dr. Neslihan Alp, Director, 423-425-4032, Fax: 423-425-5229, E-mail: neslihan-alp@utc.edu. *Application contact:* Dr. Jerald Ainsworth, Dean of Graduate Studies, 423-425-4478, Fax: 423-425-5223, E-mail: jerald-ainsworth@utc.edu.

The University of Texas at Austin, Graduate School, Program in Computational and Applied Mathematics, Austin, TX 78712-1111. Offers MA, PhD. Terminal master's awarded for partial completion of doctoral program. *Degree requirements:* For master's, thesis optional; for doctorate, thesis/dissertation, 3 area qualifying exams. Electronic applications accepted.

The University of Texas at El Paso, Graduate School, College of Science, Computational Science Program, El Paso, TX 79968-0001. Offers MS, PhD. *Students:* 16 (2 women); includes 1 Black or African American, non-Hispanic/Latino; 5 Hispanic/Latino, 10 international. *Degree requirements:* For master's, thesis or internship; for doctorate, thesis/dissertation. *Entrance requirements:* For doctorate, GRE, statement of purpose, letters of recommendation. Additional exam requirements/recommendations for international students: Required—TOEFL; Recommended—IELTS. *Application deadline:* For fall admission, 8/1 for domestic students, 3/1 for international students; for spring admission, 11/1 for domestic students, 9/1 for international students. Applications are processed on a rolling basis. Application fee: $45 ($80 for international students). Electronic applications accepted. *Financial support:* Fellowships with partial tuition reimbursements, research assistantships with partial tuition reimbursements, teaching assistantships with partial tuition reimbursements, institutionally sponsored loans, scholarships/grants, health care benefits, tuition waivers (partial), and unspecified assistantships available. Support available to part-time students. Financial award application deadline: 3/15; financial award applicants required to submit FAFSA. *Unit head:* Dr. Leticia Velazquez, Director, 915-747-6768, Fax: 915-747-6502, E-mail: leti@utep.edu. *Application contact:* Dr. Patricia D. Witherspoon, Dean of the Graduate School, 915-747-5491, Fax: 915-747-5788, E-mail: withersp@utep.edu.

University of Utah, Graduate School, College of Engineering, School of Computing, Computational Engineering and Science Program, Salt Lake City, UT 84112. Offers MS. *Faculty:* 8 full-time (0 women). *Students:* 80 full-time (12 women), 28 part-time (3 women); includes 2 minority (both Asian, non-Hispanic/Latino), 52 international. Average age 29. 21 applicants, 48% accepted, 8 enrolled. In 2010, 1 master's awarded. *Degree requirements:* For master's, comprehensive exam, thesis (for some programs). *Entrance requirements:* For master's, minimum GPA of 3.0. Additional exam requirements/recommendations for international students: Required—TOEFL (minimum score 500 paper-based; 173 computer-based; 61 iBT), IELTS (minimum score 6). *Application deadline:* For fall admission, 1/15 priority date for domestic and international students. Application fee: $55 ($65 for international students). Electronic applications accepted. *Expenses:* Contact institution. *Financial support:* In 2010–11, 1 student received support, including 1 fellowship (averaging $15,000 per year), 2 research assistantships with full tuition reimbursements available (averaging $12,000 per year), 1 teaching assistantship with full tuition reimbursement available (averaging $12,000 per year); health care benefits and unspecified assistantships also available. Financial award application deadline: 12/15; financial award applicants required to submit FAFSA. *Faculty research:* Mathematical modeling, the formulation of the numerical methodology for solving the problem, the selection of the appropriate computer architecture and algorithms, and the effective interpretation of the results through visualization and/or statistical reduction. *Unit head:* Dr. Kris Sikorski, Director, 801-581-8579, Fax: 801-581-5843, E-mail: sikorski@cs.utah.edu. *Application contact:* Ann Carlstrom, Graduate Advisor, 801-581-7631, Fax: 801-581-5843, E-mail: annc@cs.utah.edu.

University of Utah, Graduate School, Professional Master of Science and Technology Program, Salt Lake City, UT 84112-1107. Offers biotechnology (PSM); computational science (PSM); environmental science (PSM); science instrumentation (PSM). Part-time programs available. *Faculty:* 2 full-time (0 women). *Students:* 32 full-time (17 women), 38 part-time (13 women); includes 1 Black or African American, non-Hispanic/Latino; 3 Asian, non-Hispanic/Latino; 1 Hispanic/Latino, 19 international. Average age 31. 66 applicants, 48% accepted, 16 enrolled. In 2010, 7 master's awarded. *Degree requirements:* For master's, internship. *Entrance requirements:* For master's, GRE (recommended), minimum undergraduate GPA of 3.0, bachelor's degree from accredited university or college. Additional exam requirements/recommendations for international students: Required—TOEFL (minimum score 500 paper-based; 173 computer-based; 61 iBT), IELTS (minimum score 6). *Application deadline:* For fall admission, 3/1 for domestic and international students. Application fee: $55 ($65 for international students). Electronic applications accepted. *Expenses:* Tuition, area resident: Part-time $179.19 per credit hour. Tuition, state resident: full-time $4384. Tuition, nonresident: full-time $16,684; part-time $630.67 per credit hour. Required fees: $350 per semester. Tuition and fees vary according to course load, degree level and program. *Financial support:* In 2010–11, 8 students received support, including 5 fellowships with full and partial tuition reimbursements available (averaging $16,800 per year), 2 research assistantships (averaging $6,200 per year); unspecified assistantships also available. Financial award applicants required to submit FAFSA. *Faculty research:* Drug delivery systems, in vitro erythroid expansion and HRE (Hypoxia responsive element). *Unit head:* Jennifer Schmidt, Program Director, 801-585-5630, E-mail: jennifer.schmidt@gradschool.utah.edu. *Application contact:* Amy Kimball, Project Coordinator, 801-585-3650, Fax: 801-585-6749, E-mail: amy.kimball@gradschool.utah.edu.

University of Washington, Graduate School, College of Arts and Sciences, Department of Mathematics, Seattle, WA 98195. Offers mathematics (MA, MS, PhD); numerical analysis (MS); optimization (MS). Part-time programs available. Terminal master's awarded for partial completion of doctoral program. *Degree requirements:* For master's, thesis optional; for doctorate, 2 foreign languages, thesis/dissertation. *Entrance requirements:* For master's, GRE, minimum GPA of 3.0; for doctorate, GRE General Test, GRE Subject Test (mathematics), minimum GPA of 3.0. Additional exam requirements/recommendations for international students: Required—

Computational Sciences

University of Washington (continued)
TOEFL. Electronic applications accepted. *Faculty research:* Algebra, analysis, probability, combinatorics and geometry.

Western Kentucky University, Graduate Studies, Ogden College of Science and Engineering, Department of Mathematics and Computer Science, Bowling Green, KY 42101. Offers computational mathematics (MS); computer science (MS); mathematics (MA, MS). *Degree requirements:* For master's, comprehensive exam, thesis optional, written exam. *Entrance requirements:* For master's, GRE General Test, minimum GPA of 2.75. Additional exam requirements/recommendations for international students: Required—TOEFL (minimum score 555 paper-based; 213 computer-based; 79 iBT). *Faculty research:* Differential equations numerical analysis, probability statistics, algebra, typology, knot theory.

Western Michigan University, Graduate College, College of Arts and Sciences, Department of Mathematics, Program in Applied and Computational Mathematics, Kalamazoo, MI 49008. Offers MS.

Mathematical and Computational Finance

Bernard M. Baruch College of the City University of New York, Weissman School of Arts and Sciences, Program in Financial Engineering, New York, NY 10010-5585. Offers MS. *Entrance requirements:* For master's, GRE General Test or GMAT, 3 recommendations. Additional exam requirements/recommendations for international students: Required—TOEFL, TWE.

Boston University, School of Management, Boston, MA 02215. Offers business administration (MBA); executive business administration (EMBA); investment management (MS); management (PhD); mathematical finance (MS, PhD); JD/MBA; MBA/MA; MBA/MPH; MBA/MS; MBA/MSIS; MD/MBA; MS/MBA. *Accreditation:* AACSB. Part-time and evening/weekend programs available. *Faculty:* 185 full-time (49 women), 60 part-time/adjunct (15 women). *Students:* 525 full-time (206 women), 743 part-time (272 women); includes 14 Black or African American, non-Hispanic/Latino; 134 Asian, non-Hispanic/Latino; 19 Hispanic/Latino, 247 international. Average age 30. 1,387 applicants, 28% accepted, 160 enrolled. In 2010, 532 master's, 5 doctorates awarded. *Degree requirements:* For doctorate, comprehensive exam, thesis/dissertation. *Entrance requirements:* For master's, GMAT (for MBA and MS in investment management); GMAT or GRE General Test (for MS in mathematical finance), resume, 2 letters of recommendation; for doctorate, GMAT or GRE General Test, resume, personal statement, 3 letters of recommendation, 3 essays, official transcripts. *Application deadline:* For fall admission, 1/5 for domestic and international students; for spring admission, 11/1 for domestic students. Application fee: $125. Electronic applications accepted. *Expenses:* Tuition: Full-time $39,314; part-time $1228 per credit. Required fees: $40 per semester. *Financial support:* Career-related internships or fieldwork, Federal Work-Study, institutionally sponsored loans, scholarships/grants, and tuition waivers (partial) available. Financial award applicants required to submit FAFSA. *Faculty research:* Innovation policy and productivity, corporate social responsibility, risk management, information systems, entrepreneurship, clean energy, sustainability. *Unit head:* Kenneth W. Freeman, Allen Questrom Professor and Dean, 617-353-9720, Fax: 617-353-5581, E-mail: kfreeman@bu.edu. *Application contact:* Patti Cudney, Assistant Dean, Graduate Admissions, 617-353-2670, Fax: 617-353-7368, E-mail: mba@bu.edu.

Carnegie Mellon University, Mellon College of Science, Department of Mathematical Sciences, Pittsburgh, PA 15213-3891. Offers algorithms, combinatorics, and optimization (PhD); applied mathematics (PhD); computational finance (MS); mathematical finance (PhD); mathematical sciences (MS, DA, PhD); pure and applied logic (PhD). Part-time programs available. Terminal master's awarded for partial completion of doctoral program. *Degree requirements:* For doctorate, thesis/dissertation. *Entrance requirements:* For master's and doctorate, GRE General Test, GRE Subject Test. Additional exam requirements/recommendations for international students: Required—TOEFL. Electronic applications accepted. *Faculty research:* Continuum mechanics, discrete mathematics, applied and computational mathematics.

Carnegie Mellon University, Tepper School of Business, Pittsburgh, PA 15213-3891. Offers accounting (PhD); algorithms, combinatorics, and optimization (MS, PhD); business management and software engineering (MBMSE); civil engineering and industrial management (MS); computational finance (MSCF); economics (MS, PhD); electronic commerce (MS); environmental engineering and management (MEEM); finance (PhD); financial economics (PhD); industrial administration (MBA), including administration and public management; information systems (PhD); management of manufacturing and automation (PhD); marketing (PhD); mathematical finance (PhD); operations research (PhD); organizational behavior and theory (PhD); political economy (PhD); production and operations management (PhD); public policy and management (MS, MSED); software engineering and business management (MS); JD/MS; JD/MSIA; M Div/MS; MOM/MSIA; MSCF/MSIA. JD/MSIA offered jointly with University of Pittsburgh. Part-time programs available. Terminal master's awarded for partial completion of doctoral program. *Degree requirements:* For doctorate, thesis/dissertation. *Entrance requirements:* For master's, GMAT. Additional exam requirements/recommendations for international students: Required—TOEFL. *Expenses:* Contact institution.

DePaul University, Charles H. Kellstadt Graduate School of Business, Department of Finance, Chicago, IL 60604-2287. Offers behavioral finance (MBA); computational finance (MS); finance (MBA, MSF); financial analysis (MBA); financial management and control (MBA); international marketing and finance (MBA); managerial finance (MBA); real estate (MS); real estate finance and investment (MBA); strategy, execution and valuation (MBA). Part-time and evening/weekend programs available. *Faculty:* 26 full-time (5 women), 23 part-time/adjunct (2 women). *Students:* 454 full-time (138 women), 190 part-time (41 women); includes 85 minority (13 Black or African American, non-Hispanic/Latino; 53 Asian, non-Hispanic/Latino; 17 Hispanic/Latino; 2 Two or more races, non-Hispanic/Latino), 129 international. In 2010, 239 master's awarded. *Entrance requirements:* For master's, GMAT, 2 letters of recommendation, resume. Additional exam requirements/recommendations for international students: Required—TOEFL (minimum score 550 paper-based; 213 computer-based; 80 iBT). *Application deadline:* For fall admission, 7/1 for domestic students, 6/1 for international students; for winter admission, 10/1 for domestic students, 9/1 for international students; for spring admission, 2/1 for domestic students, 1/1 for international students. Applications are processed on a rolling basis. Application fee: $60. Electronic applications accepted. *Financial support:* In 2010–11, 8 students received support, including 6 research assistantships with partial tuition reimbursements available (averaging $4,340 per year); scholarships/grants and unspecified assistantships also available. Financial award application deadline: 4/1; financial award applicants required to submit FAFSA. *Faculty research:* Derivatives, valuation, international finance, real estate, corporate finance. *Unit head:* Ali M. Fatemi, Professor and Chair, 312-362-8826, Fax: 312-362-6566, E-mail: afatemi@depaul.edu. *Application contact:* Christopher E. Kinsella, Director of Cohort MBA Programs, 312-362-8810, Fax: 312-362-6677, E-mail: kgsb@depaul.edu.

DePaul University, College of Computing and Digital Media, Chicago, IL 60604. Offers animation (MA, MFA); applied technology (MS); business information technology (MS); cinema (MFA); cinema production (MS); computational finance (MS); computer and information sciences (PhD); computer game development (MS); computer graphics and motion technology (MS); computer information and network security (MS); computer science (MS); e-commerce technology (MS); human-computer interaction (MS); information systems (MS); information technology (MA); information technology project management (MS); network engineering and management (MS); predictive analytics (MS); screenwriting (MFA); software engineering (MS); JD/MA; JD/MS. Part-time and evening/weekend programs available. Postbaccalaureate distance learning degree programs offered (no on-campus study). *Faculty:* 51 full-time (11 women), 50 part-time/adjunct (9 women). *Students:* 952 full-time (230 women), 927 part-time (226 women); includes 557 minority (205 Black or African American, non-Hispanic/Latino; 2 American Indian or Alaska Native, non-Hispanic/Latino; 167 Asian, non-Hispanic/Latino; 136 Hispanic/Latino; 7 Native Hawaiian or other Pacific Islander, non-Hispanic/Latino; 40 Two or more races, non-Hispanic/Latino), 292 international. Average age 31. 896 applicants, 70% accepted, 324 enrolled. In 2010, 417 master's, 6 doctorates awarded. *Degree requirements:* For master's, thesis (for some programs); for doctorate, comprehensive exam, thesis/dissertation. *Entrance requirements:* For master's, GRE or GMAT (MS in computational finance only), bachelor's degree, resume (MS in predictive analytics only), IT experience (MS in information technology project management only), portfolio review (MFA); for doctorate, GRE, master's degree in computer science. Additional exam requirements/recommendations for international students: Required—TOEFL (minimum score 550 paper-based; 213 computer-based; 80 iBT), IELTS (minimum score 6.5), Pearson Test of English (minimum score 53). *Application deadline:* For fall admission, 8/15 priority date for domestic students, 6/1 priority date for international students; for winter admission, 12/15 priority date for domestic students, 9/15 priority date for international students; for spring admission, 3/1 priority date for domestic students, 12/15 priority date for international students. Applications are processed on a rolling basis. Application fee: $25. Electronic applications accepted. *Expenses:* Contact institution. *Financial support:* In 2010–11, 102 students received support, including 4 fellowships with full tuition reimbursements available (averaging $24,435 per year), 6 research assistantships (averaging $21,100 per year), 92 teaching assistantships with full and partial tuition reimbursements available (averaging $6,904 per year); Federal Work-Study, scholarships/grants, tuition waivers (full and partial), and unspecified assistantships also available. Support available to part-time students. Financial award application deadline: 4/30; financial award applicants required to submit FAFSA. *Faculty research:* Bioinformatics, visual computing, graphics and animation, high performance and scientific computing, databases. Total annual research expenditures: $1.4 million. *Unit head:* Dr. David Miller, Dean, 312-362-8381, Fax: 312-362-5185. *Application contact:* Dr. Liz Friedman, Assistant Dean of Student Services, 312-362-8714, Fax: 312-362-5179, E-mail: efriedm2@cdm.depaul.edu.

Florida State University, The Graduate School, College of Arts and Sciences, Department of Mathematics, Tallahassee, FL 32306-4510. Offers applied computational mathematics (MS, PhD); biomedical mathematics (MS, PhD); financial mathematics (MS, PhD); pure mathematics (MS, PhD). Part-time programs available. *Faculty:* 46 full-time (11 women), 2 part-time/adjunct (both women). *Students:* 139 full-time (35 women), 7 part-time (0 women); includes 3 Black or African American, non-Hispanic/Latino; 3 Asian, non-Hispanic/Latino; 4 Hispanic/Latino, 92 international. Average age 26. 342 applicants, 40% accepted, 39 enrolled. In 2010, 42 master's, 8 doctorates awarded. Terminal master's awarded for partial completion of doctoral program. *Degree requirements:* For master's, comprehensive exam (for some programs), thesis optional; for doctorate, comprehensive exam (for some programs), thesis/dissertation, candidacy exam including written qualifying examinations which differ by degree concentrations. *Entrance requirements:* For master's and doctorate, GRE General Test, minimum upper-division GPA of 3.0, 4-year bachelor's degree. Additional exam requirements/recommendations for international students: Required—TOEFL (minimum score 213 computer-based; 80 iBT), IELTS (minimum score 6.5). *Application deadline:* For fall admission, 1/3 priority date for domestic students, 12/15 priority date for international students; for spring admission, 11/1 for domestic and international students. Applications are processed on a rolling basis. Application fee: $30. Electronic applications accepted. *Expenses:* Tuition, state resident: full-time $8238.24. *Financial support:* In 2010–11, 102 students received support, including 6 fellowships with full tuition reimbursements available (averaging $19,000 per year), 15 research assistantships with full tuition reimbursements available (averaging $20,000 per year), 75 teaching assistantships with full tuition reimbursements available (averaging $18,000 per year); career-related internships or fieldwork, institutionally sponsored loans, scholarships/grants, health care benefits, tuition waivers (full and partial), and unspecified assistantships also available. *Faculty research:* Geometric topology, algebraic geometry, fluid dynamics, financial mathematics, biomedical mathematics. *Unit head:* Dr. Philip L. Bowers, Chairperson, 850-645-3338, Fax: 850-644-4053, E-mail: bowers@math.fsu.edu. *Application contact:* Dr. Bettye Anne Case, Associate Chair for Graduate Studies, 850-644-1586, Fax: 850-644-4053, E-mail: case@math.fsu.edu.

Georgia Institute of Technology, Graduate Studies and Research, College of Management, Program in Management, Atlanta, GA 30332-0001. Offers accounting (PhD); finance (PhD); information technology management (PhD); marketing (PhD); operations management (PhD); organizational behavior (PhD); quantitative and computational finance (MS); strategic management (PhD). *Accreditation:* AACSB. *Degree requirements:* For doctorate, comprehensive exam, thesis/dissertation, oral exams. *Entrance requirements:* For master's and doctorate, GMAT. Additional exam requirements/recommendations for international students: Required—TOEFL. *Faculty research:* MIS, management of technology, international business, entrepreneurship, operations management.

Georgia Institute of Technology, Graduate Studies and Research, College of Sciences, School of Mathematics, Atlanta, GA 30332-0001. Offers algorithms, combinatorics, and optimization (PhD); applied mathematics (MS); bioinformatics (PhD); mathematics (PhD); quantitative and computational finance (MS); statistics (MS Stat). Terminal master's awarded for partial completion of doctoral program. *Degree requirements:* For master's, thesis or alternative; for doctorate, one foreign language, thesis/dissertation. *Entrance requirements:* For master's, GRE General Test, minimum GPA of 3.0; for doctorate, GRE General Test, GRE Subject Test, minimum GPA of 3.0. Additional exam requirements/recommendations for international students: Required—TOEFL. Electronic applications accepted. *Faculty research:* Dynamical systems, discrete mathematics, probability and statistics, mathematical physics.

Illinois Institute of Technology, Stuart School of Business, Program in Mathematical Finance, Chicago, IL 60616-3793. Offers MMF. Part-time and evening/weekend programs available. *Faculty:* 37 full-time (4 women), 21 part-time/adjunct (5 women). *Students:* 20 full-time (6 women), 2 part-time (0 women); includes 2 minority (both Asian, non-Hispanic/Latino), 19 international. Average age 24. 138 applicants, 53% accepted, 15 enrolled. In 2010, 5 master's awarded. *Entrance requirements:* For master's, GRE (minimum score 1200). Additional exam requirements/recommendations for international students: Required—TOEFL (minimum score 600 paper-based; 85 iBT); Recommended—IELTS (minimum score 7). *Application deadline:* For fall admission, 8/1 for domestic students, 5/1 for international students; for spring admission,

12/15 for domestic students, 10/15 for international students. Applications are processed on a rolling basis. Application fee: $75. Electronic applications accepted. *Expenses:* Contact institution. *Financial support:* Career-related internships or fieldwork, Federal Work-Study, institutionally sponsored loans, scholarships/grants, traineeships, health care benefits, and tuition waivers (partial) available. Support available to part-time students. Financial award applicants required to submit FAFSA. *Faculty research:* Factor models for investment management, credit rating and credit risk management, hedge fund performance analysis, option trading and risk management, global asset allocation strategies. *Unit head:* Tomasz Bielecki, Professor, 312-567-3165, Fax: 312-567-3135, E-mail: bielecki@iit.edu. *Application contact:* Deborah Gibson, Director, Graduate Admission, 866-472-3448, Fax: 312-567-3138, E-mail: inquiry.grad@iit.edu.

The Johns Hopkins University, G. W. C. Whiting School of Engineering, Department of Applied Mathematics and Statistics, Baltimore, MD 21218-2699. Offers computational medicine (PhD); discrete mathematics (MA, MSE, PhD); financial mathematics (MSE); operations research/optimization/decision science (MA, MSE, PhD); statistics/probability/stochastic processes (MA, MSE, PhD). *Faculty:* 17 full-time (3 women), 4 part-time/adjunct (0 women). *Students:* 72 full-time (27 women), 3 part-time (0 women); includes 10 minority (1 Black or African American, non-Hispanic/Latino; 7 Asian, non-Hispanic/Latino; 2 Two or more races, non-Hispanic/Latino), 51 international. Average age 25. 306 applicants, 47% accepted, 36 enrolled. In 2010, 26 master's, 7 doctorates awarded. Terminal master's awarded for partial completion of doctoral program. *Degree requirements:* For master's, thesis (for some programs); for doctorate, thesis/dissertation, oral exam, introductory exam. *Entrance requirements:* For master's and doctorate, GRE General Test, GRE Subject Test. Additional exam requirements/recommendations for international students: Required—TOEFL (minimum score 600 paper-based; 250 computer-based; 100 iBT). *Application deadline:* For fall admission, 1/15 for domestic and international students; for spring admission, 9/15 for domestic and international students. Application fee: $75. Electronic applications accepted. *Financial support:* In 2010–11, 40 students received support, including 9 fellowships with full tuition reimbursements available (averaging $19,800 per year), 19 research assistantships with full tuition reimbursements available (averaging $1,800 per year), 9 teaching assistantships with full tuition reimbursements available (averaging $1,800 per year); Federal Work-Study, institutionally sponsored loans, scholarships/grants, health care benefits, tuition waivers (partial), and unspecified assistantships also available. Financial award application deadline: 1/15. *Faculty research:* Discrete mathematics, probability, statistics, optimization and operations research, scientific computation, financial mathematics. Total annual research expenditures: $1.3 million. *Unit head:* Dr. Daniel Q. Naiman, Chair, 410-516-7203, Fax: 410-516-7459, E-mail: daniel.naiman@jhu.edu. *Application contact:* Kristin Bechtel, Academic Program Coordinator, 410-516-7198, Fax: 410-516-7459, E-mail: kbechtel@jhu.edu.

Monmouth University, The Graduate School, Department of Mathematics, West Long Branch, NJ 07764-1898. Offers financial mathematics (MS). Part-time and evening/weekend programs available. *Faculty:* 2 full-time (0 women). *Students:* 5 full-time (2 women), 9 part-time (4 women); includes 1 Black or African American, non-Hispanic/Latino; 2 Asian, non-Hispanic/Latino; 2 Hispanic/Latino; 1 Two or more races, non-Hispanic/Latino, 2 international. Average age 31. 15 applicants, 60% accepted, 4 enrolled. *Degree requirements:* For master's, 6 credits of financial mathematics practicum. *Entrance requirements:* For master's, minimum GPA of 3.0 in major, 2.5 overall; undergraduate degree in mathematics or related field with substantial component of math; coursework in calculus, linear algebra, differential equations (with some exposure to partial differential equations), and a course in calculus-based statistics. Additional exam requirements/recommendations for international students: Required—TOEFL (minimum score 550 paper-based; 213 computer-based; 79 iBT), IELTS (minimum score 5) or Michigan English Language Assessment Battery (minimum score 77), Cambridge A, B, C. *Application deadline:* For fall admission, 7/15 priority date for domestic students, 6/1 for international students; for spring admission, 10/15 priority date for domestic students, 11/1 for international students. Application fee: $50. *Expenses:* Tuition: Full-time $19,572; part-time $816 per credit. Required fees: $628; $157 per semester. *Financial support:* In 2010–11, 10 students received support, including 10 fellowships (averaging $2,860 per year), 2 research assistantships (averaging $8,442 per year); career-related internships or fieldwork, scholarships/grants, and unspecified assistantships also available. Support available to part-time students. Financial award applicants required to submit FAFSA. *Faculty research:* Mathematics and computational finance, economics, Monte Carlo methods. *Unit head:* Dr. Joseph Coyle, Program Director, 732-263-5306, E-mail: jcoyle@monmouth.edu. *Application contact:* Kevin Roane, Director, Office of Graduate Admission, 732-571-3452, Fax: 732-263-5123, E-mail: gradadm@monmouth.edu.

New York University, Graduate School of Arts and Science, Courant Institute of Mathematical Sciences, Department of Mathematics, New York, NY 10012-1019. Offers atmosphere ocean science and mathematics (PhD); mathematics (MS, PhD); mathematics and statistics/operations research (MS); mathematics in finance (MS); scientific computing (MS). Part-time and evening/weekend programs available. *Faculty:* 46 full-time (0 women). *Students:* 199 full-time (35 women), 114 part-time (23 women); includes 3 Black or African American, non-Hispanic/Latino; 1 American Indian or Alaska Native, non-Hispanic/Latino; 41 Asian, non-Hispanic/Latino; 4 Hispanic/Latino, 164 international. Average age 28. 1,273 applicants, 29% accepted, 118 enrolled. In 2010, 66 master's, 16 doctorates awarded. *Degree requirements:* For master's, thesis optional; for doctorate, one foreign language, thesis/dissertation, oral and written exams. *Entrance requirements:* For master's and doctorate, GRE General Test, GRE Subject Test. Additional exam requirements/recommendations for international students: Required—TOEFL. *Application deadline:* For fall admission, 1/4 for domestic students; for spring admission, 11/1 for domestic students. Application fee: $90. *Financial support:* Fellowships with tuition reimbursements, research assistantships with tuition reimbursements, teaching assistantships with tuition reimbursements, Federal Work-Study, institutionally sponsored loans, scholarships/grants, health care benefits, and unspecified assistantships available. Financial award application deadline: 1/4; financial award applicants required to submit FAFSA. *Faculty research:* Partial differential equations, computational science, applied mathematics, geometry and topology, probability and stochastic processes. *Unit head:* Fedor Bogomolov, Director of Graduate Studies, 212-998-3238, Fax: 212-995-4121, E-mail: admissions@math.nyu.edu. *Application contact:* Tamar Arnon, Program Administrator, 212-998-3238, Fax: 212-995-4121, E-mail: admissions@math.nyu.edu.

North Carolina State University, Graduate School, College of Agriculture and Life Sciences and College of Engineering and College of Physical and Mathematical Sciences, Program in Financial Mathematics, Raleigh, NC 27695. Offers MFM. Part-time programs available. *Degree requirements:* For master's, thesis optional, project/internship. *Entrance requirements:* For master's, GRE General Test. Additional exam requirements/recommendations for international students: Required—TOEFL (minimum score 550 paper-based; 213 computer-based). Electronic applications accepted. *Faculty research:* Financial mathematics modeling and computation, futures, options and commodities markets, real options, credit risk, portfolio optimization.

Polytechnic Institute of NYU, Department of Finance and Risk Engineering, Brooklyn, NY 11201-2990. Offers financial engineering (MS, Advanced Certificate), including capital markets (MS), computational finance (MS), financial technology (MS); financial technology management (Advanced Certificate); organizational behavior (Advanced Certificate); risk management (Advanced Certificate); technology management (Advanced Certificate). Part-time and evening/weekend programs available. *Faculty:* 6 full-time (1 woman), 24 part-time/adjunct (5 women). *Students:* 126 full-time (45 women), 61 part-time (15 women); includes 4 Black or African American, non-Hispanic/Latino; 17 Asian, non-Hispanic/Latino; 1 Hispanic/Latino, 130 international. Average age 27. 528 applicants, 44% accepted, 67 enrolled. In 2010, 154 master's awarded. *Degree requirements:* For master's, comprehensive exam (for some programs), thesis (for some programs). *Entrance requirements:* For master's, GMAT, minimum B average in undergraduate course work. Additional exam requirements/recommendations for international students: Required—TOEFL (minimum score 550 paper-based; 213 computer-based; 80 iBT); Recommended—IELTS (minimum score 6.5). *Application deadline:* For fall admission, 7/31 priority date for domestic students, 4/30 priority date for international students; for spring admission, 12/31 priority date for domestic students, 11/30 priority date for international students. Applications are processed on a rolling basis. Application fee: $75. Electronic applications accepted. *Expenses:* Tuition: Full-time $21,492; part-time $1194 per credit. Required fees: $385 per semester. Tuition and fees vary according to course load. *Financial support:* Institutionally sponsored loans, scholarships/grants, and unspecified assistantships available. Support available to part-time students. Financial award applicants required to submit FAFSA. *Unit head:* Prof. Charles S. Tapiero, Academic Director, 718-260-3653, Fax: 718-260-3874, E-mail: ctapiero@poly.edu. *Application contact:* JeanCarlo Bonilla, Director, Graduate Enrollment Management, 718-260-3182, Fax: 718-260-3624.

Polytechnic Institute of NYU, Westchester Graduate Center, Graduate Programs, Department of Finance and Risk Engineering, Major in Financial Engineering, Hawthorne, NY 10532-1507. Offers capital markets (MS); computational finance (MS); financial engineering (AC); financial technology (MS); financial technology management (AC); information management (AC). *Students:* 1 (woman) part-time, all international. Average age 25. In 2010, 8 master's awarded. *Degree requirements:* For master's, comprehensive exam (for some programs), thesis (for some programs). *Entrance requirements:* Additional exam requirements/recommendations for international students: Required—TOEFL (minimum score 550 paper-based; 213 computer-based; 80 iBT); Recommended—IELTS (minimum score 6.5). *Application deadline:* For fall admission, 7/31 priority date for domestic students, 4/30 priority date for international students; for spring admission, 12/31 priority date for domestic students, 11/30 priority date for international students. Applications are processed on a rolling basis. Application fee: $75. Electronic applications accepted. *Expenses:* Tuition: Full-time $21,492; part-time $1194 per credit. Required fees: $385 per semester. Tuition and fees vary according to course load. *Financial support:* Institutionally sponsored loans, scholarships/grants, and unspecified assistantships available. Support available to part-time students. *Unit head:* Dr. Charles S. Tapiero, Department Head, 718-260-3653, E-mail: ctapiero@poly.edu. *Application contact:* JeanCarlo Bonilla, Director of Graduate Enrollment Management, 718-260-3182, Fax: 718-260-3624, E-mail: gradinfo@poly.edu.

Rice University, Graduate Programs, George R. Brown School of Engineering, Department of Statistics, Houston, TX 77251-1892. Offers bioinformatics (PhD); biostatistics (PhD); computational finance (PhD); general statistics (PhD); statistics (M Stat, MA); MBA/M Stat. Part-time programs available. *Degree requirements:* For master's, comprehensive exam; for doctorate, comprehensive exam, thesis/dissertation. *Entrance requirements:* For master's and doctorate, GRE General Test, minimum GPA of 3.0. Additional exam requirements/recommendations for international students: Required—TOEFL (minimum score 630 paper-based; 250 computer-based; 90 iBT). Electronic applications accepted. *Faculty research:* Statistical genetics, non parametric function estimation, computational statistics and visualization, stochastic processes.

Santa Clara University, School of Engineering, Program in Applied Mathematics, Santa Clara, CA 95053. Offers applied mathematics (MS); mathematical finance (MS). Part-time and evening/weekend programs available. *Students:* 8 full-time (2 women), 17 part-time (7 women); includes 6 minority (all Asian, non-Hispanic/Latino), 2 international. Average age 30. 8 applicants, 75% accepted, 3 enrolled. In 2010, 1 master's awarded. *Degree requirements:* For master's, thesis (for some programs). *Entrance requirements:* For master's, GRE (waiver may be available), transcript. Additional exam requirements/recommendations for international students: Required—TOEFL (minimum score 550 paper-based; 213 computer-based; 79 iBT). *Application deadline:* For fall admission, 8/12 for domestic students, 7/15 for international students; for winter admission, 10/28 for domestic students, 9/23 for international students; for spring admission, 2/25 for domestic students, 1/21 for international students. Applications are processed on a rolling basis. Application fee: $60. Electronic applications accepted. *Expenses:* Contact institution. *Financial support:* Research assistantships, teaching assistantships available. Financial award application deadline: 3/2; financial award applicants required to submit FAFSA. *Unit head:* Dr. Alex Zecevic, Associate Dean for Graduate Studies, 408-554-2394, E-mail: azecevic@scu.edu. *Application contact:* Stacey Tinker, Director of Admissions, Graduate Engineering, 408-554-4748, Fax: 408-554-4323, E-mail: stinker@scu.edu.

Stanford University, School of Humanities and Sciences, Department of Mathematics, Stanford, CA 94305-9991. Offers financial mathematics (MS); mathematics (MS, PhD). Terminal master's awarded for partial completion of doctoral program. *Degree requirements:* For doctorate, 2 foreign languages, thesis/dissertation, oral exam. *Entrance requirements:* For master's, GRE General Test; for doctorate, GRE General Test, GRE Subject Test. Additional exam requirements/recommendations for international students: Required—TOEFL. Electronic applications accepted. *Expenses:* Tuition: Full-time $38,700; part-time $860 per unit. One-time fee: $200 full-time.

Université de Montréal, Faculty of Arts and Sciences, Department of Economic Sciences, Montréal, QC H3C 3J7, Canada. Offers economics (M Sc, PhD); mathematical and computational finance (M Sc). *Degree requirements:* For master's, one foreign language, thesis; for doctorate, one foreign language, thesis/dissertation, general exam. Electronic applications accepted. *Faculty research:* Applied and economic theory, public choice, international trade, labor economics, industrial organization.

Université de Montréal, Faculty of Arts and Sciences, Department of Mathematics and Statistics, Montréal, QC H3C 3J7, Canada. Offers mathematical and computational finance (M Sc, DESS); mathematics (M Sc, PhD); statistics (M Sc, PhD). *Degree requirements:* For master's, thesis; for doctorate, thesis/dissertation, general exam. *Entrance requirements:* For master's and doctorate, proficiency in French. Electronic applications accepted. *Faculty research:* Pure and applied mathematics, actuarial mathematics.

University of Alberta, Faculty of Graduate Studies and Research, Department of Mathematical and Statistical Sciences, Edmonton, AB T6G 2E1, Canada. Offers applied mathematics (M Sc, PhD); biostatistics (M Sc); mathematical finance (M Sc, PhD); mathematical physics (M Sc, PhD); mathematics (M Sc, PhD); statistics (M Sc, PhD, Postgraduate Diploma). Part-time programs available. Terminal master's awarded for partial completion of doctoral program. *Degree requirements:* For master's, thesis (for some programs); for doctorate, comprehensive exam, thesis/dissertation. *Entrance requirements:* Additional exam requirements/recommendations for international students: Required—TOEFL (minimum score 580 paper-based; 237 computer-based). Electronic applications accepted. *Faculty research:* Classical and functional analysis, algebra, differential equations, geometry.

University of California, Santa Barbara, Graduate Division, College of Letters and Sciences, Division of Mathematics, Life, and Physical Sciences, Department of Statistics and Applied Probability, Santa Barbara, CA 93106-3110. Offers financial mathematics and statistics (PhD); quantitative methods in the social sciences (PhD); statistics (MA), including applied statistics, mathematical statistics; statistics and applied probability (PhD); MA/PhD. *Faculty:* 11 full-time (3 women). *Students:* 49 full-time (17 women); includes 30 Asian, non-Hispanic/Latino; 2 Hispanic/Latino. Average age 29. 195 applicants, 20% accepted, 14 enrolled. In 2010, 16 master's, 2 doctorates awarded. Terminal master's awarded for partial completion of doctoral program. *Degree requirements:* For master's, comprehensive exam, thesis (for some programs); for doctorate, comprehensive exam, thesis/dissertation. *Entrance requirements:* For master's and doctorate, GRE General Test. Additional exam requirements/recommendations for international students: Required—TOEFL (minimum score 550 paper-based; 80 iBT), IELTS (minimum score 7). *Application deadline:* For fall admission, 1/1 priority date for domestic and

Mathematical and Computational Finance

University of California, Santa Barbara (continued)
international students; for winter admission, 11/1 priority date for domestic and international students; for spring admission, 2/1 priority date for domestic and international students. Application fee: $70 ($90 for international students). Electronic applications accepted. *Financial support:* In 2010–11, 23 students received support, including 6 fellowships with full tuition reimbursements available (averaging $11,285 per year), 1 research assistantship with full and partial tuition reimbursement available (averaging $2,790 per year), 28 teaching assistantships with partial tuition reimbursements available (averaging $14,557 per year). Financial award application deadline: 1/1; financial award applicants required to submit FAFSA. *Faculty research:* Bayesian inference, financial mathematics, stochastic processes, environmental statistics, biostatistical modeling. Total annual research expenditures: $139,480. *Unit head:* Dr. Yuedong Wang, Chair, 805-893-4870, E-mail: yeudong@pstat.ucsb.edu. *Application contact:* Rickie R. Smith, Graduate Program Assistant, 805-893-2129, Fax: 805-893-2334, E-mail: smith@pstat.ucsb.edu.

University of Chicago, Division of the Physical Sciences, Department of Mathematics, Program in Financial Mathematics, Chicago, IL 60637. Offers MS. Part-time and evening/weekend programs available. *Faculty:* 1 full-time (0 women), 13 part-time/adjunct (1 woman). *Students:* 68 full-time (21 women), 30 part-time (0 women); includes 1 Black or African American, non-Hispanic/Latino; 12 Asian, non-Hispanic/Latino; 1 Hispanic/Latino. Average age 30. 492 applicants, 47% accepted, 99 enrolled. In 2010, 120 master's awarded. *Entrance requirements:* For master's, GRE General Test, GRE Math Subject Test. Additional exam requirements/recommendations for international students: Required—TOEFL (minimum score 600 paper-based; 250 computer-based). *Application deadline:* For fall admission, 1/7 priority date for domestic and international students. Application fee: $55. Electronic applications accepted. *Financial support:* Fellowships, research assistantships, teaching assistantships, institutionally sponsored loans available. Financial award applicants required to submit FAFSA. *Unit head:* William DeRonne, Executive Director, 773-702-1458, E-mail: bderonne@uchicago.edu. *Application contact:* Ashley Doss, Program Administrator, 773-834-0785, Fax: 773-834-4386, E-mail: adoss@uchicago.edu.

University of Connecticut, Graduate School, College of Liberal Arts and Sciences, Department of Mathematics, Field of Applied Financial Mathematics, Storrs, CT 06269. Offers MS. *Degree requirements:* For master's, comprehensive exam. *Entrance requirements:* Additional exam requirements/recommendations for international students: Required—TOEFL (minimum score 550 paper-based; 213 computer-based). Electronic applications accepted.

University of Dayton, Graduate School, College of Arts and Sciences, Department of Mathematics, Dayton, OH 45469-1300. Offers applied mathematics (MAS); financial mathematics (MFM); mathematics education (MME). Part-time and evening/weekend programs available. *Faculty:* 15 full-time (5 women). *Students:* 17 full-time (10 women), 8 part-time (1 woman); includes 2 minority (1 Black or African American, non-Hispanic/Latino; 1 Two or more races, non-Hispanic/Latino), 13 international. Average age 27. 42 applicants, 88% accepted, 11 enrolled. In 2010, 8 master's awarded. *Entrance requirements:* For master's, minimum undergraduate GPA of 2.8 (MAS), 3.0 (MFM, MME). Additional exam requirements/recommendations for international students: Required—TOEFL (minimum score 550 paper-based; 213 computer-based; 80 iBT). *Application deadline:* For fall admission, 3/1 priority date for domestic students, 7/1 priority date for international students; for winter admission, 7/1 priority date for international students; for spring admission, 1/1 priority date for international students. Application fee: $0 ($50 for international students). Electronic applications accepted. *Expenses:* Tuition: Full-time $7800; part-time $650 per credit hour. *Financial support:* In 2010–11, 6 teaching assistantships with full tuition reimbursements (averaging $13,400 per year) were awarded; institutionally sponsored loans, health care benefits, and unspecified assistantships also available. Financial award applicants required to submit FAFSA. *Faculty research:* Differential equations, integral equations, general topology, measure theory, graph theory, financial math, math education, numerical analysis. *Unit head:* Dr. Joe D. Mashburn, Chair, 937-229-2511, Fax: 937-229-2566, E-mail: joe.mashburn@notes.udayton.edu. *Application contact:* Alexander Popovski, Associate Director of Graduate and International Admissions, 937-229-2357, Fax: 937-229-4729, E-mail: alex.popovski@notes.udayton.edu.

University of Illinois at Chicago, Graduate College, College of Liberal Arts and Sciences, Department of Mathematics, Statistics, and Computer Science, Chicago, IL 60607-7128. Offers applied mathematics (MS, PhD); computational finance (MS, PhD); computer science (MS, PhD); mathematics (DA); mathematics and information sciences for industry (MS); probability and statistics (PhD); pure mathematics (MS, PhD); statistics (MS); teaching of mathematics (MST), including elementary, secondary. Part-time programs available. *Faculty:* 36 full-time (3 women). *Students:* 150 full-time (54 women), 31 part-time (18 women); includes 3 Black or African American, non-Hispanic/Latino; 1 Asian, non-Hispanic/Latino; 8 Hispanic/Latino, 62 international. Average age 26. 224 applicants, 56% accepted, 43 enrolled. In 2010, 34 master's, 17 doctorates awarded. *Degree requirements:* For master's, comprehensive exam; for doctorate, one foreign language, thesis/dissertation. *Entrance requirements:* For master's and doctorate, GRE General Test, minimum GPA of 3.0. Additional exam requirements/recommendations for international students: Required—TOEFL (minimum score 100 iBT). *Application deadline:* For fall admission, 1/1 for domestic and international students; for spring admission, 10/1 for domestic students, 7/15 for international students. Applications are processed on a rolling basis. Application fee: $60. Electronic applications accepted. *Financial support:* In 2010–11, 109 students received support, including 2 fellowships with full tuition reimbursements available (averaging $20,000 per year), 8 research assistantships with full tuition reimbursements available (averaging $17,000 per year), 87 teaching assistantships with full tuition reimbursements available (averaging $17,000 per year); Federal Work-Study, scholarships/grants, and tuition waivers (full) also available. Financial award application deadline: 1/1. *Unit head:* Lawrence Ein, Head, 312-996-3044, E-mail: ein@math.uic.edu. *Application contact:* Brooke Shipley, Director of Graduate Studies, 312-996-5119, E-mail: dgs@math.uic.edu.

The University of Manchester, School of Mathematics, Manchester, United Kingdom. Offers actuarial science (PhD); applied mathematics (M Phil, PhD); applied numerical computing (M Phil, PhD); financial mathematics (M Phil, PhD); mathematical logic (M Phil); probability (M Phil, PhD); pure mathematics (M Phil, PhD); statistics (M Phil, PhD).

The University of North Carolina at Charlotte, Graduate School, Belk College of Business, Program in Mathematical Finance, Charlotte, NC 28223-0001. Offers MS. Part-time and evening/weekend programs available. *Faculty:* 12 full-time (1 woman), 1 part-time/adjunct (0 women). *Students:* 29 full-time (6 women), 27 part-time (4 women); includes 9 minority (3 Black or African American, non-Hispanic/Latino; 6 Asian, non-Hispanic/Latino), 23 international. Average age 29. 94 applicants, 86% accepted, 23 enrolled. In 2010, 34 master's awarded. *Degree requirements:* For master's, thesis or alternative. *Entrance requirements:* For master's, GRE General Test or GMAT, minimum GPA of 2.75 overall. Additional exam requirements/recommendations for international students: Required—TOEFL (minimum score 557 paper-based; 220 computer-based; 83 iBT). *Application deadline:* For fall admission, 7/15 for domestic students, 5/1 for international students; for spring admission, 11/15 for domestic students, 10/1 for international students. Applications are processed on a rolling basis. Application fee: $55. Electronic applications accepted. *Expenses:* Tuition, state resident: full-time $3464. Tuition, nonresident: full-time $14,297. Required fees: $2094. Tuition and fees vary according to course load. *Financial support:* Career-related internships or fieldwork, Federal Work-Study, institutionally sponsored loans, scholarships/grants, and unspecified assistantships available. Support available to part-time students. Financial award application deadline: 4/1; financial award applicants required to submit FAFSA. *Unit head:* Dr. Judson Russell, Director, 704-687-7618, Fax: 704-687-4014, E-mail: belkgradprograms@uncc.edu. *Application contact:* Kathy B. Giddings, Director of Graduate Admissions, 704-687-5503, Fax: 704-687-3279, E-mail: gradadm@uncc.edu.

University of Southern California, Graduate School, Dana and David Dornsife College of Letters, Arts and Sciences, Department of Economics, Los Angeles, CA 90089. Offers economic development programming (MA, PhD); mathematical finance (MS); M Pl/MA; MA/JD. *Faculty:* 20 full-time (2 women), 9 part-time/adjunct (0 women). *Students:* 106 full-time (41 women), 6 part-time (0 women); includes 7 minority (5 Asian, non-Hispanic/Latino; 2 Two or more races, non-Hispanic/Latino), 89 international. 417 applicants, 19% accepted, 40 enrolled. In 2010, 34 master's, 9 doctorates awarded. Terminal master's awarded for partial completion of doctoral program. *Degree requirements:* For master's, comprehensive exam; for doctorate, comprehensive exam, thesis/dissertation. *Entrance requirements:* For master's and doctorate, GRE. Additional exam requirements/recommendations for international students: Required—TOEFL (minimum score 93 iBT). *Application deadline:* For fall admission, 12/1 priority date for domestic and international students. Application fee: $85. Electronic applications accepted. *Expenses:* Tuition: Full-time $31,240; part-time $1420 per unit. Required fees: $600. One-time fee: $35 full-time. Full-time tuition and fees vary according to degree level and program. *Financial support:* In 2010–11, 53 students received support, including 24 fellowships with full tuition reimbursements available (averaging $21,000 per year), 3 research assistantships with full tuition reimbursements available (averaging $21,000 per year), 27 teaching assistantships with full tuition reimbursements available (averaging $21,000 per year). Financial award application deadline: 12/1. *Faculty research:* Macro theory, development economics, econometrics. *Unit head:* Prof. Simon Wilkie, Chair, 213-740-8335, Fax: 213-740-8543, E-mail: swilkie@usc.edu. *Application contact:* Morgan Ponder, Assistant Director, 213-740-3507, Fax: 213-740-8543, E-mail: ponder@dornsife.usc.edu.

University of Southern California, Graduate School, Dana and David Dornsife College of Letters, Arts and Sciences, Department of Mathematics, Los Angeles, CA 90089. Offers applied mathematics (MA, MS, PhD); mathematical finance (MS); mathematics (MA, PhD); statistics (MS). Part-time programs available. *Faculty:* 48 full-time (6 women). *Students:* 103 full-time (33 women), 14 part-time (6 women); includes 11 minority (8 Asian, non-Hispanic/Latino; 1 Hispanic/Latino; 2 Two or more races, non-Hispanic/Latino), 85 international. 559 applicants, 20% accepted, 32 enrolled. In 2010, 37 master's, 7 doctorates awarded. Terminal master's awarded for partial completion of doctoral program. *Degree requirements:* For master's, comprehensive exam (for some programs), thesis (for some programs); for doctorate, one foreign language, comprehensive exam, thesis/dissertation. *Entrance requirements:* For master's, GRE General Test, GMAT; for doctorate, GRE—General and Subject in Mathematics. Additional exam requirements/recommendations for international students: Required—TOEFL (minimum score 100 iBT). *Application deadline:* For fall and spring admission, 12/1 for domestic and international students. Applications are processed on a rolling basis. Application fee: $85. Electronic applications accepted. *Expenses:* Tuition: Full-time $31,240; part-time $1420 per unit. Required fees: $600. One-time fee: $35 full-time. Full-time tuition and fees vary according to degree level and program. *Financial support:* In 2010–11, 68 students received support, including 5 fellowships with full tuition reimbursements available (averaging $19,250 per year), 3 research assistantships with full tuition reimbursements available (averaging $19,250 per year), 58 teaching assistantships with full tuition reimbursements available (averaging $19,250 per year). Financial award application deadline: 12/1. *Faculty research:* Algebra, algebraic geometry and number theory, analysis/partial differential equations, applied mathematics, financial mathematics, probability, combinatorics and statistics. Total annual research expenditures: $1.7 million. *Unit head:* Prof. Gary Rosen, Chair, 213-740-1717, Fax: 213-740-2424, E-mail: grosen@usc.edu. *Application contact:* Amy Yung, Department Coordinator, 213-740-8168, Fax: 213-740-2424, E-mail: amy@usc.edu.

University of Toronto, School of Graduate Studies, Physical Sciences Division, Program in Mathematical Finance, Toronto, ON M5S 1A1, Canada. Offers MMF.

Mathematics

Alabama State University, Department of Mathematics and Computer Science, Montgomery, AL 36101-0271. Offers mathematics (M Ed, MS, Ed S). Part-time programs available. *Degree requirements:* For Ed S, thesis. *Entrance requirements:* For master's, GRE, GRE Subject Test, graduate writing competence test; for Ed S, GRE General Test, MAT, graduate writing competency test. Additional exam requirements/recommendations for international students: Required—TOEFL (minimum score 500 paper-based; 173 computer-based). *Faculty research:* Discrete mathematics, symbolic dynamics, mathematical social sciences.

American University, College of Arts and Sciences, Department of Mathematics and Statistics, Washington, DC 22016-8050. Offers applied statistics (Certificate); mathematics (MA); statistics (MS). Part-time and evening/weekend programs available. *Faculty:* 25 full-time (7 women), 12 part-time/adjunct (0 women). *Students:* 9 full-time (2 women), 12 part-time (7 women); includes 2 minority (1 Black or African American, non-Hispanic/Latino; 1 Asian, non-Hispanic/Latino), 3 international. Average age 29. 38 applicants, 68% accepted, 7 enrolled. In 2010, 6 master's awarded. *Degree requirements:* For master's, comprehensive exam, thesis or alternative, tools of research in foreign language or computer language. *Entrance requirements:* For master's, GRE; for Certificate, bachelor's degree. Additional exam requirements/recommendations for international students: Required—TOEFL. *Application deadline:* For fall admission, 2/1 for domestic students; for spring admission, 10/1 for domestic students. Application fee: $80. *Financial support:* Fellowships, research assistantships, teaching assistantships, career-related internships or fieldwork, Federal Work-Study, institutionally sponsored loans, and unspecified assistantships available. Support available to part-time students. Financial award application deadline: 2/1. *Faculty research:* Logic, random processes, probability analysis, biostatistics, statistical computing. *Unit head:* Dr. Mary W. Gray, Chair, 202-885-3171, Fax: 202-885-3155, E-mail: mgray@american.edu. *Application contact:* Kathleen Clowery, Director, Graduate Admissions, 202-885-3621, Fax: 202-885-1505.

American University of Beirut, Graduate Programs, Faculty of Arts and Sciences, Beirut, Lebanon. Offers anthropology (MA); Arabic language and literature (MA); archaeology (MA); biology (MS); chemistry (MS); computational science (MS); computer science (MS); economics (MA); education (MA); English language (MA); English literature (MA); environmental policy planning (MSES); financial economics (MAFE); geology (MS); history (MA); mathematics (MA, MS); Middle Eastern studies (MA); philosophy (MA); physics (MS); political studies (MA); psychology (MA); public administration (MA); sociology (MA); statistics (MA, MS). Part-time

programs available. *Faculty:* 229 full-time (98 women), 136 part-time/adjunct (79 women). *Students:* 158 full-time (104 women), 263 part-time (171 women). Average age 25. 356 applicants, 59% accepted, 127 enrolled. In 2010, 57 master's awarded. *Degree requirements:* For master's, one foreign language, comprehensive exam, thesis (for some programs). *Entrance requirements:* For master's, GRE, letter of recommendation. Additional exam requirements/recommendations for international students: Required—TOEFL (minimum score 600 paper-based; 250 computer-based; 97 iBT), IELTS (minimum score 7). *Application deadline:* For fall admission, 4/30 for domestic and international students; for spring admission, 11/1 for domestic and international students. Application fee: $50. *Expenses:* Tuition: Full-time $12,294; part-time $683 per credit. Required fees: $499; $499 per credit. Tuition and fees vary according to course load and program. *Financial support:* In 2010–11, 33 students received support. Career-related internships or fieldwork, institutionally sponsored loans, scholarships/grants, health care benefits, and unspecified assistantships available. Financial award application deadline: 2/4; financial award applicants required to submit FAFSA. *Faculty research:* Modern and contemporary world theatre; mineralogy, petrology, and geochemistry; cell differentiation and transformation; combinatorial technologies; philosophy of action; continental philosophy; Phoenician epigraphy; nascent complex societies and urbanism; the economies of the Arab world; environmental economics; tectonophysics; host-parasite interactions; innate immunity; insect-plant interactions; history of the Ottoman archives; decentralization; transparency and corruption. Total annual research expenditures: $622,243. *Unit head:* Dr. Patrick McGreevy, Dean, 961-137-4374 Ext. 3800, Fax: 961-174-4461, E-mail: pm07@aub.edu.lb. *Application contact:* Dr. Salim Kanaan, Director, Admissions Office, 961-135-0000 Ext. 2594, Fax: 961-175-0775, E-mail: sk00@aub.edu.lb.

Andrews University, School of Graduate Studies, College of Arts and Sciences, Interdisciplinary Studies in Mathematics and Physical Science Program, Berrien Springs, MI 49104. Offers MS.

Appalachian State University, Cratis D. Williams Graduate School, Department of Mathematical Sciences, Boone, NC 28608. Offers mathematics (MA); mathematics education (MA). Part-time programs available. Postbaccalaureate distance learning degree programs offered (no on-campus study). *Faculty:* 22 full-time (9 women), 2 part-time/adjunct (1 woman). *Students:* 15 full-time (9 women), 5 part-time (4 women). 22 applicants, 91% accepted, 13 enrolled. In 2010, 11 master's awarded. *Degree requirements:* For master's, comprehensive exam, thesis optional. *Entrance requirements:* For master's, GRE General Test, 3 letters of recommendation. Additional exam requirements/recommendations for international students: Required—TOEFL (minimum score 570 paper-based; 230 computer-based; 79 iBT), IELTS (minimum score 6.5). *Application deadline:* For fall admission, 7/1 for domestic students, 2/1 for international students; for spring admission, 11/1 for domestic students, 7/1 for international students. Applications are processed on a rolling basis. Application fee: $55. Electronic applications accepted. *Expenses:* Tuition, state resident: full-time $3428; part-time $428 per unit. Tuition, nonresident: full-time $14,518; part-time $1814 per unit. Required fees: $2320; $344 per unit. Tuition and fees vary according to campus/location. *Financial support:* In 2010–11, 14 teaching assistantships (averaging $9,500 per year) were awarded; fellowships, research assistantships, career-related internships or fieldwork, Federal Work-Study, scholarships/grants, and unspecified assistantships also available. Financial award application deadline: 4/1; financial award applicants required to submit FAFSA. *Faculty research:* Graph theory, differential equations, logic, geometry, complex analysis, topology, algebra, mathematics education. Total annual research expenditures: $402,000. *Unit head:* Dr. Mark Ginn, Chair, 828-262-3050, Fax: 828-265-8617, E-mail: ginnmc@appstate.edu. *Application contact:* Dr. Trina Palmer, Graduate Director, 828-262-3050, E-mail: palmerk@appstate.edu.

Arizona State University, College of Liberal Arts and Sciences, Department of Mathematics and Statistics, Tempe, AZ 85287-1804. Offers applied mathematics (PhD); computational biosciences (PhD); mathematics (MA, MNS, PhD); mathematics education (PhD); statistics (PhD). Part-time programs available. *Faculty:* 94 full-time (32 women), 4 part-time/adjunct (1 woman). *Students:* 72 full-time (21 women), 23 part-time (10 women); includes 9 minority (2 Black or African American, non-Hispanic/Latino; 3 Asian, non-Hispanic/Latino; 4 Hispanic/Latino), 24 international. Average age 30. 168 applicants, 48% accepted, 26 enrolled. In 2010, 17 master's, 19 doctorates awarded. Terminal master's awarded for partial completion of doctoral program. *Median time to degree:* Of those who began their doctoral program in fall 2002, 69% received their degree in 8 years or less. *Degree requirements:* For master's, thesis or alternative, interactive Program of Study (iPOS) submitted before completing 50 percent of required credit hours; for doctorate, comprehensive exam, thesis/dissertation, interactive Program of Study (iPOS) submitted before completing 50 percent of required credit hours. *Entrance requirements:* For master's and doctorate, GRE General Test, minimum GPA of 3.0 or equivalent in last 2 years of work leading to bachelor's degree. Additional exam requirements/recommendations for international students: Required—TOEFL, IELTS, or Pearson Test of English. *Application deadline:* For fall admission, 1/1 for domestic and international students. Applications are processed on a rolling basis. Application fee: $70 ($90 for international students). Electronic applications accepted. *Expenses:* Contact institution. *Financial support:* In 2010–11, 12 research assistantships with full and partial tuition reimbursements (averaging $18,559 per year), 55 teaching assistantships with full and partial tuition reimbursements (averaging $17,743 per year) were awarded; fellowships with full tuition reimbursements, career-related internships or fieldwork, Federal Work-Study, institutionally sponsored loans, scholarships/grants, and tuition waivers (partial) also available. Financial award application deadline: 3/1; financial award applicants required to submit FAFSA. Total annual research expenditures: $4.5 million. *Unit head:* Dr. Wayne Raskind, Director, 480-965-3951, E-mail: raskind@asu.edu. *Application contact:* Graduate Admissions, 480-965-6113.

Arkansas State University, Graduate School, College of Sciences and Mathematics, Department of Mathematics and Statistics, Jonesboro, State University, AR 72467. Offers mathematics (MS); mathematics education (MSE). Part-time programs available. *Faculty:* 7 full-time (2 women). *Students:* 11 full-time (8 women), 8 part-time (5 women); includes 1 minority (Hispanic/Latino), 3 international. Average age 30. 14 applicants, 64% accepted, 9 enrolled. In 2010, 2 master's awarded. *Degree requirements:* For master's, comprehensive exam, thesis or alternative. *Entrance requirements:* For master's, GRE General Test or MAT, appropriate bachelor's degree, official transcripts, immunization records, valid teaching certificate (MSE). Additional exam requirements/recommendations for international students: Required—TOEFL (minimum score 550 paper-based; 213 computer-based; 79 iBT), IELTS (minimum score 6), PTE: Pearson Test of English Academic (56). *Application deadline:* For fall admission, 7/1 for domestic and international students; for spring admission, 11/15 for domestic students, 11/14 for international students. Applications are processed on a rolling basis. Application fee: $30 ($40 for international students). Electronic applications accepted. *Expenses:* Tuition, state resident: full-time $3888; part-time $216 per credit hour. Tuition, nonresident: full-time $9918; part-time $551 per credit hour. International tuition: $8376 full-time. Required fees: $932; $49 per credit hour. $25 per term. One-time fee: $30. Tuition and fees vary according to course load and program. *Financial support:* In 2010–11, 9 students received support; teaching assistantships, career-related internships or fieldwork, scholarships/grants, and unspecified assistantships available. Financial award application deadline: 7/1; financial award applicants required to submit FAFSA. *Unit head:* Dr. Debra Ingram, Chair, 870-972-3090, Fax: 870-972-3950, E-mail: dingram@astate.edu. *Application contact:* Dr. Andrew Sustich, Dean of the Graduate School, 870-972-3029, Fax: 870-972-3857, E-mail: sustich@astate.edu.

Auburn University, Graduate School, College of Sciences and Mathematics, Department of Mathematics and Statistics, Auburn University, AL 36849. Offers applied mathematics (MAM, MS); mathematics (MS, PhD); probability and statistics (M Prob S); statistics (MS). *Faculty:* 54 full-time (8 women), 4 part-time/adjunct (1 woman). *Students:* 50 full-time (8 women), 44 part-time (17 women); includes 2 Black or African American, non-Hispanic/Latino; 1 Asian, non-Hispanic/Latino; 1 Hispanic/Latino, 46 international. Average age 28. 212 applicants, 52% accepted, 20 enrolled. In 2010, 16 master's, 10 doctorates awarded. *Degree requirements:* For doctorate, thesis/dissertation. *Entrance requirements:* For master's, GRE General Test, undergraduate mathematics background; for doctorate, GRE General Test, GRE Subject Test. *Application deadline:* For fall admission, 7/7 priority date for domestic students; for spring admission, 11/24 for domestic students. Applications are processed on a rolling basis. Application fee: $50 ($60 for international students). Electronic applications accepted. *Expenses:* Tuition, state resident: full-time $7002. Tuition, nonresident: full-time $21,898. International tuition: $22,116 full-time. Required fees: $892. Tuition and fees vary according to course load and program. *Financial support:* Fellowships, teaching assistantships available. Financial award applicants required to submit FAFSA. *Faculty research:* Pure and applied mathematics. *Unit head:* Dr. Michel Smith, Chair, 334-844-4290, Fax: 334-844-6655. *Application contact:* Dr. George Flowers, Dean of the Graduate School, 334-844-2125.

Aurora University, College of Arts and Sciences, Aurora, IL 60506-4892. Offers elementary math and science (MATL); life science (MATL); mathematics (MATL, MS). Part-time and evening/weekend programs available. *Faculty:* 6 full-time (3 women), 4 part-time/adjunct (2 women). *Students:* 3 full-time (0 women), 118 part-time (77 women); includes 1 Black or African American, non-Hispanic/Latino; 2 Asian, non-Hispanic/Latino; 9 Hispanic/Latino. Average age 35. 18 applicants, 94% accepted, 12 enrolled. In 2010, 10 master's awarded. *Entrance requirements:* Additional exam requirements/recommendations for international students: Required—TOEFL (minimum score 550 paper-based; 213 computer-based). *Application deadline:* For fall admission, 7/15 priority date for domestic students, 3/1 for international students; for spring admission, 12/15 for domestic students, 7/1 for international students. Applications are processed on a rolling basis. Application fee: $25. Electronic applications accepted. *Expenses:* Contact institution. *Financial support:* Teaching assistantships, Federal Work-Study, scholarships/grants, and unspecified assistantships available. Support available to part-time students. Financial award application deadline: 4/15; financial award applicants required to submit FAFSA. *Unit head:* Dr. Saib Othman, Dean, 630-844-4229, E-mail: sothman@aurora.edu. *Application contact:* Marcia Koenen, Director of Adult and Graduate Studies, 800-742-5281, Fax: 630-844-6854, E-mail: auadmission@aurora.edu.

Ball State University, Graduate School, College of Sciences and Humanities, Department of Mathematical Sciences, Program in Mathematics, Muncie, IN 47306-1099. Offers mathematics (MA, MS); mathematics education (MA). *Students:* 6 full-time (2 women), 17 part-time (13 women), 5 international. Average age 39. 19 applicants, 74% accepted, 5 enrolled. In 2010, 3 master's awarded. Application fee: $50. *Expenses:* Tuition, state resident: full-time $6160; part-time $299 per credit hour. Tuition, nonresident: full-time $16,020; part-time $783 per credit hour. Required fees: $2278; $95 per credit hour. *Financial support:* In 2010–11, 7 teaching assistantships with tuition reimbursements (averaging $11,261 per year) were awarded. Financial award application deadline: 3/1. *Unit head:* Dr. Sheryl Stump, Director, 765-285-8662, Fax: 765-285-1721. *Application contact:* Dr. Hanspeter Fischer, Director, 765-285-8640, Fax: 765-285-1721, E-mail: mali@bsu.edu.

Baylor University, Graduate School, College of Arts and Sciences, Department of Mathematics, Waco, TX 76798. Offers MS, PhD. *Students:* 24 full-time (6 women); includes 2 minority (1 Asian, non-Hispanic/Latino; 1 Hispanic/Latino), 5 international. In 2010, 2 master's, 2 doctorates awarded. *Degree requirements:* For master's, final oral exam. *Entrance requirements:* For master's, GRE General Test. *Application deadline:* For fall admission, 8/1 for domestic students. Applications are processed on a rolling basis. Application fee: $25. *Financial support:* Teaching assistantships, career-related internships or fieldwork, Federal Work-Study, and institutionally sponsored loans available. Support available to part-time students. Financial award application deadline: 5/1. *Faculty research:* Algebra, statistics, probability, applied mathematics, numerical analysis. *Unit head:* Dr. Ronald Stanke, Graduate Program Director, 254-710-6577, Fax: 254-710-3569, E-mail: ronald_stanke@baylor.edu. *Application contact:* Rita Massey, Administrative Assistant, 254-710-3146, Fax: 254-710-3870, E-mail: rita_massey@baylor.edu.

Bemidji State University, School of Graduate Studies, Bemidji, MN 56601-2699. Offers biology (MS); counseling psychology (MS); education (M Ed, MS); English (MA, MS); environmental studies (MS); mathematics (MS); mathematics (elementary and middle level education) (MS); special education (M Sp Ed, MS). Part-time programs available. Postbaccalaureate distance learning degree programs offered (no on-campus study). *Faculty:* 142 full-time (61 women), 37 part-time/adjunct (22 women). *Students:* 82 full-time (51 women), 350 part-time (210 women); includes 21 minority (6 Black or African American, non-Hispanic/Latino; 3 American Indian or Alaska Native, non-Hispanic/Latino; 6 Asian, non-Hispanic/Latino; 6 Hispanic/Latino), 8 international. Average age 35. 491 applicants, 93% accepted, 307 enrolled. In 2010, 97 master's awarded. *Degree requirements:* For master's, comprehensive exam, thesis (for some programs). *Entrance requirements:* For master's, GRE, letters of recommendation, letters of interest. Additional exam requirements/recommendations for international students: Required—TOEFL (minimum score 550 paper-based; 213 computer-based; 80 iBT). *Application deadline:* Applications are processed on a rolling basis. Application fee: $20. Electronic applications accepted. *Expenses:* Tuition, state resident: full-time $6605; part-time $330 per credit. Tuition, nonresident: full-time $6605; part-time $330 per credit. Required fees: $107.97 per credit. *Financial support:* In 2010–11, 110 students received support, including 40 research assistantships with partial tuition reimbursements available (averaging $7,196 per year), 40 teaching assistantships with partial tuition reimbursements available (averaging $7,196 per year); career-related internships or fieldwork, Federal Work-Study, scholarships/grants, health care benefits, and unspecified assistantships also available. Support available to part-time students. Financial award application deadline: 4/15; financial award applicants required to submit FAFSA. *Unit head:* Dr. Patricia Rogers, Dean, 218-755-2027, Fax: 218-755-2258, E-mail: progers@bemidjistate.edu. *Application contact:* Joan Miller, Senior Office and Administrative Specialist, 218-755-2027, Fax: 218-755-2258, E-mail: jmiller@bemidjistate.edu.

Boston College, Graduate School of Arts and Sciences, Department of Mathematics, Chestnut Hill, MA 02467-3800. Offers PhD, MBA/MA. Part-time programs available. *Entrance requirements:* Additional exam requirements/recommendations for international students: Required—TOEFL (minimum score 600 paper-based; 250 computer-based; 100 iBT). Electronic applications accepted. *Faculty research:* Abstract algebra and number theory, topology, probability and statistics, computer science, analysis.

Boston University, Graduate School of Arts and Sciences, Department of Mathematics and Statistics, Boston, MA 02215. Offers mathematics (MA, PhD). *Students:* 48 full-time (13 women), 2 part-time (0 women); includes 3 minority (1 Black or African American, non-Hispanic/Latino; 1 Asian, non-Hispanic/Latino; 1 Hispanic/Latino), 24 international. Average age 27. 198 applicants, 17% accepted, 12 enrolled. In 2010, 71 master's, 8 doctorates awarded. Terminal master's awarded for partial completion of doctoral program. *Degree requirements:* For master's, one foreign language, comprehensive exam; for doctorate, one foreign language, comprehensive exam, thesis/dissertation. *Entrance requirements:* For master's and doctorate, GRE General Test, GRE Subject Test, 3 letters of recommendation. Additional exam requirements/recommendations for international students: Required—TOEFL (minimum score 600 paper-based; 250 computer-based). *Application deadline:* For fall admission, 1/15 for domestic and international students; for spring admission, 10/15 for domestic and international students. Application fee: $70. Electronic applications accepted. *Expenses:* Tuition: Full-time $39,314; part-time $1228 per credit. Required fees: $40 per semester. *Financial support:* In 2010–11, 4 fellowships with full tuition reimbursements (averaging $19,300 per year), 10 research assistantships with full tuition reimbursements (averaging $18,800 per year), 30 teaching assistantships with full tuition reimbursements (averaging $18,800 per year) were awarded; Federal Work-Study and scholarships/grants also available. Support available to part-time students. Financial award application deadline: 1/15; financial award applicants required to submit FAFSA. *Unit head:* Ralph D'Agostino, Chairman, 617-353-2767, Fax: 617-353-8100, E-mail: ralph@bu.edu.

Peterson's Graduate Programs in the Physical Sciences, Mathematics, Agricultural Sciences, the Environment & Natural Resources 2012

www.facebook.com/petersonspublishing **259**

Mathematics

Boston University (continued)
Application contact: Kathleen Heavey, Staff Coordinator, 617-353-2560, Fax: 617-353-8100, E-mail: kheavey@bu.edu.

Bowling Green State University, Graduate College, College of Arts and Sciences, Department of Mathematics and Statistics, Bowling Green, OH 43403. Offers applied statistics (MS); mathematics (MA, MAT, PhD); statistics (PhD). Part-time programs available. *Degree requirements:* For master's, thesis or alternative; for doctorate, comprehensive exam, thesis/dissertation. *Entrance requirements:* For master's and doctorate, GRE General Test. Additional exam requirements/recommendations for international students: Required—TOEFL. Electronic applications accepted. *Faculty research:* Statistics and probability, algebra, analysis.

Brandeis University, Graduate School of Arts and Sciences, Department of Mathematics, Waltham, MA 02454-9110. Offers MA, PhD, Postbaccalaureate Certificate. Part-time programs available. *Faculty:* 14 full-time (2 women). *Students:* 38 full-time (10 women), 1 part-time (0 women); includes 1 Hispanic/Latino, 17 international. 116 applicants, 19% accepted, 11 enrolled. In 2010, 1 master's, 3 doctorates awarded. *Degree requirements:* For doctorate, 2 foreign languages, thesis/dissertation. *Entrance requirements:* For master's, GRE General Test and GRE Subject Test (recommended), resume, letters of recommendation; for doctorate, GRE General Test, GRE Subject Test, resume, letters of recommendation. Additional exam requirements/recommendations for international students: Required—TOEFL (minimum score 600 paper-based; 250 computer-based; 100 iBT); Recommended—IELTS (minimum score 7). *Application deadline:* For fall admission, 1/15 priority date for domestic students. Applications are processed on a rolling basis. Application fee: $75. Electronic applications accepted. *Financial support:* In 2010–11, 25 fellowships with full tuition reimbursements (averaging $20,000 per year), 2 teaching assistantships with partial tuition reimbursements (averaging $3,200 per year) were awarded; scholarships/grants, health care benefits, and tuition waivers (full) also available. Financial award application deadline: 4/15; financial award applicants required to submit FAFSA. *Faculty research:* Algebra, analysis, number theory, combinatorics, topology. *Unit head:* Prof. Dmitry Kleinbock, Director of Graduate Studies, 781-736-3059, Fax: 781-736-3085, E-mail: kleinboc@brandeis.edu. *Application contact:* Janet Ledda, Department Administrator, 781-736-3051, Fax: 781-736-3085, E-mail: ledda@brandeis.edu.

Brigham Young University, Graduate Studies, College of Physical and Mathematical Sciences, Department of Mathematics, Provo, UT 84602-1001. Offers MS, PhD. Part-time programs available. *Faculty:* 32 full-time (2 women). *Students:* 12 full-time (2 women), 28 part-time (6 women); includes 5 minority (4 Asian, non-Hispanic/Latino; 1 Hispanic/Latino). Average age 23. 18 applicants, 83% accepted, 14 enrolled. In 2010, 6 master's, 4 doctorates awarded. Terminal master's awarded for partial completion of doctoral program. *Degree requirements:* For master's, comprehensive exam, thesis (for some programs), project; written exams; for doctorate, one foreign language, comprehensive exam, thesis/dissertation, qualifying exams. *Entrance requirements:* For master's, GRE General Test, GRE Subject Test (math), minimum GPA of 3.0 in last 60 hours, bachelor's degree in mathematics; for doctorate, GRE General Test, GRE Subject Test (math), master's degree in mathematics or related field. Additional exam requirements/recommendations for international students: Required—TOEFL (minimum score 600 paper-based; 240 computer-based; 85 iBT). *Application deadline:* For fall admission, 3/1 priority date for domestic and international students; for winter admission, 9/15 for domestic students, 3/1 priority date for international students; for spring admission, 2/15 for domestic and international students. Applications are processed on a rolling basis. Application fee: $50. Electronic applications accepted. *Expenses:* Tuition: Full-time $5580; part-time $310 per credit hour. Tuition and fees vary according to program and student's religious affiliation. *Financial support:* In 2010–11, 30 students received support, including 20 research assistantships (averaging $12,000 per year), 30 teaching assistantships with full tuition reimbursements available (averaging $17,000 per year); institutionally sponsored loans also available. Support available to part-time students. Financial award application deadline: 3/1. *Faculty research:* Algebraic geometry/number theory, applied math/nonlinear PDEs, combinatorics/matrix theory, geometric group theory/topology. Total annual research expenditures: $781,845. *Unit head:* Dr. Tyler J. Jarvis, Chairperson, 801-422-5925, Fax: 801-422-0504, E-mail: jarvis@math.byu.edu. *Application contact:* Lonette Stoddard, Graduate Secretary, 801-422-2062, Fax: 801-422-0504, E-mail: gradschool@math.byu.edu.

Brock University, Faculty of Graduate Studies, Faculty of Mathematics and Science, Program in Mathematics and Statistics, St. Catharines, ON L2S 3A1, Canada. Offers M Sc. Part-time programs available. *Degree requirements:* For master's, thesis or project. *Entrance requirements:* For master's, honors degree. Additional exam requirements/recommendations for international students: Required—TOEFL (minimum score 550 paper-based; 213 computer-based; 80 iBT), IELTS (minimum score 6.5), TWE (minimum score 4). Electronic applications accepted.

Brooklyn College of the City University of New York, Division of Graduate Studies, Department of Mathematics, Brooklyn, NY 11210-2889. Offers mathematics (MA, PhD). Part-time and evening/weekend programs available. *Degree requirements:* For master's, comprehensive exam (mathematics). *Entrance requirements:* For master's, minimum GPA of 3.0, 2 letters of recommendation. Additional exam requirements/recommendations for international students: Required—TOEFL (minimum score 500 paper-based; 173 computer-based; 61 iBT). *Application deadline:* For fall admission, 3/1 priority date for domestic students, 2/1 priority date for international students; for spring admission, 11/1 priority date for domestic students, 10/1 priority date for international students. Applications are processed on a rolling basis. Application fee: $125. Electronic applications accepted. *Expenses:* Tuition, state resident: full-time $7360; part-time $310 per credit hour. Tuition, nonresident: full-time $13,800; part-time $575 per credit hour. Required fees: $190 per semester. *Financial support:* Federal Work-Study, institutionally sponsored loans, and scholarships/grants available. Support available to part-time students. Financial award application deadline: 5/1; financial award applicants required to submit FAFSA. *Faculty research:* Differential geometry, gauge theory, complex analysis, orthogonal functions. *Unit head:* Dr. Jun Hu, Chairperson, 718-951-5246, E-mail: junhu@brooklyn.cuny.edu. *Application contact:* Hernan Sierra, Graduate Admissions Coordinator, 718-951-4536, Fax: 718-951-4506, E-mail: grads@brooklyn.cuny.edu.

Brown University, Graduate School, Department of Mathematics, Providence, RI 02912. Offers M Sc, MA, PhD. *Faculty:* 26 full-time (5 women). *Students:* 46 full-time (10 women); includes 2 minority (both Asian, non-Hispanic/Latino), 27 international. Average age 25. 251 applicants, 13% accepted, 9 enrolled. In 2010, 7 master's, 3 doctorates awarded. *Degree requirements:* For doctorate, one foreign language, thesis/dissertation. *Entrance requirements:* For doctorate, GRE. Additional exam requirements/recommendations for international students: Required—TOEFL (minimum paper-based score 590, iBT 100) or IELTS (7.5). *Application deadline:* For fall admission, 1/10 priority date for domestic and international students. Application fee: $75. Electronic applications accepted. *Financial support:* In 2010–11, 46 students received support, including 20 fellowships with full tuition reimbursements available (averaging $19,500 per year), 7 research assistantships with full tuition reimbursements available (averaging $19,500 per year), 19 teaching assistantships with full tuition reimbursements available (averaging $19,500 per year); Federal Work-Study, institutionally sponsored loans, and tuition waivers (full and partial) also available. Financial award application deadline: 1/10; financial award applicants required to submit FAFSA. *Faculty research:* Algebraic geometry, number theory, functional analysis, geometry, topology, theoretical PDE. Total annual research expenditures: $1.1 million. *Unit head:* Prof. Jeffrey Hoffstein, Chair, 401-863-3319, Fax: 401-863-9471, E-mail: jhoff@math.brown.edu. *Application contact:* Prof. Dan Abramovich, Director of Graduate Studies, 401-863-7968, Fax: 401-863-9471, E-mail: abrmovic@math.brown.edu.

Bryn Mawr College, Graduate School of Arts and Sciences, Department of Mathematics, Bryn Mawr, PA 19010-2899. Offers MA, PhD. Part-time programs available. *Faculty:* 6. *Students:* 3 full-time (0 women), 1 (woman) part-time. Average age 25. 10 applicants, 30% accepted, 2 enrolled. In 2010, 3 doctorates awarded. *Degree requirements:* For master's, one foreign language, thesis; for doctorate, 2 foreign languages, comprehensive exam, thesis/dissertation. *Entrance requirements:* For master's and doctorate, GRE General Test. Additional exam requirements/recommendations for international students: Required—TOEFL (minimum score 600 paper-based; 200 computer-based). *Application deadline:* For fall admission, 1/3 for domestic and international students. Application fee: $50. *Financial support:* In 2010–11, 1 research assistantship with full tuition reimbursement (averaging $15,000 per year), 4 teaching assistantships with partial tuition reimbursements (averaging $14,000 per year) were awarded; Federal Work-Study, scholarships/grants, tuition waivers (full and partial), unspecified assistantships, and tuition awards also available. Support available to part-time students. Financial award application deadline: 1/3. *Unit head:* Dr. Leslie C Cheng, Chair, 610-526-5349, E-mail: lcheng@brynmawr.edu. *Application contact:* Teri R. Lobo, Administrative Assistant to the Graduate School of Arts and Sciences Dean, 610-526-5074, Fax: 610-526-5076, E-mail: lrmiller@brynmawr.edu.

See Display on next page and Close-Up on page 303.

Bucknell University, Graduate Studies, College of Arts and Sciences, Department of Mathematics, Lewisburg, PA 17837. Offers MA, MS. Part-time programs available. *Entrance requirements:* For master's, GRE General Test, GRE Subject Test, minimum GPA of 2.8. Additional exam requirements/recommendations for international students: Required—TOEFL. *Expenses:* Tuition: Full-time $36,992; part-time $4624 per course.

California Institute of Technology, Division of Physics, Mathematics and Astronomy, Department of Mathematics, Pasadena, CA 91125-0001. Offers PhD. *Degree requirements:* For doctorate, one foreign language, thesis/dissertation, candidacy and final exams. *Entrance requirements:* For doctorate, GRE General Test, GRE Subject Test. Additional exam requirements/recommendations for international students: Required—TOEFL. *Faculty research:* Number theory, combinatorics, differential geometry, dynamical systems, finite groups.

California Polytechnic State University, San Luis Obispo, College of Science and Mathematics, Department of Mathematics, San Luis Obispo, CA 93407. Offers MS. Part-time programs available. *Faculty:* 1 full-time (0 women). *Students:* 9 full-time (4 women), 10 part-time (4 women); includes 4 minority (1 Asian, non-Hispanic/Latino; 3 Hispanic/Latino). Average age 24. 31 applicants, 35% accepted, 7 enrolled. In 2010, 5 master's awarded. *Degree requirements:* For master's, comprehensive exam, qualifying exams. *Entrance requirements:* For master's, minimum GPA of 2.5 in last 90 quarter units of course work. Additional exam requirements/recommendations for international students: Required—TOEFL (minimum score 550 paper-based; 213 computer-based) or IELTS (minimum score 6). *Application deadline:* For fall admission, 7/1 for domestic students, 11/30 for international students; for winter admission, 11/1 for domestic students, 6/30 for international students; for spring admission, 2/1 for domestic students. Applications are processed on a rolling basis. Application fee: $55. *Expenses:* Tuition, state resident: full-time $5386; part-time $3124 per year. Tuition, nonresident: full-time $11,160; part-time $248 per unit. Required fees: $2250; $614 per term. One-time fee: $2250 full-time; $1842 part-time. *Financial support:* Fellowships, teaching assistantships, career-related internships or fieldwork, Federal Work-Study, and scholarships/grants available. Support available to part-time students. Financial award application deadline: 3/2; financial award applicants required to submit FAFSA. *Faculty research:* Combinatorics, dynamical systems, ordinary and partial differential equations, operator theory, topology. *Unit head:* Dr. Dylan Retsek, Graduate Coordinator, 805-756-2072, Fax: 805-756-6537, E-mail: dretsek@calpoly.edu. *Application contact:* Dr. Dylan Retsek, Graduate Coordinator, 805-756-2072, Fax: 805-756-6537, E-mail: dretsek@calpoly.edu.

California State Polytechnic University, Pomona, Academic Affairs, College of Science, Program in Mathematics, Pomona, CA 91768-2557. Offers applied mathematics (MS); pure mathematics (MS). Part-time programs available. *Students:* 16 full-time (7 women), 38 part-time (21 women); includes 22 minority (2 Black or African American, non-Hispanic/Latino; 13 Asian, non-Hispanic/Latino; 7 Hispanic/Latino), 4 international. Average age 32. 76 applicants, 51% accepted, 11 enrolled. In 2010, 16 master's awarded. *Degree requirements:* For master's, thesis or alternative. *Entrance requirements:* For master's, GRE General Test. *Application deadline:* For fall admission, 5/1 priority date for domestic students; for winter admission, 10/15 priority date for domestic students; for spring admission, 1/20 priority date for domestic students. Applications are processed on a rolling basis. Application fee: $55. Electronic applications accepted. *Expenses:* Tuition, state resident: full-time $5386; part-time $2850 per year. Tuition, nonresident: full-time $12,082; part-time $248 per credit. Required fees: $577; $248 per credit. $577 per year. Tuition and fees vary according to course load and program. *Financial support:* Career-related internships or fieldwork, Federal Work-Study, and institutionally sponsored loans available. Support available to part-time students. Financial award application deadline: 3/2; financial award applicants required to submit FAFSA. *Unit head:* Dr. Amber Rosin, Graduate Coordinator, 909-869-2426, Fax: 909-869-4904, E-mail: arrosin@csupomona.edu. *Application contact:* Scott J. Duncan, Director, Admissions, 909-869-3258, Fax: 909-869-4529, E-mail: sjduncan@csupomona.edu.

California State University Channel Islands, Extended Education, Program in Mathematics, Camarillo, CA 93012. Offers MS. Part-time and evening/weekend programs available. *Degree requirements:* For master's, thesis. *Entrance requirements:* For master's, BA in math. Additional exam requirements/recommendations for international students: Required—TOEFL (minimum score 550 paper-based).

California State University, East Bay, Office of Academic Programs and Graduate Studies, College of Science, Department of Mathematics and Computer Science, Mathematics Program, Hayward, CA 94542-3000. Offers applied math (MS); mathematics (MS); mathematics teaching (MS). Part-time and evening/weekend programs available. *Faculty:* 6 full-time (4 women). *Students:* 19 full-time (7 women), 60 part-time (27 women); includes 28 minority (3 Black or African American, non-Hispanic/Latino; 1 American Indian or Alaska Native, non-Hispanic/Latino; 19 Asian, non-Hispanic/Latino; 2 Hispanic/Latino; 1 Native Hawaiian or other Pacific Islander, non-Hispanic/Latino; 2 Two or more races, non-Hispanic/Latino), 3 international. Average age 36. 115 applicants, 22% accepted, 14 enrolled. In 2010, 16 master's awarded. *Degree requirements:* For master's, comprehensive exam or thesis. *Entrance requirements:* For master's, minimum GPA of 3.0 in field. Additional exam requirements/recommendations for international students: Required—TOEFL (minimum score 550 paper-based; 213 computer-based). *Application deadline:* For fall admission, 6/30 for domestic and international students. Application fee: $55. Electronic applications accepted. *Financial support:* Fellowships, teaching assistantships, Federal Work-Study, institutionally sponsored loans, and scholarships/grants available. Support available to part-time students. Financial award application deadline: 3/1; financial award applicants required to submit FAFSA. *Unit head:* Prof. Edna Reiter, Chair, 510-885-3414, Fax: 510-885-4169, E-mail: edna.reiter@csueastbay.edu. *Application contact:* Dr. Donna Wiley, Interim Associate Director, 510-885-2928, Fax: 510-885-4777, E-mail: donna.wiley@csueastbay.edu.

California State University, Fresno, Division of Graduate Studies, College of Science and Mathematics, Department of Mathematics, Fresno, CA 93740-8027. Offers mathematics (MA); teaching (MA). Part-time programs available. *Degree requirements:* For master's, thesis or alternative. *Entrance requirements:* For master's, GRE General Test. Additional exam requirements/recommendations for international students: Required—TOEFL. Electronic applications accepted. *Faculty research:* Diagnostic testing project.

California State University, Fullerton, Graduate Studies, College of Natural Science and Mathematics, Department of Mathematics, Fullerton, CA 92834-9480. Offers applied mathematics (MA); mathematics (MA); mathematics for secondary school teachers (MA).

260 www.facebook.com/petersonspublishing

Peterson's Graduate Programs in the Physical Sciences, Mathematics, Agricultural Sciences, the Environment & Natural Resources 2012

BRYN MAWR
COLLEGE

Graduate Program in Mathematics

Why Bryn Mawr Mathematics?

Supportive environment

Excellent research opportunities

Diverse and progressive teaching experiences

A liberal-arts-college setting near the City of Philadelphia

Discover for yourself what Bryn Mawr has to offer!

plan your visit at:

www.brynmawr.edu/math/graduate

Part-time programs available. *Students:* 17 full-time (4 women), 64 part-time (32 women); includes 1 Black or African American, non-Hispanic/Latino; 24 Asian, non-Hispanic/Latino; 9 Hispanic/Latino; 2 Two or more races, non-Hispanic/Latino, 1 international. Average age 30. 104 applicants, 62% accepted, 38 enrolled. In 2010, 28 master's awarded. *Degree requirements:* For master's, comprehensive exam or project. *Entrance requirements:* For master's, minimum GPA of 2.5 in last 60 units of course work, major in mathematics or related field. Application fee: $55. *Financial support:* Research assistantships, teaching assistantships, career-related internships or fieldwork, Federal Work-Study, institutionally sponsored loans, and scholarships/grants available. Support available to part-time students. Financial award application deadline: 3/1; financial award applicants required to submit FAFSA. *Unit head:* Dr. Paul Deland, Chair, 657-278-3631. *Application contact:* Admissions/Applications, 657-278-2371.

California State University, Long Beach, Graduate Studies, College of Natural Sciences and Mathematics, Department of Mathematics and Statistics, Long Beach, CA 90840. Offers mathematics (MS), including applied mathematics, applied statistics, mathematics education for secondary school teachers. Part-time programs available. *Faculty:* 18 full-time (7 women), 3 part-time/adjunct (2 women). *Students:* 53 full-time (19 women), 107 part-time (35 women); includes 4 Black or African American, non-Hispanic/Latino; 52 Asian, non-Hispanic/Latino; 24 Hispanic/Latino, 13 international. Average age 30. 175 applicants, 71% accepted, 80 enrolled. In 2010, 28 master's awarded. *Degree requirements:* For master's, comprehensive exam or thesis. *Application deadline:* For fall admission, 7/1 for domestic students; for spring admission, 12/1 for domestic students. Applications are processed on a rolling basis. Application fee: $55. Electronic applications accepted. *Financial support:* Teaching assistantships, Federal Work-Study, institutionally sponsored loans, scholarships/grants, and traineeships available. Financial award application deadline: 3/2. *Faculty research:* Algebra, functional analysis, partial differential equations, operator theory, numerical analysis. *Unit head:* Dr. Robert Mena, Chair, 562-985-4721, Fax: 562-985-8227, E-mail: rmena@csulb.edu. *Application contact:* Dr. Ngo Viet, Graduate Associate Chair, 562-985-4721, Fax: 562-985-8227, E-mail: viet@csulb.edu.

California State University, Los Angeles, Graduate Studies, College of Natural and Social Sciences, Department of Mathematics, Los Angeles, CA 90032-8530. Offers mathematics (MS), including applied mathematics, mathematics. Part-time and evening/weekend programs available. *Faculty:* 4 full-time (1 woman). *Students:* 31 full-time (15 women), 29 part-time (9 women); includes 31 minority (1 Black or African American, non-Hispanic/Latino; 17 Asian, non-Hispanic/Latino; 9 Hispanic/Latino; 4 Two or more races, non-Hispanic/Latino), 9 international. Average age 34. 41 applicants, 100% accepted, 23 enrolled. In 2010, 25 master's awarded. *Degree requirements:* For master's, comprehensive exam or thesis. *Entrance requirements:* For master's, previous course work in mathematics. Additional exam requirements/recommendations for international students: Required—TOEFL (minimum score 500 paper-based; 173 computer-based). *Application deadline:* For fall admission, 5/1 for domestic and international students. Applications are processed on a rolling basis. Application fee: $55. Electronic applications accepted. *Financial support:* Teaching assistantships, Federal Work-Study available. Support available to part-time students. Financial award application deadline: 3/1. *Faculty research:* Group theory, functional analysis, convexity theory, ordered geometry. *Unit head:* Dr. Silva Heubach, Chair, 323-343-2150, Fax: 323-343-5071, E-mail: sheubac@calstatela.edu. *Application contact:* Dr. Alan Muchlinski, Dean of Graduate Studies, 323-343-3820, Fax: 323-343-5653, E-mail: amuchli@exchange.calstatela.edu.

California State University, Northridge, Graduate Studies, College of Science and Mathematics, Department of Mathematics, Northridge, CA 91330. Offers applied mathematics (MS); mathematics (MS); mathematics for educational careers (MS). Part-time and evening/weekend programs available. *Degree requirements:* For master's, thesis (for some programs). *Entrance requirements:* For master's, GRE (if cumulative undergraduate GPA less than 3.0). Additional exam requirements/recommendations for international students: Required—TOEFL.

California State University, Sacramento, Graduate Studies, College of Natural Sciences and Mathematics, Department of Mathematics and Statistics, Sacramento, CA 95819. Offers MA. Part-time programs available. *Degree requirements:* For master's, thesis or alternative, writing proficiency exam. *Entrance requirements:* For master's, minimum GPA of 3.0 in mathematics, 2.5 overall during previous 2 years; BA in mathematics or equivalent. Additional exam requirements/recommendations for international students: Required—TOEFL. Electronic applications accepted.

California State University, San Bernardino, Graduate Studies, College of Natural Sciences, Department of Mathematics, San Bernardino, CA 92407-2397. Offers mathematics (MA); teaching mathematics (MAT). Part-time programs available. *Degree requirements:* For master's, advancement to candidacy. *Entrance requirements:* For master's, writing exam, minimum GPA of 3.0 in math courses. *Faculty research:* Mathematics education, technology in education, algebra, combinatorics, real analysis.

California State University, San Marcos, College of Arts and Sciences, Program in Mathematics, San Marcos, CA 92096-0001. Offers MS. Part-time and evening/weekend programs available. *Degree requirements:* For master's, thesis optional. *Entrance requirements:* Additional exam requirements/recommendations for international students: Required—TOEFL, TWE. *Faculty research:* Combinatorics, graph theory, partial differential equations, numerical analysis, computational linear algebra.

Carleton University, Faculty of Graduate Studies, Faculty of Science, School of Mathematics and Statistics, Ottawa, ON K1S 5B6, Canada. Offers mathematics (M Sc). Programs offered jointly with University of Ottawa. *Degree requirements:* For master's, thesis optional; for doctorate, one foreign language, comprehensive exam, thesis/dissertation. *Entrance requirements:* For master's, honors degree; for doctorate, master's degree. Additional exam requirements/recommendations for international students: Required—TOEFL. *Faculty research:* Pure mathematics, applied mathematics, probability and statistics.

Carnegie Mellon University, Mellon College of Science, Department of Mathematical Sciences, Pittsburgh, PA 15213-3891. Offers algorithms, combinatorics, and optimization (PhD); applied mathematics (PhD); computational finance (MS); mathematical finance (PhD); mathematical sciences (MS, DA, PhD); pure and applied logic (PhD). Part-time programs available. Terminal master's awarded for partial completion of doctoral program. *Degree requirements:* For doctorate, thesis/dissertation. *Entrance requirements:* For master's and doctorate, GRE General Test, GRE Subject Test. Additional exam requirements/recommendations for international students: Required—TOEFL. Electronic applications accepted. *Faculty research:* Continuum mechanics, discrete mathematics, applied and computational mathematics.

Case Western Reserve University, School of Graduate Studies, Department of Mathematics, Cleveland, OH 44106. Offers applied mathematics (MS, PhD); mathematics (MS, PhD). Part-time programs available. *Faculty:* 18 full-time (5 women), 1 part-time/adjunct (0 women). *Students:* 16 full-time (7 women), 4 part-time (3 women), 9 international. Average age 27. 84 applicants, 14% accepted, 4 enrolled. In 2010, 3 master's, 2 doctorates awarded. Terminal master's awarded for partial completion of doctoral program. *Degree requirements:* For master's, thesis or alternative, thesis (applied mathematics); for doctorate, thesis/dissertation. *Entrance requirements:* For master's and doctorate, GRE General Test. Additional exam requirements/recommendations for international students: Required—TOEFL (minimum score 550 paper-based; 213 computer-based; 79 iBT). *Application deadline:* For fall admission, 1/15 priority date for domestic students; for spring admission, 11/12 for domestic students. Applications are processed on a rolling basis. Application fee: $50. Electronic applications accepted. *Financial support:* Research assistantships, teaching assistantships available. Financial award application deadline: 1/15. *Faculty research:* Probability theory, convexity and high-dimensional phenomena,

Peterson's Graduate Programs in the Physical Sciences, Mathematics, Agricultural Sciences, the Environment & Natural Resources 2012

www.facebook.com/petersonspublishing   **261**

Mathematics

Case Western Reserve University (continued)
imaging, geometric evaluation of curves, dynamical systems, large scale scientific computing, life sciences. *Unit head:* Daniela Calvetti, Chair, 216-368-2880, Fax: 216-368-5163, E-mail: daniela.calvetti@case.edu. *Application contact:* Gaythresa Lewis, Admissions, 216-368-5014, Fax: 216-368-5163, E-mail: gxl34@case.edu.

Central Connecticut State University, School of Graduate Studies, School of Arts and Sciences, Department of Mathematical Sciences, New Britain, CT 06050-4010. Offers data mining (MS, Certificate); mathematics (MA, MS, Certificate, Sixth Year Certificate), including actuarial science (MA), computer science (MA), statistics (MA). Part-time and evening/weekend programs available. *Faculty:* 33 full-time (10 women), 65 part-time/adjunct (28 women). *Students:* 20 full-time (10 women), 131 part-time (74 women); includes 18 minority (5 Black or African American, non-Hispanic/Latino; 5 Asian, non-Hispanic/Latino; 6 Hispanic/Latino; 2 Two or more races, non-Hispanic/Latino), 8 international. Average age 37. 76 applicants, 59% accepted, 28 enrolled. In 2010, 29 master's, 4 other advanced degrees awarded. *Degree requirements:* For master's, comprehensive exam, thesis or alternative; for other advanced degree, qualifying exam. *Entrance requirements:* For master's, minimum undergraduate GPA of 2.7. Additional exam requirements/recommendations for international students: Required—TOEFL. *Application deadline:* For fall admission, 7/1 for domestic students; for spring admission, 12/1 for domestic students. Applications are processed on a rolling basis. Application fee: $50. Electronic applications accepted. *Expenses:* Tuition, area resident: Full-time $5012; part-time $470 per credit. Tuition, state resident: full-time $7518; part-time $482 per credit. Tuition, nonresident: full-time $13,962; part-time $482 per credit. Required fees: $3772. One-time fee: $62 part-time. *Financial support:* In 2010–11, 6 students received support, including 2 research assistantships; career-related internships or fieldwork, Federal Work-Study, scholarships/grants, and unspecified assistantships also available. Support available to part-time students. Financial award application deadline: 2/15; financial award applicants required to submit FAFSA. *Faculty research:* Statistics, actuarial mathematics, computer systems and engineering, computer programming techniques, operations research. *Unit head:* Dr. Jeffrey McGowan, Chair, 860-832-2835. *Application contact:* Dr. Jeffrey McGowan, Chair, 860-832-2835.

Central Michigan University, College of Graduate Studies, College of Science and Technology, Department of Mathematics, Mount Pleasant, MI 48859. Offers mathematics (MA, PhD), including teaching of college mathematics (PhD). Part-time programs available. *Faculty:* 24 full-time (8 women). *Students:* 23 full-time (5 women), 28 part-time (11 women); includes 1 Black or African American, non-Hispanic/Latino; 1 Asian, non-Hispanic/Latino; 1 Hispanic/Latino, 28 international. Average age 30. *Degree requirements:* For master's, thesis or alternative; for doctorate, thesis/dissertation. *Entrance requirements:* For master's, minimum GPA of 2.7, 20 hours of course work in mathematics; for doctorate, GRE, minimum GPA of 3.0, 20 hours of course work in mathematics. *Application deadline:* For fall admission, 6/1 for international students; for spring admission, 10/1 for international students. Applications are processed on a rolling basis. Application fee: $35 ($45 for international students). Electronic applications accepted. *Expenses:* Tuition, state resident: full-time $8208; part-time $456 per credit hour. Tuition, nonresident: full-time $13,788; part-time $766 per credit hour. One-time fee: $25. *Financial support:* Fellowships with tuition reimbursements, research assistantships with tuition reimbursements, teaching assistantships with tuition reimbursements, career-related internships or fieldwork, Federal Work-Study, unspecified assistantships, and out-of-state merit awards, non-resident graduate awards available. *Faculty research:* Combinatorics, approximation theory, applied mathematics, statistics, functional analysis and operator theory. *Unit head:* Dr. En-Bing Lin, Chairperson, 989-774-3596, Fax: 989-774-2414, E-mail: lin1e@cmich.edu. *Application contact:* Dr. Jungsywan Sepanski, Graduate Program Coordinator, 989-774-3639, Fax: 989-774-2414, E-mail: sepan1jh@cmich.edu.

Central Washington University, Graduate Studies and Research, College of the Sciences, Department of Mathematics, Ellensburg, WA 98926. Offers MAT. Program offered during summer only. *Degree requirements:* For master's, thesis or alternative. *Entrance requirements:* For master's, minimum GPA of 3.0. Additional exam requirements/recommendations for international students: Required—TOEFL (minimum score 550 paper-based; 213 computer-based; 79 iBT). Electronic applications accepted.

Chicago State University, School of Graduate and Professional Studies, College of Arts and Sciences, Department of Mathematics and Computer Science, Chicago, IL 60628. Offers computer science (MS); mathematics (MS). *Degree requirements:* For master's, thesis optional, oral exam. *Entrance requirements:* For master's, minimum GPA of 2.75.

City College of the City University of New York, Graduate School, College of Liberal Arts and Science, Division of Science, Department of Mathematics, New York, NY 10031-9198. Offers MA. Part-time programs available. *Degree requirements:* For master's, one foreign language. *Entrance requirements:* Additional exam requirements/recommendations for international students: Required—TOEFL (minimum score 500 paper-based; 61 iBT). Electronic applications accepted. *Faculty research:* Group theory, number theory, logic, statistics, computational geometry.

Claremont Graduate University, Graduate Programs, School of Mathematical Sciences, Claremont, CA 91711-6160. Offers computational and systems biology (PhD); computational mathematics and numerical analysis (MA, MS); computational science (PhD); engineering and industrial applied mathematics (PhD); mathematics (PhD); operations research and statistics (MA, MS); physical applied mathematics (MA, MS); pure mathematics (MA, MS); scientific computing (MA, MS); systems and control theory (MA, MS). Part-time programs available. *Faculty:* 6 full-time (0 women). *Students:* 50 full-time (15 women), 11 part-time (1 woman); includes 2 Black or African American, non-Hispanic/Latino; 9 Asian, non-Hispanic/Latino; 7 Hispanic/Latino; 3 Two or more races, non-Hispanic/Latino, 13 international. Average age 36. In 2010, 17 master's, 11 doctorates awarded. Terminal master's awarded for partial completion of doctoral program. *Entrance requirements:* For master's and doctorate, GRE General Test. Additional exam requirements/recommendations for international students: Required—TOEFL (minimum score 550 paper-based; 213 computer-based; 80 iBT). *Application deadline:* For fall admission, 2/1 priority date for domestic students. Applications are processed on a rolling basis. Application fee: $60. Electronic applications accepted. *Expenses:* Tuition: Full-time $35,748; part-time $1554 per unit. Required fees: $215 per semester. *Financial support:* Fellowships, research assistantships, Federal Work-Study, institutionally sponsored loans, scholarships/grants, and tuition waivers (full and partial) available. Support available to part-time students. Financial award application deadline: 2/15; financial award applicants required to submit FAFSA. *Unit head:* John Angus, Dean, 909-621-8080, Fax: 909-607-8261, E-mail: john.angus@cgu.edu. *Application contact:* Susan Townzen, Program Coordinator, 909-621-8080, Fax: 909-607-8261, E-mail: susan.n.townzen@cgu.edu.

Clark Atlanta University, School of Arts and Sciences, Department of Mathematical Sciences, Atlanta, GA 30314. Offers MS. Part-time programs available. *Faculty:* 2 full-time (1 woman), 1 part-time/adjunct (0 women). *Students:* 2 full-time (both women), 1 (woman) part-time; includes 2 Black or African American, non-Hispanic/Latino, 1 international. Average age 32. 3 applicants, 100% accepted, 1 enrolled. *Degree requirements:* For master's, one foreign language, thesis optional. *Entrance requirements:* For master's, GRE General Test, minimum GPA of 2.5. Additional exam requirements/recommendations for international students: Required—TOEFL (minimum score 500 paper-based; 173 computer-based; 61 iBT). *Application deadline:* For fall admission, 4/1 for domestic and international students; for spring admission, 11/1 for domestic and international students. Applications are processed on a rolling basis. Application fee: $40 ($55 for international students). *Expenses:* Tuition: Full-time $12,942; part-time $719 per credit hour. Required fees: $710; $355 per semester. *Financial support:* In 2010–11, 3 fellowships were awarded; scholarships/grants and unspecified assistantships

also available. Financial award application deadline: 4/30; financial award applicants required to submit FAFSA. *Faculty research:* Numerical methods for operator equations, Ada language development. *Unit head:* Dr. Charles Pierre, Chairperson, 404-880-8195, E-mail: cpierre@cau.edu. *Application contact:* Michelle Clark-Davis, Graduate Program Admissions, 404-880-6605, E-mail: cauadmissions@cau.edu.

Clarkson University, Graduate School, School of Arts and Sciences, Department of Mathematics, Potsdam, NY 13699. Offers MS, PhD. Part-time programs available. *Faculty:* 14 full-time (4 women), 1 part-time/adjunct (0 women). *Students:* 22 full-time (4 women), 12 international. Average age 27. 26 applicants, 54% accepted, 5 enrolled. In 2010, 4 master's, 1 doctorate awarded. Terminal master's awarded for partial completion of doctoral program. *Degree requirements:* For doctorate, thesis/dissertation, departmental qualifying exam. *Entrance requirements:* For master's and doctorate, GRE, transcripts of all college coursework, three letters of recommendation; resume and personal statement (recommended). Additional exam requirements/recommendations for international students: Required—TOEFL, TSE recommended. *Application deadline:* For fall admission, 1/30 priority date for domestic and international students; for spring admission, 9/1 priority date for domestic and international students. Applications are processed on a rolling basis. Application fee: $25 ($35 for international students). Electronic applications accepted. *Expenses:* Tuition: Part-time $1136 per credit hour. *Financial support:* In 2010–11, 22 students received support, including 1 fellowship with full tuition reimbursement available (averaging $21,580 per year), 10 research assistantships with full tuition reimbursements available (averaging $21,580 per year), 12 teaching assistantships with full tuition reimbursements available (averaging $21,580 per year); scholarships/grants and unspecified assistantships also available. *Faculty research:* Multilinear algebra, almost conjugacy, heat tansport, spacial scales. Total annual research expenditures: $1 million. *Unit head:* Dr. Christopher Lynch, Chair, 315-268-2395, Fax: 315-268-2371, E-mail: clynch@clarkson.edu. *Application contact:* Jennifer Reed, Graduate School Coordinator, School of Arts and Sciences, 315-268-3802, Fax: 315-268-3989, E-mail: sciencegrad@clarkson.edu.

Clemson University, Graduate School, College of Engineering and Science, Department of Mathematical Sciences, Clemson, SC 29634. Offers applied and pure mathematics (MS, PhD); computational mathematics (MS, PhD); operations research (MS, PhD); statistics (MS, PhD). Part-time programs available. *Faculty:* 48 full-time (13 women), 12 part-time/adjunct (4 women). *Students:* 127 full-time (51 women), 5 part-time (2 women); includes 2 Black or African American, non-Hispanic/Latino; 1 American Indian or Alaska Native, non-Hispanic/Latino; 1 Two or more races, non-Hispanic/Latino, 36 international. Average age 26. 163 applicants, 79% accepted, 51 enrolled. In 2010, 27 master's, 5 doctorates awarded. *Degree requirements:* For master's, thesis optional, final project; for doctorate, thesis/dissertation, qualifying exams. *Entrance requirements:* For master's and doctorate, GRE General Test. Additional exam requirements/recommendations for international students: Required—TOEFL. *Application deadline:* For fall admission, 1/15 priority date for domestic and international students; for spring admission, 10/1 priority date for domestic students; 9/15 priority date for international students. Applications are processed on a rolling basis. Application fee: $70 ($80 for international students). Electronic applications accepted. *Expenses:* Tuition, state resident: full-time $6492; part-time $400 per credit hour. Tuition, nonresident: full-time $13,634; part-time $800 per credit hour. Required fees: $262 per semester. Part-time tuition and fees vary according to course load and program. *Financial support:* In 2010–11, 110 students received support, including 2 fellowships with full and partial tuition reimbursements available (averaging $6,000 per year), 8 research assistantships with partial tuition reimbursements available (averaging $19,823 per year), 101 teaching assistantships with partial tuition reimbursements available (averaging $17,582 per year); career-related internships or fieldwork, institutionally sponsored loans, scholarships/grants, health care benefits, and unspecified assistantships also available. Support available to part-time students. Financial award application deadline: 4/15. *Faculty research:* Applied and computational analysis, cryptography, discrete mathematics, optimization, statistics. Total annual research expenditures: $823,404. *Unit head:* Dr. Robert L. Taylor, Chair, 864-656-5240, Fax: 864-656-5230, E-mail: rtaylo2@clemson.edu. *Application contact:* Dr. K.B. Kulasekera, Graduate Coordinator, 864-656-5231, Fax: 864-656-5230, E-mail: kk@clemson.edu.

Cleveland State University, College of Graduate Studies, College of Sciences and Health Professions, Department of Mathematics, Cleveland, OH 44115. Offers MA, MS. Part-time programs available. *Faculty:* 18 full-time (8 women). *Students:* 12 full-time (2 women), 17 part-time (7 women); includes 1 Black or African American, non-Hispanic/Latino; 1 Asian, non-Hispanic/Latino; 1 Hispanic/Latino, 2 international. Average age 31. 26 applicants, 73% accepted, 10 enrolled. In 2010, 8 master's awarded. *Degree requirements:* For master's, exit project. *Entrance requirements:* For master's, GRE. Additional exam requirements/recommendations for international students: Required—TOEFL (minimum score 515 paper-based; 197 computer-based). *Application deadline:* For fall admission, 6/15 priority date for domestic and international students. Applications are processed on a rolling basis. Application fee: $30. Electronic applications accepted. *Expenses:* Tuition, state resident: full-time $8447; part-time $469 per credit hour. Tuition, nonresident: full-time $16,020; part-time $890 per credit hour. Required fees: $50. *Financial support:* In 2010–11, 6 students received support, including 3 teaching assistantships with full tuition reimbursements available (averaging $9,000 per year); Federal Work-Study, institutionally sponsored loans, scholarships/grants, and tuition waivers (full and partial) also available. Financial award application deadline: 3/15. *Faculty research:* Algebraic topology, probability and statistics, differential equations, geometry. *Unit head:* Dr. John Peter Holcomb, Chairperson, 216-687-4681, Fax: 216-523-7340, E-mail: j.p.holcomb@csuohio.edu. *Application contact:* Dr. John F. Oprea, Graduate Program Director, 216-687-4702, Fax: 216-523-7340, E-mail: j.oprea@csuohio.edu.

The College at Brockport, State University of New York, School of Science and Mathematics, Department of Mathematics, Brockport, NY 14420-2997. Offers MA. Part-time programs available. *Students:* 5 full-time (2 women), 3 part-time (1 woman). 8 applicants, 63% accepted, 3 enrolled. In 2010, 4 master's awarded. *Degree requirements:* For master's, comprehensive exam. *Entrance requirements:* For master's, minimum GPA of 3.0, letters of recommendation; statement of objectives. Additional exam requirements/recommendations for international students: Required—TOEFL (minimum score 550 paper-based; 213 computer-based; 79 iBT). *Application deadline:* For fall admission, 7/15 priority date for domestic and international students; for spring admission, 11/15 priority date for domestic and international students. Application fee: $50. Electronic applications accepted. *Financial support:* In 2010–11, 3 teaching assistantships with full tuition reimbursements (averaging $6,000 per year) were awarded; Federal Work-Study, scholarships/grants, and unspecified assistantships also available. Support available to part-time students. Financial award application deadline: 3/15; financial award applicants required to submit FAFSA. *Faculty research:* Mathematical modeling, dynamical systems, complex/functional analysis, graph theory and combinations, algebra and number theory. *Unit head:* Dr. Mihail Barbosu, Chairperson, 585-395-2036, Fax: 585-395-2304, E-mail: mbarbosu@brockport.edu. *Application contact:* Dr. Howard Skogman, Graduate Director, 585-395-2046, Fax: 585-395-2304, E-mail: hskogman@brockport.edu.

College of Charleston, Graduate School, School of Sciences and Mathematics, Program in Mathematics, Charleston, SC 29424-0001. Offers mathematics (MS). Part-time and evening/weekend programs available. *Faculty:* 31 full-time (10 women), 1 part-time/adjunct (0 women). *Students:* 9 full-time (4 women), 5 part-time (2 women); includes 1 minority (Two or more races, non-Hispanic/Latino), 3 international. Average age 27. 11 applicants, 73% accepted, 8 enrolled. In 2010, 8 master's, 2 other advanced degrees awarded. *Degree requirements:* For master's, thesis optional. *Entrance requirements:* For master's, GRE, BS in mathematics or equivalent, 2 letters of recommendation. Additional exam requirements/recommendations for international students: Required—TOEFL (minimum score 81 iBT). *Application deadline:* For fall admission, 7/1 priority date for domestic students; for spring admission, 11/1 priority date

for domestic students. Applications are processed on a rolling basis. Application fee: $45. Electronic applications accepted. *Financial support:* In 2010–11, research assistantships (averaging $12,400 per year), teaching assistantships (averaging $13,300 per year) were awarded; Federal Work-Study, scholarships/grants, and unspecified assistantships also available. Support available to part-time students. Financial award application deadline: 4/1; financial award applicants required to submit FAFSA. *Faculty research:* Algebra, dynamical systems, probability, analysis and topology, combinatorics. *Unit head:* Dr. Ben Cox, Director, 843-953-5715, Fax: 843-953-1410, E-mail: coxbl@cofc.edu. *Application contact:* Susan Hallatt, Director of Graduate Admissions, 843-953-5614, Fax: 843-953-1434, E-mail: hallatts@cofc.edu.

Colorado School of Mines, Graduate School, Department of Mathematical and Computer Sciences, Golden, CO 80401. Offers MS, PhD. Part-time programs available. *Faculty:* 33 full-time (14 women), 6 part-time/adjunct (1 woman). *Students:* 54 full-time (16 women), 8 part-time (1 woman); includes 1 Black or African American, non-Hispanic/Latino; 1 American Indian or Alaska Native, non-Hispanic/Latino; 2 Asian, non-Hispanic/Latino; 1 Hispanic/Latino, 11 international. Average age 28. 80 applicants, 66% accepted, 24 enrolled. In 2010, 15 master's, 1 doctorate awarded. *Degree requirements:* For master's, thesis (for some programs); for doctorate, comprehensive exam, thesis/dissertation. *Entrance requirements:* For master's and doctorate, GRE General Test. Additional exam requirements/recommendations for international students: Required—TOEFL (minimum score 550 paper-based; 213 computer-based; 80 iBT). *Application deadline:* For fall admission, 1/15 priority date for domestic and international students; for spring admission, 10/15 priority date for domestic and international students. Application fee: $50 ($70 for international students). Electronic applications accepted. *Expenses:* Tuition, state resident: full-time $11,550; part-time $641 per credit. Tuition, nonresident: full-time $25,980; part-time $1444 per credit. Required fees: $1874; $937 per semester. *Financial support:* In 2010–11, 38 students received support, including 6 fellowships with full tuition reimbursements available (averaging $20,000 per year), 19 research assistantships with full tuition reimbursements available (averaging $20,000 per year), 13 teaching assistantships with full tuition reimbursements available (averaging $20,000 per year); scholarships/grants, health care benefits, and unspecified assistantships also available. Financial award application deadline: 1/15; financial award applicants required to submit FAFSA. *Faculty research:* Applied statistics, numerical computation, artificial intelligence, linear optimization. Total annual research expenditures: $660,064. *Unit head:* Dr. Tracy Camp, Interim Department Head, 303-273-2184, Fax: 303-273-3875, E-mail: tcamp@mines.edu. *Application contact:* William Navidi, Professor, 303-273-3489, Fax: 303-273-3875, E-mail: wnavidi@mines.edu.

Colorado State University, Graduate School, College of Natural Sciences, Department of Mathematics, Fort Collins, CO 80523-1874. Offers MAT, MS, PhD. Postbaccalaureate distance learning degree programs offered (no on-campus study). *Faculty:* 23 full-time (5 women). *Students:* 32 full-time (12 women), 19 part-time (7 women); includes 5 minority (2 Black or African American, non-Hispanic/Latino; 1 Asian, non-Hispanic/Latino; 2 Hispanic/Latino), 6 international. Average age 28. 69 applicants, 52% accepted, 9 enrolled. In 2010, 7 master's, 9 doctorates awarded. Terminal master's awarded for partial completion of doctoral program. *Degree requirements:* For master's, comprehensive exam (for some programs), thesis (for some programs); for doctorate, comprehensive exam, thesis/dissertation. *Entrance requirements:* For master's and doctorate, GRE General Test or GMAT, minimum GPA of 3.0, 3 letters of recommendation. Additional exam requirements/recommendations for international students: Required—TOEFL (minimum score 550 paper-based; 213 computer-based; 80 iBT). *Application deadline:* For fall admission, 2/15 priority date for domestic and international students; for spring admission, 7/15 priority date for domestic and international students. Applications are processed on a rolling basis. Application fee: $50. Electronic applications accepted. *Expenses:* Tuition, state resident: full-time $7434; part-time $413 per credit. Tuition, nonresident: full-time $19,022; part-time $1057 per credit. Required fees: $1729; $88 per credit. *Financial support:* In 2010–11, 6 fellowships (averaging $45,362 per year), 12 research assistantships with full tuition reimbursements (averaging $9,752 per year), 35 teaching assistantships with full tuition reimbursements (averaging $14,388 per year) were awarded; health care benefits also available. Financial award application deadline: 1/15; financial award applicants required to submit FAFSA. *Faculty research:* Numerical analysis, algebraic geometry, combinatorics, number theory, computational mathematics. Total annual research expenditures: $1.5 million. *Unit head:* Dr. Simon Tavener, Chair, 970-491-6452, Fax: 970-491-2161, E-mail: tavener@math.colostate.edu. *Application contact:* Bryan Elder, Graduate Coordinator, 970-491-7925, Fax: 970-491-2161, E-mail: elder@math.colostate.edu.

Columbia University, Graduate School of Arts and Sciences, Division of Natural Sciences, Department of Mathematics, New York, NY 10027. Offers M Phil, MA, PhD. *Degree requirements:* For master's, written exam; for doctorate, 2 foreign languages, thesis/dissertation. *Entrance requirements:* For master's and doctorate, GRE General Test, major in mathematics. Additional exam requirements/recommendations for international students: Required—TOEFL. *Faculty research:* Algebra, topology, analysis.

Concordia University, School of Graduate Studies, Faculty of Arts and Science, Department of Mathematics and Statistics, Montréal, QC H3G 1M8, Canada. Offers mathematics (M Sc, MA, PhD); teaching of mathematics (MTM). *Degree requirements:* For master's, thesis optional; for doctorate, comprehensive exam, thesis/dissertation. *Entrance requirements:* For master's, honors degree in mathematics or equivalent. *Faculty research:* Number theory, computational algebra, mathematical physics, differential geometry, dynamical systems and statistics.

Cornell University, Graduate School, Graduate Fields of Arts and Sciences, Field of Mathematics, Ithaca, NY 14853-0001. Offers PhD. *Faculty:* 48 full-time (4 women). *Students:* 65 full-time (24 women); includes 2 Asian, non-Hispanic/Latino, 36 international. Average age 25. 302 applicants, 9% accepted, 8 enrolled. In 2010, 9 doctorates awarded. *Degree requirements:* For doctorate, one foreign language, comprehensive exam, thesis/dissertation, teaching experience. *Entrance requirements:* For doctorate, GRE General Test, GRE Subject Test (mathematics), 3 letters of recommendation. Additional exam requirements/recommendations for international students: Required—TOEFL (minimum score 600 paper-based; 250 computer-based; 95 iBT). *Application deadline:* For fall admission, 1/15 for domestic students. Application fee: $80. Electronic applications accepted. *Expenses:* Tuition: Full-time $29,500. Required fees: $76. Tuition and fees vary according to degree level and program. *Financial support:* In 2010–11, 6 fellowships with full tuition reimbursements, 3 research assistantships with full tuition reimbursements, 51 teaching assistantships with full tuition reimbursements were awarded; institutionally sponsored loans, scholarships/grants, health care benefits, tuition waivers (full and partial), and unspecified assistantships also available. Financial award applicants required to submit FAFSA. *Faculty research:* Analysis, dynamical systems, Lie theory, logic, topology and geometry. *Unit head:* Director of Graduate Studies, 607-255-6757, Fax: 607-255-7149. *Application contact:* Graduate Field Assistant, 607-255-6757, Fax: 607-255-7149, E-mail: gradinfo@math.cornell.edu.

Dalhousie University, Faculty of Science, Department of Mathematics and Statistics, Program in Mathematics, Halifax, NS B3H 4R2, Canada. Offers M Sc, PhD. *Degree requirements:* For master's, thesis; for doctorate, thesis/dissertation. *Entrance requirements:* Additional exam requirements/recommendations for international students: Required—TOEFL, IELTS, CANTEST, CAEL, or Michigan English Language Assessment Battery. Electronic applications accepted. *Faculty research:* Applied mathematics, category theory, algebra, analysis, graph theory.

Dartmouth College, Arts and Sciences Graduate Programs, Department of Mathematics, Hanover, NH 03755. Offers PhD. *Degree requirements:* For doctorate, 2 foreign languages, thesis/dissertation. *Entrance requirements:* For doctorate, GRE General Test, GRE Subject Test. Additional exam requirements/recommendations for international students: Required—TOEFL. *Faculty research:* Mathematical logic, set theory, combinations, number theory.

Delaware State University, Graduate Programs, Department of Mathematics, Program in Mathematics, Dover, DE 19901-2277. Offers MS. *Entrance requirements:* Additional exam requirements/recommendations for international students: Required—TOEFL (minimum score 550 paper-based). Electronic applications accepted.

DePaul University, College of Liberal Arts and Sciences, Department of Mathematical Sciences, Chicago, IL 60614. Offers applied mathematics (MS), including actuarial science or statistics; applied statistics (MS, Certificate); mathematics education (MA). Part-time and evening/weekend programs available. *Faculty:* 23 full-time (6 women), 18 part-time/adjunct (5 women). *Students:* 111 full-time (60 women), 66 part-time (30 women); includes 16 Black or African American, non-Hispanic/Latino; 17 Asian, non-Hispanic/Latino; 16 Hispanic/Latino; 2 Two or more races, non-Hispanic/Latino, 10 international. Average age 30. 40 applicants, 100% accepted. In 2010, 30 master's awarded. *Degree requirements:* For master's, comprehensive exam. *Entrance requirements:* Additional exam requirements/recommendations for international students: Required—TOEFL. *Application deadline:* For fall admission, 7/30 for domestic students, 6/30 for international students; for winter admission, 11/30 for domestic students, 10/31 for international students; for spring admission, 2/15 for domestic students. Applications are processed on a rolling basis. Application fee: $25. *Financial support:* In 2010–11, 12 students received support, including research assistantships with partial tuition reimbursements available (averaging $6,000 per year); teaching assistantships, tuition waivers (full) also available. Financial award application deadline: 4/30. *Faculty research:* Verbally prime algebras, enveloping algebras of Lie, superalgebras and related rings, harmonic analysis, estimation theory. *Unit head:* Dr. Ahmed I. Zayed, Chairperson, 773-325-7806, Fax: 773-325-7807, E-mail: azayed@depaul.edu. *Application contact:* Ann Spittle, Director of Graduate Admissions, 312-362-8300, Fax: 312-362-5749, E-mail: admitdpu@depaul.edu.

Dowling College, Programs in Arts and Sciences, Oakdale, NY 11769-1999. Offers integrated math and science (MS); liberal studies (MA). Part-time and evening/weekend programs available. *Faculty:* 6 full-time (1 woman). *Students:* 3 full-time (2 women), 9 part-time (6 women); includes 1 minority (Asian, non-Hispanic/Latino). Average age 33. 14 applicants, 79% accepted, 6 enrolled. In 2010, 1 master's awarded. *Degree requirements:* For master's, comprehensive exam, thesis. *Entrance requirements:* For master's, minimum undergraduate GPA of 3.0, 2 letters of recommendation. Additional exam requirements/recommendations for international students: Required—TOEFL (minimum score 550 paper-based). *Application deadline:* For fall admission, 9/1 priority date for domestic students; for winter admission, 1/1 priority date for domestic students; for spring admission, 2/1 priority date for domestic students. Applications are processed on a rolling basis. Application fee: $50. Electronic applications accepted. *Expenses:* Tuition: Part-time $884 per credit hour. Part-time tuition and fees vary according to degree level and campus/location. *Financial support:* Federal Work-Study available. Support available to part-time students. Financial award application deadline: 6/30; financial award applicants required to submit FAFSA. *Unit head:* Dr. Paul Abramson, Dean, 631-244-3162, Fax: 631-244-1035, E-mail: abramsop@dowling.edu. *Application contact:* Ronnie S. Macdonald, Assistant Vice President for Enrollment Services/Dean of Admissions, 631-244-3357, Fax: 631-244-1059, E-mail: macdonar@dowling.edu.

Drexel University, College of Arts and Sciences, Department of Mathematics, Program in Mathematics, Philadelphia, PA 19104-2875. Offers MS, PhD. *Degree requirements:* For doctorate, one foreign language, thesis/dissertation. *Entrance requirements:* For master's and doctorate, GRE. Additional exam requirements/recommendations for international students: Required—TOEFL. Electronic applications accepted.

Duke University, Graduate School, Department of Mathematics, Durham, NC 27708. Offers PhD. *Faculty:* 27 full-time. *Students:* 48 full-time (10 women); includes 2 Asian, non-Hispanic/Latino; 2 Hispanic/Latino, 17 international. 174 applicants, 17% accepted, 11 enrolled. In 2010, 3 doctorates awarded. *Degree requirements:* For doctorate, 2 foreign languages, thesis/dissertation. *Entrance requirements:* For doctorate, GRE General Test, GRE Subject Test. Additional exam requirements/recommendations for international students: Required—TOEFL (minimum score 550 paper-based; 213 computer-based; 83 iBT), IELTS (minimum score 7). *Application deadline:* For fall admission, 12/8 priority date for domestic and international students. Application fee: $75. Electronic applications accepted. *Financial support:* Fellowships, research assistantships, teaching assistantships, Federal Work-Study available. Financial award application deadline: 12/8. *Unit head:* Thomas Witelski, Director of Graduate Studies, 919-660-2801, Fax: 919-660-2821, E-mail: sholder@math.duke.edu. *Application contact:* Elizabeth Hutton, Director of Admissions, 919-684-3913, Fax: 919-684-2277, E-mail: grad-admissions@duke.edu.

Duquesne University, Graduate School of Liberal Arts, Program in Computational Mathematics, Pittsburgh, PA 15282-0001. Offers MA, MS. *Faculty:* 18 full-time (5 women), 19 part-time/adjunct (7 women). *Students:* 13 full-time (4 women), 2 part-time (0 women), 5 international. Average age 23. 15 applicants, 100% accepted, 5 enrolled. In 2010, 5 master's awarded. *Degree requirements:* For master's, thesis. *Entrance requirements:* For master's, GRE General Test. Additional exam requirements/recommendations for international students: Required—TOEFL. *Application deadline:* For fall admission, 8/1 for domestic students, 5/1 for international students. Applications are processed on a rolling basis. Electronic applications accepted. *Expenses:* Tuition: Part-time $884 per credit. Required fees: $84 per credit. Tuition and fees vary according to course load. *Financial support:* In 2010–11, 2 teaching assistantships with full tuition reimbursements (averaging $10,000 per year) were awarded; Federal Work-Study, institutionally sponsored loans, scholarships/grants, and unspecified assistantships also available. Financial award application deadline: 5/1. *Unit head:* Dr. Jeff Jackson, Chair, 412-396-6467. *Application contact:* Dr. Donald Simon, Professor, 412-396-6472, E-mail: compmath@mathcs.duq.edu.

East Carolina University, Graduate School, Thomas Harriot College of Arts and Sciences, Department of Mathematics, Greenville, NC 27858-4353. Offers applied mathematics (MA); mathematics (MA). Part-time and evening/weekend programs available. *Degree requirements:* For master's, comprehensive exam. *Entrance requirements:* For master's, GRE General Test, MAT. Additional exam requirements/recommendations for international students: Required—TOEFL. *Expenses:* Tuition, state resident: full-time $3130; part-time $391.25 per credit hour. Tuition, nonresident: full-time $13,817; part-time $1727.13 per credit hour. Required fees: $1916; $239.50 per credit hour. Tuition and fees vary according to campus/location and program.

Eastern Illinois University, Graduate School, College of Sciences, Department of Mathematics and Computer Science, Charleston, IL 61920-3099. Offers mathematics (MA); mathematics education (MA). *Entrance requirements:* For master's, GRE General Test.

Eastern Kentucky University, The Graduate School, College of Arts and Sciences, Department of Mathematics and Statistics, Richmond, KY 40475-3102. Offers mathematical sciences (MS). Part-time programs available. *Degree requirements:* For master's, comprehensive exam. *Entrance requirements:* For master's, GRE General Test, minimum GPA of 2.5. *Faculty research:* Graph theory, number theory, ring theory, topology, statistics, Abstract Algebra.

Eastern Michigan University, Graduate School, College of Arts and Sciences, Department of Mathematics, Ypsilanti, MI 48197. Offers applied statistics (MA); computer science (MA); mathematics (MA); mathematics education (MA). Part-time and evening/weekend programs available. Postbaccalaureate distance learning degree programs offered (minimal on-campus study). *Faculty:* 22 full-time (7 women). *Students:* 5 full-time (3 women), 50 part-time (26 women); includes 7 minority (4 Black or African American, non-Hispanic/Latino; 2 Asian, non-Hispanic/Latino; 1 Hispanic/Latino), 10 international. Average age 35. 35 applicants, 54% accepted, 15 enrolled. In 2010, 19 master's awarded. *Degree requirements:* For master's,

Mathematics

Eastern Michigan University (continued)
thesis optional. *Entrance requirements:* Additional exam requirements/recommendations for international students: Required—TOEFL. *Application deadline:* Applications are processed on a rolling basis. Application fee: $35. *Financial support:* Fellowships, research assistantships with full tuition reimbursements, teaching assistantships with full tuition reimbursements, career-related internships or fieldwork, Federal Work-Study, institutionally sponsored loans, scholarships/grants, tuition waivers (partial), and unspecified assistantships available. Support available to part-time students. Financial award applicants required to submit FAFSA. *Unit head:* Dr. Christopher Gardiner, Department Head, 734-487-1444, Fax: 734-487-2489, E-mail: cgardiner@emich.edu. *Application contact:* Dr. Bingwu Wang, Graduate Coordinator, 734-487-5044, Fax: 734-487-2489, E-mail: bwang@emich.edu.

Eastern New Mexico University, Graduate School, College of Liberal Arts and Sciences, Department of Mathematical Sciences, Portales, NM 88130. Offers MA. Part-time programs available. *Faculty:* 7 full-time (3 women). *Students:* 3 full-time (1 woman); includes 1 minority (Two or more races, non-Hispanic/Latino). Average age 26. 1 applicant, 100% accepted, 1 enrolled. *Degree requirements:* For master's, comprehensive exam, thesis optional, 3 comprehensive exams, one course in analysis, one sequence of algebra or partial differential equations. *Entrance requirements:* For master's, minimum GPA of 3.0, completion of standard calculus sequence and courses in linear algebra, differential equations, and abstract algebra. Additional exam requirements/recommendations for international students: Required—TOEFL (minimum score 550 paper-based; 213 computer-based; 79 iBT), IELTS (minimum score 6). *Application deadline:* For fall admission, 7/20 priority date for domestic students, 6/20 for international students; for spring admission, 12/15 priority date for domestic students, 11/15 priority date for international students. Applications are processed on a rolling basis. Application fee: $10. Electronic applications accepted. *Expenses:* Tuition, state resident: full-time $3210; part-time $130 per credit hour. Tuition, nonresident: full-time $8652; part-time $360.50 per credit hour. Required fees: $1212; $50.50 per credit hour. Tuition and fees vary according to course load. *Financial support:* In 2010–11, 1 fellowship with partial tuition reimbursement (averaging $5,312 per year), 3 teaching assistantships with partial tuition reimbursements (averaging $8,500 per year) were awarded; career-related internships or fieldwork, tuition waivers (partial), and unspecified assistantships also available. Support available to part-time students. Financial award applicants required to submit FAFSA. *Unit head:* Dr. Kristi Jarman, Graduate Coordinator, 575-562-2336, Fax: 575-562-2555, E-mail: kristi.jarman@enmu.edu. *Application contact:* Leslie Schroeder, Department Secretary, 575-562-2309, Fax: 575-562-2555, E-mail: leslie.schroeder@enmu.edu.

Eastern Washington University, Graduate Studies, College of Science, Health and Engineering, Department of Mathematics, Cheney, WA 99004-2431. Offers mathematics (MS); teaching mathematics (MA). *Accreditation:* NCATE. Part-time programs available. *Degree requirements:* For master's, comprehensive exam, thesis (for some programs). *Entrance requirements:* For master's, GRE General Test, departmental qualifying exam, minimum GPA of 3.0.

East Tennessee State University, School of Graduate Studies, College of Arts and Sciences, Department of Mathematics, Johnson City, TN 37614. Offers MS. Part-time and evening/weekend programs available. *Faculty:* 14 full-time (4 women). *Students:* 11 full-time (4 women), 2 part-time (0 women); includes 1 minority (Black or African American, non-Hispanic/Latino), 1 international. Average age 28. 18 applicants, 44% accepted, 4 enrolled. In 2010, 10 master's awarded. *Degree requirements:* For master's, comprehensive exam, thesis. *Entrance requirements:* For master's, GRE General Test, bachelor's degree in math or related area. Additional exam requirements/recommendations for international students: Required—TOEFL (minimum score 550 paper-based; 213 computer-based; 79 iBT). *Application deadline:* For fall admission, 6/1 priority date for domestic students, 4/30 for international students; for spring admission, 11/1 for domestic students, 11/30 for international students. Application fee: $25 ($35 for international students). Electronic applications accepted. *Financial support:* In 2010–11, 12 teaching assistantships with full tuition reimbursements (averaging $7,700 per year) were awarded; research assistantships with full tuition reimbursements, career-related internships or fieldwork, institutionally sponsored loans, scholarships/grants, unspecified assistantships, and laboratory assistantships also available. Financial award application deadline: 7/1; financial award applicants required to submit FAFSA. *Faculty research:* Graph theory and combinatorics, probability and statistics, analysis, numerical and applied math, algebra. Total annual research expenditures: $197,750. *Unit head:* Dr. Anant Godbole, Chair, 423-439-5359, Fax: 423-439-8361, E-mail: godbolea@etsu.edu. *Application contact:* Admissions and Records Clerk, 423-439-4221, Fax: 423-439-5624, E-mail: gradsch@etsu.edu.

Elizabeth City State University, School of Mathematics, Science and Technology, Program in Mathematics, Elizabeth City, NC 27909-7806. Offers MS. Part-time and evening/weekend programs available. *Degree requirements:* For master's, thesis. *Entrance requirements:* For master's, MAT and/or GRE. Additional exam requirements/recommendations for international students: Required—TOEFL. Electronic applications accepted. *Faculty research:* Oceanic temperature effects, mathematics strategies in elementary schools, multimedia, Antarctic temperature mapping, computer networks, water quality, remote sensing, polar ice, satellite imagery.

Emory University, Laney Graduate School, Department of Mathematics and Computer Science, Atlanta, GA 30322-1100. Offers computer science (MS, PhD); mathematics (MS, PhD). Terminal master's awarded for partial completion of doctoral program. *Degree requirements:* For master's, thesis; for doctorate, one foreign language, comprehensive exam, thesis/dissertation. *Entrance requirements:* For master's and doctorate, GRE General Test. Electronic applications accepted. *Expenses:* Tuition: Full-time $33,800. Required fees: $1300.

Emporia State University, Graduate School, College of Liberal Arts and Sciences, Department of Mathematics, Computer Science and Economics, Emporia, KS 66801-5087. Offers mathematics (MS). Part-time programs available. *Faculty:* 14 full-time (2 women), 1 (woman) part-time/adjunct. *Students:* 8 full-time (3 women), 14 part-time (9 women); includes 1 minority (Native Hawaiian or other Pacific Islander, non-Hispanic/Latino), 5 international. 10 applicants, 100% accepted, 8 enrolled. In 2010, 5 master's awarded. *Degree requirements:* For master's, comprehensive exam or thesis. *Entrance requirements:* For master's, appropriate undergraduate degree. Additional exam requirements/recommendations for international students: Required—TOEFL (minimum score 520 paper-based; 133 computer-based; 68 iBT). *Application deadline:* For fall admission, 8/15 priority date for domestic students. Applications are processed on a rolling basis. Application fee: $30 ($75 for international students). Electronic applications accepted. *Expenses:* Tuition, state resident: full-time $4382; part-time $183 per credit hour. Tuition, nonresident: full-time $13,572; part-time $566 per credit hour. Required fees: $1022; $62 per credit hour. Tuition and fees vary according to course level, course load and campus/location. *Financial support:* In 2010–11, 1 research assistantship (averaging $7,059 per year), 4 teaching assistantships with full tuition reimbursements (averaging $6,833 per year) were awarded; career-related internships or fieldwork, Federal Work-Study, institutionally sponsored loans, health care benefits, and unspecified assistantships also available. Financial award application deadline: 3/15; financial award applicants required to submit FAFSA. *Unit head:* Dr. H. Joe Yanik, Chair, 620-341-5281, Fax: 620-341-6055, E-mail: hyanik@emporia.edu. *Application contact:* Dr. H. Joe Yanik, Graduate Coordinator, 620-341-5639, E-mail: hyanik@emporia.edu.

Fairfield University, College of Arts and Sciences, Fairfield, CT 06824-5195. Offers American studies (MA); communication (MA); creative writing (MFA); mathematics (MS). Part-time and evening/weekend programs available. Postbaccalaureate distance learning degree programs offered (minimal on-campus study). *Faculty:* 46 full-time (20 women), 15 part-time/adjunct (7 women). *Students:* 96 full-time (65 women), 97 part-time (63 women); includes 7 Black or African American, non-Hispanic/Latino; 5 Hispanic/Latino; 2 Two or more races, non-Hispanic/Latino, 7 international. Average age 41. 114 applicants, 62% accepted, 38 enrolled. In 2010, 36 master's awarded. *Degree requirements:* For master's, capstone research course. *Entrance requirements:* For master's, minimum GPA of 3.0, 2 letters of recommendation, resume. Additional exam requirements/recommendations for international students: Required—TOEFL (minimum score 550 paper-based; 213 computer-based; 80 iBT). *Application deadline:* For fall admission, 5/15 for international students; for spring admission, 10/15 for international students. Applications are processed on a rolling basis. Application fee: $60. Electronic applications accepted. *Expenses:* Tuition: Part-time $600 per hour. Part-time tuition and fees vary according to degree level and program. *Financial support:* In 2010–11, 19 students received support. Unspecified assistantships available. Financial award applicants required to submit FAFSA. *Faculty research:* Non-commutative algebra, partial differential equations, writing (fiction, non-fiction and poetry), communication for social change, comparative media systems, negotiation and management. *Unit head:* Dr. Robbin Crabtree, Dean, 203-254-4000 Ext. 3263, Fax: 203-254-4119, E-mail: rcrabtree@fairfield.edu. *Application contact:* Marianne Gumpper, Director of Graduate and Continuing Studies Admissions, 203-254-4184, Fax: 203-254-4073, E-mail: gradadmis@fairfield.edu.

Fairleigh Dickinson University, Metropolitan Campus, University College: Arts, Sciences, and Professional Studies, School of Computer Sciences and Engineering, Program in Mathematical Foundation, Teaneck, NJ 07666-1914. Offers MS. *Students:* 1 (woman) full-time, 21 part-time (17 women). Average age 37. 3 applicants, 100% accepted, 2 enrolled. In 2010, 10 master's awarded. *Application deadline:* Applications are processed on a rolling basis. Application fee: $40. *Application contact:* Susan Brooman, University Director of Graduate Admissions, 201-692-2554, Fax: 201-692-2560, E-mail: globaleducation@fdu.edu.

Fayetteville State University, Graduate School, Department of Mathematics and Computer Science, Fayetteville, NC 28301-4298. Offers mathematics (MS). Part-time and evening/weekend programs available. *Faculty:* 17 full-time (3 women). *Students:* 2 full-time (0 women), 2 part-time (0 women); includes 3 minority (1 Black or African American, non-Hispanic/Latino; 1 Asian, non-Hispanic/Latino; 1 Native Hawaiian or other Pacific Islander, non-Hispanic/Latino). Average age 35. In 2010, 2 master's awarded. *Degree requirements:* For master's, comprehensive exam, thesis or alternative, internship. *Entrance requirements:* For master's, GRE General Test. *Application deadline:* For fall admission, 4/15 for domestic students; for spring admission, 10/15 for domestic students. Applications are processed on a rolling basis. Application fee: $35. Electronic applications accepted. *Unit head:* Dr. Dwight House, Chairperson, 910-672-1664, E-mail: dhouse@uncfsu.edu. *Application contact:* Katrina Hoffman, Graduate Admissions Officer, 910-672-1374, Fax: 910-672-1470, E-mail: khoffma1@uncfsu.edu.

Florida Atlantic University, Charles E. Schmidt College of Science, Department of Mathematical Sciences, Boca Raton, FL 33431-0991. Offers applied mathematics and statistics (MS); mathematical sciences (MS, MST, PhD). Part-time programs available. *Faculty:* 37 full-time (5 women), 4 part-time/adjunct (0 women). *Students:* 49 full-time (7 women), 25 part-time (15 women); includes 17 minority (6 Black or African American, non-Hispanic/Latino; 9 Asian, non-Hispanic/Latino; 2 Hispanic/Latino), 29 international. Average age 31. 73 applicants, 41% accepted, 22 enrolled. In 2010, 26 master's, 8 doctorates awarded. Terminal master's awarded for partial completion of doctoral program. *Degree requirements:* For master's, comprehensive exam (for some programs), thesis (for some programs); for doctorate, comprehensive exam, thesis/dissertation. *Entrance requirements:* For master's and doctorate, GRE General Test, minimum GPA of 3.0. Additional exam requirements/recommendations for international students: Required—TOEFL (minimum score 500 paper-based; 173 computer-based). *Application deadline:* For fall admission, 7/1 priority date for domestic students, 2/15 priority date for international students; for spring admission, 11/1 priority date for domestic students, 7/15 priority date for international students. Applications are processed on a rolling basis. Application fee: $30. Electronic applications accepted. *Expenses:* Tuition, area resident: Part-time $319.96 per credit. Tuition, state resident: part-time $319.96 per credit. Tuition, nonresident: part-time $926.42 per credit. *Financial support:* In 2010–11, fellowships with partial tuition reimbursements (averaging $20,000 per year), teaching assistantships with partial tuition reimbursements (averaging $20,000 per year) were awarded; Federal Work-Study also available. Financial award application deadline: 4/1. *Faculty research:* Cryptography, statistics, algebra, analysis, combinatorics. *Unit head:* Dr. Lee Klingler, Chair, 561-297-0274, Fax: 561-297-2436, E-mail: klingler@fau.edu. *Application contact:* Dr. Heinrich Niederhausen, Graduate Director, 561-297-3237, Fax: 561-297-2436, E-mail: niederha@fau.edu.

Florida International University, College of Arts and Sciences, Department of Mathematics and Statistics, Program in Mathematical Sciences, Miami, FL 33199. Offers MS. Part-time and evening/weekend programs available. *Students:* 9 full-time (4 women), 3 part-time (0 women); includes 2 Black or African American, non-Hispanic/Latino; 1 Asian, non-Hispanic/Latino; 4 Hispanic/Latino, 5 international. Average age 25. 34 applicants, 29% accepted, 7 enrolled. In 2010, 5 master's awarded. *Entrance requirements:* For master's, GRE, letter of intent; three letters of recommendation; minimum GPA of 3.0 in upper-division mathematics courses. Additional exam requirements/recommendations for international students: Required—TOEFL (minimum score 550 paper-based; 80 iBT). *Application deadline:* For fall admission, 6/1 for domestic students, 3/1 for international students; for spring admission, 10/1 for domestic students, 9/1 for international students. Applications are processed on a rolling basis. Application fee: $30. Electronic applications accepted. *Financial support:* Institutionally sponsored loans and scholarships/grants available. Financial award application deadline: 3/1; financial award applicants required to submit FAFSA. *Unit head:* Dr. Bao Qin Li, Chair, Mathematics and Statistics Department, 305-348-2743, Fax: 305-348-6158, E-mail: bao.li@fiu.edu. *Application contact:* Dr. Zhenmin Chen, Graduate Director, 305-348-2743, Fax: 305-348-6158, E-mail: gradadm@fiu.edu.

Florida State University, The Graduate School, College of Arts and Sciences, Department of Mathematics, Tallahassee, FL 32306-4510. Offers applied computational mathematics (MS, PhD); biomedical mathematics (MS, PhD); financial mathematics (MS, PhD); pure mathematics (MS, PhD). Part-time programs available. *Faculty:* 46 full-time (11 women), 2 part-time/adjunct (both women). *Students:* 139 full-time (35 women), 7 part-time (0 women); includes 3 Black or African American, non-Hispanic/Latino; 3 Asian, non-Hispanic/Latino; 4 Hispanic/Latino, 92 international. Average age 26. 342 applicants, 40% accepted, 39 enrolled. In 2010, 42 master's, 8 doctorates awarded. Terminal master's awarded for partial completion of doctoral program. *Degree requirements:* For master's, comprehensive exam (for some programs), thesis optional; for doctorate, comprehensive exam (for some programs), thesis/dissertation, candidacy exam including written qualifying examinations which differ by degree concentrations. *Entrance requirements:* For master's and doctorate, GRE General Test, minimum upper-division GPA of 3.0, 4-year bachelor's degree. Additional exam requirements/recommendations for international students: Required—TOEFL (minimum score 213 computer-based; 80 iBT), IELTS (minimum score 6.5). *Application deadline:* For fall admission, 1/3 priority date for domestic students, 12/15 priority date for international students; for spring admission, 11/1 for domestic and international students. Applications are processed on a rolling basis. Application fee: $30. Electronic applications accepted. *Expenses:* Tuition, state resident: full-time $8238.24. *Financial support:* In 2010–11, 102 students received support, including 6 fellowships with full tuition reimbursements available (averaging $19,000 per year), 15 research assistantships with full tuition reimbursements available (averaging $20,000 per year), 75 teaching assistantships with full tuition reimbursements available (averaging $18,000 per year); career-related internships or fieldwork, institutionally sponsored loans, scholarships/grants, health care benefits, tuition waivers (full and partial), and unspecified assistantships also available. *Faculty research:* Geometric topology, algebraic geometry, fluid dynamics, financial mathematics, biomedical mathematics. *Unit head:* Dr. Philip L. Bowers, Chairperson, 850-645-3338, Fax: 850-644-

4053, E-mail: bowers@math.fsu.edu. *Application contact:* Dr. Bettye Anne Case, Associate Chair for Graduate Studies, 850-644-1586, Fax: 850-644-4053, E-mail: case@math.fsu.edu.

George Mason University, College of Science, Department of Mathematical Sciences, Fairfax, VA 22030. Offers actuarial sciences (Certificate); mathematics (MS, PhD). Evening/weekend programs available. *Faculty:* 30 full-time (7 women), 10 part-time/adjunct (4 women). *Students:* 10 full-time (2 women), 40 part-time (9 women); includes 8 minority (2 Black or African American, non-Hispanic/Latino; 3 Asian, non-Hispanic/Latino; 3 Hispanic/Latino), 4 international. Average age 31. 61 applicants, 48% accepted, 12 enrolled. In 2010, 1 doctorate, 6 other advanced degrees awarded. *Degree requirements:* For master's, comprehensive exam, thesis optional. *Entrance requirements:* For master's, minimum GPA of 3.0 in last 60 hours of course work. Additional exam requirements/recommendations for international students: Required—TOEFL (minimum score 570 paper-based; 230 computer-based; 88 iBT). *Application deadline:* For fall admission, 5/1 for domestic students; for spring admission, 11/1 for domestic students. Application fee: $100. Electronic applications accepted. *Expenses:* Tuition, state resident: full-time $8192; part-time $440 per credit hour. Tuition, nonresident: full-time $22,952; part-time $1055 per credit hour. Required fees: $2364; $99 per credit hour. *Financial support:* In 2010–11, 19 students received support, including 3 fellowships (averaging $18,000 per year), 4 research assistantships (averaging $16,067 per year), 12 teaching assistantships (averaging $15,748 per year); career-related internships or fieldwork, Federal Work-Study, scholarships/grants, unspecified assistantships, and health care benefits (full-time research or teaching assistantship recipients) also available. Financial award application deadline: 3/1; financial award applicants required to submit FAFSA. *Faculty research:* Nonlinear dynamics and topology, with an emphasis on global bifurcations and chaos; numerical and theoretical methods of dynamical systems. Total annual research expenditures: $522,044. *Unit head:* Klaus Fischer, Chair, 703-993-1462, Fax: 703-993-1491. *Application contact:* Dr. David Walnut, Graduate Coordinator, 703-993-1478, E-mail: dwalnut@gmu.edu.

Georgetown University, Graduate School of Arts and Sciences, Department of Mathematics, Washington, DC 20057. Offers mathematics and statistics (MS).

The George Washington University, Columbian College of Arts and Sciences, Department of Mathematics, Washington, DC 20052. Offers applied mathematics (MA, MS, PhD); pure mathematics (MA, MS, PhD). Part-time and evening/weekend programs available. *Faculty:* 18 full-time (3 women), 6 part-time/adjunct (2 women). *Students:* 17 full-time (5 women), 6 part-time (2 women); includes 1 Black or African American, non-Hispanic/Latino; 1 Asian, non-Hispanic/Latino; 1 Hispanic/Latino, 8 international. Average age 27. 73 applicants, 79% accepted, 9 enrolled. In 2010, 7 master's, 4 doctorates awarded. Terminal master's awarded for partial completion of doctoral program. *Degree requirements:* For master's, comprehensive exam; for doctorate, one foreign language, thesis/dissertation, general exam. *Entrance requirements:* For master's and doctorate, GRE General Test, minimum GPA of 3.0, interview. Additional exam requirements/recommendations for international students: Required—TOEFL (minimum score 550 paper-based; 213 computer-based; 80 iBT). *Application deadline:* For fall admission, 1/15 priority date for domestic and international students; for spring admission, 10/1 priority date for domestic students, 9/1 priority date for international students. Applications are processed on a rolling basis. Application fee: $75. Electronic applications accepted. *Financial support:* In 2010–11, 17 students received support; fellowships with full tuition reimbursements available, teaching assistantships with tuition reimbursements available, Federal Work-Study and tuition waivers available. Financial award application deadline: 1/15. *Unit head:* John B. Conway, Chair, 202-994-0553, E-mail: conway@gwu.edu. *Application contact:* John B. Conway, Chair, 202-994-0553, E-mail: conway@gwu.edu.

Georgia Institute of Technology, Graduate Studies and Research, College of Sciences, School of Mathematics, Atlanta, GA 30332-0001. Offers algorithms, combinatorics, and optimization (PhD); applied mathematics (MS); bioinformatics (PhD); mathematics (PhD); quantitative and computational finance (MS); statistics (MS Stat). Terminal master's awarded for partial completion of doctoral program. *Degree requirements:* For master's, thesis or alternative; for doctorate, one foreign language, thesis/dissertation. *Entrance requirements:* For master's, GRE General Test, minimum GPA of 3.0; for doctorate, GRE General Test, GRE Subject Test, minimum GPA of 3.0. Additional exam requirements/recommendations for international students: Required—TOEFL. Electronic applications accepted. *Faculty research:* Dynamical systems, discrete mathematics, probability and statistics, mathematical physics.

Georgia Institute of Technology, Graduate Studies and Research, Multidisciplinary Program in Algorithms, Combinatorics, and Optimization, Atlanta, GA 30332-0001. Offers PhD. *Degree requirements:* For doctorate, thesis/dissertation. *Entrance requirements:* For doctorate, GRE General Test, GRE Subject Test (computer science or mathematics). Additional exam requirements/recommendations for international students: Required—TOEFL. Electronic applications accepted. *Faculty research:* Complexity, graph minors, combinatorial optimization, mathematical programming, probabilistic methods.

Georgian Court University, School of Arts and Sciences, Lakewood, NJ 08701-2697. Offers biology (MA); Catholic school leadership (Certificate); clinical mental health counseling (MA); holistic health studies (MA); mathematics (MA); pastoral ministry (Certificate); religious education (Certificate); school psychology (Certificate); theology (MA, Certificate). Part-time and evening/weekend programs available. *Faculty:* 19 full-time (11 women), 7 part-time/adjunct (5 women). *Students:* 61 full-time (59 women), 143 part-time (113 women); includes 20 minority (5 Black or African American, non-Hispanic/Latino; 3 Asian, non-Hispanic/Latino; 11 Hispanic/Latino; 1 Two or more races, non-Hispanic/Latino), 1 international. Average age 39. 139 applicants, 59% accepted, 50 enrolled. In 2010, 5 master's awarded. *Degree requirements:* For master's, comprehensive exam (for some programs), thesis (for some programs). *Entrance requirements:* For master's, GRE, MAT, or NTE/PRAXIS, 3 letters of recommendation. Additional exam requirements/recommendations for international students: Required—TOEFL (minimum score 550 paper-based; 213 computer-based). *Application deadline:* For fall admission, 8/1 priority date for domestic students, 4/1 for international students; for spring admission, 1/1 priority date for domestic students, 7/1 for international students. Applications are processed on a rolling basis. Application fee: $40. Electronic applications accepted. *Expenses:* Tuition: Full-time $12,510; part-time $695 per credit. Required fees: $416 per year. Tuition and fees vary according to campus/location and program. *Financial support:* Scholarships/grants, health care benefits, and unspecified assistantships available. Financial award application deadline: 4/15; financial award applicants required to submit FAFSA. *Unit head:* Dr. Linda James, Dean, 732-987-2617, Fax: 732-987-2007. *Application contact:* Patrick Givens, Assistant Director of Admissions, 732-987-2736, Fax: 732-987-2084, E-mail: graduateadmissions@georgian.edu.

Georgia Southern University, Jack N. Averitt College of Graduate Studies, Allen E. Paulson College of Science and Technology, Department of Mathematical Sciences, Statesboro, GA 30460. Offers mathematics (MS). Part-time programs available. *Students:* 23 full-time (7 women), 4 part-time (0 women); includes 5 Black or African American, non-Hispanic/Latino, 13 international. Average age 29. 18 applicants, 100% accepted, 12 enrolled. In 2010, 16 master's awarded. *Degree requirements:* For master's, comprehensive exam, thesis, terminal exam, project. *Entrance requirements:* For master's, GRE, BS in engineering, science, or mathematics; course work in calculus, probability, linear algebra; proficiency in a computer programming language. Additional exam requirements/recommendations for international students: Required—TOEFL (minimum score 550 paper-based; 213 computer-based; 80 iBT). *Application deadline:* For fall admission, 3/1 priority date for domestic and international students; for spring admission, 10/1 priority date for domestic students, 10/1 for international students. Applications are processed on a rolling basis. Application fee: $50. Electronic applications accepted. *Expenses:* Tuition, state resident: full-time $6000; part-time $250 per semester hour. Tuition, nonresident: full-time $23,976; part-time $999 per semester hour. Required fees: $1644. *Financial support:* In 2010–11, 27 students received support, including research assistantships with partial tuition reimbursements available (averaging $7,200 per year), teaching assistantships with partial tuition reimbursements available (averaging $7,200 per year); career-related internships or fieldwork, Federal Work-Study, scholarships/grants, tuition waivers (partial), and unspecified assistantships also available. Support available to part-time students. Financial award application deadline: 4/15; financial award applicants required to submit FAFSA. *Faculty research:* Optimization, approximation theory, computed tomography, matrix analysis, applied statistics. Total annual research expenditures: $2,200. *Unit head:* Dr. Martha Abell, Chair, 912-478-5132, Fax: 912-478-0654, E-mail: martha@georgiasouthern.edu. *Application contact:* Dr. Charles Ziglar, Coordinator for Graduate Student Recruitment, 912-478-5635, Fax: 912-478-0740, E-mail: gradadmissions@georgiasouthern.edu.

Georgia State University, College of Arts and Sciences, Department of Mathematics and Statistics, Atlanta, GA 30302-3083. Offers mathematics (MA, MS); mathematics and statistics (PhD). Part-time and evening/weekend programs available. *Degree requirements:* For master's, comprehensive exam (for some programs), thesis (for some programs), exam; for doctorate, comprehensive exam, thesis/dissertation. *Entrance requirements:* For master's and doctorate, GRE. Additional exam requirements/recommendations for international students: Required—TOEFL. Electronic applications accepted. *Faculty research:* Analysis, biostatistics, discrete mathematics, linear algebra, statistics.

Graduate School and University Center of the City University of New York, Graduate Studies, Program in Mathematics, New York, NY 10016-4039. Offers PhD. *Degree requirements:* For doctorate, 2 foreign languages, thesis/dissertation. *Entrance requirements:* For doctorate, GRE General Test. Additional exam requirements/recommendations for international students: Required—TOEFL. Electronic applications accepted.

Hardin-Simmons University, Graduate School, Holland School of Sciences and Mathematics, Abilene, TX 79698-0001. Offers MS, DPT. Part-time programs available. *Faculty:* 5 full-time (0 women). *Students:* 8 full-time (5 women), 4 part-time (1 woman); includes 1 Hispanic/Latino, 1 international. Average age 27. 4 applicants, 100% accepted, 4 enrolled. In 2010, 5 master's awarded. *Degree requirements:* For master's, comprehensive exam, thesis or alternative, internship; for doctorate, comprehensive exam, thesis/dissertation or alternative. *Entrance requirements:* For master's, minimum undergraduate GPA of 3.0 in major, 2.7 overall; 2 semesters of course work each in biology, chemistry and geology; interview; writing sample; occupational experience; for doctorate, letters of recommendation, interview, writing sample. Additional exam requirements/recommendations for international students: Required—TOEFL (minimum score 550 paper-based; 213 computer-based; 75 iBT). *Application deadline:* For fall admission, 8/15 priority date for domestic students, 4/1 for international students; for spring admission, 1/5 priority date for domestic students, 9/1 for international students. Applications are processed on a rolling basis. Application fee: $50. *Expenses:* Tuition: Full-time $12,150; part-time $675 per credit hour. Required fees: $650; $110 per semester. Tuition and fees vary according to degree level. *Financial support:* In 2010–11, 12 students received support; fellowships, career-related internships or fieldwork and scholarships/grants available. Support available to part-time students. Financial award application deadline: 6/30; financial award applicants required to submit FAFSA. *Unit head:* Dr. Christopher McNair, Dean, 325-670-1401, Fax: 325-670-1385, E-mail: cmcnair@hsutx.edu. *Application contact:* Dr. Nancy Kucinski, Dean of Graduate Studies, 325-670-1298, Fax: 325-670-1564, E-mail: gradoff@hsutx.edu.

Harvard University, Graduate School of Arts and Sciences, Department of Mathematics, Cambridge, MA 02138. Offers PhD. *Degree requirements:* For doctorate, 2 foreign languages, thesis/dissertation, qualifying exam. *Entrance requirements:* For doctorate, GRE General Test, GRE Subject Test. Additional exam requirements/recommendations for international students: Required—TOEFL. *Expenses:* Tuition: Full-time $34,976. Required fees: $1166. Full-time tuition and fees vary according to program.

Howard University, Graduate School, Department of Mathematics, Washington, DC 20059-0002. Offers applied mathematics (MS, PhD); mathematics (MS, PhD). Part-time programs available. Terminal master's awarded for partial completion of doctoral program. *Degree requirements:* For master's, comprehensive exam, thesis or alternative, qualifying exam; for doctorate, 2 foreign languages, comprehensive exam, thesis/dissertation, qualifying exams. *Entrance requirements:* For master's, GRE General Test, minimum GPA of 3.0; for doctorate, GRE General Test. Additional exam requirements/recommendations for international students: Required—TOEFL. Electronic applications accepted.

Hunter College of the City University of New York, Graduate School, School of Arts and Sciences, Department of Mathematics and Statistics, New York, NY 10021-5085. Offers applied mathematics (MA); mathematics for secondary education (MA); pure mathematics (MA). Part-time and evening/weekend programs available. *Faculty:* 5 full-time (0 women), 2 part-time/adjunct (1 woman). *Students:* 8 full-time (4 women), 82 part-time (31 women); includes 2 Black or African American, non-Hispanic/Latino; 23 Asian, non-Hispanic/Latino; 5 Hispanic/Latino, 9 international. Average age 31. 58 applicants, 52% accepted, 21 enrolled. In 2010, 15 master's awarded. *Degree requirements:* For master's, one foreign language, comprehensive exam, thesis (for some programs). *Entrance requirements:* For master's, GRE General Test, 24 credits in mathematics. Additional exam requirements/recommendations for international students: Required—TOEFL. *Application deadline:* For fall admission, 4/1 for domestic students, 2/1 for international students; for spring admission, 11/1 for domestic students, 9/1 for international students. Application fee: $125. *Financial support:* Federal Work-Study, institutionally sponsored loans, scholarships/grants, and tuition waivers (partial) available. Support available to part-time students. *Faculty research:* Data analysis, dynamical systems, computer graphics, topology, statistical decision theory. *Unit head:* Ada Peluso, Chairperson, 212-772-5300, Fax: 212-772-4858, E-mail: peluso@math.hunter.cuny.edu. *Application contact:* William Zlata, Director for Graduate Admissions, 212-772-4482, Fax: 212-650-3336, E-mail: admissions@hunter.cuny.edu.

Idaho State University, Office of Graduate Studies, College of Arts and Sciences, Department of Mathematics, Pocatello, ID 83209-8085. Offers mathematics (MS, DA); mathematics for secondary teachers (MA). Part-time programs available. *Degree requirements:* For master's, comprehensive exam, thesis (for some programs), oral and written exams; for doctorate, comprehensive exam, thesis/dissertation, teaching internships. *Entrance requirements:* For master's, GRE General Test, GRE Subject Test, course work in modern algebra, differential equations, advanced calculus, introductory analysis; for doctorate, GRE General Test, GRE Subject Test, minimum graduate GPA of 3.5, MS in mathematics, teaching experience, 3 letters of recommendation. Additional exam requirements/recommendations for international students: Required—TOEFL (minimum score 550 paper-based; 213 computer-based; 80 iBT). Electronic applications accepted. *Faculty research:* Algebra, analysis geometry, statistics, applied mathematics.

Illinois State University, Graduate School, College of Arts and Sciences, Department of Mathematics, Program in Mathematics, Normal, IL 61790-2200. Offers MA, MS. *Degree requirements:* For master's, thesis or alternative. *Entrance requirements:* For master's, GRE General Test, minimum GPA of 2.8 in last 60 hours of course work.

Indiana State University, College of Graduate and Professional Studies, College of Arts and Sciences, Department of Mathematics and Computer Science, Terre Haute, IN 47809. Offers math teaching (MA, MS); mathematics and computer science (MA); mathematics and computer sciences (MS). Part-time programs available. *Degree requirements:* For master's, thesis or alternative. *Entrance requirements:* For master's, 24 semester hours of course work in undergraduate mathematics. Electronic applications accepted.

Indiana University Bloomington, University Graduate School, College of Arts and Sciences, Department of Mathematics, Bloomington, IN 47405-7000. Offers applied mathematics-

Peterson's Graduate Programs in the Physical Sciences, Mathematics, Agricultural Sciences, the Environment & Natural Resources 2012

www.facebook.com/petersonspublishing 265

Mathematics

Indiana University Bloomington *(continued)*
numerical analysis (MA, PhD); mathematics education (MAT); probability-statistics (MA, PhD); pure mathematics (MA). *Faculty:* 46 full-time (3 women). *Students:* 130 full-time (25 women), 1 part-time (0 women); includes 11 minority (1 Black or African American, non-Hispanic/Latino; 1 American Indian or Alaska Native, non-Hispanic/Latino; 8 Asian, non-Hispanic/Latino; 1 Hispanic/Latino), 72 international. Average age 27. 223 applicants, 25% accepted, 27 enrolled. In 2010, 12 master's, 13 doctorates awarded. Terminal master's awarded for partial completion of doctoral program. *Degree requirements:* For doctorate, one foreign language, thesis/dissertation. *Entrance requirements:* For master's and doctorate, GRE General Test, GRE Subject Test. Additional exam requirements/recommendations for international students: Required—TOEFL. *Application deadline:* For fall admission, 1/15 priority date for domestic and international students. Applications are processed on a rolling basis. Application fee: $55 ($65 for international students). Electronic applications accepted. *Financial support:* In 2010–11, 2 students received support, including 9 fellowships with full tuition reimbursements available (averaging $21,450 per year), 11 research assistantships with full tuition reimbursements available (averaging $16,045 per year), 96 teaching assistantships with full tuition reimbursements available (averaging $15,870 per year); scholarships/grants, health care benefits, and unspecified assistantships also available. Financial award application deadline: 1/15. *Faculty research:* Topology, geometry, algebra, applied, analysis. *Unit head:* Kevin Zumbrun, Chair, 812-855-2200. *Application contact:* Kate Bowman, Graduate Secretary, 812-855-2645, Fax: 812-855-0046, E-mail: gradmath@indiana.edu.

Indiana University of Pennsylvania, School of Graduate Studies and Research, College of Natural Sciences and Mathematics, Department of Mathematics, Indiana, PA 15705-1087. Offers applied mathematics (MS); elementary and middle school mathematics education (M Ed); mathematics education (M Ed). Part-time programs available. *Faculty:* 9 full-time (4 women). *Students:* 19 full-time (6 women), 16 part-time (13 women); includes 6 minority (2 Black or African American, non-Hispanic/Latino; 3 Asian, non-Hispanic/Latino; 1 Two or more races, non-Hispanic/Latino), 4 international. Average age 28. 41 applicants, 51% accepted, 13 enrolled. In 2010, 22 master's awarded. *Degree requirements:* For master's, thesis optional. *Entrance requirements:* For master's, 2 letters of recommendation. Additional exam requirements/recommendations for international students: Required—TOEFL. *Application deadline:* For fall admission, 7/1 priority date for domestic students; for spring admission, 11/1 for domestic students. Applications are processed on a rolling basis. Application fee: $40. *Financial support:* In 2010–11, 14 research assistantships with full and partial tuition reimbursements (averaging $3,120 per year) were awarded; career-related internships or fieldwork and Federal Work-Study also available. Support available to part-time students. Financial award application deadline: 3/15; financial award applicants required to submit FAFSA. *Unit head:* Dr. Gary S. Stoudt, Chairperson, 724-357-2608, E-mail: gsstoudt@iup.edu. *Application contact:* Dr. Jacqueline Gorman, Dean's Associate, 724-357-2609, E-mail: jgorman@iup.edu.

Indiana University–Purdue University Fort Wayne, College of Arts and Sciences, Department of Mathematical Sciences, Fort Wayne, IN 46805-1499. Offers applied mathematics (MS); applied statistics (Certificate); mathematics (MS); operations research (MS); teaching (MAT). Part-time and evening/weekend programs available. *Faculty:* 18 full-time (4 women), 1 (woman) part-time/adjunct. *Students:* 3 full-time (0 women), 17 part-time (6 women). Average age 33. 12 applicants, 100% accepted, 12 enrolled. In 2010, 4 master's, 3 other advanced degrees awarded. *Entrance requirements:* For master's, minimum GPA of 3.0, major or minor in mathematics, three letters of recommendation. Additional exam requirements/recommendations for international students: Required—TOEFL (minimum score 550 paper-based; 213 computer-based; 77 iBT); Recommended—TWE. *Application deadline:* For fall admission, 8/1 priority date for domestic students, 7/1 priority date for international students; for spring admission, 12/1 for domestic students, 10/1 for international students. Applications are processed on a rolling basis. Application fee: $55 ($60 for international students). Electronic applications accepted. *Expenses:* Tuition, state resident: full-time $4824; part-time $268 per credit. Tuition, nonresident: full-time $11,625; part-time $646 per credit. Required fees: $555; $30.85 per credit. Tuition and fees vary according to course load. *Financial support:* In 2010–11, 9 teaching assistantships with partial tuition reimbursements (averaging $12,740 per year) were awarded; scholarships/grants and unspecified assistantships also available. Support available to part-time students. Financial award application deadline: 3/1; financial award applicants required to submit FAFSA. *Faculty research:* Axis-supported external fields, discipline of doubt, t-design graphs. *Unit head:* Dr. David A. Legg, Chair, 260-481-6222, Fax: 260-481-0155, E-mail: legg@ipfw.edu. *Application contact:* Dr. W. Douglas Weakley, Director of Graduate Studies, 260-481-6233, Fax: 260-481-0155, E-mail: weakley@ipfw.edu.

Indiana University–Purdue University Indianapolis, School of Science, Department of Mathematical Sciences, Doctoral Program in Mathematics, Indianapolis, IN 46202-2896. Offers applied mathematics (PhD); mathematics (PhD). *Students:* 13 full-time (6 women), 6 part-time; includes 2 minority (1 Black or African American, non-Hispanic/Latino; 1 Hispanic/Latino), 8 international. Average age 29. 13 applicants, 62% accepted, 7 enrolled. Application fee: $55 ($65 for international students). *Unit head:* Slawomir Klimek, Director of Graduate Programs, 317-274-6918, E-mail: grad-program@math.iupui.edu. *Application contact:* Slawomir Klimek, Director of Graduate Programs, 317-274-6918, E-mail: grad-program@math.iupui.edu.

Indiana University–Purdue University Indianapolis, School of Science, Department of Mathematical Sciences, Master's Program in Mathematics, Indianapolis, IN 46202-2896. Offers applied mathematics (MS); applied statistics (MS); mathematics (MS). *Students:* 6 full-time (1 woman), 18 part-time (7 women); includes 5 minority (1 Black or African American, non-Hispanic/Latino; 3 Asian, non-Hispanic/Latino; 1 Hispanic/Latino), 3 international. Average age 36. 4 applicants, 75% accepted, 3 enrolled. In 2010, 10 master's awarded. Application fee: $55 ($65 for international students). *Unit head:* Slawomir Klimek, Director of Graduate Programs, 317-274-6918, E-mail: grad-program@math.iupui.edu. *Application contact:* Slawomir Klimek, Director of Graduate Programs, 317-274-6918, E-mail: grad-program@math.iupui.edu.

Instituto Tecnologico de Santo Domingo, Graduate School, Area of Basic And Environmental Sciences, Santo Domingo, Dominican Republic. Offers environmental science (M En S), including environmental education, environmental management, marine resources, natural resources management; mathematics (MS, PhD); renewable energy technology (MS, Certificate).

Iowa State University of Science and Technology, Graduate College, College of Liberal Arts and Sciences, Department of Mathematics, Ames, IA 50011. Offers applied mathematics (MS, PhD); mathematics (MS, PhD); school mathematics (MSM). *Faculty:* 43 full-time (6 women), 2 part-time/adjunct (1 woman). *Students:* 82 full-time (24 women), 14 part-time (4 women); includes 3 Black or African American, non-Hispanic/Latino; 3 Asian, non-Hispanic/Latino; 5 Hispanic/Latino, 38 international. 150 applicants, 21% accepted, 15 enrolled. In 2010, 9 master's, 7 doctorates awarded. *Degree requirements:* For master's, thesis or alternative; for doctorate, thesis/dissertation. *Entrance requirements:* For master's and doctorate, GRE General Test. Additional exam requirements/recommendations for international students: Required—TOEFL (minimum score 550 paper-based; 79 iBT), IELTS (minimum score 6.5). *Application deadline:* For fall admission, 2/1 priority date for domestic and international students; for spring admission, 10/1 priority date for domestic and international students. Application fee: $40 ($90 for international students). Electronic applications accepted. *Financial support:* In 2010–11, 7 research assistantships with full and partial tuition reimbursements (averaging $7,827 per year), 67 teaching assistantships with full and partial tuition reimbursements (averaging $11,732 per year) were awarded; fellowships, scholarships/grants, health care benefits, and unspecified assistantships also available. *Unit head:* Dr. Wolfgang Kliemann, Chair, 515-294-1752, Fax: 515-294-5454, E-mail: gradmath@iastate.edu. *Application contact:* Dr. Paul Sacks, Director of Graduate Education, 515-294-0393, E-mail: gradmath@iastate.edu.

Jackson State University, Graduate School, College of Science, Engineering and Technology, Department of Mathematics, Jackson, MS 39217. Offers mathematics (MS). Part-time and evening/weekend programs available. *Faculty:* 7 full-time (1 woman), 1 (woman) part-time/adjunct. *Students:* 8 full-time (2 women), 2 part-time (both women); includes 8 Black or African American, non-Hispanic/Latino. Average age 31. In 2010, 1 master's awarded. *Degree requirements:* For master's, comprehensive exam, thesis (for some programs). *Entrance requirements:* For master's, GRE General Test. Additional exam requirements/recommendations for international students: Required—TOEFL (minimum score 520 paper-based; 195 computer-based; 67 iBT). *Application deadline:* For fall admission, 3/1 priority date for domestic students, 3/1 for international students; for spring admission, 10/1 for domestic and international students. Applications are processed on a rolling basis. Application fee: $25. *Expenses:* Tuition, state resident: full-time $5050; part-time $281 per credit hour. Tuition, nonresident: full-time $12,380; part-time $689 per credit hour. *Financial support:* Career-related internships or fieldwork, Federal Work-Study, scholarships/grants, and unspecified assistantships available. Support available to part-time students. Financial award application deadline: 3/1; financial award applicants required to submit FAFSA. *Unit head:* Dr. Tor A. Kwembe, Chair, 601-979-2161, E-mail: tor.a.kwembe@jsums.edu. *Application contact:* Sharlene Wilson, Admissions Coordinator, 601-979-2455, Fax: 601-979-4325, E-mail: sharlene.f.wilson@jsums.edu.

Jacksonville State University, College of Graduate Studies and Continuing Education, College of Arts and Sciences, Department of Mathematics, Jacksonville, AL 36265-1602. Offers MS. Part-time and evening/weekend programs available. *Degree requirements:* For master's, comprehensive exam, thesis (for some programs). *Entrance requirements:* For master's, GRE General Test or MAT. Electronic applications accepted.

James Madison University, The Graduate School, College of Science and Mathematics, Department of Mathematics and Statistics, Harrisonburg, VA 22807. Offers M Ed. Part-time programs available. *Faculty:* 2 full-time (1 woman). *Students:* 5 part-time (3 women). Average age 27. In 2010, 2 master's awarded. *Degree requirements:* For master's, comprehensive exam. *Entrance requirements:* For master's, undergraduate major in mathematics. *Application deadline:* For fall admission, 5/1 priority date for domestic students; for spring admission, 9/1 priority date for domestic students. Application fee: $55. *Financial support:* Application deadline: 3/1. *Unit head:* Dr. David C. Carothers, Academic Unit Head, 540-568-6184, E-mail: carothdc@jmu.edu. *Application contact:* Lynette M. Bible, Director of Graduate Admissions, 540-568-6395, Fax: 540-568-7860, E-mail: biblelm@jmu.edu.

John Carroll University, Graduate School, Department of Mathematics, University Heights, OH 44118-4581. Offers MA, MS. Part-time and evening/weekend programs available. *Degree requirements:* For master's, comprehensive exam, thesis (for some programs), research essay. *Entrance requirements:* For master's, minimum GPA of 2.5, teaching certificate (MA). Electronic applications accepted. *Faculty research:* Algebraic topology, algebra, differential geometry, combinatorics, Lie groups.

The Johns Hopkins University, Zanvyl Krieger School of Arts and Sciences, Department of Mathematics, Baltimore, MD 21218-2699. Offers PhD. *Faculty:* 25 full-time (5 women), 11 part-time/adjunct (3 women). *Students:* 35 full-time (9 women); includes 1 minority (Asian, non-Hispanic/Latino), 22 international. Average age 24. 103 applicants, 11% accepted, 11 enrolled. In 2010, 3 doctorates awarded. *Degree requirements:* For doctorate, one foreign language, thesis/dissertation, 3 qualifying exams. *Entrance requirements:* For doctorate, GRE General Test, GRE Subject Test. Additional exam requirements/recommendations for international students: Required—TOEFL (minimum score 600 paper-based; 250 computer-based; 100 iBT), IELTS. *Application deadline:* For fall admission, 1/15 for domestic and international students. Application fee: $75. Electronic applications accepted. *Financial support:* In 2010–11, 32 teaching assistantships with full tuition reimbursements were awarded; fellowships with full tuition reimbursements, research assistantships, Federal Work-Study and institutionally sponsored loans also available. Financial award application deadline: 4/15; financial award applicants required to submit FAFSA. *Faculty research:* Algebraic geometry, number theory, algebraic topology, differential geometry, partial differential equations. Total annual research expenditures: $907,848. *Unit head:* Dr. Richard Wentworth, Chair, 410-516-4518, Fax: 410-516-5549, E-mail: cmese@math.jhu.edu. *Application contact:* Sabrina Raymond, Graduate Program Coordinator, 410-516-4178, Fax: 410-516-5549, E-mail: sraymond@jhu.edu.

Kansas State University, Graduate School, College of Arts and Sciences, Department of Mathematics, Manhattan, KS 66506. Offers MS, PhD. Part-time programs available. Terminal master's awarded for partial completion of doctoral program. *Degree requirements:* For master's, thesis or alternative; for doctorate, one foreign language, thesis/dissertation. *Entrance requirements:* For master's, GRE, bachelor's degree in mathematics; for doctorate, master's degree in mathematics. Additional exam requirements/recommendations for international students: Required—TOEFL (minimum score 600 paper-based; 250 computer-based). Electronic applications accepted. *Faculty research:* Low-dimensional topology, geometry, complex and harmonic analysis, group and representation theory, noncommunicative spaces.

Kent State University, College of Arts and Sciences, Department of Mathematical Sciences, Kent, OH 44242-0001. Offers applied mathematics (MA, MS, PhD); pure mathematics (MA, MS, PhD). Part-time programs available. *Degree requirements:* For master's, thesis optional; for doctorate, one foreign language, thesis/dissertation. Electronic applications accepted. *Expenses:* Tuition, state resident: full-time $7866; part-time $437 per credit hour. Tuition, nonresident: full-time $14,022; part-time $779 per credit hour. *Faculty research:* Approximation theory, measure theory, ring theory, functional analysis, complex analysis.

Kent State University, Graduate School of Education, Health, and Human Services, School of Teaching, Learning and Curriculum Studies, Program in Math Specialization, Kent, OH 44242-0001. Offers M Ed, MA. Part-time programs available. *Faculty:* 4 full-time (2 women). *Students:* 11 part-time (all women). 3 applicants, 100% accepted. In 2010, 5 master's awarded. *Entrance requirements:* Additional exam requirements/recommendations for international students: Required—TOEFL. *Application deadline:* Applications are processed on a rolling basis. Application fee: $30 ($60 for international students). Electronic applications accepted. *Expenses:* Tuition, state resident: full-time $7866; part-time $437 per credit hour. Tuition, nonresident: full-time $14,022; part-time $779 per credit hour. *Financial support:* In 2010–11, research assistantships (averaging $9,000 per year). *Unit head:* Dr. Trish Koontz, Coordinator, 330-672-0640, E-mail: tkoontz@kent.edu. *Application contact:* Nancy Miller, Academic Program Coordinator, Office of Graduate Student Services, 330-672-2576, Fax: 330-672-9162, E-mail: ogs@kent.edu.

Lakehead University, Graduate Studies, School of Mathematical Sciences, Thunder Bay, ON P7B 5E1, Canada. Offers computer science (M Sc); mathematical science (MA). Part-time and evening/weekend programs available. *Degree requirements:* For master's, thesis optional. *Entrance requirements:* For master's, minimum B average, honours degree in mathematics or computer science. Additional exam requirements/recommendations for international students: Required—TOEFL. *Faculty research:* Numerical analysis, classical analysis, theoretical computer science, abstract harmonic analysis, functional analysis.

Lamar University, College of Graduate Studies, College of Arts and Sciences, Department of Mathematics, Beaumont, TX 77710. Offers MS. *Faculty:* 6 full-time (1 woman). *Students:* 6 full-time (4 women), 3 part-time (1 woman); includes 1 Black or African American, non-Hispanic/Latino; 1 Asian, non-Hispanic/Latino; 1 Hispanic/Latino, 2 international. Average age 24. 12 applicants, 50% accepted, 3 enrolled. In 2010, 4 master's awarded. *Degree requirements:* For master's, comprehensive exam (for some programs), thesis optional. *Entrance requirements:* For master's, GRE General Test, minimum GPA of 2.5 in last 60 hours of undergraduate course work. Additional exam requirements/recommendations for international students:

Required—TOEFL. *Application deadline:* For fall admission, 5/15 priority date for domestic students; for spring admission, 10/1 priority date for domestic students. Applications are processed on a rolling basis. Application fee: $25 ($50 for international students). *Expenses:* Tuition, state resident: full-time $4160; part-time $208 per credit hour. Tuition, nonresident: full-time $10,360; part-time $518 per credit hour. *Financial support:* In 2010–11, 4 teaching assistantships (averaging $12,000 per year) were awarded; fellowships, research assistantships also available. Financial award application deadline: 4/1. *Faculty research:* Complex analysis, differential equations, algebra, topology statistics. Total annual research expenditures: $43,585. *Unit head:* Charles F. Coppin, Chair, 409-880-8792, Fax: 409-880-8794, E-mail: chair@math.lamar.edu. *Application contact:* Dr. Paul Chiou, Professor, 409-880-8800, Fax: 409-880-8794, E-mail: chiou@math.lamar.edu.

Lehigh University, College of Arts and Sciences, Department of Mathematics, Bethlehem, PA 18015. Offers applied mathematics (MS, PhD); mathematics (MS, PhD); statistics (MS). Part-time programs available. *Faculty:* 21 full-time (1 woman). *Students:* 37 full-time (20 women), 3 part-time (0 women); includes 2 minority (1 Asian, non-Hispanic/Latino; 1 Hispanic/Latino), 17 international. Average age 25. 105 applicants, 50% accepted, 11 enrolled. In 2010, 6 master's, 5 doctorates awarded. Terminal master's awarded for partial completion of doctoral program. *Degree requirements:* For master's, comprehensive exam, thesis optional; for doctorate, comprehensive exam, thesis/dissertation, qualifying exams, general exam. *Entrance requirements:* For master's and doctorate, minimum undergraduate GPA of 2.75, 3.0 for last two semesters; adequate background in math. Additional exam requirements/recommendations for international students: Required—TOEFL (minimum score 550 paper-based; 213 computer-based; 85 iBT). *Application deadline:* For fall admission, 1/15 priority date for domestic and international students; for spring admission, 12/1 priority date for domestic and international students. Applications are processed on a rolling basis. Application fee: $75. Electronic applications accepted. *Financial support:* In 2010–11, 35 students received support, including 2 fellowships with full tuition reimbursements available (averaging $25,000 per year), 23 teaching assistantships with full tuition reimbursements available (averaging $17,500 per year); research assistantships with full tuition reimbursements available, scholarships/grants and tuition waivers (partial) also available. Financial award application deadline: 1/15. *Faculty research:* Probability and statistics, geometry and topology, number theory, algebra, differential equations. Total annual research expenditures: $192,998. *Unit head:* Dr. Wei-Min Huang, Chairman, 610-758-3730, Fax: 610-758-3767, E-mail: wh02@lehigh.edu. *Application contact:* Dr. Terry Napier, Graduate Coordinator, 610-758-3755, E-mail: mathgrad@lehigh.edu.

Lehman College of the City University of New York, Division of Natural and Social Sciences, Department of Mathematics and Computer Science, Program in Mathematics, Bronx, NY 10468-1589. Offers MA. Part-time and evening/weekend programs available. *Degree requirements:* For master's, one foreign language, thesis or alternative.

Long Island University, C.W. Post Campus, College of Liberal Arts and Sciences, Department of Mathematics, Brookville, NY 11548-1300. Offers applied mathematics (MS); mathematics education (MS); mathematics for secondary school teachers (MS). Part-time and evening/weekend programs available. *Degree requirements:* For master's, thesis or alternative, oral presentation. *Entrance requirements:* Additional exam requirements/recommendations for international students: Required—TOEFL. Electronic applications accepted. *Faculty research:* Differential geometry, topological groups, general topology, number theory, analysis and statistics, numerical analysis.

Louisiana State University and Agricultural and Mechanical College, Graduate School, College of Basic Sciences, Department of Mathematics, Baton Rouge, LA 70803. Offers MS, PhD. *Faculty:* 56 full-time (4 women), 1 part-time/adjunct (0 women). *Students:* 96 full-time (24 women), 2 part-time (0 women); includes 2 Black or African American, non-Hispanic/Latino; 3 Hispanic/Latino; 2 Two or more races, non-Hispanic/Latino, 42 international. Average age 27. 104 applicants, 66% accepted, 23 enrolled. In 2010, 23 master's, 12 doctorates awarded. Terminal master's awarded for partial completion of doctoral program. *Degree requirements:* For doctorate, 2 foreign languages, thesis/dissertation. *Entrance requirements:* For master's and doctorate, GRE General Test, minimum GPA of 3.0. Additional exam requirements/recommendations for international students: Required—TOEFL (minimum score 550 paper-based; 213 computer-based; 79 iBT) or IELTS (minimum score 6.5). *Application deadline:* For fall admission, 1/25 priority date for domestic students, 5/15 for international students; for spring admission, 10/15 for international students. Applications are processed on a rolling basis. Application fee: $50 ($70 for international students). Electronic applications accepted. *Financial support:* In 2010–11, 92 students received support, including 23 fellowships with full and partial tuition reimbursements available (averaging $14,656 per year), 8 research assistantships with full and partial tuition reimbursements available (averaging $19,640 per year), 60 teaching assistantships with full and partial tuition reimbursements available (averaging $17,325 per year); Federal Work-Study, institutionally sponsored loans, scholarships/grants, health care benefits, tuition waivers (full), and unspecified assistantships also available. Financial award application deadline: 3/1; financial award applicants required to submit FAFSA. *Faculty research:* Algebra, graph theory and combinatorics, algebraic topology, analysis and probability, topological algebra. Total annual research expenditures: $1.5 million. *Unit head:* Dr. Lawrence Smolinksy, Chair, 225-578-1570, Fax: 225-578-4276, E-mail: mmsmol@lsu.edu. *Application contact:* Dr. Leonard F. Richardson, Director of Graduate Studies and Assistant Chairman, 225-578-1568, Fax: 225-578-4276, E-mail: rich@math.lsu.edu.

Louisiana Tech University, Graduate School, College of Engineering and Science, Department of Mathematics and Statistics, Ruston, LA 71272. Offers MS. Part-time programs available. *Degree requirements:* For master's, thesis or alternative. *Entrance requirements:* For master's, GRE General Test, minimum GPA of 3.0 in last 60 hours. Additional exam requirements/recommendations for international students: Required—TOEFL.

Loyola University Chicago, Graduate School, Department of Mathematical Sciences and Statistics, Chicago, IL 60660. Offers applied statistics (MS); mathematics and statistics (MS), including pure mathematics. Part-time programs available. *Faculty:* 19 full-time (4 women). *Students:* 29 full-time (20 women), 6 part-time (2 women); includes 11 minority (1 Black or African American, non-Hispanic/Latino; 6 Asian, non-Hispanic/Latino; 3 Hispanic/Latino; 1 Two or more races, non-Hispanic/Latino), 6 international. Average age 28. 64 applicants, 75% accepted, 23 enrolled. In 2010, 21 master's awarded. *Entrance requirements:* For master's, GRE General Test. Additional exam requirements/recommendations for international students: Required—TOEFL. *Application deadline:* For fall admission, 8/1 for domestic students; for spring admission, 12/1 for domestic students. Applications are processed on a rolling basis. Application fee: $0. Electronic applications accepted. *Expenses:* Tuition: Full-time $14,940; part-time $830 per credit hour. Required fees: $87 per semester. Part-time tuition and fees vary according to course load and program. *Financial support:* In 2010–11, 13 students received support, including 6 teaching assistantships with tuition reimbursements available (averaging $10,000 per year); career-related internships or fieldwork, Federal Work-Study, institutionally sponsored loans, and tuition waivers (partial) also available. Financial award application deadline: 3/15. *Faculty research:* Probability and statistics, differential equations, algebra, combinations. Total annual research expenditures: $10,000. *Unit head:* Dr. Robert Jensen, Chair, 773-508-3578, Fax: 773-508-2123, E-mail: rjensen@luc.edu. *Application contact:* Dr. W. Cary Huffman, Graduate Program Director, Mathematics, 773-508-3563, Fax: 773-508-2123, E-mail: whuffma@luc.edu.

Marquette University, Graduate School, College of Arts and Sciences, Department of Mathematics, Statistics, and Computer Science, Milwaukee, WI 53201-1881. Offers bioinformatics (MS); computational sciences (MS, PhD); computing (MS); mathematics education (MS). Part-time and evening/weekend programs available. Postbaccalaureate distance learning degree programs offered (minimal on-campus study). *Faculty:* 27 full-time (9 women), 8 part-time/adjunct (3 women). *Students:* 13 full-time (2 women), 26 part-time (7 women); includes 2 minority (1 Black or African American, non-Hispanic/Latino; 1 Asian, non-Hispanic/Latino), 15 international. Average age 31. 57 applicants, 42% accepted, 10 enrolled. In 2010, 9 master's awarded. Terminal master's awarded for partial completion of doctoral program. *Degree requirements:* For master's, thesis or alternative, Master's essay with oral presentation; for doctorate, comprehensive exam, thesis/dissertation, Qualifying Examination. *Entrance requirements:* For master's, official transcripts from all current and previous colleges/universities except Marquette, three letters of recommendation; for doctorate, GRE General Test, official transcripts from all current and previous colleges/universities except Marquette, three letters of recommendation, English-language publications authored by applicant (if applicable, strongly recommended). Additional exam requirements/recommendations for international students: Required—TOEFL (minimum score 530 paper-based; 78 computer-based). *Application deadline:* For fall admission, 1/15 for domestic and international students. Applications are processed on a rolling basis. Application fee: $50. Electronic applications accepted. *Expenses:* Tuition: Full-time $16,290; part-time $905 per credit hour. Tuition and fees vary according to program. *Financial support:* In 2010–11, 4 fellowships, 6 research assistantships, 15 teaching assistantships were awarded; Federal Work-Study, institutionally sponsored loans, scholarships/grants, and tuition waivers (full and partial) also available. Support available to part-time students. Financial award application deadline: 2/15. *Faculty research:* Models of physiological systems, mathematical immunology, computational group theory, mathematical logic, computational science. Total annual research expenditures: $696,366. *Unit head:* Dr. Gary Krenz, Chair, 414-288-7573, Fax: 414-288-1578. *Application contact:* Dr. Francis Pastijn, Director of Graduate Studies, 414-288-5229.

Marshall University, Academic Affairs Division, College of Science, Department of Mathematics, Huntington, WV 25755. Offers MA, MS. *Faculty:* 23 full-time (6 women), 1 part-time/adjunct (0 women). *Students:* 17 full-time (6 women), 1 part-time (0 women); includes 1 Hispanic/Latino, 7 international. Average age 27. In 2010, 5 master's awarded. *Degree requirements:* For master's, thesis (for some programs). *Entrance requirements:* For master's, GRE General Test. Application fee: $40. *Unit head:* Dr. Ralph Oberste-Vorth, Chairperson, 304-696-6010, E-mail: oberstevorth@marshall.edu. *Application contact:* Dr. Alfred Akinsete, Information Contact, 304-696-4646, Fax: 304-746-1902, E-mail: akinsete@marshall.edu.

Massachusetts Institute of Technology, School of Science, Department of Mathematics, Cambridge, MA 02139-4307. Offers PhD. *Faculty:* 45 full-time (4 women), 2 part-time/adjunct (0 women). *Students:* 105 full-time (20 women); includes 8 minority (all Asian, non-Hispanic/Latino), 54 international. Average age 25. 456 applicants, 10% accepted, 21 enrolled. In 2010, 22 doctorates awarded. *Degree requirements:* For doctorate, comprehensive exam, thesis/dissertation. *Entrance requirements:* For doctorate, GRE General Test, GRE Subject Test (mathematics). Additional exam requirements/recommendations for international students: Required—IELTS (minimum score 6). *Application deadline:* For fall admission, 12/15 for domestic and international students. Application fee: $75. Electronic applications accepted. *Expenses:* Tuition: Full-time $38,940; part-time $605 per unit. Required fees: $272. *Financial support:* In 2010–11, 101 students received support, including 49 fellowships with tuition reimbursements available (averaging $28,890 per year), 15 research assistantships with tuition reimbursements available (averaging $30,190 per year), 39 teaching assistantships with tuition reimbursements available (averaging $31,181 per year); Federal Work-Study, institutionally sponsored loans, scholarships/grants, health care benefits, and unspecified assistantships also available. *Faculty research:* Analysis, geometry and topology; algebra and number theory; representation theory; combinatorics, theoretical computer science and computational biology; physical applied mathematics and computational science. Total annual research expenditures: $4.9 million. *Unit head:* Prof. Michael Sipser, Department Head, 617-253-4381, Fax: 617-253-4358, E-mail: math@mit.edu. *Application contact:* Graduate Education, 617-253-2689, Fax: 617-253-4358, E-mail: gradofc@math.mit.edu.

McGill University, Faculty of Graduate and Postdoctoral Studies, Faculty of Science, Department of Mathematics and Statistics, Montréal, QC H3A 2T5, Canada. Offers computational science and engineering (M Sc); mathematics and statistics (M Sc, MA, PhD), including applied mathematics (M Sc, MA), pure mathematics (M Sc, MA), statistics (M Sc, MA).

McMaster University, School of Graduate Studies, Faculty of Science, Department of Mathematics and Statistics, Hamilton, ON L8S 4M2, Canada. Offers mathematics (M Sc, PhD); statistics (M Sc), including applied statistics, medical statistics, statistical theory. Part-time programs available. *Degree requirements:* For master's, thesis or alternative, oral exam; for doctorate, comprehensive exam, thesis/dissertation. *Entrance requirements:* For master's, minimum B+ average in last year of honors degree; for doctorate, minimum B+ average, M Sc in mathematics or statistics. Additional exam requirements/recommendations for international students: Required—TOEFL (minimum score 550 paper-based; 213 computer-based). *Faculty research:* Algebra, analysis, applied mathematics, geometry and topology, probability and statistics.

McNeese State University, Doré School of Graduate Studies, College of Science, Department of Mathematics, Computer Science, and Statistics, Lake Charles, LA 70609. Offers computer science (MS); mathematics (MS); statistics (MS). Evening/weekend programs available. *Faculty:* 11 full-time (3 women). *Students:* 25 full-time (9 women), 13 part-time (5 women); includes 3 minority (1 Black or African American, non-Hispanic/Latino; 1 Asian, non-Hispanic/Latino; 1 Hispanic/Latino), 27 international. In 2010, 17 master's awarded. *Degree requirements:* For master's, comprehensive exam, thesis or alternative, written exam. *Entrance requirements:* For master's, GRE. *Application deadline:* For fall admission, 5/15 priority date for domestic and international students; for spring admission, 10/15 priority date for domestic and international students. Applications are processed on a rolling basis. Application fee: $20 ($30 for international students). Tuition and fees vary according to course load. *Financial support:* Teaching assistantships available. Financial award application deadline: 5/1. *Unit head:* Sid Bradley, Head, 337-475-5788, Fax: 337-475-5799, E-mail: sbradley@mcneese.edu. *Application contact:* Dr. George F. Mead, Interim Dean of Dore' School of Graduate Studies, 337-475-5396, Fax: 337-475-5397, E-mail: admissions@mcneese.edu.

Memorial University of Newfoundland, School of Graduate Studies, Department of Mathematics and Statistics, St. John's, NL A1C 5S7, Canada. Offers mathematics (M Sc, PhD); statistics (M Sc, MAS, PhD). Part-time programs available. *Degree requirements:* For master's, thesis, practicum and report (MAS); for doctorate, comprehensive exam, thesis/dissertation, oral defense of thesis. *Entrance requirements:* For master's, 2nd class honors degree (MAS); for doctorate, MAS or M Sc in mathematics and statistics. Electronic applications accepted. *Faculty research:* Algebra, topology, applied mathematics, mathematical statistics, applied statistics and probability.

Miami University, Graduate School, College of Arts and Science, Department of Mathematics, Oxford, OH 45056. Offers MA, MAT, MS. *Students:* 23 full-time (7 women), 3 part-time (2 women), 2 international. Average age 25. In 2010, 14 master's awarded. *Entrance requirements:* Additional exam requirements/recommendations for international students: Required—TOEFL. Application fee: $50. *Expenses:* Tuition, state resident: full-time $11,616; part-time $484 per credit hour. Tuition, nonresident: full-time $25,656; part-time $1069 per credit hour. Required fees: $528. *Financial support:* Research assistantships, teaching assistantships, health care benefits and unspecified assistantships available. Financial award application deadline: 3/1; financial award applicants required to submit FAFSA. *Unit head:* Dr. Patrick Dowling, Department Chair, 513-529-5818, E-mail: dowlinpn@muohio.edu. *Application contact:* Dr. Doug Ward, Director of Graduate Studies, 513-529-3534, E-mail: wardde@muohio.edu.

Michigan State University, The Graduate School, College of Natural Science, Department of Mathematics, East Lansing, MI 48824. Offers applied mathematics (MS, PhD); industrial

Mathematics

Michigan State University (continued)
mathematics (MS); mathematics (MAT, MS, PhD). *Entrance requirements:* Additional exam requirements/recommendations for international students: Required—TOEFL. Electronic applications accepted.

Michigan Technological University, Graduate School, College of Sciences and Arts, Department of Mathematical Sciences, Houghton, MI 49931. Offers MS, PhD. Part-time programs available. Terminal master's awarded for partial completion of doctoral program. *Degree requirements:* For master's, comprehensive exam (for some programs), thesis (for some programs); for doctorate, comprehensive exam, thesis/dissertation, proficiency exam. *Entrance requirements:* For master's and doctorate, GRE General Test, GRE Subject Test (recommended). Additional exam requirements/recommendations for international students: Required—TOEFL (minimum score 550 paper-based; 213 computer-based). Electronic applications accepted. *Faculty research:* Fluid dynamics, mathematical modeling, design theory, coding theory, statistical genetics.

Middle Tennessee State University, College of Graduate Studies, College of Basic and Applied Sciences, Department of Mathematical Sciences, Murfreesboro, TN 37132. Offers mathematics (MS, MST, PhD). Part-time and evening/weekend programs available. Postbaccalaureate distance learning degree programs offered. *Faculty:* 21 full-time (9 women). *Students:* 6 full-time (2 women), 24 part-time (13 women); includes 2 Black or African American, non-Hispanic/Latino; 6 Asian, non-Hispanic/Latino; 1 Hispanic/Latino. Average age 32. 17 applicants, 82% accepted, 14 enrolled. In 2010, 15 master's awarded. *Degree requirements:* For master's, comprehensive exam. *Entrance requirements:* For master's, GRE General Test or MAT. Additional exam requirements/recommendations for international students: Required—TOEFL (minimum score 525 paper-based; 195 computer-based; 71 iBT) or IELTS (minimum score 6). *Application deadline:* For fall admission, 6/1 for domestic and international students. Applications are processed on a rolling basis. Application fee: $25 ($30 for international students). Electronic applications accepted. *Expenses:* Tuition, state resident: full-time $4632. Tuition, nonresident: full-time $11,520. *Financial support:* In 2010–11, 11 students received support. Institutionally sponsored loans available. Support available to part-time students. Financial award application deadline: 5/1; financial award applicants required to submit FAFSA. *Unit head:* Dr. Donald Nelson, Interim Chair, 615-898-2669, Fax: 615-898-5422, E-mail: dnelson@mtsu.edu. *Application contact:* Dr. Michael Allen, Dean and Vice Provost for Research, 615-898-2840, Fax: 615-904-8020, E-mail: mallen@mtsu.edu.

Minnesota State University Mankato, College of Graduate Studies, College of Science, Engineering and Technology, Department of Mathematics and Statistics, Program in Mathematics, Mankato, MN 56001. Offers MA, MS. *Students:* 9 full-time (6 women), 11 part-time (4 women). *Degree requirements:* For master's, one foreign language, comprehensive exam, thesis or alternative. *Entrance requirements:* For master's, GRE General Test, minimum GPA of 3.0 during previous 2 years. Additional exam requirements/recommendations for international students: Required—TOEFL. *Application deadline:* For fall admission, 7/1 priority date for domestic students; for spring admission, 11/1 for domestic students. Applications are processed on a rolling basis. Application fee: $40. Electronic applications accepted. *Financial support:* Research assistantships with partial tuition reimbursements, teaching assistantships with partial tuition reimbursements, unspecified assistantships available. Financial award application deadline: 3/15; financial award applicants required to submit FAFSA. *Unit head:* Dr. Deepak Sanjel, Graduate Coordinator, 507-389-2319. *Application contact:* 507-389-2321, E-mail: grad@mnsu.edu.

Mississippi College, Graduate School, College of Arts and Sciences, School of Science and Mathematics, Department of Mathematics, Clinton, MS 39058. Offers M Ed, MCS, MS. Part-time programs available. *Degree requirements:* For master's, comprehensive exam, thesis optional. *Entrance requirements:* For master's, GRE or NTE, minimum GPA of 2.5. Additional exam requirements/recommendations for international students: Recommended—IELTS. Electronic applications accepted.

Mississippi State University, College of Arts and Sciences, Department of Mathematics and Statistics, Mississippi State, MS 39762. Offers mathematical sciences (PhD); mathematics (MS); statistics (MS). Part-time programs available. *Faculty:* 20 full-time (4 women). *Students:* 40 full-time (23 women), 3 part-time (1 woman); includes 6 minority (3 Black or African American, non-Hispanic/Latino; 2 Asian, non-Hispanic/Latino; 1 Two or more races, non-Hispanic/Latino), 23 international. Average age 28. 54 applicants, 52% accepted, 16 enrolled. In 2010, 7 master's, 1 doctorate awarded. Terminal master's awarded for partial completion of doctoral program. *Degree requirements:* For master's, thesis optional, comprehensive oral or written exam; for doctorate, one foreign language, thesis/dissertation, comprehensive oral and written exam. *Entrance requirements:* For master's, minimum GPA of 2.75 on last two years of undergraduate courses; for doctorate, GRE. Additional exam requirements/recommendations for international students: Required—TOEFL (minimum score 475 paper-based; 153 computer-based; 53 iBT); Recommended—IELTS (minimum score 4.5). *Application deadline:* For fall admission, 3/15 priority date for domestic students, 5/1 for international students; for spring admission, 11/1 for domestic students, 9/1 for international students. Applications are processed on a rolling basis. Application fee: $40. Electronic applications accepted. *Expenses:* Tuition, state resident: full-time $2730.50; part-time $304 per credit hour. Tuition, nonresident: full-time $6901; part-time $767 per credit hour. *Financial support:* In 2010–11, 29 teaching assistantships with full tuition reimbursements (averaging $13,472 per year) were awarded; Federal Work-Study, institutionally sponsored loans, tuition waivers (partial), and unspecified assistantships also available. Financial award application deadline: 4/1; financial award applicants required to submit FAFSA. *Faculty research:* Differential equations, algebra, numerical analysis, functional analysis, applied statistics. Total annual research expenditures: $1.7 million. *Unit head:* Dr. Mohsen Razzaghi, Interim Head, 662-325-3414, Fax: 662-325-0005, E-mail: razzaghi@math.msstate.edu. *Application contact:* Dr. Corlis Johnson, Associate Department Head/Graduate Coordinator, 662-325-3414, Fax: 662-325-0005, E-mail: cjohnson@math.msstate.edu.

Missouri State University, Graduate College, College of Natural and Applied Sciences, Department of Mathematics, Springfield, MO 65897. Offers mathematics (MS); natural and applied science (MNAS), including mathematics (MNAS, MS Ed); secondary education (MS Ed), including mathematics (MNAS, MS Ed). Part-time programs available. *Degree requirements:* For master's, comprehensive exam, thesis or alternative. *Entrance requirements:* For master's, GRE (MS, MNAS), minimum undergraduate GPA of 3.0 (MS, MNAS), 9-12 teacher certification (MS Ed). Additional exam requirements/recommendations for international students: Required—TOEFL (minimum score 550 paper-based; 213 computer-based; 79 iBT). Electronic applications accepted. *Expenses:* Tuition, state resident: full-time $3348; part-time $186 per credit hour. Tuition, nonresident: full-time $6696; part-time $372 per credit hour. Required fees: $238 per semester. Tuition and fees vary according to course level, course load and program. *Faculty research:* Harmonic analysis, commutative algebra, number theory, K-theory, probability.

Missouri University of Science and Technology, Graduate School, Department of Mathematics and Statistics, Rolla, MO 65409. Offers applied mathematics (MS); mathematics (MST, PhD), including mathematics (PhD), mathematics education (MST), statistics (PhD). Terminal master's awarded for partial completion of doctoral program. *Degree requirements:* For master's, thesis or alternative; for doctorate, one foreign language, thesis/dissertation. *Entrance requirements:* For master's and doctorate, GRE General Test, GRE Subject Test. Electronic applications accepted. *Faculty research:* Analysis, differential equations, topology, statistics.

Montana State University, College of Graduate Studies, College of Letters and Science, Department of Mathematical Sciences, Bozeman, MT 59717. Offers mathematics (MS, PhD), including mathematics education option (MS); statistics (MS, PhD). Part-time programs available. Postbaccalaureate distance learning degree programs offered (minimal on-campus study). *Faculty:* 32 full-time (10 women), 12 part-time/adjunct (5 women). *Students:* 8 full-time (1 woman), 70 part-time (34 women); includes 3 minority (1 Asian, non-Hispanic/Latino; 1 Hispanic/Latino; 1 Two or more races, non-Hispanic/Latino), 6 international. Average age 31. 32 applicants, 50% accepted, 11 enrolled. In 2010, 24 master's, 6 doctorates awarded. *Degree requirements:* For master's, comprehensive exam, thesis (for some programs); for doctorate, comprehensive exam, thesis/dissertation. *Entrance requirements:* For master's and doctorate, GRE General Test. Additional exam requirements/recommendations for international students: Required—TOEFL (minimum score 550 paper-based; 213 computer-based). *Application deadline:* For fall admission, 7/15 priority date for domestic students, 5/15 priority date for international students; for spring admission, 12/1 priority date for domestic students, 10/1 priority date for international students. Applications are processed on a rolling basis. Application fee: $30. Electronic applications accepted. *Expenses:* Tuition, state resident: full-time $5553.90. Tuition, nonresident: full-time $14,646. Required fees: $1233. *Financial support:* In 2010–11, 55 students received support, including 2 research assistantships with tuition reimbursements available (averaging $14,450 per year), 53 teaching assistantships with tuition reimbursements available (averaging $14,250 per year); career-related internships or fieldwork, scholarships/grants, tuition waivers (full), and unspecified assistantships also available. Support available to part-time students. Financial award application deadline: 3/1; financial award applicants required to submit FAFSA. *Faculty research:* Applied mathematics, dynamical systems, statistics, mathematics education, mathematical and computational biology. Total annual research expenditures: $899,316. *Unit head:* Dr. Kenneth Bowers, Head, 406-994-3604, Fax: 406-994-1789, E-mail: bowers@math.montana.edu. *Application contact:* Dr. Carl A. Fox, Vice Provost for Graduate Education, 406-994-4145, Fax: 406-994-7433, E-mail: gradstudy@montana.edu.

Morgan State University, School of Graduate Studies, School of Computer, Mathematical, and Natural Sciences, Department of Mathematics, Baltimore, MD 21251. Offers MA. Part-time and evening/weekend programs available. *Degree requirements:* For master's, comprehensive exam, thesis. *Entrance requirements:* For master's, GRE. Additional exam requirements/recommendations for international students: Required—TOEFL (minimum score 550 paper-based; 213 computer-based). *Faculty research:* Number theory, semigroups, analysis, operations research.

Murray State University, College of Science, Engineering and Technology, Program in Mathematics and Statistics, Murray, KY 42071. Offers MA, MAT, MS. Part-time programs available. *Degree requirements:* For master's, comprehensive exam, thesis optional. *Entrance requirements:* For master's, GRE General Test. Additional exam requirements/recommendations for international students: Required—TOEFL. *Faculty research:* Algebraic structures, mathematical biology, topolgy.

Naval Postgraduate School, Graduate Programs, Department of Mathematics, Monterey, CA 93943. Offers applied mathematics (MS, PhD). Program only open to commissioned officers of the United States and friendly nations and selected United States federal civilian employees. Part-time programs available. *Degree requirements:* For master's, thesis; for doctorate, one foreign language, thesis/dissertation.

New Jersey Institute of Technology, Office of Graduate Studies, College of Science and Liberal Arts, Department of Mathematical Science, Program in Mathematics Science, Newark, NJ 07102. Offers PhD. Part-time and evening/weekend programs available. *Students:* 8 full-time (3 women); includes 1 Black or African American, non-Hispanic/Latino, 4 international. Average age 24. 58 applicants, 31% accepted, 8 enrolled. *Entrance requirements:* For doctorate, GRE General Test, minimum graduate GPA of 3.5. Additional exam requirements/recommendations for international students: Required—TOEFL (minimum score 550 paper-based; 213 computer-based; 79 iBT). *Application deadline:* For fall admission, 6/5 priority date for domestic students, 4/1 for international students; for spring admission, 11/15 for domestic and international students. Applications are processed on a rolling basis. Application fee: $65. Electronic applications accepted. *Expenses:* Tuition, state resident: full-time $14,724; part-time $818 per credit. Tuition, nonresident: full-time $20,304; part-time $1128 per credit. Required fees: $2272; $209 per credit. $103 per semester. One-time fee: $312 full-time; $212 part-time. *Financial support:* Fellowships with full and partial tuition reimbursements, research assistantships with full and partial tuition reimbursements, teaching assistantships with full and partial tuition reimbursements, career-related internships or fieldwork, Federal Work-Study, institutionally sponsored loans, and unspecified assistantships available. Financial award application deadline: 3/15. *Unit head:* Dr. Daljit S. Ahluwalia, Chair, 973-596-8465, E-mail: daljit.ahluwalia@njit.edu. *Application contact:* Kathryn Kelly, Director of Admissions, 973-596-3300, Fax: 973-596-3461, E-mail: admissions@njit.edu.

New Mexico Institute of Mining and Technology, Graduate Studies, Department of Mathematics, Socorro, NM 87801. Offers applied math (PhD); mathematics (MS); operations research (MS). *Degree requirements:* For master's, thesis optional; for doctorate, thesis/dissertation. *Entrance requirements:* For master's, GRE General Test. Additional exam requirements/recommendations for international students: Required—TOEFL (minimum score 540 paper-based; 207 computer-based). *Faculty research:* Applied mathematics, differential equations, industrial mathematics, numerical analysis, stochastic processes.

New Mexico State University, Graduate School, College of Arts and Sciences, Department of Mathematical Sciences, Las Cruces, NM 88003-8001. Offers MS, PhD. Part-time programs available. *Faculty:* 13 full-time (2 women). *Students:* 39 full-time (9 women), 4 part-time (3 women); includes 6 minority (1 Black or African American, non-Hispanic/Latino; 5 Hispanic/Latino), 24 international. Average age 32. 74 applicants, 82% accepted, 12 enrolled. In 2010, 7 master's, 7 doctorates awarded. *Degree requirements:* For master's, thesis optional, final oral exam; for doctorate, one foreign language, comprehensive exam, thesis/dissertation, final oral exam. *Entrance requirements:* Additional exam requirements/recommendations for international students: Required—TOEFL (minimum score 530 paper-based; 197 computer-based). *Application deadline:* For fall admission, 2/1 priority date for domestic and international students; for spring admission, 10/1 for domestic and international students. Applications are processed on a rolling basis. Application fee: $30 ($50 for international students). Electronic applications accepted. *Expenses:* Tuition, state resident: full-time $4536; part-time $242 per credit. Tuition, nonresident: full-time $15,816; part-time $712 per credit. Required fees: $636 per term. *Financial support:* In 2010–11, 2 research assistantships (averaging $20,810 per year), 33 teaching assistantships (averaging $14,907 per year) were awarded; fellowships, scholarships/grants, health care benefits, and unspecified assistantships also available. Financial award application deadline: 2/1. *Faculty research:* Commutative algebra, dynamical systems, harmonic analysis and applications, algebraic topology, statistics. *Unit head:* Dr. Joseph Lakey, Head, 575-646-3901, Fax: 575-646-1064, E-mail: jlakey@nmsu.edu. *Application contact:* Dr. David Finston, Professor, 575-646-2637, Fax: 575-646-1064, E-mail: dfinston@nmsu.edu.

New York University, Graduate School of Arts and Science, Courant Institute of Mathematical Sciences, Department of Mathematics, New York, NY 10012-1019. Offers atmosphere ocean science and mathematics (PhD); mathematics (MS, PhD); mathematics and statistics/operations research (MS); mathematics in finance (MS); scientific computing (MS). Part-time and evening/weekend programs available. *Faculty:* 46 full-time (0 women). *Students:* 199 full-time (35 women), 114 part-time (23 women); includes 3 Black or African American, non-Hispanic/Latino; 1 American Indian or Alaska Native, non-Hispanic/Latino; 41 Asian, non-Hispanic/Latino; 4 Hispanic/Latino, 164 international. Average age 28. 1,273 applicants, 29% accepted, 118 enrolled. In 2010, 66 master's, 16 doctorates awarded. *Degree requirements:* For master's, thesis optional; for doctorate, one foreign language, thesis/dissertation, oral and written exams. *Entrance requirements:* For master's and doctorate, GRE General Test, GRE

Subject Test. Additional exam requirements/recommendations for international students: Required—TOEFL. *Application deadline:* For fall admission, 1/4 for domestic students; for spring admission, 11/1 for domestic students. Application fee: $90. *Financial support:* Fellowships with tuition reimbursements, research assistantships with tuition reimbursements, teaching assistantships with tuition reimbursements, Federal Work-Study, institutionally sponsored loans, scholarships/grants, health care benefits, and unspecified assistantships available. Financial award application deadline: 1/4; financial award applicants required to submit FAFSA. *Faculty research:* Partial differential equations, computational science, applied mathematics, geometry and topology, probability and stochastic processes. *Unit head:* Fedor Bogomolov, Director of Graduate Studies, 212-998-3238, Fax: 212-995-4121, E-mail: admissions@math.nyu.edu. *Application contact:* Tamar Arnon, Program Administrator, 212-998-3238, Fax: 212-995-4121, E-mail: admissions@math.nyu.edu.

Nicholls State University, Graduate Studies, College of Arts and Sciences, Department of Mathematics and Computer Science, Thibodaux, LA 70310. Offers community/technical college mathematics (MS). Part-time and evening/weekend programs available. *Degree requirements:* For master's, comprehensive exam. *Entrance requirements:* For master's, GRE General Test. Electronic applications accepted. *Faculty research:* Operations research, statistics, numerical analysis, algebra, topology.

North Carolina Central University, Division of Academic Affairs, College of Science and Technology, Department of Mathematics and Computer Science, Durham, NC 27707-3129. Offers applied mathematics (MS); mathematics education (MS); pure mathematics (MS). Part-time and evening/weekend programs available. *Degree requirements:* For master's, one foreign language, comprehensive exam, thesis. *Entrance requirements:* For master's, minimum GPA of 3.0 in major, 2.5 overall. Additional exam requirements/recommendations for international students: Required—TOEFL. *Faculty research:* Structure theorems for Lie algebra, Kleene monoids and semi-groups, theoretical computer science, mathematics education.

North Carolina State University, Graduate School, College of Agriculture and Life Sciences and College of Engineering and College of Physical and Mathematical Sciences, Program in Financial Mathematics, Raleigh, NC 27695. Offers MFM. Part-time programs available. *Degree requirements:* For master's, thesis optional, project/internship. *Entrance requirements:* For master's, GRE General Test. Additional exam requirements/recommendations for international students: Required—TOEFL (minimum score 550 paper-based; 213 computer-based). Electronic applications accepted. *Faculty research:* Financial mathematics modeling and computation, futures, options and commodities markets, real options, credit risk, portfolio optimization.

North Carolina State University, Graduate School, College of Physical and Mathematical Sciences, Department of Mathematics, Program in Mathematics, Raleigh, NC 27695. Offers MS, PhD. *Degree requirements:* For master's, thesis (for some programs); for doctorate, thesis/dissertation. *Entrance requirements:* For master's and doctorate, GRE, GRE Subject Test (recommended). Electronic applications accepted.

North Dakota State University, College of Graduate and Interdisciplinary Studies, College of Science and Mathematics, Department of Mathematics, Fargo, ND 58108. Offers applied mathematics (MS, PhD); mathematics (MS, PhD). *Faculty:* 15 full-time, 4 part-time/adjunct. *Students:* 24 full-time (7 women), 2 part-time (1 woman); includes 1 Two or more races, non-Hispanic/Latino, 6 international. Average age 28. 26 applicants, 35% accepted, 5 enrolled. In 2010, 3 master's, 2 doctorates awarded. *Degree requirements:* For master's, comprehensive exam, thesis; for doctorate, one foreign language, comprehensive exam, thesis/dissertation, computer proficiency. *Entrance requirements:* For master's and doctorate, GRE General Test. Additional exam requirements/recommendations for international students: Required—TOEFL (minimum score 525 paper-based; 197 computer-based; 71 iBT), IELTS. *Application deadline:* For fall admission, 5/1 priority date for domestic and international students; for spring admission, 8/1 for domestic students, 8/1 priority date for international students. Applications are processed on a rolling basis. Application fee: $45 ($60 for international students). Electronic applications accepted. *Financial support:* In 2010–11, 5 fellowships with full tuition reimbursements (averaging $18,000 per year), 1 research assistantship with tuition reimbursement (averaging $14,000 per year), 17 teaching assistantships with full tuition reimbursements (averaging $9,300 per year) were awarded; Federal Work-Study, institutionally sponsored loans, and tuition waivers (full) also available. Support available to part-time students. Financial award application deadline: 3/31. *Faculty research:* Discrete mathematics, number theory, analysis theory, algebra, applied math. Total annual research expenditures: $33,227. *Unit head:* Dr. Warren Shreve, Chair, 701-231-8171, Fax: 701-231-7598, E-mail: warren.shreve@ndsu.edu. *Application contact:* Dr. Jim Coykendall, Graduate Program Director, 701-231-8079, Fax: 701-231-7598, E-mail: jim.coykendall@ndsu.edu.

Northeastern Illinois University, Graduate College, College of Arts and Sciences, Department of Mathematics, Programs in Mathematics, Chicago, IL 60625-4699. Offers mathematics (MS); mathematics for elementary school teachers (MA). Part-time and evening/weekend programs available. *Faculty:* 16 full-time (5 women), 13 part-time/adjunct (5 women). *Students:* 12 full-time (3 women), 37 part-time (16 women); includes 9 minority (3 Black or African American, non-Hispanic/Latino; 4 Asian, non-Hispanic/Latino; 2 Hispanic/Latino), 2 international. Average age 35. 35 applicants, 71% accepted, 12 enrolled. In 2010, 19 master's awarded. *Degree requirements:* For master's, comprehensive exam, thesis optional, project. *Entrance requirements:* For master's, minimum GPA of 2.75, 6 undergraduate courses in mathematics. Additional exam requirements/recommendations for international students: Required—TOEFL (minimum score 550 paper-based; 213 computer-based; 79 iBT). *Application deadline:* Applications are processed on a rolling basis. Application fee: $30. Electronic applications accepted. *Financial support:* In 2010–11, 1 research assistantship with full and partial tuition reimbursement (averaging $6,600 per year) was awarded; career-related internships or fieldwork, Federal Work-Study, institutionally sponsored loans, scholarships/grants, tuition waivers (full and partial), and unspecified assistantships also available. Support available to part-time students. Financial award applicants required to submit FAFSA. *Faculty research:* Numerical analysis, mathematical biology, operations research, statistics, geometry and mathematics of finance. *Unit head:* Dr. Paul P. O'Hara, Department Chair. *Application contact:* Dr. Paul P. O'Hara, Department Chair.

Northeastern University, College of Science, Department of Mathematics, Boston, MA 02115-5096. Offers applied mathematics (MS); mathematics (MS, PhD); operations research (MSOR). Part-time and evening/weekend programs available. *Faculty:* 39 full-time (5 women), 15 part-time/adjunct (7 women). *Students:* 52 full-time (16 women), 3 part-time (2 women). 164 applicants, 58% accepted, 14 enrolled. In 2010, 6 master's, 7 doctorates awarded. *Degree requirements:* For master's, thesis (for some programs); for doctorate, thesis/dissertation, qualifying exams. *Entrance requirements:* For master's and doctorate, GRE Subject Test, GRE General Test. Additional exam requirements/recommendations for international students: Required—TOEFL. *Application deadline:* For fall admission, 2/1 priority date for domestic and international students. Applications are processed on a rolling basis. Application fee: $50. Electronic applications accepted. *Financial support:* In 2010–11, 26 teaching assistantships with tuition reimbursements (averaging $17,345 per year) were awarded; research assistantships with tuition reimbursements, Federal Work-Study, institutionally sponsored loans, tuition waivers (full and partial), and unspecified assistantships also available. Financial award application deadline: 3/1; financial award applicants required to submit FAFSA. *Faculty research:* Algebra and singularities, combinatorics, topology, probability and statistics, geometric analysis and partial differential equations. *Unit head:* Dr. Jerzy Weyman, Graduate Coordinator, 617-373-5513, Fax: 617-373-5658, E-mail: j.weyman@neu.edu. *Application contact:* Jo-Anne Dickinson, Admissions Contact, 617-373-5990, Fax: 617-373-7281, E-mail: gsas@neu.edu.

Northern Arizona University, Graduate College, College of Engineering, Forestry and Natural Sciences, Department of Mathematics and Statistics, Flagstaff, AZ 86011. Offers applied statistics (Certificate); mathematics (MAT, MS); statistics (MS). Part-time programs available. *Faculty:* 42 full-time (12 women). *Students:* 23 full-time (10 women), 18 part-time (11 women); includes 8 minority (3 Black or African American, non-Hispanic/Latino; 1 Asian, non-Hispanic/Latino; 4 Hispanic/Latino), 1 international. Average age 28. 33 applicants, 61% accepted, 12 enrolled. In 2010, 15 master's, 1 other advanced degree awarded. *Degree requirements:* For master's, comprehensive exam (for some programs), thesis (for some programs). *Entrance requirements:* For master's, minimum GPA of 3.0. Additional exam requirements/recommendations for international students: Required—TOEFL (minimum score 550 paper-based; 213 computer-based; 80 iBT), IELTS (minimum score 7). *Application deadline:* For fall admission, 3/15 priority date for domestic and international students; for spring admission, 10/15 priority date for domestic and international students. Applications are processed on a rolling basis. Application fee: $65. Electronic applications accepted. *Financial support:* In 2010–11, 22 teaching assistantships with partial tuition reimbursements (averaging $14,051 per year) were awarded; Federal Work-Study, scholarships/grants, health care benefits, tuition waivers (full and partial), and unspecified assistantships also available. Financial award applicants required to submit FAFSA. *Faculty research:* Topology, statistics, groups, ring theory, number theory. *Unit head:* Dr. Janet M. McShane, Chair, 928-523-1252, Fax: 928-523-5847, E-mail: janet.mcshane@nau.edu. *Application contact:* Sharon O'Connor, Chair, 928-523-3481, Fax: 928-523-5847, E-mail: math.grad@nau.edu.

Northern Illinois University, Graduate School, College of Liberal Arts and Sciences, Department of Mathematical Sciences, De Kalb, IL 60115-2854. Offers mathematical sciences (PhD); mathematics (MS); statistics (MS). Part-time programs available. *Faculty:* 43 full-time (10 women), 4 part-time/adjunct (0 women). *Students:* 58 full-time (22 women), 32 part-time (13 women); includes 12 minority (3 Black or African American, non-Hispanic/Latino; 6 Asian, non-Hispanic/Latino; 1 Hispanic/Latino; 1 Native Hawaiian or other Pacific Islander, non-Hispanic/Latino; 1 Two or more races, non-Hispanic/Latino), 20 international. Average age 29. 65 applicants, 63% accepted, 14 enrolled. In 2010, 7 master's, 3 doctorates awarded. Terminal master's awarded for partial completion of doctoral program. *Degree requirements:* For master's, comprehensive exam, thesis optional; for doctorate, one foreign language, thesis/dissertation, candidacy exam, dissertation defense, internship. *Entrance requirements:* For master's, GRE General Test, minimum GPA of 2.75; for doctorate, GRE General Test, minimum GPA of 2.75 (undergraduate), 3.2 (graduate). Additional exam requirements/recommendations for international students: Required—TOEFL (minimum score 550 paper-based; 213 computer-based). *Application deadline:* For fall admission, 6/1 for domestic students, 5/1 for international students; for spring admission, 11/1 for domestic students, 10/1 for international students. Applications are processed on a rolling basis. Application fee: $30. Electronic applications accepted. *Expenses:* Tuition, state resident: full-time $7200; part-time $300 per credit hour. Tuition, nonresident: full-time $14,400; part-time $600 per credit hour. Required fees: $79 per credit hour. *Financial support:* In 2010–11, 43 teaching assistantships with full tuition reimbursements were awarded; fellowships with full tuition reimbursements, research assistantships with full tuition reimbursements, career-related internships or fieldwork, Federal Work-Study, scholarships/grants, tuition waivers (full), and unspecified assistantships also available. Support available to part-time students. Financial award applicants required to submit FAFSA. *Faculty research:* Numerical linear algebra, noncommutative rings, nonlineal partial differential equations, finite group theory, abstract harmonic analysis. *Unit head:* Dr. William D. Blair, Chair, 815-753-0566, Fax: 815-753-1112, E-mail: blair@math.niu.edu. *Application contact:* Dr. Bernard Harris, Director, Graduate Studies, 815-753-6775, E-mail: harris@math.niu.edu.

Northwestern University, The Graduate School, Judd A. and Marjorie Weinberg College of Arts and Sciences, Department of Mathematics, Evanston, IL 60208. Offers PhD. Admissions and degrees offered through The Graduate School. Part-time programs available. *Degree requirements:* For doctorate, thesis/dissertation, preliminary exam. *Entrance requirements:* For doctorate, GRE General Test, GRE Subject Test. Additional exam requirements/recommendations for international students: Required—TOEFL. *Faculty research:* Algebra, algebraic topology, analysis dynamical systems, partial differential equations.

Oakland University, Graduate Study and Lifelong Learning, College of Arts and Sciences, Department of Mathematics and Statistics, Program in Mathematics, Rochester, MI 48309-4401. Offers MA. *Entrance requirements:* Additional exam requirements/recommendations for international students: Required—TOEFL (minimum score 550 paper-based; 213 computer-based). Electronic applications accepted. *Expenses:* Contact institution.

The Ohio State University, Graduate School, College of Arts and Sciences, Division of Natural and Mathematical Sciences, Department of Mathematics, Columbus, OH 43210. Offers MA, MS, PhD. *Faculty:* 68. *Students:* 49 full-time (9 women), 81 part-time (17 women); includes 1 Black or African American, non-Hispanic/Latino; 4 Hispanic/Latino, 60 international. Average age 27. In 2010, 7 master's, 18 doctorates awarded. *Degree requirements:* For master's, thesis optional; for doctorate, 2 foreign languages, thesis/dissertation. *Entrance requirements:* For master's and doctorate, GRE General Test, GRE Subject Test (mathematics). Additional exam requirements/recommendations for international students: Required—TOEFL. *Application deadline:* For fall admission, 8/15 priority date for domestic students, 7/1 priority date for international students; for winter admission, 12/1 priority date for domestic students, 11/1 priority date for international students; for spring admission, 3/1 priority date for domestic students, 2/1 priority date for international students. Applications are processed on a rolling basis. Application fee: $40 ($50 for international students). Electronic applications accepted. *Expenses:* Tuition, state resident: full-time $10,605. Tuition, nonresident: full-time $26,535. Tuition and fees vary according to course load and program. *Financial support:* Fellowships, research assistantships, teaching assistantships, Federal Work-Study, institutionally sponsored loans, and unspecified assistantships available. Support available to part-time students. *Unit head:* Luis Casian, Chair, 614-292-7173, E-mail: casian@math.ohio-state.edu. *Application contact:* 614-292-9444, Fax: 614-292-3895, E-mail: domestic.grad@osu.edu.

Ohio University, Graduate College, College of Arts and Sciences, Department of Mathematics, Athens, OH 45701-2979. Offers MS, PhD. Part-time and evening/weekend programs available. *Students:* 45 full-time (8 women), 1 part-time (0 women); includes 3 minority (1 American Indian or Alaska Native, non-Hispanic/Latino; 2 Asian, non-Hispanic/Latino), 19 international. 89 applicants, 69% accepted, 15 enrolled. In 2010, 9 master's, 4 doctorates awarded. Terminal master's awarded for partial completion of doctoral program. *Degree requirements:* For master's, thesis optional; for doctorate, comprehensive exam, thesis/dissertation. *Entrance requirements:* For master's and doctorate, minimum GPA of 3.0. Additional exam requirements/recommendations for international students: Required—TOEFL (minimum score 550 paper-based; 80 iBT) or IELTS (minimum score 6.5). *Application deadline:* For fall admission, 2/1 priority date for domestic and international students. Applications are processed on a rolling basis. Application fee: $50 ($55 for international students). Electronic applications accepted. *Financial support:* Fellowships with full tuition reimbursements, teaching assistantships with full tuition reimbursements, Federal Work-Study and institutionally sponsored loans available. Financial award application deadline: 2/1. *Faculty research:* Algebra (group and ring theory), functional analysis, topology, differential equations, computational math. *Unit head:* Dr. Jeff Connor, Chair, 740-593-1254, Fax: 740-593-9805, E-mail: connor@math.ohiou.edu. *Application contact:* Dr. Martin Mohlenkamp, Graduate Chair, 740-593-1259, Fax: 740-593-9805, E-mail: mjm@math.ohiou.edu.

Oklahoma State University, College of Arts and Sciences, Department of Mathematics, Stillwater, OK 74078. Offers applied mathematics (MS, PhD); mathematics education (MS, PhD); pure mathematics (MS, PhD). *Faculty:* 37 full-time (7 women), 5 part-time/adjunct (4 women). *Students:* 4 full-time (1 woman), 26 part-time (6 women); includes 1 Asian, non-Hispanic/Latino, 20 international. Average age 31. 69 applicants, 16% accepted, 6 enrolled. In 2010, 2 doctorates awarded. *Degree requirements:* For master's, thesis, creative component,

Mathematics

Oklahoma State University (continued)

or report; for doctorate, comprehensive exam, thesis/dissertation. *Entrance requirements:* For master's and doctorate, GRE (recommended). Additional exam requirements/recommendations for international students: Required—TOEFL (minimum score 550 paper-based; 79 iBT). *Application deadline:* For fall admission, 3/1 for domestic and international students; for spring admission, 10/15 for domestic students, 10/15 priority date for international students. Applications are processed on a rolling basis. Application fee: $40 ($75 for international students). Electronic applications accepted. *Expenses:* Tuition, state resident: full-time $3716; part-time $154.85 per credit hour. Tuition, nonresident: full-time $14,892; part-time $621 per credit hour. Required fees: $2044; $85.20 per credit hour. One-time fee: $50. Tuition and fees vary according to course load and campus/location. *Financial support:* In 2010–11, 29 teaching assistantships (averaging $18,431 per year) were awarded; health care benefits and tuition waivers (partial) also available. Financial award application deadline: 3/1; financial award applicants required to submit FAFSA. *Unit head:* Dr. Dale Alspach, Head, 405-744-5688, Fax: 405-744-8275. *Application contact:* Dr. Mark Payton, Dean, 405-744-6368, Fax: 405-744-0355, E-mail: grad-i@okstate.edu.

Old Dominion University, College of Sciences, Programs in Computational and Applied Mathematics, Norfolk, VA 23529. Offers MS, PhD. Part-time programs available. *Faculty:* 22 full-time (0 women), 2 part-time/adjunct (0 women). *Students:* 20 full-time (8 women), 9 part-time (7 women); includes 5 minority (2 Black or African American, non-Hispanic/Latino; 2 Asian, non-Hispanic/Latino; 1 Two or more races, non-Hispanic/Latino), 14 international. Average age 29. 31 applicants, 55% accepted, 8 enrolled. In 2010, 6 master's, 7 doctorates awarded. Terminal master's awarded for partial completion of doctoral program. *Degree requirements:* For master's, project; for doctorate, comprehensive exam, thesis/dissertation, candidacy exam. *Entrance requirements:* For master's, minimum GPA of 3.0 in major, 2.5 overall; for doctorate, GRE General Test, 3 recommendation letters, transcripts, essay. Additional exam requirements/recommendations for international students: Required—TOEFL. *Application deadline:* For fall admission, 6/1 for domestic students, 5/15 for international students; for winter admission, 11/1 for domestic students, 10/1 for international students; for spring admission, 3/1 for domestic students, 2/1 for international students. Applications are processed on a rolling basis. Application fee: $40. Electronic applications accepted. *Expenses:* Tuition, state resident: full-time $8592; part-time $358 per credit. Tuition, nonresident: full-time $21,672; part-time $903 per credit. Required fees: $119 per semester. One-time fee: $50. *Financial support:* In 2010–11, 4 fellowships with full tuition reimbursements (averaging $17,000 per year), 4 research assistantships with full tuition reimbursements (averaging $16,000 per year), 12 teaching assistantships with full tuition reimbursements (averaging $15,000 per year) were awarded; scholarships/grants also available. Financial award application deadline: 2/15; financial award applicants required to submit FAFSA. *Faculty research:* Numerical analysis, integral equations, continuum mechanics. Total annual research expenditures: $506,890. *Unit head:* Dr. Richard Noren, Graduate Program Director, 757-683-3882, Fax: 757-683-3885, E-mail: rnoren@odu.edu. *Application contact:* Dr. Richard Noren, Graduate Program Director, 757-683-3882, Fax: 757-683-3885, E-mail: rnoren@odu.edu.

Oregon State University, Graduate School, College of Science, Department of Mathematics, Corvallis, OR 97331. Offers MA, MAIS, MS, PhD. Terminal master's awarded for partial completion of doctoral program. *Degree requirements:* For master's, variable foreign language requirement, thesis or alternative; for doctorate, one foreign language, thesis/dissertation, qualifying exams. *Entrance requirements:* For master's and doctorate, minimum GPA of 3.0 in last 90 hours. Additional exam requirements/recommendations for international students: Required—TOEFL.

Penn State University Park, Graduate School, Eberly College of Science, Department of Mathematics, State College, University Park, PA 16802-1503. Offers mathematics (MA), including applied mathematics. *Unit head:* Dr. John Roe, Head, 814-865-7527, Fax: 814-865-3735, E-mail: roe@math.psu.edu. *Application contact:* Dr. Dimitri Burago, Associate Head of Graduate Studies, 814-865-7741, E-mail: burago@math.psu.edu.

Pittsburg State University, Graduate School, College of Arts and Sciences, Department of Mathematics, Pittsburg, KS 66762. Offers MS. *Degree requirements:* For master's, thesis or alternative. *Faculty research:* Operations research, numerical analysis, applied analysis, applied algebra.

Polytechnic Institute of NYU, Department of Mathematics, Brooklyn, NY 11201-2990. Offers MS, PhD. Part-time and evening/weekend programs available. *Faculty:* 3 full-time (0 women), 1 part-time/adjunct (0 women). *Students:* 16 full-time (6 women), 13 part-time (2 women); includes 1 Asian, non-Hispanic/Latino; 2 Hispanic/Latino, 14 international. Average age 32. 58 applicants, 57% accepted, 9 enrolled. In 2010, 5 master's, 2 doctorates awarded. *Degree requirements:* For master's, comprehensive exam (for some programs), thesis (for some programs); for doctorate, comprehensive exam, thesis/dissertation. *Entrance requirements:* Additional exam requirements/recommendations for international students: Required—TOEFL (minimum score 550 paper-based; 213 computer-based; 80 iBT); Recommended—IELTS (minimum score 6.5). *Application deadline:* For fall admission, 7/31 priority date for domestic students, 4/30 priority date for international students; for spring admission, 12/31 priority date for domestic students, 11/30 priority date for international students. Applications are processed on a rolling basis. Application fee: $75. Electronic applications accepted. *Expenses:* Tuition: Full-time $21,492; part-time $1194 per credit. Required fees: $385 per semester. Tuition and fees vary according to course load. *Financial support:* In 2010–11, 5 fellowships (averaging $35,280 per year), 5 teaching assistantships (averaging $47,554 per year) were awarded; research assistantships, institutionally sponsored loans, scholarships/grants, and unspecified assistantships also available. Support available to part-time students. Financial award applicants required to submit FAFSA. Total annual research expenditures: $207,212. *Unit head:* Dr. Erwin Lutwak, Head, 718-260-3366, Fax: 718-260-3139, E-mail: lutwak@magnus.poly.edu. *Application contact:* JeanCarlo Bonilla, Director of Graduate Enrollment Management, 718-260-3182, Fax: 718-260-3624, E-mail: gradinfo@poly.edu.

Portland State University, Graduate Studies, College of Liberal Arts and Sciences, Department of Mathematics and Statistics, Portland, OR 97207-0751. Offers mathematical sciences (PhD); mathematics education (PhD); statistics (MS); MA/MS. *Faculty:* 31 full-time (10 women), 14 part-time/adjunct (6 women). *Students:* 57 full-time (19 women), 55 part-time (24 women); includes 1 Black or African American, non-Hispanic/Latino; 5 Asian, non-Hispanic/Latino; 8 Hispanic/Latino, 9 international. Average age 32. 79 applicants, 78% accepted, 33 enrolled. In 2010, 18 master's, 2 doctorates awarded. *Degree requirements:* For master's, thesis or alternative, exams; for doctorate, 2 foreign languages, thesis/dissertation, exams. *Entrance requirements:* For master's, GRE General Test, GRE Subject Test, minimum GPA of 3.0 in upper-division course work or 2.75 overall; for doctorate, GRE General Test. Additional exam requirements/recommendations for international students: Required—TOEFL (minimum score 550 paper-based; 213 computer-based). *Application deadline:* For fall admission, 4/1 for domestic students, 3/1 for international students; for winter admission, 9/1 for domestic students, 8/1 for international students; for spring admission, 11/1 for domestic and international students. Applications are processed on a rolling basis. Application fee: $50. *Expenses:* Tuition, state resident: full-time $8505; part-time $315 per credit. Tuition, nonresident: full-time $13,284; part-time $492 per credit. Required fees: $1482; $21 per credit. $99 per term. One-time fee: $120. Part-time tuition and fees vary according to course load and program. *Financial support:* In 2010–11, 1 research assistantship (averaging $19,448 per year), 24 teaching assistantships with full tuition reimbursements (averaging $12,545 per year) were awarded; Federal Work-Study, scholarships/grants, tuition waivers (partial), and unspecified assistantships also available. Support available to part-time students. Financial award application deadline: 3/1; financial award applicants required to submit FAFSA. *Faculty research:* Algebra, topology, statistical distribution theory, control theory, statistical robustness. Total annual research expenditures: $430,663. *Unit head:* J.J.P. Veerman, Chair, 503-725-8187, Fax: 503-725-3661, E-mail: mthchair@pdx.edu. *Application contact:* John Erdman, Coordinator, 503-725-3621, Fax: 503-725-3661, E-mail: erdman@pdx.edu.

Portland State University, Graduate Studies, Systems Science Program, Portland, OR 97207-0751. Offers computational intelligence (Certificate); computer modeling and simulation (Certificate); systems science (MS); systems science/anthropology (PhD); systems science/business administration (PhD); systems science/civil engineering (PhD); systems science/economics (PhD); systems science/engineering management (PhD); systems science/general (PhD); systems science/mathematical sciences (PhD); systems science/mechanical engineering (PhD); systems science/psychology (PhD); systems science/sociology (PhD). *Faculty:* 4 full-time (0 women), 1 part-time/adjunct (0 women). *Students:* 15 full-time (4 women), 35 part-time (11 women); includes 1 American Indian or Alaska Native, non-Hispanic/Latino; 1 Asian, non-Hispanic/Latino; 1 Two or more races, non-Hispanic/Latino, 4 international. Average age 39. 8 applicants, 88% accepted, 5 enrolled. In 2010, 2 master's, 4 doctorates awarded. *Degree requirements:* For doctorate, variable foreign language requirement, thesis/dissertation. *Entrance requirements:* For master's, 2 letters of recommendation; for doctorate, GMAT, GRE General Test, minimum undergraduate GPA of 3.0. Additional exam requirements/recommendations for international students: Required—TOEFL. *Application deadline:* For fall admission, 2/1 for domestic students; for spring admission, 11/1 for domestic students. Application fee: $50. *Expenses:* Tuition, state resident: full-time $8505; part-time $315 per credit. Tuition, nonresident: full-time $13,284; part-time $492 per credit. Required fees: $1482; $21 per credit. $99 per term. One-time fee: $120. Part-time tuition and fees vary according to course load and program. *Financial support:* In 2010–11, 1 research assistantship with full tuition reimbursement (averaging $7,704 per year) was awarded; teaching assistantships with full tuition reimbursements, career-related internships or fieldwork, Federal Work-Study, scholarships/grants, and unspecified assistantships also available. Support available to part-time students. Financial award application deadline: 3/1; financial award applicants required to submit FAFSA. *Faculty research:* Systems theory and methodology, artificial intelligence neural networks, information theory, nonlinear dynamics/chaos, modeling and simulation. *Unit head:* George Lendaris, Acting Director, 503-725-4960. *Application contact:* Dawn Sharafi, Administrative Assistant, 503-725-4960, E-mail: dawn@sysc.pdx.edu.

Prairie View A&M University, College of Arts and Sciences, Department of Mathematics, Prairie View, TX 77446-0519. Offers MS. Part-time and evening/weekend programs available. *Faculty:* 2 full-time (1 woman). *Students:* 6 full-time (4 women), 6 part-time (1 woman); includes 8 Black or African American, non-Hispanic/Latino; 1 Hispanic/Latino. Average age 40. 3 applicants, 100% accepted, 3 enrolled. In 2010, 1 master's awarded. *Degree requirements:* For master's, comprehensive exam, thesis. *Entrance requirements:* For master's, GRE General Test, bachelor's degree in mathematics. *Application deadline:* Applications are processed on a rolling basis. Application fee: $50. *Expenses:* Tuition, state resident: full-time $3586.14; part-time $119.06 per credit hour. Tuition, nonresident: part-time $511.23 per credit hour. *Financial support:* In 2010–11, 1 student received support, including 1 research assistantship (averaging $17,618 per year); career-related internships or fieldwork, Federal Work-Study, and institutionally sponsored loans also available. Support available to part-time students. Financial award application deadline: 4/1; financial award applicants required to submit FAFSA. *Faculty research:* Stochastic processor, queuing theory, waveler numeric analyses, delay systems mathematic modeling. Total annual research expenditures: $43,413. *Unit head:* Dr. Aliakbar Montazer Haghighi, Head, 936-261-1970, Fax: 936-261-2088, E-mail: amhaghighi@pvamu.edu. *Application contact:* Dr. Arona R. Davies, Graduate Advisor, 936-261-1972, Fax: 936-261-2088, E-mail: andavies@pvamu.edu.

Princeton University, Graduate School, Department of Mathematics, Princeton, NJ 08544-1019. Offers PhD. *Degree requirements:* For doctorate, 2 foreign languages, thesis/dissertation. *Entrance requirements:* For doctorate, GRE General Test, GRE Subject Test, 3 letters of recommendation. Additional exam requirements/recommendations for international students: Required—TOEFL (minimum score 600 paper-based; 250 computer-based). Electronic applications accepted.

Purdue University, Graduate School, College of Science, Department of Mathematics, West Lafayette, IN 47907. Offers MS, PhD. Terminal master's awarded for partial completion of doctoral program. *Degree requirements:* For doctorate, one foreign language, thesis/dissertation, oral and written exams. *Entrance requirements:* For master's and doctorate, GRE. Additional exam requirements/recommendations for international students: Required—TOEFL (minimum score 570 paper-based; 230 computer-based). Electronic applications accepted. *Faculty research:* Algebra, analysis, topology, differential equations, applied mathematics.

Purdue University Calumet, Graduate Studies Office, School of Engineering, Mathematics, and Science, Department of Mathematics, Computer Science, and Statistics, Hammond, IN 46323-2094. Offers computer science (MS); mathematics (MAT, MS). Part-time programs available. *Faculty:* 8 full-time (2 women). *Students:* 3 full-time (1 woman), 14 part-time (6 women); includes 2 Black or African American, non-Hispanic/Latino. Average age 29. 6 applicants, 100% accepted. *Entrance requirements:* Additional exam requirements/recommendations for international students: Required—TOEFL. *Application deadline:* For fall admission, 5/1 priority date for domestic students; for spring admission, 11/1 priority date for domestic students. Applications are processed on a rolling basis. Application fee: $30. *Expenses:* Tuition, state resident: full-time $6867. Tuition, nonresident: full-time $14,157. *Financial support:* In 2010–11, 5 students received support, including 1 research assistantship with partial tuition reimbursement available (averaging $7,000 per year), 4 teaching assistantships with partial tuition reimbursements available (averaging $7,000 per year). Financial award application deadline: 3/1. *Faculty research:* Topology, analysis, algebra, mathematics education. Total annual research expenditures: $55,000. *Unit head:* Dr. C. M. Murphy, Head, 219-989-2270, Fax: 219-989-2165, E-mail: cmmurphy@purduecal.edu. *Application contact:* Dr. Catherine M. Murphy, Graduate Advisor, 219-989-2270, E-mail: cmmurphy@purduecal.edu.

Queens College of the City University of New York, Division of Graduate Studies, Mathematics and Natural Sciences Division, Department of Mathematics, Flushing, NY 11367-1597. Offers MA. Part-time and evening/weekend programs available. *Faculty:* 31 full-time (6 women). *Students:* 2 full-time (both women), 50 part-time (25 women); includes 2 Black or African American, non-Hispanic/Latino; 17 Asian, non-Hispanic/Latino; 2 Hispanic/Latino, 10 international. 49 applicants, 47% accepted, 16 enrolled. In 2010, 15 master's awarded. *Degree requirements:* For master's, comprehensive exam. *Entrance requirements:* For master's, minimum GPA of 3.0. Additional exam requirements/recommendations for international students: Required—TOEFL. *Application deadline:* For fall admission, 4/1 for domestic students; for spring admission, 11/1 for domestic students. Applications are processed on a rolling basis. Application fee: $125. *Financial support:* Career-related internships or fieldwork, Federal Work-Study, institutionally sponsored loans, and tuition waivers (partial) available. Support available to part-time students. Financial award application deadline: 4/1; financial award applicants required to submit FAFSA. *Faculty research:* Topology, differential equations, combinatorics. *Unit head:* Dr. Wallace Goldberg, Chairperson, 718-997-5800, E-mail: wallace_goldberg@qc.edu. *Application contact:* Dr. Nick Metas, Graduate Adviser, 718-997-5800, E-mail: nick_metas@qc.edu.

Queen's University at Kingston, School of Graduate Studies and Research, Faculty of Arts and Sciences, Department of Mathematics and Statistics, Kingston, ON K7L 3N6, Canada. Offers mathematics (M Sc, M Sc Eng, PhD); statistics (M Sc, M Sc Eng, PhD). Part-time programs available. *Degree requirements:* For master's, thesis; for doctorate, comprehensive exam, thesis/dissertation. *Entrance requirements:* Additional exam requirements/

270 www.facebook.com/petersonspublishing

Peterson's Graduate Programs in the Physical Sciences, Mathematics, Agricultural Sciences, the Environment & Natural Resources 2012

recommendations for international students: Required—TOEFL. *Faculty research:* Algebra, analysis, applied mathematics, statistics.

Rensselaer Polytechnic Institute, Graduate School, School of Science, Program in Mathematics, Troy, NY 12180-3590. Offers MS, PhD. Part-time programs available. *Faculty:* 23 full-time (3 women), 4 part-time/adjunct (1 woman). *Students:* 51 full-time (17 women), 3 part-time (1 woman); includes 1 Black or African American, non-Hispanic/Latino; 3 Asian, non-Hispanic/Latino; 1 Hispanic/Latino, 8 international. Average age 22. 123 applicants, 37% accepted, 16 enrolled. In 2010, 11 master's, 8 doctorates awarded. Terminal master's awarded for partial completion of doctoral program. *Degree requirements:* For doctorate, comprehensive exam, thesis/dissertation, preliminary exam, candidacy presentation. *Entrance requirements:* For master's and doctorate, GRE General Test. Additional exam requirements/recommendations for international students: Required—TOEFL. *Application deadline:* For fall admission, 1/15 priority date for domestic students, 1/15 for international students. Applications are processed on a rolling basis. Application fee: $75. Electronic applications accepted. *Expenses:* Tuition: Full-time $39,600; part-time $1650 per credit. Required fees: $1896. *Financial support:* In 2010–11, 42 students received support, including fellowships with full tuition reimbursements available (averaging $23,000 per year), 5 research assistantships with full tuition reimbursements available (averaging $21,000 per year), 34 teaching assistantships with full tuition reimbursements available (averaging $17,500 per year); institutionally sponsored loans also available. Financial award application deadline: 2/1. *Faculty research:* Inverse problems, biomathematics, operations research, applied mathematics, mathematical modeling. *Unit head:* Dr. Donald A. Drew, Chair, 518-276-6345, Fax: 518-276-4824, E-mail: drewd@rpi.edu. *Application contact:* Dawnmarie Robens, Graduate Student Coordinator, 518-276-6414, Fax: 518-276-4824, E-mail: robensd@rpi.edu.

Rhode Island College, School of Graduate Studies, Faculty of Arts and Sciences, Department of Mathematics and Computer Science, Providence, RI 02908-1991. Offers mathematics (MA); mathematics content specialist (CGS). Part-time and evening/weekend programs available. *Faculty:* 4 full-time (2 women). *Students:* 4 part-time (2 women). Average age 31. In 2010, 1 master's awarded. *Degree requirements:* For master's, comprehensive exam. *Entrance requirements:* For master's, GRE General Test or MAT, minimum of 30 hours beyond pre-calculus math, 3 letters of recommendation, interview. Additional exam requirements/recommendations for international students: Recommended—TOEFL (minimum score 550 paper-based; 213 computer-based; 79 iBT). *Application deadline:* For fall admission, 3/1 for domestic students; for spring admission, 11/1 for domestic students. Applications are processed on a rolling basis. Application fee: $50. *Expenses:* Tuition, state resident: full-time $8208; part-time $342 per credit hour. Tuition, nonresident: full-time $16,080; part-time $670 per credit hour. Required fees: $554; $20 per credit. $72 per term. *Financial support:* In 2010–11, 2 teaching assistantships with full tuition reimbursements (averaging $4,550 per year) were awarded; Federal Work-Study, scholarships/grants, health care benefits, and unspecified assistantships also available. Support available to part-time students. Financial award application deadline: 5/15; financial award applicants required to submit FAFSA. *Unit head:* Dr. Raimundo Kovac, Chair, 401-456-8038. *Application contact:* Graduate Studies, 401-456-8700.

Rice University, Graduate Programs, Wiess School of Natural Sciences, Department of Mathematics, Houston, TX 77251-1892. Offers PhD. Terminal master's awarded for partial completion of doctoral program. *Degree requirements:* For doctorate, one foreign language, comprehensive exam, thesis/dissertation. *Entrance requirements:* For doctorate, GRE Subject Test, GRE General Test. Additional exam requirements/recommendations for international students: Required—TOEFL (minimum score 600 paper-based; 90 iBT). Electronic applications accepted. *Faculty research:* Algebraic geometry/algebra, complex analysis and Teichmuller theory, dynamical systems and Ergodic theory, topology, differential geometry and geometric analysis.

Rivier College, School of Graduate Studies, Department of Computer Science and Mathematics, Nashua, NH 03060. Offers computer science (MS); mathematics (MAT). Part-time and evening/weekend programs available. *Faculty:* 5 full-time (3 women), 3 part-time/adjunct (0 women). *Students:* 16 full-time (9 women), 36 part-time (17 women); includes 2 Black or African American, non-Hispanic/Latino; 20 Asian, non-Hispanic/Latino. Average age 36. 26 applicants, 50% accepted, 8 enrolled. In 2010, 16 master's awarded. *Entrance requirements:* For master's, GRE Subject Test. *Application deadline:* Applications are processed on a rolling basis. Application fee: $25. Electronic applications accepted. *Expenses:* Tuition: Part-time $456 per credit. *Financial support:* Available to part-time students. Application deadline: 2/1. *Unit head:* Dr. Paul Cunningham, Director, 603-897-8272, E-mail: pcunningham@rivier.edu. *Application contact:* Mathew Kittredge, Director of Graduate Admissions, 603-897-8229, Fax: 603-897-8810, E-mail: mkittredge@rivier.edu.

Roosevelt University, Graduate Division, College of Arts and Sciences, Department of Mathematics and Actuarial Science, Program in Mathematics, Chicago, IL 60605. Offers mathematical sciences (MS), including actuarial science. Part-time and evening/weekend programs available. *Faculty research:* Statistics, mathematics education, finite groups, computers in mathematics.

Rowan University, Graduate School, College of Liberal Arts and Sciences, Department of Mathematics, Glassboro, NJ 08028-1701. Offers MA. Part-time and evening/weekend programs available. *Faculty:* 4 full-time (1 woman), 2 part-time/adjunct (1 woman). *Students:* 5 full-time (0 women), 19 part-time (11 women); includes 3 Black or African American, non-Hispanic/Latino; 1 Hispanic/Latino. Average age 31. 20 applicants, 100% accepted, 14 enrolled. In 2010, 2 master's awarded. *Degree requirements:* For master's, thesis. *Entrance requirements:* For master's, GRE General Test. Additional exam requirements/recommendations for international students: Required—TOEFL. *Application deadline:* Applications are processed on a rolling basis. Application fee: $65 ($200 for international students). Electronic applications accepted. *Expenses:* Tuition, area resident: Part-time $602 per semester hour. Tuition, nonresident: part-time $602 per semester hour. Required fees: $100 per semester hour. One-time fee: $10 part-time. *Financial support:* Career-related internships or fieldwork, scholarships/grants, health care benefits, and unspecified assistantships available. Support available to part-time students. *Unit head:* Dr. Horacio Sosa, Dean, College of Graduate and Continuing Education, 856-256-4747, Fax: 856-256-5638, E-mail: sosa@rowan.edu. *Application contact:* Karen Haynes, Graduate Coordinator, 856-256-4052, Fax: 856-256-4436, E-mail: haynes@rowan.edu.

Royal Military College of Canada, Division of Graduate Studies and Research, Science Division, Department of Mathematics and Computer Science, Kingston, ON K7K 7B4, Canada. Offers computer science (M Sc); mathematics (M Sc). *Degree requirements:* For master's, thesis. *Entrance requirements:* For master's, honours degree with second-class standing. Electronic applications accepted.

Rutgers, The State University of New Jersey, Camden, Graduate School of Arts and Sciences, Program in Mathematical Sciences, Camden, NJ 08102. Offers mathematics (MS). Part-time and evening/weekend programs available. *Faculty:* 15 full-time (2 women), 1 part-time/adjunct (0 women). *Students:* 7 full-time (3 women), 18 part-time (7 women); includes 3 Black or African American, non-Hispanic/Latino; 5 Asian, non-Hispanic/Latino; 1 Hispanic/Latino, 1 international. Average age 31. 26 applicants, 100% accepted, 14 enrolled. In 2010, 15 master's awarded. *Degree requirements:* For master's, comprehensive exam, thesis optional, survey paper, 30 credits. *Entrance requirements:* For master's, GRE, BS/BA in math or related subject, 2 letters of recommendation. Additional exam requirements/recommendations for international students: Required—TOEFL (minimum score 550 paper-based; 213 computer-based), IELTS. *Application deadline:* For fall admission, 3/1 priority date for domestic students, 4/1 priority date for international students; for spring admission, 12/1 priority date for domestic

students, 11/1 priority date for international students. Applications are processed on a rolling basis. Application fee: $65. Electronic applications accepted. *Expenses:* Tuition, state resident: full-time $4963; part-time $319 per credit. Tuition, nonresident: full-time $10,493; part-time $680 per credit. *Financial support:* In 2010–11, 1 student received support, including 17 fellowships with partial tuition reimbursements available (averaging $282 per year), 1 teaching assistantship with full tuition reimbursement available (averaging $26,000 per year); Federal Work-Study, scholarships/grants, and tuition waivers (partial) also available. Financial award application deadline: 3/15; financial award applicants required to submit FAFSA. *Faculty research:* Differential geometry, dynamical systems, vertex operator algebra, automorphic forms, CR-structures. Total annual research expenditures: $90,759. *Unit head:* Dr. Haydee Herrera, Director, 856-258-6076, Fax: 856-225-6602, E-mail: haydeeh@camden.rutgers.edu. *Application contact:* Dr. Haydee Herrera, Director, 856-258-6076, Fax: 856-225-6602, E-mail: haydeeh@camden.rutgers.edu.

Rutgers, The State University of New Jersey, Newark, Graduate School, Program in Mathematical Sciences, Newark, NJ 07102. Offers PhD. *Faculty:* 14 full-time (2 women). *Students:* 10 full-time (3 women); includes 6 Asian, non-Hispanic/Latino; 1 Hispanic/Latino. 16 applicants, 6% accepted, 0 enrolled. In 2010, 1 doctorate awarded. *Degree requirements:* For doctorate, thesis/dissertation, written qualifying exam. *Entrance requirements:* For doctorate, GRE General Test, minimum B average. Additional exam requirements/recommendations for international students: Required—TOEFL. *Application deadline:* For fall admission, 6/15 priority date for domestic students. Applications are processed on a rolling basis. Application fee: $60. Electronic applications accepted. *Expenses:* Tuition, state resident: part-time $600 per credit. Tuition, nonresident: full-time $10,694. *Financial support:* In 2010–11, 1 fellowship (averaging $18,000 per year), 2 research assistantships with full and partial tuition reimbursements (averaging $23,112 per year), 8 teaching assistantships with full and partial tuition reimbursements (averaging $23,112 per year) were awarded; tuition waivers (full and partial) also available. Financial award application deadline: 3/1. *Faculty research:* Number theory, automorphic form, low-dimensional topology, Kleinian groups, representation theory. *Unit head:* Dr. Zhengya Mao, Program Coordinator, 973-353-5156 Ext. 20, Fax: 973-353-5270, E-mail: zmao@andromeda.rutgers.edu. *Application contact:* Jason Hand, Director of Admissions, 973-353-5205, Fax: 973-353-1440.

Rutgers, The State University of New Jersey, New Brunswick, Graduate School-New Brunswick, Department of Mathematics, Piscataway, NJ 08854-8097. Offers applied mathematics (MS, PhD); mathematics (MS, PhD). Part-time programs available. *Degree requirements:* For doctorate, one foreign language, comprehensive exam, thesis/dissertation. *Entrance requirements:* For master's and doctorate, GRE General Test, GRE Subject Test. Additional exam requirements/recommendations for international students: Required—TOEFL. *Expenses:* Tuition, state resident: full-time $7200; part-time $600 per credit. Tuition, nonresident: full-time $11,124; part-time $927 per credit. *Faculty research:* Logic and set theory, number theory, mathematical physics, control theory, partial differential equations.

St. Cloud State University, School of Graduate Studies, College of Science and Engineering, Department of Mathematics, St. Cloud, MN 56301-4498. Offers MS. *Degree requirements:* For master's, comprehensive exam (for some programs), thesis or alternative. *Entrance requirements:* For master's, GRE General Test, minimum GPA of 2.75. Additional exam requirements/recommendations for international students: Required—Michigan English Language Assessment Battery; Recommended—TOEFL (minimum score 550 paper-based; 213 computer-based), IELTS (minimum score 6.5). Electronic applications accepted.

St. John's University, St. John's College of Liberal Arts and Sciences, Department of Mathematics and Computer Science, Queens, NY 11439. Offers algebra (MA); analysis (MA); applied mathematics (MA); computer science (MA); geometry-topology (MA); logic and foundations (MA); probability and statistics (MA). Part-time and evening/weekend programs available. *Students:* 4 full-time (1 woman), 3 part-time (1 woman); includes 3 minority (1 Black or African American, non-Hispanic/Latino; 1 Asian, non-Hispanic/Latino; 1 Hispanic/Latino). Average age 25. 19 applicants, 42% accepted, 5 enrolled. In 2010, 3 master's awarded. *Degree requirements:* For master's, comprehensive exam, thesis optional. *Entrance requirements:* For master's, minimum GPA of 3.0. Additional exam requirements/recommendations for international students: Required—TOEFL (minimum score 600 paper-based; 250 computer-based; 100 iBT), IELTS (minimum score 5.5). *Application deadline:* For fall admission, 5/1 priority date for domestic and international students; for spring admission, 11/1 priority date for domestic and international students. Applications are processed on a rolling basis. Application fee: $70. Electronic applications accepted. *Expenses:* Tuition: Full-time $17,100; part-time $950 per credit. Required fees: $340; $170 per semester. Tuition and fees vary according to program. *Financial support:* Research assistantships, scholarships/grants available. Support available to part-time students. Financial award application deadline: 3/1; financial award applicants required to submit FAFSA. *Faculty research:* Functional analysis and operator theory, algebraic K-theory, applied mathematics, measure theory, differential geometry and mathematics education. *Unit head:* Dr. Charles Traina, Chair, 718-990-6166, E-mail: trainac@stjohns.edu. *Application contact:* Kathleen Davis, Director of Graduate Admission, 718-990-1601, Fax: 718-990-5686, E-mail: gradhelp@stjohns.edu.

Saint Joseph's University, College of Arts and Sciences, Department of Mathematics and Computer Science, Philadelphia, PA 19131-1395. Offers computer science (MS); mathematics and computer science (Post-Master's Certificate). Part-time and evening/weekend programs available. *Faculty:* 8 full-time (4 women), 2 part-time/adjunct (1 woman). *Students:* 45 full-time (12 women), 22 part-time (4 women); includes 3 Black or African American, non-Hispanic/Latino; 3 Asian, non-Hispanic/Latino, 54 international. Average age 27. 49 applicants, 61% accepted, 23 enrolled. In 2010, 25 master's awarded. *Entrance requirements:* For master's, 2 letters of recommendation. *Application deadline:* For fall admission, 7/15 priority date for domestic students, 4/15 for international students; for winter admission, 4/15 for domestic students, 1/15 for international students; for spring admission, 11/15 priority date for domestic students, 10/15 for international students. Applications are processed on a rolling basis. Application fee: $35. Electronic applications accepted. *Expenses:* Tuition: Part-time $729 per credit. Tuition and fees vary according to course load, degree level and program. *Financial support:* Teaching assistantships with partial tuition reimbursements, unspecified assistantships available. Financial award applicants required to submit FAFSA. *Faculty research:* Computer vision, pathways to careers. Total annual research expenditures: $175,000. *Unit head:* Dr. Jonathan Hodgson, Director, Graduate Computer Science, 610-660-1517, Fax: 610-660-3082, E-mail: jhodgson@sju.edu. *Application contact:* Kate McConnell, Director, Graduate College of Arts and Sciences Admissions and Retention, 610-660-3184, Fax: 610-660-3230, E-mail: kate.mcconnell@sju.edu.

Saint Louis University, Graduate Education, College of Arts and Sciences and Graduate Education, Department of Mathematics and Computer Science, St. Louis, MO 63103-2097. Offers mathematics (MA, MA-R, PhD). Part-time programs available. *Degree requirements:* For master's, comprehensive exam, thesis (for some programs); for doctorate, one foreign language, thesis/dissertation, preliminary exams. *Entrance requirements:* For master's, GRE General Test, letters of recommendation, resume, interview; for doctorate, GRE General Test, letters of recommendation, resumé, interview, transcripts, goal statement. Additional exam requirements/recommendations for international students: Required—TOEFL (minimum score 525 paper-based; 194 computer-based). Electronic applications accepted. *Faculty research:* Algebra, groups and rings, analysis, differential geometry, topology.

Saint Xavier University, Graduate Studies, School of Arts and Sciences, Department of Mathematics and Computer Science, Chicago, IL 60655-3105. Offers applied computer science in Internet information systems (MS); mathematics and computer science (MA); MBA/MS. *Degree requirements:* For master's, thesis optional.

Peterson's Graduate Programs in the Physical Sciences, Mathematics, Agricultural Sciences, the Environment & Natural Resources 2012

www.facebook.com/petersonspublishing　**271**

Mathematics

Salem State University, School of Graduate Studies, Program in Mathematics, Salem, MA 01970-5353. Offers MAT, MS. Part-time and evening/weekend programs available. *Students:* 1 (woman) full-time, 8 part-time (2 women); includes 1 Asian, non-Hispanic/Latino, 2 international. Average age 32. 1 applicant, 100% accepted, 1 enrolled. In 2010, 3 master's awarded. *Entrance requirements:* For master's, GRE or MAT. Additional exam requirements/recommendations for international students: Required—TOEFL (minimum score 550 paper-based; 80 iBT) or IELTS (minimum score 5.5). *Application deadline:* For fall admission, 5/1 for domestic students; for spring admission, 10/1 for domestic students. Applications are processed on a rolling basis. Application fee: $50. *Expenses:* Tuition, state resident: full-time $2520; part-time $290 per credit hour. Tuition, nonresident: full-time $4140; part-time $380 per credit hour. Required fees: $2700. *Financial support:* Career-related internships or fieldwork, Federal Work-Study, scholarships/grants, health care benefits, and unspecified assistantships available. Financial award application deadline: 5/1; financial award applicants required to submit FAFSA. *Unit head:* Julie Belock, Program Coordinator, 978-542-6321, Fax: 978-542-7175, E-mail: jbelock@salemstate.edu. *Application contact:* Dr. Lee A. Brossoit, Assistant Dean of Graduate Admissions, 978-542-6675, Fax: 978-542-7215, E-mail: lbrossoit@salemstate.edu.

Sam Houston State University, College of Arts and Sciences, Department of Mathematics and Statistics, Huntsville, TX 77341. Offers mathematics (MA, MS); statistics (MS). Part-time programs available. *Faculty:* 12 full-time (3 women). *Students:* 26 full-time (11 women), 7 part-time (5 women); includes 2 Hispanic/Latino, 11 international. Average age 30. 24 applicants, 92% accepted, 10 enrolled. In 2010, 8 master's awarded. *Entrance requirements:* For master's, GRE General Test. Additional exam requirements/recommendations for international students: Required—TOEFL (minimum score 550 paper-based; 213 computer-based; 79 iBT). *Application deadline:* For fall admission, 8/1 for domestic and international students; for spring admission, 12/1 for domestic and international students. Applications are processed on a rolling basis. Application fee: $20. *Expenses:* Tuition, state resident: full-time $1363; part-time $163 per credit hour. Tuition, nonresident: full-time $3856; part-time $473 per credit hour. *Financial support:* Teaching assistantships, institutionally sponsored loans available. Support available to part-time students. Financial award application deadline: 5/31; financial award applicants required to submit FAFSA. *Unit head:* Dr. Mark Klespis, Chair, 936-294-1577, Fax: 936-294-1882, E-mail: klespis@shsu.edu. *Application contact:* Dr. Jianzhong Wang, Advisor, 936-294-3521, Fax: 936-294-1882, E-mail: mth_jxw@shsu.edu.

San Diego State University, Graduate and Research Affairs, College of Sciences, Department of Mathematics and Statistics, San Diego, CA 92182. Offers applied mathematics (MS); mathematics (MA); mathematics and science education (PhD); statistics (MS). PhD offered jointly wtih University of California, San Diego. Part-time programs available. *Degree requirements:* For doctorate, thesis/dissertation. *Entrance requirements:* For master's, GRE General Test; for doctorate, GRE, minimum GPA of 3.25 in last 30 undergraduate semester units, minimum graduate GPA of 3.5, MSE recommendation form, 3 letters of recommendation. Additional exam requirements/recommendations for international students: Required—TOEFL. Electronic applications accepted. *Faculty research:* Teacher education in mathematics.

San Francisco State University, Division of Graduate Studies, College of Science and Engineering, Department of Mathematics, San Francisco, CA 94132-1722. Offers MA. *Application deadline:* Applications are processed on a rolling basis. *Unit head:* Dr. David Bao, Chair, 415-338-2251, E-mail: statmath@math.sfsu.edu. *Application contact:* Dr. Eric Hayashi, Graduate Coordinator, 415-338-2251, E-mail: hayashi@math.sfsu.edu.

San Jose State University, Graduate Studies and Research, College of Science, Department of Mathematics, San Jose, CA 95192-0001. Offers applied mathematics (MS); mathematics (MA, MS); mathematics education (MA); statistics (MA). Part-time and evening/weekend programs available. *Degree requirements:* For master's, comprehensive exam, thesis (for some programs). *Entrance requirements:* For master's, GRE Subject Test. Electronic applications accepted. *Faculty research:* Artificial intelligence, algorithms, numerical analysis, software database, number theory.

Simon Fraser University, Graduate Studies, Faculty of Science, Department of Mathematics, Burnaby, BC V5A 1S6, Canada. Offers applied and computational mathematics (M Sc, PhD); mathematics (M Sc, PhD). *Degree requirements:* For master's, thesis; for doctorate, thesis/dissertation. *Entrance requirements:* For master's, GRE General Test, minimum GPA of 3.0, 3 letters of reference; for doctorate, GRE General Test, minimum GPA of 3.5, 3 letters of reference. Additional exam requirements/recommendations for international students: Required—TWE or IELTS. Electronic applications accepted. *Faculty research:* Semi-groups, number theory, optimization, combinations.

Smith College, Graduate and Special Programs, Center for Women in Mathematics Post-Baccalaureate Program, Northampton, MA 01063. Offers Postbaccalaureate Certificate. Part-time programs available. *Faculty:* 12 full-time (5 women). *Students:* 10 full-time (all women); includes 1 Black or African American, non-Hispanic/Latino; 1 Asian, non-Hispanic/Latino; 1 Hispanic/Latino. Average age 26. 17 applicants, 59% accepted, 8 enrolled. In 2010, 7 Postbaccalaureate Certificates awarded. *Entrance requirements:* Additional exam requirements/recommendations for international students: Required—TOEFL. *Application deadline:* For fall admission, 7/1 for domestic students; for spring admission, 12/15 for domestic students. Applications are processed on a rolling basis. Application fee: $60. *Expenses:* Tuition: Full-time $14,520; part-time $1210 per credit. *Financial support:* In 2010–11, 10 students received support. Scholarships/grants and tuition waivers (full) available. Support available to part-time students. *Unit head:* Ruth Haas, Director, 413-585-3872, E-mail: rhaas@smith.edu. *Application contact:* Jim Henle, Director, 413-585-3867, E-mail: jhenle@smith.edu.

South Dakota State University, Graduate School, College of Engineering, Department of Mathematics and Statistics, Brookings, SD 57007. Offers computational science and statistics (PhD); mathematics (MS); statistics (MS). Part-time programs available. *Faculty:* 12 full-time (1 woman). *Students:* 30 full-time (10 women), 12 part-time (4 women); includes 14 minority (all Asian, non-Hispanic/Latino). 25 applicants, 72% accepted, 12 enrolled. In 2010, 12 master's, 3 doctorates awarded. Terminal master's awarded for partial completion of doctoral program. *Degree requirements:* For master's, thesis (for some programs), oral exam; for doctorate, comprehensive exam, thesis/dissertation, oral and written exams. *Entrance requirements:* Additional exam requirements/recommendations for international students: Required—TOEFL (minimum score 550 paper-based; 213 computer-based; 80 iBT); Recommended—IELTS. *Application deadline:* For fall admission, 4/1 for domestic and international students. Applications are processed on a rolling basis. Application fee: $35. *Financial support:* In 2010–11, 5 fellowships with partial tuition reimbursements (averaging $22,847 per year), 9 research assistantships with partial tuition reimbursements (averaging $20,580 per year), 16 teaching assistantships with partial tuition reimbursements (averaging $17,135 per year) were awarded; unspecified assistantships also available. *Faculty research:* Financial mathematics, predictive analytics, operations research, bioinformatics, biostatistics, computational science, statistics, number theory, abstract algebra. Total annual research expenditures: $310,000. *Unit head:* Dr. Kurt Cogswell, Head, 605-688-6196, Fax: 605-688-5880, E-mail: kurt.cogswell@sdstate.edu. *Application contact:* Dr. Don Vestal, Graduate Coordinator, 605-688-6196, Fax: 605-688-5880, E-mail: don.vestal@sdstate.edu.

Southeastern Louisiana University, College of Science and Technology, Program in Integrated Science and Technology, Hammond, LA 70402. Offers chemistry (MS); computer science (MS); information technology (MS); mathematics (MS); physics (MS). Part-time and evening/weekend programs available. *Faculty:* 11 full-time (3 women). *Students:* 13 full-time (5 women), 11 part-time (2 women); includes 1 minority (Asian, non-Hispanic/Latino), 8 international. Average age 32. 13 applicants, 46% accepted, 4 enrolled. In 2010, 5 master's awarded. *Degree requirements:* For master's, thesis (for some programs), 33-36 hours. *Entrance requirements:* For master's, GRE (minimum combined score 850), 2 letters of reference; minimum GPA of 2.75; 30 hours of course work including chemistry, physics, industrial technology, or mathematics. Additional exam requirements/recommendations for international students: Required—TOEFL (minimum score 500 paper-based; 173 computer-based; 61 iBT). *Application deadline:* For fall admission, 7/15 priority date for domestic students, 6/1 priority date for international students; for spring admission, 12/1 priority date for domestic students, 10/1 priority date for international students. Applications are processed on a rolling basis. Application fee: $20 ($30 for international students). Electronic applications accepted. *Expenses:* Tuition, state resident: full-time $3533. Tuition, nonresident: full-time $12,002. Required fees: $907. Tuition and fees vary according to degree level. *Financial support:* In 2010–11, 7 students received support, including 7 research assistantships (averaging $10,100 per year); career-related internships or fieldwork, Federal Work-Study, institutionally sponsored loans, and unspecified assistantships also available. Support available to part-time students. Financial award application deadline: 5/1; financial award applicants required to submit FAFSA. *Faculty research:* Computational statistics, medicinal chemistry, machine learning, optical interferometry,strength of materials and structure. *Unit head:* Dr. Ken Li, Coordinator, 985-549-3822, Fax: 985-549-2099, E-mail: kli@selu.edu. *Application contact:* Sandra Meyers, Graduate Admissions Analyst, 985-549-5620, Fax: 985-549-5632, E-mail: admissions@selu.edu.

Southeast Missouri State University, School of Graduate Studies, Department of Mathematics, Cape Girardeau, MO 63701-4799. Offers MNS. Part-time and evening/weekend programs available. Postbaccalaureate distance learning degree programs offered (minimal on-campus study). *Faculty:* 7 full-time (2 women), 3 part-time/adjunct (2 women). *Students:* 6 full-time (2 women), 9 part-time (5 women); includes 1 minority (Asian, non-Hispanic/Latino), 2 international. Average age 32. 11 applicants, 100% accepted, 6 enrolled. In 2010, 5 master's awarded. *Degree requirements:* For master's, comprehensive exam (for some programs), thesis (for some programs), scholarly paper. *Entrance requirements:* For master's, minimum undergraduate GPA of 2.75 in last 30 hours in mathematics or science; major in mathematics or completion of certain courses; 2 letters of recommendation. Additional exam requirements/recommendations for international students: Required—TOEFL (minimum score 550 paper-based; 213 computer-based; 79 iBT); Recommended—IELTS (minimum score 6). *Application deadline:* For fall admission, 8/1 for domestic students, 6/1 for international students; for spring admission, 11/21 for domestic students, 10/1 for international students. Applications are processed on a rolling basis. Application fee: $25 ($35 for international students). Electronic applications accepted. *Expenses:* Tuition, state resident: full-time $4698; part-time $261 per credit hour. Tuition, nonresident: full-time $8379; part-time $465.50 per credit hour. *Financial support:* In 2010–11, 5 students received support, including 6 teaching assistantships with full tuition reimbursements available (averaging $7,600 per year); career-related internships or fieldwork, Federal Work-Study, institutionally sponsored loans, scholarships/grants, tuition waivers (full), and unspecified assistantships also available. Financial award application deadline: 6/30; financial award applicants required to submit FAFSA. *Faculty research:* Applied mathematics, algebraic geometry, differential equations, mathematics education, statistics. *Unit head:* Dr. Tamela Hanebrink, Chairperson, 573-651-2165, Fax: 573-986-6811, E-mail: thanbrink@semo.edu. *Application contact:* Gail Amick, Administrative Secretary, 573-651-2049, Fax: 573-651-2001, E-mail: gamick@semo.edu.

Southern Connecticut State University, School of Graduate Studies, School of Arts and Sciences, Department of Mathematics, New Haven, CT 06515-1355. Offers MS. Part-time and evening/weekend programs available. *Faculty:* 22 full-time (7 women). *Students:* 7 full-time (4 women), 18 part-time (14 women); includes 1 Black or African American, non-Hispanic/Latino. 46 applicants, 13% accepted, 3 enrolled. In 2010, 1 master's awarded. *Degree requirements:* For master's, thesis or alternative. *Entrance requirements:* For master's, interview. *Application deadline:* For fall admission, 7/15 priority date for domestic students. Applications are processed on a rolling basis. Application fee: $50. Electronic applications accepted. *Expenses:* Tuition, state resident: full-time $5137; part-time $518 per credit. Tuition, nonresident: part-time $542 per credit. Required fees: $4008; $55 per semester. Tuition and fees vary according to program. *Financial support:* Application deadline: 4/15. *Unit head:* Dr. Alain D'Amour, Chairperson, 203-392-5579, Fax: 203-392-6805, E-mail: damoura1@southernct.edu. *Application contact:* Dr. Therese Bennett, Graduate Coordinator, 203-392-6997, Fax: 203-392-6805, E-mail: bennettt1@southernct.edu.

Southern Illinois University Carbondale, Graduate School, College of Science, Department of Mathematics, Carbondale, IL 62901-4701. Offers mathematics (MA, MS, PhD); statistics (MS). PhD offered jointly with Southeast Missouri State University. Part-time programs available. *Degree requirements:* For master's, thesis; for doctorate, 2 foreign languages, thesis/dissertation. *Entrance requirements:* For master's, minimum GPA of 2.7; for doctorate, minimum GPA of 3.25. Additional exam requirements/recommendations for international students: Required—TOEFL. *Faculty research:* Differential equations, combinatorics, probability, algebra, numerical analysis.

Southern Illinois University Edwardsville, Graduate School, College of Arts and Sciences, Department of Mathematics and Statistics, Edwardsville, IL 62026. Offers mathematics (MS). Part-time programs available. *Faculty:* 18 full-time (6 women). *Students:* 13 full-time (7 women), 22 part-time (10 women); includes 1 minority (Black or African American, non-Hispanic/Latino), 11 international. Average age 26. 29 applicants, 83% accepted. In 2010, 5 master's awarded. *Degree requirements:* For master's, thesis (for some programs), research paper/project. *Entrance requirements:* Additional exam requirements/recommendations for international students: Required—TOEFL (minimum score 550 paper-based; 213 computer-based; 79 iBT), IELTS (minimum score 6.5). *Application deadline:* For fall admission, 7/22 for domestic students, 6/1 for international students; for spring admission, 12/9 for domestic students, 10/1 for international students. Applications are processed on a rolling basis. Application fee: $30. Electronic applications accepted. *Expenses:* Tuition, state resident: full-time $6012; part-time $1503 per semester. Tuition, nonresident: full-time $15,030; part-time $3758 per semester. Required fees: $1711; $675 per semester. *Financial support:* In 2010–11, 1 research assistantship with full tuition reimbursement (averaging $8,064 per year), 22 teaching assistantships with full tuition reimbursements (averaging $8,064 per year) were awarded; fellowships with full tuition reimbursements, career-related internships or fieldwork, Federal Work-Study, institutionally sponsored loans, scholarships/grants, traineeships, and unspecified assistantships also available. Support available to part-time students. Financial award application deadline: 3/1; financial award applicants required to submit FAFSA. *Unit head:* Dr. Krzysztof Jarosz, Chair, 618-650-2354, E-mail: kjarosz@siue.edu. *Application contact:* Dr. Adam Weyhaupt, Director, 618-650-2220, E-mail: aweyhau@siue.edu.

Southern Methodist University, Dedman College, Department of Mathematics, Dallas, TX 75275. Offers computational and applied mathematics (MS, PhD). *Faculty:* 17 full-time (2 women), 3 part-time/adjunct (2 women). *Students:* 18 full-time (7 women); includes 1 Black or African American, non-Hispanic/Latino; 1 Asian, non-Hispanic/Latino; 2 Hispanic/Latino, 7 international. Average age 27. 25 applicants, 28% accepted, 6 enrolled. In 2010, 4 master's, 3 doctorates awarded. *Degree requirements:* For master's, oral exams; for doctorate, thesis/dissertation, oral and written exams. *Entrance requirements:* For master's and doctorate, GRE General Test, minimum GPA of 3.0, 18 undergraduate hours in mathematics beyond first and second year calculus. Additional exam requirements/recommendations for international students: Required—TOEFL. *Application deadline:* For fall admission, 2/1 priority date for domestic students, 2/1 for international students; for spring admission, 11/30 for domestic students. Applications are processed on a rolling basis. Application fee: $75. Electronic applications accepted. *Financial support:* In 2010–11, 18 students received support, including 5 research assistantships with full tuition reimbursements available (averaging $18,000 per year), 13 teaching assistantships with full tuition reimbursements available (averaging $16,500 per year); career-related internships or fieldwork, scholarships/grants, health care benefits, tuition

272 www.facebook.com/petersonspublishing

Peterson's Graduate Programs in the Physical Sciences, Mathematics, Agricultural Sciences, the Environment & Natural Resources 2012

waivers, and unspecified assistantships also available. Support available to part-time students. Financial award application deadline: 2/1; financial award applicants required to submit FAFSA. *Faculty research:* Numerical analysis and scientific computation, fluid dynamics, optics, wave propagation, mathematical biology. Total annual research expenditures: $369,480. *Unit head:* Dr. Douglas A. Reinelt, Chairman, 214-768-2506, Fax: 214-768-2355, E-mail: mathchair@mail.smu.edu. *Application contact:* Dr. Thomas W. Carr, Director of Graduate Studies, 214-768-3460, E-mail: math@mail.smu.edu.

Southern University and Agricultural and Mechanical College, Graduate School, College of Sciences, Department of Mathematics, Baton Rouge, LA 70813. Offers MS. *Degree requirements:* For master's, comprehensive exam, thesis optional. *Entrance requirements:* For master's, GMAT, GRE General Test. Additional exam requirements/recommendations for international students: Required—TOEFL. *Faculty research:* Algebraic number theory, abstract algebra, computer analysis, probability, mathematics education.

Stanford University, School of Engineering, Program in Scientific Computing and Computational Mathematics, Stanford, CA 94305-9991. Offers MS, PhD. Terminal master's awarded for partial completion of doctoral program. *Degree requirements:* For doctorate, thesis/dissertation, qualifying exam. *Entrance requirements:* For master's, GRE General Test; for doctorate, GRE General Test, GRE Subject Test. Additional exam requirements/recommendations for international students: Required—TOEFL. Electronic applications accepted. *Expenses:* Tuition: Full-time $38,700; part-time $860 per unit. One-time fee: $200 full-time.

Stanford University, School of Humanities and Sciences, Department of Mathematics, Stanford, CA 94305-9991. Offers financial mathematics (MS); mathematics (MS, PhD). Terminal master's awarded for partial completion of doctoral program. *Degree requirements:* For doctorate, 2 foreign languages, thesis/dissertation, oral exam. *Entrance requirements:* For master's, GRE General Test; for doctorate, GRE General Test, GRE Subject Test. Additional exam requirements/recommendations for international students: Required—TOEFL. Electronic applications accepted. *Expenses:* Tuition: Full-time $38,700; part-time $860 per unit. One-time fee: $200 full-time.

State University of New York at Binghamton, Graduate School, School of Arts and Sciences, Department of Mathematical Sciences, Binghamton, NY 13902-6000. Offers computer science (MA, PhD); probability and statistics (MA, PhD). Part-time programs available. *Faculty:* 26 full-time (5 women), 13 part-time/adjunct (5 women). *Students:* 42 full-time (13 women), 24 part-time (8 women); includes 3 Black or African American, non-Hispanic/Latino; 1 Asian, non-Hispanic/Latino; 2 Hispanic/Latino, 27 international. Average age 27. 82 applicants, 28% accepted, 16 enrolled. In 2010, 15 master's, 6 doctorates awarded. Terminal master's awarded for partial completion of doctoral program. *Degree requirements:* For master's, thesis or alternative; for doctorate, 2 foreign languages, thesis/dissertation. *Entrance requirements:* For master's and doctorate, GRE General Test, GRE Subject Test. Additional exam requirements/recommendations for international students: Required—TOEFL (minimum score 550 paper-based; 213 computer-based; 80 iBT). *Application deadline:* For fall admission, 4/15 priority date for domestic and international students; for spring admission, 11/30 priority date for domestic and international students. Applications are processed on a rolling basis. Application fee: $60. Electronic applications accepted. *Financial support:* In 2010–11, 51 students received support, including 4 fellowships with full tuition reimbursements available (averaging $16,500 per year), 1 research assistantship with full tuition reimbursement available (averaging $16,500 per year), 48 teaching assistantships with full tuition reimbursements available (averaging $16,500 per year); career-related internships or fieldwork, Federal Work-Study, institutionally sponsored loans, scholarships/grants, health care benefits, tuition waivers (full and partial), and unspecified assistantships also available. Financial award application deadline: 2/15; financial award applicants required to submit FAFSA. *Unit head:* Dr. Fernando Guzman, Chairperson, 607-777-2148, E-mail: fer@math.binghamton.edu. *Application contact:* Catherine Smith, Recruiting and Admissions Coordinator, 607-777-2151, Fax: 607-777-2501, E-mail: cmsmith@binghamton.edu.

State University of New York at Fredonia, Graduate Studies, Department of Mathematical Sciences, Fredonia, NY 14063-1136. Offers MS Ed. Part-time and evening/weekend programs available. *Degree requirements:* For master's, thesis optional. *Expenses:* Tuition, state resident: full-time $8370; part-time $349 per credit hour. Tuition, nonresident: full-time $13,250; part-time $552 per credit hour. Required fees: $1328; $55.15 per credit hour.

State University of New York College at Cortland, Graduate Studies, School of Arts and Sciences, Department of Mathematics, Cortland, NY 13045. Offers MAT, MS Ed.

State University of New York College at Potsdam, School of Arts and Sciences, Department of Mathematics, Potsdam, NY 13676. Offers MA. Part-time and evening/weekend programs available. *Faculty:* 6 full-time (2 women). *Students:* 1 full-time (0 women). 1 applicant, 100% accepted, 1 enrolled. In 2010, 6 master's awarded. *Degree requirements:* For master's, comprehensive exam. *Entrance requirements:* For master's, minimum GPA of 3.0 in all undergraduate math courses, 2.75 in last 60 hours of undergraduate coursework. Additional exam requirements/recommendations for international students: Required—TOEFL (minimum score 550 paper-based; 213 computer-based; 80 iBT), IELTS (minimum score 6). *Application deadline:* For fall admission, 4/1 priority date for domestic and international students; for winter admission, 10/15 for domestic and international students; for spring admission, 3/1 priority date for domestic and international students. Applications are processed on a rolling basis. Application fee: $50. *Financial support:* Teaching assistantships with full tuition reimbursements, Federal Work-Study and unspecified assistantships available. Support available to part-time students. Financial award application deadline: 3/1; financial award applicants required to submit FAFSA. *Unit head:* Dr. Joel Foisy, Chairperson, 315-267-2084, Fax: 315-267-3176, E-mail: foisyjs@potsdam.edu. *Application contact:* Peter Cutler, Graduate Admissions Counselor, 315-267-3154, Fax: 315-267-4802, E-mail: cutlerpj@potsdam.edu.

Stephen F. Austin State University, Graduate School, College of Sciences and Mathematics, Department of Mathematics and Statistics, Nacogdoches, TX 75962. Offers mathematics (MS); mathematics education (MS); statistics (MS). *Degree requirements:* For master's, comprehensive exam, thesis optional. *Entrance requirements:* For master's, GRE General Test, minimum GPA of 2.8 in last 60 hours, 2.5 overall. Additional exam requirements/recommendations for international students: Required—TOEFL. *Faculty research:* Kernel type estimators, fractal mappings, spline curve fitting, robust regression continua theory.

Stevens Institute of Technology, Graduate School, Charles V. Schaefer Jr. School of Engineering, Department of Mathematical Sciences, Program in Mathematics, Hoboken, NJ 07030. Offers MS, PhD. *Students:* 21 full-time (6 women), 8 part-time (0 women); includes 5 Asian, non-Hispanic/Latino; 2 Hispanic/Latino, 11 international. Average age 31. 10 applicants, 80% accepted. *Degree requirements:* For master's, thesis optional; for doctorate, one foreign language, thesis/dissertation. *Entrance requirements:* For master's and doctorate, GRE. Additional exam requirements/recommendations for international students: Required—TOEFL. *Application deadline:* Applications are processed on a rolling basis. Application fee: $50. Electronic applications accepted. *Unit head:* Dr. Robert Gilman, Director, 201-216-5449, Fax: 201-216-8321. *Application contact:* Dr. Milos Dostal, Professor, 201-216-5426.

Stony Brook University, State University of New York, Graduate School, College of Arts and Sciences, Department of Mathematics, Stony Brook, NY 11794. Offers MA, MAT, PhD. *Faculty:* 28 full-time (5 women), 2 part-time/adjunct (1 woman). *Students:* 70 full-time (13 women), 35 part-time (25 women); includes 3 Asian, non-Hispanic/Latino; 3 Hispanic/Latino; 1 Two or more races, non-Hispanic/Latino, 44 international. Average age 27. 244 applicants, 11% accepted, 20 enrolled. In 2010, 18 master's, 5 doctorates awarded. *Degree requirements:* For doctorate, 2 foreign languages, thesis/dissertation. *Entrance requirements:* For master's and doctorate, GRE General Test. Additional exam requirements/recommendations for international students: Required—TOEFL. *Application deadline:* For fall admission, 1/15 for domestic students. Application fee: $100. *Expenses:* Tuition, state resident: full-time $8370; part-time $349 per credit. Tuition, nonresident: full-time $13,780; part-time $574 per credit. Required fees: $994. *Financial support:* In 2010–11, 15 research assistantships, 48 teaching assistantships were awarded; fellowships also available. *Faculty research:* Real analysis, relativity and mathematical physics, complex analysis, topology, combinatorics. Total annual research expenditures: $1.6 million. *Unit head:* Dr. David Ebin, Chair, 631-632-8290. *Application contact:* Dr. Leon Takhtajan, Director, 631-632-8258, Fax: 631-632-7631, E-mail: leontak@math.sunysb.edu.

Syracuse University, College of Arts and Sciences, Program in Mathematics, Syracuse, NY 13244. Offers MS, PhD. Part-time programs available. *Students:* 44 full-time (13 women), 2 part-time (0 women), 11 international. Average age 26. 75 applicants, 35% accepted, 15 enrolled. In 2010, 10 master's, 3 doctorates awarded. Terminal master's awarded for partial completion of doctoral program. *Degree requirements:* For doctorate, 2 foreign languages, thesis/dissertation, qualifying exam. *Entrance requirements:* For master's and doctorate, GRE General Test, GRE Subject Test (recommended). Additional exam requirements/recommendations for international students: Required—TOEFL (minimum score 100 iBT). *Application deadline:* For fall admission, 2/1 priority date for domestic and international students. Application fee: $75. Electronic applications accepted. *Expenses:* Tuition: Part-time $1162 per credit. *Financial support:* Fellowships with full tuition reimbursements, research assistantships with full tuition reimbursements, teaching assistantships with full and partial tuition reimbursements, tuition waivers (partial) available. Financial award application deadline: 1/1; financial award applicants required to submit FAFSA. *Faculty research:* Pure mathematics, numerical mathematics, computing statistics. *Unit head:* Dr. Mark Kleiner, Associate Chair for Graduate Studies, 315-443-1499, Fax: 315-443-1475. *Application contact:* Dr. Mark Kleiner, Associate Chair for Graduate Studies, 315-443-1499, Fax: 315-443-1475, E-mail: mkleiner@syr.edu.

Tarleton State University, College of Graduate Studies, College of Science and Technology, Department of Mathematics, Stephenville, TX 76402. Offers mathematics (MS). Part-time and evening/weekend programs available. *Degree requirements:* For master's, comprehensive exam, thesis (for some programs). *Entrance requirements:* For master's, GRE General Test, minimum GPA of 3.0. Additional exam requirements/recommendations for international students: Required—TOEFL (minimum score 550 paper-based; 213 computer-based; 80 iBT). Electronic applications accepted.

Temple University, College of Science and Technology, Department of Mathematics, Philadelphia, PA 19122-6096. Offers applied mathematics (MA); mathematics (PhD); pure mathematics (MA). Part-time and evening/weekend programs available. *Faculty:* 16 full-time (1 woman). *Students:* 20 full-time (2 women), 7 part-time (3 women), 5 international. 59 applicants, 24% accepted, 6 enrolled. In 2010, 7 master's, 3 doctorates awarded. Terminal master's awarded for partial completion of doctoral program. *Degree requirements:* For master's, thesis optional, written exam; for doctorate, 2 foreign languages, thesis/dissertation, oral and written exams. *Entrance requirements:* For master's, GRE General Test, minimum GPA of 3.0; for doctorate, GRE General Test, GRE Subject Test, minimum GPA of 3.0. Additional exam requirements/recommendations for international students: Required—TOEFL (minimum score 550 paper-based; 213 computer-based; 79 iBT). *Application deadline:* For fall admission, 2/15 priority date for domestic students, 12/15 for international students; for spring admission, 11/15 priority date for domestic students, 8/1 for international students. Applications are processed on a rolling basis. Application fee: $50. Electronic applications accepted. *Financial support:* Fellowships, research assistantships, teaching assistantships, Federal Work-Study and institutionally sponsored loans available. Financial award application deadline: 1/15; financial award applicants required to submit FAFSA. *Faculty research:* Differential geometry, numerical analysis. *Unit head:* Dr. Edward Letzter, Chair, 215-204-4650, Fax: 215-204-6433, E-mail: mathematics@temple.edu. *Application contact:* Dr. Edward Letzter, Chair, 215-204-4650, Fax: 215-204-6433, E-mail: mathematics@temple.edu.

Tennessee State University, The School of Graduate Studies and Research, College of Arts and Sciences, Department of Physics and Mathematics, Nashville, TN 37209-1561. Offers mathematical sciences (MS). *Entrance requirements:* For master's, GRE General Test. Electronic applications accepted.

Tennessee Technological University, Graduate School, College of Arts and Sciences, Department of Mathematics, Cookeville, TN 38505. Offers MS. Part-time programs available. *Faculty:* 17 full-time (4 women). *Students:* 9 full-time (1 woman), 2 part-time (both women); includes 3 Asian, non-Hispanic/Latino. Average age 27. 10 applicants, 60% accepted, 3 enrolled. In 2010, 2 master's awarded. *Degree requirements:* For master's, thesis or alternative. *Entrance requirements:* For master's, GRE General Test. Additional exam requirements/recommendations for international students: Required—TOEFL (minimum score 550 paper-based; 79 iBT); IELTS (minimum score 5.5). *Application deadline:* For fall admission, 8/1 for domestic students, 5/1 for international students; for spring admission, 12/1 for domestic students, 10/1 for international students. Application fee: $25 ($30 for international students). Electronic applications accepted. *Expenses:* Tuition, state resident: full-time $7934; part-time $388 per credit hour. Tuition, nonresident: full-time $19,758; part-time $962 per credit hour. *Financial support:* In 2010–11, 3 research assistantships (averaging $7,500 per year), 7 teaching assistantships (averaging $7,500 per year) were awarded. Financial award application deadline: 4/1. *Unit head:* Dr. Allan Mills, Interim Chairperson, 931-372-3441, Fax: 931-372-6353. *Application contact:* Shelia K. Kendrick, Coordinator of Graduate Admissions, 931-372-3808, Fax: 931-372-3497, E-mail: skendrick@tntech.edu.

Texas A&M International University, Office of Graduate Studies and Research, College of Arts and Sciences, Department of Mathematical and Physical Science, Laredo, TX 78041-1900. Offers MA. *Faculty:* 3 full-time (0 women). *Students:* 9 full-time (1 woman), 5 part-time (1 woman); includes 34 Hispanic/Latino, 1 international. Average age 33. 22 applicants, 77% accepted, 13 enrolled. *Entrance requirements:* For master's, GRE General Test. Additional exam requirements/recommendations for international students: Required—TOEFL (minimum score 550 paper-based; 213 computer-based). *Application deadline:* For fall admission, 4/30 priority date for domestic students; for spring admission, 11/30 for domestic students, 10/1 for international students. Applications are processed on a rolling basis. Application fee: $25. *Financial support:* In 2010–11, 1 student received support, including 4 research assistantships (averaging $9,100 per year). Financial award application deadline: 11/1. *Unit head:* Dr. Rafic Bachnak, Chair, 956-326-2408, Fax: 956-326-2439, E-mail: rbachnak@tamiu.edu. *Application contact:* Suzanne Hansen-Alford, Director of Graduate Recruiting, 956-326-3023, Fax: 956-326-3021, E-mail: graduateschool@tamiu.edu.

Texas A&M University, College of Science, Department of Mathematics, College Station, TX 77843. Offers MS, PhD. Part-time programs available. Postbaccalaureate distance learning degree programs offered (minimal on-campus study). *Faculty:* 51. *Students:* 112 full-time (35 women), 24 part-time (12 women); includes 1 Black or African American, non-Hispanic/Latino; 6 Asian, non-Hispanic/Latino; 7 Hispanic/Latino, 68 international. Average age 27. In 2010, 27 master's, 14 doctorates awarded. Terminal master's awarded for partial completion of doctoral program. *Degree requirements:* For master's, comprehensive exam, thesis optional; for doctorate, one foreign language, comprehensive exam, thesis/dissertation. *Entrance requirements:* For master's and doctorate, GRE General Test. Additional exam requirements/recommendations for international students: Required—TOEFL (minimum score 550 paper-based; 213 computer-based). *Application deadline:* For fall admission, 3/1 for domestic and international students; for spring admission, 8/1 for domestic and international students. Applications are processed on a rolling basis. Application fee: $50 ($75 for international students). Electronic applications accepted. *Financial support:* In 2010–11, fellowships with partial tuition reimbursements (averaging $17,850 per year), research assistantships with partial tuition reimbursements

Mathematics

Texas A&M University *(continued)*
(averaging $17,850 per year), teaching assistantships with partial tuition reimbursements (averaging $17,850 per year) were awarded; career-related internships or fieldwork, institutionally sponsored loans, scholarships/grants, and unspecified assistantships also available. Financial award application deadline: 3/1; financial award applicants required to submit FAFSA. *Faculty research:* Functional analysis, numerical analysis, algebra, geometry/topology, applied mathematics. *Unit head:* Dr. Albert Boggess, Head, 979-845-9424, Fax: 979-845-6028, E-mail: boggess@math.tamu.edu. *Application contact:* Monique Stewart, Academic Advisor I, 979-862-4137, Fax: 979-862-4190, E-mail: stewart@math.tamu.edu.

Texas A&M University–Commerce, Graduate School, College of Arts and Sciences, Department of Mathematics, Commerce, TX 75429-3011. Offers MA, MS. Part-time programs available. *Degree requirements:* For master's, comprehensive exam, thesis (for some programs). *Entrance requirements:* For master's, GRE General Test. Electronic applications accepted.

Texas A&M University–Corpus Christi, Graduate Studies and Research, College of Science and Technology, Program in Mathematics, Corpus Christi, TX 78412-5503. Offers applied and computational mathematics (MS); curriculum content (MS). Part-time programs available. *Degree requirements:* For master's, thesis (for some programs). *Entrance requirements:* For master's, 2 letters of recommendation.

Texas A&M University–Kingsville, College of Graduate Studies, College of Arts and Sciences, Department of Mathematics, Kingsville, TX 78363. Offers MS. Part-time programs available. *Degree requirements:* For master's, comprehensive exam, thesis or alternative. *Entrance requirements:* For master's, GRE General Test. Additional exam requirements/recommendations for international students: Required—TOEFL. *Faculty research:* Complex analysis, multivariate analysis, algebra, numerical analysis, applied statistics.

Texas Christian University, College of Science and Engineering, Department of Mathematics, Fort Worth, TX 76129-0002. Offers MAT, MS, PhD. Part-time and evening/weekend programs available. *Faculty:* 12 full-time (2 women). *Students:* 8 full-time (3 women), 5 part-time (2 women); includes 2 Asian, non-Hispanic/Latino; 1 Hispanic/Latino. In 2010, 4 master's awarded. Terminal master's awarded for partial completion of doctoral program. *Degree requirements:* For master's, thesis optional; for doctorate, comprehensive exam, thesis/dissertation, 72 hours of full-time study with minimum GPA of 2.75. *Entrance requirements:* For master's and doctorate, GRE, 24 hours of math, including courses in elementary calculus of one and several variables, linear algebra, abstract algebra and real analysis. Additional exam requirements/recommendations for international students: Required—TOEFL. *Application deadline:* For fall admission, 3/1 priority date for domestic students, 3/1 for international students; for spring admission, 10/15 priority date for domestic students, 12/1 for international students. Applications are processed on a rolling basis. Application fee: $50. Electronic applications accepted. *Expenses:* Tuition: Full-time $18,720; part-time $1040 per credit hour. Tuition and fees vary according to course load and program. *Financial support:* In 2010–11, 11 students received support, including 7 teaching assistantships (averaging $16,000 per year); tuition waivers (full) also available. Financial award application deadline: 3/1. *Faculty research:* Topology, analysis, number theory. *Unit head:* Dr. Bob Doran, Chairperson, 817-257-7335, E-mail: r.doran@tcu.edu. *Application contact:* Dr. Ken Richardson, Director of TCU Mathematics Graduate Program, 817-257-6128, E-mail: k.richardson@tcu.edu.

Texas Southern University, School of Science and Technology, Department of Mathematics, Houston, TX 77004-4584. Offers MS. Part-time and evening/weekend programs available. *Faculty:* 8 full-time (2 women). *Students:* 2 full-time (0 women), 6 part-time (4 women); includes 6 Black or African American, non-Hispanic/Latino; 2 Asian, non-Hispanic/Latino. Average age 36. 2 applicants, 100% accepted, 2 enrolled. In 2010, 2 master's awarded. *Degree requirements:* For master's, comprehensive exam, thesis. *Entrance requirements:* For master's, GRE General Test, minimum GPA of 2.5. Additional exam requirements/recommendations for international students: Required—TOEFL. *Application deadline:* For fall admission, 7/1 for domestic and international students; for spring admission, 11/1 for domestic and international students. Applications are processed on a rolling basis. Application fee: $50 ($75 for international students). Electronic applications accepted. *Expenses:* Tuition, state resident: full-time $1875; part-time $100 per credit hour. Tuition, nonresident: full-time $6641; part-time $343 per credit hour. Tuition and fees vary according to course level, course load and degree level. *Financial support:* In 2010–11, 1 teaching assistantship (averaging $5,600 per year) was awarded; fellowships, research assistantships, scholarships/grants and unspecified assistantships also available. Financial award application deadline: 5/1. *Faculty research:* Statistics, number theory, topology, differential equations, numerical analysis. *Unit head:* Dr. Azime Saydam, Chair, 713-313-1396, E-mail: saydamas@tsu.edu. *Application contact:* Nia Eakins, Administrative Assistant, 713-313-7002, E-mail: eakinsnm@tsu.edu.

Texas State University–San Marcos, Graduate School, College of Science, Department of Mathematics, San Marcos, TX 78666. Offers industrial mathematics (MS); mathematics (MS); mathematics education (PhD); middle school mathematics teaching (M Ed). Part-time programs available. *Faculty:* 16 full-time (7 women), 1 part-time/adjunct (0 women). *Students:* 30 full-time (17 women), 35 part-time (22 women); includes 18 minority (5 Black or African American, non-Hispanic/Latino; 3 Asian, non-Hispanic/Latino; 9 Hispanic/Latino; 1 Two or more races, non-Hispanic/Latino), 2 international. Average age 34. 30 applicants, 67% accepted, 12 enrolled. In 2010, 22 master's, 1 doctorate awarded. *Degree requirements:* For master's, comprehensive exam, thesis (for some programs). *Entrance requirements:* For master's, GRE General Test, minimum GPA of 2.75 in last 60 hours of course work. Additional exam requirements/recommendations for international students: Required—TOEFL (minimum score 550 paper-based; 213 computer-based; 78 iBT). *Application deadline:* For fall admission, 6/15 priority date for domestic students, 6/1 priority date for international students; for spring admission, 10/15 priority date for domestic students, 10/1 priority date for international students. Applications are processed on a rolling basis. Application fee: $40 ($90 for international students). Electronic applications accepted. *Expenses:* Tuition, state resident: full-time $6024; part-time $251 per credit hour. Tuition, nonresident: full-time $13,536; part-time $564 per credit hour. Required fees: $1776; $50 per credit hour. $306 per semester. *Financial support:* In 2010–11, 59 students received support, including 5 research assistantships (averaging $3,795 per year), 22 teaching assistantships (averaging $5,106 per year); Federal Work-Study and institutionally sponsored loans also available. Support available to part-time students. Financial award application deadline: 4/1; financial award applicants required to submit FAFSA. *Faculty research:* Dynamic geometry, mathematics education, Route Protocos, Mathworks 3m podcast. Total annual research expenditures: $1.5 million. *Unit head:* Dr. Nathaniel Dean, Chair, 512-245-3555, Fax: 512-245-3425, E-mail: nd17@txstate.edu. *Application contact:* Dr. Gregory Passty, Graduate Adviser, 512-245-3446, Fax: 512-245-3425, E-mail: passty@txstate.edu.

Texas Tech University, Graduate School, College of Arts and Sciences, Department of Mathematics and Statistics, Lubbock, TX 79409. Offers mathematics (MA, MS, PhD); statistics (MS). Part-time programs available. *Faculty:* 38 full-time (6 women). *Students:* 106 full-time (44 women), 15 part-time (10 women); includes 1 Black or African American, non-Hispanic/Latino; 1 Asian, non-Hispanic/Latino; 7 Hispanic/Latino; 1 Two or more races, non-Hispanic/Latino, 67 international. Average age 27. 109 applicants, 79% accepted, 30 enrolled. In 2010, 40 master's, 3 doctorates awarded. *Degree requirements:* For master's, thesis or alternative; for doctorate, one foreign language, thesis/dissertation. *Entrance requirements:* For master's and doctorate, GRE General Test. Additional exam requirements/recommendations for international students: Required—TOEFL (minimum score 550 paper-based; 213 computer-based; 79 iBT). *Application deadline:* For fall admission, 6/1 priority date for domestic students, 1/15 priority date for international students; for spring admission, 9/1 priority date for domestic students, 6/15 priority date for international students. Applications are processed on a rolling

basis. Application fee: $50 ($75 for international students). Electronic applications accepted. *Expenses:* Tuition, state resident: full-time $5495.76; part-time $228.99 per credit hour. Tuition, nonresident: full-time $12,936; part-time $538.99 per credit hour. Required fees: $2674; $36 per credit hour. $905 per semester. *Financial support:* In 2010–11, 103 students received support, including 3 research assistantships with partial tuition reimbursements available (averaging $2,321 per year), 44 teaching assistantships with partial tuition reimbursements available (averaging $7,308 per year); fellowships also available. Financial award application deadline: 4/15; financial award applicants required to submit FAFSA. *Faculty research:* Numerical analysis, mathematical biology, complex analysis, algebra and geometry; ordinary and partial differential equations. Total annual research expenditures: $1.6 million. *Unit head:* Dr. Kent Pearce, Chair, 806-742-2566, Fax: 806-742-1112, E-mail: kent.pearce@ttu.edu. *Application contact:* Dr. Ram Iyer, Graduate Adviser, 806-742-2566, Fax: 806-742-1112, E-mail: ram.iyer@ttu.edu.

Texas Woman's University, Graduate School, College of Arts and Sciences, Department of Mathematics and Computer Science, Denton, TX 76201. Offers mathematics (MA, MS); mathematics teaching (MS). Part-time and evening/weekend programs available. *Faculty:* 14 full-time (10 women), 1 part-time/adjunct (0 women). *Students:* 9 full-time (6 women), 32 part-time (24 women); includes 2 Black or African American, non-Hispanic/Latino; 5 Asian, non-Hispanic/Latino; 5 Hispanic/Latino, 4 international. Average age 34. 13 applicants, 92% accepted, 9 enrolled. In 2010, 3 master's awarded. *Degree requirements:* For master's, comprehensive exam, thesis (for some programs). *Entrance requirements:* For master's, 2 letters of reference. Additional exam requirements/recommendations for international students: Required—TOEFL (minimum score 550 paper-based; 213 computer-based; 79 iBT). *Application deadline:* For fall admission, 7/1 priority date for domestic students, 3/1 for international students; for spring admission, 12/1 priority date for domestic students, 7/1 for international students. Applications are processed on a rolling basis. Application fee: $50 ($75 for international students). Electronic applications accepted. *Expenses:* Tuition, state resident: full-time $3834; part-time $213 per credit hour. Tuition, nonresident: full-time $9468; part-time $526 per credit hour. Required fees: $1247; $220 per credit hour. *Financial support:* In 2010–11, 14 students received support, including 6 research assistantships (averaging $11,520 per year), 9 teaching assistantships (averaging $11,520 per year); career-related internships or fieldwork, Federal Work-Study, institutionally sponsored loans, scholarships/grants, traineeships, health care benefits, and unspecified assistantships also available. Support available to part-time students. Financial award application deadline: 3/1; financial award applicants required to submit FAFSA. *Faculty research:* Biopharmaceutical statistics, dynamic systems and control theory, Bayesian inference, math and computer science curriculum innovation, computer modeling of physical phenomenon. *Unit head:* Dr. Don E. Edwards, Chair, 940-898-2166, Fax: 940-898-2179, E-mail: mathcs@twu.edu. *Application contact:* Dr. Samuel Wheeler, Assistant Director of Admissions, 940-898-3188, Fax: 940-898-3081, E-mail: wheelersr@twu.edu.

Tufts University, Graduate School of Arts and Sciences, Department of Mathematics, Medford, MA 02155. Offers MA, MS, PhD. Terminal master's awarded for partial completion of doctoral program. *Degree requirements:* For master's, one foreign language, thesis; for doctorate, 2 foreign languages, thesis/dissertation. *Entrance requirements:* For master's, GRE General Test; for doctorate, GRE General Test, GRE Subject Tests. Additional exam requirements/recommendations for international students: Required—TOEFL (minimum score 550 paper-based; 213 computer-based; 80 iBT). Electronic applications accepted. *Expenses:* Tuition: Full-time $39,624; part-time $3962 per course. Required fees: $40 per year. Full-time tuition and fees vary according to degree level, program and student level. Part-time tuition and fees vary according to course load.

Tulane University, School of Science and Engineering, Department of Mathematics, New Orleans, LA 70118-5669. Offers applied mathematics (MS); mathematics (MS, PhD); statistics (MS). *Degree requirements:* For master's, thesis (for some programs); for doctorate, thesis/dissertation. *Entrance requirements:* For master's, GRE General Test, minimum B average in undergraduate course work; for doctorate, GRE General Test. Additional exam requirements/recommendations for international students: Required—TOEFL. Electronic applications accepted.

Université de Moncton, Faculty of Science, Department of Mathematics and Statistics, Moncton, NB E1A 3E9, Canada. Offers mathematics (M Sc). *Degree requirements:* For master's, one foreign language, thesis. *Entrance requirements:* For master's, minimum GPA of 3.0. Electronic applications accepted. *Faculty research:* Statistics, numerical analysis, fixed point theory, mathematical physics.

Université de Montréal, Faculty of Arts and Sciences, Department of Mathematics and Statistics, Montréal, QC H3C 3J7, Canada. Offers mathematical and computational finance (M Sc, DESS); mathematics (M Sc, PhD); statistics (M Sc, PhD). *Degree requirements:* For master's, thesis; for doctorate, thesis/dissertation, general exam. *Entrance requirements:* For master's and doctorate, proficiency in French. Electronic applications accepted. *Faculty research:* Pure and applied mathematics, actuarial mathematics.

Université de Sherbrooke, Faculty of Sciences, Department of Mathematics, Sherbrooke, QC J1K 2R1, Canada. Offers M Sc, PhD. *Degree requirements:* For master's, thesis; for doctorate, comprehensive exam, thesis/dissertation. *Entrance requirements:* For doctorate, master's degree. Electronic applications accepted. *Faculty research:* Measure theory, differential equations, probability, statistics, error control codes.

Université du Québec à Montréal, Graduate Programs, Program in Mathematics, Montréal, QC H3C 3P8, Canada. Offers M Sc, PhD. Part-time programs available. *Degree requirements:* For master's, thesis; for doctorate, thesis/dissertation. *Entrance requirements:* For master's, appropriate bachelor's degree or equivalent, proficiency in French; for doctorate, appropriate master's degree or equivalent, proficiency in French.

Université du Québec à Trois-Rivières, Graduate Programs, Program in Mathematics and Computer Science, Trois-Rivières, QC G9A 5H7, Canada. Offers M Sc. *Faculty research:* Probability, statistics.

Université Laval, Faculty of Sciences and Engineering, Department of Mathematics and Statistics, Programs in Mathematics, Québec, QC G1K 7P4, Canada. Offers M Sc, PhD. Terminal master's awarded for partial completion of doctoral program. *Degree requirements:* For master's, thesis (for some programs); for doctorate, comprehensive exam, thesis/dissertation. *Entrance requirements:* For master's and doctorate, knowledge of French and English. Electronic applications accepted.

University at Albany, State University of New York, College of Arts and Sciences, Department of Mathematics and Statistics, Albany, NY 12222-0001. Offers mathematics (PhD); secondary teaching (MA); statistics (MA). *Degree requirements:* For doctorate, one foreign language, thesis/dissertation. *Entrance requirements:* For doctorate, GRE General Test. Additional exam requirements/recommendations for international students: Required—TOEFL (minimum score 550 paper-based; 213 computer-based). Electronic applications accepted.

University at Buffalo, the State University of New York, Graduate School, College of Arts and Sciences, Department of Mathematics, Buffalo, NY 14260. Offers MA, PhD. *Faculty:* 33 full-time (2 women), 12 part-time/adjunct (3 women). *Students:* 70 full-time (34 women); includes 26 minority (25 Asian, non-Hispanic/Latino; 1 Hispanic/Latino), 1 international. Average age 29. 103 applicants, 44% accepted, 18 enrolled. In 2010, 41 master's, 9 doctorates awarded. Terminal master's awarded for partial completion of doctoral program. *Degree requirements:* For master's, comprehensive exam (for some programs), thesis (for some programs), project (for some programs); for doctorate, comprehensive exam, thesis/dissertation. *Entrance requirements:* Additional exam requirements/recommendations for international

274 www.facebook.com/petersonspublishing

Peterson's Graduate Programs in the Physical Sciences, Mathematics, Agricultural Sciences, the Environment & Natural Resources 2012

students: Required—TOEFL (minimum score 550 paper-based; 213 computer-based; 79 iBT). *Application deadline:* For fall admission, 1/15 priority date for domestic and international students; for spring admission, 9/15 priority date for domestic and international students. Applications are processed on a rolling basis. Application fee: $75. Electronic applications accepted. *Financial support:* In 2010–11, 33 students received support, including fellowships with full tuition reimbursements available (averaging $4,000 per year), 50 teaching assistantships with full tuition reimbursements available (averaging $16,188 per year); research assistantships, Federal Work-Study, institutionally sponsored loans, and unspecified assistantships also available. Financial award application deadline: 1/15; financial award applicants required to submit FAFSA. *Faculty research:* Algebra, analysis, applied mathematics, logic, number theory, topology. Total annual research expenditures: $354,932. *Unit head:* Dr. Brian D. Hassard, Chairman, 716-645-8780, Fax: 716-645-5039, E-mail: chair@math.buffalo.edu. *Application contact:* Dr. Clifford Bloom, Director of Graduate Studies, 716-645-8783, Fax: 716-645-5039, E-mail: graduatedirector@math.buffalo.edu.

The University of Akron, Graduate School, Buchtel College of Arts and Sciences, Department of Theoretical and Applied Mathematics, Program in Mathematics, Akron, OH 44325. Offers MS. Part-time and evening/weekend programs available. *Students:* 17 full-time (4 women), 3 part-time (2 women); includes 2 Black or African American, non-Hispanic/Latino. Average age 24. 10 applicants, 80% accepted, 3 enrolled. In 2010, 3 master's awarded. *Degree requirements:* For master's, thesis optional, seminar and comprehensive exam or thesis. *Entrance requirements:* For master's, minimum GPA of 2.75, three letters of recommendation, statement of purpose. Additional exam requirements/recommendations for international students: Required—TOEFL (minimum score 550 paper-based; 213 computer-based; 79 iBT). *Application deadline:* Applications are processed on a rolling basis. Application fee: $30 ($40 for international students). Electronic applications accepted. *Expenses:* Tuition, state resident: full-time $6800; part-time $378 per credit hour. Tuition, nonresident: full-time $11,644; part-time $647 per credit hour. Required fees: $1265. One-time fee: $30 full-time. *Unit head:* Dr. Gerald Young, Coordinator, 330-972-5731, E-mail: gyoung1@uakron.edu. *Application contact:* Associate Dean.

The University of Alabama, Graduate School, College of Arts and Sciences, Department of Mathematics, Tuscaloosa, AL 35487. Offers applied mathematics (PhD); mathematics (MA, PhD); pure mathematics (PhD). *Faculty:* 26 full-time (0 women). *Students:* 31 full-time (13 women), 21 part-time (3 women); includes 4 minority (3 Black or African American, non-Hispanic/Latino; 1 Two or more races, non-Hispanic/Latino), 26 international. Average age 28. 51 applicants, 59% accepted, 14 enrolled. In 2010, 8 master's, 1 doctorate awarded. Terminal master's awarded for partial completion of doctoral program. *Degree requirements:* For master's, thesis or alternative; for doctorate, thesis/dissertation. *Entrance requirements:* For master's and doctorate, GRE General Test, minimum GPA of 3.0. Additional exam requirements/recommendations for international students: Required—TOEFL (minimum score 550 paper-based; 79 iBT). *Application deadline:* For fall admission, 7/1 for domestic students, 5/31 for international students; for spring admission, 11/30 for domestic students, 10/31 for international students. Applications are processed on a rolling basis. Application fee: $50 ($60 for international students). Electronic applications accepted. *Expenses:* Tuition, state resident: full-time $7900. Tuition, nonresident: full-time $20,500. *Financial support:* In 2010–11, 1 fellowship with full tuition reimbursement (averaging $30,000 per year), 35 teaching assistantships with full tuition reimbursements (averaging $12,258 per year) were awarded; research assistantships with full tuition reimbursements, Federal Work-Study, institutionally sponsored loans, scholarships/grants, and unspecified assistantships also available. Support available to part-time students. Financial award application deadline: 7/1. *Faculty research:* Analysis, topology, algebra, fluid mechanics and system control theory, optimization, stochastic processes, numerical analysis. Total annual research expenditures: $13,050. *Unit head:* Dr. Zhijian Wu, Chairperson and Professor, 205-348-5080, Fax: 205-348-7067, E-mail: zwu@as.ua.edu. *Application contact:* Dr. Vo Liem, Director, 205-348-4898, Fax: 205-348-7067, E-mail: vliem@as.ua.edu.

The University of Alabama at Birmingham, College of Arts and Sciences, Program in Mathematics, Birmingham, AL 35294. Offers MS. *Students:* 10 full-time (3 women), 1 part-time (0 women); includes 1 Black or African American, non-Hispanic/Latino, 1 international. Average age 27. 5 applicants, 80% accepted, 1 enrolled. In 2010, 10 master's awarded. Terminal master's awarded for partial completion of doctoral program. *Degree requirements:* For master's, thesis optional. *Entrance requirements:* For master's, GRE General Test. *Application deadline:* Applications are processed on a rolling basis. Electronic applications accepted. *Expenses:* Tuition, state resident: full-time $5482. Tuition, nonresident: full-time $12,430. Tuition and fees vary according to program. *Financial support:* In 2010–11, 17 fellowships with full tuition reimbursements (averaging $17,000 per year), 14 teaching assistantships with full tuition reimbursements (averaging $14,400 per year) were awarded; research assistantships, career-related internships or fieldwork, Federal Work-Study, institutionally sponsored loans, scholarships/grants, traineeships, health care benefits, tuition waivers (full and partial), and unspecified assistantships also available. Support available to part-time students. Financial award application deadline: 8/1; financial award applicants required to submit FAFSA. *Faculty research:* Differential equations, topology, mathematical physics, dynamic systems. *Unit head:* Dr. Rudi Weikard, Chair, 205-934-2154, Fax: 205-934-9025, E-mail: weikard@uab.edu. *Application contact:* Dr. Gunter Stolz, Graduate Recruitment Coordinator/Professor, 205-934-2154, Fax: 205-934-9025, E-mail: stolz@math.uab.edu.

The University of Alabama in Huntsville, School of Graduate Studies, College of Science, Department of Mathematical Sciences, Huntsville, AL 35899. Offers applied mathematics (PhD); mathematics (MA, MS). PhD offered jointly with The University of Alabama (Tuscaloosa), The University of Alabama at Birmingham. Part-time and evening/weekend programs available. *Faculty:* 13 full-time (0 women). *Students:* 16 full-time (9 women), 16 part-time (6 women); includes 7 minority (4 Black or African American, non-Hispanic/Latino; 3 Asian, non-Hispanic/Latino), 6 international. Average age 29. 28 applicants, 50% accepted, 10 enrolled. In 2010, 4 master's, 1 doctorate awarded. *Degree requirements:* For master's, comprehensive exam, thesis or alternative, oral and written exams; for doctorate, comprehensive exam, thesis/dissertation, oral and written exams. *Entrance requirements:* For master's and doctorate, GRE General Test, minimum GPA of 3.0. Additional exam requirements/recommendations for international students: Required—TOEFL (minimum score 550 paper-based; 213 computer-based; 62 iBT). *Application deadline:* For fall admission, 7/15 for domestic students, 4/1 for international students; for spring admission, 11/30 for domestic students, 9/1 for international students. Applications are processed on a rolling basis. Application fee: $40 ($50 for international students). Electronic applications accepted. *Expenses:* Tuition, state resident: full-time $7250; part-time $407.75 per credit hour. Tuition, nonresident: full-time $17,358; part-time $970.05 per credit hour. Required fees: $246.80 per semester. Tuition and fees vary according to course load and program. *Financial support:* In 2010–11, 13 students received support, including 16 teaching assistantships with full and partial tuition reimbursements available (averaging $10,575 per year); career-related internships or fieldwork, Federal Work-Study, institutionally sponsored loans, scholarships/grants, health care benefits, and unspecified assistantships also available. Support available to part-time students. Financial award application deadline: 4/1; financial award applicants required to submit FAFSA. *Faculty research:* Dynamical systems, mathematical biology, stochastic processes, numerical analysis, combinatorics. Total annual research expenditures: $277,636. *Unit head:* Dr. Jia Li, Chair, 256-824-6470, Fax: 256-824-6173, E-mail: li@math.uah.edu. *Application contact:* Kathy Biggs, Graduate Studies Admissions Manager, 256-824-6199, Fax: 256-824-6405, E-mail: deangrad@uah.edu.

University of Alaska Fairbanks, College of Natural Sciences and Mathematics, Department of Mathematics and Statistics, Fairbanks, AK 99775-6660. Offers mathematics (MAT, PhD); statistics (MS). Part-time programs available. *Faculty:* 15 full-time (7 women). *Students:* 8 full-time (2 women), 6 part-time (3 women); includes 2 minority (both Asian, non-Hispanic/Latino), 1 international. Average age 31. 16 applicants, 38% accepted, 4 enrolled. In 2010, 4 master's, 2 doctorates awarded. Terminal master's awarded for partial completion of doctoral program. *Degree requirements:* For master's, comprehensive exam, thesis or alternative; for doctorate, comprehensive exam, thesis/dissertation, oral defense. *Entrance requirements:* Additional exam requirements/recommendations for international students: Required—TOEFL (minimum score 550 paper-based; 213 computer-based; 80 iBT). *Application deadline:* For fall admission, 6/1 for domestic students, 3/1 for international students; for spring admission, 10/15 for domestic students, 9/1 for international students. Applications are processed on a rolling basis. Application fee: $60. Electronic applications accepted. *Expenses:* Tuition, state resident: full-time $5688; part-time $316 per credit. Tuition, nonresident: full-time $11,628; part-time $646 per credit. Required fees: $289 per semester. Tuition and fees vary according to course load and reciprocity agreements. *Financial support:* In 2010–11, 2 research assistantships with tuition reimbursements (averaging $10,360 per year), 6 teaching assistantships with tuition reimbursements (averaging $17,088 per year) were awarded; fellowships with tuition reimbursements, career-related internships or fieldwork, Federal Work-Study, scholarships/grants, health care benefits, and unspecified assistantships also available. Support available to part-time students. Financial award application deadline: 2/15; financial award applicants required to submit FAFSA. *Faculty research:* Kriging, arrangements of hyperplanes, bifurcation analysis of time-periodic differential-delay equations, inverse problems, phylogenic tree construction. *Unit head:* Dr. John Rhodes, Department Chair, 907-474-7332, Fax: 907-474-5394, E-mail: fymath@uaf.edu. *Application contact:* Dr. John Rhodes, Department Chair, 907-474-7332, Fax: 907-474-5394, E-mail: fymath@uaf.edu.

University of Alberta, Faculty of Graduate Studies and Research, Department of Mathematical and Statistical Sciences, Edmonton, AB T6G 2E1, Canada. Offers applied mathematics (M Sc, PhD); biostatistics (M Sc); mathematical finance (M Sc, PhD); mathematical physics (M Sc, PhD); mathematics (M Sc, PhD); statistics (M Sc, PhD, Postgraduate Diploma). Part-time programs available. Terminal master's awarded for partial completion of doctoral program. *Degree requirements:* For master's, thesis (for some programs); for doctorate, comprehensive exam, thesis/dissertation. *Entrance requirements:* Additional exam requirements/recommendations for international students: Required—TOEFL (minimum score 580 paper-based; 237 computer-based). Electronic applications accepted. *Faculty research:* Classical and functional analysis, algebra, differential equations, geometry.

The University of Arizona, College of Science, Department of Mathematics, Tucson, AZ 85721. Offers mathematical sciences (PMS), including applied science and business; mathematics (MA, MS, PhD). Part-time programs available. *Faculty:* 52 full-time (7 women), 5 part-time/adjunct (1 woman). *Students:* 48 full-time (11 women), 51 part-time (35 women); includes 26 minority (1 Black or African American, non-Hispanic/Latino; 2 Asian, non-Hispanic/Latino; 17 Hispanic/Latino; 6 Two or more races, non-Hispanic/Latino), 12 international. Average age 32. 98 applicants, 31% accepted, 13 enrolled. In 2010, 4 master's, 4 doctorates awarded. *Degree requirements:* For master's, thesis; for doctorate, 2 foreign languages, thesis/dissertation. *Entrance requirements:* For master's, GRE; for doctorate, GRE, statement of purpose. Additional exam requirements/recommendations for international students: Required—TOEFL (minimum score 550 paper-based; 213 computer-based; 79 iBT). *Application deadline:* For fall admission, 2/1 for domestic students, 12/1 for international students; for spring admission, 10/1 for domestic students, 6/1 for international students. Applications are processed on a rolling basis. Application fee: $75. Electronic applications accepted. *Expenses:* Tuition, state resident: full-time $7692. *Financial support:* In 2010–11, 26 research assistantships (averaging $21,837 per year), 52 teaching assistantships (averaging $21,556 per year) were awarded; scholarships/grants, health care benefits, tuition waivers (full and partial), and unspecified assistantships also available. Financial award application deadline: 3/5. *Faculty research:* Algebra/number theory, computational science, dynamical systems, geometry, analysis. Total annual research expenditures: $6.8 million. *Unit head:* Department Head's Office, 520-621-2713. *Application contact:* Sandy Sutton, Graduate Coordinator, 520-621-2068, Fax: 520-621-8322, E-mail: gradoffice@math.arizona.edu.

The University of Arizona, Graduate Interdisciplinary Programs, Graduate Interdisciplinary Program in Applied Mathematics, Tucson, AZ 85721. Offers applied mathematics (MS, PhD); mathematical sciences (PMS). *Faculty:* 1. *Students:* 39 full-time (10 women); includes 1 Asian, non-Hispanic/Latino; 4 Hispanic/Latino; 1 Two or more races, non-Hispanic/Latino, 4 international. Average age 28. 108 applicants, 10% accepted, 11 enrolled. In 2010, 9 master's, 7 doctorates awarded. Terminal master's awarded for partial completion of doctoral program. *Degree requirements:* For master's, thesis (for some programs); for doctorate, comprehensive exam, thesis/dissertation. *Entrance requirements:* For master's, GRE, 3 letters of recommendation; for doctorate, GRE, 3 letters of recommendation, statement of purpose. Additional exam requirements/recommendations for international students: Required—TOEFL (minimum score 575 paper-based; 230 computer-based; 80 iBT). *Application deadline:* For fall admission, 1/15 for domestic students, 1/30 for international students. Applications are processed on a rolling basis. Application fee: $65. Electronic applications accepted. *Expenses:* Tuition, state resident: full-time $7692. *Financial support:* In 2010–11, 1 research assistantship with full tuition reimbursement (averaging $17,120 per year) was awarded; institutionally sponsored loans, scholarships/grants, health care benefits, tuition waivers (full), and unspecified assistantships also available. Financial award application deadline: 3/1; financial award applicants required to submit FAFSA. *Faculty research:* Dynamical systems and chaos, partial differential equations, pattern formation, fluid dynamics and turbulence, scientific computation, mathematical physics, mathematical biology, medical imaging, applied probability and stochastic processes. Total annual research expenditures: $22,526. *Unit head:* Dr. Michael Tabor, Head, 520-621-4664, Fax: 520-626-5048, E-mail: tabor@math.arizona.edu. *Application contact:* Graduate Coordinator, 520-621-2016, Fax: 520-626-5048, E-mail: applmath@u.arizona.edu.

University of Arkansas, Graduate School, J. William Fulbright College of Arts and Sciences, Department of Mathematical Sciences, Program in Mathematics, Fayetteville, AR 72701-1201. Offers MS, PhD. *Students:* 26 full-time (9 women), 21 part-time (10 women); includes 4 minority (2 Black or African American, non-Hispanic/Latino; 2 Hispanic/Latino), 14 international. 23 applicants, 57% accepted. In 2010, 1 master's, 2 doctorates awarded. *Degree requirements:* For master's, thesis or alternative; for doctorate, 2 foreign languages, thesis/dissertation. *Application deadline:* For fall admission, 4/1 for international students; for spring admission, 10/1 for international students. Applications are processed on a rolling basis. Application fee: $40 ($50 for international students). Electronic applications accepted. *Financial support:* In 2010–11, 3 fellowships with tuition reimbursements, 6 research assistantships, 39 teaching assistantships were awarded; career-related internships or fieldwork and Federal Work-Study also available. Support available to part-time students. Financial award application deadline: 4/1; financial award applicants required to submit FAFSA. *Unit head:* Dr. Chaim Goodman-Strauss, Chair, 479-575-3351, Fax: 479-575-8630, E-mail: strauss@uark.edu. *Application contact:* Dr. John Ryan, Graduate Coordinator, 479-575-3351, Fax: 479-575-8630, E-mail: jryan@uark.edu.

University of Arkansas at Little Rock, Graduate School, College of Science and Mathematics, Department of Mathematics and Statistics, Little Rock, AR 72204-1099. Offers applied statistics (Graduate Certificate); mathematical sciences (MS). Part-time and evening/weekend programs available. *Degree requirements:* For master's, comprehensive exam. *Entrance requirements:* For master's, GRE General Test, GRE Subject Test, minimum GPA of 2.7, previous course work in advanced mathematics.

University of Arkansas at Little Rock, Graduate School, College of Science and Mathematics, Program in Integrated Science and Mathematics, Little Rock, AR 72204-1099. Offers MS.

Peterson's Graduate Programs in the Physical Sciences, Mathematics, Agricultural Sciences, the Environment & Natural Resources 2012

www.facebook.com/petersonspublishing 275

Mathematics

The University of British Columbia, Faculty of Science, Program in Mathematics, Vancouver, BC V6T 1Z2, Canada. Offers M Sc, MA, PhD. Part-time programs available. *Degree requirements:* For master's, thesis or alternative, essay, qualifying exam; for doctorate, comprehensive exam, thesis/dissertation, qualifying exam, thesis proposal. *Entrance requirements:* Additional exam requirements/recommendations for international students: Required—TOEFL (minimum score 600 paper-based; 250 computer-based; 100 iBT). Electronic applications accepted. Tuition charges are reported in Canadian dollars. *Expenses:* Tuition, area resident: Full-time $4179 Canadian dollars. International tuition: $7344 Canadian dollars full-time. *Faculty research:* Applied mathematics, financial mathematics, pure mathematics.

University of Calgary, Faculty of Graduate Studies, Faculty of Science, Department of Mathematics and Statistics, Calgary, AB T2N 1N4, Canada. Offers M Sc, PhD. *Degree requirements:* For master's, comprehensive exam, thesis; for doctorate, thesis/dissertation, candidacy exam, preliminary exams. *Entrance requirements:* For master's, honors degree in applied math, pure math, or statistics; for doctorate, MA or M Sc. Additional exam requirements/recommendations for international students: Required—TOEFL (minimum score 600 paper-based; 250 computer-based), IELTS (minimum score 7), TOEFL (paper-based 600; computer-based 250) or IELTS (paper-based 7). *Faculty research:* Combinatorics, applied mathematics, statistics, probability, analysis.

University of California, Berkeley, Graduate Division, College of Letters and Science, Department of Mathematics, Berkeley, CA 94720-1500. Offers applied mathematics (PhD); mathematics (MA, PhD). Terminal master's awarded for partial completion of doctoral program. *Degree requirements:* For master's, exam or thesis; for doctorate, 2 foreign languages, thesis/dissertation, qualifying exam. *Entrance requirements:* For master's and doctorate, GRE General Test, GRE Subject Test, minimum GPA of 3.0, 3 letters of recommendation. *Faculty research:* Algebra, analysis, logic, geometry/topology.

University of California, Davis, Graduate Studies, Program in Mathematics, Davis, CA 95616. Offers MA, MAT, PhD. Terminal master's awarded for partial completion of doctoral program. *Degree requirements:* For master's, comprehensive exam; for doctorate, one foreign language, thesis/dissertation. *Entrance requirements:* For master's and doctorate, GRE General Test, GRE Subject Test, minimum GPA of 3.0. Additional exam requirements/recommendations for international students: Required—TOEFL (minimum score 550 paper-based; 213 computer-based). Electronic applications accepted. *Faculty research:* Mathematical physics, geometric topology, probability, partial differential equations, applied mathematics.

University of California, Irvine, School of Physical Sciences, Department of Mathematics, Irvine, CA 92697. Offers MS, PhD. *Students:* 106 full-time (27 women); includes 22 minority (2 Black or African American, non-Hispanic/Latino; 17 Asian, non-Hispanic/Latino; 1 Hispanic/Latino; 2 Two or more races, non-Hispanic/Latino), 44 international. Average age 28. 174 applicants, 36% accepted, 23 enrolled. In 2010, 15 master's, 11 doctorates awarded. *Degree requirements:* For doctorate, thesis/dissertation. *Entrance requirements:* For master's and doctorate, GRE General Test, GRE Subject Test, minimum GPA of 3.0. Additional exam requirements/recommendations for international students: Required—TOEFL (minimum score 550 paper-based; 213 computer-based). *Application deadline:* For fall admission, 1/15 priority date for domestic and international students. Applications are processed on a rolling basis. Application fee: $80 ($100 for international students). Electronic applications accepted. *Financial support:* Fellowships, research assistantships with full tuition reimbursements, teaching assistantships, institutionally sponsored loans, traineeships, health care benefits, and unspecified assistantships available. Financial award application deadline: 3/1; financial award applicants required to submit FAFSA. *Faculty research:* Algebra and logic, geometry and topology, probability, mathematical physics. *Unit head:* Prof. Frederic Yui-Ming Wan, Professor, 949-824-5529, Fax: 949-824-7993, E-mail: fwan@uci.edu. *Application contact:* Donna M. McConnell, Graduate Affairs Officer, 949-824-5544, Fax: 949-824-7993, E-mail: dmcconne@uci.edu.

University of California, Los Angeles, Graduate Division, College of Letters and Science, Department of Mathematics, Los Angeles, CA 90095. Offers MA, MAT, PhD. *Faculty:* 52 full-time (48 women). *Students:* 164 full-time (26 women); includes 25 minority (1 Black or African American, non-Hispanic/Latino; 18 Asian, non-Hispanic/Latino; 6 Hispanic/Latino), 53 international. Average age 26. 379 applicants, 18% accepted, 27 enrolled. In 2010, 17 master's, 31 doctorates awarded. Terminal master's awarded for partial completion of doctoral program. *Degree requirements:* For master's, comprehensive exam or thesis; for doctorate, one foreign language, thesis/dissertation, oral and written qualifying exams. *Entrance requirements:* For master's, GRE General Test, GRE Subject Test, minimum GPA of 3.2 in mathematics, 12 quarter courses of upper division math; for doctorate, GRE General Test, GRE Subject Test, minimum GPA of 3.5 in mathematics, 12 quarter courses of upper division math. *Application deadline:* For fall admission, 12/15 for domestic students, 11/15 for international students. Application fee: $70 ($90 for international students). Electronic applications accepted. *Financial support:* In 2010–11, 138 fellowships with full and partial tuition reimbursements, 87 research assistantships with full and partial tuition reimbursements, 126 teaching assistantships with full and partial tuition reimbursements were awarded; Federal Work-Study, institutionally sponsored loans, scholarships/grants, health care benefits, tuition waivers (full and partial), and unspecified assistantships also available. Financial award application deadline: 3/1; financial award applicants required to submit FAFSA. *Unit head:* Dr. Sorin Popa, Chair, 310-825-8502, E-mail: popa@math.ucla.edu. *Application contact:* Department Office, 310-825-4971, E-mail: gradapps@math.ucla.edu.

University of California, Riverside, Graduate Division, Department of Mathematics, Riverside, CA 92521-0102. Offers MA, MS, PhD. Part-time programs available. Terminal master's awarded for partial completion of doctoral program. *Degree requirements:* For master's, comprehensive exam; for doctorate, thesis/dissertation, qualifying exams. *Entrance requirements:* For master's and doctorate, GRE General Test, minimum GPA of 3.2. Additional exam requirements/recommendations for international students: Required—TOEFL (minimum score 550 paper-based; 213 computer-based; 80 iBT). Electronic applications accepted. *Faculty research:* Algebraic geometry, commutative algebra, Lie algebra, differential equations, differential geometry.

University of California, San Diego, Office of Graduate Studies, Department of Mathematics, La Jolla, CA 92093. Offers applied mathematics (MA); mathematics (MA, PhD); statistics (MS). *Degree requirements:* For doctorate, thesis/dissertation. *Entrance requirements:* For master's and doctorate, GRE General Test, GRE Subject Test. Electronic applications accepted.

University of California, Santa Barbara, Graduate Division, College of Letters and Sciences, Division of Mathematics, Life, and Physical Sciences, Department of Mathematics, Santa Barbara, CA 93106-3080. Offers applied mathematics (MA), including computational science and engineering; mathematics (MA, PhD), including computational science and engineering; MA/PhD. *Faculty:* 29 full-time (3 women). *Students:* 50 full-time (11 women); includes 2 Black or African American, non-Hispanic/Latino; 6 Asian, non-Hispanic/Latino; 6 Hispanic/Latino. Average age 26. 151 applicants, 21% accepted, 9 enrolled. In 2010, 7 master's, 10 doctorates awarded. Terminal master's awarded for partial completion of doctoral program. *Degree requirements:* For master's, comprehensive exam (for some programs), thesis (for some programs); for doctorate, comprehensive exam, thesis/dissertation. *Entrance requirements:* For master's and doctorate, GRE General Test, GRE Subject Test (math). Additional exam requirements/recommendations for international students: Required—TOEFL (minimum score 575 paper-based; 80 iBT), IELTS (minimum score 7). *Application deadline:* For fall admission, 1/1 priority date for domestic and international students. Application fee: $70 ($90 for international students). Electronic applications accepted. *Financial support:* In 2010–11, 50 students received support, including 15 fellowships with full tuition reimbursements available (averaging $11,684 per year), 11 research assistantships with full tuition reimbursements available (averaging $7,984 per year), 42 teaching assistantships with partial tuition reimbursements available (averaging $16,637 per year); Federal Work-Study, institutionally sponsored loans, health care benefits, and tuition waivers (full and partial) also available. Financial award application deadline: 3/2; financial award applicants required to submit FAFSA. *Faculty research:* Topology, differential geometry, algebra, applied mathematics, partial differential equations. Total annual research expenditures: $205,000. *Unit head:* Prof. Martin Scharlemann, Chair, 805-893-8340, Fax: 805-893-2385, E-mail: mgscharl@math.ucsb.edu. *Application contact:* Medina Price, Graduate Advisor, 805-893-8192, Fax: 805-893-2385, E-mail: price@math.ucsb.edu.

University of California, Santa Cruz, Division of Graduate Studies, Division of Physical and Biological Sciences, Department of Mathematics, Santa Cruz, CA 95064. Offers MA, PhD. *Students:* 35 full-time (8 women); includes 3 minority (2 Asian, non-Hispanic/Latino; 1 Hispanic/Latino), 11 international. Average age 27. 67 applicants, 27% accepted, 10 enrolled. In 2010, 6 master's, 1 doctorate awarded. Terminal master's awarded for partial completion of doctoral program. *Degree requirements:* For master's, thesis; for doctorate, one foreign language, thesis/dissertation, qualifying exam. *Entrance requirements:* For doctorate, GRE General Test, GRE Subject Test. Additional exam requirements/recommendations for international students: Required—TOEFL (minimum score 550 paper-based; 220 computer-based; 83 iBT); Recommended—IELTS (minimum score 8). *Application deadline:* For fall admission, 1/15 for domestic and international students. Application fee: $70 ($90 for international students). Electronic applications accepted. *Financial support:* Fellowships, research assistantships, teaching assistantships, institutionally sponsored loans and tuition waivers available. Financial award applicants required to submit FAFSA. *Faculty research:* Vertex operator algebras, algebraic topology, elliptic cohomology, quantum field theory, automorphic forms, dynamical systems, celestial mechanics, geometric mechanics, bifurcation theory, control theory, representations of Lie and p-adic groups, applications to number theory, Bessel functions, Rankin-Selberg integrals, Gelfand-Graev models, differential geometry, nonlinear analysis, harmonic maps, Ginzburg-Landau problem. *Unit head:* Sandra Yates, Graduate Program Coordinator, 831-459-5461, E-mail: syates1@ucsc.edu. *Application contact:* Sandra Yates, Graduate Program Coordinator, 831-459-5461, E-mail: syates1@ucsc.edu.

University of Central Arkansas, Graduate School, College of Natural Sciences and Math, Department of Mathematics, Conway, AR 72035-0001. Offers applied mathematics (MS); math education (MA). Part-time programs available. *Faculty:* 16 full-time (4 women). *Students:* 10 full-time (4 women), 3 part-time (2 women); includes 1 minority (Asian, non-Hispanic/Latino), 3 international. Average age 29. 8 applicants, 100% accepted, 4 enrolled. In 2010, 7 master's awarded. *Degree requirements:* For master's, comprehensive exam, thesis optional. *Entrance requirements:* For master's, GRE General Test, minimum GPA of 2.7. Additional exam requirements/recommendations for international students: Required—TOEFL (minimum score 550 paper-based; 213 computer-based). *Application deadline:* For fall admission, 3/1 priority date for domestic students; for spring admission, 10/1 priority date for domestic students. Applications are processed on a rolling basis. Application fee: $25 ($50 for international students). *Financial support:* In 2010–11, 11 teaching assistantships with partial tuition reimbursements (averaging $8,500 per year) were awarded; Federal Work-Study, scholarships/grants, and unspecified assistantships also available. Financial award application deadline: 2/15; financial award applicants required to submit FAFSA. *Unit head:* Dr. Ramesh Garimella, Chair, 501-450-3147, Fax: 501-450-5662, E-mail: rameshg@uca.edu. *Application contact:* Susan Wood, Admissions Assistant, 501-450-3124, Fax: 501-450-5678, E-mail: swood@uca.edu.

University of Central Florida, College of Sciences, Department of Mathematics, Orlando, FL 32816. Offers applied mathematics (Certificate); mathematical science (MS); mathematics (PhD). Part-time and evening/weekend programs available. *Faculty:* 46 full-time (10 women), 8 part-time/adjunct (0 women). *Students:* 45 full-time (15 women), 22 part-time (10 women); includes 6 Black or African American, non-Hispanic/Latino; 3 Asian, non-Hispanic/Latino; 5 Hispanic/Latino, 13 international. Average age 32. 77 applicants, 71% accepted, 24 enrolled. In 2010, 3 master's, 2 doctorates awarded. *Degree requirements:* For master's, thesis or alternative; for doctorate, thesis/dissertation, candidacy exam. *Entrance requirements:* For master's, GRE General Test, minimum GPA of 3.0 in last 60 hours; for doctorate, GRE Subject Test, minimum GPA of 3.0 in last 60 hours or master's qualifying exam. Additional exam requirements/recommendations for international students: Required—TOEFL. *Application deadline:* For fall admission, 7/15 for domestic students; for spring admission, 12/1 for domestic students. Application fee: $30. Electronic applications accepted. *Expenses:* Tuition, state resident: part-time $256.56 per credit hour. Tuition, nonresident: part-time $1011.52 per credit hour. Part-time tuition and fees vary according to program. *Financial support:* In 2010–11, 36 students received support, including 7 fellowships with partial tuition reimbursements available (averaging $8,200 per year), 4 research assistantships with partial tuition reimbursements available (averaging $4,400 per year), 38 teaching assistantships with partial tuition reimbursements available (averaging $12,400 per year); career-related internships or fieldwork, Federal Work-Study, institutionally sponsored loans, tuition waivers (partial), and unspecified assistantships also available. Financial award application deadline: 3/1; financial award applicants required to submit FAFSA. *Faculty research:* Applied mathematics, analysis, approximation theory, graph theory, mathematical statistics. *Unit head:* Dr. Piotr Mikusinski, Chair, 407-823-0445, Fax: 407-823-6253, E-mail: piotrm@mail.ucf.edu. *Application contact:* Dr. Piotr Mikusinski, Chair, 407-823-0445, Fax: 407-823-6253, E-mail: piotrm@mail.ucf.edu.

University of Central Missouri, The Graduate School, College of Science and Technology, Warrensburg, MO 64093. Offers applied mathematics (MS); aviation safety (MS); biology (MS); computer science (MS); environmental studies (MA); industrial management (MS); mathematics (MS); technology (MS); technology management (PhD). PhD is offered jointly with Indiana State University. Part-time programs available. Postbaccalaureate distance learning degree programs offered. *Entrance requirements:* Additional exam requirements/recommendations for international students: Required—TOEFL (minimum score 550 paper-based; 79 computer-based). Electronic applications accepted.

University of Central Oklahoma, College of Graduate Studies and Research, College of Mathematics and Science, Department of Mathematics and Statistics, Edmond, OK 73034-5209. Offers applied mathematical sciences (MS), including computer science, mathematics, mathematics/computer science teaching, statistics. Part-time programs available. *Degree requirements:* For master's, thesis. *Entrance requirements:* Additional exam requirements/recommendations for international students: Required—TOEFL (minimum score 550 paper-based; 213 computer-based). Electronic applications accepted. *Faculty research:* Curvature, FAA, math education.

University of Chicago, Division of the Physical Sciences, Department of Mathematics, Chicago, IL 60637-1513. Offers applied mathematics (SM, PhD); financial mathematics (MS); mathematics (SM, PhD). *Faculty:* 57 full-time (7 women). *Students:* 88 full-time (20 women), 40 international. 403 applicants, 12% accepted, 16 enrolled. In 2010, 17 master's, 10 doctorates awarded. *Degree requirements:* For master's, one foreign language; for doctorate, one foreign language, thesis/dissertation, 2 qualifying exams, oral topic presentation. *Entrance requirements:* For master's and doctorate, GRE General Test, GRE Subject Test. Additional exam requirements/recommendations for international students: Required—TOEFL (minimum score 600 paper-based; 250 computer-based). *Application deadline:* For fall admission, 1/5 for domestic and international students. Application fee: $55. Electronic applications accepted. *Financial support:* In 2010–11, 26 fellowships, 62 teaching assistantships were awarded; research assistantships, career-related internships or fieldwork, institutionally sponsored loans, and scholarships/grants also available. Financial award application deadline: 1/5; financial award applicants required to submit CSS PROFILE or FAFSA. *Faculty research:* Analysis, differential geometry,

algebra number theory, topology, algebraic geometry. *Unit head:* Dr. Peter Constantin, Chair, 773-702-7399, Fax: 773-702-9787. *Application contact:* Laurie Wail, Graduate Studies Assistant, 773-702-7358, Fax: 773-702-9787, E-mail: lwail@math.uchicago.edu.

University of Cincinnati, Graduate School, McMicken College of Arts and Sciences, Department of Mathematical Sciences, Cincinnati, OH 45221. Offers applied mathematics (MS, PhD); mathematics education (MAT); pure mathematics (MS, PhD); statistics (MS, PhD). Part-time programs available. Terminal master's awarded for partial completion of doctoral program. *Degree requirements:* For master's, comprehensive exam, thesis or alternative; for doctorate, one foreign language, comprehensive exam, thesis/dissertation. *Entrance requirements:* For master's, GRE, teacher certification (MAT); for doctorate, GRE. Additional exam requirements/recommendations for international students: Required—TOEFL. Electronic applications accepted. *Faculty research:* Algebra, analysis, differential equations, numerical analysis, statistics.

University of Colorado at Colorado Springs, College of Letters, Arts and Sciences, Department of Mathematics, Colorado Springs, CO 80933-7150. Offers applied mathematics (MS); applied science (PhD); mathematics (M Sc). Part-time and evening/weekend programs available. *Faculty:* 11 full-time (1 woman), 1 (woman) part-time/adjunct. *Students:* 10 full-time (3 women), 10 part-time (6 women), 2 international. Average age 34. 9 applicants, 78% accepted, 6 enrolled. In 2010, 2 master's awarded. *Degree requirements:* For master's, thesis, qualifying exam. *Entrance requirements:* For master's, GRE General Test, minimum GPA of 3.0. Additional exam requirements/recommendations for international students: Required—TOEFL. *Application deadline:* For fall admission, 6/15 for domestic students. Applications are processed on a rolling basis. Application fee: $60 ($75 for international students). *Expenses:* Tuition, state resident: full-time $7916. Tuition, nonresident: full-time $16,610. Tuition and fees vary according to course load, degree level, program, reciprocity agreements and student level. *Financial support:* Teaching assistantships, Federal Work-Study and scholarships/grants available. Support available to part-time students. Financial award application deadline: 3/1; financial award applicants required to submit FAFSA. *Faculty research:* Abelian groups and noncommutative rings, hormone analysis and computer vision, probability and mathematical physics, stochastic dynamics, probability models. *Unit head:* Dr. Sarbarish Chakravarty, Chair, 719-255-3549, Fax: 719-255-3605, E-mail: schakrav@uccs.edu. *Application contact:* Elizabeth Buzo, Graduate Liaison, 719-255-3554, Fax: 719-255-3605, E-mail: ebuzo@uccs.edu.

University of Colorado at Colorado Springs, College of Letters, Arts and Sciences, Master of Sciences Program, Colorado Springs, CO 80933-7150. Offers applied science—bioscience (M Sc); applied science—physics (M Sc); biology (M Sc); chemistry (M Sc); health promotion (M Sc); mathematics (M Sc); physics (M Sc); sports medicine (M Sc); sports nutrition (M Sc). Part-time programs available. *Students:* 19 full-time (10 women), 11 part-time (4 women); includes 2 Asian, non-Hispanic/Latino; 3 Hispanic/Latino. Average age 34. 20 applicants, 55% accepted, 7 enrolled. In 2010, 14 master's awarded. *Degree requirements:* For master's, thesis or alternative. *Entrance requirements:* For master's, minimum GPA of 2.75. *Application deadline:* For fall admission, 6/1 priority date for domestic students; for spring admission, 12/1 for domestic students. Application fee: $60 ($75 for international students). *Expenses:* Contact institution. *Financial support:* Fellowships, research assistantships, teaching assistantships, career-related internships or fieldwork, Federal Work-Study, and scholarships/grants available. Support available to part-time students. Financial award application deadline: 3/1; financial award applicants required to submit FAFSA. *Faculty research:* Biomechanics and physiology of elite athletic training, genetic engineering in yeast and bacteria including phage display and DNA repair, immunology and cell biology, synthetic organic chemistry. *Application contact:* Michael Sanderson, Information Contact, 719-255-3417, Fax: 719-255-3037, E-mail: gradschl@uccs.edu.

University of Colorado Boulder, Graduate School, College of Arts and Sciences, Department of Mathematics, Boulder, CO 80309. Offers MA, MS, PhD. *Faculty:* 26 full-time (4 women). *Students:* 68 full-time (18 women), 3 part-time (0 women); includes 7 minority (1 Black or African American, non-Hispanic/Latino; 1 American Indian or Alaska Native, non-Hispanic/Latino; 2 Asian, non-Hispanic/Latino; 3 Hispanic/Latino), 10 international. Average age 27. 143 applicants, 20 enrolled. In 2010, 17 master's, 7 doctorates awarded. Terminal master's awarded for partial completion of doctoral program. *Degree requirements:* For master's, comprehensive exam, thesis or alternative; for doctorate, one foreign language, comprehensive exam, thesis/dissertation, 2 preliminary exams. *Entrance requirements:* For master's, minimum undergraduate GPA of 3.0. *Application deadline:* For fall admission, 1/15 priority date for domestic students, 1/15 for international students; for spring admission, 11/1 for domestic and international students. Applications are processed on a rolling basis. Application fee: $50 ($60 for international students). *Financial support:* In 2010–11, 42 fellowships (averaging $6,054 per year), 10 research assistantships (averaging $6,092 per year) were awarded; scholarships/grants and tuition waivers (full) also available. Support available to part-time students. Financial award application deadline: 2/1. *Faculty research:* Pure mathematics, applied mathematics and mathematical physics (including algebra, algebraic geometry, differential equations, differential geometry, logic and foundations). Total annual research expenditures: $293,333.

University of Colorado Denver, College of Liberal Arts and Sciences, Program in Integrated Sciences, Denver, CO 80217-3364. Offers applied science (MIS); computer science (MIS); mathematics (MIS). Part-time and evening/weekend programs available. *Students:* 4 full-time (1 woman), 3 part-time (1 woman); includes 1 Hispanic/Latino. Average age 41. 4 applicants, 100% accepted, 2 enrolled. In 2010, 1 master's awarded. *Degree requirements:* For master's, thesis or alternative, 30 credit hours; thesis or project. *Entrance requirements:* For master's, GRE if undergraduate GPA is 2.75 or less, minimum of 40 semester hours in mathematics, computer science, physics, biology, chemistry and/or geology. *Application deadline:* For fall admission, 4/15 for domestic students; for spring admission, 10/15 for domestic students. Application fee: $50 ($75 for international students). Electronic applications accepted. *Expenses:* Tuition, state resident: full-time $7332; part-time $355 per credit hour. Tuition, nonresident: full-time $18,990; part-time $1055 per credit hour. Required fees: $998. Tuition and fees vary according to course level, course load, degree level, campus/location, program, reciprocity agreements and student level. *Financial support:* Application deadline: 4/1. *Faculty research:* Computer science, applied science, mathematics.

University of Connecticut, Graduate School, College of Liberal Arts and Sciences, Department of Mathematics, Field of Mathematics, Storrs, CT 06269. Offers actuarial science (MS, PhD); mathematics (MS, PhD). Terminal master's awarded for partial completion of doctoral program. *Degree requirements:* For master's, comprehensive exam; for doctorate, thesis/dissertation. *Entrance requirements:* For master's and doctorate, GRE General Test. Additional exam requirements/recommendations for international students: Required—TOEFL (minimum score 550 paper-based; 213 computer-based). Electronic applications accepted.

University of Delaware, College of Arts and Sciences, Department of Mathematical Sciences, Newark, DE 19716. Offers applied mathematics (MS, PhD); mathematics (MS, PhD). Part-time programs available. Terminal master's awarded for partial completion of doctoral program. *Degree requirements:* For master's, thesis (for some programs); for doctorate, one foreign language, thesis/dissertation, qualifying exam. *Entrance requirements:* For master's and doctorate, GRE General Test. Additional exam requirements/recommendations for international students: Required—TOEFL. Electronic applications accepted. *Faculty research:* Scattering theory, inverse problems, fluid dynamics, numerical analysis, combinatorics.

University of Denver, Faculty of Natural Sciences and Mathematics, Department of Mathematics, Denver, CO 80208. Offers MA, MS, PhD. Part-time programs available. *Faculty:* 15 full-time (4 women), 2 part-time/adjunct (1 woman). *Students:* 1 (woman) full-time, 19 part-time (3 women); includes 2 minority (1 Asian, non-Hispanic/Latino; 1 Hispanic/Latino), 7 international. Average age 27. 31 applicants, 81% accepted, 9 enrolled. In 2010, 3 master's, 2

doctorates awarded. Terminal master's awarded for partial completion of doctoral program. *Degree requirements:* For master's, computer language, foreign language, or laboratory experience; for doctorate, one foreign language, comprehensive exam, thesis/dissertation, oral and written exams. *Entrance requirements:* For master's, GRE General Test, BA or BS in mathematics or related field; for doctorate, GRE General Test. Additional exam requirements/recommendations for international students: Required—TOEFL (minimum score 550 paper-based; 80 iBT). *Application deadline:* Applications are processed on a rolling basis. Application fee: $60. Electronic applications accepted. *Expenses:* Tuition: Full-time $35,604; part-time $29,670 per year. Required fees: $687 per year. Tuition and fees vary according to program. *Financial support:* In 2010–11, 12 teaching assistantships with full and partial tuition reimbursements (averaging $17,453 per year) were awarded; career-related internships or fieldwork, Federal Work-Study, institutionally sponsored loans, scholarships/grants, and unspecified assistantships also available. Support available to part-time students. Financial award application deadline: 3/1; financial award applicants required to submit FAFSA. *Faculty research:* Real-time software, convex bodies, multidimensional data, parallel computer clusters. *Unit head:* Dr. Alvaro Arias, Chairperson, 303-871-3559, Fax: 303-871-3173, E-mail: aarias@math.du.edu. *Application contact:* Information Contact, 303-871-2911, Fax: 303-871-3173, E-mail: info@math.du.edu.

University of Florida, Graduate School, College of Liberal Arts and Sciences, Department of Mathematics, Gainesville, FL 32611. Offers MA, MAT, MS, MST, PhD. Part-time programs available. *Faculty:* 42 full-time (3 women), 1 part-time/adjunct (0 women). *Students:* 118 full-time (42 women), 4 part-time (0 women); includes 3 Black or African American, non-Hispanic/Latino; 8 Asian, non-Hispanic/Latino; 10 Hispanic/Latino, 40 international. Average age 27. 233 applicants, 34% accepted, 18 enrolled. In 2010, 11 master's, 8 doctorates awarded. Terminal master's awarded for partial completion of doctoral program. *Degree requirements:* For master's, comprehensive exam, thesis optional, First year exam; for doctorate, one foreign language, comprehensive exam, thesis/dissertation. *Entrance requirements:* For master's and doctorate, GRE General Test, minimum GPA of 3.0. Additional exam requirements/recommendations for international students: Required—TOEFL (minimum score 550 paper-based; 213 computer-based; 80 iBT), IELTS (minimum score 6). *Application deadline:* For fall admission, 6/1 priority date for domestic students. Applications are processed on a rolling basis. Application fee: $30. Electronic applications accepted. *Expenses:* Tuition, state resident: full-time $10,915.92. Tuition, nonresident: full-time $28,309. *Financial support:* In 2010–11, 109 students received support, including 23 fellowships, 3 research assistantships (averaging $17,522 per year), 83 teaching assistantships (averaging $20,449 per year); career-related internships or fieldwork and unspecified assistantships also available. Financial award applicants required to submit FAFSA. *Faculty research:* Combinatorics and number theory, group theory, probability theory, logic, differential geometry and mathematical physics. *Unit head:* James E. Keesling, PhD, Chairman, 352-392-0281 Ext. 224, Fax: 352-392-8357, E-mail: kees@ufl.edu. *Application contact:* Paul L. Robinson, PhD, Graduate Coordinator, 352-392-0281 Ext. 223, Fax: 352-392-8357, E-mail: paulr@ufl.edu.

University of Georgia, College of Arts and Sciences, Department of Mathematics, Athens, GA 30602. Offers applied mathematical science (MAMS); mathematics (MA, PhD). *Faculty:* 31 full-time (4 women). *Students:* 48 full-time (14 women); includes 1 Black or African American, non-Hispanic/Latino; 1 Asian, non-Hispanic/Latino; 2 Hispanic/Latino, 12 international. 117 applicants, 14% accepted, 7 enrolled. In 2010, 4 master's, 3 doctorates awarded. *Degree requirements:* For master's, one foreign language, thesis (for some programs); for doctorate, 2 foreign languages, thesis/dissertation. *Entrance requirements:* For master's and doctorate, GRE General Test. *Application deadline:* For fall admission, 7/1 priority date for domestic students; for spring admission, 11/15 for domestic students. Application fee: $50. Electronic applications accepted. *Expenses:* Tuition, state resident: full-time $7200; part-time $344 per credit hour. Tuition, nonresident: full-time $21,900; part-time $944 per credit hour. Tuition and fees vary according to course load and program. *Financial support:* Fellowships, research assistantships, teaching assistantships, unspecified assistantships available. *Unit head:* Dr. Malcolm Adams, Head, 706-542-2564, E-mail: fu@math.uga.edu. *Application contact:* Dr. Brian D. Boe, Graduate Coordinator, 706-542-2547, Fax: 706-542-2573, E-mail: grad@math.uga.edu.

University of Guelph, Graduate Studies, College of Physical and Engineering Science, Department of Mathematics and Statistics, Guelph, ON N1G 2W1, Canada. Offers applied mathematics (PhD); applied statistics (PhD); mathematics and statistics (M Sc). Part-time programs available. *Degree requirements:* For master's, thesis (for some programs); for doctorate, thesis/dissertation. *Entrance requirements:* For master's, minimum B- average during previous 2 years of course work; for doctorate, minimum B average. Additional exam requirements/recommendations for international students: Required—TOEFL (minimum score 550 paper-based; 213 computer-based; 89 iBT), IELTS (minimum score 6.5). *Faculty research:* Dynamical systems, mathematical biology, numerical analysis, linear and nonlinear models, reliability and bioassay.

University of Hawaii at Manoa, Graduate Division, College of Natural Sciences, Department of Mathematics, Honolulu, HI 96822. Offers MA, PhD. Part-time programs available. *Faculty:* 31 full-time (4 women). *Students:* 25 full-time (7 women), 13 part-time (6 women); includes 1 Black or African American, non-Hispanic/Latino; 9 Asian, non-Hispanic/Latino; 1 Hispanic/Latino; 2 Two or more races, non-Hispanic/Latino, 5 international. Average age 30. 43 applicants, 63% accepted, 13 enrolled. In 2010, 5 master's, 1 doctorate awarded. *Degree requirements:* For doctorate, one foreign language, comprehensive exam, thesis/dissertation. *Entrance requirements:* For master's and doctorate, GRE General Test, minimum GPA of 3.0. Additional exam requirements/recommendations for international students: Required—TOEFL (minimum score 500 paper-based; 173 computer-based; 61 iBT), IELTS (minimum score 5). *Application deadline:* For fall admission, 3/1 for domestic students, 2/1 for international students; for spring admission, 9/1 for domestic students, 8/1 for international students. Applications are processed on a rolling basis. Application fee: $60. *Financial support:* In 2010–11, 8 fellowships (averaging $2,000 per year), 1 research assistantship (averaging $16,176 per year), 17 teaching assistantships (averaging $16,154 per year) were awarded; institutionally sponsored loans, tuition waivers (full and partial), and unspecified assistantships also available. Support available to part-time students. Financial award application deadline: 3/1. *Faculty research:* Analysis, algebra, lattice theory, logic topology, differential geometry. Total annual research expenditures: $492,000. *Application contact:* James Nation, Graduate Chair, 808-956-7951, Fax: 808-956-9139, E-mail: jb@math.hawaii.edu.

University of Houston, College of Natural Sciences and Mathematics, Department of Mathematics, Houston, TX 77204. Offers applied mathematics (MS); mathematics (MA, PhD). Part-time programs available. *Faculty:* 29 full-time (2 women), 1 (woman) part-time/adjunct. *Students:* 87 full-time (37 women), 41 part-time (21 women); includes 3 Black or African American, non-Hispanic/Latino; 12 Asian, non-Hispanic/Latino; 9 Hispanic/Latino; 1 Two or more races, non-Hispanic/Latino, 55 international. Average age 31. 42 applicants, 83% accepted, 18 enrolled. In 2010, 23 master's, 12 doctorates awarded. *Degree requirements:* For master's, thesis optional. *Entrance requirements:* For master's and doctorate, GRE V-Q . Additional exam requirements/recommendations for international students: Required—TOEFL (minimum score 550 paper-based; 79 iBT), IELTS (minimum score 6.5). *Application deadline:* For fall admission, 7/3 for domestic students, 5/1 for international students; for spring admission, 12/4 for domestic students, 10/1 for international students. Applications are processed on a rolling basis. Application fee: $0 ($75 for international students). Electronic applications accepted. *Expenses:* Tuition, state resident: full-time $8592; part-time $358 per credit hour. Tuition, nonresident: full-time $16,032; part-time $668 per credit hour. Required fees: $2889. Tuition and fees vary according to course load and program. *Financial support:* In 2010–11, 14 research assistantships with partial tuition reimbursements (averaging $8,720 per year), 23

Peterson's Graduate Programs in the Physical Sciences, Mathematics, Agricultural Sciences, the Environment & Natural Resources 2012

www.facebook.com/petersonspublishing   **277**

Mathematics

University of Houston (continued)
teaching assistantships with partial tuition reimbursements (averaging $13,184 per year) were awarded; career-related internships or fieldwork, Federal Work-Study, institutionally sponsored loans, scholarships/grants, health care benefits, and unspecified assistantships also available. Support available to part-time students. Financial award application deadline: 2/1. *Faculty research:* Applied mathematics, modern analysis, computational science, geometry, dynamical systems. *Unit head:* Dr. Jeffery E. Morgan, Chairperson, 713-743-3500, Fax: 713-743-3505, E-mail: jmorgan@math.uh.edu. *Application contact:* Dr. Jeffery E. Morgan, Chairperson, 713-743-3500, Fax: 713-743-3505, E-mail: jmorgan@math.uh.edu.

University of Houston–Clear Lake, School of Science and Computer Engineering, Program in Mathematical Sciences, Houston, TX 77058-1098. Offers MS. Part-time and evening/weekend programs available. *Entrance requirements:* For master's, GRE General Test. Additional exam requirements/recommendations for international students: Required—TOEFL (minimum score 550 paper-based; 213 computer-based).

University of Idaho, College of Graduate Studies, College of Science, Department of Mathematics, Moscow, ID 83844-2282. Offers MAT, MS, PhD. *Faculty:* 5 full-time, 1 part-time/adjunct. *Students:* 19 full-time, 13 part-time. Average age 36. In 2010, 15 master's, 1 doctorate awarded. *Degree requirements:* For doctorate, 2 foreign languages, thesis/dissertation. *Entrance requirements:* For master's, minimum GPA of 2.8; for doctorate, minimum undergraduate GPA of 2.8, 3.0 graduate. *Application deadline:* For fall admission, 8/1 for domestic students; for spring admission, 12/15 for domestic students. Applications are processed on a rolling basis. Application fee: $60. Electronic applications accepted. *Expenses:* Tuition, nonresident: part-time $580 per credit. Required fees: $306 per credit. *Financial support:* Research assistantships, teaching assistantships available. Financial award applicants required to submit FAFSA. *Faculty research:* Bioinformatics and mathematical biology, analysis and differential equations, combinatorics, probability and stochastic processes, discrete geometry. *Unit head:* Dr. Monte Boisen, Chair, 208-885-6742, E-mail: math@uidaho.edu. *Application contact:* Dr. Monte Boisen, Chair, 208-885-6742, E-mail: math@uidaho.edu.

University of Illinois at Chicago, Graduate College, College of Liberal Arts and Sciences, Department of Mathematics, Statistics, and Computer Science, Chicago, IL 60607-7128. Offers applied mathematics (MS, PhD); computational finance (MS, PhD); computer science (MS, PhD); mathematics (DA); mathematics and information sciences for industry (MS); probability and statistics (PhD); pure mathematics (MS, PhD); statistics (MS); teaching of mathematics (MST), including elementary, secondary. Part-time programs available. *Faculty:* 36 full-time (3 women). *Students:* 150 full-time (54 women), 31 part-time (18 women); includes 3 Black or African American, non-Hispanic/Latino; 1 Asian, non-Hispanic/Latino; 8 Hispanic/Latino, 62 international. Average age 26. 224 applicants, 56% accepted, 43 enrolled. In 2010, 34 master's, 17 doctorates awarded. *Degree requirements:* For master's, comprehensive exam; for doctorate, one foreign language, thesis/dissertation. *Entrance requirements:* For master's and doctorate, GRE General Test, minimum GPA of 3.0. Additional exam requirements/recommendations for international students: Required—TOEFL (minimum score 100 iBT). *Application deadline:* For fall admission, 1/1 for domestic and international students; for spring admission, 10/1 for domestic students, 7/15 for international students. Applications are processed on a rolling basis. Application fee: $60. Electronic applications accepted. *Financial support:* In 2010–11, 109 students received support, including 2 fellowships with full tuition reimbursements available (averaging $20,000 per year), 8 research assistantships with full tuition reimbursements available (averaging $17,000 per year), 87 teaching assistantships with full tuition reimbursements available (averaging $17,000 per year); Federal Work-Study, scholarships/grants, and tuition waivers (full) also available. Financial award application deadline: 1/1. *Unit head:* Lawrence Ein, Head, 312-996-3044, E-mail: ein@math.uic.edu. *Application contact:* Brooke Shipley, Director of Graduate Studies, 312-996-5119, E-mail: dgs@math.uic.edu.

University of Illinois at Urbana–Champaign, Graduate College, College of Liberal Arts and Sciences, Department of Mathematics, Champaign, IL 61820. Offers applied mathematics (MS); applied mathematics: actuarial science (MS); mathematics (MA, MS, PhD); teaching of mathematics (MS). *Faculty:* 65 full-time (5 women), 4 part-time/adjunct (0 women). *Students:* 159 full-time (45 women), 35 part-time (10 women); includes 13 minority (7 Asian, non-Hispanic/Latino; 4 Hispanic/Latino; 2 Two or more races, non-Hispanic/Latino), 105 international. 454 applicants, 22% accepted, 50 enrolled. In 2010, 48 master's, 19 doctorates awarded. *Entrance requirements:* For master's, GRE General Test, GRE Subject Test (mathematics), minimum GPA of 3.0; for doctorate, GRE General Test, GRE Subject Test (math), minimum GPA of 3.0. Additional exam requirements/recommendations for international students: Required—TOEFL (minimum score 550 paper-based; 213 computer-based). *Application deadline:* Applications are processed on a rolling basis. Application fee: $75 ($90 for international students). Electronic applications accepted. *Financial support:* In 2010–11, 26 fellowships, 40 research assistantships, 146 teaching assistantships were awarded; tuition waivers (full and partial) also available. *Unit head:* Sheldon Katz, Chair, 217-265-6258, Fax: 217-333-9576, E-mail: katzs@illinois.edu. *Application contact:* Marci Blocher, Office Support Specialist, 217-333-3350, Fax: 217-333-9576, E-mail: mblocher@illinois.edu.

The University of Iowa, Graduate College, College of Liberal Arts and Sciences, Department of Mathematics, Iowa City, IA 52242-1316. Offers MS, PhD. *Degree requirements:* For master's, thesis optional, exam; for doctorate, comprehensive exam, thesis/dissertation. *Entrance requirements:* For master's and doctorate, GRE General Test, minimum GPA of 3.0. Additional exam requirements/recommendations for international students: Required—TOEFL (minimum score 620 paper-based; 260 computer-based; 105 iBT). Electronic applications accepted.

The University of Kansas, Graduate Studies, College of Liberal Arts and Sciences, Department of Mathematics, Lawrence, KS 66045. Offers mathematics (MA, PhD). *Faculty:* 38 full-time (8 women). *Students:* 65 full-time (10 women), 11 part-time (0 women); includes 5 minority (1 Black or African American, non-Hispanic/Latino; 2 Asian, non-Hispanic/Latino; 1 Hispanic/Latino; 1 Two or more races, non-Hispanic/Latino), 32 international. Average age 28. 117 applicants, 32% accepted, 21 enrolled. In 2010, 12 master's, 2 doctorates awarded. Terminal master's awarded for partial completion of doctoral program. *Degree requirements:* For master's, comprehensive exam, thesis or alternative; for doctorate, one foreign language, comprehensive exam, thesis/dissertation, 1 computer language. *Entrance requirements:* For master's and doctorate, GRE. Additional exam requirements/recommendations for international students: Required—TOEFL, minimum for both TOEFL and IELTS based on Graduate Studies minimum requirements. *Application deadline:* For fall admission, 1/31 priority date for domestic and international students. Applications are processed on a rolling basis. Application fee: $55 ($65 for international students). Electronic applications accepted. *Expenses:* Tuition, state resident: full-time $7092; part-time $295.50 per credit hour. Tuition, nonresident: full-time $16,590; part-time $691.25 per credit hour. Required fees: $858; $71.49 per credit hour. Tuition and fees vary according to course load, campus/location and program. *Financial support:* Fellowships with full tuition reimbursements, research assistantships with full and partial tuition reimbursements, teaching assistantships with full tuition reimbursements, institutionally sponsored loans, scholarships/grants, health care benefits, and unspecified assistantships available. Support available to part-time students. Financial award application deadline: 1/31. *Faculty research:* Commutative algebra, algebraic geometry, combinatronics, stochastic adaptive control, probability analysis, operator algebras, harmonic analysis, PDES, numerical analysis, dynamical systems, topology, set theory. *Unit head:* Prof. Satya Mandal, Chair, 785-864-3651, Fax: 785-864-5255, E-mail: mandal@math.ku.edu. *Application contact:* Prof. Milena Stanislavova, Admissions Director of Graduate Studies, 785-864-3651, E-mail: stanis@math.ku.edu.

University of Kentucky, Graduate School, College of Arts and Sciences, Program in Mathematics, Lexington, KY 40506-0032. Offers applied mathematics (MS); mathematics (MA, MS, PhD). *Degree requirements:* For master's, comprehensive exam, thesis optional; for doctorate, one foreign language, comprehensive exam, thesis/dissertation. *Entrance requirements:* For master's, GRE General Test, minimum undergraduate GPA of 2.75; for doctorate, GRE General Test, minimum graduate GPA of 3.0. Additional exam requirements/recommendations for international students: Required—TOEFL (minimum score 550 paper-based; 213 computer-based). Electronic applications accepted. *Faculty research:* Numerical analysis, combinatorics, partial differential equations, algebra and number theory, real and complex analysis.

University of Lethbridge, School of Graduate Studies, Lethbridge, AB T1K 3M4, Canada. Offers accounting (MScM); addictions counseling (M Sc); agricultural biotechnology (M Sc); agricultural studies (M Sc, MA); anthropology (MA); archaeology (MA); art (MA, MFA); biochemistry (M Sc); biological sciences (M Sc); biomolecular science (PhD); biosystems and biodiversity (PhD); Canadian studies (MA); chemistry (M Sc); computer science (M Sc); computer science and geographical information science (M Sc); counseling psychology (M Ed); dramatic arts (MA); earth, space, and physical science (PhD); economics (MA); educational leadership (M Ed); English (MA); environmental science (M Sc); evolution and behavior (PhD); exercise science (M Sc); finance (MScM); French (MA); French/German (MA); French/Spanish (MA); general education (M Ed); general management (MScM); geography (M Sc, MA); German (MA); health science (M Sc); history (MA); human resource management and labour relations (MScM); individualized multidisciplinary (M Sc, MA); information systems (MScM); international management (MScM); kinesiology (M Sc, MA); management (M Sc, MA); marketing (MScM); mathematics (M Sc); music (M Mus, MA); Native American studies (MA); neuroscience (M Sc, PhD); new media (MA); nursing (M Sc); philosophy (MA); physics (M Sc); policy and strategy (MScM); political science (MA); psychology (M Sc, MA); religious studies (MA); social sciences (MA); sociology (MA); theatre and dramatic arts (MFA); theoretical and computational science (PhD); urban and regional studies (MA); women's studies (MA). Part-time and evening/weekend programs available. *Degree requirements:* For doctorate, comprehensive exam, thesis/dissertation. *Entrance requirements:* For master's, GMAT (M Sc in management), bachelor's degree in related field, minimum GPA of 3.0 during previous 20 graded semester courses, 2 years teaching or related experience (M Ed); for doctorate, master's degree, minimum graduate GPA of 3.5. Additional exam requirements/recommendations for international students: Required—TOEFL. *Faculty research:* Movement and brain plasticity, gibberellin physiology, photosynthesis, carbon cycling, molecular properties of main-group ring components.

University of Louisiana at Lafayette, College of Sciences, Department of Mathematics, Lafayette, LA 70504. Offers MS, PhD. Terminal master's awarded for partial completion of doctoral program. *Degree requirements:* For master's, thesis or alternative; for doctorate, 2 foreign languages, comprehensive exam, thesis/dissertation. *Entrance requirements:* For master's, GRE General Test, minimum GPA of 2.75; for doctorate, GRE General Test, minimum GPA of 3.0. Additional exam requirements/recommendations for international students: Required—TOEFL (minimum score 550 paper-based; 213 computer-based). Electronic applications accepted. *Faculty research:* Topology, algebra, applied mathematics, analysis.

University of Louisville, Graduate School, College of Arts and Sciences, Department of Mathematics, Louisville, KY 40292. Offers applied and industrial mathematics (PhD); mathematics (MA). Part-time programs available. *Faculty:* 30 full-time (8 women), 3 part-time/adjunct (1 woman). *Students:* 34 full-time (13 women), 6 part-time (2 women); includes 2 Black or African American, non-Hispanic/Latino; 1 Hispanic/Latino, 9 international. Average age 29. 31 applicants, 77% accepted, 10 enrolled. In 2010, 3 master's, 1 doctorate awarded. Terminal master's awarded for partial completion of doctoral program. *Degree requirements:* For master's, comprehensive exam (for some programs), thesis optional; for doctorate, comprehensive exam, thesis/dissertation, internship, project. *Entrance requirements:* For master's and doctorate, GRE General Test. Additional exam requirements/recommendations for international students: Required—TOEFL (minimum score 550 paper-based; 215 computer-based; 79 iBT). *Application deadline:* For fall admission, 3/15 priority date for domestic and international students; for winter admission, 8/15 priority date for domestic and international students. Applications are processed on a rolling basis. Application fee: $50. Electronic applications accepted. *Expenses:* Tuition, state resident: full-time $9144; part-time $508 per credit hour. Tuition, nonresident: full-time $19,026; part-time $1057 per credit hour. Tuition and fees vary according to program and reciprocity agreements. *Financial support:* In 2010–11, 25 students received support, including 2 fellowships with full tuition reimbursements available (averaging $20,000 per year), 1 research assistantship (averaging $20,000 per year), 25 teaching assistantships with full tuition reimbursements available (averaging $20,000 per year); health care benefits and unspecified assistantships also available. Financial award application deadline: 3/15. *Faculty research:* Algebra, analysis, bio-mathematics, combinatorics and graph theory, coding theory, consesus theory, financial mathematics, functional equations, partial differential equations. Total annual research expenditures: $77,000. *Unit head:* Dr. Thomas Riedel, Chair, 502-852-6826, Fax: 502-852-7132, E-mail: thomas.riedel@louisville.edu. *Application contact:* Dr. Bingtuan Li, Graduate Studies Director, 502-852-6826, Fax: 502-852-7132, E-mail: bing.li@louisville.edu.

University of Maine, Graduate School, College of Liberal Arts and Sciences, Department of Mathematics and Statistics, Orono, ME 04469. Offers mathematics (MA). *Faculty:* 16 full-time (3 women), 8 part-time/adjunct (4 women). *Students:* 10 full-time (2 women), 1 part-time (0 women), 1 international. Average age 27. 11 applicants, 64% accepted, 5 enrolled. In 2010, 6 master's awarded. *Degree requirements:* For master's, thesis optional. *Entrance requirements:* For master's, GRE General Test. Additional exam requirements/recommendations for international students: Required—TOEFL. *Application deadline:* For fall admission, 2/1 priority date for domestic students. Applications are processed on a rolling basis. Application fee: $65. Electronic applications accepted. *Expenses:* Tuition, state resident: full-time $400. Tuition, nonresident: full-time $1050. *Financial support:* In 2010–11, 7 teaching assistantships with tuition reimbursements (averaging $12,790 per year) were awarded; tuition waivers (full and partial) also available. Financial award application deadline: 3/1. *Unit head:* Dr. David Bradley, Chair, 207-581-3920, Fax: 207-581-4977. *Application contact:* Scott G. Delcourt, Associate Dean of the Graduate School, 207-581-3291, Fax: 207-581-3232, E-mail: graduate@maine.edu.

The University of Manchester, School of Mathematics, Manchester, United Kingdom. Offers actuarial science (PhD); applied mathematics (M Phil, PhD); applied numerical computing (M Phil, PhD); financial mathematics (M Phil, PhD); mathematical logic (M Phil); probability (M Phil, PhD); pure mathematics (M Phil, PhD); statistics (M Phil, PhD).

University of Manitoba, Faculty of Graduate Studies, Faculty of Science, Department of Mathematics, Winnipeg, MB R3T 2N2, Canada. Offers M Sc, PhD. *Degree requirements:* For master's, one foreign language, thesis or alternative; for doctorate, one foreign language, thesis/dissertation.

University of Manitoba, Faculty of Graduate Studies, Faculty of Science, Program in Mathematical, Computational and Statistical Sciences, Winnipeg, MB R3T 2N2, Canada. Offers MMCSS.

University of Maryland, College Park, Academic Affairs, College of Computer, Mathematical and Natural Sciences, Department of Mathematics, Program in Mathematics, College Park, MD 20742. Offers MA, PhD. Part-time and evening/weekend programs available. *Students:* 71 full-time (12 women), 8 part-time (0 women); includes 8 minority (4 Asian, non-Hispanic/Latino; 3 Hispanic/Latino; 1 Two or more races, non-Hispanic/Latino), 22 international. 279 applicants, 11% accepted, 13 enrolled. In 2010, 6 master's, 11 doctorates awarded. Terminal master's awarded for partial completion of doctoral program. *Degree requirements:* For master's, thesis or alternative; for doctorate, one foreign language, thesis/dissertation, written exam, oral exam. *Entrance requirements:* For master's, GRE General Test, GRE Subject Test, minimum GPA of 3.0, 3 letters of recommendation; for doctorate, GRE General Test, GRE Subject Test, 3 letters of recommendation. *Application deadline:* For fall admission, 1/15 priority date for

domestic students, 1/15 for international students; for spring admission, 10/1 for domestic students, 6/1 for international students. Applications are processed on a rolling basis. Application fee: $75. Electronic applications accepted. *Expenses:* Tuition, area resident: Part-time $471 per credit hour. Tuition, state resident: part-time $471 per credit hour. Tuition, nonresident: part-time $1016 per credit hour. Required fees: $337 per term. *Financial support:* In 2010–11, 6 fellowships with full and partial tuition reimbursements (averaging $15,208 per year), 11 research assistantships (averaging $19,505 per year), 48 teaching assistantships (averaging $17,278 per year) were awarded. Financial award applicants required to submit FAFSA. *Unit head:* James Yorke, 301-405-5048, E-mail: yorke@umd.edu. *Application contact:* Dr. Charles A. Caramello, Dean of Graduate School, 301-405-0358, Fax: 301-314-9305, E-mail: ccaramel@umd.edu.

University of Massachusetts Amherst, Graduate School, College of Natural Sciences, Department of Mathematics and Statistics, Program in Mathematics and Statistics, Amherst, MA 01003. Offers MS, PhD. *Students:* 52 full-time (14 women), 1 (woman) part-time; includes 5 minority (1 Black or African American, non-Hispanic/Latino; 1 Asian, non-Hispanic/Latino; 1 Hispanic/Latino; 2 Two or more races, non-Hispanic/Latino), 22 international. Average age 28. 253 applicants, 18% accepted, 18 enrolled. In 2010, 16 master's, 7 doctorates awarded. Terminal master's awarded for partial completion of doctoral program. *Degree requirements:* For master's, thesis or alternative; for doctorate, comprehensive exam, thesis/dissertation. *Entrance requirements:* For master's and doctorate, GRE General Test, GRE Subject Test (mathematics). Additional exam requirements/recommendations for international students: Required—TOEFL (minimum score 550 paper-based; 213 computer-based; 80 iBT), IELTS (minimum score 6.5). *Application deadline:* For fall admission, 2/1 for domestic and international students; for spring admission, 10/1 for domestic and international students. Applications are processed on a rolling basis. Application fee: $50 ($65 for international students). Electronic applications accepted. *Expenses:* Tuition, state resident: full-time $2640. Required fees: $8282. One-time fee: $357 full-time. *Financial support:* Fellowships, research assistantships, teaching assistantships, career-related internships or fieldwork, Federal Work-Study, scholarships/grants, traineeships, health care benefits, tuition waivers (full), and unspecified assistantships available. Support available to part-time students. Financial award application deadline: 2/1; financial award applicants required to submit FAFSA. *Unit head:* Dr. Siman Wong, Graduate Program Director, 413-545-2282, Fax: 413-545-1801. *Application contact:* Jean M. Ames, Supervisor of Admissions, 413-545-0722, Fax: 413-577-0010, E-mail: gradadm@grad.umass.edu.

University of Massachusetts Lowell, College of Arts and Sciences, Department of Mathematical Sciences, Lowell, MA 01854-2881. Offers applied mathematics (MS); computational mathematics (PhD); mathematics (MS). Part-time programs available. *Entrance requirements:* For master's, GRE General Test.

University of Memphis, Graduate School, College of Arts and Sciences, Department of Mathematical Sciences, Memphis, TN 38152. Offers applied mathematics (MS); applied statistics (PhD); bioinformatics (MS); computer science (PhD); computer sciences (MS); mathematics (MS, PhD); statistics (MS, PhD). Part-time programs available. *Faculty:* 19 full-time (4 women), 3 part-time/adjunct (0 women). *Students:* 38 full-time (12 women), 21 part-time (12 women); includes 8 minority (5 Black or African American, non-Hispanic/Latino; 2 Asian, non-Hispanic/Latino; 1 Hispanic/Latino), 25 international. Average age 34. 49 applicants, 55% accepted, 9 enrolled. In 2010, 6 master's, 5 doctorates awarded. Terminal master's awarded for partial completion of doctoral program. *Degree requirements:* For master's, comprehensive exam; for doctorate, one foreign language, thesis/dissertation, oral exams. *Entrance requirements:* For master's and doctorate, GRE General Test, minimum GPA of 2.5. Additional exam requirements/recommendations for international students: Required—TOEFL (minimum score 550 paper-based; 210 computer-based). *Application deadline:* For fall admission, 8/1 for domestic students, 5/1 priority date for international students; for spring admission, 12/1 for domestic students, 9/1 priority date for international students. Applications are processed on a rolling basis. Application fee: $35 ($60 for international students). Electronic applications accepted. *Financial support:* In 2010–11, 22 students received support; fellowships with full tuition reimbursements available, research assistantships with full tuition reimbursements available, teaching assistantships with full tuition reimbursements available, career-related internships or fieldwork, Federal Work-Study, scholarships/grants, and unspecified assistantships available. Financial award application deadline: 2/15; financial award applicants required to submit FAFSA. *Faculty research:* Combinatorics, ergodic theory, graph theory, Ramsey theory, applied statistics. *Unit head:* Dr. James E. Jamison, Chairman, 901-678-2482, Fax: 901-678-2480, E-mail: jjamison@memphis.edu. *Application contact:* Dr. Anna Kaminska, Coordinator of Graduate Studies, 901-678-2494, Fax: 901-678-2480.

University of Miami, Graduate School, College of Arts and Sciences, Department of Mathematics, Coral Gables, FL 33124. Offers MA, MS, PhD. Part-time and evening/weekend programs available. Terminal master's awarded for partial completion of doctoral program. *Degree requirements:* For master's, comprehensive exam, qualifying exams; for doctorate, one foreign language, thesis/dissertation, qualifying exams. *Entrance requirements:* For master's and doctorate, GRE General Test, minimum GPA of 3.0. Additional exam requirements/recommendations for international students: Required—TOEFL (minimum score 550 paper-based; 213 computer-based; 59 iBT). Electronic applications accepted. *Faculty research:* Applied mathematics, probability, geometric analysis, differential equations, algebraic combinatorics.

University of Michigan, Horace H. Rackham School of Graduate Studies, College of Literature, Science, and the Arts, Department of Mathematics, Ann Arbor, MI 48109. Offers applied and interdisciplinary mathematics (AM, MS, PhD); mathematics (AM, MS, PhD). Part-time programs available. *Faculty:* 64 full-time (10 women). *Students:* 144 full-time (37 women), 1 part-time (0 women); includes 15 minority (1 Black or African American, non-Hispanic/Latino; 6 Asian, non-Hispanic/Latino; 5 Hispanic/Latino; 1 Native Hawaiian or other Pacific Islander, non-Hispanic/Latino; 2 Two or more races, non-Hispanic/Latino), 61 international. Average age 26. 545 applicants, 15% accepted, 33 enrolled. In 2010, 30 master's, 23 doctorates awarded. *Degree requirements:* For doctorate, one foreign language, comprehensive exam, thesis/dissertation, oral defense of dissertation, preliminary exam. *Entrance requirements:* For master's and doctorate, GRE General Test, GRE Subject Test. Additional exam requirements/recommendations for international students: Required—TOEFL (minimum score 580 paper-based; 220 computer-based; 84 iBT). *Application deadline:* For fall admission, 1/15 for domestic and international students. Applications are processed on a rolling basis. Application fee: $65 ($75 for international students). Electronic applications accepted. *Expenses:* Tuition, state resident: full-time $17,784; part-time $1116 per credit hour. Tuition, nonresident: full-time $35,944; part-time $2125 per credit hour. International tuition: $35,994 full-time. Required fees: $95 per semester. Tuition and fees vary according to course load, degree level and program. *Financial support:* In 2010–11, 131 students received support, including 24 fellowships with full tuition reimbursements available (averaging $25,000 per year), 15 research assistantships with full tuition reimbursements available (averaging $17,270 per year), 92 teaching assistantships with full tuition reimbursements available (averaging $17,270 per year). Financial award application deadline: 3/15. *Faculty research:* Algebra, analysis, topology, applied mathematics, geometry. *Unit head:* Prof. Mel Hochster, Chair, 734-936-1310, Fax: 734-763-0937, E-mail: math-chair@umich.edu. *Application contact:* Prof. Alejandro Uribe, Associate Chairman for Graduate Studies, 734-764-7436, Fax: 734-763-0937, E-mail: math.acgs@umich.edu.

University of Minnesota, Twin Cities Campus, Institute of Technology, School of Mathematics, Minneapolis, MN 55455-0213. Offers MS, PhD. Part-time programs available. Terminal master's awarded for partial completion of doctoral program. *Degree requirements:* For master's, thesis (for some programs); for doctorate, 2 foreign languages, thesis/dissertation. *Entrance requirements:* For master's, GRE Subject Test (recommended); for doctorate, GRE Subject Test. Additional exam requirements/recommendations for international students: Required—TOEFL. *Faculty research:* Partial and ordinary differential equations, algebra and number theory, geometry, combinatorics, numerical analysis.

University of Mississippi, Graduate School, College of Liberal Arts, Department of Mathematics, Oxford, University, MS 38677. Offers MA, MS, PhD. *Students:* 30 full-time (13 women), 2 part-time (1 woman); includes 4 Black or African American, non-Hispanic/Latino; 6 Asian, non-Hispanic/Latino. In 2010, 1 master's, 1 doctorate awarded. *Degree requirements:* For master's, thesis (for some programs); for doctorate, thesis/dissertation. *Entrance requirements:* For master's, GRE General Test, minimum GPA of 3.0; for doctorate, GRE General Test. Additional exam requirements/recommendations for international students: Required—TOEFL. *Application deadline:* For fall admission, 4/1 for domestic students; for spring admission, 10/1 for domestic students. Applications are processed on a rolling basis. Application fee: $25. Electronic applications accepted. *Financial support:* Scholarships/grants available. Financial award application deadline: 3/1; financial award applicants required to submit FAFSA. *Unit head:* Dr. Iwo M. Labuda, Interim Chairman, 662-915-7071, Fax: 662-915-5491, E-mail: mdepart@olemiss.edu. *Application contact:* Dr. Christy M. Wyandt, Associate Dean, 662-915-7474, Fax: 662-915-7577, E-mail: cwyandt@olemiss.edu.

University of Missouri, Graduate School, College of Arts and Sciences, Department of Mathematics, Columbia, MO 65211. Offers applied mathematics (MS); mathematics (MA, MST, PhD). *Faculty:* 47 full-time (9 women), 11 part-time/adjunct (6 women). *Students:* 60 full-time (12 women), 9 part-time (0 women); includes 2 minority (1 Hispanic/Latino; 1 Two or more races, non-Hispanic/Latino), 23 international. Average age 27. 138 applicants, 13% accepted, 15 enrolled. In 2010, 7 master's, 7 doctorates awarded. *Degree requirements:* For doctorate, 2 foreign languages, comprehensive exam, thesis/dissertation. *Entrance requirements:* For master's and doctorate, GRE General Test, minimum GPA of 3.0; bachelor's degree from accredited institution. Additional exam requirements/recommendations for international students: Required—TOEFL (minimum score 500 paper-based; 173 computer-based; 61 iBT). *Application deadline:* For fall admission, 1/15 for domestic students. Applications are processed on a rolling basis. Application fee: $45 ($60 for international students). Electronic applications accepted. *Financial support:* In 2010–11, 7 fellowships with full tuition reimbursements, 4 research assistantships with full tuition reimbursements, 64 teaching assistantships with full tuition reimbursements were awarded; institutionally sponsored loans, health care benefits, and unspecified assistantships also available. Financial award applicants required to submit FAFSA. *Faculty research:* Algebraic geometry, analysis (real, complex, functional and harmonic), analytic functions, applied mathematics, financial mathematics and mathematics of insurance, commutative rings, scattering theory, differential equations (ordinary and partial), differential geometry, dynamical systems, general relativity, mathematical physics, number theory, probabilistic analysis and topology. *Unit head:* Dr. Glen Himmelberg, Department Chair, 573-882-6222, E-mail: himmelbergg@missouri.edu. *Application contact:* Amy Crews, Administrative Assistant, 573-882-6222, E-mail: crewsae@missouri.edu.

University of Missouri–Kansas City, College of Arts and Sciences, Department of Mathematics and Statistics, Kansas City, MO 64110-2499. Offers MA, MS, PhD. PhD (interdisciplinary) offered through the School of Graduate Studies. Part-time programs available. *Faculty:* 12 full-time (3 women), 8 part-time/adjunct (2 women). *Students:* 3 full-time (2 women), 31 part-time (11 women); includes 1 minority (Asian, non-Hispanic/Latino), 6 international. Average age 30. 45 applicants, 67% accepted, 14 enrolled. In 2010, 10 master's awarded. Terminal master's awarded for partial completion of doctoral program. *Degree requirements:* For master's, written exam; for doctorate, 2 foreign languages, thesis/dissertation, oral and written exams. *Entrance requirements:* For master's, bachelor's degree in mathematics, minimum GPA of 3.0; for doctorate, GMAT or GRE General Test. Additional exam requirements/recommendations for international students: Required—TOEFL (minimum score 550 paper-based; 213 computer-based; 80 iBT). *Application deadline:* For fall admission, 3/15 for domestic students, 3/15 priority date for international students; for spring admission, 10/15 for domestic and international students. Applications are processed on a rolling basis. Application fee: $45 ($50 for international students). Electronic applications accepted. *Expenses:* Tuition, state resident: full-time $5522.40; part-time $306.80 per credit hour. Tuition, nonresident: full-time $7128; part-time $792 per credit hour. Required fees: $261.15 per term. *Financial support:* In 2010–11, 2 research assistantships (averaging $13,300 per year), 10 teaching assistantships with full tuition reimbursements (averaging $17,175 per year) were awarded; Federal Work-Study, institutionally sponsored loans, and tuition waivers (full and partial) also available. Support available to part-time students. Financial award application deadline: 3/1; financial award applicants required to submit FAFSA. *Faculty research:* Numerical analysis, statistics, biostatistics commutative algebra, differential equations. Total annual research expenditures: $6,878. *Unit head:* Dr. Jie Chen, Chair/Professor, 816-235-1641, Fax: 816-235-5517, E-mail: umkcmathdept@umkc.edu. *Application contact:* Dr. Hristo Voulov, Associate Professor, 816-235-1641, Fax: 816-235-5517, E-mail: umkcmathdept@umkc.edu.

University of Missouri–St. Louis, College of Arts and Sciences, Department of Mathematics and Computer Science, St. Louis, MO 63121. Offers applied mathematics (PhD), including computer science, mathematics; computer science (MS); mathematics (MA). Part-time and evening/weekend programs available. *Faculty:* 16 full-time (2 women), 1 part-time/adjunct (0 women). *Students:* 21 full-time (8 women), 43 part-time (13 women); includes 9 minority (5 Black or African American, non-Hispanic/Latino; 2 American Indian or Alaska Native, non-Hispanic/Latino; 2 Asian, non-Hispanic/Latino), 17 international. Average age 32. 98 applicants, 49% accepted, 12 enrolled. In 2010, 18 master's awarded. *Degree requirements:* For master's, thesis optional; for doctorate, thesis/dissertation. *Entrance requirements:* For master's, GRE (for TA assistantships), 2 letters of recommendation; C programming, C++ or Java (for computer science); for doctorate, GRE General Test, 3 letters of recommendation. Additional exam requirements/recommendations for international students: Required—TOEFL (minimum score 550 paper-based; 213 computer-based). *Application deadline:* For fall admission, 7/1 priority date for domestic and international students; for spring admission, 12/1 priority date for domestic and international students. Applications are processed on a rolling basis. Application fee: $35 ($40 for international students). Electronic applications accepted. *Expenses:* Tuition, state resident: full-time $5522; part-time $306.80 per credit hour. Tuition, nonresident: full-time $14,253; part-time $792.10 per credit hour. Required fees: $658; $49 per credit hour. One-time fee: $12. Tuition and fees vary according to program. *Financial support:* In 2010–11, 5 research assistantships with full and partial tuition reimbursements (averaging $10,845 per year), 7 teaching assistantships with full and partial tuition reimbursements (averaging $13,285 per year) were awarded; fellowships with full tuition reimbursements also available. Financial award applicants required to submit FAFSA. *Faculty research:* Statistics, algebra, analysis. *Unit head:* Dr. Shiying Zhao, Director of Graduate Studies, 314-516-5741, Fax: 314-516-5400, E-mail: zhao@arch.cs.umsl.edu. *Application contact:* 314-516-5458, Fax: 314-516-6996, E-mail: gradadm@umsl.edu.

The University of Montana, Graduate School, College of Arts and Sciences, Department of Mathematical Sciences, Missoula, MT 59812-0002. Offers mathematics (MA, PhD), including college teaching (PhD), traditional mathematics research (PhD); mathematics education (MA). Part-time programs available. Terminal master's awarded for partial completion of doctoral program. *Degree requirements:* For doctorate, thesis/dissertation. *Entrance requirements:* For master's and doctorate, GRE General Test. Additional exam requirements/recommendations for international students: Required—TOEFL (minimum score 525 paper-based; 195 computer-based).

University of Nebraska at Omaha, Graduate Studies, College of Arts and Sciences, Department of Mathematics, Omaha, NE 68182. Offers MA, MAT, MS. Part-time programs available.

Peterson's Graduate Programs in the Physical Sciences, Mathematics, Agricultural Sciences, the Environment & Natural Resources 2012

www.facebook.com/petersonspublishing 279

Mathematics

University of Nebraska at Omaha (continued)

Faculty: 14 full-time (2 women). *Students:* 16 full-time (3 women), 33 part-time (9 women); includes 3 minority (1 Black or African American, non-Hispanic/Latino; 1 Asian, non-Hispanic/Latino; 1 Hispanic/Latino), 7 international. Average age 33. 24 applicants, 54% accepted, 9 enrolled. In 2010, 13 master's awarded. *Degree requirements:* For master's, comprehensive exam, thesis (for some programs). *Entrance requirements:* For master's, minimum GPA of 3.0, 15 undergraduate math hours. Additional exam requirements/recommendations for international students: Required—TOEFL (minimum score 500 paper-based; 173 computer-based; 61 iBT). *Application deadline:* For fall admission, 7/1 priority date for domestic students; for spring admission, 12/1 priority date for domestic students. Applications are processed on a rolling basis. Application fee: $45. Electronic applications accepted. *Financial support:* In 2010–11, 21 students received support; research assistantships with tuition reimbursements available, teaching assistantships with tuition reimbursements available, Federal Work-Study, institutionally sponsored loans, traineeships, tuition waivers (partial), and unspecified assistantships available. Support available to part-time students. Financial award application deadline: 3/1; financial award applicants required to submit FAFSA. *Unit head:* Dr. Jack W. Heidel, Chairperson, 402-554-3430. *Application contact:* Dr. Steve From, 402-554-2341, Fax: 402-554-3143, E-mail: graduate@unomaha.edu.

University of Nebraska–Lincoln, Graduate College, College of Arts and Sciences, Department of Mathematics, Lincoln, NE 68588. Offers mathematics (MA, MAT, MS, PhD); mathematics and computer science (PhD). *Degree requirements:* For master's, thesis optional; for doctorate, variable foreign language requirement, comprehensive exam, thesis/dissertation. *Entrance requirements:* Additional exam requirements/recommendations for international students: Required—TOEFL (minimum score 550 paper-based; 213 computer-based), GRE General Test. Electronic applications accepted. *Faculty research:* Applied mathematics, commutative algebra, algebraic geometry, Bayesian statistics, biostatistics.

University of Nevada, Las Vegas, Graduate College, College of Science, Department of Mathematical Sciences, Las Vegas, NV 89154-4020. Offers MS, PhD. Part-time programs available. *Faculty:* 31 full-time (5 women). *Students:* 47 full-time (16 women), 13 part-time (4 women); includes 12 minority (2 Asian, non-Hispanic/Latino; 1 Hispanic/Latino; 9 Two or more races, non-Hispanic/Latino), 24 international. Average age 29. 50 applicants, 50% accepted, 13 enrolled. In 2010, 8 master's, 1 doctorate awarded. *Degree requirements:* For master's, comprehensive exam (for some programs), thesis (for some programs), oral exam. *Entrance requirements:* For master's and doctorate, GRE General Test. Additional exam requirements/recommendations for international students: Required—TOEFL (minimum score 550 paper-based; 213 computer-based; 80 iBT), IELTS (minimum score 7). *Application deadline:* For fall admission, 3/15 priority date for domestic and international students. Applications are processed on a rolling basis. Application fee: $60 ($75 for international students). Electronic applications accepted. *Expenses:* Tuition, area resident: Part-time $239.50 per credit. Tuition, state resident: part-time $239.50 per credit. Tuition, nonresident: part-time $503 per credit. Required fees: $108 per semester. Tuition and fees vary according to course load, program and reciprocity agreements. *Financial support:* In 2010–11, 46 teaching assistantships with partial tuition reimbursements (averaging $10,739 per year) were awarded; institutionally sponsored loans, scholarships/grants, health care benefits, and unspecified assistantships also available. Financial award application deadline: 3/1. *Faculty research:* Statistics and biostatistics, numerical analysis and scientific computing, partial differential equations, number theory, mathematical logic. Total annual research expenditures: $100,596. *Unit head:* Dr. Derrick Dubose, Chair/ Professor, 702-895-0382, Fax: 702-895-4343, E-mail: dubose@unlv.nevada.edu. *Application contact:* Graduate College Admissions Evaluator, 702-895-3320, Fax: 702-895-4180, E-mail: gradcollege@unlv.edu.

University of Nevada, Reno, Graduate School, College of Science, Department of Mathematics and Statistics, Reno, NV 89557. Offers mathematics (MS); teaching mathematics (MATM). *Degree requirements:* For master's, thesis optional. *Entrance requirements:* For master's, GRE General Test, minimum GPA of 2.75. Additional exam requirements/recommendations for international students: Required—TOEFL (minimum score 500 paper-based; 173 computer-based; 61 iBT), IELTS (minimum score 6). Electronic applications accepted. *Expenses:* Tuition, state resident: full-time $2219; part-time $246 per credit. Tuition, nonresident: part-time $510 per credit. International tuition: $9009 full-time. Required fees: $59 per term. One-time fee: $101. Tuition and fees vary according to course load. *Faculty research:* Operator algebra, nonlinear systems, differential equations.

University of New Brunswick Fredericton, School of Graduate Studies, Faculty of Science, Department of Mathematics and Statistics, Fredericton, NB E3B 5A3, Canada. Offers M Sc, PhD. *Faculty:* 10 full-time (0 women), 1 part-time/adjunct (0 women). *Students:* 22 full-time (8 women), 2 part-time (1 woman). In 2010, 2 master's, 1 doctorate awarded. *Degree requirements:* For master's, thesis; for doctorate, comprehensive exam, thesis/dissertation. *Entrance requirements:* For master's and doctorate, minimum GPA of 3.0. Additional exam requirements/recommendations for international students: Required—TOEFL (minimum score 550 paper-based; 80 computer-based), TWE (minimum score 4); Recommended—IELTS (minimum score 7). *Application deadline:* For fall admission, 3/1 priority date for domestic students. Applications are processed on a rolling basis. Application fee: $50 Canadian dollars. *Expenses:* Tuition, area resident: Full-time $3708; part-time $927 per term. International tuition: $6300 full-time. Required fees: $50 per term. *Financial support:* In 2010–11, 8 fellowships, 19 research assistantships (averaging $12,000 per year), 20 teaching assistantships (averaging $4,996 per year) were awarded. *Faculty research:* Algebra, general relativity, mathematical biology, quantum field theory, pure math, data analysis, experimental design. *Unit head:* Dr. James Watmough, Director of Graduate Studies, 506-458-7363, Fax: 506-453-4705, E-mail: watmough@unb.ca. *Application contact:* Marilyn Hetherington, Graduate Secretary, 506-458-7373, Fax: 506-453-4705, E-mail: mhetheri@unb.ca.

University of New Hampshire, Graduate School, College of Engineering and Physical Sciences, Department of Mathematics and Statistics, Durham, NH 03824. Offers applied mathematics (MS); industrial statistics (Postbaccalaureate Certificate); mathematics (MS, MST, PhD); mathematics education (PhD); statistics (MS). *Faculty:* 21 full-time (5 women). *Students:* 31 full-time (13 women), 25 part-time (10 women); includes 2 minority (both Two or more races, non-Hispanic/Latino), 17 international. Average age 31. 71 applicants, 49% accepted, 19 enrolled. In 2010, 17 master's, 6 doctorates, 3 other advanced degrees awarded. Terminal master's awarded for partial completion of doctoral program. *Degree requirements:* For doctorate, 2 foreign languages, thesis/dissertation. *Entrance requirements:* Additional exam requirements/recommendations for international students: Required—TOEFL (minimum score 550 paper-based; 213 computer-based; 80 iBT). *Application deadline:* For fall admission, 4/1 priority date for domestic students, 4/1 for international students; for spring admission, 12/1 for domestic students. Applications are processed on a rolling basis. Application fee: $65. Electronic applications accepted. *Financial support:* In 2010–11, 40 students received support, including 3 fellowships, 2 research assistantships, 34 teaching assistantships; Federal Work-Study, scholarships/grants, and tuition waivers (full and partial) also available. Support available to part-time students. Financial award application deadline: 2/15. *Faculty research:* Operator theory, complex analysis, algebra, nonlinear dynamics, statistics. *Unit head:* Dr. Edward Hindon, Chairperson, 603-862-2320. *Application contact:* Jan Jankowski, Administrative Assistant, 603-862-2320, E-mail: jan.jankowski@unh.edu.

University of New Mexico, Graduate School, College of Arts and Sciences, Department of Mathematics and Statistics, Albuquerque, NM 87131-2039. Offers mathematics (MS, PhD); statistics (MS, PhD). Part-time programs available. *Faculty:* 87 full-time (33 women), 59 part-time/adjunct (22 women). *Students:* 55 full-time (19 women), 19 part-time (3 women); includes 1 American Indian or Alaska Native, non-Hispanic/Latino; 3 Asian, non-Hispanic/Latino; 12 Hispanic/Latino, 23 international. Average age 33. 99 applicants, 45% accepted, 14 enrolled. In 2010, 17 master's, 5 doctorates awarded. Terminal master's awarded for partial completion of doctoral program. *Degree requirements:* For master's, comprehensive exam (for some programs), thesis or alternative; for doctorate, one foreign language, comprehensive exam, thesis/dissertation, 4 department seminars. *Entrance requirements:* For master's and doctorate, minimum GPA of 3.0, 3 letters of recommendation, letter of intent. Additional exam requirements/recommendations for international students: Required—TOEFL (minimum score 550 paper-based; 213 computer-based). *Application deadline:* For fall admission, 2/15 priority date for domestic students; for spring admission, 11/1 priority date for domestic students. Application fee: $50. Electronic applications accepted. *Expenses:* Tuition, state resident: full-time $5991; part-time $251 per credit hour. Tuition, nonresident: full-time $14,405; part-time $800.20 per credit hour. Tuition and fees vary according to course level, course load, program and reciprocity agreements. *Financial support:* In 2010–11, 59 students received support, including 15 research assistantships with tuition reimbursements available (averaging $8,419 per year), 46 teaching assistantships with tuition reimbursements available (averaging $14,812 per year); health care benefits and unspecified assistantships also available. Financial award application deadline: 2/15; financial award applicants required to submit FAFSA. *Faculty research:* Pure and applied mathematics, applied statistics, numerical analysis, biostatistics, differential geometry, fluid dynamics, nonparametric curve estimation. Total annual research expenditures: $1.5 million. *Unit head:* Dr. Alexander Stone, Chair, 505-277-4613, Fax: 505-277-5505, E-mail: astone@math.unm.edu. *Application contact:* Ana Parra Lombard, Coordinator, Program Advisement, 505-277-5250, Fax: 505-277-5505, E-mail: aparra@math.unm.edu.

University of New Orleans, Graduate School, College of Sciences, Department of Mathematics, New Orleans, LA 70148. Offers MS. Part-time programs available. *Entrance requirements:* For master's, BA or BS in mathematics. Additional exam requirements/recommendations for international students: Required—TOEFL (minimum score 550 paper-based; 213 computer-based; 79 iBT). Electronic applications accepted. *Faculty research:* Differential equations, combinatorics, statistics, complex analysis, algebra.

The University of North Carolina at Chapel Hill, Graduate School, College of Arts and Sciences, Department of Mathematics, Chapel Hill, NC 27599. Offers MA, MS, PhD. *Degree requirements:* For master's, comprehensive exam, thesis or alternative, computer proficiency; for doctorate, 2 foreign languages, thesis/dissertation, 3 comprehensive exams, computer proficiency. *Entrance requirements:* For master's and doctorate, GRE General Test, minimum GPA of 3.0. Additional exam requirements/recommendations for international students: Required—TOEFL. Electronic applications accepted. *Faculty research:* Algebraic geometry, topology, analysis, lie theory, applied math.

The University of North Carolina at Charlotte, Graduate School, College of Arts and Sciences, Department of Mathematics and Statistics, Charlotte, NC 28223-0001. Offers applied mathematics (MS, PhD); mathematics (MS); mathematics education (MA). Part-time and evening/weekend programs available. *Faculty:* 43 full-time (5 women). *Students:* 51 full-time (16 women), 30 part-time (14 women); includes 13 minority (9 Black or African American, non-Hispanic/Latino; 3 Asian, non-Hispanic/Latino; 1 Hispanic/Latino), 38 international. Average age 29. 63 applicants, 95% accepted, 23 enrolled. In 2010, 16 master's, 4 doctorates awarded. *Degree requirements:* For master's, comprehensive exam, thesis or alternative; for doctorate, thesis/dissertation. *Entrance requirements:* For master's, GRE General Test, minimum GPA of 3.0 in undergraduate major, 2.75 overall; for doctorate, GRE General Test, minimum overall GPA of 3.0. Additional exam requirements/recommendations for international students: Required—TOEFL (minimum score: 557 paper-based; 220 computer-based; or 83 iBT), Michigan English Language Assessment Battery (minimum score 78), IELTS (minimum score 6.5), or post-secondary degree earned in a country or province where English is the primary spoken language. *Application deadline:* For fall admission, 7/1 for domestic students, 5/1 for international students; for spring admission, 11/1 for domestic students, 10/1 for international students. Applications are processed on a rolling basis. Application fee: $55. Electronic applications accepted. *Expenses:* Tuition, state resident: full-time $3464. Tuition, nonresident: full-time $14,297. Required fees: $2094. Tuition and fees vary according to course load. *Financial support:* In 2010–11, 50 students received support, including 6 fellowships (averaging $37,414 per year), 8 research assistantships (averaging $14,738 per year), 36 teaching assistantships (averaging $13,340 per year); career-related internships or fieldwork, Federal Work-Study, institutionally sponsored loans, scholarships/grants, and unspecified assistantships also available. Support available to part-time students. Financial award application deadline: 4/1; financial award applicants required to submit FAFSA. *Faculty research:* Numerical analysis, differential equations, probability, algebra, analysis, mathematics education, statistics. Total annual research expenditures: $1.3 million. *Unit head:* Dr. Alan S. Dow, Chair, 704-687-4560, Fax: 704-687-6415, E-mail: adow@uncc.edu. *Application contact:* Kathy B. Giddings, Director of Graduate Admissions, 704-687-5503, Fax: 704-687-3279, E-mail: gradadm@uncc.edu.

The University of North Carolina at Charlotte, Graduate School, College of Arts and Sciences, Department of Sociology, Charlotte, NC 28223-0001. Offers health research (MA); mathematical sociology and quantitative methods (MA); organizations, occupations, and work (MA); political sociology (MA); race and gender (MA); social psychology (MA); social theory (MA); sociology of education (MA); stratification (MA). Part-time and evening/weekend programs available. *Faculty:* 18 full-time (10 women). *Students:* 11 full-time (7 women), 14 part-time (8 women); includes 6 minority (4 Black or African American, non-Hispanic/Latino; 2 Asian, non-Hispanic/Latino). Average age 29. 20 applicants, 60% accepted, 8 enrolled. In 2010, 2 master's awarded. *Degree requirements:* For master's, thesis or alternative, thesis or comprehensive exam. *Entrance requirements:* For master's, GRE or MAT, minimum GPA of 3.0 in last 2 years, 2.75 overall. Additional exam requirements/recommendations for international students: Required—TOEFL (minimum score 557 paper-based; 220 computer-based; 83 iBT). *Application deadline:* For fall admission, 7/1 for domestic students, 5/1 for international students; for spring admission, 11/1 for domestic students, 10/1 for international students. Applications are processed on a rolling basis. Application fee: $55. Electronic applications accepted. *Expenses:* Tuition, state resident: full-time $3464. Tuition, nonresident: full-time $14,297. Required fees: $2094. Tuition and fees vary according to course load. *Financial support:* In 2010–11, 6 students received support, including 1 fellowship (averaging $60,000 per year), 1 research assistantship (averaging $9,000 per year), 1 teaching assistantship (averaging $9,000 per year); career-related internships or fieldwork, institutionally sponsored loans, scholarships/grants, and unspecified assistantships also available. Support available to part-time students. Financial award application deadline: 4/1; financial award applicants required to submit FAFSA. *Faculty research:* Social psychology, sociology of education, social gerontology, quantitative methodology, medical sociology. Total annual research expenditures: $61,382. *Unit head:* Dr. Lisa Rachotte, Chair, 704-687-2288, Fax: 704-687-3091, E-mail: lrashott@uncc.edu. *Application contact:* Kathy B. Giddings, Director of Graduate Admissions, 704-687-5503, Fax: 704-687-3279, E-mail: gradadm@uncc.edu.

The University of North Carolina at Greensboro, Graduate School, College of Arts and Sciences, Department of Mathematics and Statistics, Greensboro, NC 27412-5001. Offers mathematics (MA, PhD). Part-time programs available. *Degree requirements:* For master's, comprehensive exam, thesis (for some programs). *Entrance requirements:* For master's, GRE General Test. Additional exam requirements/recommendations for international students: Required—TOEFL. Electronic applications accepted. *Faculty research:* General and geometric topology, statistics, computer networks, symbolic logic, mathematics education.

The University of North Carolina Wilmington, College of Arts and Sciences, Department of Mathematical Sciences, Wilmington, NC 28403-3297. Offers MS. *Faculty:* 21 full-time (5 women). *Students:* 10 full-time (2 women), 18 part-time (12 women); includes 1 Black or African American, non-Hispanic/Latino; 1 Hispanic/Latino; 1 Two or more races, non-Hispanic/

280 www.facebook.com/petersonspublishing

Peterson's Graduate Programs in the Physical Sciences, Mathematics, Agricultural Sciences, the Environment & Natural Resources 2012

Latino. Average age 30. 15 applicants, 67% accepted, 10 enrolled. In 2010, 13 master's awarded. *Degree requirements:* For master's, comprehensive exam, thesis. *Entrance requirements:* For master's, GRE General Test, GRE Subject Test, minimum B average in undergraduate major. Additional exam requirements/recommendations for international students: Required—TOEFL (minimum score 550 paper-based; 217 computer-based; 79 iBT), IELTS (minimum score 6.5). *Application deadline:* For fall admission, 3/15 for domestic students. Applications are processed on a rolling basis. Application fee: $60. *Financial support:* In 2010–11, 13 teaching assistantships with full and partial tuition reimbursements (averaging $10,000 per year) were awarded; career-related internships or fieldwork and Federal Work-Study also available. Support available to part-time students. Financial award application deadline: 3/15. *Unit head:* Dr. Matthew Tenhuisen, Department Chair, 910-962-3294, Fax: 910-962-7107, E-mail: tenhuisenm@uncw.edu. *Application contact:* Dr. John Karlof, Graduate Coordinator, 910-962-3384, E-mail: karlofj@uncw.edu.

University of North Dakota, Graduate School, College of Arts and Sciences, Department of Mathematics, Grand Forks, ND 58202. Offers M Ed, MS. Part-time programs available. *Faculty:* 16 full-time (3 women). *Students:* 6 full-time (4 women), 1 part-time (0 women), 2 international. Average age 29. 11 applicants, 73% accepted, 4 enrolled. In 2010, 3 master's awarded. *Degree requirements:* For master's, thesis or alternative, final exam. *Entrance requirements:* For master's, minimum GPA of 3.0. Additional exam requirements/recommendations for international students: Required—TOEFL (minimum score 550 paper-based; 213 computer-based; 79 iBT), IELTS (minimum score 6.5). *Application deadline:* For fall admission, 3/15 priority date for domestic and international students. Applications are processed on a rolling basis. Application fee: $35. Electronic applications accepted. *Expenses:* Tuition, state resident: full-time $5857; part-time $306.74 per credit. Tuition, nonresident: full-time $15,666; part-time $729.77 per credit. Required fees: $53.42 per credit. Tuition and fees vary according to course load, program and reciprocity agreements. *Financial support:* In 2010–11, 4 students received support, including 4 teaching assistantships with full tuition reimbursements available (averaging $11,570 per year); fellowships with full and partial tuition reimbursements available, research assistantships with full and partial tuition reimbursements available, Federal Work-Study, institutionally sponsored loans, scholarships/grants, health care benefits, tuition waivers (full and partial), and unspecified assistantships also available. Support available to part-time students. Financial award application deadline: 3/15; financial award applicants required to submit FAFSA. *Faculty research:* Statistics, measure theory, topological vector spaces, algebra, applied math. Total annual research expenditures: $6,296. *Unit head:* Dr. Richard P. Millspaugh, Chairperson, 701-777-2881, Fax: 701-777-3619, E-mail: richard_millspaugh@und.nodak.edu. *Application contact:* Matt Anderson, Admissions Specialist, 701-777-2947, Fax: 701-777-3618, E-mail: matthew.anderson@gradschool.und.edu.

University of Northern British Columbia, Office of Graduate Studies, Prince George, BC V2N 4Z9, Canada. Offers business administration (Diploma); community health science (M Sc); disability management (MA); education (M Ed); first nations studies (MA); gender studies (MA); history (MA); interdisciplinary studies (MA); international studies (MA); mathematical, computer and physical sciences (M Sc); natural resources and environmental studies (M Sc, MA, MNRES, PhD); political science (MA); psychology (M Sc, PhD); social work (MSW). Part-time and evening/weekend programs available. Postbaccalaureate distance learning degree programs offered (no on-campus study). *Degree requirements:* For master's, thesis; for doctorate, thesis/dissertation. *Entrance requirements:* For master's, GRE, minimum B average in undergraduate course work; for doctorate, candidacy exam, minimum A average in graduate course work.

University of Northern Colorado, Graduate School, College of Natural and Health Sciences, School of Mathematical Sciences, Greeley, CO 80639. Offers mathematical teaching (MA); mathematics (MA, PhD); mathematics education (PhD); mathematics: liberal arts (MA). Part-time programs available. *Faculty:* 16 full-time (5 women). *Students:* 17 full-time (9 women), 21 part-time (14 women); includes 2 Asian, non-Hispanic/Latino; 1 Hispanic/Latino, 3 international. Average age 35. 13 applicants, 38% accepted, 3 enrolled. In 2010, 5 master's, 3 doctorates awarded. *Degree requirements:* For master's, comprehensive exam, thesis or alternative; for doctorate, comprehensive exam, thesis/dissertation. *Entrance requirements:* For master's, GRE General Test (liberal arts), 3 letters of recommendation; for doctorate, GRE General Test, 3 letters of recommendation. *Application deadline:* Applications are processed on a rolling basis. Application fee: $50 ($60 for international students). Electronic applications accepted. *Expenses:* Tuition, state resident: full-time $6199; part-time $344 per credit hour. Tuition, nonresident: full-time $14,834; part-time $824 per credit hour. Required fees: $1091; $60.60 per credit hour. Tuition and fees vary according to course load, degree level and program. *Financial support:* In 2010–11, 11 research assistantships (averaging $3,092 per year), 12 teaching assistantships (averaging $12,823 per year) were awarded; fellowships, unspecified assistantships also available. Financial award application deadline: 3/1; financial award applicants required to submit FAFSA. *Unit head:* Dr. Dean Allison, Director, 970-351-2820, Fax: 970-351-2155. *Application contact:* Linda Sisson, Graduate Student Admission Coordinator, 970-351-1807, Fax: 970-351-2371, E-mail: linda.sisson@unco.edu.

University of Northern Iowa, Graduate College, College of Natural Sciences, Department of Mathematics, Cedar Falls, IA 50614. Offers industrial mathematics (PSM), including actuarial science, continuous quality improvement, mathematical computing and modeling; mathematics (MA), including mathematics, secondary; mathematics for middle grades 4-8 (MA). Part-time programs available. *Students:* 19 full-time (13 women), 22 part-time (17 women); includes 2 minority (1 Asian, non-Hispanic/Latino; 1 Two or more races, non-Hispanic/Latino), 5 international. 20 applicants, 40% accepted, 6 enrolled. In 2010, 18 master's awarded. *Degree requirements:* For master's, comprehensive exam (for some programs), thesis or alternative. *Entrance requirements:* For master's, minimum GPA of 3.0. Additional exam requirements/recommendations for international students: Required—TOEFL (minimum score 600 paper-based; 250 computer-based; 100 iBT). *Application deadline:* For fall admission, 8/1 priority date for domestic students. Applications are processed on a rolling basis. Application fee: $50 ($70 for international students). Electronic applications accepted. *Financial support:* Career-related internships or fieldwork, Federal Work-Study, scholarships/grants, and tuition waivers (full and partial) available. Support available to part-time students. Financial award application deadline: 2/1. *Unit head:* Dr. Douglas Mupasiri, Interim Head, 319-273-2012, Fax: 319-273-2546, E-mail: douglas.mupasiri@uni.edu. *Application contact:* Laurie S. Russell, Record Analyst, 319-273-2623, Fax: 319-273-2885, E-mail: laurie.russell@uni.edu.

University of North Florida, College of Arts and Sciences, Department of Mathematics and Statistics, Jacksonville, FL 32224. Offers mathematical sciences (MS); statistics (MS). Part-time and evening/weekend programs available. *Faculty:* 21 full-time (8 women). *Students:* 12 full-time (3 women), 8 part-time (3 women); includes 2 Black or African American, non-Hispanic/Latino, 6 international. Average age 29. 34 applicants, 38% accepted, 7 enrolled. In 2010, 7 master's awarded. *Degree requirements:* For master's, comprehensive exam, thesis optional. *Entrance requirements:* For master's, GRE General Test, minimum GPA of 3.0 in last 60 hours of course work. Additional exam requirements/recommendations for international students: Required—TOEFL (minimum score 500 paper-based; 173 computer-based; 61 iBT). *Application deadline:* For fall admission, 7/1 priority date for domestic students, 6/1 for international students; for spring admission, 11/1 priority date for domestic students, 10/1 for international students. Applications are processed on a rolling basis. Application fee: $30. Electronic applications accepted. *Expenses:* Tuition, state resident: full-time $7646.40; part-time $318.60 per credit hour. Tuition, nonresident: full-time $23,502; part-time $979.24 per credit hour. Required fees: $1208.88; $50.37 per credit hour. Tuition and fees vary according to course load and program. *Financial support:* In 2010–11, 12 students received support, including 9 teaching assistantships (averaging $6,100 per year); Federal Work-Study, scholarships/grants, tuition waivers (partial), and unspecified assistantships also available. Support available to part-time students. Financial award application deadline: 4/1; financial award applicants required to submit FAFSA. *Faculty research:* Real analysis, number theory, Euclidean geometry. Total annual research expenditures: $53,523. *Unit head:* Dr. Scott H. Hochwald, Chair, 904-620-2653, Fax: 904-620-2818, E-mail: shochwal@unf.edu. *Application contact:* Lillith Richardson, Assistant Director, The Graduate School, 904-620-1360, Fax: 904-620-1362, E-mail: graduateschool@unf.edu.

University of North Texas, Toulouse Graduate School, College of Arts and Sciences, Department of Mathematics, Denton, TX 76203. Offers MA, MS, PhD. Part-time programs available. Terminal master's awarded for partial completion of doctoral program. *Degree requirements:* For master's, thesis (for some programs); for doctorate, one foreign language, comprehensive exam, thesis/dissertation. *Entrance requirements:* For master's and doctorate, GRE General Test. Additional exam requirements/recommendations for international students: Recommended—TOEFL (minimum score 550 paper-based; 213 computer-based). *Application deadline:* For fall admission, 7/15 for domestic students; for spring admission, 11/15 for domestic students. *Expenses:* Tuition, state resident: full-time $4298; part-time $239 per credit hour. Tuition, nonresident: full-time $10,782; part-time $549 per credit hour. Required fees: $1292; $270 per credit hour. *Financial support:* Fellowships with tuition reimbursements, research assistantships, teaching assistantships, Federal Work-Study and institutionally sponsored loans available. Financial award application deadline: 4/1; financial award applicants required to submit FAFSA. *Faculty research:* Differential equations, descriptive set theory, combinatorics, functional analysis, algebra. *Application contact:* Graduate Advisor, 940-565-4304, Fax: 940-565-4805, E-mail: brojovic@unt.edu.

University of Notre Dame, Graduate School, College of Science, Department of Mathematics, Notre Dame, IN 46556. Offers algebra (PhD); algebraic geometry (PhD); applied mathematics (MSAM); complex analysis (PhD); differential geometry (PhD); logic (PhD); partial differential equations (PhD); topology (PhD). Terminal master's awarded for partial completion of doctoral program. *Degree requirements:* For doctorate, one foreign language, thesis/dissertation, qualifying exam. *Entrance requirements:* For master's and doctorate, GRE General Test, GRE Subject Test. Additional exam requirements/recommendations for international students: Required—TOEFL (minimum score 600 paper-based; 250 computer-based; 80 iBT). Electronic applications accepted. *Faculty research:* Algebra, analysis, geometry/topology, logic, applied math.

University of Oklahoma, College of Arts and Sciences, Department of Mathematics, Norman, OK 73019. Offers MA, MS, PhD, MBA/MS. Part-time programs available. *Faculty:* 33 full-time (3 women). *Students:* 61 full-time (23 women), 13 part-time (6 women); includes 7 minority (2 Black or African American, non-Hispanic/Latino; 1 American Indian or Alaska Native, non-Hispanic/Latino; 3 Asian, non-Hispanic/Latino; 1 Two or more races, non-Hispanic/Latino), 28 international. Average age 30. 20 applicants, 65% accepted, 8 enrolled. In 2010, 5 master's, 5 doctorates awarded. Terminal master's awarded for partial completion of doctoral program. *Degree requirements:* For master's, comprehensive exam, thesis optional; for doctorate, 2 foreign languages, thesis/dissertation, qualifying exam. *Entrance requirements:* Additional exam requirements/recommendations for international students: Required—TOEFL (minimum score 550 paper-based; 213 computer-based; 79 iBT). *Application deadline:* For fall admission, 4/1 priority date for domestic students, 4/1 for international students; for spring admission, 11/1 for domestic students, 9/1 for international students. Applications are processed on a rolling basis. Application fee: $40 ($90 for international students). Electronic applications accepted. *Expenses:* Tuition, state resident: full-time $3892.80; part-time $162.20 per credit hour. Tuition, nonresident: full-time $14,167; part-time $590.30 per credit hour. Required fees: $2523.40; $94.60 per credit hour. Tuition and fees vary according to course load and degree level. *Financial support:* In 2010–11, 72 students received support, including 12 fellowships with full tuition reimbursements available (averaging $3,783 per year), 59 teaching assistantships with partial tuition reimbursements available (averaging $14,946 per year); scholarships/grants, health care benefits, and unspecified assistantships also available. Financial award applicants required to submit FAFSA. *Faculty research:* Topology, geometry, algebra, analysis, mathematics pedagogy. Total annual research expenditures: $376,758. *Unit head:* Paul Goodey, Chair, 405-325-6711, Fax: 405-325-7484, E-mail: pgoodey@ou.edu. *Application contact:* Anne Jones, Assistant to Graduate Director, 405-325-6711, Fax: 405-325-7484, E-mail: ajones@math.ou.edu.

See Display on next page and Close-Up on page 311.

University of Oregon, Graduate School, College of Arts and Sciences, Department of Mathematics, Eugene, OR 97403. Offers MA, MS, PhD. Part-time programs available. Terminal master's awarded for partial completion of doctoral program. *Degree requirements:* For doctorate, 2 foreign languages, thesis/dissertation. *Entrance requirements:* For master's and doctorate, GRE General Test, GRE Subject Test. Additional exam requirements/recommendations for international students: Required—TOEFL. *Faculty research:* Algebra, topology, analytic geometry, numerical analysis, statistics.

University of Ottawa, Faculty of Graduate and Postdoctoral Studies, Faculty of Science, Ottawa-Carleton Institute of Mathematics and Statistics, Ottawa, ON K1N 6N5, Canada. Offers M Sc, PhD. M Sc, PhD offered jointly with Carleton University. Part-time programs available. *Degree requirements:* For master's, thesis optional; for doctorate, one foreign language, comprehensive exam, thesis/dissertation. *Entrance requirements:* For master's, honors B Sc degree or equivalent, minimum B average; for doctorate, M Sc, minimum B+ average. Electronic applications accepted. *Faculty research:* Pure mathematics, applied mathematics, probability and statistics.

University of Pennsylvania, School of Arts and Sciences, Graduate Group in Mathematics, Philadelphia, PA 19104. Offers AM, PhD. *Faculty:* 29 full-time (2 women), 5 part-time/adjunct (0 women). *Students:* 60 full-time (9 women), 1 part-time (0 women); includes 5 Asian, non-Hispanic/Latino, 33 international. 290 applicants, 7% accepted, 8 enrolled. In 2010, 8 master's, 8 doctorates awarded. Terminal master's awarded for partial completion of doctoral program. *Degree requirements:* For master's, one foreign language, thesis or alternative; for doctorate, 2 foreign languages, thesis/dissertation. *Entrance requirements:* For master's and doctorate, GRE General Test, GRE Subject Test. Additional exam requirements/recommendations for international students: Required—TOEFL. *Application deadline:* For fall admission, 12/1 priority date for domestic students. Application fee: $70. Electronic applications accepted. *Expenses:* Tuition: Full-time $25,660; part-time $4758 per course. Required fees: $2152; $270 per course. Tuition and fees vary according to course load, degree level and program. *Financial support:* In 2010–11, 13 fellowships, 27 teaching assistantships were awarded; institutionally sponsored loans, scholarships/grants, traineeships, health care benefits, and unspecified assistantships also available. Financial award application deadline: 12/15. *Faculty research:* Geometry-topology, analysis, algebra, logic, combinatorics. *Unit head:* Jonathan Block, Department Chair, Mathematics, 215-898-8468, E-mail: blockj@math.upenn.edu. *Application contact:* Jonathan Block, Department Chair, Mathematics, 215-898-8468, E-mail: blockj@math.upenn.edu.

University of Pittsburgh, School of Arts and Sciences, Department of Mathematics, Pittsburgh, PA 15260. Offers applied mathematics (MA, MS); mathematics (MA, MS, PhD). Part-time programs available. *Faculty:* 33 full-time (5 women), 16 part-time/adjunct (2 women). *Students:* 79 full-time (24 women), 4 part-time (2 women); includes 2 Black or African American, non-Hispanic/Latino; 1 Native Hawaiian or other Pacific Islander, non-Hispanic/Latino, 42 international. 266 applicants, 15% accepted, 21 enrolled. In 2010, 17 master's, 12 doctorates awarded. Terminal master's awarded for partial completion of doctoral program. *Degree requirements:* For master's, comprehensive exam, thesis (for some programs); for doctorate, comprehensive exam, thesis/dissertation, preliminary exams, defense of dissertation. *Entrance*

Department of Mathematics
The University of Oklahoma

Thank you for your interest in our department and in the University of Oklahoma! The **Mathematics Department** at the University of Oklahoma has a long and rich academic tradition dating back to the mid-1890s. We awarded our first master's degree in 1927 and our first doctorate in 1947. We offer a wide range of options leading to the Master of Arts, Master of Science, and Ph.D. degrees. You will be able to select from a broad **range of options** in pure and applied mathematics and in research in mathematics education for your graduate degree:

1. **Algebra and Number Theory.** Algebraic Geometry, Algebraic Groups, Combinatorics, Modular Forms, Representation Theory (real, p-adic, Lie, automorphic).
2. **Analysis.** Global Analysis, Harmonic Analysis, Integrable Systems, PDEs, Signal Processing, Spectral Theory, Wavelets and Frames.
3. **Applied Mathematics and Mathematical Physics.** Control Theory, Dynamical Systems, Modeling.
4. **Geometry.** Convexity, Harmonic Maps, Riemannian Geometry, Group Actions and Non-negative Curvature.
5. **RUME.** Research in Undergraduate Mathematics Education, Diversity and Equity, International Comparative Education.
6. **Topology.** Algebraic and Geometric Topology, Dimension Theory, Geometric Group Theory, Hyperbolic Geometry, Low Dimensional Topology, Teichmuller Theory.

For more information, contact:
Cristin Sloan, Assistant to the Graduate Director
Department of Mathematics
The University of Oklahoma
Norman, OK 73019
csloan@ou.edu
www.math.ou.edu/grad/

University of Pittsburgh (continued)

requirements: For master's, GRE General Test, GRE Subject Test (recommended), minimum GPA of 3.0; for doctorate, GRE General Test, GRE Subject Test (recommended), minimum GPA of 3.0, minimum QPA of 3.25 in math curriculum. Additional exam requirements/recommendations for international students: Required—TOEFL (minimum score 550 paper-based; 213 computer-based; 80 iBT), IELTS (minimum score 6.5). *Application deadline:* For fall admission, 1/15 priority date for domestic and international students; for spring admission, 9/1 priority date for domestic students; 9/1 for international students. Applications are processed on a rolling basis. Application fee: $50. Electronic applications accepted. *Expenses:* Tuition, state resident: full-time $17,304; part-time $701 per credit. Tuition, nonresident: full-time $29,554; part-time $1210 per credit. Required fees: $740; $214 per term. Tuition and fees vary according to program. *Financial support:* In 2010–11, 84 students received support, including 8 fellowships with full and partial tuition reimbursements available (averaging $18,350 per year), 11 research assistantships with full and partial tuition reimbursements available (averaging $16,000 per year), 53 teaching assistantships with full and partial tuition reimbursements available (averaging $15,830 per year); institutionally sponsored loans, scholarships/grants, traineeships, health care benefits, tuition waivers (partial), and unspecified assistantships also available. Financial award application deadline: 1/15. *Faculty research:* Algebra, analysis, computational math, geometry/topology, math biology. Total annual research expenditures: $1.8 million. *Unit head:* Ivan Yotov, Chair, 412-624-8361, Fax: 412-624-8397, E-mail: yotov@math.pitt.edu. *Application contact:* Molly Williams, Administrator, 412-624-1175, Fax: 412-624-8397, E-mail: mollyw@pitt.edu.

University of Puerto Rico, Mayagüez Campus, Graduate Studies, College of Arts and Sciences, Department of Mathematical Sciences, Mayagüez, PR 00681-9000. Offers applied mathematics (MS); pure mathematics (MS); scientific computation (MS); statistics (MS). Part-time programs available. *Students:* 40 full-time (11 women), 1 part-time (0 women); includes 7 Hispanic/Latino, 34 international. 19 applicants, 26% accepted, 3 enrolled. In 2010, 7 master's awarded. *Degree requirements:* For master's, one foreign language, comprehensive exam, thesis optional. *Entrance requirements:* For master's, undergraduate degree in mathematics or its equivalent. *Application deadline:* For fall admission, 2/15 for domestic and international students; for spring admission, 9/15 for domestic and international students. Applications are processed on a rolling basis. Application fee: $25. *Expenses:* Tuition, state resident: full-time $1188. Tuition, nonresident: full-time $1188. International tuition: $6126 full-time. Tuition and fees vary according to course level and course load. *Financial support:* In 2010–11, 39 students received support, including fellowships (averaging $12,000 per year), 20 research assistantships (averaging $15,000 per year), 39 teaching assistantships (averaging $8,500 per year); Federal Work-Study and institutionally sponsored loans also available. *Faculty research:* Automata theory, linear algebra, logic. Total annual research expenditures: $2.7 million. *Unit head:* Prof. Silvestre Col??n, Director, 787-832-4040 Ext. 3848, Fax: 787-265-5454, E-mail: silvestre.colon@upr.edu. *Application contact:* Prof. Silvestre Col??n, Director, 787-832-4040 Ext. 3848, Fax: 787-265-5454, E-mail: silvestre.colon@upr.edu.

University of Puerto Rico, Río Piedras, College of Natural Sciences, Department of Mathematics, San Juan, PR 00931-3300. Offers MS, PhD. Part-time programs available. *Degree requirements:* For master's, comprehensive exam, thesis; for doctorate, comprehensive exam, thesis/dissertation. *Entrance requirements:* For master's and doctorate, GRE General Test and GRE Subject Test, interview, minimum GPA of 3.0, 3 letters of recommendation. *Faculty research:* Investigation of database logistics, cryptograph systems, distribution and spectral theory, Boolean function, differential equations.

University of Regina, Faculty of Graduate Studies and Research, Faculty of Science, Department of Mathematics and Statistics, Regina, SK S4S 0A2, Canada. Offers mathematics (M Sc, MA, PhD); statistics (M Sc, MA, PhD). *Faculty:* 17 full-time (3 women). *Students:* 17 full-time (4 women), 1 (woman) part-time. 16 applicants, 44% accepted. In 2010, 5 master's, 3 doctorates awarded. *Degree requirements:* For master's, thesis; for doctorate, comprehensive exam, thesis/dissertation. *Entrance requirements:* Additional exam requirements/recommendations for international students: Required—TOEFL (minimum score 580 paper-based; 80 iBT). *Application deadline:* Applications are processed on a rolling basis. Application fee: $100. Electronic applications accepted. Tuition and fees charges are reported in Canadian dollars. *Expenses:* Tuition, area resident: Full-time $3244.50 Canadian dollars; part-time $180.25 Canadian dollars per credit hour. International tuition: $4744.50 Canadian dollars full-time. Required fees: $494 Canadian dollars; $115.25 Canadian dollars per credit hour. $115.25 Canadian dollars per semester. Tuition and fees vary according to program. *Financial support:* In 2010–11, 3 fellowships (averaging $20,000 per year), 1 research assistantship (averaging $18,000 per year), 3 teaching assistantships (averaging $6,978 per year) were awarded; scholarships/grants also available. Financial award application deadline: 6/15. *Faculty research:* Discrete mathematics, actuarial science and statistics, matrix theory, mathematical science, numerical analysis. *Unit head:* Dr. Allen Herman, Head, 306-585-4487, Fax: 306-585-4020, E-mail: allen.herman@uregina.ca. *Application contact:* Dr. Martin Argerami, Graduate Program Coordinator, 306-585-4340, Fax: 306-585-4020, E-mail: martin.argerami@math.uregina.ca.

University of Rhode Island, Graduate School, College of Arts and Sciences, Department of Mathematics, Kingston, RI 02881. Offers applied mathematical sciences (MS, PhD); mathematics (MS, PhD). Part-time programs available. *Faculty:* 19 full-time (4 women), 1 part-time/adjunct (0 women). *Students:* 23 full-time (10 women), 10 part-time (1 woman), 2 international. In 2010, 7 master's, 2 doctorates awarded. *Degree requirements:* For master's, comprehensive exam (for some programs), thesis optional; for doctorate, one foreign language, comprehensive exam, thesis/dissertation optional. *Entrance requirements:* For master's and doctorate, 2 letters of recommendation. Additional exam requirements/recommendations for international students: Required—TOEFL (minimum score 550 paper-based; 213 computer-based). *Application deadline:* For fall admission, 7/15 for domestic students, 2/1 for international students; for spring admission, 11/15 for domestic students, 7/15 for international students. Application fee: $65. Electronic applications accepted. *Expenses:* Tuition, state resident: full-time $9588; part-time $533 per credit hour. Tuition, nonresident: full-time $22,968; part-time $1276 per credit hour. Required fees: $1282; $68 per semester. Tuition and fees vary according to program. *Financial support:* In 2010–11, 2 research assistantships with full tuition reimbursements (averaging $13,894 per year), 13 teaching assistantships with full and partial tuition reimbursements (averaging $13,560 per year) were awarded. Financial award application deadline: 7/15; financial award applicants required to submit FAFSA. *Unit head:* Dr. Nancy Eaton, Chairman, 401-874-2709, Fax: 401-874-4454, E-mail: eaton@math.uri.edu. *Application contact:* Dr. Woong Kook, Director of Graduate Studies, 401-874-4421, Fax: 401-874-4454, E-mail: andrewk@math.uri.edu.

University of Rochester, School of Arts and Sciences, Department of Mathematics, Program in Mathematical Methods, Rochester, NY 14627.

University of Rochester, School of Arts and Sciences, Department of Mathematics, Programs in Mathematics, Rochester, NY 14627.

University of Saskatchewan, College of Graduate Studies and Research, College of Arts and Sciences, Department of Mathematics and Statistics, Saskatoon, SK S7N 5A2, Canada.

282   www.facebook.com/petersonspublishing

Peterson's Graduate Programs in the Physical Sciences, Mathematics, Agricultural Sciences, the Environment & Natural Resources 2012

Offers M Math, MA, PhD. *Degree requirements:* For master's, thesis (for some programs); for doctorate, comprehensive exam (for some programs), thesis/dissertation. *Entrance requirements:* Additional exam requirements/recommendations for international students: Required—TOEFL (minimum score 80 iBT); Recommended—IELTS (minimum score 6.5). Electronic applications accepted.

University of South Alabama, Graduate School, College of Arts and Sciences, Department of Mathematics and Statistics, Mobile, AL 36688. Offers mathematics (MS). Part-time and evening/weekend programs available. *Faculty:* 18 full-time (5 women). *Students:* 8 full-time (5 women), 1 part-time (0 women); includes 1 Asian, non-Hispanic/Latino, 1 international. 13 applicants, 69% accepted, 4 enrolled. In 2010, 2 master's awarded. *Degree requirements:* For master's, comprehensive exam, thesis optional. *Entrance requirements:* For master's, GRE, BS in mathematics or a mathematics-related field. Additional exam requirements/recommendations for international students: Required—TOEFL. *Application deadline:* For fall admission, 7/15 priority date for domestic students, 6/15 priority date for international students; for spring admission, 12/1 priority date for domestic students, 11/1 priority date for international students. Applications are processed on a rolling basis. Application fee: $35. *Expenses:* Tuition, state resident: part-time $300 per credit hour. Tuition, nonresident: part-time $600 per credit hour. Required fees: $150 per semester. *Financial support:* Fellowships, research assistantships available. Support available to part-time students. Financial award application deadline: 4/1. *Faculty research:* Knot theory, chaos theory. *Unit head:* Dr. Scott Carter, Chair, 251-460-6264, Fax: 251-460-7969. *Application contact:* Dr. Dan Silver, Graduate Coordinator, 251-460-6264.

University of South Carolina, The Graduate School, College of Arts and Sciences, Department of Mathematics, Columbia, SC 29208. Offers mathematics (MA, MS, PhD); mathematics education (M Math, MAT). MAT offered in cooperation with the College of Education. Part-time programs available. Terminal master's awarded for partial completion of doctoral program. *Degree requirements:* For master's, comprehensive exam, thesis (for some programs); for doctorate, one foreign language, comprehensive exam, thesis/dissertation, admission to candidacy exam, residency. *Entrance requirements:* For master's and doctorate, GRE General Test. Additional exam requirements/recommendations for international students: Required—TOEFL (minimum score 600 paper-based; 250 computer-based; 100 iBT). Electronic applications accepted. *Faculty research:* Computational mathematics, analysis (classical/modern), discrete mathematics, algebra, number theory.

The University of South Dakota, Graduate School, College of Arts and Sciences, Department of Mathematics, Vermillion, SD 57069-2390. Offers MA, MNS, MS. Part-time programs available. *Degree requirements:* For master's, thesis (for some programs). *Entrance requirements:* For master's, GRE, minimum GPA of 2.7. Additional exam requirements/recommendations for international students: Required—TOEFL (minimum score 550 paper-based; 213 computer-based; 79 iBT). Electronic applications accepted.

University of Southern California, Graduate School, Dana and David Dornsife College of Letters, Arts and Sciences, Department of Mathematics, Los Angeles, CA 90089. Offers applied mathematics (MA, MS, PhD); mathematical finance (MS); mathematics (MA, PhD); statistics (MS). Part-time programs available. *Faculty:* 48 full-time (6 women). *Students:* 103 full-time (33 women), 14 part-time (6 women); includes 11 minority (8 Asian, non-Hispanic/Latino; 1 Hispanic/Latino; 2 Two or more races, non-Hispanic/Latino), 85 international. 559 applicants, 20% accepted, 32 enrolled. In 2010, 37 master's, 7 doctorates awarded. Terminal master's awarded for partial completion of doctoral program. *Degree requirements:* For master's, comprehensive exam (for some programs), thesis (for some programs); for doctorate, one foreign language, comprehensive exam, thesis/dissertation. *Entrance requirements:* For master's, GRE General Test, GMAT; for doctorate, GRE—General and Subject in Mathematics. Additional exam requirements/recommendations for international students: Required—TOEFL (minimum score 100 iBT). *Application deadline:* For fall and spring admission, 12/1 for domestic and international students. Applications are processed on a rolling basis. Application fee: $85. Electronic applications accepted. *Expenses:* Tuition: Full-time $31,240; part-time $1420 per unit. Required fees: $600. One-time fee: $35 full-time. Full-time tuition and fees vary according to degree level and program. *Financial support:* In 2010–11, 68 students received support, including 5 fellowships with full tuition reimbursements available (averaging $19,250 per year), 3 research assistantships with full tuition reimbursements available (averaging $19,250 per year), 58 teaching assistantships with full tuition reimbursements available (averaging $19,250 per year). Financial award application deadline: 12/1. *Faculty research:* Algebra, algebraic geometry and number theory, analysis/partial differential equations, applied mathematics, financial mathematics, probability, combinatorics and statistics. Total annual research expenditures: $1.7 million. *Unit head:* Prof. Gary Rosen, Chair, 213-740-1717, Fax: 213-740-2424, E-mail: grosen@usc.edu. *Application contact:* Amy Yung, Department Coordinator, 213-740-8168, Fax: 213-740-2424, E-mail: amy@usc.edu.

University of Southern Mississippi, Graduate School, College of Science and Technology, Department of Mathematics, Hattiesburg, MS 39406-0001. Offers computational science (PhD); mathematics (MS). Part-time programs available. *Faculty:* 11 full-time (3 women), 1 part-time/adjunct (0 women). *Students:* 11 full-time (8 women), 2 part-time (0 women); includes 3 Black or African American, non-Hispanic/Latino; 1 Asian, non-Hispanic/Latino, 3 international. Average age 29. 12 applicants, 83% accepted, 5 enrolled. In 2010, 1 master's awarded. *Degree requirements:* For master's, comprehensive exam, thesis or alternative; for doctorate, comprehensive exam, thesis/dissertation. *Entrance requirements:* For master's, GRE General Test, minimum GPA of 2.75 in last 60 hours; for doctorate, GRE General Test, minimum GPA of 3.5. Additional exam requirements/recommendations for international students: Required—TOEFL, IELTS. *Application deadline:* For fall admission, 3/15 priority date for domestic and international students; for spring admission, 1/10 priority date for domestic and international students. Applications are processed on a rolling basis. Application fee: $50. Electronic applications accepted. *Financial support:* In 2010–11, 1 fellowship (averaging $18,000 per year), research assistantships with full tuition reimbursements (averaging $11,500 per year), 11,500 teaching assistantships with full tuition reimbursements (averaging $11,408 per year) were awarded; Federal Work-Study, scholarships/grants, health care benefits, and unspecified assistantships also available. Financial award application deadline: 3/15; financial award applicants required to submit FAFSA. *Faculty research:* Dynamical systems, numerical analysis and multigrid methods, random number generation, matrix theory, group theory. *Unit head:* Dr. Joseph Kolibal, Interim Chair, 601-266-4289, Fax: 601-266-5818. *Application contact:* Dr. James Lambers, Director, Graduate Admissions, 601-266-4289, Fax: 601-266-5818.

University of South Florida, Graduate School, College of Arts and Sciences, Department of Mathematics and Statistics, Tampa, FL 33620-9951. Offers mathematics (MA, PhD); statistics (MA). Part-time and evening/weekend programs available. *Faculty:* 15 full-time (0 women), 6 part-time/adjunct (all women). *Students:* 73 full-time (24 women), 16 part-time (4 women); includes 2 Black or African American, non-Hispanic/Latino; 5 Asian, non-Hispanic/Latino; 6 Hispanic/Latino; 2 Two or more races, non-Hispanic/Latino, 40 international. Average age 32. 73 applicants, 63% accepted, 21 enrolled. In 2010, 17 master's, 6 doctorates awarded. Terminal master's awarded for partial completion of doctoral program. *Degree requirements:* For master's, one foreign language, comprehensive exam, thesis optional; for doctorate, 2 foreign languages, comprehensive exam, thesis/dissertation. *Entrance requirements:* For master's, GRE General Test, minimum GPA of 3.0; for doctorate, GRE General Test, minimum GPA of 3.5 in undergraduate/graduate mathematics courses. Additional exam requirements/recommendations for international students: Required—TOEFL (minimum score 550 paper-based; 213 computer-based; 79 iBT). *Application deadline:* For fall admission, 2/1 for domestic students, 1/2 for international students; for spring admission, 8/1 for domestic students, 6/1 for international students. Application fee: $30. Electronic applications accepted. *Financial support:* In 2010–11, 57 students received support, including 6 research assistantships (averaging $13,555 per year), 57 teaching assistantships with partial tuition reimbursements available (averaging $13,634 per year); unspecified assistantships also available. Financial award application deadline: 2/1. *Faculty research:* Approximation theory, differential equations, discrete mathematics, functional analysis topology. Total annual research expenditures: $520,926. *Unit head:* Dr. Marcus McWaters, Chairperson, 813-974-3838, Fax: 813-974-2700, E-mail: mmm@usf.edu. *Application contact:* Dr. Xiang-Dong Hou, Graduate Admissions Director, 813-974-2561, Fax: 813-974-2700, E-mail: xhou@cas.usf.edu.

The University of Tennessee, Graduate School, College of Arts and Sciences, Department of Mathematics, Knoxville, TN 37996. Offers applied mathematics (MS); mathematical ecology (PhD); mathematics (M Math, MS, PhD). Part-time programs available. *Degree requirements:* For master's, thesis or alternative; for doctorate, one foreign language, thesis/dissertation. *Entrance requirements:* For master's and doctorate, minimum GPA of 2.7. Additional exam requirements/recommendations for international students: Required—TOEFL. Electronic applications accepted. *Expenses:* Tuition, state resident: full-time $7440; part-time $414 per credit hour. Tuition, nonresident: full-time $22,478; part-time $1250 per credit hour. Required fees: $922; $43 per credit hour. Tuition and fees vary according to program.

The University of Texas at Arlington, Graduate School, College of Science, Department of Mathematics, Arlington, TX 76019. Offers applied math (MS); mathematics (PhD); mathematics education (MA). Part-time and evening/weekend programs available. *Faculty:* 26 full-time (7 women). *Students:* 54 full-time (19 women), 75 part-time (32 women); includes 13 Black or African American, non-Hispanic/Latino; 7 Asian, non-Hispanic/Latino; 12 Hispanic/Latino, 31 international. 86 applicants, 99% accepted, 63 enrolled. In 2010, 11 master's, 9 doctorates awarded. *Degree requirements:* For master's, comprehensive exam, thesis or alternative; for doctorate, comprehensive exam, thesis/dissertation, preliminary examinations. *Entrance requirements:* For master's, GRE General Test (minimum score 350 verbal, 650 quantitative); for doctorate, GRE General Test (minimum score: 350 verbal, 700 quantitative), 30 hours of graduate course work in mathematics, minimum GPA of 3.0 in last 60 hours of course work. Additional exam requirements/recommendations for international students: Required—TOEFL (minimum score 550 paper-based; 213 computer-based; 79 iBT). *Application deadline:* For fall admission, 6/1 priority date for domestic students, 4/1 for international students; for winter admission, 10/15 priority date for domestic students, 9/15 for international students. Applications are processed on a rolling basis. Application fee: $35 ($50 for international students). Electronic applications accepted. *Expenses:* Tuition, state resident: full-time $7500. Tuition, nonresident: full-time $13,080. International tuition: $13,250 full-time. *Financial support:* In 2010–11, 36 students received support, including 17 fellowships with full tuition reimbursements available (averaging $27,500 per year), 2 research assistantships with partial tuition reimbursements available, 23 teaching assistantships with partial tuition reimbursements available (averaging $20,750 per year); Federal Work-Study, institutionally sponsored loans, scholarships/grants, health care benefits, and unspecified assistantships also available. Financial award application deadline: 6/1; financial award applicants required to submit FAFSA. *Faculty research:* Algebra, combinatorics and geometry, applied mathematics and mathematical biology, computational mathematics, mathematics education, probability and statistics. *Unit head:* Dr. Zhu Jiaping, Chair, 817-272-1114, E-mail: jpzhu@uta.edu. *Application contact:* Dr. Jianzhong Su, Graduate Advisor, 817-272-5684, Fax: 817-272-5802, E-mail: su@uta.edu.

The University of Texas at Austin, Graduate School, College of Natural Sciences, Department of Mathematics, Austin, TX 78712-1111. Offers mathematics (MA, PhD); statistics (MS Stat). *Entrance requirements:* For master's and doctorate, GRE General Test. Electronic applications accepted.

The University of Texas at Brownsville, Graduate Studies, College of Science, Mathematics and Technology, Brownsville, TX 78520-4991. Offers biological sciences (MS, MSIS); mathematics (MS); physics (MS). Part-time and evening/weekend programs available. *Degree requirements:* For master's, comprehensive exam, thesis optional. *Entrance requirements:* For master's, GRE General Test. Additional exam requirements/recommendations for international students: Required—TOEFL. *Faculty research:* Fish, insects, barrier islands, algae, curlits.

The University of Texas at Dallas, School of Natural Sciences and Mathematics, Department of Mathematical Sciences, Richardson, TX 75080. Offers applied mathematics (MS, PhD); engineering mathematics (MS); mathematical science (MS); statistics (MS, PhD). Part-time and evening/weekend programs available. *Faculty:* 15 full-time (2 women). *Students:* 43 full-time (16 women), 22 part-time (6 women); includes 20 minority (6 Black or African American, non-Hispanic/Latino; 11 Asian, non-Hispanic/Latino; 3 Hispanic/Latino), 23 international. Average age 32. 147 applicants, 32% accepted, 9 enrolled. In 2010, 18 master's, 6 doctorates awarded. *Degree requirements:* For master's, thesis optional; for doctorate, thesis/dissertation. *Entrance requirements:* For master's, GRE General Test, minimum GPA of 3.0 in upper-level course work in field; for doctorate, GRE General Test, minimum GPA of 3.5 in upper-level course work in field. Additional exam requirements/recommendations for international students: Required—TOEFL (minimum score 550 paper-based; 215 computer-based). *Application deadline:* For fall admission, 7/15 for domestic students, 5/1 priority date for international students; for spring admission, 11/15 for domestic students, 9/1 priority date for international students. Applications are processed on a rolling basis. Application fee: $50 ($100 for international students). Electronic applications accepted. *Expenses:* Tuition, state resident: full-time $10,248; part-time $569 per credit hour. Tuition, nonresident: full-time $18,544; part-time $1030 per credit hour. Tuition and fees vary according to course load. *Financial support:* In 2010–11, 39 students received support, including 2 research assistantships (averaging $15,750 per year), 31 teaching assistantships with partial tuition reimbursements available (averaging $13,933 per year); career-related internships or fieldwork, Federal Work-Study, institutionally sponsored loans, scholarships/grants, and unspecified assistantships also available. Support available to part-time students. Financial award application deadline: 4/30; financial award applicants required to submit FAFSA. *Faculty research:* Sequential analysis, applications in semiconductor manufacturing, medical image analysis, computational anatomy, information theory, probability theory. *Unit head:* Dr. Wieslaw Z. Krawcewicz, Department Head, 972-883-6820, Fax: 972-883-6622, E-mail: wieslaw@utdallas.edu. *Application contact:* Dr. Wieslaw Z. Krawcewicz, Department Head, 972-883-6820, Fax: 972-883-6622, E-mail: wieslaw@utdallas.edu.

The University of Texas at El Paso, Graduate School, College of Science, Department of Mathematical Sciences, El Paso, TX 79968-0001. Offers mathematical sciences (MS); mathematics (teaching) (MAT); statistics (MS). Part-time and evening/weekend programs available. *Students:* 61 (30 women); includes 1 Asian, non-Hispanic/Latino; 38 Hispanic/Latino, 13 international. Average age 34. In 2010, 17 master's awarded. *Degree requirements:* For master's, thesis optional. *Entrance requirements:* For master's, minimum GPA of 3.0, letters of recommendation. Additional exam requirements/recommendations for international students: Required—TOEFL; Recommended—IELTS. *Application deadline:* For fall admission, 8/1 priority date for domestic students, 3/1 for international students; for spring admission, 11/1 priority date for domestic students, 9/1 for international students. Applications are processed on a rolling basis. Application fee: $45 ($80 for international students). Electronic applications accepted. *Financial support:* In 2010–11, research assistantships with partial tuition reimbursements (averaging $21,812 per year), teaching assistantships with partial tuition reimbursements (averaging $17,450 per year) were awarded; fellowships with tuition reimbursements, institutionally sponsored loans, scholarships/grants, health care benefits, tuition waivers (partial), and unspecified assistantships also available. Support available to part-time students. Financial award application deadline: 3/15; financial award applicants required to submit FAFSA. *Unit head:* Dr. Maria C. Mariani, Chair, 915-747-5761, Fax: 915-747-6502, E-mail: mcmariani@utep.edu. *Application contact:* Dr. Patricia D. Witherspoon, Dean of the Graduate School, 915-747-5491, Fax: 915-747-5788, E-mail: withersp@utep.edu.

Peterson's Graduate Programs in the Physical Sciences, Mathematics, Agricultural Sciences, the Environment & Natural Resources 2012

www.facebook.com/petersonspublishing 283

Mathematics

The University of Texas at San Antonio, College of Sciences, Department of Mathematics, San Antonio, TX 78249-0617. Offers applied mathematics-industrial mathematics (MS); mathematics (MS); mathematics education (MS). Part-time and evening/weekend programs available. *Faculty:* 9 full-time (1 woman). *Students:* 22 full-time (8 women), 45 part-time (20 women); includes 30 minority (2 Black or African American, non-Hispanic/Latino; 4 Asian, non-Hispanic/Latino; 22 Hispanic/Latino; 2 Two or more races, non-Hispanic/Latino), 9 international. Average age 30. 41 applicants, 76% accepted, 23 enrolled. In 2010, 11 master's awarded. *Degree requirements:* For master's, comprehensive exam (for some programs), thesis (for some programs). *Entrance requirements:* For master's, GRE General Test, minimum GPA of 3.0 in last 60 hours. Additional exam requirements/recommendations for international students: Required—TOEFL (minimum score 500 paper-based; 173 computer-based; 61 iBT), IELTS (minimum score 5). *Application deadline:* For fall admission, 7/1 for domestic students, 4/1 for international students; for spring admission, 11/1 for domestic students, 9/1 for international students. Applications are processed on a rolling basis. Application fee: $45 ($80 for international students). Electronic applications accepted. *Expenses:* Tuition, state resident: full-time $4172; part-time $231.75 per credit hour. Tuition, nonresident: full-time $15,332; part-time $851.75 per credit hour. *Financial support:* In 2010–11, 9 students received support, including 1 research assistantship (averaging $22,800 per year), 25 teaching assistantships (averaging $11,536 per year); scholarships/grants, tuition waivers, and unspecified assistantships also available. Support available to part-time students. *Faculty research:* Computational statistics, deterministic and stochastic differential equations, applications of mathematics to architecture and urbanism, mathematical biology, numerical analysis. Total annual research expenditures: $117,596. *Unit head:* Dr. Francis A. Norman, Department Chair, 210-458-5735, Fax: 210-458-4439, E-mail: sandy.norman@utsa.edu. *Application contact:* Veronica Ramirez, Assistant Dean of the Graduate School, 210-458-4330, Fax: 210-458-4332, E-mail: graduatestudies@utsa.edu.

The University of Texas at Tyler, College of Arts and Sciences, Department of Mathematics, Tyler, TX 75799-0001. Offers MS, MSIS. *Degree requirements:* For master's, comprehensive exam, thesis optional. *Entrance requirements:* For master's, GRE General Test. Additional exam requirements/recommendations for international students: Required—TOEFL (minimum score 79 computer-based). *Faculty research:* Discrete geometry, knot theory, commutative algebra, noncommutative rings, group theory, mathematical biology, mathematical physics.

The University of Texas–Pan American, College of Science and Engineering, Department of Mathematics, Edinburg, TX 78539. Offers mathematical science (MS); mathematics teaching (MS). Part-time and evening/weekend programs available. *Degree requirements:* For master's, comprehensive exam. *Entrance requirements:* For master's, GRE General Test, minimum GPA of 3.0. *Faculty research:* Boundary value problems in differential equations, training of public school teachers in methods of presenting mathematics, harmonic analysis, inverse problems, commulative algebra.

University of the Incarnate Word, School of Graduate Studies and Research, School of Mathematics, Science, and Engineering, Program in Mathematics, San Antonio, TX 78209-6397. Offers mathematics teaching (MA); research statistics (MS). Part-time and evening/weekend programs available. *Faculty:* 7 full-time (4 women). *Students:* 1 full-time (0 women), 2 part-time (both women); includes 2 Hispanic/Latino, 1 international. Average age 49. In 2010, 2 master's awarded. *Degree requirements:* For master's, capstone or prerequisite knowledge (for research statistics). *Entrance requirements:* For master's, GRE (minimum score 800 verbal and quantitative), 18 hours of undergraduate mathematics with minimum GPA of 3.0; letter of recommendation by a professional in the field, writing sample, teaching experience at the precollege level. Additional exam requirements/recommendations for international students: Required—TOEFL (minimum score 560 paper-based; 220 computer-based; 83 iBT). *Application deadline:* Applications are processed on a rolling basis. Application fee: $20. Electronic applications accepted. *Expenses:* Tuition: Part-time $725 per contact hour. Required fees: $890 per semester. *Financial support:* Federal Work-Study and scholarships/grants available. Financial award applicants required to submit FAFSA. *Faculty research:* Nearness spaces in mathematical constructs, professional development of mathematics teachers. *Unit head:* Dr. Zhanbo Yang, Graduate Programs Coordinator, 210-283-5008, Fax: 210-829-3153, E-mail: yang@uiwtx.edu. *Application contact:* Andrea Cyterski-Acosta, Dean of Enrollment, 210-829-6005, Fax: 210-829-3921, E-mail: admis@uiwtx.edu.

The University of Toledo, College of Graduate Studies, College of Natural Sciences and Mathematics, Department of Mathematics, Toledo, OH 43606-3390. Offers applied mathematics (MS, PhD); mathematics (MA, PhD); statistics (MS, PhD). Part-time programs available. *Faculty:* 25. *Students:* 44 full-time (12 women), 13 part-time (7 women), 44 international. Average age 30. 84 applicants, 43% accepted, 19 enrolled. In 2010, 15 master's, 2 doctorates awarded. *Degree requirements:* For master's, thesis; for doctorate, 2 foreign languages, thesis/dissertation. *Entrance requirements:* For master's and doctorate, GRE General Test, GRE Subject Test, A minimum 2.7 cumulative point-hour ratio (on a 4.0 scale) for all previous academic work. Three letters of recommendation, a statement of purpose, and transcripts from all prior institutions attended. Additional exam requirements/recommendations for international students: Required—TOEFL (minimum score 550 paper-based; 213 computer-based; 80 iBT), IELTS (minimum score 6.5). *Application deadline:* For fall admission, 1/15 priority date for domestic and international students. Applications are processed on a rolling basis. Application fee: $45 ($75 for international students). Electronic applications accepted. *Expenses:* Tuition, state resident: full-time $11,426; part-time $476 per credit hour. Tuition, nonresident: full-time $21,660; part-time $903 per credit hour. One-time fee: $62. *Financial support:* Research assistantships with full tuition reimbursements, teaching assistantships with full tuition reimbursements, Federal Work-Study, institutionally sponsored loans, scholarships/grants, and unspecified assistantships available. Support available to part-time students. *Faculty research:* Topology. *Unit head:* Dr. Paul Hewitt, Chair, 419-530-2568, E-mail: paul.hewitt@utoledo.edu. *Application contact:* Graduate School Office, 419-530-4723, Fax: 419-530-4723, E-mail: grdsch@utnet.utoledo.edu.

University of Toronto, School of Graduate Studies, Physical Sciences Division, Department of Mathematics, Toronto, ON M5S 1A1, Canada. Offers M Sc, MMF, PhD. Part-time programs available. *Degree requirements:* For master's, thesis optional, research project; for doctorate, thesis/dissertation. *Entrance requirements:* For master's, minimum B average in final year, bachelor's degree in mathematics or a related area, 3 letters of reference; for doctorate, master's degree in mathematics or a related area, minimum A– average, 3 letters of reference.

University of Tulsa, Graduate School, College of Arts and Sciences, School of Education, Program in Teaching Arts, Tulsa, OK 74104-3189. Offers art (MTA); biology (MTA); English (MTA); history (MTA); mathematics (MTA); theatre (MTA). Part-time programs available. *Students:* 2 part-time (both women); includes 1 minority (American Indian or Alaska Native, non-Hispanic/Latino). Average age 31. 1 applicant, 0% accepted, 0 enrolled. In 2010, 2 master's awarded. *Entrance requirements:* For master's, GRE General Test. Additional exam requirements/recommendations for international students: Required—TOEFL (minimum score 575 paper-based; 231 computer-based), IELTS (minimum score 6.5). *Application deadline:* Applications are processed on a rolling basis. Application fee: $40. Electronic applications accepted. *Expenses:* Tuition: Full-time $16,902; part-time $939 per credit hour. Required fees: $1020; $4 per credit hour. Tuition and fees vary according to course load. *Financial support:* In 2010–11, 2 students received support, including 2 fellowships with full and partial tuition reimbursements available (averaging $2,191 per year); research assistantships with full and partial tuition reimbursements available, teaching assistantships with full and partial tuition reimbursements available, Federal Work-Study, scholarships/grants, and tuition waivers (full and partial) also available. Support available to part-time students. Financial award application deadline: 2/1; financial award applicants required to submit FAFSA. *Unit head:* Dr. David Brown, Advisor, 918-631-2719, Fax: 918-631-2133, E-mail: david-brown@utulsa.edu. *Application contact:* Dr. David Brown, Advisor, 918-631-2719, Fax: 918-631-2133, E-mail: david-brown@utulsa.edu.

University of Tulsa, Graduate School, College of Engineering and Natural Sciences, Department of Mathematical and Computer Sciences, Program in Mathematical Sciences, Tulsa, OK 74104-3189. Offers MS, MTA, MSF/MSAM. Part-time programs available. *Faculty:* 11 full-time (2 women). *Students:* 4 full-time (3 women), 2 part-time (1 woman), 1 international. Average age 26. 6 applicants, 67% accepted, 3 enrolled. In 2010, 5 master's awarded. *Degree requirements:* For master's, thesis (for some programs). *Entrance requirements:* For master's, GRE General Test. Additional exam requirements/recommendations for international students: Required—TOEFL (minimum score 550 paper-based; 213 computer-based; 80 iBT), IELTS (minimum score 6). *Application deadline:* Applications are processed on a rolling basis. Application fee: $40. Electronic applications accepted. *Expenses:* Tuition: Full-time $16,902; part-time $939 per credit hour. Required fees: $1020; $4 per credit hour. Tuition and fees vary according to course load. *Financial support:* In 2010–11, 1 fellowship with full and partial tuition reimbursement (averaging $3,756 per year), 2 research assistantships with full and partial tuition reimbursements (averaging $2,250 per year), 6 teaching assistantships with full and partial tuition reimbursements (averaging $10,056 per year) were awarded; Federal Work-Study, scholarships/grants, health care benefits, tuition waivers (full and partial), and unspecified assistantships also available. Financial award application deadline: 2/1; financial award applicants required to submit FAFSA. *Faculty research:* Optimization theory, numerical analysis, mathematical physics, modeling, Bayesian statistical inference. *Application contact:* Dr. Shirley Pomeranz, Advisor, 918-631-2990, Fax: 918-631-3077, E-mail: shirley-pomeranz@utulsa.edu.

University of Utah, Graduate School, College of Science, Department of Mathematics, Salt Lake City, UT 84112-0090. Offers M Stat, MA, MS, PhD. Part-time programs available. *Faculty:* 46 full-time (5 women), 1 part-time/adjunct (0 women). *Students:* 84 full-time (20 women), 35 part-time (20 women); includes 11 minority (2 Black or African American, non-Hispanic/Latino; 1 Asian, non-Hispanic/Latino; 5 Hispanic/Latino; 1 Native Hawaiian or other Pacific Islander, non-Hispanic/Latino; 2 Two or more races, non-Hispanic/Latino), 23 international. Average age 30. 203 applicants, 20% accepted, 30 enrolled. In 2010, 11 master's, 10 doctorates awarded. *Degree requirements:* For master's, thesis or alternative, written or oral exam; for doctorate, comprehensive exam, thesis/dissertation, written and oral exams. *Entrance requirements:* For master's and doctorate, GRE MATH SUBJECT EXAM, minimum undergraduate GPA of 3.0. Additional exam requirements/recommendations for international students: Required—TOEFL (minimum score 500 paper-based; 173 computer-based; 61 iBT). *Application deadline:* For fall admission, 1/15 for domestic and international students; for spring admission, 11/1 for domestic and international students. Application fee: $55 ($65 for international students). Electronic applications accepted. *Expenses:* Tuition, area resident: Part-time $179.19 per credit hour. Tuition, state resident: full-time $4384. Tuition, nonresident: full-time $16,684; part-time $630.67 per credit hour. Required fees: $350 per semester. Tuition and fees vary according to course load, degree level and program. *Financial support:* In 2010–11, 71 students received support, including 19 research assistantships with full tuition reimbursements available (averaging $15,800 per year), 52 teaching assistantships with full tuition reimbursements available (averaging $15,300 per year); fellowships also available. Financial award application deadline: 1/15. *Faculty research:* Algebraic geometry; geometry and topology materials and microstructure; mathematical biology; probability and statistics. Total annual research expenditures: $3.2 million. *Unit head:* Dr. Aaron Bertram, Chairman, 801-581-6851, Fax: 801-581-4148, E-mail: bertram@math.utah.edu. *Application contact:* Dr. Andrejs Treibergs, Graduate Advisor, 801-581-8350, Fax: 801-581-4148, E-mail: treiberg@math.utah.edu.

University of Utah, Graduate School, Interdepartmental Program in Statistics, Salt Lake City, UT 84112-1107. Offers biostatistics (M Stat); econometrics (M Stat); educational psychology (M Stat); mathematics (M Stat); sociology (M Stat); statistics (M Stat). Part-time programs available. *Students:* 28 full-time (11 women), 17 part-time (9 women); includes 2 Black or African American, non-Hispanic/Latino; 2 Asian, non-Hispanic/Latino; 2 Hispanic/Latino, 10 international. Average age 30. 59 applicants, 44% accepted, 12 enrolled. In 2010, 15 master's awarded. *Degree requirements:* For master's, comprehensive exam, projects. *Entrance requirements:* For master's, GRE General Test (sociology and educational psychology), minimum GPA of 3.0; course work in calculus, matrix theory, statistics. Additional exam requirements/recommendations for international students: Required—TOEFL (minimum score 500 paper-based; 173 computer-based). *Application deadline:* For fall admission, 7/1 for domestic students, 4/1 for international students. Applications are processed on a rolling basis. Application fee: $55 ($65 for international students). *Expenses:* Tuition, area resident: Part-time $179.19 per credit hour. Tuition, state resident: full-time $4384. Tuition, nonresident: full-time $16,684; part-time $630.67 per credit hour. Required fees: $350 per semester. Tuition and fees vary according to course load, degree level and program. *Financial support:* Career-related internships or fieldwork available. *Faculty research:* Biostatistics, management, economics, educational psychology, mathematics. *Unit head:* Tariq Mughal, Chair, University Statistics Committee, 801-585-9547, E-mail: tariaq.mughal@business.utah.edu. *Application contact:* Laura Egbert, MSTAT Program Coordinator, 801-585-6853, E-mail: laura.demattia@utah.edu.

University of Vermont, Graduate College, College of Engineering and Mathematics, Department of Mathematics and Statistics, Program in Mathematics, Burlington, VT 05405. Offers mathematics (MS, PhD); mathematics education (MST). *Students:* 23 (6 women), 2 international. 46 applicants, 57% accepted, 11 enrolled. In 2010, 4 master's, 4 doctorates awarded. *Degree requirements:* For doctorate, thesis/dissertation. *Entrance requirements:* For master's and doctorate, GRE General Test. Additional exam requirements/recommendations for international students: Required—TOEFL (minimum score 550 paper-based; 213 computer-based; 80 iBT). *Application deadline:* For fall admission, 4/1 priority date for domestic students. Applications are processed on a rolling basis. Application fee: $40. Electronic applications accepted. *Expenses:* Tuition, state resident: part-time $537 per credit hour. Tuition, nonresident: part-time $1355 per credit hour. *Financial support:* Fellowships, research assistantships, teaching assistantships available. Financial award application deadline: 3/1. *Unit head:* Dr. M. Wilson, Coordinator, 802-656-2940. *Application contact:* Dr. M. Wilson, Coordinator, 802-656-2940.

University of Victoria, Faculty of Graduate Studies, Faculty of Science, Department of Mathematics and Statistics, Victoria, BC V8W 2Y2, Canada. Offers M Sc, MA, PhD. Part-time programs available. *Degree requirements:* For master's, thesis; for doctorate, one foreign language, thesis/dissertation, 3 qualifying exams, candidacy exam. *Entrance requirements:* Additional exam requirements/recommendations for international students: Required—TOEFL (minimum score 575 paper-based; 233 computer-based), IELTS (minimum score 7). Electronic applications accepted. *Faculty research:* Functional analysis and operator theory, applied ordinary and partial differential equations, discrete mathematics and graph theory.

University of Virginia, College and Graduate School of Arts and Sciences, Department of Mathematics, Charlottesville, VA 22903. Offers math education (MA); mathematics (MA, MS, PhD). *Faculty:* 25 full-time (5 women), 1 (woman) part-time/adjunct. *Students:* 50 full-time (13 women); includes 2 Asian, non-Hispanic/Latino; 1 Hispanic/Latino, 10 international. Average age 26. 101 applicants, 12% accepted, 6 enrolled. In 2010, 8 master's, 5 doctorates awarded. *Degree requirements:* For master's, one foreign language, comprehensive exam, thesis optional; for doctorate, one foreign language, comprehensive exam, thesis/dissertation. *Entrance requirements:* For master's and doctorate, GRE General Test, GRE Subject Test, 2-3 letters of recommendation. Additional exam requirements/recommendations for international students: Required—TOEFL (minimum score 600 paper-based; 250 computer-based; 90 iBT), IELTS. *Application deadline:* For fall admission, 1/15 for domestic and international students. Applications are processed on a rolling basis. Application fee: $60. Electronic applications accepted. *Financial support:* Fellowships, teaching assistantships, unspecified assistantships available. Financial award application deadline: 1/15; financial award applicants required to submit

FAFSA. *Unit head:* Brian Parshall, Chair, 434-924-4919, Fax: 434-982-3084, E-mail: math-help@virginia.edu. *Application contact:* Brian Parshall, Chair, 434-924-4919, Fax: 434-982-3084, E-mail: math-help@virginia.edu.

University of Washington, Graduate School, College of Arts and Sciences, Department of Mathematics, Seattle, WA 98195. Offers mathematics (MA, MS, PhD); numerical analysis (MS); optimization (MS). Part-time programs available. Terminal master's awarded for partial completion of doctoral program. *Degree requirements:* For master's, thesis optional; for doctorate, 2 foreign languages, thesis/dissertation. *Entrance requirements:* For master's, GRE, minimum GPA of 3.0; for doctorate, GRE General Test, GRE Subject Test (mathematics), minimum GPA of 3.0. Additional exam requirements/recommendations for international students: Required—TOEFL. Electronic applications accepted. *Faculty research:* Algebra, analysis, probability, combinatorics and geometry.

University of Washington, Graduate School, Interdisciplinary Graduate Program in Quantitative Ecology and Resource Management, Seattle, WA 98195. Offers MS, PhD. *Degree requirements:* For master's, thesis; for doctorate, thesis/dissertation. *Entrance requirements:* For master's and doctorate, GRE General Test, minimum GPA of 3.0. Additional exam requirements/recommendations for international students: Required—TOEFL. Electronic applications accepted. *Faculty research:* Population dynamics, statistical analysis, ecological modeling and systems analysis of aquatic and terrestrial ecosystems.

University of Waterloo, Graduate Studies, Faculty of Mathematics, Department of Combinatorics and Optimization, Waterloo, ON N2L 3G1, Canada. Offers M Math, PhD. *Degree requirements:* For master's, research paper or thesis; for doctorate, comprehensive exam, thesis/dissertation. *Entrance requirements:* For master's, GRE General Test, honors degree in field, minimum B+ average; for doctorate, GRE General Test, master's degree, minimum A average. Additional exam requirements/recommendations for international students: Required—TOEFL, TWE. Electronic applications accepted. *Faculty research:* Algebraic and enumerative combinatorics, continuous optimization, cryptography, discrete optimization and graph theory.

University of Waterloo, Graduate Studies, Faculty of Mathematics, Department of Pure Mathematics, Waterloo, ON N2L 3G1, Canada. Offers M Math, PhD. Part-time programs available. Terminal master's awarded for partial completion of doctoral program. *Degree requirements:* For master's, thesis optional; for doctorate, comprehensive exam, thesis/dissertation. *Entrance requirements:* For master's, honors degree in field, minimum B+ average; for doctorate, master's degree, minimum B+ average. Additional exam requirements/recommendations for international students: Required—TOEFL (minimum score 580 paper-based; 237 computer-based; 92 iBT), TWE (minimum score 4). Electronic applications accepted. *Faculty research:* Algebra, algebraic and differential geometry, functional and harmonic analysis, logic and universal algebra, number theory.

The University of Western Ontario, Faculty of Graduate Studies, Physical Sciences Division, Department of Mathematics, London, ON N6A 5B8, Canada. Offers M Sc, PhD. Terminal master's awarded for partial completion of doctoral program. *Degree requirements:* For master's, thesis or alternative; for doctorate, one foreign language, comprehensive exam, thesis/dissertation, qualifying exam. *Entrance requirements:* For master's, minimum B average, honors degree; for doctorate, master's degree. Additional exam requirements/recommendations for international students: Required—TOEFL (minimum score 550 paper-based; 213 computer-based). *Faculty research:* Algebra and number theory, analysis, geometry and topology.

University of West Florida, College of Arts and Sciences: Sciences, Department of Mathematics and Statistics, Pensacola, FL 32514-5750. Offers applied statistics (MS); mathematical sciences (MS). Part-time and evening/weekend programs available. *Faculty:* 8 full-time (1 woman). *Students:* 17 full-time (6 women), 47 part-time (29 women); includes 5 Black or African American, non-Hispanic/Latino; 2 Asian, non-Hispanic/Latino; 3 Hispanic/Latino; 1 Two or more races, non-Hispanic/Latino, 1 international. Average age 33. 41 applicants, 95% accepted, 32 enrolled. In 2010, 13 master's awarded. *Degree requirements:* For master's, thesis optional. *Entrance requirements:* For master's, GRE General Test, minimum GPA of 3.0. Additional exam requirements/recommendations for international students: Required—TOEFL (minimum score 550 paper-based; 213 computer-based). *Application deadline:* For fall admission, 6/1 for domestic students, 5/15 for international students; for spring admission, 10/1 for domestic and international students. Applications are processed on a rolling basis. Application fee: $30. *Expenses:* Tuition, state resident: full-time $4982; part-time $208 per credit hour. Tuition, nonresident: full-time $20,059; part-time $836 per credit hour. Required fees: $1365; $57 per credit hour. *Financial support:* In 2010–11, 25 fellowships with partial tuition reimbursements (averaging $421 per year), 4 research assistantships with partial tuition reimbursements (averaging $3,280 per year), 7 teaching assistantships with partial tuition reimbursements (averaging $5,141 per year) were awarded; unspecified assistantships also available. Financial award application deadline: 4/15; financial award applicants required to submit FAFSA. *Unit head:* Dr. Kuiyuan Li, Chairperson, 850-474-2287, E-mail: mathstat@uwf.edu. *Application contact:* Terry McCray, Assistant Director of Graduate Admissions, 850-473-7718, Fax: 850-473-7714, E-mail: gradadmissions@uwf.edu.

University of West Georgia, College of Arts and Sciences, Department of Mathematics, Carrollton, GA 30118. Offers mathematics (MSM); teaching and applied mathematics (MS). *Faculty:* 13 full-time (2 women). *Students:* 5 part-time (2 women). Average age 26. 8 applicants, 50% accepted, 0 enrolled. *Degree requirements:* For master's, comprehensive exam, thesis optional, 36 credit hours. *Entrance requirements:* For master's, GRE. Additional exam requirements/recommendations for international students: Required—TOEFL (minimum score 523 paper-based; 193 computer-based; 69 iBT). *Application deadline:* For fall admission, 7/17 for domestic students, 6/6 for international students; for spring admission, 11/20 for domestic students, 10/3 for international students. Applications are processed on a rolling basis. Application fee: $30. Electronic applications accepted. *Expenses:* Tuition, state resident: full-time $4130; part-time $173 per semester hour. Tuition, nonresident: full-time $16,524; part-time $689 per semester hour. Required fees: $1586; $44.01 per semester hour. $397 per semester. Tuition and fees vary according to program. *Financial support:* In 2010–11, 3 students received support, including 3 teaching assistantships (averaging $6,800 per year); unspecified assistantships also available. *Unit head:* Dr. Minh Nguyen, Interim Chair, 678-839-6489, E-mail: vnguyen@westga.edu. *Application contact:* Dr. Charles W. Clark, Dean, 678-839-6508, E-mail: cclark@westga.edu.

University of Windsor, Faculty of Graduate Studies, Faculty of Science, Department of Mathematics and Statistics, Windsor, ON N9B 3P4, Canada. Offers mathematics (M Sc); statistics (M Sc, PhD). *Degree requirements:* For master's, thesis or alternative; for doctorate, comprehensive exam, thesis/dissertation. *Entrance requirements:* For master's, minimum B average; for doctorate, minimum A average. Additional exam requirements/recommendations for international students: Required—TOEFL (minimum score 560 paper-based; 220 computer-based). Electronic applications accepted. *Faculty research:* Applied mathematics, operational research, fluid dynamics.

University of Wisconsin–Madison, Graduate School, College of Letters and Science, Department of Mathematics, Madison, WI 53706. Offers PhD. *Faculty:* 47 full-time (3 women). *Students:* 114 full-time (30 women); includes 1 Black or African American, non-Hispanic/Latino; 1 American Indian or Alaska Native, non-Hispanic/Latino; 47 Asian, non-Hispanic/Latino; 2 Hispanic/Latino. Average age 24. 472 applicants, 15% accepted, 19 enrolled. In 2010, 21 doctorates awarded. *Degree requirements:* For doctorate, comprehensive exam, thesis/dissertation, classes in a minor field; minimum GPA of 3.3. *Entrance requirements:* For doctorate, GRE General Test, GRE Subject Test (math). Additional exam requirements/recommendations for international students: Required—TOEFL (minimum score 580 paper-based; 237 computer-based; 92 iBT), IELTS. *Application deadline:* For fall admission, 12/31 priority date for domestic and international students. Application fee: $56. Electronic applications accepted. *Expenses:* Tuition, state resident: full-time $9887.36; part-time $617.96 per credit. Tuition, nonresident: full-time $24,054; part-time $1503.40 per credit. Required fees: $67.63 per credit. Tuition and fees vary according to reciprocity agreements. *Financial support:* In 2010–11, 20 research assistantships with full tuition reimbursements (averaging $16,000 per year), 120 teaching assistantships with full tuition reimbursements (averaging $14,088 per year) were awarded; institutionally sponsored loans, scholarships/grants, and unspecified assistantships also available. Financial award application deadline: 12/31. *Faculty research:* Analysis, applied/computational mathematics, geometry/topology, logic, algebra/number theory, probability. Total annual research expenditures: $2.3 million. *Unit head:* Shi Jin, Chair, 608-263-3051, Fax: 608-263-8891, E-mail: jin@math.wisc.edu. *Application contact:* Mary Rice, Graduate Program Administrator, 608-263-8884, Fax: 608-263-8891, E-mail: grad_program@math.wisc.edu.

University of Wisconsin–Milwaukee, Graduate School, College of Letters and Sciences, Department of Mathematical Sciences, Milwaukee, WI 53201-0413. Offers mathematics (MS, PhD). *Faculty:* 36 full-time (4 women). *Students:* 71 full-time (19 women), 17 part-time (9 women); includes 2 Black or African American, non-Hispanic/Latino; 1 American Indian or Alaska Native, non-Hispanic/Latino; 3 Asian, non-Hispanic/Latino; 1 Hispanic/Latino, 22 international. Average age 31. 80 applicants, 58% accepted, 26 enrolled. In 2010, 25 master's, 5 doctorates awarded. *Degree requirements:* For master's, comprehensive exam, thesis optional; for doctorate, 2 foreign languages, thesis/dissertation. *Entrance requirements:* Additional exam requirements/recommendations for international students: Required—TOEFL (minimum score 550 paper-based; 79 iBT), IELTS (minimum score 6.5). *Application deadline:* For fall admission, 1/1 priority date for domestic students; for spring admission, 9/1 for domestic students. Applications are processed on a rolling basis. Application fee: $56 ($96 for international students). Electronic applications accepted. *Financial support:* In 2010–11, 23 fellowships, 9 research assistantships, 56 teaching assistantships were awarded; career-related internships or fieldwork, health care benefits, and unspecified assistantships also available. Support available to part-time students. Financial award application deadline: 4/15; financial award applicants required to submit FAFSA. *Faculty research:* Algebra, applied mathematics, atmospheric science, probability and statistics, topology. Total annual research expenditures: $948,956. *Unit head:* Craig Guilbault, Representative, 414-229-5110, Fax: 414-229-4907, E-mail: craigg@uwm.edu. *Application contact:* General Information Contact, 414-229-4982, Fax: 414-229-6967, E-mail: gradschool@uwm.edu.

University of Wyoming, College of Arts and Sciences, Department of Mathematics, Laramie, WY 82071. Offers mathematics (MA, MAT, MS, MST, PhD); mathematics/computer science (PhD). Part-time programs available. Terminal master's awarded for partial completion of doctoral program. *Degree requirements:* For master's, comprehensive exam, thesis, qualifying exam; for doctorate, comprehensive exam, thesis/dissertation, preliminary exam. *Entrance requirements:* For master's and doctorate, GRE General Test, minimum GPA of 3.0. Additional exam requirements/recommendations for international students: Required—TOEFL (minimum score 540 paper-based; 76 iBT). *Faculty research:* Numerical analysis, classical analysis, mathematical modeling, algebraic combinations.

Utah State University, School of Graduate Studies, College of Science, Department of Mathematics and Statistics, Logan, UT 84322. Offers industrial mathematics (MS); mathematical sciences (PhD); mathematics (M Math, MS); statistics (MS). Part-time programs available. Terminal master's awarded for partial completion of doctoral program. *Degree requirements:* For master's, thesis optional, qualifying exam; for doctorate, one foreign language, comprehensive exam, thesis/dissertation. *Entrance requirements:* For master's and doctorate, GRE General Test, minimum GPA of 3.0. Additional exam requirements/recommendations for international students: Required—TOEFL. *Faculty research:* Differential equations, computational mathematics, dynamical systems, probability and statistics, pure mathematics.

Vanderbilt University, Graduate School, Department of Mathematics, Nashville, TN 37240-1001. Offers MA, MAT, MS, PhD. *Faculty:* 33 full-time (3 women). *Students:* 33 full-time (10 women), 2 part-time (1 woman); includes 1 Hispanic/Latino; 1 Two or more races, non-Hispanic/Latino. Average age 27. 144 applicants, 10% accepted, 5 enrolled. In 2010, 5 master's, 2 doctorates awarded. *Degree requirements:* For master's, one foreign language, thesis or alternative; for doctorate, one foreign language, comprehensive exam, thesis/dissertation. *Entrance requirements:* For master's and doctorate, GRE General Test, GRE Subject Test. Additional exam requirements/recommendations for international students: Required—TOEFL (minimum score 570 paper-based; 230 computer-based; 88 iBT). *Application deadline:* For fall admission, 1/15 for domestic and international students. Application fee: $0. Electronic applications accepted. *Financial support:* Fellowships with full and partial tuition reimbursements, research assistantships with full tuition reimbursements, teaching assistantships with full tuition reimbursements, Federal Work-Study, institutionally sponsored loans, scholarships/grants, and health care benefits available. Financial award application deadline: 1/15; financial award applicants required to submit CSS PROFILE or FAFSA. *Faculty research:* Algebra, topology, applied mathematics, graph theory, analytical mathematics. *Unit head:* Dietmar Bisch, PhD, Chair, 615-322-1999, Fax: 615-343-0215, E-mail: dietmar.bisch@vanderbilt.edu. *Application contact:* Mike Neamtu, PhD, Director of Graduate Studies, 615-322-6655, Fax: 315-343-0215, E-mail: marian.neamtu@vanderbilt.edu.

Villanova University, Graduate School of Liberal Arts and Sciences, Department of Mathematical Sciences, Program in Mathematical Sciences, Villanova, PA 19085-1699. Offers MA. Part-time and evening/weekend programs available. *Students:* 18 full-time (6 women), 13 part-time (3 women). Average age 31. 16 applicants, 100% accepted, 6 enrolled. In 2010, 17 master's awarded. *Degree requirements:* For master's, comprehensive exam. *Entrance requirements:* For master's, GRE, minimum GPA of 3.0. Additional exam requirements/recommendations for international students: Required—TOEFL. *Application deadline:* For fall admission, 3/1 priority date for domestic and international students; for spring admission, 11/15 priority date for domestic and international students. Applications are processed on a rolling basis. Application fee: $50. Electronic applications accepted. *Expenses:* Tuition: Part-time $700 per credit. Part-time tuition and fees vary according to degree level and program. *Financial support:* Research assistantships, Federal Work-Study available. Financial award applicants required to submit FAFSA. *Unit head:* Dr. Douglas Norton, Chair, 610-519-4850. *Application contact:* Dr. Adele Lindenmeyr, Dean, Graduate School of Liberal Arts and Sciences, 610-519-7093, Fax: 610-519-7096.

Virginia Commonwealth University, Graduate School, College of Humanities and Sciences, Department of Mathematics and Applied Mathematics, Richmond, VA 23284-9005. Offers applied mathematics (MS); mathematics (MS); operations research (MS); statistical sciences and operations research (MS). *Students:* 21 full-time (11 women), 23 part-time (9 women); includes 6 minority (3 Black or African American, non-Hispanic/Latino; 2 Asian, non-Hispanic/Latino; 1 Two or more races, non-Hispanic/Latino), 6 international. 29 applicants, 72% accepted, 17 enrolled. In 2010, 14 master's awarded. *Degree requirements:* For master's, thesis optional. *Entrance requirements:* For master's, GRE General Test, GRE Subject Test, 30 undergraduate semester credits in the mathematical sciences or closely-related fields. Additional exam requirements/recommendations for international students: Required—TOEFL (minimum score 600 paper-based; 250 computer-based; 100 iBT); Recommended—IELTS (minimum score 6.5). *Application deadline:* For fall admission, 3/1 for domestic students; for spring admission, 10/1 for domestic students. Applications are processed on a rolling basis. Application fee: $50. Electronic applications accepted. *Expenses:* Tuition, state resident: full-time $4308; part-time $479 per credit hour. Tuition, nonresident: full-time $8942; part-time $994 per credit hour. Required fees: $2000; $85 per credit hour. Tuition and fees vary according to course level,

Mathematics

Virginia Commonwealth University (continued)

course load, degree level, campus/location and program. *Financial support:* Fellowships, research assistantships, teaching assistantships, Federal Work-Study and institutionally sponsored loans available. Support available to part-time students. Financial award applicants required to submit FAFSA. *Faculty research:* Mathematics, applied mathematics. *Unit head:* Dr. Andrew M. Lewis, Chair, 804-828-1301 Ext. 128, Fax: 804-828-8785, E-mail: amlewis@vcu.edu. *Application contact:* Dr. John F. Berglund, Graduate Program Director, 804-828-1301, E-mail: jfberglu@vcu.edu.

Virginia Polytechnic Institute and State University, Graduate School, College of Science, Department of Mathematics, Blacksburg, VA 24061. Offers MS, PhD. *Faculty:* 61 full-time (18 women), 1 (woman) part-time/adjunct. *Students:* 59 full-time (14 women), 4 part-time (1 woman); includes 1 Black or African American, non-Hispanic/Latino; 2 Asian, non-Hispanic/Latino; 1 Hispanic/Latino, 30 international. Average age 29. 121 applicants, 21% accepted, 13 enrolled. In 2010, 17 master's, 8 doctorates awarded. *Degree requirements:* For master's, comprehensive exam (for some programs), thesis (for some programs); for doctorate, comprehensive exam (for some programs), thesis/dissertation (for some programs). *Entrance requirements:* For master's and doctorate, GRE. Additional exam requirements/recommendations for international students: Required—TOEFL (minimum score 550 paper-based; 213 computer-based). *Application deadline:* For fall admission, 7/1 for domestic and international students; for spring admission, 12/1 for domestic and international students. Applications are processed on a rolling basis. Application fee: $65. Electronic applications accepted. *Expenses:* Tuition, area resident: Full-time $9399; part-time $488 per credit hour. Tuition, state resident: full-time $9399; part-time $488 per credit hour. Tuition, nonresident: full-time $17,854; part-time $957.75 per credit hour. International tuition: $17,854 full-time. Required fees: $1534. Full-time tuition and fees vary according to program. *Financial support:* In 2010–11, 2 fellowships with full tuition reimbursements (averaging $2,483 per year), 6 research assistantships with full tuition reimbursements (averaging $16,903 per year), 37 teaching assistantships with full tuition reimbursements (averaging $16,562 per year) were awarded; career-related internships or fieldwork, Federal Work-Study, scholarships/grants, health care benefits, and unspecified assistantships also available. Financial award application deadline: 1/15. *Faculty research:* Differential equations, operator theory, numerical analysis, algebra, control theory. Total annual research expenditures: $1.5 million. *Unit head:* Dr. Peter E. Haskell, UNIT HEAD, 540-231-6536, Fax: 540-231-5960, E-mail: phaskell@vt.edu. *Application contact:* Jeff Borggaard, Contact, 540-231-7667, Fax: 540-231-5960, E-mail: jborggaard@vt.edu.

Virginia State University, School of Graduate Studies, Research, and Outreach, School of Engineering, Science and Technology, Department of Mathematics and Computer Science, Petersburg, VA 23806-0001. Offers computer science (MS); mathematics (MS); mathematics education (M Ed). *Degree requirements:* For master's, thesis (for some programs). *Expenses:* Tuition, state resident: full-time $5576; part-time $335 per credit hour. Tuition, nonresident: full-time $13,402; part-time $670 per credit hour.

Wake Forest University, Graduate School of Arts and Sciences, Department of Mathematics, Winston-Salem, NC 27109. Offers MA. Part-time programs available. *Degree requirements:* For master's, one foreign language, thesis optional. *Entrance requirements:* For master's, GRE General Test. Additional exam requirements/recommendations for international students: Required—TOEFL (minimum score 213 computer-based; 79 iBT). Electronic applications accepted. *Faculty research:* Algebra, ring theory, topology, differential equations.

Washington State University, Graduate School, College of Sciences, Department of Mathematics, Pullman, WA 99164. Offers applied mathematics (MS, PhD); mathematics teaching (MS, PhD). Part-time programs available. *Faculty:* 26. *Students:* 33 full-time (11 women), 5 part-time (3 women); includes 1 Black or African American, non-Hispanic/Latino; 2 Asian, non-Hispanic/Latino, 10 international. Average age 29. 84 applicants, 29% accepted, 9 enrolled. In 2010, 7 master's, 1 doctorate awarded. *Degree requirements:* For master's, comprehensive exam (for some programs), thesis (for some programs), oral exam, project; for doctorate, 2 foreign languages, comprehensive exam, thesis/dissertation, oral exam, written exam. *Entrance requirements:* For master's and doctorate, minimum GPA of 3.0, 3 letters of recommendation. Additional exam requirements/recommendations for international students: Required—TOEFL (minimum score 600 paper-based; 250 computer-based), IELTS. *Application deadline:* For fall admission, 1/10 for domestic and international students; for spring admission, 7/1 for domestic and international students. Applications are processed on a rolling basis. Application fee: $50. Electronic applications accepted. *Expenses:* Tuition, state resident: full-time $8552; part-time $443 per credit. Tuition, nonresident: full-time $21,650; part-time $1083 per credit. Required fees: $846. *Financial support:* In 2010–11, 33 students received support, including 2 fellowships with tuition reimbursements available (averaging $2,500 per year), 3 research assistantships with full and partial tuition reimbursements available (averaging $14,634 per year), 27 teaching assistantships with full and partial tuition reimbursements available (averaging $13,383 per year); career-related internships or fieldwork, Federal Work-Study, institutionally sponsored loans, health care benefits, and tuition waivers (partial) also available. Financial award application deadline: 2/15; financial award applicants required to submit FAFSA. *Faculty research:* Computational mathematics, operations research, modeling in the natural sciences, applied statistics. *Unit head:* Dr. K.A. Ariyawansa, Chair, 509-335-4918, Fax: 509-335-1188, E-mail: ari@wsu.edu. *Application contact:* Graduate School Admissions, 800-GRADWSU, Fax: 509-335-1949, E-mail: gradsch@wsu.edu.

Washington University in St. Louis, Graduate School of Arts and Sciences, Department of Mathematics, St. Louis, MO 63130-4899. Offers mathematics (MA, PhD); statistics (MA). Terminal master's awarded for partial completion of doctoral program. *Degree requirements:* For master's, thesis or alternative; for doctorate, thesis/dissertation. *Entrance requirements:* For master's and doctorate, GRE General Test. Electronic applications accepted.

Washington University in St. Louis, School of Engineering and Applied Science, Department of Electrical and Systems Engineering, St. Louis, MO 63130-4899. Offers electrical engineering (MS, D Sc, PhD); systems science and mathematics (MS, D Sc, PhD). Part-time programs available. *Faculty:* 16 full-time (2 women), 5 part-time/adjunct (0 women). *Students:* 63 full-time (12 women), 18 part-time (1 woman); includes 1 Black or African American, non-Hispanic/Latino; 15 Asian, non-Hispanic/Latino; 2 Hispanic/Latino, 45 international. Average age 23. 299 applicants, 18% accepted, 18 enrolled. In 2010, 21 master's, 6 doctorates awarded. Terminal master's awarded for partial completion of doctoral program. *Degree requirements:* For master's, thesis or alternative; for doctorate, comprehensive exam, thesis/dissertation. *Entrance requirements:* For master's, minimum GPA of 3.0 in the last 2 years of undergraduate course work; for doctorate, GRE. Additional exam requirements/recommendations for international students: Required—TOEFL (minimum score 550 paper-based; 213 computer-based; 80 iBT). *Application deadline:* For fall admission, 1/15 for domestic and international students. Applications are processed on a rolling basis. Application fee: $60. Electronic applications accepted. *Financial support:* In 2010–11, 12 fellowships with full tuition reimbursements (averaging $20,000 per year), 32 research assistantships with full tuition reimbursements (averaging $26,950 per year) were awarded; teaching assistantships with full tuition reimbursements, career-related internships or fieldwork, Federal Work-Study, institutionally sponsored loans, scholarships/grants, and unspecified assistantships also available. Financial award application deadline: 1/15; financial award applicants required to submit FAFSA. *Faculty research:* Applied physics and electronics, signal and image processing, systems analysis, biomedicine, and energy. Total annual research expenditures: $2 million. *Unit head:* Dr. Arye Nehorai, Chair, 314-935-5565, Fax: 314-935-7500, E-mail: nehorai@ese.wustl.edu. *Application contact:* Shauna Dollison, Director of Graduate Programs, 314-935-4830, Fax: 314-935-7500, E-mail: sdollison@ese.wustl.edu.

Wayne State University, College of Liberal Arts and Sciences, Department of Mathematics, Program in Mathematics, Detroit, MI 48202. Offers MA, MS, PhD. *Students:* 28 full-time (5 women), 21 part-time (7 women); includes 2 Black or African American, non-Hispanic/Latino, 24 international. Average age 29. 62 applicants, 45% accepted, 14 enrolled. In 2010, 8 master's, 2 doctorates awarded. *Degree requirements:* For master's, thesis or alternative; for doctorate, 2 foreign languages, thesis/dissertation. *Entrance requirements:* For master's, successful completion of 12 semester credits in mathematics beyond sophomore calculus; for doctorate, master's degree in mathematics or equivalent level of advancement. Additional exam requirements/recommendations for international students: Required—TOEFL (minimum score 550 paper-based; 213 computer-based); Recommended—TWE (minimum score 6). *Application deadline:* For fall admission, 7/1 for domestic students, 6/1 for international students; for winter admission, 10/1 for international students; for spring admission, 2/1 for international students. Applications are processed on a rolling basis. Application fee: $30 ($50 for international students). Electronic applications accepted. *Expenses:* Tuition, state resident: full-time $7662; part-time $478.85 per credit hour. Tuition, nonresident: full-time $16,920; part-time $1057.55 per credit hour. Required fees: $571.20; $35.70 per credit hour. $188.05 per semester. Tuition and fees vary according to course load and program. *Unit head:* Lowell Hansen, Chair, 313-577-7596, E-mail: lowell@math.wayne.edu. *Application contact:* Bert Schreiber, Professor, 313-577-8838, E-mail: bschreiber@wayne.edu.

Wesleyan University, Graduate Programs, Department of Mathematics and Computer Science, Middletown, CT 06459. Offers MA, PhD. *Faculty:* 16 full-time (4 women). *Students:* 21 full-time (9 women); includes 1 Asian, non-Hispanic/Latino; 3 Hispanic/Latino, 4 international. Average age 28. 44 applicants, 9% accepted, 4 enrolled. In 2010, 2 master's, 1 doctorate awarded. Terminal master's awarded for partial completion of doctoral program. *Degree requirements:* For master's, one foreign language, thesis; for doctorate, 2 foreign languages, thesis/dissertation. *Entrance requirements:* For master's, GRE General Test, GRE Subject Test; for doctorate, GRE Subject Test. Additional exam requirements/recommendations for international students: Required—TOEFL. *Application deadline:* For fall admission, 2/15 for domestic and international students. Applications are processed on a rolling basis. Application fee: $0. Electronic applications accepted. *Expenses:* Tuition: Full-time $43,404. Required fees: $830. *Financial support:* In 2010–11, 18 teaching assistantships with full tuition reimbursements were awarded; tuition waivers (full and partial) also available. Financial award application deadline: 4/15; financial award applicants required to submit FAFSA. *Faculty research:* Topology, analysis. *Unit head:* Dr. Mark Hovey, Chair, 860-685-2169, E-mail: mhovey@wesleyan.edu. *Application contact:* Caryn Canalia, Administrative Assistant, 860-685-2182, Fax: 860-685-2571, E-mail: ccanalia@wesleyan.edu.

See Display on next page and Close-Up on page 313.

West Chester University of Pennsylvania, Office of Graduate Studies, College of Arts and Sciences, Department of Mathematics, West Chester, PA 19383. Offers applied statistics (MS, Certificate); mathematics (MA, Teaching Certificate). Part-time and evening/weekend programs available. *Students:* 17 full-time (7 women), 61 part-time (25 women); includes 22 minority (10 Black or African American, non-Hispanic/Latino; 10 Asian, non-Hispanic/Latino; 2 Hispanic/Latino), 9 international. Average age 31. 50 applicants, 80% accepted, 15 enrolled. In 2010, 31 master's, 1 other advanced degree awarded. *Degree requirements:* For master's, thesis optional. *Entrance requirements:* For master's, GMAT, GRE General Test, or MAT are required for Mathematics MA, optional for Applied Statistics Program, interview; for other advanced degree, GMAT, GRE General Test, or MAT are required for Mathematics Teaching Certificate, optional for Applied Statistics Program. Additional exam requirements/recommendations for international students: Required—TOEFL (minimum score 550 paper-based; 213 computer-based; 80 iBT). *Application deadline:* For fall admission, 4/15 priority date for domestic students, 3/15 for international students; for spring admission, 10/15 for domestic students, 9/1 for international students. Applications are processed on a rolling basis. Application fee: $35. Electronic applications accepted. *Expenses:* Tuition, state resident: full-time $6966; part-time $387 per credit. Tuition, nonresident: full-time $11,146; part-time $619 per credit. Required fees: $1614.40; $133.24 per credit. Part-time tuition and fees vary according to campus/location. *Financial support:* Unspecified assistantships available. Support available to part-time students. Financial award application deadline: 2/15; financial award applicants required to submit FAFSA. *Faculty research:* Teachers teaching with technology in service training program, biostatistics, hierarchial linear models, clustered bionary outcome date. *Unit head:* Dr. Kathleen Jackson, Chair, 610-436-2537, E-mail: kjackson@wcupa.edu. *Application contact:* Dr. Gail Gallitano, Graduate Coordinator for Mathematics, 610-436-2452, E-mail: ggallitano@wcupa.edu.

Western Carolina University, Graduate School, College of Arts and Sciences, Department of Mathematics and Computer Science, Cullowhee, NC 28723. Offers applied mathematics (MS). Part-time and evening/weekend programs available. *Degree requirements:* For master's, thesis or alternative. *Entrance requirements:* For master's, GRE General Test, appropriate undergraduate degree, 3 letters of recommendation. Additional exam requirements/recommendations for international students: Required—TOEFL (minimum score 550 paper-based; 270 computer-based; 79 iBT).

Western Connecticut State University, Division of Graduate Studies and External Programs, School of Arts and Sciences, Department of Mathematics, Danbury, CT 06810-6885. Offers mathematics (MA); theoretical mathematics (MA). Part-time programs available. *Students:* 1 full-time (0 women), 8 part-time (2 women). Average age 32. In 2010, 3 master's awarded. *Degree requirements:* For master's, thesis or research project, completion of program in 6 years. *Entrance requirements:* For master's, minimum GPA of 2.5. Additional exam requirements/recommendations for international students: Recommended—TOEFL (minimum score 550 paper-based; 213 computer-based; 79 iBT), IELTS (minimum score 6). *Application deadline:* For fall admission, 8/5 priority date for domestic students; for spring admission, 1/5 priority date for domestic students. Applications are processed on a rolling basis. Application fee: $50. *Expenses:* Tuition, state resident: full-time $5012; part-time $417 per credit hour. Tuition, nonresident: full-time $13,962; part-time $423 per credit hour. Required fees: $3886. Full-time tuition and fees vary according to course load, degree level and program. *Financial support:* Application deadline: 5/1. *Unit head:* Dr. Sam Lightwood, Graduate Coordinator, 203-837-9369, Fax: 203-837-8525, E-mail: lightwoods@wcsu.edu. *Application contact:* Chris Shankle, Associate Director of Graduate Studies, 203-837-9005, Fax: 203-837-8326, E-mail: shanklec@wcsu.edu.

Western Illinois University, School of Graduate Studies, College of Arts and Sciences, Department of Mathematics, Macomb, IL 61455-1390. Offers applied math (Certificate); mathematics (MS). Part-time programs available. *Students:* 10 full-time (3 women), 2 part-time (both women), 4 international. Average age 30. 9 applicants, 67% accepted. In 2010, 8 master's, 3 other advanced degrees awarded. *Degree requirements:* For master's, thesis or alternative. *Entrance requirements:* Additional exam requirements/recommendations for international students: Required—TOEFL (minimum score 500 paper-based; 173 computer-based; 61 iBT). *Application deadline:* Applications are processed on a rolling basis. Application fee: $30. Electronic applications accepted. *Expenses:* Tuition, state resident: full-time $6370; part-time $265.40 per credit hour. Tuition, nonresident: full-time $12,740; part-time $530.80 per credit hour. Required fees: $75.67 per credit hour. *Financial support:* In 2010–11, 10 students received support, including 6 research assistantships with full tuition reimbursements available (averaging $7,280 per year), 4 teaching assistantships with full tuition reimbursements available (averaging $8,400 per year). Financial award applicants required to submit FAFSA. *Unit head:* Dr. Iraj Kalantari, Chairperson, 309-298-1054. *Application contact:* Evelyn Hoing, Assistant Director of Graduate Studies, 309-298-1806, Fax: 309-298-2345, E-mail: grad-office@wiu.edu.

Western Kentucky University, Graduate Studies, Ogden College of Science and Engineering, Department of Mathematics and Computer Science, Bowling Green, KY 42101. Offers

WESLEYAN UNIVERSITY
DEPARTMENT OF MATHEMATICS AND COMPUTER SCIENCE

- Graduate programs include a Ph. D. program in mathematics and M.A. programs in mathematics and in computer science.

- Research emphasis at Wesleyan is in pure mathematics and theoretical computer science.

- A distinctive feature of our department is the close interaction between the computer science faculty and the mathematics faculty, particularly those in logic and discrete mathematics.

For more information, contact,

Caryn Canalia, Administrative Assistant
Department of Mathematics and Computer Science
Wesleyan University
265 Church Street
Middletown, CT 06459
ccanalia@wesleyan.edu

http://www.math.wesleyan.edu/

computational mathematics (MS); computer science (MS); mathematics (MA, MS). *Degree requirements:* For master's, comprehensive exam, thesis optional, written exam. *Entrance requirements:* For master's, GRE General Test, minimum GPA of 2.75. Additional exam requirements/recommendations for international students: Required—TOEFL (minimum score 555 paper-based; 213 computer-based; 79 iBT). *Faculty research:* Differential equations numerical analysis, probability statistics, algebra, typology, knot theory.

Western Michigan University, Graduate College, College of Arts and Sciences, Department of Mathematics, Programs in Mathematics, Kalamazoo, MI 49008. Offers mathematics (MA, PhD); mathematics education (MA, PhD). *Degree requirements:* For master's, oral exams; for doctorate, one foreign language, thesis/dissertation, oral exams, 3 comprehensive exams, internship. *Entrance requirements:* For doctorate, GRE General Test.

Western Washington University, Graduate School, College of Sciences and Technology, Department of Mathematics, Bellingham, WA 98225-5996. Offers MS. Part-time programs available. *Degree requirements:* For master's, thesis (for some programs), project, qualifying examination. *Entrance requirements:* For master's, GRE General Test, minimum GPA of 3.0 in last 60 semester hours or last 90 quarter hours. Additional exam requirements/recommendations for international students: Required—TOEFL (minimum score 550 paper-based; 227 computer-based). Electronic applications accepted. *Faculty research:* Numerical analysis, combinatorics, harmonic analysis, inverse problems, reliability testing.

West Texas A&M University, College of Agriculture, Nursing, and Natural Sciences, Department of Mathematics, Physical Sciences and Engineering Technology, Program in Mathematics, Canyon, TX 79016-0001. Offers MS. Part-time programs available. *Degree requirements:* For master's, comprehensive exam, thesis optional. *Entrance requirements:* For master's, GRE General Test. Additional exam requirements/recommendations for international students: Required—TOEFL (minimum score 550 paper-based). Electronic applications accepted.

West Virginia University, Eberly College of Arts and Sciences, Department of Mathematics, Morgantown, WV 26506. Offers applied mathematics (MS, PhD); discrete mathematics (PhD); interdisciplinary mathematics (MS); mathematics for secondary education (MS); pure mathematics (MS). Part-time programs available. Terminal master's awarded for partial completion of doctoral program. *Degree requirements:* For master's, comprehensive exam (for some programs), thesis optional; for doctorate, one foreign language, comprehensive exam, thesis/dissertation. *Entrance requirements:* For master's, GRE Subject Test (recommended), minimum GPA of 2.5; for doctorate, GRE Subject Test (recommended), master's degree in mathematics. Additional exam requirements/recommendations for international students: Required—TOEFL (paper-based 550; computer-based 213) or IELTS (paper-based 6). *Faculty research:* Combinatorics and graph theory, differential equations, applied and computational mathematics.

Wichita State University, Graduate School, Fairmount College of Liberal Arts and Sciences, Department of Mathematics and Statistics, Wichita, KS 67260. Offers applied mathematics (PhD); mathematics (MS). Part-time programs available. *Unit head:* Dr. Buma Fridman, Chair, 316-978-3160, Fax: 316-978-3748, E-mail: buma.fridman@wichita.edu. *Application contact:* Dr. Kenneth Miller, Graduate Coordinator, 316-978-3160, Fax: 316-978-3748, E-mail: kenneth. miller@wichita.edu.

Wilfrid Laurier University, Faculty of Graduate and Postdoctoral Studies, Faculty of Science, Department of Mathematics, Waterloo, ON N2L 3C5, Canada. Offers mathematics for science and finance (M Sc). Part-time programs available. *Faculty:* 16 full-time (3 women), 2 part-time/

adjunct (0 women). *Students:* 11 full-time (6 women). 20 applicants, 65% accepted, 10 enrolled. In 2010, 11 master's awarded. *Degree requirements:* For master's, thesis optional. *Entrance requirements:* For master's, 4-year honors degree in mathematics, minimum B+ average. Additional exam requirements/recommendations for international students: Required—TOEFL (minimum score 89 iBT). *Application deadline:* For fall admission, 2/1 priority date for domestic and international students. Application fee: $100. Electronic applications accepted. Tuition and fees charges are reported in Canadian dollars. *Expenses:* Tuition, area resident: Full-time $15,300 Canadian dollars; part-time $1200 Canadian dollars per credit. International tuition: $21,300 Canadian dollars full-time. Required fees: $650 Canadian dollars; $100 Canadian dollars per credit. Tuition and fees vary according to course load, degree level, campus/location and program. *Financial support:* In 2010–11, 21 fellowships, 11 research assistantships, 21 teaching assistantships were awarded; career-related internships or fieldwork, scholarships/grants, health care benefits, and unspecified assistantships also available. *Faculty research:* Modeling, analysis, resolution, and generalization of financial and scientific problems. *Unit head:* Dr. Roman Makarov, Graduate Co-ordinator, 519-884-0710 Ext. 3017, Fax: 519-884-9738, E-mail: rmakarov@wlu.ca. *Application contact:* Rosemary Springett, Graduate Admissions and Records Officer, 519-884-0710 Ext. 3078, Fax: 519-884-1020, E-mail: gradstudies@wlu.ca.

Wilkes University, College of Graduate and Professional Studies, College of Science and Engineering, Department of Mathematics and Computer Science, Wilkes-Barre, PA 18766-0002. Offers mathematics (MS, MS Ed). Part-time programs available. *Students:* 1 full-time (0 women), 3 part-time (0 women). Average age 33. In 2010, 1 master's awarded. *Degree requirements:* For master's, thesis or alternative. *Entrance requirements:* For master's, GRE General Test. Additional exam requirements/recommendations for international students: Required—TOEFL (minimum score 550 paper-based; 213 computer-based; 79 iBT). *Application deadline:* Applications are processed on a rolling basis. Application fee: $45 ($65 for international students). Electronic applications accepted. Tuition and fees vary according to course level and program. *Financial support:* Federal Work-Study and unspecified assistantships available. Financial award application deadline: 3/1; financial award applicants required to submit FAFSA. *Unit head:* Dr. Vee Ming Lew, Chair, 570-408-4844, Fax: 570-408-7883, E-mail: veeming.lew@wilkes.edu. *Application contact:* Kathleen Houlihan, Director of Graduate Studies, 570-408-3235, Fax: 570-408-7846, E-mail: kathleen.houlihan@wilkes.edu.

Worcester Polytechnic Institute, Graduate Studies and Research, Department of Mathematical Sciences, Worcester, MA 01609-2280. Offers applied mathematics (MS); applied statistics (MS); financial mathematics (MS); industrial mathematics (MS); mathematical sciences (PhD, Graduate Certificate); mathematics (MME). Part-time and evening/weekend programs available. *Faculty:* 17 full-time (1 woman), 6 part-time/adjunct (2 women). *Students:* 48 full-time (20 women), 27 part-time (11 women); includes 3 Black or African American, non-Hispanic/Latino; 2 Hispanic/Latino; 2 Native Hawaiian or other Pacific Islander, non-Hispanic/Latino, 38 international. 230 applicants, 56% accepted, 26 enrolled. In 2010, 21 master's, 2 doctorates awarded. *Degree requirements:* For master's, thesis (for some programs); for doctorate, comprehensive exam, thesis/dissertation. *Entrance requirements:* For master's and doctorate, GRE General Test, GRE Subject Test in math (recommended), 3 letters of recommendation. Additional exam requirements/recommendations for international students: Required—TOEFL (minimum score 550 paper-based; 213 computer-based; 79 iBT), IELTS (minimum score 6.5). *Application deadline:* For fall admission, 1/1 priority date for domestic students, 1/1 for international students; for spring admission, 10/1 priority date for domestic students, 10/1 for international students. Applications are processed on a rolling basis. Application fee: $70.

Peterson's Graduate Programs in the Physical Sciences, Mathematics, Agricultural Sciences, the Environment & Natural Resources 2012

www.facebook.com/petersonspublishing　　**287**

Mathematics

Worcester Polytechnic Institute (continued)
Electronic applications accepted. *Expenses:* Tuition: Full-time $20,862; part-time $1159 per term. One-time fee: $15. *Financial support:* Career-related internships or fieldwork, institutionally sponsored loans, scholarships/grants, and unspecified assistantships available. Financial award application deadline: 1/1; financial award applicants required to submit FAFSA. *Faculty research:* Applied analysis and differential equations, computational mathematics, discrete mathematics, applied and computational statistics, industrial and financial mathematics, mathematical biology. *Unit head:* Dr. Bogdan Vernescu, Head, 508-831-5241, Fax: 508-831-5824, E-mail: vernescu@wpi.edu. *Application contact:* Dr. Joseph Petruccelli, Graduate Coordinator, 508-831-5241, Fax: 508-831-5824, E-mail: jdp@wpi.edu.

Wright State University, School of Graduate Studies, College of Science and Mathematics, Department of Mathematics and Statistics, Program in Mathematics, Dayton, OH 45435. Offers MS. *Degree requirements:* For master's, comprehensive exam. *Entrance requirements:* For master's, previous course work in mathematics beyond calculus. Additional exam requirements/recommendations for international students: Required—TOEFL. *Faculty research:* Analysis, algebraic combinatorics, graph theory, operator theory.

Yale University, Graduate School of Arts and Sciences, Department of Mathematics, New Haven, CT 06520. Offers M Phil, MS, PhD. *Degree requirements:* For doctorate, 2 foreign languages, thesis/dissertation. *Entrance requirements:* For doctorate, GRE General Test, GRE Subject Test.

York University, Faculty of Graduate Studies, Faculty of Science and Engineering, Program in Mathematics and Statistics, Toronto, ON M3J 1P3, Canada. Offers industrial and applied mathematics (M Sc); mathematics and statistics (MA, PhD). Part-time programs available. *Degree requirements:* For master's, thesis optional; for doctorate, one foreign language, comprehensive exam, thesis/dissertation. Electronic applications accepted.

Youngstown State University, Graduate School, College of Science, Technology, Engineering and Mathematics, Department of Mathematics and Statistics, Youngstown, OH 44555-0001. Offers applied mathematics (MS); computer science (MS); secondary mathematics (MS); statistics (MS). Part-time programs available. *Degree requirements:* For master's, comprehensive exam, thesis optional. *Entrance requirements:* For master's, minimum GPA of 2.7 in computer science and mathematics. Additional exam requirements/recommendations for international students: Required—TOEFL. *Faculty research:* Regression analysis, numerical analysis, statistics, Markov chain, topology and fuzzy sets.

Statistics

Acadia University, Faculty of Pure and Applied Science, Department of Mathematics and Statistics, Wolfville, NS B4P 2R6, Canada. Offers applied mathematics and statistics (M Sc). *Faculty:* 12 full-time (3 women), 2 part-time/adjunct (0 women). *Students:* 5 full-time (2 women), 2 part-time (1 woman). 8 applicants, 63% accepted, 3 enrolled. *Degree requirements:* For master's, thesis. *Entrance requirements:* For master's, honors degree in mathematics, statistics or equivalent. Additional exam requirements/recommendations for international students: Required—TOEFL (minimum score 580 paper-based; 237 computer-based; 93 iBT), IELTS (minimum score 6.5). *Application deadline:* For fall admission, 2/1 priority date for domestic and international students. Applications are processed on a rolling basis. Application fee: $50. *Financial support:* Fellowships, research assistantships, teaching assistantships, career-related internships or fieldwork and unspecified assistantships available. Financial award application deadline: 2/1. *Faculty research:* Geophysical fluid dynamics, machine scheduling problems, control theory, stochastic optimization, survival analysis. *Unit head:* Dr. Jeff Hooper, Head, 902-585-1382, Fax: 902-585-1074, E-mail: jeff.hooper@acadiau.ca. *Application contact:* Dr. Richard Karsten, Graduate Coordinator, 902-585-1608, Fax: 902-585-1074, E-mail: richard.karsten@acadiau.ca.

American University, College of Arts and Sciences, Department of Mathematics and Statistics, Washington, DC 22016-8050. Offers applied statistics (Certificate); mathematics (MA); statistics (MS). Part-time and evening/weekend programs available. *Faculty:* 25 full-time (7 women), 12 part-time/adjunct (0 women). *Students:* 9 full-time (2 women), 12 part-time (7 women); includes 2 minority (1 Black or African American, non-Hispanic/Latino; 1 Asian, non-Hispanic/Latino), 3 international. Average age 29. 38 applicants, 68% accepted, 7 enrolled. In 2010, 6 master's awarded. *Degree requirements:* For master's, comprehensive exam, thesis or alternative, tools of research in foreign language or computer language. *Entrance requirements:* For master's, GRE; for Certificate, bachelor's degree. Additional exam requirements/recommendations for international students: Required—TOEFL. *Application deadline:* For fall admission, 2/1 for domestic students; for spring admission, 10/1 for domestic students. Application fee: $80. *Financial support:* Fellowships, research assistantships, teaching assistantships, career-related internships or fieldwork, Federal Work-Study, institutionally sponsored loans, and unspecified assistantships available. Support available to part-time students. Financial award application deadline: 2/1. *Faculty research:* Logic, random processes, probability analysis, biostatistics, statistical computing. *Unit head:* Dr. Mary W. Gray, Chair, 202-885-3171, Fax: 202-885-3155, E-mail: mgray@american.edu. *Application contact:* Kathleen Clowery, Director, Graduate Admissions, 202-885-3621, Fax: 202-885-1505.

American University of Beirut, Graduate Programs, Faculty of Arts and Sciences, Beirut, Lebanon. Offers anthropology (MA); Arabic language and literature (MA); archaeology (MA); biology (MS); chemistry (MS); computational science (MS); computer science (MS); economics (MA); education (MA); English language (MA); English literature (MA); environmental policy planning (MSES); financial economics (MAFE); geology (MS); history (MA); mathematics (MA, MS); Middle Eastern studies (MA); philosophy (MA); physics (MS); political studies (MA); psychology (MA); public administration (MA); sociology (MA); statistics (MA, MS). Part-time programs available. *Faculty:* 229 full-time (98 women), 136 part-time/adjunct (79 women). *Students:* 158 full-time (104 women), 263 part-time (171 women). Average age 25. 356 applicants, 59% accepted, 127 enrolled. In 2010, 57 master's awarded. *Degree requirements:* For master's, one foreign language, comprehensive exam, thesis (for some programs). *Entrance requirements:* For master's, GRE, letter of recommendation. Additional exam requirements/recommendations for international students: Required—TOEFL (minimum score 600 paper-based; 250 computer-based; 97 iBT), IELTS (minimum score 7). *Application deadline:* For fall admission, 4/30 for domestic and international students; for spring admission, 11/1 for domestic and international students. Application fee: $50. *Expenses:* Tuition: Full-time $12,294; part-time $683 per credit. Required fees: $499; $499 per credit. Tuition and fees vary according to course load and program. *Financial support:* In 2010–11, 33 students received support. Career-related internships or fieldwork, institutionally sponsored loans, scholarships/grants, health care benefits, and unspecified assistantships available. Financial award application deadline: 2/4; financial award applicants required to submit FAFSA. *Faculty research:* Modern and contemporary world theatre; mineralogy, petrology, and geochemistry; cell differentiation and transformation; combinatorial technologies; philosophy of action; continental philosophy; Phoenician epigraphy; nascent complex societies and urbanism; the economies of the Arab world; environmental economics; tectonophysics; host-parasite interactions; innate immunity; insect-plant interactions; history of the Ottoman archives; decentralization; transparency and corruption. Total annual research expenditures: $622,243. *Unit head:* Dr. Patrick McGreevy, Dean, 961-137-4374 Ext. 3800, Fax: 961-174-4461, E-mail: pm07@aub.edu.lb. *Application contact:* Dr. Salim Kanaan, Director, Admissions Office, 961-135-0000 Ext. 2594, Fax: 961-175-0775, E-mail: sk00@aub.edu.lb.

Arizona State University, College of Liberal Arts and Sciences, Department of Mathematics and Statistics, Tempe, AZ 85287-1804. Offers applied mathematics (PhD); computational biosciences (PhD); mathematics (MA, MNS, PhD); mathematics education (PhD); statistics (PhD). Part-time programs available. *Faculty:* 94 full-time (32 women), 4 part-time/adjunct (1 woman). *Students:* 72 full-time (21 women), 23 part-time (10 women); includes 9 minority (2 Black or African American, non-Hispanic/Latino; 3 Asian, non-Hispanic/Latino; 4 Hispanic/Latino), 24 international. Average age 30. 168 applicants, 48% accepted, 26 enrolled. In 2010, 17 master's, 19 doctorates awarded. Terminal master's awarded for partial completion of doctoral program. *Median time to degree:* Of those who began their doctoral program in fall 2002, 69% received their degree in 8 years or less. *Degree requirements:* For master's, thesis or alternative, interactive Program of Study (iPOS) submitted before completing 50 percent of required credit hours; for doctorate, comprehensive exam, thesis/dissertation, interactive Program of Study (iPOS) submitted before completing 50 percent of required credit hours. *Entrance*

requirements: For master's and doctorate, GRE General Test, minimum GPA of 3.0 or equivalent in last 2 years of work leading to bachelor's degree. Additional exam requirements/recommendations for international students: Required—TOEFL, IELTS, or Pearson Test of English. *Application deadline:* For fall admission, 1/1 for domestic and international students. Applications are processed on a rolling basis. Application fee: $70 ($90 for international students). Electronic applications accepted. *Expenses:* Contact institution. *Financial support:* In 2010–11, 12 research assistantships with full and partial tuition reimbursements (averaging $18,559 per year), 55 teaching assistantships with full and partial tuition reimbursements (averaging $17,743 per year) were awarded; fellowships with full tuition reimbursements, career-related internships or fieldwork, Federal Work-Study, institutionally sponsored loans, scholarships/grants, and tuition waivers (partial) also available. Financial award application deadline: 3/1; financial award applicants required to submit FAFSA. Total annual research expenditures: $4.5 million. *Unit head:* Dr. Wayne Raskind, Director, 480-965-3951, E-mail: raskind@asu.edu. *Application contact:* Graduate Admissions, 480-965-6113.

Arizona State University, Graduate College, Interdisciplinary Program in Statistics, Tempe, AZ 85287-1003. Offers MS, Graduate Certificate. Part-time and evening/weekend programs available. Postbaccalaureate distance learning degree programs offered (minimal on-campus study). *Faculty:* 19 full-time (6 women). *Students:* 13 full-time (10 women), 11 part-time (6 women); includes 6 minority (5 Asian, non-Hispanic/Latino; 1 Native Hawaiian or other Pacific Islander, non-Hispanic/Latino), 9 international. Average age 31. 67 applicants, 70% accepted. In 2010, 11 master's, 17 other advanced degrees awarded. *Degree requirements:* For master's, thesis and oral defense/examination or applied project with oral defense/examination; interactive Program of Study (iPOS) submitted before completing 50 percent of required credit hours. *Entrance requirements:* For master's, minimum GPA of 3.0 in the last 2 years of work leading to the bachelor's degree, 3 letters of recommendation, statement of goals; for Graduate Certificate, bachelor's degree, completion of intro to applied statistics, 1 semester of calculus. Additional exam requirements/recommendations for international students: Required—TOEFL (minimum score 550 paper-based; 213 computer-based; 80 iBT), IELTS (minimum score 6.5). *Application deadline:* For fall admission, 7/1 for domestic and international students; for spring admission, 11/15 for domestic and international students. Application fee: $70 ($90 for international students). Electronic applications accepted. *Expenses:* Tuition, state resident: full-time $8510; part-time $608 per credit. Tuition, nonresident: full-time $16,542; part-time $919 per credit. Required fees: $339; $110 per credit. Part-time tuition and fees vary according to course load. *Financial support:* In 2010–11, 2 research assistantships with partial tuition reimbursements (averaging $14,369 per year) were awarded; teaching assistantships with partial tuition reimbursements, institutionally sponsored loans, scholarships/grants, and tuition waivers (partial) also available. Financial award application deadline: 3/1; financial award applicants required to submit FAFSA. *Unit head:* Dr. Maria T. Allison, University Vice Provost and Dean, Graduate College, 480-965-7279, E-mail: statistics@asu.edu. *Application contact:* Graduate Admissions, 480-965-6113.

Auburn University, Graduate School, College of Sciences and Mathematics, Department of Mathematics and Statistics, Auburn University, AL 36849. Offers applied mathematics (MAM, MS); mathematics (MS, PhD); probability and statistics (M Prob S); statistics (MS). *Faculty:* 54 full-time (8 women), 4 part-time/adjunct (1 woman). *Students:* 50 full-time (8 women), 44 part-time (17 women); includes 2 Black or African American, non-Hispanic/Latino; 1 Asian, non-Hispanic/Latino; 1 Hispanic/Latino, 46 international. Average age 28. 212 applicants, 52% accepted, 20 enrolled. In 2010, 16 master's, 10 doctorates awarded. *Degree requirements:* For doctorate, thesis/dissertation. *Entrance requirements:* For master's, GRE General Test, undergraduate mathematics background; for doctorate, GRE General Test, GRE Subject Test. *Application deadline:* For fall admission, 7/7 priority date for domestic students; for spring admission, 11/24 for domestic students. Applications are processed on a rolling basis. Application fee: $50 ($60 for international students). Electronic applications accepted. *Expenses:* Tuition, state resident: full-time $7002. Tuition, nonresident: full-time $21,898. International tuition: $22,116 full-time. Required fees: $892. Tuition and fees vary according to course load and program. *Financial support:* Fellowships, teaching assistantships available. Financial award applicants required to submit FAFSA. *Faculty research:* Pure and applied mathematics. *Unit head:* Dr. Michel Smith, Chair, 334-844-4290, Fax: 334-844-6655. *Application contact:* Dr. George Flowers, Dean of the Graduate School, 334-844-2125.

Ball State University, Graduate School, College of Sciences and Humanities, Department of Mathematical Sciences, Program in Statistics, Muncie, IN 47306-1099. Offers MA. *Students:* 11 full-time (1 woman), 4 part-time (2 women); includes 2 Black or African American, non-Hispanic/Latino; 1 Asian, non-Hispanic/Latino, 6 international. Average age 27. 15 applicants, 87% accepted, 8 enrolled. Application fee: $50. *Expenses:* Tuition, state resident: full-time $6160; part-time $299 per credit hour. Tuition, nonresident: full-time $16,020; part-time $783 per credit hour. Required fees: $2278; $95 per credit hour. *Financial support:* In 2010–11, 8 teaching assistantships with tuition reimbursements (averaging $11,179 per year) were awarded. Financial award application deadline: 3/1. *Faculty research:* Robust methods. *Unit head:* Dr. Sheryl Stump, Director, 765-285-8662, Fax: 765-285-1721. *Application contact:* Dr. Hanspeter Fischer, Director, 765-285-8640, Fax: 765-285-1721, E-mail: mali@bsu.edu.

Baylor University, Graduate School, College of Arts and Sciences, Department of Statistics, Waco, TX 76798. Offers MA, PhD. *Faculty:* 7 full-time (1 woman), 4 part-time/adjunct (1 woman). *Students:* 26 full-time (18 women), 1 part-time (0 women); includes 4 minority (2 Black or African American, non-Hispanic/Latino; 2 Asian, non-Hispanic/Latino), 5 international. Average age 24. 38 applicants, 16% accepted. In 2010, 5 master's, 5 doctorates awarded. *Degree requirements:* For doctorate, thesis/dissertation. *Entrance requirements:* For master's, GRE General Test, 3 semesters of course work in calculus; for doctorate, GRE General Test.

Peterson's Graduate Programs in the Physical Sciences, Mathematics, Agricultural Sciences, the Environment & Natural Resources 2012

Application deadline: Applications are processed on a rolling basis. Application fee: $25. *Financial support:* In 2010–11, 1 fellowship, 5 research assistantships, 7 teaching assistantships were awarded; institutionally sponsored loans also available. *Faculty research:* Mathematical statistics, probability theory, biostatistics, linear models, time series. *Unit head:* Dr. James Stamey, Graduate Program Director, 254-710-7405, E-mail: james_stamey@baylor.edu. *Application contact:* Dr. James Stamey, Graduate Program Director, 254-710-7405, E-mail: james_stamey@baylor.edu.

Bernard M. Baruch College of the City University of New York, Zicklin School of Business, Department of Statistics and Computer Information Systems, Program in Statistics, New York, NY 10010-5585. Offers MBA, MS. Part-time and evening/weekend programs available. *Entrance requirements:* For master's, GMAT, 2 letters of recommendation, resume, 2 years of work experience. Additional exam requirements/recommendations for international students: Required—TOEFL (minimum score 590 paper-based; 243 computer-based), TWE.

Bowling Green State University, Graduate College, College of Arts and Sciences, Department of Mathematics and Statistics, Bowling Green, OH 43403. Offers applied statistics (MS); mathematics (MA, MAT, PhD); statistics (PhD). Part-time programs available. *Degree requirements:* For master's, thesis or alternative; for doctorate, comprehensive exam, thesis/dissertation. *Entrance requirements:* For master's and doctorate, GRE General Test. Additional exam requirements/recommendations for international students: Required—TOEFL. Electronic applications accepted. *Faculty research:* Statistics and probability, algebra, analysis.

Brigham Young University, Graduate Studies, College of Physical and Mathematical Sciences, Department of Statistics, Provo, UT 84602-1001. Offers applied statistics (MS). *Faculty:* 16 full-time (3 women). *Students:* 26 full-time (8 women); includes 1 minority (Asian, non-Hispanic/Latino). Average age 26. 26 applicants, 69% accepted, 14 enrolled. In 2010, 6 master's awarded. *Degree requirements:* For master's, comprehensive exam, thesis (for some programs). *Entrance requirements:* For master's, GRE General Test, minimum undergraduate GPA of 3.3; course work in statistical methods, theory, multivariable calculus, and linear algebra with minimum B– average. Additional exam requirements/recommendations for international students: Required—TOEFL (minimum score 580 paper-based; 237 computer-based; 85 iBT). *Application deadline:* For fall admission, 2/1 for domestic and international students. Application fee: $50. Electronic applications accepted. *Expenses:* Tuition: Full-time $5580; part-time $310 per credit hour. Tuition and fees vary according to program and student's religious affiliation. *Financial support:* In 2010–11, 20 students received support, including 8 research assistantships with full and partial tuition reimbursements available (averaging $10,000 per year), 18 teaching assistantships with full and partial tuition reimbursements available (averaging $10,000 per year); scholarships/grants and unspecified assistantships also available. Financial award application deadline: 2/1. *Faculty research:* Statistical genetics, reliability and pollution monitoring, Bayesian methods. Total annual research expenditures: $42,000. *Unit head:* Dr. Del T. Scott, Chair, 801-422-7054, Fax: 801-422-0635, E-mail: scottd@byu.edu. *Application contact:* Dr. Christopher Shane Reese, Graduate Coordinator, 801-422-9250, Fax: 801-422-0635, E-mail: reese@stat.byu.edu.

Brock University, Faculty of Graduate Studies, Faculty of Mathematics and Science, Program in Mathematics and Statistics, St. Catharines, ON L2S 3A1, Canada. Offers M Sc. Part-time programs available. *Degree requirements:* For master's, thesis or project. *Entrance requirements:* For master's, honors degree. Additional exam requirements/recommendations for international students: Required—TOEFL (minimum score 550 paper-based; 213 computer-based; 80 iBT), IELTS (minimum score 6.5), TWE (minimum score 4). Electronic applications accepted.

California State University, East Bay, Office of Academic Programs and Graduate Studies, College of Science, Department of Statistics and Biostatistics, Statistics Program, Hayward, CA 94542-3000. Offers MS. Part-time and evening/weekend programs available. *Faculty:* 7 full-time (3 women). *Students:* 20 full-time (7 women), 84 part-time (41 women); includes 5 Black or African American, non-Hispanic/Latino; 32 Asian, non-Hispanic/Latino; 6 Hispanic/Latino; 1 Two or more races, non-Hispanic/Latino, 35 international. Average age 31. 135 applicants, 47% accepted, 36 enrolled. In 2010, 30 master's awarded. *Degree requirements:* For master's, comprehensive exam. *Entrance requirements:* For master's, letters of recommendation, minimum GPA of 3.0, math through lower-division calculus. Additional exam requirements/recommendations for international students: Required—TOEFL (minimum score 550 paper-based; 213 computer-based). *Application deadline:* For fall admission, 6/30 for domestic and international students. Application fee: $55. Electronic applications accepted. *Financial support:* Fellowships, career-related internships or fieldwork, Federal Work-Study, institutionally sponsored loans, scholarships/grants, and unspecified assistantships available. Support available to part-time students. Financial award application deadline: 3/2; financial award applicants required to submit FAFSA. *Unit head:* Dr. Eric Suess, Chair, 510-885-3435, Fax: 510-885-4714, E-mail: eric.suess@csueastbay.edu. *Application contact:* Donna Wiley, Interim Associate Director, 510-885-3286, Fax: 510-885-4777, E-mail: donna.wiley@csueastbay.edu.

California State University, Sacramento, Graduate Studies, College of Natural Sciences and Mathematics, Department of Mathematics and Statistics, Sacramento, CA 95819. Offers MA. Part-time programs available. *Degree requirements:* For master's, thesis or alternative, writing proficiency exam. *Entrance requirements:* For master's, minimum GPA of 3.0 in mathematics, 2.5 overall during previous 2 years; BA in mathematics or equivalent. Additional exam requirements/recommendations for international students: Required—TOEFL. Electronic applications accepted.

Carnegie Mellon University, College of Humanities and Social Sciences, Department of Statistics, Pittsburgh, PA 15213-3891. Offers machine learning and statistics (PhD); mathematical finance (PhD); statistics (MS, PhD), including applied statistics (PhD), computational statistics (PhD), theoretical statistics (PhD); statistics and public policy (PhD). Terminal master's awarded for partial completion of doctoral program. *Degree requirements:* For doctorate, comprehensive exam, thesis/dissertation. *Entrance requirements:* For master's and doctorate, GRE General Test. Additional exam requirements/recommendations for international students: Required—TOEFL. *Faculty research:* Stochastic processes, Bayesian statistics, statistical computing, decision theory, psychiatric statistics.

Case Western Reserve University, School of Graduate Studies, Department of Statistics, Cleveland, OH 44106. Offers MS, PhD. *Faculty:* 4 full-time (2 women), 6 part-time/adjunct (1 woman). *Students:* 17 full-time (7 women), 6 part-time (2 women); includes 3 Asian, non-Hispanic/Latino, 14 international. Average age 33. 20 applicants, 0% accepted, 0 enrolled. In 2010, 1 master's, 3 doctorates awarded. *Degree requirements:* For master's, thesis (for some programs); for doctorate, thesis/dissertation. *Entrance requirements:* Additional exam requirements/recommendations for international students: Required—TOEFL (minimum score 550 paper-based; 213 computer-based; 79 iBT). *Application deadline:* For fall admission, 3/1 priority date for domestic students. Application fee: $50. Electronic applications accepted. *Financial support:* Teaching assistantships, career-related internships or fieldwork available. Support available to part-time students. Financial award application deadline: 3/1. *Faculty research:* Generalized linear models, asymptotics for restricted MLE Bayesian inference, sample survey theory, statistical computing, nonparametric inference, projection pursuit, stochastic processes, dynamical systems and chaotic behavior. *Unit head:* Jill Korbin, Interim Chair, 216-368-6942, Fax: 216-368-0252, E-mail: jill.korbin@case.edu. *Application contact:* Sharon Dingess, Admissions, 216-368-6941, Fax: 216-368-0252, E-mail: skd@case.edu.

Central Connecticut State University, School of Graduate Studies, School of Arts and Sciences, Department of Mathematical Sciences, New Britain, CT 06050-4010. Offers data mining (MS, Certificate); mathematics (MA, MS, Certificate, Sixth Year Certificate), including

actuarial science (MA), computer science (MA), statistics (MA). Part-time and evening/weekend programs available. *Faculty:* 33 full-time (10 women), 65 part-time/adjunct (28 women). *Students:* 20 full-time (10 women), 131 part-time (74 women); includes 18 minority (5 Black or African American, non-Hispanic/Latino; 5 Asian, non-Hispanic/Latino; 6 Hispanic/Latino; 2 Two or more races, non-Hispanic/Latino), 8 international. Average age 37. 76 applicants, 59% accepted, 28 enrolled. In 2010, 29 master's, 4 other advanced degrees awarded. *Degree requirements:* For master's, comprehensive exam, thesis or alternative; for other advanced degree, qualifying exam. *Entrance requirements:* For master's, minimum undergraduate GPA of 2.7. Additional exam requirements/recommendations for international students: Required—TOEFL. *Application deadline:* For fall admission, 7/1 for domestic students; for spring admission, 12/1 for domestic students. Applications are processed on a rolling basis. Application fee: $50. Electronic applications accepted. *Expenses:* Tuition, area resident: Full-time $5012; part-time $470 per credit. Tuition, state resident: full-time $7518; part-time $482 per credit. Tuition, nonresident: full-time $13,962; part-time $482 per credit. Required fees: $3772. One-time fee: $62 part-time. *Financial support:* In 2010–11, 6 students received support, including 2 research assistantships; career-related internships or fieldwork, Federal Work-Study, scholarships/grants, and unspecified assistantships also available. Support available to part-time students. Financial award application deadline: 2/15; financial award applicants required to submit FAFSA. *Faculty research:* Statistics, actuarial mathematics, computer systems and engineering, computer programming techniques, operations research. *Unit head:* Dr. Jeffrey McGowan, Chair, 860-832-2835. *Application contact:* Dr. Jeffrey McGowan, Chair, 860-832-2835.

Claremont Graduate University, Graduate Programs, School of Mathematical Sciences, Claremont, CA 91711-6160. Offers computational and systems biology (PhD); computational mathematics and numerical analysis (MA, MS); computational science (PhD); engineering and industrial applied mathematics (PhD); mathematics (PhD); operations research and statistics (MA, MS); physical applied mathematics (MA, MS); pure mathematics (MA, MS); scientific computing (MA, MS); systems and control theory (MA, MS). Part-time programs available. *Faculty:* 6 full-time (0 women). *Students:* 50 full-time (15 women), 11 part-time (1 woman); includes 2 Black or African American, non-Hispanic/Latino; 9 Asian, non-Hispanic/Latino; 7 Hispanic/Latino; 3 Two or more races, non-Hispanic/Latino, 13 international. Average age 36. In 2010, 17 master's, 11 doctorates awarded. Terminal master's awarded for partial completion of doctoral program. *Entrance requirements:* For master's and doctorate, GRE General Test. Additional exam requirements/recommendations for international students: Required—TOEFL (minimum score 550 paper-based; 213 computer-based; 80 iBT). *Application deadline:* For fall admission, 2/1 priority date for domestic students. Applications are processed on a rolling basis. Application fee: $60. Electronic applications accepted. *Expenses:* Tuition: Full-time $35,748; part-time $1554 per unit. Required fees: $215 per semester. *Financial support:* Fellowships, research assistantships, Federal Work-Study, institutionally sponsored loans, scholarships/grants, and tuition waivers (full and partial) available. Support available to part-time students. Financial award application deadline: 2/15; financial award applicants required to submit FAFSA. *Unit head:* John Angus, Dean, 909-621-8080, Fax: 909-607-8261, E-mail: john.angus@cgu.edu. *Application contact:* Susan Townzen, Program Coordinator, 909-621-8080, Fax: 909-607-8261, E-mail: susan.n.townzen@cgu.edu.

Clemson University, Graduate School, College of Business and Behavioral Science, Department of Economics, Program in Applied Economics and Statistics, Clemson, SC 29634. Offers MS, PhD. *Faculty:* 20 full-time (5 women). *Students:* 34 full-time (14 women), 6 part-time (1 woman); includes 1 minority (Asian, non-Hispanic/Latino), 7 international. Average age 30. 127 applicants, 65% accepted, 17 enrolled. In 2010, 1 master's, 14 doctorates awarded. *Degree requirements:* For master's, thesis optional. *Entrance requirements:* For master's, GRE General Test, minimum GPA of 3.0. Additional exam requirements/recommendations for international students: Required—TOEFL. *Application deadline:* For fall admission, 5/1 for domestic students, 4/15 for international students; for spring admission, 10/1 for domestic students, 9/15 for international students. Applications are processed on a rolling basis. Application fee: $70 ($80 for international students). Electronic applications accepted. *Expenses:* Contact institution. *Financial support:* In 2010–11, 27 students received support, including 7 research assistantships with partial tuition reimbursements available (averaging $13,268 per year), 25 teaching assistantships with partial tuition reimbursements available (averaging $16,379 per year); fellowships with full and partial tuition reimbursements available, institutionally sponsored loans, scholarships/grants, and unspecified assistantships also available. Financial award application deadline: 3/1; financial award applicants required to submit FAFSA. *Faculty research:* Agricultural policy, agricultural production, agricultural marketing, natural resource economics, regional economic development. Total annual research expenditures: $489,768. *Unit head:* Dr. Hoke Hill, Chair, 864-656-3225, E-mail: hhill@clemson.edu. *Application contact:* Ellen Reneke, Staff Assistant for Graduate Programs, 864-656-5791, Fax: 864-656-5776, E-mail: ereneke@clemson.edu.

Clemson University, Graduate School, College of Engineering and Science, Department of Mathematical Sciences, Clemson, SC 29634. Offers applied and pure mathematics (MS, PhD); computational mathematics (MS, PhD); operations research (MS, PhD); statistics (MS, PhD). Part-time programs available. *Faculty:* 48 full-time (13 women), 12 part-time/adjunct (4 women). *Students:* 127 full-time (51 women), 5 part-time (2 women); includes 2 Black or African American, non-Hispanic/Latino; 1 American Indian or Alaska Native, non-Hispanic/Latino; 1 Two or more races, non-Hispanic/Latino, 36 international. Average age 26. 163 applicants, 79% accepted, 51 enrolled. In 2010, 27 master's, 5 doctorates awarded. *Degree requirements:* For master's, thesis optional, final project; for doctorate, thesis/dissertation, qualifying exams. *Entrance requirements:* For master's and doctorate, GRE General Test. Additional exam requirements/recommendations for international students: Required—TOEFL. *Application deadline:* For fall admission, 1/15 priority date for domestic and international students; for spring admission, 10/1 priority date for domestic students, 9/15 priority date for international students. Applications are processed on a rolling basis. Application fee: $70 ($80 for international students). Electronic applications accepted. *Expenses:* Tuition, state resident: full-time $6492; part-time $400 per credit hour. Tuition, nonresident: full-time $13,634; part-time $800 per credit hour. Required fees: $262 per semester. Part-time tuition and fees vary according to course load and program. *Financial support:* In 2010–11, 110 students received support, including 2 fellowships with full and partial tuition reimbursements available (averaging $6,000 per year), 8 research assistantships with partial tuition reimbursements available (averaging $19,823 per year), 101 teaching assistantships with partial tuition reimbursements available (averaging $17,582 per year); career-related internships or fieldwork, institutionally sponsored loans, scholarships/grants, health care benefits, and unspecified assistantships also available. Support available to part-time students. Financial award application deadline: 4/15. *Faculty research:* Applied and computational analysis, cryptography, discrete mathematics, optimization, statistics. Total annual research expenditures: $823,404. *Unit head:* Dr. Robert L. Taylor, Chair, 864-656-5240, Fax: 864-656-5230, E-mail: rtaylo2@clemson.edu. *Application contact:* Dr. K.B. Kulasekera, Graduate Coordinator, 864-656-5231, Fax: 864-656-5230, E-mail: kk@clemson.edu.

Colorado State University, Graduate School, College of Natural Sciences, Department of Statistics, Fort Collins, CO 80523-1877. Offers MS, PhD. Postbaccalaureate distance learning degree programs offered (no on-campus study). *Faculty:* 10 full-time (4 women), 1 part-time/adjunct (0 women). *Students:* 31 full-time (12 women), 52 part-time (20 women); includes 9 minority (5 Asian, non-Hispanic/Latino; 3 Hispanic/Latino; 1 Two or more races, non-Hispanic/Latino), 19 international. Average age 33. 115 applicants, 27% accepted, 20 enrolled. In 2010, 19 master's, 4 doctorates awarded. Terminal master's awarded for partial completion of doctoral program. *Degree requirements:* For master's, comprehensive exam (for some programs), thesis (for some programs), project, seminar; for doctorate, comprehensive exam, thesis/dissertation, candidacy exam, preliminary exam, seminar. *Entrance requirements:* For master's and doctorate, GRE General Test, minimum GPA of 3.0, background in math and

Peterson's Graduate Programs in the Physical Sciences, Mathematics, Agricultural Sciences, the Environment & Natural Resources 2012

www.facebook.com/petersonspublishing   **289**

Statistics

Colorado State University (continued)

statistics. Additional exam requirements/recommendations for international students: Required—TOEFL (minimum score 550 paper-based; 213 computer-based; 80 iBT). *Application deadline:* For fall admission, 2/1 priority date for domestic and international students. Application fee: $50. Electronic applications accepted. *Expenses:* Tuition, state resident: full-time $7434; part-time $413 per credit. Tuition, nonresident: full-time $19,022; part-time $1057 per credit. Required fees: $1729; $88 per credit. *Financial support:* In 2010–11, 35 students received support, including 8 research assistantships with full tuition reimbursements available (averaging $8,229 per year), 27 teaching assistantships with full tuition reimbursements available (averaging $13,309 per year); fellowships, health care benefits also available. Financial award application deadline: 1/15; financial award applicants required to submit FAFSA. *Faculty research:* Applied probability, linear models and experimental design, time-series analysis, non-parametric statistical inference, statistical consulting. Total annual research expenditures: $350,028. *Unit head:* Dr. Jean Opsomer, Professor and Chair, 970-491-3841, Fax: 970-491-7895, E-mail: jean.opsomer@colostate.edu. *Application contact:* Jennifer Tallchief, Graduate Admissions Coordinator, 970-491-5269, Fax: 970-491-7895, E-mail: tallchie@stat.colostate.edu.

Columbia University, Graduate School of Arts and Sciences, Division of Natural Sciences, Department of Statistics, New York, NY 10027. Offers M Phil, MA, PhD, MD/PhD. Part-time programs available. *Degree requirements:* For doctorate, thesis/dissertation. *Entrance requirements:* For master's and doctorate, GRE General Test, GRE Subject Test. Additional exam requirements/recommendations for international students: Required—TOEFL.

Columbia University, Graduate School of Arts and Sciences, Program in Quantitative Methods in the Social Sciences, New York, NY 10027. Offers MA. Part-time programs available.

Cornell University, Graduate School, Graduate Fields of Engineering, Field of Operations Research and Information Engineering, Ithaca, NY 14853. Offers applied probability and statistics (PhD); manufacturing systems engineering (PhD); mathematical programming (PhD); operations research and industrial engineering (M Eng). *Faculty:* 35 full-time (5 women). *Students:* 162 full-time (46 women); includes 3 Black or African American, non-Hispanic/Latino; 14 Asian, non-Hispanic/Latino; 3 Hispanic/Latino, 117 international. Average age 23. 1,076 applicants, 34% accepted, 139 enrolled. In 2010, 85 master's, 6 doctorates awarded. *Degree requirements:* For doctorate, comprehensive exam, thesis/dissertation. *Entrance requirements:* For master's and doctorate, GRE General Test, 3 letters of recommendation. Additional exam requirements/recommendations for international students: Required—TOEFL (minimum score 600 paper-based; 250 computer-based; 100 iBT). *Application deadline:* For fall admission, 12/15 for domestic students. Application fee: $70. Electronic applications accepted. *Expenses:* Tuition: Full-time $29,500. Required fees: $76. Tuition and fees vary according to degree level and program. *Financial support:* In 2010–11, 44 students received support, including 12 fellowships with full tuition reimbursements available, 9 research assistantships with full tuition reimbursements available, 24 teaching assistantships with full tuition reimbursements available; institutionally sponsored loans, scholarships/grants, health care benefits, tuition waivers (full and partial), and unspecified assistantships also available. Financial award applicants required to submit FAFSA. *Faculty research:* Mathematical programming and combinatorial optimization, statistics, stochastic processes, mathematical finance, simulation, manufacturing, e-commerce. *Unit head:* Director of Graduate Studies, 607-255-9128, Fax: 607-255-9129. *Application contact:* Graduate Field Assistant, 607-255-9128, Fax: 607-255-9129, E-mail: orie@cornell.edu.

Cornell University, Graduate School, Graduate Fields of Engineering, Field of Statistics, Ithaca, NY 14853-0001. Offers applied statistics (MPS); biometry (MS, PhD); decision theory (MS, PhD); economic and social statistics (MS, PhD); engineering statistics (MS, PhD); experimental design (MS, PhD); mathematical statistics (MS, PhD); probability (MS, PhD); sampling (MS, PhD); statistical computing (MS, PhD); stochastic processes (MS, PhD). *Faculty:* 21 full-time (2 women). *Students:* 76 full-time (37 women); includes 4 Asian, non-Hispanic/Latino; 2 Hispanic/Latino, 53 international. Average age 24. 429 applicants, 27% accepted, 50 enrolled. In 2010, 36 master's, 3 doctorates awarded. Terminal master's awarded for partial completion of doctoral program. *Degree requirements:* For master's, project (MPS), thesis (MS); for doctorate, one foreign language, thesis/dissertation. *Entrance requirements:* For master's, GRE General Test (MS), 2 letters of recommendation (MS, MPS); for doctorate, GRE General Test, 2 letters of recommendation. Additional exam requirements/recommendations for international students: Required—TOEFL (minimum score 550 paper-based; 213 computer-based; 77 iBT). *Application deadline:* For fall admission, 1/15 for domestic students. Applications are processed on a rolling basis. Application fee: $70. Electronic applications accepted. *Expenses:* Tuition: Full-time $29,500. Required fees: $76. Tuition and fees vary according to degree level and program. *Financial support:* In 2010–11, 26 students received support, including 3 fellowships with full tuition reimbursements available, 9 research assistantships with full tuition reimbursements available, 17 teaching assistantships with full tuition reimbursements available; institutionally sponsored loans, scholarships/grants, tuition waivers (full and partial), and unspecified assistantships also available. Financial award applicants required to submit FAFSA. *Faculty research:* Bayesian analysis, survival analysis, nonparametric statistics, stochastic processes, mathematical statistics. *Unit head:* Director of Graduate Studies, 607-255-8066. *Application contact:* Graduate Field Assistant, 607-255-8066, E-mail: csc@cornell.edu.

Dalhousie University, Faculty of Science, Department of Mathematics and Statistics, Program in Statistics, Halifax, NS B3H 4R2, Canada. Offers M Sc, PhD. *Degree requirements:* For master's, thesis, 50 hours of consulting; for doctorate, thesis/dissertation, 50 hours of consulting. *Entrance requirements:* Additional exam requirements/recommendations for international students: Required—TOEFL, IELTS, CANTEST, CAEL, or Michigan English Language Assessment Battery. Electronic applications accepted. *Faculty research:* Data analysis, multivariate analysis, robustness, time series, statistical genetics.

Duke University, Graduate School, Department of Statistical Science, Durham, NC 27708. Offers PhD. Part-time programs available. *Faculty:* 20 full-time. *Students:* 36 full-time (13 women); includes 1 Black or African American, non-Hispanic/Latino; 1 American Indian or Alaska Native, non-Hispanic/Latino; 1 Asian, non-Hispanic/Latino, 21 international. 182 applicants, 7% accepted, 10 enrolled. In 2010, 9 doctorates awarded. *Degree requirements:* For doctorate, thesis/dissertation. *Entrance requirements:* For doctorate, GRE General Test. Additional exam requirements/recommendations for international students: Required—TOEFL (minimum score 550 paper-based; 213 computer-based; 83 iBT), IELTS (minimum score 7). *Application deadline:* For fall admission, 12/8 priority date for domestic and international students. Application fee: $75. Electronic applications accepted. *Financial support:* Fellowships, research assistantships, teaching assistantships available. Financial award application deadline: 12/8. *Unit head:* Mike West, Director of Graduate Studies, 919-684-8029, Fax: 919-684-8594, E-mail: karen@stat.duke.edu. *Application contact:* Elizabeth Hutton, 919-684-3913, Fax: 919-684-2277, E-mail: grad-admissions@duke.edu.

Florida Atlantic University, Charles E. Schmidt College of Science, Department of Mathematical Sciences, Boca Raton, FL 33431-0991. Offers applied mathematics and statistics (MS); mathematical sciences (MS, MST, PhD). Part-time programs available. *Faculty:* 37 full-time (5 women), 4 part-time/adjunct (0 women). *Students:* 49 full-time (7 women), 25 part-time (15 women); includes 17 minority (6 Black or African American, non-Hispanic/Latino; 9 Asian, non-Hispanic/Latino; 2 Hispanic/Latino), 29 international. Average age 31. 73 applicants, 41% accepted, 22 enrolled. In 2010, 26 master's, 8 doctorates awarded. Terminal master's awarded for partial completion of doctoral program. *Degree requirements:* For master's, comprehensive exam (for some programs), thesis (for some programs); for doctorate, comprehensive exam, thesis/dissertation. *Entrance requirements:* For master's and doctorate, GRE General Test, minimum GPA of 3.0. Additional exam requirements/recommendations for international students: Required—TOEFL (minimum score 500 paper-based; 173 computer-based). *Application deadline:* For fall admission, 7/1 priority date for domestic students, 2/15 priority date for international students; for spring admission, 11/1 priority date for domestic students, 7/15 priority date for international students. Applications are processed on a rolling basis. Application fee: $30. Electronic applications accepted. *Expenses:* Tuition, area resident: Part-time $319.96 per credit. Tuition, state resident: part-time $319.96 per credit. Tuition, nonresident: part-time $926.42 per credit. *Financial support:* In 2010–11, fellowships with partial tuition reimbursements (averaging $20,000 per year), teaching assistantships with partial tuition reimbursements (averaging $20,000 per year) were awarded; Federal Work-Study also available. Financial award application deadline: 4/1. *Faculty research:* Cryptography, statistics, algebra, analysis, combinatorics. *Unit head:* Dr. Lee Klingler, Chair, 561-297-0274, Fax: 561-297-2436, E-mail: klingler@fau.edu. *Application contact:* Dr. Heinrich Niederhausen, Graduate Director, 561-297-3237, Fax: 561-297-2436, E-mail: niederha@fau.edu.

Florida International University, College of Arts and Sciences, Department of Mathematics and Statistics, Program in Statistics, Miami, FL 33199. Offers MS. Part-time and evening/weekend programs available. *Students:* 9 full-time (3 women), 7 part-time (4 women); includes 2 Asian, non-Hispanic/Latino; 4 Hispanic/Latino, 7 international. Average age 34. 23 applicants, 17% accepted, 4 enrolled. In 2010, 4 master's awarded. *Degree requirements:* For master's, thesis optional. *Entrance requirements:* For master's, GRE General Test, minimum GPA of 3.0, 3 letters of recommendation, resume. Additional exam requirements/recommendations for international students: Required—TOEFL (minimum score 550 paper-based; 80 iBT). *Application deadline:* For fall admission, 6/1 for domestic students, 4/1 for international students; for spring admission, 10/1 for domestic students, 9/1 for international students. Applications are processed on a rolling basis. Application fee: $30. Electronic applications accepted. *Financial support:* Institutionally sponsored loans and scholarships/grants available. Financial award application deadline: 3/1; financial award applicants required to submit FAFSA. *Unit head:* Dr. Bao Qin Li, Chair, Mathematics and Statistics Department, 305-348-2743, Fax: 305-348-6158, E-mail: bao.li@fiu.edu. *Application contact:* Dr. Zhenmin Chen, Director of Graduate Programs, 305-348-2743, Fax: 305-348-6158, E-mail: Zhenmin.Chen@fiu.edu.

Florida State University, The Graduate School, College of Arts and Sciences, Department of Statistics, Tallahassee, FL 32306-4330. Offers applied statistics (MS); biostatistics (MS, PhD); mathematical statistics (MS, PhD). Part-time programs available. *Faculty:* 15 full-time (2 women). *Students:* 52 full-time (21 women), 20 part-time (8 women); includes 10 Black or African American, non-Hispanic/Latino; 5 Asian, non-Hispanic/Latino; 8 Hispanic/Latino, 27 international. Average age 29. 182 applicants, 15% accepted, 18 enrolled. In 2010, 4 master's, 10 doctorates awarded. Terminal master's awarded for partial completion of doctoral program. *Degree requirements:* For doctorate, thesis/dissertation, departmental qualifying exam. *Entrance requirements:* For master's, GRE General Test, previous course work in calculus, minimum GPA of 3.0; for doctorate, GRE General Test, minimum GPA of 3.0, 1 course in linear algebra (preferred), calculus I-III, real analysis. Additional exam requirements/recommendations for international students: Required—TOEFL (minimum score 600 paper-based; 250 computer-based; 100 iBT). *Application deadline:* For fall admission, 7/1 for domestic and international students; for spring admission, 11/1 for domestic and international students. Applications are processed on a rolling basis. Application fee: $30. Electronic applications accepted. *Expenses:* Tuition, state resident: full-time $8238.24. *Financial support:* In 2010–11, 49 students received support, including 1 fellowship with full tuition reimbursement available (averaging $19,000 per year), 10 research assistantships with full tuition reimbursements available (averaging $22,185 per year), 41 teaching assistantships with full tuition reimbursements available (averaging $19,653 per year); Federal Work-Study, institutionally sponsored loans, scholarships/grants, health care benefits, and unspecified assistantships also available. Support available to part-time students. Financial award application deadline: 2/15; financial award applicants required to submit FAFSA. *Faculty research:* Statistical inference, probability theory, biostatistics, nonparametric estimation, automatic target recognition. *Unit head:* Dr. Dan McGee, Chairman, 850-644-3218, Fax: 850-644-5271, E-mail: info@stat.fsu.edu. *Application contact:* Chauncey Richburg, Academic Support Assistant, 850-644-3514, Fax: 850-644-5271, E-mail: richburg@stat.fsu.edu.

Florida State University, The Graduate School, College of Education, Department of Educational Psychology and Learning Systems, Program in Measurement and Statistics, Tallahassee, FL 32306. Offers MS, PhD, Ed S. *Faculty:* 5 full-time (3 women). *Students:* 28 full-time (17 women), 4 part-time (2 women); includes 4 minority (2 Black or African American, non-Hispanic/Latino; 1 Asian, non-Hispanic/Latino; 1 Hispanic/Latino), 21 international. Average age 32. 26 applicants, 58% accepted, 7 enrolled. In 2010, 8 master's, 1 doctorate awarded. *Degree requirements:* For master's, comprehensive exam; for doctorate, thesis/dissertation, preliminary exam, prospectus. *Entrance requirements:* Additional exam requirements/recommendations for international students: Required—TOEFL (minimum score 550 paper-based; 213 computer-based; 80 iBT). *Application deadline:* For fall admission, 7/1 for domestic and international students; for winter admission, 11/1 for domestic and international students; for spring admission, 3/1 for domestic and international students. Application fee: $30. Electronic applications accepted. *Expenses:* Tuition, state resident: full-time $8238.24. *Financial support:* Fellowships with full and partial tuition reimbursements, research assistantships with full and partial tuition reimbursements, teaching assistantships with full and partial tuition reimbursements available. *Faculty research:* Methods for meta analysis; IRT/mixIRT; CBT; modeling, especially of large data sets. *Unit head:* Dr. Betsy Becker, Program Leader, 850-645-2371, Fax: 850-644-8776, E-mail: bbecker@fsu.edu. *Application contact:* Peggy Lollie, Program Assistant, 850-644-8786, Fax: 850-644-8776, E-mail: plollie@fsu.edu.

George Mason University, Volgenau School of Engineering, Department of Statistics, Fairfax, VA 22030. Offers biostatistics (Certificate); federal statistics (Certificate); statistical science (MS, PhD). Part-time and evening/weekend programs available. *Faculty:* 11 full-time (2 women), 5 part-time/adjunct (0 women). *Students:* 14 full-time (9 women), 55 part-time (23 women); includes 2 Black or African American, non-Hispanic/Latino; 11 Asian, non-Hispanic/Latino; 3 Hispanic/Latino, 17 international. Average age 32. 61 applicants, 77% accepted, 19 enrolled. In 2010, 17 master's, 2 doctorates, 1 other advanced degree awarded. Terminal master's awarded for partial completion of doctoral program. *Degree requirements:* For master's, comprehensive exam, thesis optional, qualifying exams; for doctorate, comprehensive exam, thesis/dissertation, qualifying exams. *Entrance requirements:* For master's, GRE (recommended), letters of recommendation, resume; for doctorate, GRE (recommended), personal goal statement, resume, 2 transcripts, letters of recommendation. Additional exam requirements/recommendations for international students: Required—TOEFL (minimum score 570 paper-based; 230 computer-based; 88 iBT), IELTS (minimum score 6.5). *Application deadline:* For fall admission, 3/15 priority date for domestic students, 12/15 priority date for international students; for spring admission, 10/1 for domestic and international students. Applications are processed on a rolling basis. Application fee: $100. Electronic applications accepted. *Expenses:* Tuition, state resident: full-time $8192; part-time $440 per credit hour. Tuition, nonresident: full-time $22,952; part-time $1055 per credit hour. Required fees: $2364; $99 per credit hour. *Financial support:* In 2010–11, 22 students received support, including 2 fellowships with full tuition reimbursements available (averaging $18,000 per year), 5 research assistantships with full and partial tuition reimbursements available (averaging $15,170 per year), 15 teaching assistantships with full and partial tuition reimbursements available (averaging $11,180 per year); Federal Work-Study, scholarships/grants, unspecified assistantships, and health care benefits (full-time research or teaching assistantship recipients) also available. Financial award application deadline: 3/1; financial award applicants required to submit FAFSA. *Faculty research:* Computational statistics, nonparametric function estimation, scientific and statistical visualization, statistical applications to engineering, survey research. Total annual research expenditures: $179,978. *Unit head:* Dr. William Rosenberger, Chair, 703-993-3645, Fax: 703-993-1700,

290 www.facebook.com/petersonspublishing

Peterson's Graduate Programs in the Physical Sciences, Mathematics, Agricultural Sciences, the Environment & Natural Resources 2012

E-mail: satistics@gmu.edu. *Application contact:* Elizabeth Quigley, Administrative Assistant, 703-993-9107, E-mail: equigley@gmu.edu.

Georgetown University, Graduate School of Arts and Sciences, Department of Mathematics, Washington, DC 20057. Offers mathematics and statistics (MS).

The George Washington University, Columbian College of Arts and Sciences, Department of Statistics, Washington, DC 20052. Offers statistics (MS, PhD); survey design and data analysis (Graduate Certificate). Part-time and evening/weekend programs available. *Faculty:* 17 full-time (5 women), 14 part-time/adjunct (2 women). *Students:* 40 full-time (24 women), 75 part-time (33 women); includes 8 Black or African American, non-Hispanic/Latino; 8 Asian, non-Hispanic/Latino; 3 Hispanic/Latino, 50 international. Average age 29. 220 applicants, 87% accepted, 38 enrolled. In 2010, 8 master's, 2 doctorates, 14 other advanced degrees awarded. Terminal master's awarded for partial completion of doctoral program. *Degree requirements:* For master's, comprehensive exam; for doctorate, thesis/dissertation, general exam. *Entrance requirements:* For master's and doctorate, GRE General Test, interview, minimum GPA of 3.0. Additional exam requirements/recommendations for international students: Required—TOEFL (minimum score 550 paper-based; 213 computer-based; 80 iBT). *Application deadline:* For fall admission, 1/15 priority date for domestic and international students; for spring admission, 10/1 priority date for domestic students, 9/1 priority date for international students. Applications are processed on a rolling basis. Application fee: $75. Electronic applications accepted. *Financial support:* In 2010–11, 13 students received support; fellowships with tuition reimbursements available, teaching assistantships with tuition reimbursements available, Federal Work-Study and tuition waivers available. Financial award application deadline: 1/15. *Unit head:* Dr. Reza Modarres, Chair, 202-994-6888, E-mail: reza@gwu.edu. *Application contact:* Information Contact, 202-994-6356, Fax: 202-994-6917.

Georgia Institute of Technology, Graduate Studies and Research, College of Sciences, School of Mathematics, Atlanta, GA 30332-0001. Offers algorithms, combinatorics, and optimization (PhD); applied mathematics (MS); bioinformatics (PhD); mathematics (PhD); quantitative and computational finance (MS); statistics (MS Stat). Terminal master's awarded for partial completion of doctoral program. *Degree requirements:* For master's, thesis or alternative; for doctorate, one foreign language, thesis/dissertation. *Entrance requirements:* For master's, GRE General Test, minimum GPA of 3.0; for doctorate, GRE General Test, GRE Subject Test, minimum GPA of 3.0. Additional exam requirements/recommendations for international students: Required—TOEFL. Electronic applications accepted. *Faculty research:* Dynamical systems, discrete mathematics, probability and statistics, mathematical physics.

Georgia Institute of Technology, Graduate Studies and Research, Multidisciplinary Program in Statistics, Atlanta, GA 30332-0001. Offers MS Stat. Part-time programs available. *Degree requirements:* For master's, thesis optional. *Entrance requirements:* For master's, GRE General Test, minimum GPA of 3.0. Additional exam requirements/recommendations for international students: Required—TOEFL. *Faculty research:* Statistical control procedures, statistical modeling of transportation systems.

Georgia State University, College of Arts and Sciences, Department of Mathematics and Statistics, Atlanta, GA 30302-3083. Offers mathematics (MA, MS); mathematics and statistics (PhD). Part-time and evening/weekend programs available. *Degree requirements:* For master's, comprehensive exam (for some programs), thesis (for some programs), exam; for doctorate, comprehensive exam, thesis/dissertation. *Entrance requirements:* For master's and doctorate, GRE. Additional exam requirements/recommendations for international students: Required—TOEFL. Electronic applications accepted. *Faculty research:* Analysis, biostatistics, discrete mathematics, linear algebra, statistics.

Hampton University, Graduate College, Program in Applied Mathematics, Hampton, VA 23668. Offers computational mathematics (MS); nonlinear science (MS); statistics and probability (MS). *Degree requirements:* For master's, thesis optional. *Entrance requirements:* For master's, GRE General Test.

Harvard University, Graduate School of Arts and Sciences, Department of Statistics, Cambridge, MA 02138. Offers AM, PhD. Terminal master's awarded for partial completion of doctoral program. *Degree requirements:* For master's, one foreign language; for doctorate, one foreign language, thesis/dissertation, exam, qualifying paper. *Entrance requirements:* For master's and doctorate, GRE General Test, GRE Subject Test (recommended). Additional exam requirements/recommendations for international students: Required—TOEFL. *Expenses:* Tuition: Full-time $34,976. Required fees: $1166. Full-time tuition and fees vary according to program. *Faculty research:* Interactive graphic analysis of multidimensional data, data analysis, modeling and inference, statistical modeling of U.S. economic time series.

Indiana University Bloomington, University Graduate School, College of Arts and Sciences, Department of Mathematics, Bloomington, IN 47405-7000. Offers applied mathematics-numerical analysis (MA, PhD); mathematics education (MAT); probability-statistics (MA, PhD); pure mathematics (MA). *Faculty:* 46 full-time (3 women). *Students:* 130 full-time (25 women), 1 part-time (0 women); includes 11 minority (1 Black or African American, non-Hispanic/Latino; 1 American Indian or Alaska Native, non-Hispanic/Latino; 8 Asian, non-Hispanic/Latino; 1 Hispanic/Latino), 72 international. Average age 27. 223 applicants, 25% accepted, 27 enrolled. In 2010, 12 master's, 13 doctorates awarded. Terminal master's awarded for partial completion of doctoral program. *Degree requirements:* For doctorate, one foreign language, thesis/dissertation. *Entrance requirements:* For master's and doctorate, GRE General Test, GRE Subject Test. Additional exam requirements/recommendations for international students: Required—TOEFL. *Application deadline:* For fall admission, 1/15 priority date for domestic and international students. Applications are processed on a rolling basis. Application fee: $55 ($65 for international students). Electronic applications accepted. *Financial support:* In 2010–11, 2 students received support, including 9 fellowships with full tuition reimbursements available (averaging $21,450 per year), 11 research assistantships with full tuition reimbursements available (averaging $16,045 per year), 96 teaching assistantships with full tuition reimbursements available (averaging $15,870 per year); scholarships/grants, health care benefits, and unspecified assistantships also available. Financial award application deadline: 1/15. *Faculty research:* Topology, geometry, algebra, applied, analysis. *Unit head:* Kevin Zumbrun, Chair, 812-855-2200. *Application contact:* Kate Bowman, Graduate Secretary, 812-855-2645, Fax: 812-855-0046, E-mail: gradmath@indiana.edu.

Iowa State University of Science and Technology, Graduate College, College of Liberal Arts and Sciences, Department of Statistics, Ames, IA 50011. Offers MS, PhD, MBA/MS. *Faculty:* 37 full-time (11 women). *Students:* 134 full-time (53 women), 41 part-time (19 women); includes 17 Black or African American, non-Hispanic/Latino; 1 American Indian or Alaska Native, non-Hispanic/Latino; 8 Asian, non-Hispanic/Latino, 68 international. 373 applicants, 10% accepted, 20 enrolled. In 2010, 22 master's, 13 doctorates awarded. *Degree requirements:* For master's, thesis or alternative; for doctorate, thesis/dissertation. *Entrance requirements:* For master's and doctorate, GRE General Test. Additional exam requirements/recommendations for international students: Required—TOEFL (minimum score 550 paper-based; 80 iBT), IELTS (minimum score 6.5). *Application deadline:* For fall admission, 3/15 priority date for domestic and international students; for spring admission, 10/31 for domestic and international students. Applications are processed on a rolling basis. Application fee: $40 ($90 for international students). *Financial support:* In 2010–11, 58 research assistantships with full and partial tuition reimbursements (averaging $11,583 per year), 63 teaching assistantships with full and partial tuition reimbursements (averaging $14,112 per year) were awarded; fellowships, scholarships/grants, health care benefits, and unspecified assistantships also available. *Unit head:* Dr. Kenneth Koehler, Chair, 515-294-4181, Fax: 515-294-4040, E-mail: statistics@iastate.edu. *Application contact:* Dr. Alicia Carriguiry, Director of Graduate Education, 515-294-3440, E-mail: statistics@iastate.edu.

James Madison University, The Graduate School, College of Science and Mathematics, Department of Mathematics and Statistics, Harrisonburg, VA 22807. Offers M Ed. Part-time programs available. *Faculty:* 2 full-time (1 woman). *Students:* 5 part-time (3 women). Average age 27. In 2010, 2 master's awarded. *Degree requirements:* For master's, comprehensive exam. *Entrance requirements:* For master's, undergraduate major in mathematics. *Application deadline:* For fall admission, 5/1 priority date for domestic students; for spring admission, 9/1 priority date for domestic students. Application fee: $55. *Financial support:* Application deadline: 3/1. *Unit head:* Dr. David C. Carothers, Academic Unit Head, 540-568-6184, E-mail: carothdc@jmu.edu. *Application contact:* Lynette M. Bible, Director of Graduate Admissions, 540-568-6395, Fax: 540-568-7860, E-mail: biblelm@jmu.edu.

The Johns Hopkins University, G. W. C. Whiting School of Engineering, Department of Applied Mathematics and Statistics, Baltimore, MD 21218-2699. Offers computational medicine (PhD); discrete mathematics (MA, MSE, PhD); financial mathematics (MSE); operations research/optimization/decision science (MA, MSE, PhD); statistics/probability/stochastic processes (MA, MSE, PhD). *Faculty:* 17 full-time (3 women), 4 part-time/adjunct (0 women). *Students:* 72 full-time (27 women), 3 part-time (0 women); includes 10 minority (1 Black or African American, non-Hispanic/Latino; 7 Asian, non-Hispanic/Latino; 2 Two or more races, non-Hispanic/Latino), 51 international. Average age 25. 306 applicants, 47% accepted, 36 enrolled. In 2010, 26 master's, 7 doctorates awarded. Terminal master's awarded for partial completion of doctoral program. *Degree requirements:* For master's, thesis (for some programs); for doctorate, thesis/dissertation, oral exam, introductory exam. *Entrance requirements:* For master's and doctorate, GRE General Test, GRE Subject Test. Additional exam requirements/recommendations for international students: Required—TOEFL (minimum score 600 paper-based; 250 computer-based; 100 iBT). *Application deadline:* For fall admission, 1/15 for domestic and international students; for spring admission, 9/15 for domestic and international students. Application fee: $75. Electronic applications accepted. *Financial support:* In 2010–11, 40 students received support, including 9 fellowships with full tuition reimbursements available (averaging $19,800 per year), 19 research assistantships with full tuition reimbursements available (averaging $1,800 per year), 9 teaching assistantships with full tuition reimbursements available (averaging $1,800 per year); Federal Work-Study, institutionally sponsored loans, scholarships/grants, health care benefits, tuition waivers (partial), and unspecified assistantships also available. Financial award application deadline: 1/15. *Faculty research:* Discrete mathematics, probability, statistics, optimization and operations research, scientific computation, financial mathematics. Total annual research expenditures: $1.3 million. *Unit head:* Dr. Daniel Q. Naiman, Chair, 410-516-7203, Fax: 410-516-7459, E-mail: daniel.naiman@jhu.edu. *Application contact:* Kristin Bechtel, Academic Program Coordinator, 410-516-7198, Fax: 410-516-7459, E-mail: kbechtel@jhu.edu.

The Johns Hopkins University, G. W. C. Whiting School of Engineering, Program in Engineering Management, Baltimore, MD 21218-2699. Offers biomaterials (MSEM); communications science (MSEM); computer science (MSEM); fluid mechanics (MSEM); materials science and engineering (MSEM); mechanical engineering (MSEM); mechanics and materials (MSEM); nano-biotechnology (MSEM); nanomaterials and nanotechnology (MSEM); probability and statistics (MSEM); smart product and device design (MSEM); systems analysis, management and environmental policy (MSEM). *Students:* 32 full-time (5 women), 4 part-time (0 women); includes 7 minority (3 Black or African American, non-Hispanic/Latino; 3 Asian, non-Hispanic/Latino; 1 Hispanic/Latino), 11 international. Average age 23. 110 applicants, 60% accepted, 27 enrolled. In 2010, 6 master's awarded. *Entrance requirements:* For master's, GRE, 3 letters of recommendation, resume. Additional exam requirements/recommendations for international students: Required—TOEFL (minimum score 600 paper-based; 250 computer-based; 100 iBT) or IELTS (minimum score 7). *Application deadline:* For fall admission, 1/15 priority date for domestic students, 1/15 for international students; for spring admission, 9/15 priority date for domestic students, 9/15 for international students. Applications are processed on a rolling basis. Application fee: $75. Electronic applications accepted. *Financial support:* Fellowships, health care benefits available. *Unit head:* Dr. Edward R. Scheinerman, Interim Director/Vice Dean for Education, School of Engineering/Professor, Applied Mathematics and Statistics, 410-516-7395, Fax: 410-516-4880, E-mail: ers@jhu.edu. *Application contact:* Dennis McIver, Coordinator of Graduate Admissions, 410-516-8174, Fax: 410-516-0780, E-mail: graduateadmissions@jhu.edu.

Kansas State University, Graduate School, College of Arts and Sciences, Department of Statistics, Manhattan, KS 66506. Offers MS, PhD. Terminal master's awarded for partial completion of doctoral program. *Degree requirements:* For master's, thesis optional; for doctorate, thesis/dissertation, qualifying and preliminary exams. *Entrance requirements:* For master's, GRE; for doctorate, previous course work in statistics and mathematics. Additional exam requirements/recommendations for international students: Required—TOEFL (minimum score 550 paper-based; 213 computer-based). Electronic applications accepted. *Faculty research:* Linear and nonlinear statistical models, design analysis of experiments, nonparametric methods for reliability and survival data, resampling methods and their application, categorical data analysis.

Lehigh University, College of Arts and Sciences, Department of Mathematics, Bethlehem, PA 18015. Offers applied mathematics (MS, PhD); mathematics (MS, PhD); statistics (MS). Part-time programs available. *Faculty:* 21 full-time (1 woman). *Students:* 37 full-time (20 women), 3 part-time (0 women); includes 2 minority (1 Asian, non-Hispanic/Latino; 1 Hispanic/Latino), 17 international. Average age 25. 105 applicants, 50% accepted, 11 enrolled. In 2010, 6 master's, 5 doctorates awarded. Terminal master's awarded for partial completion of doctoral program. *Degree requirements:* For master's, comprehensive exam, thesis optional; for doctorate, comprehensive exam, thesis/dissertation, qualifying exams, general exam. *Entrance requirements:* For master's and doctorate, minimum undergraduate GPA of 2.75, 3.0 for last two semesters; adequate background in math. Additional exam requirements/recommendations for international students: Required—TOEFL (minimum score 550 paper-based; 213 computer-based; 85 iBT). *Application deadline:* For fall admission, 1/15 priority date for domestic and international students; for spring admission, 12/1 priority date for domestic and international students. Applications are processed on a rolling basis. Application fee: $75. Electronic applications accepted. *Financial support:* In 2010–11, 35 students received support, including 2 fellowships with full tuition reimbursements available (averaging $25,000 per year), 23 teaching assistantships with full tuition reimbursements available (averaging $17,500 per year); research assistantships with full tuition reimbursements available, scholarships/grants and tuition waivers (partial) also available. Financial award application deadline: 1/15. *Faculty research:* Probability and statistics, geometry and topology, number theory, algebra, differential equations. Total annual research expenditures: $192,998. *Unit head:* Dr. Wei-Min Huang, Chairman, 610-758-3730, Fax: 610-758-3767, E-mail: wh02@lehigh.edu. *Application contact:* Dr. Terry Napier, Graduate Coordinator, 610-758-3755, E-mail: mathgrad@lehigh.edu.

Louisiana State University and Agricultural and Mechanical College, Graduate School, College of Agriculture, Department of Experimental Statistics, Baton Rouge, LA 70803. Offers applied statistics (M App St). Part-time programs available. *Faculty:* 9 full-time (1 woman). *Students:* 15 full-time (12 women), 4 part-time (2 women); includes 2 Asian, non-Hispanic/Latino, 11 international. Average age 29. 23 applicants, 57% accepted, 4 enrolled. In 2010, 8 master's awarded. *Degree requirements:* For master's, project. *Entrance requirements:* For master's, GRE General Test, minimum GPA of 3.0. Additional exam requirements/recommendations for international students: Required—TOEFL (minimum score 550 paper-based; 213 computer-based; 79 iBT) or IELTS (minimum score 6.5). *Application deadline:* For fall admission, 1/25 priority date for domestic students, 5/15 for international students; for

Statistics

Louisiana State University and Agricultural and Mechanical College (continued)
spring admission, 10/15 priority date for domestic students, 10/15 for international students. Applications are processed on a rolling basis. Application fee: $50 ($70 for international students). Electronic applications accepted. *Financial support:* In 2010–11, 14 students received support, including 2 research assistantships with partial tuition reimbursements available (averaging $14,700 per year), 10 teaching assistantships with partial tuition reimbursements available (averaging $10,085 per year); fellowships, career-related internships or fieldwork, Federal Work-Study, institutionally sponsored loans, tuition waivers (full and partial), and unspecified assistantships also available. Financial award application deadline: 4/1; financial award applicants required to submit FAFSA. *Faculty research:* Linear models, statistical computing, ecological statistics. *Unit head:* Dr. James Geaghan, Head, 225-578-8303, Fax: 225-578-8344, E-mail: head@stat.lsu.edu. *Application contact:* Dr. James Geaghan, Graduate Adviser, 225-578-8303, E-mail: jgeaghan@lsu.edu.

Louisiana Tech University, Graduate School, College of Engineering and Science, Department of Mathematics and Statistics, Ruston, LA 71272. Offers MS. Part-time programs available. *Degree requirements:* For master's, thesis or alternative. *Entrance requirements:* For master's, GRE General Test, minimum GPA of 3.0 in last 60 hours. Additional exam requirements/recommendations for international students: Required—TOEFL.

Loyola University Chicago, Graduate School, Department of Mathematical Sciences and Statistics, Chicago, IL 60660. Offers applied statistics (MS); mathematics and statistics (MS), including pure mathematics. Part-time programs available. *Faculty:* 19 full-time (4 women). *Students:* 29 full-time (20 women), 6 part-time (2 women); includes 11 minority (1 Black or African American, non-Hispanic/Latino; 6 Asian, non-Hispanic/Latino; 3 Hispanic/Latino; 1 Two or more races, non-Hispanic/Latino), 6 international. Average age 28. 64 applicants, 75% accepted, 23 enrolled. In 2010, 21 master's awarded. *Entrance requirements:* For master's, GRE General Test. Additional exam requirements/recommendations for international students: Required—TOEFL. *Application deadline:* For fall admission, 8/1 for domestic students; for spring admission, 12/1 for domestic students. Applications are processed on a rolling basis. Application fee: $0. Electronic applications accepted. *Expenses:* Tuition: Full-time $14,940; part-time $830 per credit hour. Required fees: $87 per semester. Part-time tuition and fees vary according to course load and program. *Financial support:* In 2010–11, 13 students received support, including 6 teaching assistantships with tuition reimbursements available (averaging $10,000 per year); career-related internships or fieldwork, Federal Work-Study, institutionally sponsored loans, and tuition waivers (partial) also available. Financial award application deadline: 3/15. *Faculty research:* Probability and statistics, differential equations, algebra, combinations. Total annual research expenditures: $10,000. *Unit head:* Dr. Robert Jensen, Chair, 773-508-3578, Fax: 773-508-2123, E-mail: rjensen@luc.edu. *Application contact:* Dr. W. Cary Huffman, Graduate Program Director, Mathematics, 773-508-3563, Fax: 773-508-2123, E-mail: whuffma@luc.edu.

McGill University, Faculty of Graduate and Postdoctoral Studies, Faculty of Arts, Department of Economics, Montréal, QC H3A 2T5, Canada. Offers economics (MA, PhD); social statistics (MA).

McGill University, Faculty of Graduate and Postdoctoral Studies, Faculty of Arts, Department of Sociology, Montréal, QC H3A 2T5, Canada. Offers medical sociology (MA); neo-tropical environment (MA); social statistics (MA); sociology (MA, PhD, Diploma).

McGill University, Faculty of Graduate and Postdoctoral Studies, Faculty of Science, Department of Mathematics and Statistics, Montréal, QC H3A 2T5, Canada. Offers computational science and engineering (M Sc); mathematics and statistics (M Sc, MA, PhD), including applied mathematics (M Sc, MA), pure mathematics (M Sc, MA), statistics (M Sc, MA).

McMaster University, School of Graduate Studies, Faculty of Science, Department of Mathematics and Statistics, Program in Statistics, Hamilton, ON L8S 4M2, Canada. Offers applied statistics (M Sc); medical statistics (M Sc); statistical theory (M Sc). *Degree requirements:* For master's, thesis or alternative. *Entrance requirements:* For master's, honors degree background in mathematics and statistics. Additional exam requirements/recommendations for international students: Required—TOEFL (minimum score 550 paper-based; 213 computer-based). *Faculty research:* Development of polymer production technology, quality of life in patients who use pharmaceutical agents, mathematical modeling, order statistics from progressively censored samples, nonlinear stochastic model in genetics.

McNeese State University, Doré School of Graduate Studies, College of Science, Department of Mathematics, Computer Science, and Statistics, Lake Charles, LA 70609. Offers computer science (MS); mathematics (MS); statistics (MS). Evening/weekend programs available. *Faculty:* 11 full-time (3 women). *Students:* 25 full-time (9 women), 13 part-time (5 women); includes 3 minority (1 Black or African American, non-Hispanic/Latino; 1 Asian, non-Hispanic/Latino; 1 Hispanic/Latino), 27 international. In 2010, 17 master's awarded. *Degree requirements:* For master's, comprehensive exam, thesis or alternative, written exam. *Entrance requirements:* For master's, GRE. *Application deadline:* For fall admission, 5/15 priority date for domestic and international students; for spring admission, 10/15 priority date for domestic and international students. Applications are processed on a rolling basis. Application fee: $20 ($30 for international students). Tuition and fees vary according to course load. *Financial support:* Teaching assistantships available. Financial award application deadline: 5/1. *Unit head:* Sid Bradley, Head, 337-475-5788, Fax: 337-475-5799, E-mail: sbradley@mcneese.edu. *Application contact:* Dr. George F. Mead, Interim Dean of Dore' School of Graduate Studies, 337-475-5396, Fax: 337-475-5397, E-mail: admissions@mcneese.edu.

Memorial University of Newfoundland, School of Graduate Studies, Department of Mathematics and Statistics, St. John's, NL A1C 5S7, Canada. Offers mathematics (M Sc, PhD); statistics (M Sc, MAS, PhD). Part-time programs available. *Degree requirements:* For master's, thesis, practicum and report (MAS); for doctorate, comprehensive exam, thesis/dissertation, oral defense of thesis. *Entrance requirements:* For master's, 2nd class honors degree (MAS); for doctorate, MAS or M Sc in mathematics and statistics. Electronic applications accepted. *Faculty research:* Algebra, topology, applied mathematics, mathematical statistics, applied statistics and probability.

Miami University, Graduate School, College of Arts and Science, Department of Statistics, Oxford, OH 45056. Offers MS. *Students:* 17 full-time (9 women); includes 3 minority (all Asian, non-Hispanic/Latino), 7 international. Average age 26. In 2010, 6 master's awarded. *Entrance requirements:* Additional exam requirements/recommendations for international students: Required—TOEFL. Application fee: $50. *Expenses:* Tuition, state resident: full-time $11,616; part-time $484 per credit hour. Tuition, nonresident: full-time $25,656; part-time $1069 per credit hour. Required fees: $528. *Financial support:* Research assistantships, teaching assistantships, health care benefits and unspecified assistantships available. Financial award application deadline: 3/1; financial award applicants required to submit FAFSA. *Unit head:* Dr. A. John Bailer, Professor/Chair, 513-529-3538, E-mail: baileraj@muohio.edu. *Application contact:* Dr. David J. Groggel, Associate Professor and Director of Graduate Studies, 513-529-6087, E-mail: groggedj@muohio.edu.

Michigan State University, The Graduate School, College of Natural Science, Department of Statistics and Probability, East Lansing, MI 48824. Offers applied statistics (MS); statistics (MS, PhD). *Entrance requirements:* Additional exam requirements/recommendations for international students: Required—TOEFL. Electronic applications accepted.

Minnesota State University Mankato, College of Graduate Studies, College of Science, Engineering and Technology, Department of Mathematics and Statistics, Program in Statistics, Mankato, MN 56001. Offers MS. *Students:* 4 full-time (2 women), 3 part-time (0 women). *Degree requirements:* For master's, one foreign language, comprehensive exam, thesis or alternative. *Entrance requirements:* For master's, GRE General Test, minimum GPA of 3.0 during previous 2 years. Additional exam requirements/recommendations for international students: Required—TOEFL. *Application deadline:* For fall admission, 7/1 priority date for domestic students; for spring admission, 11/1 for domestic students. Applications are processed on a rolling basis. Application fee: $40. Electronic applications accepted. *Financial support:* Research assistantships with partial tuition reimbursements, teaching assistantships with partial tuition reimbursements, unspecified assistantships available. Financial award application deadline: 3/15; financial award applicants required to submit FAFSA. *Unit head:* Dr. Brian Martensen, Chairperson, 507-389-1453. *Application contact:* 507-389-2321, E-mail: grad@mnsu.edu.

Mississippi State University, College of Arts and Sciences, Department of Mathematics and Statistics, Mississippi State, MS 39762. Offers mathematical sciences (PhD); mathematics (MS); statistics (MS). Part-time programs available. *Faculty:* 20 full-time (4 women). *Students:* 40 full-time (23 women), 3 part-time (1 woman); includes 6 minority (3 Black or African American, non-Hispanic/Latino; 2 Asian, non-Hispanic/Latino; 1 Two or more races, non-Hispanic/Latino), 23 international. Average age 28. 54 applicants, 52% accepted, 16 enrolled. In 2010, 7 master's, 1 doctorate awarded. Terminal master's awarded for partial completion of doctoral program. *Degree requirements:* For master's, thesis optional, comprehensive oral or written exam; for doctorate, one foreign language, thesis/dissertation, comprehensive oral and written exam. *Entrance requirements:* For master's, minimum GPA of 2.75 on last two years of undergraduate courses; for doctorate, GRE. Additional exam requirements/recommendations for international students: Required—TOEFL (minimum score 475 paper-based; 153 computer-based; 53 iBT); Recommended—IELTS (minimum score 4.5). *Application deadline:* For fall admission, 3/15 priority date for domestic students, 5/1 for international students; for spring admission, 11/1 for domestic students, 9/1 for international students. Applications are processed on a rolling basis. Application fee: $40. Electronic applications accepted. *Expenses:* Tuition, state resident: full-time $2730.50; part-time $304 per credit hour. Tuition, nonresident: full-time $6901; part-time $767 per credit hour. *Financial support:* In 2010–11, 29 teaching assistantships with full tuition reimbursements (averaging $13,472 per year) were awarded; Federal Work-Study, institutionally sponsored loans, tuition waivers (partial), and unspecified assistantships also available. Financial award application deadline: 4/1; financial award applicants required to submit FAFSA. *Faculty research:* Differential equations, algebra, numerical analysis, functional analysis, applied statistics. Total annual research expenditures: $1.7 million. *Unit head:* Dr. Mohsen Razzaghi, Interim Head, 662-325-3414, Fax: 662-325-0005, E-mail: razzaghi@math.msstate.edu. *Application contact:* Dr. Corlis Johnson, Associate Department Head/Graduate Coordinator, 662-325-3414, Fax: 662-325-0005, E-mail: cjohnson@math.msstate.edu.

Missouri University of Science and Technology, Graduate School, Department of Mathematics and Statistics, Rolla, MO 65409. Offers applied mathematics (MS); mathematics (MST, PhD), including mathematics (PhD), mathematics education (MST), statistics (PhD). Terminal master's awarded for partial completion of doctoral program. *Degree requirements:* For master's, thesis or alternative; for doctorate, one foreign language, thesis/dissertation. *Entrance requirements:* For master's and doctorate, GRE General Test, GRE Subject Test. Electronic applications accepted. *Faculty research:* Analysis, differential equations, topology, statistics.

Montana State University, College of Graduate Studies, College of Letters and Science, Department of Ecology, Bozeman, MT 59717. Offers ecological and environmental statistics (MS); ecology and environmental sciences (PhD); fish and wildlife biology (PhD); fish and wildlife management (MS). Part-time programs available. *Faculty:* 12 full-time (2 women), 2 part-time/adjunct (0 women). *Students:* 3 full-time (2 women), 46 part-time (16 women). Average age 31. 11 applicants, 27% accepted, 3 enrolled. In 2010, 3 master's, 1 doctorate awarded. *Degree requirements:* For master's, comprehensive exam, thesis (for some programs); for doctorate, comprehensive exam, thesis/dissertation. *Entrance requirements:* For master's and doctorate, GRE, minimum GPA of 3.0, letters of recommendation, essay. Additional exam requirements/recommendations for international students: Required—TOEFL (minimum score 550 paper-based; 213 computer-based). *Application deadline:* For fall admission, 7/15 priority date for domestic students, 5/15 priority date for international students; for spring admission, 12/1 priority date for domestic students, 10/1 priority date for international students. Applications are processed on a rolling basis. Application fee: $30. Electronic applications accepted. *Expenses:* Tuition, state resident: full-time $5553.90. Tuition, nonresident: full-time $14,646. Required fees: $1233. *Financial support:* In 2010–11, 46 students received support, including 1 fellowship with full and partial tuition reimbursement available (averaging $19,200 per year), 32 research assistantships with full and partial tuition reimbursements available (averaging $18,000 per year), 16 teaching assistantships with full tuition reimbursements available (averaging $10,862 per year); career-related internships or fieldwork, institutionally sponsored loans, scholarships/grants, traineeships, health care benefits, tuition waivers (partial), and unspecified assistantships also available. Support available to part-time students. Financial award application deadline: 3/1; financial award applicants required to submit FAFSA. *Faculty research:* Community ecology, population ecology, land-use effects, management and conservation, environmental modeling. Total annual research expenditures: $2.6 million. *Unit head:* Dr. David Roberts, Head, 406-994-4548, Fax: 406-994-3190, E-mail: droberts@montana.edu. *Application contact:* Dr. Carl A. Fox, Vice Provost for Graduate Education, 406-994-4145, Fax: 406-994-7433, E-mail: gradstudy@montana.edu.

Montana State University, College of Graduate Studies, College of Letters and Science, Department of Mathematical Sciences, Bozeman, MT 59717. Offers mathematics (MS, PhD), including mathematics education option (MS); statistics (MS, PhD). Part-time programs available. Postbaccalaureate distance learning degree programs offered (minimal on-campus study). *Faculty:* 32 full-time (10 women), 12 part-time/adjunct (5 women). *Students:* 8 full-time (1 woman), 70 part-time (34 women); includes 3 minority (1 Asian, non-Hispanic/Latino; 1 Hispanic/Latino; 1 Two or more races, non-Hispanic/Latino), 6 international. Average age 31. 32 applicants, 50% accepted, 11 enrolled. In 2010, 24 master's, 6 doctorates awarded. *Degree requirements:* For master's, comprehensive exam, thesis (for some programs); for doctorate, comprehensive exam, thesis/dissertation. *Entrance requirements:* For master's and doctorate, GRE General Test. Additional exam requirements/recommendations for international students: Required—TOEFL (minimum score 550 paper-based; 213 computer-based). *Application deadline:* For fall admission, 7/15 priority date for domestic students, 5/15 priority date for international students; for spring admission, 12/1 priority date for domestic students, 10/1 priority date for international students. Applications are processed on a rolling basis. Application fee: $30. Electronic applications accepted. *Expenses:* Tuition, state resident: full-time $5553.90. Tuition, nonresident: full-time $14,646. Required fees: $1233. *Financial support:* In 2010–11, 55 students received support, including 2 research assistantships with tuition reimbursements available (averaging $14,450 per year), 53 teaching assistantships with tuition reimbursements available (averaging $14,250 per year); career-related internships or fieldwork, scholarships/grants, tuition waivers (full), and unspecified assistantships also available. Support available to part-time students. Financial award application deadline: 3/1; financial award applicants required to submit FAFSA. *Faculty research:* Applied mathematics, dynamical systems, statistics, mathematics education, mathematical and computational biology. Total annual research expenditures: $899,316. *Unit head:* Dr. Kenneth Bowers, Head, 406-994-3604, Fax: 406-994-1789, E-mail: bowers@math.montana.edu. *Application contact:* Dr. Carl A. Fox, Vice Provost for Graduate Education, 406-994-4145, Fax: 406-994-7433, E-mail: gradstudy@montana.edu.

Montclair State University, The Graduate School, College of Science and Mathematics, Department of Mathematics, Montclair, NJ 07043-1624. Offers math education (Ed D);

mathematics (Certificate); physical science (Certificate); statistics (MS), including mathematics education, pure and applied mathematics; teaching middle grades math (MA, Certificate). Part-time and evening/weekend programs available. *Faculty:* 32 full-time (10 women), 30 part-time/adjunct (14 women). *Students:* 21 full-time (9 women), 109 part-time (81 women); includes 9 Black or African American, non-Hispanic/Latino; 5 Asian, non-Hispanic/Latino; 9 Hispanic/Latino; 2 Two or more races, non-Hispanic/Latino, 1 international. Average age 34. 36 applicants, 81% accepted, 20 enrolled. In 2010, 28 master's, 2 doctorates, 7 other advanced degrees awarded. *Degree requirements:* For master's, comprehensive exam. *Entrance requirements:* For master's, GRE General Test, 2 letters of recommendation. Additional exam requirements/recommendations for international students: Required—TOEFL (minimum iBT score of 83) or IELTS. *Application deadline:* For fall admission, 6/1 for international students; for spring admission, 10/1 for international students. Applications are processed on a rolling basis. Application fee: $60. *Expenses:* Tuition, state resident: part-time $501.34 per credit. Tuition, nonresident: part-time $773.88 per credit. Required fees: $71.15 per credit. *Financial support:* In 2010–11, 8 research assistantships with full tuition reimbursements (averaging $7,000 per year), 1 teaching assistantship with full tuition reimbursement (averaging $15,000 per year) were awarded; Federal Work-Study, scholarships/grants, and unspecified assistantships also available. Support available to part-time students. Financial award application deadline: 3/1; financial award applicants required to submit FAFSA. *Faculty research:* Mathematical sciences, math education. Total annual research expenditures: $1.2 million. *Unit head:* Dr. Helen Roberts, Chairperson, 973-655-5132. *Application contact:* Amy Aiello, Director of Graduate Admissions and Operations, 973-655-5147, Fax: 973-655-7869, E-mail: graduate.school@montclair.edu.

Murray State University, College of Science, Engineering and Technology, Program in Mathematics and Statistics, Murray, KY 42071. Offers MA, MAT, MS. Part-time programs available. *Degree requirements:* For master's, comprehensive exam, thesis optional. *Entrance requirements:* For master's, GRE General Test. Additional exam requirements/recommendations for international students: Required—TOEFL. *Faculty research:* Algebraic structures, mathematical biology, topolgy.

New York University, Leonard N. Stern School of Business, Department of Information, Operations and Management Sciences, New York, NY 10012-1019. Offers information systems (MBA, PhD); operations management (MBA, PhD); statistics (MBA, PhD). *Faculty research:* Knowledge management, economics of information, computer-supported groups and communities financial information systems, data mining and business intelligence.

North Carolina State University, Graduate School, College of Physical and Mathematical Sciences, Department of Statistics, Raleigh, NC 27695. Offers M Stat, MS, PhD. Part-time programs available. *Degree requirements:* For master's, comprehensive exam, thesis (for some programs), final oral exam; for doctorate, thesis/dissertation, final oral and written exams, written and oral preliminary exams. *Entrance requirements:* For master's and doctorate, GRE General Test. Additional exam requirements/recommendations for international students: Required—TOEFL. Electronic applications accepted. *Faculty research:* Biostatistics; time series; spatial, inference, environmental, industrial, genetics applications; nonlinear models; DOE.

North Dakota State University, College of Graduate and Interdisciplinary Studies, College of Science and Mathematics, Department of Statistics, Fargo, ND 58108. Offers applied statistics (MS, Certificate); statistics (PhD); MS/MS. *Faculty:* 4 full-time (2 women), 1 part-time/adjunct (0 women). *Students:* 1 (woman) full-time, 3 part-time (2 women), 1 international. Average age 24. 8 applicants, 100% accepted, 1 enrolled. In 2010, 2 doctorates awarded. *Degree requirements:* For master's, comprehensive exam, thesis; for doctorate, comprehensive exam, thesis/dissertation. *Entrance requirements:* For master's and doctorate, minimum GPA of 3.0. Additional exam requirements/recommendations for international students: Required—TOEFL (minimum score 550 paper-based; 213 computer-based; 79 iBT). *Application deadline:* Applications are processed on a rolling basis. Application fee: $45 ($60 for international students). *Financial support:* In 2010–11, 2 fellowships with full tuition reimbursements, 7 research assistantships with full tuition reimbursements, 9 teaching assistantships with full tuition reimbursements were awarded; career-related internships or fieldwork, Federal Work-Study, institutionally sponsored loans, and tuition waivers (full) also available. Financial award application deadline: 4/15. *Faculty research:* Nonparametric statistics, survival analysis, multivariate analysis, distribution theory, inference modeling, biostatistics. *Unit head:* Dr. Rhonda Magel, Chair, 701-231-7532, Fax: 701-231-8734, E-mail: ndsu.stats@ndsu.edu. *Application contact:* Judy Normann, Academic Assistant, 701-231-7532, Fax: 702-231-8734, E-mail: ndsu.stats@ndsu.edu.

Northern Arizona University, Graduate College, College of Engineering, Forestry and Natural Sciences, Department of Mathematics and Statistics, Flagstaff, AZ 86011. Offers applied statistics (Certificate); mathematics (MAT, MS); statistics (MS). Part-time programs available. *Faculty:* 42 full-time (12 women). *Students:* 23 full-time (10 women), 18 part-time (11 women); includes 8 minority (3 Black or African American, non-Hispanic/Latino; 1 Asian, non-Hispanic/Latino; 4 Hispanic/Latino), 1 international. Average age 28. 33 applicants, 61% accepted, 12 enrolled. In 2010, 15 master's, 1 other advanced degree awarded. *Degree requirements:* For master's, comprehensive exam (for some programs), thesis (for some programs). *Entrance requirements:* For master's, minimum GPA of 3.0. Additional exam requirements/recommendations for international students: Required—TOEFL (minimum score 550 paper-based; 213 computer-based; 80 iBT), IELTS (minimum score 7). *Application deadline:* For fall admission, 3/15 priority date for domestic and international students; for spring admission, 10/15 priority date for domestic and international students. Applications are processed on a rolling basis. Application fee: $65. Electronic applications accepted. *Financial support:* In 2010–11, 22 teaching assistantships with partial tuition reimbursements (averaging $14,051 per year) were awarded; Federal Work-Study, scholarships/grants, health care benefits, tuition waivers (full and partial), and unspecified assistantships also available. Financial award applicants required to submit FAFSA. *Faculty research:* Topology, statistics, groups, ring theory, number theory. *Unit head:* Dr. Janet M. McShane, Chair, 928-523-1252, Fax: 928-523-5847, E-mail: janet.mcshane@nau.edu. *Application contact:* Sharon O'Connor, Chair, 928-523-3481, Fax: 928-523-5847, E-mail: math.grad@nau.edu.

Northern Illinois University, Graduate School, College of Liberal Arts and Sciences, Department of Mathematical Sciences, Division of Statistics, De Kalb, IL 60115-2854. Offers MS. Part-time programs available. *Faculty:* 8 full-time (1 woman), 1 part-time/adjunct (0 women). *Students:* 12 full-time (5 women), 4 part-time (3 women); includes 2 Asian, non-Hispanic/Latino, 8 international. Average age 29. 28 applicants, 68% accepted, 9 enrolled. In 2010, 6 master's awarded. *Degree requirements:* For master's, comprehensive exam, thesis optional. *Entrance requirements:* For master's, GRE General Test, minimum GPA of 2.75, course work in statistics, calculus, linear algebra. Additional exam requirements/recommendations for international students: Required—TOEFL (minimum score 550 paper-based; 213 computer-based). *Application deadline:* For fall admission, 6/1 for domestic students, 5/1 for international students; for spring admission, 11/1 for domestic students, 10/1 for international students. Applications are processed on a rolling basis. Application fee: $30. Electronic applications accepted. *Expenses:* Tuition, state resident: full-time $7200; part-time $300 per credit hour. Tuition, nonresident: full-time $14,400; part-time $600 per credit hour. Required fees: $79 per credit hour. *Financial support:* In 2010–11, 1 research assistantship with full tuition reimbursement, 18 teaching assistantships with full tuition reimbursements were awarded; fellowships with full tuition reimbursements, career-related internships or fieldwork, Federal Work-Study, scholarships/grants, tuition waivers (full), and unspecified assistantships also available. Support available to part-time students. Financial award applicants required to submit FAFSA. *Faculty research:* Reality and life testing, quality control, statistical inference from stochastic process, nonparametric statistics. *Unit head:* Dr. Rama T. Lingham, Director, 815-753-6773, Fax: 815-753-6776. *Application contact:* Dr. Alan Polansky, Director, Graduate Studies, 815-753-6864, E-mail: polansky@math.niu.edu.

Northwestern University, The Graduate School, Judd A. and Marjorie Weinberg College of Arts and Sciences, Department of Statistics, Evanston, IL 60208. Offers MS, PhD. Admissions and degrees offered through The Graduate School. Part-time programs available. Terminal master's awarded for partial completion of doctoral program. *Degree requirements:* For master's, final exam; for doctorate, thesis/dissertation, preliminary exam, final exam. *Entrance requirements:* For master's and doctorate, GRE General Test. Additional exam requirements/recommendations for international students: Required—TOEFL. *Faculty research:* Theoretical statistics, applied statistics, computational methods, statistical designs, complex models.

Oakland University, Graduate Study and Lifelong Learning, College of Arts and Sciences, Department of Mathematics and Statistics, Program in Statistical Methods, Rochester, MI 48309-4401. Offers Certificate. *Entrance requirements:* Additional exam requirements/recommendations for international students: Required—TOEFL (minimum score 550 paper-based; 213 computer-based). *Expenses:* Contact institution.

The Ohio State University, Graduate School, College of Arts and Sciences, Division of Natural and Mathematical Sciences, Department of Statistics, Columbus, OH 43210. Offers biostatistics (PhD); statistics (M Appl Stat, MS, PhD). *Faculty:* 29. *Students:* 77 full-time (32 women), 40 part-time (18 women); includes 2 Black or African American, non-Hispanic/Latino; 5 Asian, non-Hispanic/Latino, 55 international. Average age 27. In 2010, 44 master's, 11 doctorates awarded. *Degree requirements:* For master's, thesis optional; for doctorate, thesis/dissertation. *Entrance requirements:* For master's and doctorate, GRE General Test. Additional exam requirements/recommendations for international students: Required—TOEFL (minimum score 600 paper-based; 250 computer-based). *Application deadline:* For fall admission, 8/15 priority date for domestic students, 7/1 priority date for international students; for winter admission, 12/1 priority date for domestic students, 11/1 priority date for international students; for spring admission, 3/1 priority date for domestic students, 2/1 priority date for international students. Applications are processed on a rolling basis. Application fee: $40 ($50 for international students). Electronic applications accepted. *Expenses:* Tuition, state resident: full-time $10,605. Tuition, nonresident: full-time $26,535. Tuition and fees vary according to course load and program. *Financial support:* Fellowships, research assistantships, teaching assistantships, Federal Work-Study and institutionally sponsored loans available. Support available to part-time students. *Unit head:* Doug Wolfe, Chair, 614-292-0293, Fax: 614-292-2096, E-mail: wolfe.9@osu.edu. *Application contact:* 614-292-9444, Fax: 614-292-3895, E-mail: domestic.grad@osu.edu.

Oklahoma State University, College of Arts and Sciences, Department of Statistics, Stillwater, OK 74078. Offers MS, PhD. *Faculty:* 7 full-time (3 women), 2 part-time/adjunct (1 woman). *Students:* 13 full-time (6 women), 13 part-time (5 women); includes 2 Asian, non-Hispanic/Latino, 15 international. Average age 31. 63 applicants, 38% accepted, 7 enrolled. In 2010, 4 master's, 1 doctorate awarded. *Degree requirements:* For master's, comprehensive exam, thesis optional; for doctorate, comprehensive exam, thesis/dissertation. *Entrance requirements:* For master's and doctorate, GRE. Additional exam requirements/recommendations for international students: Required—TOEFL (minimum score 550 paper-based), IELTS (minimum score 7). *Application deadline:* For fall admission, 3/1 priority date for international students; for spring admission, 8/1 priority date for international students. Applications are processed on a rolling basis. Application fee: $40 ($75 for international students). Electronic applications accepted. *Expenses:* Tuition, state resident: full-time $3716; part-time $154.85 per credit hour. Tuition, nonresident: full-time $14,892; part-time $621 per credit hour. Required fees: $2044; $85.20 per credit hour. One-time fee: $50. Tuition and fees vary according to course load and campus/location. *Financial support:* In 2010–11, 1 research assistantship (averaging $14,874 per year), 21 teaching assistantships (averaging $16,211 per year) were awarded; career-related internships or fieldwork, Federal Work-Study, scholarships/grants, health care benefits, tuition waivers (partial), and unspecified assistantships also available. Support available to part-time students. Financial award application deadline: 3/1; financial award applicants required to submit FAFSA. *Faculty research:* Linear models, sampling methods, ranking and selections procedures, categorical data, multiple comparisons. *Unit head:* Dr. Ibrahim Ahmad, Head, 405-744-5684, Fax: 405-744-3533. *Application contact:* Dr. Gordon Emslie, Dean, 405-744-6368, Fax: 405-744-0355, E-mail: grad-i@okstate.edu.

Oregon State University, Graduate School, College of Science, Department of Statistics, Corvallis, OR 97331. Offers operations research (MA, MS); statistics (MA, MS, PhD). Part-time programs available. *Degree requirements:* For master's, consulting experience; for doctorate, thesis/dissertation, consulting experience. *Entrance requirements:* For master's and doctorate, minimum GPA of 3.0 in last 90 hours. Additional exam requirements/recommendations for international students: Required—TOEFL. *Faculty research:* Analysis of enumerative data, nonparametric statistics, asymptotics, experimental design, generalized regression models, linear model theory, reliability theory, survival analysis, wildlife and general survey methodology.

Penn State University Park, Graduate School, Eberly College of Science, Department of Statistics, State College, University Park, PA 16802-1503. Offers MA, MAS, MS, PhD. *Unit head:* Dr. Bruce G. Lindsay, Head, 814-865-1348, Fax: 814-863-7114, E-mail: bgl@psu.edu. *Application contact:* Information Contact, 814-865-8630, E-mail: b2a@psu.edu.

Portland State University, Graduate Studies, College of Liberal Arts and Sciences, Department of Mathematics and Statistics, Portland, OR 97207-0751. Offers mathematical sciences (PhD); mathematics education (PhD); statistics (MS); MA/MS. *Faculty:* 31 full-time (10 women), 14 part-time/adjunct (6 women). *Students:* 57 full-time (19 women), 55 part-time (24 women); includes 1 Black or African American, non-Hispanic/Latino; 5 Asian, non-Hispanic/Latino; 8 Hispanic/Latino, 9 international. Average age 32. 79 applicants, 78% accepted, 33 enrolled. In 2010, 18 master's, 2 doctorates awarded. *Degree requirements:* For master's, thesis or alternative, exams; for doctorate, 2 foreign languages, thesis/dissertation, exams. *Entrance requirements:* For master's, GRE General Test, GRE Subject Test, minimum GPA of 3.0 in upper-division course work or 2.75 overall; for doctorate, GRE General Test. Additional exam requirements/recommendations for international students: Required—TOEFL (minimum score 550 paper-based; 213 computer-based). *Application deadline:* For fall admission, 4/1 for domestic students, 3/1 for international students; for winter admission, 9/1 for domestic students, 8/1 for international students; for spring admission, 11/1 for domestic and international students. Applications are processed on a rolling basis. Application fee: $50. *Expenses:* Tuition, state resident: full-time $8505; part-time $315 per credit. Tuition, nonresident: full-time $13,284; part-time $492 per credit. Required fees: $1482; $21 per credit. $99 per term. One-time fee: $120. Part-time tuition and fees vary according to course load and program. *Financial support:* In 2010–11, 1 research assistantship (averaging $19,448 per year), 24 teaching assistantships with full tuition reimbursements (averaging $12,545 per year) were awarded; Federal Work-Study, scholarships/grants, tuition waivers (partial), and unspecified assistantships also available. Support available to part-time students. Financial award application deadline: 3/1; financial award applicants required to submit FAFSA. *Faculty research:* Algebra, topology, statistical distribution theory, control theory, statistical robustness. Total annual research expenditures: $430,663. *Unit head:* J.J.P. Veerman, Chair, 503-725-8187, Fax: 503-725-3661, E-mail: mthchair@pdx.edu. *Application contact:* John Erdman, Coordinator, 503-725-3621, Fax: 503-725-3661, E-mail: erdman@pdx.edu.

Purdue University, Graduate School, College of Science, Department of Statistics, West Lafayette, IN 47909. Offers MS, PhD, Certificate. Part-time programs available. *Faculty:* 48 full-time (16 women). *Students:* 108 full-time (49 women); includes 5 Black or African American, non-Hispanic/Latino; 1 American Indian or Alaska Native, non-Hispanic/Latino; 84 Asian, non-Hispanic/Latino; 1 Hispanic/Latino, 77 international. Average age 27. 473 applicants, 8%

Statistics

Purdue University (continued)
accepted, 32 enrolled. In 2010, 27 master's, 10 doctorates awarded. Terminal master's awarded for partial completion of doctoral program. *Degree requirements:* For master's, comprehensive exam; for doctorate, thesis/dissertation, qualifying exams. *Entrance requirements:* For master's and doctorate, GRE General Test. Additional exam requirements/recommendations for international students: Required—TOEFL (minimum score 100 computer-based); Recommended—IELTS. *Application deadline:* For fall admission, 1/15 for domestic and international students; for spring admission, 10/15 for domestic students, 9/15 for international students. Application fee: $55 ($65 for international students). Electronic applications accepted. *Financial support:* In 2010–11, 4 students received support, including 4 fellowships with full tuition reimbursements available (averaging $20,000 per year), 2 research assistantships with full tuition reimbursements available (averaging $20,000 per year), 5 teaching assistantships with full tuition reimbursements available (averaging $20,000 per year); career-related internships or fieldwork and unspecified assistantships also available. Support available to part-time students. Financial award application deadline: 1/15; financial award applicants required to submit FAFSA. *Faculty research:* Nonparametric models, computational finance, design of experiments, probability theory, bioinformatics. *Unit head:* Dr. Rebecca W. Doerge, Head, 765-494-3141, Fax: 765-494-0558, E-mail: doerge@purdue.edu. *Application contact:* Becca Miller, Graduate Secretary, 765-494-5794, Fax: 765-494-0558, E-mail: rlmitche@purdue.edu.

Queen's University at Kingston, School of Graduate Studies and Research, Faculty of Arts and Sciences, Department of Mathematics and Statistics, Kingston, ON K7L 3N6, Canada. Offers mathematics (M Sc, M Sc Eng, PhD); statistics (M Sc, M Sc Eng, PhD). Part-time programs available. *Degree requirements:* For master's, thesis; for doctorate, comprehensive exam, thesis/dissertation. *Entrance requirements:* Additional exam requirements/recommendations for international students: Required—TOEFL. *Faculty research:* Algebra, analysis, applied mathematics, statistics.

Rice University, Graduate Programs, George R. Brown School of Engineering, Department of Statistics, Houston, TX 77251-1892. Offers bioinformatics (PhD); biostatistics (PhD); computational finance (PhD); general statistics (PhD); statistics (M Stat, MA); MBA/M Stat. Part-time programs available. *Degree requirements:* For master's, comprehensive exam; for doctorate, comprehensive exam, thesis/dissertation. *Entrance requirements:* For master's and doctorate, GRE General Test, minimum GPA of 3.0. Additional exam requirements/recommendations for international students: Required—TOEFL (minimum score 630 paper-based; 250 computer-based; 90 iBT). Electronic applications accepted. *Faculty research:* Statistical genetics, non parametric function estimation, computational statistics and visualization, stochastic processes.

Rochester Institute of Technology, Graduate Enrollment Services, Kate Gleason College of Engineering, Center of Quality and Applied Statistics, Rochester, NY 14623-5603. Offers applied statistics (MS); statistical quality (AC). Part-time and evening/weekend programs available. Postbaccalaureate distance learning degree programs offered (no on-campus study). *Students:* 19 full-time (12 women), 39 part-time (12 women); includes 5 Asian, non-Hispanic/Latino; 3 Hispanic/Latino, 11 international. Average age 34. 38 applicants, 61% accepted, 15 enrolled. In 2010, 18 master's, 1 other advanced degree awarded. *Degree requirements:* For master's, oral exam. *Entrance requirements:* For master's, course work in calculus, minimum GPA of 3.0. Additional exam requirements/recommendations for international students: Required—TOEFL (minimum score 570 paper-based; 230 computer-based; 88 iBT) or IELTS (minimum score 6.5). *Application deadline:* For fall admission, 2/15 priority date for domestic and international students; for winter admission, 10/15 for domestic students; for spring admission, 2/1 for domestic students. Applications are processed on a rolling basis. Application fee: $50. *Expenses:* Tuition: Full-time $33,234; part-time $924 per credit hour. Required fees: $219. *Financial support:* In 2010–11, 33 students received support; research assistantships with partial tuition reimbursements available, career-related internships or fieldwork, institutionally sponsored loans, scholarships/grants, and unspecified assistantships available. Support available to part-time students. Financial award applicants required to submit FAFSA. *Faculty research:* Industrial statistics, quality control. *Unit head:* Dr. Donald Baker, Director, 585-475-6990, Fax: 585-475-5959, E-mail: cqas@rit.edu. *Application contact:* Diane Ellison, Assistant Vice President, Graduate Enrollment Services, 585-475-2229, Fax: 585-475-7164, E-mail: gradinfo@rit.edu.

Rutgers, The State University of New Jersey, New Brunswick, Graduate School-New Brunswick, Program in Statistics, Piscataway, NJ 08854-8097. Offers applied statistics (MS); biostatistics (MS); data mining (MS); quality and productivity management (MS); statistics (MS, PhD). Part-time programs available. Terminal master's awarded for partial completion of doctoral program. *Degree requirements:* For master's, comprehensive exam, essay, exam, non-thesis essay paper; for doctorate, one foreign language, thesis/dissertation, qualifying oral and written exams. *Entrance requirements:* For master's, GRE General Test; for doctorate, GRE General Test, GRE Subject Test (recommended). Additional exam requirements/recommendations for international students: Required—TOEFL (minimum score 550 paper-based; 213 computer-based). Electronic applications accepted. *Expenses:* Tuition, state resident: full-time $7200; part-time $600 per credit. Tuition, nonresident: full-time $11,124; part-time $927 per credit. *Faculty research:* Probability, decision theory, linear models, multivariate statistics, statistical computing.

St. John's University, St. John's College of Liberal Arts and Sciences, Department of Mathematics and Computer Science, Queens, NY 11439. Offers algebra (MA); analysis (MA); applied mathematics (MA); computer science (MA); geometry-topology (MA); logic and foundations (MA); probability and statistics (MA). Part-time and evening/weekend programs available. *Students:* 4 full-time (1 woman), 3 part-time (1 woman); includes 3 minority (1 Black or African American, non-Hispanic/Latino; 1 Asian, non-Hispanic/Latino; 1 Hispanic/Latino). Average age 25. 19 applicants, 42% accepted, 5 enrolled. In 2010, 3 master's awarded. *Degree requirements:* For master's, comprehensive exam, thesis optional. *Entrance requirements:* For master's, minimum GPA of 3.0. Additional exam requirements/recommendations for international students: Required—TOEFL (minimum score 600 paper-based; 250 computer-based; 100 iBT), IELTS (minimum score 5.5). *Application deadline:* For fall admission, 5/1 priority date for domestic and international students; for spring admission, 11/1 priority date for domestic and international students. Applications are processed on a rolling basis. Application fee: $70. Electronic applications accepted. *Expenses:* Tuition: Full-time $17,100; part-time $950 per credit. Required fees: $340; $170 per semester. Tuition and fees vary according to program. *Financial support:* Research assistantships, scholarships/grants available. Support available to part-time students. Financial award application deadline: 3/1; financial award applicants required to submit FAFSA. *Faculty research:* Functional analysis and operator theory, algebraic K-theory, applied mathematics, measure theory, differential geometry and mathematics education. *Unit head:* Dr. Charles Traina, Chair, 718-990-6166, E-mail: trainac@stjohns.edu. *Application contact:* Kathleen Davis, Director of Graduate Admission, 718-990-1601, Fax: 718-990-5686, E-mail: gradhelp@stjohns.edu.

Sam Houston State University, College of Arts and Sciences, Department of Mathematics and Statistics, Huntsville, TX 77341. Offers mathematics (MA, MS); statistics (MS). Part-time programs available. *Faculty:* 12 full-time (3 women). *Students:* 26 full-time (11 women), 7 part-time (5 women); includes 2 Hispanic/Latino, 11 international. Average age 30. 24 applicants, 92% accepted, 10 enrolled. In 2010, 8 master's awarded. *Entrance requirements:* For master's, GRE General Test. Additional exam requirements/recommendations for international students: Required—TOEFL (minimum score 550 paper-based; 213 computer-based; 79 iBT). *Application deadline:* For fall admission, 8/1 for domestic and international students; for spring admission, 12/1 for domestic and international students. Applications are processed on a rolling basis. Application fee: $20. *Expenses:* Tuition, state resident: full-time $1363; part-time $163 per credit hour. Tuition, nonresident: full-time $3856; part-time $473 per credit hour. *Financial support:* Teaching assistantships, institutionally sponsored loans available. Support available to part-time students. Financial award application deadline: 5/31; financial award applicants required to submit FAFSA. *Unit head:* Dr. Mark Klespis, Chair, 936-294-1577, Fax: 936-294-1882, E-mail: klespis@shsu.edu. *Application contact:* Dr. Jianzhong Wang, Advisor, 936-294-3521, Fax: 936-294-1882, E-mail: mth_jxw@shsu.edu.

San Diego State University, Graduate and Research Affairs, College of Sciences, Department of Mathematics and Statistics, Program in Statistics, San Diego, CA 92182. Offers MS. Part-time programs available. *Degree requirements:* For master's, comprehensive exam. *Entrance requirements:* For master's, GRE General Test. Additional exam requirements/recommendations for international students: Required—TOEFL. Electronic applications accepted.

San Jose State University, Graduate Studies and Research, College of Science, Department of Mathematics, San Jose, CA 95192-0001. Offers applied mathematics (MS); mathematics (MA, MS); mathematics education (MA); statistics (MA). Part-time and evening/weekend programs available. *Degree requirements:* For master's, comprehensive exam, thesis (for some programs). *Entrance requirements:* For master's, GRE Subject Test. Electronic applications accepted. *Faculty research:* Artificial intelligence, algorithms, numerical analysis, software database, number theory.

Simon Fraser University, Graduate Studies, Faculty of Science, Department of Statistics and Actuarial Science, Burnaby, BC V5A 1S6, Canada. Offers M Sc, PhD. Part-time programs available. *Degree requirements:* For master's, participation in consulting, project; for doctorate, comprehensive exam, thesis/dissertation. *Entrance requirements:* For master's, minimum GPA of 3.0; for doctorate, minimum GPA of 3.5. Additional exam requirements/recommendations for international students: Required—TOEFL. Electronic applications accepted. *Faculty research:* Biostatistics, experimental design, envirometrics, statistical computing, statistical theory.

South Dakota State University, Graduate School, College of Engineering, Department of Mathematics and Statistics, Brookings, SD 57007. Offers computational science and statistics (PhD); mathematics (MS); statistics (MS). Part-time programs available. *Faculty:* 12 full-time (1 woman). *Students:* 30 full-time (10 women), 12 part-time (4 women); includes 14 minority (all Asian, non-Hispanic/Latino). 25 applicants, 72% accepted, 12 enrolled. In 2010, 12 master's, 3 doctorates awarded. Terminal master's awarded for partial completion of doctoral program. *Degree requirements:* For master's, thesis (for some programs), oral exam; for doctorate, comprehensive exam, thesis/dissertation, oral and written exams. *Entrance requirements:* Additional exam requirements/recommendations for international students: Required—TOEFL (minimum score 550 paper-based; 213 computer-based; 80 iBT); Recommended—IELTS. *Application deadline:* For fall admission, 4/1 for domestic and international students. Applications are processed on a rolling basis. Application fee: $35. *Financial support:* In 2010–11, 5 fellowships with partial tuition reimbursements (averaging $22,847 per year), 9 research assistantships with partial tuition reimbursements (averaging $20,580 per year), 16 teaching assistantships with partial tuition reimbursements (averaging $17,135 per year) were awarded; unspecified assistantships also available. *Faculty research:* Financial mathematics, predictive analytics, operations research, bioinformatics, biostatistics, computational science, statistics, number theory, abstract algebra. Total annual research expenditures: $310,000. *Unit head:* Dr. Kurt Cogswell, Head, 605-688-6196, Fax: 605-688-5880, E-mail: kurt.cogswell@sdstate.edu. *Application contact:* Dr. Don Vestal, Graduate Coordinator, 605-688-6196, Fax: 605-688-5880, E-mail: don.vestal@sdstate.edu.

Southern Illinois University Carbondale, Graduate School, College of Science, Department of Mathematics, Carbondale, IL 62901-4701. Offers mathematics (MA, MS, PhD); statistics (MS). PhD offered jointly with Southeast Missouri State University. Part-time programs available. *Degree requirements:* For master's, thesis; for doctorate, 2 foreign languages, thesis/dissertation. *Entrance requirements:* For master's, minimum GPA of 2.7; for doctorate, minimum GPA of 3.25. Additional exam requirements/recommendations for international students: Required—TOEFL. *Faculty research:* Differential equations, combinatorics, probability, algebra, numerical analysis.

Southern Methodist University, Dedman College, Department of Statistical Science, Dallas, TX 75275-0332. Offers MS, PhD. Part-time programs available. *Faculty:* 10 full-time (4 women), 2 part-time/adjunct (1 woman). *Students:* 28 full-time (11 women), 1 part-time (0 women); includes 3 Asian, non-Hispanic/Latino, 21 international. Average age 27. 68 applicants, 53% accepted, 7 enrolled. In 2010, 5 master's, 4 doctorates awarded. *Degree requirements:* For master's, thesis, oral and written exams; for doctorate, thesis/dissertation, oral and written exams. *Entrance requirements:* For master's, GRE General Test, 12 hours of advanced math courses; for doctorate, GRE General Test, minimum GPA of 3.0. Additional exam requirements/recommendations for international students: Required—TOEFL. *Application deadline:* For fall admission, 6/30 priority date for domestic students; for spring admission, 11/30 priority date for domestic students. Applications are processed on a rolling basis. Application fee: $60. Electronic applications accepted. *Financial support:* In 2010–11, 23 students received support, including 5 research assistantships with full tuition reimbursements available (averaging $18,000 per year), 23 teaching assistantships with full tuition reimbursements available (averaging $15,000 per year); health care benefits also available. Financial award application deadline: 4/1. *Faculty research:* Regression, time series, linear models sampling, nonparametrics, biostatistics. Total annual research expenditures: $250,000. *Unit head:* Dr. Wayne A. Woodward, Chair, 214-768-2457, Fax: 214-768-4035, E-mail: waynew@mail.smu.edu. *Application contact:* Dr. Richard Gunst, Graduate Advisor, 214-768-2441, Fax: 214-768-4035, E-mail: rgunst@smu.edu.

Stanford University, School of Humanities and Sciences, Department of Statistics, Stanford, CA 94305-9991. Offers MS, PhD. Terminal master's awarded for partial completion of doctoral program. *Degree requirements:* For doctorate, thesis/dissertation, oral exam, qualifying exams. *Entrance requirements:* For master's, GRE General Test; for doctorate, GRE General Test, GRE Subject Test. Additional exam requirements/recommendations for international students: Required—TOEFL. Electronic applications accepted. *Expenses:* Tuition: Full-time $38,700; part-time $860 per unit. One-time fee: $200 full-time.

State University of New York at Binghamton, Graduate School, School of Arts and Sciences, Department of Mathematical Sciences, Binghamton, NY 13902-6000. Offers computer science (MA, PhD); probability and statistics (MA, PhD). Part-time programs available. *Faculty:* 26 full-time (5 women), 13 part-time/adjunct (5 women). *Students:* 42 full-time (13 women), 24 part-time (8 women); includes 3 Black or African American, non-Hispanic/Latino; 1 Asian, non-Hispanic/Latino; 2 Hispanic/Latino, 27 international. Average age 27. 82 applicants, 28% accepted, 16 enrolled. In 2010, 15 master's, 6 doctorates awarded. Terminal master's awarded for partial completion of doctoral program. *Degree requirements:* For master's, thesis or alternative; for doctorate, 2 foreign languages, thesis/dissertation. *Entrance requirements:* For master's and doctorate, GRE General Test, GRE Subject Test. Additional exam requirements/recommendations for international students: Required—TOEFL (minimum score 550 paper-based; 213 computer-based; 80 iBT). *Application deadline:* For fall admission, 4/15 priority date for domestic and international students; for spring admission, 11/30 priority date for domestic and international students. Applications are processed on a rolling basis. Application fee: $60. Electronic applications accepted. *Financial support:* In 2010–11, 51 students received support, including 4 fellowships with full tuition reimbursements available (averaging $16,500 per year), 1 research assistantship with full tuition reimbursement available (averaging $16,500 per year), 48 teaching assistantships with full tuition reimbursements available (averaging $16,500 per year); career-related internships or fieldwork, Federal Work-Study, institutionally sponsored loans, scholarships/grants, health care benefits, tuition waivers (full and partial), and unspecified assistantships also available. Financial award application deadline: 2/15; financial award applicants required to submit FAFSA. *Unit head:* Dr. Fernando Guzman,

Chairperson, 607-777-2148, E-mail: fer@math.binghamton.edu. *Application contact:* Catherine Smith, Recruiting and Admissions Coordinator, 607-777-2151, Fax: 607-777-2501, E-mail: cmsmith@binghamton.edu.

Stephen F. Austin State University, Graduate School, College of Sciences and Mathematics, Department of Mathematics and Statistics, Nacogdoches, TX 75962. Offers mathematics (MS); mathematics education (MS); statistics (MS). *Degree requirements:* For master's, comprehensive exam, thesis optional. *Entrance requirements:* For master's, GRE General Test, minimum GPA of 2.8 in last 60 hours, 2.5 overall. Additional exam requirements/recommendations for international students: Required—TOEFL. *Faculty research:* Kernel type estimators, fractal mappings, spline curve fitting, robust regression continua theory.

Stevens Institute of Technology, Graduate School, Charles V. Schaefer Jr. School of Engineering, Department of Mathematical Sciences, Program in Stochastic Systems, Hoboken, NJ 07030. Offers MS, Certificate. *Students:* 1 full-time (0 women). Average age 27. *Unit head:* Darinka Dentcheva, Head, 201-216-8640. *Application contact:* Dr. Milos Dostal, Professor, 201-216-5426.

Stony Brook University, State University of New York, Graduate School, College of Engineering and Applied Sciences, Department of Applied Mathematics and Statistics, Stony Brook, NY 11794. Offers MS, PhD. *Faculty:* 20 full-time (3 women), 3 part-time/adjunct (1 woman). *Students:* 271 full-time (108 women), 13 part-time (3 women); includes 3 Black or African American, non-Hispanic/Latino; 21 Asian, non-Hispanic/Latino; 8 Hispanic/Latino; 1 Two or more races, non-Hispanic/Latino, 208 international. Average age 28. 483 applicants, 79% accepted, 116 enrolled. In 2010, 46 master's, 16 doctorates awarded. *Degree requirements:* For master's, thesis or alternative; for doctorate, one foreign language, comprehensive exam, thesis/dissertation. *Entrance requirements:* For master's and doctorate, GRE General Test. Additional exam requirements/recommendations for international students: Required—TOEFL. *Application deadline:* For fall admission, 1/15 for domestic students. Application fee: $100. *Expenses:* Tuition, state resident: full-time $8370; part-time $349 per credit. Tuition, nonresident: full-time $13,780; part-time $574 per credit. Required fees: $994. *Financial support:* In 2010–11, 44 research assistantships, 47 teaching assistantships were awarded; fellowships also available. *Faculty research:* Biostatistics, combinatorial analysis, differential equations, modeling. Total annual research expenditures: $3.7 million. *Unit head:* Dr. Jim Glimm, Chairman, 631-632-8360. *Application contact:* Dr. Xiaolin Li, Graduate Director, 631-632-8354, Fax: 631-632-8490, E-mail: linli@ams.sunysb.edu.

Temple University, Fox School of Business, Doctoral Programs in Business, Philadelphia, PA 19122-6096. Offers accounting (PhD); entrepreneurship (PhD); finance (PhD); international business (PhD); management information systems (PhD); marketing (PhD); risk management and insurance (PhD); statistics (PhD); strategic management (PhD); tourism and sport (PhD). *Accreditation:* AACSB. *Degree requirements:* For doctorate, thesis/dissertation. *Entrance requirements:* For doctorate, GRE General Test, GMAT, minimum GPA of 3.0, master's degree. Additional exam requirements/recommendations for international students: Required—TOEFL (minimum score 600 paper-based; 250 computer-based; 100 iBT), IELTS (minimum score 7.5). Electronic applications accepted.

Temple University, Fox School of Business, Specialized Master's Programs, Philadelphia, PA 19122-6096. Offers accountancy (MS); actuarial science (MS); finance (MS); financial engineering (MS); human resource management (MS); marketing (MS); statistics (MS). *Accreditation:* AACSB. Part-time programs available. *Entrance requirements:* For master's, GRE General Test or GMAT, minimum undergraduate GPA of 3.0. Additional exam requirements/recommendations for international students: Required—TOEFL (minimum score 600 paper-based; 250 computer-based; 100 iBT), IELTS (minimum score 7.5).

Texas A&M University, College of Science, Department of Statistics, College Station, TX 77843. Offers MS, PhD. Part-time programs available. *Faculty:* 31. *Students:* 86 full-time (39 women), 84 part-time (32 women); includes 5 Black or African American, non-Hispanic/Latino; 19 Asian, non-Hispanic/Latino; 4 Hispanic/Latino, 62 international. Average age 29. In 2010, 19 master's, 11 doctorates awarded. Terminal master's awarded for partial completion of doctoral program. *Degree requirements:* For doctorate, thesis/dissertation. *Entrance requirements:* For master's and doctorate, GRE General Test. Additional exam requirements/recommendations for international students: Required—TOEFL. *Application deadline:* For fall admission, 3/1 priority date for domestic students; for spring admission, 8/1 for domestic students. Applications are processed on a rolling basis. Application fee: $50 ($75 for international students). *Financial support:* Fellowships, research assistantships, teaching assistantships, career-related internships or fieldwork available. Financial award application deadline: 3/1. *Faculty research:* Time series, chemometrics, biometrics, smoothing, linear models. *Unit head:* Dr. Simon Sheather, Head, 979-845-3141, Fax: 979-845-3144, E-mail: sheather@stat.tamu.edu. *Application contact:* P. Fred Dahm, Graduate Director, 979-845-7251, Fax: 979-845-3144, E-mail: fdahm@stat.tamu.edu.

Texas Tech University, Graduate School, College of Arts and Sciences, Department of Mathematics and Statistics, Lubbock, TX 79409. Offers mathematics (MA, MS, PhD); statistics (MS). Part-time programs available. *Faculty:* 38 full-time (6 women). *Students:* 106 full-time (44 women), 15 part-time (10 women); includes 1 Black or African American, non-Hispanic/Latino; 1 Asian, non-Hispanic/Latino; 7 Hispanic/Latino; 1 Two or more races, non-Hispanic/Latino, 67 international. Average age 27. 109 applicants, 79% accepted, 30 enrolled. In 2010, 40 master's, 3 doctorates awarded. *Degree requirements:* For master's, thesis or alternative; for doctorate, one foreign language, thesis/dissertation. *Entrance requirements:* For master's and doctorate, GRE General Test. Additional exam requirements/recommendations for international students: Required—TOEFL (minimum score 550 paper-based; 213 computer-based; 79 iBT). *Application deadline:* For fall admission, 6/1 priority date for domestic students, 1/15 priority date for international students; for spring admission, 9/1 priority date for domestic students, 6/15 priority date for international students. Applications are processed on a rolling basis. Application fee: $50 ($75 for international students). Electronic applications accepted. *Expenses:* Tuition, state resident: full-time $5495.76; part-time $228.99 per credit hour. Tuition, nonresident: full-time $12,936; part-time $538.99 per credit hour. Required fees: $2674; $36 per credit hour. $905 per semester. *Financial support:* In 2010–11, 103 students received support, including 3 research assistantships with partial tuition reimbursements available (averaging $2,321 per year), 44 teaching assistantships with partial tuition reimbursements available (averaging $7,308 per year); fellowships also available. Financial award application deadline: 4/15; financial award applicants required to submit FAFSA. *Faculty research:* Numerical analysis, mathematical biology, complex analysis, algebra and geometry; ordinary and partial differential equations. Total annual research expenditures: $1.6 million. *Unit head:* Dr. Kent Pearce, Chair, 806-742-2566, Fax: 806-742-1112, E-mail: kent.pearce@ttu.edu. *Application contact:* Dr. Ram Iyer, Graduate Adviser, 806-742-2566, Fax: 806-742-1112, E-mail: ram.iyer@ttu.edu.

Texas Tech University, Graduate School, Jerry S. Rawls College of Business Administration, Programs in Business Administration, Lubbock, TX 79409. Offers agricultural business (MBA); business administration (IMBA); business statistics (MBA); entrepreneurship and innovation (MBA); general business (MBA); health organization management (MBA); international business (MBA); management and leadership skills (MBA); management information systems (MBA); marketing (MBA); real estate (MBA); JD/MBA; MBA/M Arch; MBA/MA; MBA/MD; MBA/MS; MBA/Pharm D. Part-time and evening/weekend programs available. *Faculty:* 47 full-time (8 women), 5 part-time/adjunct (0 women). *Students:* 52 full-time (13 women), 531 part-time (152 women); includes 121 minority (28 Black or African American, non-Hispanic/Latino; 3 American Indian or Alaska Native, non-Hispanic/Latino; 31 Asian, non-Hispanic/Latino; 53 Hispanic/Latino; 6 Two or more races, non-Hispanic/Latino), 49 international. Average age 30. 437 applicants, 77% accepted, 258 enrolled. In 2010, 228 master's awarded. *Degree requirements:* For master's, capstone course. *Entrance requirements:* For master's, GMAT, holistic review of academic credentials. Additional exam requirements/recommendations for international students: Required—TOEFL (minimum score 550 paper-based; 213 computer-based; 79 iBT). *Application deadline:* For fall admission, 4/1 priority date for domestic students, 1/15 for international students; for spring admission, 9/1 priority date for domestic students, 6/15 for international students. Applications are processed on a rolling basis. Application fee: $50 ($75 for international students). Electronic applications accepted. *Expenses:* Tuition, state resident: full-time $5495.76; part-time $228.99 per credit hour. Tuition, nonresident: full-time $12,936; part-time $538.99 per credit hour. Required fees: $2674; $36 per credit hour. $905 per semester. *Financial support:* In 2010–11, 25 research assistantships (averaging $8,800 per year) were awarded; teaching assistantships, career-related internships or fieldwork, Federal Work-Study, scholarships/grants, health care benefits, and unspecified assistantships also available. Support available to part-time students. Financial award applicants required to submit FAFSA. *Unit head:* Dr. W. Jay Conover, Director, 806-742-1546, Fax: 806-742-3958, E-mail: jay.conover@ttu.edu. *Application contact:* Cynthia D. Barnes, Director, Graduate Services Center, 806-742-3184, Fax: 806-742-3958, E-mail: ba_grad@ttu.edu.

Tulane University, School of Science and Engineering, Department of Mathematics, New Orleans, LA 70118-5669. Offers applied mathematics (MS); mathematics (MS, PhD); statistics (MS). *Degree requirements:* For master's, thesis (for some programs); for doctorate, thesis/dissertation. *Entrance requirements:* For master's, GRE General Test, minimum B average in undergraduate course work; for doctorate, GRE General Test. Additional exam requirements/recommendations for international students: Required—TOEFL. Electronic applications accepted.

Université de Montréal, Faculty of Arts and Sciences, Department of Mathematics and Statistics, Montréal, QC H3C 3J7, Canada. Offers mathematical and computational finance (M Sc, DESS); mathematics (M Sc, PhD); statistics (M Sc, PhD). *Degree requirements:* For master's, thesis; for doctorate, thesis/dissertation, general exam. *Entrance requirements:* For master's and doctorate, proficiency in French. Electronic applications accepted. *Faculty research:* Pure and applied mathematics, actuarial mathematics.

Université Laval, Faculty of Sciences and Engineering, Department of Mathematics and Statistics, Program in Statistics, Québec, QC G1K 7P4, Canada. Offers M Sc. *Degree requirements:* For master's, thesis (for some programs). *Entrance requirements:* For master's, knowledge of French and English. Electronic applications accepted.

University at Albany, State University of New York, College of Arts and Sciences, Department of Mathematics and Statistics, Albany, NY 12222-0001. Offers mathematics (PhD); secondary teaching (MA); statistics (MA). *Degree requirements:* For doctorate, one foreign language, thesis/dissertation. *Entrance requirements:* For doctorate, GRE General Test. Additional exam requirements/recommendations for international students: Required—TOEFL (minimum score 550 paper-based; 213 computer-based). Electronic applications accepted.

University at Albany, State University of New York, School of Education, Department of Educational and Counseling Psychology, Albany, NY 12222-0001. Offers counseling psychology (MS, PhD, CAS); educational psychology (Ed D); educational psychology and statistics (MS); measurements and evaluation (Ed D); rehabilitation counseling (MS), including counseling psychology; school counselor (CAS); school psychology (Psy D, CAS); special education (MS); statistics and research design (Ed D). *Accreditation:* APA (one or more programs are accredited). Evening/weekend programs available. *Degree requirements:* For doctorate, thesis/dissertation. *Entrance requirements:* For doctorate, GRE General Test. Additional exam requirements/recommendations for international students: Required—TOEFL (minimum score 550 paper-based; 213 computer-based). Electronic applications accepted.

The University of Akron, Graduate School, Buchtel College of Arts and Sciences, Department of Statistics, Akron, OH 44325. Offers MS. Part-time and evening/weekend programs available. *Faculty:* 11 full-time (4 women), 4 part-time/adjunct (2 women). *Students:* 21 full-time (8 women), 3 part-time (1 woman), 13 international. Average age 29. 36 applicants, 83% accepted, 7 enrolled. In 2010, 7 master's awarded. *Degree requirements:* For master's, comprehensive exam, thesis optional. *Entrance requirements:* For master's, minimum GPA of 2.75, hold a baccalaureate degree in statistics, mathematics, or a related area, three letters of recommendation, one semester of applied statistics, completion of three semesters of calculus, linear algebra, or equivalent. Additional exam requirements/recommendations for international students: Required—TOEFL (minimum score 550 paper-based; 213 computer-based; 79 iBT). *Application deadline:* Applications are processed on a rolling basis. Application fee: $30 ($40 for international students). Electronic applications accepted. *Expenses:* Tuition, state resident: full-time $6800; part-time $378 per credit hour. Tuition, nonresident: full-time $11,644; part-time $647 per credit hour. Required fees: $1265. One-time fee: $30 full-time. *Financial support:* In 2010–11, 2 research assistantships, 12 teaching assistantships with full tuition reimbursements were awarded. *Faculty research:* Experimental design, sampling, actuarial science, biostatistics. Total annual research expenditures: $41,155. *Unit head:* Dr. David Stark, Interim Chair, 330-972-8008, E-mail: dstark1@uakron.edu. *Application contact:* Associate Dean.

University of Alaska Fairbanks, College of Natural Sciences and Mathematics, Department of Mathematics and Statistics, Fairbanks, AK 99775-6660. Offers mathematics (MAT, PhD); statistics (MS). Part-time programs available. *Faculty:* 15 full-time (7 women). *Students:* 8 full-time (2 women), 6 part-time (3 women); includes 2 minority (both Asian, non-Hispanic/Latino), 1 international. Average age 31. 16 applicants, 38% accepted, 4 enrolled. In 2010, 4 master's, 2 doctorates awarded. Terminal master's awarded for partial completion of doctoral program. *Degree requirements:* For master's, comprehensive exam, thesis or alternative; for doctorate, comprehensive exam, thesis/dissertation, oral defense. *Entrance requirements:* Additional exam requirements/recommendations for international students: Required—TOEFL (minimum score 550 paper-based; 213 computer-based; 80 iBT). *Application deadline:* For fall admission, 6/1 for domestic students, 3/1 for international students; for spring admission, 10/15 for domestic students, 9/1 for international students. Applications are processed on a rolling basis. Application fee: $60. Electronic applications accepted. *Expenses:* Tuition, state resident: full-time $5688; part-time $316 per credit. Tuition, nonresident: full-time $11,628; part-time $646 per credit. Required fees: $289 per semester. Tuition and fees vary according to course load and reciprocity agreements. *Financial support:* In 2010–11, 2 research assistantships with tuition reimbursements (averaging $10,360 per year), 6 teaching assistantships with tuition reimbursements (averaging $17,088 per year) were awarded; fellowships with tuition reimbursements, career-related internships or fieldwork, Federal Work-Study, scholarships/grants, health care benefits, and unspecified assistantships also available. Support available to part-time students. Financial award application deadline: 2/15; financial award applicants required to submit FAFSA. *Faculty research:* Kriging, arrangements of hyperplanes, bifurcation analysis of time-periodic differential-delay equations, inverse problems, phylogenic tree construction. *Unit head:* Dr. John Rhodes, Department Chair, 907-474-7332, Fax: 907-474-5394, E-mail: fymath@uaf.edu. *Application contact:* Dr. John Rhodes, Department Chair, 907-474-7332, Fax: 907-474-5394, E-mail: fymath@uaf.edu.

University of Alberta, Faculty of Graduate Studies and Research, Department of Mathematical and Statistical Sciences, Edmonton, AB T6G 2E1, Canada. Offers applied mathematics (M Sc, PhD); biostatistics (M Sc); mathematical finance (M Sc, PhD); mathematical physics (M Sc, PhD); mathematics (M Sc, PhD); statistics (M Sc, PhD, Postgraduate Diploma). Part-time programs available. Terminal master's awarded for partial completion of doctoral program. *Degree requirements:* For master's, thesis (for some programs); for doctorate, comprehensive exam, thesis/dissertation. *Entrance requirements:* Additional exam requirements/recommendations for international students: Required—TOEFL (minimum score 580 paper-

Statistics

University of Alberta (continued)

based; 237 computer-based). Electronic applications accepted. *Faculty research:* Classical and functional analysis, algebra, differential equations, geometry.

The University of Arizona, Graduate Interdisciplinary Programs, Graduate Interdisciplinary Program in Statistics, Tucson, AZ 85721. Offers MS, PhD. *Students:* 13 full-time (5 women), 4 part-time (2 women); includes 1 Asian, non-Hispanic/Latino; 1 Hispanic/Latino, 5 international. Average age 33. 19 applicants, 63% accepted, 5 enrolled. *Application deadline:* For fall admission, 2/1 for domestic and international students; for spring admission, 8/1 for domestic and international students. *Expenses:* Tuition, state resident: full-time $7692. *Application contact:* Jolene M. Gruener, Associate Director, 520-621-8368, E-mail: gidp@email.arizona.edu.

University of Arkansas, Graduate School, J. William Fulbright College of Arts and Sciences, Department of Mathematical Sciences, Program in Statistics, Fayetteville, AR 72701-1201. Offers MS. *Students:* 14 full-time (7 women); includes 2 minority (both Black or African American, non-Hispanic/Latino), 10 international. 13 applicants, 77% accepted. In 2010, 8 master's awarded. *Degree requirements:* For master's, thesis. *Application deadline:* For fall admission, 4/1 for international students; for spring admission, 10/1 for international students. Applications are processed on a rolling basis. Application fee: $40 ($50 for international students). Electronic applications accepted. *Financial support:* In 2010–11, 6 research assistantships, 5 teaching assistantships were awarded; fellowships, career-related internships or fieldwork and Federal Work-Study also available. Support available to part-time students. Financial award application deadline: 4/1; financial award applicants required to submit FAFSA. *Unit head:* Dr. Laurie Meaux, Chair of Studies, 479-575-3352, Fax: 479-575-8630, E-mail: lmeaux@uark.edu. *Application contact:* Dr. John Ryan, Graduate Coordinator, 479-575-3351, Fax: 479-575-8630, E-mail: jryan@uark.edu.

The University of British Columbia, Faculty of Science, Department of Statistics, Vancouver, BC V6T 1Z2, Canada. Offers M Sc, PhD. *Faculty:* 16 full-time (4 women), 6 part-time/adjunct (1 woman). *Students:* 41 full-time (13 women); includes 33 Asian, non-Hispanic/Latino; 1 Hispanic/Latino, 1 international. Average age 28. 79 applicants, 49% accepted, 22 enrolled. In 2010, 5 master's, 5 doctorates awarded. *Degree requirements:* For master's, thesis or alternative, Departmental Seminar; for doctorate, comprehensive exam, thesis/dissertation. *Entrance requirements:* Additional exam requirements/recommendations for international students: Required—TOEFL (minimum score 600 paper-based; 250 computer-based; 100 iBT), IELTS (minimum score 7.5). *Application deadline:* For fall admission, 2/7 priority date for domestic students, 2/1 for international students. Applications are processed on a rolling basis. Application fee: $90 Canadian dollars ($150 Canadian dollars for international students). Electronic applications accepted. Tuition charges are reported in Canadian dollars. *Expenses:* Tuition, area resident: Full-time $4179 Canadian dollars. International tuition: $7344 Canadian dollars full-time. *Financial support:* In 2010–11, 37 students received support, including 20 research assistantships (averaging $15,000 per year), 17 teaching assistantships (averaging $10,000 per year); fellowships, career-related internships or fieldwork, Federal Work-Study, and tuition waivers (partial) also available. Financial award application deadline: 2/28. *Faculty research:* Theoretical, applied, biostatistical, and computational statistics. *Unit head:* Dr. Nancy Heckman, Head, 604-822-6844, Fax: 604-822-6960, E-mail: head@stat.ubc.ca. *Application contact:* Andrea Sollberger, Graduate Admissions, 604-822-4821, Fax: 604-822-6960, E-mail: gradinfo@stat.ubc.ca.

University of Calgary, Faculty of Graduate Studies, Faculty of Science, Department of Mathematics and Statistics, Calgary, AB T2N 1N4, Canada. Offers M Sc, PhD. *Degree requirements:* For master's, comprehensive exam, thesis; for doctorate, thesis/dissertation, candidacy exam, preliminary exams. *Entrance requirements:* For master's, honors degree in applied math, pure math, or statistics; for doctorate, MA or M Sc. Additional exam requirements/recommendations for international students: Required—TOEFL (minimum score 600 paper-based; 250 computer-based), IELTS (minimum score 7), TOEFL (paper-based 600; computer-based 250) or IELTS (paper-based 7). *Faculty research:* Combinatorics, applied mathematics, statistics, probability, analysis.

University of California, Berkeley, Graduate Division, College of Letters and Science, Department of Statistics, Berkeley, CA 94720-1500. Offers MA, PhD. *Degree requirements:* For doctorate, thesis/dissertation, qualifying exam, written preliminary exam. *Entrance requirements:* For master's and doctorate, GRE General Test, minimum GPA of 3.0, 3 letters of recommendation.

University of California, Davis, Graduate Studies, Program in Statistics, Davis, CA 95616. Offers MS, PhD. Terminal master's awarded for partial completion of doctoral program. *Degree requirements:* For master's, comprehensive exam; for doctorate, thesis/dissertation. *Entrance requirements:* For master's and doctorate, GRE General Test, minimum GPA of 3.0. Additional exam requirements/recommendations for international students: Required—TOEFL (minimum score 550 paper-based; 213 computer-based). Electronic applications accepted. *Faculty research:* Nonparametric analysis, time series analysis, biostatistics, curve estimation, reliability.

University of California, Irvine, Donald Bren School of Information and Computer Sciences, Department of Statistics, Irvine, CA 92697. Offers MS, PhD. *Students:* 29 full-time (10 women), 1 (woman) part-time; includes 6 minority (all Asian, non-Hispanic/Latino), 16 international. Average age 28. 147 applicants, 24% accepted, 8 enrolled. In 2010, 4 master's, 1 doctorate awarded. Application fee: $80 ($100 for international students). *Unit head:* Jessica M. Utts, Chair, 949-824-0649, Fax: 949-824-9863, E-mail: jutts@uci.edu. *Application contact:* Kris Bolcer, Assistant Director, Graduate Affairs, 949-824-5156, Fax: 949-824-4163, E-mail: kbolcer@uci.edu.

University of California, Los Angeles, Graduate Division, College of Letters and Science, Department of Statistics, Los Angeles, CA 90095. Offers MS, PhD. *Faculty:* 11 full-time (1 woman). *Students:* 81 full-time (27 women); includes 19 minority (15 Asian, non-Hispanic/Latino; 2 Hispanic/Latino; 1 Native Hawaiian or other Pacific Islander, non-Hispanic/Latino; 1 Two or more races, non-Hispanic/Latino), 29 international. Average age 28. 280 applicants, 28% accepted, 31 enrolled. In 2010, 19 master's, 8 doctorates awarded. Terminal master's awarded for partial completion of doctoral program. *Degree requirements:* For master's, comprehensive exam or thesis; for doctorate, thesis/dissertation, oral and written exams, student teaching. *Entrance requirements:* For master's, GRE General Test, minimum GPA of 3.2, 12 quarter or 8 semester courses in upper-division quantitative work; for doctorate, GRE General Test, minimum GPA of 3.5, 12 quarter or 8 semester courses in upper-division quantitative work. Application fee: $70 ($90 for international students). Electronic applications accepted. *Financial support:* In 2010–11, 32 fellowships with full and partial tuition reimbursements, 30 research assistantships with full and partial tuition reimbursements, 42 teaching assistantships with full and partial tuition reimbursements were awarded; Federal Work-Study, institutionally sponsored loans, scholarships/grants, health care benefits, tuition waivers (full and partial), and unspecified assistantships also available. Financial award application deadline: 3/1; financial award applicants required to submit FAFSA. *Unit head:* Dr. Jan DeLeeuw, Chair, 310-825-9550, E-mail: deleeuw@stat.ucla.edu. *Application contact:* Department Office, 310-206-3742, E-mail: glenda@stat.ucla.edu.

University of California, Riverside, Graduate Division, Department of Statistics, Riverside, CA 92521-0102. Offers applied statistics (PhD); statistics (MS). Terminal master's awarded for partial completion of doctoral program. *Degree requirements:* For master's, comprehensive exam; for doctorate, comprehensive exam, thesis/dissertation. *Entrance requirements:* For master's and doctorate, GRE General Test. Additional exam requirements/recommendations for international students: Required—TOEFL (minimum score 550 paper-based; 213 computer-based; 80 iBT). Electronic applications accepted. *Faculty research:* Design and analysis of

gene expression experiments using DNA microarrays, statistical design and analysis of experiments, linear models, probability models and statistical inference, SNP/SFP discovery using DNA microarray, genetic mapping.

University of California, San Diego, Office of Graduate Studies, Department of Mathematics, La Jolla, CA 92093. Offers applied mathematics (MA); mathematics (MA, PhD); statistics (MS). *Degree requirements:* For doctorate, thesis/dissertation. *Entrance requirements:* For master's and doctorate, GRE General Test, GRE Subject Test. Electronic applications accepted.

University of California, Santa Barbara, Graduate Division, College of Letters and Sciences, Division of Mathematics, Life, and Physical Sciences, Department of Statistics and Applied Probability, Santa Barbara, CA 93106-3110. Offers financial mathematics and statistics (PhD); quantitative methods in the social sciences (PhD); statistics (MA), including applied statistics, mathematical statistics; statistics and applied probability (PhD); MA/PhD. *Faculty:* 11 full-time (3 women). *Students:* 49 full-time (17 women); includes 30 Asian, non-Hispanic/Latino; 2 Hispanic/Latino. Average age 29. 195 applicants, 20% accepted, 14 enrolled. In 2010, 16 master's, 2 doctorates awarded. Terminal master's awarded for partial completion of doctoral program. *Degree requirements:* For master's, comprehensive exam, thesis (for some programs); for doctorate, comprehensive exam, thesis/dissertation. *Entrance requirements:* For master's and doctorate, GRE General Test. Additional exam requirements/recommendations for international students: Required—TOEFL (minimum score 550 paper-based; 80 iBT), IELTS (minimum score 7). *Application deadline:* For fall admission, 1/1 priority date for domestic and international students; for winter admission, 11/1 priority date for domestic and international students; for spring admission, 2/1 priority date for domestic and international students. Application fee: $70 ($90 for international students). Electronic applications accepted. *Financial support:* In 2010–11, 23 students received support, including 6 fellowships with full tuition reimbursements available (averaging $11,285 per year), 1 research assistantship with full and partial tuition reimbursement available (averaging $2,790 per year), 28 teaching assistantships with partial tuition reimbursements available (averaging $14,557 per year). Financial award application deadline: 1/1; financial award applicants required to submit FAFSA. *Faculty research:* Bayesian inference, financial mathematics, stochastic processes, environmental statistics, biostatistical modeling. Total annual research expenditures: $139,480. *Unit head:* Dr. Yuedong Wang, Chair, 805-893-4870, E-mail: yeudong@pstat.ucsb.edu. *Application contact:* Rickie R. Smith, Graduate Program Assistant, 805-893-2129, Fax: 805-893-2334, E-mail: smith@pstat.ucsb.edu.

University of California, Santa Cruz, Division of Graduate Studies, Jack Baskin School of Engineering, Program in Statistics and Applied Mathematics, Santa Cruz, CA 95064. Offers MS, PhD. *Students:* 38 full-time (22 women), 7 part-time (0 women); includes 8 minority (2 Asian, non-Hispanic/Latino; 6 Hispanic/Latino), 11 international. Average age 30. 64 applicants, 44% accepted, 12 enrolled. In 2010, 2 doctorates awarded. Terminal master's awarded for partial completion of doctoral program. *Degree requirements:* For master's, seminar, qualifying exam, capstone project; for doctorate, thesis/dissertation, seminar, qualifying exam. *Entrance requirements:* For master's and doctorate, GRE General Test; GRE Subject Test in math (recommended). Additional exam requirements/recommendations for international students: Required—TOEFL (minimum score 570 paper-based; 230 computer-based; 89 iBT); Recommended—IELTS (minimum score 8). *Application deadline:* For fall admission, 1/3 for domestic and international students. Application fee: $70 ($90 for international students). Electronic applications accepted. *Financial support:* Fellowships, research assistantships, teaching assistantships, institutionally sponsored loans and tuition waivers available. Financial award applicants required to submit FAFSA. *Faculty research:* Bayesian nonparametric methods; computationally intensive Bayesian inference, prediction, and decision-making; envirometrics; fluid mechanics; mathematical biology. *Unit head:* Tracie Tucker, Graduate Program Coordinator, 831-459-5737, E-mail: ttucker@soe.ucsc.edu. *Application contact:* Tracie Tucker, Graduate Program Coordinator, 831-459-5737, E-mail: ttucker@soe.ucsc.edu.

University of Central Florida, College of Sciences, Department of Statistics and Actuarial Science, Orlando, FL 32816. Offers SAS data mining (Certificate); statistical computing (MS). Part-time and evening/weekend programs available. *Faculty:* 10 full-time (3 women), 2 part-time/adjunct (0 women). *Students:* 29 full-time (12 women), 13 part-time (4 women); includes 3 Black or African American, non-Hispanic/Latino; 3 Asian, non-Hispanic/Latino; 1 Hispanic/Latino, 19 international. Average age 30. 59 applicants, 90% accepted, 26 enrolled. In 2010, 22 master's, 7 other advanced degrees awarded. *Degree requirements:* For master's, comprehensive exam. *Entrance requirements:* For master's, GRE General Test, minimum GPA of 3.0 in last 60 hours. Additional exam requirements/recommendations for international students: Required—TOEFL. *Application deadline:* For fall admission, 7/15 for domestic students; for spring admission, 12/1 for domestic students. Application fee: $30. Electronic applications accepted. *Expenses:* Tuition, state resident: part-time $256.56 per credit hour. Tuition, nonresident: part-time $1011.52 per credit hour. Part-time tuition and fees vary according to program. *Financial support:* In 2010–11, 13 students received support, including 1 fellowship with partial tuition reimbursement available (averaging $4,000 per year), 1 research assistantship with partial tuition reimbursement available (averaging $9,400 per year), 12 teaching assistantships with partial tuition reimbursements available (averaging $11,100 per year); career-related internships or fieldwork, Federal Work-Study, institutionally sponsored loans, tuition waivers (partial), and unspecified assistantships also available. Financial award application deadline: 3/1; financial award applicants required to submit FAFSA. *Faculty research:* Multivariate analysis, quality control, shrinkage estimation. *Unit head:* Dr. David Nickerson, Chair, 407-823-2289, Fax: 407-823-5419, E-mail: nickerson@mail.ucf.edu. *Application contact:* Dr. David Nickerson, Chair, 407-823-2289, Fax: 407-823-5419, E-mail: nickerson@mail.ucf.edu.

University of Central Oklahoma, College of Graduate Studies and Research, College of Mathematics and Science, Department of Mathematics and Statistics, Edmond, OK 73034-5209. Offers applied mathematical sciences (MS), including computer science, mathematics, mathematics/computer science teaching, statistics. Part-time programs available. *Degree requirements:* For master's, thesis. *Entrance requirements:* Additional exam requirements/recommendations for international students: Required—TOEFL (minimum score 550 paper-based; 213 computer-based). Electronic applications accepted. *Faculty research:* Curvature, FAA, math education.

University of Chicago, Booth School of Business, Full-Time MBA Program, Chicago, IL 60637. Offers accounting (MBA); analytic finance (MBA); analytic management (MBA); econometrics and statistics (MBA); economics (MBA); entrepreneurship (MBA); finance (MBA); general management (MBA); human resource management (MBA); international business (MBA); managerial and organizational behavior (MBA); marketing management (MBA); operations management (MBA); strategic management (MBA); MBA/AM; MBA/JD; MBA/MA; MBA/MD; MBA/MPP. *Accreditation:* AACSB. Part-time and evening/weekend programs available. *Faculty:* 157 full-time, 35 part-time/adjunct. *Students:* 1,177 full-time (417 women); includes 301 minority (62 Black or African American, non-Hispanic/Latino; 1 American Indian or Alaska Native, non-Hispanic/Latino; 164 Asian, non-Hispanic/Latino; 55 Hispanic/Latino; 19 Two or more races, non-Hispanic/Latino), 403 international. Average age 28. 4,299 applicants, 22% accepted, 579 enrolled. In 2010, 1,374 master's awarded. *Entrance requirements:* For master's, GMAT, 2 letters of recommendation, 3 essays, resume, interview; transcripts. Additional exam requirements/recommendations for international students: Required—TOEFL (minimum score 600 paper-based; 250 computer-based), IELTS. *Application deadline:* For fall admission, 10/10 priority date for domestic students, 10/13 priority date for international students; for winter admission, 1/5 for domestic and international students; for spring admission, 4/13 for domestic and international students. Application fee: $200. Electronic applications accepted. *Expenses:* Contact institution. *Financial support:* Fellowships available. Financial award applicants required to submit FAFSA. *Faculty research:* Finance, economics, entrepreneurship,

strategy, management. *Unit head:* Stacey Kole, Deputy Dean, 773-702-7121. *Application contact:* Kurt Ahlm, Associate Dean of Admissions and Financial Aid, 773-702-7369, Fax: 773-702-9085, E-mail: admissions@chicagobooth.edu.

University of Chicago, Division of the Physical Sciences, Department of Statistics, Chicago, IL 60637. Offers SM, PhD. Part-time programs available. *Faculty:* 24 full-time (3 women), 1 part-time/adjunct (0 women). *Students:* 101 full-time (46 women), 8 part-time (4 women); includes 1 Black or African American, non-Hispanic/Latino; 11 Asian, non-Hispanic/Latino, 79 international. Average age 27. 392 applicants, 22% accepted, 41 enrolled. In 2010, 11 master's, 3 doctorates awarded. Terminal master's awarded for partial completion of doctoral program. *Degree requirements:* For master's, thesis; for doctorate, thesis/dissertation. *Entrance requirements:* For master's and doctorate, GRE General Test, GRE Subject Test. Additional exam requirements/recommendations for international students: Required—TOEFL. *Application deadline:* For fall admission, 6/15 for domestic and international students. Applications are processed on a rolling basis. Application fee: $55. Electronic applications accepted. *Financial support:* In 2010–11, fellowships with full tuition reimbursements (averaging $21,030 per year), research assistantships with full tuition reimbursements (averaging $21,030 per year), teaching assistantships with full tuition reimbursements (averaging $21,030 per year) were awarded; tuition waivers (partial) also available. Financial award application deadline: 2/1. *Faculty research:* Genetics, econometrics, generalized linear models, history of statistics, probability theory. *Unit head:* Kathryn Kraynik, Department Administrator, 773-702-8335, E-mail: kraynik@galton.uchicago.edu. *Application contact:* Sandra Romero, Admissions Specialist, 773-702-0541, E-mail: sandra@galton.uchicago.edu.

University of Cincinnati, Graduate School, McMicken College of Arts and Sciences, Department of Mathematical Sciences, Cincinnati, OH 45221. Offers applied mathematics (MS, PhD); mathematics education (MAT); pure mathematics (MS, PhD); statistics (MS, PhD). Part-time programs available. Terminal master's awarded for partial completion of doctoral program. *Degree requirements:* For master's, comprehensive exam, thesis or alternative; for doctorate, one foreign language, comprehensive exam, thesis/dissertation. *Entrance requirements:* For master's, GRE, teacher certification (MAT); for doctorate, GRE. Additional exam requirements/recommendations for international students: Required—TOEFL. Electronic applications accepted. *Faculty research:* Algebra, analysis, differential equations, numerical analysis, statistics.

University of Connecticut, Graduate School, College of Liberal Arts and Sciences, Department of Statistics, Storrs, CT 06269. Offers MS, PhD. Terminal master's awarded for partial completion of doctoral program. *Degree requirements:* For master's, comprehensive exam; for doctorate, thesis/dissertation. *Entrance requirements:* For master's and doctorate, GRE General Test. Additional exam requirements/recommendations for international students: Required—TOEFL (minimum score 550 paper-based; 213 computer-based). Electronic applications accepted.

University of Delaware, College of Agriculture and Natural Resources, Program in Statistics, Newark, DE 19716. Offers MS. Part-time programs available. *Entrance requirements:* For master's, GRE General Test, 3 letters of recommendation. Additional exam requirements/recommendations for international students: Required—TOEFL (minimum score 550 paper-based; 213 computer-based). Electronic applications accepted.

University of Denver, Daniels College of Business, Department of Statistics and Operations Technology, Denver, CO 80208. Offers business intelligence (MS); data mining (MS). *Faculty:* 7 full-time (2 women). *Entrance requirements:* Additional exam requirements/recommendations for international students: Required—TOEFL (minimum score 570 paper-based; 88 iBT). *Application deadline:* For fall admission, 1/15 priority date for domestic students. Applications are processed on a rolling basis. Application fee: $60. Electronic applications accepted. *Expenses:* Tuition: Full-time $35,604; part-time $29,670 per year. Required fees: $687 per year. Tuition and fees vary according to program. *Financial support:* Career-related internships or fieldwork, Federal Work-Study, institutionally sponsored loans, and scholarships/grants available. Support available to part-time students. Financial award application deadline: 2/15; financial award applicants required to submit FAFSA. *Unit head:* Dr. Anthony Hayter, Professor, 303-871-4341, E-mail: anthony.hayter@du.edu. *Application contact:* Information Contact, 303-871-3416.

University of Florida, Graduate School, College of Liberal Arts and Sciences, Department of Statistics, Gainesville, FL 32611. Offers M Stat, MS Stat, PhD. Part-time programs available. *Faculty:* 10 full-time (0 women). *Students:* 97 full-time (32 women), 3 part-time (2 women); includes 3 Asian, non-Hispanic/Latino; 3 Hispanic/Latino, 68 international. Average age 28. 418 applicants, 3% accepted, 12 enrolled. In 2010, 8 master's, 3 doctorates awarded. Terminal master's awarded for partial completion of doctoral program. *Degree requirements:* For master's, variable foreign language requirement, comprehensive exam, thesis (for some programs), final oral exam. Thesis required for Masters of Science degree; for doctorate, comprehensive exam, thesis/dissertation. *Entrance requirements:* For master's and doctorate, GRE General Test, minimum GPA of 3.0. Additional exam requirements/recommendations for international students: Required—TOEFL (minimum score 550 paper-based; 213 computer-based; 80 iBT), IELTS (minimum score 6). *Application deadline:* For fall admission, 2/1 priority date for domestic students, 2/1 for international students. Applications are processed on a rolling basis. Application fee: $30. Electronic applications accepted. *Expenses:* Tuition, state resident: full-time $10,915.92. Tuition, nonresident: full-time $28,309. *Financial support:* In 2010–11, 61 students received support, including 20 fellowships, 4 research assistantships (averaging $14,938 per year), 37 teaching assistantships (averaging $20,205 per year); unspecified assistantships also available. Financial award application deadline: 2/1; financial award applicants required to submit FAFSA. *Faculty research:* Bayesian statistics, biostatistics, Markov Chain Monte Carlo (MCMC), nonparametric statistics, statistical genetics/genomics. Total annual research expenditures: $701,961. *Unit head:* Michael J. Daniels, PhD, Chair, 352-273-1845, Fax: 352-392-5175, E-mail: mdaniels@stat.ufl.edu. *Application contact:* James P. Hobert, PhD, Coordinator, 352-392-1941, Fax: 352-392-5175, E-mail: jhobert@stat.ufl.edu.

University of Georgia, College of Arts and Sciences, Department of Statistics, Athens, GA 30602. Offers MS, PhD. *Faculty:* 16 full-time (5 women). *Students:* 52 full-time (19 women), 8 part-time (6 women); includes 1 Black or African American, non-Hispanic/Latino; 3 Asian, non-Hispanic/Latino, 37 international. 151 applicants, 38% accepted, 18 enrolled. In 2010, 19 master's, 3 doctorates awarded. *Degree requirements:* For master's, thesis (for some programs); for doctorate, one foreign language, thesis/dissertation. *Entrance requirements:* For master's and doctorate, GRE General Test. *Application deadline:* For fall admission, 7/1 priority date for domestic students; for spring admission, 11/15 for domestic students. Application fee: $50. Electronic applications accepted. *Expenses:* Tuition, state resident: full-time $7200; part-time $344 per credit hour. Tuition, nonresident: full-time $21,900; part-time $944 per credit hour. Tuition and fees vary according to course load and program. *Financial support:* Fellowships, research assistantships, teaching assistantships, unspecified assistantships available. *Unit head:* Dr. John Stufken, Head, 706-542-8218, Fax: 706-542-3391, E-mail: jstufken@stat.uga.edu. *Application contact:* Dr. Lynn Seymour, Graduate Coordinator, 706-542-3307, Fax: 706-542-3391, E-mail: seymour@stat.uga.edu.

University of Guelph, Graduate Studies, College of Physical and Engineering Science, Department of Mathematics and Statistics, Guelph, ON N1G 2W1, Canada. Offers applied mathematics (PhD); applied statistics (PhD); mathematics and statistics (M Sc). Part-time programs available. *Degree requirements:* For master's, thesis (for some programs); for doctorate, thesis/dissertation. *Entrance requirements:* For master's, minimum B- average during previous 2 years of course work; for doctorate, minimum B average. Additional exam requirements/recommendations for international students: Required—TOEFL (minimum score 550 paper-based; 213 computer-based; 89 iBT), IELTS (minimum score 6.5). *Faculty research:* Dynamical systems, mathematical biology, numerical analysis, linear and nonlinear models, reliability and bioassay.

University of Houston–Clear Lake, School of Science and Computer Engineering, Program in Statistics, Houston, TX 77058-1098. Offers MS. *Entrance requirements:* For master's, GRE General Test. Additional exam requirements/recommendations for international students: Required—TOEFL (minimum score 550 paper-based; 213 computer-based).

University of Idaho, College of Graduate Studies, College of Science, Department of Statistics, Moscow, ID 83844-2282. Offers MS. *Faculty:* 5 full-time. *Students:* 14 full-time. Average age 28. In 2010, 5 master's awarded. *Degree requirements:* For master's, thesis or alternative. *Entrance requirements:* For master's, minimum GPA of 2.8. *Application deadline:* For fall admission, 8/1 for domestic students; for spring admission, 12/15 for domestic students. Applications are processed on a rolling basis. Application fee: $60. Electronic applications accepted. *Expenses:* Tuition, nonresident: part-time $580 per credit. Required fees: $306 per credit. *Financial support:* Research assistantships, teaching assistantships available. Financial award applicants required to submit FAFSA. *Faculty research:* Statistical genetics, biostatistics, nonlinear population dynamics, multivariate and computational statistics, Six Sigma innovation and design. *Unit head:* Dr. Rick Edgeman, Chair, 208-885-2929, E-mail: stat@uidaho.edu. *Application contact:* Dr. Rick Edgeman, Chair, 208-885-2929, E-mail: stat@uidaho.edu.

University of Illinois at Chicago, Graduate College, College of Liberal Arts and Sciences, Department of Mathematics, Statistics, and Computer Science, Chicago, IL 60607-7128. Offers applied mathematics (MS, PhD); computational finance (MS, PhD); computer science (MS, PhD); mathematics (DA); mathematics and information sciences for industry (MS); probability and statistics (PhD); pure mathematics (MS, PhD); statistics (MS); teaching of mathematics (MST), including elementary, secondary. Part-time programs available. *Faculty:* 36 full-time (3 women). *Students:* 150 full-time (54 women), 31 part-time (18 women); includes 3 Black or African American, non-Hispanic/Latino; 1 Asian, non-Hispanic/Latino; 8 Hispanic/Latino, 62 international. Average age 26. 224 applicants, 56% accepted, 43 enrolled. In 2010, 34 master's, 17 doctorates awarded. *Degree requirements:* For master's, comprehensive exam; for doctorate, one foreign language, thesis/dissertation. *Entrance requirements:* For master's and doctorate, GRE General Test, minimum GPA of 3.0. Additional exam requirements/recommendations for international students: Required—TOEFL (minimum score 100 iBT). *Application deadline:* For fall admission, 1/1 for domestic and international students; for spring admission, 10/1 for domestic students, 7/15 for international students. Applications are processed on a rolling basis. Application fee: $60. Electronic applications accepted. *Financial support:* In 2010–11, 109 students received support, including 2 fellowships with full tuition reimbursements available (averaging $20,000 per year), 8 research assistantships with full tuition reimbursements available (averaging $17,000 per year), 87 teaching assistantships with full tuition reimbursements available (averaging $17,000 per year); Federal Work-Study, scholarships/grants, and tuition waivers (full) also available. Financial award application deadline: 1/1. *Unit head:* Lawrence Ein, Head, 312-996-3044, E-mail: ein@math.uic.edu. *Application contact:* Brooke Shipley, Director of Graduate Studies, 312-996-5119, E-mail: dgs@math.uic.edu.

University of Illinois at Urbana–Champaign, Graduate College, College of Liberal Arts and Sciences, Department of Statistics, Champaign, IL 61820. Offers applied statistics (MS); statistics (PhD). *Faculty:* 11 full-time (4 women). *Students:* 50 full-time (26 women), 12 part-time (5 women); includes 5 minority (1 Black or African American, non-Hispanic/Latino; 4 Asian, non-Hispanic/Latino), 44 international. 299 applicants, 14% accepted, 18 enrolled. In 2010, 41 master's, 3 doctorates awarded. *Entrance requirements:* For master's and doctorate, GRE, minimum GPA of 3.0. Additional exam requirements/recommendations for international students: Required—TOEFL (minimum score 590 paper-based; 243 computer-based). *Application deadline:* Applications are processed on a rolling basis. Application fee: $75 ($90 for international students). Electronic applications accepted. *Financial support:* In 2010–11, 1 fellowship, 29 research assistantships, 33 teaching assistantships were awarded; tuition waivers (full and partial) also available. *Faculty research:* Statistical decision theory, sequential analysis, computer-aided stochastic modeling. *Unit head:* Douglas G. Simpson, Chair, 217-244-0885, Fax: 217-244-7190, E-mail: dgs@illinois.edu. *Application contact:* Melissa Banks, Office Support Specialist, 217-333-2167, Fax: 217-244-7190, E-mail: mdbanks@illinois.edu.

The University of Iowa, Graduate College, College of Education, Department of Psychological and Quantitative Foundations, Iowa City, IA 52242-1316. Offers counseling psychology (PhD); educational measurement and statistics (MA, PhD); educational psychology (MA, PhD); school psychology (PhD, Ed S); JD/PhD. *Accreditation:* APA. *Degree requirements:* For master's, thesis optional, exam; for doctorate, comprehensive exam, thesis/dissertation; for Ed S, exam. *Entrance requirements:* For master's, doctorate, and Ed S, GRE General Test, minimum GPA of 3.0. Additional exam requirements/recommendations for international students: Required—TOEFL (minimum score 550 paper-based; 213 computer-based; 81 iBT). Electronic applications accepted.

The University of Iowa, Graduate College, College of Liberal Arts and Sciences, Department of Statistics and Actuarial Science, Iowa City, IA 52242-1316. Offers MS, PhD. *Degree requirements:* For master's, thesis optional, exam; for doctorate, comprehensive exam, thesis/dissertation. *Entrance requirements:* For master's and doctorate, GRE General Test, minimum GPA of 3.0. Additional exam requirements/recommendations for international students: Required—TOEFL (minimum score 550 paper-based; 213 computer-based; 81 iBT). Electronic applications accepted.

University of Kentucky, Graduate School, College of Arts and Sciences, Program in Statistics, Lexington, KY 40506-0032. Offers MS, PhD. *Degree requirements:* For master's, comprehensive exam, thesis optional; for doctorate, comprehensive exam, thesis/dissertation. *Entrance requirements:* For master's, GRE General Test, minimum undergraduate GPA of 2.75; for doctorate, GRE General Test, minimum graduate GPA of 3.0. Additional exam requirements/recommendations for international students: Required—TOEFL (minimum score 550 paper-based; 213 computer-based). Electronic applications accepted. *Faculty research:* Computer intensive statistical inference, biostatistics, mathematical and applied statistics, applied probability.

The University of Manchester, School of Mathematics, Manchester, United Kingdom. Offers actuarial science (PhD); applied mathematics (M Phil, PhD); applied numerical computing (M Phil, PhD); financial mathematics (M Phil, PhD); mathematical logic (M Phil); probability (M Phil, PhD); pure mathematics (M Phil, PhD); statistics (M Phil, PhD).

The University of Manchester, School of Social Sciences, Manchester, United Kingdom. Offers ethnographic documentary (M Phil); interdisciplinary study of culture (PhD); philosophy (PhD); politics (PhD); social anthropology (PhD); social anthropology with visual media (PhD); social change (PhD); social statistics (PhD); sociology (PhD); visual anthropology (M Phil).

University of Manitoba, Faculty of Graduate Studies, Faculty of Science, Department of Statistics, Winnipeg, MB R3T 2N2, Canada. Offers M Sc, PhD. *Degree requirements:* For master's, thesis or alternative; for doctorate, one foreign language, thesis/dissertation.

University of Manitoba, Faculty of Graduate Studies, Faculty of Science, Program in Mathematical, Computational and Statistical Sciences, Winnipeg, MB R3T 2N2, Canada. Offers MMCSS.

University of Maryland, Baltimore County, Graduate School, College of Natural and Mathematical Sciences, Department of Mathematics and Statistics, Program in Statistics, Baltimore, MD 21250. Offers biostatistics (PhD); environmental statistics (MS); statistics (MS, PhD). Part-time and evening/weekend programs available. *Faculty:* 8 full-time (3 women). *Students:* 31 full-time (14 women), 24 part-time (14 women); includes 14 minority (5 Black or

Statistics

University of Maryland, Baltimore County *(continued)*
African American, non-Hispanic/Latino; 9 Asian, non-Hispanic/Latino, 17 international. Average age 30. 54 applicants, 80% accepted, 15 enrolled. In 2010, 9 master's, 2 doctorates awarded. Terminal master's awarded for partial completion of doctoral program. *Degree requirements:* For master's, comprehensive exam (for some programs), thesis (for some programs); for doctorate, comprehensive exam, thesis/dissertation. *Entrance requirements:* For master's and doctorate, GRE General Test, minimum GPA of 3.0. Additional exam requirements/recommendations for international students: Required—TOEFL (minimum score 600 paper-based; 250 computer-based; 100 iBT). *Application deadline:* For fall admission, 2/15 priority date for domestic students, 1/1 priority date for international students; for spring admission, 10/15 priority date for domestic students, 5/1 priority date for international students. Applications are processed on a rolling basis. Application fee: $50. Electronic applications accepted. *Financial support:* In 2010–11, 22 students received support, including 6 research assistantships with full tuition reimbursements available (averaging $15,500 per year), 16 teaching assistantships with full tuition reimbursements available (averaging $15,500 per year); fellowships with full tuition reimbursements available, career-related internships or fieldwork, scholarships/grants, health care benefits, tuition waivers (full and partial), and unspecified assistantships also available. Support available to part-time students. Financial award application deadline: 2/15. *Faculty research:* Design of experiments, statistical decision theory and inference, time series analysis, biostatistics and environmental statistics, bioinformatics. Total annual research expenditures: $2.8 million. *Unit head:* Dr. Anindya Roy, Director, 410-455-2435, Fax: 410-455-1066, E-mail: anindya@math.umbc.edu. *Application contact:* Dr. Anindya Roy, Director, 410-455-2435, Fax: 410-455-1066, E-mail: anindya@math.umbc.edu.

University of Maryland, College Park, Academic Affairs, College of Computer, Mathematical and Natural Sciences, Department of Mathematics, Program in Mathematical Statistics, College Park, MD 20742. Offers MA, PhD. Part-time and evening/weekend programs available. *Students:* 22 full-time (12 women), 13 part-time (7 women); includes 10 minority (2 Black or African American, non-Hispanic/Latino; 8 Asian, non-Hispanic/Latino), 17 international. 141 applicants, 10% accepted, 8 enrolled. In 2010, 4 master's, 2 doctorates awarded. Terminal master's awarded for partial completion of doctoral program. *Degree requirements:* For master's, thesis or comprehensive exams, scholarly paper; for doctorate, one foreign language, thesis/dissertation, written and oral exams. *Entrance requirements:* For master's and doctorate, GRE General Test, GRE Subject Test (mathematics), minimum GPA of 3.0, 3 letters of recommendation. *Application deadline:* For fall admission, 5/1 for domestic students, 2/1 for international students; for spring admission, 10/1 for domestic students, 6/1 for international students. Applications are processed on a rolling basis. Application fee: $75. Electronic applications accepted. *Expenses:* Tuition, area resident: Part-time $471 per credit hour. Tuition, state resident: part-time $471 per credit hour. Tuition, nonresident: part-time $1016 per credit hour. Required fees: $337 per term. *Financial support:* In 2010–11, 2 fellowships (averaging $13,400 per year), 11 teaching assistantships (averaging $16,855 per year) were awarded; research assistantships. Financial award applicants required to submit FAFSA. *Faculty research:* Statistics and probability, stochastic processes, nonparametric statistics, space-time statistics. *Unit head:* Dr. Paul Smith, Director, 301-405-5061, Fax: 301-314-0827, E-mail: pjs@math.umd.edu. *Application contact:* Dr. Charles A. Caramello, Dean of Graduate School, 301-405-0358, Fax: 301-314-9305, E-mail: ccaramel@umd.edu.

University of Massachusetts Amherst, Graduate School, College of Natural Sciences, Department of Mathematics and Statistics, Program in Mathematics and Statistics, Amherst, MA 01003. Offers MS, PhD. *Students:* 52 full-time (14 women), 1 (woman) part-time; includes 5 minority (1 Black or African American, non-Hispanic/Latino; 1 Asian, non-Hispanic/Latino; 1 Hispanic/Latino; 2 Two or more races, non-Hispanic/Latino), 22 international. Average age 28. 253 applicants, 18% accepted, 18 enrolled. In 2010, 16 master's, 7 doctorates awarded. Terminal master's awarded for partial completion of doctoral program. *Degree requirements:* For master's, thesis or alternative; for doctorate, comprehensive exam, thesis/dissertation. *Entrance requirements:* For master's and doctorate, GRE General Test, GRE Subject Test (mathematics). Additional exam requirements/recommendations for international students: Required—TOEFL (minimum score 550 paper-based; 213 computer-based; 80 iBT), IELTS (minimum score 6.5). *Application deadline:* For fall admission, 2/1 for domestic and international students; for spring admission, 10/1 for domestic and international students. Applications are processed on a rolling basis. Application fee: $50 ($65 for international students). Electronic applications accepted. *Expenses:* Tuition, state resident: full-time $2640. Required fees: $8282. One-time fee: $357 full-time. *Financial support:* Fellowships, research assistantships, teaching assistantships, career-related internships or fieldwork, Federal Work-Study, scholarships/grants, traineeships, health care benefits, tuition waivers (full), and unspecified assistantships available. Support available to part-time students. Financial award application deadline: 2/1; financial award applicants required to submit FAFSA. *Unit head:* Dr. Siman Wong, Graduate Program Director, 413-545-2282, Fax: 413-545-1801. *Application contact:* Jean M. Ames, Supervisor of Admissions, 413-545-0722, Fax: 413-577-0010, E-mail: gradadm@grad.umass.edu.

University of Memphis, Graduate School, College of Arts and Sciences, Department of Mathematical Sciences, Memphis, TN 38152. Offers applied mathematics (MS); applied statistics (PhD); bioinformatics (MS); computer science (PhD); computer sciences (MS); mathematics (MS, PhD); statistics (MS, PhD). Part-time programs available. *Faculty:* 19 full-time (4 women), 3 part-time/adjunct (0 women). *Students:* 38 full-time (12 women), 21 part-time (12 women); includes 8 minority (5 Black or African American, non-Hispanic/Latino; 2 Asian, non-Hispanic/Latino; 1 Hispanic/Latino), 25 international. Average age 34. 49 applicants, 55% accepted, 9 enrolled. In 2010, 6 master's, 5 doctorates awarded. Terminal master's awarded for partial completion of doctoral program. *Degree requirements:* For master's, comprehensive exam; for doctorate, one foreign language, thesis/dissertation, oral exams. *Entrance requirements:* For master's and doctorate, GRE General Test, minimum GPA of 2.5. Additional exam requirements/recommendations for international students: Required—TOEFL (minimum score 550 paper-based; 210 computer-based). *Application deadline:* For fall admission, 8/1 for domestic students, 5/1 priority date for international students; for spring admission, 12/1 for domestic students, 9/1 priority date for international students. Applications are processed on a rolling basis. Application fee: $35 ($60 for international students). Electronic applications accepted. *Financial support:* In 2010–11, 22 students received support; fellowships with full tuition reimbursements available, research assistantships with full tuition reimbursements available, teaching assistantships with full tuition reimbursements available, career-related internships or fieldwork, Federal Work-Study, scholarships/grants, and unspecified assistantships available. Financial award application deadline: 2/15; financial award applicants required to submit FAFSA. *Faculty research:* Combinatorics, ergodic theory, graph theory, Ramsey theory, applied statistics. *Unit head:* Dr. James E. Jamison, Chairman, 901-678-2482, Fax: 901-678-2480, E-mail: jjamison@memphis.edu. *Application contact:* Dr. Anna Kaminska, Coordinator of Graduate Studies, 901-678-2494, Fax: 901-678-2480.

University of Michigan, Horace H. Rackham School of Graduate Studies, College of Literature, Science, and the Arts, Department of Statistics, Ann Arbor, MI 48109. Offers applied statistics (AM); statistics (AM, PhD). *Faculty:* 33 full-time (8 women), 1 part-time/adjunct (0 women). *Students:* 113 full-time (49 women); includes 1 American Indian or Alaska Native, non-Hispanic/Latino; 3 Asian, non-Hispanic/Latino; 1 Hispanic/Latino, 76 international. Average age 27. 413 applicants, 20% accepted, 38 enrolled. In 2010, 37 master's, 6 doctorates awarded. Terminal master's awarded for partial completion of doctoral program. *Degree requirements:* For master's, thesis; for doctorate, thesis/dissertation, oral defense of dissertation, preliminary exam. *Entrance requirements:* For master's and doctorate, GRE General Test. Additional exam requirements/recommendations for international students: Required—TOEFL (minimum score 560 paper-based; 220 computer-based; 84 iBT), IELTS (minimum score 6.5). *Application deadline:* For

fall admission, 1/31 priority date for domestic students, 1/15 priority date for international students. Applications are processed on a rolling basis. Application fee: $65 ($75 for international students). Electronic applications accepted. *Expenses:* Tuition, state resident: full-time $17,784; part-time $1116 per credit hour. Tuition, nonresident: full-time $35,944; part-time $2125 per credit hour. International tuition: $35,994 full-time. Required fees: $95 per semester. Tuition and fees vary according to course load, degree level and program. *Financial support:* In 2010–11, 62 students received support, including 3 fellowships with full and partial tuition reimbursements available (averaging $25,000 per year), 17 research assistantships with full and partial tuition reimbursements available (averaging $17,270 per year), 42 teaching assistantships with full and partial tuition reimbursements available (averaging $17,270 per year); career-related internships or fieldwork, Federal Work-Study, institutionally sponsored loans, scholarships/grants, health care benefits, and unspecified assistantships also available. Financial award application deadline: 1/31. *Faculty research:* Reliability and degradation modeling, biological and legal applications, bioinformatics, statistical computing, covariance estimation. *Unit head:* Prof. Tailen Hsing, Chair, 734-763-3519, Fax: 734-763-4676, E-mail: statchair@umich.edu. *Application contact:* Lu Ann Custer, Graduate Secretary, 734-763-3520, Fax: 734-763-4676, E-mail: stat-admiss-ques@umich.edu.

University of Minnesota, Twin Cities Campus, Graduate School, College of Liberal Arts, School of Statistics, Minneapolis, MN 55455-0213. Offers MS, PhD. Part-time programs available. Terminal master's awarded for partial completion of doctoral program. *Degree requirements:* For doctorate, comprehensive exam, thesis/dissertation. *Entrance requirements:* For master's and doctorate, GRE General Test. Additional exam requirements/recommendations for international students: Required—TOEFL (minimum score 100 iBT). Electronic applications accepted. *Faculty research:* Data analysis, statistical computing, experimental design, probability theory, Bayesian inference.

University of Missouri, Graduate School, College of Arts and Sciences, Department of Statistics, Columbia, MO 65211. Offers MA, PhD. *Degree requirements:* For doctorate, comprehensive exam, thesis/dissertation. *Entrance requirements:* For master's, GRE General Test, minimum GPA of 3.0 in math and statistics courses; bachelor's degree from accredited college/university in related area; for doctorate, GRE General Test, minimum GPA of 3.0, 3.5 in math/statistics. Additional exam requirements/recommendations for international students: Required—TOEFL (minimum score 535 paper-based; 200 computer-based; 73 iBT). Electronic applications accepted. *Faculty research:* Statistical problems in the fields of ecology, genetics, economics, meteorology, wildlife management, epidemiology, AIDS research, geophysics, and climatology.

University of Missouri–Kansas City, College of Arts and Sciences, Department of Mathematics and Statistics, Kansas City, MO 64110-2499. Offers MA, MS, PhD. PhD (interdisciplinary) offered through the School of Graduate Studies. Part-time programs available. *Faculty:* 12 full-time (3 women), 8 part-time/adjunct (2 women). *Students:* 3 full-time (2 women), 31 part-time (11 women); includes 1 minority (Asian, non-Hispanic/Latino), 6 international. Average age 30. 45 applicants, 67% accepted, 14 enrolled. In 2010, 10 master's awarded. Terminal master's awarded for partial completion of doctoral program. *Degree requirements:* For master's, written exam; for doctorate, 2 foreign languages, thesis/dissertation, oral and written exams. *Entrance requirements:* For master's, bachelor's degree in mathematics, minimum GPA of 3.0; for doctorate, GMAT or GRE General Test. Additional exam requirements/recommendations for international students: Required—TOEFL (minimum score 550 paper-based; 213 computer-based; 80 iBT). *Application deadline:* For fall admission, 3/15 for domestic students, 3/15 priority date for international students; for spring admission, 10/15 for domestic and international students. Applications are processed on a rolling basis. Application fee: $45 ($50 for international students). Electronic applications accepted. *Expenses:* Tuition, state resident: full-time $5522.40; part-time $306.80 per credit hour. Tuition, nonresident: full-time $7128; part-time $792 per credit hour. Required fees: $261.15 per term. *Financial support:* In 2010–11, 2 research assistantships (averaging $13,300 per year), 10 teaching assistantships with full tuition reimbursements (averaging $17,175 per year) were awarded; Federal Work-Study, institutionally sponsored loans, and tuition waivers (full and partial) also available. Support available to part-time students. Financial award application deadline: 3/1; financial award applicants required to submit FAFSA. *Faculty research:* Numerical analysis, statistics, biostatistics commutative algebra, differential equations. Total annual research expenditures: $6,878. *Unit head:* Dr. Jie Chen, Chair/Professor, 816-235-1641, Fax: 816-235-5517, E-mail: umkcmathdept@umkc.edu. *Application contact:* Dr. Hristo Voulov, Associate Professor, 816-235-1641, Fax: 816-235-5517, E-mail: umkcmathdept@umkc.edu.

University of Nebraska–Lincoln, Graduate College, College of Agricultural Sciences and Natural Resources, Department of Statistics, Lincoln, NE 68588. Offers MS, PhD. *Degree requirements:* For master's, thesis optional. *Entrance requirements:* For master's, GRE General Test. Additional exam requirements/recommendations for international students: Required—TOEFL (minimum score 550 paper-based; 213 computer-based). Electronic applications accepted. *Faculty research:* Design of experiments, linear models, spatial variability, statistical modeling and inference, sampling.

University of New Brunswick Fredericton, School of Graduate Studies, Faculty of Science, Department of Mathematics and Statistics, Fredericton, NB E3B 5A3, Canada. Offers M Sc, PhD. *Faculty:* 10 full-time (0 women), 1 part-time/adjunct (0 women). *Students:* 22 full-time (8 women), 2 part-time (1 woman). In 2010, 2 master's, 1 doctorate awarded. *Degree requirements:* For master's, thesis; for doctorate, comprehensive exam, thesis/dissertation. *Entrance requirements:* For master's and doctorate, minimum GPA of 3.0. Additional exam requirements/recommendations for international students: Required—TOEFL (minimum score 550 paper-based; 80 computer-based), TWE (minimum score 4); Recommended—IELTS (minimum score 7). *Application deadline:* For fall admission, 3/1 priority date for domestic students. Applications are processed on a rolling basis. Application fee: $50 Canadian dollars. *Expenses:* Tuition, area resident: Full-time $3708; part-time $927 per term. International tuition: $6300 full-time. Required fees: $50 per term. *Financial support:* In 2010–11, 8 fellowships, 19 research assistantships (averaging $12,000 per year), 20 teaching assistantships (averaging $4,996 per year) were awarded. *Faculty research:* Algebra, general relativity, mathematical biology, quantum field theory, pure math, data analysis, experimental design. *Unit head:* Dr. James Watmough, Director of Graduate Studies, 506-458-7363, Fax: 506-453-4705, E-mail: watmough@unb.ca. *Application contact:* Marilyn Hetherington, Graduate Secretary, 506-458-7373, Fax: 506-453-4705, E-mail: mhetheri@unb.ca.

University of New Hampshire, Center for Graduate and Professional Studies, Manchester, NH 03101. Offers business administration (MBA); counseling (M Ed); education (M Ed, MAT); educational administration and supervision (M Ed, Ed S); industrial statistics (Certificate); public administration (MPA); public health (MPH, Certificate); social work (MSW); software systems engineering (Certificate). Part-time and evening/weekend programs available. *Students:* 97 full-time (65 women), 159 part-time (85 women); includes 20 minority (11 Black or African American, non-Hispanic/Latino; 1 American Indian or Alaska Native, non-Hispanic/Latino; 6 Asian, non-Hispanic/Latino; 2 Hispanic/Latino), 2 international. 119 applicants, 71% accepted, 61 enrolled. In 2010, 79 master's, 1 other advanced degree awarded. *Degree requirements:* For master's, thesis or alternative. *Entrance requirements:* Additional exam requirements/recommendations for international students: Required—TOEFL (minimum score 550 paper-based; 213 computer-based; 80 iBT). *Application deadline:* For fall admission, 6/1 for domestic students, 4/1 for international students; for spring admission, 12/1 for domestic students. Applications are processed on a rolling basis. Application fee: $65. Electronic applications accepted. *Financial support:* In 2010–11, 21 students received support, including 1 fellowship, 1 teaching assistantship; research assistantships, Federal Work-Study, scholarships/grants, health care benefits, and unspecified assistantships also available. Support available to part-time

students. Financial award application deadline: 3/1; financial award applicants required to submit FAFSA. *Unit head:* Kate Ferreira, Director, 603-641-4313, E-mail: unhm.gradcenter@unh.edu. *Application contact:* Graduate Admissions Office, 603-862-3000, Fax: 603-862-0275, E-mail: grad.school@unh.edu.

University of New Hampshire, Graduate School, College of Engineering and Physical Sciences, Department of Mathematics and Statistics, Durham, NH 03824. Offers applied mathematics (MS); industrial statistics (Postbaccalaureate Certificate); mathematics (MS, MST, PhD); mathematics education (PhD); statistics (MS). *Faculty:* 21 full-time (5 women). *Students:* 31 full-time (13 women), 25 part-time (10 women); includes 2 minority (both Two or more races, non-Hispanic/Latino), 17 international. Average age 31. 71 applicants, 49% accepted, 19 enrolled. In 2010, 17 master's, 6 doctorates, 3 other advanced degrees awarded. Terminal master's awarded for partial completion of doctoral program. *Degree requirements:* For doctorate, 2 foreign languages, thesis/dissertation. *Entrance requirements:* Additional exam requirements/recommendations for international students: Required—TOEFL (minimum score 550 paper-based; 213 computer-based; 80 iBT). *Application deadline:* For fall admission, 4/1 priority date for domestic students, 4/1 for international students; for spring admission, 12/1 for domestic students. Applications are processed on a rolling basis. Application fee: $65. Electronic applications accepted. *Financial support:* In 2010–11, 40 students received support, including 3 fellowships, 2 research assistantships, 34 teaching assistantships; Federal Work-Study, scholarships/grants, and tuition waivers (full and partial) also available. Support available to part-time students. Financial award application deadline: 2/15. *Faculty research:* Operator theory, complex analysis, algebra, nonlinear dynamics, statistics. *Unit head:* Dr. Edward Hindon, Chairperson, 603-862-2320. *Application contact:* Jan Jankowski, Administrative Assistant, 603-862-2320, E-mail: jan.jankowski@unh.edu.

University of New Mexico, Graduate School, College of Arts and Sciences, Department of Mathematics and Statistics, Albuquerque, NM 87131-2039. Offers mathematics (MS, PhD); statistics (MS, PhD). Part-time programs available. *Faculty:* 87 full-time (33 women), 59 part-time/adjunct (22 women). *Students:* 55 full-time (19 women), 19 part-time (3 women); includes 1 American Indian or Alaska Native, non-Hispanic/Latino; 3 Asian, non-Hispanic/Latino; 12 Hispanic/Latino, 23 international. Average age 33. 99 applicants, 45% accepted, 14 enrolled. In 2010, 17 master's, 5 doctorates awarded. Terminal master's awarded for partial completion of doctoral program. *Degree requirements:* For master's, comprehensive exam (for some programs), thesis or alternative; for doctorate, one foreign language, comprehensive exam, thesis/dissertation, 4 department seminars. *Entrance requirements:* For master's and doctorate, minimum GPA of 3.0, 3 letters of recommendation, letter of intent. Additional exam requirements/recommendations for international students: Required—TOEFL (minimum score 550 paper-based; 213 computer-based). *Application deadline:* For fall admission, 2/15 priority date for domestic students; for spring admission, 11/1 priority date for domestic students. Application fee: $50. Electronic applications accepted. *Expenses:* Tuition, state resident: full-time $5991; part-time $251 per credit hour. Tuition, nonresident: full-time $14,405; part-time $800.20 per credit hour. Tuition and fees vary according to course level, course load, program and reciprocity agreements. *Financial support:* In 2010–11, 59 students received support, including 15 research assistantships with tuition reimbursements available (averaging $8,419 per year), 46 teaching assistantships with tuition reimbursements available (averaging $14,812 per year); health care benefits and unspecified assistantships also available. Financial award application deadline: 2/15; financial award applicants required to submit FAFSA. *Faculty research:* Pure and applied mathematics, applied statistics, numerical analysis, biostatistics, differential geometry, fluid dynamics, nonparametric curve estimation. Total annual research expenditures: $1.5 million. *Unit head:* Dr. Alexander Stone, Chair, 505-277-4613, Fax: 505-277-5505, E-mail: astone@math.unm.edu. *Application contact:* Ana Parra Lombard, Coordinator, Program Advisement, 505-277-5250, Fax: 505-277-5505, E-mail: aparra@math.unm.edu.

The University of North Carolina at Chapel Hill, Graduate School, College of Arts and Sciences, Department of Statistics, Chapel Hill, NC 27599. Offers MS, PhD. *Degree requirements:* For master's, comprehensive exam, essay or thesis; for doctorate, comprehensive exam, thesis/dissertation. *Entrance requirements:* For master's and doctorate, GRE General Test, GRE Subject Test, minimum GPA of 3.0. Additional exam requirements/recommendations for international students: Required—TOEFL.

University of North Florida, College of Arts and Sciences, Department of Mathematics and Statistics, Jacksonville, FL 32224. Offers mathematical sciences (MS); statistics (MS). Part-time and evening/weekend programs available. *Faculty:* 21 full-time (8 women). *Students:* 12 full-time (3 women), 8 part-time (3 women); includes 2 Black or African American, non-Hispanic/Latino, 6 international. Average age 29. 34 applicants, 38% accepted, 7 enrolled. In 2010, 7 master's awarded. *Degree requirements:* For master's, comprehensive exam, thesis optional. *Entrance requirements:* For master's, GRE General Test, minimum GPA of 3.0 in last 60 hours of course work. Additional exam requirements/recommendations for international students: Required—TOEFL (minimum score 500 paper-based; 173 computer-based; 61 iBT). *Application deadline:* For fall admission, 7/1 priority date for domestic students, 6/1 for international students; for spring admission, 11/1 priority date for domestic students, 10/1 for international students. Applications are processed on a rolling basis. Application fee: $30. Electronic applications accepted. *Expenses:* Tuition, state resident: full-time $7646.40; part-time $318.60 per credit hour. Tuition, nonresident: full-time $23,502; part-time $979.24 per credit hour. Required fees: $1208.88; $50.37 per credit hour. Tuition and fees vary according to course load and program. *Financial support:* In 2010–11, 12 students received support, including 9 teaching assistantships (averaging $6,100 per year); Federal Work-Study, scholarships/grants, tuition waivers (partial), and unspecified assistantships also available. Support available to part-time students. Financial award application deadline: 4/1; financial award applicants required to submit FAFSA. *Faculty research:* Real analysis, number theory, Euclidean geometry. Total annual research expenditures: $53,523. *Unit head:* Dr. Scott H. Hochwald, Chair, 904-620-2653, Fax: 904-620-2818, E-mail: shochwal@unf.edu. *Application contact:* Lillith Richardson, Assistant Director, The Graduate School, 904-620-1360, Fax: 904-620-1362, E-mail: graduateschool@unf.edu.

University of Ottawa, Faculty of Graduate and Postdoctoral Studies, Faculty of Science, Ottawa-Carleton Institute of Mathematics and Statistics, Ottawa, ON K1N 6N5, Canada. Offers M Sc, PhD. M Sc, PhD offered jointly with Carleton University. Part-time programs available. *Degree requirements:* For master's, thesis optional; for doctorate, one foreign language, comprehensive exam, thesis/dissertation. *Entrance requirements:* For master's, honors B Sc degree or equivalent, minimum B average; for doctorate, M Sc, minimum B+ average. Electronic applications accepted. *Faculty research:* Pure mathematics, applied mathematics, probability and statistics.

University of Pennsylvania, Wharton School, Department of Statistics, Philadelphia, PA 19104. Offers MBA, PhD. *Degree requirements:* For doctorate, comprehensive exam, thesis/dissertation. *Entrance requirements:* For master's and doctorate, GRE. Additional exam requirements/recommendations for international students: Required—TOEFL, TWE. *Expenses:* Tuition: Full-time $25,660; part-time $4758 per course. Required fees: $2152; $270 per course. Tuition and fees vary according to course load, degree level and program. *Faculty research:* Nonparametric function estimation, analysis of algorithms, time series analysis, observational studies, inference.

University of Pittsburgh, School of Arts and Sciences, Department of Statistics, Pittsburgh, PA 15260. Offers applied statistics (MA, MS); statistics (MA, MS, PhD). Part-time programs available. *Faculty:* 7 full-time (1 woman). *Students:* 34 full-time (19 women), 4 part-time (0 women); includes 1 Black or African American, non-Hispanic/Latino, 30 international. Average age 23. 309 applicants, 19% accepted, 16 enrolled. In 2010, 7 master's, 2 doctorates awarded. Terminal master's awarded for partial completion of doctoral program. *Degree requirements:* For master's, comprehensive exam, thesis (for some programs); for doctorate, comprehensive exam, thesis/dissertation. *Entrance requirements:* For master's, 3 semesters of calculus, 1 semester of linear algebra, 1 year of mathematical statistics; for doctorate, 3 semesters of calculus, 1 semester of linear algebra, 1 year of mathematical statistics, 1 semester of advanced calculus. Additional exam requirements/recommendations for international students: Required—TOEFL (minimum score 550 paper-based; 213 computer-based; 80 iBT). *Application deadline:* For fall admission, 1/15 priority date for domestic and international students; for spring admission, 10/1 priority date for domestic students, 9/1 priority date for international students. Application fee: $50. Electronic applications accepted. *Expenses:* Tuition, state resident: full-time $17,304; part-time $701 per credit. Tuition, nonresident: full-time $29,554; part-time $1210 per credit. Required fees: $740; $214 per term. Tuition and fees vary according to program. *Financial support:* In 2010–11, 1 fellowship with full tuition reimbursement (averaging $18,546 per year), 7 research assistantships with full tuition reimbursements (averaging $16,140 per year), 13 teaching assistantships with full tuition reimbursements (averaging $15,520 per year) were awarded; career-related internships or fieldwork, Federal Work-Study, institutionally sponsored loans, scholarships/grants, health care benefits, and unspecified assistantships also available. Financial award application deadline: 1/15. *Faculty research:* Multivariate statistics, time series, reliability, meta-analysis, linear and nonlinear regression modeling. *Unit head:* Satish Iyengar, Chair, 412-624-8341, Fax: 412-648-8814, E-mail: sii@pitt.edu. *Application contact:* Leon J. Gleser, Director of Graduate Studies, 412-624-3925, Fax: 412-648-8814, E-mail: gleser@pitt.edu.

University of Puerto Rico, Mayagüez Campus, Graduate Studies, College of Arts and Sciences, Department of Mathematical Sciences, Mayagüez, PR 00681-9000. Offers applied mathematics (MS); pure mathematics (MS); scientific computation (MS); statistics (MS). Part-time programs available. *Students:* 40 full-time (11 women), 1 part-time (0 women); includes 7 Hispanic/Latino, 34 international. 19 applicants, 26% accepted, 3 enrolled. In 2010, 7 master's awarded. *Degree requirements:* For master's, one foreign language, comprehensive exam, thesis optional. *Entrance requirements:* For master's, undergraduate degree in mathematics or its equivalent. *Application deadline:* For fall admission, 2/15 for domestic and international students; for spring admission, 9/15 for domestic and international students. Applications are processed on a rolling basis. Application fee: $25. *Expenses:* Tuition, state resident: full-time $1188. Tuition, nonresident: full-time $1188. International tuition: $6126 full-time. Tuition and fees vary according to course level and course load. *Financial support:* In 2010–11, 39 students received support, including fellowships (averaging $12,000 per year), 20 research assistantships (averaging $15,000 per year), 39 teaching assistantships (averaging $8,500 per year); Federal Work-Study and institutionally sponsored loans also available. *Faculty research:* Automata theory, linear algebra, logic. Total annual research expenditures: $2.7 million. *Unit head:* Prof. Silvestre Col??n, Director, 787-832-4040 Ext. 3848, Fax: 787-265-5454, E-mail: silvestre.colon@upr.edu. *Application contact:* Prof. Silvestre Col??n, Director, 787-832-4040 Ext. 3848, Fax: 787-265-5454, E-mail: silvestre.colon@upr.edu.

University of Regina, Faculty of Graduate Studies and Research, Faculty of Science, Department of Mathematics and Statistics, Regina, SK S4S 0A2, Canada. Offers mathematics (M Sc, MA, PhD); statistics (M Sc, MA, PhD). *Faculty:* 17 full-time (3 women). *Students:* 17 full-time (4 women), 1 (woman) part-time. 16 applicants, 44% accepted. In 2010, 5 master's, 3 doctorates awarded. *Degree requirements:* For master's, thesis; for doctorate, comprehensive exam, thesis/dissertation. *Entrance requirements:* Additional exam requirements/recommendations for international students: Required—TOEFL (minimum score 580 paper-based; 80 iBT). *Application deadline:* Applications are processed on a rolling basis. Application fee: $100. Electronic applications accepted. Tuition and fees charges are reported in Canadian dollars. *Expenses:* Tuition, area resident: Full-time $3244.50 Canadian dollars; part-time $180.25 Canadian dollars per credit hour. International tuition: $4744.50 Canadian dollars full-time. Required fees: $494 Canadian dollars; $115.25 Canadian dollars per credit hour. $115.25 Canadian dollars per semester. Tuition and fees vary according to program. *Financial support:* In 2010–11, 3 fellowships (averaging $20,000 per year), 1 research assistantship (averaging $18,000 per year), 3 teaching assistantships (averaging $6,978 per year) were awarded; scholarships/grants also available. Financial award application deadline: 6/15. *Faculty research:* Discrete mathematics, actuarial science and statistics, matrix theory, mathematical science, numerical analysis. *Unit head:* Dr. Allen Herman, Head, 306-585-4487, Fax: 306-585-4020, E-mail: allen.herman@uregina.ca. *Application contact:* Dr. Martin Argerami, Graduate Program Coordinator, 306-585-4340, Fax: 306-585-4020, E-mail: martin.argerami@math.uregina.ca.

University of Rhode Island, Graduate School, College of Arts and Sciences, Department of Computer Science and Statistics, Kingston, RI 02881. Offers applied mathematics (PhD), including computer science, statistics; computer science (MS, PhD); digital forensics (Graduate Certificate); statistics (MS). Part-time programs available. *Faculty:* 10 full-time (3 women), 2 part-time/adjunct (0 women). *Students:* 39 full-time (10 women), 44 part-time (11 women); includes 16 minority (2 Black or African American, non-Hispanic/Latino; 2 American Indian or Alaska Native, non-Hispanic/Latino; 2 Asian, non-Hispanic/Latino; 2 Hispanic/Latino; 8 Native Hawaiian or other Pacific Islander, non-Hispanic/Latino), 8 international. In 2010, 5 master's awarded. *Degree requirements:* For master's, comprehensive exam (for some programs), thesis optional; for doctorate, comprehensive exam, thesis/dissertation. *Entrance requirements:* For master's and doctorate, GRE, 2 letters of recommendation. Additional exam requirements/recommendations for international students: Required—TOEFL (minimum score 550 paper-based; 213 computer-based). *Application deadline:* For fall admission, 7/15 for domestic students, 2/1 for international students; for spring admission, 11/15 for domestic students, 7/15 for international students. Application fee: $65. Electronic applications accepted. *Expenses:* Tuition, state resident: full-time $9588; part-time $533 per credit hour. Tuition, nonresident: full-time $22,968; part-time $1276 per credit hour. Required fees: $1282; $68 per semester. Tuition and fees vary according to program. *Financial support:* In 2010–11, 1 research assistantship (averaging $5,210 per year), 10 teaching assistantships with full and partial tuition reimbursements (averaging $10,456 per year) were awarded. Financial award application deadline: 2/1; financial award applicants required to submit FAFSA. *Faculty research:* Bioinformatics, computer and digital forensics, behavioral model of pedestrian dynamics, real-time distributed object computing, cryptography. Total annual research expenditures: $962,948. *Unit head:* Dr. James G. Kowalski, Chair, 401-874-2510, Fax: 401-874-4617, E-mail: kowalski@cs.uri.edu. *Application contact:* Dr. Victor Fay-Wolfe, Director of Graduate Studies, 401-874-2701, Fax: 401-874-4617, E-mail: wolfe@cs.uri.edu.

University of Rochester, School of Arts and Sciences, Department of Mathematics, Program in Statistics, Rochester, NY 14627.

University of Rochester, School of Medicine and Dentistry, Graduate Programs in Medicine and Dentistry, Department of Biostatistics and Computational Biology, Rochester, NY 14627. Offers medical statistics (MS); statistics (MA, PhD). Terminal master's awarded for partial completion of doctoral program. *Degree requirements:* For doctorate, thesis/dissertation, qualifying exam. *Entrance requirements:* For master's and doctorate, GRE General Test. Additional exam requirements/recommendations for international students: Required—TOEFL.

University of Saskatchewan, College of Graduate Studies and Research, College of Arts and Sciences, Department of Mathematics and Statistics, Saskatoon, SK S7N 5A2, Canada. Offers M Math, MA, PhD. *Degree requirements:* For master's, thesis (for some programs); for doctorate, comprehensive exam (for some programs), thesis/dissertation. *Entrance requirements:* Additional exam requirements/recommendations for international students: Required—TOEFL (minimum score 80 iBT); Recommended—IELTS (minimum score 6.5). Electronic applications accepted.

Peterson's Graduate Programs in the Physical Sciences, Mathematics, Agricultural Sciences, the Environment & Natural Resources 2012

www.facebook.com/petersonspublishing 299

Statistics

University of South Africa, College of Economic and Management Sciences, Pretoria, South Africa. Offers accounting (D Admin, D Com); accounting science (DA); auditing (D Admin, D Com); business administration (M Tech); business economics (D Admin); business leadership (DBL); business management (D Admin, D Com); economic management analysis (M Tech); economics (D Admin, D Com, PhD); human resource development (M Tech); industrial psychology (D Admin, D Com, PhD); logistics (D Com); marketing (M Tech); public administration (D Admin, D Com, DPA, PhD); public management (M Tech); quantitative management (D Admin, D Com); real estate (M Tech); statistics (D Admin, PhD); tourism management (D Admin, D Com); transport economics (D Admin, D Com).

University of South Carolina, The Graduate School, College of Arts and Sciences, Department of Statistics, Columbia, SC 29208. Offers applied statistics (CAS); industrial statistics (MIS); statistics (MS, PhD). Part-time and evening/weekend programs available. Postbaccalaureate distance learning degree programs offered (minimal on-campus study). Terminal master's awarded for partial completion of doctoral program. *Degree requirements:* For master's, thesis; for doctorate, comprehensive exam, thesis/dissertation. *Entrance requirements:* For master's, GRE General Test or GMAT, 2 years of work experience (MIS); for doctorate, GRE General Test; for CAS, GRE General Test or GMAT. Additional exam requirements/recommendations for international students: Required—TOEFL (minimum score 600 paper-based; 250 computer-based; 100 iBT). Electronic applications accepted. *Expenses:* Contact institution. *Faculty research:* Reliability, environmentrics, statistics computing, psychometrics, bioinformatics.

The University of South Dakota, Graduate School, College of Arts and Sciences, Department of Computer Science, Vermillion, SD 57069-2390. Offers computational sciences and statistics (PhD); computer science (MS). Part-time programs available. *Degree requirements:* For master's, thesis optional. *Entrance requirements:* For master's, GRE General Test, GRE Subject Test (recommended), minimum GPA of 2.7. Additional exam requirements/recommendations for international students: Required—TOEFL (minimum score 550 paper-based; 213 computer-based; 79 iBT). Electronic applications accepted.

University of Southern California, Graduate School, Dana and David Dornsife College of Letters, Arts and Sciences, Department of Mathematics, Los Angeles, CA 90089. Offers applied mathematics (MA, MS, PhD); mathematical finance (MS); mathematics (MA, PhD); statistics (MS). Part-time programs available. *Faculty:* 48 full-time (6 women). *Students:* 103 full-time (33 women), 14 part-time (6 women); includes 11 minority (8 Asian, non-Hispanic/Latino; 1 Hispanic/Latino; 2 Two or more races, non-Hispanic/Latino), 85 international. 559 applicants, 20% accepted, 32 enrolled. In 2010, 37 master's, 7 doctorates awarded. Terminal master's awarded for partial completion of doctoral program. *Degree requirements:* For master's, comprehensive exam (for some programs), thesis (for some programs); for doctorate, one foreign language, comprehensive exam, thesis/dissertation. *Entrance requirements:* For master's, GRE General Test, GMAT; for doctorate, GRE—General and Subject in Mathematics. Additional exam requirements/recommendations for international students: Required—TOEFL (minimum score 100 iBT). *Application deadline:* For fall and spring admission, 12/1 for domestic and international students. Applications are processed on a rolling basis. Application fee: $85. Electronic applications accepted. *Expenses:* Tuition: Full-time $31,240; part-time $1420 per unit. Required fees: $600. One-time fee: $35 full-time. Full-time tuition and fees vary according to degree level and program. *Financial support:* In 2010–11, 68 students received support, including 5 fellowships with full tuition reimbursements available (averaging $19,250 per year), 3 research assistantships with full tuition reimbursements available (averaging $19,250 per year), 58 teaching assistantships with full tuition reimbursements available (averaging $19,250 per year). Financial award application deadline: 12/1. *Faculty research:* Algebra, algebraic geometry and number theory, analysis/partial differential equations, applied mathematics, financial mathematics, probability, combinatorics and statistics. Total annual research expenditures: $1.7 million. *Unit head:* Prof. Gary Rosen, Chair, 213-740-1717, Fax: 213-740-2424, E-mail: grosen@usc.edu. *Application contact:* Amy Yung, Department Coordinator, 213-740-8168, Fax: 213-740-2424, E-mail: amy@usc.edu.

University of Southern Maine, College of Arts and Sciences, Program in Statistics, Portland, ME 04104-9300. Offers MS.

University of South Florida, Graduate School, College of Arts and Sciences, Department of Mathematics and Statistics, Tampa, FL 33620-9951. Offers mathematics (MA, PhD); statistics (MA). Part-time and evening/weekend programs available. *Faculty:* 15 full-time (0 women), 6 part-time/adjunct (all women). *Students:* 73 full-time (24 women), 16 part-time (4 women); includes 2 Black or African American, non-Hispanic/Latino; 5 Asian, non-Hispanic/Latino; 6 Hispanic/Latino; 2 Two or more races, non-Hispanic/Latino, 40 international. Average age 32. 73 applicants, 63% accepted, 21 enrolled. In 2010, 17 master's, 6 doctorates awarded. Terminal master's awarded for partial completion of doctoral program. *Degree requirements:* For master's, one foreign language, comprehensive exam, thesis optional; for doctorate, 2 foreign languages, comprehensive exam, thesis/dissertation. *Entrance requirements:* For master's, GRE General Test, minimum GPA of 3.0; for doctorate, GRE General Test, minimum GPA of 3.5 in undergraduate/graduate mathematics courses. Additional exam requirements/recommendations for international students: Required—TOEFL (minimum score 550 paper-based; 213 computer-based; 79 iBT). *Application deadline:* For fall admission, 2/1 for domestic students, 1/2 for international students; for spring admission, 8/1 for domestic students, 6/1 for international students. Application fee: $30. Electronic applications accepted. *Financial support:* In 2010–11, 57 students received support, including 6 research assistantships (averaging $13,555 per year), 57 teaching assistantships with partial tuition reimbursements available (averaging $13,634 per year); unspecified assistantships also available. Financial award application deadline: 2/1. *Faculty research:* Approximation theory, differential equations, discrete mathematics, functional analysis topology. Total annual research expenditures: $520,926. *Unit head:* Dr. Marcus McWaters, Chairperson, 813-974-3838, Fax: 813-974-2700, E-mail: mmm@usf.edu. *Application contact:* Dr. Xiang-Dong Hou, Graduate Admissions Director, 813-974-2561, Fax: 813-974-2700, E-mail: xhou@cas.usf.edu.

The University of Tennessee, Graduate School, College of Business Administration, Department of Statistics, Knoxville, TN 37996. Offers industrial statistics (MS); statistics (MS). Part-time programs available. *Degree requirements:* For master's, thesis or alternative. *Entrance requirements:* For master's, GMAT or GRE General Test, minimum GPA of 2.7. Additional exam requirements/recommendations for international students: Required—TOEFL. Electronic applications accepted. *Expenses:* Tuition, state resident: full-time $7440; part-time $414 per credit hour. Tuition, nonresident: full-time $22,478; part-time $1250 per credit hour. Required fees: $922; $43 per credit hour. Tuition and fees vary according to program.

The University of Tennessee, Graduate School, College of Business Administration, Program in Business Administration, Knoxville, TN 37996. Offers accounting (PhD); finance (MBA, PhD); logistics and transportation (MBA, PhD); management (PhD); marketing (MBA, PhD); operations management (MBA); professional business administration (MBA); statistics (PhD); JD/MBA; MS/MBA. *Accreditation:* AACSB. Postbaccalaureate distance learning degree programs offered. *Degree requirements:* For master's, thesis or alternative; for doctorate, thesis/dissertation. *Entrance requirements:* For master's and doctorate, GMAT, minimum GPA of 2.7. Additional exam requirements/recommendations for international students: Required—TOEFL. Electronic applications accepted. *Expenses:* Tuition, state resident: full-time $7440; part-time $414 per credit hour. Tuition, nonresident: full-time $22,478; part-time $1250 per credit hour. Required fees: $922; $43 per credit hour. Tuition and fees vary according to program.

The University of Texas at Austin, Graduate School, College of Natural Sciences, Department of Mathematics, Program in Statistics, Austin, TX 78712-1111. Offers MS Stat. *Entrance requirements:* For master's, GRE General Test.

The University of Texas at Dallas, School of Natural Sciences and Mathematics, Department of Mathematical Sciences, Richardson, TX 75080. Offers applied mathematics (MS, PhD); engineering mathematics (MS); mathematical science (MS); statistics (MS, PhD). Part-time and evening/weekend programs available. *Faculty:* 15 full-time (2 women). *Students:* 43 full-time (16 women), 22 part-time (6 women); includes 20 minority (6 Black or African American, non-Hispanic/Latino; 11 Asian, non-Hispanic/Latino; 3 Hispanic/Latino), 23 international. Average age 32. 147 applicants, 32% accepted, 9 enrolled. In 2010, 18 master's, 6 doctorates awarded. *Degree requirements:* For master's, thesis optional; for doctorate, thesis/dissertation. *Entrance requirements:* For master's, GRE General Test, minimum GPA of 3.0 in upper-level course work in field; for doctorate, GRE General Test, minimum GPA of 3.5 in upper-level course work in field. Additional exam requirements/recommendations for international students: Required—TOEFL (minimum score 550 paper-based; 215 computer-based). *Application deadline:* For fall admission, 7/15 for domestic students, 5/1 priority date for international students; for spring admission, 11/15 for domestic students, 9/1 priority date for international students. Applications are processed on a rolling basis. Application fee: $50 ($100 for international students). Electronic applications accepted. *Expenses:* Tuition, state resident: full-time $10,248; part-time $569 per credit hour. Tuition, nonresident: full-time $18,544; part-time $1030 per credit hour. Tuition and fees vary according to course load. *Financial support:* In 2010–11, 39 students received support, including 2 research assistantships (averaging $15,750 per year), 31 teaching assistantships with partial tuition reimbursements available (averaging $13,933 per year); career-related internships or fieldwork, Federal Work-Study, institutionally sponsored loans, scholarships/grants, and unspecified assistantships also available. Support available to part-time students. Financial award application deadline: 4/30; financial award applicants required to submit FAFSA. *Faculty research:* Sequential analysis, applications in semiconductor manufacturing, medical image analysis, computational anatomy, information theory, probability theory. *Unit head:* Dr. Wieslaw Z. Krawcewicz, Department Head, 972-883-6820, Fax: 972-883-6622, E-mail: wieslaw@utdallas.edu. *Application contact:* Dr. Wieslaw Z. Krawcewicz, Department Head, 972-883-6820, Fax: 972-883-6622, E-mail: wieslaw@utdallas.edu.

The University of Texas at El Paso, Graduate School, College of Science, Department of Mathematical Sciences, El Paso, TX 79968-0001. Offers mathematical sciences (MS); mathematics (teaching) (MAT); statistics (MS). Part-time and evening/weekend programs available. *Students:* 61 (30 women); includes 1 Asian, non-Hispanic/Latino; 38 Hispanic/Latino, 13 international. Average age 34. In 2010, 17 master's awarded. *Degree requirements:* For master's, thesis optional. *Entrance requirements:* For master's, minimum GPA of 3.0, letters of recommendation. Additional exam requirements/recommendations for international students: Required—TOEFL; Recommended—IELTS. *Application deadline:* For fall admission, 8/1 priority date for domestic students, 3/1 for international students; for spring admission, 11/1 priority date for domestic students, 9/1 for international students. Applications are processed on a rolling basis. Application fee: $45 ($80 for international students). Electronic applications accepted. *Financial support:* In 2010–11, research assistantships with partial tuition reimbursements (averaging $21,812 per year), teaching assistantships with partial tuition reimbursements (averaging $17,450 per year) were awarded; fellowships with tuition reimbursements, institutionally sponsored loans, scholarships/grants, health care benefits, tuition waivers (partial), and unspecified assistantships also available. Support available to part-time students. Financial award application deadline: 3/15; financial award applicants required to submit FAFSA. *Unit head:* Dr. Maria C. Mariani, Chair, 915-747-5761, Fax: 915-747-6502, E-mail: mcmariani@utep.edu. *Application contact:* Dr. Patricia D. Witherspoon, Dean of the Graduate School, 915-747-5491, Fax: 915-747-5788, E-mail: withersp@utep.edu.

The University of Texas at San Antonio, College of Business, Department of Management Science and Statistics, San Antonio, TX 78249-0617. Offers applied statistics (MS, PhD); management science (MBA). *Accreditation:* AACSB. Part-time and evening/weekend programs available. *Faculty:* 15 full-time (4 women), 1 part-time/adjunct (0 women). *Students:* 34 full-time (12 women), 23 part-time (6 women); includes 13 minority (2 Black or African American, non-Hispanic/Latino; 5 Asian, non-Hispanic/Latino; 5 Hispanic/Latino; 1 Native Hawaiian or other Pacific Islander, non-Hispanic/Latino), 16 international. Average age 31. 51 applicants, 67% accepted, 25 enrolled. In 2010, 15 master's, 1 doctorate awarded. *Degree requirements:* For master's, comprehensive exam (for some programs), thesis (for some programs). *Entrance requirements:* For master's, GMAT, minimum GPA of 3.0. Additional exam requirements/recommendations for international students: Required—TOEFL (minimum score 500 paper-based; 173 computer-based; 61 iBT). *Application deadline:* For fall admission, 7/1 for domestic students, 4/1 for international students; for spring admission, 11/1 for domestic students, 9/1 for international students. Applications are processed on a rolling basis. Application fee: $45 ($80 for international students). Electronic applications accepted. *Expenses:* Tuition, state resident: full-time $4172; part-time $231.75 per credit hour. Tuition, nonresident: full-time $15,332; part-time $851.75 per credit hour. *Financial support:* In 2010–11, 13 students received support, including 1 fellowship (averaging $45,000 per year), 79 research assistantships (averaging $13,264 per year), 8 teaching assistantships (averaging $8,000 per year). *Faculty research:* Applied statistics, biostatistics, supply chain management. Total annual research expenditures: $23,518. *Unit head:* Dr. Raydel Tullous, PhD, Department Chair, 210-458-6345, Fax: 210-458-6350, E-mail: raydel.tullous@utsa.edu. *Application contact:* Veronica Ramirez, Assistant Dean of the Graduate School, 210-458-7841, Fax: 210-458-4332, E-mail: graduatestudies@utsa.edu.

University of the Incarnate Word, School of Graduate Studies and Research, School of Mathematics, Science, and Engineering, Program in Mathematics, San Antonio, TX 78209-6397. Offers mathematics teaching (MA); research statistics (MS). Part-time and evening/weekend programs available. *Faculty:* 7 full-time (4 women). *Students:* 1 full-time (0 women), 2 part-time (both women); includes 2 Hispanic/Latino, 1 international. Average age 49. In 2010, 2 master's awarded. *Degree requirements:* For master's, capstone or prerequisite knowledge (for research statistics). *Entrance requirements:* For master's, GRE (minimum score 800 verbal and quantitative), 18 hours of undergraduate mathematics with minimum GPA of 3.0; letter of recommendation by a professional in the field, writing sample, teaching experience at the precollege level. Additional exam requirements/recommendations for international students: Required—TOEFL (minimum score 560 paper-based; 220 computer-based; 83 iBT). *Application deadline:* Applications are processed on a rolling basis. Application fee: $20. Electronic applications accepted. *Expenses:* Tuition: Part-time $725 per contact hour. Required fees: $890 per semester. *Financial support:* Federal Work-Study and scholarships/grants available. Financial award applicants required to submit FAFSA. *Faculty research:* Nearness spaces in mathematical constructs, professional development of mathematics teachers. *Unit head:* Dr. Zhanbo Yang, Graduate Programs Coordinator, 210-283-5008, Fax: 210-829-3153, E-mail: yang@uiwtx.edu. *Application contact:* Andrea Cyterski-Acosta, Dean of Enrollment, 210-829-6005, Fax: 210-829-3921, E-mail: admis@uiwtx.edu.

University of the Incarnate Word, School of Graduate Studies and Research, School of Mathematics, Science, and Engineering, Program in Research Statistics, San Antonio, TX 78209-6397. Offers MS. *Faculty:* 4 full-time (1 woman). *Students:* 11 part-time (8 women); includes 1 Black or African American, non-Hispanic/Latino; 1 Asian, non-Hispanic/Latino; 6 Hispanic/Latino. *Expenses:* Tuition: Part-time $725 per contact hour. Required fees: $890 per semester. *Faculty research:* Biomedical statistical research, solar and wind powered systems. *Unit head:* Dr. Glenn Edward James, Dean, 210-829-3152, Fax: 210-829-3153, E-mail: gjames@uiwtx.edu. *Application contact:* Andrea Cyterski-Acosta, Dean of Enrollment, 210-829-6005, Fax: 210-829-3921, E-mail: admis@uiwtx.edu.

The University of Toledo, College of Graduate Studies, College of Natural Sciences and Mathematics, Department of Mathematics, Toledo, OH 43606-3390. Offers applied mathematics (MS, PhD); mathematics (MA, PhD); statistics (MS, PhD). Part-time programs available. *Faculty:* 25. *Students:* 44 full-time (12 women), 13 part-time (7 women), 44 international.

Average age 30. 84 applicants, 43% accepted, 19 enrolled. In 2010, 15 master's, 2 doctorates awarded. *Degree requirements:* For master's, thesis; for doctorate, 2 foreign languages, thesis/dissertation. *Entrance requirements:* For master's and doctorate, GRE General Test, GRE Subject Test, A minimum 2.7 cumulative point-hour ratio (on a 4.0 scale) for all previous academic work. Three letters of recommendation, a statement of purpose, and transcripts from all prior institutions attended. Additional exam requirements/recommendations for international students: Required—TOEFL (minimum score 550 paper-based; 213 computer-based; 80 iBT), IELTS (minimum score 6.5). *Application deadline:* For fall admission, 1/15 priority date for domestic and international students. Applications are processed on a rolling basis. Application fee: $45 ($75 for international students). Electronic applications accepted. *Expenses:* Tuition, state resident: full-time $11,426; part-time $476 per credit hour. Tuition, nonresident: full-time $21,660; part-time $903 per credit hour. One-time fee: $62. *Financial support:* Research assistantships with full tuition reimbursements, teaching assistantships with full tuition reimbursements, Federal Work-Study, institutionally sponsored loans, scholarships/grants, and unspecified assistantships available. Support available to part-time students. *Faculty research:* Topology. *Unit head:* Dr. Paul Hewitt, Chair, 419-530-2568, E-mail: paul.hewitt@utoledo.edu. *Application contact:* Graduate School Office, 419-530-4723, Fax: 419-530-4723, E-mail: grdsch@utnet.utoledo.edu.

University of Toronto, School of Graduate Studies, Physical Sciences Division, Department of Statistics, Toronto, ON M5S 1A1, Canada. Offers M Sc, PhD. Part-time programs available. *Degree requirements:* For doctorate, comprehensive exam, thesis/dissertation. *Entrance requirements:* For master's, GRE (recommended for students educated outside of Canada), 3 letters of reference; for doctorate, GRE (recommended for students educated outside of Canada), 3 letters of reference, M Stat or equivalent, minimum B+ average.

University of Utah, Graduate School, College of Education, Department of Educational Psychology, Salt Lake City, UT 84112. Offers counseling psychology (PhD); educational psychology (MA); instructional design and educational technology (M Ed); learning and cognition (MS, PhD); professional counseling (MS); professional psychology (M Ed); reading and literacy (M Ed, PhD); school counseling (M Ed, MS); school psychology (MS, PhD); statistics (M Stat). *Accreditation:* APA (one or more programs are accredited). Evening/weekend programs available. Postbaccalaureate distance learning degree programs offered (minimal on-campus study). *Faculty:* 20 full-time (10 women), 6 part-time/adjunct (4 women). *Students:* 119 full-time (96 women), 105 part-time (72 women); includes 25 minority (1 American Indian or Alaska Native, non-Hispanic/Latino; 6 Asian, non-Hispanic/Latino; 13 Hispanic/Latino; 1 Native Hawaiian or other Pacific Islander, non-Hispanic/Latino; 4 Two or more races, non-Hispanic/Latino), 3 international. Average age 33. 238 applicants, 34% accepted, 60 enrolled. In 2010, 40 master's, 18 doctorates awarded. *Degree requirements:* For master's, variable foreign language requirement, comprehensive exam, thesis (for some programs); for doctorate, variable foreign language requirement, thesis/dissertation, oral exam. *Entrance requirements:* For master's and doctorate, GRE General Test, minimum GPA of 3.0. Additional exam requirements/recommendations for international students: Required—TOEFL (minimum score 500 paper-based; 173 computer-based). *Application deadline:* For fall admission, 4/1 for domestic and international students; for spring admission, 11/1 for domestic and international students. Application fee: $55 ($65 for international students). *Expenses:* Contact institution. *Financial support:* In 2010–11, 90 students received support, including 45 fellowships with full and partial tuition reimbursements available (averaging $11,500 per year), 13 research assistantships with full and partial tuition reimbursements available (averaging $11,500 per year), 32 teaching assistantships with full and partial tuition reimbursements available (averaging $11,500 per year); career-related internships or fieldwork, Federal Work-Study, institutionally sponsored loans, scholarships/grants, and unspecified assistantships also available. Financial award application deadline: 2/1; financial award applicants required to submit FAFSA. *Faculty research:* Autism, computer technology and instruction, cognitive behavior, aging, group counseling. Total annual research expenditures: $902,082. *Unit head:* Dr. Elaine Clark, Chair, 801-581-7148, Fax: 801-581-5566, E-mail: clark@ed.utah.edu. *Application contact:* Kendra Lee Wiebke, Academic Program Specialist, 801-581-7148, Fax: 801-581-5566, E-mail: kendra.wiebke@utah.edu.

University of Utah, Graduate School, David Eccles School of Business, Business Administration Program, Salt Lake City, UT 84112. Offers accounting (PhD); business administration (EMBA, MBA, PMBA); statistics (M Stat). Part-time and evening/weekend programs available. *Faculty:* 18 full-time (8 women). *Students:* 608 full-time (118 women), 31 part-time (9 women); includes 53 minority (4 Black or African American, non-Hispanic/Latino; 2 American Indian or Alaska Native, non-Hispanic/Latino; 27 Asian, non-Hispanic/Latino; 15 Hispanic/Latino; 5 Two or more races, non-Hispanic/Latino), 47 international. Average age 32. 930 applicants, 45% accepted, 311 enrolled. In 2010, 256 master's, 8 doctorates awarded. Terminal master's awarded for partial completion of doctoral program. *Degree requirements:* For doctorate, thesis/dissertation, oral qualifying exams, written qualifying exams. *Entrance requirements:* For master's, GMAT, statistics course with minimum B grade, minimum undergraduate GPA of 3.0; for doctorate, GMAT or GRE General Test. Additional exam requirements/recommendations for international students: Required—TOEFL (minimum score 600 paper-based; 250 computer-based; 100 iBT), IELTS (minimum score 7). *Application deadline:* For fall admission, 2/15 priority date for domestic and international students. Applications are processed on a rolling basis. Application fee: $55 ($65 for international students). Electronic applications accepted. *Expenses:* Contact institution. *Financial support:* In 2010–11, 20 students received support, including 1 fellowship with partial tuition reimbursement available (averaging $9,000 per year), 58 teaching assistantships with partial tuition reimbursements available (averaging $6,350 per year); scholarships/grants and unspecified assistantships also available. Financial award application deadline: 2/15; financial award applicants required to submit FAFSA. *Faculty research:* Corporate finance, strategy services, consumer behavior, financial disclosures, operations. Total annual research expenditures: $60,805. *Unit head:* Linda Wells, Program Director of MBA Program, Fax: 801-581-3666. *Application contact:* Andrea Chmelik, Coordinator, 801-581-1719, Fax: 801-581-3666, E-mail: andrea.chmelik@business.utah.edu.

University of Utah, Graduate School, Interdepartmental Program in Statistics, Salt Lake City, UT 84112-1107. Offers biostatistics (M Stat); econometrics (M Stat); educational psychology (M Stat); mathematics (M Stat); sociology (M Stat); statistics (M Stat). Part-time programs available. *Students:* 28 full-time (11 women), 17 part-time (9 women); includes 2 Black or African American, non-Hispanic/Latino; 2 Asian, non-Hispanic/Latino; 2 Hispanic/Latino, 10 international. Average age 30. 59 applicants, 44% accepted, 12 enrolled. In 2010, 15 master's awarded. *Degree requirements:* For master's, comprehensive exam, projects. *Entrance requirements:* For master's, GRE General Test (sociology and educational psychology), minimum GPA of 3.0; course work in calculus, matrix theory, statistics. Additional exam requirements/recommendations for international students: Required—TOEFL (minimum score 500 paper-based; 173 computer-based). *Application deadline:* For fall admission, 7/1 for domestic students, 4/1 for international students. Applications are processed on a rolling basis. Application fee: $55 ($65 for international students). *Expenses:* Tuition, area resident: Part-time $179.19 per credit hour. Tuition, state resident: full-time $4384. Tuition, nonresident: full-time $16,684; part-time $630.67 per credit hour. Required fees: $350 per semester. Tuition and fees vary according to course load, degree level and program. *Financial support:* Career-related internships or fieldwork available. *Faculty research:* Biostatistics, management, economics, educational psychology, mathematics. *Unit head:* Tariq Mughal, Chair, University Statistics Committee, 801-585-9547, E-mail: tariaq.mughal@business.utah.edu. *Application contact:* Laura Egbert, MSTAT Program Coordinator, 801-585-6853, E-mail: laura.demattia@utah.edu.

University of Utah, Graduate School, Professional Master of Science and Technology Program, Salt Lake City, UT 84112-1107. Offers biotechnology (PSM); computational science (PSM); environmental science (PSM); science instrumentation (PSM). Part-time programs available. *Faculty:* 2 full-time (0 women). *Students:* 32 full-time (17 women), 38 part-time (13 women); includes 1 Black or African American, non-Hispanic/Latino; 3 Asian, non-Hispanic/Latino; 1 Hispanic/Latino, 19 international. Average age 31. 66 applicants, 48% accepted, 16 enrolled. In 2010, 7 master's awarded. *Degree requirements:* For master's, internship. *Entrance requirements:* For master's, GRE (recommended), minimum undergraduate GPA of 3.0, bachelor's degree from accredited university or college. Additional exam requirements/recommendations for international students: Required—TOEFL (minimum score 500 paper-based; 173 computer-based; 61 iBT), IELTS (minimum score 6). *Application deadline:* For fall admission, 3/1 for domestic and international students. Application fee: $55 ($65 for international students). Electronic applications accepted. *Expenses:* Tuition, area resident: Part-time $179.19 per credit hour. Tuition, state resident: full-time $4384. Tuition, nonresident: full-time $16,684; part-time $630.67 per credit hour. Required fees: $350 per semester. Tuition and fees vary according to course load, degree level and program. *Financial support:* In 2010–11, 8 students received support, including 5 fellowships with full and partial tuition reimbursements available (averaging $16,800 per year), 2 research assistantships (averaging $6,200 per year); unspecified assistantships also available. Financial award applicants required to submit FAFSA. *Faculty research:* Drug delivery systems, in vitro erythroid expansion and HRE (Hypoxia responsive element). *Unit head:* Jennifer Schmidt, Program Director, 801-585-5630, E-mail: jennifer.schmidt@gradschool.utah.edu. *Application contact:* Amy Kimball, Project Coordinator, 801-585-3650, Fax: 801-585-6749, E-mail: amy.kimball@gradschool.utah.edu.

University of Vermont, Graduate College, College of Engineering and Mathematics, Department of Mathematics and Statistics, Program in Statistics, Burlington, VT 05405. Offers MS. *Students:* 6 (2 women); includes 1 Asian, non-Hispanic/Latino, 4 international. 19 applicants, 58% accepted, 1 enrolled. In 2010, 8 master's awarded. *Entrance requirements:* Additional exam requirements/recommendations for international students: Required—TOEFL (minimum score 550 paper-based; 213 computer-based). *Application deadline:* For fall admission, 4/1 priority date for domestic students. Applications are processed on a rolling basis. Application fee: $40. Electronic applications accepted. *Expenses:* Tuition, state resident: part-time $537 per credit hour. Tuition, nonresident: part-time $1355 per credit hour. *Financial support:* Fellowships, research assistantships, teaching assistantships available. Financial award application deadline: 3/1. *Faculty research:* Applied statistics. *Unit head:* Dr. Jeff Buzas, Coordinator, 802-656-2940. *Application contact:* Dr. Jeff Buzas, Coordinator, 802-656-2940.

University of Victoria, Faculty of Graduate Studies, Faculty of Science, Department of Mathematics and Statistics, Victoria, BC V8W 2Y2, Canada. Offers M Sc, MA, PhD. Part-time programs available. *Degree requirements:* For master's, thesis; for doctorate, one foreign language, thesis/dissertation, 3 qualifying exams, candidacy exam. *Entrance requirements:* Additional exam requirements/recommendations for international students: Required—TOEFL (minimum score 575 paper-based; 233 computer-based), IELTS (minimum score 7). Electronic applications accepted. *Faculty research:* Functional analysis and operator theory, applied ordinary and partial differential equations, discrete mathematics and graph theory.

University of Virginia, College and Graduate School of Arts and Sciences, Department of Statistics, Charlottesville, VA 22903. Offers MS, PhD. *Faculty:* 8 full-time (2 women). *Students:* 41 full-time (19 women), 2 part-time (0 women); includes 4 Asian, non-Hispanic/Latino, 28 international. Average age 25. 126 applicants, 34% accepted, 21 enrolled. In 2010, 11 master's, 4 doctorates awarded. *Degree requirements:* For master's, exam; for doctorate, comprehensive exam, thesis/dissertation. *Entrance requirements:* For master's and doctorate, GRE General Test, 3 letters of recommendation. Additional exam requirements/recommendations for international students: Required—TOEFL (minimum score 600 paper-based; 250 computer-based; 90 iBT), IELTS (minimum score 7). *Application deadline:* For fall admission, 2/1 for domestic and international students. Applications are processed on a rolling basis. Application fee: $60. Electronic applications accepted. *Financial support:* Fellowships, teaching assistantships available. Financial award applicants required to submit FAFSA. *Unit head:* Ted Chang, Chairman, 434-924-3222, Fax: 434-924-3076, E-mail: gradapp1@pitman.stat.virginia.edu. *Application contact:* Feifang Hu, Director of Graduate Program, 434-924-3222, Fax: 434-924-3076, E-mail: gradapp1@pitman.stat.virginia.edu.

University of Washington, Graduate School, College of Arts and Sciences, Department of Statistics, Seattle, WA 98195. Offers MS, PhD. Terminal master's awarded for partial completion of doctoral program. *Degree requirements:* For master's, thesis optional; for doctorate, one foreign language, thesis/dissertation. *Entrance requirements:* For master's and doctorate, GRE General Test, minimum GPA of 3.0. Additional exam requirements/recommendations for international students: Required—TOEFL. *Faculty research:* Mathematical statistics, stochastic modeling, spatial statistics, statistical computing.

University of Washington, Graduate School, School of Public Health, Department of Biostatistics, Seattle, WA 98195. Offers biostatistics (MPH, MS, PhD); clinical research (MS), including biostatistics; statistical genetics (PhD). *Faculty:* 46 full-time (22 women), 6 part-time/adjunct (1 woman). *Students:* 74 full-time (39 women), 6 part-time (5 women); includes 7 Asian, non-Hispanic/Latino; 1 Hispanic/Latino, 27 international. Average age 28. 202 applicants, 14% accepted, 15 enrolled. In 2010, 14 master's, 8 doctorates awarded. Terminal master's awarded for partial completion of doctoral program. *Degree requirements:* For master's, comprehensive exam, thesis, computer proficiency, consulting, departmental qualifying exams; for doctorate, comprehensive exam, thesis/dissertation, computer proficiency, consulting, departmental qualifying exams. *Entrance requirements:* For master's, GRE General Test; for doctorate, GRE General Test, Master's degree. Additional exam requirements/recommendations for international students: Required—TOEFL. *Application deadline:* For fall admission, 1/2 for domestic students. Application fee: $75. Electronic applications accepted. *Financial support:* In 2010–11, 80 research assistantships with full and partial tuition reimbursements (averaging $21,000 per year), 12 teaching assistantships with full and partial tuition reimbursements (averaging $21,000 per year) were awarded; scholarships/grants, traineeships, and health care benefits also available. *Faculty research:* Statistical methods for survival data analysis, clinical trials, epidemiological case control and cohort studies, statistical genetics. *Unit head:* Dr. Bruce Weir, Department Chair, 206-543-1044. *Application contact:* Alex Mackenzie, Counseling Services Coordinator, 206-543-1044, Fax: 206-543-3286, E-mail: alexam@u.washington.edu.

University of Waterloo, Graduate Studies, Faculty of Mathematics, Department of Statistics and Actuarial Science, Waterloo, ON N2L 3G1, Canada. Offers actuarial science (M Math, PhD); biostatistics (PhD); statistics (M Math, PhD); statistics-biostatistics (M Math); statistics-computing (M Math); statistics-finance (M Math). *Degree requirements:* For master's, research paper or thesis; for doctorate, comprehensive exam, thesis/dissertation. *Entrance requirements:* For master's, honors degree in field, minimum B+ average; for doctorate, master's degree, minimum B+ average. Additional exam requirements/recommendations for international students: Required—TOEFL (minimum score 600 paper-based; 250 computer-based; 90 iBT), TWE (minimum score 4.5). Electronic applications accepted. *Faculty research:* Data analysis, risk theory, inference, stochastic processes, quantitative finance.

The University of Western Ontario, Faculty of Graduate Studies, Physical Sciences Division, Department of Statistical and Actuarial Sciences, London, ON N6A 5B8, Canada. Offers M Sc, PhD. *Degree requirements:* For master's, thesis (for some programs); for doctorate, comprehensive exam, thesis/dissertation. *Entrance requirements:* For master's, honours BA with B+ average. Additional exam requirements/recommendations for international students: Required—TOEFL. *Faculty research:* Statistical theory, statistical applications, probability, actuarial science.

University of Windsor, Faculty of Graduate Studies, Faculty of Science, Department of Mathematics and Statistics, Windsor, ON N9B 3P4, Canada. Offers mathematics (M Sc);

Statistics

University of Windsor (continued)
statistics (M Sc, PhD). *Degree requirements:* For master's, thesis or alternative; for doctorate, comprehensive exam, thesis/dissertation. *Entrance requirements:* For master's, minimum B average; for doctorate, minimum A average. Additional exam requirements/recommendations for international students: Required—TOEFL (minimum score 560 paper-based; 220 computer-based). Electronic applications accepted. *Faculty research:* Applied mathematics, operational research, fluid dynamics.

University of Wisconsin–Madison, Graduate School, College of Letters and Science, Department of Statistics, Madison, WI 53706-1380. Offers biometry (MS); statistics (MS, PhD). Part-time programs available. *Degree requirements:* For master's, exam; for doctorate, thesis/dissertation. *Entrance requirements:* For master's and doctorate, GRE. Additional exam requirements/recommendations for international students: Required—TOEFL. Electronic applications accepted. *Expenses:* Tuition, state resident: full-time $9887.36; part-time $617.96 per credit. Tuition, nonresident: full-time $24,054; part-time $1503.40 per credit. Required fees: $67.63 per credit. Tuition and fees vary according to reciprocity agreements. *Faculty research:* Biostatistics, bootstrap and other resampling theory and methods, linear and nonlinear models, nonparametrics, time series and stochastic processes.

University of Wyoming, College of Arts and Sciences, Department of Statistics, Laramie, WY 82070. Offers MS, PhD. Terminal master's awarded for partial completion of doctoral program. *Degree requirements:* For master's, comprehensive exam (for some programs), thesis (for some programs); for doctorate, comprehensive exam, thesis/dissertation. *Entrance requirements:* For master's, GMAT, GRE General Test, minimum GPA of 3.0; for doctorate, GRE General Test, minimum GPA of 3.0. Additional exam requirements/recommendations for international students: Required—TOEFL; Recommended—TWE. Electronic applications accepted. *Faculty research:* Linear models categorical, Baysain, spatial biological sciences and engineering, multi-variate.

Utah State University, School of Graduate Studies, College of Science, Department of Mathematics and Statistics, Logan, UT 84322. Offers industrial mathematics (MS); mathematical sciences (PhD); mathematics (M Math, MS); statistics (MS). Part-time programs available. Terminal master's awarded for partial completion of doctoral program. *Degree requirements:* For master's, thesis optional, qualifying exam; for doctorate, one foreign language, comprehensive exam, thesis/dissertation. *Entrance requirements:* For master's and doctorate, GRE General Test, minimum GPA of 3.0. Additional exam requirements/recommendations for international students: Required—TOEFL. *Faculty research:* Differential equations, computational mathematics, dynamical systems, probability and statistics, pure mathematics.

Virginia Commonwealth University, Graduate School, College of Humanities and Sciences, Department of Mathematics and Applied Mathematics, Program in Statistical Sciences and Operations Research, Richmond, VA 23284-9005. Offers MS. *Students:* 20 applicants, 70% accepted, 11 enrolled. *Entrance requirements:* For master's, GRE General Test, 30 undergraduate credits in mathematics, statistics, or operations research, including calculus I and II, multivariate calculus, linear algebra, probability and statistics. Additional exam requirements/recommendations for international students: Required—TOEFL (minimum score 600 paper-based; 250 computer-based; 100 iBT); Recommended—IELTS (minimum score 6.5). *Application deadline:* For fall admission, 3/1 for domestic students; for spring admission, 10/15 for domestic students. Applications are processed on a rolling basis. Application fee: $50. Electronic applications accepted. *Expenses:* Tuition, state resident: full-time $4308; part-time $479 per credit hour. Tuition, nonresident: full-time $8942; part-time $994 per credit hour. Required fees: $2000; $85 per credit hour. Tuition and fees vary according to course level, course load, degree level, campus/location and program. *Unit head:* Dr. D'Arcy P. Mays, Chair, 804-828-1301 Ext. 151. *Application contact:* Dr. Edward L. Boone, Director, Master???s Programs in Statistical Sciences and Operations Research, 804-828-4637, E-mail: jawood@vcu.edu.

Virginia Polytechnic Institute and State University, Graduate School, College of Science, Department of Statistics, Blacksburg, VA 24061. Offers MS, PhD. *Faculty:* 16 full-time (4 women). *Students:* 63 full-time (24 women), 5 part-time (1 woman); includes 1 Black or African American, non-Hispanic/Latino; 2 Asian, non-Hispanic/Latino, 40 international. Average age 28. 64 applicants, 36% accepted, 17 enrolled. In 2010, 15 master's, 5 doctorates awarded. *Degree requirements:* For master's, comprehensive exam (for some programs), thesis (for some programs); for doctorate, comprehensive exam (for some programs), thesis/dissertation (for some programs). *Entrance requirements:* For master's and doctorate, GRE. Additional exam requirements/recommendations for international students: Required—TOEFL (minimum score 550 paper-based; 213 computer-based). *Application deadline:* For fall admission, 7/1 for domestic and international students; for spring admission, 12/1 for domestic and international students. Applications are processed on a rolling basis. Application fee: $65. Electronic applications accepted. *Expenses:* Tuition, area resident: Full-time $9399; part-time $488 per credit hour. Tuition, state resident: full-time $9399; part-time $488 per credit hour. Tuition, nonresident: full-time $17,854; part-time $957.75 per credit hour. International tuition: $17,854 full-time. Required fees: $1534. Full-time tuition and fees vary according to program. *Financial support:* In 2010–11, 6 research assistantships with full tuition reimbursements (averaging $18,662 per year), 29 teaching assistantships with full tuition reimbursements (averaging $15,922 per year) were awarded; career-related internships or fieldwork, Federal Work-Study, scholarships/grants, health care benefits, and unspecified assistantships also available. Financial award application deadline: 1/15. *Faculty research:* Design and sampling theory, computing and simulation, nonparametric statistics, robust and multivariate methods, biostatistics quality. Total annual research expenditures: $378,013. *Unit head:* Dr. Eric P. Smith, UNIT HEAD, 540-231-5657, Fax: 540-231-3863, E-mail: epsmith@vt.edu. *Application contact:* Jeffrey Birch, Contact, 540-231-7934, Fax: 540-231-3863, E-mail: jbbirch@vt.edu.

Washington State University, Graduate School, College of Agricultural, Human, and Natural Resource Sciences, Department of Statistics, Pullman, WA 99164. Offers applied statistics (MS); theoretical statistics (MS). *Faculty:* 7. *Students:* 12 full-time (7 women), 1 part-time (0 women), 12 international. Average age 29. 35 applicants, 26% accepted, 3 enrolled. In 2010, 12 master's awarded. *Degree requirements:* For master's, comprehensive exam (for some programs), thesis (for some programs), project. *Entrance requirements:* For master's, GRE, three letters of reference; official copies of all college transcripts. Additional exam requirements/recommendations for international students: Required—TOEFL (minimum score 560 paper-based; 220 computer-based), IELTS. *Application deadline:* For fall admission, 1/10 for domestic and international students; for spring admission, 7/1 for domestic and international students. Application fee: $50. *Expenses:* Tuition, state resident: full-time $8552; part-time $443 per credit. Tuition, nonresident: full-time $21,650; part-time $1083 per credit. Required fees: $846. *Financial support:* In 2010–11, 10 students received support, including 4 teaching assistantships with tuition reimbursements available (averaging $18,204 per year). *Faculty research:* Environmental statistics, logistic regression, statistical methods for ecology and wildlife, spatial data analysis, linear and non-linear models. Total annual research expenditures: $9,000. *Unit head:* Dr. Michael A. Jacroux, Professor/Chair, 509-335-8645, Fax: 509-335-8369, E-mail: jacroux@wsu.edu. *Application contact:* Graduate School Admissions, 800-GRADWSU, Fax: 509-335-1949, E-mail: gradsch@wsu.edu.

Washington University in St. Louis, Graduate School of Arts and Sciences, Department of Mathematics, St. Louis, MO 63130-4899. Offers mathematics (MA, PhD); statistics (MA). Terminal master's awarded for partial completion of doctoral program. *Degree requirements:* For master's, thesis or alternative; for doctorate, thesis/dissertation. *Entrance requirements:* For master's and doctorate, GRE General Test. Electronic applications accepted.

Wayne State University, College of Liberal Arts and Sciences, Department of Mathematics, Program in Mathematical Statistics, Detroit, MI 48202. Offers MA, PhD. *Faculty:* 20 full-time (2 women). *Students:* 2 full-time (0 women), 6 part-time (3 women); includes 3 minority (2 Black or African American, non-Hispanic/Latino; 1 Asian, non-Hispanic/Latino), 2 international. Average age 36. 5 applicants, 60% accepted, 2 enrolled. In 2010, 6 master's awarded. *Degree requirements:* For doctorate, thesis/dissertation. *Entrance requirements:* Additional exam requirements/recommendations for international students: Required—TOEFL (minimum score 550 paper-based; 213 computer-based); Recommended—TWE (minimum score 6). *Application deadline:* For fall admission, 7/1 for domestic students, 6/1 for international students; for winter admission, 10/1 for international students; for spring admission, 2/1 for international students. Applications are processed on a rolling basis. Application fee: $30 ($50 for international students). Electronic applications accepted. *Expenses:* Tuition, state resident: full-time $7662; part-time $478.85 per credit hour. Tuition, nonresident: full-time $16,920; part-time $1057.55 per credit hour. Required fees: $571.20; $35.70 per credit hour. $188.05 per semester. Tuition and fees vary according to course load and program. *Unit head:* Lowell Hansen, Chair, 313-577-7596, E-mail: lowell@math.wayne.edu. *Application contact:* Bert Schreiber, Professor, 313-577-8838, E-mail: bschreiber@wayne.edu.

Western Michigan University, Graduate College, College of Arts and Sciences, Department of Statistics, Kalamazoo, MI 49008. Offers MS, PhD.

West Virginia University, College of Business and Economics, Division of Economics and Finance, Morgantown, WV 26506. Offers business analysis (MA); developmental financial economics (PhD); environmental and resource economics (PhD); international economics (PhD); mathematical economics (MA); monetary economics (PhD); public finance (PhD); public policy (MA); regional and urban economics (PhD); statistics and economics (MA). Terminal master's awarded for partial completion of doctoral program. *Degree requirements:* For master's, thesis optional; for doctorate, comprehensive exam, thesis/dissertation. *Entrance requirements:* For master's and doctorate, GRE General Test, minimum GPA of 3.0; course work in intermediate microeconomics, intermediate macroeconomics, calculus, and statistics. Additional exam requirements/recommendations for international students: Required—TOEFL. Electronic applications accepted. *Faculty research:* Financial economics, regional/urban development, public economics, international trade/international finance/development economics, monetary economics.

West Virginia University, Eberly College of Arts and Sciences, Department of Statistics, Morgantown, WV 26506. Offers MS. *Degree requirements:* For master's, comprehensive exam, thesis. *Entrance requirements:* For master's, minimum GPA of 3.0, course work in linear algebra and multivariable calculus. Additional exam requirements/recommendations for international students: Required—TOEFL. *Faculty research:* Linear models, categorical data analysis, statistical computing, experimental design, non parametric analysis.

Yale University, Graduate School of Arts and Sciences, Department of Statistics, New Haven, CT 06520. Offers MA, PhD. Terminal master's awarded for partial completion of doctoral program. *Degree requirements:* For doctorate, thesis/dissertation. *Entrance requirements:* For doctorate, GRE General Test, GRE Subject Test.

York University, Faculty of Graduate Studies, Faculty of Science and Engineering, Program in Mathematics and Statistics, Toronto, ON M3J 1P3, Canada. Offers industrial and applied mathematics (M Sc); mathematics and statistics (MA, PhD). Part-time programs available. *Degree requirements:* For master's, thesis optional; for doctorate, one foreign language, comprehensive exam, thesis/dissertation. Electronic applications accepted.

Youngstown State University, Graduate School, College of Science, Technology, Engineering and Mathematics, Department of Mathematics and Statistics, Youngstown, OH 44555-0001. Offers applied mathematics (MS); computer science (MS); secondary mathematics (MS); statistics (MS). Part-time programs available. *Degree requirements:* For master's, comprehensive exam, thesis optional. *Entrance requirements:* For master's, minimum GPA of 2.7 in computer science and mathematics. Additional exam requirements/recommendations for international students: Required—TOEFL. *Faculty research:* Regression analysis, numerical analysis, statistics, Markov chain, topology and fuzzy sets.

BRYN MAWR

BRYN MAWR COLLEGE

Graduate Program in Mathematics

Programs of Study

Bryn Mawr's Graduate Program in Mathematics offers university-quality research training that leads to M.A. and Ph.D. degrees in the supportive environment of a liberal arts college. For students interested in well-rounded training that includes serious attention to teaching as well as research, Bryn Mawr provides an alternative to large research-oriented universities. The program is part of the Graduate School of Arts and Sciences, a coeducational school that is part of Bryn Mawr College, a world renowned women's college.

Research Facilities

Students have access to first-class library resources, including Scifinder Scholar; a campus collection composed of over 1 million volumes, including books, documents, microform, and multimedia material; a tri-college collection with Haverford College and Swarthmore College of over 1 million titles; and more than 550 journal subscriptions in the sciences with Internet access to the most recent issues.

Financial Aid

The Bryn Mawr Mathematics Department views graduate student teaching assistantships as an important facet of each graduate student's education. In general, all graduate students are supported with teaching assistantships, as long as they are making satisfactory progress towards their degrees. In addition, at least 1 advanced mathematics graduate student each year is awarded a research assistantship, allowing for a year of research without teaching duties.

A typical financial package includes a teaching assistantship and summer stipend ($18,000), plus tuition coverage and a health insurance subsidy (approximately $25,500); for a total financial package of $43,500.

Cost of Study

Full-time tuition in 2011–12, consisting of six courses per year, is $34,110. Part-time tuition is $5685 for one unit; $11,370 for two units. Units of supervised work cost $910, and the fee for continuing enrollment is $460 per semester.

Living and Housing Costs

Students live locally or in Philadelphia. Shared apartments can be rented for $600 to $900 per month; studio apartments begin at $800 per month. Other expenses include transportation (about $165 per month if commuting from Philadelphia) and health insurance (approximately $2500 per year for domestic students and approximately $1500 for international students). Complete information about Bryn Mawr's cost of attendance may be found online at http://www.brynmawr.edu/sfs/cost/graduate_students.html.

Student Group

In the 2010–11 academic year, there were 16 graduate students in the graduate program in mathematics; 5 of whom were men. Students have the opportunity to be part of Bryn Mawr's Graduate Group in Science and Mathematics, an interdisciplinary group including graduate programs in chemistry, mathematics, and physics. The group facilitates scholarly and social interactions among graduate students, promotes interdisciplinary research projects, and provides a mentoring program by graduate students.

Student Outcomes

After completing the program at Bryn Mawr, graduate students have gone on to academic positions at the University of Arizona, Penn State, DeSales University, Eastern University, and Ohio University; and positions in industry at companies such as GlaxoSmithKline, PricewaterhouseCoopers, and Lockheed Martin.

Location

Bryn Mawr is a suburb of Philadelphia, the fifth-largest city in the United States. It is well served by rail lines (the Main Line) and by bus. Philadelphia is renowned for music, museums, and sports, and it is also a culinary mecca with restaurants serving many cuisines. The metropolitan area has more than 100 museums and fifty colleges and universities, with a total population of 250,000 students.

The College

Bryn Mawr is a liberal arts college for women with two coeducational graduate schools: the Graduate School of Arts and Sciences and the Graduate School of Social Work and Social Research. Founded in 1885, Bryn Mawr was the first institution in the United States to offer the Ph.D. to women, and graduate education continues to be a significant part of its mission. Graduate students number approximately 400, out of a total enrollment of approximately 1,750 including undergraduates.

Applying

Students may apply to the Graduate Program in Mathematics online at: https://app.applyyourself.com/?id=brynmawrg. Students who have questions and are interested in applying to the Department of Mathematics are encouraged to complete the contact form online at http://www.brynmawr.edu/admissions/graduate/GSAS_INFO_REQUEST_MATH.shtml.

Correspondence and Information

Department of Mathematics
Bryn Mawr College
101 North Merion Avenue
Bryn Mawr, Pennsylvania 19010-2899

Phone: 610-526-5348
E-mail: admissions@brynmawr.edu
Web site: http://www.brynmawr.edu/math/graduate

Peterson's Graduate Programs in the Physical Sciences, Mathematics, Agricultural Sciences, the Environment & Natural Resources 2012

www.facebook.com/petersonspublishing   **303**

Bryn Mawr College

THE FACULTY AND THEIR RESEARCH

Victor J. Donnay, Professor; Ph.D., NYU, 1986. Dynamical systems, ergodic theory, differential geometry, math education.

Helen G. Grundman, Professor and Graduate Adviser; Ph.D., Berkeley, 1989. Algebra, algebraic number theory, analytic number theory.

Paul M. Melvin, Rachel C. Hale Professor of the Sciences and Mathematics, Professor, and Chair; Ph.D., Berkeley, 1977. Geometric topology, low-dimensional manifolds, quantum topology.

Lisa Traynor, Professor; Ph.D., SUNY at Stony Brook, 1992. Symplectic topology, differential geometry and topology.

Leslie C. Cheng, Associate Professor; Ph.D., Pittsburgh, 1998. Fourier analysis on Euclidean spaces, oscillatory integrals, singular integrals, Hardy spaces.

304 www.facebook.com/petersonspublishing

Peterson's Graduate Programs in the Physical Sciences, Mathematics, Agricultural Sciences, the Environment & Natural Resources 2012

MEDICAL COLLEGE OF WISCONSIN

Graduate School of Biomedical Sciences
Division of Biostatistics

Program of Study

The Division of Biostatistics offers a Ph.D. degree program designed for students with strong undergraduate preparation in mathematics and trains students in biostatistical methodology, theory, and practice. Emphasis is placed on sound theoretical understanding of statistical principles, research in the development of applied methodology, and collaborative research with biomedical scientists and clinicians. In addition, students gain substantial training and experience in statistical computing and in the use of software packages. Courses in the program are offered in collaboration with the Department of Mathematics at the University of Wisconsin–Milwaukee. The degree requirements, including dissertation research, are typically completed in five years beyond a bachelor's degree.

Faculty members are engaged in a number of collaborative research projects at the Center for International Blood and Marrow Transplant Research, the Clinical and Translational Science Institute, the Center for Patient Care and Outcomes Research, the Human and Molecular Genetics Center, the Clinical Cancer Center, and Marquette University. Dissertation research topics in statistical methodology often evolve from the faculty collaborative research projects, and students usually become coauthors on professional periodicals.

Research Facilities

The Division of Biostatistics is located within the Institute for Health and Society at the Medical College of Wisconsin (MCW). The Medical College has extensive research laboratories and facilities available for faculty and student use. The Division has an up-to-date network of Sun workstations, PCs, and peripherals. The Division's network is equipped with all leading statistical software and tools needed for the development of statistical methodology. Students are afforded access to multiple library collections including MCW, the University of Wisconsin–Milwaukee, and the Division of Biostatistics. The Epidemiology Data Service provides access to national data on health, health care, and special clinical data sets collected locally. The Medical College is a repository for the National Center for Health Statistics. The Biostatistics program also houses the Biostatistics Consulting Service, which affords students the opportunity to experience extensive biomedical research.

Financial Aid

Students are supported by fellowships for the first 18 months and then by research assistantships. Each includes tuition, stipend, and health insurance. The stipend for 2010–11 was $26,777 per year. The research assistantships provide students with the opportunity to gain experience in statistical consulting and collaborative research.

Living and Housing Costs

Many rental units are available in pleasant residential neighborhoods surrounding the Medical College. Housing costs begin at about $550 per month for a shared apartment.

Student Group

There are more than 1,270 students enrolled in educational programs at the Medical College. This includes 820 medical students and more than 450 graduate students. A low student-faculty ratio fosters individual attention and a close working relationship between students and faculty members.

Alumni of the MCW Biostatistics program are typically employed in academia and biomedical sciences. Alumni are employed at Georgia State University, Johns Hopkins University, the University of Pittsburgh, the Medical College of Wisconsin, GlaxoSmithKline, Takeda Global Research and Development, Teva Pharmaceuticals, and many other private- and public-sector organizations.

Location

Milwaukee has long been noted for its old-world image. Its many ethnic traditions, especially from Middle Europe, give the city this distinction. Cultural opportunities are numerous and include museums, concert halls, art centers, and theaters. Milwaukee has a well-administered government, a low crime rate, and excellent schools. It borders Lake Michigan and lies within commuting distance of 200 inland lakes. Outdoor activities may be pursued year-round.

The College

Founded in 1893, the College became the Marquette University School of Medicine in 1913. It was reorganized in 1967 as an independent corporation and renamed the Medical College of Wisconsin in 1970. There are more than 1,300 faculty members. MCW is one of six organizations working in partnership on the Milwaukee Regional Medical Complex (MRMC) campus. Full-time students in any department may enroll in graduate courses in other departments and in programs of the University of Wisconsin–Milwaukee and Marquette University without any increase in basic tuition. The College ranks in the top 34 percent of U.S. medical schools in National Institute of Health research funding.

Applying

Prerequisites include an undergraduate degree in mathematics or closely related fields, an overall grade point average of B or better, B average or better in mathematics and science, and an average of 60th percentile score on the quantitative and verbal sections of the GRE. Foreign students are also required to submit their TOEFL score (Institution Code: 1519, Department Code: 99). The application deadline is February 15 but students are encouraged to complete applications by early January.

Correspondence and Information

Division of Biostatistics
Medical College of Wisconsin
8701 Watertown Plank Road
Milwaukee, Wisconsin 53226
Phone: 414-955-8280
E-mail: biostat@mcw.edu
Web site: http://www.mcw.edu/biostatistics.htm

For application forms and information:
Graduate School of Biomedical Sciences
Medical College of Wisconsin
8701 Watertown Plank Road
Milwaukee, Wisconsin 53226
Phone: 414-955-8218
E-mail: gradschool@mcw.edu
Web site: http://www.mcw.edu/gradschool

Peterson's Graduate Programs in the Physical Sciences, Mathematics, Agricultural Sciences, the Environment & Natural Resources 2012

www.facebook.com/petersonspublishing   **305**

Medical College of Wisconsin

THE FACULTY AND THEIR RESEARCH

Kwang Woo Ahn, Assistant Professor, Ph.D., Iowa.
   Web site: http://www.mcw.edu/biostatistics/Faculty/Faculty/KwangWooAhnPhD.htm.
Ruta Bajorunaite, Assistant Professor; Ph.D., Medical College of Wisconsin.
   Web site: http://www.mcw.edu/biostatistics/Faculty/Faculty/RutaBajorunaitePhD.htm.
John P. Klein, Professor and Director; Ph.D., Missouri–Columbia.
   Web site: http://www.mcw.edu/biostatistics/Faculty/Faculty/JohnPKleinPhD.htm.
Purushottam (Prakash) W. Laud, Professor; Ph.D., Missouri–Columbia.
   Web site: http://www.mcw.edu/biostatistics/Faculty/Faculty/PrakashLaudPhD.htm.
Jennifer Le-Rademacher, Assistant Professor, Ph.D., Georgia.
   Web site: http://www.mcw.edu/biostatistics/Faculty/Faculty/JenniferLeRademacherPhD.htm.
Jessica Pruszynski, Assistant Professor; Ph.D., Baylor.
   Web site: http://www.mcw.edu/biostatistics/Faculty/Faculty/JessicaPruszynskiPhD.htm.
Brent R. Logan, Associate Professor; Ph.D., Northwestern.
   Web site: http://www.mcw.edu/biostatistics/Faculty/Faculty/BrentLoganPhD.htm.
Aniko Szabo, Associate Professor; Ph.D., Memphis.
   Web site: http://www.mcw.edu/biostatistics/Faculty/Faculty/AnikoSzaboPhD.htm.
Sergey Tarima, Assistant Professor; Ph.D., Kentucky.
   Web site: http://www.mcw.edu/biostatistics/Faculty/Faculty/SergeyTarimaPhD.htm.
Tao Wang, Associate Professor; Ph.D., North Carolina State.
   Web site: http://www.mcw.edu/biostatistics/Faculty/Faculty/TaoWangPhD.htm.
Mei-Jie Zhang, Professor; Ph.D., Florida State.
   Web site: http://www.mcw.edu/biostatistics/Faculty/Faculty/MeiJieZhangPhD.htm.

Adjunct Faculty (University of Wisconsin–Milwaukee and Marquette University)
Jay Beder, Professor; Ph.D., George Washington.
   Web site: https://pantherfile.uwm.edu/beder/www/.
Vytaras Brazauskas, Associate Professor; Ph.D., Texas at Dallas.
   Web site: https://pantherfile.uwm.edu/vytaras/www/.
Daniel Gervini, Associate Professor; Ph.D., Buenos Aires.
   Web site: https://pantherfile.uwm.edu/gervini/www/.
Jugal Ghorai, Professor; Ph.D., Purdue.
   Web site: https://pantherfile.uwm.edu/jugal/www/.
Eric Key, Professor; Ph.D., Cornell.
   Web site: http://www.uwm.edu/~ericskey/.
Tom O'Bryan, Associate Professor; Ph.D., Michigan State.
   Web site: http://www4.uwm.edu/letsci/math/people/faculty/obryan.cfm.
Daniel B. Rowe, Associate Professor, Ph.D., California, Riverside.
   Web site: http://www.marquette.edu/mscs/facstaff-rowe.shtml.
Gilbert Walter, Professor Emeritus; Ph.D., Wisconsin–Madison.
   Web site: https://pantherfile.uwm.edu/ggw/www/.

306   www.facebook.com/petersonspublishing

*Peterson's Graduate Programs in the Physical Sciences, Mathematics,
Agricultural Sciences, the Environment & Natural Resources 2012*

UNIVERSITY OF CALIFORNIA, LOS ANGELES

School of Medicine
Department of Biomathematics

Programs of Study

The Department of Biomathematics offers a graduate program leading to the Master of Science and Doctor of Philosophy degrees in biomathematics. The goal of the doctoral program is to train creative, fully independent investigators in mathematical and computational biology who can initiate research in both applied mathematics and their chosen biomedical specialty. The Department's orientation is away from abstract modeling and toward theoretical and applied research that is vital to the advancement of current biomedical frontiers. This is reflected in a curriculum providing a high level of competence in biology or biomedicine; substantial training in applied mathematics, statistics, and computing; and appropriate biomathematics courses and research experience. A low student-faculty ratio permits close and frequent contact between students and faculty members throughout the training and research years. The Systems and Integrative Biology Training Program, which is housed in biomathematics (http://dragon.nuc.ucla.edu/sibtp/), provides additional links to research and advising through more than two dozen participating faculty members from a range of UCLA departments and programs.

Entering students come from a variety of backgrounds in mathematics, biology, the physical sciences, and computer science. Some of the students are enrolled in the UCLA M.D./Ph.D. program. Doctoral students generally use the first two years to take the core sequence and electives in biomathematics, to broaden their backgrounds in biology and mathematics, and to begin directed individual study or research. Comprehensive examinations in biomathematics are taken after this period, generally followed by the choice of a major field and dissertation area. Individualized programs permit students to select graduate courses in relevant areas such as applied mathematics, physics, statistics, and engineering, along with advanced training in their field of special emphasis in biology. Prospective students should visit http://www.gdnet.ucla.edu/gasaa/library/pgmrqintro.htm for program requirement details.

The master's program can be a step to further graduate work in biomathematics, but it also can be adapted to the needs of researchers desiring supplemental biomathematical training or of individuals wishing to provide methodologic support to biomedical researchers. The M.S. program requires at least five graduate biomathematics courses and either a thesis or comprehensive examination plan. The master's degree can be completed in one or two years.

Research Facilities

The Department is situated in the Center for the Health Sciences, close to UCLA's rich research and educational resources in the School of Medicine; the Departments of Mathematics, Biology, Computer Science, Engineering, Chemistry, and Physics; the Institute for Pure and Applied Mathematics; and the Molecular Biology Institute. The Department has for many years housed multidisciplinary research programs comprising innovative modeling, statistical, and computing methods directed to many areas of biomedical research. It was the original home of the BMDP statistical programs and has an active consulting clinic for biomedical researchers. Modern computer resources are readily available. The Biomedical Library is one of the finest libraries of its kind in the country, and nearby are the Engineering and Mathematical Sciences Library and other subject libraries of the renowned nineteen-branch University Library. The Department maintains a small library with selected titles in mathematical biology and statistics.

Financial Aid

Financial support is provided from a variety of sources, including University-sponsored fellowships, affiliated training grants, research assistantships, and other merit-based funds. Supplementation is also possible from consulting and teaching assistantships.

Cost of Study

The 2011–12 registration and other fees for California residents are estimated at $13,548 and for nonresidents at $28,651 (includes nonresident supplemental tuition projected to be $15,102). Domestic students may attain residency status after one year. The University's fee proposal is subject to change based on state budget decisions.

Living and Housing Costs

The estimated cost of living varies. (The cost of living is in addition to the cost of study.) For additional housing information, students can go to the Web site (http://www.housing.ucla.edu/housing_site/index.htm).

Student Group

Currently, 12 graduate students are enrolled in the Department's program. An NIH predoctoral training grant supports up to 6 students. The other students are also receiving financial support and/or are employed on campus in the area of their research. Many graduates hold tenure-track appointments at leading universities, research appointments at the National Institutes of Health, or positions in industry.

Location

UCLA's 411 acres are cradled in rolling green hills just 5 miles inland from the ocean, in one of the most attractive areas of southern California. The campus is bordered on the north by the protected wilderness of the Santa Monica Mountains and at its southern gate by Westwood Village, one of the entertainment magnets of Los Angeles.

The University

UCLA is one of America's most prestigious and influential public universities, serving almost 40,000 students. The Department of Biomathematics is one of ten basic science departments in the School of Medicine. The medical school, which is regarded by many to be among the best in the nation, is situated on the south side of the UCLA campus, adjacent to the Life Sciences Building and the Court of Sciences. For more information, students can visit the University's Web site (http://www.ucla.edu).

Applying

Most students enter in the fall quarter, but applications for winter- or spring-quarter entry are considered. However, it is important that candidates applying for financial support initiate the application by the middle of January for decisions for the following fall. The Department expects applicants for direct admission to the doctoral program to submit scores on the General Test of the Graduate Record Examinations and on one GRE Subject Test of the student's choice. Inquiries are welcome from students early in their undergraduate training. The Department supports minority recruitment.

Correspondence and Information

Admissions Committee Chair
Department of Biomathematics
UCLA School of Medicine
Los Angeles, California 90095-1766
Phone: 310-825-5554
Fax: 310-825-8685
E-mail: gradprog@biomath.ucla.edu
Web site: http://www.biomath.ucla.edu/

Peterson's Graduate Programs in the Physical Sciences, Mathematics, Agricultural Sciences, the Environment & Natural Resources 2012

www.facebook.com/petersonspublishing   **307**

University of California, Los Angeles

THE FACULTY AND THEIR RESEARCH

A. A. Afifi, Professor of Biostatistics and Biomathematics; Ph.D. (statistics), Berkeley, 1965. Multivariate statistical analysis, with applications to biomedical and public health problems; longitudinal and correlated data analysis.

Tom Chou, Professor of Biomathematics and Mathematics; Ph.D. (physics), Harvard, 1995. Applied mathematics, theoretical biophysics, cellular and molecular modeling, stochastic processes.

Robert M. Elashoff, Professor of Biomathematics and Biostatistics and Chair of Biostatistics; Ph.D. (statistics), Harvard, 1963. Markov renewal models in survival analysis, random coefficient regression models, adaptive designs.

Eli Engel, Adjunct Associate Professor of Biomathematics; M.D., Buffalo, 1951; Ph.D. (physiology), UCLA, 1975. Mechanisms for acid neutralization in gastric mucus, facilitated transport of oxygen, theory of intracellular microelectrodes.

Sung-Cheng (Henry) Huang, Professor of Medical Pharmacology and Biomathematics; D.Sc. (electrical engineering), Washington (St. Louis), 1973. Positron emission computed tomography and physiological modeling.

Robert I. Jennrich, Professor of Mathematics, Biomathematics, and Biostatistics (Emeritus); Ph.D. (mathematics), UCLA, 1960. Statistical methodology, computational algorithms, nonlinear regression, factor analysis, compartment analysis.

Elliot M. Landaw, Professor and Chair of Biomathematics; M.D., Chicago, 1972; Ph.D. (biomathematics), UCLA, 1980. Identifiability and optimal experiment design for compartmental models; nonlinear regression; modeling/estimation applications in pharmacokinetics, ligand-receptor analysis, transport, and molecular biology.

Kenneth L. Lange, Professor of Biomathematics and Chair of Human Genetics; Ph.D. (mathematics), MIT, 1971. Statistical and mathematical methods for human genetics, demography, medical imaging, probability, optimization theory.

Carol M. Newton, Professor of Biomathematics and Radiation Oncology (Emeritus); Ph.D. (physics and mathematics), Stanford, 1956; M.D., Chicago, 1960. Simulation; cellular models for hematopoiesis, cancer treatment strategies, and optimization; interactive graphics for modeling; model-based exploration of complex data structures.

Michael E. Phelps, Norton Simon Professor; Chair, Department of Molecular and Medical Pharmacology; Professor of Biomathematics; Director, Institute for Molecular Medicine; and Director, Crump Institute for Molecular Imaging; Ph.D. (nuclear chemistry), Washington (St. Louis), 1970. Positron emission tomography (PET), tracer kinetic modeling of biochemical and pharmacokinetic processes, molecular imaging of human disease.

Steven Piantadosi, Professor of Biomathematics; M.D., North Carolina, 1977; Ph.D. (biomathematics), M.I.T., 1982. Clinical trials methodology, adaptive designs, translational and dose-finding studies in cancer.

Van M. Savage, Assistant Professor of Biomathematics; Ph.D. (physics), Washington (St. Louis), 2001. Physiological models of vascular systems, sleep, tumor growth, allometric scaling, ecological interactions and biodiversity.

Janet S. Sinsheimer, Professor of Biomathematics, Biostatistics, and Human Genetics; Ph.D. (biomathematics), UCLA, 1994. Statistical models of molecular evolution and genetics.

Marc A. Suchard, Associate Professor of Biomathematics, Biostatistics, and Human Genetics; Ph.D. (biomathematics), 2002, M.D., 2004, UCLA. Evolutionary reconstruction, sequence analysis, medical time series.

308 www.facebook.com/petersonspublishing

Peterson's Graduate Programs in the Physical Sciences, Mathematics, Agricultural Sciences, the Environment & Natural Resources 2012

University of California, Los Angeles

SELECTED PUBLICATIONS

Tom Chou

Diffusion-dependent mechanisms of receptor engagement and viral entry. *J. Phys. Chem. B.* 114(46):15403–12, 2010.

Arrival times in a zero-range process with injection and decay. *J. Phys. A: Math. Theor.* 43(30): 305003, 2010.

Reconstruction of potential energy profiles from multiple rupture time distributions. *Proc. Math. Phys. Eng. Sci.* 466(2124): 3479–99, 2010.

A mathematical model for intercellular signaling during epithelial wound healing. *J. Theor. Biol.* 266(1):70–8, 2010.

Frequency-dependent chemolocation and chemotactic target selection. *Phys. Biol.* 7(2): 026003, 2010.

Fluctuation theorems for entropy production and heat dissipation in periodically driven Markov chains. *J. Stat. Phys.* 137(1):165–88, 2009.

Optimal cytoplasmic transport in viral infections. *PLoS One* 4(12):e8165, 2009.

Enhancement of charged macromolecule capture by nanopores in a salt gradient. *J. Chem. Phys.* 131(3):034703, 2009.

Accelerated search kinetics mediated by redox reactions of DNA repair enzymes. *Biophys. J.* 96(10):3949–58, 2009.

Mechanisms of receptor/coreceptor–mediated entry of enveloped viruses. *Biophys. J.* 96(7):2624–36, 2009.

A quantitative affinity-profiling system that reveals distinct CD4/CCR5 usage patterns among human immunodeficiency virus type 1 and simian immunodeficiency virus strains. *J. Virol.* 83(21):11016–26, 2009.

Interface growth driven by surface kinetics and convection. *SIAM J. Appl. Math.* 70(1):24–39, 2009.

Exact steady-state velocity of ratchets driven by random sequential adsorption. *J. Phys. A: Math. Theor.* 40(21):5575–84, 2007.

Modeling the emergence of the 'hot zones': Tuberculosis and the amplification dynamics of drug resistance. *Nat. Med.* 10(10):1111–6, 2004.

Clustered bottlenecks in mRNA translation and protein synthesis. *Phys. Rev. Lett.* 93(19):198101, 2004.

Physical mechanisms of gas and perfluron retinopexy and sub-retinal fluid displacement. *Phys. Med. Biol.* 49(13):2989–97, 2004.

Robert M. Elashoff

Non-parametric inference for assessing treatment efficacy in randomized clinical trials with a time-to-event outcome and all-or-none compliance. *Biometrika*, in press.

Robust inference for longitudinal data analysis with non-ignorable and non-monotonic missing values. *Statistics and Its Interface*, in press.

Predicting treatment outcomes and responder subsets in scleroderma-related interstitial lung disease. *Arthritis. Rheum.*, in press.

Lung cancer chemoprevention with celecoxib in former smokers. *Cancer Prevention Research* 4:984–91, 2011.

Phase II study of bevacizumab plus temozolomide during and after radiation therapy for patients with newly diagnosed glioblastoma multiforme. *J. Clin. Oncol.* 29(2):142–8, 2011.

Pancreatitis, pancreatic, and thyroid cancer with glucagon-like peptide-1–based thearpies and cancer with glucagons like peptide-1 based therapies. *Gastroenterology* 141(1):150–6, 2011.

A general joint model for longitudinal measurements and competing risks survival data with heterogeneous random effects. *Lifetime Data Anal.* 17(1):80–100, 2011.

Value of the new bone classification system in pediatric renal osteodystrophy. *Clin. J. Am. Soc. Nephrol.* 5(10):1860–6, 2010.

The impact on morbidity and length of stay of early versus delayed complete lymphadenectomy in melanoma: Results of the Multicenter Selective Lymphadenectomy Trial (I). *Ann. Surg. Oncol.* 17(12):3324–9, 2010.

Protection against bronchiolitis obliterans syndrome is associated with allograft CCR7+ CD45RA- T regulatory cells. *PLoS One* 5(6):e11354, 2010.

Differential response of triple-negative breast cancer to a docetaxel and carboplatin-based neoadjuvant treatment. *Cancer* 116(8):4227–37, 2010.

The calcemic response to continuous parathyroid hormone (PTH)(1-34) infusion in end-stage kidney disease varies according to bone turnover: A potential role for PTH(7-84). *J. Clin. Endocrinol. Metab.* 95(6):2772–80, 2010. PMID: 20382692.

International randomized clinical trial, stroke inpatient rehabilitation with reinforcement of walking speed (SIRROWS), improves outcomes. *Neurorehabilitation and Neural Repair* 24(3):235–42, 2010.

Eli Engel

Intestinal alkaline phosphatase regulates protective surface microclimate pH in rat duodenum. *J. Physiol.* PMID:19451200, 2009.

CFTR inhibition augments NHE3 activity during luminal high CO_2 exposure in rat duodenal mucosa. *Am. J. Physiol. Gastrointest. Liver Physiol.* 294(6):G1318–27, 2008.

Solute diffusion through stripped mouse duodenum. *J. Physiol. Pharmacol.* 58:767–91, 2007.

When policy meets statistics: The very real effect that questionable statistical analysis has on limiting health-care access for bariatric surgery. *Arch. Surg.* 142(10):979–87, 2007.

Duodenal brush border intestinal alkaline phosphatase activity affects bicarbonate secretion in rats. *Am. J. Physiol. Gastrointest. Liver Physiol.* 293:G1223–33, 2007.

Carbonic anhydrases and mucosal vanilloid receptors help mediate the hyperemic response to luminal CO_2 in rat duodenum. *Gastroenterology* 131(1):142–52, 2006.

Epithelial carbonic anhydrases facilitate PCO_2 and pH regulation in rat duodenal mucosa. *J. Physiol.* 573(3):827–42, 2006.

Role of gastric mast cells in the regulation of central TRH analog-induced hyperemia in rats. *Peptides* 26(9):1580–9, 2005.

Mechanism of augmented duodenal HCO_3^- secretion after elevation of luminal CO_2. *Am. J. Physiol. Gastrointest. Liver Physiol.* 288(3):G557–63, 2005.

Barrier function of the gastric mucus gel. *Am. J. Physiol. Gastrointest. Liver Physiol.* 269:G994–9, 1995.

Sung-Cheng (Henry) Huang

Effects of administration route, dietary condition, and blood glucose level on kinetics and uptake of ^{18}F-FDG in mice. *J. Nucl. Med.* 52(5):800–7, 2011.

Movement correction method for human brain PET images: Application to quantitative analysis of dynamic ^{18}F-FDDNP scans. *J. Nucl. Med.* 51(2):210–18, 2010.

FDDNP binding using MR derived cortical surface maps. *NeuroImage* 49(1):240–8, 2010.

Functional expression of SGLTs in rat brain. *Am. J. Physiol. Cell Physiol.* 299(6):C1277–84, 2010.

Positron emission tomography imaging of DMBA/TPA mouse skin multi-step tumorigenesis. *Mol. Oncol.* 4(2):119–25, 2010.

Kinetics of 3'-deoxy-3'-^{18}F-fluorothymidine during treatment monitoring of recurrent high-grade glioma. *J. Nucl. Med.* 51(5):720–7, 2010.

Derivation of a compartmental model for quantifying ^{64}Cu-RGD peptide kinetics in tumor bearing mice. *J. Nucl. Med.* 50:250–8, 2009. doi:10.2967/jnumed.108.054049

FLT-PET imaging of radiation responses in murine tumors. *Mol. Imag. Biol.* 10(6):325–34, 2008.

^{18}F-FDOPA kinetics in brain tumors. *J. Nucl. Med.* 48:1651–61, 2007.

Estimation of the ^{18}F-FDG input function in mice by use of dynamic small-animal PET and minimal blood sample data. *J. Nucl. Med.* 48:2037–45, 2007.

Non-invasive measurement of cardiovascular function in mice with ultra-high temporal resolution small animal PET. *J. Nucl. Med.* 47:974–80, 2006.

PET of brain amyloid and tau in mild cognitive impairment. *New Engl. J. Med.* 355:2652–63, 2006.

An Internet-based kinetic imaging system (KIS) for microPET. *Mol. Imaging Biol.* 7:330–41, 2005.

Subcorticle white matter metabolic changes remote from focal hemorrhagic lesions suggest diffuse injury following human traumatic brain injury (TBI). *Neurosurgery* 55(6):1306–17, 2004.

Accuracy of a method using short inhalation of ^{15}O-O_2 for measuring cerebral oxygen extraction fraction with PET in healthy humans. *J. Nucl. Med.* 45:765–70, 2004.

Elliot M. Landaw

Rapid antimicrobial susceptibility determination of uropathogens in clinical urine specimens by use of ATP bioluminescence. *J. Clin. Microbiol.* 46(4):1213–9, 2008.

CREB is a critical regulator of normal hematopoiesis and leukemogenesis. *Blood* 1;111(3):1182–92, 2008.

Development of an advanced electrochemical DNA biosensor for bacterial pathogen detection. *J. Mol. Diagn.* 9(2):158–68, 2007.

Phosphorylation of the ATP-binding loop directs oncogenicity of drug-resistant BCR-ABL mutants. *Proc. Natl. Acad. Sci. U.S.A.* 103(51):19466–71, 2006.

Use of electrochemical DNA biosensors for rapid molecular identification of uropathogens in clinical urine specimens. *J. Clin. Microbiol.* 44(2):561–70, 2006.

Initial high-dose nasal allergen exposure prevents allergic sensitization to a neoantigen. *J. Immunol.* 174(11):7440–5, 2005.

The role of CREB as a proto-oncogene in hematopoiesis and in acute myeloid leukemia. *Canc. Cell* 7(4):351–62, 2005.

Toxicokinetic interaction of 2,5-hexanedione and methyl ethyl ketone. *Arch. Toxicol.* 75:643–52, 2002.

Acute upregulation of blood-brain barrier glucose transporter activity in seizures. *Am. J. Physiol. Heart Circ. Physiol.* 279(3):H1346–54, 2000.

A model-based approach for assessing in vivo combination therapy interactions. *Proc. Natl. Acad. Sci. U.S.A.* 96:13023–8, 1999.

Testing the fit of a quantal model of neurotransmission. *Biophys. J.* 76:1847–55, 1999.

An analysis of a class of DNA sequence reading molecules. *J. Comput. Biol.* 5:571–83, 1998.

The theoretical limits of DNA sequence discrimination by linked polyamides. *Proc. Natl. Acad. Sci. U.S.A.* 95:4315–20, 1998.

Estimation of the DNA sequence discriminatory ability of hairpin-linked lexitropsins. *Proc. Natl. Acad. Sci. U.S.A.* 94:5634–9, 1997.

Kenneth L. Lange

Unifying ideas for non-parametric linkage analysis. *Hum. Hered.*, in press.

Extinction models for cancer stem cell therapy. *Math. Biosciences,* in press.

A quasi-Newton acceleration for high-dimensional optimization algorithms. *Stat. Comput.* 21(2):261–73, 2011.

A fast procedure for calculating importance weights in bootstrap sampling. *Comput. Stat. Data Anal.* 55(1):26–33, 2011.

Linkage analysis without defined pedigrees. *Genet. Epidemiol.* 35(5)360–70, 2011.

Penalized regression for genome-wide association screening of sequence data. In *Biocomputing 2011: Proceedings of the Pacific Symposium* Hackensack: World Scientific Publishing Company, 2011.

A cross-population extended haplotype-based homozygosity score test to detect positive selection in genome-wide scans. *Statistics and Its Interface* 4:51–63, 2011.

Intelligence in Williams Syndrome is related to STX1A, which encodes a component of the presynaptic SNARE complex. *PLoS ONE* 5(4):e10292, 2010. doi:10.1371.

Peterson's Graduate Programs in the Physical Sciences, Mathematics, Agricultural Sciences, the Environment & Natural Resources 2012

www.facebook.com/petersonspublishing **309**

University of California, Los Angeles

A powerful score test to detect positive selection in genome-wide scans. *Eur. J. Hum. Genet.* 18(10):1148–59, 2010.

Reconstructing DNA copy number by penalized estimation and imputation. *Ann. Appl. Stat.* 4:1749–73, 2010.

A Poisson model for random multigraphs. *Bioinformatics* 26(16):2004–11, 2010.

Association screening of common and rare genetic variants by penalized regression. *Bioinformatics* 26(19):2357–82, 2010.

Graphics processing units and high-dimensional optimization. *Stat. Sci.* 25(3):311–24, 2010.

Numerical Analysis for Statisticians, 2nd ed. New York: Springer, 2010.

Optimization. New York: Springer, 2004.

Applied Probability, 2nd ed. New York: Springer, 2010.

Mathematical and Statistical Methods for Genetic Analysis, 2nd ed. New York: Springer, 2002.

Michael E. Phelps

Reduction of glucose metabolic activity is more accurate than change in size at predicting histopathologic response to neoadjuvant therapy in high-grade soft-tissue sarcomas. *Clin. Cancer Res.* 14(3):715–20, 2008.

Positron emission tomography with computed tomography imaging of neuroinflammation in experimental autoimmune encephalomyelitis. *Proc. Natl. Acad. Sci. U.S.A.* 104:1937–42, 2007.

PET of brain amyloid and tau in mild cognitive impairment. *New Engl. J. Med.* 355:2652–63, 2006.

Systems biology and new technologies enable predictive and preventative medicine. *Science* 306:640–3, 2004.

Measurement of the global lumped constant for FDG in normal human brain using [^{15}O]water and FDG PET imaging: A new method with validation based on multiple methodologies. *Mol. Imaging Biol.* 5:32–41, 2003.

Monitoring gene therapy with reporter gene imaging. *Semin. Nucl. Med.* 31(4):312–20, 2001.

Positron emission tomography in evaluation of dementia: Regional brain metabolism and long term outcome. *J. Am. Med. Assoc.* 286:2120–7, 2001.

Positron emission tomography provides molecular imaging of biological processes. *Proc. Natl. Acad. Sci. U.S.A.* 97:9226–33, 2000.

Quantification of target gene expression by imaging reporter gene expression in living animals. *Nature Med.* 6(8):933–7, 2000.

Van M. Savage

Systematic variation in the temperature dependence of physiological and ecological traits. *Proc. Natl. Acad. Sci. U.S.A.* 108(26):10591–6, 2011.

Curvature in metabolic scaling: A reply to Mackay. *J. Theor. Biol.* 280(15):197–8, 2011.

Hydraulic trade-offs and space filling enable better predictions of vascular structure and function in plants. *Proc. Natl. Acad. Sci. U.S.A.* 107(52):22722–7, 2010.

Curvature in metabolic scaling. *Nature* 464(7289):753–6, 2010.

An integrative framework for stochastic, size-structured community assembly. *Proc. Natl. Acad. Sci.* 106(15):6170–5, 2009.

Sizing up allometric scaling theory. *PLoS Computational Biology* 4(9):e1000171, 2008.

A general trait-based framework for studying the effects of biodiversity on ecosystem functioning. *J. Theor. Biol.* 247:213–29, 2007.

Setting the absolute tempo of biodiversity dynamics. *Ecol. Lett.* 10:637–46, 2007.

A general model for allometric covariation in botanical form and function. *Proc. Natl. Acad. Sci., U.S.A.,* 104(32):13204–9, 2007.

A quantitative, theoretical framework for understanding mammalian sleep. *Proc. Natl. Acad. Sci., U.S.A.,* 104(3):1051–6, 2007.

Scaling of number, size, and metabolic rate of cells with body size in mammals. *Proc. Natl. Acad. Sci., U.S.A.,* 104(11):4718–23, 2007.

Kinetic effects of temperature on rates of genetic divergence and speciation. *Proc. Natl. Acad. Sci., U.S.A.,* 103(24) :9130–5, 2006.

Effects of body size and temperature on population growth. *Am. Nat.* 163(3), 429–41, 2004.

Improved approximations to scaling relationships for species, populations, and ecosystems across latitudinal and elevational gradients. *J. Theor. Biol.* 227(4), 525–34, 2004.

The predominance of quarter-power scaling in biology. *Funct. Ecol.* 18(2), 257–82, 2004.

Toward a metabolic theory of ecology (MacArthur award paper). *Ecology* 85(7), 1771–89, 2004.

Effects of size and temperature on metabolic rate. *Science* 293, 2248–51, 2001.

Janet S. Sinsheimer

Penalized regression for genome-wide association screening of sequence data. In *Biocomputing 2011: Proceedings of the Pacific Symposium* Hackensack: World Scientific Publishing Company, 2011.

Association screening of common and rare genetic variants by penalized regression. *Bioinformatics* 26(19):2375–82, 2010.

Prioritizing GWAS results: A review of statistical methods and recommendations for their application. *Am. J. Hum. Genet.* 86(1):6–22, 2010.

Modeling maternal-offspring gene-gene interactions: The extended-MFG test. *Genet. Epidemiol.* 34(5):512–21, 2010.

Reuse, recycle, reweigh: Combating influenza through efficient sequential Bayesian computation for massive data. *Ann. Appl. Stat.* 4(4):1722–48, 2010.

A heterozygote-homozygote test of Hardy-Weinberg equilibrium. *Eur. J. Hum. Genet.* 17(11):1495–500, 2010.

Differential destruction of stem cells: Implications for targeted cancer stem cell therapy. *Canc. Res.* 69(24):9481–9, 2009.

Associations between single nucleotide polymorphisms (SNPs) in double strand DNA repair pathway genes and familial breast cancer. *Clin. Canc. Res.* 15:2192–203, 2009.

Estimating ethnic admixture from pedigree data. *Am. J. Hum. Genet.* 82(3):748–75, 2008.

Mixed effects models for quantitative trait loci mapping with inbred strains. *Genetics* 180:1743–61, 2008.

Detecting maternal-fetal genotype incompatibilities using non-codominant data. *Ann. Hum. Genet.* 70:541–53, 2006.

The v-MFG test: Investigating maternal, offspring, and maternal-fetal genetic incompatibilities effects on disease and viability. *Genet. Epidemiol.* 30:333–47, 2006.

Allowing for missing data at highly polymorphic genes when testing for maternal, offspring and maternal-fetal genotype incompatibility effects. *Hum. Hered.* 62:165–74, 2006.

A conditional-on-exchangeable-parental-genotypes likelihood that remains unbiased under multiple-affected-sibling ascertainment. *Genet. Epidemiol.* 29:87–90, 2005.

Fishing for pleiotropic QTLs in a polygenic sea. *Ann. Hum. Genet.* 69:590–611, 2005.

An exact maternal-fetal genotype incompatibility (MFG) test. *Genet. Epidemiol.* 28:83–95, 2005.

Models for estimating Bayes factors with applications to phylogeny and tests of monophyly. *Biometrics* 61:665–73, 2005.

Marc A. Suchard

Graphical processing units and high-dimensional optimization. *Stat. Sci.* 25(3), 311–24, 2010.

Reuse, recycle, reweigh: Combating influenza through efficient sequential Bayesian computation for massive data. *Ann. Appl. Stat.* 4(4): 1722–48, 2010.

Bayesian phylogeography finds its roots. *PLoS Computational Biology* 5(9): e1000520, 2009.

Alignment uncertainty and genomic analysis. *Science* 319:473–6, 2008.

Counting labeled transitions in continuous-time Markov models of evolution. *J. Math. Biol.* 56:391–412, 2008.

Phylogenetic mapping of recombination hotspots in human immunodeficiency virus via spatially smoothed change-point processes. *Genetics* 175:1773–85, 2007.

Use of electrochemical DNA biosensors for rapid molecular identification of uropathogens in clinical urine specimens. *J. Clin. Microbiol.* 44:561–70, 2006.

Models for estimating Bayes factors with applications to phylogeny and tests of monophyly. *Biometrics* 61:665–73, 2005.

Stochastic models for horizontal gene transfer: Taking a random walk through tree space. *Genetics* 170:419–31, 2005.

Joint Bayesian estimation of alignment and phylogeny. *Syst. Biol.* 54:401–18, 2005.

Evolution of human immunodeficiency virus type 1 coreceptor usage during antiretroviral therapy: A Bayesian approach. *J. Virol.* 78:11296–302, 2004.

Alterations in dynamics of circulating ghrelin, adiponectin and leptin in human obesity. *Proc. Natl. Acad. Sci. U.S.A.* 101:10435–9, 2004.

Hierarchical phylogenetic models for analyzing multipartite sequence data. *Syst. Biol.* 52:649–64, 2003.

Inferring spatial phylogenetic variation along nucleotide sequences: A multiple change-point model. *J. Am. Stat. Assoc.* 98:427–37, 2003.

Are you my mother? Bayesian phylogenetic models to detect recombination among putative parental strains. *Appl. Bioinformatics* 2:131–44, 2003.

Oh brother, where art thou? A Bayes factor test for recombination with uncertain heritage. *Syst. Biol.* 51:715–28, 2002.

Bayesian selection of continuous-time Markov chain evolutionary models. *Mol. Biol. Evol.* 18:1001–13, 2001.

Are general practitioners willing and able to provide genetic services for common diseases? *J. Genet. Counsel.* 8:301–11, 1999.

310 www.facebook.com/petersonspublishing

Peterson's Graduate Programs in the Physical Sciences, Mathematics, Agricultural Sciences, the Environment & Natural Resources 2012

UNIVERSITY OF OKLAHOMA

Department of Mathematics

Programs of Study

While the Mathematics Department at the University of Oklahoma (OU) offers three different graduate degrees—M.S., M.A., and Ph.D.—students are considered to be on either two tracks, the M.S. track or the M.A./Ph.D. track.

The M.A./Ph.D track is the standard program for most students seeking a Ph.D. in mathematics. All students in the program (regardless of their future specialization) need to pass the three Ph.D. qualifying examinations in algebra, analysis, and topology. Each of these exams is associated with a two-semester graduate course sequence that forms the core of the M.A. degree and also count toward the Ph.D. degree. Students who pass all three qualifying examinations can go into the Ph.D. program in one of the following two options.

Ph.D. program (traditional option): This is essentially the same as the M.A./Ph.D. program above. The main difference is that students who already have a master's degree in mathematics may apply directly to this program. Students with a baccalaureate degree apply to the M.A./Ph.D. program and move into to the Ph.D. program on successful completion of the Ph.D. qualifying examinations. The student's ultimate goal in this program is to write and defend a dissertation representing an original contribution to research in mathematics.

Ph.D. program (RUME—research in undergraduate mathematics—option): As is the case with the traditional option, students who already have a master's degree in mathematics may apply to this program, while students with a baccalaureate degree apply to the M.A./Ph.D. program. The student's ultimate goal in this program is to write and defend a dissertation representing an original contribution to research in undergraduate mathematics education.

Students with strong mathematical backgrounds are encouraged to take "free shot" attempts at the Ph.D. qualifying examinations, usually held in August, the week before classes start. These attempts are only offered to students when they first enter the program, and results do not go on the student's record unless they pass.

The M.S. track (Master of Science program) is offered by the Mathematics Department for students who want to pursue studies in mathematics beyond the undergraduate level, but who do not plan to obtain a doctorate in mathematics. Recent graduates of the M.S. program have gone on to careers as actuaries, statistical analysts, and software engineers. Some become mathematics teachers in settings ranging from middle school to two- and four-year colleges. Still others have gone on to obtain doctorates and academic positions in fields other than mathematics, such as economics, mathematics education, and computer science.

Students will be able to select from a broad range of options in pure and applied mathematics and in research in undergraduate mathematics education as they pursue their graduate degree, including: (1) Algebra and Number Theory: algebraic geometry, algebraic groups, combinatorics, modular forms, representation theory (real, p-adic, Lie, automorphic); (2) Analysis: global analysis, harmonic analysis, integrable systems, PDEs, signal processing, spectral theory, wavelets and frames; (3) Applied Mathematics and Mathematical Physics: control theory, dynamical systems, modeling; (4) Geometry: convexity, harmonic maps, Riemannian geometry, group actions, non-negative curvature; (5) RUME: research in undergraduate mathematics education, diversity and equity, international comparative education; (6) Topology: algebraic and geometric topology, dimension theory, geometric group theory, hyperbolic geometry, low-dimensional topology, Teichmuller theory.

Additional information about the University's graduate programs in mathematics can be found at http://math.ou.edu/grad/programs.html.

Research Facilities

Students in the Department have a wide range of facilities and resources to support their study and research efforts. The department maintains two servers, Aftermath and Zeus, both of which run the Linux operating system. The Aftermath server hosts login shells and some software, while Zeus is the primary file server and provides NFS service to workstations throughout the department. The file system is protected by a RAID backup system. The systems manager should be able to recover a user's lost data for up to three or four weeks. There are two workstation clusters for graduate students in the department.

The library's LORA system gives students access to MathSciNet, the definitive database of mathematics literature reviews and bibliographical information (available in BibTeX format); JSTOR, and numerous other online databases and resources from off-campus locations.

Financial Aid

Most students are employed as graduate teaching assistants while earning their degrees. The students' transition into their new roles as educators is facilitated by a lighter course load in the first year and participation in the Department's graduate teaching seminar. Other graduate teaching assistant duties include grading, working in the Mathematics Help Center, and assisting in multisection courses.

During the 2009–10 academic year, stipends for graduate teaching assistants who were fully English-language qualified to teach ranged from $15,038 to $16,187. Stipends for graduate teaching assistants who were not fully English-language qualified started at $14,030.

Other opportunities include graduate assistantships. A variable number of teaching assistantships are available for the summer semester in June and July each year, with a stipend of approximately $2500. Several faculty members also provide support for research assistants using funds from research grants. Research assistants usually participate in research-related projects under the supervision of the faculty member. Further details regarding financial support for graduate students can be found at http://math.ou.edu/grad/finance.html.

Cost of Study

In the 2010–11 academic year, tuition and fees for graduate students totaled $292.95 per credit hour for Oklahoma students and $721.05 per credit hour for nonresident students.

Living and Housing Costs

The University offers several on-campus apartment choices. In addition, there are a large number of privately owned apartments, duplexes, and houses available in Norman. Many off-campus housing locations are served by CART, the Cleveland Area Rapid Transit system, which is free for OU students.

Student Group

The OU mathematics graduate program is comprised of about 70 students, representing over a dozen different countries from around the globe. There is an active Mathematics Graduate Student Association which provides guidance and mentoring and organizes various events for graduate students. Additional details about the association can be found online at http://math.ou.edu/~mgsa/.

Location

As part of the dynamic Southwest, Oklahoma benefits from both its rich historic heritage and the vital and modern growth of its metropolitan areas. Although by location a suburb of Oklahoma City, Norman is an independent community with a permanent population of more than 95,000. Norman residents enjoy extensive parks and recreation programs and a 10,000-acre lake and park area. *Money* magazine named Norman as the nation's sixth best place to live in the 2008 edition of its annual rankings.

The University and The Department

The Mathematics Department at the University of Oklahoma has a long and rich academic tradition dating back to the mid-1890s. Students who pursue a graduate degree in mathematics at OU become part of a team that is responsible for the instruction of 10,000–12,000 OU undergraduate students annually. The Department's faculty members strive to maintain a vibrant and collegial research atmosphere and also serve as sources of inspiration, mentoring, and advice. The strong sense of community is enhanced by having faculty, postdoctoral, and student offices, as well as a common room and instructional classrooms, all housed in the same building. Prospective graduate students can experience the Mathematics Department in person during OU MathFest, an annual two-day open house for prospective graduate students. Dates, schedules, and a registration form for MathFest are available at http://www.math.ou.edu/grad/mathfest/2010/ou_mathfest_2010.html.

Applying

Prospective students should submit the Mathematics Department graduate application form online, or may also download, print, and mail the form with the required materials listed below to the Mathematics Department. To ensure full consideration, the complete application and all supporting material needs to be received by the Department by January 31, 2012. The Department will forward everything to the Office of Admissions. Applications after this date will be considered, but those received after May 31 are rarely considered. International applicants are subject to the University's April 1 deadline. In addition to the application form, students must submit official transcripts from all colleges and universities attended, GRE scores, TOEFL scores (if English is not the student's native language), and letters of reference from 3 people familiar with the student's work in mathematics (using the form found at http://math.ou.edu/grad/gradapp/Reference_Request.pdf). While the University's forms indicate an application fee is necessary, the Mathematics Department prescreens all applications and makes qualified applicants an offer; the application fee can be submitted then.

Correspondence and Information

Director of Graduate Studies
University of Oklahoma
Department of Mathematics
601 Elm Street, PHSC 423
Norman, Oklahoma 73019

Phone: 800-522-0772 (toll-free)
E-mail: mathgraddir@ou.edu
Web site: http://www.math.ou.edu

Peterson's Graduate Programs in the Physical Sciences, Mathematics, Agricultural Sciences, the Environment & Natural Resources 2012

www.facebook.com/petersonspublishing

311

University of Oklahoma

AREAS OF INSTRUCTION

The Mathematics Department at the University of Oklahoma has 34 permanent faculty members, 8 visiting faculty members, and a support staff of 6 (including a full-time undergraduate adviser). Virtually all of the department's faculty have active research programs (many externally funded) and regularly publish articles in mathematical journals and participate in conferences around the world.

Additional details regarding the Mathematics Department faculty can be found at http://www.math.ou.edu/people/faculty_research.html.

Students walk to class on the Norman campus.

312 www.facebook.com/petersonspublishing

Peterson's Graduate Programs in the Physical Sciences, Mathematics, Agricultural Sciences, the Environment & Natural Resources 2012

WESLEYAN UNIVERSITY

Department of Mathematics and Computer Science

Programs of Study

The Department offers a program of courses and research leading to the degrees of Master of Arts and Doctor of Philosophy.

The Ph.D. degree demands breadth of knowledge, intensive specialization in one field, original contribution to that field, and expository skill. First-year courses are designed to provide a strong foundation in algebra, analysis, and topology. Written preliminary examinations are taken after the first year. During the second year, the student continues with a variety of courses, sampling areas of possible concentration. The student must choose a thesis adviser by the end of the second year and pass the special preliminary examination, which is an oral exam managed by the student's adviser and examination committee, by the end of the third year. Also required is the ability to read mathematics in at least two of the following languages: French, German, and Russian. The usual time required for completion of all requirements for a Ph.D., including the dissertation, is five years.

During their time in the program, most Ph.D. candidates teach two courses per year, typically small sections (fewer than 20 students) of calculus.

The M.A. degree is designed to ensure basic knowledge and the capacity for sustained scholarly study; requirements are six semester courses at the graduate level and the writing and oral presentation of a thesis. The thesis requires (at least) independent search and study of the literature.

Students are also involved in a variety of Departmental activities, including seminars and colloquiums. The small size of the program contributes to an atmosphere of informality and accessibility.

The emphasis at Wesleyan is in pure mathematics and theoretical computer science, and most Wesleyan Ph.D.'s have chosen academic careers.

Research Facilities

The Department is housed in the Science Center, where all graduate students and faculty members have offices. Computer facilities are available for both learning and research purposes. The Science Library collection has about 120,000 volumes, with extensive mathematics holdings; there are more than 200 subscriptions to mathematics journals, and approximately sixty new mathematics books arrive each month. The proximity of students and faculty and the daily gatherings at teatime are also key elements of the research environment.

Financial Aid

Each applicant for admission is automatically considered for appointment to an assistantship. For the 2011–12 academic year, a nine-month stipend is $18,000, plus a dependency allowance when appropriate, and an additional three-month stipend of $6000 is usually available for the student who wishes to remain on campus to study during the summer. Costs of tuition and health fees are borne by the University. All students in good standing are given financial support for the duration of their studies.

Cost of Study

The only academic costs to the student are books and other educational materials.

Living and Housing Costs

The University provides some subsidized housing and assists in finding private housing. The monthly rent of a single student's housing (a private room in a 2- or 4-person house, with common kitchen and living area) is about $640.

Student Group

The number of graduate students in mathematics ranges from 18 to 22, with an entering class of 3 to 5 each year. There have always been both male and female students, graduates of small colleges and large universities, and U.S. and international students, including, in recent years, students from Bulgaria, Chile, China, Germany, India, Iran, and Sri Lanka.

Location

Middletown, Connecticut, is a small city of 40,000 by the Connecticut River, about 19 miles southeast of Hartford and 25 miles northeast of New Haven, midway between New York and Boston. The University provides many cultural and recreational opportunities, supplemented by those in the countryside and in larger cities nearby.

The University

Founded in 1831, Wesleyan is an independent coeducational institution of liberal arts and sciences, with Ph.D. programs in biology, chemistry, ethnomusicology, mathematics, and physics and master's programs in a number of departments. Current enrollments show about 2,800 undergraduates and 145 graduate students.

Applying

No specific courses are required for admission, but it is expected that the equivalent of an undergraduate major in mathematics will have been completed. The complete application consists of the application form, transcripts of all previous academic work at or beyond the college level, letters of recommendation from 3 college instructors familiar with the applicant's mathematical ability and performance, and GRE scores (if available). Applications should be submitted by February 15 in order to receive adequate consideration, but requests for admission from outstanding candidates are welcome at any time. Preference is given to Ph.D. candidates.

Correspondence and Information

Department of Mathematics and Computer Science
Graduate Education Committee
Wesleyan University
Middletown, Connecticut 06459-0128
Phone: 860-685-2620
E-mail: ccanalia@wesleyan.edu
Web site: http://www.math.wesleyan.edu

*Peterson's Graduate Programs in the Physical Sciences, Mathematics,
Agricultural Sciences, the Environment & Natural Resources 2012*

www.facebook.com/petersonspublishing　　**313**

Wesleyan University

THE FACULTY AND THEIR RESEARCH

Professors
Wai Kiu Chan, Ph.D., Ohio State. Number theory, quadratic forms.
Karen Collins, Ph.D., MIT. Combinatorics.
Adam Fieldsteel, Ph.D., Berkeley. Ergodic theory.
Mark Hovey, Ph.D., MIT. Algebraic topology and homological algebra.
Michael S. Keane, Dr.rer.nat., Erlangen-Nuremberg. Ergodic theory, random walks, statistical physics.
Philip H. Scowcroft, Ph.D., Cornell. Foundations of mathematics, model-theoretic algebra.
Carol Wood, Ph.D., Yale. Mathematical logic, applications of model theory to algebra.

Associate Professors
Petra Bonfert-Taylor, Ph.D., Berlin Technical. Complex analysis, complex dynamics, geometric function theory, discrete groups.
David Pollack, Ph.D., Harvard. Number theory, automorphic forms, representation of p-adic groups.
Edward C. Taylor, Ph.D., SUNY at Stony Brook. Analysis, low-dimensional geometry and topology.

Assistant Professors
Constance Leidy, Ph.D., Rice. Knot theory, low-dimensional topology.
Christopher Rasmussen, Ph.D., Arizona. Algebraic geometry.

Professors of Computer Science
Danny Krizanc, Ph.D., Harvard. Theoretical computer science.
Michael Rice, Ph.D., Wesleyan. Parallel computing, formal specification methods.

Associate Professors of Computer Science
James Lipton, Ph.D., Cornell. Logic and computation, logic programming, type theory, linear logic.
Norman Danner, Ph.D., Indiana Bloomington. Logic, theoretical computer science.

Assistant Professor of Computer Science
Eric Aaron, Ph.D., Cornell. Intelligent virtual agents, reasoning about navigation, hybrid systems, game artificial intelligence, behavioral animation/robotics, applied logic, cognitive modeling, attention, automated verification, tumor modeling.

Professors Emeriti
W. Wistar Comfort, Ph.D., Washington (Seattle). Point-set topology, ultrafilters, set theory, topological groups.
Ethan M. Coven, Ph.D., Yale. Dynamical systems.
Anthony W. Hager, Ph.D., Penn State. Lattice-ordered algebraic structures, general and categorical topology.
F. E. J. Linton, Ph.D., Columbia. Categorical algebra, functorial semantics, topoi.
James D. Reid, Ph.D., Washington (Seattle). Abelian groups, module theory.
Lewis C. Robertson, Ph.D., UCLA. Lie groups, topological groups, representation theory.
Robert A. Rosenbaum, Ph.D., Yale. Geometry, mathematics and science education.

Faculty-student conferences, daily gatherings at teatime, and discussions in graduate students' offices are key ingredients of the research environment in the Department of Mathematics.

314   www.facebook.com/petersonspublishing

Peterson's Graduate Programs in the Physical Sciences, Mathematics,
Agricultural Sciences, the Environment & Natural Resources 2012

ACADEMIC AND PROFESSIONAL PROGRAMS IN THE AGRICULTURAL SCIENCES

Section 8
Agricultural and Food Sciences

This section contains a directory of institutions offering graduate work in agricultural and food sciences, followed by an in-depth entry submitted by an institution that chose to prepare a detailed program description. Additional information about programs listed in the directory may be obtained by writing directly to the dean of a graduate school or chair of a department at the address given in the directory.

For programs offering related work, see also in this book *Natural Resources*. In the other guides in this series:

Graduate Programs in the Humanities, Arts & Social Sciences
See *Architecture (Landscape Architecture)* and *Economics (Agricultural Economics and Agribusiness)*

Graduate Programs in the Biological Sciences
See *Biological and Biomedical Sciences; Botany and Plant Biology; Ecology, Environmental Biology, and Evolutionary Biology; Entomology; Genetics, Developmental Biology, and Reproductive Biology; Nutrition; Pathology and Pathobiology; Physiology;* and *Zoology*

Graduate Programs in Engineering & Applied Sciences
See *Agricultural Engineering and Bioengineering* and *Biomedical Engineering and Biotechnology*

Graduate Programs in Business, Education, Health, Information Studies, Law & Social Work
See *Education (Agricultural Education)* and *Veterinary Medicine and Sciences*

CONTENTS

Program Directories

Agricultural Sciences—General

Alabama Agricultural and Mechanical University, School of Graduate Studies, School of Agricultural and Environmental Sciences, Huntsville, AL 35811. Offers MS, MURP, PhD. Part-time and evening/weekend programs available. Terminal master's awarded for partial completion of doctoral program. *Degree requirements:* For doctorate, one foreign language, thesis/dissertation. *Entrance requirements:* For master's, GRE General Test; for doctorate, GRE General Test, MS. Additional exam requirements/recommendations for international students: Required—TOEFL (minimum score 500 paper-based; 173 computer-based; 61 iBT). Electronic applications accepted. *Faculty research:* Remote sensing, environmental pollutants, food biotechnology, plant growth.

Alcorn State University, School of Graduate Studies, School of Agriculture and Applied Science, Alcorn State, MS 39096-7500. Offers agricultural economics (MS Ag); agronomy (MS Ag); animal science (MS Ag). *Degree requirements:* For master's, thesis optional. *Faculty research:* Aquatic systems, dairy herd improvement, fruit production, alternative farming practices.

Angelo State University, College of Graduate Studies, College of Sciences, Department of Agriculture, San Angelo, TX 76909. Offers animal science (MS). Part-time and evening/weekend programs available. *Faculty:* 4 full-time (0 women). *Students:* 16 full-time (6 women), 8 part-time (4 women); includes 1 Hispanic/Latino. Average age 23. 7 applicants, 100% accepted, 7 enrolled. In 2010, 11 master's awarded. *Degree requirements:* For master's, comprehensive exam, thesis optional. *Entrance requirements:* For master's, GRE General Test, essay. Additional exam requirements/recommendations for international students: Required—TOEFL or IELTS. *Application deadline:* For fall admission, 7/15 priority date for domestic students, 6/10 for international students; for spring admission, 12/1 priority date for domestic students, 11/1 for international students. Applications are processed on a rolling basis. Application fee: $40 ($50 for international students). Electronic applications accepted. *Expenses:* Tuition, state resident: full-time $4560; part-time $152 per credit hour. Tuition, nonresident: full-time $13,860; part-time $462 per credit hour. Required fees: $2132. Tuition and fees vary according to course load. *Financial support:* In 2010–11, 10 students received support, including 9 research assistantships (averaging $9,887 per year); Federal Work-Study, scholarships/grants, and unspecified assistantships also available. Support available to part-time students. Financial award application deadline: 3/1. *Faculty research:* Effect of protein and energy on feedlot performance, bitterweed toxicosis in sheep, meat laboratory, North Concho watershed project, baseline vegetation. *Unit head:* Dr. Gilbert R. Engdahl, Department Head, 325-942-2027 Ext. 227, E-mail: gil.engdahl@angelo.edu. *Application contact:* Dr. Cody B. Scott, Graduate Advisor, 325-942-2027 Ext. 284, E-mail: cody.scott@angelo.edu.

Arkansas State University, Graduate School, College of Agriculture and Technology, Jonesboro, State University, AR 72467. Offers agricultural education (SCCT); agriculture (MSA); vocational-technical administration (SCCT). Part-time programs available. *Faculty:* 8 full-time (0 women), 3 part-time/adjunct (1 woman). *Students:* 12 full-time (4 women), 26 part-time (13 women); includes 14 minority (2 Black or African American, non-Hispanic/Latino; 12 Hispanic/Latino). Average age 32. 14 applicants, 93% accepted, 7 enrolled. In 2010, 7 master's awarded. *Degree requirements:* For master's, comprehensive exam, thesis or alternative; for SCCT, comprehensive exam. *Entrance requirements:* For master's, GRE General Test or MAT, appropriate bachelor's degree, official transcripts, immunization records; for SCCT, GRE General Test or MAT, interview, master's degree, official transcript, immunization records. Additional exam requirements/recommendations for international students: Required—TOEFL (minimum score 550 paper-based; 213 computer-based; 79 iBT), IELTS (minimum score 6), PTE: Pearson Test of English Academic (56). *Application deadline:* For fall admission, 7/1 for domestic and international students; for spring admission, 11/15 for domestic students, 11/14 for international students. Applications are processed on a rolling basis. Application fee: $30 ($40 for international students). Electronic applications accepted. *Expenses:* Tuition, state resident: full-time $3888; part-time $216 per credit hour. Tuition, nonresident: full-time $9918; part-time $551 per credit hour. International tuition: $8376 full-time. Required fees: $932; $49 per credit hour. $25 per term. One-time fee: $30. Tuition and fees vary according to course load and program. *Financial support:* In 2010–11, 4 students received support; teaching assistantships, career-related internships or fieldwork, scholarships/grants, and unspecified assistantships available. Financial award application deadline: 7/1; financial award applicants required to submit FAFSA. *Unit head:* Dr. Gregory Phillips, Dean, 870-972-2085, Fax: 870-972-3885, E-mail: gphillips@astate.edu. *Application contact:* Dr. Andrew Sustich, Dean of the Graduate School, 870-972-3029, Fax: 870-972-3857, E-mail: sustich@astate.edu.

Auburn University, Graduate School, College of Agriculture, Auburn University, AL 36849. Offers M Ag, M Aq, MS, PhD. Part-time programs available. *Faculty:* 150 full-time (30 women), 1 part-time/adjunct (0 women). *Students:* 133 full-time (54 women), 123 part-time (48 women); includes 8 Black or African American, non-Hispanic/Latino; 2 American Indian or Alaska Native, non-Hispanic/Latino; 6 Asian, non-Hispanic/Latino; 3 Hispanic/Latino, 106 international. Average age 29. 204 applicants, 45% accepted, 55 enrolled. In 2010, 48 master's, 17 doctorates awarded. *Degree requirements:* For doctorate, thesis/dissertation. *Entrance requirements:* For master's and doctorate, GRE General Test. *Application deadline:* For fall admission, 7/7 for domestic students; for spring admission, 11/24 for domestic students. Applications are processed on a rolling basis. Application fee: $50 ($60 for international students). Electronic applications accepted. *Expenses:* Tuition, state resident: full-time $7002. Tuition, nonresident: full-time $21,898. International tuition: $22,116 full-time. Required fees: $892. Tuition and fees vary according to course load and program. *Financial support:* Fellowships, research assistantships, teaching assistantships, Federal Work-Study available. Support available to part-time students. Financial award application deadline: 3/15; financial award applicants required to submit FAFSA. *Unit head:* William Batchelor, Dean, 334-844-2345. *Application contact:* Dr. George Flowers, Dean of the Graduate School, 334-844-2125.

Brigham Young University, Graduate Studies, College of Life Sciences, Provo, UT 84602-1001. Offers MPH, MS, PhD. *Faculty:* 127 full-time (16 women), 3 part-time/adjunct (1 woman). *Students:* 213 full-time (100 women), 31 part-time (13 women); includes 29 minority (2 Black or African American, non-Hispanic/Latino; 14 Asian, non-Hispanic/Latino; 12 Hispanic/Latino; 1 Native Hawaiian or other Pacific Islander, non-Hispanic/Latino). Average age 27. 169 applicants, 51% accepted, 73 enrolled. In 2010, 62 master's, 9 doctorates awarded. *Degree requirements:* For master's, comprehensive exam, thesis; for doctorate, comprehensive exam, thesis/dissertation. *Entrance requirements:* For master's and doctorate, GRE General Test, minimum GPA of 3.0 for last 60 hours of course work. Additional exam requirements/recommendations for international students: Required—TOEFL (minimum score 530 paper-based; 237 computer-based; 85 iBT), IELTS. *Application deadline:* For fall admission, 2/1 for domestic and international students. Electronic applications accepted. *Expenses:* Tuition: Full-time $5580; part-time $310 per credit hour. Tuition and fees vary according to program and student's religious affiliation. *Financial support:* In 2010–11, 183 students received support, including 21 fellowships with full and partial tuition reimbursements available (averaging $4,630 per year), 52 research assistantships with full and partial tuition reimbursements available (averaging $12,840 per year), 9 teaching assistantships with full and partial tuition reimbursements available (averaging $15,996 per year); scholarships/grants and tuition waivers (partial) also available. Financial award application deadline: 2/1. Total annual research expenditures: $4.5 million. *Unit head:* Dr. Rodney J. Brown, Dean, 801-422-3963, Fax: 801-422-0050. *Application contact:* Sue Pratley, Application Contact, 801-422-3963, Fax: 801-422-0050, E-mail: sue_pratley@byu.edu.

California Polytechnic State University, San Luis Obispo, College of Agriculture, Food and Environmental Sciences, Department of Agriculture, San Luis Obispo, CA 93407. Offers MS. Part-time programs available. *Faculty:* 5 full-time (1 woman). *Students:* 45 full-time (33 women), 36 part-time (23 women); includes 9 minority (1 American Indian or Alaska Native, non-Hispanic/Latino; 5 Hispanic/Latino; 3 Two or more races, non-Hispanic/Latino), 6 international. Average age 28. 77 applicants, 55% accepted, 35 enrolled. In 2010, 33 master's awarded. *Degree requirements:* For master's, comprehensive exam, thesis. *Entrance requirements:* For master's, GRE, minimum GPA of 2.75 in last 90 quarter units of course work. Additional exam requirements/recommendations for international students: Required—TOEFL (minimum score 550 paper-based; 213 computer-based) or IELTS (minimum score 6). *Application deadline:* For fall admission, 4/1 for domestic students, 11/30 for international students; for winter admission, 10/1 for domestic students, 6/30 for international students; for spring admission, 10/1 for domestic students. Applications are processed on a rolling basis. Application fee: $55. Electronic applications accepted. *Expenses:* Tuition, state resident: full-time $5386; part-time $3124 per year. Tuition, nonresident: full-time $11,160; part-time $248 per unit. Required fees: $2250; $614 per term. One-time fee: $2250 full-time; $1842 part-time. *Financial support:* Fellowships, research assistantships, teaching assistantships, career-related internships or fieldwork, Federal Work-Study, institutionally sponsored loans, scholarships/grants, and unspecified assistantships available. Support available to part-time students. Financial award application deadline: 3/2; financial award applicants required to submit FAFSA. *Unit head:* Dr. Mark Shelton, Associate Dean/Graduate Coordinator, 805-756-2161, Fax: 805-756-6577, E-mail: mshelton@calpoly.edu. *Application contact:* Dr. Mark Shelton, Associate Dean/Graduate Coordinator, 805-756-2161, Fax: 805-756-6577, E-mail: mshelton@calpoly.edu.

California State Polytechnic University, Pomona, Academic Affairs, College of Agriculture, Pomona, CA 91768-2557. Offers MS. Part-time programs available. *Faculty:* 28 full-time (9 women), 21 part-time/adjunct (14 women). *Students:* 15 full-time (14 women), 45 part-time (36 women); includes 24 minority (3 Black or African American, non-Hispanic/Latino; 3 American Indian or Alaska Native, non-Hispanic/Latino; 8 Asian, non-Hispanic/Latino; 7 Hispanic/Latino; 3 Two or more races, non-Hispanic/Latino), 6 international. Average age 29. 68 applicants, 37% accepted, 22 enrolled. In 2010, 16 master's awarded. *Degree requirements:* For master's, thesis or alternative. *Application deadline:* For fall admission, 5/1 priority date for domestic students; for winter admission, 10/15 priority date for domestic students; for spring admission, 1/2 priority date for domestic students. Applications are processed on a rolling basis. Application fee: $55. Electronic applications accepted. *Expenses:* Tuition, state resident: full-time $5386; part-time $2850 per year. Tuition, nonresident: full-time $12,082; part-time $248 per credit. Required fees: $577; $248 per credit. $577 per year. Tuition and fees vary according to course load and program. *Financial support:* Career-related internships or fieldwork, Federal Work-Study, and institutionally sponsored loans available. Support available to part-time students. Financial award application deadline: 3/2; financial award applicants required to submit FAFSA. *Faculty research:* Equine nutrition, physiology, and reproduction; leadership development; bioartificial pancreas; plant science; ruminant and human nutrition. *Unit head:* Dr. Lester C. Young, Dean, 909-869-2203, E-mail: lcyoung@csupomona.edu. *Application contact:* Dan Hostetler, Chair/Professor, 909-869-2189, Fax: 909-869-5036, E-mail: dghostetler@csupomona.edu.

Clemson University, Graduate School, College of Agriculture, Forestry and Life Sciences, Clemson, SC 29634. Offers M Ag Ed, MFR, MS, PhD. Part-time programs available. *Faculty:* 180 full-time (52 women), 20 part-time/adjunct (7 women). *Students:* 291 full-time (158 women), 78 part-time (41 women); includes 21 minority (10 Black or African American, non-Hispanic/Latino; 4 Asian, non-Hispanic/Latino; 5 Hispanic/Latino; 2 Two or more races, non-Hispanic/Latino), 87 international. Average age 30. 431 applicants, 39% accepted, 118 enrolled. In 2010, 80 master's, 23 doctorates awarded. Terminal master's awarded for partial completion of doctoral program. *Degree requirements:* For master's, thesis (for some programs); for doctorate, thesis/dissertation. *Entrance requirements:* For master's and doctorate, GRE General Test. Additional exam requirements/recommendations for international students: Required—TOEFL. *Application deadline:* For fall admission, 4/15 for domestic and international students; for spring admission, 10/1 for domestic students, 9/15 for international students. Applications are processed on a rolling basis. Application fee: $70 ($80 for international students). Electronic applications accepted. *Expenses:* Contact institution. *Financial support:* In 2010–11, 259 students received support, including 41 fellowships with full and partial tuition reimbursements available, 159 research assistantships with partial tuition reimbursements available, 162 teaching assistantships with partial tuition reimbursements available; career-related internships or fieldwork, Federal Work-Study, institutionally sponsored loans, scholarships/grants, and unspecified assistantships also available. Financial award applicants required to submit FAFSA. Total annual research expenditures: $10.6 million. *Unit head:* Dr. Thomas Scott, Dean, 864-656-7592, Fax: 864-656-1286. *Application contact:* Dr. Joseph Culin, Associate Dean for Research and Graduate Studies, 864-656-2810, E-mail: jculin@clemson.edu.

Colorado State University, Graduate School, College of Agricultural Sciences, Fort Collins, CO 80523-1101. Offers M Agr, MLA, MS, PhD. Part-time and evening/weekend programs available. Postbaccalaureate distance learning degree programs offered (no on-campus study). *Faculty:* 100 full-time (18 women), 2 part-time/adjunct (0 women). *Students:* 160 full-time (73 women), 153 part-time (73 women); includes 26 minority (3 Black or African American, non-Hispanic/Latino; 6 American Indian or Alaska Native, non-Hispanic/Latino; 12 Hispanic/Latino; 5 Two or more races, non-Hispanic/Latino), 53 international. Average age 31. 253 applicants, 67% accepted, 95 enrolled. In 2010, 41 master's, 21 doctorates awarded. *Degree requirements:* For master's, thesis (for some programs); for doctorate, comprehensive exam (for some programs), thesis/dissertation. *Entrance requirements:* For master's and doctorate, GRE General Test, minimum GPA of 3.0, 3 letters of recommendation, bachelor's degree. Additional exam requirements/recommendations for international students: Recommended—TOEFL (minimum score 550 paper-based; 150 computer-based). *Application deadline:* For fall admission, 7/1 for domestic and international students; for spring admission, 1/1 for domestic and international students. Applications are processed on a rolling basis. Application fee: $50. Electronic applications accepted. *Expenses:* Tuition, state resident: full-time $7434; part-time $413 per credit. Tuition, nonresident: full-time $19,022; part-time $1057 per credit. Required fees: $1729; $88 per credit. *Financial support:* In 2010–11, 148 students received support, including 15 fellowships (averaging $29,039 per year), 103 research assistantships (averaging $14,170 per year), 30 teaching assistantships (averaging $10,272 per year); scholarships/grants and unspecified assistantships also available. Financial award applicants required to submit FAFSA. *Faculty research:* Systems methodology, biotechnology, plant and animal breeding, water management, plant protection. Total annual research expenditures: $13.3 million. *Unit head:* Dr. Craig Beyrouty, Dean, 970-491-6274, Fax: 970-491-4895, E-mail: craig.beyrouty@colostate.edu. *Application contact:* Pam Schell, Administrative Assistant, 970-491-2410, Fax: 970-491-4895, E-mail: pam.schell@colostate.edu.

Dalhousie University, Faculty of Graduate Studies, Nova Scotia Agricultural College, Truro, NS B2N 5E3, Canada. Offers M Sc. Part-time programs available. *Degree requirements:* For master's, thesis, candidacy exam. *Entrance requirements:* For master's, minimum GPA of 3.0. Additional exam requirements/recommendations for international students: Required—TOEFL, IELTS, 1 of the following 5 approved tests: TOEFL, IELTS, CANTEST, CAEL, Michigan English Language Assessment Battery. Electronic applications accepted. *Faculty research:* Agribiology, soil science, animal science, plant science, and agricultural chemistry.

Florida Agricultural and Mechanical University, Division of Graduate Studies, Research, and Continuing Education, College of Engineering Science, Technology, and Agriculture, Division of Agricultural Sciences, Tallahassee, FL 32307-3200. Offers agribusiness (MS); animal science (MS); engineering technology (MS); entomology (MS); food science (MS);

international programs (MS); plant science (MS). *Degree requirements:* For master's, thesis. *Entrance requirements:* For master's, GRE General Test, minimum GPA of 3.0. Additional exam requirements/recommendations for international students: Required—TOEFL (minimum score 500 paper-based).

Illinois State University, Graduate School, College of Applied Science and Technology, Department of Agriculture, Normal, IL 61790-2200. Offers agribusiness (MS). *Degree requirements:* For master's, thesis optional. *Entrance requirements:* For master's, GRE General Test, minimum GPA of 3.0 in last 60 hours. *Faculty research:* Engineering-economic system models for rural ethanol production facilities, development and evaluation of a propane-fueled, production scale, on-site thermal destruction system C-FAR 2007; field scale evaluation and technology transfer of economically, ecologically systems; sound liquid swine manure treatment and application.

Instituto Tecnológico y de Estudios Superiores de Monterrey, Campus Monterrey, Graduate and Research Division, Program in Agriculture, Monterrey, Mexico. Offers agricultural parasitology (PhD); agricultural sciences (MS); farming productivity (MS); food processing engineering (MS); phytopathology (MS). Part-time programs available. *Degree requirements:* For master's, one foreign language, thesis; for doctorate, one foreign language, thesis/dissertation. *Entrance requirements:* For master's, EXADEP; for doctorate, GMAT or GRE, master's degree in related field. Additional exam requirements/recommendations for international students: Required—TOEFL. *Faculty research:* Animal embryos and reproduction, crop entomology, tropical agriculture, agricultural productivity, induced mutation in oleaginous plants.

Iowa State University of Science and Technology, Graduate College, College of Agriculture, Ames, IA 50011. Offers M Ag, MS, PhD. Part-time programs available. Postbaccalaureate distance learning degree programs offered (no on-campus study). *Faculty:* 271 full-time (47 women), 26 part-time/adjunct (11 women). *Students:* 439 full-time (193 women), 308 part-time (116 women); includes 17 Black or African American, non-Hispanic/Latino; 2 American Indian or Alaska Native, non-Hispanic/Latino; 11 Asian, non-Hispanic/Latino; 10 Hispanic/Latino, 213 international. 416 applicants, 32% accepted, 88 enrolled. In 2010, 101 master's, 50 doctorates awarded. *Degree requirements:* For doctorate, thesis/dissertation. *Entrance requirements:* Additional exam requirements/recommendations for international students: Required—TOEFL. *Application deadline:* Applications are processed on a rolling basis. Application fee: $40 ($90 for international students). Electronic applications accepted. *Financial support:* In 2010–11, 305 research assistantships with full and partial tuition reimbursements (averaging $16,922 per year), 13 teaching assistantships with full and partial tuition reimbursements (averaging $12,294 per year) were awarded; fellowships, Federal Work-Study, scholarships/grants, health care benefits, and unspecified assistantships also available. Support available to part-time students. *Unit head:* Dr. Wendy Wintersteen, Dean, 515-294-2518, Fax: 515-294-6800. *Application contact:* Information Contact, 515-294-5836, Fax: 515-294-2592, E-mail: grad_admissions@iastate.edu.

Iowa State University of Science and Technology, Graduate College, Interdisciplinary Programs, Program in Sustainable Agriculture, Ames, IA 50011. Offers MS, PhD. *Students:* 35 full-time (21 women), 8 part-time (3 women); includes 3 Black or African American, non-Hispanic/Latino; 2 Asian, non-Hispanic/Latino; 2 Hispanic/Latino, 7 international. In 2010, 4 master's, 3 doctorates awarded. *Degree requirements:* For master's, thesis or alternative; for doctorate, thesis/dissertation. *Entrance requirements:* For master's and doctorate, GRE General Test. Additional exam requirements/recommendations for international students: Required—TOEFL (minimum score 570 paper-based; 80 iBT), IELTS (minimum score 6.5). *Application deadline:* For fall admission, 2/1 for domestic and international students; for spring admission, 6/1 priority date for domestic and international students. Application fee: $40 ($90 for international students). *Financial support:* In 2010–11, 20 research assistantships with full and partial tuition reimbursements (averaging $15,362 per year), 3 teaching assistantships with full and partial tuition reimbursements (averaging $11,088 per year) were awarded. *Unit head:* Dr. Mary Wiedenhoeft, Chair, Supervising Committee, 515-294-6518, E-mail: gpsa@iastate.edu. *Application contact:* Charles Sauer, Information Contact, 515-294-6518, E-mail: gpsa@iastate.edu.

Kansas State University, Graduate School, College of Agriculture, Manhattan, KS 66506. Offers MAB, MS, PhD. Part-time programs available. Postbaccalaureate distance learning degree programs offered (minimal on-campus study). Terminal master's awarded for partial completion of doctoral program. *Degree requirements:* For doctorate, thesis/dissertation. *Entrance requirements:* For master's, GRE, minimum undergraduate GPA of 3.0; for doctorate, GRE, minimum undergraduate GPA of 3.5. Additional exam requirements/recommendations for international students: Required—TOEFL (minimum score 550 paper-based; 213 computer-based). Electronic applications accepted.

Louisiana State University and Agricultural and Mechanical College, Graduate School, College of Agriculture, Baton Rouge, LA 70803. Offers M App St, MS, MSBAE, PhD. Part-time programs available. *Students:* 355 full-time (172 women), 149 part-time (88 women); includes 29 Black or African American, non-Hispanic/Latino; 6 Asian, non-Hispanic/Latino; 16 Hispanic/Latino; 2 Two or more races, non-Hispanic/Latino, 167 international. Average age 31. 282 applicants, 50% accepted, 52 enrolled. In 2010, 95 master's, 42 doctorates awarded. Terminal master's awarded for partial completion of doctoral program. *Degree requirements:* For doctorate, thesis/dissertation. *Entrance requirements:* For master's and doctorate, GRE General Test, minimum GPA of 3.0. Additional exam requirements/recommendations for international students: Required—TOEFL (minimum score 550 paper-based; 213 computer-based; 79 iBT) or IELTS (minimum score 6.5). *Application deadline:* For fall admission, 5/15 for domestic and international students; for spring admission, 10/15 for domestic and international students. Applications are processed on a rolling basis. Application fee: $50 ($70 for international students). Electronic applications accepted. *Financial support:* In 2010–11, 414 students received support, including 8 fellowships with full tuition reimbursements available (averaging $2,030 per year), 233 research assistantships with partial tuition reimbursements available (averaging $17,686 per year), 47 teaching assistantships with partial tuition reimbursements available (averaging $12,661 per year); career-related internships or fieldwork, Federal Work-Study, institutionally sponsored loans, health care benefits, tuition waivers (full), and unspecified assistantships also available. Support available to part-time students. Financial award applicants required to submit FAFSA. *Faculty research:* Biotechnology, resource economics and marketing, aquaculture, food science and technology. Total annual research expenditures: $503,274. *Unit head:* Dr. Kenneth Koonce, Dean, 225-578-2362, Fax: 225-578-2526, E-mail: kkoonce@lsu.edu. *Application contact:* Paula Beecher, Recruiting Coordinator, 225-578-2468, E-mail: pbeeche@lsu.edu.

McGill University, Faculty of Graduate and Postdoctoral Studies, Faculty of Agricultural and Environmental Sciences, Montréal, QC H3A 2T5, Canada. Offers M Sc, M Sc A, PhD, Certificate, Graduate Diploma.

McNeese State University, Doré School of Graduate Studies, College of Science, Department of Agricultural Sciences, Program in Environmental and Chemical Sciences, Lake Charles, LA 70609. Offers agricultural sciences (MS); environmental science (MS). Evening/weekend programs available. *Faculty:* 12 full-time (0 women). *Students:* 21 full-time (9 women), 13 part-time (8 women); includes 2 minority (1 Black or African American, non-Hispanic/Latino; 1 American Indian or Alaska Native, non-Hispanic/Latino), 2 international. In 2010, 9 master's awarded. *Degree requirements:* For master's, comprehensive exam, thesis or alternative. *Entrance requirements:* For master's, GRE. *Application deadline:* For fall admission, 5/15 priority date for domestic and international students; for spring admission, 10/15 priority date for domestic and international students. Applications are processed on a rolling basis. Application fee: $20 ($30 for international students). Tuition and fees vary according to course load. *Financial support:* Application deadline: 5/1. *Unit head:* Dr. Bruce C. Wyman, Coordinator, 337-475-5669, Fax: 337-475-5677, E-mail: wyman@mcneese.edu. *Application contact:* Dr. Bruce C. Wyman, Coordinator, 337-475-5669, Fax: 337-475-5677, E-mail: wyman@mcneese.edu.

Michigan State University, The Graduate School, College of Agriculture and Natural Resources, East Lansing, MI 48824. Offers MA, MIPS, MS, MURP, PhD. *Faculty research:* Plant science, animal sciences, forestry, fisheries and wildlife, recreation and tourism.

Mississippi State University, College of Agriculture and Life Sciences, Department of Biochemistry and Molecular Biology, Mississippi State, MS 39762. Offers agriculture life sciences (MS), including biochemistry; molecular biology (PhD). *Faculty:* 6 full-time (0 women). *Students:* 23 full-time (12 women), 2 part-time (1 woman); includes 3 minority (2 Black or African American, non-Hispanic/Latino; 1 Two or more races, non-Hispanic/Latino), 11 international. Average age 27. 25 applicants, 28% accepted, 4 enrolled. In 2010, 3 master's, 4 doctorates awarded. Terminal master's awarded for partial completion of doctoral program. *Degree requirements:* For master's, thesis (for some programs), comprehensive oral or written exam; for doctorate, thesis/dissertation, comprehensive oral and written exam. *Entrance requirements:* For master's, GRE General Test, minimum GPA of 2.75; for doctorate, GRE. Additional exam requirements/recommendations for international students: Required—TOEFL (minimum score 550 paper-based; 213 computer-based; 79 iBT); Recommended—IELTS (minimum score 6.5). *Application deadline:* For fall admission, 7/1 for domestic students, 5/1 for international students; for spring admission, 11/1 for domestic students, 9/1 for international students. Applications are processed on a rolling basis. Application fee: $40. Electronic applications accepted. *Expenses:* Tuition, state resident: full-time $2730.50; part-time $304 per credit hour. Tuition, nonresident: full-time $6901; part-time $767 per credit hour. *Financial support:* In 2010–11, 15 research assistantships with full tuition reimbursements (averaging $13,530 per year) were awarded; Federal Work-Study, institutionally sponsored loans, and unspecified assistantships also available. Financial award application deadline: 4/1; financial award applicants required to submit FAFSA. *Faculty research:* Fish nutrition, plant and animal molecular biology, plant biochemistry, enzymology, lipid metabolism. *Unit head:* Dr. Scott T. Willard, Professor and Department Head, 662-325-2640, Fax: 662-325-8664, E-mail: swilliard@ads.msstate.edu. *Application contact:* Dr. Din-Pow Ma, Professor/Graduate Coordinator, 662-325-7739, Fax: 662-325-8664, E-mail: dm1@ra.msstate.edu.

Mississippi State University, College of Agriculture and Life Sciences, Department of Entomology and Plant Pathology, Mississippi State, MS 39762. Offers agricultural life sciences (MS), including entomology and plant pathology (MS, PhD); life sciences (PhD), including entomology and plant pathology (MS, PhD). *Faculty:* 20 full-time (1 woman). *Students:* 19 full-time (4 women), 10 part-time (5 women); includes 2 minority (1 Black or African American, non-Hispanic/Latino; 1 Hispanic/Latino), 2 international. Average age 32. 17 applicants, 47% accepted, 7 enrolled. In 2010, 2 master's, 4 doctorates awarded. *Degree requirements:* For master's, thesis; for doctorate, thesis/dissertation. *Entrance requirements:* For master's, GRE General Test, minimum GPA of 2.75; for doctorate, GRE General Test. Additional exam requirements/recommendations for international students: Required—TOEFL (minimum score 475 paper-based; 153 computer-based; 53 iBT); Recommended—IELTS (minimum score 4.5). *Application deadline:* For fall admission, 7/1 for domestic students, 5/1 for international students; for spring admission, 11/1 for domestic students, 9/1 for international students. Applications are processed on a rolling basis. Application fee: $40. Electronic applications accepted. *Expenses:* Tuition, state resident: full-time $2730.50; part-time $304 per credit hour. Tuition, nonresident: full-time $6901; part-time $767 per credit hour. *Financial support:* In 2010–11, 20 research assistantships (averaging $16,783 per year) were awarded; Federal Work-Study, institutionally sponsored loans, and unspecified assistantships also available. Financial award application deadline: 4/1; financial award applicants required to submit FAFSA. *Unit head:* Dr. Scott T. Willard, Professor and Department Head, 662-325-2640, Fax: 662-325-8837, E-mail: swillard@bch.msstate.edu. *Application contact:* Dr. Michael Caprio, Professor and Graduate Coordinator, 662-325-2085, Fax: 662-325-8837, E-mail: mcaprio@entomology.msstate.edu.

Mississippi State University, College of Agriculture and Life Sciences, Department of Plant and Soil Sciences, Mississippi State, MS 39762. Offers agricultural sciences (PhD), including agronomy (MS, PhD), horticulture (MS, PhD), weed science (MS, PhD); agriculture (MS), including agronomy (MS, PhD), horticulture (MS, PhD), weed science (MS, PhD). *Faculty:* 31 full-time (1 woman), 1 part-time/adjunct (0 women). *Students:* 33 full-time (10 women), 22 part-time (7 women); includes 2 minority (both American Indian or Alaska Native, non-Hispanic/Latino), 18 international. Average age 31. 23 applicants, 39% accepted, 7 enrolled. In 2010, 11 master's, 6 doctorates awarded. *Degree requirements:* For master's, thesis, exit seminar describing thesis research; for doctorate, comprehensive exam, thesis/dissertation, two departmental seminars. *Entrance requirements:* For master's, GRE (weed science), minimum GPA of 2.75 (agronomy/horticulture), 3.0 (weed science); for doctorate, GRE (weed science), minimum GPA of 3.0 (agronomy/horticulture), 3.25 (weed science). Additional exam requirements/recommendations for international students: Required—TOEFL (minimum score 550 paper-based; 213 computer-based; 79 iBT); Recommended—IELTS (minimum score 6.5). *Application deadline:* For fall admission, 7/1 for domestic students, 5/1 for international students; for spring admission, 10/1 for domestic students, 9/1 for international students. Applications are processed on a rolling basis. Application fee: $40. Electronic applications accepted. *Expenses:* Tuition, state resident: full-time $2730.50; part-time $304 per credit hour. Tuition, nonresident: full-time $6901; part-time $767 per credit hour. *Financial support:* In 2010–11, 29 research assistantships (averaging $14,353 per year), 2 teaching assistantships (averaging $15,542 per year) were awarded; Federal Work-Study, institutionally sponsored loans, scholarships/grants, and unspecified assistantships also available. Financial award application deadline: 4/1; financial award applicants required to submit FAFSA. *Unit head:* Dr. Daniel Reynolds, Professor/Interim Department Head, 662-325-2311, Fax: 662-325-8742, E-mail: dreynolds@pss.msstate.edu. *Application contact:* Dr. William Kingery, Graduate Coordinator, 662-325-2748, Fax: 662-325-8742, E-mail: wkingery@pss.msstate.edu.

Mississippi State University, College of Agriculture and Life Sciences, Department of Poultry Science, Mississippi State, MS 39762. Offers agriculture (MS), including poultry science (MS, PhD); agriculture sciences (PhD), including poultry science (MS, PhD). *Faculty:* 2 full-time (0 women). *Students:* 9 full-time (2 women), 4 international. Average age 27. 4 applicants, 25% accepted, 1 enrolled. In 2010, 3 master's awarded. *Degree requirements:* For master's, comprehensive exam, thesis optional; for doctorate, comprehensive exam, thesis/dissertation. *Entrance requirements:* Additional exam requirements/recommendations for international students: Required—TOEFL (minimum score 475 paper-based; 153 computer-based; 53 iBT); Recommended—IELTS (minimum score 4.5). *Application deadline:* For fall admission, 7/1 for domestic students, 5/1 for international students; for spring admission, 10/1 for domestic students, 11/1 for international students. Applications are processed on a rolling basis. Application fee: $40. Electronic applications accepted. *Expenses:* Tuition, state resident: full-time $2730.50; part-time $304 per credit hour. Tuition, nonresident: full-time $6901; part-time $767 per credit hour. *Financial support:* In 2010–11, 8 research assistantships with partial tuition reimbursements (averaging $14,520 per year), 1 teaching assistantship with partial tuition reimbursement (averaging $9,816 per year) were awarded; Federal Work-Study, institutionally sponsored loans, scholarships/grants, and unspecified assistantships also available. Financial award application deadline: 4/1; financial award applicants required to submit FAFSA. *Unit head:* Dr. Benjy Mikel, Interim Department Head and Professor, 662-325-5508, Fax: 662-325-8292, E-mail: wbm50@.msstate.edu. *Application contact:* Dr. Chris McDaniel, Professor and Graduate Coordinator, 662-325-1839, Fax: 662-325-8292, E-mail: cmcdaniel@poultry.msstate.edu.

Agricultural Sciences—General

Mississippi State University, College of Agriculture and Life Sciences, School of Human Sciences, Mississippi State, MS 39762. Offers agricultural sciences (PhD), including agriculture and extension education; agriculture and extension education (MS). *Accreditation:* NCATE (one or more programs are accredited). Part-time programs available. *Faculty:* 15 full-time (8 women). *Students:* 9 full-time (4 women), 51 part-time (35 women); includes 14 minority (all Black or African American, non-Hispanic/Latino), 1 international. Average age 37. 20 applicants, 85% accepted, 15 enrolled. In 2010, 18 master's awarded. *Degree requirements:* For master's, thesis optional, comprehensive oral or written exam. *Entrance requirements:* For master's, GRE, minimum GPA of 2.75 in last 4 semesters of course work; for doctorate, minimum GPA of 3.0 on prior graduate work. Additional exam requirements/recommendations for international students: Required—TOEFL (minimum score 475 paper-based; 153 computer-based; 53 iBT); Recommended—IELTS (minimum score 4.5). *Application deadline:* For fall admission, 7/1 for domestic students, 5/1 for international students; for spring admission, 11/1 for domestic students, 9/1 for international students. Applications are processed on a rolling basis. Application fee: $40. Electronic applications accepted. *Expenses:* Tuition, state resident: full-time $2730.50; part-time $304 per credit hour. Tuition, nonresident: full-time $6901; part-time $767 per credit hour. *Financial support:* In 2010–11, 1 research assistantship (averaging $9,872 per year), 5 teaching assistantships with full tuition reimbursements (averaging $12,126 per year) were awarded; Federal Work-Study, institutionally sponsored loans, and unspecified assistantships also available. Financial award application deadline: 4/1; financial award applicants required to submit FAFSA. *Faculty research:* Animal welfare, agroscience, information technology, learning styles, problem solving. *Unit head:* Dr. Walter Taylor, Interim Director, 662-325-8593, E-mail: wntaylor@ais.msstate.edu. *Application contact:* Dr. Jacquelyn Deeds, Professor and Graduate Coordinator, 662-325-7834, E-mail: jdeeds@ais.msstate.edu.

Missouri State University, Graduate College, College of Natural and Applied Sciences, Department of Agriculture, Springfield, MO 65897. Offers natural and applied science (MNAS), including agriculture (MNAS, MS Ed); plant science (MS); secondary education (MS Ed), including agriculture (MNAS, MS Ed). Part-time programs available. *Degree requirements:* For master's, comprehensive exam, thesis or alternative. *Entrance requirements:* For master's, GRE (MS plant science, MNAS), 9-12 teacher certification (MS Ed), minimum GPA of 3.0 (MS plant science, MNAS). Additional exam requirements/recommendations for international students: Required—TOEFL (minimum score 550 paper-based; 213 computer-based; 79 iBT). Electronic applications accepted. *Expenses:* Tuition, state resident: full-time $3348; part-time $186 per credit hour. Tuition, nonresident: full-time $6696; part-time $372 per credit hour. Required fees: $238 per semester. Tuition and fees vary according to course level, course load and program. *Faculty research:* Grapevine biotechnology, agricultural marketing, Asian elephant reproduction, poultry science, integrated pest management.

Montana State University, College of Graduate Studies, College of Agriculture, Bozeman, MT 59717. Offers MS, PhD. Part-time programs available. Postbaccalaureate distance learning degree programs offered (minimal on-campus study). *Faculty:* 90 full-time (21 women), 15 part-time/adjunct (4 women). *Students:* 26 full-time (7 women), 95 part-time (45 women); includes 9 minority (3 American Indian or Alaska Native, non-Hispanic/Latino; 1 Asian, non-Hispanic/Latino; 4 Hispanic/Latino; 1 Two or more races, non-Hispanic/Latino), 12 international. Average age 30. 88 applicants, 42% accepted, 30 enrolled. In 2010, 28 master's, 7 doctorates awarded. *Degree requirements:* For master's, comprehensive exam; for doctorate, comprehensive exam, thesis/dissertation. *Entrance requirements:* For master's and doctorate, GRE General Test. Additional exam requirements/recommendations for international students: Required—TOEFL (minimum score 550 paper-based; 213 computer-based). *Application deadline:* For fall admission, 7/15 priority date for domestic students, 5/15 priority date for international students; for spring admission, 12/1 priority date for domestic students, 10/1 priority date for international students. Applications are processed on a rolling basis. Application fee: $30. Electronic applications accepted. *Expenses:* Tuition, state resident: full-time $5553.90. Tuition, nonresident: full-time $14,646. Required fees: $1233. *Financial support:* Application deadline: 3/1. Total annual research expenditures: $20.7 million. *Unit head:* Dr. Jeffrey S. Jacobsen, Dean, 406-994-7060, Fax: 406-994-3933, E-mail: jefj@montana.edu. *Application contact:* Dr. Carl A. Fox, Vice Provost for Graduate Education, 406-994-4145, Fax: 406-994-7433, E-mail: gradstudy@montana.edu.

Morehead State University, Graduate Programs, College of Science and Technology, Department of Agricultural Sciences, Morehead, KY 40351. Offers career and technical agricultural education (MS). Part-time and evening/weekend programs available. *Degree requirements:* For master's, comprehensive exam, thesis or alternative, exit exam. *Entrance requirements:* For master's, GRE, minimum GPA of 3.0 for undergraduate major. Additional exam requirements/recommendations for international students: Required—TOEFL (minimum score 500 paper-based; 173 computer-based). Electronic applications accepted.

Murray State University, School of Agriculture, Murray, KY 42071. Offers agriculture (MS); agriculture education (MS). Evening/weekend programs available. Postbaccalaureate distance learning degree programs offered (minimal on-campus study). *Degree requirements:* For master's, comprehensive exam, thesis (for some programs). *Entrance requirements:* Additional exam requirements/recommendations for international students: Required—TOEFL. *Faculty research:* Ultrasound in beef, corn and soybean research, tobacco research.

New Mexico State University, Graduate School, College of Agricultural, Consumer and Environmental Sciences, Department of Entomology, Plant Pathology and Weed Science, Las Cruces, NM 88003-8001. Offers agricultural biology (MS). Part-time programs available. *Faculty:* 7 full-time (2 women). *Students:* 11 full-time (5 women), 4 part-time (2 women); includes 5 minority (4 Hispanic/Latino; 1 Two or more races, non-Hispanic/Latino), 2 international. Average age 27. 14 applicants, 79% accepted, 9 enrolled. In 2010, 5 master's awarded. *Degree requirements:* For master's, comprehensive exam, thesis. *Entrance requirements:* For master's, GRE General Test. *Application deadline:* For fall admission, 7/1 priority date for domestic students; for spring admission, 11/1 priority date for domestic students. Applications are processed on a rolling basis. Application fee: $30 ($50 for international students). Electronic applications accepted. *Expenses:* Tuition, state resident: full-time $4536; part-time $242 per credit. Tuition, nonresident: full-time $15,816; part-time $712 per credit. Required fees: $636 per term. *Financial support:* In 2010–11, 8 students received support, including 6 research assistantships with full tuition reimbursements available (averaging $20,550 per year), 2 teaching assistantships with partial tuition reimbursements available (averaging $14,225 per year); career-related internships or fieldwork and health care benefits also available. Financial award application deadline: 3/1. *Faculty research:* Integrated pest management, pesticide application and safety, livestock ectoparasite research, biotechnology, nematology. *Unit head:* Dr. Jill Schroeder, Interim Head, 575-646-3225, Fax: 575-646-8087, E-mail: jischroe@nmsu.edu. *Application contact:* Cindy Bullard, Intermediate Administrative Assistant, 575-646-1145, Fax: 575-646-8087, E-mail: cbullard@nmsu.edu.

North Carolina Agricultural and Technical State University, Graduate School, School of Agriculture and Environmental Sciences, Greensboro, NC 27411. Offers MS. Part-time and evening/weekend programs available. *Degree requirements:* For master's, comprehensive exam, qualifying exam. *Entrance requirements:* For master's, GRE General Test. *Faculty research:* Aid for small farmers, agricultural technology, housing, food science, nutrition.

North Carolina State University, Graduate School, College of Agriculture and Life Sciences, Raleigh, NC 27695. Offers M Tox, MAE, MB, MBAE, MFG, MFM, MFS, MG, MMB, MN, MP, MS, MZS, Ed D, PhD, Certificate. Part-time programs available. Electronic applications accepted.

North Dakota State University, College of Graduate and Interdisciplinary Studies, College of Agriculture, Food Systems, and Natural Resources, Fargo, ND 58108. Offers MS, PhD. Part-time programs available. *Students:* 110 full-time (50 women), 45 part-time (20 women); includes 4 Black or African American, non-Hispanic/Latino; 1 American Indian or Alaska Native, non-Hispanic/Latino; 17 Asian, non-Hispanic/Latino; 9 Hispanic/Latino, 30 international. *Degree requirements:* For doctorate, thesis/dissertation. *Entrance requirements:* Additional exam requirements/recommendations for international students: Required—TOEFL. *Application deadline:* Applications are processed on a rolling basis. Application fee: $45 ($60 for international students). Electronic applications accepted. *Financial support:* Fellowships with full tuition reimbursements, research assistantships with full tuition reimbursements, teaching assistantships with full tuition reimbursements, career-related internships or fieldwork, Federal Work-Study, and institutionally sponsored loans available. Support available to part-time students. *Faculty research:* Horticulture and forestry, plant and wheat breeding, diseases of insects, animal and range sciences, soil science, veterinary medicine. *Unit head:* Dr. Kenneth F. Grafton, Dean, 701-231-8790, Fax: 701-231-8520, E-mail: k.grafton@ndsu.edu. *Application contact:* Dr. Kenneth F. Grafton, Dean, 701-231-8790, Fax: 701-231-8520, E-mail: k.grafton@ndsu.edu.

Northwest Missouri State University, Graduate School, Melvin and Valorie Booth College of Business and Professional Studies, Department of Agriculture, Maryville, MO 64468-6001. Offers agricultural economics (MBA); agriculture (MS); teaching agriculture (MS Ed). Part-time programs available. *Faculty:* 7 full-time (2 women). *Students:* 8 full-time (2 women), 2 part-time (1 woman); includes 1 Two or more races, non-Hispanic/Latino. 8 applicants, 88% accepted, 3 enrolled. In 2010, 5 master's awarded. *Degree requirements:* For master's, comprehensive exam, thesis (for some programs). *Entrance requirements:* For master's, GRE General Test, minimum undergraduate GPA of 2.5, writing sample. Additional exam requirements/recommendations for international students: Required—TOEFL (minimum score 550 paper-based; 213 computer-based). *Application deadline:* For fall admission, 7/1 for domestic and international students; for spring admission, 11/15 for domestic and international students. Applications are processed on a rolling basis. Application fee: $0 ($50 for international students). *Financial support:* In 2010–11, 3 research assistantships with full tuition reimbursements (averaging $6,000 per year), 2 teaching assistantships with full tuition reimbursements (averaging $6,000 per year) were awarded; unspecified assistantships also available. Financial award application deadline: 4/1; financial award applicants required to submit FAFSA. *Unit head:* Dr. Arley Larson, Chairperson, 660-562-1161. *Application contact:* Dr. Gregory Haddock, Dean of Graduate School, 660-562-1145, Fax: 660-562-1096, E-mail: gradsch@nwmissouri.edu.

Nova Scotia Agricultural College, Research and Graduate Studies, Truro, NS B2N 5E3, Canada. Offers agriculture (M Sc), including air quality, animal behavior, animal molecular genetics, animal nutrition, animal technology, aquaculture, botany, crop management, crop physiology, ecology, environmental microbiology, food science, horticulture, nutrient management, pest management, physiology, plant biotechnology, plant pathology, soil chemistry, soil fertility, waste management and composting, water quality. Program offered jointly with Dalhousie University. Part-time programs available. *Degree requirements:* For master's, thesis, ATC Exam Teaching Assistantship. *Entrance requirements:* For master's, honors B Sc, minimum GPA of 3.0. Additional exam requirements/recommendations for international students: Required—TOEFL (minimum score 580 paper-based; 237 computer-based; 92 iBT), IELTS, Michigan English Language Assessment Battery, CanTEST, CAEL. *Faculty research:* Bio-product development, organic agriculture, nutrient management, air and water quality, agricultural biotechnology.

The Ohio State University, Graduate School, College of Food, Agricultural, and Environmental Sciences, Columbus, OH 43210. Offers M Ed, MS, PhD. Part-time programs available. *Faculty:* 313. *Students:* 407 full-time (232 women), 138 part-time (64 women); includes 12 Black or African American, non-Hispanic/Latino; 16 Asian, non-Hispanic/Latino; 15 Hispanic/Latino; 1 Two or more races, non-Hispanic/Latino, 203 international. Average age 28. In 2010, 93 master's, 49 doctorates awarded. *Degree requirements:* For doctorate, thesis/dissertation. *Entrance requirements:* Additional exam requirements/recommendations for international students: Required—TOEFL (minimum score 550 paper-based; 213 computer-based), IELTS (minimum score 7), or Michigan English Language Assessment Battery (minimum score 83). *Application deadline:* For fall admission, 8/15 priority date for domestic students, 7/1 priority date for international students; for winter admission, 12/1 priority date for domestic students, 11/1 priority date for international students; for spring admission, 3/1 priority date for domestic students, 2/1 priority date for international students. Applications are processed on a rolling basis. Application fee: $40 ($50 for international students). Electronic applications accepted. *Expenses:* Tuition, state resident: full-time $10,605. Tuition, nonresident: full-time $26,535. Tuition and fees vary according to course load and program. *Financial support:* Fellowships, research assistantships, teaching assistantships, career-related internships or fieldwork, Federal Work-Study, institutionally sponsored loans, and unspecified assistantships available. Support available to part-time students. *Unit head:* Dr. Bobby Moser, Dean, 614-292-6891, Fax: 614-292-1218, E-mail: moser.2@osu.edu. *Application contact:* Graduate Admissions, 614-292-9444, Fax: 614-292-3895, E-mail: domestic.grad@osu.edu.

Oklahoma State University, College of Agricultural Science and Natural Resources, Stillwater, OK 74078. Offers M Ag, MS, PhD. Postbaccalaureate distance learning degree programs offered. *Faculty:* 244 full-time (57 women), 18 part-time/adjunct (2 women). *Students:* 175 full-time (86 women), 317 part-time (150 women); includes 7 Black or African American, non-Hispanic/Latino; 18 American Indian or Alaska Native, non-Hispanic/Latino; 6 Asian, non-Hispanic/Latino; 7 Hispanic/Latino, 196 international. Average age 29. 516 applicants, 35% accepted, 104 enrolled. In 2010, 103 master's, 32 doctorates awarded. *Degree requirements:* For master's, thesis (for some programs); for doctorate, comprehensive exam, thesis/dissertation. *Entrance requirements:* For master's and doctorate, GRE or GMAT. Additional exam requirements/recommendations for international students: Required—TOEFL (minimum score 550 paper-based; 79 iBT). *Application deadline:* For fall admission, 3/1 priority date for international students; for spring admission, 8/1 priority date for international students. Applications are processed on a rolling basis. Application fee: $40 ($75 for international students). Electronic applications accepted. *Expenses:* Tuition, state resident: full-time $3716; part-time $154.85 per credit hour. Tuition, nonresident: full-time $14,892; part-time $621 per credit hour. Required fees: $2044; $85.20 per credit hour. One-time fee: $50. Tuition and fees vary according to course load and campus/location. *Financial support:* In 2010–11, 299 research assistantships (averaging $15,727 per year), 20 teaching assistantships (averaging $15,655 per year) were awarded; fellowships, career-related internships or fieldwork, Federal Work-Study, scholarships/grants, health care benefits, tuition waivers (partial), and unspecified assistantships also available. Support available to part-time students. Financial award application deadline: 3/1; financial award applicants required to submit FAFSA. *Unit head:* Dr. Robert E. Whitson, Dean, 405-744-5398, Fax: 405-744-2480. *Application contact:* Dr. Gordon Emslie, Dean, 405-744-6368, Fax: 405-744-0355, E-mail: grad-i@okstate.edu.

Oregon State University, Graduate School, College of Agricultural Sciences, Corvallis, OR 97331. Offers M Ag, M Agr, MA, MAIS, MAT, MS, PhD. Part-time programs available. Terminal master's awarded for partial completion of doctoral program. *Degree requirements:* For doctorate, thesis/dissertation. *Entrance requirements:* For master's and doctorate, GRE, minimum GPA of 3.0 in last 90 hours of course work. Additional exam requirements/recommendations for international students: Required—TOEFL. *Faculty research:* Fish and wildlife biology, food science, soil/water/plant relationships, natural resources, animal biochemistry.

Penn State University Park, Graduate School, College of Agricultural Sciences, State College, University Park, PA 16802-1503. Offers M Agr, M Ed, MFR, MPS, MS, PhD. *Students:* 336 full-time (192 women), 31 part-time (16 women). Average age 29. 528 applicants, 30% accepted, 91 enrolled. In 2010, 65 master's, 40 doctorates awarded. *Entrance requirements:* Additional exam requirements/recommendations for international students: Required—TOEFL (minimum score 550 paper-based; 213 computer-based; 80 iBT). *Application deadline:* Applica-

tions are processed on a rolling basis. Application fee: $65. Electronic applications accepted. *Financial support:* Fellowships, research assistantships, teaching assistantships available. Financial award applicants required to submit FAFSA. *Unit head:* Dr. Bruce A. McPheron, Dean, 814-865-2541, Fax: 814-865-3103, E-mail: bam10@psu.edu. *Application contact:* Cynthia E. Nicosia, Director Graduate Enrollment Services, 814-865-1834, E-mail: cey1@psu.edu.

Prairie View A&M University, College of Agriculture and Human Sciences, Prairie View, TX 77446-0519. Offers agricultural economics (MS); animal sciences (MS); interdisciplinary human sciences (MS); soil science (MS). Part-time and evening/weekend programs available. *Faculty:* 11 full-time (2 women). *Students:* 47 full-time (33 women), 34 part-time (26 women); includes 62 Black or African American, non-Hispanic/Latino; 2 Asian, non-Hispanic/Latino; 2 Hispanic/Latino, 5 international. Average age 30. 147 applicants, 100% accepted. In 2010, 21 master's awarded. *Degree requirements:* For master's, comprehensive exam, thesis (for some programs), field placement. *Entrance requirements:* For master's, GRE General Test, minimum GPA of 2.45. Additional exam requirements/recommendations for international students: Required—TOEFL (minimum score 550 paper-based). *Application deadline:* For fall admission, 6/1 for domestic and international students; for spring admission, 10/1 for domestic and international students. Applications are processed on a rolling basis. Application fee: $50. *Expenses:* Tuition, state resident: full-time $3586.14; part-time $119.06 per credit hour. Tuition, nonresident: part-time $511.23 per credit hour. *Financial support:* In 2010–11, 57 students received support, including 8 fellowships with tuition reimbursements available (averaging $12,000 per year), 10 research assistantships with tuition reimbursements available (averaging $15,000 per year); career-related internships or fieldwork, Federal Work-Study, institutionally sponsored loans, scholarships/grants, tuition waivers (partial), and unspecified assistantships also available. Support available to part-time students. Financial award application deadline: 4/1; financial award applicants required to submit FAFSA. *Faculty research:* Domestic violence prevention, water quality, food growth regulators, wetland dynamics, biochemistry, obesity and nutrition, family therapy. Total annual research expenditures: $4 million. *Unit head:* Dr. Freddie Richards, Dean, 936-261-2528, Fax: 936-261-5143, E-mail: flrichards@pvamu.edu. *Application contact:* Dr. Richard W. Griffin, Interim Department Head, 936-261-5019, Fax: 936-261-5148, E-mail: rwgriffin@pvamu.edu.

Purdue University, Graduate School, College of Agriculture, West Lafayette, IN 47907. Offers EMBA, M Agr, MA, MS, MSF, PhD. Part-time programs available. *Degree requirements:* For doctorate, thesis/dissertation. *Entrance requirements:* Additional exam requirements/recommendations for international students: Required—TOEFL. Electronic applications accepted.

Sam Houston State University, College of Arts and Sciences, Department of Agricultural Sciences, Huntsville, TX 77341. Offers agriculture (MS); industrial technology (MA). Part-time and evening/weekend programs available. *Students:* 28 full-time (9 women), 21 part-time (13 women); includes 1 Hispanic/Latino, 1 international. Average age 27. 18 applicants, 100% accepted, 17 enrolled. In 2010, 12 master's awarded. *Degree requirements:* For master's, thesis optional. *Entrance requirements:* For master's, GRE General Test, minimum GPA of 2.5. Additional exam requirements/recommendations for international students: Required—TOEFL (minimum score 550 paper-based; 213 computer-based; 79 iBT). *Application deadline:* For fall admission, 8/1 for domestic and international students; for spring admission, 12/1 for domestic and international students. Application fee: $20. Electronic applications accepted. *Expenses:* Tuition, state resident: full-time $1363; part-time $163 per credit hour. Tuition, nonresident: full-time $3856; part-time $473 per credit hour. *Financial support:* Teaching assistantships, career-related internships or fieldwork available. Financial award application deadline: 5/31; financial award applicants required to submit FAFSA. *Unit head:* Dr. Stanley F. Kelley, Chair, 936-294-1189, Fax: 936-294-1232, E-mail: sfkelley@shsu.edu. *Application contact:* Tammy Gray, Advisor, 936-294-1230, E-mail: dca_tag@shsu.edu.

South Dakota State University, Graduate School, College of Agriculture and Biological Sciences, Brookings, SD 57007. Offers MS, PhD. Part-time programs available. *Degree requirements:* For master's, thesis, oral exam; for doctorate, thesis/dissertation, preliminary oral and written exams. *Entrance requirements:* Additional exam requirements/recommendations for international students: Required—TOEFL.

Southern Arkansas University–Magnolia, Graduate Programs, Magnolia, AR 71753. Offers agriculture (MS); business administration (MBA); computer and information sciences (MS); education (M Ed), including counseling and development, curriculum and instruction emphasis, educational administration and supervision, elementary education, middle level emphasis, reading emphasis, secondary education, TESOL emphasis; kinesiology (M Ed); library media and information specialist (M Ed); mental health and clinical counseling (MS); public administration (MPA); school counseling (M Ed); teaching (MAT). *Accreditation:* NCATE. Part-time and evening/weekend programs available. *Faculty:* 32 full-time (16 women), 6 part-time/adjunct (5 women). *Students:* 71 full-time (43 women), 364 part-time (275 women); includes 109 Black or African American, non-Hispanic/Latino; 1 American Indian or Alaska Native, non-Hispanic/Latino; 3 Asian, non-Hispanic/Latino, 19 international. Average age 33. 107 applicants, 71% accepted, 69 enrolled. In 2010, 157 master's awarded. *Degree requirements:* For master's, comprehensive exam, thesis optional. *Entrance requirements:* For master's, GRE, MAT or GMAT, minimum GPA of 2.75. *Application deadline:* For fall admission, 7/31 for domestic students; for winter admission, 12/1 for domestic students; for spring admission, 12/1 for domestic students. Applications are processed on a rolling basis. Application fee: $25. *Expenses:* Tuition, state resident: part-time $221 per hour. Tuition, nonresident: part-time $325 per hour. *Financial support:* Career-related internships or fieldwork, Federal Work-Study, scholarships/grants, tuition waivers (full), and unspecified assistantships available. Financial award applicants required to submit FAFSA. *Faculty research:* Alternative certification for teachers, supervision of instruction, instructional leadership, counseling. *Unit head:* Dr. Kim Bloss, Dean, Graduate Studies, 870-235-4150, Fax: 870-235-5227, E-mail: kkbloss@saumag.edu. *Application contact:* Dr. Kim Bloss, Dean, Graduate Studies, 870-235-4150, Fax: 870-235-5227, E-mail: kkbloss@saumag.edu.

Southern Illinois University Carbondale, Graduate School, College of Agriculture, Carbondale, IL 62901-4701. Offers MS, MBA/MS. Part-time programs available. *Entrance requirements:* For master's, minimum GPA of 2.7. Additional exam requirements/recommendations for international students: Required—TOEFL. *Faculty research:* Production and studies in crops, animal nutrition, agribusiness economics and management, forest biology and ecology, microcomputers in agriculture.

Southern University and Agricultural and Mechanical College, Graduate School, College of Agricultural, Family and Consumer Sciences, Baton Rouge, LA 70813. Offers urban forestry (MS). *Degree requirements:* For master's, thesis. *Entrance requirements:* For master's, GRE, minimum GPA of 3.0. Additional exam requirements/recommendations for international students: Required—TOEFL (minimum score 525 paper-based; 193 computer-based). *Faculty research:* Urban forest interactions with environment, social and economic impacts of urban forests, tree biology/pathology, development of urban forest management tools.

Tarleton State University, College of Graduate Studies, College of Agriculture and Human Sciences, Department of Agribusiness, Agronomy, Horticulture, and Range Management, Stephenville, TX 76402. Offers agriculture (MS). Part-time and evening/weekend programs available. *Degree requirements:* For master's, comprehensive exam. *Entrance requirements:* For master's, GRE, minimum GPA of 3.0. Additional exam requirements/recommendations for international students: Required—TOEFL (minimum score 550 paper-based; 213 computer-based; 80 iBT). Electronic applications accepted.

Tarleton State University, College of Graduate Studies, College of Agriculture and Human Sciences, Department of Agricultural Services and Development, Stephenville, TX 76402. Offers agriculture education (MS). Part-time and evening/weekend programs available. Post-baccalaureate distance learning degree programs offered (minimal on-campus study). *Degree requirements:* For master's, comprehensive exam. *Entrance requirements:* For master's, GRE General Test, minimum GPA of 3.0. Additional exam requirements/recommendations for international students: Required—TOEFL (minimum score 550 paper-based; 213 computer-based; 80 iBT). Electronic applications accepted.

Tennessee State University, The School of Graduate Studies and Research, School of Agriculture and Consumer Sciences, Nashville, TN 37209-1561. Offers agricultural sciences (MS), including agribusiness, agricultural education, animal science, plant science. Part-time and evening/weekend programs available. *Degree requirements:* For master's, thesis. *Entrance requirements:* For master's, GRE General Test, GRE Subject Test, MAT. *Faculty research:* Small farm economics, ornamental horticulture, beef cattle production, rural elderly.

Texas A&M University, College of Agriculture and Life Sciences, College Station, TX 77843. Offers M Agr, M Ed, M Eng, MAB, MS, DE, Ed D, PhD. Part-time programs available. Post-baccalaureate distance learning degree programs offered (minimal on-campus study). *Faculty:* 326. *Students:* 1,103 full-time (550 women), 299 part-time (134 women); includes 188 minority (43 Black or African American, non-Hispanic/Latino; 6 American Indian or Alaska Native, non-Hispanic/Latino; 25 Asian, non-Hispanic/Latino; 114 Hispanic/Latino), 432 international. Average age 29. In 2010, 157 master's, 78 doctorates awarded. *Entrance requirements:* Additional exam requirements/recommendations for international students: Required—TOEFL (minimum score 550 paper-based; 213 computer-based). *Application deadline:* For fall admission, 7/21 priority date for domestic students, 6/1 priority date for international students; for spring admission, 12/1 priority date for domestic students, 10/1 priority date for international students. Applications are processed on a rolling basis. Application fee: $50 ($75 for international students). Electronic applications accepted. *Financial support:* Fellowships, research assistantships, teaching assistantships, career-related internships or fieldwork, Federal Work-Study, institutionally sponsored loans, scholarships/grants, tuition waivers (partial), and unspecified assistantships available. Support available to part-time students. Financial award applicants required to submit FAFSA. *Faculty research:* Plant sciences, animal sciences, environmental natural resources, biological and agricultural engineering, agricultural economics. *Unit head:* Dr. Mark Hussey, Vice Chancellor/Dean, 979-845-4747, Fax: 979-845-9938, E-mail: mhussey@tamu.edu. *Application contact:* Graduate Admissions, 979-845-1044, E-mail: admissions@tamu.edu.

Texas A&M University–Commerce, Graduate School, College of Arts and Sciences, Department of Agriculture, Commerce, TX 75429-3011. Offers agricultural education (M Ed, MS); agricultural sciences (M Ed, MS). Part-time programs available. *Degree requirements:* For master's, comprehensive exam, thesis (for some programs). *Entrance requirements:* For master's, GRE General Test. Electronic applications accepted. *Faculty research:* Soil conservation, retention.

Texas A&M University–Kingsville, College of Graduate Studies, College of Agriculture and Home Economics, Kingsville, TX 78363. Offers MS, PhD. Part-time and evening/weekend programs available. *Degree requirements:* For master's, comprehensive exam, thesis or alternative; for doctorate, one foreign language, comprehensive exam, thesis/dissertation. *Entrance requirements:* For master's, GRE General Test, minimum GPA of 3.0; for doctorate, GRE General Test, minimum GPA of 3.5. Additional exam requirements/recommendations for international students: Required—TOEFL. *Faculty research:* Mesquite cloning; genesis of soil salinity; dove management; bone development; egg, meat, and milk consumption versus price.

Texas Tech University, Graduate School, College of Agricultural Sciences and Natural Resources, Lubbock, TX 79409. Offers M Agr, MAB, MLA, MS, Ed D, PhD, JD/MS. Part-time programs available. Postbaccalaureate distance learning degree programs offered (minimal on-campus study). *Faculty:* 57 full-time (8 women), 7 part-time/adjunct (0 women). *Students:* 245 full-time (110 women), 103 part-time (41 women); includes 5 Black or African American, non-Hispanic/Latino; 3 American Indian or Alaska Native, non-Hispanic/Latino; 1 Asian, non-Hispanic/Latino; 13 Hispanic/Latino; 3 Two or more races, non-Hispanic/Latino, 85 international. Average age 28. 257 applicants, 49% accepted, 87 enrolled. In 2010, 63 master's, 31 doctorates awarded. *Degree requirements:* For master's, thesis or alternative; for doctorate, thesis/dissertation. *Entrance requirements:* For master's and doctorate, GRE General Test, formal approval from departmental committee. Additional exam requirements/recommendations for international students: Required—TOEFL (minimum score 550 paper-based; 213 computer-based; 79 iBT). *Application deadline:* For fall admission, 6/1 priority date for domestic students, 1/15 priority date for international students; for spring admission, 9/1 priority date for domestic students, 6/15 priority date for international students. Applications are processed on a rolling basis. Application fee: $50 ($75 for international students). Electronic applications accepted. *Expenses:* Contact institution. *Financial support:* In 2010–11, 211 students received support, including 81 research assistantships with partial tuition reimbursements available (averaging $5,146 per year), 8 teaching assistantships with partial tuition reimbursements available (averaging $7,149 per year); career-related internships or fieldwork, Federal Work-Study, institutionally sponsored loans, scholarships/grants, traineeships, health care benefits, and unspecified assistantships also available. Support available to part-time students. Financial award application deadline: 4/15; financial award applicants required to submit FAFSA. *Faculty research:* Biotechnology and genomics, water management, food safety, policy, ecology. Total annual research expenditures: $14.9 million. *Unit head:* Dr. John M. Burns, Dean, 806-742-2810, E-mail: john.burns@ttu.edu. *Application contact:* Dr. Cindy Akers, Director, Student Services Center, 806-742-2808, Fax: 806-742-2836, E-mail: cindy.akers@ttu.edu.

Tropical Agriculture Research and Higher Education Center, Graduate School, Turrialba, Costa Rica. Offers agribusiness management (MS); agroforestry systems (PhD); development practices (MS); ecological agriculture (MS); environmental socioeconomics (MS); forestry in tropical and subtropical zones (PhD); integrated watershed management (MS); international sustainable tourism (MS); management and conservation of tropical rainforests and biodiversity (MS); tropical agriculture (PhD); tropical agroforestry (MS). *Entrance requirements:* For master's, GRE, 2 years of related professional experience, letters of recommendation; for doctorate, GRE, 4 letters of recommendation, letter of support from employing organization, master's degree in agronomy, biological sciences, forestry, natural resources or related field. Additional exam requirements/recommendations for international students: Required—TOEFL (minimum score 550 paper-based; 213 computer-based). Electronic applications accepted. *Faculty research:* Biodiversity in fragmented landscapes, ecosystem management, integrated pest management, environmental livestock production, biotechnology carbon balances in diverse land uses.

Universidad Nacional Pedro Henriquez Urena, Graduate School, Santo Domingo, Dominican Republic. Offers agricultural diversity (MS), including horticultural/fruit production, tropical animal production; conservation of monuments and cultural assets (M Arch); ecology and environment (MS); environmental engineering (MEE); international relations (MA); natural resource management (MS); political science (MA); project optimization (MPM); project feasibility (MPM); project management (MPM); sanitation engineering (ME); science for teachers (MS); tropical Caribbean architecture (M Arch).

Université Laval, Faculty of Agricultural and Food Sciences, Québec, QC G1K 7P4, Canada. Offers M Sc, PhD, Diploma. Part-time programs available. *Degree requirements:* For doctorate, comprehensive exam, thesis/dissertation. Electronic applications accepted.

University of Alberta, Faculty of Graduate Studies and Research, Department of Agricultural, Food and Nutritional Science, Edmonton, AB T6G 2E1, Canada. Offers M Ag, M Eng, M Sc,

Agricultural Sciences—General

University of Alberta (continued)
PhD, MBA/M Ag. *Degree requirements:* For master's, thesis; for doctorate, comprehensive exam, thesis/dissertation. *Entrance requirements:* For master's, minimum GPA of 3.3; for doctorate, minimum GPA of 3.5. Additional exam requirements/recommendations for international students: Required—IELTS (minimum score 6.5), TOEFL (minimum score of 550 paper-based or a total iBT score of 88 with a score of at least 20 on each of the individual skill areas), Michigan English Language Assessment Battery (minimum score 85); CAEL (overall minimum score 60). *Faculty research:* Animal science, food science, nutrition and metabolism, bioresource engineering, plant science and range management.

The University of Arizona, College of Agriculture and Life Sciences, Tucson, AZ 85721. Offers M Ag Ed, MHE Ed, MS, PhD. Part-time programs available. *Faculty:* 120 full-time (36 women), 5 part-time/adjunct (1 woman). *Students:* 305 full-time (169 women), 91 part-time (52 women); includes 9 Black or African American, non-Hispanic/Latino; 1 American Indian or Alaska Native, non-Hispanic/Latino; 6 Asian, non-Hispanic/Latino; 39 Hispanic/Latino; 29 Two or more races, non-Hispanic/Latino, 97 international. Average age 31. 358 applicants, 37% accepted, 66 enrolled. In 2010, 73 master's, 32 doctorates awarded. *Degree requirements:* For doctorate, thesis/dissertation. *Entrance requirements:* For master's, GRE, GMAT, or MAT, bachelor's degree or equivalent, minimum GPA of 3.0. Additional exam requirements/recommendations for international students: Required—TOEFL. *Application deadline:* For fall admission, 1/1 for domestic students, 12/1 for international students. Applications are processed on a rolling basis. Application fee: $75. Electronic applications accepted. *Expenses:* Tuition, state resident: full-time $7692. *Financial support:* In 2010–11, 126 research assistantships with full and partial tuition reimbursements (averaging $16,919 per year), 47 teaching assistantships with full and partial tuition reimbursements (averaging $15,942 per year) were awarded; fellowships with full and partial tuition reimbursements, career-related internships or fieldwork, Federal Work-Study, institutionally sponsored loans, scholarships/grants, traineeships, health care benefits, tuition waivers (full and partial), and unspecified assistantships also available. *Faculty research:* Regulation of skeletal muscle mass during growth, bone health and osteoporosis prevention, regulation of gene expression, development of new crops for arid and semi-arid lands, molecular genetics and pathogenesis of the opportunistic pathogen. Total annual research expenditures: $36.4 million. *Unit head:* Dr. Eugene G. Sander, Dean, 520-621-7621, Fax: 520-621-7196. *Application contact:* Dr. David E. Cox, Associate Dean, 520-621-3612, Fax: 520-621-8662.

University of Arkansas, Graduate School, Dale Bumpers College of Agricultural, Food and Life Sciences, Fayetteville, AR 72701-1201. Offers MS, PhD. *Students:* 113 full-time (53 women), 196 part-time (103 women); includes 16 minority (8 Black or African American, non-Hispanic/Latino; 2 American Indian or Alaska Native, non-Hispanic/Latino; 2 Asian, non-Hispanic/Latino; 4 Hispanic/Latino), 88 international. 164 applicants, 59% accepted. In 2010, 81 master's, 18 doctorates awarded. *Degree requirements:* For doctorate, thesis/dissertation. *Application deadline:* For fall admission, 4/1 for international students; for spring admission, 10/1 for international students. Applications are processed on a rolling basis. Application fee: $40 ($50 for international students). Electronic applications accepted. *Financial support:* In 2010–11, 14 fellowships with tuition reimbursements, 168 research assistantships, 8 teaching assistantships were awarded; career-related internships or fieldwork, Federal Work-Study, scholarships/grants, and unspecified assistantships also available. Support available to part-time students. Financial award application deadline: 4/1; financial award applicants required to submit FAFSA. *Unit head:* Dr. Michael E. Vayda, Dean, 479-575-2034, Fax: 479-575-7273, E-mail: mvayda@uark.edu. *Application contact:* Graduate Admissions, 479-575-6246, Fax: 479-575-5908, E-mail: gradinfo@uark.edu.

The University of British Columbia, Faculty of Land and Food Systems, Vancouver, BC V6T 1Z1, Canada. Offers M Sc, MFS, PhD. *Degree requirements:* For master's, thesis; for doctorate, comprehensive exam, thesis/dissertation. *Entrance requirements:* Additional exam requirements/recommendations for international students: Required—TOEFL (minimum score 577 paper-based; 233 computer-based; 90 iBT), IELTS (minimum score 6.5). Electronic applications accepted. Tuition charges are reported in Canadian dollars. *Expenses:* Tuition, area resident: Full-time $4179 Canadian dollars. International tuition: $7344 Canadian dollars full-time.

University of California, Davis, Graduate Studies, Graduate Group in International Agricultural Development, Davis, CA 95616. Offers MS. *Degree requirements:* For master's, comprehensive exam (for some programs), thesis (for some programs). *Entrance requirements:* For master's, GRE General Test, minimum GPA of 3.0. Additional exam requirements/recommendations for international students: Required—TOEFL (minimum score 550 paper-based; 213 computer-based). Electronic applications accepted. *Faculty research:* Aspects of agricultural, environmental and social sciences on agriculture and related issues in developing countries.

University of Connecticut, Graduate School, College of Agriculture and Natural Resources, Storrs, CT 06269. Offers MS, PhD. Terminal master's awarded for partial completion of doctoral program. *Degree requirements:* For master's, comprehensive exam; for doctorate, comprehensive exam, thesis/dissertation. *Entrance requirements:* For master's and doctorate, GRE General Test. Additional exam requirements/recommendations for international students: Required—TOEFL (minimum score 550 paper-based; 213 computer-based). Electronic applications accepted.

University of Delaware, College of Agriculture and Natural Resources, Newark, DE 19716. Offers MA, MS, PhD. Part-time programs available. *Degree requirements:* For master's, thesis; for doctorate, thesis/dissertation. *Entrance requirements:* For master's and doctorate, GRE General Test. Electronic applications accepted.

University of Florida, Graduate School, College of Agricultural and Life Sciences, Gainesville, FL 32611. Offers M Ag, MAB, MFAS, MFRC, MFYCS, MS, DPM, PhD, JD/MFRC, JD/MS, JD/PhD. Part-time programs available. *Faculty:* 346 full-time (93 women), 12 part-time/adjunct (4 women). *Students:* 904 full-time (447 women), 268 part-time (158 women); includes 25 Black or African American, non-Hispanic/Latino; 5 American Indian or Alaska Native, non-Hispanic/Latino; 40 Asian, non-Hispanic/Latino; 61 Hispanic/Latino, 387 international. Average age 30. 614 applicants, 43% accepted, 192 enrolled. In 2010, 217 master's, 129 doctorates awarded. *Degree requirements:* For master's, comprehensive exam (for some programs), thesis (for some programs); for doctorate, comprehensive exam, thesis/dissertation. *Entrance requirements:* For master's and doctorate, GRE General Test, minimum GPA of 3.0. Additional exam requirements/recommendations for international students: Required—TOEFL (minimum score 550 paper-based; 213 computer-based; 80 iBT), IELTS (minimum score 6). *Application deadline:* Applications are processed on a rolling basis. Application fee: $30. Electronic applications accepted. *Expenses:* Tuition, state resident: full-time $10,915.92. Tuition, nonresident: full-time $28,309. *Financial support:* In 2010–11, 744 students received support, including 155 fellowships with tuition reimbursements available, 515 research assistantships with tuition reimbursements available (averaging $17,173 per year), 74 teaching assistantships with tuition reimbursements available (averaging $17,409 per year); career-related internships or fieldwork, Federal Work-Study, institutionally sponsored loans, and unspecified assistantships also available. Support available to part-time students. Financial award application deadline: 2/1; financial award applicants required to submit FAFSA. *Faculty research:* Institute of Food and Agricultural Science: agriculture, human and natural resources, and the life sciences to enhance and sustain the quality of human life. Total annual research expenditures: $145.9 million. *Unit head:* Allen F. Wysocki, PhD, Interim Associate Dean, 352-392-1963, Fax: 352-392-8988, E-mail: wysocki@ufl.edu. *Application contact:* Jane E. Luzar, PhD, Associate Dean for Academic Programs, 352-392-2251, Fax: 352-392-8988, E-mail: ejluzar@ufl.edu.

University of Georgia, College of Agricultural and Environmental Sciences, Athens, GA 30602. Offers MA Ext, MADS, MAE, MAL, MCCS, MFT, MPPPM, MS, PhD. *Faculty:* 207 full-time (37 women), 18 part-time/adjunct (4 women). *Students:* 343 full-time (170 women), 84 part-time (31 women); includes 21 Black or African American, non-Hispanic/Latino; 9 Asian, non-Hispanic/Latino; 8 Hispanic/Latino; 2 Two or more races, non-Hispanic/Latino, 155 international. 386 applicants, 44% accepted, 104 enrolled. In 2010, 96 master's, 29 doctorates awarded. *Degree requirements:* For doctorate, thesis/dissertation. *Entrance requirements:* For master's and doctorate, GRE General Test. *Application deadline:* For fall admission, 7/1 priority date for domestic students; for spring admission, 11/15 for domestic students. Application fee: $50. Electronic applications accepted. *Expenses:* Tuition, state resident: full-time $7200; part-time $344 per credit hour. Tuition, nonresident: full-time $21,900; part-time $944 per credit hour. Tuition and fees vary according to course load and program. *Financial support:* Fellowships, research assistantships, teaching assistantships, career-related internships or fieldwork and unspecified assistantships available. *Unit head:* Dr. J. Scott Angle, Dean, 706-542-3924, Fax: 706-542-0803, E-mail: caesdean@uga.edu. *Application contact:* Krista Haynes, Director of Enrolled Student Services, 706-425-1789, Fax: 706-425-3094, E-mail: gradoff@uga.edu.

University of Guelph, Graduate Studies, Ontario Agricultural College, Guelph, ON N1G 2W1, Canada. Offers M Sc, MLA, PhD, Diploma, MA/M Sc. Part-time programs available. Postbaccalaureate distance learning degree programs offered (minimal on-campus study). *Degree requirements:* For doctorate, thesis/dissertation.

University of Hawaii at Manoa, Graduate Division, College of Tropical Agriculture and Human Resources, Honolulu, HI 96822. Offers MS, PhD. Part-time programs available. *Students:* 197 full-time (99 women), 54 part-time (26 women); includes 78 minority (1 Black or African American, non-Hispanic/Latino; 1 American Indian or Alaska Native, non-Hispanic/Latino; 44 Asian, non-Hispanic/Latino; 3 Hispanic/Latino; 13 Native Hawaiian or other Pacific Islander, non-Hispanic/Latino; 16 Two or more races, non-Hispanic/Latino), 90 international. Average age 34. 240 applicants, 57% accepted, 93 enrolled. In 2010, 30 master's, 10 doctorates awarded. *Entrance requirements:* Additional exam requirements/recommendations for international students: Required—TOEFL or IELTS. *Financial support:* In 2010–11, 12 students received support, including 37 fellowships, 129 research assistantships, 16 teaching assistantships; career-related internships or fieldwork, Federal Work-Study, institutionally sponsored loans, tuition waivers (full and partial), and unspecified assistantships also available. Total annual research expenditures: $11.7 million. *Unit head:* Sylvia Yuen, Interim Dean, 808-956-8234, Fax: 808-956-9105, E-mail: syuen@hawaii.edu. *Application contact:* Sylvia Yuen, Interim Dean, 808-956-8234, Fax: 808-956-9105, E-mail: syuen@hawaii.edu.

University of Illinois at Urbana–Champaign, Graduate College, College of Agricultural, Consumer and Environmental Sciences, Program in Agricultural Production, Champaign, IL 61820. Offers MS. Applications are only accepted for the fall semester. Part-time programs available. *Students:* 7 full-time (4 women); includes 1 Hispanic/Latino. 7 applicants, 71% accepted, 4 enrolled. *Degree requirements:* For master's, internship. *Entrance requirements:* For master's, GRE, minimum GPA of 3.0 for last 60 hours of undergraduate work and any graduate study. Additional exam requirements/recommendations for international students: Required—TOEFL (minimum score 590 paper-based; 243 computer-based). Application fee: $75 ($90 for international students). *Unit head:* Bryan White, Director, 217-333-1044. *Application contact:* Bryan White, Director, 217-333-1044.

University of Kentucky, Graduate School, College of Agriculture, Lexington, KY 40506-0032. Offers MS, MSFAM, MSFOR, PhD. Part-time programs available. Terminal master's awarded for partial completion of doctoral program. *Degree requirements:* For master's, comprehensive exam, thesis (for some programs); for doctorate, comprehensive exam, thesis/dissertation. *Entrance requirements:* For master's, GRE General Test, minimum undergraduate GPA of 2.75; for doctorate, GRE General Test, minimum undergraduate GPA of 2.75, graduate 3.0. Additional exam requirements/recommendations for international students: Required—TOEFL (minimum score 550 paper-based; 213 computer-based). Electronic applications accepted.

University of Lethbridge, School of Graduate Studies, Lethbridge, AB T1K 3M4, Canada. Offers accounting (MScM); addictions counseling (M Sc); agricultural biotechnology (M Sc); agricultural studies (M Sc, MA); anthropology (MA); archaeology (MA); art (MA, MFA); biochemistry (M Sc); biological sciences (M Sc); biomolecular science (PhD); biosystems and biodiversity (PhD); Canadian studies (MA); chemistry (M Sc); computer science (M Sc); computer science and geographical information science (M Sc); counseling psychology (M Ed); dramatic arts (MA); earth, space, and physical science (PhD); economics (MA); educational leadership (M Ed); English (MA); environmental science (M Sc); evolution and behavior (PhD); exercise science (M Sc); finance (MScM); French (MA); French/German (MA); French/Spanish (MA); general education (M Ed); general management (MScM); geography (M Sc, MA); German (MA); health science (M Sc); history (MA); human resource management and labour relations (MScM); individualized multidisciplinary (M Sc, MA); information systems (MScM); international management (MScM); kinesiology (M Sc, MA); management (M Sc, MA); marketing (MScM); mathematics (M Sc); music (M Mus, MA); Native American studies (MA); neuroscience (M Sc, PhD); new media (MA); nursing (M Sc); philosophy (MA); physics (M Sc); policy and strategy (MScM); political science (MA); psychology (M Sc, MA); religious studies (MA); social sciences (MA); sociology (MA); theatre and dramatic arts (MFA); theoretical and computational science (PhD); urban and regional studies (MA); women's studies (MA). Part-time and evening/weekend programs available. *Degree requirements:* For doctorate, comprehensive exam, thesis/dissertation. *Entrance requirements:* For master's, GMAT (M Sc in management), bachelor's degree in related field, minimum GPA of 3.0 during previous 20 graded semester courses, 2 years teaching or related experience (M Ed); for doctorate, master's degree, minimum graduate GPA of 3.5. Additional exam requirements/recommendations for international students: Required—TOEFL. *Faculty research:* Movement and brain plasticity, gibberellin physiology, photosynthesis, carbon cycling, molecular properties of main-group ring components.

University of Maine, Graduate School, College of Natural Sciences, Forestry, and Agriculture, Orono, ME 04469. Offers MF, MPS, MS, MWC, PhD, CAS. *Accreditation:* SAF (one or more programs are accredited). Part-time and evening/weekend programs available. *Faculty:* 152 full-time (54 women), 43 part-time/adjunct (26 women). *Students:* 259 full-time (145 women), 91 part-time (53 women); includes 10 minority (2 American Indian or Alaska Native, non-Hispanic/Latino; 6 Asian, non-Hispanic/Latino; 1 Hispanic/Latino; 1 Two or more races, non-Hispanic/Latino), 47 international. Average age 30. 456 applicants, 27% accepted, 98 enrolled. In 2010, 77 master's, 17 doctorates, 1 other advanced degree awarded. *Degree requirements:* For doctorate, thesis/dissertation. *Entrance requirements:* For master's and doctorate, GRE General Test. Additional exam requirements/recommendations for international students: Required—TOEFL. *Application deadline:* For fall admission, 2/1 priority date for domestic students. Applications are processed on a rolling basis. Application fee: $65. Electronic applications accepted. *Expenses:* Tuition, state resident: full-time $400. Tuition, nonresident: full-time $1050. *Financial support:* Career-related internships or fieldwork, Federal Work-Study, institutionally sponsored loans, scholarships/grants, tuition waivers (full and partial), and unspecified assistantships available. Support available to part-time students. Financial award application deadline: 3/1. *Unit head:* Dr. Edward Ashworth, Dean, 207-581-3206, Fax: 207-581-3207. *Application contact:* Scott G. Delcourt, Associate Dean of the Graduate School, 207-581-3291, Fax: 207-581-3232, E-mail: graduate@maine.edu.

University of Manitoba, Faculty of Graduate Studies, Faculty of Agricultural and Food Sciences, Winnipeg, MB R3T 2N2, Canada. Offers M Sc, PhD. *Degree requirements:* For master's, thesis or alternative; for doctorate, variable foreign language requirement, thesis/dissertation.

University of Maryland, College Park, Academic Affairs, College of Agriculture and Natural Resources, College Park, MD 20742. Offers DVM, MS, PhD. Part-time and evening/weekend programs available. *Faculty:* 320 full-time (139 women), 40 part-time/adjunct (21 women). *Students:* 338 full-time (211 women), 21 part-time (12 women); includes 9 Black or African

American, non-Hispanic/Latino; 21 Asian, non-Hispanic/Latino; 13 Hispanic/Latino; 1 Native Hawaiian or other Pacific Islander, non-Hispanic/Latino; 3 Two or more races, non-Hispanic/Latino, 95 international. 546 applicants, 26% accepted, 82 enrolled. In 2010, 28 first professional degrees, 27 master's, 23 doctorates awarded. *Degree requirements:* For doctorate, thesis/dissertation; for DVM, thesis/dissertation, oral exam, public seminar. *Entrance requirements:* For DVM, GRE General Test; for master's, minimum GPA of 3.0. Additional exam requirements/recommendations for international students: Required—TOEFL. *Application deadline:* For fall admission, 12/15 for domestic and international students; for spring admission, 6/1 for international students. Applications are processed on a rolling basis. Application fee: $75. Electronic applications accepted. *Expenses:* Tuition, area resident: Part-time $471 per credit hour. Tuition, state resident: part-time $471 per credit hour. Tuition, nonresident: part-time $1016 per credit hour. Required fees: $337 per term. *Financial support:* In 2010–11, 4 fellowships with full and partial tuition reimbursements (averaging $16,452 per year), 88 research assistantships with tuition reimbursements (averaging $17,447 per year), 84 teaching assistantships with tuition reimbursements (averaging $16,542 per year) were awarded; career-related internships or fieldwork, Federal Work-Study, and scholarships/grants also available. Support available to part-time students. Financial award applicants required to submit FAFSA. Total annual research expenditures: $36.8 million. *Unit head:* Dr. Cheng-i Wei, Dean, 301-405-2072, Fax: 301-314-9146, E-mail: wei@umd.edu. *Application contact:* Dr. Charles A. Caramello, Dean of Graduate School, 301-405-0358, Fax: 301-314-9305, E-mail: ccaramel@umd.edu.

University of Maryland Eastern Shore, Graduate Programs, Department of Agriculture, Princess Anne, MD 21853-1299. Offers food and agricultural sciences (MS); food science and technology (PhD). *Degree requirements:* For master's, comprehensive exam, thesis (for some programs), oral exam; for doctorate, comprehensive exam, thesis/dissertation. *Entrance requirements:* For master's, GRE, minimum GPA of 3.0. Additional exam requirements/recommendations for international students: Required—TOEFL (minimum score 213 computer-based; 80 iBT). Electronic applications accepted. *Faculty research:* Poultry and swine nutrition and management, soybean specialty products, farm management practices, aquaculture technology.

University of Minnesota, Twin Cities Campus, Graduate School, College of Food, Agricultural and Natural Resource Sciences, Saint Paul, MN 55108. Offers MS, PhD. Part-time programs available. *Faculty:* 713 full-time (172 women). *Students:* 480 full-time (253 women), 52 part-time (20 women); includes 64 minority (5 Black or African American, non-Hispanic/Latino; 1 American Indian or Alaska Native, non-Hispanic/Latino; 36 Asian, non-Hispanic/Latino; 16 Hispanic/Latino; 6 Two or more races, non-Hispanic/Latino), 152 international. Average age 30. 850 applicants, 29% accepted, 170 enrolled. In 2010, 71 master's, 43 doctorates awarded. Terminal master's awarded for partial completion of doctoral program. *Degree requirements:* For master's, comprehensive exam, thesis; for doctorate, comprehensive exam, thesis/dissertation. *Entrance requirements:* For master's and doctorate, GRE general test. Additional exam requirements/recommendations for international students: Required—TOEFL (minimum score 550 paper-based; 213 computer-based; 79 iBT). *Application deadline:* For fall admission, 12/15 priority date for domestic and international students; for spring admission, 10/15 for domestic and international students. Applications are processed on a rolling basis. Application fee: $75 ($95 for international students). Electronic applications accepted. *Financial support:* In 2010–11, fellowships with full tuition reimbursements (averaging $23,500 per year), research assistantships with full and partial tuition reimbursements (averaging $18,000 per year), teaching assistantships with full and partial tuition reimbursements (averaging $18,000 per year) were awarded; career-related internships or fieldwork, institutionally sponsored loans, scholarships/grants, health care benefits, tuition waivers (full), and unspecified assistantships also available. Support available to part-time students. Financial award application deadline: 12/15. Total annual research expenditures: $38.9 million. *Unit head:* Dr. F. Abel Ponce de Leon, Senior Associate Dean, 612-625-4772, Fax: 612-625-1260, E-mail: apl@umn.edu. *Application contact:* Lisa Wiley, Graduate Programs Coordinator, 612-624-2748, Fax: 612-625-1260, E-mail: lwiley@umn.edu.

University of Missouri, Graduate School, College of Agriculture, Food and Natural Resources, Columbia, MO 65211. Offers MS, PhD, Graduate Certificate, MD/PhD. Part-time programs available. Terminal master's awarded for partial completion of doctoral program. *Degree requirements:* For master's, thesis (for some programs); for doctorate, variable foreign language requirement, comprehensive exam (for some programs), thesis/dissertation. *Entrance requirements:* For master's and doctorate, GRE General Test, minimum GPA of 3.0. Additional exam requirements/recommendations for international students: Required—TOEFL (minimum score 500 paper-based; 173 computer-based; 61 iBT), IELTS (minimum score 5.5). Electronic applications accepted.

University of Nebraska–Lincoln, Graduate College, College of Agricultural Sciences and Natural Resources, Lincoln, NE 68588. Offers M Ag, MA, MBA, MS, PhD. *Degree requirements:* For doctorate, comprehensive exam, thesis/dissertation. *Entrance requirements:* Additional exam requirements/recommendations for international students: Required—TOEFL. Electronic applications accepted. *Faculty research:* Environmental sciences, animal sciences, human resources and family sciences, plant breeding and genetics, food and nutrition.

University of Nevada, Reno, Graduate School, College of Agriculture, Biotechnology and Natural Resources, Reno, NV 89557. Offers MS, PhD. Terminal master's awarded for partial completion of doctoral program. *Degree requirements:* For master's, thesis optional; for doctorate, thesis/dissertation. *Entrance requirements:* For master's, GRE General Test, minimum GPA of 2.75; for doctorate, GRE General Test, minimum GPA of 3.0. Additional exam requirements/recommendations for international students: Required—TOEFL (minimum score 500 paper-based; 173 computer-based; 61 iBT), IELTS (minimum score 6). Electronic applications accepted. *Expenses:* Tuition, state resident: full-time $2219; part-time $246 per credit. Tuition, nonresident: part-time $510 per credit. International tuition: $9009 full-time. Required fees: $59 per term. One-time fee: $101. Tuition and fees vary according to course load.

University of Puerto Rico, Mayagüez Campus, Graduate Studies, College of Agricultural Sciences, Mayagüez, PR 00681-9000. Offers MS. Part-time programs available. *Students:* 144 full-time (74 women), 14 part-time (3 women); includes 72 Hispanic/Latino, 8 international. 33 applicants, 76% accepted, 12 enrolled. In 2010, 14 master's awarded. *Degree requirements:* For master's, comprehensive exam, thesis. *Application deadline:* For fall admission, 2/15 for domestic and international students; for spring admission, 9/15 for domestic and international students. Applications are processed on a rolling basis. Application fee: $25. *Expenses:* Tuition, state resident: full-time $1188. Tuition, nonresident: full-time $1188. International tuition: $6126 full-time. Tuition and fees vary according to course level and course load. *Financial support:* In 2010–11, 60 research assistantships with tuition reimbursements (averaging $15,000 per year), 44 teaching assistantships with tuition reimbursements (averaging $8,500 per year) were awarded; career-related internships or fieldwork, Federal Work-Study, and institutionally sponsored loans also available. Total annual research expenditures: $459,210. *Unit head:* Prof. Aristides Armstrong, Associate Dean, 787-832-4040 Ext. 2181, E-mail: aristides.armstrong@upr.edu. *Application contact:* Carmen Figueroa, Student Affairs Official, 787-265-3809, Fax: 787-265-5489, E-mail: carmen.figueroa11@upr.edu.

University of Saskatchewan, College of Graduate Studies and Research, College of Agriculture, Saskatoon, SK S7N 5A2, Canada. Offers M Ag, M Sc, MA, PhD, Diploma, PGD. Part-time programs available. *Degree requirements:* For master's, thesis (for some programs); for doctorate, comprehensive exam (for some programs), thesis/dissertation. *Entrance requirements:* Additional exam requirements/recommendations for international students: Required—TOEFL (minimum score 80 iBT); Recommended—IELTS (minimum score 6.5).

University of South Africa, College of Agriculture and Environmental Sciences, Pretoria, South Africa. Offers agriculture (MS); consumer science (MCS); environmental management (MA, MS, PhD); environmental science (MA, MS, PhD); geography (MA, MS, PhD); horticulture (M Tech); human ecology (MHE); life sciences (MS); nature conservation (M Tech).

The University of Tennessee, Graduate School, College of Agricultural Sciences and Natural Resources, Knoxville, TN 37996. Offers MS, PhD. Part-time programs available. Postbaccalaureate distance learning degree programs offered (minimal on-campus study). *Degree requirements:* For master's, thesis (for some programs); for doctorate, thesis/dissertation. *Entrance requirements:* For master's and doctorate, minimum GPA of 2.7. Additional exam requirements/recommendations for international students: Required—TOEFL. Electronic applications accepted. *Expenses:* Tuition, state resident: full-time $7440; part-time $414 per credit hour. Tuition, nonresident: full-time $22,478; part-time $1250 per credit hour. Required fees: $922; $43 per credit hour. Tuition and fees vary according to program.

The University of Tennessee at Martin, Graduate Programs, College of Agriculture and Applied Sciences, Program in Agricultural and Natural Resources Management, Martin, TN 38238-1000. Offers MSANR. Part-time programs available. Postbaccalaureate distance learning degree programs offered (no on-campus study). *Faculty:* 26. *Students:* 37 (13 women); includes 3 Black or African American, non-Hispanic/Latino, 1 international. 18 applicants, 94% accepted, 12 enrolled. In 2010, 8 master's awarded. *Degree requirements:* For master's, comprehensive exam, thesis optional. *Entrance requirements:* For master's, GRE General Test, minimum GPA of 2.5. Additional exam requirements/recommendations for international students: Required—TOEFL (minimum score 525 paper-based; 197 computer-based; 71 iBT). *Application deadline:* For fall admission, 8/1 priority date for domestic students, 7/15 priority date for international students; for spring admission, 12/15 priority date for domestic students, 12/1 priority date for international students. Applications are processed on a rolling basis. Application fee: $30 ($130 for international students). Electronic applications accepted. *Expenses:* Tuition, state resident: full-time $7164; part-time $400 per credit hour. Tuition, nonresident: full-time $19,574; part-time $1090 per credit hour. Required fees: $1044; $60 per credit hour. *Financial support:* In 2010–11, 1 student received support, including 1 research assistantship with full tuition reimbursement available (averaging $7,920 per year); scholarships/grants and unspecified assistantships also available. Support available to part-time students. Financial award application deadline: 2/15; financial award applicants required to submit FAFSA. *Unit head:* Dr. Tim Burcham, Coordinator, 731-881-7275, Fax: 731-881-7968, E-mail: tburcham@utm.edu. *Application contact:* Linda S. Arant, Student Services Specialist, 731-881-7012, Fax: 731-881-7499, E-mail: larant@utm.edu.

University of Vermont, Graduate College, College of Agriculture and Life Sciences, Burlington, VT 05405. Offers MPA, MS, MSD, PhD, MD/MS, MD/PhD. Part-time programs available. *Students:* 146 (81 women); includes 1 Black or African American, non-Hispanic/Latino; 6 Asian, non-Hispanic/Latino; 1 Hispanic/Latino, 19 international. 206 applicants, 43% accepted, 32 enrolled. In 2010, 42 master's, 4 doctorates awarded. *Degree requirements:* For doctorate, one foreign language, thesis/dissertation. *Entrance requirements:* For master's and doctorate, GRE General Test. Additional exam requirements/recommendations for international students: Required—TOEFL (minimum score 550 paper-based; 213 computer-based; 80 iBT). Application fee: $40. Electronic applications accepted. *Expenses:* Tuition, state resident: part-time $537 per credit hour. Tuition, nonresident: part-time $1355 per credit hour. *Financial support:* Fellowships, research assistantships, teaching assistantships, career-related internships or fieldwork, Federal Work-Study, and tuition waivers (full and partial) available. Financial award application deadline: 3/1. *Unit head:* Dr. Thomas C. Vogelmann, Dean, 802-656-2980. *Application contact:* Dr. Thomas C. Vogelmann, Dean, 802-656-2980.

University of Wisconsin–Madison, Graduate School, College of Agricultural and Life Sciences, Madison, WI 53706-1380. Offers MA, MPS, MS, PhD. Part-time programs available. *Entrance requirements:* For master's and doctorate, GRE. Additional exam requirements/recommendations for international students: Required—TOEFL. Electronic applications accepted. *Expenses:* Tuition, state resident: full-time $9887.36; part-time $617.96 per credit. Tuition, nonresident: full-time $24,054; part-time $1503.40 per credit. Required fees: $67.63 per credit. Tuition and fees vary according to reciprocity agreements.

University of Wisconsin–River Falls, Outreach and Graduate Studies, College of Agriculture, Food, and Environmental Sciences, River Falls, WI 54022. Offers MS. Part-time programs available. *Degree requirements:* For master's, comprehensive exam, thesis (for some programs). *Entrance requirements:* For master's, minimum GPA of 2.75. Additional exam requirements/recommendations for international students: Required—TOEFL (minimum score 500 paper-based; 65 iBT), IELTS (minimum score 5.4). Electronic applications accepted.

University of Wyoming, College of Agriculture and Natural Resources, Laramie, WY 82070. Offers MA, MS, PhD. Part-time programs available. Terminal master's awarded for partial completion of doctoral program. *Degree requirements:* For doctorate, thesis/dissertation. *Entrance requirements:* For master's and doctorate, GRE General Test, minimum GPA of 3.0. Electronic applications accepted. *Faculty research:* Nutrition, molecular biology, animal science, plant science, entomology.

Utah State University, School of Graduate Studies, College of Agriculture, Logan, UT 84322. Offers MDA, MFMS, MS, PhD. Part-time programs available. Postbaccalaureate distance learning degree programs offered (minimal on-campus study). Terminal master's awarded for partial completion of doctoral program. *Degree requirements:* For doctorate, thesis/dissertation. *Entrance requirements:* For master's and doctorate, GRE General Test, minimum GPA of 3.0. Additional exam requirements/recommendations for international students: Required—TOEFL. *Faculty research:* Low-input agriculture, anti-viral chemotherapy, lactic culture, environmental biophysics and climate.

Virginia Polytechnic Institute and State University, Graduate School, College of Agriculture and Life Sciences, Department of Agriculture, Human and Natural Resources Information Technology, Blacksburg, VA 24061. Offers agricultural and life sciences (MS, MSLFS). *Students:* 45 full-time (24 women), 3 part-time (2 women); includes 7 Black or African American, non-Hispanic/Latino; 1 American Indian or Alaska Native, non-Hispanic/Latino, 1 international. Average age 36. 11 applicants, 73% accepted, 5 enrolled. In 2010, 7 master's awarded. *Degree requirements:* For master's, comprehensive exam (for some programs), thesis (for some programs). *Entrance requirements:* For master's, GRE. Additional exam requirements/recommendations for international students: Required—TOEFL (minimum score 550 paper-based; 213 computer-based). *Application deadline:* For fall admission, 7/1 for domestic and international students; for spring admission, 12/1 for domestic and international students. Applications are processed on a rolling basis. Application fee: $65. Electronic applications accepted. *Expenses:* Tuition, area resident: Full-time $9399; part-time $488 per credit hour. Tuition, state resident: full-time $9399; part-time $488 per credit hour. Tuition, nonresident: full-time $17,854; part-time $957.75 per credit hour. International tuition: $17,854 full-time. Required fees: $1534. Full-time tuition and fees vary according to program. *Financial support:* Career-related internships or fieldwork, Federal Work-Study, scholarships/grants, health care benefits, and unspecified assistantships available. *Unit head:* Dr. Roy C. Woods, UNIT HEAD, 540-231-6879, Fax: 540-231-3857, E-mail: rcwoods@vt.edu. *Application contact:* Belinda Carroll, Contact, 540-231-2443, Fax: 540-231-3857, E-mail: moth@vt.edu.

Virginia State University, School of Graduate Studies, Research, and Outreach, School of Agriculture, Petersburg, VA 23806-0001. Offers MS. *Expenses:* Tuition, state resident: full-time $5576; part-time $335 per credit hour. Tuition, nonresident: full-time $13,402; part-time $670 per credit hour.

Agricultural Sciences—General

Washington State University, Graduate School, College of Agricultural, Human, and Natural Resource Sciences, Department of Crop and Soil Sciences, Program in Agriculture, Pullman, WA 99164. Offers MS. *Faculty:* 25. *Students:* 2 full-time (1 woman), 16 part-time (9 women); includes 1 minority (American Indian or Alaska Native, non-Hispanic/Latino). Average age 34. 19 applicants, 26% accepted, 3 enrolled. In 2010, 12 master's awarded. *Degree requirements:* For master's, comprehensive exam (for some programs), thesis (for some programs), oral defense. *Entrance requirements:* For master's, transcripts of all college course work, three letters of reference, personal statement describing intent and interest area(s). Additional exam requirements/recommendations for international students: Required—TOEFL, IELTS. *Application deadline:* For fall admission, 1/10 for domestic and international students; for spring admission, 7/1 for domestic and international students. Application fee: $50. *Expenses:* Tuition, state resident: full-time $8552; part-time $443 per credit. Tuition, nonresident: full-time $21,650; part-time $1083 per credit. Required fees: $846. *Financial support:* In 2010–11, 1 fellowship (averaging $2,850 per year), research assistantships (averaging $18,204 per year), teaching assistantships (averaging $18,204 per year) were awarded. Total annual research expenditures: $6.2 million. *Unit head:* Dr. Richard Koenig, Interim Director, 509-335-2726, Fax: 509-335-8674, E-mail: richk@wsu.edu. *Application contact:* Graduate School Admissions, 800-GRADWSU, Fax: 509-335-1949, E-mail: gradsch@wsu.edu.

Western Kentucky University, Graduate Studies, Ogden College of Science and Engineering, Department of Agriculture, Bowling Green, KY 42101. Offers MA Ed, MS. Part-time and evening/weekend programs available. *Degree requirements:* For master's, comprehensive exam, thesis optional. *Entrance requirements:* For master's, GRE General Test, minimum GPA of 2.75. Additional exam requirements/recommendations for international students: Required—TOEFL (minimum score 555 paper-based; 213 computer-based; 79 iBT). *Faculty research:* Establishment of warm season grasses, heat composting, enrichment activities in agricultural education.

West Texas A&M University, College of Agriculture, Nursing, and Natural Sciences, Division of Agriculture, Canyon, TX 79016-0001. Offers agricultural business and economics (MS); agriculture (PhD); animal science (MS); plant science (MS). Part-time programs available. *Degree requirements:* For master's, comprehensive exam, thesis optional. *Entrance requirements:* For master's, GRE General Test. Additional exam requirements/recommendations for international students: Required—TOEFL (minimum score 550 paper-based). Electronic applications accepted.

West Virginia University, Davis College of Agriculture, Forestry and Consumer Sciences, Morgantown, WV 26506. Offers M Agr, MS, MSF, PhD. Part-time programs available. *Degree requirements:* For master's, thesis; for doctorate, thesis/dissertation. *Entrance requirements:* Additional exam requirements/recommendations for international students: Required—TOEFL. Electronic applications accepted. *Faculty research:* Reproductive physiology, soil and water quality, human nutrition, aquaculture, wildlife management.

Agronomy and Soil Sciences

Alabama Agricultural and Mechanical University, School of Graduate Studies, School of Agricultural and Environmental Sciences, Department of Plant and Soil Science, Huntsville, AL 35811. Offers animal sciences (MS); environmental science (MS); plant and soil science (PhD). Evening/weekend programs available. Terminal master's awarded for partial completion of doctoral program. *Degree requirements:* For master's, thesis; for doctorate, one foreign language, thesis/dissertation. *Entrance requirements:* For master's, GRE General Test, BS in agriculture; for doctorate, GRE General Test, master's degree. Additional exam requirements/recommendations for international students: Required—TOEFL (minimum score 500 paper-based; 173 computer-based; 61 iBT). Electronic applications accepted. *Faculty research:* Plant breeding, cytogenetics, crop production, soil chemistry and fertility, remote sensing.

Alcorn State University, School of Graduate Studies, School of Agriculture and Applied Science, Alcorn State, MS 39096-7500. Offers agricultural economics (MS Ag); agronomy (MS Ag); animal science (MS Ag). *Degree requirements:* For master's, thesis optional. *Faculty research:* Aquatic systems, dairy herd improvement, fruit production, alternative farming practices.

American University of Beirut, Graduate Programs, Faculty of Agricultural and Food Sciences, Beirut, Lebanon. Offers agricultural economics (MS); animal sciences (MS); ecosystem management (MSES); food technology (MS); irrigation (MS); mechanization (MS); nutrition (MS); plant protection (MS); plant science (MS); poultry science (MS); soils (MS). Part-time programs available. *Faculty:* 22 full-time (6 women). *Students:* 6 full-time (3 women), 86 part-time (77 women). Average age 24. 94 applicants, 60% accepted, 15 enrolled. In 2010, 28 master's awarded. *Degree requirements:* For master's, one foreign language, comprehensive exam, thesis (for some programs). *Entrance requirements:* Additional exam requirements/recommendations for international students: Required—TOEFL (minimum score 600 paper-based; 250 computer-based; 100 iBT), IELTS (minimum score 7.5). *Application deadline:* For fall admission, 4/30 for domestic and international students; for spring admission, 11/1 for domestic and international students. Applications are processed on a rolling basis. Application fee: $50. Electronic applications accepted. *Expenses:* Tuition: Full-time $12,294; part-time $683 per credit. Required fees: $499; $499 per credit. Tuition and fees vary according to course load and program. *Financial support:* In 2010–11, 18 research assistantships with partial tuition reimbursements (averaging $13,132 per year), 42 teaching assistantships with full and partial tuition reimbursements (averaging $1,000 per year) were awarded; scholarships/grants, health care benefits, and unspecified assistantships also available. Financial award application deadline: 2/2. *Faculty research:* Community and therapeutic nutrition; food safety and food microbiology; landscape planning, nature and rural heritage conservation; pathology, immunology and control of poultry and animal diseases; agricultural economics and development. Total annual research expenditures: $900,000. *Unit head:* Prof. Nahla Hwalla, Dean, 961-134-3002 Ext. 4400, Fax: 961-174-4460, E-mail: nahla@aub.edu.lb. *Application contact:* Dr. Salim Kanaan, Director, Admissions Office, 961-135-0000 Ext. 2594, Fax: 961-175-0775, E-mail: sk00@aub.edu.lb.

Auburn University, Graduate School, College of Agriculture, Department of Agronomy and Soils, Auburn University, AL 36849. Offers M Ag, MS, PhD. Part-time programs available. *Faculty:* 26 full-time (6 women). *Students:* 20 full-time (7 women), 21 part-time (5 women); includes 1 Asian, non-Hispanic/Latino, 20 international. Average age 28. 19 applicants, 47% accepted, 7 enrolled. In 2010, 11 master's, 4 doctorates awarded. *Degree requirements:* For master's, thesis (for some programs); for doctorate, thesis/dissertation. *Entrance requirements:* For master's and doctorate, GRE General Test. *Application deadline:* For fall admission, 7/7 for domestic students; for spring admission, 11/24 for domestic students. Applications are processed on a rolling basis. Application fee: $50 ($60 for international students). Electronic applications accepted. *Expenses:* Tuition, state resident: full-time $7002. Tuition, nonresident: full-time $21,898. International tuition: $22,116 full-time. Required fees: $892. Tuition and fees vary according to course load and program. *Financial support:* Research assistantships, teaching assistantships, Federal Work-Study available. Support available to part-time students. Financial award application deadline: 3/15; financial award applicants required to submit FAFSA. *Faculty research:* Plant breeding and genetics; weed science; crop production; soil fertility and plant nutrition; soil genesis, morphology, and classification. *Unit head:* Dr. Joseph T. Touchton, Head, 334-844-4100, E-mail: jtouchto@ag.auburn.edu. *Application contact:* Dr. George Flowers, Dean of the Graduate School, 334-844-2125.

Colorado State University, Graduate School, College of Agricultural Sciences, Department of Soil and Crop Sciences, Fort Collins, CO 80523-1170. Offers MS, PhD. Part-time programs available. *Faculty:* 20 full-time (4 women), 2 part-time/adjunct (0 women). *Students:* 23 full-time (8 women), 16 part-time (3 women); includes 2 minority (both Black or African American, non-Hispanic/Latino), 15 international. Average age 33. 12 applicants, 75% accepted, 7 enrolled. In 2010, 2 master's, 2 doctorates awarded. Terminal master's awarded for partial completion of doctoral program. *Degree requirements:* For master's, thesis; for doctorate, comprehensive exam, thesis/dissertation, student teaching. *Entrance requirements:* For master's, GRE, minimum GPA of 3.0, appropriate bachelor's degree, letters of recommendation, statement of purpose; for doctorate, GRE, minimum GPA of 3.0, appropriate master's degree, letters of recommendation. Additional exam requirements/recommendations for international students: Required—TOEFL (minimum score 550 paper-based; 213 computer-based; 80 iBT). *Application deadline:* For fall admission, 4/1 priority date for domestic students, 5/1 priority date for international students; for spring admission, 9/1 priority date for domestic students, 10/1 priority date for international students. Application fee: $50. Electronic applications accepted. *Expenses:* Tuition, state resident: full-time $7434; part-time $413 per credit. Tuition, nonresident: full-time $19,022; part-time $1057 per credit. Required fees: $1729; $88 per credit. *Financial support:* In 2010–11, 26 students received support, including 3 fellowships with full tuition reimbursements available (averaging $22,940 per year), 21 research assistantships with full tuition reimbursements available (averaging $17,231 per year), 2 teaching assistantships with full tuition reimbursements available (averaging $8,331 per year); scholarships/grants, unspecified assistantships, and fellowships also available. Financial award application deadline: 2/15; financial award applicants required to submit FAFSA. *Faculty research:* Water quality, soil fertility, soil/plant ecosystems, plant breeding and genetics, cropping systems. Total annual research expenditures: $3.6 million. *Unit head:* Dr. Gary A. Peterson, Head, 970-491-6501, Fax: 970-491-0564, E-mail: gary.peterson@colostate.edu. *Application contact:* Karen Allison, Graduate Contact, 970-491-6295, Fax: 970-491-0564, E-mail: karen.allison@colostate.edu.

Cornell University, Graduate School, Graduate Fields of Agriculture and Life Sciences, Field of Soil and Crop Sciences, Ithaca, NY 14853-0001. Offers agronomy (MS, PhD); environmental information science (MS, PhD); environmental management (MPS); field crop science (MS, PhD); soil science (MS, PhD). *Faculty:* 39 full-time (9 women). *Students:* 29 full-time (13 women); includes 6 Hispanic/Latino, 9 international. Average age 29. 45 applicants, 24% accepted, 7 enrolled. In 2010, 3 master's, 4 doctorates awarded. *Degree requirements:* For master's, thesis (MS); for doctorate, comprehensive exam, thesis/dissertation. *Entrance requirements:* For master's and doctorate, GRE General Test, 2 letters of recommendation. Additional exam requirements/recommendations for international students: Required—TOEFL (minimum score 550 paper-based; 213 computer-based; 77 iBT). *Application deadline:* For fall admission, 2/1 priority date for domestic students. Applications are processed on a rolling basis. Application fee: $70. Electronic applications accepted. *Expenses:* Tuition: Full-time $29,500. Required fees: $76. Tuition and fees vary according to degree level and program. *Financial support:* In 2010–11, 6 fellowships with full tuition reimbursements, 11 research assistantships with full tuition reimbursements, 6 teaching assistantships with full tuition reimbursements were awarded; institutionally sponsored loans, traineeships, health care benefits, tuition waivers (full and partial), and unspecified assistantships also available. *Faculty research:* Soil chemistry, physics and biology; crop physiology and management; environmental information science and modeling; international agriculture; weed science. *Unit head:* Director of Graduate Studies, 607-255-3267, Fax: 607-255-8615. *Application contact:* Graduate Field Assistant, 607-255-3267, Fax: 607-255-8615, E-mail: ljh4@cornell.edu.

Iowa State University of Science and Technology, Graduate College, College of Agriculture, Department of Agronomy, Ames, IA 50011. Offers agricultural meteorology (MS, PhD); agronomy (MS); crop production and physiology (MS, PhD); plant breeding (MS, PhD); soil science (MS, PhD). Postbaccalaureate distance learning degree programs offered (no on-campus study). *Faculty:* 67 full-time (10 women), 5 part-time/adjunct (1 woman). *Students:* 104 full-time (33 women), 142 part-time (42 women); includes 4 Black or African American, non-Hispanic/Latino; 5 Asian, non-Hispanic/Latino; 4 Hispanic/Latino, 51 international. 86 applicants, 63% accepted, 39 enrolled. In 2010, 29 master's, 3 doctorates awarded. *Degree requirements:* For master's, thesis or alternative; for doctorate, thesis/dissertation. *Entrance requirements:* Additional exam requirements/recommendations for international students: Recommended—TOEFL (minimum score 550 paper-based; 79 iBT), IELTS (minimum score 6.5). *Application deadline:* For fall admission, 4/15 priority date for domestic and international students; for spring admission, 10/1 priority date for domestic and international students. Applications are processed on a rolling basis. Application fee: $40 ($90 for international students). Electronic applications accepted. *Financial support:* In 2010–11, 67 research assistantships with full and partial tuition reimbursements (averaging $17,362 per year), 5 teaching assistantships with full and partial tuition reimbursements (averaging $14,270 per year) were awarded; fellowships, scholarships/grants, health care benefits, and unspecified assistantships also available. *Unit head:* Dr. Kendall Lamkey, Head, 515-294-7636, Fax: 515-294-3163. *Application contact:* Dr. Thomas E. Loynachan, Director of Graduate Education, 515-294-2999, E-mail: gradprograms@agron.iastate.edu.

Kansas State University, Graduate School, College of Agriculture, Department of Agronomy, Manhattan, KS 66506. Offers crop science (MS, PhD); range management (MS, PhD); soil science (MS, PhD); weed science (MS, PhD). Part-time programs available. Terminal master's awarded for partial completion of doctoral program. *Degree requirements:* For master's, thesis or alternative, oral exam; for doctorate, thesis/dissertation, preliminary exams. *Entrance requirements:* For master's, minimum GPA of 3.0 in BS; for doctorate, minimum GPA of 3.5 in master's program. Additional exam requirements/recommendations for international students: Required—TOEFL (minimum score 500 paper-based; 250 computer-based). Electronic applications accepted. *Faculty research:* Range and forage science, soil and environmental science, crop physiology, weed science, plant breeding and genetics.

Louisiana State University and Agricultural and Mechanical College, Graduate School, College of Agriculture, School of Plant, Environmental and Soil Science, Department of Agronomy and Environmental Management, Baton Rouge, LA 70803. Offers agronomy (MS, PhD). Part-time programs available. *Faculty:* 32 full-time (4 women). *Students:* 39 full-time (11 women), 5 part-time (1 woman); includes 1 Asian, non-Hispanic/Latino; 2 Hispanic/Latino; 1 Two or more races, non-Hispanic/Latino, 19 international. Average age 29. 27 applicants, 37% accepted, 4 enrolled. In 2010, 3 master's, 5 doctorates awarded. *Degree requirements:* For master's, thesis or alternative; for doctorate, thesis/dissertation. *Entrance requirements:* For master's and doctorate, GRE General Test, minimum GPA of 3.0. Additional exam requirements/

recommendations for international students: Required—TOEFL (minimum score 550 paper-based; 213 computer-based; 79 iBT) or IELTS (minimum score 6.5). *Application deadline:* For fall admission, 1/25 priority date for domestic students, 5/15 for international students; for spring admission, 10/15 for international students. Applications are processed on a rolling basis. Application fee: $50 ($70 for international students). Electronic applications accepted. *Financial support:* In 2010–11, 41 students received support, including 34 research assistantships with partial tuition reimbursements available (averaging $19,212 per year), 1 teaching assistantship with partial tuition reimbursement available (averaging $16,000 per year); fellowships, Federal Work-Study, scholarships/grants, tuition waivers (full), and unspecified assistantships also available. Support available to part-time students. Financial award applicants required to submit FAFSA. *Faculty research:* Crop production, resource management, environmental studies, soil science, plant genetics. Total annual research expenditures: $54,474. *Unit head:* Dr. Don LaBonte, Director, 225-578-2110, Fax: 225-578-1403, E-mail: dlabont@lsu.edu. *Application contact:* Dr. David Weindofr, Graduate Coordinator, 225-578-0396, Fax: 225-578-1403, E-mail: dweindorf@agcenter.lsu.edu.

McGill University, Faculty of Graduate and Postdoctoral Studies, Faculty of Agricultural and Environmental Sciences, Department of Bioresource Engineering, Montréal, QC H3A 2T5, Canada. Offers computer applications (M Sc, M Sc A, PhD); food engineering (M Sc, M Sc A, PhD); grain drying (M Sc, M Sc A, PhD); irrigation and drainage (M Sc, M Sc A, PhD); machinery (M Sc, M Sc A, PhD); pollution control (M Sc, M Sc A, PhD); post-harvest technology (M Sc, M Sc A, PhD); soil dynamics (M Sc, M Sc A, PhD); structure and environment (M Sc, M Sc A, PhD); vegetable and fruit storage (M Sc, M Sc A, PhD).

McGill University, Faculty of Graduate and Postdoctoral Studies, Faculty of Agricultural and Environmental Sciences, Department of Natural Resource Sciences, Montréal, QC H3A 2T5, Canada. Offers entomology (M Sc, PhD); environmental assessment (M Sc); forest science (M Sc, PhD); microbiology (M Sc, PhD); micrometeorology (M Sc, PhD); neotropical environment (M Sc, PhD); soil science (M Sc, PhD); wildlife biology (M Sc, PhD).

Michigan State University, The Graduate School, College of Agriculture and Natural Resources, Department of Crop and Soil Sciences, East Lansing, MI 48824. Offers crop and soil sciences (MS, PhD); crop and soil sciences-environmental toxicology (PhD); plant breeding and genetics-crop and soil sciences (MS); plant breeding, genetics and biotechnology-crop and soil sciences (PhD). *Entrance requirements:* Additional exam requirements/recommendations for international students: Required—TOEFL (minimum score 550 paper-based; 213 computer-based), Michigan State University ELT (minimum score 85), Michigan Michigan English Language Assessment Battery (minimum score 83). Electronic applications accepted.

Michigan State University, The Graduate School, College of Agriculture and Natural Resources, MSU-DOE Plant Research Laboratory, East Lansing, MI 48824. Offers biochemistry and molecular biology (PhD); cellular and molecular biology (PhD); crop and soil sciences (PhD); genetics (PhD); microbiology and molecular genetics (PhD); plant biology (PhD); plant physiology (PhD). Offered jointly with the Department of Energy. *Degree requirements:* For doctorate, comprehensive exam, thesis/dissertation, laboratory rotation, defense of dissertation. *Entrance requirements:* For doctorate, GRE General Test, acceptance into one of the affiliated department programs; 3 letters of recommendation; bachelor's degree or equivalent in life sciences, chemistry, biochemistry, or biophysics; research experience. Electronic applications accepted. *Faculty research:* Role of hormones in the regulation of plant development and physiology, molecular mechanisms associated with signal recognition, development and application of genetic methods and materials, protein routing and function.

Mississippi State University, College of Agriculture and Life Sciences, Department of Plant and Soil Sciences, Mississippi State, MS 39762. Offers agricultural sciences (PhD), including agronomy (MS, PhD), horticulture (MS, PhD), weed science (MS, PhD); agriculture (MS), including agronomy (MS, PhD), horticulture (MS, PhD), weed science (MS, PhD). *Faculty:* 31 full-time (1 woman), 1 part-time/adjunct (0 women). *Students:* 33 full-time (10 women), 22 part-time (7 women); includes 2 minority (both American Indian or Alaska Native, non-Hispanic/Latino), 18 international. Average age 31. 23 applicants, 39% accepted, 7 enrolled. In 2010, 11 master's, 6 doctorates awarded. *Degree requirements:* For master's, thesis, exit seminar describing thesis research; for doctorate, comprehensive exam, thesis/dissertation, two departmental seminars. *Entrance requirements:* For master's, GRE (weed science), minimum GPA of 2.75 (agronomy/horticulture), 3.0 (weed science); for doctorate, GRE (weed science), minimum GPA of 3.0 (agronomy/horticulture), 3.25 (weed science). Additional exam requirements/recommendations for international students: Required—TOEFL (minimum score 550 paper-based; 213 computer-based; 79 iBT); Recommended—IELTS (minimum score 6.5). *Application deadline:* For fall admission, 7/1 for domestic students, 5/1 for international students; for spring admission, 10/1 for domestic students, 9/1 for international students. Applications are processed on a rolling basis. Application fee: $40. Electronic applications accepted. *Expenses:* Tuition, state resident: full-time $2730.50; part-time $304 per credit hour. Tuition, nonresident: full-time $6901; part-time $767 per credit hour. *Financial support:* In 2010–11, 29 research assistantships (averaging $14,353 per year), 2 teaching assistantships (averaging $15,542 per year) were awarded; Federal Work-Study, institutionally sponsored loans, scholarships/grants, and unspecified assistantships also available. Financial award application deadline: 4/1; financial award applicants required to submit FAFSA. *Unit head:* Dr. Daniel Reynolds, Professor/Interim Department Head, 662-325-2311, Fax: 662-325-8742, E-mail: dreynolds@pss.msstate.edu. *Application contact:* Dr. William Kingery, Graduate Coordinator, 662-325-2748, Fax: 662-325-8742, E-mail: wkingery@pss.msstate.edu.

North Carolina Agricultural and Technical State University, Graduate School, School of Agriculture and Environmental Sciences, Department of Natural Resources and Environmental Design, Greensboro, NC 27411. Offers plant, soil and environmental science (MS). Part-time and evening/weekend programs available. *Degree requirements:* For master's, comprehensive exam, thesis optional, qualifying exam. *Entrance requirements:* For master's, GRE General Test, minimum GPA of 3.0. *Faculty research:* Soil parameters and compaction of forest site, controlled traffic effects on soil, improving soybean and vegetable crops.

North Carolina State University, Graduate School, College of Agriculture and Life Sciences, Department of Crop Science, Raleigh, NC 27695. Offers MS, PhD. Part-time programs available. Terminal master's awarded for partial completion of doctoral program. *Degree requirements:* For master's, thesis; for doctorate, thesis/dissertation. *Entrance requirements:* For master's and doctorate, GRE. Electronic applications accepted. *Faculty research:* Crop breeding and genetics, application of biotechnology to crop improvement, plant physiology, crop physiology and management, agroecology.

North Carolina State University, Graduate School, College of Agriculture and Life Sciences, Department of Soil Science, Raleigh, NC 27695. Offers MS, PhD. Part-time programs available. Postbaccalaureate distance learning degree programs offered. *Degree requirements:* For master's, thesis (for some programs); for doctorate, thesis/dissertation. *Entrance requirements:* For master's and doctorate, GRE, minimum GPA of 3.0. Additional exam requirements/recommendations for international students: Required—TOEFL (minimum score 75 iBT). Electronic applications accepted. *Faculty research:* Soil management, soil-environmental relations, chemical and physical properties of soils, nutrient and water management, land use.

North Dakota State University, College of Graduate and Interdisciplinary Studies, College of Agriculture, Food Systems, and Natural Resources, Department of Soil Science, Fargo, ND 58108. Offers environmental and conservation science (PhD); environmental conservation science (MS); natural resource management (MS, PhD); soil sciences (MS, PhD). Part-time programs available. *Faculty:* 8 full-time (1 woman), 6 part-time/adjunct (0 women). *Students:* 7 full-time (5 women), 1 part-time (0 women). Average age 23. 3 applicants, 67% accepted, 2 enrolled. In 2010, 2 master's, 1 doctorate awarded. *Degree requirements:* For master's, comprehensive exam, thesis, classroom teaching; for doctorate, comprehensive exam, thesis/dissertation, classroom teaching. *Entrance requirements:* Additional exam requirements/recommendations for international students: Required—TOEFL (minimum score 525 paper-based; 193 computer-based; 71 iBT). *Application deadline:* Applications are processed on a rolling basis. Application fee: $45 ($60 for international students). Electronic applications accepted. *Financial support:* In 2010–11, 7 research assistantships with full tuition reimbursements (averaging $14,300 per year) were awarded; fellowships, Federal Work-Study, institutionally sponsored loans, and scholarships/grants also available. Financial award application deadline: 3/15. *Faculty research:* Microclimate, nitrogen management, landscape studies, water quality, soil management. *Unit head:* Dr. Donald Kirby, Interim Chair, 701-231-8901, Fax: 701 231 7861. *Application contact:* Dr. Donald Kirby, Interim Chair, 701-231-8901, Fax: 701-231-7861.

Nova Scotia Agricultural College, Research and Graduate Studies, Truro, NS B2N 5E3, Canada. Offers agriculture (M Sc), including air quality, animal behavior, animal molecular genetics, animal nutrition, animal technology, aquaculture, botany, crop management, crop physiology, ecology, environmental microbiology, food science, horticulture, nutrient management, pest management, physiology, plant biotechnology, plant pathology, soil chemistry, soil fertility, waste management and composting, water quality. Program offered jointly with Dalhousie University. Part-time programs available. *Degree requirements:* For master's, thesis, ATC Exam Teaching Assistantship. *Entrance requirements:* For master's, honors B Sc, minimum GPA of 3.0. Additional exam requirements/recommendations for international students: Required—TOEFL (minimum score 580 paper-based; 237 computer-based; 92 iBT), IELTS, Michigan English Language Assessment Battery, CanTEST, CAEL. *Faculty research:* Bio-product development, organic agriculture, nutrient management, air and water quality, agricultural biotechnology.

The Ohio State University, Graduate School, College of Food, Agricultural, and Environmental Sciences, School of Environment and Natural Resources, Program in Soil Science, Columbus, OH 43210. Offers MS, PhD. *Faculty:* 17. *Students:* 2 full-time (1 woman), 3 part-time (2 women); includes 1 Hispanic/Latino, 1 international. Average age 30. In 2010, 1 master's, 1 doctorate awarded. *Degree requirements:* For doctorate, thesis/dissertation. *Entrance requirements:* For master's and doctorate, GRE General Test. Additional exam requirements/recommendations for international students: Required—TOEFL (minimum score 550 paper-based; 213 computer-based), IELTS (minimum score 7), or Michigan English Language Assessment Battery (minimum score 90). *Application deadline:* For fall admission, 8/15 priority date for domestic students, 7/1 priority date for international students; for winter admission, 12/1 priority date for domestic students, 11/1 priority date for international students; for spring admission, 3/1 priority date for domestic students, 2/1 priority date for international students. Applications are processed on a rolling basis. Application fee: $40 ($50 for international students). Electronic applications accepted. *Expenses:* Tuition, state resident: full-time $10,605. Tuition, nonresident: full-time $26,535. Tuition and fees vary according to course load and program. *Unit head:* Richard Dick, Graduate Studies Committee Chair, 614-263-3877, Fax: 614-292-7432, E-mail: dick.78@osu.edu. *Application contact:* 614-292-9444, Fax: 614-292-3895, E-mail: domestic.grad@osu.edu.

Oklahoma State University, College of Agricultural Science and Natural Resources, Department of Horticulture and Landscape Architecture, Stillwater, OK 74078. Offers agriculture (M Ag); crop science (PhD); environmental science (PhD); horticulture (MS); plant science (PhD). *Faculty:* 21 full-time (2 women), 1 (woman) part-time/adjunct. *Students:* 1 (woman) full-time, 16 part-time (8 women); includes 1 Black or African American, non-Hispanic/Latino; 1 American Indian or Alaska Native, non-Hispanic/Latino; 1 Hispanic/Latino, 9 international. Average age 30. 12 applicants, 33% accepted, 4 enrolled. In 2010, 3 master's awarded. *Degree requirements:* For master's, thesis (for some programs); for doctorate, comprehensive exam, thesis/dissertation. *Entrance requirements:* For master's and doctorate, GRE or GMAT. Additional exam requirements/recommendations for international students: Required—TOEFL (minimum score 550 paper-based; 79 iBT). *Application deadline:* For fall admission, 3/1 priority date for international students; for spring admission, 8/1 priority date for international students. Applications are processed on a rolling basis. Application fee: $40 ($75 for international students). Electronic applications accepted. *Expenses:* Tuition, state resident: full-time $3716; part-time $154.85 per credit hour. Tuition, nonresident: full-time $14,892; part-time $621 per credit hour. Required fees: $2044; $85.20 per credit hour. One-time fee: $50. Tuition and fees vary according to course load and campus/location. *Financial support:* In 2010–11, 14 research assistantships (averaging $14,037 per year) were awarded; career-related internships or fieldwork, Federal Work-Study, scholarships/grants, health care benefits, tuition waivers (partial), and unspecified assistantships also available. Support available to part-time students. Financial award application deadline: 3/1; financial award applicants required to submit FAFSA. *Faculty research:* Stress and postharvest physiology; water utilization and runoff; IPM systems and nursery, turf, floriculture, vegetable, net and fruit produces and natural resources, food extraction, and processing; public garden management. *Unit head:* Dr. Dale Maronek, Head, 405-744-5414, Fax: 405-744-9709. *Application contact:* Dr. Gordon Emslie, Dean, 405-744-6368, Fax: 405-744-0355, E-mail: grad-i@okstate.edu.

Oklahoma State University, College of Agricultural Science and Natural Resources, Department of Plant and Soil Sciences, Stillwater, OK 74078. Offers crop science (PhD); environmental science (PhD); plant and soil sciences (MS); plant science (PhD); soil science (M Ag, PhD). *Faculty:* 30 full-time (4 women), 4 part-time/adjunct (1 woman). *Students:* 20 full-time (6 women), 42 part-time (19 women); includes 1 Black or African American, non-Hispanic/Latino; 1 American Indian or Alaska Native, non-Hispanic/Latino; 1 Asian, non-Hispanic/Latino, 31 international. Average age 28. 48 applicants, 33% accepted, 11 enrolled. In 2010, 11 master's, 1 doctorate awarded. *Degree requirements:* For master's, thesis; for doctorate, comprehensive exam, thesis/dissertation. *Entrance requirements:* For master's and doctorate, GRE or GMAT. Additional exam requirements/recommendations for international students: Required—TOEFL (minimum score 550 paper-based; 79 iBT). *Application deadline:* For fall admission, 3/1 priority date for international students; for spring admission, 8/1 priority date for international students. Applications are processed on a rolling basis. Application fee: $40 ($75 for international students). Electronic applications accepted. *Expenses:* Tuition, state resident: full-time $3716; part-time $154.85 per credit hour. Tuition, nonresident: full-time $14,892; part-time $621 per credit hour. Required fees: $2044; $85.20 per credit hour. One-time fee: $50. Tuition and fees vary according to course load and campus/location. *Financial support:* In 2010–11, 48 research assistantships (averaging $14,676 per year) were awarded; career-related internships or fieldwork, Federal Work-Study, scholarships/grants, health care benefits, tuition waivers (partial), and unspecified assistantships also available. Support available to part-time students. Financial award application deadline: 3/1; financial award applicants required to submit FAFSA. *Faculty research:* Crop science, weed science, rangeland ecology and management, biotechnology, breeding and genetics. *Unit head:* Dr. David R. Porter, Head, 405-744-6130, Fax: 405-744-5269. *Application contact:* Dr. Gordon Emslie, Dean, 405-744-6368, Fax: 405-744-0355, E-mail: grad-i@okstate.edu.

Oregon State University, Graduate School, College of Agricultural Sciences, Department of Crop and Soil Science, Program in Crop Science, Corvallis, OR 97331. Offers M Agr, MAIS, MS, PhD. Part-time programs available. *Degree requirements:* For master's, thesis (for some programs); for doctorate, variable foreign language requirement, thesis/dissertation. *Entrance requirements:* For master's and doctorate, GRE, minimum GPA of 3.0 in last 90 hours of course work. Additional exam requirements/recommendations for international students: Required—TOEFL. *Faculty research:* Cereal and new crops breeding and genetics; weed science; seed technology and production; potato, new crops, and general crop production; plant physiology.

Agronomy and Soil Sciences

Oregon State University, Graduate School, College of Agricultural Sciences, Department of Crop and Soil Science, Program in Soil Science, Corvallis, OR 97331. Offers M Agr, MAIS, MS, PhD. Part-time programs available. *Degree requirements:* For master's, thesis (for some programs); for doctorate, variable foreign language requirement, thesis/dissertation. *Entrance requirements:* For master's and doctorate, GRE, minimum GPA of 3.0 in last 90 hours of course work. Additional exam requirements/recommendations for international students: Required—TOEFL. *Faculty research:* Soil physics, chemistry, biology, fertility, and genesis.

Penn State University Park, Graduate School, College of Agricultural Sciences, Department of Crop and Soil Sciences, State College, University Park, PA 16802-1503. Offers MS, PhD.

Prairie View A&M University, College of Agriculture and Human Sciences, Prairie View, TX 77446-0519. Offers agricultural economics (MS); animal sciences (MS); interdisciplinary human sciences (MS); soil science (MS). Part-time and evening/weekend programs available. *Faculty:* 11 full-time (2 women). *Students:* 47 full-time (33 women), 34 part-time (26 women); includes 62 Black or African American, non-Hispanic/Latino; 2 Asian, non-Hispanic/Latino; 2 Hispanic/Latino, 5 international. Average age 30. 147 applicants, 100% accepted. In 2010, 21 master's awarded. *Degree requirements:* For master's, comprehensive exam, thesis (for some programs), field placement. *Entrance requirements:* For master's, GRE General Test, minimum GPA of 2.45. Additional exam requirements/recommendations for international students: Required—TOEFL (minimum score 550 paper-based). *Application deadline:* For fall admission, 6/1 for domestic and international students; for spring admission, 10/1 for domestic and international students. Applications are processed on a rolling basis. Application fee: $50. *Expenses:* Tuition, state resident: full-time $3586.14; part-time $119.06 per credit hour. Tuition, nonresident: part-time $511.23 per credit hour. *Financial support:* In 2010–11, 57 students received support, including 8 fellowships with tuition reimbursements available (averaging $12,000 per year), 10 research assistantships with tuition reimbursements available (averaging $15,000 per year); career-related internships or fieldwork, Federal Work-Study, institutionally sponsored loans, scholarships/grants, tuition waivers (partial), and unspecified assistantships also available. Support available to part-time students. Financial award application deadline: 4/1; financial award applicants required to submit FAFSA. *Faculty research:* Domestic violence prevention, water quality, food growth regulators, wetland dynamics, biochemistry, obesity and nutrition, family therapy. Total annual research expenditures: $4 million. *Unit head:* Dr. Freddie Richards, Dean, 936-261-2528, Fax: 936-261-5143, E-mail: flrichards@pvamu.edu. *Application contact:* Dr. Richard W. Griffin, Interim Department Head, 936-261-5019, Fax: 936-261-5148, E-mail: rwgriffin@pvamu.edu.

Purdue University, Graduate School, College of Agriculture, Department of Agronomy, West Lafayette, IN 47907. Offers MS, PhD. Part-time programs available. *Degree requirements:* For doctorate, thesis/dissertation. *Entrance requirements:* For master's and doctorate, GRE General Test. Electronic applications accepted. *Faculty research:* Plant genetics and breeding, crop physiology and ecology, agricultural meteorology, soil microbiology.

South Dakota State University, Graduate School, College of Agriculture and Biological Sciences, Department of Plant Science, Brookings, SD 57007. Offers agronomy (PhD); biological sciences (PhD); plant science (MS). *Degree requirements:* For master's, thesis (for some programs), oral exam; for doctorate, comprehensive exam, thesis/dissertation, preliminary oral and written exams. *Entrance requirements:* Additional exam requirements/recommendations for international students: Required—TOEFL (minimum score 560 paper-based; 220 computer-based; 83 iBT).

Southern Illinois University Carbondale, Graduate School, College of Agriculture, Department of Plant, Soil, and General Agriculture, Carbondale, IL 62901-4701. Offers horticultural science (MS); plant and soil science (MS). *Degree requirements:* For master's, thesis. *Entrance requirements:* For master's, minimum GPA of 2.7. Additional exam requirements/recommendations for international students: Required—TOEFL. *Faculty research:* Herbicides, fertilizers, agriculture education, landscape design, plant breeding.

Texas A&M University, College of Agriculture and Life Sciences, Department of Soil and Crop Sciences, College Station, TX 77843. Offers agronomy (M Agr, MS, PhD); food science and technology (MS, PhD); genetics (PhD); molecular and environmental plant sciences (MS, PhD); plant breeding (MS, PhD); soil science (MS, PhD). *Faculty:* 36. *Students:* 94 full-time (35 women), 30 part-time (7 women); includes 14 minority (3 Black or African American, non-Hispanic/Latino; 1 American Indian or Alaska Native, non-Hispanic/Latino; 3 Asian, non-Hispanic/Latino; 7 Hispanic/Latino), 36 international. Average age 26. In 2010, 11 master's, 3 doctorates awarded. *Degree requirements:* For master's, thesis; for doctorate, thesis/dissertation. *Entrance requirements:* For master's and doctorate, GRE General Test. Additional exam requirements/recommendations for international students: Required—TOEFL. *Application deadline:* For fall admission, 3/1 priority date for domestic students; for spring admission, 8/1 for domestic students. Applications are processed on a rolling basis. Application fee: $50 ($75 for international students). *Financial support:* In 2010–11, fellowships (averaging $16,000 per year), research assistantships with partial tuition reimbursements (averaging $15,000 per year) were awarded; career-related internships or fieldwork, Federal Work-Study, and institutionally sponsored loans also available. *Faculty research:* Soil and crop management, turfgrass science, weed science, cereal chemistry, food protein chemistry. *Unit head:* Dr. David D. Baltensperger, Department Head, 979-845-3001, E-mail: dbaltensperger@ag.tamu.edu. *Application contact:* Dr. David D. Baltensperger, Department Head, 979-845-3001, E-mail: dbaltensperger@ag.tamu.edu.

Texas A&M University–Kingsville, College of Graduate Studies, College of Agriculture and Home Economics, Program in Plant and Soil Sciences, Kingsville, TX 78363. Offers MS, PhD. *Degree requirements:* For master's, comprehensive exam, thesis or alternative. *Entrance requirements:* For master's, GRE General Test, minimum GPA of 3.0. Additional exam requirements/recommendations for international students: Required—TOEFL.

Texas Tech University, Graduate School, College of Agricultural Sciences and Natural Resources, Department of Plant and Soil Science, Lubbock, TX 79409. Offers crop science (MS); horticulture (MS); plant and soil science (PhD); plant protection (MS); soil science (MS); JD/MS. Part-time programs available. Postbaccalaureate distance learning degree programs offered (no on-campus study). *Faculty:* 14 full-time (3 women), 6 part-time/adjunct (0 women). *Students:* 57 full-time (23 women), 42 part-time (20 women); includes 3 Black or African American, non-Hispanic/Latino; 1 Asian, non-Hispanic/Latino; 4 Hispanic/Latino, 31 international. Average age 30. 64 applicants, 52% accepted, 22 enrolled. In 2010, 13 master's, 7 doctorates awarded. *Degree requirements:* For master's, thesis or alternative; for doctorate, thesis/dissertation. *Entrance requirements:* For master's and doctorate, GRE General Test, formal approval from departmental committee. Additional exam requirements/recommendations for international students: Required—TOEFL (minimum score 550 paper-based; 213 computer-based; 79 iBT). *Application deadline:* For fall admission, 6/1 priority date for domestic students, 1/15 priority date for international students; for spring admission, 9/1 priority date for domestic students, 6/15 priority date for international students. Applications are processed on a rolling basis. Application fee: $50 ($75 for international students). Electronic applications accepted. *Expenses:* Tuition, state resident: full-time $5495.76; part-time $228.99 per credit hour. Tuition, nonresident: full-time $12,936; part-time $538.99 per credit hour. Required fees: $2674; $36 per credit hour. $905 per semester. *Financial support:* In 2010–11, 55 students received support, including 18 research assistantships with partial tuition reimbursements available (averaging $3,594 per year), 2 teaching assistantships with partial tuition reimbursements available (averaging $5,398 per year). Financial award application deadline: 4/15; financial award applicants required to submit FAFSA. *Faculty research:* Molecular and cellular biology of plant stress, physiology/genetics of crop production in semiarid conditions, agricultural bioterrorism, improvement of native plants, soil science and management. Total annual research expenditures: $4.9 million. *Unit head:* Dr. Richard Zartman, Chair, 806-742-2838, Fax: 806-742-0775, E-mail: richard.zartman@ttu.edu. *Application contact:* Dr. Eric Hequet, Graduate Adviser, 806-742-2837, Fax: 806-742-0775, E-mail: eric.hequet@ttu.edu.

Tuskegee University, Graduate Programs, College of Agricultural, Environmental and Natural Sciences, Department of Agricultural Sciences, Program in Plant and Soil Sciences, Tuskegee, AL 36088. Offers MS. *Faculty:* 13 full-time (1 woman), 2 part-time/adjunct (1 woman). *Students:* 2 full-time (both women), 2 part-time (both women); includes 3 Black or African American, non-Hispanic/Latino, 1 international. Average age 30. In 2010, 6 master's awarded. *Degree requirements:* For master's, thesis. *Entrance requirements:* For master's, GRE General Test. Additional exam requirements/recommendations for international students: Required—TOEFL (minimum score 500 paper-based; 69 computer-based). *Application deadline:* For fall admission, 7/15 for domestic students. Applications are processed on a rolling basis. Application fee: $25 ($35 for international students). *Expenses:* Tuition: Full-time $16,100; part-time $665 per credit hour. Required fees: $650. *Financial support:* Application deadline: 4/15. *Application contact:* Dr. Robert L. Laney, Vice President/Director Admissions and Enrollment Management, 334-727-8580, Fax: 334-727-5750, E-mail: planey@tuskegee.edu.

Université Laval, Faculty of Agricultural and Food Sciences, Department of Soils and Agricultural Engineering, Programs in Soils and Environment Science, Québec, QC G1K 7P4, Canada. Offers environmental technology (M Sc); soils and environment science (M Sc, PhD). Terminal master's awarded for partial completion of doctoral program. *Degree requirements:* For master's, thesis (for some programs); for doctorate, comprehensive exam, thesis/dissertation. *Entrance requirements:* For master's and doctorate, knowledge of French and English. Electronic applications accepted.

Université Laval, Faculty of Forestry and Geomatics, Program in Agroforestry, Québec, QC G1K 7P4, Canada. Offers M Sc. *Degree requirements:* For master's, thesis (for some programs). *Entrance requirements:* For master's, English exam (comprehension of English), knowledge of French, knowledge of a third language. Electronic applications accepted.

University of Alberta, Faculty of Graduate Studies and Research, Department of Renewable Resources, Edmonton, AB T6G 2E1, Canada. Offers agroforestry (M Ag, M Sc, MF); conservation biology (M Sc, PhD); forest biology and management (M Sc, PhD); land reclamation and remediation (M Sc, PhD); protected areas and wildlands management (M Sc, PhD); soil science (M Ag, M Sc, PhD); water and land resources (M Ag, M Sc, PhD); wildlife ecology and management (M Sc, PhD); MBA/M Ag; MBA/MF. Part-time programs available. *Degree requirements:* For master's, thesis (for some programs); for doctorate, comprehensive exam, thesis/dissertation. *Entrance requirements:* For master's, minimum 2 years of relevant professional experiences, minimum GPA of 3.0; for doctorate, minimum GPA of 3.0. Additional exam requirements/recommendations for international students: Required—TOEFL (minimum score 550 paper-based; 213 computer-based). Electronic applications accepted. *Faculty research:* Natural and managed landscapes.

The University of Arizona, College of Agriculture and Life Sciences, Department of Soil, Water and Environmental Science, Tucson, AZ 85721. Offers MS, PhD. *Faculty:* 10 full-time (2 women). *Students:* 57 full-time (40 women), 6 part-time (3 women); includes 2 Black or African American, non-Hispanic/Latino; 1 American Indian or Alaska Native, non-Hispanic/Latino; 1 Asian, non-Hispanic/Latino; 11 Hispanic/Latino; 4 Two or more races, non-Hispanic/Latino, 18 international. Average age 33. 37 applicants, 54% accepted, 13 enrolled. In 2010, 12 master's, 6 doctorates awarded. *Degree requirements:* For master's, thesis; for doctorate, comprehensive exam, thesis/dissertation. *Entrance requirements:* For master's, GRE (recommended), minimum GPA of 3.0, letter of interest, 3 letters of recommendation; for doctorate, GRE (recommended), MS, minimum GPA of 3.0, letter of interest, 3 letters of recommendation. Additional exam requirements/recommendations for international students: Required—TOEFL (minimum score 550 paper-based; 213 computer-based; 80 iBT). *Application deadline:* For fall admission, 6/1 for domestic students, 12/1 for international students; for spring admission, 10/1 for domestic students, 6/1 for international students. Applications are processed on a rolling basis. Application fee: $75. *Expenses:* Tuition, state resident: full-time $7692. *Financial support:* In 2010–11, 14 students received support, including 32 research assistantships with full and partial tuition reimbursements available (averaging $18,538 per year), 4 teaching assistantships with full and partial tuition reimbursements available (averaging $18,275 per year); fellowships, Federal Work-Study, institutionally sponsored loans, scholarships/grants, health care benefits, tuition waivers (full and partial), and unspecified assistantships also available. Financial award application deadline: 5/1. *Faculty research:* Plant production, environmental microbiology, contaminant flow and transport, aquaculture. Total annual research expenditures: $3.6 million. *Unit head:* Dr. Jeffery C. Silvertooth, Head, 520-621-7228, Fax: 520-621-1647, E-mail: silver@ag.arizona.edu. *Application contact:* Alicia Velasquez, 520-621-1606, Fax: 520-621-1647, E-mail: avelasqu@ag.arizona.edu.

University of Arkansas, Graduate School, Dale Bumpers College of Agricultural, Food and Life Sciences, Department of Crop, Soil and Environmental Sciences, Fayetteville, AR 72701-1201. Offers agronomy (MS, PhD). *Students:* 12 full-time (1 woman), 30 part-time (10 women), 19 international. 14 applicants, 64% accepted. In 2010, 18 master's, 5 doctorates awarded. *Degree requirements:* For master's, thesis optional; for doctorate, variable foreign language requirement, thesis/dissertation. *Application deadline:* For fall admission, 4/1 for international students; for spring admission, 10/1 for international students. Applications are processed on a rolling basis. Application fee: $40 ($50 for international students). Electronic applications accepted. *Financial support:* In 2010–11, 33 research assistantships were awarded; fellowships with tuition reimbursements, teaching assistantships, career-related internships or fieldwork and Federal Work-Study also available. Support available to part-time students. Financial award application deadline: 4/1; financial award applicants required to submit FAFSA. *Unit head:* Dr. Robert Bacon, Interim Departmental Chairperson, 479-575-2347, Fax: 479-575-7465, E-mail: rbacon@uark.edu. *Application contact:* Dr. Kristofor Brye, Graduate Coordinator, 479-575-5742, E-mail: kbrye@uark.edu.

The University of British Columbia, Faculty of Land and Food Systems, Program in Soil Science, Vancouver, BC V6T 1Z1, Canada. Offers M Sc, PhD. *Degree requirements:* For master's, thesis; for doctorate, comprehensive exam, thesis/dissertation. *Entrance requirements:* Additional exam requirements/recommendations for international students: Required—TOEFL (minimum score 577 paper-based; 233 computer-based; 90 iBT), IELTS (minimum score 6.5). Electronic applications accepted. Tuition charges are reported in Canadian dollars. *Expenses:* Tuition, area resident: Full-time $4179 Canadian dollars. International tuition: $7344 Canadian dollars full-time. *Faculty research:* Soil and water conservation, land use, land use and land classification, soil physics, soil chemistry and mineralogy.

University of California, Davis, Graduate Studies, Graduate Group in Horticulture and Agronomy, Davis, CA 95616. Offers MS. *Degree requirements:* For master's, comprehensive exam (for some programs), thesis (for some programs). *Entrance requirements:* For master's, GRE General Test. Additional exam requirements/recommendations for international students: Required—TOEFL (minimum score 550 paper-based; 213 computer-based). Electronic applications accepted. *Faculty research:* Postharvest physiology, mineral nutrition, crop improvement, plant growth and development.

University of California, Davis, Graduate Studies, Graduate Group in Soils and Biogeochemistry, Davis, CA 95616. Offers MS, PhD. Terminal master's awarded for partial completion of doctoral program. *Degree requirements:* For master's, comprehensive exam (for some programs), thesis (for some programs); for doctorate, thesis/dissertation. *Entrance requirements:* For master's, minimum GPA of 3.3; for doctorate, GRE, minimum GPA of 3.3. Additional exam requirements/recommendations for international students: Required—TOEFL (minimum score

550 paper-based; 213 computer-based). Electronic applications accepted. *Faculty research:* Rhizosphere ecology, soil transport processes, biogeochemical cycling, sustainable agriculture.

University of California, Riverside, Graduate Division, Program in Soil and Water Sciences, Riverside, CA 92521-0102. Offers MS, PhD. *Faculty:* 27 full-time (4 women). *Students:* 17 full-time (10 women). Average age 29. 63 applicants, 19% accepted, 9 enrolled. In 2010, 4 master's awarded. *Entrance requirements:* For master's and doctorate, minimum GPA of 3.2. Additional exam requirements/recommendations for international students: Required—TOEFL (minimum score 550 paper-based; 213 computer-based; 80 iBT). *Application deadline:* For fall admission, 5/1 for domestic students, 2/1 for international students; for winter admission, 9/1 for domestic students, 7/1 for international students; for spring admission, 12/1 for domestic students, 10/1 for international students. Application fee: $60 ($75 for international students). Electronic applications accepted. *Financial support:* In 2010–11, fellowships with tuition reimbursements (averaging $12,000 per year), research assistantships with tuition reimbursements (averaging $18,000 per year) were awarded. *Unit head:* Dr. Jay Gan, Chair, 951-827-2712, Fax: 951-827-3993. *Application contact:* Mari Ridgeway, Program Assistant, 951-827-5103, Fax: 951-827-3993, E-mail: soilwater@ucr.edu.

University of Connecticut, Graduate School, College of Agriculture and Natural Resources, Department of Plant Science, Storrs, CT 06269. Offers plant and soil sciences (MS, PhD). Terminal master's awarded for partial completion of doctoral program. *Degree requirements:* For master's, comprehensive exam; for doctorate, thesis/dissertation. *Entrance requirements:* For master's and doctorate, GRE General Test, GRE Subject Test. Additional exam requirements/recommendations for international students: Required—TOEFL (minimum score 550 paper-based; 213 computer-based). Electronic applications accepted.

University of Delaware, College of Agriculture and Natural Resources, Department of Plant and Soil Sciences, Newark, DE 19716. Offers MS, PhD. Part-time programs available. Terminal master's awarded for partial completion of doctoral program. *Degree requirements:* For master's, thesis; for doctorate, thesis/dissertation. *Entrance requirements:* For master's and doctorate, GRE General Test. Additional exam requirements/recommendations for international students: Required—TOEFL (minimum score 550 paper-based; 213 computer-based). Electronic applications accepted. *Faculty research:* Soil chemistry, plant and cell tissue culture, plant breeding and genetics, soil physics, soil biochemistry, plant molecular biology, soil microbiology.

University of Florida, Graduate School, College of Agricultural and Life Sciences, Department of Agronomy, Gainesville, FL 32611. Offers M Ag, MS, PhD. Part-time programs available. *Faculty:* 15 full-time (4 women). *Students:* 35 full-time (13 women), 2 part-time (0 women); includes 1 Asian, non-Hispanic/Latino; 1 Hispanic/Latino, 20 international. Average age 28. 11 applicants, 36% accepted, 4 enrolled. In 2010, 6 master's, 4 doctorates awarded. Terminal master's awarded for partial completion of doctoral program. *Degree requirements:* For master's, thesis (for some programs); for doctorate, comprehensive exam, thesis/dissertation (for some programs). *Entrance requirements:* For master's and doctorate, GRE General Test, minimum GPA of 3.0. Additional exam requirements/recommendations for international students: Required—TOEFL (minimum score 550 paper-based; 213 computer-based; 80 iBT), IELTS (minimum score 6). *Application deadline:* For fall admission, 6/1 priority date for domestic students, 5/1 for international students; for spring admission, 9/1 for domestic students, 8/1 for international students. Applications are processed on a rolling basis. Application fee: $30. Electronic applications accepted. *Expenses:* Tuition, state resident: full-time $10,915.92. Tuition, nonresident: full-time $28,309. *Financial support:* In 2010–11, 34 students received support, including 5 fellowships, 29 research assistantships (averaging $17,570 per year); career-related internships or fieldwork, institutionally sponsored loans, and unspecified assistantships also available. Financial award application deadline: 1/1; financial award applicants required to submit FAFSA. *Faculty research:* Plant breeding and genetics weed science, crop physiology and ecology, crop management and nutrition. Total annual research expenditures: $2.3 million. *Unit head:* Dr. Maria Gallo, Chair, 352-392-1811 Ext. 206, Fax: 352-392-1840, E-mail: mgm@ufl.edu. *Application contact:* Dr. Jerry M. Bennett, Graduate Coordinator, 352-273-1811 Ext. 230, Fax: 352-392-1840, E-mail: jmbt@ufl.edu.

University of Florida, Graduate School, College of Agricultural and Life Sciences, Department of Soil and Water Science, Gainesville, FL 32611. Offers MS, PhD. Part-time and evening/weekend programs available. Postbaccalaureate distance learning degree programs offered (no on-campus study). *Faculty:* 20 full-time (3 women). *Students:* 66 full-time (32 women), 59 part-time (30 women); includes 2 Black or African American, non-Hispanic/Latino; 1 Asian, non-Hispanic/Latino; 1 Hispanic/Latino, 43 international. Average age 31. 64 applicants, 50% accepted, 6 enrolled. In 2010, 14 master's, 11 doctorates awarded. Terminal master's awarded for partial completion of doctoral program. *Degree requirements:* For master's, thesis (for some programs), Thesis and non-thesis Master's Program; for doctorate, comprehensive exam, thesis/dissertation. *Entrance requirements:* For master's and doctorate, GRE General Test minimum score 1000. (GRE expires 5 years from test date), minimum GPA of 3.0. Additional exam requirements/recommendations for international students: Required—TOEFL (minimum score 550 paper-based; 213 computer-based; 80 iBT), IELTS (minimum score 6). *Application deadline:* For fall admission, 3/1 priority date for domestic students, 3/1 for international students; for spring admission, 10/1 for domestic and international students. Applications are processed on a rolling basis. Application fee: $30. Electronic applications accepted. *Expenses:* Tuition, state resident: full-time $10,915.92. Tuition, nonresident: full-time $28,309. *Financial support:* In 2010–11, 51 students received support, including 10 fellowships, 40 research assistantships (averaging $16,291 per year), 1 teaching assistantship (averaging $15,450 per year); career-related internships or fieldwork, Federal Work-Study, institutionally sponsored loans, and unspecified assistantships also available. Support available to part-time students. Financial award applicants required to submit FAFSA. *Faculty research:* Nutrient, pesticide, and waste management; soil, water, and aquifer remediation; carbon dynamics and ecosystem services; landscape analysis and modeling; wetlands and aquatic ecosystems. *Unit head:* K. Ramesh Reddy, PhD, Chair, 352-392-1804 Ext. 317, Fax: 352-392-3399, E-mail: krr@ufl.edu. *Application contact:* Andrew Ogram, PhD, Graduate Coordinator, 352-392-1951 Ext. 211, Fax: 352-392-3902, E-mail: aogram@ufl.edu.

University of Georgia, College of Agricultural and Environmental Sciences, Department of Crop and Soil Sciences, Athens, GA 30602. Offers crop and soil science (MS, PhD); crop and soil sciences (MCCS); plant protection and pest management (MPPPM). Part-time programs available. *Faculty:* 30 full-time (2 women), 4 part-time/adjunct (1 woman). *Students:* 31 full-time (10 women), 9 part-time (0 women); includes 1 Black or African American, non-Hispanic/Latino; 1 Asian, non-Hispanic/Latino, 12 international. Average age 24. 24 applicants, 50% accepted, 9 enrolled. In 2010, 8 master's awarded. *Degree requirements:* For master's, thesis (MS); for doctorate, comprehensive exam, thesis/dissertation. *Entrance requirements:* For master's and doctorate, GRE General Test. Additional exam requirements/recommendations for international students: Required—TOEFL (minimum score 550 paper-based; 213 computer-based). *Application deadline:* For fall admission, 7/1 priority date for domestic students, 4/15 priority date for international students; for spring admission, 11/15 for domestic students, 10/15 priority date for international students. Applications are processed on a rolling basis. Application fee: $50. Electronic applications accepted. *Expenses:* Tuition, state resident: full-time $7200; part-time $344 per credit hour. Tuition, nonresident: full-time $21,900; part-time $944 per credit hour. Tuition and fees vary according to course load and program. *Financial support:* In 2010–11, research assistantships with full tuition reimbursements (averaging $14,600 per year), teaching assistantships with full tuition reimbursements (averaging $15,350 per year) were awarded; fellowships, scholarships/grants, tuition waivers (full), and unspecified assistantships also available. *Faculty research:* Plant breeding, genomics, nutrient management, water quality, soil chemistry. *Unit head:* Dr. Donn Graham Shilling, Head, 706-542-2461, Fax: 706-542-0914, E-mail: dgs@uga.edu. *Application contact:* Dr. Miguel L. Cabrera, Graduate Coordinator, 706-542-1242, Fax: 706-542-0914, E-mail: mcabrera@uga.edu.

University of Guelph, Graduate Studies, Ontario Agricultural College, Department of Land Resource Science, Guelph, ON N1G 2W1, Canada. Offers atmospheric science (M Sc, PhD); environmental and agricultural earth sciences (M Sc, PhD); land resources management (M Sc, PhD); soil science (M Sc, PhD). Part-time programs available. *Degree requirements:* For master's, thesis (for some programs), research project (non-thesis track); for doctorate, comprehensive exam, thesis/dissertation. *Entrance requirements:* For master's, minimum B-average during previous 2 years of course work; for doctorate, minimum B average during previous 2 years of course work. Additional exam requirements/recommendations for international students: Required—TOEFL (minimum score 550 paper-based; 213 computer-based). Electronic applications accepted. *Faculty research:* Soil science, environmental earth science, land resource management.

University of Idaho, College of Graduate Studies, College of Agricultural and Life Sciences, Department of Plant, Soil, and Entomological Sciences, Program in Soil and Land Resources, Moscow, ID 83844-2282. Offers MS, PhD. *Students:* 8 full-time, 3 part-time. Average age 27. In 2010, 1 doctorate awarded. *Degree requirements:* For doctorate, thesis/dissertation. *Entrance requirements:* For master's and doctorate, GRE General Test, minimum GPA of 3.0. *Application deadline:* For fall admission, 8/1 for domestic students; for spring admission, 12/15 for domestic students. Applications are processed on a rolling basis. Application fee: $60. Electronic applications accepted. *Expenses:* Tuition, nonresident: part-time $580 per credit. Required fees: $306 per credit. *Financial support:* Applicants required to submit FAFSA. *Faculty research:* Pedology, soil biology and biochemistry, soil chemistry, soil fertility and plant nutrition, soil physics. *Unit head:* Dr. James B. Johnson, Department Head, 208-885-6274, E-mail: nthompson@uidaho.edu. *Application contact:* Dr. James B. Johnson, Department Head, 208-885-6274, E-mail: nthompson@uidaho.edu.

University of Illinois at Urbana–Champaign, Graduate College, College of Agricultural, Consumer and Environmental Sciences, Department of Crop Sciences, Champaign, IL 61820. Offers bioinformatics: crop sciences (MS); crop sciences (MS, PhD). Postbaccalaureate distance learning degree programs offered (no on-campus study). *Faculty:* 46 full-time (6 women), 1 (woman) part-time/adjunct. *Students:* 87 full-time (22 women), 39 part-time (10 women); includes 3 Asian, non-Hispanic/Latino; 2 Hispanic/Latino, 46 international. 101 applicants, 46% accepted, 34 enrolled. In 2010, 11 master's, 4 doctorates awarded. *Entrance requirements:* For master's and doctorate, GRE, minimum GPA of 3.0. Additional exam requirements/recommendations for international students: Required—TOEFL (minimum score 570 paper-based). *Application deadline:* Applications are processed on a rolling basis. Application fee: $75 ($90 for international students). Electronic applications accepted. *Financial support:* In 2010–11, 48 fellowships, 78 research assistantships, 17 teaching assistantships were awarded; tuition waivers (full and partial) also available. *Faculty research:* Plant breeding and genetics, molecular biology, crop production, plant physiology, weed science. *Unit head:* German A. Bollero, Head, 217-333-9475, Fax: 217-333-9817, E-mail: gbollero@illinois.edu. *Application contact:* S. Dianne Carson, Secretary, 217-244-0396, Fax: 217-333-9817, E-mail: sdcarson@illinois.edu.

University of Kentucky, Graduate School, College of Agriculture, Program in Crop Science, Lexington, KY 40506-0032. Offers MS, PhD. *Degree requirements:* For master's, comprehensive exam, thesis optional; for doctorate, comprehensive exam, thesis/dissertation. *Entrance requirements:* For master's, GRE General Test, minimum GPA of 2.75; for doctorate, GRE General Test, minimum GPA of 3.0. Additional exam requirements/recommendations for international students: Required—TOEFL (minimum score 550 paper-based; 213 computer-based). Electronic applications accepted. *Faculty research:* Crop physiology, crop ecology, crop management, crop breeding and genetics, weed science.

University of Kentucky, Graduate School, College of Agriculture, Program in Plant and Soil Science, Lexington, KY 40506-0032. Offers MS. *Degree requirements:* For master's, comprehensive exam, thesis optional. *Entrance requirements:* For master's, GRE General Test, minimum undergraduate GPA of 2.75, graduate 3.0. Additional exam requirements/recommendations for international students: Required—TOEFL (minimum score 550 paper-based; 213 computer-based). Electronic applications accepted.

University of Kentucky, Graduate School, College of Agriculture, Program in Soil Science, Lexington, KY 40506-0032. Offers PhD. *Degree requirements:* For doctorate, comprehensive exam, thesis/dissertation. *Entrance requirements:* For doctorate, GRE General Test, minimum graduate GPA of 3.0, undergraduate 2.75. Additional exam requirements/recommendations for international students: Required—TOEFL (minimum score 550 paper-based; 213 computer-based). Electronic applications accepted. *Faculty research:* Soil fertility and plant nutrition, soil chemistry and physics, soil genesis and morphology, soil management and conservation, water and environmental quality.

University of Maine, Graduate School, College of Natural Sciences, Forestry, and Agriculture, Department of Plant, Soil, and Environmental Sciences, Orono, ME 04469. Offers biological sciences (PhD); ecology and environmental sciences (MS, PhD); forest resources (PhD); horticulture (MS); plant science (PhD); plant, soil, and environmental sciences (MS); resource utilization (MS). *Faculty:* 9 full-time (3 women), 7 part-time/adjunct (3 women). *Students:* 6 full-time (2 women), 2 part-time (1 woman), 2 international. Average age 31. 9 applicants, 22% accepted, 0 enrolled. In 2010, 2 master's awarded. *Entrance requirements:* For master's and doctorate, GRE General Test. Additional exam requirements/recommendations for international students: Required—TOEFL. *Application deadline:* Applications are processed on a rolling basis. Application fee: $65. Electronic applications accepted. *Expenses:* Tuition, state resident: full-time $400. Tuition, nonresident: full-time $1050. *Financial support:* In 2010–11, 16 research assistantships with tuition reimbursements (averaging $16,260 per year), 3 teaching assistantships with tuition reimbursements (averaging $12,790 per year) were awarded; scholarships/grants, tuition waivers (full and partial), and unspecified assistantships also available. *Unit head:* Dr. Gregory Porter, Chair, 207-581-2943, Fax: 207-581-3207. *Application contact:* Scott G. Delcourt, Associate Dean of the Graduate School, 207-581-3291, Fax: 207-581-3232, E-mail: graduate@maine.edu.

University of Manitoba, Faculty of Graduate Studies, Faculty of Agricultural and Food Sciences, Department of Plant Science, Winnipeg, MB R3T 2N2, Canada. Offers agronomy and plant protection (M Sc, PhD); horticulture (M Sc, PhD); plant breeding and genetics (M Sc, PhD); plant physiology-biochemistry (M Sc, PhD). *Degree requirements:* For master's, thesis; for doctorate, one foreign language, thesis/dissertation.

University of Manitoba, Faculty of Graduate Studies, Faculty of Agricultural and Food Sciences, Department of Soil Science, Winnipeg, MB R3T 2N2, Canada. Offers M Sc, PhD. *Degree requirements:* For master's, thesis; for doctorate, one foreign language, thesis/dissertation.

University of Massachusetts Amherst, Graduate School, College of Natural Sciences, Department of Plant, Soil and Insect Sciences, Program in Plant and Soil Sciences, Amherst, MA 01003. Offers plant and soil sciences (MS, PhD); soil science (MS). Postbaccalaureate distance learning degree programs offered (minimal on-campus study). *Faculty:* 27 full-time (7 women). *Students:* 21 full-time (12 women), 16 part-time (8 women); includes 1 minority (Asian, non-Hispanic/Latino), 18 international. Average age 34. 28 applicants, 29% accepted, 7 enrolled. In 2010, 7 master's, 1 doctorate awarded. Terminal master's awarded for partial completion of doctoral program. *Degree requirements:* For master's, thesis or alternative; for doctorate, comprehensive exam, thesis/dissertation. *Entrance requirements:* For master's and doctorate, GRE General Test. Additional exam requirements/recommendations for inter-

Agronomy and Soil Sciences

University of Massachusetts Amherst (continued)
national students: Required—TOEFL (minimum score 550 paper-based; 213 computer-based; 80 iBT), IELTS (minimum score 6.5). *Application deadline:* For fall admission, 1/7 for domestic and international students; for spring admission, 10/1 for domestic and international students. Applications are processed on a rolling basis. Application fee: $50 ($65 for international students). Electronic applications accepted. *Expenses:* Tuition, state resident: full-time $2640. Required fees: $8282. One-time fee: $357 full-time. *Financial support:* Fellowships, research assistantships, teaching assistantships, career-related internships or fieldwork, Federal Work-Study, scholarships/grants, traineeships, health care benefits, tuition waivers (full), and unspecified assistantships available. Support available to part-time students. Financial award application deadline: 1/2; financial award applicants required to submit FAFSA. *Unit head:* Dr. Geunhwa Jung, Graduate Program Director, 413-545-1059, Fax: 413-545-2115. *Application contact:* Jean M. Ames, Supervisor of Admissions, 413-545-0722, Fax: 413-577-0010, E-mail: gradadm@grad.umass.edu.

University of Minnesota, Twin Cities Campus, Graduate School, College of Food, Agricultural and Natural Resource Sciences, Land and Atmospheric Science Graduate Program, Saint Paul, MN 55108. Offers MS, PhD. *Faculty:* 45 full-time (7 women). *Students:* 18 full-time (8 women), 1 part-time (0 women); includes 3 minority (1 Black or African American, non-Hispanic/Latino; 1 Hispanic/Latino; 1 Two or more races, non-Hispanic/Latino), 5 international. Average age 30. 30 applicants, 43% accepted, 7 enrolled. In 2010, 3 master's awarded. Terminal master's awarded for partial completion of doctoral program. *Degree requirements:* For master's, comprehensive exam, thesis; for doctorate, comprehensive exam, thesis/dissertation. *Entrance requirements:* For master's and doctorate, GRE General Test, minimum GPA of 3.0. Additional exam requirements/recommendations for international students: Required—TOEFL (minimum score 550 paper-based; 213 computer-based; 79 iBT). *Application deadline:* For fall admission, 12/15 priority date for domestic students, 12/15 for international students; for spring admission, 10/15 priority date for domestic students, 10/15 for international students. Applications are processed on a rolling basis. Application fee: $75 ($95 for international students). Electronic applications accepted. *Financial support:* In 2010–11, fellowships with full tuition reimbursements (averaging $23,500 per year), research assistantships with full and partial tuition reimbursements (averaging $17,000 per year), teaching assistantships with full and partial tuition reimbursements (averaging $17,000 per year) were awarded; scholarships/grants, health care benefits, tuition waivers (full), and unspecified assistantships also available. Support available to part-time students. *Faculty research:* Soil water and atmospheric resources, soil physical management, agricultural chemicals and their management, plant nutrient management, biological nitrogen fixation. *Unit head:* Dr. Timothy Griffis, Co-Director of Graduate Studies, 612-625-3117, Fax: 612-625-2208, E-mail: tgriffis@umn.edu. *Application contact:* Kari Jarco, Program Coordinator, 612-625-5251, Fax: 612-625-2208, E-mail: kjarcho@umn.edu.

University of Missouri, Graduate School, College of Agriculture, Food and Natural Resources, Division of Plant Sciences, Columbia, MO 65211. Offers crop, soil and pest management (MS, PhD); entomology (MS, PhD); horticulture (MS, PhD); plant biology and genetics (MS, PhD); plant stress biology (MS, PhD). *Faculty:* 103 full-time (24 women), 5 part-time/adjunct (1 woman). *Students:* 61 full-time (29 women), 13 part-time (7 women); includes 2 minority (1 Black or African American, non-Hispanic/Latino; 1 American Indian or Alaska Native, non-Hispanic/Latino), 25 international. Average age 28. 65 applicants, 31% accepted, 18 enrolled. In 2010, 4 master's, 10 doctorates awarded. Terminal master's awarded for partial completion of doctoral program. *Degree requirements:* For master's, thesis; for doctorate, comprehensive exam, thesis/dissertation. *Entrance requirements:* For master's and doctorate, GRE General Test, minimum GPA of 3.0; bachelor's degree from accredited college. Additional exam requirements/recommendations for international students: Required—TOEFL (minimum score 500 paper-based; 173 computer-based; 61 iBT), IELTS (minimum score 5.5). *Application deadline:* For fall admission, 1/15 priority date for domestic students. Applications are processed on a rolling basis. Application fee: $45 ($60 for international students). Electronic applications accepted. *Financial support:* In 2010–11, 2 fellowships with tuition reimbursements, 59 research assistantships with tuition reimbursements, 1 teaching assistantship with tuition reimbursement were awarded; institutionally sponsored loans, scholarships/grants, health care benefits, and unspecified assistantships also available. Support available to part-time students. *Faculty research:* Crop, soil and pest management; entomology; horticulture; plant biology and genetics; plant microbiology and pathology. *Unit head:* Dr. Michael Collins, Director, 573-882-1957, E-mail: collinsm@missouri.edu. *Application contact:* Dr. James Schoelz, Director of Graduate Studies, 573-882-1185, E-mail: schoelzj@missouri.edu.

University of Missouri, Graduate School, School of Natural Resources, Department of Soil, Environmental, and Atmospheric Sciences, Columbia, MO 65211. Offers atmospheric science (MS, PhD); soil science (MS, PhD). *Degree requirements:* For doctorate, thesis/dissertation. *Entrance requirements:* For master's and doctorate, GRE General Test, minimum GPA of 3.0. Additional exam requirements/recommendations for international students: Required—TOEFL (minimum score 530 paper-based; 197 computer-based; 71 iBT).

University of Nebraska–Lincoln, Graduate College, College of Agricultural Sciences and Natural Resources, Department of Agronomy and Horticulture, Program in Agronomy, Lincoln, NE 68588. Offers MS, PhD. *Degree requirements:* For master's, thesis; for doctorate, comprehensive exam, thesis/dissertation. *Entrance requirements:* Additional exam requirements/recommendations for international students: Required—TOEFL (minimum score 500 paper-based; 173 computer-based). Electronic applications accepted. *Faculty research:* Crop physiology and production, plant breeding and genetics, range and forage management, soil and water science, weed science.

University of Puerto Rico, Mayagüez Campus, Graduate Studies, College of Agricultural Sciences, Department of Agronomy and Soils, Mayagüez, PR 00681-9000. Offers agronomy (MS); soils (MS). Part-time programs available. *Students:* 33 full-time (15 women), 2 part-time (0 women); includes 16 Hispanic/Latino, 7 international. 10 applicants, 60% accepted, 5 enrolled. In 2010, 1 master's awarded. *Degree requirements:* For master's, comprehensive exam, thesis. *Application deadline:* For fall admission, 2/15 for domestic and international students; for spring admission, 9/15 for domestic and international students. Applications are processed on a rolling basis. Application fee: $25. *Expenses:* Tuition, state resident: full-time $1188. Tuition, nonresident: full-time $1188. International tuition: $6126 full-time. Tuition and fees vary according to course level and course load. *Financial support:* In 2010–11, 32 students received support, including 37 research assistantships with tuition reimbursements available (averaging $15,000 per year), 21 teaching assistantships with tuition reimbursements available (averaging $8,500 per year); Federal Work-Study and institutionally sponsored loans also available. *Faculty research:* Soil physics and chemistry, soil management, plant physiology, ecology, plant breeding. Total annual research expenditures: $330,000. *Unit head:* Dr. Hipolito O'Farrill, Director, 787-265-3851, E-mail: hipolito.ofarrill@upr.edu. *Application contact:* Carmen Figueroa, Student Affairs Official, 787-265-3809, Fax: 787-265-5489, E-mail: carmen.figueroa11@upr.edu.

University of Puerto Rico, Mayagüez Campus, Graduate Studies, College of Agricultural Sciences, Department of Crop Protection, Mayagüez, PR 00681-9000. Offers MS. Part-time programs available. *Students:* 18 full-time (11 women), 1 part-time (0 women); includes 17 Hispanic/Latino, 2 international. 7 applicants, 71% accepted, 4 enrolled. In 2010, 3 master's awarded. *Degree requirements:* For master's, comprehensive exam, thesis. *Entrance requirements:* For master's, minimum GPA of 2.75, BS in agricultural science or its equivalent. *Application deadline:* For fall admission, 2/15 for domestic and international students; for spring admission, 9/15 for domestic and international students. Applications are processed on a rolling basis. Application fee: $25. *Expenses:* Tuition, state resident: full-time $1188. Tuition, nonresident: full-time $1188. International tuition: $6126 full-time. Tuition and fees vary according to course level and course load. *Financial support:* In 2010–11, fellowships (averaging $12,000 per year), research assistantships with tuition reimbursements (averaging $15,000 per year), teaching assistantships with tuition reimbursements (averaging $8,500 per year) were awarded; career-related internships or fieldwork, Federal Work-Study, and institutionally sponsored loans also available. Financial award application deadline: 5/30. *Faculty research:* Nematology, virology, plant pathology, weed control, peas and soybean seed diseases. *Unit head:* Dr. Hip??lito O'Farrill, Director, 787-265-3859, Fax: 787-265-5490, E-mail: hipolito.ofarrill@upr.edu. *Application contact:* Prof. Nydia Vicente, Coordinator, 787-832-4040 Ext. 3104, Fax: 787-265-5490, E-mail: nvicente@uprm.edu.

University of Saskatchewan, College of Graduate Studies and Research, College of Agriculture, Department of Soil Science, Saskatoon, SK S7N 5A2, Canada. Offers M Ag, M Sc, PhD, Diploma. *Degree requirements:* For master's, thesis (for some programs); for doctorate, comprehensive exam (for some programs), thesis/dissertation. *Entrance requirements:* Additional exam requirements/recommendations for international students: Required—TOEFL (minimum score 80 iBT); Recommended—IELTS (minimum score 6.5).

University of Vermont, Graduate College, College of Agriculture and Life Sciences, Department of Plant and Soil Science, Burlington, VT 05405. Offers MS, PhD. *Students:* 24 (13 women), 3 international. 26 applicants, 12% accepted, 1 enrolled. In 2010, 3 master's, 1 doctorate awarded. *Degree requirements:* For master's, thesis; for doctorate, one foreign language, thesis/dissertation. *Entrance requirements:* For master's and doctorate, GRE General Test. Additional exam requirements/recommendations for international students: Required—TOEFL (minimum score 550 paper-based; 213 computer-based; 80 iBT). *Application deadline:* For fall admission, 3/1 priority date for domestic students. Applications are processed on a rolling basis. Application fee: $40. Electronic applications accepted. *Expenses:* Tuition, state resident: part-time $537 per credit hour. Tuition, nonresident: part-time $1355 per credit hour. *Financial support:* Fellowships, research assistantships, teaching assistantships available. Financial award application deadline: 3/1. *Faculty research:* Soil chemistry, plant nutrition. *Unit head:* Dr. Deborah Neher, Chairperson, 802-656-2630. *Application contact:* Dr. Josef Gorres, Coordinator, 802-656-2630.

University of Wisconsin–Madison, Graduate School, College of Agricultural and Life Sciences, Department of Agronomy, Madison, WI 53706-1380. Offers agronomy (MS, PhD). *Degree requirements:* For master's, thesis or alternative; for doctorate, thesis/dissertation. *Entrance requirements:* For master's and doctorate, GRE, minimum GPA of 3.0. Additional exam requirements/recommendations for international students: Required—TOEFL (minimum score 580 paper-based; 213 computer-based). Electronic applications accepted. *Expenses:* Tuition, state resident: full-time $9887.36; part-time $617.96 per credit. Tuition, nonresident: full-time $24,054; part-time $1503.40 per credit. Required fees: $67.63 per credit. Tuition and fees vary according to reciprocity agreements. *Faculty research:* Plant breeding and genetics, plant molecular biology and physiology, cropping systems and management, weed science.

University of Wisconsin–Madison, Graduate School, College of Agricultural and Life Sciences, Department of Soil Science, Madison, WI 53706. Offers MS, PhD. *Faculty:* 17 full-time (2 women). *Students:* 20 full-time (10 women), 2 part-time (1 woman); includes 2 Asian, non-Hispanic/Latino; 2 Hispanic/Latino. Average age 25. 32 applicants, 19% accepted, 4 enrolled. In 2010, 3 master's, 1 doctorate awarded. *Degree requirements:* For master's, comprehensive exam, thesis; for doctorate, comprehensive exam, thesis/dissertation. *Entrance requirements:* For master's and doctorate, GRE General Test. Additional exam requirements/recommendations for international students: Required—TOEFL. *Application deadline:* Applications are processed on a rolling basis. Application fee: $56. Electronic applications accepted. *Expenses:* Tuition, state resident: full-time $9887.36; part-time $617.96 per credit. Tuition, nonresident: full-time $24,054; part-time $1503.40 per credit. Required fees: $67.63 per credit. Tuition and fees vary according to reciprocity agreements. *Financial support:* In 2010–11, 12 research assistantships with full tuition reimbursements (averaging $16,000 per year), 2 teaching assistantships (averaging $16,000 per year) were awarded. *Faculty research:* Soil characterization and mapping, fate of toxicants in the environment, soil microbiology, permafrost, water quality and quantity. Total annual research expenditures: $1.5 million. *Unit head:* William Bland, Chair, 608-263-5691, Fax: 608-265-2595, E-mail: wlbland@wisc.edu. *Application contact:* Carol J. Duffy, Program Assistant, 608-262-0485, Fax: 608-265-2595, E-mail: cjduffy@wisc.edu.

University of Wyoming, College of Agriculture and Natural Resources, Department of Plant Sciences, Laramie, WY 82070. Offers agronomy (MS, PhD). *Degree requirements:* For master's, thesis; for doctorate, thesis/dissertation. *Entrance requirements:* For master's and doctorate, GRE General Test, minimum GPA of 3.0. Additional exam requirements/recommendations for international students: Required—TOEFL (minimum score 525 paper-based; 197 computer-based). Electronic applications accepted. *Faculty research:* Crops, weeds, plant diseases.

University of Wyoming, College of Agriculture and Natural Resources, Department of Renewable Resources, Laramie, WY 82070. Offers agroecology (MS); entomology (MS, PhD); entomology/water resources (MS, PhD); rangeland ecology and watershed management (MS, PhD), including soil sciences (PhD), soil sciences and water resources (MS); rangeland ecology and watershed management/water resources (MS, PhD); soil science (MS); soil science/water resources (PhD). Part-time programs available. *Degree requirements:* For master's, comprehensive exam, thesis, oral examination; for doctorate, comprehensive exam, thesis/dissertation, preliminary oral and written exam, oral final exam. *Entrance requirements:* For master's and doctorate, GRE General Test, minimum GPA of 3.0. Additional exam requirements/recommendations for international students: Required—TOEFL. Electronic applications accepted. *Faculty research:* Plant control, grazing management, riparian restoration, riparian management, reclamation.

Utah State University, School of Graduate Studies, College of Agriculture, Department of Plants, Soils, and Biometeorology, Logan, UT 84322. Offers biometeorology (MS, PhD); ecology (MS, PhD); plant science (MS, PhD); soil science (MS, PhD). Part-time programs available. Terminal master's awarded for partial completion of doctoral program. *Degree requirements:* For master's, thesis; for doctorate, thesis/dissertation. *Entrance requirements:* For master's, GRE General Test, BS in plant, soil, atmospheric science, or related field; minimum GPA of 3.0; for doctorate, GRE General Test, minimum GPA of 3.0. Additional exam requirements/recommendations for international students: Required—TOEFL. Electronic applications accepted. *Faculty research:* Biotechnology and genomics, plant physiology and biology, nutrient and water efficient landscapes, physical-chemical-biological processes in soil, environmental biophysics and climate.

Virginia Polytechnic Institute and State University, Graduate School, College of Agriculture and Life Sciences, Department of Crop and Soil Environmental Sciences, Blacksburg, VA 24061. Offers MS, PhD. *Faculty:* 19 full-time (2 women). *Students:* 34 full-time (16 women), 7 part-time (3 women); includes 1 Black or African American, non-Hispanic/Latino, 5 international. Average age 26. 25 applicants, 40% accepted, 8 enrolled. In 2010, 4 master's, 3 doctorates awarded. *Degree requirements:* For master's, comprehensive exam (for some programs), thesis (for some programs); for doctorate, comprehensive exam (for some programs), thesis/dissertation (for some programs). *Entrance requirements:* For master's and doctorate, GRE. Additional exam requirements/recommendations for international students: Required—TOEFL (minimum score 550 paper-based; 213 computer-based). *Application deadline:* For fall admission, 7/1 for domestic and international students; for spring admission, 12/1 for domestic and international students. Applications are processed on a rolling basis. Application fee: $65. Electronic applications accepted. *Expenses:* Tuition, area resident: Full-time $9399; part-time $488 per credit hour. Tuition, state resident: full-time $9399; part-time $488 per credit hour. Tuition, nonresident: full-time $17,854; part-time $957.75 per credit hour. International tuition:

$17,854 full-time. Required fees: $1534. Full-time tuition and fees vary according to program. *Financial support:* In 2010–11, 21 research assistantships with full tuition reimbursements (averaging $21,513 per year), 5 teaching assistantships with full tuition reimbursements (averaging $15,381 per year) were awarded; career-related internships or fieldwork, Federal Work-Study, scholarships/grants, health care benefits, and unspecified assistantships also available. Financial award application deadline: 1/15. *Faculty research:* Environmental soil chemistry, waste management, soil fertility, plant molecular genetics, turfgrass management. Total annual research expenditures: $2.9 million. *Unit head:* Dr. James R. McKenna, Unit Head, 540-231-6305, Fax: 540-231-3431, E-mail: hodges@vt.edu. *Application contact:* Lee Daniels, Contact, 540-231-7175, Fax: 540-231-3431, E-mail: wdaniels@vt.edu.

Washington State University, Graduate School, College of Agricultural, Human, and Natural Resource Sciences, Department of Crop and Soil Sciences, Program in Crop Sciences, Pullman, WA 99164. Offers MS, PhD. *Faculty:* 25. *Students:* 30 full-time (17 women), 4 part-time (1 woman); includes 1 minority (Asian, non-Hispanic/Latino), 14 international. Average age 30. 73 applicants, 21% accepted, 15 enrolled. In 2010, 3 master's, 3 doctorates awarded. Terminal master's awarded for partial completion of doctoral program. *Degree requirements:* For master's, comprehensive exam (for some programs), thesis (for some programs), oral exam; for doctorate, comprehensive exam, thesis/dissertation, oral exam, written exam. *Entrance requirements:* For master's and doctorate, GRE General Test, personal statement of educational goals and professional expectations. Additional exam requirements/recommendations for international students: Required—TOEFL (minimum score 550 paper-based; 213 computer-based), IELTS. *Application deadline:* For fall admission, 1/10 priority date for domestic and international students; for spring admission, 7/1 priority date for domestic and international students. Applications are processed on a rolling basis. Application fee: $50. Electronic applications accepted. *Expenses:* Tuition, state resident: full-time $8552; part-time $443 per credit. Tuition, nonresident: full-time $21,650; part-time $1083 per credit. Required fees: $846. *Financial support:* In 2010–11, 5 fellowships (averaging $7,580 per year), 15 research assistantships with full and partial tuition reimbursements (averaging $18,204 per year), 1 teaching assistantship with full and partial tuition reimbursement (averaging $18,204 per year) were awarded; career-related internships or fieldwork, Federal Work-Study, institutionally sponsored loans, tuition waivers (partial), and teaching associateships also available. Financial award application deadline: 2/1; financial award applicants required to submit FAFSA. *Faculty research:* Barley genetics, soil biology, soil fertility, winter wheat breeding, weed science. Total annual research expenditures: $6.2 million. *Unit head:* Dr. Richard Koenig, Chair, 509-335-2726, Fax: 509-335-8674, E-mail: richk@wsu.edu. *Application contact:* Graduate School Admissions, 800-GRADWSU, Fax: 509-335-1949, E-mail: gradsch@wsu.edu.

Washington State University, Graduate School, College of Agricultural, Human, and Natural Resource Sciences, Department of Crop and Soil Sciences, Program in Soil Sciences, Pullman, WA 99164. Offers MS, PhD. *Faculty:* 25. *Students:* 22 full-time (10 women), 5 part-time (1 woman); includes 2 minority (1 American Indian or Alaska Native, non-Hispanic/Latino; 1 Asian, non-Hispanic/Latino), 5 international. Average age 30. 34 applicants, 21% accepted, 5 enrolled. In 2010, 5 master's, 1 doctorate awarded. Terminal master's awarded for partial completion of doctoral program. *Degree requirements:* For master's, comprehensive exam (for some programs), thesis (for some programs), oral exam; for doctorate, comprehensive exam, thesis/dissertation, oral exam, written exam. *Entrance requirements:* For master's and doctorate, GRE. Additional exam requirements/recommendations for international students: Required—TOEFL (minimum score 550 paper-based; 213 computer-based), IELTS. *Application deadline:* For fall admission, 1/10 priority date for domestic and international students; for spring admission, 7/1 priority date for domestic and international students. Applications are processed on a rolling basis. Application fee: $50. Electronic applications accepted. *Expenses:* Tuition, state resident: full-time $8552; part-time $443 per credit. Tuition, nonresident: full-time $21,650; part-time $1083 per credit. Required fees: $846. *Financial support:* In 2010–11, 1 fellowship (averaging $4,000 per year), 11 research assistantships with full and partial tuition reimbursements (averaging $18,204 per year), 1 teaching assistantship with tuition reimbursement (averaging $18,204 per year) were awarded; career-related internships or fieldwork, Federal Work-Study, institutionally sponsored loans, and tuition waivers (partial) also available. Financial award application deadline: 4/1; financial award applicants required to submit FAFSA. *Faculty research:* Environmental soils, soil/water quality, soil microbiology, soil physics. Total annual research expenditures: $6.2 million. *Unit head:* Dr. Richard Koenig, Interim Director, 509-335-2726, Fax: 509-335-8674, E-mail: richk@wsu.edu. *Application contact:* Graduate School Admissions, 800-GRADWSU, Fax: 509-335-1949, E-mail: gradsch@wsu.edu.

West Virginia University, Davis College of Agriculture, Forestry and Consumer Sciences, Division of Plant and Soil Sciences, Program in Agricultural Sciences, Morgantown, WV 26506. Offers animal and food sciences (PhD); plant and soil sciences (PhD). *Degree requirements:* For doctorate, thesis/dissertation, oral and written exams. *Entrance requirements:* Additional exam requirements/recommendations for international students: Required—TOEFL. *Faculty research:* Ruminant nutrition, metabolism, forage utilization, physiology, reproduction.

Animal Sciences

Alabama Agricultural and Mechanical University, School of Graduate Studies, School of Agricultural and Environmental Sciences, Department of Plant and Soil Science, Huntsville, AL 35811. Offers animal sciences (MS); environmental science (MS); plant and soil science (PhD). Evening/weekend programs available. Terminal master's awarded for partial completion of doctoral program. *Degree requirements:* For master's, thesis; for doctorate, one foreign language, thesis/dissertation. *Entrance requirements:* For master's, GRE General Test, BS in agriculture; for doctorate, GRE General Test, master's degree. Additional exam requirements/recommendations for international students: Required—TOEFL (minimum score 500 paper-based; 173 computer-based; 61 iBT). Electronic applications accepted. *Faculty research:* Plant breeding, cytogenetics, crop production, soil chemistry and fertility, remote sensing.

Alcorn State University, School of Graduate Studies, School of Agriculture and Applied Science, Alcorn State, MS 39096-7500. Offers agricultural economics (MS Ag); agronomy (MS Ag); animal science (MS Ag). *Degree requirements:* For master's, thesis optional. *Faculty research:* Aquatic systems, dairy herd improvement, fruit production, alternative farming practices.

American University of Beirut, Graduate Programs, Faculty of Agricultural and Food Sciences, Beirut, Lebanon. Offers agricultural economics (MS); animal sciences (MS); ecosystem management (MSES); food technology (MS); irrigation (MS); mechanization (MS); nutrition (MS); plant protection (MS); plant science (MS); poultry science (MS); soils (MS). Part-time programs available. *Faculty:* 22 full-time (6 women). *Students:* 6 full-time (3 women), 86 part-time (77 women). Average age 24. 94 applicants, 60% accepted, 15 enrolled. In 2010, 28 master's awarded. *Degree requirements:* For master's, one foreign language, comprehensive exam, thesis (for some programs). *Entrance requirements:* Additional exam requirements/recommendations for international students: Required—TOEFL (minimum score 600 paper-based; 250 computer-based; 100 iBT), IELTS (minimum score 7.5). *Application deadline:* For fall admission, 4/30 for domestic and international students; for spring admission, 11/1 for domestic and international students. Applications are processed on a rolling basis. Application fee: $50. Electronic applications accepted. *Expenses:* Tuition: Full-time $12,294; part-time $683 per credit. Required fees: $499; $499 per credit. Tuition and fees vary according to course load and program. *Financial support:* In 2010–11, 18 research assistantships with partial tuition reimbursements (averaging $13,132 per year), 42 teaching assistantships with full and partial tuition reimbursements (averaging $1,000 per year) were awarded; scholarships/grants, health care benefits, and unspecified assistantships also available. Financial award application deadline: 2/2. *Faculty research:* Community and therapeutic nutrition; food safety and food microbiology; landscape planning, nature and rural heritage conservation; pathology, immunology and control of poultry and animal diseases; agricultural economics and development. Total annual research expenditures: $900,000. *Unit head:* Prof. Nahla Hwalla, Dean, 961-134-3002 Ext. 4400, Fax: 961-174-4460, E-mail: nahla@aub.edu.lb. *Application contact:* Dr. Salim Kanaan, Director, Admissions Office, 961-135-0000 Ext. 2594, Fax: 961-175-0775, E-mail: sk00@aub.edu.lb.

Angelo State University, College of Graduate Studies, College of Sciences, Department of Agriculture, San Angelo, TX 76909. Offers animal science (MS). Part-time and evening/weekend programs available. *Faculty:* 4 full-time (0 women). *Students:* 16 full-time (6 women), 8 part-time (4 women); includes 1 Hispanic/Latino. Average age 23. 7 applicants, 100% accepted, 7 enrolled. In 2010, 11 master's awarded. *Degree requirements:* For master's, comprehensive exam, thesis optional. *Entrance requirements:* For master's, GRE General Test, essay. Additional exam requirements/recommendations for international students: Required—TOEFL or IELTS. *Application deadline:* For fall admission, 7/15 priority date for domestic students, 6/10 for international students; for spring admission, 12/1 priority date for domestic students, 11/1 for international students. Applications are processed on a rolling basis. Application fee: $40 ($50 for international students). Electronic applications accepted. *Expenses:* Tuition, state resident: full-time $4560; part-time $152 per credit hour. Tuition, nonresident: full-time $13,860; part-time $462 per credit hour. Required fees: $2132. Tuition and fees vary according to course load. *Financial support:* In 2010–11, 10 students received support, including 9 research assistantships (averaging $9,887 per year); Federal Work-Study, scholarships/grants, and unspecified assistantships also available. Support available to part-time students. Financial award application deadline: 3/1. *Faculty research:* Effect of protein and energy on feedlot performance, bitterweed toxicosis in sheep, meat laboratory, North Concho watershed project, baseline vegetation. *Unit head:* Dr. Gilbert R. Engdahl, Department Head, 325-942-2027 Ext. 227, E-mail: gil.engdahl@angelo.edu. *Application contact:* Dr. Cody B. Scott, Graduate Advisor, 325-942-2027 Ext. 284, E-mail: cody.scott@angelo.edu.

Auburn University, Graduate School, College of Agriculture, Department of Animal Sciences, Auburn University, AL 36849. Offers M Ag, MS, PhD. Part-time programs available. *Faculty:* 23 full-time (5 women), 1 part-time/adjunct (0 women). *Students:* 5 full-time (2 women), 20 part-time (11 women); includes 2 Black or African American, non-Hispanic/Latino; 1 American Indian or Alaska Native, non-Hispanic/Latino; 1 Hispanic/Latino. Average age 27. 28 applicants, 14% accepted, 2 enrolled. In 2010, 8 master's awarded. *Degree requirements:* For master's, thesis (for some programs); for doctorate, thesis/dissertation. *Entrance requirements:* For master's and doctorate, GRE General Test. *Application deadline:* For fall admission, 7/7 for domestic students; for spring admission, 11/24 for domestic students. Applications are processed on a rolling basis. Application fee: $50 ($60 for international students). Electronic applications accepted. *Expenses:* Tuition, state resident: full-time $7002. Tuition, nonresident: full-time $21,898. International tuition: $22,116 full-time. Required fees: $892. Tuition and fees vary according to course load and program. *Financial support:* Research assistantships, teaching assistantships, Federal Work-Study available. Support available to part-time students. Financial award application deadline: 3/15; financial award applicants required to submit FAFSA. *Faculty research:* Animal breeding and genetics, animal biochemistry and nutrition, physiology of reproduction, animal production. *Unit head:* Dr. L. Wayne Greene, Head, 334-844-1528. *Application contact:* Dr. George Flowers, Dean of the Graduate School, 334-844-2125.

Auburn University, Graduate School, College of Agriculture, Department of Poultry Science, Auburn University, AL 36849. Offers M Ag, MS, PhD. Part-time programs available. *Faculty:* 16 full-time (3 women). *Students:* 9 full-time (3 women), 9 part-time (all women); includes 2 Asian, non-Hispanic/Latino, 7 international. Average age 29. 12 applicants, 33% accepted, 3 enrolled. In 2010, 3 master's, 3 doctorates awarded. *Degree requirements:* For master's, thesis (for some programs); for doctorate, thesis/dissertation. *Entrance requirements:* For master's, GRE General Test; for doctorate, GRE General Test, MS. *Application deadline:* For fall admission, 7/7 for domestic students; for spring admission, 11/24 for domestic students. Applications are processed on a rolling basis. Application fee: $50 ($60 for international students). Electronic applications accepted. *Expenses:* Tuition, state resident: full-time $7002. Tuition, nonresident: full-time $21,898. International tuition: $22,116 full-time. Required fees: $892. Tuition and fees vary according to course load and program. *Financial support:* Research assistantships, Federal Work-Study available. Support available to part-time students. Financial award application deadline: 3/15; financial award applicants required to submit FAFSA. *Faculty research:* Poultry nutrition, poultry breeding, poultry physiology, poultry diseases and parasites, processing/food science. *Unit head:* Dr. Donald E. Conner, Head, 334-844-4133, E-mail: connede@auburn.edu. *Application contact:* Dr. George Flowers, Dean of the Graduate School, 334-844-2125.

Boise State University, Graduate College, College of Arts and Sciences, Department of Biology, Program in Raptor Biology, Boise, ID 83725-0399. Offers MS. Part-time programs available. *Degree requirements:* For master's, thesis. *Entrance requirements:* For master's, GRE General Test, minimum GPA of 3.0. Electronic applications accepted. *Faculty research:* Avian ecology.

Brigham Young University, Graduate Studies, College of Life Sciences, Department of Plant and Wildlife Sciences, Provo, UT 84602-1001. Offers environmental science (MS); genetics and biotechnology (MS); wildlife and wildlands conservation (MS, PhD). *Faculty:* 26 full-time (2 women). *Students:* 63 full-time (23 women); includes 2 Asian, non-Hispanic/Latino; 1 Hispanic/Latino; 1 Native Hawaiian or other Pacific Islander, non-Hispanic/Latino, 5 international. Average age 25. 33 applicants, 55% accepted, 18 enrolled. *Degree requirements:* For master's, thesis; for doctorate, comprehensive exam, thesis/dissertation, minimum GPA of 3.2, 54 hours (18 dissertation, 36 coursework). *Entrance requirements:* For master's, GRE General Test, minimum GPA of 3.2 during last 60 hours of course work; for doctorate, GRE, minimum GPA of 3.2. Additional exam requirements/recommendations for international students: Required—TOEFL (minimum score 580 paper-based; 237 computer-based; 85 iBT). *Application deadline:* 2/1 for domestic and international students. Applications are processed on a rolling basis. Application fee: $0. Electronic applications accepted. *Expenses:* Tuition: Full-time $5580; part-time $310 per credit hour. Tuition and fees vary according to program and student's religious affiliation. *Financial support:* In 2010–11, 63 students received support, including 2 research assistantships with partial tuition reimbursements available (averaging $16,650 per year), 37 teaching assistantships with partial tuition reimbursements available (averaging $16,650 per year); scholarships/grants and tuition waivers (partial) also available. Financial award application deadline: 2/1. *Faculty research:* environmental science, plant genetics, plant ecology, plant

Animal Sciences

Brigham Young University (continued)
nutrition and pathology, wildlife and wildlands conservation. *Unit head:* Dr. Val J. Anderson, Chair, 801-422-3527, Fax: 801-422-0008, E-mail: val_anderson@byu.edu. *Application contact:* Dr. Loreen Allphin, Graduate Coordinator, 801-422-5603, Fax: 801-422-0008, E-mail: loreen_allphin@byu.edu.

California State University, Fresno, Division of Graduate Studies, College of Agricultural Sciences and Technology, Department of Animal Science and Agricultural Education, Fresno, CA 93740-8027. Offers animal science (MS). Part-time and evening/weekend programs available. *Degree requirements:* For master's, thesis. *Entrance requirements:* For master's, GRE General Test, minimum GPA of 3.0 in last 60 hours. Additional exam requirements/recommendations for international students: Required—TOEFL. Electronic applications accepted. *Faculty research:* Horse nutrition, animal health and welfare, electronic monitoring.

Clemson University, Graduate School, College of Agriculture, Forestry and Life Sciences, Department of Animal and Veterinary Sciences, Clemson, SC 29634. Offers animal and veterinary sciences (MS, PhD). *Faculty:* 13 full-time (5 women), 1 part-time/adjunct (0 women). *Students:* 11 full-time (8 women), 1 part-time (0 women); includes 1 Black or African American, non-Hispanic/Latino, 2 international. Average age 28. 17 applicants, 59% accepted, 3 enrolled. In 2010, 9 master's, 1 doctorate awarded. *Degree requirements:* For doctorate, thesis/dissertation. *Entrance requirements:* For master's and doctorate, GRE General Test. Additional exam requirements/recommendations for international students: Required—TOEFL. *Application deadline:* For fall admission, 4/15 for international students; for spring admission, 9/15 for international students. Applications are processed on a rolling basis. Application fee: $70 ($80 for international students). Electronic applications accepted. *Expenses:* Contact institution. *Financial support:* In 2010–11, 8 students received support, including 3 fellowships with full and partial tuition reimbursements available (averaging $9,667 per year), 4 research assistantships with partial tuition reimbursements available (averaging $16,750 per year), 4 teaching assistantships with partial tuition reimbursements available (averaging $15,000 per year); career-related internships or fieldwork, Federal Work-Study, institutionally sponsored loans, scholarships/grants, and unspecified assistantships also available. Financial award applicants required to submit FAFSA. Total annual research expenditures: $737,056. *Unit head:* Dr. Susan K. Duckett, Chair, 864-656-2570, Fax: 864-656-3131, E-mail: sducket@clemson.edu. *Application contact:* Dr. Denzil Maurice, 864-656-4023, E-mail: dmrc@clemson.edu.

Colorado State University, Graduate School, College of Agricultural Sciences, Department of Animal Sciences, Fort Collins, CO 80523-1171. Offers MS, PhD. *Faculty:* 21 full-time (3 women). *Students:* 42 full-time (23 women), 22 part-time (13 women); includes 1 American Indian or Alaska Native, non-Hispanic/Latino; 1 Hispanic/Latino, 11 international. Average age 28. 58 applicants, 26% accepted, 15 enrolled. In 2010, 12 master's, 10 doctorates awarded. *Degree requirements:* For master's, variable foreign language requirement, comprehensive exam, thesis, one article prepared for publication in a refereed scientific journal with degree candidate as senior author and approval of on-campus graduate committee consisting of three faculty members; for doctorate, variable foreign language requirement, comprehensive exam, thesis/dissertation, two articles prepared for publication in refereed scientific publication with degree candidate as senior author and approval of on-campus graduate committee consisting of three faculty members. *Entrance requirements:* For master's, GRE General Test (minimum score 1000 verbal and quantitative), minimum GPA of 3.0; reference letters; department questionnaire; for doctorate, GRE General Test (combined minimum score of 1000 on the Verbal and Quantitative sections), minimum GPA of 3.0; reference letters; department questionnaire. Additional exam requirements/recommendations for international students: Required—TOEFL (minimum score 525 paper-based; 71 computer-based; 80 iBT), IELTS (minimum score 6.5). *Application deadline:* For fall admission, 4/1 for domestic and international students; for spring admission, 10/1 for domestic and international students. Applications are processed on a rolling basis. Application fee: $50. Electronic applications accepted. *Expenses:* Tuition, state resident: full-time $7434; part-time $413 per credit. Tuition, nonresident: full-time $19,022; part-time $1057 per credit. Required fees: $1729; $88 per credit. *Financial support:* In 2010–11, 47 students received support, including 2 fellowships with full tuition reimbursements available (averaging $37,000 per year), 39 research assistantships with full tuition reimbursements available (averaging $12,660 per year), 6 teaching assistantships with full tuition reimbursements available (averaging $10,995 per year); scholarships/grants and unspecified assistantships also available. Financial award applicants required to submit FAFSA. *Faculty research:* Meat science, food safety, Livestock management systems, equine science, breeding and genetics. Total annual research expenditures: $2.9 million. *Unit head:* Dr. William R. Wailes, Department Head, 970-491-5390, Fax: 970-491-5326, E-mail: w.wailes@colostate.edu. *Application contact:* Melissa Weiss, Administrative Assistant, 970-491-1442, Fax: 970-491-5326, E-mail: m.weiss@colostate.edu.

Cornell University, Graduate School, Graduate Fields of Agriculture and Life Sciences, Field of Animal Science, Ithaca, NY 14853-0001. Offers animal breeding (MS, PhD); animal genetics (MS, PhD). *Faculty:* 32 full-time (9 women). *Students:* 38 full-time (22 women); includes 1 Asian, non-Hispanic/Latino; 2 Hispanic/Latino, 14 international. Average age 28. 34 applicants, 29% accepted, 10 enrolled. In 2010, 5 master's, 2 doctorates awarded. *Degree requirements:* For master's, thesis, teaching experience; for doctorate, comprehensive exam, thesis/dissertation, teaching experience. *Entrance requirements:* For master's and doctorate, 2 letters of recommendation. Additional exam requirements/recommendations for international students: Required—TOEFL (minimum score 550 paper-based; 213 computer-based; 77 iBT). *Application deadline:* For fall admission, 4/1 for domestic students; for spring admission, 9/1 for domestic students. Application fee: $70. Electronic applications accepted. *Expenses:* Tuition: Full-time $29,500. Required fees: $76. Tuition and fees vary according to degree level and program. *Financial support:* In 2010–11, 4 fellowships with full tuition reimbursements, 15 research assistantships with full tuition reimbursements, 11 teaching assistantships with full tuition reimbursements were awarded; institutionally sponsored loans, scholarships/grants, health care benefits, tuition waivers (full and partial), and unspecified assistantships also available. Financial award applicants required to submit FAFSA. *Faculty research:* Quantitative genetics, genetic improvement of animal populations, statistical genetics. *Unit head:* Director of Graduate Studies, 607-255-4416, Fax: 607-254-5413, E-mail: shh4@cornell.edu. *Application contact:* Graduate Field Assistant, 607-255-4416, Fax: 607-254-5413, E-mail: shh4@cornell.edu.

Florida Agricultural and Mechanical University, Division of Graduate Studies, Research, and Continuing Education, College of Engineering Science, Technology, and Agriculture, Division of Agricultural Sciences, Tallahassee, FL 32307-3200. Offers agribusiness (MS); animal science (MS); engineering technology (MS); entomology (MS); food science (MS); international programs (MS); plant science (MS). *Degree requirements:* For master's, thesis. *Entrance requirements:* For master's, GRE General Test, minimum GPA of 3.0. Additional exam requirements/recommendations for international students: Required—TOEFL (minimum score 500 paper-based).

Fort Valley State University, College of Graduate Studies and Extended Education, Program in Animal Science, Fort Valley, GA 31030. Offers MS. *Degree requirements:* For master's, thesis. *Entrance requirements:* For master's, GRE General Test.

Iowa State University of Science and Technology, Graduate College, College of Agriculture, Department of Animal Science, Ames, IA 50011. Offers animal breeding and genetics (MS, PhD); animal physiology (MS); animal psychology (PhD); animal science (MS, PhD); meat science (MS, PhD). *Faculty:* 58 full-time (9 women), 2 part-time/adjunct (0 women). *Students:* 66 full-time (36 women), 31 part-time (12 women); includes 2 Black or African American, non-Hispanic/Latino; 1 Hispanic/Latino, 29 international. 45 applicants, 24% accepted, 9 enrolled. In 2010, 21 master's, 6 doctorates awarded. *Degree requirements:* For master's, thesis or alternative; for doctorate, thesis/dissertation. *Entrance requirements:* For master's and doctorate, GRE General Test. Additional exam requirements/recommendations for international students: Required—TOEFL (minimum score 550 paper-based; 80 iBT), IELTS (minimum score 6.5). *Application deadline:* For fall admission, 2/1 priority date for domestic and international students; for spring admission, 9/1 priority date for domestic and international students. Application fee: $40 ($90 for international students). Electronic applications accepted. *Financial support:* In 2010–11, 58 research assistantships with full and partial tuition reimbursements (averaging $16,771 per year), 2 teaching assistantships with full and partial tuition reimbursements (averaging $12,945 per year) were awarded; fellowships, scholarships/grants, health care benefits, and unspecified assistantships also available. *Faculty research:* Animal breeding, animal nutrition, meat science, muscle biology, nutritional physiology. *Unit head:* Dr. Maynard Hogberg, Head, 515-294-2160, Fax: 515-294-6994. *Application contact:* Dr. Joseph Sebranek, Director of Graduate Education, 515-294-2160.

Kansas State University, Graduate School, College of Agriculture, Department of Animal Sciences and Industry, Manhattan, KS 66506. Offers animal breeding and genetics (MS, PhD); meat science (MS, PhD); monogastric nutrition (MS, PhD); physiology (MS, PhD); ruminant nutrition (MS, PhD). *Degree requirements:* For master's, thesis, oral exam; for doctorate, thesis/dissertation, preliminary exams. *Entrance requirements:* Additional exam requirements/recommendations for international students: Required—TOEFL (minimum score 550 paper-based; 213 computer-based). Electronic applications accepted. *Faculty research:* Animal nutrition, animal physiology, meat science, animal genetics.

Louisiana State University and Agricultural and Mechanical College, Graduate School, College of Agriculture, School of Animal Sciences, Baton Rouge, LA 70803. Offers MS, PhD. Part-time programs available. *Faculty:* 17 full-time (2 women). *Students:* 32 full-time (21 women), 11 part-time (6 women); includes 1 Black or African American, non-Hispanic/Latino; 2 Hispanic/Latino, 10 international. Average age 27. 16 applicants, 69% accepted, 4 enrolled. In 2010, 7 master's, 1 doctorate awarded. Terminal master's awarded for partial completion of doctoral program. *Degree requirements:* For master's, thesis; for doctorate, thesis/dissertation. *Entrance requirements:* For master's and doctorate, GRE General Test, minimum GPA of 3.0. Additional exam requirements/recommendations for international students: Required—TOEFL (minimum score 550 paper-based; 213 computer-based; 79 iBT) or IELTS (minimum score 6.5). *Application deadline:* For fall admission, 1/25 priority date for domestic students, 5/15 for international students; for spring admission, 10/15 for international students. Applications are processed on a rolling basis. Application fee: $50 ($70 for international students). Electronic applications accepted. *Financial support:* In 2010–11, 36 students received support, including 1 fellowship (averaging $6,261 per year), 3 research assistantships with partial tuition reimbursements available (averaging $15,000 per year), 21 teaching assistantships with partial tuition reimbursements available (averaging $14,642 per year); Federal Work-Study, institutionally sponsored loans, scholarships/grants, health care benefits, tuition waivers (full and partial), and unspecified assistantships also available. Support available to part-time students. Financial award applicants required to submit FAFSA. *Faculty research:* Reproductive physiology, biotechnology, meats, non-ruminant and ruminant nutrition, daily science. Total annual research expenditures: $25,643. *Unit head:* Dr. Gary Hay, Head, 225-578-3241, Fax: 225-578-3279, E-mail: ghay@agctr.lsu.edu. *Application contact:* Dr. Donald L. Thompson, Graduate Coordinator, 225-578-3445, Fax: 225-578-3279, E-mail: dthomp1@lsu.edu.

McGill University, Faculty of Graduate and Postdoctoral Studies, Faculty of Agricultural and Environmental Sciences, Department of Animal Science, Montréal, QC H3A 2T5, Canada. Offers M Sc, M Sc A, PhD.

Michigan State University, College of Veterinary Medicine and The Graduate School, Graduate Programs in Veterinary Medicine, Department of Large Animal Clinical Sciences, East Lansing, MI 48824. Offers MS, PhD. *Entrance requirements:* Additional exam requirements/recommendations for international students: Required—TOEFL (minimum score 550 paper-based; 213 computer-based), Michigan State University ELT (minimum score 85), Michigan English Language Assessment Battery (minimum score 83). Electronic applications accepted.

Michigan State University, College of Veterinary Medicine and The Graduate School, Graduate Programs in Veterinary Medicine, Department of Small Animal Clinical Sciences, East Lansing, MI 48824. Offers MS. *Degree requirements:* For master's, thesis. *Entrance requirements:* Additional exam requirements/recommendations for international students: Required—TOEFL, Michigan State University ELT (minimum score 85), Michigan English Language Assessment Battery (minimum score 83).

Michigan State University, The Graduate School, College of Agriculture and Natural Resources, Department of Animal Science, East Lansing, MI 48824. Offers animal science (MS, PhD); animal science-environmental toxicology (PhD). *Entrance requirements:* Additional exam requirements/recommendations for international students: Required—TOEFL (minimum score 550 paper-based; 213 computer-based), Michigan State University ELT (minimum score 85), Michigan English Language Assessment Battery (minimum score 83). Electronic applications accepted.

Mississippi State University, College of Agriculture and Life Sciences, Department of Animal Dairy Sciences, Mississippi State, MS 39762. Offers agricultural life sciences (MS), including animal physiology (MS, PhD), genetics (MS, PhD); agricultural science (PhD), including animal dairy sciences, animal nutrition (MS, PhD); agriculture (MS), including animal dairy science, animal nutrition (MS, PhD); life sciences (PhD), including animal physiology (MS, PhD), genetics (MS, PhD). *Faculty:* 12 full-time (5 women). *Students:* 24 full-time (12 women), 11 part-time (6 women); includes 4 minority (2 Black or African American, non-Hispanic/Latino; 2 Hispanic/Latino), 6 international. Average age 29. 22 applicants, 55% accepted, 7 enrolled. In 2010, 6 master's, 1 doctorate awarded. *Degree requirements:* For master's, thesis, comprehensive oral or written exam; for doctorate, thesis/dissertation, comprehensive oral or written exam. *Entrance requirements:* For master's, GRE General Test, minimum GPA of 3.0; for doctorate, GRE General Test. Additional exam requirements/recommendations for international students: Required—TOEFL (minimum score 575 paper-based). *Application deadline:* For fall admission, 7/1 for domestic students, 5/1 for international students; for spring admission, 11/1 for domestic students, 9/1 for international students. Applications are processed on a rolling basis. Application fee: $40. Electronic applications accepted. *Expenses:* Tuition, state resident: full-time $2730.50; part-time $304 per credit hour. Tuition, nonresident: full-time $6901; part-time $767 per credit hour. *Financial support:* In 2010–11, 16 research assistantships (averaging $12,464 per year), 2 teaching assistantships (averaging $10,324 per year) were awarded; Federal Work-Study, institutionally sponsored loans, and unspecified assistantships also available. Financial award application deadline: 4/1; financial award applicants required to submit FAFSA. *Faculty research:* Ecology and population dynamics, physiology, biochemistry and behavior, systematics. *Unit head:* Dr. Terry Kiser, Professor and Department Head, 662-325-2802, Fax: 662-325-8873, E-mail: tkiser@ads.msstate.edu. *Application contact:* Dr. Peter Ryan, Graduate Coordinator, 662-325-2802, Fax: 662-325-8873, E-mail: ryan@cvm.msstate.edu.

Mississippi State University, College of Agriculture and Life Sciences, Department of Poultry Science, Mississippi State, MS 39762. Offers agriculture (MS), including poultry science (MS, PhD); agriculture sciences (PhD), including poultry science (MS, PhD). *Faculty:* 2 full-time (0 women). *Students:* 9 full-time (2 women), 4 international. Average age 27. 4 applicants, 25% accepted, 1 enrolled. In 2010, 3 master's awarded. *Degree requirements:* For master's, comprehensive exam, thesis optional; for doctorate, comprehensive exam, thesis/dissertation. *Entrance requirements:* Additional exam requirements/recommendations for international students: Required—TOEFL (minimum score 475 paper-based; 153 computer-based; 53 iBT); Recommended—IELTS (minimum score 4.5). *Application deadline:* For fall admission, 7/1 for

domestic students, 5/1 for international students; for spring admission, 10/1 for domestic students, 11/1 for international students. Applications are processed on a rolling basis. Application fee: $40. Electronic applications accepted. *Expenses:* Tuition, state resident: full-time $2730.50; part-time $304 per credit hour. Tuition, nonresident: full-time $6901; part-time $767 per credit hour. *Financial support:* In 2010–11, 8 research assistantships with partial tuition reimbursements (averaging $14,520 per year), 1 teaching assistantship with partial tuition reimbursement (averaging $9,816 per year) were awarded; Federal Work-Study, institutionally sponsored loans, scholarships/grants, and unspecified assistantships also available. Financial award application deadline: 4/1; financial award applicants required to submit FAFSA. *Unit head:* Dr. Benjy Mikel, Interim Department Head and Professor, 662-325-5508, Fax: 662-325-8292, E-mail: wbm50@.msstate.edu. *Application contact:* Dr. Chris McDaniel, Professor and Graduate Coordinator, 662-325-1839, Fax: 662-325-8292, E-mail: cmcdaniel@poultry.msstate.edu.

Montana State University, College of Graduate Studies, College of Agriculture, Department of Animal and Range Sciences, Bozeman, MT 59717. Offers MS, PhD. Part-time programs available. *Faculty:* 13 full-time (4 women), 4 part-time/adjunct (1 woman). *Students:* 5 full-time (2 women), 13 part-time (6 women), 1 international. Average age 31. 13 applicants, 38% accepted, 4 enrolled. In 2010, 5 master's, 2 doctorates awarded. *Degree requirements:* For master's, comprehensive exam; for doctorate, comprehensive exam, thesis/dissertation. *Entrance requirements:* For master's, GRE, minimum GPA of 3.0; undergraduate coursework in animal science, range science or closely-related field; faculty adviser; for doctorate, GRE. Additional exam requirements/recommendations for international students: Required—TOEFL (minimum score 550 paper-based; 213 computer-based; 80 iBT). *Application deadline:* For fall admission, 7/15 priority date for domestic students, 5/15 priority date for international students; for spring admission, 12/1 priority date for domestic students, 10/1 priority date for international students. Applications are processed on a rolling basis. Application fee: $30. Electronic applications accepted. *Expenses:* Tuition, state resident: full-time $5553.90. Tuition, nonresident: full-time $14,646. Required fees: $1233. *Financial support:* In 2010–11, 6 students received support, including 3 research assistantships (averaging $31,000 per year), 3 teaching assistantships (averaging $14,500 per year); tuition waivers (full) also available. Financial award application deadline: 3/1; financial award applicants required to submit FAFSA. *Faculty research:* Rangeland ecology, wildlife habitat management, residual feed intake, post-partum effect of bulls, increasing efficiency of sheep production systems. Total annual research expenditures: $1.5 million. *Unit head:* Dr. Glenn Duff, Department Head, 406-994-4850, Fax: 406-994-5589, E-mail: glenn.duff@montana.edu. *Application contact:* Dr. Carl A. Fox, Vice Provost for Graduate Education, 406-994-4145, Fax: 406-994-7433, E-mail: gradstudy@montana.edu.

New Mexico State University, Graduate School, College of Agricultural, Consumer and Environmental Sciences, Department of Animal and Range Sciences, Las Cruces, NM 88003-8001. Offers animal science (MS, PhD); domestic animal biology (M Ag); range science (M Ag, MS, PhD). Part-time programs available. *Faculty:* 9 full-time (2 women). *Students:* 36 full-time (23 women), 9 part-time (2 women); includes 6 minority (1 American Indian or Alaska Native, non-Hispanic/Latino; 4 Hispanic/Latino; 1 Two or more races, non-Hispanic/Latino), 7 international. Average age 27. 27 applicants, 81% accepted, 16 enrolled. In 2010, 11 master's, 2 doctorates awarded. Terminal master's awarded for partial completion of doctoral program. *Degree requirements:* For master's, thesis, seminar, experimental statistics; for doctorate, thesis/dissertation, research tool. *Entrance requirements:* For master's, minimum GPA of 3.0 in last 60 hours of undergraduate course work (MS); for doctorate, minimum graduate GPA of 3.2. Additional exam requirements/recommendations for international students: Required—TOEFL (minimum score 530 paper-based; 71 computer-based), IELTS (minimum score 6). *Application deadline:* For fall admission, 7/1 priority date for domestic students, 7/1 for international students; for spring admission, 11/1 for domestic and international students. Applications are processed on a rolling basis. Application fee: $30 ($50 for international students). Electronic applications accepted. *Expenses:* Tuition, state resident: full-time $4536; part-time $242 per credit. Tuition, nonresident: full-time $15,816; part-time $712 per credit. Required fees: $636 per term. *Financial support:* In 2010–11, 25 students received support, including 3 research assistantships (averaging $12,823 per year), 24 teaching assistantships (averaging $20,008 per year); Federal Work-Study and health care benefits also available. Support available to part-time students. Financial award application deadline: 3/1. *Faculty research:* Reproductive physiology, ruminant nutrition, nutrition toxicology, range ecology, wildland hydrology. *Unit head:* Dr. Tim Ross, Interim Head, 575-646-2514, Fax: 575-646-5441, E-mail: tross@nmsu.edu. *Application contact:* Dr. Tim Ross, Interim Head, 575-646-2514, Fax: 575-646-5441, E-mail: tross@nmsu.edu.

North Carolina Agricultural and Technical State University, Graduate School, School of Agriculture and Environmental Sciences, Department of Animal Sciences, Greensboro, NC 27411. Offers animal health science (MS).

North Carolina State University, Graduate School, College of Agriculture and Life Sciences, Department of Animal Science, Raleigh, NC 27695. Offers animal and poultry science (PhD); animal science (MS). *Degree requirements:* For master's, thesis optional. *Entrance requirements:* For master's, GRE, minimum GPA of 3.0. Electronic applications accepted. *Faculty research:* Nutrient utilization, mineral nutrition, genomics, endocrinology, reproductive physiology.

North Carolina State University, Graduate School, College of Agriculture and Life Sciences, Department of Poultry Science, Raleigh, NC 27695. Offers MS. Part-time programs available. *Degree requirements:* For master's, thesis. Electronic applications accepted. *Faculty research:* Reproductive physiology, nutrition, toxicology, immunology, molecular biology.

North Dakota State University, College of Graduate and Interdisciplinary Studies, College of Agriculture, Food Systems, and Natural Resources, Department of Animal and Range Sciences, Fargo, ND 58108. Offers animal science (MS, PhD); natural resource management (MS, PhD); range sciences (MS, PhD). *Students:* 19 full-time (14 women), 7 part-time (4 women); includes 1 American Indian or Alaska Native, non-Hispanic/Latino; 1 Asian, non-Hispanic/Latino. Average age 25. 13 applicants, 62% accepted. In 2010, 17 master's, 2 doctorates awarded. *Degree requirements:* For master's, thesis; for doctorate, comprehensive exam, thesis/dissertation. *Entrance requirements:* For master's and doctorate, GRE General Test. Additional exam requirements/recommendations for international students: Required—TOEFL (minimum score 71 iBT). *Application deadline:* Applications are processed on a rolling basis. Application fee: $45 ($60 for international students). *Financial support:* In 2010–11, 1 fellowship with tuition reimbursement (averaging $18,000 per year), 29 research assistantships with tuition reimbursements (averaging $13,000 per year) were awarded; teaching assistantships, Federal Work-Study, institutionally sponsored loans, and tuition waivers (partial) also available. Financial award application deadline: 3/15. *Faculty research:* Reproduction, nutrition, meat and muscle biology, breeding/genetics. Total annual research expenditures: $1.5 million. *Unit head:* Dr. David Buchanan, Chair, 701-231-7643, Fax: 701-231-7590, E-mail: david.buchanan@ndsu.edu. *Application contact:* Dr. David Buchanan, Chair, 701-231-7643, Fax: 701-231-7590, E-mail: david.buchanan@ndsu.edu.

Nova Scotia Agricultural College, Research and Graduate Studies, Truro, NS B2N 5E3, Canada. Offers agriculture (M Sc), including air quality, animal behavior, animal molecular genetics, animal nutrition, animal technology, aquaculture, botany, crop management, crop physiology, ecology, environmental microbiology, food science, horticulture, nutrient management, pest management, physiology, plant biotechnology, plant pathology, soil chemistry, soil fertility, waste management and composting, water quality. Program offered jointly with Dalhousie University. Part-time programs available. *Degree requirements:* For master's, thesis, ATC Exam Teaching Assistantship. *Entrance requirements:* For master's, honors B Sc, minimum GPA of 3.0. Additional exam requirements/recommendations for international students: Required—TOEFL (minimum score 580 paper-based; 237 computer-based; 92 iBT), IELTS, Michigan English Language Assessment Battery, CanTEST, CAEL. *Faculty research:* Bio-product development, organic agriculture, nutrient management, air and water quality, agricultural biotechnology.

The Ohio State University, Graduate School, College of Food, Agricultural, and Environmental Sciences, Department of Animal Sciences, Columbus, OH 43210. Offers MS, PhD. *Faculty:* 47. *Students:* 36 full-time (26 women), 11 part-time (6 women); includes 2 Black or African American, non-Hispanic/Latino; 4 Hispanic/Latino, 15 international. Average age 27. In 2010, 9 master's, 4 doctorates awarded. *Degree requirements:* For master's, thesis; for doctorate, thesis/dissertation. *Entrance requirements:* For master's and doctorate, GRE General Test. Additional exam requirements/recommendations for international students: Required—TOEFL (minimum score 550 paper-based; 213 computer-based), IELTS (minimum score 7), or Michigan English Language Assessment Battery (minimum score 84). *Application deadline:* For fall admission, 8/15 priority date for domestic students, 7/1 priority date for international students; for winter admission, 12/1 priority date for domestic students, 11/1 priority date for international students; for spring admission, 3/1 priority date for domestic students, 2/1 priority date for international students. Applications are processed on a rolling basis. Application fee: $40 ($50 for international students). Electronic applications accepted. *Expenses:* Tuition, state resident: full-time $10,605. Tuition, nonresident: full-time $26,535. Tuition and fees vary according to course load and program. *Financial support:* Fellowships, research assistantships, teaching assistantships, Federal Work-Study and institutionally sponsored loans available. Support available to part-time students. *Unit head:* Joseph Hogan, Chair, 330-263-3801, Fax: 614-292-2929, E-mail: hogan.4@osu.edu. *Application contact:* Graduate Admissions, 614-292-9444, Fax: 614-292-3895, E-mail: domestic.grad@osu.edu.

Oklahoma State University, College of Agricultural Science and Natural Resources, Department of Animal Science, Stillwater, OK 74078. Offers animal sciences (M Ag, MS); food science (MS, PhD). *Faculty:* 28 full-time (6 women), 4 part-time/adjunct (0 women). *Students:* 25 full-time (19 women), 49 part-time (24 women); includes 1 Black or African American, non-Hispanic/Latino; 3 Hispanic/Latino, 30 international. Average age 27. 105 applicants, 12% accepted, 12 enrolled. In 2010, 17 master's, 5 doctorates awarded. *Degree requirements:* For master's, thesis; for doctorate, comprehensive exam, thesis/dissertation. *Entrance requirements:* For master's and doctorate, GRE or GMAT. Additional exam requirements/recommendations for international students: Required—TOEFL (minimum score 550 paper-based; 79 iBT). *Application deadline:* For fall admission, 3/1 priority date for international students; for spring admission, 8/1 priority date for international students. Applications are processed on a rolling basis. Application fee: $40 ($75 for international students). Electronic applications accepted. *Expenses:* Tuition, state resident: full-time $3716; part-time $154.85 per credit hour. Tuition, nonresident: full-time $14,892; part-time $621 per credit hour. Required fees: $2044; $85.20 per credit hour. One-time fee: $50. Tuition and fees vary according to course load and campus/location. *Financial support:* In 2010–11, 38 research assistantships (averaging $14,013 per year), 1 teaching assistantship (averaging $11,064 per year) were awarded; career-related internships or fieldwork, Federal Work-Study, scholarships/grants, health care benefits, tuition waivers (partial), and unspecified assistantships also available. Support available to part-time students. Financial award application deadline: 3/1; financial award applicants required to submit FAFSA. *Faculty research:* Quantitative trait loci identification for economical traits in swing/beef; waste management strategies in livestock; endocrine control of reproductive processes in farm animals; cholesterol synthesis, inhibition, and reduction; food safety research. *Unit head:* Dr. Ronald Kensinger, Head, 405-744-6062, Fax: 405-744-7390. *Application contact:* Dr. Gerald Horn, Information Contact, 405-744-6070, Fax: 405-744-6621, E-mail: gerald.horn@okstate.edu.

Oregon State University, Graduate School, College of Agricultural Sciences, Department of Animal Sciences, Corvallis, OR 97331. Offers animal science (M Agr, MAIS, MS, PhD), poultry science (M Agr, MAIS, MS, PhD). Terminal master's awarded for partial completion of doctoral program. *Degree requirements:* For master's, thesis (for some programs); for doctorate, thesis/dissertation. *Entrance requirements:* For master's and doctorate, GRE General Test, minimum GPA of 3.0 in last 90 hours. Additional exam requirements/recommendations for international students: Required—TOEFL. *Faculty research:* Reproductive physiology, population genetics, general nutrition of ruminants and nonruminants, embryo physiology, endocrinology.

Penn State University Park, Graduate School, College of Agricultural Sciences, Department of Dairy and Animal Science, State College, University Park, PA 16802-1503. Offers MPS, MS, PhD.

Prairie View A&M University, College of Agriculture and Human Sciences, Prairie View, TX 77446-0519. Offers agricultural economics (MS); animal sciences (MS); interdisciplinary human sciences (MS); soil science (MS). Part-time and evening/weekend programs available. *Faculty:* 11 full-time (2 women). *Students:* 47 full-time (33 women), 34 part-time (26 women); includes 62 Black or African American, non-Hispanic/Latino; 2 Asian, non-Hispanic/Latino; 2 Hispanic/Latino, 5 international. Average age 30. 147 applicants, 100% accepted. In 2010, 21 master's awarded. *Degree requirements:* For master's, comprehensive exam, thesis (for some programs), field placement. *Entrance requirements:* For master's, GRE General Test, minimum GPA of 2.45. Additional exam requirements/recommendations for international students: Required—TOEFL (minimum score 550 paper-based). *Application deadline:* For fall admission, 6/1 for domestic and international students; for spring admission, 10/1 for domestic and international students. Applications are processed on a rolling basis. Application fee: $50. *Expenses:* Tuition, state resident: full-time $3586.14; part-time $119.06 per credit hour. Tuition, nonresident: part-time $511.23 per credit hour. *Financial support:* In 2010–11, 57 students received support, including 8 fellowships with tuition reimbursements available (averaging $12,000 per year), 10 research assistantships with tuition reimbursements available (averaging $15,000 per year); career-related internships or fieldwork, Federal Work-Study, institutionally sponsored loans, scholarships/grants, tuition waivers (partial), and unspecified assistantships also available. Support available to part-time students. Financial award application deadline: 4/1; financial award applicants required to submit FAFSA. *Faculty research:* Domestic violence prevention, water quality, food growth regulators, wetland dynamics, biochemistry, obesity and nutrition, family therapy. Total annual research expenditures: $4 million. *Unit head:* Dr. Freddie Richards, Dean, 936-261-2528, Fax: 936-261-5143, E-mail: flrichards@pvamu.edu. *Application contact:* Dr. Richard W. Griffin, Interim Department Head, 936-261-5019, Fax: 936-261-5148, E-mail: rwgriffin@pvamu.edu.

Purdue University, Graduate School, College of Agriculture, Department of Animal Sciences, West Lafayette, IN 47907. Offers MS, PhD. Part-time programs available. Terminal master's awarded for partial completion of doctoral program. *Degree requirements:* For master's, thesis optional; for doctorate, thesis/dissertation. *Entrance requirements:* For master's and doctorate, GRE General Test. Additional exam requirements/recommendations for international students: Required—TOEFL; Recommended—TWE. Electronic applications accepted. *Faculty research:* Genetics, meat science, nutrition, management, ethology.

Rutgers, The State University of New Jersey, New Brunswick, Graduate School-New Brunswick, Program in Endocrinology and Animal Biosciences, Piscataway, NJ 08854-8097. Offers MS, PhD. Terminal master's awarded for partial completion of doctoral program. *Degree requirements:* For master's, thesis; for doctorate, comprehensive exam, thesis/dissertation. *Entrance requirements:* For master's and doctorate, GRE General Test. Additional exam requirements/recommendations for international students: Required—TOEFL. Electronic applications accepted. *Expenses:* Tuition, state resident: full-time $7200; part-time $600 per credit. Tuition, nonresident: full-time $11,124; part-time $927 per credit. *Faculty research:* Comparative and behavioral endocrinology, epigenetic regulation of the endocrine system, exercise physiology

Animal Sciences

Rutgers, The State University of New Jersey, New Brunswick (continued)
and immunology, fetal and neonatal developmental programming, mammary gland biology and breast cancer, neuroendocrinology and alcohol studies, reproductive and developmental toxicology.

South Dakota State University, Graduate School, College of Agriculture and Biological Sciences, Department of Animal and Range Sciences, Brookings, SD 57007. Offers animal science (MS, PhD); biological sciences (PhD). Part-time programs available. *Degree requirements:* For master's, thesis, oral exam; for doctorate, comprehensive exam, thesis/dissertation, preliminary oral and written exams. *Entrance requirements:* Additional exam requirements/recommendations for international students: Required—TOEFL (minimum score 550 paper-based; 213 computer-based; 79 iBT). *Faculty research:* Ruminant and nonruminant nutrition, meat science, reproductive physiology, range utilization, ecology genetics, muscle biology, animal production.

South Dakota State University, Graduate School, College of Agriculture and Biological Sciences, Department of Dairy Science, Brookings, SD 57007. Offers animal sciences (MS, PhD); biological sciences (MS, PhD). Part-time programs available. *Degree requirements:* For master's, thesis, oral exam; for doctorate, comprehensive exam, thesis/dissertation, preliminary oral and written exams. *Entrance requirements:* Additional exam requirements/recommendations for international students: Required—TOEFL (minimum score 550 paper-based; 213 computer-based). *Faculty research:* Dairy cattle nutrition, energy metabolism, food safety, dairy processing technology.

Southern Illinois University Carbondale, Graduate School, College of Agriculture, Department of Animal Science, Food and Nutrition, Program in Animal Science, Carbondale, IL 62901-4701. Offers MS. *Degree requirements:* For master's, thesis. *Entrance requirements:* For master's, minimum GPA of 2.7. Additional exam requirements/recommendations for international students: Required—TOEFL. *Faculty research:* Nutrition, reproductive physiology, animal biotechnology, phytoestrogens and animal reproduction.

Sul Ross State University, Division of Agricultural and Natural Resource Science, Program in Animal Science, Alpine, TX 79832. Offers M Ag, MS. Part-time programs available. *Degree requirements:* For master's, thesis (for some programs). *Entrance requirements:* For master's, GRE General Test, minimum GPA of 2.5 in last 60 hours of undergraduate work. *Faculty research:* Reproductive physiology, meat processing, animal nutrition, equine foot and motion studies, Spanish goat and Barbido sheep studies.

Texas A&M University, College of Agriculture and Life Sciences, Department of Animal Science, College Station, TX 77843. Offers M Agr, MS, PhD. *Faculty:* 31. *Students:* 94 full-time (55 women), 26 part-time (16 women); includes 12 minority (3 Black or African American, non-Hispanic/Latino; 2 Asian, non-Hispanic/Latino; 7 Hispanic/Latino), 10 international. Average age 26. In 2010, 22 master's, 4 doctorates awarded. *Degree requirements:* For master's, thesis; for doctorate, thesis/dissertation. *Entrance requirements:* For master's and doctorate, GRE General Test. Additional exam requirements/recommendations for international students: Required—TOEFL. *Application deadline:* For fall admission, 2/1 priority date for domestic students; for spring admission, 10/1 priority date for domestic students. Applications are processed on a rolling basis. Application fee: $50 ($75 for international students). *Financial support:* In 2010–11, fellowships (averaging $15,000 per year), research assistantships (averaging $12,950 per year), teaching assistantships (averaging $11,500 per year) were awarded; career-related internships or fieldwork, Federal Work-Study, institutionally sponsored loans, and scholarships/grants also available. Financial award application deadline: 2/1; financial award applicants required to submit FAFSA. *Faculty research:* Genetic engineering/gene markers, dietary effects on colon cancer, biotechnology. *Unit head:* Dr. H. Russell Cross, Interim Head, 979-845-1543, Fax: 979-845-6433, E-mail: hrcross@tamu.edu. *Application contact:* Dr. H. Russell Cross, Interim Head, 979-845-1543, Fax: 979-845-6433, E-mail: hrcross@tamu.edu.

Texas A&M University, College of Agriculture and Life Sciences, Department of Poultry Science, College Station, TX 77843. Offers M Agr, MS, PhD. Part-time and evening/weekend programs available. Postbaccalaureate distance learning degree programs offered (no on-campus study). *Faculty:* 15. *Students:* 42 full-time (20 women), 11 part-time (6 women); includes 11 minority (2 Black or African American, non-Hispanic/Latino; 1 American Indian or Alaska Native, non-Hispanic/Latino; 4 Asian, non-Hispanic/Latino; 4 Hispanic/Latino), 25 international. Average age 29. In 2010, 3 master's, 1 doctorate awarded. Terminal master's awarded for partial completion of doctoral program. *Degree requirements:* For master's, thesis (for some programs); for doctorate, thesis/dissertation. *Entrance requirements:* For master's and doctorate, GRE General Test. Additional exam requirements/recommendations for international students: Required—TOEFL. Application fee: $50 ($75 for international students). Electronic applications accepted. *Financial support:* In 2010–11, fellowships with partial tuition reimbursements (averaging $18,000 per year); research assistantships with partial tuition reimbursements, teaching assistantships, scholarships/grants and unspecified assistantships also available. Financial award application deadline: 4/1; financial award applicants required to submit FAFSA. *Faculty research:* Poultry diseases and immunology, avian genetics and physiology, nutrition and metabolism, poultry processing and food safety, waste management. *Unit head:* Dr. John B. Carey, Head, 979-845-1931, E-mail: jcarey@poultry.tamu.edu. *Application contact:* Jennifer Allen, Academic Advisor II, 979-845-1654, E-mail: jallen@poultry.tamu.edu.

Texas A&M University–Kingsville, College of Graduate Studies, College of Agriculture and Home Economics, Program in Animal Sciences, Kingsville, TX 78363. Offers MS. *Degree requirements:* For master's, comprehensive exam, thesis or alternative. *Entrance requirements:* For master's, GRE General Test, minimum GPA of 3.0. Additional exam requirements/recommendations for international students: Required—TOEFL.

Texas Tech University, Graduate School, College of Agricultural Sciences and Natural Resources, Department of Animal and Food Sciences, Lubbock, TX 79409-2141. Offers animal science (MS, PhD); food science (MS). *Faculty:* 10 full-time (3 women). *Students:* 56 full-time (27 women), 11 part-time (4 women); includes 1 Hispanic/Latino; 1 Two or more races, non-Hispanic/Latino, 13 international. Average age 26. 70 applicants, 34% accepted, 21 enrolled. In 2010, 16 master's, 9 doctorates awarded. *Degree requirements:* For master's, thesis or alternative, internship (M Agr); for doctorate, thesis/dissertation. *Entrance requirements:* For master's and doctorate, GRE General Test, formal approval from departmental committee. Additional exam requirements/recommendations for international students: Required—TOEFL (minimum score 550 paper-based; 213 computer-based; 79 iBT). *Application deadline:* For fall admission, 6/1 priority date for domestic students, 1/15 priority date for international students; for spring admission, 9/1 priority date for domestic students, 6/15 priority date for international students. Applications are processed on a rolling basis. Application fee: $50 ($75 for international students). Electronic applications accepted. *Expenses:* Tuition, state resident: full-time $5495.76; part-time $228.99 per credit hour. Tuition, nonresident: full-time $12,936; part-time $538.99 per credit hour. Required fees: $2674; $36 per credit hour. $905 per semester. *Financial support:* In 2010–11, 54 students received support, including 23 research assistantships with partial tuition reimbursements available (averaging $5,040 per year), 2 teaching assistantships with partial tuition reimbursements available (averaging $5,011 per year). Financial award application deadline: 4/15; financial award applicants required to submit FAFSA. *Faculty research:* Animal growth composition and product acceptability, animal nutrition and utilization, animal physiology and adaptation to stress, food microbiology, meat science safety and security. Total annual research expenditures: $4.6 million. *Unit head:* Dr. Leslie D. Thompson, Chairman, 806-742-2805 Ext. 223, Fax: 806-742-0898, E-mail: leslie.thompson@ttu.edu. *Application contact:* Sandy Gellner, Graduate Secretary, 806-742-2805 Ext. 221, Fax: 806-742-0898, E-mail: sandra.gellner@ttu.edu.

Tufts University, Cummings School of Veterinary Medicine, Program in Conservation Medicine, Medford, MA 02155. Offers MS. *Degree requirements:* For master's, case study, preceptorship. *Entrance requirements:* For master's, GRE, official transcripts, curriculum vitae. Additional exam requirements/recommendations for international students: Required—TOEFL or IELTS. Electronic applications accepted. *Expenses:* Tuition: Full-time $39,624; part-time $3962 per course. Required fees: $40 per year. Full-time tuition and fees vary according to degree level, program and student level. Part-time tuition and fees vary according to course load.

Tuskegee University, Graduate Programs, College of Agricultural, Environmental and Natural Sciences, Department of Agricultural Sciences, Program in Animal and Poultry Sciences, Tuskegee, AL 36088. Offers MS. *Faculty:* 13 full-time (1 woman), 2 part-time/adjunct (1 woman). *Students:* 13 full-time (7 women), 2 part-time (both women); includes 8 Black or African American, non-Hispanic/Latino; 11 Hispanic/Latino, 2 international. Average age 27. In 2010, 4 master's awarded. *Degree requirements:* For master's, thesis. *Entrance requirements:* For master's, GRE General Test. Additional exam requirements/recommendations for international students: Required—TOEFL (minimum score 500 paper-based; 69 computer-based). *Application deadline:* For fall admission, 7/15 for domestic students. Applications are processed on a rolling basis. Application fee: $25 ($35 for international students). *Expenses:* Tuition: Full-time $16,100; part-time $665 per credit hour. Required fees: $650. *Financial support:* Application deadline: 4/15. *Unit head:* Dr. P. K. Biswas, Head, 334-727-8446. *Application contact:* Dr. Robert L. Laney, Vice President/Director of Admissions and Enrollment Management, 334-727-8580, Fax: 334-727-5750, E-mail: planey@tuskegee.edu.

Universidad Nacional Pedro Henriquez Urena, Graduate School, Santo Domingo, Dominican Republic. Offers agricultural diversity (MS), including horticultural/fruit production, tropical animal production; conservation of monuments and cultural assets (M Arch); ecology and environment (MS); environmental engineering (MEE); international relations (MA); natural resource management (MS); political science (MA); project optimization (MPM); project feasibility (MPM); project management (MPM); sanitation engineering (ME); science for teachers (MS); tropical Caribbean architecture (M Arch).

Université Laval, Faculty of Agricultural and Food Sciences, Department of Animal Sciences, Programs in Animal Sciences, Québec, QC G1K 7P4, Canada. Offers M Sc, PhD. Part-time programs available. Terminal master's awarded for partial completion of doctoral program. *Degree requirements:* For master's, thesis; for doctorate, comprehensive exam, thesis/dissertation. *Entrance requirements:* For master's and doctorate, knowledge of French and English. Electronic applications accepted.

The University of Arizona, College of Agriculture and Life Sciences, Department of Animal Sciences, Tucson, AZ 85721. Offers MS, PhD. Part-time programs available. *Faculty:* 7 full-time (1 woman). *Students:* 16 full-time (6 women), 7 part-time (5 women); includes 1 Black or African American, non-Hispanic/Latino; 1 Asian, non-Hispanic/Latino; 2 Hispanic/Latino; 2 Two or more races, non-Hispanic/Latino, 4 international. Average age 28. 26 applicants, 65% accepted, 12 enrolled. In 2010, 6 master's, 1 doctorate awarded. *Degree requirements:* For master's, thesis; for doctorate, thesis/dissertation. *Entrance requirements:* For master's, GRE Subject Test, 3 letters of recommendation, minimum GPA of 3.0; for doctorate, GRE Subject Test (biology or chemistry recommended), 3 letters of recommendation, statement of purpose, minimum GPA of 3.0. Additional exam requirements/recommendations for international students: Required—TOEFL (minimum score 550 paper-based; 213 computer-based; 80 iBT). *Application deadline:* Applications are processed on a rolling basis. Application fee: $75. *Expenses:* Tuition, state resident: full-time $7692. *Financial support:* In 2010–11, 10 students received support, including 8 research assistantships with partial tuition reimbursements available (averaging $19,830 per year); fellowships, teaching assistantships with partial tuition reimbursements available, scholarships/grants, health care benefits, and unspecified assistantships also available. Financial award application deadline: 4/1. *Faculty research:* Nutrition of beef and dairy cattle, reproduction and breeding, muscle growth and function, animal stress, meat science. Total annual research expenditures: $793,069. *Unit head:* Dr. Ronald E. Allen, Professor and Head, 520-621-7626, Fax: 520-621-9435, E-mail: rallen@ag.arizona.edu. *Application contact:* Dr. Lance Baumgard, Grad, Committee Chair, 520-621-1487, Fax: 520-621-9435, E-mail: baumgard@ag.arizona.edu.

University of Arkansas, Graduate School, Dale Bumpers College of Agricultural, Food and Life Sciences, Department of Animal Science, Fayetteville, AR 72701-1201. Offers MS, PhD. *Students:* 15 full-time (8 women), 14 part-time (6 women), 3 international. 18 applicants, 50% accepted. In 2010, 6 master's, 1 doctorate awarded. *Degree requirements:* For master's, thesis; for doctorate, variable foreign language requirement, thesis/dissertation. *Entrance requirements:* For master's, GRE General Test or minimum GPA of 2.7. *Application deadline:* For fall admission, 4/1 for international students; for spring admission, 10/1 for international students. Applications are processed on a rolling basis. Application fee: $40 ($50 for international students). Electronic applications accepted. *Financial support:* In 2010–11, 1 fellowship with tuition reimbursement, 19 research assistantships, 1 teaching assistantship were awarded; career-related internships or fieldwork and Federal Work-Study also available. Support available to part-time students. Financial award application deadline: 4/1; financial award applicants required to submit FAFSA. *Unit head:* Dr. Keith Lusby, Chair, 479-575-4351, E-mail: klusby@uark.edu. *Application contact:* Dr. David Kreider, Graduate Coordinator, 479-575-6323, E-mail: dkreider@uark.edu.

University of Arkansas, Graduate School, Dale Bumpers College of Agricultural, Food and Life Sciences, Department of Poultry Science, Fayetteville, AR 72701-1201. Offers MS, PhD. *Faculty:* 15 full-time (3 women). *Students:* 12 full-time (3 women), 29 part-time (16 women); includes 4 minority (1 Black or African American, non-Hispanic/Latino; 3 Hispanic/Latino), 17 international. 8 applicants, 75% accepted. In 2010, 2 master's, 3 doctorates awarded. *Degree requirements:* For master's, thesis; for doctorate, variable foreign language requirement, thesis/dissertation. *Application deadline:* For fall admission, 4/1 for international students; for spring admission, 10/1 for international students. Applications are processed on a rolling basis. Application fee: $40 ($50 for international students). Electronic applications accepted. *Financial support:* In 2010–11, 2 fellowships with tuition reimbursements, 26 research assistantships were awarded; teaching assistantships, career-related internships or fieldwork and Federal Work-Study also available. Support available to part-time students. Financial award application deadline: 4/1; financial award applicants required to submit FAFSA. *Unit head:* Dr. Mike Kidd, Department Head, 479-575-4952, E-mail: mkidd@uark.edu. *Application contact:* Dr. Mike Slavik, Graduate Coordinator, 479-575-4952, E-mail: mslavik@uark.edu.

The University of British Columbia, Faculty of Land and Food Systems, Animal Science Graduate Program, Vancouver, BC V6T 1Z1, Canada. Offers M Sc, PhD. *Degree requirements:* For master's, thesis; for doctorate, comprehensive exam, thesis/dissertation. *Entrance requirements:* Additional exam requirements/recommendations for international students: Required—TOEFL (minimum score 577 paper-based; 233 computer-based; 90 iBT), IELTS (minimum score 6.5). Electronic applications accepted. Tuition charges are reported in Canadian dollars. *Expenses:* Tuition, area resident: Full-time $4179 Canadian dollars. International tuition: $7344 Canadian dollars full-time. *Faculty research:* Animal production, animal behavior and welfare, reproductive physiology, animal genetics, aquaculture and fish physiology.

University of California, Davis, Graduate Studies, Graduate Group in Animal Biology, Davis, CA 95616. Offers MAM, MS, PhD. Terminal master's awarded for partial completion of doctoral program. *Degree requirements:* For master's, comprehensive exam (for some programs), thesis (for some programs); for doctorate, thesis/dissertation. *Entrance requirements:* For master's, GRE General Test, minimum GPA of 3.0. Additional exam requirements/recommendations for international students: Required—TOEFL (minimum score 550 paper-

based; 213 computer-based). Electronic applications accepted. *Faculty research:* Genetics, nutrition, physiology and behavior in domestic and aquatic animals.

University of Connecticut, Graduate School, College of Agriculture and Natural Resources, Department of Animal Science, Storrs, CT 06269. Offers MS, PhD. Terminal master's awarded for partial completion of doctoral program. *Degree requirements:* For master's, comprehensive exam, thesis; for doctorate, comprehensive exam, thesis/dissertation. *Entrance requirements:* For master's and doctorate, GRE General Test, GRE Subject Test. Additional exam requirements/recommendations for international students: Required—TOEFL (minimum score 550 paper-based, 213 computer-based). Electronic applications accepted.

University of Delaware, College of Agriculture and Natural Resources, Department of Animal and Food Sciences, Newark, DE 19716. Offers animal sciences (MS, PhD); food sciences (MS). Part-time programs available. Terminal master's awarded for partial completion of doctoral program. *Degree requirements:* For master's, thesis; for doctorate, comprehensive exam, thesis/dissertation. *Entrance requirements:* For master's and doctorate, GRE General Test. Additional exam requirements/recommendations for international students: Required—TOEFL. Electronic applications accepted. *Faculty research:* Food chemistry, food microbiology, process engineering technology, packaging, food analysis, microbial genetics, molecular endocrinology, growth physiology, avian immunology and virology, monogastric nutrition, avian genomics.

University of Florida, Graduate School, College of Agricultural and Life Sciences, Department of Animal Sciences, Gainesville, FL 32611. Offers MS, PhD. Part-time programs available. *Faculty:* 24 full-time (5 women). *Students:* 48 full-time (27 women), 4 part-time (3 women); includes 1 Black or African American, non-Hispanic/Latino; 2 Hispanic/Latino, 22 international. Average age 27. 50 applicants, 54% accepted, 25 enrolled. In 2010, 20 master's, 3 doctorates awarded. *Degree requirements:* For master's, variable foreign language requirement, comprehensive exam (for some programs), thesis (for some programs), One departmental and one exit seminar required. Thesis and non-thesis options; for doctorate, comprehensive exam, thesis/dissertation, Two departmental seminars and one exit seminar required. *Entrance requirements:* For master's and doctorate, GRE General Test, minimum GPA of 3.0. Additional exam requirements/recommendations for international students: Required—TOEFL (minimum score 550 paper-based; 213 computer-based; 80 iBT), IELTS (minimum score 6). *Application deadline:* For fall admission, 3/1 priority date for domestic students, 2/1 for international students; for winter admission, 9/1 for domestic students, 8/1 for international students; for spring admission, 1/1 for domestic students, 12/1 for international students. Applications are processed on a rolling basis. Application fee: $30. Electronic applications accepted. *Expenses:* Tuition, state resident: full-time $10,915.92. Tuition, nonresident: full-time $28,309. *Financial support:* In 2010–11, 34 students received support, including 11 fellowships, 23 research assistantships (averaging $15,502 per year). Financial award applicants required to submit FAFSA. *Faculty research:* Ruminal metabolism and fermentation, enteric greenhouse gas emissions, beef cattle nutrition; embryonic development, fertility, uterine biology, dairy cattle, heat stress; genetic and genomic evaluation of animals in multibreed populations; prostaglandin and immune response to lipopolysaccharides in dairy cattle, dietary fatty acids and their effects on reproduction, immunity and energy metabolism; metabolic influences of nutrients on reproduction. Total annual research expenditures: $563,225. *Unit head:* Dr. Geoffrey Dahl, Chair, 352-392-1981 Ext. 221, Fax: 352-392-5595, E-mail: gdahl@ufl.edu. *Application contact:* Dr. Joel H. Brendemuhl, Graduate Coordinator, 352-392-8073, Fax: 352-392-1913, E-mail: brendj@ufl.edu.

University of Florida, Interdisciplinary Concentration in Animal Molecular and Cellular Biology, Gainesville, FL 32611. Offers MS, PhD. Program offered jointly with College of Agricultural and Life Sciences, College of Liberal Arts and Sciences, College of Medicine, and College of Veterinary Medicine. *Students:* 2 full-time (both women), 2 international. Average age 27. 5 applicants, 80% accepted, 4 enrolled. *Entrance requirements:* For master's and doctorate, GRE General Test of 1000, minimum GPA of 3.0. Additional exam requirements/recommendations for international students: Required—TOEFL (minimum score 550 paper-based; 213 computer-based; 80 iBT), IELTS (minimum score 6). Application fee: $30. Electronic applications accepted. *Expenses:* Tuition, state resident: full-time $10,915.92. Tuition, nonresident: full-time $28,309. *Financial support:* In 2010–11, 2 students received support, including 1 fellowship, 1 research assistantship (averaging $25,749 per year). Financial award applicants required to submit FAFSA. *Unit head:* Geoffrey E. Dahl, PhD, Chair, Animal Sciences, 352-392-1981 Ext. 221, Fax: 352-392-5595, E-mail: gdahl@ufl.edu. *Application contact:* Dr. Joel H. Brendemuhl, Assistant Chair, 352-392-8073, Fax: 352-392-5595, E-mail: brendj@ufl.edu.

University of Georgia, College of Agricultural and Environmental Sciences, Department of Animal and Dairy Sciences, Athens, GA 30602. Offers animal and dairy science (PhD); animal and dairy sciences (MADS); animal science (MS); dairy science (MS). *Faculty:* 19 full-time (2 women), 1 part-time/adjunct (0 women). *Students:* 25 full-time (19 women), 7 part-time (5 women); includes 2 Black or African American, non-Hispanic/Latino, 6 international. 26 applicants, 23% accepted, 4 enrolled. In 2010, 11 master's, 4 doctorates awarded. *Degree requirements:* For master's, thesis; for doctorate, one foreign language, thesis/dissertation. *Entrance requirements:* For master's and doctorate, GRE General Test. *Application deadline:* For fall admission, 7/1 priority date for domestic students; for spring admission, 11/15 for domestic students. Application fee: $50. Electronic applications accepted. *Expenses:* Tuition, state resident: full-time $7200; part-time $344 per credit hour. Tuition, nonresident: full-time $21,900; part-time $944 per credit hour. Tuition and fees vary according to course load and program. *Financial support:* Fellowships, research assistantships, teaching assistantships, unspecified assistantships available. *Unit head:* Dr. J. Keith Bertrand, Interim Head, 706-542-6259, Fax: 706-542-2465, E-mail: adshead@uga.edu. *Application contact:* Dr. Michael J. Azain, Graduate Coordinator, 706-542-0963, Fax: 706-583-0274, E-mail: mazain@uga.edu.

University of Georgia, College of Agricultural and Environmental Sciences, Department of Poultry Science, Athens, GA 30602. Offers animal nutrition (PhD); poultry science (MS, PhD). *Faculty:* 14 full-time (3 women), 3 part-time/adjunct (1 woman). *Students:* 23 full-time (13 women), 1 part-time (0 women); includes 1 Asian, non-Hispanic/Latino, 2 Hispanic/Latino, 6 international. 1 applicant, 100% accepted, 0 enrolled. In 2010, 6 master's, 2 doctorates awarded. *Degree requirements:* For master's, thesis; for doctorate, one foreign language, thesis/dissertation. *Entrance requirements:* For master's and doctorate, GRE General Test. *Application deadline:* For fall admission, 7/1 priority date for domestic students; for spring admission, 11/15 for domestic students. Application fee: $50. Electronic applications accepted. *Expenses:* Tuition, state resident: full-time $7200; part-time $344 per credit hour. Tuition, nonresident: full-time $21,900; part-time $944 per credit hour. Tuition and fees vary according to course load and program. *Financial support:* Fellowships, research assistantships, teaching assistantships, unspecified assistantships available. *Unit head:* Dr. Michael Lacy, Head, 706-542-1351, E-mail: mlacy@uga.edu. *Application contact:* Dr. Larry R. McDougald, Graduate Coordinator, 706-542-1337, Fax: 706-542-1827, E-mail: lrmcd@uga.edu.

University of Guelph, Graduate Studies, Ontario Agricultural College, Department of Animal and Poultry Science, Guelph, ON N1G 2W1, Canada. Offers M Sc, PhD. Part-time programs available. *Degree requirements:* For master's, thesis (for some programs); for doctorate, comprehensive exam, thesis/dissertation. *Entrance requirements:* For master's, minimum B- average during previous 2 years of course work; for doctorate, minimum B- average. Additional exam requirements/recommendations for international students: Required—TOEFL (minimum score 550 paper-based; 213 computer-based; 89 iBT), IELTS (minimum score 6.5). *Faculty research:* Animal breeding and genetics (quantitative or molecular), animal nutrition (monogastric or ruminant), animal physiology (environmental, reproductive or behavioral), behavior and welfare.

University of Hawaii at Manoa, Graduate Division, College of Tropical Agriculture and Human Resources, Department of Human Nutrition, Food and Animal Sciences, Program in Animal Sciences, Honolulu, HI 96822. Offers MS. Part-time programs available. *Faculty:* 19 full-time (6 women), 4 part-time/adjunct (2 women). *Students:* 3 full-time (all women), 7 part-time (5 women); includes 3 Asian, non-Hispanic/Latino; 2 Two or more races, non-Hispanic/Latino, 1 international. Average age 28. 6 applicants, 33% accepted, 2 enrolled. In 2010, 1 master's awarded. *Entrance requirements:* For master's, GRE General Test. Additional exam requirements/recommendations for international students: Required—TOEFL (minimum score 580 paper-based; 100 iBT), IELTS (minimum score 5). *Application deadline:* For fall admission, 2/1 for domestic and international students; for spring admission, 9/1 for domestic and international students. Application fee: $60. *Financial support:* In 2010–11, 6 students received support, including 2 fellowships (averaging $1,250 per year), 2 research assistantships with full tuition reimbursements available (averaging $16,824 per year); tuition waivers (full) also available. Financial award applicants required to submit FAFSA. *Faculty research:* Nutritional biochemistry, food composition, nutrition education, nutritional epidemiology, international nutrition, food toxicology. Total annual research expenditures: $413,000. *Application contact:* Jinzeng Yang, Graduate Chairperson, 808-956-7095, Fax: 808-956-4024, E-mail: jinzeng@hawaii.edu.

University of Idaho, College of Graduate Studies, College of Agricultural and Life Sciences, Department of Animal and Veterinary Science, Moscow, ID 83844-2282. Offers animal physiology (PhD); animal science (MS), including production. *Faculty:* 4 full-time, 1 part-time/adjunct. *Students:* 18 full-time, 17 part-time. Average age 29. In 2010, 3 master's, 1 doctorate awarded. *Degree requirements:* For doctorate, thesis/dissertation. *Entrance requirements:* For master's, GRE General Test, minimum GPA of 2.8; for doctorate, minimum undergraduate GPA of 2.8, graduate 3.0. *Application deadline:* For fall admission, 8/1 for domestic students; for spring admission, 12/15 for domestic students. Applications are processed on a rolling basis. Application fee: $60. Electronic applications accepted. *Expenses:* Tuition, nonresident: part-time $580 per credit. Required fees: $306 per credit. *Financial support:* Research assistantships, teaching assistantships available. Financial award applicants required to submit FAFSA. *Faculty research:* Reproductive biology, muscle and growth physiology, meat science, aquaculture, ruminant nutrition. *Unit head:* Dr. Carl W. Hunt, Head, 208-885-6345, E-mail: angelac@uidaho.edu. *Application contact:* Dr. Carl W. Hunt, Head, 208-885-6345, E-mail: angelac@uidaho.edu.

University of Illinois at Urbana–Champaign, Graduate College, College of Agricultural, Consumer and Environmental Sciences, Department of Animal Sciences, Champaign, IL 61820. Offers animal sciences (MS, PhD); bioinformatics: animal sciences (MS). *Faculty:* 37 full-time (5 women), 1 part-time/adjunct (0 women). *Students:* 106 full-time (49 women), 6 part-time (3 women); includes 1 Black or African American, non-Hispanic/Latino; 1 Asian, non-Hispanic/Latino; 2 Hispanic/Latino, 45 international. 65 applicants, 51% accepted, 27 enrolled. In 2010, 24 master's, 16 doctorates awarded. *Entrance requirements:* For master's and doctorate, GRE General Test, GRE Subject Test (biology), minimum GPA of 3.0. Additional exam requirements/recommendations for international students: Required—TOEFL (minimum score 590 paper-based; 243 computer-based), TWE. *Application deadline:* Applications are processed on a rolling basis. Application fee: $75 ($90 for international students). Electronic applications accepted. *Financial support:* In 2010–11, 19 fellowships, 89 research assistantships, 16 teaching assistantships were awarded; tuition waivers (full and partial) also available. *Unit head:* Neal R. Merchen, Head, 217-333-3462, Fax: 217-244-2871, E-mail: nmerchen@illinois.edu. *Application contact:* Allison Mosley, Resource and Policy Analyst, 217-333-1044, Fax: 217-333-5044, E-mail: amosley@illinois.edu.

University of Kentucky, Graduate School, College of Agriculture, Program in Animal Sciences, Lexington, KY 40506-0032. Offers MS, PhD. Terminal master's awarded for partial completion of doctoral program. *Degree requirements:* For master's, comprehensive exam, thesis optional; for doctorate, comprehensive exam, thesis/dissertation. *Entrance requirements:* For master's, GRE General Test, minimum undergraduate GPA of 2.75; for doctorate, GRE General Test, minimum graduate GPA of 3.0. Additional exam requirements/recommendations for international students: Required—TOEFL (minimum score 550 paper-based; 213 computer-based). Electronic applications accepted. *Faculty research:* Nutrition of horses, cattle, swine, poultry, and sheep; physiology of reproduction and lactation; food science; microbiology.

University of Maine, Graduate School, College of Natural Sciences, Forestry, and Agriculture, Department of Animal and Veterinary Sciences, Orono, ME 04469. Offers animal sciences (MPS, MS). Part-time programs available. *Faculty:* 6 full-time (0 women), 2 part-time/adjunct (1 woman). *Students:* 3 full-time (2 women), 2 part-time (both women). Average age 37. 7 applicants, 14% accepted, 1 enrolled. In 2010, 1 master's awarded. *Entrance requirements:* For master's, GRE General Test. Additional exam requirements/recommendations for international students: Required—TOEFL. *Application deadline:* For fall admission, 2/1 priority date for domestic students. Applications are processed on a rolling basis. Application fee: $65. Electronic applications accepted. *Expenses:* Tuition, state resident: full-time $400. Tuition, nonresident: full-time $1050. *Financial support:* In 2010–11, 3 research assistantships with tuition reimbursements (averaging $14,887 per year), 1 teaching assistantship with tuition reimbursement (averaging $12,790 per year) were awarded; Federal Work-Study, institutionally sponsored loans, and tuition waivers (full and partial) also available. Financial award application deadline: 3/1. *Faculty research:* Animal nutrition, parasitology, veterinary pathology, reproductive physiology, marine life nutrition and management. *Unit head:* Dr. Martin Stokes, Chair, 207-581-2770, Fax: 207-581-2770. *Application contact:* Scott G. Delcourt, Associate Dean of the Graduate School, 207-581-3291, Fax: 207-581-3232, E-mail: graduate@maine.edu.

University of Manitoba, Faculty of Graduate Studies, Faculty of Agricultural and Food Sciences, Department of Animal Science, Winnipeg, MB R3T 2N2, Canada. Offers M Sc, PhD. *Degree requirements:* For master's, thesis; for doctorate, one foreign language, thesis/dissertation.

University of Maryland, College Park, Academic Affairs, College of Agriculture and Natural Resources, Department of Animal and Avian Sciences, Program in Animal Sciences, College Park, MD 20742. Offers MS, PhD. *Students:* 32 full-time (19 women), 3 part-time (2 women); includes 1 Hispanic/Latino, 14 international. 60 applicants, 13% accepted, 8 enrolled. In 2010, 3 master's, 3 doctorates awarded. *Degree requirements:* For master's, thesis, oral exam or written comprehensive exam; for doctorate, thesis/dissertation, journal publication, scientific paper. *Entrance requirements:* For master's, GRE General Test, minimum GPA of 3.0; for doctorate, GRE General Test. Additional exam requirements/recommendations for international students: Required—TOEFL. *Application deadline:* For fall admission, 5/15 for domestic students, 2/1 for international students; for spring admission, 10/1 for domestic students, 6/1 for international students. Applications are processed on a rolling basis. Application fee: $75. Electronic applications accepted. *Expenses:* Tuition, area resident: Part-time $471 per credit hour. Tuition, state resident: part-time $471 per credit hour. Tuition, nonresident: part-time $1016 per credit hour. Required fees: $337 per term. *Financial support:* In 2010–11, 1 research assistantship (averaging $17,805 per year), 30 teaching assistantships (averaging $16,500 per year) were awarded; fellowships also available. Financial award applicants required to submit FAFSA. *Faculty research:* Animal physiology, cell biology and biochemistry, reproduction, biometrics, animal behavior. *Unit head:* Dr. Tom Porter, Chairman, 301-405-1366, Fax: 301-314-9059, E-mail: teporter@umd.edu. *Application contact:* Dr. Charles A Caramello, Dean of Graduate School, 301-405-0358, Fax: 301-314-9305, E-mail: ccaramel@umd.edu.

University of Massachusetts Amherst, Graduate School, College of Natural Sciences, Department of Animal Biotechnology and Biomedical Sciences, Amherst, MA 01003. Offers MS, PhD. Part-time programs available. *Faculty:* 22 full-time (9 women). *Students:* 28 full-time (17 women), 1 (woman) part-time; includes 1 minority (Hispanic/Latino), 8 international. Average

Animal Sciences

University of Massachusetts Amherst (continued)
age 28. 52 applicants, 21% accepted, 10 enrolled. In 2010, 3 master's, 2 doctorates awarded. Terminal master's awarded for partial completion of doctoral program. *Degree requirements:* For master's, thesis or alternative; for doctorate, comprehensive exam, thesis/dissertation. *Entrance requirements:* For master's and doctorate, GRE General Test. Additional exam requirements/recommendations for international students: Required—TOEFL (minimum score 550 paper-based; 213 computer-based; 80 iBT), IELTS (minimum score 6.5). *Application deadline:* For fall admission, 2/1 for domestic and international students; for spring admission, 10/1 for domestic and international students. Applications are processed on a rolling basis. Application fee: $50 ($65 for international students). Electronic applications accepted. *Expenses:* Tuition, state resident: full-time $2640. Required fees: $8282. One-time fee: $357 full-time. *Financial support:* In 2010–11, 1 fellowship (averaging $1,731 per year), 40 research assistantships with full tuition reimbursements (averaging $12,032 per year), 13 teaching assistantships with full tuition reimbursements (averaging $9,586 per year) were awarded; career-related internships or fieldwork, Federal Work-Study, scholarships/grants, traineeships, health care benefits, tuition waivers (full), and unspecified assistantships also available. Support available to part-time students. Financial award application deadline: 2/1; financial award applicants required to submit FAFSA. *Unit head:* Dr. Pablo E. Visconti, Graduate Program Director, 413-577-1193, Fax: 413-577-1150. *Application contact:* Jean M. Ames, Supervisor of Admissions, 413-545-0722, Fax: 413-577-0010, E-mail: gradadm@grad.umass.edu.

University of Minnesota, Twin Cities Campus, Graduate School, College of Food, Agricultural and Natural Resource Sciences, Program in Animal Science, Minneapolis, MN 55455-0213. Offers MS, PhD. Part-time programs available. *Faculty:* 39 full-time (9 women). *Students:* 32 full-time (21 women); includes 1 minority (Asian, non-Hispanic/Latino), 10 international. Average age 30. 22 applicants, 45% accepted, 6 enrolled. In 2010, 3 master's, 1 doctorate awarded. Terminal master's awarded for partial completion of doctoral program. *Degree requirements:* For master's, comprehensive exam, thesis; for doctorate, comprehensive exam, thesis/dissertation. *Entrance requirements:* For master's and doctorate, GRE. Additional exam requirements/recommendations for international students: Required—TOEFL (minimum score 550 paper-based; 213 computer-based; 79 iBT). *Application deadline:* For fall admission, 12/15 priority date for domestic and international students; for spring admission, 10/15 priority date for domestic and international students. Applications are processed on a rolling basis. Application fee: $75 ($95 for international students). Electronic applications accepted. *Financial support:* In 2010–11, fellowships with full tuition reimbursements (averaging $23,500 per year), research assistantships with full tuition reimbursements (averaging $20,800 per year), teaching assistantships with full tuition reimbursements (averaging $20,800 per year) were awarded; scholarships/grants and unspecified assistantships also available. Support available to part-time students. *Faculty research:* Physiology, growth biology, nutrition, genetics, production systems. Total annual research expenditures: $1.1 million. *Unit head:* Dr. William Dayton, Director of Graduate Studies, 612-624-2234, Fax: 612-625-5789, E-mail: wdayton@umn.edu. *Application contact:* Kim Reno, Assistant to the Director of Graduate Studies, 612-624-3491, E-mail: renox001@umn.edu.

University of Missouri, Graduate School, College of Agriculture, Food and Natural Resources, Department of Animal Sciences, Columbia, MO 65211. Offers MS, PhD. *Faculty:* 71 full-time (12 women), 6 part-time/adjunct (1 woman). *Students:* 43 full-time (25 women), 8 part-time (3 women); includes 1 minority (Hispanic/Latino), 7 international. Average age 26. 41 applicants, 24% accepted, 8 enrolled. In 2010, 12 master's, 3 doctorates awarded. Terminal master's awarded for partial completion of doctoral program. *Degree requirements:* For doctorate, 2 foreign languages, comprehensive exam, thesis/dissertation. *Entrance requirements:* For master's, GRE General Test, minimum GPA of 3.0; for doctorate, GRE General Test (minimum score: Verbal 400, Quantitative 550), minimum GPA of 3.0. Additional exam requirements/recommendations for international students: Required—TOEFL (minimum score 500 paper-based; 173 computer-based; 61 iBT), IELTS (minimum score 5.5). *Application deadline:* Applications are processed on a rolling basis. Application fee: $45 ($60 for international students). Electronic applications accepted. *Financial support:* Fellowships, research assistantships with tuition reimbursements, teaching assistantships with tuition reimbursements, institutionally sponsored loans, scholarships/grants, health care benefits, and unspecified assistantships available. Support available to part-time students. Financial award applicants required to submit FAFSA. *Faculty research:* Reproductive and environmental physiology, ruminant and monogastric nutrition, genetics/genomics, meat science and livestock production across swine, dairy cattle, beef cattle, poultry, companion animals and horses. *Unit head:* Dr. Rod Geisert, Department Chair, 573-884-0934, E-mail: geisertr@missouri.edu. *Application contact:* Cinda Hudlow, Administrative Assistant, 573-882-7446, E-mail: hudlowc@missouri.edu.

University of Nebraska–Lincoln, Graduate College, College of Agricultural Sciences and Natural Resources, Department of Animal Science, Lincoln, NE 68588. Offers MS, PhD. *Degree requirements:* For master's, thesis; for doctorate, comprehensive exam, thesis/dissertation. *Entrance requirements:* For master's and doctorate, GRE General Test. Additional exam requirements/recommendations for international students: Required—TOEFL (minimum score 525 paper-based; 195 computer-based). Electronic applications accepted. *Faculty research:* Animal breeding and genetics, meat and poultry products, nonruminant and ruminant nutrition, physiology.

University of Nevada, Reno, Graduate School, College of Agriculture, Biotechnology and Natural Resources, Department of Animal Science, Reno, NV 89557. Offers MS. *Degree requirements:* For master's, thesis optional. *Entrance requirements:* For master's, GRE, minimum GPA of 2.75. Additional exam requirements/recommendations for international students: Required—TOEFL (minimum score 500 paper-based; 173 computer-based; 61 iBT), IELTS (minimum score 6). Electronic applications accepted. *Expenses:* Tuition, state resident: full-time $2219; part-time $246 per credit. Tuition, nonresident: part-time $510 per credit. International tuition: $9009 full-time. Required fees: $59 per term. One-time fee: $101. Tuition and fees vary according to course load. *Faculty research:* Sperm fertility, embryo development, ruminant utilization of forages.

University of New Hampshire, Graduate School, College of Life Sciences and Agriculture, Department of Biological Sciences, Program in Animal Science, Durham, NH 03824. Offers MS. Part-time programs available. *Faculty:* 23 full-time. *Students:* 5 full-time (4 women), 4 part-time (3 women); includes 1 Hispanic/Latino. Average age 29. 16 applicants, 19% accepted, 2 enrolled. In 2010, 2 master's awarded. *Entrance requirements:* For master's, GRE General Test. Additional exam requirements/recommendations for international students: Required—TOEFL (minimum score 550 paper-based; 213 computer-based; 80 iBT). *Application deadline:* For fall admission, 6/1 priority date for domestic students, 4/1 for international students; for spring admission, 12/1 for domestic students. Applications are processed on a rolling basis. Application fee: $65. Electronic applications accepted. *Financial support:* In 2010–11, 6 students received support, including 2 research assistantships, 4 teaching assistantships; fellowships, career-related internships or fieldwork, Federal Work-Study, scholarships/grants, and tuition waivers (full and partial) also available. Support available to part-time students. Financial award application deadline: 2/15. *Unit head:* Dr. Chris Neefus, Chair, 603-862-3205. *Application contact:* Diane Lavalliere, Administrative Assistant, 603-862-2100.

University of New Hampshire, Graduate School, College of Life Sciences and Agriculture, Department of Molecular, Cellular and Biomedical Sciences, Program in Animal and Nutritional Sciences, Durham, NH 03824. Offers PhD. Part-time programs available. *Faculty:* 23 full-time. *Students:* 6 full-time (2 women), 1 (woman) part-time. Average age 39. 7 applicants, 29% accepted, 2 enrolled. *Entrance requirements:* For doctorate, GRE. Additional exam requirements/recommendations for international students: Required—TOEFL (minimum score 550 paper-based; 213 computer-based; 80 iBT). *Application deadline:* For fall admission, 6/1 priority date for domestic students, 4/1 priority date for international students; for spring admission, 12/1 for domestic students. Application fee: $65. Electronic applications accepted. *Financial support:* In 2010–11, 4 students received support, including 4 teaching assistantships; fellowships, research assistantships, scholarships/grants, traineeships, and unspecified assistantships also available. Support available to part-time students. *Unit head:* Dr. Rick Cote, Chairperson, 603-862-2458. *Application contact:* Flora Joyal, Administrative Assistant, 603-862-4095, E-mail: ansc.grad.program.info@unh.edu.

University of Puerto Rico, Mayagüez Campus, Graduate Studies, College of Agricultural Sciences, Department of Animal Industries, Mayagüez, PR 00681-9000. Offers MS. Part-time programs available. *Students:* 22 full-time (11 women); includes 21 Hispanic/Latino, 1 international. 1 applicant, 100% accepted, 0 enrolled. In 2010, 2 master's awarded. *Degree requirements:* For master's, comprehensive exam, thesis. *Entrance requirements:* For master's, minimum GPA of 2.75, BS in agricultural science or closely-related field. *Application deadline:* For fall admission, 2/15 for domestic and international students; for spring admission, 9/15 for domestic and international students. Applications are processed on a rolling basis. Application fee: $25. *Expenses:* Tuition, state resident: full-time $1188. Tuition, nonresident: full-time $1188. International tuition: $6126 full-time. Tuition and fees vary according to course level and course load. *Financial support:* In 2010–11, 7 research assistantships with tuition reimbursements (averaging $15,000 per year), 15 teaching assistantships with tuition reimbursements (averaging $8,500 per year) were awarded; fellowships, Federal Work-Study and institutionally sponsored loans also available. *Faculty research:* Swine production and nutrition, poultry production, dairy science and technology, microbiology. *Unit head:* Dr. Jose LaTorre, Director, 787-265-3854, Fax: 787-834-4548, E-mail: jlatorre@uprm.edu. *Application contact:* Dr. Teodoro Ruiz, Coordinator, 787-832-4040 Ext. 2574, Fax: 787-834-4548, E-mail: truiz@uprm.edu.

University of Rhode Island, Graduate School, College of the Environment and Life Sciences, Department of Fisheries, Animal and Veterinary Science, Kingston, RI 02881. Offers animal health and disease (MS); animal science (MS); aquaculture (MS); aquatic pathology (MS); environmental sciences (PhD), including animal science, aquacultural science, aquatic pathology, fisheries science; fisheries (MS). *Faculty:* 10 full-time (4 women). *Students:* 14 full-time (7 women), 6 part-time (1 woman); includes 4 minority (2 Black or African American, non-Hispanic/Latino; 2 Hispanic/Latino), 3 international. In 2010, 3 master's, 2 doctorates awarded. *Degree requirements:* For master's, comprehensive exam (for some programs), thesis optional; for doctorate, comprehensive exam, thesis/dissertation. *Entrance requirements:* For master's and doctorate, GRE, 2 letters of recommendation. Additional exam requirements/recommendations for international students: Required—TOEFL (minimum score 550 paper-based; 213 computer-based). *Application deadline:* For fall admission, 7/15 for domestic students, 2/1 for international students; for spring admission, 11/15 for domestic students, 7/15 for international students. Application fee: $65. Electronic applications accepted. *Expenses:* Tuition, state resident: full-time $9588; part-time $533 per credit hour. Tuition, nonresident: full-time $22,968; part-time $1276 per credit hour. Required fees: $1282; $68 per semester. Tuition and fees vary according to program. *Financial support:* In 2010–11, 9 research assistantships with full and partial tuition reimbursements (averaging $11,492 per year), 3 teaching assistantships with full and partial tuition reimbursements (averaging $12,894 per year) were awarded. Financial award application deadline: 7/15; financial award applicants required to submit FAFSA. Total annual research expenditures: $1.8 million. *Unit head:* Dr. David Bengtson, Chair, 401-874-2668, Fax: 401-874-7575, E-mail: bengtson@uri.edu. *Application contact:* Dr. Marta Gomez-Chiarri, Director of Graduate Studies, 401-874-2917, Fax: 401-874-7575, E-mail: gomezchi@uri.edu.

University of Saskatchewan, College of Graduate Studies and Research, College of Agriculture, Department of Animal and Poultry Science, Saskatoon, SK S7N 5A2, Canada. Offers M Ag, M Sc, PhD. *Degree requirements:* For master's, thesis; for doctorate, thesis/dissertation. *Entrance requirements:* Additional exam requirements/recommendations for international students: Required—TOEFL.

University of Saskatchewan, Western College of Veterinary Medicine and College of Graduate Studies and Research, Graduate Programs in Veterinary Medicine, Department of Large Animal Clinical Sciences, Saskatoon, SK S7N 5A2, Canada. Offers M Sc, M Vet Sc, PhD. *Faculty:* 10 full-time (3 women), 1 part-time/adjunct (0 women). *Students:* 23 full-time (13 women); includes 1 Black or African American, non-Hispanic/Latino. In 2010, 3 master's, 1 doctorate awarded. *Degree requirements:* For master's, thesis (for some programs); for doctorate, comprehensive exam (for some programs), thesis/dissertation. *Entrance requirements:* Additional exam requirements/recommendations for international students: Required—TOEFL (minimum score 80 iBT); Recommended—IELTS (minimum score 6.5). Electronic applications accepted. *Faculty research:* Reproduction, infectious diseases, epidemiology, food safety. *Unit head:* Dr. John Campbell, Head, 306-966-7145, Fax: 306-966-7159, E-mail: john.campbell@usask.ca. *Application contact:* Dr. Joseph Stookey, Associate Dean, Research, 306-966-7145, Fax: 306-966-7159, E-mail: joseph.stookey@usask.ca.

University of Saskatchewan, Western College of Veterinary Medicine and College of Graduate Studies and Research, Graduate Programs in Veterinary Medicine, Department of Small Animal Clinical Sciences, Saskatoon, SK S7N 5A2, Canada. Offers small animal clinical sciences (M Sc, PhD); veterinary anesthesiology, radiology and surgery (M Vet Sc); veterinary internal medicine (M Vet Sc). *Faculty:* 9 full-time (6 women). *Students:* 10 full-time (8 women). In 2010, 1 master's awarded. *Degree requirements:* For master's, thesis (for some programs); for doctorate, comprehensive exam (for some programs), thesis/dissertation. *Entrance requirements:* Additional exam requirements/recommendations for international students: Required—TOEFL (minimum score 80 iBT); Recommended—IELTS (minimum score 6.5). Electronic applications accepted. *Faculty research:* Orthopedics, wildlife, cardiovascular exercise/myelopathy, ophthalmology. *Unit head:* Dr. Klaas Post, Head, 306-966-7084, Fax: 306-966-7174, E-mail: klaas.post@usask.ca. *Application contact:* Dr. Klaas Post, Graduate Chair, 306-966-7084, Fax: 306-966-7174, E-mail: klaas.post@usask.ca.

The University of Tennessee, Graduate School, College of Agricultural Sciences and Natural Resources, Department of Animal Science, Knoxville, TN 37996. Offers animal anatomy (PhD); breeding (MS, PhD); management (MS, PhD); nutrition (MS, PhD); physiology (MS, PhD). Part-time programs available. *Degree requirements:* For master's, thesis; for doctorate, thesis/dissertation. *Entrance requirements:* For master's and doctorate, GRE General Test, minimum GPA of 2.7. Additional exam requirements/recommendations for international students: Required—TOEFL. Electronic applications accepted. *Expenses:* Tuition, state resident: full-time $7440; part-time $414 per credit hour. Tuition, nonresident: full-time $22,478; part-time $1250 per credit hour. Required fees: $922; $43 per credit hour. Tuition and fees vary according to program.

University of Vermont, Graduate College, College of Agriculture and Life Sciences, Department of Animal Sciences, Burlington, VT 05405. Offers MS, PhD. *Students:* 5 (2 women), 1 international. 5 applicants, 20% accepted, 1 enrolled. In 2010, 2 master's awarded. *Degree requirements:* For master's, thesis; for doctorate, one foreign language, thesis/dissertation. *Entrance requirements:* For master's and doctorate, GRE General Test. Additional exam requirements/recommendations for international students: Required—TOEFL (minimum score 550 paper-based; 213 computer-based; 80 iBT). *Application deadline:* For fall admission, 4/1 priority date for domestic students. Applications are processed on a rolling basis. Application fee: $40. Electronic applications accepted. *Expenses:* Tuition, state resident: part-time $537 per credit hour. Tuition, nonresident: part-time $1355 per credit hour. *Financial support:* Fellowships, research assistantships, teaching assistantships available. Financial award application deadline: 3/1. *Faculty research:* Animal nutrition, dairy production. *Unit head:* Dr. John M. Burke, Interim Chairperson, 802-656-2070. *Application contact:* Dr. David Kerr, Coordinator, 802-656-2070.

University of Vermont, Graduate College, College of Agriculture and Life Sciences, Program in Animal, Nutrition and Food Sciences, Burlington, VT 05405. Offers PhD. *Students:* 18 (7 women); includes 2 Asian, non-Hispanic/Latino, 10 international. 18 applicants, 44% accepted, 5 enrolled. In 2010, 2 doctorates awarded. *Degree requirements:* For doctorate, one foreign language, thesis/dissertation. *Entrance requirements:* For doctorate, GRE General Test. Additional exam requirements/recommendations for international students: Required—TOEFL (minimum score 550 paper-based; 213 computer-based; 80 iBT). *Application deadline:* For fall admission, 4/1 priority date for domestic students. Applications are processed on a rolling basis. Application fee: $40. Electronic applications accepted. *Expenses:* Tuition, state resident: part-time $537 per credit hour. Tuition, nonresident: part-time $1355 per credit hour. *Financial support:* Application deadline: 3/1. *Unit head:* Dr. R. K. Johnson, Dean, 802-656-2070. *Application contact:* Dr. David Kerr, Coordinator, 802-656-2070.

University of Wisconsin–Madison, Graduate School, College of Agricultural and Life Sciences, Department of Animal Sciences, Madison, WI 53706-1380. Offers MS, PhD. Part-time programs available. *Faculty:* 18 full-time (2 women), 5 part-time/adjunct (0 women). *Students:* 26 full-time (9 women), 7 part-time (3 women); includes 1 Asian, non-Hispanic/Latino; 1 Hispanic/Latino, 11 international. Average age 28. 50 applicants, 16% accepted, 8 enrolled. In 2010, 4 master's, 2 doctorates awarded. Terminal master's awarded for partial completion of doctoral program. *Degree requirements:* For master's, thesis; for doctorate, thesis/dissertation. *Entrance requirements:* For master's and doctorate, GRE General Test. Additional exam requirements/recommendations for international students: Required—TOEFL (minimum score 550 paper-based; 213 computer-based; 80 iBT). *Application deadline:* Applications are processed on a rolling basis. Application fee: $56. Electronic applications accepted. *Expenses:* Tuition, state resident: full-time $9887.36; part-time $617.96 per credit. Tuition, nonresident: full-time $24,054; part-time $1503.40 per credit. Required fees: $67.63 per credit. Tuition and fees vary according to reciprocity agreements. *Financial support:* In 2010–11, 22 students received support, including 1 fellowship with full tuition reimbursement available (averaging $20,160 per year), 19 research assistantships with full tuition reimbursements available (averaging $20,400 per year), 2 teaching assistantships with full tuition reimbursements available (averaging $14,087 per year); Federal Work-Study also available. Support available to part-time students. *Faculty research:* Animal biology, immunity and toxicology, endocrinology and reproductive physiology, genetics-animal breeding, meat science, muscle biology. *Unit head:* Dr. Daniel M. Schaefer, Chair, 608-263-4513, Fax: 608-262-5157, E-mail: schaeferd@ansci.wisc.edu. *Application contact:* Kathy A. Monson, Student Services Coordinator, 608-263-5225, Fax: 608-262-5157, E-mail: kamonson@wisc.edu.

University of Wisconsin–Madison, Graduate School, College of Agricultural and Life Sciences, Department of Dairy Science, Madison, WI 53706-1380. Offers MS, PhD. Part-time programs available. *Faculty:* 12 full-time (1 woman). *Students:* 37 full-time (15 women), 2 part-time (both women); includes 1 Black or African American, non-Hispanic/Latino, 22 international. Average age 29. 27 applicants, 30% accepted, 8 enrolled. In 2010, 2 master's, 3 doctorates awarded. Terminal master's awarded for partial completion of doctoral program. *Degree requirements:* For master's, thesis; for doctorate, thesis/dissertation. *Entrance requirements:* For master's and doctorate, GRE General Test. Additional exam requirements/recommendations for international students: Required—TOEFL (minimum score 550 paper-based; 213 computer-based; 80 iBT). *Application deadline:* Applications are processed on a rolling basis. Application fee: $56. Electronic applications accepted. *Expenses:* Tuition, state resident: full-time $9887.36; part-time $617.96 per credit. Tuition, nonresident: full-time $24,054; part-time $1503.40 per credit. Required fees: $67.63 per credit. Tuition and fees vary according to reciprocity agreements. *Financial support:* In 2010–11, 35 students received support, including 1 fellowship with full tuition reimbursement available (averaging $20,400 per year), 33 research assistantships with full tuition reimbursements available (averaging $20,400 per year); Federal Work-Study also available. Support available to part-time students. *Faculty research:* Genetics, nutrition, lactation, reproduction, management of dairy cattle. *Unit head:* Dr. Kent A. Weigel, Chair, 608-263-3308, Fax: 608-263-9412, E-mail: kweigel@wisc.edu. *Application contact:* Kathy A. Monson, Student Services Coordintor, 608-263-4300, Fax: 608-262-5157, E-mail: kamonson@wisc.edu.

University of Wyoming, College of Agriculture and Natural Resources, Department of Animal Sciences, Program in Animal Sciences, Laramie, WY 82070. Offers MS, PhD. *Degree requirements:* For master's, comprehensive exam, thesis; for doctorate, comprehensive exam, thesis/dissertation. *Entrance requirements:* For master's, GRE General Test, minimum GPA of 3.0; for doctorate, GRE General Test or MS degree, minimum GPA of 3.0. Additional exam requirements/recommendations for international students: Required—TOEFL (minimum score 525 paper-based). *Faculty research:* Reproductive biology, ruminant nutrition meat science, muscle biology, food microbiology, lipid metabolism.

Utah State University, School of Graduate Studies, College of Agriculture, Department of Animal, Dairy and Veterinary Sciences, Logan, UT 84322. Offers animal science (MS, PhD); bioveterinary science (MS, PhD); dairy science (MS). Part-time programs available. *Degree requirements:* For master's, thesis (for some programs); for doctorate, comprehensive exam, thesis/dissertation. *Entrance requirements:* For master's and doctorate, GRE General Test, minimum GPA of 3.0. Additional exam requirements/recommendations for international students: Required—TOEFL. Electronic applications accepted. *Faculty research:* Monoclonal antibodies, antiviral chemotherapy, management systems, biotechnology, rumen fermentation manipulation.

Virginia Polytechnic Institute and State University, Graduate School, College of Agriculture and Life Sciences, Department of Animal and Poultry Sciences, Blacksburg, VA 24061. Offers MS, PhD. *Faculty:* 18 full-time (6 women). *Students:* 38 full-time (24 women), 5 part-time (3 women); includes 1 American Indian or Alaska Native, non-Hispanic/Latino; 1 Asian, non-Hispanic/Latino; 1 Hispanic/Latino, 12 international. Average age 27. 31 applicants, 55% accepted, 11 enrolled. In 2010, 7 master's, 3 doctorates awarded. *Degree requirements:* For master's, comprehensive exam (for some programs), thesis (for some programs); for doctorate, comprehensive exam (for some programs), thesis/dissertation (for some programs). *Entrance requirements:* For master's and doctorate, GRE. Additional exam requirements/recommendations for international students: Required—TOEFL (minimum score 550 paper-based; 213 computer-based). *Application deadline:* For fall admission, 7/1 for domestic and international students; for spring admission, 12/1 for domestic and international students. Applications are processed on a rolling basis. Application fee: $65. Electronic applications accepted. *Expenses:* Tuition, area resident: Full-time $9399; part-time $488 per credit hour. Tuition, state resident: full-time $9399; part-time $488 per credit hour. Tuition, nonresident: full-time $17,854; part-time $957.75 per credit hour. International tuition: $17,854 full-time. Required fees: $1534. Full-time tuition and fees vary according to program. *Financial support:* In 2010–11, 10 fellowships with full tuition reimbursements (averaging $7,414 per year), 32 research assistantships with full tuition reimbursements (averaging $23,486 per year), 11 teaching assistantships with full tuition reimbursements (averaging $13,606 per year) were awarded; career-related internships or fieldwork, Federal Work-Study, scholarships/grants, health care benefits, and unspecified assistantships also available. Financial award application deadline: 1/15. *Faculty research:* Quantitative genetics of cattle and sheep, swine nutrition and management, animal molecular biology, nutrition of grazing livestock. Total annual research expenditures: $2.9 million. *Unit head:* Dr. David E. Gerrard, Unit Head, 540-231-9157, Fax: 540-231-3010, E-mail: dgerrard@vt.edu. *Application contact:* David Notter, Contact, 540-231-5135, Fax: 540-231-3010, E-mail: drnotter@vt.edu.

Virginia Polytechnic Institute and State University, Graduate School, College of Agriculture and Life Sciences, Department of Dairy Science, Blacksburg, VA 24061. Offers MS, PhD. *Faculty:* 9 full-time (3 women). *Students:* 17 full-time (13 women); includes 1 Hispanic/Latino, 6 international. Average age 26. 12 applicants, 33% accepted, 3 enrolled. In 2010, 4 master's, 2 doctorates awarded. *Degree requirements:* For master's, comprehensive exam (for some programs), thesis (for some programs); for doctorate, comprehensive exam (for some programs), thesis/dissertation (for some programs). *Entrance requirements:* For master's and doctorate, GRE. Additional exam requirements/recommendations for international students: Required—TOEFL (minimum score 550 paper-based; 213 computer-based). *Application deadline:* For fall admission, 7/1 for domestic and international students; for spring admission, 12/1 for domestic and international students. Applications are processed on a rolling basis. Application fee: $65. Electronic applications accepted. *Expenses:* Tuition, area resident: Full-time $9399; part-time $488 per credit hour. Tuition, state resident: full-time $9399; part-time $488 per credit hour. Tuition, nonresident: full-time $17,854; part-time $957.75 per credit hour. International tuition: $17,854 full-time. Required fees: $1534. Full-time tuition and fees vary according to program. *Financial support:* In 2010–11, 5 fellowships with full tuition reimbursements (averaging $7,424 per year), 10 research assistantships with full tuition reimbursements (averaging $16,972 per year), 2 teaching assistantships with full tuition reimbursements (averaging $13,868 per year) were awarded; career-related internships or fieldwork, Federal Work-Study, scholarships/grants, health care benefits, and unspecified assistantships also available. Financial award application deadline: 1/15. *Faculty research:* Genetics, nutrition, reproduction, lactation. Total annual research expenditures: $2.9 million. *Unit head:* Dr. Michael Akers, UNIT HEAD, 540-231-4757, Fax: 540-231-3010, E-mail: akers@vt.edu. *Application contact:* Isis Mullarky, Contact, 540-231-2410, Fax: 540-231-3010, E-mail: mullarky@vt.edu.

Washington State University, Graduate School, College of Agricultural, Human, and Natural Resource Sciences, Department of Animal Sciences, Pullman, WA 99164. Offers MS, PhD. Part-time programs available. *Faculty:* 29. *Students:* 14 full-time (10 women), 2 part-time (1 woman); includes 6 minority (2 Black or African American, non-Hispanic/Latino; 1 American Indian or Alaska Native, non-Hispanic/Latino; 1 Asian, non-Hispanic/Latino; 1 Hispanic/Latino; 1 Two or more races, non-Hispanic/Latino), 2 international. Average age 27. 35 applicants, 34% accepted, 8 enrolled. In 2010, 4 master's, 1 doctorate awarded. *Degree requirements:* For master's, comprehensive exam (for some programs), thesis (for some programs), oral exam; for doctorate, comprehensive exam, thesis/dissertation, oral and written exam. *Entrance requirements:* For master's, GRE, minimum GPA of 3.0, 3 letters of recommendation, department questionnaire; for doctorate, GRE General Test, minimum GPA of 3.0. Additional exam requirements/recommendations for international students: Required—TOEFL, IELTS. *Application deadline:* For fall admission, 1/10 priority date for domestic students, 1/10 for international students; for spring admission, 7/1 priority date for domestic students, 7/1 for international students. Applications are processed on a rolling basis. Application fee: $50. Electronic applications accepted. *Expenses:* Tuition, state resident: full-time $8552; part-time $443 per credit. Tuition, nonresident: full-time $21,650; part-time $1083 per credit. Required fees: $846. *Financial support:* In 2010–11, fellowships (averaging $5,000 per year), research assistantships with full and partial tuition reimbursements (averaging $18,204 per year), teaching assistantships with full and partial tuition reimbursements (averaging $18,204 per year) were awarded; career-related internships or fieldwork, Federal Work-Study, institutionally sponsored loans, scholarships/grants, health care benefits, tuition waivers (partial), and teaching associateships also available. Financial award application deadline: 4/1; financial award applicants required to submit FAFSA. *Faculty research:* Reproduction, genetics, equine cytokines, fish diseases and vaccines. Total annual research expenditures: $682,000. *Unit head:* Dr. Margaret Benson, Professor and Chair, 509-335-5523, Fax: 509-335-1082, E-mail: m_benson@wsu.edu. *Application contact:* Graduate School Admissions, 800-GRADWSU, Fax: 509-335-1949, E-mail: gradsch@wsu.edu.

West Texas A&M University, College of Agriculture, Nursing, and Natural Sciences, Division of Agriculture, Emphasis in Animal Science, Canyon, TX 79016-0001. Offers MS. Part-time programs available. *Degree requirements:* For master's, comprehensive exam, thesis optional. *Entrance requirements:* For master's, GRE General Test. Additional exam requirements/recommendations for international students: Required—TOEFL (minimum score 550 paper-based). Electronic applications accepted. *Faculty research:* Nutrition, animal breeding, meat science, reproduction physiology, feedlots.

West Virginia University, Davis College of Agriculture, Forestry and Consumer Sciences, Division of Animal and Nutritional Sciences, Program in Animal and Nutritional Sciences, Morgantown, WV 26506. Offers breeding (MS); food sciences (MS); nutrition (MS); physiology (MS); production management (MS); reproduction (MS). Part-time programs available. *Degree requirements:* For master's, thesis, oral and written exams. *Entrance requirements:* For master's, GRE, minimum GPA of 2.5. Additional exam requirements/recommendations for international students: Required—TOEFL. *Faculty research:* Animal nutrition, reproductive physiology, food science.

West Virginia University, Davis College of Agriculture, Forestry and Consumer Sciences, Division of Plant and Soil Sciences, Program in Agricultural Sciences, Morgantown, WV 26506. Offers animal and food sciences (PhD); plant and soil sciences (PhD). *Degree requirements:* For doctorate, thesis/dissertation, oral and written exams. *Entrance requirements:* Additional exam requirements/recommendations for international students: Required—TOEFL. *Faculty research:* Ruminant nutrition, metabolism, forage utilization, physiology, reproduction.

Aquaculture

American University of Beirut, Graduate Programs, Faculty of Agricultural and Food Sciences, Beirut, Lebanon. Offers agricultural economics (MS); animal sciences (MS); ecosystem management (MSES); food technology (MS); irrigation (MS); mechanization (MS); nutrition (MS); plant protection (MS); plant science (MS); poultry science (MS); soils (MS). Part-time programs available. *Faculty:* 22 full-time (6 women). *Students:* 6 full-time (3 women), 86 part-time (77 women). Average age 24. 94 applicants, 60% accepted, 15 enrolled. In 2010, 28 master's awarded. *Degree requirements:* For master's, one foreign language, comprehensive exam, thesis (for some programs). *Entrance requirements:* Additional exam requirements/recommendations for international students: Required—TOEFL (minimum score 600 paper-based; 250 computer-based; 100 iBT), IELTS (minimum score 7.5). *Application deadline:* For fall admission, 4/30 for domestic and international students; for spring admission, 11/1 for domestic and international students. Applications are processed on a rolling basis. Application fee: $50. Electronic applications accepted. *Expenses:* Tuition: Full-time $12,294; part-time $683 per credit. Required fees: $499; $499 per credit. Tuition and fees vary according to course load and program. *Financial support:* In 2010–11, 18 research assistantships with partial tuition reimbursements (averaging $13,132 per year), 42 teaching assistantships with

Aquaculture

American University of Beirut (continued)

full and partial tuition reimbursements (averaging $1,000 per year) were awarded; scholarships/grants, health care benefits, and unspecified assistantships also available. Financial award application deadline: 2/2. *Faculty research:* Community and therapeutic nutrition; food safety and food microbiology; landscape planning, nature and rural heritage conservation; pathology, immunology and control of poultry and animal diseases; agricultural economics and development. Total annual research expenditures: $900,000. *Unit head:* Prof. Nahla Hwalla, Dean, 961-134-3002 Ext. 4400, Fax: 961-174-4460, E-mail: nahla@aub.edu.lb. *Application contact:* Dr. Salim Kanaan, Director, Admissions Office, 961-135-0000 Ext. 2594, Fax: 961-175-0775, E-mail: sk00@aub.edu.lb.

Auburn University, Graduate School, College of Agriculture, Department of Fisheries and Allied Aquacultures, Auburn University, AL 36849. Offers M Aq, MS, PhD. Part-time programs available. *Faculty:* 20 full-time (3 women). *Students:* 37 full-time (16 women), 31 part-time (10 women); includes 2 Black or African American, non-Hispanic/Latino; 1 American Indian or Alaska Native, non-Hispanic/Latino; 1 Hispanic/Latino, 33 international. Average age 28. 49 applicants, 49% accepted, 21 enrolled. In 2010, 12 master's, 5 doctorates awarded. *Degree requirements:* For master's, thesis (for some programs); for doctorate, 2 foreign languages, thesis/dissertation. *Entrance requirements:* For master's and doctorate, GRE General Test. *Application deadline:* For fall admission, 7/7 for domestic students; for spring admission, 11/24 for domestic students. Applications are processed on a rolling basis. Application fee: $50 ($60 for international students). Electronic applications accepted. *Expenses:* Tuition, state resident: full-time $7002. Tuition, nonresident: full-time $21,898. International tuition: $22,116 full-time. Required fees: $892. Tuition and fees vary according to course load and program. *Financial support:* Fellowships, research assistantships, teaching assistantships, Federal Work-Study available. Support available to part-time students. Financial award application deadline: 3/15; financial award applicants required to submit FAFSA. *Faculty research:* Channel catfish production; aquatic animal health; community and population ecology; pond management; production hatching, breeding and genetics. Total annual research expenditures: $8 million. *Unit head:* Dr. David B. Rouse, Head, 334-844-4786. *Application contact:* Dr. George Flowers, Dean of the Graduate School, 334-844-2125.

Clemson University, Graduate School, College of Agriculture, Forestry and Life Sciences, Department of Forestry and Natural Resources, Program in Wildlife and Fisheries Biology, Clemson, SC 29634. Offers MS, PhD. *Students:* 26 full-time (17 women), 7 part-time (5 women); includes 3 Black or African American, non-Hispanic/Latino, 1 international. Average age 31. 18 applicants, 56% accepted, 6 enrolled. In 2010, 10 master's, 5 doctorates awarded. *Degree requirements:* For master's, thesis; for doctorate, thesis/dissertation. *Entrance requirements:* For master's, GRE General Test, minimum undergraduate GPA of 3.0; for doctorate, GRE General Test. Additional exam requirements/recommendations for international students: Required—TOEFL, IELTS. *Application deadline:* For fall admission, 6/1 for domestic students, 4/15 for international students; for spring admission, 9/15 for international students. Applications are processed on a rolling basis. Application fee: $70 ($80 for international students). Electronic applications accepted. *Expenses:* Contact institution. *Financial support:* In 2010–11, 26 students received support, including 5 fellowships with full and partial tuition reimbursements available (averaging $12,144 per year), 18 research assistantships with partial tuition reimbursements available (averaging $15,743 per year), 7 teaching assistantships with partial tuition reimbursements available (averaging $11,583 per year); career-related internships or fieldwork, institutionally sponsored loans, scholarships/grants, health care benefits, and unspecified assistantships also available. Support available to part-time students. Financial award applicants required to submit FAFSA. *Faculty research:* Intensive freshwater culture systems, conservation biology, stream management, applied wildlife management. *Unit head:* Dr. Patricia Layton, Chair, 864-656-3303, Fax: 864-656-3304, E-mail: playton@clemson.edu. *Application contact:* Dr. David Guynn, Graduate Program Coordinator, 864-656-4830, Fax: 864-656-5344, E-mail: dguynn@clemson.edu.

Kentucky State University, College of Mathematics, Sciences, Technology and Health, Frankfort, KY 40601. Offers aquaculture (MS); computer science (MS), including computer science theory, information assurance, information technology; environmental science (MS). Part-time and evening/weekend programs available. *Faculty:* 10 full-time (1 woman), 1 part-time/adjunct (0 women). *Students:* 34 full-time (16 women), 32 part-time (6 women); includes 22 minority (15 Black or African American, non-Hispanic/Latino; 3 Asian, non-Hispanic/Latino; 1 Hispanic/Latino; 1 Native Hawaiian or other Pacific Islander, non-Hispanic/Latino; 2 Two or more races, non-Hispanic/Latino), 12 international. Average age 34. 55 applicants, 51% accepted, 18 enrolled. In 2010, 16 master's awarded. *Degree requirements:* For master's, comprehensive exam, thesis optional. *Entrance requirements:* For master's, GRE, GMAT. Additional exam requirements/recommendations for international students: Required—TOEFL (minimum score 525 paper-based; 173 computer-based). *Application deadline:* Applications are processed on a rolling basis. Application fee: $30 ($100 for international students). Electronic applications accepted. *Expenses:* Tuition, state resident: full-time $5886; part-time $352 per credit hour. Tuition, nonresident: full-time $9054; part-time $528 per credit hour. Required fees: $450; $26 per credit hour. *Financial support:* In 2010–11, 41 students received support, including 18 research assistantships (averaging $11,378 per year); career-related internships or fieldwork, scholarships/grants, tuition waivers (partial), and unspecified assistantships also available. Financial award application deadline: 4/15; financial award applicants required to submit FAFSA. *Unit head:* Dr. Charles Bennett, Dean, 502-597-6926, E-mail: charles.bennett@kysu.edu. *Application contact:* Dr. Titilayo Ufomata, Acting Director of Graduate Studies, 502-597-6443, E-mail: titilayo.ufomata@kysu.edu.

Memorial University of Newfoundland, School of Graduate Studies, Interdisciplinary Program in Aquaculture, St. John's, NL A1C 5S7, Canada. Offers M Sc. Part-time programs available. *Degree requirements:* For master's, thesis, seminar or thesis topic. *Entrance requirements:* For master's, honors B Sc or diploma in aquaculture from the Marine Institute of Memorial University of Newfoundland. Electronic applications accepted. *Faculty research:* Marine fish larval biology, fin fish nutrition, shellfish culture, fin fish virology, fin fish reproductive biology.

Nova Scotia Agricultural College, Research and Graduate Studies, Truro, NS B2N 5E3, Canada. Offers agriculture (M Sc), including air quality, animal behavior, animal molecular genetics, animal nutrition, animal technology, aquaculture, botany, crop management, crop physiology, ecology, environmental microbiology, food science, horticulture, nutrient management, pest management, physiology, plant biotechnology, plant pathology, soil chemistry, soil fertility, waste management and composting, water quality. Program offered jointly with Dalhousie University. Part-time programs available. *Degree requirements:* For master's, thesis, ATC Exam Teaching Assistantship. *Entrance requirements:* For master's, honors B Sc, minimum GPA of 3.0. Additional exam requirements/recommendations for international students: Required—TOEFL (minimum score 580 paper-based; 237 computer-based; 92 iBT), IELTS, Michigan English Language Assessment Battery, CanTEST, CAEL. *Faculty research:* Bio-product development, organic agriculture, nutrient management, air and water quality, agricultural biotechnology.

Purdue University, Graduate School, College of Agriculture, Department of Forestry and Natural Resources, West Lafayette, IN 47907. Offers aquaculture, fisheries, aquatic science (MSF); aquaculture, fisheries, aquatic sciences (MS, PhD); forest biology (MS, MSF, PhD); natural resources and environmental policy (MS, MSF); natural resources environmental policy (PhD); quantitative resource analysis (MS, MSF, PhD); wildlife science (MS, MSF, PhD); wood science and technology (MS, MSF, PhD). *Degree requirements:* For master's, thesis; for doctorate, thesis/dissertation. *Entrance requirements:* For master's and doctorate, GRE General Test, minimum B+ average in undergraduate course work. Additional exam requirements/recommendations for international students: Required—TOEFL. Electronic applications accepted. *Faculty research:* Wildlife management, forest management, forest ecology, forest soils, limnology.

Texas A&M University–Corpus Christi, Graduate Studies and Research, College of Science and Technology, Program in Mariculture, Corpus Christi, TX 78412-5503. Offers MS.

University of Arkansas at Pine Bluff, School of Agriculture, Fisheries and Human Sciences, Pine Bluff, AR 71601-2799. Offers aquaculture and fisheries (MS).

University of Florida, Graduate School, College of Agricultural and Life Sciences, Department of Fisheries and Aquatic Sciences, Gainesville, FL 32611. Offers MFAS, MS, PhD. Part-time programs available. *Students:* 5 full-time (2 women), 2 part-time (1 woman), 1 international. Average age 29. 34 applicants, 26% accepted, 8 enrolled. In 2010, 1 master's awarded. *Degree requirements:* For master's, thesis (for some programs), Thesis required for Masters of Science. Technical paper required for MFAS degree; for doctorate, comprehensive exam, thesis/dissertation. *Entrance requirements:* For master's and doctorate, GRE General Test, minimum GPA of 3.0. Additional exam requirements/recommendations for international students: Required—TOEFL (minimum score 550 paper-based; 213 computer-based; 80 iBT), IELTS (minimum score 6). *Application deadline:* For fall admission, 6/1 for domestic students, 3/1 for international students; for spring admission, 10/1 for domestic students, 8/1 for international students. Applications are processed on a rolling basis. Application fee: $30. Electronic applications accepted. *Expenses:* Tuition, state resident: full-time $10,915.92. Tuition, nonresident: full-time $28,309. *Financial support:* In 2010–11, 4 students received support, including 1 fellowship, 3 research assistantships (averaging $20,141 per year); unspecified assistantships also available. Financial award application deadline: 1/31; financial award applicants required to submit FAFSA. *Faculty research:* Conservation and management of aquatic ecosystems; aquatic animal health; water quality, nutrients, and eutrophication; sustainable and quantitative fisheries; aquaculture or ornamental fish, marine baitfish, and shellfish. Total annual research expenditures: $10 million. *Unit head:* Nancy J. Peterson, PhD, Associate Director, 352-846-0848, Fax: 352-846-1277, E-mail: njp@ufl.edu. *Application contact:* Charles Cichra, PhD, Graduate Coordinator, 352-273-3621, Fax: 352-392-3672, E-mail: cecichra@ufl.edu.

University of Guelph, Graduate Studies, Ontario Agricultural College, Program in Aquaculture, Guelph, ON N1G 2W1, Canada. Offers M Sc. *Degree requirements:* For master's, practicum, research project. *Entrance requirements:* For master's, minimum B- average during previous 2 years of course work. *Faculty research:* Protein and amino acid metabolism, genetics, gamete cryogenics, pathology, epidemiology.

University of Rhode Island, Graduate School, College of the Environment and Life Sciences, Department of Fisheries, Animal and Veterinary Science, Kingston, RI 02881. Offers animal health and disease (MS); animal science (MS); aquaculture (MS); aquatic pathology (MS); environmental sciences (PhD), including animal science, aquacultural science, aquatic pathology, fisheries science; fisheries (MS). *Faculty:* 10 full-time (4 women). *Students:* 14 full-time (7 women), 6 part-time (1 woman); includes 4 minority (2 Black or African American, non-Hispanic/Latino; 2 Hispanic/Latino), 3 international. In 2010, 3 master's, 2 doctorates awarded. *Degree requirements:* For master's, comprehensive exam (for some programs), thesis optional; for doctorate, comprehensive exam, thesis/dissertation. *Entrance requirements:* For master's and doctorate, GRE, 2 letters of recommendation. Additional exam requirements/recommendations for international students: Required—TOEFL (minimum score 550 paper-based; 213 computer-based). *Application deadline:* For fall admission, 7/15 for domestic students, 2/1 for international students; for spring admission, 11/15 for domestic students, 7/15 for international students. Application fee: $65. Electronic applications accepted. *Expenses:* Tuition, state resident: full-time $9588; part-time $533 per credit hour. Tuition, nonresident: full-time $22,968; part-time $1276 per credit hour. Required fees: $1282; $68 per semester. Tuition and fees vary according to program. *Financial support:* In 2010–11, 9 research assistantships with full and partial tuition reimbursements (averaging $11,492 per year), 3 teaching assistantships with full and partial tuition reimbursements (averaging $12,894 per year) were awarded. Financial award application deadline: 7/15; financial award applicants required to submit FAFSA. Total annual research expenditures: $1.8 million. *Unit head:* Dr. David Bengtson, Chair, 401-874-2668, Fax: 401-874-7575, E-mail: bengtson@uri.edu. *Application contact:* Dr. Marta Gomez-Chiarri, Director of Graduate Studies, 401-874-2917, Fax: 401-874-7575, E-mail: gomezchi@uri.edu.

Food Science and Technology

Alabama Agricultural and Mechanical University, School of Graduate Studies, School of Agricultural and Environmental Sciences, Department of Family and Consumer Sciences, Huntsville, AL 35811. Offers family and consumer sciences (MS); food science (MS, PhD). Part-time and evening/weekend programs available. *Degree requirements:* For master's, comprehensive exam, thesis optional; for doctorate, one foreign language, thesis/dissertation. *Entrance requirements:* For master's, GRE General Test; for doctorate, GRE General Test, MS. Additional exam requirements/recommendations for international students: Required—TOEFL (minimum score 500 paper-based; 173 computer-based; 61 iBT). Electronic applications accepted. *Faculty research:* Food biotechnology, nutrition, food microbiology, food engineering, food chemistry.

Alabama Agricultural and Mechanical University, School of Graduate Studies, School of Agricultural and Environmental Sciences, Department of Food and Animal Sciences, Huntsville, AL 35811. Offers food science (MS, PhD). *Entrance requirements:* Additional exam requirements/recommendations for international students: Required—TOEFL (minimum score 500 paper-based; 173 computer-based; 61 iBT).

American University of Beirut, Graduate Programs, Faculty of Agricultural and Food Sciences, Beirut, Lebanon. Offers agricultural economics (MS); animal sciences (MS); ecosystem management (MSES); food technology (MS); irrigation (MS); mechanization (MS); nutrition (MS); plant protection (MS); plant science (MS); poultry science (MS); soils (MS). Part-time programs available. *Faculty:* 22 full-time (6 women). *Students:* 6 full-time (3 women), 86 part-time (77 women). Average age 24. 94 applicants, 60% accepted, 15 enrolled. In 2010, 28 master's awarded. *Degree requirements:* For master's, one foreign language, comprehensive exam, thesis (for some programs). *Entrance requirements:* Additional exam requirements/recommendations for international students: Required—TOEFL (minimum score 600 paper-based; 250 computer-based; 100 iBT), IELTS (minimum score 7.5). *Application deadline:* For fall admission, 4/30 for domestic and international students; for spring admission, 11/1 for

domestic and international students. Applications are processed on a rolling basis. Application fee: $50. Electronic applications accepted. *Expenses:* Tuition: Full-time $12,294; part-time $683 per credit. Required fees: $499; $499 per credit. Tuition and fees vary according to course load and program. *Financial support:* In 2010–11, 18 research assistantships with partial tuition reimbursements (averaging $13,132 per year), 42 teaching assistantships with full and partial tuition reimbursements (averaging $1,000 per year) were awarded; scholarships/grants, health care benefits, and unspecified assistantships also available. Financial award application deadline: 2/2. *Faculty research:* Community and therapeutic nutrition; food safety and food microbiology; landscape planning, nature and rural heritage conservation; pathology, immunology and control of poultry and animal diseases; agricultural economics and development. Total annual research expenditures: $900,000. *Unit head:* Prof. Nahla Hwalla, Dean, 961-134-3002 Ext. 4400, Fax: 961-174-4460, E-mail: nahla@aub.edu.lb. *Application contact:* Dr. Salim Kanaan, Director, Admissions Office, 961-135-0000 Ext. 2594, Fax: 961-175-0775, E-mail: sk00@aub.edu.lb.

Auburn University, Graduate School, College of Human Sciences, Department of Nutrition and Food Science, Auburn University, AL 36849. Offers MS, PhD. Part-time programs available. *Faculty:* 16 full-time (7 women). *Students:* 16 full-time (11 women), 13 part-time (6 women); includes 4 Black or African American, non-Hispanic/Latino, 7 international. Average age 31. 79 applicants, 37% accepted, 9 enrolled. In 2010, 10 master's, 5 doctorates awarded. *Degree requirements:* For master's, thesis (for some programs); for doctorate, thesis/dissertation. *Entrance requirements:* For master's and doctorate, GRE General Test. *Application deadline:* For fall admission, 7/7 for domestic students; for spring admission, 11/24 for domestic students. Applications are processed on a rolling basis. Application fee: $50 ($60 for international students). Electronic applications accepted. *Expenses:* Tuition, state resident: full-time $7002. Tuition, nonresident: full-time $21,898. International tuition: $22,116 full-time. Required fees: $892. Tuition and fees vary according to course load and program. *Financial support:* Research assistantships, teaching assistantships, career-related internships or fieldwork and Federal Work-Study available. Support available to part-time students. Financial award application deadline: 3/15; financial award applicants required to submit FAFSA. *Faculty research:* Food quality and safety, diet, food supply, physical activity in maintenance of health, prevention of selected chronic disease states. *Unit head:* Dr. Douglas B. White, Head, 334-844-3266. *Application contact:* Dr. George Flowers, Dean of the Graduate School, 334-844-2125.

Boston University, Metropolitan College, Program in Gastronomy, Boston, MA 02215. Offers business (MLA); communications (MLA); food policy (MLA); history and culture (MLA). Part-time and evening/weekend programs available. *Faculty:* 1 (woman) full-time, 11 part-time/adjunct (5 women). *Students:* 7 full-time (all women), 64 part-time (52 women); includes 13 minority (3 Black or African American, non-Hispanic/Latino; 1 American Indian or Alaska Native, non-Hispanic/Latino; 6 Asian, non-Hispanic/Latino; 1 Hispanic/Latino; 2 Two or more races, non-Hispanic/Latino), 2 international. Average age 29. 30 applicants, 93% accepted, 26 enrolled. In 2010, 9 master's awarded. *Degree requirements:* For master's, thesis optional. *Entrance requirements:* Additional exam requirements/recommendations for international students: Required—TOEFL. *Application deadline:* Applications are processed on a rolling basis. Application fee: $70. Electronic applications accepted. *Expenses:* Tuition: Full-time $39,314; part-time $1228 per credit. Required fees: $40 per semester. *Financial support:* In 2010–11, 4 research assistantships with partial tuition reimbursements (averaging $2,500 per year), 1 teaching assistantship (averaging $2,500 per year) were awarded; career-related internships or fieldwork, scholarships/grants, and unspecified assistantships also available. Support available to part-time students. Financial award applicants required to submit FAFSA. *Faculty research:* Food studies. *Unit head:* Dr. Rachel Black, Assistant Professor, 617-353-6291, Fax: 617-353-4130, E-mail: rblack@bu.edu. *Application contact:* Dr. Rachel Black, Assistant Professor, 617-353-6291, Fax: 617-353-4130, E-mail: rblack@bu.edu.

Brigham Young University, Graduate Studies, College of Life Sciences, Department of Nutrition, Dietetics and Food Science, Provo, UT 84602-1001. Offers food science (MS); nutrition (MS). *Faculty:* 13 full-time (5 women). *Students:* 14 full-time (9 women), 2 part-time (both women); includes 1 Black or African American, non-Hispanic/Latino; 1 Asian, non-Hispanic/Latino. Average age 24. 5 applicants, 60% accepted, 1 enrolled. In 2010, 6 master's awarded. *Degree requirements:* For master's, comprehensive exam, thesis. *Entrance requirements:* For master's, GRE General Test. Additional exam requirements/recommendations for international students: Required—TOEFL (minimum score 550 paper-based; 213 computer-based). *Application deadline:* For fall admission, 2/1 for domestic students, 2/1 priority date for international students; for winter admission, 6/30 for domestic students, 6/30 priority date for international students. Application fee: $50. Electronic applications accepted. *Expenses:* Tuition: Full-time $5580; part-time $310 per credit hour. Tuition and fees vary according to program and student's religious affiliation. *Financial support:* In 2010–11, 9 students received support, including 4 research assistantships (averaging $20,325 per year), 3 teaching assistantships (averaging $20,325 per year); career-related internships or fieldwork, institutionally sponsored loans, and scholarships/grants also available. Financial award application deadline: 4/1. *Faculty research:* Dairy foods, lipid oxidation, food processes, magnesium and selenium nutrition, nutrient effect on gene expression. Total annual research expenditures: $312,604. *Unit head:* Dr. Michael L. Dunn, Chair, 801-422-6670, Fax: 801-422-0258, E-mail: michael_dunn@byu.edu. *Application contact:* Dr. Susan Fullmer, Graduate Coordinator, 801-422-3349, Fax: 801-422-0258, E-mail: susan_fullmer@byu.edu.

California State University, Fresno, Division of Graduate Studies, College of Agricultural Sciences and Technology, Department of Food Science and Nutritional Sciences, Fresno, CA 93740-8027. Offers MS. Part-time programs available. *Degree requirements:* For master's, thesis. *Entrance requirements:* For master's, GRE General Test, minimum GPA of 3.0 in last 60 units. Additional exam requirements/recommendations for international students: Required—TOEFL. Electronic applications accepted. *Faculty research:* Liquid foods, analysis, mushrooms, gaseous ozone, natamycin.

California State University, Long Beach, Graduate Studies, College of Health and Human Services, Department of Family and Consumer Sciences, Master of Science in Nutritional Science Program, Long Beach, CA 90840. Offers food science (MS); hospitality foodservice and hotel management (MS); nutritional science (MS). Part-time programs available. *Students:* 30 full-time (all women), 19 part-time (18 women); includes 1 Black or African American, non-Hispanic/Latino; 7 Asian, non-Hispanic/Latino; 4 Hispanic/Latino. Average age 26. 119 applicants, 39% accepted, 23 enrolled. In 2010, 11 master's awarded. *Degree requirements:* For master's, thesis, oral presentation of thesis or directed project. *Entrance requirements:* For master's, GRE, minimum GPA of 2.5 in last 60 units. *Application deadline:* For fall admission, 5/1 for domestic students. Applications are processed on a rolling basis. Application fee: $55. Electronic applications accepted. *Financial support:* Federal Work-Study, institutionally sponsored loans, and scholarships/grants available. Financial award application deadline: 3/2. *Faculty research:* Protein and water-soluble vitamins, sensory evaluation of foods, mineral deficiencies in humans, child nutrition, minerals and blood pressure. *Unit head:* Dr. M. Sue Stanley, Chair, 562-985-4484, Fax: 562-985-4414, E-mail: stanleym@csulb.edu. *Application contact:* Dr. Mary Jacob, Graduate Coordinator, 562-985-4484, Fax: 562-985-4414, E-mail: marjacob@csulb.edu.

Chapman University, Graduate Studies, Schmid College of Science, Food Science Program, Orange, CA 92866. Offers MS, MBA/MS. Part-time and evening/weekend programs available. *Faculty:* 3 full-time (2 women), 4 part-time/adjunct (3 women). *Students:* 9 full-time (7 women), 34 part-time (27 women); includes 15 minority (1 Black or African American, non-Hispanic/Latino; 12 Asian, non-Hispanic/Latino; 2 Hispanic/Latino), 13 international. Average age 27. 45 applicants, 69% accepted, 19 enrolled. In 2010, 14 master's awarded. *Degree requirements:* For master's, comprehensive exam, thesis optional. *Entrance requirements:* For master's, GRE or GMAT, minimum undergraduate GPA of 3.0. Additional exam requirements/

recommendations for international students: Required—TOEFL (minimum score 550 paper-based; 213 computer-based; 80 iBT). *Application deadline:* For fall admission, 5/2 priority date for domestic students; for spring admission, 11/1 priority date for domestic students. Application fee: $60. Electronic applications accepted. *Financial support:* Fellowships, Federal Work-Study and scholarships/grants available. Financial award applicants required to submit FAFSA. *Unit head:* Dr. Anuradha Prakash, Program Director, 714-744-7895, E-mail: prakash@chapman.edu. *Application contact:* Gianne Diosomito, Graduate Admission Counselor, 714-997-6711, E-mail: diosomit@chapman.edu.

Clemson University, Graduate School, College of Agriculture, Forestry and Life Sciences, Department of Food, Nutrition and Packaging Sciences, Program in Food, Nutrition, and Culinary Science, Clemson, SC 29634. Offers MS. *Students:* 27 full-time (18 women), 5 part-time (2 women); includes 2 Hispanic/Latino, 14 international. Average age 29. 54 applicants, 28% accepted, 12 enrolled. In 2010, 8 master's awarded. *Degree requirements:* For master's, thesis. *Entrance requirements:* For master's, GRE General Test. Additional exam requirements/recommendations for international students: Required—TOEFL, IELTS. *Application deadline:* For fall admission, 6/1 for domestic students, 4/15 for international students; for spring admission, 9/15 for international students. Applications are processed on a rolling basis. Application fee: $70 ($80 for international students). Electronic applications accepted. *Expenses:* Contact institution. *Financial support:* In 2010–11, 18 students received support, including 11 research assistantships with partial tuition reimbursements available (averaging $9,871 per year), 13 teaching assistantships with partial tuition reimbursements available (averaging $6,692 per year); fellowships with full and partial tuition reimbursements available, career-related internships or fieldwork, institutionally sponsored loans, scholarships/grants, health care benefits, and unspecified assistantships also available. Support available to part-time students. Financial award applicants required to submit FAFSA. *Unit head:* Dr. Anthony L. Pometto, Chair, 864-656-4382, Fax: 864-656-3131, E-mail: pometto@clemson.edu. *Application contact:* Dr. Paul Dawson, Coordinator, 864-656-1138, Fax: 864-656-3131, E-mail: pdawson@clemson.edu.

Clemson University, Graduate School, College of Agriculture, Forestry and Life Sciences, Department of Food, Nutrition and Packaging Sciences and Department of Animal and Veterinary Sciences, Program in Food Technology, Clemson, SC 29634. Offers PhD. *Students:* 7 full-time (6 women), 8 part-time (3 women); includes 2 Black or African American, non-Hispanic/Latino; 1 Asian, non-Hispanic/Latino, 5 international. Average age 38. 21 applicants, 29% accepted, 3 enrolled. In 2010, 2 doctorates awarded. *Degree requirements:* For doctorate, thesis/dissertation. *Entrance requirements:* For doctorate, GRE General Test. Additional exam requirements/recommendations for international students: Required—TOEFL, IELTS. *Application deadline:* For fall admission, 6/1 for domestic students, 4/15 for international students; for spring admission, 9/15 for international students. Applications are processed on a rolling basis. Application fee: $70 ($80 for international students). Electronic applications accepted. *Expenses:* Contact institution. *Financial support:* In 2010–11, 7 students received support, including 3 research assistantships with partial tuition reimbursements available (averaging $18,833 per year), 5 teaching assistantships with partial tuition reimbursements available (averaging $12,600 per year); fellowships with full and partial tuition reimbursements available, career-related internships or fieldwork, institutionally sponsored loans, scholarships/grants, health care benefits, and unspecified assistantships also available. Support available to part-time students. Financial award applicants required to submit FAFSA. *Unit head:* Dr. Anthony Pometto, Coordinator, 864-656-4382, Fax: 864-656-3131, E-mail: pometto@clemson.edu. *Application contact:* Dr. Paul Dawson, Coordinator, 864-656-1138, Fax: 864-656-3131, E-mail: pdawson@clemson.edu.

Colorado State University, Graduate School, College of Applied Human Sciences, Department of Food Science and Human Nutrition, Fort Collins, CO 80523-1571. Offers MS, PhD. *Accreditation:* ADtA. Part-time programs available. *Faculty:* 16 full-time (7 women), 2 part-time/adjunct (1 woman). *Students:* 54 full-time (45 women), 33 part-time (22 women); includes 7 minority (3 Asian, non-Hispanic/Latino; 3 Hispanic/Latino; 1 Two or more races, non-Hispanic/Latino), 5 international. Average age 29. 142 applicants, 39% accepted, 24 enrolled. In 2010, 30 master's, 2 doctorates awarded. *Degree requirements:* For master's, thesis; for doctorate, thesis/dissertation. *Entrance requirements:* For master's and doctorate, GRE General Test, minimum GPA of 3.0, resume, 3 letters of recommendation. Additional exam requirements/recommendations for international students: Required—TOEFL (minimum score 550 paper-based; 213 computer-based; 80 iBT). *Application deadline:* For fall admission, 2/15 priority date for domestic and international students; for spring admission, 7/15 priority date for domestic and international students. Application fee: $50. Electronic applications accepted. *Expenses:* Tuition, state resident: full-time $7434; part-time $413 per credit. Tuition, nonresident: full-time $19,022; part-time $1057 per credit. Required fees: $1729; $88 per credit. *Financial support:* In 2010–11, 18 students received support, including 9 research assistantships with full and partial tuition reimbursements available (averaging $9,201 per year), 9 teaching assistantships with full and partial tuition reimbursements available (averaging $7,533 per year); fellowships, Federal Work-Study, scholarships/grants, and unspecified assistantships also available. Financial award application deadline: 3/1; financial award applicants required to submit FAFSA. *Faculty research:* Metabolic regulation, nutrition education, food safety, obesity and diabetes, metabolism. Total annual research expenditures: $5 million. *Unit head:* Dr. Christopher Melby, Head, 970-491-6736, Fax: 970-491-7252, E-mail: christopher.melby@colostate.edu. *Application contact:* Paula Coleman, Graduate Coordinator, 970-491-3819, Fax: 970-491-3875, E-mail: pcoleman@cahs.colostate.edu.

Cornell University, Graduate School, Graduate Fields of Agriculture and Life Sciences, Field of Food Science and Technology, Ithaca, NY 14853-0001. Offers dairy science (MPS, MS, PhD); food chemistry (MPS, MS, PhD); food engineering (MPS, MS, PhD); food microbiology (MPS, MS, PhD); food processing waste technology (MPS, MS, PhD); food science (MFS, MPS, MS, PhD); international food science (MPS, MS, PhD); sensory evaluation (MPS, MS, PhD). *Faculty:* 43 full-time (10 women). *Students:* 85 full-time (51 women); includes 3 Black or African American, non-Hispanic/Latino; 5 Asian, non-Hispanic/Latino; 1 Hispanic/Latino, 47 international. Average age 26. 192 applicants, 23% accepted, 40 enrolled. In 2010, 4 master's, 12 doctorates awarded. Terminal master's awarded for partial completion of doctoral program. *Degree requirements:* For master's, thesis (MS), teaching experience; for doctorate, comprehensive exam, thesis/dissertation, teaching experience. *Entrance requirements:* For master's and doctorate, GRE General Test, 3 letters of recommendation. Additional exam requirements/recommendations for international students: Required—TOEFL (minimum score 550 paper-based; 213 computer-based; 77 iBT). *Application deadline:* For fall admission, 1/30 priority date for domestic students. Application fee: $70. Electronic applications accepted. *Expenses:* Tuition: Full-time $29,500. Required fees: $76. Tuition and fees vary according to degree level and program. *Financial support:* In 2010–11, 10 fellowships with full tuition reimbursements, 37 research assistantships with full tuition reimbursements, 12 teaching assistantships with full tuition reimbursements were awarded; institutionally sponsored loans, scholarships/grants, health care benefits, tuition waivers (full and partial), and unspecified assistantships also available. Financial award applicants required to submit FAFSA. *Faculty research:* Food microbiology/biotechnology, food engineering/processing, food safety/toxicology, sensory science/flavor chemistry, food packaging. *Unit head:* Director of Graduate Studies, 607-255-7637, Fax: 607-254-4868. *Application contact:* Graduate Field Assistant, 607-255-7637, Fax: 607-254-4868, E-mail: fdscigrad@cornell.edu.

Dalhousie University, Faculty of Engineering, Department of Food Science and Technology, Halifax, NS B3J 1Z1, Canada. Offers M Sc, PhD. *Degree requirements:* For master's, thesis; for doctorate, thesis/dissertation. *Entrance requirements:* Additional exam requirements/recommendations for international students: Required—TOEFL, IELTS, CANTEST, CAEL, or Michigan English Language Assessment Battery. Electronic applications accepted. *Faculty research:* Food microbiology, food safety/HALLP, rheology and rheometry, food processing, seafood processing.

Peterson's Graduate Programs in the Physical Sciences, Mathematics, Agricultural Sciences, the Environment & Natural Resources 2012

www.facebook.com/petersonspublishing **337**

Food Science and Technology

Drexel University, School of Technology and Professional Studies, Philadelphia, PA 19104-2875. Offers construction management (MS); engineering technology (MS); food science (MS); hospitality management (MS); professional studies: creativity studies (MS); professional studies: e-learning leadership (MS); professional studies: homeland security management (MS); project management (MS); property management (MS); sport management (MS). Post-baccalaureate distance learning degree programs offered.

Florida Agricultural and Mechanical University, Division of Graduate Studies, Research, and Continuing Education, College of Engineering Science, Technology, and Agriculture, Division of Agricultural Sciences, Tallahassee, FL 32307-3200. Offers agribusiness (MS); animal science (MS); engineering technology (MS); entomology (MS); food science (MS); international programs (MS); plant science (MS). *Degree requirements:* For master's, thesis. *Entrance requirements:* For master's, GRE General Test, minimum GPA of 3.0. Additional exam requirements/recommendations for international students: Required—TOEFL (minimum score 500 paper-based).

Florida State University, The Graduate School, College of Human Sciences, Department of Nutrition, Food, and Exercise Sciences, Tallahassee, FL 32306-1493. Offers exercise science (MS, PhD), including exercise physiology, sports sciences (MS); nutrition and food sciences (MS, PhD), including clinical nutrition (MS), food science, human nutrition (PhD), nutrition and sport (MS), nutrition science (MS), nutrition, education and health promotion (MS). Part-time programs available. *Faculty:* 19 full-time (11 women). *Students:* 135 full-time (87 women), 34 part-time (26 women); includes 18 minority (7 Black or African American, non-Hispanic/Latino; 4 Asian, non-Hispanic/Latino; 6 Hispanic/Latino; 1 Two or more races, non-Hispanic/Latino), 28 international. 155 applicants, 37% accepted, 34 enrolled. In 2010, 30 master's, 7 doctorates awarded. *Degree requirements:* For master's, comprehensive exam (for some programs), thesis optional; for doctorate, thesis/dissertation. *Entrance requirements:* For master's, GRE General Test, minimum upper-division GPA of 3.0; for doctorate, GRE General Test, minimum upper-division GPA of 3.0, MS. Additional exam requirements/recommendations for international students: Required—TOEFL (minimum score 550 paper-based; 80 iBT). *Application deadline:* For fall admission, 7/1 for domestic students, 3/1 for international students; for spring admission, 11/1 for domestic students, 5/1 for international students. Applications are processed on a rolling basis. Application fee: $30. Electronic applications accepted. *Expenses:* Tuition, state resident: full-time $8238.24. *Financial support:* In 2010–11, 62 students received support, including 1 fellowship with partial tuition reimbursement available (averaging $10,000 per year), 13 research assistantships with partial tuition reimbursements available (averaging $8,000 per year), 42 teaching assistantships with partial tuition reimbursements available (averaging $8,000 per year); career-related internships or fieldwork, Federal Work-Study, institutionally sponsored loans, scholarships/grants, and unspecified assistantships also available. Financial award application deadline: 1/15; financial award applicants required to submit FAFSA. *Faculty research:* Body composition, functional food, chronic disease and aging response; food safety, food allergy, and safety/quality detection methods; sports nutrition, energy and human performance; strength training, functional performance, cardiovascular physiology, sarcopenia. *Unit head:* Dr. Bahram H. Arjmandi, Professor/Chair, 850-645-1517, Fax: 850-645-5000, E-mail: barjmandi@fsu.edu. *Application contact:* Joseph J. Carroll, Administrative Support Assistant, 850-644-4800, Fax: 850-645-5000, E-mail: jjcarroll@admin.fsu.edu.

Framingham State University, Division of Graduate and Continuing Education, Programs in Food and Nutrition, Food Science and Nutrition Science Program, Framingham, MA 01701-9101. Offers MS. Part-time and evening/weekend programs available. *Entrance requirements:* For master's, GRE General Test.

Illinois Institute of Technology, Graduate College, College of Science and Letters, Program in Food Safety and Technology, Chicago, IL 60616-3793. Offers MFPE, MFST, MS. Part-time programs available. *Faculty:* 7 full-time (1 woman), 1 part-time/adjunct (0 women). *Students:* 47 full-time (33 women), 9 part-time (3 women); includes 6 minority (2 Black or African American, non-Hispanic/Latino; 3 Asian, non-Hispanic/Latino; 1 Two or more races, non-Hispanic/Latino), 47 international. Average age 26. 76 applicants, 74% accepted, 31 enrolled. In 2010, 15 master's awarded. *Degree requirements:* For master's, comprehensive exam (for some programs), thesis (for some programs). *Entrance requirements:* For master's, GRE General Test, minimum undergraduate GPA of 3.0. Additional exam requirements/recommendations for international students: Required—TOEFL (minimum score 523 paper-based; 213 computer-based; 70 iBT). *Application deadline:* For fall admission, 5/1 for domestic and international students; for spring admission, 10/15 for domestic and international students. Applications are processed on a rolling basis. Application fee: $50. Electronic applications accepted. *Expenses:* Tuition: Full-time $18,576; part-time $1032 per credit hour. Required fees: $583 per semester. One-time fee: $150. Tuition and fees vary according to program and student level. *Financial support:* In 2010–11, 11 research assistantships with full and partial tuition reimbursements (averaging $1,573 per year) were awarded; fellowships with partial tuition reimbursements, Federal Work-Study, institutionally sponsored loans, scholarships/grants, health care benefits, and unspecified assistantships also available. Support available to part-time students. Financial award applicants required to submit FAFSA. *Faculty research:* Microbial food safety and security, food virology, interfacial colloidial phenomena, development of DNA-based methods for detection, differentiation and tracking of foodborne pathogens in food systems and environment, appetite and obesity management and vascular disease. Total annual research expenditures: $8 million. *Unit head:* Dr. Robert E. Brackett, Vice President and Director, 708-563-1533, E-mail: rbrackett@iit.edu. *Application contact:* Deborah Gibson, Director, Graduate Admission, 866-472-3448, Fax: 312-567-3138, E-mail: inquiry.grad@iit.edu.

Iowa State University of Science and Technology, Graduate College, College of Human Sciences and College of Agriculture, Department of Food Science and Human Nutrition, Ames, IA 50011. Offers food science and technology (MS, PhD); nutrition (MS, PhD). *Faculty:* 49 full-time (27 women), 3 part-time/adjunct (2 women). *Students:* 39 full-time (25 women), 11 part-time (10 women); includes 4 Black or African American, non-Hispanic/Latino; 2 Asian, non-Hispanic/Latino; 1 Hispanic/Latino, 21 international. 58 applicants, 16% accepted, 6 enrolled. In 2010, 9 master's, 4 doctorates awarded. *Degree requirements:* For master's, thesis; for doctorate, thesis/dissertation. *Entrance requirements:* For master's and doctorate, GRE General Test. Additional exam requirements/recommendations for international students: Required—TOEFL (minimum score 550 paper-based; 79 iBT), IELTS (minimum score 6.5). *Application deadline:* For fall admission, 1/15 priority date for domestic and international students. Applications are processed on a rolling basis. Application fee: $40 ($90 for international students). Electronic applications accepted. *Financial support:* In 2010–11, 47 research assistantships with full and partial tuition reimbursements (averaging $15,342 per year), 1 teaching assistantship with full and partial tuition reimbursement (averaging $9,111 per year) were awarded; fellowships, scholarships/grants also available. *Unit head:* Dr. Ruth S. MacDonald, Chair, 515-294-5991, Fax: 515-294-8181, E-mail: ruthmacd@iastate.edu. *Application contact:* Dr. Patricia Murphy, Director of Graduate Education, 515-294-6442, E-mail: gradsecretary@iastate.edu.

Kansas State University, Graduate School, College of Agriculture, Food Science Institute, Manhattan, KS 66506. Offers MS, PhD. Part-time programs available. Postbaccalaureate distance learning degree programs offered (minimal on-campus study). *Degree requirements:* For master's, thesis, residency; for doctorate, thesis/dissertation, preliminary exams, residency. *Entrance requirements:* For master's, GRE General Test, minimum GPA of 3.0 in undergraduate course work, course work in mathematics; for doctorate, GRE General Test, minimum GPA of 3.5 in master's course work. Additional exam requirements/recommendations for international students: Required—TOEFL (minimum score 550 paper-based; 213 computer-based). Electronic applications accepted. *Faculty research:* Systems to insure food safety and security, determining nutrients and bioactive compounds, evaluate new processes and agricultural ingredients into higher food values, sensory evaluation strategies for foods.

Louisiana State University and Agricultural and Mechanical College, Graduate School, College of Agriculture, Department of Food Science, Baton Rouge, LA 70803. Offers MS, PhD. Part-time programs available. *Faculty:* 12 full-time (5 women). *Students:* 42 full-time (23 women), 3 part-time (2 women); includes 2 Black or African American, non-Hispanic/Latino; 1 Hispanic/Latino, 33 international. Average age 28. 61 applicants, 25% accepted, 8 enrolled. In 2010, 7 master's, 4 doctorates awarded. *Degree requirements:* For master's, thesis; for doctorate, thesis/dissertation. *Entrance requirements:* For master's and doctorate, GRE General Test, minimum GPA of 3.0. Additional exam requirements/recommendations for international students: Required—TOEFL (minimum score 550 paper-based; 213 computer-based; 79 iBT), IELTS (minimum score 6.5). *Application deadline:* For fall admission, 1/25 priority date for domestic students, 5/15 for international students; for spring admission, 10/15 for international students. Applications are processed on a rolling basis. Application fee: $50 ($70 for international students). Electronic applications accepted. *Financial support:* In 2010–11, 45 students received support, including 1 fellowship (averaging $29,011 per year), 38 research assistantships with partial tuition reimbursements available (averaging $16,605 per year), 2 teaching assistantships with partial tuition reimbursements available (averaging $15,750 per year); Federal Work-Study, institutionally sponsored loans, scholarships/grants, health care benefits, tuition waivers (full and partial), and unspecified assistantships also available. Support available to part-time students. Financial award application deadline: 4/1; financial award applicants required to submit FAFSA. *Faculty research:* Food chemistry/analysis, food microbiology, food processing/engineering, sensory science, product development. Total annual research expenditures: $74,876. *Unit head:* Dr. John W. Finley, Head, 225-578-5206, Fax: 225-578-5300, E-mail: jfinley@agcenter.lsu.edu. *Application contact:* Dr. Kenneth McMillan, Graduate Coordinator, 225-578-5207, Fax: 225-578-5300, E-mail: kmcmill@agcenter.lsu.edu.

McGill University, Faculty of Graduate and Postdoctoral Studies, Faculty of Agricultural and Environmental Sciences, Department of Food Science and Agricultural Chemistry, Montréal, QC H3A 2T5, Canada. Offers M Sc, PhD.

Memorial University of Newfoundland, School of Graduate Studies, Department of Biochemistry, St. John's, NL A1C 5S7, Canada. Offers biochemistry (M Sc, PhD); food science (M Sc, PhD). Part-time programs available. *Degree requirements:* For master's, thesis; for doctorate, comprehensive exam, thesis/dissertation, oral defense of thesis. *Entrance requirements:* For master's, 2nd class degree in related field; for doctorate, M Sc. Electronic applications accepted. *Faculty research:* Toxicology, cell and molecular biology, food engineering, marine biotechnology, lipid biology.

Michigan State University, College of Veterinary Medicine and The Graduate School, Graduate Programs in Veterinary Medicine, National Food Safety and Toxicology Center, East Lansing, MI 48824. Offers food safety (MS). *Entrance requirements:* Additional exam requirements/recommendations for international students: Required—TOEFL, Michigan State University ELT (minimum score 85), Michigan English Language Assessment Battery (minimum score 83). Electronic applications accepted.

Michigan State University, The Graduate School, College of Agriculture and Natural Resources and College of Natural Science, Department of Food Science and Human Nutrition, East Lansing, MI 48824. Offers food science (MS, PhD); food science—environmental toxicology (PhD); human nutrition (MS, PhD); human nutrition-environmental toxicology (PhD). *Entrance requirements:* Additional exam requirements/recommendations for international students: Required—TOEFL (minimum score 550 paper-based; 213 computer-based), Michigan State University ELT (minimum score 85), Michigan English Language Assessment Battery (minimum score 83). Electronic applications accepted.

Middle Tennessee State University, College of Graduate Studies, College of Behavioral and Health Sciences, Department of Human Sciences, Murfreesboro, TN 37132. Offers child development and family studies (MS); nutrition and food science (MS). Part-time and evening/weekend programs available. Postbaccalaureate distance learning degree programs offered. *Faculty:* 7 full-time (all women). *Students:* 24 part-time (23 women); includes 4 Black or African American, non-Hispanic/Latino; 2 Asian, non-Hispanic/Latino; 1 Hispanic/Latino. Average age 31. 22 applicants, 82% accepted, 18 enrolled. In 2010, 5 master's awarded. *Degree requirements:* For master's, comprehensive exam, thesis. *Entrance requirements:* For master's, GRE or MAT. Additional exam requirements/recommendations for international students: Required—TOEFL (minimum score 525 paper-based; 195 computer-based; 71 iBT) or IELTS (minimum score 6). *Application deadline:* For fall admission, 6/1 for domestic and international students. Applications are processed on a rolling basis. Application fee: $25 ($30 for international students). Electronic applications accepted. *Expenses:* Tuition, state resident: full-time $4632. Tuition, nonresident: full-time $11,520. *Financial support:* In 2010–11, 5 students received support. Application deadline: 5/1. *Faculty research:* Courtship relationships, feminist methodology and epistemology in family studies, school uniforms, body fat in elderly, asynchronous distance education. *Unit head:* Dr. Deborah G. Belcher, Interim Chair, 615-898-2884, Fax: 615-898-5130, E-mail: dbelcher@mtsu.edu. *Application contact:* Dr. Michael Allen, Dean and Vice Provost for Research, 615-898-2840, Fax: 615-904-8020, E-mail: mallen@mtsu.edu.

Mississippi State University, College of Agriculture and Life Sciences, Department of Food Science, Nutrition and Health Promotion, Mississippi State, MS 39762. Offers food science and technology (MS, PhD); health promotion (MS); nutrition (MS, PhD). Postbaccalaureate distance learning degree programs offered (no on-campus study). *Faculty:* 11 full-time (4 women), 1 part-time/adjunct (0 women). *Students:* 48 full-time (32 women), 37 part-time (28 women); includes 12 minority (10 Black or African American, non-Hispanic/Latino; 2 Hispanic/Latino), 16 international. Average age 29. 97 applicants, 53% accepted, 29 enrolled. In 2010, 23 master's, 7 doctorates awarded. *Degree requirements:* For master's, comprehensive exam, thesis; for doctorate, comprehensive exam, thesis/dissertation. *Entrance requirements:* For master's, GRE General Test, minimum GPA of 2.8; for doctorate, GRE General Test, minimum GPA of 3.0. Additional exam requirements/recommendations for international students: Required—TOEFL (minimum score 475 paper-based; 153 computer-based; 53 iBT); Recommended—IELTS (minimum score 4.5). *Application deadline:* For fall admission, 7/1 for domestic students, 5/1 for international students; for spring admission, 11/1 for domestic students, 9/1 for international students. Applications are processed on a rolling basis. Application fee: $40. Electronic applications accepted. *Expenses:* Tuition, state resident: full-time $2730.50; part-time $304 per credit hour. Tuition, nonresident: full-time $6901; part-time $767 per credit hour. *Financial support:* In 2010–11, 12 research assistantships with full tuition reimbursements (averaging $12,115 per year), 4 teaching assistantships with full tuition reimbursements (averaging $13,380 per year) were awarded; Federal Work-Study, institutionally sponsored loans, scholarships/grants, and unspecified assistantships also available. Financial award application deadline: 4/1; financial award applicants required to submit FAFSA. *Faculty research:* Food preservation, food chemistry, food safety, food processing, product development. *Unit head:* Dr. Benjy Mikel, Professor and Head, 662-325-3200, Fax: 662-325-8728, E-mail: wmikel@fsnhp.msstate.edu. *Application contact:* Dr. Juan Silva, Professor and Graduate Coordinator, 662-325-3200, Fax: 662-325-8728, E-mail: jls@ra.msstate.edu.

Montclair State University, The Graduate School, College of Education and Human Services, Department of Health and Nutrition Sciences, Montclair, NJ 07043-1624. Offers American Dietetic Association (Certificate); food safety instructor (Certificate); health education (MA); nutrition and exercise science (Certificate); nutrition and food science (MS); public health (MPH), including community health education. Part-time and evening/weekend programs available. *Faculty:* 16 full-time (11 women), 59 part-time/adjunct (46 women). *Students:* 62

full-time (52 women), 63 part-time (56 women); includes 15 Black or African American, non-Hispanic/Latino; 9 Asian, non-Hispanic/Latino; 9 Hispanic/Latino; 1 Native Hawaiian or other Pacific Islander, non-Hispanic/Latino, 5 international. Average age 31. 75 applicants, 56% accepted, 31 enrolled. In 2010, 32 master's, 12 other advanced degrees awarded. *Degree requirements:* For master's, comprehensive exam, thesis optional. *Entrance requirements:* For master's, GRE, 2 letters of recommendation. Additional exam requirements/recommendations for international students: Required—TOEFL (minimum iBT score of 83) or IELTS. *Application deadline:* For fall admission, 6/1 for international students; for spring admission, 10/1 for international students. Application fee: $60. *Expenses:* Tuition, state resident: part-time $501.34 per credit. Tuition, nonresident: part-time $773.88 per credit. Required fees: $71.15 per credit. *Financial support:* In 2010–11, 8 research assistantships with full tuition reimbursements (averaging $7,000 per year), 1 teaching assistantship with full tuition reimbursement (averaging $7,000 per year) were awarded; Federal Work-Study, scholarships/grants, and unspecified assistantships also available. Support available to part-time students. Financial award application deadline: 3/1; financial award applicants required to submit FAFSA. *Faculty research:* Improving health via improved nutrition, nutrition epidemiology: assessing health behaviors, mechanisms or pathways to reduce health disparities in underserved or nutritionally at-risk populations, dietary behaviors and theories, psychosocial determinants. Total annual research expenditures: $688,174. *Unit head:* Dr. Eva Goldfarb, Chairperson, 973-655-4154. *Application contact:* Amy Aiello, Director of Graduate Admissions and Operations, 973-655-5147, Fax: 973-655-7869, E-mail: graduate.school@montclair.edu.

New York University, Steinhardt School of Culture, Education, and Human Development, Department of Nutrition, Food Studies, and Public Health, Program in Food Studies and Food Management, New York, NY 10012-1019. Offers food studies (MA), including food culture, food systems; food studies and food management (PhD). Part-time programs available. *Faculty:* 6 full-time (5 women). *Students:* 21 full-time (18 women), 138 part-time (117 women); includes 4 Black or African American, non-Hispanic/Latino; 15 Asian, non-Hispanic/Latino; 7 Hispanic/Latino, 13 international. Average age 31. 163 applicants, 45% accepted, 50 enrolled. In 2010, 26 master's awarded. *Degree requirements:* For master's, thesis (for some programs); for doctorate, thesis/dissertation. *Entrance requirements:* For doctorate, GRE General Test, interview. Additional exam requirements/recommendations for international students: Required—TOEFL. *Application deadline:* For fall admission, 12/1 priority date for domestic students, 12/1 for international students; for spring admission, 11/1 for domestic and international students. Applications are processed on a rolling basis. Application fee: $75. Electronic applications accepted. *Financial support:* Fellowships with full and partial tuition reimbursements, career-related internships or fieldwork, Federal Work-Study, institutionally sponsored loans, scholarships/grants, tuition waivers (partial), and unspecified assistantships available. Financial award application deadline: 2/1; financial award applicants required to submit FAFSA. *Faculty research:* Cultural and social history of food, food systems and agriculture, food and aesthetics, political economy of food. *Unit head:* Dr. Jennifer Berg, Director, 212-998-5580, Fax: 212-995-4194. *Application contact:* 212-998-5030, Fax: 212-995-4328, E-mail: steinhardt.gradadmissions@nyu.edu.

North Carolina State University, Graduate School, College of Agriculture and Life Sciences, Department of Food Science, Raleigh, NC 27695. Offers MFS, MS, PhD. *Degree requirements:* For master's, thesis (for some programs); for doctorate, thesis/dissertation. *Entrance requirements:* For master's and doctorate, GRE. Electronic applications accepted. *Faculty research:* Food safety, value-added food products, environmental quality, nutrition and health, biotechnology.

North Dakota State University, College of Graduate and Interdisciplinary Studies, College of Agriculture, Food Systems, and Natural Resources, Department of Cereal and Food Sciences, Fargo, ND 58108. Offers cereal science (MS, PhD). Part-time programs available. *Faculty:* 8 full-time (2 women), 2 part-time/adjunct (0 women). *Students:* 7 full-time (3 women), 6 part-time (4 women), 11 international. 5 applicants, 20% accepted, 1 enrolled. In 2010, 2 master's awarded. Terminal master's awarded for partial completion of doctoral program. *Degree requirements:* For master's, comprehensive exam, thesis; for doctorate, comprehensive exam, thesis/dissertation. *Entrance requirements:* Additional exam requirements/recommendations for international students: Required—TOEFL (minimum score 550 paper-based; 213 computer-based; 79 iBT), IELTS (minimum score 6). *Application deadline:* For fall admission, 5/1 priority date for domestic students. Application fee: $45 ($60 for international students). *Financial support:* In 2010–11, 15 research assistantships with full tuition reimbursements (averaging $12,000 per year) were awarded; career-related internships or fieldwork and unspecified assistantships also available. Support available to part-time students. *Faculty research:* Legume food products, cereal proteins and product quality, oilseeds functional components. Total annual research expenditures: $500,000. *Unit head:* Dr. Deland Myers, Chair, 701-231-7711, Fax: 701-231-5171, E-mail: deland.myers@ndsu.edu. *Application contact:* Dr. Deland Myers, Chair, 701-231-7711, Fax: 701-231-5171, E-mail: deland.myers@ndsu.edu.

North Dakota State University, College of Graduate and Interdisciplinary Studies, Interdisciplinary Program in Food Safety, Fargo, ND 58108. Offers MS, PhD. Part-time programs available. Postbaccalaureate distance learning degree programs offered (minimal on-campus study). *Faculty:* 10 full-time (5 women), 3 part-time/adjunct (2 women). *Students:* 8 full-time (5 women), 3 part-time (all women), 7 international. Average age 25. 18 applicants, 17% accepted, 3 enrolled. In 2010, 1 master's awarded. Terminal master's awarded for partial completion of doctoral program. *Degree requirements:* For master's, thesis; for doctorate, comprehensive exam, thesis/dissertation. *Entrance requirements:* Additional exam requirements/recommendations for international students: Required—TOEFL (minimum score 525 paper-based; 197 computer-based; 71 iBT), TWE (minimum score 5). *Application deadline:* Applications are processed on a rolling basis. Application fee: $45 ($60 for international students). Electronic applications accepted. *Financial support:* In 2010–11, 9 research assistantships with full tuition reimbursements (averaging $16,000 per year) were awarded; scholarships/grants also available. *Faculty research:* Mycotoxins in grain, pathogens in meat systems, sensor development for food pathogens. *Unit head:* Dr. Clifford Hall, Associate Director, 701-231-6359, Fax: 701-231-5171, E-mail: clifford.hall@ndsu.edu. *Application contact:* Dr. Clifford Hall, Associate Director, 701-231-6359, Fax: 701-231-5171, E-mail: clifford.hall@ndsu.edu.

Nova Scotia Agricultural College, Research and Graduate Studies, Truro, NS B2N 5E3, Canada. Offers agriculture (M Sc), including air quality, animal behavior, animal molecular genetics, animal nutrition, animal technology, aquaculture, botany, crop management, crop physiology, ecology, environmental microbiology, food science, horticulture, nutrient management, pest management, physiology, plant biotechnology, plant pathology, soil chemistry, soil fertility, waste management and composting, water quality. Program offered jointly with Dalhousie University. Part-time programs available. *Degree requirements:* For master's, thesis, ATC Exam Teaching Assistantship. *Entrance requirements:* For master's, honors B Sc, minimum GPA of 3.0. Additional exam requirements/recommendations for international students: Required—TOEFL (minimum score 580 paper-based; 237 computer-based; 92 iBT), IELTS, Michigan English Language Assessment Battery, CanTEST, CAEL. *Faculty research:* Bio-product development, organic agriculture, nutrient management, air and water quality, agricultural biotechnology.

The Ohio State University, Graduate School, College of Food, Agricultural, and Environmental Sciences, Department of Food Science and Nutrition, Columbus, OH 43210. Offers food science (MS, PhD). *Accreditation:* ADtA. *Faculty:* 23. *Students:* 53 full-time (37 women), 22 part-time (8 women); includes 5 Black or African American, non-Hispanic/Latino; 6 Asian, non-Hispanic/Latino; 2 Hispanic/Latino, 34 international. Average age 28. In 2010, 14 master's, 9 doctorates awarded. *Degree requirements:* For master's, thesis optional; for doctorate, thesis/dissertation. *Entrance requirements:* For master's and doctorate, GRE General Test. Additional exam requirements/recommendations for international students: Required—TOEFL (minimum score 550 paper-based; 213 computer-based), IELTS (minimum score 7), or Michigan English Language Assessment Battery (minimum score 89). *Application deadline:* For fall admission, 8/15 priority date for domestic students, 7/1 priority date for international students; for winter admission, 12/1 priority date for domestic students, 11/1 priority date for international students; for spring admission, 3/1 priority date for domestic students, 2/1 priority date for international students. Applications are processed on a rolling basis. Application fee: $40 ($50 for international students). Electronic applications accepted. *Expenses:* Tuition, state resident: full-time $10,605. Tuition, nonresident: full-time $26,535. Tuition and fees vary according to course load and program. *Financial support:* Fellowships, research assistantships, Federal Work-Study and institutionally sponsored loans available. Support available to part-time students. *Unit head:* Mike Mangino, Interim Chair, 614-292-7769, E-mail: mangino.2@osu.edu. *Application contact:* Graduate Admissions, 614-292-9444, Fax: 614-292-3895, E-mail: domestic.grad@osu.edu.

Oklahoma State University, College of Agricultural Science and Natural Resources, Department of Animal Science, Stillwater, OK 74078. Offers animal sciences (M Ag, MS); food science (MS, PhD). *Faculty:* 28 full-time (6 women), 4 part-time/adjunct (0 women). *Students:* 25 full-time (19 women), 49 part-time (24 women); includes 1 Black or African American, non-Hispanic/Latino; 3 Hispanic/Latino, 30 international. Average age 27. 105 applicants, 12% accepted, 12 enrolled. In 2010, 17 master's, 5 doctorates awarded. *Degree requirements:* For master's, thesis; for doctorate, comprehensive exam, thesis/dissertation. *Entrance requirements:* For master's and doctorate, GRE or GMAT. Additional exam requirements/recommendations for international students: Required—TOEFL (minimum score 550 paper-based; 79 iBT). *Application deadline:* For fall admission, 3/1 priority date for international students; for spring admission, 8/1 priority date for international students. Applications are processed on a rolling basis. Application fee: $40 ($75 for international students). Electronic applications accepted. *Expenses:* Tuition, state resident: full-time $3716; part-time $154.85 per credit hour. Tuition, nonresident: full-time $14,892; part-time $621 per credit hour. Required fees: $2044; $85.20 per credit hour. One-time fee: $50. Tuition and fees vary according to course load and campus/location. *Financial support:* In 2010–11, 38 research assistantships (averaging $14,013 per year), 1 teaching assistantship (averaging $11,064 per year) were awarded; career-related internships or fieldwork, Federal Work-Study, scholarships/grants, health care benefits, tuition waivers (partial), and unspecified assistantships also available. Support available to part-time students. Financial award application deadline: 3/1; financial award applicants required to submit FAFSA. *Faculty research:* Quantitative trait loci identification for economical traits in swing/beef; waste management strategies in livestock; endocrine control of reproductive processes in farm animals; cholesterol synthesis, inhibition, and reduction; food safety research. *Unit head:* Dr. Ronald Kensinger, Head, 405-744-6062, Fax: 405-744-7390. *Application contact:* Dr. Gerald Horn, Information Contact, 405-744-6070, Fax: 405-744-6621, E-mail: gerald.horn@okstate.edu.

Oregon State University, Graduate School, College of Agricultural Sciences, Department of Food Science and Technology, Corvallis, OR 97331. Offers M Agr, MAIS, MS, PhD. *Degree requirements:* For master's, thesis (for some programs); for doctorate, thesis/dissertation. *Entrance requirements:* For master's and doctorate, GRE General Test, minimum GPA of 3.0 in last 90 hours. Additional exam requirements/recommendations for international students: Required—TOEFL. *Faculty research:* Diet, cancer, and anticarcinogenesis; sensory analysis; chemistry and biochemistry.

Penn State University Park, Graduate School, College of Agricultural Sciences, Department of Food Science, State College, University Park, PA 16802-1503. Offers MS, PhD.

Purdue University, Graduate School, College of Agriculture, Department of Food Science, West Lafayette, IN 47907. Offers MS, PhD. *Degree requirements:* For master's, thesis (for some programs); for doctorate, thesis/dissertation, teaching assistantship. *Entrance requirements:* For master's and doctorate, GRE General Test. Additional exam requirements/recommendations for international students: Required—TOEFL, TWE. Electronic applications accepted. *Faculty research:* Processing, technology, microbiology, chemistry of foods, carbohydrate chemistry.

Rutgers, The State University of New Jersey, New Brunswick, Graduate School-New Brunswick, Program in Food Science, Piscataway, NJ 08854-8097. Offers M Phil, MS, PhD. Part-time and evening/weekend programs available. Postbaccalaureate distance learning degree programs offered (minimal on-campus study). *Degree requirements:* For master's, thesis or alternative; for doctorate, thesis/dissertation. *Entrance requirements:* For master's and doctorate, GRE General Test. *Expenses:* Tuition, state resident: full-time $7200; part-time $600 per credit. Tuition, nonresident: full-time $11,124; part-time $927 per credit. *Faculty research:* Nutraceuticals and functional foods, food and flavor analysis, food chemistry and biochemistry, food nanotechnology, food engineering and processing.

South Dakota State University, Graduate School, College of Education and Human Sciences, Department of Nutrition, Food Science and Hospitality, Brookings, SD 57007. Offers dietetics (MS); nutrition, food science and hospitality (MFCS); nutritional sciences (MS, PhD). Part-time programs available. *Degree requirements:* For master's, comprehensive exam (for some programs), thesis (for some programs), oral exam. *Entrance requirements:* Additional exam requirements/recommendations for international students: Required—TOEFL (minimum score 525 paper-based). *Faculty research:* Food chemistry, bone density, functional food, nutrition education, nutrition biochemistry.

Texas A&M University, College of Agriculture and Life Sciences, Department of Nutrition and Food Science, College Station, TX 77843. Offers food science and technology (M Agr); nutrition (MS, PhD). *Faculty:* 17. *Students:* 74 full-time (52 women), 10 part-time (9 women); includes 11 minority (1 Black or African American, non-Hispanic/Latino; 5 Asian, non-Hispanic/Latino; 5 Hispanic/Latino), 30 international. *Degree requirements:* For master's, thesis; for doctorate, thesis/dissertation. *Entrance requirements:* For master's and doctorate, GRE General Test. Additional exam requirements/recommendations for international students: Required—TOEFL. *Application deadline:* For fall admission, 2/1 priority date for domestic students; for spring admission, 10/1 priority date for domestic students. Applications are processed on a rolling basis. Application fee: $50 ($75 for international students). *Financial support:* Fellowships, research assistantships, teaching assistantships, career-related internships or fieldwork and scholarships/grants available. *Faculty research:* Food safety, microbiology, product development. *Unit head:* Dr. Jimmy T. Keeton, Department Head, 979-458-3428, E-mail: jkeeton@tamu.edu. *Application contact:* Dr. Jimmy T. Keeton, Department Head, 979-458-3428, E-mail: jkeeton@tamu.edu.

Texas A&M University, College of Agriculture and Life Sciences, Department of Soil and Crop Sciences, College Station, TX 77843. Offers agronomy (M Agr, MS, PhD); food science and technology (MS, PhD); genetics (PhD); molecular and environmental plant sciences (MS, PhD); plant breeding (MS, PhD); soil science (MS, PhD). *Faculty:* 36. *Students:* 94 full-time (35 women), 30 part-time (7 women); includes 14 minority (3 Black or African American, non-Hispanic/Latino; 1 American Indian or Alaska Native, non-Hispanic/Latino; 3 Asian, non-Hispanic/Latino; 7 Hispanic/Latino), 36 international. Average age 26. In 2010, 11 master's, 3 doctorates awarded. *Degree requirements:* For master's, thesis; for doctorate, thesis/dissertation. *Entrance requirements:* For master's and doctorate, GRE General Test. Additional exam requirements/recommendations for international students: Required—TOEFL. *Application deadline:* For fall admission, 3/1 priority date for domestic students; for spring admission, 8/1 for domestic students. Applications are processed on a rolling basis. Application fee: $50 ($75 for international students). *Financial support:* In 2010–11, fellowships (averaging $16,000 per year), research assistantships with partial tuition reimbursements (averaging $15,000 per year) were awarded; career-related internships or fieldwork, Federal Work-Study, and institutionally

Food Science and Technology

Texas A&M University (continued)
sponsored loans also available. *Faculty research:* Soil and crop management, turfgrass science, weed science, cereal chemistry, food protein chemistry. *Unit head:* Dr. David D. Baltensperger, Department Head, 979-845-3001, E-mail: dbaltensperger@ag.tamu.edu. *Application contact:* Dr. David D. Baltensperger, Department Head, 979-845-3001, E-mail: dbaltensperger@ag.tamu.edu.

Texas Tech University, Graduate School, College of Agricultural Sciences and Natural Resources, Department of Animal and Food Sciences, Lubbock, TX 79409-2141. Offers animal science (MS, PhD); food science (MS). *Faculty:* 10 full-time (3 women). *Students:* 56 full-time (27 women), 11 part-time (4 women); includes 1 Hispanic/Latino; 1 Two or more races, non-Hispanic/Latino, 13 international. Average age 26. 70 applicants, 34% accepted, 21 enrolled. In 2010, 16 master's, 9 doctorates awarded. *Degree requirements:* For master's, thesis or alternative, internship (M Agr); for doctorate, thesis/dissertation. *Entrance requirements:* For master's and doctorate, GRE General Test, formal approval from departmental committee. Additional exam requirements/recommendations for international students: Required—TOEFL (minimum score 550 paper-based; 213 computer-based; 79 iBT). *Application deadline:* For fall admission, 6/1 priority date for domestic students, 1/15 priority date for international students; for spring admission, 9/1 priority date for domestic students, 6/15 priority date for international students. Applications are processed on a rolling basis. Application fee: $50 ($75 for international students). Electronic applications accepted. *Expenses:* Tuition, state resident: full-time $5495.76; part-time $228.99 per credit hour. Tuition, nonresident: full-time $12,936; part-time $538.99 per credit hour. Required fees: $2674; $36 per credit hour. $905 per semester. *Financial support:* In 2010–11, 54 students received support, including 23 research assistantships with partial tuition reimbursements available (averaging $5,040 per year), 2 teaching assistantships with partial tuition reimbursements available (averaging $5,011 per year). Financial award application deadline: 4/15; financial award applicants required to submit FAFSA. *Faculty research:* Animal growth composition and product acceptability, animal nutrition and utilization, animal physiology and adaptation to stress, food microbiology, meat science safety and security. Total annual research expenditures: $4.6 million. *Unit head:* Dr. Leslie D. Thompson, Chairman, 806-742-2805 Ext. 223, Fax: 806-742-0898, E-mail: leslie.thompson@ttu.edu. *Application contact:* Sandy Gellner, Graduate Secretary, 806-742-2805 Ext. 221, Fax: 806-742-0898, E-mail: sandra.gellner@ttu.edu.

Texas Woman's University, Graduate School, College of Health Sciences, Department of Nutrition and Food Sciences, Denton, TX 76201. Offers food science (MS); food systems administration (MS); nutrition (MS, PhD). Part-time and evening/weekend programs available. *Faculty:* 17 full-time (9 women). *Students:* 94 full-time (87 women), 97 part-time (89 women); includes 11 Black or African American, non-Hispanic/Latino; 21 Asian, non-Hispanic/Latino; 17 Hispanic/Latino, 24 international. Average age 28. 114 applicants, 73% accepted, 51 enrolled. In 2010, 72 master's, 6 doctorates awarded. *Degree requirements:* For master's, comprehensive exam; for doctorate, comprehensive exam, thesis/dissertation, qualifying exam. *Entrance requirements:* For master's, GRE General Test (preferred minimum score 350 Verbal, 450 Quantitative), minimum GPA of 3.25, resume; for doctorate, GRE General Test (preferred minimum score 450 Verbal, 550 Quantitative), minimum GPA of 3.5, 2 letters of reference, resume. Additional exam requirements/recommendations for international students: Required—TOEFL (minimum score 550 paper-based; 213 computer-based; 79 iBT). *Application deadline:* For fall admission, 7/1 priority date for domestic students, 3/1 for international students; for spring admission, 12/1 priority date for domestic students, 7/1 for international students. Applications are processed on a rolling basis. Application fee: $50 ($75 for international students). Electronic applications accepted. *Expenses:* Tuition, state resident: full-time $3834; part-time $213 per credit hour. Tuition, nonresident: full-time $9468; part-time $526 per credit hour. Required fees: $1247; $220 per credit hour. *Financial support:* In 2010–11, 64 students received support, including 33 research assistantships (averaging $12,942 per year), 1 teaching assistantship (averaging $12,942 per year); career-related internships or fieldwork, Federal Work-Study, institutionally sponsored loans, scholarships/grants, traineeships, health care benefits, and unspecified assistantships also available. Support available to part-time students. Financial award application deadline: 3/1; financial award applicants required to submit FAFSA. *Faculty research:* Bioactive food components and cancer, nutraceuticals and functional foods in diabetes, obesity and bone health, food safety, dietary modulation of dyslipidemia, childhood obesity prevention. Total annual research expenditures: $1.1 million. *Unit head:* Dr. Chandan Prasad, Chair, 940-898-2636, Fax: 940-898-2634, E-mail: nutrfdsci@twu.edu. *Application contact:* Dr. Samuel Wheeler, Assistant Director of Admissions, 940-898-3188, Fax: 940-898-3081, E-mail: wheelersr@twu.edu.

Tuskegee University, Graduate Programs, College of Agricultural, Environmental and Natural Sciences, Department of Food and Nutritional Sciences, Tuskegee, AL 36088. Offers MS. *Faculty:* 4 full-time (3 women). *Students:* 9 full-time (all women); includes 7 Black or African American, non-Hispanic/Latino, 1 international. Average age 28. In 2010, 6 master's awarded. *Degree requirements:* For master's, thesis. *Entrance requirements:* For master's, GRE General Test. Additional exam requirements/recommendations for international students: Required—TOEFL (minimum score 500 paper-based; 69 computer-based). *Application deadline:* For fall admission, 7/15 for domestic students. Applications are processed on a rolling basis. Application fee: $25 ($35 for international students). *Expenses:* Tuition: Full-time $16,100; part-time $665 per credit hour. Required fees: $650. *Financial support:* Application deadline: 4/15. *Unit head:* Dr. Ralphenia Pace, Head, 334-727-8162. *Application contact:* Dr. Robert L. Laney, Vice President/Director Admissions and Enrollment Management, 334-727-8580, Fax: 334-727-5750, E-mail: planey@tuskegee.edu.

Universidad de las Américas–Puebla, Division of Graduate Studies, School of Engineering, Program in Chemical Engineering, Puebla, Mexico. Offers chemical engineering (MS); food technology (MS). Part-time and evening/weekend programs available. *Degree requirements:* For master's, one foreign language, thesis. *Faculty research:* Food science, reactors, oil industry, biotechnology.

Universidad de las Américas–Puebla, Division of Graduate Studies, School of Engineering, Program in Food Sciences, Puebla, Mexico. Offers MS.

Université de Moncton, School of Food Science, Nutrition and Family Studies, Moncton, NB E1A 3E9, Canada. Offers foods/nutrition (M Sc). Part-time programs available. *Degree requirements:* For master's, one foreign language, thesis. *Entrance requirements:* For master's, previous course work in statistics. Electronic applications accepted. *Faculty research:* Clinic nutrition (anemia, elderly, osteoporosis), applied nutrition, metabolic activities of lactic bacteria, solubility of low density lipoproteins, bile acids.

Université Laval, Faculty of Agricultural and Food Sciences, Department of Food Sciences and Nutrition, Programs in Food Sciences and Technology, Québec, QC G1K 7P4, Canada. Offers M Sc, PhD. Terminal master's awarded for partial completion of doctoral program. *Degree requirements:* For master's, thesis (for some programs); for doctorate, comprehensive exam, thesis/dissertation. *Entrance requirements:* For master's and doctorate, knowledge of French and English. Electronic applications accepted.

University of Arkansas, Graduate School, Dale Bumpers College of Agricultural, Food and Life Sciences, Department of Food Science, Fayetteville, AR 72701-1201. Offers MS, PhD. *Students:* 12 full-time (6 women), 30 part-time (19 women); includes 1 minority (Black or African American, non-Hispanic/Latino), 21 international. 45 applicants, 24% accepted. In 2010, 6 master's, 4 doctorates awarded. *Degree requirements:* For master's, thesis; for doctorate, thesis/dissertation. *Application deadline:* For fall admission, 4/1 for international students; for spring admission, 10/1 for international students. Applications are processed on a rolling basis. Application fee: $40 ($50 for international students). Electronic applications accepted. *Financial support:* In 2010–11, 2 fellowships with tuition reimbursements, 30 research assistantships were awarded; teaching assistantships, career-related internships or fieldwork, Federal Work-Study, scholarships/grants, and unspecified assistantships also available. Support available to part-time students. Financial award application deadline: 4/1; financial award applicants required to submit FAFSA. *Unit head:* Dr. Jean-Francois Meullenet, Department Head, 479-575-4605, E-mail: jfmeull@uark.edu. *Application contact:* Dr. Jean-Francois Meullenet, Department Head, 479-575-4605, E-mail: jfmeull@uark.edu.

University of Arkansas, Graduate School, Dale Bumpers College of Agricultural, Food and Life Sciences, Program in Agricultural, Food and Life Sciences, Fayetteville, AR 72701-1201. Offers MS. Part-time and evening/weekend programs available. Postbaccalaureate distance learning degree programs offered (minimal on-campus study). *Students:* 2 full-time (1 woman), 25 part-time (13 women); includes 2 minority (1 American Indian or Alaska Native, non-Hispanic/Latino; 1 Hispanic/Latino). 4 applicants, 100% accepted. In 2010, 7 master's awarded. *Degree requirements:* For master's, thesis optional. *Application deadline:* For fall admission, 4/1 for international students; for spring admission, 10/1 for international students. Applications are processed on a rolling basis. Application fee: $40 ($50 for international students). Electronic applications accepted. *Financial support:* Fellowships, research assistantships, teaching assistantships, career-related internships or fieldwork and Federal Work-Study available. Support available to part-time students. Financial award application deadline: 4/1; financial award applicants required to submit FAFSA. *Unit head:* Dr. Michael E. Vayda, Dean, 479-575-2034, E-mail: mvayda@uark.edu. *Application contact:* Diana Bisbee, Program Coordinator, 479-575-2025, E-mail: dbisbee@uark.edu.

The University of British Columbia, Faculty of Land and Food Systems, Program in Food Science, Vancouver, BC V6T 1Z1, Canada. Offers M Sc, MFS, PhD. *Degree requirements:* For master's, thesis; for doctorate, comprehensive exam, thesis/dissertation. *Entrance requirements:* Additional exam requirements/recommendations for international students: Required—TOEFL (minimum score 577 paper-based; 233 computer-based; 90 iBT), IELTS (minimum score 6.5). Electronic applications accepted. Tuition charges are reported in Canadian dollars. *Expenses:* Tuition, area resident: Full-time $4179 Canadian dollars. International tuition: $7344 Canadian dollars full-time. *Faculty research:* Food chemistry and biochemistry, food process science, food toxicology and safety, food microbiology, food biotechnology.

University of California, Davis, Graduate Studies, Graduate Group in Food Science, Davis, CA 95616. Offers MS, PhD. Terminal master's awarded for partial completion of doctoral program. *Degree requirements:* For master's, comprehensive exam (for some programs), thesis (for some programs); for doctorate, thesis/dissertation. *Entrance requirements:* For master's and doctorate, GRE General Test, minimum GPA of 3.0. Additional exam requirements/recommendations for international students: Required—TOEFL (minimum score 550 paper-based; 213 computer-based). Electronic applications accepted.

University of Delaware, College of Agriculture and Natural Resources, Department of Animal and Food Sciences, Newark, DE 19716. Offers animal sciences (MS, PhD); food sciences (MS). Part-time programs available. Terminal master's awarded for partial completion of doctoral program. *Degree requirements:* For master's, thesis; for doctorate, comprehensive exam, thesis/dissertation. *Entrance requirements:* For master's and doctorate, GRE General Test. Additional exam requirements/recommendations for international students: Required—TOEFL. Electronic applications accepted. *Faculty research:* Food chemistry, food microbiology, process engineering technology, packaging, food analysis, microbial genetics, molecular endocrinology, growth physiology, avian immunology and virology, monogastric nutrition, avian genomics.

University of Florida, Graduate School, College of Agricultural and Life Sciences, Department of Food Science and Human Nutrition, Gainesville, FL 32611. Offers food science (MS, PhD); nutritional sciences (MS, PhD). *Degree requirements:* For master's, thesis optional; for doctorate, thesis/dissertation. *Entrance requirements:* For master's and doctorate, GRE General Test, minimum GPA of 3.0. Additional exam requirements/recommendations for international students: Required—TOEFL. Electronic applications accepted. *Expenses:* Tuition, state resident: full-time $10,915.92. Tuition, nonresident: full-time $28,309. *Faculty research:* Pesticide research, nutritional biochemistry and microbiology, food safety and toxicology assessment and dietetics, food chemistry.

University of Georgia, College of Agricultural and Environmental Sciences, Department of Food Science and Technology, Athens, GA 30602. Offers food science (MS, PhD); food technology (MFT). Part-time programs available. *Faculty:* 18 full-time (6 women), 2 part-time/adjunct (0 women). *Students:* 54 full-time (38 women), 18 part-time (9 women); includes 4 Black or African American, non-Hispanic/Latino; 6 Asian, non-Hispanic/Latino; 3 Hispanic/Latino; 1 Two or more races, non-Hispanic/Latino, 29 international. 124 applicants, 35% accepted, 20 enrolled. In 2010, 11 master's, 7 doctorates awarded. *Degree requirements:* For master's, thesis; for doctorate, thesis/dissertation. *Entrance requirements:* For master's and doctorate, GRE General Test. Additional exam requirements/recommendations for international students: Required—TOEFL (minimum score 550 paper-based; 213 computer-based). *Application deadline:* For fall admission, 7/1 for domestic students, 5/1 priority date for international students; for spring admission, 11/15 for domestic students, 10/1 priority date for international students. Applications are processed on a rolling basis. Application fee: $50. Electronic applications accepted. *Expenses:* Tuition, state resident: full-time $7200; part-time $344 per credit hour. Tuition, nonresident: full-time $21,900; part-time $944 per credit hour. Tuition and fees vary according to course load and program. *Financial support:* Fellowships, research assistantships, teaching assistantships, unspecified assistantships available. Total annual research expenditures: $1.5 million. *Unit head:* Dr. Rakesh K. Singh, Head, 706-542-2286, E-mail: rsingh@uga.edu. *Application contact:* Dr. Mark A. Harrison, Graduate Coordinator, 706-542-1088, Fax: 706-542-1050, E-mail: mahfst@uga.edu.

University of Guelph, Graduate Studies, Ontario Agricultural College, Department of Food Science, Guelph, ON N1G 2W1, Canada. Offers food safety and quality assurance (M Sc); food science (M Sc, PhD). *Degree requirements:* For master's, thesis; for doctorate, comprehensive exam, thesis/dissertation. *Entrance requirements:* For master's, minimum B-average during previous 2 years of honors B Sc degree; for doctorate, minimum B average. Additional exam requirements/recommendations for international students: Required—TOEFL (minimum score 550 paper-based; 213 computer-based), IELTS (minimum score 6.5). Electronic applications accepted. *Faculty research:* Food chemistry, food microbiology, food processing, preservation and utilization.

University of Hawaii at Manoa, Graduate Division, College of Tropical Agriculture and Human Resources, Department of Human Nutrition, Food and Animal Sciences, Program in Food Science, Honolulu, HI 96822. Offers MS. Part-time programs available. *Faculty:* 17 full-time (2 women), 1 part-time/adjunct (0 women). *Students:* 4 full-time (3 women); includes 1 Asian, non-Hispanic/Latino, 2 international. Average age 34. 7 applicants, 57% accepted, 1 enrolled. In 2010, 1 master's awarded. *Degree requirements:* For master's, thesis optional. *Entrance requirements:* For master's, GRE General Test. Additional exam requirements/recommendations for international students: Required—TOEFL (minimum score 580 paper-based; 237 computer-based; 92 iBT), IELTS (minimum score 5). *Application deadline:* For fall admission, 2/1 for domestic and international students; for spring admission, 9/1 for domestic and international students. Application fee: $50. *Financial support:* In 2010–11, 3 students received support, including 1 fellowship (averaging $4,000 per year), 1 research assistantship (averaging $18,198 per year), 1 teaching assistantship (averaging $14,382 per year). *Faculty research:* Biochemistry of natural products, sensory evaluation, food processing, food chemistry, food safety. Total annual research expenditures: $10,000. *Application contact:* Yong Li, Graduate Chairperson, 808-956-8356, Fax: 808-956-4024, E-mail: liyong@hawaii.edu.

University of Idaho, College of Graduate Studies, College of Agricultural and Life Sciences, Bistate School of Food Science, Moscow, ID 83844-2282. Offers MS, PhD. *Faculty:* 3 full-time. *Students:* 7 full-time, 5 part-time. Average age 28. *Entrance requirements:* For master's, minimum GPA of 2.8. *Application deadline:* For fall admission, 8/1 for domestic students; for spring admission, 12/15 for domestic students. Applications are processed on a rolling basis. Application fee: $60. Electronic applications accepted. *Expenses:* Tuition, nonresident: part-time $580 per credit. Required fees: $306 per credit. *Financial support:* Research assistantships, teaching assistantships available. Financial award applicants required to submit FAFSA. *Faculty research:* Food biotechnology, food and environmental toxicology, bio-preservation of food products, conversion of biomass. *Unit head:* Dr. Denise Smith, Director, 208-885-0707, E-mail: foodscience@uidaho.edu. *Application contact:* Dr. Denise Smith, Director, 208-885-0707, E-mail: foodscience@uidaho.edu.

University of Illinois at Urbana–Champaign, Graduate College, College of Agricultural, Consumer and Environmental Sciences, Department of Food Science and Human Nutrition, Champaign, IL 61820. Offers food science (MS); food science and human nutrition (MS, PhD), including professional science (MS); human nutrition (MS). Part-time programs available. Postbaccalaureate distance learning degree programs offered (minimal on-campus study). *Faculty:* 26 full-time (12 women), 1 (woman) part-time/adjunct. *Students:* 63 full-time (41 women), 18 part-time (10 women); includes 9 minority (2 Black or African American, non-Hispanic/Latino; 6 Asian, non-Hispanic/Latino; 1 Two or more races, non-Hispanic/Latino), 37 international. 153 applicants, 16% accepted, 18 enrolled. In 2010, 20 master's, 4 doctorates awarded. *Entrance requirements:* For master's and doctorate, GRE, minimum GPA of 3.0. Additional exam requirements/recommendations for international students: Required—TOEFL (minimum score 550 paper-based; 213 computer-based; 79 iBT) or IELTS (minimum score 6.5). *Application deadline:* Applications are processed on a rolling basis. Application fee: $75 ($90 for international students). Electronic applications accepted. *Financial support:* In 2010–11, 14 fellowships, 36 research assistantships, 16 teaching assistantships were awarded; tuition waivers (full and partial) also available. *Unit head:* Faye L. Dong, Head, 217-244-4498, Fax: 217-265-0925, E-mail: fayedong@illinois.edu. *Application contact:* Barb J. Vandeventer, Office Administrator, 217-333-1324, Fax: 217-265-0925, E-mail: vandvntr@illinois.edu.

University of Maine, Graduate School, College of Natural Sciences, Forestry, and Agriculture, Department of Food Science and Human Nutrition, Orono, ME 04469. Offers food and nutritional sciences (PhD); food science and human nutrition (MS). Part-time programs available. *Faculty:* 7 full-time (6 women), 2 part-time/adjunct (1 woman). *Students:* 35 full-time (28 women), 3 part-time (all women); includes 1 American Indian or Alaska Native, non-Hispanic/Latino; 1 Asian, non-Hispanic/Latino, 4 international. Average age 27. 53 applicants, 34% accepted, 15 enrolled. In 2010, 17 master's awarded. *Degree requirements:* For master's, thesis; for doctorate, thesis/dissertation. *Entrance requirements:* For master's, GRE General Test, minimum GPA of 3.0; for doctorate, GRE General Test. Additional exam requirements/recommendations for international students: Required—TOEFL. *Application deadline:* For fall admission, 2/1 priority date for domestic students. Applications are processed on a rolling basis. Application fee: $65. Electronic applications accepted. *Expenses:* Tuition, state resident: full-time $400. Tuition, nonresident: full-time $1050. *Financial support:* In 2010–11, 9 research assistantships with tuition reimbursements (averaging $13,500 per year), 4 teaching assistantships with tuition reimbursements (averaging $12,000 per year) were awarded; scholarships/grants and tuition waivers (full and partial) also available. Financial award application deadline: 3/1. *Faculty research:* Product development of fruit and vegetables, lipid oxidation in fish and meat, analytical methods development, metabolism of potato glycoalkaloids, seafood quality. *Unit head:* Dr. Denise Skonberg, 207-581-1639. *Application contact:* Scott G. Delcourt, Associate Dean of the Graduate School, 207-581-3291, Fax: 207-581-3232, E-mail: graduate@maine.edu.

University of Manitoba, Faculty of Graduate Studies, Faculty of Agricultural and Food Sciences, Department of Food Science, Winnipeg, MB R3T 2N2, Canada. Offers food and nutritional sciences (PhD); food science (M Sc); foods and nutrition (M Sc). *Degree requirements:* For master's, thesis.

University of Maryland, College Park, Academic Affairs, College of Agriculture and Natural Resources, Department of Nutrition and Food Science, Program in Food Science, College Park, MD 20742. Offers MS, PhD. *Students:* 22 full-time (9 women), 4 part-time (all women); includes 3 Black or African American, non-Hispanic/Latino; 1 Asian, non-Hispanic/Latino; 2 Hispanic/Latino, 15 international. 37 applicants, 14% accepted, 4 enrolled. In 2010, 2 master's awarded. *Degree requirements:* For master's, comprehensive exam, research-based thesis or equivalent paper; for doctorate, comprehensive exam, thesis/dissertation. *Entrance requirements:* For master's, GRE General Test, minimum GPA of 3.0, professional experience, 3 letters of recommendation; for doctorate, GRE General Test, minimum GPA of 3.0. Additional exam requirements/recommendations for international students: Required—TOEFL. *Application deadline:* For fall admission, 12/15 for domestic and international students; for spring admission, 6/1 for domestic and international students. Applications are processed on a rolling basis. Application fee: $75. Electronic applications accepted. *Expenses:* Tuition, area resident: Part-time $471 per credit hour. Tuition, state resident: part-time $471 per credit hour. Tuition, nonresident: part-time $1016 per credit hour. Required fees: $337 per term. *Financial support:* In 2010–11, 2 fellowships (averaging $15,800 per year), 10 research assistantships (averaging $16,178 per year), 13 teaching assistantships (averaging $15,877 per year) were awarded. Financial award applicants required to submit FAFSA. *Faculty research:* Food chemistry, engineering, microbiology, and processing technology; quality assurance; membrane separations, rheology and texture measurement. *Unit head:* Lucy Yu, Acting Chair, 301-405-0773, E-mail: lyu5@umd.edu. *Application contact:* Dr. Charles A. Caramello, Dean of Graduate School, 301-405-0358, Fax: 301-314-9305, E-mail: ccaramel@umd.edu.

University of Maryland Eastern Shore, Graduate Programs, Department of Agriculture, Program in Food and Agricultural Sciences, Princess Anne, MD 21853-1299. Offers MS. *Degree requirements:* For master's, comprehensive exam, thesis or alternative, oral exams. *Entrance requirements:* For master's, GRE General Test, minimum GPA of 3.0. Additional exam requirements/recommendations for international students: Required—TOEFL (minimum score 213 computer-based; 80 iBT). Electronic applications accepted. *Faculty research:* Poultry and swine nutrition and management, soybean specialty products, farm management practices, agriculture technology.

University of Maryland Eastern Shore, Graduate Programs, Department of Agriculture, Program in Food Science and Technology, Princess Anne, MD 21853-1299. Offers PhD. *Degree requirements:* For doctorate, comprehensive exam, thesis/dissertation. *Entrance requirements:* For doctorate, minimum GPA of 3.0, strong background in food science and related fields, intended dissertation research. Additional exam requirements/recommendations for international students: Required—TOEFL (minimum score 213 computer-based; 80 iBT). Electronic applications accepted. *Faculty research:* Prevalence, growth, survival and control of listeria; microbial models of the effect of storage temperature.

University of Massachusetts Amherst, Graduate School, College of Natural Sciences, Department of Food Science, Amherst, MA 01003. Offers MS, PhD. Part-time programs available. *Faculty:* 15 full-time (3 women). *Students:* 27 full-time (18 women), 11 part-time (6 women); includes 1 minority (Black or African American, non-Hispanic/Latino), 25 international. Average age 28. 100 applicants, 28% accepted, 14 enrolled. In 2010, 4 master's, 1 doctorate awarded. Terminal master's awarded for partial completion of doctoral program. *Degree requirements:* For master's, thesis or alternative; for doctorate, comprehensive exam, thesis/dissertation. *Entrance requirements:* For master's and doctorate, GRE General Test. Additional exam requirements/recommendations for international students: Required—TOEFL (minimum score 550 paper-based; 213 computer-based; 80 iBT), IELTS (minimum score 6.5). *Application deadline:* For fall admission, 2/1 for domestic and international students; for spring admission, 10/1 for domestic and international students. Applications are processed on a rolling basis. Application fee: $50 ($65 for international students). Electronic applications accepted. *Expenses:* Tuition, state resident: full-time $2640. Required fees: $8282. One-time fee: $357 full-time. *Financial support:* In 2010–11, 1 fellowship with full tuition reimbursement (averaging $7,000 per year), 21 research assistantships with full tuition reimbursements (averaging $9,526 per year), 8 teaching assistantships with full tuition reimbursements (averaging $6,759 per year) were awarded; career-related internships or fieldwork, Federal Work-Study, scholarships/grants, traineeships, health care benefits, tuition waivers (full), and unspecified assistantships also available. Support available to part-time students. Financial award application deadline: 2/1; financial award applicants required to submit FAFSA. *Unit head:* Dr. Ronald G. Labbe, Graduate Program Director, 413-545-2276, Fax: 413-545-1262. *Application contact:* Jean M. Ames, Supervisor of Admissions, 413-545-0721, Fax: 413-577-0010, E-mail: gradadm@grad.umass.edu.

University of Minnesota, Twin Cities Campus, Graduate School, College of Food, Agricultural and Natural Resource Sciences, Program in Food Science, Minneapolis, MN 55455-0213. Offers MS, PhD. Part-time programs available. *Faculty:* 24 full-time (7 women). *Students:* 30 full-time (20 women), 13 part-time (6 women); includes 17 minority (1 Black or African American, non-Hispanic/Latino; 14 Asian, non-Hispanic/Latino; 2 Hispanic/Latino), 23 international. Average age 30. 110 applicants, 30% accepted, 9 enrolled. In 2010, 2 master's, 2 doctorates awarded. Terminal master's awarded for partial completion of doctoral program. *Degree requirements:* For master's, comprehensive exam, thesis; for doctorate, comprehensive exam, thesis/dissertation. *Entrance requirements:* For master's and doctorate, GRE General Test, previous course work in general chemistry, organic chemistry, calculus, physics, and biology. Additional exam requirements/recommendations for international students: Required—TOEFL (minimum score 550 paper-based; 213 computer-based; 79 iBT). *Application deadline:* For fall admission, 12/15 for domestic and international students; for spring admission, 10/15 for domestic and international students. Applications are processed on a rolling basis. Application fee: $75 ($95 for international students). Electronic applications accepted. *Financial support:* In 2010–11, fellowships with full tuition reimbursements (averaging $23,500 per year), research assistantships with full and partial tuition reimbursements (averaging $17,500 per year), teaching assistantships with full and partial tuition reimbursements (averaging $17,500 per year) were awarded; career-related internships or fieldwork, scholarships/grants, traineeships, health care benefits, and unspecified assistantships also available. Support available to part-time students. *Faculty research:* Food chemistry, food microbiology, food technology, grain science, dairy science, food safety. Total annual research expenditures: $2.1 million. *Unit head:* Dr. David E. Smith, Director of Graduate Studies, 612-624-3260, Fax: 612-625-5272, E-mail: desmith@umn.edu. *Application contact:* Nancy L. Toedt, Program Coordinator, 612-624-6753, Fax: 612-625-5272, E-mail: ntoedt@umn.edu.

University of Missouri, Graduate School, College of Agriculture, Food and Natural Resources, Department of Food Science, Columbia, MO 65211. Offers food science (MS, PhD); foods and food systems management (MS); human nutrition (MS). *Faculty:* 17 full-time (4 women), 2 part-time/adjunct (0 women). *Students:* 28 full-time (12 women), 8 part-time (4 women); includes 1 minority (Hispanic/Latino), 19 international. Average age 27. 53 applicants, 40% accepted, 6 enrolled. In 2010, 9 master's, 2 doctorates awarded. Terminal master's awarded for partial completion of doctoral program. *Degree requirements:* For doctorate, comprehensive exam, thesis/dissertation. *Entrance requirements:* For master's, GRE General Test (minimum score: Verbal and Quantitative 1000 with neither section below 400, Analytical 3.5), minimum GPA of 3.0; BS in food science from accredited university; for doctorate, GRE General Test (minimum score: Verbal and Quantitative 1000 with neither section below 400, Analytical 3.5), minimum GPA of 3.0; BS and MS in food science from accredited university. Additional exam requirements/recommendations for international students: Required—TOEFL (minimum score 550 paper-based; 79 iBT). *Application deadline:* For fall admission, 4/1 priority date for domestic students; for winter admission, 10/1 priority date for domestic students. Applications are processed on a rolling basis. Application fee: $45 ($60 for international students). Electronic applications accepted. *Financial support:* Fellowships, research assistantships with tuition reimbursements, teaching assistantships with tuition reimbursements, institutionally sponsored loans, scholarships/grants, health care benefits, and unspecified assistantships available. Support available to part-time students. *Faculty research:* Food chemistry, food analysis, food microbiology, food engineering and process control, functional foods, meat science and processing technology. *Unit head:* Dr. Jinglu Tan, Department Chair, 573-882-2369, E-mail: tanj@missouri.edu. *Application contact:* JoAnn Lewis, 573-882-4113, E-mail: lewisj@missouri.edu.

University of Nebraska–Lincoln, Graduate College, College of Agricultural Sciences and Natural Resources, Department of Food Science and Technology, Lincoln, NE 68588. Offers MS, PhD. *Degree requirements:* For master's, thesis optional; for doctorate, comprehensive exam, thesis/dissertation. *Entrance requirements:* For master's and doctorate, GRE General Test. Additional exam requirements/recommendations for international students: Required—TOEFL (minimum score 505 paper-based; 213 computer-based). Electronic applications accepted. *Faculty research:* Food chemistry, microbiology, processing, engineering, and biotechnology.

University of Puerto Rico, Mayagüez Campus, Graduate Studies, College of Agricultural Sciences, Department of Food Science and Technology, Mayagüez, PR 00681-9000. Offers MS. Part-time programs available. *Students:* 31 full-time (20 women); includes 20 Hispanic/Latino, 11 international. 6 applicants, 100% accepted, 3 enrolled. In 2010, 1 master's awarded. *Degree requirements:* For master's, comprehensive exam, thesis. *Entrance requirements:* For master's, minimum GPA of 2.5. *Application deadline:* For fall admission, 2/15 for domestic and international students; for spring admission, 9/15 for domestic and international students. Applications are processed on a rolling basis. Application fee: $25. *Expenses:* Tuition, state resident: full-time $1188. Tuition, nonresident: full-time $1188. International tuition: $6126 full-time. Tuition and fees vary according to course level and course load. *Financial support:* In 2010–11, 2 students received support, including 1 research assistantship (averaging $15,000 per year), 1 teaching assistantship (averaging $8,500 per year); Federal Work-Study and institutionally sponsored loans also available. *Faculty research:* Food microbiology, food science, seafood technology, food engineering and packaging, fermentation. Total annual research expenditures: $128,100. *Unit head:* Dr. Edna Negron, Director, 787-265-5410, Fax: 787-265-5410, E-mail: enegron@uprm.edu. *Application contact:* Ivette Vissepo, Secretary, 787-832-4040 Ext. 3078, Fax: 787-265-5410, E-mail: ivissepo@uprm.edu.

University of Rhode Island, Graduate School, College of the Environment and Life Sciences, Department of Nutrition and Food Sciences, Kingston, RI 02881. Offers food science (MS, PhD); nutrition (MS, PhD). Part-time programs available. *Faculty:* 8 full-time (5 women), 1 (woman) part-time/adjunct. *Students:* 18 full-time (15 women), 10 part-time (all women); includes 1 minority (Asian, non-Hispanic/Latino), 1 international. In 2010, 11 master's awarded. *Degree requirements:* For master's, comprehensive exam (for some programs), thesis optional; for doctorate, thesis/dissertation. *Entrance requirements:* For master's and doctorate, GRE, 2 letters of recommendation. Additional exam requirements/recommendations for international students: Required—TOEFL (minimum score 550 paper-based; 213 computer-based). *Application deadline:* For fall admission, 7/15 for domestic students, 2/1 for international students; for spring admission, 11/15 for domestic students, 7/15 for international students. Application fee: $65. Electronic applications accepted. *Expenses:* Tuition, state resident: full-time $9588; part-time $533 per credit hour. Tuition, nonresident: full-time $22,968; part-time $1276 per credit hour. Required fees: $1282; $68 per semester. Tuition and fees vary according to program. *Financial support:* In 2010–11, 9 research assistantships with full and partial tuition reimbursements (averaging $13,122 per year), 5 teaching assistantships with full and partial tuition reimbursements (averaging $11,578 per year) were awarded. Financial award application

Food Science and Technology

University of Rhode Island (continued)

deadline: 7/15; financial award applicants required to submit FAFSA. *Faculty research:* Food safety and quality, marine resource utilization, nutrition in underserved populations, eating behavior, lipid metabolism. Total annual research expenditures: $2.2 million. *Unit head:* Dr. Catherine English, Chair, 401-874-5869, Fax: 401-874-5974, E-mail: cathy@uri.edu. *Application contact:* Dr. Geoffrey Greene, Director of Graduate Studies, 401-874-4028, E-mail: gwg@uri.edu.

University of Saskatchewan, College of Graduate Studies and Research, College of Agriculture, Department of Applied Microbiology and Food Science, Saskatoon, SK S7N 5A2, Canada. Offers M Ag, M Sc, PhD. *Degree requirements:* For master's, thesis; for doctorate, comprehensive exam (for some programs), thesis/dissertation. *Entrance requirements:* Additional exam requirements/recommendations for international students: Required—TOEFL (minimum score 80 iBT); Recommended—IELTS (minimum score 6.5).

University of Southern California, Graduate School, School of Pharmacy, Regulatory Science Programs, Los Angeles, CA 90089. Offers clinical research design and management (Graduate Certificate); food safety (Graduate Certificate); patient and product safety (Graduate Certificate); preclinical drug development (Graduate Certificate); regulatory and clinical affairs (Graduate Certificate); regulatory science (MS, DRSc). Part-time and evening/weekend programs available. Postbaccalaureate distance learning degree programs offered (minimal on-campus study). *Faculty:* 6 full-time (2 women), 7 part-time/adjunct (5 women). *Students:* 22 full-time (13 women), 50 part-time (26 women); includes 21 minority (3 Black or African American, non-Hispanic/Latino; 13 Asian, non-Hispanic/Latino; 4 Hispanic/Latino; 1 Two or more races, non-Hispanic/Latino), 13 international. 57 applicants, 54% accepted, 31 enrolled. In 2010, 32 master's, 28 other advanced degrees awarded. Terminal master's awarded for partial completion of doctoral program. *Degree requirements:* For master's, thesis optional; for doctorate, comprehensive exam, thesis/dissertation. *Entrance requirements:* For master's, GRE. Additional exam requirements/recommendations for international students: Required—TOEFL (minimum score 603 paper-based; 250 computer-based; 100 iBT). *Application deadline:* For fall admission, 6/15 priority date for domestic and international students; for winter admission, 2/15 priority date for domestic and international students; for spring admission, 10/15 priority date for domestic and international students. Application fee: $85. Electronic applications accepted. *Expenses:* Tuition: Full-time $31,240; part-time $1420 per unit. Required fees: $600. One-time fee: $35 full-time. Full-time tuition and fees vary according to degree level and program. *Unit head:* Dr. Frances J.R. Richmond, Director, Regulatory Science Programs, 323-442-3531, Fax: 323-442-2333, E-mail: fjr@hsc.usc.edu. *Application contact:* Dr. Kathy Rolle, Program Manager, Regulatory Science Programs, 323-442-3102, Fax: 323-442-2333, E-mail: regsci@usc.edu.

The University of Tennessee, Graduate School, College of Agricultural Sciences and Natural Resources, Department of Food Science and Technology, Knoxville, TN 37996. Offers food science and technology (MS, PhD), including food chemistry (PhD), food microbiology (PhD), food processing (PhD), sensory evaluation of foods (PhD). Part-time programs available. *Degree requirements:* For master's, thesis or alternative; for doctorate, thesis/dissertation. *Entrance requirements:* For master's and doctorate, GRE General Test, minimum GPA of 2.7. Additional exam requirements/recommendations for international students: Required—TOEFL. Electronic applications accepted. *Expenses:* Tuition, state resident: full-time $7440; part-time $414 per credit hour. Tuition, nonresident: full-time $22,478; part-time $1250 per credit hour. Required fees: $922; $43 per credit hour. Tuition and fees vary according to program.

The University of Tennessee at Martin, Graduate Programs, College of Agriculture and Applied Sciences, Department of Family and Consumer Sciences, Martin, TN 38238-1000. Offers dietetics (MSFCS); general family and consumer sciences (MSFCS). Part-time programs available. Postbaccalaureate distance learning degree programs offered (minimal on-campus study). *Faculty:* 8. *Students:* 40 (38 women); includes 6 Black or African American, non-Hispanic/Latino; 2 Hispanic/Latino; 1 Two or more races, non-Hispanic/Latino, 1 international. 45 applicants, 69% accepted, 12 enrolled. In 2010, 10 master's awarded. *Degree requirements:* For master's, comprehensive exam, thesis optional. *Entrance requirements:* For master's, GRE General Test, minimum GPA of 2.5. Additional exam requirements/recommendations for international students: Required—TOEFL (minimum score 525 paper-based; 197 computer-based; 71 iBT). *Application deadline:* For fall admission, 8/1 priority date for domestic students, 6/15 priority date for international students; for spring admission, 12/15 priority date for domestic students, 12/1 priority date for international students. Applications are processed on a rolling basis. Application fee: $30 ($130 for international students). Electronic applications accepted. *Expenses:* Tuition, state resident: full-time $7164; part-time $400 per credit hour. Tuition, nonresident: full-time $19,574; part-time $1090 per credit hour. Required fees: $1044; $60 per credit hour. *Financial support:* In 2010–11, 2 students received support, including 2 research assistantships with full tuition reimbursements available (averaging $7,893 per year); scholarships/grants and unspecified assistantships also available. Support available to part-time students. Financial award application deadline: 2/15; financial award applicants required to submit FAFSA. *Faculty research:* Children with developmental disabilities, regional food product development and marketing, parent education. *Unit head:* Dr. Lisa LeBleu, Coordinator, 731-881-7116, Fax: 731-881-7106, E-mail: llebleu@utm.edu. *Application contact:* Linda S. Arant, Student Services Specialist, 731-881-7012, Fax: 731-881-7499, E-mail: larant@utm.edu.

University of Vermont, Graduate College, College of Agriculture and Life Sciences, Program in Animal, Nutrition and Food Sciences, Burlington, VT 05405. Offers PhD. *Students:* 18 (7 women); includes 2 Asian, non-Hispanic/Latino, 10 international. 18 applicants, 44% accepted, 5 enrolled. In 2010, 2 doctorates awarded. *Degree requirements:* For doctorate, one foreign language, thesis/dissertation. *Entrance requirements:* For doctorate, GRE General Test. Additional exam requirements/recommendations for international students: Required—TOEFL (minimum score 550 paper-based; 213 computer-based; 80 iBT). *Application deadline:* For fall admission, 4/1 priority date for domestic students. Applications are processed on a rolling basis. Application fee: $40. Electronic applications accepted. *Expenses:* Tuition, state resident: part-time $537 per credit hour. Tuition, nonresident: part-time $1355 per credit hour. *Financial support:* Application deadline: 3/1. *Unit head:* Dr. R. K. Johnson, Dean, 802-656-2070. *Application contact:* Dr. David Kerr, Coordinator, 802-656-2070.

University of Wisconsin–Madison, Graduate School, College of Agricultural and Life Sciences, Department of Food Science, Madison, WI 53706-1380. Offers MS, PhD. Part-time programs available. *Degree requirements:* For master's, thesis; for doctorate, thesis/dissertation. *Entrance requirements:* For master's and doctorate, GRE General Test. Additional exam requirements/recommendations for international students: Required—TOEFL. Electronic applications accepted. *Expenses:* Tuition, state resident: full-time $9887.36; part-time $617.96 per credit. Tuition, nonresident: full-time $24,054; part-time $1503.40 per credit. Required fees: $67.63 per credit. Tuition and fees vary according to reciprocity agreements. *Faculty research:* Food chemistry, food engineering, food microbiology, food processing.

University of Wisconsin–Stout, Graduate School, College of Human Development, Program in Food and Nutritional Sciences, Menomonie, WI 54751. Offers MS. Part-time programs available. *Degree requirements:* For master's, thesis. *Entrance requirements:* For master's, minimum GPA of 3.0. Additional exam requirements/recommendations for international students: Required—TOEFL (minimum score 500 paper-based; 173 computer-based; 61 iBT). Electronic applications accepted. *Faculty research:* Disease states and nutrition, childhood obesity, nutraceuticals, food safety, nanotechnology.

University of Wyoming, College of Agriculture and Natural Resources, Department of Animal Sciences, Program in Food Science and Human Nutrition, Laramie, WY 82070. Offers MS. *Degree requirements:* For master's, thesis. *Entrance requirements:* For master's, GRE General Test, minimum GPA of 3.0. Additional exam requirements/recommendations for international students: Required—TOEFL (minimum score 525 paper-based). Electronic applications accepted. *Faculty research:* Protein and lipid metabolism, food microbiology, food safety, meat science.

Utah State University, School of Graduate Studies, College of Agriculture, Department of Nutrition and Food Sciences, Logan, UT 84322. Offers dietetic administration (MDA); food microbiology and safety (MFMS); nutrition and food sciences (MS, PhD); nutrition science (MS, PhD), including molecular biology. Postbaccalaureate distance learning degree programs offered. *Degree requirements:* For master's, thesis; for doctorate, comprehensive exam, thesis/dissertation, teaching experience. *Entrance requirements:* For master's, GRE General Test, minimum GPA of 3.0, course work in chemistry, biochemistry, physics, math, bacteriology, physiology; for doctorate, GRE General Test, minimum GPA of 3.2, course work in chemistry, MS or manuscript in referred journal. Additional exam requirements/recommendations for international students: Required—TOEFL (minimum score 550 paper-based). Electronic applications accepted. *Faculty research:* Mineral balance, meat microbiology and nitrate interactions, milk ultrafiltration, lactic culture, milk coagulation.

Virginia Polytechnic Institute and State University, Graduate School, College of Agriculture and Life Sciences, Department of Food Science and Technology, Blacksburg, VA 24061. Offers food science and technology (PhD); health product risk management (Certificate); produce food safety (Certificate). *Faculty:* 8 full-time (3 women). *Students:* 24 full-time (16 women), 9 part-time (4 women); includes 2 Black or African American, non-Hispanic/Latino; 1 Asian, non-Hispanic/Latino; 2 Hispanic/Latino, 7 international. Average age 29. 54 applicants, 30% accepted, 4 enrolled. In 2010, 10 master's, 6 doctorates awarded. *Degree requirements:* For master's, comprehensive exam (for some programs), thesis (for some programs); for doctorate, comprehensive exam (for some programs), thesis/dissertation (for some programs). *Entrance requirements:* For master's and doctorate, GRE. Additional exam requirements/recommendations for international students: Required—TOEFL (minimum score 550 paper-based; 213 computer-based). *Application deadline:* For fall admission, 7/1 for domestic and international students; for spring admission, 12/1 for domestic and international students. Applications are processed on a rolling basis. Application fee: $65. Electronic applications accepted. *Expenses:* Tuition, area resident: Full-time $9399; part-time $488 per credit hour. Tuition, state resident: full-time $9399; part-time $488 per credit hour. Tuition, nonresident: full-time $17,854; part-time $957.75 per credit hour. International tuition: $17,854 full-time. Required fees: $1534. Full-time tuition and fees vary according to program. *Financial support:* In 2010–11, 10 research assistantships with full tuition reimbursements (averaging $26,279 per year), 10 teaching assistantships with full tuition reimbursements (averaging $13,893 per year) were awarded; career-related internships or fieldwork, Federal Work-Study, scholarships/grants, health care benefits, and unspecified assistantships also available. Financial award application deadline: 1/15. *Faculty research:* Food microbiology, food chemistry, food processing, engineering, muscle foods. *Unit head:* Dr. Joseph E. Marcy, UNIT HEAD, 540-231-6806, Fax: 540-231-9293, E-mail: jmarcy@vt.edu. *Application contact:* Joe Eifert, Contact, 540-231-3658, Fax: 540-231-9293, E-mail: jeifert@vt.edu.

Washington State University, Graduate School, College of Agricultural, Human, and Natural Resource Sciences, Department of Food Science and Human Nutrition, Program in Food Science, Pullman, WA 99164. Offers MS, PhD. *Faculty:* 7. *Students:* 33 full-time (19 women), 3 part-time (1 woman), 16 international. Average age 27. 135 applicants, 10% accepted, 12 enrolled. In 2010, 5 master's awarded. *Degree requirements:* For master's, comprehensive exam (for some programs), thesis (for some programs), oral exam, written exam; for doctorate, comprehensive exam, thesis/dissertation, oral exam, written exam. *Entrance requirements:* For master's, GRE General Test, official transcripts; letter of interest; resume; minimum GPA of 3.0; resume; 3 letters of recommendation, 1 from major advisor; for doctorate, GRE General Test, MS demonstrating ability to conduct and report research; minimum GPA of 3.0; resume; 3 letters of recommendation, 1 from major advisor. Additional exam requirements/recommendations for international students: Required—TOEFL (minimum score 550 paper-based; 213 computer-based; 80 iBT), IELTS. *Application deadline:* For fall admission, 1/10 priority date for domestic students, 1/10 for international students; for spring admission, 7/1 priority date for domestic students, 7/1 for international students. Applications are processed on a rolling basis. Application fee: $50. Electronic applications accepted. *Expenses:* Tuition, state resident: full-time $8552; part-time $443 per credit. Tuition, nonresident: full-time $21,650; part-time $1083 per credit. Required fees: $846. *Financial support:* In 2010–11, 21 students received support, including fellowships with tuition reimbursements available (averaging $4,250 per year), 9 research assistantships with full and partial tuition reimbursements available (averaging $18,204 per year), 1 teaching assistantship with full and partial tuition reimbursement available (averaging $18,204 per year); career-related internships or fieldwork, Federal Work-Study, institutionally sponsored loans, scholarships/grants, tuition waivers (partial), and unspecified assistantships also available. Financial award application deadline: 2/1; financial award applicants required to submit FAFSA. *Faculty research:* Sports anemia, lipid chemistry, malfunction of edible oils and fats, malolactic fermentation, wine microbiology. Total annual research expenditures: $570,000. *Unit head:* Dr. Denise Smith, Director, 509-335-2101, Fax: 509-335-4815, E-mail: denise.smith@wsu.edu. *Application contact:* Graduate School Admissions, 800-GRADWSU, Fax: 509-335-1949, E-mail: gradsch@wsu.edu.

Wayne State University, College of Liberal Arts and Sciences, Department of Nutrition and Food Science, Detroit, MI 48202. Offers MA, MS, PhD. *Faculty:* 10 full-time (7 women). *Students:* 43 full-time (36 women), 14 part-time (13 women); includes 11 minority (3 Black or African American, non-Hispanic/Latino; 8 Asian, non-Hispanic/Latino), 19 international. Average age 30. 49 applicants, 65% accepted, 16 enrolled. In 2010, 5 master's, 2 doctorates awarded. Terminal master's awarded for partial completion of doctoral program. *Degree requirements:* For master's, thesis (for some programs); for doctorate, thesis/dissertation. *Entrance requirements:* For master's, GRE General Test, minimum GPA of 3.0; for doctorate, GRE General Test, minimum GPA of 3.0; letters of recommendation; personal statement. Additional exam requirements/recommendations for international students: Required—TOEFL (minimum score 550 paper-based; 213 computer-based); Recommended—TWE (minimum score 6). *Application deadline:* For fall admission, 7/1 for domestic students, 6/1 for international students; for winter admission, 10/1 for international students; for spring admission, 2/1 for international students. Applications are processed on a rolling basis. Application fee: $30 ($50 for international students). Electronic applications accepted. *Expenses:* Tuition, state resident: full-time $7662; part-time $478.85 per credit hour. Tuition, nonresident: full-time $16,920; part-time $1057.55 per credit hour. Required fees: $571.20; $35.70 per credit hour. $188.05 per semester. Tuition and fees vary according to course load and program. *Financial support:* In 2010–11, 10 students received support, including 2 fellowships with tuition reimbursements available (averaging $16,875 per year), 2 research assistantships (averaging $18,788 per year), 8 teaching assistantships (averaging $16,984 per year); career-related internships or fieldwork and Federal Work-Study also available. Financial award application deadline: 4/1. *Faculty research:* Nutrition, cancer and gene expression, food microbiology and food safety, lipids, lipoprotein and cholesterol metabolism, obesity and diabetes, metabolomics. *Unit head:* Dr. K.L. Catherine Jen, Chair, 313-577-2500, E-mail: cjen@sun.science.wayne.edu. *Application contact:* Pramod Khosla, Assistant Professor, 313-577-9055, Fax: 313-577-8616, E-mail: pkhosla@sun.science.wayne.edu.

West Virginia University, Davis College of Agriculture, Forestry and Consumer Sciences, Division of Animal and Nutritional Sciences, Program in Animal and Nutritional Sciences, Morgantown, WV 26506. Offers breeding (MS); food sciences (MS); nutrition (MS); physiology (MS); production management (MS); reproduction (MS). Part-time programs available. *Degree requirements:* For master's, thesis, oral and written exams. *Entrance requirements:* For master's,

GRE, minimum GPA of 2.5. Additional exam requirements/recommendations for international students: Required—TOEFL. *Faculty research:* Animal nutrition, reproductive physiology, food science.

West Virginia University, Davis College of Agriculture, Forestry and Consumer Sciences, Division of Plant and Soil Sciences, Program in Agricultural Sciences, Morgantown, WV 26506. Offers animal and food sciences (PhD); plant and soil sciences (PhD). *Degree requirements:* For doctorate, thesis/dissertation, oral and written exams. *Entrance requirements:* Additional exam requirements/recommendations for international students: Required—TOEFL. *Faculty research:* Ruminant nutrition, metabolism, forage utilization, physiology, reproduction.

Horticulture

Auburn University, Graduate School, College of Agriculture, Department of Horticulture, Auburn University, AL 36849. Offers M Ag, MS, PhD. Part-time programs available. *Faculty:* 19 full-time (4 women). *Students:* 10 full-time (7 women), 24 part-time (6 women); includes 2 Black or African American, non-Hispanic/Latino; 1 Hispanic/Latino, 5 international. Average age 29. 20 applicants, 45% accepted, 6 enrolled. In 2010, 6 master's, 3 doctorates awarded. *Degree requirements:* For master's, thesis (for some programs); for doctorate, thesis/dissertation. *Entrance requirements:* For master's and doctorate, GRE General Test. *Application deadline:* For fall admission, 7/7 for domestic students; for spring admission, 11/24 for domestic students. Applications are processed on a rolling basis. Application fee: $50 ($60 for international students). Electronic applications accepted. *Expenses:* Tuition, state resident: full-time $7002. Tuition, nonresident: full-time $21,898. International tuition: $22,116 full-time. Required fees: $892. Tuition and fees vary according to course load and program. *Financial support:* Research assistantships, teaching assistantships, Federal Work-Study available. Support available to part-time students. Financial award application deadline: 3/15; financial award applicants required to submit FAFSA. *Faculty research:* Environmental regulators, water quality, weed control, growth regulators, plasticulture. *Unit head:* Dr. J. David Williams, Chair, 334-844-4862. *Application contact:* Dr. George Flowers, Dean of the Graduate School, 334-844-2125.

Colorado State University, Graduate School, College of Agricultural Sciences, Department of Horticulture and Landscape Architecture, Fort Collins, CO 80523-1173. Offers horticulture (MS, PhD); landscape architecture (MLA). Part-time programs available. *Faculty:* 24 full-time (4 women). *Students:* 16 full-time (5 women), 12 part-time (4 women); includes 5 minority (1 Black or African American, non-Hispanic/Latino; 1 American Indian or Alaska Native, non-Hispanic/Latino; 1 Hispanic/Latino; 2 Two or more races, non-Hispanic/Latino), 6 international. Average age 33. 22 applicants, 68% accepted, 8 enrolled. In 2010, 3 master's, 5 doctorates awarded. *Degree requirements:* For master's, thesis (for some programs); for doctorate, comprehensive exam, thesis/dissertation. *Entrance requirements:* For master's, GRE General Test (minimum upper 50th percentile, minimum score 1100 verbal and quantitative), minimum GPA of 3.0, letters of reference, related bachelor's degree or experience; for doctorate, GRE General Test (upper 50th percentile and combined minimum score of 1100 for the Verbal and Quantitative sections), minimum GPA of 3.0, letters of reference, statement of purpose, related bachelor's degree or experience. Additional exam requirements/recommendations for international students: Required—TOEFL (minimum score 550 paper-based; 213 computer-based; 80 iBT). *Application deadline:* Applications are processed on a rolling basis. Application fee: $50. Electronic applications accepted. *Expenses:* Tuition, state resident: full-time $7434; part-time $413 per credit. Tuition, nonresident: full-time $19,022; part-time $1057 per credit. Required fees: $1729; $88 per credit. *Financial support:* In 2010–11, 12 students received support, including 2 fellowships with full tuition reimbursements available (averaging $16,489 per year), 6 research assistantships with partial tuition reimbursements available (averaging $7,679 per year), 4 teaching assistantships with partial tuition reimbursements available (averaging $8,657 per year); scholarships/grants, unspecified assistantships, and fellowships also available. Financial award applicants required to submit FAFSA. *Faculty research:* Antioxidants in food crops, environmental physiology, water conservation, tissue culture, rhizosphere biology, cancer prevention through dietary intervention. Total annual research expenditures: $2.5 million. *Unit head:* Dr. Stephen J. Wallner, Head, 970-491-7018, Fax: 970-491-7745, E-mail: stephen.wallner@colostate.edu. *Application contact:* Kathi Nietfeld, Coordinator, 970-491-7018, Fax: 970-491-7745, E-mail: kathi.nietfeld@colostate.edu.

Cornell University, Graduate School, Graduate Fields of Agriculture and Life Sciences, Field of Horticulture, Ithaca, NY 14853-0001. Offers controlled environment agriculture (MPS, PhD); controlled environment horticulture (MS); greenhouse crops (MPS, MS, PhD); horticultural business management (MPS, MS, PhD); horticultural physiology (MPS, MS, PhD); landscape horticulture (MPS, MS, PhD); nursery crops (MPS, MS, PhD); nutrition of horticultural crops (MPS, MS, PhD); plant propagation (MPS, MS, PhD); public garden management (MPS, MS, PhD); restoration ecology (MPS, MS, PhD); taxonomy of ornamental plants (MPS, MS, PhD); turfgrass science (MPS, MS, PhD); urban horticulture (MPS, MS, PhD); weed science (MPS, MS, PhD). *Faculty:* 48 full-time (13 women). *Students:* 35 full-time (18 women); includes 2 Hispanic/Latino, 12 international. Average age 28. 54 applicants, 26% accepted, 14 enrolled. In 2010, 6 master's, 3 doctorates awarded. *Degree requirements:* For master's, thesis (MS); for doctorate, comprehensive exam, thesis/dissertation. *Entrance requirements:* For master's and doctorate, GRE General Test, 3 letters of recommendation. Additional exam requirements/recommendations for international students: Required—TOEFL (minimum score 550 paper-based; 213 computer-based; 77 iBT). *Application deadline:* For fall admission, 1/15 for domestic students; for spring admission, 8/15 for domestic students. Application fee: $70. Electronic applications accepted. *Expenses:* Tuition: Full-time $29,500. Required fees: $76. Tuition and fees vary according to degree level and program. *Financial support:* In 2010–11, 3 fellowships with full tuition reimbursements, 17 research assistantships with full tuition reimbursements, 9 teaching assistantships with full tuition reimbursements were awarded; institutionally sponsored loans, scholarships/grants, health care benefits, tuition waivers (full and partial), and unspecified assistantships also available. Financial award applicants required to submit FAFSA. *Faculty research:* Plant selection/plant materials, greenhouse management, greenhouse crop production, urban landscape management, turfgrass management. *Unit head:* Director of Graduate Studies, 607-255-4568, Fax: 607-255-0599. *Application contact:* Graduate Field Assistant, 607-255-4568, Fax: 607-255-0599, E-mail: hortgrad@cornell.edu.

Iowa State University of Science and Technology, Graduate College, College of Agriculture, Department of Horticulture, Ames, IA 50011. Offers MS, PhD. *Faculty:* 17 full-time (4 women), 2 part-time/adjunct (both women). *Students:* 11 full-time (4 women), 6 part-time (3 women), 6 international. 8 applicants, 25% accepted, 0 enrolled. In 2010, 3 master's, 4 doctorates awarded. *Degree requirements:* For master's, thesis; for doctorate, thesis/dissertation. *Entrance requirements:* For master's and doctorate, GRE General Test. Additional exam requirements/recommendations for international students: Required—TOEFL (minimum score 550 paper-based; 79 iBT), IELTS (minimum score 6.5). *Application deadline:* Applications are processed on a rolling basis. Application fee: $40 ($90 for international students). Electronic applications accepted. *Financial support:* In 2010–11, 16 research assistantships with partial tuition reimbursements (averaging $14,835 per year) were awarded; fellowships, teaching assistantships with full and partial tuition reimbursements, scholarships/grants, health care benefits, and unspecified assistantships also available. *Unit head:* Dr. Jeffrey Iles, Head, 515-294-3718, E-mail: hortgrad@iastate.edu. *Application contact:* Dr. William R. Graves, Director of Graduate Education, 515-294-2751, E-mail: hortgrade@iastate.edu.

Kansas State University, Graduate School, College of Agriculture, Department of Horticulture, Forestry and Recreation Resources, Manhattan, KS 66506. Offers horticulture (MS, PhD). *Degree requirements:* For master's, thesis, oral exam; for doctorate, thesis/dissertation, preliminary exams. *Entrance requirements:* For master's and doctorate, GRE General Test. Additional exam requirements/recommendations for international students: Required—TOEFL (minimum score 550 paper-based; 213 computer-based). Electronic applications accepted. *Faculty research:* Environmental stress, phytochemicals and health, crop nutrition, sustainable horticulture, turfgrass science.

Louisiana State University and Agricultural and Mechanical College, Graduate School, College of Agriculture, School of Plant, Environmental and Soil Science, Department of Horticulture, Baton Rouge, LA 70803. Offers MS, PhD. Part-time programs available. *Faculty:* 10 full-time (1 woman). *Students:* 4 full-time (1 woman), 3 part-time (2 women); includes 1 Black or African American, non-Hispanic/Latino, 2 international. Average age 32. 4 applicants, 25% accepted, 0 enrolled. In 2010, 1 master's awarded. Terminal master's awarded for partial completion of doctoral program. *Degree requirements:* For master's, thesis (for some programs); for doctorate, thesis/dissertation. *Entrance requirements:* For master's and doctorate, GRE General Test, minimum GPA of 3.0. Additional exam requirements/recommendations for international students: Required—TOEFL (minimum score 550 paper-based; 213 computer-based; 79 iBT) or IELTS (minimum score 6.5). *Application deadline:* For fall admission, 7/1 priority date for domestic students, 5/15 for international students; for spring admission, 10/15 for international students. Applications are processed on a rolling basis. Application fee: $50 ($70 for international students). Electronic applications accepted. *Financial support:* In 2010–11, 5 students received support, including 3 research assistantships with partial tuition reimbursements available (averaging $19,333 per year); fellowships, Federal Work-Study, health care benefits, tuition waivers (full and partial), and unspecified assistantships also available. Financial award application deadline: 4/15; financial award applicants required to submit FAFSA. *Faculty research:* Plant breeding, stress physiology, postharvest physiology, biotechnology. *Unit head:* Dr. Don LaBonte, Director, 225-578-1043, Fax: 225-578-1068, E-mail: dlabont@lsu.edu. *Application contact:* Dr. David Weindorf, Graduate Coordinator, 225-578-0396, Fax: 225-578-1068, E-mail: dweindorf@agcenter.lsu.edu.

Michigan State University, The Graduate School, College of Agriculture and Natural Resources, Department of Horticulture, East Lansing, MI 48824. Offers horticulture (MS, PhD); plant breeding, genetics and biotechnology-horticulture (MS, PhD). *Entrance requirements:* Additional exam requirements/recommendations for international students: Required—TOEFL. Electronic applications accepted.

Mississippi State University, College of Agriculture and Life Sciences, Department of Plant and Soil Sciences, Mississippi State, MS 39762. Offers agricultural sciences (PhD), including agronomy (MS, PhD), horticulture (MS, PhD), weed science (MS, PhD); agriculture (MS), including agronomy (MS, PhD), horticulture (MS, PhD), weed science (MS, PhD). *Faculty:* 31 full-time (1 woman), 1 part-time/adjunct (0 women). *Students:* 33 full-time (10 women), 22 part-time (7 women); includes 2 minority (both American Indian or Alaska Native, non-Hispanic/Latino), 18 international. Average age 31. 23 applicants, 39% accepted, 7 enrolled. In 2010, 11 master's, 6 doctorates awarded. *Degree requirements:* For master's, thesis, exit seminar describing thesis research; for doctorate, comprehensive exam, thesis/dissertation, two departmental seminars. *Entrance requirements:* For master's, GRE (weed science), minimum GPA of 2.75 (agronomy/horticulture), 3.0 (weed science); for doctorate, GRE (weed science), minimum GPA of 3.0 (agronomy/horticulture), 3.25 (weed science). Additional exam requirements/recommendations for international students: Required—TOEFL (minimum score 550 paper-based; 213 computer-based; 79 iBT); Recommended—IELTS (minimum score 6.5). *Application deadline:* For fall admission, 7/1 for domestic students, 5/1 for international students; for spring admission, 10/1 for domestic students, 9/1 for international students. Applications are processed on a rolling basis. Application fee: $40. Electronic applications accepted. *Expenses:* Tuition, state resident: full-time $2730.50; part-time $304 per credit hour. Tuition, nonresident: full-time $6901; part-time $767 per credit hour. *Financial support:* In 2010–11, 29 research assistantships (averaging $14,353 per year), 2 teaching assistantships (averaging $15,542 per year) were awarded; Federal Work-Study, institutionally sponsored loans, scholarships/grants, and unspecified assistantships also available. Financial award application deadline: 4/1; financial award applicants required to submit FAFSA. *Unit head:* Dr. Daniel Reynolds, Professor/Interim Department Head, 662-325-2311, Fax: 662-325-8742, E-mail: dreynolds@pss.msstate.edu. *Application contact:* Dr. William Kingery, Graduate Coordinator, 662-325-2748, Fax: 662-325-8742, E-mail: wkingery@pss.msstate.edu.

New Mexico State University, Graduate School, College of Agricultural, Consumer and Environmental Sciences, Department of Plant and Environmental Sciences, Las Cruces, NM 88003-8001. Offers horticulture (MS); plant and environmental sciences (MS, PhD). Part-time programs available. *Faculty:* 19 full-time (4 women). *Students:* 48 full-time (20 women), 8 part-time (3 women); includes 12 minority (1 American Indian or Alaska Native, non-Hispanic/Latino; 10 Hispanic/Latino; 1 Two or more races, non-Hispanic/Latino), 21 international. Average age 31. 29 applicants, 86% accepted, 15 enrolled. In 2010, 11 master's, 4 doctorates awarded. Terminal master's awarded for partial completion of doctoral program. *Degree requirements:* For master's, thesis; for doctorate, one foreign language, comprehensive exam, thesis/dissertation. *Entrance requirements:* For master's, minimum GPA of 3.0; for doctorate, minimum GPA of 3.3. Additional exam requirements/recommendations for international students: Required—TOEFL. *Application deadline:* For fall admission, 7/1 priority date for domestic students; for spring admission, 11/1 priority date for domestic students. Applications are processed on a rolling basis. Application fee: $30 ($50 for international students). Electronic applications accepted. *Expenses:* Tuition, state resident: full-time $4536; part-time $242 per credit. Tuition, nonresident: full-time $15,816; part-time $712 per credit. Required fees: $636 per term. *Financial support:* In 2010–11, 11 students received support, including 30 research assistantships with partial tuition reimbursements available (averaging $22,214 per year), 10 teaching assistantships with partial tuition reimbursements available (averaging $14,330 per year); career-related internships or fieldwork, Federal Work-Study, scholarships/grants, health care benefits, and unspecified assistantships also available. Support available to part-time students. Financial award application deadline: 3/1. *Faculty research:* Plant breeding and genetics, molecular biology, plant physiology, soil science and environmental remediation, urban horticulture and turfgrass management. *Unit head:* Dr. Richard Pratt, Head, 575-646-3406, Fax: 575-646-6041, E-mail: ricpratt@nmsu.edu. *Application contact:* Esther Ramirez, Information Contact, 575-646-3406, Fax: 575-646-6041, E-mail: esramire@nmsu.edu.

North Carolina State University, Graduate School, College of Agriculture and Life Sciences, Department of Horticultural Science, Raleigh, NC 27695. Offers MS, PhD, Certificate. Postbaccalaureate distance learning degree programs offered. Terminal master's awarded for

Horticulture

North Carolina State University (continued)

partial completion of doctoral program. *Degree requirements:* For master's, thesis (for some programs); for doctorate, thesis/dissertation. *Entrance requirements:* For master's and doctorate, GRE General Test, bachelor's degree in agriculture or biology, minimum GPA of 3.0. Electronic applications accepted. *Faculty research:* Plant physiology, breeding and genetics, tissue culture, herbicide physiology, propagation.

Nova Scotia Agricultural College, Research and Graduate Studies, Truro, NS B2N 5E3, Canada. Offers agriculture (M Sc), including air quality, animal behavior, animal molecular genetics, animal nutrition, animal technology, aquaculture, botany, crop management, crop physiology, ecology, environmental microbiology, food science, horticulture, nutrient management, pest management, physiology, plant biotechnology, plant pathology, soil chemistry, soil fertility, waste management and composting, water quality. Program offered jointly with Dalhousie University. Part-time programs available. *Degree requirements:* For master's, thesis, ATC Exam Teaching Assistantship. *Entrance requirements:* For master's, honors B Sc, minimum GPA of 3.0. Additional exam requirements/recommendations for international students: Required—TOEFL (minimum score 580 paper-based; 237 computer-based; 92 iBT), IELTS, Michigan English Language Assessment Battery, CanTEST, CAEL. *Faculty research:* Bio-product development, organic agriculture, nutrient management, air and water quality, agricultural biotechnology.

The Ohio State University, Graduate School, College of Food, Agricultural, and Environmental Sciences, Department of Horticulture and Crop Science, Columbus, OH 43210. Offers MS, PhD. *Faculty:* 51. *Students:* 43 full-time (22 women), 15 part-time (8 women); includes 1 Hispanic/Latino, 25 international. Average age 30. In 2010, 5 master's, 2 doctorates awarded. *Degree requirements:* For master's, thesis optional; for doctorate, thesis/dissertation. *Entrance requirements:* For master's and doctorate, GRE General Test. Additional exam requirements/recommendations for international students: Required—TOEFL (minimum score 550 paper-based; 213 computer-based), IELTS (minimum score 7), or Michigan English Language Assessment Battery (minimum score 86). *Application deadline:* For fall admission, 8/15 priority date for domestic students, 7/1 priority date for international students; for winter admission, 12/1 priority date for domestic students, 11/1 priority date for international students; for spring admission, 3/1 priority date for domestic students, 2/1 priority date for international students. Applications are processed on a rolling basis. Application fee: $40 ($50 for international students). Electronic applications accepted. *Expenses:* Tuition, state resident: full-time $10,605. Tuition, nonresident: full-time $26,535. Tuition and fees vary according to course load and program. *Financial support:* Fellowships, research assistantships, teaching assistantships, Federal Work-Study and institutionally sponsored loans available. Support available to part-time students. *Unit head:* Bill Randle, Chair, 614-247-7718, E-mail: randle.15@osu.edu. *Application contact:* Graduate Admissions, 614-292-9444, Fax: 614-292-3895, E-mail: domestic.grad@osu.edu.

Oklahoma State University, College of Agricultural Science and Natural Resources, Department of Horticulture and Landscape Architecture, Stillwater, OK 74078. Offers agriculture (M Ag); crop science (PhD); environmental science (PhD); horticulture (MS); plant science (PhD). *Faculty:* 21 full-time (2 women), 1 (woman) part-time/adjunct. *Students:* 1 (woman) full-time, 16 part-time (8 women); includes 1 Black or African American, non-Hispanic/Latino; 1 American Indian or Alaska Native, non-Hispanic/Latino; 1 Hispanic/Latino, 9 international. Average age 30. 12 applicants, 33% accepted, 4 enrolled. In 2010, 3 master's awarded. *Degree requirements:* For master's, thesis (for some programs); for doctorate, comprehensive exam, thesis/dissertation. *Entrance requirements:* For master's and doctorate, GRE or GMAT. Additional exam requirements/recommendations for international students: Required—TOEFL (minimum score 550 paper-based; 79 iBT). *Application deadline:* For fall admission, 3/1 priority date for international students; for spring admission, 8/1 priority date for international students. Applications are processed on a rolling basis. Application fee: $40 ($75 for international students). Electronic applications accepted. *Expenses:* Tuition, state resident: full-time $3716; part-time $154.85 per credit hour. Tuition, nonresident: full-time $14,892; part-time $621 per credit hour. Required fees: $2044; $85.20 per credit hour. One-time fee: $50. Tuition and fees vary according to course load and campus/location. *Financial support:* In 2010–11, 14 research assistantships (averaging $14,037 per year) were awarded; career-related internships or fieldwork, Federal Work-Study, scholarships/grants, health care benefits, tuition waivers (partial), and unspecified assistantships also available. Support available to part-time students. Financial award application deadline: 3/1; financial award applicants required to submit FAFSA. *Faculty research:* Stress and postharvest physiology; water utilization and runoff; IPM systems and nursery, turf, floriculture, vegetable, net and fruit produces and natural resources, food extraction, and processing; public garden management. *Unit head:* Dr. Dale Maronek, Head, 405-744-5414, Fax: 405-744-9709. *Application contact:* Dr. Gordon Emslie, Dean, 405-744-6368, Fax: 405-744-0355, E-mail: grad-i@okstate.edu.

Oregon State University, Graduate School, College of Agricultural Sciences, Department of Horticulture, Corvallis, OR 97331. Offers M Ag, MAIS, MS, PhD. *Degree requirements:* For master's, thesis (for some programs); for doctorate, thesis/dissertation. *Entrance requirements:* For master's and doctorate, GRE General Test, minimum GPA of 3.0 in last 90 hours. Additional exam requirements/recommendations for international students: Required—TOEFL.

Penn State University Park, Graduate School, College of Agricultural Sciences, Department of Horticulture, State College, University Park, PA 16802-1503. Offers M Agr, MS, PhD.

Purdue University, Graduate School, College of Agriculture, Department of Horticulture and Landscape Architecture, West Lafayette, IN 47907. Offers horticulture (M Agr, MS, PhD). Part-time programs available. Terminal master's awarded for partial completion of doctoral program. *Degree requirements:* For doctorate, thesis/dissertation. *Entrance requirements:* For master's and doctorate, GRE. Additional exam requirements/recommendations for international students: Required—TOEFL. Electronic applications accepted. *Faculty research:* Plant physiology, plant genetics and breeding, plant molecular biology and cell physiology, environmental and production horticulture.

Rutgers, The State University of New Jersey, New Brunswick, Graduate School-New Brunswick, Program in Plant Biology, Piscataway, NJ 08854-8097. Offers horticulture and plant technology (MS, PhD); molecular and cellular biology (MS, PhD); organismal and population biology (MS, PhD); plant pathology (MS, PhD). Part-time programs available. Terminal master's awarded for partial completion of doctoral program. *Degree requirements:* For master's, comprehensive exam, thesis or alternative; for doctorate, comprehensive exam, thesis/dissertation. *Entrance requirements:* For master's and doctorate, GRE General Test, GRE Subject Test (recommended). Additional exam requirements/recommendations for international students: Required—TOEFL (minimum score 600 paper-based; 250 computer-based). Electronic applications accepted. *Expenses:* Tuition, state resident: full-time $7200; part-time $600 per credit. Tuition, nonresident: full-time $11,124; part-time $927 per credit. *Faculty research:* Molecular biology and biochemistry of plants, plant development and genomics, plant protection, plant improvement, plant management of horticultural and field crops.

Southern Illinois University Carbondale, Graduate School, College of Agriculture, Department of Plant, Soil, and General Agriculture, Carbondale, IL 62901-4701. Offers horticultural science (MS); plant and soil science (MS). *Degree requirements:* For master's, thesis. *Entrance requirements:* For master's, minimum GPA of 2.7. Additional exam requirements/recommendations for international students: Required—TOEFL. *Faculty research:* Herbicides, fertilizers, agriculture education, landscape design, plant breeding.

Texas A&M University, College of Agriculture and Life Sciences, Department of Horticultural Sciences, College Station, TX 77843. Offers M Agr, MS, PhD. *Faculty:* 17. *Students:* 33 full-time (16 women), 9 part-time (3 women); includes 2 minority (1 Asian, non-Hispanic/Latino; 1 Hispanic/Latino), 24 international. Average age 29. In 2010, 7 master's awarded. Terminal master's awarded for partial completion of doctoral program. *Degree requirements:* For master's, thesis (for some programs), professional internship; for doctorate, thesis/dissertation. *Entrance requirements:* For master's and doctorate, GRE General Test. Additional exam requirements/recommendations for international students: Required—TOEFL. Application fee: $50 ($75 for international students). Electronic applications accepted. *Financial support:* In 2010–11, 30 students received support, including fellowships with full tuition reimbursements available (averaging $15,000 per year), research assistantships with partial tuition reimbursements available (averaging $14,000 per year), teaching assistantships with partial tuition reimbursements available (averaging $14,000 per year); career-related internships or fieldwork and tuition waivers (partial) also available. Financial award application deadline: 4/1. *Faculty research:* Plant breeding, molecular biology, plant nutrition, postharvest physiology, plant physiology. *Unit head:* Tim Davis, Head, 979-458-2048, Fax: 979-845-0627, E-mail: t-davis5@tamu.edu. *Application contact:* Dr. Michael Arnold, Professor, 979-845-1499, Fax: 979-845-0627, E-mail: ma-arnold@tamu.edu.

Texas Tech University, Graduate School, College of Agricultural Sciences and Natural Resources, Department of Plant and Soil Science, Lubbock, TX 79409. Offers crop science (MS); horticulture (MS); plant and soil science (PhD); plant protection (MS); soil science (MS); JD/MS. Part-time programs available. Postbaccalaureate distance learning degree programs offered (no on-campus study). *Faculty:* 14 full-time (3 women), 6 part-time/adjunct (0 women). *Students:* 57 full-time (23 women), 42 part-time (20 women); includes 3 Black or African American, non-Hispanic/Latino; 1 Asian, non-Hispanic/Latino; 4 Hispanic/Latino, 31 international. Average age 30. 64 applicants, 52% accepted, 22 enrolled. In 2010, 13 master's, 7 doctorates awarded. *Degree requirements:* For master's, thesis or alternative; for doctorate, thesis/dissertation. *Entrance requirements:* For master's and doctorate, GRE General Test, formal approval from departmental committee. Additional exam requirements/recommendations for international students: Required—TOEFL (minimum score 550 paper-based; 213 computer-based; 79 iBT). *Application deadline:* For fall admission, 6/1 priority date for domestic students, 1/15 priority date for international students; for spring admission, 9/1 priority date for domestic students, 6/15 priority date for international students. Applications are processed on a rolling basis. Application fee: $50 ($75 for international students). Electronic applications accepted. *Expenses:* Tuition, state resident: full-time $5495.76; part-time $228.99 per credit hour. Tuition, nonresident: full-time $12,936; part-time $538.99 per credit hour. Required fees: $2674; $36 per credit hour. $905 per semester. *Financial support:* In 2010–11, 55 students received support, including 18 research assistantships with partial tuition reimbursements available (averaging $3,594 per year), 2 teaching assistantships with partial tuition reimbursements available (averaging $5,398 per year). Financial award application deadline: 4/15; financial award applicants required to submit FAFSA. *Faculty research:* Molecular and cellular biology of plant stress, physiology/genetics of crop production in semiarid conditions, agricultural bioterrorism, improvement of native plants, soil science and management. Total annual research expenditures: $4.9 million. *Unit head:* Dr. Richard Zartman, Chair, 806-742-2838, Fax: 806-742-0775, E-mail: richard.zartman@ttu.edu. *Application contact:* Dr. Eric Hequet, Graduate Adviser, 806-742-2837, Fax: 806-742-0775, E-mail: eric.hequet@ttu.edu.

Universidad Nacional Pedro Henriquez Urena, Graduate School, Santo Domingo, Dominican Republic. Offers agricultural diversity (MS), including horticultural/fruit production, tropical animal production; conservation of monuments and cultural assets (M Arch); ecology and environment (MS); environmental engineering (MEE); international relations (MA); natural resource management (MS); political science (MA); project optimization (MPM); project feasibility (MPM); project management (MPM); sanitation engineering (ME); science for teachers (MS); tropical Caribbean architecture (M Arch).

University of Arkansas, Graduate School, Dale Bumpers College of Agricultural, Food and Life Sciences, Department of Horticulture, Fayetteville, AR 72701-1201. Offers MS. *Students:* 1 full-time (0 women), 8 part-time (4 women), 3 international. 6 applicants, 50% accepted. In 2010, 4 master's awarded. *Degree requirements:* For master's, thesis. *Application deadline:* For fall admission, 4/1 for international students; for spring admission, 10/1 for international students. Applications are processed on a rolling basis. Application fee: $40 ($50 for international students). Electronic applications accepted. *Financial support:* In 2010–11, 6 research assistantships were awarded; fellowships, teaching assistantships, career-related internships or fieldwork and Federal Work-Study also available. Support available to part-time students. Financial award application deadline: 4/1; financial award applicants required to submit FAFSA. *Unit head:* Dr. David Hensley, Department Head, 479-575-2603, E-mail: dhensley@uark.edu. *Application contact:* Dr. J. Brad Murphy, Graduate Coordinator, 479-575-2603, E-mail: jbmurph@comp.uark.edu.

University of California, Davis, Graduate Studies, Graduate Group in Horticulture and Agronomy, Davis, CA 95616. Offers MS. *Degree requirements:* For master's, comprehensive exam (for some programs), thesis (for some programs). *Entrance requirements:* For master's, GRE General Test. Additional exam requirements/recommendations for international students: Required—TOEFL (minimum score 550 paper-based; 213 computer-based). Electronic applications accepted. *Faculty research:* Postharvest physiology, mineral nutrition, crop improvement, plant growth and development.

University of Delaware, College of Agriculture and Natural Resources, Longwood Graduate Program in Public Horticulture, Newark, DE 19716. Offers MS. *Degree requirements:* For master's, thesis, internship. *Entrance requirements:* For master's, GRE General Test, introductory taxonomy course. Additional exam requirements/recommendations for international students: Required—TOEFL. Electronic applications accepted. *Faculty research:* Management and development of publicly oriented horticultural institutions.

University of Florida, Graduate School, College of Agricultural and Life Sciences, Department of Environmental Horticulture, Gainesville, FL 32611. Offers anatomy and development (MS, PhD); breeding and genetics (MS, PhD); ecology (MS, PhD); plant biotechnology (MS, PhD); stress physiology (MS, PhD); taxonomy (MS, PhD); tissue culture (MS, PhD). Postbaccalaureate distance learning degree programs offered (no on-campus study). *Faculty:* 17 full-time (3 women), 1 (woman) part-time/adjunct. *Students:* 30 full-time (11 women), 8 part-time (5 women); includes 1 Black or African American, non-Hispanic/Latino; 3 Hispanic/Latino, 8 international. Average age 32. 30 applicants, 47% accepted, 11 enrolled. In 2010, 6 master's, 1 doctorate awarded. *Degree requirements:* For master's, comprehensive exam, thesis optional, Thesis optional for Master's degree. Teaching experience; for doctorate, comprehensive exam, thesis/dissertation, teaching experience. *Entrance requirements:* For master's and doctorate, GRE General Test, minimum GPA of 3.0. Additional exam requirements/recommendations for international students: Required—TOEFL (minimum score 550 paper-based; 213 computer-based; 80 iBT), IELTS (minimum score 6). *Application deadline:* For fall admission, 1/15 priority date for domestic students, 1/15 for international students; for spring admission, 9/1 for domestic and international students. Applications are processed on a rolling basis. Application fee: $30. Electronic applications accepted. *Expenses:* Tuition, state resident: full-time $10,915.92. Tuition, nonresident: full-time $28,309. *Financial support:* In 2010–11, 26 students received support, including 4 fellowships, 22 research assistantships (averaging $17,406 per year); teaching assistantships, unspecified assistantships also available. Financial award application deadline: 2/1; financial award applicants required to submit FAFSA. *Faculty research:* Breeding and genetics, conservation horticulture landscape design and ecology, floriculture, nursery and foliage crop production, turfgrasses, urban horticulture. Total annual research expenditures: $1.5 million. *Unit head:* Dr. Terril A. Nell, Chair, 352-273-4583, Fax: 352-392-3870, E-mail: tanell@ufl.edu. *Application contact:* Dr. Charles L. Guy, Graduate Coordinator, 352-392-1831 Ext. 222, Fax: 352-392-3870, E-mail: clguy@ufl.edu.

University of Florida, Graduate School, College of Agricultural and Life Sciences, Department of Horticultural Sciences, Gainesville, FL 32611. Offers plant breeding and genetics (MS, PhD); plant production and nutrient management (MS, PhD); postharvest biology (MS, PhD); sustainable/organic practice (MS, PhD); weed science (MS, PhD). *Faculty:* 29 full-time (9 women), 1 part-time/adjunct (0 women). *Students:* 44 full-time (21 women), 6 part-time (3 women); includes 3 Hispanic/Latino, 31 international. Average age 29. 36 applicants, 36% accepted, 12 enrolled. In 2010, 10 master's, 7 doctorates awarded. *Degree requirements:* For master's, thesis optional, Thesis and non-thesis options for Masters Degree; for doctorate, comprehensive exam, thesis/dissertation. *Entrance requirements:* For master's and doctorate, GRE General Test, minimum GPA of 3.0. Additional exam requirements/recommendations for international students: Required—TOEFL (minimum score 550 paper-based; 213 computer-based; 80 iBT), IELTS (minimum score 6). *Application deadline:* For fall admission, 1/1 priority date for domestic students, 1/1 for international students; for spring admission, 8/1 for domestic and international students. Applications are processed on a rolling basis. Application fee: $30. Electronic applications accepted. *Expenses:* Tuition, state resident: full-time $10,915.92. Tuition, nonresident: full-time $28,309. *Financial support:* In 2010–11, 38 students received support, including 38 research assistantships (averaging $17,926 per year); institutionally sponsored loans also available. Financial award application deadline: 6/1; financial award applicants required to submit FAFSA. *Faculty research:* Breeding and genetics, crop production, organic/sustainable agriculture and nutrition, physiology and biochemistry, plant molecular and cellularbiology, postharvest biology. Total annual research expenditures: $15.6 million. *Unit head:* Dr. Daniel J. Cantliffe, Chair, 352-273-4766, Fax: 352-392-6479, E-mail: djcant@ufl.edu. *Application contact:* Dr. Steven A. Sargent, Graduate Coordinator, 352-273-4780, E-mail: sasa@ufl.edu.

University of Georgia, College of Agricultural and Environmental Sciences, Department of Horticulture, Athens, GA 30602. Offers horticulture (MS, PhD); plant protection and pest management (MPPPM). Part-time programs available. *Faculty:* 24 full-time (6 women). *Students:* 19 full-time (8 women), 3 part-time (1 woman); includes 1 Hispanic/Latino, 9 international. 18 applicants, 44% accepted, 7 enrolled. In 2010, 3 master's, 1 doctorate awarded. *Degree requirements:* For master's, thesis (MS); for doctorate, one foreign language, thesis/dissertation. *Entrance requirements:* For master's and doctorate, GRE General Test. *Application deadline:* For fall admission, 7/1 priority date for domestic students; for spring admission, 11/15 for domestic students. Application fee: $50. Electronic applications accepted. *Expenses:* Tuition, state resident: full-time $7200; part-time $344 per credit hour. Tuition, nonresident: full-time $21,900; part-time $944 per credit hour. Tuition and fees vary according to course load and program. *Financial support:* In 2010–11, fellowships with partial tuition reimbursements (averaging $1,338 per year), research assistantships with partial tuition reimbursements (averaging $1,338 per year), teaching assistantships with partial tuition reimbursements (averaging $1,338 per year) were awarded; unspecified assistantships also available. *Unit head:* Dr. Douglas A. Bailey, Head, 706-542-2471, Fax: 706-542-0624, E-mail: dabailey@uga.edu. *Application contact:* Dr. Marc van Iersel, Graduate Coordinator, 706-583-0284, Fax: 706-542-0624, E-mail: mvanier@uga.edu.

University of Guelph, Graduate Studies, Ontario Agricultural College, Department of Plant Agriculture, Guelph, ON N1G 2W1, Canada. Offers M Sc, PhD. Part-time programs available. *Degree requirements:* For master's, thesis; for doctorate, comprehensive exam, thesis/dissertation. *Entrance requirements:* For master's, minimum B average during previous 2 years of course work; for doctorate, minimum B average. Additional exam requirements/recommendations for international students: Required—TOEFL (minimum score 550 paper-based; 213 computer-based; 89 iBT), IELTS (minimum score 6.5), Michigan English Language Assessment Battery (minimum score: 85). Electronic applications accepted. *Faculty research:* Plant physiology, biochemistry, taxonomy, morphology, genetics, production, ecology, breeding and biotechnology.

University of Hawaii at Manoa, Graduate Division, College of Tropical Agriculture and Human Resources, Department of Tropical Plant and Soil Sciences, Honolulu, HI 96822. Offers MS, PhD. Part-time programs available. *Faculty:* 34 full-time (6 women), 10 part-time/adjunct (5 women). *Students:* 20 full-time (9 women), 8 part-time (3 women); includes 9 minority (3 Asian, non-Hispanic/Latino; 5 Native Hawaiian or other Pacific Islander, non-Hispanic/Latino; 1 Two or more races, non-Hispanic/Latino), 10 international. Average age 34. 25 applicants, 56% accepted, 11 enrolled. In 2010, 2 master's awarded. *Degree requirements:* For master's, thesis optional; for doctorate, comprehensive exam, thesis/dissertation. *Entrance requirements:* For master's and doctorate, GRE General Test. Additional exam requirements/recommendations for international students: Required—TOEFL (minimum score 520 paper-based; 213 computer-based; 79 iBT), IELTS (minimum score 5). *Application deadline:* For fall admission, 3/1 for domestic students, 1/15 for international students; for spring admission, 9/1 for domestic students, 8/1 for international students. Application fee: $60. *Financial support:* In 2010–11, 1 fellowship (averaging $3,500 per year), 17 research assistantships (averaging $17,461 per year) were awarded; tuition waivers (full and partial) also available. *Faculty research:* Genetics and breeding; physiology, culture, and management; weed science; turfgrass and landscape; sensory evaluation. Total annual research expenditures: $2.5 million. *Application contact:* Kent Kobayashi, Graduate Chair, 808-956-5900, Fax: 808-956-3894, E-mail: kentko@hawaii.edu.

University of Maine, Graduate School, College of Natural Sciences, Forestry, and Agriculture, Department of Plant, Soil, and Environmental Sciences, Program in Horticulture, Orono, ME 04469. Offers MS. *Students:* 1 full-time (0 women), 2 part-time (1 woman), 2 international. Average age 32. In 2010, 2 master's awarded. *Entrance requirements:* For master's, GRE General Test. Additional exam requirements/recommendations for international students: Required—TOEFL. *Application deadline:* For fall admission, 2/1 priority date for domestic students. Applications are processed on a rolling basis. Application fee: $65. Electronic applications accepted. *Expenses:* Tuition, state resident: full-time $400. Tuition, nonresident: full-time $1050. *Financial support:* Tuition waivers (full and partial) available. Financial award application deadline: 3/1. *Unit head:* Dr. Tsutomu Ohno, Coordinator, 207-584-2975. *Application contact:* Scott G. Delcourt, Associate Dean of the Graduate School, 207-581-3291, Fax: 207-581-3232, E-mail: graduate@maine.edu.

University of Manitoba, Faculty of Graduate Studies, Faculty of Agricultural and Food Sciences, Department of Plant Science, Winnipeg, MB R3T 2N2, Canada. Offers agronomy and plant protection (M Sc, PhD); horticulture (M Sc, PhD); plant breeding and genetics (M Sc, PhD); plant physiology-biochemistry (M Sc, PhD). *Degree requirements:* For master's, thesis; for doctorate, one foreign language, thesis/dissertation.

University of Maryland, College Park, Academic Affairs, College of Agriculture and Natural Resources, Department of Plant Science and Landscape Architecture, Program in Horticulture, College Park, MD 20742. Offers MS, PhD. *Students:* 8 full-time (5 women), 2 international. 36 applicants, 42% accepted, 8 enrolled. *Entrance requirements:* For doctorate, GRE General Test. Additional exam requirements/recommendations for international students: Required—TOEFL. *Application deadline:* For fall admission, 2/1 for domestic and international students; for spring admission, 6/1 for domestic and international students. Applications are processed on a rolling basis. Application fee: $75. Electronic applications accepted. *Expenses:* Tuition, area resident: Part-time $471 per credit hour. Tuition, state resident: part-time $471 per credit hour. Tuition, nonresident: part-time $1016 per credit hour. Required fees: $337 per term. *Financial support:* In 2010–11, 5 research assistantships (averaging $16,803 per year), 3 teaching assistantships (averaging $16,363 per year) were awarded; fellowships, career-related internships or fieldwork also available. Financial award applicants required to submit FAFSA. *Faculty research:* Mineral nutrition, genetics and breeding, chemical growth, histochemistry, postharvest physiology. *Unit head:* Dr. Gary Coleman, Coordinator, 301-405-4371, Fax: 301-314-9308, E-mail: wkenwort@umd.edu. *Application contact:* Dr. Charles A. Caramello, Dean of Graduate School, 301-405-0358, Fax: 301-314-9305, E-mail: ccaramel@umd.edu.

University of Missouri, Graduate School, College of Agriculture, Food and Natural Resources, Division of Plant Sciences, Program in Horticulture, Columbia, MO 65211. Offers MS, PhD. *Degree requirements:* For master's, thesis; for doctorate, variable foreign language requirement, thesis/dissertation. *Entrance requirements:* For master's and doctorate, GRE General Test, minimum GPA of 3.0. *Application deadline:* Applications are processed on a rolling basis. Application fee: $45 ($60 for international students). *Financial support:* Research assistantships, teaching assistantships, institutionally sponsored loans available. *Application contact:* Dr. Jeanne Mihail, Director of Graduate Studies, 573-882-0574, E-mail: mihailj@missouri.edu.

University of Nebraska–Lincoln, Graduate College, College of Agricultural Sciences and Natural Resources, Department of Agronomy and Horticulture, Program in Horticulture, Lincoln, NE 68588. Offers MS, PhD. *Degree requirements:* For master's, thesis optional. *Entrance requirements:* For master's, GRE General Test. Additional exam requirements/recommendations for international students: Required—TOEFL (minimum score 600 paper-based; 250 computer-based). Electronic applications accepted. *Faculty research:* Horticultural crops: production, management, cultural, and ecological aspects; tissue and cell culture; plant nutrition and anatomy; postharvest physiology and ecology.

University of Puerto Rico, Mayagüez Campus, Graduate Studies, College of Agricultural Sciences, Department of Horticulture, Mayagüez, PR 00681-9000. Offers MS. Part-time programs available. *Students:* 12 full-time (5 women), 3 part-time (0 women); includes 14 Hispanic/Latino. 2 applicants, 100% accepted, 0 enrolled. In 2010, 3 master's awarded. *Degree requirements:* For master's, comprehensive exam, thesis. *Entrance requirements:* For master's, BS in agricultural science or its equivalent. *Application deadline:* For fall admission, 2/15 for domestic and international students; for spring admission, 9/15 for domestic and international students. Applications are processed on a rolling basis. Application fee: $25. *Expenses:* Tuition, state resident: full-time $1188. Tuition, nonresident: full-time $1188. International tuition: $6126 full-time. Tuition and fees vary according to course level and course load. *Financial support:* Federal Work-Study and institutionally sponsored loans available. *Faculty research:* Growth regulators, floriculture, starchy crops, coffee and fruit technology. *Unit head:* Prof. Hipolito O'Farrill, Director, 787-265-3852, Fax: 787-265-0860, E-mail: hipolito.ofarrill@upr.edu. *Application contact:* Janice Perez, Secretary, 787-832-4040 Ext. 3511, E-mail: japerez@uprm.edu.

University of South Africa, College of Agriculture and Environmental Sciences, Pretoria, South Africa. Offers agriculture (MS); consumer science (MCS); environmental management (MA, MS, PhD); environmental science (MA, MS, PhD); geography (MA, MS, PhD); horticulture (M Tech); human ecology (MHE); life sciences (MS); nature conservation (M Tech).

University of Vermont, Graduate College, College of Agriculture and Life Sciences, Department of Plant and Soil Science, Burlington, VT 05405. Offers MS, PhD. *Students:* 24 (13 women), 3 international. 26 applicants, 12% accepted, 1 enrolled. In 2010, 3 master's, 1 doctorate awarded. *Degree requirements:* For master's, thesis; for doctorate, one foreign language, thesis/dissertation. *Entrance requirements:* For master's and doctorate, GRE General Test. Additional exam requirements/recommendations for international students: Required—TOEFL (minimum score 550 paper-based; 213 computer-based; 80 iBT). *Application deadline:* For fall admission, 3/1 priority date for domestic students. Applications are processed on a rolling basis. Application fee: $40. Electronic applications accepted. *Expenses:* Tuition, state resident: part-time $537 per credit hour. Tuition, nonresident: part-time $1355 per credit hour. *Financial support:* Fellowships, research assistantships, teaching assistantships available. Financial award application deadline: 3/1. *Faculty research:* Soil chemistry, plant nutrition. *Unit head:* Dr. Deborah Neher, Chairperson, 802-656-2630. *Application contact:* Dr. Josef Gorres, Coordinator, 802-656-2630.

University of Washington, Graduate School, College of Forest Resources, Seattle, WA 98195. Offers bioresource science and engineering (MS, PhD); environmental horticulture (MEH); environmental horticulture and urban forestry (MS, PhD); forest ecology (MS, PhD); forest management (MFR); forest soils (MS, PhD); forest systems and bioenergy (MS, PhD); restoration ecology (MS, PhD); social sciences (MS, PhD); sustainable resource management (MS, PhD); wildlife science (MS, PhD); MFR/MAIS; MPA/MS. *Accreditation:* SAF. *Degree requirements:* For master's, thesis (for some programs); for doctorate, comprehensive exam (for some programs), thesis/dissertation. *Entrance requirements:* For master's and doctorate, GRE, minimum GPA of 3.0. Additional exam requirements/recommendations for international students: Required—TOEFL. Electronic applications accepted. *Faculty research:* Ecosystem analysis, silviculture and forest protection, paper science and engineering, environmental horticulture and urban forestry, natural resource policy and economics.

University of Wisconsin–Madison, Graduate School, College of Agricultural and Life Sciences, Department of Horticulture, Madison, WI 53706-1380. Offers horticulture (MS, PhD); plant breeding and genetics (MS, PhD). Part-time programs available. Terminal master's awarded for partial completion of doctoral program. *Degree requirements:* For master's, comprehensive exam, thesis (for some programs); for doctorate, comprehensive exam, thesis/dissertation. *Entrance requirements:* For master's and doctorate, minimum GPA of 3.0. Additional exam requirements/recommendations for international students: Required—TOEFL (minimum score 580 paper-based; 213 computer-based). Electronic applications accepted. *Expenses:* Tuition, state resident: full-time $9887.36; part-time $617.96 per credit. Tuition, nonresident: full-time $24,054; part-time $1503.40 per credit. Required fees: $67.63 per credit. Tuition and fees vary according to reciprocity agreements. *Faculty research:* Biotechnology, crop breeding/genetics, environmental physiology, crop management, cytogenetics.

Virginia Polytechnic Institute and State University, Graduate School, College of Agriculture and Life Sciences, Department of Horticulture, Blacksburg, VA 24061. Offers MS, PhD. *Faculty:* 11 full-time (3 women). *Students:* 24 full-time (6 women), 7 part-time (5 women); includes 1 Asian, non-Hispanic/Latino; 1 Hispanic/Latino, 10 international. Average age 33. 10 applicants, 60% accepted, 4 enrolled. In 2010, 3 master's, 1 doctorate awarded. *Degree requirements:* For master's, comprehensive exam (for some programs), thesis (for some programs); for doctorate, comprehensive exam (for some programs), thesis/dissertation (for some programs). *Entrance requirements:* For master's and doctorate, GRE. Additional exam requirements/recommendations for international students: Required—TOEFL (minimum score 550 paper-based; 213 computer-based). *Application deadline:* For fall admission, 7/1 for domestic and international students; for spring admission, 12/1 for domestic and international students. Applications are processed on a rolling basis. Application fee: $65. Electronic applications accepted. *Expenses:* Tuition, area resident: Full-time $9399; part-time $488 per credit hour. Tuition, state resident: full-time $9399; part-time $488 per credit hour. Tuition, nonresident: full-time $17,854; part-time $957.75 per credit hour. International tuition: $17,854 full-time. Required fees: $1534. Full-time tuition and fees vary according to program. *Financial support:* In 2010–11, 8 research assistantships with full tuition reimbursements (averaging $19,017 per year), 4 teaching assistantships with full tuition reimbursements (averaging $14,475 per year) were awarded; career-related internships or fieldwork, Federal Work-Study, scholarships/grants, health care benefits, and unspecified assistantships also available. Financial award application deadline: 1/15. Total annual research expenditures: $913,388. *Unit head:* Dr. Jerzy Nowak, UNIT HEAD, 540-231-5451, Fax: 540-231-3083, E-mail: jenowak@vt.edu. *Application contact:* Roger Harris, Contact, 540-231-4026, Fax: 540-231-3083, E-mail: rharris@vt.edu.

Washington State University, Graduate School, College of Agricultural, Human, and Natural Resource Sciences, Department of Horticulture and Landscape Architecture, Pullman, WA

Horticulture

Washington State University (continued)
99164. Offers horticulture (MS, PhD); landscape architecture (MSLA). Part-time programs available. *Faculty:* 18. *Students:* 26 full-time (21 women), 1 (woman) part-time; includes 1 minority (Black or African American, non-Hispanic/Latino), 10 international. Average age 28. 43 applicants, 33% accepted, 10 enrolled. In 2010, 7 master's awarded. *Degree requirements:* For master's, comprehensive exam (for some programs), thesis (for some programs), oral exam; for doctorate, comprehensive exam, thesis/dissertation, oral exam, written exam. *Entrance requirements:* For master's and doctorate, GRE General Test, GRE Subject Test, minimum GPA of 3.0, 3 letters of recommendation. Additional exam requirements/recommendations for international students: Required—TOEFL (minimum score 550 paper-based). *Application deadline:* For fall admission, 2/1 priority date for domestic students, 3/1 for international students; for spring admission, 9/1 for domestic students, 7/1 for international students. Applications are processed on a rolling basis. Application fee: $50. Electronic applications accepted. *Expenses:* Tuition, state resident: full-time $8552; part-time $443 per credit. Tuition, nonresident: full-time $21,650; part-time $1083 per credit. Required fees: $846. *Financial support:* In 2010–11, 16 students received support, including fellowships (averaging $2,275 per year), 10 research assistantships with full and partial tuition reimbursements available (averaging $18,204 per year), 2 teaching assistantships with full and partial tuition reimbursements available (averaging $18,204 per year); career-related internships or fieldwork, Federal Work-Study, institutionally sponsored loans, and health care benefits also available. Financial award application deadline: 4/1; financial award applicants required to submit FAFSA. *Faculty research:* Post-harvest physiology, genetics/plant breeding, molecular biology. Total annual research expenditures: $3.9 million. *Unit head:* Dr. N. Richard Knowles, Chair, 509-335-9502, Fax: 509-335-8690, E-mail: rknowles@wsu.edu. *Application contact:* Graduate School Admissions, 800-GRADWSU, Fax: 509-335-1949, E-mail: gradsch@wsu.edu.

West Virginia University, Davis College of Agriculture, Forestry and Consumer Sciences, Division of Plant and Soil Sciences, Morgantown, WV 26506. Offers agricultural sciences (PhD), including animal and food sciences, plant and soil sciences; agronomy (MS); entomology (MS); environmental microbiology (MS); horticulture (MS); plant pathology (MS). *Degree requirements:* For master's, thesis. *Entrance requirements:* For master's, GRE, minimum GPA of 2.5. Additional exam requirements/recommendations for international students: Required—TOEFL. *Faculty research:* Water quality, reclamation of disturbed land, crop production, pest control, environmental protection.

Plant Sciences

Alabama Agricultural and Mechanical University, School of Graduate Studies, School of Agricultural and Environmental Sciences, Department of Plant and Soil Science, Huntsville, AL 35811. Offers animal sciences (MS); environmental science (MS); plant and soil science (PhD). Evening/weekend programs available. Terminal master's awarded for partial completion of doctoral program. *Degree requirements:* For master's, thesis; for doctorate, one foreign language, thesis/dissertation. *Entrance requirements:* For master's, GRE General Test, BS in agriculture; for doctorate, GRE General Test, master's degree. Additional exam requirements/recommendations for international students: Required—TOEFL (minimum score 500 paper-based; 173 computer-based; 61 iBT). Electronic applications accepted. *Faculty research:* Plant breeding, cytogenetics, crop production, soil chemistry and fertility, remote sensing.

American University of Beirut, Graduate Programs, Faculty of Agricultural and Food Sciences, Beirut, Lebanon. Offers agricultural economics (MS); animal sciences (MS); ecosystem management (MSES); food technology (MS); irrigation (MS); mechanization (MS); nutrition (MS); plant protection (MS); plant science (MS); poultry science (MS); soils (MS). Part-time programs available. *Faculty:* 22 full-time (6 women). *Students:* 6 full-time (3 women), 86 part-time (77 women). Average age 24. 94 applicants, 60% accepted, 15 enrolled. In 2010, 28 master's awarded. *Degree requirements:* For master's, one foreign language, comprehensive exam, thesis (for some programs). *Entrance requirements:* Additional exam requirements/recommendations for international students: Required—TOEFL (minimum score 600 paper-based; 250 computer-based; 100 iBT), IELTS (minimum score 7.5). *Application deadline:* For fall admission, 4/30 for domestic and international students; for spring admission, 11/1 for domestic and international students. Applications are processed on a rolling basis. Application fee: $50. Electronic applications accepted. *Expenses:* Tuition: Full-time $12,294; part-time $683 per credit. Required fees: $499; $499 per credit. Tuition and fees vary according to course load and program. *Financial support:* In 2010–11, 18 research assistantships with partial tuition reimbursements (averaging $13,132 per year), 42 teaching assistantships with full and partial tuition reimbursements (averaging $1,000 per year) were awarded; scholarships/grants, health care benefits, and unspecified assistantships also available. Financial award application deadline: 2/2. *Faculty research:* Community and therapeutic nutrition; food safety and food microbiology; landscape planning, nature and rural heritage conservation; pathology, immunology and control of poultry and animal diseases; agricultural economics and development. Total annual research expenditures: $900,000. *Unit head:* Prof. Nahla Hwalla, Dean, 961-134-3002 Ext. 4400, Fax: 961-174-4460, E-mail: nahla@aub.edu.lb. *Application contact:* Dr. Salim Kanaan, Director, Admissions Office, 961-135-0000 Ext. 2594, Fax: 961-175-0775, E-mail: sk00@aub.edu.lb.

Brigham Young University, Graduate Studies, College of Life Sciences, Department of Plant and Wildlife Sciences, Provo, UT 84602-1001. Offers environmental science (MS); genetics and biotechnology (MS); wildlife and wildlands conservation (MS, PhD). *Faculty:* 26 full-time (2 women). *Students:* 63 full-time (23 women); includes 2 Asian, non-Hispanic/Latino; 1 Hispanic/Latino; 1 Native Hawaiian or other Pacific Islander, non-Hispanic/Latino, 5 international. Average age 25. 33 applicants, 55% accepted, 18 enrolled. *Degree requirements:* For master's, thesis; for doctorate, comprehensive exam, thesis/dissertation, minimum GPA of 3.2, 54 hours (18 dissertation, 36 coursework). *Entrance requirements:* For master's, GRE General Test, minimum GPA of 3.2 during last 60 hours of course work; for doctorate, GRE, minimum GPA of 3.2. Additional exam requirements/recommendations for international students: Required—TOEFL (minimum score 580 paper-based; 237 computer-based; 85 iBT). *Application deadline:* 2/1 for domestic and international students. Applications are processed on a rolling basis. Application fee: $0. Electronic applications accepted. *Expenses:* Tuition: Full-time $5580; part-time $310 per credit hour. Tuition and fees vary according to program and student's religious affiliation. *Financial support:* In 2010–11, 63 students received support, including 2 research assistantships with partial tuition reimbursements available (averaging $16,650 per year), 37 teaching assistantships with partial tuition reimbursements available (averaging $16,650 per year); scholarships/grants and tuition waivers (partial) also available. Financial award application deadline: 2/1. *Faculty research:* environmental science, plant genetics, plant ecology, plant nutrition and pathology, wildlife and wildlands conservation. *Unit head:* Dr. Val J. Anderson, Chair, 801-422-3527, Fax: 801-422-0008, E-mail: val_anderson@byu.edu. *Application contact:* Dr. Loreen Allphin, Graduate Coordinator, 801-422-5603, Fax: 801-422-0008, E-mail: loreen_allphin@byu.edu.

California State University, Fresno, Division of Graduate Studies, College of Agricultural Sciences and Technology, Department of Plant Science, Fresno, CA 93740-8027. Offers MS. Part-time programs available. *Degree requirements:* For master's, thesis. *Entrance requirements:* For master's, GRE General Test, minimum GPA of 2.5. Additional exam requirements/recommendations for international students: Required—TOEFL. Electronic applications accepted. *Faculty research:* Crop patterns, small watershed management, electronic monitoring of feedlot cattle, disease control, dairy operations.

Clemson University, Graduate School, College of Agriculture, Forestry and Life Sciences, Department of Forestry and Natural Resources, Program in Plant and Environmental Sciences, Clemson, SC 29634. Offers MS, PhD. *Students:* 34 full-time (10 women), 10 part-time (2 women); includes 1 Hispanic/Latino, 14 international. Average age 31. 32 applicants, 53% accepted, 12 enrolled. In 2010, 7 master's awarded. *Degree requirements:* For master's, thesis; for doctorate, thesis/dissertation. *Entrance requirements:* For master's, GRE General Test, bachelor's degree in biological science or chemistry; for doctorate, GRE General Test. Additional exam requirements/recommendations for international students: Required—TOEFL, IELTS. *Application deadline:* Applications are processed on a rolling basis. Application fee: $70 ($80 for international students). Electronic applications accepted. *Expenses:* Contact institution. *Financial support:* In 2010–11, 31 students received support, including 4 fellowships with full and partial tuition reimbursements available (averaging $6,635 per year), 26 research assistantships with partial tuition reimbursements available (averaging $16,445 per year), 8 teaching assistantships with partial tuition reimbursements available (averaging $11,000 per year); career-related internships or fieldwork, institutionally sponsored loans, scholarships/grants, health care benefits, and unspecified assistantships also available. Support available to part-time students. Financial award application deadline: 3/15; financial award applicants required to submit FAFSA. *Faculty research:* Systematics, aquatic botany, plant ecology, plant-fungus interactions, plant developmental genetics. *Unit head:* Dr. Patricia A. Zungoli, Chair, 864-656-3137, Fax: 864-656-5065, E-mail: pzngl@clemson.edu. *Application contact:* Dr. Halina Knap, Plant and Environmental Sciences Graduate Coordinator, 864-656-3102, Fax: 864-656-5065, E-mail: hskrpsk@clemson.edu.

Colorado State University, Graduate School, College of Agricultural Sciences, Department of Bioagricultural Sciences and Pest Management, Fort Collins, CO 80523-1177. Offers entomology (MS, PhD); plant pathology and weed science (MS, PhD). Part-time programs available. *Faculty:* 19 full-time (4 women). *Students:* 20 full-time (9 women), 21 part-time (10 women); includes 4 minority (2 American Indian or Alaska Native, non-Hispanic/Latino; 1 Hispanic/Latino; 1 Two or more races, non-Hispanic/Latino), 4 international. Average age 32. 15 applicants, 73% accepted, 9 enrolled. In 2010, 5 master's, 1 doctorate awarded. *Degree requirements:* For master's, comprehensive exam, thesis; for doctorate, comprehensive exam, thesis/dissertation. *Entrance requirements:* For master's, GRE General Test, minimum GPA of 3.0, letters of recommendation; for doctorate, GRE General Test, minimum GPA of 3.0, letters of recommendation, essay. Additional exam requirements/recommendations for international students: Required—TOEFL (minimum score 550 paper-based; 213 computer-based; 80 iBT). *Application deadline:* For fall admission, 1/15 priority date for domestic students, 1/1 priority date for international students; for spring admission, 9/1 priority date for domestic and international students. Applications are processed on a rolling basis. Application fee: $50. Electronic applications accepted. *Expenses:* Tuition, state resident: full-time $7434; part-time $413 per credit. Tuition, nonresident: full-time $19,022; part-time $1057 per credit. Required fees: $1729; $88 per credit. *Financial support:* In 2010–11, 8 fellowships with partial tuition reimbursements (averaging $32,474 per year), 27 research assistantships with full tuition reimbursements (averaging $15,270 per year), 12 teaching assistantships with full tuition reimbursements (averaging $9,900 per year) were awarded; unspecified assistantships and fellowships also available. Financial award application deadline: 1/15; financial award applicants required to submit FAFSA. *Faculty research:* Entomology specialization, plant pathology specialization, weed science specialization, ecology and biodiversity, integrated pest management. Total annual research expenditures: $2.7 million. *Unit head:* Dr. Thomas O. Holtzer, Head, 970-491-5261, Fax: 970-491-3862, E-mail: tholtzer@lamar.colostate.edu. *Application contact:* Janet Dill, Education Coordinator, 970-491-0402, Fax: 970-491-3862, E-mail: janet.dill@colostate.edu.

Colorado State University, Graduate School, College of Agricultural Sciences, Department of Soil and Crop Sciences, Fort Collins, CO 80523-1170. Offers MS, PhD. Part-time programs available. *Faculty:* 20 full-time (4 women), 2 part-time/adjunct (0 women). *Students:* 23 full-time (8 women), 16 part-time (3 women); includes 2 minority (both Black or African American, non-Hispanic/Latino), 15 international. Average age 33. 12 applicants, 75% accepted, 7 enrolled. In 2010, 2 master's, 2 doctorates awarded. Terminal master's awarded for partial completion of doctoral program. *Degree requirements:* For master's, thesis; for doctorate, comprehensive exam, thesis/dissertation, student teaching. *Entrance requirements:* For master's, GRE, minimum GPA of 3.0, appropriate bachelor's degree, letters of recommendation, statement of purpose; for doctorate, GRE, minimum GPA of 3.0, appropriate master's degree, letters of recommendation. Additional exam requirements/recommendations for international students: Required—TOEFL (minimum score 550 paper-based; 213 computer-based; 80 iBT). *Application deadline:* For fall admission, 4/1 priority date for domestic students, 5/1 priority date for international students; for spring admission, 9/1 priority date for domestic students, 10/1 priority date for international students. Application fee: $50. Electronic applications accepted. *Expenses:* Tuition, state resident: full-time $7434; part-time $413 per credit. Tuition, nonresident: full-time $19,022; part-time $1057 per credit. Required fees: $1729; $88 per credit. *Financial support:* In 2010–11, 26 students received support, including 3 fellowships with full tuition reimbursements available (averaging $22,940 per year), 21 research assistantships with full tuition reimbursements available (averaging $17,231 per year), 2 teaching assistantships with full tuition reimbursements available (averaging $8,331 per year); scholarships/grants, unspecified assistantships, and fellowships also available. Financial award application deadline: 2/15; financial award applicants required to submit FAFSA. *Faculty research:* Water quality, soil fertility, soil/plant ecosystems, plant breeding and genetics, cropping systems. Total annual research expenditures: $3.6 million. *Unit head:* Dr. Gary A. Peterson, Head, 970-491-6501, Fax: 970-491-0564, E-mail: gary.peterson@colostate.edu. *Application contact:* Karen Allison, Graduate Contact, 970-491-6295, Fax: 970-491-0564, E-mail: karen.allison@colostate.edu.

Cornell University, Graduate School, Graduate Fields of Agriculture and Life Sciences, Field of Plant Breeding, Ithaca, NY 14853-0001. Offers plant breeding (MPS, MS, PhD); plant genetics (MPS, MS, PhD). *Faculty:* 29 full-time (7 women). *Students:* 33 full-time (19 women); includes 2 Asian, non-Hispanic/Latino; 1 Hispanic/Latino, 16 international. Average age 25. 63 applicants, 27% accepted, 15 enrolled. In 2010, 3 master's, 9 doctorates awarded. Terminal master's awarded for partial completion of doctoral program. *Degree requirements:* For master's, thesis (MS), project paper (MPS); for doctorate, comprehensive exam, thesis/dissertation. *Entrance requirements:* For master's and doctorate, GRE General Test, GRE Subject Test (recommended), 3 letters of recommendation. Additional exam requirements/recommendations for international students: Required—TOEFL (minimum score 550 paper-based; 213 computer-based; 77 iBT). *Application deadline:* For fall admission, 1/15 priority date for domestic students. Application fee: $70. Electronic applications accepted. *Expenses:* Tuition: Full-time $29,500. Required fees: $76. Tuition and fees vary according to degree level and program.

Financial support: In 2010–11, 3 fellowships with full tuition reimbursements, 18 research assistantships with full tuition reimbursements, 2 teaching assistantships with full tuition reimbursements were awarded; institutionally sponsored loans, scholarships/grants, health care benefits, tuition waivers (full and partial), and unspecified assistantships also available. Financial award applicants required to submit FAFSA. *Faculty research:* Crop breeding for improved yield, stress resistance and quality; genetics and genomics of crop plants; applications of molecular biology and bioinformatics to crop improvement; genetic diversity and utilization of wild germplasm; international agriculture. *Unit head:* Director of Graduate Studies, 607-255-2180. *Application contact:* Graduate Field Assistant, 607-255-2180, E-mail: plbrgrad@cornell.edu.

Cornell University, Graduate School, Graduate Fields of Agriculture and Life Sciences, Field of Plant Protection, Ithaca, NY 14853-0001. Offers MPS. *Faculty:* 21 full-time (4 women). *Students:* 1 applicant, 0% accepted, 0 enrolled. *Degree requirements:* For master's, internship, final exam. *Entrance requirements:* For master's, GRE General Test, 3 letters of recommendation. Additional exam requirements/recommendations for international students: Required—TOEFL (minimum score 550 paper-based; 213 computer-based; 77 iBT). *Application deadline:* For fall admission, 4/1 for domestic students. Application fee: $70. Electronic applications accepted. *Expenses:* Tuition: Full-time $29,500. Required fees: $76. Tuition and fees vary according to degree level and program. *Financial support:* Fellowships with full tuition reimbursements, research assistantships with full tuition reimbursements, teaching assistantships with full tuition reimbursements, institutionally sponsored loans, scholarships/grants, health care benefits, tuition waivers (full and partial), and unspecified assistantships available. Financial award applicants required to submit FAFSA. *Faculty research:* Fruit and vegetable crop insects and diseases, systems modeling, biological control, plant protection economics, integrated pest management. *Unit head:* Director of Graduate Studies, 315-787-2323, Fax: 315-787-2326. *Application contact:* Graduate Field Assistant, 315-787-2323, Fax: 315-787-2326, E-mail: plprotection@cornell.edu.

Delaware State University, Graduate Programs, Department of Agriculture and Natural Resources, Program in Plant Science, Dover, DE 19901-2277. Offers MS. *Entrance requirements:* For master's, GRE. Additional exam requirements/recommendations for international students: Required—TOEFL (minimum score 550 paper-based).

Florida Agricultural and Mechanical University, Division of Graduate Studies, Research, and Continuing Education, College of Engineering Science, Technology, and Agriculture, Division of Agricultural Sciences, Tallahassee, FL 32307-3200. Offers agribusiness (MS); animal science (MS); engineering technology (MS); entomology (MS); food science (MS); international programs (MS); plant science (MS). *Degree requirements:* For master's, thesis. *Entrance requirements:* For master's, GRE General Test, minimum GPA of 3.0. Additional exam requirements/recommendations for international students: Required—TOEFL (minimum score 500 paper-based).

Illinois State University, Graduate School, College of Arts and Sciences, Department of Biological Sciences, Normal, IL 61790-2200. Offers animal behavior (MS); bacteriology (MS); biochemistry (MS); biological sciences (MS); biology (PhD); biophysics (MS); biotechnology (MS); botany (MS, PhD); cell biology (MS); conservation biology (MS); developmental biology (MS); ecology (MS, PhD); entomology (MS); evolutionary biology (MS); genetics (MS, PhD); immunology (MS); microbiology (MS, PhD); molecular biology (MS); molecular genetics (MS); neurobiology (MS); neuroscience (MS); parasitology (MS); physiology (MS, PhD); plant biology (MS, PhD); plant molecular biology (MS); plant sciences (MS); structural biology (MS); zoology (MS, PhD). Part-time programs available. *Degree requirements:* For master's, thesis or alternative; for doctorate, variable foreign language requirement, thesis/dissertation, 2 terms of residency. *Entrance requirements:* For master's, GRE General Test, minimum GPA of 2.6 in last 60 hours of course work; for doctorate, GRE General Test. *Faculty research:* Redox balance and drug development in schistosoma mansoni, control of the growth of listeria monocytogenes at low temperature, regulation of cell expansion and microtubule function by SPRI, CRUI: physiology and fitness consequences of different life history phenotypes.

Lehman College of the City University of New York, Division of Natural and Social Sciences, Department of Biological Sciences, Program in Plant Sciences, Bronx, NY 10468-1589. Offers PhD. *Degree requirements:* For doctorate, 2 foreign languages, thesis/dissertation. *Entrance requirements:* For doctorate, GRE General Test.

McGill University, Faculty of Graduate and Postdoctoral Studies, Faculty of Agricultural and Environmental Sciences, Department of Plant Science, Montréal, QC H3A 2T5, Canada. Offers M Sc, M Sc A, PhD, Certificate.

Miami University, Graduate School, College of Arts and Science, Department of Botany, Oxford, OH 45056. Offers MA, MAT, MS, PhD. *Students:* 48 full-time (28 women), 131 part-time (96 women); includes 6 minority (2 Black or African American, non-Hispanic/Latino; 2 Asian, non-Hispanic/Latino; 2 Two or more races, non-Hispanic/Latino), 15 international. Average age 35. In 2010, 17 master's, 4 doctorates awarded. *Entrance requirements:* For master's, GRE General Test, GRE Subject Test (recommended), minimum undergraduate GPA of 3.0 during previous 2 years or 2.75 overall; for doctorate, GRE General Test, GRE Subject Test (recommended), minimum undergraduate GPA of 2.75, 3.0 graduate. Additional exam requirements/recommendations for international students: Required—TOEFL (minimum score 550 paper-based). *Application deadline:* Applications are processed on a rolling basis. Application fee: $50. Electronic applications accepted. *Expenses:* Tuition, state resident: full-time $11,616; part-time $484 per credit hour. Tuition, nonresident: full-time $25,656; part-time $1069 per credit hour. Required fees: $528. *Financial support:* Research assistantships, teaching assistantships with full tuition reimbursements, Federal Work-Study, institutionally sponsored loans, health care benefits, and unspecified assistantships available. Financial award application deadline: 3/1; financial award applicants required to submit FAFSA. *Faculty research:* Evolution of plants, fungi and algae; bioinformatics; molecular biology of plants and cyanobacteria; food web dynamics; plant science education. *Unit head:* Dr. John Kiss, Chair, 513-529-4200, E-mail: kissjz@muohio.edu. *Application contact:* Dr. Richard C. Moore, Graduate Coordinator, 513-529-4278, E-mail: moorerc@muohio.edu.

Michigan State University, The Graduate School, College of Agriculture and Natural Resources, MSU-DOE Plant Research Laboratory, East Lansing, MI 48824. Offers biochemistry and molecular biology (PhD); cellular and molecular biology (PhD); crop and soil sciences (PhD); genetics (PhD); microbiology and molecular genetics (PhD); plant biology (PhD); plant physiology (PhD). Offered jointly with the Department of Energy. *Degree requirements:* For doctorate, comprehensive exam, thesis/dissertation, laboratory rotation, defense of dissertation. *Entrance requirements:* For doctorate, GRE General Test, acceptance into one of the affiliated department programs; 3 letters of recommendation; bachelor's degree or equivalent in life sciences, chemistry, biochemistry, or biophysics; research experience. Electronic applications accepted. *Faculty research:* Role of hormones in the regulation of plant development and physiology, molecular mechanisms associated with signal recognition, development and application of genetic methods and materials, protein routing and function.

Michigan State University, The Graduate School, College of Agriculture and Natural Resources, Program in Plant Breeding and Genetics, East Lansing, MI 48824. Offers MS, PhD. *Entrance requirements:* Additional exam requirements/recommendations for international students: Required—TOEFL. Electronic applications accepted. *Faculty research:* Applied plant breeding and genetics; disease, insect and herbicide resistances; gene isolation and genomics; abiotic stress factors; molecular mapping.

Mississippi State University, College of Agriculture and Life Sciences, Department of Plant and Soil Sciences, Mississippi State, MS 39762. Offers agricultural sciences (PhD), including agronomy (MS, PhD), horticulture (MS, PhD), weed science (MS, PhD); agriculture (MS), including agronomy (MS, PhD), horticulture (MS, PhD), weed science (MS, PhD). *Faculty:* 31 full-time (1 woman), 1 part-time/adjunct (0 women). *Students:* 33 full-time (10 women), 22 part-time (7 women); includes 2 minority (both American Indian or Alaska Native, non-Hispanic/Latino), 18 international. Average age 31. 23 applicants, 39% accepted, 7 enrolled. In 2010, 11 master's, 6 doctorates awarded. *Degree requirements:* For master's, thesis, exit seminar describing thesis research; for doctorate, comprehensive exam, thesis/dissertation, two departmental seminars. *Entrance requirements:* For master's, GRE (weed science), minimum GPA of 2.75 (agronomy/horticulture), 3.0 (weed science); for doctorate, GRE (weed science), minimum GPA of 3.0 (agronomy/horticulture), 3.25 (weed science). Additional exam requirements/recommendations for international students: Required—TOEFL (minimum score 550 paper-based; 213 computer-based; 79 iBT); Recommended—IELTS (minimum score 6.5). *Application deadline:* For fall admission, 7/1 for domestic students, 5/1 for international students; for spring admission, 10/1 for domestic students, 9/1 for international students. Applications are processed on a rolling basis. Application fee: $40. Electronic applications accepted. *Expenses:* Tuition, state resident: full-time $2730.50; part-time $304 per credit hour. Tuition, nonresident: full-time $6901; part-time $767 per credit hour. *Financial support:* In 2010–11, 29 research assistantships (averaging $14,353 per year), 2 teaching assistantships (averaging $15,542 per year) were awarded; Federal Work-Study, institutionally sponsored loans, scholarships/grants, and unspecified assistantships also available. Financial award application deadline: 4/1; financial award applicants required to submit FAFSA. *Unit head:* Dr. Daniel Reynolds, Professor/Interim Department Head, 662-325-2311, Fax: 662-325-8742, E-mail: dreynolds@pss.msstate.edu. *Application contact:* Dr. William Kingery, Graduate Coordinator, 662-325-2748, Fax: 662-325-8742, E-mail: wkingery@pss.msstate.edu.

Missouri State University, Graduate College, College of Natural and Applied Sciences, Department of Agriculture, Springfield, MO 65897. Offers natural and applied science (MNAS), including agriculture (MNAS, MS Ed); plant science (MS); secondary education (MS Ed), including agriculture (MNAS, MS Ed). Part-time programs available. *Degree requirements:* For master's, comprehensive exam, thesis or alternative. *Entrance requirements:* For master's, GRE (MS plant science, MNAS), 9-12 teacher certification (MS Ed), minimum GPA of 3.0 (MS plant science, MNAS). Additional exam requirements/recommendations for international students: Required—TOEFL (minimum score 550 paper-based; 213 computer-based; 79 iBT). Electronic applications accepted. *Expenses:* Tuition, state resident: full-time $3348; part-time $186 per credit hour. Tuition, nonresident: full-time $6696; part-time $372 per credit hour. Required fees: $238 per semester. Tuition and fees vary according to course level, course load and program. *Faculty research:* Grapevine biotechnology, agricultural marketing, Asian elephant reproduction, poultry science, integrated pest management.

Montana State University, College of Graduate Studies, College of Agriculture, Department of Plant Sciences and Plant Pathology, Bozeman, MT 59717. Offers plant pathology (MS); plant sciences (MS, PhD), including plant genetics (PhD), plant pathology (PhD). Part-time programs available. *Faculty:* 24 full-time (5 women), 2 part-time/adjunct (0 women). *Students:* 3 full-time (1 woman), 14 part-time (6 women); includes 2 minority (1 Asian, non-Hispanic/Latino; 1 Two or more races, non-Hispanic/Latino), 5 international. Average age 29. 17 applicants, 41% accepted, 6 enrolled. In 2010, 5 master's awarded. *Degree requirements:* For master's, comprehensive exam; for doctorate, comprehensive exam, thesis/dissertation. *Entrance requirements:* For master's, GRE General Test, minimum GPA of 3.0; for doctorate, GRE General Test. Additional exam requirements/recommendations for international students: Required—TOEFL (minimum score 550 paper-based; 213 computer-based). *Application deadline:* For fall admission, 7/15 priority date for domestic students, 5/15 priority date for international students; for spring admission, 12/1 priority date for domestic students, 10/1 priority date for international students. Applications are processed on a rolling basis. Application fee: $30. Electronic applications accepted. *Expenses:* Tuition, state resident: full-time $5553.90. Tuition, nonresident: full-time $14,646. Required fees: $1233. *Financial support:* In 2010–11, 9 students received support, including 4 research assistantships with tuition reimbursements available (averaging $32,665 per year), 5 teaching assistantships with tuition reimbursements available (averaging $16,271 per year); health care benefits and unspecified assistantships also available. Financial award application deadline: 3/1; financial award applicants required to submit FAFSA. *Faculty research:* Plant genetics, plant metabolism, plant microbe interactions, plant pathology, entomology research. Total annual research expenditures: $3.2 million. *Unit head:* Dr. John Sherwood, Head, 406-994-5153, Fax: 406-994-7600, E-mail: sherwood@montana.edu. *Application contact:* Dr. Carl A. Fox, Vice Provost for Graduate Education, 406-994-4145, Fax: 406-994-7433, E-mail: gradstudy@montana.edu.

New Mexico State University, Graduate School, College of Agricultural, Consumer and Environmental Sciences, Department of Entomology, Plant Pathology and Weed Science, Las Cruces, NM 88003-8001. Offers agricultural biology (MS). Part-time programs available. *Faculty:* 7 full-time (2 women). *Students:* 11 full-time (5 women), 4 part-time (2 women); includes 5 minority (4 Hispanic/Latino; 1 Two or more races, non-Hispanic/Latino), 2 international. Average age 27. 14 applicants, 79% accepted, 9 enrolled. In 2010, 5 master's awarded. *Degree requirements:* For master's, comprehensive exam, thesis. *Entrance requirements:* For master's, GRE General Test. *Application deadline:* For fall admission, 7/1 priority date for domestic students; for spring admission, 11/1 priority date for domestic students. Applications are processed on a rolling basis. Application fee: $30 ($50 for international students). Electronic applications accepted. *Expenses:* Tuition, state resident: full-time $4536; part-time $242 per credit. Tuition, nonresident: full-time $15,816; part-time $712 per credit. Required fees: $636 per term. *Financial support:* In 2010–11, 8 students received support, including 6 research assistantships with full tuition reimbursements available (averaging $20,550 per year), 2 teaching assistantships with partial tuition reimbursements available (averaging $14,225 per year); career-related internships or fieldwork and health care benefits also available. Financial award application deadline: 3/1. *Faculty research:* Integrated pest management, pesticide application and safety, livestock ectoparasite research, biotechnology, nematology. *Unit head:* Dr. Jill Schroeder, Interim Head, 575-646-3225, Fax: 575-646-8087, E-mail: jischroe@nmsu.edu. *Application contact:* Cindy Bullard, Intermediate Administrative Assistant, 575-646-1145, Fax: 575-646-8087, E-mail: cbullard@nmsu.edu.

New Mexico State University, Graduate School, College of Agricultural, Consumer and Environmental Sciences, Department of Plant and Environmental Sciences, Las Cruces, NM 88003-8001. Offers horticulture (MS); plant and environmental sciences (MS, PhD). Part-time programs available. *Faculty:* 19 full-time (4 women). *Students:* 48 full-time (20 women), 8 part-time (3 women); includes 12 minority (1 American Indian or Alaska Native, non-Hispanic/Latino; 10 Hispanic/Latino; 1 Two or more races, non-Hispanic/Latino), 21 international. Average age 31. 29 applicants, 86% accepted, 15 enrolled. In 2010, 11 master's, 4 doctorates awarded. Terminal master's awarded for partial completion of doctoral program. *Degree requirements:* For master's, thesis; for doctorate, one foreign language, comprehensive exam, thesis/dissertation. *Entrance requirements:* For master's, minimum GPA of 3.0; for doctorate, minimum GPA of 3.3. Additional exam requirements/recommendations for international students: Required—TOEFL. *Application deadline:* For fall admission, 7/1 priority date for domestic students; for spring admission, 11/1 priority date for domestic students. Applications are processed on a rolling basis. Application fee: $30 ($50 for international students). Electronic applications accepted. *Expenses:* Tuition, state resident: full-time $4536; part-time $242 per credit. Tuition, nonresident: full-time $15,816; part-time $712 per credit. Required fees: $636 per term. *Financial support:* In 2010–11, 11 students received support, including 30 research assistantships with partial tuition reimbursements available (averaging $22,214 per year), 10 teaching assistantships with partial tuition reimbursements available (averaging $14,330 per year); career-related internships or fieldwork, Federal Work-Study, scholarships/grants, health care benefits, and unspecified assistantships also available. Support available to part-time students. Financial award application deadline: 3/1. *Faculty research:* Plant breeding and

Plant Sciences

New Mexico State University (continued)
genetics, molecular biology, plant physiology, soil science and environmental remediation, urban horticulture and turfgrass management. *Unit head:* Dr. Richard Pratt, Head, 575-646-3406, Fax: 575-646-6041, E-mail: ricpratt@nmsu.edu. *Application contact:* Esther Ramirez, Information Contact, 575-646-3406, Fax: 575-646-6041, E-mail: esramire@nmsu.edu.

North Carolina Agricultural and Technical State University, Graduate School, School of Agriculture and Environmental Sciences, Department of Natural Resources and Environmental Design, Greensboro, NC 27411. Offers plant, soil and environmental science (MS). Part-time and evening/weekend programs available. *Degree requirements:* For master's, comprehensive exam, thesis optional, qualifying exam. *Entrance requirements:* For master's, GRE General Test, minimum GPA of 3.0. *Faculty research:* Soil parameters and compaction of forest site, controlled traffic effects on soil, improving soybean and vegetable crops.

North Dakota State University, College of Graduate and Interdisciplinary Studies, College of Agriculture, Food Systems, and Natural Resources, Department of Plant Sciences, Fargo, ND 58108. Offers crop and weed sciences (MS); horticulture (MS); natural resource management (MS); plant sciences (PhD). Part-time programs available. *Faculty:* 36 full-time (3 women), 23 part-time/adjunct (3 women). *Students:* 44 full-time (14 women), 16 part-time (7 women); includes 4 Hispanic/Latino, 19 international. Average age 26. 44 applicants, 45% accepted. In 2010, 11 master's, 6 doctorates awarded. *Degree requirements:* For master's, thesis; for doctorate, thesis/dissertation. *Entrance requirements:* Additional exam requirements/recommendations for international students: Required—TOEFL (minimum score 525 paper-based; 197 computer-based; 71 iBT). *Application deadline:* Applications are processed on a rolling basis. Application fee: $45 ($60 for international students). Electronic applications accepted. *Financial support:* In 2010–11, 2 fellowships (averaging $19,950 per year), 64 research assistantships were awarded; teaching assistantships, Federal Work-Study and institutionally sponsored loans also available. Financial award application deadline: 4/15. *Faculty research:* Biotechnology, weed control science, plant breeding, plant genetics, crop physiology. Total annual research expenditures: $880,000. *Unit head:* Dr. Al Schneiter, Head, 701-231-7971, Fax: 701-231-8474, E-mail: albert.schneiter@ndsu.edu. *Application contact:* Dr. Al Schneiter, Head, 701-231-7971, Fax: 701-231-8474, E-mail: albert.schneiter@ndsu.edu.

Oklahoma State University, College of Agricultural Science and Natural Resources, Department of Horticulture and Landscape Architecture, Stillwater, OK 74078. Offers agriculture (M Ag); crop science (PhD); environmental science (PhD); horticulture (MS); plant science (PhD). *Faculty:* 21 full-time (2 women), 1 (woman) part-time/adjunct. *Students:* 1 (woman) full-time, 16 part-time (8 women); includes 1 Black or African American, non-Hispanic/Latino; 1 American Indian or Alaska Native, non-Hispanic/Latino; 1 Hispanic/Latino, 9 international. Average age 30. 12 applicants, 33% accepted, 4 enrolled. In 2010, 3 master's awarded. *Degree requirements:* For master's, thesis (for some programs); for doctorate, comprehensive exam, thesis/dissertation. *Entrance requirements:* For master's and doctorate, GRE or GMAT. Additional exam requirements/recommendations for international students: Required—TOEFL (minimum score 550 paper-based; 79 iBT). *Application deadline:* For fall admission, 3/1 priority date for international students; for spring admission, 8/1 priority date for international students. Applications are processed on a rolling basis. Application fee: $40 ($75 for international students). Electronic applications accepted. *Expenses:* Tuition, state resident: full-time $3716; part-time $154.85 per credit hour. Tuition, nonresident: full-time $14,892; part-time $621 per credit hour. Required fees: $2044; $85.20 per credit hour. One-time fee: $50. Tuition and fees vary according to course load and campus/location. *Financial support:* In 2010–11, 14 research assistantships (averaging $14,037 per year) were awarded; career-related internships or fieldwork, Federal Work-Study, scholarships/grants, health care benefits, tuition waivers (partial), and unspecified assistantships also available. Support available to part-time students. Financial award application deadline: 3/1; financial award applicants required to submit FAFSA. *Faculty research:* Stress and postharvest physiology; water utilization and runoff; IPM systems and nursery, turf, floriculture, vegetable, net and fruit produces and natural resources, food extraction, and processing; public garden management. *Unit head:* Dr. Dale Maronek, Head, 405-744-5414, Fax: 405-744-9709. *Application contact:* Dr. Gordon Emslie, Dean, 405-744-6368, Fax: 405-744-0355, E-mail: grad-i@okstate.edu.

Oklahoma State University, College of Agricultural Science and Natural Resources, Department of Plant and Soil Sciences, Stillwater, OK 74078. Offers crop science (PhD); environmental science (PhD); plant and soil sciences (MS); plant science (PhD); soil science (M Ag, PhD). *Faculty:* 30 full-time (4 women), 4 part-time/adjunct (1 woman). *Students:* 20 full-time (6 women), 42 part-time (19 women); includes 1 Black or African American, non-Hispanic/Latino; 1 American Indian or Alaska Native, non-Hispanic/Latino; 1 Asian, non-Hispanic/Latino, 31 international. Average age 28. 48 applicants, 33% accepted, 11 enrolled. In 2010, 11 master's, 1 doctorate awarded. *Degree requirements:* For master's, thesis; for doctorate, comprehensive exam, thesis/dissertation. *Entrance requirements:* For master's and doctorate, GRE or GMAT. Additional exam requirements/recommendations for international students: Required—TOEFL (minimum score 550 paper-based; 79 iBT). *Application deadline:* For fall admission, 3/1 priority date for international students; for spring admission, 8/1 priority date for international students. Applications are processed on a rolling basis. Application fee: $40 ($75 for international students). Electronic applications accepted. *Expenses:* Tuition, state resident: full-time $3716; part-time $154.85 per credit hour. Tuition, nonresident: full-time $14,892; part-time $621 per credit hour. Required fees: $2044; $85.20 per credit hour. One-time fee: $50. Tuition and fees vary according to course load and campus/location. *Financial support:* In 2010–11, 48 research assistantships (averaging $14,676 per year) were awarded; career-related internships or fieldwork, Federal Work-Study, scholarships/grants, health care benefits, tuition waivers (partial), and unspecified assistantships also available. Support available to part-time students. Financial award application deadline: 3/1; financial award applicants required to submit FAFSA. *Faculty research:* Crop science, weed science, rangeland ecology and management, biotechnology, breeding and genetics. *Unit head:* Dr. David R. Porter, Head, 405-744-6130, Fax: 405-744-5269. *Application contact:* Dr. Gordon Emslie, Dean, 405-744-6368, Fax: 405-744-0355, E-mail: grad-i@okstate.edu.

Oklahoma State University, College of Arts and Sciences, Department of Botany, Stillwater, OK 74078. Offers botany (MS); environmental science (MS, PhD); plant science (PhD). *Faculty:* 13 full-time (4 women), 1 (woman) part-time/adjunct. *Students:* 12 part-time (5 women); includes 1 American Indian or Alaska Native, non-Hispanic/Latino; 1 Hispanic/Latino, 2 international. Average age 29. 5 applicants, 80% accepted, 3 enrolled. In 2010, 3 master's awarded. *Degree requirements:* For master's, thesis; for doctorate, comprehensive exam, thesis/dissertation. *Entrance requirements:* For master's and doctorate, GRE or GMAT. Additional exam requirements/recommendations for international students: Required—TOEFL (minimum score 550 paper-based; 79 iBT). *Application deadline:* For fall admission, 3/1 priority date for international students; for spring admission, 8/1 priority date for international students. Applications are processed on a rolling basis. Application fee: $40 ($75 for international students). Electronic applications accepted. *Expenses:* Tuition, state resident: full-time $3716; part-time $154.85 per credit hour. Tuition, nonresident: full-time $14,892; part-time $621 per credit hour. Required fees: $2044; $85.20 per credit hour. One-time fee: $50. Tuition and fees vary according to course load and campus/location. *Financial support:* In 2010–11, 4 research assistantships (averaging $16,635 per year), 12 teaching assistantships (averaging $14,896 per year) were awarded; career-related internships or fieldwork, Federal Work-Study, scholarships/grants, health care benefits, tuition waivers (partial), and unspecified assistantships also available. Support available to part-time students. Financial award application deadline: 3/1; financial award applicants required to submit FAFSA. *Faculty research:* Ethnobotany, developmental genetics of Arabidopsis, biological roles of Plasmodesmata, community ecology and biodiversity, nutrient cycling in grassland ecosystems. *Unit head:* Dr. Linda Watson, Head, 405-744-5559, Fax: 405-744-7074. *Application contact:* Dr. Gordon Emslie, Dean, 405-744-6368, Fax: 405-744-0355, E-mail: grad-i@okstate.edu.

Oklahoma State University, Graduate College, Stillwater, OK 74078. Offers environmental science (MS); international studies (MS); natural and applied science (MS); photonics (PhD); plant science (PhD). Programs are interdisciplinary. *Faculty:* 2 full-time (1 woman). *Students:* 69 full-time (40 women), 131 part-time (68 women); includes 13 Black or African American, non-Hispanic/Latino; 15 American Indian or Alaska Native, non-Hispanic/Latino; 8 Asian, non-Hispanic/Latino; 8 Hispanic/Latino, 70 international. Average age 30. 690 applicants, 74% accepted, 75 enrolled. In 2010, 66 master's, 7 doctorates awarded. *Degree requirements:* For master's, thesis (for some programs); for doctorate, comprehensive exam, thesis/dissertation. *Entrance requirements:* For master's and doctorate, GRE or GMAT. Additional exam requirements/recommendations for international students: Required—TOEFL (minimum score 550 paper-based; 79 iBT). *Application deadline:* For fall admission, 3/1 priority date for international students; for spring admission, 8/1 priority date for international students. Applications are processed on a rolling basis. Application fee: $40 ($75 for international students). Electronic applications accepted. *Expenses:* Tuition, state resident: full-time $3716; part-time $154.85 per credit hour. Tuition, nonresident: full-time $14,892; part-time $621 per credit hour. Required fees: $2044; $85.20 per credit hour. One-time fee: $50. Tuition and fees vary according to course load and campus/location. *Financial support:* In 2010–11, 2 research assistantships (averaging $12,900 per year) were awarded; career-related internships or fieldwork, Federal Work-Study, scholarships/grants, health care benefits, tuition waivers (partial), and unspecified assistantships also available. Support available to part-time students. Financial award application deadline: 3/1; financial award applicants required to submit FAFSA. *Unit head:* Dr. Gordon Emslie, Dean, 405-744-6368, Fax: 405-744-0355, E-mail: grad-i@okstate.edu. *Application contact:* Dr. Susan Mathew, Coordinator of Admissions, 405-744-6368, Fax: 405-744-0355, E-mail: grad-i@okstate.edu.

South Dakota State University, Graduate School, College of Agriculture and Biological Sciences, Department of Plant Science, Brookings, SD 57007. Offers agronomy (PhD); biological sciences (PhD); plant science (MS). *Degree requirements:* For master's, thesis (for some programs), oral exam; for doctorate, comprehensive exam, thesis/dissertation, preliminary oral and written exams. *Entrance requirements:* Additional exam requirements/recommendations for international students: Required—TOEFL (minimum score 560 paper-based; 220 computer-based; 83 iBT).

Southern Illinois University Carbondale, Graduate School, College of Agriculture, Department of Plant, Soil, and General Agriculture, Carbondale, IL 62901-4701. Offers horticultural science (MS); plant and soil science (MS). *Degree requirements:* For master's, thesis. *Entrance requirements:* For master's, minimum GPA of 2.7. Additional exam requirements/recommendations for international students: Required—TOEFL. *Faculty research:* Herbicides, fertilizers, agriculture education, landscape design, plant breeding.

State University of New York College of Environmental Science and Forestry, Department of Environmental and Forest Biology, Syracuse, NY 13210-2779. Offers applied ecology (MPS); chemical ecology (MPS, MS, PhD); conservation biology (MPS, MS, PhD); ecology (MPS, MS, PhD); entomology (MPS, MS, PhD); environmental interpretation (MPS, MS, PhD); environmental physiology (MPS, MS, PhD); fish and wildlife biology and management (MPS, MS, PhD); forest pathology and mycology (MPS, MS, PhD); plant biotechnology (MPS); plant science and biotechnology (MPS, MS, PhD). *Degree requirements:* For master's, thesis (for some programs); for doctorate, comprehensive exam, thesis/dissertation. *Entrance requirements:* For master's and doctorate, GRE General Test, GRE Subject Test, minimum GPA of 3.0. Additional exam requirements/recommendations for international students: Required—TOEFL (minimum score 550 paper-based; 213 computer-based; 80 iBT), IELTS (minimum score 6). *Expenses:* Tuition, state resident: full-time $8370; part-time $349 per credit hour. Tuition, nonresident: full-time $13,780. Required fees: $30.30 per credit hour. $20 per year. *Faculty research:* Ecology, fish and wildlife biology and management, plant science, entomology.

Texas A&M University, College of Agriculture and Life Sciences, Department of Soil and Crop Sciences, College Station, TX 77843. Offers agronomy (M Agr, MS, PhD); food science and technology (MS, PhD); genetics (PhD); molecular and environmental plant sciences (MS, PhD); plant breeding (MS, PhD); soil science (MS, PhD). *Faculty:* 36. *Students:* 94 full-time (35 women), 30 part-time (7 women); includes 14 minority (3 Black or African American, non-Hispanic/Latino; 1 American Indian or Alaska Native, non-Hispanic/Latino; 3 Asian, non-Hispanic/Latino; 7 Hispanic/Latino), 36 international. Average age 26. In 2010, 11 master's, 3 doctorates awarded. *Degree requirements:* For master's, thesis; for doctorate, thesis/dissertation. *Entrance requirements:* For master's and doctorate, GRE General Test. Additional exam requirements/recommendations for international students: Required—TOEFL. *Application deadline:* For fall admission, 3/1 priority date for domestic students; for spring admission, 8/1 for domestic students. Applications are processed on a rolling basis. Application fee: $50 ($75 for international students). *Financial support:* In 2010–11, fellowships (averaging $16,000 per year), research assistantships with partial tuition reimbursements (averaging $15,000 per year) were awarded; career-related internships or fieldwork, Federal Work-Study, and institutionally sponsored loans also available. *Faculty research:* Soil and crop management, turfgrass science, weed science, cereal chemistry, food protein chemistry. *Unit head:* Dr. David D. Baltensperger, Department Head, 979-845-3001, E-mail: dbaltensperger@ag.tamu.edu. *Application contact:* Dr. David D. Baltensperger, Department Head, 979-845-3001, E-mail: dbaltensperger@ag.tamu.edu.

Texas A&M University–Kingsville, College of Graduate Studies, College of Agriculture and Home Economics, Program in Plant and Soil Sciences, Kingsville, TX 78363. Offers MS, PhD. *Degree requirements:* For master's, comprehensive exam, thesis or alternative. *Entrance requirements:* For master's, GRE General Test, minimum GPA of 3.0. Additional exam requirements/recommendations for international students: Required—TOEFL.

Texas Tech University, Graduate School, College of Agricultural Sciences and Natural Resources, Department of Plant and Soil Science, Lubbock, TX 79409. Offers crop science (MS); horticulture (MS); plant and soil science (PhD); plant protection (MS); soil science (MS); JD/MS. Part-time programs available. Postbaccalaureate distance learning degree programs offered (no on-campus study). *Faculty:* 14 full-time (3 women), 6 part-time/adjunct (0 women). *Students:* 57 full-time (23 women), 42 part-time (20 women); includes 3 Black or African American, non-Hispanic/Latino; 1 Asian, non-Hispanic/Latino; 4 Hispanic/Latino, 31 international. Average age 30. 64 applicants, 52% accepted, 22 enrolled. In 2010, 13 master's, 7 doctorates awarded. *Degree requirements:* For master's, thesis or alternative; for doctorate, thesis/dissertation. *Entrance requirements:* For master's and doctorate, GRE General Test, formal approval from departmental committee. Additional exam requirements/recommendations for international students: Required—TOEFL (minimum score 550 paper-based; 213 computer-based; 79 iBT). *Application deadline:* For fall admission, 6/1 priority date for domestic students, 1/15 priority date for international students; for spring admission, 9/1 priority date for domestic students, 6/15 priority date for international students. Applications are processed on a rolling basis. Application fee: $50 ($75 for international students). Electronic applications accepted. *Expenses:* Tuition, state resident: full-time $5495.76; part-time $228.99 per credit hour. Tuition, nonresident: full-time $12,936; part-time $538.99 per credit hour. Required fees: $2674; $36 per credit hour. $905 per semester. *Financial support:* In 2010–11, 55 students received support, including 18 research assistantships with partial tuition reimbursements available (averaging $3,594 per year), 2 teaching assistantships with partial tuition reimbursements available (averaging $5,398 per year). Financial award application deadline: 4/15; financial award applicants required to submit FAFSA. *Faculty research:* Molecular and cellular biology of plant stress, physiology/genetics of crop production in semiarid conditions, agricultural bioterrorism, improvement of native plants, soil science and management. Total annual research

expenditures: $4.9 million. *Unit head:* Dr. Richard Zartman, Chair, 806-742-2838, Fax: 806-742-0775, E-mail: richard.zartman@ttu.edu. *Application contact:* Dr. Eric Hequet, Graduate Adviser, 806-742-2837, Fax: 806-742-0775, E-mail: eric.hequet@ttu.edu.

Tuskegee University, Graduate Programs, College of Agricultural, Environmental and Natural Sciences, Department of Agricultural Sciences, Program in Plant and Soil Sciences, Tuskegee, AL 36088. Offers MS. *Faculty:* 13 full-time (1 woman), 2 part-time/adjunct (1 woman). *Students:* 2 full-time (both women), 2 part-time (both women); includes 3 Black or African American, non-Hispanic/Latino, 1 international. Average age 30. In 2010, 6 master's awarded. *Degree requirements:* For master's, thesis. *Entrance requirements:* For master's, GRE General Test. Additional exam requirements/recommendations for international students: Required—TOEFL (minimum score 500 paper-based; 60 computer-based). *Application deadline:* For fall admission, 7/15 for domestic students. Applications are processed on a rolling basis. Application fee: $25 ($35 for international students). *Expenses:* Tuition: Full-time $16,100; part-time $665 per credit hour. Required fees: $650. *Financial support:* Application deadline: 4/15. *Application contact:* Dr. Robert L. Laney, Vice President/Director Admissions and Enrollment Management, 334-727-8580, Fax: 334-727-5750, E-mail: planey@tuskegee.edu.

The University of Arizona, College of Agriculture and Life Sciences, Department of Plant Sciences, Tucson, AZ 85721. Offers plant pathology (PhD); plant sciences (MS, PhD). Part-time programs available. *Faculty:* 18 full-time (6 women), 1 (woman) part-time/adjunct. *Students:* 24 full-time (11 women), 1 part-time (0 women); includes 1 Asian, non-Hispanic/Latino; 1 Hispanic/Latino; 2 Two or more races, non-Hispanic/Latino, 11 international. Average age 30. 41 applicants, 22% accepted, 5 enrolled. In 2010, 3 master's, 4 doctorates awarded. *Degree requirements:* For master's, thesis or alternative; for doctorate, thesis/dissertation. *Entrance requirements:* For master's, GRE General Test, GRE Subject Test (biology or chemistry recommended), minimum GPA of 3.0, academic resume, 3 letters of recommendation; for doctorate, GRE General Test, GRE Subject Test (biology or chemistry recommended), minimum GPA of 3.0, academic resume, statement of interest, 3 letters of recommendation. Additional exam requirements/recommendations for international students: Required—TOEFL. *Application deadline:* For fall admission, 12/1 for domestic and international students; for spring admission, 6/1 for domestic and international students. Applications are processed on a rolling basis. Application fee: $75. Electronic applications accepted. *Expenses:* Tuition, state resident: full-time $7692. *Financial support:* In 2010–11, 16 research assistantships with full tuition reimbursements (averaging $19,238 per year), 5 teaching assistantships with full tuition reimbursements (averaging $20,831 per year) were awarded; fellowships, career-related internships or fieldwork, Federal Work-Study, scholarships/grants, health care benefits, tuition waivers (partial), and unspecified assistantships also available. *Faculty research:* Molecular/cell biology, plant genetics and physiology, agronomic and horticultural production (including turf and ornamentals). Total annual research expenditures: $6.8 million. *Unit head:* Dr. Robert T. Leonard, Head, 520-621-1945. *Application contact:* Dr. Rachel W. Pfister, Graduate Coordinator/Advisor, 520-621-8423, Fax: 520-621-7186, E-mail: pfister@ag.arizona.edu.

University of Arkansas, Graduate School, Dale Bumpers College of Agricultural, Food and Life Sciences, Interdepartmental Program in Plant Science, Fayetteville, AR 72701-1201. Offers PhD. *Students:* 3 full-time (1 woman), 10 part-time (4 women), 6 international. 9 applicants, 22% accepted. In 2010, 3 doctorates awarded. *Degree requirements:* For doctorate, thesis/dissertation. *Application deadline:* For fall admission, 4/1 for international students; for spring admission, 10/1 for international students. Applications are processed on a rolling basis. Application fee: $40 ($50 for international students). Electronic applications accepted. *Financial support:* In 2010–11, 12 research assistantships were awarded; fellowships with tuition reimbursements, teaching assistantships, career-related internships or fieldwork and Federal Work-Study also available. Support available to part-time students. Financial award application deadline: 4/1; financial award applicants required to submit FAFSA. *Unit head:* Dr. A. Rick Bennett, Department Head, 479-575-2445, E-mail: rbennett@uark.edu. *Application contact:* Dr. Ioannis Tzanetakis, Graduate Coordinator, 479-575-3180, E-mail: itzaneta@uark.edu.

The University of British Columbia, Faculty of Land and Food Systems, Plant Science Program, Vancouver, BC V6T 1Z1, Canada. Offers M Sc, PhD. Part-time programs available. *Degree requirements:* For master's, thesis; for doctorate, comprehensive exam, thesis/dissertation. *Entrance requirements:* Additional exam requirements/recommendations for international students: Required—TOEFL (minimum score 577 paper-based; 233 computer-based; 90 iBT), IELTS (minimum score 6.5). Electronic applications accepted. Tuition charges are reported in Canadian dollars. *Expenses:* Tuition, area resident: Full-time $4179 Canadian dollars. International tuition: $7344 Canadian dollars full-time. *Faculty research:* Plant physiology and biochemistry, biotechnology, plant protection (insect, weeds, and diseases), plant breeding, plant-environment interaction.

University of California, Riverside, Graduate Division, Department of Botany and Plant Sciences, Riverside, CA 92521-0102. Offers plant biology (MS, PhD), including plant genetics (PhD). Part-time programs available. Terminal master's awarded for partial completion of doctoral program. *Degree requirements:* For master's, comprehensive exams or thesis; for doctorate, thesis/dissertation, qualifying exams. *Entrance requirements:* For master's and doctorate, GRE General Test, minimum GPA of 3.2. Additional exam requirements/recommendations for international students: Required—TOEFL (minimum score 550 paper-based; 213 computer-based; 80 iBT). Electronic applications accepted. *Faculty research:* Agricultural plant biology; biochemistry and physiology; cellular, molecular and developmental biology; ecology, evolution, systematics and ethnobotany; genetics, genomics and bioinformatics.

University of Connecticut, Graduate School, College of Agriculture and Natural Resources, Department of Plant Science, Storrs, CT 06269. Offers plant and soil sciences (MS, PhD). Terminal master's awarded for partial completion of doctoral program. *Degree requirements:* For master's, comprehensive exam; for doctorate, thesis/dissertation. *Entrance requirements:* For master's and doctorate, GRE General Test, GRE Subject Test. Additional exam requirements/recommendations for international students: Required—TOEFL (minimum score 550 paper-based; 213 computer-based). Electronic applications accepted.

University of Delaware, College of Agriculture and Natural Resources, Department of Plant and Soil Sciences, Newark, DE 19716. Offers MS, PhD. Part-time programs available. Terminal master's awarded for partial completion of doctoral program. *Degree requirements:* For master's, thesis; for doctorate, thesis/dissertation. *Entrance requirements:* For master's and doctorate, GRE General Test. Additional exam requirements/recommendations for international students: Required—TOEFL (minimum score 550 paper-based; 213 computer-based). Electronic applications accepted. *Faculty research:* Soil chemistry, plant and cell tissue culture, plant breeding and genetics, soil physics, soil biochemistry, plant molecular biology, soil microbiology.

University of Florida, Graduate School, College of Agricultural and Life Sciences, Program in Plant Medicine, Gainesville, FL 32611. Offers DPM. Part-time programs available. *Students:* 26 full-time (11 women), 2 part-time (0 women); includes 3 Hispanic/Latino, 9 international. Average age 29. 16 applicants, 56% accepted, 9 enrolled. In 2010, 6 doctorates awarded. *Degree requirements:* For doctorate, comprehensive exam, thesis/dissertation. *Entrance requirements:* For doctorate, GRE Test, minimum GPA of 3.0. Additional exam requirements/recommendations for international students: Required—TOEFL (minimum score 550 paper-based; 213 computer-based; 80 iBT), IELTS (minimum score 6). *Application deadline:* For fall admission, 6/15 for domestic and international students; for spring admission, 9/15 for domestic and international students. Application fee: $30. *Expenses:* Tuition, state resident: full-time $10,915.92. Tuition, nonresident: full-time $28,309. *Financial support:* In 2010–11, 16 students received support, including 10 fellowships, 6 research assistantships (averaging $15,013 per year). Financial award applicants required to submit FAFSA. Total annual research expenditures: $120,571. *Unit head:* Eric Triplett, PhD, Director, 352-392-5430, Fax: 352-392-7348, E-mail: ewt@ufl.edu. *Application contact:* Robert J. McGovern, PhD, Graduate Coordinator, 352-392-3631 Ext. 213, Fax: 352-392-8988, E-mail: rjmcgov@ufl.edu.

University of Georgia, College of Agricultural and Environmental Sciences, Institute of Plant Breeding, Genetics and Genomics, Athens, GA 30602. Offers MS, PhD. *Students:* 22 full-time (7 women), 5 part-time (1 woman), 12 international. 17 applicants, 24% accepted, 3 enrolled. In 2010, 3 master's awarded. *Expenses:* Tuition, state resident: full-time $7200; part-time $344 per credit hour. Tuition, nonresident: full-time $21,900; part-time $944 per credit hour. Tuition and fees vary according to course load and program. *Financial support:* Tuition waivers and unspecified assistantships available. *Unit head:* Dr. E. Charles Brummer, Director, 706-542-8847, Fax: 706-583-8120, E-mail: pbgg@uga.edu. *Application contact:* Dr. Dayton Wilde, Graduate Coordinator, 706-542-5607, E-mail: pbgg@uga.edu.

University of Hawaii at Manoa, Graduate Division, College of Tropical Agriculture and Human Resources, Department of Plant and Environmental Protection Sciences, Honolulu, HI 96822. Offers entomology (MS, PhD); tropical plant pathology (MS, PhD). Part-time programs available. *Faculty:* 48 full-time (9 women), 12 part-time/adjunct (6 women). *Students:* 26 full-time (13 women), 5 part-time (1 woman); includes 6 minority (3 Asian, non-Hispanic/Latino; 3 Two or more races, non-Hispanic/Latino), 16 international. Average age 33. 28 applicants, 64% accepted, 9 enrolled. In 2010, 2 master's awarded. Terminal master's awarded for partial completion of doctoral program. *Degree requirements:* For master's, thesis optional; for doctorate, comprehensive exam, thesis/dissertation. *Entrance requirements:* For master's and doctorate, GRE General Test. Additional exam requirements/recommendations for international students: Required—TOEFL (minimum score 500 paper-based; 173 computer-based; 61 iBT), IELTS (minimum score 5). *Application deadline:* For fall admission, 3/1 for domestic and international students; for spring admission, 10/1 for domestic and international students. *Financial support:* In 2010–11, 7 fellowships, 24 research assistantships were awarded; teaching assistantships, tuition waivers (full) also available. *Faculty research:* Nematology, virology, mycology, bacteriology, epidemiology. *Unit head:* Dr. J. Kenneth Grace, Chair, 808-956-7076, Fax: 808-956-2428. *Application contact:* Dr. J. Kenneth Grace, Chair, 808-956-7076, Fax: 808-956-2428.

University of Idaho, College of Graduate Studies, College of Agricultural and Life Sciences, Department of Plant, Soil, and Entomological Sciences, Program in Plant Science, Moscow, ID 83844-2282. Offers MS, PhD. *Students:* 11 full-time, 5 part-time. Average age 35. In 2010, 2 master's awarded. *Degree requirements:* For doctorate, thesis/dissertation. *Entrance requirements:* For master's and doctorate, GRE General Test, minimum GPA of 3.0. *Application deadline:* For fall admission, 8/1 for domestic students; for spring admission, 12/15 for domestic students. Application fee: $60. *Expenses:* Tuition, nonresident: part-time $580 per credit. Required fees: $306 per credit. *Financial support:* Applicants required to submit FAFSA. *Faculty research:* Controlling root diseases in wheat and barley, sustainable agriculture, horticulture and urban landscape management, reduced herbicide rates control weeds in grain, wheat breeding program. *Unit head:* Dr. James B. Johnson, Chair, 208-885-6274, E-mail: nthompson@uidaho.edu. *Application contact:* Dr. James B. Johnson, Chair, 208-885-6274, E-mail: nthompson@uidaho.edu.

University of Kentucky, Graduate School, College of Agriculture, Program in Plant and Soil Science, Lexington, KY 40506-0032. Offers MS. *Degree requirements:* For master's, comprehensive exam, thesis optional. *Entrance requirements:* For master's, GRE General Test, minimum undergraduate GPA of 2.75, graduate 3.0. Additional exam requirements/recommendations for international students: Required—TOEFL (minimum score 550 paper-based; 213 computer-based). Electronic applications accepted.

University of Maine, Graduate School, College of Natural Sciences, Forestry, and Agriculture, Department of Biological Sciences, Orono, ME 04469. Offers biological sciences (PhD); botany and plant pathology (MS); ecology and environmental science (MS, PhD), including water resources; entomology (MS); plant science (PhD); zoology (MS, PhD). Part-time programs available. *Faculty:* 22 full-time (8 women), 4 part-time/adjunct (2 women). *Students:* 48 full-time (32 women), 14 part-time (11 women); includes 1 minority (Asian, non-Hispanic/Latino), 4 international. Average age 30. 121 applicants, 17% accepted, 18 enrolled. In 2010, 8 master's, 4 doctorates awarded. *Degree requirements:* For doctorate, thesis/dissertation. *Entrance requirements:* For master's and doctorate, GRE General Test. Additional exam requirements/recommendations for international students: Required—TOEFL. *Application deadline:* For fall admission, 2/1 priority date for domestic students. Applications are processed on a rolling basis. Application fee: $65. Electronic applications accepted. *Expenses:* Tuition, state resident: full-time $400. Tuition, nonresident: full-time $1050. *Financial support:* In 2010–11, 5 research assistantships with tuition reimbursements (averaging $17,995 per year), 19 teaching assistantships with tuition reimbursements (averaging $12,790 per year) were awarded; career-related internships or fieldwork, Federal Work-Study, institutionally sponsored loans, and tuition waivers (full and partial) also available. Financial award application deadline: 3/1. *Unit head:* Dr. Jody Jellison, Chair, 207-581-2551, Fax: 207-581-2537. *Application contact:* Scott G. Delcourt, Associate Dean of the Graduate School, 207-581-3291, Fax: 207-581-3232, E-mail: graduate@maine.edu.

University of Maine, Graduate School, College of Natural Sciences, Forestry, and Agriculture, Department of Plant, Soil, and Environmental Sciences, Orono, ME 04469. Offers biological sciences (PhD); ecology and environmental sciences (MS, PhD); forest resources (PhD); horticulture (MS); plant science (PhD); plant, soil, and environmental sciences (MS); resource utilization (MS). *Faculty:* 9 full-time (3 women), 7 part-time/adjunct (3 women). *Students:* 6 full-time (2 women), 2 part-time (1 woman), 2 international. Average age 31. 9 applicants, 22% accepted, 0 enrolled. In 2010, 2 master's awarded. *Entrance requirements:* For master's and doctorate, GRE General Test. Additional exam requirements/recommendations for international students: Required—TOEFL. *Application deadline:* Applications are processed on a rolling basis. Application fee: $65. Electronic applications accepted. *Expenses:* Tuition, state resident: full-time $400. Tuition, nonresident: full-time $1050. *Financial support:* In 2010–11, 16 research assistantships with tuition reimbursements (averaging $16,260 per year), 3 teaching assistantships with tuition reimbursements (averaging $12,790 per year) were awarded; scholarships/grants, tuition waivers (full and partial), and unspecified assistantships also available. *Unit head:* Dr. Gregory Porter, Chair, 207-581-2943, Fax: 207-581-3207. *Application contact:* Scott G. Delcourt, Associate Dean of the Graduate School, 207-581-3291, Fax: 207-581-3232, E-mail: graduate@maine.edu.

The University of Manchester, Faculty of Life Sciences, Manchester, United Kingdom. Offers adaptive organismal biology (M Phil, PhD); animal biology (M Phil, PhD); biochemistry (M Phil, PhD); bioinformatics (M Phil, PhD); biomolecular sciences (M Phil, PhD); biotechnology (M Phil, PhD); cell biology (M Phil, PhD); cell matrix research (M Phil, PhD); channels and transporters (M Phil, PhD); developmental biology (M Phil, PhD); Egyptology (M Phil, PhD); environmental biology (M Phil, PhD); evolutionary biology (M Phil, PhD); gene expression (M Phil, PhD); genetics (M Phil, PhD); history of science, technology and medicine (M Phil, PhD); immunology (M Phil, PhD); integrative neurobiology and behavior (M Phil, PhD); membrane trafficking (M Phil, PhD); microbiology (M Phil, PhD); molecular and cellular neuroscience (M Phil, PhD); molecular biology (M Phil, PhD); molecular cancer studies (M Phil, PhD); neuroscience (M Phil, PhD); ophthalmology (M Phil, PhD); optometry (M Phil, PhD); organelle function (M Phil, PhD); pharmacology (M Phil, PhD); physiology (M Phil, PhD); plant sciences (M Phil, PhD); stem cell research (M Phil, PhD); structural biology (M Phil, PhD); systems neuroscience (M Phil, PhD); toxicology (M Phil, PhD).

University of Manitoba, Faculty of Graduate Studies, Faculty of Agricultural and Food Sciences, Department of Plant Science, Winnipeg, MB R3T 2N2, Canada. Offers agronomy and plant protection (M Sc, PhD); horticulture (M Sc, PhD); plant breeding and genetics (M Sc,

Plant Sciences

University of Manitoba (continued)
PhD); plant physiology-biochemistry (M Sc, PhD). *Degree requirements:* For master's, thesis; for doctorate, one foreign language, thesis/dissertation.

University of Massachusetts Amherst, Graduate School, College of Natural Sciences, Department of Plant, Soil and Insect Sciences, Program in Plant and Soil Sciences, Amherst, MA 01003. Offers plant and soil sciences (MS, PhD); soil science (MS). Postbaccalaureate distance learning degree programs offered (minimal on-campus study). *Faculty:* 27 full-time (7 women). *Students:* 21 full-time (12 women), 16 part-time (8 women); includes 1 minority (Asian, non-Hispanic/Latino), 18 international. Average age 34. 28 applicants, 29% accepted, 7 enrolled. In 2010, 7 master's, 1 doctorate awarded. Terminal master's awarded for partial completion of doctoral program. *Degree requirements:* For master's, thesis or alternative; for doctorate, comprehensive exam, thesis/dissertation. *Entrance requirements:* For master's and doctorate, GRE General Test. Additional exam requirements/recommendations for international students: Required—TOEFL (minimum score 550 paper-based; 213 computer-based; 80 iBT), IELTS (minimum score 6.5). *Application deadline:* For fall admission, 1/7 for domestic and international students; for spring admission, 10/1 for domestic and international students. Applications are processed on a rolling basis. Application fee: $50 ($65 for international students). Electronic applications accepted. *Expenses:* Tuition, state resident: full-time $2640. Required fees: $8282. One-time fee: $357 full-time. *Financial support:* Fellowships, research assistantships, teaching assistantships, career-related internships or fieldwork, Federal Work-Study, scholarships/grants, traineeships, health care benefits, tuition waivers (full), and unspecified assistantships available. Support available to part-time students. Financial award application deadline: 1/2; financial award applicants required to submit FAFSA. *Unit head:* Dr. Geunhwa Jung, Graduate Program Director, 413-545-1059, Fax: 413-545-2115. *Application contact:* Jean M. Ames, Supervisor of Admissions, 413-545-0722, Fax: 413-577-0010, E-mail: gradadm@grad.umass.edu.

University of Massachusetts Amherst, Graduate School, Interdisciplinary Programs, Program in Plant Biology, Amherst, MA 01003. Offers biochemistry and metabolism (MS, PhD); cell biology and physiology (MS, PhD); environmental, ecological and integrative (PhD); environmental, ecological and integrative biology (MS); genetics and evolution (MS, PhD). *Students:* 18 full-time (8 women); includes 1 minority (Asian, non-Hispanic/Latino), 7 international. Average age 29. 27 applicants, 41% accepted, 6 enrolled. In 2010, 3 doctorates awarded. *Degree requirements:* For master's, thesis; for doctorate, 2 foreign languages, comprehensive exam, thesis/dissertation. *Entrance requirements:* For master's and doctorate, GRE General Test. Additional exam requirements/recommendations for international students: Required—TOEFL (minimum score 550 paper-based; 213 computer-based; 80 iBT), IELTS (minimum score 6.5). *Application deadline:* For fall admission, 12/15 for domestic and international students; for spring admission, 10/1 for domestic and international students. Applications are processed on a rolling basis. Application fee: $50 ($65 for international students). Electronic applications accepted. *Expenses:* Tuition, state resident: full-time $2640. Required fees: $8282. One-time fee: $357 full-time. *Financial support:* In 2010–11, 12 research assistantships with full tuition reimbursements (averaging $11,651 per year) were awarded; fellowships, teaching assistantships, career-related internships or fieldwork, Federal Work-Study, scholarships/grants, traineeships, health care benefits, tuition waivers (full), and unspecified assistantships also available. Support available to part-time students. Financial award application deadline: 12/15; financial award applicants required to submit FAFSA. *Unit head:* Dr. Elsbeth L. Walker, Graduate Program Director, 413-577-3217, Fax: 413-545-3243. *Application contact:* Jean M. Ames, Supervisor of Admissions, 413-545—0722, Fax: 413-577-0010, E-mail: gradadm@grad.umass.edu.

University of Minnesota, Twin Cities Campus, Graduate School, College of Food, Agricultural and Natural Resource Sciences, Program in Applied Plant Sciences, Minneapolis, MN 55455-0213. Offers MS, PhD. Part-time programs available. *Faculty:* 57 full-time (12 women). *Students:* 49 full-time (24 women), 3 part-time (1 woman); includes 6 minority (2 Asian, non-Hispanic/Latino; 4 Hispanic/Latino), 7 international. Average age 30. 50 applicants, 32% accepted, 15 enrolled. In 2010, 8 master's, 8 doctorates awarded. Terminal master's awarded for partial completion of doctoral program. *Degree requirements:* For master's, comprehensive exam, thesis; for doctorate, comprehensive exam, thesis/dissertation. *Entrance requirements:* For master's and doctorate, GRE General Test. Additional exam requirements/recommendations for international students: Required—TOEFL (minimum score 550 paper-based; 213 computer-based; 79 iBT). *Application deadline:* For fall admission, 12/1 priority date for domestic and international students; for spring admission, 10/15 priority date for domestic and international students. Applications are processed on a rolling basis. Application fee: $75 ($95 for international students). Electronic applications accepted. *Financial support:* In 2010–11, fellowships with full tuition reimbursements (averaging $24,000 per year), research assistantships with full and partial tuition reimbursements (averaging $21,000 per year) were awarded; teaching assistantships, scholarships/grants, health care benefits, and unspecified assistantships also available. *Faculty research:* Weed science, horticulture, crop management, sustainable agriculture, biotechnology, plant breeding. Total annual research expenditures: $5.6 million. *Unit head:* Dr. Jim Anderson, Director of Graduate Studies, 612-625-9763, Fax: 612-625-1268, E-mail: ander319@umn.edu. *Application contact:* Lynne Medgaarden, Assistant to the Director of Graduate Studies, 612-625-4742, Fax: 612-625-1268, E-mail: medga001@umn.edu.

University of Missouri, Graduate School, College of Agriculture, Food and Natural Resources, Division of Plant Sciences, Program in Plant Biology and Genetics, Columbia, MO 65211. Offers MS, PhD. Terminal master's awarded for partial completion of doctoral program. *Degree requirements:* For master's, thesis; for doctorate, thesis/dissertation. *Entrance requirements:* For master's and doctorate, GRE General Test, minimum GPA of 3.0. *Application deadline:* For fall admission, 3/1 priority date for domestic students. Applications are processed on a rolling basis. Application fee: $45 ($60 for international students). *Financial support:* Research assistantships, teaching assistantships, institutionally sponsored loans available. *Unit head:* Dr. Jeanne Mihail, Director of Graduate Studies, 573-882-0574, E-mail: mihailj@missouri.edu. *Application contact:* Dr. Jeanne Mihail, Director of Graduate Studies, 573-882-0574, E-mail: mihailj@missouri.edu.

University of Rhode Island, Graduate School, College of the Environment and Life Sciences, Department of Plant Sciences, Kingston, RI 02881. Offers entomology (MS, PhD); plant sciences (MS, PhD). Part-time programs available. *Faculty:* 9 full-time (2 women), 1 part-time/adjunct (0 women). *Degree requirements:* For master's, comprehensive exam (for some programs), thesis optional; for doctorate, comprehensive exam, thesis/dissertation. *Entrance requirements:* For master's and doctorate, GRE, 2 letters of recommendation. Additional exam requirements/recommendations for international students: Required—TOEFL (minimum score 550 paper-based; 213 computer-based). *Application deadline:* For fall admission, 7/15 for domestic students, 2/1 for international students; for spring admission, 11/15 for domestic students, 7/15 for international students. Application fee: $65. Electronic applications accepted. *Expenses:* Tuition, state resident: full-time $9588; part-time $533 per credit hour. Tuition, nonresident: full-time $22,968; part-time $1276 per credit hour. Required fees: $1282; $68 per semester. Tuition and fees vary according to program. *Financial support:* In 2010–11, 3 research assistantships with full and partial tuition reimbursements (averaging $10,612 per year), 1 teaching assistantship with full and partial tuition reimbursement (averaging $6,974 per year) were awarded. Financial award application deadline: 7/15; financial award applicants required to submit FAFSA. *Faculty research:* Plant development and management; pest management; tick biology, ecology, and control; identification and replacement of invasive ornamentals. Total annual research expenditures: $1.3 million. *Unit head:* Dr. Brian K. Maynard, Interim Chair, 401-874-2928, Fax: 401-874-2494, E-mail: bmaynard@uri.edu. *Application contact:* Dr. Thomas Mather, Director of Graduate Studies, 401-874-5616, Fax: 401-874-2494, E-mail: tmather@uri.edu.

University of Saskatchewan, College of Graduate Studies and Research, College of Agriculture, Department of Plant Sciences, Saskatoon, SK S7N 5A2, Canada. Offers M Sc, PhD. *Degree requirements:* For master's, thesis; for doctorate, comprehensive exam (for some programs), thesis/dissertation. *Entrance requirements:* Additional exam requirements/recommendations for international students: Required—TOEFL (minimum score 80 iBT); Recommended—IELTS (minimum score 6.5).

The University of Tennessee, Graduate School, College of Agricultural Sciences and Natural Resources, Department of Plant Sciences, Knoxville, TN 37996. Offers floriculture (MS); landscape design (MS); public horticulture (MS); turfgrass (MS); woody ornamentals (MS). Part-time programs available. *Degree requirements:* For master's, thesis or alternative. *Entrance requirements:* For master's, minimum GPA of 2.7. Additional exam requirements/recommendations for international students: Required—TOEFL. Electronic applications accepted. *Expenses:* Tuition, state resident: full-time $7440; part-time $414 per credit hour. Tuition, nonresident: full-time $22,478; part-time $1250 per credit hour. Required fees: $922; $43 per credit hour. Tuition and fees vary according to program.

University of Vermont, Graduate College, College of Agriculture and Life Sciences, Department of Plant and Soil Science, Burlington, VT 05405. Offers MS, PhD. *Students:* 24 (13 women), 3 international. 26 applicants, 12% accepted, 1 enrolled. In 2010, 3 master's, 1 doctorate awarded. *Degree requirements:* For master's, thesis; for doctorate, one foreign language, thesis/dissertation. *Entrance requirements:* For master's and doctorate, GRE General Test. Additional exam requirements/recommendations for international students: Required—TOEFL (minimum score 550 paper-based; 213 computer-based; 80 iBT). *Application deadline:* For fall admission, 3/1 priority date for domestic students. Applications are processed on a rolling basis. Application fee: $40. Electronic applications accepted. *Expenses:* Tuition, state resident: part-time $537 per credit hour. Tuition, nonresident: part-time $1355 per credit hour. *Financial support:* Fellowships, research assistantships, teaching assistantships available. Financial award application deadline: 3/1. *Faculty research:* Soil chemistry, plant nutrition. *Unit head:* Dr. Deborah Neher, Chairperson, 802-656-2630. *Application contact:* Dr. Josef Gorres, Coordinator, 802-656-2630.

The University of Western Ontario, Faculty of Graduate Studies, Biosciences Division, Department of Plant Sciences, London, ON N6A 5B8, Canada. Offers plant and environmental sciences (M Sc); plant sciences (M Sc, PhD); plant sciences and environmental sciences (PhD); plant sciences and molecular biology (M Sc, PhD). *Degree requirements:* For master's, thesis; for doctorate, thesis/dissertation. *Entrance requirements:* For doctorate, M Sc or equivalent. Additional exam requirements/recommendations for international students: Required—TOEFL. *Faculty research:* Ecology systematics, plant biochemistry and physiology, yeast genetics, molecular biology.

University of Wisconsin–Madison, Graduate School, College of Agricultural and Life Sciences, Department of Horticulture, Madison, WI 53706-1380. Offers horticulture (MS, PhD); plant breeding and genetics (MS, PhD). Part-time programs available. Terminal master's awarded for partial completion of doctoral program. *Degree requirements:* For master's, comprehensive exam, thesis (for some programs); for doctorate, comprehensive exam, thesis/dissertation. *Entrance requirements:* For master's and doctorate, minimum GPA of 3.0. Additional exam requirements/recommendations for international students: Required—TOEFL (minimum score 580 paper-based; 213 computer-based). Electronic applications accepted. *Expenses:* Tuition, state resident: full-time $9887.36; part-time $617.96 per credit. Tuition, nonresident: full-time $24,054; part-time $1503.40 per credit. Required fees: $67.63 per credit. Tuition and fees vary according to reciprocity agreements. *Faculty research:* Biotechnology, crop breeding/genetics, environmental physiology, crop management, cytogenetics.

Utah State University, School of Graduate Studies, College of Agriculture, Department of Plants, Soils, and Biometeorology, Logan, UT 84322. Offers biometeorology (MS, PhD); ecology (MS, PhD); plant science (MS, PhD); soil science (MS, PhD). Part-time programs available. Terminal master's awarded for partial completion of doctoral program. *Degree requirements:* For master's, thesis; for doctorate, thesis/dissertation. *Entrance requirements:* For master's, GRE General Test, BS in plant, soil, atmospheric science, or related field; minimum GPA of 3.0; for doctorate, GRE General Test, minimum GPA of 3.0. Additional exam requirements/recommendations for international students: Required—TOEFL. Electronic applications accepted. *Faculty research:* Biotechnology and genomics, plant physiology and biology, nutrient and water efficient landscapes, physical-chemical-biological processes in soil, environmental biophysics and climate.

Virginia State University, School of Graduate Studies, Research, and Outreach, School of Agriculture, Department of Agriculture and Human Ecology, Petersburg, VA 23806-0001. Offers plant science (MS). *Expenses:* Tuition, state resident: full-time $5576; part-time $335 per credit hour. Tuition, nonresident: full-time $13,402; part-time $670 per credit hour.

West Texas A&M University, College of Agriculture, Nursing, and Natural Sciences, Division of Agriculture, Emphasis in Plant Science, Canyon, TX 79016-0001. Offers MS. Part-time programs available. *Degree requirements:* For master's, comprehensive exam, thesis optional. *Entrance requirements:* For master's, GRE General Test. Additional exam requirements/recommendations for international students: Required—TOEFL (minimum score 550 paper-based). Electronic applications accepted. *Faculty research:* Crop and soil disciplines.

West Virginia University, Davis College of Agriculture, Forestry and Consumer Sciences, Division of Plant and Soil Sciences, Program in Agricultural Sciences, Morgantown, WV 26506. Offers animal and food sciences (PhD); plant and soil sciences (PhD). *Degree requirements:* For doctorate, thesis/dissertation, oral and written exams. *Entrance requirements:* Additional exam requirements/recommendations for international students: Required—TOEFL. *Faculty research:* Ruminant nutrition, metabolism, forage utilization, physiology, reproduction.

Viticulture and Enology

California State University, Fresno, Division of Graduate Studies, College of Agricultural Sciences and Technology, Department of Viticulture and Enology, Fresno, CA 93740-8027. Offers MS. Part-time and evening/weekend programs available. *Degree requirements:* For master's, comprehensive exam (for some programs), thesis (for some programs). *Entrance requirements:* For master's, GRE General Test, minimum GPA of 2.5. Additional exam requirements/recommendations for international students: Required—TOEFL. Electronic applications accepted. *Faculty research:* Ethel carbonate formation, clinical an physiological characterization, grape and wine quality.

University of California, Davis, Graduate Studies, Graduate Group in Viticulture and Enology, Davis, CA 95616. Offers MS, PhD. *Degree requirements:* For master's, comprehensive exam (for some programs), thesis (for some programs). *Entrance requirements:* Additional exam requirements/recommendations for international students: Required—TOEFL (minimum score 550 paper-based; 213 computer-based).

Peterson's Graduate Programs in the Physical Sciences, Mathematics, Agricultural Sciences, the Environment & Natural Resources 2012

www.facebook.com/petersonspublishing   **351**

ACADEMIC AND PROFESSIONAL PROGRAMS IN THE ENVIRONMENT AND NATURAL RESOURCES

Section 9
Environmental Sciences and Management

This section contains a directory of institutions offering graduate work in environmental sciences and management, followed by in-depth entries submitted by institutions that chose to prepare detailed program descriptions. Additional informantion about programs listed in the directory but not augmented by an in-depth entry may be obtained by writing directly to the dean of a graduate school or chair of a department at the address given in the directory.

For programs offering related work, see also in this book *Natural Resources*. In the other guides in this series:

Graduate Programs in the Humanities, Arts & Social Sciences
See *Political Science and International Affairs* and *Public, Regional, and Industrial Affairs*

Graduate Programs in the Biological Sciences
See *Ecology, Environmental Biology,* and *Evolutionary Biology*

Graduate Programs in Engineering & Applied Sciences
See *Management of Engineering* and *Technology*

CONTENTS

Environmental Management and Policy

Adelphi University, Graduate School of Arts and Sciences, Program in Environmental Studies, Garden City, NY 11530-0701. Offers MS. *Students:* 7 full-time (3 women), 13 part-time (6 women); includes 3 Black or African American, non-Hispanic/Latino; 1 Hispanic/Latino, 1 international. Average age 27. In 2010, 8 master's awarded. *Degree requirements:* For master's, thesis optional. *Entrance requirements:* For master's, GRE General Test, 2 letters of recommendation; course work in microeconomics, political science, statistics/calculus, and either chemistry or physics; computer literacy. Additional exam requirements/recommendations for international students: Required—TOEFL (minimum score 550 paper-based; 213 computer-based; 80 iBT). *Application deadline:* For fall admission, 5/1 for international students; for spring admission, 11/1 for international students. Applications are processed on a rolling basis. Application fee: $50. Electronic applications accepted. *Financial support:* Research assistantships with full and partial tuition reimbursements, teaching assistantships, career-related internships or fieldwork, Federal Work-Study, institutionally sponsored loans, and unspecified assistantships available. Financial award application deadline: 2/15; financial award applicants required to submit FAFSA. *Faculty research:* Contaminates sites, workplace exposure level of contaminants, climate change and human health. *Unit head:* Dr. Anagnostis Agelarakis, Director, 516-877-4112, E-mail: agelarak@adelphi.edu. *Application contact:* Christine Murphy, Director of Admissions, 516-877-3050, Fax: 516-877-3039, E-mail: graduateadmissions@adelphi.edu.

See Close-Up on page 393.

Air Force Institute of Technology, Graduate School of Engineering and Management, Department of Systems and Engineering Management, Dayton, OH 45433-7765. Offers cost analysis (MS); environmental and engineering management (MS); environmental engineering science (MS); information resource/systems management (MS). *Accreditation:* ABET. Part-time programs available. *Degree requirements:* For master's, thesis. *Entrance requirements:* For master's, GRE, GMAT, minimum GPA of 3.0.

American Public University System, AMU/APU Graduate Programs, Charles Town, WV 25414. Offers accounting (MBA); administration and supervision (M Ed); air warfare (MA Military Studies); asymmetrical warfare (MA Military Studies); criminal justice (MA); emergency and disaster management (MA); entrepreneurship (MBA); environmental policy and management (MS); finance (MBA); general (MBA); global business management (MBA); guidance and counseling (M Ed); history (MA); homeland security (MA); homeland security resource allocation (MBA); humanities (MA); information technology (MS); information technology management (MBA); intelligence studies (MA); international relations and conflict resolution (MA); joint warfare (MA Military Studies); land warfare (MA Military Studies); legal studies (MA); management (MA), including defense mangement, general, human resource management, organizational leadership, public administration; marketing (MBA); military history (MA); national security studies (MA); naval warfare (MA Military Studies); nonprofit management (MBA); political science (MA); psychology (MA); public administration (MA); public health (MA); security management (MA); space studies (MS); sports management (MS); strategic leadership (MA Military Studies); teaching (M Ed), including elementary, secondary social sciences; transportation and logistics management (MA). Programs offered via distance learning only. Part-time and evening/weekend programs available. Postbaccalaureate distance learning degree programs offered (no on-campus study). *Faculty:* 253 full-time (134 women), 1,208 part-time/adjunct (570 women). *Students:* 956 full-time (422 women), 8,476 part-time (2,821 women); includes 2,511 minority (1,218 Black or African American, non-Hispanic/Latino; 68 American Indian or Alaska Native, non-Hispanic/Latino; 219 Asian, non-Hispanic/Latino; 705 Hispanic/Latino; 46 Native Hawaiian or other Pacific Islander, non-Hispanic/Latino; 255 Two or more races, non-Hispanic/Latino), 107 international. Average age 35. 9,550 applicants, 100% accepted. In 2010, 1,688 master's awarded. *Degree requirements:* For master's, comprehensive exam or practicum. *Entrance requirements:* For master's, official transcript showing earned bachelor's degree from institution accredited by recognized accrediting body. Additional exam requirements/recommendations for international students: Required—TOEFL (minimum score 550 paper-based; 213 computer-based), IELTS (minimum score 6.5). *Application deadline:* Applications are processed on a rolling basis. Application fee: $0. Electronic applications accepted. *Financial support:* Applicants required to submit FAFSA. *Faculty research:* Military history, criminal justice, management performance, national security. *Unit head:* Dr. Frank McCluskey, Provost, 877-468-6268, Fax: 304-724-3780. *Application contact:* Terry Grant, Director of Enrollment Management, 877-468-6268, Fax: 304-724-3780, E-mail: info@apus.edu.

American University, College of Arts and Sciences, Department of Environmental Science, Washington, DC 20016-8001. Offers environmental assessment (Graduate Certificate); environmental science (MS). *Degree requirements:* For master's, comprehensive exam, thesis (for some programs). *Entrance requirements:* For master's, GRE General Test, GRE Subject Test, minimum GPA of 3.0. Additional exam requirements/recommendations for international students: Required—TOEFL.

American University, School of International Service, Washington, DC 20016-8071. Offers comparative and regional studies (Certificate); cross-cultural communication (Certificate); development management (MS); ethics, peace, and global affairs (MA); European studies (Certificate); global environmental policy (MA, Certificate); international affairs (MA), including comparative and regional studies, environmental policy, international economic policy, international politics, natural resources and sustainable development, U. S. foreign policy; international communication (MA, Certificate); international development (MA, Certificate); international development management (Certificate); international economic policy (Certificate); international economic relations (Certificate); international media (MA); international peace and conflict resolution (MA, Certificate); international relations (PhD); international service (MIS); peace building (Certificate); the Americas (Certificate); United States foreign policy (Certificate); JD/MA. Part-time and evening/weekend programs available. *Faculty:* 91 full-time (35 women), 48 part-time/adjunct (16 women). *Students:* 591 full-time (383 women), 367 part-time (229 women); includes 164 minority (51 Black or African American, non-Hispanic/Latino; 4 American Indian or Alaska Native, non-Hispanic/Latino; 42 Asian, non-Hispanic/Latino; 63 Hispanic/Latino; 4 Two or more races, non-Hispanic/Latino), 94 international. Average age 27. 2,115 applicants, 59% accepted, 360 enrolled. In 2010, 370 master's, 7 doctorates awarded. Terminal master's awarded for partial completion of doctoral program. *Degree requirements:* For master's, one foreign language, comprehensive exam, thesis or alternative; for doctorate, one foreign language, comprehensive exam, thesis/dissertation, research practicum; for Certificate, minimum 15 credit hours related course work. *Entrance requirements:* For master's, GRE, 24 credits of course work in related social sciences, minimum GPA of 3.5, 2 letters of recommendation, bachelor's degree, resume; for doctorate, GRE, 2 letters of recommendation, 24 credits in related social sciences; for Certificate, bachelor's degree. Additional exam requirements/recommendations for international students: Required—TOEFL (minimum score 600 paper-based; 250 computer-based; 100 iBT). *Application deadline:* For fall admission, 1/15 priority date for domestic students; for spring admission, 10/1 priority date for domestic students. Applications are processed on a rolling basis. Application fee: $50. *Financial support:* Career-related internships or fieldwork, Federal Work-Study, and institutionally sponsored loans available. Financial award application deadline: 1/15. *Faculty research:* International intellectual property, international environmental issues, international law and legal order, international telecommunications/technology, international sustainable development. *Unit head:* Dr. Louis W. Goodman, Dean, 202-885-1600, Fax: 202-885-2494. *Application contact:* Yasmin Quianzon, Director of Graduate Admissions and Financial Aid, 202-885-2496, Fax: 202-885-1109.

American University of Beirut, Graduate Programs, Faculty of Arts and Sciences, Beirut, Lebanon. Offers anthropology (MA); Arabic language and literature (MA); archaeology (MA); biology (MS); chemistry (MS); computational science (MS); computer science (MS); economics (MA); education (MA); English language (MA); English literature (MA); environmental policy planning (MSES); financial economics (MAFE); geology (MS); history (MA); mathematics (MA, MS); Middle Eastern studies (MA); philosophy (MA); physics (MS); political studies (MA); psychology (MA); public administration (MA); sociology (MA); statistics (MA, MS). Part-time programs available. *Faculty:* 229 full-time (98 women), 136 part-time/adjunct (79 women). *Students:* 158 full-time (104 women), 263 part-time (171 women). Average age 25. 356 applicants, 59% accepted, 127 enrolled. In 2010, 57 master's awarded. *Degree requirements:* For master's, one foreign language, comprehensive exam, thesis (for some programs). *Entrance requirements:* For master's, GRE, letter of recommendation. Additional exam requirements/recommendations for international students: Required—TOEFL (minimum score 600 paper-based; 250 computer-based; 97 iBT), IELTS (minimum score 7). *Application deadline:* For fall admission, 4/30 for domestic and international students; for spring admission, 11/1 for domestic and international students. Application fee: $50. *Expenses:* Tuition: Full-time $12,294; part-time $683 per credit. Required fees: $499; $499 per credit. Tuition and fees vary according to course load and program. *Financial support:* In 2010–11, 33 students received support. Career-related internships or fieldwork, institutionally sponsored loans, scholarships/grants, health care benefits, and unspecified assistantships available. Financial award application deadline: 2/4; financial award applicants required to submit FAFSA. *Faculty research:* Modern and contemporary world theatre; mineralogy, petrology, and geochemistry; cell differentiation and transformation; combinatorial technologies; philosophy of action; continental philosophy; Phoenician epigraphy; nascent complex societies and urbanism; the economies of the Arab world; environmental economics; tectonophysics; host-parasite interactions; innate immunity; insect-plant interactions; history of the Ottoman archives; decentralization; transparency and corruption. Total annual research expenditures: $622,243. *Unit head:* Dr. Patrick McGreevy, Dean, 961-137-4374 Ext. 3800, Fax: 961-174-4461, E-mail: pm07@aub.edu.lb. *Application contact:* Dr. Salim Kanaan, Director, Admissions Office, 961-135-0000 Ext. 2594, Fax: 961-175-0775, E-mail: sk00@aub.edu.lb.

Antioch University New England, Graduate School, Department of Environmental Studies, Doctoral Program in Environmental Studies, Keene, NH 03431-3552. Offers PhD. *Degree requirements:* For doctorate, thesis/dissertation, practicum. *Entrance requirements:* For doctorate, master's degree and previous experience in the environmental field. Additional exam requirements/recommendations for international students: Required—TOEFL (minimum score 600 paper-based; 250 computer-based). Electronic applications accepted. *Expenses:* Contact institution. *Faculty research:* Environmental history, green politics, ecopsychology.

Antioch University New England, Graduate School, Department of Environmental Studies, Individualized Program, Keene, NH 03431-3552. Offers MS. *Degree requirements:* For master's, practicum, seminar, thesis or project. *Entrance requirements:* For master's, detailed proposal.

Antioch University New England, Graduate School, Department of Environmental Studies, Program in Environmental Advocacy and Organizing, Keene, NH 03431-3552. Offers MS. *Degree requirements:* For master's, practicum, seminar. *Entrance requirements:* For master's, samples of written work, portfolio, letters of recommendation, interview.

Antioch University New England, Graduate School, Department of Environmental Studies, Program in Resource Management and Conservation, Keene, NH 03431-3552. Offers MS. *Degree requirements:* For master's, thesis optional, practicum. *Entrance requirements:* For master's, previous undergraduate course work in science and math. Additional exam requirements/recommendations for international students: Required—TOEFL (minimum score 600 paper-based; 250 computer-based). Electronic applications accepted. *Expenses:* Contact institution. *Faculty research:* Waste management, land use.

Antioch University New England, Graduate School, Department of Organization and Management, Program in Organizational and Environmental Sustainability (Green MBA), Keene, NH 03431-3552. Offers MBA. Part-time programs available. *Entrance requirements:* For master's, GRE, resume, 3 letters of recommendation. Additional exam requirements/recommendations for international students: Required—TOEFL (minimum score 600 paper-based; 250 computer-based).

Antioch University Seattle, Graduate Programs, Center for Creative Change, Seattle, WA 98121-1814. Offers environment and community (MA); management (MS); organizational psychology (MA); strategic communications (MA); whole system design (MA). Evening/weekend programs available. Electronic applications accepted. *Expenses:* Contact institution.

Appalachian State University, Cratis D. Williams Graduate School, Department of Government and Justice Studies, Boone, NC 28608. Offers criminal justice (MS); political science (MA), including American government, environmental politics and policy analysis, international relations; public administration (MPA), including public management, town, city and county management. Part-time programs available. Postbaccalaureate distance learning degree programs offered (no on-campus study). *Faculty:* 24 full-time (5 women), 3 part-time/adjunct (2 women). *Students:* 72 full-time (29 women), 53 part-time (25 women); includes 6 Black or African American, non-Hispanic/Latino; 1 Asian, non-Hispanic/Latino; 3 Hispanic/Latino; 1 Two or more races, non-Hispanic/Latino. 86 applicants, 86% accepted, 58 enrolled. In 2010, 49 master's awarded. *Degree requirements:* For master's, variable foreign language requirement, comprehensive exam, thesis optional. *Entrance requirements:* For master's, GRE General Test, 3 letters of recommendation. Additional exam requirements/recommendations for international students: Required—TOEFL (minimum score 570 paper-based; 230 computer-based; 79 iBT), IELTS (minimum score 6.5). *Application deadline:* For fall admission, 7/1 for domestic students, 2/1 for international students; for spring admission, 11/1 for domestic students, 7/1 for international students. Applications are processed on a rolling basis. Application fee: $55. Electronic applications accepted. *Expenses:* Tuition, state resident: full-time $3428; part-time $428 per unit. Tuition, nonresident: full-time $14,518; part-time $1814 per unit. Required fees: $2320; $344 per unit. Tuition and fees vary according to campus/location. *Financial support:* In 2010–11, 20 research assistantships (averaging $8,000 per year) were awarded; fellowships, teaching assistantships, career-related internships or fieldwork, Federal Work-Study, scholarships/grants, and unspecified assistantships also available. Financial award application deadline: 4/1; financial award applicants required to submit FAFSA. *Faculty research:* Campaign finance, emerging democracies, bureaucratic politics, judicial behavior, administration of justice. Total annual research expenditures: $143,000. *Unit head:* Dr. Brian Ellison, Chairperson, 828-262-3085, E-mail: ellisonba@appstate.edu. *Application contact:* Sandy Krause, Director of Admissions and Recruiting, 828-262-2130, Fax: 828-262-2709, E-mail: krausesl@appstate.edu.

Arizona State University, College of Technology and Innovation, Department of Technology Management, Mesa, AZ 85212. Offers technology (aviation management and human factors) (MS); technology (environmental technology management) (MS); technology (global technology and development) (MS); technology (graphic information technology) (MS); technology (management of technology) (MS). Part-time and evening/weekend programs available. Postbaccalaureate distance learning degree programs offered (minimal on-campus study). *Faculty:* 13 full-time (3 women), 6 part-time/adjunct (2 women). *Students:* 56 full-time (16 women), 212 part-time (95 women); includes 61 minority (14 Black or African American, non-Hispanic/Latino; 8 American Indian or Alaska Native, non-Hispanic/Latino; 14 Asian, non-Hispanic/Latino; 21 Hispanic/Latino; 4 Two or more races, non-Hispanic/Latino), 27 international. Average age 36. 124 applicants, 77% accepted, 58 enrolled. In 2010, 35 master's awarded. *Degree requirements:* For master's, thesis or applied project and oral defense; interactive Program of Study (iPOS) submitted before completing 50 percent of required credit hours. *Entrance*

requirements: For master's, GRE, minimum GPA of 3.0 or equivalent in last 2 years of work leading to bachelor's degree. Additional exam requirements/recommendations for international students: Required—TOEFL, IELTS, or Pearson Test of English. *Application deadline:* For fall admission, 7/1 for domestic and international students; for spring admission, 12/1 for domestic and international students. Applications are processed on a rolling basis. Application fee: $70 ($90 for international students). Electronic applications accepted. *Expenses:* Tuition, state resident: full-time $8510; part-time $608 per credit. Tuition, nonresident: full-time $16,542; part-time $919 per credit. Required fees: $339; $110 per credit. Part-time tuition and fees vary according to course load. *Financial support:* In 2010–11, 3 research assistantships with full and partial tuition reimbursements (averaging $12,729 per year), 1 teaching assistantship with full and partial tuition reimbursement (averaging $14,125 per year) were awarded; career-related internships or fieldwork, Federal Work-Study, scholarships/grants, health care benefits, tuition waivers (full and partial), and unspecified assistantships also available. Support available to part-time students. Financial award application deadline: 3/1; financial award applicants required to submit FAFSA. *Faculty research:* Digital imaging, digital publishing, Internet development/e-commerce, information aviation human factors, pilot selection, databases, multimedia, commercial digital photography, digital workflow, computer graphics modeling and animation, information design, sociotechnology, visual and technical literacy, environmental management, quality management, project management, industrial ethics, hazardous materials, environmental chemistry. Total annual research expenditures: $755,686. *Unit head:* Dr. Mitzi Montoya, Vice Provost and Dean, 480-727-1955, Fax: 480-727-1538, E-mail: mitzi.montoya@asu.edu. *Application contact:* Graduate Admissions, 480-965-6113.

Arizona State University, W.P. Carey School of Business, Morrison School of Agribusiness and Resource Management, Mesa, AZ 85212. Offers agribusiness (MS). Part-time and evening/weekend programs available. *Faculty:* 12 full-time (1 woman), 1 part-time/adjunct (0 women). *Students:* 8 full-time (3 women), 3 part-time (2 women); includes 3 minority (1 American Indian or Alaska Native, non-Hispanic/Latino; 2 Hispanic/Latino), 2 international. Average age 29. 6 applicants, 83% accepted, 3 enrolled. In 2010, 18 master's awarded. *Degree requirements:* For master's, thesis, oral defense, interactive Program of Study (iPOS) submitted before completing 50 percent of required credit hours. *Entrance requirements:* For master's, GMAT or GRE General Test, minimum GPA of 3.0 in last 2 years of work leading to bachelor's degree, 3 letters of recommendation, resume, official transcripts, statement of intent. Additional exam requirements/recommendations for international students: Required—TOEFL (minimum score 550 paper-based; 213 computer-based; 80 iBT), IELTS (minimum score 6.5); Recommended—TWE. *Application deadline:* For fall admission, 2/1 priority date for domestic and international students; for spring admission, 10/15 priority date for domestic and international students. Applications are processed on a rolling basis. Application fee: $70 ($90 for international students). Electronic applications accepted. *Expenses:* Tuition, state resident: full-time $8510; part-time $608 per credit. Tuition, nonresident: full-time $16,542; part-time $919 per credit. Required fees: $339; $110 per credit. Part-time tuition and fees vary according to course load. *Financial support:* In 2010–11, 2 research assistantships with partial tuition reimbursements (averaging $4,988 per year) were awarded; fellowships with full and partial tuition reimbursements, teaching assistantships with partial tuition reimbursements, career-related internships or fieldwork, institutionally sponsored loans, scholarships/grants, and tuition waivers (full and partial) also available. Financial award application deadline: 3/1; financial award applicants required to submit CSS PROFILE or FAFSA. *Faculty research:* Consumer behavior and marketing strategies in food markets, supply-chain management, derivatives and risk management, and international agricultural trade and policy. Total annual research expenditures: $365,322. *Unit head:* Dr. Timothy Richards, Chair, 480-727-1488, Fax: 480-727-1186, E-mail: trichards@asu.edu. *Application contact:* Graduate Admissions, 480-965-6113.

Bard College, Bard Center for Environmental Policy, Annandale-on-Hudson, NY 12504. Offers climate science and policy (MS, Professional Certificate), including agriculture (MS), ecosystems (MS); environmental policy (MS, Professional Certificate); sustainability (MBA); MS/JD; MS/MAT. Part-time programs available. *Faculty:* 10 full-time (5 women), 6 part-time/adjunct (3 women). *Students:* 58 full-time (41 women). Average age 26. 75 applicants, 77% accepted, 28 enrolled. In 2010, 13 master's awarded. *Degree requirements:* For master's, thesis, 4-month, full-time internship. *Entrance requirements:* For master's, GRE, coursework in statistics, chemistry and one other semester of college science; personal statement; curriculum vitae; 3 letters of recommendation; sample of written work. Additional exam requirements/recommendations for international students: Required—TOEFL (minimum score 600 paper-based; 250 computer-based; 100 iBT). *Application deadline:* For winter admission, 1/15 priority date for domestic and international students; for spring admission, 5/15 for domestic and international students. Applications are processed on a rolling basis. Application fee: $65. Electronic applications accepted. *Expenses:* Contact institution. *Financial support:* In 2010–11, 58 students received support, including 58 fellowships (averaging $7,000 per year), 6 research assistantships (averaging $6,000 per year), 1 teaching assistantship (averaging $6,000 per year); career-related internships or fieldwork, scholarships/grants, tuition waivers (full), and unspecified assistantships also available. Support available to part-time students. Financial award application deadline: 2/15; financial award applicants required to submit FAFSA. *Faculty research:* Climate and agriculture, alternative energy, environmental economics, environmental toxicology, EPA law, sustainable development, international relations, literature and composition, human rights, agronomy, advocacy, leadership. *Unit head:* Dr. Eban Goodstein, Director, 845-758-7067, Fax: 845-758-7636, E-mail: ebangood@bard.edu. *Application contact:* Molly Williams, Admissions Coordinator, 845-758-7071, Fax: 845-758-7636, E-mail: mwilliam@bard.edu.

Baylor University, Graduate School, College of Arts and Sciences, Department of Environmental Studies, Waco, TX 76798. Offers MES, MS. *Students:* 11 full-time (6 women); includes 2 minority (1 Black or African American, non-Hispanic/Latino; 1 Hispanic/Latino), 3 international. In 2010, 2 master's awarded. *Degree requirements:* For master's, thesis. *Entrance requirements:* For master's, GRE General Test. *Application deadline:* For fall admission, 8/1 priority date for domestic students; for spring admission, 1/1 for domestic students. Applications are processed on a rolling basis. Application fee: $25. *Financial support:* Research assistantships, teaching assistantships, career-related internships or fieldwork, Federal Work-Study, and institutionally sponsored loans available. *Faculty research:* Renewable energy/waste management policies, Third World environmental problem solving, ecotourism. *Unit head:* Dr. Joe Yelderman, Graduate Program Director, 254-710-1385, Fax: 254-710-3409, E-mail: joe_yelderman@baylor.edu. *Application contact:* Glenda Plemons, Administrative Assistant, 254-710-3405, Fax: 254-710-3870, E-mail: glenda_plemons@baylor.edu.

Baylor University, Graduate School, College of Arts and Sciences, Program in Air Science and Environment, Waco, TX 76798. Offers IMES. *Application contact:* Suzanne Keener, Administrative Assistant, 254-710-3588, Fax: 254-710-3870.

Bemidji State University, School of Graduate Studies, Bemidji, MN 56601-2699. Offers biology (MS); counseling psychology (MS); education (M Ed, MS); English (MA, MS); environmental studies (MS); mathematics (MS); mathematics (elementary and middle level education) (MS); special education (M Sp Ed, MS). Part-time programs available. Postbaccalaureate distance learning degree programs offered (no on-campus study). *Faculty:* 142 full-time (61 women), 37 part-time/adjunct (22 women). *Students:* 82 full-time (51 women), 350 part-time (210 women); includes 21 minority (6 Black or African American, non-Hispanic/Latino; 3 American Indian or Alaska Native, non-Hispanic/Latino; 6 Asian, non-Hispanic/Latino; 6 Hispanic/Latino), 8 international. Average age 35. 491 applicants, 93% accepted, 307 enrolled. In 2010, 97 master's awarded. *Degree requirements:* For master's, comprehensive exam, thesis (for some programs). *Entrance requirements:* For master's, GRE, letters of recommendation, letters of interest. Additional exam requirements/recommendations for international students: Required—TOEFL (minimum score 550 paper-based; 213 computer-based; 80 iBT). *Application deadline:* Applications are processed on a rolling basis. Application fee: $20. Electronic applications accepted. *Expenses:* Tuition, state resident: full-time $6605; part-time $330 per credit. Tuition, nonresident: full-time $6605; part-time $330 per credit. Required fees: $107.97 per credit. *Financial support:* In 2010–11, 110 students received support, including 40 research assistantships with partial tuition reimbursements available (averaging $7,196 per year), 40 teaching assistantships with partial tuition reimbursements available (averaging $7,196 per year); career-related internships or fieldwork, Federal Work-Study, scholarships/grants, health care benefits, and unspecified assistantships also available. Support available to part-time students. Financial award application deadline: 4/15; financial award applicants required to submit FAFSA. *Unit head:* Dr. Patricia Rogers, Dean, 218-755-2027, Fax: 218-755-2258, E-mail: progers@bemidjistate.edu. *Application contact:* Joan Miller, Senior Office and Administrative Specialist, 218-755-2027, Fax: 218-755-2258, E-mail: jmiller@bemidjistate.edu.

Boise State University, Graduate College, College of Social Sciences and Public Affairs, Department of Public Policy and Administration, Boise, ID 83725-0399. Offers environmental and natural resources policy and administration (MPA); general public administration (MPA); state and local government policy and administration (MPA). *Accreditation:* NASPAA. Part-time programs available. *Degree requirements:* For master's, comprehensive exam, directed research project, internship. *Entrance requirements:* For master's, GRE General Test, minimum GPA of 3.0. Additional exam requirements/recommendations for international students: Required—TOEFL. Electronic applications accepted.

Boston University, Graduate School of Arts and Sciences, Department of Geography and Environment, Boston, MA 02215. Offers energy and environmental analysis (MA); environmental remote sensing and GIs (MA); geography (MA); geography and environment (PhD); international relations and environmental policy (MA). *Students:* 55 full-time (23 women), 10 part-time (3 women); includes 3 minority (1 Asian, non-Hispanic/Latino; 1 Hispanic/Latino; 1 Two or more races, non-Hispanic/Latino), 17 international. Average age 28. 64 applicants, 23% accepted, 5 enrolled. In 2010, 1 master's, 2 doctorates awarded. Terminal master's awarded for partial completion of doctoral program. *Degree requirements:* For master's, one foreign language, comprehensive exam, thesis; for doctorate, one foreign language, comprehensive exam, thesis/dissertation. *Entrance requirements:* For master's and doctorate, GRE General Test, GRE Subject Test, 3 letters of recommendation. Additional exam requirements/recommendations for international students: Required—TOEFL (minimum score 600 paper-based; 250 computer-based). *Application deadline:* For fall admission, 7/1 for domestic and international students; for spring admission, 11/15 for domestic and international students. Application fee: $70. Electronic applications accepted. *Expenses:* Tuition: Full-time $39,314; part-time $1228 per credit. Required fees: $40 per semester. *Financial support:* In 2010–11, 33 students received support, including 2 fellowships with full tuition reimbursements available (averaging $19,300 per year), 20 research assistantships with full tuition reimbursements available (averaging $18,800 per year), 11 teaching assistantships with full tuition reimbursements available (averaging $18,800 per year); Federal Work-Study and unspecified assistantships also available. Support available to part-time students. Financial award application deadline: 1/15; financial award applicants required to submit FAFSA. Total annual research expenditures: $1.2 million. *Unit head:* Robert Kaufmann, Chairman, 617-353-3940, Fax: 617-353-8399, E-mail: kaufmann@bu.edu. *Application contact:* Christopher DeVits, Graduate Program Coordinator, 617-353-7554, Fax: 617-353-8399, E-mail: cdevits@bu.edu.

Boston University, Graduate School of Arts and Sciences, Department of International Relations, Boston, MA 02215. Offers African studies (Certificate); international relations (MA); international relations and environmental policy management (MA); international relations and international communication (MA); JD/MA; MBA/MA. *Students:* 49 full-time (36 women), 12 part-time (7 women); includes 10 minority (2 Black or African American, non-Hispanic/Latino; 5 Asian, non-Hispanic/Latino; 1 Hispanic/Latino; 2 Two or more races, non-Hispanic/Latino), 10 international. Average age 26. 417 applicants, 59% accepted, 50 enrolled. In 2010, 41 master's awarded. *Degree requirements:* For master's, one foreign language, comprehensive exam, thesis. *Entrance requirements:* For master's, GRE General Test, 3 letters of recommendation; for Certificate, GRE General Test. Additional exam requirements/recommendations for international students: Required—TOEFL (minimum score 600 paper-based; 250 computer-based). *Application deadline:* For fall admission, 4/15 for domestic and international students; for spring admission, 10/15 for domestic and international students. Application fee: $70. Electronic applications accepted. *Expenses:* Tuition: Full-time $39,314; part-time $1228 per credit. Required fees: $40 per semester. *Financial support:* In 2010–11, 19 students received support. Federal Work-Study, scholarships/grants, and unspecified assistantships available. Support available to part-time students. Financial award application deadline: 1/15; financial award applicants required to submit FAFSA. *Unit head:* William Grimes, Chairman, 617-353-9420, Fax: 617-353-9290, E-mail: wgrimes@bu.edu. *Application contact:* Michael Williams, Graduate Program Administrator, 617-353-9349, Fax: 617-353-9290, E-mail: mawillia@bu.edu.

Brown University, Graduate School, Center for Environmental Studies, Providence, RI 02912. Offers AM. Part-time programs available. *Degree requirements:* For master's, thesis. *Entrance requirements:* For master's, GRE, writing sample. Additional exam requirements/recommendations for international students: Required—TOEFL. Electronic applications accepted. *Faculty research:* Solid waste management, risk management policy (environmental health), resource management policy (water/fisheries), climate change, environmental justice, sustainable design, marine ecosystems.

California State University, Fullerton, Graduate Studies, College of Humanities and Social Sciences, Program in Environmental Studies, Fullerton, CA 92834-9480. Offers environmental sciences (MS). Part-time programs available. *Students:* 28 full-time (18 women), 38 part-time (19 women); includes 16 minority (2 Black or African American, non-Hispanic/Latino; 5 Asian, non-Hispanic/Latino; 6 Hispanic/Latino; 3 Two or more races, non-Hispanic/Latino), 2 international. Average age 29. 95 applicants, 45% accepted, 28 enrolled. In 2010, 25 master's awarded. *Degree requirements:* For master's, thesis. *Entrance requirements:* For master's, minimum GPA of 2.5 in last 60 units of course work. Application fee: $55. *Financial support:* Career-related internships or fieldwork, Federal Work-Study, institutionally sponsored loans, and scholarships/grants available. Support available to part-time students. Financial award application deadline: 3/1; financial award applicants required to submit FAFSA. *Unit head:* Dr. John Bock, Coordinator, 657-278-4373. *Application contact:* Admissions/Applications, 657-278-2371.

Central European University, Graduate Studies, Department of Environmental Sciences and Policy, Budapest, Hungary. Offers MS, PhD. Part-time programs available. *Faculty:* 9 full-time (2 women), 2 part-time/adjunct (both women). *Students:* 119 full-time (70 women), 8 part-time (4 women). Average age 29. 1,099 applicants, 5% accepted, 52 enrolled. In 2010, 47 master's, 2 doctorates awarded. Terminal master's awarded for partial completion of doctoral program. *Degree requirements:* For master's, one foreign language, thesis; for doctorate, one foreign language, comprehensive exam, thesis/dissertation. *Entrance requirements:* For master's and doctorate, interview. Additional exam requirements/recommendations for international students: Required—TOEFL (minimum score 570 paper-based; 230 computer-based). *Application deadline:* For fall admission, 1/5 for domestic and international students. Application fee: $0. Electronic applications accepted. Tuition and fees charges are reported in euros. *Expenses:* Tuition: Full-time 11,000 euros. Required fees: 250 euros. One-time fee: 200 euros full-time. Tuition and fees vary according to degree level, program, reciprocity agreements and student level. *Financial support:* In 2010–11, 52 students received support, including 32 fellowships with full and partial tuition reimbursements available (averaging $6,000 per year); career-related internships or fieldwork, institutionally sponsored loans, scholarships/grants, and tuition waivers (full and partial) also available. Financial award application deadline: 1/5. *Faculty research:* Management of ecological systems, environmental impact assessment, energy

Environmental Management and Policy

Central European University (continued)
conservation, climate change policy, forest policy in countries in transition. Total annual research expenditures: $16,127. *Unit head:* Dr. Alan Watt, Head of Department, 361-327-3021, Fax: 361-327-3031, E-mail: envsci@ceu.hu. *Application contact:* Krisztina Szabados, Department Coordinator, 361-327-3021, Fax: 361-327-3031, E-mail: envsci@ceu.hu.

Clark University, Graduate School, Department of International Development, Community, and Environment, Program in Environmental Science and Policy, Worcester, MA 01610-1477. Offers MA, MA/MBA. Part-time programs available. *Students:* 40 full-time (23 women), 8 part-time (3 women); includes 1 minority (Black or African American, non-Hispanic/Latino), 21 international. Average age 28. 94 applicants, 74% accepted, 29 enrolled. In 2010, 25 master's awarded. *Degree requirements:* For master's, thesis. *Entrance requirements:* For master's, 3 references, resume or curriculum vitae. Additional exam requirements/recommendations for international students: Required—TOEFL (minimum score 575 paper-based; 233 computer-based; 90 iBT) or IELTS (minimum score 6.5). *Application deadline:* For fall admission, 1/15 for domestic students. Application fee: $50. *Expenses:* Tuition: Full-time $37,000; part-time $1156 per credit hour. Required fees: $30; $1156 per credit hour. *Financial support:* In 2010–11, research assistantships with partial tuition reimbursements (averaging $5,000 per year), teaching assistantships with partial tuition reimbursements (averaging $5,000 per year) were awarded; fellowships with partial tuition reimbursements, institutionally sponsored loans and scholarships/grants also available. *Faculty research:* Environmental justice, health and risk assessment, media content analysis of energy technologies, uncertainty-risk analysis, inventory of major sources of greenhouse gas emissions. *Unit head:* Dr. William F. Fisher, Director, 508-421-3765, Fax: 508-793-8820, E-mail: wfisher@clarku.edu. *Application contact:* Paula Hall, IDCE Graduate Admissions, 508-793-7201, Fax: 508-793-8820, E-mail: idce@clarku.edu.

Clark University, Graduate School, Department of International Development, Community, and Environment, Program in Geographic Information Science for Development and Environment, Worcester, MA 01610-1477. Offers MA. *Students:* 41 full-time (19 women), 1 part-time (0 women); includes 2 minority (1 Asian, non-Hispanic/Latino; 1 Hispanic/Latino), 22 international. Average age 26. 80 applicants, 44% accepted, 19 enrolled. In 2010, 7 master's awarded. *Degree requirements:* For master's, thesis. *Entrance requirements:* For master's, 3 references, resume or curriculum vitae. Additional exam requirements/recommendations for international students: Required—TOEFL (minimum score 575 paper-based; 233 computer-based; 90 iBT) or IELTS (minimum score 6.5). *Application deadline:* For fall admission, 1/15 for domestic students. Application fee: $50. *Expenses:* Tuition: Full-time $37,000; part-time $1156 per credit hour. Required fees: $30; $1156 per credit hour. *Financial support:* In 2010–11, research assistantships with partial tuition reimbursements (averaging $5,000 per year), teaching assistantships with partial tuition reimbursements (averaging $5,000 per year) were awarded; fellowships with partial tuition reimbursements, institutionally sponsored loans and scholarships/grants also available. *Faculty research:* Land-use change, the effects of environmental influences on child health and development, quantitative methods, watershed management, brownfields redevelopment, human/environment interactions, biodiversity conservation, climate change. *Unit head:* IDCE, 508-793-7201, Fax: 508-793-8820. *Application contact:* Paula Hall, IDCE Graduate Admissions Office, 508-793-7205, E-mail: idce@clarku.edu.

Clemson University, Graduate School, College of Agriculture, Forestry and Life Sciences, Department of Forestry and Natural Resources, Program in Plant and Environmental Sciences, Clemson, SC 29634. Offers MS, PhD. *Students:* 34 full-time (10 women), 10 part-time (2 women); includes 1 Hispanic/Latino, 14 international. Average age 31. 32 applicants, 53% accepted, 12 enrolled. In 2010, 7 master's awarded. *Degree requirements:* For master's, thesis; for doctorate, thesis/dissertation. *Entrance requirements:* For master's, GRE General Test, bachelor's degree in biological science or chemistry; for doctorate, GRE General Test. Additional exam requirements/recommendations for international students: Required—TOEFL, IELTS. *Application deadline:* Applications are processed on a rolling basis. Application fee: $70 ($80 for international students). Electronic applications accepted. *Expenses:* Contact institution. *Financial support:* In 2010–11, 31 students received support, including 4 fellowships with full and partial tuition reimbursements available (averaging $6,635 per year), 26 research assistantships with partial tuition reimbursements available (averaging $16,445 per year), 8 teaching assistantships with partial tuition reimbursements available (averaging $11,000 per year); career-related internships or fieldwork, institutionally sponsored loans, scholarships/grants, health care benefits, and unspecified assistantships also available. Support available to part-time students. Financial award application deadline: 3/15; financial award applicants required to submit FAFSA. *Faculty research:* Systematics, aquatic botany, plant ecology, plant-fungus interactions, plant developmental genetics. *Unit head:* Dr. Patricia A. Zungoli, Chair, 864-656-3137, Fax: 864-656-5065, E-mail: pzngl@clemson.edu. *Application contact:* Dr. Halina Knap, Plant and Environmental Sciences Graduate Coordinator, 864-656-3102, Fax: 864-656-5065, E-mail: hskrpsk@clemson.edu.

Cleveland State University, College of Graduate Studies, Maxine Goodman Levin College of Urban Affairs, Program in Environmental Studies, Cleveland, OH 44115. Offers environmental studies (MAES); geographic information systems (Certificate); urban real estate development and finance (Certificate); JD/MAES. Part-time and evening/weekend programs available. *Faculty:* 26 full-time (10 women), 3 part-time/adjunct (0 women). *Students:* 12 full-time (5 women), 23 part-time (12 women); includes 1 Asian, non-Hispanic/Latino, 4 international. 16 applicants, 50% accepted, 6 enrolled. In 2010, 7 master's awarded. *Degree requirements:* For master's, thesis or alternative, exit project. *Entrance requirements:* For master's, GRE General Test (minimum score: verbal and quantitative 40th percentile, analytical writing 4.0), minimum GPA of 3.0. Additional exam requirements/recommendations for international students: Required—TOEFL (minimum score 525 paper-based; 197 computer-based; 65 iBT). *Application deadline:* For fall admission, 7/15 priority date for domestic students, 5/15 for international students; for spring admission, 11/1 for international students. Applications are processed on a rolling basis. Application fee: $30. Electronic applications accepted. *Expenses:* Tuition, state resident: full-time $8447; part-time $469 per credit hour. Tuition, nonresident: full-time $16,020; part-time $890 per credit hour. Required fees: $50. *Financial support:* In 2010–11, 1 student received support, including 1 research assistantship with full and partial tuition reimbursement available (averaging $6,960 per year); career-related internships or fieldwork, Federal Work-Study, scholarships/grants, tuition waivers (full and partial), and unspecified assistantships also available. Support available to part-time students. Financial award application deadline: 3/1; financial award applicants required to submit FAFSA. *Faculty research:* Environmental policy and administration, environmental planning, geographic information systems (GIS), urban sustainability planning and management, energy policy, land re-use. *Unit head:* Dr. Sanda Kaufman, Director, 216-687-2367, Fax: 216-687-9342, E-mail: s.kaufman@csuohio.edu. *Application contact:* Joan Demko, Graduate Academic Support Specialist, 216-523-7522, Fax: 216-687-5398, E-mail: urbanprograms@csuohio.edu.

College of the Atlantic, Program in Human Ecology, Bar Harbor, ME 04609-1198. Offers M Phil. *Degree requirements:* For master's, thesis. *Faculty research:* Conservation of endangered species, public policy/community planning, environmental education, history, philosophy.

Columbia University, Graduate School of Arts and Sciences, Program in Climate and Society, New York, NY 10027. Offers MA.

Columbia University, School of International and Public Affairs, Program in Environmental Science and Policy, New York, NY 10027. Offers MPA. Program admits applicants for late May/early June start only. *Degree requirements:* For master's, workshops. *Entrance requirements:* For master's, GRE (recommended), previous course work in biology and chemistry, earth sciences (recommended), economics (strongly recommended). Additional exam requirements/recommendations for international students: Required—TOEFL. Electronic applications accepted. *Faculty research:* Ecological management of enclosed ecosystems vegetation dynamics, environmental policy and management, energy policy, nuclear waste policy, environmental and natural resource economics and policy, carbon sequestration, urban planning, environmental risk assessment/toxicology, environmental justice.

See Display on page 375 and Close-Up on page 395.

Concordia University, School of Graduate Studies, Faculty of Arts and Science, Department of Geography, Planning and Environment, Montréal, QC H3G 1M8, Canada. Offers environmental impact assessment (Diploma); geography, urban and environmental studies (M Sc).

Cornell University, Graduate School, Graduate Fields of Agriculture and Life Sciences, Field of Natural Resources, Ithaca, NY 14853-0001. Offers aquatic science (MPS, MS, PhD); environmental management (MPS); fishery science (MPS, MS, PhD); forest science (MPS, MS, PhD); resource policy and management (MPS, MS, PhD); wildlife science (MPS, MS, PhD). *Faculty:* 36 full-time (7 women). *Students:* 48 full-time (21 women); includes 1 Asian, non-Hispanic/Latino; 1 Hispanic/Latino, 11 international. Average age 30. 52 applicants, 27% accepted, 11 enrolled. In 2010, 8 master's, 6 doctorates awarded. *Degree requirements:* For master's, thesis (MS); project paper (MPS); for doctorate, comprehensive exam, thesis/dissertation. *Entrance requirements:* For master's and doctorate, GRE General Test, 2 letters of recommendation. Additional exam requirements/recommendations for international students: Required—TOEFL (minimum score 550 paper-based; 213 computer-based; 77 iBT). *Application deadline:* For spring admission, 10/30 for domestic students. Applications are processed on a rolling basis. Application fee: $70. Electronic applications accepted. *Expenses:* Tuition: Full-time $29,500. Required fees: $76. Tuition and fees vary according to degree level and program. *Financial support:* In 2010–11, 9 fellowships with full tuition reimbursements, 16 research assistantships with full tuition reimbursements, 15 teaching assistantships with full tuition reimbursements were awarded; institutionally sponsored loans, scholarships/grants, health care benefits, tuition waivers (full and partial), and unspecified assistantships also available. Financial award applicants required to submit FAFSA. *Faculty research:* Ecosystem-level dynamics, systems modeling, conservation biology/management, resource management's human dimensions, biogeochemistry. *Unit head:* Director of Graduate Studies, 607-255-2807, Fax: 607-255-0349. *Application contact:* Graduate Field Assistant, 607-255-2807, Fax: 607-255-0349, E-mail: nrgrad@cornell.edu.

Cornell University, Graduate School, Graduate Fields of Agriculture and Life Sciences, Field of Soil and Crop Sciences, Ithaca, NY 14853-0001. Offers agronomy (MS, PhD); environmental information science (MS, PhD); environmental management (MPS); field crop science (MS, PhD); soil science (MS, PhD). *Faculty:* 39 full-time (9 women). *Students:* 29 full-time (13 women); includes 6 Hispanic/Latino, 9 international. Average age 29. 45 applicants, 24% accepted, 7 enrolled. In 2010, 3 master's, 4 doctorates awarded. *Degree requirements:* For master's, thesis (MS); for doctorate, comprehensive exam, thesis/dissertation. *Entrance requirements:* For master's and doctorate, GRE General Test, 2 letters of recommendation. Additional exam requirements/recommendations for international students: Required—TOEFL (minimum score 550 paper-based; 213 computer-based; 77 iBT). *Application deadline:* For fall admission, 2/1 priority date for domestic students. Applications are processed on a rolling basis. Application fee: $70. Electronic applications accepted. *Expenses:* Tuition: Full-time $29,500. Required fees: $76. Tuition and fees vary according to degree level and program. *Financial support:* In 2010–11, 6 fellowships with full tuition reimbursements, 11 research assistantships with full tuition reimbursements, 6 teaching assistantships with full tuition reimbursements were awarded; institutionally sponsored loans, traineeships, health care benefits, tuition waivers (full and partial), and unspecified assistantships also available. *Faculty research:* Soil chemistry, physics and biology; crop physiology and management; environmental information science and modeling; international agriculture; weed science. *Unit head:* Director of Graduate Studies, 607-255-3267, Fax: 607-255-8615. *Application contact:* Graduate Field Assistant, 607-255-3267, Fax: 607-255-8615, E-mail: ljh4@cornell.edu.

Cornell University, Graduate School, Graduate Fields of Architecture, Art and Planning, Field of Regional Science, Ithaca, NY 14853-0001. Offers environmental studies (MA, MS, PhD); international spatial problems (MA, MS, PhD); location theory (MA, MS, PhD); multiregional economic analysis (MA, MS, PhD); peace science (MA, MS, PhD); planning methods (MA, MS, PhD); urban and regional economics (MA, MS, PhD). *Faculty:* 22 full-time (6 women). *Students:* 20 full-time (6 women); includes 1 Black or African American, non-Hispanic/Latino, 18 international. Average age 31. 5 applicants, 80% accepted, 4 enrolled. In 2010, 3 doctorates awarded. Terminal master's awarded for partial completion of doctoral program. *Degree requirements:* For master's, thesis; for doctorate, comprehensive exam, thesis/dissertation. *Entrance requirements:* For master's and doctorate, GRE General Test, 2 letters of recommendation. Additional exam requirements/recommendations for international students: Required—TOEFL (minimum score 600 paper-based; 250 computer-based; 77 iBT). *Application deadline:* For fall admission, 1/15 priority date for domestic students. Application fee: $70. Electronic applications accepted. *Expenses:* Tuition: Full-time $29,500. Required fees: $76. Tuition and fees vary according to degree level and program. *Financial support:* In 2010–11, 1 research assistantship with full tuition reimbursement, 2 teaching assistantships with full tuition reimbursements were awarded; fellowships with full tuition reimbursements, institutionally sponsored loans, scholarships/grants, health care benefits, tuition waivers (full and partial), and unspecified assistantships also available. Financial award applicants required to submit FAFSA. *Faculty research:* Urban and regional growth, spatial economics, formation of spatial patterns by socioeconomic systems, non-linear dynamics and complex systems, environmental-economic systems. *Unit head:* Director of Graduate Studies, 607-255-6848, Fax: 607-255-1971. *Application contact:* Graduate Field Assistant, 607-255-6848, Fax: 607-255-1971, E-mail: regsci@cornell.edu.

Cornell University, Graduate School, Graduate Fields of Arts and Sciences, Field of Archaeology, Ithaca, NY 14853-0001. Offers environmental archaeology (MA); historical archaeology (MA); Latin American archaeology (MA); medieval archaeology (MA); Mediterranean and Near Eastern archaeology (MA); Stone Age archaeology (MA). *Faculty:* 18 full-time (5 women). *Students:* 8 full-time (7 women); includes 1 Hispanic/Latino. Average age 24. 23 applicants, 30% accepted, 3 enrolled. *Degree requirements:* For master's, one foreign language, thesis. *Entrance requirements:* For master's, GRE General Test, 3 letters of recommendation, sample of written work. Additional exam requirements/recommendations for international students: Required—TOEFL (minimum score 550 paper-based; 213 computer-based; 77 iBT). *Application deadline:* For fall admission, 1/15 for domestic students. Application fee: $80. Electronic applications accepted. *Expenses:* Tuition: Full-time $29,500. Required fees: $76. Tuition and fees vary according to degree level and program. *Financial support:* In 2010–11, 1 fellowship with full tuition reimbursement, 3 teaching assistantships with full tuition reimbursements were awarded; research assistantships with full tuition reimbursements, institutionally sponsored loans, scholarships/grants, health care benefits, tuition waivers (full and partial), and unspecified assistantships also available. Financial award applicants required to submit FAFSA. *Faculty research:* Anatolia, Lydia, Sardis, classical and Hellenistic Greece; science in archaeology; North American Indians; Stone Age Africa; Mayan trade. *Unit head:* Director of Graduate Studies, 607-255-6768, E-mail: blj7@cornell.edu. *Application contact:* Graduate Field Assistant, 607-255-6768, E-mail: dsd6@cornell.edu.

Dalhousie University, Faculty of Management, School for Resource and Environmental Studies, Halifax, NS B3H 3J5, Canada. Offers MES, MREM, MLIS/MREM. Part-time programs available. *Degree requirements:* For master's, thesis. *Entrance requirements:* For master's, honors degree. Additional exam requirements/recommendations for international students: Required—TOEFL, IELTS, CANTEST, CAEL, or Michigan English Language Assessment Battery. Electronic applications accepted. *Faculty research:* Resource management and ecology, aboriginal resource rights, management of toxic substances, environmental impact assessment, forest management, policy, coastal zone management.

Drexel University, College of Arts and Sciences, Program in Environmental Policy, Philadelphia, PA 19104-2875. Offers MS. Part-time and evening/weekend programs available. *Degree requirements:* For master's, thesis optional. Electronic applications accepted.

Duke University, Graduate School, Department of Environment, Durham, NC 27708. Offers natural resource economics/policy (PhD); natural resource science/ecology (PhD); natural resource systems science (PhD); JD/AM. Part-time programs available. *Faculty:* 28 full-time. *Students:* 59 full-time (33 women); includes 2 Black or African American, non-Hispanic/Latino; 1 Asian, non-Hispanic/Latino, 17 international. 84 applicants, 13% accepted, 6 enrolled. In 2010, 14 doctorates awarded. *Degree requirements:* For doctorate, variable foreign language requirement, thesis/dissertation. *Entrance requirements:* For doctorate, GRE General Test. Additional exam requirements/recommendations for international students: Required—TOEFL (minimum score 550 paper-based; 213 computer-based; 83 iBT), IELTS (minimum score 7). *Application deadline:* For fall admission, 12/8 priority date for domestic and international students. Application fee: $75. Electronic applications accepted. *Financial support:* Fellowships, research assistantships, teaching assistantships, Federal Work-Study available. Financial award application deadline: 12/8. *Unit head:* Gaby Katul, Director of Graduate Studies, 919-613-8002, Fax: 919-613-8061, E-mail: meg.stephens@duke.edu. *Application contact:* Elizabeth Hutton, Director, Graduate Admissions, 919-684-3913, Fax: 919-684-2277, E-mail: grad-admissions@duke.edu.

Duke University, Graduate School, Program in Environmental Policy, Durham, NC 27708. Offers PhD. *Faculty:* 29 full-time. *Students:* 4 full-time (1 woman), 2 international. 48 applicants, 17% accepted, 4 enrolled. *Degree requirements:* For doctorate, comprehensive exam, thesis/dissertation. *Entrance requirements:* For doctorate, GRE General. Additional exam requirements/recommendations for international students: Required—TOEFL (minimum score 550 paper-based; 213 computer-based; 83 iBT), IELTS (minimum score 7). *Application deadline:* For fall admission, 12/8 priority date for domestic and international students. Application fee: $75. Electronic applications accepted. *Financial support:* Fellowships, research assistantships, teaching assistantships available. Financial award application deadline: 12/8. *Unit head:* Jeff Vincent, Dean, 919-613-8002, Fax: 919-613-8061, E-mail: meg.stephens@duke.edu. *Application contact:* Elizabeth Hutton, Director of Admissions, 919-684-3913, E-mail: grad-admissions@duke.edu.

Duke University, Nicholas School of the Environment, Durham, NC 27708-0328. Offers coastal environmental management (MEM); DEL-environmental leadership (MEM); energy and environment (MEM); environmental economics and policy (MEM); environmental health and security (MEM); forest resource management (MF); global environmental change (MEM); resource ecology (MEM); water and air resources (MEM); JD/AM; JD/MEM; JD/MF; MAT/MEM; MBA/MEM; MBA/MF; MEM/MPP; MF/MPP. *Accreditation:* SAF (one or more programs are accredited). Part-time programs available. *Degree requirements:* For master's, thesis. *Entrance requirements:* For master's, GRE General Test, previous course work in biology or ecology, calculus, statistics, and microeconomics; computer familiarity with word processing and data analysis. Additional exam requirements/recommendations for international students: Required—TOEFL (minimum score 550 paper-based; 213 computer-based). Electronic applications accepted. *Expenses:* Contact institution. *Faculty research:* Ecosystem management, conservation ecology, earth systems, risk assessment.

Duquesne University, Bayer School of Natural and Environmental Sciences, Environmental Science and Management Program, Pittsburgh, PA 15282-0001. Offers environmental management (MEM, Certificate); environmental science (Certificate); environmental science and management (MS); JD/MS; MBA/MS; MS/MS. Part-time and evening/weekend programs available. Postbaccalaureate distance learning degree programs offered (minimal on-campus study). *Faculty:* 4 full-time (0 women), 8 part-time/adjunct (0 women). *Students:* 22 full-time (9 women), 17 part-time (12 women), 6 international. Average age 27. 28 applicants, 96% accepted, 17 enrolled. In 2010, 15 master's awarded. *Degree requirements:* For master's, thesis (for some programs), minimum of 36 credit hours; for Certificate, minimum of 18 credit hours. *Entrance requirements:* For master's, GRE General Test, course work in biology, chemistry, and calculus or statistics; 3 letters of reference. Additional exam requirements/recommendations for international students: Required—TOEFL (minimum score 80 iBT). *Application deadline:* For fall admission, 4/1 priority date for domestic students, 4/1 for international students; for spring admission, 10/1 priority date for domestic students, 10/1 for international students. Applications are processed on a rolling basis. Application fee: $40. *Expenses:* Contact institution. *Financial support:* In 2010–11, 8 students received support, including 1 fellowship (averaging $17,000 per year), 2 research assistantships (averaging $16,000 per year), 3 teaching assistantships with full and partial tuition reimbursements available (averaging $10,875 per year); career-related internships or fieldwork, scholarships/grants, tuition waivers (partial), and unspecified assistantships also available. Financial award application deadline: 5/31. *Faculty research:* Watershed management systems, environmental analytical chemistry, environmental endocrinology, environmental microbiology, aquatic biology. *Unit head:* Dr. John Stolz, Director, 412-396-4367, Fax: 412-396-4092, E-mail: stolz@duq.edu. *Application contact:* Heather Costello, Graduate Academic Advisor, 412-396-6339, Fax: 412-396-4881, E-mail: costelloh@duq.edu.

The Evergreen State College, Graduate Programs, Program in Environmental Studies, Olympia, WA 98505. Offers MES. Part-time and evening/weekend programs available. *Faculty:* 4 full-time (2 women), 4 part-time/adjunct (1 woman). *Students:* 42 full-time (18 women), 44 part-time (25 women); includes 1 Black or African American, non-Hispanic/Latino; 3 Asian, non-Hispanic/Latino; 3 Hispanic/Latino; 1 Native Hawaiian or other Pacific Islander, non-Hispanic/Latino. Average age 32. 61 applicants, 98% accepted, 32 enrolled. In 2010, 21 master's awarded. *Degree requirements:* For master's, thesis. *Entrance requirements:* For master's, GRE, BA or BS; minimum GPA of 3.0 in last 90 quarter hours toward BA/BS; 15 quarter hours in social sciences and biological or physical science; 4 in statistics, biology, and microeconomics; 3 letters of recommendation; evidence of writing, analytical and general communication skills of high quality and at level appropriate for graduate study. Additional exam requirements/recommendations for international students: Required—TOEFL (minimum score 600 paper-based; 250 computer-based). *Application deadline:* For fall admission, 11/15 priority date for domestic and international students. Applications are processed on a rolling basis. Application fee: $50. Electronic applications accepted. *Expenses:* Contact institution. *Financial support:* In 2010–11, 47 students received support, including 9 fellowships (averaging $1,558 per year); research assistantships, career-related internships or fieldwork, Federal Work-Study, scholarships/grants, tuition waivers (partial), and unspecified assistantships also available. Support available to part-time students. Financial award application deadline: 3/15; financial award applicants required to submit FAFSA. *Faculty research:* Oceanography, marine biology, geography, fluvial geomorphology, forest ecology, computer science, political science, economics, energy, climate change. *Unit head:* Dr. Martha Henderson, Director, 360-867-6225, Fax: 360-867-5430, E-mail: mhenders@evergreen.edu. *Application contact:* Gail Wootan, Assistant Director, 360-867-6225, Fax: 360-867-5430, E-mail: wootang@evergreen.edu.

Florida Atlantic University, Dorothy F. Schmidt College of Arts and Letters, Department of History, Boca Raton, FL 33431-0991. Offers environmental studies (Certificate); history (MA). Part-time programs available. *Faculty:* 20 full-time (10 women), 1 part-time/adjunct (0 women). *Students:* 19 full-time (7 women), 15 part-time (3 women); includes 3 minority (1 Black or African American, non-Hispanic/Latino; 2 Hispanic/Latino), 1 international. Average age 33. 33 applicants, 45% accepted, 12 enrolled. In 2010, 6 master's awarded. *Degree requirements:* For master's, one foreign language, thesis optional. *Entrance requirements:* For master's, GRE General Test, minimum GPA of 3.0. *Application deadline:* For fall admission, 6/1 priority date for domestic students, 2/15 for international students; for spring admission, 10/15 for domestic students, 8/15 for international students. Applications are processed on a rolling basis. Application fee: $30. Electronic applications accepted. *Expenses:* Tuition, area resident: Part-time $319.96 per credit. Tuition, state resident: part-time $319.96 per credit. Tuition, nonresident: part-time $926.42 per credit. *Financial support:* Fellowships, research assistantships, teaching assistantships with tuition reimbursements, career-related internships or fieldwork, Federal Work-Study, and tuition waivers (partial) available. Support available to part-time students. Financial award application deadline: 3/1. *Faculty research:* Twentieth century America, U. S. urban history, Florida history, history of socialism, Latin America. *Unit head:* Dr. Patricia Kollander, Chair, 561-297-3841, Fax: 561-297-2704, E-mail: kollande@fau.edu. *Application contact:* Ben Lowe, Director of Graduate Programs, 561-297-3846, Fax: 561-297-2704, E-mail: bplowe@fau.edu.

Florida Gulf Coast University, College of Professional Studies, Program in Public Administration, Fort Myers, FL 33965-6565. Offers criminal justice (MPA); environmental policy (MPA); general public administration (MPA); management (MPA). *Accreditation:* NASPAA. Part-time programs available. *Faculty:* 35 full-time (15 women), 34 part-time/adjunct (12 women). *Students:* 71 full-time (46 women), 20 part-time (11 women); includes 10 Black or African American, non-Hispanic/Latino; 1 American Indian or Alaska Native, non-Hispanic/Latino; 7 Hispanic/Latino, 2 international. Average age 31. 46 applicants, 67% accepted, 26 enrolled. In 2010, 11 master's awarded. *Entrance requirements:* For master's, GRE General Test, MAT, minimum GPA of 3.0. Additional exam requirements/recommendations for international students: Required—TOEFL (minimum score 550 paper-based; 213 computer-based). *Application deadline:* For fall admission, 7/1 priority date for domestic students; for spring admission, 11/15 for domestic students. Applications are processed on a rolling basis. Application fee: $30. Electronic applications accepted. *Expenses:* Tuition, state resident: part-time $322.08 per credit hour. Tuition, nonresident: part-time $1117.08 per credit hour. *Financial support:* In 2010–11, 5 research assistantships were awarded; career-related internships or fieldwork and tuition waivers (full and partial) also available. Support available to part-time students. *Faculty research:* Personnel, public policy, public finance, housing policy. *Unit head:* Terry Busson, Chair, 239-590-7704, E-mail: tbusson@fgcu.edu. *Application contact:* Roger Green, Information Contact, 239-590-7838, Fax: 239-590-7846.

Florida Institute of Technology, Graduate Programs, College of Engineering, Department of Marine and Environmental Systems, Melbourne, FL 32901-6975. Offers earth remote sensing (MS); environmental resource management (MS); environmental science (MS, PhD); meteorology (MS); ocean engineering (MS, PhD); oceanography (MS, PhD). Part-time programs available. *Faculty:* 11 full-time (0 women), 3 part-time/adjunct (0 women). *Students:* 47 full-time (16 women), 15 part-time (5 women); includes 4 minority (1 Black or African American, non-Hispanic/Latino; 1 Asian, non-Hispanic/Latino; 1 Hispanic/Latino; 1 Two or more races, non-Hispanic/Latino), 10 international. Average age 27. 118 applicants, 49% accepted, 19 enrolled. In 2010, 21 master's, 1 doctorate awarded. *Degree requirements:* For master's, comprehensive exam (for some programs), thesis (for some programs), seminar, field project, written final exam, internship, technical paper, oral presentation or internship; for doctorate, comprehensive exam, thesis/dissertation, seminar, internships (oceanography and environmental science), publications. *Entrance requirements:* For master's, GRE General Test (environmental science, oceanography, environmental resource management, meteorology, earth remote sensing), 3 letters of recommendation, minimum GPA of 3.0, resume, transcripts, statement of objectives; for doctorate, GRE General Test (oceanography, environmental science), resume, 3 letters of recommendation, minimum GPA of 3.3, statement of objectives, on campus interview (highly recommended). Additional exam requirements/recommendations for international students: Required—TOEFL (minimum score 550 paper-based; 213 computer-based; 79 iBT). *Application deadline:* For fall admission, 4/1 for international students; for spring admission, 9/30 for international students. Applications are processed on a rolling basis. Application fee: $50. Electronic applications accepted. *Expenses:* Tuition: Part-time $1040 per credit hour. Tuition and fees vary according to campus/location. *Financial support:* In 2010–11, 5 fellowships with full and partial tuition reimbursements (averaging $7,240 per year), 5 research assistantships with full and partial tuition reimbursements (averaging $3,664 per year), 10 teaching assistantships with full and partial tuition reimbursements (averaging $6,670 per year) were awarded; career-related internships or fieldwork, institutionally sponsored loans, tuition waivers (partial), unspecified assistantships, and tuition remissions also available. Support available to part-time students. Financial award application deadline: 3/1; financial award applicants required to submit FAFSA. Total annual research expenditures: $1.7 million. *Unit head:* Dr. George Maul, Department Head, 321-674-7453, Fax: 321-674-7212, E-mail: gmaul@fit.edu. *Application contact:* Cheryl A. Brown, Associate Director of Graduate Admissions, 321-674-7581, Fax: 321-723-9468, E-mail: cbrown@fit.edu.

Florida International University, College of Arts and Sciences, Department of Earth and Environment, Program in Environmental Studies, Miami, FL 33199. Offers MS. Part-time programs available. *Students:* 28 full-time (15 women), 12 part-time (6 women); includes 1 American Indian or Alaska Native, non-Hispanic/Latino; 1 Asian, non-Hispanic/Latino; 7 Hispanic/Latino, 9 international. Average age 28. 45 applicants, 36% accepted, 16 enrolled. In 2010, 17 master's awarded. *Degree requirements:* For master's, thesis or alternative. *Entrance requirements:* For master's, GRE General Test, minimum GPA of 3.0, 3 letters of recommendation, letter of intent. Additional exam requirements/recommendations for international students: Required—TOEFL (minimum score 550 paper-based; 80 iBT). *Application deadline:* For fall admission, 3/1 for domestic and international students; for spring admission, 10/1 for domestic students, 9/1 for international students. Applications are processed on a rolling basis. Application fee: $30. Electronic applications accepted. *Financial support:* Institutionally sponsored loans and scholarships/grants available. Financial award application deadline: 3/1; financial award applicants required to submit FAFSA. *Unit head:* Dr. Rosemary Hickey-Vargas, Chair, Earth and Environment Department, 305-348-1930, Fax: 305-348-6137, E-mail: rosemary.hickey-vargas@fiu.edu. *Application contact:* Dr. Krishnaswamy Jayachandran, Director, Graduate Program, 305-348-1930, Fax: 305-348-6137, E-mail: jayachan@fiu.edu.

George Mason University, College of Science, Department of Environmental Science and Policy, Fairfax, VA 22030. Offers environmental management (Certificate); environmental science and policy (MS); environmental science and public policy (PhD). Part-time programs available. *Faculty:* 20 full-time (7 women), 4 part-time/adjunct (3 women). *Students:* 20 full-time (13 women), 147 part-time (78 women); includes 7 Black or African American, non-Hispanic/Latino; 7 Asian, non-Hispanic/Latino; 9 Hispanic/Latino, 18 international. Average age 36. 85 applicants, 55% accepted, 37 enrolled. In 2010, 21 master's, 7 doctorates, 1 other advanced degree awarded. *Degree requirements:* For doctorate, thesis/dissertation, internship. *Entrance requirements:* For doctorate, GRE General Test, GRE Subject Test. Additional exam requirements/recommendations for international students: Required—TOEFL (minimum score 570 paper-based; 230 computer-based; 88 iBT). *Application deadline:* For fall admission, 5/1 for domestic students; for spring admission, 11/1 for domestic students. Application fee: $100. Electronic applications accepted. *Expenses:* Tuition, state resident: full-time $8192; part-time $440 per credit hour. Tuition, nonresident: full-time $22,952; part-time $1055 per credit hour. Required fees: $2364; $99 per credit hour. *Financial support:* In 2010–11, 47 students received support, including 2 fellowships (averaging $18,000 per year), 9 research assistantships (averaging $16,408 per year), 36 teaching assistantships (averaging $12,478 per year); career-related internships or fieldwork, Federal Work-Study, scholarships/grants, unspecified assistantships, and health care benefits (full-time research or teaching assistantship recipients) also available. Financial award application deadline: 3/1; financial award applicants required to submit FAFSA. Total annual research expenditures: $425,538. *Unit head:* Dr. R. Christian Jones, Interim Director, 703-993-1127, Fax: 703-993-1046, E-mail: rcjones@gmu.edu. *Application contact:* Dr. Albert Torzilli, Graduate Coordinator, 703-993-1062, E-mail: atorzill@gmu.edu.

The George Washington University, Columbian College of Arts and Sciences, Program in Environmental and Resource Policy, Washington, DC 20052. Offers MA. *Students:* 3 full-time

Environmental Management and Policy

The George Washington University *(continued)*
(2 women), 17 part-time (14 women); includes 4 minority (1 Black or African American, non-Hispanic/Latino; 2 Asian, non-Hispanic/Latino; 1 Hispanic/Latino). Average age 28. 38 applicants, 68% accepted, 5 enrolled. In 2010, 6 master's awarded. *Degree requirements:* For master's, capstone course. *Entrance requirements:* For master's, GRE General Test, minimum GPA of 3.0, two letters of recommendation. Additional exam requirements/recommendations for international students: Required—TOEFL (minimum score 600 paper-based; 250 computer-based; 100 iBT). *Application deadline:* For fall admission, 4/1 priority date for domestic and international students; for spring admission, 10/1 priority date for domestic students, 9/1 priority date for international students. Applications are processed on a rolling basis. Application fee: $60. Electronic applications accepted. *Financial support:* In 2010–11, 2 students received support; fellowships with tuition reimbursements available, institutionally sponsored loans and tuition waivers available. Financial award application deadline: 1/15. *Unit head:* Prof. Henry Teng, Chair, 202-994-1008. *Application contact:* Prof. Henry Teng, Chair, 202-994-1008.

Georgia Institute of Technology, Graduate Studies and Research, College of Architecture, City and Regional Planning Program, Atlanta, GA 30332-0001. Offers city and regional planning (PhD); economic development (MCRP); environmental planning and management (MCRP); geographic information systems (MCRP); land and community development (MCRP); land use planning (MCRP); transportation (MCRP); urban design (MCRP); MCP/MSCE. *Accreditation:* ACSP. *Degree requirements:* For master's, thesis, internship. *Entrance requirements:* For master's, GRE General Test, minimum GPA of 2.7. Additional exam requirements/recommendations for international students: Required—TOEFL. Electronic applications accepted.

Goddard College, Graduate Division, Master of Arts in Individualized Studies Program, Plainfield, VT 05667-9432. Offers consciousness studies (MA); environmental studies (MA); transformative language arts (MA). Postbaccalaureate distance learning degree programs offered (minimal on-campus study). *Degree requirements:* For master's, thesis. *Entrance requirements:* For master's, 3 letters of recommendation, study plan, bibliography/resource list, interview. Electronic applications accepted. *Expenses:* Contact institution.

Green Mountain College, Program in Environmental Studies, Poultney, VT 05764-1199. Offers MS. Distance learning only. Part-time and evening/weekend programs available. Postbaccalaureate distance learning degree programs offered (no on-campus study). *Entrance requirements:* For master's, portfolio, curriculum vitae, 3 recommendations. Electronic applications accepted. *Faculty research:* Herbarium specimen, solar electricity's value, environmental politics.

Hardin-Simmons University, Graduate School, Holland School of Sciences and Mathematics, Program in Environmental Management, Abilene, TX 79698-0001. Offers MS. Part-time programs available. *Faculty:* 5 full-time (0 women). *Students:* 8 full-time (5 women), 4 part-time (1 woman); includes 1 Hispanic/Latino, 1 international. Average age 27. 4 applicants, 100% accepted, 4 enrolled. In 2010, 5 master's awarded. *Degree requirements:* For master's, comprehensive exam, thesis or alternative, internship. *Entrance requirements:* For master's, minimum undergraduate GPA of 3.0 in major, 2.7 overall; 2 semesters of course work each in biology, chemistry, and geology; interview; writing sample; occupational experience. Additional exam requirements/recommendations for international students: Required—TOEFL (minimum score 550 paper-based; 213 computer-based; 75 iBT). *Application deadline:* For fall admission, 8/15 priority date for domestic students, 4/1 for international students; for spring admission, 1/5 priority date for domestic students, 9/1 for international students. Applications are processed on a rolling basis. Application fee: $50. *Expenses:* Tuition: Full-time $12,150; part-time $675 per credit hour. Required fees: $650; $110 per semester. Tuition and fees vary according to degree level. *Financial support:* Fellowships, career-related internships or fieldwork and scholarships/grants available. Support available to part-time students. Financial award application deadline: 6/30; financial award applicants required to submit FAFSA. *Faculty research:* South American history, herpetology, geology, environmental education, petroleum biodegradation, environmental ecology and microbiology. *Unit head:* Dr. Mark Ouimette, Director, 325-670-1383, Fax: 325-670-1391, E-mail: ouimette@hsutx.edu. *Application contact:* Dr. Nancy Kucinski, Dean of Graduate Studies, 325-670-1298, Fax: 325-670-1564, E-mail: gradoff@hsutx.edu.

Harvard University, Extension School, Cambridge, MA 02138-3722. Offers applied sciences (CAS); biotechnology (ALM); educational technologies (ALM); educational technology (CET); English for graduate and professional studies (DGP); environmental management (ALM, CEM); information technology (ALM); journalism (ALM); liberal arts (ALM); management (ALM, CM); mathematics for teaching (ALM); museum studies (ALM); premedical studies (Diploma); publication and communication (CPC). Part-time and evening/weekend programs available. *Degree requirements:* For master's, thesis. *Entrance requirements:* For master's, 3 completed graduate courses with grade of B or higher. Additional exam requirements/recommendations for international students: Required—TOEFL (minimum score 600 paper-based; 250 computer-based), TWE (minimum score 5). *Expenses:* Contact institution.

Humboldt State University, Academic Programs, College of Natural Resources and Sciences, Programs in Environmental Systems, Arcata, CA 95521-8299. Offers environmental systems (MS), including energy, environment and society, environmental resources engineering, geology, math modeling. *Students:* 35 full-time (12 women), 6 part-time (0 women); includes 4 minority (1 Asian, non-Hispanic/Latino; 3 Hispanic/Latino), 2 international. Average age 28. 72 applicants, 29% accepted, 15 enrolled. In 2010, 21 master's awarded. *Degree requirements:* For master's, thesis. *Entrance requirements:* For master's, GRE, appropriate bachelor's degree, minimum GPA of 2.5, 3 letters of recommendation. Additional exam requirements/recommendations for international students: Required—TOEFL. *Application deadline:* For fall admission, 2/15 for domestic students; for spring admission, 10/15 for domestic students. Applications are processed on a rolling basis. Application fee: $55. Tuition and fees vary according to program. *Financial support:* Application deadline: 3/1. *Faculty research:* Mathematical modeling, international development technology, geology, environmental resources engineering. *Unit head:* Dr. Chris Dugaw, Chair, 707-826-4251, Fax: 707-826-4145, E-mail: dugaw@humboldt.edu. *Application contact:* Julie Tucker, Administrative Support, 707-826-3256, Fax: 707-826-3140, E-mail: jlt7002@humboldt.edu.

Idaho State University, Office of Graduate Studies, College of Engineering, Civil and Environmental Engineering Department, Pocatello, ID 83209-8060. Offers civil engineering (MS); environmental engineering (MS); environmental science and management (MS). Part-time programs available. *Degree requirements:* For master's, comprehensive exam (for some programs), thesis optional, thesis project, 2 semesters of seminar. *Entrance requirements:* For master's, GRE. Additional exam requirements/recommendations for international students: Required—TOEFL (minimum score 550 paper-based; 213 computer-based; 80 iBT). Electronic applications accepted. *Faculty research:* Floor vibration investigations, earthquake engineering, base isolation systems and seismic risk assessment, infrastructure revitalization (building foundations and damage, bridge structures, highways, and dams), slope stability and soil erosion, pavement rehabilitation, computational fluid dynamics and flood control structures, microbial fuel cells, water treatment and water quality modeling, environmental risk assessment, biotechnology, nanotechnology.

Illinois Institute of Technology, Stuart School of Business, Program in Environmental Management and Sustainability, Chicago, IL 60661. Offers MS, JD/MS, MBA/MS. Part-time and evening/weekend programs available. *Faculty:* 37 full-time (4 women), 21 part-time/adjunct (5 women). *Students:* 29 full-time (15 women), 42 part-time (22 women); includes 4 minority (2 Black or African American, non-Hispanic/Latino; 1 Asian, non-Hispanic/Latino; 1 Two or more races, non-Hispanic/Latino), 14 international. Average age 32. 36 applicants, 81% accepted, 16 enrolled. In 2010, 26 master's awarded. *Entrance requirements:* For master's, GRE (minimum score 1000) or GMAT (500). Additional exam requirements/recommendations for international

students: Required—TOEFL (minimum score 600 paper-based; 85 iBT); Recommended—IELTS (minimum score 7). *Application deadline:* For fall admission, 8/1 for domestic students, 5/1 for international students; for spring admission, 12/15 for domestic students, 10/15 for international students. Applications are processed on a rolling basis. Application fee: $75. Electronic applications accepted. *Expenses:* Contact institution. *Financial support:* In 2010–11, 2 research assistantships with partial tuition reimbursements (averaging $4,850 per year) were awarded; career-related internships or fieldwork, Federal Work-Study, institutionally sponsored loans, scholarships/grants, traineeships, health care benefits, and tuition waivers (partial) also available. Support available to part-time students. Financial award applicants required to submit FAFSA. *Faculty research:* Wind energy, carbon footprint reduction, critical asset management, solar energy, water quality management. *Unit head:* Dr. George P. Nassos, Director, Center for Sustainable Enterprise, 312-906-6543, Fax: 312-906-6549, E-mail: gnassos@stuart.iit.edu. *Application contact:* Deborah Gibson, Director, Graduate Admission, 866-472-3448, Fax: 312-567-3138, E-mail: inquiry.grad@iit.edu.

Indiana University Bloomington, School of Public and Environmental Affairs, Public Affairs Programs, Bloomington, IN 47405-7000. Offers comparative and international affairs (MPA); economic development (MPA); energy (MPA); environmental policy (PhD); environmental policy and natural resource management (MPA); information systems (MPA); local government management (MPA); nonprofit management (MPA, Certificate); policy analysis (MPA); public finance (PhD); public financial administration (MPA); public management (MPA, PhD); public policy analysis (PhD); specialized public affairs (MPA); sustainability and sustainable development (MPA); JD/MPA; MPA/MIS; MPA/MLS; MSES/MPA. *Accreditation:* NASPAA (one or more programs are accredited). Part-time programs available. *Faculty:* 31 full-time, 15 part-time/adjunct. *Students:* 466 full-time (261 women); includes 11 Black or African American, non-Hispanic/Latino; 2 American Indian or Alaska Native, non-Hispanic/Latino; 42 Asian, non-Hispanic/Latino; 1 Hispanic/Latino, 65 international. Average age 26. 650 applicants, 218 enrolled. In 2010, 166 master's, 10 doctorates awarded. *Degree requirements:* For master's, Core classes and capstone; for doctorate, comprehensive exam, thesis/dissertation. *Entrance requirements:* For master's, GRE General Test or GMAT, official transcripts, 3 letters of recommendation, resume, personal statement, departmental questions; for doctorate, GRE General Test or LSAT and TOEFL (intl), official transcripts, 3 letters of recommendation, resume or curriculum vitae, statement of purpose, application, application fee, residence classification (Intl.). Additional exam requirements/recommendations for international students: Required—TOEFL (minimum score 600 paper-based; 96 iBT); Recommended—IELTS (minimum score 7). *Application deadline:* For fall admission, 5/1 priority date for domestic students, 12/1 priority date for international students. Applications are processed on a rolling basis. Application fee: $55 ($65 for international students). Electronic applications accepted. *Financial support:* Fellowships with partial tuition reimbursements, research assistantships with partial tuition reimbursements, teaching assistantships with partial tuition reimbursements, career-related internships or fieldwork, Federal Work-Study, scholarships/grants, health care benefits, unspecified assistantships, and Service Corps programs available. Financial award application deadline: 2/1; financial award applicants required to submit FAFSA. *Faculty research:* Comparative and international affairs, environmental policy and resource management, policy analysis, public finance, public management, urban management, nonprofit management, energy policy, social policy, public finance. *Unit head:* Jennifer Forney, Director of Graduate Student Services, 812-855-9485, Fax: 812-856-3665, E-mail: speampo@indiana.edu. *Application contact:* Audrey Whitaker, Admissions Assistant, 812-855-2840, E-mail: speaapps@indiana.edu.

Instituto Tecnologico de Santo Domingo, Graduate School, Area of Basic And Environmental Sciences, Santo Domingo, Dominican Republic. Offers environmental science (M En S), including environmental education, environmental management, marine resources, natural resources management; mathematics (MS, PhD); renewable energy technology (MS, Certificate).

Instituto Tecnológico y de Estudios Superiores de Monterrey, Campus Estado de México, Professional and Graduate Division, Estado de Mexico, Mexico. Offers administration of information technologies (MITA); architecture (M Arch); business administration (GMBA, MBA); computer sciences (MCS, PhD); education (M Ed); educational institution administration (MAD); educational technology and innovation (PhD); electronic commerce (MEC); environmental systems (MS); finance (MAF); humanistic studies (MHS); information sciences and knowledge management (MISKM); information systems (MS); manufacturing systems (MS); marketing (MEM); quality systems and productivity (MS); science and materials engineering (PhD); telecommunications management (MTM). Part-time programs available. Postbaccalaureate distance learning degree programs offered (minimal on-campus study). *Degree requirements:* For master's, one foreign language, thesis (for some programs); for doctorate, one foreign language, thesis/dissertation. *Entrance requirements:* For master's, E-PAEP 500, interview; for doctorate, E-PAEP 500, research proposal. Additional exam requirements/recommendations for international students: Required—TOEFL (minimum score 550 paper-based). *Faculty research:* Surface treatments by plasmas, mechanical properties, robotics, graphical computing, mechatronics security protocols.

Instituto Tecnológico y de Estudios Superiores de Monterrey, Campus Irapuato, Graduate Programs, Irapuato, Mexico. Offers administration (MBA); administration of information technology (MAIT); administration of telecommunications (MAT); architecture (M Arch); computer science (MCS); education (M Ed); educational administration (MEA); educational innovation and technology (DEIT); educational technology (MET); electronic commerce (MBA); environmental administration and planning (MEAP); environmental systems (MES); finances (MBA); humanistic studies (MHS); international management for Latin American executives (MIMLAE); library and information science (MLIS); manufacturing quality management (MMQM); marketing research (MBA).

Inter American University of Puerto Rico, Metropolitan Campus, Graduate Programs, Program in Environmental Evaluation and Protection, San Juan, PR 00919-1293. Offers MS.

The Johns Hopkins University, Engineering for Professionals, Part-Time Program in Environmental Planning and Management, Baltimore, MD 21218-2699. Offers MS, Post-Master's Certificate. Part-time and evening/weekend programs available. Postbaccalaureate distance learning degree programs offered (no on-campus study). *Students:* 4 full-time (3 women), 64 part-time (35 women); includes 19 minority (5 Black or African American, non-Hispanic/Latino; 5 Asian, non-Hispanic/Latino; 8 Hispanic/Latino; 1 Two or more races, non-Hispanic/Latino), 3 international. Average age 31. 25 applicants, 100% accepted, 15 enrolled. In 2010, 7 master's awarded. Application fee: $75. *Unit head:* Dr. Hedy Alavi, Program Chair, 410-516-7091, Fax: 410-516-8996, E-mail: hedy.alavi@jhu.edu. *Application contact:* Priyanka Dwivedi, Admissions Manager, 410-516-2300, Fax: 410-579-8049, E-mail: pdwived1@jhu.edu.

The Johns Hopkins University, G. W. C. Whiting School of Engineering, Program in Engineering Management, Baltimore, MD 21218-2699. Offers biomaterials (MSEM); communications science (MSEM); computer science (MSEM); fluid mechanics (MSEM); materials science and engineering (MSEM); mechanical engineering (MSEM); mechanics and materials (MSEM); nano-biotechnology (MSEM); nanomaterials and nanotechnology (MSEM); probability and statistics (MSEM); smart product and device design (MSEM); systems analysis, management and environmental policy (MSEM). *Students:* 32 full-time (5 women), 4 part-time (0 women); includes 7 minority (3 Black or African American, non-Hispanic/Latino; 3 Asian, non-Hispanic/Latino; 1 Hispanic/Latino), 11 international. Average age 23. 110 applicants, 60% accepted, 27 enrolled. In 2010, 6 master's awarded. *Entrance requirements:* For master's, GRE, 3 letters of recommendation, resume. Additional exam requirements/recommendations for international students: Required—TOEFL (minimum score 600 paper-based; 250 computer-based; 100 iBT) or IELTS (minimum score 7). *Application deadline:* For fall admission, 1/15 priority date for domestic students, 1/15 for international students; for spring admission, 9/15 priority date for domestic students, 9/15 for international students. Applications are processed

on a rolling basis. Application fee: $75. Electronic applications accepted. *Financial support:* Fellowships, health care benefits available. *Unit head:* Dr. Edward R. Scheinerman, Interim Director/Vice Dean for Education, School of Engineering/Professor, Applied Mathematics and Statistics, 410-516-7395, Fax: 410-516-4880, E-mail: ers@jhu.edu. *Application contact:* Dennis McIver, Coordinator of Graduate Admissions, 410-516-8174, Fax: 410-516-0780, E-mail: graduateadmissions@jhu.edu.

The Johns Hopkins University, Zanvyl Krieger School of Arts and Sciences, Advanced Academic Programs, Program in Environmental Sciences and Policy, Baltimore, MD 21218-2699. Offers MS. Part-time and evening/weekend programs available. Postbaccalaureate distance learning degree programs offered (minimal on-campus study). *Faculty:* 1 (woman) full-time, 37 part-time/adjunct (3 women). *Students:* 20 full-time (10 women), 224 part-time (134 women); includes 28 minority (10 Black or African American, non-Hispanic/Latino; 9 Asian, non-Hispanic/Latino; 3 Hispanic/Latino; 6 Two or more races, non-Hispanic/Latino), 11 international. Average age 31. 126 applicants, 63% accepted, 55 enrolled. In 2010, 81 master's awarded. *Degree requirements:* For master's, thesis (for some programs). *Entrance requirements:* For master's, minimum GPA of 3.0, coursework in chemistry and calculus. Additional exam requirements/recommendations for international students: Required—TOEFL (minimum score 250 computer-based). *Application deadline:* For fall admission, 5/31 priority date for domestic students, 4/30 priority date for international students; for spring admission, 10/31 priority date for domestic and international students. Application fee: $75. *Financial support:* Applicants required to submit FAFSA. *Unit head:* Dr. Eileen McGurty, Associate Program Chair, 410-516-7049, E-mail: emgurty@jhu.edu. *Application contact:* Valana M. McMickens, Admissions Manager, 202-452-1941, Fax: 202-452-1970, E-mail: aapadmissions@jhu.edu.

Kean University, College of Business and Public Management, Program in Public Administration, Union, NJ 07083. Offers environmental management (MPA); health services administration (MPA); non-profit management (MPA); public administration (MPA). *Accreditation:* NASPAA. Part-time and evening/weekend programs available. *Faculty:* 7 full-time (4 women). *Students:* 61 full-time (41 women), 82 part-time (48 women); includes 61 Black or African American, non-Hispanic/Latino; 7 Asian, non-Hispanic/Latino; 19 Hispanic/Latino, 5 international. Average age 31. 70 applicants, 76% accepted, 36 enrolled. In 2010, 44 master's awarded. *Degree requirements:* For master's, thesis, internship, research seminar. *Entrance requirements:* For master's, minimum GPA of 3.0, 2 letters of recommendation, interview, writing sample, transcripts. *Application deadline:* For fall admission, 6/1 for domestic students; for spring admission, 11/1 for domestic students. Application fee: $75 ($150 for international students). Electronic applications accepted. *Expenses:* Tuition, state resident: full-time $10,872; part-time $500 per credit. Tuition, nonresident: full-time $14,736; part-time $614 per credit. Required fees: $2740.80; $125 per credit. Part-time tuition and fees vary according to course load and degree level. *Financial support:* In 2010–11, 11 research assistantships with full tuition reimbursements (averaging $3,263 per year) were awarded; unspecified assistantships also available. Financial award applicants required to submit FAFSA. *Unit head:* Dr. Patricia Moore, Program Coordinator, 908-737-4314, E-mail: pmoore@kean.edu. *Application contact:* Reenat Hasan, Pre-Admissions Coordinator, 908-737-5923, Fax: 908-737-5925, E-mail: hasanr@kean.edu.

Lamar University, College of Graduate Studies, College of Engineering, Department of Civil Engineering, Beaumont, TX 77710. Offers civil engineering (ME, MES, DE); environmental engineering (MS); environmental studies (MS). Part-time programs available. *Faculty:* 5 full-time (1 woman), 1 part-time/adjunct (0 women). *Students:* 31 full-time (6 women), 18 part-time (7 women); includes 1 Black or African American, non-Hispanic/Latino; 3 Asian, non-Hispanic/Latino, 28 international. Average age 29. 37 applicants, 65% accepted, 7 enrolled. In 2010, 42 master's, 1 doctorate awarded. *Degree requirements:* For master's, thesis optional; for doctorate, thesis/dissertation. *Entrance requirements:* For master's and doctorate, GRE General Test. Additional exam requirements/recommendations for international students: Required—TOEFL. *Application deadline:* For fall admission, 5/15 priority date for domestic students; for spring admission, 10/1 priority date for domestic students. Applications are processed on a rolling basis. Application fee: $25 ($50 for international students). *Expenses:* Tuition, state resident: full-time $4160; part-time $208 per credit hour. Tuition, nonresident: full-time $10,360; part-time $518 per credit hour. *Financial support:* In 2010–11, 45 fellowships with partial tuition reimbursements (averaging $1,000 per year), 10 research assistantships with partial tuition reimbursements (averaging $7,200 per year), 3 teaching assistantships with partial tuition reimbursements (averaging $7,200 per year) were awarded; scholarships/grants and tuition waivers (partial) also available. Financial award application deadline: 4/1. *Faculty research:* Environmental remediations, construction productivity, geotechnical soil stabilization, lake/reservoir hydrodynamics, air pollution. *Unit head:* Dr. Enno Koehn, Chair, 409-880-8759, Fax: 409-880-8121, E-mail: koehneu@hal.lamar.edu. *Application contact:* Sandy Drane, Coordinator of Graduate Admissions, 409-880-8356, Fax: 409-880-8414, E-mail: gradmissions@hal.lamar.edu.

Lehigh University, College of Arts and Sciences, Program in Environmental Initiative, Bethlehem, PA 18015. Offers environmental law and policy (Graduate Certificate); environmental policy design (MA). Part-time programs available. *Students:* 6 full-time (3 women), 5 part-time (4 women). Average age 26. 8 applicants, 63% accepted, 4 enrolled. In 2010, 1 master's awarded. *Degree requirements:* For master's, thesis optional, thesis or additional course work. *Entrance requirements:* For master's, GRE, minimum GPA of 2.75, 3.0 for last two undergraduate semesters. Additional exam requirements/recommendations for international students: Required—TOEFL. *Application deadline:* For fall admission, 1/15 for domestic and international students; for spring admission, 12/1 for domestic and international students. Applications are processed on a rolling basis. Application fee: $75. Electronic applications accepted. *Financial support:* In 2010–11, 9 students received support, including 1 teaching assistantship with full tuition reimbursement available (averaging $17,900 per year); scholarships/grants and tuition waivers (partial) also available. Financial award application deadline: 1/15; financial award applicants required to submit FAFSA. *Faculty research:* Environmental law, politics, policy (national and local). *Unit head:* Dr. John Gilroy, Director, 610-758-5964, Fax: 610-758-6377, E-mail: ei@lehigh.edu. *Application contact:* Terry Harnett, Academic Coordinator, 610-758-4745, Fax: 610-758-6232, E-mail: mth204@lehigh.edu.

Long Island University, C.W. Post Campus, College of Liberal Arts and Sciences, Department of Earth and Environmental Science, Brookville, NY 11548-1300. Offers earth science (MS); earth science education (MS); environmental studies (MS).

Louisiana State University and Agricultural and Mechanical College, Graduate School, School of the Coast and Environment, Department of Environmental Sciences, Baton Rouge, LA 70803. Offers environmental planning and management (MS); environmental toxicology (MS). *Faculty:* 9 full-time (3 women). *Students:* 26 full-time (17 women), 7 part-time (2 women); includes 5 Black or African American, non-Hispanic/Latino; 2 Asian, non-Hispanic/Latino, 6 international. Average age 26. 19 applicants, 84% accepted, 10 enrolled. In 2010, 6 master's awarded. *Degree requirements:* For master's, thesis (for some programs). *Entrance requirements:* For master's, GRE General Test, minimum GPA of 3.0. Additional exam requirements/recommendations for international students: Required—TOEFL (minimum score 550 paper-based; 213 computer-based; 79 iBT) or IELTS (minimum score 6.5). *Application deadline:* For fall admission, 1/25 priority date for domestic students, 5/15 for international students; for spring admission, 10/15 for international students. Applications are processed on a rolling basis. Application fee: $50 ($70 for international students). Electronic applications accepted. *Financial support:* In 2010–11, 27 students received support, including 1 fellowship with full and partial tuition reimbursement available (averaging $17,831 per year), 19 research assistantships with full and partial tuition reimbursements available (averaging $14,842 per year), 1 teaching assistantship with full and partial tuition reimbursement available (averaging $15,740 per year); career-related internships or fieldwork, Federal Work-Study, institutionally sponsored loans, scholarships/grants, health care benefits, and unspecified assistantships also available. Support available to part-time students. Financial award applicants required to submit FAFSA. *Faculty research:* Environmental toxicology, environmental policy and law, microbial ecology, bioremediation, genetic toxicology. Total annual research expenditures: $921,141. *Unit head:* Dr. Ed Laws, Chair, 225-578-8521, Fax: 225-578-4286, E-mail: edlaws@lsu.edu. *Application contact:* Charlotte G. St. Romain, Academic Coordinator, 225-578-8522, Fax: 225-578-4286, E-mail: cstrom4@lsu.edu.

Marylhurst University, Department of Business Administration, Marylhurst, OR 97036-0261. Offers finance (MBA); general management (MBA); government policy and administration (MBA); green development (MBA); health care management (MBA); marketing (MBA); natural and organic resources (MBA); nonprofit management (MBA); organizational behavior (MBA); real estate (MBA); renewable energy (MBA); sustainable business (MBA). Part-time and evening/weekend programs available. Postbaccalaureate distance learning degree programs offered (no on-campus study). *Faculty:* 3 full-time (0 women), 36 part-time/adjunct (6 women). *Students:* 27 full-time (13 women), 727 part-time (373 women); includes 167 minority (47 Black or African American, non-Hispanic/Latino; 6 American Indian or Alaska Native, non-Hispanic/Latino; 36 Asian, non-Hispanic/Latino; 51 Hispanic/Latino; 6 Native Hawaiian or other Pacific Islander, non-Hispanic/Latino; 21 Two or more races, non-Hispanic/Latino), 7 international. Average age 38. 262 applicants, 91% accepted, 194 enrolled. In 2010, 289 master's awarded. *Degree requirements:* For master's, comprehensive exam, capstone course. *Entrance requirements:* For master's, GMAT (if GPA less than 3.0 and fewer than 5 years of work experience), interview, resume, 2 letters of recommendation. Additional exam requirements/recommendations for international students: Recommended—TOEFL (minimum score 550 paper-based; 213 computer-based; 80 iBT). *Application deadline:* For fall admission, 9/11 priority date for domestic and international students; for winter admission, 12/15 priority date for domestic and international students; for spring admission, 3/15 priority date for domestic students, 3/17 priority date for international students. Applications are processed on a rolling basis. Application fee: $50. Electronic applications accepted. *Expenses:* Tuition: Full-time $13,932; part-time $516 per credit. Tuition and fees vary according to course load and program. *Financial support:* Scholarships/grants available. Support available to part-time students. Financial award applicants required to submit FAFSA. *Unit head:* Bob Hanks, Director of Business and Real Estate Programs, 503-636-8141, Fax: 503-697-5597, E-mail: mba@marylhurst.edu. *Application contact:* Maruska Lynch, Graduate Admissions Specialist, 800-634-9982 Ext. 6322, Fax: 503-699-6320, E-mail: admissions@marylhurst.edu.

McGill University, Faculty of Graduate and Postdoctoral Studies, Faculty of Agricultural and Environmental Sciences, Department of Natural Resource Sciences, Montréal, QC H3A 2T5, Canada. Offers entomology (M Sc, PhD); environmental assessment (M Sc); forest science (M Sc, PhD); microbiology (M Sc, PhD); micrometeorology (M Sc, PhD); neotropical environment (M Sc, PhD); soil science (M Sc, PhD); wildlife biology (M Sc, PhD).

Michigan Technological University, Graduate School, College of Sciences and Arts, Department of Social Sciences, Program in Environmental and Energy Policy, Houghton, MI 49931. Offers PhD. *Entrance requirements:* For doctorate, GRE, BS or BA, and MS (preferably), in environmental policy or related field. Additional exam requirements/recommendations for international students: Required—TOEFL (minimum score 79 iBT).

Michigan Technological University, Graduate School, College of Sciences and Arts, Department of Social Sciences, Program in Environmental Policy, Houghton, MI 49931. Offers MS. Part-time programs available. *Degree requirements:* For master's, comprehensive exam, project or thesis. *Entrance requirements:* Additional exam requirements/recommendations for international students: Required—TOEFL (minimum score 550 paper-based; 213 computer-based). Electronic applications accepted.

Missouri State University, Graduate College, Interdisciplinary Program in Administrative Studies, Springfield, MO 65897. Offers applied communication (MS); criminal justice (MS); environmental management (MS); project management (MS); sports management (MS). Part-time and evening/weekend programs available. Postbaccalaureate distance learning degree programs offered (no on-campus study). *Degree requirements:* For master's, comprehensive exam, thesis or alternative. *Entrance requirements:* For master's, GRE, GMAT, 3 years of work experience. Additional exam requirements/recommendations for international students: Required—TOEFL (minimum score 550 paper-based; 213 computer-based; 79 iBT). Electronic applications accepted. *Expenses:* Tuition, state resident: full-time $3348; part-time $186 per credit hour. Tuition, nonresident: full-time $6696; part-time $372 per credit hour. Required fees: $238 per semester. Tuition and fees vary according to course level, course load and program.

Montclair State University, The Graduate School, College of Science and Mathematics, Department of Earth and Environmental Studies, Program in Environmental Management, Montclair, NJ 07043-1624. Offers MA, PhD. *Faculty:* 16 full-time (2 women), 20 part-time/adjunct (7 women). *Students:* 39 full-time (19 women), 59 part-time (29 women); includes 3 Black or African American, non-Hispanic/Latino; 1 Asian, non-Hispanic/Latino; 4 Hispanic/Latino, 17 international. Average age 34. 43 applicants, 65% accepted, 21 enrolled. In 2010, 23 master's, 1 doctorate awarded. *Degree requirements:* For master's, comprehensive exam. *Entrance requirements:* For master's, GRE General Test, 2 letters of recommendation; for doctorate, GRE General Test, 3 letters of recommendation. Additional exam requirements/recommendations for international students: Required—TOEFL (minimum iBT score of 83) or IELTS. Application fee: $60. *Expenses:* Tuition, state resident: part-time $501.34 per credit. Tuition, nonresident: part-time $773.88 per credit. Required fees: $71.15 per credit. *Financial support:* Tuition waivers (full) and unspecified assistantships available. *Faculty research:* Spatial environmental data analysis, water resource management in northern New Jersey and Long Island drainage basins, marine geochemistry of the Newark Bay and New York Harbor. *Unit head:* Dr. Michael Kruge, Director, 973-655-5423, Fax: 973-655-6810. *Application contact:* Dr. Michael Kruge, Director, 973-655-5423, Fax: 973-655-6810.

Monterey Institute of International Studies, Graduate School of International Policy and Management, Program in International Environmental Policy, Monterey, CA 93940-2691. Offers MA. *Degree requirements:* For master's, one foreign language. *Entrance requirements:* For master's, minimum GPA of 3.0, proficiency in a foreign language. Additional exam requirements/recommendations for international students: Required—TOEFL (minimum score 550 paper-based; 213 computer-based; 80 iBT). Electronic applications accepted. *Expenses:* Tuition: Full-time $32,000; part-time $1525 per credit hour. Required fees: $56.

Morehead State University, Graduate Programs, College of Science and Technology, Department of Biology and Chemistry, Morehead, KY 40351. Offers biology (MS); biology regional analysis (MS). Part-time programs available. *Degree requirements:* For master's, comprehensive exam, thesis optional, oral and written final exams. *Entrance requirements:* For master's, GRE General Test, minimum GPA of 3.0 in biology, 2.5 overall; undergraduate major/minor in biology, environmental science, or equivalent. Additional exam requirements/recommendations for international students: Required—TOEFL (minimum score 525 paper-based; 173 computer-based). Electronic applications accepted. *Faculty research:* Atherosclerosis, RNA evolution, cancer biology, water quality/ecology, immunoparasitology.

Naropa University, Graduate Programs, Program in Environmental Leadership, Boulder, CO 80302-6697. Offers MA. *Faculty:* 2 full-time (both women), 13 part-time/adjunct (7 women). *Students:* 28 full-time (19 women), 1 (woman) part-time, 3 international. Average age 30. 30 applicants, 83% accepted, 14 enrolled. In 2010, 8 master's awarded. *Degree requirements:* For master's, comprehensive exam, applied leadership project. *Entrance requirements:* For master's, in-person interview, writing sample, letter of interest, resume, 3 letters of recommendation. Additional exam requirements/recommendations for international students:

Environmental Management and Policy

Naropa University (continued)

Required—TOEFL (minimum score 600 paper-based; 250 computer-based). *Application deadline:* For fall admission, 1/15 priority date for domestic and international students. Applications are processed on a rolling basis. Application fee: $60. Electronic applications accepted. *Expenses:* Tuition: Full-time $17,820; part-time $810 per credit. Required fees: $305 per semester. Tuition and fees vary according to course load, program and reciprocity agreements. *Financial support:* In 2010–11, 13 students received support, including 4 research assistantships with partial tuition reimbursements available (averaging $2,175 per year), 2 teaching assistantships with partial tuition reimbursements available (averaging $2,175 per year); Federal Work-Study, scholarships/grants, tuition waivers (partial), and unspecified assistantships also available. Support available to part-time students. Financial award application deadline: 3/1; financial award applicants required to submit FAFSA. *Unit head:* Dr. Jeanine Canty, Director, School of Natural and Social Sciences, 303-245-4735, E-mail: jcanty@naropa.edu. *Application contact:* Roslynn Regnery, Graduate Admissions Counselor, 303-546-3598, Fax: 303-546-3583, E-mail: rregnery@naropa.edu.

New Jersey Institute of Technology, Office of Graduate Studies, College of Science and Liberal Arts, Department of Chemistry and Environmental Science, Program in Environmental Policy Studies, Newark, NJ 07102. Offers MS. Part-time and evening/weekend programs available. *Students:* 6 part-time (4 women); includes 1 Black or African American, non-Hispanic/Latino; 3 Asian, non-Hispanic/Latino. Average age 33. 8 applicants, 63% accepted, 2 enrolled. In 2010, 8 master's awarded. Terminal master's awarded for partial completion of doctoral program. *Degree requirements:* For master's, thesis or alternative. *Entrance requirements:* For master's, GRE General Test. Additional exam requirements/recommendations for international students: Required—TOEFL (minimum score 550 paper-based; 213 computer-based; 79 iBT). *Application deadline:* For fall admission, 6/5 priority date for domestic students, 4/1 for international students; for spring admission, 11/15 for domestic and international students. Applications are processed on a rolling basis. Application fee: $65. Electronic applications accepted. *Expenses:* Tuition, state resident: full-time $14,724; part-time $818 per credit. Tuition, nonresident: full-time $20,304; part-time $1128 per credit. Required fees: $2272; $209 per credit. $103 per semester. One-time fee: $312 full-time; $212 part-time. *Financial support:* Fellowships with full and partial tuition reimbursements, research assistantships with full and partial tuition reimbursements, teaching assistantships with full and partial tuition reimbursements, career-related internships or fieldwork, Federal Work-Study, institutionally sponsored loans, and unspecified assistantships available. Financial award application deadline: 3/15. *Unit head:* Dr. Nancy L. Jackson, Director, 973-596-8467, E-mail: nancy.jackson@njit.edu. *Application contact:* Kathryn Kelly, Director of Admissions, 973-596-3300, Fax: 973-596-3461, E-mail: admissions@njit.edu.

The New School: A University, Milano The New School for Management and Urban Policy, Program in Environmental Policy and Sustainability Management, New York, NY 10011. Offers MS.

New York Institute of Technology, Graduate Division, School of Engineering and Computing Sciences, Program in Energy Management, Old Westbury, NY 11568-8000. Offers energy management (MS); energy technology (Advanced Certificate); environmental management (Advanced Certificate); facilities management (Advanced Certificate). Part-time and evening/weekend programs available. Postbaccalaureate distance learning degree programs offered. *Students:* 57 full-time (12 women), 104 part-time (17 women); includes 31 minority (12 Black or African American, non-Hispanic/Latino; 2 American Indian or Alaska Native, non-Hispanic/Latino; 6 Asian, non-Hispanic/Latino; 11 Hispanic/Latino), 38 international. Average age 32. In 2010, 48 master's, 34 other advanced degrees awarded. *Degree requirements:* For master's, comprehensive exam, thesis or alternative. *Entrance requirements:* For master's, minimum QPA of 2.85. Additional exam requirements/recommendations for international students: Required—TOEFL (minimum score 550 paper-based; 213 computer-based). *Application deadline:* For fall admission, 7/1 priority date for domestic students; for spring admission, 12/1 priority date for domestic students. Applications are processed on a rolling basis. Application fee: $50. Electronic applications accepted. *Expenses:* Tuition: Part-time $835 per credit. *Financial support:* Fellowships, research assistantships with partial tuition reimbursements, institutionally sponsored loans, tuition waivers (full and partial), and unspecified assistantships available. Support available to part-time students. Financial award applicants required to submit FAFSA. *Unit head:* Dr. Robert Amundsen, Director, 516-686-7578, E-mail: ramundse@nyit.edu. *Application contact:* Dr. Jacquelyn Nealon, Vice President for Enrollment Services, 516-686-7925, Fax: 516-686-7597, E-mail: jnealon@nyit.edu.

New York University, School of Continuing and Professional Studies, Center for Global Affairs, New York, NY 10012-1019. Offers global affairs (MS), including environment/energy policy, human rights and humanitarian assistance, international law, dispute settlement, and institutions, international relations, peace building, private sector: international business, economics, and development, transnational security. Part-time and evening/weekend programs available. *Faculty:* 10 full-time (3 women), 29 part-time/adjunct (14 women). *Students:* 92 full-time (62 women), 119 part-time (90 women); includes 12 Black or African American, non-Hispanic/Latino; 1 American Indian or Alaska Native, non-Hispanic/Latino; 14 Asian, non-Hispanic/Latino; 10 Hispanic/Latino, 32 international. Average age 30. 419 applicants, 58% accepted, 81 enrolled. In 2010, 113 master's awarded. *Degree requirements:* For master's, thesis. *Entrance requirements:* For master's, GRE General Test or GMAT (for recent graduates), 2 letters of recommendation, resume, essay, professional experience. Additional exam requirements/recommendations for international students: Required—TOEFL (minimum score 600 paper-based; 250 computer-based; 100 iBT). *Application deadline:* For fall admission, 2/1 priority date for domestic and international students; for spring admission, 10/15 priority date for domestic students, 8/15 priority date for international students. Applications are processed on a rolling basis. Application fee: $75. Electronic applications accepted. *Financial support:* In 2010–11, 163 students received support, including 163 fellowships (averaging $2,554 per year); institutionally sponsored loans, scholarships/grants, and tuition waivers (partial) also available. Support available to part-time students. Financial award application deadline: 3/1; financial award applicants required to submit FAFSA. *Unit head:* Dr. Vera Jelinek, Divisional Dean and Clinical Associate Professor, 212-992-8380, Fax: 212-995-4597, E-mail: vera.jelinek@nyu.edu. *Application contact:* Cori Epstein, Associate Director, 212-992-8380, Fax: 212-995-4597, E-mail: graduate.global.affairs@nyu.edu.

Northeastern Illinois University, Graduate College, College of Arts and Sciences, Department of Geography, Environmental Studies and Economics, Program in Geography and Environmental Studies, Chicago, IL 60625-4699. Offers MA. Part-time and evening/weekend programs available. *Faculty:* 6 full-time (0 women), 3 part-time/adjunct (2 women). *Students:* 13 full-time (6 women), 31 part-time (18 women); includes 7 minority (3 Black or African American, non-Hispanic/Latino; 1 Asian, non-Hispanic/Latino; 2 Hispanic/Latino; 1 Two or more races, non-Hispanic/Latino), 1 international. Average age 34. 14 applicants, 86% accepted, 8 enrolled. In 2010, 8 master's awarded. *Degree requirements:* For master's, comprehensive exam, thesis optional. *Entrance requirements:* For master's, undergraduate minor in geography or environmental studies, minimum GPA of 2.75. Additional exam requirements/recommendations for international students: Required—TOEFL (minimum score 550 paper-based; 213 computer-based; 79 iBT). *Application deadline:* For fall admission, 4/1 priority date for domestic students; for spring admission, 8/15 for domestic students. Applications are processed on a rolling basis. Application fee: $30. Electronic applications accepted. *Financial support:* In 2010–11, 2 research assistantships with full tuition reimbursements (averaging $6,600 per year) were awarded; career-related internships or fieldwork, Federal Work-Study, institutionally sponsored loans, scholarships/grants, tuition waivers (full and partial), and unspecified assistantships also available. Support available to part-time students. Financial award applicants required to submit FAFSA. *Faculty research:* Segregation and urbanization of minority groups in the Chicago area, scale dependence and parameterization in nonpoint source pollution modeling, ecological land classification and mapping, ecosystem restoration, soil-vegetation relationships. *Unit head:* Dr. Dennis Grammenos, Department Chair. *Application contact:* Dr. Dennis Grammenos, Department Chair.

Northern Arizona University, Graduate College, College of Engineering, Forestry and Natural Sciences, School of Earth Sciences and Environmental Sustainability, Flagstaff, AZ 86011. Offers climate science and solutions (MS); earth science (MS); environmental sciences and policy (MS); geology (MS). *Faculty:* 27 full-time (7 women). *Students:* 50 full-time (22 women), 18 part-time (9 women); includes 4 minority (1 American Indian or Alaska Native, non-Hispanic/Latino; 1 Asian, non-Hispanic/Latino; 2 Hispanic/Latino), 2 international. 113 applicants, 31% accepted, 27 enrolled. In 2010, 21 master's awarded. *Degree requirements:* For master's, comprehensive exam (for some programs), thesis (for some programs). *Entrance requirements:* Additional exam requirements/recommendations for international students: Required—TOEFL (minimum score 550 paper-based; 213 computer-based; 80 iBT), IELTS (minimum score 7). *Application deadline:* For fall admission, 2/1 priority date for domestic and international students. Applications are processed on a rolling basis. Application fee: $65. Electronic applications accepted. *Financial support:* In 2010–11, 6 fellowships, 7 research assistantships with partial tuition reimbursements (averaging $12,866 per year), 28 teaching assistantships with partial tuition reimbursements (averaging $12,477 per year) were awarded; career-related internships or fieldwork, Federal Work-Study, scholarships/grants, health care benefits, tuition waivers (full and partial), and unspecified assistantships also available. Financial award applicants required to submit FAFSA. *Unit head:* Dr. Abe Springer, Director, 928-523-7198. *Application contact:* Dr. Abe Springer, Director, 928-523-7198.

Nova Scotia Agricultural College, Research and Graduate Studies, Truro, NS B2N 5E3, Canada. Offers agriculture (M Sc), including air quality, animal behavior, animal molecular genetics, animal nutrition, animal technology, aquaculture, botany, crop management, crop physiology, ecology, environmental microbiology, food science, horticulture, nutrient management, pest management, physiology, plant biotechnology, plant pathology, soil chemistry, soil fertility, waste management and composting, water quality. Program offered jointly with Dalhousie University. Part-time programs available. *Degree requirements:* For master's, thesis, ATC Exam Teaching Assistantship. *Entrance requirements:* For master's, honors B Sc, minimum GPA of 3.0. Additional exam requirements/recommendations for international students: Required—TOEFL (minimum score 580 paper-based; 237 computer-based; 92 iBT), IELTS, Michigan English Language Assessment Battery, CanTEST, CAEL. *Faculty research:* Bio-product development, organic agriculture, nutrient management, air and water quality, agricultural biotechnology.

Ohio University, Graduate College, College of Arts and Sciences, Department of Geological Sciences, Athens, OH 45701-2979. Offers environmental geochemistry (MS); environmental geology (MS); environmental/hydrology (MS); geology (MS); geology education (MS); geomorphology/surficial processes (MS); geophysics (MS); hydrogeology (MS); sedimentology (MS); structure/tectonics (MS). Part-time programs available. *Students:* 14 full-time (8 women), 1 (woman) part-time. 15 applicants, 60% accepted, 8 enrolled. In 2010, 7 master's awarded. *Degree requirements:* For master's, thesis. *Entrance requirements:* Additional exam requirements/recommendations for international students: Required—TOEFL (minimum score 550 paper-based; 80 iBT) or IELTS (minimum score 6.5). *Application deadline:* For fall admission, 2/1 priority date for domestic and international students. Application fee: $50 ($55 for international students). Electronic applications accepted. *Financial support:* Research assistantships with full tuition reimbursements, teaching assistantships with full tuition reimbursements, Federal Work-Study, institutionally sponsored loans, scholarships/grants, tuition waivers (partial), and unspecified assistantships available. Financial award application deadline: 2/1. *Faculty research:* Geoscience education, tectonics, fluvial geomorphology, invertebrate paleontology, mine/hydrology. Total annual research expenditures: $649,020. *Unit head:* Dr. Gregory Nadon, Chair, 740-593-4212, Fax: 740-593-0486, E-mail: nadon@ohio.edu. *Application contact:* Dr. Douglas Green, Graduate Chair, 740-593-1843, Fax: 740-593-0486, E-mail: green@ohio.edu.

Ohio University, Graduate College, College of Arts and Sciences, Program in Environmental Studies, Athens, OH 45701-2979. Offers MS. Part-time programs available. *Students:* 25 full-time (15 women), 6 part-time (4 women); includes 1 minority (Two or more races, non-Hispanic/Latino), 4 international. Average age 28. 43 applicants, 51% accepted, 13 enrolled. In 2010, 19 master's awarded. *Degree requirements:* For master's, comprehensive exam (for some programs), written exams or thesis, research project. *Entrance requirements:* For master's, minimum GPA of 3.0. Additional exam requirements/recommendations for international students: Required—TOEFL (minimum score 600 paper-based; 100 iBT) or IELTS (minimum score 7). *Application deadline:* For fall admission, 1/1 priority date for domestic and international students; for winter admission, 10/1 for domestic and international students; for spring admission, 2/1 for domestic and international students. Application fee: $50 ($55 for international students). Electronic applications accepted. *Financial support:* Fellowships with tuition reimbursements, research assistantships with tuition reimbursements, teaching assistantships with tuition reimbursements, career-related internships or fieldwork, Federal Work-Study, institutionally sponsored loans, scholarships/grants, tuition waivers (full and partial), and unspecified assistantships available. Financial award application deadline: 1/1. *Faculty research:* Air quality modeling, conservation biology, environmental policy, geographical information systems, land management and watershed restoration. *Unit head:* Dr. Michele Morrone, Director, 740-593-9549, Fax: 740-593-0924, E-mail: morrone@ohio.edu. *Application contact:* Graduate Admissions, 740-593-2800, E-mail: graduate@ohio.edu.

Pace University, Dyson College of Arts and Sciences, Department of Public Administration, New York, NY 10038. Offers environmental management (MPA); government management (MPA); health care administration (MPA); management for public safety and homeland security (MA); nonprofit management (MPA); JD/MPA. Offered at White Plains, NY location only. Part-time and evening/weekend programs available. *Degree requirements:* For master's, capstone project. *Entrance requirements:* For master's, GRE General Test. Additional exam requirements/recommendations for international students: Required—TOEFL. Electronic applications accepted.

Penn State University Park, Graduate School, Intercollege Graduate Programs, Intercollege Program in Environmental Pollution Control, State College, University Park, PA 16802-1503. Offers MEPC, MS. *Unit head:* Dr. Herschel A. Elliott, Chair, 814-865-1417, Fax: 814-863-1031, E-mail: helliott3@psu.edu. *Application contact:* Dr. Herschel A. Elliott, Chair, 814-865-1417, Fax: 814-863-1031, E-mail: helliott3@psu.edu.

Plymouth State University, College of Graduate Studies, Graduate Studies in Education, Program in Science, Plymouth, NH 03264-1595. Offers applied meteorology (MS); environmental science and policy (MS); science education (MS).

Point Park University, School of Arts and Sciences, Department of Natural Science and Engineering Technology, Pittsburgh, PA 15222-1984. Offers engineering management (MS); environmental studies (MS). Part-time and evening/weekend programs available. *Faculty:* 4 full-time, 4 part-time/adjunct. *Students:* 7 full-time (4 women), 17 part-time (6 women); includes 5 minority (4 Black or African American, non-Hispanic/Latino; 1 Hispanic/Latino), 2 international. Average age 35. 36 applicants, 69% accepted, 11 enrolled. In 2010, 18 master's awarded. *Degree requirements:* For master's, comprehensive exam (for some programs), thesis or alternative. *Entrance requirements:* For master's, minimum QPA of 2.75, 2 letters of recommendation, minimum B average in engineering technology or a related field, official undergraduate transcript, statement of intent, resume. Additional exam requirements/recommendations for international students: Required—TOEFL. *Application deadline:* Applications are processed on a rolling basis. Application fee: $30. Electronic applications accepted.

Expenses: Tuition: Full-time $12,456; part-time $692 per credit. Required fees: $630; $35 per credit. *Financial support:* In 2010–11, 16 students received support, including 1 teaching assistantship with full tuition reimbursement available (averaging $6,400 per year); scholarships/grants also available. Financial award application deadline: 4/15; financial award applicants required to submit FAFSA. *Unit head:* Dr. Mark Farrell, Chair, 412-392-3879, Fax: 421-392-3962, E-mail: mfarrell@pointpark.edu. *Application contact:* Misty Williams, Recruiter/Counselor, 412-392-3826, Fax: 412-392-6164, E-mail: mdwilliams@pointpark.edu.

Polytechnic University of Puerto Rico, Graduate School, Hato Rey, PR 00919. Offers business administration (MBA), including computer information systems, general management, management of information systems, management of international enterprises; civil engineering (ME, MS); computer engineering (ME, MS); computer science (MCS, MS); electrical engineering (ME, MS); engineering management (MEM); environmental management (MEM); landscape architecture (M Land Arch); manufacturing competitiveness (MMC, MS); manufacturing engineering (ME, MS); mechanical engineering (M Mech E). Part-time and evening/weekend programs available. *Entrance requirements:* For master's, 3 letters of recommendation.

Polytechnic University of Puerto Rico, Miami Campus, Graduate School, Miami, FL 33166. Offers accounting (MBA); business administration (MBA); construction management (MEM); environmental management (MEM); finance (MBA); human resources management (MBA); logistics and supply chain management (MBA); management of international enterprises (MBA); manufacturing management (MEM); marketing management (MBA); project management (MBA). Part-time and evening/weekend programs available. Postbaccalaureate distance learning degree programs offered (no on-campus study). *Entrance requirements:* For master's, minimum GPA of 3.0. Electronic applications accepted.

Polytechnic University of Puerto Rico, Orlando Campus, Graduate School, Winter Park, FL 32792. Offers accounting (MBA); business administration (MBA); construction management (MEM); engineering management (MEM); environmental management (MEM); finance (MBA); human resources management (MBA); management of international enterprises (MBA); management of technology (MBA); manufacturing management (MEM). Part-time and evening/weekend programs available. Postbaccalaureate distance learning degree programs offered (no on-campus study). *Entrance requirements:* For master's, minimum GPA of 3.0. Electronic applications accepted.

Portland State University, Graduate Studies, College of Liberal Arts and Sciences, Program in Environmental Sciences and Management, Portland, OR 97207-0751. Offers environmental management (MEM); environmental sciences/biology (PhD); environmental sciences/chemistry (PhD); environmental sciences/civil engineering (PhD); environmental sciences/geography (PhD); environmental sciences/geology (PhD); environmental sciences/physics (PhD); environmental studies (MS); science/environmental science (MST). Part-time programs available. *Faculty:* 14 full-time (6 women), 7 part-time/adjunct (5 women). *Students:* 57 full-time (31 women), 48 part-time (23 women); includes 5 minority (1 Black or African American, non-Hispanic/Latino; 2 Asian, non-Hispanic/Latino; 2 Hispanic/Latino), 6 international. Average age 34. 89 applicants, 56% accepted, 34 enrolled. In 2010, 14 master's, 3 doctorates awarded. *Degree requirements:* For master's, thesis or alternative; for doctorate, variable foreign language requirement, comprehensive exam, thesis/dissertation, oral and qualifying exams. *Entrance requirements:* For master's, GRE General Test, 3 letters of recommendation; for doctorate, minimum GPA of 3.0 in upper-division course work or 2.75 overall. Additional exam requirements/recommendations for international students: Required—TOEFL (minimum score 550 paper-based; 213 computer-based). *Application deadline:* For fall admission, 2/1 for domestic and international students. Applications are processed on a rolling basis. Application fee: $50. *Expenses:* Tuition, state resident: full-time $8505; part-time $315 per credit. Tuition, nonresident: full-time $13,284; part-time $492 per credit. Required fees: $1482; $21 per credit. $99 per term. One-time fee: $120. Part-time tuition and fees vary according to course load and program. *Financial support:* In 2010–11, 4 research assistantships with full tuition reimbursements (averaging $10,480 per year), 6 teaching assistantships with full tuition reimbursements (averaging $10,267 per year) were awarded; Federal Work-Study, scholarships/grants, tuition waivers (partial), and unspecified assistantships also available. Support available to part-time students. Financial award application deadline: 3/1; financial award applicants required to submit FAFSA. *Faculty research:* Environmental aspects of biology, chemistry, civil engineering, geology, physics. Total annual research expenditures: $1.2 million. *Unit head:* Dr. Mark Sytsma, Chair, 503-725-8038, Fax: 503-725-3888, E-mail: sytsmam@pdx.edu. *Application contact:* Dr. Mark Sytsma, Chair, 503-725-8038, Fax: 503-725-3888, E-mail: sytsmam@pdx.edu.

Prescott College, Graduate Programs, Program in Environmental Studies, Prescott, AZ 86301. Offers environmental studies (MA); student-directed independent study (MA). Part-time programs available. Postbaccalaureate distance learning degree programs offered (minimal on-campus study). *Faculty:* 1 full-time (0 women), 29 part-time/adjunct (12 women). *Students:* 11 full-time (8 women), 34 part-time (23 women); includes 7 minority (2 Black or African American, non-Hispanic/Latino; 1 American Indian or Alaska Native, non-Hispanic/Latino; 1 Asian, non-Hispanic/Latino; 1 Hispanic/Latino; 2 Two or more races, non-Hispanic/Latino), 2 international. Average age 35. 23 applicants, 70% accepted, 8 enrolled. In 2010, 8 master's awarded. *Degree requirements:* For master's, thesis, fieldwork or internship, practicum. *Entrance requirements:* For master's, 2 letters of recommendation, resume. Additional exam requirements/recommendations for international students: Required—TOEFL (minimum score 500 paper-based; 173 computer-based). *Application deadline:* For fall admission, 4/15 priority date for domestic and international students; for spring admission, 9/15 priority date for domestic and international students. Applications are processed on a rolling basis. Application fee: $40. Electronic applications accepted. *Expenses:* Tuition: Full-time $15,600; part-time $650 per credit. Required fees: $50 per term. One-time fee: $190. Tuition and fees vary according to course load and degree level. *Financial support:* Career-related internships or fieldwork, Federal Work-Study, and scholarships/grants available. Financial award applicants required to submit FAFSA. *Unit head:* Peter Sherman, Interim Chair, 928-350-1014, Fax: 928-776-5151, E-mail: psherman@prescott.edu. *Application contact:* Kerstin Alicki, Admissions Counselor, 877-412-8705, Fax: 928-277-4695, E-mail: admissions@prescott.edu.

Purdue University, Graduate School, College of Agriculture, Department of Forestry and Natural Resources, West Lafayette, IN 47907. Offers aquaculture, fisheries, aquatic science (MSF); aquaculture, fisheries, aquatic sciences (MS, PhD); forest biology (MS, MSF, PhD); natural resources and environmental policy (MS, MSF); natural resources environmental policy (PhD); quantitative resource analysis (MS, MSF, PhD); wildlife science (MS, MSF, PhD); wood science and technology (MS, MSF, PhD). *Degree requirements:* For master's, thesis; for doctorate, thesis/dissertation. *Entrance requirements:* For master's and doctorate, GRE General Test, minimum B+ average in undergraduate course work. Additional exam requirements/recommendations for international students: Required—TOEFL. Electronic applications accepted. *Faculty research:* Wildlife management, forest management, forest ecology, forest soils, limnology.

Rensselaer Polytechnic Institute, Graduate School, School of Humanities, Arts, and Social Sciences, Program in Ecological Economics, Troy, NY 12180-3590. Offers PhD. Part-time programs available. *Faculty:* 8 full-time (1 woman). *Students:* 11 full-time (7 women); includes 4 Asian, non-Hispanic/Latino; 3 Hispanic/Latino. Average age 26. 25 applicants, 24% accepted, 3 enrolled. In 2010, 3 doctorates awarded. *Degree requirements:* For doctorate, comprehensive exam, thesis/dissertation. *Entrance requirements:* For doctorate, GRE General Test or GMAT, writing sample, statement of background goals, 2 recommendation letters, resume or curriculum vitae. Additional exam requirements/recommendations for international students: Required—TOEFL (minimum score 600 paper-based; 250 computer-based; 100 iBT), IELTS. *Application deadline:* For fall admission, 1/15 priority date for domestic and international students. Applications are processed on a rolling basis. Application fee: $75. Electronic applications accepted. *Expenses:* Tuition: Full-time $39,600; part-time $1650 per credit. Required fees: $1896. *Financial support:* In 2010–11, 9 students received support, including 2 fellowships with full tuition reimbursements available (averaging $22,000 per year), 3 research assistantships with full tuition reimbursements available (averaging $17,500 per year), 4 teaching assistantships (averaging $17,500 per year); scholarships/grants and unspecified assistantships also available. Financial award application deadline: 1/15. *Faculty research:* Economic development and trade with a focus on technology, lifestyles, and environment; input-output analysis; pollution policy in the electric power sector; electricity market design; renewable energy integration in the power grid; experimental economics; law and economics; environmental economics; behavioral economics; technology change; applied econometrics. Total annual research expenditures: $100,000. *Unit head:* Prof. Faye Duchin, Professor of Economics/Director, 518-276-2038, Fax: 518-276-2235, E-mail: duchin@rpi.edu. *Application contact:* Betty Jean Kaufman, Administrative Assistant, 518-276-6387, Fax: 518-276-2235, E-mail: kaufmb@rpi.edu.

Rice University, Graduate Programs, Wiess School–Professional Science Master's Programs, Professional Master's Program in Environmental Analysis and Decision Making, Houston, TX 77251-1892. Offers MS. Part-time programs available. *Degree requirements:* For master's, internship. *Entrance requirements:* For master's, GRE General Test, letters of recommendation (4). Additional exam requirements/recommendations for international students: Required—TOEFL (minimum score 600 paper-based; 250 computer-based; 90 iBT). Electronic applications accepted. *Faculty research:* Environmental biotechnology, environmental nanochemistry, environmental statistics, remote sensing.

Rochester Institute of Technology, Graduate Enrollment Services, College of Applied Science and Technology, Department of Civil Engineering Technology, Environmental Management and Safety, Rochester, NY 14623-5603. Offers MS. Part-time and evening/weekend programs available. Postbaccalaureate distance learning degree programs offered (minimal on-campus study). *Students:* 20 full-time (9 women), 36 part-time (14 women); includes 5 Black or African American, non-Hispanic/Latino; 1 American Indian or Alaska Native, non-Hispanic/Latino; 4 Asian, non-Hispanic/Latino; 1 Hispanic/Latino, 15 international. Average age 36. 31 applicants, 52% accepted, 12 enrolled. In 2010, 14 master's awarded. *Degree requirements:* For master's, thesis or project. *Entrance requirements:* For master's, minimum GPA of 3.0. Additional exam requirements/recommendations for international students: Required—TOEFL (minimum score 550 paper-based; 213 computer-based; 79 iBT) or IELTS (minimum score 6.5). *Application deadline:* For fall admission, 2/15 priority date for domestic and international students; for winter admission, 11/1 priority date for domestic students; for spring admission, 2/1 priority date for domestic students, 1/1 priority date for international students. Applications are processed on a rolling basis. Electronic applications accepted. *Expenses:* Tuition: Full-time $33,234; part-time $924 per credit hour. Required fees: $219. *Financial support:* In 2010–11, 31 students received support; research assistantships with partial tuition reimbursements available, teaching assistantships with partial tuition reimbursements available, career-related internships or fieldwork, scholarships/grants, and unspecified assistantships available. Support available to part-time students. Financial award applicants required to submit FAFSA. *Faculty research:* Environmental, health and safety (EHS) issues; regulatory, voluntary and business drivers for EHS programs; design and implementation of effective EHS management systems and programs; design and implementation of performance measurement processes. *Unit head:* Dr. John Morelli, Department Chair, 585-475-7213, E-mail: john.morelli@rit.edu. *Application contact:* Diane Ellison, Assistant Vice President, Graduate Enrollment Services, 585-475-2229, Fax: 585-475-7164, E-mail: gradinfo@rit.edu.

Royal Roads University, Graduate Studies, Environment and Sustainability Program, Victoria, BC V9B 5Y2, Canada. Offers environment and management (M Sc, MA); environmental education and communication (MA, G Dip, Graduate Certificate); MA/MS. Postbaccalaureate distance learning degree programs offered (minimal on-campus study). *Degree requirements:* For master's, thesis. *Entrance requirements:* For master's, 5-7 years of related work experience. Electronic applications accepted. *Faculty research:* Sustainable development, atmospheric processes, sustainable communities, chemical fate and transport of persistent organic pollutants, educational technology.

St. Cloud State University, School of Graduate Studies, College of Science and Engineering, Department of Environmental and Technological Studies, St. Cloud, MN 56301-4498. Offers MS. *Degree requirements:* For master's, thesis or alternative. *Entrance requirements:* For master's, minimum GPA of 2.75. Additional exam requirements/recommendations for international students: Required—TOEFL (minimum score 550 paper-based; 213 computer-based), Michigan English Language Assessment Battery; Recommended—IELTS (minimum score 6.5). Electronic applications accepted.

Saint Mary-of-the-Woods College, Program in Earth Literacy, Saint Mary-of-the-Woods, IN 47876. Offers MA. Part-time programs available. Postbaccalaureate distance learning degree programs offered (minimal on-campus study). *Degree requirements:* For master's, thesis. Electronic applications accepted. *Faculty research:* Ecology, art, spirituality.

Samford University, Howard College of Arts and Sciences, Birmingham, AL 35229. Offers MSEM, JD/MSEM. Part-time and evening/weekend programs available. *Faculty:* 6 full-time (1 woman), 6 part-time/adjunct (0 women). *Students:* 21 full-time (10 women), 13 part-time (8 women); includes 7 minority (4 Black or African American, non-Hispanic/Latino; 1 American Indian or Alaska Native, non-Hispanic/Latino; 2 Asian, non-Hispanic/Latino), 9 international. Average age 31. 26 applicants, 96% accepted, 22 enrolled. In 2010, 14 master's awarded. *Entrance requirements:* For master's, GRE General Test (minimum score 1000) or MAT (minimum score 50), minimum GPA of 3.0, 3 years of work experience. Additional exam requirements/recommendations for international students: Required—TOEFL (minimum score 550 paper-based; 213 computer-based; 80 iBT). *Application deadline:* For fall admission, 8/1 for domestic and international students; for winter admission, 2/1 for domestic students; for spring admission, 1/2 for domestic students, 12/14 for international students. Applications are processed on a rolling basis. Application fee: $35. *Expenses:* Contact institution. *Financial support:* In 2010–11, 1 student received support. *Faculty research:* Mosquito fish as an environmental model for pollutants, PCB contamination, environmental epidemiology and toxicology, GIS, geology and natural resource management. *Unit head:* Dean David W. Chapman, Dean, 205-726-2771, Fax: 205-726-2279. *Application contact:* Dr. Ronald N. Hunsinger, Professor/Chair, 205-726-2944, Fax: 205-726-2479, E-mail: rnhunsin@samford.edu.

San Francisco State University, Division of Graduate Studies, College of Behavioral and Social Sciences, Department of Geography and Human Environmental Studies, San Francisco, CA 94132-1722. Offers geographic information science (MS); geography (MA), including resource management and environmental planning. *Unit head:* Dr. Jerry Davis, Chair, 415-338-2049, E-mail: jerry@sfsu.edu. *Application contact:* Nancy Wilkinson, Graduate Coordinator, 415-338-2049.

San Jose State University, Graduate Studies and Research, College of Social Sciences, Department of Environmental Studies, San Jose, CA 95192-0001. Offers MS. Part-time programs available. *Degree requirements:* For master's, comprehensive exam, thesis or alternative. *Entrance requirements:* Additional exam requirements/recommendations for international students: Required—TOEFL (minimum score 580 paper-based). Electronic applications accepted. *Faculty research:* Remote sensing, land use/land cover mapping.

Shippensburg University of Pennsylvania, School of Graduate Studies, College of Arts and Sciences, Department of Geography and Earth Science, Shippensburg, PA 17257-2299. Offers geoenvironmental studies (MS). Part-time and evening/weekend programs available. *Faculty:* 11 full-time (4 women), 1 part-time/adjunct (0 women). *Students:* 19 full-time (5

Environmental Management and Policy

Shippensburg University of Pennsylvania (continued)
women), 14 part-time (5 women). Average age 29. 25 applicants, 80% accepted, 11 enrolled. In 2010, 20 master's awarded. *Degree requirements:* For master's, comprehensive exam, thesis optional, thesis (6 credits) or a 1 semester research project (3 credits) and internship (6 credits), departmental practicum exam. *Entrance requirements:* For master's, GRE (if GPA less than 2.75), 12 credit hours in geography or earth sciences or 15 credit hours each in social sciences (including 6 hours in geography) and natural sciences (including 6 in the earth sciences) or a combined total of 18 credits in geography and earth science. Additional exam requirements/recommendations for international students: Required—TOEFL (minimum score 580 paper-based; 237 computer-based); Recommended—IELTS (minimum score 6). *Application deadline:* For fall admission, 3/1 for international students; for spring admission, 7/1 for international students. Applications are processed on a rolling basis. Application fee: $30. Electronic applications accepted. *Expenses:* Tuition, state resident: full-time $6966. Tuition, nonresident: full-time $11,146. Required fees: $1802. *Financial support:* In 2010–11, 9 research assistantships with full tuition reimbursements (averaging $5,000 per year) were awarded; career-related internships or fieldwork, scholarships/grants, unspecified assistantships, and resident hall director and student payroll positions also available. Support available to part-time students. Financial award application deadline: 3/1; financial award applicants required to submit FAFSA. *Unit head:* Dr. Tim Hawkins, Associate Professor, 717-477-1685, Fax: 717-477-4029, E-mail: twhawk@ship.edu. *Application contact:* Jeremy R. Goshorn, Associate Dean of Graduate Admissions, 717-477-1231, Fax: 717-477-4016, E-mail: jrgoshorn@ship.edu.

Shippensburg University of Pennsylvania, School of Graduate Studies, College of Arts and Sciences, Department of Sociology and Anthropology, Shippensburg, PA 17257-2299. Offers organizational development and leadership (MS), including business, communications, education, environmental management, higher education, historical administration, individual and organizational development, public organizations, social structures and organizations. Part-time and evening/weekend programs available. *Faculty:* 3 full-time (all women). *Students:* 18 full-time (13 women), 46 part-time (33 women); includes 11 minority (6 Black or African American, non-Hispanic/Latino; 3 Asian, non-Hispanic/Latino; 2 Two or more races, non-Hispanic/Latino), 2 international. Average age 32. 56 applicants, 55% accepted, 20 enrolled. In 2010, 28 master's awarded. *Degree requirements:* For master's, capstone experience including internship. *Entrance requirements:* For master's, interview (if GPA less than 2.75), resume, personal goals statement. Additional exam requirements/recommendations for international students: Required—TOEFL (minimum score 580 paper-based; 237 computer-based); Recommended—IELTS (minimum score 6). *Application deadline:* For fall admission, 3/1 for international students; for spring admission, 7/1 for international students. Applications are processed on a rolling basis. Application fee: $30. Electronic applications accepted. *Expenses:* Tuition, state resident: full-time $6966. Tuition, nonresident: full-time $11,146. Required fees: $1802. *Financial support:* In 2010–11, 8 research assistantships with full tuition reimbursements (averaging $5,000 per year) were awarded; career-related internships or fieldwork, scholarships/grants, unspecified assistantships, and resident hall director and student payroll positions also available. Support available to part-time students. Financial award applicants required to submit FAFSA. *Unit head:* Dr. Barbara Denison, Chairperson, 717-477-1735, Fax: 717-477-4011, E-mail: bjdeni@ship.edu. *Application contact:* Jeremy R. Goshorn, Associate Dean of Graduate Admissions, 717-477-1231, Fax: 717-477-4016, E-mail: jrgoshorn@ship.edu.

Simon Fraser University, Graduate Studies, Faculty of Applied Sciences, School of Resource and Environmental Management, Burnaby, BC V5A 1S6, Canada. Offers MRM, PhD. *Degree requirements:* For master's, thesis or alternative, research project; for doctorate, comprehensive exam, thesis/dissertation. *Entrance requirements:* For master's, minimum GPA of 3.0; for doctorate, GRE Writing Assessment, minimum GPA of 3.5. Additional exam requirements/recommendations for international students: Required—TOEFL or IELTS. *Faculty research:* Management of resources, resource economics, regional planning, public policy analysis, tourism and parks.

Slippery Rock University of Pennsylvania, Graduate Studies (Recruitment), College of Health, Environment, and Science, Department of Parks, Recreation, and Environmental Education, Slippery Rock, PA 16057-1383. Offers environmental education (M Ed); resource management (MS). Part-time and evening/weekend programs available. Postbaccalaureate distance learning degree programs offered. *Faculty:* 4 full-time (1 woman), 3 part-time/adjunct (2 women). *Students:* 21 full-time (12 women), 74 part-time (33 women); includes 6 minority (2 Black or African American, non-Hispanic/Latino; 1 American Indian or Alaska Native, non-Hispanic/Latino; 3 Hispanic/Latino). Average age 29. 62 applicants, 79% accepted, 34 enrolled. In 2010, 31 master's awarded. *Degree requirements:* For master's, comprehensive exam (for some programs), thesis (for some programs). *Entrance requirements:* For master's, GRE General Test, MAT, minimum GPA of 2.75. Additional exam requirements/recommendations for international students: Required—TOEFL (minimum score 550 paper-based; 213 computer-based; 80 iBT). *Application deadline:* For fall admission, 3/1 priority date for domestic students, 5/1 priority date for international students; for spring admission, 11/1 priority date for domestic students, 9/1 priority date for international students. Applications are processed on a rolling basis. Application fee: $25 ($30 for international students). Electronic applications accepted. *Expenses:* Tuition, state resident: full-time $6966; part-time $387 per credit. Tuition, nonresident: full-time $11,146; part-time $619 per credit. Required fees: $2388; $202 per credit. *Financial support:* Career-related internships or fieldwork, Federal Work-Study, institutionally sponsored loans, scholarships/grants, tuition waivers (partial), and unspecified assistantships available. Support available to part-time students. Financial award application deadline: 5/1; financial award applicants required to submit FAFSA. *Unit head:* Dr. Daniel Dziubek, Graduate Coordinator, 724-738-2958, Fax: 724-738-2938, E-mail: daniel.dziubek@sru.edu. *Application contact:* Angela Piverotto, Interim Director of Graduate Studies, 724-738-2051, Fax: 724-738-2146, E-mail: graduate.admissions@sru.edu.

Southeast Missouri State University, School of Graduate Studies, Department of Human Environmental Studies, Cape Girardeau, MO 63701-4799. Offers human environmental studies (MA). Part-time programs available. *Faculty:* 12 full-time (10 women). *Students:* 12 full-time (9 women), 14 part-time (all women); includes 2 minority (1 Black or African American, non-Hispanic/Latino; 1 Asian, non-Hispanic/Latino). Average age 26. 19 applicants, 89% accepted, 12 enrolled. In 2010, 7 master's awarded. *Degree requirements:* For master's, internship. *Entrance requirements:* For master's, MAT or GRE General Test, minimum undergraduate GPA of 2.75; 15 undergraduate hours in field. Additional exam requirements/recommendations for international students: Required—TOEFL (minimum score 550 paper-based; 213 computer-based; 79 iBT); Recommended—IELTS (minimum score 6). *Application deadline:* For fall admission, 8/1 for domestic students, 6/1 for international students; for spring admission, 11/21 for domestic students, 10/1 for international students. Applications are processed on a rolling basis. Application fee: $25 ($35 for international students). Electronic applications accepted. *Expenses:* Tuition, state resident: full-time $4698; part-time $261 per credit hour. Tuition, nonresident: full-time $8379; part-time $465.50 per credit hour. *Financial support:* In 2010–11, 8 students received support, including 6 teaching assistantships with full tuition reimbursements available (averaging $7,600 per year); career-related internships or fieldwork, Federal Work-Study, institutionally sponsored loans, scholarships/grants, tuition waivers (full), and unspecified assistantships also available. Financial award application deadline: 6/30; financial award applicants required to submit FAFSA. *Unit head:* Dr. Shelba Y. Branscum, 573-651-2729, Fax: 573-651-2949, E-mail: sybranscum@semo.edu. *Application contact:* Gail Amick, Administrative Secretary, 573-651-2049, Fax: 573-651-2001, E-mail: gamick@semo.edu.

Southeast Missouri State University, School of Graduate Studies, Harrison College of Business, Cape Girardeau, MO 63701-4799. Offers accounting (MBA); entrepreneurship (MBA); environmental management (MBA); financial management (MBA); general management (MBA); health administration (MBA); industrial management (MBA); international business (MBA); sport management (MBA). *Accreditation:* AACSB. Part-time and evening/weekend programs available. Postbaccalaureate distance learning degree programs offered (no on-campus study). *Faculty:* 31 full-time (10 women). *Students:* 51 full-time (24 women), 72 part-time (34 women); includes 4 minority (1 American Indian or Alaska Native, non-Hispanic/Latino; 3 Asian, non-Hispanic/Latino), 32 international. Average age 28. 71 applicants, 83% accepted, 33 enrolled. In 2010, 46 master's awarded. *Degree requirements:* For master's, variable foreign language requirement, applied research project; foreign language or 9 credit hours (for international business). *Entrance requirements:* For master's, GMAT (minimum score 400), minimum undergraduate GPA of 2.5, prerequisite courses for non-business undergraduate majors. Additional exam requirements/recommendations for international students: Required—TOEFL (minimum score 550 paper-based; 213 computer-based; 79 iBT); Recommended—IELTS (minimum score 6). *Application deadline:* For fall admission, 8/1 for domestic students, 6/1 for international students; for spring admission, 11/21 for domestic students, 10/1 for international students. Applications are processed on a rolling basis. Application fee: $25 ($35 for international students). Electronic applications accepted. *Expenses:* Tuition, state resident: full-time $4698; part-time $261 per credit hour. Tuition, nonresident: full-time $8379; part-time $465.50 per credit hour. *Financial support:* In 2010–11, 52 students received support, including 10 teaching assistantships with full tuition reimbursements available (averaging $7,600 per year); career-related internships or fieldwork, Federal Work-Study, institutionally sponsored loans, scholarships/grants, tuition waivers (full), and unspecified assistantships also available. Financial award application deadline: 6/30; financial award applicants required to submit FAFSA. *Faculty research:* Human resources, laws impacting accounting, advertising. *Unit head:* Dr. Kenneth A. Heischmidt, Director, Graduate Programs in Business, 573-651-5116, Fax: 573-651-5032, E-mail: kheischmidt@semo.edu. *Application contact:* Gail Amick, Administrative Secretary, 573-651-2049, Fax: 573-651-2001, E-mail: gamick@semo.edu.

Southern Illinois University Edwardsville, Graduate School, College of Arts and Sciences, Program in Environmental Science Management, Edwardsville, IL 62026-0001. Offers MS. Part-time and evening/weekend programs available. *Students:* 5 full-time (3 women), 4 part-time (3 women); includes 5 minority (1 Black or African American, non-Hispanic/Latino; 1 Asian, non-Hispanic/Latino; 1 Hispanic/Latino; 2 Native Hawaiian or other Pacific Islander, non-Hispanic/Latino). Average age 26. 15 applicants, 80% accepted. In 2010, 1 master's awarded. *Degree requirements:* For master's, thesis, internship. *Entrance requirements:* For master's, GRE. Additional exam requirements/recommendations for international students: Required—TOEFL (minimum score 550 paper-based; 213 computer-based; 79 iBT), IELTS (minimum score 6.5). *Application deadline:* For fall admission, 7/22 for domestic students, 6/1 for international students; for spring admission, 12/9 for domestic students, 10/1 for international students. Applications are processed on a rolling basis. Application fee: $30. Electronic applications accepted. *Expenses:* Tuition, state resident: full-time $6012; part-time $1503 per semester. Tuition, nonresident: full-time $15,030; part-time $3758 per semester. Required fees: $1711; $675 per semester. *Financial support:* In 2010–11, 1 teaching assistantship with full tuition reimbursement (averaging $8,064 per year) was awarded; fellowships with full tuition reimbursements, research assistantships with full tuition reimbursements, career-related internships or fieldwork, Federal Work-Study, institutionally sponsored loans, scholarships/grants, traineeships, and unspecified assistantships also available. Support available to part-time students. Financial award application deadline: 3/1; financial award applicants required to submit FAFSA. *Unit head:* Dr. Kevin Johnson, Program Director, 618-650-5934, E-mail: kevjohn@siue.edu. *Application contact:* Dr. Kevin Johnson, Program Director, 618-650-5934, E-mail: kevjohn@siue.edu.

Stanford University, School of Earth Sciences, Earth Systems Program, Stanford, CA 94305-9991. Offers MS. Students admitted at the undergraduate level. Electronic applications accepted. *Expenses:* Tuition: Full-time $38,700; part-time $860 per unit. One-time fee: $200 full-time.

State University of New York College of Environmental Science and Forestry, Department of Environmental Resources Engineering, Syracuse, NY 13210-2779. Offers ecological engineering (MS, PhD); environmental and resources engineering (MPS, MS, PhD); environmental management (MPS); geospatial information science and engineering (MS, PhD); mapping sciences (MPS); water resources engineering (MS, PhD). *Degree requirements:* For master's, thesis (for some programs); for doctorate, comprehensive exam, thesis/dissertation. *Entrance requirements:* For master's and doctorate, GRE General Test, minimum GPA of 3.0. Additional exam requirements/recommendations for international students: Required—TOEFL (minimum score 550 paper-based; 213 computer-based; 80 iBT), IELTS (minimum score 6). *Expenses:* Tuition, state resident: full-time $8370; part-time $349 per credit hour. Tuition, nonresident: full-time $13,780. Required fees: $30.30 per credit hour. $20 per year. *Faculty research:* Forest engineering, paper science and engineering, wood products engineering.

State University of New York College of Environmental Science and Forestry, Department of Environmental Studies, Syracuse, NY 13210-2779. Offers MPS, MS. *Degree requirements:* For master's, thesis (for some programs). *Entrance requirements:* For master's, GRE General Test. *Expenses:* Tuition, state resident: full-time $8370; part-time $349 per credit hour. Tuition, nonresident: full-time $13,780. Required fees: $30.30 per credit hour. $20 per year.

State University of New York College of Environmental Science and Forestry, Department of Forest and Natural Resources Management, Syracuse, NY 13210-2779. Offers ecology and ecosystems (MPS, MS, PhD); economics, governance and human dimensions (MPS, MS, PhD); environmental and natural resource policy (PhD); forest resources management (MF); monitoring, analysis and modeling (MPS, MS, PhD); natural resources management (MPS, MS, PhD). *Accreditation:* SAF. *Degree requirements:* For master's, thesis (for some programs); for doctorate, comprehensive exam, thesis/dissertation. *Entrance requirements:* For master's and doctorate, GRE General Test, minimum GPA of 3.0. Additional exam requirements/recommendations for international students: Required—TOEFL (minimum score 550 paper-based; 213 computer-based; 80 iBT), IELTS (minimum score 6). *Expenses:* Tuition, state resident: full-time $8370; part-time $349 per credit hour. Tuition, nonresident: full-time $13,780. Required fees: $30.30 per credit hour. $20 per year. *Faculty research:* Silviculture recreation management, tree improvement, operations management, economics.

State University of New York College of Environmental Science and Forestry, Program in Environmental Science, Syracuse, NY 13210-2779. Offers environmental and community land planning (MPS, MS, PhD); environmental and natural resources policy (PhD); environmental communication and participatory processes (MPS, MS, PhD); environmental policy and democratic processes (MPS, MS, PhD); environmental systems and risk management (MPS, MS, PhD); water and wetland resource studies (MPS, MS, PhD). Part-time programs available. *Degree requirements:* For master's, thesis (for some programs); for doctorate, comprehensive exam, thesis/dissertation. *Entrance requirements:* For master's and doctorate, GRE General Test, minimum GPA of 3.0. Additional exam requirements/recommendations for international students: Required—TOEFL (minimum score 550 paper-based; 213 computer-based; 80 iBT), IELTS (minimum score 6). *Expenses:* Tuition, state resident: full-time $8370; part-time $349 per credit hour. Tuition, nonresident: full-time $13,780. Required fees: $30.30 per credit hour. $20 per year. *Faculty research:* Environmental education/communications, water resources, land resources, waste management.

Stony Brook University, State University of New York, Graduate School, College of Engineering and Applied Sciences, Department of Technology and Society, Program in Energy and Environmental Systems, Stony Brook, NY 11794. Offers MS, Advanced Certificate. Part-time programs available. *Degree requirements:* For master's, thesis, project. *Application deadline:* For fall admission, 2/1 for domestic students; for spring admission, 10/1 for domestic students. Electronic applications accepted. *Expenses:* Tuition, state resident: full-time $8370; part-time

$349 per credit. Tuition, nonresident: full-time $13,780; part-time $574 per credit. Required fees: $994. *Financial support:* Research assistantships, teaching assistantships, career-related internships or fieldwork available. *Unit head:* Dr. David Ferguson, Chairman, 631-632-8770, E-mail: david.ferguson@stonybrook.edu. *Application contact:* Dr. Sheldon Reaven, 631-632-8770, E-mail: sheldon.raven@sunysb.edu.

Stony Brook University, State University of New York, School of Professional Development, Stony Brook, NY 11794. Offers biology-grade 7-12 (MAT); chemistry-grade 7-12 (MAT); coaching (Graduate Certificate); coaching online (Graduate Certificate); computer integrated engineering (Graduate Certificate); earth science-grade 7-12 (MAT); educational computing (Graduate Certificate); educational leadership (Advanced Certificate); English-grade 7-12 (MAT); environmental management (Graduate Certificate); environmental/occupational health and safety (Graduate Certificate); French-grade 7-12 (MAT); German-grade 7-12 (MAT); human resource management (Graduate Certificate); human resource management online (Graduate Certificate); information systems management (Graduate Certificate); Italian-grade 7-12 (MAT); liberal studies (MA); liberal studies online (MAT); mathematics-grade 7-12 (MAT); operation research (Graduate Certificate); physics-grade 7-12 (MAT); professional studies online (MPS); school administration and supervision (Graduate Certificate); school building leadership (Graduate Certificate); school district administration (Graduate Certificate); school district business leadership (Advanced Certificate); school district leadership (Graduate Certificate); social science and the professions (MPS), including environmental waste management, human resource management; social studies-grade 7-12 (MAT); Spanish-grade 7-12 (MAT); waste management (Graduate Certificate). Part-time and evening/weekend programs available. Postbaccalaureate distance learning degree programs offered. *Faculty:* 25 full-time (10 women), 105 part-time/adjunct (40 women). *Students:* 360 full-time (228 women), 1,097 part-time (729 women); includes 180 minority (65 Black or African American, non-Hispanic/Latino; 2 American Indian or Alaska Native, non-Hispanic/Latino; 30 Asian, non-Hispanic/Latino; 81 Hispanic/Latino; 1 Native Hawaiian or other Pacific Islander, non-Hispanic/Latino; 1 Two or more races, non-Hispanic/Latino), 10 international. Average age 28. In 2010, 505 master's, 187 other advanced degrees awarded. *Degree requirements:* For master's, one foreign language, thesis or alternative. *Application deadline:* Applications are processed on a rolling basis. Application fee: $100. *Expenses:* Tuition, state resident: full-time $8370; part-time $349 per credit. Tuition, nonresident: full-time $13,780; part-time $574 per credit. Required fees: $994. *Financial support:* In 2010–11, 1 teaching assistantship was awarded; fellowships, research assistantships, career-related internships or fieldwork also available. Support available to part-time students. *Unit head:* Dr. Paul J. Edelson, Dean, 631-632-7052, Fax: 631-632-9046, E-mail: paul.edelson@stonybrook.edu. *Application contact:* Dr. Paul J. Edelson, Dean, 631-632-7052, Fax: 631-632-9046, E-mail: paul.edelson@stonybrook.edu.

Texas Southern University, School of Public Affairs, Program in Urban Planning and Environmental Policy, Houston, TX 77004-4584. Offers MS, PhD. *Accreditation:* ACSP. Part-time and evening/weekend programs available. *Faculty:* 4 full-time (2 women). *Students:* 44 full-time (21 women), 35 part-time (20 women); includes 62 Black or African American, non-Hispanic/Latino; 7 Asian, non-Hispanic/Latino; 3 Hispanic/Latino, 1 international. Average age 37. 27 applicants, 100% accepted, 20 enrolled. In 2010, 1 master's, 3 doctorates awarded. *Degree requirements:* For master's, comprehensive exam, thesis optional. *Entrance requirements:* For master's, GRE General Test, minimum GPA of 2.5. Additional exam requirements/recommendations for international students: Required—TOEFL. *Application deadline:* For fall admission, 7/1 priority date for domestic students, 7/1 for international students; for spring admission, 11/1 for domestic and international students. Applications are processed on a rolling basis. Application fee: $50 ($75 for international students). Electronic applications accepted. *Expenses:* Tuition, state resident: full-time $1875; part-time $100 per credit hour. Tuition, nonresident: full-time $6641; part-time $343 per credit hour. Tuition and fees vary according to course level, course load and degree level. *Financial support:* In 2010–11, 6 research assistantships (averaging $4,122 per year), 1 teaching assistantship (averaging $6,000 per year) were awarded; fellowships, career-related internships or fieldwork, Federal Work-Study, and institutionally sponsored loans also available. Financial award application deadline: 5/1; financial award applicants required to submit FAFSA. *Unit head:* Dr. Qisheng Pan, Chair, 713-313-7221, E-mail: taylor_sa@tsu.edu. *Application contact:* Sheila Taylor, Secretary, 713-313-6842, E-mail: randell_bj@tsu.edu.

Texas State University–San Marcos, Graduate School, College of Liberal Arts, Department of Geography, Program in Resource and Environmental Studies, San Marcos, TX 78666. Offers MAG. Part-time and evening/weekend programs available. *Faculty:* 5 full-time (3 women), 2 part-time/adjunct (0 women). *Students:* 16 full-time (8 women), 14 part-time (8 women); includes 2 minority (both Hispanic/Latino). Average age 30. 8 applicants, 88% accepted, 6 enrolled. In 2010, 5 master's awarded. *Degree requirements:* For master's, comprehensive exam. *Entrance requirements:* For master's, GRE General Test, minimum GPA of 3.0 in last 60 hours of course work, letter of interest, 2 letters of recommendation, curriculum vitae/resume. Additional exam requirements/recommendations for international students: Required—TOEFL (minimum score 550 paper-based; 213 computer-based; 78 iBT). *Application deadline:* For fall admission, 5/1 priority date for domestic students, 4/15 for international students; for spring admission, 10/15 priority date for domestic students, 10/1 for international students. Applications are processed on a rolling basis. Application fee: $40 ($90 for international students). *Expenses:* Tuition, state resident: full-time $6024; part-time $251 per credit hour. Tuition, nonresident: full-time $13,536; part-time $564 per credit hour. Required fees: $1776; $50 per credit hour. $306 per semester. *Financial support:* In 2010–11, 15 students received support, including 2 research assistantships (averaging $5,238 per year), 5 teaching assistantships (averaging $4,563 per year); career-related internships or fieldwork, Federal Work-Study, institutionally sponsored loans, and scholarships/grants also available. Support available to part-time students. Financial award application deadline: 4/1; financial award applicants required to submit FAFSA. *Unit head:* Dr. David Butler, Graduate Adviser, 512-245-2170, Fax: 512-245-8353, E-mail: db25@txstate.edu. *Application contact:* Dr. J. Michael Willoughby, Dean of Graduate School, 512-245-2581, Fax: 512-245-8365, E-mail: gradcollege@txstate.edu.

Texas Tech University, Graduate School, College of Architecture, PhD Program in Land-Use Planning, Management, and Design, Lubbock, TX 79409. Offers PhD. *Students:* 5 full-time (2 women), 3 part-time (1 woman), 2 international. Average age 41. 12 applicants, 17% accepted, 0 enrolled. *Degree requirements:* For doctorate, comprehensive exam, thesis/dissertation. *Entrance requirements:* For doctorate, GRE General Test. Additional exam requirements/recommendations for international students: Required—TOEFL (minimum score 550 paper-based; 213 computer-based; 79 iBT). *Application deadline:* For fall admission, 6/1 priority date for domestic students, 1/15 priority date for international students; for spring admission, 9/1 priority date for domestic students, 6/15 priority date for international students. Applications are processed on a rolling basis. Application fee: $50 ($75 for international students). Electronic applications accepted. *Expenses:* Tuition, state resident: full-time $5495.76; part-time $228.99 per credit hour. Tuition, nonresident: full-time $12,936; part-time $538.99 per credit hour. Required fees: $2674; $36 per credit hour. $905 per semester. *Financial support:* Application deadline: 4/15. *Faculty research:* Architecture, landscape architecture, geography, urban planning, environmental policy. *Unit head:* Dr. Saif Haq, Program Director, 806-742-3136 Ext. 284, Fax: 806-742-4604, E-mail: saif.haq@ttu.edu. *Application contact:* Lori Rodriguez, Academic Program Assistant, 806-742-3136 Ext. 247, Fax: 806-742-1400, E-mail: lori.rodriguez@ttu.edu.

Towson University, Program in Geography and Environmental Planning, Towson, MD 21252-0001. Offers MA. Part-time and evening/weekend programs available. *Students:* 8 full-time (4 women), 26 part-time (17 women); includes 2 minority (both Black or African American, non-Hispanic/Latino), 1 international. Average age 30. In 2010, 3 master's awarded. *Degree requirements:* For master's, thesis optional. *Entrance requirements:* For master's, 9 credits of course work in geography, minimum GPA of 3.0 in geography, 2 narrative letters of recommendation. Additional exam requirements/recommendations for international students: Required—TOEFL. *Application deadline:* Applications are processed on a rolling basis. Application fee: $50. Electronic applications accepted. *Expenses:* Tuition, state resident: part-time $324 per credit. Tuition, nonresident: part-time $681 per credit. Required fees: $95 per term. *Financial support:* In 2010–11, 1 teaching assistantship with full tuition reimbursement (averaging $4,000 per year) was awarded; Federal Work-Study and unspecified assistantships also available. Financial award application deadline: 4/1; financial award applicants required to submit FAFSA. *Faculty research:* Geographic information systems, regional planning, hazards, development issues, urban fluvial systems. *Unit head:* Martin Roberge, Graduate Program Director, 410-704-5011, Fax: 410-704-3880, E-mail: mroberge@towson.edu. *Application contact:* 410-704-2501, Fax: 410-704-4675, E-mail: grads@towson.edu.

Trent University, Graduate Studies, Program in Environmental and Life Sciences, Environmental and Resource Studies Program, Peterborough, ON K9J 7B8, Canada. Offers M Sc, PhD. *Degree requirements:* For master's, thesis; for doctorate, thesis/dissertation. *Entrance requirements:* For master's, honours degree; for doctorate, master's degree. *Faculty research:* Environmental biogeochemistry, aquatic organic contaminants, fisheries, wetland ecology, renewable resource management.

Tropical Agriculture Research and Higher Education Center, Graduate School, Turrialba, Costa Rica. Offers agribusiness management (MS); agroforestry systems (PhD); development practices (MS); ecological agriculture (MS); environmental socioeconomics (MS); forestry in tropical and subtropical zones (PhD); integrated watershed management (MS); international sustainable tourism (MS); management and conservation of tropical rainforests and biodiversity (MS); tropical agriculture (PhD); tropical agroforestry (MS). *Entrance requirements:* For master's, GRE, 2 years of related professional experience, letters of recommendation; for doctorate, GRE, 4 letters of recommendation, letter of support from employing organization, master's degree in agronomy, biological sciences, forestry, natural resources or related field. Additional exam requirements/recommendations for international students: Required—TOEFL (minimum score 550 paper-based; 213 computer-based). Electronic applications accepted. *Faculty research:* Biodiversity in fragmented landscapes, ecosystem management, integrated pest management, environmental livestock production, biotechnology carbon balances in diverse land uses.

Troy University, Graduate School, College of Arts and Sciences, Program in Environmental Analysis and Management, Troy, AL 36082. Offers MS. Part-time and evening/weekend programs available. *Students:* 8 full-time (5 women), 22 part-time (13 women); includes 7 minority (2 Black or African American, non-Hispanic/Latino; 2 Asian, non-Hispanic/Latino; 3 Hispanic/Latino). Average age 25. 65 applicants, 63% accepted. In 2010, 16 master's awarded. *Degree requirements:* For master's, comprehensive exam or thesis, minimum GPA of 3.0, admission to candidacy. *Entrance requirements:* For master's, GRE (minimum score of 850) or MAT (minimum score of 385), minimum undergraduate GPA of 2.5, 2 letters of recommendation. Additional exam requirements/recommendations for international students: Required—TOEFL (minimum score 523 paper-based; 193 computer-based; 70 iBT), IELTS (minimum score 6). *Application deadline:* Applications are processed on a rolling basis. Application fee: $50. Electronic applications accepted. *Expenses:* Tuition, state resident: full-time $4428; part-time $246 per credit hour. Tuition, nonresident: full-time $8856; part-time $492 per credit hour. Required fees: $432; $24 per credit hour. $50 per term. Tuition and fees vary according to program. *Unit head:* Dr. Glenn Cohen, Chairman, 334-670-3660, Fax: 334-670-3662, E-mail: gcohen@troy.edu. *Application contact:* Brenda K. Campbell, Director of Graduate Admissions, 334-670-3178, Fax: 334-670-3733, E-mail: bcamp@troy.edu.

Troy University, Graduate School, College of Arts and Sciences, Program in Public Administration, Troy, AL 36082. Offers education (MPA); environmental management (MPA); government contracting (MPA); health care administration (MPA); justice administration (MPA); national security affairs (MPA); nonprofit management (MPA); public human resources management (MPA); public management (MPA). *Accreditation:* NASPAA. Part-time and evening/weekend programs available. Postbaccalaureate distance learning degree programs offered (no on-campus study). *Degree requirements:* For master's, capstone course, research methodologies course. *Entrance requirements:* For master's, GRE, MAT or GMAT, minimum undergraduate GPA of 2.5, letter of recommendation, essay. Additional exam requirements/recommendations for international students: Required—TOEFL (minimum score 523 paper-based; 193 computer-based; 70 iBT), IELTS (minimum score 6). *Application deadline:* Applications are processed on a rolling basis. Application fee: $50. Electronic applications accepted. *Expenses:* Tuition, state resident: full-time $4428; part-time $246 per credit hour. Tuition, nonresident: full-time $8856; part-time $492 per credit hour. Required fees: $432; $24 per credit hour. $50 per term. Tuition and fees vary according to program. *Financial support:* Available to part-time students. Applicants required to submit FAFSA. *Unit head:* Dr. Ellen Rosell, Chairman, 334-670-3758, Fax: 334-670-5647, E-mail: erosell@troy.edu. *Application contact:* Brenda K. Campbell, Director of Graduate Admissions, 334-670-3178, Fax: 334-670-3733, E-mail: bcamp@troy.edu.

Tufts University, Graduate School of Arts and Sciences, Department of Urban and Environmental Policy and Planning, Medford, MA 02155. Offers community development (MA); environmental policy (MA); health and human welfare (MA); housing policy (MA); international environment/development policy (MA); public policy (MPP); MA/MS; MALD/MA. *Accreditation:* ACSP (one or more programs are accredited). Part-time programs available. *Degree requirements:* For master's, thesis, internship. *Entrance requirements:* For master's, GRE General Test. Additional exam requirements/recommendations for international students: Required—TOEFL (minimum score 550 paper-based; 213 computer-based; 80 iBT). Electronic applications accepted. *Expenses:* Contact institution.

Tufts University, Graduate School of Arts and Sciences, Graduate Certificate Programs, Community Environmental Studies Program, Medford, MA 02155. Offers Certificate. Part-time and evening/weekend programs available. Electronic applications accepted. *Expenses:* Contact institution.

Tufts University, Graduate School of Arts and Sciences, Graduate Certificate Programs, Environmental Management Program, Medford, MA 02155. Offers Certificate. Part-time and evening/weekend programs available. Electronic applications accepted. *Expenses:* Tuition: Full-time $39,624; part-time $3962 per course. Required fees: $40 per year. Full-time tuition and fees vary according to degree level, program and student level. Part-time tuition and fees vary according to course load.

Tufts University, School of Engineering, Department of Civil and Environmental Engineering, Medford, MA 02155. Offers civil engineering (ME, MS, PhD), including geotechnical engineering, structural engineering; environmental engineering (ME, MS, PhD), including environmental engineering and environmental sciences, environmental geotechnology, environmental health, environmental science and management, hazardous materials management, water resources engineering. Part-time programs available. Terminal master's awarded for partial completion of doctoral program. *Degree requirements:* For master's, thesis or alternative; for doctorate, thesis/dissertation. *Entrance requirements:* For master's and doctorate, GRE General Test. Additional exam requirements/recommendations for international students: Required—TOEFL (minimum score 550 paper-based; 213 computer-based; 80 iBT). Electronic applications accepted. *Expenses:* Tuition: Full-time $39,624; part-time $3962 per course. Required fees: $40 per year. Full-time tuition and fees vary according to degree level, program and student level. Part-time tuition and fees vary according to course load.

Environmental Management and Policy

Universidad Autonoma de Guadalajara, Graduate Programs, Guadalajara, Mexico. Offers administrative law and justice (LL M); advertising and corporate communications (MA); architecture (M Arch); business (MBA); computational science (MCC); education (Ed M, Ed D); English-Spanish translation (MA); entrepreneurship and management (MBA); integrated management of digital animation (MA); international business (MIB); international corporate law (LL M); internet technologies (MS); manufacturing systems (MMS); occupational health (MS); philosophy (MA, PhD); power electronics (MS); quality systems (MQS); renewable energy (MS); social evaluation of projects (MBA); strategic market research (MBA); tax law (MA); teaching mathematics (MA).

Universidad del Turabo, Graduate Programs, Programs in Science and Technology, Gurabo, PR 00778-3030. Offers environmental analysis (MSE), including environmental chemistry; environmental management (MSE), including pollution management; environmental science (D Sc), including environmental biology. *Entrance requirements:* For master's, GRE, EXADEP, interview.

Universidad Metropolitana, School of Environmental Affairs, Program in Environmental Planning, San Juan, PR 00928-1150. Offers MP. Part-time programs available. *Degree requirements:* For master's, thesis. *Entrance requirements:* For master's, EXADEP, interview. Electronic applications accepted.

Universidad Metropolitana, School of Environmental Affairs, Program in Environmental Studies, San Juan, PR 00928-1150. Offers MAES. Part-time programs available. *Degree requirements:* For master's, thesis or alternative. *Entrance requirements:* For master's, EXADEP, interview. Electronic applications accepted.

Université de Montréal, Faculty of Medicine, Programs in Environment and Prevention, Montréal, QC H3C 3J7, Canada. Offers environment, health and disaster management (DESS). Electronic applications accepted. *Faculty research:* Health, environment, pollutants, protection, waste.

Université du Québec à Chicoutimi, Graduate Programs, Program in Renewable Resources, Chicoutimi, QC G7H 2B1, Canada. Offers M Sc. Part-time programs available. *Degree requirements:* For master's, thesis. *Entrance requirements:* For master's, appropriate bachelor's degree, proficiency in French.

Université du Québec, Institut National de la Recherche Scientifique, Graduate Programs, Research Center—Water, Earth and Environment, Québec, QC G1K 9A9, Canada. Offers earth sciences (M Sc, PhD); earth sciences-environmental technologies (M Sc); water sciences (M Sc, PhD). Part-time programs available. *Faculty:* 41. *Students:* 196 full-time (79 women), 17 part-time (5 women), 94 international. Average age 30. In 2010, 19 master's, 17 doctorates awarded. *Degree requirements:* For master's, thesis optional; for doctorate, thesis/dissertation. *Entrance requirements:* For master's, appropriate bachelor's degree, proficiency in French; for doctorate, appropriate master's degree, proficiency in French. *Application deadline:* For fall admission, 3/30 for domestic and international students; for winter admission, 11/1 for domestic and international students; for spring admission, 3/1 for domestic and international students. Application fee: $30. *Financial support:* Fellowships, research assistantships, teaching assistantships available. *Faculty research:* Land use, impacts of climate change, adaptation to climate change, integrated management of resources (mineral and water). *Unit head:* Yves Begin, Director, 418-654-2524, Fax: 418-654-2600, E-mail: info@ete.inrs.ca. *Application contact:* Yvonne Boisvert, Registrar, 418-654-3861, Fax: 418-654-3858, E-mail: registrariat@adm.inrs.ca.

Université Laval, Faculty of Administrative Sciences, Programs in Business Administration, Québec, QC G1K 7P4, Canada. Offers accounting (MBA); agri-food management (MBA); electronic business (MBA, Diploma); factory management and logistics (MBA); finance (MBA); firm management (MBA); geomatic management (MBA); information technology management (MBA); international management (MBA); management (MBA); management accounting (MBA, Diploma); marketing (MBA); modeling and organizational decision (MBA); occupational health and safety management (MBA); pharmacy management (MBA); social and environmental responsibility (MBA); technological entrepreneurship (Diploma). *Accreditation:* AACSB. Part-time and evening/weekend programs available. Postbaccalaureate distance learning degree programs offered (no on-campus study). *Entrance requirements:* For master's and Diploma, knowledge of French and English. Electronic applications accepted.

Université Laval, Faculty of Agricultural and Food Sciences, Department of Soils and Agricultural Engineering, Programs in Agri-Food Engineering, Québec, QC G1K 7P4, Canada. Offers agri-food engineering (M Sc); environmental technology (M Sc). *Degree requirements:* For master's, thesis (for some programs). *Entrance requirements:* For master's, knowledge of French. Electronic applications accepted.

Université Laval, Faculty of Agricultural and Food Sciences, Department of Soils and Agricultural Engineering, Programs in Soils and Environment Science, Québec, QC G1K 7P4, Canada. Offers environmental technology (M Sc); soils and environment science (M Sc, PhD). Terminal master's awarded for partial completion of doctoral program. *Degree requirements:* For master's, thesis (for some programs); for doctorate, comprehensive exam, thesis/dissertation. *Entrance requirements:* For master's and doctorate, knowledge of French and English. Electronic applications accepted.

University at Albany, State University of New York, College of Arts and Sciences, Department of Biological Sciences, Program in Biodiversity, Conservation, and Policy, Albany, NY 12222-0001. Offers MS. *Degree requirements:* For master's, one foreign language. *Entrance requirements:* For master's, GRE General Test. *Faculty research:* Aquatic ecology, plant community ecology, biodiversity and public policy, restoration ecology, coastal and estuarine science.

University of Alaska Fairbanks, College of Engineering and Mines, Department of Civil and Environmental Engineering, Program in Environmental Engineering, Fairbanks, AK 99775-5900. Offers engineering (PhD), including environmental engineering; environmental engineering (MS), including environmental contaminants, environmental science and management, water supply and waste treatment. Part-time programs available. *Students:* 3 full-time (all women), 3 part-time (2 women). Average age 28. 5 applicants, 60% accepted, 1 enrolled. In 2010, 3 master's, 1 doctorate awarded. *Degree requirements:* For master's, comprehensive exam, thesis or alternative; for doctorate, comprehensive exam, thesis/dissertation, oral exam, oral defense. *Entrance requirements:* For master's, basic computer techniques; for doctorate, GRE General Test. Additional exam requirements/recommendations for international students: Required—TOEFL (minimum score 575 paper-based; 213 computer-based). *Application deadline:* For fall admission, 6/1 for domestic students, 3/1 for international students; for spring admission, 10/15 for domestic students, 9/1 for international students. Applications are processed on a rolling basis. Application fee: $60. Electronic applications accepted. *Expenses:* Tuition, state resident: full-time $5688; part-time $316 per credit. Tuition, nonresident: full-time $11,628; part-time $646 per credit. Required fees: $289 per semester. Tuition and fees vary according to course load and reciprocity agreements. *Financial support:* In 2010–11, 4 research assistantships (averaging $13,290 per year), 1 teaching assistantship (averaging $7,088 per year) were awarded; fellowships, career-related internships or fieldwork, Federal Work-Study, scholarships/grants, health care benefits, and unspecified assistantships also available. Support available to part-time students. Financial award application deadline: 7/1; financial award applicants required to submit FAFSA. *Unit head:* Dr. David Barnes, Department Chair, 907-474-7241, Fax: 907-474-6087, E-mail: fyeqe@uaf.edu. *Application contact:* Dr. David Barnes, Department Chair, 907-474-7241, Fax: 907-474-6087, E-mail: fyeqe@uaf.edu.

University of Alaska Fairbanks, College of Liberal Arts, Department of Northern Studies, Fairbanks, AK 99775-6460. Offers environmental politics and policy (MA); Northern history (MA). Part-time programs available. *Students:* 15 full-time (9 women), 21 part-time (13 women); includes 6 minority (1 Black or African American, non-Hispanic/Latino; 2 American Indian or Alaska Native, non-Hispanic/Latino; 1 Hispanic/Latino; 2 Two or more races, non-Hispanic/Latino), 2 international. Average age 39. 14 applicants, 57% accepted, 8 enrolled. In 2010, 9 master's awarded. *Degree requirements:* For master's, comprehensive exam, thesis or alternative. *Entrance requirements:* Additional exam requirements/recommendations for international students: Required—TOEFL (minimum score 550 paper-based; 213 computer-based; 80 iBT). *Application deadline:* For fall admission, 6/1 for domestic students, 3/1 for international students; for spring admission, 10/15 for domestic students, 9/1 for international students. Applications are processed on a rolling basis. Application fee: $60. Electronic applications accepted. *Expenses:* Tuition, state resident: full-time $5688; part-time $316 per credit. Tuition, nonresident: full-time $11,628; part-time $646 per credit. Required fees: $289 per semester. Tuition and fees vary according to course load and reciprocity agreements. *Financial support:* In 2010–11, 9 teaching assistantships with tuition reimbursements (averaging $7,462 per year) were awarded; fellowships with tuition reimbursements, research assistantships with tuition reimbursements, career-related internships or fieldwork, Federal Work-Study, scholarships/grants, health care benefits, and unspecified assistantships also available. Support available to part-time students. Financial award application deadline: 1/1; financial award applicants required to submit FAFSA. *Faculty research:* Canadian history, environmental history, Native Alaskan history and art, fetal alcohol syndrome. *Unit head:* Mary Ehrlander, Director, 907-474-7126, Fax: 907-474-5817, E-mail: fynors@uaf.edu. *Application contact:* Mary Ehrlander, Director, 907-474-7126, Fax: 907-474-5817, E-mail: fynors@uaf.edu.

University of Alberta, Faculty of Graduate Studies and Research, Department of Economics, Edmonton, AB T6G 2E1, Canada. Offers economics (MA, PhD); economics and finance (MA); environmental and natural resource economics (PhD). Part-time programs available. *Degree requirements:* For doctorate, thesis/dissertation. *Entrance requirements:* For master's and doctorate, GRE. Additional exam requirements/recommendations for international students: Required—TOEFL. *Faculty research:* Public finance, international trade, industrial organization, Pacific Rim economics, monetary economics.

University of Calgary, Faculty of Graduate Studies, Interdisciplinary Graduate Programs, Calgary, AB T2N 1N4, Canada. Offers interdisciplinary research (M Sc, MA, PhD); resources and the environment (M Sc, MA, PhD). Part-time programs available. *Degree requirements:* For master's, thesis; for doctorate, thesis/dissertation, written and oral candidacy exam. *Entrance requirements:* Additional exam requirements/recommendations for international students: Required—TOEFL (minimum score 600 paper-based; 250 computer-based).

University of Calgary, Faculty of Law, Programs in Natural Resources, Energy and Environmental Law, Calgary, AB T2N 1N4, Canada. Offers LL M, Postbaccalaureate Certificate. Part-time and evening/weekend programs available. *Faculty:* 13 full-time (7 women). *Students:* 35 full-time (23 women), 8 part-time (5 women); includes 4 Black or African American, non-Hispanic/Latino; 1 Hispanic/Latino. Average age 33. 50 applicants, 26% accepted, 11 enrolled. In 2010, 8 master's awarded. *Degree requirements:* For master's, thesis (for some programs), thesis is required for LLM thesis-based program—not required for LLM course-based program. *Entrance requirements:* For master's, JD or LLB degree. Additional exam requirements/recommendations for international students: Required—TOEFL (minimum score 100 iBT), IELTS (minimum score 7). *Application deadline:* For fall admission, 12/15 priority date for domestic and international students; for winter admission, 7/15 priority date for domestic students. Application fee: $100 ($130 for international students). Electronic applications accepted. *Financial support:* In 2010–11, 14 students received support, including 11 fellowships (averaging $15,000 per year); scholarships/grants also available. Financial award application deadline: 5/1. *Faculty research:* Natural resources law and regulations; environmental law, ethics and policies; oil and gas and energy law; water and municipal law; Aboriginal law. Total annual research expenditures: $362,000. *Unit head:* Alastair Lucas, Dean, 403-220-5447, Fax: 403-282-8325, E-mail: lawdean@ucalgary.ca. *Application contact:* Brenda Tschanz, Graduate Program Administrator and Admissions Assistant, 403-210-8718, Fax: 403-210-9662, E-mail: tschanz@ucalgary.ca.

University of California, Berkeley, Graduate Division, College of Natural Resources, Department of Environmental Science, Policy, and Management, Berkeley, CA 94720-1500. Offers environmental science, policy, and management (MS, PhD); forestry (MF). Terminal master's awarded for partial completion of doctoral program. *Degree requirements:* For master's, thesis optional; for doctorate, thesis/dissertation, qualifying exam. *Entrance requirements:* For master's and doctorate, GRE General Test, minimum GPA of 3.0, 3 letters of recommendation. Additional exam requirements/recommendations for international students: Required—TOEFL. Electronic applications accepted. *Faculty research:* Biology and ecology of insects; ecosystem function and environmental issues of soils; plant health/interactions from molecular to ecosystem levels; range management and ecology; forest and resource policy, sustainability, and management.

University of California, Berkeley, UC Berkeley Extension, Certificate Programs in Sustainability Studies, Berkeley, CA 94720-1500. Offers leadership in sustainability and environmental management (Professional Certificate); solar energy and green building (Professional Certificate); sustainable design (Professional Certificate).

University of California, Santa Barbara, Graduate Division, College of Letters and Sciences, Division of Social Sciences, Department of Global and International Studies, Santa Barbara, CA 93106-7065. Offers global culture and religion (MA); global government and human rights (MA); political economy, sustainable development, and the environment (MA). *Faculty:* 14 full-time (5 women), 4 part-time/adjunct (1 woman). *Students:* 37 full-time (25 women); includes 6 Asian, non-Hispanic/Latino; 2 Hispanic/Latino; 1 Native Hawaiian or other Pacific Islander, non-Hispanic/Latino. Average age 28. 55 applicants, 42% accepted, 12 enrolled. In 2010, 14 master's awarded. *Degree requirements:* For master's, one foreign language, thesis or alternative, 2 years of a second language. *Entrance requirements:* For master's, GRE, 2 years of a second language with minimum B grade, 3 letters of recommendation, resume/curriculum vitae. Additional exam requirements/recommendations for international students: Required—TOEFL (minimum score 600 paper-based; 80 iBT), IELTS (minimum score 7). *Application deadline:* For fall admission, 12/15 for domestic and international students. Application fee: $70 ($90 for international students). Electronic applications accepted. *Financial support:* In 2010–11, 36 students received support, including 29 fellowships with partial tuition reimbursements available (averaging $6,805 per year), 31 teaching assistantships with partial tuition reimbursements available (averaging $8,175 per year); career-related internships or fieldwork also available. Financial award application deadline: 12/15; financial award applicants required to submit FAFSA. *Faculty research:* Global culture religion, global governance human rights, political rconomy, environment, sustainable development. Total annual research expenditures: $240,000. *Unit head:* Prof. Giles Gunn, Chair, 805-893-4299, Fax: 805-893-8003, E-mail: ggunn@global.ucsb.edu. *Application contact:* Jessea Gay Marie, Graduate Program Advisor/Internship Assistance Officer, 805-893-4668, Fax: 805-893-8003, E-mail: gd-global@global.ucsb.edu.

University of California, Santa Barbara, Graduate Division, Donald Bren School of Environmental Science and Management, Santa Barbara, CA 93106-5131. Offers economics and environmental science (PhD); environmental science and management (MESM, PhD); technology and society (PhD). *Faculty:* 17 full-time (3 women), 2 part-time/adjunct (0 women). *Students:* 219 full-time (128 women); includes 1 Black or African American, non-Hispanic/Latino; 1 American Indian or Alaska Native, non-Hispanic/Latino; 33 Asian, non-Hispanic/Latino; 11 Hispanic/Latino. Average age 28. 521 applicants, 40% accepted, 82 enrolled. In

2010, 75 master's awarded. *Degree requirements:* For master's, thesis; for doctorate, thesis/dissertation. *Entrance requirements:* For master's and doctorate, GRE. Additional exam requirements/recommendations for international students: Required—TOEFL (minimum score 550 paper-based; 80 iBT), IELTS (minimum score 7). *Application deadline:* For fall admission, 12/15 priority date for domestic and international students. Application fee: $70 ($90 for international students). Electronic applications accepted. *Financial support:* In 2010–11, 105 students received support, including 83 fellowships with full and partial tuition reimbursements available (averaging $6,929 per year), 27 research assistantships with full and partial tuition reimbursements available (averaging $8,918 per year), 32 teaching assistantships with partial tuition reimbursements available (averaging $8,112 per year); career-related internships or fieldwork and tuition waivers (full and partial) also available. Financial award application deadline: 12/15; financial award applicants required to submit FAFSA. *Faculty research:* Coastal marine resources management, conservation planning, corporate environmental management, economics and politics of the environment, energy and climate, pollution prevention and remediation, water resources management. *Unit head:* Bryant Wieneke, Assistant Dean, Planning and Administration, 805-893-2212, Fax: 805-893-7612, E-mail: bryant@bren.ucsb.edu. *Application contact:* Graduate Advisor, 805-893-7611, Fax: 805-893-7612, E-mail: admissions@bren.ucsb.edu.

University of California, Santa Cruz, Division of Graduate Studies, Division of Social Sciences, Program in Environmental Studies, Santa Cruz, CA 95064. Offers PhD. *Students:* 37 full-time (23 women), 4 part-time (2 women); includes 1 Black or African American, non-Hispanic/Latino; 1 Asian, non-Hispanic/Latino, 4 international. Average age 33. 39 applicants, 21% accepted, 2 enrolled. In 2010, 2 doctorates awarded. *Degree requirements:* For doctorate, thesis/dissertation, qualifying exam. *Entrance requirements:* For doctorate, GRE General Test. Additional exam requirements/recommendations for international students: Required—TOEFL (minimum score 550 paper-based; 220 computer-based; 83 iBT); Recommended—IELTS (minimum score 8). *Application deadline:* For fall admission, 12/15 for domestic and international students. Application fee: $70 ($90 for international students). Electronic applications accepted. *Financial support:* Fellowships, research assistantships, teaching assistantships, institutionally sponsored loans and tuition waivers available. Financial award applicants required to submit FAFSA. *Faculty research:* Political economy and sustainability, conservation biology, agroecology, environmental policy analysis. *Unit head:* Marissa Maciel, Graduate Program Coordinator, 831-459-4136, E-mail: maciel@ucsc.edu. *Application contact:* Marissa Maciel, Graduate Program Coordinator, 831-459-4136, E-mail: maciel@ucsc.edu.

University of Central Missouri, The Graduate School, College of Science and Technology, Warrensburg, MO 64093. Offers applied mathematics (MS); aviation safety (MS); biology (MS); computer science (MS); environmental studies (MA); industrial management (MS); mathematics (MS); technology (MS); technology management (PhD). PhD is offered jointly with Indiana State University. Part-time programs available. Postbaccalaureate distance learning degree programs offered. *Entrance requirements:* Additional exam requirements/recommendations for international students: Required—TOEFL (minimum score 550 paper-based; 79 computer-based). Electronic applications accepted.

University of Chicago, Irving B. Harris Graduate School of Public Policy Studies, Chicago, IL 60637-1513. Offers environmental science and policy (MS); public policy studies (AM, MPP, PhD); JD/MPP; MBA/MPP; MPP/M Div; MPP/MA. Part-time programs available. *Degree requirements:* For doctorate, thesis/dissertation. *Entrance requirements:* Additional exam requirements/recommendations for international students: Required—TOEFL. Electronic applications accepted. *Expenses:* Contact institution. *Faculty research:* Family and child policy, international security, health policy, social policy.

University of Colorado Boulder, Graduate School, College of Arts and Sciences, Program in Environmental Studies, Boulder, CO 80309. Offers MS, PhD. *Faculty:* 6 full-time (3 women). *Students:* 42 full-time (25 women), 12 part-time (7 women); includes 8 minority (1 Black or African American, non-Hispanic/Latino; 4 American Indian or Alaska Native, non-Hispanic/Latino; 3 Asian, non-Hispanic/Latino). Average age 31. 279 applicants, 14 enrolled. In 2010, 14 master's, 1 doctorate awarded. *Entrance requirements:* For master's, minimum undergraduate GPA of 3.0. *Application deadline:* For fall admission, 1/15 for domestic students, 12/1 for international students. *Financial support:* In 2010–11, 19 fellowships (averaging $13,158 per year), 13 research assistantships (averaging $13,454 per year) were awarded. *Faculty research:* Climate and atmospheric chemistry, water sciences, environmental policy and sustainability, waste management and environmental remediation, biogeochemical cycles. Total annual research expenditures: $1.1 million.

University of Colorado Denver, College of Architecture and Planning, Program in Urban and Regional Planning, Denver, CO 80217-3364. Offers economic and community development planning (MURP); land use and environmental planning (MURP); urban place making (MURP). *Accreditation:* ACSP. Part-time programs available. *Students:* 125 full-time (57 women), 5 part-time (3 women); includes 1 Black or African American, non-Hispanic/Latino; 2 American Indian or Alaska Native, non-Hispanic/Latino; 3 Asian, non-Hispanic/Latino; 8 Hispanic/Latino, 9 international. Average age 30. 145 applicants, 68% accepted, 38 enrolled. In 2010, 47 master's awarded. *Degree requirements:* For master's, thesis optional, minimum of 51 semester hours. *Entrance requirements:* For master's, GRE if GPA below 3.0, writing sample. Additional exam requirements/recommendations for international students: Required—TOEFL (minimum score 550 paper-based; 213 computer-based). *Application deadline:* For fall admission, 2/15 for domestic students; for spring admission, 10/1 for domestic students. Application fee: $50 ($75 for international students). Electronic applications accepted. *Expenses:* Contact institution. *Financial support:* Career-related internships or fieldwork, Federal Work-Study, and scholarships/grants available. Financial award application deadline: 4/1; financial award applicants required to submit FAFSA. *Faculty research:* Physical planning, environmental planning, economic development planning. *Unit head:* Brian Muller, Associate Professor and Chair, 303-556-5967, E-mail: brian.muller@ucdenver.edu. *Application contact:* Brian Muller, Associate Professor and Chair, 303-556-5967, E-mail: brian.muller@ucdenver.edu.

University of Colorado Denver, College of Liberal Arts and Sciences, Program in Humanities, Denver, CO 80217-3364. Offers community health science (MSS); humanities (MH); international studies (MSS); social science (MSS); society and the environment (MSS); women's and gender studies (MSS). Part-time and evening/weekend programs available. *Students:* 53 full-time (39 women), 35 part-time (22 women); includes 4 Black or African American, non-Hispanic/Latino; 1 American Indian or Alaska Native, non-Hispanic/Latino; 3 Asian, non-Hispanic/Latino; 7 Hispanic/Latino, 1 international. Average age 33. 41 applicants, 54% accepted, 19 enrolled. In 2010, 29 master's awarded. *Degree requirements:* For master's, thesis or alternative, 36 credit hours, project or thesis. *Entrance requirements:* For master's, writing sample, statement of purpose/letter of intent. Additional exam requirements/recommendations for international students: Required—TOEFL (minimum score 525 paper-based). *Application deadline:* For fall admission, 5/15 priority date for domestic students; for spring admission, 10/15 priority date for domestic students. Application fee: $50 ($75 for international students). Electronic applications accepted. *Expenses:* Tuition, state resident: full-time $7332; part-time $355 per credit hour. Tuition, nonresident: full-time $18,990; part-time $1055 per credit hour. Required fees: $998. Tuition and fees vary according to course level, course load, degree level, campus/location, program, reciprocity agreements and student level. *Financial support:* Federal Work-Study and scholarships/grants available. Financial award application deadline: 4/1; financial award applicants required to submit FAFSA. *Faculty research:* Women and gender in the classical Mediterranean, communication theory and democracy, relationship between psychology and philosophy. *Unit head:* Myra Bookman, Associate Director of Humanities and Social Science, 303-556-2496, Fax: 303-556-8100, E-mail: myra.bookman@ucdenver.edu. *Application contact:* Catherine Osmundson, Program Assistant, 303-556-2305, E-mail: catherine.osmundson@ucdenver.edu.

University of Colorado Denver, School of Public Affairs, Program in Public Affairs and Administration, Denver, CO 80127. Offers public administration (MPA), including domestic violence, emergency management and homeland security, environmental policy, management and law, homeland security and defense, local government, nonprofit management, public administration; public affairs (PhD). *Accreditation:* NASPAA. Part-time and evening/weekend programs available. Postbaccalaureate distance learning degree programs offered (no on-campus study). *Faculty:* 19 full-time (9 women), 14 part-time/adjunct (5 women). *Students:* 317 full-time (181 women), 167 part-time (100 women); includes 15 Black or African American, non-Hispanic/Latino; 2 American Indian or Alaska Native, non-Hispanic/Latino; 18 Asian, non-Hispanic/Latino; 29 Hispanic/Latino; 1 Two or more races, non-Hispanic/Latino, 36 international. Average age 30. 270 applicants, 66% accepted, 118 enrolled. In 2010, 119 master's, 4 doctorates awarded. *Degree requirements:* For master's, thesis or alternative, 36-39 credit hours; for doctorate, comprehensive exam, thesis/dissertation, minimum of 66 semester hours, including at least 30 hours of doctoral dissertation credits. *Entrance requirements:* For master's and doctorate, GRE, resume, essay, transcripts, recommendations. Additional exam requirements/recommendations for international students: Required—TOEFL (minimum score 550 paper-based; 223 computer-based). *Application deadline:* For fall admission, 2/1 for domestic students; for spring admission, 10/15 priority date for domestic students. Application fee: $50 ($75 for international students). Electronic applications accepted. *Expenses:* Contact institution. *Financial support:* Fellowships with partial tuition reimbursements, research assistantships with partial tuition reimbursements, teaching assistantships with partial tuition reimbursements, Federal Work-Study and scholarships/grants available. Support available to part-time students. Financial award application deadline: 4/1; financial award applicants required to submit FAFSA. *Faculty research:* Housing, education and the social and economic issues of vulnerable populations; nonprofit governance and management; education finance, effectiveness and reform; P-20 (preschool through graduate school) education initiatives; municipal government accountability. *Unit head:* Dr. Mary Guy, Program Director, 303-315-2007, Fax: 303-315-2229, E-mail: mary.guy@ucdenver.edu. *Application contact:* Annie Davies, Director of Marketing, Community Outreach and Alumni Affairs, 303-315-2896, Fax: 303-315-2229, E-mail: annie.davies@ucdenver.edu.

University of Dayton, Graduate School, School of Engineering, Department of Mechanical and Aerospace Engineering, Dayton, OH 45469-1300. Offers aerospace engineering (MSAE, DE, PhD); mechanical engineering (MSME, DE, PhD); renewable and clean energy (MS). Part-time programs available. Postbaccalaureate distance learning degree programs offered (no on-campus study). *Faculty:* 16 full-time (2 women), 11 part-time/adjunct (1 woman). *Students:* 113 full-time (22 women), 26 part-time (6 women); includes 15 minority (6 Black or African American, non-Hispanic/Latino; 3 Asian, non-Hispanic/Latino; 6 Hispanic/Latino), 47 international. Average age 28. 113 applicants, 84% accepted, 50 enrolled. In 2010, 30 master's, 7 doctorates awarded. Terminal master's awarded for partial completion of doctoral program. *Degree requirements:* For master's, thesis optional; for doctorate, variable foreign language requirement, thesis/dissertation, departmental qualifying exam. *Entrance requirements:* Additional exam requirements/recommendations for international students: Required—TOEFL (minimum score 550 paper-based; 213 computer-based; 80 iBT). *Application deadline:* For fall admission, 8/1 priority date for domestic students, 6/1 priority date for international students; for winter admission, 9/1 priority date for international students; for spring admission, 3/1 priority date for international students. Applications are processed on a rolling basis. Application fee: $0. Electronic applications accepted. *Expenses:* Tuition: Full-time $7800; part-time $650 per credit hour. *Financial support:* In 2010–11, 25 students received support, including 29 research assistantships with full tuition reimbursements available (averaging $11,000 per year), 7 teaching assistantships with full tuition reimbursements available (averaging $9,100 per year). Financial award applicants required to submit FAFSA. *Faculty research:* Jet engine combustion, surface coating friction and wear, aircraft thermal management, aerospace fuels, energy efficient buildings, energy efficient manufacturing, renewable energy. Total annual research expenditures: $1.2 million. *Unit head:* Dr. Kelly Kissock, Chair, 937-229-2999, Fax: 937-229-4766, E-mail: kelly.kissock@udayton.edu. *Application contact:* Dr. Vinod Jain, Graduate Program Director, 937-229-2992, Fax: 937-229-4766, E-mail: vinod.jain@notes.udayton.edu.

University of Delaware, College of Human Services, Education and Public Policy, Center for Energy and Environmental Policy, Newark, DE 19716. Offers environmental and energy policy (MEEP, PhD); urban affairs and public policy (MA, PhD), including community development and nonprofit leadership (MA), energy and environmental policy (MA), governance, planning and management (PhD), historic preservation (MA), social and urban policy (PhD), technology, environment and society (PhD). *Degree requirements:* For master's, analytical paper or thesis; for doctorate, comprehensive exam, thesis/dissertation. *Entrance requirements:* For master's, GRE General Test, minimum GPA of 3.0; for doctorate, GRE General Test, minimum GPA of 3.5. Additional exam requirements/recommendations for international students: Required—TOEFL. Electronic applications accepted. *Faculty research:* Sustainable development, renewable energy, climate change, environmental policy, environmental justice, disaster policy.

University of Denver, University College, Denver, CO 80208. Offers arts and culture (MLS, Certificate), including art, literature, and culture, arts development and program management (Certificate), creative writing; environmental policy and management (MAS, Certificate), including energy and sustainability (Certificate), environmental assessment of nuclear power (Certificate), environmental health and safety (Certificate), environmental management, natural resource management (Certificate); geographic information systems (MAS, Certificate); global affairs (MLS, Certificate), including translation studies, world history and culture; healthcare leadership (MPH, Certificate), including healthcare policy, law, and ethics, medical and healthcare information technologies, strategic management of healthcare; information and communications technology (MCIS, Certificate), including database design and administration (Certificate), geographic information systems (MCIS), information security systems security (Certificate), information systems security (MCIS), project management (MCIS, MPS, Certificate), software design and administration (Certificate), software design and programming (MCIS), technology management, telecommunications technology (MCIS), Web design and development; leadership and organizations (MPS, Certificate), including human capital in organizations, philanthropic leadership, project management (MCIS, MPS, Certificate), strategic innovation and change; organizational and professional communication (MPS, Certificate), including alternative dispute resolution, organizational communication, organizational development and training, public relations and marketing; security management (MAS, Certificate), including emergency planning and response, information security (MAS), organizational security; strategic human resource management (MPS, Certificate), including global human resources (MPS), human resource management and development (MPS). Part-time and evening/weekend programs available. Postbaccalaureate distance learning degree programs offered (no on-campus study). *Faculty:* 7 full-time (2 women), 212 part-time/adjunct (83 women). *Students:* 52 full-time (19 women), 1,044 part-time (625 women); includes 196 minority (81 Black or African American, non-Hispanic/Latino; 7 American Indian or Alaska Native, non-Hispanic/Latino; 30 Asian, non-Hispanic/Latino; 66 Hispanic/Latino; 3 Native Hawaiian or other Pacific Islander, non-Hispanic/Latino; 9 Two or more races, non-Hispanic/Latino), 76 international. Average age 36. 488 applicants, 91% accepted, 339 enrolled. In 2010, 286 master's, 130 other advanced degrees awarded. *Entrance requirements:* Additional exam requirements/recommendations for international students: Required—TOEFL (minimum score 550 paper-based; 80 iBT). *Application deadline:* For fall admission, 6/22 priority date for domestic students, 6/10 priority date for international students; for winter admission, 9/15 priority date for domestic students, 9/6 priority date for international students; for spring admission, 2/3 priority date for domestic students, 12/15 priority date for international students. Applications are processed on a rolling basis. Application fee: $75. Electronic applications accepted. *Expenses:* Contact institution. *Financial support:* Applicants required to submit FAFSA. *Unit head:* Dr. James Davis, Dean, 303-871-2291, Fax: 303-871-4047, E-mail: jdavis@du.edu. *Application contact:* Information Contact, 303-871-3155, Fax: 303-871-4047, E-mail: ucolinfo@du.edu.

Environmental Management and Policy

The University of Findlay, Graduate and Professional Studies, College of Sciences, Master of Science Program in Environmental, Safety and Health Management, Findlay, OH 45840-3653. Offers MSEM. Part-time and evening/weekend programs available. Postbaccalaureate distance learning degree programs offered (no on-campus study). *Faculty:* 11 full-time (3 women), 3 part-time/adjunct (2 women). *Students:* 3 full-time (1 woman), 87 part-time (34 women); includes 10 minority (4 Black or African American, non-Hispanic/Latino; 1 American Indian or Alaska Native, non-Hispanic/Latino; 5 Asian, non-Hispanic/Latino), 28 international. Average age 35. 25 applicants, 84% accepted, 14 enrolled. In 2010, 30 master's awarded. *Degree requirements:* For master's, thesis, cumulative project. *Entrance requirements:* For master's, GRE, minimum undergraduate GPA of 3.0 in last 60 hours of course work. Additional exam requirements/recommendations for international students: Required—TOEFL (minimum score 550 paper-based; 213 computer-based; 80 iBT). *Application deadline:* Applications are processed on a rolling basis. Application fee: $25. Electronic applications accepted. *Expenses:* Tuition: Full-time $17,000; part-time $700 per semester hour. Required fees: $680; $35 per semester hour. Tuition and fees vary according to course load and program. *Financial support:* In 2010–11, 1 research assistantship with full and partial tuition reimbursement (averaging $4,200 per year), 1 teaching assistantship with full and partial tuition reimbursement (averaging $6,000 per year) were awarded; career-related internships or fieldwork, Federal Work-Study, health care benefits, and unspecified assistantships also available. Financial award application deadline: 4/1; financial award applicants required to submit FAFSA. *Unit head:* William Doyle, PhD, Director, 419-434-5747, Fax: 419-434-4822, E-mail: doyle@findlay.edu. *Application contact:* Heather Riffle, Assistant Director, Graduate and Professional Studies, 419-434-4640, Fax: 419-434-5517, E-mail: riffle@findlay.edu.

University of Guelph, Graduate Studies, Ontario Agricultural College, Department of Land Resource Science, Guelph, ON N1G 2W1, Canada. Offers atmospheric science (M Sc, PhD); environmental and agricultural earth sciences (M Sc, PhD); land resources management (M Sc, PhD); soil science (M Sc, PhD). Part-time programs available. *Degree requirements:* For master's, thesis (for some programs), research project (non-thesis track); for doctorate, comprehensive exam, thesis/dissertation. *Entrance requirements:* For master's, minimum B-average during previous 2 years of course work; for doctorate, minimum B average during previous 2 years of course work. Additional exam requirements/recommendations for international students: Required—TOEFL (minimum score 550 paper-based; 213 computer-based). Electronic applications accepted. *Faculty research:* Soil science, environmental earth science, land resource management.

University of Hawaii at Manoa, Graduate Division, College of Social Sciences, Department of Urban and Regional Planning, Honolulu, HI 96822. Offers community planning and social policy (MURP); disaster preparedness and emergency management (Graduate Certificate); environmental planning and management (MURP); land use and infrastructure planning (MURP); urban and regional planning (PhD, Graduate Certificate); urban and regional planning in Asia and Pacific (MURP). *Accreditation:* ACSP. Part-time programs available. *Faculty:* 28 full-time (9 women), 11 part-time/adjunct (2 women). *Students:* 63 full-time (35 women), 25 part-time (12 women); includes 24 minority (1 Black or African American, non-Hispanic/Latino; 6 Asian, non-Hispanic/Latino; 1 Hispanic/Latino; 9 Native Hawaiian or other Pacific Islander, non-Hispanic/Latino; 7 Two or more races, non-Hispanic/Latino), 30 international. Average age 33. 89 applicants, 63% accepted, 32 enrolled. In 2010, 30 master's, 3 doctorates, 1 other advanced degree awarded. *Entrance requirements:* For master's, GRE General Test, minimum GPA of 3.0; for doctorate, GRE General Test. Additional exam requirements/recommendations for international students: Required—TOEFL (minimum score 500 paper-based; 173 computer-based; 61 iBT), IELTS (minimum score 5). *Application deadline:* For fall admission, 3/1 for domestic and international students; for spring admission, 9/1 for domestic and international students. Application fee: $60. *Financial support:* In 2010–11, 11 fellowships (averaging $2,314 per year), 28 research assistantships (averaging $16,718 per year), 2 teaching assistantships (averaging $14,382 per year) were awarded; career-related internships or fieldwork, Federal Work-Study, institutionally sponsored loans, and tuition waivers (full) also available. Total annual research expenditures: $423,000. *Application contact:* Dolores Foley, Graduate Chair, 808-956-7381, Fax: 808-956-6870, E-mail: dolores@hawaii.edu.

University of Hawaii at Manoa, Graduate Division, College of Tropical Agriculture and Human Resources, Department of Natural Resources and Environmental Management, Honolulu, HI 96822. Offers MS, PhD. Part-time programs available. *Faculty:* 31 full-time (5 women), 2 part-time/adjunct (1 woman). *Students:* 53 full-time (31 women), 19 part-time (7 women); includes 15 minority (7 Asian, non-Hispanic/Latino; 2 Hispanic/Latino; 2 Native Hawaiian or other Pacific Islander, non-Hispanic/Latino; 4 Two or more races, non-Hispanic/Latino), 21 international. Average age 32. 82 applicants, 56% accepted, 32 enrolled. In 2010, 7 master's, 5 doctorates awarded. Terminal master's awarded for partial completion of doctoral program. *Degree requirements:* For master's, thesis optional; for doctorate, comprehensive exam, thesis/dissertation. *Entrance requirements:* For master's and doctorate, GRE General Test, minimum GPA of 3.0 in last 4 semesters of course work. Additional exam requirements/recommendations for international students: Required—TOEFL (minimum score 600 paper-based; 250 computer-based; 100 iBT), IELTS (minimum score 7). *Application deadline:* For fall admission, 3/1 for domestic students, 1/15 for international students; for spring admission, 9/1 for domestic students, 8/1 for international students. Applications are processed on a rolling basis. Application fee: $60. *Financial support:* In 2010–11, 10 fellowships (averaging $1,822 per year), 22 research assistantships (averaging $19,469 per year), 4 teaching assistantships (averaging $14,820 per year) were awarded; career-related internships or fieldwork and tuition waivers (full and partial) also available. *Faculty research:* Bioeconomics, natural resource management. Total annual research expenditures: $3.1 million. *Application contact:* John Yanagida, Graduate Chair, 808-956-7530, Fax: 808-956-6539, E-mail: jyanagid@hawaii.edu.

University of Houston–Clear Lake, School of Business, Program in Administrative Science, Houston, TX 77058-1098. Offers environmental management (MS); human resource management (MA). *Accreditation:* CAHME (one or more programs are accredited). Part-time and evening/weekend programs available. *Degree requirements:* For master's, thesis optional. *Entrance requirements:* For master's, GMAT. Additional exam requirements/recommendations for international students: Required—TOEFL (minimum score 550 paper-based; 213 computer-based). Electronic applications accepted.

University of Illinois at Springfield, Graduate Programs, College of Public Affairs and Administration, Program in Environmental Studies, Springfield, IL 62703-5407. Offers environmental science (MS); environmental studies (MA). Part-time and evening/weekend programs available. Postbaccalaureate distance learning degree programs offered (no on-campus study). *Degree requirements:* For master's, thesis or project. *Entrance requirements:* For master's, minimum undergraduate GPA of 3.0, 2 letters of recommendation. Additional exam requirements/recommendations for international students: Required—TOEFL (minimum score 500 paper-based; 176 computer-based; 61 iBT). Electronic applications accepted. *Expenses:* Tuition, state resident: full-time $6774; part-time $282.25 per credit hour. Tuition, nonresident: full-time $15,078; part-time $628.25 per credit hour. Required fees: $15.25 per credit hour. $492 per term.

University of Maine, Graduate School, College of Liberal Arts and Sciences, Department of History, Orono, ME 04469. Offers American studies (MA, PhD); Canadian studies (MA, PhD); East Asian (MA); environmental (MA); European (MA); technology (MA). *Faculty:* 11 full-time (1 woman), 2 part-time/adjunct (1 woman). *Students:* 24 full-time (8 women), 35 part-time (13 women); includes 4 minority (2 American Indian or Alaska Native, non-Hispanic/Latino; 2 Hispanic/Latino). Average age 38. 43 applicants, 40% accepted, 15 enrolled. In 2010, 5 master's, 3 doctorates awarded. Terminal master's awarded for partial completion of doctoral program. *Degree requirements:* For master's, variable foreign language requirement, thesis optional; for doctorate, one foreign language, thesis/dissertation. *Entrance requirements:* For master's and doctorate, GRE General Test. Additional exam requirements/recommendations for international students: Required—TOEFL. *Application deadline:* For fall admission, 2/1 priority date for domestic students. Applications are processed on a rolling basis. Application fee: $65. Electronic applications accepted. *Expenses:* Tuition, state resident: full-time $400. Tuition, nonresident: full-time $1050. *Financial support:* In 2010–11, 9 teaching assistantships with tuition reimbursements (averaging $12,790 per year) were awarded; career-related internships or fieldwork, Federal Work-Study, and tuition waivers (full and partial) also available. Support available to part-time students. Financial award application deadline: 3/1. *Faculty research:* Canadian labor and working classes; American social, cultural, and urban history. *Unit head:* Dr. Nathan Godfried, Chair, 207-581-1923, Fax: 207-581-1817. *Application contact:* Scott G. Delcourt, Associate Dean of the Graduate School, 207-581-3291, Fax: 207-581-3232, E-mail: graduate@maine.edu.

The University of Manchester, School of Environment and Development, Manchester, United Kingdom. Offers architecture (M Phil, PhD); development policy and management (M Phil, PhD); human geography (M Phil, PhD); physical geography (M Phil, PhD); planning and landscape (M Phil, PhD).

University of Maryland, Baltimore County, Graduate School, College of Arts, Humanities and Social Sciences, Department of Geography and Environmental Systems, Program in Geography and Environmental Systems, Baltimore, MD 21250. Offers MS, PhD. *Faculty:* 11 full-time (4 women), 6 part-time/adjunct (1 woman). *Students:* 19 full-time (12 women), 5 part-time (4 women); includes 2 Black or African American, non-Hispanic/Latino; 1 Asian, non-Hispanic/Latino, 2 international. Average age 32. 25 applicants, 56% accepted, 6 enrolled. Terminal master's awarded for partial completion of doctoral program. *Degree requirements:* For master's, thesis optional, annual faculty evaluation, research paper; for doctorate, comprehensive exam, thesis/dissertation, annual faculty evaluation, qualifying exams, proposal and dissertation defense. *Entrance requirements:* For master's and doctorate, GRE, minimum GPA of 3.0 overall, 3.3 in major. Additional exam requirements/recommendations for international students: Required—TOEFL (minimum score 550 paper-based; 213 computer-based; 80 iBT). *Application deadline:* For fall admission, 2/1 for domestic and international students. Application fee: $50. Electronic applications accepted. *Financial support:* In 2010–11, 15 students received support, including 1 fellowship with full tuition reimbursement available (averaging $30,000 per year), 8 research assistantships with full tuition reimbursements available (averaging $18,392 per year), 6 teaching assistantships with full tuition reimbursements available (averaging $18,392 per year); scholarships/grants, traineeships, and unspecified assistantships also available. Financial award application deadline: 2/1. *Faculty research:* Watershed processes, climate and weather systems; ecology and biogeography; landscape ecology and land-use change; human geography, urban sustainability and environmental health; environmental policy; geographic information science and remote sensing. *Unit head:* Dr. Christopher M. Swan, Graduate Program Director, 410-455-2002, E-mail: gpd.ges@umbc.edu. *Application contact:* Kathryn Nee, Coordinator of Domestic Admissions, 410-455-2944, E-mail: nee@umbc.edu.

University of Maryland University College, Graduate School of Management and Technology, Program in Environmental Management, Adelphi, MD 20783. Offers MS, Certificate. Offered evenings and weekends only. Part-time and evening/weekend programs available. Postbaccalaureate distance learning degree programs offered (no on-campus study). *Students:* 14 full-time (9 women), 446 part-time (232 women); includes 129 minority (77 Black or African American, non-Hispanic/Latino; 4 American Indian or Alaska Native, non-Hispanic/Latino; 13 Asian, non-Hispanic/Latino; 32 Hispanic/Latino; 3 Two or more races, non-Hispanic/Latino), 8 international. Average age 34. 162 applicants, 100% accepted, 78 enrolled. In 2010, 63 master's, 10 other advanced degrees awarded. *Degree requirements:* For master's, thesis or alternative, capstone course. *Application deadline:* Applications are processed on a rolling basis. Application fee: $50. Electronic applications accepted. *Financial support:* Federal Work-Study and scholarships/grants available. Support available to part-time students. Financial award application deadline: 6/1; financial award applicants required to submit FAFSA. *Unit head:* Dr. Robert Beauchamp, Director, 240-684-2400, Fax: 240-684-2401, E-mail: rbeauchamp@umuc.edu. *Application contact:* Coordinator, Graduate Admissions, 800-888-8682, Fax: 240-684-2151, E-mail: newgrad@umuc.edu.

University of Massachusetts Amherst, Graduate School, College of Natural Sciences, Department of Environmental Conservation, Amherst, MA 01003. Offers building systems (MS, PhD); environmental policy and human dimensions (MS, PhD); forest resources (MS, PhD); water, wetlands and watersheds (MS, PhD); wildlife and fisheries conservation (MS, PhD). Part-time programs available. *Faculty:* 51 full-time (7 women). *Students:* 55 full-time (30 women), 35 part-time (16 women); includes 5 minority (2 Black or African American, non-Hispanic/Latino; 3 Hispanic/Latino), 10 international. Average age 32. 73 applicants, 41% accepted, 23 enrolled. In 2010, 8 master's, 4 doctorates awarded. Terminal master's awarded for partial completion of doctoral program. *Degree requirements:* For master's, thesis or alternative; for doctorate, comprehensive exam, thesis/dissertation. *Entrance requirements:* For master's and doctorate, GRE General Test. Additional exam requirements/recommendations for international students: Required—TOEFL (minimum score 550 paper-based; 213 computer-based; 80 iBT), IELTS (minimum score 6.5). *Application deadline:* For fall admission, 2/1 for domestic and international students; for spring admission, 10/1 for domestic and international students. Applications are processed on a rolling basis. Application fee: $50 ($65 for international students). Electronic applications accepted. *Expenses:* Tuition, state resident: full-time $2640. Required fees: $8282. One-time fee: $357 full-time. *Financial support:* In 2010–11, 6 fellowships with full tuition reimbursements (averaging $14,507 per year), 62 research assistantships with full tuition reimbursements (averaging $9,977 per year), 33 teaching assistantships with full tuition reimbursements (averaging $6,243 per year) were awarded; career-related internships or fieldwork, Federal Work-Study, scholarships/grants, traineeships, health care benefits, tuition waivers (full), and unspecified assistantships also available. Support available to part-time students. Financial award application deadline: 2/1; financial award applicants required to submit FAFSA. *Unit head:* Dr. Matt Kelty, Graduate Program Director, 413-545-2666, Fax: 413-545-4358. *Application contact:* Jean M. Ames, Supervisor of Admissions, 413-545-0721, Fax: 413-577-0100, E-mail: gradadm@grad.umass.edu.

University of Massachusetts Dartmouth, Graduate School, School of Education, Public Policy, and Civic Engagement, Department of Public Policy, North Dartmouth, MA 02747-2300. Offers environmental policy (Postbaccalaureate Certificate); public policy (MPP). Part-time programs available. Postbaccalaureate distance learning degree programs offered (minimal on-campus study). *Faculty:* 5 full-time (2 women), 1 (woman) part-time/adjunct. *Students:* 13 full-time (7 women), 28 part-time (16 women); includes 1 Black or African American, non-Hispanic/Latino; 1 Hispanic/Latino. Average age 32. 26 applicants, 77% accepted, 7 enrolled. In 2010, 10 master's awarded. *Entrance requirements:* For master's, GRE or GMAT. Additional exam requirements/recommendations for international students: Required—TOEFL (minimum score 500 paper-based; 213 computer-based). *Application deadline:* For fall admission, 4/20 for domestic students, 2/20 for international students; for spring admission, 11/15 for domestic students, 9/15 for international students. Applications are processed on a rolling basis. Application fee: $40 ($60 for international students). Electronic applications accepted. *Expenses:* Tuition, state resident: full-time $2071; part-time $86 per credit. Tuition, nonresident: full-time $8099; part-time $337 per credit. Required fees: $9446; $394 per credit. One-time fee: $75. Part-time tuition and fees vary according to class time, course load, degree level and reciprocity agreements. *Financial support:* In 2010–11, 3 research assistantships with full tuition reimbursements (averaging $5,333 per year) were awarded; Federal Work-Study and unspecified assistantships also available. Support available to part-time students. Financial award application deadline: 3/1. *Faculty research:* Demographic analysis, legal and regulatory framework. Total

annual research expenditures: $82,244. *Unit head:* Dr. Michael Goodman, 508-990-9660, E-mail: mgoodman@umassd.edu. *Application contact:* Elan Turcotte-Shamski, Graduate Admissions Officer, 508-999-8604, Fax: 508-999-8183, E-mail: graduate@umassd.edu.

University of Massachusetts Lowell, School of Health and Environment, Department of Work Environment, Lowell, MA 01854-2881. Offers cleaner production and pollution prevention (MS, Sc D); environmental risk assessment (Certificate); epidemiology (MS, Sc D); ergonomics and safety (MS, Sc D); identification and control of ergonomic hazards (Certificate); job stress and healthy job redesign (Certificate); occupational and environmental hygiene (MS, Sc D); radiological health physics and general work environment protection (Certificate); work environment policy (MS, Sc D). *Accreditation:* ABET (one or more programs are accredited). Part-time programs available. Terminal master's awarded for partial completion of doctoral program. *Degree requirements:* For master's, thesis optional; for doctorate, thesis/dissertation. *Entrance requirements:* For master's and doctorate, GRE General Test. Additional exam requirements/recommendations for international students: Required—TOEFL.

University of Miami, Graduate School, School of Business Administration, Department of Economics, Coral Gables, FL 33124. Offers economic development (MA, PhD); environmental economics (PhD); human resource economics (MA, PhD); international economics (MA, PhD); macroeconomics (PhD). Students admitted every two years in the fall semester. Terminal master's awarded for partial completion of doctoral program. *Degree requirements:* For master's, comprehensive exam; for doctorate, comprehensive exam, thesis/dissertation. *Entrance requirements:* For master's and doctorate, GRE General Test, minimum GPA of 3.0. Additional exam requirements/recommendations for international students: Required—TOEFL (minimum score 550 paper-based). *Faculty research:* International economics/trade, applied microeconomics, development.

University of Michigan, School of Natural Resources and Environment, Program in Natural Resources and Environment, Ann Arbor, MI 48109. Offers aquatic sciences: research and management (MS); behavior, education and communication (MS); conservation biology (MS); conservation ecology (MS); environmental informatics (MS); environmental justice (MS); environmental policy and planning (MS); natural resources and environment (PhD); sustainable systems (MS); terrestrial ecosystems (MS); MS/AM; MS/JD; MS/MBA. *Faculty:* 42 full-time, 23 part-time/adjunct. *Students:* 450 full-time (254 women); includes 7 Black or African American, non-Hispanic/Latino; 2 American Indian or Alaska Native, non-Hispanic/Latino; 35 Asian, non-Hispanic/Latino; 13 Hispanic/Latino; 6 Two or more races, non-Hispanic/Latino, 50 international. Average age 27. 692 applicants. In 2010, 133 master's, 11 doctorates awarded. Terminal master's awarded for partial completion of doctoral program. *Degree requirements:* For master's, practicum or group project; for doctorate, comprehensive exam, thesis/dissertation, oral defense of dissertation, preliminary exam. *Entrance requirements:* For master's, GRE General Test; for doctorate, GRE General Test, master's degree. Additional exam requirements/recommendations for international students: Required—TOEFL (minimum score 560 paper-based; 220 computer-based; 84 iBT). *Application deadline:* For fall admission, 1/5 priority date for domestic and international students. Applications are processed on a rolling basis. Application fee: $65 ($75 for international students). Electronic applications accepted. *Expenses:* Tuition, state resident: full-time $17,784; part-time $1116 per credit hour. Tuition, nonresident: full-time $35,944; part-time $2125 per credit hour. International tuition: $35,994 full-time. Required fees: $95 per semester. Tuition and fees vary according to course load, degree level and program. *Financial support:* Fellowships with tuition reimbursements, research assistantships with tuition reimbursements, teaching assistantships with tuition reimbursements, career-related internships or fieldwork, Federal Work-Study, institutionally sponsored loans, scholarships/grants, health care benefits, and unspecified assistantships available. Support available to part-time students. Financial award application deadline: 1/5; financial award applicants required to submit FAFSA. *Faculty research:* Stream ecology, plant-insect interactions, fish biology, resource control and reproductive success, remote sensing, conservation ecology. *Application contact:* Graduate Admissions Team, 734-764-6453, Fax: 734-936-2195, E-mail: snre.admissions@umich.edu.

University of Minnesota, Twin Cities Campus, Graduate School, Hubert H. Humphrey School of Public Affairs, Program in Science, Technology, and Environmental Policy, Minneapolis, MN 55455-0213. Offers MS, JD/MS. Part-time programs available. *Degree requirements:* For master's, thesis. *Entrance requirements:* For master's, GRE General Test, undergraduate training in the biological or physical sciences or engineering, minimum undergraduate GPA of 3.0. Additional exam requirements/recommendations for international students: Required—TOEFL (minimum score 600 paper-based; 250 computer-based; 100 iBT). Electronic applications accepted. *Faculty research:* Economics, history, philosophy, and politics of science and technology; organization and management of science and technology.

The University of Montana, Graduate School, College of Arts and Sciences, Program in Environmental Studies (EVST), Missoula, MT 59812-0002. Offers MS, JD/MS. Part-time programs available. *Faculty:* 6 full-time (2 women), 2 part-time/adjunct (0 women). *Students:* 39 full-time (28 women), 23 part-time (16 women); includes 1 Hispanic/Latino, 1 international. Average age 30. 69 applicants, 72% accepted, 22 enrolled. In 2010, 31 master's awarded. *Degree requirements:* For master's, thesis, portfolio or professional paper. *Entrance requirements:* For master's, GRE General Test (minimum score: 500 verbal). Additional exam requirements/recommendations for international students: Required—TOEFL (minimum score 580 paper-based; 237 computer-based; 92 iBT). *Application deadline:* For fall admission, 2/1 priority date for domestic and international students. Application fee: $51. *Financial support:* In 2010–11, 18 students received support, including 4 fellowships with partial tuition reimbursements available (averaging $5,000 per year), 6 teaching assistantships with full tuition reimbursements available (averaging $9,000 per year). Financial award application deadline: 4/15. *Faculty research:* Pollution ecology, sustainable agriculture, environmental writing, environmental policy, environmental justice, habitat-land management. Total annual research expenditures: $86,108. *Unit head:* Dr. Len Broberg, Director, 406-243-5209, Fax: 406-243-6090, E-mail: len.broberg@mso.umt.edu. *Application contact:* Karen Hurd, Administrative Assistant, 406-243-6273, Fax: 406-243-6090, E-mail: karen.hurd@mso.umt.edu.

University of Nevada, Reno, Graduate School, College of Science, Mackay School of Earth Sciences and Engineering, Department of Geography, Program in Land Use Planning, Reno, NV 89557. Offers MS. *Degree requirements:* For master's, thesis. *Entrance requirements:* For master's, GRE General Test, minimum GPA of 3.0. Additional exam requirements/recommendations for international students: Required—TOEFL (minimum score 500 paper-based; 173 computer-based; 61 iBT), IELTS (minimum score 6). Electronic applications accepted. *Expenses:* Tuition, state resident: full-time $2219; part-time $246 per credit. Tuition, nonresident: part-time $510 per credit. International tuition: $9009 full-time. Required fees: $59 per term. One-time fee: $101. Tuition and fees vary according to course load. *Faculty research:* Contemporary planning, environmental planning.

University of New Brunswick Fredericton, School of Graduate Studies, Faculty of Engineering, Department of Chemical Engineering, Fredericton, NB E3B 5A3, Canada. Offers chemical engineering (M Eng, M Sc E, PhD); environmental studies (M Eng). Part-time programs available. *Faculty:* 11 full-time (3 women), 1 part-time/adjunct (0 women). *Students:* 59 full-time (24 women), 6 part-time (0 women). In 2010, 10 master's, 3 doctorates awarded. *Degree requirements:* For master's, thesis; for doctorate, comprehensive exam, thesis/dissertation, qualifying exam. *Entrance requirements:* For master's and doctorate, minimum GPA of 3.0. Additional exam requirements/recommendations for international students: Required—TOEFL (minimum score 580 paper-based), TWE (minimum score 4). *Application deadline:* For fall admission, 3/1 priority date for domestic students. Application fee: $50 Canadian dollars. Electronic applications accepted. *Expenses:* Tuition, area resident: Full-time $3708; part-time $927 per term. International tuition: $6300 full-time. Required fees: $50 per term. *Financial support:* In 2010–11, 109 research assistantships with tuition reimbursements (averaging $18,000 per year), 51 teaching assistantships (averaging $1,500 per year) were awarded. *Faculty research:* Processing and characterizing nanoengineered composite materials based on carbon nanotubes, enhanced oil recovery processes and oil sweep strategies for conventional and heavy oils, pulp and paper, waste-water treatment, chemistry and corrosion of high and lower temperature water systems. *Unit head:* Dr. Kecheng Li, Director of Graduate Studies, 506-451-6861, Fax: 506-453-3591, E-mail: kecheng@unb.ca. *Application contact:* Sylvia Demerson, Graduate Secretary, 506-453-4520, Fax: 506-453-3591, E-mail: sdemerso@unb.ca.

University of New Brunswick Fredericton, School of Graduate Studies, Faculty of Engineering, Department of Civil Engineering, Fredericton, NB E3B 5A3, Canada. Offers construction engineering and management (M Eng, M Sc E, PhD); environmental engineering (M Eng, M Sc E, PhD); environmental studies (M Eng); geotechnical engineering (M Eng, M Sc E, PhD); groundwater/hydrology (M Eng, M Sc E, PhD); materials (M Eng, M Sc E, PhD); pavements (M Eng, M Sc E, PhD); structures (M Eng, M Sc E, PhD); transportation (M Eng, M Sc E, PhD). Part-time programs available. *Faculty:* 13 full-time (1 woman), 7 part-time/adjunct (1 woman). *Students:* 34 full-time (8 women), 16 part-time (2 women). In 2010, 16 master's, 6 doctorates awarded. *Degree requirements:* For master's, thesis, proposal; for doctorate, comprehensive exam, thesis/dissertation, qualifying exam; proposal; 27 credit hours of courses. *Entrance requirements:* For master's, minimum GPA of 3.0; B Sc E in civil engineering or related engineering degree; for doctorate, minimum GPA of 3.0; graduate degree in engineering or applied science. Additional exam requirements/recommendations for international students: Required—TWE (minimum score 4), TOEFL (minimum score 580 paper-based; 237 computer-based) or IELTS (minimum score 7.5). *Application deadline:* For fall admission, 5/1 priority date for domestic students; for winter admission, 11/1 priority date for domestic students. Applications are processed on a rolling basis. Application fee: $50 Canadian dollars. *Expenses:* Tuition, area resident: Full-time $3708; part-time $927 per term. International tuition: $6300 full-time. Required fees: $50 per term. *Financial support:* In 2010–11, 52 research assistantships (averaging $7,000 per year), 46 teaching assistantships (averaging $2,000 per year) were awarded; career-related internships or fieldwork and scholarships/grants also available. *Faculty research:* Construction engineering and management; materials and infrastructure renewal; highway and pavement research; structures and solid mechanics; geotechnical, soil; structure interaction; transportation and planning; environment, solid waste management. *Unit head:* Dr. Eric Hildebrand, Director of Graduate Studies, 506-453-5113, Fax: 506-453-3568, E-mail: edh@unb.ca. *Application contact:* Joyce Moore, Graduate Secretary, 506-452-6127, Fax: 506-453-3568, E-mail: civil-grad@unb.ca.

University of New Brunswick Fredericton, School of Graduate Studies, Faculty of Forestry and Environmental Management, Fredericton, NB E3B 5A3, Canada. Offers ecological foundations of forest management (PhD); environmental management (MEM); forest engineering (M Sc FE, MFE); forest products marketing (MBA); forest resources (M Sc F, MF, PhD). Part-time programs available. *Faculty:* 22 full-time (3 women), 1 part-time/adjunct (0 women). *Students:* 68 full-time (29 women), 7 part-time (2 women). In 2010, 20 master's, 4 doctorates awarded. *Degree requirements:* For master's, thesis; for doctorate, thesis/dissertation. *Entrance requirements:* For master's and doctorate, minimum GPA of 3.0. Additional exam requirements/recommendations for international students: Required—TWE (minimum score 4), TOEFL (minimum score 580 paper-based) or IELTS. *Application deadline:* For fall admission, 3/1 priority date for domestic students. Application fee: $50 Canadian dollars. Electronic applications accepted. *Expenses:* Tuition, area resident: Full-time $3708; part-time $927 per term. International tuition: $6300 full-time. Required fees: $50 per term. *Financial support:* In 2010–11, 54 research assistantships, 46 teaching assistantships were awarded. *Faculty research:* Forest machines, soils, and ecosystems; integrated forest management; forest meteorology; wood engineering, stream ecosystems dynamics; forest and natural resources policy; forest operations planning; wood technology and mechanics; forest road construction and engineering; forest, wildlife, insect, bird, and fire ecology; remote sensing; insect impacts; Silviculture; LiDAR analytics; integrated pest management; forest tree genetics; genetic resource conservation and sustainable management. *Unit head:* Dr. John Kershaw, Director of Graduate Studies, 506-453-4933, Fax: 506-453-3538, E-mail: kershaw@unb.ca. *Application contact:* Faith Sharpe, Graduate Secretary, 506-458-7520, Fax: 506-453-3538, E-mail: fsharpe@unb.ca.

University of New Hampshire, Graduate School, College of Life Sciences and Agriculture, Department of Natural Resources, Durham, NH 03824. Offers environmental conservation (MS); forestry (MS); integrated coastal ecosystem science, policy, management (MS); natural resources (MS); water resources (MS); wildlife (MS). Part-time programs available. *Faculty:* 40 full-time. *Students:* 22 full-time (8 women), 27 part-time (15 women); includes 1 Asian, non-Hispanic/Latino; 1 Hispanic/Latino, 1 international. Average age 30. 54 applicants, 39% accepted, 14 enrolled. In 2010, 13 master's awarded. *Degree requirements:* For master's, thesis or alternative. *Entrance requirements:* For master's, GRE General Test. Additional exam requirements/recommendations for international students: Required—TOEFL (minimum score 550 paper-based; 213 computer-based; 80 iBT). *Application deadline:* For fall admission, 6/1 for domestic students, 4/1 for international students; for spring admission, 12/1 for domestic students. Applications are processed on a rolling basis. Application fee: $65. Electronic applications accepted. *Financial support:* In 2010–11, 23 students received support, including 3 fellowships, 6 research assistantships, 14 teaching assistantships; career-related internships or fieldwork, Federal Work-Study, scholarships/grants, and tuition waivers (full and partial) also available. Support available to part-time students. Financial award application deadline: 2/15. *Unit head:* Dr. John Halstead, Chairperson, 603-862-3950, E-mail: natural.resources@unh.edu. *Application contact:* Linda Scogin, Administrative Assistant, 603-862-3932, E-mail: natural.resources@unh.edu.

University of New Haven, Graduate School, College of Arts and Sciences, Program in Environmental Sciences, West Haven, CT 06516-1916. Offers environmental ecology (Certificate); environmental geoscience (MS); environmental health and management (MS); environmental science (MS); geographical information systems (Certificate). Part-time and evening/weekend programs available. *Students:* 13 full-time (5 women), 24 part-time (10 women); includes 2 Black or African American, non-Hispanic/Latino; 1 American Indian or Alaska Native, non-Hispanic/Latino; 1 Asian, non-Hispanic/Latino; 1 Hispanic/Latino, 4 international. Average age 27. 29 applicants, 100% accepted, 14 enrolled. In 2010, 13 master's, 1 other advanced degree awarded. *Degree requirements:* For master's, thesis or alternative. *Application deadline:* For fall admission, 5/31 for international students; for winter admission, 10/15 for international students; for spring admission, 1/15 for international students. Applications are processed on a rolling basis. Application fee: $50. Electronic applications accepted. *Financial support:* Research assistantships with partial tuition reimbursements, teaching assistantships with partial tuition reimbursements, career-related internships or fieldwork, Federal Work-Study, scholarships/grants, tuition waivers, and unspecified assistantships available. Support available to part-time students. Financial award applicants required to submit FAFSA. *Faculty research:* Mapping and assessing geological and living resources in Long Island Sound, geology, San Salvador Island, Bahamas. *Unit head:* Dr. Roman Zajac, Coordinator, 203-932-7108. *Application contact:* Eloise Gormley, Director of Graduate Admissions, 203-932-7449, Fax: 203-932-7137, E-mail: gradinfo@newhaven.edu.

University of New Mexico, Graduate School, Water Resources Program, Albuquerque, NM 87131-2039. Offers hydroscience (MWR); policy management (MWR). Part-time programs available. *Faculty:* 1 full-time (0 women). *Students:* 14 full-time (9 women), 24 part-time (15 women); includes 7 American Indian or Alaska Native, non-Hispanic/Latino; 1 Asian, non-Hispanic/Latino; 7 Hispanic/Latino. Average age 37. 26 applicants, 54% accepted, 9 enrolled. In 2010, 6 master's awarded. *Degree requirements:* For master's, professional project. *Entrance*

Environmental Management and Policy

University of New Mexico (continued)

requirements: For master's, minimum GPA of 3.0 during last 2 years of undergraduate work, 3 letters of reference. Additional exam requirements/recommendations for international students: Required—TOEFL (minimum score 550 paper-based; 213 computer-based). *Application deadline:* For fall admission, 7/15 for domestic students; for spring admission, 11/15 for domestic students. Applications are processed on a rolling basis. Application fee: $50. Electronic applications accepted. *Expenses:* Tuition, state resident: full-time $5991; part-time $251 per credit hour. Tuition, nonresident: full-time $14,405; part-time $800.20 per credit hour. Tuition and fees vary according to course level, course load, program and reciprocity agreements. *Financial support:* In 2010–11, 24 students received support, including 3 research assistantships with full and partial tuition reimbursements available (averaging $5,791 per year); career-related internships or fieldwork, institutionally sponsored loans, scholarships/grants, and unspecified assistantships also available. Financial award application deadline: 3/1; financial award applicants required to submit FAFSA. *Faculty research:* Sustainable water resources, transboundary water resources, economics, water law, hydrology, developing countries, hydrogeology. Total annual research expenditures: $150,557. *Unit head:* Dr. Bruce M. Thomson, Director, 505-277-5249, Fax: 505-277-5226, E-mail: bthomson@unm.edu. *Application contact:* Annamarie Cordova, Administrative Assistant II, 505-277-7759, Fax: 505-277-5226, E-mail: acordova@unm.edu.

The University of North Carolina at Chapel Hill, Graduate School, School of Public Health, Department of Environmental Sciences and Engineering, Chapel Hill, NC 27599. Offers air, radiation and industrial hygiene (MPH, MS, MSEE, MSPH, PhD); aquatic and atmospheric sciences (MPH, MS, MSPH, PhD); environmental engineering (MPH, MS, MSEE, MSPH, PhD); environmental health sciences (MPH, MS, MSPH, PhD); environmental management and policy (MPH, MS, MSPH, PhD). Terminal master's awarded for partial completion of doctoral program. *Degree requirements:* For master's, comprehensive exam, thesis (for some programs), research paper; for doctorate, comprehensive exam, thesis/dissertation. *Entrance requirements:* For master's and doctorate, GRE General Test, minimum GPA of 3.0. Additional exam requirements/recommendations for international students: Required—TOEFL. Electronic applications accepted. *Faculty research:* Air, radiation and industrial hygiene, aquatic and atmospheric sciences, environmental health sciences, environmental management and policy, water resources engineering.

The University of North Carolina Wilmington, College of Arts and Sciences, Department of Environmental Studies, Wilmington, NC 28403-3297. Offers coastal management (MA); environmental education and interpretation (MA); environmental management (MA); individualized study (MA). Part-time programs available. *Faculty:* 9 full-time (0 women). *Students:* 18 full-time (15 women), 19 part-time (13 women); includes 1 Hispanic/Latino, 1 international. Average age 30. 25 applicants, 92% accepted, 21 enrolled. In 2010, 14 master's awarded. *Degree requirements:* For master's, comprehensive exam, thesis or alternative, final project, practicum. *Entrance requirements:* For master's, GRE, 3 letters of recommendation. Additional exam requirements/recommendations for international students: Required—TOEFL (minimum score 550 paper-based; 217 computer-based; 79 iBT), IELTS (minimum score 6.5). *Application deadline:* For fall admission, 4/15 for domestic and international students; for spring admission, 10/15 for domestic and international students. Application fee: $60. Electronic applications accepted. *Financial support:* In 2010–11, 5 fellowships with full tuition reimbursements (averaging $1,000 per year), 5 teaching assistantships with full and partial tuition reimbursements (averaging $10,000 per year) were awarded; research assistantships, career-related internships or fieldwork, scholarships/grants, and unspecified assistantships also available. *Faculty research:* Coastal management, environmental management, environmental education, environmental law, natural resource management. *Unit head:* Dr. Jack Hall, 910-962-3488, Fax: 910-962-7634, E-mail: hallj@uncw.edu. *Application contact:* Dr. Jeffery Hill, Graduate Program Coordinator, 910-962-3264, Fax: 910-962-7634, E-mail: hillj@uncw.edu.

University of Northern British Columbia, Office of Graduate Studies, Prince George, BC V2N 4Z9, Canada. Offers business administration (Diploma); community health science (M Sc); disability management (MA); education (M Ed); first nations studies (MA); gender studies (MA); history (MA); interdisciplinary studies (MA); international studies (MA); mathematical, computer and physical sciences (M Sc); natural resources and environmental studies (M Sc, MA, MNRES, PhD); political science (MA); psychology (M Sc, PhD); social work (MSW). Part-time and evening/weekend programs available. Postbaccalaureate distance learning degree programs offered (no on-campus study). *Degree requirements:* For master's, thesis; for doctorate, thesis/dissertation. *Entrance requirements:* For master's, GRE, minimum B average in undergraduate course work; for doctorate, candidacy exam, minimum A average in graduate course work.

University of Oregon, Graduate School, College of Arts and Sciences, Environmental Studies Program, Eugene, OR 97403. Offers environmental science, studies, and policy (PhD); environmental studies (MA, MS). *Degree requirements:* For master's, one foreign language, thesis; for doctorate, comprehensive exam, thesis/dissertation. *Entrance requirements:* For master's, GRE General Test, minimum GPA of 3.0; for doctorate, GRE General Test. Additional exam requirements/recommendations for international students: Required—TOEFL (minimum score 550 paper-based; 213 computer-based). Electronic applications accepted.

University of Pennsylvania, School of Arts and Sciences, College of Liberal and Professional Studies, Philadelphia, PA 19104. Offers environmental studies (MES); individualized study (MLA). *Students:* 97 full-time (63 women), 256 part-time (165 women); includes 15 Black or African American, non-Hispanic/Latino; 1 American Indian or Alaska Native, non-Hispanic/Latino; 16 Asian, non-Hispanic/Latino; 15 Hispanic/Latino, 33 international. 600 applicants, 46% accepted, 213 enrolled. In 2010, 151 master's awarded. *Application deadline:* For fall admission, 12/1 priority date for domestic students. Application fee: $70. Electronic applications accepted. *Expenses:* Tuition: Full-time $25,660; part-time $4758 per course. Required fees: $2152; $270 per course. Tuition and fees vary according to course load, degree level and program. *Unit head:* Dr. Kristine Billmyer, Associate Dean and Director, College of Liberal and Professional Studies, 215-898-8681, E-mail: gdasdmis@sas.upenn.edu. *Application contact:* Patricia Rea, Coordinator for Admissions, 215-573-5816, Fax: 215-573-8068, E-mail: gdasadmis@sas.upenn.edu.

University of Pittsburgh, Graduate School of Public and International Affairs, Division of International Development, Pittsburgh, PA 15260. Offers development planning and environmental sustainability (MID); human security (MID); nongovernmental organizations and civil society (MID); MID/JD; MID/MBA; MID/MPH; MID/MPIA; MID/MSIS; MID/MSW. Part-time programs available. *Faculty:* 30 full-time (12 women), 67 part-time/adjunct (25 women). *Students:* 66 full-time (46 women), 7 part-time (5 women); includes 7 minority (1 Black or African American, non-Hispanic/Latino; 3 Asian, non-Hispanic/Latino; 3 Hispanic/Latino), 11 international. Average age 25. 125 applicants, 82% accepted, 39 enrolled. In 2010, 35 master's awarded. *Degree requirements:* For master's, thesis optional, internship, capstone seminar. *Entrance requirements:* For master's, GRE General Test, 3 letters of recommendation, recommended minimum GPA of 3.2. Additional exam requirements/recommendations for international students: Required—TOEFL (minimum score 550 paper-based; 213 computer-based; 80 iBT), TWE (minimum score 4); Recommended—IELTS (minimum score 7). *Application deadline:* For fall admission, 2/1 for domestic students, 1/5 for international students; for spring admission, 11/1 for domestic students, 8/1 for international students. Application fee: $50. Electronic applications accepted. *Expenses:* Tuition, state resident: full-time $17,304; part-time $701 per credit. Tuition, nonresident: full-time $29,554; part-time $1210 per credit. Required fees: $740; $214 per term. Tuition and fees vary according to program. *Financial support:* In 2010–11, 28 students received support. Scholarships/grants, tuition waivers (full and partial), unspecified assistantships, and student employment available. Financial award application deadline: 2/1. *Faculty research:* Nongovernmental organizations, religion and civil society, international development, development economics and policy, human rights and development, humanitarian intervention, ethnic conflict and civil war, post-conflict peace-building, corruption and transnational governance, civil society and public affairs, political constraints on rural development. Total annual research expenditures: $892,349. *Unit head:* Dr. Paul J Nelson, Director, 412-648-7645, Fax: 412-648-2605, E-mail: pjnelson@pitt.edu. *Application contact:* Elizabeth Hruby, Graduate Enrollment Counselor, 412-648-7640, Fax: 412-648-7641, E-mail: eah44@pitt.edu.

University of Puerto Rico, Río Piedras, Graduate School of Planning, San Juan, PR 00931-3300. Offers economic planning systems (MP); environmental planning (MP); social policy and planning (MP); urban and territorial planning (MP). *Accreditation:* ACSP. Part-time programs available. *Degree requirements:* For master's, comprehensive exam, thesis, planning project defense. *Entrance requirements:* For master's, PAEG, GRE, minimum GPA of 3.0, 2 letters of recommendation. *Faculty research:* Municipalities, historic Atlas, Puerto Rico, economic future.

University of Rhode Island, Graduate School, College of the Environment and Life Sciences, Department of Environmental and Natural Resource Economics, Kingston, RI 02881. Offers MESM, MS, PhD. Part-time programs available. *Faculty:* 6 full-time (2 women), 3 part-time/adjunct (1 woman). *Students:* 37 full-time (17 women), 4 part-time (2 women); includes 3 minority (1 Asian, non-Hispanic/Latino; 2 Hispanic/Latino), 13 international. In 2010, 4 master's, 4 doctorates awarded. *Degree requirements:* For master's, comprehensive exam (for some programs), thesis optional; for doctorate, comprehensive exam, thesis/dissertation. *Entrance requirements:* For master's, GRE, 2 letters of recommendation; for doctorate, GRE, 3 letters of recommendation. Additional exam requirements/recommendations for international students: Required—TOEFL (minimum score 550 paper-based; 213 computer-based). *Application deadline:* For fall admission, 7/15 for domestic students, 2/1 for international students; for spring admission, 11/15 for domestic students, 7/15 for international students. Application fee: $65. Electronic applications accepted. *Expenses:* Tuition, state resident: full-time $9588; part-time $533 per credit hour. Tuition, nonresident: full-time $22,968; part-time $1276 per credit hour. Required fees: $1282; $68 per semester. Tuition and fees vary according to program. *Financial support:* In 2010–11, 10 research assistantships with partial tuition reimbursements (averaging $12,990 per year), 2 teaching assistantships with full and partial tuition reimbursements (averaging $6,985 per year) were awarded. Financial award application deadline: 7/15; financial award applicants required to submit FAFSA. *Faculty research:* Policy Simulation Laboratory: utilizes computer technologies to help understand the consequences of policy actions, experimental economics. Total annual research expenditures: $637,583. *Unit head:* Dr. James Opaluch, Chair, 401-874-4590, Fax: 401-874-4766, E-mail: jimo@uri.edu. *Application contact:* Dr. James Opaluch, Graduate Admission Committee, 401-874-4590, Fax: 401-874-4766, E-mail: jimo@uri.edu.

University of South Africa, College of Agriculture and Environmental Sciences, Pretoria, South Africa. Offers agriculture (MS); consumer science (MCS); environmental management (MA, MS, PhD); environmental science (MA, MS, PhD); geography (MA, MS, PhD); horticulture (M Tech); human ecology (MHE); life sciences (MS); nature conservation (M Tech).

University of South Carolina, The Graduate School, School of the Environment, Program in Earth and Environmental Resources Management, Columbia, SC 29208. Offers MEERM, JD/MEERM. Part-time programs available. Postbaccalaureate distance learning degree programs offered (no on-campus study). *Degree requirements:* For master's, thesis optional. *Entrance requirements:* For master's, GRE General Test. Additional exam requirements/recommendations for international students: Required—TOEFL. Electronic applications accepted. *Faculty research:* Hydrology, sustainable development, environmental geology and engineering, energy/environmental resources management.

University of South Florida, Graduate School, College of Arts and Sciences, Department of Environmental Science and Policy, Tampa, FL 33620-9951. Offers MS. *Students:* 12 full-time (7 women), 14 part-time (8 women); includes 3 Hispanic/Latino; 1 Two or more races, non-Hispanic/Latino, 2 international. Average age 30. 26 applicants, 54% accepted, 8 enrolled. In 2010, 11 master's awarded. *Degree requirements:* For master's, comprehensive exam, thesis (for some programs). *Entrance requirements:* For master's, minimum GPA of 3.0. Additional exam requirements/recommendations for international students: Required—TOEFL (minimum score 600 paper-based; 213 computer-based). *Application deadline:* For fall admission, 2/15 for domestic students, 1/2 for international students; for spring admission, 10/15 for domestic students. Application fee: $30. *Financial support:* Scholarships/grants and unspecified assistantships available. Support available to part-time students. Financial award application deadline: 5/1. Total annual research expenditures: $163,893. *Unit head:* Robert Brinkmann, Interim Director, 813-974-4939, Fax: 813-974-4808, E-mail: rbrinkmann@cas.usf.edu. *Application contact:* Philip Van Beynen, Program Director, 813-974-3026, Fax: 813-974-4808, E-mail: vanbeyne@cas.usf.edu.

The University of Tennessee, Graduate School, College of Arts and Sciences, Department of Sociology, Knoxville, TN 37996. Offers criminology (MA, PhD); energy, environment, and resource policy (MA, PhD); political economy (MA, PhD). Part-time programs available. *Degree requirements:* For master's, thesis or alternative; for doctorate, thesis/dissertation. *Entrance requirements:* For master's, GRE General Test, minimum GPA of 3.0; for doctorate, GRE General Test, minimum GPA of 3.5. Additional exam requirements/recommendations for international students: Required—TOEFL. Electronic applications accepted. *Expenses:* Tuition, state resident: full-time $7440; part-time $414 per credit hour. Tuition, nonresident: full-time $22,478; part-time $1250 per credit hour. Required fees: $922; $43 per credit hour. Tuition and fees vary according to program.

University of Washington, Graduate School, Interdisciplinary Graduate Program in Quantitative Ecology and Resource Management, Seattle, WA 98195. Offers MS, PhD. *Degree requirements:* For master's, thesis; for doctorate, thesis/dissertation. *Entrance requirements:* For master's and doctorate, GRE General Test, minimum GPA of 3.0. Additional exam requirements/recommendations for international students: Required—TOEFL. Electronic applications accepted. *Faculty research:* Population dynamics, statistical analysis, ecological modeling and systems analysis of aquatic and terrestrial ecosystems.

University of Waterloo, Graduate Studies, Faculty of Environmental Studies, Department of Environment and Resource Studies, Waterloo, ON N2L 3G1, Canada. Offers MES. Part-time programs available. *Degree requirements:* For master's, thesis. *Entrance requirements:* For master's, honors degree, minimum B average, resume. Additional exam requirements/recommendations for international students: Required—TOEFL, TWE. Electronic applications accepted. *Faculty research:* Applied sustainability; sustainable water policy; food, agriculture, and the environment; biology studies; environment and business; ecological monitoring; soil ecosystem dynamics; urban water demand management; demand response.

University of Waterloo, Graduate Studies, Faculty of Environmental Studies, Program in Tourism Policy and Planning, Waterloo, ON N2L 3G1, Canada. Offers MAES. Part-time programs available. *Degree requirements:* For master's, research paper. *Entrance requirements:* For master's, honors degree in related field, minimum B average. Additional exam requirements/recommendations for international students: Required—TOEFL, TWE. Electronic applications accepted. *Faculty research:* Urban and regional economics, regional economic development, strategic planning, environmental economics, economic geography.

University of Wisconsin–Green Bay, Graduate Studies, Program in Environmental Science and Policy, Green Bay, WI 54311-7001. Offers MS. Part-time programs available. *Faculty:* 10 full-time (3 women), 2 part-time/adjunct (0 women). *Students:* 16 full-time (12 women), 18 part-time (9 women); includes 6 minority (1 Black or African American, non-Hispanic/Latino; 3

American Indian or Alaska Native, non-Hispanic/Latino; 1 Asian, non-Hispanic/Latino; 1 Hispanic/Latino). Average age 29. 27 applicants, 85% accepted, 16 enrolled. In 2010, 11 master's awarded. *Degree requirements:* For master's, thesis. *Entrance requirements:* For master's, GRE General Test, minimum GPA of 3.0. *Application deadline:* For fall admission, 8/1 for domestic students; for spring admission, 11/1 for domestic students. Applications are processed on a rolling basis. Application fee: $56. Electronic applications accepted. *Expenses:* Tuition, state resident: full-time $7001; part-time $389 per credit. Tuition, nonresident: full-time $16,771; part-time $932 per credit. Required fees: $1314; $110 per credit. Tuition and fees vary according to reciprocity agreements. *Financial support:* In 2010–11, 1 research assistantship with full tuition reimbursement, 4 teaching assistantships with full tuition reimbursements were awarded; career-related internships or fieldwork, Federal Work-Study, and institutionally sponsored loans also available. Financial award application deadline: 7/15; financial award applicants required to submit FAFSA. *Faculty research:* Bald eagle, parasitic population of domestic and wild animals, resource recovery, anaerobic digestion of organic waste. *Unit head:* Dr. Patricia Terry, Coordinator, 920-465-2749, E-mail: terryp@uwgb.edu. *Application contact:* Pam Harvey-Jacobs, Director of Admissions, 920-465-2111, E-mail: harveyp@uwgb.edu.

Utah State University, School of Graduate Studies, College of Natural Resources, Department of Environment and Society, Logan, UT 84322. Offers bioregional planning (MS); geography (MA, MS); human dimensions of ecosystem science and management (MS, PhD); recreation resource management (MS, PhD). *Degree requirements:* For master's, comprehensive exam, thesis (for some programs). *Entrance requirements:* For master's and doctorate, GRE General Test, minimum GPA of 3.0. Additional exam requirements/recommendations for international students: Required—TOEFL. Electronic applications accepted. *Faculty research:* Geographic information systems/geographic and environmental education, bioregional planning, natural resource and environmental policy, outdoor recreation and tourism, natural resource and environmental management.

Vanderbilt University, School of Engineering, Department of Civil and Environmental Engineering, Program in Environmental Engineering, Nashville, TN 37240-1001. Offers environmental engineering (M Eng); environmental management (MS, PhD). MS and PhD offered through the Graduate School. Part-time programs available. *Faculty:* 9 full-time (0 women), 1 (woman) part-time/adjunct. *Students:* 27 full-time (15 women); includes 2 Black or African American, non-Hispanic/Latino; 1 Asian, non-Hispanic/Latino, 4 international. Average age 30. 75 applicants, 17% accepted, 8 enrolled. In 2010, 10 master's, 3 doctorates awarded. Terminal master's awarded for partial completion of doctoral program. *Degree requirements:* For master's, thesis or alternative; for doctorate, thesis/dissertation. *Entrance requirements:* For master's and doctorate, GRE General Test. Additional exam requirements/recommendations for international students: Required—TOEFL. *Application deadline:* For fall admission, 1/15 for domestic students; for spring admission, 11/1 for domestic students. Applications are processed on a rolling basis. Application fee: $0. Electronic applications accepted. *Financial support:* In 2010–11, 5 fellowships with full tuition reimbursements (averaging $30,000 per year), 12 research assistantships with full tuition reimbursements (averaging $25,200 per year), 7 teaching assistantships with full tuition reimbursements (averaging $21,600 per year) were awarded; career-related internships or fieldwork, institutionally sponsored loans, scholarships/grants, traineeships, and tuition waivers (full and partial) also available. Financial award application deadline: 1/15. *Faculty research:* Waste treatment, hazardous waste management, chemical waste treatment, water quality. *Unit head:* Dr. David S. Kosson, Chair, 615-322-2697, Fax: 615-322-3365, E-mail: david.kosson@vanderbilt.edu. *Application contact:* Dr. James H. Clarke, Graduate Program Administrator, 615-322-3897, Fax: 615-322-3365.

Vermont Law School, Law School, Environmental Law Center, South Royalton, VT 05068-0096. Offers LL M, MELP, JD/MELP. Part-time programs available. *Faculty:* 11 full-time (3 women), 13 part-time/adjunct (7 women). *Students:* 64 full-time (35 women); includes 2 Black or African American, non-Hispanic/Latino; 1 American Indian or Alaska Native, non-Hispanic/Latino; 1 Two or more races, non-Hispanic/Latino. Average age 30. 92 applicants, 91% accepted, 48 enrolled. In 2010, 65 master's awarded. *Entrance requirements:* Additional exam requirements/recommendations for international students: Required—TOEFL. *Application deadline:* For fall admission, 3/1 priority date for domestic students. Applications are processed on a rolling basis. Application fee: $60. *Financial support:* In 2010–11, 2 fellowships with full tuition reimbursements (averaging $5,000 per year) were awarded; career-related internships or fieldwork, Federal Work-Study, institutionally sponsored loans, scholarships/grants, and tuition waivers (partial) also available. Support available to part-time students. Financial award application deadline: 3/1; financial award applicants required to submit FAFSA. *Faculty research:* Environment and technology; takings; international environmental law; interaction among science, law, and environmental policy; air pollution. Total annual research expenditures: $52,000. *Unit head:* Marc Mihaly, Associate Dean, 802-831-1342, Fax: 802-763-2490, E-mail: admiss@vermontlaw.edu. *Application contact:* Anne Mansfield, Associate Director, 802-831-1338, Fax: 802-763-2940, E-mail: admiss@vermontlaw.edu.

Virginia Commonwealth University, Graduate School, School of Life Sciences, Center for Environmental Studies, Richmond, VA 23284-9005. Offers M Env Sc, MS. *Students:* 22 full-time (10 women), 34 part-time (16 women); includes 10 minority (5 Black or African American, non-Hispanic/Latino; 3 Asian, non-Hispanic/Latino; 1 Hispanic/Latino; 1 Two or more races, non-Hispanic/Latino), 1 international. Average age 33. 32 applicants, 69% accepted, 16 enrolled. In 2010, 15 master's awarded. *Degree requirements:* For master's, thesis. *Entrance requirements:* For master's, GRE General Test. Additional exam requirements/recommendations for international students: Required—TOEFL (minimum score 600 paper-based; 250 computer-based; 100 iBT). *Application deadline:* For fall admission, 7/1 for domestic students; for spring admission, 12/1 for domestic students. Application fee: $50. Electronic applications accepted. *Expenses:* Tuition, state resident: full-time $4308; part-time $479 per credit hour. Tuition, nonresident: full-time $8942; part-time $994 per credit hour. Required fees: $2000; $85 per credit hour. Tuition and fees vary according to course level, course load, degree level, campus/location and program. *Financial support:* Applicants required to submit FAFSA. *Unit head:* Dr. Gregory C. Garman, Director, 804-828-1574, Fax: 804-828-0503, E-mail: gcgarman@vcu.edu. *Application contact:* Dr. Gregory C. Garman, Director, 804-828-1574, Fax: 804-828-0503, E-mail: gcgarman@vcu.edu.

Virginia Polytechnic Institute and State University, Graduate School, College of Architecture and Urban Studies, School of Public and International Affairs, Blacksburg, VA 24061. Offers economic development (Certificate); government and international affairs (MPIA, PhD); homeland security policy (Certificate); local government management (Certificate); metropolitan studies (MAIA); nonprofit and nongovernmental organization management (Certificate); planning, governance and globalization (PhD); public administration and public affairs (MPA, PhD); urban and regional planning (MURPL). *Accreditation:* ACSP. *Faculty:* 31 full-time (9 women). *Students:* 114 full-time (66 women), 105 part-time (54 women); includes 11 Black or African American, non-Hispanic/Latino; 1 American Indian or Alaska Native, non-Hispanic/Latino; 7 Asian, non-Hispanic/Latino; 8 Hispanic/Latino, 19 international. Average age 31. 166 applicants, 67% accepted, 53 enrolled. In 2010, 41 master's, 3 doctorates awarded. *Degree requirements:* For master's, comprehensive exam (for some programs), thesis (for some programs); for doctorate, comprehensive exam (for some programs), thesis/dissertation (for some programs). *Entrance requirements:* For master's and doctorate, GRE. Additional exam requirements/recommendations for international students: Required—TOEFL (minimum score 550 paper-based; 213 computer-based). *Application deadline:* For fall admission, 7/1 for domestic and international students; for spring admission, 12/1 for domestic and international students. Applications are processed on a rolling basis. Application fee: $65. Electronic applications accepted. *Expenses:* Tuition, area resident: Full-time $9399; part-time $488 per credit hour. Tuition, state resident: full-time $9399; part-time $488 per credit hour. Tuition, nonresident: full-time $17,854; part-time $957.75 per credit hour. International tuition: $17,854 full-time. Required fees: $1534. Full-time tuition and fees vary according to program. *Financial support:* In 2010–11, 1 teaching assistantship with full tuition reimbursement (averaging $21,395 per year) was awarded; career-related internships or fieldwork, Federal Work-Study, scholarships/grants, health care benefits, and unspecified assistantships also available. Financial award application deadline: 1/15. *Faculty research:* Design theory, environmental planning, town planning, transportation planning. Total annual research expenditures: $610,749. *Unit head:* Dr. Karen M. Hult, UNIT HEAD, 540-231-5351, Fax: 540-231-9938, E-mail: khult@vt.edu. *Application contact:* Krystal D. Wright, Contact, 540-231-2291, Fax: 540-231-9938, E-mail: garch@vt.edu.

Virginia Polytechnic Institute and State University, Graduate School, College of Liberal Arts and Human Sciences, Department of Political Science, Blacksburg, VA 24061. Offers environmental politics and policy (Certificate); foundations of political analysis (Certificate); information policy and society (Certificate); political science (MA); security studies (Certificate). *Faculty:* 22 full-time (6 women), 1 (woman) part-time/adjunct. *Students:* 40 full-time (15 women), 49 part-time (19 women); includes 1 Black or African American, non-Hispanic/Latino; 1 American Indian or Alaska Native, non-Hispanic/Latino; 3 Asian, non-Hispanic/Latino; 4 Hispanic/Latino, 10 international. Average age 32. 49 applicants, 47% accepted, 13 enrolled. In 2010, 12 master's awarded. *Degree requirements:* For master's, comprehensive exam (for some programs), thesis (for some programs). *Entrance requirements:* For master's, GRE. Additional exam requirements/recommendations for international students: Required—TOEFL (minimum score 550 paper-based; 213 computer-based). *Application deadline:* For fall admission, 7/1 for domestic and international students; for spring admission, 12/1 for domestic and international students. Applications are processed on a rolling basis. Application fee: $65. Electronic applications accepted. *Expenses:* Tuition, area resident: Full-time $9399; part-time $488 per credit hour. Tuition, state resident: full-time $9399; part-time $488 per credit hour. Tuition, nonresident: full-time $17,854; part-time $957.75 per credit hour. International tuition: $17,854 full-time. Required fees: $1534. Full-time tuition and fees vary according to program. *Financial support:* In 2010–11, 12 teaching assistantships with full tuition reimbursements (averaging $12,972 per year) were awarded; career-related internships or fieldwork, Federal Work-Study, scholarships/grants, health care benefits, and unspecified assistantships also available. Financial award application deadline: 1/15. *Faculty research:* Comparative politics, international relations, American government and politics, research methods. Total annual research expenditures: $24,854. *Unit head:* Dr. Ilja A. Luciak, UNIT HEAD, 540-231-6571, Fax: 540-231-6078, E-mail: iluciak@vt.edu. *Application contact:* Tim Luke, Contact, 540-231-6633, Fax: 540-231-6078, E-mail: twluke@vt.edu.

Virginia Polytechnic Institute and State University, VT Online, Blacksburg, VA 24061. Offers aerospace engineering (MS); business information systems (Graduate Certificate); career and technical education (MS); computer engineering (M Eng, MS); decision support systems (Graduate Certificate); eLearning leadership (MA); electrical engineering (M Eng, MS); engineering administration (MEA); environmental politics and policy (Graduate Certificate); foundations of political analysis (Graduate Certificate); health product risk management (Graduate Certificate); information policy and society (Graduate Certificate); information security (Graduate Certificate); instructional technology (MA); liberal arts (Graduate Certificate); life sciences: health product risk management (MS); natural resources (MNR, Graduate Certificate); networking (Graduate Certificate); nonprofit and nongovernmental organization management (Graduate Certificate); ocean engineering (MS); political science (MA); security studies (Graduate Certificate); software development (Graduate Certificate). *Expenses:* Tuition, area resident: Full-time $9399; part-time $488 per credit hour. Tuition, state resident: full-time $9399; part-time $488 per credit hour. Tuition, nonresident: full-time $17,854; part-time $957.75 per credit hour. International tuition: $17,854 full-time. Required fees: $1534. Full-time tuition and fees vary according to program.

Webster University, College of Arts and Sciences, Department of Biological Sciences, St. Louis, MO 63119-3194. Offers environmental management (MS); nurse anesthesia (MS); professional science management and leadership (MA). Part-time programs available. Postbaccalaureate distance learning degree programs offered (no on-campus study). *Degree requirements:* For master's, comprehensive exam (for some programs), thesis (for some programs). *Entrance requirements:* Additional exam requirements/recommendations for international students: Required—TOEFL. *Expenses:* Tuition: Part-time $585 per credit hour. Tuition and fees vary according to degree level, campus/location and program.

Webster University, George Herbert Walker School of Business and Technology, Department of Business, St. Louis, MO 63119-3194. Offers business (MA); business and organizational security management (MBA); computer resources and information management (MBA); environmental management (MBA); finance (MA, MBA); health services management (MBA); human resources development (MBA); human resources management (MBA); international business (MA, MBA); management and leadership (MBA); marketing (MBA); procurement and acquisitions management (MBA); telecommunications management (MBA). *Accreditation:* ACBSP. Part-time and evening/weekend programs available. Postbaccalaureate distance learning degree programs offered (no on-campus study). *Degree requirements:* For master's, comprehensive exam (for some programs), thesis (for some programs). *Entrance requirements:* Additional exam requirements/recommendations for international students: Required—TOEFL. *Expenses:* Tuition: Part-time $585 per credit hour. Tuition and fees vary according to degree level, campus/location and program.

Webster University, George Herbert Walker School of Business and Technology, Department of Management, St. Louis, MO 63119-3194. Offers business and organizational security management (MA); computer resources and information management (MA); environmental management (MS); government contracting (Certificate); health care management (MA); health services management (MA); human resources development (MA); human resources management (MA); management (DM); management and leadership (MA); marketing (MA); nonprofit management (Certificate); procurement and acquisitions management (MA); public administration (MA); quality management (MA); space systems operations management (MS); telecommunications management (MA). *Accreditation:* ACBSP. Part-time and evening/weekend programs available. Postbaccalaureate distance learning degree programs offered (no on-campus study). *Degree requirements:* For master's, thesis (for some programs); for doctorate, thesis/dissertation, written exam. *Entrance requirements:* For doctorate, GMAT, 3 years of work experience, MBA. Additional exam requirements/recommendations for international students: Required—TOEFL. *Expenses:* Tuition: Part-time $585 per credit hour. Tuition and fees vary according to degree level, campus/location and program.

Wesley College, Business Program, Dover, DE 19901-3875. Offers environmental management (MBA); executive leadership (MBA); management (MBA). Executive leadership concentration also offered at New Castle, DE location. Part-time and evening/weekend programs available. *Entrance requirements:* For master's, GMAT or GRE, minimum undergraduate GPA of 2.75.

Wesley College, Environmental Studies Program, Dover, DE 19901-3875. Offers MS. Part-time and evening/weekend programs available. *Entrance requirements:* For master's, BA/BSM in science or engineering field, portfolio.

West Virginia University, Davis College of Agriculture, Forestry and Consumer Sciences, Division of Resource Management and Sustainable Development, Morgantown, WV 26506. Offers agricultural and extension education (MS, PhD), including agricultural and extension education, teaching vocational-agriculture (MS); agricultural and resource economics (MS); human and community development (PhD); natural resource economics (PhD); resource management (PhD); resource management and sustainable development (PhD). Part-time programs available. *Degree requirements:* For master's, thesis; for doctorate, comprehensive

Environmental Management and Policy

West Virginia University (continued)

exam, thesis/dissertation. *Entrance requirements:* For master's, GRE General Test. Additional exam requirements/recommendations for international students: Required—TOEFL. *Faculty research:* Environmental economics, energy economics, agriculture.

West Virginia University, Eberly College of Arts and Sciences, Department of Geology and Geography, Program in Geography, Morgantown, WV 26506. Offers energy and environmental resources (MA); geographic information systems (PhD); geography-regional development (PhD); GIS/cartographic analysis (MA); regional development (MA). Part-time programs available. *Degree requirements:* For master's, thesis, oral and written exams; for doctorate, comprehensive exam, thesis/dissertation, oral and written exams. *Entrance requirements:* For master's and doctorate, GRE General Test, minimum GPA of 3.0. Additional exam requirements/recommendations for international students: Required—TOEFL. Electronic applications accepted. *Faculty research:* Space, place and development, geographic information science, environmental geography.

Wilfrid Laurier University, Faculty of Graduate and Postdoctoral Studies, Faculty of Arts, Department of Geography and Environmental Studies, Waterloo, ON N2L 3C5, Canada. Offers environmental and resource management (MA, MES, PhD); environmental science (M Sc, MES, PhD); geomatics (M Sc, MES, PhD); human geography (MES, PhD). Part-time programs available. *Faculty:* 17 full-time (5 women). *Students:* 47 full-time (20 women), 12 part-time (6 women), 4 international. 78 applicants, 40% accepted, 18 enrolled. In 2010, 11 master's, 7 doctorates awarded. *Degree requirements:* For master's, thesis optional; for doctorate, thesis/dissertation. *Entrance requirements:* For master's, honors BA in geography, minimum B average in undergraduate course work; honors BSc with minimum B+ or honors BES or BA in physical geography, environmental or earth sciences or the equivalent; for doctorate, MA in geography, minimum A- average. Additional exam requirements/recommendations for international students: Required—TOEFL (minimum score 89 iBT). *Application deadline:* For fall admission, 2/1 priority date for domestic and international students. Application fee: $100. Electronic applications accepted. Tuition and fees charges are reported in Canadian dollars. *Expenses:* Tuition, area resident: Full-time $15,300 Canadian dollars; part-time $1200 Canadian dollars per credit. International tuition: $21,300 Canadian dollars full-time. Required fees: $650 Canadian dollars; $100 Canadian dollars per credit. Tuition and fees vary according to course load, degree level, campus/location and program. *Financial support:* In 2010–11, 51 fellowships, 8 research assistantships, 51 teaching assistantships were awarded; career-related internships or fieldwork, scholarships/grants, health care benefits, and unspecified assistantships also available. *Faculty research:* Resources management, urban, economic, physical, cultural, earth surfaces, geomatics, historical, regional, spatial data handling. *Unit head:* Dr. Houston Saunderson, Graduate Co-ordinator, 519-884-0710 Ext. 2573, Fax: 519-725-1342, E-mail: hsaunderson@wlu.ca. *Application contact:* Jennifer Williams, Graduate Admissions and Records Officer, 519-884-0710 Ext. 3536, Fax: 519-884-1020, E-mail: gradstudies@wlu.ca.

Wilfrid Laurier University, Faculty of Graduate and Postdoctoral Studies, Faculty of Arts and School of Business and Economics, International Public Policy Program, Waterloo, ON N2L 3C5, Canada. Offers global governance (MIPP); human security (MIPP); international economic relations (MIPP); international environmental policy (MIPP). *Faculty:* 17 full-time (8 women). *Students:* 16 full-time (9 women), 2 international. 90 applicants, 30% accepted, 14 enrolled. In 2010, 15 master's awarded. *Entrance requirements:* For master's, honours BA with minimum B average. Additional exam requirements/recommendations for international students: Required—TOEFL (minimum score 89 iBT). *Application deadline:* For fall admission, 2/1 priority date for domestic and international students. Application fee: $100. Electronic applications accepted. Tuition and fees charges are reported in Canadian dollars. *Expenses:* Tuition, area resident: Full-time $15,300 Canadian dollars; part-time $1200 Canadian dollars per credit. International tuition: $21,300 Canadian dollars full-time. Required fees: $650 Canadian dollars; $100 Canadian dollars per credit. Tuition and fees vary according to course load, degree level, campus/location and program. *Financial support:* In 2010–11, 5 fellowships, 5 teaching assistantships were awarded; career-related internships or fieldwork, scholarships/grants, health care benefits, and unspecified assistantships also available. *Faculty research:* International environmental policy, international economic relations, human security, global governance. *Unit head:* Terry Snodden, EdD, Graduate Co-ordinator, 519-884-0710 Ext. 2945, Fax: 519-884-8854, E-mail: tlevesque@wlu.ca. *Application contact:* Jennifer Williams, Graduate Admissions and Records Officer, 519-884-0710 Ext. 3536, Fax: 519-884-1020, E-mail: gradstudies@wlu.ca.

Willamette University, Graduate School of Education, Salem, OR 97301-3931. Offers environmental literacy (M Ed); reading (M Ed); special education (M Ed); teaching (MAT). *Accreditation:* NCATE. Evening/weekend programs available. *Students:* 139 full-time (79 women), 2 part-time (both women). *Degree requirements:* For master's, leadership project (action research). *Entrance requirements:* For master's, California Basic Educational Skills Test, Multiple Subject Assessment for Teachers, PRAXIS, minimum GPA of 3.0, classroom experience, 2 letters of reference. *Application deadline:* Applications are processed on a rolling basis. Application fee: $50. Electronic applications accepted. *Expenses:* Contact institution. *Financial support:* Fellowships, career-related internships or fieldwork, institutionally sponsored loans, scholarships/grants, and tuition waivers (partial) available. Financial award application deadline: 2/1; financial award applicants required to submit FAFSA. *Faculty research:* Educational leadership, multicultural education, middle school education, clinical supervision, educational technology. *Unit head:* Julie Gess-Newsome, Dean, 503-370-6798, Fax: 503-375-5478, E-mail: jgessnew@willamette.edu. *Application contact:* Heather Daniels, Director of Admission, 503-375-5453, Fax: 503-375-5478, E-mail: hdaniels@willamette.edu.

Yale University, Graduate School of Arts and Sciences, Department of Forestry and Environmental Studies, New Haven, CT 06520. Offers environmental sciences (PhD); forestry (PhD). *Degree requirements:* For doctorate, thesis/dissertation. *Entrance requirements:* For doctorate, GRE General Test.

Yale University, School of Forestry and Environmental Studies, New Haven, CT 06511. Offers MEM, MES, MF, MFS, PhD, JD/MEM, MBA/MEM, MBA/MF, MEM/M Arch, MEM/MA, MEM/MPH, MF/MA. *Accreditation:* SAF (one or more programs are accredited). Part-time programs available. Terminal master's awarded for partial completion of doctoral program. *Degree requirements:* For master's, thesis (for some programs); for doctorate, thesis/dissertation. *Entrance requirements:* For master's, GRE General Test, GMAT or LSAT; for doctorate, GRE General Test. Additional exam requirements/recommendations for international students: Required—TOEFL (minimum score 600 paper-based; 250 computer-based; 100 iBT). Electronic applications accepted. *Expenses:* Contact institution. *Faculty research:* Environmental policy, social ecology, industrial environmental management, forestry, environmental health, urban ecology, water science policy.

York University, Faculty of Graduate Studies, Program in Environmental Studies, Toronto, ON M3J 1P3, Canada. Offers MES, PhD, MES/LL B, MES/MA. Part-time programs available. *Degree requirements:* For master's, thesis optional; for doctorate, comprehensive exam, thesis/dissertation, research seminar. Electronic applications accepted.

Youngstown State University, Graduate School, College of Liberal Arts and Social Sciences, Program in Environmental Studies, Youngstown, OH 44555-0001. Offers environmental studies (MS); industrial/institutional management (Certificate); risk management (Certificate). *Degree requirements:* For master's, comprehensive exam, thesis, oral defense of dissertation. *Entrance requirements:* For master's, GRE General Test or minimum GPA of 2.7. Additional exam requirements/recommendations for international students: Required—TOEFL.

Environmental Sciences

Alabama Agricultural and Mechanical University, School of Graduate Studies, School of Agricultural and Environmental Sciences, Department of Plant and Soil Science, Huntsville, AL 35811. Offers animal sciences (MS); environmental science (MS); plant and soil science (PhD). Evening/weekend programs available. Terminal master's awarded for partial completion of doctoral program. *Degree requirements:* For master's, thesis; for doctorate, one foreign language, thesis/dissertation. *Entrance requirements:* For master's, GRE General Test, BS in agriculture; for doctorate, GRE General Test, master's degree. Additional exam requirements/recommendations for international students: Required—TOEFL (minimum score 500 paper-based; 173 computer-based; 61 iBT). Electronic applications accepted. *Faculty research:* Plant breeding, cytogenetics, crop production, soil chemistry and fertility, remote sensing.

Alabama State University, Department of Earth and Environmental Sciences, Montgomery, AL 36101-0271. Offers MS, PhD. *Degree requirements:* For master's, one foreign language, thesis or alternative; for doctorate, one foreign language, thesis/dissertation. *Entrance requirements:* For master's, GRE General Test, minimum B average in undergraduate course work; for doctorate, GRE General Test. Additional exam requirements/recommendations for international students: Required—TOEFL. Electronic applications accepted. *Faculty research:* Sedimentation, isotopes, biogeochemistry, marine geology, structural geology.

Alaska Pacific University, Graduate Programs, Environmental Science Department, Program in Environmental Science, Anchorage, AK 99508-4672. Offers MSES. Part-time programs available. *Degree requirements:* For master's, thesis. *Entrance requirements:* For master's, GRE General Test, minimum GPA of 3.0. Additional exam requirements/recommendations for international students: Required—TOEFL (minimum score 550 paper-based; 213 computer-based).

American University, College of Arts and Sciences, Department of Biology, Washington, DC 20016-8007. Offers applied science (MS); biology (MA, MS); environmental science (MS), including environmental science, marine science. Part-time programs available. *Faculty:* 9 full-time (3 women), 3 part-time/adjunct (0 women). *Students:* 8 full-time (2 women), 8 part-time (6 women); includes 3 minority (1 Black or African American, non-Hispanic/Latino; 2 Asian, non-Hispanic/Latino), 2 international. Average age 25. 40 applicants, 53% accepted, 3 enrolled. In 2010, 10 master's awarded. *Degree requirements:* For master's, comprehensive exam, thesis (for some programs). *Entrance requirements:* For master's, GRE General Test, GRE Subject Test. Additional exam requirements/recommendations for international students: Required—TOEFL. *Application deadline:* For fall admission, 2/1 for domestic students; for spring admission, 10/1 for domestic students. Application fee: $80. *Financial support:* Fellowships, research assistantships with tuition reimbursements, teaching assistantships with tuition reimbursements, career-related internships or fieldwork, Federal Work-Study, and institutionally sponsored loans available. Financial award application deadline: 2/1. *Faculty research:* Neurobiology, cave biology, population genetics, vertebrate physiology. *Unit head:* Dr. David Carlini, Chair, 202-885-2194, Fax: 202-885-2182, E-mail: carlini@american.edu. *Application contact:* Kathleen Clowery, Director, Graduate Admissions, 202-885-3621, Fax: 202-885-1505.

American University, College of Arts and Sciences, Department of Environmental Science, Washington, DC 20016-8001. Offers environmental assessment (Graduate Certificate); environmental science (MS). *Degree requirements:* For master's, comprehensive exam, thesis (for some programs). *Entrance requirements:* For master's, GRE General Test, GRE Subject Test, minimum GPA of 3.0. Additional exam requirements/recommendations for international students: Required—TOEFL.

American University of Beirut, Graduate Programs, Faculty of Agricultural and Food Sciences, Beirut, Lebanon. Offers agricultural economics (MS); animal sciences (MS); ecosystem management (MSES); food technology (MS); irrigation (MS); mechanization (MS); nutrition (MS); plant protection (MS); plant science (MS); poultry science (MS); soils (MS). Part-time programs available. *Faculty:* 22 full-time (6 women). *Students:* 6 full-time (3 women), 86 part-time (77 women). Average age 24. 94 applicants, 60% accepted, 15 enrolled. In 2010, 28 master's awarded. *Degree requirements:* For master's, one foreign language, comprehensive exam, thesis (for some programs). *Entrance requirements:* Additional exam requirements/recommendations for international students: Required—TOEFL (minimum score 600 paper-based; 250 computer-based; 100 iBT), IELTS (minimum score 7.5). *Application deadline:* For fall admission, 4/30 for domestic and international students; for spring admission, 11/1 for domestic and international students. Applications are processed on a rolling basis. Application fee: $50. Electronic applications accepted. *Expenses:* Tuition: Full-time $12,294; part-time $683 per credit. Required fees: $499; $499 per credit. Tuition and fees vary according to course load and program. *Financial support:* In 2010–11, 18 research assistantships with partial tuition reimbursements (averaging $13,132 per year), 42 teaching assistantships with full and partial tuition reimbursements (averaging $1,000 per year) were awarded; scholarships/grants, health care benefits, and unspecified assistantships also available. Financial award application deadline: 2/2. *Faculty research:* Community and therapeutic nutrition; food safety and food microbiology; landscape planning, nature and rural heritage conservation; pathology, immunology and control of poultry and animal diseases; agricultural economics and development. Total annual research expenditures: $900,000. *Unit head:* Prof. Nahla Hwalla, Dean, 961-134-3002 Ext. 4400, Fax: 961-174-4460, E-mail: nahla@aub.edu.lb. *Application contact:* Dr. Salim Kanaan, Director, Admissions Office, 961-135-0000 Ext. 2594, Fax: 961-175-0775, E-mail: sk00@aub.edu.lb.

American University of Beirut, Graduate Programs, Faculty of Engineering and Architecture, Beirut, Lebanon. Offers applied energy (MME); civil engineering (ME, PhD); electrical and computer engineering (ME, PhD); engineering management (MEM); environmental and water resources (ME); environmental and water resources engineering (PhD); environmental technology (MSES); mechanical engineering (ME, PhD); urban design (MUD); urban planning and policy (MUP). Part-time programs available. *Faculty:* 57 full-time (12 women), 3 part-time/adjunct (0 women). *Students:* 261 full-time (92 women), 58 part-time (20 women). Average age 25. 272 applicants, 79% accepted, 108 enrolled. In 2010, 70 master's, 1 doctorate awarded. *Degree requirements:* For master's, one foreign language, comprehensive exam, thesis (for some programs); for doctorate, one foreign language, comprehensive exam, thesis/dissertation, publications. *Entrance requirements:* For master's, GRE (for electrical and computer engineering), letters of recommendation; for doctorate, GRE, letters of recommendation, master's degree, transcripts, curriculum vitae, interview. Additional exam requirements/

recommendations for international students: Required—TOEFL (minimum score 600 paper-based; 250 computer-based; 100 iBT), IELTS (minimum score 7.5). *Application deadline:* For fall admission, 2/5 priority date for domestic and international students; for spring admission, 11/1 priority date for domestic students, 11/1 for international students. Applications are processed on a rolling basis. Application fee: $50. Electronic applications accepted. *Expenses:* Tuition: Full-time $12,294; part-time $683 per credit. Required fees: $499; $499 per credit. Tuition and fees vary according to course load and program. *Financial support:* In 2010–11, 10 fellowships with full tuition reimbursements (averaging $24,800 per year), 33 research assistantships with full tuition reimbursements (averaging $24,800 per year), 70 teaching assistantships with full tuition reimbursements (averaging $9,800 per year) were awarded; career-related internships or fieldwork, institutionally sponsored loans, scholarships/grants, health care benefits, and unspecified assistantships also available. Total annual research expenditures: $586,131. *Unit head:* Fadl H. Moukalled, Acting Dean, 961-135-0000 Ext. 3400, Fax: 961-174-4462, E-mail: memouk@aub.edu.lb. *Application contact:* Dr. Salim Kanaan, Director, Admissions Office, 961-135-0000 Ext. 2594, Fax: 961-175-0775, E-mail: sk00@aub.edu.lb.

American University of Beirut, Graduate Programs, Faculty of Health Sciences, Beirut, Lebanon. Offers environmental sciences (MSES), including environmental health; epidemiology (MS); epidemiology and biostatistics (MPH); health management and policy (MPH); health promotion and community health (MPH); population health (MS). Part-time programs available. *Faculty:* 33 full-time (23 women), 8 part-time/adjunct (3 women). *Students:* 64 full-time (55 women), 111 part-time (85 women). Average age 26. 209 applicants, 67% accepted, 75 enrolled. In 2010, 54 master's awarded. *Degree requirements:* For master's, one foreign language, comprehensive exam, thesis (for some programs). *Entrance requirements:* For master's, 2 letters of recommendation, personal statement, transcripts. Additional exam requirements/recommendations for international students: Required—TOEFL (minimum score 600 paper-based; 250 computer-based; 97 iBT), IELTS (minimum score 7). *Application deadline:* For fall admission, 2/20 for domestic and international students; for spring admission, 11/1 for domestic and international students. Application fee: $50. Electronic applications accepted. *Expenses:* Tuition: Full-time $12,294; part-time $683 per credit. Required fees: $499; $499 per credit. Tuition and fees vary according to course load and program. *Financial support:* In 2010–11, 65 students received support. Scholarships/grants, health care benefits, and unspecified assistantships available. Financial award application deadline: 2/20. *Faculty research:* Tobacco control; health of the elderly; youth health; mental health; women's health; reproductive and sexual health, including HIV/AIDS; water quality; health systems; quality in health care delivery; health human resources; health policy; occupational and environmental health; social inequality; social determinants of health; chronic diseases. Total annual research expenditures: $1.5 million. *Unit head:* Iman Adel Nuwayhid, Dean, 961-134-0119, Fax: 961-174-4470, E-mail: nuwayhid@aub.edu.lb. *Application contact:* Mitra Tauk, Assistant for Graduate Student Affairs, 961-135-0000 Ext. 4687, Fax: 961-174-4470, E-mail: mt12@aub.edu.lb.

Antioch University New England, Graduate School, Department of Environmental Studies, Doctoral Program in Environmental Studies, Keene, NH 03431-3552. Offers PhD. *Degree requirements:* For doctorate, thesis/dissertation, practicum. *Entrance requirements:* For doctorate, master's degree and previous experience in the environmental field. Additional exam requirements/recommendations for international students: Required—TOEFL (minimum score 600 paper-based; 250 computer-based). Electronic applications accepted. *Expenses:* Contact institution. *Faculty research:* Environmental history, green politics, ecopsychology.

Antioch University New England, Graduate School, Department of Environmental Studies, Program in Environmental Education, Keene, NH 03431-3552. Offers MS. *Degree requirements:* For master's, practicum. *Entrance requirements:* For master's, previous undergraduate course work in biology, chemistry, mathematics (environmental biology); resume; 3 letters of recommendation. Additional exam requirements/recommendations for international students: Required—TOEFL (minimum score 550 paper-based; 213 computer-based). Electronic applications accepted. *Expenses:* Contact institution. *Faculty research:* Sustainability, natural resources inventory.

Arizona State University, College of Liberal Arts and Sciences, School of Human Evolution and Social Change, Tempe, AZ 85287-2402. Offers anthropology (PhD); anthropology (archaeology) (PhD); anthropology (bioarchaeology) (PhD); anthropology (museum studies) (MA); anthropology (physical) (PhD); applied mathematics for the life and social sciences (PhD); environmental social science (PhD); environmental social science (urbanism) (PhD); global health (MA); global health (health and culture) (PhD); global health (urbanism) (PhD); immigration studies (Graduate Certificate). *Faculty:* 52 full-time (19 women), 4 part-time/adjunct (2 women). *Students:* 127 full-time (77 women), 52 part-time (37 women); includes 43 minority (8 Black or African American, non-Hispanic/Latino; 4 American Indian or Alaska Native, non-Hispanic/Latino; 4 Asian, non-Hispanic/Latino; 26 Hispanic/Latino; 1 Two or more races, non-Hispanic/Latino), 19 international. Average age 32. 250 applicants, 24% accepted, 25 enrolled. In 2010, 8 master's, 18 doctorates, 7 other advanced degrees awarded. Terminal master's awarded for partial completion of doctoral program. *Degree requirements:* For master's, thesis or alternative, interactive Program of Study (iPOS) submitted before completing 50 percent of required credit hours; for doctorate, comprehensive exam, thesis/dissertation, interactive Program of Study (iPOS) submitted before completing 50 percent of required credit hours. *Entrance requirements:* For master's and doctorate, GRE, minimum GPA of 3.0 or equivalent in last 2 years of work leading to bachelor's degree. Additional exam requirements/recommendations for international students: Required—TOEFL, IELTS, or Pearson Test of English. *Application deadline:* For fall admission, 12/15 for domestic students, 12/1 for international students. Applications are processed on a rolling basis. Application fee: $70 ($90 for international students). Electronic applications accepted. *Expenses:* Tuition, state resident: full-time $8510; part-time $608 per credit. Tuition, nonresident: full-time $16,542; part-time $919 per credit. Required fees: $339; $110 per credit. Part-time tuition and fees vary according to course load. *Financial support:* In 2010–11, 30 research assistantships with full and partial tuition reimbursements (averaging $14,993 per year), 63 teaching assistantships with full and partial tuition reimbursements (averaging $15,266 per year) were awarded; fellowships with full tuition reimbursements, career-related internships or fieldwork, Federal Work-Study, institutionally sponsored loans, scholarships/grants, and tuition waivers (full and partial) also available. Financial award application deadline: 3/1; financial award applicants required to submit FAFSA. Total annual research expenditures: $3.8 million. *Unit head:* Dr. Sander van der Leeuw, Director, 480-965-6214, E-mail: vanderle@asu.edu. *Application contact:* Graduate Admissions, 480-965-6113.

Arkansas State University, Graduate School, College of Sciences and Mathematics, Program in Environmental Sciences, Jonesboro, State University, AR 72467. Offers MS, PhD. Part-time programs available. *Faculty:* 2 full-time (1 woman), 1 (woman) part-time/adjunct. *Students:* 16 full-time (8 women), 8 part-time (3 women); includes 3 minority (2 Black or African American, non-Hispanic/Latino; 1 Hispanic/Latino), 5 international. Average age 33. 15 applicants, 60% accepted, 6 enrolled. In 2010, 39 master's, 1 doctorate awarded. *Degree requirements:* For master's, comprehensive exam, thesis (for some programs); for doctorate, comprehensive exam, thesis/dissertation. *Entrance requirements:* For master's, GRE General Test, appropriate bachelor's degree, letters of reference, interview, official transcript, immunization records, letter of intent; for doctorate, GRE, appropriate bachelor's or master's degree, interview, letters of reference, personal statement, official transcript, immunization records. Additional exam requirements/recommendations for international students: Required—TOEFL (minimum score 550 paper-based; 213 computer-based; 79 iBT), IELTS (minimum score 6), PTE: Pearson Test of English Academic (56). *Application deadline:* For fall admission, 2/15 for domestic and international students; for spring admission, 8/15 for domestic and international students. Applications are processed on a rolling basis. Application fee: $50. Electronic applications accepted. *Expenses:* Tuition, state resident: full-time $3888; part-time $216 per credit hour. Tuition, nonresident: full-time $9918; part-time $551 per credit hour. International tuition: $8376 full-time. Required fees: $932; $49 per credit hour. $25 per term. One-time fee: $30. Tuition and fees vary according to course load and program. *Financial support:* In 2010–11, 9 students received support; fellowships, research assistantships, teaching assistantships, career-related internships or fieldwork, scholarships/grants, and unspecified assistantships available. Financial award application deadline: 7/1; financial award applicants required to submit FAFSA. *Unit head:* Dr. Thomas Risch, Director, 870-972-2007, Fax: 870-972-2008, E-mail: trisch@astate.edu. *Application contact:* Dr. Andrew Sustich, Dean of the Graduate School, 870-972-3029, Fax: 870-972-3857, E-mail: sustich@astate.edu.

Baylor University, Graduate School, College of Arts and Sciences, The Institute of Ecological, Earth and Environmental Sciences, Waco, TX 76798. Offers PhD. *Students:* 7 full-time (3 women); includes 1 minority (Two or more races, non-Hispanic/Latino), 5 international. In 2010, 1 doctorate awarded. *Unit head:* Dr. Joseph D. White, Director, 254-710-2911, E-mail: joseph_d_white@baylor.edu. *Application contact:* Suzanne Keener, Administrative Assistant, 254-710-3588, Fax: 254-710-3870.

Brigham Young University, Graduate Studies, College of Life Sciences, Department of Plant and Wildlife Sciences, Provo, UT 84602-1001. Offers environmental science (MS); genetics and biotechnology (MS); wildlife and wildlands conservation (MS, PhD). *Faculty:* 26 full-time (2 women). *Students:* 63 full-time (23 women); includes 2 Asian, non-Hispanic/Latino; 1 Hispanic/Latino; 1 Native Hawaiian or other Pacific Islander, non-Hispanic/Latino, 5 international. Average age 25. 33 applicants, 55% accepted, 18 enrolled. *Degree requirements:* For master's, thesis; for doctorate, comprehensive exam, thesis/dissertation, minimum GPA of 3.2, 54 hours (18 dissertation, 36 coursework). *Entrance requirements:* For master's, GRE General Test, minimum GPA of 3.2 during last 60 hours of course work; for doctorate, GRE, minimum GPA of 3.2. Additional exam requirements/recommendations for international students: Required—TOEFL (minimum score 580 paper-based; 237 computer-based; 85 iBT). *Application deadline:* 2/1 for domestic and international students. Applications are processed on a rolling basis. Application fee: $0. Electronic applications accepted. *Expenses:* Tuition: Full-time $5580; part-time $310 per credit hour. Tuition and fees vary according to program and student's religious affiliation. *Financial support:* In 2010–11, 63 students received support, including 2 research assistantships with partial tuition reimbursements available (averaging $16,650 per year), 37 teaching assistantships with partial tuition reimbursements available (averaging $16,650 per year); scholarships/grants and tuition waivers (partial) also available. Financial award application deadline: 2/1. *Faculty research:* environmental science, plant genetics, plant ecology, plant nutrition and pathology, wildlife and wildlands conservation. *Unit head:* Dr. Val J. Anderson, Chair, 801-422-3527, Fax: 801-422-0008, E-mail: val_anderson@byu.edu. *Application contact:* Dr. Loreen Allphin, Graduate Coordinator, 801-422-5603, Fax: 801-422-0008, E-mail: loreen_allphin@byu.edu.

California State Polytechnic University, Pomona, Academic Affairs, College of Environmental Design, John T. Lyle Center for Regenerative Studies, Pomona, CA 91768-2557. Offers MS. Part-time programs available. *Students:* 19 full-time (12 women), 19 part-time (12 women); includes 8 minority (1 Asian, non-Hispanic/Latino; 4 Hispanic/Latino; 3 Two or more races, non-Hispanic/Latino), 1 international. Average age 31. 34 applicants, 62% accepted, 14 enrolled. In 2010, 6 master's awarded. *Application deadline:* For fall admission, 5/1 priority date for domestic students; for winter admission, 10/15 priority date for domestic students; for spring admission, 1/20 priority date for domestic students. Applications are processed on a rolling basis. Application fee: $55. Electronic applications accepted. *Expenses:* Tuition, state resident: full-time $5386; part-time $2850 per year. Tuition, nonresident: full-time $12,082; part-time $248 per credit. Required fees: $577; $248 per credit. $577 per year. Tuition and fees vary according to course load and program. *Financial support:* Application deadline: 3/2. *Unit head:* Dr. Kyle D. Brown, Director, 909-869-5178, E-mail: kdbrown@csupomona.edu. *Application contact:* Scott J. Duncan, Director, Admissions, 909-869-3258, Fax: 909-869-4529, E-mail: sjduncan@csupomona.edu.

California State University, Chico, Graduate School, College of Natural Sciences, Department of Geological and Environmental Sciences, Program in Environmental Science, Chico, CA 95929-0722. Offers MS. Part-time programs available. *Students:* 8 full-time (3 women), 6 part-time (3 women); includes 1 Hispanic/Latino, 1 international. Average age 33. 15 applicants, 60% accepted, 5 enrolled. In 2010, 1 master's awarded. *Degree requirements:* For master's, thesis. *Entrance requirements:* For master's, GRE. Additional exam requirements/recommendations for international students: Required—TOEFL (minimum score 550 paper-based; 213 computer-based; 80 iBT), IELTS (minimum score 6.5). *Application deadline:* For fall admission, 3/1 priority date for domestic students, 3/1 for international students; for spring admission, 9/15 priority date for domestic students, 9/15 for international students. Applications are processed on a rolling basis. Application fee: $55. Electronic applications accepted. *Unit head:* Dr. William Murphy, Graduate Coordinator, 530-898-5163. *Application contact:* Dr. William Murphy, Graduate Coordinator, 530-898-5163.

California State University, Dominguez Hills, College of Natural and Behavioral Sciences, Program in Environmental Science, Carson, CA 90747-0001. Offers MS. *Faculty:* 2 full-time (0 women). *Students:* 4 full-time (1 woman), 9 part-time (3 women); includes 3 Black or African American, non-Hispanic/Latino; 2 Hispanic/Latino, 2 international. Average age 33. 12 applicants, 92% accepted, 7 enrolled.Application fee: $55. *Unit head:* Dr. John Keyantash, Chair, 310-243-2363, E-mail: jkeyantash@csudh.edu. *Application contact:* Brandy McLelland, Interim Director, Student Information Services, 310-243-3645, E-mail: bmclelland@csudh.edu.

California State University, East Bay, Office of Academic Programs and Graduate Studies, College of Science, Department of Earth and Environmental Sciences, Hayward, CA 94542-3000. Offers geology (MS). Evening/weekend programs available. *Faculty:* 3 full-time (0 women), 2 part-time/adjunct (1 woman). *Students:* 4 full-time (3 women), 10 part-time (4 women); includes 1 Hispanic/Latino, 2 international. Average age 34. 11 applicants, 45% accepted, 2 enrolled. In 2010, 1 master's awarded. *Degree requirements:* For master's, thesis. *Entrance requirements:* For master's, GRE, minimum GPA of 2.75 in field, 2.5 overall. Additional exam requirements/recommendations for international students: Required—TOEFL (minimum score 550 paper-based; 213 computer-based). *Application deadline:* For fall admission, 6/30 for domestic and international students. Application fee: $55. Electronic applications accepted. *Financial support:* Career-related internships or fieldwork, Federal Work-Study, and institutionally sponsored loans available. Support available to part-time students. Financial award application deadline: 3/2; financial award applicants required to submit FAFSA. *Unit head:* Dr. Jeffrey Seitz, Chair/Graduate Coordinator, 510-885-3486, Fax: 510-885-2526, E-mail: jeffrey.seitz@csueastbay.edu. *Application contact:* Dr. Donna Wiley, Interim Associate Director, 510-885-2928, Fax: 510-885-4777, E-mail: donna.wiley@csueastbay.edu.

California State University, Fullerton, Graduate Studies, College of Humanities and Social Sciences, Program in Environmental Studies, Fullerton, CA 92834-9480. Offers environmental sciences (MS). Part-time programs available. *Students:* 28 full-time (18 women), 38 part-time (19 women); includes 16 minority (2 Black or African American, non-Hispanic/Latino; 5 Asian, non-Hispanic/Latino; 6 Hispanic/Latino; 3 Two or more races, non-Hispanic/Latino), 2 international. Average age 29. 95 applicants, 45% accepted, 28 enrolled. In 2010, 25 master's awarded. *Degree requirements:* For master's, thesis. *Entrance requirements:* For master's, minimum GPA of 2.5 in last 60 units of course work. Application fee: $55. *Financial support:* Career-related internships or fieldwork, Federal Work-Study, institutionally sponsored loans, and scholarships/grants available. Support available to part-time students. Financial award application deadline: 3/1; financial award applicants required to submit FAFSA. *Unit head:* Dr. John Bock, Coordinator, 657-278-4373. *Application contact:* Admissions/Applications, 657-278-2371.

Environmental Sciences

California State University, Northridge, Graduate Studies, College of Science and Mathematics, Department of Chemistry and Biochemistry, Northridge, CA 91330. Offers biochemistry (MS); chemistry (MS), including chemistry, environmental chemistry. *Degree requirements:* For master's, thesis. *Entrance requirements:* For master's, GRE General Test or minimum GPA of 3.0. Additional exam requirements/recommendations for international students: Required—TOEFL. Electronic applications accepted.

California State University, San Bernardino, Graduate Studies, College of Social and Behavioral Sciences, Program in Environmental Sciences, San Bernardino, CA 92407-2397. Offers MS.

Christopher Newport University, Graduate Studies, Department of Biology, Chemistry and Environmental Science, Newport News, VA 23606-2998. Offers environmental science (MS). Part-time and evening/weekend programs available. *Faculty:* 8 full-time (3 women), 1 part-time/adjunct (0 women). *Students:* 10 full-time (6 women), 19 part-time (10 women); includes 6 minority (1 Black or African American, non-Hispanic/Latino; 3 Hispanic/Latino; 1 Native Hawaiian or other Pacific Islander, non-Hispanic/Latino; 1 Two or more races, non-Hispanic/Latino). Average age 27. 8 applicants, 75% accepted, 3 enrolled. In 2010, 10 master's awarded. *Degree requirements:* For master's, comprehensive exam, thesis optional. *Entrance requirements:* For master's, GRE General Test, minimum GPA of 3.0. Additional exam requirements/recommendations for international students: Required—TOEFL (minimum score 580 paper-based; 237 computer-based; 92 iBT). *Application deadline:* For fall admission, 8/15 priority date for domestic students, 4/1 for international students; for spring admission, 10/15 for domestic students, 10/1 for international students. Applications are processed on a rolling basis. Application fee: $50. Electronic applications accepted. *Expenses:* Tuition, state resident: part-time $418 per credit hour. Tuition, nonresident: part-time $769 per credit hour. *Financial support:* In 2010–11, 6 students received support, including 3 research assistantships with full tuition reimbursements available (averaging $2,000 per year); fellowships with full tuition reimbursements available, teaching assistantships, career-related internships or fieldwork, Federal Work-Study, institutionally sponsored loans, scholarships/grants, and unspecified assistantships also available. Support available to part-time students. Financial award application deadline: 3/1; financial award applicants required to submit FAFSA. *Faculty research:* Wetlands ecology and restoration, aquatic ecology, wetlands mitigation, greenhouse gases. *Unit head:* Dr. Gary Whiting, Coordinator, 757-594-7613, Fax: 757-594-7209, E-mail: gwhiting@cnu.edu. *Application contact:* Lyn Sawyer, Associate Director, Graduate Admissions and Records, 757-594-7544, Fax: 757-594-7649, E-mail: gradstdy@cnu.edu.

City College of the City University of New York, Graduate School, College of Liberal Arts and Science, Division of Science, Department of Earth and Atmospheric Sciences, New York, NY 10031-9198. Offers earth and environmental science (PhD); earth systems science (MA). PhD program offered jointly with Graduate School and University Center of the City University of New York. *Degree requirements:* For master's, comprehensive exam, thesis. *Entrance requirements:* Additional exam requirements/recommendations for international students: Required—TOEFL (minimum score 500 paper-based; 61 iBT). Electronic applications accepted. *Faculty research:* Water resources, high-temperature geochemistry, sedimentary basin analysis, tectonics.

Clarkson University, Graduate School, Institute for a Sustainable Environment, Program in Environmental Science and Engineering, Potsdam, NY 13699. Offers MS, PhD. Part-time programs available. *Students:* 30 full-time (16 women), 1 (woman) part-time, 16 international. Average age 27. 7 applicants, 100% accepted, 7 enrolled. In 2010, 5 master's, 2 doctorates awarded. Terminal master's awarded for partial completion of doctoral program. *Degree requirements:* For master's, thesis; for doctorate, comprehensive exam, thesis/dissertation, proposal/defense. *Entrance requirements:* For master's and doctorate, GRE, transcripts of all college coursework, resume, personal statement, three letters of recommendation. Additional exam requirements/recommendations for international students: Required—TOEFL (minimum score 550 paper-based; 213 computer-based; 80 iBT), IELTS (minimum score 6.5). *Application deadline:* For fall admission, 1/30 priority date for domestic and international students; for spring admission, 9/1 priority date for domestic and international students. Applications are processed on a rolling basis. Application fee: $25 ($35 for international students). Electronic applications accepted. *Expenses:* Tuition: Part-time $1136 per credit hour. *Financial support:* In 2010–11, 29 students received support, including fellowships with full tuition reimbursements available (averaging $21,580 per year), 17 research assistantships with full tuition reimbursements available (averaging $21,580 per year), 10 teaching assistantships with full tuition reimbursements available (averaging $21,580 per year); scholarships/grants, tuition waivers (partial), and unspecified assistantships also available. *Faculty research:* Biological, chemical, physical and social systems; renewable energy; environmental health. *Unit head:* Dr. Philip Hopke, Director, 315-268-3856, Fax: 315-268-4291, E-mail: hopkepk@clarkson.edu. *Application contact:* Suzann Cheney, Administrative Secretary, 315-268-3856, Fax: 315-268-4291, E-mail: scheney@clarkson.edu.

Clemson University, Graduate School, College of Agriculture, Forestry and Life Sciences, Program in Environmental Toxicology, Clemson, SC 29634. Offers MS, PhD. *Students:* 22 full-time (10 women), 2 part-time (0 women); includes 1 Hispanic/Latino, 7 international. Average age 30. 37 applicants, 35% accepted, 6 enrolled. In 2010, 8 master's, 2 doctorates awarded. *Degree requirements:* For master's, thesis; for doctorate, one foreign language, thesis/dissertation. *Entrance requirements:* For master's and doctorate, GRE General Test. Additional exam requirements/recommendations for international students: Required—TOEFL. *Application deadline:* For fall admission, 2/1 for domestic and international students; for spring admission, 9/15 for domestic and international students. Applications are processed on a rolling basis. Application fee: $70 ($80 for international students). Electronic applications accepted. *Expenses:* Contact institution. *Financial support:* In 2010–11, 21 students received support, including 3 fellowships with full and partial tuition reimbursements available (averaging $13,960 per year), 13 research assistantships with partial tuition reimbursements available (averaging $13,738 per year), 17 teaching assistantships with partial tuition reimbursements available (averaging $9,676 per year); career-related internships or fieldwork, Federal Work-Study, institutionally sponsored loans, scholarships/grants, health care benefits, and unspecified assistantships also available. Financial award applicants required to submit FAFSA. *Faculty research:* Biochemical toxicology, analytical toxicology, ecological risk assessment, wildlife toxicology, mathematical modeling. Total annual research expenditures: $3 million. *Unit head:* Dr. Lisa Bain, Graduate Program Director, 864-656-5050, E-mail: lbain@clemson.edu. *Application contact:* Dr. Lisa J. Bain, Graduate Program Director, 864-656-5050, E-mail: lbain@clemson.edu.

Cleveland State University, College of Graduate Studies, College of Sciences and Health Professions, Department of Biological, Geological, and Environmental Sciences, Cleveland, OH 44115. Offers biology (MS); environmental science (MS); museum studies for natural historians (MS); regulatory biology (PhD); JD/MS. Part-time programs available. *Faculty:* 11 full-time (3 women), 6 part-time/adjunct (3 women). *Students:* 74 full-time (42 women), 35 part-time (19 women); includes 2 Black or African American, non-Hispanic/Latino; 2 Asian, non-Hispanic/Latino; 3 Hispanic/Latino, 41 international. Average age 30. 64 applicants, 13% accepted, 5 enrolled. In 2010, 12 master's, 2 doctorates awarded. Terminal master's awarded for partial completion of doctoral program. *Degree requirements:* For master's, comprehensive exam (for some programs), thesis (for some programs); for doctorate, comprehensive exam, thesis/dissertation. *Entrance requirements:* For master's, GRE General Test, 2 letters of recommendation; for doctorate, GRE General Test, 2 letters of recommendation; 1-2 page essay; statement of career goals and research interests. Additional exam requirements/recommendations for international students: Required—TOEFL (minimum score 525 paper-based; 197 computer-based). *Application deadline:* For fall admission, 4/1 priority date for domestic and international students; for spring admission, 12/1 priority date for domestic students. Applications are processed on a rolling basis. Application fee: $30. Electronic applications accepted. *Expenses:* Tuition, state resident: full-time $8447; part-time $469 per credit hour. Tuition, nonresident: full-time $16,020; part-time $890 per credit hour. Required fees: $50. *Financial support:* In 2010–11, 29 students received support, including research assistantships with full and partial tuition reimbursements available (averaging $16,500 per year), teaching assistantships with full and partial tuition reimbursements available (averaging $16,500 per year); institutionally sponsored loans and unspecified assistantships also available. *Faculty research:* Molecular and cell biology, immunology, urban ecology. *Unit head:* Dr. Jeffrey Dean, Chair, 216-687-2120, Fax: 216-687-6972, E-mail: j.dean@csuohio.edu. *Application contact:* Dr. Jeffrey Dean, Chair, 216-687-2120, Fax: 216-687-6972, E-mail: j.dean@csuohio.edu.

The College at Brockport, State University of New York, School of Science and Mathematics, Department of Environmental Science and Biology, Brockport, NY 14420-2997. Offers MS. Part-time programs available. *Students:* 10 full-time (2 women), 18 part-time (8 women); includes 1 Asian, non-Hispanic/Latino; 1 Hispanic/Latino. 19 applicants, 58% accepted, 9 enrolled. In 2010, 1 master's awarded. *Degree requirements:* For master's, comprehensive exam, thesis. *Entrance requirements:* For master's, minimum GPA of 3.0, letters of recommendation, sample of scientific writing; statement of objectives. Additional exam requirements/recommendations for international students: Required—TOEFL (minimum score 550 paper-based; 213 computer-based; 79 iBT). *Application deadline:* For fall admission, 4/15 priority date for domestic and international students; for spring admission, 11/15 priority date for domestic and international students. Application fee: $50. Electronic applications accepted. *Financial support:* In 2010–11, 1 research assistantship with full tuition reimbursement was awarded; Federal Work-Study, scholarships/grants, and unspecified assistantships also available. Support available to part-time students. Financial award application deadline: 3/15; financial award applicants required to submit FAFSA. *Faculty research:* Aquatic and terrestrial ecology/organismal biology, watersheds and wetlands, persistent toxic chemicals, soil-plant interactions, aquaculture. *Unit head:* Dr. James Haynes, Chairperson, 585-395-5975, Fax: 585-395-5969, E-mail: jhaynes@brockport.edu. *Application contact:* Dr. Christopher Norment, Graduate Director, 585-395-5748, Fax: 585-395-5969, E-mail: cnorment@brockport.edu.

College of Charleston, Graduate School, School of Sciences and Mathematics, Program in Environmental Studies, Charleston, SC 29424-0001. Offers MS. Part-time and evening/weekend programs available. *Faculty:* 26 full-time (8 women), 5 part-time/adjunct (3 women). *Students:* 46 full-time (36 women), 31 part-time (19 women); includes 2 minority (1 Asian, non-Hispanic/Latino; 1 Hispanic/Latino). Average age 27. 51 applicants, 63% accepted, 20 enrolled. In 2010, 27 master's awarded. *Degree requirements:* For master's, thesis optional, thesis or research internship. *Entrance requirements:* For master's, GRE, minimum GPA of 3.0, 3 letters of recommendation. Additional exam requirements/recommendations for international students: Required—TOEFL (minimum score 81 iBT). *Application deadline:* For fall admission, 3/1 for domestic students; for spring admission, 11/1 for domestic students. Application fee: $45. Electronic applications accepted. *Expenses:* Contact institution. *Financial support:* In 2010–11, 5 research assistantships (averaging $17,000 per year), 6 teaching assistantships (averaging $16,000 per year) were awarded; fellowships, career-related internships or fieldwork, Federal Work-Study, scholarships/grants, and unspecified assistantships also available. Support available to part-time students. Financial award application deadline: 4/1; financial award applicants required to submit FAFSA. *Unit head:* Dr. Timothy Callahan, Director, 843-953-2000, Fax: 843-953-2001, E-mail: callahant@cofc.edu. *Application contact:* Susan Hallatt, Director of Graduate Admissions, 843-953-5614, Fax: 843-953-1434, E-mail: hallatts@cofc.edu.

College of Staten Island of the City University of New York, Graduate Programs, Center for Environmental Science, Staten Island, NY 10314-6600. Offers MS. Part-time and evening/weekend programs available. *Faculty:* 5 full-time (3 women), 4 part-time/adjunct (2 women). *Students:* 33 part-time (17 women); includes 9 minority (3 Black or African American, non-Hispanic/Latino; 5 Asian, non-Hispanic/Latino; 1 Hispanic/Latino), 4 international. Average age 30. 19 applicants, 84% accepted, 7 enrolled. In 2010, 6 master's awarded. Terminal master's awarded for partial completion of doctoral program. *Degree requirements:* For master's, thesis. *Entrance requirements:* For master's, GRE General Test, 1 year of course work in chemistry, physics, calculus, and ecology; minimum GPA of 3.0 in undergraduate science and engineering; bachelor's degree in a natural science or engineering; interview. Additional exam requirements/recommendations for international students: Required—TOEFL (minimum score 550 paper-based; 213 computer-based; 79 iBT), IELTS (minimum score 6.5). *Application deadline:* Applications are processed on a rolling basis. Application fee: $125. Electronic applications accepted. *Expenses:* Tuition, state resident: full-time $7730; part-time $325 per credit. Tuition, nonresident: full-time $14,520; part-time $605 per credit. Required fees: $378. *Financial support:* In 2010–11, 6 research assistantships (averaging $2,000 per year) were awarded; career-related internships or fieldwork, Federal Work-Study, and scholarships/grants also available. Support available to part-time students. Financial award applicants required to submit FAFSA. Total annual research expenditures: $38,000. *Unit head:* Dr. Alfred Levine, Director, 718-982-2822, Fax: 718-982-3923, E-mail: envirscimasters@mail.csi.cuny.edu. *Application contact:* Sasha Spence, Assistant Director of Graduate Recruitment and Admissions, 718-982-2699, Fax: 718-982-2500, E-mail: sasha.spence@csi.cuny.edu.

Colorado School of Mines, Graduate School, Division of Environmental Science and Engineering, Golden, CO 80401. Offers MS, PhD. Part-time programs available. *Faculty:* 22 full-time (5 women), 8 part-time/adjunct (3 women). *Students:* 90 full-time (45 women), 22 part-time (12 women); includes 3 Black or African American, non-Hispanic/Latino; 3 Asian, non-Hispanic/Latino; 8 Hispanic/Latino; 1 Two or more races, non-Hispanic/Latino, 9 international. Average age 28. 154 applicants, 54% accepted, 36 enrolled. In 2010, 37 master's, 4 doctorates awarded. *Degree requirements:* For master's, thesis (for some programs); for doctorate, comprehensive exam, thesis/dissertation. *Entrance requirements:* For master's and doctorate, GRE General Test. Additional exam requirements/recommendations for international students: Required—TOEFL (minimum score 550 paper-based; 213 computer-based; 80 iBT). *Application deadline:* For fall admission, 1/15 priority date for domestic and international students; for spring admission, 10/15 priority date for domestic and international students. Application fee: $50 ($70 for international students). Electronic applications accepted. *Expenses:* Tuition, state resident: full-time $11,550; part-time $641 per credit. Tuition, nonresident: full-time $25,980; part-time $1444 per credit. Required fees: $1874; $937 per semester. *Financial support:* In 2010–11, 41 students received support, including 1 fellowship with full tuition reimbursement available (averaging $20,000 per year), 38 research assistantships with full tuition reimbursements available (averaging $20,000 per year), 2 teaching assistantships with full tuition reimbursements available (averaging $20,000 per year); scholarships/grants, health care benefits, and unspecified assistantships also available. Financial award application deadline: 1/15; financial award applicants required to submit FAFSA. *Faculty research:* Treatment of water and wastes, environmental law: policy and practice, natural environment systems, hazardous waste management, environmental data analysis. Total annual research expenditures: $4.1 million. *Unit head:* Dr. John McCray, Division Director, 303-384-3490, Fax: 303-273-3413, E-mail: jmccray@mines.edu. *Application contact:* Tim VanHaverbeke, Research Faculty, 303-273-3467, Fax: 303-273-3413, E-mail: tvanhave@mines.edu.

Columbia University, Graduate School of Arts and Sciences, Program in Climate and Society, New York, NY 10027. Offers MA.

Columbia University, School of International and Public Affairs, Program in Environmental Science and Policy, New York, NY 10027. Offers MPA. Program admits applicants for late May/early June start only. *Degree requirements:* For master's, workshops. *Entrance requirements:* For master's, GRE (recommended), previous course work in biology and

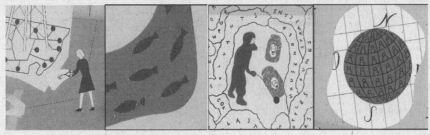
chemistry, earth sciences (recommended), economics (strongly recommended). Additional exam requirements/recommendations for international students: Required—TOEFL. Electronic applications accepted. *Faculty research:* Ecological management of enclosed ecosystems vegetation dynamics, environmental policy and management, energy policy, nuclear waste policy, environmental and natural resource economics and policy, carbon sequestration, urban planning, environmental risk assessment/toxicology, environmental justice.

See Close-Up on page 395.

Columbus State University, Graduate Studies, College of Letters and Sciences, Environmental Science Program, Columbus, GA 31907-5645. Offers MS. Part-time and evening/weekend programs available. *Faculty:* 5 full-time (0 women), 3 part-time/adjunct (1 woman). *Students:* 11 full-time (8 women), 11 part-time (6 women); includes 7 minority (3 Black or African American, non-Hispanic/Latino; 2 Hispanic/Latino; 1 Native Hawaiian or other Pacific Islander, non-Hispanic/Latino; 1 Two or more races, non-Hispanic/Latino), 1 international. Average age 31. 13 applicants, 77% accepted, 6 enrolled. In 2010, 9 master's awarded. *Degree requirements:* For master's, thesis. *Entrance requirements:* For master's, GRE General Test, minimum GPA of 3.0. Additional exam requirements/recommendations for international students: Required—TOEFL (minimum score 550 paper-based; 213 computer-based; 79 iBT). *Application deadline:* For fall admission, 6/30 priority date for domestic students, 5/1 for international students; for spring admission, 11/1 for domestic and international students. Applications are processed on a rolling basis. Application fee: $30. Electronic applications accepted. *Expenses:* Tuition, state resident: full-time $5573; part-time $232 per semester hour. Tuition, nonresident: full-time $13,968; part-time $582 per semester hour. Required fees: $1300; $650 per semester. Tuition and fees vary according to degree level and program. *Financial support:* In 2010–11, 10 students received support, including 12 research assistantships with partial tuition reimbursements available (averaging $3,000 per year); career-related internships or fieldwork, Federal Work-Study, institutionally sponsored loans, scholarships/grants, and unspecified assistantships also available. Support available to part-time students. Financial award application deadline: 5/1; financial award applicants required to submit FAFSA. *Unit head:* Dr. Shawn Cruzen, Department Chair, 706-649-1785, E-mail: cruzen_shawn@colstate.edu. *Application contact:* Katie Thornton, Graduate Admissions Specialist, 706-568-2035, Fax: 706-568-2462, E-mail: thornton_katie@colstate.edu.

Cornell University, Graduate School, Graduate Fields of Agriculture and Life Sciences, Field of Soil and Crop Sciences, Ithaca, NY 14853-0001. Offers agronomy (MS, PhD); environmental information science (MS, PhD); environmental management (MPS); field crop science (MS, PhD); soil science (MS, PhD). *Faculty:* 39 full-time (9 women). *Students:* 29 full-time (13 women); includes 6 Hispanic/Latino, 9 international. Average age 29. 45 applicants, 24% accepted, 7 enrolled. In 2010, 3 master's, 4 doctorates awarded. *Degree requirements:* For master's, thesis (MS); for doctorate, comprehensive exam, thesis/dissertation. *Entrance requirements:* For master's and doctorate, GRE General Test, 2 letters of recommendation. Additional exam requirements/recommendations for international students: Required—TOEFL (minimum score 550 paper-based; 213 computer-based; 77 iBT). *Application deadline:* For fall admission, 2/1 priority date for domestic students. Applications are processed on a rolling basis. Application fee: $70. Electronic applications accepted. *Expenses:* Tuition: Full-time $29,500. Required fees: $76. Tuition and fees vary according to degree level and program. *Financial support:* In 2010–11, 6 fellowships with full tuition reimbursements, 11 research assistantships with full tuition reimbursements, 6 teaching assistantships with full tuition reimbursements were awarded; institutionally sponsored loans, traineeships, health care benefits, tuition waivers (full and partial), and unspecified assistantships also available. *Faculty research:* Soil chemistry, physics and biology; crop physiology and management; environmental information science and modeling; international agriculture; weed science. *Unit head:* Director of Graduate Studies, 607-255-3267, Fax: 607-255-8615. *Application contact:* Graduate Field Assistant, 607-255-3267, Fax: 607-255-8615, E-mail: ljh4@cornell.edu.

Drexel University, College of Arts and Sciences, Program in Environmental Science, Philadelphia, PA 19104-2875. Offers MS, PhD. Part-time and evening/weekend programs available. Terminal master's awarded for partial completion of doctoral program. *Degree requirements:* For master's, thesis optional; for doctorate, thesis/dissertation. Electronic applications accepted.

Duke University, Graduate School, Department of Environment, Durham, NC 27708. Offers natural resource economics/policy (PhD); natural resource science/ecology (PhD); natural resource systems science (PhD); JD/AM. Part-time programs available. *Faculty:* 28 full-time. *Students:* 59 full-time (33 women); includes 2 Black or African American, non-Hispanic/Latino; 1 Asian, non-Hispanic/Latino, 17 international. 84 applicants, 13% accepted, 6 enrolled. In 2010, 14 doctorates awarded. *Degree requirements:* For doctorate, variable foreign language requirement, thesis/dissertation. *Entrance requirements:* For doctorate, GRE General Test. Additional exam requirements/recommendations for international students: Required—TOEFL (minimum score 550 paper-based; 213 computer-based; 83 iBT), IELTS (minimum score 7). *Application deadline:* For fall admission, 12/8 priority date for domestic and international students. Application fee: $75. Electronic applications accepted. *Financial support:* Fellowships, research assistantships, teaching assistantships, Federal Work-Study available. Financial award application deadline: 12/8. *Unit head:* Gaby Katul, Director of Graduate Studies, 919-613-8002, Fax: 919-613-8061, E-mail: meg.stephens@duke.edu. *Application contact:* Elizabeth Hutton, Director, Graduate Admissions, 919-684-3913, Fax: 919-684-2277, E-mail: grad-admissions@duke.edu.

Duke University, Nicholas School of the Environment, Durham, NC 27708-0328. Offers coastal environmental management (MEM); DEL-environmental leadership (MEM); energy and environment (MEM); environmental economics and policy (MEM); environmental health and security (MEM); forest resource management (MF); global environmental change (MEM); resource ecology (MEM); water and air resources (MEM); JD/AM; JD/MEM; JD/MF; MAT/MEM; MBA/MEM; MBA/MF; MEM/MPP; MF/MPP. *Accreditation:* SAF (one or more programs are accredited). Part-time programs available. *Degree requirements:* For master's, thesis. *Entrance requirements:* For master's, GRE General Test, previous course work in biology or ecology, calculus, statistics, and microeconomics; computer familiarity with word processing and data analysis. Additional exam requirements/recommendations for international students: Required—TOEFL (minimum score 550 paper-based; 213 computer-based). Electronic applications accepted. *Expenses:* Contact institution. *Faculty research:* Ecosystem management, conservation ecology, earth systems, risk assessment.

Duquesne University, Bayer School of Natural and Environmental Sciences, Environmental Science and Management Program, Pittsburgh, PA 15282-0001. Offers environmental management (MEM, Certificate); environmental science (Certificate); environmental science and management (MS); JD/MS; MBA/MS; MS/MS. Part-time and evening/weekend programs available. Postbaccalaureate distance learning degree programs offered (minimal on-campus study). *Faculty:* 4 full-time (0 women), 8 part-time/adjunct (0 women). *Students:* 22 full-time (9 women), 17 part-time (12 women), 6 international. Average age 27. 28 applicants, 96% accepted, 17 enrolled. In 2010, 15 master's awarded. *Degree requirements:* For master's, thesis (for some programs), minimum of 36 credit hours; for Certificate, minimum of 18 credit hours. *Entrance requirements:* For master's, GRE General Test, course work in biology, chemistry, and calculus or statistics; 3 letters of reference. Additional exam requirements/

Peterson's Graduate Programs in the Physical Sciences, Mathematics, Agricultural Sciences, the Environment & Natural Resources 2012

www.facebook.com/petersonspublishing

375

Environmental Sciences

Duquesne University (continued)

recommendations for international students: Required—TOEFL (minimum score 80 iBT). *Application deadline:* For fall admission, 4/1 priority date for domestic students, 4/1 for international students; for spring admission, 10/1 priority date for domestic students, 10/1 for international students. Applications are processed on a rolling basis. Application fee: $40. *Expenses:* Contact institution. *Financial support:* In 2010–11, 8 students received support, including 1 fellowship (averaging $17,000 per year), 2 research assistantships (averaging $16,000 per year), 3 teaching assistantships with full and partial tuition reimbursements available (averaging $10,875 per year); career-related internships or fieldwork, scholarships/grants, tuition waivers (partial), and unspecified assistantships also available. Financial award application deadline: 5/31. *Faculty research:* Watershed management systems, environmental analytical chemistry, environmental endocrinology, environmental microbiology, aquatic biology. *Unit head:* Dr. John Stolz, Director, 412-396-4367, Fax: 412-396-4092, E-mail: stolz@duq.edu. *Application contact:* Heather Costello, Graduate Academic Advisor, 412-396-6339, Fax: 412-396-4881, E-mail: costelloh@duq.edu.

Florida Agricultural and Mechanical University, Environmental Sciences Institute, Tallahassee, FL 32307. Offers MS, PhD. *Faculty:* 10 full-time (2 women). *Students:* 26 full-time (23 women), 3 part-time (0 women); includes 20 Black or African American, non-Hispanic/Latino; 3 Asian, non-Hispanic/Latino; 2 Hispanic/Latino, 3 international. Average age 25. 21 applicants, 14% accepted, 3 enrolled. In 2010, 3 master's, 2 doctorates awarded. *Degree requirements:* For master's, thesis; for doctorate, comprehensive exam, thesis/dissertation, oral exam. *Entrance requirements:* For master's and doctorate, GRE General Test, minimum GPA of 3.0. Additional exam requirements/recommendations for international students: Required—TOEFL. *Application deadline:* For fall admission, 6/1 priority date for domestic students, 4/1 priority date for international students; for spring admission, 11/1 priority date for domestic and international students. Application fee: $9 for international students. *Financial support:* In 2010–11, 28 students received support, including 10 fellowships with full and partial tuition reimbursements available, 18 research assistantships with tuition reimbursements available; career-related internships or fieldwork, institutionally sponsored loans, scholarships/grants, and unspecified assistantships also available. Financial award application deadline: 6/10; financial award applicants required to submit FAFSA. *Faculty research:* Environmental chemistry, environmental policy and risk management, aquatic and terrestrial ecology, biomolecular sciences. *Unit head:* Dr. Michael Abazinge, Director, 850-599-3550, Fax: 850-599-8183, E-mail: michael.abazinge@famu.edu. *Application contact:* Ora S. Mukes, Coordinator Academic Support Services, 850-561-2641, Fax: 850-412-5504, E-mail: ora.mukes@famu.edu.

Florida Atlantic University, Charles E. Schmidt College of Science, Environmental Sciences Program, Boca Raton, FL 33431-0991. Offers MS. *Students:* 17 full-time (9 women), 7 part-time (3 women); includes 4 minority (1 Black or African American, non-Hispanic/Latino; 3 Hispanic/Latino), 1 international. Average age 27. 21 applicants, 57% accepted, 9 enrolled. In 2010, 3 master's awarded. *Degree requirements:* For master's, thesis. *Entrance requirements:* For master's, GRE General Test, minimum GPA of 3.0. Additional exam requirements/recommendations for international students: Required—TOEFL. *Application deadline:* For fall admission, 3/15 for domestic and international students; for spring admission, 10/1 for domestic and international students. Application fee: $30. *Expenses:* Tuition, area resident: Part-time $319.96 per credit. Tuition, state resident: part-time $319.96 per credit. Tuition, nonresident: part-time $926.42 per credit. *Financial support:* Teaching assistantships, career-related internships or fieldwork and Federal Work-Study available. *Faculty research:* Tropical and terrestrial ecology, coastal/marine/wetlands ecology, hydrogeology, tropical botany. *Unit head:* Dr. Dale Gawlik, Director, 561-297-3333, Fax: 561-297-2067, E-mail: dgawlik@fau.edu. *Application contact:* Dr. Dale Gawlik, Director, 561-297-3333, Fax: 561-297-2067, E-mail: dgawlik@fau.edu.

Florida Gulf Coast University, College of Arts and Sciences, Program in Environmental Science, Fort Myers, FL 33965-6565. Offers MS. Part-time programs available. *Faculty:* 187 full-time (78 women), 177 part-time/adjunct (70 women). *Students:* 30 full-time (22 women), 6 part-time (2 women); includes 1 Hispanic/Latino, 1 international. Average age 30. 19 applicants, 58% accepted, 7 enrolled. In 2010, 6 master's awarded. *Entrance requirements:* For master's, GRE General Test, minimum GPA of 3.0. Additional exam requirements/recommendations for international students: Required—TOEFL (minimum score 550 paper-based; 213 computer-based). *Application deadline:* For fall admission, 2/15 priority date for domestic students. Applications are processed on a rolling basis. Application fee: $30. Electronic applications accepted. *Expenses:* Tuition, state resident: part-time $322.08 per credit hour. Tuition, nonresident: part-time $1117.08 per credit hour. *Faculty research:* Political issues in environmental science, recycling, environmentally-friendly buildings, pathophysiology, immunotoxicology of marine organisms. *Unit head:* Dr. Aswani Volety, Chair, 239-590-7216, Fax: 239-590-7200, E-mail: avolety@fgcu.edu. *Application contact:* Patricia Price, Executive Secretary, 239-590-7196, Fax: 239-590-7200, E-mail: price@fgcu.edu.

Florida Institute of Technology, Graduate Programs, College of Engineering, Department of Marine and Environmental Systems, Melbourne, FL 32901-6975. Offers earth remote sensing (MS); environmental resource management (MS); environmental science (MS, PhD); meteorology (MS); ocean engineering (MS, PhD); oceanography (MS, PhD). Part-time programs available. *Faculty:* 11 full-time (0 women), 3 part-time/adjunct (0 women). *Students:* 47 full-time (16 women), 15 part-time (5 women); includes 4 minority (1 Black or African American, non-Hispanic/Latino; 1 Asian, non-Hispanic/Latino; 1 Hispanic/Latino; 1 Two or more races, non-Hispanic/Latino), 10 international. Average age 27. 118 applicants, 49% accepted, 19 enrolled. In 2010, 21 master's, 1 doctorate awarded. *Degree requirements:* For master's, comprehensive exam (for some programs), thesis (for some programs), seminar, field project, written final exam, internship, technical paper, oral presentation or internship; for doctorate, comprehensive exam, thesis/dissertation, seminar, internships (oceanography and environmental science), publications. *Entrance requirements:* For master's, GRE General Test (environmental science, oceanography, environmental resource management, meteorology, earth remote sensing), 3 letters of recommendation, minimum GPA of 3.0, resume, transcripts, statement of objectives; for doctorate, GRE General Test (oceanography, environmental science), resume, 3 letters of recommendation, minimum GPA of 3.3, statement of objectives, on campus interview (highly recommended). Additional exam requirements/recommendations for international students: Required—TOEFL (minimum score 550 paper-based; 213 computer-based; 79 iBT). *Application deadline:* For fall admission, 4/1 for international students; for spring admission, 9/30 for international students. Applications are processed on a rolling basis. Application fee: $50. Electronic applications accepted. *Expenses:* Tuition: Part-time $1040 per credit hour. Tuition and fees vary according to campus/location. *Financial support:* In 2010–11, 5 fellowships with full and partial tuition reimbursements (averaging $7,240 per year), 5 research assistantships with full and partial tuition reimbursements (averaging $3,664 per year), 10 teaching assistantships with full and partial tuition reimbursements (averaging $6,670 per year) were awarded; career-related internships or fieldwork, institutionally sponsored loans, tuition waivers (partial), unspecified assistantships, and tuition remissions also available. Support available to part-time students. Financial award application deadline: 3/1; financial award applicants required to submit FAFSA. Total annual research expenditures: $1.7 million. *Unit head:* Dr. George Maul, Department Head, 321-674-7453, Fax: 321-674-7212, E-mail: gmaul@fit.edu. *Application contact:* Cheryl A. Brown, Associate Director of Graduate Admissions, 321-674-7581, Fax: 321-723-9468, E-mail: cbrown@fit.edu.

Florida International University, College of Arts and Sciences, Department of Earth and Environment, Program in Environmental Studies, Miami, FL 33199. Offers MS. Part-time programs available. *Students:* 28 full-time (15 women), 12 part-time (6 women); includes 1 American Indian or Alaska Native, non-Hispanic/Latino; 1 Asian, non-Hispanic/Latino; 7 Hispanic/Latino, 9 international. Average age 28. 45 applicants, 36% accepted, 16 enrolled. In 2010, 17 master's awarded. *Degree requirements:* For master's, thesis or alternative. *Entrance requirements:* For master's, GRE General Test, minimum GPA of 3.0, 3 letters of recommendation, letter of intent. Additional exam requirements/recommendations for international students: Required—TOEFL (minimum score 550 paper-based; 80 iBT). *Application deadline:* For fall admission, 3/1 for domestic and international students; for spring admission, 10/1 for domestic students, 9/1 for international students. Applications are processed on a rolling basis. Application fee: $30. Electronic applications accepted. *Financial support:* Institutionally sponsored loans and scholarships/grants available. Financial award application deadline: 3/1; financial award applicants required to submit FAFSA. *Unit head:* Dr. Rosemary Hickey-Vargas, Chair, Earth and Environment Department, 305-348-1930, Fax: 305-348-6137, E-mail: rosemary.hickey-vargas@fiu.edu. *Application contact:* Dr. Krishnaswamy Jayachandran, Director, Graduate Program, 305-348-1930, Fax: 305-348-6137, E-mail: jayachan@fiu.edu.

Florida State University, The Graduate School, College of Arts and Sciences, Department of Earth, Ocean and Atmospheric Science, Program in Oceanography, Tallahassee, FL 32306-4320. Offers aquatic environmental science (MS); oceanography (MS, PhD). *Faculty:* 15 full-time (1 woman). *Students:* 48 full-time (24 women); includes 1 Black or African American, non-Hispanic/Latino; 3 Asian, non-Hispanic/Latino, 9 international. Average age 27. 61 applicants, 36% accepted, 10 enrolled. In 2010, 8 master's, 4 doctorates awarded. *Median time to degree:* Of those who began their doctoral program in fall 2002, 100% received their degree in 8 years or less. *Degree requirements:* For master's, thesis; for doctorate, comprehensive exam, thesis/dissertation. *Entrance requirements:* For master's and doctorate, GRE General Test. Additional exam requirements/recommendations for international students: Required—TOEFL (minimum score 550 paper-based; 213 computer-based; 80 iBT). *Application deadline:* For fall admission, 2/15 priority date for domestic and international students; for spring admission, 7/15 priority date for domestic and international students. Applications are processed on a rolling basis. Application fee: $35. Electronic applications accepted. *Expenses:* Tuition, state resident: full-time $8238.24. *Financial support:* In 2010–11, 41 students received support, including 1 fellowship with full tuition reimbursement available, 26 research assistantships with full tuition reimbursements available, 14 teaching assistantships with full tuition reimbursements available. Financial award application deadline: 2/15; financial award applicants required to submit FAFSA. *Faculty research:* Trace metals in seawater, currents and waves, modeling, benthic ecology, marine biogeochemistry. *Unit head:* Dr. Jeffrey Chanton, Area Coordinator, 850-644-6700, Fax: 850-644-2581, E-mail: chanton@ocean.fsu.edu. *Application contact:* Michaela Lupiani, Academic Coordinator, 850-644-6700, Fax: 850-644-2581, E-mail: admissions@ocean.fsu.edu.

Gannon University, School of Graduate Studies, College of Engineering and Business, School of Engineering and Computer Science, Program in Environmental and Occupational Science and Health, Erie, PA 16541-0001. Offers Certificate. Part-time and evening/weekend programs available. *Entrance requirements:* Additional exam requirements/recommendations for international students: Required—TOEFL (minimum score 79 iBT). *Application deadline:* Applications are processed on a rolling basis. Application fee: $25. Electronic applications accepted. *Expenses:* Tuition: Full-time $14,670; part-time $815 per credit. Required fees: $430; $18 per credit. Tuition and fees vary according to class time, course load, degree level, campus/location and program. *Financial support:* Scholarships/grants available. Financial award application deadline: 7/1; financial award applicants required to submit FAFSA. *Unit head:* Dr. Harry Diz, Chair, 814-871-7633, E-mail: diz001@gannon.edu. *Application contact:* Kara Morgan, Assistant Director of Graduate Admissions, 814-871-5831, Fax: 814-871-5827, E-mail: graduate@gannon.edu.

Gannon University, School of Graduate Studies, College of Engineering and Business, School of Engineering and Computer Science, Program in Environmental Science and Engineering, Erie, PA 16541-0001. Offers MS. Part-time and evening/weekend programs available. *Students:* 12 full-time (5 women), 5 part-time (4 women), 3 international. Average age 28. 32 applicants, 63% accepted, 3 enrolled. In 2010, 4 master's awarded. *Degree requirements:* For master's, thesis, internship, research paper or project. *Entrance requirements:* For master's, GRE. Additional exam requirements/recommendations for international students: Required—TOEFL (minimum score 79 iBT). *Application deadline:* Applications are processed on a rolling basis. Application fee: $25. Electronic applications accepted. *Expenses:* Tuition: Full-time $14,670; part-time $815 per credit. Required fees: $430; $18 per credit. Tuition and fees vary according to class time, course load, degree level, campus/location and program. *Financial support:* Scholarships/grants and unspecified assistantships available. Financial award application deadline: 7/1; financial award applicants required to submit FAFSA. *Faculty research:* Water quality, air quality, biomass energy, industrial waste treatment, environmental risk assessment. *Unit head:* Dr. Harry Diz, Chair, 814-871-7633, E-mail: diz001@gannon.edu. *Application contact:* Kara Morgan, Assistant Director of Graduate Admissions, 814-871-5831, Fax: 814-871-5827, E-mail: graduate@gannon.edu.

George Mason University, College of Science, Department of Environmental Science and Policy, Fairfax, VA 22030. Offers environmental management (Certificate); environmental science and policy (MS); environmental science and public policy (PhD). Part-time programs available. *Faculty:* 20 full-time (7 women), 4 part-time/adjunct (3 women). *Students:* 20 full-time (13 women), 147 part-time (78 women); includes 7 Black or African American, non-Hispanic/Latino; 7 Asian, non-Hispanic/Latino; 9 Hispanic/Latino, 18 international. Average age 36. 85 applicants, 55% accepted, 37 enrolled. In 2010, 21 master's, 7 doctorates, 1 other advanced degree awarded. *Degree requirements:* For doctorate, thesis/dissertation, internship. *Entrance requirements:* For doctorate, GRE General Test, GRE Subject Test. Additional exam requirements/recommendations for international students: Required—TOEFL (minimum score 570 paper-based; 230 computer-based; 88 iBT). *Application deadline:* For fall admission, 5/1 for domestic students; for spring admission, 11/1 for domestic students. Application fee: $100. Electronic applications accepted. *Expenses:* Tuition, state resident: full-time $8192; part-time $440 per credit hour. Tuition, nonresident: full-time $22,952; part-time $1055 per credit hour. Required fees: $2364; $99 per credit hour. *Financial support:* In 2010–11, 47 students received support, including 2 fellowships (averaging $18,000 per year), 9 research assistantships (averaging $16,408 per year), 36 teaching assistantships (averaging $12,478 per year); career-related internships or fieldwork, Federal Work-Study, scholarships/grants, unspecified assistantships, and health care benefits (full-time research or teaching assistantship recipients) also available. Financial award application deadline: 3/1; financial award applicants required to submit FAFSA. Total annual research expenditures: $425,538. *Unit head:* Dr. R. Christian Jones, Interim Director, 703-993-1127, Fax: 703-993-1046, E-mail: rcjones@gmu.edu. *Application contact:* Dr. Albert Torzilli, Graduate Coordinator, 703-993-1062, E-mail: atorzill@gmu.edu.

Georgia Institute of Technology, Graduate Studies and Research, College of Sciences, School of Earth and Atmospheric Sciences, Atlanta, GA 30332-0340. Offers atmospheric chemistry, aerosols and clouds (MS, PhD); dynamics of weather and climate (MS, PhD); geochemistry (MS, PhD); geophysics (MS, PhD); oceanography (MS, PhD); paleoclimate (MS, PhD); planetary science (MS, PhD); remote sensing (MS, PhD). Part-time programs available. Terminal master's awarded for partial completion of doctoral program. *Degree requirements:* For master's, thesis or alternative; for doctorate, comprehensive exam, thesis/dissertation. *Entrance requirements:* For master's, GRE, letters of recommendation; for doctorate, GRE, academic transcripts, letters of recommendation, personal statement. Additional exam requirements/recommendations for international students: Required—TOEFL (minimum score 550 paper-based; 213 computer-based; 79 iBT). *Faculty research:* Geophysics; atmospheric chemistry, aerosols and clouds; dynamics of weather and climate; geochemistry; oceanography; paleoclimate; planetary science; remote sensing.

Graduate School and University Center of the City University of New York, Graduate Studies, Program in Earth and Environmental Sciences, New York, NY 10016-4039. Offers

PhD. *Degree requirements:* For doctorate, one foreign language, comprehensive exam, thesis/dissertation. *Entrance requirements:* For doctorate, GRE General Test. Additional exam requirements/recommendations for international students: Required—TOEFL. Electronic applications accepted.

Harvard University, Cyprus International Institute for the Environment and Public Health in Association with Harvard School of Public Health, Cambridge, MA 02138. Offers environmental health (MS). *Entrance requirements:* For master's, GRE, resume, 3 letters of recommendation, BA or BS. Additional exam requirements/recommendations for international students: Required—TOEFL (minimum score 220 computer-based), IELTS (minimum score 7). Electronic applications accepted. *Expenses:* Tuition: Full-time $34,976. Required fees: $1166. Full-time tuition and fees vary according to program. *Faculty research:* Air pollution, climate change, biostatistics, sustainable development, environmental management.

Howard University, Graduate School, Department of Chemistry, Washington, DC 20059-0002. Offers analytical chemistry (MS, PhD); atmospheric (MS, PhD); biochemistry (MS, PhD); environmental (MS, PhD); inorganic chemistry (MS, PhD); organic chemistry (MS, PhD); physical chemistry (MS, PhD). Terminal master's awarded for partial completion of doctoral program. *Degree requirements:* For master's, comprehensive exam, thesis, teaching experience; for doctorate, comprehensive exam, thesis/dissertation, teaching experience. *Entrance requirements:* For master's, GRE General Test, minimum GPA of 2.7; for doctorate, GRE General Test, minimum GPA of 3.0. Additional exam requirements/recommendations for international students: Required—TOEFL. Electronic applications accepted. *Faculty research:* Synthetic organics, materials, natural products, mass spectrometry.

Humboldt State University, Academic Programs, College of Natural Resources and Sciences, Programs in Environmental Systems, Arcata, CA 95521-8299. Offers environmental systems (MS), including energy, environment and society, environmental resources engineering, geology, math modeling. *Students:* 35 full-time (12 women), 6 part-time (0 women); includes 4 minority (1 Asian, non-Hispanic/Latino; 3 Hispanic/Latino), 2 international. Average age 28. 72 applicants, 29% accepted, 15 enrolled. In 2010, 21 master's awarded. *Degree requirements:* For master's, thesis. *Entrance requirements:* For master's, GRE, appropriate bachelor's degree, minimum GPA of 2.5, 3 letters of recommendation. Additional exam requirements/recommendations for international students: Required—TOEFL. *Application deadline:* For fall admission, 2/15 for domestic students; for spring admission, 10/15 for domestic students. Applications are processed on a rolling basis. Application fee: $55. Tuition and fees vary according to program. *Financial support:* Application deadline: 3/1. *Faculty research:* Mathematical modeling, international development technology, geology, environmental resources engineering. *Unit head:* Dr. Chris Dugaw, Chair, 707-826-4251, Fax: 707-826-4145, E-mail: dugaw@humboldt.edu. *Application contact:* Julie Tucker, Administrative Support, 707-826-3256, Fax: 707-826-3140, E-mail: jlt7002@humboldt.edu.

Hunter College of the City University of New York, Graduate School, School of Arts and Sciences, Department of Geography, New York, NY 10021-5085. Offers analytical geography (MA); earth system science (MA); environmental and social issues (MA); geographic information science (Certificate); geographic information systems (MA); teaching earth science (MA). Part-time and evening/weekend programs available. *Faculty:* 13 full-time (7 women), 8 part-time/adjunct (1 woman). *Students:* 2 full-time (both women), 50 part-time (23 women); includes 5 Black or African American, non-Hispanic/Latino; 4 Asian, non-Hispanic/Latino; 5 Hispanic/Latino. Average age 31. 22 applicants, 82% accepted, 12 enrolled. In 2010, 15 master's, 3 other advanced degrees awarded. *Degree requirements:* For master's, comprehensive exam or thesis. *Entrance requirements:* For master's, GRE General Test, minimum B average in major, B- overall; 18 credits of course work in geography; 2 letters of recommendation; for Certificate, minimum B average in major, B- overall. Additional exam requirements/recommendations for international students: Required—TOEFL. *Application deadline:* For fall admission, 4/1 for domestic students; for spring admission, 11/1 for domestic students. Applications are processed on a rolling basis. Application fee: $125. *Financial support:* In 2010–11, 1 fellowship (averaging $3,000 per year), 2 research assistantships (averaging $10,000 per year), 10 teaching assistantships (averaging $6,000 per year) were awarded; career-related internships or fieldwork, Federal Work-Study, institutionally sponsored loans, and unspecified assistantships also available. Financial award application deadline: 3/1. *Faculty research:* Urban geography, economic geography, geographic information science, demographic methods, climate change. *Unit head:* Prof. William Solecki, Chair, 212-772-4536, Fax: 212-772-5268, E-mail: wsolecki@hunter.cuny.edu. *Application contact:* Prof. Marianna Pavlovskaya, Graduate Adviser, 212-772-5320, Fax: 212-772-5268, E-mail: mpavlov@geo.hunter.cuny.edu.

Idaho State University, Office of Graduate Studies, College of Arts and Sciences, Department of Geosciences, Pocatello, ID 83209-8072. Offers geographic information science (MS); geology (MNS, MS); geology with emphasis in environmental geoscience (MS); geophysics/hydrology/geology (MS); geotechnology (Postbaccalaureate Certificate). Part-time programs available. *Degree requirements:* For master's, comprehensive exam, thesis, oral colloquium; for Postbaccalaureate Certificate, thesis optional, minimum 19 credits. *Entrance requirements:* For master's, GRE General Test (minimum 50th percentile in 2 sections), 3 letters of recommendation; for Postbaccalaureate Certificate, GRE General Test, 3 letters of recommendation, bachelor's degree, statement of goals. Additional exam requirements/recommendations for international students: Required—TOEFL (minimum score 550 paper-based; 213 computer-based; 80 iBT). Electronic applications accepted. *Faculty research:* Quantitative field mapping and sampling: microscopic, geochemical, and isotopic analysis of rocks, minerals and water; remote sensing, geographic information systems, and global positioning systems: environmental and watershed management; surficial and fluvial processes: landscape change; regional tectonics, structural geology; planetary geology.

Idaho State University, Office of Graduate Studies, College of Engineering, Civil and Environmental Engineering Department, Pocatello, ID 83209-8060. Offers civil engineering (MS); environmental engineering (MS); environmental science and management (MS). Part-time programs available. *Degree requirements:* For master's, comprehensive exam (for some programs), thesis optional, thesis project, 2 semesters of seminar. *Entrance requirements:* For master's, GRE. Additional exam requirements/recommendations for international students: Required—TOEFL (minimum score 550 paper-based; 213 computer-based; 80 iBT). Electronic applications accepted. *Faculty research:* Floor vibration investigations, earthquake engineering, base isolation systems and seismic risk assessment, infrastructure revitalization (building foundations and damage, bridge structures, highways, and dams), slope stability and soil erosion, pavement rehabilitation, computational fluid dynamics and flood control structures, microbial fuel cells, water treatment and water quality modeling, environmental risk assessment, biotechnology, nanotechnology.

Idaho State University, Office of Graduate Studies, Department of Interdisciplinary Studies, Pocatello, ID 83209. Offers general interdisciplinary (M Ed, MA, MNS); waste management and environmental science (MS). Part-time programs available. *Degree requirements:* For master's, comprehensive exam, thesis optional. *Entrance requirements:* For master's, GRE General Test or MAT, minimum GPA of 3.0. Additional exam requirements/recommendations for international students: Required—TOEFL (minimum score 550 paper-based; 213 computer-based; 80 iBT).

Indiana University Bloomington, School of Public and Environmental Affairs, Environmental Science Programs, Bloomington, IN 47405-7000. Offers applied ecology (MSES); energy (MSES); environmental chemistry, toxicology, and risk assessment (MSES); environmental science (PhD); specialized environmental science (MSES); water resources (MSES); JD/MSES; MSES/MS. Part-time programs available. *Faculty:* 17 full-time, 8 part-time/adjunct. *Students:* 87 full-time (49 women), 2 part-time (1 woman); includes 1 Black or African American, non-Hispanic/Latino; 1 American Indian or Alaska Native, non-Hispanic/Latino; 10 Asian, non-Hispanic/Latino; 5 Hispanic/Latino, 11 international. Average age 26. 79 applicants, 29 enrolled. In 2010, 53 master's, 10 doctorates awarded. Terminal master's awarded for partial completion of doctoral program. *Degree requirements:* For master's, thesis optional; for doctorate, comprehensive exam, thesis/dissertation. *Entrance requirements:* For master's, GRE General Test or GMAT, official transcripts, 3 letters of recommendation, resume, personal statement, departmental questions; for doctorate, GRE General Test or LSAT and TOEFL (Intl.), official transcripts, 3 letters of recommendation, resume or curriculum vitae, statement of purpose, application, application fee, residence classification (Intl.). Additional exam requirements/recommendations for international students: Required—TOEFL (minimum score 600 paper-based; 96 iBT); Recommended—IELTS (minimum score 7). *Application deadline:* For fall admission, 5/1 for domestic students, 12/1 for international students; for spring admission, 11/1 for domestic and international students. Applications are processed on a rolling basis. Application fee: $55 ($65 for international students). Electronic applications accepted. *Financial support:* Fellowships with partial tuition reimbursements, research assistantships with partial tuition reimbursements, teaching assistantships with partial tuition reimbursements, career-related internships or fieldwork, Federal Work-Study, scholarships/grants, health care benefits, and unspecified assistantships available. Financial award application deadline: 2/1; financial award applicants required to submit FAFSA. *Faculty research:* Applied ecology, bio-geo chemistry, toxicology, wetlands ecology, environmental microbiology, forest ecology, environmental chemistry. *Unit head:* Jennifer J. Forney, Director, Graduate Student Servies, 812-855-9485, Fax: 812-856-3665, E-mail: speampo@indiana.edu. *Application contact:* Audrey Whittaker, Admissions Assistant, 812-855-2840, Fax: 812-856-3665, E-mail: speaapps@indiana.edu.

See Close-Up on page 397.

Indiana University Northwest, School of Public and Environmental Affairs, Gary, IN 46408-1197. Offers criminal justice (MPA); environmental affairs (Graduate Certificate); health services administration (MPA); human services administration (MPA); nonprofit management (Graduate Certificate); public management (MPA, Graduate Certificate). *Accreditation:* NASPAA (one or more programs are accredited). Part-time programs available. *Faculty:* 5 full-time (3 women). *Students:* 9 full-time (6 women), 127 part-time (96 women); includes 96 minority (81 Black or African American, non-Hispanic/Latino; 1 American Indian or Alaska Native, non-Hispanic/Latino; 2 Asian, non-Hispanic/Latino; 10 Hispanic/Latino; 2 Two or more races, non-Hispanic/Latino). Average age 38. 43 applicants, 95% accepted, 40 enrolled. In 2010, 37 master's, 24 other advanced degrees awarded. *Entrance requirements:* For master's, GRE General Test or GMAT, letters of recommendation. *Application deadline:* For fall admission, 8/15 priority date for domestic students. Applications are processed on a rolling basis. Application fee: $25. *Financial support:* Career-related internships or fieldwork, Federal Work-Study, and tuition waivers (partial) available. Support available to part-time students. Financial award application deadline: 3/1. *Faculty research:* Employment in income security policies, evidence in criminal justice, equal employment law, social welfare policy and welfare reform, public finance in developing countries. *Unit head:* George Assibey-Mensah, Interim Dean/Division Director, 219-980-6695, Fax: 219-980-6737. *Application contact:* Sandra Hall Smith, Secretary, 219-980-6695, Fax: 219-980-6737, E-mail: shsmith@iun.edu.

Instituto Tecnologico de Santo Domingo, Graduate School, Area of Basic And Environmental Sciences, Santo Domingo, Dominican Republic. Offers environmental science (M En S), including environmental education, environmental management, marine resources, natural resources management; mathematics (MS, PhD); renewable energy technology (MS, Certificate).

Instituto Tecnológico y de Estudios Superiores de Monterrey, Campus Ciudad de México, Virtual University Division, Ciudad de Mexico, Mexico. Offers administration of information technologies (MA); computer sciences (MA); education (MA, PhD); educational technology (MA); environmental engineering (MA); environmental systems (MA); humanistic studies (MA); industrial engineering (MA); international business for Latin America (MA); quality systems (MA); quality systems and productivity (MA). Part-time and evening/weekend programs available. Postbaccalaureate distance learning degree programs offered (minimal on-campus study). *Entrance requirements:* For master's and doctorate, Instituto entrance exam. Additional exam requirements/recommendations for international students: Required—TOEFL.

Inter American University of Puerto Rico, San Germán Campus, Graduate Studies Center, Program in Environmental Sciences, San Germán, PR 00683-5008. Offers environmental biology (MS); environmental chemistry (MS); water analysis (MS). Part-time and evening/weekend programs available. *Degree requirements:* For master's, comprehensive exam, thesis. *Entrance requirements:* For master's, GRE General Test or EXADEP, minimum GPA of 3.0. *Expenses:* Tuition: Part-time $202 per credit. Required fees: $258 per semester. *Faculty research:* Environmental biology, environmental chemistry, water resources and unit operations.

Iowa State University of Science and Technology, Graduate College, College of Liberal Arts and Sciences, Department of Geological and Atmospheric Sciences, Ames, IA 50011. Offers earth science (MS, PhD); environmental science (MS, PhD); geology (MS, PhD); meteorology (MS, PhD). *Faculty:* 20 full-time (2 women). *Students:* 33 full-time (8 women), 8 part-time (3 women); includes 1 Asian, non-Hispanic/Latino, 3 international. 45 applicants, 49% accepted, 9 enrolled. In 2010, 9 master's, 5 doctorates awarded. *Degree requirements:* For master's, thesis (for some programs); for doctorate, thesis/dissertation. *Entrance requirements:* For master's and doctorate, GRE General Test. Additional exam requirements/recommendations for international students: Required—TOEFL (minimum score 550 paper-based; 79 iBT), IELTS (minimum score 6.5). *Application deadline:* For fall admission, 1/1 priority date for domestic students. Applications are processed on a rolling basis. Application fee: $40 ($90 for international students). Electronic applications accepted. *Financial support:* In 2010–11, 23 research assistantships with full and partial tuition reimbursements (averaging $12,780 per year), 8 teaching assistantships with full and partial tuition reimbursements (averaging $6,806 per year) were awarded; fellowships, scholarships/grants, health care benefits, and unspecified assistantships also available. *Unit head:* Dr. Carl E. Jacobson, Chair, 515-294-4477. *Application contact:* Dr. Carl E. Jacobson, Chair, 515-294-4477.

Iowa State University of Science and Technology, Graduate College, Interdisciplinary Programs, Program in Environmental Sciences, Ames, IA 50011. Offers MS, PhD. *Students:* 16 full-time (8 women), 14 part-time (9 women); includes 4 Black or African American, non-Hispanic/Latino; 1 American Indian or Alaska Native, non-Hispanic/Latino, 12 international. In 2010, 7 master's, 4 doctorates awarded. *Degree requirements:* For master's, thesis; for doctorate, thesis/dissertation. *Entrance requirements:* For master's and doctorate, GRE General Test. Additional exam requirements/recommendations for international students: Required—TOEFL (minimum score 550 paper-based; 79 iBT), IELTS (minimum score 6.5). *Application deadline:* For fall admission, 2/1 for domestic and international students; for spring admission, 6/1 for domestic and international students. Applications are processed on a rolling basis. Application fee: $40 ($90 for international students). Electronic applications accepted. *Financial support:* In 2010–11, 13 research assistantships with partial tuition reimbursements (averaging $16,036 per year), 1 teaching assistantship with partial tuition reimbursement (averaging $21,825 per year) were awarded; scholarships/grants, health care benefits, and unspecified assistantships also available. *Unit head:* Dr. John Downing, Supervisory Committee Chair, 515-294-6518, Fax: 515-294-9573. *Application contact:* Charles Sauer, Information Contact, 515-294-6518, E-mail: eeboffice@iastate.edu.

Jackson State University, Graduate School, College of Science, Engineering and Technology, Department of Biology, Jackson, MS 39217. Offers environmental science (MS, PhD). Part-time and evening/weekend programs available. *Faculty:* 14 full-time (2 women). *Students:* 24 full-time (16 women), 26 part-time (17 women); includes 39 Black or African American, non-Hispanic/Latino, 4 international. Average age 37. In 2010, 13 master's, 7 doctorates

Environmental Sciences

Jackson State University (continued)

awarded. *Degree requirements:* For master's, comprehensive exam, thesis (alternative accepted for MST); for doctorate, comprehensive exam, thesis/dissertation. *Entrance requirements:* For master's, GRE General Test; for doctorate, MAT. Additional exam requirements/recommendations for international students: Required—TOEFL (minimum score 520 paper-based; 195 computer-based; 67 iBT). *Application deadline:* For fall admission, 3/1 priority date for domestic students, 3/1 for international students; for spring admission, 10/15 for domestic students, 10/1 for international students. Applications are processed on a rolling basis. Application fee: $25. *Expenses:* Tuition, state resident: full-time $5050; part-time $281 per credit hour. Tuition, nonresident: full-time $12,380; part-time $689 per credit hour. *Financial support:* Career-related internships or fieldwork, Federal Work-Study, scholarships/grants, and unspecified assistantships available. Support available to part-time students. Financial award application deadline: 3/1; financial award applicants required to submit FAFSA. *Faculty research:* Comparative studies on the carbohydrate composition of marine macroalgae, host-parasite relationship between the spruce budworm and entomepathogen fungus. *Unit head:* Dr. Gregorio Begonia, Acting Chair, 601-979-2586, Fax: 601-979-5853, E-mail: gregorieo.begonia@jsums.edu. *Application contact:* Sharlene Wilson, Director of Graduate Admissions, 601-979-2455, Fax: 601-979-4325, E-mail: sharlene.f.wilson@jsums.edu.

The Johns Hopkins University, Zanvyl Krieger School of Arts and Sciences, Advanced Academic Programs, Program in Environmental Sciences and Policy, Baltimore, MD 21218-2699. Offers MS. Part-time and evening/weekend programs available. Postbaccalaureate distance learning degree programs offered (minimal on-campus study). *Faculty:* 1 (woman) full-time, 37 part-time/adjunct (3 women). *Students:* 20 full-time (10 women), 224 part-time (134 women); includes 28 minority (10 Black or African American, non-Hispanic/Latino; 9 Asian, non-Hispanic/Latino; 3 Hispanic/Latino; 6 Two or more races, non-Hispanic/Latino), 11 international. Average age 31. 126 applicants, 63% accepted, 55 enrolled. In 2010, 81 master's awarded. *Degree requirements:* For master's, thesis (for some programs). *Entrance requirements:* For master's, minimum GPA of 3.0, coursework in chemistry and calculus. Additional exam requirements/recommendations for international students: Required—TOEFL (minimum score 250 computer-based). *Application deadline:* For fall admission, 5/31 priority date for domestic students, 4/30 priority date for international students; for spring admission, 10/31 priority date for domestic and international students. Application fee: $75. *Financial support:* Applicants required to submit FAFSA. *Unit head:* Dr. Eileen McGurty, Associate Program Chair, 410-516-7049, E-mail: emgurty@jhu.edu. *Application contact:* Valana M. McMickens, Admissions Manager, 202-452-1941, Fax: 202-452-1970, E-mail: aapadmissions@jhu.edu.

Kentucky State University, College of Mathematics, Sciences, Technology and Health, Frankfort, KY 40601. Offers aquaculture (MS); computer science (MS), including computer science theory, information assurance, information technology; environmental science (MS). Part-time and evening/weekend programs available. *Faculty:* 10 full-time (1 woman), 1 part-time/adjunct (0 women). *Students:* 34 full-time (16 women), 32 part-time (6 women); includes 22 minority (15 Black or African American, non-Hispanic/Latino; 3 Asian, non-Hispanic/Latino; 1 Hispanic/Latino; 1 Native Hawaiian or other Pacific Islander, non-Hispanic/Latino; 2 Two or more races, non-Hispanic/Latino), 12 international. Average age 34. 55 applicants, 51% accepted, 18 enrolled. In 2010, 16 master's awarded. *Degree requirements:* For master's, comprehensive exam, thesis optional. *Entrance requirements:* For master's, GRE, GMAT. Additional exam requirements/recommendations for international students: Required—TOEFL (minimum score 525 paper-based; 173 computer-based). *Application deadline:* Applications are processed on a rolling basis. Application fee: $30 ($100 for international students). Electronic applications accepted. *Expenses:* Tuition, state resident: full-time $5886; part-time $352 per credit hour. Tuition, nonresident: full-time $9054; part-time $528 per credit hour. Required fees: $450; $26 per credit hour. *Financial support:* In 2010–11, 41 students received support, including 18 research assistantships (averaging $11,378 per year); career-related internships or fieldwork, scholarships/grants, tuition waivers (partial), and unspecified assistantships also available. Financial award application deadline: 4/15; financial award applicants required to submit FAFSA. *Unit head:* Dr. Charles Bennett, Dean, 502-597-6926, E-mail: charles.bennett@kysu.edu. *Application contact:* Dr. Titilayo Ufomata, Acting Director of Graduate Studies, 502-597-6443, E-mail: titilayo.ufomata@kysu.edu.

Laurentian University, School of Graduate Studies and Research, Programme in Chemistry and Biochemistry, Sudbury, ON P3E 2C6, Canada. Offers analytical chemistry (M Sc); biochemistry (M Sc); environmental chemistry (M Sc); organic chemistry (M Sc); physical/theoretical chemistry (M Sc). Part-time programs available. *Degree requirements:* For master's, thesis or alternative. *Entrance requirements:* For master's, honors degree with minimum second class. *Faculty research:* Cell cycle checkpoints, kinetic modeling, toxicology to metal stress, quantum chemistry, biogeochemistry metal speciation.

Lehigh University, College of Arts and Sciences, Department of Earth and Environmental Sciences, Bethlehem, PA 18015. Offers MS, PhD. *Faculty:* 14 full-time (1 woman), 1 (woman) part-time/adjunct. *Students:* 26 full-time (10 women), 2 part-time (1 woman), 4 international. Average age 27. 57 applicants, 23% accepted, 10 enrolled. In 2010, 10 master's, 1 doctorate awarded. Terminal master's awarded for partial completion of doctoral program. *Degree requirements:* For master's, thesis; for doctorate, thesis/dissertation. *Entrance requirements:* For master's and doctorate, GRE General Test, transcripts, recommendation letters, research statement, faculty advocates. Additional exam requirements/recommendations for international students: Required—TOEFL (minimum score 85 iBT). *Application deadline:* For fall admission, 1/15 for domestic and international students. Applications are processed on a rolling basis. Application fee: $75. Electronic applications accepted. *Financial support:* In 2010–11, 13 students received support, including 3 fellowships with full tuition reimbursements available (averaging $15,400 per year), 12 research assistantships with full tuition reimbursements available (averaging $15,400 per year), 10 teaching assistantships with full tuition reimbursements available (averaging $15,400 per year); career-related internships or fieldwork, Federal Work-Study, institutionally sponsored loans, scholarships/grants, tuition waivers (full and partial), and unspecified assistantships also available. Support available to part-time students. Financial award application deadline: 1/15. *Faculty research:* Tectonics, surficial processes, ecology, environmental change. Total annual research expenditures: $1.1 million. *Unit head:* Dr. Frank J. Pazzaglia, Chairman, 610-758-3667, Fax: 610-758-3677, E-mail: fjp3@lehigh.edu. *Application contact:* Dr. Zicheng Yu, Graduate Coordinator, 610-758-6751, Fax: 610-758-3677, E-mail: ziy2@lehigh.edu.

Louisiana State University and Agricultural and Mechanical College, Graduate School, College of Agriculture, School of Renewable Natural Resources, Baton Rouge, LA 70803. Offers fisheries (MS); forestry (MS, PhD); wildlife (MS); wildlife and fisheries science (PhD). *Faculty:* 33 full-time (5 women). *Students:* 65 full-time (16 women), 8 part-time (3 women); includes 2 Hispanic/Latino, 22 international. Average age 29. 28 applicants, 39% accepted, 8 enrolled. In 2010, 17 master's, 4 doctorates awarded. *Degree requirements:* For master's, thesis; for doctorate, thesis/dissertation. *Entrance requirements:* For master's, GRE General Test, minimum GPA of 3.0; for doctorate, GRE General Test, MS, minimum GPA of 3.0. Additional exam requirements/recommendations for international students: Required—TOEFL (minimum score 550 paper-based; 213 computer-based; 79 iBT), IELTS (minimum score 6.5). *Application deadline:* For fall admission, 1/25 priority date for domestic students, 5/15 for international students; for spring admission, 10/15 for international students. Applications are processed on a rolling basis. Application fee: $50 ($70 for international students). Electronic applications accepted. *Financial support:* In 2010–11, 69 students received support, including 7 fellowships (averaging $36,514 per year), 60 research assistantships with partial tuition reimbursements available (averaging $19,070 per year); Federal Work-Study, institutionally sponsored loans, scholarships/grants, health care benefits, tuition waivers (full and partial), and unspecified assistantships also available. Financial award application deadline: 4/15; financial award applicants required to submit FAFSA. *Faculty research:* Forest biology and management, aquaculture, fisheries biology and ecology, upland and wetlands wildlife. Total annual research expenditures: $3,080. *Unit head:* Dr. Allen Rutherford, Director, 225-578-4131, Fax: 225-578-4227, E-mail: druther@lsu.edu. *Application contact:* Dr. William Kelso, Coordinator of Graduate Studies, 225-578-4176, Fax: 225-578-4227, E-mail: wkelso@lsu.edu.

Louisiana State University and Agricultural and Mechanical College, Graduate School, School of the Coast and Environment, Department of Environmental Sciences, Baton Rouge, LA 70803. Offers environmental planning and management (MS); environmental toxicology (MS). *Faculty:* 9 full-time (3 women). *Students:* 26 full-time (17 women), 7 part-time (2 women); includes 5 Black or African American, non-Hispanic/Latino; 2 Asian, non-Hispanic/Latino, 6 international. Average age 26. 19 applicants, 84% accepted, 10 enrolled. In 2010, 6 master's awarded. *Degree requirements:* For master's, thesis (for some programs). *Entrance requirements:* For master's, GRE General Test, minimum GPA of 3.0. Additional exam requirements/recommendations for international students: Required—TOEFL (minimum score 550 paper-based; 213 computer-based; 79 iBT) or IELTS (minimum score 6.5). *Application deadline:* For fall admission, 1/25 priority date for domestic students, 5/15 for international students; for spring admission, 10/15 for international students. Applications are processed on a rolling basis. Application fee: $50 ($70 for international students). Electronic applications accepted. *Financial support:* In 2010–11, 27 students received support, including 1 fellowship with full and partial tuition reimbursement available (averaging $17,831 per year), 19 research assistantships with full and partial tuition reimbursements available (averaging $14,842 per year), 1 teaching assistantship with full and partial tuition reimbursement available (averaging $15,740 per year); career-related internships or fieldwork, Federal Work-Study, institutionally sponsored loans, scholarships/grants, health care benefits, and unspecified assistantships also available. Support available to part-time students. Financial award applicants required to submit FAFSA. *Faculty research:* Environmental toxicology, environmental policy and law, microbial ecology, bioremediation, genetic toxicology. Total annual research expenditures: $921,141. *Unit head:* Dr. Ed Laws, Chair, 225-578-8521, Fax: 225-578-4286, E-mail: edlaws@lsu.edu. *Application contact:* Charlotte G. St. Romain, Academic Coordinator, 225-578-8522, Fax: 225-578-4286, E-mail: cstrom4@lsu.edu.

Loyola Marymount University, College of Science and Engineering, Department of Civil Engineering and Environmental Science, Program in Environmental Science, Los Angeles, CA 90045. Offers MS. Part-time programs available. *Faculty:* 6 full-time (1 woman), 4 part-time/adjunct (0 women). *Students:* 10 full-time (6 women), 23 part-time (13 women); includes 2 Black or African American, non-Hispanic/Latino; 8 Asian, non-Hispanic/Latino; 5 Hispanic/Latino, 2 international. Average age 29. 25 applicants, 92% accepted, 16 enrolled. In 2010, 2 master's awarded. *Degree requirements:* For master's, comprehensive exam, thesis or alternative. *Entrance requirements:* For master's, 2 letters of recommendation; BS or undergraduate engineering degree; 3 semester hours of general chemistry; course work in mathematics through one year of college calculus; 12 semester hours or 4 courses in science including biology, microbiology, chemistry, or physics. Additional exam requirements/recommendations for international students: Required—TOEFL (minimum score 550 paper-based; 213 computer-based; 80 iBT). *Application deadline:* Applications are processed on a rolling basis. Application fee: $50. Electronic applications accepted. *Financial support:* In 2010–11, 7 students received support. Scholarships/grants and unspecified assistantships available. Support available to part-time students. Financial award application deadline: 6/1; financial award applicants required to submit FAFSA. Total annual research expenditures: $6,004. *Unit head:* Prof. Joe J. Reichenberger, Graduate Director, 310-338-2830, E-mail: jreichenberger@lmu.edu. *Application contact:* Chake H. Kouyoumjian, Associate Dean of Graduate Studies, 310-338-2721, Fax: 310-338-6086, E-mail: ckouyoum@lmu.edu.

Marshall University, Academic Affairs Division, College of Information Technology and Engineering, Division of Applied Science and Technology, Program in Environmental Science, Huntington, WV 25755. Offers MS. Part-time and evening/weekend programs available. *Students:* 17 full-time (3 women), 14 part-time (6 women); includes 1 Black or African American, non-Hispanic/Latino, 5 international. Average age 31. In 2010, 13 master's awarded. *Degree requirements:* For master's, final project, oral exam. *Entrance requirements:* For master's, GRE General Test or MAT, minimum GPA of 2.5, course work in calculus. Application fee: $40. *Financial support:* Tuition waivers (full) available. Support available to part-time students. Financial award application deadline: 8/1; financial award applicants required to submit FAFSA. *Unit head:* Dr. D. Scott Simonton, Associate Professor, 304-746-2045, E-mail: simonton@marshall.edu. *Application contact:* Information Contact, 304-746-1900, Fax: 304-746-1902, E-mail: services@marshall.edu.

Massachusetts Institute of Technology, School of Engineering, Department of Civil and Environmental Engineering, Cambridge, MA 02139. Offers biological oceanography (PhD, Sc D); chemical oceanography (PhD, Sc D); civil and environmental engineering (M Eng, SM, PhD, Sc D); civil and environmental systems (PhD, Sc D); civil engineering (PhD, Sc D, CE); coastal engineering (PhD, Sc D); construction engineering and management (PhD, Sc D); environmental biology (PhD, Sc D); environmental chemistry (PhD, Sc D); environmental engineering (PhD, Sc D); environmental fluid mechanics (PhD, Sc D); geotechnical and geoenvironmental engineering (PhD, Sc D); hydrology (PhD, Sc D); information technology (PhD, Sc D); oceanographic engineering (PhD, Sc D); structures and materials (PhD, Sc D); transportation (PhD, Sc D); SM/MBA. *Faculty:* 36 full-time (6 women). *Students:* 181 full-time (56 women); includes 27 minority (3 Black or African American, non-Hispanic/Latino; 10 Asian, non-Hispanic/Latino; 10 Hispanic/Latino; 4 Two or more races, non-Hispanic/Latino), 93 international. Average age 26. 525 applicants, 29% accepted, 74 enrolled. In 2010, 85 master's, 18 doctorates, 2 other advanced degrees awarded. *Degree requirements:* For master's and CE, thesis; for doctorate, comprehensive exam, thesis/dissertation. *Entrance requirements:* For master's and doctorate, GRE General Test. Additional exam requirements/recommendations for international students: Required—TOEFL (minimum score 577 paper-based; 233 computer-based; 90 iBT), IELTS (minimum score 7). *Application deadline:* For fall admission, 1/2 for domestic and international students. Application fee: $75. Electronic applications accepted. *Expenses:* Tuition: Full-time $38,940; part-time $605 per unit. Required fees: $272. *Financial support:* In 2010–11, 146 students received support, including 50 fellowships with tuition reimbursements available (averaging $21,808 per year), 90 research assistantships with tuition reimbursements available (averaging $28,452 per year), 20 teaching assistantships with tuition reimbursements available (averaging $27,842 per year); career-related internships or fieldwork, Federal Work-Study, institutionally sponsored loans, scholarships/grants, health care benefits, and unspecified assistantships also available. *Faculty research:* Environmental chemistry; environmental microbiology; environmental fluid mechanics and coastal engineering; geotechnical engineering and geomechanics; hydrology and hydroclimatology; mechanics of materials and structures; operations research/supply chain; transportation. Total annual research expenditures: $19.5 million. *Unit head:* Prof. Andrew Whittle, Department Head, 617-253-7101. *Application contact:* Patricia Glidden, Graduate Admissions Coordinator, 617-253-7119, Fax: 617-258-6775, E-mail: cee-admissions@mit.edu.

McNeese State University, Doré School of Graduate Studies, College of Science, Department of Agricultural Sciences, Program in Environmental and Chemical Sciences, Lake Charles, LA 70609. Offers agricultural sciences (MS); environmental science (MS). Evening/weekend programs available. *Faculty:* 12 full-time (0 women). *Students:* 21 full-time (9 women), 13 part-time (8 women); includes 2 minority (1 Black or African American, non-Hispanic/Latino; 1 American Indian or Alaska Native, non-Hispanic/Latino), 2 international. In 2010, 9 master's awarded. *Degree requirements:* For master's, comprehensive exam, thesis or alternative. *Entrance requirements:* For master's, GRE. *Application deadline:* For fall admission, 5/15 priority date for domestic and international students; for spring admission, 10/15 priority date

for domestic and international students. Applications are processed on a rolling basis. Application fee: $20 ($30 for international students). Tuition and fees vary according to course load. *Financial support:* Application deadline: 5/1. *Unit head:* Dr. Bruce C. Wyman, Coordinator, 337-475-5669, Fax: 337-475-5677, E-mail: wyman@mcneese.edu. *Application contact:* Dr. Bruce C. Wyman, Coordinator, 337-475-5669, Fax: 337-475-5677, E-mail: wyman@mcneese.edu.

Memorial University of Newfoundland, School of Graduate Studies, Interdisciplinary Program in Environmental Science, St. John's, NL A1C 5S7, Canada. Offers M Env Sc, M Sc. Part-time programs available. *Degree requirements:* For master's, thesis (M Sc), project (M Env Sci). *Entrance requirements:* For master's, honors B Sc or 2nd class B Eng. Electronic applications accepted. *Faculty research:* Earth and ocean systems, environmental chemistry and toxicology, environmental engineering.

Mercer University, Graduate Studies, Macon Campus, School of Engineering, Macon, GA 31207-0003. Offers biomedical engineering (MSE); computer engineering (MSE); electrical engineering (MSE); engineering management (MSE); environmental engineering (MSE); environmental systems (MS); mechanical engineering (MSE); software engineering (MSE); software systems (MS); technical communications management (MS); technical management (MS). Part-time and evening/weekend programs available. Postbaccalaureate distance learning degree programs offered (no on-campus study). *Faculty:* 18 full-time (4 women), 1 part-time/adjunct (0 women). *Students:* 11 full-time (2 women), 100 part-time (22 women); includes 26 minority (13 Black or African American, non-Hispanic/Latino; 12 Asian, non-Hispanic/Latino; 1 Hispanic/Latino), 3 international. Average age 32. In 2010, 46 master's awarded. *Degree requirements:* For master's, thesis or alternative. *Entrance requirements:* For master's, minimum undergraduate GPA of 3.0. Additional exam requirements/recommendations for international students: Required—TOEFL. *Application deadline:* For fall admission, 7/1 for domestic students; for spring admission, 11/15 for domestic students. Applications are processed on a rolling basis. Application fee: $35 ($50 for international students). Electronic applications accepted. *Expenses:* Contact institution. *Financial support:* Federal Work-Study available. *Unit head:* Dr. Wade H. Shaw, Dean, 478-301-2459, Fax: 478-301-5593, E-mail: shaw_wh@mercer.edu. *Application contact:* Greg Lofton, Graduate Program Coordinator, 478-301-5480, Fax: 478-301-5434, E-mail: lofton_g@mercer.edu.

Miami University, Graduate School, Institute of Environmental Sciences, Oxford, OH 45056. Offers M En. Part-time programs available. *Students:* 53 full-time (33 women), 6 part-time (3 women); includes 4 minority (1 Black or African American, non-Hispanic/Latino; 1 American Indian or Alaska Native, non-Hispanic/Latino; 1 Asian, non-Hispanic/Latino; 1 Two or more races, non-Hispanic/Latino), 5 international. Average age 29. In 2010, 14 master's awarded. *Entrance requirements:* For master's, minimum undergraduate GPA of 3.0 during previous 2 years or 2.75 overall. Additional exam requirements/recommendations for international students: Required—TOEFL. Application fee: $50. *Expenses:* Tuition, state resident: full-time $11,616; part-time $484 per credit hour. Tuition, nonresident: full-time $25,656; part-time $1069 per credit hour. Required fees: $528. *Financial support:* Fellowships with tuition reimbursements, research assistantships, teaching assistantships, career-related internships or fieldwork, Federal Work-Study, health care benefits, tuition waivers (full), and unspecified assistantships available. Financial award application deadline: 3/1; financial award applicants required to submit FAFSA. *Unit head:* Dr. Doug Miekle, Co-Director, 513-529-5811, Fax: 513-529-5814, E-mail: ies@muohio.edu. *Application contact:* Dr. Doug Miekle, Co-Director, 513-529-5811, Fax: 513-529-5814, E-mail: ies@muohio.edu.

Michigan State University, The Graduate School, College of Natural Science, Department of Geological Sciences, East Lansing, MI 48824. Offers environmental geosciences (MS, PhD); environmental geosciences-environmental toxicology (PhD); geological sciences (MS, PhD). *Degree requirements:* For master's, thesis (for those without prior thesis work); for doctorate, thesis/dissertation. *Entrance requirements:* For master's, GRE General Test, minimum GPA of 3.0, course work in geoscience, 3 letters of recommendation; for doctorate, GRE General Test, 3 letters of recommendation. Additional exam requirements/recommendations for international students: Required—TOEFL (minimum score 550 paper-based; 213 computer-based), Michigan State University ELT (minimum score 85), Michigan English Language Assessment Battery (minimum score 83). Electronic applications accepted. *Faculty research:* Water in the environment, global and biological change, crystal dynamics.

Minnesota State University Mankato, College of Graduate Studies, College of Science, Engineering and Technology, Department of Biological Sciences, Program in Environmental Sciences, Mankato, MN 56001. Offers MS. *Students:* 4 full-time (3 women), 9 part-time (2 women). *Degree requirements:* For master's, one foreign language, comprehensive exam, thesis or alternative. *Entrance requirements:* For master's, minimum GPA of 3.0 during previous 2 years. Additional exam requirements/recommendations for international students: Required—TOEFL. *Application deadline:* For fall admission, 7/1 priority date for domestic students; for spring admission, 11/1 for domestic students. Applications are processed on a rolling basis. Application fee: $40. Electronic applications accepted. *Financial support:* Research assistantships with partial tuition reimbursements, teaching assistantships with partial tuition reimbursements, career-related internships or fieldwork, Federal Work-Study, institutionally sponsored loans, and unspecified assistantships available. Financial award application deadline: 3/15; financial award applicants required to submit FAFSA. *Unit head:* Dr. Beth Proctor, Graduate Coordinator, 507-389-5697. *Application contact:* 507-389-2321, E-mail: grad@mnsu.edu.

Montana State University, College of Graduate Studies, College of Agriculture, Department of Land Resources and Environmental Sciences, Bozeman, MT 59717. Offers land rehabilitation (interdisciplinary) (MS); land resources and environmental sciences (MS), including land rehabilitation (interdisciplinary), land resources and environmental sciences. Part-time programs available. *Faculty:* 24 full-time (6 women), 1 part-time/adjunct (0 women). *Students:* 7 full-time (3 women), 38 part-time (14 women); includes 3 minority (2 American Indian or Alaska Native, non-Hispanic/Latino; 1 Hispanic/Latino), 2 international. Average age 32. 21 applicants, 24% accepted, 4 enrolled. In 2010, 7 master's awarded. *Degree requirements:* For master's, comprehensive exam. *Entrance requirements:* For master's, GRE General Test. Additional exam requirements/recommendations for international students: Required—TOEFL (minimum score 550 paper-based; 213 computer-based). *Application deadline:* For fall admission, 7/15 priority date for domestic students, 5/15 priority date for international students; for spring admission, 12/1 priority date for domestic students, 10/1 priority date for international students. Applications are processed on a rolling basis. Application fee: $30. Electronic applications accepted. *Expenses:* Tuition, state resident: full-time $5553.90. Tuition, nonresident: full-time $14,646. Required fees: $1233. *Financial support:* In 2010–11, 5 fellowships with partial tuition reimbursements (averaging $25,000 per year), 38 research assistantships with full and partial tuition reimbursements (averaging $17,000 per year), 15 teaching assistantships with full and partial tuition reimbursements (averaging $2,000 per year) were awarded; scholarships/grants, health care benefits, tuition waivers (partial), and unspecified assistantships also available. Financial award application deadline: 3/1; financial award applicants required to submit FAFSA. *Faculty research:* Soil nutrient management and plant nutrition, isotope biogeochemistry of soils, biodegradation of hydrocarbons in soils and natural waters, remote sensing, GIS systems, managed and natural ecosystems, microbial and metabolic diversity in geothermally heated soils, integrated management of weeds, diversified cropping systems, insect behavior and ecology, river ecology, microbial biogeochemistry, weed ecology. Total annual research expenditures: $5.5 million. *Unit head:* Dr. Tracy M. Sterling, Head, 406-994-7060, Fax: 406-994-3933, E-mail: tracy.sterling@montana.edu. *Application contact:* Dr. Carl A. Fox, Vice Provost for Graduate Education, 406-994-4145, Fax: 406-994-7433, E-mail: gradstudy@montana.edu.

Montana State University, College of Graduate Studies, College of Letters and Science, Department of Ecology, Bozeman, MT 59717. Offers ecological and environmental statistics (MS); ecology and environmental sciences (PhD); fish and wildlife biology (PhD); fish and wildlife management (MS). Part-time programs available. *Faculty:* 12 full-time (2 women), 2 part-time/adjunct (0 women). *Students:* 3 full-time (2 women), 46 part-time (16 women). Average age 31. 11 applicants, 27% accepted, 3 enrolled. In 2010, 3 master's, 1 doctorate awarded. *Degree requirements:* For master's, comprehensive exam, thesis (for some programs); for doctorate, comprehensive exam, thesis/dissertation. *Entrance requirements:* For master's and doctorate, GRE, minimum GPA of 3.0, letters of recommendation, essay. Additional exam requirements/recommendations for international students: Required—TOEFL (minimum score 550 paper-based; 213 computer-based). *Application deadline:* For fall admission, 7/15 priority date for domestic students, 5/15 priority date for international students; for spring admission, 12/1 priority date for domestic students, 10/1 priority date for international students. Applications are processed on a rolling basis. Application fee: $30. Electronic applications accepted. *Expenses:* Tuition, state resident: full-time $5553.90. Tuition, nonresident: full-time $14,646. Required fees: $1233. *Financial support:* In 2010–11, 46 students received support, including 1 fellowship with full and partial tuition reimbursement available (averaging $19,200 per year), 32 research assistantships with full and partial tuition reimbursements available (averaging $18,000 per year), 16 teaching assistantships with full tuition reimbursements available (averaging $10,862 per year); career-related internships or fieldwork, institutionally sponsored loans, scholarships/grants, traineeships, health care benefits, tuition waivers (partial), and unspecified assistantships also available. Support available to part-time students. Financial award application deadline: 3/1; financial award applicants required to submit FAFSA. *Faculty research:* Community ecology, population ecology, land-use effects, management and conservation, environmental modeling. Total annual research expenditures: $2.6 million. *Unit head:* Dr. David Roberts, Head, 406-994-4548, Fax: 406-994-3190, E-mail: droberts@montana.edu. *Application contact:* Dr. Carl A. Fox, Vice Provost for Graduate Education, 406-994-4145, Fax: 406-994-7433, E-mail: gradstudy@montana.edu.

Montclair State University, The Graduate School, College of Science and Mathematics, Department of Earth and Environmental Studies, Montclair, NJ 07043-1624. Offers earth science (Certificate); environmental management (MA, PhD); environmental studies (MS), including environmental education, environmental management, environmental science; geographic information science (Certificate); geoscience (MS), including geoscience. Part-time and evening/weekend programs available. *Faculty:* 16 full-time (2 women), 20 part-time/adjunct (7 women). *Students:* 39 full-time (19 women), 59 part-time (29 women); includes 3 Black or African American, non-Hispanic/Latino; 1 Asian, non-Hispanic/Latino; 4 Hispanic/Latino, 17 international. Average age 34. 43 applicants, 65% accepted, 21 enrolled. In 2010, 23 master's, 1 doctorate, 2 other advanced degrees awarded. *Degree requirements:* For master's, comprehensive exam, thesis or alternative; for doctorate, thesis/dissertation. *Entrance requirements:* For master's, GRE General Test, 2 letters of recommendation; for doctorate, GRE General Test, 3 letters of recommendation. Additional exam requirements/recommendations for international students: Required—TOEFL (minimum score: 83 iBT) or IELTS. *Application deadline:* For fall admission, 6/1 for international students; for spring admission, 10/1 for international students. Applications are processed on a rolling basis. Application fee: $60. Electronic applications accepted. *Expenses:* Tuition, state resident: part-time $501.34 per credit. Tuition, nonresident: part-time $773.88 per credit. Required fees: $71.15 per credit. *Financial support:* In 2010–11, 3 fellowships (averaging $15,000 per year), 9 research assistantships with full tuition reimbursements (averaging $7,000 per year), 13 teaching assistantships with full tuition reimbursements (averaging $15,000 per year) were awarded; Federal Work-Study, scholarships/grants, and unspecified assistantships also available. Support available to part-time students. Financial award application deadline: 3/1; financial award applicants required to submit FAFSA. *Faculty research:* Antarctica, carbon pools, contaminated sediments, wetlands. Total annual research expenditures: $712,648. *Unit head:* Dr. Matthew Gorring, Chairperson, 973-655-5409. *Application contact:* Amy Aiello, Director of Graduate Admissions and Operations, 973-655-5147, Fax: 973-655-7869, E-mail: graduate.school@montclair.edu.

Murray State University, College of Health Sciences and Human Services, Program in Occupational Safety and Health, Murray, KY 42071. Offers environmental science (MS); industrial hygiene (MS); safety management (MS). *Accreditation:* ABET. Part-time programs available. *Degree requirements:* For master's, comprehensive exam, thesis optional, professional internship. Electronic applications accepted. *Faculty research:* Light effects on plant growth, ergonomics, toxic effects of pets' pesticides, traffic safety.

New Jersey Institute of Technology, Office of Graduate Studies, College of Science and Liberal Arts, Department of Chemistry and Environmental Science, Program in Environmental Science, Newark, NJ 07102. Offers MS, PhD. Part-time and evening/weekend programs available. *Students:* 16 full-time (11 women), 20 part-time (9 women); includes 3 Black or African American, non-Hispanic/Latino; 1 American Indian or Alaska Native, non-Hispanic/Latino; 3 Asian, non-Hispanic/Latino, 13 international. Average age 32. 37 applicants, 43% accepted, 10 enrolled. In 2010, 16 master's, 3 doctorates awarded. *Degree requirements:* For doctorate, thesis/dissertation. *Entrance requirements:* For master's, GRE General Test; for doctorate, GRE General Test, minimum graduate GPA of 3.5. Additional exam requirements/recommendations for international students: Required—TOEFL (minimum score 550 paper-based; 213 computer-based; 79 iBT). *Application deadline:* For fall admission, 6/5 priority date for domestic students; for spring admission, 11/15 for domestic and international students. Applications are processed on a rolling basis. Application fee: $65. Electronic applications accepted. *Expenses:* Tuition, state resident: full-time $14,724; part-time $818 per credit. Tuition, nonresident: full-time $20,304; part-time $1128 per credit. Required fees: $2272; $209 per credit. $103 per semester. One-time fee: $312 full-time; $212 part-time. *Financial support:* Fellowships with full and partial tuition reimbursements, research assistantships with full and partial tuition reimbursements, teaching assistantships with full and partial tuition reimbursements, career-related internships or fieldwork, Federal Work-Study, institutionally sponsored loans, and unspecified assistantships available. Financial award application deadline: 3/15. *Unit head:* Dr. Somenath Mitra, Chair, 673-596-5611, E-mail: mitra@njit.edu. *Application contact:* Kathryn Kelly, Director of Admissions, 973-596-3300, Fax: 973-596-3461, E-mail: admissions@njit.edu.

New Mexico Institute of Mining and Technology, Graduate Studies, Department of Chemistry, Socorro, NM 87801. Offers biochemistry (MS); chemistry (MS); environmental chemistry (PhD); explosives technology and atmospheric chemistry (PhD). Part-time programs available. *Degree requirements:* For master's, thesis; for doctorate, thesis/dissertation. *Entrance requirements:* For master's, GRE General Test; for doctorate, GRE General Test, GRE Subject Test. Additional exam requirements/recommendations for international students: Required—TOEFL (minimum score 540 paper-based; 207 computer-based). Electronic applications accepted. *Faculty research:* Organic, analytical, environmental, and explosives chemistry.

New Mexico State University, Graduate School, College of Agricultural, Consumer and Environmental Sciences, Department of Plant and Environmental Sciences, Las Cruces, NM 88003-8001. Offers horticulture (MS); plant and environmental sciences (MS, PhD). Part-time programs available. *Faculty:* 19 full-time (4 women). *Students:* 48 full-time (20 women), 8 part-time (3 women); includes 12 minority (1 American Indian or Alaska Native, non-Hispanic/Latino; 10 Hispanic/Latino; 1 Two or more races, non-Hispanic/Latino), 21 international. Average age 31. 29 applicants, 86% accepted, 15 enrolled. In 2010, 11 master's, 4 doctorates awarded. Terminal master's awarded for partial completion of doctoral program. *Degree requirements:* For master's, thesis; for doctorate, one foreign language, comprehensive exam, thesis/dissertation. *Entrance requirements:* For master's, minimum GPA of 3.0; for doctorate, minimum GPA of 3.3. Additional exam requirements/recommendations for international students: Required—TOEFL. *Application deadline:* For fall admission, 7/1 priority date for domestic

Environmental Sciences

New Mexico State University (continued)
students; for spring admission, 11/1 priority date for domestic students. Applications are processed on a rolling basis. Application fee: $30 ($50 for international students). Electronic applications accepted. *Expenses:* Tuition, state resident: full-time $4536; part-time $242 per credit. Tuition, nonresident: full-time $15,816; part-time $712 per credit. Required fees: $636 per term. *Financial support:* In 2010–11, 11 students received support, including 30 research assistantships with partial tuition reimbursements available (averaging $22,214 per year), 10 teaching assistantships with partial tuition reimbursements available (averaging $14,330 per year); career-related internships or fieldwork, Federal Work-Study, scholarships/grants, health care benefits, and unspecified assistantships also available. Support available to part-time students. Financial award application deadline: 3/1. *Faculty research:* Plant breeding and genetics, molecular biology, plant physiology, soil science and environmental remediation, urban horticulture and turfgrass management. *Unit head:* Dr. Richard Pratt, Head, 575-646-3406, Fax: 575-646-6041, E-mail: ricpratt@nmsu.edu. *Application contact:* Esther Ramirez, Information Contact, 575-646-3406, Fax: 575-646-6041, E-mail: esramire@nmsu.edu.

North Carolina Agricultural and Technical State University, Graduate School, School of Agriculture and Environmental Sciences, Greensboro, NC 27411. Offers MS. Part-time and evening/weekend programs available. *Degree requirements:* For master's, comprehensive exam, qualifying exam. *Entrance requirements:* For master's, GRE General Test. *Faculty research:* Aid for small farmers, agricultural technology, housing, food science, nutrition.

North Dakota State University, College of Graduate and Interdisciplinary Studies, College of Agriculture, Food Systems, and Natural Resources, Department of Soil Science, Fargo, ND 58108. Offers environmental and conservation science (PhD); environmental conservation science (MS); natural resource management (MS, PhD); soil sciences (MS, PhD). Part-time programs available. *Faculty:* 8 full-time (1 woman), 6 part-time/adjunct (0 women). *Students:* 7 full-time (5 women), 1 part-time (0 women). Average age 23. 3 applicants, 67% accepted, 2 enrolled. In 2010, 2 master's, 1 doctorate awarded. *Degree requirements:* For master's, comprehensive exam, thesis, classroom teaching; for doctorate, comprehensive exam, thesis/dissertation, classroom teaching. *Entrance requirements:* Additional exam requirements/recommendations for international students: Required—TOEFL (minimum score 525 paper-based; 193 computer-based; 71 iBT). *Application deadline:* Applications are processed on a rolling basis. Application fee: $45 ($60 for international students). Electronic applications accepted. *Financial support:* In 2010–11, 7 research assistantships with full tuition reimbursements (averaging $14,300 per year) were awarded; fellowships, Federal Work-Study, institutionally sponsored loans, and scholarships/grants also available. Financial award application deadline: 3/15. *Faculty research:* Microclimate, nitrogen management, landscape studies, water quality, soil management. *Unit head:* Dr. Donald Kirby, Interim Chair, 701-231-8901, Fax: 701-231-7861. *Application contact:* Dr. Donald Kirby, Interim Chair, 701-231-8901, Fax: 701-231-7861.

North Dakota State University, College of Graduate and Interdisciplinary Studies, College of Science and Mathematics, Department of Biological Sciences, Fargo, ND 58108. Offers biology (MS); botany (MS, PhD); cellular and molecular biology (PhD); environmental and conservation sciences (MS, PhD); genomics (PhD); natural resources management (MS, PhD); zoology (MS, PhD). *Students:* 18 full-time (8 women), 5 part-time (3 women); includes 2 American Indian or Alaska Native, non-Hispanic/Latino, 2 international. 17 applicants, 35% accepted. In 2010, 12 master's, 9 doctorates awarded. *Degree requirements:* For master's, thesis; for doctorate, thesis/dissertation. *Entrance requirements:* For master's and doctorate, GRE General Test. Additional exam requirements/recommendations for international students: Required—TOEFL. *Application deadline:* For fall admission, 3/15 priority date for domestic students; for spring admission, 10/30 priority date for domestic students. Applications are processed on a rolling basis. Application fee: $45 ($60 for international students). Electronic applications accepted. *Financial support:* Fellowships with full tuition reimbursements, research assistantships with full tuition reimbursements, teaching assistantships with full tuition reimbursements, career-related internships or fieldwork, Federal Work-Study, institutionally sponsored loans, scholarships/grants, tuition waivers (full), and unspecified assistantships available. Support available to part-time students. Financial award application deadline: 4/15; financial award applicants required to submit FAFSA. *Faculty research:* Comparative endocrinology, physiology, behavioral ecology, plant cell biology, aquatic biology. Total annual research expenditures: $675,000. *Unit head:* Dr. Marinus L. Otte, Head, 701-231-7087, E-mail: marinus.otte@ndsu.edu. *Application contact:* Dr. Marinus L. Otte, Head, 701-231-7087, E-mail: marinus.otte@ndsu.edu.

North Dakota State University, College of Graduate and Interdisciplinary Studies, Interdisciplinary Program in Environmental and Conservation Sciences, Fargo, ND 58108. Offers MS, PhD. *Faculty:* 59. *Students:* 27 full-time (12 women), 9 part-time (3 women), 18 international. 12 applicants, 92% accepted, 9 enrolled. In 2010, 3 master's awarded. *Degree requirements:* For master's, comprehensive exam, thesis. *Entrance requirements:* Additional exam requirements/recommendations for international students: Required—TOEFL (minimum score 550 paper-based; 213 computer-based; 79 iBT). *Application deadline:* For fall admission, 5/1 for international students; for spring admission, 8/1 for international students. Application fee: $35. *Unit head:* Dr. Craig Stockwell, Director, 701-231-8449, Fax: 701-231-7149, E-mail: craig.stockwell@ndsu.edu. *Application contact:* Madonna Fitzgerald, Administrative Assistant, 701-231-6456, E-mail: madonna.fitzgerald@ndsu.edu.

Northern Arizona University, Graduate College, College of Engineering, Forestry and Natural Sciences, School of Earth Sciences and Environmental Sustainability, Flagstaff, AZ 86011. Offers climate science and solutions (MS); earth science (MS); environmental sciences and policy (MS); geology (MS). *Faculty:* 27 full-time (7 women). *Students:* 50 full-time (22 women), 18 part-time (9 women); includes 4 minority (1 American Indian or Alaska Native, non-Hispanic/Latino; 1 Asian, non-Hispanic/Latino; 2 Hispanic/Latino), 2 international. 113 applicants, 31% accepted, 27 enrolled. In 2010, 21 master's awarded. *Degree requirements:* For master's, comprehensive exam (for some programs), thesis (for some programs). *Entrance requirements:* Additional exam requirements/recommendations for international students: Required—TOEFL (minimum score 550 paper-based; 213 computer-based; 80 iBT), IELTS (minimum score 7). *Application deadline:* For fall admission, 2/1 priority date for domestic and international students. Applications are processed on a rolling basis. Application fee: $65. Electronic applications accepted. *Financial support:* In 2010–11, 6 fellowships, 7 research assistantships with partial tuition reimbursements (averaging $12,866 per year), 28 teaching assistantships with partial tuition reimbursements (averaging $12,477 per year) were awarded; career-related internships or fieldwork, Federal Work-Study, scholarships/grants, health care benefits, tuition waivers (full and partial), and unspecified assistantships also available. Financial award applicants required to submit FAFSA. *Unit head:* Dr. Abe Springer, Director, 928-523-7198. *Application contact:* Dr. Abe Springer, Director, 928-523-7198.

Nova Scotia Agricultural College, Research and Graduate Studies, Truro, NS B2N 5E3, Canada. Offers agriculture (M Sc), including air quality, animal behavior, animal molecular genetics, animal nutrition, animal technology, aquaculture, botany, crop management, crop physiology, ecology, environmental microbiology, food science, horticulture, nutrient management, pest management, physiology, plant biotechnology, plant pathology, soil chemistry, soil fertility, waste management and composting, water quality. Program offered jointly with Dalhousie University. Part-time programs available. *Degree requirements:* For master's, thesis, ATC Exam Teaching Assistantship. *Entrance requirements:* For master's, honors B Sc, minimum GPA of 3.0. Additional exam requirements/recommendations for international students: Required—TOEFL (minimum score 580 paper-based; 237 computer-based; 92 iBT), IELTS, Michigan English Language Assessment Battery, CanTEST, CAEL. *Faculty research:* Bio-product development, organic agriculture, nutrient management, air and water quality, agricultural biotechnology.

Nova Southeastern University, Oceanographic Center, Program in Marine Environmental Science, Fort Lauderdale, FL 33314-7796. Offers MS. *Faculty:* 15 full-time (1 woman), 5 part-time/adjunct (0 women). *Students:* 4 full-time (all women), 5 part-time (3 women); includes 2 Hispanic/Latino. Average age 25. 14 applicants, 64% accepted, 6 enrolled. In 2010, 2 master's awarded. *Degree requirements:* For master's, thesis. *Entrance requirements:* For master's, GRE. Additional exam requirements/recommendations for international students: Required—TOEFL (minimum score 550 paper-based). *Application deadline:* Applications are processed on a rolling basis. Application fee: $50. *Unit head:* Dr. Richard Dodge, Dean, 954-262-3600, Fax: 954-262-4020, E-mail: dodge@nsu.nova.edu. *Application contact:* Dr. Richard Spieler, Director of Academic Programs, 954-262-3600, Fax: 954-262-4020, E-mail: spieler@nova.edu.

Oakland University, Graduate Study and Lifelong Learning, College of Arts and Sciences, Department of Chemistry, Rochester, MI 48309-4401. Offers biological sciences: health and environmental chemistry (PhD); chemistry (MS). *Degree requirements:* For master's, thesis; for doctorate, thesis/dissertation. *Entrance requirements:* For master's, minimum GPA of 3.0 for unconditional admission; for doctorate, GRE Subject Test, minimum GPA of 3.0 for unconditional admission. Additional exam requirements/recommendations for international students: Required—TOEFL (minimum score 550 paper-based; 213 computer-based). Electronic applications accepted. *Faculty research:* Chemistry of free radical species generated from biological intermediates; fate of toxic organic compounds in the environment; electroanalytical and surface chemistry at solid/liquid interface; computational modeling of intermolecular interactions and surface phenomena; metabolism and biological activity of modified fatty acids and xenobiotic carboxylic acids; physiologic and pathologic mechanisms that modulate immune responses.

OGI School of Science & Engineering at Oregon Health & Science University, Graduate Studies, Department of Environmental and Biomolecular Systems, Beaverton, OR 97006-8921. Offers biochemistry and molecular biology (MS, PhD); environmental health systems (MS); environmental information technology (MS, PhD); environmental science and engineering (MS, PhD). Part-time programs available. Terminal master's awarded for partial completion of doctoral program. *Degree requirements:* For master's, thesis optional; for doctorate, comprehensive exam, oral defense of dissertation. *Entrance requirements:* For master's and doctorate, GRE General Test. Additional exam requirements/recommendations for international students: Required—TOEFL. Electronic applications accepted. *Faculty research:* Air and water science, hydrogeology, estuarine and coastal modeling, environmental microbiology, contaminant transport, biochemistry, biomolecular systems.

The Ohio State University, Graduate School, College of Food, Agricultural, and Environmental Sciences, School of Environment and Natural Resources, Columbus, OH 43210. Offers MS, PhD. *Students:* 70 full-time (39 women), 18 part-time (9 women); includes 2 Asian, non-Hispanic/Latino; 4 Hispanic/Latino; 1 Two or more races, non-Hispanic/Latino, 11 international. Average age 28. In 2010, 12 master's, 4 doctorates awarded. *Degree requirements:* For master's, thesis; for doctorate, thesis/dissertation. *Entrance requirements:* For master's and doctorate, GRE. Additional exam requirements/recommendations for international students: Required—TOEFL. *Application deadline:* Applications are processed on a rolling basis. Application fee: $40 ($50 for international students). Electronic applications accepted. *Expenses:* Tuition, state resident: full-time $10,605. Tuition, nonresident: full-time $26,535. Tuition and fees vary according to course load and program. *Unit head:* Ronald Hendrick, Director, 614-292-8522, E-mail: hendrick.15@osu.edu. *Application contact:* Graduate Admissions, 614-292-9444, Fax: 614-292-3895, E-mail: domestic.grad@osu.edu.

Oklahoma State University, College of Agricultural Science and Natural Resources, Department of Horticulture and Landscape Architecture, Stillwater, OK 74078. Offers agriculture (M Ag); crop science (PhD); environmental science (PhD); horticulture (MS); plant science (PhD). *Faculty:* 21 full-time (2 women), 1 (woman) part-time/adjunct. *Students:* 1 (woman) full-time, 16 part-time (8 women); includes 1 Black or African American, non-Hispanic/Latino; 1 American Indian or Alaska Native, non-Hispanic/Latino; 1 Hispanic/Latino, 9 international. Average age 30. 12 applicants, 33% accepted, 4 enrolled. In 2010, 3 master's awarded. *Degree requirements:* For master's, thesis (for some programs); for doctorate, comprehensive exam, thesis/dissertation. *Entrance requirements:* For master's and doctorate, GRE or GMAT. Additional exam requirements/recommendations for international students: Required—TOEFL (minimum score 550 paper-based; 79 iBT). *Application deadline:* For fall admission, 3/1 priority date for international students; for spring admission, 8/1 priority date for international students. Applications are processed on a rolling basis. Application fee: $40 ($75 for international students). Electronic applications accepted. *Expenses:* Tuition, state resident: full-time $3716; part-time $154.85 per credit hour. Tuition, nonresident: full-time $14,892; part-time $621 per credit hour. Required fees: $2044; $85.20 per credit hour. One-time fee: $50. Tuition and fees vary according to course load and campus/location. *Financial support:* In 2010–11, 14 research assistantships (averaging $14,037 per year) were awarded; career-related internships or fieldwork, Federal Work-Study, scholarships/grants, health care benefits, tuition waivers (partial), and unspecified assistantships also available. Support available to part-time students. Financial award application deadline: 3/1; financial award applicants required to submit FAFSA. *Faculty research:* Stress and postharvest physiology; water utilization and runoff; IPM systems and nursery, turf, floriculture, vegetable, net and fruit produces and natural resources, food extraction, and processing; public garden management. *Unit head:* Dr. Dale Maronek, Head, 405-744-5414, Fax: 405-744-9709. *Application contact:* Dr. Gordon Emslie, Dean, 405-744-6368, Fax: 405-744-0355, E-mail: grad-i@okstate.edu.

Oklahoma State University, College of Agricultural Science and Natural Resources, Department of Plant and Soil Sciences, Stillwater, OK 74078. Offers crop science (PhD); environmental science (PhD); plant and soil sciences (MS); plant science (PhD); soil science (M Ag, PhD). *Faculty:* 30 full-time (4 women), 4 part-time/adjunct (1 woman). *Students:* 20 full-time (6 women), 42 part-time (19 women); includes 1 Black or African American, non-Hispanic/Latino; 1 American Indian or Alaska Native, non-Hispanic/Latino; 1 Asian, non-Hispanic/Latino, 31 international. Average age 28. 48 applicants, 33% accepted, 11 enrolled. In 2010, 11 master's, 1 doctorate awarded. *Degree requirements:* For master's, thesis; for doctorate, comprehensive exam, thesis/dissertation. *Entrance requirements:* For master's and doctorate, GRE or GMAT. Additional exam requirements/recommendations for international students: Required—TOEFL (minimum score 550 paper-based; 79 iBT). *Application deadline:* For fall admission, 3/1 priority date for international students; for spring admission, 8/1 priority date for international students. Applications are processed on a rolling basis. Application fee: $40 ($75 for international students). Electronic applications accepted. *Expenses:* Tuition, state resident: full-time $3716; part-time $154.85 per credit hour. Tuition, nonresident: full-time $14,892; part-time $621 per credit hour. Required fees: $2044; $85.20 per credit hour. One-time fee: $50. Tuition and fees vary according to course load and campus/location. *Financial support:* In 2010–11, 48 research assistantships (averaging $14,676 per year) were awarded; career-related internships or fieldwork, Federal Work-Study, scholarships/grants, health care benefits, tuition waivers (partial), and unspecified assistantships also available. Support available to part-time students. Financial award application deadline: 3/1; financial award applicants required to submit FAFSA. *Faculty research:* Crop science, weed science, rangeland ecology and management, biotechnology, breeding and genetics. *Unit head:* Dr. David R. Porter, Head, 405-744-6130, Fax: 405-744-5269. *Application contact:* Dr. Gordon Emslie, Dean, 405-744-6368, Fax: 405-744-0355, E-mail: grad-i@okstate.edu.

Oklahoma State University, College of Arts and Sciences, Department of Botany, Stillwater, OK 74078. Offers botany (MS); environmental science (MS, PhD); plant science (PhD). *Faculty:* 13 full-time (4 women), 1 (woman) part-time/adjunct. *Students:* 12 part-time (5 women); includes 1 American Indian or Alaska Native, non-Hispanic/Latino; 1 Hispanic/Latino, 2

international. Average age 29. 5 applicants, 80% accepted, 3 enrolled. In 2010, 3 master's awarded. *Degree requirements:* For master's, thesis; for doctorate, comprehensive exam, thesis/dissertation. *Entrance requirements:* For master's and doctorate, GRE or GMAT. Additional exam requirements/recommendations for international students: Required—TOEFL (minimum score 550 paper-based; 79 iBT). *Application deadline:* For fall admission, 3/1 priority date for international students; for spring admission, 8/1 priority date for international students. Applications are processed on a rolling basis. Application fee: $40 ($75 for international students). Electronic applications accepted. *Expenses:* Tuition, state resident: full-time $3716; part-time $154.85 per credit hour. Tuition, nonresident: full-time $14,892; part-time $621 per credit hour. Required fees: $2044; $85.20 per credit hour. One-time fee: $50. Tuition and fees vary according to course load and campus/location. *Financial support:* In 2010–11, 4 research assistantships (averaging $16,635 per year), 12 teaching assistantships (averaging $14,896 per year) were awarded; career-related internships or fieldwork, Federal Work-Study, scholarships/grants, health care benefits, tuition waivers (partial), and unspecified assistantships also available. Support available to part-time students. Financial award application deadline: 3/1; financial award applicants required to submit FAFSA. *Faculty research:* Ethnobotany, developmental genetics of Arabidopsis, biological roles of Plasmodesmata, community ecology and biodiversity, nutrient cycling in grassland ecosystems. *Unit head:* Dr. Linda Watson, Head, 405-744-5559, Fax: 405-744-7074. *Application contact:* Dr. Gordon Emslie, Dean, 405-744-6368, Fax: 405-744-0355, E-mail: grad-i@okstate.edu.

Oklahoma State University, Graduate College, Stillwater, OK 74078. Offers environmental science (MS); international studies (MS); natural and applied science (MS); photonics (PhD); plant science (PhD). Programs are interdisciplinary. *Faculty:* 2 full-time (1 woman). *Students:* 69 full-time (40 women), 131 part-time (68 women); includes 13 Black or African American, non-Hispanic/Latino; 15 American Indian or Alaska Native, non-Hispanic/Latino; 8 Asian, non-Hispanic/Latino; 8 Hispanic/Latino, 70 international. Average age 30. 690 applicants, 74% accepted, 75 enrolled. In 2010, 66 master's, 7 doctorates awarded. *Degree requirements:* For master's, thesis (for some programs); for doctorate, comprehensive exam, thesis/dissertation. *Entrance requirements:* For master's and doctorate, GRE or GMAT. Additional exam requirements/recommendations for international students: Required—TOEFL (minimum score 550 paper-based; 79 iBT). *Application deadline:* For fall admission, 3/1 priority date for international students; for spring admission, 8/1 priority date for international students. Applications are processed on a rolling basis. Application fee: $40 ($75 for international students). Electronic applications accepted. *Expenses:* Tuition, state resident: full-time $3716; part-time $154.85 per credit hour. Tuition, nonresident: full-time $14,892; part-time $621 per credit hour. Required fees: $2044; $85.20 per credit hour. One-time fee: $50. Tuition and fees vary according to course load and campus/location. *Financial support:* In 2010–11, 2 research assistantships (averaging $12,900 per year) were awarded; career-related internships or fieldwork, Federal Work-Study, scholarships/grants, health care benefits, tuition waivers (partial), and unspecified assistantships also available. Support available to part-time students. Financial award application deadline: 3/1; financial award applicants required to submit FAFSA. *Unit head:* Dr. Gordon Emslie, Dean, 405-744-6368, Fax: 405-744-0355, E-mail: grad-i@okstate.edu. *Application contact:* Dr. Susan Mathew, Coordinator of Admissions, 405-744-6368, Fax: 405-744-0355, E-mail: grad-i@okstate.edu.

Oregon Health & Science University, School of Medicine, Graduate Programs in Medicine, Department of Environmental and Biomolecular Systems, Portland, OR 97239-3098. Offers biochemistry and molecular biology (MS, PhD); environmental science and engineering (MS, PhD). Part-time programs available. *Faculty:* 14 full-time (4 women), 1 (woman) part-time/adjunct. *Students:* 21 full-time (12 women), 25 part-time (12 women); includes 1 Black or African American, non-Hispanic/Latino; 3 American Indian or Alaska Native, non-Hispanic/Latino; 5 Asian, non-Hispanic/Latino; 3 Hispanic/Latino, 8 international. Average age 33. 45 applicants, 60% accepted, 11 enrolled. In 2010, 8 master's, 2 doctorates awarded. Terminal master's awarded for partial completion of doctoral program. *Degree requirements:* For master's, thesis (for some programs); for doctorate, comprehensive exam, thesis/dissertation. *Entrance requirements:* For master's and doctorate, GRE General Test (minimum scores: 500 Verbal/600 Quantitative/4.5 Analytical) or MCAT (for some programs). Additional exam requirements/recommendations for international students: Required—TOEFL. *Application deadline:* For fall admission, 7/15 for domestic students, 5/15 for international students; for winter admission, 10/15 for domestic students, 9/15 for international students; for spring admission, 1/15 for domestic students, 12/15 for international students. Applications are processed on a rolling basis. Application fee: $65. Electronic applications accepted. *Financial support:* Health care benefits and full tuition and stipends available. *Unit head:* Paul Tratnyek, PhD, Program Director, 503-748-1070, E-mail: info@ebs.ogi.edu. *Application contact:* Nancy Christie, Program Coordinator, 503-748-1070, E-mail: info@ebs.ogi.edu.

Oregon State University, Graduate School, College of Agricultural Sciences, Department of Environmental and Molecular Toxicology, Corvallis, OR 97331. Offers toxicology (MS, PhD).

Oregon State University, Graduate School, Program in Environmental Sciences, Corvallis, OR 97331. Offers MA, MS, PhD.

Pace University, Dyson College of Arts and Sciences, Program in Environmental Science, New York, NY 10038. Offers MS. Offered at Pleasantville, NY location only. *Degree requirements:* For master's, research project. *Entrance requirements:* For master's, GRE. Additional exam requirements/recommendations for international students: Required—TOEFL. Electronic applications accepted.

Penn State Harrisburg, Graduate School, School of Science, Engineering and Technology, Middletown, PA 17057-4898. Offers M Eng, MEPC, MPS, MS, MEPC/JD. Evening/weekend programs available. *Unit head:* Dr. Omid Ansary, Director, 717-948-6353, E-mail: axa8@psu.edu. *Application contact:* Robert Coffman, Director of Admissions, 717-948-6250, Fax: 717-948-6325, E-mail: ric1@psu.edu.

Penn State University Park, Graduate School, Intercollege Graduate Programs, Intercollege Program in Environmental Pollution Control, State College, University Park, PA 16802-1503. Offers MEPC, MS. *Unit head:* Dr. Herschel A. Elliott, Chair, 814-865-1417, Fax: 814-863-1031, E-mail: helliott3@psu.edu. *Application contact:* Dr. Herschel A. Elliott, Chair, 814-865-1417, Fax: 814-863-1031, E-mail: helliott3@psu.edu.

Polytechnic Institute of NYU, Department of Civil Engineering, Major in Environmental Science, Brooklyn, NY 11201-2990. Offers MS. Part-time and evening/weekend programs available. *Students:* 3 full-time (2 women), 1 (woman) part-time; includes 2 Black or African American, non-Hispanic/Latino, 2 international. 16 applicants, 63% accepted, 4 enrolled. In 2010, 1 master's awarded. *Degree requirements:* For master's, comprehensive exam (for some programs), thesis (for some programs). *Entrance requirements:* Additional exam requirements/recommendations for international students: Required—TOEFL (minimum score 550 paper-based; 213 computer-based; 80 iBT); Recommended—IELTS (minimum score 6.5). *Application deadline:* For fall admission, 7/31 priority date for domestic students, 4/30 priority date for international students; for spring admission, 12/31 priority date for domestic students, 10/30 priority date for international students. Applications are processed on a rolling basis. Application fee: $75. Electronic applications accepted. *Expenses:* Tuition: Full-time $21,492; part-time $1194 per credit. Required fees: $385 per semester. Tuition and fees vary according to course load. *Financial support:* Fellowships, research assistantships, teaching assistantships, institutionally sponsored loans, scholarships/grants, and unspecified assistantships available. Support available to part-time students. Financial award applicants required to submit FAFSA. *Unit head:* Dr. Lawrence Chiarelli, Head, 718-260-4040, Fax: 718-260-3433, E-mail: lchiarel@poly.edu. *Application contact:* JeanCarlo Bonilla, Director of Graduate Enrollment Management, 718-260-3182, Fax: 718-260-3624, E-mail: gradinfo@poly.edu.

Pontifical Catholic University of Puerto Rico, College of Sciences, Department of Biology, Ponce, PR 00717-0777. Offers environmental sciences (MS). *Degree requirements:* For master's, thesis. *Entrance requirements:* For master's, GRE, 2 letters of recommendation, interview, minimum GPA of 2.75.

Portland State University, Graduate Studies, College of Liberal Arts and Sciences, Department of Geology, Portland, OR 97207-0751. Offers environmental sciences and resources (PhD); geology (MA, MS); science/geology (MAT, MST). Part-time programs available. *Faculty:* 10 full-time (2 women), 3 part-time/adjunct (2 women). *Students:* 15 full-time (6 women), 26 part-time (5 women); includes 1 American Indian or Alaska Native, non-Hispanic/Latino. Average age 30. 20 applicants, 90% accepted, 8 enrolled. In 2010, 4 master's awarded. *Degree requirements:* For master's, comprehensive exam, thesis, field comprehensive; for doctorate, thesis/dissertation, 2 years of residency. *Entrance requirements:* For master's, GRE General Test, GRE Subject Test, BA/BS in geology, minimum GPA of 3.0 in upper-division course work or 2.75 overall. Additional exam requirements/recommendations for international students: Required—TOEFL (minimum score 550 paper-based; 213 computer-based). *Application deadline:* 1/31 priority date for domestic and international students. Applications are processed on a rolling basis. Application fee: $50. *Expenses:* Tuition, state resident: full-time $8505; part-time $315 per credit. Tuition, nonresident: full-time $13,284; part-time $492 per credit. Required fees: $1482; $21 per credit. $99 per term. One-time fee: $120. Part-time tuition and fees vary according to course load and program. *Financial support:* In 2010–11, 8 teaching assistantships with full tuition reimbursements (averaging $11,702 per year) were awarded; research assistantships with full tuition reimbursements, career-related internships or fieldwork, Federal Work-Study, scholarships/grants, and unspecified assistantships also available. Support available to part-time students. Financial award application deadline: 3/1; financial award applicants required to submit FAFSA. *Faculty research:* Sediment transport, volcanic environmental geology, coastal and fluvial processes. Total annual research expenditures: $1.8 million. *Unit head:* Dr. Andrew Fountain, Chair, 503-725-3386, Fax: 503-725-3025, E-mail: andrew@pdx.edu. *Application contact:* Nancy Eriksson, Office Coordinator, 503-725-3022, Fax: 503-725-3025, E-mail: nancye@pdx.edu.

Portland State University, Graduate Studies, College of Liberal Arts and Sciences, Program in Environmental Sciences and Management, Portland, OR 97207-0751. Offers environmental management (MEM); environmental sciences/biology (PhD); environmental sciences/chemistry (PhD); environmental sciences/civil engineering (PhD); environmental sciences/geography (PhD); environmental sciences/geology (PhD); environmental sciences/physics (PhD); environmental studies (MS); science/environmental science (MST). Part-time programs available. *Faculty:* 14 full-time (6 women), 7 part-time/adjunct (5 women). *Students:* 57 full-time (31 women), 48 part-time (23 women); includes 5 minority (1 Black or African American, non-Hispanic/Latino; 2 Asian, non-Hispanic/Latino; 2 Hispanic/Latino), 6 international. Average age 34. 89 applicants, 56% accepted, 34 enrolled. In 2010, 14 master's, 3 doctorates awarded. *Degree requirements:* For master's, thesis or alternative; for doctorate, variable foreign language requirement, comprehensive exam, thesis/dissertation, oral and qualifying exams. *Entrance requirements:* For master's, GRE General Test, 3 letters of recommendation; for doctorate, minimum GPA of 3.0 in upper-division course work or 2.75 overall. Additional exam requirements/recommendations for international students: Required—TOEFL (minimum score 550 paper-based; 213 computer-based). *Application deadline:* For fall admission, 2/1 for domestic and international students. Applications are processed on a rolling basis. Application fee: $50. *Expenses:* Tuition, state resident: full-time $8505; part-time $315 per credit. Tuition, nonresident: full-time $13,284; part-time $492 per credit. Required fees: $1482; $21 per credit. $99 per term. One-time fee: $120. Part-time tuition and fees vary according to course load and program. *Financial support:* In 2010–11, 4 research assistantships with full tuition reimbursements (averaging $10,480 per year), 6 teaching assistantships with full tuition reimbursements (averaging $10,267 per year) were awarded; Federal Work-Study, scholarships/grants, tuition waivers (partial), and unspecified assistantships also available. Support available to part-time students. Financial award application deadline: 3/1; financial award applicants required to submit FAFSA. *Faculty research:* Environmental aspects of biology, chemistry, civil engineering, geology, physics. Total annual research expenditures: $1.2 million. *Unit head:* Dr. Mark Sytsma, Chair, 503-725-8038, Fax: 503-725-3888, E-mail: sytsmam@pdx.edu. *Application contact:* Dr. Mark Sytsma, Chair, 503-725-8038, Fax: 503-725-3888, E-mail: sytsmam@pdx.edu.

Queens College of the City University of New York, Division of Graduate Studies, Mathematics and Natural Sciences Division, School of Earth and Environmental Sciences, Flushing, NY 11367-1597. Offers MA. Part-time and evening/weekend programs available. *Faculty:* 14 full-time (4 women). *Students:* 1 (woman) full-time, 17 part-time (11 women); includes 2 Asian, non-Hispanic/Latino; 3 Hispanic/Latino, 2 international. 13 applicants, 38% accepted, 3 enrolled. *Degree requirements:* For master's, comprehensive exam, thesis. *Entrance requirements:* For master's, GRE, previous course work in calculus, physics, and chemistry; minimum GPA of 3.0. Additional exam requirements/recommendations for international students: Required—TOEFL. *Application deadline:* For fall admission, 4/1 for domestic students; for spring admission, 11/1 for domestic students. Applications are processed on a rolling basis. Application fee: $125. *Financial support:* Career-related internships or fieldwork, Federal Work-Study, institutionally sponsored loans, tuition waivers (partial), and unspecified assistantships available. Support available to part-time students. Financial award application deadline: 4/1; financial award applicants required to submit FAFSA. *Faculty research:* Sedimentology/stratigraphy, paleontology, field petrology. *Unit head:* Dr. Yan Zheng, Chairperson, 718-997-3300. *Application contact:* Dr. Hannes Brueckner, Graduate Adviser, 718-997-3300, E-mail: hannes_brueckner@qc.edu.

Rice University, Graduate Programs, George R. Brown School of Engineering, Department of Civil and Environmental Engineering, Houston, TX 77251-1892. Offers civil engineering (MCE, MS, PhD); environmental engineering (MEE, MES, MS, PhD); environmental science (MEE, MES, MS, PhD). Part-time programs available. *Degree requirements:* For master's, thesis (for some programs); for doctorate, thesis/dissertation. *Entrance requirements:* For master's and doctorate, GRE General Test, GRE Subject Test, minimum GPA of 3.25. Additional exam requirements/recommendations for international students: Required—TOEFL (minimum score 600 paper-based; 250 computer-based; 90 iBT). Electronic applications accepted. *Faculty research:* Biology and chemistry of groundwater, pollutant fate in groundwater systems, water quality monitoring, urban storm water runoff, urban air quality.

Rice University, Graduate Programs, Wiess School–Professional Science Master's Programs, Houston, TX 77251-1892. Offers MS.

The Richard Stockton College of New Jersey, School of Graduate and Continuing Studies, Program in Environmental Science, Pomona, NJ 08240-0195. Offers PSM. Part-time and evening/weekend programs available. *Faculty:* 7 full-time (1 woman). *Students:* 4 full-time (0 women), 17 part-time (5 women). Average age 30. 9 applicants, 89% accepted, 7 enrolled. *Degree requirements:* For master's, thesis optional. *Entrance requirements:* For master's, GRE. Additional exam requirements/recommendations for international students: Required—TOEFL. *Application deadline:* For fall admission, 7/1 for domestic and international students; for spring admission, 12/1 for domestic and international students. Applications are processed on a rolling basis. Application fee: $50. Electronic applications accepted. *Expenses:* Tuition, state resident: full-time $9310; part-time $517.25 per credit. Tuition, nonresident: full-time $14,332; part-time $796.23 per credit. Required fees: $2600; $144 per credit. $70 per semester. Tuition and fees vary according to degree level. *Financial support:* In 2010–11, 5 students received support, including 5 research assistantships; Federal Work-Study, scholarships/grants, and unspecified assistantships also available. Financial award application deadline: 3/1; financial award applicants required to submit FAFSA. *Unit head:* Dr. Tait Chirenje, Program Director, 609-652-4588, E-mail: tait.chirenje@stockton.edu. *Application contact:* Tara Williams,

Environmental Sciences

The Richard Stockton College of New Jersey (continued)
Assistant Director of Graduate Enrollment Management, 609-626-3640, Fax: 609-626-6050, E-mail: gradschool@stockton.edu.

Rochester Institute of Technology, Graduate Enrollment Services, College of Science, Health Sciences and Sustainability, Department of Biological Sciences, Program in Environmental Science, Rochester, NY 14623-5603. Offers MS. Part-time and evening/weekend programs available. *Students:* 10 full-time (4 women), 5 part-time (4 women), 1 international. Average age 27. 21 applicants, 43% accepted, 7 enrolled. In 2010, 2 master's awarded. *Degree requirements:* For master's, thesis. *Entrance requirements:* For master's, GRE General Test (recommended), minimum GPA of 3.0. Additional exam requirements/recommendations for international students: Required—TOEFL (minimum score 550 paper-based; 213 computer-based; 79 iBT) or IELTS (minimum score 6.5). *Application deadline:* For fall admission, 2/15 priority date for domestic and international students; for winter admission, 11/1 for domestic students; for spring admission, 2/1 for domestic students. Applications are processed on a rolling basis. Application fee: $50. Electronic applications accepted. *Expenses:* Tuition: Full-time $33,234; part-time $924 per credit hour. Required fees: $219. *Financial support:* In 2010–11, 7 students received support; fellowships with partial tuition reimbursements available, research assistantships with partial tuition reimbursements available, teaching assistantships with partial tuition reimbursements available, career-related internships or fieldwork, scholarships/grants, and unspecified assistantships available. Support available to part-time students. Financial award applicants required to submit FAFSA. *Faculty research:* Environmental chemistry, digital imaging, environmental biology, remote sensing, mathematics and statistics, environmental public policy, environmental economics. *Unit head:* Dr. Karl Korfmacher, Graduate Program Director, 585-475-5554, Fax: 585-475-5000, E-mail: kfkscl@rit.edu. *Application contact:* Diane Ellison, Assistant Vice President, Graduate Enrollment Services, 585-475-2229, Fax: 585-475-7164, E-mail: gradinfo@rit.edu.

Royal Military College of Canada, Division of Graduate Studies and Research, Engineering Division, Program in Environmental Science, Kingston, ON K7K 7B4, Canada. Offers M Sc, PhD. *Degree requirements:* For master's, thesis; for doctorate, comprehensive exam, thesis/dissertation. *Entrance requirements:* For master's, honours degree with second-class standing; for doctorate, master's degree. Electronic applications accepted.

Rutgers, The State University of New Jersey, Newark, Graduate School, Program in Environmental Science, Newark, NJ 07102. Offers MS, PhD. MS, PhD offered jointly with New Jersey Institute of Technology. *Faculty:* 7 full-time (3 women). *Students:* 13 full-time (7 women), 13 part-time (6 women); includes 5 Black or African American, non-Hispanic/Latino; 5 Asian, non-Hispanic/Latino; 2 Hispanic/Latino. 23 applicants, 48% accepted, 5 enrolled. In 2010, 1 doctorate awarded. *Entrance requirements:* For master's and doctorate, GRE, minimum B average. *Application deadline:* For fall admission, 4/1 for domestic students; for spring admission, 12/1 for domestic students. Application fee: $60. *Expenses:* Tuition, state resident: part-time $600 per credit. Tuition, nonresident: full-time $10,694. *Financial support:* In 2010–11, 1 fellowship (averaging $18,000 per year), 1 research assistantship with full and partial tuition reimbursement (averaging $23,112 per year), 7 teaching assistantships with full and partial tuition reimbursements (averaging $23,112 per year) were awarded; Federal Work-Study and tuition waivers (full and partial) also available. Support available to part-time students. *Unit head:* Dr. Alex Gates, Program Coordinator and Adviser, 973-353-5034, Fax: 973-353-5100, E-mail: agates@andromeda.rutgers.edu. *Application contact:* Jason Hand, Director of Admissions, 973-353-5205, Fax: 973-353-1440.

Rutgers, The State University of New Jersey, New Brunswick, Graduate School-New Brunswick, Department of Environmental Sciences, Piscataway, NJ 08854-8097. Offers air pollution and resources (MS, PhD); aquatic biology (MS, PhD); aquatic chemistry (MS, PhD); atmospheric science (MS, PhD); chemistry and physics of aerosol and hydrosol systems (MS, PhD); environmental chemistry (MS, PhD); environmental microbiology (MS, PhD); environmental toxicology (PhD); exposure assessment (PhD); fate and effects of pollutants (MS, PhD); pollution prevention and control (MS, PhD); water and wastewater treatment (MS, PhD); water resources (MS, PhD). Terminal master's awarded for partial completion of doctoral program. *Degree requirements:* For master's, comprehensive exam, thesis or alternative, oral final exam; for doctorate, comprehensive exam, thesis/dissertation, thesis defense, qualifying exam. *Entrance requirements:* For master's and doctorate, GRE General Test. Additional exam requirements/recommendations for international students: Required—TOEFL. Electronic applications accepted. *Expenses:* Tuition, state resident: full-time $7200; part-time $600 per credit. Tuition, nonresident: full-time $11,124; part-time $927 per credit. *Faculty research:* Biological waste treatment; contaminant fate and transport; air, soil and water quality.

South Dakota School of Mines and Technology, Graduate Division, PhD Program in Atmospheric and Environmental Sciences, Rapid City, SD 57701-3995. Offers PhD. Program offered jointly with South Dakota State University. *Degree requirements:* For doctorate, comprehensive exam, thesis/dissertation. *Entrance requirements:* For doctorate, GRE General Test, GRE Subject Test. Additional exam requirements/recommendations for international students: Required—TOEFL, TWE. Electronic applications accepted.

Southeast Missouri State University, School of Graduate Studies, Program in Environmental Science, Cape Girardeau, MO 63701-4799. Offers MS. *Faculty:* 15 full-time (3 women). *Students:* 2 full-time (both women), 2 part-time (1 woman). Average age 31. 3 applicants, 100% accepted, 3 enrolled. *Degree requirements:* For master's, comprehensive exam (for some programs), thesis (for some programs), oral defense; internship, scholarly paper (for some programs). *Entrance requirements:* For master's, GRE, minimum undergraduate GPA of 3.0; goals and objectives; 2 letters of recommendation; criminal background check. Additional exam requirements/recommendations for international students: Required—TOEFL (minimum score 550 paper-based; 213 computer-based; 79 iBT); Recommended—IELTS (minimum score 6). *Application deadline:* For fall admission, 8/1 for domestic students, 6/1 for international students; for spring admission, 11/21 for domestic students, 10/1 for international students. Applications are processed on a rolling basis. Application fee: $25 ($35 for international students). Electronic applications accepted. *Expenses:* Tuition, state resident: full-time $4698; part-time $261 per credit hour. Tuition, nonresident: full-time $8379; part-time $465.50 per credit hour. *Financial support:* In 2010–11, 4 students received support, including 2 teaching assistantships with full tuition reimbursements available (averaging $7,600 per year); career-related internships or fieldwork, Federal Work-Study, institutionally sponsored loans, scholarships/grants, tuition waivers (full), and unspecified assistantships also available. Financial award application deadline: 6/30; financial award applicants required to submit FAFSA. *Faculty research:* Contamination of soils and water with environmental chemicals, influence of environmental factors on respiratory health, determination of energy related pollutants in environmental samples, economic valuation of water resources, impacts of environmental chemicals on wildlife species. Total annual research expenditures: $100,000. *Unit head:* Dr. Stephen R. Overmann, Program Director, 573-651-2386, E-mail: srovermann@semo.edu. *Application contact:* Gail Amick, Administrative Secretary, 573-651-2049, Fax: 573-651-2001, E-mail: gamick@semo.edu.

Southern Illinois University Carbondale, Graduate School, College of Science, Department of Geology and Department of Geography, Program in Environmental Resources and Policy, Carbondale, IL 62901-4701. Offers PhD. *Entrance requirements:* For doctorate, GRE.

Southern Illinois University Edwardsville, Graduate School, College of Arts and Sciences, Program in Environmental Sciences, Edwardsville, IL 62026-0001. Offers MS. Part-time and evening/weekend programs available. *Students:* 9 full-time (4 women), 26 part-time (14 women); includes 2 minority (1 American Indian or Alaska Native, non-Hispanic/Latino; 1 Two or more races, non-Hispanic/Latino), 5 international. Average age 26. 38 applicants, 32% accepted, 0 enrolled. In 2010, 10 master's awarded. *Degree requirements:* For master's, thesis (for some programs), final exam, oral exam. *Entrance requirements:* For master's, GRE. Additional exam requirements/recommendations for international students: Required—TOEFL (minimum score 550 paper-based; 213 computer-based; 79 iBT), IELTS (minimum score 6.5). *Application deadline:* For fall admission, 7/22 for domestic students, 6/1 for international students; for spring admission, 12/9 for domestic students, 10/1 for international students. Applications are processed on a rolling basis. Application fee: $30. Electronic applications accepted. *Expenses:* Tuition, state resident: full-time $6012; part-time $1503 per semester. Tuition, nonresident: full-time $15,030; part-time $3758 per semester. Required fees: $1711; $675 per semester. *Financial support:* In 2010–11, 1 fellowship with full tuition reimbursement (averaging $8,370 per year), research assistantships with full tuition reimbursements (averaging $8,064 per year), 11 teaching assistantships with full tuition reimbursements (averaging $8,064 per year) were awarded; career-related internships or fieldwork, Federal Work-Study, institutionally sponsored loans, scholarships/grants, traineeships, and unspecified assistantships also available. Support available to part-time students. Financial award application deadline: 3/1; financial award applicants required to submit FAFSA. *Unit head:* Dr. Kevin Johnson, Program Director, 618-650-5934, E-mail: kevjohn@siue.edu. *Application contact:* Dr. Kevin Johnson, Program Director, 618-650-5934, E-mail: kevjohn@siue.edu.

Southern Methodist University, Bobby B. Lyle School of Engineering, Department of Environmental and Civil Engineering, Dallas, TX 75275-0340. Offers applied science (MS, PhD); civil and environmental engineering (PhD); civil engineering (MS); environmental engineering (MS); environmental science (MS), including environmental systems management. Part-time and evening/weekend programs available. Postbaccalaureate distance learning degree programs offered (no on-campus study). *Faculty:* 6 full-time (0 women), 11 part-time/adjunct (3 women). *Students:* 11 full-time (8 women), 47 part-time (21 women); includes 5 Black or African American, non-Hispanic/Latino; 2 Asian, non-Hispanic/Latino; 3 Hispanic/Latino, 6 international. Average age 37. 50 applicants, 86% accepted, 28 enrolled. In 2010, 26 master's awarded. Terminal master's awarded for partial completion of doctoral program. *Degree requirements:* For master's, thesis optional; for doctorate, thesis/dissertation, oral and written qualifying exams. *Entrance requirements:* For master's, GRE General Test, minimum GPA of 3.0 in last 2 years; bachelor's degree in engineering, mathematics, or sciences; for doctorate, GRE, BS and MS in related field, minimum GPA of 3.3. Additional exam requirements/recommendations for international students: Required—TOEFL. *Application deadline:* For fall admission, 7/1 for domestic students, 5/15 for international students; for spring admission, 11/15 for domestic students, 9/1 for international students. Applications are processed on a rolling basis. Application fee: $75. Electronic applications accepted. *Financial support:* In 2010–11, 9 students received support, including 2 research assistantships with full tuition reimbursements available (averaging $18,000 per year), 7 teaching assistantships with full tuition reimbursements available (averaging $18,000 per year); unspecified assistantships also available. *Faculty research:* Human and environmental health effects of endocrine disrupters, development of air pollution control systems for diesel engines, structural analysis and design, modeling and design of waste treatment systems. Total annual research expenditures: $100,000. *Unit head:* Prof. Khaled Abdelghany, Associate Chair, 214-768-3894, Fax: 214-768-2164, E-mail: khaled@lyle.smu.edu. *Application contact:* Marc Valerin, Director of Graduate and Executive Admissions, 214-768-3042, Fax: 214-768-3778, E-mail: valerin@lyle.smu.edu.

Southern University and Agricultural and Mechanical College, Graduate School, College of Sciences, Department of Chemistry, Baton Rouge, LA 70813. Offers analytical chemistry (MS); biochemistry (MS); environmental sciences (MS); inorganic chemistry (MS); organic chemistry (MS); physical chemistry (MS). *Degree requirements:* For master's, thesis. *Entrance requirements:* For master's, GMAT or GRE General Test. Additional exam requirements/recommendations for international students: Required—TOEFL (minimum score 525 paper-based; 193 computer-based). *Faculty research:* Synthesis of macrocyclic ligands, latex accelerators, anticancer drugs, biosensors, absorption isotheums, isolation of specific enzymes from plants.

Stanford University, School of Earth Sciences, Department of Geological and Environmental Sciences, Stanford, CA 94305-9991. Offers MS, PhD, Eng. Terminal master's awarded for partial completion of doctoral program. *Degree requirements:* For master's and Eng, thesis; for doctorate, thesis/dissertation. *Entrance requirements:* For master's, doctorate, and Eng, GRE General Test. Additional exam requirements/recommendations for international students: Required—TOEFL. Electronic applications accepted. *Expenses:* Tuition: Full-time $38,700; part-time $860 per unit. One-time fee: $200 full-time.

Stanford University, School of Earth Sciences, Earth Systems Program, Stanford, CA 94305-9991. Offers MS. Students admitted at the undergraduate level. Electronic applications accepted. *Expenses:* Tuition: Full-time $38,700; part-time $860 per unit. One-time fee: $200 full-time.

State University of New York College of Environmental Science and Forestry, Department of Environmental and Forest Biology, Syracuse, NY 13210-2779. Offers applied ecology (MPS); chemical ecology (MPS, MS, PhD); conservation biology (MPS, MS, PhD); ecology (MPS, MS, PhD); entomology (MPS, MS, PhD); environmental interpretation (MPS, MS, PhD); environmental physiology (MPS, MS, PhD); fish and wildlife biology and management (MPS, MS, PhD); forest pathology and mycology (MPS, MS, PhD); plant biotechnology (MPS); plant science and biotechnology (MPS, MS, PhD). *Degree requirements:* For master's, thesis (for some programs); for doctorate, comprehensive exam, thesis/dissertation. *Entrance requirements:* For master's and doctorate, GRE General Test, GRE Subject Test, minimum GPA of 3.0. Additional exam requirements/recommendations for international students: Required—TOEFL (minimum score 550 paper-based; 213 computer-based; 80 iBT), IELTS (minimum score 6). *Expenses:* Tuition, state resident: full-time $8370; part-time $349 per credit hour. Tuition, nonresident: full-time $13,780. Required fees: $30.30 per credit hour. $20 per year. *Faculty research:* Ecology, fish and wildlife biology and management, plant science, entomology.

State University of New York College of Environmental Science and Forestry, Program in Environmental Science, Syracuse, NY 13210-2779. Offers environmental and community land planning (MPS, MS, PhD); environmental and natural resources policy (PhD); environmental communication and participatory processes (MPS, MS, PhD); environmental policy and democratic processes (MPS, MS, PhD); environmental systems and risk management (MPS, MS, PhD); water and wetland resource studies (MPS, MS, PhD). Part-time programs available. *Degree requirements:* For master's, thesis (for some programs); for doctorate, comprehensive exam, thesis/dissertation. *Entrance requirements:* For master's and doctorate, GRE General Test, minimum GPA of 3.0. Additional exam requirements/recommendations for international students: Required—TOEFL (minimum score 550 paper-based; 213 computer-based; 80 iBT), IELTS (minimum score 6). *Expenses:* Tuition, state resident: full-time $8370; part-time $349 per credit hour. Tuition, nonresident: full-time $13,780. Required fees: $30.30 per credit hour. $20 per year. *Faculty research:* Environmental education/communications, water resources, land resources, waste management.

Stephen F. Austin State University, Graduate School, College of Sciences and Mathematics, Division of Environmental Science, Nacogdoches, TX 75962. Offers MS. *Degree requirements:* For master's, comprehensive exam. *Entrance requirements:* For master's, GRE General Test, minimum GPA of 2.8 in last 60 hours, 2.5 overall. Additional exam requirements/recommendations for international students: Required—TOEFL.

Tarleton State University, College of Graduate Studies, College of Science and Technology, Department of Chemistry, Geosciences and Environmental Sciences, Stephenville, TX 76402. Offers environmental science (MS). Part-time and evening/weekend programs available. *Degree requirements:* For master's, comprehensive exam, thesis optional. *Entrance requirements:* For master's, GRE General Test, minimum GPA of 3.0. Additional exam requirements/

recommendations for international students: Required—TOEFL (minimum score 550 paper-based; 213 computer-based; 80 iBT). Electronic applications accepted.

Taylor University, Master of Environmental Science Program, Upland, IN 46989-1001. Offers MES. *Faculty:* 3 part-time/adjunct (0 women). *Students:* 16 full-time (8 women), 2 part-time (both women), 1 international. Average age 26. 35 applicants, 31% accepted, 8 enrolled. In 2010, 8 master's awarded. *Degree requirements:* For master's, thesis (for some programs). *Application deadline:* Applications are processed on a rolling basis. Application fee: $0. *Expenses:* Contact institution. *Financial support:* In 2010–11, 18 fellowships (averaging $10,000 per year), 5 teaching assistantships (averaging $6,000 per year) were awarded; scholarships/grants also available. Financial award applicants required to submit FAFSA. *Faculty research:* Environmental assessment. *Unit head:* Dr. Edwin Richard Squiers, Chair, 765-998-5386, Fax: 765-998-4976, E-mail: rcsquiers@taylor.edu. *Application contact:* Becky Taylor, Program Assistant, 765-998-4960, Fax: 765-998-4976, E-mail: mes@taylor.edu.

Tennessee Technological University, Graduate School, College of Arts and Sciences, Department of Environmental Sciences, Cookeville, TN 38505. Offers biology (PhD); chemistry (PhD). *Students:* 9 full-time (4 women), 6 part-time (2 women); includes 3 Black or African American, non-Hispanic/Latino; 2 Asian, non-Hispanic/Latino; 2 Hispanic/Latino. 14 applicants, 21% accepted, 1 enrolled. In 2010, 4 doctorates awarded. *Degree requirements:* For doctorate, comprehensive exam, thesis/dissertation. *Entrance requirements:* For doctorate, GRE. Additional exam requirements/recommendations for international students: Required—TOEFL (minimum score 550 paper-based; 79 iBT), IELTS (minimum score 5.5). *Application deadline:* For fall admission, 8/1 for domestic students, 5/1 for international students; for spring admission, 12/1 for domestic students, 10/2 for international students. Application fee: $25 ($30 for international students). Electronic applications accepted. *Expenses:* Tuition, state resident: full-time $7934; part-time $388 per credit hour. Tuition, nonresident: full-time $19,758; part-time $962 per credit hour. *Financial support:* In 2010–11, 5 research assistantships (averaging $10,000 per year), 3 teaching assistantships (averaging $10,000 per year) were awarded; fellowships also available. Financial award application deadline: 4/1. *Unit head:* Dr. Dal Ensor, Director. *Application contact:* Shelia K. Kendrick, Coordinator of Graduate Admissions, 931-372-3808, Fax: 931-372-3497, E-mail: skendrick@tntech.edu.

Texas A&M University–Corpus Christi, Graduate Studies and Research, College of Science and Technology, Program in Environmental Science, Corpus Christi, TX 78412-5503. Offers MS. Part-time and evening/weekend programs available. *Degree requirements:* For master's, comprehensive exam, thesis (for some programs). *Entrance requirements:* For master's, GRE General Test. Additional exam requirements/recommendations for international students: Required—TOEFL. Electronic applications accepted.

Texas Christian University, College of Science and Engineering, Department of Environmental Science, Fort Worth, TX 76129-0002. Offers MA, MEM, MS, MBA/MEM. Part-time programs available. *Degree requirements:* For master's, comprehensive exam, thesis (MS). *Entrance requirements:* For master's, GRE General Test, 1 year each of course work in biology and chemistry, 1 semester each in calculus and statistics. Additional exam requirements/recommendations for international students: Required—TOEFL (minimum score 550 paper-based; 213 computer-based; 80 iBT). *Application deadline:* For fall admission, 2/28 for domestic and international students. Applications are processed on a rolling basis. Application fee: $50. *Expenses:* Tuition: Full-time $18,720; part-time $1040 per credit hour. Tuition and fees vary according to course load and program. *Financial support:* In 2010–11, 8 teaching assistantships with full and partial tuition reimbursements (averaging $14,000 per year) were awarded; career-related internships or fieldwork, tuition waivers, and unspecified assistantships also available. Support available to part-time students. Financial award application deadline: 2/28. *Unit head:* Dr. Ken Morgan, Director, 817 257 7270. *Application contact:* Dr. Mike Slattery, Professor, 817-257-7506.

Texas Christian University, College of Science and Engineering, School of Geology, Energy and the Environment, Fort Worth, TX 76129-0002. Offers environmental science (MS); geology (MS); MBA/MEM. *Expenses:* Tuition: Full-time $18,720; part-time $1040 per credit hour. Tuition and fees vary according to course load and program. *Unit head:* Dr. Demitris Kouris, Dean, 817-257-7727, E-mail: d.kouris@tcu.edu. *Application contact:* Dr. Magnus Rittby, Associate Dean for Administration and Graduate Programs, 817-257-7729, Fax: 817-257-7736, E-mail: m.rittby@tcu.edu.

Texas Tech University, Graduate School, College of Arts and Sciences, Department of Environmental Toxicology, Lubbock, TX 79409. Offers MS, PhD, JD/MS, MBA/MS, MS/MPA. Part-time programs available. *Faculty:* 10 full-time (1 woman), 1 part-time/adjunct (0 women). *Students:* 53 full-time (26 women), 2 part-time (1 woman); includes 1 Black or African American, non-Hispanic/Latino; 1 Asian, non-Hispanic/Latino; 1 Hispanic/Latino; 1 Two or more races, non-Hispanic/Latino, 23 international. Average age 26. 51 applicants, 45% accepted, 13 enrolled. In 2010, 4 master's, 4 doctorates awarded. *Degree requirements:* For master's, thesis; for doctorate, thesis/dissertation. *Entrance requirements:* For master's and doctorate, GRE General Test. Additional exam requirements/recommendations for international students: Required—TOEFL (minimum score 550 paper-based; 213 computer-based; 79 iBT). *Application deadline:* For fall admission, 6/1 priority date for domestic students, 1/15 priority date for international students; for spring admission, 9/1 priority date for domestic students, 6/15 priority date for international students. Applications are processed on a rolling basis. Application fee: $50 ($75 for international students). Electronic applications accepted. *Expenses:* Tuition, state resident: full-time $5495.76; part-time $228.99 per credit hour. Tuition, nonresident: full-time $12,936; part-time $538.99 per credit hour. Required fees: $2674; $36 per credit hour. $905 per semester. *Financial support:* In 2010–11, 50 students received support, including 19 research assistantships (averaging $7,129 per year), 5 teaching assistantships with partial tuition reimbursements available (averaging $5,581 per year). Financial award application deadline: 4/15; financial award applicants required to submit FAFSA. *Faculty research:* Terrestrial and aquatic toxicology, biochemical and developmental toxicology, advanced materials, countermeasures to biologic and chemical threats, molecular epidemiology and modeling. Total annual research expenditures: $1.9 million. *Unit head:* Dr. Ronald J. Kendall, Director and Chairman, 806-885-4567, Fax: 806-885-2132, E-mail: ron.kendall@tiehh.ttu.edu. *Application contact:* Ryan Bounds, Assistant Managing Director, 806-885-4567, Fax: 806-885-2132, E-mail: ryan.bounds@ttu.edu.

Thompson Rivers University, Program in Environmental Science, Kamloops, BC V2C 5N3, Canada. Offers MS. *Entrance requirements:* For master's, personal resume, 2 letters of recommendation. Additional exam requirements/recommendations for international students: Required—TOEFL.

Towson University, Program in Environmental Science, Towson, MD 21252-0001. Offers MS, Certificate. Part-time and evening/weekend programs available. *Students:* 5 full-time (3 women), 29 part-time (16 women); includes 5 minority (1 Black or African American, non-Hispanic/Latino; 1 American Indian or Alaska Native, non-Hispanic/Latino; 2 Asian, non-Hispanic/Latino; 1 Hispanic/Latino), 2 international. Average age 31. In 2010, 11 master's awarded. *Entrance requirements:* For master's, GRE (recommended), bachelor's degree in related field, minimum GPA of 3.0. *Application deadline:* Applications are processed on a rolling basis. Application fee: $50. Electronic applications accepted. *Expenses:* Tuition, state resident: part-time $324 per credit. Tuition, nonresident: part-time $681 per credit. Required fees: $95 per term. *Financial support:* Application deadline: 4/1. *Unit head:* Dr. Steven Lev, Graduate Program Director, 410-704-2744, Fax: 410-704-2604, E-mail: slev@towson.edu. *Application contact:* 410-704-2501, Fax: 410-704-4675, E-mail: grads@towson.edu.

Tufts University, School of Engineering, Department of Civil and Environmental Engineering, Medford, MA 02155. Offers civil engineering (ME, MS, PhD), including geotechnical engineering, structural engineering; environmental engineering (ME, MS, PhD), including environmental engineering and environmental sciences, environmental geotechnology, environmental health, environmental science and management, hazardous materials management, water resources engineering. Part-time programs available. Terminal master's awarded for partial completion of doctoral program. *Degree requirements:* For master's, thesis or alternative; for doctorate, thesis/dissertation. *Entrance requirements:* For master's and doctorate, GRE General Test. Additional exam requirements/recommendations for international students: Required—TOEFL (minimum score 550 paper-based; 213 computer-based; 80 iBT). Electronic applications accepted. *Expenses:* Tuition: Full-time $39,624; part-time $3962 per course. Required fees: $40 per year. Full-time tuition and fees vary according to degree level, program and student level. Part-time tuition and fees vary according to course load.

Tuskegee University, Graduate Programs, College of Agricultural, Environmental and Natural Sciences, Department of Agricultural Sciences, Program in Environmental Sciences, Tuskegee, AL 36088. Offers MS. *Faculty:* 13 full-time (1 woman), 2 part-time/adjunct (1 woman). In 2010, 4 master's awarded. *Degree requirements:* For master's, thesis. *Entrance requirements:* For master's, GRE General Test. Additional exam requirements/recommendations for international students: Required—TOEFL (minimum score 500 paper-based; 69 computer-based). *Application deadline:* For fall admission, 7/15 for domestic students. Applications are processed on a rolling basis. Application fee: $25 ($35 for international students). *Expenses:* Tuition: Full-time $16,100; part-time $665 per credit hour. Required fees: $650. *Financial support:* Application deadline: 4/15. *Unit head:* Dr. P. K. Biswas, Head, 334-727-8446. *Application contact:* Dr. Robert L. Laney, Vice President/Director of Admissions and Enrollment Management, 334-727-8580, Fax: 334-727-5750, E-mail: planey@tuskegee.edu.

Universidad del Turabo, Graduate Programs, Programs in Science and Technology, Gurabo, PR 00778-3030. Offers environmental analysis (MSE), including environmental chemistry; environmental management (MSE), including pollution management; environmental science (D Sc), including environmental biology. *Entrance requirements:* For master's, GRE, EXADEP, interview.

Universidad Nacional Pedro Henriquez Urena, Graduate School, Santo Domingo, Dominican Republic. Offers agricultural diversity (MS), including horticultural/fruit production, tropical animal production; conservation of monuments and cultural assets (M Arch); ecology and environment (MS); environmental engineering (MEE); international relations (MA); natural resource management (MS); political science (MA); project optimization (MPM); project feasibility (MPM); project management (MPM); sanitation engineering (ME); science for teachers (MS); tropical Caribbean architecture (M Arch).

Université de Sherbrooke, Faculty of Sciences, Centre Universitaire de Formation en Environnement, Sherbrooke, QC J1K 2R1, Canada. Offers M Sc, Diploma. Postbaccalaureate distance learning degree programs offered (no on-campus study). Electronic applications accepted. *Faculty research:* Environmental studies.

Université du Québec à Montréal, Graduate Programs, Program in Environmental Sciences, Montréal, QC H3C 3P8, Canada. Offers M Sc, PhD, Certificate. Part-time programs available. *Degree requirements:* For master's, research report; for doctorate, thesis/dissertation. *Entrance requirements:* For master's, appropriate bachelor's degree or equivalent, proficiency in French; for doctorate, appropriate master's degree or equivalent, proficiency in French.

Université du Québec à Trois-Rivières, Graduate Programs, Program in Environmental Sciences, Trois-Rivières, QC G9A 5H7, Canada. Offers M Sc, PhD. Part-time programs available. *Degree requirements:* For master's, thesis. *Entrance requirements:* For master's, appropriate bachelor's degree, proficiency in French.

Université du Québec en Abitibi-Témiscamingue, Graduate Programs, Program in Environmental Sciences, Rouyn-Noranda, QC J9X 5E4, Canada. Offers biology (MS); environmental sciences (PhD); sustainable forest ecosystem management (MS).

Université Laval, Faculty of Sciences and Engineering, Department of Geology and Geological Engineering, Programs in Earth Sciences, Québec, QC G1K 7P4, Canada. Offers earth sciences (M Sc, PhD); environmental technologies (M Sc). Offered jointly with INRS-Géressources. Terminal master's awarded for partial completion of doctoral program. *Degree requirements:* For master's, thesis (for some programs); for doctorate, comprehensive exam, thesis/dissertation. *Entrance requirements:* For master's and doctorate, knowledge of French. Electronic applications accepted.

University at Albany, State University of New York, College of Arts and Sciences, Department of Biological Sciences, Program in Biodiversity, Conservation, and Policy, Albany, NY 12222-0001. Offers MS. *Degree requirements:* For master's, one foreign language. *Entrance requirements:* For master's, GRE General Test. *Faculty research:* Aquatic ecology, plant community ecology, biodiversity and public policy, restoration ecology, coastal and estuarine science.

University at Buffalo, the State University of New York, Graduate School, College of Arts and Sciences, Department of Geography, Buffalo, NY 14260. Offers earth systems science (MA); economic geography and international business and world trade (MA); environmental and earth systems science (MS); environmental modeling and analysis (MA); geographic information science (MA, Certificate); geographic information systems and science (MS); geography (MA, PhD); urban and regional geography (MA); MA/MBA. *Faculty:* 14 full-time (6 women), 1 part-time/adjunct (0 women). *Students:* 60 full-time (24 women), 49 part-time (13 women); includes 1 Black or African American, non-Hispanic/Latino; 46 Asian, non-Hispanic/Latino; 4 Hispanic/Latino, 1 international. 162 applicants, 46% accepted, 38 enrolled. In 2010, 21 master's, 5 doctorates awarded. Terminal master's awarded for partial completion of doctoral program. *Degree requirements:* For master's, thesis (for some programs), project; for doctorate, thesis/dissertation. *Entrance requirements:* For master's, GRE General Test, minimum GPA of 2.9; for doctorate, GRE General Test, minimum GPA of 3.0. Additional exam requirements/recommendations for international students: Required—TOEFL (minimum score 550 paper-based; 213 computer-based; 79 iBT). *Application deadline:* For fall admission, 7/1 priority date for domestic students, 1/10 priority date for international students; for spring admission, 12/1 priority date for domestic students, 10/1 priority date for international students. Applications are processed on a rolling basis. Application fee: $75. Electronic applications accepted. *Financial support:* In 2010–11, 19 students received support, including 7 fellowships with full tuition reimbursements available (averaging $5,714 per year), 14 teaching assistantships with full tuition reimbursements available (averaging $13,520 per year); research assistantships with full tuition reimbursements available, career-related internships or fieldwork, Federal Work-Study, institutionally sponsored loans, traineeships, health care benefits, and unspecified assistantships also available. Financial award application deadline: 1/10. *Faculty research:* International business and world trade, geographic information systems and cartography, transportation, urban and regional analysis, physical and environmental geography. Total annual research expenditures: $944,614. *Unit head:* Dr. Sharmistha Bagchi-Sen, Chairman, 716-645-0473, Fax: 716-645-2329, E-mail: geosbs@buffalo.edu. *Application contact:* Betsy Abraham, Graduate Secretary, 716-645-0471, Fax: 716-645-2329, E-mail: babraham@buffalo.edu.

The University of Alabama in Huntsville, School of Graduate Studies, College of Science, Department of Atmospheric and Environmental Science, Huntsville, AL 35899. Offers MS, PhD. Part-time and evening/weekend programs available. *Faculty:* 9 full-time (0 women), 3 part-time/adjunct (2 women). *Students:* 26 full-time (12 women), 7 part-time (3 women);

Environmental Sciences

The University of Alabama in Huntsville (continued)
includes 1 minority (Black or African American, non-Hispanic/Latino), 7 international. Average age 27. 30 applicants, 53% accepted, 10 enrolled. In 2010, 11 master's, 5 doctorates awarded. *Degree requirements:* For master's, comprehensive exam, thesis or alternative, oral and written exams; for doctorate, comprehensive exam, thesis/dissertation, oral and written exams. *Entrance requirements:* For master's, GRE General Test, minimum GPA of 3.0; sequence of courses in calculus (including the calculus of vector-valued functions); courses in linear algebra and ordinary differential equations; two semesters each of chemistry and calculus-based physics; proficiency in at least one high-level computer programming language; for doctorate, GRE General Test, minimum GPA of 3.0. Additional exam requirements/recommendations for international students: Required—TOEFL (minimum score 550 paper-based; 213 computer-based; 62 iBT). *Application deadline:* For fall admission, 7/15 for domestic students, 4/1 for international students; for spring admission, 11/30 for domestic students, 9/1 for international students. Applications are processed on a rolling basis. Application fee: $40 ($50 for international students). Electronic applications accepted. *Expenses:* Tuition, state resident: full-time $7250; part-time $407.75 per credit hour. Tuition, nonresident: full-time $17,358; part-time $970.05 per credit hour. Required fees: $246.80 per semester. Tuition and fees vary according to course load and program. *Financial support:* In 2010–11, 25 students received support, including 24 research assistantships with full and partial tuition reimbursements available (averaging $14,325 per year), 1 teaching assistantship with full and partial tuition reimbursement available (averaging $13,500 per year); career-related internships or fieldwork, Federal Work-Study, institutionally sponsored loans, scholarships/grants, health care benefits, tuition waivers, and unspecified assistantships also available. Support available to part-time students. Financial award application deadline: 4/1; financial award applicants required to submit FAFSA. *Faculty research:* Satellite remote sensing, severe weather, meso-scale modeling, atmospheric chemistry, data assimilation. Total annual research expenditures: $9.8 million. *Unit head:* Dr. Sundar Christopher, Chair, 256-922-7872, Fax: 256-922-7755, E-mail: sundar@nsstc.uah.edu. *Application contact:* Kathy Biggs, Graduate Studies Admissions Manager, 256-824-6199, Fax: 256-824-6405, E-mail: deangrad@uah.edu.

University of Alaska Anchorage, School of Engineering, Program in Applied Environmental Science and Technology, Anchorage, AK 99508. Offers M AEST, MS. Part-time and evening/weekend programs available. *Degree requirements:* For master's, comprehensive exam, thesis (for some programs). *Entrance requirements:* For master's, GRE General Test. Additional exam requirements/recommendations for international students: Required—TOEFL (minimum score 550 paper-based; 213 computer-based). *Faculty research:* Wastewater treatment, environmental regulations, water resources management, justification of public facilities, rural sanitation, biological treatment process.

University of Alaska Fairbanks, College of Engineering and Mines, Department of Civil and Environmental Engineering, Program in Environmental Engineering, Fairbanks, AK 99775-5900. Offers engineering (PhD), including environmental engineering; environmental engineering (MS), including environmental contaminants, environmental science and management, water supply and waste treatment. Part-time programs available. *Students:* 3 full-time (all women), 3 part-time (2 women). Average age 28. 5 applicants, 60% accepted, 1 enrolled. In 2010, 3 master's, 1 doctorate awarded. *Degree requirements:* For master's, comprehensive exam, thesis or alternative; for doctorate, comprehensive exam, thesis/dissertation, oral exam, oral defense. *Entrance requirements:* For master's, basic computer techniques; for doctorate, GRE General Test. Additional exam requirements/recommendations for international students: Required—TOEFL (minimum score 575 paper-based; 213 computer-based). *Application deadline:* For fall admission, 6/1 for domestic students, 3/1 for international students; for spring admission, 10/15 for domestic students, 9/1 for international students. Applications are processed on a rolling basis. Application fee: $60. Electronic applications accepted. *Expenses:* Tuition, state resident: full-time $5688; part-time $316 per credit. Tuition, nonresident: full-time $11,628; part-time $646 per credit. Required fees: $289 per semester. Tuition and fees vary according to course load and reciprocity agreements. *Financial support:* In 2010–11, 4 research assistantships (averaging $13,290 per year), 1 teaching assistantship (averaging $7,088 per year) were awarded; fellowships, career-related internships or fieldwork, Federal Work-Study, scholarships/grants, health care benefits, and unspecified assistantships also available. Support available to part-time students. Financial award application deadline: 7/1; financial award applicants required to submit FAFSA. *Unit head:* Dr. David Barnes, Department Chair, 907-474-7241, Fax: 907-474-6087, E-mail: fyeqe@uaf.edu. *Application contact:* Dr. David Barnes, Department Chair, 907-474-7241, Fax: 907-474-6087, E-mail: fyeqe@uaf.edu.

University of Alaska Fairbanks, College of Engineering and Mines, Department of Civil and Environmental Engineering, Program in Environmental Quality Science, Fairbanks, AK 99775-5900. Offers MS. Part-time programs available. *Students:* 2 full-time (both women). Average age 24. 2 applicants, 0% accepted, 0 enrolled. *Degree requirements:* For master's, comprehensive exam, thesis or alternative. *Entrance requirements:* For master's, calculus, chemistry, basic computer techniques. Additional exam requirements/recommendations for international students: Required—TOEFL (minimum score 575 paper-based; 213 computer-based). *Application deadline:* For fall admission, 6/1 for domestic students, 3/1 for international students; for spring admission, 10/15 for domestic students, 9/1 for international students. Applications are processed on a rolling basis. Application fee: $60. Electronic applications accepted. *Expenses:* Tuition, state resident: full-time $5688; part-time $316 per credit. Tuition, nonresident: full-time $11,628; part-time $646 per credit. Required fees: $289 per semester. Tuition and fees vary according to course load and reciprocity agreements. *Financial support:* Fellowships, research assistantships, teaching assistantships, career-related internships or fieldwork, Federal Work-Study, scholarships/grants, health care benefits, and unspecified assistantships available. Support available to part-time students. Financial award application deadline: 7/1; financial award applicants required to submit FAFSA. *Unit head:* Dr. David Barnes, Department Chair, 907-474-7241, Fax: 907-474-6087, E-mail: fyeqe@uaf.edu. *Application contact:* Dr. David Barnes, Department Chair, 907-474-7241, Fax: 907-474-6087, E-mail: fyeqe@uaf.edu.

University of Alaska Fairbanks, College of Natural Sciences and Mathematics, Department of Chemistry and Biochemistry, Fairbanks, AK 99775-6160. Offers biochemistry and molecular biology (MS, PhD); chemistry (MA, MS); environmental chemistry (MS, PhD). Part-time programs available. *Faculty:* 9 full-time (1 woman). *Students:* 33 full-time (17 women), 4 part-time (2 women); includes 8 minority (1 Black or African American, non-Hispanic/Latino; 2 American Indian or Alaska Native, non-Hispanic/Latino; 2 Asian, non-Hispanic/Latino; 3 Two or more races, non-Hispanic/Latino), 6 international. Average age 31. 38 applicants, 34% accepted, 10 enrolled. In 2010, 3 master's, 4 doctorates awarded. *Degree requirements:* For master's, comprehensive exam, thesis or alternative; for doctorate, comprehensive exam, thesis/dissertation, oral defense. *Entrance requirements:* Additional exam requirements/recommendations for international students: Required—TOEFL (minimum score 550 paper-based; 213 computer-based). *Application deadline:* For fall admission, 6/1 for domestic students, 3/1 for international students; for spring admission, 10/15 for domestic students, 9/1 for international students. Applications are processed on a rolling basis. Application fee: $60. Electronic applications accepted. *Expenses:* Tuition, state resident: full-time $5688; part-time $316 per credit. Tuition, nonresident: full-time $11,628; part-time $646 per credit. Required fees: $289 per semester. Tuition and fees vary according to course load and reciprocity agreements. *Financial support:* In 2010–11, 15 research assistantships with tuition reimbursements (averaging $12,459 per year), 16 teaching assistantships with tuition reimbursements (averaging $14,968 per year) were awarded; fellowships with tuition reimbursements, Federal Work-Study, scholarships/grants, health care benefits, and unspecified assistantships also available. Support available to part-time students. Financial award application deadline: 7/1; financial award applicants required to submit FAFSA. *Faculty research:* Atmospheric aerosols, cold adaptation, hibernation and neuroprotection, liganogated ion channels, arctic contaminants. *Unit head:* Bill Simpson, Department Chair, 907-474-5510, Fax: 907-474-5640, E-mail: fychem@uaf.edu. *Application contact:* Bill Simpson, Department Chair, 907-474-5510, Fax: 907-474-5640, E-mail: fychem@uaf.edu.

University of Alberta, Faculty of Graduate Studies and Research, Department of Civil and Environmental Engineering, Edmonton, AB T6G 2E1, Canada. Offers construction engineering and management (M Eng, M Sc, PhD); environmental engineering (M Eng, M Sc, PhD); environmental science (M Sc, PhD); geoenvironmental engineering (M Eng, M Sc, PhD); geotechnical engineering (M Eng, M Sc, PhD); mining engineering (M Eng, M Sc, PhD); petroleum engineering (M Eng, M Sc, PhD); structural engineering (M Eng, M Sc, PhD); water resources (M Eng, M Sc, PhD). Part-time programs available. Postbaccalaureate distance learning degree programs offered (minimal on-campus study). *Degree requirements:* For master's, thesis (for some programs); for doctorate, thesis/dissertation. *Entrance requirements:* For master's, minimum GPA of 3.0 in last 2 years of undergraduate studies; for doctorate, minimum GPA of 3.0. Additional exam requirements/recommendations for international students: Required—TOEFL (minimum score 550 paper-based; 213 computer-based). Electronic applications accepted. *Faculty research:* Mining.

The University of Arizona, College of Agriculture and Life Sciences, Department of Soil, Water and Environmental Science, Tucson, AZ 85721. Offers MS, PhD. *Faculty:* 10 full-time (2 women). *Students:* 57 full-time (40 women), 6 part-time (3 women); includes 2 Black or African American, non-Hispanic/Latino; 1 American Indian or Alaska Native, non-Hispanic/Latino; 1 Asian, non-Hispanic/Latino; 11 Hispanic/Latino; 4 Two or more races, non-Hispanic/Latino, 18 international. Average age 33. 37 applicants, 54% accepted, 13 enrolled. In 2010, 12 master's, 6 doctorates awarded. *Degree requirements:* For master's, thesis; for doctorate, comprehensive exam, thesis/dissertation. *Entrance requirements:* For master's, GRE (recommended), minimum GPA of 3.0, letter of interest, 3 letters of recommendation; for doctorate, GRE (recommended), MS, minimum GPA of 3.0, letter of interest, 3 letters of recommendation. Additional exam requirements/recommendations for international students: Required—TOEFL (minimum score 550 paper-based; 213 computer-based; 80 iBT). *Application deadline:* For fall admission, 6/1 for domestic students, 12/1 for international students; for spring admission, 10/1 for domestic students, 6/1 for international students. Applications are processed on a rolling basis. Application fee: $75. *Expenses:* Tuition, state resident: full-time $7692. *Financial support:* In 2010–11, 14 students received support, including 32 research assistantships with full and partial tuition reimbursements available (averaging $18,538 per year), 4 teaching assistantships with full and partial tuition reimbursements available (averaging $18,275 per year); fellowships, Federal Work-Study, institutionally sponsored loans, scholarships/grants, health care benefits, tuition waivers (full and partial), and unspecified assistantships also available. Financial award application deadline: 5/1. *Faculty research:* Plant production, environmental microbiology, contaminant flow and transport, aquaculture. Total annual research expenditures: $3.6 million. *Unit head:* Dr. Jeffery C. Silvertooth, Head, 520-621-7228, Fax: 520-621-1647, E-mail: silver@ag.arizona.edu. *Application contact:* Alicia Velasquez, 520-621-1606, Fax: 520-621-1647, E-mail: avelasqu@ag.arizona.edu.

The University of Arizona, College of Agriculture and Life Sciences, Graduate Interdisciplinary Program in Arid Lands Resource Sciences, Tucson, AZ 85721. Offers PhD. *Faculty:* 5. *Students:* 19 full-time (9 women), 5 part-time (1 woman); includes 5 Two or more races, non-Hispanic/Latino, 9 international. Average age 43. 7 applicants, 57% accepted, 4 enrolled. *Degree requirements:* For doctorate, one foreign language, comprehensive exam, thesis/dissertation. *Entrance requirements:* For doctorate, GRE. Additional exam requirements/recommendations for international students: Required—TOEFL (minimum score 550 paper-based; 213 computer-based). *Application deadline:* For fall admission, 2/15 priority date for domestic and international students; for spring admission, 8/1 priority date for domestic students, 8/15 priority date for international students. Applications are processed on a rolling basis. Application fee: $75. *Expenses:* Tuition, state resident: full-time $7692. *Financial support:* In 2010–11, 2 research assistantships with full tuition reimbursements (averaging $14,670 per year), 1 teaching assistantship with full tuition reimbursement (averaging $14,164 per year) were awarded; fellowships, career-related internships or fieldwork, scholarships/grants, health care benefits, and unspecified assistantships also available. Financial award application deadline: 4/1. *Faculty research:* International development; famine, famine early warning systems, and food security; land use, history, change, degradation, desertification, management, and policy; sustainable agriculture and farming systems; remote sensing and spatial analysis; carbon sequestration; political-ecology of natural resources; ethnoecology and other ethno-sciences; economic and agricultural policy and development; economic botany; borderlands issues; globalization; civil conflict; urban development. Total annual research expenditures: $2.3 million. *Unit head:* Dr. Stuart E. Marsh, Chair, 520-621-8574, E-mail: smarsh@ag.arizona.edu. *Application contact:* Anita E. Finnell, Graduate Coordinator, 520-621-9111, Fax: 520-621-3816, E-mail: alrsgidp@email.arizona.edu.

University of California, Berkeley, Graduate Division, College of Natural Resources, Department of Environmental Science, Policy, and Management, Berkeley, CA 94720-1500. Offers environmental science, policy, and management (MS, PhD); forestry (MF). Terminal master's awarded for partial completion of doctoral program. *Degree requirements:* For master's, thesis optional; for doctorate, thesis/dissertation, qualifying exam. *Entrance requirements:* For master's and doctorate, GRE General Test, minimum GPA of 3.0, 3 letters of recommendation. Additional exam requirements/recommendations for international students: Required—TOEFL. Electronic applications accepted. *Faculty research:* Biology and ecology of insects; ecosystem function and environmental issues of soils; plant health/interactions from molecular to ecosystem levels; range management and ecology; forest and resource policy, sustainability, and management.

University of California, Davis, Graduate Studies, Graduate Group in Soils and Biogeochemistry, Davis, CA 95616. Offers MS, PhD. Terminal master's awarded for partial completion of doctoral program. *Degree requirements:* For master's, comprehensive exam (for some programs), thesis (for some programs); for doctorate, thesis/dissertation. *Entrance requirements:* For master's, minimum GPA of 3.3; for doctorate, GRE, minimum GPA of 3.3. Additional exam requirements/recommendations for international students: Required—TOEFL (minimum score 550 paper-based; 213 computer-based). Electronic applications accepted. *Faculty research:* Rhizosphere ecology, soil transport processes, biogeochemical cycling, sustainable agriculture.

University of California, Los Angeles, Graduate Division, School of Public Health, Department of Environmental Health Sciences, Los Angeles, CA 90095. Offers environmental health sciences (MS, PhD); environmental science and engineering (D Env); molecular toxicology (PhD); JD/MPH. *Accreditation:* ABET (one or more programs are accredited). *Degree requirements:* For master's, comprehensive exam or thesis; for doctorate, thesis/dissertation, oral and written qualifying exams. *Entrance requirements:* For master's, GRE General Test, minimum GPA of 3.0; for doctorate, GRE General Test, minimum undergraduate GPA of 3.0. Electronic applications accepted.

University of California, Los Angeles, Graduate Division, School of Public Health, Program in Environmental Science and Engineering, Los Angeles, CA 90095. Offers D Env. *Degree requirements:* For doctorate, thesis/dissertation, oral and written qualifying exams. *Entrance requirements:* For doctorate, GRE General Test, minimum undergraduate GPA of 3.0, master's degree or equivalent in a natural science, engineering, or public health. *Faculty research:* Toxic and hazardous substances, air and water pollution, risk assessment/management, water resources, marine science.

University of California, Merced, Division of Graduate Studies, School of Natural Sciences, Merced, CA 95343. Offers applied mathematics (MS, PhD); biological engineering and small-

scale technologies (MS, PhD); environmental systems (MS, PhD); mechanical engineering and applied mechanics (MS, PhD); physics and chemistry (PhD); quantitative and systems biology (MS, PhD).

University of California, Riverside, Graduate Division, Graduate Materials Science and Engineering Program, Riverside, CA 92521. Offers MS, PhD. *Faculty:* 40. *Students:* 15 full-time (5 women); includes 1 Black or African American, non-Hispanic/Latino; 6 Asian, non-Hispanic/Latino. Average age 27. 60 applicants, 30% accepted, 8 enrolled. *Entrance requirements:* For master's and doctorate, GRE. Additional exam requirements/recommendations for international students: Required—TOEFL (minimum score 550 paper-based; 213 computer-based; 80 iBT). *Application deadline:* For fall admission, 1/5 priority date for domestic students. Application fee: $0 ($100 for international students). Electronic applications accepted. *Financial support:* In 2010–11, 8 students received support; fellowships, research assistantships, teaching assistantships, scholarships/grants, health care benefits, and unspecified assistantships available. Financial award application deadline: 1/5. *Unit head:* MSE Program Office, 951-827-3392, Fax: 951-827-3188, E-mail: mse-program@engr.ucr.edu. *Application contact:* Graduate Admissions, 951-827-3392, Fax: 951-827-3188, E-mail: mse-program@engr.ucr.edu.

University of California, Santa Barbara, Graduate Division, College of Letters and Sciences, Division of Social Sciences, Department of Economics, Santa Barbara, CA 93106-9210. Offers economics (MA, PhD); economics and environmental science (PhD); MA/PhD. *Faculty:* 30 full-time (4 women), 14 part-time/adjunct (4 women). *Students:* 104 full-time (41 women); includes 31 Asian, non-Hispanic/Latino; 11 Hispanic/Latino. Average age 26. 318 applicants, 55% accepted, 57 enrolled. In 2010, 34 master's, 10 doctorates awarded. Terminal master's awarded for partial completion of doctoral program. *Degree requirements:* For master's, comprehensive exam, thesis; for doctorate, comprehensive exam, thesis/dissertation. *Entrance requirements:* For master's, GRE General Test, 3 letters of recommendation, resume/curriculum vitae; for doctorate, GRE General Test, 3 letters of recommendation, statement of purpose, personal achievements/contributions statement, resume/curriculum vitae, transcripts for post-secondary institutions attended. Additional exam requirements/recommendations for international students: Required—TOEFL (minimum score 550 paper-based; 80 iBT), IELTS (minimum score 7). *Application deadline:* For fall admission, 12/1 priority date for domestic and international students. Application fee: $70 ($90 for international students). Electronic applications accepted. *Financial support:* In 2010–11, 65 students received support, including 24 fellowships with full and partial tuition reimbursements available (averaging $12,105 per year), 7 research assistantships with full and partial tuition reimbursements available (averaging $9,616 per year), 56 teaching assistantships with partial tuition reimbursements available (averaging $12,114 per year); Federal Work-Study, institutionally sponsored loans, scholarships/grants, health care benefits, tuition waivers (full and partial), and unspecified assistantships also available. Support available to part-time students. Financial award application deadline: 12/1; financial award applicants required to submit FAFSA. *Faculty research:* Labor economics, econometrics, macroeconomic theory and policy, environmental and natural resources economics (EES), experimental and behavioral economics. *Unit head:* Prof. Perry Shapiro, Chair, 805-893-2253, Fax: 805-893-8830, E-mail: pxshap@econ.ucsb.edu. *Application contact:* Mark Patterson, Staff Graduate Advisor, 805-893-2205, Fax: 805-893-8830, E-mail: mark@econ.ucsb.edu.

University of California, Santa Barbara, Graduate Division, Donald Bren School of Environmental Science and Management, Santa Barbara, CA 93106-5131. Offers economics and environmental science (PhD); environmental science and management (MESM, PhD); technology and society (PhD). *Faculty:* 17 full-time (3 women), 2 part-time/adjunct (0 women). *Students:* 219 full-time (128 women); includes 1 Black or African American, non-Hispanic/Latino; 1 American Indian or Alaska Native, non-Hispanic/Latino; 33 Asian, non-Hispanic/Latino; 11 Hispanic/Latino. Average age 28. 521 applicants, 40% accepted, 82 enrolled. In 2010, 75 master's awarded. *Degree requirements:* For master's, thesis; for doctorate, thesis/dissertation. *Entrance requirements:* For master's and doctorate, GRE. Additional exam requirements/recommendations for international students: Required—TOEFL (minimum score 550 paper-based; 80 iBT), IELTS (minimum score 7). *Application deadline:* For fall admission, 12/15 priority date for domestic and international students. Application fee: $70 ($90 for international students). Electronic applications accepted. *Financial support:* In 2010–11, 105 students received support, including 83 fellowships with full and partial tuition reimbursements available (averaging $6,929 per year), 27 research assistantships with full and partial tuition reimbursements available (averaging $8,918 per year), 32 teaching assistantships with partial tuition reimbursements available (averaging $8,112 per year); career-related internships or fieldwork and tuition waivers (full and partial) also available. Financial award application deadline: 12/15; financial award applicants required to submit FAFSA. *Faculty research:* Coastal marine resources management, conservation planning, corporate environmental management, economics and politics of the environment, energy and climate, pollution prevention and remediation, water resources management. *Unit head:* Bryant Wieneke, Assistant Dean, Planning and Administration, 805-893-2212, Fax: 805-893-7612, E-mail: bryant@bren.ucsb.edu. *Application contact:* Graduate Advisor, 805-893-7611, Fax: 805-893-7612, E-mail: admissions@bren.ucsb.edu.

University of Chicago, Irving B. Harris Graduate School of Public Policy Studies, Chicago, IL 60637-1513. Offers environmental science and policy (MS); public policy studies (AM, MPP, PhD); JD/MPP; MBA/MPP; MPP/M Div; MPP/MA. Part-time programs available. *Degree requirements:* For doctorate, thesis/dissertation. *Entrance requirements:* Additional exam requirements/recommendations for international students: Required—TOEFL. Electronic applications accepted. *Expenses:* Contact institution. *Faculty research:* Family and child policy, international security, health policy, social policy.

University of Cincinnati, Graduate School, College of Engineering, Department of Civil and Environmental Engineering, Program in Environmental Sciences, Cincinnati, OH 45221. Offers MS, PhD. Part-time programs available. *Degree requirements:* For master's, thesis or alternative; for doctorate, one foreign language, thesis/dissertation. *Entrance requirements:* For master's and doctorate, GRE General Test. Additional exam requirements/recommendations for international students: Required—TOEFL (minimum score 580 paper-based; 237 computer-based; 92 iBT). Electronic applications accepted. *Faculty research:* Environmental microbiology, solid-waste management, air pollution control, water pollution control, aerosols.

University of Colorado at Colorado Springs, College of Letters, Arts and Sciences, Department of Geography and Environmental Studies, Colorado Springs, CO 80933-7150. Offers MA. Part-time programs available. *Faculty:* 11 full-time (2 women). *Students:* 14 full-time (5 women), 4 part-time (2 women); includes 1 Hispanic/Latino. Average age 36. 13 applicants, 77% accepted, 6 enrolled. In 2010, 7 master's awarded. *Degree requirements:* For master's, comprehensive exam (for some programs), thesis (for some programs). *Entrance requirements:* For master's, GRE. *Application deadline:* For fall admission, 4/1 priority date for domestic students. Applications are processed on a rolling basis. Application fee: $60 ($75 for international students). *Expenses:* Tuition, state resident: full-time $7916. Tuition, nonresident: full-time $16,610. Tuition and fees vary according to course load, degree level, program, reciprocity agreements and student level. *Financial support:* Federal Work-Study and scholarships/grants available. Support available to part-time students. Financial award application deadline: 3/1; financial award applicants required to submit FAFSA. *Faculty research:* Natural hazard mitigation and policy issues, applied geography, geographic information systems, population geography. Total annual research expenditures: $106,415. *Unit head:* Dr. Emily Skop, Associate Professor, 719-255-3789, Fax: 719-255-4066, E-mail: eskop@uccs.edu. *Application contact:* Mary McGill, Program Assistant, 719-255-3016, E-mail: mmcgill@uccs.edu.

University of Colorado Denver, College of Liberal Arts and Sciences, Department of Geography and Environmental Sciences, Denver, CO 80217. Offers environmental sciences (MS), including air quality, ecosystems, environmental health, environmental science education, environmental sciences, geo-spatial analysis, hazardous waste, water quality. Part-time and evening/weekend programs available. *Students:* 48 full-time (28 women), 4 part-time (3 women); includes 2 Black or African American, non-Hispanic/Latino; 2 Asian, non-Hispanic/Latino; 3 Hispanic/Latino, 8 international. Average age 29. 44 applicants, 52% accepted, 14 enrolled. In 2010, 17 master's awarded. *Degree requirements:* For master's, thesis or alternative. *Entrance requirements:* For master's, GRE General Test, BA in one of the natural/physical sciences or engineering (or equivalent background); prerequisite coursework in calculus and physics (one semester each), general chemistry with lab and general biology with lab (two semesters each). Additional exam requirements/recommendations for international students: Required—TOEFL (minimum score 525 paper-based; 197 computer-based). *Application deadline:* For fall admission, 4/1 for domestic students; for spring admission, 10/1 for domestic students. Application fee: $50 ($75 for international students). Electronic applications accepted. *Expenses:* Tuition, state resident: full-time $7332; part-time $355 per credit hour. Tuition, nonresident: full-time $18,990; part-time $1055 per credit hour. Required fees: $998. Tuition and fees vary according to course level, course load, degree level, campus/location, program, reciprocity agreements and student level. *Financial support:* Research assistantships, teaching assistantships, Federal Work-Study available. Financial award application deadline: 4/1; financial award applicants required to submit FAFSA. *Faculty research:* Air quality, environmental health, ecosystems, hazardous waste, water quality, geo-spatial analysis and environmental science education. *Unit head:* Dr. John Wyckoff, Director, 303-556-2590, Fax: 303-556-6197, E-mail: john.wyckoff@cudenver.edu. *Application contact:* Dr. John Wyckoff, Director, 303-556-2590, Fax: 303-556-6197, E-mail: john.wyckoff@cudenver.edu.

University of Guam, Office of Graduate Studies, College of Natural and Applied Sciences, Program in Environmental Science, Mangilao, GU 96923. Offers MS. Part-time programs available. *Degree requirements:* For master's, thesis. *Entrance requirements:* For master's, GRE General Test. Additional exam requirements/recommendations for international students: Required—TOEFL. *Faculty research:* Water resources, ecology, karst formations, hydrogeology, meteorology.

University of Guelph, Graduate Studies, Ontario Agricultural College, Department of Land Resource Science, Guelph, ON N1G 2W1, Canada. Offers atmospheric science (M Sc, PhD); environmental and agricultural earth sciences (M Sc, PhD); land resources management (M Sc, PhD); soil science (M Sc, PhD). Part-time programs available. *Degree requirements:* For master's, thesis (for some programs), research project (non-thesis track); for doctorate, comprehensive exam, thesis/dissertation. *Entrance requirements:* For master's, minimum B-average during previous 2 years of course work; for doctorate, minimum B average during previous 2 years of course work. Additional exam requirements/recommendations for international students: Required—TOEFL (minimum score 550 paper-based; 213 computer-based). Electronic applications accepted. *Faculty research:* Soil science, environmental earth science, land resource management.

University of Hawaii at Hilo, Program in Tropical Conservation Biology and Environmental Science, Hilo, HI 96720-4091. Offers MS.

University of Houston–Clear Lake, School of Science and Computer Engineering, Program in Environmental Science, Houston, TX 77058-1098. Offers MS. Part-time and evening/weekend programs available. *Entrance requirements:* For master's, GRE General Test. Additional exam requirements/recommendations for international students: Required—TOEFL (minimum score 550 paper-based; 213 computer-based).

University of Idaho, College of Graduate Studies, Program in Environmental Science, Moscow, ID 83844-2282. Offers MS, PhD. *Students:* 50 full-time (24 women), 37 part-time (23 women). Average age 33. In 2010, 16 master's, 3 doctorates awarded. *Application deadline:* For fall admission, 8/1 for domestic students; for spring admission, 12/15 for domestic students. Applications are processed on a rolling basis. Application fee: $60. Electronic applications accepted. *Expenses:* Tuition, nonresident: part-time $580 per credit. Required fees: $306 per credit. *Financial support:* Research assistantships, teaching assistantships available. Financial award applicants required to submit FAFSA. *Unit head:* Dr. Stephen S. Mulkey, Director, 208-885-6113, Fax: 208-885-4674, E-mail: envs@uidaho.edu. *Application contact:* Dr. Stephen S. Mulkey, Director, 208-885-6113, Fax: 208-885-4674, E-mail: envs@uidaho.edu.

University of Illinois at Springfield, Graduate Programs, College of Public Affairs and Administration, Program in Environmental Studies, Springfield, IL 62703-5407. Offers environmental science (MS); environmental studies (MA). Part-time and evening/weekend programs available. Postbaccalaureate distance learning degree programs offered (no on-campus study). *Degree requirements:* For master's, thesis or project. *Entrance requirements:* For master's, minimum undergraduate GPA of 3.0, 2 letters of recommendation. Additional exam requirements/recommendations for international students: Required—TOEFL (minimum score 500 paper-based; 176 computer-based; 61 iBT). Electronic applications accepted. *Expenses:* Tuition, state resident: full-time $6774; part-time $282.25 per credit hour. Tuition, nonresident: full-time $15,078; part-time $628.25 per credit hour. Required fees: $15.25 per credit hour. $492 per term.

University of Illinois at Urbana–Champaign, Graduate College, College of Agricultural, Consumer and Environmental Sciences, Department of Natural Resources and Environmental Science, Champaign, IL 61820. Offers MS, PhD, MS/JD. Part-time programs available. Postbaccalaureate distance learning degree programs offered (no on-campus study). *Faculty:* 22 full-time (6 women), 1 part-time/adjunct (0 women). *Students:* 44 full-time (19 women), 77 part-time (32 women); includes 2 Asian, non-Hispanic/Latino; 5 Hispanic/Latino; 1 Two or more races, non-Hispanic/Latino, 18 international. 120 applicants, 43% accepted, 38 enrolled. In 2010, 27 master's, 4 doctorates awarded. *Entrance requirements:* For master's and doctorate, GRE, minimum GPA of 3.0. Additional exam requirements/recommendations for international students: Required—TOEFL (minimum score 600 paper-based; 250 computer-based). *Application deadline:* Applications are processed on a rolling basis. Application fee: $75 ($90 for international students). Electronic applications accepted. *Financial support:* In 2010–11, 7 fellowships, 60 research assistantships, 13 teaching assistantships were awarded; tuition waivers (full and partial) also available. *Unit head:* Jeffrey D. Brawn, Head, 217-244-5937, Fax: 217-244-3219, E-mail: jbrawn@illinois.edu. *Application contact:* Karen M. Claus, Secretary, 217-333-5824, Fax: 217-244-3219, E-mail: kclaus@illinois.edu.

University of Illinois at Urbana–Champaign, Graduate College, College of Engineering, Department of Civil and Environmental Engineering, Champaign, IL 61820. Offers civil engineering (MS); environmental engineering in civil engineering (MS, PhD); environmental science in civil engineering (MS, PhD); M Arch/MS; MBA/MS. *Faculty:* 46 full-time (7 women), 1 part-time/adjunct (0 women). *Students:* 380 full-time (103 women), 79 part-time (18 women); includes 2 Black or African American, non-Hispanic/Latino; 27 Asian, non-Hispanic/Latino; 15 Hispanic/Latino; 4 Two or more races, non-Hispanic/Latino, 248 international. 961 applicants, 38% accepted, 159 enrolled. In 2010, 119 master's, 45 doctorates awarded. *Entrance requirements:* For master's and doctorate, GRE. Additional exam requirements/recommendations for international students: Required—TOEFL (minimum score 550 paper-based; 213 computer-based; 79 iBT) or IELTS (minimum score 6.5). *Application deadline:* Applications are processed on a rolling basis. Application fee: $75 ($90 for international students). Electronic applications accepted. *Financial support:* In 2010–11, 60 fellowships, 260 research assistantships, 77 teaching assistantships were awarded; tuition waivers (full and partial) also available. *Unit head:* Amr S. Elnashai, Head, 217-265-5497, Fax: 217-265-8040, E-mail: aelnash@illinois.edu.

Environmental Sciences

University of Illinois at Urbana–Champaign (continued)
Application contact: Mary Pearson, Administrative Secretary, 217-333-3811, Fax: 217-333-9464, E-mail: mkpearso@illinois.edu.

The University of Kansas, Graduate Studies, School of Engineering, Department of Civil, Environmental, and Architectural Engineering, Program in Environmental Science, Lawrence, KS 66045. Offers MS, PhD. Part-time programs available. *Faculty:* 9 full-time (1 woman), 1 part-time/adjunct (0 women). *Students:* 5 full-time (2 women), 4 part-time (2 women); includes 2 minority (1 Asian, non-Hispanic/Latino; 1 Hispanic/Latino). Average age 27. 8 applicants, 75% accepted, 3 enrolled. In 2010, 3 master's awarded. *Degree requirements:* For master's, thesis or alternative, exam; for doctorate, comprehensive exam, thesis/dissertation. *Entrance requirements:* For master's, GRE, minimum GPA of 3.0; for doctorate, GRE, minimum GPA of 3.5. Additional exam requirements/recommendations for international students: Required—TOEFL. *Application deadline:* For fall admission, 3/1 priority date for domestic and international students; for spring admission, 12/1 priority date for domestic students, 8/15 priority date for international students. Applications are processed on a rolling basis. Application fee: $55 ($65 for international students). Electronic applications accepted. *Expenses:* Tuition, state resident: full-time $7092; part-time $295.50 per credit hour. Tuition, nonresident: full-time $16,590; part-time $691.25 per credit hour. Required fees: $858; $71.49 per credit hour. Tuition and fees vary according to course load, campus/location and program. *Financial support:* Fellowships with full tuition reimbursements, research assistantships with full tuition reimbursements, teaching assistantships, career-related internships or fieldwork available. Financial award application deadline: 2/7. *Faculty research:* Water quality, water treatment, wastewater treatment, air quality, air pollution control, solid waste, hazardous waste, water resources engineering, water resources science. *Unit head:* Craig D. Adams, Professor and Chair, 785-864-2700, Fax: 785-864-5631, E-mail: adamscd@ku.edu. *Application contact:* Bruce M. McEnroe, Professor and Graduate Advisor, 785-864-2925, Fax: 785-864-2925, E-mail: mcenroe@ku.edu.

University of Lethbridge, School of Graduate Studies, Lethbridge, AB T1K 3M4, Canada. Offers accounting (MScM); addictions counseling (M Sc); agricultural biotechnology (M Sc); agricultural studies (M Sc, MA); anthropology (MA); archaeology (MA); art (MA, MFA); biochemistry (M Sc); biological sciences (M Sc); biomolecular science (PhD); biosystems and biodiversity (PhD); Canadian studies (MA); chemistry (M Sc); computer science (M Sc); computer science and geographical information science (M Sc); counseling psychology (M Ed); dramatic arts (MA); earth, space, and physical science (PhD); economics (MA); educational leadership (M Ed); English (MA); environmental science (M Sc); evolution and behavior (PhD); exercise science (M Sc); finance (MScM); French (MA); French/German (MA); French/Spanish (MA); general education (M Ed); general management (MScM); geography (M Sc, MA); German (MA); health science (M Sc); history (MA); human resource management and labour relations (MScM); individualized multidisciplinary (M Sc, MA); information systems (MScM); international management (MScM); kinesiology (M Sc, MA); management (M Sc, MA); marketing (MScM); mathematics (M Sc); music (M Mus, MA); Native American studies (MA); neuroscience (M Sc, PhD); new media (MA); nursing (M Sc); philosophy (MA); physics (M Sc); policy and strategy (MScM); political science (MA); psychology (M Sc, MA); religious studies (MA); social sciences (MA); sociology (MA); theatre and dramatic arts (MFA); theoretical and computational science (PhD); urban and regional studies (MA); women's studies (MA). Part-time and evening/weekend programs available. *Degree requirements:* For doctorate, comprehensive exam, thesis/dissertation. *Entrance requirements:* For master's, GMAT (M Sc in management), bachelor's degree in related field, minimum GPA of 3.0 during previous 20 graded semester courses, 2 years teaching or related experience (M Ed); for doctorate, master's degree, minimum graduate GPA of 3.5. Additional exam requirements/recommendations for international students: Required—TOEFL. *Faculty research:* Movement and brain plasticity, gibberellin physiology, photosynthesis, carbon cycling, molecular properties of main-group ring components.

University of Maine, Graduate School, College of Natural Sciences, Forestry, and Agriculture, Department of Biological Sciences, Program in Ecology and Environmental Science, Orono, ME 04469. Offers water resources (PhD). Part-time programs available. *Students:* 41 full-time (30 women), 11 part-time (6 women), 1 international. Average age 31. 84 applicants, 20% accepted, 15 enrolled. In 2010, 11 master's, 4 doctorates awarded. *Degree requirements:* For doctorate, thesis/dissertation. *Entrance requirements:* For master's and doctorate, GRE General Test. Additional exam requirements/recommendations for international students: Required—TOEFL. *Application deadline:* For fall admission, 2/1 priority date for domestic students. Applications are processed on a rolling basis. Application fee: $65. Electronic applications accepted. *Expenses:* Tuition, state resident: full-time $400. Tuition, nonresident: full-time $1050. *Financial support:* Career-related internships or fieldwork, Federal Work-Study, institutionally sponsored loans, and tuition waivers (full) available. Financial award application deadline: 3/1. *Unit head:* Dr. Chris Cronan, Coordinator, 207-581-3235. *Application contact:* Scott G. Delcourt, Associate Dean of the Graduate School, 207-581-3291, Fax: 207-581-3232, E-mail: graduate@maine.edu.

University of Maine, Graduate School, College of Natural Sciences, Forestry, and Agriculture, Department of Plant, Soil, and Environmental Sciences, Orono, ME 04469. Offers biological sciences (PhD); ecology and environmental sciences (MS, PhD); forest resources (PhD); horticulture (MS); plant science (PhD); plant, soil, and environmental sciences (MS); resource utilization (MS). *Faculty:* 9 full-time (3 women), 7 part-time/adjunct (3 women). *Students:* 6 full-time (2 women), 2 part-time (1 woman), 2 international. Average age 31. 9 applicants, 22% accepted, 0 enrolled. In 2010, 2 master's awarded. *Entrance requirements:* For master's and doctorate, GRE General Test. Additional exam requirements/recommendations for international students: Required—TOEFL. *Application deadline:* Applications are processed on a rolling basis. Application fee: $65. Electronic applications accepted. *Expenses:* Tuition, state resident: full-time $400. Tuition, nonresident: full-time $1050. *Financial support:* In 2010–11, 16 research assistantships with tuition reimbursements (averaging $16,260 per year), 3 teaching assistantships with tuition reimbursements (averaging $12,790 per year) were awarded; scholarships/grants, tuition waivers (full and partial), and unspecified assistantships also available. *Unit head:* Dr. Gregory Porter, Chair, 207-581-2943, Fax: 207-581-3207. *Application contact:* Scott G. Delcourt, Associate Dean of the Graduate School, 207-581-3291, Fax: 207-581-3232, E-mail: graduate@maine.edu.

The University of Manchester, School of Earth, Atmospheric and Environmental Sciences, Manchester, United Kingdom. Offers atmospheric sciences (M Phil, M Sc, PhD); basin studies and petroleum geosciences (M Phil, M Sc, PhD); earth, atmospheric and environmental sciences (M Phil, M Sc, PhD); environmental geochemistry and cosmochemistry (M Phil, M Sc, PhD); isotope geochemistry and cosmochemistry (M Phil, M Sc, PhD); paleontology (M Phil, M Sc, PhD); physics and chemistry of minerals and fluids (M Phil, M Sc, PhD); structural and petrological geosciences (M Phil, M Sc, PhD).

University of Manitoba, Faculty of Graduate Studies, Clayton H. Riddell Faculty of Environment, Earth, and Resources, Department of Environment and Geography, Winnipeg, MB R3T 2N2, Canada. Offers environment (M Env); environment and geography (M Sc); geography (MA, PhD). *Degree requirements:* For master's, thesis; for doctorate, one foreign language, thesis/dissertation.

University of Maryland, Baltimore, Graduate School, Program in Marine-Estuarine-Environmental Sciences, Baltimore, MD 21201. Offers MS, PhD. Part-time programs available. *Faculty:* 7. *Students:* 1 (woman) full-time, all international. 1 applicant, 0% accepted, 0 enrolled. Terminal master's awarded for partial completion of doctoral program. *Degree requirements:* For master's, thesis, oral defense; for doctorate, comprehensive exam, thesis/dissertation, proposal defense, oral defense. *Entrance requirements:* For master's and doctorate, GRE General Test, minimum GPA of 3.0. Additional exam requirements/recommendations for international students: Required—TOEFL. *Application deadline:* For fall admission, 2/1 for domestic students, 1/1 for international students; for spring admission, 9/1 for domestic students. Applications are processed on a rolling basis. Application fee: $50. Electronic applications accepted. Part-time tuition and fees vary according to course load, degree level and program. *Financial support:* In 2010–11, 1 research assistantship with tuition reimbursement was awarded; fellowships with tuition reimbursements, teaching assistantships with tuition reimbursements, scholarships/grants and unspecified assistantships also available. *Unit head:* Dr. Kennedy T. Paynter, Director, Marine-Estuarine-Environmental Science Graduate Program, 301-405-6938, Fax: 301-314-4139, E-mail: mees@umd.edu. *Application contact:* Dr. Kennedy T. Paynter, Director, Marine-Estuarine-Environmental Science Graduate Program, 301-405-6938, Fax: 301-314-4139, E-mail: mees@umd.edu.

University of Maryland, Baltimore County, Graduate School, Marine-Estuarine-Environmental Sciences Graduate Program, Baltimore, MD 21250. Offers MS, PhD. Part-time programs available. *Faculty:* 14. *Students:* 5 full-time (3 women), 1 part-time (0 women); includes 1 Black or African American, non-Hispanic/Latino; 1 Hispanic/Latino. 8 applicants, 0% accepted, 0 enrolled. In 2010, 1 master's, 1 doctorate awarded. *Degree requirements:* For master's, thesis, oral defense; for doctorate, comprehensive exam, thesis/dissertation, proposal defense, oral defense. *Entrance requirements:* For master's and doctorate, GRE General Test, minimum GPA of 3.0. Additional exam requirements/recommendations for international students: Required—TOEFL. *Application deadline:* For fall admission, 2/1 for domestic students, 1/1 for international students; for spring admission, 9/1 for domestic students. Applications are processed on a rolling basis. Application fee: $50. Electronic applications accepted. *Financial support:* In 2010–11, 2 fellowships with tuition reimbursements (averaging $22,500 per year), 1 research assistantship with tuition reimbursement (averaging $21,000 per year), 1 teaching assistantship with tuition reimbursement (averaging $20,000 per year) were awarded; career-related internships or fieldwork, scholarships/grants, and unspecified assistantships also available. Financial award application deadline: 12/1. *Unit head:* Dr. Kennedy T. Paynter, Director, 301-405-6938, Fax: 301-314-4139, E-mail: mees@umd.edu. *Application contact:* Dr. Kennedy T. Paynter, Director, 301-405-6938, Fax: 301-314-4139, E-mail: mees@umd.edu.

University of Maryland, College Park, Academic Affairs, College of Agriculture and Natural Resources, Department of Environmental Science and Technology, College Park, MD 20742. Offers MS, PhD. *Faculty:* 26 full-time (3 women), 7 part-time/adjunct (3 women). *Students:* 31 full-time (17 women), 3 part-time (1 woman); includes 3 Black or African American, non-Hispanic/Latino; 1 Hispanic/Latino; 1 Two or more races, non-Hispanic/Latino, 4 international. 82 applicants, 29% accepted, 8 enrolled. In 2010, 2 master's, 3 doctorates awarded. *Application deadline:* For fall admission, 1/15 for domestic students, 2/1 for international students; for spring admission, 8/15 for domestic students, 6/1 for international students. Application fee: $75. *Expenses:* Tuition, area resident: Part-time $471 per credit hour. Tuition, state resident: part-time $471 per credit hour. Tuition, nonresident: part-time $1016 per credit hour. Required fees: $337 per term. *Financial support:* In 2010–11, 19 research assistantships (averaging $17,044 per year), 6 teaching assistantships (averaging $16,789 per year) were awarded; fellowships with full tuition reimbursements also available. Total annual research expenditures: $5 million. *Unit head:* Dr. Frank Coale, Chair, 301-405-1306, E-mail: fjcoale@umd.edu. *Application contact:* Dr. Charles A. Caramello, Dean of Graduate School, 301-405-0358, Fax: 301-314-9305, E-mail: ccaramel@umd.edu.

University of Maryland, College Park, Academic Affairs, College of Computer, Mathematical and Natural Sciences, Program in Marine-Estuarine-Environmental Sciences, College Park, MD 20742. Offers MS, PhD. Intercampus, interdisciplinary program. Part-time programs available. *Faculty:* 132. *Students:* 122 (78 women); includes 4 Black or African American, non-Hispanic/Latino; 2 Asian, non-Hispanic/Latino; 4 Hispanic/Latino, 27 international. 131 applicants, 32% accepted, 32 enrolled. In 2010, 11 master's, 7 doctorates awarded. Terminal master's awarded for partial completion of doctoral program. *Degree requirements:* For master's, thesis, oral defense; for doctorate, comprehensive exam, thesis/dissertation, proposal defense, oral defense. *Entrance requirements:* For master's and doctorate, GRE General Test, minimum GPA of 3.0. Additional exam requirements/recommendations for international students: Required—TOEFL. *Application deadline:* For fall admission, 2/1 for domestic and international students; for spring admission, 9/1 for domestic students, 6/1 for international students. Applications are processed on a rolling basis. Application fee: $60. Electronic applications accepted. *Expenses:* Tuition, area resident: Part-time $471 per credit hour. Tuition, state resident: part-time $471 per credit hour. Tuition, nonresident: part-time $1016 per credit hour. Required fees: $337 per term. *Financial support:* In 2010–11, 9 teaching assistantships with full tuition reimbursements were awarded; fellowships with full tuition reimbursements, research assistantships with full tuition reimbursements, Federal Work-Study, scholarships/grants, traineeships, health care benefits, and unspecified assistantships also available. Financial award application deadline: 1/1; financial award applicants required to submit FAFSA. *Faculty research:* Marine and estuarine organisms, terrestrial and freshwater ecology, remote environmental sensing, fisheries science, oceanography, environmental chemistry. *Unit head:* Dr. Kennedy T. Paynter, Director, 301-405-6938, Fax: 301-314-4139, E-mail: mees@umd.edu. *Application contact:* Dr. Kennedy T. Paynter, Director, 301-405-6938, Fax: 301-314-4139, E-mail: mees@umd.edu.

University of Maryland Eastern Shore, Graduate Programs, Department of Natural Sciences, Program in Marine-Estuarine-Environmental Sciences, Princess Anne, MD 21853-1299. Offers MS, PhD. Part-time programs available. *Faculty:* 26. *Students:* 29 (17 women); includes 13 Black or African American, non-Hispanic/Latino; 1 Asian, non-Hispanic/Latino, 10 international. 16 applicants, 25% accepted, 4 enrolled. In 2010, 2 master's, 2 doctorates awarded. *Degree requirements:* For master's, thesis; for doctorate, comprehensive exam, thesis/dissertation, proposal defense. *Entrance requirements:* For master's and doctorate, GRE General Test, minimum GPA of 3.0. Additional exam requirements/recommendations for international students: Required—TOEFL. *Application deadline:* For fall admission, 2/1 for domestic and international students; for spring admission, 9/1 for domestic students, 8/1 for international students. Applications are processed on a rolling basis. Application fee: $30. Electronic applications accepted. *Financial support:* In 2010–11, 30 students received support; fellowships with tuition reimbursements available, research assistantships with tuition reimbursements available, teaching assistantships with tuition reimbursements available, career-related internships or fieldwork, scholarships/grants, and unspecified assistantships available. Support available to part-time students. Financial award application deadline: 1/1. *Unit head:* Dr. Kennedy T. Paynter, Director, 301-405-6938, Fax: 301-314-4139, E-mail: mees@umd.edu. *Application contact:* Dr. Kennedy T. Paynter, Director, 301-405-6938, Fax: 301-314-4139, E-mail: mees@umd.edu.

University of Massachusetts Boston, Office of Graduate Studies, College of Science and Mathematics, Department of Environmental, Earth and Ocean Sciences, Track in Environmental, Earth and Ocean Sciences, Boston, MA 02125-3393. Offers PhD. Part-time and evening/weekend programs available. *Degree requirements:* For doctorate, comprehensive exam, thesis/dissertation, oral exams. *Entrance requirements:* For doctorate, GRE General Test, minimum GPA of 2.75. *Faculty research:* Conservation genetics, anthropogenic and natural influences on community structures of coral reef factors, geographical variation in mitochondrial DNA, protein chemistry and enzymology pertaining to insect cuticle.

University of Massachusetts Lowell, College of Arts and Sciences, Department of Chemistry, Lowell, MA 01854-2881. Offers analytical chemistry (PhD); biochemistry (PhD); chemistry (MS, PhD); environmental studies (PhD); green chemistry (PhD); inorganic chemistry (PhD); organic chemistry (PhD); polymer science (MS). Terminal master's awarded for partial completion of doctoral program. *Degree requirements:* For master's, thesis; for doctorate, 2 foreign

languages, thesis/dissertation. *Entrance requirements:* For master's and doctorate, GRE General Test. Electronic applications accepted.

University of Massachusetts Lowell, James B. Francis College of Engineering, Department of Civil and Environmental Engineering and College of Arts and Sciences, Program in Environmental Studies, Lowell, MA 01854-2881. Offers environmental engineering (MSES); environmental studies (PhD, Certificate). Part-time programs available. *Degree requirements:* For master's, thesis optional. *Entrance requirements:* For master's, GRE General Test. *Faculty research:* Remote sensing of air pollutants, atmospheric deposition of toxic metals, contaminant transport in groundwater, soil remediation.

University of Massachusetts Lowell, School of Health and Environment, Department of Work Environment, Lowell, MA 01854-2881. Offers cleaner production and pollution prevention (MS, Sc D); environmental risk assessment (Certificate); epidemiology (MS, Sc D); ergonomics and safety (MS, Sc D); identification and control of ergonomic hazards (Certificate); job stress and healthy job redesign (Certificate); occupational and environmental hygiene (MS, Sc D); radiological health physics and general work environment protection (Certificate); work environment policy (MS, Sc D). *Accreditation:* ABET (one or more programs are accredited). Part-time programs available. Terminal master's awarded for partial completion of doctoral program. *Degree requirements:* For master's, thesis optional; for doctorate, thesis/dissertation. *Entrance requirements:* For master's and doctorate, GRE General Test. Additional exam requirements/recommendations for international students: Required—TOEFL.

University of Medicine and Dentistry of New Jersey, Graduate School of Biomedical Sciences, Graduate Programs in Biomedical Sciences–Piscataway, Program in Environmental Sciences/Exposure Assessment, Piscataway, NJ 08854-5635. Offers PhD, MD/PhD. PhD offered jointly with Rutgers, The State University of New Jersey, New Brunswick. *Entrance requirements:* Additional exam requirements/recommendations for international students: Required—TOEFL. Electronic applications accepted.

University of Michigan, School of Natural Resources and Environment, Program in Natural Resources and Environment, Ann Arbor, MI 48109. Offers aquatic sciences: research and management (MS); behavior, education and communication (MS); conservation biology (MS); conservation ecology (MS); environmental informatics (MS); environmental justice (MS); environmental policy and planning (MS); natural resources and environment (PhD); sustainable systems (MS); terrestrial ecosystems (MS); MS/AM; MS/JD; MS/MBA. *Faculty:* 42 full-time, 23 part-time/adjunct. *Students:* 450 full-time (254 women); includes 7 Black or African American, non-Hispanic/Latino; 2 American Indian or Alaska Native, non-Hispanic/Latino; 35 Asian, non-Hispanic/Latino; 13 Hispanic/Latino; 6 Two or more races, non-Hispanic/Latino, 50 international. Average age 27. 692 applicants. In 2010, 133 master's, 11 doctorates awarded. Terminal master's awarded for partial completion of doctoral program. *Degree requirements:* For master's, practicum or group project; for doctorate, comprehensive exam, thesis/dissertation, oral defense of dissertation, preliminary exam. *Entrance requirements:* For master's, GRE General Test; for doctorate, GRE General Test, master's degree. Additional exam requirements/recommendations for international students: Required—TOEFL (minimum score 560 paper-based; 220 computer-based; 84 iBT). *Application deadline:* For fall admission, 1/5 priority date for domestic and international students. Applications are processed on a rolling basis. Application fee: $65 ($75 for international students). Electronic applications accepted. *Expenses:* Tuition, state resident: full-time $17,784; part-time $1116 per credit hour. Tuition, nonresident: full-time $35,944; part-time $2125 per credit hour. International tuition: $35,994 full-time. Required fees: $95 per semester. Tuition and fees vary according to course load, degree level and program. *Financial support:* Fellowships with tuition reimbursements, research assistantships with tuition reimbursements, teaching assistantships with tuition reimbursements, career-related internships or fieldwork, Federal Work-Study, institutionally sponsored loans, scholarships/grants, health care benefits, and unspecified assistantships available. Support available to part-time students. Financial award application deadline: 1/5; financial award applicants required to submit FAFSA. *Faculty research:* Stream ecology, plant-insect interactions, fish biology, resource control and reproductive success, remote sensing, conservation ecology. *Application contact:* Graduate Admissions Team, 734-764-6453, Fax: 734-936-2195, E-mail: snre.admissions@umich.edu.

University of Michigan–Dearborn, College of Arts, Sciences, and Letters, Master of Science in Environmental Science Program, Dearborn, MI 48128. Offers MS. Part-time and evening/weekend programs available. *Faculty:* 9 full-time (2 women), 3 part-time/adjunct (0 women). *Students:* 6 full-time (2 women), 22 part-time (13 women); includes 2 Black or African American, non-Hispanic/Latino; 1 Asian, non-Hispanic/Latino; 1 Hispanic/Latino. Average age 31. 7 applicants, 71% accepted, 5 enrolled. In 2010, 2 master's awarded. *Degree requirements:* For master's, thesis optional. *Entrance requirements:* For master's, 2 letters of reference, minimum GPA of 3.0. Additional exam requirements/recommendations for international students: Required—TOEFL (minimum score 560 paper-based; 220 computer-based). *Application deadline:* For fall admission, 8/1 priority date for domestic students, 4/1 for international students; for winter admission, 12/1 priority date for domestic students, 11/1 for international students; for spring admission, 4/1 for domestic students, 3/1 for international students. Applications are processed on a rolling basis. Application fee: $60 ($75 for international students). *Financial support:* In 2010–11, 1 fellowship (averaging $2,500 per year), 2 research assistantships (averaging $2,500 per year) were awarded. Financial award application deadline: 4/1; financial award applicants required to submit FAFSA. *Faculty research:* Heavy metal and PAH containment/remediation, land use and impact on ground water and surface water quality, ecosystems and management, natural resources, plant and animal diversity. *Unit head:* Dr. Sonia Tiquia, Director, 313-593-5148, E-mail: smtiquia@umich.edu. *Application contact:* Carol Ligienza, Administrative Coordinator, CASL Graduate Programs, 313-593-1183, Fax: 313-583-6700, E-mail: caslgrad@umd.umich.edu.

The University of Montana, Graduate School, College of Arts and Sciences, Program in Environmental Studies (EVST), Missoula, MT 59812-0002. Offers MS, JD/MS. Part-time programs available. *Faculty:* 6 full-time (2 women), 2 part-time/adjunct (0 women). *Students:* 39 full-time (28 women), 23 part-time (16 women); includes 1 Hispanic/Latino, 1 international. Average age 30. 69 applicants, 72% accepted, 22 enrolled. In 2010, 31 master's awarded. *Degree requirements:* For master's, thesis, portfolio or professional paper. *Entrance requirements:* For master's, GRE General Test (minimum score: 500 verbal). Additional exam requirements/recommendations for international students: Required—TOEFL (minimum score 580 paper-based; 237 computer-based; 92 iBT). *Application deadline:* For fall admission, 2/1 priority date for domestic and international students. Application fee: $51. *Financial support:* In 2010–11, 18 students received support, including 4 fellowships with partial tuition reimbursements available (averaging $5,000 per year), 6 teaching assistantships with full tuition reimbursements available (averaging $9,000 per year). Financial award application deadline: 4/15. *Faculty research:* Pollution ecology, sustainable agriculture, environmental writing, environmental policy, environmental justice, habitat-land management. Total annual research expenditures: $86,108. *Unit head:* Dr. Len Broberg, Director, 406-243-5209, Fax: 406-243-6090, E-mail: len.broberg@mso.umt.edu. *Application contact:* Karen Hurd, Administrative Assistant, 406-243-6273, Fax: 406-243-6090, E-mail: karen.hurd@mso.umt.edu.

University of Nevada, Las Vegas, Graduate College, Greenspun College of Urban Affairs, School of Environmental and Public Affairs, Las Vegas, NV 89154-4030. Offers crisis and emergency management (MS); environmental science (MS, PhD); non-profit management (Certificate); public administration (MPA); public affairs (PhD); public management (Certificate). Part-time programs available. *Faculty:* 6 full-time (2 women). *Students:* 55 full-time (27 women), 95 part-time (55 women); includes 63 minority (17 Black or African American, non-Hispanic/Latino; 2 American Indian or Alaska Native, non-Hispanic/Latino; 5 Asian, non-Hispanic/Latino; 20 Hispanic/Latino; 19 Two or more races, non-Hispanic/Latino), 8 international. Average age 35. 67 applicants, 72% accepted, 35 enrolled. In 2010, 61 master's, 2 doctorates, 24 other advanced degrees awarded. *Degree requirements:* For master's, comprehensive exam (for some programs), thesis; for doctorate, comprehensive exam (for some programs), thesis/dissertation. *Entrance requirements:* Additional exam requirements/recommendations for international students: Required—TOEFL (minimum score 550 paper-based; 213 computer-based; 80 iBT), IELTS (minimum score 7). *Application deadline:* For fall admission, 2/15 priority date for domestic and international students; for spring admission, 11/15 priority date for domestic and international students. Applications are processed on a rolling basis. Application fee: $60 ($95 for international students). Electronic applications accepted. *Expenses:* Tuition, area resident: Part-time $239.50 per credit. Tuition, state resident: part-time $239.50 per credit. Tuition, nonresident: part-time $503 per credit. Required fees: $108 per semester. Tuition and fees vary according to course load, program and reciprocity agreements. *Financial support:* In 2010–11, 9 students received support, including 6 research assistantships with partial tuition reimbursements available (averaging $13,850 per year), 3 teaching assistantships with partial tuition reimbursements available (averaging $10,666 per year); institutionally sponsored loans, scholarships/grants, health care benefits, and unspecified assistantships also available. Financial award application deadline: 3/1. *Faculty research:* Environmental decision-making and management; budgeting and human resource/workforce management; urban design, sustainability and governance; participatory simulation modeling of environmental issues; public and non-profit management. Total annual research expenditures: $1.1 million. *Unit head:* Dr. Ed Weber, Chair/Associate Professor, 702-895-4440, Fax: 702-895-4436, E-mail: edward.weber@unlv.edu. *Application contact:* Graduate College Admissions Evaluator, 702-895-3320, Fax: 702-895-4180, E-mail: gradcollege@unlv.edu.

University of Nevada, Reno, Graduate School, College of Agriculture, Biotechnology and Natural Resources, Department of Natural Resources and Environmental Sciences, Reno, NV 89557. Offers MS. *Degree requirements:* For master's, thesis optional. *Entrance requirements:* For master's, GRE, minimum GPA of 2.75. Additional exam requirements/recommendations for international students: Required—TOEFL (minimum score 500 paper-based; 173 computer-based; 61 iBT), IELTS (minimum score 6). Electronic applications accepted. *Expenses:* Tuition, state resident: full-time $2219; part-time $246 per credit. Tuition, nonresident: part-time $510 per credit. International tuition: $9009 full-time. Required fees: $59 per term. One-time fee: $101. Tuition and fees vary according to course load. *Faculty research:* Range management, plant physiology, remote sensing, soils, wildlife.

University of Nevada, Reno, Graduate School, Interdisciplinary Program in Environmental Sciences and Health, Reno, NV 89557. Offers MS, PhD. Terminal master's awarded for partial completion of doctoral program. *Degree requirements:* For master's, thesis; for doctorate, thesis/dissertation. *Entrance requirements:* For master's, GRE General Test, minimum GPA of 2.75; for doctorate, GRE General Test, minimum GPA of 3.0. Additional exam requirements/recommendations for international students: Required—TOEFL (minimum score 500 paper-based; 173 computer-based; 61 iBT), IELTS (minimum score 6). Electronic applications accepted. *Expenses:* Tuition, state resident: full-time $2219; part-time $246 per credit. Tuition, nonresident: part-time $510 per credit. International tuition: $9009 full-time. Required fees: $59 per term. One-time fee: $101. Tuition and fees vary according to course load. *Faculty research:* Environmental chemistry, environmental toxicology, ecological toxicology.

University of New Haven, Graduate School, College of Arts and Sciences, Program in Environmental Sciences, West Haven, CT 06516-1916. Offers environmental ecology (Certificate); environmental geoscience (MS); environmental health and management (MS); environmental science (MS); geographical information systems (Certificate). Part-time and evening/weekend programs available. *Students:* 13 full-time (5 women), 24 part-time (10 women); includes 2 Black or African American, non-Hispanic/Latino; 1 American Indian or Alaska Native, non-Hispanic/Latino; 1 Asian, non-Hispanic/Latino; 1 Hispanic/Latino, 4 international. Average age 27. 29 applicants, 100% accepted, 14 enrolled. In 2010, 13 master's, 1 other advanced degree awarded. *Degree requirements:* For master's, thesis or alternative. *Application deadline:* For fall admission, 5/31 for international students; for winter admission, 10/15 for international students; for spring admission, 1/15 for international students. Applications are processed on a rolling basis. Application fee: $50. Electronic applications accepted. *Financial support:* Research assistantships with partial tuition reimbursements, teaching assistantships with partial tuition reimbursements, career-related internships or fieldwork, Federal Work-Study, scholarships/grants, tuition waivers, and unspecified assistantships available. Support available to part-time students. Financial award applicants required to submit FAFSA. *Faculty research:* Mapping and assessing geological and living resources in Long Island Sound, geology, San Salvador Island, Bahamas. *Unit head:* Dr. Roman Zajac, Coordinator, 203-932-7108. *Application contact:* Eloise Gormley, Director of Graduate Admissions, 203-932-7449, Fax: 203-932-7137, E-mail: gradinfo@newhaven.edu.

University of New Orleans, Graduate School, College of Sciences, Department of Earth and Environmental Sciences, New Orleans, LA 70148. Offers MS. Evening/weekend programs available. *Degree requirements:* For master's, thesis. *Entrance requirements:* For master's, GRE General Test. Additional exam requirements/recommendations for international students: Required—TOEFL (minimum score 550 paper-based; 213 computer-based; 79 iBT). Electronic applications accepted. *Faculty research:* Continental margin structure and seismology, burial diagenesis of siliclastic sediments, tectonics at convergent plate margins, continental shelf sediment stability, early diagenesis of carbonates.

The University of North Carolina at Chapel Hill, Graduate School, School of Public Health, Department of Environmental Sciences and Engineering, Chapel Hill, NC 27599. Offers air, radiation and industrial hygiene (MPH, MS, MSEE, MSPH, PhD); aquatic and atmospheric sciences (MPH, MS, MSPH, PhD); environmental engineering (MPH, MS, MSEE, MSPH, PhD); environmental health sciences (MPH, MS, MSPH, PhD); environmental management and policy (MPH, MS, MSPH, PhD). Terminal master's awarded for partial completion of doctoral program. *Degree requirements:* For master's, comprehensive exam, thesis (for some programs), research paper; for doctorate, comprehensive exam, thesis/dissertation. *Entrance requirements:* For master's and doctorate, GRE General Test, minimum GPA of 3.0. Additional exam requirements/recommendations for international students: Required—TOEFL. Electronic applications accepted. *Faculty research:* Air, radiation and industrial hygiene, aquatic and atmospheric sciences, environmental health sciences, environmental management and policy, water resources engineering.

University of Northern Iowa, Graduate College, College of Natural Sciences, Environmental Programs, Cedar Falls, IA 50614. Offers environmental health (MS); environmental science (MS). *Students:* 5 full-time (4 women), 7 part-time (4 women), 4 international. 14 applicants, 14% accepted, 2 enrolled. In 2010, 2 master's awarded. *Degree requirements:* For master's, comprehensive exam, thesis or alternative. *Entrance requirements:* For master's, minimum GPA of 3.0; 3 letters of recommendation. Additional exam requirements/recommendations for international students: Required—TOEFL (minimum score 500 paper-based; 180 computer-based; 61 iBT). *Application deadline:* For fall admission, 8/1 priority date for domestic students. Applications are processed on a rolling basis. Application fee: $50 ($70 for international students). Electronic applications accepted. *Financial support:* Application deadline: 2/1. *Unit head:* Dr. Maureen Clayton, Head, 319-273-7147, Fax: 319-273-7125, E-mail: maureen.clayton@uni.edu. *Application contact:* Laurie S. Russell, Record Analyst, 319-273-2623, Fax: 319-273-2885, E-mail: laurie.russell@uni.edu.

University of North Texas, Toulouse Graduate School, College of Arts and Sciences, Department of Biological Sciences, Program in Environmental Science, Denton, TX 76203. Offers MS, PhD. *Degree requirements:* For master's, oral defense of thesis; for doctorate, one foreign language, comprehensive exam, thesis/dissertation. *Entrance requirements:* For master's and doctorate, GRE General Test. Additional exam requirements/recommendations for inter-

Environmental Sciences

University of North Texas (continued)
national students: Recommended—TOEFL (minimum score 550 paper-based; 213 computer-based; 79 iBT). *Expenses:* Tuition, state resident: full-time $4298; part-time $239 per credit hour. Tuition, nonresident: full-time $10,782; part-time $549 per credit hour. Required fees: $1292; $270 per credit hour. *Financial support:* Applicants required to submit FAFSA. *Application contact:* Graduate Advisor, 940-565-2011, Fax: 940-565-3821.

University of Oklahoma, College of Engineering, School of Civil Engineering and Environmental Science, Program in Environmental Science, Norman, OK 73019-0390. Offers air (M Env Sc); environmental science (PhD). Part-time programs available. *Students:* 8 full-time (5 women), 8 part-time (5 women); includes 2 minority (both American Indian or Alaska Native, non-Hispanic/Latino), 2 international. Average age 30. 7 applicants, 14% accepted, 1 enrolled. In 2010, 2 master's, 1 doctorate awarded. Terminal master's awarded for partial completion of doctoral program. *Degree requirements:* For master's, comprehensive exam, oral exams; for doctorate, comprehensive exam, thesis/dissertation, oral and qualifying exams. *Entrance requirements:* For master's, minimum GPA of 3.0; for doctorate, minimum graduate GPA of 3.5. Additional exam requirements/recommendations for international students: Required—TOEFL (minimum score 600 paper-based; 250 computer-based; 100 iBT). *Application deadline:* For fall admission, 4/1 priority date for domestic students, 4/1 for international students; for spring admission, 11/1 for domestic students, 9/1 for international students. Applications are processed on a rolling basis. Application fee: $40 ($90 for international students). Electronic applications accepted. *Expenses:* Tuition, state resident: full-time $3892.80; part-time $162.20 per credit hour. Tuition, nonresident: full-time $14,167; part-time $590.30 per credit hour. Required fees: $2523.40; $94.60 per credit hour. Tuition and fees vary according to course load and degree level. *Financial support:* In 2010–11, 9 students received support. Scholarships/grants available. Financial award application deadline: 3/1; financial award applicants required to submit FAFSA. *Faculty research:* Constructed wetlands, sustainable water treatment technologies, subsurface transport and fate of chemicals. *Unit head:* Robert C. Knox, Director, 405-325-5911, Fax: 405-325-4217, E-mail: rknox@ou.edu. *Application contact:* Susan Williams, Graduate Programs Assistant, 405-325-2344, Fax: 405-325-4147, E-mail: srwilliams@ou.edu.

University of Pennsylvania, School of Arts and Sciences, Graduate Group in Earth and Environmental Science, Philadelphia, PA 19104. Offers MS, PhD. Part-time programs available. *Faculty:* 8 full-time (1 woman), 4 part-time/adjunct (0 women). *Students:* 18 full-time (11 women), 4 international. 36 applicants, 17% accepted, 6 enrolled. In 2010, 2 doctorates awarded. *Degree requirements:* For master's, one foreign language, thesis; for doctorate, one foreign language, thesis/dissertation. *Entrance requirements:* For master's and doctorate, GRE General Test. Additional exam requirements/recommendations for international students: Required—TOEFL. *Application deadline:* For fall admission, 12/1 priority date for domestic students. Application fee: $70. Electronic applications accepted. *Expenses:* Tuition: Full-time $25,660; part-time $4758 per course. Required fees: $2152; $270 per course. Tuition and fees vary according to course load, degree level and program. *Financial support:* Fellowships, research assistantships, teaching assistantships, institutionally sponsored loans, scholarships/grants, traineeships, health care benefits, and unspecified assistantships available. Financial award application deadline: 12/15. *Faculty research:* Isotope geochemistry, regional tectonics, environmental geology, metamorphic and igneous petrology, paleontology.

University of Puerto Rico, Río Piedras, College of Natural Sciences, Department of Environmental Sciences, San Juan, PR 00931-3300. Offers MS, PhD.

University of Rhode Island, Graduate School, College of the Environment and Life Sciences, Department of Fisheries, Animal and Veterinary Science, Kingston, RI 02881. Offers animal health and disease (MS); animal science (MS); aquaculture (MS); aquatic pathology (MS); environmental sciences (PhD), including animal science, aquacultural science, aquatic pathology, fisheries science; fisheries (MS). *Faculty:* 10 full-time (4 women). *Students:* 14 full-time (7 women), 6 part-time (1 woman); includes 4 minority (2 Black or African American, non-Hispanic/Latino; 2 Hispanic/Latino), 3 international. In 2010, 3 master's, 2 doctorates awarded. *Degree requirements:* For master's, comprehensive exam (for some programs), thesis optional; for doctorate, comprehensive exam, thesis/dissertation. *Entrance requirements:* For master's and doctorate, GRE, 2 letters of recommendation. Additional exam requirements/recommendations for international students: Required—TOEFL (minimum score 550 paper-based; 213 computer-based). *Application deadline:* For fall admission, 7/15 for domestic students, 2/1 for international students; for spring admission, 11/15 for domestic students, 7/15 for international students. Application fee: $65. Electronic applications accepted. *Expenses:* Tuition, state resident: full-time $9588; part-time $533 per credit hour. Tuition, nonresident: full-time $22,968; part-time $1276 per credit hour. Required fees: $1282; $68 per semester. Tuition and fees vary according to program. *Financial support:* In 2010–11, 9 research assistantships with full and partial tuition reimbursements (averaging $11,492 per year), 3 teaching assistantships with full and partial tuition reimbursements (averaging $12,894 per year) were awarded. Financial award application deadline: 7/15; financial award applicants required to submit FAFSA. Total annual research expenditures: $1.8 million. *Unit head:* Dr. David Bengtson, Chair, 401-874-2668, Fax: 401-874-7575, E-mail: bengtson@uri.edu. *Application contact:* Dr. Marta Gomez-Chiarri, Director of Graduate Studies, 401-874-2917, Fax: 401-874-7575, E-mail: gomezchi@uri.edu.

University of Saskatchewan, College of Graduate Studies and Research, School of Environment and Sustainability, Saskatoon, SK S7N 5A2, Canada. Offers MES.

University of South Africa, College of Agriculture and Environmental Sciences, Pretoria, South Africa. Offers agriculture (MS); consumer science (MCS); environmental management (MA, MS, PhD); environmental science (MA, MS, PhD); geography (MA, MS, PhD); horticulture (M Tech); human ecology (MHE); life sciences (MS); nature conservation (M Tech).

University of South Florida, Graduate School, College of Arts and Sciences, Department of Chemistry, Tampa, FL 33620-9951. Offers analytical chemistry (MS, PhD); biochemistry (MS, PhD); computational chemistry (MS, PhD); environmental chemistry (MS, PhD); inorganic chemistry (MS, PhD); organic chemistry (MS); physical chemistry (MS, PhD); polymer chemistry (PhD). Part-time programs available. *Faculty:* 15 full-time (1 woman). *Students:* 120 full-time (42 women), 9 part-time (2 women); includes 7 Black or African American, non-Hispanic/Latino; 8 Asian, non-Hispanic/Latino; 8 Hispanic/Latino, 62 international. Average age 29. 1,118 applicants, 4% accepted, 20 enrolled. In 2010, 4 master's, 14 doctorates awarded. Terminal master's awarded for partial completion of doctoral program. *Degree requirements:* For master's, comprehensive exam, thesis (for some programs); for doctorate, 2 foreign languages, comprehensive exam, thesis/dissertation. *Entrance requirements:* For master's, GRE General Test or GMAT, minimum GPA of 3.0. Additional exam requirements/recommendations for international students: Required—TOEFL (minimum score 550 paper-based; 213 computer-based). *Application deadline:* For fall admission, 2/15 priority date for domestic students, 1/2 priority date for international students; for spring admission, 10/1 priority date for domestic students, 6/1 priority date for international students. Applications are processed on a rolling basis. Application fee: $30. Electronic applications accepted. *Financial support:* In 2010–11, 39 research assistantships (averaging $14,359 per year), 99 teaching assistantships with tuition reimbursements (averaging $15,094 per year) were awarded; unspecified assistantships also available. Financial award application deadline: 6/30. *Faculty research:* Synthesis, bio-organic chemistry, bioinorganic chemistry, environmental chemistry, NMR. Total annual research expenditures: $3.9 million. *Unit head:* Dr. Randy Larsen, Chairperson, 813-974-4129, Fax: 813-974-3203, E-mail: rlarsen@cas.usf.edu. *Application contact:* Patricia Muisener, Director, 813-974-1730, Fax: 813-974-3203, E-mail: muisener@cas.usf.edu.

University of South Florida, Graduate School, College of Arts and Sciences, Department of Environmental Science and Policy, Tampa, FL 33620-9951. Offers MS. *Students:* 12 full-time (7 women), 14 part-time (8 women); includes 3 Hispanic/Latino; 1 Two or more races, non-Hispanic/Latino, 2 international. Average age 30. 26 applicants, 54% accepted, 8 enrolled. In 2010, 11 master's awarded. *Degree requirements:* For master's, comprehensive exam, thesis (for some programs). *Entrance requirements:* For master's, minimum GPA of 3.0. Additional exam requirements/recommendations for international students: Required—TOEFL (minimum score 600 paper-based; 213 computer-based). *Application deadline:* For fall admission, 2/15 for domestic students, 1/2 for international students; for spring admission, 10/15 for domestic students. Application fee: $30. *Financial support:* Scholarships/grants and unspecified assistantships available. Support available to part-time students. Financial award application deadline: 5/1. Total annual research expenditures: $163,893. *Unit head:* Robert Brinkmann, Interim Director, 813-974-4939, Fax: 813-974-4808, E-mail: rbrinkmann@cas.usf.edu. *Application contact:* Philip Van Beynen, Program Director, 813-974-3026, Fax: 813-974-4808, E-mail: vanbeyne@cas.usf.edu.

The University of Tennessee at Chattanooga, Graduate School, College of Arts and Sciences, Department of Biological and Environmental Sciences, Chattanooga, TN 37403. Offers environmental sciences (MS). Part-time and evening/weekend programs available. *Faculty:* 8 full-time (1 woman). *Students:* 16 full-time (11 women), 19 part-time (10 women); includes 1 minority (Black or African American, non-Hispanic/Latino), 1 international. Average age 29. 18 applicants, 83% accepted, 9 enrolled. In 2010, 5 master's awarded. *Degree requirements:* For master's, thesis optional. *Entrance requirements:* For master's, GRE General Test, minimum undergraduate GPA of 2.75; undergraduate course work in ecology or knowledge equivalent. Additional exam requirements/recommendations for international students: Required—TOEFL (minimum score 550 paper-based; 213 computer-based; 79 iBT), IELTS (minimum score 6). *Application deadline:* For fall admission, 8/1 priority date for domestic students, 6/1 for international students; for spring admission, 12/1 priority date for domestic students, 10/1 for international students. Applications are processed on a rolling basis. Application fee: $35. Electronic applications accepted. *Financial support:* In 2010–11, 5 research assistantships with full and partial tuition reimbursements (averaging $5,500 per year), 6 teaching assistantships with full and partial tuition reimbursements (averaging $5,500 per year) were awarded; career-related internships or fieldwork, scholarships/grants, and unspecified assistantships also available. Support available to part-time students. *Faculty research:* Bioremediation, stream fish ecology and conservation, environmental law and policy, avian conservation and management. Total annual research expenditures: $574,605. *Unit head:* Dr. John Tucker, Department Head, 423-425-4341, Fax: 423-425-2285, E-mail: john-tucker@utc.edu. *Application contact:* Dr. Jerald Ainsworth, Dean of Graduate Studies, 423-425-4478, Fax: 423-425-5223, E-mail: Jerald-Ainsworth@utc.edu.

The University of Texas at Arlington, Graduate School, College of Science, Department of Earth and Environmental Sciences, Program in Environmental and Earth Sciences, Arlington, TX 76019. Offers environmental science (MS, PhD); geology (MS, PhD). Part-time and evening/weekend programs available. *Faculty:* 5 full-time (0 women), 1 part-time/adjunct (0 women). *Students:* 22 full-time (13 women), 25 part-time (12 women); includes 2 Black or African American, non-Hispanic/Latino; 1 American Indian or Alaska Native, non-Hispanic/Latino; 2 Asian, non-Hispanic/Latino; 4 Hispanic/Latino, 11 international. 23 applicants, 74% accepted, 10 enrolled. In 2010, 11 master's, 1 doctorate awarded. Terminal master's awarded for partial completion of doctoral program. *Degree requirements:* For master's, thesis optional; for doctorate, comprehensive exam, thesis/dissertation. *Entrance requirements:* For master's, GRE General Test. Additional exam requirements/recommendations for international students: Required—TOEFL (minimum score 550 paper-based; 213 computer-based). *Application deadline:* Applications are processed on a rolling basis. Application fee: $35 ($50 for international students). Electronic applications accepted. *Expenses:* Tuition, state resident: full-time $7500. Tuition, nonresident: full-time $13,080. International tuition: $13,250 full-time. *Financial support:* In 2010–11, 4 fellowships (averaging $1,000 per year), 7 teaching assistantships (averaging $14,700 per year) were awarded; career-related internships or fieldwork, Federal Work-Study, institutionally sponsored loans, scholarships/grants, health care benefits, and unspecified assistantships also available. Financial award applicants required to submit FAFSA. *Unit head:* Dr. John S. Wickham, Chair, 817-272-2987, Fax: 817-272-2628, E-mail: wickham@uta.edu. *Application contact:* Dr. Andrew Hunt, Graduate Advisor, 817-272-2987, Fax: 817-272-2628, E-mail: hunt@uta.edu.

The University of Texas at El Paso, Graduate School, College of Science, Environmental Science Program, El Paso, TX 79968-0001. Offers MS. *Degree requirements:* For master's, thesis. *Entrance requirements:* For master's, GRE, bachelor's degree in a science or engineering discipline, 3 letters of recommendation. Additional exam requirements/recommendations for international students: Required—TOEFL. *Unit head:* Dr. Carl Lieb, Program Director, 915-747-5554, Fax: 915-747-5990. *Application contact:* Joel Gilbert, Program Coordinator, 915-747-5554, Fax: 915-747-5990, E-mail: esci@utep.edu.

The University of Texas at El Paso, Graduate School, Interdisciplinary Program in Environmental Science and Engineering, El Paso, TX 79968-0001. Offers PhD. Part-time and evening/weekend programs available. *Students:* 41 (15 women); includes 3 Asian, non-Hispanic/Latino; 10 Hispanic/Latino, 21 international. Average age 34. In 2010, 4 doctorates awarded. *Degree requirements:* For doctorate, thesis/dissertation. *Entrance requirements:* For doctorate, GRE, letters of recommendation. Additional exam requirements/recommendations for international students: Required—TOEFL; Recommended—IELTS. *Application deadline:* For fall admission, 8/1 for domestic students, 3/1 for international students; for spring admission, 11/1 for domestic students, 9/1 for international students. Applications are processed on a rolling basis. Application fee: $45 ($80 for international students). Electronic applications accepted. *Financial support:* In 2010–11, research assistantships with partial tuition reimbursements (averaging $22,500 per year), teaching assistantships with partial tuition reimbursements (averaging $18,000 per year) were awarded; fellowships with partial tuition reimbursements, institutionally sponsored loans, scholarships/grants, health care benefits, tuition waivers (partial), and unspecified assistantships also available. Support available to part-time students. Financial award application deadline: 3/15; financial award applicants required to submit FAFSA. *Unit head:* Dr. Barry A. Benedict, Director, 915-747-5604, Fax: 915-747-5145, E-mail: babenedict@utep.edu. *Application contact:* Dr. Patricia D. Witherspoon, Dean of the Graduate School, 915-747-5491, Fax: 915-747-5788, E-mail: withersp@utep.edu.

The University of Texas at San Antonio, College of Engineering, Department of Civil and Environmental Engineering, San Antonio, TX 78249-0617. Offers civil engineering (MS, MSCE); environmental science and engineering (PhD). Part-time and evening/weekend programs available. *Faculty:* 11 full-time (2 women). *Students:* 43 full-time (11 women), 34 part-time (8 women); includes 25 minority (5 Black or African American, non-Hispanic/Latino; 4 Asian, non-Hispanic/Latino; 15 Hispanic/Latino; 1 Two or more races, non-Hispanic/Latino), 24 international. Average age 32. 56 applicants, 50% accepted, 21 enrolled. In 2010, 12 master's, 4 doctorates awarded. *Degree requirements:* For master's, comprehensive exam (for some programs), thesis (for some programs); for doctorate, comprehensive exam, thesis/dissertation. *Entrance requirements:* For master's, GRE General Test, minimum GPA of 3.0 in last 60 hours of undergraduate degree. Additional exam requirements/recommendations for international students: Required—TOEFL (minimum score 500 paper-based; 173 computer-based; 61 iBT), IELTS (minimum score 5). *Application deadline:* For fall admission, 7/1 for domestic students, 4/1 for international students; for spring admission, 11/1 for domestic students, 9/1 for international students. Applications are processed on a rolling basis. Application fee: $45 ($80 for international students). Electronic applications accepted. *Expenses:* Tuition, state resident: full-time $4172; part-time $231.75 per credit hour. Tuition, nonresident: full-time $15,332; part-time $851.75 per credit hour. *Financial support:* In 2010–11, 29 students received support,

UTSA Engineering
PH.D. IN ENVIRONMENTAL SCIENCE & ENGINEERING

Program Overview:

A multidisciplinary program administered by the Civil and Environmental Engineering (CEE) Department. It encompasses faculty and facilities from the college of Sciences and the CEE Department. Areas of research emphasis include water resources, environmental quality, environmental remediation, pollution control, conservation ecology, spatial analysis, remote sensing, and hydrometeorology.

Major Research Facilities:

*Concrete Lab

*Environmental Engineering Lab

*Bio-Environmental Lab

*Superpave Lab (AASHTO-accredited)

*Geotechnical Lab

*Hydraulics Lab

*Structural Dynamics Lab

Please visit us at
http://engineering.utsa.edu/CE/deptInfo.html
or email to coegradinfo@utsa.edu

---

including 20 research assistantships (averaging $15,462 per year); career-related internships or fieldwork, scholarships/grants, tuition waivers, and unspecified assistantships also available. Support available to part-time students. Financial award application deadline: 3/31. Total annual research expenditures: $475,434. *Unit head:* Dr. Athanassio T. Papagiannakis, Chair, 210-458-7517, Fax: 210-458-6475, E-mail: at.papagiannakis@utsa.edu. *Application contact:* Veronica Ramirez, Assistant Dean of the Graduate School, 210-458-4330, Fax: 210-458-4332, E-mail: graduatestudies@utsa.edu.

The University of Texas at San Antonio, College of Sciences, Department of Geological Sciences, San Antonio, TX 78249-0617. Offers MS. Part-time programs available. *Faculty:* 7 full-time (2 women), 1 part-time/adjunct (0 women). *Students:* 8 full-time (4 women), 7 part-time (1 woman); includes 3 minority (2 Hispanic/Latino; 1 Two or more races, non-Hispanic/Latino), 2 international. Average age 29. 16 applicants, 75% accepted, 7 enrolled. In 2010, 2 master's awarded. *Degree requirements:* For master's, comprehensive exam (for some programs), thesis (for some programs). *Entrance requirements:* For master's, GRE General Test, minimum GPA of 3.0 in last 60 hours. Additional exam requirements/recommendations for international students: Required—TOEFL (minimum score 500 paper-based; 173 computer-based; 61 iBT), IELTS (minimum score 5). *Application deadline:* For fall admission, 7/1 for domestic students, 4/1 for international students; for spring admission, 11/1 for domestic students, 9/1 for international students. Applications are processed on a rolling basis. Application fee: $45 ($80 for international students). Electronic applications accepted. *Expenses:* Tuition, state resident: full-time $4172; part-time $231.75 per credit hour. Tuition, nonresident: full-time $15,332; part-time $851.75 per credit hour. *Financial support:* In 2010–11, 7 students received support, including 2 fellowships (averaging $38,000 per year), 8 teaching assistantships (averaging $11,125 per year); scholarships/grants, tuition waivers, and unspecified assistantships also available. Support available to part-time students. *Faculty research:* Water resources/hydrogeology, low-temperature geochemistry, petrology and tectonics, energy resources, paleoclimatology, landscape dynamics. Total annual research expenditures: $396,687. *Unit head:* Dr. Allan R. Dutton, Interim Department Chair, 210-458-4455, Fax: 210-458-4469, E-mail: allan.dutton@utsa.edu. *Application contact:* Veronica Ramirez, Assistant Dean of the Graduate School, 210-458-4330, Fax: 210-458-4332, E-mail: graduatestudies@utsa.edu.

See Close-Up on page 399.

University of the Virgin Islands, Graduate Programs, Division of Science and Mathematics, Program in Environmental and Marine Science, Saint Thomas, VI 00802-9990. Offers MS. *Entrance requirements:* For master's, GRE. Additional exam requirements/recommendations for international students: Required—TOEFL (minimum score 550 paper-based; 213 computer-based).

The University of Toledo, College of Graduate Studies, College of Natural Sciences and Mathematics, Department of Environmental Sciences, Toledo, OH 43606-3390. Offers geology (MS), including earth surface processes, general geology. Part-time programs available. *Faculty:* 30. *Students:* 9 full-time (5 women), 1 (woman) part-time; includes 1 minority (Black or African American, non-Hispanic/Latino), 1 international. Average age 30. 9 applicants, 56% accepted, 5 enrolled. In 2010, 2 master's awarded. *Degree requirements:* For master's, thesis. *Entrance requirements:* For master's, GRE General Test, A minimum 2.7 cumulative point-hour ratio (on a 4.0 scale) for all previous academic work. Three letters of recommendation, a statement of purpose, and transcripts from all prior institutions attended. Additional exam requirements/recommendations for international students: Required—TOEFL (minimum score 550 paper-based; 213 computer-based; 80 iBT), IELTS (minimum score 6.5). *Application deadline:* For fall admission, 1/15 priority date for domestic and international students. Applications are processed on a rolling basis. Application fee: $45 ($75 for international students). Electronic applications accepted. *Expenses:* Tuition, state resident: full-time $11,426; part-time $476 per credit hour. Tuition, nonresident: full-time $21,660; part-time $903 per credit hour. One-time fee: $62. *Financial support:* Research assistantships with tuition reimbursements, teaching assistantships with tuition reimbursements, Federal Work-Study, institutionally sponsored loans, scholarships/grants, tuition waivers (full), and unspecified assistantships available. Support available to part-time students. *Faculty research:* Environmental geochemistry, geophysics, petrology and mineralogy, paleontology, geohydrology. *Unit head:* Dr. Timothy G. Fisher, Chair, 419-530-2883, E-mail: timothy.fisher@utoledo.edu. *Application contact:* Graduate School Office, 419-530-4723, Fax: 419-530-4724, E-mail: grdsch@utnet.utoledo.edu.

University of Toronto, School of Graduate Studies, Physical Sciences Division, Department of Physical and Environmental Sciences, Toronto, ON M5S 1A1, Canada. Offers environmental science (M Env Sc, PhD).

University of Utah, Graduate School, Professional Master of Science and Technology Program, Salt Lake City, UT 84112-1107. Offers biotechnology (PSM); computational science (PSM); environmental science (PSM); science instrumentation (PSM). Part-time programs available. *Faculty:* 2 full-time (0 women). *Students:* 32 full-time (17 women), 38 part-time (13 women); includes 1 Black or African American, non-Hispanic/Latino; 3 Asian, non-Hispanic/Latino; 1 Hispanic/Latino, 19 international. Average age 31. 66 applicants, 48% accepted, 16 enrolled. In 2010, 7 master's awarded. *Degree requirements:* For master's, internship. *Entrance requirements:* For master's, GRE (recommended), minimum undergraduate GPA of 3.0, bachelor's degree from accredited university or college. Additional exam requirements/recommendations for international students: Required—TOEFL (minimum score 500 paper-based; 173 computer-based; 61 iBT), IELTS (minimum score 6). *Application deadline:* For fall admission, 3/1 for domestic and international students. Application fee: $55 ($65 for international students). Electronic applications accepted. *Expenses:* Tuition, area resident: Part-time $179.19 per credit hour. Tuition, state resident: full-time $4384. Tuition, nonresident: full-time $16,684; part-time $630.67 per credit hour. Required fees: $350 per semester. Tuition and fees vary according to course load, degree level and program. *Financial support:* In 2010–11, 8 students received support, including 5 fellowships with full and partial tuition reimbursements available (averaging $16,800 per year), 2 research assistantships (averaging $6,200 per year); unspecified assistantships also available. Financial award applicants required to submit FAFSA. *Faculty research:* Drug delivery systems, in vitro erythroid expansion and HRE (Hypoxia responsive element). *Unit head:* Jennifer Schmidt, Program Director, 801-585-5630, E-mail: jennifer.schmidt@gradschool.utah.edu. *Application contact:* Amy Kimball, Project Coordinator, 801-585-3650, Fax: 801-585-6749, E-mail: amy.kimball@gradschool.utah.edu.

University of Virginia, College and Graduate School of Arts and Sciences, Department of Environmental Sciences, Charlottesville, VA 22903. Offers MA, MS, PhD. *Faculty:* 29 full-time (4 women), 2 part-time/adjunct (both women). *Students:* 73 full-time (41 women), 1 (woman) part-time; includes 2 Asian, non-Hispanic/Latino, 9 international. Average age 29. 103 applicants, 31% accepted, 18 enrolled. In 2010, 13 master's, 8 doctorates awarded. *Degree requirements:* For master's, thesis; for doctorate, comprehensive exam, thesis/dissertation. *Entrance requirements:* For master's and doctorate, GRE General Test, 2 letters of recommendation. Additional exam requirements/recommendations for international students: Required—TOEFL (minimum score 600 paper-based; 250 computer-based; 90 iBT), IELTS (minimum score 7). *Application deadline:* For fall admission, 12/1 for domestic and international students; for winter admission, 10/15 for domestic and international students. Applications are processed on a rolling basis. Application fee: $60. Electronic applications accepted. *Financial support:* Fellowships, research assistantships, teaching assistantships available. Financial award application deadline: 12/1; financial award applicants required to submit FAFSA. *Unit head:* Patricia Wiberg, Chairman, 434-924-7761, Fax: 434-982-2137, E-mail: jcz@virginia.edu. *Application contact:* Graduate Admissions Chair, 434-924-7761, Fax: 434-982-2137.

The University of Western Ontario, Faculty of Graduate Studies, Biosciences Division, Department of Plant Sciences, London, ON N6A 5B8, Canada. Offers plant and environmental

Peterson's Graduate Programs in the Physical Sciences, Mathematics, Agricultural Sciences, the Environment & Natural Resources 2012

www.facebook.com/petersonspublishing

389

Environmental Sciences

The University of Western Ontario (continued)
sciences (M Sc); plant sciences (M Sc, PhD); plant sciences and environmental sciences (PhD); plant sciences and molecular biology (M Sc, PhD). *Degree requirements:* For master's, thesis; for doctorate, thesis/dissertation. *Entrance requirements:* For doctorate, M Sc or equivalent. Additional exam requirements/recommendations for international students: Required—TOEFL. *Faculty research:* Ecology systematics, plant biochemistry and physiology, yeast genetics, molecular biology.

The University of Western Ontario, Faculty of Graduate Studies, Physical Sciences Division, Department of Earth Sciences, London, ON N6A 5B8, Canada. Offers environment and sustainability (MES); geology (M Sc, PhD); geology and environmental science (M Sc, PhD); geophysics (M Sc, PhD); geophysics and environmental science (M Sc, PhD). *Degree requirements:* For master's, thesis; for doctorate, thesis/dissertation, qualifying exam. *Entrance requirements:* For master's, honors in B Sc; for doctorate, M Sc. Additional exam requirements/recommendations for international students: Required—TOEFL. *Faculty research:* Geophysics, geochemistry, paleontology, sedimentology/stratigraphy, glaciology/quaternary.

University of West Florida, College of Arts and Sciences: Sciences, Department of Environmental Studies, Pensacola, FL 32514-5750. Offers environmental science (MS). Part-time programs available. *Faculty:* 5 full-time (0 women), 1 part-time/adjunct (0 women). *Students:* 9 full-time (4 women), 15 part-time (9 women); includes 1 Black or African American, non-Hispanic/Latino; 1 Two or more races, non-Hispanic/Latino, 1 international. Average age 30. 12 applicants, 67% accepted, 5 enrolled. In 2010, 9 master's awarded. *Entrance requirements:* For master's, GRE General Test. Additional exam requirements/recommendations for international students: Required—TOEFL (minimum score 550 paper-based; 213 computer-based). *Application deadline:* For fall admission, 6/1 for domestic students, 5/15 for international students; for spring admission, 10/1 for domestic and international students. Application fee: $30. *Expenses:* Tuition, state resident: full-time $4982; part-time $208 per credit hour. Tuition, nonresident: full-time $20,059; part-time $836 per credit hour. Required fees: $1365; $57 per credit hour. *Financial support:* In 2010–11, 3 fellowships with partial tuition reimbursements (averaging $1,000 per year), 11 research assistantships with partial tuition reimbursements (averaging $4,100 per year), 4 teaching assistantships with partial tuition reimbursements (averaging $5,450 per year) were awarded; unspecified assistantships also available. Financial award application deadline: 4/15; financial award applicants required to submit FAFSA. *Unit head:* Dr. Matthew C. Schwartz, Chairperson, 850-474-3469. *Application contact:* Terry McCray, Assistant Director of Graduate Admissions, 850-473-7718, Fax: 850-473-7714, E-mail: gradadmissions@uwf.edu.

University of Windsor, Faculty of Graduate Studies, GLIER-Great Lakes Institute for Environmental Research, Windsor, ON N9B 3P4, Canada. Offers environmental science (M Sc, PhD). *Degree requirements:* For master's, thesis; for doctorate, thesis/dissertation. *Entrance requirements:* For master's, minimum B+ average; for doctorate, M Sc degree, minimum B+ average. Additional exam requirements/recommendations for international students: Required—TOEFL (minimum score 560 paper-based; 220 computer-based). Electronic applications accepted. *Faculty research:* Environmental chemistry and toxicology, conservation and resource management, iron formation geochemistry.

University of Wisconsin–Green Bay, Graduate Studies, Program in Environmental Science and Policy, Green Bay, WI 54311-7001. Offers MS. Part-time programs available. *Faculty:* 10 full-time (3 women), 2 part-time/adjunct (0 women). *Students:* 16 full-time (12 women), 18 part-time (9 women); includes 6 minority (1 Black or African American, non-Hispanic/Latino; 3 American Indian or Alaska Native, non-Hispanic/Latino; 1 Asian, non-Hispanic/Latino; 1 Hispanic/Latino). Average age 29. 27 applicants, 85% accepted, 16 enrolled. In 2010, 11 master's awarded. *Degree requirements:* For master's, thesis. *Entrance requirements:* For master's, GRE General Test, minimum GPA of 3.0. *Application deadline:* For fall admission, 8/1 for domestic students; for spring admission, 11/1 for domestic students. Applications are processed on a rolling basis. Application fee: $56. Electronic applications accepted. *Expenses:* Tuition, state resident: full-time $7001; part-time $389 per credit. Tuition, nonresident: full-time $16,771; part-time $932 per credit. Required fees: $1314; $110 per credit. Tuition and fees vary according to reciprocity agreements. *Financial support:* In 2010–11, 1 research assistantship with full tuition reimbursement, 4 teaching assistantships with full tuition reimbursements were awarded; career-related internships or fieldwork, Federal Work-Study, and institutionally sponsored loans also available. Financial award application deadline: 7/15; financial award applicants required to submit FAFSA. *Faculty research:* Bald eagle, parasitic population of domestic and wild animals, resource recovery, anaerobic digestion of organic waste. *Unit head:* Dr. Patricia Terry, Coordinator, 920-465-2749, E-mail: terryp@uwgb.edu. *Application contact:* Pam Harvey-Jacobs, Director of Admissions, 920-465-2111, E-mail: harveyp@uwgb.edu.

University of Wisconsin–Madison, Graduate School, Gaylord Nelson Institute for Environmental Studies, Environmental Monitoring Program, Madison, WI 53706-1380. Offers MS, PhD. Part-time programs available. *Faculty:* 1 full-time (0 women), 1 part-time/adjunct (0 women). *Students:* 3 (2 women), 1 international. Average age 39. *Degree requirements:* For master's, thesis or alternative; for doctorate, thesis/dissertation. *Expenses:* Tuition, state resident: full-time $9887.36; part-time $617.96 per credit. Tuition, nonresident: full-time $24,054; part-time $1503.40 per credit. Required fees: $67.63 per credit. Tuition and fees vary according to reciprocity agreements. *Financial support:* In 2010–11, 1 student received support, including fellowships with full tuition reimbursements available (averaging $18,756 per year), 1 research assistantship with full tuition reimbursement available (averaging $14,960 per year), teaching assistantships with full tuition reimbursements available (averaging $9,392 per year); career-related internships or fieldwork, Federal Work-Study, scholarships/grants, health care benefits, unspecified assistantships, and project assistantships also available. *Faculty research:* Remote sensing, geographic information systems, climate modeling, natural resource management. *Unit head:* Stephen J. Ventura, Chair, 608-262-6416, Fax: 608-262-2273, E-mail: sventura@wisc.edu. *Application contact:* Jim Miller, Student Services Coordinator, 608-263-4373, Fax: 608-262-2273, E-mail: jemiller@wisc.edu.

Vanderbilt University, Graduate School, Department of Earth and Environmental Sciences, Nashville, TN 37240-1001. Offers MAT, MS. *Faculty:* 8 full-time (2 women). *Students:* 11 full-time (4 women); includes 1 Hispanic/Latino. Average age 26. 27 applicants, 37% accepted, 5 enrolled. In 2010, 4 master's awarded. *Degree requirements:* For master's, thesis. *Entrance requirements:* For master's, GRE General Test, GRE Subject Test (recommended). Additional exam requirements/recommendations for international students: Required—TOEFL (minimum score 570 paper-based; 230 computer-based; 88 iBT). *Application deadline:* For fall admission, 1/15 for domestic and international students. Application fee: $0. Electronic applications accepted. *Financial support:* Fellowships with full and partial tuition reimbursements, research assistantships with full and partial tuition reimbursements, teaching assistantships with full tuition reimbursements, career-related internships or fieldwork, Federal Work-Study, institutionally sponsored loans, and health care benefits available. Financial award application deadline: 1/15; financial award applicants required to submit CSS PROFILE or FAFSA. *Faculty research:* Geochemical processes, magmatic processes and crustal evolution, paleoecology and paleoenvironments, sedimentary systems, transport phenomena, environmental policy. *Unit head:* Dr. David J. Furbish, Chair, 615-322-2137, Fax: 615-322-2138, E-mail: david.j.furbish@vanderbilt.edu. *Application contact:* Calvin F. Miller, Director of Graduate Studies, 615-322-2232, Fax: 615-322-2138, E-mail: calvin.f.miller@vanderbilt.edu.

Virginia Polytechnic Institute and State University, Graduate School, College of Engineering, Department of Civil and Environmental Engineering, Blacksburg, VA 24061. Offers civil engineering (M Eng, MS, PhD); civil infrastructure systems (Certificate); environmental engineering (MS); environmental sciences and engineering (MS); transportation systems engineering (Certificate); treatment process engineering (Certificate); urban hydrology and stormwater management (Certificate); water quality management (Certificate). *Accreditation:* ABET (one or more programs are accredited). *Faculty:* 44 full-time (8 women), 1 part-time/adjunct (0 women). *Students:* 320 full-time (108 women), 70 part-time (20 women); includes 9 Black or African American, non-Hispanic/Latino; 15 Asian, non-Hispanic/Latino; 13 Hispanic/Latino, 126 international. Average age 27. 639 applicants, 44% accepted, 121 enrolled. In 2010, 97 master's, 18 doctorates awarded. *Degree requirements:* For master's, comprehensive exam (for some programs), thesis (for some programs); for doctorate, comprehensive exam (for some programs), thesis/dissertation (for some programs). *Entrance requirements:* For master's and doctorate, GRE. Additional exam requirements/recommendations for international students: Required—TOEFL (minimum score 550 paper-based; 213 computer-based). *Application deadline:* For fall admission, 7/1 for domestic and international students; for spring admission, 12/1 for domestic and international students. Applications are processed on a rolling basis. Application fee: $65. Electronic applications accepted. *Expenses:* Tuition, area resident: Full-time $9399; part-time $488 per credit hour. Tuition, state resident: full-time $9399; part-time $488 per credit hour. Tuition, nonresident: full-time $17,854; part-time $957.75 per credit hour. International tuition: $17,854 full-time. Required fees: $1534. Full-time tuition and fees vary according to program. *Financial support:* In 2010–11, 35 fellowships with full tuition reimbursements (averaging $5,861 per year), 82 research assistantships with full tuition reimbursements (averaging $20,397 per year), 33 teaching assistantships with full tuition reimbursements (averaging $14,542 per year) were awarded; career-related internships or fieldwork, Federal Work-Study, scholarships/grants, health care benefits, and unspecified assistantships also available. Financial award application deadline: 1/15. *Faculty research:* Construction, environmental geotechnical hydrosystems, structures and transportation engineering. Total annual research expenditures: $12.2 million. *Unit head:* Dr. Sam Easterling, UNIT HEAD, 540-231-5143, Fax: 540-231-7532, E-mail: seaster@vt.edu. *Application contact:* Marc Widdowson, Contact, 540-231-7153, Fax: 540-231-7532, E-mail: mwiddows@vt.edu.

Virginia Polytechnic Institute and State University, Graduate School, College of Natural Resources and Environment, Department of Geography, Program in Geospatial and Environmental Analysis, Blacksburg, VA 24061. Offers PhD. *Expenses:* Tuition, area resident: Full-time $9399; part-time $488 per credit hour. Tuition, state resident: full-time $9399; part-time $488 per credit hour. Tuition, nonresident: full-time $17,854; part-time $957.75 per credit hour. International tuition: $17,854 full-time. Required fees: $1534. Full-time tuition and fees vary according to program.

Washington State University, Graduate School, College of Sciences, Programs in Environmental Science and Regional Planning, Program in Environmental and Natural Resource Sciences, Pullman, WA 99164. Offers PhD. Application fee: $50. *Expenses:* Tuition, state resident: full-time $8552; part-time $443 per credit. Tuition, nonresident: full-time $21,650; part-time $1083 per credit. Required fees: $846. *Unit head:* Dr. Keith A. Blatner, Chair, 509-335-6166, E-mail: blatner@wsu.edu. *Application contact:* Graduate School Admissions, 800-GRADWSU, Fax: 509-335-1949, E-mail: gradsch@wsu.edu.

Washington State University, Graduate School, College of Sciences, School of Earth and Environmental Sciences, Pullman, WA 99164. Offers MS, PhD. Application fee: $50. *Expenses:* Tuition, state resident: full-time $8552; part-time $443 per credit. Tuition, nonresident: full-time $21,650; part-time $1083 per credit. Required fees: $846. *Unit head:* Dr. Steve Bollens, Director, 509-335-3009, E-mail: bollens@vancouver.wsu.edu. *Application contact:* Graduate School Admissions, 800-GRADWSU, Fax: 509-335-1949, E-mail: gradsch@wsu.edu.

Washington State University, Graduate School, College of Sciences, School of Earth and Environmental Sciences, Department of Natural Resource Sciences, Program in Environmental Science, Pullman, WA 99164. Offers environmental and natural resource sciences (PhD); environmental science (MS). *Faculty:* 7. *Students:* 42 full-time (24 women), 34 part-time (17 women); includes 1 Black or African American, non-Hispanic/Latino; 2 American Indian or Alaska Native, non-Hispanic/Latino; 3 Asian, non-Hispanic/Latino; 2 Hispanic/Latino, 2 international. Average age 29. 76 applicants, 32% accepted, 18 enrolled. In 2010, 15 master's awarded. *Degree requirements:* For master's, comprehensive exam (for some programs), thesis (for some programs), oral exam; for doctorate, comprehensive exam, thesis/dissertation, oral exam, written exam. *Entrance requirements:* For master's, 3 undergraduate semester hours each in sociology or cultural anthropology, environmental science, biological sciences, and calculus or statistics; 4 in general ecology; and 6 in general chemistry or general physics; for doctorate, minimum GPA of 3.0. Additional exam requirements/recommendations for international students: Required—TOEFL, IELTS. *Application deadline:* For fall admission, 1/10 priority date for domestic students, 1/10 for international students. Applications are processed on a rolling basis. Application fee: $50. *Expenses:* Tuition, state resident: full-time $8552; part-time $443 per credit. Tuition, nonresident: full-time $21,650; part-time $1083 per credit. Required fees: $846. *Financial support:* In 2010–11, 16 students received support, including 1 fellowship (averaging $3,000 per year), 4 research assistantships with full and partial tuition reimbursements available (averaging $13,917 per year), 4 teaching assistantships with full and partial tuition reimbursements available (averaging $13,506 per year); Federal Work-Study, institutionally sponsored loans, and tuition waivers (partial) also available. Financial award application deadline: 2/15; financial award applicants required to submit FAFSA. *Unit head:* Dr. John A. Wolff, Head, 509-335-2825, E-mail: jawolff@mail.wsu.edu. *Application contact:* Graduate School Admissions, 800-GRADWSU, Fax: 509-335-1949, E-mail: gradsch@wsu.edu.

Washington State University Tri-Cities, Graduate Programs, Program in Environmental Science, Richland, WA 99352-1671. Offers applied environmental science (MS); environmental science (PhD). Part-time programs available. *Faculty:* 40. *Students:* 5 full-time (1 woman), 37 part-time (17 women); includes 1 Black or African American, non-Hispanic/Latino; 1 American Indian or Alaska Native, non-Hispanic/Latino; 1 Hispanic/Latino. *Degree requirements:* For master's, comprehensive exam, thesis (for some programs), oral exam; for doctorate, comprehensive exam, thesis/dissertation. *Entrance requirements:* For master's, GRE General Test, minimum GPA of 3.0, 3 letters of recommendation. Additional exam requirements/recommendations for international students: Required—TOEFL (minimum score 550 paper-based; 213 computer-based). *Application deadline:* For fall admission, 1/10 priority date for domestic students, 1/10 for international students; for spring admission, 7/1 priority date for domestic students, 7/1 for international students. Application fee: $50. *Financial support:* In 2010–11, 8 students received support, including research assistantships with full and partial tuition reimbursements available (averaging $14,634 per year), teaching assistantships with full and partial tuition reimbursements available (averaging $13,383 per year); fellowships, Federal Work-Study, scholarships/grants, health care benefits, and unspecified assistantships also available. Financial award application deadline: 1/15. *Faculty research:* Radiation ecology, cytogenetics. *Unit head:* John Strand, Graduate Advisor, 509-372-7326, E-mail: jstrand@tricity.wsu.edu. *Application contact:* Bonnie Bates, Graduate School Admissions, 800-GRADWSU, Fax: 509-372-7171, E-mail: bbates@tricity.wsu.edu.

Washington State University Vancouver, Graduate Programs, Program in Environmental Science, Vancouver, WA 98686. Offers MS. *Faculty:* 16. *Students:* 22 full-time (12 women); includes 1 American Indian or Alaska Native, non-Hispanic/Latino; 1 Asian, non-Hispanic/Latino; 1 Hispanic/Latino. Average age 38. In 2010, 5 master's awarded. *Degree requirements:* For master's, comprehensive exam, thesis (for some programs). *Entrance requirements:* For master's, GRE General Test, minimum GPA of 3.0, 3 letters of recommendation. Additional exam requirements/recommendations for international students: Required—TOEFL (minimum score 550 paper-based; 213 computer-based). *Application deadline:* For fall admission, 1/10 priority date for domestic students, 1/10 for international students; for spring admission, 7/1

priority date for domestic students, 7/1 for international students. Application fee: $50. *Financial support:* In 2010–11, research assistantships with tuition reimbursements (averaging $14,634 per year), teaching assistantships (averaging $13,383 per year) were awarded. Financial award application deadline: 2/15. *Faculty research:* Conservation biology, environmental chemistry. *Unit head:* Dr. Stephen Bollens, Graduate Program Coordinator, 360-546-9611, Fax: 360-546-9064, E-mail: tissot@vancouver.wsu.edu. *Application contact:* Dawn Banker, Academic Coordinator, 360-546-9478, Fax: 360-546-9064, E-mail: bankerd@vancouver.wsu.edu.

Wesleyan University, Graduate Programs, Department of Earth and Environmental Sciences, Middletown, CT 06459. Offers MA. *Faculty:* 3 full-time (1 woman), 1 (woman) part-time/adjunct. *Students:* 6 full-time (1 woman); includes 1 American Indian or Alaska Native, non-Hispanic/Latino; 1 Hispanic/Latino. Average age 25. 5 applicants, 60% accepted, 2 enrolled. In 2010, 4 master's awarded. *Degree requirements:* For master's, thesis. *Entrance requirements:* For master's, GRE General Test, GRE Subject Test. Additional exam requirements/recommendations for international students: Required—TOEFL. *Application deadline:* For fall admission, 1/15 for domestic and international students. Applications are processed on a rolling basis. Application fee: $0. Electronic applications accepted. *Expenses:* Tuition: Full-time $43,404. Required fees: $830. *Financial support:* In 2010–11, 4 teaching assistantships with full tuition reimbursements were awarded; tuition waivers (full and partial) also available. Financial award application deadline: 4/15; financial award applicants required to submit FAFSA. *Faculty research:* Tectonics, volcanology, stratigraphy, coastal processes, geochemistry. *Unit head:* Dr. Peter Patton, Chair, 860-685-2268, E-mail: ppatton@wesleyan.edu. *Application contact:* Ginny Harris, Administrative Assistant, 860-685-2244, E-mail: vharris@wesleyan.edu.

Western Connecticut State University, Division of Graduate Studies and External Programs, School of Arts and Sciences, Department of Biological and Environmental Sciences, Danbury, CT 06810-6885. Offers MA. Part-time programs available. *Students:* 1 full-time (0 women), 8 part-time (7 women); includes 1 minority (Black or African American, non-Hispanic/Latino). Average age 34. In 2010, 10 master's awarded. *Degree requirements:* For master's, comprehensive exam or thesis, completion of program in 6 years. *Entrance requirements:* For master's, minimum GPA of 2.5. Additional exam requirements/recommendations for international students: Recommended—TOEFL (minimum score 550 paper-based; 213 computer-based; 79 iBT), IELTS (minimum score 6). *Application deadline:* For fall admission, 8/5 priority date for domestic students; for spring admission, 1/5 priority date for domestic students. Applications are processed on a rolling basis. Application fee: $50. *Expenses:* Tuition, state resident: full-time $5012; part-time $417 per credit hour. Tuition, nonresident: full-time $13,962; part-time $423 per credit hour. Required fees: $3886. Full-time tuition and fees vary according to course load, degree level and program. *Financial support:* Application deadline: 5/1. *Unit head:* Dr. Richard Halliburton, Graduate Coordinator, 203-837-8233, Fax: 203-837-8525, E-mail: halliburtonr@wcsu.edu. *Application contact:* Chris Shankle, Associate Director of Graduate Studies, 203-837-9005, Fax: 203-837-8326, E-mail: shanklec@wcsu.edu.

Western Washington University, Graduate School, Huxley College of the Environment, Department of Environmental Sciences, Bellingham, WA 98225-5996. Offers environmental science (MS); marine and estuarine science (MS). Part-time programs available. *Degree requirements:* For master's, thesis. *Entrance requirements:* For master's, GRE General Test, minimum GPA of 3.0 in last 60 semester hours or last 90 quarter hours. Additional exam requirements/recommendations for international students: Required—TOEFL (minimum score 567 paper-based; 227 computer-based). Electronic applications accepted. *Faculty research:* Landscape ecology, climate change, watershed studies, environmental toxicology and risk assessment, aquatic toxicology, toxic algae, invasive species.

Western Washington University, Graduate School, Huxley College of the Environment, Department of Environmental Studies, Bellingham, WA 98225-5996. Offers environmental education (M Ed); geography (MS). Part-time programs available. *Degree requirements:* For master's, thesis. *Entrance requirements:* For master's, GRE General Test, minimum GPA of 3.0 in last 60 semester hours or last 90 quarter hours. Additional exam requirements/recommendations for international students: Required—TOEFL (minimum score 567 paper-based; 227 computer-based). Electronic applications accepted. *Faculty research:* Geomorphology; pedogenesis; quaternary studies and climate change in the western U.S. landscape ecology, biogeography, pyrogeography, and spatial analysis.

West Texas A&M University, College of Agriculture, Nursing, and Natural Sciences, Department of Life, Earth, and Environmental Sciences, Program in Environmental Science, Canyon, TX 79016-0001. Offers MS. Part-time programs available. *Degree requirements:* For master's, comprehensive exam, thesis optional. *Entrance requirements:* For master's, GRE General Test. Additional exam requirements/recommendations for international students: Required—TOEFL (minimum score 550 paper-based). Electronic applications accepted. *Faculty research:* Degradation of presistant pesticides in soils and ground water, air quality.

Wichita State University, Graduate School, Fairmount College of Liberal Arts and Sciences, Department of Geology, Wichita, KS 67260. Offers earth, environmental, and physical sciences (MS). Part-time programs available. *Unit head:* Dr. William Parcell, Chair, 316-978-3140, E-mail: william.parcell@wichita.edu. *Application contact:* Dr. Collette Burke, Graduate Coordinator, 316-978-3140, E-mail: collette.burke@wichita.edu.

Wilfrid Laurier University, Faculty of Graduate and Postdoctoral Studies, Faculty of Arts, Department of Geography and Environmental Studies, Waterloo, ON N2L 3C5, Canada. Offers environmental and resource management (MA, MES, PhD); environmental science (M Sc, MES, PhD); geomatics (M Sc, MES, PhD); human geography (MES, PhD). Part-time programs available. *Faculty:* 17 full-time (5 women). *Students:* 47 full-time (20 women), 12 part-time (6 women), 4 international. 78 applicants, 40% accepted, 18 enrolled. In 2010, 11 master's, 7 doctorates awarded. *Degree requirements:* For master's, thesis optional; for doctorate, thesis/dissertation. *Entrance requirements:* For master's, honors BA in geography, minimum B average in undergraduate course work; honors BSc with minimum B+ or honors BES or BA in physical geography, environmental or earth sciences or the equivalent; for doctorate, MA in geography, minimum A- average. Additional exam requirements/recommendations for international students: Required—TOEFL (minimum score 89 iBT). *Application deadline:* For fall admission, 2/1 priority date for domestic and international students. Application fee: $100. Electronic applications accepted. Tuition and fees charges are reported in Canadian dollars. *Expenses:* Tuition, area resident: Full-time $15,300 Canadian dollars; part-time $1200 Canadian dollars per credit. International tuition: $21,300 Canadian dollars full-time. Required fees: $650 Canadian dollars; $100 Canadian dollars per credit. Tuition and fees vary according to course load, degree level, campus/location and program. *Financial support:* In 2010–11, 51 fellowships, 8 research assistantships, 51 teaching assistantships were awarded; career-related internships or fieldwork, scholarships/grants, health care benefits, and unspecified assistantships also available. *Faculty research:* Resources management, urban, economic, physical, cultural, earth surfaces, geomatics, historical, regional, spatial data handling. *Unit head:* Dr. Houston Saunderson, Graduate Co-ordinator, 519-884-0710 Ext. 2573, Fax: 519-725-1342, E-mail: hsaunderson@wlu.ca. *Application contact:* Jennifer Williams, Graduate Admissions and Records Officer, 519-884-0710 Ext. 3536, Fax: 519-884-1020, E-mail: gradstudies@wlu.ca.

Wright State University, School of Graduate Studies, College of Science and Mathematics, Department of Biological Sciences, Dayton, OH 45435. Offers biological sciences (MS); environmental sciences (MS). *Degree requirements:* For master's, thesis optional. *Entrance requirements:* Additional exam requirements/recommendations for international students: Required—TOEFL.

Wright State University, School of Graduate Studies, College of Science and Mathematics, Department of Chemistry, Dayton, OH 45435. Offers chemistry (MS); environmental sciences (MS). Part-time and evening/weekend programs available. *Degree requirements:* For master's, oral defense of thesis, seminar. *Entrance requirements:* Additional exam requirements/recommendations for international students: Required—TOEFL. *Faculty research:* Polymer synthesis and characterization, laser kinetics, organic and inorganic synthesis, analytical and environmental chemistry.

Wright State University, School of Graduate Studies, College of Science and Mathematics, Program in Environmental Sciences, Dayton, OH 45435. Offers PhD.

Yale University, Graduate School of Arts and Sciences, Department of Forestry and Environmental Studies, New Haven, CT 06520. Offers environmental sciences (PhD); forestry (PhD). *Degree requirements:* For doctorate, thesis/dissertation. *Entrance requirements:* For doctorate, GRE General Test.

Yale University, School of Forestry and Environmental Studies, New Haven, CT 06511. Offers MEM, MES, MF, MFS, PhD, JD/MEM, MBA/MEM, MBA/MF, MEM/M Arch, MEM/MA, MEM/MPH, MF/MA. *Accreditation:* SAF (one or more programs are accredited). Part-time programs available. Terminal master's awarded for partial completion of doctoral program. *Degree requirements:* For master's, thesis (for some programs); for doctorate, thesis/dissertation. *Entrance requirements:* For master's, GRE General Test, GMAT or LSAT; for doctorate, GRE General Test. Additional exam requirements/recommendations for international students: Required—TOEFL (minimum score 600 paper-based; 250 computer-based; 100 iBT). Electronic applications accepted. *Expenses:* Contact institution. *Faculty research:* Environmental policy, social ecology, industrial environmental management, forestry, environmental health, urban ecology, water science policy.

Marine Affairs

Dalhousie University, Faculty of Management, Marine Affairs Program, Halifax, NS B3H 3J5, Canada. Offers MMM. *Degree requirements:* For master's, project. *Entrance requirements:* For master's, minimum GPA of 3.0. Additional exam requirements/recommendations for international students: Required—TOEFL, IELTS, CANTEST, CAEL, or Michigan English Language Assessment Battery. Electronic applications accepted. *Faculty research:* Coastal zone management, sea use planning, development of non-living resources, protection and preservation of the coastal and marine environment, marine law and policy, fisheries management, maritime transport, conflict management.

Duke University, Nicholas School of the Environment, Durham, NC 27708-0328. Offers coastal environmental management (MEM); DEL-environmental leadership (MEM); energy and environment (MEM); environmental economics and policy (MEM); environmental health and security (MEM); forest resource management (MF); global environmental change (MEM); resource ecology (MEM); water and air resources (MEM); JD/AM; JD/MEM; JD/MF; MAT/MEM; MBA/MEM; MBA/MF; MEM/MPP; MF/MPP. *Accreditation:* SAF (one or more programs are accredited). Part-time programs available. *Degree requirements:* For master's, thesis. *Entrance requirements:* For master's, GRE General Test, previous course work in biology or ecology, calculus, statistics, and microeconomics; computer familiarity with word processing and data analysis. Additional exam requirements/recommendations for international students: Required—TOEFL (minimum score 550 paper-based; 213 computer-based). Electronic applications accepted. *Expenses:* Contact institution. *Faculty research:* Ecosystem management, conservation ecology, earth systems, risk assessment.

East Carolina University, Graduate School, Program in Coastal Resources Management, Greenville, NC 27858-4353. Offers PhD. *Degree requirements:* For doctorate, comprehensive exam, thesis/dissertation, internship. *Entrance requirements:* For doctorate, GRE. Additional exam requirements/recommendations for international students: Required—TOEFL. *Expenses:* Tuition, state resident: full-time $3130; part-time $391.25 per credit hour. Tuition, nonresident: full-time $13,817; part-time $1727.13 per credit hour. Required fees: $1916; $239.50 per credit hour. Tuition and fees vary according to campus/location and program. *Faculty research:* Coastal geology, wetlands and coastal ecology, ecological and social networks, submerged cultural resources, coastal resources economics.

Louisiana State University and Agricultural and Mechanical College, Graduate School, School of the Coast and Environment, Department of Oceanography and Coastal Sciences, Baton Rouge, LA 70803. Offers MS, PhD. *Faculty:* 29 full-time (4 women), 2 part-time/adjunct (0 women). *Students:* 51 full-time (30 women), 4 part-time (2 women); includes 1 Hispanic/Latino, 12 international. Average age 29. 37 applicants, 22% accepted, 7 enrolled. In 2010, 7 master's, 7 doctorates awarded. *Degree requirements:* For master's, thesis (for some programs); for doctorate, one foreign language, thesis/dissertation. *Entrance requirements:* For master's, GRE General Test, minimum GPA of 3.0; for doctorate, GRE General Test, MA or MS, minimum GPA of 3.0. Additional exam requirements/recommendations for international students: Required—TOEFL (minimum score 550 paper-based; 213 computer-based; 79 iBT) or IELTS (minimum score 6.5). *Application deadline:* For fall admission, 1/25 priority date for domestic students, 5/15 for international students; for spring admission, 10/15 for international students. Applications are processed on a rolling basis. Application fee: $50 ($70 for international students). *Financial support:* In 2010–11, 54 students received support, including 8 fellowships (averaging $17,589 per year), 44 research assistantships with full and partial tuition reimbursements available (averaging $19,606 per year); teaching assistantships with full and partial tuition reimbursements available, Federal Work-Study, institutionally sponsored loans, scholarships/grants, health care benefits, tuition waivers (full and partial), and unspecified assistantships also available. Support available to part-time students. Financial award applicants required to submit FAFSA. *Faculty research:* Physical and geological oceanography, wetland sustainability and restoration fisheries, coastal ecology and biogeochemistry. Total annual research expenditures: $8.1 million. *Unit head:* Dr. Donald Baltz, Chair, 225-578-6308, Fax: 225-578-6307, E-mail: dbaltz@lsu.edu. *Application contact:* Dr. Charles Lindau, Graduate Adviser, 225-578-8766, Fax: 225-578-6423, E-mail: clinda1@lsu.edu.

Memorial University of Newfoundland, School of Graduate Studies, Department of Sociology, St. John's, NL A1C 5S7, Canada. Offers gender (PhD); maritime sociology (PhD); sociology (M Phil, MA); work and development (PhD). Part-time programs available. *Degree requirements:* For master's, comprehensive exam, thesis optional, program journal (M Phil); for doctorate, one foreign language, comprehensive exam, thesis/dissertation, oral defense of thesis. *Entrance requirements:* For master's, 2nd class degree from university of recognized standing in area of

Marine Affairs

Memorial University of Newfoundland (continued)
study; for doctorate, MA, M Phil, or equivalent. Electronic applications accepted. *Faculty research:* Work and development, gender, maritime sociology.

Memorial University of Newfoundland, School of Graduate Studies, Interdisciplinary Program in Marine Studies, St. John's, NL A1C 5S7, Canada. Offers fisheries resource management (MMS, Advanced Diploma). Part-time programs available. *Degree requirements:* For master's, report. *Entrance requirements:* For master's and Advanced Diploma, high 2nd class degree from a recognized university. *Faculty research:* Biological, ecological and oceanographic aspects of world fisheries; economics; political science; sociology.

Nova Southeastern University, Oceanographic Center, Program in Coastal Zone Management, Dania Beach, FL 33004. Offers MS. *Faculty:* 15 full-time (1 woman), 5 part-time/adjunct (0 women). *Students:* 21 full-time (14 women), 20 part-time (14 women); includes 1 American Indian or Alaska Native, non-Hispanic/Latino; 4 Hispanic/Latino, 1 international. Average age 30. 44 applicants, 52% accepted, 2 enrolled. In 2010, 12 master's awarded. *Degree requirements:* For master's, thesis. *Entrance requirements:* For master's, GRE. Additional exam requirements/recommendations for international students: Required—TOEFL (minimum score 550 paper-based). *Application deadline:* Applications are processed on a rolling basis. Application fee: $50. *Financial support:* Career-related internships or fieldwork, Federal Work-Study, scholarships/grants, and unspecified assistantships available. Financial award applicants required to submit FAFSA. *Unit head:* Dr. Richard Spieler, Director of Academic Programs, 954-262-3600, Fax: 954-262-4020, E-mail: spieler@nova.edu. *Application contact:* Dr. Richard Spieler, Director of Academic Programs, 954-262-3600, Fax: 954-262-4020, E-mail: spieler@nova.edu.

Old Dominion University, College of Business and Public Administration, MBA Program, Norfolk, VA 23529. Offers business and economic forecasting (MBA); financial analysis and valuation (MBA); information technology and enterprise integration (MBA); international business (MBA); maritime and port management (MBA); public administration (MBA). *Accreditation:* AACSB. Part-time and evening/weekend programs available. *Faculty:* 66 full-time (15 women), 6 part-time/adjunct (1 woman). *Students:* 74 full-time (32 women), 166 part-time (62 women); includes 45 minority (21 Black or African American, non-Hispanic/Latino; 1 American Indian or Alaska Native, non-Hispanic/Latino; 8 Asian, non-Hispanic/Latino; 10 Hispanic/Latino; 1 Native Hawaiian or other Pacific Islander, non-Hispanic/Latino; 4 Two or more races, non-Hispanic/Latino), 19 international. Average age 31. 169 applicants, 52% accepted, 61 enrolled. In 2010, 100 master's awarded. *Entrance requirements:* For master's, GMAT, letter of reference, resume, coursework in calculus, essay. Additional exam requirements/recommendations for international students: Required—TOEFL (minimum score 550 paper-based; 213 computer-based; 80 iBT). *Application deadline:* For fall admission, 6/1 priority date for domestic students, 4/15 priority date for international students; for spring admission, 11/1 priority date for domestic students, 10/1 priority date for international students. Applications are processed on a rolling basis. Application fee: $50. Electronic applications accepted. *Expenses:* Tuition, state resident: full-time $8592; part-time $358 per credit. Tuition, nonresident: full-time $21,672; part-time $903 per credit. Required fees: $119 per semester. One-time fee: $50. *Financial support:* In 2010–11, 44 students received support, including 90 research assistantships with partial tuition reimbursements available (averaging $3,200 per year); career-related internships or fieldwork, scholarships/grants, and unspecified assistantships also available. Support available to part-time students. Financial award application deadline: 2/15; financial award applicants required to submit FAFSA. *Faculty research:* International business, buyer behavior, financial markets, strategy, operations research. *Unit head:* Dr. Larry Filer, Graduate Program Director, 757-683-3585, Fax: 757-683-5750, E-mail: mbainfo@odu.edu. *Application contact:* Shanna Wood, MBA Program Manager, 757-683-3585, Fax: 757-683-5750, E-mail: mbainfo@odu.edu.

Oregon State University, Graduate School, College of Oceanic and Atmospheric Sciences, Program in Marine Resource Management, Corvallis, OR 97331. Offers MA, MS. *Degree requirements:* For master's, thesis optional. *Entrance requirements:* For master's, GRE General Test, minimum GPA of 3.0 in last 90 hours of course work. Additional exam requirements/recommendations for international students: Required—TOEFL. *Faculty research:* Ocean and coastal resources, fisheries resources, marine pollution, marine recreation and tourism.

Stevens Institute of Technology, Graduate School, Charles V. Schaefer Jr. School of Engineering, Department of Civil, Environmental, and Ocean Engineering, Program in Maritime Systems, Hoboken, NJ 07030. Offers MS. *Students:* 3 full-time (0 women), 4 part-time (1 woman), 1 international. Average age 32. 4 applicants, 100% accepted.Application fee: $50. *Unit head:* Dr. Michael S. Bruno, Information Contact, 201-216-5338, Fax: 201-216-8214, E-mail: mbruno@stevens-tech.edu. *Application contact:* Dr. Michael S. Bruno, Information Contact, 201-216-5338, Fax: 201-216-8214, E-mail: mbruno@stevens-tech.edu.

Stony Brook University, State University of New York, Graduate School, School of Marine and Atmospheric Sciences, Program in Marine Conservation and Policy, Stony Brook, NY 11794. Offers MA. *Students:* 8 full-time (4 women). 10 applicants, 80% accepted, 7 enrolled. *Degree requirements:* For master's, capstone project or internship. *Entrance requirements:* For master's, minimum GPA of 3.0; one semester of college-level biology and three additional semester courses in college-level math or science; personal statement; 3 letters of reference; official transcripts. *Application deadline:* For fall admission, 7/15 for domestic students. Electronic applications accepted. *Expenses:* Tuition, state resident: full-time $8370; part-time $349 per credit. Tuition, nonresident: full-time $13,780; part-time $574 per credit. Required fees: $994. *Unit head:* Dr. Robert Cerrato, Director, 631-632-8666, E-mail: robert.cerrato@stonybrook.edu. *Application contact:* Dr. Anne McElroy, Assistant Director, 631-632-8488, Fax: 631-632-8200, E-mail: amcelroy@notes.cc.sunysb.edu.

Université du Québec à Rimouski, Graduate Programs, Program in Management of Marine Resources, Rimouski, QC G5L 3A1, Canada. Offers M Sc, Diploma. Part-time programs available. *Entrance requirements:* For master's, appropriate bachelor's degree, proficiency in French.

University of Delaware, College of Earth, Ocean, and Environment, School of Marine Science and Policy, Newark, DE 19716. Offers marine policy (MMP); marine studies (MS, PhD), including marine biosciences, oceanography, physical ocean science and engineering; oceanography (PhD).

University of Maine, Graduate School, College of Natural Sciences, Forestry, and Agriculture, School of Marine Sciences, Program in Marine Policy, Orono, ME 04469. Offers MS. *Students:* 6 full-time (4 women), 3 part-time (1 woman), 1 international. Average age 29. 24 applicants, 8% accepted, 2 enrolled. In 2010, 2 master's awarded. *Degree requirements:* For master's, thesis. *Entrance requirements:* For master's, GRE General Test. Additional exam requirements/recommendations for international students: Required—TOEFL. *Application deadline:* For fall admission, 2/1 priority date for domestic students. Applications are processed on a rolling basis. Application fee: $65. Electronic applications accepted. *Expenses:* Tuition, state resident: full-time $400. Tuition, nonresident: full-time $1050. *Financial support:* Fellowships with tuition reimbursements, research assistantships with tuition reimbursements, teaching assistantships with tuition reimbursements, career-related internships or fieldwork, Federal Work-Study, and tuition waivers (full and partial) available. Support available to part-time students. Financial award application deadline: 3/1. *Unit head:* Dr. James Wilson, Coordinator, 207-581-4368. *Application contact:* Scott G. Delcourt, Associate Dean of the Graduate School, 207-581-3219, Fax: 207-581-3232, E-mail: graduate@maine.edu.

University of Miami, Graduate School, Rosenstiel School of Marine and Atmospheric Science, Division of Marine Affairs and Policy, Coral Gables, FL 33124. Offers MA, MS, JD/MA. Part-time programs available. *Degree requirements:* For master's, comprehensive exam, thesis (for some programs), internship, paper. *Entrance requirements:* For master's, GRE General Test. Additional exam requirements/recommendations for international students: Required—TOEFL (minimum score 550 paper-based; 213 computer-based). Electronic applications accepted.

University of Rhode Island, Graduate School, College of the Environment and Life Sciences, Department of Marine Affairs, Kingston, RI 02881. Offers MA, MESM, MMA, PhD, JD/MMA. Part-time programs available. *Faculty:* 7 full-time (1 woman). *Students:* 34 full-time (16 women), 17 part-time (12 women); includes 3 minority (1 Asian, non-Hispanic/Latino; 2 Hispanic/Latino), 4 international. In 2010, 10 master's, 2 doctorates awarded. *Degree requirements:* For master's, comprehensive exam (for some programs), thesis optional; for doctorate, comprehensive exam, thesis/dissertation. *Entrance requirements:* For master's, GRE (for MA), 2 letters of recommendation (for MMA); for doctorate, GRE, 2 letters of recommendation, writing sample. Additional exam requirements/recommendations for international students: Required—TOEFL (minimum score 550 paper-based; 213 computer-based). *Application deadline:* For fall admission, 4/7 for domestic students, 2/1 for international students. Application fee: $65. Electronic applications accepted. *Expenses:* Tuition, state resident: full-time $9588; part-time $533 per credit hour. Tuition, nonresident: full-time $22,968; part-time $1276 per credit hour. Required fees: $1282; $68 per semester. Tuition and fees vary according to program. *Financial support:* In 2010–11, 3 research assistantships with full tuition reimbursements (averaging $14,198 per year), 4 teaching assistantships with full and partial tuition reimbursements (averaging $6,513 per year) were awarded. Financial award application deadline: 2/1; financial award applicants required to submit FAFSA. *Faculty research:* Assessing change in coastal ecosystems and its impact to society. Total annual research expenditures: $188,228. *Unit head:* Dr. Robert Thompson, Chair, 401-874-4485, Fax: 401-874-2156, E-mail: rob@uri.edu. *Application contact:* Dr. Richard Burroughs, Director of Master's Studies, 401-874-4045, Fax: 401-874-2156, E-mail: rburroughs@uri.edu.

University of San Diego, College of Arts and Sciences, Department of Marine Science and Environmental Studies, San Diego, CA 92110-2492. Offers marine science (MS). Part-time programs available. *Faculty:* 3 full-time (1 woman). *Students:* 9 full-time (7 women), 8 part-time (5 women); includes 1 Black or African American, non-Hispanic/Latino; 2 Hispanic/Latino; 2 Two or more races, non-Hispanic/Latino. Average age 25. 23 applicants, 52% accepted, 8 enrolled. In 2010, 7 master's awarded. *Degree requirements:* For master's, thesis. *Entrance requirements:* For master's, GRE General Test, minimum GPA of 3.0, undergraduate major in science. Additional exam requirements/recommendations for international students: Required—TOEFL (minimum score 580 paper-based; 237 computer-based; 83 iBT), TWE. *Application deadline:* For fall admission, 4/1 for domestic and international students. Applications are processed on a rolling basis. Application fee: $45. Electronic applications accepted. *Expenses:* Tuition: Full-time $21,744; part-time $1208 per unit. Required fees: $224. Full-time tuition and fees vary according to course load and degree level. *Financial support:* In 2010–11, 11 students received support. Career-related internships or fieldwork, Federal Work-Study, institutionally sponsored loans, and unspecified assistantships available. Support available to part-time students. Financial award application deadline: 4/1; financial award applicants required to submit FAFSA. *Faculty research:* Marine ecology, environmental geology and geochemistry, climatology, physiological ecology, fisheries and aquaculture. *Unit head:* Dr. Ronald S. Kaufmann, Director, 619-260-5904, Fax: 619-260-6874, E-mail: kaufmann@sandiego.edu. *Application contact:* Stephen Pultz, Director of Admissions and Enrollment, 619-260-4506, Fax: 619-260-6836, E-mail: admissions@sandiego.edu.

University of Washington, Graduate School, College of Ocean and Fishery Sciences, School of Marine Affairs, Seattle, WA 98195. Offers MMA, Graduate Certificate. *Degree requirements:* For master's, thesis. *Entrance requirements:* For master's, GRE General Test, minimum GPA of 3.0. Additional exam requirements/recommendations for international students: Required—TOEFL. Electronic applications accepted. *Faculty research:* Marine pollution, port authorities, fisheries management, global climate change, marine environmental protection.

University of West Florida, College of Arts and Sciences: Sciences, School of Allied Health and Life Sciences, Department of Biology, Pensacola, FL 32514-5750. Offers biological chemistry (MS); biology (MS); biology education (MST); biotechnology (MS); coastal zone studies (MS); environmental biology (MS). *Faculty:* 10 full-time (2 women). *Students:* 6 full-time (4 women), 32 part-time (18 women); includes 1 Black or African American, non-Hispanic/Latino; 1 Asian, non-Hispanic/Latino; 1 Hispanic/Latino, 1 international. Average age 28. 17 applicants, 53% accepted, 7 enrolled. In 2010, 3 master's awarded. *Degree requirements:* For master's, thesis. *Entrance requirements:* For master's, GRE General Test. Additional exam requirements/recommendations for international students: Required—TOEFL (minimum score 550 paper-based; 213 computer-based). *Application deadline:* For fall admission, 6/1 for domestic students, 5/15 for international students; for spring admission, 10/1 for domestic and international students. Applications are processed on a rolling basis. Application fee: $30. *Expenses:* Tuition, state resident: full-time $4982; part-time $208 per credit hour. Tuition, nonresident: full-time $20,059; part-time $836 per credit hour. Required fees: $1365; $57 per credit hour. *Financial support:* In 2010–11, 20 fellowships with partial tuition reimbursements (averaging $523 per year), 18 research assistantships with partial tuition reimbursements (averaging $5,700 per year), 12 teaching assistantships with partial tuition reimbursements (averaging $8,042 per year) were awarded; unspecified assistantships also available. Financial award application deadline: 4/15; financial award applicants required to submit FAFSA. *Unit head:* Dr. George L. Stewart, Chairperson, 850-474-2748. *Application contact:* Terry McCray, Assistant Director of Graduate Admissions, 850-473-7718, Fax: 850-473-7714, E-mail: gradadmissions@uwf.edu.

ADELPHI UNIVERSITY

College of the Arts and Sciences
Program in Environmental Studies

Program of Study	The Master of Science in environmental studies comprises 36 credits of course work, incorporating classroom, laboratory, and field opportunities and an optional thesis or internship. The thesis provides additional flexibility for the student with more specific career or educational goals. Full-time students can anticipate three semesters of 12 credits each. Field classes, internships, and research are also offered during the summer months.
	The program is organized into a common course area and two areas of concentration—the global human environment and the global physical environment—and one area of integration, environmental education. In recognition of the context of both areas of concentration in the contemporary world, courses are required from the common area for all students. These offerings are fundamental to both concentrations and provide insights into the social, political, institutional, economic, and physical applications of environmental issues. Within each concentration, opportunities exist for the student to make program selections that reflect areas of faculty and student interest. For example, such selections could focus on the physical, chemical, biological, and biochemical aspects of pollutant detection; the cultural, societal, epidemiological, public health, paleontological, and paleopathological effects of environmental perturbations; or the economic, governmental, and social interactions consequent to environmental concerns. It is also possible for a student to elect sufficient courses from all areas to achieve a broader focus on environmental studies, leading to certification for teaching purposes. In the future, the program expects to add distinct areas of concentration. Additional opportunities are provided for the student in the form of technical field and laboratory experiences as well as special topic courses that might not be available on a regular basis.
	The faculty members draw their expertise from a wide spectrum of disciplines. Instructors are committed to involving participants fully in the multidisciplinary nature of environmental problems and the search for solutions. The environmental studies program provides firm, integrated foundations in both the social-political-cultural and the scientific-technical areas. This preparation makes students environmentally aware members of society in many professions, in graduate study in environmental studies/sciences, or in both.
Research Facilities	The University's primary research holdings are at Swirbul Library and include 600,000 volumes (including bound periodicals and government publications), 806,000 items in microformats, 33,000 audiovisual items, and access to over 61,000 electronic journal titles. Online access is provided to more than 221 research databases.
Financial Aid	The program offers a number of stipends and financial assistance awards to teaching and research assistants on a yearly basis. Further opportunities for financial support over the course of every academic year, including the summers, are offered through the research projects and activities of faculty members.
Cost of Study	For the 2011–12 academic year, the tuition rate is $835 per credit. University fees ranged from $275 to $410 per semester.
Living and Housing Costs	The University assists single and married students in finding suitable accommodations whenever possible. The cost of living is dependent on location and the number of rooms rented.
Location	Located in historic Garden City, New York, 45 minutes from Manhattan and 20 minutes from Queens, Adelphi's 75-acre suburban campus is known for the beauty of its landscape and architecture. The campus is a short walk from the Long Island Railroad and is convenient to New York's major airports and several major highways. Off-campus centers are located in Manhattan, Hauppauge, and Poughkeepsie.
The University and The College	Founded in 1896, Adelphi is a fully accredited, private university with nearly 8,000 undergraduate, graduate, and returning-adult students in the arts and sciences, business, clinical psychology, education, nursing, and social work. Students come from forty-one states and forty-eight countries. The *Fiske Guide to Colleges* recognized Adelphi as a "Best Buy" in higher education for the fifth year in a row. The University is one of only twenty-four private institutions in the nation to earn this recognition.
	Mindful of the cultural inheritance of the past, the College of Arts and Sciences encompasses those realms of inquiry that have characterized the modern pursuit of knowledge. The faculty members of the College place a high priority on their students' intellectual development in and out of the classroom and structure programs and opportunities to foster that growth. Students analyze original research or other creative work, develop firsthand facility with creative or research methodologies, undertake collaborative work with peers and mentors, engage in serious internships, and hone communicative skills.
Applying	Students should have a bachelor's degree in environmental studies or a related field and a demonstrated promise of successful achievement in the field. A student must submit the completed application form, the $50 application fee, and official college transcripts. For more information, students should contact the graduate coordinator.
Correspondence and Information	Beth Christensen, Graduate Coordinator and Associate Professor Program in Environmental Studies College of Arts and Sciences Science Building, Room 118 Adelphi University Garden City, New York 11530 Phone: 516-877-4174 Fax: 516-877-4485 E-mail: christensen@adelphi.edu Web site: http://academics.adelphi.edu/artsci/env/graduate-environmental-studies.php

Peterson's Graduate Programs in the Physical Sciences, Mathematics,
Agricultural Sciences, the Environment & Natural Resources 2012

www.facebook.com/petersonspublishing **393**

Adelphi University

THE FACULTY AND THEIR RESEARCH

Anagnostis Agelarakis, Professor of Anthropology and Director, Environmental Studies Program; Ph.D., Columbia, 1989. Plio-Pleistocene human evolution, human ecology, paleopathology, paleoenvironments, forensics, field methods.

Regina Axelrod, Professor of Political Science; Ph.D., CUNY, 1978. Environmental and energy policy in the United States, the European Union, and Central and Eastern Europe.

Sean Bentley, Associate Professor of Physics, Ph.D., Rochester, 2004. Mathematical methods of physics, quantum mechanics, circuits, optics.

Beth Christensen, Graduate Coordinator and Associate Professor of Earth Sciences; Ph.D., South Carolina, 1997. Cenozoic climate and sea-level change, influence of African climate on hominid evolution, New Jersey margin geology.

Anthony Cok, Professor of Earth Sciences; Ph.D., Dalhousic, 1970. Glacial marine science sediments, marine resources and pollution.

John Dooher, Professor of Physics; Ph.D., Stevens, 1965. Energy, pollution issues, and physics.

Laraine Fletcher, Professor of Anthropology and Sociology; Ph.D., SUNY at Stony Brook, 1978.

Matthias Foellmer, Assistant Professor of Biology; Ph.D., Concordia, 2004. Evolutionary ecology: significance of extreme sexual size dimorphism (SSD); differences in reproductive roles between the sexes.

Martin H. Garrell, Professor of Physics; Ph.D., Illinois, 1966. Energy studies, environmental problem solving, marine conservation issues.

David Gleicher, Associate Professor of Accounting, Finance, and Economics; Ph.D., Columbia, 1984. Maritime history, social semiotics.

Hannah Kim, Assistant Professor of Anthropology and Sociology; Ph.D., Columbia, 2001. Cultural anthropology, anthropology of religion, ethnographic survey of Asia.

Katie Laatikainen, Associate Professor of Political Science and International Studies; Ph.D., South Carolina, 2001. The growing role of the European Union common foreign and security policy in the United Nations context.

Joseph Landesberg, Professor of Chemistry; Ph.D., Harvard, 1965. Synthetic organic chemistry and organic-iron carbonyl systems.

David P. Machlis, Associate Professor of Accounting, Finance, and Economics; Ph.D., Rutgers, 1971. Environmental economics.

Gottipaty Rao, Professor of Physics; Ph.D., Algarh Muslim (India), 1963. Light principles and statistics.

Lawrence Sullivan, Associate Professor of Political Science, Ph.D, Michigan. Chinese politics, international relations in East Asia, political theory.

Mariano Torras, Professor of Economics; Ph.D., Massachusetts, Amherst, 2000. Well-being assessment, environmental and natural resource accounting, dematerialization trends, links between power inequality and health outcomes as well as other socioeconomic variables.

Andrea Ward, Assistant Professor of Biology; Ph.D., Massachusetts Amherst, 2005. Evolution of the elongate body form in fishes, developmental origin of body elongation, effect of body elongation on locomotion.

Benjamin Weeks, Associate Professor of Biology; Ph.D., Connecticut, 1988. Immunotoxicity and neurotoxicity of pyrethroid pesticide.

Justyna Widera, Assistant Professor of Chemistry; Ph.D., Warsaw (Poland), 2000. Nanotechnology, quantum dots, sensors, molecular machines.

Adelphi's campus in historic Garden City, Long Island, New York.

A registered arboretum, Adelphi is truly a green campus.

394 www.facebook.com/petersonspublishing

Peterson's Graduate Programs in the Physical Sciences, Mathematics, Agricultural Sciences, the Environment & Natural Resources 2012

COLUMBIA UNIVERSITY

Program in Environmental Science and Policy

Programs of Study	Students enrolled in the Master of Public Administration in Environmental Science and Policy program are awarded an M.P.A. degree from Columbia University's School of International and Public Affairs (SIPA) after a single year of intensive study. The program is affiliated with The Earth Institute, a Columbia University research institution dedicated to finding solutions for sustainable development and addressing some of the world's most difficult problems. The curriculum, designed by The Earth Institute and SIPA, requires students complete a total of 54 points over three semesters, starting the day after Memorial Day (summer term).
	The intensive study begins with natural science courses, including ecology and urban ecology, climate and water, and environmental chemistry and toxicology. In the autumn and spring, students take the core curriculum, which focuses on sustainability management, financial management, microeconomics, and quantitative techniques, all of which provides the skills for developing policy and managing public organizations. Physical and social sciences are also linked throughout the program so that students gain an integrated understanding of earth systems and sustainable development. This program requires more environmental science than any other public policy master's degree in the world.
	Graduates of the M.P.A. program are skilled at understanding complex environmental problems and developing sustainable solutions. They are protecting the environment as analysts, managers, educators, communicators, advocates, and consultants.
Research Facilities	Columbia's libraries, with over 10 million volumes and an extensive collection of electronic resources, manuscripts, rare books, microforms, and other nonprint formats, rank as one of the top five academic library systems in the nation. Lehman Library, located within the School of International and Public Affairs, is an excellent resource for materials in political science, sociology, social and cultural anthropology, political geography, journalism, and environmental science. As part of a program cosponsored by The Earth Institute, M.P.A. in Environmental Science and Policy students have access to the Lamont-Doherty Observatory, a world-renowned research facility operated by Columbia University. The Earth Institute's unique structure facilitates links between the earth scientists at the observatory and the engineers, economists, and social and political scientists within the other units of the institute. The new cross-disciplinary research teams that are born from these interactions allow for the building of powerful connections between understanding the Earth's systems and devising applications that benefit humankind directly.
Financial Aid	Fellowships are available; however, they are partial and must be used toward tuition. Fellowships awards are dispersed in three installments at the beginning of each semester. Candidates seeking a fellowship should fill out the fellowship application form when they apply for the program. Notification regarding fellowship status will be received at the same time as notification of acceptance. If the candidate applies before the early deadline, notification regarding the fellowship will be provided by December 1. The final deadline for admission with fellowship consideration is January 15.
Cost of Study	The program's tuition and fees for 2011–12 total $63,192.
Living and Housing Costs	Living expenses are estimated at around $21,057; personal expenses and books cost about $10,205. However, costs may vary according to personal choices. Housing is available for entering full-time M.P.A. students in Columbia University owned buildings in the Morningside Heights and Washington Heights neighborhoods near SIPA, but it is not guaranteed.
Student Group	The class of 2012 comprises 64 students hailing from North America, Europe, Africa, South America, and Asia. The program accepts individuals from a variety of academic backgrounds and with experience in various fields including engineering, business, education, government, sciences, and nonprofit. This diversity reflects the systems-based approach and communications emphases of the program. The University strives to have a large mix of students from varying backgrounds to enhance dialogue and broaden perspectives on environmental issues.
Student Outcomes	Seventy-nine percent of alumni are currently working in environmental and sustainable development fields in the public sector (e.g., the City of New York, Metropolitan Transit Authority, and U.S. Environmental Protection Agency), private sector (e.g., AIG, ICF International, and Deutsche Bank), and the nonprofit sector (e.g., the National Resources Defense Council, The Nature Conservancy, and the American Public Power Association).
Location	Columbia University is located on the Upper West Side of Manhattan. The Morningside Heights campus houses three undergraduate schools—Columbia College, the Fu Foundation School of Engineering and Applied Science, and the School of General Studies—as well as graduate and professional schools for arts and sciences, architecture, the arts, business, international affairs, journalism, law, and social work.
The University and The Department	Founded in 1754, Columbia University is the oldest university in New York, and the fifth oldest in the country. The urban location of the campus has long attracted intellectuals of all kinds, as is evidenced by the list of diverse and successful alumni and faculty. Total enrollment for fall 2010 was 27,606; approximately 70 percent of these students are working toward graduate degrees. The students and faculty represent a wide variety of religious, racial, and ethnic backgrounds, with 23 percent qualifying as international students.
Applying	The early notification deadline for the program is November 1. Those who submit their application to the program and for fellowship consideration early are guaranteed an answer about the program and their fellowship application by December 1. Otherwise, application forms for the program and fellowship consideration can be submitted by January 15. The final deadline for applying to the program without fellowship consideration is February 15. Students will be notified whether they have been admitted by early March.
Correspondence and Information	Sarah Tweedie, Assistant Director M.P.A. Program in Environmental Science and Policy Columbia University School of International and Public Affairs 1408 International Affairs Building 420 West 118th Street Mail code: 3328 New York, New York 10027 Phone: 212-854-3142 Fax: 212-854-3010 E-mail: st2745@columbia.edu Web site: http://www.columbia.edu/cu/mpaenvironment/index.html

Peterson's Graduate Programs in the Physical Sciences, Mathematics, Agricultural Sciences, the Environment & Natural Resources 2012

www.facebook.com/petersonspublishing   **395**

Columbia University

THE FACULTY AND THEIR RESEARCH

Howard N. Apsan, Adjunct Professor; Ph.D., Columbia, 1985. Organizational management and leadership, environmental health and safety, risk management.

Kathleen Callahan, Deputy Director for Research Management, Lamont-Doherty Earth Observatory; Adjunct Lecturer, School of International and Public Affairs; B.A., CUNY, Hunter.

Steven A. Cohen, Director, M.P.A. Program in Environmental Science and Policy; Executive Director, the Earth Institute at Columbia University; Ph.D., Buffalo, SUNY, 1979. Environmental policy and management, energy policy, nuclear waste policy, urban policy and politics, public management, management effectiveness.

Nancy Degnan, Lecturer; Ph.D., Columbia. Community-based initiatives in education, sustainable development and redevelopment, microfinance and enterprise development.

Olle Folke, Assistant Professor; M.A., SLU (Sweden), 2005. Income and education, environmental and anti-immigration party election strategies, ninteenth- and twentieth-century U.S. politics: spoils system, policy of the demand for cars.

Adela J. Gondek, Adjunct Professor; Ph.D., Harvard, 1981. Concept of the person in modern liberalism, forms of justice and the formation of political coalitions in the U.S., politics and public ethics.

Sophia N. Johnson, Adjunct Associate Professor; Ph.D., Rutgers, 2009. International political economy, theories of comparative analysis, political economy of development, South Asian politics, economic liberalization reforms, theories of the state, governance and globalization, democracy and development, environmental politics, environmental governance, environmental policy, North-South relations, foreign policy analysis, cooperation and diplomacy.

Lloyd Kass, Adjunct Assistant Professor; M.P.A., Columbia, 1998.

Felix Lam, Adjunct Professor; Postgraduate Program Certificate, Pennsylvania (Wharton), 2001. Chief financial officer of the New York City Housing Authority (NYCHA), responsible for all financial planning, accounting, insurance, investment activities, and energy management of the nation's largest public housing authority with more than $3 billion in net assets.

Juerg M. Matter, Adjunct Assistant Professor; Ph.D. (natural sciences), ETH Zurich (Switzerland), 2001. Carbon capture and storage as a climate change mitigation technology.

Michael P. Musso, Adjunct Professor; M.P.H. (environmental health science), Columbia, 2007.

Suresh Naidu, Assistant Professor; Ph.D. (economics), Berkeley, 2008. Political economy, economic history, development economics.

Irene Nielson, Lecturer; M.P.A. (environmental science and policy), Columbia, 2005.

Matthew I. Palmer, Adjunct Assistant Professor; Ph.D., Rutgers, 2005. Plant community ecology with emphases on conservation, restoration, and ecosystem function.

Michael Puma, Associate Research Scientist; Ph.D. (civil and environmental engineering), Princeton, 2006. Interactions of the hydrologic cycle with climate, terrestrial ecosystems, and society; improving the water and land dynamics of the Goddard Institute for Space Studies' climate model.

Louise Rosen, Associate Director, M.P.A. Program in Environmental Science and Policy, the Earth Institute, and the School of International and Public Affairs; M.S. (journalism), Columbia, 1999. Economic and political development, environmental justice.

Jeffrey D. Sachs, Director, the Earth Institute at Columbia University; Ph.D., Harvard 1980. Health and development, economic geography, globalization, transition to market economies in Eastern Europe and the former Soviet Union, international financial markets, international macroeconomic policy coordination, emerging markets, economic development and growth, global competitiveness, macroeconomic policies in developing and developed countries.

Jason E. Smerdon, Adjunct Assistant Professor; Ph.D. (applied physics), Michigan, 2004. Reconstructing the climate of the Common Era and understanding the dynamics of climate variability during that time period.

Martha Stark, Adjunct Lecturer, Master of Public Administration in Environmental Science and Policy, School of International and Public Affairs.

E. Gail Suchman, Adjunct Professor; J.D., Boston College, 1979.

Sara Tjossem, Associate Director for M.P.A. EnvironmentalScience and Policy Curriculum; Ph.D. (history of science), Cornell, 1994. Intersection of science and society, history of twentieth-century biology, history of ecology and agriculture, marine science, development of environmental movements.

Bogdan Vasi, Assistant Professor; Ph.D., Cornell, 2004. Adoption and implementation of local programs to address global climate change, development of the wind energy industry, strategies for coping with tragedies of the commons.

396   www.facebook.com/petersonspublishing

Peterson's Graduate Programs in the Physical Sciences, Mathematics,
Agricultural Sciences, the Environment & Natural Resources 2012

INDIANA UNIVERSITY BLOOMINGTON

School of Public and Environmental Affairs
Environmental Science Graduate Programs

Programs of Study
The School of Public and Environmental Affairs (SPEA) offers a Master of Science in Environmental Science (M.S.E.S.) degree.

The M.S.E.S. program educates professionals who combine specialization in an area of environmental science with the analytical and policy skills necessary to apply that knowledge in a broader context. This degree program includes an experiential requirement, usually fulfilled by an internship, but also allows for a research focus culminating in a traditional master's thesis.

For students desiring more in-depth study in environmental science, the M.S.E.S. program is an excellent preparation for entry into the Ph.D. in environmental science program. Alternatively, students desiring more in-depth preparation in policy, law, or other related fields can combine their M.S.E.S. with a degree in public affairs (M.P.A./M.S.E.S.), law (M.S.E.S./J.D.), or a number of other disciplines in biology, chemistry, physics, geography, geological sciences, or journalism.

The M.S.E.S. program requires 48 credit hours distributed among four sets of courses: science courses, policy and management courses, tool-skill courses, and an experiential requirement. There are no required courses per se; however, each student is expected to demonstrate several competencies, depending on his or her concentration. These competencies include relevant natural and physical sciences, economics, policy or law, and quantitative problem solving. Concentrations include applied ecology; energy; environmental chemistry, toxicology, and risk assessment; and water resources. Faculty advisers work with the student to ensure that these competencies are met and that the student is pursuing a suitable plan of study. This curriculum provides students with a general knowledge of environmental science, including tool skills to allow them to apply that knowledge within a specialized area of expertise.

Research Facilities
Complementing the School's own resources, Indiana University maintains eight nationally prominent area studies centers and sixty language programs to facilitate international research and career interests. SPEA has affiliations with several research centers on both the Bloomington and Indianapolis campuses, including the Center for Research in Environmental Science; the Indiana University Research and Teaching Preserve; and the Center for the Study of Institutions, Population, and Environmental Change. Additionally, IU's new multidisciplinary science building opened in October 2009, a 65,000-square-foot, five-story building that brings together IU researchers in environmental science, biogeochemistry, and other life sciences that cross disciplinary boundaries.

SPEA is committed to meeting the research needs of its students. PCs, mainframe computers, and a geographic information system (GIS) computing laboratory are available. More than forty additional computing sites on the Bloomington campus are available for student use.

SPEA houses its own newly renovated Information Commons, which provides convenient access to individual and group workstations, student-focused services that support individual and collaborative learning and research, and access to rich library resources shared with the Kelley School of Business. The Indiana University Bloomington Libraries have been recognized by peers as the top university library in the country, according to the Association of College and Research Libraries, 2010.

Financial Aid
Departmental assistance for qualified students is awarded on a competitive basis and is determined by merit. Awards include fellowships, scholarships, and teaching and research assistantships. Prospective students may apply for merit-based awards by checking the appropriate box on the admission application form. Students may apply for need-based aid through the University Office of Student Financial Assistance (OSFA).

SPEA hosts a one-of-a-kind, collaborative program called Service Corps, which enables M.S.E.S. and M.P.A. students to apply their classroom learning directly to the field in both the public and nonprofit sectors. Service Corps is a financial aid mechanism that offers students real-world experience working in an array of governmental and nonprofit agencies while concurrently pursuing their academic plans. The program is a partnership among the University, the School, and a number of valued external stakeholders in the community and region. Students are selected for participation during the merit aid allocation process.

SPEA also houses a brand new AmeriCorps VISTA program, in which SPEA graduate students take a hiatus from their graduate studies to serve a one-year term as full-time AmeriCorps VISTA members. Students will have the opportunity to serve at a variety of nonprofit and government agencies working on capacity-building projects. SPEA VISTA Fellows receive 3 credit hours for their year of service, which also fulfills the master's program's experiential requirement. Additionally, AmeriCorps VISTA members receive an annual living allowance, health benefits, and all benefits associated with AmeriCorps VISTA service, including an education award of $5550. Members also gain a civil service benefit, authorizing noncompetitive eligibility for federal jobs for one year following service.

Cost of Study
In-state residents pay $415 per credit hour and nonresidents pay $902 per credit hour for master's programs in 2011–12.

Living and Housing Costs
The 1,200 on-campus apartments for graduate students range in monthly rent from $519 for a furnished efficiency to $1164 for an unfurnished three-bedroom apartment. Rates include all utilities as well as local telephone service, cable TV, and Internet connection.

A variety of off-campus apartments and rental houses are available near the University. Rents are generally inexpensive, with the average two-bedroom unit renting for $550 to $800 per month. Free campus and municipal bus systems serve most apartment complexes. Recently named the number-one small transit system in North America by the American Public Transportation Association, the Bloomington Transit system provides easy transportation to SPEA and many other areas of Bloomington.

Student Group
About 322 students are enrolled in the M.P.A. program, with 100 students pursuing the dual M.P.A./M.S.E.S. program and 71 students enrolled in the Ph.D. programs in public affairs or public policy. About 27 percent of these students are international, more than one half are women, and more than 5 percent are members of underrepresented populations.

SPEA recognizes service in AmeriCorps, Teach for America, and Peace Corps, hosting both the Peace Corps' Coverdell Fellows/USA and Master's International (MI) programs. Volunteers receive a waiver of the experiential component which is a part of the academic design and a reduction of the total number of credit hours required for degree completion. Peace Corps Fellows and MIs also receive a competitive merit aid package in addition to the benefits described above.

Student Outcomes
SPEA maintains an outstanding placement record, attributed to a well-rounded curriculum, national prestige, and strong alumni support. Within six months of the close of the 2008–09 academic year, approximately 76 percent of students responding to SPEA's annual employment survey indicated that they had procured full-time professional positions or were continuing their education. The SPEA Office of Career Services (OCS) is staffed with professionals who assist graduate students with all of their career development needs. With so many resources at their disposal, SPEA students annually compete for many of the most prestigious and competitive positions in federal and state government and top-tier nonprofits and foundations. Recent placements include positions with the Environmental Protection Agency; Department of State; National Forest Service; National Oceanographic and Atmospheric Institute; Nature Conservancy; Indiana Department of Environmental Management; U.S. Geological Survey; U.S. Agency for International Development; U.S. Department of Agriculture; Federal Highway Administration; ICF International; National Park Service; ABT Associates, Inc.; GEI Consultants, Inc.; Tetra Tech, Inc.; Federal Energy Regulatory Commission; U.S. Department of Energy; U.S. Peace Corps; NTH Consultants, Ltd.; and U.S. Fish and Wildlife Service.

Location
Bloomington, a college town with a population of 110,000, was chosen as one of the top 10 college towns in America for its "rich mixture of atmospherics and academia" by Edward Fiske, former education editor of the *New York Times*. It is a culturally vibrant community settled among southern Indiana's rolling hills just 45 miles south of Indianapolis, the state capital. Mild winters and warm summers are ideal for outdoor recreation in the two state forests, one national forest, three state parks, and an array of lakes and streams that surround Bloomington.

The University and The School
Established in 1820, Indiana University has more than 9,000 graduate students and a total of nearly 42,500 students enrolled on the Bloomington campus. SPEA is the top-ranked graduate program on the campus. Fifty-five other academic departments are ranked in the top 20 in the country, including music, business, biology, foreign languages, political science, and chemistry. Attractions include nearly 1,000 musical performances each year, including eight full-length operas and professional Broadway plays; the IU Art Museum, designed by I. M. Pei, with more than 30,000 art objects; fifty campus and community volunteer agencies; more than 700 student clubs and organizations; two indoor student recreational facilities; and Big Ten athletics.

SPEA, founded in 1972, was the first school to combine public management, policy, and administration with the environmental sciences.

Applying
Application files must include the SPEA admission application form, transcripts, GRE General Test scores, and three letters of recommendation. Priority is given to applications received by February 1. Students applying for awards must submit a complete application file by the priority deadline, February 1. School visits are encouraged to determine program fit. Applicants can access the School's Web site at http://www.spea.indiana.edu.

Correspondence and Information

For master's programs:
Master's Program Office
SPEA 260
Indiana University
Bloomington, Indiana 47405

Phone: 812-855-2840
    800-765-7755 (toll-free in U.S. only)
E-mail: speainfo@indiana.edu
Web site: http://www.spea.indiana.edu

For doctoral programs:
Doctoral Program Office
SPEA 441
Indiana University
Bloomington, Indiana 47405

Phone: 812-855-2457
    800-765-7755 (toll-free in U.S. only)
E-mail: bsnedega@indiana.edu

Peterson's Graduate Programs in the Physical Sciences, Mathematics, Agricultural Sciences, the Environment & Natural Resources 2012

www.facebook.com/petersonspublishing   397

Indiana University Bloomington

THE FACULTY AND THEIR RESEARCH

Osita G. Afoaku, Ph.D., Washington State, 1991. Human rights, sustainable development, democratization, and state reconstruction in Africa; U.S.-African/Third World relations; U.N. Security Council reform.

David B. Audretsch, Ph.D., Wisconsin, 1980. Economics policy, entrepreneurship, innovation, globalization, regional economic policy, industrial restructuring and government policy, small enterprises in Europe and the United States.

Matthew R. Auer, Ph.D., Yale, 1996. Intersection of foreign aid and sustainable development, international forest politics, energy efficiency, environmental education.

Mathew Baggetta, Ph.D., Harvard, 2009. Civil society, voluntary associations, civic engagement, social capital.

James Barnes, J.D., Harvard, 1967. Environmental law, domestic and international environmental policy, ethics and the public official, mediation and alternative dispute resolution, law and public policy.

Lisa Blomgren Bingham, J.D., Connecticut, 1979. Collaborative governance, comparative governance, dispute resolution, dispute system design, mediation, administrative law, labor and employment law.

Jennifer N. Brass, Ph.D., Berkeley, 2010. African politics, nongovernmental organizations (NGOs), energy and international development, comparative public administration, governance, civil society, political economy of development.

Sanya Carley, Ph.D. North Carolina at Chapel Hill, 2010. Energy policy and economics, electricity technology innovation policy, applied econometrics, policy instruments.

Joyce Y. Chang, Ph.D. candidate, J.D., Ohio State, 2003. Environmental policy, public policy, political theory and methodology, public law.

Melissa A. L. Clark, M.S., Indiana, 1999. Aquatic and terrestrial habitats, working closely with the Indiana Clean Lakes Program, water resources and water quality, implementing sustainability initiatives on campus and community.

Christopher B. Craft, Ph.D., North Carolina State, 1987. Wetland restoration and ecosystem development, wetlands and water quality, wetlands and climate change, including carbon sequestration and peat accretion.

Brian L. DeLong, M.A., Wake Forest. National and international security policies from an argumentation, rhetorical, and critical cultural perspective.

Sameeksha Desai, Ph.D., George Mason, 2008. Entrepreneurship, innovation, and economic development policy; political economy and allocation of entrepreneurship in areas of political instability, conflict, and disaster; postconflict reconstruction; social entrepreneurship.

Denvil R. Duncan, Ph.D., Georgia State, 2010. Public economics, labor economics, economic development.

Sébastien Dusanter, Ph.D., Université Lille 1 (France), 2002. Advancing knowledge of the oxidative capacity of the atmosphere through laboratory studies and field measurements to improve the chemical mechanisms included in atmospheric models to tackle fundamental issues related to climate change and air quality.

Michael A. Edwards, Ph.D., North Dakota State, 1999. Atmospheric chemistry research: mechanistic studies of terpenes reacting with ozone, future regulation of hydrogen storage materials.

Sergio Fernandez, Ph.D., Georgia, 2004. Public management and organization theory, privatization and contracting out, public-sector leadership, organizational change.

Burnell C. Fischer, Ph.D., Purdue, 1974. Forestry, particularly silviculture and urban forestry; growth and development of Central Hardwood forest stands and response to various silvicultural practices; community and urban forestry issues; forest resources policy and state government management; human factors relating to forests and forest products, particularly with regard to collaborative forestry.

Seth Freedman, Ph.D., Maryland, College Park, 2010. Health economics, public economics, labor economics.

Beth Gazley, Ph.D., Georgia, 2004. Nonprofit management and governance, volunteerism, collaboration, intersectoral relations and the role of the voluntary sector in emergency planning.

David Good, Ph.D., Pennsylvania, 1985. Quantitative policy modeling, productivity measurement in public and regulated industries, urban policy analysis.

John D. Graham, Ph.D., Carnegie-Mellon,1983. Government reform, energy and the environment, the future of the automobile in both developed and developing countries.

Kirsten Grønbjerg, Ph.D., Chicago, 1974. Nonprofit and public-sector relationships, examining scope and community dimensions of the Indiana nonprofit sector, the American welfare system, nonprofit funding relations, nonprofit data sources.

Hendrik M. Haitjema, Ph.D., Minnesota, 1982. Groundwater flow modeling, including regional groundwater flow systems, conjunctive surface-water and groundwater flow modeling, 3-D groundwater flow, and saltwater intrusion problems, with emphasis on application of analytic functions to modeling groundwater flow, specifically analytic-element method.

Bradley T. Heim, Ph.D., Northwestern, 2002. Behavioral impact of tax policies on labor supply, consumption, income and earnings, employment mode, health insurance purchases, charitable giving, and retirement savings; analysis of labor, business, and household income dynamics.

Diane S. Henshel, Ph.D., Washington (St. Louis), 1987. Sublethal health effects of environmental pollutants, especially pollutant effects on the developing organism, including the effects of polychlorinated dibenzo-p-dioxins (PCDDs) and related congeners on the developing nervous system of birds exposed in the wild and under controlled laboratory conditions.

Monika Herzig, D.M.E., Indiana, 1997. Touring jazz pianist, concert promotion, music industry, jazz education.

Ronald Hites, Ph.D., MIT, 1968. Applying organic analytical chemistry techniques to the analysis of trace levels of toxic pollutants, such as polychlorinated biphenyls and pesticides, with focus on understanding behavior of these compounds in the atmosphere and in the Great Lakes.

Cheryl K. Hughes, M.B.A., Indiana Wesleyan, 2002. Human resource management/training and development.

Christopher Hunt, M.A., Cambridge, 1961. Programming and presentation of the performing and visual arts and entertainment.

Chaman Jain, Ph.D., Indiana, 1975. Governmental and non-profit accounting and reporting, financial management in nonprofit organizations, governmental budgeting and finance, financial (corporate) management.

Craig Johnson, Ph.D., SUNY at Albany, 1993. Capital markets and financial intermediation, financial management, public budgeting and finance, financing e-government, financing economic development, environmental and infrastructure finance.

William W. Jones, M.S., Wisconsin–Madison, 1977. Lake and watershed management, especially diagnosing lake and watershed water-quality problems; preparing management plans to address problems identified; stream ecology.

Haeil Jung, Ph.D., Chicago, 2009. Applied econometrics and program evaluation, crime policy, public policy for low-income families.

Kerry Krutilla, Ph.D., Duke, 1988. Theory and practice of benefit-cost analysis, environmental policy analysis, program evaluation of environmental programs, natural resource management in developing countries.

Marc L. Lame, Ph.D., Arizona State, 1992. Implementation of integrated pest-management programs in schools and day-care facilities.

Leslie Lenkowsky, Ph.D., Harvard, 1982. Nonprofits and public policy, civil society in comparative perspective, institutional grant makers, volunteering and civic engagement, education and social welfare policy, social entrepreneurship.

Alvin (Al) Lyons, Ph.D., Indiana–Purdue at Indianapolis, 2009. Philanthropic studies; nonprofit management, fund development, strategic planning, and board development; social entrepreneurship; programs for nonprofit organizations, with an emphasis on hospitals.

Joyce Y. Man, Ph.D., Johns Hopkins, 1993. Public finance, urban and regional economics, international trade, economic development, public budgeting and financial management.

Michael McGuire, Ph.D., Indiana, 1995. Intergovernmental and interorganizational collaboration and networks, federalism and intergovernmental relations, public management, emergency management.

Vicky J. Meretsky, Ph.D., Arizona, 1995. Ecology and management of rare species, biocomplexity, landscape-level species and community conservation, temporal patterns in biodiversity, integrating ecosystem research and endangered species management within adaptive management.

John L. Mikesell, Ph.D., Illinois, 1969. Governmental finance, especially questions of policy and administration of sales and property taxation; state lotteries; public budgeting; public finance in countries of the former Soviet Union.

Ashlyn Aiko Nelson, Ph.D., Stanford, 2005. Housing finance, education finance, education policy, the mortgage crisis.

Patrick O'Meara, Ph.D., Indiana, 1970. Comparative politics and development, Southern African politics, ethics and politics.

Clinton V. Oster Jr., Ph.D., Harvard, 1978. Aviation safety, airline economics and competition policy, international aviation, aviation infrastructure, environmental and natural resource policy, government regulation, business-government relations.

Elinor Ostrom, Ph.D., UCLA, 1965. Exploring how institutional rules affect the structure of action situations within which individuals face incentives, make choices, and jointly affect each other; problems involving collective goods and common-pool resource systems; how various types of institutions enhance or detract from the capabilities of individuals to achieve equitable, workable, and efficient solutions.

James Perry, Ph.D., Syracuse, 1974. Public service motivation, government and civil service reform, public management, public human resource management, national and community service, performance-related pay, public organizational behavior.

Flynn W. Picardal, Ph.D., Arizona, 1992. Bioremediation, environmental microbiology, and biogeochemistry, with a focus on the microbial reduction of iron oxides and nitrate, transformation of metals and chlorinated hydrocarbons, and combined microbial-geochemical interactions.

Maureen A. Pirog, Ph.D., Pennsylvania, 1981. Poverty and income maintenance, child support enforcement, welfare reform, adolescent parenting.

Orville W. Powell, M.P.A., Penn State, 1963. Local government and the U.S. Constitution.

Daniel Preston, M.A.L.D., Tufts (Fletcher), 2005. Global environment, international affairs, politics, poverty alleviation, corporate and public sector strategy, country competitiveness, financial markets, economic development, education, good governance, public policy.

Jonathan D. Raff, Ph.D., Indiana Bloomington, 2007. Applying interdisciplinary approaches to understand how thermal and photochemical reactions on surfaces affect the fate of pollutants in the environment and impact global climate.

J. C. Randolph, Ph.D., Carleton (Ottawa), 1972. Forest ecology; ecological aspects of global environmental change, with particular interests in forestry and agriculture; applications of geographic information systems (GIS) and remote sensing in environmental and natural resources management; landscape ecology and regional-scale modeling; physiological ecology of woody plants and of small mammals.

David A. Reingold, Ph.D., Chicago, 1996. Urban poverty, economic development, social welfare policy, low-income housing policy, government performance.

Terri L. Renner, M.B.A., Indiana, 1985. Financial management, information systems, entrepreneurship.

Rafael Reuveny, Ph.D., Indiana, 1997. International political economy; globalization; rise and fall of major powers; political conflict and how it interacts with international trade, democracy, and the environment; sustainable development; Middle East political economy.

Kenneth R. Richards, J.D./Ph.D., Pennsylvania, 1997. Domestic and international climate change policy, environmental policy implementation, carbon sequestration economics and law, energy law, U.S. Forest Service organizational design and management.

Evan J. Ringquist, Ph.D., Wisconsin–Madison, 1990. Public policy (environmental, energy, natural resources, and regulation), research methodology, American political institutions.

Justin Ross, Ph.D., West Virginia, 2007. Public economics, urban/regional economics, spatial econometrics, applied microeconomics, quantile regressions, public finance, political economy, game theory.

Todd V. Royer, Ph.D., Idaho State, 1999. Aquatic biogeochemistry, water resources, nutrient and carbon cycling in streams and rivers, water quality and nutrient standards.

Barry Rubin, Ph.D., Wisconsin–Madison, 1977. Urban and regional economic development and impact analysis, quantitative analysis of local government management and labor relations issues, statistics and quantitative methods, econometric modeling, public management information systems, strategic planning and management.

Michael Rushton, Ph.D., British Columbia, 1990. Cultural economics, policy and administration, nonprofit and public organizations and management, tax policy, government funding for the arts and other policies toward nonprofit organizations, cultural districts, the relationships between the arts and economic growth.

Adrian Sargeant, Ph.D., Exeter (England). Nonprofit marketing, including the arts, education, health care. and philanthropy; fundraising and philanthropy.

Kristin Seefeldt, Ph.D., Michigan, 2010. Poverty and low-income families in the United States, housing instability, implementation of programs serving low-income families.

Yue (Jen) Shang, Ph.D., Indiana, 2008. Nonprofit marketing, marketing communications for nonprofit organizations, donor behavior, fund development, philanthropic psychology.

Joseph Shaw, Ph.D., Kentucky, 2001. Environmental toxicology, environmental genomics, comparative physiology.

Daniel Simon, Ph.D., Maryland, College Park, 1999. Variety of issues linking government policies and firm behavior with individual outcomes and firm performance.

Kosali Simon, Ph.D., Maryland, College Park, 1999. Health economics and policy, the impact of state and federal regulations attempting to ease the availability of private and public health insurance for vulnerable populations on health insurance, health, and labor market outcomes.

Nan Stager, M.S., Indiana, 1978. Mediation, negotiation, alternative dispute resolution, public input processes.

Philip S. Stevens, Ph.D., Harvard, 1990. Characterization of chemical mechanisms that influence regional air quality and global climate change.

Anh Tran, Ph.D., Harvard, 2009. Institutions and behavior of bureaucrats, entrepreneurs and workers in developing countries.

Terry Usrey, M.S., Indiana, 1983. E-government, information technology policy, information technology management.

Henry K. Wakhungu, Ph.D., Indiana, 2004. Development of growth simulation models for sustainable management of indigenous community forests; experimental designs in tropical forestry research; how preservice teachers conceptualize mathematics (philosophically), indexed with mathematics learning and teaching.

Jeffrey R. White, Ph.D., Syracuse, 1984. Environmental biogeochemistry, aquatic chemistry, limnology.

Lois R. Wise, Ph.D., Indiana, 1982. Public management and employment policies and practices.

Wenli Yan, Ph.D., Kentucky, 2008. Public and nonprofit financial management, state and local government finance, quantitative methods.

C. Kurt Zorn, Ph.D., Syracuse, 1981. State and local finance, transportation safety, economic development, gaming policy.

THE UNIVERSITY OF TEXAS AT SAN ANTONIO

Ph.D. Program in Environmental Sciences and Engineering

Programs of Study
The Civil and Environmental Engineering (CEE) Department at the University of Texas at San Antonio (UTSA) offers the opportunity for advanced study and research leading to the Doctor of Philosophy degree in environmental science and engineering. The educational objective of this program is to produce graduates who are capable of conducting original research in the industry or academia as well as assuming a leadership role in their elected employment field. This is a multidisciplinary program administered by the CEE Department. It encompasses faculty members and facilities from the College of Sciences and the CEE Department, as well as individual faculty members from other UTSA departments. Areas of research emphasis include water resources, environmental quality, environmental remediation, pollution control, conservation ecology, spatial analysis, remote sensing, cold regions environment and change, and natural hazards. More information on the curriculum can be found at http://engineering.utsa.edu/CE/curriculum.html

Research Facilities
The CEE Department has state-of-the-art instructional and laboratory facilities including structural, environmental, bioenvironmental, GIS, and geomaterials. The geomaterials lab has full Superpave capabilities and is AASHTO-accredited. Additional information regarding research facilities can be found at http://engineering.utsa.edu/CE/labs.html

Financial Aid
Funding is available through teaching assistantships and research assistantships. A list of recent research projects is available at http://engineering.utsa.edu/CE/researchfunding.html. Students may also take advantage of scholarship opportunities listed at http://engineering.utsa.edu/scholarships/index.php.

Cost of Study
For the 2011–12 academic year, tuition and fees for a full-time graduate degree student (9 semester hours) are approximately $3149 per semester for Texas residents and $8783 per semester for nonresidents. Some courses and programs have additional fees. Please view the following Web sites for more information: http://www.utsa.edu/fiscalservices/tuition.html and http://www.graduateschool.utsa.edu/prospective_students/detail/graduate_tuition_and_fees.

Living and Housing Costs
University on-campus housing is available and includes apartment-style living at four complexes—Chisholm Hall, University Oaks, Laurel Village, and Chaparral Village. Off-campus housing is also available and includes many apartments adjacent to the University as well as a large number located within a 5-mile drive. The rate for a one-bedroom apartment is approximately $500 per month.

Student Group
In the 2010 fall semester, the University enrolled more than 30,000 students, of whom more than 4,000 were graduate students. The CEE Department enrolls over 75 full- and part-time graduate students per year.

Location
San Antonio, with a population of 1.5 million, is one of the nation's major metropolitan areas. As the home of the Alamo and numerous other missions built by the Franciscans, the city is historically and culturally diverse. The Guadalupe Cultural Arts Center, McNay Art Museum, the San Antonio Museum of Art, and the Witte Museum enrich the city. The performing arts are represented by the San Antonio Symphony, the annual Tejano Music Festival and Tejano Music Awards, and performances by opera and ballet companies. Also notable are Sea World, Six Flags Fiesta Texas, Brackenridge Park, the Botanical Gardens, and the downtown Riverwalk. The San Antonio Zoo has the third-largest collection in North America. A city landmark is the Tower of the Americas, which was built for the 1968 World's Fair. San Antonio is home to the National Basketball Association's Spurs, league champions in 2000, 2003, 2005, and 2007. Numerous nearby lakes allow almost year-round outdoor activity, and the beaches of the Texas Gulf coast are within a 2-hour drive. San Antonio is home to numerous festivals throughout the year, including the Fiesta San Antonio and the Rodeo with activities such as parades, fairs, and concerts.

The University
The University was founded in 1969 and has since become a comprehensive metropolitan institution. Its research expenditures place it in the top 25 percent of public universities in Texas. The University has entered a new building and recruitment phase with a view to greatly expand the research effort in the biosciences. The UTSA Roadrunners football team will compete as an NCAA Division I FCS independent in August 2011 and is expected to make the transition to a Division I FBS subdivision team by 2013.

Applying
Applicants for admission as postgraduate degree-seeking students may apply as early as nine months before the beginning of the semester in which they wish to begin graduate study. Because of the time needed to prepare graduate summaries, applicants are encouraged to have their admission file completed at least one month before the application deadline. Application forms and instructions are available on the Graduate School Web site at www.graduateschool.utsa.edu or from the Graduate School. The completed application form, a nonrefundable application fee, and all required supporting documents must be on file with the Graduate School by the appropriate application deadline.

Correspondence and Information
For application information:
The Graduate School
The University of Texas at San Antonio
One UTSA Circle
San Antonio, Texas 78249
Phone: 210-458-4330
Web site: http://www.graduateschool.utsa.edu

For program information:
Department of Civil and Environmental Engineering
The University of Texas at San Antonio
One UTSA Circle
San Antonio, Texas 78249
Phone: 210-458-7571
E-mail: John.Strubelt@usta.edu
Web site: http://engineering.utsa.edu/CE/deptInfo.html

The University of Texas at San Antonio

THE FACULTY AND THEIR RESEARCH

G. Alberto Arroyo, Professor. Structures, forensic analysis.

Sazzad Bin-Shafique, Associate Professor. Beneficial use of wastes and industrial by-products, solidification and stabilization of soil and waste, waste geotechnics, remediation geotechnics, leachability testing, groundwater and contaminant transport modeling.

Samer Desouky, Assistant Professor. Asphalt pavement materials.

Manuel Diaz, Associate Professor. Structures, bridges.

Richard French, Professor. Hydrology and hydraulics of semiarid lands.

Jie Huang, Assistant Professor. Geotechnical engineering, full-scale instrumentation and numerical modeling.

Drew Johnson, Associate Professor. Research and development of novel membrane separation and transfer processes for air and water systems; research and development of biological, physical, and chemical processes for water, wastewater, and waste treatment; water conveyance and conservation.

Xiaofeng Liu, Assistant Professor. Environmental fluid mechanics, sediment transport, multiphase flow, computational fluid dynamics (CFD), water quality modeling.

A. T. Papagiannakis, Professor and Department Chair. Pavement-vehicle interaction, pavement traffic loading, micromechanical analysis of asphalt concretes.

Ruoting Pei, Assistant Professor. Applied environmental microbiology, antibiotic resistance, microbial indicator, molecular microbial ecology, biological remediation, environmental toxicology.

Hatim Sharif, Associate Professor. Hydrologic analysis, modeling, and prediction; land-atmosphere interactions; remote sensing application in hydrometeorology; application of geographic information systems (GIS) in water resources.

Les Shephard, Professor and Director of SERI. Energy and environmental quality.

Heather Shipley, Assistant Professor. Fate, transport, and reactivity of chemicals in natural systems; contaminant adsorption/desorption involving nanoparticles.

Jose Weismann, Professor. Transportation infrastructure management, pavement materials.

400 www.facebook.com/petersonspublishing

Peterson's Graduate Programs in the Physical Sciences, Mathematics, Agricultural Sciences, the Environment & Natural Resources 2012

Section 10
Natural Resources

This section contains a directory of institutions offering graduate work in natural resources, followed by an in-depth entry submitted by an institution that chose to prepare a detailed program description. Additional information about programs listed in the directory may be obtained by writing directly to the dean of a graduate school or chair of a department at the address given in the directory.

For programs offering related work, see also in this book *Environmental Sciences and Management* and *Meteorology and Atmospheric Sciences.* In the other guides in this series:

Graduate Programs in the Humanities, Arts & Social Sciences
See *Architecture (Landscape Architecture)* and *Public, Regional, and Industrial Affairs*

Graduate Programs in the Biological Sciences
See *Biological and Biomedical Sciences; Botany and Plant Biology; Ecology, Environmental Biology, and Evolutionary Biology; Entomology; Genetics, Developmental Biology, and Reproductive Biology; Nutrition; Pathology and Pathobiology; Pharmacology and Toxicology; Physiology;* and *Zoology*

Graduate Programs in Engineering & Applied Sciences
See *Agricultural Engineering and Bioengineering; Civil and Environmental Engineering; Geological, Mineral/Mining, and Petroleum Engineering; Management of Engineering and Technology;* and *Ocean Engineering*

Graduate Programs in Business, Education, Health, Information Studies, Law & Social Work
See *Veterinary Medicine and Sciences*

CONTENTS

Program Directories

Fish, Game, and Wildlife Management

Arkansas Tech University, Graduate College, College of Natural and Health Sciences, Russellville, AR 72801. Offers fisheries and wildlife biology (MS); health informatics (MS); nursing (MSN). *Students:* 9 full-time (4 women), 25 part-time (21 women); includes 1 minority (Black or African American, non-Hispanic/Latino), 2 international. Average age 36. In 2010, 9 master's awarded. *Degree requirements:* For master's, thesis, project. *Entrance requirements:* For master's, GRE General Test. Additional exam requirements/recommendations for international students: Required—TOEFL (minimum score 550 paper-based; 213 computer-based; 79 iBT), IELTS (minimum score 6). *Application deadline:* For fall admission, 3/1 priority date for domestic students, 5/1 priority date for international students; for spring admission, 10/1 priority date for domestic and international students. Applications are processed on a rolling basis. Application fee: $0 ($30 for international students). Electronic applications accepted. *Expenses:* Tuition, state resident: full-time $4680; part-time $195 per credit hour. Tuition, nonresident: full-time $9360; part-time $390 per credit hour. Required fees: $714; $14 per credit hour. One-time fee: $326 part-time. Tuition and fees vary according to course load. *Financial support:* In 2010–11, teaching assistantships with full tuition reimbursements (averaging $4,000 per year); research assistantships, career-related internships or fieldwork, Federal Work-Study, scholarships/grants, health care benefits, and unspecified assistantships also available. Support available to part-time students. Financial award application deadline: 4/15; financial award applicants required to submit FAFSA. *Faculty research:* Fisheries, warblers, fish movement, darter populations, bob white studies. *Unit head:* Dr. Richard Cohoon, Dean, 479-964-0816, E-mail: richard.cohoon@atu.edu. *Application contact:* Dr. Mary B. Gunter, Dean of Graduate College, 479-968-0398, Fax: 479-964-0542, E-mail: graduate.school@atu.edu.

Auburn University, Graduate School, College of Agriculture, Department of Fisheries and Allied Aquacultures, Auburn University, AL 36849. Offers M Aq, MS, PhD. Part-time programs available. *Faculty:* 20 full-time (3 women). *Students:* 37 full-time (16 women), 31 part-time (10 women); includes 2 Black or African American, non-Hispanic/Latino; 1 American Indian or Alaska Native, non-Hispanic/Latino; 1 Hispanic/Latino, 33 international. Average age 28. 49 applicants, 49% accepted, 21 enrolled. In 2010, 12 master's, 5 doctorates awarded. *Degree requirements:* For master's, thesis (for some programs); for doctorate, 2 foreign languages, thesis/dissertation. *Entrance requirements:* For master's and doctorate, GRE General Test. *Application deadline:* For fall admission, 7/7 for domestic students; for spring admission, 11/24 for domestic students. Applications are processed on a rolling basis. Application fee: $50 ($60 for international students). Electronic applications accepted. *Expenses:* Tuition, state resident: full-time $7002. Tuition, nonresident: full-time $21,898. International tuition: $22,116 full-time. Required fees: $892. Tuition and fees vary according to course load and program. *Financial support:* Fellowships, research assistantships, teaching assistantships, Federal Work-Study available. Support available to part-time students. Financial award application deadline: 3/15; financial award applicants required to submit FAFSA. *Faculty research:* Channel catfish production; aquatic animal health; community and population ecology; pond management; production hatching, breeding and genetics. Total annual research expenditures: $8 million. *Unit head:* Dr. David B. Rouse, Head, 334-844-4786. *Application contact:* Dr. George Flowers, Dean of the Graduate School, 334-844-2125.

Auburn University, Graduate School, School of Forestry and Wildlife Sciences, Auburn University, AL 36849. Offers forest economics (PhD); forestry (MS, PhD); natural resource conservation (MNR); wildlife sciences (MS, PhD). *Accreditation:* SAF. Part-time programs available. *Faculty:* 28 full-time (5 women), 2 part-time/adjunct (0 women). *Students:* 29 full-time (12 women), 53 part-time (17 women); includes 1 Black or African American, non-Hispanic/Latino; 1 Asian, non-Hispanic/Latino; 1 Hispanic/Latino, 28 international. Average age 28. 55 applicants, 44% accepted, 17 enrolled. In 2010, 5 master's, 3 doctorates awarded. *Degree requirements:* For master's, thesis (MS); for doctorate, thesis/dissertation. *Entrance requirements:* For master's and doctorate, GRE General Test. *Application deadline:* For fall admission, 7/7 for domestic students; for spring admission, 11/24 for domestic students. Applications are processed on a rolling basis. Application fee: $50 ($60 for international students). Electronic applications accepted. *Expenses:* Tuition, state resident: full-time $7002. Tuition, nonresident: full-time $21,898. International tuition: $22,116 full-time. Required fees: $892. Tuition and fees vary according to course load and program. *Financial support:* Fellowships, research assistantships, teaching assistantships, Federal Work-Study available. Support available to part-time students. Financial award application deadline: 3/15; financial award applicants required to submit FAFSA. *Faculty research:* Forest nursery management, silviculture and vegetation management, biological processes and ecological relationships, growth and yield of plantations and natural stands, urban forestry, forest taxation, law and policy. *Unit head:* Dr. James P. Shepard, Dean, 334-844-4000, Fax: 334-844-1084, E-mail: brinker@forestry.auburn.edu. *Application contact:* Dr. George Flowers, Dean of the Graduate School, 334-844-2125.

Brigham Young University, Graduate Studies, College of Life Sciences, Department of Plant and Wildlife Sciences, Provo, UT 84602-1001. Offers environmental science (MS); genetics and biotechnology (MS); wildlife and wildlands conservation (MS, PhD). *Faculty:* 26 full-time (2 women). *Students:* 63 full-time (23 women); includes 2 Asian, non-Hispanic/Latino; 1 Hispanic/Latino; 1 Native Hawaiian or other Pacific Islander, non-Hispanic/Latino, 5 international. Average age 25. 33 applicants, 55% accepted, 18 enrolled. *Degree requirements:* For master's, thesis; for doctorate, comprehensive exam, thesis/dissertation, minimum GPA of 3.2, 54 hours (18 dissertation, 36 coursework). *Entrance requirements:* For master's, GRE General Test, minimum GPA of 3.2 during last 60 hours of course work; for doctorate, GRE, minimum GPA of 3.2. Additional exam requirements/recommendations for international students: Required—TOEFL (minimum score 580 paper-based; 237 computer-based; 85 iBT). *Application deadline:* 2/1 for domestic and international students. Applications are processed on a rolling basis. Application fee: $0. Electronic applications accepted. *Expenses:* Tuition: Full-time $5580; part-time $310 per credit hour. Tuition and fees vary according to program and student's religious affiliation. *Financial support:* In 2010–11, 63 students received support, including 2 research assistantships with partial tuition reimbursements available (averaging $16,650 per year), 37 teaching assistantships with partial tuition reimbursements available (averaging $16,650 per year); scholarships/grants and tuition waivers (partial) also available. Financial award application deadline: 2/1. *Faculty research:* environmental science, plant genetics, plant ecology, plant nutrition and pathology, wildlife and wildlands conservation. *Unit head:* Dr. Val J. Anderson, Chair, 801-422-3527, Fax: 801-422-0008, E-mail: val_anderson@byu.edu. *Application contact:* Dr. Loreen Allphin, Graduate Coordinator, 801-422-5603, Fax: 801-422-0008, E-mail: loreen_allphin@byu.edu.

Clemson University, Graduate School, College of Agriculture, Forestry and Life Sciences, Department of Forestry and Natural Resources, Program in Wildlife and Fisheries Biology, Clemson, SC 29634. Offers MS, PhD. *Students:* 26 full-time (17 women), 7 part-time (5 women); includes 3 Black or African American, non-Hispanic/Latino, 1 international. Average age 31. 18 applicants, 56% accepted, 6 enrolled. In 2010, 10 master's, 5 doctorates awarded. *Degree requirements:* For master's, thesis; for doctorate, thesis/dissertation. *Entrance requirements:* For master's, GRE General Test, minimum undergraduate GPA of 3.0; for doctorate, GRE General Test. Additional exam requirements/recommendations for international students: Required—TOEFL, IELTS. *Application deadline:* For fall admission, 6/1 for domestic students, 4/15 for international students; for spring admission, 9/15 for international students. Applications are processed on a rolling basis. Application fee: $70 ($80 for international students). Electronic applications accepted. *Expenses:* Contact institution. *Financial support:* In 2010–11, 26 students received support, including 5 fellowships with full and partial tuition reimbursements available (averaging $12,144 per year), 18 research assistantships with partial tuition reimbursements available (averaging $15,743 per year), 7 teaching assistantships with partial tuition reimbursements available (averaging $11,583 per year); career-related internships or fieldwork, institutionally sponsored loans, scholarships/grants, health care benefits, and unspecified assistantships also available. Support available to part-time students. Financial award applicants required to submit FAFSA. *Faculty research:* Intensive freshwater culture systems, conservation biology, stream management, applied wildlife management. *Unit head:* Dr. Patricia Layton, Chair, 864-656-3303, Fax: 864-656-3304, E-mail: playton@clemson.edu. *Application contact:* Dr. David Guynn, Graduate Program Coordinator, 864-656-4830, Fax: 864-656-5344, E-mail: dguynn@clemson.edu.

Colorado State University, Graduate School, Warner College of Natural Resources, Department of Fishery and Wildlife Biology, Fort Collins, CO 80523-1474. Offers fish, wildlife and conservation biology (MFWCB); fishery and wildlife biology (MFWB, MS, PhD). *Faculty:* 15 full-time (4 women). *Students:* 13 full-time (3 women), 15 part-time (5 women); includes 1 minority (Hispanic/Latino). Average age 31. 7 applicants, 86% accepted, 6 enrolled. In 2010, 4 master's, 1 doctorate awarded. Terminal master's awarded for partial completion of doctoral program. *Degree requirements:* For master's, comprehensive exam, thesis (for some programs); for doctorate, comprehensive exam, thesis/dissertation. *Entrance requirements:* For master's, GRE General Test (combined minimum score of 1200 on the Verbal and Quantitative sections), minimum GPA of 3.0, BA or BS in related field, letters of recommendation, personal narrative, resume, transcripts; for doctorate, GRE General Test (minimum score 1000 verbal and quantitative), minimum GPA of 3.0, MS in related field. Additional exam requirements/recommendations for international students: Required—TOEFL (minimum score 550 paper-based; 213 computer-based; 80 iBT). *Application deadline:* For fall admission, 2/15 priority date for domestic and international students. Applications are processed on a rolling basis. Application fee: $50. Electronic applications accepted. *Expenses:* Tuition, state resident: full-time $7434; part-time $413 per credit. Tuition, nonresident: full-time $19,022; part-time $1057 per credit. Required fees: $1729; $88 per credit. *Financial support:* In 2010–11, 4 fellowships with full and partial tuition reimbursements (averaging $37,058 per year), 17 research assistantships with full and partial tuition reimbursements (averaging $12,477 per year), 11 teaching assistantships with full and partial tuition reimbursements (averaging $7,568 per year) were awarded; tuition waivers (full and partial) and unspecified assistantships also available. Financial award application deadline: 2/15; financial award applicants required to submit FAFSA. *Faculty research:* Conservation biology, aquatic ecology, animal behavior, population modeling, habitat evaluation and management. Total annual research expenditures: $3.6 million. *Unit head:* Dr. Kenneth R. Wilson, Head, 970-491-7755, Fax: 970-491-5091, E-mail: kenneth.wilson@colostate.edu. *Application contact:* Joyce Pratt, Graduate Contact, 970-491-5020, Fax: 970-491-5091, E-mail: joyce.pratt@colostate.edu.

Cornell University, Graduate School, Graduate Fields of Agriculture and Life Sciences, Field of Natural Resources, Ithaca, NY 14853-0001. Offers aquatic science (MPS, MS, PhD); environmental management (MPS); fishery science (MPS, MS, PhD); forest science (MPS, MS, PhD); resource policy and management (MPS, MS, PhD); wildlife science (MPS, MS, PhD). *Faculty:* 36 full-time (7 women). *Students:* 48 full-time (21 women); includes 1 Asian, non-Hispanic/Latino; 1 Hispanic/Latino, 11 international. Average age 30. 52 applicants, 27% accepted, 11 enrolled. In 2010, 8 master's, 6 doctorates awarded. *Degree requirements:* For master's, thesis (MS), project paper (MPS); for doctorate, comprehensive exam, thesis/dissertation. *Entrance requirements:* For master's and doctorate, GRE General Test, 2 letters of recommendation. Additional exam requirements/recommendations for international students: Required—TOEFL (minimum score 550 paper-based; 213 computer-based; 77 iBT). *Application deadline:* For spring admission, 10/30 for domestic students. Applications are processed on a rolling basis. Application fee: $70. Electronic applications accepted. *Expenses:* Tuition: Full-time $29,500. Required fees: $76. Tuition and fees vary according to degree level and program. *Financial support:* In 2010–11, 9 fellowships with full tuition reimbursements, 16 research assistantships with full tuition reimbursements, 15 teaching assistantships with full tuition reimbursements were awarded; institutionally sponsored loans, scholarships/grants, health care benefits, tuition waivers (full and partial), and unspecified assistantships also available. Financial award applicants required to submit FAFSA. *Faculty research:* Ecosystem-level dynamics, systems modeling, conservation biology/management, resource management's human dimensions, biogeochemistry. *Unit head:* Director of Graduate Studies, 607-255-2807, Fax: 607-255-0349. *Application contact:* Graduate Field Assistant, 607-255-2807, Fax: 607-255-0349, E-mail: nrgrad@cornell.edu.

Frostburg State University, Graduate School, College of Liberal Arts and Sciences, Department of Biology, Program in Fisheries and Wildlife Management, Frostburg, MD 21532-1099. Offers MS. Part-time and evening/weekend programs available. *Degree requirements:* For master's, thesis. *Entrance requirements:* For master's, GRE General Test, resume. Additional exam requirements/recommendations for international students: Required—TOEFL. Electronic applications accepted. *Faculty research:* Evolution and systematics of freshwater fishes, biochemical mechanisms of temperature adaptation in freshwater fishes, wildlife and fish parasitology, biology of freshwater invertebrates, remote sensing.

Humboldt State University, Academic Programs, College of Natural Resources and Sciences, Programs in Natural Resources, Arcata, CA 95521-8299. Offers natural resources (MS), including fisheries, forestry, natural resources planning and interpretation, rangeland resources and wildland soils, wastewater utilization, watershed management, wildlife. *Students:* 62 full-time (27 women), 21 part-time (7 women); includes 4 minority (1 Asian, non-Hispanic/Latino; 2 Hispanic/Latino; 1 Two or more races, non-Hispanic/Latino), 2 international. Average age 29. 117 applicants, 47% accepted, 33 enrolled. In 2010, 23 master's awarded. *Degree requirements:* For master's, thesis or alternative. *Entrance requirements:* For master's, GRE, appropriate bachelor's degree, minimum GPA of 2.5, 3 letters of recommendation, resume. Additional exam requirements/recommendations for international students: Required—TOEFL (minimum score 500 paper-based; 173 computer-based). *Application deadline:* For fall admission, 2/1 for domestic and international students; for spring admission, 9/30 for domestic and international students. Applications are processed on a rolling basis. Application fee: $55. Tuition and fees vary according to program. *Financial support:* Fellowships, career-related internships or fieldwork and Federal Work-Study available. Support available to part-time students. Financial award application deadline: 3/1; financial award applicants required to submit FAFSA. *Faculty research:* Spotted owl habitat, pre-settlement vegetation, hardwood utilization, tree physiology, fisheries. *Unit head:* Dr. Gary Hendrickson, Coordinator, 707-826-4233, E-mail: thiesfel@humboldt.edu. *Application contact:* Julie Tucker, Administrative Support Coordinator, 707-826-3256, E-mail: jlt7002@humboldt.edu.

Iowa State University of Science and Technology, Graduate College, College of Agriculture, Department of Natural Resource Ecology and Management, Ames, IA 50011. Offers forestry (MS, PhD); wildlife ecology (MS). *Faculty:* 20 full-time (5 women), 11 part-time/adjunct (3 women). *Students:* 38 full-time (14 women), 11 part-time (3 women); includes 1 American Indian or Alaska Native, non-Hispanic/Latino; 1 Hispanic/Latino, 10 international. 16 applicants, 25% accepted, 3 enrolled. In 2010, 7 master's, 2 doctorates awarded. *Degree requirements:* For master's, thesis (for some programs); for doctorate, thesis/dissertation. *Entrance requirements:* For master's and doctorate, GRE General Test. Additional exam requirements/recommendations for international students: Required—TOEFL (minimum score 550 paper-based; 79 iBT), IELTS (minimum score 6.5). *Application deadline:* For fall admission, 4/1 priority date for domestic and international students; for spring admission, 10/1 priority date for domestic and international students. Application fee: $40 ($90 for international students). Electronic applications accepted. *Financial support:* In 2010–11, 28 research assistantships with full and partial tuition reimbursements (averaging $15,773 per year), 3 teaching assistantships with full and partial tuition reimbursements (averaging $11,171 per year) were awarded.

Unit head: Dr. Stephen Jungst, Interim Chair, 515-294-1166. *Application contact:* Dr. Janette Thompson, Director of Graduate Education, 515-294-1626, E-mail: nremgrad@iastate.edu.

Louisiana State University and Agricultural and Mechanical College, Graduate School, College of Agriculture, School of Renewable Natural Resources, Baton Rouge, LA 70803. Offers fisheries (MS); forestry (MS, PhD); wildlife (MS); wildlife and fisheries science (PhD). *Faculty:* 33 full-time (5 women). *Students:* 65 full-time (16 women), 8 part-time (3 women); includes 2 Hispanic/Latino, 22 international. Average age 29. 28 applicants, 39% accepted, 8 enrolled. In 2010, 17 master's, 4 doctorates awarded. *Degree requirements:* For master's, thesis; for doctorate, thesis/dissertation. *Entrance requirements:* For master's, GRE General Test, minimum GPA of 3.0; for doctorate, GRE General Test, MS, minimum GPA of 3.0. Additional exam requirements/recommendations for international students: Required—TOEFL (minimum score 550 paper-based; 213 computer-based; 79 iBT), IELTS (minimum score 6.5). *Application deadline:* For fall admission, 1/25 priority date for domestic students, 5/15 for international students; for spring admission, 10/15 for international students. Applications are processed on a rolling basis. Application fee: $50 ($70 for international students). Electronic applications accepted. *Financial support:* In 2010–11, 69 students received support, including 7 fellowships (averaging $36,514 per year), 60 research assistantships with partial tuition reimbursements available (averaging $19,070 per year); Federal Work-Study, institutionally sponsored loans, scholarships/grants, health care benefits, tuition waivers (full and partial), and unspecified assistantships also available. Financial award application deadline: 4/15; financial award applicants required to submit FAFSA. *Faculty research:* Forest biology and management, aquaculture, fisheries biology and ecology, upland and wetlands wildlife. Total annual research expenditures: $3,080. *Unit head:* Dr. Allen Rutherford, Director, 225-578-4131, Fax: 225-578-4227, E-mail: druther@lsu.edu. *Application contact:* Dr. William Kelso, Coordinator of Graduate Studies, 225-578-4176, Fax: 225-578-4227, E-mail: wkelso@lsu.edu.

McGill University, Faculty of Graduate and Postdoctoral Studies, Faculty of Agricultural and Environmental Sciences, Department of Natural Resource Sciences, Montréal, QC H3A 2T5, Canada. Offers entomology (M Sc, PhD); environmental assessment (M Sc); forest science (M Sc, PhD); microbiology (M Sc, PhD); micrometeorology (M Sc, PhD); neotropical environment (M Sc, PhD); soil science (M Sc, PhD); wildlife biology (M Sc, PhD).

Memorial University of Newfoundland, School of Graduate Studies, Interdisciplinary Program in Marine Studies, St. John's, NL A1C 5S7, Canada. Offers fisheries resource management (MMS, Advanced Diploma). Part-time programs available. *Degree requirements:* For master's, report. *Entrance requirements:* For master's and Advanced Diploma, high 2nd class degree from a recognized university. *Faculty research:* Biological, ecological and oceanographic aspects of world fisheries; economics; political science; sociology.

Michigan State University, The Graduate School, College of Agriculture and Natural Resources, Department of Fisheries and Wildlife, East Lansing, MI 48824. Offers fisheries and wildlife (MS, PhD); fisheries and wildlife—environmental toxicology (PhD). *Entrance requirements:* Additional exam requirements/recommendations for international students: Required—TOEFL (minimum score 550 paper-based; 213 computer-based), Michigan State University ELT (minimum score 85), Michigan English Language Assessment Battery (minimum score 83). Electronic applications accepted.

Mississippi State University, College of Forest Resources, Department of Wildlife, Fisheries and Aquaculture, Mississippi State, MS 39762. Offers forest resources (PhD), including wildlife and fisheries; wildlife and fisheries science (MS). Part-time programs available. *Faculty:* 21 full-time (1 woman), 1 part-time/adjunct (0 women). *Students:* 63 full-time (16 women), 15 part-time (5 women); includes 5 minority (1 Black or African American, non-Hispanic/Latino; 3 Hispanic/Latino; 1 Two or more races, non-Hispanic/Latino), 6 international. Average age 29. 39 applicants, 56% accepted, 20 enrolled. In 2010, 13 master's, 2 doctorates awarded. *Degree requirements:* For master's, thesis, comprehensive oral or written exam; for doctorate, comprehensive exam, thesis/dissertation. *Entrance requirements:* For master's, GRE or minimum GPA of 3.0 on last 60 hours of undergraduate courses, bachelor's degree; for doctorate, GRE or minimum GPA of 3.2 on prior graduate studies, master's degree. Additional exam requirements/recommendations for international students: Required—TOEFL (minimum score 550 paper-based; 213 computer-based; 79 iBT); Recommended—IELTS (minimum score 6.5). *Application deadline:* For fall admission, 7/1 for domestic students, 5/1 for international students; for spring admission, 11/1 for domestic students, 9/1 for international students. Applications are processed on a rolling basis. Application fee: $40. Electronic applications accepted. *Expenses:* Tuition, state resident: full-time $2730.50; part-time $304 per credit hour. Tuition, nonresident: full-time $6901; part-time $767 per credit hour. *Financial support:* In 2010–11, 51 research assistantships with partial tuition reimbursements (averaging $13,981 per year) were awarded; Federal Work-Study, institutionally sponsored loans, and unspecified assistantships also available. Financial award application deadline: 4/1; financial award applicants required to submit FAFSA. *Faculty research:* Spatial technology, habitat restoration, aquaculture, fisheries, wildlife management. *Unit head:* Dr. Bruce D. Leopold, Department Head and Graduate Coordinator, 662-325-2619, Fax: 662-325-8726, E-mail: bleopold@cfr.msstate.edu. *Application contact:* Dr. Eric Dibble, Professor and Coordinator of Graduate Studies, 662-325-7494, Fax: 662-325-8726, E-mail: edibble@cfr.msstate.edu.

Montana State University, College of Graduate Studies, College of Letters and Science, Department of Ecology, Bozeman, MT 59717. Offers ecological and environmental statistics (MS); ecology and environmental sciences (PhD); fish and wildlife biology (PhD); fish and wildlife management (MS). Part-time programs available. *Faculty:* 12 full-time (2 women), 2 part-time/adjunct (0 women). *Students:* 3 full-time (2 women), 46 part-time (16 women). Average age 31. 11 applicants, 27% accepted, 3 enrolled. In 2010, 3 master's, 1 doctorate awarded. *Degree requirements:* For master's, comprehensive exam, thesis (for some programs); for doctorate, comprehensive exam, thesis/dissertation. *Entrance requirements:* For master's and doctorate, GRE, minimum GPA of 3.0, letters of recommendation, essay. Additional exam requirements/recommendations for international students: Required—TOEFL (minimum score 550 paper-based; 213 computer-based). *Application deadline:* For fall admission, 7/15 priority date for domestic students, 5/15 priority date for international students; for spring admission, 12/1 priority date for domestic students, 10/1 priority date for international students. Applications are processed on a rolling basis. Application fee: $30. Electronic applications accepted. *Expenses:* Tuition, state resident: full-time $5553.90. Tuition, nonresident: full-time $14,646. Required fees: $1233. *Financial support:* In 2010–11, 46 students received support, including 1 fellowship with full and partial tuition reimbursement available (averaging $19,200 per year), 32 research assistantships with full and partial tuition reimbursements available (averaging $18,000 per year), 16 teaching assistantships with full tuition reimbursements available (averaging $10,862 per year); career-related internships or fieldwork, institutionally sponsored loans, scholarships/grants, traineeships, health care benefits, tuition waivers (partial), and unspecified assistantships also available. Support available to part-time students. Financial award application deadline: 3/1; financial award applicants required to submit FAFSA. *Faculty research:* Community ecology, population ecology, land-use effects, management and conservation, environmental modeling. Total annual research expenditures: $2.6 million. *Unit head:* Dr. David Roberts, Head, 406-994-4548, Fax: 406-994-3190, E-mail: droberts@montana.edu. *Application contact:* Dr. Carl A. Fox, Vice Provost for Graduate Education, 406-994-4145, Fax: 406-994-7433, E-mail: gradstudy@montana.edu.

New Mexico Highlands University, Graduate Studies, College of Arts and Sciences, Department of Natural Sciences, Las Vegas, NM 87701. Offers chemistry (MS); life science (MS). Part-time programs available. *Faculty:* 21 full-time (10 women). *Students:* 23 full-time (8 women), 11 part-time (6 women); includes 1 American Indian or Alaska Native, non-Hispanic/Latino; 20 Hispanic/Latino, 11 international. Average age 28. 14 applicants, 93% accepted, 7 enrolled. In 2010, 4 master's awarded. *Degree requirements:* For master's, comprehensive exam, thesis. *Entrance requirements:* For master's, minimum undergraduate GPA of 3.0. Additional exam requirements/recommendations for international students: Required—TOEFL (minimum score 540 paper-based; 207 computer-based). *Application deadline:* For fall admission, 8/1 priority date for domestic students. Applications are processed on a rolling basis. Application fee: $15. *Expenses:* Tuition, state resident: full-time $2544. Required fees: $624; $132 per credit hour. *Financial support:* In 2010–11, 17 students received support. Career-related internships or fieldwork, Federal Work-Study, institutionally sponsored loans, scholarships/grants, tuition waivers (full and partial), and unspecified assistantships available. Support available to part-time students. Financial award application deadline: 3/1. *Faculty research:* Invasive organisms in managed and wildland ecosystems, juniper and pinyon ecology and management, vegetation and community structure, big game management, quantitative forestry. *Unit head:* Dr. Mary Shaw, Department Head, 505-454-3407, E-mail: shaw_mary@nmhu.edu. *Application contact:* Diane Trujillo, Administrative Assistant, Graduate Studies, 505-454-3266, Fax: 505-426-2117, E-mail: dtrujillo@nmhu.edu.

New Mexico State University, Graduate School, College of Agricultural, Consumer and Environmental Sciences, Department of Fish, Wildlife and Conservation Ecology, Las Cruces, NM 88003. Offers wildlife science (MS). *Faculty:* 6 full-time (3 women), 1 (woman) part-time/adjunct. *Students:* 18 full-time (7 women), 5 part-time (2 women); includes 3 minority (all Hispanic/Latino), 1 international. Average age 27. 17 applicants, 94% accepted, 7 enrolled. In 2010, 9 master's awarded. *Degree requirements:* For master's, thesis (for some programs). *Entrance requirements:* For master's, GRE General Test, minimum GPA of 3.0. Additional exam requirements/recommendations for international students: Required—TOEFL. *Application deadline:* For fall admission, 4/1 priority date for domestic students; for spring admission, 11/1 priority date for domestic students. Applications are processed on a rolling basis. Application fee: $30 ($50 for international students). Electronic applications accepted. *Expenses:* Tuition, state resident: full-time $4536; part-time $242 per credit. Tuition, nonresident: full-time $15,816; part-time $712 per credit. Required fees: $636 per term. *Financial support:* In 2010–11, 12 research assistantships with partial tuition reimbursements (averaging $19,196 per year), 5 teaching assistantships with partial tuition reimbursements (averaging $7,900 per year) were awarded; career-related internships or fieldwork, Federal Work-Study, scholarships/grants, health care benefits, and unspecified assistantships also available. Support available to part-time students. Financial award application deadline: 4/1. *Faculty research:* Ecosystems analyses, landscape and wildlife ecology, wildlife and fish population dynamics, management models, wildlife and fish habitat relationships. *Unit head:* Dr. Martha J. Desmond, Interim Head, 575-646-1217, Fax: 575-646-1281, E-mail: mdesmond@nmsu.edu. *Application contact:* Doris J. Morgan, Interim Administrative Assistant, 575-646-7051, Fax: 575-646-1281, E-mail: domorgan@nmsu.edu.

North Carolina State University, Graduate School, College of Natural Resources, Program in Fisheries and Wildlife Sciences, Raleigh, NC 27695. Offers MFWS, MS, PhD. *Degree requirements:* For master's, thesis optional. *Entrance requirements:* For master's, GRE General Test. Additional exam requirements/recommendations for international students: Required—TOEFL. Electronic applications accepted. *Faculty research:* Fisheries biology; ecology of marine, estuarine, and anadromous fishes; aquaculture pond water quality; larviculture of freshwater and marine finfish; predator/prey interactions.

Oregon State University, Graduate School, College of Agricultural Sciences, Department of Fisheries and Wildlife, Program in Fisheries Science, Corvallis, OR 97331. Offers M Agr, MAIS, MS, PhD. Part-time programs available. *Degree requirements:* For master's, thesis (for some programs); for doctorate, thesis/dissertation. *Entrance requirements:* For master's and doctorate, GRE, minimum GPA of 3.0 in last 90 hours. Additional exam requirements/recommendations for international students: Required—TOEFL. *Faculty research:* Fisheries ecology, fish toxicology, stream ecology, quantitative analyses of marine and freshwater fish populations.

Oregon State University, Graduate School, College of Agricultural Sciences, Department of Fisheries and Wildlife, Program in Wildlife Science, Corvallis, OR 97331. Offers MAIS, MS, PhD. *Degree requirements:* For master's, thesis (for some programs); for doctorate, thesis/dissertation. *Entrance requirements:* For master's and doctorate, GRE, minimum GPA of 3.0 in last 90 hours. Additional exam requirements/recommendations for international students: Required—TOEFL.

Purdue University, Graduate School, College of Agriculture, Department of Forestry and Natural Resources, West Lafayette, IN 47907. Offers aquaculture, fisheries, aquatic science (MSF); aquaculture, fisheries, aquatic sciences (MS, PhD); forest biology (MS, MSF, PhD); natural resources and environmental policy (MS, MSF); natural resources environmental policy (PhD); quantitative resource analysis (MS, MSF, PhD); wildlife science (MS, MSF, PhD); wood science and technology (MS, MSF, PhD). *Degree requirements:* For master's, thesis; for doctorate, thesis/dissertation. *Entrance requirements:* For master's and doctorate, GRE General Test, minimum B+ average in undergraduate course work. Additional exam requirements/recommendations for international students: Required—TOEFL. Electronic applications accepted. *Faculty research:* Wildlife management, forest management, forest ecology, forest soils, limnology.

South Dakota State University, Graduate School, College of Agriculture and Biological Sciences, Department of Wildlife and Fisheries Sciences, Brookings, SD 57007. Offers MS, PhD. Part-time programs available. *Degree requirements:* For master's, thesis, oral exam; for doctorate, comprehensive exam, thesis/dissertation, interim exam, oral and written comprehensive exams. *Entrance requirements:* For master's and doctorate, GRE. Additional exam requirements/recommendations for international students: Required—TOEFL (minimum score 525 paper-based; 197 computer-based; 71 iBT). *Faculty research:* Agriculture interactions, wetland conservation, biostress, wildlife and fisheries ecology and techniques.

State University of New York College of Environmental Science and Forestry, Department of Environmental and Forest Biology, Syracuse, NY 13210-2779. Offers applied ecology (MPS); chemical ecology (MPS, MS, PhD); conservation biology (MPS, MS, PhD); ecology (MPS, MS, PhD); entomology (MPS, MS, PhD); environmental interpretation (MPS, MS, PhD); environmental physiology (MPS, MS, PhD); fish and wildlife biology and management (MPS, MS, PhD); forest pathology and mycology (MPS, MS, PhD); plant biotechnology (MPS); plant science and biotechnology (MPS, MS, PhD). *Degree requirements:* For master's, thesis (for some programs); for doctorate, comprehensive exam, thesis/dissertation. *Entrance requirements:* For master's and doctorate, GRE General Test, GRE Subject Test, minimum GPA of 3.0. Additional exam requirements/recommendations for international students: Required—TOEFL (minimum score 550 paper-based; 213 computer-based; 80 iBT), IELTS (minimum score 6). *Expenses:* Tuition, state resident: full-time $8370; part-time $349 per credit hour. Tuition, nonresident: full-time $13,780. Required fees: $30.30 per credit hour. $20 per year. *Faculty research:* Ecology, fish and wildlife biology and management, plant science, entomology.

Sul Ross State University, Division of Agricultural and Natural Resource Science, Program in Range and Wildlife Management, Alpine, TX 79832. Offers M Ag, MS. Part-time programs available. *Degree requirements:* For master's, thesis (for some programs). *Entrance requirements:* For master's, GRE General Test, minimum undergraduate GPA of 2.5 in last 60 hours.

Tennessee Technological University, Graduate School, College of Arts and Sciences, Department of Biology, Cookeville, TN 38505. Offers fish, game, and wildlife management (MS). Part-time programs available. *Faculty:* 22 full-time (2 women). *Students:* 11 full-time (5 women), 11 part-time (6 women); includes 1 Black or African American, non-Hispanic/Latino. Average age 25. 17 applicants, 35% accepted, 4 enrolled. In 2010, 8 master's awarded.

Fish, Game, and Wildlife Management

Tennessee Technological University (continued)
Degree requirements: For master's, thesis. *Entrance requirements:* For master's, GRE. Additional exam requirements/recommendations for international students: Required—TOEFL (minimum score 550 paper-based; 79 iBT), IELTS (minimum score 5.5). *Application deadline:* For fall admission, 8/1 for domestic students, 5/1 for international students; for spring admission, 12/1 for domestic students, 10/1 for international students. Application fee: $25 ($30 for international students). Electronic applications accepted. *Expenses:* Tuition, state resident: full-time $7934; part-time $388 per credit hour. Tuition, nonresident: full-time $19,758; part-time $962 per credit hour. *Financial support:* In 2010–11, 17 research assistantships (averaging $9,000 per year), 8 teaching assistantships (averaging $7,500 per year) were awarded. Financial award application deadline: 4/1. *Faculty research:* Aquatics, environmental studies. *Unit head:* Dr. Daniel Combs, Interim Chairperson, 931-372-3134, Fax: 931-372-6257, E-mail: dcombs@tntech.edu. *Application contact:* Shelia K. Kendrick, Coordinator of Graduate Admissions, 931-372-3808, Fax: 931-372-3497, E-mail: skendrick@tntech.edu.

Texas A&M University, College of Agriculture and Life Sciences, Department of Wildlife and Fisheries Sciences, College Station, TX 77843. Offers MS, PhD. Part-time programs available. Postbaccalaureate distance learning degree programs offered (no on-campus study). *Faculty:* 30. *Students:* 89 full-time (57 women), 58 part-time (30 women); includes 34 minority (4 Black or African American, non-Hispanic/Latino; 2 American Indian or Alaska Native, non-Hispanic/Latino; 1 Asian, non-Hispanic/Latino; 27 Hispanic/Latino), 19 international. Average age 26. In 2010, 18 master's, 6 doctorates awarded. Terminal master's awarded for partial completion of doctoral program. *Degree requirements:* For master's, thesis, final oral defense; for doctorate, thesis/dissertation, final oral defense. *Entrance requirements:* For master's and doctorate, GRE General Test, minimum GPA of 3.0. Additional exam requirements/recommendations for international students: Required—TOEFL (minimum score 550 paper-based; 213 computer-based). *Application deadline:* For fall admission, 3/1 for international students; for spring admission, 8/1 for international students. Applications are processed on a rolling basis. Application fee: $50 ($75 for international students). Electronic applications accepted. *Financial support:* In 2010–11, fellowships with partial tuition reimbursements (averaging $22,000 per year), research assistantships (averaging $14,400 per year), teaching assistantships (averaging $14,400 per year) were awarded; career-related internships or fieldwork, institutionally sponsored loans, and scholarships/grants also available. Financial award application deadline: 3/1; financial award applicants required to submit FAFSA. *Faculty research:* Wildlife ecology and management, fisheries ecology and management, aquaculture, biological inventories and museum collections, biosystematics and genome analysis. *Unit head:* Dr. Thomas E. Lacher, Professor and Head, 979-845-5777, Fax: 979-845-3786, E-mail: tlacher@tamu.edu. *Application contact:* Felix Arnold, Academic Advisor II, 979-845-5768, Fax: 979-845-3786, E-mail: fwarnold@tamu.edu.

Texas A&M University–Kingsville, College of Graduate Studies, College of Agriculture and Home Economics, Program in Range and Wildlife Management, Kingsville, TX 78363. Offers MS. *Degree requirements:* For master's, comprehensive exam, thesis or alternative. *Entrance requirements:* For master's, GRE General Test, minimum GPA of 3.0. Additional exam requirements/recommendations for international students: Required—TOEFL.

Texas A&M University–Kingsville, College of Graduate Studies, College of Agriculture and Home Economics, Program in Wildlife Science, Kingsville, TX 78363. Offers PhD. *Degree requirements:* For doctorate, one foreign language, comprehensive exam, thesis/dissertation. *Entrance requirements:* For doctorate, GRE General Test, minimum GPA of 3.5.

Texas State University–San Marcos, Graduate School, College of Science, Department of Biology, Program in Wildlife Ecology, San Marcos, TX 78666. Offers MS. *Faculty:* 7 full-time (1 woman), 2 part-time/adjunct (0 women). *Students:* 27 full-time (18 women), 14 part-time (6 women); includes 11 minority (1 Black or African American, non-Hispanic/Latino; 2 Asian, non-Hispanic/Latino; 8 Hispanic/Latino), 1 international. Average age 27. 13 applicants, 100% accepted, 12 enrolled. In 2010, 8 master's awarded. *Degree requirements:* For master's, thesis. *Entrance requirements:* For master's, GRE General Test (preferred minimum combined score of 1000 Verbal and Quantitative), bachelor's degree in biology or related discipline, minimum GPA of 3.0 in last 60 hours of undergraduate work. Additional exam requirements/recommendations for international students: Required—TOEFL (minimum score 550 paper-based; 213 computer-based; 78 iBT). *Application deadline:* For fall admission, 6/15 priority date for domestic students, 6/1 priority date for international students; for spring admission, 10/15 priority date for domestic students, 10/1 priority date for international students. Applications are processed on a rolling basis. Application fee: $40 ($90 for international students). Electronic applications accepted. *Expenses:* Tuition, state resident: full-time $6024; part-time $251 per credit hour. Tuition, nonresident: full-time $13,536; part-time $564 per credit hour. Required fees: $1776; $50 per credit hour. $306 per semester. *Financial support:* In 2010–11, 13 students received support, including 1 research assistantship (averaging $5,625 per year), 31 teaching assistantships (averaging $4,573 per year); Federal Work-Study and institutionally sponsored loans also available. Support available to part-time students. Financial award application deadline: 4/1; financial award applicants required to submit FAFSA. *Unit head:* Dr. John Baccus, Graduate Advisor, 512-245-2178, Fax: 512-245-8713, E-mail: jb02@txstate.edu. *Application contact:* Dr. J. Michael Willoughby, Dean of the Graduate School, 512-245-2581, Fax: 512-245-8365, E-mail: jw02@swt.edu.

Texas Tech University, Graduate School, College of Agricultural Sciences and Natural Resources, Department of Natural Resources Management, Lubbock, TX 79409. Offers fisheries science (MS, PhD); range science (MS, PhD); wildlife science (MS, PhD); wildlife, aquatic, and wildlands science and management (MS, PhD). Part-time programs available. *Faculty:* 9 full-time (0 women), 1 part-time/adjunct (0 women). *Students:* 47 full-time (14 women), 3 part-time (1 woman); includes 1 American Indian or Alaska Native, non-Hispanic/Latino; 1 Hispanic/Latino; 2 Two or more races, non-Hispanic/Latino, 7 international. Average age 27. 23 applicants, 61% accepted, 12 enrolled. In 2010, 5 master's, 2 doctorates awarded. *Degree requirements:* For master's, thesis; for doctorate, thesis/dissertation. *Entrance requirements:* For master's and doctorate, GRE General Test, formal approval from departmental committee. Additional exam requirements/recommendations for international students: Required—TOEFL (minimum score 550 paper-based; 213 computer-based; 79 iBT). *Application deadline:* For fall admission, 6/1 priority date for domestic students, 1/15 priority date for international students; for spring admission, 9/1 priority date for domestic students, 6/15 priority date for international students. Applications are processed on a rolling basis. Application fee: $50 ($75 for international students). Electronic applications accepted. *Expenses:* Tuition, state resident: full-time $5495.76; part-time $228.99 per credit hour. Tuition, nonresident: full-time $12,936; part-time $538.99 per credit hour. Required fees: $2674; $36 per credit hour. $905 per semester. *Financial support:* In 2010–11, 43 students received support, including 19 research assistantships with partial tuition reimbursements available (averaging $6,023 per year), 2 teaching assistantships with partial tuition reimbursements available (averaging $4,994 per year). Financial award application deadline: 4/15; financial award applicants required to submit FAFSA. *Faculty research:* Use of fire on range lands, big game, upland game, and waterfowl; playa lakes in the southern Great Plains; conservation biology; fish ecology and physiology. Total annual research expenditures: $921,668. *Unit head:* Dr. Mark Wallace, Interim Chairman, 806-742-2841, Fax: 806-742-2280, E-mail: mark.wallace@ttu.edu. *Application contact:* Renee Dillon, Sr. Business Assistant, 806-742-2841, E-mail: renee.dillon@ttu.edu.

Université du Québec à Rimouski, Graduate Programs, Program in Wildlife Resources Management, Rimouski, QC G5L 3A1, Canada. Offers biology (PhD); wildlife resources management (M Sc, Diploma). PhD offered jointly with Université du Québec à Montréal, Université du Québec à Trois-Rivières, and Université du Québec en Abitibi-Témiscamingue. *Entrance requirements:* For degree, appropriate bachelor's degree, proficiency in French.

University of Alaska Fairbanks, College of Natural Sciences and Mathematics, Department of Biology and Wildlife, Fairbanks, AK 99775-6100. Offers biological sciences (MS, PhD), including biology, botany, wildlife biology (PhD), zoology; biology (MAT, MS); wildlife biology (MS). Part-time programs available. *Faculty:* 22 full-time (10 women). *Students:* 80 full-time (46 women), 42 part-time (26 women); includes 13 minority (2 American Indian or Alaska Native, non-Hispanic/Latino; 3 Asian, non-Hispanic/Latino; 2 Hispanic/Latino; 6 Two or more races, non-Hispanic/Latino), 6 international. Average age 31. 53 applicants, 30% accepted, 15 enrolled. In 2010, 11 master's, 10 doctorates awarded. *Degree requirements:* For master's, comprehensive exam, thesis, oral exam, oral defense; for doctorate, comprehensive exam, thesis/dissertation, oral exam, oral defense. *Entrance requirements:* For master's and doctorate, GRE General Test, GRE Subject Test (biology). Additional exam requirements/recommendations for international students: Required—TOEFL (minimum score 550 paper-based; 213 computer-based; 80 iBT), TWE. *Application deadline:* For fall admission, 6/1 for domestic students, 3/1 for international students; for spring admission, 10/15 for domestic students, 9/1 for international students. Applications are processed on a rolling basis. Application fee: $60. Electronic applications accepted. *Expenses:* Tuition, state resident: full-time $5688; part-time $316 per credit. Tuition, nonresident: full-time $11,628; part-time $646 per credit. Required fees: $289 per semester. Tuition and fees vary according to course load and reciprocity agreements. *Financial support:* In 2010–11, 38 research assistantships with tuition reimbursements (averaging $11,087 per year), 20 teaching assistantships with tuition reimbursements (averaging $8,587 per year) were awarded; fellowships with tuition reimbursements, career-related internships or fieldwork, Federal Work-Study, scholarships/grants, health care benefits, and unspecified assistantships also available. Support available to part-time students. Financial award application deadline: 7/1; financial award applicants required to submit FAFSA. *Faculty research:* Plant-herbivore interactions, plant metabolic defenses, insect manufacture of glycerol, ice nucleators, structure and functions of arctic and subarctic freshwater ecosystems. *Unit head:* Christa Mulder, Department Chair, 907-474-7671, Fax: 907-474-6716, E-mail: fybio@uaf.edu. *Application contact:* Christa Mulder, Department Chair, 907-474-7671, Fax: 907-474-6716, E-mail: fybio@uaf.edu.

University of Alaska Fairbanks, School of Fisheries and Ocean Sciences, Program in Marine Sciences and Limnology, Fairbanks, AK 99775-7220. Offers marine biology (MS, PhD); oceanography (PhD), including biological oceanography, chemical oceanography, fisheries, geological oceanography, physical oceanography. Part-time programs available. *Faculty:* 8 full-time (4 women). *Students:* 40 full-time (26 women), 12 part-time (7 women); includes 3 minority (2 Asian, non-Hispanic/Latino; 1 Hispanic/Latino), 3 international. Average age 31. 54 applicants, 26% accepted, 14 enrolled. In 2010, 6 master's, 1 doctorate awarded. *Degree requirements:* For master's, comprehensive exam, thesis, oral defense; for doctorate, comprehensive exam, thesis/dissertation, oral defense. *Entrance requirements:* For master's and doctorate, GRE General Test. Additional exam requirements/recommendations for international students: Required—TOEFL (minimum score 550 paper-based; 213 computer-based; 80 iBT). *Application deadline:* For fall admission, 6/1 for domestic students, 3/1 for international students; for spring admission, 10/15 for domestic students, 8/1 for international students. Applications are processed on a rolling basis. Application fee: $60. Electronic applications accepted. *Expenses:* Tuition, state resident: full-time $5688; part-time $316 per credit. Tuition, nonresident: full-time $11,628; part-time $646 per credit. Required fees: $289 per semester. Tuition and fees vary according to course load and reciprocity agreements. *Financial support:* In 2010–11, 24 research assistantships with tuition reimbursements (averaging $11,704 per year), 9 teaching assistantships with tuition reimbursements (averaging $11,008 per year) were awarded; fellowships with tuition reimbursements, career-related internships or fieldwork, Federal Work-Study, scholarships/grants, health care benefits, and unspecified assistantships also available. Support available to part-time students. Financial award application deadline: 7/1; financial award applicants required to submit FAFSA. *Unit head:* Katrin Iken, Co-Chair, 907-474-7289, Fax: 907-474-5863, E-mail: academics@sfos.uaf.edu. *Application contact:* Christina Neumann, Academic Manager, 907-474-7289, Fax: 907-474-5863, E-mail: clneumann@alaska.edu.

The University of Arizona, College of Agriculture and Life Sciences, School of Natural Resources, Program in Wildlife, Fisheries Conservation, and Management, Tucson, AZ 85721. Offers MS, PhD. *Students:* 3 full-time (1 woman), 4 part-time (0 women), 2 international. Average age 40. *Degree requirements:* For master's, thesis; for doctorate, comprehensive exam, thesis/dissertation. *Entrance requirements:* For master's, GRE General Test, GRE Subject Test (biology), minimum GPA of 3.0, 3 letters of recommendation; for doctorate, GRE General Test, GRE Subject Test (biology), minimum GPA of 3.0, 3 letters of recommendation, MA or MS. Additional exam requirements/recommendations for international students: Required—TOEFL (minimum score 550 paper-based; 213 computer-based). *Application deadline:* For fall admission, 8/1 priority date for domestic students, 12/1 for international students; for spring admission, 7/1 for international students. Applications are processed on a rolling basis. Application fee: $75. *Expenses:* Tuition, state resident: full-time $7692. *Financial support:* Research assistantships with partial tuition reimbursements, teaching assistantships with partial tuition reimbursements, scholarships/grants, health care benefits, tuition waivers (partial), and unspecified assistantships available. *Faculty research:* Short-term effects of artificial oases on Arizona wildlife, elk response to cattle in northern Arizona, effect of reservoir operation on tailwaters, conservation of wildlife. *Unit head:* Dr. R. William Mannan, Chair, 520-621-7283, E-mail: mannan@ag.arizona.edu. *Application contact:* Cheryl L. Craddock, Academic Coordinator, 520-621-7260, Fax: 520-621-8801, E-mail: ccraddoc@email.arizona.edu.

University of Arkansas at Pine Bluff, School of Agriculture, Fisheries and Human Sciences, Pine Bluff, AR 71601-2799. Offers aquaculture and fisheries (MS).

University of Delaware, College of Agriculture and Natural Resources, Department of Entomology and Wildlife Ecology, Newark, DE 19716. Offers entomology and applied ecology (MS, PhD), including avian ecology, evolution and taxonomy, insect biological control, insect ecology and behavior (MS), insect genetics, pest management, plant-insect interactions, wildlife ecology and management. Part-time programs available. *Degree requirements:* For master's, comprehensive exam, thesis, oral exam, seminar; for doctorate, comprehensive exam, thesis/dissertation, qualifying exam, seminar. *Entrance requirements:* For master's, GRE General Test, minimum GPA of 3.0 in field, 2.8 overall; for doctorate, GRE General Test, GRE Subject Test (biology), minimum GPA of 3.0 in field, 2.8 overall. Additional exam requirements/recommendations for international students: Required—TOEFL. Electronic applications accepted. *Faculty research:* Ecology and evolution of plant-insect interactions, ecology of wildlife conservation management, habitat restoration, biological control, applied ecosystem management.

University of Florida, Graduate School, College of Agricultural and Life Sciences, Department of Wildlife Ecology and Conservation, Gainesville, FL 32611. Offers MS, PhD. *Faculty:* 16 full-time (4 women), 1 part-time/adjunct (0 women). *Students:* 36 full-time (19 women), 9 part-time (4 women); includes 1 Black or African American, non-Hispanic/Latino; 1 Asian, non-Hispanic/Latino; 3 Hispanic/Latino, 11 international. Average age 31. 50 applicants, 8% accepted, 4 enrolled. In 2010, 11 master's, 7 doctorates awarded. *Degree requirements:* For master's, comprehensive exam, thesis optional, Thesis and non-thesis options for MS degree; for doctorate, comprehensive exam, thesis/dissertation. *Entrance requirements:* For master's and doctorate, GRE General Test, minimum GPA of 3.3. Additional exam requirements/recommendations for international students: Required—TOEFL (minimum score 550 paper-based; 213 computer-based; 80 iBT), IELTS (minimum score 6). *Application deadline:* For fall admission, 6/1 priority date for domestic students; for spring admission, 12/1 for domestic students. Applications are processed on a rolling basis. Application fee: $30. Electronic applications accepted. *Expenses:* Tuition, state resident: full-time $10,915.92. Tuition, nonresident: full-time $28,309. *Financial support:* In 2010–11, 33 students received support, including 8

fellowships, 16 research assistantships (averaging $21,203 per year), 9 teaching assistantships (averaging $21,685 per year); institutionally sponsored loans also available. Financial award applicants required to submit FAFSA. *Faculty research:* Wildlife biology and management, tropical ecology and conservation, conservation biology, landscape ecology and restoration, conservation education. *Unit head:* John P. Hayes, PhD, Department Chair, 352-846-0552, E-mail: hayesj@ufl.edu. *Application contact:* Wiley Kitchens, PhD, Graduate Coordinator, 352-846-0536, Fax: 352-846-0841, E-mail: wiley01@ufl.edu.

University of Idaho, College of Graduate Studies, College of Natural Resources, Department of Fish and Wildlife Resources, Moscow, ID 83844-2282. Offers natural resources (MS, PhD). *Faculty:* 13 full-time, 1 part-time/adjunct. *Students:* 8 full-time, 3 part-time. Average age 28. In 2010, 7 master's awarded. *Degree requirements:* For doctorate, thesis/dissertation. *Entrance requirements:* For master's, minimum GPA of 2.8; for doctorate, minimum undergraduate GPA of 2.8, 3.0 graduate. *Application deadline:* For fall admission, 8/1 for domestic students; for spring admission, 12/15 for domestic students. Applications are processed on a rolling basis. Application fee: $60. Electronic applications accepted. *Expenses:* Tuition, nonresident: part-time $580 per credit. Required fees: $306 per credit. *Financial support:* Research assistantships, teaching assistantships available. Financial award applicants required to submit FAFSA. *Faculty research:* Waterfowl and wetland ecology, lake restoration and management, sustainable aquaculture production, riparian ecology and river restoration, wildlife ecology and management. *Unit head:* Dr. Kerry Reese, Department Head, 208-885-6434, E-mail: fish_wildlife@uidaho.edu. *Application contact:* Dr. Kerry Reese, Department Head, 208-885-6434, E-mail: fish_wildlife@uidaho.edu.

University of Maine, Graduate School, College of Natural Sciences, Forestry, and Agriculture, Department of Wildlife Ecology, Orono, ME 04469. Offers wildlife conservation (MWC); wildlife ecology (MS, PhD). Part-time programs available. *Faculty:* 7 full-time (3 women), 1 (woman) part-time/adjunct. *Students:* 10 full-time (3 women), 8 part-time (3 women); includes 1 minority (Asian, non-Hispanic/Latino), 1 international. Average age 36. 9 applicants, 0% accepted, 0 enrolled. In 2010, 2 master's awarded. *Degree requirements:* For master's, thesis (for some programs); for doctorate, one foreign language, thesis/dissertation. *Entrance requirements:* For master's and doctorate, GRE General Test. Additional exam requirements/recommendations for international students: Required—TOEFL. *Application deadline:* For fall admission, 2/1 priority date for domestic students. Applications are processed on a rolling basis. Application fee: $65. Electronic applications accepted. *Expenses:* Tuition, state resident: full-time $400. Tuition, nonresident: full-time $1050. *Financial support:* In 2010–11, 19 research assistantships with tuition reimbursements (averaging $18,218 per year), 2 teaching assistantships with tuition reimbursements (averaging $12,790 per year) were awarded; career-related internships or fieldwork, Federal Work-Study, institutionally sponsored loans, and tuition waivers (full and partial) also available. Financial award application deadline: 3/1. *Faculty research:* Integration of wildlife and forest management; population dynamics; behavior, physiology and nutrition; wetland ecology and influence of environmental disturbances. *Unit head:* Dr. James Gilbert, Chair, 207-581-2872, Fax: 207-581-2858. *Application contact:* Scott G. Delcourt, Associate Dean of the Graduate School, 207-581-3291, Fax: 207-581-3232, E-mail: graduate@maine.edu.

University of Massachusetts Amherst, Graduate School, College of Natural Sciences, Department of Environmental Conservation, Program in Wildlife and Fisheries Conservation, Amherst, MA 01003. Offers MS, PhD. Part-time programs available. *Students:* 32 full-time (17 women), 32 part-time (11 women); includes 1 Black or African American, non-Hispanic/Latino; 1 American Indian or Alaska Native, non-Hispanic/Latino, 10 international. Average age 32. 43 applicants, 26% accepted, 9 enrolled. In 2010, 8 master's, 3 doctorates awarded. Terminal master's awarded for partial completion of doctoral program. *Degree requirements:* For master's, thesis optional; for doctorate, comprehensive exam, thesis/dissertation. *Entrance requirements:* For master's and doctorate, GRE General Test. Additional exam requirements/recommendations for international students: Required—TOEFL (minimum score 550 paper-based; 213 computer-based; 80 iBT), IELTS (minimum score 6.5). *Application deadline:* For fall admission, 2/1 for domestic and international students; for spring admission, 10/1 for domestic and international students. Applications are processed on a rolling basis. Application fee: $50 ($65 for international students). Electronic applications accepted. *Expenses:* Tuition, state resident: full-time $2640. Required fees: $8282. One-time fee: $357 full-time. *Financial support:* Fellowships, research assistantships, teaching assistantships, career-related internships or fieldwork, Federal Work-Study, scholarships/grants, traineeships, health care benefits, tuition waivers (full), and unspecified assistantships available. Support available to part-time students. Financial award application deadline: 2/1. *Unit head:* Dr. Kevin McGarigal, Graduate Program Director, 413-545-2666, Fax: 413-545-4358. *Application contact:* Jean M. Ames, Supervisor of Admissions, 413-545-0722, Fax: 413-577-0010, E-mail: gradadm@grad.umass.edu.

University of Miami, Graduate School, Rosenstiel School of Marine and Atmospheric Science, Division of Marine Biology and Fisheries, Coral Gables, FL 33124. Offers MA, MS, PhD. Terminal master's awarded for partial completion of doctoral program. *Degree requirements:* For master's, comprehensive exam, thesis; for doctorate, comprehensive exam, thesis/dissertation. *Entrance requirements:* For master's and doctorate, GRE General Test. Additional exam requirements/recommendations for international students: Required—TOEFL (minimum score 550 paper-based; 213 computer-based). Electronic applications accepted. *Faculty research:* Biochemistry, physiology, plankton, coral, biology.

University of Missouri, Graduate School, School of Natural Resources, Department of Fisheries and Wildlife, Columbia, MO 65211. Offers MS, PhD. *Degree requirements:* For doctorate, thesis/dissertation. *Entrance requirements:* For master's and doctorate, GRE General Test, minimum GPA of 3.0. Additional exam requirements/recommendations for international students: Required—TOEFL (minimum score 550 paper-based; 213 computer-based; 79 iBT).

The University of Montana, Graduate School, College of Forestry and Conservation, Missoula, MT 59812-0002. Offers ecosystem management (MEM, MS); fish and wildlife biology (PhD); forestry (MS, PhD); recreation management (MS); resource conservation (MS); wildlife biology (MS). *Degree requirements:* For doctorate, thesis/dissertation. *Entrance requirements:* For master's and doctorate, GRE General Test. Additional exam requirements/recommendations for international students: Required—TOEFL (minimum score 575 paper-based; 213 computer-based).

University of New Hampshire, Graduate School, College of Life Sciences and Agriculture, Department of Natural Resources, Durham, NH 03824. Offers environmental conservation (MS); forestry (MS); integrated coastal ecosystem science, policy, management (MS); natural resources (MS); water resources (MS); wildlife (MS). Part-time programs available. *Faculty:* 40 full-time. *Students:* 22 full-time (8 women), 27 part-time (15 women); includes 1 Asian, non-Hispanic/Latino; 1 Hispanic/Latino, 1 international. Average age 30. 54 applicants, 39% accepted, 14 enrolled. In 2010, 13 master's awarded. *Degree requirements:* For master's, thesis or alternative. *Entrance requirements:* For master's, GRE General Test. Additional exam requirements/recommendations for international students: Required—TOEFL (minimum score 550 paper-based; 213 computer-based; 80 iBT). *Application deadline:* For fall admission, 6/1 for domestic students, 4/1 for international students; for spring admission, 12/1 for domestic students. Applications are processed on a rolling basis. Application fee: $65. Electronic applications accepted. *Financial support:* In 2010–11, 23 students received support, including 3 fellowships, 6 research assistantships, 14 teaching assistantships; career-related internships or fieldwork, Federal Work-Study, scholarships/grants, and tuition waivers (full and partial) also available. Support available to part-time students. Financial award application deadline: 2/15. *Unit head:* Dr. John Halstead, Chairperson, 603-862-3950, E-mail: natural.resources@unh.edu. *Application contact:* Linda Scogin, Administrative Assistant, 603-862-3932, E-mail: natural.resources@unh.edu.

University of North Dakota, Graduate School, College of Arts and Sciences, Department of Biology, Grand Forks, ND 58202. Offers botany (MS, PhD); ecology (MS, PhD); entomology (MS, PhD); environmental biology (MS, PhD); fisheries/wildlife (MS, PhD); genetics (MS, PhD); zoology (MS, PhD). *Faculty:* 17 full-time (5 women), 6 part-time/adjunct (1 woman). *Students:* 19 full-time (6 women), 8 part-time (2 women); includes 4 minority (3 American Indian or Alaska Native, non-Hispanic/Latino; 1 Asian, non-Hispanic/Latino), 1 international. Average age 28. 21 applicants, 33% accepted, 4 enrolled. In 2010, 1 master's awarded. Terminal master's awarded for partial completion of doctoral program. *Degree requirements:* For master's, thesis, final exam; for doctorate, comprehensive exam, thesis/dissertation, final exam. *Entrance requirements:* For master's, GRE General Test, GRE Subject Test, minimum GPA of 3.0; for doctorate, GRE General Test, GRE Subject Test, minimum GPA of 3.5. Additional exam requirements/recommendations for international students: Required—TOEFL (minimum score 550 paper-based; 213 computer-based; 79 iBT), IELTS (minimum score 6.5). *Application deadline:* For fall admission, 2/15 for domestic and international students; for spring admission, 10/15 for domestic and international students. Application fee: $35. Electronic applications accepted. *Expenses:* Tuition, state resident: full-time $5857; part-time $306.74 per credit. Tuition, nonresident: full-time $15,666; part-time $729.77 per credit. Required fees: $53.42 per credit. Tuition and fees vary according to course load, program and reciprocity agreements. *Financial support:* In 2010–11, 22 students received support, including 5 research assistantships with full and partial tuition reimbursements available (averaging $11,375 per year), 17 teaching assistantships with full and partial tuition reimbursements available (averaging $10,813 per year); fellowships with full and partial tuition reimbursements available, Federal Work-Study, institutionally sponsored loans, scholarships/grants, health care benefits, tuition waivers (full and partial), and unspecified assistantships also available. Support available to part-time students. Financial award application deadline: 3/15; financial award applicants required to submit FAFSA. *Faculty research:* Population biology, wildlife ecology, RNA processing, hormonal control of behavior. Total annual research expenditures: $736,510. *Unit head:* Dr. Brett Goodwin, Graduate Director, 701-777-2621, Fax: 701-777-2623, E-mail: brett.goodwin@mail.und.edu. *Application contact:* Matthew Anderson, Admissions Specialist, 701-777-2947, Fax: 701-777-3619, E-mail: matthew.anderson@gradschool.und.eu.

University of Rhode Island, Graduate School, College of the Environment and Life Sciences, Department of Fisheries, Animal and Veterinary Science, Kingston, RI 02881. Offers animal health and disease (MS); animal science (MS); aquaculture (MS); aquatic pathology (MS); environmental sciences (PhD), including animal science, aquacultural science, aquatic pathology, fisheries science; fisheries (MS). *Faculty:* 10 full-time (4 women). *Students:* 14 full-time (7 women), 6 part-time (1 woman); includes 4 minority (2 Black or African American, non-Hispanic/Latino; 2 Hispanic/Latino), 3 international. In 2010, 3 master's, 2 doctorates awarded. *Degree requirements:* For master's, comprehensive exam (for some programs), thesis optional; for doctorate, comprehensive exam, thesis/dissertation. *Entrance requirements:* For master's and doctorate, GRE, 2 letters of recommendation. Additional exam requirements/recommendations for international students: Required—TOEFL (minimum score 550 paper-based; 213 computer-based). *Application deadline:* For fall admission, 7/15 for domestic students, 2/1 for international students; for spring admission, 11/15 for domestic students, 7/15 for international students. Application fee: $65. Electronic applications accepted. *Expenses:* Tuition, state resident: full-time $9588; part-time $533 per credit hour. Tuition, nonresident: full-time $22,968; part-time $1276 per credit hour. Required fees: $1282; $68 per semester. Tuition and fees vary according to program. *Financial support:* In 2010–11, 9 research assistantships with full and partial tuition reimbursements (averaging $11,492 per year), 3 teaching assistantships with full and partial tuition reimbursements (averaging $12,894 per year) were awarded. Financial award application deadline: 7/15; financial award applicants required to submit FAFSA. Total annual research expenditures: $1.8 million. *Unit head:* Dr. David Bengtson, Chair, 401-874-2668, Fax: 401-874-7575, E-mail: bengtson@uri.edu. *Application contact:* Dr. Marta Gomez-Chiarri, Director of Graduate Studies, 401-874-2917, Fax: 401-874-7575, E-mail: gomezchi@uri.edu.

The University of Tennessee, Graduate School, College of Agricultural Sciences and Natural Resources, Department of Forestry, Wildlife, and Fisheries, Program in Wildlife and Fisheries Science, Knoxville, TN 37996. Offers MS. *Degree requirements:* For master's, thesis. *Entrance requirements:* For master's, GRE General Test, minimum GPA of 2.7. Additional exam requirements/recommendations for international students: Required—TOEFL. Electronic applications accepted. *Expenses:* Tuition, state resident: full-time $7440; part-time $414 per credit hour. Tuition, nonresident: full-time $22,478; part-time $1250 per credit hour. Required fees: $922; $43 per credit hour. Tuition and fees vary according to program.

University of Washington, Graduate School, College of Forest Resources, Seattle, WA 98195. Offers bioresource science and engineering (MS, PhD); environmental horticulture (MEH); environmental horticulture and urban forestry (MS, PhD); forest ecology (MS, PhD); forest management (MFR); forest soils (MS, PhD); forest systems and bioenergy (MS, PhD); restoration ecology (MS, PhD); social sciences (MS, PhD); sustainable resource management (MS, PhD); wildlife science (MS, PhD); MFR/MAIS; MPA/MS. *Accreditation:* SAF. *Degree requirements:* For master's, thesis (for some programs); for doctorate, comprehensive exam (for some programs), thesis/dissertation. *Entrance requirements:* For master's and doctorate, GRE, minimum GPA of 3.0. Additional exam requirements/recommendations for international students: Required—TOEFL. Electronic applications accepted. *Faculty research:* Ecosystem analysis, silviculture and forest protection, paper science and engineering, environmental horticulture and urban forestry, natural resource policy and economics.

University of Washington, Graduate School, College of Ocean and Fishery Sciences, School of Aquatic and Fishery Sciences, Seattle, WA 98195. Offers MS, PhD. *Degree requirements:* For master's, thesis; for doctorate, thesis/dissertation. *Entrance requirements:* For master's and doctorate, GRE General Test, minimum GPA of 3.0. Additional exam requirements/recommendations for international students: Required—TOEFL. Electronic applications accepted. *Faculty research:* Fish and shellfish ecology, fisheries management, aquatic ecology, conservation biology, genetics.

University of Wisconsin–Madison, Graduate School, College of Agricultural and Life Sciences, Department of Forest and Wildlife Ecology, Program in Wildlife Ecology, Madison, WI 53706-1380. Offers MS, PhD. *Expenses:* Tuition, state resident: full-time $9887.36; part-time $617.96 per credit. Tuition, nonresident: full-time $24,054; part-time $1503.40 per credit. Required fees: $67.63 per credit. Tuition and fees vary according to reciprocity agreements.

Utah State University, School of Graduate Studies, College of Natural Resources, Department of Aquatic, Watershed, and Earth Resources, Logan, UT 84322. Offers ecology (MS, PhD); fisheries biology (MS, PhD); watershed science (MS, PhD). *Degree requirements:* For master's, thesis (for some programs); for doctorate, thesis/dissertation. *Entrance requirements:* For master's and doctorate, GRE General Test, minimum GPA of 3.2. Additional exam requirements/recommendations for international students: Required—TOEFL. Electronic applications accepted. *Faculty research:* Behavior, population ecology, habitat, conservation biology, restoration, aquatic ecology, fisheries management, fluvial geomorphology, remote sensing, conservation biology.

Utah State University, School of Graduate Studies, College of Natural Resources, Department of Wildland Resources, Logan, UT 84322. Offers ecology (MS, PhD); forestry (MS, PhD); range science (MS, PhD); wildlife biology (MS, PhD). Part-time programs available. *Degree requirements:* For master's, thesis; for doctorate, comprehensive exam, thesis/dissertation. *Entrance requirements:* For master's and doctorate, GRE General Test, minimum GPA of 3.0. Additional exam requirements/recommendations for international students: Required—TOEFL. *Faculty research:* Range plant ecophysiology, plant community ecology, ruminant nutrition, population ecology.

Fish, Game, and Wildlife Management

Virginia Polytechnic Institute and State University, Graduate School, College of Natural Resources and Environment, Department of Fisheries and Wildlife Sciences, Blacksburg, VA 24061. Offers MS, PhD. *Faculty:* 14 full-time (6 women). *Students:* 39 full-time (23 women), 8 part-time (6 women); includes 1 Black or African American, non-Hispanic/Latino; 1 American Indian or Alaska Native, non-Hispanic/Latino; 1 Asian, non-Hispanic/Latino, 10 international. Average age 30. 31 applicants, 26% accepted, 8 enrolled. In 2010, 5 master's, 1 doctorate awarded. *Degree requirements:* For master's, comprehensive exam (for some programs), thesis (for some programs); for doctorate, comprehensive exam (for some programs), thesis/dissertation (for some programs). *Entrance requirements:* For master's and doctorate, GRE. Additional exam requirements/recommendations for international students: Required—TOEFL (minimum score 550 paper-based; 213 computer-based). *Application deadline:* For fall admission, 7/1 for domestic and international students; for spring admission, 12/1 for domestic and international students. Applications are processed on a rolling basis. Application fee: $65. Electronic applications accepted. *Expenses:* Tuition, area resident: Full-time $9399; part-time $488 per credit hour. Tuition, state resident: full-time $9399; part-time $488 per credit hour. Tuition, nonresident: full-time $17,854; part-time $957.75 per credit hour. International tuition: $17,854 full-time. Required fees: $1534. Full-time tuition and fees vary according to program. *Financial support:* In 2010–11, 27 research assistantships with full tuition reimbursements (averaging $18,066 per year), 4 teaching assistantships with full tuition reimbursements (averaging $13,813 per year) were awarded; career-related internships or fieldwork, Federal Work-Study, scholarships/grants, health care benefits, and unspecified assistantships also available. Financial award application deadline: 1/15. *Faculty research:* Fisheries management, wildlife management, wildlife toxicology and physiology, endangered species, computer applications. Total annual research expenditures: $3.1 million. *Unit head:* Dr. Eric M. Hallerman, UNIT HEAD, 540-231-5573, Fax: 540-231-7580, E-mail: ehallem@vt.edu. *Application contact:* Steve McMullin, Contact, 540-231-8847, Fax: 540-231-7580, E-mail: smcmulli@vt.edu.

West Virginia University, Davis College of Agriculture, Forestry and Consumer Sciences, Division of Forestry, Program in Wildlife and Fisheries Resources, Morgantown, WV 26506. Offers MS. Part-time programs available. *Degree requirements:* For master's, comprehensive exam, thesis. *Entrance requirements:* For master's, GRE, minimum GPA of 3.0. Additional exam requirements/recommendations for international students: Required—TOEFL. Electronic applications accepted. *Faculty research:* Managing habitat for game, nongame, and fish; fish ecology; wildlife ecology.

Forestry

Auburn University, Graduate School, School of Forestry and Wildlife Sciences, Auburn University, AL 36849. Offers forest economics (PhD); forestry (MS, PhD); natural resource conservation (MNR); wildlife sciences (MS, PhD). *Accreditation:* SAF. Part-time programs available. *Faculty:* 28 full-time (5 women), 2 part-time/adjunct (0 women). *Students:* 29 full-time (12 women), 53 part-time (17 women); includes 1 Black or African American, non-Hispanic/Latino; 1 Asian, non-Hispanic/Latino; 1 Hispanic/Latino, 28 international. Average age 28. 55 applicants, 44% accepted, 17 enrolled. In 2010, 5 master's, 3 doctorates awarded. *Degree requirements:* For master's, thesis (MS); for doctorate, thesis/dissertation. *Entrance requirements:* For master's and doctorate, GRE General Test. *Application deadline:* For fall admission, 7/7 for domestic students; for spring admission, 11/24 for domestic students. Applications are processed on a rolling basis. Application fee: $50 ($60 for international students). Electronic applications accepted. *Expenses:* Tuition, state resident: full-time $7002. Tuition, nonresident: full-time $21,898. International tuition: $22,116 full-time. Required fees: $892. Tuition and fees vary according to course load and program. *Financial support:* Fellowships, research assistantships, teaching assistantships, Federal Work-Study available. Support available to part-time students. Financial award application deadline: 3/15; financial award applicants required to submit FAFSA. *Faculty research:* Forest nursery management, silviculture and vegetation management, biological processes and ecological relationships, growth and yield of plantations and natural stands, urban forestry, forest taxation, law and policy. *Unit head:* Dr. James P. Shepard, Dean, 334-844-4000, Fax: 334-844-1084, E-mail: brinker@forestry.auburn.edu. *Application contact:* Dr. George Flowers, Dean of the Graduate School, 334-844-2125.

California Polytechnic State University, San Luis Obispo, College of Agriculture, Food and Environmental Sciences, Department of Natural Resources Management, San Luis Obispo, CA 93407. Offers forestry sciences (MS). Part-time programs available. *Faculty:* 1 full-time (0 women). *Students:* 2 full-time (0 women), 2 part-time (0 women); includes 1 minority (Hispanic/Latino). Average age 37. 6 applicants, 33% accepted, 2 enrolled. In 2010, 4 master's awarded. *Degree requirements:* For master's, comprehensive exam, thesis. *Entrance requirements:* For master's, minimum GPA of 2.75 in last 90 quarter units of course work. Additional exam requirements/recommendations for international students: Required—TOEFL (minimum score 550 paper-based; 213 computer-based) or IELTS (minimum score 6). *Application deadline:* For fall admission, 4/1 for domestic students, 11/30 for international students; for winter admission, 10/1 for domestic students, 6/30 for international students; for spring admission, 10/1 for domestic students. Applications are processed on a rolling basis. Application fee: $55. Electronic applications accepted. *Expenses:* Tuition, state resident: full-time $5386; part-time $3124 per year. Tuition, nonresident: full-time $11,160; part-time $248 per unit. Required fees: $2250; $614 per term. One-time fee: $2250 full-time; $1842 part-time. *Financial support:* Fellowships, research assistantships, career-related internships or fieldwork, Federal Work-Study, institutionally sponsored loans, scholarships/grants, and unspecified assistantships available. Support available to part-time students. Financial award application deadline: 3/2; financial award applicants required to submit FAFSA. *Faculty research:* Hydrology, biometrics, forest health and management, fire science, urban and community forestry. *Unit head:* Dr. Doug Piirto, Department Head/Graduate Coordinator, 805-756-2968, Fax: 805-756-1402, E-mail: dpiirto@calpoly.edu. *Application contact:* Dr. Mark Shelton, Associate Dean/Graduate Coordinator, 805-756-2161, Fax: 805-756-6577, E-mail: mshelton@calpoly.edu.

Clemson University, Graduate School, College of Agriculture, Forestry and Life Sciences, Department of Forestry and Natural Resources, Program in Forest Resources, Clemson, SC 29634. Offers MFR, MS, PhD. Part-time programs available. *Students:* 34 full-time (7 women), 5 part-time (1 woman); includes 1 Black or African American, non-Hispanic/Latino; 2 Two or more races, non-Hispanic/Latino, 4 international. Average age 31. 27 applicants, 59% accepted, 12 enrolled. In 2010, 10 master's, 1 doctorate awarded. *Degree requirements:* For master's, thesis; for doctorate, thesis/dissertation. *Entrance requirements:* For master's, GRE General Test, minimum B average in last 2 years of undergraduate course work; for doctorate, GRE General Test, minimum B average in graduate course work. Additional exam requirements/recommendations for international students: Required—TOEFL, IELTS. *Application deadline:* For fall admission, 3/1 priority date for domestic students, 4/15 for international students; for spring admission, 10/1 for domestic students, 9/15 for international students. Applications are processed on a rolling basis. Application fee: $70 ($80 for international students). Electronic applications accepted. *Expenses:* Contact institution. *Financial support:* In 2010–11, 23 students received support, including 3 fellowships with full and partial tuition reimbursements available (averaging $7,667 per year), 19 research assistantships with partial tuition reimbursements available (averaging $12,799 per year), 7 teaching assistantships with partial tuition reimbursements available (averaging $7,105 per year); career-related internships or fieldwork, institutionally sponsored loans, scholarships/grants, health care benefits, and unspecified assistantships also available. Support available to part-time students. Financial award application deadline: 5/1; financial award applicants required to submit FAFSA. *Faculty research:* Wetlands management, wood technology, forest management, silviculture, economics. *Unit head:* Dr. Patricia Layton, Chair, 864-656-3303, Fax: 864-656-3304, E-mail: playton@clemson.edu. *Application contact:* Dr. David Guynn, Graduate Program Coordinator, 864-656-4830, E-mail: dguynn@clemson.edu.

Colorado State University, Graduate School, Warner College of Natural Resources, Department of Forest, Rangeland, and Watershed Stewardship, Fort Collins, CO 80523-1472. Offers forest sciences (MS, PhD); natural resources stewardship (MNRS); rangeland ecosystem science (MS, PhD); watershed science (MS). Part-time programs available. Postbaccalaureate distance learning degree programs offered (no on-campus study). *Faculty:* 18 full-time (5 women), 2 part-time/adjunct (0 women). *Students:* 45 full-time (21 women), 90 part-time (31 women); includes 9 minority (3 American Indian or Alaska Native, non-Hispanic/Latino; 1 Asian, non-Hispanic/Latino; 5 Hispanic/Latino), 9 international. Average age 34. 59 applicants, 76% accepted, 28 enrolled. In 2010, 27 master's, 2 doctorates awarded. *Degree requirements:* For master's, thesis (for some programs); for doctorate, comprehensive exam, thesis/dissertation. *Entrance requirements:* For master's, GRE General Test (minimum score 1000 verbal and quantitative), minimum GPA of 3.0, 3 letters of recommendation; for doctorate, GRE General Test (combined minimum score of 1100 on the Verbal and Quantitative sections), minimum GPA of 3.0, 3 letters of recommendation, statement of research interest. Additional exam requirements/recommendations for international students: Required—TOEFL (minimum score 550 paper-based; 213 computer-based; 80 iBT), IELTS (minimum score 6.5). *Application deadline:* For fall admission, 2/15 priority date for domestic and international students; for spring admission, 7/15 priority date for domestic and international students. Applications are processed on a rolling basis. Application fee: $50. Electronic applications accepted. *Expenses:* Tuition, state resident: full-time $7434; part-time $413 per credit. Tuition, nonresident: full-time $19,022; part-time $1057 per credit. Required fees: $1729; $88 per credit. *Financial support:* In 2010–11, 46 students received support, including 1 fellowship (averaging $23,971 per year), 32 research assistantships with full and partial tuition reimbursements available (averaging $15,871 per year), 13 teaching assistantships with full and partial tuition reimbursements available (averaging $7,106 per year); Federal Work-Study, scholarships/grants, and unspecified assistantships also available. Financial award application deadline: 2/15; financial award applicants required to submit FAFSA. *Faculty research:* Ecology, natural resource management, hydrology, restoration, human dimensions. Total annual research expenditures: $2.4 million. *Unit head:* Dr. Frederick Smith, Interim Department Head, 970-491-7505, Fax: 970-491-6754, E-mail: fwsmith@colostate.edu. *Application contact:* Sonya LeFebre, Coordinator, 970-491-1907, Fax: 970-491-6754, E-mail: sonya.lefebre@colostate.edu.

Cornell University, Graduate School, Graduate Fields of Agriculture and Life Sciences, Field of Natural Resources, Ithaca, NY 14853-0001. Offers aquatic science (MPS, MS, PhD); environmental management (MPS); fishery science (MPS, MS, PhD); forest science (MPS, MS, PhD); resource policy and management (MPS, MS, PhD); wildlife science (MPS, MS, PhD). *Faculty:* 36 full-time (7 women). *Students:* 48 full-time (21 women); includes 1 Asian, non-Hispanic/Latino; 1 Hispanic/Latino, 11 international. Average age 30. 52 applicants, 27% accepted, 11 enrolled. In 2010, 8 master's, 6 doctorates awarded. *Degree requirements:* For master's, thesis (MS), project paper (MPS); for doctorate, comprehensive exam, thesis/dissertation. *Entrance requirements:* For master's and doctorate, GRE General Test, 2 letters of recommendation. Additional exam requirements/recommendations for international students: Required—TOEFL (minimum score 550 paper-based; 213 computer-based; 77 iBT). *Application deadline:* For spring admission, 10/30 for domestic students. Applications are processed on a rolling basis. Application fee: $70. Electronic applications accepted. *Expenses:* Tuition: Full-time $29,500. Required fees: $76. Tuition and fees vary according to degree level and program. *Financial support:* In 2010–11, 9 fellowships with full tuition reimbursements, 16 research assistantships with full tuition reimbursements, 15 teaching assistantships with full tuition reimbursements were awarded; institutionally sponsored loans, scholarships/grants, health care benefits, tuition waivers (full and partial), and unspecified assistantships also available. Financial award applicants required to submit FAFSA. *Faculty research:* Ecosystem-level dynamics, systems modeling, conservation biology/management, resource management's human dimensions, biogeochemistry. *Unit head:* Director of Graduate Studies, 607-255-2807, Fax: 607-255-0349. *Application contact:* Graduate Field Assistant, 607-255-2807, Fax: 607-255-0349, E-mail: nrgrad@cornell.edu.

Duke University, Nicholas School of the Environment, Durham, NC 27708-0328. Offers coastal environmental management (MEM); DEL-environmental leadership (MEM); energy and environment (MEM); environmental economics and policy (MEM); environmental health and security (MEM); forest resource management (MF); global environmental change (MEM); resource ecology (MEM); water and air resources (MEM); JD/AM; JD/MEM; JD/MF; MAT/MEM; MBA/MEM; MBA/MF; MEM/MPP; MF/MPP. *Accreditation:* SAF (one or more programs are accredited). Part-time programs available. *Degree requirements:* For master's, thesis. *Entrance requirements:* For master's, GRE General Test, previous course work in biology or ecology, calculus, statistics, and microeconomics; computer familiarity with word processing and data analysis. Additional exam requirements/recommendations for international students: Required—TOEFL (minimum score 550 paper-based; 213 computer-based). Electronic applications accepted. *Expenses:* Contact institution. *Faculty research:* Ecosystem management, conservation ecology, earth systems, risk assessment.

Harvard University, Graduate School of Arts and Sciences, Department of Forestry, Cambridge, MA 02138. Offers forest science (MFS). *Degree requirements:* For master's, thesis. *Entrance requirements:* For master's, GRE General Test, bachelor's degree in biology or forestry. Additional exam requirements/recommendations for international students: Required—TOEFL. *Expenses:* Tuition: Full-time $34,976. Required fees: $1166. Full-time tuition and fees vary according to program. *Faculty research:* Forest ecology, planning, and physiology; forest microbiology.

Humboldt State University, Academic Programs, College of Natural Resources and Sciences, Programs in Natural Resources, Arcata, CA 95521-8299. Offers natural resources (MS), including fisheries, forestry, natural resources planning and interpretation, rangeland resources and wildland soils, wastewater utilization, watershed management, wildlife. *Students:* 62 full-time (27 women), 21 part-time (7 women); includes 4 minority (1 Asian, non-Hispanic/Latino; 2 Hispanic/Latino; 1 Two or more races, non-Hispanic/Latino), 2 international. Average age 29. 117 applicants, 47% accepted, 33 enrolled. In 2010, 23 master's awarded. *Degree requirements:* For master's, thesis or alternative. *Entrance requirements:* For master's, GRE, appropriate bachelor's degree, minimum GPA of 2.5, 3 letters of recommendation, resume. Additional exam requirements/recommendations for international students: Required—TOEFL (minimum score 500 paper-based; 173 computer-based). *Application deadline:* For fall admission, 2/1 for domestic and international students; for spring admission, 9/30 for domestic and

international students. Applications are processed on a rolling basis. Application fee: $55. Tuition and fees vary according to program. *Financial support:* Fellowships, career-related internships or fieldwork and Federal Work-Study available. Support available to part-time students. Financial award application deadline: 3/1; financial award applicants required to submit FAFSA. *Faculty research:* Spotted owl habitat, pre-settlement vegetation, hardwood utilization, tree physiology, fisheries. *Unit head:* Dr. Gary Hendrickson, Coordinator, 707-826-4233, E-mail: thiesfel@humboldt.edu. *Application contact:* Julie Tucker, Administrative Support Coordinator, 707-826-3256, E-mail: jlt7002@humboldt.edu.

Iowa State University of Science and Technology, Graduate College, College of Agriculture, Department of Natural Resource Ecology and Management, Ames, IA 50011. Offers forestry (MS, PhD); wildlife ecology (MS). *Faculty:* 20 full-time (5 women), 11 part-time/adjunct (3 women). *Students:* 38 full-time (14 women), 11 part-time (3 women); includes 1 American Indian or Alaska Native, non-Hispanic/Latino; 1 Hispanic/Latino, 10 international. 16 applicants, 25% accepted, 3 enrolled. In 2010, 7 master's, 2 doctorates awarded. *Degree requirements:* For master's, thesis (for some programs); for doctorate, thesis/dissertation. *Entrance requirements:* For master's and doctorate, GRE General Test. Additional exam requirements/recommendations for international students: Required—TOEFL (minimum score 550 paper-based; 79 iBT), IELTS (minimum score 6.5). *Application deadline:* For fall admission, 4/1 priority date for domestic and international students; for spring admission, 10/1 priority date for domestic and international students. Application fee: $40 ($90 for international students). Electronic applications accepted. *Financial support:* In 2010–11, 28 research assistantships with full and partial tuition reimbursements (averaging $15,773 per year), 3 teaching assistantships with full and partial tuition reimbursements (averaging $11,171 per year) were awarded. *Unit head:* Dr. Stephen Jungst, Interim Chair, 515-294-1166. *Application contact:* Dr. Janette Thompson, Director of Graduate Education, 515-294-1626, E-mail: nremgrad@iastate.edu.

Lakehead University, Graduate Studies, Faculty of Forestry, Thunder Bay, ON P7B 5E1, Canada. Offers forest sciences (PhD); forestry (M Sc F, MF). Part-time programs available. *Degree requirements:* For master's, report (MF), thesis (M Sc F). *Entrance requirements:* For master's, minimum B average. Additional exam requirements/recommendations for international students: Required—TOEFL. *Faculty research:* Soils, silviculture, wildlife, ecology, genetics.

Louisiana State University and Agricultural and Mechanical College, Graduate School, College of Agriculture, School of Renewable Natural Resources, Baton Rouge, LA 70803. Offers fisheries (MS); forestry (MS, PhD); wildlife (MS); wildlife and fisheries science (PhD). *Faculty:* 33 full-time (5 women). *Students:* 65 full-time (16 women), 8 part-time (3 women); includes 2 Hispanic/Latino, 22 international. Average age 29. 28 applicants, 39% accepted, 8 enrolled. In 2010, 17 master's, 4 doctorates awarded. *Degree requirements:* For master's, thesis; for doctorate, thesis/dissertation. *Entrance requirements:* For master's, GRE General Test, minimum GPA of 3.0; for doctorate, GRE General Test, MS, minimum GPA of 3.0. Additional exam requirements/recommendations for international students: Required—TOEFL (minimum score 550 paper-based; 213 computer-based; 79 iBT), IELTS (minimum score 6.5). *Application deadline:* For fall admission, 1/25 priority date for domestic students, 5/15 for international students; for spring admission, 10/15 for international students. Applications are processed on a rolling basis. Application fee: $50 ($70 for international students). Electronic applications accepted. *Financial support:* In 2010–11, 69 students received support, including 7 fellowships (averaging $36,514 per year), 60 research assistantships with partial tuition reimbursements available (averaging $19,070 per year); Federal Work-Study, institutionally sponsored loans, scholarships/grants, health care benefits, tuition waivers (full and partial), and unspecified assistantships also available. Financial award application deadline: 4/15; financial award applicants required to submit FAFSA. *Faculty research:* Forest biology and management, aquaculture, fisheries biology and ecology, upland and wetlands wildlife. Total annual research expenditures: $3,080. *Unit head:* Dr. Allen Rutherford, Director, 225-578-4131, Fax: 225-578-4227, E-mail: druther@lsu.edu. *Application contact:* Dr. William Kelso, Coordinator of Graduate Studies, 225-578-4176, Fax: 225-578-4227, E-mail: wkelso@lsu.edu.

McGill University, Faculty of Graduate and Postdoctoral Studies, Faculty of Agricultural and Environmental Sciences, Department of Natural Resource Sciences, Montréal, QC H3A 2T5, Canada. Offers entomology (M Sc, PhD); environmental assessment (M Sc); forest science (M Sc, PhD); microbiology (M Sc, PhD); micrometeorology (M Sc, PhD); neotropical environment (M Sc, PhD); soil science (M Sc, PhD); wildlife biology (M Sc, PhD).

Michigan State University, The Graduate School, College of Agriculture and Natural Resources, Department of Forestry, East Lansing, MI 48824. Offers forestry (MS, PhD); forestry-environmental toxicology (PhD); plant breeding, genetics and biotechnology-forestry (MS, PhD). *Entrance requirements:* Additional exam requirements/recommendations for international students: Required—TOEFL (minimum score 550 paper-based; 213 computer-based), Michigan State University ELT (minimum score 85), Michigan English Language Assessment Battery (minimum score 83). Electronic applications accepted.

Michigan Technological University, Graduate School, School of Forest Resources and Environmental Science, Program in Forest Ecology and Management, Houghton, MI 49931. Offers MS. Part-time programs available. *Degree requirements:* For master's, thesis (for some programs). *Entrance requirements:* For master's, GRE. Additional exam requirements/recommendations for international students: Required—TOEFL (minimum score 550 paper-based; 213 computer-based). Electronic applications accepted.

Michigan Technological University, Graduate School, School of Forest Resources and Environmental Science, Program in Forest Molecular Genetics and Biotechnology, Houghton, MI 49931. Offers MS, PhD. Part-time programs available. Terminal master's awarded for partial completion of doctoral program. *Degree requirements:* For master's, thesis (for some programs); for doctorate, comprehensive exam, thesis/dissertation. *Entrance requirements:* For master's, GRE. Additional exam requirements/recommendations for international students: Required—TOEFL (minimum score 550 paper-based; 213 computer-based). Electronic applications accepted.

Michigan Technological University, Graduate School, School of Forest Resources and Environmental Science, Program in Forestry, Houghton, MI 49931. Offers MF, MS. Part-time programs available. *Degree requirements:* For master's, thesis (for some programs). *Entrance requirements:* For master's, GRE. Additional exam requirements/recommendations for international students: Required—TOEFL (minimum score 550 paper-based; 213 computer-based). Electronic applications accepted.

Michigan Technological University, Graduate School, School of Forest Resources and Environmental Science, Program in Forest Science, Houghton, MI 49931. Offers PhD. Part-time programs available. *Degree requirements:* For doctorate, comprehensive exam, thesis/dissertation. *Entrance requirements:* Additional exam requirements/recommendations for international students: Required—TOEFL (minimum score 550 paper-based; 213 computer-based). Electronic applications accepted.

Mississippi State University, College of Forest Resources, Department of Forest Products, Mississippi State, MS 39762. Offers forest products (MS); forest resources (PhD), including forest products. *Faculty:* 12 full-time (2 women), 2 part-time/adjunct (0 women). *Students:* 26 full-time (12 women), 6 part-time (1 woman); includes 2 minority (1 Asian, non-Hispanic/Latino; 1 Hispanic/Latino), 18 international. Average age 30. 20 applicants, 35% accepted, 7 enrolled. In 2010, 9 master's, 7 doctorates awarded. *Degree requirements:* For master's, thesis optional; for doctorate, comprehensive exam, thesis/dissertation. *Entrance requirements:* For master's, GRE (if undergraduate GPA of last two years less than 3.0); for doctorate, GRE if undergraduate GPA of last two years is below 3.0. Additional exam requirements/recommendations for international students: Required—TOEFL (minimum score 550 paper-based; 213 computer-based; 79 iBT); Recommended—IELTS (minimum score 6.5). *Application deadline:* For fall admission, 7/1 for domestic students, 5/1 for international students; for spring admission, 11/1 for domestic students, 9/1 for international students. Applications are processed on a rolling basis. Application fee: $40. Electronic applications accepted. *Expenses:* Tuition, state resident: full-time $2730.50; part-time $304 per credit hour. Tuition, nonresident: full-time $6901; part-time $767 per credit hour. *Financial support:* In 2010–11, 23 research assistantships with full tuition reimbursements (averaging $14,575 per year) were awarded; Federal Work-Study, institutionally sponsored loans, and unspecified assistantships also available. Financial award application deadline: 4/1; financial award applicants required to submit FAFSA. *Faculty research:* Wood property enhancement and durability, environmental science and chemistry, wood-based composites, primary wood production, furniture manufacturing and management. *Unit head:* Dr. Robin Shmulsky, Department Head and Graduate Coordinator, 662-325-2116, Fax: 662-325-8126, E-mail: rshmulsky@cfr.msstate.edu. *Application contact:* Dr. Robin Shmulsky, Department Head and Graduate Coordinator, 662-325-2116, Fax: 662-325-8126, E-mail: rshmulsky@cfr.msstate.edu.

Mississippi State University, College of Forest Resources, Department of Forestry, Mississippi State, MS 39762. Offers forest resources (PhD), including forestry; forestry (MS). Part-time programs available. *Faculty:* 18 full-time (3 women), 1 part-time/adjunct (0 women). *Students:* 36 full-time (6 women), 26 part-time (4 women); includes 3 minority (1 Black or African American, non-Hispanic/Latino; 1 American Indian or Alaska Native, non-Hispanic/Latino; 1 Native Hawaiian or other Pacific Islander, non-Hispanic/Latino), 12 international. Average age 32. 37 applicants, 73% accepted, 22 enrolled. In 2010, 6 master's, 2 doctorates awarded. *Degree requirements:* For master's, thesis optional, comprehensive oral or written exam; for doctorate, comprehensive exam, thesis/dissertation. *Entrance requirements:* For master's, GRE (if undergraduate GPA of last two years less than 3.0), minimum GPA of 2.5; for doctorate, minimum GPA of 3.1 on prior graduate courses. Additional exam requirements/recommendations for international students: Required—TOEFL (minimum score 550 paper-based; 213 computer-based; 79 iBT); Recommended—IELTS (minimum score 6.5). *Application deadline:* For fall admission, 7/1 for domestic students, 5/1 for international students; for spring admission, 11/1 for domestic students, 9/1 for international students. Applications are processed on a rolling basis. Application fee: $40. Electronic applications accepted. *Expenses:* Tuition, state resident: full-time $2730.50; part-time $304 per credit hour. Tuition, nonresident: full-time $6901; part-time $767 per credit hour. *Financial support:* In 2010–11, 28 research assistantships with full tuition reimbursements (averaging $14,629 per year), 4 teaching assistantships with full tuition reimbursements (averaging $13,395 per year) were awarded; Federal Work-Study, institutionally sponsored loans, and unspecified assistantships also available. Financial award application deadline: 4/1; financial award applicants required to submit FAFSA. *Faculty research:* Forest hydrology, forest biometry, forest management/economics, forest biology, industrial forest operations. *Unit head:* Dr. Andrew Ezell, Professor/Head/Graduate Coordinator, 662-325-2949, Fax: 662-325-8126, E-mail: aezell@cfr.msstate.edu. *Application contact:* Dr. Andrew Ezell, Professor/Head/Graduate Coordinator, 662-325-2949, Fax: 662-325-8126, E-mail: aezell@cfr.msstate.edu.

Mississippi State University, College of Forest Resources, Department of Wildlife, Fisheries and Aquaculture, Mississippi State, MS 39762. Offers forest resources (PhD), including wildlife and fisheries; wildlife and fisheries science (MS). Part-time programs available. *Faculty:* 21 full-time (1 woman), 1 part-time/adjunct (0 women). *Students:* 63 full-time (16 women), 15 part-time (5 women); includes 5 minority (1 Black or African American, non-Hispanic/Latino; 3 Hispanic/Latino; 1 Two or more races, non-Hispanic/Latino), 6 international. Average age 29. 39 applicants, 56% accepted, 20 enrolled. In 2010, 13 master's, 2 doctorates awarded. *Degree requirements:* For master's, thesis, comprehensive oral or written exam; for doctorate, comprehensive exam, thesis/dissertation. *Entrance requirements:* For master's, GRE or minimum GPA of 3.0 on last 60 hours of undergraduate courses, bachelor's degree; for doctorate, GRE or minimum GPA of 3.2 on prior graduate studies, master's degree. Additional exam requirements/recommendations for international students: Required—TOEFL (minimum score 550 paper-based; 213 computer-based; 79 iBT); Recommended—IELTS (minimum score 6.5). *Application deadline:* For fall admission, 7/1 for domestic students, 5/1 for international students; for spring admission, 11/1 for domestic students, 9/1 for international students. Applications are processed on a rolling basis. Application fee: $40. Electronic applications accepted. *Expenses:* Tuition, state resident: full-time $2730.50; part-time $304 per credit hour. Tuition, nonresident: full-time $6901; part-time $767 per credit hour. *Financial support:* In 2010–11, 51 research assistantships with partial tuition reimbursements (averaging $13,981 per year) were awarded; Federal Work-Study, institutionally sponsored loans, and unspecified assistantships also available. Financial award application deadline: 4/1; financial award applicants required to submit FAFSA. *Faculty research:* Spatial technology, habitat restoration, aquaculture, fisheries, wildlife management. *Unit head:* Dr. Bruce D. Leopold, Department Head and Graduate Coordinator, 662-325-2619, Fax: 662-325-8726, E-mail: bleopold@cfr.msstate.edu. *Application contact:* Dr. Eric Dibble, Professor and Coordinator of Graduate Studies, 662-325-7494, Fax: 662-325-8726, E-mail: edibble@cfr.msstate.edu.

North Carolina State University, Graduate School, College of Natural Resources, Department of Forestry and Environmental Resources, Raleigh, NC 27695. Offers MF, MS, PhD. Part-time programs available. *Degree requirements:* For master's, thesis (for some programs), teaching experience; for doctorate, thesis/dissertation, teaching experience. *Entrance requirements:* For master's and doctorate, GRE General Test. Additional exam requirements/recommendations for international students: Required—TOEFL. Electronic applications accepted. *Faculty research:* Forest genetics, forest ecology and silviculture, forest economics/management/policy, international forestry, remote sensing/geographic information systems.

Northern Arizona University, Graduate College, College of Engineering, Forestry and Natural Sciences, School of Forestry, Flagstaff, AZ 86011. Offers forest science (MF, MSF); forestry (PhD). Part-time programs available. *Faculty:* 20 full-time (9 women). *Students:* 48 full-time (21 women), 13 part-time (7 women); includes 6 minority (1 Asian, non-Hispanic/Latino; 4 Hispanic/Latino; 1 Two or more races, non-Hispanic/Latino), 2 international. Average age 33. 23 applicants, 52% accepted, 9 enrolled. In 2010, 17 master's, 5 doctorates awarded. *Degree requirements:* For master's, thesis optional; for doctorate, comprehensive exam, thesis/dissertation. *Entrance requirements:* For master's, GRE General Test; for doctorate, GRE General Test. Additional exam requirements/recommendations for international students: Required—TOEFL (minimum score 550 paper-based; 213 computer-based; 80 iBT), IELTS (minimum score 7). *Application deadline:* For fall admission, 3/15 priority date for domestic and international students; for spring admission, 10/15 priority date for domestic and international students. Applications are processed on a rolling basis. Application fee: $65. Electronic applications accepted. *Financial support:* In 2010–11, 19 research assistantships (averaging $18,996 per year) were awarded; career-related internships or fieldwork, Federal Work-Study, scholarships/grants, traineeships, health care benefits, tuition waivers (full and partial), and unspecified assistantships also available. Financial award applicants required to submit FAFSA. *Faculty research:* Multiresource management, ecology, entomology, recreation, hydrology. Total annual research expenditures: $1.4 million. *Unit head:* Dr. James Allen, Chair, 928-523-5894, Fax: 928-523-1080, E-mail: james.allen@nau.edu. *Application contact:* April Sandoval, Administrative Associate, 928-523-6666, Fax: 928-523-1080, E-mail: forestrygraduatestudies@xdl.nau.edu.

Oklahoma State University, College of Agricultural Science and Natural Resources, Department of Natural Resource Ecology and Management, Stillwater, OK 74078. Offers M Ag, MS, PhD. *Faculty:* 30 full-time (4 women). *Students:* 1 (woman) full-time, 45 part-time (15 women); includes 1 Black or African American, non-Hispanic/Latino; 3 American Indian or Alaska Native, non-Hispanic/Latino; 1 Asian, non-Hispanic/Latino, 6 international. Average age 30. 17

Peterson's Graduate Programs in the Physical Sciences, Mathematics, Agricultural Sciences, the Environment & Natural Resources 2012

www.facebook.com/petersonspublishing 407

Forestry

Oklahoma State University (continued)
applicants, 29% accepted, 5 enrolled. In 2010, 11 master's, 3 doctorates awarded. *Degree requirements:* For master's, comprehensive exam (for some programs), thesis; for doctorate, comprehensive exam, thesis/dissertation. *Entrance requirements:* For master's and doctorate, GRE or GMAT. Additional exam requirements/recommendations for international students: Required—TOEFL (minimum score 550 paper-based; 79 iBT). *Application deadline:* For fall admission, 3/1 priority date for international students; for spring admission, 8/1 priority date for international students. Applications are processed on a rolling basis. Application fee: $40 ($75 for international students). Electronic applications accepted. *Expenses:* Tuition, state resident: full-time $3716; part-time $154.85 per credit hour. Tuition, nonresident: full-time $14,892; part-time $621 per credit hour. Required fees: $2044; $85.20 per credit hour. One-time fee: $50. Tuition and fees vary according to course load and campus/location. *Financial support:* In 2010–11, 34 research assistantships (averaging $15,811 per year), 1 teaching assistantship (averaging $17,496 per year) were awarded; career-related internships or fieldwork, Federal Work-Study, scholarships/grants, health care benefits, tuition waivers (partial), and unspecified assistantships also available. Support available to part-time students. Financial award application deadline: 3/1; financial award applicants required to submit FAFSA. *Faculty research:* Forest ecology, upland bird ecology, forest ecophysiology, urban forestry, molecular forest genetics/biotechnology/tree breeding. *Unit head:* Dr. Keith Owens, Head, 405-744-5438, Fax: 405-744-3530. *Application contact:* Dr. Gordon Emslie, Dean, 405-744-6368, Fax: 405-744-0355, E-mail: grad-i@okstate.edu.

Oregon State University, Graduate School, College of Forestry, Department of Forest Ecosystems and Society, Corvallis, OR 97331. Offers MAIS, MF, MS, PhD. *Accreditation:* SAF (one or more programs are accredited). Part-time programs available. *Degree requirements:* For master's, thesis (for some programs); for doctorate, thesis/dissertation. *Entrance requirements:* For master's and doctorate, GRE General Test, minimum GPA of 3.0 in last 90 hours. Additional exam requirements/recommendations for international students: Required—TOEFL. *Faculty research:* Ecosystem structure and function, nutrient cycling, biotechnology, vegetation management, integrated forest protection.

Oregon State University, Graduate School, College of Forestry, Department of Forest Engineering, Resources and Management, Corvallis, OR 97331. Offers forest engineering (MF, MS); forest hydrology (MF, MS, PhD); forest operations (MF); forest soil science (MF, MS, PhD); timber harvesting (PhD).

Oregon State University, Graduate School, College of Forestry, Department of Wood Science and Engineering, Corvallis, OR 97331. Offers forest products (MAIS, MF, MS, PhD); wood science and technology (MF, MS, PhD). *Accreditation:* SAF (one or more programs are accredited). Part-time programs available. *Degree requirements:* For master's, thesis (for some programs); for doctorate, thesis/dissertation. *Entrance requirements:* For master's and doctorate, GRE General Test, minimum GPA of 3.0 in last 90 hours. Additional exam requirements/recommendations for international students: Required—TOEFL. *Faculty research:* Biodeterioration and preservation, timber engineering, process engineering and control, composite materials science, anatomy, chemistry and physical properties.

Penn State University Park, Graduate School, College of Agricultural Sciences, School of Forest Resources, State College, University Park, PA 16802-1503. Offers M Agr, MFR, MS, PhD.

Purdue University, Graduate School, College of Agriculture, Department of Forestry and Natural Resources, West Lafayette, IN 47907. Offers aquaculture, fisheries, aquatic science (MSF); aquaculture, fisheries, aquatic sciences (MS, PhD); forest biology (MS, MSF, PhD); natural resources and environmental policy (MS, MSF); natural resources environmental policy (PhD); quantitative resource analysis (MS, MSF, PhD); wildlife science (MS, MSF, PhD); wood science and technology (MS, MSF, PhD). *Degree requirements:* For master's, thesis; for doctorate, thesis/dissertation. *Entrance requirements:* For master's and doctorate, GRE General Test, minimum B+ average in undergraduate course work. Additional exam requirements/recommendations for international students: Required—TOEFL. Electronic applications accepted. *Faculty research:* Wildlife management, forest management, forest ecology, forest soils, limnology.

Southern Illinois University Carbondale, Graduate School, College of Agriculture, Department of Forestry, Carbondale, IL 62901-4701. Offers MS. Part-time programs available. *Degree requirements:* For master's, thesis. *Entrance requirements:* For master's, minimum GPA of 2.7. Additional exam requirements/recommendations for international students: Required—TOEFL. *Faculty research:* Forest recreation, forest ecology, remote sensing, forest management and economics.

Southern University and Agricultural and Mechanical College, Graduate School, College of Agricultural, Family and Consumer Sciences, Department of Urban Forestry, Baton Rouge, LA 70813. Offers MS. *Degree requirements:* For master's, thesis. *Entrance requirements:* For master's, GRE, minimum GPA of 3.0. Additional exam requirements/recommendations for international students: Required—TOEFL (minimum score 525 paper-based; 193 computer-based). *Faculty research:* Biology of plant pathogen, water resources, plant pathology.

State University of New York College of Environmental Science and Forestry, Department of Environmental and Forest Biology, Syracuse, NY 13210-2779. Offers applied ecology (MPS); chemical ecology (MPS, MS, PhD); conservation biology (MPS, MS, PhD); ecology (MPS, MS, PhD); entomology (MPS, MS, PhD); environmental interpretation (MPS, MS, PhD); environmental physiology (MPS, MS, PhD); fish and wildlife biology and management (MPS, MS, PhD); forest pathology and mycology (MPS, MS, PhD); plant biotechnology (MPS); plant science and biotechnology (MPS, MS, PhD). *Degree requirements:* For master's, thesis (for some programs); for doctorate, comprehensive exam, thesis/dissertation. *Entrance requirements:* For master's and doctorate, GRE General Test, GRE Subject Test, minimum GPA of 3.0. Additional exam requirements/recommendations for international students: Required—TOEFL (minimum score 550 paper-based; 213 computer-based; 80 iBT), IELTS (minimum score 6). *Expenses:* Tuition, state resident: full-time $8370; part-time $349 per credit hour. Tuition, nonresident: full-time $13,780. Required fees: $30.30 per credit hour. $20 per year. *Faculty research:* Ecology, fish and wildlife biology and management, plant science, entomology.

State University of New York College of Environmental Science and Forestry, Department of Forest and Natural Resources Management, Syracuse, NY 13210-2779. Offers ecology and ecosystems (MPS, MS, PhD); economics, governance and human dimensions (MPS, MS, PhD); environmental and natural resource policy (PhD); forest resources management (MF); monitoring, analysis and modeling (MPS, MS, PhD); natural resources management (MPS, MS, PhD). *Accreditation:* SAF. *Degree requirements:* For master's, thesis (for some programs); for doctorate, comprehensive exam, thesis/dissertation. *Entrance requirements:* For master's and doctorate, GRE General Test, minimum GPA of 3.0. Additional exam requirements/recommendations for international students: Required—TOEFL (minimum score 550 paper-based; 213 computer-based; 80 iBT), IELTS (minimum score 6). *Expenses:* Tuition, state resident: full-time $8370; part-time $349 per credit hour. Tuition, nonresident: full-time $13,780. Required fees: $30.30 per credit hour. $20 per year. *Faculty research:* Silviculture recreation management, tree improvement, operations management, economics.

State University of New York College of Environmental Science and Forestry, Department of Sustainable Construction Management and Engineering, Syracuse, NY 13210-2779. Offers construction management (MPS, MS, PhD); engineered wood products and structures (MPS, MS, PhD); tropical timbers wood science and technology (MPS, MS, PhD); wood anatomy and ultrastructure (MPS, MS, PhD); wood treatments (MPS, MS, PhD). *Degree requirements:* For

master's, thesis (for some programs); for doctorate, comprehensive exam, thesis/dissertation. *Entrance requirements:* For master's and doctorate, GRE General Test, minimum GPA of 3.0. Additional exam requirements/recommendations for international students: Required—TOEFL (minimum score 550 paper-based; 213 computer-based; 80 iBT), IELTS (minimum score 6). *Expenses:* Tuition, state resident: full-time $8370; part-time $349 per credit hour. Tuition, nonresident: full-time $13,780. Required fees: $30.30 per credit hour. $20 per year.

Stephen F. Austin State University, Graduate School, College of Forestry and Agriculture, Department of Forestry, Nacogdoches, TX 75962. Offers MF, MS, PhD. Part-time programs available. *Degree requirements:* For master's, thesis; for doctorate, thesis/dissertation. *Entrance requirements:* For master's and doctorate, GRE General Test. Additional exam requirements/recommendations for international students: Required—TOEFL. *Faculty research:* Wildlife management, basic plant science, forest recreation, multipurpose land management.

Texas A&M University, College of Agriculture and Life Sciences, Department of Ecosystem Science and Management, College Station, TX 77843. Offers forestry (MS, PhD); rangeland ecology and management (M Agr, MS, PhD). Part-time programs available. *Faculty:* 24. *Students:* 59 full-time (31 women), 28 part-time (12 women); includes 16 minority (2 Black or African American, non-Hispanic/Latino; 1 Asian, non-Hispanic/Latino; 13 Hispanic/Latino), 12 international. Average age 27. In 2010, 9 master's, 3 doctorates awarded. Terminal master's awarded for partial completion of doctoral program. *Degree requirements:* For master's, thesis (for some programs); for doctorate, thesis/dissertation. *Entrance requirements:* For master's and doctorate, GRE General Test. Additional exam requirements/recommendations for international students: Required—TOEFL. *Application deadline:* For fall admission, 3/1 priority date for domestic students; for spring admission, 11/1 priority date for domestic students. Applications are processed on a rolling basis. Application fee: $50 ($75 for international students). Electronic applications accepted. *Financial support:* In 2010–11, fellowships with partial tuition reimbursements (averaging $15,000 per year), research assistantships with partial tuition reimbursements (averaging $15,000 per year), teaching assistantships with partial tuition reimbursements (averaging $15,000 per year) were awarded; career-related internships or fieldwork and institutionally sponsored loans also available. Support available to part-time students. Financial award application deadline: 3/1; financial award applicants required to submit FAFSA. *Faculty research:* Expert systems, geographic information systems, economics, biology, genetics. *Unit head:* Dr. Steve Whisenant, Professor and Head, 979-845-5000, Fax: 979-845-6049, E-mail: s-whisenant@tamu.edu. *Application contact:* Dr. Carol Loopstra, Associate Professor, 979-862-2200, Fax: 979-845-6049, E-mail: c-loopstra@tamu.edu.

Tropical Agriculture Research and Higher Education Center, Graduate School, Turrialba, Costa Rica. Offers agribusiness management (MS); agroforestry systems (PhD); development practices (MS); ecological agriculture (MS); environmental socioeconomics (MS); forestry in tropical and subtropical zones (PhD); integrated watershed management (MS); international sustainable tourism (MS); management and conservation of tropical rainforests and biodiversity (MS); tropical agriculture (PhD); tropical agroforestry (MS). *Entrance requirements:* For master's, GRE, 2 years of related professional experience, letters of recommendation; for doctorate, GRE, 4 letters of recommendation, letter of support from employing organization, master's degree in agronomy, biological sciences, forestry, natural resources or related field. Additional exam requirements/recommendations for international students: Required—TOEFL (minimum score 550 paper-based; 213 computer-based). Electronic applications accepted. *Faculty research:* Biodiversity in fragmented landscapes, ecosystem management, integrated pest management, environmental livestock production, biotechnology carbon balances in diverse land uses.

Université du Québec en Abitibi-Témiscamingue, Graduate Programs, Program in Environmental Sciences, Rouyn-Noranda, QC J9X 5E4, Canada. Offers biology (MS); environmental sciences (PhD); sustainable forest ecosystem management (MS).

Université Laval, Faculty of Forestry and Geomatics, Department of Wood and Forest Sciences, Programs in Forestry Sciences, Québec, QC G1K 7P4, Canada. Offers M Sc, PhD. Terminal master's awarded for partial completion of doctoral program. *Degree requirements:* For master's, thesis (for some programs); for doctorate, comprehensive exam, thesis/dissertation. *Entrance requirements:* For master's and doctorate, knowledge of French. Additional exam requirements/recommendations for international students: Required—TOEIC or TOEFL. Electronic applications accepted.

Université Laval, Faculty of Forestry and Geomatics, Department of Wood and Forest Sciences, Programs in Wood Sciences, Québec, QC G1K 7P4, Canada. Offers M Sc, PhD. Terminal master's awarded for partial completion of doctoral program. *Degree requirements:* For master's, thesis; for doctorate, comprehensive exam, thesis/dissertation. *Entrance requirements:* For master's and doctorate, knowledge of French. Electronic applications accepted.

Université Laval, Faculty of Forestry and Geomatics, Program in Agroforestry, Québec, QC G1K 7P4, Canada. Offers M Sc. *Degree requirements:* For master's, thesis (for some programs). *Entrance requirements:* For master's, English exam (comprehension of English), knowledge of French, knowledge of a third language. Electronic applications accepted.

University of Alberta, Faculty of Graduate Studies and Research, Department of Rural Economy, Edmonton, AB T6G 2E1, Canada. Offers agricultural economics (M Ag, M Sc, PhD); forest economics (M Ag, M Sc, PhD); rural sociology (M Ag, M Sc); MBA/M Ag. Part-time programs available. *Degree requirements:* For doctorate, thesis/dissertation. *Entrance requirements:* Additional exam requirements/recommendations for international students: Required—TOEFL. *Faculty research:* Agroforestry, development, extension education, marketing and trade, natural resources and environment, policy, production economics.

The University of Arizona, College of Agriculture and Life Sciences, School of Natural Resources, Watershed Resources Program, Tucson, AZ 85721. Offers MS, PhD. *Students:* 1 full-time (0 women), 6 part-time (4 women); includes 1 Asian, non-Hispanic/Latino; 2 Hispanic/Latino. Average age 40. *Degree requirements:* For master's, thesis; for doctorate, comprehensive exam, thesis/dissertation. *Entrance requirements:* For master's, GRE General Test, minimum GPA of 3.0, 3 letters of recommendation; for doctorate, GRE General Test, minimum GPA of 3.0, 3 letters of recommendation, MA or MS. Additional exam requirements/recommendations for international students: Required—TOEFL (minimum score 550 paper-based; 213 computer-based). *Application deadline:* For fall admission, 8/1 priority date for domestic students, 12/1 for international students; for spring admission, 7/1 for international students. Applications are processed on a rolling basis. Application fee: $75. *Expenses:* Tuition, state resident: full-time $7692. *Financial support:* Research assistantships with partial tuition reimbursements, teaching assistantships with partial tuition reimbursements, career-related internships or fieldwork, scholarships/grants, health care benefits, tuition waivers (partial), and unspecified assistantships available. *Faculty research:* Forest fuel characteristics, prescribed fire, tree ring-fire scar analysis, erosion, sedimentation. *Unit head:* Dr. Joseph G. Hiller, Chair, 520-621-7255, Fax: 520-621-8801, E-mail: jghiller@cals.arizona.edu. *Application contact:* Cheryl L. Craddock, Academic Coordinator, 520-621-7260, Fax: 520-621-8801, E-mail: ccraddoc@email.arizona.edu.

University of Arkansas at Monticello, School of Forest Resources, Monticello, AR 71656. Offers MS. Part-time programs available. *Degree requirements:* For master's, comprehensive exam, thesis. *Entrance requirements:* For master's, GRE General Test, minimum GPA of 2.7. Additional exam requirements/recommendations for international students: Required—TOEFL (minimum score 550 paper-based; 213 computer-based). Electronic applications accepted. *Faculty research:* Geographic information systems/remote sensing, forest ecology, wildlife ecology and management.

The University of British Columbia, Faculty of Forestry, Vancouver, BC V6T 1Z1, Canada. Offers M Sc, MA Sc, MF, PhD. Part-time programs available. *Degree requirements:* For master's, thesis (for some programs); for doctorate, comprehensive exam, thesis/dissertation, thesis exam. *Entrance requirements:* Additional exam requirements/recommendations for international students: Required—TOEFL (minimum score 550 paper-based; 213 computer-based; 80 iBT). Electronic applications accepted. Tuition charges are reported in Canadian dollars. *Expenses:* Tuition, area resident: Full-time $4179 Canadian dollars. International tuition: $7344 Canadian dollars full-time. *Faculty research:* Forest sciences, forest resources management, forest operations, wood sciences, conservation, forests and society.

University of California, Berkeley, Graduate Division, College of Natural Resources, Department of Environmental Science, Policy, and Management, Berkeley, CA 94720-1500. Offers environmental science, policy, and management (MS, PhD); forestry (MF). Terminal master's awarded for partial completion of doctoral program. *Degree requirements:* For master's, thesis optional; for doctorate, thesis/dissertation, qualifying exam. *Entrance requirements:* For master's and doctorate, GRE General Test, minimum GPA of 3.0, 3 letters of recommendation. Additional exam requirements/recommendations for international students: Required—TOEFL. Electronic applications accepted. *Faculty research:* Biology and ecology of insects; ecosystem function and environmental issues of soils; plant health/interactions from molecular to ecosystem levels; range management and ecology; forest and resource policy, sustainability, and management.

University of Florida, Graduate School, College of Agricultural and Life Sciences, School of Forest Resources and Conservation, Gainesville, FL 32611. Offers MFRC, MS, PhD, JD/MFRC, JD/MS, JD/PhD. Part-time and evening/weekend programs available. Postbaccalaureate distance learning degree programs offered. *Faculty:* 39 full-time (6 women), 6 part-time/adjunct (2 women). *Students:* 91 full-time (38 women), 36 part-time (20 women); includes 1 Black or African American, non-Hispanic/Latino; 1 American Indian or Alaska Native, non-Hispanic/Latino; 4 Asian, non-Hispanic/Latino; 5 Hispanic/Latino, 26 international. Average age 29. 77 applicants, 42% accepted, 29 enrolled. In 2010, 23 master's, 13 doctorates awarded. Terminal master's awarded for partial completion of doctoral program. *Degree requirements:* For master's, comprehensive exam, thesis optional, MS with thesis and non-thesis option. Project (no thesis) required for MFRC degree; for doctorate, comprehensive exam, thesis/dissertation. *Entrance requirements:* For master's, GRE General Test score at least 1000, minimum GPA of 3.0; for doctorate, GRE General Test, minimum GPA of 3.25. Additional exam requirements/recommendations for international students: Required—TOEFL (minimum score 550 paper-based; 213 computer-based; 80 iBT), IELTS (minimum score 6). *Application deadline:* For fall admission, 1/3 priority date for domestic students, 1/3 for international students; for spring admission, 8/1 for domestic and international students. Applications are processed on a rolling basis. Application fee: $30. Electronic applications accepted. *Expenses:* Tuition, state resident: full-time $10,915.92. Tuition, nonresident: full-time $28,309. *Financial support:* In 2010–11, 84 students received support, including 22 fellowships with full tuition reimbursements available, 61 research assistantships with full tuition reimbursements available (averaging $17,379 per year), 1 teaching assistantship with full tuition reimbursement available (averaging $20,431 per year); Federal Work-Study and institutionally sponsored loans also available. Support available to part-time students. Financial award application deadline: 1/3; financial award applicants required to submit FAFSA. *Faculty research:* Forest biology and ecology; natural resource economics and management; human dimensions and resource policy; tropical forestry and agroforestry; geomatics: geospatial, GIS, and Remote Sensing. Total annual research expenditures: $3.4 million. *Unit head:* Dr. Tim White, PhD, Director, 352-846-0850, Fax: 352-392-1707, E-mail: tlwhite@ufl.edu. *Application contact:* Taylor Stein, PhD, Graduate Coordinator, 352-846-0860, Fax: 352-846-1277, E-mail: tstein@ufl.edu.

University of Georgia, School of Forestry and Natural Resources, Athens, GA 30602. Offers MFR, MS, PhD. *Faculty:* 41 full-time (6 women), 7 part-time/adjunct (1 woman). *Students:* 145 full-time (63 women), 28 part-time (6 women); includes 1 Black or African American, non-Hispanic/Latino; 1 Asian, non-Hispanic/Latino; 1 Two or more races, non-Hispanic/Latino, 18 international. 91 applicants, 66% accepted, 46 enrolled. In 2010, 45 master's, 15 doctorates awarded. *Degree requirements:* For master's, thesis (MS); for doctorate, one foreign language, thesis/dissertation. *Entrance requirements:* For master's and doctorate, GRE General Test. *Application deadline:* For fall admission, 7/1 priority date for domestic students; for spring admission, 11/15 for domestic students. Application fee: $50. Electronic applications accepted. *Expenses:* Tuition, state resident: full-time $7200; part-time $344 per credit hour. Tuition, nonresident: full-time $21,900; part-time $944 per credit hour. Tuition and fees vary according to course load and program. *Financial support:* Fellowships, research assistantships, teaching assistantships, unspecified assistantships available. *Application contact:* Dr. Laurence Schimleck, Graduate Coordinator, 706-542-0464, Fax: 706-542-8356, E-mail: lschimlect@warnell.uga.edu.

University of Kentucky, Graduate School, College of Agriculture, Program in Forestry, Lexington, KY 40506-0032. Offers MSFOR. *Degree requirements:* For master's, comprehensive exam, thesis optional. *Entrance requirements:* For master's, GRE General Test, minimum undergraduate GPA of 2.75. Additional exam requirements/recommendations for international students: Required—TOEFL (minimum score 550 paper-based; 213 computer-based). Electronic applications accepted. *Faculty research:* Forest ecology, silviculture, watershed management, forest products utilization, wildlife habitat management.

University of Maine, Graduate School, College of Natural Sciences, Forestry, and Agriculture, Department of Forest Management and Forest Ecosystem Science, Orono, ME 04469. Offers forest resources (PhD); forestry (MF, MS). *Accreditation:* SAF (one or more programs are accredited). Part-time programs available. *Faculty:* 20 full-time (1 woman). *Students:* 39 full-time (13 women), 8 part-time (3 women), 10 international. Average age 29. 55 applicants, 36% accepted, 16 enrolled. In 2010, 10 master's, 1 doctorate awarded. *Degree requirements:* For master's, thesis; for doctorate, one foreign language, thesis/dissertation. *Entrance requirements:* For master's and doctorate, GRE General Test. Additional exam requirements/recommendations for international students: Required—TOEFL. *Application deadline:* For fall admission, 2/1 priority date for domestic students. Applications are processed on a rolling basis. Application fee: $65. Electronic applications accepted. *Expenses:* Tuition, state resident: full-time $400. Tuition, nonresident: full-time $1050. *Financial support:* In 2010–11, 28 research assistantships with tuition reimbursements (averaging $17,487 per year), 7 teaching assistantships with tuition reimbursements (averaging $12,790 per year) were awarded; career-related internships or fieldwork, Federal Work-Study, and institutionally sponsored loans also available. Financial award application deadline: 3/1. *Faculty research:* Forest economics, engineering and operations analysis, biometrics and remote sensing, timber management, wood technology. *Unit head:* Dr. Robert Wagner, Chair, 207-581-4737. *Application contact:* Scott G. Delcourt, Associate Dean of the Graduate School, 207-581-3291, Fax: 207-581-3232, E-mail: graduate@maine.edu.

University of Maine, Graduate School, College of Natural Sciences, Forestry, and Agriculture, Department of Plant, Soil, and Environmental Sciences, Orono, ME 04469. Offers biological sciences (PhD); ecology and environmental sciences (MS, PhD); forest resources (PhD); horticulture (MS); plant science (PhD); plant, soil, and environmental sciences (MS); resource utilization (MS). *Faculty:* 9 full-time (3 women), 7 part-time/adjunct (3 women). *Students:* 6 full-time (2 women), 2 part-time (1 woman), 2 international. Average age 31. 9 applicants, 22% accepted, 0 enrolled. In 2010, 2 master's awarded. *Entrance requirements:* For master's and doctorate, GRE General Test. Additional exam requirements/recommendations for international students: Required—TOEFL. *Application deadline:* Applications are processed on a rolling basis. Application fee: $65. Electronic applications accepted. *Expenses:* Tuition, state resident: full-time $400. Tuition, nonresident: full-time $1050. *Financial support:* In 2010–11, 16 research assistantships with tuition reimbursements (averaging $16,260 per year), 3 teaching assistantships with tuition reimbursements (averaging $12,790 per year) were awarded; scholarships/grants, tuition waivers (full and partial), and unspecified assistantships also available. *Unit head:* Dr. Gregory Porter, Chair, 207-581-2943, Fax: 207-581-3207. *Application contact:* Scott G. Delcourt, Associate Dean of the Graduate School, 207-581-3291, Fax: 207-581-3232, E-mail: graduate@maine.edu.

University of Massachusetts Amherst, Graduate School, College of Natural Sciences, Department of Environmental Conservation, Program in Forest Resources, Amherst, MA 01003. Offers MS, PhD. Part-time programs available. *Students:* 16 full-time (9 women), 7 part-time (3 women); includes 1 Black or African American, non-Hispanic/Latino; 1 Hispanic/Latino, 3 international. Average age 31. 24 applicants, 63% accepted, 11 enrolled. In 2010, 2 master's, 2 doctorates awarded. Terminal master's awarded for partial completion of doctoral program. *Degree requirements:* For master's, thesis or alternative; for doctorate, comprehensive exam, thesis/dissertation. *Entrance requirements:* For master's and doctorate, GRE General Test. Additional exam requirements/recommendations for international students: Required—TOEFL (minimum score 550 paper-based; 213 computer-based; 80 iBT), IELTS (minimum score 6.5). *Application deadline:* For fall admission, 2/1 for domestic and international students; for spring admission, 10/1 for domestic and international students. Applications are processed on a rolling basis. Application fee: $50 ($65 for international students). Electronic applications accepted. *Expenses:* Tuition, state resident: full-time $2640. Required fees: $8282. One-time fee: $357 full-time. *Financial support:* Fellowships, research assistantships, teaching assistantships, career-related internships or fieldwork, Federal Work-Study, scholarships/grants, traineeships, health care benefits, tuition waivers (full), and unspecified assistantships available. Support available to part-time students. Financial award application deadline: 2/1. *Unit head:* Dr. Brian C.P. Kane, Graduate Program Director, 413-545-2666, Fax: 413-545-4358. *Application contact:* Jean M. Ames, Supervisor of Admissions, 413-545-0722, Fax: 413-577-0010, E-mail: gradadm@grad.umass.edu.

University of Missouri, Graduate School, School of Natural Resources, Department of Forestry, Columbia, MO 65211. Offers MS, PhD. Terminal master's awarded for partial completion of doctoral program. *Degree requirements:* For master's, thesis; for doctorate, thesis/dissertation. *Entrance requirements:* For master's and doctorate, GRE General Test, minimum GPA of 3.0. Additional exam requirements/recommendations for international students: Required—TOEFL (minimum score 500 paper-based; 173 computer-based; 61 iBT).

The University of Montana, Graduate School, College of Forestry and Conservation, Missoula, MT 59812-0002. Offers ecosystem management (MEM, MS); fish and wildlife biology (PhD); forestry (MS, PhD); recreation management (MS); resource conservation (MS); wildlife biology (MS). *Degree requirements:* For doctorate, thesis/dissertation. *Entrance requirements:* For master's and doctorate, GRE General Test. Additional exam requirements/recommendations for international students: Required—TOEFL (minimum score 575 paper-based; 213 computer-based).

University of New Brunswick Fredericton, School of Graduate Studies, Faculty of Forestry and Environmental Management, Fredericton, NB E3B 5A3, Canada. Offers ecological foundations of forest management (PhD); environmental management (MEM); forest engineering (M Sc FE, MFE); forest products marketing (MBA); forest resources (M Sc F, MF, PhD). Part-time programs available. *Faculty:* 22 full-time (3 women), 1 part-time/adjunct (0 women). *Students:* 68 full-time (29 women), 7 part-time (2 women). In 2010, 20 master's, 4 doctorates awarded. *Degree requirements:* For master's, thesis; for doctorate, thesis/dissertation. *Entrance requirements:* For master's and doctorate, minimum GPA of 3.0. Additional exam requirements/recommendations for international students: Required—TWE (minimum score 4), TOEFL (minimum score 580 paper-based) or IELTS. *Application deadline:* For fall admission, 3/1 priority date for domestic students. Application fee: $50 Canadian dollars. Electronic applications accepted. *Expenses:* Tuition, area resident: Full-time $3708; part-time $927 per term. International tuition: $6300 full-time. Required fees: $50 per term. *Financial support:* In 2010–11, 54 research assistantships, 46 teaching assistantships were awarded. *Faculty research:* Forest machines, soils, and ecosystems; integrated forest management; forest meteorology; wood engineering; stream ecosystems dynamics; forest and natural resources policy; forest operations planning; wood technology and mechanics; forest road construction and engineering; forest, wildlife, insect, bird, and fire ecology; remote sensing; insect impacts; Silviculture; LiDAR analytics; integrated pest management; forest tree genetics; genetic resource conservation and sustainable management. *Unit head:* Dr. John Kershaw, Director of Graduate Studies, 506-453-4933, Fax: 506-453-3538, E-mail: kershaw@unb.ca. *Application contact:* Faith Sharpe, Graduate Secretary, 506-458-7520, Fax: 506-453-3538, E-mail: fsharpe@unb.ca.

University of New Hampshire, Graduate School, College of Life Sciences and Agriculture, Department of Natural Resources, Durham, NH 03824. Offers environmental conservation (MS); forestry (MS); integrated coastal ecosystem science, policy, management (MS); natural resources (MS); water resources (MS); wildlife (MS). Part-time programs available. *Faculty:* 40 full-time. *Students:* 22 full-time (8 women), 27 part-time (15 women); includes 1 Asian, non-Hispanic/Latino; 1 Hispanic/Latino, 1 international. Average age 30. 54 applicants, 39% accepted, 14 enrolled. In 2010, 13 master's awarded. *Degree requirements:* For master's, thesis or alternative. *Entrance requirements:* For master's, GRE General Test. Additional exam requirements/recommendations for international students: Required—TOEFL (minimum score 550 paper-based; 213 computer-based; 80 iBT). *Application deadline:* For fall admission, 6/1 for domestic students, 4/1 for international students; for spring admission, 12/1 for domestic students. Applications are processed on a rolling basis. Application fee: $65. Electronic applications accepted. *Financial support:* In 2010–11, 23 students received support, including 3 fellowships, 6 research assistantships, 14 teaching assistantships; career-related internships or fieldwork, Federal Work-Study, scholarships/grants, and tuition waivers (full and partial) also available. Support available to part-time students. Financial award application deadline: 2/15. *Unit head:* Dr. John Halstead, Chairperson, 603-862-3950, E-mail: natural.resources@unh.edu. *Application contact:* Linda Scogin, Administrative Assistant, 603-862-3932, E-mail: natural.resources@unh.edu.

The University of Tennessee, Graduate School, College of Agricultural Sciences and Natural Resources, Department of Forestry, Wildlife, and Fisheries, Program in Forestry, Knoxville, TN 37996. Offers MS. *Degree requirements:* For master's, thesis or alternative. *Entrance requirements:* For master's, GRE General Test, minimum GPA of 2.7. Additional exam requirements/recommendations for international students: Required—TOEFL. Electronic applications accepted. *Expenses:* Tuition, state resident: full-time $7440; part-time $414 per credit hour. Tuition, nonresident: full-time $22,478; part-time $1250 per credit hour. Required fees: $922; $43 per credit hour. Tuition and fees vary according to program.

University of Toronto, School of Graduate Studies, Life Sciences Division, Faculty of Forestry, Toronto, ON M5S 1A1, Canada. Offers M Sc F, MFC, PhD. *Degree requirements:* For master's, comprehensive exam, thesis, oral thesis/research paper defense; for doctorate, thesis/dissertation, oral defense of thesis. *Entrance requirements:* For master's, bachelor's degree in a related area, minimum B average in final year (M Sc F), final 2 years (MFC); resume, 3 letters of reference; for doctorate, writing sample, minimum A– average, master's in a related area, 3 letters of reference, resumé.

University of Vermont, Graduate College, The Rubenstein School of Environment and Natural Resources, Program in Natural Resources, Burlington, VT 05405. Offers natural resources (MS, PhD), including aquatic ecology and watershed science (MS), environment thought and culture (MS), environment, science and public affairs (MS), forestry (MS). *Students:* 102 (54 women); includes 2 Black or African American, non-Hispanic/Latino; 2 American Indian or Alaska Native, non-Hispanic/Latino; 7 Asian, non-Hispanic/Latino; 4 Hispanic/Latino, 5

Forestry

University of Vermont (continued)

international. 140 applicants, 32% accepted, 22 enrolled. In 2010, 22 master's, 8 doctorates awarded. *Degree requirements:* For master's, thesis or alternative; for doctorate, thesis/dissertation. *Entrance requirements:* For master's and doctorate, GRE General Test. Additional exam requirements/recommendations for international students: Required—TOEFL (minimum score 550 paper-based; 213 computer-based; 80 iBT). *Application deadline:* For fall admission, 3/1 priority date for domestic students. Applications are processed on a rolling basis. Application fee: $40. Electronic applications accepted. *Expenses:* Tuition, state resident: part-time $537 per credit hour. Tuition, nonresident: part-time $1355 per credit hour. *Financial support:* Fellowships, research assistantships, teaching assistantships available. Financial award application deadline: 3/1. *Unit head:* Dr. Mary Watzin, Coordinator, 802-656-2620. *Application contact:* Dr. Mary Watzin, Coordinator, 802-656-2620.

University of Washington, Graduate School, College of Forest Resources, Seattle, WA 98195. Offers bioresource science and engineering (MS, PhD); environmental horticulture (MEH); environmental horticulture and urban forestry (MS, PhD); forest ecology (MS, PhD); forest management (MFR); forest soils (MS, PhD); forest systems and bioenergy (MS, PhD); restoration ecology (MS, PhD); social sciences (MS, PhD); sustainable resource management (MS, PhD); wildlife science (MS, PhD); MFR/MAIS; MPA/MS. *Accreditation:* SAF. *Degree requirements:* For master's, thesis (for some programs); for doctorate, comprehensive exam (for some programs), thesis/dissertation. *Entrance requirements:* For master's and doctorate, GRE, minimum GPA of 3.0. Additional exam requirements/recommendations for international students: Required—TOEFL. Electronic applications accepted. *Faculty research:* Ecosystem analysis, silviculture and forest protection, paper science and engineering, environmental horticulture and urban forestry, natural resource policy and economics.

University of Wisconsin–Madison, Graduate School, College of Agricultural and Life Sciences, Department of Forest and Wildlife Ecology, Program in Forestry, Madison, WI 53706-1380. Offers MS, PhD. *Expenses:* Tuition, state resident: full-time $9887.36; part-time $617.96 per credit. Tuition, nonresident: full-time $24,054; part-time $1503.40 per credit. Required fees: $67.63 per credit. Tuition and fees vary according to reciprocity agreements.

Utah State University, School of Graduate Studies, College of Natural Resources, Department of Wildland Resources, Logan, UT 84322. Offers ecology (MS, PhD); forestry (MS, PhD); range science (MS, PhD); wildlife biology (MS, PhD). Part-time programs available. *Degree requirements:* For master's, thesis; for doctorate, comprehensive exam, thesis/dissertation. *Entrance requirements:* For master's and doctorate, GRE General Test, minimum GPA of 3.0. Additional exam requirements/recommendations for international students: Required—TOEFL. *Faculty research:* Range plant ecophysiology, plant community ecology, ruminant nutrition, population ecology.

Virginia Polytechnic Institute and State University, Graduate School, College of Natural Resources and Environment, Department of Forestry, Blacksburg, VA 24061. Offers forestry (MS, PhD); watershed management (Certificate). *Faculty:* 24 full-time (5 women). *Students:* 54 full-time (21 women), 12 part-time (5 women); includes 2 Hispanic/Latino, 16 international. Average age 29. 48 applicants, 52% accepted, 23 enrolled. In 2010, 16 master's, 6 doctorates awarded. *Degree requirements:* For master's, comprehensive exam (for some programs), thesis (for some programs); for doctorate, comprehensive exam (for some programs), thesis/dissertation (for some programs). *Entrance requirements:* For master's and doctorate, GRE. Additional exam requirements/recommendations for international students: Required—TOEFL (minimum score 550 paper-based; 213 computer-based). *Application deadline:* For fall admission, 7/1 for domestic and international students; for spring admission, 12/1 for domestic and international students. Applications are processed on a rolling basis. Application fee: $65. Electronic applications accepted. *Expenses:* Tuition, area resident: Full-time $9399; part-time $488 per credit hour. Tuition, state resident: full-time $9399; part-time $488 per credit hour. Tuition, nonresident: full-time $17,854; part-time $957.75 per credit hour. International tuition: $17,854 full-time. Required fees: $1534. Full-time tuition and fees vary according to program. *Financial support:* In 2010–11, 31 research assistantships with full tuition reimbursements (averaging $18,274 per year), 8 teaching assistantships with full tuition reimbursements (averaging $15,016 per year) were awarded; career-related internships or fieldwork, Federal Work-Study, scholarships/grants, health care benefits, and unspecified assistantships also available. Financial award application deadline: 1/15. Total annual research expenditures: $4.8 million. *Unit head:* Dr. Janaki Alavalapati, UNIT HEAD, 540-231-5676, Fax: 540-231-3698, E-mail: jrra@vt.edu. *Application contact:* Dr. Janaki Alavalapati, UNIT HEAD, 540-231-5676, Fax: 540-231-3698, E-mail: jrra@vt.edu.

Virginia Polytechnic Institute and State University, Graduate School, College of Natural Resources and Environment, Department of Wood Science and Forest Products, Blacksburg, VA 24061. Offers MF, MS, PhD. *Faculty:* 13 full-time (2 women). *Students:* 17 full-time (7 women), 3 part-time (1 woman), 9 international. Average age 33. 18 applicants, 50% accepted, 2 enrolled. In 2010, 4 master's, 3 doctorates awarded. *Degree requirements:* For master's, comprehensive exam (for some programs), thesis (for some programs); for doctorate, comprehensive exam (for some programs), thesis/dissertation (for some programs). *Entrance requirements:* For master's and doctorate, GRE. Additional exam requirements/recommendations for international students: Required—TOEFL (minimum score 550 paper-based; 213 computer-based). *Application deadline:* For fall admission, 7/1 for domestic and international students; for spring admission, 12/1 for domestic and international students. Applications are processed on a rolling basis. Application fee: $65. Electronic applications accepted. *Expenses:* Tuition, area resident: Full-time $9399; part-time $488 per credit hour. Tuition, state resident: full-time $9399; part-time $488 per credit hour. Tuition, nonresident: full-time $17,854; part-time $957.75 per credit hour. International tuition: $17,854 full-time. Required fees: $1534. Full-time tuition and fees vary according to program. *Financial support:* In 2010–11, 17 research assistantships with full tuition reimbursements (averaging $18,098 per year), 2 teaching assistantships with full tuition reimbursements (averaging $14,858 per year) were awarded; career-related internships or fieldwork, Federal Work-Study, scholarships/grants, health care benefits, and unspecified assistantships also available. Financial award application deadline: 1/15. *Faculty research:* Wood chemistry, wood engineering, wood composites, wood processing, forest products marketing/management, recycling. *Unit head:* Dr. Barry M. Goodell, UNIT HEAD, 540-231-8853, Fax: 540-231-8176, E-mail: oodell@vt.edu. *Application contact:* Debbie Garnard, Contact, 540-231-8853, Fax: 540-231-8176, E-mail: garnandd@vt.edu.

West Virginia University, Davis College of Agriculture, Forestry and Consumer Sciences, Division of Forestry, Program in Forest Resource Science, Morgantown, WV 26506. Offers PhD. *Degree requirements:* For doctorate, comprehensive exam, thesis/dissertation. *Entrance requirements:* For doctorate, GRE, minimum GPA of 3.0. Additional exam requirements/recommendations for international students: Required—TOEFL. *Faculty research:* Impact of management on wildlife and fish, forest sampling designs, forest economics and policy, oak regeneration.

West Virginia University, Davis College of Agriculture, Forestry and Consumer Sciences, Division of Forestry, Program in Forestry, Morgantown, WV 26506. Offers MSF. *Degree requirements:* For master's, thesis. *Entrance requirements:* For master's, GRE, minimum GPA of 3.0. Additional exam requirements/recommendations for international students: Required—TOEFL. *Faculty research:* Health and productivity on Appalachian forests, wood industries in Appalachian forests, role of forestry in regional economics.

Yale University, Graduate School of Arts and Sciences, Department of Forestry and Environmental Studies, New Haven, CT 06520. Offers environmental sciences (PhD); forestry (PhD). *Degree requirements:* For doctorate, thesis/dissertation. *Entrance requirements:* For doctorate, GRE General Test.

Yale University, School of Forestry and Environmental Studies, New Haven, CT 06511. Offers MEM, MES, MF, MFS, PhD, JD/MEM, MBA/MEM, MBA/MF, MEM/M Arch, MEM/MA, MEM/MPH, MF/MA. *Accreditation:* SAF (one or more programs are accredited). Part-time programs available. Terminal master's awarded for partial completion of doctoral program. *Degree requirements:* For master's, thesis (for some programs); for doctorate, thesis/dissertation. *Entrance requirements:* For master's, GRE General Test, GMAT or LSAT; for doctorate, GRE General Test. Additional exam requirements/recommendations for international students: Required—TOEFL (minimum score 600 paper-based; 250 computer-based; 100 iBT). Electronic applications accepted. *Expenses:* Contact institution. *Faculty research:* Environmental policy, social ecology, industrial environmental management, forestry, environmental health, urban ecology, water science policy.

Natural Resources

American University, School of International Service, Washington, DC 20016-8071. Offers comparative and regional studies (Certificate); cross-cultural communication (Certificate); development management (MS); ethics, peace, and global affairs (MA); European studies (Certificate); global environmental policy (MA, Certificate); international affairs (MA), including comparative and regional studies, environmental policy, international economic policy, international politics, natural resources and sustainable development, U. S. foreign policy; international communication (MA, Certificate); international development (MA, Certificate); international development management (Certificate); international economic policy (Certificate); international economic relations (Certificate); international media (MA); international peace and conflict resolution (MA, Certificate); international relations (PhD); international service (MIS); peace building (Certificate); the Americas (Certificate); United States foreign policy (Certificate); JD/MA. Part-time and evening/weekend programs available. *Faculty:* 91 full-time (35 women), 48 part-time/adjunct (16 women). *Students:* 591 full-time (383 women), 367 part-time (229 women); includes 164 minority (51 Black or African American, non-Hispanic/Latino; 4 American Indian or Alaska Native, non-Hispanic/Latino; 42 Asian, non-Hispanic/Latino; 63 Hispanic/Latino; 4 Two or more races, non-Hispanic/Latino), 94 international. Average age 27. 2,115 applicants, 59% accepted, 360 enrolled. In 2010, 370 master's, 7 doctorates awarded. Terminal master's awarded for partial completion of doctoral program. *Degree requirements:* For master's, one foreign language, comprehensive exam, thesis or alternative; for doctorate, one foreign language, comprehensive exam, thesis/dissertation, research practicum; for Certificate, minimum 15 credit hours related course work. *Entrance requirements:* For master's, GRE, 24 credits of course work in related social sciences, minimum GPA of 3.5, 2 letters of recommendation, bachelor's degree, resume; for doctorate, GRE, 2 letters of recommendation, 24 credits in related social sciences; for Certificate, bachelor's degree. Additional exam requirements/recommendations for international students: Required—TOEFL (minimum score 600 paper-based; 250 computer-based; 100 iBT). *Application deadline:* For fall admission, 1/15 priority date for domestic students; for spring admission, 10/1 priority date for domestic students. Applications are processed on a rolling basis. Application fee: $50. *Financial support:* Career-related internships or fieldwork, Federal Work-Study, and institutionally sponsored loans available. Financial award application deadline: 1/15. *Faculty research:* International intellectual property, international environmental issues, international law and legal order, international telecommunications/technology, international sustainable development. *Unit head:* Dr. Louis W. Goodman, Dean, 202-885-1600, Fax: 202-885-2494. *Application contact:* Yasmin Quianzon, Director of Graduate Admissions and Financial Aid, 202-885-2496, Fax: 202-885-1109.

Auburn University, Graduate School, School of Forestry and Wildlife Sciences, Auburn University, AL 36849. Offers forest economics (PhD); forestry (MS, PhD); natural resource conservation (MNR); wildlife sciences (MS, PhD). *Accreditation:* SAF. Part-time programs available. *Faculty:* 28 full-time (5 women), 2 part-time/adjunct (0 women). *Students:* 29 full-time (12 women), 53 part-time (17 women); includes 1 Black or African American, non-Hispanic/Latino; 1 Asian, non-Hispanic/Latino; 1 Hispanic/Latino, 28 international. Average age 28. 55 applicants, 44% accepted, 17 enrolled. In 2010, 5 master's, 3 doctorates awarded. *Degree requirements:* For master's, thesis (MS); for doctorate, thesis/dissertation. *Entrance requirements:* For master's and doctorate, GRE General Test. *Application deadline:* For fall admission, 7/7 for domestic students; for spring admission, 11/24 for domestic students. Applications are processed on a rolling basis. Application fee: $50 ($60 for international students). Electronic applications accepted. *Expenses:* Tuition, state resident: full-time $7002. Tuition, nonresident: full-time $21,898. International tuition: $22,116 full-time. Required fees: $892. Tuition and fees vary according to course load and program. *Financial support:* Fellowships, research assistantships, teaching assistantships, Federal Work-Study available. Support available to part-time students. Financial award application deadline: 3/15; financial award applicants required to submit FAFSA. *Faculty research:* Forest nursery management, silviculture and vegetation management, biological processes and ecological relationships, growth and yield of plantations and natural stands, urban forestry, forest taxation, law and policy. *Unit head:* Dr. James P. Shepard, Dean, 334-844-4000, Fax: 334-844-1084, E-mail: brinker@forestry.auburn.edu. *Application contact:* Dr. George Flowers, Dean of the Graduate School, 334-844-2125.

Ball State University, Graduate School, College of Sciences and Humanities, Department of Natural Resources, Muncie, IN 47306-1099. Offers MA, MS. *Faculty:* 12. *Students:* 10 full-time (5 women), 9 part-time (1 woman); includes 1 Hispanic/Latino. Average age 25. 14 applicants, 64% accepted, 7 enrolled. In 2010, 4 master's awarded. *Entrance requirements:* For master's, GRE General Test. Application fee: $50. *Expenses:* Tuition, state resident: full-time $6160; part-time $299 per credit hour. Tuition, nonresident: full-time $16,020; part-time $783 per credit hour. Required fees: $2278; $95 per credit hour. *Financial support:* In 2010–11, 4 teaching assistantships with full tuition reimbursements (averaging $10,691 per year) were awarded; research assistantships with full tuition reimbursements, career-related internships or fieldwork also available. Financial award application deadline: 3/1. *Faculty research:* Acid rain, indoor air pollution, land reclamation. *Unit head:* Dr. James Eflin, Chairman, 765-285-5780, Fax: 765-285-2606. *Application contact:* Dr. Robert Morris, Associate Provost for Research and Dean of the Graduate School, 765-285-1300, E-mail: rmorris@bsu.edu.

California Polytechnic State University, San Luis Obispo, College of Agriculture, Food and Environmental Sciences, Department of Natural Resources Management, San Luis Obispo, CA 93407. Offers forestry sciences (MS). Part-time programs available. *Faculty:* 1 full-time (0 women). *Students:* 2 full-time (0 women), 2 part-time (0 women); includes 1 minority (Hispanic/

Latino). Average age 37. 6 applicants, 33% accepted, 2 enrolled. In 2010, 4 master's awarded. *Degree requirements:* For master's, comprehensive exam, thesis. *Entrance requirements:* For master's, minimum GPA of 2.75 in last 90 quarter units of course work. Additional exam requirements/recommendations for international students: Required—TOEFL (minimum score 550 paper-based; 213 computer-based) or IELTS (minimum score 6). *Application deadline:* For fall admission, 4/1 for domestic students, 11/30 for international students; for winter admission, 10/1 for domestic students, 6/30 for international students; for spring admission, 10/1 for domestic students. Applications are processed on a rolling basis. Application fee: $55. Electronic applications accepted. *Expenses:* Tuition, state resident: full-time $5386; part-time $3124 per year. Tuition, nonresident: full-time $11,160; part-time $248 per unit. Required fees: $2250; $614 per term. One-time fee: $2250 full-time; $1842 part-time. *Financial support:* Fellowships, research assistantships, career-related internships or fieldwork, Federal Work-Study, institutionally sponsored loans, scholarships/grants, and unspecified assistantships available. Support available to part-time students. Financial award application deadline: 3/2; financial award applicants required to submit FAFSA. *Faculty research:* Hydrology, biometrics, forest health and management, fire science, urban and community forestry. *Unit head:* Dr. Doug Piirto, Department Head/Graduate Coordinator, 805-756-2968, Fax: 805-756-1402, E-mail: dpiirto@calpoly.edu. *Application contact:* Dr. Mark Shelton, Associate Dean/Graduate Coordinator, 805-756-2161, Fax: 805-756-6577, E-mail: mshelton@calpoly.edu.

Central Washington University, Graduate Studies and Research, College of the Sciences, Program in Resource Management, Ellensburg, WA 98926. Offers MS. *Degree requirements:* For master's, thesis. *Entrance requirements:* For master's, minimum GPA of 3.0. Additional exam requirements/recommendations for international students: Required—TOEFL (minimum score 550 paper-based; 213 computer-based; 79 iBT). Electronic applications accepted.

Colorado State University, Graduate School, Warner College of Natural Resources, Department of Forest, Rangeland, and Watershed Stewardship, Fort Collins, CO 80523-1472. Offers forest sciences (MS, PhD); natural resources stewardship (MNRS); rangeland ecosystem science (MS, PhD); watershed science (MS). Part-time programs available. Postbaccalaureate distance learning degree programs offered (no on-campus study). *Faculty:* 18 full-time (5 women), 2 part-time/adjunct (0 women). *Students:* 45 full-time (21 women), 90 part-time (31 women); includes 9 minority (3 American Indian or Alaska Native, non-Hispanic/Latino; 1 Asian, non-Hispanic/Latino; 5 Hispanic/Latino), 9 international. Average age 34. 59 applicants, 76% accepted, 28 enrolled. In 2010, 27 master's, 2 doctorates awarded. *Degree requirements:* For master's, thesis (for some programs); for doctorate, comprehensive exam, thesis/dissertation. *Entrance requirements:* For master's, GRE General Test (minimum score 1000 verbal and quantitative), minimum GPA of 3.0, 3 letters of recommendation; for doctorate, GRE General Test (combined minimum score of 1100 on the Verbal and Quantitative sections), minimum GPA of 3.0, 3 letters of recommendation, statement of research interest. Additional exam requirements/recommendations for international students: Required—TOEFL (minimum score 550 paper-based; 213 computer-based; 80 iBT), IELTS (minimum score 6.5). *Application deadline:* For fall admission, 2/15 priority date for domestic and international students; for spring admission, 7/15 priority date for domestic and international students. Applications are processed on a rolling basis. Application fee: $50. Electronic applications accepted. *Expenses:* Tuition, state resident: full-time $7434; part-time $413 per credit. Tuition, nonresident: full-time $19,022; part-time $1057 per credit. Required fees: $1729; $88 per credit. *Financial support:* In 2010–11, 46 students received support, including 1 fellowship (averaging $23,971 per year), 32 research assistantships with full and partial tuition reimbursements available (averaging $15,871 per year), 13 teaching assistantships with full and partial tuition reimbursements available (averaging $7,106 per year); Federal Work-Study, scholarships/grants, and unspecified assistantships also available. Financial award application deadline: 2/15; financial award applicants required to submit FAFSA. *Faculty research:* Ecology, natural resource management, hydrology, restoration, human dimensions. Total annual research expenditures: $2.4 million. *Unit head:* Dr. Frederick Smith, Interim Department Head, 970-491-7505, Fax: 970-491-6754, E-mail: fwsmith@colostate.edu. *Application contact:* Sonya LeFebre, Coordinator, 970-491-1907, Fax: 970-491-6754, E-mail: sonya.lefebre@colostate.edu.

Colorado State University, Graduate School, Warner College of Natural Resources, Department of Human Dimensions of Natural Resources, Fort Collins, CO 80523-1480. Offers MS, PhD. Part-time programs available. *Faculty:* 11 full-time (3 women). *Students:* 43 full-time (25 women), 18 part-time (7 women); includes 10 minority (1 Black or African American, non-Hispanic/Latino; 1 Asian, non-Hispanic/Latino; 7 Hispanic/Latino; 1 Two or more races, non-Hispanic/Latino), 7 international. Average age 30. 68 applicants, 54% accepted, 32 enrolled. In 2010, 10 master's, 3 doctorates awarded. Terminal master's awarded for partial completion of doctoral program. *Degree requirements:* For master's, comprehensive exam, thesis or alternative; for doctorate, comprehensive exam, thesis/dissertation. *Entrance requirements:* For master's, GRE General Test, minimum GPA of 3.0, 3 letters of recommendation, statement of interest; for doctorate, GRE General Test (combined minimum score of 1000 on the Verbal and Quantitative sections), minimum GPA of 3.0, 3 letters of recommendation, copy of master's thesis or professional paper, interview, statement of interest. Additional exam requirements/recommendations for international students: Required—TOEFL (minimum score 550 paper-based; 213 computer-based; 80 iBT). *Application deadline:* For fall admission, 2/1 priority date for domestic students, 2/1 for international students. Application fee: $50. Electronic applications accepted. *Expenses:* Tuition, state resident: full-time $7434; part-time $413 per credit. Tuition, nonresident: full-time $19,022; part-time $1057 per credit. Required fees: $1729; $88 per credit. *Financial support:* In 2010–11, 31 students received support, including 2 fellowships (averaging $10,494 per year), 18 research assistantships with tuition reimbursements available (averaging $12,631 per year), 11 teaching assistantships with tuition reimbursements available (averaging $9,205 per year); career-related internships or fieldwork, Federal Work-Study, scholarships/grants, traineeships, and unspecified assistantships also available. Support available to part-time students. Financial award application deadline: 2/15; financial award applicants required to submit FAFSA. *Faculty research:* International tourism, wilderness preservation, resource interpretation, human dimensions in natural resources, protected areas management. Total annual research expenditures: $1.1 million. *Unit head:* Dr. Michael J. Manfredo, Head, 970-491-0474, Fax: 970-491-2255, E-mail: manfredo@cnr.colostate.edu. *Application contact:* Linda Adams, Coordinator of Administration, 970-491-6591, Fax: 970-491-2255, E-mail: linda.adams@colostate.edu.

Cornell University, Graduate School, Graduate Fields of Agriculture and Life Sciences, Field of Natural Resources, Ithaca, NY 14853-0001. Offers aquatic science (MPS, MS, PhD); environmental management (MPS); fishery science (MPS, MS, PhD); forest science (MPS, MS, PhD); resource policy and management (MPS, MS, PhD); wildlife science (MPS, MS, PhD). *Faculty:* 36 full-time (7 women). *Students:* 48 full-time (21 women); includes 1 Asian, non-Hispanic/Latino; 1 Hispanic/Latino, 11 international. Average age 30. 52 applicants, 27% accepted, 11 enrolled. In 2010, 8 master's, 6 doctorates awarded. *Degree requirements:* For master's, thesis (MS), project paper (MPS); for doctorate, comprehensive exam, thesis/dissertation. *Entrance requirements:* For master's and doctorate, GRE General Test, 2 letters of recommendation. Additional exam requirements/recommendations for international students: Required—TOEFL (minimum score 550 paper-based; 213 computer-based; 77 iBT). *Application deadline:* For spring admission, 10/30 for domestic students. Applications are processed on a rolling basis. Application fee: $70. Electronic applications accepted. *Expenses:* Tuition: Full-time $29,500. Required fees: $76. Tuition and fees vary according to degree level and program. *Financial support:* In 2010–11, 9 fellowships with full tuition reimbursements, 16 research assistantships with full tuition reimbursements, 15 teaching assistantships with full tuition reimbursements were awarded; institutionally sponsored loans, scholarships/grants, health care benefits, tuition waivers (full and partial), and unspecified assistantships also available. Financial award applicants required to submit FAFSA. *Faculty research:* Ecosystem-level dynamics, systems modeling, conservation biology/management, resource management's human dimensions, biogeochemistry. *Unit head:* Director of Graduate Studies, 607-255-2807, Fax: 607-255-0349. *Application contact:* Graduate Field Assistant, 607-255-2807, Fax: 607-255-0349, E-mail: nrgrad@cornell.edu.

Dalhousie University, Faculty of Management, Centre for Advanced Management Education, Halifax, NS B3H 3J5, Canada. Offers financial services (MBA); information management (MIM); management (MPA); natural resources (MBA). Part-time programs available. Postbaccalaureate distance learning degree programs offered. *Entrance requirements:* For master's, GMAT, minimum GPA of 3.0, resume. Additional exam requirements/recommendations for international students: Required—TOEFL, IELTS, CANTEST, CAEL, or Michigan English Language Assessment Battery. Electronic applications accepted.

Delaware State University, Graduate Programs, Department of Agriculture and Natural Resources, Program in Natural Resources, Dover, DE 19901-2277. Offers MS. *Entrance requirements:* For master's, GRE. Additional exam requirements/recommendations for international students: Required—TOEFL (minimum score 550 paper-based).

Duke University, Graduate School, Department of Environment, Durham, NC 27708. Offers natural resource economics/policy (PhD); natural resource science/ecology (PhD); natural resource systems science (PhD); JD/AM. Part-time programs available. *Faculty:* 28 full-time. *Students:* 59 full-time (33 women); includes 2 Black or African American, non-Hispanic/Latino; 1 Asian, non-Hispanic/Latino, 17 international. 84 applicants, 13% accepted, 6 enrolled. In 2010, 14 doctorates awarded. *Degree requirements:* For doctorate, variable foreign language requirement, thesis/dissertation. *Entrance requirements:* For doctorate, GRE General Test. Additional exam requirements/recommendations for international students: Required—TOEFL (minimum score 550 paper-based; 213 computer-based; 83 iBT), IELTS (minimum score 7). *Application deadline:* For fall admission, 12/8 priority date for domestic and international students. Application fee: $75. Electronic applications accepted. *Financial support:* Fellowships, research assistantships, teaching assistantships, Federal Work-Study available. Financial award application deadline: 12/8. *Unit head:* Gaby Katul, Director of Graduate Studies, 919-613-8002, Fax: 919-613-8061, E-mail: meg.stephens@duke.edu. *Application contact:* Elizabeth Hutton, Director, Graduate Admissions, 919-684-3913, Fax: 919-684-2277, E-mail: grad-admissions@duke.edu.

Duke University, Nicholas School of the Environment, Durham, NC 27708-0328. Offers coastal environmental management (MEM); DEL-environmental leadership (MEM); energy and environment (MEM); environmental economics and policy (MEM); environmental health and security (MEM); forest resource management (MF); global environmental change (MEM); resource ecology (MEM); water and air resources (MEM); JD/AM; JD/MEM; JD/MF; MAT/MEM; MBA/MEM; MBA/MF; MEM/MPP; MF/MPP. *Accreditation:* SAF (one or more programs are accredited). Part-time programs available. *Degree requirements:* For master's, thesis. *Entrance requirements:* For master's, GRE General Test, previous course work in biology or ecology, calculus, statistics, and microeconomics; computer familiarity with word processing and data analysis. Additional exam requirements/recommendations for international students: Required—TOEFL (minimum score 550 paper-based; 213 computer-based). Electronic applications accepted. *Expenses:* Contact institution. *Faculty research:* Ecosystem management, conservation ecology, earth systems, risk assessment.

East Carolina University, Graduate School, Program in Coastal Resources Management, Greenville, NC 27858-4353. Offers PhD. *Degree requirements:* For doctorate, comprehensive exam, thesis/dissertation, internship. *Entrance requirements:* For doctorate, GRE. Additional exam requirements/recommendations for international students: Required—TOEFL. *Expenses:* Tuition, state resident: full-time $3130; part-time $391.25 per credit hour. Tuition, nonresident: full-time $13,817; part-time $1727.13 per credit hour. Required fees: $1916; $239.50 per credit hour. Tuition and fees vary according to campus/location and program. *Faculty research:* Coastal geology, wetlands and coastal ecology, ecological and social networks, submerged cultural resources, coastal resources economics.

Georgia Institute of Technology, Graduate Studies and Research, College of Engineering, School of Chemical and Biomolecular Engineering, Atlanta, GA 30332-0001. Offers bioengineering (MS Bio E, PhD); chemical engineering (MS Ch E, PhD); paper science and engineering (MS, PhD); polymers (MS Poly). *Degree requirements:* For master's, thesis; for doctorate, comprehensive exam, thesis/dissertation. *Entrance requirements:* For master's and doctorate, GRE, minimum GPA of 3.0. Additional exam requirements/recommendations for international students: Required—TOEFL (minimum score 550 paper-based; 213 computer-based). Electronic applications accepted. *Faculty research:* Biochemical engineering; process modeling, synthesis, and control; polymer science and engineering; thermodynamics and separations; surface and particle science.

Humboldt State University, Academic Programs, College of Natural Resources and Sciences, Programs in Natural Resources, Arcata, CA 95521-8299. Offers natural resources (MS), including fisheries, forestry, natural resources planning and interpretation, rangeland resources and wildland soils, wastewater utilization, watershed management, wildlife. *Students:* 62 full-time (27 women), 21 part-time (7 women); includes 4 minority (1 Asian, non-Hispanic/Latino; 2 Hispanic/Latino; 1 Two or more races, non-Hispanic/Latino), 2 international. Average age 29. 117 applicants, 47% accepted, 33 enrolled. In 2010, 23 master's awarded. *Degree requirements:* For master's, thesis or alternative. *Entrance requirements:* For master's, GRE, appropriate bachelor's degree, minimum GPA of 2.5, 3 letters of recommendation, resume. Additional exam requirements/recommendations for international students: Required—TOEFL (minimum score 500 paper-based; 173 computer-based). *Application deadline:* For fall admission, 2/1 for domestic and international students; for spring admission, 9/30 for domestic and international students. Applications are processed on a rolling basis. Application fee: $55. Tuition and fees vary according to program. *Financial support:* Fellowships, career-related internships or fieldwork and Federal Work-Study available. Support available to part-time students. Financial award application deadline: 3/1; financial award applicants required to submit FAFSA. *Faculty research:* Spotted owl habitat, pre-settlement vegetation, hardwood utilization, tree physiology, fisheries. *Unit head:* Dr. Gary Hendrickson, Coordinator, 707-826-4233, E-mail: thlesfel@humboldt.edu. *Application contact:* Julie Tucker, Administrative Support Coordinator, 707-826-3256, E-mail: jlt7002@humboldt.edu.

Instituto Tecnologico de Santo Domingo, Graduate School, Area of Basic And Environmental Sciences, Santo Domingo, Dominican Republic. Offers environmental science (M En S), including environmental education, environmental management, marine resources, natural resources management; mathematics (MS, PhD); renewable energy technology (MS, Certificate).

Iowa State University of Science and Technology, Graduate College, College of Agriculture, Department of Natural Resource Ecology and Management, Ames, IA 50011. Offers forestry (MS, PhD); wildlife ecology (MS). *Faculty:* 20 full-time (5 women), 11 part-time/adjunct (3 women). *Students:* 38 full-time (14 women), 11 part-time (3 women); includes 1 American Indian or Alaska Native, non-Hispanic/Latino; 1 Hispanic/Latino, 10 international. 16 applicants, 25% accepted, 3 enrolled. In 2010, 7 master's, 2 doctorates awarded. *Degree requirements:* For master's, thesis (for some programs); for doctorate, thesis/dissertation. *Entrance requirements:* For master's and doctorate, GRE General Test. Additional exam requirements/recommendations for international students: Required—TOEFL (minimum score 550 paper-based; 79 iBT), IELTS (minimum score 6.5). *Application deadline:* For fall admission, 4/1 priority date for domestic and international students; for spring admission, 10/1 priority date for domestic and international students. Application fee: $40 ($90 for international students). Electronic applications accepted. *Financial support:* In 2010–11, 28 research assistantships with full and partial tuition reimbursements (averaging $15,773 per year), 3 teaching assistantships with full and partial tuition reimbursements (averaging $11,171 per year) were awarded.

Natural Resources

Iowa State University of Science and Technology (continued)
Unit head: Dr. Stephen Jungst, Interim Chair, 515-294-1166. *Application contact:* Dr. Janette Thompson, Director of Graduate Education, 515-294-1626, E-mail: nremgrad@iastate.edu.

Iowa State University of Science and Technology, Graduate College, Interdisciplinary Programs, Program in Biorenewable Resources and Technology, Ames, IA 50011. Offers MS, PhD. *Students:* 19 full-time (6 women), 7 part-time (1 woman), 9 international. In 2010, 8 master's, 5 doctorates awarded. *Degree requirements:* For master's, thesis or alternative; for doctorate, thesis/dissertation. *Entrance requirements:* For master's and doctorate, GRE General Test. Additional exam requirements/recommendations for international students: Required—TOEFL (minimum score 550 paper-based; 79 iBT), IELTS (minimum score 6.5). *Application deadline:* For fall admission, 1/1 priority date for domestic and international students; for spring admission, 9/1 for domestic and international students. Applications are processed on a rolling basis. Application fee: $40 ($90 for international students). *Financial support:* In 2010–11, 4 research assistantships with full and partial tuition reimbursements (averaging $12,681 per year) were awarded. *Unit head:* Dr. Raj Raman, Chair, Supervising Committee, 515-294-6555, E-mail: brtgrad@iastate.edu. *Application contact:* Dr. Raj Raman, Chair, Supervising Committee, 515-294-6555, E-mail: brtgrad@iastate.edu.

Laurentian University, School of Graduate Studies and Research, School of Engineering, Sudbury, ON P3E 2C6, Canada. Offers mineral resources engineering (M Eng, MA Sc); natural resources engineering (PhD). Part-time programs available. *Faculty research:* Mining engineering, rock mechanics (tunneling, rockbursts, rock support), metallurgy (mineral processing, hydro and pyrometallurgy), simulations and remote mining, simulations and scheduling.

Louisiana State University and Agricultural and Mechanical College, Graduate School, College of Agriculture, School of Renewable Natural Resources, Baton Rouge, LA 70803. Offers fisheries (MS); forestry (MS, PhD); wildlife (MS); wildlife and fisheries science (PhD). *Faculty:* 33 full-time (5 women). *Students:* 65 full-time (16 women), 8 part-time (3 women); includes 2 Hispanic/Latino, 22 international. Average age 29. 28 applicants, 39% accepted, 8 enrolled. In 2010, 17 master's, 4 doctorates awarded. *Degree requirements:* For master's, thesis; for doctorate, thesis/dissertation. *Entrance requirements:* For master's, GRE General Test, minimum GPA of 3.0; for doctorate, GRE General Test, MS, minimum GPA of 3.0. Additional exam requirements/recommendations for international students: Required—TOEFL (minimum score 550 paper-based; 213 computer-based; 79 iBT), IELTS (minimum score 6.5). *Application deadline:* For fall admission, 1/25 priority date for domestic students, 5/15 for international students; for spring admission, 10/15 for international students. Applications are processed on a rolling basis. Application fee: $50 ($70 for international students). Electronic applications accepted. *Financial support:* In 2010–11, 69 students received support, including 7 fellowships (averaging $36,514 per year), 60 research assistantships with partial tuition reimbursements available (averaging $19,070 per year); Federal Work-Study, institutionally sponsored loans, scholarships/grants, health care benefits, tuition waivers (full and partial), and unspecified assistantships also available. Financial award application deadline: 4/15; financial award applicants required to submit FAFSA. *Faculty research:* Forest biology and management, aquaculture, fisheries biology and ecology, upland and wetlands wildlife. Total annual research expenditures: $3,080. *Unit head:* Dr. Allen Rutherford, Director, 225-578-4131, Fax: 225-578-4227, E-mail: druther@lsu.edu. *Application contact:* Dr. William Kelso, Coordinator of Graduate Studies, 225-578-4176, Fax: 225-578-4227, E-mail: wkelso@lsu.edu.

Marylhurst University, Department of Business Administration, Marylhurst, OR 97036-0261. Offers finance (MBA); general management (MBA); government policy and administration (MBA); green development (MBA); health care management (MBA); marketing (MBA); natural and organic resources (MBA); nonprofit management (MBA); organizational behavior (MBA); real estate (MBA); renewable energy (MBA); sustainable business (MBA). Part-time and evening/weekend programs available. Postbaccalaureate distance learning degree programs offered (no on-campus study). *Faculty:* 3 full-time (0 women), 36 part-time/adjunct (6 women). *Students:* 27 full-time (13 women), 727 part-time (373 women); includes 167 minority (47 Black or African American, non-Hispanic/Latino; 6 American Indian or Alaska Native, non-Hispanic/Latino; 36 Asian, non-Hispanic/Latino; 51 Hispanic/Latino; 6 Native Hawaiian or other Pacific Islander, non-Hispanic/Latino; 21 Two or more races, non-Hispanic/Latino), 7 international. Average age 38. 262 applicants, 91% accepted, 194 enrolled. In 2010, 289 master's awarded. *Degree requirements:* For master's, comprehensive exam, capstone course. *Entrance requirements:* For master's, GMAT (if GPA less than 3.0 and fewer than 5 years of work experience), interview, resume, 2 letters of recommendation. Additional exam requirements/recommendations for international students: Recommended—TOEFL (minimum score 550 paper-based; 213 computer-based; 80 iBT). *Application deadline:* For fall admission, 9/11 priority date for domestic and international students; for winter admission, 12/15 priority date for domestic and international students; for spring admission, 3/15 priority date for domestic students, 3/17 priority date for international students. Applications are processed on a rolling basis. Application fee: $50. Electronic applications accepted. *Expenses:* Tuition: Full-time $13,932; part-time $516 per credit. Tuition and fees vary according to course load and program. *Financial support:* Scholarships/grants available. Support available to part-time students. Financial award applicants required to submit FAFSA. *Unit head:* Bob Hanks, Director of Business and Real Estate Programs, 503-636-8141, Fax: 503-697-5597, E-mail: mba@marylhurst.edu. *Application contact:* Maruska Lynch, Graduate Admissions Specialist, 800-634-9982 Ext. 6322, Fax: 503-699-6320, E-mail: admissions@marylhurst.edu.

McGill University, Faculty of Graduate and Postdoctoral Studies, Faculty of Agricultural and Environmental Sciences, Department of Natural Resource Sciences, Montréal, QC H3A 2T5, Canada. Offers entomology (M Sc, PhD); environmental assessment (M Sc); forest science (M Sc, PhD); microbiology (M Sc, PhD); micrometeorology (M Sc, PhD); neotropical environment (M Sc, PhD); soil science (M Sc, PhD); wildlife biology (M Sc, PhD).

Michigan State University, The Graduate School, College of Agriculture and Natural Resources, Department of Community, Agriculture, Recreation, and Resource Studies, East Lansing, MI 48824. Offers MS, PhD. *Entrance requirements:* Additional exam requirements/recommendations for international students: Required—TOEFL. Electronic applications accepted.

Missouri State University, Graduate College, College of Natural and Applied Sciences, Department of Geography, Geology, and Planning, Springfield, MO 65897. Offers geospatial sciences (MS); natural and applied science (MNAS), including geography, geology and planning; secondary education (MS Ed), including earth science, geography. Part-time and evening/weekend programs available. *Degree requirements:* For master's, comprehensive exam, thesis (for some programs). *Entrance requirements:* For master's, GRE General Test (MS, MNAS), minimum undergraduate GPA of 3.0 (MS, MNAS), 9-12 teacher certification (MS Ed). Additional exam requirements/recommendations for international students: Required—TOEFL (minimum score 550 paper-based; 213 computer-based; 79 iBT). Electronic applications accepted. *Expenses:* Tuition, state resident: full-time $3348; part-time $186 per credit hour. Tuition, nonresident: full-time $6696; part-time $372 per credit hour. Required fees: $238 per semester. Tuition and fees vary according to course level, course load and program. *Faculty research:* Stratigraphy and ancient meteorite impacts, environmental geochemistry of karst, hyper-spectral image processing, water quality, small town planning.

Montana State University, College of Graduate Studies, College of Agriculture, Department of Land Resources and Environmental Sciences, Bozeman, MT 59717. Offers land rehabilitation (interdisciplinary) (MS); land resources and environmental sciences (MS), including land rehabilitation (interdisciplinary), land resources and environmental sciences. Part-time programs available. *Faculty:* 24 full-time (6 women), 1 part-time/adjunct (0 women). *Students:* 7 full-time (3 women), 38 part-time (14 women); includes 3 minority (2 American Indian or Alaska Native,

non-Hispanic/Latino; 1 Hispanic/Latino), 2 international. Average age 32. 21 applicants, 24% accepted, 4 enrolled. In 2010, 7 master's awarded. *Degree requirements:* For master's, comprehensive exam. *Entrance requirements:* For master's, GRE General Test. Additional exam requirements/recommendations for international students: Required—TOEFL (minimum score 550 paper-based; 213 computer-based). *Application deadline:* For fall admission, 7/15 priority date for domestic students, 5/15 priority date for international students; for spring admission, 12/1 priority date for domestic students, 10/1 priority date for international students. Applications are processed on a rolling basis. Application fee: $30. Electronic applications accepted. *Expenses:* Tuition, state resident: full-time $5553.90. Tuition, nonresident: full-time $14,646. Required fees: $1233. *Financial support:* In 2010–11, 5 fellowships with partial tuition reimbursements (averaging $25,000 per year), 38 research assistantships with full and partial tuition reimbursements (averaging $17,000 per year), 15 teaching assistantships with full and partial tuition reimbursements (averaging $2,000 per year) were awarded; scholarships/grants, health care benefits, tuition waivers (partial), and unspecified assistantships also available. Financial award application deadline: 3/1; financial award applicants required to submit FAFSA. *Faculty research:* Soil nutrient management and plant nutrition, isotope biogeochemistry of soils, biodegradation of hydrocarbons in soils and natural waters, remote sensing, GIS systems, managed and natural ecosystems, microbial and metabolic diversity in geothermally heated soils, integrated management of weeds, diversified cropping systems, insect behavior and ecology, river ecology, microbial biogeochemistry, weed ecology. Total annual research expenditures: $5.5 million. *Unit head:* Dr. Tracy M. Sterling, Head, 406-994-7060, Fax: 406-994-3933, E-mail: tracy.sterling@montana.edu. *Application contact:* Dr. Carl A. Fox, Vice Provost for Graduate Education, 406-994-4145, Fax: 406-994-7433, E-mail: gradstudy@montana.edu.

North Carolina State University, Graduate School, College of Natural Resources, Department of Parks, Recreation and Tourism Management, Raleigh, NC 27695. Offers natural resource management (MPRTM, MS); park and recreation management (MPRTM, MS); parks, recreation and tourism management (PhD); recreational sport management (MPRTM, MS); spatial information science (MPRTM, MS); tourism policy and development (MPRTM, MS). *Degree requirements:* For master's, thesis (for some programs); for doctorate, thesis/dissertation. *Entrance requirements:* For master's and doctorate, GRE General Test. Additional exam requirements/recommendations for international students: Required—TOEFL. Electronic applications accepted. *Faculty research:* Tourism policy and development, spatial information systems, natural resource management, recreational sports management, park and recreation management.

North Carolina State University, Graduate School, College of Natural Resources and College of Agriculture and Life Sciences, Program in Natural Resources, Raleigh, NC 27695. Offers MNR, MS. *Degree requirements:* For master's, thesis optional. *Entrance requirements:* For master's, GRE. Electronic applications accepted.

North Dakota State University, College of Graduate and Interdisciplinary Studies, College of Agriculture, Food Systems, and Natural Resources, Department of Agribusiness and Applied Economics, Fargo, ND 58108. Offers agribusiness and applied economics (MS); international agribusiness (MS); natural resource management (MS). Part-time programs available. *Faculty:* 16 full-time (3 women), 5 part-time/adjunct (1 woman). *Students:* 10 full-time (5 women), 4 part-time (0 women); includes 3 Black or African American, non-Hispanic/Latino; 4 Asian, non-Hispanic/Latino; 1 Hispanic/Latino. Average age 24. 28 applicants, 68% accepted, 12 enrolled. In 2010, 13 master's awarded. *Degree requirements:* For master's, thesis. *Entrance requirements:* For master's, minimum GPA of 3.0. Additional exam requirements/recommendations for international students: Required—TOEFL (minimum score 525 paper-based; 225 computer-based; 71 iBT). *Application deadline:* For fall admission, 2/1 priority date for domestic students, 3/1 priority date for international students. Applications are processed on a rolling basis. Application fee: $45 ($60 for international students). Electronic applications accepted. *Financial support:* In 2010–11, 8 research assistantships with tuition reimbursements (averaging $14,520 per year) were awarded; Federal Work-Study and institutionally sponsored loans also available. Financial award application deadline: 4/15. *Faculty research:* Agribusiness, transportation, marketing, microeconomics, trade. Total annual research expenditures: $1 million. *Unit head:* Dr. Thomas I. Wahl, Chair, 701-231-7470, Fax: 701-231-7400. *Application contact:* Dr. Thomas I. Wahl, Chair, 701-231-7470, Fax: 701-231-7400.

North Dakota State University, College of Graduate and Interdisciplinary Studies, College of Agriculture, Food Systems, and Natural Resources, Department of Animal and Range Sciences, Fargo, ND 58108. Offers animal science (MS, PhD); natural resource management (MS, PhD); range sciences (MS, PhD). *Students:* 19 full-time (14 women), 7 part-time (4 women); includes 1 American Indian or Alaska Native, non-Hispanic/Latino; 1 Asian, non-Hispanic/Latino. Average age 25. 13 applicants, 62% accepted. In 2010, 17 master's, 2 doctorates awarded. *Degree requirements:* For master's, thesis; for doctorate, comprehensive exam, thesis/dissertation. *Entrance requirements:* For master's and doctorate, GRE General Test. Additional exam requirements/recommendations for international students: Required—TOEFL (minimum score 71 iBT). *Application deadline:* Applications are processed on a rolling basis. Application fee: $45 ($60 for international students). *Financial support:* In 2010–11, 1 fellowship with tuition reimbursement (averaging $18,000 per year), 29 research assistantships with tuition reimbursements (averaging $13,000 per year) were awarded; teaching assistantships, Federal Work-Study, institutionally sponsored loans, and tuition waivers (partial) also available. Financial award application deadline: 3/15. *Faculty research:* Reproduction, nutrition, meat and muscle biology, breeding/genetics. Total annual research expenditures: $1.5 million. *Unit head:* Dr. David Buchanan, Chair, 701-231-7643, Fax: 701-231-7590, E-mail: david.buchanan@ndsu.edu. *Application contact:* Dr. David Buchanan, Chair, 701-231-7643, Fax: 701-231-7590, E-mail: david.buchanan@ndsu.edu.

North Dakota State University, College of Graduate and Interdisciplinary Studies, College of Agriculture, Food Systems, and Natural Resources, Department of Entomology, Fargo, ND 58108. Offers entomology (MS, PhD); environment and conservation science (MS, PhD); natural resource management (MS, PhD). Part-time programs available. *Faculty:* 7 full-time (3 women), 8 part-time/adjunct (0 women). *Students:* 6 full-time (3 women), 5 part-time (2 women), 3 international. Average age 34. 2 applicants, 50% accepted, 0 enrolled. In 2010, 1 master's, 1 doctorate awarded. *Degree requirements:* For master's, thesis; for doctorate, comprehensive exam, thesis/dissertation. *Entrance requirements:* For master's and doctorate, minimum GPA of 3.0. Additional exam requirements/recommendations for international students: Required—TOEFL (minimum score 550 paper-based; 213 computer-based; 79 iBT). *Application deadline:* Applications are processed on a rolling basis. Application fee: $45 ($60 for international students). Electronic applications accepted. *Financial support:* In 2010–11, 11 research assistantships with full tuition reimbursements (averaging $13,800 per year) were awarded; Federal Work-Study, institutionally sponsored loans, and unspecified assistantships also available. Financial award application deadline: 4/15. *Faculty research:* Insect systematics, conservation biology, integrated pest management, insect behavior, insect biology. *Unit head:* Dr. David A. Rider, Chair, 701-231-7908, Fax: 701-231-8557, E-mail: david.rider@ndsu.edu. *Application contact:* Dr. David A. Rider, Chair, 701-231-7908, Fax: 701-231-8557, E-mail: david.rider@ndsu.edu.

North Dakota State University, College of Graduate and Interdisciplinary Studies, College of Agriculture, Food Systems, and Natural Resources, Department of Plant Sciences, Fargo, ND 58108. Offers crop and weed sciences (MS); horticulture (MS); natural resource management (MS); plant sciences (PhD). Part-time programs available. *Faculty:* 36 full-time (3 women), 23 part-time/adjunct (3 women). *Students:* 44 full-time (14 women), 16 part-time (7 women); includes 4 Hispanic/Latino, 19 international. Average age 26. 44 applicants, 45% accepted. In 2010, 11 master's, 6 doctorates awarded. *Degree requirements:* For master's, thesis; for

doctorate, thesis/dissertation. *Entrance requirements:* Additional exam requirements/recommendations for international students: Required—TOEFL (minimum score 525 paper-based; 197 computer-based; 71 iBT). *Application deadline:* Applications are processed on a rolling basis. Application fee: $45 ($60 for international students). Electronic applications accepted. *Financial support:* In 2010–11, 2 fellowships (averaging $19,950 per year), 64 research assistantships were awarded; teaching assistantships, Federal Work-Study and institutionally sponsored loans also available. Financial award application deadline: 4/15. *Faculty research:* Biotechnology, weed control science, plant breeding, plant genetics, crop physiology. Total annual research expenditures: $880,000. *Unit head:* Dr. Al Schneiter, Head, 701-231-7971, Fax: 701-231-8474, E-mail: albert.schneiter@ndsu.edu. *Application contact:* Dr. Al Schneiter, Head, 701-231-7971, Fax: 701-231-8474, E-mail: albert.schneiter@ndsu.edu.

North Dakota State University, College of Graduate and Interdisciplinary Studies, College of Agriculture, Food Systems, and Natural Resources, Department of Soil Science, Fargo, ND 58108. Offers environmental and conservation science (PhD); environmental conservation science (MS); natural resource management (MS, PhD); soil sciences (MS, PhD). Part-time programs available. *Faculty:* 8 full-time (1 woman), 6 part-time/adjunct (0 women). *Students:* 7 full-time (5 women), 1 part-time (0 women). Average age 23. 3 applicants, 67% accepted, 2 enrolled. In 2010, 2 master's, 1 doctorate awarded. *Degree requirements:* For master's, comprehensive exam, thesis, classroom teaching; for doctorate, comprehensive exam, thesis/dissertation, classroom teaching. *Entrance requirements:* Additional exam requirements/recommendations for international students: Required—TOEFL (minimum score 525 paper-based; 193 computer-based; 71 iBT). *Application deadline:* Applications are processed on a rolling basis. Application fee: $45 ($60 for international students). Electronic applications accepted. *Financial support:* In 2010–11, 7 research assistantships with full tuition reimbursements (averaging $14,300 per year) were awarded; fellowships, Federal Work-Study, institutionally sponsored loans, and scholarships/grants also available. Financial award application deadline: 3/15. *Faculty research:* Microclimate, nitrogen management, landscape studies, water quality, soil management. *Unit head:* Dr. Donald Kirby, Interim Chair, 701-231-8901, Fax: 701-231-7861. *Application contact:* Dr. Donald Kirby, Interim Chair, 701-231-8901, Fax: 701-231-7861.

North Dakota State University, College of Graduate and Interdisciplinary Studies, College of Science and Mathematics, Department of Biological Sciences, Fargo, ND 58108. Offers biology (MS); botany (MS, PhD); cellular and molecular biology (PhD); environmental and conservation sciences (MS, PhD); genomics (PhD); natural resources management (MS, PhD); zoology (MS, PhD). *Students:* 18 full-time (8 women), 5 part-time (3 women); includes 2 American Indian or Alaska Native, non-Hispanic/Latino, 2 international. 17 applicants, 35% accepted. In 2010, 12 master's, 9 doctorates awarded. *Degree requirements:* For master's, thesis; for doctorate, thesis/dissertation. *Entrance requirements:* For master's and doctorate, GRE General Test. Additional exam requirements/recommendations for international students: Required—TOEFL. *Application deadline:* For fall admission, 3/15 priority date for domestic students; for spring admission, 10/30 priority date for domestic students. Applications are processed on a rolling basis. Application fee: $45 ($60 for international students). Electronic applications accepted. *Financial support:* Fellowships with full tuition reimbursements, research assistantships with full tuition reimbursements, teaching assistantships with full tuition reimbursements, career-related internships or fieldwork, Federal Work-Study, institutionally sponsored loans, scholarships/grants, tuition waivers (full), and unspecified assistantships available. Support available to part-time students. Financial award application deadline: 4/15; financial award applicants required to submit FAFSA. *Faculty research:* Comparative endocrinology, physiology, behavioral ecology, plant cell biology, aquatic biology. Total annual research expenditures: $675,000. *Unit head:* Dr. Marinus L. Otte, Head, 701-231-7087, E-mail: marinus.otte@ndsu.edu. *Application contact:* Dr. Marinus L. Otte, Head, 701-231-7087, E-mail: marinus.otte@ndsu.edu.

North Dakota State University, College of Graduate and Interdisciplinary Studies, Interdisciplinary Program in Natural Resources Management, Fargo, ND 58108. Offers MS, PhD. Part-time programs available. *Students:* 41 full-time (15 women), 15 part-time (5 women); includes 1 Black or African American, non-Hispanic/Latino, 5 international. 25 applicants, 64% accepted, 14 enrolled. In 2010, 9 master's, 2 doctorates awarded. *Degree requirements:* For master's, thesis; for doctorate, comprehensive exam, thesis/dissertation. *Entrance requirements:* Additional exam requirements/recommendations for international students: Required—TOEFL (minimum score 525 paper-based; 197 computer-based; 71 iBT). *Application deadline:* Applications are processed on a rolling basis. Application fee: $45 ($60 for international students). Electronic applications accepted. *Financial support:* In 2010–11, 25 students received support; research assistantships with full tuition reimbursements available, teaching assistantships with full tuition reimbursements available available. Support available to part-time students. Financial award application deadline: 3/15. *Faculty research:* Natural resources economics, wetlands issues, wildlife, prairie ecology, range management. Total annual research expenditures: $500,000. *Unit head:* Dr. Carolyn E. Grygiel, Director, 701-231-8180, Fax: 701-231-7590, E-mail: carolyn.grygiel@ndsu.edu. *Application contact:* Dr. Carolyn E. Grygiel, Director, 701-231-8180, Fax: 701-231-7590, E-mail: carolyn.grygiel@ndsu.edu.

The Ohio State University, Graduate School, College of Food, Agricultural, and Environmental Sciences, School of Environment and Natural Resources, Columbus, OH 43210. Offers MS, PhD. *Students:* 70 full-time (39 women), 18 part-time (9 women); includes 2 Asian, non-Hispanic/Latino; 4 Hispanic/Latino; 1 Two or more races, non-Hispanic/Latino, 11 international. Average age 28. In 2010, 12 master's, 4 doctorates awarded. *Degree requirements:* For master's, thesis; for doctorate, thesis/dissertation. *Entrance requirements:* For master's and doctorate, GRE. Additional exam requirements/recommendations for international students: Required—TOEFL. *Application deadline:* Applications are processed on a rolling basis. Application fee: $40 ($50 for international students). Electronic applications accepted. *Expenses:* Tuition, state resident: full-time $10,605. Tuition, nonresident: full-time $26,535. Tuition and fees vary according to course load and program. *Unit head:* Ronald Hendrick, Director, 614-292-8522, E-mail: hendrick.15@osu.edu. *Application contact:* Graduate Admissions, 614-292-9444, Fax: 614-292-3895, E-mail: domestic.grad@osu.edu.

Oklahoma State University, College of Agricultural Science and Natural Resources, Stillwater, OK 74078. Offers M Ag, MS, PhD. Postbaccalaureate distance learning degree programs offered. *Faculty:* 244 full-time (57 women), 18 part-time/adjunct (2 women). *Students:* 175 full-time (86 women), 317 part-time (150 women); includes 7 Black or African American, non-Hispanic/Latino; 18 American Indian or Alaska Native, non-Hispanic/Latino; 6 Asian, non-Hispanic/Latino; 7 Hispanic/Latino, 196 international. Average age 29. 516 applicants, 35% accepted, 104 enrolled. In 2010, 103 master's, 32 doctorates awarded. *Degree requirements:* For master's, thesis (for some programs); for doctorate, comprehensive exam, thesis/dissertation. *Entrance requirements:* For master's and doctorate, GRE or GMAT. Additional exam requirements/recommendations for international students: Required—TOEFL (minimum score 550 paper-based; 79 iBT). *Application deadline:* For fall admission, 3/1 priority date for international students; for spring admission, 8/1 priority date for international students. Applications are processed on a rolling basis. Application fee: $40 ($75 for international students). Electronic applications accepted. *Expenses:* Tuition, state resident: full-time $3716; part-time $154.85 per credit hour. Tuition, nonresident: full-time $14,892; part-time $621 per credit hour. Required fees: $2044; $85.20 per credit hour. One-time fee: $50. Tuition and fees vary according to course load and campus/location. *Financial support:* In 2010–11, 299 research assistantships (averaging $15,727 per year), 20 teaching assistantships (averaging $15,655 per year) were awarded; fellowships, career-related internships or fieldwork, Federal Work-Study, scholarships/grants, health care benefits, tuition waivers (partial), and unspecified assistantships also available. Support available to part-time students. Financial award application deadline: 3/1; financial award applicants required to submit FAFSA. *Unit head:* Dr. Robert E. Whitson, Dean, 405-744-5398, Fax: 405-744-2480. *Application contact:* Dr. Gordon Emslie, Dean, 405-744-6368, Fax: 405-744-0355, E-mail: grad-i@okstate.edu.

Purdue University, Graduate School, College of Agriculture, Department of Forestry and Natural Resources, West Lafayette, IN 47907. Offers aquaculture, fisheries, aquatic science (MSF); aquaculture, fisheries, aquatic sciences (MS, PhD); forest biology (MS, MSF, PhD); natural resources and environmental policy (MS, MSF); natural resources environmental policy (PhD); quantitative resource analysis (MS, MSF, PhD); wildlife science (MS, MSF, PhD); wood science and technology (MS, MSF, PhD). *Degree requirements:* For master's, thesis; for doctorate, thesis/dissertation. *Entrance requirements:* For master's and doctorate, GRE General Test, minimum B+ average in undergraduate course work. Additional exam requirements/recommendations for international students: Required—TOEFL. Electronic applications accepted. *Faculty research:* Wildlife management, forest management, forest ecology, forest soils, limnology.

San Francisco State University, Division of Graduate Studies, College of Behavioral and Social Sciences, Department of Geography and Human Environmental Studies, San Francisco, CA 94132-1722. Offers geographic information science (MS); geography (MA), including resource management and environmental planning. *Unit head:* Dr. Jerry Davis, Chair, 415-338-2049, E-mail: jerry@sfsu.edu. *Application contact:* Nancy Wilkinson, Graduate Coordinator, 415-338-2049.

State University of New York College of Environmental Science and Forestry, Department of Environmental Resources Engineering, Syracuse, NY 13210-2779. Offers ecological engineering (MS, PhD); environmental and resources engineering (MPS, MS, PhD); environmental management (MPS); geospatial information science and engineering (MS, PhD); mapping sciences (MPS); water resources engineering (MS, PhD). *Degree requirements:* For master's, thesis (for some programs); for doctorate, comprehensive exam, thesis/dissertation. *Entrance requirements:* For master's and doctorate, GRE General Test, minimum GPA of 3.0. Additional exam requirements/recommendations for international students: Required—TOEFL (minimum score 550 paper-based; 213 computer-based; 80 iBT), IELTS (minimum score 6). *Expenses:* Tuition, state resident: full-time $8370; part-time $349 per credit hour. Tuition, nonresident: full-time $13,780. Required fees: $30.30 per credit hour. $20 per year. *Faculty research:* Forest engineering, paper science and engineering, wood products engineering.

State University of New York College of Environmental Science and Forestry, Department of Forest and Natural Resources Management, Syracuse, NY 13210-2779. Offers ecology and ecosystems (MPS, MS, PhD); economics, governance and human dimensions (MPS, MS, PhD); environmental and natural resource policy (PhD); forest resources management (MF); monitoring, analysis and modeling (MPS, MS, PhD); natural resources management (MPS, MS, PhD). *Accreditation:* SAF. *Degree requirements:* For master's, thesis (for some programs); for doctorate, comprehensive exam, thesis/dissertation. *Entrance requirements:* For master's and doctorate, GRE General Test, minimum GPA of 3.0. Additional exam requirements/recommendations for international students: Required—TOEFL (minimum score 550 paper-based; 213 computer-based; 80 iBT), IELTS (minimum score 6). *Expenses:* Tuition, state resident: full-time $8370; part-time $349 per credit hour. Tuition, nonresident: full-time $13,780. Required fees: $30.30 per credit hour. $20 per year. *Faculty research:* Silviculture recreation management, tree improvement, operations management, economics.

State University of New York College of Environmental Science and Forestry, Department of Sustainable Construction Management and Engineering, Syracuse, NY 13210-2779. Offers construction management (MPS, MS, PhD); engineered wood products and structures (MPS, MS, PhD); tropical timbers wood science and technology (MPS, MS, PhD); wood anatomy and ultrastructure (MPS, MS, PhD); wood treatments (MPS, MS, PhD). *Degree requirements:* For master's, thesis (for some programs); for doctorate, comprehensive exam, thesis/dissertation. *Entrance requirements:* For master's and doctorate, GRE General Test, minimum GPA of 3.0. Additional exam requirements/recommendations for international students: Required—TOEFL (minimum score 550 paper-based; 213 computer-based; 80 iBT), IELTS (minimum score 6). *Expenses:* Tuition, state resident: full-time $8370; part-time $349 per credit hour. Tuition, nonresident: full-time $13,780. Required fees: $30.30 per credit hour. $20 per year.

Texas A&M University, College of Agriculture and Life Sciences, Department of Ecosystem Science and Management, College Station, TX 77843. Offers forestry (MS, PhD); rangeland ecology and management (M Agr, MS, PhD). Part-time programs available. *Faculty:* 24. *Students:* 59 full-time (31 women), 28 part-time (12 women); includes 16 minority (2 Black or African American, non-Hispanic/Latino; 1 Asian, non-Hispanic/Latino; 13 Hispanic/Latino), 12 international. Average age 27. In 2010, 9 master's, 3 doctorates awarded. Terminal master's awarded for partial completion of doctoral program. *Degree requirements:* For master's, thesis (for some programs); for doctorate, thesis/dissertation. *Entrance requirements:* For master's and doctorate, GRE General Test. Additional exam requirements/recommendations for international students: Required—TOEFL. *Application deadline:* For fall admission, 3/1 priority date for domestic students; for spring admission, 11/1 priority date for domestic students. Applications are processed on a rolling basis. Application fee: $50 ($75 for international students). Electronic applications accepted. *Financial support:* In 2010–11, fellowships with partial tuition reimbursements (averaging $15,000 per year), research assistantships with partial tuition reimbursements (averaging $15,000 per year), teaching assistantships with partial tuition reimbursements (averaging $15,000 per year) were awarded; career-related internships or fieldwork and institutionally sponsored loans also available. Support available to part-time students. Financial award application deadline: 3/1; financial award applicants required to submit FAFSA. *Faculty research:* Expert systems, geographic information systems, economics, biology, genetics. *Unit head:* Dr. Steve Whisenant, Professor and Head, 979-845-5000, Fax: 979-845-6049, E-mail: s-whisenant@tamu.edu. *Application contact:* Dr. Carol Loopstra, Associate Professor, 979-862-2200, Fax: 979-845-6049, E-mail: c-loopstra@tamu.edu.

Texas A&M University, College of Agriculture and Life Sciences, Department of Recreation, Park and Tourism Sciences, College Station, TX 77843. Offers natural resources development (M Agr); recreation resources development (M Agr); recreation, park, and tourism sciences (MS, PhD). *Faculty:* 16. *Students:* 64 full-time (37 women), 8 part-time (all women); includes 10 minority (5 Black or African American, non-Hispanic/Latino; 1 American Indian or Alaska Native, non-Hispanic/Latino; 4 Hispanic/Latino), 25 international. Average age 28. In 2010, 6 master's, 7 doctorates awarded. *Degree requirements:* For master's, thesis (for some programs), internship and professional paper (M Agr); for doctorate, thesis/dissertation. *Entrance requirements:* For master's and doctorate, GRE General Test. Additional exam requirements/recommendations for international students: Required—TOEFL. *Application deadline:* For fall admission, 4/15 priority date for domestic students; for spring admission, 10/15 priority date for domestic students. Applications are processed on a rolling basis. Application fee: $50 ($75 for international students). Electronic applications accepted. *Financial support:* Fellowships, research assistantships, teaching assistantships, career-related internships or fieldwork, institutionally sponsored loans, and scholarships/grants available. Financial award application deadline: 4/15; financial award applicants required to submit FAFSA. *Faculty research:* Administration and tourism, outdoor recreation, commercial recreation, environmental law, system planning. *Unit head:* Dr. Gary Ellis, Head, 979-845-7324. *Application contact:* Dr. Gary Ellis, Head, 979-845-7324.

Texas Tech University, Graduate School, College of Agricultural Sciences and Natural Resources, Department of Natural Resources Management, Lubbock, TX 79409. Offers fisheries science (MS, PhD); range science (MS, PhD); wildlife science (MS, PhD); wildlife, aquatic, and wildlands science and management (MS, PhD). Part-time programs available. *Faculty:* 9 full-time (0 women), 1 part-time/adjunct (0 women). *Students:* 47 full-time (14 women), 3 part-time (1 woman); includes 1 American Indian or Alaska Native, non-Hispanic/Latino; 1

Natural Resources

Texas Tech University (continued)
Hispanic/Latino; 2 Two or more races, non-Hispanic/Latino, 7 international. Average age 27. 23 applicants, 61% accepted, 12 enrolled. In 2010, 5 master's, 2 doctorates awarded. *Degree requirements:* For master's, thesis; for doctorate, thesis/dissertation. *Entrance requirements:* For master's and doctorate, GRE General Test, formal approval from departmental committee. Additional exam requirements/recommendations for international students: Required—TOEFL (minimum score 550 paper-based; 213 computer-based; 79 iBT). *Application deadline:* For fall admission, 6/1 priority date for domestic students, 1/15 priority date for international students; for spring admission, 9/1 priority date for domestic students, 6/15 priority date for international students. Applications are processed on a rolling basis. Application fee: $50 ($75 for international students). Electronic applications accepted. *Expenses:* Tuition, state resident: full-time $5495.76; part-time $228.99 per credit hour. Tuition, nonresident: full-time $12,936; part-time $538.99 per credit hour. Required fees: $2674; $36 per credit hour. $905 per semester. *Financial support:* In 2010–11, 43 students received support, including 19 research assistantships with partial tuition reimbursements available (averaging $6,023 per year), 2 teaching assistantships with partial tuition reimbursements available (averaging $4,994 per year). Financial award application deadline: 4/15; financial award applicants required to submit FAFSA. *Faculty research:* Use of fire on range lands, big game, upland game, and waterfowl; playa lakes in the southern Great Plains; conservation biology; fish ecology and physiology. Total annual research expenditures: $921,668. *Unit head:* Dr. Mark Wallace, Interim Chairman, 806-742-2841, Fax: 806-742-2280, E-mail: mark.wallace@ttu.edu. *Application contact:* Renee Dillon, Sr. Business Assistant, 806-742-2841, E-mail: renee.dillon@ttu.edu.

Universidad Metropolitana, School of Environmental Affairs, Program in Environmental Management, San Juan, PR 00928-1150. Offers MSEM. Part-time programs available. *Degree requirements:* For master's, thesis. Electronic applications accepted.

Universidad Nacional Pedro Henriquez Urena, Graduate School, Santo Domingo, Dominican Republic. Offers agricultural diversity (MS), including horticultural/fruit production, tropical animal production; conservation of monuments and cultural assets (M Arch); ecology and environment (MS); environmental engineering (MEE); international relations (MA); natural resource management (MS); political science (MA); project optimization (MPM); project feasibility (MPM); project management (MPM); sanitation engineering (ME); science for teachers (MS); tropical Caribbean architecture (M Arch).

Université du Québec à Montréal, Graduate Programs, Program in Earth Sciences, Montreal, QC H3C 3P8, Canada. Offers earth sciences (M Sc); mineral resources (PhD); non-renewable resources (DESS). Part-time programs available. Terminal master's awarded for partial completion of doctoral program. *Degree requirements:* For master's, thesis (for some programs); for doctorate, thesis/dissertation. *Entrance requirements:* For master's, appropriate bachelor's degree or equivalent, proficiency in French. *Faculty research:* Economic geology, structural geology, geochemistry, Quaternary geology, isotopic geochemistry.

Université du Québec en Abitibi-Témiscamingue, Graduate Programs, Program in Environmental Sciences, Rouyn-Noranda, QC J9X 5E4, Canada. Offers biology (MS); environmental sciences (PhD); sustainable forest ecosystem management (MS).

University of Alaska Fairbanks, School of Natural Resources and Agricultural Sciences, Fairbanks, AK 99775-7140. Offers natural resource and sustainability (PhD); natural resource management (MS); natural resource management and geography (MNRM, MS). Part-time programs available. *Faculty:* 37 full-time (12 women), 5 part-time/adjunct (4 women). *Students:* 31 full-time (22 women), 24 part-time (10 women); includes 5 minority (2 American Indian or Alaska Native, non-Hispanic/Latino; 1 Hispanic/Latino; 2 Two or more races, non-Hispanic/Latino), 6 international. Average age 33. 42 applicants, 26% accepted, 8 enrolled. In 2010, 3 master's, 2 doctorates awarded. *Degree requirements:* For master's, comprehensive exam, thesis or alternative. *Entrance requirements:* For master's, GRE General Test. Additional exam requirements/recommendations for international students: Required—TOEFL (minimum score 550 paper-based; 213 computer-based). *Application deadline:* For fall admission, 6/1 for domestic students, 3/1 for international students; for spring admission, 10/15 for domestic students, 9/1 for international students. Applications are processed on a rolling basis. Application fee: $60. Electronic applications accepted. *Expenses:* Tuition, state resident: full-time $5688; part-time $316 per credit. Tuition, nonresident: full-time $11,628; part-time $646 per credit. Required fees: $289 per semester. Tuition and fees vary according to course load and reciprocity agreements. *Financial support:* In 2010–11, 17 research assistantships (averaging $11,187 per year), 4 teaching assistantships (averaging $8,943 per year) were awarded; fellowships, career-related internships or fieldwork, Federal Work-Study, scholarships/grants, health care benefits, and unspecified assistantships also available. Support available to part-time students. Financial award application deadline: 2/15; financial award applicants required to submit FAFSA. *Faculty research:* Conservation biology, soil/water conservation, land use policy and planning in the arctic and subarctic, forest ecosystem management, subarctic agricultural production. Total annual research expenditures: $5.6 million. *Unit head:* Dr. Carol E. Lewis, Dean, 907-474-7083, Fax: 907-474-6567, E-mail: fysnras@uaf.edu. *Application contact:* Veazey David, Director of Enrollment Management, 907-474-5276, Fax: 907-474-6567, E-mail: dave.veazey@alaska.edu.

University of Alberta, Faculty of Graduate Studies and Research, Department of Renewable Resources, Edmonton, AB T6G 2E1, Canada. Offers agroforestry (M Ag, M Sc, MF); conservation biology (M Sc, PhD); forest biology and management (M Sc, PhD); land reclamation and remediation (M Sc, PhD); protected areas and wildlands management (M Sc, PhD); soil science (M Ag, M Sc, PhD); water and land resources (M Ag, M Sc, PhD); wildlife ecology and management (M Sc, PhD); MBA/M Ag; MBA/MF. Part-time programs available. *Degree requirements:* For master's, thesis (for some programs); for doctorate, comprehensive exam, thesis/dissertation. *Entrance requirements:* For master's, minimum 2 years of relevant professional experiences, minimum GPA of 3.0; for doctorate, minimum GPA of 3.0. Additional exam requirements/recommendations for international students: Required—TOEFL (minimum score 550 paper-based; 213 computer-based). Electronic applications accepted. *Faculty research:* Natural and managed landscapes.

University of Alberta, Faculty of Graduate Studies and Research, Program in Business Administration, Edmonton, AB T6G 2E1, Canada. Offers international business (MBA); leisure and sport management (MBA); natural resources and energy (MBA); technology commercialization (MBA); MBA/LL B; MBA/M Ag; MBA/M Eng; MBA/MF; MBA/PhD. *Accreditation:* AACSB. Part-time and evening/weekend programs available. *Degree requirements:* For master's, thesis or alternative. *Entrance requirements:* For master's, GMAT. Additional exam requirements/recommendations for international students: Required—TOEFL (minimum score 600 paper-based; 250 computer-based). Electronic applications accepted. *Faculty research:* Natural resources and energy/management and policy/family enterprise/international business/healthcare research management.

University of Arkansas at Monticello, School of Forest Resources, Monticello, AR 71656. Offers MS. Part-time programs available. *Degree requirements:* For master's, comprehensive exam, thesis. *Entrance requirements:* For master's, GRE General Test, minimum GPA of 2.7. Additional exam requirements/recommendations for international students: Required—TOEFL (minimum score 550 paper-based; 213 computer-based). Electronic applications accepted. *Faculty research:* Geographic information systems/remote sensing, forest ecology, wildlife ecology and management.

The University of British Columbia, Program in Resource Management and Environmental Studies, Vancouver, BC, BC V6T 1Z4, Canada. Offers M Sc, MA, PhD. *Degree requirements:* For master's, thesis; for doctorate, comprehensive exam, thesis/dissertation. *Entrance requirements:* Additional exam requirements/recommendations for international students: Required—TOEFL (minimum score 600 paper-based; 250 computer-based; 100 iBT), GRE (optional). Electronic applications accepted. Tuition charges are reported in Canadian dollars. *Expenses:* Tuition, area resident: Full-time $4179 Canadian dollars. International tuition: $7344 Canadian dollars full-time. *Faculty research:* Land management, water resources, energy, environmental assessment, risk evaluation.

University of California, Berkeley, Graduate Division, Group in Energy and Resources, Berkeley, CA 94720-1500. Offers MA, MS, PhD. *Degree requirements:* For master's, project or thesis; for doctorate, one foreign language, thesis/dissertation, qualifying exam. *Entrance requirements:* For master's and doctorate, GRE General Test, minimum GPA of 3.0, 3 letters of recommendation. *Faculty research:* Technical, economic, environmental, and institutional aspects of energy conservation in residential and commercial buildings; international patterns of energy use; renewable energy sources; assessment of valuation of energy and environmental resources pricing.

University of Connecticut, Graduate School, College of Agriculture and Natural Resources, Department of Natural Resources Management and Engineering, Storrs, CT 06269. Offers MS, PhD. Terminal master's awarded for partial completion of doctoral program. *Degree requirements:* For master's, comprehensive exam. *Entrance requirements:* For master's, GRE General Test, GRE Subject Test. Additional exam requirements/recommendations for international students: Required—TOEFL (minimum score 550 paper-based; 213 computer-based). Electronic applications accepted. *Faculty research:* Forest management, forest protection, water resources, biometeorology.

University of Delaware, College of Agriculture and Natural Resources, Department of Bioresources Engineering, Newark, DE 19716. Offers MS.

University of Denver, University College, Denver, CO 80208. Offers arts and culture (MLS, Certificate), including art, literature, and culture, arts development and program management (Certificate), creative writing; environmental policy and management (MAS, Certificate), including energy and sustainability (Certificate), environmental assessment of nuclear power (Certificate), environmental health and safety (Certificate), environmental management, natural resource management (Certificate); geographic information systems (MAS, Certificate); global affairs (MLS, Certificate), including translation studies, world history and culture; healthcare leadership (MPH, Certificate), including healthcare policy, law, and ethics, medical and healthcare information technologies, strategic management of healthcare; information and communications technology (MCIS, Certificate), including database design and administration (Certificate), geographic information systems (MCIS), information security systems security (Certificate), information systems security (MCIS), project management (MCIS, MPS, Certificate), software design and administration (Certificate), software design and programming (MCIS), technology management, telecommunications technology (MCIS), Web design and development; leadership and organizations (MPS, Certificate), including human capital in organizations, philanthropic leadership, project management (MCIS, MPS, Certificate), strategic innovation and change; organizational and professional communication (MPS, Certificate), including alternative dispute resolution, organizational communication, organizational development and training, public relations and marketing; security management (MAS, Certificate), including emergency planning and response, information security (MAS), organizational security; strategic human resource management (MPS, Certificate), including global human resources (MPS), human resource management and development (MPS). Part-time and evening/weekend programs available. Postbaccalaureate distance learning degree programs offered (no on-campus study). *Faculty:* 7 full-time (2 women), 212 part-time/adjunct (83 women). *Students:* 52 full-time (19 women), 1,044 part-time (625 women); includes 196 minority (81 Black or African American, non-Hispanic/Latino; 7 American Indian or Alaska Native, non-Hispanic/Latino; 30 Asian, non-Hispanic/Latino; 66 Hispanic/Latino; 3 Native Hawaiian or other Pacific Islander, non-Hispanic/Latino; 9 Two or more races, non-Hispanic/Latino), 76 international. Average age 36. 488 applicants, 91% accepted, 339 enrolled. In 2010, 286 master's, 130 other advanced degrees awarded. *Entrance requirements:* Additional exam requirements/recommendations for international students: Required—TOEFL (minimum score 550 paper-based; 80 iBT). *Application deadline:* For fall admission, 6/22 priority date for domestic students, 6/10 priority date for international students; for winter admission, 9/15 priority date for domestic students, 9/6 priority date for international students; for spring admission, 2/3 priority date for domestic students, 12/15 priority date for international students. Applications are processed on a rolling basis. Application fee: $75. Electronic applications accepted. *Expenses:* Contact institution. *Financial support:* Applicants required to submit FAFSA. *Unit head:* Dr. James Davis, Dean, 303-871-2291, Fax: 303-871-4047, E-mail: jdavis@du.edu. *Application contact:* Information Contact, 303-871-3155, Fax: 303-871-4047, E-mail: ucolinfo@du.edu.

University of Florida, Graduate School, College of Agricultural and Life Sciences, School of Forest Resources and Conservation, Gainesville, FL 32611. Offers MFRC, MS, PhD, JD/MFRC, JD/MS, JD/PhD. Part-time and evening/weekend programs available. Postbaccalaureate distance learning degree programs offered. *Faculty:* 39 full-time (6 women), 6 part-time/adjunct (2 women). *Students:* 91 full-time (38 women), 36 part-time (20 women); includes 1 Black or African American, non-Hispanic/Latino; 1 American Indian or Alaska Native, non-Hispanic/Latino; 4 Asian, non-Hispanic/Latino; 5 Hispanic/Latino, 26 international. Average age 29. 77 applicants, 42% accepted, 29 enrolled. In 2010, 23 master's, 13 doctorates awarded. Terminal master's awarded for partial completion of doctoral program. *Degree requirements:* For master's, comprehensive exam, thesis optional, MS with thesis and non-thesis option. Project (no thesis) required for MFRC degree; for doctorate, comprehensive exam, thesis/dissertation. *Entrance requirements:* For master's, GRE General Test score at least 1000, minimum GPA of 3.0; for doctorate, GRE General Test, minimum GPA of 3.25. Additional exam requirements/recommendations for international students: Required—TOEFL (minimum score 550 paper-based; 213 computer-based; 80 iBT), IELTS (minimum score 6). *Application deadline:* For fall admission, 1/3 priority date for domestic students, 1/3 for international students; for spring admission, 8/1 for domestic and international students. Applications are processed on a rolling basis. Application fee: $30. Electronic applications accepted. *Expenses:* Tuition, state resident: full-time $10,915.92. Tuition, nonresident: full-time $28,309. *Financial support:* In 2010–11, 84 students received support, including 22 fellowships with full tuition reimbursements available, 61 research assistantships with full tuition reimbursements available (averaging $17,379 per year), 1 teaching assistantship with full tuition reimbursement available (averaging $20,431 per year); Federal Work-Study and institutionally sponsored loans also available. Support available to part-time students. Financial award application deadline: 1/3; financial award applicants required to submit FAFSA. *Faculty research:* Forest biology and ecology; natural resource economics and management; human dimensions and resource policy; tropical forestry and agroforestry; geomatics: geospatial, GIS, and Remote Sensing. Total annual research expenditures: $3.4 million. *Unit head:* Dr. Tim White, PhD, Director, 352-846-0850, Fax: 352-392-1707, E-mail: tlwhite@ufl.edu. *Application contact:* Taylor Stein, PhD, Graduate Coordinator, 352-846-0860, Fax: 352-846-1277, E-mail: tstein@ufl.edu.

University of Florida, Graduate School, School of Natural Resources and Environment, Gainesville, FL 32611. Offers interdisciplinary ecology (MS, PhD). *Students:* 101 full-time (55 women), 29 part-time (15 women); includes 2 Black or African American, non-Hispanic/Latino; 1 American Indian or Alaska Native, non-Hispanic/Latino; 4 Asian, non-Hispanic/Latino; 7 Hispanic/Latino, 38 international. 65 applicants, 34% accepted, 18 enrolled. In 2010, 12 master's, 11 doctorates awarded. *Degree requirements:* For master's, comprehensive exam, thesis; for doctorate, comprehensive exam, thesis/dissertation. *Entrance requirements:* For master's and doctorate, GRE General Test, minimum GPA of 3.0. Additional exam requirements/recommendations for international students: Required—TOEFL (minimum score 550 paper-based; 213 computer-based; 80 iBT), IELTS (minimum score 6). *Application deadline:* For fall

admission, 2/1 priority date for domestic students, 2/1 for international students. Applications are processed on a rolling basis. Application fee: $30. Electronic applications accepted. *Expenses:* Tuition, state resident: full-time $10,915.92. Tuition, nonresident: full-time $28,309. *Financial support:* In 2010–11, 96 students received support, including 27 fellowships, 50 research assistantships (averaging $12,679 per year), 19 teaching assistantships (averaging $17,101 per year). Financial award applicants required to submit FAFSA. *Faculty research:* Natural sciences, social sciences, sustainability studies, research design and methods. *Unit head:* Stephen R. Humphrey, PhD, Director and Graduate Coordinator, 352-392-9230, Fax: 352-392-9748, E-mail: humphrey@ufl.edu. *Application contact:* Stephen R. Humphrey, PhD, Director and Graduate Coordinator, 352-392-9230, Fax: 352-392-9748, E-mail: humphrey@ufl.edu.

University of Georgia, School of Forestry and Natural Resources, Athens, GA 30602. Offers MFR, MS, PhD. *Faculty:* 41 full-time (6 women), 7 part-time/adjunct (1 woman). *Students:* 145 full-time (63 women), 28 part-time (6 women); includes 1 Black or African American, non-Hispanic/Latino; 1 Asian, non-Hispanic/Latino; 1 Two or more races, non-Hispanic/Latino, 18 international. 91 applicants, 66% accepted, 46 enrolled. In 2010, 45 master's, 15 doctorates awarded. *Degree requirements:* For master's, thesis (MS); for doctorate, one foreign language, thesis/dissertation. *Entrance requirements:* For master's and doctorate, GRE General Test. *Application deadline:* For fall admission, 7/1 priority date for domestic students; for spring admission, 11/15 for domestic students. Application fee: $50. Electronic applications accepted. *Expenses:* Tuition, state resident: full-time $7200; part-time $344 per credit hour. Tuition, nonresident: full-time $21,900; part-time $944 per credit hour. Tuition and fees vary according to course load and program. *Financial support:* Fellowships, research assistantships, teaching assistantships, unspecified assistantships available. *Application contact:* Dr. Laurence Schimleck, Graduate Coordinator, 706-542-0464, Fax: 706-542-8356, E-mail: lschimlect@warnell.uga.edu.

University of Guelph, Graduate Studies, Ontario Agricultural College, Department of Land Resource Science, Guelph, ON N1G 2W1, Canada. Offers atmospheric science (M Sc, PhD); environmental and agricultural earth sciences (M Sc, PhD); land resources management (M Sc, PhD); soil science (M Sc, PhD). Part-time programs available. *Degree requirements:* For master's, thesis (for some programs), research project (non-thesis track); for doctorate, comprehensive exam, thesis/dissertation. *Entrance requirements:* For master's, minimum B-average during previous 2 years of course work; for doctorate, minimum B average during previous 2 years of course work. Additional exam requirements/recommendations for international students: Required—TOEFL (minimum score 550 paper-based; 213 computer-based). Electronic applications accepted. *Faculty research:* Soil science, environmental earth science, land resource management.

University of Hawaii at Manoa, Graduate Division, College of Tropical Agriculture and Human Resources, Department of Natural Resources and Environmental Management, Honolulu, HI 96822. Offers MS, PhD. Part-time programs available. *Faculty:* 31 full-time (5 women), 2 part-time/adjunct (1 woman). *Students:* 53 full-time (31 women), 19 part-time (7 women); includes 15 minority (7 Asian, non-Hispanic/Latino; 2 Hispanic/Latino; 2 Native Hawaiian or other Pacific Islander, non-Hispanic/Latino; 4 Two or more races, non-Hispanic/Latino), 21 international. Average age 32. 82 applicants, 56% accepted, 32 enrolled. In 2010, 7 master's, 5 doctorates awarded. Terminal master's awarded for partial completion of doctoral program. *Degree requirements:* For master's, thesis optional; for doctorate, comprehensive exam, thesis/dissertation. *Entrance requirements:* For master's and doctorate, GRE General Test, minimum GPA of 3.0 in last 4 semesters of course work. Additional exam requirements/recommendations for international students: Required—TOEFL (minimum score 600 paper-based; 250 computer-based; 100 iBT), IELTS (minimum score 7). *Application deadline:* For fall admission, 3/1 for domestic students, 1/15 for international students; for spring admission, 9/1 for domestic students, 8/1 for international students. Applications are processed on a rolling basis. Application fee: $60. *Financial support:* In 2010–11, 10 fellowships (averaging $1,822 per year), 22 research assistantships (averaging $19,469 per year), 4 teaching assistantships (averaging $14,820 per year) were awarded; career-related internships or fieldwork and tuition waivers (full and partial) also available. *Faculty research:* Bioeconomics, natural resource management. Total annual research expenditures: $3.1 million. *Application contact:* John Yanagida, Graduate Chair, 808-956-7530, Fax: 808-956-6539, E-mail: jyanagid@hawaii.edu.

University of Idaho, College of Graduate Studies, College of Natural Resources, Department of Conservation Social Sciences, Moscow, ID 83844-2282. Offers natural resources (MS, PhD). *Faculty:* 13 full-time. *Students:* 16 full-time, 4 part-time. Average age 27. In 2010, 5 master's awarded. *Degree requirements:* For doctorate, thesis/dissertation. *Entrance requirements:* For master's, minimum GPA of 2.8; for doctorate, minimum undergraduate GPA of 2.8, 3.0 graduate. *Application deadline:* For fall admission, 8/1 for domestic students; for spring admission, 12/15 for domestic students. Applications are processed on a rolling basis. Application fee: $60. Electronic applications accepted. *Expenses:* Tuition, nonresident: part-time $580 per credit. Required fees: $306 per credit. *Financial support:* Research assistantships, teaching assistantships available. Financial award applicants required to submit FAFSA. *Faculty research:* Parks, wilderness and protected areas policy, planning and management, recreation and tourism planning, urban and community forestry, resource-based tourism, ecotourism, human dimensions of ecosystem management. *Unit head:* Dr. Larry Young, Department Head, 208-885-7911, E-mail: css@uidaho.edu. *Application contact:* Dr. Larry Young, Department Head, 208-885-7911, E-mail: css@uidaho.edu.

University of Idaho, College of Graduate Studies, College of Natural Resources, Department of Fish and Wildlife Resources, Moscow, ID 83844-2282. Offers natural resources (MS, PhD). *Faculty:* 13 full-time, 1 part-time/adjunct. *Students:* 8 full-time, 3 part-time. Average age 28. In 2010, 7 master's awarded. *Degree requirements:* For doctorate, thesis/dissertation. *Entrance requirements:* For master's, minimum GPA of 2.8; for doctorate, minimum undergraduate GPA of 2.8, 3.0 graduate. *Application deadline:* For fall admission, 8/1 for domestic students; for spring admission, 12/15 for domestic students. Applications are processed on a rolling basis. Application fee: $60. Electronic applications accepted. *Expenses:* Tuition, nonresident: part-time $580 per credit. Required fees: $306 per credit. *Financial support:* Research assistantships, teaching assistantships available. Financial award applicants required to submit FAFSA. *Faculty research:* Waterfowl and wetland ecology, lake restoration and management, sustainable aquaculture production, riparian ecology and river restoration, wildlife ecology and management. *Unit head:* Dr. Kerry Reese, Department Head, 208-885-6434, E-mail: fish_wildlife@uidaho.edu. *Application contact:* Dr. Kerry Reese, Department Head, 208-885-6434, E-mail: fish_wildlife@uidaho.edu.

University of Idaho, College of Graduate Studies, College of Natural Resources, Program in Natural Resources, Moscow, ID 83844-2282. Offers MNR, MS, PhD. *Faculty:* 8 full-time, 1 part-time/adjunct. *Students:* 90 full-time, 60 part-time. Average age 33. In 2010, 17 master's, 9 doctorates awarded. *Application deadline:* Applications are processed on a rolling basis. Application fee: $60. Electronic applications accepted. *Expenses:* Tuition, nonresident: part-time $580 per credit. Required fees: $306 per credit. *Financial support:* Applicants required to submit FAFSA. *Unit head:* Dr. Kurt Scott Pregitzer, Dean, 208-885-8981, Fax: 208-885-5534, E-mail: cnr@uidaho.edu. *Application contact:* Dr. Kurt Scott Pregitzer, Dean, 208-885-8981, Fax: 208-885-5534, E-mail: cnr@uidaho.edu.

University of Illinois at Urbana–Champaign, Graduate College, College of Agricultural, Consumer and Environmental Sciences, Department of Natural Resources and Environmental Science, Champaign, IL 61820. Offers MS, PhD, MS/JD. Part-time programs available. Post-baccalaureate distance learning degree programs offered (no on-campus study). *Faculty:* 22 full-time (6 women), 1 part-time/adjunct (0 women). *Students:* 44 full-time (19 women), 77 part-time (32 women); includes 2 Asian, non-Hispanic/Latino; 5 Hispanic/Latino; 1 Two or more races, non-Hispanic/Latino, 18 international. 120 applicants, 43% accepted, 38 enrolled. In 2010, 27 master's, 4 doctorates awarded. *Entrance requirements:* For master's and doctorate, GRE, minimum GPA of 3.0. Additional exam requirements/recommendations for international students: Required—TOEFL (minimum score 600 paper-based; 250 computer-based). *Application deadline:* Applications are processed on a rolling basis. Application fee: $75 ($90 for international students). Electronic applications accepted. *Financial support:* In 2010–11, 7 fellowships, 60 research assistantships, 13 teaching assistantships were awarded; tuition waivers (full and partial) also available. *Unit head:* Jeffrey D. Brawn, Head, 217-244-5937, Fax: 217-244-3219, E-mail: jbrawn@illinois.edu. *Application contact:* Karen M. Claus, Secretary, 217-333-5824, Fax: 217-244-3219, E-mail: kclaus@illinois.edu.

University of Maine, Graduate School, College of Natural Sciences, Forestry, and Agriculture, Department of Forest Management and Forest Ecosystem Science, Orono, ME 04469. Offers forest resources (PhD); forestry (MF, MS). *Accreditation:* SAF (one or more programs are accredited). Part-time programs available. *Faculty:* 20 full-time (1 woman). *Students:* 39 full-time (13 women), 8 part-time (3 women), 10 international. Average age 29. 55 applicants, 36% accepted, 16 enrolled. In 2010, 10 master's, 1 doctorate awarded. *Degree requirements:* For master's, thesis; for doctorate, one foreign language, thesis/dissertation. *Entrance requirements:* For master's and doctorate, GRE General Test. Additional exam requirements/recommendations for international students: Required—TOEFL. *Application deadline:* For fall admission, 2/1 priority date for domestic students. Applications are processed on a rolling basis. Application fee: $65. Electronic applications accepted. *Expenses:* Tuition, state resident: full-time $400. Tuition, nonresident: full-time $1050. *Financial support:* In 2010–11, 28 research assistantships with tuition reimbursements (averaging $17,487 per year), 7 teaching assistantships with tuition reimbursements (averaging $12,790 per year) were awarded; career-related internships or fieldwork, Federal Work-Study, and institutionally sponsored loans also available. Financial award application deadline: 3/1. *Faculty research:* Forest economics, engineering and operations analysis, biometrics and remote sensing, timber management, wood technology. *Unit head:* Dr. Robert Wagner, Chair, 207-581-4737. *Application contact:* Scott G. Delcourt, Associate Dean of the Graduate School, 207-581-3291, Fax: 207-581-3232, E-mail: graduate@maine.edu.

University of Maine, Graduate School, College of Natural Sciences, Forestry, and Agriculture, Department of Plant, Soil, and Environmental Sciences, Orono, ME 04469. Offers biological sciences (PhD); ecology and environmental sciences (MS, PhD); forest resources (PhD); horticulture (MS); plant science (PhD); plant, soil, and environmental sciences (MS); resource utilization (MS). *Faculty:* 9 full-time (3 women), 7 part-time/adjunct (3 women). *Students:* 6 full-time (2 women), 2 part-time (1 woman), 2 international. Average age 31. 9 applicants, 22% accepted, 0 enrolled. In 2010, 2 master's awarded. *Entrance requirements:* For master's and doctorate, GRE General Test. Additional exam requirements/recommendations for international students: Required—TOEFL. *Application deadline:* Applications are processed on a rolling basis. Application fee: $65. Electronic applications accepted. *Expenses:* Tuition, state resident: full-time $400. Tuition, nonresident: full-time $1050. *Financial support:* In 2010–11, 16 research assistantships with tuition reimbursements (averaging $16,260 per year), 3 teaching assistantships with tuition reimbursements (averaging $12,790 per year) were awarded; scholarships/grants, tuition waivers (full and partial), and unspecified assistantships also available. *Unit head:* Dr. Gregory Porter, Chair, 207-581-2943, Fax: 207-581-3207. *Application contact:* Scott G. Delcourt, Associate Dean of the Graduate School, 207-581-3291, Fax: 207-581-3232, E-mail: graduate@maine.edu.

The University of Manchester, School of Materials, Manchester, United Kingdom. Offers advanced aerospace materials engineering (M Sc); advanced metallic systems (PhD); biomedical materials (M Phil, M Sc, PhD); ceramics and glass (M Phil, M Sc, PhD); composite materials (M Sc, PhD); corrosion and protection (M Phil, M Sc, PhD); materials (M Phil, PhD); metallic materials (M Phil, M Sc, PhD); nanostructural materials (M Phil, M Sc, PhD); paper science (M Phil, M Sc, PhD); polymer science and engineering (M Phil, M Sc, PhD); technical textiles (M Sc); textile design, fashion and management (M Phil, M Sc, PhD); textile science and technology (M Phil, M Sc, PhD); textiles (M Phil, PhD); textiles and fashion (M Ent).

University of Manitoba, Faculty of Graduate Studies, Clayton H. Riddell Faculty of Environment, Earth, and Resources, Natural Resources Institute, Winnipeg, MB R3T 2N2, Canada. Offers natural resources and environmental management (PhD); natural resources management (MNRM).

University of Maryland, College Park, Academic Affairs, College of Agriculture and Natural Resources, Department of Plant Science and Landscape Architecture, Natural Resource Sciences Program, College Park, MD 20742. Offers MS, PhD. *Students:* 17 full-time (10 women), 2 part-time (1 woman); includes 1 Black or African American, non-Hispanic/Latino; 3 Hispanic/Latino, 3 international. 13 applicants, 62% accepted, 6 enrolled. In 2010, 5 master's, 2 doctorates awarded. *Degree requirements:* For master's, thesis optional; for doctorate, thesis/dissertation. *Entrance requirements:* For master's, GRE General Test, minimum GPA of 3.0, 3 letters of recommendation; for doctorate, GRE General Test. *Application deadline:* For fall admission, 1/15 for domestic students, 2/1 for international students; for spring admission, 8/1 for domestic students, 6/1 for international students. Applications are processed on a rolling basis. Application fee: $75. Electronic applications accepted. *Expenses:* Tuition, area resident: Part-time $471 per credit hour. Tuition, state resident: part-time $471 per credit hour. Tuition, nonresident: part-time $1016 per credit hour. Required fees: $337 per term. *Financial support:* In 2010–11, 12 research assistantships (averaging $17,586 per year), 2 teaching assistantships (averaging $17,884 per year) were awarded; fellowships also available. *Faculty research:* Wetland soils, acid mine drainage, acid sulfate soil. *Unit head:* Dr. William Kenworthy, Chair, 301-405-6244, Fax: 301-314-9308, E-mail: wkenwort@umd.edu. *Application contact:* Dr. Charles A. Caramello, Dean of Graduate School, 301-405-0358, Fax: 301-314-9305, E-mail: ccaramel@umd.edu.

University of Michigan, School of Natural Resources and Environment, Program in Natural Resources and Environment, Ann Arbor, MI 48109. Offers aquatic sciences: research and management (MS); behavior, education and communication (MS); conservation biology (MS); conservation ecology (MS); environmental informatics (MS); environmental justice (MS); environmental policy and planning (MS); natural resources and environment (PhD); sustainable systems (MS); terrestrial ecosystems (MS); MS/AM; MS/JD; MS/MBA. *Faculty:* 42 full-time, 23 part-time/adjunct. *Students:* 450 full-time (254 women); includes 7 Black or African American, non-Hispanic/Latino; 2 American Indian or Alaska Native, non-Hispanic/Latino; 35 Asian, non-Hispanic/Latino; 13 Hispanic/Latino; 6 Two or more races, non-Hispanic/Latino, 50 international. Average age 27. 692 applicants. In 2010, 133 master's, 11 doctorates awarded. Terminal master's awarded for partial completion of doctoral program. *Degree requirements:* For master's, practicum or group project; for doctorate, comprehensive exam, thesis/dissertation, oral defense of dissertation, preliminary exam. *Entrance requirements:* For master's, GRE General Test; for doctorate, GRE General Test, master's degree. Additional exam requirements/recommendations for international students: Required—TOEFL (minimum score 560 paper-based; 220 computer-based; 84 iBT). *Application deadline:* For fall admission, 1/5 priority date for domestic and international students. Applications are processed on a rolling basis. Application fee: $65 ($75 for international students). Electronic applications accepted. *Expenses:* Tuition, state resident: full-time $17,784; part-time $1116 per credit hour. Tuition, nonresident: full-time $35,944; part-time $2125 per credit hour. International tuition: $35,994 full-time. Required fees: $95 per semester. Tuition and fees vary according to course load, degree level and program. *Financial support:* Fellowships with tuition reimbursements, research assistantships with tuition reimbursements, teaching assistantships with tuition reimbursements, career-related internships or fieldwork, Federal Work-Study, institutionally sponsored loans, scholarships/grants, health care benefits, and unspecified assistantships available. Support available to part-time students. Financial award application deadline: 1/5; financial award applicants required

Natural Resources

University of Michigan (continued)
to submit FAFSA. *Faculty research:* Stream ecology, plant-insect interactions, fish biology, resource control and reproductive success, remote sensing, conservation ecology. *Application contact:* Graduate Admissions Team, 734-764-6453, Fax: 734-936-2195, E-mail: snre.admissions@umich.edu.

University of Minnesota, Twin Cities Campus, Graduate School, College of Food, Agricultural and Natural Resource Sciences, Program in Natural Resources Science and Management, Minneapolis, MN 55455-0213. Offers MS, PhD. Part-time programs available. *Faculty:* 120 full-time (22 women). *Students:* 75 full-time (39 women), 9 part-time (3 women); includes 6 minority (1 Black or African American, non-Hispanic/Latino; 1 American Indian or Alaska Native, non-Hispanic/Latino; 3 Asian, non-Hispanic/Latino; 1 Hispanic/Latino), 13 international. Average age 30. 101 applicants, 36% accepted, 29 enrolled. In 2010, 16 master's, 5 doctorates awarded. Terminal master's awarded for partial completion of doctoral program. *Degree requirements:* For master's, comprehensive exam, thesis; for doctorate, comprehensive exam, thesis/dissertation. *Entrance requirements:* For master's, GRE general test; for doctorate, GRE. Additional exam requirements/recommendations for international students: Required—TOEFL (minimum score 500 paper-based; 213 computer-based; 79 iBT). *Application deadline:* For fall admission, 12/15 priority date for domestic and international students; for spring admission, 10/15 for domestic and international students. Applications are processed on a rolling basis. Application fee: $75 ($95 for international students). Electronic applications accepted. *Financial support:* In 2010–11, fellowships with full tuition reimbursements (averaging $23,500 per year), research assistantships with full tuition reimbursements (averaging $19,000 per year), teaching assistantships with full tuition reimbursements (averaging $19,000 per year) were awarded; scholarships/grants, health care benefits, tuition waivers (partial), and unspecified assistantships also available. *Faculty research:* Paper science, forestry, recreation resource management, wildlife ecology, environmental education, hydrology, conservation, tourism, economics, policy, watershed management, GIS, forest products. Total annual research expenditures: $6 million. *Unit head:* Dr. Michael Kilgore, Director of Graduate Studies, 612-624-6298, E-mail: mkilgore@umn.edu. *Application contact:* Jennifer Welsh, Program Coordinator, 612-624-7683, Fax: 612-625-5212, E-mail: jwelsh@umn.edu.

University of Missouri, Graduate School, School of Natural Resources, Natural Resources Master's Degree Program, Columbia, MO 65211. Offers MNR.

The University of Montana, Graduate School, College of Forestry and Conservation, Missoula, MT 59812-0002. Offers ecosystem management (MEM, MS); fish and wildlife biology (PhD); forestry (MS, PhD); recreation management (MS); resource conservation (MS); wildlife biology (MS). *Degree requirements:* For doctorate, thesis/dissertation. *Entrance requirements:* For master's and doctorate, GRE General Test. Additional exam requirements/recommendations for international students: Required—TOEFL (minimum score 575 paper-based; 213 computer-based).

University of Nebraska–Lincoln, Graduate College, College of Agricultural Sciences and Natural Resources, Department of Agricultural Economics, Lincoln, NE 68588. Offers agribusiness (MBA); agricultural economics (MS, PhD); community development (M Ag). *Degree requirements:* For master's, thesis optional; for doctorate, comprehensive exam, thesis/dissertation. *Entrance requirements:* For master's and doctorate, GRE General Test. Additional exam requirements/recommendations for international students: Required—TOEFL (minimum score 550 paper-based; 213 computer-based). Electronic applications accepted. *Faculty research:* Marketing and agribusiness, production economics, resource law, international trade and development, rural policy and revitalization.

University of Nebraska–Lincoln, Graduate College, College of Agricultural Sciences and Natural Resources, School of Natural Resources, Lincoln, NE 68588. Offers geography (PhD); natural resources (MS, PhD). *Degree requirements:* For master's, thesis optional. *Entrance requirements:* For master's, GRE General Test. Additional exam requirements/recommendations for international students: Required—TOEFL. Electronic applications accepted. *Faculty research:* Wildlife biology, aquatic sciences, landscape ecology, agroforestry.

University of New Brunswick Saint John, Faculty of Business, Saint John, NB E2L 4L5, Canada. Offers administration (MBA); electronic commerce (MBA); international business (MBA); natural resource management (MBA). Part-time programs available. *Faculty:* 19 full-time (4 women), 14 part-time/adjunct (8 women). *Students:* 47 full-time (18 women), 55 part-time (21 women). 93 applicants, 78% accepted, 25 enrolled. In 2010, 36 master's awarded. *Entrance requirements:* For master's, GMAT, minimum GPA of 3.0. Additional exam requirements/recommendations for international students: Required—TOEFL (minimum score 580 paper-based; 237 computer-based), IELTS (minimum score 7), TWE (minimum score 4.5). *Application deadline:* For fall admission, 5/15 for domestic and international students. Applications are processed on a rolling basis. Application fee: $100. Electronic applications accepted. *Expenses:* Contact institution. *Financial support:* In 2010–11, 4 students received support. Career-related internships or fieldwork and scholarships/grants available. *Faculty research:* Business use of weblogs and podcasts to communicate, corporate governance, high-involvement work systems, international competitiveness, supply chain management and logistics. *Unit head:* Henryk Sterniczuk, Director of Graduate Studies, 506-648-5573, Fax: 506-648-5574, E-mail: sternicz@unbsj.ca. *Application contact:* Tammy Morin, Secretary, 506-648-5746, Fax: 506-648-5574, E-mail: tmorin@unbsj.ca.

University of New Hampshire, Graduate School, College of Life Sciences and Agriculture, Department of Natural Resources, Durham, NH 03824. Offers environmental conservation (MS); forestry (MS); integrated coastal ecosystem science, policy, management (MS); natural resources (MS); water resources (MS); wildlife (MS). Part-time programs available. *Faculty:* 40 full-time. *Students:* 22 full-time (8 women), 27 part-time (15 women); includes 1 Asian, non-Hispanic/Latino; 1 Hispanic/Latino, 1 international. Average age 30. 54 applicants, 39% accepted, 14 enrolled. In 2010, 13 master's awarded. *Degree requirements:* For master's, thesis or alternative. *Entrance requirements:* For master's, GRE General Test. Additional exam requirements/recommendations for international students: Required—TOEFL (minimum score 550 paper-based; 213 computer-based; 80 iBT). *Application deadline:* For fall admission, 6/1 for domestic students, 4/1 for international students; for spring admission, 12/1 for domestic students. Applications are processed on a rolling basis. Application fee: $65. Electronic applications accepted. *Financial support:* In 2010–11, 23 students received support, including 3 fellowships, 6 research assistantships, 14 teaching assistantships; career-related internships or fieldwork, Federal Work-Study, scholarships/grants, and tuition waivers (full and partial) also available. Support available to part-time students. Financial award application deadline: 2/15. *Unit head:* Dr. John Halstead, Chairperson, 603-862-3950, E-mail: natural.resources@unh.edu. *Application contact:* Linda Scogin, Administrative Assistant, 603-862-3932, E-mail: natural.resources@unh.edu.

University of New Hampshire, Graduate School, College of Life Sciences and Agriculture, Department of Resource Economics and Development, Program in Resource Administration, Durham, NH 03824. Offers MS. Part-time programs available. *Faculty:* 4 full-time (0 women), 1 (woman) part-time/adjunct. *Students:* 3 full-time (all women), 3 part-time (2 women); includes 1 Asian, non-Hispanic/Latino. Average age 28. 5 applicants, 100% accepted, 3 enrolled. In 2010, 2 master's awarded. *Degree requirements:* For master's, thesis or alternative. *Entrance requirements:* For master's, GRE General Test. Additional exam requirements/recommendations for international students: Required—TOEFL (minimum score 550 paper-based; 213 computer-based; 80 iBT). *Application deadline:* For fall admission, 6/1 priority date for domestic students, 4/1 for international students; for spring admission, 12/1 for domestic students. Applications are processed on a rolling basis. Application fee: $65. Electronic applications accepted. *Financial support:* In 2010–11, 4 students received support, including 4 teaching assistantships; fellowships, research assistantships, career-related internships or fieldwork, Federal Work-Study, and scholarships/grants also available. Support available to part-time students. Financial award application deadline: 2/15.

University of New Hampshire, Graduate School, College of Life Sciences and Agriculture, Department of Resource Economics and Development, Program in Resource Economics, Durham, NH 03824. Offers MS. Part-time programs available. *Faculty:* 6 full-time. *Students:* 3 applicants, 33% accepted, 0 enrolled. *Degree requirements:* For master's, thesis or alternative. *Entrance requirements:* For master's, GRE General Test. Additional exam requirements/recommendations for international students: Required—TOEFL (minimum score 550 paper-based; 213 computer-based; 80 iBT). *Application deadline:* For fall admission, 6/1 for domestic students, 4/1 for international students; for spring admission, 12/1 for domestic students. Applications are processed on a rolling basis. Application fee: $65. Electronic applications accepted. *Financial support:* Fellowships, research assistantships, teaching assistantships, career-related internships or fieldwork and Federal Work-Study available. Support available to part-time students. Financial award application deadline: 2/15. *Unit head:* Dr. John Halstea, Chairperson, 603-862-3914. *Application contact:* Dr. John Halstea, Chairperson, 603-862-3914.

University of New Hampshire, Graduate School, Interdisciplinary Programs, Doctoral Program in Natural Resources and Earth System Science, Durham, NH 03824. Offers earth and environmental science (PhD), including geology, oceanography; natural resources and environmental studies (PhD). *Faculty:* 59 full-time (11 women). *Students:* 61 full-time (35 women), 13 part-time (6 women); includes 3 Asian, non-Hispanic/Latino, 12 international. Average age 33. 44 applicants, 36% accepted, 8 enrolled. In 2010, 8 doctorates awarded. *Degree requirements:* For doctorate, thesis/dissertation. *Entrance requirements:* For doctorate, GRE (if from a non-US university). Additional exam requirements/recommendations for international students: Required—TOEFL (minimum score 550 paper-based; 213 computer-based; 80 iBT). *Application deadline:* For fall admission, 6/1 priority date for domestic students, 4/1 for international students; for spring admission, 12/1 for domestic students. Applications are processed on a rolling basis. Application fee: $65. Electronic applications accepted. *Financial support:* In 2010–11, 46 students received support, including 10 fellowships, 21 research assistantships, 9 teaching assistantships; Federal Work-Study, scholarships/grants, and tuition waivers (full and partial) also available. Financial award application deadline: 2/15. *Faculty research:* Environmental and natural resource studies and management. *Unit head:* Dr. John Halstead, Chairperson, 603-862-3914. *Application contact:* Dr. Linda Scogin, Administrative Assistant, 603-862-3932, E-mail: nress.phd.program@unh.edu.

University of New Mexico, Graduate School, College of Arts and Sciences, Department of Economics, Albuquerque, NM 87131-2039. Offers environmental/natural resources (MA, PhD); international/development (MA, PhD); labor/human resources (MA, PhD); public finance (MA, PhD). Part-time programs available. *Faculty:* 26 full-time (9 women), 7 part-time/adjunct (1 woman). *Students:* 47 full-time (14 women), 17 part-time (5 women); includes 2 American Indian or Alaska Native, non-Hispanic/Latino; 2 Asian, non-Hispanic/Latino; 8 Hispanic/Latino, 18 international. Average age 34. 75 applicants, 51% accepted, 15 enrolled. In 2010, 14 master's, 1 doctorate awarded. Terminal master's awarded for partial completion of doctoral program. *Degree requirements:* For master's, comprehensive exam, thesis (for some programs); for doctorate, comprehensive exam, thesis/dissertation. *Entrance requirements:* For master's and doctorate, GRE General Test, 3 letters of recommendation, letter of intent. Additional exam requirements/recommendations for international students: Required—TOEFL (minimum score 520 paper-based; 190 computer-based; 68 iBT). *Application deadline:* For fall admission, 3/1 priority date for domestic students, 3/1 for international students. Applications are processed on a rolling basis. Application fee: $50. Electronic applications accepted. *Expenses:* Tuition, state resident: full-time $5991; part-time $251 per credit hour. Tuition, nonresident: full-time $14,405; part-time $800.20 per credit hour. Tuition and fees vary according to course level, course load, program and reciprocity agreements. *Financial support:* In 2010–11, 47 students received support, including 3 fellowships with tuition reimbursements available (averaging $3,611 per year), 14 research assistantships with tuition reimbursements available (averaging $7,791 per year), 15 teaching assistantships (averaging $7,467 per year); career-related internships or fieldwork, Federal Work-Study, scholarships/grants, health care benefits, and unspecified assistantships also available. Support available to part-time students. Financial award application deadline: 3/1; financial award applicants required to submit FAFSA. *Faculty research:* Core theory, econometrics, public finance, international/development economics, labor/human resource economics, environmental/natural resource economics. Total annual research expenditures: $1.8 million. *Unit head:* Dr. Robert Berrens, Chair, 505-277-5304, Fax: 505-277-9445, E-mail: rberrens@unm.edu. *Application contact:* Shoshana Handel, Academic Advisor, 505-277-3056, Fax: 505-277-9445, E-mail: shandel@unm.edu.

University of Northern British Columbia, Office of Graduate Studies, Prince George, BC V2N 4Z9, Canada. Offers business administration (Diploma); community health science (M Sc); disability management (MA); education (M Ed); first nations studies (MA); gender studies (MA); history (MA); interdisciplinary studies (MA); international studies (MA); mathematical, computer and physical sciences (M Sc); natural resources and environmental studies (M Sc, MA, MNRES, PhD); political science (MA); psychology (M Sc, PhD); social work (MSW). Part-time and evening/weekend programs available. Postbaccalaureate distance learning degree programs offered (no on-campus study). *Degree requirements:* For master's, thesis; for doctorate, thesis/dissertation. *Entrance requirements:* For master's, GRE, minimum B average in undergraduate course work; for doctorate, candidacy exam, minimum A average in graduate course work.

University of Northern Iowa, Graduate College, College of Natural Sciences, Department of Biology, Cedar Falls, IA 50614. Offers biology (MA, MS); biotechnology (PSM); ecosystem management (PSM). Part-time programs available. *Students:* 21 full-time (9 women), 7 part-time (2 women); includes 2 minority (1 Hispanic/Latino; 1 Two or more races, non-Hispanic/Latino), 1 international. 39 applicants, 49% accepted, 13 enrolled. In 2010, 17 master's awarded. *Degree requirements:* For master's, comprehensive exam (for some programs), thesis or alternative. *Entrance requirements:* For master's, minimum GPA of 3.0; 3 letters of recommendation. Additional exam requirements/recommendations for international students: Required—TOEFL (minimum score 500 paper-based; 180 computer-based; 61 iBT). *Application deadline:* For fall admission, 8/1 priority date for domestic students. Applications are processed on a rolling basis. Application fee: $50 ($70 for international students). Electronic applications accepted. *Financial support:* Scholarships/grants available. Financial award application deadline: 2/1. *Unit head:* Dr. David Saunders, Head, 319-273-2456, Fax: 319-273-7125, E-mail: david.saunders@uni.edu. *Application contact:* Laurie S. Russell, Record Analyst, 319-273-2623, Fax: 319-273-2885, E-mail: laurie.russell@uni.edu.

University of Oklahoma, College of Earth and Energy, School of Petroleum and Geological Engineering, Program in Petroleum Engineering, Norman, OK 73019-0390. Offers natural gas engineering and management (MS); petroleum engineering (MS, PhD). Part-time programs available. *Students:* 83 full-time (16 women), 40 part-time (7 women); includes 5 minority (4 Black or African American, non-Hispanic/Latino; 1 Hispanic/Latino), 106 international. Average age 28. 143 applicants, 27% accepted, 26 enrolled. In 2010, 11 master's, 3 doctorates awarded. Terminal master's awarded for partial completion of doctoral program. *Degree requirements:* For master's, thesis optional, industrial team project or thesis; for doctorate, thesis/dissertation. *Entrance requirements:* For master's, GRE General Test, bachelor's degree in engineering, 3 letters of recommendation, minimum GPA of 3.0 during final 60 hours of undergraduate course work; for doctorate, GRE General Test, minimum GPA of 3.0, 3 letters of recommendation. Additional exam requirements/recommendations for international students: Required—TOEFL (minimum score 550 paper-based; 213 computer-based; 79 iBT). *Application*

deadline: For fall admission, 6/1 priority date for domestic students, 4/1 for international students; for spring admission, 11/1 for domestic students, 9/1 for international students. Applications are processed on a rolling basis. Application fee: $40 ($90 for international students). Electronic applications accepted. *Expenses:* Tuition, state resident: full-time $3892.80; part-time $162.20 per credit hour. Tuition, nonresident: full-time $14,167; part-time $590.30 per credit hour. Required fees: $2523.40; $94.60 per credit hour. Tuition and fees vary according to course load and degree level. *Financial support:* In 2010–11, 96 students received support. Traineeships available. Financial award application deadline: 4/15; financial award applicants required to submit FAFSA. *Faculty research:* Petrophysics, shale gas, reservoir simulation coiled tubing, poro-mechanics, enhanced oil recovery. *Unit head:* Dr. Chandra Rai, Director, 405-325-2921, Fax: 405-325-7477, E-mail: crai@ou.edu. *Application contact:* Shalli Young, Executive Assistant to the Graduate Liaison, 405-325-2921, Fax: 405-325-7477, E-mail: syoung@ou.edu.

University of Rhode Island, Graduate School, College of the Environment and Life Sciences, Department of Environmental and Natural Resource Economics, Kingston, RI 02881. Offers MESM, MS, PhD. Part-time programs available. *Faculty:* 6 full-time (2 women), 3 part-time/adjunct (1 woman). *Students:* 37 full-time (17 women), 4 part-time (2 women); includes 3 minority (1 Asian, non-Hispanic/Latino; 2 Hispanic/Latino), 13 international. In 2010, 4 master's, 4 doctorates awarded. *Degree requirements:* For master's, comprehensive exam (for some programs), thesis optional; for doctorate, comprehensive exam, thesis/dissertation. *Entrance requirements:* For master's, GRE, 2 letters of recommendation; for doctorate, GRE, 3 letters of recommendation. Additional exam requirements/recommendations for international students: Required—TOEFL (minimum score 550 paper-based; 213 computer-based). *Application deadline:* For fall admission, 7/15 for domestic students, 2/1 for international students; for spring admission, 11/15 for domestic students, 7/15 for international students. Application fee: $65. Electronic applications accepted. *Expenses:* Tuition, state resident: full-time $9588; part-time $533 per credit hour. Tuition, nonresident: full-time $22,968; part-time $1276 per credit hour. Required fees: $1282; $68 per semester. Tuition and fees vary according to program. *Financial support:* In 2010–11, 10 research assistantships with partial tuition reimbursements (averaging $12,990 per year), 2 teaching assistantships with full and partial tuition reimbursements (averaging $6,985 per year) were awarded. Financial award application deadline: 7/15; financial award applicants required to submit FAFSA. *Faculty research:* Policy Simulation Laboratory: utilizes computer technologies to help understand the consequences of policy actions, experimental economics. Total annual research expenditures: $637,583. *Unit head:* Dr. James Opaluch, Chair, 401-874-4590, Fax: 401-874-4766, E-mail: jimo@uri.edu. *Application contact:* Dr. James Opaluch, Graduate Admission Committee, 401-874-4590, Fax: 401-874-4766, E-mail: jimo@uri.edu.

University of Rhode Island, Graduate School, College of the Environment and Life Sciences, Department of Natural Resources Science, Kingston, RI 02881. Offers MESM, MS, PhD. Part-time programs available. *Faculty:* 11 full-time (1 woman). *Students:* 34 full-time (22 women), 9 part-time (8 women); includes 2 minority (1 Asian, non-Hispanic/Latino; 1 Hispanic/Latino). In 2010, 8 master's, 7 doctorates awarded. *Degree requirements:* For master's, comprehensive exam (for some programs), thesis optional; for doctorate, comprehensive exam, thesis/dissertation. *Entrance requirements:* For master's and doctorate, GRE, 2 letters of recommendation. Additional exam requirements/recommendations for international students: Required—TOEFL (minimum score 550 paper-based; 213 computer-based). *Application deadline:* For fall admission, 7/15 for domestic students, 2/1 for international students; for spring admission, 11/15 for domestic students, 7/15 for international students. Application fee: $65. Electronic applications accepted. *Expenses:* Tuition, state resident: full-time $9588; part-time $533 per credit hour. Tuition, nonresident: full-time $22,968; part-time $1276 per credit hour. Required fees: $1282; $68 per semester. Tuition and fees vary according to program. *Financial support:* In 2010–11, 14 research assistantships with full and partial tuition reimbursements (averaging $13,120 per year), 3 teaching assistantships with full and partial tuition reimbursements (averaging $10,535 per year) were awarded. Financial award application deadline: 7/15; financial award applicants required to submit FAFSA. *Faculty research:* Spatial data modeling, ecological mapping, data integration for environmental applications. Total annual research expenditures: $4.3 million. *Unit head:* Dr. Peter Paton, Chair, 401-874-2986, Fax: 401-874-4561, E-mail: ppaton@uri.edu. *Application contact:* Dr. Graham Forrester, Director of Graduate Studies, 401-874-7054, Fax: 401-874-4561, E-mail: gforrester@mail.uri.edu.

University of San Francisco, College of Arts and Sciences, Program in Environmental Management, San Francisco, CA 94117-1080. Offers MS. Evening/weekend programs available. *Degree requirements:* For master's, thesis, project. *Entrance requirements:* For master's, 3 semesters of course work in chemistry, minimum GPA of 2.7, work experience in environmental field. *Application deadline:* For fall admission, 3/1 priority date for domestic students. Applications are processed on a rolling basis. Application fee: $55 ($65 for international students). *Expenses:* Tuition: Full-time $20,070; part-time $1115 per credit hour. Tuition and fees vary according to course load, degree level and program. *Financial support:* Teaching assistantships, career-related internships or fieldwork available. Financial award application deadline: 3/2; financial award applicants required to submit FAFSA. *Faculty research:* Problems of environmental managers, water quality, hazardous materials, environmental health. *Unit head:* Dr. Robert Toia, Chair, 415-422-5927, Fax: 415-422-6387. *Application contact:* Dr. Robert Toia, Chair, 415-422-5927, Fax: 415-422-6387.

University of South Africa, College of Agriculture and Environmental Sciences, Pretoria, South Africa. Offers agriculture (MS); consumer science (MCS); environmental management (MA, MS, PhD); environmental science (MA, MS, PhD); geography (MA, MS, PhD); horticulture (M Tech); human ecology (MHE); life sciences (MS); nature conservation (M Tech).

The University of Texas at Austin, Graduate School, Cockrell School of Engineering, Department of Petroleum and Geosystems Engineering, Program in Energy and Earth Resources, Austin, TX 78712-1111. Offers MA. *Degree requirements:* For master's, thesis, seminar. *Entrance requirements:* For master's, GRE General Test. Additional exam requirements/recommendations for international students: Required—TOEFL. Electronic applications accepted.

University of Vermont, Graduate College, The Rubenstein School of Environment and Natural Resources, Program in Natural Resources, Burlington, VT 05405. Offers natural resources (MS, PhD), including aquatic ecology and watershed science (MS), environment thought and culture (MS), environment, science and public affairs (MS), forestry (MS). *Students:* 102 (54 women); includes 2 Black or African American, non-Hispanic/Latino; 2 American Indian or Alaska Native, non-Hispanic/Latino; 7 Asian, non-Hispanic/Latino; 4 Hispanic/Latino, 5 international. 140 applicants, 32% accepted, 22 enrolled. In 2010, 22 master's, 8 doctorates awarded. *Degree requirements:* For master's, thesis or alternative; for doctorate, thesis/dissertation. *Entrance requirements:* For master's and doctorate, GRE General Test. Additional exam requirements/recommendations for international students: Required—TOEFL (minimum score 550 paper-based; 213 computer-based; 80 iBT). *Application deadline:* For fall admission, 3/1 priority date for domestic students. Applications are processed on a rolling basis. Application fee: $40. Electronic applications accepted. *Expenses:* Tuition, state resident: part-time $537 per credit hour. Tuition, nonresident: part-time $1355 per credit hour. *Financial support:* Fellowships, research assistantships, teaching assistantships available. Financial award application deadline: 3/1. *Unit head:* Dr. Mary Watzin, Coordinator, 802-656-2620. *Application contact:* Dr. Mary Watzin, Coordinator, 802-656-2620.

University of Washington, Graduate School, College of Forest Resources, Seattle, WA 98195. Offers bioresource science and engineering (MS, PhD); environmental horticulture (MEH); environmental horticulture and urban forestry (MS, PhD); forest ecology (MS, PhD); forest management (MFR); forest soils (MS, PhD); forest systems and bioenergy (MS, PhD); restoration ecology (MS, PhD); social sciences (MS, PhD); sustainable resource management (MS, PhD); wildlife science (MS, PhD); MFR/MAIS; MPA/MS. *Accreditation:* SAF. *Degree requirements:* For master's, thesis (for some programs); for doctorate, comprehensive exam (for some programs), thesis/dissertation. *Entrance requirements:* For master's and doctorate, GRE, minimum GPA of 3.0. Additional exam requirements/recommendations for international students: Required—TOEFL. Electronic applications accepted. *Faculty research:* Ecosystem analysis, silviculture and forest protection, paper science and engineering, environmental horticulture and urban forestry, natural resource policy and economics.

University of Wisconsin–Madison, Graduate School, Gaylord Nelson Institute for Environmental Studies, Environment and Resources Program, Madison, WI 53706-1380. Offers MS, PhD. Part-time programs available. *Faculty:* 15 full-time (2 women), 50 part-time/adjunct (14 women). *Students:* 115 (69 women); includes 3 Black or African American, non-Hispanic/Latino; 2 American Indian or Alaska Native, non-Hispanic/Latino; 4 Asian, non-Hispanic/Latino; 3 Hispanic/Latino, 12 international. Average age 32. 215 applicants, 31% accepted, 29 enrolled. In 2010, 13 master's, 8 doctorates awarded. *Degree requirements:* For master's, thesis; for doctorate, thesis/dissertation. *Entrance requirements:* For master's and doctorate, GRE General Test. Additional exam requirements/recommendations for international students: Required—TOEFL (minimum score 550 paper-based; 213 computer-based; 80 iBT). *Application deadline:* For fall admission, 1/15 for domestic and international students; for spring admission, 10/15 for domestic and international students. Application fee: $56. Electronic applications accepted. *Expenses:* Tuition, state resident: full-time $9887.36; part-time $617.96 per credit. Tuition, nonresident: full-time $24,054; part-time $1503.40 per credit. Required fees: $67.63 per credit. Tuition and fees vary according to reciprocity agreements. *Financial support:* In 2010–11, 73 students received support, including 16 fellowships with full tuition reimbursements available (averaging $18,756 per year), 28 research assistantships with full tuition reimbursements available (averaging $14,960 per year), 16 teaching assistantships with full tuition reimbursements available (averaging $9,392 per year); career-related internships or fieldwork, Federal Work-Study, scholarships/grants, traineeships, health care benefits, unspecified assistantships, and project assistantships also available. Financial award application deadline: 1/2. *Faculty research:* Land use issues, soil science/watershed management, geographic information systems, environmental law/justice, waste management, restoration ecology, agroecology, energy resources. *Unit head:* Paul H. Zedler, Chair, 608-265-8018, Fax: 608-262-2273, E-mail: phzedler@wisc.edu. *Application contact:* Jim Miller, Student Services Coordinator, 608-263-4373, Fax: 608-262-2273, E-mail: jemiller@wisc.edu.

University of Wisconsin–Stevens Point, College of Natural Resources, Stevens Point, WI 54481-3897. Offers MS. Part-time programs available. *Degree requirements:* For master's, thesis or alternative. *Entrance requirements:* For master's, GRE. *Faculty research:* Wildlife management, environmental education, fisheries, forestry, resource policy and planning.

University of Wyoming, College of Agriculture and Natural Resources, Department of Renewable Resources, Laramie, WY 82070. Offers agroecology (MS); entomology (MS, PhD); entomology/water resources (MS, PhD); rangeland ecology and watershed management (MS, PhD), including soil sciences (PhD), soil sciences and water resources (MS); rangeland ecology and watershed management/water resources (MS, PhD); soil science (MS); soil science/water resources (PhD). Part-time programs available. *Degree requirements:* For master's, comprehensive exam, thesis, oral examination; for doctorate, comprehensive exam, thesis/dissertation, preliminary oral and written exam, oral final exam. *Entrance requirements:* For master's and doctorate, GRE General Test, minimum GPA of 3.0. Additional exam requirements/recommendations for international students: Required—TOEFL. Electronic applications accepted. *Faculty research:* Plant control, grazing management, riparian restoration, riparian management, reclamation.

University of Wyoming, College of Arts and Sciences, Department of Geography, Program in Rural Planning and Natural Resources, Laramie, WY 82070. Offers community and regional planning and natural resources (MP). *Degree requirements:* For master's, thesis or alternative. *Entrance requirements:* For master's, GRE General Test, minimum GPA of 3.0. Additional exam requirements/recommendations for international students: Required—TOEFL. *Faculty research:* Rural and small town planning, public land management.

Utah State University, School of Graduate Studies, College of Natural Resources, Interdisciplinary Program in Natural Resources, Logan, UT 84322. Offers MNR. *Entrance requirements:* For master's, GRE General Test, minimum GPA of 3.0. Additional exam requirements/recommendations for international students: Required—TOEFL. *Faculty research:* Ecosystem management, human dimensions, quantitative methods, informative management.

Virginia Polytechnic Institute and State University, Graduate School, College of Natural Resources and Environment, Program in Natural Resources, Blacksburg, VA 24061. Offers MNR, Certificate. *Students:* 11 full-time (6 women), 5 part-time (2 women); includes 1 Asian, non-Hispanic/Latino, 7 international. Average age 33. 13 applicants, 15% accepted, 2 enrolled. *Degree requirements:* For master's, comprehensive exam (for some programs), thesis (for some programs). *Entrance requirements:* For master's, GRE. Additional exam requirements/recommendations for international students: Required—TOEFL (minimum score 550 paper-based; 213 computer-based). *Application deadline:* For fall admission, 7/1 for domestic and international students; for spring admission, 12/1 for domestic and international students. Applications are processed on a rolling basis. Application fee: $65. Electronic applications accepted. *Expenses:* Tuition, area resident: Full-time $9399; part-time $488 per credit hour. Tuition, state resident: full-time $9399; part-time $488 per credit hour. Tuition, nonresident: full-time $17,854; part-time $957.75 per credit hour. International tuition: $17,854 full-time. Required fees: $1534. Full-time tuition and fees vary according to program. *Financial support:* In 2010–11, 1 research assistantship with full tuition reimbursement (averaging $13,483 per year) was awarded; career-related internships or fieldwork, Federal Work-Study, scholarships/grants, health care benefits, and unspecified assistantships also available. Financial award application deadline: 1/15. Total annual research expenditures: $255,144. *Unit head:* Dr. Paul M. Winistorfer, UNIT HEAD, 540-231-8834, Fax: 540-231-5481, E-mail: pwinisto@vt.edu. *Application contact:* Peggy Quarterman, Contact, 540-231-5481, Fax: 540-231-5481, E-mail: pquarter@vt.edu.

Virginia Polytechnic Institute and State University, VT Online, Blacksburg, VA 24061. Offers aerospace engineering (MS); business information systems (Graduate Certificate); career and technical education (MS); computer engineering (M Eng, MS); decision support systems (Graduate Certificate); eLearning leadership (MA); electrical engineering (M Eng, MS); engineering administration (MEA); environmental politics and policy (Graduate Certificate); foundations of political analysis (Graduate Certificate); health product risk management (Graduate Certificate); information policy and society (Graduate Certificate); information security (Graduate Certificate); instructional technology (MA); liberal arts (Graduate Certificate); life sciences: health product risk management (MS); natural resources (MNR, Graduate Certificate); networking (Graduate Certificate); nonprofit and nongovernmental organization management (Graduate Certificate); ocean engineering (MS); political science (MA); security studies (Graduate Certificate); software development (Graduate Certificate). *Expenses:* Tuition, area resident: Full-time $9399; part-time $488 per credit hour. Tuition, state resident: full-time $9399; part-time $488 per credit hour. Tuition, nonresident: full-time $17,854; part-time $957.75 per credit hour. International tuition: $17,854 full-time. Required fees: $1534. Full-time tuition and fees vary according to program.

Washington State University, Graduate School, College of Sciences, Programs in Environmental Science and Regional Planning, Program in Environmental and Natural Resource Sciences, Pullman, WA 99164. Offers PhD. Application fee: $50. *Expenses:* Tuition, state resident: full-time $8552; part-time $443 per credit. Tuition, nonresident: full-time $21,650; part-time $1083 per credit. Required fees: $846. *Unit head:* Dr. Keith A. Blatner, Chair,

Natural Resources

Washington State University (continued)
509-335-6166, E-mail: blatner@wsu.edu. *Application contact:* Graduate School Admissions, 800-GRADWSU, Fax: 509-335-1949, E-mail: gradsch@wsu.edu.

Washington State University, Graduate School, College of Sciences, School of Earth and Environmental Sciences, Department of Natural Resource Sciences, Program in Environmental Science, Pullman, WA 99164. Offers environmental and natural resource sciences (PhD); environmental science (MS). *Faculty:* 7. *Students:* 42 full-time (24 women), 34 part-time (17 women); includes 1 Black or African American, non-Hispanic/Latino; 2 American Indian or Alaska Native, non-Hispanic/Latino; 3 Asian, non-Hispanic/Latino; 2 Hispanic/Latino, 2 international. Average age 29. 76 applicants, 32% accepted, 18 enrolled. In 2010, 15 master's awarded. *Degree requirements:* For master's, comprehensive exam (for some programs), thesis (for some programs), oral exam; for doctorate, comprehensive exam, thesis/dissertation, oral exam, written exam. *Entrance requirements:* For master's, 3 undergraduate semester hours each in sociology or cultural anthropology, environmental science, biological sciences, and calculus or statistics; 4 in general ecology; and 6 in general chemistry or general physics; for doctorate, minimum GPA of 3.0. Additional exam requirements/recommendations for international students: Required—TOEFL, IELTS. *Application deadline:* For fall admission, 1/10 priority date for domestic students, 1/10 for international students. Applications are processed on a rolling basis. Application fee: $50. *Expenses:* Tuition, state resident: full-time $8552; part-time $443 per credit. Tuition, nonresident: full-time $21,650; part-time $1083 per credit. Required fees: $846. *Financial support:* In 2010–11, 16 students received support, including 1 fellowship (averaging $3,000 per year), 4 research assistantships with full and partial tuition reimbursements available (averaging $13,917 per year), 4 teaching assistantships with full and partial tuition reimbursements available (averaging $13,506 per year); Federal Work-

Study, institutionally sponsored loans, and tuition waivers (partial) also available. Financial award application deadline: 2/15; financial award applicants required to submit FAFSA. *Unit head:* Dr. John A. Wolff, Head, 509-335-2825, E-mail: jawolff@mail.wsu.edu. *Application contact:* Graduate School Admissions, 800-GRADWSU, Fax: 509-335-1949, E-mail: gradsch@wsu.edu.

West Virginia University, College of Business and Economics, Division of Economics and Finance, Morgantown, WV 26506. Offers business analysis (MA); developmental financial economics (PhD); environmental and resource economics (PhD); international economics (PhD); mathematical economics (MA); monetary economics (PhD); public finance (PhD); public policy (MA); regional and urban economics (PhD); statistics and economics (MA). Terminal master's awarded for partial completion of doctoral program. *Degree requirements:* For master's, thesis optional; for doctorate, comprehensive exam, thesis/dissertation. *Entrance requirements:* For master's and doctorate, GRE General Test, minimum GPA of 3.0; course work in intermediate microeconomics, intermediate macroeconomics, calculus, and statistics. Additional exam requirements/recommendations for international students: Required—TOEFL. Electronic applications accepted. *Faculty research:* Financial economics, regional/urban development, public economics, international trade/international finance/development economics, monetary economics.

West Virginia University, Davis College of Agriculture, Forestry and Consumer Sciences, Division of Resource Management and Sustainable Development, Program in Resource Management and Sustainable Development, Morgantown, WV 26506. Offers PhD. Part-time programs available. *Degree requirements:* For doctorate, thesis/dissertation. *Entrance requirements:* For doctorate, GRE General Test. Additional exam requirements/recommendations for international students: Required—TOEFL.

Range Science

Colorado State University, Graduate School, Warner College of Natural Resources, Department of Forest, Rangeland, and Watershed Stewardship, Fort Collins, CO 80523-1472. Offers forest sciences (MS, PhD); natural resources stewardship (MNRS); rangeland ecosystem science (MS, PhD); watershed science (MS). Part-time programs available: Postbaccalaureate distance learning degree programs offered (no on-campus study). *Faculty:* 18 full-time (5 women), 2 part-time/adjunct (0 women). *Students:* 45 full-time (21 women), 90 part-time (31 women); includes 9 minority (3 American Indian or Alaska Native, non-Hispanic/Latino; 1 Asian, non-Hispanic/Latino; 5 Hispanic/Latino), 9 international. Average age 34. 59 applicants, 76% accepted, 28 enrolled. In 2010, 27 master's, 2 doctorates awarded. *Degree requirements:* For master's, thesis (for some programs); for doctorate, comprehensive exam, thesis/dissertation. *Entrance requirements:* For master's, GRE General Test (minimum score 1000 verbal and quantitative), minimum GPA of 3.0, 3 letters of recommendation; for doctorate, GRE General Test (combined minimum score of 1100 on the Verbal and Quantitative sections), minimum GPA of 3.0, 3 letters of recommendation, statement of research interest. Additional exam requirements/recommendations for international students: Required—TOEFL (minimum score 550 paper-based; 213 computer-based; 80 iBT), IELTS (minimum score 6.5). *Application deadline:* For fall admission, 2/15 priority date for domestic and international students; for spring admission, 7/15 priority date for domestic and international students. Applications are processed on a rolling basis. Application fee: $50. Electronic applications accepted. *Expenses:* Tuition, state resident: full-time $7434; part-time $413 per credit. Tuition, nonresident: full-time $19,022; part-time $1057 per credit. Required fees: $1729; $88 per credit. *Financial support:* In 2010–11, 46 students received support, including 1 fellowship (averaging $23,971 per year), 32 research assistantships with full and partial tuition reimbursements available (averaging $15,871 per year), 13 teaching assistantships with full and partial tuition reimbursements available (averaging $7,106 per year); Federal Work-Study, scholarships/grants, and unspecified assistantships also available. Financial award application deadline: 2/15; financial award applicants required to submit FAFSA. *Faculty research:* Ecology, natural resource management, hydrology, restoration, human dimensions. Total annual research expenditures: $2.4 million. *Unit head:* Dr. Frederick Smith, Interim Department Head, 970-491-7505, Fax: 970-491-6754, E-mail: fwsmith@colostate.edu. *Application contact:* Sonya LeFebre, Coordinator, 970-491-1907, Fax: 970-491-6754, E-mail: sonya.lefebre@colostate.edu.

Kansas State University, Graduate School, College of Agriculture, Department of Agronomy, Manhattan, KS 66506. Offers crop science (MS, PhD); range management (MS, PhD); soil science (MS, PhD); weed science (MS, PhD). Part-time programs available. Terminal master's awarded for partial completion of doctoral program. *Degree requirements:* For master's, thesis or alternative, oral exam; for doctorate, thesis/dissertation, preliminary exams. *Entrance requirements:* For master's, minimum GPA of 3.0 in BS; for doctorate, minimum GPA of 3.5 in master's program. Additional exam requirements/recommendations for international students: Required—TOEFL (minimum score 500 paper-based; 250 computer-based). Electronic applications accepted. *Faculty research:* Range and forage science, soil and environmental science, crop physiology, weed science, plant breeding and genetics.

Montana State University, College of Graduate Studies, College of Agriculture, Department of Animal and Range Sciences, Bozeman, MT 59717. Offers MS, PhD. Part-time programs available. *Faculty:* 13 full-time (4 women), 4 part-time/adjunct (1 woman). *Students:* 5 full-time (2 women), 13 part-time (6 women), 1 international. Average age 31. 13 applicants, 38% accepted, 4 enrolled. In 2010, 5 master's, 2 doctorates awarded. *Degree requirements:* For master's, comprehensive exam; for doctorate, comprehensive exam, thesis/dissertation. *Entrance requirements:* For master's, GRE, minimum GPA of 3.0; undergraduate coursework in animal science, range science or closely-related field; faculty adviser; for doctorate, GRE. Additional exam requirements/recommendations for international students: Required—TOEFL (minimum score 550 paper-based; 213 computer-based; 80 iBT). *Application deadline:* For fall admission, 7/15 priority date for domestic students, 5/15 priority date for international students; for spring admission, 12/1 priority date for domestic students, 10/1 priority date for international students. Applications are processed on a rolling basis. Application fee: $30. Electronic applications accepted. *Expenses:* Tuition, state resident: full-time $5553.90. Tuition, nonresident: full-time $14,646. Required fees: $1233. *Financial support:* In 2010–11, 6 students received support, including 3 research assistantships (averaging $31,000 per year), 3 teaching assistantships (averaging $14,500 per year); tuition waivers (full) also available. Financial award application deadline: 3/1; financial award applicants required to submit FAFSA. *Faculty research:* Rangeland ecology, wildlife habitat management, residual feed intake, post-partum effect of bulls, increasing efficiency of sheep production systems. Total annual research expenditures: $1.5 million. *Unit head:* Dr. Glenn Duff, Department Head, 406-994-4850, Fax: 406-994-5589, E-mail: glenn.duff@montana.edu. *Application contact:* Dr. Carl A. Fox, Vice Provost for Graduate Education, 406-994-4145, Fax: 406-994-7433, E-mail: gradstudy@montana.edu.

New Mexico State University, Graduate School, College of Agricultural, Consumer and Environmental Sciences, Department of Animal and Range Sciences, Las Cruces, NM 88003-8001. Offers animal science (MS, PhD); domestic animal biology (M Ag); range science (M Ag, MS, PhD). Part-time programs available. *Faculty:* 9 full-time (2 women). *Students:* 36 full-time (23 women), 9 part-time (2 women); includes 6 minority (1 American Indian or Alaska Native,

non-Hispanic/Latino; 4 Hispanic/Latino; 1 Two or more races, non-Hispanic/Latino), 7 international. Average age 27. 27 applicants, 81% accepted, 16 enrolled. In 2010, 11 master's, 2 doctorates awarded. Terminal master's awarded for partial completion of doctoral program. *Degree requirements:* For master's, thesis, seminar, experimental statistics; for doctorate, thesis/dissertation, research tool. *Entrance requirements:* For master's, minimum GPA of 3.0 in last 60 hours of undergraduate course work (MS); for doctorate, minimum graduate GPA of 3.2. Additional exam requirements/recommendations for international students: Required—TOEFL (minimum score 530 paper-based; 71 computer-based), IELTS (minimum score 6). *Application deadline:* For fall admission, 7/1 priority date for domestic students, 7/1 for international students; for spring admission, 11/1 for domestic and international students. Applications are processed on a rolling basis. Application fee: $30 ($50 for international students). Electronic applications accepted. *Expenses:* Tuition, state resident: full-time $4536; part-time $242 per credit. Tuition, nonresident: full-time $15,816; part-time $712 per credit. Required fees: $636 per term. *Financial support:* In 2010–11, 25 students received support, including 3 research assistantships (averaging $12,823 per year), 24 teaching assistantships (averaging $20,008 per year); Federal Work-Study and health care benefits also available. Support available to part-time students. Financial award application deadline: 3/1. *Faculty research:* Reproductive physiology, ruminant nutrition, nutrition toxicology, range ecology, wildland hydrology. *Unit head:* Dr. Tim Ross, Interim Head, 575-646-2514, Fax: 575-646-5441, E-mail: tross@nmsu.edu. *Application contact:* Dr. Tim Ross, Interim Head, 575-646-2514, Fax: 575-646-5441, E-mail: tross@nmsu.edu.

North Dakota State University, College of Graduate and Interdisciplinary Studies, College of Agriculture, Food Systems, and Natural Resources, Department of Animal and Range Sciences, Fargo, ND 58108. Offers animal science (MS, PhD); natural resource management (MS, PhD); range sciences (MS, PhD). *Students:* 19 full-time (14 women), 7 part-time (4 women); includes 1 American Indian or Alaska Native, non-Hispanic/Latino; 1 Asian, non-Hispanic/Latino. Average age 25. 13 applicants, 62% accepted. In 2010, 17 master's, 2 doctorates awarded. *Degree requirements:* For master's, thesis; for doctorate, comprehensive exam, thesis/dissertation. *Entrance requirements:* For master's and doctorate, GRE General Test. Additional exam requirements/recommendations for international students: Required—TOEFL (minimum score 71 iBT). *Application deadline:* Applications are processed on a rolling basis. Application fee: $45 ($60 for international students). *Financial support:* In 2010–11, 1 fellowship with tuition reimbursement (averaging $18,000 per year), 29 research assistantships with tuition reimbursements (averaging $13,000 per year) were awarded; teaching assistantships, Federal Work-Study, institutionally sponsored loans, and tuition waivers (partial) also available. Financial award application deadline: 3/15. *Faculty research:* Reproduction, nutrition, meat and muscle biology, breeding/genetics. Total annual research expenditures: $1.5 million. *Unit head:* Dr. David Buchanan, Chair, 701-231-7643, Fax: 701-231-7590, E-mail: david.buchanan@ndsu.edu. *Application contact:* Dr. David Buchanan, Chair, 701-231-7643, Fax: 701-231-7590, E-mail: david.buchanan@ndsu.edu.

Oregon State University, Graduate School, College of Agricultural Sciences, Department of Rangeland Ecology and Management, Corvallis, OR 97331. Offers M Agr, MAIS, MS, PhD. Terminal master's awarded for partial completion of doctoral program. *Degree requirements:* For master's, thesis (for some programs); for doctorate, thesis/dissertation. *Entrance requirements:* For master's and doctorate, GRE, minimum GPA of 3.0 in last 90 hours of course work. Additional exam requirements/recommendations for international students: Required—TOEFL. *Faculty research:* Range ecology, watershed science, animal grazing, agroforestry.

Sul Ross State University, Division of Agricultural and Natural Resource Science, Program in Range and Wildlife Management, Alpine, TX 79832. Offers M Ag, MS. Part-time programs available. *Degree requirements:* For master's, thesis (for some programs). *Entrance requirements:* For master's, GRE General Test, minimum undergraduate GPA of 2.5 in last 60 hours.

Texas A&M University, College of Agriculture and Life Sciences, Department of Ecosystem Science and Management, College Station, TX 77843. Offers forestry (MS, PhD); rangeland ecology and management (M Agr, MS, PhD). Part-time programs available. *Faculty:* 24. *Students:* 59 full-time (31 women), 28 part-time (12 women); includes 16 minority (2 Black or African American, non-Hispanic/Latino; 1 Asian, non-Hispanic/Latino; 13 Hispanic/Latino), 12 international. Average age 27. In 2010, 9 master's, 3 doctorates awarded. Terminal master's awarded for partial completion of doctoral program. *Degree requirements:* For master's, thesis (for some programs); for doctorate, thesis/dissertation. *Entrance requirements:* For master's and doctorate, GRE General Test. Additional exam requirements/recommendations for international students: Required—TOEFL. *Application deadline:* For fall admission, 3/1 priority date for domestic students; for spring admission, 11/1 priority date for domestic students. Applications are processed on a rolling basis. Application fee: $50 ($75 for international students). Electronic applications accepted. *Financial support:* In 2010–11, fellowships with partial tuition reimbursements (averaging $15,000 per year), research assistantships with partial tuition reimbursements (averaging $15,000 per year), teaching assistantships with partial tuition reimbursements (averaging $15,000 per year) were awarded; career-related internships or

fieldwork and institutionally sponsored loans also available. Support available to part-time students. Financial award application deadline: 3/1; financial award applicants required to submit FAFSA. *Faculty research:* Expert systems, geographic information systems, economics, biology, genetics. *Unit head:* Dr. Steve Whisenant, Professor and Head, 979-845-5000, Fax: 979-845-6049, E-mail: s-whisenant@tamu.edu. *Application contact:* Dr. Carol Loopstra, Associate Professor, 979-862-2200, Fax: 979-845-6049, E-mail: c-loopstra@tamu.edu.

Texas A&M University–Kingsville, College of Graduate Studies, College of Agriculture and Home Economics, Program in Range and Wildlife Management, Kingsville, TX 78363. Offers MS. *Degree requirements:* For master's, comprehensive exam, thesis or alternative. *Entrance requirements:* For master's, GRE General Test, minimum GPA of 3.0. Additional exam requirements/recommendations for international students: Required—TOEFL.

Texas Tech University, Graduate School, College of Agricultural Sciences and Natural Resources, Department of Natural Resources Management, Lubbock, TX 79409. Offers fisheries science (MS, PhD); range science (MS, PhD); wildlife science (MS, PhD); wildlife, aquatic, and wildlands science and management (MS, PhD). Part-time programs available. *Faculty:* 9 full-time (0 women), 1 part-time/adjunct (0 women). *Students:* 47 full-time (14 women), 3 part-time (1 woman); includes 1 American Indian or Alaska Native, non-Hispanic/Latino; 1 Hispanic/Latino; 2 Two or more races, non-Hispanic/Latino, 7 international. Average age 27. 23 applicants, 61% accepted, 12 enrolled. In 2010, 5 master's, 2 doctorates awarded. *Degree requirements:* For master's, thesis; for doctorate, thesis/dissertation. *Entrance requirements:* For master's and doctorate, GRE General Test, formal approval from departmental committee. Additional exam requirements/recommendations for international students: Required—TOEFL (minimum score 550 paper-based; 213 computer-based; 79 iBT). *Application deadline:* For fall admission, 6/1 priority date for domestic students, 1/15 priority date for international students; for spring admission, 9/1 priority date for domestic students, 6/15 priority date for international students. Applications are processed on a rolling basis. Application fee: $50 ($75 for international students). Electronic applications accepted. *Expenses:* Tuition, state resident: full-time $5495.76; part-time $228.99 per credit hour. Tuition, nonresident: full-time $12,936; part-time $538.99 per credit hour. Required fees: $2674; $36 per credit hour. $905 per semester. *Financial support:* In 2010–11, 43 students received support, including 19 research assistantships with partial tuition reimbursements available (averaging $6,023 per year), 2 teaching assistantships with partial tuition reimbursements available (averaging $4,994 per year). Financial award application deadline: 4/15; financial award applicants required to submit FAFSA. *Faculty research:* Use of fire on range lands, big game, upland game, and waterfowl; playa lakes in the southern Great Plains; conservation biology; fish ecology and physiology. Total annual research expenditures: $921,668. *Unit head:* Dr. Mark Wallace, Interim Chairman, 806-742-2841, Fax: 806-742-2280, E-mail: mark.wallace@ttu.edu. *Application contact:* Renee Dillon, Sr. Business Assistant, 806-742-2841, E-mail: renee.dillon@ttu.edu.

The University of Arizona, College of Agriculture and Life Sciences, School of Natural Resources, Program in Rangeland Science and Management, Tucson, AZ 85721. Offers MS, PhD. *Students:* 69 full-time (37 women), 31 part-time (20 women); includes 11 Hispanic/Latino; 7 Two or more races, non-Hispanic/Latino, 12 international. Average age 33. *Degree requirements:* For master's, thesis; for doctorate, comprehensive exam, thesis/dissertation. *Entrance requirements:* For master's and doctorate, GRE General Test, minimum GPA of 3.0. Additional exam requirements/recommendations for international students: Required—TOEFL (minimum score 550 paper-based; 213 computer-based). *Application deadline:* Applications are processed on a rolling basis. Application fee: $75. *Expenses:* Tuition, state resident: full-time $7692. *Financial support:* Research assistantships, teaching assistantships, career-related internships or fieldwork, scholarships/grants, health care benefits, tuition waivers (partial), and unspecified assistantships available. *Faculty research:* Criteria for defining, mapping, and evaluating range sites; methods of establishing forage plants on southwestern range lands; plants for pollution and erosion control, beautification, and browse. *Application contact:* Cheryl L. Craddock, Academic Coordinator, 520-621-7260, Fax: 520-621-8801, E-mail: ccraddoc@email.arizona.edu.

University of California, Berkeley, Graduate Division, College of Natural Resources, Group in Range Management, Berkeley, CA 94720-1500. Offers MS. *Degree requirements:* For master's, thesis. *Entrance requirements:* For master's, GRE General Test, minimum GPA of 3.0, 3 letters of recommendation. Additional exam requirements/recommendations for international students: Required—TOEFL. *Faculty research:* Grassland and savannah ecology, wetland ecology, oak woodland classification, wildlife habitat management.

University of Wyoming, College of Agriculture and Natural Resources, Department of Renewable Resources, Laramie, WY 82070. Offers agroecology (MS); entomology (MS, PhD); entomology/water resources (MS, PhD); rangeland ecology and watershed management (MS, PhD), including soil sciences (PhD), soil sciences and water resources (MS); rangeland ecology and watershed management/water resources (MS, PhD); soil science (MS); soil science/water resources (PhD). Part-time programs available. *Degree requirements:* For master's, comprehensive exam, thesis, oral examination; for doctorate, comprehensive exam, thesis/dissertation, preliminary oral and written exam, oral final exam. *Entrance requirements:* For master's and doctorate, GRE General Test, minimum GPA of 3.0. Additional exam requirements/recommendations for international students: Required—TOEFL. Electronic applications accepted. *Faculty research:* Plant control, grazing management, riparian restoration, riparian management, reclamation.

Utah State University, School of Graduate Studies, College of Natural Resources, Department of Wildland Resources, Logan, UT 84322. Offers ecology (MS, PhD); forestry (MS, PhD); range science (MS, PhD); wildlife biology (MS, PhD). Part-time programs available. *Degree requirements:* For master's, thesis; for doctorate, comprehensive exam, thesis/dissertation. *Entrance requirements:* For master's and doctorate, GRE General Test, minimum GPA of 3.0. Additional exam requirements/recommendations for international students: Required—TOEFL. *Faculty research:* Range plant ecophysiology, plant community ecology, ruminant nutrition, population ecology.

Water Resources

Albany State University, College of Arts and Humanities, Program in Public Administration, Albany, GA 31705-2717. Offers community and economic development administration (MPA); criminal justice administration (MPA); fiscal management (MPA); general management (MPA); health administration and policy (MPA); human resources management (MPA); public policy (MPA); water resource management and policy (MPA). *Accreditation:* NASPAA. *Faculty:* 3 full-time (1 woman), 2 part-time/adjunct (0 women). *Students:* 13 full-time (7 women), 49 part-time (32 women); includes 60 Black or African American, non-Hispanic/Latino, 1 international. Average age 34. 18 applicants, 78% accepted, 12 enrolled. In 2010, 12 master's awarded. *Degree requirements:* For master's, professional public service internship, professional portfolio, capstone research project. *Entrance requirements:* For master's, GRE, MAT, or GMAT, baccalaureate degree from accredited college or university, two letters of recommendation, ASU medical and immunization form. *Application deadline:* For fall admission, 7/15 for domestic students, 5/15 for international students; for spring admission, 11/15 for domestic students, 9/15 for international students. Applications are processed on a rolling basis. Application fee: $20. Electronic applications accepted. *Expenses:* Tuition, state resident: full-time $3060; part-time $170 per credit hour. Tuition, nonresident: full-time $12,204; part-time $678 per credit hour. Required fees: $1160. Part-time tuition and fees vary according to course load. *Financial support:* Application deadline: 4/15. *Faculty research:* Public policy, strategic public human resources and human capital management, diversity management in the public sector and collective bargaining and labor relations in the public sector, e-government and public sector information systems, public administration pedagogy and business process modeling simulation, community development, nonprofit organizations, civic engagement and civic participation, healthcare disparities among minorities, poverty. Total annual research expenditures: $250. *Unit head:* Dr. Peter Ngwafu, Director, 229-430-4760, Fax: 229-430-7895, E-mail: peter.ngwafu@asurams.edu. *Application contact:* Dr. Rani George, Dean, Graduate School, 229-430-5118, Fax: 229-430-6398, E-mail: rani.george@asurams.edu.

California State University, Monterey Bay, College of Science, Media Arts and Technology, Program in Coastal and Watershed Science and Policy, Seaside, CA 93955-8001. Offers MS, PSM. Part-time programs available. *Degree requirements:* For master's, thesis, thesis defense. *Entrance requirements:* For master's, GRE, recommendations, interview. Additional exam requirements/recommendations for international students: Required—TOEFL (minimum score 525 paper-based; 213 computer-based; 71 iBT). Electronic applications accepted. *Faculty research:* Remote sensing and geospatial technology, MPA design, efficacy and management, marine science and ecology, watershed process, hydrology, restoration, sedim entology, ecosystem modeling.

Colorado State University, Graduate School, Warner College of Natural Resources, Department of Forest, Rangeland, and Watershed Stewardship, Fort Collins, CO 80523-1472. Offers forest sciences (MS, PhD); natural resources stewardship (MNRS); rangeland ecosystem science (MS, PhD); watershed science (MS). Part-time programs available. Postbaccalaureate distance learning degree programs offered (no on-campus study). *Faculty:* 18 full-time (5 women), 2 part-time/adjunct (0 women). *Students:* 45 full-time (21 women), 90 part-time (31 women); includes 9 minority (3 American Indian or Alaska Native, non-Hispanic/Latino; 1 Asian, non-Hispanic/Latino; 5 Hispanic/Latino), 9 international. Average age 34. 59 applicants, 76% accepted, 28 enrolled. In 2010, 27 master's, 2 doctorates awarded. *Degree requirements:* For master's, thesis (for some programs); for doctorate, comprehensive exam, thesis/dissertation. *Entrance requirements:* For master's, GRE General Test (minimum score 1000 verbal and quantitative), minimum GPA of 3.0, 3 letters of recommendation; for doctorate, GRE General Test (combined minimum score of 1100 on the Verbal and Quantitative sections), minimum GPA of 3.0, 3 letters of recommendation, statement of research interest. Additional exam requirements/recommendations for international students: Required—TOEFL (minimum score 550 paper-based; 213 computer-based; 80 iBT), IELTS (minimum score 6.5). *Application deadline:* For fall admission, 2/15 priority date for domestic and international students; for spring admission, 7/15 priority date for domestic and international students. Applications are processed on a rolling basis. Application fee: $50. Electronic applications accepted. *Expenses:* Tuition, state resident: full-time $7434; part-time $413 per credit. Tuition, nonresident: full-time $19,022; part-time $1057 per credit. Required fees: $1729; $88 per credit. *Financial support:* In 2010–11, 46 students received support, including 1 fellowship (averaging $23,971 per year), 32 research assistantships with full and partial tuition reimbursements available (averaging $15,871 per year), 13 teaching assistantships with full and partial tuition reimbursements available (averaging $7,106 per year); Federal Work-Study, scholarships/grants, and unspecified assistantships also available. Financial award application deadline: 2/15; financial award applicants required to submit FAFSA. *Faculty research:* Ecology, natural resource management, hydrology, restoration, human dimensions. Total annual research expenditures: $2.4 million. *Unit head:* Dr. Frederick Smith, Interim Department Head, 970-491-7505, Fax: 970-491-6754, E-mail: fwsmith@colostate.edu. *Application contact:* Sonya LeFebre, Coordinator, 970-491-1907, Fax: 970-491-6754, E-mail: sonya.lefebre@colostate.edu.

Duke University, Nicholas School of the Environment, Durham, NC 27708-0328. Offers coastal environmental management (MEM); DEL-environmental leadership (MEM); energy and environment (MEM); environmental economics and policy (MEM); environmental health and security (MEM); forest resource management (MF); global environmental change (MEM); resource ecology (MEM); water and air resources (MEM); JD/AM; JD/MEM; JD/MF; MAT/MEM; MBA/MEM; MBA/MF; MEM/MPP; MF/MPP. *Accreditation:* SAF (one or more programs are accredited). Part-time programs available. *Degree requirements:* For master's, thesis. *Entrance requirements:* For master's, GRE General Test, previous course work in biology or ecology, calculus, statistics, and microeconomics; computer familiarity with word processing and data analysis. Additional exam requirements/recommendations for international students: Required—TOEFL (minimum score 550 paper-based; 213 computer-based). Electronic applications accepted. *Expenses:* Contact institution. *Faculty research:* Ecosystem management, conservation ecology, earth systems, risk assessment.

Eastern Michigan University, Graduate School, College of Arts and Sciences, Department of Biology, Ypsilanti, MI 48197. Offers cell and molecular biology (MS); community college biology teaching (MS); ecology and organismal biology (MS); general biology (MS); water resources (MS). Part-time and evening/weekend programs available. Postbaccalaureate distance learning degree programs offered (minimal on-campus study). *Faculty:* 20 full-time (4 women). *Students:* 18 full-time (13 women), 35 part-time (19 women); includes 4 minority (2 Black or African American, non-Hispanic/Latino; 2 Two or more races, non-Hispanic/Latino), 13 international. Average age 27. 55 applicants, 47% accepted, 17 enrolled. In 2010, 10 master's awarded. *Entrance requirements:* For master's, GRE General Test, GRE Subject Test. Additional exam requirements/recommendations for international students: Required—TOEFL. *Application deadline:* Applications are processed on a rolling basis. Application fee: $35. *Financial support:* Fellowships, research assistantships with full tuition reimbursements, teaching assistantships with full tuition reimbursements, career-related internships or fieldwork, Federal Work-Study, institutionally sponsored loans, scholarships/grants, tuition waivers (partial), and unspecified assistantships available. Support available to part-time students. Financial award applicants required to submit FAFSA. *Unit head:* Dr. Marianne Laporte, Department Head, 734-487-4242, Fax: 734-487-9235, E-mail: mlaporte@emich.edu. *Application contact:* Dr. Marianne Laporte, Department Head, 734-487-4242, Fax: 734-487-9235, E-mail: mlaporte@emich.edu.

Eastern Michigan University, Graduate School, College of Arts and Sciences, Department of Geography and Geology, Programs in Geography and Geology, Ypsilanti, MI 48197. Offers geography (MA, MS); water resources (Graduate Certificate). Part-time and evening/weekend programs available. Postbaccalaureate distance learning degree programs offered (minimal on-campus study). *Students:* 1 full-time (0 women). Average age 27. *Degree requirements:* For master's, thesis optional. *Entrance requirements:* Additional exam requirements/recommendations for international students: Required—TOEFL. *Application deadline:* Applications are processed on a rolling basis. Application fee: $35. *Financial support:* Fellowships, research assistantships with full tuition reimbursements, teaching assistantships with full tuition reimbursements, career-related internships or fieldwork, Federal Work-Study, institutionally

Water Resources

Eastern Michigan University (continued)
sponsored loans, traineeships, and unspecified assistantships available. Support available to part-time students. Financial award applicants required to submit FAFSA. *Application contact:* Dr. Andrew Nazzaro, Program Advisor, 734-487-8486, Fax: 734-487-6979, E-mail: andrew.nazzaro@emich.edu.

Humboldt State University, Academic Programs, College of Natural Resources and Sciences, Programs in Natural Resources, Arcata, CA 95521-8299. Offers natural resources (MS), including fisheries, forestry, natural resources planning and interpretation, rangeland resources and wildland soils, wastewater utilization, watershed management, wildlife. *Students:* 62 full-time (27 women), 21 part-time (7 women); includes 4 minority (1 Asian, non-Hispanic/Latino; 2 Hispanic/Latino; 1 Two or more races, non-Hispanic/Latino), 2 international. Average age 29. 117 applicants, 47% accepted, 33 enrolled. In 2010, 23 master's awarded. *Degree requirements:* For master's, thesis or alternative. *Entrance requirements:* For master's, GRE, appropriate bachelor's degree, minimum GPA of 2.5, 3 letters of recommendation, resume. Additional exam requirements/recommendations for international students: Required—TOEFL (minimum score 500 paper-based; 173 computer-based). *Application deadline:* For fall admission, 2/1 for domestic and international students; for spring admission, 9/30 for domestic and international students. Applications are processed on a rolling basis. Application fee: $55. Tuition and fees vary according to program. *Financial support:* Fellowships, career-related internships or fieldwork and Federal Work-Study available. Support available to part-time students. Financial award application deadline: 3/1; financial award applicants required to submit FAFSA. *Faculty research:* Spotted owl habitat, pre-settlement vegetation, hardwood utilization, tree physiology, fisheries. *Unit head:* Dr. Gary Hendrickson, Coordinator, 707-826-4233, E-mail: thiesfel@humboldt.edu. *Application contact:* Julie Tucker, Administrative Support Coordinator, 707-826-3256, E-mail: jlt7002@humboldt.edu.

Inter American University of Puerto Rico, San Germán Campus, Graduate Studies Center, Program in Environmental Sciences, San Germán, PR 00683-5008. Offers environmental biology (MS); environmental chemistry (MS); water analysis (MS). Part-time and evening/weekend programs available. *Degree requirements:* For master's, comprehensive exam, thesis. *Entrance requirements:* For master's, GRE General Test or EXADEP, minimum GPA of 3.0. *Expenses:* Tuition: Part-time $202 per credit. Required fees: $258 per semester. *Faculty research:* Environmental biology, environmental chemistry, water resources and unit operations.

Marquette University, Graduate School, College of Engineering, Department of Civil and Environmental Engineering, Milwaukee, WI 53201-1881. Offers construction and public works management (MS, PhD); construction engineering and management (Certificate); environmental/water resources engineering (MS, PhD); structural design (Certificate); structural/geotechnical engineering (MS, PhD); transportation planning and engineering (MS, PhD); waste and wastewater treatment processes (Certificate). Part-time and evening/weekend programs available. *Faculty:* 13 full-time (0 women), 3 part-time/adjunct (0 women). *Students:* 20 full-time (4 women), 12 part-time (1 woman); includes 1 minority (Black or African American, non-Hispanic/Latino), 12 international. Average age 27. 66 applicants, 64% accepted, 9 enrolled. In 2010, 8 master's, 1 doctorate awarded. Terminal master's awarded for partial completion of doctoral program. *Degree requirements:* For master's, comprehensive exam, thesis or alternative; for doctorate, thesis/dissertation. *Entrance requirements:* For master's, GRE General Test (recommended), minimum GPA of 3.0, official transcripts from all current and previous colleges/universities except Marquette, three letters of recommendation; for doctorate, GRE General Test, minimum GPA of 3.0, official transcripts from all current and previous colleges/universities except Marquette, three letters of recommendation, brief statement of purpose, submission of any English-language publications authored by applicant (strongly recommended). Additional exam requirements/recommendations for international students: Required—TOEFL (minimum score 530 paper-based; 78 computer-based). *Application deadline:* For fall admission, 6/1 priority date for domestic students. Applications are processed on a rolling basis. Application fee: $50. Electronic applications accepted. *Expenses:* Tuition: Full-time $16,290; part-time $905 per credit hour. Tuition and fees vary according to program. *Financial support:* In 2010–11, 13 students received support, including 4 fellowships with tuition reimbursements available, 4 research assistantships with tuition reimbursements available, 10 teaching assistantships with tuition reimbursements available; Federal Work-Study, institutionally sponsored loans, scholarships/grants, and tuition waivers (full and partial) also available. Support available to part-time students. Financial award application deadline: 2/15. *Faculty research:* Highway safety, highway performance, and intelligent transportation systems; surface mount technology; watershed management. Total annual research expenditures: $662,392. *Unit head:* Dr. Thomas Wenzel, Chair, 414-288-7030, Fax: 414-288-7521, E-mail: thomas.wenzel@marquette.edu. *Application contact:* Dr. Stephen M. Heinrich, Director of Graduate Studies, 414-288-5466, E-mail: stephen.heinrich@marquette.edu.

Missouri University of Science and Technology, Graduate School, Department of Geological Sciences and Engineering, Rolla, MO 65409. Offers geological engineering (MS, DE, PhD); geology and geophysics (MS, PhD), including geochemistry, geology, geophysics, groundwater and environmental geology; petroleum engineering (MS, DE, PhD). Part-time programs available. *Degree requirements:* For master's, thesis optional; for doctorate, comprehensive exam, thesis/dissertation. *Entrance requirements:* For master's, GRE General Test (minimum score 600 quantitative, writing 3.5), minimum GPA of 3.0 in last 4 semesters; for doctorate, GRE General Test (minimum: Q 600, GRE WR 3.5). Additional exam requirements/recommendations for international students: Required—TOEFL. Electronic applications accepted. *Faculty research:* Digital image processing and geographic information systems, mineralogy, igneous and sedimentary petrology-geochemistry, sedimentology groundwater hydrology and contaminant transport.

Nova Scotia Agricultural College, Research and Graduate Studies, Truro, NS B2N 5E3, Canada. Offers agriculture (M Sc), including air quality, animal behavior, animal molecular genetics, animal nutrition, animal technology, aquaculture, botany, crop management, crop physiology, ecology, environmental microbiology, food science, horticulture, nutrient management, pest management, physiology, plant biotechnology, plant pathology, soil chemistry, soil fertility, waste management and composting, water quality. Program offered jointly with Dalhousie University. Part-time programs available. *Degree requirements:* For master's, thesis, ATC Exam Teaching Assistantship. *Entrance requirements:* For master's, honors B Sc, minimum GPA of 3.0. Additional exam requirements/recommendations for international students: Required—TOEFL (minimum score 580 paper-based; 237 computer-based; 92 iBT), IELTS, Michigan English Language Assessment Battery, CanTEST, CAEL. *Faculty research:* Bio-product development, organic agriculture, nutrient management, air and water quality, agricultural biotechnology.

Rutgers, The State University of New Jersey, New Brunswick, Graduate School-New Brunswick, Department of Environmental Sciences, Piscataway, NJ 08854-8097. Offers air pollution and resources (MS, PhD); aquatic biology (MS, PhD); aquatic chemistry (MS, PhD); atmospheric science (MS, PhD); chemistry and physics of aerosol and hydrosol systems (MS, PhD); environmental chemistry (MS, PhD); environmental microbiology (MS, PhD); environmental toxicology (PhD); exposure assessment (PhD); fate and effects of pollutants (MS, PhD); pollution prevention and control (MS, PhD); water and wastewater treatment (MS, PhD); water resources (MS, PhD). Terminal master's awarded for partial completion of doctoral program. *Degree requirements:* For master's, comprehensive exam, thesis or alternative, oral final exam; for doctorate, comprehensive exam, thesis/dissertation, thesis defense, qualifying exam. *Entrance requirements:* For master's and doctorate, GRE General Test. Additional exam requirements/recommendations for international students: Required—TOEFL. Electronic applications accepted. *Expenses:* Tuition, state resident: full-time $7200; part-time $600 per credit. Tuition, nonresident: full-time $11,124; part-time $927 per credit. *Faculty research:* Biological waste treatment; contaminant fate and transport; air, soil and water quality.

State University of New York College of Environmental Science and Forestry, Program in Environmental Science, Syracuse, NY 13210-2779. Offers environmental and community land planning (MPS, MS, PhD); environmental and natural resources policy (PhD); environmental communication and participatory processes (MPS, MS, PhD); environmental policy and democratic processes (MPS, MS, PhD); environmental systems and risk management (MPS, MS, PhD); water and wetland resource studies (MPS, MS, PhD). Part-time programs available. *Degree requirements:* For master's, thesis (for some programs); for doctorate, comprehensive exam, thesis/dissertation. *Entrance requirements:* For master's and doctorate, GRE General Test, minimum GPA of 3.0. Additional exam requirements/recommendations for international students: Required—TOEFL (minimum score 550 paper-based; 213 computer-based; 80 iBT), IELTS (minimum score 6). *Expenses:* Tuition, state resident: full-time $8370; part-time $349 per credit hour. Tuition, nonresident: full-time $13,780. Required fees: $30.30 per credit hour. $20 per year. *Faculty research:* Environmental education/communications, water resources, land resources, waste management.

Tropical Agriculture Research and Higher Education Center, Graduate School, Turrialba, Costa Rica. Offers agribusiness management (MS); agroforestry systems (PhD); development practices (MS); ecological agriculture (MS); environmental socioeconomics (MS); forestry in tropical and subtropical zones (PhD); integrated watershed management (MS); international sustainable tourism (MS); management and conservation of tropical rainforests and biodiversity (MS); tropical agriculture (PhD); tropical agroforestry (MS). *Entrance requirements:* For master's, GRE, 2 years of related professional experience, letters of recommendation; for doctorate, GRE, 4 letters of recommendation, letter of support from employing organization, master's degree in agronomy, biological sciences, forestry, natural resources or related field. Additional exam requirements/recommendations for international students: Required—TOEFL (minimum score 550 paper-based; 213 computer-based). Electronic applications accepted. *Faculty research:* Biodiversity in fragmented landscapes, ecosystem management, integrated pest management, environmental livestock production, biotechnology carbon balances in diverse land uses.

University of Alaska Fairbanks, College of Engineering and Mines, Department of Civil and Environmental Engineering, Program in Environmental Engineering, Fairbanks, AK 99775-5900. Offers engineering (PhD), including environmental engineering; environmental engineering (MS), including environmental contaminants, environmental science and management, water supply and waste treatment. Part-time programs available. *Students:* 3 full-time (all women), 3 part-time (2 women). Average age 28. 5 applicants, 60% accepted, 1 enrolled. In 2010, 3 master's, 1 doctorate awarded. *Degree requirements:* For master's, comprehensive exam, thesis or alternative; for doctorate, comprehensive exam, thesis/dissertation, oral exam, oral defense. *Entrance requirements:* For master's, basic computer techniques; for doctorate, GRE General Test. Additional exam requirements/recommendations for international students: Required—TOEFL (minimum score 575 paper-based; 213 computer-based). *Application deadline:* For fall admission, 6/1 for domestic students, 3/1 for international students; for spring admission, 10/15 for domestic students, 9/1 for international students. Applications are processed on a rolling basis. Application fee: $60. Electronic applications accepted. *Expenses:* Tuition, state resident: full-time $5688; part-time $316 per credit. Tuition, nonresident: full-time $11,628; part-time $646 per credit. Required fees: $289 per semester. Tuition and fees vary according to course load and reciprocity agreements. *Financial support:* In 2010–11, 4 research assistantships (averaging $13,290 per year), 1 teaching assistantship (averaging $7,088 per year) were awarded; fellowships, career-related internships or fieldwork, Federal Work-Study, scholarships/grants, health care benefits, and unspecified assistantships also available. Support available to part-time students. Financial award application deadline: 7/1; financial award applicants required to submit FAFSA. *Unit head:* Dr. David Barnes, Department Chair, 907-474-7241, Fax: 907-474-6087, E-mail: fyeqe@uaf.edu. *Application contact:* Dr. David Barnes, Department Chair, 907-474-7241, Fax: 907-474-6087, E-mail: fyeqe@uaf.edu.

The University of Arizona, College of Agriculture and Life Sciences, Department of Soil, Water and Environmental Science, Tucson, AZ 85721. Offers MS, PhD. *Faculty:* 10 full-time (2 women). *Students:* 57 full-time (40 women), 6 part-time (3 women); includes 2 Black or African American, non-Hispanic/Latino; 1 American Indian or Alaska Native, non-Hispanic/Latino; 1 Asian, non-Hispanic/Latino; 11 Hispanic/Latino; 4 Two or more races, non-Hispanic/Latino, 18 international. Average age 33. 37 applicants, 54% accepted, 13 enrolled. In 2010, 12 master's, 6 doctorates awarded. *Degree requirements:* For master's, thesis; for doctorate, comprehensive exam, thesis/dissertation. *Entrance requirements:* For master's, GRE (recommended), minimum GPA of 3.0, letter of interest, 3 letters of recommendation; for doctorate, GRE (recommended), MS, minimum GPA of 3.0, letter of interest, 3 letters of recommendation. Additional exam requirements/recommendations for international students: Required—TOEFL (minimum score 550 paper-based; 213 computer-based; 80 iBT). *Application deadline:* For fall admission, 6/1 for domestic students, 12/1 for international students; for spring admission, 10/1 for domestic students, 6/1 for international students. Applications are processed on a rolling basis. Application fee: $75. *Expenses:* Tuition, state resident: full-time $7692. *Financial support:* In 2010–11, 14 students received support, including 32 research assistantships with full and partial tuition reimbursements available (averaging $18,538 per year), 4 teaching assistantships with full and partial tuition reimbursements available (averaging $18,275 per year); fellowships, Federal Work-Study, institutionally sponsored loans, scholarships/grants, health care benefits, tuition waivers (full and partial), and unspecified assistantships also available. Financial award application deadline: 5/1. *Faculty research:* Plant production, environmental microbiology, contaminant flow and transport, aquaculture. Total annual research expenditures: $3.6 million. *Unit head:* Dr. Jeffery C. Silvertooth, Head, 520-621-7228, Fax: 520-621-1647, E-mail: silver@ag.arizona.edu. *Application contact:* Alicia Velasquez, 520-621-1606, Fax: 520-621-1647, E-mail: avelasqu@ag.arizona.edu.

The University of Arizona, College of Agriculture and Life Sciences, School of Natural Resources, Watershed Resources Program, Tucson, AZ 85721. Offers MS, PhD. *Students:* 1 full-time (0 women), 6 part-time (4 women); includes 1 Asian, non-Hispanic/Latino; 2 Hispanic/Latino. Average age 40. *Degree requirements:* For master's, thesis; for doctorate, comprehensive exam, thesis/dissertation. *Entrance requirements:* For master's, GRE General Test, minimum GPA of 3.0, 3 letters of recommendation; for doctorate, GRE General Test, minimum GPA of 3.0, 3 letters of recommendation, MA or MS. Additional exam requirements/recommendations for international students: Required—TOEFL (minimum score 550 paper-based; 213 computer-based). *Application deadline:* For fall admission, 8/1 priority date for domestic students, 12/1 for international students; for spring admission, 7/1 for international students. Applications are processed on a rolling basis. Application fee: $75. *Expenses:* Tuition, state resident: full-time $7692. *Financial support:* Research assistantships with partial tuition reimbursements, teaching assistantships with partial tuition reimbursements, career-related internships or fieldwork, scholarships/grants, health care benefits, tuition waivers (partial), and unspecified assistantships available. *Faculty research:* Forest fuel characteristics, prescribed fire, tree ring-fire scar analysis, erosion, sedimentation. *Unit head:* Dr. Joseph G. Hiller, Chair, 520-621-7255, Fax: 520-621-8801, E-mail: jghiller@cals.arizona.edu. *Application contact:* Cheryl L. Craddock, Academic Coordinator, 520-621-7260, Fax: 520-621-8801, E-mail: ccraddoc@email.arizona.edu.

The University of Arizona, College of Science, Department of Hydrology and Water Resources, Tucson, AZ 85721. Offers MS, PhD. Part-time programs available. *Faculty:* 15 full-time (2 women). *Students:* 37 full-time (10 women), 11 part-time (4 women); includes 5 Hispanic/Latino; 3 Two or more races, non-Hispanic/Latino, 10 international. Average age 33. 66 applicants, 14% accepted, 9 enrolled. In 2010, 6 master's, 4 doctorates awarded. *Degree requirements:* For master's, thesis; for doctorate, thesis/dissertation. *Entrance requirements:*

For master's, GRE General Test, 3 letters of recommendation, bachelor's degree in related field; for doctorate, GRE General Test, minimum undergraduate GPA of 3.2, graduate 3.4; 3 letters of recommendation; master's degree in related field; master's thesis abstract. Additional exam requirements/recommendations for international students: Required—TOEFL (minimum score 550 paper-based; 213 computer-based; 79 iBT). *Application deadline:* For fall admission, 5/1 for domestic students, 12/1 for international students; for spring admission, 10/1 for domestic students, 6/1 for international students. Applications are processed on a rolling basis. Application fee: $75. Electronic applications accepted. *Expenses:* Tuition, state resident: full-time $7692. *Financial support:* In 2010–11, 20 research assistantships with full tuition reimbursements (averaging $23,223 per year), 4 teaching assistantships with full tuition reimbursements (averaging $23,586 per year) were awarded; institutionally sponsored loans, scholarships/grants, health care benefits, and unspecified assistantships also available. Financial award application deadline: 1/31. *Faculty research:* Subsurface and surface hydrology, hydrometeorology/climatology, applied remote sensing, water resource systems, environmental hydrology and water quality. Total annual research expenditures: $5.5 million. *Unit head:* Thomas Maddock, Department Head, 520-621-7120, E-mail: maddock@hwr.arizona.edu. *Application contact:* Terrie Thompson, Academic Advising Coordinator, 520-621-3131, Fax: 520-621-1422, E-mail: programs@hwr.arizona.edu.

University of California, Riverside, Graduate Division, Program in Soil and Water Sciences, Riverside, CA 92521-0102. Offers MS, PhD. *Faculty:* 27 full-time (4 women). *Students:* 17 full-time (10 women). Average age 29. 63 applicants, 19% accepted, 9 enrolled. In 2010, 4 master's awarded. *Entrance requirements:* For master's and doctorate, minimum GPA of 3.2. Additional exam requirements/recommendations for international students: Required—TOEFL (minimum score 550 paper-based; 213 computer-based; 80 iBT). *Application deadline:* For fall admission, 5/1 for domestic students, 2/1 for international students; for winter admission, 9/1 for domestic students, 7/1 for international students; for spring admission, 12/1 for domestic students, 10/1 for international students. Application fee: $60 ($75 for international students). Electronic applications accepted. *Financial support:* In 2010–11, fellowships with tuition reimbursements (averaging $12,000 per year), research assistantships with tuition reimbursements (averaging $18,000 per year) were awarded. *Unit head:* Dr. Jay Gan, Chair, 951-827-2712, Fax: 951-827-3993. *Application contact:* Mari Ridgeway, Program Assistant, 951-827-5103, Fax: 951-827-3993, E-mail: soilwater@ucr.edu.

University of Colorado Denver, College of Liberal Arts and Sciences, Department of Geography and Environmental Sciences, Denver, CO 80217. Offers environmental sciences (MS), including air quality, ecosystems, environmental health, environmental science education, environmental sciences, geo-spatial analysis, hazardous waste, water quality. Part-time and evening/weekend programs available. *Students:* 48 full-time (28 women), 4 part-time (3 women); includes 2 Black or African American, non-Hispanic/Latino; 2 Asian, non-Hispanic/Latino; 3 Hispanic/Latino, 8 international. Average age 29. 44 applicants, 52% accepted, 14 enrolled. In 2010, 17 master's awarded. *Degree requirements:* For master's, thesis or alternative. *Entrance requirements:* For master's, GRE General Test, BA in one of the natural/physical sciences or engineering (or equivalent background); prerequisite coursework in calculus and physics (one semester each), general chemistry with lab and general biology with lab (two semesters each). Additional exam requirements/recommendations for international students: Required—TOEFL (minimum score 525 paper-based; 197 computer-based). *Application deadline:* For fall admission, 4/1 for domestic students; for spring admission, 10/1 for domestic students. Application fee: $50 ($75 for international students). Electronic applications accepted. *Expenses:* Tuition, state resident: full-time $7332; part-time $355 per credit hour. Tuition, nonresident: full-time $18,990; part-time $1055 per credit hour. Required fees: $998. Tuition and fees vary according to course level, course load, degree level, campus/location, program, reciprocity agreements and student level. *Financial support:* Research assistantships, teaching assistantships, Federal Work-Study available. Financial award application deadline: 4/1; financial award applicants required to submit FAFSA. *Faculty research:* Air quality, environmental health, ecosystems, hazardous waste, water quality, geo-spatial analysis and environmental science education. *Unit head:* Dr. John Wyckoff, Director, 303-556-2590, Fax: 303-556-6197, E-mail: john.wyckoff@cudenver.edu. *Application contact:* Dr. John Wyckoff, Director, 303-556-2590, Fax: 303-556-6197, E-mail: john.wyckoff@cudenver.edu.

University of Florida, Graduate School, College of Agricultural and Life Sciences, Department of Soil and Water Science, Gainesville, FL 32611. Offers MS, PhD. Part-time and evening/weekend programs available. Postbaccalaureate distance learning degree programs offered (no on-campus study). *Faculty:* 20 full-time (3 women). *Students:* 66 full-time (32 women), 59 part-time (30 women); includes 2 Black or African American, non-Hispanic/Latino; 1 Asian, non-Hispanic/Latino; 1 Hispanic/Latino, 43 international. Average age 31. 64 applicants, 50% accepted, 6 enrolled. In 2010, 14 master's, 11 doctorates awarded. Terminal master's awarded for partial completion of doctoral program. *Degree requirements:* For master's, thesis (for some programs), Thesis and non-thesis Master's Program; for doctorate, comprehensive exam, thesis/dissertation. *Entrance requirements:* For master's and doctorate, GRE General Test minimum score 1000. (GRE expires 5 years from test date), minimum GPA of 3.0. Additional exam requirements/recommendations for international students: Required—TOEFL (minimum score 550 paper-based; 213 computer-based; 80 iBT), IELTS (minimum score 6). *Application deadline:* For fall admission, 3/1 priority date for domestic students, 3/1 for international students; for spring admission, 10/1 for domestic and international students. Applications are processed on a rolling basis. Application fee: $30. Electronic applications accepted. *Expenses:* Tuition, state resident: full-time $10,915.92. Tuition, nonresident: full-time $28,309. *Financial support:* In 2010–11, 51 students received support, including 10 fellowships, 40 research assistantships (averaging $16,291 per year), 1 teaching assistantship (averaging $15,450 per year); career-related internships or fieldwork, Federal Work-Study, institutionally sponsored loans, and unspecified assistantships also available. Support available to part-time students. Financial award applicants required to submit FAFSA. *Faculty research:* Nutrient, pesticide, and waste management; soil, water, and aquifer remediation; carbon dynamics and ecosystem services; landscape analysis and modeling; wetlands and aquatic ecosystems. *Unit head:* K. Ramesh Reddy, PhD, Chair, 352-392-1804 Ext. 317, Fax: 352-392-3399, E-mail: krr@ufl.edu. *Application contact:* Andrew Ogram, PhD, Graduate Coordinator, 352-392-1951 Ext. 211, Fax: 352-392-3902, E-mail: aogram@ufl.edu.

University of Idaho, College of Graduate Studies, Department of Water Resources, Moscow, ID 83844-2282. Offers MS, PhD. *Faculty:* 16 full-time. *Students:* 31 full-time, 15 part-time. Average age 33. In 2010, 2 master's awarded. *Application deadline:* Applications are processed on a rolling basis. Application fee: $60. Electronic applications accepted. *Expenses:* Tuition, nonresident: part-time $580 per credit. Required fees: $306 per credit. *Financial support:* Applicants required to submit FAFSA. *Faculty research:* Water resource systems, biological wastewater treatment and water reclamation, invasive species, aquatics ecosystem restoration, watershed science and management. *Unit head:* Dr. Jan Boll, Director, 208-885-9694, E-mail: water@uidaho.edu. *Application contact:* Dr. Jan Boll, Director, 208-885-9694, E-mail: water@uidaho.edu.

University of Maine, Graduate School, College of Natural Sciences, Forestry, and Agriculture, Department of Biological Sciences, Program in Ecology and Environmental Science, Orono, ME 04469. Offers water resources (PhD). Part-time programs available. *Students:* 41 full-time (30 women), 11 part-time (6 women), 1 international. Average age 31. 84 applicants, 20% accepted, 15 enrolled. In 2010, 11 master's, 4 doctorates awarded. *Degree requirements:* For doctorate, thesis/dissertation. *Entrance requirements:* For master's and doctorate, GRE General Test. Additional exam requirements/recommendations for international students: Required—TOEFL. *Application deadline:* For fall admission, 2/1 priority date for domestic students. Applications are processed on a rolling basis. Application fee: $65. Electronic applications accepted. *Expenses:* Tuition, state resident: full-time $400. Tuition, nonresident: full-time $1050. *Financial support:* Career-related internships or fieldwork, Federal Work-Study, institutionally sponsored loans, and tuition waivers (full) available. Financial award application deadline: 3/1. *Unit head:* Dr. Chris Cronan, Coordinator, 207-581-3235. *Application contact:* Scott G. Delcourt, Associate Dean of the Graduate School, 207-581-3291, Fax: 207-581-3232, E-mail: graduate@maine.edu.

University of Maine, Graduate School, College of Natural Sciences, Forestry, and Agriculture, Department of Earth Sciences, Orono, ME 04469. Offers water resources (MS, PhD). Part-time programs available. *Faculty:* 10 full-time (2 women), 4 part-time/adjunct (1 woman). *Students:* 21 full-time (11 women), 10 part-time (4 women), 6 international. Average age 29. 37 applicants, 51% accepted, 11 enrolled. In 2010, 3 master's, 4 doctorates awarded. *Degree requirements:* For master's, thesis; for doctorate, one foreign language, thesis/dissertation. *Entrance requirements:* For master's and doctorate, GRE General Test. Additional exam requirements/recommendations for international students: Required—TOEFL. *Application deadline:* For fall admission, 2/1 priority date for domestic students. Applications are processed on a rolling basis. Application fee: $65. Electronic applications accepted. *Expenses:* Tuition, state resident: full-time $400. Tuition, nonresident: full-time $1050. *Financial support:* In 2010–11, 5 research assistantships with tuition reimbursements (averaging $16,130 per year), 6 teaching assistantships with tuition reimbursements (averaging $12,790 per year) were awarded; Federal Work-Study, institutionally sponsored loans, and tuition waivers (full and partial) also available. Financial award application deadline: 3/1. *Faculty research:* Appalachian bedrock geology, Quaternary studies, marine geology. *Unit head:* Dr. Joseph Kelley, Chair, 207-581-2162, Fax: 207-581-2202. *Application contact:* Scott G. Delcourt, Associate Dean of the Graduate School, 207-581-3291, Fax: 207-581-3232, E-mail: graduate@maine.edu.

University of Massachusetts Amherst, Graduate School, College of Natural Sciences, Department of Environmental Conservation, Amherst, MA 01003. Offers building systems (MS, PhD); environmental policy and human dimensions (MS, PhD); forest resources (MS, PhD); water, wetlands and watersheds (MS, PhD); wildlife and fisheries conservation (MS, PhD). Part-time programs available. *Faculty:* 51 full-time (7 women). *Students:* 55 full-time (30 women), 35 part-time (16 women); includes 5 minority (2 Black or African American, non-Hispanic/Latino; 3 Hispanic/Latino), 10 international. Average age 32. 73 applicants, 41% accepted, 23 enrolled. In 2010, 8 master's, 4 doctorates awarded. Terminal master's awarded for partial completion of doctoral program. *Degree requirements:* For master's, thesis or alternative; for doctorate, comprehensive exam, thesis/dissertation. *Entrance requirements:* For master's and doctorate, GRE General Test. Additional exam requirements/recommendations for international students: Required—TOEFL (minimum score 550 paper-based; 213 computer-based; 80 iBT), IELTS (minimum score 6.5). *Application deadline:* For fall admission, 2/1 for domestic and international students; for spring admission, 10/1 for domestic and international students. Applications are processed on a rolling basis. Application fee: $50 ($65 for international students). Electronic applications accepted. *Expenses:* Tuition, state resident: full-time $2640. Required fees: $8282. One-time fee: $357 full-time. *Financial support:* In 2010–11, 6 fellowships with full tuition reimbursements (averaging $14,507 per year), 62 research assistantships with full tuition reimbursements (averaging $9,977 per year), 33 teaching assistantships with full tuition reimbursements (averaging $6,243 per year) were awarded; career-related internships or fieldwork, Federal Work-Study, scholarships/grants, traineeships, health care benefits, tuition waivers (full), and unspecified assistantships also available. Support available to part-time students. Financial award application deadline: 2/1; financial award applicants required to submit FAFSA. *Unit head:* Dr. Matt Kelty, Graduate Program Director, 413-545-2666, Fax: 413-545-4358. *Application contact:* Jean M. Ames, Supervisor of Admissions, 413-545-0721, Fax: 413-577-0100, E-mail: gradadm@grad.umass.edu.

University of Minnesota, Twin Cities Campus, Graduate School, College of Food, Agricultural and Natural Resource Sciences, Program in Water Resources Science, Minneapolis, MN 55455-0213. Offers MS, PhD. Part-time programs available. *Faculty:* 120 full-time (23 women). *Students:* 29 full-time (18 women), 4 part-time (2 women), 3 international. Average age 30. 59 applicants, 29% accepted, 15 enrolled. In 2010, 12 master's, 4 doctorates awarded. *Degree requirements:* For master's, comprehensive exam, thesis; for doctorate, comprehensive exam, thesis/dissertation. *Entrance requirements:* For master's and doctorate, GRE, minimum GPA of 3.0, calculus, chemistry, biology, physics. Additional exam requirements/recommendations for international students: Required—TOEFL (minimum score 550 paper-based; 213 computer-based; 79 iBT). *Application deadline:* For fall and spring admission, 12/15 priority date for domestic and international students. Applications are processed on a rolling basis. Application fee: $75 ($95 for international students). Electronic applications accepted. *Financial support:* In 2010–11, fellowships with full tuition reimbursements (averaging $23,500 per year), research assistantships with full and partial tuition reimbursements (averaging $19,000 per year) were awarded; scholarships/grants, health care benefits, and unspecified assistantships also available. Financial award application deadline: 12/15. *Faculty research:* Hydrology, limnology, water policy and economics, water quality, water chemistry. Total annual research expenditures: $442,254. *Unit head:* Dr. Ray Newman, Director of Graduate Studies, 612-624-7456, E-mail: rnewman@umn.edu. *Application contact:* Bonnie R Anderson, Director of Graduate Studies Assistant, 612-624-7456, Fax: 612-625-1263, E-mail: ander742@umn.edu.

University of Nevada, Las Vegas, Graduate College, College of Science, Program in Water Resources Management, Las Vegas, NV 89154-4029. Offers MS. Part-time programs available. *Faculty:* 2 part-time/adjunct (0 women). *Students:* 4 full-time (3 women), 7 part-time (4 women); includes 3 minority (1 Hispanic/Latino; 2 Two or more races, non-Hispanic/Latino), 2 international. Average age 30. 8 applicants, 38% accepted, 2 enrolled. In 2010, 4 master's awarded. *Degree requirements:* For master's, comprehensive exam, thesis. *Entrance requirements:* For master's, GRE Subject Test. Additional exam requirements/recommendations for international students: Required—TOEFL (minimum score 550 paper-based; 213 computer-based; 80 iBT), IELTS (minimum score 7). *Application deadline:* For fall admission, 2/1 priority date for domestic and international students; for spring admission, 10/1 priority date for domestic and international students. Applications are processed on a rolling basis. Application fee: $60 ($95 for international students). Electronic applications accepted. *Expenses:* Tuition, area resident: Part-time $239.50 per credit. Tuition, state resident: part-time $239.50 per credit. Tuition, nonresident: part-time $503 per credit. Required fees: $108 per semester. Tuition and fees vary according to course load, program and reciprocity agreements. *Financial support:* In 2010–11, 1 student received support, including 1 research assistantship with partial tuition reimbursement available (averaging $14,000 per year); institutionally sponsored loans, scholarships/grants, health care benefits, and unspecified assistantships also available. Financial award application deadline: 3/1. *Faculty research:* Hydrogeology, water conservation, environmental chemistry, water resources planning, hydrology, waste management: hazardous materials management. *Unit head:* Dr. Michael Nicholl, Chair/Associate Professor, 702-895-4616, Fax: 702-895-4064, E-mail: michael.nicholl@unlv.edu. *Application contact:* Graduate College Admissions Evaluator, 702-895-3320, Fax: 702-895-4180, E-mail: gradcollege@unlv.edu.

University of New Brunswick Fredericton, School of Graduate Studies, Faculty of Engineering, Department of Civil Engineering, Fredericton, NB E3B 5A3, Canada. Offers construction engineering and management (M Eng, M Sc E, PhD); environmental engineering (M Eng, M Sc E, PhD); environmental studies (M Eng); geotechnical engineering (M Eng, M Sc E, PhD); groundwater/hydrology (M Eng, M Sc E, PhD); materials (M Eng, M Sc E, PhD); pavements (M Eng, M Sc E, PhD); structures (M Eng, M Sc E, PhD); transportation (M Eng, M Sc E, PhD). Part-time programs available. *Faculty:* 13 full-time (1 woman), 7 part-time/adjunct (1 woman). *Students:* 34 full-time (8 women), 16 part-time (2 women). In 2010, 16 master's, 6 doctorates awarded. *Degree requirements:* For master's, thesis, proposal; for doctorate, comprehensive exam, thesis/dissertation, qualifying exam; proposal; 27 credit hours of courses. *Entrance requirements:* For master's, minimum GPA of 3.0; B Sc E in civil engineering or related engineering degree; for doctorate, minimum GPA of 3.0; graduate degree in engineering

Water Resources

University of New Brunswick Fredericton (continued)

or applied science. Additional exam requirements/recommendations for international students: Required—TWE (minimum score 4), TOEFL (minimum score 580 paper-based; 237 computer-based) or IELTS (minimum score 7.5). *Application deadline:* For fall admission, 5/1 priority date for domestic students; for winter admission, 11/1 priority date for domestic students. Applications are processed on a rolling basis. Application fee: $50 Canadian dollars. *Expenses:* Tuition, area resident: Full-time $3708; part-time $927 per term. International tuition: $6300 full-time. Required fees: $50 per term. *Financial support:* In 2010–11, 52 research assistantships (averaging $7,000 per year), 46 teaching assistantships (averaging $2,000 per year) were awarded; career-related internships or fieldwork and scholarships/grants also available. *Faculty research:* Construction engineering and management; materials and infrastructure renewal; highway and pavement research; structures and solid mechanics; geotechnical, soil; structure interaction; transportation and planning; environment, solid waste management. *Unit head:* Dr. Eric Hildebrand, Director of Graduate Studies, 506-453-5113, Fax: 506-453-3568, E-mail: edh@unb.ca. *Application contact:* Joyce Moore, Graduate Secretary, 506-452-6127, Fax: 506-453-3568, E-mail: civil-grad@unb.ca.

University of New Hampshire, Graduate School, College of Life Sciences and Agriculture, Department of Natural Resources, Durham, NH 03824. Offers environmental conservation (MS); forestry (MS); integrated coastal ecosystem science, policy, management (MS); natural resources (MS); water resources (MS); wildlife (MS). Part-time programs available. *Faculty:* 40 full-time. *Students:* 22 full-time (8 women), 27 part-time (15 women); includes 1 Asian, non-Hispanic/Latino; 1 Hispanic/Latino, 1 international. Average age 30. 54 applicants, 39% accepted, 14 enrolled. In 2010, 13 master's awarded. *Degree requirements:* For master's, thesis or alternative. *Entrance requirements:* For master's, GRE General Test. Additional exam requirements/recommendations for international students: Required—TOEFL (minimum score 550 paper-based; 213 computer-based; 80 iBT). *Application deadline:* For fall admission, 6/1 for domestic students, 4/1 for international students; for spring admission, 12/1 for domestic students. Applications are processed on a rolling basis. Application fee: $65. Electronic applications accepted. *Financial support:* In 2010–11, 23 students received support, including 3 fellowships, 6 research assistantships, 14 teaching assistantships; career-related internships or fieldwork, Federal Work-Study, scholarships/grants, and tuition waivers (full and partial) also available. Support available to part-time students. Financial award application deadline: 2/15. *Unit head:* Dr. John Halstead, Chairperson, 603-862-3950, E-mail: natural.resources@unh.edu. *Application contact:* Linda Scogin, Administrative Assistant, 603-862-3932, E-mail: natural.resources@unh.edu.

University of New Mexico, Graduate School, Water Resources Program, Albuquerque, NM 87131-2039. Offers hydroscience (MWR); policy management (MWR). Part-time programs available. *Faculty:* 1 full-time (0 women). *Students:* 14 full-time (9 women), 24 part-time (15 women); includes 7 American Indian or Alaska Native, non-Hispanic/Latino; 1 Asian, non-Hispanic/Latino; 7 Hispanic/Latino. Average age 37. 26 applicants, 54% accepted, 9 enrolled. In 2010, 6 master's awarded. *Degree requirements:* For master's, professional project. *Entrance requirements:* For master's, minimum GPA of 3.0 during last 2 years of undergraduate work, 3 letters of reference. Additional exam requirements/recommendations for international students: Required—TOEFL (minimum score 550 paper-based; 213 computer-based). *Application deadline:* For fall admission, 7/15 for domestic students; for spring admission, 11/15 for domestic students. Applications are processed on a rolling basis. Application fee: $50. Electronic applications accepted. *Expenses:* Tuition, state resident: full-time $5991; part-time $251 per credit hour. Tuition, nonresident: full-time $14,405; part-time $800.20 per credit hour. Tuition and fees vary according to course level, course load, program and reciprocity agreements. *Financial support:* In 2010–11, 24 students received support, including 3 research assistantships with full and partial tuition reimbursements available (averaging $5,791 per year); career-related internships or fieldwork, institutionally sponsored loans, scholarships/grants, and unspecified assistantships also available. Financial award application deadline: 3/1; financial award applicants required to submit FAFSA. *Faculty research:* Sustainable water resources, transboundary water resources, economics, water law, hydrology, developing countries, hydrogeology. Total annual research expenditures: $150,557. *Unit head:* Dr. Bruce M. Thomson, Director, 505-277-5249, Fax: 505-277-5226, E-mail: bthomson@unm.edu. *Application contact:* Annamarie Cordova, Administrative Assistant II, 505-277-7759, Fax: 505-277-5226, E-mail: acordova@unm.edu.

University of Southern California, Graduate School, Viterbi School of Engineering, Sonny Astani Department of Civil Engineering, Los Angeles, CA 90089. Offers applied mechanics (MS); civil engineering (MS, PhD); computer-aided engineering (ME, Graduate Certificate); construction management (MCM); engineering technology commercialization (Graduate Certificate); environmental engineering (MS, PhD); environmental quality management (ME); structural design (ME); sustainable cities (Graduate Certificate); transportation systems (MS, Graduate Certificate); water and waste management (MS). Part-time and evening/weekend programs available. *Faculty:* 16 full-time (2 women), 35 part-time/adjunct (5 women). *Students:* 190 full-time (52 women), 81 part-time (20 women); includes 54 minority (2 Black or African American, non-Hispanic/Latino; 42 Asian, non-Hispanic/Latino; 9 Hispanic/Latino; 1 Two or more races, non-Hispanic/Latino), 149 international. 541 applicants, 43% accepted, 100 enrolled. In 2010, 74 master's, 10 doctorates awarded. Terminal master's awarded for partial completion of doctoral program. *Degree requirements:* For master's, thesis optional; for doctorate, thesis/dissertation. *Entrance requirements:* For master's and doctorate, GRE General Test. *Application deadline:* For fall admission, 12/1 priority date for domestic and international students; for spring admission, 9/15 for domestic students, 9/15 priority date for international students. Applications are processed on a rolling basis. Application fee: $85. Electronic applications accepted. *Expenses:* Tuition: Full-time $31,240; part-time $1420 per unit. Required fees: $600. One-time fee: $35 full-time. Full-time tuition and fees vary according to degree level and program. *Financial support:* In 2010–11, fellowships with full tuition reimbursements (averaging $30,000 per year), research assistantships with full tuition reimbursements (averaging $20,000 per year), teaching assistantships with full tuition reimbursements (averaging $20,000 per year) were awarded; career-related internships or fieldwork, scholarships/grants, health care benefits, and unspecified assistantships also available. Financial award application deadline: 12/1; financial award applicants required to submit CSS PROFILE or FAFSA. *Faculty research:* Geotechnical engineering, transportation engineering, structural engineering, construction management, environmental engineering, water resources. Total annual research expenditures: $5 million. *Unit head:* Dr. Jean-Pierre Bardet, Chair, 213-740-0603, Fax: 213-744-1426, E-mail: ceedept@usc.edu. *Application contact:* Jennifer A. Gerson, Director of Student Affairs, 213-740-0573, Fax: 213-740-8662, E-mail: jgerson@usc.edu.

University of the Pacific, McGeorge School of Law, Sacramento, CA 95817. Offers advocacy (JD); criminal justice (JD); experiential law teaching (LL M); intellectual property (JD); international legal studies (JD); international water resources law (LL M, JSD); law (JD); public law and policy (JD); public policy and law (LL M); tax (JD); transnational business practice (LL M); JD/MBA; JD/MPPA. *Accreditation:* ABA. Part-time and evening/weekend programs available. *Faculty:* 49 full-time (22 women), 45 part-time/adjunct (15 women). *Students:* 756 full-time (362 women), 303 part-time (148 women); includes 27 Black or African American, non-Hispanic/Latino; 19 American Indian or Alaska Native, non-Hispanic/Latino; 150 Asian, non-Hispanic/Latino; 60 Hispanic/Latino, 27 international. Average age 27. 3,209 applicants, 42% accepted, 344 enrolled. In 2010, 307 first professional degrees, 36 master's awarded. *Degree requirements:* For master's, thesis (for some programs); for doctorate, thesis/dissertation. *Entrance requirements:* For JD, LSAT; for master's, JD; for doctorate, LL M. Additional exam requirements/recommendations for international students: Required—TOEFL (minimum score 600 paper-based; 250 computer-based; 100 iBT). *Application deadline:* For fall admission, 3/15 priority date for domestic students. Applications are processed on a rolling basis. Application fee: $50. Electronic applications accepted. *Expenses:* Contact institution. *Financial support:* Fellowships, research assistantships, teaching assistantships, career-related internships or fieldwork, Federal Work-Study, institutionally sponsored loans, and scholarships/grants available. Support available to part-time students. Financial award applicants required to submit FAFSA. *Faculty research:* International legal studies, public policy and law, advocacy, intellectual property law, taxation, criminal law. *Unit head:* Elizabeth Rindskopf Parker, Dean, 916-739-7151, E-mail: elizabeth@pacific.edu. *Application contact:* 916-739-7105, Fax: 916-739-7301, E-mail: mcgeorge@pacific.edu.

University of Wisconsin–Madison, Graduate School, Gaylord Nelson Institute for Environmental Studies, Water Resources Management Program, Madison, WI 53706-1380. Offers MS. Part-time programs available. *Faculty:* 2 full-time (0 women), 10 part-time/adjunct (4 women). *Students:* 31 (20 women); includes 1 American Indian or Alaska Native, non-Hispanic/Latino; 2 Asian, non-Hispanic/Latino; 1 Hispanic/Latino, 4 international. Average age 27. 49 applicants, 78% accepted, 15 enrolled. In 2010, 20 master's awarded. *Degree requirements:* For master's, practicum. *Entrance requirements:* For master's, GRE General Test. Additional exam requirements/recommendations for international students: Required—TOEFL (minimum score 550 paper-based; 213 computer-based; 80 iBT). *Application deadline:* For fall admission, 1/15 for domestic and international students; for spring admission, 10/15 for domestic and international students. Application fee: $56. Electronic applications accepted. *Expenses:* Tuition, state resident: full-time $9887.36; part-time $617.96 per credit. Tuition, nonresident: full-time $24,054; part-time $1503.40 per credit. Required fees: $67.63 per credit. Tuition and fees vary according to reciprocity agreements. *Financial support:* In 2010–11, 11 students received support, including 2 fellowships with full tuition reimbursements available (averaging $18,756 per year), 2 research assistantships with full tuition reimbursements available (averaging $14,960 per year), 4 teaching assistantships with full tuition reimbursements available (averaging $9,392 per year); career-related internships or fieldwork, Federal Work-Study, scholarships/grants, health care benefits, unspecified assistantships, and project assistantships also available. Financial award application deadline: 1/2. *Faculty research:* Geology, hydrogeology, water chemistry, limnology, oceanography, aquatic ecology, rural sociology, water law and policy. *Unit head:* Kenneth W. Potter, Chair, 608-262-0040, Fax: 608-262-2273, E-mail: kwpotter@wisc.edu. *Application contact:* Jim Miller, Student Services Coordinator, 608-263-4373, Fax: 608-262-2273, E-mail: jemiller@wisc.edu.

University of Wisconsin–Milwaukee, Graduate School, School of Freshwater Sciences, Milwaukee, WI 53201-0413. Offers freshwater sciences (PhD); freshwater sciences and technology (MS). *Faculty:* 3 full-time (0 women). *Students:* 11 full-time (4 women); includes 1 Two or more races, non-Hispanic/Latino, 1 international. Average age 33. 13 applicants, 62% accepted, 7 enrolled.Application fee: $56 ($96 for international students). *Financial support:* Fellowships, research assistantships, teaching assistantships, unspecified assistantships available. Financial award applicants required to submit FAFSA. Total annual research expenditures: $5.8 million. *Unit head:* Dr. Mark Harris, Acting Dean, 414-382-1700, E-mail: mtharris@uwm.edu. *Application contact:* General Information Contact, 414-229-4982, Fax: 414-229-6967, E-mail: gradschool@uwm.edu.

University of Wyoming, College of Agriculture and Natural Resources, Department of Renewable Resources, Laramie, WY 82070. Offers agroecology (MS); entomology (MS, PhD); entomology/water resources (MS, PhD); rangeland ecology and watershed management (MS, PhD), including soil sciences (PhD), soil sciences and water resources (MS); rangeland ecology and watershed management/water resources (MS, PhD); soil science (MS); soil science/water resources (PhD). Part-time programs available. *Degree requirements:* For master's, comprehensive exam, thesis, oral examination; for doctorate, comprehensive exam, thesis/dissertation, preliminary oral and written exam, oral final exam. *Entrance requirements:* For master's and doctorate, GRE General Test, minimum GPA of 3.0. Additional exam requirements/recommendations for international students: Required—TOEFL. Electronic applications accepted. *Faculty research:* Plant control, grazing management, riparian restoration, riparian management, reclamation.

Utah State University, School of Graduate Studies, College of Natural Resources, Department of Aquatic, Watershed, and Earth Resources, Logan, UT 84322. Offers ecology (MS, PhD); fisheries biology (MS, PhD); watershed science (MS, PhD). *Degree requirements:* For master's, thesis (for some programs); for doctorate, thesis/dissertation. *Entrance requirements:* For master's and doctorate, GRE General Test, minimum GPA of 3.2. Additional exam requirements/recommendations for international students: Required—TOEFL. Electronic applications accepted. *Faculty research:* Behavior, population ecology, habitat, conservation biology, restoration, aquatic ecology, fisheries management, fluvial geomorphology, remote sensing, conservation biology.

Virginia Polytechnic Institute and State University, Graduate School, College of Natural Resources and Environment, Department of Forestry, Blacksburg, VA 24061. Offers forestry (MS, PhD); watershed management (Certificate). *Faculty:* 24 full-time (5 women). *Students:* 54 full-time (21 women), 12 part-time (5 women); includes 2 Hispanic/Latino, 16 international. Average age 29. 48 applicants, 52% accepted, 23 enrolled. In 2010, 16 master's, 6 doctorates awarded. *Degree requirements:* For master's, comprehensive exam (for some programs), thesis (for some programs); for doctorate, comprehensive exam (for some programs), thesis/dissertation (for some programs). *Entrance requirements:* For master's and doctorate, GRE. Additional exam requirements/recommendations for international students: Required—TOEFL (minimum score 550 paper-based; 213 computer-based). *Application deadline:* For fall admission, 7/1 for domestic and international students; for spring admission, 12/1 for domestic and international students. Applications are processed on a rolling basis. Application fee: $65. Electronic applications accepted. *Expenses:* Tuition, area resident: Full-time $9399; part-time $488 per credit hour. Tuition, state resident: full-time $9399; part-time $488 per credit hour. Tuition, nonresident: full-time $17,854; part-time $957.75 per credit hour. International tuition: $17,854 full-time. Required fees: $1534. Full-time tuition and fees vary according to program. *Financial support:* In 2010–11, 31 research assistantships with full tuition reimbursements (averaging $18,274 per year), 8 teaching assistantships with full tuition reimbursements (averaging $15,016 per year) were awarded; career-related internships or fieldwork, Federal Work-Study, scholarships/grants, health care benefits, and unspecified assistantships also available. Financial award application deadline: 1/15. Total annual research expenditures: $4.8 million. *Unit head:* Dr. Janaki Alavalapati, UNIT HEAD, 540-231-5676, Fax: 540-231-3698, E-mail: jrra@vt.edu. *Application contact:* Dr. Janaki Alavalapati, UNIT HEAD, 540-231-5676, Fax: 540-231-3698, E-mail: jrra@vt.edu.

APPENDIXES

Institutional Changes
Since the 2011 Edition

Following is an alphabetical listing of institutions that have recently closed, merged with other institutions, or changed their names or status. In the case of a name change, the former name appears first, followed by the new name.

Alliance Theological Seminary (Nyack, NY): now listed as a unit of Nyack College (Nyack, NY)

American InterContinental University (Houston, TX): name changed to American InterContinental University Houston

American InterContinental University Buckhead Campus (Atlanta, GA): closed

American InterContinental University Dunwoody Campus (Atlanta, GA): name changed to American InterContinental University Atlanta

American InterContinental University–London (London, United Kingdom): name changed to American InterContinental University London

Arkansas State University - Jonesboro (State University, AR): name changed to Arkansas State University

Bard Graduate Center for Studies in the Decorative Arts, Design, and Culture (New York, NY): name changed to Bard Graduate Center: Decorative Arts, Design History, Material Culture

Birmingham-Southern College (Birmingham, AL): no longer offers graduate degrees

California School of Podiatric Medicine at Samuel Merritt College (Oakland, CA): name changed to California School of Podiatric Medicine at Samuel Merritt University

Church of God Theological Seminary (Cleveland, TN): name changed to Pentecostal Theological Seminary

Clarke College (Dubuque, IA): name changed to Clarke University

College of Santa Fe (Santa Fe, NM): name changed to Santa Fe University of Art and Design and no longer offers graduate degrees

Dongguk Royal University (Los Angeles, CA): name changed to Dongguk University Los Angeles

Embry-Riddle Aeronautical University (Prescott, AZ): name changed to Embry-Riddle Aeronautical University–Prescott

Embry-Riddle Aeronautical University (Daytona Beach, FL): name changed to Embry-Riddle Aeronautical University–Daytona

Embry-Riddle Aeronautical University Worldwide (Daytona Beach, FL): name changed to Embry-Riddle Aeronautical University—Worldwide

Emily Carr Institute of Art & Design (Vancouver, BC, Canada): name changed to Emily Carr University of Art & Design

Emmanuel School of Religion (Johnson City, TN): name changed to Emmanuel Christian Seminary

Everest University (Clearwater, FL): no longer a campus of Everest University

Framingham State College (Framingham, MA): name changed to Framingham State University

Hannibal-LaGrange College (Hannibal, MO): name changed to Hannibal-LaGrange University

Hebrew Union College–Jewish Institute of Religion (Los Angeles, CA): merged into a single entry for Hebrew Union College–Jewish Institute of Religion (New York, NY) by request from the institution

Hebrew Union College–Jewish Institute of Religion (Cincinnati, OH): merged into a single entry for Hebrew Union College–Jewish

Institute of Religion (New York, NY) by request from the institution

Jesuit School of Theology at Berkeley (Berkeley, CA): now listed as a unit of Santa Clara University (Santa Clara, CA)

Johnson Bible College (Knoxville, TN): name changed to Johnson University

Keller Graduate School of Management (Long Island City, NY): now listed as a unit of DeVry College of New York (Long Island City, NY)

Keller Graduate School of Management (New York, NY): now listed as a unit of DeVry University Manhattan Extension Site (New York, NY)

Lancaster Bible College & Graduate School (Lancaster, PA): name changed to Lancaster Bible College

Medical College of Georgia (Augusta, GA): name changed to Georgia Health Sciences University

Mennonite Brethren Biblical Seminary (Fresno, CA): name changed to Fresno Pacific Biblical Seminary and now a unit of Fresno Pacific University (Fresno, CA)

Meritus University (Fredericton, NB, Canada): closed

Mount Mercy College (Cedar Rapids, IA): name changed to Mount Mercy University

Mount Sinai School of Medicine of New York University (New York, NY): name changed to Mount Sinai School of Medicine

Northeastern Ohio Universities College of Medicine and Pharmacy (Rootstown, OH): name changed to Northeastern Ohio Universities Colleges of Medicine and Pharmacy

Polytechnic University of the Americas–Miami Campus (Miami, FL): name changed to Polytechnic University of Puerto Rico, Miami Campus

Polytechnic University of the Americas–Orlando Campus (Winter Park, FL): name changed to Polytechnic University of Puerto Rico, Orlando Campus

Salem State College (Salem, MA): name changed to Salem State University

Sherman College of Straight Chiropractic (Spartanburg, SC): name changed to Sherman College of Chiropractic

Union Theological Seminary and Presbyterian School of Christian Education (Richmond, VA): name changed to Union Presbyterian Seminary

University of Colorado at Boulder (Boulder, CO): name changed to University of Colorado Boulder

University of Phoenix–Western Washington Campus (Tukwila, WA): merged into a single entry for University of Phoenix–Washington Campus (Seattle, WA)

Vassar College (Poughkeepsie, NY): no longer offers graduate degrees

Western New England College (Springfield, MA): name changed to Western New England University

Western States Chiropractic College (Portland, OR): name changed to University of Western States

Westfield State College (Westfield, MA): name changed to Westfield State University

Westminster Choir College of Rider University (Princeton, NJ): name changed to Westminster Choir College and now a unit of Rider University (Lawrenceville, NJ)

West Suburban College of Nursing (Oak Park, IL): name changed to Resurrection University

Worcester State College (Worcester, MA): name changed to Worcester State University

Abbreviations Used in the Guides

The following list includes abbreviations of degree names used in the profiles in the 2012 edition of the guides. Because some degrees (e.g., Doctor of Education) can be abbreviated in more than one way (e.g., D.Ed. or Ed.D.), and because the abbreviations used in the guides reflect the preferences of the individual colleges and universities, the list may include two or more abbreviations for a single degree.

Degrees

A Mus D	Doctor of Musical Arts
AC	Advanced Certificate
AD	Artist's Diploma Doctor of Arts
ADP	Artist's Diploma
Adv C	Advanced Certificate
Adv M	Advanced Master
AGC	Advanced Graduate Certificate
AGSC	Advanced Graduate Specialist Certificate
ALM	Master of Liberal Arts
AM	Master of Arts
AMBA	Accelerated Master of Business Administration Aviation Master of Business Administration
AMRS	Master of Arts in Religious Studies
APC	Advanced Professional Certificate
APMPH	Advanced Professional Master of Public Health
App Sc	Applied Scientist
App Sc D	Doctor of Applied Science
Au D	Doctor of Audiology
B Th	Bachelor of Theology
CAES	Certificate of Advanced Educational Specialization
CAGS	Certificate of Advanced Graduate Studies
CAL	Certificate in Applied Linguistics
CALS	Certificate of Advanced Liberal Studies
CAMS	Certificate of Advanced Management Studies
CAPS	Certificate of Advanced Professional Studies
CAS	Certificate of Advanced Studies
CASPA	Certificate of Advanced Study in Public Administration
CASR	Certificate in Advanced Social Research
CATS	Certificate of Achievement in Theological Studies
CBHS	Certificate in Basic Health Sciences
CBS	Graduate Certificate in Biblical Studies
CCJA	Certificate in Criminal Justice Administration
CCSA	Certificate in Catholic School Administration

CCTS	Certificate in Clinical and Translational Science
CE	Civil Engineer
CEM	Certificate of Environmental Management
CET	Certificate in Educational Technologies
CGS	Certificate of Graduate Studies
Ch E	Chemical Engineer
CM	Certificate in Management
CMH	Certificate in Medical Humanities
CMM	Master of Church Ministries
CMS	Certificate in Ministerial Studies
CNM	Certificate in Nonprofit Management
CP	Certificate in Performance
CPASF	Certificate Program for Advanced Study in Finance
CPC	Certificate in Professional Counseling Certificate in Publication and Communication
CPH	Certificate in Public Health
CPM	Certificate in Public Management
CPS	Certificate of Professional Studies
CScD	Doctor of Clinical Science
CSD	Certificate in Spiritual Direction
CSS	Certificate of Special Studies
CTS	Certificate of Theological Studies
CURP	Certificate in Urban and Regional Planning
D Admin	Doctor of Administration
D Arch	Doctor of Architecture
D Com	Doctor of Commerce
D Couns	Doctor of Counseling
D Div	Doctor of Divinity
D Ed	Doctor of Education
D Ed Min	Doctor of Educational Ministry
D Eng	Doctor of Engineering
D Engr	Doctor of Engineering
D Ent	Doctor of Enterprise
D Env	Doctor of Environment
D Law	Doctor of Law
D Litt	Doctor of Letters
D Med Sc	Doctor of Medical Science
D Min	Doctor of Ministry
D Miss	Doctor of Missiology

D Mus	Doctor of Music	DH Sc	Doctor of Health Sciences
D Mus A	Doctor of Musical Arts	DHA	Doctor of Health Administration
D Phil	Doctor of Philosophy	DHCE	Doctor of Health Care Ethics
D Prof	Doctor of Professional Studies	DHL	Doctor of Hebrew Letters
D Ps	Doctor of Psychology		Doctor of Hebrew Literature
D Sc	Doctor of Science	DHS	Doctor of Health Science
D Sc D	Doctor of Science in Dentistry	DHSc	Doctor of Health Science
D Sc IS	Doctor of Science in Information Systems	Dip CS	Diploma in Christian Studies
D Sc PA	Doctor of Science in Physician Assistant Studies	DIT	Doctor of Industrial Technology
D Th	Doctor of Theology	DJ Ed	Doctor of Jewish Education
D Th P	Doctor of Practical Theology	DJS	Doctor of Jewish Studies
DA	Doctor of Accounting	DLS	Doctor of Liberal Studies
	Doctor of Arts	DM	Doctor of Management
DA Ed	Doctor of Arts in Education		Doctor of Music
DAH	Doctor of Arts in Humanities	DMA	Doctor of Musical Arts
DAOM	Doctorate in Acupuncture and Oriental Medicine	DMD	Doctor of Dental Medicine
DAST	Diploma of Advanced Studies in Teaching	DME	Doctor of Manufacturing Management
DBA	Doctor of Business Administration		Doctor of Music Education
DBH	Doctor of Behavioral Health	DMEd	Doctor of Music Education
DBL	Doctor of Business Leadership	DMFT	Doctor of Marital and Family Therapy
DBS	Doctor of Buddhist Studies	DMH	Doctor of Medical Humanities
DC	Doctor of Chiropractic	DML	Doctor of Modern Languages
DCC	Doctor of Computer Science	DMP	Doctorate in Medical Physics
DCD	Doctor of Communications Design	DMPNA	Doctor of Management Practice in Nurse Anesthesia
DCL	Doctor of Civil Law	DN Sc	Doctor of Nursing Science
	Doctor of Comparative Law	DNAP	Doctor of Nurse Anesthesia Practice
DCM	Doctor of Church Music	DNP	Doctor of Nursing Practice
DCN	Doctor of Clinical Nutrition	DNS	Doctor of Nursing Science
DCS	Doctor of Computer Science	DO	Doctor of Osteopathy
DDN	Diplôme du Droit Notarial	DOT	Doctor of Occupational Therapy
DDS	Doctor of Dental Surgery	DPA	Doctor of Public Administration
DE	Doctor of Education	DPC	Doctor of Pastoral Counseling
	Doctor of Engineering	DPDS	Doctor of Planning and Development Studies
DED	Doctor of Economic Development	DPH	Doctor of Public Health
DEIT	Doctor of Educational Innovation and Technology	DPM	Doctor of Plant Medicine
DEL	Doctor of Executive Leadership		Doctor of Podiatric Medicine
DEM	Doctor of Educational Ministry	DPPD	Doctor of Policy, Planning, and Development
DEPD	Diplôme Études Spécialisées	DPS	Doctor of Professional Studies
DES	Doctor of Engineering Science	DPT	Doctor of Physical Therapy
DESS	Diplôme Études Supérieures Spécialisées	DPTSc	Doctor of Physical Therapy Science
DFA	Doctor of Fine Arts	Dr DES	Doctor of Design
DGP	Diploma in Graduate and Professional Studies	Dr OT	Doctor of Occupational Therapy
DH Ed	Doctor of Health Education	Dr PH	Doctor of Public Health

Peterson's Graduate Programs in the Physical Sciences, Mathematics, Agricultural Sciences, the Environment & Natural Resources 2012

Dr Sc PT	Doctor of Science in Physical Therapy		**G Dip**	Graduate Diploma
DRSc	Doctor of Regulatory Science		**GBC**	Graduate Business Certificate
DS	Doctor of Science		**GCE**	Graduate Certificate in Education
DS Sc	Doctor of Social Science		**GDM**	Graduate Diploma in Management
DSJS	Doctor of Science in Jewish Studies		**GDPA**	Graduate Diploma in Public Administration
DSL	Doctor of Strategic Leadership		**GDRE**	Graduate Diploma in Religious Education
DSW	Doctor of Social Work		**GEMBA**	Global Executive Master of Business Administration
DTL	Doctor of Talmudic Law		**GEMPA**	Gulf Executive Master of Public Administration
DV Sc	Doctor of Veterinary Science		**GM Acc**	Graduate Master of Accountancy
DVM	Doctor of Veterinary Medicine		**GMBA**	Global Master of Business Administration
DWS	Doctor of Worship Studies		**GPD**	Graduate Performance Diploma
EAA	Engineer in Aeronautics and Astronautics		**GSS**	Graduate Special Certificate for Students in Special Situations
ECS	Engineer in Computer Science		**IEMBA**	International Executive Master of Business Administration
Ed D	Doctor of Education		**IM Acc**	Integrated Master of Accountancy
Ed DCT	Doctor of Education in College Teaching		**IMA**	Interdisciplinary Master of Arts
Ed L D	Doctor of Education Leadership		**IMBA**	International Master of Business Administration
Ed M	Master of Education		**IMES**	International Master's in Environmental Studies
Ed S	Specialist in Education		**Ingeniero**	Engineer
Ed Sp	Specialist in Education		**JCD**	Doctor of Canon Law
EDB	Executive Doctorate in Business		**JCL**	Licentiate in Canon Law
EDM	Executive Doctorate in Management		**JD**	Juris Doctor
EDSPC	Education Specialist		**JSD**	Doctor of Juridical Science Doctor of Jurisprudence Doctor of the Science of Law
EE	Electrical Engineer		**JSM**	Master of Science of Law
EJD	Executive Juris Doctor		**L Th**	Licenciate in Theology
EMBA	Executive Master of Business Administration		**LL B**	Bachelor of Laws
EMFA	Executive Master of Forensic Accounting		**LL CM**	Master of Laws in Comparative Law
EMHA	Executive Master of Health Administration		**LL D**	Doctor of Laws
EMIB	Executive Master of International Business		**LL M**	Master of Laws
EML	Executive Master of Leadership		**LL M in Tax**	Master of Laws in Taxation
EMPA	Executive Master of Public Administration		**LL M CL**	Master of Laws (Common Law)
EMPP	Executive Master's of Public Policy		**M Ac**	Master of Accountancy Master of Accounting Master of Acupuncture
EMS	Executive Master of Science		**M Ac OM**	Master of Acupuncture and Oriental Medicine
EMTM	Executive Master of Technology Management		**M Acc**	Master of Accountancy Master of Accounting
Eng	Engineer		**M Acct**	Master of Accountancy Master of Accounting
Eng Sc D	Doctor of Engineering Science		**M Accy**	Master of Accountancy
Engr	Engineer		**M Actg**	Master of Accounting
Ex Doc	Executive Doctor of Pharmacy			
Exec Ed D	Executive Doctor of Education			
Exec MBA	Executive Master of Business Administration			
Exec MPA	Executive Master of Public Administration			
Exec MPH	Executive Master of Public Health			
Exec MS	Executive Master of Science			

M Acy	Master of Accountancy	M Econ	Master of Economics
M Ad	Master of Administration	M Ed	Master of Education
M Ad Ed	Master of Adult Education	M Ed T	Master of Education in Teaching
M Adm	Master of Administration	M En	Master of Engineering
M Adm Mgt	Master of Administrative Management		Master of Environmental Science
M Admin	Master of Administration	M En S	Master of Environmental Sciences
M ADU	Master of Architectural Design and Urbanism	M Eng	Master of Engineering
M Adv	Master of Advertising	M Eng Mgt	Master of Engineering Management
M Aero E	Master of Aerospace Engineering	M Engr	Master of Engineering
M AEST	Master of Applied Environmental Science and Technology	M Ent	Master of Enterprise
		M Env	Master of Environment
M Ag	Master of Agriculture	M Env Des	Master of Environmental Design
M Ag Ed	Master of Agricultural Education	M Env E	Master of Environmental Engineering
M Agr	Master of Agriculture	M Env Sc	Master of Environmental Science
M Anesth Ed	Master of Anesthesiology Education	M Fin	Master of Finance
M App Comp Sc	Master of Applied Computer Science	M Geo E	Master of Geological Engineering
M App St	Master of Applied Statistics	M Geoenv E	Master of Geoenvironmental Engineering
M Appl Stat	Master of Applied Statistics	M Geog	Master of Geography
M Aq	Master of Aquaculture	M Hum	Master of Humanities
M Arc	Master of Architecture	M Hum Svcs	Master of Human Services
M Arch	Master of Architecture	M IBD	Master of Integrated Building Delivery
M Arch I	Master of Architecture I	M IDST	Master's in Interdisciplinary Studies
M Arch II	Master of Architecture II	M Kin	Master of Kinesiology
M Arch E	Master of Architectural Engineering	M Land Arch	Master of Landscape Architecture
M Arch H	Master of Architectural History	M Litt	Master of Letters
M Bioethics	Master in Bioethics	M Mat SE	Master of Material Science and Engineering
M Biomath	Master of Biomathematics	M Math	Master of Mathematics
M Ch	Master of Chemistry	M Mech E	Master of Mechanical Engineering
M Ch E	Master of Chemical Engineering	M Med Sc	Master of Medical Science
M Chem	Master of Chemistry	M Mgmt	Master of Management
M Cl D	Master of Clinical Dentistry	M Mgt	Master of Management
M Cl Sc	Master of Clinical Science	M Min	Master of Ministries
M Comp	Master of Computing	M Mtl E	Master of Materials Engineering
M Comp E	Master of Computer Engineering	M Mu	Master of Music
M Comp Sc	Master of Computer Science	M Mus	Master of Music
M Coun	Master of Counseling	M Mus Ed	Master of Music Education
M Dent	Master of Dentistry	M Music	Master of Music
M Dent Sci	Master of Dental Sciences	M Nat Sci	Master of Natural Science
M Des	Master of Design	M Oc E	Master of Oceanographic Engineering
M Des S	Master of Design Studies	M Pet E	Master of Petroleum Engineering
M Div	Master of Divinity	M Pharm	Master of Pharmacy
M Ec	Master of Economics	M Phil	Master of Philosophy

Peterson's Graduate Programs in the Physical Sciences, Mathematics, Agricultural Sciences, the Environment & Natural Resources 2012

M Phil F	Master of Philosophical Foundations
M Pl	Master of Planning
M Plan	Master of Planning
M Pol	Master of Political Science
M Pr Met	Master of Professional Meteorology
M Prob S	Master of Probability and Statistics
M Psych	Master of Psychology
M Pub	Master of Publishing
M Rel	Master of Religion
M S Ed	Master of Science Education
M Sc	Master of Science
M Sc A	Master of Science (Applied)
M Sc AHN	Master of Science in Applied Human Nutrition
M Sc BMC	Master of Science in Biomedical Communications
M Sc CS	Master of Science in Computer Science
M Sc E	Master of Science in Engineering
M Sc Eng	Master of Science in Engineering
M Sc Engr	Master of Science in Engineering
M Sc F	Master of Science in Forestry
M Sc FE	Master of Science in Forest Engineering
M Sc Geogr	Master of Science in Geography
M Sc N	Master of Science in Nursing
M Sc OT	Master of Science in Occupational Therapy
M Sc P	Master of Science in Planning
M Sc Pl	Master of Science in Planning
M Sc PT	Master of Science in Physical Therapy
M Sc T	Master of Science in Teaching
M SEM	Master of Sustainable Environmental Management
M Serv Soc	Master of Social Service
M Soc	Master of Sociology
M Sp Ed	Master of Special Education
M Stat	Master of Statistics
M Sys Sc	Master of Systems Science
M Tax	Master of Taxation
M Tech	Master of Technology
M Th	Master of Theology
M Tox	Master of Toxicology
M Trans E	Master of Transportation Engineering
M Urb	Master of Urban Planning
M Vet Sc	Master of Veterinary Science

MA	Master of Accounting
	Master of Administration
	Master of Arts
MA Missions	Master of Arts in Missions
MA Comm	Master of Arts in Communication
MA Ed	Master of Arts in Education
MA Ed Ad	Master of Arts in Educational Administration
MA Ext	Master of Agricultural Extension
MA Islamic	Master of Arts in Islamic Studies
MA Military Studies	Master of Arts in Military Studies
MA Min	Master of Arts in Ministry
MA Miss	Master of Arts in Missiology
MA Past St	Master of Arts in Pastoral Studies
MA Ph	Master of Arts in Philosophy
MA Psych	Master of Arts in Psychology
MA Sc	Master of Applied Science
MA Sp	Master of Arts (Spirituality)
MA Th	Master of Arts in Theology
MA-R	Master of Arts (Research)
MAA	Master of Administrative Arts
	Master of Applied Anthropology
	Master of Applied Arts
	Master of Arts in Administration
MAAA	Master of Arts in Arts Administration
MAAAP	Master of Arts Administration and Policy
MAAE	Master of Arts in Art Education
MAAT	Master of Arts in Applied Theology
	Master of Arts in Art Therapy
MAB	Master of Agribusiness
MABC	Master of Arts in Biblical Counseling
	Master of Arts in Business Communication
MABE	Master of Arts in Bible Exposition
MABL	Master of Arts in Biblical Languages
MABM	Master of Agribusiness Management
MABS	Master of Arts in Biblical Studies
MABT	Master of Arts in Bible Teaching
MAC	Master of Accountancy
	Master of Accounting
	Master of Arts in Communication
	Master of Arts in Counseling
MACC	Master of Arts in Christian Counseling
	Master of Arts in Clinical Counseling
MACCM	Master of Arts in Church and Community Ministry
MACCT	Master of Accounting

MACD	Master of Arts in Christian Doctrine
MACE	Master of Arts in Christian Education
MACFM	Master of Arts in Children's and Family Ministry
MACH	Master of Arts in Church History
MACI	Master of Arts in Curriculum and Instruction
MACIS	Master of Accounting and Information Systems
MACJ	Master of Arts in Criminal Justice
MACL	Master of Arts in Christian Leadership
MACM	Master of Arts in Christian Ministries
	Master of Arts in Christian Ministry
	Master of Arts in Church Music
	Master of Arts in Counseling Ministries
MACN	Master of Arts in Counseling
MACO	Master of Arts in Counseling
MAcOM	Master of Acupuncture and Oriental Medicine
MACP	Master of Arts in Counseling Psychology
MACS	Master of Arts in Catholic Studies
MACSE	Master of Arts in Christian School Education
MACT	Master of Arts in Christian Thought
	Master of Arts in Communications and Technology
MAD	Master in Educational Institution Administration
	Master of Art and Design
MADR	Master of Arts in Dispute Resolution
MADS	Master of Animal and Dairy Science
	Master of Applied Disability Studies
MAE	Master of Aerospace Engineering
	Master of Agricultural Economics
	Master of Agricultural Education
	Master of Architectural Engineering
	Master of Art Education
	Master of Arts in Education
	Master of Arts in English
MAEd	Master of Arts Education
MAEL	Master of Arts in Educational Leadership
MAEM	Master of Arts in Educational Ministries
MAEN	Master of Arts in English
MAEP	Master of Arts in Economic Policy
MAES	Master of Arts in Environmental Sciences
MAET	Master of Arts in English Teaching
MAF	Master of Arts in Finance
MAFE	Master of Arts in Financial Economics
MAFLL	Master of Arts in Foreign Language and Literature
MAFM	Master of Accounting and Financial Management
MAFS	Master of Arts in Family Studies
MAG	Master of Applied Geography
MAGU	Master of Urban Analysis and Management

MAH	Master of Arts in Humanities
MAHA	Master of Arts in Humanitarian Assistance
	Master of Arts in Humanitarian Studies
MAHCM	Master of Arts in Health Care Mission
MAHG	Master of American History and Government
MAHL	Master of Arts in Hebrew Letters
MAHN	Master of Applied Human Nutrition
MAHSR	Master of Applied Health Services Research
MAIA	Master of Arts in International Administration
MAIB	Master of Arts in International Business
MAICS	Master of Arts in Intercultural Studies
MAIDM	Master of Arts in Interior Design and Merchandising
MAIH	Master of Arts in Interdisciplinary Humanities
MAIOP	Master of Arts in Industrial/Organizational Psychology
MAIPCR	Master of Arts in International Peace and Conflict Management
MAIS	Master of Arts in Intercultural Studies
	Master of Arts in Interdisciplinary Studies
	Master of Arts in International Studies
MAIT	Master of Administration in Information Technology
	Master of Applied Information Technology
MAJ	Master of Arts in Journalism
MAJ Ed	Master of Arts in Jewish Education
MAJCS	Master of Arts in Jewish Communal Service
MAJE	Master of Arts in Jewish Education
MAJS	Master of Arts in Jewish Studies
MAL	Master in Agricultural Leadership
MALA	Master of Arts in Liberal Arts
MALD	Master of Arts in Law and Diplomacy
MALER	Master of Arts in Labor and Employment Relations
MALM	Master of Arts in Leadership Evangelical Mobilization
MALP	Master of Arts in Language Pedagogy
MALPS	Master of Arts in Liberal and Professional Studies
MALS	Master of Arts in Liberal Studies
MALT	Master of Arts in Learning and Teaching
MAM	Master of Acquisition Management
	Master of Agriculture and Management
	Master of Applied Mathematics
	Master of Arts in Management
	Master of Arts in Ministry
	Master of Arts Management
	Master of Avian Medicine
MAMB	Master of Applied Molecular Biology

Peterson's Graduate Programs in the Physical Sciences, Mathematics, Agricultural Sciences, the Environment & Natural Resources 2012

MAMC	Master of Arts in Mass Communication
	Master of Arts in Ministry and Culture
	Master of Arts in Ministry for a Multicultural Church
	Master of Arts in Missional Christianity
MAME	Master of Arts in Missions/Evangelism
MAMFC	Master of Arts in Marriage and Family Counseling
MAMFCC	Master of Arts in Marriage, Family, and Child Counseling
MAMFT	Master of Arts in Marriage and Family Therapy
MAMHC	Master of Arts in Mental Health Counseling
MAMI	Master of Arts in Missions
MAMS	Master of Applied Mathematical Sciences
	Master of Arts in Ministerial Studies
	Master of Arts in Ministry and Spirituality
MAMT	Master of Arts in Mathematics Teaching
MAN	Master of Applied Nutrition
MANP	Master of Applied Natural Products
MANT	Master of Arts in New Testament
MAOL	Master of Arts in Organizational Leadership
MAOM	Master of Acupuncture and Oriental Medicine
	Master of Arts in Organizational Management
MAOT	Master of Arts in Old Testament
MAP	Master of Applied Psychology
	Master of Arts in Planning
	Master of Psychology
	Master of Public Administration
MAP Min	Master of Arts in Pastoral Ministry
MAPA	Master of Arts in Public Administration
MAPC	Master of Arts in Pastoral Counseling
	Master of Arts in Professional Counseling
MAPE	Master of Arts in Political Economy
MAPL	Master of Arts in Pastoral Leadership
MAPM	Master of Arts in Pastoral Ministry
	Master of Arts in Pastoral Music
	Master of Arts in Practical Ministry
MAPP	Master of Arts in Public Policy
MAPPS	Master of Arts in Asia Pacific Policy Studies
MAPS	Master of Arts in Pastoral Counseling/Spiritual Formation
	Master of Arts in Pastoral Studies
	Master of Arts in Public Service
MAPT	Master of Practical Theology
MAPW	Master of Arts in Professional Writing
MAR	Master of Arts in Religion
Mar Eng	Marine Engineer
MARC	Master of Arts in Rehabilitation Counseling
MARE	Master of Arts in Religious Education

MARL	Master of Arts in Religious Leadership
MARS	Master of Arts in Religious Studies
MAS	Master of Accounting Science
	Master of Actuarial Science
	Master of Administrative Science
	Master of Advanced Study
	Master of Aeronautical Science
	Master of American Studies
	Master of Applied Science
	Master of Applied Statistics
	Master of Archival Studies
MASA	Master of Advanced Studies in Architecture
MASD	Master of Arts in Spiritual Direction
MASE	Master of Arts in Special Education
MASF	Master of Arts in Spiritual Formation
MASJ	Master of Arts in Systems of Justice
MASL	Master of Arts in School Leadership
MASLA	Master of Advanced Studies in Landscape Architecture
MASM	Master of Aging Services Management
	Master of Arts in Specialized Ministries
MASP	Master of Applied Social Psychology
	Master of Arts in School Psychology
MASPAA	Master of Arts in Sports and Athletic Administration
MASS	Master of Applied Social Science
	Master of Arts in Social Science
MAST	Master of Arts in Science Teaching
MASW	Master of Aboriginal Social Work
MAT	Master of Arts in Teaching
	Master of Arts in Theology
	Master of Athletic Training
	Master's in Administration of Telecommunications
Mat E	Materials Engineer
MATCM	Master of Acupuncture and Traditional Chinese Medicine
MATDE	Master of Arts in Theology, Development, and Evangelism
MATDR	Master of Territorial Management and Regional Development
MATE	Master of Arts for the Teaching of English
MATESL	Master of Arts in Teaching English as a Second Language
MATESOL	Master of Arts in Teaching English to Speakers of Other Languages
MATF	Master of Arts in Teaching English as a Foreign Language/Intercultural Studies
MATFL	Master of Arts in Teaching Foreign Language
MATH	Master of Arts in Therapy

MATI	Master of Administration of Information Technology
MATL	Master of Arts in Teacher Leadership Master of Arts in Teaching of Languages Master of Arts in Transformational Leadership
MATM	Master of Arts in Teaching of Mathematics
MATS	Master of Arts in Theological Studies Master of Arts in Transforming Spirituality
MATSL	Master of Arts in Teaching a Second Language
MAUA	Master of Arts in Urban Affairs
MAUD	Master of Arts in Urban Design
MAURP	Master of Arts in Urban and Regional Planning
MAWSHP	Master of Arts in Worship
MAYM	Master of Arts in Youth Ministry
MB	Master of Bioinformatics Master of Biology
MBA	Master of Business Administration
MBA-AM	Master of Business Administration in Aviation Management
MBA-EP	Master of Business Administration–Experienced Professionals
MBAA	Master of Business Administration in Aviation
MBAE	Master of Biological and Agricultural Engineering Master of Biosystems and Agricultural Engineering
MBAH	Master of Business Administration in Health
MBAi	Master of Business Administration–International
MBAICT	Master of Business Administration in Information and Communication Technology
MBATM	Master of Business Administration in Technology Management
MBC	Master of Building Construction
MBE	Master of Bilingual Education Master of Bioengineering Master of Bioethics Master of Biological Engineering Master of Biomedical Engineering Master of Business and Engineering Master of Business Economics Master of Business Education
MBET	Master of Business, Entrepreneurship and Technology
MBiotech	Master of Biotechnology
MBIT	Master of Business Information Technology
MBL	Master of Business Law Master of Business Leadership
MBLE	Master in Business Logistics Engineering
MBMI	Master of Biomedical Imaging and Signals
MBMSE	Master of Business Management and Software Engineering
MBOE	Master of Business Operational Excellence
MBS	Master of Biblical Studies Master of Biological Science Master of Biomedical Sciences Master of Bioscience Master of Building Science
MBT	Master of Biblical and Theological Studies Master of Biomedical Technology Master of Biotechnology Master of Business Taxation
MC	Master of Communication Master of Counseling Master of Cybersecurity
MC Ed	Master of Continuing Education
MC Sc	Master of Computer Science
MCA	Master of Arts in Applied Criminology Master of Commercial Aviation
MCAM	Master of Computational and Applied Mathematics
MCC	Master of Computer Science
MCCS	Master of Crop and Soil Sciences
MCD	Master of Communications Disorders Master of Community Development
MCE	Master in Electronic Commerce Master of Christian Education Master of Civil Engineering Master of Control Engineering
MCEM	Master of Construction Engineering Management
MCH	Master of Chemical Engineering
MCHE	Master of Chemical Engineering
MCIS	Master of Communication and Information Studies Master of Computer and Information Science Master of Computer Information Systems
MCIT	Master of Computer and Information Technology
MCJ	Master of Criminal Justice
MCJA	Master of Criminal Justice Administration
MCL	Master in Communication Leadership Master of Canon Law Master of Comparative Law
MCM	Master of Christian Ministry Master of Church Music Master of City Management Master of Communication Management Master of Community Medicine Master of Construction Management Master of Contract Management Master of Corporate Media
MCMP	Master of City and Metropolitan Planning
MCMS	Master of Clinical Medical Science

432 www.facebook.com/petersonspublishing

Peterson's Graduate Programs in the Physical Sciences, Mathematics, Agricultural Sciences, the Environment & Natural Resources 2012

MCN	Master of Clinical Nutrition
MCP	Master of City Planning
	Master of Community Planning
	Master of Counseling Psychology
	Master of Cytopathology Practice
	Master of Science in Quality Systems and Productivity
MCPC	Master of Arts in Chaplaincy and Pastoral Care
MCPD	Master of Community Planning and Development
MCR	Master in Clinical Research
MCRP	Master of City and Regional Planning
MCRS	Master of City and Regional Studies
MCS	Master of Christian Studies
	Master of Clinical Science
	Master of Combined Sciences
	Master of Communication Studies
	Master of Computer Science
	Master of Consumer Science
MCSE	Master of Computer Science and Engineering
MCSL	Master of Catholic School Leadership
MCSM	Master of Construction Science/Management
MCST	Master of Science in Computer Science and Information Technology
MCTP	Master of Communication Technology and Policy
MCTS	Master of Clinical and Translational Science
MCVS	Master of Cardiovascular Science
MD	Doctor of Medicine
MDA	Master of Development Administration
	Master of Dietetic Administration
MDB	Master of Design-Build
MDE	Master of Developmental Economics
	Master of Distance Education
	Master of the Education of the Deaf
MDH	Master of Dental Hygiene
MDM	Master of Design Methods
	Master of Digital Media
MDP	Master of Development Practice
MDR	Master of Dispute Resolution
MDS	Master of Dental Surgery
ME	Master of Education
	Master of Engineering
	Master of Entrepreneurship
	Master of Evangelism
ME Sc	Master of Engineering Science
MEA	Master of Educational Administration
	Master of Engineering Administration
MEAP	Master of Environmental Administration and Planning
MEBT	Master in Electronic Business Technologies
MEC	Master of Electronic Commerce
MECE	Master of Electrical and Computer Engineering
Mech E	Mechanical Engineer
MED	Master of Education of the Deaf
MEDS	Master of Environmental Design Studies
MEE	Master in Education
	Master of Electrical Engineering
	Master of Energy Engineering
	Master of Environmental Engineering
MEEM	Master of Environmental Engineering and Management
MEENE	Master of Engineering in Environmental Engineering
MEEP	Master of Environmental and Energy Policy
MEERM	Master of Earth and Environmental Resource Management
MEH	Master in Humanistic Studies
	Master of Environmental Horticulture
MEHS	Master of Environmental Health and Safety
MEIM	Master of Entertainment Industry Management
MEL	Master of Educational Leadership
	Master of English Literature
MELP	Master of Environmental Law and Policy
MEM	Master of Ecosystem Management
	Master of Electricity Markets
	Master of Engineering Management
	Master of Environmental Management
	Master of Marketing
MEME	Master of Engineering in Manufacturing Engineering
	Master of Engineering in Mechanical Engineering
MENG	Master of Arts in English
MENVEGR	Master of Environmental Engineering
MEP	Master of Engineering Physics
MEPC	Master of Environmental Pollution Control
MEPD	Master of Education–Professional Development
	Master of Environmental Planning and Design
MER	Master of Employment Relations
MES	Master of Education and Science
	Master of Engineering Science
	Master of Environment and Sustainability
	Master of Environmental Science
	Master of Environmental Studies
	Master of Environmental Systems
	Master of Special Education
MESM	Master of Environmental Science and Management
MET	Master of Educational Technology
	Master of Engineering Technology
	Master of Entertainment Technology
	Master of Environmental Toxicology

Peterson's Graduate Programs in the Physical Sciences, Mathematics, Agricultural Sciences, the Environment & Natural Resources 2012

www.facebook.com/petersonspublishing **433**

Met E	Metallurgical Engineer
METM	Master of Engineering and Technology Management
MF	Master of Finance Master of Forestry
MFA	Master of Fine Arts
MFAM	Master in Food Animal Medicine
MFAS	Master of Fisheries and Aquatic Science
MFAW	Master of Fine Arts in Writing
MFC	Master of Forest Conservation
MFCS	Master of Family and Consumer Sciences
MFE	Master of Financial Economics Master of Financial Engineering Master of Forest Engineering
MFG	Master of Functional Genomics
MFHD	Master of Family and Human Development
MFM	Master of Financial Mathematics
MFMS	Master's in Food Microbiology and Safety
MFPE	Master of Food Process Engineering
MFR	Master of Forest Resources
MFRC	Master of Forest Resources and Conservation
MFS	Master of Food Science Master of Forensic Sciences Master of Forest Science Master of Forest Studies Master of French Studies
MFST	Master of Food Safety and Technology
MFT	Master of Family Therapy Master of Food Technology
MFWB	Master of Fishery and Wildlife Biology
MFWCB	Master of Fish, Wildlife and Conservation Biology
MFWS	Master of Fisheries and Wildlife Sciences
MFYCS	Master of Family, Youth and Community Sciences
MG	Master of Genetics
MGA	Master of Global Affairs Master of Governmental Administration
MGC	Master of Genetic Counseling
MGD	Master of Graphic Design
MGE	Master of Geotechnical Engineering
MGEM	Master of Global Entrepreneurship and Management
MGH	Master of Geriatric Health
MGIS	Master of Geographic Information Science Master of Geographic Information Systems
MGM	Master of Global Management
MGP	Master of Gestion de Projet
MGPS	Master of Global Policy Studies
MGREM	Master of Global Real Estate Management
MGS	Master of Gerontological Studies Master of Global Studies
MH	Master of Humanities
MH Ed	Master of Health Education
MH Sc	Master of Health Sciences
MHA	Master of Health Administration Master of Healthcare Administration Master of Hospital Administration Master of Hospitality Administration
MHA/MCRP	Master of Healthcare Administration/Master of City and Regional Planning
MHAD	Master of Health Administration
MHB	Master of Human Behavior
MHCA	Master of Health Care Administration
MHCI	Master of Human-Computer Interaction
MHCL	Master of Health Care Leadership
MHE	Master of Health Education Master of Human Ecology
MHE Ed	Master of Home Economics Education
MHEA	Master of Higher Education Administration
MHHS	Master of Health and Human Services
MHI	Master of Health Informatics Master of Healthcare Innovation
MHIIM	Master of Health Informatics and Information Management
MHIS	Master of Health Information Systems
MHK	Master of Human Kinetics
MHL	Master of Hebrew Literature
MHM	Master of Healthcare Management
MHMS	Master of Health Management Systems
MHP	Master of Health Physics Master of Heritage Preservation Master of Historic Preservation
MHPA	Master of Heath Policy and Administration
MHPE	Master of Health Professions Education
MHR	Master of Human Resources
MHRD	Master in Human Resource Development
MHRIR	Master of Human Resources and Industrial Relations
MHRLR	Master of Human Resources and Labor Relations

434 www.facebook.com/petersonspublishing

Peterson's Graduate Programs in the Physical Sciences, Mathematics, Agricultural Sciences, the Environment & Natural Resources 2012

MHRM	Master of Human Resources Management
MHS	Master of Health Science Master of Health Sciences Master of Health Studies Master of Hispanic Studies Master of Human Services Master of Humanistic Studies
MHSA	Master of Health Services Administration
MHSM	Master of Health Systems Management
MI	Master of Instruction
MI Arch	Master of Interior Architecture
MI St	Master of Information Studies
MIA	Master of Interior Architecture Master of International Affairs
MIAA	Master of International Affairs and Administration
MIAM	Master of International Agribusiness Management
MIB	Master of International Business
MIBA	Master of International Business Administration
MICM	Master of International Construction Management
MID	Master of Industrial Design Master of Industrial Distribution Master of Interior Design Master of International Development
MIE	Master of Industrial Engineering
MIH	Master of Integrative Health
MIHTM	Master of International Hospitality and Tourism Management
MIJ	Master of International Journalism
MILR	Master of Industrial and Labor Relations
MiM	Master in Management
MIM	Master of Industrial Management Master of Information Management Master of International Management
MIMLAE	Master of International Management for Latin American Executives
MIMS	Master of Information Management and Systems Master of Integrated Manufacturing Systems
MIP	Master of Infrastructure Planning Master of Intellectual Property
MIPER	Master of International Political Economy of Resources
MIPP	Master of International Policy and Practice Master of International Public Policy
MIPS	Master of International Planning Studies
MIR	Master of Industrial Relations Master of International Relations
MIS	Master of Industrial Statistics Master of Information Science Master of Information Systems Master of Integrated Science Master of Interdisciplinary Studies Master of International Service Master of International Studies
MISE	Master of Industrial and Systems Engineering
MISKM	Master of Information Sciences and Knowledge Management
MISM	Master of Information Systems Management
MIT	Master in Teaching Master of Industrial Technology Master of Information Technology Master of Initial Teaching Master of International Trade Master of Internet Technology
MITA	Master of Information Technology Administration
MITM	Master of Information Technology and Management
MITO	Master of Industrial Technology and Operations
MJ	Master of Journalism Master of Jurisprudence
MJ Ed	Master of Jewish Education
MJA	Master of Justice Administration
MJM	Master of Justice Management
MJS	Master of Judicial Studies Master of Juridical Science
MKM	Master of Knowledge Management
ML	Master of Latin
ML Arch	Master of Landscape Architecture
MLA	Master of Landscape Architecture Master of Liberal Arts
MLAS	Master of Laboratory Animal Science Master of Liberal Arts and Sciences
MLAUD	Master of Landscape Architecture in Urban Development
MLD	Master of Leadership Development
MLE	Master of Applied Linguistics and Exegesis
MLER	Master of Labor and Employment Relations
MLHR	Master of Labor and Human Resources
MLI Sc	Master of Library and Information Science
MLIS	Master of Library and Information Science Master of Library and Information Studies

MLM	Master of Library Media
MLRHR	Master of Labor Relations and Human Resources
MLS	Master of Leadership Studies
	Master of Legal Studies
	Master of Liberal Studies
	Master of Library Science
	Master of Life Sciences
MLSP	Master of Law and Social Policy
MLT	Master of Language Technologies
MLTCA	Master of Long Term Care Administration
MM	Master of Management
	Master of Ministry
	Master of Missiology
	Master of Music
MM Ed	Master of Music Education
MM Sc	Master of Medical Science
MM St	Master of Museum Studies
MMA	Master of Marine Affairs
	Master of Media Arts
	Master of Musical Arts
MMAE	Master of Mechanical and Aerospace Engineering
MMAS	Master of Military Art and Science
MMB	Master of Microbial Biotechnology
MMBA	Managerial Master of Business Administration
MMC	Master of Manufacturing Competitiveness
	Master of Mass Communications
	Master of Music Conducting
MMCM	Master of Music in Church Music
MMCSS	Master of Mathematical Computational and Statistical Sciences
MME	Master of Manufacturing Engineering
	Master of Mathematics Education
	Master of Mathematics for Educators
	Master of Mechanical Engineering
	Master of Medical Engineering
	Master of Mining Engineering
	Master of Music Education
MMF	Master of Mathematical Finance
MMFT	Master of Marriage and Family Therapy
MMG	Master of Management
MMH	Master of Management in Hospitality
	Master of Medical Humanities
MMI	Master of Management of Innovation
MMIS	Master of Management Information Systems
MMM	Master of Manufacturing Management
	Master of Marine Management
	Master of Medical Management
MMME	Master of Metallurgical and Materials Engineering

MMP	Master of Management Practice
	Master of Marine Policy
	Master of Medical Physics
	Master of Music Performance
MMPA	Master of Management and Professional Accounting
MMQM	Master of Manufacturing Quality Management
MMR	Master of Marketing Research
MMRM	Master of Marine Resources Management
MMS	Master of Management Science
	Master of Management Studies
	Master of Manufacturing Systems
	Master of Marine Studies
	Master of Materials Science
	Master of Medical Science
	Master of Medieval Studies
	Master of Modern Studies
MMSE	Master of Manufacturing Systems Engineering
MMSM	Master of Music in Sacred Music
MMT	Master in Marketing
	Master of Management
	Master of Math for Teaching
	Master of Music Teaching
	Master of Music Therapy
	Master's in Marketing Technology
MMus	Master of Music
MN	Master of Nursing
	Master of Nutrition
MN NP	Master of Nursing in Nurse Practitioner
MNA	Master of Nonprofit Administration
	Master of Nurse Anesthesia
MNAL	Master of Nonprofit Administration and Leadership
MNAS	Master of Natural and Applied Science
MNCM	Master of Network and Communications Management
MNE	Master of Network Engineering
	Master of Nuclear Engineering
MNL	Master in International Business for Latin America
MNM	Master of Nonprofit Management
MNO	Master of Nonprofit Organization
MNPL	Master of Not-for-Profit Leadership
MNpS	Master of Nonprofit Studies
MNR	Master of Natural Resources
MNRES	Master of Natural Resources and Environmental Studies
MNRM	Master of Natural Resource Management
MNRS	Master of Natural Resource Stewardship
MNS	Master of Natural Science
MO	Master of Oceanography

MOD	Master of Organizational Development
MOGS	Master of Oil and Gas Studies
MOH	Master of Occupational Health
MOL	Master of Organizational Leadership
MOM	Master of Oriental Medicine
MOR	Master of Operations Research
MOT	Master of Occupational Therapy
MP	Master of Physiology Master of Planning
MP Ac	Master of Professional Accountancy
MP Acc	Master of Professional Accountancy Master of Professional Accounting Master of Public Accounting
MP Aff	Master of Public Affairs
MP Th	Master of Pastoral Theology
MPA	Master of Physician Assistant Master of Professional Accountancy Master of Professional Accounting Master of Public Administration Master of Public Affairs
MPAC	Master of Professional Accounting
MPAID	Master of Public Administration and International Development
MPAP	Master of Physician Assistant Practice Master of Public Affairs and Politics
MPAS	Master of Physician Assistant Science Master of Physician Assistant Studies
MPC	Master of Pastoral Counseling Master of Professional Communication Master of Professional Counseling
MPD	Master of Product Development Master of Public Diplomacy
MPDS	Master of Planning and Development Studies
MPE	Master of Physical Education Master of Power Engineering
MPEM	Master of Project Engineering and Management
MPH	Master of Public Health
MPH/MCRP	Master of Public Health/Mster of Community and Regional Planning
MPHE	Master of Public Health Education
MPHTM	Master of Public Health and Tropical Medicine
MPIA	Master in International Affairs Master of Public and International Affairs
MPM	Master of Pastoral Ministry Master of Pest Management Master of Policy Management Master of Practical Ministries Master of Project Management Master of Public Management
MPNA	Master of Public and Nonprofit Administration
MPO	Master of Prosthetics and Orthotics
MPOD	Master of Positive Organizational Development
MPP	Master of Public Policy
MPPA	Master of Public Policy Administration Master of Public Policy and Administration
MPPAL	Master of Public Policy, Administration and Law
MPPM	Master of Public and Private Management Master of Public Policy and Management
MPPPM	Master of Plant Protection and Pest Management
MPRTM	Master of Parks, Recreation, and Tourism Management
MPS	Master of Pastoral Studies Master of Perfusion Science Master of Planning Studies Master of Political Science Master of Preservation Studies Master of Prevention Science Master of Professional Studies Master of Public Service
MPSA	Master of Public Service Administration
MPSRE	Master of Professional Studies in Real Estate
MPT	Master of Pastoral Theology Master of Physical Therapy
MPVM	Master of Preventive Veterinary Medicine
MPW	Master of Professional Writing Master of Public Works
MQM	Master of Quality Management
MQS	Master of Quality Systems
MR	Master of Recreation Master of Retailing
MRA	Master in Research Administration
MRC	Master of Rehabilitation Counseling
MRCP	Master of Regional and City Planning Master of Regional and Community Planning
MRD	Master of Rural Development
MRE	Master of Real Estate Master of Religious Education
MRED	Master of Real Estate Development
MREM	Master of Resource and Environmental Management
MRLS	Master of Resources Law Studies
MRM	Master of Resources Management
MRP	Master of Regional Planning
MRS	Master of Religious Studies
MRSc	Master of Rehabilitation Science
MS	Master of Science
MS Cmp E	Master of Science in Computer Engineering
MS Kin	Master of Science in Kinesiology

Peterson's Graduate Programs in the Physical Sciences, Mathematics, Agricultural Sciences, the Environment & Natural Resources 2012

www.facebook.com/petersonspublishing **437**

MS Acct	Master of Science in Accounting
MS Accy	Master of Science in Accountancy
MS Aero E	Master of Science in Aerospace Engineering
MS Ag	Master of Science in Agriculture
MS Arch	Master of Science in Architecture
MS Arch St	Master of Science in Architectural Studies
MS Bio E	Master of Science in Bioengineering
	Master of Science in Biomedical Engineering
MS Bm E	Master of Science in Biomedical Engineering
MS Ch E	Master of Science in Chemical Engineering
MS Chem	Master of Science in Chemistry
MS Cp E	Master of Science in Computer Engineering
MS Eco	Master of Science in Economics
MS Econ	Master of Science in Economics
MS Ed	Master of Science in Education
MS El	Master of Science in Educational Leadership and Administration
MS En E	Master of Science in Environmental Engineering
MS Eng	Master of Science in Engineering
MS Engr	Master of Science in Engineering
MS Env E	Master of Science in Environmental Engineering
MS Exp Surg	Master of Science in Experimental Surgery
MS Int A	Master of Science in International Affairs
MS Mat E	Master of Science in Materials Engineering
MS Mat SE	Master of Science in Material Science and Engineering
MS Met E	Master of Science in Metallurgical Engineering
MS Mgt	Master of Science in Management
MS Min	Master of Science in Mining
MS Min E	Master of Science in Mining Engineering
MS Mt E	Master of Science in Materials Engineering
MS Otal	Master of Science in Otalrynology
MS Pet E	Master of Science in Petroleum Engineering
MS Phys	Master of Science in Physics
MS Poly	Master of Science in Polymers
MS Psy	Master of Science in Psychology
MS Pub P	Master of Science in Public Policy
MS Sc	Master of Science in Social Science
MS Sp Ed	Master of Science in Special Education
MS Stat	Master of Science in Statistics
MS Surg	Master of Science in Surgery
MS Tax	Master of Science in Taxation

MS Tc E	Master of Science in Telecommunications Engineering
MS-R	Master of Science (Research)
MSA	Master of School Administration
	Master of Science Administration
	Master of Science in Accountancy
	Master of Science in Accounting
	Master of Science in Administration
	Master of Science in Aeronautics
	Master of Science in Agriculture
	Master of Science in Anesthesia
	Master of Science in Architecture
	Master of Science in Aviation
	Master of Sports Administration
MSA Phy	Master of Science in Applied Physics
MSAA	Master of Science in Astronautics and Aeronautics
MSAAE	Master of Science in Aeronautical and Astronautical Engineering
MSABE	Master of Science in Agricultural and Biological Engineering
MSAC	Master of Science in Acupuncture
MSACC	Master of Science in Accounting
MSaCS	Master of Science in Applied Computer Science
MSAE	Master of Science in Aeronautical Engineering
	Master of Science in Aerospace Engineering
	Master of Science in Applied Economics
	Master of Science in Applied Engineering
	Master of Science in Architectural Engineering
	Master of Science in Art Education
MSAH	Master of Science in Allied Health
MSAL	Master of Sport Administration and Leadership
MSAM	Master of Science in Applied Mathematics
MSANR	Master of Science in Agriculture and Natural Resources Systems Management
MSAPM	Master of Security Analysis and Portfolio Management
MSAS	Master of Science in Applied Statistics
	Master of Science in Architectural Studies
MSAT	Master of Science in Accounting and Taxation
	Master of Science in Advanced Technology
	Master of Science in Athletic Training
MSB	Master of Science in Bible
	Master of Science in Business
MSBA	Master of Science in Business Administration
	Master of Science in Business Analysis
MSBAE	Master of Science in Biological and Agricultural Engineering
	Master of Science in Biosystems and Agricultural Engineering
MSBC	Master of Science in Building Construction

Peterson's Graduate Programs in the Physical Sciences, Mathematics, Agricultural Sciences, the Environment & Natural Resources 2012

MSBE	Master of Science in Biological Engineering
	Master of Science in Biomedical Engineering
MSBENG	Master of Science in Bioengineering
MSBIT	Master of Science in Business Information Technology
MSBM	Master of Sport Business Management
MSBME	Master of Science in Biomedical Engineering
MSBMS	Master of Science in Basic Medical Science
MSBS	Master of Science in Biomedical Sciences
MSC	Master of Science in Commerce
	Master of Science in Communication
	Master of Science in Computers
	Master of Science in Counseling
	Master of Science in Criminology
MSCC	Master of Science in Christian Counseling
	Master of Science in Community Counseling
MSCD	Master of Science in Communication Disorders
	Master of Science in Community Development
MSCE	Master of Science in Civil Engineering
	Master of Science in Clinical Epidemiology
	Master of Science in Computer Engineering
	Master of Science in Continuing Education
MSCEE	Master of Science in Civil and Environmental Engineering
MSCF	Master of Science in Computational Finance
MSChE	Master of Science in Chemical Engineering
MSCI	Master of Science in Clinical Investigation
	Master of Science in Curriculum and Instruction
MSCIS	Master of Science in Computer and Information Systems
	Master of Science in Computer Information Science
	Master of Science in Computer Information Systems
MSCIT	Master of Science in Computer Information Technology
MSCJ	Master of Science in Criminal Justice
MSCJA	Master of Science in Criminal Justice Administration
MSCJPS	Master of Science in Criminal Justice and Public Safety
MSCJS	Master of Science in Crime and Justice Studies
MSCL	Master of Science in Collaborative Leadership
MSCLS	Master of Science in Clinical Laboratory Studies
MSCM	Master of Science in Church Management
	Master of Science in Conflict Management
	Master of Science in Construction Management
MScM	Master of Science in Management
MSCM	Master of Supply Chain Management
MSCNU	Master of Science in Clinical Nutrition

MSCP	Master of Science in Clinical Psychology
	Master of Science in Computer Engineering
	Master of Science in Counseling Psychology
MSCPE	Master of Science in Computer Engineering
MSCPharm	Master of Science in Pharmacy
MSCPI	Master in Strategic Planning for Critical Infrastructures
MSCR	Master of Science in Clinical Research
MSCRP	Master of Science in City and Regional Planning
	Master of Science in Community and Regional Planning
MSCS	Master of Science in Clinical Science
	Master of Science in Computer Science
MSCSD	Master of Science in Communication Sciences and Disorders
MSCSE	Master of Science in Computer Science and Engineering
MSCTE	Master of Science in Career and Technical Education
MSD	Master of Science in Dentistry
	Master of Science in Design
	Master of Science in Dietetics
MSDR	Master of Dispute Resolution
MSE	Master of Science Education
	Master of Science in Economics
	Master of Science in Education
	Master of Science in Engineering
	Master of Science in Engineering Management
	Master of Software Engineering
	Master of Special Education
	Master of Structural Engineering
MSECE	Master of Science in Electrical and Computer Engineering
MSED	Master of Sustainable Economic Development
MSEE	Master of Science in Electrical Engineering
	Master of Science in Environmental Engineering
MSEH	Master of Science in Environmental Health
MSEL	Master of Science in Educational Leadership
MSEM	Master of Science in Engineering Management
	Master of Science in Engineering Mechanics
	Master of Science in Environmental Management
MSENE	Master of Science in Environmental Engineering
MSEO	Master of Science in Electro-Optics
MSEP	Master of Science in Economic Policy
MSEPA	Master of Science in Economics and Policy Analysis
MSES	Master of Science in Embedded Software Engineering
	Master of Science in Engineering Science
	Master of Science in Environmental Science
	Master of Science in Environmental Studies

Peterson's Graduate Programs in the Physical Sciences, Mathematics, Agricultural Sciences, the Environment & Natural Resources 2012

www.facebook.com/petersonspublishing **439**

MSESM	Master of Science in Engineering Science and Mechanics
MSET	Master of Science in Educational Technology Master of Science in Engineering Technology
MSEV	Master of Science in Environmental Engineering
MSEVH	Master of Science in Environmental Health and Safety
MSF	Master of Science in Finance Master of Science in Forestry Master of Spiritual Formation
MSFA	Master of Science in Financial Analysis
MSFAM	Master of Science in Family Studies
MSFCS	Master of Science in Family and Consumer Science
MSFE	Master of Science in Financial Engineering
MSFOR	Master of Science in Forestry
MSFP	Master of Science in Financial Planning
MSFS	Master of Science in Financial Sciences Master of Science in Forensic Science
MSFSB	Master of Science in Financial Services and Banking
MSFT	Master of Science in Family Therapy
MSGC	Master of Science in Genetic Counseling
MSH	Master of Science in Health Master of Science in Hospice
MSHA	Master of Science in Health Administration
MSHCA	Master of Science in Health Care Administration
MSHCI	Master of Science in Human Computer Interaction
MSHCPM	Master of Science in Health Care Policy and Management
MSHE	Master of Science in Health Education
MSHES	Master of Science in Human Environmental Sciences
MSHFID	Master of Science in Human Factors in Information Design
MSHFS	Master of Science in Human Factors and Systems
MSHI	Master of Science in Health Informatics
MSHP	Master of Science in Health Professions Master of Science in Health Promotion
MSHR	Master of Science in Human Resources
MSHRL	Master of Science in Human Resource Leadership
MSHRM	Master of Science in Human Resource Management
MSHROD	Master of Science in Human Resources and Organizational Development
MSHS	Master of Science in Health Science Master of Science in Health Services Master of Science in Health Systems Master of Science in Homeland Security
MSHT	Master of Science in History of Technology
MSI	Master of Science in Information Master of Science in Instruction
MSIA	Master of Science in Industrial Administration Master of Science in Information Assurance and Computer Security
MSIB	Master of Science in International Business
MSIDM	Master of Science in Interior Design and Merchandising
MSIDT	Master of Science in Information Design and Technology
MSIE	Master of Science in Industrial Engineering Master of Science in International Economics
MSIEM	Master of Science in Information Engineering and Management
MSIID	Master of Science in Information and Instructional Design
MSIM	Master of Science in Information Management Master of Science in International Management
MSIMC	Master of Science in Integrated Marketing Communications
MSIR	Master of Science in Industrial Relations
MSIS	Master of Science in Information Science Master of Science in Information Systems Master of Science in Interdisciplinary Studies
MSISE	Master of Science in Infrastructure Systems Engineering
MSISM	Master of Science in Information Systems Management
MSISPM	Master of Science in Information Security Policy and Management
MSIST	Master of Science in Information Systems Technology
MSIT	Master of Science in Industrial Technology Master of Science in Information Technology Master of Science in Instructional Technology
MSITM	Master of Science in Information Technology Management
MSJ	Master of Science in Journalism Master of Science in Jurisprudence
MSJC	Master of Social Justice and Criminology
MSJE	Master of Science in Jewish Education
MSJFP	Master of Science in Juvenile Forensic Psychology
MSJJ	Master of Science in Juvenile Justice
MSJPS	Master of Science in Justice and Public Safety

MSJS	Master of Science in Jewish Studies	**MSNE**	Master of Science in Nuclear Engineering
MSK	Master of Science in Kinesiology	**MSNED**	Master of Science in Nurse Education
MSL	Master of School Leadership	**MSNM**	Master of Science in Nonprofit Management
	Master of Science in Leadership	**MSNS**	Master of Science in Natural Science
	Master of Science in Limnology		Master of Science in Nutritional Science
	Master of Strategic Leadership	**MSOD**	Master of Science in Organizational Development
	Master of Studies in Law	**MSOEE**	Master of Science in Outdoor and Environmental
MSLA	Master of Science in Landscape Architecture		Education
	Master of Science in Legal Administration	**MSOES**	Master of Science in Occupational Ergonomics
MSLD	Master of Science in Land Development		and Safety
MSLFS	Master of Science in Life Sciences	**MSOH**	Master of Science in Occupational Health
MSLP	Master of Speech-Language Pathology	**MSOL**	Master of Science in Organizational Leadership
MSLS	Master of Science in Library Science	**MSOM**	Master of Science in Operations Management
MSLSCM	Master of Science in Logistics and Supply Chain Management		Master of Science in Organization and Management
MSLT	Master of Second Language Teaching		Master of Science in Oriental Medicine
MSM	Master of Sacred Ministry	**MSOR**	Master of Science in Operations Research
	Master of Sacred Music	**MSOT**	Master of Science in Occupational Technology
	Master of School Mathematics		Master of Science in Occupational Therapy
	Master of Science in Management	**MSP**	Master of Science in Pharmacy
	Master of Science in Mathematics		Master of Science in Planning
	Master of Science in Organization Management		Master of Science in Psychology
	Master of Security Management		Master of Speech Pathology
MSMA	Master of Science in Marketing Analysis	**MSPA**	Master of Science in Physician Assistant
MSMAE	Master of Science in Materials Engineering		Master of Science in Professional Accountancy
MSMC	Master of Science in Mass Communications	**MSPAS**	Master of Science in Physician Assistant Studies
MSME	Master of Science in Mathematics Education	**MSPC**	Master of Science in Professional Communications
	Master of Science in Mechanical Engineering		Master of Science in Professional Counseling
MSMFE	Master of Science in Manufacturing Engineering	**MSPE**	Master of Science in Petroleum Engineering
MSMFT	Master of Science in Marriage and Family Therapy	**MSPG**	Master of Science in Psychology
MSMIS	Master of Science in Management Information Systems	**MSPH**	Master of Science in Public Health
MSMIT	Master of Science in Management and Information Technology	**MSPH/M Ed**	Master of Science in Public Health/Master of Education
MSMOT	Master of Science in Management of Technology	**MSPH/MCRP**	Master of Science in Public Health/Msater of City and Regional Planning
MSMS	Master of Science in Management Science	**MSPH/MSIS**	Master of Science in Public Health/Master of Science in Information Science
	Master of Science in Medical Sciences	**MSPH/MSLS**	Master of Science in Public Health/Master of Science in Library Science
MSMSE	Master of Science in Manufacturing Systems Engineering	**MSPHR**	Master of Science in Pharmacy
	Master of Science in Material Science and Engineering	**MSPM**	Master of Science in Professional Management
	Master of Science in Mathematics and Science Education		Master of Science in Project Management
MSMT	Master of Science in Management and Technology	**MSPNGE**	Master of Science in Petroleum and Natural Gas Engineering
	Master of Science in Medical Technology	**MSPS**	Master of Science in Pharmaceutical Science
MSMus	Master of Sacred Music		Master of Science in Political Science
MSN	Master of Science in Nursing		Master of Science in Psychological Services
MSN-R	Master of Science in Nursing (Research)	**MSPT**	Master of Science in Physical Therapy
MSNA	Master of Science in Nurse Anesthesia	**MSpVM**	Master of Specialized Veterinary Medicine

Peterson's Graduate Programs in the Physical Sciences, Mathematics, Agricultural Sciences, the Environment & Natural Resources 2012

www.facebook.com/petersonspublishing   **441**

MSR	Master of Science in Radiology
	Master of Science in Reading
MSRA	Master of Science in Recreation Administration
MSRC	Master of Science in Resource Conservation
MSRE	Master of Science in Real Estate
	Master of Science in Religious Education
MSRED	Master of Science in Real Estate Development
MSRLS	Master of Science in Recreation and Leisure Studies
MSRMP	Master of Science in Radiological Medical Physics
MSRS	Master of Science in Rehabilitation Science
MSS	Master of Science in Software
	Master of Social Science
	Master of Social Services
	Master of Software Systems
	Master of Sports Science
	Master of Strategic Studies
MSSA	Master of Science in Social Administration
MSSCP	Master of Science in Science Content and Process
MSSD	Master of Science in Sustainable Design
MSSE	Master of Science in Software Engineering
	Master of Science in Space Education
	Master of Science in Special Education
MSSEM	Master of Science in Systems and Engineering Management
MSSI	Master of Science in Security Informatics
	Master of Science in Strategic Intelligence
MSSL	Master of Science in School Leadership
	Master of Science in Strategic Leadership
MSSLP	Master of Science in Speech-Language Pathology
MSSM	Master of Science in Sports Medicine
MSSP	Master of Science in Social Policy
MSSPA	Master of Science in Student Personnel Administration
MSSS	Master of Science in Safety Science
	Master of Science in Systems Science
MSST	Master of Science in Security Technologies
MSSW	Master of Science in Social Work
MSSWE	Master of Science in Software Engineering
MST	Master of Science and Technology
	Master of Science in Taxation
	Master of Science in Teaching
	Master of Science in Technology
	Master of Science in Telecommunications
	Master of Science Teaching
MSTC	Master of Science in Technical Communication
	Master of Science in Telecommunications
MSTCM	Master of Science in Traditional Chinese Medicine

MSTE	Master of Science in Telecommunications Engineering
	Master of Science in Transportation Engineering
MSTM	Master of Science in Technical Management
MSTOM	Master of Science in Traditional Oriental Medicine
MSUD	Master of Science in Urban Design
MSW	Master of Social Work
MSWE	Master of Software Engineering
MSWREE	Master of Science in Water Resources and Environmental Engineering
MSX	Master of Science in Exercise Science
MT	Master of Taxation
	Master of Teaching
	Master of Technology
	Master of Textiles
MTA	Master of Tax Accounting
	Master of Teaching Arts
	Master of Tourism Administration
MTCM	Master of Traditional Chinese Medicine
MTD	Master of Training and Development
MTE	Master in Educational Technology
MTESOL	Master in Teaching English to Speakers of Other Languages
MTHM	Master of Tourism and Hospitality Management
MTI	Master of Information Technology
MTIM	Master of Trust and Investment Management
MTL	Master of Talmudic Law
MTM	Master of Technology Management
	Master of Telecommunications Management
	Master of the Teaching of Mathematics
MTMH	Master of Tropical Medicine and Hygiene
MTOM	Master of Traditional Oriental Medicine
MTP	Master of Transpersonal Psychology
MTPC	Master of Technical and Professional Communication
MTR	Master of Translational Research
MTS	Master of Theological Studies
MTSC	Master of Technical and Scientific Communication
MTSE	Master of Telecommunications and Software Engineering
MTT	Master in Technology Management
MTX	Master of Taxation
MUA	Master of Urban Affairs
MUD	Master of Urban Design
MUEP	Master of Urban and Environmental Planning
MUP	Master of Urban Planning

Peterson's Graduate Programs in the Physical Sciences, Mathematics, Agricultural Sciences, the Environment & Natural Resources 2012

MUPDD	Master of Urban Planning, Design, and Development
MUPP	Master of Urban Planning and Policy
MUPRED	Master of Urban Planning and Real Estate Development
MURP	Master of Urban and Regional Planning Master of Urban and Rural Planning
MURPL	Master of Urban and Regional Planning
MUS	Master of Urban Studies'
MVM	Master of VLSI and Microelectronics
MVP	Master of Voice Pedagogy
MVPH	Master of Veterinary Public Health
MVS	Master of Visual Studies
MWC	Master of Wildlife Conservation
MWE	Master in Welding Engineering
MWPS	Master of Wood and Paper Science
MWR	Master of Water Resources
MWS	Master of Women's Studies Master of Worship Studies
MZS	Master of Zoological Science
Nav Arch	Naval Architecture
Naval E	Naval Engineer
ND	Doctor of Naturopathic Medicine
NE	Nuclear Engineer
Nuc E	Nuclear Engineer
OD	Doctor of Optometry
OTD	Doctor of Occupational Therapy
PBME	Professional Master of Biomedical Engineering
PD	Professional Diploma
PGC	Post-Graduate Certificate
PGD	Postgraduate Diploma
Ph L	Licentiate of Philosophy
Pharm D	Doctor of Pharmacy
PhD	Doctor of Philosophy
PhD Otal	Doctor of Philosophy in Otalrynology
PhD Surg	Doctor of Philosophy in Surgery
PhDEE	Doctor of Philosophy in Electrical Engineering
PM Sc	Professional Master of Science
PMBA	Professional Master of Business Administration
PMC	Post Master Certificate
PMD	Post-Master's Diploma
PMS	Professional Master of Science Professional Master's

Post-Doctoral	
MS	Post-Doctoral Master of Science
Post-MSN Certificate	Post-Master of Science in Nursing Certificate
PPDPT	Postprofessional Doctor of Physical Therapy
PSM	Professional Master of Science Professional Science Master's
Psy D	Doctor of Psychology
Psy M	Master of Psychology
Psy S	Specialist in Psychology
Psya D	Doctor of Psychoanalysis
Re Dir	Director of Recreation
Rh D	Doctor of Rehabilitation
S Psy S	Specialist in Psychological Services
Sc D	Doctor of Science
Sc M	Master of Science
SCCT	Specialist in Community College Teaching
ScDPT	Doctor of Physical Therapy Science
SD	Doctor of Science Specialist Degree
SJD	Doctor of Juridical Science
SLPD	Doctor of Speech-Language Pathology
SM	Master of Science
SM Arch S	Master of Science in Architectural Studies
SM Vis S	Master of Science in Visual Studies
SMBT	Master of Science in Building Technology
SP	Specialist Degree
Sp C	Specialist in Counseling
Sp Ed	Specialist in Education
Sp LIS	Specialist in Library and Information Science
SPA	Specialist in Arts
SPCM	Special in Church Music
Spec	Specialist's Certificate
Spec M	Specialist in Music
SPEM	Special in Educational Ministries
SPS	School Psychology Specialist
Spt	Specialist Degree
SPTH	Special in Theology
SSP	Specialist in School Psychology
STB	Bachelor of Sacred Theology
STD	Doctor of Sacred Theology
STL	Licentiate of Sacred Theology
STM	Master of Sacred Theology

Peterson's Graduate Programs in the Physical Sciences, Mathematics, Agricultural Sciences, the Environment & Natural Resources 2012

www.facebook.com/petersonspublishing **443**

TDPT	Transitional Doctor of Physical Therapy	**WEMBA**	Weekend Executive Master of Business Administration
Th D	Doctor of Theology	**XMA**	Executive Master of Arts
Th M	Master of Theology	**XMBA**	Executive Master of Business Administration
VMD	Doctor of Veterinary Medicine		

INDEXES

Close-Ups and Displays

Directories and Subject Areas

Following is an alphabetical listing of directories and subject areas. Also listed are cross-references for subject area names not used in the directory structure of the guides, for example, "Arabic (*see* Near and Middle Eastern Languages)."

Graduate Programs in the Humanities, Arts & Social Sciences

Addictions/Substance Abuse Counseling
Administration (*see* Arts Administration; Public Administration)
African-American Studies
African Languages and Literatures (*see* African Studies)
African Studies
Agribusiness (*see* Agricultural Economics and Agribusiness)
Agricultural Economics and Agribusiness
Alcohol Abuse Counseling (*see* Addictions/Substance Abuse Counseling)
American Indian/Native American Studies
American Studies
Anthropology
Applied Arts and Design—General
Applied Behavior Analysis
Applied Economics
Applied History (*see* Public History)
Applied Psychology
Applied Social Research
Arabic (*see* Near and Middle Eastern Languages)
Arab Studies (*see* Near and Middle Eastern Studies)
Archaeology
Architectural History
Architecture
Archives Administration (*see* Public History)
Area and Cultural Studies (*see* African-American Studies; African Studies; American Indian/Native American Studies; American Studies; Asian-American Studies; Asian Studies; Canadian Studies; Cultural Studies; East European and Russian Studies; Ethnic Studies; Folklore; Gender Studies; Hispanic Studies; Holocaust Studies; Jewish Studies; Latin American Studies; Near and Middle Eastern Studies; Northern Studies; Pacific Area/ Pacific Rim Studies; Western European Studies; Women's Studies)
Art/Fine Arts
Art History
Arts Administration
Arts Journalism
Art Therapy
Asian-American Studies
Asian Languages
Asian Studies
Behavioral Sciences (*see* Psychology)
Bible Studies (*see* Religion; Theology)
Biological Anthropology
Black Studies (*see* African-American Studies)
Broadcasting (*see* Communication; Film, Television, and Video Production)
Broadcast Journalism
Building Science
Canadian Studies
Celtic Languages
Ceramics (*see* Art/Fine Arts)
Child and Family Studies
Child Development
Chinese
Chinese Studies (*see* Asian Languages; Asian Studies)

Christian Studies (*see* Missions and Missiology; Religion; Theology)
Cinema (*see* Film, Television, and Video Production)
City and Regional Planning (*see* Urban and Regional Planning)
Classical Languages and Literatures (*see* Classics)
Classics
Clinical Psychology
Clothing and Textiles
Cognitive Psychology (*see* Psychology—General; Cognitive Sciences)
Cognitive Sciences
Communication—General
Community Affairs (*see* Urban and Regional Planning; Urban Studies)
Community Planning (*see* Architecture; Environmental Design; Urban and Regional Planning; Urban Design; Urban Studies)
Community Psychology (*see* Social Psychology)
Comparative and Interdisciplinary Arts
Comparative Literature
Composition (*see* Music)
Computer Art and Design
Conflict Resolution and Mediation/Peace Studies
Consumer Economics
Corporate and Organizational Communication
Corrections (*see* Criminal Justice and Criminology)
Counseling (*see* Counseling Psychology; Pastoral Ministry and Counseling)
Counseling Psychology
Crafts (*see* Art/Fine Arts)
Creative Arts Therapies (*see* Art Therapy; Therapies—Dance, Drama, and Music)
Criminal Justice and Criminology
Cultural Anthropology
Cultural Studies
Dance
Decorative Arts
Demography and Population Studies
Design (*see* Applied Arts and Design; Architecture; Art/Fine Arts; Environmental Design; Graphic Design; Industrial Design; Interior Design; Textile Design; Urban Design)
Developmental Psychology
Diplomacy (*see* International Affairs)
Disability Studies
Drama Therapy (*see* Therapies—Dance, Drama, and Music)
Dramatic Arts (*see* Theater)
Drawing (*see* Art/Fine Arts)
Drug Abuse Counseling (*see* Addictions/Substance Abuse Counseling)
Drug and Alcohol Abuse Counseling (*see* Addictions/Substance Abuse Counseling)
East Asian Studies (*see* Asian Studies)
East European and Russian Studies
Economic Development
Economics
Educational Theater (*see* Theater; Therapies—Dance, Drama, and Music)
Emergency Management
English
Environmental Design
Ethics
Ethnic Studies
Ethnomusicology (*see* Music)
Experimental Psychology
Family and Consumer Sciences—General
Family Studies (*see* Child and Family Studies)
Family Therapy (*see* Child and Family Studies; Clinical Psychology; Counseling Psychology; Marriage and Family Therapy)
Filmmaking (*see* Film, Television, and Video Production)
Film Studies (*see* Film, Television, and Video Production)
Film, Television, and Video Production

Film, Television, and Video Theory and Criticism
Fine Arts (*see* Art/Fine Arts)
Folklore
Foreign Languages (*see* specific language)
Foreign Service (*see* International Affairs; International
   Development)
Forensic Psychology
Forensic Sciences
Forensics (*see* Speech and Interpersonal Communication)
French
Gender Studies
General Studies (*see* Liberal Studies)
Genetic Counseling
Geographic Information Systems
Geography
German
Gerontology
Graphic Design
Greek (*see* Classics)
Health Communication
Health Psychology
Hebrew (*see* Near and Middle Eastern Languages)
Hebrew Studies (*see* Jewish Studies)
Hispanic and Latin American Languages
Hispanic Studies
Historic Preservation
History
History of Art (*see* Art History)
History of Medicine
History of Science and Technology
Holocaust and Genocide Studies
Home Economics (*see* Family and Consumer Sciences—General)
Homeland Security
Household Economics, Sciences, and Management (*see* Family and
   Consumer Sciences—General)
Human Development
Humanities
Illustration
Industrial and Labor Relations
Industrial and Organizational Psychology
Industrial Design
Interdisciplinary Studies
Interior Design
International Affairs
International Development
International Economics
International Service (*see* International Affairs; International
   Development)
International Trade Policy
Internet and Interactive Multimedia
Interpersonal Communication (*see* Speech and Interpersonal
   Communication)
Interpretation (*see* Translation and Interpretation)
Islamic Studies (*see* Near and Middle Eastern Studies; Religion)
Italian
Japanese
Japanese Studies (*see* Asian Languages; Asian Studies; Japanese)
Jewelry (*see* Art/Fine Arts)
Jewish Studies
Journalism
Judaic Studies (*see* Jewish Studies; Religion)
Labor Relations (*see* Industrial and Labor Relations)
Landscape Architecture
Latin American Studies
Latin (*see* Classics)
Law Enforcement (*see* Criminal Justice and Criminology)
Liberal Studies
Lighting Design
Linguistics
Literature (*see* Classics; Comparative Literature; specific language)
Marriage and Family Therapy
Mass Communication
Media Studies
Medical Illustration

Medieval and Renaissance Studies
Metalsmithing (*see* Art/Fine Arts)
Middle Eastern Studies (*see* Near and Middle Eastern Studies)
Military and Defense Studies
Mineral Economics
Ministry (*see* Pastoral Ministry and Counseling; Theology)
Missions and Missiology
Motion Pictures (*see* Film, Television, and Video Production)
Museum Studies
Music
Musicology (*see* Music)
Music Therapy (*see* Therapies—Dance, Drama, and Music)
National Security
Native American Studies (*see* American Indian/Native American
   Studies)
Near and Middle Eastern Languages
Near and Middle Eastern Studies
Near Environment (*see* Family and Consumer Sciences)
Northern Studies
Organizational Psychology (*see* Industrial and Organizational
   Psychology)
Oriental Languages (*see* Asian Languages)
Oriental Studies (*see* Asian Studies)
Pacific Area/Pacific Rim Studies
Painting (*see* Art/Fine Arts)
Pastoral Ministry and Counseling
Philanthropic Studies
Philosophy
Photography
Playwriting (*see* Theater; Writing)
Policy Studies (*see* Public Policy)
Political Science
Population Studies (*see* Demography and Population Studies)
Portuguese
Printmaking (*see* Art/Fine Arts)
Product Design (*see* Industrial Design)
Psychoanalysis and Psychotherapy
Psychology—General
Public Administration
Public Affairs
Public History
Public Policy
Public Speaking (*see* Mass Communication; Rhetoric; Speech and
   Interpersonal Communication)
Publishing
Regional Planning (*see* Architecture; Urban and Regional Planning;
   Urban Design; Urban Studies)
Rehabilitation Counseling
Religion
Renaissance Studies (*see* Medieval and Renaissance Studies)
Rhetoric
Romance Languages
Romance Literatures (*see* Romance Languages)
Rural Planning and Studies
Rural Sociology
Russian
Scandinavian Languages
School Psychology
Sculpture (*see* Art/Fine Arts)
Security Administration (*see* Criminal Justice and Criminology)
Slavic Languages
Slavic Studies (*see* East European and Russian Studies; Slavic
   Languages)
Social Psychology
Social Sciences
Sociology
Southeast Asian Studies (*see* Asian Studies)
Soviet Studies (*see* East European and Russian Studies; Russian)
Spanish
Speech and Interpersonal Communication
Sport Psychology
Studio Art (*see* Art/Fine Arts)
Substance Abuse Counseling (*see* Addictions/Substance Abuse
   Counseling)

448   www.facebook.com/petersonspublishing

*Peterson's Graduate Programs in the Physical Sciences, Mathematics,
Agricultural Sciences, the Environment & Natural Resources 2012*

Survey Methodology
Sustainable Development
Technical Communication
Technical Writing
Telecommunications (*see* Film, Television, and Video Production)
Television (*see* Film, Television, and Video Production)
Textile Design
Textiles (*see* Clothing and Textiles; Textile Design)
Thanatology
Theater
Theater Arts (*see* Theater)
Theology
Therapies—Dance, Drama, and Music
Translation and Interpretation
Transpersonal and Humanistic Psychology
Urban and Regional Planning
Urban Design
Urban Planning (*see* Architecture; Urban and Regional Planning; Urban Design; Urban Studies)
Urban Studies
Video (*see* Film, Television, and Video Production)
Visual Arts (*see* Applied Arts and Design; Art/Fine Arts; Film, Television, and Video Production; Graphic Design; Illustration; Photography)
Western European Studies
Women's Studies
World Wide Web (*see* Internet and Interactive Multimedia)
Writing

Graduate Programs in the Biological Sciences

Anatomy
Animal Behavior
Bacteriology
Behavioral Sciences (*see* Biopsychology; Neuroscience; Zoology)
Biochemistry
Biological and Biomedical Sciences—General
Biological Chemistry (*see* Biochemistry)
Biological Oceanography (*see* Marine Biology)
Biophysics
Biopsychology
Botany
Breeding (*see* Botany; Plant Biology; Genetics)
Cancer Biology/Oncology
Cardiovascular Sciences
Cell Biology
Cellular Physiology (*see* Cell Biology; Physiology)
Computational Biology
Conservation (*see* Conservation Biology; Environmental Biology)
Conservation Biology
Crop Sciences (*see* Botany; Plant Biology)
Cytology (*see* Cell Biology)
Developmental Biology
Dietetics (*see* Nutrition)
Ecology
Embryology (*see* Developmental Biology)
Endocrinology (*see* Physiology)
Entomology
Environmental Biology
Evolutionary Biology
Foods (*see* Nutrition)
Genetics
Genomic Sciences
Histology (*see* Anatomy; Cell Biology)
Human Genetics
Immunology
Infectious Diseases
Laboratory Medicine (*see* Immunology; Microbiology; Pathology)
Life Sciences (*see* Biological and Biomedical Sciences)

Marine Biology
Medical Microbiology
Medical Sciences (*see* Biological and Biomedical Sciences)
Medical Science Training Programs (*see* Biological and Biomedical Sciences)
Microbiology
Molecular Biology
Molecular Biophysics
Molecular Genetics
Molecular Medicine
Molecular Pathogenesis
Molecular Pathology
Molecular Pharmacology
Molecular Physiology
Molecular Toxicology
Neural Sciences (*see* Biopsychology; Neurobiology; Neuroscience)
Neurobiology
Neuroendocrinology (*see* Biopsychology; Neurobiology; Neuroscience; Physiology)
Neuropharmacology (*see* Biopsychology; Neurobiology; Neuroscience; Pharmacology)
Neurophysiology (*see* Biopsychology; Neurobiology; Neuroscience; Physiology)
Neuroscience
Nutrition
Oncology (*see* Cancer Biology/Oncology)
Organismal Biology (*see* Biological and Biomedical Sciences; Zoology)
Parasitology
Pathobiology
Pathology
Pharmacology
Photobiology of Cells and Organelles (*see* Botany; Cell Biology; Plant Biology)
Physiological Optics (*see* Physiology)
Physiology
Plant Biology
Plant Molecular Biology
Plant Pathology
Plant Physiology
Pomology (*see* Botany; Plant Biology)
Psychobiology (*see* Biopsychology)
Psychopharmacology (*see* Biopsychology; Neuroscience; Pharmacology)
Radiation Biology
Reproductive Biology
Sociobiology (*see* Evolutionary Biology)
Structural Biology
Systems Biology
Teratology
Theoretical Biology (*see* Biological and Biomedical Sciences)
Therapeutics (*see* Pharmacology)
Toxicology
Translational Biology
Tropical Medicine (*see* Parasitology)
Virology
Wildlife Biology (*see* Zoology)
Zoology

Graduate Programs in the Physical Sciences, Mathematics, Agricultural Sciences, the Environment & Natural Resources

Acoustics
Agricultural Sciences
Agronomy and Soil Sciences
Analytical Chemistry

Peterson's Graduate Programs in the Physical Sciences, Mathematics, Agricultural Sciences, the Environment & Natural Resources 2012

www.facebook.com/petersonspublishing **449**

Animal Sciences
Applied Mathematics
Applied Physics
Applied Statistics
Aquaculture
Astronomy
Astrophysical Sciences (*see* Astrophysics; Atmospheric Sciences; Meteorology; Planetary and Space Sciences)
Astrophysics
Atmospheric Sciences
Biological Oceanography (*see* Marine Affairs; Marine Sciences; Oceanography)
Biomathematics
Biometry
Biostatistics
Chemical Physics
Chemistry
Computational Sciences
Condensed Matter Physics
Dairy Science (*see* Animal Sciences)
Earth Sciences (*see* Geosciences)
Environmental Management and Policy
Environmental Sciences
Environmental Studies (*see* Environmental Management and Policy)
Experimental Statistics (*see* Statistics)
Fish, Game, and Wildlife Management
Food Science and Technology
Forestry
General Science (*see* specific topics)
Geochemistry
Geodetic Sciences
Geological Engineering (*see* Geology)
Geological Sciences (*see* Geology)
Geology
Geophysical Fluid Dynamics (*see* Geophysics)
Geophysics
Geosciences
Horticulture
Hydrogeology
Hydrology
Inorganic Chemistry
Limnology
Marine Affairs
Marine Geology
Marine Sciences
Marine Studies (*see* Marine Affairs; Marine Geology; Marine Sciences; Oceanography)
Mathematical and Computational Finance
Mathematical Physics
Mathematical Statistics (*see* Applied Statistics; Statistics)
Mathematics
Meteorology
Mineralogy
Natural Resource Management (*see* Environmental Management and Policy; Natural Resources)
Natural Resources
Nuclear Physics (*see* Physics)
Ocean Engineering (*see* Marine Affairs; Marine Geology; Marine Sciences; Oceanography)
Oceanography
Optical Sciences
Optical Technologies (*see* Optical Sciences)
Optics (*see* Applied Physics; Optical Sciences; Physics)
Organic Chemistry
Paleontology
Paper Chemistry (*see* Chemistry)
Photonics
Physical Chemistry
Physics
Planetary and Space Sciences
Plant Sciences
Plasma Physics
Poultry Science (*see* Animal Sciences)
Radiological Physics (*see* Physics)

Range Management (*see* Range Science)
Range Science
Resource Management (*see* Environmental Management and Policy; Natural Resources)
Solid-Earth Sciences (*see* Geosciences)
Space Sciences (*see* Planetary and Space Sciences)
Statistics
Theoretical Chemistry
Theoretical Physics
Viticulture and Enology
Water Resources

Graduate Programs in Engineering & Applied Sciences

Aeronautical Engineering (*see* Aerospace/Aeronautical Engineering)
Aerospace/Aeronautical Engineering
Aerospace Studies (*see* Aerospace/Aeronautical Engineering)
Agricultural Engineering
Applied Mechanics (*see* Mechanics)
Applied Science and Technology
Architectural Engineering
Artificial Intelligence/Robotics
Astronautical Engineering (*see* Aerospace/Aeronautical Engineering)
Automotive Engineering
Aviation
Biochemical Engineering
Bioengineering
Bioinformatics
Biological Engineering (*see* Bioengineering)
Biomedical Engineering
Biosystems Engineering
Biotechnology
Ceramic Engineering (*see* Ceramic Sciences and Engineering)
Ceramic Sciences and Engineering
Ceramics (*see* Ceramic Sciences and Engineering)
Chemical Engineering
Civil Engineering
Computer and Information Systems Security
Computer Engineering
Computer Science
Computing Technology (*see* Computer Science)
Construction Engineering
Construction Management
Database Systems
Electrical Engineering
Electronic Materials
Electronics Engineering (*see* Electrical Engineering)
Energy and Power Engineering
Energy Management and Policy
Engineering and Applied Sciences
Engineering and Public Affairs (*see* Technology and Public Policy)
Engineering and Public Policy (*see* Energy Management and Policy; Technology and Public Policy)
Engineering Design
Engineering Management
Engineering Mechanics (*see* Mechanics)
Engineering Metallurgy (*see* Metallurgical Engineering and Metallurgy)
Engineering Physics
Environmental Design (*see* Environmental Engineering)
Environmental Engineering
Ergonomics and Human Factors
Financial Engineering
Fire Protection Engineering
Food Engineering (*see* Agricultural Engineering)
Game Design and Development
Gas Engineering (*see* Petroleum Engineering)
Geological Engineering
Geophysics Engineering (*see* Geological Engineering)

Peterson's Graduate Programs in the Physical Sciences, Mathematics, Agricultural Sciences, the Environment & Natural Resources 2012

Geotechnical Engineering
Hazardous Materials Management
Health Informatics
Health Systems (*see* Safety Engineering; Systems Engineering)
Highway Engineering (*see* Transportation and Highway Engineering)
Human-Computer Interaction
Human Factors (*see* Ergonomics and Human Factors)
Hydraulics
Hydrology (*see* Water Resources Engineering)
Industrial Engineering (*see* Industrial/Management Engineering)
Industrial/Management Engineering
Information Science
Internet Engineering
Macromolecular Science (*see* Polymer Science and Engineering)
Management Engineering (*see* Engineering Management; Industrial/Management Engineering)
Management of Technology
Manufacturing Engineering
Marine Engineering (*see* Civil Engineering)
Materials Engineering
Materials Sciences
Mechanical Engineering
Mechanics
Medical Informatics
Metallurgical Engineering and Metallurgy
Metallurgy (*see* Metallurgical Engineering and Metallurgy)
Mineral/Mining Engineering
Modeling and Simulation
Nanotechnology
Nuclear Engineering
Ocean Engineering
Operations Research
Paper and Pulp Engineering
Petroleum Engineering
Pharmaceutical Engineering
Plastics Engineering (*see* Polymer Science and Engineering)
Polymer Science and Engineering
Public Policy (*see* Energy Management and Policy; Technology and Public Policy)
Reliability Engineering
Robotics (*see* Artificial Intelligence/Robotics)
Safety Engineering
Software Engineering
Solid-State Sciences (*see* Materials Sciences)
Structural Engineering
Surveying Science and Engineering
Systems Analysis (*see* Systems Engineering)
Systems Engineering
Systems Science
Technology and Public Policy
Telecommunications
Telecommunications Management
Textile Sciences and Engineering
Textiles (*see* Textile Sciences and Engineering)
Transportation and Highway Engineering
Urban Systems Engineering (*see* Systems Engineering)
Waste Management (*see* Hazardous Materials Management)
Water Resources Engineering

Graduate Programs in Business, Education, Health, Information Studies, Law & Social Work

Accounting
Actuarial Science
Acupuncture and Oriental Medicine
Acute Care/Critical Care Nursing
Administration (*see* Business Administration and Management; Educational Administration; Health Services Management and Hospital Administration; Industrial and Manufacturing Management; Nursing and Healthcare Administration; Pharmaceutical Administration; Sports Management)
Adult Education
Adult Nursing
Advanced Practice Nursing (*see* Family Nurse Practitioner Studies)
Advertising and Public Relations
Agricultural Education
Alcohol Abuse Counseling (*see* Counselor Education)
Allied Health—General
Allied Health Professions (*see* Clinical Laboratory Sciences/Medical Technology; Clinical Research; Communication Disorders; Dental Hygiene; Emergency Medical Services; Occupational Therapy; Physical Therapy; Physician Assistant Studies; Rehabilitation Sciences)
Allopathic Medicine
Anesthesiologist Assistant Studies
Archival Management and Studies
Art Education
Athletics Administration (*see* Kinesiology and Movement Studies)
Athletic Training and Sports Medicine
Audiology (*see* Communication Disorders)
Aviation Management
Banking (*see* Finance and Banking)
Bioethics
Business Administration and Management—General
Business Education
Child-Care Nursing (*see* Maternal and Child/Neonatal Nursing)
Chiropractic
Clinical Laboratory Sciences/Medical Technology
Clinical Research
Communication Disorders
Community College Education
Community Health
Community Health Nursing
Computer Education
Continuing Education (*see* Adult Education)
Counseling (*see* Counselor Education)
Counselor Education
Curriculum and Instruction
Dental and Oral Surgery (*see* Oral and Dental Sciences)
Dental Assistant Studies (*see* Dental Hygiene)
Dental Hygiene
Dental Services (*see* Dental Hygiene)
Dentistry
Developmental Education
Distance Education Development
Drug Abuse Counseling (*see* Counselor Education)
Early Childhood Education
Educational Leadership and Administration
Educational Measurement and Evaluation
Educational Media/Instructional Technology
Educational Policy
Educational Psychology
Education—General
Education of the Blind (*see* Special Education)
Education of the Deaf (*see* Special Education)
Education of the Gifted
Education of the Hearing Impaired (*see* Special Education)
Education of the Learning Disabled (*see* Special Education)
Education of the Mentally Retarded (*see* Special Education)
Education of the Physically Handicapped (*see* Special Education)
Education of Students with Severe/Multiple Disabilities
Education of the Visually Handicapped (*see* Special Education)
Electronic Commerce
Elementary Education
Emergency Medical Services
English as a Second Language
English Education
Entertainment Management
Entrepreneurship
Environmental and Occupational Health
Environmental Education
Environmental Law

Peterson's Graduate Programs in the Physical Sciences, Mathematics, Agricultural Sciences, the Environment & Natural Resources 2012

www.facebook.com/petersonspublishing   **451**

Epidemiology
Exercise and Sports Science
Exercise Physiology (see Kinesiology and Movement Studies)
Facilities and Entertainment Management
Family Nurse Practitioner Studies
Finance and Banking
Food Services Management (see Hospitality Management)
Foreign Languages Education
Forensic Nursing
Foundations and Philosophy of Education
Gerontological Nursing
Guidance and Counseling (see Counselor Education)
Health Education
Health Law
Health Physics/Radiological Health
Health Promotion
Health-Related Professions (see individual allied health professions)
Health Services Management and Hospital Administration
Health Services Research
Hearing Sciences (see Communication Disorders)
Higher Education
HIV/AIDS Nursing
Home Economics Education
Hospice Nursing
Hospital Administration (see Health Services Management and Hospital Administration)
Hospitality Management
Hotel Management (see Travel and Tourism)
Human Resources Development
Human Resources Management
Human Services
Industrial Administration (see Industrial and Manufacturing Management)
Industrial and Manufacturing Management
Industrial Education (see Vocational and Technical Education)
Industrial Hygiene
Information Studies
Instructional Technology (see Educational Media/Instructional Technology)
Insurance
Intellectual Property Law
International and Comparative Education
International Business
International Commerce (see International Business)
International Economics (see International Business)
International Health
International Trade (see International Business)
Investment and Securities (see Business Administration and Management; Finance and Banking; Investment Management)
Investment Management
Junior College Education (see Community College Education)
Kinesiology and Movement Studies
Laboratory Medicine (see Clinical Laboratory Sciences/Medical Technology)
Law
Legal and Justice Studies
Leisure Services (see Recreation and Park Management)
Leisure Studies
Library Science
Logistics
Management (see Business Administration and Management)
Management Information Systems
Management Strategy and Policy
Marketing
Marketing Research
Maternal and Child Health
Maternal and Child/Neonatal Nursing
Mathematics Education
Medical Imaging
Medical Nursing (see Medical/Surgical Nursing)
Medical Physics
Medical/Surgical Nursing
Medical Technology (see Clinical Laboratory Sciences/Medical Technology)

Medicinal and Pharmaceutical Chemistry
Medicinal Chemistry (see Medicinal and Pharmaceutical Chemistry)
Medicine (see Allopathic Medicine; Naturopathic Medicine; Osteopathic Medicine; Podiatric Medicine)
Middle School Education
Midwifery (see Nurse Midwifery)
Movement Studies (see Kinesiology and Movement Studies)
Multilingual and Multicultural Education
Museum Education
Music Education
Naturopathic Medicine
Nonprofit Management
Nuclear Medical Technology (see Clinical Laboratory Sciences/Medical Technology)
Nurse Anesthesia
Nurse Midwifery
Nurse Practitioner Studies (see Family Nurse Practitioner Studies)
Nursery School Education (see Early Childhood Education)
Nursing Administration (see Nursing and Healthcare Administration)
Nursing and Healthcare Administration
Nursing Education
Nursing—General
Nursing Informatics
Occupational Education (see Vocational and Technical Education)
Occupational Health (see Environmental and Occupational Health; Occupational Health Nursing)
Occupational Health Nursing
Occupational Therapy
Oncology Nursing
Optometry
Oral and Dental Sciences
Oral Biology (see Oral and Dental Sciences)
Oral Pathology (see Oral and Dental Sciences)
Organizational Behavior
Organizational Management
Oriental Medicine and Acupuncture (see Acupuncture and Oriental Medicine)
Orthodontics (see Oral and Dental Sciences)
Osteopathic Medicine
Parks Administration (see Recreation and Park Management)
Pediatric Nursing
Pedontics (see Oral and Dental Sciences)
Perfusion
Personnel (see Human Resources Development; Human Resources Management; Organizational Behavior; Organizational Management; Student Affairs)
Pharmaceutical Administration
Pharmaceutical Chemistry (see Medicinal and Pharmaceutical Chemistry)
Pharmaceutical Sciences
Pharmacy
Philosophy of Education (see Foundations and Philosophy of Education)
Physical Education
Physical Therapy
Physician Assistant Studies
Physiological Optics (see Vision Sciences)
Podiatric Medicine
Preventive Medicine (see Community Health and Public Health)
Project Management
Psychiatric Nursing
Public Health—General
Public Health Nursing (see Community Health Nursing)
Public Relations (see Advertising and Public Relations)
Quality Management
Quantitative Analysis
Radiological Health (see Health Physics/Radiological Health)
Reading Education
Real Estate
Recreation and Park Management
Recreation Therapy (see Recreation and Park Management)
Rehabilitation Sciences
Rehabilitation Therapy (see Physical Therapy)
Religious Education

452   www.facebook.com/petersonspublishing

Peterson's Graduate Programs in the Physical Sciences, Mathematics, Agricultural Sciences, the Environment & Natural Resources 2012

Remedial Education (*see* Special Education)
Restaurant Administration (*see* Hospitality Management)
School Nursing
Science Education
Secondary Education
Social Sciences Education
Social Studies Education (*see* Social Sciences Education)
Social Work
Special Education
Speech-Language Pathology and Audiology (*see* Communication Disorders)
Sports Management
Sports Medicine (*see* Athletic Training and Sports Medicine)
Sports Psychology and Sociology (*see* Kinesiology and Movement Studies)
Student Affairs
Substance Abuse Counseling (*see* Counselor Education)
Supply Chain Management
Surgical Nursing (*see* Medical/Surgical Nursing)

Sustainability Management
Systems Management (*see* Management Information Systems)
Taxation
Teacher Education (*see* specific subject areas)
Teaching English as a Second Language (*see* English as a Second Language)
Technical Education (*see* Vocational and Technical Education)
Teratology (*see* Environmental and Occupational Health)
Therapeutics (*see* Pharmaceutical Sciences; Pharmacy)
Transcultural Nursing
Transportation Management
Travel and Tourism
Urban Education
Veterinary Medicine
Veterinary Sciences
Vision Sciences
Vocational and Technical Education
Vocational Counseling (*see* Counselor Education)
Women's Health Nursing

Peterson's Graduate Programs in the Physical Sciences, Mathematics, Agricultural Sciences, the Environment & Natural Resources 2012

www.facebook.com/petersonspublishing   **453**

Directories and Subject Areas in This Book

Special Advertising Section

Thomas Jefferson University School of Population Health

University of Medicine & Dentistry of New Jersey

Saint Louis University

St. Mary's University

The Winston Preparatory Schools

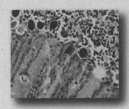

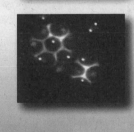
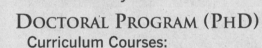

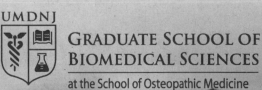

+ AMIT SOOD | sports business major

BE A BILLIKEN

Find out how the breadth and depth of the fully accredited undergraduate and graduate programs at Saint Louis University's **JOHN COOK SCHOOL OF BUSINESS** will give you the knowledge and tools necessary for success in today's global and highly technical business world.

—— + Visit **BeABilliken.com** for more information on our undergraduate business programs and to see what life is like as a Billiken.

To learn about our graduate business programs, attend an open house or visit **gradbiz.slu.edu.** +———————

SAINT LOUIS UNIVERSITY

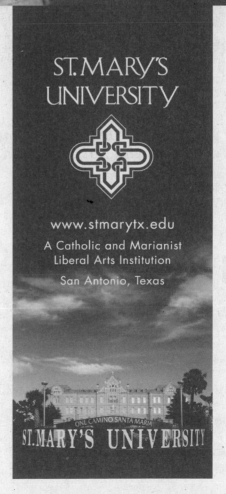

NOTES

NOTES

NOTES

NOTES

NOTES

NOTES

NOTES

NOTES

NOTES

NOTES

NOTES

NOTES

NOTES